**The definitive guide to
the global game**

ALMANACK
OF WORLD
FOOTBALL
2008

Guy Oliver

headline

First published in 2007
by HEADLINE PUBLISHING GROUP

1

Front cover photographs: (left) Cristiano Ronaldo in action for Manchester United - *Action Images*;
(centre left) Iraq celebrate winning the AFC Asian Cup - *Action Images*; (centre right) Samuel Eto'o
in action for Barcelona - *Action Images*; (right) David Beckham makes his debut
for Los Angeles Galaxy - *Action Images*;

Spine photograph: Milan celebrate winning the UEFA Champions League - *Action Images*

Back cover photographs: (left) Kaká in action for Brazil - *Action Images*; (centre left) Action from
the Copa Libertadores Final between Boca Juniors and Grêmio - *Action Images*;
(centre) Ronaldinho in action for Barcelona - *Action Images*; (centre right) Arsenal Ladies
celebrate winning the UEFA Women's Cup - *Action Images*; (right) Lionel Messi
in action for Argentina - *Action Images*;

A CIP catalogue record for this title is available from the British Library

ISBN 978 0 7553 1508 6

Design: Guy Oliver
Design consultant: Peter Ward
Cover design: Head Design Ltd

Printed and bound in Great Britain by Mackays of Chatham PLC,
Chatham, Kent

The data within the Almanack of World Football has been obtained from a variety of sources, official
and unofficial. The Author cannot vouch for the accuracy of the data in all cases.

HEADLINE PUBLISHING GROUP
An Hachette Livre UK Company
338 Euston Road
London NW1 3BH

www.headline.co.uk
www.hodderheadline.com

CONTENTS

PART ONE – FIFA AND WORLD FOOTBALL

PART TWO – THE NATIONS OF THE WORLD

4 CONTENTS

PART THREE – THE CONTINENTAL CONFEDERATIONS

ASIA

AFRICA

CENTRAL & NORTH AMERICA, THE CARIBBEAN

SOUTH AMERICA

OCEANIA

EUROPE

ALPHABETICAL LISTING OF
THE NATIONS OF THE WORLD

As the 208 member associations of FIFA are organised in the Almanack according to their trigram and not alphabetically, the following table provides a quick alphabetical reference to page numbers.

COUNTRY		PAGE	COUNTRY		PAGE
Afghanistan	AFG	59	Bhutan	BHU	133
Albania	ALB	63	Bolivia	BOL	145
Algeria	ALG	67	Bosnia-Herzegovina	BIH	135
American Samoa	ASA	94	Botswana	BOT	149
Andorra	AND	71	Brazil	BRA	152
Angola	ANG	74	British Virgin Islands	VGB	770
Anguilla	AIA	61	Brunei Darussalam	BRU	164
Antigua and Barbuda	ATG	96	Bulgaria	BUL	166
Argentina	ARG	80	Burkina Faso	BFA	127
Armenia	ARM	88	Burma (Myanmar)	MYA	531
Aruba	ARU	92	Burundi	BDI	116
Australia	AUS	98	Cambodia	CAM	170
Austria	AUT	103	Cameroon	CMR	197
Azerbaijan	AZE	107	Canada	CAN	172
Bahamas	BAH	111	Cape Verde Islands	CPV	213
Bahrain	BHR	130	Cayman Islands	CAY	175
Bangladesh	BAN	113	Central African Republic	CTA	223
Barbados	BRB	161	Chad	CHA	180
Belarus	BLR	139	Chile	CHI	182
Belgium	BEL	118	China PR	CHN	187
Belize	BLZ	143	Chinese Taipei (Taiwan)	TPE	727
Benin	BEN	122	Colombia	COL	206
Bermuda	BER	124	Comoros	COM	211

ACKNOWLEDGEMENTS

Thanks once again to Mark Gleeson for his huge efforts in getting Africa up to standard. Huge thanks also to Tom Chittick without whom you would not be reading this and to Oliver Greenleaves for his invaluable contribution inputting the stats. Thanks to Cris Freddi for casting his eye over the content to check that it made sense; to Neil McKnight, Daniel Fein, Tom Lewis, Michael Oliver and Roger Lakin for their help. My thanks also to Lorraine Jerram, David Wilson and Rhea Halford at Headline. Information from the Almanack comes from official sources on the internet, but much also comes from the brilliant RSSSF and its network of contributors - thanks to you all.

AUTHOR'S NOTE
As the Almanack sets off on its own without FIFA, I would like to say a huge thank you to everyone there who helped to get the book established. To Lars Bretscher, Helen de Haan, Andreas Herren, Marius Schneider and Jérôme Champagne thanks for your help in the past and for your continued support. The major innovation in the Almanack this year has been the inclusion of the medals tables and the maps that compliment these tables. In future we would like to include more nations but the historical information is not complete enough yet. If you feel you can help, contact me on almanack@harpastumpublishing.com.

PART ONE

FIFA AND WORLD FOOTBALL

FIFA

Fédération Internationale de Football Association

Just eight weeks after Italians worldwide celebrated the Azzurri's triumph in the FIFA World Cup final in Berlin, the people of North Korea were also celebrating a football world championship. Hot on the heels of the World Cup, Russia hosted the FIFA Women's U–20 World Championship and the tournament was full of surprises with neither of the pre tournament favourites Germany or the USA making it to the final. The Americans had beaten the Germans in the quarter-finals, but they in turn lost to China in the semi-finals who qualified to meet the real surprise package, North Korea, in the final. The triumph of the Koreans in the final was no fluke as they had been impressive throughout the tournament, winning all six games they played and conceding just one goal. In the group stage they beat Germany 2-0 and both Switzerland and Mexico 4-0, to qualify for the knock-out stage where they disposed of France and Brazil before thrashing the Chinese 5-0 in the final in Moscow. By winning the title North Korea joined an exclusive club of just 25 nations that have won a major world title. Next up on the FIFA calendar was the FIFA Club World Cup in Japan where Ronaldinho's Barcelona were expected to stroll to the title. After comfortably beating Mexico's América, Barca faced Copa Libertadores winners Internacional, from Ronaldinho's home town of Pôrto Alegre, in the

THE FIFA BIG COUNT OF 2006

	Male	Female		Total
Number of players	238 557 000	25 995 000	Referees and Assistant Referees	843 000
Professionals	113 000		Admin, Coaches, Technical, Medical	4 214 000
Amateurs 18+	15 481 000		Number of clubs	301 000
Youth under 18	21 548 000		Number of teams	1 752 000
Unregistered	226 265 000		Clubs with women's teams	26 000
Total involved in football	264 552 000		Players as % of population	4.13%

final. Clearly fired up for the encounter, Internacional were the better team, winning 1-0 with a goal from Adriano eight minutes before the end, to seal a South American triumph for the second year in a row. Hugely popular in South America where winning the Copa Libertadores is often known as 'Project Tokyo' the FIFA Club World Cup will need to broaden it's appeal to European clubs and the decision to hold future tournaments away from Japan may just do that. FIFA's final offering of the year was the FIFA U–20 World Cup which was played in Canada before large and enthusiastic crowds. Once again it was Argentina who grabbed all the headlines by winning the title for a sixth time - their fifth success in the past seven tournaments - underlining the success of a youth system which nurtures and develops the extraordinary pool of talented players that exists in the country. Off the field, Fabio Cannavaro was honoured at the FIFA World Player Gala in Zürich in December 2006 when he was crowned FIFA World Player of the Year and then at the end of May Zürich also hosted the 57th FIFA Congress which co-incided with the official opening of FIFA's plush new headquarters next to the city zoo. At the Congress, Montenegro became the 208th member of FIFA while Sepp Blatter was re-elected unopposed for a further four years as FIFA President.

Fédération Internationale de Football Association (FIFA)
FIFA-Strasse 20, PO Box, 8044 Zürich, Switzerland
Tel +41 43 222 7777   Fax +41 43 222 7878
contact@fifa.org
www.fifa.com
President: BLATTER Joseph S.
General Secretary: VALCKE Jérôme   Deputy General Secretary: KATTNER Marksu
Delegate of the President for Special Affairs: CHAMPAGNE Jérôme

FIFA EXECUTIVE COMMITTEE

President: BLATTER Joseph S. SUI   Senior Vice-President: GRONDONA Julio ARG   Vice-President: HAYATOU Issa CMR
Vice-President: CHUNG Mong Joon, Dr KOR   Vice-President: WARNER Jack A. TRI   Vice-President: VILLAR LLONA Angel Maria ESP
Vice-President: PLATINI Michel FRA   Vice-President: TEMARII Reynald TAH   Vice-President: THOMPSON Geoff ENG

ORDINARY MEMBERS OF THE EXECUTIVE COMMITTEE

D'HOOGHE Michel, Dr BEL	TEIXEIRA Ricardo Terra BRA	BIN HAMMAM Mohamed QAT
ERZIK Senes TUR	BLAZER Chuck USA	MAKUDI Worawi THA
LEOZ Nicolás, Dr PAR	KOLOSKOV Viacheslav, Dr RUS	OGURA Junji JPN
CHIBOUB Slim TUN	ADAMU Amos, Dr NGA	LEFKARITIS Marios CYP
ANOUMA Jacques CIV	BECKENBAUER Franz GER	SALGUERO Rafael GUA
	General Secretary: VALCKE Jérôme	

OTHER FIFA COMMITTEES

	Chairman	Organising Committee for...	Chairman
Emergency Committee	BLATTER Joseph S.	The FIFA World Cup	HAYATOU Issa
Finance Committee	GRONDONA Julio H.	The FIFA Confederations Cup	BLAZER Chuck
Internal Audit Committee	CARRARO Franco, Dr	The Olympic Football Tournaments	HAYATOU Issa
Referees' Committee	VILLAR LLONA Angel Maria	The FIFA U-20 World Cup	WARNER Jack A.
Technical & Development Committee	PLATINI Michel	The FIFA U-17 World Cup	WARNER Jack A.
Sports Medical Committee	D'HOOGHE Michel, Dr	Women's Football and FIFA Women's World Cup	MAKUDI Worawi
Players' Status Committee	MAYER-VORFELDER Gerhard	The U-20 and U-17 Women's World Cups	BALZER Chuck
Legal Committee	WILL David H.	Futsal and Beach Soccer Committee	TEIXEIRA Ricardo Terra
Fair Play and Social Responsibility	ERZIK Senes	The FIFA Club World Cup	KOLOSKOV Viacheslav, Dr
Media Committee	MAYER-VORFELDER Gerhard	Associations Committee	KOLOSKOV Viacheslav, Dr
Football Committee	VILLAR LLONA Angel Maria	Marketing and Television Advisory Board	GRONDONA Julio H.
Strategic Studies Committee	BLATTER Joseph S.	Goal Bureau	BIN HAMMAM Mohamed
FIFA Club Task Force	CHIBOUB Slim	FIFA Medical Assessment and Research Centre	D'HOOGHE Michel, Dr
Doping Control Sub-Committee	D'HOOGHE Michel, Dr	Disciplinary Committee	MATHIER Marcel, Me.
Appeal Committee	SALGUERO Rafael	Ethics Committee	COE Sebastian

FIFA TOURNAMENTS

FIFA WORLD CUP

Year	Host Country	Winners	Score	Runners-up	Venue
1930	Uruguay	Uruguay	4-2	Argentina	Centenario, Montevideo
1934	Italy	Italy	2-1	Czechoslovakia	PNF, Rome
1938	France	Italy	4-2	Hungary	Colombes, Paris
1950	Brazil	Uruguay	2-1	Brazil	Maracana, Rio de Janeiro
1954	Switzerland	Germany FR	3-2	Hungary	Wankdorf, Berne
1958	Sweden	Brazil	5-2	Sweden	Råsunda, Stockholm
1962	Chile	Brazil	3-1	Czechoslovakia	Estadio Nacional, Santiago
1966	England	England	4-2	Germany FR	Wembley, London
1970	Mexico	Brazil	4-1	Italy	Azteca, Mexico City
1974	Germany FR	Germany FR	2-1	Netherlands	Olympiastadion, Munich
1978	Argentina	Argentina	3-1	Netherlands	Monumental, Buenos Aires
1982	Spain	Italy	3-1	Germany FR	Bernabeu, Madrid
1986	Mexico	Argentina	3-2	Germany FR	Azteca, Mexico City
1990	Italy	Germany FR	1-0	Argentina	Olimpico, Rome
1994	USA	Brazil	0-0 3-2p	Italy	Rose Bowl, Pasadena
1998	France	France	3-0	Brazil	Stade de France, Paris
2002	Korea Rep/Japan	Brazil	2-0	Germany	International Stadium, Yokohama
2006	Germany	Italy	1-1 5-3p	France	Olympiastadion, Berlin

The FIFA World Cup is the most popular single sports event in the world and ranks alongside the Olympic Games as the focus of sporting attention in the years that the two sporting festivals are held. When FIFA was founded in 1904 it reserved the right to organise a world championship for its members. However, it took more than a quarter of a century for that aim to become reality and it wasn't until the Barcelona Congress of 1929 that a resolution was passed paving the way for the first tournament to be held the following year in Uruguay. The reason the World Cup was such a long time in coming was due to the huge appeal of the Football Tournament of the Olympic Games, the winners of which were regarded as world champions. The Olympic tournament had first been officially organised in 1908 but by the late 1920s there was growing disquiet amongst the members of FIFA that, because of the amateur ethos and the surge of professionalism after 1925, especially within central Europe, the best players were no longer eligible to compete. Although FIFA was responsible for organising the Olympic Football Tournament, the then FIFA President Jules Rimet realised that the best way forward was to organise a separate tournament that was open to anyone. Just 13 teams entered the first tournament, a figure that has risen to over 200 today. It may be the dream of every footballer to take part in the FIFA World Cup but only a very select club of players and nations have won the coveted prize; seven nations and 274 players to be precise. Staged every four years, the finals have been hosted by 15 countries with Mexico, Italy, France and Germany each having been granted the honour twice. For many years the hosting would alternate between the Americas and Europe but in 2002 Asia welcomed the tournament for the first time and in 2010 South Africa will entertain as each continent is given a chance on a rotational basis. Much of the excitement of the FIFA World Cup can also be found in the qualifying tournaments, which in some parts of the world are now spread over two years. The 32 places in the finals are decided on a continental basis with the hosts, but no longer the holders, qualifying automatically. For the 2006 tournament South America had four guaranteed places, Europe 13, Africa five, Asia four and Central and North America three, with the final two places decided via a series of play-offs between all the Confederations bar Europe and Africa. For many just making it to the finals is achievement enough, although for the elite the aim remains winning the Cup itself. Not that the trophy is actually a cup anymore. For the first eight tournaments it was possible to celebrate by drinking champagne from the Jules Rimet trophy, but since 1974 the solid gold trophy is in the form of a globe, held aloft by two athletes at the moment of victory.

FIFA WORLD CUP MEDALS TABLE

	Country	G	S	B	F	SF
1	Brazil	5	2	2	7	7
2	Italy	4	2	1	6	7
3	Germany	3	4	3	7	10
4	Argentina	2	2		4	3
5	Uruguay	2			2	3
6	France	1	1	2	2	5
7	England	1			1	2
8	Czechoslovakia		2		2	2
	Hungary		2		2	2
10	Netherlands		2		2	1
11	Sweden		1	2	1	3
12	Poland			2		1
13	Austria			1		2
	Portugal			1		2
	Yugoslavia			1		2
16	Chile			1		1
	Croatia			1		1
	Turkey			1		1
	USA			1		1
20	Belgium					1
	Bulgaria					1
	Korea Republic					1
	Soviet Union					1
		18	18	19	36	60

This table represents the Gold (winners), Silver (runners-up) and Bronze (3rd place) winners of nations in the FIFA World Cup™, along with the number of appearances in the final and semi-finals

FIFA WOMEN'S WORLD CUP

Year	Host Country	Winners	Score	Runners-up	Venue
1991	China PR	USA	2-1	Norway	Tianhe, Guangzhou
1995	Sweden	Norway	2-0	Germany	Råsunda, Stockholm
1999	USA	USA	0-0 5-4p	China PR	Rose Bowl, Pasadena
2003	USA	Germany	2-1	Sweden	Home Depot Centre, Carson
2007	China PR				

With the rapid growth of women's football since the 1970s it was a logical step for FIFA to organise a World Cup for women in 1991 to replace the growing number of unofficial tournaments that were being staged around the world. As early as 1970, 40,000 fans in the Stadio Communale in Turin watched Denmark beat Italy to win the Coppa del Mondo while the following year the Danes won the Mundial 1971 in front of 110,000 fans in Mexico City's Azteca Stadium, beating the hosts in the final of a tournament that had been played to packed stadia throughout. The surge in interest in women's football in the Far East and in the Americas in the late 1980s convinced FIFA that the time was right to get involved in the women's game. In 1988 they organised the FIFA Women's Invitation Tournament in China PR. The event, won by Norway, who beat Sweden in the final in Guangzhou, was a huge success although it isn't counted as part of the FIFA Women's World Cup record. The first official tournament was held three years later, in 1991, and again hosted by China PR. The winners were the United States, a major player in the popularisation of the women's game thanks to the seven million women and girls involved with football there. Two of the tournaments since then have been held in the USA although the 2003 tournament should have been held in China but was switched to the States due to the SARS outbreak in the Far East.

FIFA WOMEN'S WORLD CUP MEDALS TABLE

	Country	G	S	B	F	SF
1	USA	2		2	2	4
2	Germany	1	1		2	3
	Norway	1	1		2	3
4	Sweden		1	1	1	2
5	China PR		1		1	2
6	Brazil			1		1
	Canada					1
		4	4	4	8	16

This table represents the Gold (winners), Silver (runners-up) and Bronze (3rd place) winners of nations in the FIFA World Cup™, along with the number of appearances in the final and semi-finals

FIFA CLUB WORLD CUP

Year	Host Country	Winners	Score	Runners-up	Venue
2000	Brazil	Corinthians, BRA	0-0 4-3p	Vasco da Gama, BRA	Maracana, Rio de Janeiro
2005	Japan	São Paulo FC, BRA	1-0	Liverpool, ENG	International, Yokohama
2006	Japan	Internacional, BRA	1-0	Barcelona, ESP	International, Yokohama
2007	Japan				

For many years fans around the world were denied the chance to watch their teams play against clubs from different Confederations and vie for the title of world champions, but since 2000 that has become a reality. European critics railed against FIFA when the FIFA Club World Cup was introduced, citing an overcrowded fixture list, but after taking on their concerns, FIFA announced that from 2005 the tournament would replace the annual Toyota Cup played between the European and South American club champions and that it would be held annually thereafter. By adopting a straight knock-out format, with the European and South American champions joining at the semi-final stage, fixtures have been kept to a minimum. From 2008 the option of playing the tournament away from Japan has been discussed but no final decision has been taken.

MEN'S OLYMPIC FOOTBALL TOURNAMENT

Year	Host City	Winners	Score	Runners-up	Venue
1896	Athens	No tournament took place			
1900	Paris	Great Britain	4-0	France	Vélodrome Municipal, Paris
1904	St Louis	Canada	4-0	USA	Francis Field, St Louis
1906	Athens	Denmark	9-0	Greece	Podilatodromino, Athens
1908	London	England (as GBR)	2-0	Denmark	White City, London
1912	Stockholm	England (as GBR)	4-2	Denmark	Stockholms Stadion, Stockholm
1916	Berlin	Games cancelled			
1920	Antwerp	Belgium	2-0	Czechoslovakia	Olympisch Stadion, Antwerp
1924	Paris	Uruguay	3-0	Switzerland	Colombes, Paris
1928	Amsterdam	Uruguay	1-1 2-1	Argentina	Olympisch Stadion, Amsterdam
1932	Los Angeles	No football tournament played			
1936	Berlin	Italy	2-1	Austria	Olympiastadion, Berlin
1940	Tokyo/Helsinki	Games cancelled			
1944	London	Games cancelled			
1948	London	Sweden	3-1	Yugoslavia	Wembley, London
1952	Helsinki	Hungary	2-0	Yugoslavia	Olympiastadion, Helsinki
1956	Melbourne	Soviet Union	1-0	Yugoslavia	Melbourne Cricket Ground
1960	Rome	Yugoslavia	3-1	Denmark	Flaminio, Rome
1964	Tokyo	Hungary	2-1	Czechoslovakia	National Stadium, Tokyo
1968	Mexico City	Hungary	4-1	Bulgaria	Azteca, Mexico City
1972	Munich	Poland	2-1	Hungary	Olympiastadion, Munich
1976	Montreal	German DR	3-1	Poland	Olympic Stadium, Montreal
1980	Moscow	Czechoslovakia	1-0	German DR	Centralny, Moscow
1984	Los Angeles	France	2-0	Brazil	Rose Bowl, Pasadena
1988	Seoul	Soviet Union	2-1	Brazil	Olympic Stadium, Seoul
1992	Barcelona	Spain	3-2	Poland	Camp Nou, Barcelona
1996	Atlanta	Nigeria	3-2	Argentina	Sanford Stadium, Athens
2000	Sydney	Cameroon	2-2 5-4p	Spain	Olympic Stadium, Sydney
2004	Athens	Argentina	1-0	Paraguay	Olympic Stadium, Athens

The history of the Men's Olympic Football Tournament can be divided into three broad phases. Before the introduction of the FIFA World Cup™ in 1930 the winners were lauded as world champions, an honour won twice by Uruguay and England (playing under the banner of Great Britain) and once by Belgium. After 1928 the tournament remained amateur in a world increasingly dominated by professionalism, a situation exploited by countries from the communist bloc who were professionals in all but name. From 1952 until 1980 teams from behind the Iron Curtain walked off with every title, notably the Hungarians, winners in 1952, 1964 and 1968. For the 1984 and 1988 tournaments the amateur restrictions were relaxed with all players who had not taken part in a World Cup eligible to compete, but in 1992 the third major phase began when it became an age-restricted tournament for under-23s although three over-age players were also permitted in the team. Sixteen nations have won Olympic football gold although it is a competition that has been dominated by Europe with only four nations from elsewhere winning the prize. After the legendary triumphs of Uruguay in the 1920s it wasn't until 2004 that another South American team – Argentina – won, and the Olympic title remains the only major title not yet won by Brazil. In 1996 Nigeria broke the duck for Africa and that was followed in Sydney four years later by Cameroon. Four previous winners no longer exist as countries – the Soviet Union, East Germany, Czechoslovakia and Yugoslavia while there is also some confusion as to the inaugural winners. The team representing Great Britain was the famous pre-World War One England amateur team that was so instrumental in spreading the game across Europe, hence the listing as England rather than Great Britain. As with the FIFA World Cup™ the finalists for the Olympics are decided by continental qualifying competitions which in 2004 resulted in four finalists from Africa and Europe (including hosts Greece), three from Asia, two from South America, two from the rest of the Americas and one from Oceania.

WOMEN'S OLYMPIC FOOTBALL TOURNAMENT

Year	Host City	Winners	Score	Runners-up	Venue
1996	Atlanta	USA	2-1	China	Sanford Stadium, Athens
2000	Sydney	Norway	3-2	USA	Sydney Football Stadium, Sydney
2004	Athens	USA	2-1	Brazil	Karaiskaki, Piraeus

Women's football is a very recent addition to the list of Olympic sports but in conjunction with the FIFA Women's World Cup it now provides the sport with a second championship of world repute, as, unlike the men's Olympic Football Tournament, the full national teams can enter. The 1996 games in Atlanta were the perfect launch pad for the Women's Olympic Football Tournament with the final between the USA and China witnessed by 76,489 in the Sanford Stadium in Athens, Georgia, while the average for all games was 39,362. The United States have remained the dominant force since winning the first final against China, losing to Norway in Sydney and then winning again in 2004 against Brazil. Whereas the participants for the 1996 tournament qualified by finishing among the top eight in the 1995 Women's World Cup, there is now a qualifying tournament run along continental lines.

FIFA CONFEDERATIONS CUP

Year	Host Country	Winners	Score	Runners-up	Venue
1992	Saudi Arabia	Argentina	3-1	Saudi Arabia	King Fahd, Riyadh
1995	Saudi Arabia	Denmark	2-0	Argentina	King Fahd, Riyadh
1997	Saudi Arabia	Brazil	6-0	Australia	King Fahd, Riyadh
1999	Mexico	Mexico	4-3	Brazil	Azteca, Mexico City
2001	Korea/Japan	France	1-0	Japan	International Stadium, Yokohama
2003	France	France	1-0	Cameroon	Stade de France, Paris
2005	Germany	Brazil	4-1	Argentina	Waldstadion, Frankfurt

Conceived in 1992, the Confederations Cup's purpose was to bring together the continental champions from around the world. Initially known as the King Fahd Cup, it was later rebranded the FIFA Confederations Cup in 1997 when it came under FIFA's control. Riyadh in Saudi Arabia staged the first three editions, but from 1999 other countries were give the opportunity to host the tournament in an effort to broaden its appeal and before the 2002 and 2006 FIFA World Cups it was used as a timely trial run in Korea Republic and Japan in 2001 and in Germany in 2005. After drawing criticism from within Europe, especially among the big clubs who complained of fixture overcrowding, FIFA responded by switching the tournament from a two year to a four year cycle. As in 2001 and 2005 it will now be used as a trial run before each FIFA World Cup with the next edition in South Africa in 2009.

FIFA FUTSAL WORLD CHAMPIONSHIP

Year	Host Country	Winners	Score	Runners-up	Venue
1989	Netherlands	Brazil	2-1	Netherlands	Rotterdam
1992	Hong Kong	Brazil	4-1	United States	Hong Kong
1996	Spain	Brazil	6-4	Spain	Barcelona
2000	Guatemala	Spain	4-3	Brazil	Guatemala City
2004	Chinese Taipei	Spain	2-1	Italy	Taipei City

Futsal, the five-a-side indoor version of football, has become an increasingly important part of FIFA's work and since 1989 there have been five FIFA Futsal World Championships. The first three were won by Brazil, the major power in the game, though that position has been challenged by Spain, who have won the past two titles. Via a series of continental qualifiers, most of which double up as continental championships, 16 teams qualify for the finals. Games consist of two periods of 20 minutes and any of seven substitutes may be brought on or taken off throughout the game as many times as desired.

FIFA U–20 WORLD CUP

Year	Host Country	Winners	Score	Runners-up	Final Venue
1977	Tunisia	Soviet Union	2-2 9-8p	Mexico	El Menzah, Tunis
1979	Japan	Argentina	3-1	Soviet Union	National Stadium, Tokyo
1981	Australia	Germany FR	4-0	Qatar	Sydney Cricket Ground
1983	Mexico	Brazil	1-0	Argentina	Azteca, Mexico City
1985	Soviet Union	Brazil	1-0	Spain	Centralny, Moscow
1987	Chile	Yugoslavia	1-1 5-4p	Germany FR	Estadio Nacional, Santiago
1989	Saudi Arabia	Portugal	2-0	Nigeria	King Fahd, Riyadh
1991	Portugal	Portugal	0-0 4-2p	Brazil	Da Luz, Lisbon
1993	Australia	Brazil	2-1	Ghana	Sydney Football Stadium, Sydney
1995	Qatar	Argentina	2-0	Brazil	Khalifa, Doha
1997	Malaysia	Argentina	2-1	Uruguay	Shahalam Stadium, Shah Alam
1999	Nigeria	Spain	4-0	Japan	Surulere, Lagos
2001	Argentina	Argentina	3-0	Ghana	Jose Amalfitani, Buenos Aires
2003	UAE	Brazil	1-0	Spain	Zayed Sports City, Abu Dhabi
2005	Netherlands	Argentina	2-1	Nigeria	Galgenwaard, Utrecht
2007	Canada	Argentina	2-1	Czech Republic	National Soccer Stadium, Toronto

As well as the Football Tournament of the Olympic Games, FIFA now organises four other major age-restricted championships. The longest established of these is the FIFA U-20 World Cup which before 2007 was known as the FIFA World Youth Championship. Since its inception in 1977 in Tunisia, the tournament has been held every two years and countries from all six Confederations have hosted the event at least once. The winners of the FIFA U-20 World Cup have all hailed from either Europe or South America, with Argentina having won six titles and Brazil four. At first, many were sceptical of the value of a youth tournament, especially with the problems associated with over-aged players, but it seems that this issue has died down, largely thanks to the harsh penalties handed out to those caught cheating. The FIFA U-20 World Cup is now seen in most countries as a vital step in the education of the top young footballers, where they can encounter high pressure tournament conditions and different styles of play early in their careers and it is surely no coincidence that countries like Brazil, Argentina and Spain, where support for the tournament is strong, consistently produce young players of a very high calibre. The first tournament, in 1977, was also the first global tournament to take place in Africa, with the Soviet Union beating Mexico 9-8 on penalties in Tunis. Through the years, many great players have graced the tournament, none more so than in 1979 when Diego Maradona lead his team to a title that was celebrated in Argentina almost as much as the FIFA World Cup win the year before. Germany's only title came two years later in Australia, when they beat Qatar, the smallest nation ever to appear in a FIFA final. Then it was the turn of Brazil, who won the 1983 and 1985 tournaments with players such as current national team coach, Dunga, and the 1994 FIFA World Cup winners Cláudio Taffarel, Jorginho and Bebeto. One of the most famous triumphs came in Chile in 1987, when a European team won a FIFA tournament on South American soil for the first and, so far, only time. The triumphant Yugoslav side contained great names such as Zvonimir Boban, Robert Prosinecki and Davor Suker. The next two tournaments, in 1989 and 1991, saw back-to-back wins for Portugal with a group of players that were soon to become known as the 'Golden Generation,' notably Figo, João Pinto, Paulo Sousa and Rui Costa. In the 1990s, Argentina rose to prominence again, winning in 1995, 1997 and 2001 under the guidance of coach Jose Pekerman, and then again in 2005 and 2007 to seal a record six titles. In-between, Spain won a first title in 1999 in Nigeria, the first time a FIFA tournament had been played in sub-Saharan Africa.

FIFA U–17 WOMEN'S WORLD CUP

Year	Host Country	Winners	Score	Runners-up	Final Venue
2008	New Zealand				

The introduction of the FIFA U–17 Women's World Cup completes the line-up of possible FIFA tournaments with the first edition taking place in New Zealand in 2008

FIFA U–17 WORLD CHAMPIONSHIP

Year	Host Country	Winners	Score	Runners-up	Final Venue
1985	China	Nigeria	2-0	Germany FR	Workers' Stadium, Beijing
1987	Canada	Soviet Union	1-1 3-1p	Nigeria	Varsity Stadium, Toronto
1989	Scotland	Saudi Arabia	2-2 5-4p	Scotland	Hampden Park, Glasgow
1991	Italy	Ghana	1-0	Spain	Comunale, Florence
1993	Japan	Nigeria	2-1	Ghana	National Stadium, Tokyo
1995	Ecuador	Ghana	3-2	Brazil	Monumental, Guayaquil
1997	Egypt	Brazil	2-1	Ghana	National Stadium, Cairo
1999	New Zealand	Brazil	0-0 8-7p	Australia	North Harbour, Auckland
2001	Trinidad	France	3-0	Nigeria	Hasely Crawford, Port of Spain
2003	Finland	Brazil	1-0	Spain	Töölö, Helsinki
2005	Peru	Mexico	3-0	Brazil	Estadio Nacional, Lima
2007	Korea Republic				

The second of the FIFA age-restricted tournaments to be introduced was the FIFA U-17 World Championship, now known as the FIFA U–17 World Cup. It has been held every two years since 1985 and countries from all six Confederations have hosted the event at least once. Brazil is the most successful nation in the history of the tournament with three titles, all won in a six year period between 1997 and 2003. Competition has been much more open than in the U–20 event, with African, Asian and North American sides all challenging the supremacy of the South Americans and Europeans by winning tournaments. Right from the start, Nigeria beat Germany 2-0 in Beijing in the final of the inaugural 1985 tournament to become the first African world champions at any level. The Nigerians reached the final again in Toronto two years later, but were beaten on penalties by the Soviet Union. In the third tournament, Saudi Arabia were the surprise winners, beating Scotland in another final decided on penalties to give Asia its first world championship. By reaching the final, the Scots were the first and so far only host nation to make it that far. African supremacy at this level was then confirmed in Italy in 1991, Japan in 1993 and in Ecuador in 1995, with Ghana appearing in all three finals, winning in 1991 and 1995 and losing to Nigeria in Tokyo in 1993. In the late 1990s, Brazil, rather belatedly, began to flex their muscles with Ronaldinho inspiring his country to its first triumph in the 1997 finals in Egypt - a title successfully defended two years later in New Zealand. France was the first European winner for 14 years when they beat Nigeria in the 2001 final in Trinidad and Tobago, but overall the European record has been poor with only France and Spain reaching the final since the start of the 1990s. Spain's first appearance in the final came in 2003, in Finland, but they were beaten by a Brazil team winning a record third title. In the 2005 final in Peru, Mexico beat Brazil to win a first world championship for the CONCACAF region, the only confederation until then, apart from Oceania, not to have won the trophy.

FIFA U–20 WOMEN'S WORLD CUP

Year	Host Country	Winners	Score	Runners-up	Final Venue
2002	Canada	United States	1-0	Canada	Commonwealth, Edmonton
2004	Thailand	Germany	2-0	China PR	Rajamangala National, Bangkok
2006	Russia	Korea DPR	5-0	China PR	Lokomotiv, Moscow

In 2002, due to the growing interest in women's football, the third of FIFA's youth tournaments was launched, the FIFA U-19 Women's World Championship. After two editions, the tournament was changed to an under 20 contest to bring it in line with the men's event and from the 2008 tournament it will be known as the FIFA U–20 Women's World Cup. The two editions of the U-19 event were played in Canada and Thailand, and the rise in standards has surprised even those involved in the women's game. The USA and Germany have dominated, with the Americans winning the inaugural event and then losing in the semi-finals to Germany in 2004; Germany going on to beat China PR in the final. There were surprise winners of the 2006 tournament, however, when North Korea won their first FIFA title by beating China 5-0 in the final.

FIFA WORLD PLAYER 2006

FIFA WORLD PLAYER 2006

Rank	Player	Club	Nat	1st	x5	2nd	x3	3rd	x1	Total
1	Fabio CANNAVARO	Real Madrid	ITA	70	350	38	114	34	34	498
2	Zinedine ZIDANE	Real Madrid	FRA	66	330	33	99	25	25	454
3	RONALDINHO	Barcelona	BRA	50	250	36	108	22	22	380
4	Thierry HENRY	Arsenal	FRA	28	140	48	144	33	33	317
5	Samuel ETO'O	Barcelona	CMR	37	185	29	87	28	28	300
6	Didier DROGBA	Chelsea	CIV	12	60	24	72	18	18	150
7	KAKA	Milan	BRA	15	75	14	42	22	22	139
8	Gianluigi BUFFON	Juventus	ITA	8	40	20	60	18	18	118
9	Andrea PIRLO	Milan	ITA	6	30	15	45	11	11	86
10	CRISTIANO RONALDO	Manchester United	POR	7	35	10	30	4	4	69
11	Michael BALLACK	Chelsea	GER	3	15	8	24	14	14	53
12	Steven GERRARD	Liverpool	ENG	5	25	5	15	8	8	48
13	Miroslav KLOSE	Werder Bremen	GER	3	15	5	15	16	16	46
14	Frank LAMPARD	Chelsea	ENG	3	15	3	9	7	7	31
15	DECO	Barcelona	POR	1	5	3	9	11	11	25
16	Luis FIGO	Internazionale	POR	1	5	5	15	0	0	20
17	Juan Roman RIQUELME	Villrreal	ARG	1	5	3	9	2	2	16
17	Franck RIBERY	Olympique Marseille	FRA	0	0	4	12	4	4	16
17	Wayne ROONEY	Manchester United	ENG	2	10	1	3	3	3	16
20	Gennaro GATTUSO	Milan	ITA	0	0	4	12	3	3	15
21	Andriy SHEVCHENKO	Chelsea	UKR	1	5	3	9	0	0	14
22	Patrick VIEIRA	Internazionale	FRA	0	0	3	9	4	4	13
22	Michael ESSIEN	Chelsea	GHA	0	0	2	6	7	7	13
24	Petr CECH	Chelsea	CZE	1	5	0	0	6	6	11
25	Alessandro NESTA	Milan	ITA	1	5	1	3	1	1	9
26	Lilian THURAM	Barcelona	FRA	1	5	0	0	3	3	8
27	Jens LEHMANN	Arsenal	GER	0	0	0	0	6	6	6
28	Philipp LAHM	Bayern München	GER	0	0	0	0	3	3	3
29	ADRIANO	Internazionale	BRA	0	0	0	0	2	2	2
30	Tomas ROSICKY	Arsenal	CZE	0	0	0	0	0	0	0

Each first placing earns five points • Each second placing earns three points • Each third placing earns one point

FIFA WOMEN'S WORLD PLAYER 2006

Rank	Player	Club	Nat	1st	x5	2nd	x3	3rd	x1	Total
1	MARTA	Umeå IK	BRA	64	320	43	129	26	26	475
2	Kristine LILLY	KIF Orebro	USA	44	220	46	138	30	30	388
3	Renate LINGOR	1.FFC Frankfurt	GER	39	195	30	90	20	20	305
4	Abby WAMBACH	Washington Freedom	USA	22	110	16	48	24	24	182
5	Kelly SMITH	Arsenal	ENG	15	75	20	60	22	22	157
6	Silke ROTTENBERG	1.FFC Frankfurt	GER	16	80	18	54	20	20	154
7	HAN Duan	Dalian	CHN	10	50	17	51	15	15	116
8	MA Xiaoxu	Umeå IK	CHN	8	40	16	48	11	11	99
9	Malin MOSTROM	Umeå IK	SWE	8	40	14	42	5	5	87
10	Lotta SCHELIN	Göteborg FC	SWE	10	50	7	21	11	11	82
11	Cynthia UWAK	FC Pietatarsaal	NGA	9	45	10	30	6	6	81
12	RI Kum Suk		PRK	10	50	3	9	5	5	64
13	Ingvild STENSLAND	Kolbotn	NOR	4	20	7	21	13	13	54
14	Laura GEORGES	Boston Eagles	FRA	5	25	4	12	11	11	48
15	Christine SINCLAIR	Vancouver Whitecaps	CAN	1	5	6	18	16	16	39
16	Monica OCAMPO	FC Indiana	MEX	1	5	6	18	11	11	34
17	Sandrine SOUBEYRAND	FCF Juvisy	FRA	2	10	3	9	12	12	31
18	Laura KALMARI	Umeå IK	FIN	3	15	2	6	3	3	24
19	Cheryl SALISBURY	New York Power	AUS	0	0	1	3	9	9	12
20	Catherine PAASKE SORENSEN	Brøndby	DEN	0	0	3	9	2	2	11

Each first placing earns five points • Each second placing earns three points • Each third placing earns one point

FIFA WORLD PLAYER 2006 – HOW THEY VOTED

Coach	1st	2nd	3rd	Captain	1st	2nd	3rd
AFG Mohammad Kargar	Zidane	Ballack	Lahm	Maroof Gulistani	Zidane	Ribery	Ballack
ALG Jean-Michel Cavalli	Zidane	Ronaldinho	Buffon	Gaouaoui Lounes	Kaká	Lampard	Zidane
AND David Rodrigo	Ronaldinho	Eto'o	Deco	Oscar Sonejee	Zidane	Ronaldinho	Cannavaro
ANG Luis Oliveira Gonçalves	Eto'o	Drogba	Ronaldinho	Paulo Figueiredo	Eto'o	Ronaldinho	Rooney
ARG Alfio Basile	Cannavaro	Drogba	Eto'o	Roberto Ayala	Zidane	Cannavaro	Henry
ARM Ian Porterfield	Cannavaro	Zidane	Henry	Sarigs Hovsepyan	Cannavaro	Drogba	Eto'o
ATG Derrick Edwards	Ronaldinho	Henry	C. Ronaldo	Nathaniel Teon	Henry	Ronaldinho	Nesta
AUS Graham Arnold	Cannavaro	Henry	Ronaldinho	Lucas Neill	Cannavaro	C. Ronaldo	Henry
AUT Josef Hickersberger	Eto'o	Cannavaro	Lehmann	Andreas Ivanschitz	Zidane	Henry	Ronaldinho
AZE Shahin Diniyev	C. Ronaldo	Zidane	Cannavaro	Aslan Karimov	C. Ronaldo	Zidane	Cannavaro
BAH Gary White	Cannavaro	Drogba	Cech	Nesley Jean	Eto'o	Drogba	Essien
BAN Bablu Hasanuzzaman	Zidane	Buffon	Ronaldinho	Huq Aminul	Buffon	Kaká	Zidane
BEL René Vandereycken	Cannavaro	Buffon	Klose	no vote	none	none	none
BER Kyle Lightbourne	Kaká	Essien	Klose	Kentione Jennings	Eto'o	Gerrard	Riquelme
BFA Traore Malo Idrissa	Ronaldinho	Eto'o	Zidane	Soulama Gbdoulaye	Zidane	Gerrard	Eto'o
BHR Hans-Peter Briegel	Eto'o	Buffon	Ronaldinho	Talal Jusuf	Eto'o	Buffon	Lehmann
BHU Kharey Basnet	Drogba	Henry	C. Ronaldo	Passang Tshering	Henry	C. Ronaldo	Klose
BIH Blaz Sliskovic	Zidane	none	none	Zlatan Bajramovic	Zidane	none	none
BLR Yuri Puntus	Henry	Zidane	Ronaldinho	Sergey Shtaniuk	Zidane	Cannavaro	Cech
BLZ Carlos Charlie Slusher	Eto'o	Ronaldinho	Klose	Vallan Dennis Symps	Ronaldinho	Henry	Essien
BOL Erwin Sanchez	Kaká	Buffon	Henry	Sergio Golarza	Kaká	Cannavaro	Eto'o
BOT Colwyn Rowe	Henry	Ronaldinho	Gerrard	Modiri Carlos Marumo	Eto'o	Drogba	Essien
BRA Carlos Dunga	Cannavaro	Buffon	Zidane	Lucio	Drogba	Henry	Buffon
BUL Hristo Stoitchkov	Eto'o	Deco	Ronaldinho	Dimitar Berbatov	Eto'o	Drogba	Henry
CAN Stephen Hart	Zidane	Cannavaro	Lehmann	Kevin McKenna	Henry	Eto'o	invalid vote
CAY Marcos A. Tinoco	Ballack	Pirlo	Klose	Frederick Wilks	Ronaldinho	Eto'o	Kaká
CGO Noël Tosi	Drogba	Zidane	Ribery	Oscar Ewolo	Drogba	Vieira	invalid vote
CHA Matoltiga O. Kalatt	Ronaldinho	Henry	Cannavaro	Valery Ndakom	Henry	Eto'o	Ronaldinho
CHI Nelson Acosta Lopez	Cannavaro	Gattuso	Vieira	Jorge Vargas Palacios	Zidane	Henry	Buffon
CHN Zhu Guanghu	Zidane	Pirlo	Cannavaro	Zheng Zhi	Zidane	Deco	Cannavaro
CIV Ulrich Stielike	Klose	Riquelme	C. Ronaldo	Didier Drogba	Zidane	Buffon	Eto'o
CMR Jules Nyongha	Rooney	Ballack	Buffon	Rigobert Song	Klose	Cannavaro	Vieira
COD Mutombo Bibey	Eto'o	Ronaldinho	Henry	Bageta Dikilo	Eto'o	Ronaldinho	Henry
COK Tim Jerks	Pirlo	Riquelme	Lahm	John Pareanga	Zidane	C. Ronaldo	Cannavaro
COL Reinaldo Rueda Rivera	Ronaldinho	Vieira	Pirlo	Oscar Cordoba Arce	Buffon	Henry	Ronaldinho
CPV José Rui Aguiaz	Eto'o	C. Ronaldo	Essien	Claudio Aguiar	Eto'o	Drogba	Henry
CRC Hernan Medford Bryan	Ronaldinho	Cannavaro	invalid vote	Jose Porras	Ronaldinho	Zidane	Pirlo
CRO Slaven Bilic	Henry	Zidane	Ronaldinho	Niko Kovac	Cannavaro	Eto'o	Lampard
CTA Jim-Fortuné Pelejopa	Eto'o	Drogba	Ronaldinho	Marcelin Tamboula	Eto'o	Drogba	Henry
CUB Raul Valentin Triana	Zidane	Cannavaro	Klose	Jeniel Marquez Molina	Zidane	Cannavaro	Pirlo
CYP Angelos Anastasiades	Lampard	Kaká	Cannavaro	Joannis Okkas	Kaká	Henry	Zidane
CZE Karel Brückner	Cannavaro	Zidane	Klose	Tomas Rosicky	Henry	Ronaldinho	Zidane
DEN Morten Olsen	Eto'o	Pirlo	Cannavaro	Thomas Helveg	Cannavaro	Ribery	Eto'o
DJI Mohamed Omar Ali	Cannavaro	Drogba	Henry	Kader Salem	Pirlo	Eto'o	Zidane
DMA Juan Emilio Mojica	Ronaldinho	Pirlo	Eto'o	Yan Carlos Berroa	C. Ronaldo	Ronaldinho	Buffon
ECU Luis Fernando Suarez	Kaká	Drogba	Eto'o	Ivan Hurtato Angulo	Ronaldinho	Eto'o	Kaká
EGY Hasan Shehata	Zidane	Eto'o	Ronaldinho	Ahmed Hasan	Zidane	Eto'o	Ronaldinho
ENG Steve McClaren	Cannavaro	Zidane	Ronaldinho	John Terry	Cannavaro	Kaká	Henry
EQG Antonio Dumas	Kaká	Drogba	Essien	Silvestre Mesaka	Lampard	Drogba	Adriano
ERI Dorian Marin	Kaká	Eto'o	Zidane	Ytdalekachw Shtmangus	Eto'o	Drogba	Kaká
ESP Luis Aragones Suarez	Eto'o	Henry	Ronaldinho	Raúl Gonzales Blanco	Cannavaro	Eto'o	Kaká
EST Jelle Goes	Cannavaro	Buffon	Kaká	Mart Poom	Zidane	Ronaldinho	Cannavaro
ETH Seyoum Abate Bekele	Drogba	C. Ronaldo	Kaká	Mulualem Regassa	Drogba	C. Ronaldo	Kaká
FIN Roy Hodgson	Pirlo	Henry	Cannavaro	Jari Litmanen	Cannavaro	Henry	Deco
FRA Raymond Domenech	Cech	Gattuso	Drogba	Patrick Vieira	Eto'o	Buffon	Deco
FRO Jogvan Martin Olsen	Zidane	Ronaldinho	Henry	Oli Johannesen	Ronaldinho	Henry	Cannavaro
GEO Klaus Toppmöller	Cannavaro	Zidane	Klose	Kakha Kaladze	Kaká	Ronaldinho	Cannavaro
GER Joachim Löw	Cannavaro	Eto'o	Henry	Michael Ballack	Henry	Cannavaro	Ronaldinho
GHA Claude Le Roy	Eto'o	Henry	invalid vote	Stephen Appiah	Cannavaro	invalid vote	C. Ronaldo
GRE Otto Rehhagel	Zidane	Klose	Ballack	Theodoros Zagorakis	Cannavaro	Zidane	Pirlo
GRN Alister Debellotte	Ronaldinho	Henry	Lampard	Franklyn Baptiste	Ronaldinho	Drogba	Lampard
GUA Hernan Dario Gomez	Cannavaro	Zidane	Vieira	no vote	none	none	none
GUM Morio Tsukitata	Lampard	Cannavaro	Deco	James Bush	Zidane	Ronaldinho	Lampard
HKG Lai Sun-Cheung	Cannavaro	Klose	Kaká	Tan Chun Zip	Zidane	Eto'o	Cannavaro

FIFA WORLD PLAYER 2006 – HOW THEY VOTED

	Coach	1st	2nd	3rd	Captain	1st	2nd	3rd
HON	Flavio Ortega	Eto'o	Kaká	Drogba	Milton Alexander Reyes	Kaká	Eto'o	Drogba
HUN	Peter Bozsik	Ronaldinho	Zidane	Pirlo	Pal Dardai	Cannavaro	Klose	Buffon
IDN	Peter Withe	Zidane	Pirlo	Ballack	Punaryo Astaman	Zidane	Nesta	Ballack
IND	Bob Houghton	Cannavaro	Buffon	Cech	Baichung Bhutia	Zidane	Cannavaro	Henry
IRL	Stephen Staunton	Riquelme	Deco	Henry	Robbie Keane	Ronaldinho	Kaká	Gerrard
IRN	Amir Ghalehnoy	Cannavaro	Kaká	Zidane	Mehdi Mahdavikia	Cannavaro	Drogba	Zidane
ISL	Eyjolfur Sverrisson	Zidane	Cannavaro	Buffon	Eidur Gudjohnsen	Ronaldinho	invalid vote	Cannavaro
ISR	Dror Kashtan	Cannavaro	Pirlo	Eto'o	Yossi Benayoun	Cannavaro	Pirlo	Zidane
ITA	Roberto Donadoni	Henry	Shevchenko	Kaká	Fabio Cannavaro	Thuram	Vieira	Eto'o
JAM	Carl Brown	Cannavaro	Buffon	Eto'o	Ricardo Fuller	Ronaldinho	Drogba	Kaká
JOR	Mahmoud El-Gohary	Cannavaro	Henry	Zidane	Faisal Suleiman	Shevchenko	Luis Figo	Ballack
JPN	Ivan Osim	Eto'o	Ronaldinho	Cannavaro	Yoshikatsu Kawaguchi	Zidane	Cannavaro	Buffon
KAZ	Arno Pijpers	Henry	Ronaldinho	Deco	Nurbol Zhumaskaliyev	Ronaldinho	Lampard	Drogba
KGZ	Nemat Zakirov	Zidane	Shevchenko	Cech	Ruslan Sydykov	Klose	Cannavaro	Buffon
KOR	Pim Verbeek	Cannavaro	Henry	Pirlo	Kim Nam Il	Zidane	Essien	Vieira
KSA	Marcos Paqueta	Zidane	Cannavaro	Klose	Hussein Abdul Ghani	Ronaldinho	Henry	Riquelme
KUW	Mihai Stoichita	Zidane	Cannavaro	Klose	Nohayer Al Shammary	Cannavaro	Zidane	Klose
LAO	Sutsakhone Oudomphet	Ronaldinho	Henry	Kaká	Valasine Dalaphone	Luis Figo	Ballack	Zidane
LBR	Frank Jerico Nagbe	Ronaldinho	Drogba	Gerrard	Solomon Grimes	Ronaldinho	Eto'o	Drogba
LBY	Abubaker Bani	Eto'o	Drogba	Henry	Tareq Eltayib	Eto'o	Ronaldinho	Gerrard
LIB	Adnan Mekdache	Zidane	Cannavaro	Ribery	Ahmad Naamani	Ronaldinho	Ballack	Buffon
LIE	Martin Andermatt	Kaká	Eto'o	Thuram	Daniel Hasler	Zidane	Eto'o	Cannavaro
LTU	Algimantas Liubinskas	Henry	Zidane	Cannavaro	Tomas Danielevicius	Henry	Cannavaro	Cech
LVA	Jurijs Andrejevs	Zidane	Pirlo	Eto'o	Vitalijs Astafjevs	Zidane	Eto'o	Ronaldinho
MAD	Jean François Dhebon	Cannavaro	Zidane	Drogba	Mamisoa Razafindrakoto	Cannavaro	Zidane	Drogba
MAR	Mhammed Fakhir	Ronaldinho	Lampard	Kaká	Talal Karkouri	Ballack	Eto'o	Henry
MAS	B. Sattananthan Nair	Cannavaro	Zidane	Pirlo	Mohd Kh. Shahabuddin	Rooney	Ronaldinho	Cannavaro
MDA	Anatolie Teslev	Cannavaro	Ronaldinho	Drogba	Rafu Rebeja	Cannavaro	Ronaldinho	Ballack
MDV	Iordan Stoykov	Drogba	Cannavaro	Henry	Assad Abdul Ghani	Gerrard	Cannavaro	Kaká
MEX	Guillermo Cantu Saenz	Pirlo	Henry	Essien	Edwin van der Sar	Cannavaro	Eto'o	Lehmann
MGL	Ishdorj Otgonbayar	Ronaldinho	Cannavaro	Henry	no vote	none	none	none
MKD	Srecko Katanec	Eto'o	Cannavaro	Henry	Lunbengaraw Donrov	Cannavaro	Ronaldinho	Zidane
MLI	Jean François Jodar	Henry	Zidane	Eto'o	Goce Seploski	Eto'o	Ronaldinho	Rooney
MLT	Dusan Fitzel	Pirlo	Henry	Eto'o	Bassala Toure	Drogba	Eto'o	Henry
MOZ	Artur Semedo	Ronaldinho	Henry	Eto'o	Gilbert Agius	Cannavaro	Zidane	Pirlo
MRI	Sarjoo Gowreesunkur	Cannavaro	Buffon	Ribery	Manuel Bucuane	Ronaldinho	Henry	Eto'o
MTN	Moustapha Sall	Ronaldinho	Zidane	Cannavaro	Cyril Mourgine	Eto'o	Drogba	Cannavaro
MYA	Sann Win	Cannavaro	Zidane	Henry	Ahmed S.	Ronaldinho	Zidane	Cannavaro
NCA	Carlos de Toro	Ronaldinho	Riquelme	Eto'o	Soe Myat Min	Cannavaro	Pirlo	Henry
NCL	Didier Chambarom	Zidane	Henry	Buffon	Carlos R. Alonso	Henry	Ronaldinho	Lampard
NED	Marco van Basten	Ronaldinho	Henry	Cannavaro	no vote	none	none	none
NGA	Augustine Eguavoen	Cannavaro	Buffon	Drogba	Nwankwo Kanu	Eto'o	Henry	Drogba
NIG	Tchanile Bannh	Ronaldinho	Zidane	Eto'o	Laminon Rabo	Eto'o	invalid vote	invalid vote
NIR	Lawrie Sanchez	Cannavaro	Henry	Klose	Aaron Hughes	Ronaldinho	Cannavaro	Eto'o
NOR	Aage Hareide	Cannavaro	Zidane	Buffon	Martin Andersen	Cannavaro	Henry	Zidane
NZL	Ricki Herbert	Cannavaro	Kaká	Eto'o	Danny Hay	Henry	C. Ronaldo	Zidane
OMA	Milan Macala	Ronaldinho	Henry	Cech	no vote	none	none	none
PAN	Alexandre Guimaraes	Ronaldinho	Pirlo	Thuram	no vote	none	none	none
PAR	Raul Amarilla	Cannavaro	Kaká	Deco	Carlos Alberto Gamarra	Cannavaro	Ronaldinho	Kaká
PER	Franco Navarro	Kaká	Zidane	Pirlo	Leao Butron	Ronaldinho	Zidane	Kaká
PHI	José Arsiton Caslib	Zidane	Cannavaro	Lehmann	Louiz Michael Casas	Zidane	Cannavaro	Lehmann
PLE	Mohamad Alsabah	Zidane	Eto'o	Buffon	Jendeya Saeb	Zidane	Eto'o	Thuram
POL	Leo Beenhakker	Zidane	Henry	Kaká	Maciej Zurawski	Ronaldinho	Henry	Zidane
POR	Luiz Felipe Scolari	Henry	Cannavaro	Kaká	Francisco da Costa	Henry	Kaká	Eto'o
PUR	Garabet Demirdjan	Eto'o	Henry	Ballack	José Sandoval	Zidane	Luis Figo	Gattuso
QAT	Dzemaludin Musovic	Cannavaro	Henry	Pirlo	no vote	none	none	none
ROU	Victor Piturca	C. Ronaldo	Kaká	Ronaldinho	Christian Chivu	Kaká	C. Ronaldo	Deco
RSA	Pitso Mosimane	Ronaldinho	Henry	Eto'o	Aaron Mokoena	Cannavaro	Drogba	Eto'o
RUS	Guus Hiddink	Zidane	Buffon	Lahm	Evgeniy Aldonin	Zidane	Ronaldinho	Drogba
RWA	Michael Nees	Ballack	Henry	Ronaldinho	Jimmy Gatele	Henry	Ballack	Cannavaro
SCO	Walter Smith	Cannavaro	Henry	Gattuso	Barry Ferguson	Buffon	Henry	Gattuso
SEN	Henri Kasperzack	Ronaldinho	Henry	Drogba	El-Hadji Diouf	Eto'o	Ronaldinho	Cannavaro
SEY	Raoul Shongu	Henry	Drogba	Eto'o	Denis Barbe	Henry	Kaká	Cannavaro
SIN	Radojko Avramovic	Henry	Pirlo	Cannavaro	Iskandar Bin Sahak	Cannavaro	Buffon	Zidane

FIFA WORLD PLAYER 2006 – HOW THEY VOTED

	Coach	1st	2nd	3rd	Captain	1st	2nd	3rd
SKN	Leonard Taylor	Drogba	Ronaldinho	Henry	Francis Devon	Ronaldinho	Cannavaro	Henry
SLV	Mauricio Alberto Alfaro	Cannavaro	Ribery	Zidane	Dennis Alas Morales	Henry	Kaká	Zidane
SMR	Giampaolo Mazza	Cannavaro	Buffon	Klose	Andy Selva	Buffon	Gattuso	Cannavaro
SOM	Abdi Farah Ali	Cannavaro	Eto'o	Zidane	Abdulkadir Omar Ibrahim	Cannavaro	Eto'o	Kaká
SRB	Javier Clemente	Cannavaro	Ribery	Deco	Dejan Stankovic	Buffon	Ronaldinho	Lampard
SRI	Jang Jung	Cannavaro	Klose	Zidane	S. Devinda	C. Ronaldo	Shevchenko	Adriano
STP	Juvenal Correia	Eto'o	Ronaldinho	Lampard	Denilson	Deco	Eto'o	Cannavaro
SUD	Ahmed Babiker Elfaki	Ronaldinho	Buffon	Henry	Hiatham Mustafa Karar	Ronaldinho	Buffon	Eto'o
SUI	Jakob Kuhn	Cannavaro	Ronaldinho	Buffon	Johann Vogel	Eto'o	Ronaldinho	Henry
SUR	Kenneth Jaliens	Pirlo	Buffon	Zidane	Clifton Sandvliet	Zidane	Cannavaro	Kaká
SVK	Dusan Galis	Cannavaro	Zidane	Drogba	Miroslav Karhan	Ronaldinho	Cannavaro	Henry
SVN	Branko Oblak	Buffon	Cannavaro	Zidane	Milenko Acimovic	Ronaldinho	Pirlo	Buffon
SWE	Lars Lagerbäck	Henry	Klose	Cannavaro	Frederik Ljungberg	Cannavaro	Henry	Gerrard
SWZ	Ayman Mohamed	Zidane	Henry	Ribery	Dennis Masina	Zidane	Cannavaro	Ronaldinho
SYR	Fajer Ebraheem	Ronaldinho	Kaká	Ballack	Maher Al Sayed	Ronaldinho	Kaká	Ballack
TAH	Eddy Etaeta	Henry	Cannavaro	Buffon	Naea Bennett	Henry	Zidane	Cannavaro
TAN	Marcio Maximo	Kaká	Gerrard	Henry	Meck Maxime	Gerrard	Ronaldinho	Henry
TCA	Charlie Cook	Cannavaro	C. Ronaldo	Pirlo	Anthony Dennis	C. Ronaldo	Cannavaro	Zidane
TGA	Kilifi Ulele	Henry	Ronaldinho	Gerrard	Kamaliele Papani	Gerrard	Ballack	Drogba
THA	Chanvit Phalajivin	Cannavaro	Zidane	Ballack	Datsakorn Thonglao	Cannavaro	Zidane	Ballack
TJK	Makhmadion Khabibulloev	Zidane	Luis Figo	Ballack	Asliddin Khabibulloev	Zidane	Luis Figo	Ballack
TKM	Rahim Kurbanmamedov	Zidane	Gerrard	Kaká	Begench Kuliyev	Zidane	Gerrard	Kaká
TOG	Kodjovi Mawuena	Zidane	C. Ronaldo	Gerrard	Dosseh Yaovi Abalo	Drogba	Henry	Essien
TPE	Toshiaki Imai	Zidane	Cannavaro	Klose	Yung Jen Cheng	Zidane	Luis Figo	Klose
TRI	Anton Corneal	Zidane	Ballack	Deco	Dwight Yorke	Zidane	Ballack	Deco
TUN	Roger Lemerre	Eto'o	Henry	Drogba	Khaled Badra	Eto'o	Henry	Drogba
TUR	Fatih Terim	Kaká	Gattuso	Eto'o	Hakan Sükür	Nesta	Drogba	Buffon
UGA	Laszlo Csaba	Drogba	Zidane	Ballack	Hanington Kalyesubula	Gerrard	Ronaldinho	Kaká
UKR	Oleg Blokhin	Buffon	Eto'o	Cannavaro	Shevchenko	Zidane	Pirlo	Buffon
URU	Oscar Washington Tabarez	Cannavaro	Ronaldinho	Drogba	Diego Lugano	Ronaldinho	Henry	Drogba
USA	Bruce Arena	Ronaldinho	Cannavaro	Henry	Claudio Reyna	Ronaldinho	Pirlo	Deco
UZB	Valeriy Nepomnyaschiy	Zidane	Cannavaro	Eto'o	Andrey Fyodorov	Zidane	Cannavaro	Henry
VEN	Richard Paèz	Zidane	Buffon	Cannavaro	Oswaldo Vizcarrondo	Cannavaro	Zidane	Ronaldinho
VGB	Avondale Williams	Gerrard	Henry	Cannavaro	Joel Fahie	Henry	Rooney	Gerrard
VIE	Alfred Riedl	Zidane	Henry	Ronaldinho	Nguyem Minh Phuong	Zidane	Pirlo	Klose
WAL	John Toshack	Buffon	Henry	Eto'o	no vote	none	none	none
ZAM	Patrick Phiri	C. Ronaldo	Ronaldinho	Rooney	Clive Hachilensa	Drogba	Eto'o	Henry

FIFA WOMEN'S WORLD PLAYER 2006 – HOW THEY VOTED

	Coach	1st	2nd	3rd	Captain	1st	2nd	3rd
ALG	Azeddine Chih	Uwak	Lingor	Lilly	Naïma Laduadi	Uwak	Lingor	Lilly
ANG	André Nzuzi	Marta	Lingor	Lilly	Lidia Lubano	Lingor	Marta	Lilly
ARG	José Carlos Borrello	Marta	Lingor	Lilly	Marisa Isabel Gerez	Marta	Rottenberg	Stensland
ARM	Mher Mikayelyan	Lingor	Marta	Georges	Gayane Konstanyan	Lingor	Marta	Georges
ARU	Gregory Engelbrecht	Ma Xiaoxu	Ocampo	Lilly	Jouraine Maduro	Ma Xiaoxu	Ocampo	Lilly
ATG	Chesley Browne	Schelin	Smith	Ocampo	O'deal Simon	Schelin	Smith	Ocampo
AUS	Tom Sermanni	Wambach	Marta	Smith	Cheryl Salisbury	Moström	Wambach	Marta
AUT	Ernst Weber	Smith	Lingor	Marta	Sonja Spieler	Lilly	Smith	Lingor
AZE	Shamil Heydarov	Marta	Moström	Soubeyrand	Kifayat Osmanova	Marta	Moström	Soubeyrand
BAH	Matthew Green	Smith	Marta	Sinclair	Talitha Wood	Marta	Uwak	Ma Xiaoxu
BAN	Mosharraf Badal	Lilly	Schelin	Ma Xiaoxu	Dalia Akter	Lilly	Stensland	Han Duan

FIFA WOMEN'S WORLD PLAYER 2006 – HOW THEY VOTED

	Coach	1st	2nd	3rd	Captain	1st	2nd	3rd
BER	Vance Brown	Marta	Wambach	Lilly	Naquita Dill	Lilly	Marta	Uwak
BHR	Hans-Peter Briegel	Wambach	Moström	Sinclair	Marwa Mohamed	Wambach	Moström	Sinclair
BIH	Devad Bekic	Schelin	Stensland	Lingor	Sabina Pehic	Marta	Lilly	Rottenberg
BLR	Oleg Volakh	Rottenberg	Schelin	Marta	Natalia Ryzhevich	Rottenberg	Marta	Moström
BOL	Nelfi Ibañez Guerra	Marta	Lilly	Lingor	Juana Mendez Barja	Marta	Lilly	Lingor
BRA	Jorge Luiz Barcellos	Ma Xiaoxu	Uwak	Ocampo	Aline Pellegrino	Ma Xiaoxu	Uwak	Ocampo
BUL	Emil Atanasov	Lingor	Smith	Rottenberg	Deyana Petrakieva	Moström	Lingor	Smith
CAN	Even Pellerud	Schelin	Lilly	Marta	Christine Sinclair	Lilly	Moström	Smith
CAY	Thiago da Cunha	Marta	Ma Xiaoxu	Smith	Judy Rivers	Lingor	Marta	Smith
CGO	Noël Tosi	Lilly	Wambach	Georges	Malouga	Soubeyrand	Lilly	Wambach
CHA	Charlotte Djimdin	Stensland	Marta	Uwak	Gisele Ali Dabou	Marta	Georges	Stensland
CHI	Manuel Rodriguez	Marta	Rottenberg	Stensland	Belen Gaete	Marta	Sinclair	Lilly
CHN	Ma Liangxing	Wambach	Marta	Lilly	Pu Wei	Lilly	Rottenberg	Smith
COK	Alex Napa	Marta	Lingor	Salisbury	Mii Piri	Marta	Sinclair	Ri Kum Suk
COL	Jhon Agudelo	Han Duan	Lilly	Marta	Carmen Rodallega	Lilly	Ma Xiaoxu	Marta
CRC	Allan Brown	Marta	Moström	Lilly	Monica Salazar Carrillo	Marta	Lilly	Wambach
CRO	Damir Ruhek	Lilly	Kalmari	Lingor	Marina Koljenik	Kalmari	Rottenberg	Wambach
CTA	François Yanguere	Lingor	Han Duan	Lilly	Jeannette Imindji	Lilly	Marta	Han Duan
CUB	Rufino Sotolongo Reyes	Rottenberg	Marta	Lilly	Yohania Ocampo	Rottenberg	Marta	Lilly
CZE	Dusan Zovinec	Marta	Moström	Smith	Eva Smeralova	Moström	Marta	Smith
DEN	Kenneth Heiner-Moeller	Smith	Marta	Lingor	Katrine Pedersen	Marta	Smith	Stensland
DJI	Ahmed Said	Marta	Wambach	Sörensen	Fathia Ali	Marta	Rottenberg	Soubeyrand
DOM	José Luis Elejalde	Lilly	Ocampo	Marta	Leonela Mojica G.	Lilly	Ocampo	Marta
ECU	Garys Casquete	Marta	Stensland	Ma Xiaoxu	Paola Bermudes	Marta	Lilly	Ma Xiaoxu
EGY	Mohamed Saad	Smith	Lilly	Marta	Marwa Ibrahim	Smith	Lilly	Marta
ENG	Hope Powell	Lingor	Moström	Rottenberg	Faye White	Lingor	Moström	Wambach
EQG	Sebastian Enga	Uwak	Lingor	Soubeyrand	Genoveva Añon Man	Uwak	Soubeyrand	Lingor
ERI	Mosazghi Ghezehey	Lilly	Rottenberg	Marta	Merhawit Tekeste	Lingor	Lilly	Marta
ESP	Ignacio Quereda Laviña	Lingor	Sörensen	Lilly	Maider Castillo	Moström	Sörensen	Lingor
EST	Jori Saar	Lingor	Han Duan	Moström	Elis Meetua	Stensland	Lilly	Ma Xiaoxu
ETH	Beletish G/Mariam	Marta	Uwak	Han Duan	Rahel Degeegen	Marta	Uwak	Han Duan
FRA	Elisabeth Loisel	Lilly	Rottenberg	Han Duan	Sonia Bompastor	Wambach	Marta	Lilly
FRO	Alvur Hansen	Stensland	Marta	Wambach	Bara Skaale Klakstein	Marta	Smith	Soubeyrand
GEO	Maia Japaridze	Lingor	Smith	Lilly	Salome Khubuluri	Georges	Han Duan	Soubeyrand
GER	Silvia Neid	Lilly	Stensland	Smith	Birgit Prinz	Lilly	Stensland	Wambach
GHA	Isaac Paha	Lingor	none	none	Grace Adjoa Bayor	none	none	none
GRE	Dimitrios Batsilas	Lilly	Marta	Wambach	Eftichia Michailidou	Marta	Lingor	Schelin
GRN	Dean Jules	Wambach	Marta	Sinclair	Delis Peters	Wambach	Marta	Sinclair
GUA	Antonio Garcia Gamboa	Marta	Lilly	Moström	no vote	none	none	none
GUI	Camara Fabert	Marta	Lilly	Rottenberg	Christine Guilavogui	Lilly	Marta	Georges
GUM	Kim Sang Hoon	Lilly	Wambach	Rottenberg	Cheri Stewart	Lilly	Wambach	Rottenberg
HKG	Chu Chi Kwong Alex	Han Duan	Wambach	Sinclair	Ho Wing Kam	Wambach	Han Duan	Sinclair
HUN	Andras Telek	Smith	Wambach	Soubeyrand	Aranka Paraoanu	Smith	Lilly	Wambach
IDN	Muhardi	Lingor	Lilly	Marta	Yakomina Swabra	Lingor	Marta	Lilly
IRL	Noel King	Wambach	Lingor	Smith	Ciara Grant	Wambach	Smith	Lingor
IRN	Shahrzad Mozafar	Lilly	Uwak	Soubeyrand	Masoumeh Jahanchi	Lingor	Wambach	Uwak
ISL	Jorundur Aki Sveinsson	Lingor	Smith	Schelin	Asthildur Helgadottir	Lingor	Smith	Stensland
ITA	Pietro Ghedin	Lingor	Sinclair	Stensland	Patrizia Panico	Stensland	Rottenberg	Marta
JAM	Vin Blaine	Wambach	Lilly	Sinclair	Nicola Bell	Smith	Wambach	Marta
JOR	Issa Al-Turk	Ri Kum Suk	Ma Xiaoxu	Han Duan	no vote	none	none	none
JPN	Hiroshi Ohashi	Lilly	Wambach	Salisbury	Hiromi Isozaki	Wambach	Ri Kum Suk	Salisbury
KAZ	Vladimir Scherbakov	Schelin	Marta	Georges	Natalya Ivanova	Smith	Lingor	Marta
KGZ	Gulbara Umatalieva	Ri Kum Suk	Han Duan	Ma Xiaoxu	Svetlana Pokachalova	Han Duan	Ri Kum Suk	Schelin
KOR	An Jong Goan	Ri Kum Suk	Ma Xiaoxu	Salisbury	Jim Suk Hee	Ri Kum Suk	Ma Xiaoxu	Salisbury
LAO	Viensavanh Sengchanh	Rottenberg	Ma Xiaoxu	Marta	no vote	none	none	none
LIB	Vatche Sarkissian	Lilly	Lingor	Han Duan	Stephany Zein	Wambach	Moström	Rottenberg
LTU	Rimas Viktoravicius	Soubeyrand	Schelin	Lingor	Justina Lavrenovaite	Schelin	Marta	Kalmari
LUX	Jean Romain	Lingor	Marta	Stensland	Joelle Leuchter	Marta	Smith	Schelin
LVA	Agris Bandolis	Rottenberg	Ri Kum Suk	Ma Xiaoxu	Diana Vanaga	Schelin	Marta	Rottenberg
MAD	Herihaja Andriatianasasoa	Rottenberg	Lilly	Georges	Rasoarimalala	Rottenberg	Lilly	Georges
MAR	Alaoui Slimani	Lilly	Lingor	Wambach	Bomahdi Lamiae	Georges	Sinclair	Lilly
MAS	Ibrahim Mohamad	Ma Xiaoxu	Moström	Rottenberg	Angela Anak Kais	Lilly	Ma Xiaoxu	Georges
MDZ	Evghenii Pusicov	Georges	Marta	Smith	Ludmila Ninicu	Lingor	Moström	Lilly
MDV	Mohamed Athif	Lingor	Rottenberg	Schelin	Mariyam Mirfath	Lingor	Schelin	Rottenberg

FIFA WOMEN'S WORLD PLAYER 2006 – HOW THEY VOTED

	Coach	1st	2nd	3rd	Captain	1st	2nd	3rd
MEX	Leonardo Cuellar	Wambach	Lilly	Salisbury	Monica Vergara Rubio	Lilly	Marta	Wambach
MGL	Ishdorj Otgonbayar	Ri Kum Suk	Han Duan	Wambach	Baapyew	Ri Kum Suk	Han Duan	Wambach
MLI	Moriba Diallo	Rottenberg	Salisbury	Wambach	Diaty N'Daye	Schelin	Sörensen	Smith
MLT	Pierre Brincat	Marta	Schelin	Georges	Rebecca D'Agostino	Marta	Schelin	Georges
MOZ	Michel Chau	Han Duan	Ma Xiaoxu	Schelin	Sara Jacob Simonie	Ma Xiaoxu	Uwak	Rottenberg
MRI	Alain Dominique Jules	Marta	Sinclair	Lilly	Martine Kelly	Sinclair	Rottenberg	Wambach
MYA	U Aye Kyu	Marta	Ma Xiaoxu	Rottenberg	San San Maw	Lilly	Han Duan	Ri Kum Suk
NCA	Eduardo Lopez Campos	Lilly	Marta	Moström	Modesta Rojas	Lilly	Marta	Sinclair
NED	Vera Pauw	Smith	Lilly	Soubeyrand	Marleen Wissink	Smith	Soubeyrand	Stensland
NGA	Ntiero Effiom Ntiero	invalid vote	Lilly	Marta	Kikelomo Ajayi	invalid vote	Moström	Rottenberg
NIG	Amina Celine André	Schelin	Lilly	Rottenberg	Hauija Issa	Schelin	Rottenberg	Lilly
NIR	Alfie Wylie	Kalmari	Smith	Marta	Sara Booth	Lilly	Lingor	Smith
NOR	Bjarne Berntsen	Lingor	Lilly	Han Duan	Ane S. Horpestad	Marta	Lingor	Wambach
NZL	Allan Jones	Han Duan	Lilly	Salisbury	Maia Jackman	Han Duan	Lilly	Salisbury
PAN	Lizandro Borboron P.	Marta	Sinclair	Ocampo	no vote	none	none	none
PAR	Augustin Torres	Marta	Rottenberg	Ocampo	Noelia Barrios	Marta	Han Duan	Smith
PER	Lorena Pastrano	Marta	Lilly	Sinclair	Adriana Davila Soracco	Lingor	Marta	Ocampo
PHI	Marlon M. Maro	Lingor	Lilly	Ri Kum Suk	Marielle Benitez	Ri Kum Suk	Lingor	Lilly
PLE	Waleed Lulu	Han Duan	Lingor	Ri Kum Suk	Hane Thaljeya	Ma Xiaoxu	Rottenberg	Schelin
POL	Jan Stepczak	Marta	Rottenberg	Smith	Maria Makowska	Marta	Lingor	Smith
POR	José Augusto	Marta	Ocampo	Schelin	Paula Santos	Lilly	Lingor	Soubeyrand
PUR	Jorge Oscar Rosa	Wambach	Ma Xiaoxu	Ocampo	Maria E. Larracuente	Lilly	Wambach	Ocampo
ROU	Gheorghe Staicu	Lingor	Smith	Schelin	Daniela Pufulete	Moström	Lingor	Rottenberg
RSA	Augustine Makalakalane	Marta	Uwak	Sinclair	Portia Modise	Marta	Uwak	Lilly
RUS	Yuri Bystritskiy	Lingor	Han Duan	Smith	Elena Fomina	Marta	Georges	Rottenberg
RWA	Kyle Beard	Wambach	Marta	Uwak	Saaba Uzamukunda	Uwak	Wambach	Marta
SCO	Anna Signeul	Lingor	Marta	Smith	Julie Fleeting	Smith	Marta	Lilly
SEN	Diaby Bassouaré	Marta	Stensland	Schelin	Seyni Ndir Seck	Marta	Smith	Stensland
SEY	Elsie Erwesta	Marta	Lilly	Lingor	Natasha Bibi	Marta	Lingor	Lilly
SIN	Abdullah Noor	Ma Xiaoxu	Lilly	Salisbury	Noor Azean Adam	Lilly	Ma Xiaoxu	Han Duan
SKN	Leonard Taylor	Lilly	Marta	Wambach	Sishauna Stanley	Marta	Lilly	Soubeyrand
SLV	Carlos Felipe Cañadas	Lilly	Ma Xiaoxu	Ocampo	Cristina Elena Caceres	Lilly	Ma Xiaoxu	Rottenberg
SOM	Hussein Ali Abdule	Uwak	Marta	Han Duan	Halima Ali	Uwak	Marta	Lingor
SRB	Perica Krstic	Moström	Marta	Kalmari	Suzana Stanojevic	Moström	Marta	Kalmari
SRI	R. M. U. Mahindapala	Han Duan	Lingor	Smith	Shanika Rajapaksha	Han Duan	Lingor	Smith
STP	Osvaldo Costa de Deus	Marta	Uwak	Georges	Jargima Vaz da Veiga	Marta	Lilly	Uwak
SUI	Béatrice von Siebenthal	Smith	Moström	Lingor	Prisca Steinegger	Lingor	Smith	Ma Xiaoxu
SUR	Arno Berrenstein	Ocampo	Lilly	Sinclair	Jennifer Buyne	Lilly	Wambach	Sörensen
SVK	Frantisek Urvay	Georges	Han Duan	Marta	Monika Matysova	Kalmari	Georges	Han Duan
SVN	Zoran Cirkvencic	Wambach	Rottenberg	Stensland	Karmen Vais	Wambach	Rottenberg	Stensland
SWE	Thomas Dennerb	Marta	Lilly	Rottenberg	Malin Moström	Marta	Han Duan	Smith
SWZ	Christian Twala	Lingor	Lilly	Ma Xiaoxu	Xolile Nxumalo	Lilly	Wambach	Uwak
SYR	Abdul Ghani Tateesh	Lingor	Ma Xiaoxu	Sinclair	Hayat Seria	Lingor	Ma Xiaoxu	Sinclair
TAH	Ralph Apuarii	Lilly	Lingor	Soubeyrand	Mimosa Marmouyet	Lilly	Lingor	Rottenberg
TCA	Charlie Cook	Smith	Rottenberg	Wambach	Sonia Bien-Aime	Wambach	Smith	Lilly
TGA	Kilfi Vele	Marta	Lilly	Rottenberg	Adelaide Tuivailala	Marta	Lilly	Sinclair
THA	Chana Yodprang	Lingor	Lilly	Stensland	Chidtawan Chawong	Lingor	Lilly	Stensland
TJK	Damir Kamelitdimov	Ri Kum Suk	Han Duan	Marta	Dilaphbuz	Lingor	Smith	Lilly
TKM	Mamedov Atamurad	Ri Kum Suk	Han Duan	Lingor	Gataulina Farida	Ri Kum Suk	Han Duan	Lingor
TOG	Sokpo Ubenyo	Marta	Lilly	Lingor	Yawo	Lingor	Han Duan	Marta
TPE	Chou Tai-Ying	Lilly	Marta	Han Duan	Yu Pei-Wen	Lilly	Marta	Han Duan
TRI	Jamaal Shabazz	Marta	Lilly	Ocampo	Jingue James	Wambach	Lilly	Smith
TUR	Hamdi Aslan	Rottenberg	Lilly	Han Duan	Bahar Özgüvenc	Wambach	Rottenberg	Moström
UGA	Laszlo Csaba	Rottenberg	Lingor	Wambach	Nantanda Majidah	Lilly	Stensland	Ri Kum Suk
UKR	Volodymyr Kulaev	Rottenberg	Ma Xiaoxu	Lingor	Olena Mazurenko	Rottenberg	Marta	Wambach
URU	Juan José Duarte	Lingor	Wambach	Marta	Carla Arrua	Marta	Ocampo	Schelin
USA	Greg Ryan	Han Duan	Lingor	Marta	Kristine Lilly	Moström	Lingor	Sinclair
UZE	Abdurakhman	Marta	Soubeyrand	Lingor	Gulnara Azamova	Georges	Han Duan	Lilly
VEN	Milaoro Infant	Lilly	Smith	Marta	Laury Marquez	Marta	Lingor	Han Duan
VGB	Wendol Williams	Smith	Lingor	Wambach	Cassandra Gregg	Wambach	Smith	Lilly
VIE	Tran Ngoc Thai Tuan	Rottenberg	Lilly	Ma Xiaoxu	Doan Thi Kim Chi	Rottenberg	Lilly	Ma Xiaoxu
VIR	Yohannes Worede	Marta	Smith	Wambach	Elizabeth C. Ferguson	Rottenberg	Schelin	Wambach
WAL	Andrew Beattie	Marta	Lilly	Lingor	Jayne Ludlow	Lingor	Kalmari	Wambach
ZAM	George Chikokola	Uwak	Georges	Lingor	Gift Lisaka	Uwak	Marta	Wambach

PAST WINNERS OF THE FIFA WOMEN'S WORLD PLAYER AWARD

WOMEN'S WORLD PLAYER 2001

		Votes
HAMM Mia	USA	154
SUN Wen	CHN	79
MILBRETT Tiffeny	USA	47
PRINZ Birgit	GER	40
FITSCHEN Doris	GER	37
SISSI	BRA	35
LJUNBERG Hanna	SWE	29
WIEGMANN Bettina	GER	17
RIISE Hege	NOR	16
MELLGREN Dagny	NOR	13

WOMEN'S WORLD PLAYER 2002

		Votes
HAMM Mia	USA	161
PRINZ Birgit	GER	96
SUN Wen	CHN	58
MILBRETT Tiffeny	USA	45
PICHON Marinette	FRA	42
SINCLAIR Christine	CAN	38
JONES Steffi	GER	19
RIISE Hege	NOR	17
SISSI	BRA	14
BAI Jie	CHN	13

WOMEN'S WORLD PLAYER 2003

		Votes
PRINZ Birgit	GER	268
HAMM Mia	USA	133
LJUNGBERG Hanna	SWE	84
SVENSSON Victoria	SWE	82
MEINERT Maren	GER	69
WIEGMANN Bettina	GER	49
MOSTROEM Malin	SWE	23
KATIA	BRA	14
LINGOR Renate	GER	14
MARTA	BRA	13

WOMEN'S WORLD PLAYER 2004

		Votes
PRINZ Birgit	GER	376
HAMM Mia	USA	286
MARTA	BRA	281
WAMBACH Abby	USA	126
LILLY Kristine	USA	109
LJUNGBERG Hanna	SWE	109
BOXX Shannon	USA	102
SVENSSON Victoria	SWE	89
LINGOR Renate	GER	89
CRISTIANE	BRA	80

WOMEN'S WORLD PLAYER 2005

		Votes
PRINZ Birgit	GER	513
MARTA	BRA	429
BOXX Shannon	USA	235
LJUNGBERG Hanna	SWE	206
LINGOR Renate	GER	170
DOMINGUEZ Maribel	MEX	115
GULBRANDSEN Solveig	NOR	97
MINNERT Sandra	GER	97
WELSH Christie	USA	78
SMITH Kelly	ENG	60

PAST WINNERS OF THE FIFA WORLD PLAYER AWARD

FIFA WORLD PLAYER 1991

		Votes
MATTHÄUS Lothar	GER	128
PAPIN Jean-Pierre	FRA	113
LINEKER Gary	ENG	40
PROSINECKI Robert	YUG	38
VAN BASTEN Marco	NED	23
BARESI Franco	ITA	12
ZAMORANO Ivan	CHI	10
BREHME Andreas	GER	9
VIALLI Gianluca	ITA	8
SCIFO Enzo	BEL	7

FIFA WORLD PLAYER 1992

		Votes
VAN BASTEN Marco	NED	151
STOICHKOV Hristo	BUL	88
HÄSSLER Thomas	GER	61
PAPIN Jean-Pierre	FRA	46
LAUDRUP Brian	DEN	44
SCHMEICHEL Peter	DEN	44
BERGKAMP Dennis	NED	29
RIJKAARD Frank	NED	23
PELE Abedi	GHA	10
BARESI Franco	ITA	10

FIFA WORLD PLAYER 1993

		Votes
VAN BASTEN Marco	NED	151
STOICHKOV Hristo	BUL	88
HÄSSLER Thomas	GER	61
PAPIN Jean-Pierre	FRA	46
LAUDRUP Brian	DEN	44
SCHMEICHEL Peter	DEN	44
BERGKAMP Dennis	NED	29
RIJKAARD Frank	NED	23
PELE Abedi	GHA	10
BARESI Franco	ITA	10

FIFA WORLD PLAYER 1994

		Votes
ROMARIO	BRA	346
STOICHKOV Hristo	BUL	100
BAGGIO Roberto	ITA	80
HAGI Georghe	ROU	50
MALDINI Paolo	ITA	40
BEBETO	BRA	16
BERGKAMP Dennis	NED	11
DUNGA Carlos	BRA	9
BARESI Franco	ITA	7
BROLIN Tomas	SWE	7

FIFA WORLD PLAYER 1995

		Votes
WEAH George	LBR	170
MALDINI Paolo	ITA	80
KLINSMANN Jürgen	GER	58
ROMARIO	BRA	50
BAGGIO Roberto	ITA	49
STOICHKOV Hristo	BUL	37
ZAMORANO Ivan	CHI	36
JUNINHO	BRA	28
SAMMER Matthias	GER	23
LAUDRUP Michael	DEN	20

FIFA WORLD PLAYER 1996

		Votes
RONALDO	BRA	329
WEAH George	LBR	140
SHEARER Alan	ENG	123
SAMMER Matthias	GER	109
KLINSMANN Jürgen	GER	54
KANU Nwankwo	NGA	32
MALDINI Paolo	ITA	25
SUKER Davor	CRO	24
BATISTUTA Gabriel	ARG	19
ROMARIO	BRA	13

FIFA WORLD PLAYER 1997

		Votes
RONALDO	BRA	480
ROBERTO CARLOS	BRA	65
BERGKAMP Dennis	NED	62
ZIDANE Zinedine	FRA	62
RAÚL	ESP	51
DEL PIERO Alessandro	ITA	27
SUKER Davor	CRO	20
BATISTUTA Gabriel	ARG	16
SHEARER Alan	ENG	16
LEONARDO	BRA	14

FIFA WORLD PLAYER 1998

		Votes
ZIDANE Zinedine	FRA	518
RONALDO	BRA	164
SUKER Davor	CRO	108
OWEN Michael	ENG	43
BATISTUTA Gabriel	ARG	40
RIVALDO	BRA	37
BERGKAMP Dennis	NED	33
DAVIDS Edgar	NED	26
DESAILLY Marcel	FRA	23
THURAM Lillian	FRA	14

FIFA WORLD PLAYER 1999

		Votes
RIVALDO	BRA	538
BECKHAM David	ENG	194
BATISTUTA Gabriel	ARG	79
ZIDANE Zinedine	FRA	68
VIERI Christian	ITA	39
FIGO Luis	POR	35
SHEVCHENKO Andriy	UKR	34
RAÚL	ESP	31
COLE Andy	ENG	24
YORKE Dwight	TRI	19

FIFA WORLD PLAYER 2000

		Votes
ZIDANE Zinedine	FRA	370
FIGO Luis	POR	329
RIVALDO	BRA	263
BATISTUTA Gabriel	ARG	57
SHEVCHENKO Andriy	UKR	48
BECKHAM David	ENG	41
HENRY Thierry	FRA	35
NESTA Alessandro	ITA	23
KLUIVERT Patrick	NED	22
TOTTI Francesco	ITA	14

FIFA WORLD PLAYER 2001

		Votes
FIGO Luis	POR	250
BECKHAM David	ENG	238
RAÚL	ESP	96
ZIDANE Zinedine	FRA	94
RIVALDO	BRA	92
VERON Juan Sebastian	ARG	71
KAHN Oliver	GER	65
OWEN Michael	ENG	61
SHEVCHENKO Andriy	UKR	46
TOTTI Francesco	ITA	40

FIFA WORLD PLAYER 2002

		Votes
RONALDO	BRA	387
KAHN Oliver	GER	171
ZIDANE Zinedine	FRA	148
ROBERTO CARLOS	BRA	114
RIVALDO	BRA	92
RAÚL	ESP	90
BALLACK Michael	GER	82
BECKHAM David	ENG	51
HENRY Thierry	FRA	38
OWEN Michael	ENG	34

FIFA WORLD PLAYER 2003

		Votes
ZIDANE Zinedine	FRA	264
HENRY Thierry	FRA	186
RONALDO	BRA	176
NEDVED Pavel	CZE	158
ROBERTO CARLOS	BRA	105
VAN NISTELROOY Ruud	NED	86
BECKHAM David	ENG	74
RAÚL	ESP	39
MALDINI Paolo	ITA	37
SHEVCHENKO Andriy	UKR	26

FIFA WORLD PLAYER 2004

		Votes
RONALDINHO	BRA	620
HENRY Thierry	FRA	552
SHEVCHENKO Andriy	UKR	253
NEDVED Pavel	CZE	178
ZIDANE Zinedine	FRA	150
ADRIANO	BRA	98
DECO	POR	96
RONALDO	BRA	96
VAN NISTELROOY Ruud	NED	67
KAKA & ROONEY Wayne		64

FIFA WORLD PLAYER 2005

		Votes
RONALDINHO	BRA	956
LAMPARD Frank	ENG	306
ETO'O Samuel	CMR	190
HENRY Thierry	FRA	172
ADRIANO	BRA	170
SHEVCHENKO Andriy	UKR	153
GERRARD Steven	ENG	131
KAKA	BRA	101
MALDINI Paolo	ITA	76
DROGBA Didier	CIV	65

RECORDS OF THE 30 PLAYERS SELECTED FOR THE 2006 AWARD

1 - FABIO CANNAVARO

13-09-1973 Naples, ITA (1.76/75)

	League			Europe			ITA	
92-93 Napoli	2	0	SA	11				
93-94 Napoli	27	0	SA	6				
94-95 Napoli	29	1	SA	7	3	0	UC r3	
95-96 Parma	29	1	SA	6	6	0	CC qf	
96-97 Parma	27	0	SA	2	0	UC r1	8	0
97-98 Parma	31	0	SA	6	7	0	CL gA	11	0
98-99 Parma	30	1	SA	4	8	0	UC W	9	0
99-00 Parma	31	2	SA	5	9	1	C/U r4	13	0
00-01 Parma	33	0	SA	4	6	0	UC r4	9	0
01-02 Parma	31	1	SA	10	9	0	C/U r4	11	0
02-03 Internazionale	28	0	SA	2	12	1	CL sf	9	0
03-04 Internazionale	22	2	SA	4	9	0	C/U qf	10	1
04-05 Juventus	38	2	SA	1	9	1	CL qf	5	0
05-06 Juventus	36	4	SA	3	9	0	CL qf	15	0
06-07 Real Madrid	32	0	PD	1	6	0	CL r2	8	0

Honours: WC 2006; UC 1999, Lge 2005 2006 (both withdrawn), Cup 1999 2002
Italy debut: 22-01-1997 v NIR • 108 caps • 1 goal

2 - ZINEDINE ZIDANE

23-06-1972 Marseille, FRA (1.85/78)

	League			Europe			FRA	
88-89 Cannes	2	0	L1	12				
89-90 Cannes	0	0	L1	11				
90-91 Cannes	28	1	L1	4				
91-92 Cannes	31	5	L1	19	4	0	UC r3	
92-93 Bordeaux	35	10	L1	4				
93-94 Bordeaux	34	6	L1	4	6	2	UC r3	
94-95 Bordeaux	37	6	L1	7	4	1	UC r2	3	2
95-96 Bordeaux	33	6	L1	16	10	1	UC F	14	3
96-97 Juventus	29	5	SA	1	13	2	CL F	9	1
97-98 Juventus	32	7	SA	1	11	3	CL F	13	5
98-99 Juventus	25	2	SA	6	10	0	CL sf	6	0
99-00 Juventus	32	4	SA	2	10	0	U/C r4	14	5
00-01 Juventus	33	6	SA	2	4	0	CL gE	7	2
01-02 Real Madrid	31	7	PD	3	9	3	CL W	9	1
02-03 Real Madrid	33	9	PD	1	14	3	CL sf	7	3
03-04 Real Madrid	33	7	PD	4	10	3	CL qf	11	4
04-05 Real Madrid	29	6	PD	2	10	0	CL r2		
05-06 Real Madrid	29	9	PD	2	4	0	CL r2	15	5

Honours: WC 1998; EC 2000; CL 2002, Lge 1997 1998 2003
France debut: 17-08-1994 v CZE • 108 caps • 31 goals

3 - RONALDINHO

21-03-1980 Porto Alegre, BRA (1.80/76)

Season	Club	League				Sth Am/Europe				BRA	
1998	Grêmio	14	1	SA	8	10	1	CL	qf		
1999	Grêmio	17	5	SA	18	5	2	MS	gE	10	7
2000	Grêmio	11	8	SA	10	4	1	MS	gB	7	1
2001	Grêmio	0	0	SA	5					4	1
01-02	PSG	28	9	L1	4	6	2	UC	r3	9	3
02-03	PSG	27	8	L1	11	4	1	UC	r3	9	2
03-04	Barcelona	32	15	PD	2	7	4	UC	r4	5	2
04-05	Barcelona	35	9	PD	1	7	4	CL	r2	16	11
05-06	Barcelona	29	19	PD	1	17	8	CL	W	8	0
06-07	Barcelona	32	21	PD	2	8	2	CL	r2	7	2

Honours: WC 2002, CA 1999, CC 2005; CL 2006 Lge 2005 2006, Cup 2001; Brazil debut: 26-06-1999 v LVA • 75 caps • 29 goals

5 - SAMUEL ETO'O

10-03-1981 Nkon, CMR (1.80/75)

Season	Club	League				Europe				CMR	
97-98	Leganés	28	3	D2	13						
98-99	Real Madrid	1	0	PD	-						
98-99	Espanyol	0	0	PD	7						
99-00	Real Madrid	2	0	PD	-	3	0	CL	W		
99-00	Mallorca	13	6	PD	10						
00-01	Mallorca	28	11	PD	3						
01-02	Mallorca	30	6	PD	16	9	3	C/U	r3		
02-03	Mallorca	30	14	PD	9						
03-04	Mallorca	32	17	PD	11	7	4	UC	r4		
04-05	Barcelona	37	24	PD	1	7	4	CL	r2		
05-06	Barcelona	34	27	PD	1	11	6	CL	W	Total	
06-07	Barcelona	19	11	PD	2	3	1	CL	r2	69	25

Honours: CN 2000 2002, Olympic Gold 2000; Lge 2005 2006, Cup 2003 • Cameroon debut: 9-08-1997 v ZAM

7 - KAKA

22-04-1982 Brasilia, BRA (1.83/73)

Season	Club	League				Europe				BRA	
2001	São Paulo	26	12	SA	qf						
2002	São Paulo	20	8	SA	qf					4	1
2003	São Paulo	10	2	SA	-					1	0
03-04	Milan	30	10	SA	1	10	2	CL	qf	11	3
04-05	Milan	36	7	SA	2	8	2	CL	F	11	4
05-06	Milan	35	14	SA	2	12	5	CL	sf	16	4
06-07	Milan	31	8	SA	4	14	10	CL	W	9	4

Honours: WC 2002, CC 2005; CL 2007, Lge 2004
Brazil debut: 31-01-2002 v BOL • 52 caps • 16 goals

9 - ANDREA PIRLO

19-05-1979 Brescia, ITA (1.77/68)

Season	Club	League				Europe				ITA	
94-95	Brescia	1	0	SA	18						
95-96	Brescia	0	0	SB	16						
96-97	Brescia	17	2	SB	1						
97-98	Brescia	29	4	SA	15						
98-99	Internazionale	18	0	SA	8	7	0	CL	qf		
99-00	Reggina	28	6	SA	12						
00-01	Internazionale	4	0	SA	-	3	0	UC	r2		
00-01	Brescia	10	0	SA	8						
01-02	Milan	18	2	SA	4	9	0	UC	sf		
02-03	Milan	27	9	SA	3	13	0	CL	W	4	0
03-04	Milan	32	6	SA	1	11	1	CL	qf	7	1
04-05	Milan	30	4	SA	2	12	1	CL	F	4	2
05-06	Milan	33	4	SA	3	12	1	CL	sf	16	2
06-07	Milan	34	2	SA	4	13	1	CL	W	7	0

Honours: WC 2006; CL 2003, Lge 2004, Cup 2003
Italy debut: 7-09-2002 v AZE • 38 caps • 5 goals

4 - THIERRY HENRY

17-08-1977 Paris, FRA (1.87/81)

Season	Club	League				Europe				FRA	
94-95	Monaco	8	3	L1	6						
95-96	Monaco	18	3	L1	3	1	0	UC	r1		
96-97	Monaco	36	9	L1	1	9	1	UC	sf		
97-98	Monaco	30	4	L1	3	9	7	CL	sf	9	3
98-99	Juventus	13	1	L1	-	5	0	UC	r3		
98-99	Arsenal	16	3	SA	6					2	0
99-00	Arsenal	31	17	PL	2	12	8	C/U	F	10	5
00-01	Arsenal	35	17	PL	2	14	4	CL	qf	8	2
01-02	Arsenal	33	24	PL	1	11	7	CL	r2	9	2
02-03	Arsenal	37	24	PL	2	12	7	CL	r2	13	10
03-04	Arsenal	37	30	PL	1	10	5	CL	qf	12	5
04-05	Arsenal	32	25	PL	2	8	5	CL	r2	7	1
05-06	Arsenal	32	27	PL	4	11	5	CL	F	15	8
06-07	Arsenal	17	10	PL	4	7	1	CL	r2	7	4

Honours: WC 1998, EC 2000, CC 2003; Lge 1997 2002 2004, Cup 2002 2003 • France debut: 11-10-1997 v RSA • 92 caps • 40 goals

6 - DIDIER DROGBA

11-03-1978 Abidjan, CIV (1.83/86)

Season	Club	League				Europe				CIV	
98-99	Le Mans	2	0	D2	17						
99-00	Le Mans	30	6	D2	8						
00-01	Le Mans	11	0	D2	14						
01-02	Le Mans	21	5	D2	5						
01-02	Guingamp	11	3	L1	16						
02-03	Guingamp	34	17	L1	7						
03-04	Oly. Marseille	35	18	L1	7	10	6	C/U	F		
04-05	Chelsea	26	10	PL	1	9	5	CL	sf		
05-06	Chelsea	29	12	PL	1	7	1	CL	r2	Total	
06-07	Chelsea	36	20	PL	2	12	6	CL	sf	40	27

Honours: Lge 2005 2006, Cup 2007, LCup 2005 2007
Côte d'Ivoire debut: 8-09-2002 v RSA

8 - GIANLUIGI BUFFON

28-01-1978 Carrara, ITA (1.90/88)

Season	Club	League				Europe				ITA	
95-96	Parma	9	-	SA	5						
96-97	Parma	27	-	SA	2	1	-	UC	r1		
97-98	Parma	32	-	SA	6	8	-	CL	r1	2	-
98-99	Parma	34	-	SA	4	11	-	UC	W	7	-
99-00	Parma	32	-	SA	5	9	-	C/U	r4	6	-
00-01	Parma	34	-	SA	4	7	-	U	r4	5	-
01-02	Juventus	34	-	SA	1	10	-	CL	r2	10	-
02-03	Juventus	32	-	SA	1	15	-	CL	F	8	-
03-04	Juventus	32	-	SA	3	6	-	CL	r2	11	-
04-05	Juventus	37	-	SA		11	-	CL	qf	8	-
05-06	Juventus	18	-	SA		4	-	CL	qf	10	-
06-07	Juventus	37	-	SB	1					8	-

Honours: WC 2006; UC 1999, Lge 2002 2003 2005, Cup 1999
Italy debut: 29-10-1997 v RUS • 75 caps

10 - CRISTIANO RONALDO

5-02-1985 Funchal, POR (1.84/78)

Season	Club	League				Europe				POR	
02-03	Sporting CP	25	3	SL	3	3	0	CL	r1		
03-04	Manchester Utd	29	4	PL	3	5	0	CL	r2	13	2
04-05	Manchester Utd	33	5	PL	3	8	0	CL	r2	10	7
05-06	Manchester Utd	33	9	PL	2	8	1	CL	r1	15	3
06-07	Manchester Utd	34	17	PL	1	11	3	CL	sf	8	5

Honours: Lge 2007, Cup 2004, LCup 2006
Portugal debut: 20-08-2003 v KAZ • 46 caps • 17 goals

11 – MICHAEL BALLACK

26-09-1976 Chemnitz, GER (1.89/80)

	League				Europe				GER	
95-96	Chemnitzer FC	15	0	B2	15					
96-97	Chemnitzer FC	34	10	B3	4					
97-98	Kaiserslautern	16	0	BL	1					
98-99	Kaiserslautern	30	4	BL	5	6	0	CL	qf	1	0
99-00	Bayer Leverkusen	23	3	BL	2	2	2	UC	r3	8	0
00-01	Bayer Leverkusen	27	7	BL	4	5	2	CL	g	8	3
01-02	Bayer Leverkusen	29	17	BL	2	16	6	CL	F	11	6
02-03	Bayern München	26	10	BL	1	7	1	CL	g	5	3
03-04	Bayern München	28	7	BL	2	8	0	CL	r2	11	8
04-05	Bayern München	27	13	BL	1	9	2	CL	qf	13	8
05-06	Bayern München	26	14	BL	1	6	1	CL	r2	13	3
06-07	Chelsea	26	5	PL	2	10	2	CL	sf	6	3

Honours: Lge 1998 2003 2005 2006, Cup 2003 2005 2006 2007, LCup 2007 • Germany debut: 28-04-1999 v SCO • 76 caps • 34 goals

14 – FRANK LAMPARD

21-06-1978 Romford, ENG (1.83/79)

	League				Europe				ENG	
95-96	West Ham Utd	2	0	PL	10					
95-96	Swansea City	9	1	D3	22					
96-97	West Ham Utd	13	0	PL	14					
97-98	West Ham Utd	31	4	PL	8					
98-99	West Ham Utd	38	5	PL	5					
99-00	West Ham Utd	34	7	PL	9	4	1	UC	r2	1	0
00-01	West Ham Utd	30	7	PL	15					1	0
01-02	Chelsea	37	5	PL	6	4	1	UC	r2	5	0
02-03	Chelsea	38	6	PL	4	2	1	UC	r1	4	0
03-04	Chelsea	38	10	PL	2	14	4	CL	sf	12	5
04-05	Chelsea	38	13	PL	1	12	4	CL	sf	9	3
05-06	Chelsea	35	16	PL	1	8	2	CL	r2	13	3
06-07	Chelsea	37	11	PL	2	11	11	CL	sf	10	1

Honours: Lge 2005 2006; Cup 2007, LCup 2005 2007
England debut: 10-10-1999 v BEL • 55 caps • 12 goals

16 – FIGO

4-11-1972 Lisbon, POR (1.80/75)

	League				Europe				POR	
89-90	Sporting CP	3	0	SL	3			UC	r1		
90-91	Sporting CP	0	0	SL	3			UC	sf		
91-92	Sporting CP	34	1	SL	4	2	0	UC	r1	7	0
92-93	Sporting CP	32	0	SL	3	2	0	UC	r1	8	1
93-94	Sporting CP	31	8	SL	3	5	0	UC	r3	1	0
94-95	Sporting CP	29	7	SL	2	2	0	UC	r1	7	3
95-96	Barcelona	35	5	PD	3	10	3	UC	sf	8	1
96-97	Barcelona	36	4	PD	2	8	1	CC	W	8	2
97-98	Barcelona	35	5	PD	3	9	1	CL	gC	4	1
98-99	Barcelona	34	7	PD	1	6	1	CL	gD	8	1
99-00	Barcelona	32	9	PD	2	13	5	CL	sf	12	6
00-01	Real Madrid	34	9	PD	1	16	5	CL	sf	9	7
01-02	Real Madrid	28	7	PD	3	11	3	CL	W	11	5
02-03	Real Madrid	32	10	PD	1	17	2	CL	sf	8	1
03-04	Real Madrid	36	9	PD	4	10	2	CL	qf	17	3
04-05	Real Madrid	32	3	PD	2	10	4	CL	r2	2	0
05-06	Internazionale	34	5	SA	1	8	1	CL	qf	15	1
06-07	Internazionale	32	2	SA	1	7	0	CL	r2		

Honours: CL 2002 CC 1997, Lge 1998 1999 2001 2003 2006 2007, Cup 1995 1997 1998 2006
Portugal debut: 12-10-1991 v LUX • 127 caps • 32 goals

12 – STEVEN GERRARD

30-05-1980 Whiston, ENG (1.87/78)

	League				Europe				ENG	
97-98	Liverpool	0	0	PL	3						
98-99	Liverpool	12	0	PL	1	1	0	UC	r1		
99-00	Liverpool	29	1	PL	4					2	0
00-01	Liverpool	33	7	PL	3	9	2	UC	W	3	0
01-02	Liverpool	28	3	PL	2	14	1	CL	qf	5	1
02-03	Liverpool	34	5	PL	5	11	0	C/U	qf	8	2
03-04	Liverpool	34	4	PL	4	8	2	UC	r4	10	1
04-05	Liverpool	30	7	PL	5	10	4	CL	W	6	2
05-06	Liverpool	32	10	PL	3	11	6	CL	r2	13	3
06-07	Liverpool	36	7	PL	3	12	3	CL	F	10	3

Honours: CL 2005, UC 2001, Cup 2001 2006, LCup 2001 2003
England debut: 31-05-2000 v UKR • 57 caps • 12 goals

13 – MIROSLAV KLOSE

9-06-1978 Oppeln, POL (1.82/74)

	League				Europe				GER	
98-99	FC Homburg	18	1								
99-00	Kaiserslautern	2	0	BL	5						
00-01	Kaiserslautern	29	9	BL	8	12	2	UC	sf	4	2
01-02	Kaiserslautern	31	16	BL	7					15	11
02-03	Kaiserslautern	32	9	BL	14					10	2
03-04	Kaiserslautern	26	10	BL	15	2	1	UC	r1	11	1
04-05	Werder Bremen	32	15	BL	3	8	2	CL	g	6	4
05-06	Werder Bremen	26	25	BL	2	9	4	CL	r2	16	9
06-07	Werder Bremen	31	13	BL	3	13	2	C/U	sf	7	4

Honours: None
Germany debut: 24-03-2001 v ALB • 69 caps • 33 goals

15 – DECO

27-08-1977 São Bernardo do Campo, BRA (1.74/75)

	League				Europe				POR	
1997	Corinthians	0	0	SA	17						
97-98	Alverca	32	13	D2	3						
98-99	Salgueiros	12	2	D1	-						
98-99	Porto	6	0	SL	1						
99-00	Porto	23	1	SL	2	11	3	CL	qf		
00-01	Porto	31	6	SL	2	10	0	C/U	qf		
01-02	Porto	30	13	SL	3	15	6	CL	r2		
02-03	Porto	30	10	SL	1	12	1	UC	W	4	1
03-04	Porto	28	2	SL	1	12	2	CL	W	15	0
04-05	Barcelona	35	7	PD	1	7	2	CL	r2	10	1
05-06	Barcelona	29	3	PD	1	11	2	CL	W	10	1
06-07	Barcelona	31	1	PD	2	8	2	CL	r2	7	0

Honours: CL 2004 2006, UC 2003, Lge 1999 2003 2004 2005 2006, Cup 2000 2001 2003 • Portugal debut: 29-03-2003 v BRA
46 caps • 3 goals

17 – JUAN ROMAN RIQUELME

24-06-1978 Buenos Aires, ARG (1.80/76)

	League				Sth Am/Europe				ARG	
96-97	Boca Juniors	22	4	PD	10/9	2	0	SC	r1		
97-98	Boca Juniors	19	0	PD	2/6	6	0	CM	qf	1	0
98-99	Boca Juniors	37	10	PD	1/1	5	0	CM	r1	5	0
99-00	Boca Juniors	24	4	PD	3/7	11	3	CL	W		
00-01	Boca Juniors	27	10	PD	1/3	12	3	CL	W		
01-02	Boca Juniors	22	10	PD	3/3	4	0	CL	qf	1	0
02-03	Barcelona	30	3	PD	6	11	2	CL	r2	3	1
03-04	Villarreal	33	8	PD	8	12	4	UC	sf	2	0
04-05	Villarreal	35	15	PD	3	9	2	UC	qf	12	5
05-06	Villarreal	25	12	PD	7	14	2	CL	sf	12	2
06-07	Boca Juniors	28	3	PD	2/2	11	8	CL	W	6	5

Honours: CL 2000 2001 2007, Lge 1999x2 2001
Argentina debut: 16-11-1997 v COL • 42 caps • 13 goals

17 - FRANCK RIBERY

7-04-1983 Boulogne-sue-Mer, FRA (1.70/62)

		League				Europe				FRA	
01-02	Boulogne	24	5	N	17						
02-03	Olympique Alès	18	1	N	15						
03-04	Stade Brestois	35	3	N	2						
04-05	FC Metz	20	2	L1	16						
04-05	Galatasaray	14	0	SL	2						
05-06	Olymp. Marseille	35	6	L1	5	7	1	UC	r4	10	1
06-07	Olymp. Marseille	25	5	L1	2	3	0	UC	r1	8	1

Honours: None
France debut: 27-05-2006 v MEX • 18 caps • 2 goals

20 - GENNARO GATTUSO

9-01-1978 Corigliano Schiavonea, ITA (1.77/77)

		League				Europe				ITA	
95-96	Perugia	2	0	SB	3						
96-97	Perugia	8	0	SA	16						
97-98	Rangers	36	7	SPL	2	2	1	CL	pr		
98-99	Rangers	4	0	SPL	-	3	1	UC	r3		
98-99	Salernitana	25	0	SA	15						
99-00	Milan	22	1	SA	3	5	0	CL	gH	2	0
00-01	Milan	24	0	SA	6	10	0	CL	r2	4	1
01-02	Milan	32	0	SA	4	10	0	UC	sf	9	0
02-03	Milan	25	0	SA	3	14	0	CL	W	4	0
03-04	Milan	33	1	SA	1	9	1	CL	qf	8	0
04-05	Milan	32	0	SA	2	11	0	CL	F	7	0
05-06	Milan	35	3	SA	3	11	0	CL	sf	13	0
06-07	Milan	30	1	SA	4	12	0	CL	W	6	0

Honours: WC 2006; CL 2003 2007, Lge 2004, Cup 2003
Italy debut: 23-02-2000 v SWE • 53 caps • 1 goal

22 - MICHAEL ESSIEN

3-12-1982 Accra, GHA (1.80/77)

		League				Europe				GHA	
99-00	Liberty										
00-01	Bastia	13	1	L1	8						
01-02	Bastia	24	4	L1	11						
02-03	Bastia	29	6	L1	12						
03-04	Oly. Lyonnais	34	3	L1	1	8	0	CL	qf		
04-05	Oly. Lyonnais	37	4	L1	1	10	5	CL	qf		
05-06	Chelsea	31	2	PL	1	6	0	CL	r2	Total	
06-07	Chelsea	33	2	PL	2	10	2	CL	sf	25	5

Honours: Lge 2004 2005 2006, Cup 2007, LCup 2007
Ghana debut: 21-01-2002 v MAR

25 - ALESSANDRO NESTA

19-03-1976 Rome, ITA (1.87/79)

		League				Europe				ITA	
93-94	Lazio	2	0	SA	4						
94-95	Lazio	11	0	SA	2						
95-96	Lazio	23	0	SA	3	3	0	UC	r2		
96-97	Lazio	25	0	SA	4	4	0	UC	r2	5	0
97-98	Lazio	30	0	SA	7	10	1	UC	F	10	0
98-99	Lazio	20	1	SA	2	4	0	CW	W	5	0
99-00	Lazio	28	0	SA	1	10	0	CL	qf	11	0
00-01	Lazio	29	0	SA	3	8	0	CL	r2	7	0
01-02	Lazio	25	0	SA	6	6	0	CL	r1	8	0
02-03	Milan	29	1	SA	3	14	0	CL	W	7	0
03-04	Milan	26	0	SA	1	7	0	CL	qf	9	0
04-05	Milan	29	0	SA	2	12	0	CL	F	5	0
05-06	Milan	30	1	SA	2	10	0	CL	sf	10	0
06-07	Milan	14	0	SA	4	8	0	CL	W	1	0

Honours: WC 2006; CL 2003 2007, CW 1999, Lge 2000 2004, Cup 1998 2000 2003; Italy debut: 5-10-1996 v MDA • 78 caps

17 - WAYNE ROONEY

24-10-1985 Liverpool, ENG (1.80/76)

		League				Europe				ENG	
02-03	Everton	33	6	PL	7					5	0
03-04	Everton	34	9	PL	17					12	9
04-05	Manchester Utd	29	11	PL	3	6	3	CL	r2	6	0
05-06	Manchester Utd	36	16	PL	2	5	1	CL	r1	10	2
06-07	Manchester Utd	35	14	PL	1	12	4	CL	sf	5	1

Honours: Lge 2007, LCup 2006
England debut: 12-02-2003 v AUS • 38 caps • 12 goals

21 - ANDRIY SHEVCHENKO

29-09-1976 Dvirkivshchyna, UKR (1.83/73)

		League				Europe				UKR	
94-95	Dynamo Kyiv	16	1	PL	1	2	1	CL	g	2	0
95-96	Dynamo Kyiv	31	16	PL	1	3	2	CL	g	2	1
96-97	Dynamo Kyiv	20	6	PL	1					6	2
97-98	Dynamo Kyiv	23	19	PL	1	10	6	CL	qf	3	2
98-99	Dynamo Kyiv	28	18	PL	1	14	10	CL	sf	9	1
99-00	Milan	32	24	SA	3	6	1	CL	g	7	3
00-01	Milan	34	24	SA	6	14	9	CL	r2	7	5
01-02	Milan	29	14	SA	4	8	3	UC	sf	6	5
02-03	Milan	24	5	SA	3	11	4	CL	W	4	2
03-04	Milan	32	24	SA	1	9	4	CL	qf	4	1
04-05	Milan	29	17	SA	2	10	6	CL	F	8	5
05-06	Milan	28	19	SA	2	12	9	CL	sf	9	4
06-07	Chelsea	30	4	PL	2	10	5	CL	sf	3	2

Honours: CL 2003, Lge 1995 1996 1997 1998 1999 2004, Cup 1996 1998 1999 2003 2007, LCup 2007
Ukraine debut: 25-03-1995 v CRO • 72 caps • 33 goals

22 - PATRICK VIEIRA

23-06-1976 Dakar, SEN (1.92/82)

		League				Europe				FRA	
93-94	Cannes	5	0	L1	6						
94-95	Cannes	31	2	L1	9	4	1	UC	r2		
95-96	Cannes	13	0	L1	14						
95-96	Milan	2	0	SA	1	2	0	UC	qf		
96-97	Arsenal	31	2	PL	3	1	0	UC	r1	5	0
97-98	Arsenal	33	2	PL	1	2	0	UC	r1	4	0
98-99	Arsenal	34	3	PL	2	3	0	CL	gE	5	0
99-00	Arsenal	30	2	PL	2	14	0	C/U	F	16	0
00-01	Arsenal	30	6	PL	2	12	0	CL	qf	14	2
01-02	Arsenal	36	2	PL	1	11	1	CL	r2	12	2
02-03	Arsenal	24	3	PL	2	12	1	CL	r2	6	1
03-04	Arsenal	29	3	PL	1	6	0	CL	qf	10	0
04-05	Arsenal	32	6	PL	2	6	0	CL	r2	7	0
05-06	Juventus	31	5	SA	-	7	0	CL	qf	15	2
06-07	Internazionale	20	1	SA	1	4	1	CL	r2	7	0

Honours: WC 1998, EC 2000 CC 2001; Lge 1998 2002 2004 2007, Cup 1998 2002 2005 • France debut: 26-02-1997 v NED • 101 caps • 6 goals

24 - PETR CECH

20-05-1982 Plzen, CZE (1.96/85)

		League				Europe				CZE	
98-99	Viktoria Plzen	0	-	L1	15						
99-00	Chmel	1	-	L1	10						
00-01	Chmel	26	-	L1	10						
01-02	Sparta Praha	26	-	L1	2					2	-
02-03	Stade Rennais	37	-	L1	15					10	-
03-04	Stade Rennais	33	-	L1	9					11	-
04-05	Chelsea	35	-	PL	1	12	-	CL	sf	9	-
05-06	Chelsea	34	-	PL	1	7	-	CL	r2	12	-
06-07	Chelsea	20	-	PL	2	8	-	CL	sf	8	-

Honours: Lge 2005 2006, Cup 2007, LCup 2005 2007
Czech Rep Debut: 12-02-2002 v HUN • 52 caps

26 – LILIAM THURAM

1-01-1972 Pointe-a-Pitre, GDP (1.82/75)

			League				Europe			FRA	
90-91	Monaco	1	0	L1	2						
91-92	Monaco	19	0	L1	2	4	0	CC	F		
92-93	Monaco	37	0	L1	3	4	0	CC	r2		
93-94	Monaco	25	1	L1	9	8	1	CL	sf		
94-95	Monaco	37	2	L1	6					2	0
95-96	Monaco	36	5	L1	3	2	0	UC	r1	1	0
96-97	Parma	34	1	SA	2	2	0	UC	r1	9	0
97-98	Parma	32	0	SA	6	8	0	CL	gA	14	2
98-99	Parma	34	0	SA	4	11	0	UC	W	8	0
99-00	Parma	33	0	SA	5	10	0	C/U	r4	15	0
00-01	Parma	30	0	SA	4	7	0	UC	r4	5	0
01-02	Juventus	30	0	SA	1	8	0	CL	r2	10	0
02-03	Juventus	27	1	SA	1	15	0	CL	F	12	0
03-04	Juventus	23	0	SA	3	5	0	CL	r2	14	0
04-05	Juventus	37	0	SA	1	11	0	CL	qf	13	0
05-06	Juventus	27	0	SA	1			CL	qf	18	0
06-07	Barcelona	23	0	PD	2	4	0	CL	r2	9	0

Honours: WC 1998, EC 2000 CC 2003; UC 1999, Lge 2002 2003 2005 2006 (last two withdrawn), Cup 1999
France debut: 17-08-1994 v CZE • 130 caps • 2 goals

28 – PHILIPP LAHM

11-11-1983 Munich, GER (1.70/61)

			League				Europe			GER	
01-02	B. München AM	27	2	RS	10						
02-03	B. München AM	34	1	RS	4	1	0	CL	gG		
03-04	VfB Stuttgart	31	1	BL	4	7	0	CL	r2	9	1
04-05	VfB Stuttgart	22	1	BL	5	6	1	UC	r3	6	0
05-06	B. München	20	0	BL	1	4	0	CL	r2	10	1
06-07	B. München	34	1	BL	4	9	0	CL	qf	9	0

Honours: Lge 2006, Cup 2006
Germany debut: 18-02-2004 v CRO • 34 caps • 2 goals

30 – TOMAS ROSICKY

4-10-1980 Plzen, CZE (1.78/67)

			League				Europe			CZE	
98-99	Sparta Praha	3	0	L1	1						
99-00	Sparta Praha	24	5	L1	1			CL	pr	6	0
00-01	Sparta Praha	14	3	L1	1	8	2	CL	gB	2	0
00-01	B. Dortmund	15	0	BL	3					5	0
01-02	B. Dortmund	30	5	BL	1	16	1	C/U	F	7	2
02-03	B. Dortmund	30	4	BL	3	7	2	CL	r2	9	4
03-04	B. Dortmund	19	2	BL	6	4	0	C/U	r2	10	2
04-05	B. Dortmund	27	4	BL	7					9	5
05-06	B. Dortmund	28	5	BL	7					9	4
06-07	Arsenal	26	3	PL	4	6	1	CL	r2	8	0

Honours: Lge 1999 2000 2001 2002
Czech debut: 23-02-2000 v IRL • 65 caps • 17 goals

27 – JENS LEHMANN

10-11-1969 Essen, GER (1.87/80)

			League				Europe			GER	
88-89	Schalke 04	13	-	B2							
89-90	Schalke 04	27	-	B2							
90-91	Schalke 04	34	-	B2							
91-92	Schalke 04	37	-	BL	11						
92-93	Schalke 04	8	-	BL	10						
93-94	Schalke 04	21	-	BL	14						
94-95	Schalke 04	34	1	BL	11						
95-96	Schalke 04	32	-	BL	3						
96-97	Schalke 04	34	-	BL	12	12	-	UC	W		
97-98	Schalke 04	34	1	BL	5	7	-	UC	qf	2	-
98-99	Milan	5	-	SA	1						
98-99	B. Dortmund	13	-	BL	4					2	-
99-00	B. Dortmund	31	-	BL	11	12	-	C/U	r4	8	-
00-01	B. Dortmund	31	-	BL	3					1	-
01-02	B. Dortmund	30	-	BL	1	17	-	C/U	F	1	-
02-03	B. Dortmund	24	-	BL	3	12	-	CL	r2	1	-
03-04	Arsenal	38	-	PL	1	10	-	CL	qf	2	-
04-05	Arsenal	28	-	PL	2	7	-	CL	r2	7	-
05-06	Arsenal	38	-	PL	4	8	-	CL	F	13	-
06-07	Arsenal	36	-	PL	4	8	-	CL	r2	8	-

Honours: UC 1997, Lge 2002 2004, Cup 2005
Germany debut: 18-02-1998 v OMA • 46 caps

29 – ADRIANO

17-02-1982 Rio de Janeiro, BRA (1.89/87)

			League				Europe			BRA	
1999	Flamengo	0	0	SA	12						
2000	Flamengo	19	7	SA	15					1	0
2001	Flamengo	17	6	SA	24						
01-02	Internazionale	8	1	SA	0	5	0	UC	qf		
01-02	Fiorentina	15	6	SA	17						
02-03	Parma	28	15	SA	6	2	2	UC	r2	5	3
03-04	Parma	9	8	SA	0	2	1	UC	r3		
03-04	Internazionale	16	9	SA	4					8	7
04-05	Internazionale	30	16	SA	3	9	10	CL	qf	11	7
05-06	Internazionale	30	13	SA	3	11	6	CL	qf	11	8
06-07	Internazionale	23	5	SA	1	3	0	CL	r2	1	0

Honours: CA 2004, CC 2005; Lge 2006 2007, Cup 2005
Brazil debut: 15-11-2000 v COL • 37 caps • 25 goals

KEY

WC = FIFA World Cup • EC = UEFA European Championship • CC = FIFA Confederations Cup • OG = Olympic gold • CA = Copa America • CN = Africa Cup of Nations • CL = UEFA Champions League or Copa Libertadores • UC = UEFA Cup • CW = Cup Winners Cup • C/U = UEFA Champions League then the UEFA Cup • LGE = Domestic league championship • CUP = Domestic Cup • LCUP = League Cup • AS = Allsvenskan (Sweden) • BL = Bundesliga (Germany) • B2 = Bundesliga 2 (Germany) • ED = Eredivisie (Netherlands) • L1 = Ligue 1 (France) • PD = Primera Division (Argentina & Spain) • PL = Premier League (England) • RS = Regionalliga Süd • SA = Serie A (Brazil and Italy) • SB = Serie B (Italy) • SL = Superliga (Portugal & Turkey) • The first line for each player gives the following information - date and place of birth, nationality, height in meters, weight in kilogrammes • The columns for each table read as follows - season, club, league appearances, league goals, name of the league, final position; continental appearances, continental goals, competition, round reached; international appearances, international goals

FIFA U–20 WOMEN'S WORLD CHAMPIONSHIP 2006

FIFA U–20 WOMEN'S WORLD CHAMPIONSHIP RUSSIA 2006

First round groups	Pts	Quarter-finals		Semi-finals			Final		
Brazil	5								
Russia	5	Korea DPR	2						
Australia	4	France	1						
New Zealand	1								
				Korea DPR	1				
	Pts			Brazil	0				
China PR	9								
Nigeria	6	Nigeria	1						
Canada	3	Brazil	2						
Finland	0								
							Korea DPR	5	
	Pts						China PR	0	
Korea DPR	9								
Germany	6	USA	4						
Mexico	3	Germany	1						
Switzerland	0								
				USA	0	4p			
	Pts			China PR	0	5p			
USA	9								
France	6	Russia	0				3rd Place Play-off		
Argentina	3	China PR	4				Brazil	0	6p
Congo DR	0						USA	0	5p

GROUP A	PL	W	D	L	F	A	GD	PTS	RUS	AUS	NZL
1 Brazil	3	1	2	0	2	0	+2	5	0-0	2-0	0-0
2 Russia	3	1	2	0	4	3	+1	5		1-1	3-2
3 Australia	3	1	1	1	4	3	1+	4			3-0
4 New Zealand	3	0	1	2	2	6	-4	1			

Petrovsky, St Petersburg
17-08-2006, 16:00, 1100, Gall HUN, Müller GER, Santuari ITA

NZL   0   3   AUS

McCallum 2 [39] [80], Shipard [93+]

NEW ZEALAND			AUSTRALIA		
1 CLANSEY Aroon			WILLIAMS Lydia 1		
2 PERCIVAL Ria			POLKINGHORNE Clare 2		
4 HOYLE Katie	67		BROGAN Danielle 3		
5 RISHWORTH Hannah			CARROLL Kim 4		
7 SMITH Merissa	65		KENNEDY Olivia 5		
8 RILEY Alexandra			(C) SHIPARD Sally [6]		
9 GREGORIUS Sarah		86	McDONNELL Sasha 9		
10 HUMPHRIES Emma			LEDBROOK Kylie 10		
11 YALLOP Kirsty (C)	85	90	BLAYNEY Leah [11]		
[14] ERCEG Abby			McCALLUM Collette [14]		
16 RENNIE Petria		69	KHAMIS Leena 19		
Tr: HARDMAN John			Tr: EDWARDS Alistair		
13 KETE Emma	65	69	TRISTRAM Jenna 7		
17 LANKSHEAR Maggie	67	86	UZUNLAR Servet 8		
20 LONGO Annalie	85	90	COOPER Caitlin 13		

Petrovsky, St Petersburg
20-08-2006, 16:00, 700, Bennett USA, Tovar MEX, Jeffery GUY

BRA   2   0   AUS

Francielle [42p], Fabiana [69]

BRAZIL			AUSTRALIA		
1 BARBARA			WILLIAMS Lydia 1		
2 DAIANE			POLKINGHORNE Clare [2]		
3 MONICA			BROGAN Danielle 3		
[4] ALIANE			CARROLL Kim 4		
5 ERIKA			KENNEDY Olivia 5		
6 DANIELLE			(C) SHIPARD Sally 6		
7 FRANCIELLE			McDONNELL Sasha 9		
8 RENATA COSTA (C)		59	LEDBROOK Kylie [10]		
9 FABIANA		80	BLAYNEY Leah 11		
11 MAURINE	80		McCALLUM Collette 14		
15 ADRIANE	46	66	KHAMIS Leena 19		
Tr: BARCELOS Jorge			Tr: EDWARDS Alistair		
16 ELIS	46	59	TRISTRAM Jenna 7		
20 STEPHANE	80	80	UZUNLAR Servet 8		
		66	CHAPMAN Amy 12		

Torpedo, Moscow
23-08-2006, 16:00, 1000, Beck GER, Müller GER, Santuari ITA

AUS   1   1   RUS

Brogan [85]   Kozhnikova [75]

AUSTRALIA			RUSSIA		
1 WILLIAMS Lydia			TODUA Elvira 1		
2 POLKINGHORNE Clare			FILISOVA Maria 2		
3 BROGAN Danielle			KOZHNIKOVA Anna 3		
4 CARROLL Kim	70		GROMOLYUK Anna 5		
5 KENNEDY Olivia			TEREKHOVA Elena 7		
6 SHIPARD Sally (C)			TITOVA Oxana [8]		
8 UZUNLAR Servet	77	93	DANILOVA Elena 9		
[9] McDONNELL Sasha			MOROZOVA Elena 11		
12 CHAPMAN Amy	62		(C) TSYBUTOVICH Ksenia 13		
14 McCALLUM Collette			STAROVOYTOVA Tamara 16		
15 JACKSON Amy	68		SHCHEGALEVA Elena [17]		
Tr: EDWARDS Alistair			Tr: GRISHIN Valentin		
7 TRISTRAM Jenna	77	70	GOMOZOVA Alexandra 4		
10 LEDBROOK Kylie	62	93	ANOKHINA Kristina 19		
13 COOPER Caitlin	68				

Petrovsky, St Petersburg
17-08-2006, 19:00, 12 200, Palmqvist SWE, Borg SWE, Lagrange FRA

RUS   0   0   BRA

RUSSIA			BRAZIL		
1 TODUA Elvira			BARBARA 1		
2 FILISOVA Maria			DAIANE 2		
3 KOZHNIKOVA Anna			MONICA 3		
4 GOMOZOVA Alexandra			ALIANE [4]		
5 GROMOLYUK Anna			ERIKA 5		
6 KHARCHENKO Nadezda	46		DANIELLE 6		
7 TEREKHOVA Elena			FRANCIELLE 7		
9 DANILOVA Elena			(C) RENATA COSTA 8		
10 PETROVA Olga	34		FABIANA 9		
11 MOROZOVA Elena		66	ADRIANE 15		
[13] TSYBUTOVICH Ksenia (C)			STEPHANE [20]		
Tr: GRISHIN Valentin			Tr: BARCELOS Jorge		
8 TITOVA Oxana	85	66	ELIS 16		
17 SHCHEGALEVA Elena	34				
19 ANOKHINA Kristina	85	46			

Petrovsky, St Petersburg
20-08-2006, 19:00, 3400, Hong KOR, Liu TPE, Yoshizawa JPN

RUS   3   2   NZL

Kozhnikova [5], Terekhova [14],   Erceg [18], Humphries [56]
Akimova [93+]

RUSSIA			NEW ZEALAND		
[1] TODUA Elvira			CLANSEY Aroon 1		
[2] FILISOVA Maria			PERCIVAL Ria 2		
3 KOZHNIKOVA Anna			HOYLE Katie [4]		
[4] GOMOZOVA Alexandra			RISHWORTH Hannah 5		
7 TEREKHOVA Elena			RILEY Alexandra 8		
8 TITOVA Oxana	85	89	GREGORIUS Sarah 9		
9 DANILOVA Elena			HUMPHRIES Emma 10		
11 MOROZOVA Elena	75		(C) YALLOP Kirsty 11		
13 TSYBUTOVICH Ksenia (C)	33		ERCEG Abby 14		
16 STAROVOYTOVA Tamara			RENNIE Petria [16]		
17 SHCHEGALEVA Elena	51		LANKSHEAR Maggie 17		
Tr: GRISHIN Valentin			Tr: HARDMAN John		
5 GROMOLYUK Anna	75	33	BROMLEY Hannah 6		
15 AKIMOVA Svetlana	85	89	COLLINS Helen 19		
		51	LONGO Annalie 20		

Podmoskovie, Moscow
23-08-2006, 16:00, 500, De Silva TRI, Riley JAM, Mohammed TRI

BRA   0   0   NZL

BRAZIL			NEW ZEALAND		
1 BARBARA			CLANSEY Aroon 1		
2 DAIANE			PERCIVAL Ria 2		
5 ERIKA			HOYLE Katie 4		
6 DANIELLE			RISHWORTH Hannah 5		
7 FRANCIELLE			BROMLEY Hannah 6		
8 RENATA COSTA (C)		92	RILEY Alexandra 8		
9 FABIANA	46		GREGORIUS Sarah 9		
11 MAURINE	75		HUMPHRIES Emma 10		
14 FERNANDA			(C) YALLOP Kirsty 11		
15 ADRIANE	61		ERCEG Abby 14		
20 STEPHANE		74	LONGO Annalie 20		
Tr: BARCELOS Jorge			Tr: HARDMAN John		
16 ELIS	61	74	LEOTA Renee 12		
17 PAMELA	46	92	COLLINS Helen 19		
18 JOCIELMA	75				

GROUP B	PL	W	D	L	F	A	GD	PTS		NGA	CAN	FIN
1 China PR	3	3	0	0	6	1	+5	9		3-0	1-0	2-1
2 Nigeria	3	2	0	1	11	5	+6	6			3-2	8-0
3 Canada	3	1	0	2	4	4	0	3				2-0
4 Finland	3	0	0	3	1	12	-11	0				

Podmoskovie, Moscow
17-08-2006, 16:00, 2000, Ferreira-James GUY, Ribeiro BRA, Canales ECU

CHN 2 1 FIN

Ma Xiaoxu 37p, Zi Jingjing 72   Yuan Fan OG 1

CHINA PR					FINLAND	
1 ZHANG Yanru					KORPELA Tinja-Riikka	1
2 ZHOU Gaoping					(C) SAARI Maija	2
3 YUAN Fan					HYYRYNEN Tuija	3
4 ZHANG Wei					HYVONEN Niina	4
8 YOU Jia					HOVI Hanna	5
9 RAO Huifang	54				BERG Neea	6
10 MA Xiaoxu (C)					SAINIO Essi	7
12 ZHU Wei	73	73			MA Xiaoxu	10
14 WANG Dongni	57				LOU Xiaoxu	11
15 YUE Min					ZHUANG Ran	13
16 ZHANG Wei Shuang	88				WENG Xiaojie	18
Tr: SHANG Ruihua					Tr: MATIKAINEN Jarmo	
7 XI Dingying	73	73			YOU Jia	8
19 ZI Jingjing	54	57			ZHANG Wei Shuang	16
		88			MA Zixiang	17

Podmoskovie, Moscow
17-08-2006, 19:00, 800, D'Coth IND, Shamsuri MAS, Yoshizawa JPN

NGA 3 2 CAN

Ishola 29, Uwak 2 82 91+   Kyle 25, Cicchini 71

NIGERIA					CANADA	
12 BULUS Christy					LABBE Stephanie	1
2 CHIKWELU Rita					SCHMIDT Sophie	3
3 SABI Akudo					VANDERPOOL Caroline	4
6 IKIDI Faith			88		KYLE Kaylyn	6
7 AKPA Gladys					CICCHINI Amanda	10
9 IWUAGWU Akudo					SCOTT Desiree	11
10 MEKULEYI Titilayo	60		46		RIVERSO Loredana	13
14 ISHOLA Tawa					JAMANI Aysha	14
16 JEROME Ulumma			72		COLLISON Lisa	15
17 AKUSOBI Blessing					BOUDREAU Taryne	16
18 UWAK Cynthia					BECKLES Vonya	19
Tr: OKONKWO Emmanuel					Tr: BRIDGE Ian	
4 EKE Maureen	60		46		ROBINSON Jodi-Ann	7
			88		ADAMS Paige	8
			72		SLEIMAN Rheanne	17

Podmoskovie, Moscow
20-08-2006, 16:00, 1200, Avdonchenko RUS, Villa ESP, Lagrange FRA

FIN 0 2 CAN

Robinson 2 39p 70

FINLAND					CANADA	
1 KORPELA Tinja-Riikka					LABBE Stephanie	1
2 SAARI Maija			77		SCHMIDT Sophie	3
3 HYYRYNEN Tuija					VANDERPOOL Caroline	4
4 HYVONEN Niina			61		KYLE Kaylyn	6
5 HOVI Hanna			82		ROBINSON Jodi-Ann	7
6 BERG Neea					CICCHINI Amanda	10
7 SAINIO Essi	65				SCOTT Desiree	11
9 LAIHANEN Taru	34				RIVERSO Loredana	13
10 PORKKA Tytti	34				JAMANI Aysha	14
11 HOKKANEN Susanna					BOUDREAU Taryne	16
13 PURANEN Leena					BECKLES Vonya	19
Tr: MATIKAINEN Jarmo					Tr: BRIDGE Ian	
14 TIILIKAINEN Heini	65	61			ADAMS Paige	8
16 WESTERLUND Anna	34	77			IACCHELLI Selenia	9
17 KIVELA Heidi	34	82			COLLISON Lisa	15

Podmoskovie, Moscow
20-08-2006, 19:00, 2000, Beck GER, Müller GER, Santuari ITA

CHN 3 0 NGA

Lou Xiaoxu 9, Ma Xiaoxu 2 31 69

CHINA PR					NIGERIA	
1 ZHANG Yanru					BULUS Christy	12
2 ZHOU Gaoping					CHIKWELU Rita	2
3 YUAN Fan					SABI Akudo	3
4 ZHANG Wei					IKIDI Faith	6
10 MA Xiaoxu	88				AKPA Gladys	7
11 LOU Xiaoxu	78	72			IWUAGWU Akudo	9
12 ZHU Wei	62	50			MEKULEYI Titilayo	10
13 ZHUANG Ran					JEROME Ulumma	16
15 YUE Min					AKUSOBI Blessing	17
16 ZHANG Wei Shuang					UWAK Cynthia	18
20 LIU Xiaoyan			39		OGIAGBEHVA Emueje	20
Tr: SHANG Ruihua					Tr: OKONKWO Emmanuel	
6 HOU Lijia	88	39			EKE Maureen	4
9 RAO Huifang	62	50			GODWIN Stella	11
19 ZI Jingjing	78	72			CHUKWUDI Ogonna	13

Torpedo, Moscow
23-08-2006, 19:00, 100, Brohet BEL, Borg SWE, Nadolska POL

CAN 0 1 CHN

Ma Xiaoxu 48

CANADA					CHINA PR	
1 LABBE Stephanie					ZHANG Yanru	1
2 RADCHUCK Katie	73				ZHOU Gaoping	2
3 SCHMIDT Sophie					YUAN Fan	3
4 VANDERPOOL Caroline					ZHANG Wei	4
6 KYLE Kaylyn	56				RAO Huifang	9
7 ROBINSON Jodi-Ann	80				MA Xiaoxu	10
9 IACCHELLI Selenia	61				LOU Xiaoxu	11
10 CICCHINI Amanda	61				ZHU Wei	12
11 SCOTT Desiree					YUE Min	15
12 COLLISON Lisa	46				ZHANG Wei Shuang	16
19 BECKLES Vonya					LIU Xiaoyan	20
Tr: BRIDGE Ian					Tr: SHANG Ruihua	
8 ADAMS Paige	56	61			XI Dingying	7
13 RIVERSO Loredana	73	61			YOU Jia	8
14 JAMANI Aysha	46	80			ZI Jingjing	19

Podmoskovie, Moscow
23-08-2006, 19:00, 400, Bennett USA, Tovar MEX, Jeffery GUY

FIN 0 8 NGA

Sabi 2 7 42, Eke 3 13 65 79, Uwak 15, Chikwelu 2 47 73

FINLAND					NIGERIA	
1 KORPELA Tinja-Riikka					OLUEHI Tochukwu	1
2 SAARI Maija			86		CHIKWELU Rita	2
3 HYYRYNEN Tuija					SABI Akudo	3
5 HOVI Hanna					EKE Maureen	4
6 BERG Neea					IKIDI Faith	6
9 LAIHANEN Taru	74				OPARAOCHA Chizoma	8
10 PORKKA Tytti			69		IWUAGWU Akudo	9
11 HOKKANEN Susanna					GODWIN Stella	11
13 PURANEN Leena	26				JEROME Ulumma	16
15 VUORELA Kaisa					AKUSOBI Blessing	17
17 KIVELA Heidi	46				UWAK Cynthia	18
Tr: MATIKAINEN Jarmo					Tr: OKONKWO Emmanuel	
8 HARKONEN Eeva	74	69			CHUKWUDI Ogonna	13
16 WESTERLUND Anna	46	86			ISHOLA Tawa	14
18 SALLSTROM Linda	26					

GROUP C	PL	W	D	L	F	A	GD	PTS		GER	MEX	SUI
1 Korea DPR	3	3	0	0	10	0	+10	9		2-0	4-0	4-0
2 Germany	3	2	0	1	15	3	+12	6			9-1	6-0
3 Mexico	3	1	0	2	5	15	-10	3				4-2
4 Switzerland	3	0	0	3	2	14	-12	0				

Dynamo, Moscow
18-08-2006, 16:00, 3500, Ogston AUS, Keen AUS, Ho AUS

SUI 2   4 MEX

Buerki 2 [12] [65]   Corral 2 [15] [47+], Gordillo [30], Ocampo [92+]

SWITZERLAND			MEXICO	
12 THALMANN Gaelle			LADRON Anjuli	1
2 ABBE Caroline			(C) GORDILLO Maria	2
3 BACHMANN Ramona			GUTIERREZ Nancy	3
4 BETSCHART Sandra	81		VILLALPANDO Leticia	4
7 BUERKI Vanessa			VALDEZ Isabel	5
10 KAUFMANN Isabelle	76		NIEVA Christine	6
11 MAENDLY Sandy	60		JUAREZ Rebecca	8
14 MEYER Isabelle			OCAMPO Monica	9
15 MOSER Martina (C)			CORRAL Charlyn	10
19 STILLHARD Francesca			MORALES Tania	11
20 ZAHNO Simone	62 83		MARTINEZ Areli	17
Tr: TADDEI Claudio			Tr: CUELLAR Leonardo	
6 BURGER Beatrice	62 76		MENDEZ Janet	7
16 RAEMY Camille	60 83		FARIAS Janelly	16
17 SARRASIN Maeva	81			

Dynamo, Moscow
18-08-2006, 19:00, 700, Gaye SEN, Oulhaj MAR, Ndah BEN

PRK 2   0 GER

Jong Pok Hui [35], Jo Yun Mi [70]

KOREA DPR			GERMANY	
1 JON Myong Hui			HOLZ Romina	12
2 JO Yun Mi			SCHIEWE Carolin	4
6 KIM Chun Hui			PETER Babett	5
7 KIM Song Hui	31		WEBER Meike	6
9 RI Song Sim			BAJRAMAJ Fatmire	7
10 JONG Pok Hui	59	65	GOESSLING Lena	8
15 KIL Son Hui			OKOYINO DA MBABI Celia	10
16 HONG Myong Gum (C)		72	LAUDEHR Simone	11
17 RI Un Hyang			HOEFLER Juliane	13
19 RI Jin Ok		56	NEUMANN Lydia	17
20 KIM Kyong Hwa			MAIER Juliane	18
Tr: CHOE Kwang Sok			Tr: MEINERT Maren	
3 RI Un Suk	31	56	KERSCHOWSKI Monique	3
4 O Kum Hui	59	72	BLAESSE Anna	14
		65	KESSLER Nadine	20

Dynamo, Moscow
21-08-2006, 16:00, 500, Gaal HUN, Borg SWE, Nadolska POL

MEX 1   9 GER

Cisneros [76]   Okoyino da Mbabi [24], Bajramaj [29], Kessler [31], Blaesse 3 [37] [44] [84], Laudehr [49], Maier [58], Oster [77]

MEXICO			GERMANY	
1 LADRON Anjuli			HOLZ Romina	12
2 GORDILLO Maria (C)			HAYE Janina	2
3 GUTIERREZ Nancy			KERSCHOWSKI Monique	3
4 VILLALPANDO Leticia			PETER Babett	5
5 VALDEZ Isabel	59		BAJRAMAJ Fatmire	7
6 NIEVA Christine			GOESSLING Lena	8
8 JUAREZ Rebecca			OKOYINO DA MBABI Celia	10
9 OCAMPO Monica	64		LAUDEHR Simone	11
16 FARIAS Janelly	32		BLAESSE Anna	14
19 GANDARILLA Nancy			MAIER Juliane	18
21 ACEVEDO Jackie	46 59		KESSLER Nadine	20
Tr: CUELLAR Leonardo			Tr: MEINERT Maren	
10 CORRAL Charlyn	46 59		ANGEL Ann-Christin	9
15 MENDEZ Norma	32 59		OSTER Jennifer	15
18 CISNEROS Monique	64 63		SCHLANKE Josephine	16

Dynamo, Moscow
21-08-2006, 19:00, 600, De Silva TRI, Riley JAM, Mohammed TRI

SUI 0   4 PRK

Jong Pok Hui [46+], Kim Ok Sim [50], Kim Song Hui 2 [78] [80]

SWITZERLAND			KOREA DPR	
12 THALMANN Gaelle			JON Myong Hui	1
2 ABBE Caroline		48	JO Yun Mi	2
3 BACHMANN Ramona		35	RI Un Suk	3
4 BETSCHART Sandra			KIM Chun Hui	6
5 BEUTLER Barbara			RI Song Sim	9
7 BUERKI Vanessa		65	JONG Pok Hui	10
8 BERNAUER Vanessa	87		KIL Son Hui	15
10 KAUFMANN Isabelle	77		(C) HONG Myong Gum	16
14 MEYER Isabelle			RI Un Hyang	17
18 SCHWARZ Flavia	83		RI Jin Ok	19
Tr: TADDEI Claudio			KIM Kyong Hwa	20
6 BURGER Beatrice	87 65		Tr: CHOE Kwang Sok	
16 RAEMY Camille	83 48		O Kum Hui	4
17 SARRASIN Maeva	77 35		KIM Song Hui	7
			KIM Ok Sim	13

Petrovsky, St Petersburg
24-08-2006, 16:00, 300, Ferreira-James GUY, Ribeiro BRA, Canales ECU

GER 6   0 SUI

Bajramaj 2 [4] [62p], Laudehr [21], Okoyino da Mbabi [45], Kessler [85], Blaesse [89]

GERMANY			SWITZERLAND	
12 HOLZ Romina			MICHEL Stenia	1
3 KERSCHOWSKI Monique			ABBE Caroline	2
4 SCHIEWE Carolin	46		BACHMANN Ramona	3
5 PETER Babett			BETSCHART Sandra	4
7 BAJRAMAJ Fatmire	75		BEUTLER Barbara	5
8 GOESSLING Lena	67		BUERKI Vanessa	7
10 OKOYINO DA MBABI Celia		28	KAUFMANN Isabelle	10
11 LAUDEHR Simone			MEYER Isabelle	14
14 BLAESSE Anna			(C) MOSER Martina	15
18 MAIER Juliane	56		STILLHARD Francesca	18
20 KESSLER Nadine		59	ZAHNO Simone	20
Tr: MEINERT Maren			Tr: TADDEI Claudio	
6 WEBER Meike	67 59		BERNAUER Vanessa	8
13 HOEFLER Juliane	46	75 82	MAENDLY Sandy	11
19 SCHROEDER Corina	56	28	SCHWARZ Flavia	18

Dynamo, Moscow
24-08-2006, 16:00, 500, Avdonchenko RUS, Villa ESP, Lagrange FRA

MEX 0   4 PRK

Kim Hyang Mi [33], Kim Kyong Hwa [35], Kil Son Hui [42], O Kum Hui [59]

MEXICO			KOREA DPR	
12 VANEGAS Erika			JON Myong Hui	1
2 GORDILLO Maria (C)			KIM Chun Hui	6
5 VALDEZ Isabel			KIM Song Hui	7
6 NIEVA Christine	46		RI Song Sim	9
9 OCAMPO Monica	34		KIM Ok Sim	13
10 CORRAL Charlyn	55 66		KIL Son Hui	15
15 MENDEZ Norma			(C) HONG Myong Gum	16
16 FARIAS Janelly			RI Un Hyang	17
17 MARTINEZ Areli	51		RI Jin Ok	19
21 ACEVEDO Jackie	69		KIM Kyong Hwa	20
Tr: CUELLAR Leonardo			KIM Hyang Mi	21
4 VILLALPANDO Leticia	46 34		Tr: CHOE Kwang Sok	
7 MENDEZ Janet	5 66	34	O Kum Hui	4
19 GANDARILLA Nancy	69 51	66	JONG Pok Hui	10
		51	RI Jin Hui	14

GROUP D	PL	W	D	L	F	A	GD	PTS		FRA	ARG	COD
1 USA	3	3	0	0	7	2	+5	9		1-0	4-1	2-1
2 France	3	2	0	1	6	1	+5	6			5-0	1-0
3 Argentina	3	1	0	2	5	9	-4	3				4-0
4 Congo DR	3	0	0	3	1	7	-6	0				

Torpedo, Moscow
18-08-2006, 16:00, 300, Brohet BEL, Villa ESP, Nadolska POL

COD 1 2 USA

Nzuzi 70

O'Hara 33, Rodriguez 65p

CONGO DR						USA
1 BUAZO Mamie					21	HAIG Joanna
2 TEZI Pitshou	46			46	2	ANGELI Jordan
4 NZUZI Tresorine					3	LOGTERMAN Stephanie
5 KIUVU Guyssie (C)				46	4	KRZYSIK Nikki
6 MAFUALA Nanu					6	(C) LOPEZ Stephanie
7 AMANI Oliva	86				7	POACH Amanda
9 NSHIMIRE Annette					11	HEATH Tobin
11 LUMBU Nanouche					12	RODRIGUEZ Amy
12 ZENGA Mify	51				13	DI MARTINO Tina
14 KUYANGISA Odile				84	14	LONG Alexandra
15 BONGO Christine					19	O'HARA Kelley
Tr: BONGANYA Poly						Tr: SCHULZ Tim
8 WADIO Olga	86	84		84	5	WAGENFUHR Sarah
17 MALEMBO Yvonne	51	46		46	16	HARDY Erin
		46		46	20	NOGUEIRA Casey

Torpedo, Moscow
18-08-2006, 19:00, 250, De Silva TRI, Riley JAM, Mohammed TRI

FRA 5 0 ARG

Boulleau 12, Delie 2 28 65, Necib 51, Houara 85

FRANCE					ARGENTINA
16 BOUHADDI Sarah				1	MINNIG Elisabeth
2 DELANNOY Sabrina				2	(C) GONZALEZ Eva
3 BOULLEAU Laure (C)				3	PEREZ Catalina
4 COURTEILLE Morgane	57			4	LEIVA Ruth
5 DUCHER Coralie				5	QUINONES Florencia
7 HOUARA Jessica			82	7	MANICLER Ludmila
9 THOMIS Elodie				8	MANDRILE Florencia
10 NECIB Louisa	80			11	PEREYRA Mercedes
13 CORDIER Elodie				16	CHAVEZ Gabriela
18 DELIE Marie-Laure			46	18	MENDIETA Emilia
20 HENRY Amandine	67		46	19	BLANCO Maria
Tr: PILARD Stephane					Tr: BORRELLO Jose Carlos
6 PIZZALA Caroline	80		46	9	POTASSA Maria
11 COUDRAY Melodie	57		82	10	HIRMBRUCHNER Analia
14 DHAOU Ines	67		46	14	BRACAMONTE Joanna

Torpedo, Moscow
21-08-2006, 16:00, 200, Gaye SEN, Oulhaj MAR, Ndah BEN

USA 4 1 ARG

Rostedt 13, Adams 38, Long 62, Nogueira 91+

Pereyra 53

USA					ARGENTINA
18 DAVIS Kelsey				1	MINNIG Elisabeth
2 ANGELI Jordan	76			2	(C) GONZALEZ Eva
3 LOGTERMAN Stephanie			46	4	LEIVA Ruth
4 KRZYSIK Nikki (C)				5	QUINONES Florencia
5 WAGENFUHR Sarah				6	FARINA Marisa
7 POACH Amanda	46			7	MANICLER Ludmila
9 ADAMS Danesha				8	MANDRILE Florencia
10 BOCK Brittany	46	76		9	POTASSA Maria
15 DEW Carrie		67		10	HIRMBRUCHNER Analia
16 HARDY Erin				11	PEREYRA Mercedes
17 ROSTEDT Jessica				16	CHAVEZ Gabriela
Tr: SCHULZ Tim					Tr: BORRELLO Jose Carlos
14 LONG Alexandra	46	46		3	PEREZ Catalina
19 O'HARA Kelley	73	46	67	19	BLANCO Maria
20 NOGUEIRA Casey	76	76		20	URBANI Amancay

Torpedo, Moscow
21-08-2006, 19:00, 130, Ogston AUS, Keen AUS, Ho AUS

COD 0 1 FRA

Henry 44

CONGO DR					FRANCE
1 BUAZO Mamie				16	BOUHADDI Sarah
2 TEZI Pitshou				2	DELANNOY Sabrina
3 MENGI Lucie				3	BOULLEAU Laure
4 NZUZI Tresorine				4	COURTEILLE Morgane
5 KIUVU Guyssie				5	DUCHER Coralie
6 MAFUALA Nanu				7	HOUARA Jessica
7 AMANI Oliva	82	81		9	THOMIS Elodie
9 NSHIMIRE Annette	52	65	65	10	NECIB Louisa
14 KUYANGISA Odile				14	DHAOU Ines
16 BONGO Christine				18	DELIE Marie-Laure
17 MALEMBO Yvonne	78			20	HENRY Amandine
Tr: BONGANYA Poly					Tr: PILARD Stephane
10 MAFUTA Arlette	78	65	65	6	PIZZALA Caroline
12 ZENGA Mify	52	81	81	17	PLU Helene
13 NSIMBA Charmante	82				

Petrovsky, St Petersburg
24-08-2006, 19:00, 450, D'Coth IND, Shamsuri MAS, Yoshizawa JPN

ARG 4 0 COD

Manicler 3 13 17 47+, Potassa 15

ARGENTINA					CONGO DR
1 MINNIG Elisabeth				1	BUAZO Mamie
2 GONZALEZ Eva (C)	46			2	TEZI Pitshou
3 PEREZ Catalina				3	MENGI Lucie
4 QUINONES Florencia				4	NZUZI Tresorine
6 FARINA Marisa				5	(C) KIUVU Guyssie
7 MANICLER Ludmila	72			6	MAFUALA Nanu
8 MANDRILE Florencia				7	AMANI Oliva
9 POTASSA Maria	89			10	MAFUTA Arlette
10 HIRMBRUCHNER Analia	54	49	49	12	ZENGA Mify
11 PEREYRA Mercedes				14	KUYANGISA Odile
16 CHAVEZ Gabriela	68			15	BONGO Christine
Tr: BORRELLO Jose Carlos					Tr: BONGANYA Poly
4 LEIVA Ruth	72	49	49	8	WADIO Olga
15 SUAREZ Mariana	89	46		11	LUMBU Nanouche
19 BLANCO Maria	54	76	76	17	MALEMBO Yvonne

Dynamo, Moscow
24-08-2006, 19:00, 300, Hong KOR, Liu TPE, Ho AUS

USA 1 0 FRA

Rostedt 61

USA					FRANCE
1 HENDERSON Val				16	BOUHADDI Sarah
2 ANGELI Jordan				2	DELANNOY Sabrina
4 KRZYSIK Nikki			74	3	BOULLEAU Laure
5 WAGENFUHR Sarah	46	42	42	5	DUCHER Coralie
6 LOPEZ Stephanie				6	PIZZALA Caroline
8 CHENEY Lauren				8	B.ABDELWAHAB Meriame
10 BOCK Brittany	58			9	THOMIS Elodie
11 HEATH Tobin				10	NECIB Louisa
12 RODRIGUEZ Amy	46			11	COUDRAY Melodie
13 DI MARTINO Tina				15	L'HUILLIER Emilie
15 DEW Carrie	63		63	20	HENRY Amandine
Tr: SCHULZ Tim					Tr: PILARD Stephane
7 POACH Amanda	46	42	42	13	CORDIER Elodie
14 LONG Alexandra	58	74	74	14	DHAOU Ines
17 ROSTEDT Jessica	46	63	63	18	DELIE Marie-Laure

QUARTER-FINALS

Torpedo, Moscow
26-08-2006, 16:00, 700, Avdonchenko RUS, Müller GER, Santuari ITA

BRA 2 1 NGA

Fabiana 47+, Adriane 95+ — Uwak 65

#	BRAZIL			NIGERIA	#
1	BARBARA		92+	OLUEHI Tochukwu	1
2	DAIANE			CHIKWELU Rita	2
3	MONICA			(C) SABI Akudo	3
4	ALIANE		94+	EKE Maureen	4
5	ERIKA			IKIDI Faith	6
6	DANIELLE			OPARAOCHA Chizoma	8
7	FRANCIELLE			IWUAGWU Akudo	9
8	RENATA COSTA (C)		56	GODWIN Stella	11
9	FABIANA			JEROME Ulumma	16
11	MAURINE		80	AKUSOBI Blessing	17
17	PAMELA	72		UWAK Cynthia	18
	Tr: BARCELOS Jorge			Tr: OKONKWO Emmanuel	
15	ADRIANE	72	94+	BULUS Christy	12
			80	AKPA Gladys	7
			56	ISHOLA Tawa	14

Torpedo, Moscow
26-08-2006, 19:00, 2000, Gaal HUN, Lagrange FRA, Nadolska POL

CHN 4 0 RUS

Zi Jingjing 8, Ma Xiaoxu 19, Zhang Wei Shuang 40, You Jia 60

#	CHINA PR			RUSSIA	#
1	ZHANG Yanru			TODUA Elvira	1
2	ZHOU Gaoping			FILISOVA Maria	2
3	YUAN Fan			KOZHNIKOVA Anna	3
4	ZHANG Wei			GOMOZOVA Alexandra	4
5	WENG Xinzhi			KHARCHENKO Nadezda	6
7	XI Dingying	46		TEREKHOVA Elena	7
10	MA Xiaoxu (C)	66		TITOVA Oxana	8
13	ZHUANG Ran		46	DANILOVA Elena	9
15	YUE Min			MOROZOVA Elena	11
16	ZHANG Wei Shuang	81		(C) TSYBUTOVICH Ksenia	13
19	ZI Jingjing			STAROVOYTOVA Tamara	16
	Tr: SHANG Ruihua			Tr: GRISHIN Valentin	
8	YOU Jia	46	46	AKIMOVA Svetlana	15
11	LOU Xiaoxu	66			
20	LIU Xiaoxu	81			

Petrovsky, St Petersburg
27-08-2006, 16:00, 550, Bennett USA, Tovar MEX, Riley JAM

PRK 2 1 FRA

Kim Kyong Hwa 46, Hong Myong Gum 90 — Thomis 62

#	KOREA DPR			FRANCE	#
1	JON Myong Hui			BOUHADDI Sarah	16
2	JO Yun Mi	69		DELANNOY Sabrina	2
6	KIM Chun Hui			(C) BOULLEAU Laure	3
7	KIM Song Hui		79	COURTEILLE Morgane	4
9	RI Song Sim		93+	DUCHER Coralie	5
15	KIL Son Hui			PIZZALA Caroline	6
16	HONG Myong Gum (C)		55	HOUARA Jessica	7
17	RI Un Hyang			NECIB Louisa	10
19	RI Jin Ok			DHAOU Ines	14
20	KIM Kyong Hwa			DELIE Marie-Laure	18
21	KIM Hyang Mi	53		HENRY Amandine	20
	Tr: CHOE Kwang Sok			Tr: PILARD Stephane	
3	RI Un Suk	69	55	THOMIS Elodie	9
4	O Kum Hui	53	79	CORDIER Elodie	13
			93+	L'HUILLIER Emilie	15

Petrovsky, St Petersburg
27-08-2006, 19:00, 750, Palmqvist SWE, Villa ESP, Borg SWE

USA 4 1 GER

O'Hara 36, Adams 2 37 70, Rodriguez 90 — Neumann 65

#	USA			GERMANY	#
1	HENDERSON Val			HOLZ Romina	12
4	KRZYSIK Nikki	78	78	HAYE Janina	2
6	LOPEZ Stephanie (C)			PETER Babett	5
7	POACH Amanda			BAJRAMAJ Fatmire	7
8	CHENEY Lauren	62		GOESSLING Lena	8
9	ADAMS Danesha			OKOYINO DA MBABI Celia	10
10	BOCK Brittany	48 76	76	LAUDEHR Simone	11
11	HEATH Tobin			HOEFLER Juliane	13
12	RODRIGUEZ Amy	33		BLAESSE Anna	14
15	DEW Carrie			MAIER Juliane	18
19	O'HARA Kelley	48		KESSLER Nadine	20
	Tr: SCHULZ Tim			Tr: MEINERT Maren	
2	ANGELI Jordan	48 78	78	ANGEL Ann-Christin	9
13	DI MARTINO Tina	62 76	76	OSTER Jennifer	15
14	LONG Alexandra	48 33		NEUMANN Lydia	17

SEMI-FINALS

Lokomotiv, Moscow
31-08-2006, 16:00, 1000, Beck GER, Nadolska POL, Müller GER

BRA 0 1 PRK

Ri Un Hyang 87

#	BRAZIL			KOREA DPR	#
1	BARBARA			JON Myong Hui	1
2	DAIANE			JO Yun Mi	2
3	MONICA		72	O Kum Hui	4
4	ALIANE			KIM Chun Hui	6
5	ERIKA		93+	KIM Song Hui	7
6	DANIELLE			RI Song Sim	9
7	FRANCIELLE			KIL Son Hui	15
8	RENATA COSTA (C)			(C) HONG Myong Gum	16
9	FABIANA			RI Un Hyang	17
11	MAURINE			RI Jin Ok	19
15	ADRIANE	59		KIM Kyong Hwa	20
	Tr: BARCELOS Jorge			Tr: CHOE Kwang Sok	
17	PAMELA	59	72	RI Un Suk	3
			93+	KIM Hyang Mi	21

Lokomotiv, Moscow
31-08-2006, 19:00, 1000, Ogston AUS, Ho AUS, Keen AUS

CHN 0 0 USA
5 PSO 4

#	CHINA PR			USA	#
1	ZHANG Yanru			HENDERSON Val	1
2	ZHOU Gaoping		46	ANGELI Jordan	2
3	YUAN Fan			LOGTERMAN Stephanie	3
4	ZHANG Wei			KRZYSIK Nikki	4
5	WENG Xinzhi		46	WAGENFUHR Sarah	5
9	RAO Huifang	62		LOPEZ Stephanie	6
10	MA Xiaoxu			CHENEY Lauren	8
11	LOU Xiaoxu			BOCK Brittany	10
13	ZHUANG Ran			DI MARTINO Tina	13
15	YUE Min			DEW Carrie	15
16	ZHANG Wei Shuang	120 66	66	ROSTEDT Jessica	17
	Tr: SHANG Ruihua			Tr: SCHULZ Tim	
12	ZHU Wei	120 46	46	POACH Amanda	7
19	ZI Jingjing	62 66	66	ADAMS Danesha	9
			46	O'HARA Kelley	19

THIRD PLACE PLAY-OFF

Lokomotiv, Moscow
3-09-2006, 16:00, Palmqvist SWE, Villa ESP, Borg SWE

BRA	0 0	USA
	6 PSO 5	

BRAZIL		USA	
1 BARBARA		HENDERSON Val	1
2 DAIANE		KRZYSIK Nikki	4
3 MONICA		(C) LOPEZ Stephanie	6
4 ALIANE		POACH Amanda	7
5 ERIKA		CHENEY Lauren	8
6 DANIELLE		HEATH Tobin	11
7 FRANCIELLE		RODRIGUEZ Amy	12
8 RENATA COSTA (C)	85	DI MARTINO Tina	13
9 FABIANA		LONG Alexandra	14
11 MAURINE		DEW Carrie	15
20 STEPHANE	46	O'HARA Kelley	19
Tr: BARCELOS Jorge		Tr: SCHULZ Tim	
17 PAMELA	85	ANGELI Jordan	2
	46	ADAMS Danesha	9

FINAL

U-20 Women's 2006 Final	Lokomotiv, Moscow	3-09-2006
Kick-off: 19:00		Attendance: 8500

KOREA DPR	5 0	CHINA PR

JO Yun Mi [29], KIM Song Hui 3 [39] [47+] [52], KIL Son Hui [56]

KOREA DPR				MATCH STATS			CHINA PR		
1	GK	JON Myong Hui					(c) ZHANG Yanru	GK	1
2	MF	JO Yun Mi	81	15	Shots	13	ZHOU Gaoping	DF	2
6	MF	KIM Chun Hui		13	Shots on Goal	5	YUAN Fan	DF	3
7	MF	KIM Song Hui		15	Fouls Committed	12	ZHANG Wei	DF	4
9	DF	RI Song Sim		8	Corner Kicks	6	WENG Xinzhi	DF	5
13	MF	KIM Ok Sim	64	4	Offside	1	46	YOU Jia	MF	8
15	FW	KIL Son Hui		58	Possession %	42	LOU Xiaoxu	FW	11
16	DF	HONG Myong Gum (c)		(C)Captain †Man of the Match			ZHUANG Ran	MF	13
17	DF	RI Un Hyang		MATCH OFFICIALS			YUE Min	DF	15
19	DF	RI Jin Ok		REFEREE		69	ZHANG Wei Shuang	MF	16
20	MF	KIM Kyong Hwa		BENNETT Jennifer USA			LIU Xiaoyan	DF	20
		Tr: CHOE Kwang Sok		ASSISTANTS			Tr: SHANG Ruihua		
		Substitutes		TOVAR Maria Isabel MEX			Substitutes		
8	GK	MIN Jong Rim		RILEY Paulette JAM			WENG Xiaojie	GK	18
18	GK	JONG Ryon Hui		4TH OFFICIAL			XU Meishuang	GK	21
3	FW	RI Un Suk	64	GAAL Gyoengyi HUN			HOU Lijia	MF	6
4	FW	O Kum Hui					XI Dingying	MF	7
5	DF	KIM Hyon Suk					RAO Huifang	MF	9
10	FW	JONG Pok Hui					46	MA Xiaoxu	FW	10
11	FW	RA Un Sim					ZHU Wei	FW	12
12	FW	RI Jong Sim	81				WANG Dongni	DF	14
14	MF	RI Jin Hui					MA Zixiang	MF	17
21	MF	KIM Hyang Mi					69	ZI Jingjing	FW	19

We showed real quality today. That was as good as it gets from us, the players sweated blood for the team today. I'm overjoyed we've been able to fulfil the expectations of our government and our fans back home. We have plenty of talented players in Korea.

Choe Kwang Sok

Midfield was our problem area, because we played the ball square too often and that's fraught with danger on a heavy pitch like todays. We opened the door to our opponents, they made chances and turned them into goals. That's why we ended up losing so heavily.

Shang Ruihua

FIFA CLUB WORLD CUP 2006

FIFA CLUB WORLD CUP JAPAN 2006

Quarter-finals			Semi-finals			Final		
Internacional	BRA	Bye						
			Internacional	BRA	2			
			Al Ahly Cairo	EGY	1			
Auckland City	NZL	0						
Al Ahly Cairo	EGY	2						
						Internacional	BRA	1
						Barcelona	ESP	0
América	MEX	1						
Jeonbuk Motors	KOR	0						
			América	MEX	0			
			Barcelona	ESP	4			
Barcelona	ESP	Bye						

Fifth Place Play-off			Third Place Play-off		
Jeonbuk Motors	KOR	3	Al Ahly Cairo	EGY	2
Auckland City	NZL	0	América	MEX	1

First Round	Toyota Stadium, Toyota	10-12-2006
Kick-off: 19:20		Attendance: 29 912

AUCKLAND CITY   0   2   AL AHLY

Flavio [51], Aboutrika [73]

AUCKLAND CITY			
1	GK	NICHOLSON Ross	
4	MF	SEAMAN Paul	
5	DF	PERRY Jonathan	
6	MF	MULROONEY Liam	56
7	DF	PRITCHETT James	
10	FW	YOUNG Grant	
11	MF	SYKES Neil (C)	
14	FW	JORDAN Keryn	56
19	MF	COOMBES Chad	
20	DF	UHLMANN Greg	
21	DF	VAN STEEDEN Riki	52
		Tr: JONES Allan	
		Substitutes	
2	MF	HAYNE Jason	56
3	DF	SIGMUND Ben	52
16	MF	IWAMOTO Teru	56

MATCH STATS		
5	Shots	21
2	Shots on Goal	8
28	Fouls Committed	8
3	Corner Kicks	2
4	Offside	1
35	Possession %	65

MATCH OFFICIALS
REFEREE
AL GHAMDI Khalil KSA
ASSISTANTS
GHULOUM Eisa UAE
AL KADRI Hamdi SYR
4TH OFFICIAL
BATRES Carlos GUA

AL AHLY			
	EL HADARY Essam	GK	1
93+	EL SHATER Islam	DF	2
	GOMAA Wael	DF	6
	(C) MOHAMED Shady	DF	7
84	EMAD MOTEAB	FW	9
89	AHMED Shadid	DF	12
	ASHOUR Hossam	MF	13
	SHAWKY Mohamed	MF	17
	MOHAMED SEDIK	DF	20
	ABOUTRIKA Mohamed	FW	22
	FLAVIO	FW	23
	Tr: MANUEL Jose		
	Substitutes		
84	SAID Tarek	DF	3
93+	AHMED SEDIK	DF	8
89	MENSAH Akwety	MF	16

We palyed very well today for an amateur club. All my players did their jobs very well, especially in the first half. We were down to ten men with an injury when they took the lead. You're obviously vulnerable when you've only got ten players on the field, although that's not to take anything away from Flavio.

Alan Jones

We were very nervous in the first half. It was basically as if we were playing against ourselves and not Auckland. In the second half, the goal gave us back our belief, we retained possession much better and looked more solid. At the end of the day, that was the decisive factor in winning.

Manuel Jose

First Round	National Stadium, Tokyo	11-12-2006
Kick-off: 19:20		Attendance: 34 197

JEONBUK MOTORS   0   1   AMERICA

Ricardo Rojas [79]

JEONBUK MOTORS			
21	GK	KWOUN Sun Tae	
2	DF	CHOI Chul Soon	85
4	DF	CHOI Jin Cheul	
5	DF	KIM Young Sun	
6	DF	KIM Hyun Su (C)	
8	MF	CHUNG Jung Kwan	
11	DF	WANG Jung Hyun	29
12	MF	JEON Kwang Hwan	
15	FW	ZECARLO	
16	DF	LIM You Hwan	83
22	MF	KIM Hyeung Bum	
		Tr: CHOI Kang Hee	
		Substitutes	
10	MF	BOTTI	29
14	MF	LEE Hyun Seung	83
20	DF	KIM In Ho	85

MATCH STATS		
7	Shots	18
2	Shots on Goal	6
16	Fouls Committed	18
4	Corner Kicks	3
0	Offside	2
37	Possession %	63

MATCH OFFICIALS
REFEREE
DAMON Jerome RSA
ASSISTANTS
MOLEFE Enock RSA
NTAGUNGIRA Celestin RWA
4TH OFFICIAL
MOHD SALLEH Subkhiddin MAS

AMERICA			
	OCHOA Guillermo	GK	1
	CASTRO Jose Antonio	DF	3
	ROJAS Oscar	DF	4
	DAVINO Duilio	DF	5
86	LOPEZ Claudio	FW	7
	CABANAS Salvador	FW	9
	(C) BLANCO Cuauhtemoc	MF	10
71	FABIANO PEREIRA	MF	11
	ROJAS Ricardo	DF	16
	VILLA German	MF	18
	ARGUELLO Alejandro	MF	20
	Tr: TENA Luis Fernando		
	Substitutes		
86	VUOSO Matias	FW	8
71	MOSQUEDA Juan	MF	13

My players gave it their best shot, but we were unable to make anything of the few chances that came our way. You need plenty of experience to become a good team, but at the moment we have a lot of young players who are short on big-tournament experience.

Choi Kang Hee

It was a very difficult match as the Koreans were very well organised. They were agile and quick. We didn't make much of the space offered to us in the first half, but as the game went on we had more of the possession and we finally translated our chances into a goal.

Luis Fernando Tena

Semi-final	National Stadium, Tokyo	13-12-2006
Kick-off: 19:20		Attendance: 33 690

AL AHLY   1   2   INTERNACIONAL

Flavio [54]

Alexandre Prato [23], Luiz Adriano [72]

		AL AHLY	
1	GK	EL HADARY Essam	82
2	DF	EL SHATER Islam	75
3	DF	SAID Tarek	
4	DF	EL NAHAS Emad	
6	DF	GOMAA Wael	
7	DF	MOHAMED Shady (C)	
13	MF	ASHOUR Hossam	
14	MF	MOSTAFA Hassan	46
17	MF	SHAWKY Mohamed	
22	FW	ABOUTRIKA Mohamed	
23	FW	FLAVIO	

Tr: MANUEL Jose

		Substitutes	
19	GK	ABDELHAMID Amir	82
8	DF	AHMED SEDIK	75
9	FW	EMAD MOTEAB	46

MATCH STATS		
10	Shots	16
4	Shots on Goal	5
12	Fouls Committed	17
4	Corner Kicks	5
1	Offside	8
51	Possession %	49

MATCH OFFICIALS

REFEREE
MOHD SALLEH Subkhiddin MAS

ASSISTANTS
AL KADRI Hamdi SYR
GHULOUM Eisa UAE

4TH OFFICIAL
AL GHAMDI Khalil KSA

	INTERNACIONAL		
	CLEMER	GK	1
	CEARA	DF	2
	INDIO	DF	3
	FABIANO ELLER	DF	4
	WELLINGTON MONTEIRO	MF	5
63	HIDALGO Martin	DF	6
	ALEX	MF	7
	EDINHO	MF	8
	(C) FERNANDAO	FW	9
82	IARLEY	FW	10
65	ALEXANDRE PATO	FW	11

Tr: BRAGA Abel

	Substitutes		
63	RUBENS CARDOSO	DF	15
82	VARGAS Fabian	MF	17
65	LUIZ ADRIANO	FW	18

I'm proud of the way my players performed today. I'm delighted, because we've shown how well an African team can play. Brazil is one of the most advanced football nations. You can't compare Brazilian and Egyptian football, but what we've seen today proves we can hold our own.

Manuel Jose

We weren't on top form and half of my players fell below their normal standard, Yet again, what we have seen here is that every team always always has a chance of winning. I think were we were probably slightly lucky winners today. Our two youngest players scored the goals and decided the game.

Abel Braga

Semi-final	International Stadium, Yokohama	14-12-2006
Kick-off: 19:20		Attendance: 62 316

AMERICA   0   4   BARCELONA

Gudjohnsen [11], Marquez [30], Ronaldinho [65], Deco [85]

		AMERICA	
1	GK	OCHOA Guillermo	
3	DF	CASTRO Jose Antonio	
4	DF	ROJAS Oscar	
5	DF	DAVINO Duilio (C)	
6	FW	LOPEZ Claudio	74
9	FW	CABANAS Salvador	46
11	MF	FABIANO PEREIRA	74
16	DF	ROJAS Ricardo	
18	MF	VILLA German	
20	MF	ARGUELLO Alejandro	
23	FW	CUEVAS Nelson	

Tr: TENA Luis Fernando

		Substitutes	
8	FW	VUOSO Matias	74
10	MF	BLANCO Cuauhtemoc	46
22	MF	MENDOZA Raul Alvin	74

MATCH STATS		
11	Shots	22
4	Shots on Goal	9
12	Fouls Committed	9
2	Corner Kicks	6
7	Offside	0
47	Possession %	53

MATCH OFFICIALS

REFEREE
RUIZ Oscar COL

ASSISTANTS
BERRIO Wilson COL
YANEZ Rafael VEN

4TH OFFICIAL
DAMON Jerome RSA

	BARCELONA		
	VICTOR VALDES	GK	1
61	MOTTA	MF	3
	MARQUEZ Rafael	DF	4
	(C) PUYOL Carlos	DF	5
66	GUDJOHNSEN Eidur	FW	7
74	GIULY Ludovic	FW	8
	RONALDINHO	FW	10
	ZAMBROTTA Gianluca	DF	11
	VAN BRONCKHORST Giovanni	DF	12
	DECO	MF	20
	INIESTA	MF	24

Tr: RIJKAARD Frank

	Substitutes		
74	BELLETTI	DF	2
61	XAVI	MF	6
66	EZQUERRO	FW	18

It was a very good but getting anything from the game was always going to be difficult. They were letting the ball do the work and they caught us on the break a couple of times in the first half. We lost our shape in the opening 45 minutes instead of taking the pace out of the game.

Luis Fernando Tena

My team needed quite a while to find their rhythm. I'm happy America weren't able to exploit this weakness. I only stopped worrying after we went 3-0 up. We were mentally stronger than América today, although we shouldn't have lost concentration after the opening goals. We're all suffering from jetlag.

Frank Rijkaard

Match for 5th Place	National Stadium, Tokyo	15-12-2006
Kick-off: 19:20		Attendance: 23 258

AUCKLAND CITY   0 3   JEONBUK MOTORS

Lee Hyun Seung [17], Kim Hyeung Bum [31], Zecarlo [73p]

AUCKLAND CITY				MATCH STATS				JEONBUK MOTORS		
1	GK	NICHOLSON Ross						KWOUN Sun Tae	GK	21
4	MF	SEAMAN Paul		8	Shots	10	88	CHOI Jin Cheul	DF	4
5	DF	PERRY Jonathan		2	Shots on Goal	7		KIM Young Sun	DF	5
6	MF	MULROONEY Liam	79	30	Fouls Committed	12	81	(C) KIM Hyun Su	DF	6
7	DF	PRITCHETT James		3	Corner Kicks	5	76	JANG Ji Hyun	MF	7
10	FW	YOUNG Grant	77	4	Offside	0		CHUNG Jung Kwan	MF	8
11	MF	SYKES Neil (C)		40	Possession %	60		LEE Hyun Seung	MF	14
14	FW	JORDAN Keryn						ZECARLO	FW	15
19	MF	COOMBES Chad			MATCH OFFICIALS			LIM You Hwan	DF	16
20	DF	UHLMANN Greg			REFEREE			KIM In Ho	DF	20
22	MF	LITTLE Bryan	59		AL GHAMDI Khalil KSA			KIM Hyeung Bum	MF	22
	Tr: JONES Allan				ASSISTANTS			Tr: CHOI Kang Hee		
	Substitutes				GHULOUM Eisa UAE			Substitutes		
2	MF	HAYNE Jason	79		AL KADRI Hamdi SYR		81	JEON Kwang Hwan	MF	12
9	FW	URLOVIC Paul	77		4TH OFFICIAL		88	SHIN Sang Hoon	MF	13
16	MF	IWAMOTO Teru	59		BATRES Carlos GUA		76	KIM Young Sin	MF	17

This competition is open to amateurs and professionals alike and I think it's fantastic. It's a genuine honour to have been able to take part in this competition. As amateurs we gave it our best shot against professional teams, but we failed to score in either game, although we did better this evening.

Allan Jones

Taking part in this competition has taught the players a great deal. We already know what it takes to win in Asia, but here I felt we came up short in various respects. Our play is way too erratic and we've got to do something about these highs and lows. We need a stronger bench too.

Choi Kang Hee

Match for 3rd Place	International Stadium, Yokohama	17-12-2006
Kick-off: 16:20		Attendance: 51 641

AL AHLY   2 1   AMERICA

Mohamed Aboutrika 2 [42 79]   Cabanas [59]

AL AHLY				MATCH STATS				AMERICA		
19	GK	ABDELHAMID Amir						OCHOA Guillermo	GK	1
2	DF	EL SHATER Islam	67	13	Shots	16		CASTRO Jose Antonio	DF	3
3	DF	SAID Tarek		3	Shots on Goal	8		ROJAS Oscar	DF	4
4	DF	EL NAHAS Emad		25	Fouls Committed	10		(C) DAVINO Duilio	DF	5
6	DF	GOMAA Wael		3	Corner Kicks	4	67	VUOSO Matias	FW	8
7	MF	MOHAMED Shady (C)		1	Offside	2		CABANAS Salvador	FW	9
9	FW	EMAD MOTEAB	75	48	Possession %	52	46	FABIANO PEREIRA	MF	11
13	MF	ASHOUR Hossam	65					MOSQUEDA Juan	MF	13
17	MF	SHAWKY Mohamed			MATCH OFFICIALS		86	ROJAS Ricardo	DF	16
22	FW	ABOUTRIKA Mohamed			REFEREE			ARGUELLO Alejandro	MF	20
23	FW	FLAVIO			DAMON Jerome RSA			CUEVAS Nelson	FW	23
	Tr: MANUEL Jose				ASSISTANTS			Tr: TENA Luis Fernando		
	Substitutes				MOLEFE Enock RSA			Substitutes		
8	DF	AHMED SEDIK	67		NTAGUNGIRA Celestin RWA		67	LOPEZ Claudio	FW	7
14	MF	MOSTAFA Hassan	65		4TH OFFICIAL		46	BLANCO Cuauhtemoc	MF	10
20	DF	MOHAMED SEDIK	75		RUIZ Oscar COL		86	MENDOZA Raul Alvin	MF	22

We put on a real high quality display. Our style this time was more European than it was last year. Every time we play a club from outside of Africa we pick up valuable experience. I wanted us to to be able to take part in this competition again so that we could show everyone the real Al Ahly, and today we did just that.

Manuel Jose

We had a poor first half. In the second we had more possession and started to create more scoring chances. After we scored the equaliser, we really went for it. We took risks going forward and that left spaces in midfield and at the back which our opponents exploited. Aboutrika really stood out for Ahly.

Luis Fernando Tena

Final	International Stadium, Yokohama	17-12-2006
Kick-off: 19:20		Attendance: 67 128

INTERNACIONAL   1   0   BARCELONA

Adriano [82]

INTERNACIONAL				MATCH STATS			BARCELONA		
1	GK	CLEMER					VICTOR VALDES	GK	1
2	DF	CEARA		10	Shots	17	59	MOTTA	MF	3
3	DF	INDIO		2	Shots on Goal	6		MARQUEZ Rafael	DF	4
4	DF	FABIANO ELLER		25	Fouls Committed	15		(C) PUYOL Carlos	DF	5
5	MF	WELLINGTON MONTEIRO		2	Corner Kicks	11	88	GUDJOHNSEN Eidur	FW	7
7	MF	ALEX	46	5	Offside	1		GIULY Ludovic	FW	8
8	MF	EDINHO		42	Possession %	58		RONALDINHO	FW	10
9	FW	FERNANDAO (C)	76				46	ZAMBROTTA Gianluca	DF	11
10	FW	IARLEY		MATCH OFFICIALS			VAN BRONCKHORST Giovanni	DF	12
11	FW	ALEXANDRE PATO	61	REFEREE			DECO	MF	20
15	DF	RUBENS CARDOSO		BATRES Carlos GUA			INIESTA	MF	24
		Tr: BRAGA Abel		ASSISTANTS			Tr: RIJKAARD Frank		
		Substitutes		PASTRANA Carlos HON			Substitutes		
16	MF	ADRIANO	76	LEAL Leonel CRC		46	BELLETTI	DF	2
17	MF	VARGAS Fabian	46	4TH OFFICIAL		59	XAVI	MF	6
18	FW	LUIZ ADRIANO	61	MOHD SALLEH Subkhiddin MAS		88	EZQUERRO	FW	18

This is a great achievement. We outlined an objective and we ran after it. Now we are champions of the world. Barcelona have an excellent team but we played with courage. The players are heroes. We played with three forwards, but were always thinking about marking - the only way to beat them.

Abel Braga

I have to congratulate Inter, who played as a team and put in a great performance. I feel that they were the better side. At no time were we in control of the game. Every time we got close to their area we ran up against a wall of players. They put in a quality performance. We're bitterly disappointed.

Frank Rijkaard

FIFA BEACH SOCCER WORLD CUP 2006

FIFA BEACH SOCCER WORLD CUP BRAZIL 2006

First round groups	USA	POL	JPN	Pts	Quarter-finals		Semi-finals		Final	
Brazil	10-6	9-2	10-2	9						
USA		4-2	4-8	3	**Brazil**	12				
Poland			8-5	3	Canada	1				
Japan				3						
							Brazil	7		
	CAN	ESP	IRN	Pts			Portugal	4		
France	8-1	7-4	6-3	9						
Canada		4-0	6-6	4	Bahrain	2				
Spain			6-1	3	**Portugal**	6				
Iran				1						
									Brazil	4
	URU	SOL	CMR	Pts					Uruguay	1
Portugal	5-4	14-2	10-3	9						
Uruguay		10-5	3-3	4	**France**	3				
Solomon Islands			5-2	3	Japan	2				
Cameroon				1						
							France	0 0p		
	BAH	NGA	ITA	Pts			**Uruguay**	0 1p		
Argentina	2-1	5-4	3-1	9						
Bahrain		5-5	4-2	4	Argentina	1		**3rd Place Play-off**		
Nigeria			4-3	4	**Uruguay**	2		**France**	6	
Italy				0				Portugal	4	

FIFA U–20 WORLD CUP CANADA 2007

FIFA U-20 WORLD CUP CANADA 2007

First round groups	Pts	Round of 16		Quarter-finals		Semi-finals		Final	
Group A	Pts								
Chile	7	**Argentina**	3						
Austria	5	Poland	1						
Congo	4			**Argentina**	1				
Canada	0			Mexico	0				
Group B	Pts	Congo	0						
Spain	7	**Mexico**	3						
Zambia	4					**Argentina**	3		
Uruguay	4					Chile	0		
Jordan	1	**Nigeria**	2						
Group C	Pts	Zambia	1						
Mexico	9			Nigeria	0				
Gambia	6			**Chile**	4				
Portugal	3	Portugal	0						
New Zealand	0	**Chile**	1						
								Argentina	2
								Czech Republic	1
Group D	Pts								
USA	7	**Austria**	2						
Poland	4	Gambia	1						
Brazil	3			**Austria**	2				
Korea Republic	2			USA	1				
Group E	Pts	Uruguay	1						
Argentina	7	**USA**	2						
Czech Republic	5					Austria	0		
Korea DPR	2					**Czech Republic**	2		
Panama	1	**Spain**	4						
Group F	Pts	Brazil	2						
Japan	7			Spain	1 3p				
Nigeria	7			**Czech Republic**	1 4p	3rd place play-off			
Costa Rica	3	Japan	2 3p			**Chile**	1		
Scotland	0	**Czech Republic**	2 4p			Austria	0		

GROUP A	PL	W	D	L	F	A	PTS
1 Chile	3	2	1	0	6	0	7
2 Austria	3	1	2	0	2	1	5
3 Congo	3	1	1	1	3	4	4
4 Canada	3	0	0	3	0	6	0

	AUT	CGO	CAN
	0-0	3-0	3-0
		1-1	1-0
			2-0

National Soccer Stadium, Toronto
1-07-2007, 19:45, 19 526, Undiano Mallenco ESP

CAN 0 3 CHI

Medina [25], Carmona [54], Grondona [81]

CANADA			CHILE	
1 BEGOVIC Asmir			TOSELLI Cristopher	1
2 ATTAKORA-GYAN Nana			SUAREZ Cristian	2
3 O'CONNOR Kent			ISLA Mauricio	3
4 EDGAR David			LARRONDO Nicolas	5
5 HABER Marcus			MEDEL Gary	6
6 B-BOURGAULT Jonathan		69	CURRIMILLA Dagoberto	8
7 PETERS Jaime		80	MEDINA Nicolas	9
9 LOMBARDO Andrea	64		VIDAL Arturo	14
10 JOHNSON Will (c)			CARMONA Carlos	15
11 JACKSON Simeon	46		CORTES Gerardo	16
15 NUNEZ Cristian		84	VIDANGOSSY Mathias	18
Tr: MITCHELL Dale			Tr: SULANTAY José	
14 RICKETTS Tosaint	46	84	GODOY Eric	4
16 ELLIOTT Alex	64	80	GRONDONA Jaime	11
		69	SEPULVEDA Christian	13

Commonwealth Stadium, Edmonton
5-07-2007, 17:45, 31 579, Buitrago COL

AUT 1 0 CAN

Okotie [47]

AUSTRIA			CANADA	
12 LUKSE Andreas			BEGOVIC Asmir (c)	1
2 PANNY Thomas			O'CONNOR Kent	3
4 PROEDL Sebastian (c)			EDGAR David	4
6 STANISLAW Michael			HABER Marcus	5
8 KAVLAK Veli		61	B-BOURGAULT Jonathan	6
9 HOFFER Erwin	72		PETERS Jaime	7
10 JUNUZOVIC Zlatko	81	81	AYRE Keegan	8
14 MORGENTHALER Bernhard			JOHNSON Will	10
15 MADL Michael			JACKSON Simeon	11
19 OKOTIE Rubin	84	25	LUMLEY Stephen	13
20 RASSWALDER Siegfried			RICKETTS Tosaint	14
Tr: GLUDOVATZ Paul			Tr: MITCHELL Dale	
3 GRAMANN Daniel	84	81	LOMBARDO Andrea	9
7 HARNIK Martin	72	61	NUNEZ Cristian	15
11 HACKMAIR Peter	81	25	D'AGOSTINO Michael	19

Commonwealth Stadium, Edmonton
8-07-2007, 18:00, 32 058, Webb ENG

CAN 0 2 CGO

Ngakosso [26], Ikouma [60]

CANADA			CONGO	
1 BEGOVIC Asmir	73		ONKA Destin	1
2 ATTAKORA-GYAN Nana			AHOUNGOU Yan	3
4 EDGAR David (c)		83	IKOUMA Gracia	5
5 HABER Marcus	73		NDINGA Delvin	8
6 B-BOURGAULT Jonathan		48	NGAKOSSO Ermejea	9
7 PETERS Jaime		76	FILANCKEMBO Cecil (c)	10
9 LOMBARDO Andrea			IBARA Franchel	11
10 JOHNSON Will			LOPARIMI Jacques	14
13 LUMLEY Stephen	57		OKIELE Mimille	15
14 RICKETTS Tosaint	46		MERECK Murhyen	17
18 OWUSU-ANSAH Kennedy			NKOUNGA Saide	18
Tr: MITCHELL Dale			Tr: HUDANSKI Eddie	
11 JACKSON Simeon	46	76	ONDJOLA Jules	4
16 ELLIOTT Alex	73	48	LAKOLO Prestone	7
17 GALA Gabriel	57	83	TCHILIMBOU Harris	13

Commonwealth Stadium, Edmonton
2-07-2007, 17:45, 19 899, Wijngaarde SUR

CGO 1 1 AUT

Ibara [59p]

Hoffer [7]

CONGO			AUSTRIA	
1 ONKA Destin			ZAGLMAIR Michael	21
3 AHOUNGOU Yan	41		PANNY Thomas	2
4 ONDJOLA Jules			PROEDL Sebastian (c)	4
5 IKOUMA Gracia			STANISLAW Michael	4
6 MBANI Oxence		76	HARNIK Martin	7
8 NDINGA Delvin			KAVLAK Veli	8
10 FILANCKEMBO Cecil (c)	89	92	HOFFER Erwin	9
11 IBARA Franchel			JUNUZOVIC Zlatko	10
12 NGUESSI Fabrice		61	HACKMAIR Peter	11
15 OKIELE Mimille			MADL Michael	15
17 MERECK Murhyen			RASSWALDER Siegfried	20
Tr: HUDANSKI Eddie			Tr: GLUDOVATZ Paul	
2 KOMBO Yann	41	76	MORGENTHALER Bernhard	14
13 TCHILIMBOU Harris	89	92	ENZENBERGER Ingo	16
		61	OKOTIE Rubin	19

Commonwealth Stadium, Edmonton
5-07-2007, 20:30, 30 352, Irmatov UZB

CHI 3 0 CGO

Sanchez [49], Medina [75], Vidal [82]

CHILE			CONGO	
1 TOSELLI Cristopher			ONKA Destin	1
2 SUAREZ Cristian		22	KOMBO Yann	2
3 ISLA Mauricio		65	IKOUMA Gracia	5
5 LARRONDO Nicolas			MBANI Oxence	6
6 MEDEL Gary			NDINGA Delvin	8
7 SANCHEZ Alexis			NGAKOSSO Ermejea	9
8 CURRIMILLA Dagoberto		65	TCHILIMBOU Harris	13
9 MEDINA Nicolas	89		OKIELE Mimille	15
14 VIDAL Arturo	84		MERECK Murhyen (c)	17
15 CARMONA Carlos (c)			NKOUNGA Saide	18
18 VIDANGOSSY Mathias	79	83	ITOUA Bovid	19
Tr: SULANTAY José			Tr: HUDANSKI Eddie	
11 GRONDONA Jaime	84	83	LAKOLO Prestone	7
13 SEPULVEDA Christian	79	65	FILANCKEMBO Cecil	10
19 SILVA Michael	89	65	KAPOLONGO Ulrich	20

National Soccer Stadium, Toronto
8-07-2007, 20:00, 19 526, Aguilar SLV

CHI 0 0 AUT

CHILE			AUSTRIA	
1 TOSELLI Cristopher			KURU Bartolomej	1
3 ISLA Mauricio			GRAMANN Daniel	3
4 GODOY Eric			PROEDL Sebastian (c)	4
5 LARRONDO Nicolas			SUTTNER Markus	5
8 CURRIMILLA Dagoberto	83		STANISLAW Michael	6
9 MEDINA Nicolas		80	HARNIK Martin	7
14 VIDAL Arturo		87	HOFFER Erwin	9
15 CARMONA Carlos (c)	29	68	JUNUZOVIC Zlatko	10
16 CORTES Gerardo			HACKMAIR Peter	11
17 MARTINEZ Hans			MORGENTHALER Bernhard	14
18 VIDANGOSSY Mathias	67		MADL Michael	15
Tr: SULANTAY José			Tr: GLUDOVATZ Paul	
2 SUAREZ Cristian	83	87	SIMKOVIC Tomas	17
6 MEDEL Gary	29	80	HINUM Thomas	18
11 GRONDONA Jaime	67	68	OKOTIE Rubin	19

GROUP B		PL	W	D	L	F	A	PTS
1	Spain	3	2	1	0	8	5	7
2	Zambia	3	1	1	1	4	3	4
3	Uruguay	3	1	1	1	3	4	4
4	Jordan	3	0	1	2	3	6	1

	ZAM	URU	JOR
Spain	2-1	2-2	4-2
Zambia		2-0	1-1
Uruguay			1-0

Swangard Stadium, Burnaby
1-07-2007, 14:15, 10 000, Vaughn USA

JOR 1 1 ZAM

Abdallah Salim 41 — Tembo 8p

JORDAN				ZAMBIA		
1	AL ASMAR Hamad			BANDA Jacob	1	
3	ZAWAHREH Ibrahim			ZIMBA Joseph	3	
6	BANI YASEEN Anas (c)			BANDA Dennis	4	
7	SULEIMAN Baha	46		PHIRI Richard	7	
8	SALIM Abdallah			NJOBVU William	8	
10	NOFAL Ahmad	12	74	TEMBO Fwayo	11	
11	HIJAH Anas			(c) MWANSA Sebastian	12	
15	HASAN Adnan			KACHINGA Goodson	14	
19	AL ZAIDEH Loiy	61		ZULU Justine	15	
20	AL BASHIR Ala	45		KOLA Rodgers	18	
21	AL JUMAH Tariq	6	61	MAYUKA Emmanuel	19	
Tr: POULSEN Jan				Tr: LWANDAMINA George		
13	AL BASHA Mohammad	12	61	LUPIYA Simon	9	61
14	FRAEH Raed	61	74	SIMUTOWE Musatwe	13	74
17	ALAWNEH Mohammad	46				

Swangard Stadium, Burnaby
1-07-2007, 17:00, 10 000, Stark GER

ESP 2 2 URU

Adrian Lopez 71, Diego Capel 93+ — Cavani 47, Luis Suarez 56

SPAIN				URUGUAY		
1	ADAN (c)			GOICOECHEA Mauro	1	
2	BARRAGAN Antonio			CACERES Martin	3	
4	MARC VALIENTE			ROMAN Marcel	5	
5	PIQUE Gerard			KAGELMACHER Gary	6	
6	MARIO SUAREZ	75		CARDACCIO Mathias	7	
7	TONI CALVO	57	66	SUAREZ Damian	8	
8	JAVI GARCIA	60		(c) CAVANI Edinson	9	
9	BUENO Alberto	53		DIAZ Juan Manuel	13	
11	CAPEL Diego			ARISMENDI Hugo	16	
12	CANELLA Roberto	60		SURRACO Juan	17	
16	MATA Juan Manuel			SUAREZ Luis	18	
Tr: MELENDEZ Gines				Tr: FERRIN Gustavo		
18	ADRIAN LOPEZ	53	60	PRIETO Mauricio	2	60
19	GARCIA Marcos	57	75	RUIZ Enzo	15	75
20	STEPHEN Sunny	60		MONTELONGO Bruno	16	66

Swangard Stadium, Burnaby
4-07-2007, 17:00, 10 000, O'Leary NZL

URU 1 0 JOR

Cavani 40

URUGUAY			JORDAN		
1	GOICOECHEA Mauro		AL ASMAR Hamad	1	
3	CACERES Martin		ZAWAHREH Ibrahim	3	
5	ROMAN Marcel		(c) BANI YASEEN Anas	6	
6	KAGELMACHER Gary		SULEIMAN Baha	7	
8	SUAREZ Damian		SALIM Abdallah	8	
9	CAVANI Edinson (c)	67	HIJAH Anas	11	
10	VONDER PUTTEN Gerardo	61	AL BASHA Mohammad	13	
13	DIAZ Juan Manuel		FRAEH Raed	14	
14	ARISMENDI Hugo	64	HASAN Adnan	15	
17	SURRACO Juan	61	AL ZAIDEH Loiy	19	61
18	SUAREZ Luis	77	AL BASHIR Ala	20	89
Tr: FERRIN Gustavo			Tr: POULSEN Jan		
7	CARDACCIO Mathias	64	AL KATATSHEH Khaled	5	89
16	MONTELONGO Bruno	77	NOFAL Ahmad	10	61
19	VIUDEZ Tabare	61 67	ALAWNEH Mohammad	17	67

Swangard Stadium, Burnaby
4-07-2007, 19:45, 10 000, Areedondo MEX

ZAM 1 2 ESP

Njobvu 74 — Mario Suarez 30p, Mata 40

ZAMBIA				SPAIN		
1	BANDA Jacob			(c) ADAN	1	
3	ZIMBA Joseph			BARRAGAN Antonio	2	
4	BANDA Dennis			CRESPO Jose	3	
5	NYAMBE Henry			MARC VALIENTE	4	
8	NJOBVU William			PIQUE Gerard	5	
10	MULENGA Clifford	79		MARIO SUAREZ	6	
11	TEMBO Fwayo	58	67	TONI CALVO	7	
12	MWANSA Sebastian (c)			CAPEL Diego	11	
14	KACHINGA Goodson		50	MATA Juan Manuel	16	
19	MAYUKA Emmanuel			ADRIAN LOPEZ	18	
20	SUNZU Stophira	60		STEPHEN Sunny	20	
Tr: LWANDAMINA George				Tr: MELENDEZ Gines		
7	PHIRI Richard	60	79	JAVI GARCIA	8	
9	LUPIYA Simon	58	50	GRANERO Esteban	10	
			67	GONZALEZ Iriome	15	

Royal Athletic Park, Victoria
7-07-2007, 14:15, 11 500, Hansson SWE

URU 0 2 ZAM

Mulenga 22p, Kola 51

URUGUAY			ZAMBIA		
1	GOICOECHEA Mauro 19		BANDA Jacob	1	
2	PRIETO Mauricio		ZIMBA Joseph	3	
3	CACERES Martin		BANDA Dennis	4	
5	ROMAN Marcel	40	NYAMBE Henry 40	5	
6	KAGELMACHER Gary		NJOBVU William	8	
7	CARDACCIO Mathias	62	MULENGA Clifford	10	
9	CAVANI Edinson (c)		(c) MWANSA Sebastian	12	
11	FIGUEROA Elias	21	KACHINGA Goodson	14	
13	DIAZ Juan Manuel	90	KOLA Rodgers	18	
14	ARISMENDI Hugo	65	MAYUKA Emmanuel	19	
16	MONTELONGO Bruno	46	SUNZU Stophira	20	
Tr: FERRIN Gustavo			Tr: LWANDAMINA George		
10	VONDER PUTTEN Gerardo	65 62	PHIRI Richard	7	62
12	IRRAZABAL Yonatan	21 90	SIMUTOWE Musatwe	13	90
18	SUAREZ Luis	46			

Swangard Stadium, Burnaby
7-07-2007, 14:15, 10 000, Buitrago COL

ESP 4 2 JOR

Adrian Lopez 3 29 32 38, Marcos Garcia 79 — Loiy Al Zaideh 48, Abdallah Salim 56

SPAIN			JORDAN		
1	ADAN (c)		AL ASMAR Hamad	1	
3	CRESPO Jose		(c) BANI YASEEN Anas	6	
5	PIQUE Gerard	43	SULEIMAN Baha	7	
8	JAVI GARCIA	62	SALIM Abdallah	8	
10	GRANERO Esteban		HIJAH Anas	11	
12	CANELLA Roberto		AL BASHA Mohammad	13	
13	GONZALEZ Adrian	68	FRAEH Raed	14	
15	GONZALEZ Iriome	65	HASAN Adnan	15	
17	ELUSTONDO Gorka	86	AL ZAIDEH Loiy	19	
18	ADRIAN LOPEZ		AL BASHIR Ala	20	
19	GARCIA Marcos		AL JUMAH Tariq	21	
Tr: MELENDEZ Gines			Tr: POULSEN Jan		
4	MARC VALIENTE	43 68	NOFAL Ahmad	10	68
11	CAPEL Diego	65 86	ALAWNEH Mohammad	17	86
20	STEPHEN Sunny	62			

GROUP C	PL	W	D	L	F	A	PTS
1 Mexico	3	3	0	0	7	2	9
2 Gambia	3	2	0	1	3	4	6
3 Portugal	3	1	0	2	4	4	3
4 New Zealand	3	0	0	3	1	5	0

	GAM	POR	NZL
	3-0	2-1	2-1
		2-1	1-0
			2-0

National Soccer Stadium, Toronto
2-07-2007, 14:15, 19 500, Buitrago COL

POR 2 0 NZL

Bruno Gama 2 [45] [61p]

PORTUGAL	#				NEW ZEALAND	#	
RUI PATRICIO	12				SPOONLEY Jacob	1	
PAULO RENATO	4				PETERS Sam	2	
NUNO COELHO	6				HOGG Ian	3	
BRUNO GAMA (c)	7	63			PEVERLEY Cole	4	
PELE	8				EDGINTON Phil	6	
ZEQUINHA	9				HENDERSON Craig	7	
FABIO COENTRAO	11				BROCKIE Jeremy	10	
ANTUNES	13	75			JENKINS Sam	11	
JOAO PEDRO	14				ROYDHOUSE Nick	12	
MANO	18	69			BOXALL Michael	14	
BRUNO PEREIRINHA	20	79			KEAT Dan (c)	15	
Tr: COUCEIRO José					Tr: JACOBS Stu		
ANDRE MARQUES	5	75	63		DRAPER Greg	9	63
VITOR GOMES	10	69					
ZEZINANDO	15	79					

National Soccer Stadium, Toronto
2-07-2007, 17:00, 19 500, Irmatov UZB

GAM 0 3 MEX

Dos Santos [57], Moreno [67], Javier Hernandez [89]

GAMBIA	#				MEXICO	#	
GOMEZ Joseph	1				BLANCO Alfonso	1	
GOMEZ Pierre	2				(c) ARAUJO Patricio	2	
NGUM Alagie	4				JUAREZ Efrain	3	
JAMMEH Ken (c)	5				MORENO Hector	5	
BOJANG Mandou	6				ESPARZA Omar	6	
JAGNE Pa Modou	9				HERNANDEZ Jorge	7	54
SOHNA Ebrima	11	86			VELA Carlos	9	80
MANSALLY Abdoulie	12	84			DOS SANTOS Giovanni	10	85
JALLOW Ousman	13				DOMINGUEZ Julio Cesar	13	
NYASSI Sainey	14	65			ALDRETE Adrian	16	
JAITEH Tijan	15				VILLALUZ Cesar	18	
Tr: JOHNSON Peter					Tr: RAMIREZ Jesus		
JATTA Paul	8	86	54		BARRERA Pablo	8	54
CONATEH Pa Landing	10	84	85		HERNANDEZ Javier	11	85
NYASSI Sanna	17	65	80		SILVA Juan Carlos	15	80

National Soccer Stadium, Toronto
5-07-2007, 17:00, 11 869, Aguilar SLV

NZL 0 1 GAM

Jallow [22]

NEW ZEALAND	#				GAMBIA	#	
SPOONLEY Jacob	1				GOMEZ Joseph	1	
PETERS Sam	2	63			GOMEZ Pierre	2	
HOGG Ian	3				NGUM Alagie	4	
PEVERLEY Cole	4	25			(c) JAMMEH Ken	5	
EDGINTON Phil	6				BOJANG Mandou	6	
HENDERSON Craig	7				JAGNE Pa Modou	9	
BROCKIE Jeremy	10	57			CONATEH Pa Landing	10	
JENKINS Sam	11	70			SOHNA Ebrima	11	
ROYDHOUSE Nick	12	84			JALLOW Ousman	13	84
BOXALL Michael	14	78			NYASSI Sainey	14	78
KEAT Dan (c)	15				JAITEH Tijan	15	
Tr: JACOBS Stu					Tr: JOHNSON Peter		
DRAPER Greg	9	25	78		MENDY Furmus	3	78
SCHAEFFERS Tim	17	63	84		JATTA Paul	8	84
CLAPHAM Aaron	21	70	57		MANSALLY Abdoulie	12	57

National Soccer Stadium, Toronto
5-07-2007, 19:45, 19 500, Webb ENG

MEX 2 1 POR

Dos Santos [48p], Barrera [66]   Antunes [89]

MEXICO	#				PORTUGAL	#	
BLANCO Alfonso	1				RUI PATRICIO	12	
ARAUJO Patricio (c)	2				PAULO RENATO	4	
JUAREZ Efrain	3				NUNO COELHO	6	
MORENO Hector	5				(c) BRUNO GAMA	7	69
ESPARZA Omar	6				PELE	8	
HERNANDEZ Jorge	7	90	74		ZEQUINHA	9	74
VELA Carlos	9				FABIO COENTRAO	11	
DOS SANTOS Giovanni	10	85			ANTUNES	13	
DOMINGUEZ Julio Cesar	13				JOAO PEDRO	14	
ALDRETE Adrian	16				MANO	18	
VILLALUZ Cesar	18	64	57		BRUNO PEREIRINHA	20	57
Tr: RAMIREZ Jesus					Tr: COUCEIRO José		
BARRERA Pablo	8	64	74		ZEZINANDO	15	74
SILVA Juan Carlos	15	90	69		FELICIANO CONDESSO	17	69
GUERRERO Jose	17	85	57		GUEDES	19	57

Le Stade Olympique, Montreal
8-07-2007, 17:15, 28 402, Stark GER

POR 1 2 GAM

Feliciano Condesso [20]   Jallow [44p], Mansally [68]

PORTUGAL	#				GAMBIA	#	
RUI PATRICIO	12				GOMEZ Joseph	1	
PEDRO CORREIA	2				GOMEZ Pierre	2	
STEVEN VITORIA	3	63			NGUM Alagie	4	
PAULO RENATO	4	59			(c) JAMMEH Ken	5	
ANDRE MARQUES	5	62			BOJANG Mandou	6	
NUNO COELHO	6	32			JATTA Paul	8	
BRUNO GAMA (c)	7	74			JAGNE Pa Modou	9	
ZEQUINHA	9				SOHNA Ebrima	11	
ZEZINANDO	15				JALLOW Ousman	13	64
FELICIANO CONDESSO	17	64			NYASSI Sainey	14	
GUEDES	19				JAITEH Tijan	15	
Tr: COUCEIRO José					Tr: JOHNSON Peter		
ANTUNES	13	62	64		MENDY Furmus	3	64
JOAO PEDRO	14	63	32		MANSALLY Abdoulie	12	32
DIOGO TAVARES	16	74					

Commonwealth Stadium, Edmonton
8-07-2007, 15:15, 29 792, Benouza ALG

NZL 1 2 MEX

Pelter [89]   Bermudez [24], Mares [78]

NEW ZEALAND	#				MEXICO	#	
SPOONLEY Jacob	1				COTA Rodolfo	12	
PEVERLEY Cole	4				LEDESMA Arturo	4	
PELTER Jack (c)	5	46			(c) HERNANDEZ Jorge	7	46
DRAPER Greg	9	57			VELA Carlos	9	57
BROCKIE Jeremy	10				HERNANDEZ Javier	11	
JENKINS Sam	11				DOMINGUEZ Julio Cesar	13	
ROYDHOUSE Nick	12	88			MARES Oscar	14	
BOXALL Michael	14				SILVA Juan Carlos	15	
SCHAEFFERS Tim	17				GUERRERO Jose	17	
PURCELL Kieran	19	81			BERMUDEZ Christian	19	81
CLAPHAM Aaron	21	83			CASTRO Alejandro	20	
Tr: JACOBS Stu					Tr: RAMIREZ Jesus		
CUNNINGHAM Michael	13	83	46		ESPARZA Omar	6	46
RICHARDSON Tim	18	88	57		BARRERA Pablo	8	57
					ALDRETE Adrian	16	81

GROUP D	PL	W	D	L	F	A	PTS
1 USA	3	2	1	0	9	3	7
2 Poland	3	1	1	1	3	7	4
3 Brazil	3	1	0	2	4	5	3
4 Korea Republic	3	0	2	1	4	5	2

	POL	BRA	KOR
POL	6-1	2-1	1-1
BRA		1-0	1-1
KOR			3-2

Le Stade Olympique, Montreal
30-07-2007, 14:15, 55 800, Webb ENG

POL 1 0 BRA

Krychowiak [23]

POLAND			BRAZIL	
1 BIALKOWSKI Bartosz			CASSIO	1
2 STAROSTA Ben			EDUARDO	2
3 FOJUT Jaroslaw			LUIZAO	3
4 KROL Krzysztof	27		DAVID MARINHO	4
5 STRUGAREK Krzysztof		78	ROBERTO	5
6 DANCH Adam			JO	9
8 MARCINIAK Artur (c)			RENATO AUGUSTO	10
9 MALECKI Patryk			ALEXANDRE PATO	11
11 JANCZYK Dawid	73	66	CARLAO	16
16 KRYCHOWIAK Grzegorz	93	66	(c) JI PARANA	17
20 CYWKA Tomasz	61		LEANDRO LIMA	20
Tr: GLOBISZ Michal			Tr: RODRIGUES Nelson	
10 JANOSZKA Lukasz	73	66	MARCELO	6
17 FETER Jakub	93	66	CARLOS EDUARDO	18
18 SACHA Mariusz	61	78	LUIZ ADRIANO	19

Le Stade Olympique, Montreal
30-07-2007, 17:00, 55 800, Aguilar SLV

KOR 1 1 USA

Shin Young Rok [38]   Szetela [16]

KOREA REPUBLIC			USA	
21 KIM Jin Hyeon			SEITZ Chris	1
2 CHOI Chul Soon			WARD Tim	2
3 SHIN Kwang Hoon			STURGIS Nathan	5
5 KI Sung Yueng			BRADLEY Michael	6
8 KIM Dong Suk	70	52	SZETELA Danny	7
9 LEE Sang Ho			ROGERS Robbie	8
10 SHIM Young Sung	84		(c) ADU Freddy	11
11 PARK Joo Ho (c)			ALTIDORE Josmer	12
14 LEE Chung Yong			ZIZZO Sal	15
18 SHIN Young Rok	59		VALENTIN Julian	16
20 BAE Seung Jin			BELTRAN Tony	19
Tr: CHO Dong Hyun			Tr: RONGEN Thomas	
16 LEE Hyun Seung	84	52	McCARTY Dax	10
17 SONG Jin Hyung	70			
19 HA Tae Goon	59			

Le Stade Olympique, Montreal
3-07-2007, 17:00, 35 801, Hansson SWE

USA 6 1 POL

Szetela 2 [9 51], Adu 3 [20 48+ 85],
Altidore [70]   Janczyk [5]

USA			POLAND	
1 SEITZ Chris			BIALKOWSKI Bartosz	1
5 STURGIS Nathan			STAROSTA Ben	2
6 BRADLEY Michael			FOJUT Jaroslaw	3
7 SZETELA Danny	73		STRUGAREK Krzysztof	5
8 ROGERS Robbie			DANCH Adam	6
11 ADU Freddy (c)		67	(c) MARCINIAK Artur	8
12 ALTIDORE Josmer	79		MALECKI Patryk	9
14 WALLACE Anthony	63		JANCZYK Dawid	11
15 ZIZZO Sal		55	KRYCHOWIAK Grzegorz	16
16 VALENTIN Julian	33	46	SACHA Mariusz	18
19 BELTRAN Tony			CYWKA Tomasz	20
Tr: RONGEN Thomas			Tr: GLOBISZ Michal	
4 IGWE Amaechi	63	55	MAREK Adrian	7
10 McCARTY Dax	79	46	SZALEK Jakub	14
13 SARKODIE Ofori	33	67	ADAMIEC Pawel	19

Le Stade Olympique, Montreal
3-07-2007, 19:45, 35 801, Kassai HUN

BRA 3 2 KOR

Amaral [35], Alexandre Pato 2 [48 59]   Shim Young Sung [83],
Shin Young Rok [89]

BRAZIL			KOREA REPUBLIC	
1 CASSIO			KIM Jin Hyeon	21
3 LUIZAO			CHOI Chul Soon	2
4 DAVID MARINHO			SHIN Kwang Hoon	3
5 ROBERTO			KI Sung Yueng	5
6 MARCELO			LEE Sang Ho	9
9 JO			SHIM Young Sung	10
10 RENATO AUGUSTO		54	(c) PARK Joo Ho	11
11 ALEXANDRE PATO	71		LEE Chung Yong	14
13 AMARAL		33	SONG Jin Hyung	17
17 JI PARANA (c)	77	66	HA Tae Goon	19
20 LEANDRO LIMA	68		BAE Seung Jin	20
Tr: RODRIGUES Nelson			Tr: CHO Dong Hyun	
7 WILLIAN	68	33	KIM Dong Suk	8
18 MARCONE	77	54	JEONG Kyung Ho	15
19 LUIZ ADRIANO	71	66	SHIN Young Rok	18

Frank Clair Stadium, Ottawa
6-07-2005, 19:45, 26 500, Undiano Mallenco ESP

BRA 1 2 USA

Leandro Lima [64]   Altidore 2 [25 81]

BRAZIL			USA	
1 CASSIO			SEITZ Chris	1
3 LUIZAO		82	STURGIS Nathan	5
5 ROBERTO			BRADLEY Michael	6
6 MARCELO			SZETELA Danny	7
9 JO		82	ROGERS Robbie	8
10 RENATO AUGUSTO	71		(c) ADU Freddy	11
11 ALEXANDRE PATO		92	ALTIDORE Josmer	12
13 AMARAL			SARKODIE Ofori	13
15 EDSON			WALLACE Anthony	14
17 JI PARANA (c)	84		ZIZZO Sal	15
20 LEANDRO LIMA	78	89	BELTRAN Tony	19
Tr: RODRIGUES Nelson			Tr: RONGEN Thomas	
7 WILLIAN	84	89	WARD Tim	2
18 CARLOS EDUARDO	71	82	IGWE Amaechi	4
19 LUIZ ADRIANO	78	92	McCARTY Dax	10

Le Stade Olympique, Montreal
6-07-2005, 19:45, 34 912, Wijngaarde SUR

POL 1 1 KOR

Janczyk [45]   Lee Sang Ho [71]

POLAND			KOREA REPUBLIC	
1 BIALKOWSKI Bartosz			KIM Jin Hyeon	21
2 STAROSTA Ben			(c) CHOI Chul Soon	2
3 FOJUT Jaroslaw			SHIN Kwang Hoon	3
4 KROL Krzysztof			KI Sung Yueng	5
5 STRUGAREK Krzysztof			LEE Sang Ho	9
6 DANCH Adam		63	SHIM Young Sung	10
7 MAREK Adrian			LEE Chung Yong	14
8 MARCINIAK Artur (c)	88	29	JEONG Kyung Ho	15
9 MALECKI Patryk			SONG Jin Hyung	17
11 JANCZYK Dawid	83	46	HA Tae Goon	19
20 CYWKA Tomasz	86		BAE Seung Jin	20
Tr: GLOBISZ Michal			Tr: CHO Dong Hyun	
14 SZALEK Jakub	88	29	PARK Jong Jin	7
15 DABROWSKI Maciej	86	63	KIM Dong Suk	8
19 ADAMIEC Pawel	83	46	SHIN Young Rok	18

GROUP E	PL	W	D	L	F	A	PTS		CZE	PRK	PAN
1 Argentina	3	2	1	0	7	0	7		0-0	1-0	6-0
2 Czech Republic	3	1	2	0	4	3	5			2-2	2-1
3 Korea DPR	3	0	2	1	2	3	2				0-0
4 Panama	3	0	1	2	1	8	1				

Frank Clair Stadium, Ottawa
30-06-2007, 16:30, 26 559, Benouza ALG

PRK 0 0 PAN

KOREA DPR			PANAMA	
1 JU Kwang Min			MEJIA Luis 1	
5 PAK Nam Chol			VASQUEZ Eric 2	
7 KIM Kum Il (c)			MITCHELL Marvin 5	
8 RI Chol Myong	74		JARAMILLO Luis 8	
12 KIM Kuk Jin	84		(c) TORRES Gabriel 9	
14 JON Kwang Ik			BARAHONA Nelson 10	
15 YUN Yong Il		46	COOPER Armando 11	
16 RI Kwang Hyok		79	GONZALEZ Pablo 13	
17 PAK Chol Min	78		DASENT Eduardo 16	
19 KIM Kyong Il			POLO Celso 19	
20 JONG Chol Min			RODRIGUEZ Carlos 20	
Tr: JO Tong Sop			Tr: DELY Julio	
9 PAK Song Chol	78	46	OVALLE Luis 3	
11 RI Hung Ryong	84	74	BROWN Josue 4	
		79	GONZALEZ Javier 7	

Frank Clair Stadium, Ottawa
30-06-2007, 19:15, 26 559

ARG 0 0 CZE

ARGENTINA			CZECH REPUBLIC	
1 ROMERO Sergio			PETR Radek 1	
2 FAZIO Federico			DOHNALEK Jakub 2	
3 INSUA Emiliano			KUBAN Lukas 3	
4 MERCADO Gabriel			MAZUCH Ondrej 4	
5 BANEGA Ever			(c) SIMUNEK Jan 5	
6 CAHAIS Matias (c)			KUDELA Ondrej 6	
7 YACOB Claudio		79	FENIN Martin 9	
9 ZARATE Mauro		88	JANDA Petr 12	
10 AGUERO Sergio			GECOV Marcel 14	
15 CABRAL Alejandro	64	58	STRESTIK Marek 15	
17 MORALEZ Maximiliano	81		SUCHY Marek 17	
Tr: TOCALLI Hugo			Tr: SOUKUP Miroslav	
19 PIATTI Pablo	64	79	OKLESTEK Tomas 11	
20 ACOSTA Lautaro	81	88	MICOLA Tomas 13	
		58	PEKHART Tomas 18	

Frank Clair Stadium, Ottawa
3-07-2007, 17:00, 22 200, Undiano Mallenco ESP

CZE 2 2 PRK

Kalouda 56, Fenin 66   Kim Kum Il 12, Jon Kwang Ik 89

CZECH REPUBLIC			KOREA DPR	
1 PETR Radek			JU Kwang Min 1	
2 DOHNALEK Jakub	46		PAK Nam Chol 5	
3 KUBAN Lukas			(c) KIM Kum Il 7	
5 SIMUNEK Jan (c)			RI Chol Myong 8	
6 KUDELA Ondrej			PAK Song Chol 9	
9 FENIN Martin	90	63	KIM Kuk Jin 12	
12 JANDA Petr			JON Kwang Ik 14	
14 GECOV Marcel			YUN Yong Il 15	
17 SUCHY Marek			RI Kwang Hyok 16	
18 PEKHART Tomas	81		KIM Kyong Il 19	
19 KALOUDA Lubos	83		JONG Chol Min 20	
Tr: SOUKUP Miroslav			Tr: JO Tong Sop	
11 OKLESTEK Tomas	83	81	RI Hung Ryong 11	
13 MICOLA Tomas	90	63	PAK Chol Min 20	
15 STRESTIK Marek	46			

Frank Clair Stadium, Ottawa
3-07-2007, 19:45, 23 500, Mohd Salleh MAS

PAN 0 6 ARG

Moralez 2 20 27, Zarate 23,
Aguero 2 25 62, Di Maria 76

PANAMA			ARGENTINA	
1 MEJIA Luis			ROMERO Sergio 1	
2 VASQUEZ Eric			FAZIO Federico 2	
3 OVALLE Luis			INSUA Emiliano 3	
5 MITCHELL Marvin	36	69	BANEGA Ever 5	
6 CASTANEDA Francisco	59		(c) CAHAIS Matias 6	
7 GONZALEZ Javier			YACOB Claudio 7	
9 TORRES Gabriel (c)			SANCHEZ Matias 8	
10 BARAHONA Nelson	64	61	ZARATE Mauro 9	
14 VERGARA Christian			AGUERO Sergio 10	
19 POLO Celso		19	ESCUDERO Damian 11	
20 RODRIGUEZ Carlos			MORALEZ Maximiliano 17	
Tr: DELY Julio			Tr: TOCALLI Hugo	
4 BROWN Josue	59	69	CABRAL Alejandro 15	
13 GONZALEZ Pablo	36	61	DI MARIA Angel 18	
18 QUINTERO Alberto	64	19	PIATTI Pablo 19	

Le Stade Olympique, Montreal
6-07-2007, 17:00, 34 912, Depiero CAN

CZE 2 1 PAN

Kalouda 79, Strestik 82   Barahona 84

CZECH REPUBLIC			PANAMA	
1 PETR Radek			MEJIA Luis 1	
3 KUBAN Lukas		93+	VASQUEZ Eric 2	
4 MAZUCH Ondrej			OVALLE Luis 3	
5 SIMUNEK Jan (c)			MITCHELL Marvin 5	
6 KUDELA Ondrej		65	CASTANEDA Francisco 6	
9 FENIN Martin	84		GONZALEZ Javier 7	
12 JANDA Petr	89		(c) TORRES Gabriel 9	
13 MICOLA Tomas	67	73	GONZALEZ Pablo 13	
15 STRESTIK Marek			VERGARA Christian 14	
17 SUCHY Marek			POLO Celso 19	
19 KALOUDA Lubos		46	RODRIGUEZ Carlos 20	
Tr: SOUKUP Miroslav			Tr: DELY Julio	
10 MARES Jakub	89	73	BARAHONA Nelson 10	
14 GECOV Marcel	67	46	COOPER Armando 11	
18 PEKHART Tomas	84	65	QUINTERO Alberto 18	

Frank Clair Stadium, Ottawa
6-07-2007, 17:00, 26 500, Kassai HUN

ARG 1 0 PRK

Aguero 35

ARGENTINA			KOREA DPR	
1 ROMERO Sergio			JU Kwang Min 1	
2 FAZIO Federico			PAK Nam Chol 5	
3 INSUA Emiliano			(c) KIM Kum Il 7	
4 MERCADO Gabriel			RI Chol Myong 8	
5 BANEGA Ever			PAK Song Chol 9	
8 SANCHEZ Matias			KIM Kuk Jin 12	
9 ZARATE Mauro			JON Kwang Ik 14	
10 AGUERO Sergio (c)	66		YUN Yong Il 15	
13 VOBORIL German			RI Kwang Hyok 16	
17 MORALEZ Maximiliano	73	65	KIM Kyong Il 19	
20 ACOSTA Lautaro	59	51	JONG Chol Min 20	
Tr: TOCALLI Hugo			Tr: JO Tong Sop	
15 CABRAL Alejandro	59	65	RI Hung Ryong 11	
16 GOMEZ Alejandro	73	51	PAK Chol Min 17	
18 DI MARIA Angel	66			

GROUP F		PL	W	D	L	F	A	PTS
1	Japan	3	2	1	0	4	1	7
2	Nigeria	3	2	1	0	3	0	7
3	Costa Rica	3	1	0	2	2	3	3
4	Scotland	3	0	0	3	2	7	0

	NGA	CRC	SCO
	0-0	1-0	3-1
		1-0	2-0
			2-1

Royal Athletic Park, Victoria
1-07-2007, 14:15, 11 500, Arredondo MEX

JPN 3 1 SCO

Morishima [43], Umesaki [57],
Oayama [79]   Campbell [82]

JAPAN				SCOTLAND
1	HAYASHI Akihiro			McNEIL Andrew 1
2	UCHIDA Atsuto			CAVE-BROWN Andrew 2
3	YASUDA Michihiro			WALLACE Lee 3
4	FUKUMOTO Yohei (c)			ADAMS Jamie 4
5	MAKINO Tomoaki			(c) CUTHBERT Scott 5
7	UMESAKI Tsukasa			REYNOLDS Mark 6
8	TANAKA Atomu	76		ELLIOT Calum 8
9	KAWAHARA Kazuhisa	68		FLETCHER Steven 9
10	KASHIWAGI Yosuke	92	75	DORRANS Graham 10
12	MORISHIMA Yasuhito		61	CONROY Ryan 11
15	AOYAMA Jun		46	LOWING Alan 19
	Tr: YOSHIDA Yasushi			Tr: GEMMILL Archie
6	MORISHIGE Masato	92	46	CAMPBELL Ross 16
14	AOKI Kota	68	61	SNODGRASS Robert 18
16	FUJITA Seiya	76	75	GILMOUR Brian 20

Royal Athletic Park, Victoria
4-07-2007, 17:00, 10 500, Stark GER

CRC 0 1 JPN

Tanaka [67]

COSTA RICA				JAPAN
1	QUESADA Alfonso			HAYASHI Akihiro 1
3	DAWSON Rudy (c)			UCHIDA Atsuto 2
4	GONZALEZ Giancarlo			YASUDA Michihiro 3
5	RODRIGUEZ Esteban			(c) MAKINO Tomoaki 5
6	CUBERO Jose	86		MAKINO Tomoaki 5
7	HERRERA Pablo			UMESAKI Tsukasa 7
8	BORGES Celso			TANAKA Atomu 8
10	PEREZ Luis	59	76	KAWAHARA Kazuhisa 9
11	SOLORZANO Jean	77	90	KASHIWAGI Yosuke 10
16	RAMOS Leslie			MORISHIMA Yasuhito 12
17	MYRIE Dave			AOYAMA Jun 15
	Tr: ALFARO Geovanni			Tr: YOSHIDA Yasushi
12	McDONALD Jonathan	77	90	MORISHIGE Masato 6
13	CAMBLE Marlon	86	76	AOKI Kota 14
14	FERNANDEZ Argenis	59	80	FUJITA Seiya 16

Royal Athletic Park, Victoria
7-07-2007, 17:00, 11 500, Arredondo MEX

JPN 0 0 NGA

JAPAN				NIGERIA
18	TAKEDA Yohei			EZENWA Ikechukwu 21
2	UCHIDA Atsuto			SODIQ Suraj 2
4	FUKUMOTO Yohei (c)			ECHIEJILE Uwa 3
6	MORISHIGE Masato			OLUFEMI Oladapo 4
8	UMESAKI Tsukasa	70		AYODEJI Adeniyi 5
11	HAVENAAR Mike			(c) BALA Ezekiel 8
13	YANAGAWA Masaki		68	OWELLO Solomon 10
16	FUJITA Seiya		54	AGBETU Akeem 11
17	OTA Kosuke		89	IDEYE Brown 15
19	HIRASHIGE Ryuichi	64		EGBETA Robert 16
20	KAGAWA Shinji	78		ADAMS Moses 20
	Tr: YOSHIDA Yasushi			Tr: BOSSO Ladan
3	YASUDA Michihiro	70	89	KOFARMATA Bello 7
12	KASHIWAGI Yosuke	78	54	OZOKWO Nduka 9
14	AOKI Kota	64	68	AKABUEZE Chukwuma 14

Royal Athletic Park, Victoria
1-07-2007, 17:00, 11 500, O'Leary NZL

NGA 1 0 CRC

Ideye [75]

NIGERIA				COSTA RICA
12	OCHEJE Moses	49		QUESADA Alfonso 1
2	SODIQ Suraj			(c) DAWSON Rudy 3
3	ECHIEJILE Uwa			GONZALEZ Giancarlo 4
4	OLUFEMI Oladapo			CUBERO Jose 6
6	AMBROSE Efe			HERRERA Pablo 7
8	BALA Ezekiel (c)			BORGES Celso 8
10	OWELLO Solomon		69	ELIZONDO Cesar 9
14	AKABUEZE Chukwuma	66	81	PEREZ Luis 10
15	IDEYE Brown		84	GONZALEZ Orlando 15
17	LATIFU Akeem			RAMOS Leslie 16
20	ADAMS Moses	84		MYRIE Dave 17
	Tr: BOSSO Ladan			Tr: ALFARO Geovanni
1	THOMAS Olufemi	49	69	SOLORZANO Jean 11
7	KOFARMATA Bello	66	84	McDONALD Jonathan 12
13	OKARDI Blessing	84	81	CAMBLE Marlon 13

Royal Athletic Park, Victoria
4-07-2007, 19:45, 10 500, Vaughn USA

SCO 0 2 NGA

Bala 2 [49] [78]

SCOTLAND				NIGERIA
1	McNEIL Andrew			THOMAS Olufemi 1
3	WALLACE Lee			SODIQ Suraj 2
4	ADAMS Jamie	64		ECHIEJILE Uwa 3
5	CUTHBERT Scott (c)			OLUFEMI Oladapo 4
6	REYNOLDS Mark		82	AMBROSE Efe 6
8	ELLIOT Calum			(c) BALA Ezekiel 8
9	FLETCHER Steven		69	OWELLO Solomon 10
13	O'LEARY Ryan		47	OKARDI Blessing 13
14	CONSIDINE Andrew		72	AKABUEZE Chukwuma 14
16	CAMPBELL Ross	64		IDEYE Brown 15
18	SNODGRASS Robert	79		LATIFU Akeem 17
	Tr: GEMMILL Archie			Tr: BOSSO Ladan
7	McGLINCHEY Michael	64	72	KOFARMATA Bello 7
10	DORRANS Graham	64	69	OZOKWO Nduka 9
11	CONROY Ryan	79	47	ADAMS Moses 20

Swangard Stadium, Burnaby
7-07-2007, 17:00, 10 000, Mohd Salleh MAS

SCO 1 2 CRC

Reynolds [18]   Herrera [57], McDonald [92+]

SCOTLAND				COSTA RICA
12	FOX Scott			QUESADA Alfonso 1
3	WALLACE Lee			(c) DAWSON Rudy 3
5	CUTHBERT Scott (c)		74	RODRIGUEZ Esteban 5
6	REYNOLDS Mark			CUBERO Jose 6
7	McGLINCHEY Michael			HERRERA Pablo 7
8	ELLIOT Calum			BORGES Celso 8
9	FLETCHER Steven		46	ELIZONDO Cesar 9
10	DORRANS Graham	62		McDONALD Jonathan 12
13	O'LEARY Ryan	66		RAMOS Leslie 16
14	CONSIDINE Andrew			MYRIE Dave 17
17	LYNCH Sean	72	89	WASTON Kendall 20
	Tr: GEMMILL Archie			Tr: ALFARO Geovanni
11	CONROY Ryan	62	46	SOLORZANO Jean 11
15	KENNETH Garry	66	89	CAMBLE Marlon 13
18	SNODGRASS Robert	72	74	FERNANDEZ Argenis 14

ROUND OF 16

National Soccer Stadium, Toronto
12-07-2007, 16:45, 19 526, Aguilar SLV

ARG 3 1 POL

Di Maria [40], Aguero 2 [46] [86] | Janczyk [33]

ARGENTINA			POLAND	
1 ROMERO Sergio			BIALKOWSKI Bartosz	1
2 FAZIO Federico			STAROSTA Ben	2
3 INSUA Emiliano			KROL Krzysztof	4
4 MERCADO Gabriel			STRUGAREK Krzysztof	5
5 BANEGA Ever			DANCH Adam	6
6 CAHAIS Matias (c)	71		MAREK Adrian	7
7 YACOB Claudio	75		(c) MARCINIAK Artur	8
10 AGUERO Sergio			MALECKI Patryk	9
17 MORALEZ Maximiliano	89	91+	JANCZYK Dawid	11
18 DI MARIA Angel	76		KRYCHOWIAK Grzegorz	16
19 PIATTI Pablo	84	77	CYWKA Tomasz	20
Tr: TOCALLI Hugo			Tr: GLOBISZ Michal	
15 CABRAL Alejandro	84	77	JANOSZKA Lukasz	10
16 GOMEZ Alejandro	89	71	RACZKA Damian	13
20 ACOSTA Lautaro	76	75	SACHA Mariusz	18

Le Stade Olympique, Montreal
12-07-2007, 19:45, 40 204, Kassai HUN

MEX 3 0 CGO

Dos Santos [23]p, Esparza [85], Barrera [94]+

MEXICO			CONGO	
1 BLANCO Alfonso			ONKA Destin	1
2 ARAUJO Patricio (c)			MBANI Oxence	6
3 JUAREZ Efrain	73		LAKOLO Prestone	7
5 MORENO Hector			NDINGA Delvin	8
6 ESPARZA Omar		74	(c) FILANCKEMBO Cecil	10
7 HERNANDEZ Jorge	55	48	IBARA Franchel	11
9 VELA Carlos	67		NGUESSI Fabrice	12
10 DOS SANTOS Giovanni	90		LOPARIMI Jacques	14
13 DOMINGUEZ Julio Cesar			OKIELE Mimille	15
16 ALDRETE Adrian			MERECK Murhyen	17
18 VILLALUZ Cesar		80	NKOUNGA Saide	18
Tr: RAMIREZ Jesus			Tr: HUDANSKI Eddie	
8 BARRERA Pablo	55	74	IKOUMA Gracia	5
11 HERNANDEZ Javier	90	73	TCHILIMBOU Harris	13
19 BERMUDEZ Christian	67	80	KAPOLONGO Ulrich	20

Frank Clair Stadium, Ottawa
12-07-2007, 16:45, 22 531, Stark GER

ZAM 1 2 NGA

Kola [33] | Echiejile [3], Akabueze [57]

ZAMBIA			NIGERIA	
1 BANDA Jacob			EZENWA Ikechukwu	21
3 ZIMBA Joseph	37		SODIQ Suraj	2
4 BANDA Dennis			ECHIEJILE Uwa	3
7 PHIRI Richard			OLUFEMI Oladapo	4
8 NJOBVU William			AMBROSE Efe	6
10 MULENGA Clifford			(c) BALA Ezekiel	8
12 MWANSA Sebastian (c)	61	81	OWELLO Solomon	10
14 KACHINGA Goodson			AKABUEZE Chukwuma	14
18 KOLA Rodgers			IDEYE Brown	15
19 MAYUKA Emmanuel			LATIFU Akeem	17
20 SUNZU Stophira	72		ADAMS Moses	20
Tr: LWANDAMINA George			Tr: BOSSO Ladan	
11 TEMBO Fwayo	72	81	OZOKWO Nduka	9
13 SIMUTOWE Musatwe	37			
15 ZULU Justine	61			

Commonwealth Stadium, Edmonton
12-07-2007, 17:45, 24 687, Mohd Salleh MAS

CHI 1 0 POR

Vidal [45]

CHILE			PORTUGAL	
1 TOSELLI Cristopher			RUI PATRICIO	12
2 SUAREZ Cristian			(c) PAULO RENATO	4
3 ISLA Mauricio (c)	70		NUNO COELHO	6
5 LARRONDO Nicolas	46		PELE	8
6 MEDEL Gary	90		ZEQUINHA	9
7 SANCHEZ Alexis	76		FABIO COENTRAO	11
8 CURRIMILLA Dagoberto			ANTUNES	13
9 MEDINA Nicolas	63		JOAO PEDRO	14
14 VIDAL Arturo	94+		FELICIANO CONDESSO	17
17 MARTINEZ Hans		90	MANO	18
18 VIDANGOSSY Mathias	86	81	BRUNO PEREIRINHA	19
Tr: SULANTAY José			Tr: COUCEIRO José	
11 GRONDONA Jaime	63	81	ANDRE MARQUES	5
13 SEPULVEDA Christian	86	46	ZEZINANDO	15
16 CORTES Gerardo	76	70	GUEDES	19

Commonwealth Stadium, Edmonton
11-07-2007, 17:45, 18 721, Benouza ALG

AUT 2 1 GAM

Proedl [46]+, Hoffer [81] | Pierre Gomez [69]

AUSTRIA			GAMBIA	
21 ZAGLMAIR Michael			GOMEZ Joseph	1
2 PANNY Thomas		85	GOMEZ Pierre	2
4 PROEDL Sebastian (c)		85	MENDY Furmus	3
6 STANISLAW Michael			NGUM Alagie	4
7 HARNIK Martin	71		BOJANG Mandou	6
8 KAVLAK Veli			JAGNE Pa Modou	9
10 JUNUZOVIC Zlatko			SOHNA Ebrima	11
11 HACKMAIR Peter	88		MANSALLY Abdoulie	12
15 MADL Michael	66		(c) JALLOW Ousman	13
19 OKOTIE Rubin	87		NYASSI Sainey	14
20 RASSWALDER Siegfried		43	JAITEH Tijan	15
Tr: GLUDOVATZ Paul			Tr: JOHNSON Peter	
3 GRAMANN Daniel	66	85	CONATEH Pa Landing	10
9 HOFFER Erwin	71	85	NYASSI Sanna	17
18 HINUM Thomas	87	88	NGUM Modou	20

National Soccer Stadium, Toronto
11-07-2007, 19:45, 19 526, Irmatov UZB

USA 2 1 URU

Cardaccio OG [87], Bradley [107] | Luis Suarez [73]

USA			URUGUAY	
18 PERK Brian			IRRAZABAL Yonatan	12
5 STURGIS Nathan	117		CACERES Martin	3
6 BRADLEY Michael			ROMAN Marcel	5
7 SZETELA Danny			KAGELMACHER Gary	6
8 ROGERS Robbie			CARDACCIO Mathias	7
11 ADU Freddy (c)			SUAREZ Damian	8
12 ALTIDORE Josmer	51		(c) CAVANI Edinson	9
14 WALLACE Anthony			DIAZ Juan Manuel	13
15 ZIZZO Sal	54		ARISMENDI Hugo	14
16 VALENTIN Julian		108	SURRACO Juan	17
19 BELTRAN Tony	81	83	SUAREZ Luis	18
Tr: RONGEN Thomas			Tr: FERRIN Gustavo	
10 McCARTY Dax	54	117	VONDER PUTTEN Gerardo	10
17 FERRARI Gabe	81	108	FIGUEROA Elias	11
20 AKPAN Andre	51	83	VIUDEZ Tabare	19

Swangard Stadium, Burnaby
11-07-2007, 20:15, 10 000, Hansson SWE

ESP 4 2 BRA

Pique [43], Javi Garcia [84], Bueno [102], Adrian Lopez [121] — Leandro Lima [39], Alexandre Pato [41]

#	SPAIN			BRAZIL	#
1	ADAN (c)			CASSIO	1
2	BARRAGAN Antonio	77		LUIZAO	3
3	CRESPO Jose			ROBERTO	5
4	MARC VALIENTE			MARCELO	6
5	PIQUE Gerard		63	WILLIAN	7
8	JAVI GARCIA		51	JO	9
11	CAPEL Diego			ALEXANDRE PATO	11
16	MATA Juan Manuel		70	AMARAL	13
18	ADRIAN LOPEZ			EDSON	15
19	GARCIA Marcos	55		(c) JI PARANA	17
20	STEPHEN Sunny	71	102	LEANDRO LIMA	20
	Tr: MELENDEZ Gines			Tr: RODRIGUES Nelson	
7	TONI CALVO	77	70	EDUARDO	2
9	BUENO Alberto	71	63	CARLOS EDUARDO	18
10	GRANERO Esteban	55	51	LUIZ ADRIANO	19

Royal Athletic Park, Victoria
11-07-2007, 20:15, 11 500, Buitrago COL

JPN 2 2 CZE   (p.s.o. 3–4)

Makino [22], Morishima [47p] — Kudela [74p], Mares [77p]

#	JAPAN			CZECH REPUBLIC	#
1	HAYASHI Akihiro			PETR Radek	1
2	UCHIDA Atsuto		91	KUBAN Lukas	3
3	YASUDA Michihiro			MAZUCH Ondrej	4
4	FUKUMOTO Yohei (c)			(c) SIMUNEK Jan	5
5	MAKINO Tomoaki			KUDELA Ondrej	6
7	UMESAKI Tsukasa	110		FENIN Martin	9
8	TANAKA Atomu	78		JANDA Petr	12
9	KAWAHARA Kazuhisa	70	46	GECOV Marcel	14
10	KASHIWAGI Yosuke		55	STRESTIK Marek	15
12	MORISHIMA Yasuhito			SUCHY Marek	17
15	AOYAMA Jun			KALOUDA Lubos	19
	Tr: YOSHIDA Yasushi			Tr: SOUKUP Miroslav	
14	AOKI Kota	70	85 46	MARES Jakub	10
16	FUJITA Seiya	78	91	OKLESTEK Tomas	11
20	KAGAWA Shinji	110	55	PEKHART Tomas	18

QUARTER-FINALS

Frank Clair Stadium, Ottawa
15-07-2007, 19:45, 26 559, Undiano Mallenco ESP

ARG 1 0 MEX

Moralez [45]

#	ARGENTINA			MEXICO	#
1	ROMERO Sergio			BLANCO Alfonso	1
2	FAZIO Federico			(c) ARAUJO Patricio	2
3	INSUA Emiliano			JUAREZ Efrain	3
4	MERCADO Gabriel			MORENO Hector	5
5	BANEGA Ever			ESPARZA Omar	6
6	CAHAIS Matias (c)		66	HERNANDEZ Jorge	7
7	YACOB Claudio		75	VELA Carlos	8
10	AGUERO Sergio	91		DOS SANTOS Giovanni	10
17	MORALEZ Maximiliano			DOMINGUEZ Julio Cesar	13
18	DI MARIA Angel	75	54	ALDRETE Adrian	16
19	PIATTI Pablo	89		VILLALUZ Cesar	18
	Tr: TOCALLI Hugo			Tr: RAMIREZ Jesus	
8	SANCHEZ Matias	89	66	BARRERA Pablo	8
9	ZARATE Mauro	91	54	GUERRERO Jose	17
20	ACOSTA Lautaro	75	75	BERMUDEZ Christian	19

Le Stade Olympique, Montreal
15-07-2007, 14:15, 46 252, Webb ENG

CHI 4 0 NGA

Grondona [96], Isla 2 [114p] [118], Vidangossy [122]

#	CHILE			NIGERIA	#
1	TOSELLI Cristopher (c)			EZENWA Ikechukwu	21
2	SUAREZ Cristian	113		SODIQ Suraj	2
3	ISLA Mauricio			ECHIEJILE Uwa	3
5	LARRONDO Nicolas			OLUFEMI Oladapo	4
6	MEDEL Gary			AMBROSE Efe	6
7	SANCHEZ Alexis	46		(c) BALA Ezekiel	8
9	CURRIMILLA Dagoberto	101		OWELLO Solomon	10
10	MEDINA Nicolas	46	106	AKABUEZE Chukwuma	14
13	SEPULVEDA Christian	89		IDEYE Brown	15
17	MARTINEZ Hans			LATIFU Akeem	17
18	VIDANGOSSY Mathias			ADAMS Moses	20
	Tr: SULANTAY José			Tr: BOSSO Ladan	
4	GODOY Eric	101	110	KOFARMATA Bello	7
11	GRONDONA Jaime	89	110 46	OZOKWO Nduka	9
15	CARMONA Carlos	46	106	AGBETU Akeem	11

National Soccer Stadium, Toronto
14-07-2007, 14:15, 19 526, Hansson SWE

AUT 2 1 USA

Okotie [43], Hoffer [105] — Altidore [15]

#	AUSTRIA			USA	#
21	ZAGLMAIR Michael			SEITZ Chris	1
2	PANNY Thomas			STURGIS Nathan	5
4	PROEDL Sebastian (c)			BRADLEY Michael	6
5	SUTTNER Markus		63	SZETELA Danny	7
6	STANISLAW Michael			ROGERS Robbie	8
8	KAVLAK Veli			(c) ADU Freddy	11
10	JUNUZOVIC Zlatko	103		ALTIDORE Josmer	12
11	HACKMAIR Peter		104	WALLACE Anthony	14
14	MORGENTHALER Bernhard	37	106	ZIZZO Sal	15
15	MADL Michael			VALENTIN Julian	16
19	OKOTIE Rubin	121	81	BELTRAN Tony	19
	Tr: GLUDOVATZ Paul			Tr: RONGEN Thomas	
7	HARNIK Martin	37	81	WARD Tim	2
9	HOFFER Erwin	103	63	McCARTY Dax	10
13	PIRKER Thomas	121	106	FERRARI Gabe	17

Commonwealth Stadium, Edmonton
14-07-2007, 17:45, 26 801, Irmatov UZB

ESP 1 1 CZE   (p.s.o. 3–4)

Mata [110] — Kalouda [103]

#	SPAIN			CZECH REPUBLIC	#
1	ADAN (c)			PETR Radek	1
2	BARRAGAN Antonio			KUBAN Lukas	3
3	CRESPO Jose			MAZUCH Ondrej	4
4	MARC VALIENTE			(c) SIMUNEK Jan	5
5	PIQUE Gerard			KUDELA Ondrej	6
6	MARIO SUAREZ	95		FENIN Martin	9
8	JAVI GARCIA		118	JANDA Petr	12
10	GRANERO Esteban	56		MICOLA Tomas	13
11	CAPEL Diego			STRESTIK Marek	15
16	MATA Juan Manuel			SUCHY Marek	17
18	ADRIAN LOPEZ	81	107	KALOUDA Lubos	19
	Tr: MELENDEZ Gines			Tr: SOUKUP Miroslav	
7	TONI CALVO	56	107	GECOV Marcel	14
9	BUENO Alberto	81	66	PEKHART Tomas	18
14	GONZALEZ Adrian	95	118	CIHLAR Tomas	20

SEMI-FINALS

National Soccer Stadium, Toronto
19-07-2007, 19:45, 19 526, Stark GER

CHI   0   3   ARG

Di Maria 12, Yacob 65, Moralez 93+

CHI	CHILE			ARGENTINA	ARG
1	TOSELLI Cristopher (c)			ROMERO Sergio	1
2	SUAREZ Cristian			FAZIO Federico	2
4	GODOY Eric			INSUA Emiliano	3
5	LARRONDO Nicolas			MERCADO Gabriel	4
6	MEDEL Gary [15]		85	BANEGA Ever	5
8	CURRIMILLA Dagoberto [77]			(c) CAHAIS Matias	6
9	MEDINA Nicolas	76		YACOB Claudio	7
14	VIDAL Arturo			AGUERO Sergio	10
16	CORTES Gerardo	59		MORALEZ Maximiliano	17
17	MARTINEZ Hans		51	DI MARIA Angel	18
18	VIDANGOSSY Mathias		80	PIATTI Pablo	19
	Tr: SULANTAY José			Tr: TOCALLI Hugo	
3	ISLA Mauricio	59	51	SANCHEZ Matias	8
7	SANCHEZ Alexis	76	85	CABRAL Alejandro	15
			80	ACOSTA Lautaro	20

Commonwealth Stadium, Edmonton
18-07-2007, 17:45, 28 401, Webb ENG

AUT   0   2   CZE

Micola 4, Fenin 15

AUT	AUSTRIA			CZECH REPUBLIC	CZE
21	ZAGLMAIR Michael			PETR Radek	1
3	GRAMANN Daniel			KUBAN Lukas	3
4	PROEDL Sebastian (c)			MAZUCH Ondrej	4
5	SUTTNER Markus			(c) SIMUNEK Jan	5
7	HARNIK Martin	46		KUDELA Ondrej	6
8	KAVLAK Veli			FENIN Martin	9
9	HOFFER Erwin		81	JANDA Petr [12]	12
11	HACKMAIR Peter		72	MICOLA Tomas	13
17	SIMKOVIC Tomas	59	61	STRESTIK Marek	15
18	HINUM Thomas			SUCHY Marek [17]	17
20	RASSWALDER Siegfried	79		KALOUDA Lubos	19
	Tr: GLUDOVATZ Paul			Tr: SOUKUP Miroslav	
10	JUNUZOVIC Zlatko	46	72	MARES Jakub	16
14	MORGENTHALER Bernhard	79	61	PEKHART Tomas [18]	18
19	OKOTIE Rubin	59	81	CIHLAR Tomas	20

3RD PLACE PLAY-OFF

National Soccer Stadium, Toronto
22-07-2007, 12:15, 19 526, Hansson SWE

AUT   0   1   CHI

Martínez 46+

AUT	AUSTRIA			CHILE	CHI
12	LUKSE Andreas			TOSELLI Cristopher	1
4	PROEDL Sebastian (c)			SUAREZ Cristian	2
5	SUTTNER Markus		74	(c) ISLA Mauricio	3
6	STANISLAW Michael	75		GODOY Eric	4
8	KAVLAK Veli			LARRONDO Nicolas	5
10	JUNUZOVIC Zlatko			MEDINA Nicolas	9
11	HACKMAIR Peter			SEPULVEDA Christian	13
15	MADL Michael [15]	68		VIDAL Arturo	14
18	HINUM Thomas	87		MARTINEZ Hans	17
19	OKOTIE Rubin			VIDANGOSSY Mathias	18
20	RASSWALDER Siegfried	62	61	SILVA Michael	19
	Tr: GLUDOVATZ Paul			Tr: SULANTAY José	
7	HARNIK Martin	62	61	CORTES Gerardo	16
9	HOFFER Erwin	75	74	PERALTA Isaias	20
13	PIRKER Thomas	87			

ROUND OF 16 PENALTY SHOOT-OUT JAPAN V CZECH REPUBLIC
CZECH REPUBLIC WON 4-3

Yasuda ✖; Fenin ✓; Aoki ✓; Kudela ✓; Makino ✖; Suchy ✓;
Morishima ✖; Pekhart ✖; Kashiwagi ✓; Oklestek ✓

QUARTER-FINAL PENALTY SHOOT-OUT SPAIN V CZECH REPUBLIC
CZECH REPUBLIC WON 4-3

Mata ✓; Fenin ✓; González ✓; Suchy ✓; Valiente ✖;
Kudela ✓; Javi Garcia ✓; Pekhart ✓; Pique ✖

FIFA U-20 WORLD CUP FINAL

National Soccer Stadium, Toronto

22-07-2007, 15:15, 19 526

ARGENTINA	**2**	**1**	CZECH REPUBLIC

Sergio Aguero [62], Mauro Zarate [86]   Martin Fenin [60]

ARGENTINA				MATCH STATS			CZECH REPUBLIC			
1	GK	ROMERO Sergio					PETR Radek	GK	1	
2	DF	FAZIO Federico		14	Shots	11	KUBAN Lukas	DF	3	
3	DF	INSUA Emiliano		8	Shots on Goal	5	MAZUCH Ondrej	DF	4	
4	DF	MERCADO Gabriel		26	Fouls Committed	23	(c) SIMUNEK Jan	DF	5	
5	MF	BANEGA Ever		11	Corner Kicks	3	KUDELA Ondrej	MF	6	
8	MF	SANCHEZ Matias		1	Offside	1	FENIN Martin	FW	9	
9	FW	ZARATE Mauro		63	Possession %	37	76	MARES Jakub	MF	10
10	FW	AGUERO Sergio (c)					MICOLA Tomas	MF	13	
14	DF	SIGALI Leonardo					83	STRESTIK Marek	FW	15
17	MF	MORALEZ Maximiliano	93+	MATCH OFFICIALS			SUCHY Marek	DF	17	
19	FW	PIATTI Pablo	80	REFEREE			KALOUDA Lubos	MF	19	
Tr: TOCALLI Hugo				UNDIANO MALLENCO Alberto ESP			Tr: SOUKUP Miroslav			
Substitutes				ASSISTANTS			Substitutes			
11	MF	ESCUDERO Damian		MARTINEZ Fermin ESP			DOHNALEK Jakub	DF	2	
12	GK	GARCIA Javier		YUSTE GIMENEZ Juan Carlos ESP			VALENTA Jiri	MF	7	
13	DF	VOBORIL German		4TH OFFICIAL			HELD Michal	DF	8	
15	MF	CABRAL Alejandro	93+	IRMATOV Ravshan UZB			OKLESTEK Tomas	MF	11	
16	MF	GOMEZ Alejandro				76	GECOV Marcel	MF	14	
18	FW	DI MARIA Angel					FRYDRYCH Ludek	GK	16	
20	FW	ACOSTA Lautaro	80			83	PEKHART Tomas	FW	18	
21	GK	CENTENO Bruno					CIHLAR Tomas	DF	20	
6	DF	CAHAIS Matias (not available)					FRYSTAK Tomas	GK	21	
7	MF	YACOB Claudio (not available)					(not available) JANDA Petr	MF	12	

Although the Czechs played to a very high level today, I was always confident in my team's ability to turn the game round. I thought we were always in control of the game. We worked hard throughout, and doubly so when we went behind.

Hugo Tocalli

The key was equalising quickly and continuing to believe in ourselves. Physically they were very big and a real handful. We really had to work hard for it.

Gabriel Mercado

We didn't let our supporters down. It was an entertaining game and we played a great part in a great final. Argentina have a very good team and they had the better of the second half. Looking back as a whole, we battled in every single game and no one had it easy against us. When we scored the first goal it was an amazing feeling, but our opponents were unforgiving and punished us for every mistake. This has been the most significant success for Czech football since independence.

Miroslav Soukup

PART TWO

THE NATIONS OF THE WORLD

AFG – AFGHANISTAN

NATIONAL TEAM RECORD
JULY 10TH 2006 TO JULY 12TH 2010

PL	W	D	L	F	A	%
0	0	0	0	0	0	0

FIFA/COCA-COLA WORLD RANKING

1993	1994	1995	1996	1997	1998	1999	2000	2001	2002	2003	2004	2005	2006	High		Low	
-	-	-	-	-	-	-	-	-	-	196	200	189	180	**174**	08/06	**204**	01/03

2006–2007											
08/06	09/06	10/06	11/06	12/06	01/07	02/07	03/07	04/07	05/07	06/07	07/07
174	175	176	175	180	178	178	179	190	187	186	188

With political events very much dominating daily life in Afghanistan, football had a low profile in the 2006-07 season, despite the encouraging progress made the year before. After the AFC Challenge Cup outing in April 2006, the national team went into hibernation, although there was some activity at youth level. The under 23 team entered the qualifiers for the Beijing Olympics and were drawn against Vietnam. It was decided that a one-off match in Nam Dinh would be played but in an example of the difficulties facing football in Afghanistan, the team failed to get to Vietnam in time for the scheduled match due to flight difficulties. Sensibly, FIFA decided to delay

INTERNATIONAL HONOURS
None

the match by a week, by which time they had arrived. It turned out to be a short adventure after they were knocked out following a 2-0 defeat. Five months earlier the under 23's had taken part in the South Asian Federation Games in Colombo, Sri Lanka. Afghanistan started encouragingly with two 0-0 draws against India and Bangladesh but then lost 5-1 to Nepal. Progress is being made at grass roots level. In May 2007, for example, 17 girls' teams took part in a football tournament in Kabul organised by the National Olympic Committee, whilst one-off tournaments are regularly organised around the country for clubs sides and are very popular with the fans.

THE FIFA BIG COUNT OF 2006

	Male	Female		Total
Number of players	526 441	340	Referees and Assistant Referees	100
Professionals	0		Admin, Coaches, Technical, Medical	45
Amateurs 18+	4928		Number of clubs	224
Youth under 18	13 188		Number of teams	500
Unregistered	4 000		Clubs with women's teams	1
Total players	526 781		Players as % of population	1.70%

Afghanistan Football Federation (AFF)
PO Box 5099, Kabul, Afghanistan
Tel +93 75 2023770   Fax +93 75 2023770
aff.kabul@gmail.com   www.aff.com.af
President: KARAMUDDIN Karim   General Secretary: RUSTAMI Mukhtar
Vice-President: MUZAFARI Sayed Zia   Treasurer: TABESH Tawab   Media Officer: MUJAB Nasrat Sayed
Men's Coach: KARGAR Mohamed   Women's Coach: WALI ZADAH Abdul Sabor
AFF formed: 1933   AFC: 1954   FIFA: 1948
Red shirts with white trimmings, Red shorts, Red socks or white shirts with red trimmings, White shorts, White socks

RECENT INTERNATIONALS PLAYED BY AFGHANISTAN

2002 Opponents	Score	Venue	Comp	Scorers	Att	Referee
No international matches played in 2002						
2003						
10-01 Sri Lanka	L 0-1	Dhaka	SAFr1			
12-01 India	L 0-4	Dhaka	SAFr1			
14-01 Pakistan	L 0-1	Dhaka	SAFr1			
16-03 Kyrgyzstan	W 2-1	Kathmandu	ACq	Sayeed Tahir [26], Farid Azimi [76]		
18-03 Nepal	L 0-4	Kathmandu	ACq			
19-11 Turkmenistan	L 0-11	Ashgabat	WCq		12 000	Busurmankulov KGZ
23-11 Turkmenistan	L 0-2	Kabul	WCq		6 000	Khan PAK
2004						
No international matches played in 2004						
2005						
9-11 Tajikistan	L 0-4	Dushanbe	Fr			
7-12 Maldives	L 1-9	Karachi	SAFr1	Sayed Maqsood [39]		
9-12 Pakistan	L 0-1	Karachi	SAFr1			
11-12 Sri Lanka	W 2-1	Karachi	SAFr1	Hafizullah Qadami [35], Abdul Maroof Gullistani [41]		
2006						
1-04 India	L 0-2	Chittagong	CCr1		2 500	Al Ghatrifi OMA
3-04 Chinese Taipei	D 2-2	Chittagong	CCr1	Hafizullah Qadami 2 [20 23]	2 500	Lee Gi Young KOR
5-04 Philippines	D 1-1	Chittagong	CCr1	Sayed Maqsood [26]	3 000	Mujghef JOR
2007						
No international matches played in 2007 before August						

SAF = South Asian Football Federation Cup • AC = Asian Cup • CC = AFC Challenge Cup • WC = FIFA World Cup
q = qualifier • r1 = first round group

AFGHANISTAN NATIONAL TEAM RECORDS AND RECORD SEQUENCES

Records			Sequence records			
Victory	2-1	KYR 2003, SRI 2005	Wins	1	2003, 2005	Clean sheets	1	
Defeat	0-11	TKM 2003	Defeats	11	1948-1975	Goals scored	3	1954-59, 1979
Player Caps	n/a		Undefeated	2	2006	Without goal	6	1941-1951
Player Goals	n/a		Without win	28	1941-2003	Goals against	21	1948-1984

RECENT LEAGUE AND CUP RECORD

Championship		Cup	
Year Champions			Winners
No championship has been organised in Afghanistan since the 1970s			

AFGHANISTAN COUNTRY INFORMATION

Capital	Kabul	Independence	1919 from the UK	GDP per Capita	$700
Population	28 513 677	Status	Islamic Republic of Afghanistan	GNP Ranking	109
Area km²	647 500	Language	Pushtu, Dari	Dialling code	+93
Population density	44 per km²	Literacy rate	36%	Internet code	.af
% in urban areas	20 %	Main religion	Sunni Muslim 80%	GMT + / –	+4.5
Towns/Cities ('000)	Kabul 3 043; Kandahar 391; Mazar-e-Sharif 303; Herat 272; Jalabad 200; Kunduz 161; Ghazni 143; Bamiyan 125; Balkh 114; Baglan 108; Ghardez 103; Khost 96; Maymaneh 79				
Neighbours (km)	Iran 936; Turkmenistan 744; Uzbekistan 137; Tajikistan 1 206; China 76; Pakistan 2 430				
Main stadia	Kabul National Stadium – Kabul 25 000				

AIA – ANGUILLA

NATIONAL TEAM RECORD
JULY 10TH 2006 TO JULY 12TH 2010

PL	W	D	L	F	A	%
3	0	0	3	5	18	0

FIFA/COCA-COLA WORLD RANKING

1993	1994	1995	1996	1997	1998	1999	2000	2001	2002	2003	2004	2005	2006	High		Low	
-	-	-	-	190	197	202	197	194	196	198	197	198	196	**189**	06/97	**202**	02/00

2006–2007											
08/06	09/06	10/06	11/06	12/06	01/07	02/07	03/07	04/07	05/07	06/07	07/07
194	196	196	196	196	197	197	197	197	196	196	196

A busy year for football in the tiny island of Anguilla saw the national team take to the field for the first time in two and a half years when they entered the Digicel Caribbean Cup. In a first qualifying round tournament in St John's, Antigua, Anguilla shipped 18 goals in three matches against Antigua, St Kitts and Barbados and the national team has now failed to win a game since beating Montserrat in 2001. Indeed their record stands at just two victories and one draw in all the 32 matches that they have played. Anguilla did manage to score five times, however, through Richard O'Connor, Girdon Connor, Gaekward St Hillaire and Kapil Assent. The under 17 and under 20

INTERNATIONAL HONOURS
None

teams entered the qualifying rounds for the FIFA tournaments in their age groups but both were on the end of some heavy double figure defeats. The gulf in class between Anguilla and the other islands at club level has meant that, unlike the national teams, clubs are unwilling to take part in Caribbean competitions. The seven team championship does, however, remain fiercely contested with Kicks United winning the title for the first time in a close battle with Attackers and defending champions Roaring Lions. Despite racking up an impressive 18-1 victory over Full Monty, Attackers had to settle for second place.

THE FIFA BIG COUNT OF 2006

	Male	Female		Total
Number of players	1 160	437	Referees and Assistant Referees	7
Professionals	10		Admin, Coaches, Technical, Medical	63
Amateurs 18+	230		Number of clubs	11
Youth under 18	662		Number of teams	16
Unregistered	195		Clubs with women's teams	4
Total players	1 597		Players as % of population	11.85%

Anguilla Football Association (AFA)
PO Box 1318, The Valley, Anguilla
Tel +1 264 497 7323   Fax +1 264 497 7324
axafa@yahoo.com   www. none
President: GUISHARD Raymond   General Secretary: HUGHES Damian
Vice-President: CARTY Diana   Treasurer: TBD   Media Officer: HUGHES Damian
Men's Coach: HODGE Vernon   Women's Coach: JOHNSON Colin
AFA formed: 1990   CONCACAF: 1996   FIFA: 1996
Colours: Turquoise & white shirts, Turquoise shorts, Turquoise socks or Orange & blue shirts, Orange shorts, Orange socks

RECENT INTERNATIONALS PLAYED BY ANGUILLA

2002	Opponents	Score	Venue	Comp	Scorers	Att	Referee
6-07	British Virgin Islands	L 1-2	Tortola	Fr			
2003							
No international matches played in 2003							
2004							
19-03	Dominican Republic	D 0-0	Santo Domingo	WCq		400	Mattus CRC
21-03	Dominican Republic	L 0-6	Santo Domingo	WCq		850	Porras CRC
2005							
No international matches played in 2005							
2006							
20-09	Antigua and Barbuda	L 3-5	St John's	CCq	St Hillaire [13], Assent [51], O'Connor [90]	300	Wijngaarde SUR
22-09	St Kitts and Nevis	L 1-6	St John's	CCq	O'Connor [22]	500	Phillips GRN
24-09	Barbados	L 1-7	St John's	CCq	Connor [48]	2 800	Wijngaarde SUR
2007							
No international matches played in 2007 before August							

Fr = Friendly match • WC = FIFA World Cup • CC = Digicel Caribbean Cup • q = qualifier

ANGUILLA NATIONAL TEAM RECORDS AND RECORD SEQUENCES

Records			Sequence records		
Victory	4-1	MSR 2001	Wins	1	
Defeat	0-14	GUY 1998	Defeats	17	1991-1998
Player Caps	n/a		Undefeated	1	
Player Goals	n/a		Without win	18	1991-1998

Sequence records		
Clean sheets	1	
Goals scored	5	2000-2002
Without goal	7	1991-1994
Goals against	27	1991-2002

RECENT LEAGUE RECORD

Year Champions

1998	Spartans International
1999	Attackers
2000	No tournament played
2001	Roaring Lions
2002	Roaring Lions
2003	Roaring Lions
2004	Spartans International
2005	Roaring Lions
2006	Kicks United

ANGUILLA 2006-07
KATEGORIA E PARE (2)

	Pl	W	D	L	F	A	Pts
Kicks United	11	9	0	2	36	10	27
Attackers	11	8	1	2	55	12	25
Roaring Lions	10	7	0	3	34	18	21
Spartan FC	10	5	1	4	27	13	16
Full Monty	10	3	0	7	17	57	9
ALHCS FC	10	1	0	9	4	34	3
Jam Boys	Withdrew after 6 matches						

Ended 25/02/2007

ANGUILLA COUNTRY INFORMATION

Capital	The Valley	Independence	Overseas territory of the UK	GDP per Capita	$8 600
Population	13 008	Status		GDP Ranking	n/a
Area km²	102	Language	English	Dialling code	+1 264
Population density	128 per km²	Literacy rate	95%	Internet code	.ai
% in urban areas	n/a	Main religion	Christian 88%	GMT +/–	-4
Towns/Cities ('000)	North Side 1; The Valley 1; Stoney Ground 1; The Quarter 1				
Neighbours (km)	Caribbean Sea 61				
Main stadia	Ronald Webster Park Annex – The Valley 1 100				

ALB – ALBANIA

ALBANIA NATIONAL TEAM RECORD
JULY 10TH 2006 TO JULY 12TH 2010

PL	W	D	L	F	A	%
9	3	3	3	11		50

FIFA/COCA-COLA WORLD RANKING

1993	1994	1995	1996	1997	1998	1999	2000	2001	2002	2003	2004	2005	2006	High	Low
92	100	91	116	116	106	83	72	96	93	89	86	82	87	**62** 08/06	**124** 08/97

2006–2007											
08/06	09/06	10/06	11/06	12/06	01/07	02/07	03/07	04/07	05/07	06/07	07/07
62	75	88	86	87	86	87	88	77	78	69	67

Under coach Shkelqim Muca, runaway leaders SK Tirana comfortably won the League for a fourth time in five seasons. The season, however, was marked by an increase in violence, especially against officials, with much of it away from the pitch. In one match - between second division Burrel and Erzeni - the former Tirana coach Sulejman Mena was attacked in the changing room whilst working for the federation and spent 15 days in intensive care. There was better news in the Cup, where, after six defeats in the final, Besa Kavajë finally got their hands on the trophy, the first silverware in the history of the club. Their opponents, neighbours Teuta Durrës, had failed to score

INTERNATIONAL HONOURS
Balkan Cup 1946

in any of their eight appearances in the final, having won their three Cups on penalties, but although they lost Teuta did score their first goals in a 3-2 defeat. The national team, with just three points from their first five UEFA Euro 2008 games, failed to live up to expectations following their encouraging FIFA World Cup campaign. Coach Otto Baric blamed the lack of first team opportunities for his foreign based stars and controversially dropped 33 year old Lazio forward Igli Tare as he sought to encourage a younger generation of home based players. The only wins for the national team came at the beginning and end of the season - against San Marino and Luxembourg.

THE FIFA BIG COUNT OF 2006

	Male	Female		Total
Number of players	149 730	15 000	Referees and Assistant Referees	1200
Professionals	550		Admin, Coaches, Technical, Medical	5000
Amateurs 18+	38 800		Number of clubs	440
Youth under 18	14 000		Number of teams	574
Unregistered	34 000		Clubs with women's teams	16
Total players	164 730		Players as % of population	4.60%

The Football Association of Albania (FSHF)
Federata Shqiptare e Futbolit, Rruga Labinoti, Pallati perballe Shkolles, "Gjuhet e Huaja", Tirana, Albania
Tel +355 43 46601   Fax +355 43 46 609
fshf@albaniaonline.net   www.fshf.org
President: DUKA Armand   General Secretary: MICI Roland
Vice-President: KASMI Bujar   Treasurer: KASMI Bujar   Media Officer: NURISHMI Lysien
Men's Coach: BARIC Otto   Women's Coach: None
FSHF formed: 1930   UEFA: 1954   FIFA: 1932
Red shirts with black trimming, Black shorts, Red socks or White shirts with red and black trimming, black shorts, White socks

RECENT INTERNATIONALS PLAYED BY ALBANIA

2002 Opponents	Score	Venue	Comp	Scorers	Att	Referee
12-10 Switzerland	D 1-1	Tirana	ECq	Murati [79]	15 000	Erdemir TUR
16-10 Russia	L 1-4	Volgograd	ECq	Duro.K [13]	18 000	Sundell SWE
2003						
12-02 Vietnam	W 5-0	Bastia Umbra - ITA	Fr	Bushi [16], Myrtaj 2 [21 38], Dragusha [53], Pinari [85]		Nikoluci ITA
29-03 Russia	W 3-1	Shkoder	ECq	Rraklli [20], Lala [79], Tare [82]	16 000	Allaerts BEL
2-04 Republic of Ireland	D 0-0	Tirana	ECq		20 000	Farina ITA
30-04 Bulgaria	L 0-2	Sofia	Fr		9 325	Vidlak CZE
7-06 Republic of Ireland	L 1-2	Dublin	ECq	Skela [8]	33 000	Mikulski POL
11-06 Switzerland	L 2-3	Geneva	ECq	Lala [23], Skela [86p]	26 000	Bennett ENG
20-08 Macedonia	L 1-3	Prilep	Fr	Skela [74]	3 000	Mihajlevic SCM
6-09 Georgia	L 0-3	Tbilisi	ECq		18 000	Vollquartz DEN
10-09 Georgia	W 3-1	Tirana	ECq	Hasi [52], Tare [54], Bushi [80]	10 500	Salomir ROM
11-10 Portugal	L 3-5	Lisbon	Fr	Aliaj 2 [13 59], Tare [43]	5 000	Garibian FRA
15-11 Estonia	W 2-0	Tirana	Fr	Aliaj [26], Bushi [81]	5 000	Douros GRE
2004						
18-02 Sweden	W 2-1	Tirana	Fr	Skela [69], Aliaj [75]	15 000	Paparesta ITA
31-03 Iceland	W 2-1	Tirana	Fr	Aliaj [42], Bushi [78]	12 000	Bertini ITA
28-04 Estonia	D 1-1	Tallinn	Fr	Aliaj [51]	1 500	Sipailo LVA
18-08 Cyprus	L 1-2	Nicosia	Fr	Rraklli [64]	200	Kapitanis CYP
4-09 Greece	W 2-1	Tirana	WCq	Murati [2], Aliaj [11]	15 800	Gonzalez ESP
8-09 Georgia	L 0-2	Tbilisi	WCq		20 000	Courtney NIR
9-10 Denmark	L 0-2	Tirana	WCq		14 500	Baskarov RUS
13-10 Kazakhstan	W 1-0	Almaty	WCq	Bushi [61]	12 300	Stuchlik AUT
2005						
9-02 Ukraine	L 0-2	Tirana	WCq		12 000	Bennett ENG
26-03 Turkey	L 0-2	Istanbul	WCq		32 000	Plautz AUT
30-03 Greece	L 0-2	Piraeus	WCq		31 700	Layec FRA
29-05 Poland	L 0-1	Szczecin	Fr		14 000	Weiner GER
4-06 Georgia	W 3-2	Tirana	WCq	Tare 2 [6 56], Skela [33]	BCD	Tudor ROM
8-06 Denmark	L 1-3	Copenhagen	WCq	Bogdani [73]	26 366	Frojdfeldt SWE
17-08 Azerbaijan	W 2-1	Tirana	Fr	Bushi [37], Cana [72]	7 300	
3-09 Kazakhstan	W 2-1	Tirana	WCq	Myrtaj [53], Bogdani [56]	3 000	Slupik POL
8-10 Ukraine	D 2-2	Dnepropetrovsk	WCq	Bogdani 2 [75 83]	24 000	Verbist BEL
12-10 Turkey	L 0-1	Tirana	WCq		8 000	Dauden Ibanez ESP
2006						
1-03 Lithuania	L 1-2	Tirana	Fr	Aliaj [38p]		Pieri ITA
22-03 Georgia	D 0-0	Tirana	Fr			
16-08 San Marino	W 3-0	Serravalle	Fr	Tare [7], Skela [23], Lala [38]		
2-09 Belarus	D 2-2	Minsk	ECq	Skela [7p], Hasi [86]	23 000	Asumaa FIN
6-09 Romania	L 0-2	Tirana	ECq		12 000	Benquerença POR
11-10 Netherlands	L 1-2	Amsterdam	ECq	Curri [67]	40 085	Yefet ISR
2007						
7-02 FYR Macedonia	L 0-1	Tirana	Fr		8 000	Bertini ITA
24-03 Slovenia	D 0-0	Shkoder	ECq		7 000	Attard MLT
28-03 Bulgaria	D 0-0	Sofia	ECq		19 800	Eriksson SWE
2-06 Luxembourg	W 2-0	Tirana	ECq	Kapllani [38], Haxhi [57]	3 000	Silgava GEO
6-06 Luxembourg	W 3-0	Luxembourg	ECq	Skella [25], Kapllani 2 [36 72]	4 325	Malzinskas LTU

Fr = Friendly match • EC = UEFA EURO 2004/2008 • WC = FIFA World Cup • q = qualifier • BCD = behind closed doors

ALBANIA NATIONAL TEAM RECORDS AND RECORD SEQUENCES

Records			Sequence records				
Victory	5-0	VIE 2003	Wins	4	1999-2000	Clean sheets	4	2007-
Defeat	0-12	HUN 1950	Defeats	10	1989-1991	Goals scored	7	1973-1980
Player Caps	73	STRAKOSHA Foto	Undefeated	4	Six times	Without goal	6	1987-88, 1990-91
Player Goals	14	BUSHI Alban	Without win	25	1985-1991	Goals against	14	1988-1991

REPUBLIKA E SHQIPERISE; REPUBLIC OF ALBANIA

Capital	Tirana	Language	Albanian			Independence	1912
Population	3 581 655	Area	28 748 km²	Density	123 per km²	% in cities	37%
GDP per cap	$4 500	Dailling code	+355	Internet	.al	GMT + / -	+1

MAJOR CITIES/TOWNS

		Population '000
1	Tirana	380
2	Durrës	124
3	Elbasan	102
4	Vlorë	90
5	Shkodër	88
6	Fier	62
7	Korçë	58
8	Berat	47
9	Lushnjë	42
10	Kavajë	29
11	Pogradec	26
12	Laç	25
13	Gjirokastër	23
14	Patos	23
15	Krujë	21
16	Lezhë	19
17	Kuçovë	18
18	Kukës	18
19	Burrel	15
20	Sarandë	15
21	Peshkopi	15
22	Cërrik	14
23	Shijak	14
24	Peqin	7

MEDALS TABLE

		Overall			League			Cup			Europe			City	Stadium	Cap'ty	DoF
		G	S	B	G	S	B	G	S	B	G	S	B				
1	SK Tiranë	35	19	11	23	13	11	12	6					Tirana	Selman Stërmasi	12 500	1920
2	Partizani Tiranë	30	26	8	15	18	8	15	8					Tirana	Qemal Stafa	19 500	1945
3	Dinamo Tiranë	29	14	10	16	9	10	13	5					Tirana	Qemal Stafa	19 500	1950
4	Vllaznia Shkodër	14	16	14	9	10	14	5	6					Shkodër	Loro Borici	16 000	1919
5	Teuta Durrës	4	11	5	1	5	5	3	6					Durrës	Niko Dovana	12 000	1922
6	SK Elbasani	4	2	1	2	1	1	2	1					Elbasan	Ruzhdi Bizhuda	8 000	1923
7	Flamurtari Vlorë	3	14	3	1	6	3	2	8					Vlorë	Flamurtari	8 500	1923
8	Besa Kavajë	1	7	9		1	9	1	6					Kavajë	Besa	8 000	1925
9	Skënderbeu Korçë	1	6	2	1	3	2		3					Korçë	Skënderbeu	8 000	1925
10	Apollonia Fier	1					1							Fier	Loni Papuçiu	6 000	1925
11	Lushnja		3						3					Lushnjë	Roza Haxhiu	12 000	1926
12	Tomori Berat	2			1									Berat	Tomori	13 350	1923
13	Albpetrol Patosi	1							1					Patosi	Alush Noga	5 000	1947
	Luftëtari Gjirokastër	1			1									Gjirokastër	Subi Bakiri	8 400	1929
15	Bylis Ballshi			1			1							Bylis	Adush Muça	6 500	1972

RECENT LEAGUE AND CUP RECORD

	Championship						Cup		
Year	Champions	Pts	Runners-up	Pts	Third	Pts	Winners	Score	Runners-up
1995	SK Tirana	44	Teuta Durrës	32	Partizani Tiranë	32	Teuta Durrës	0-0 4-3p	SK Tirana
1996	SK Tirana	55	Teuta Durrës	54	Partizani Tiranë	46	SK Tirana	1-1 4-3p	Flamurtari Vlorë
1997	SK Tirana	46	Vllaznia Shkodër	43	Flamurtari Vlorë	41	Partizani Tiranë	2-2 4-3p	Flamurtari Vlorë
1998	Vllaznia Shkodër	72	SK Tirana	65	Partizani Tiranë	64	Apolonia Fier	1-0	Lushnjë
1999	SK Tirana	61	Vllaznia Shkodër	60	Bylis Ballshi	59	SK Tirana	0-0 3-0p	Vllaznia Shkodër
2000	SK Tirana	52	Tomori Berat	52	Teuta Durrës	49	Teuta Durrës	0-0 5-4p	Lushnjë
2001	Vllaznia Shkodër	56	SK Tirana	54	Dinamo Tiranë	52	SK Tirana	5-0	Teuta Durrës
2002	Dinamo Tiranë	63	SK Tirana	62	Partizani Tiranë	46	SK Tirana	1-0	Dinamo Tiranë
2003	SK Tirana	60	Vllaznia Shkodër	49	Partizani Tiranë	46	Dinamo Tiranë	1-0	Teuta Durrës
2004	SK Tirana	80	Dinamo Tiranë	71	Vllaznia Shkodër	68	Partizani Tiranë	1-0	Dinamo Tiranë
2005	SK Tirana	84	SK Elbasani	79	Dinamo Tiranë	62	Teuta Durrës	0-0 6-5p	SK Tirana
2006	KF Elbasani	72	SK Tirana	62	Dinamo Tiranë	61	SK Tirana	1-0	Vllaznia Shkodër
2007	SK Tirana	72	Teuta Durrës	67	Vllaznia Shkodër	63	Besa Kavajë	3-2	Teuta Durrës

ALBANIA 2006-07
KATEGORIA SUPERIORE

	Pl	W	D	L	F	A	Pts	Tirana	Teuta	Vllaznia	Partizani	Dinamo	Besa	Elbasani	Kastrioti	Flamurtari	Shkumbini	Luftëtari	Apollonia
SK Tirana †	33	22	6	5	65	33	72		5-0	1-0 4-2	3-2	1-0 2-1	2-1	1-2	2-0	8-3	2-0 1-1	2-2	1-0 2-0 3-1 1-0
Teuta Durrës ‡	33	19	10	4	44	26	67	1-1 2-0		1-0	0-0 1-0 0-0 3-1	1-0	1-0	2-1	1-0 2-1	1-1	1-1 3-0 2-0 4-1		
Vllaznia Shkodër	33	18	9	6	46	28	63	1-1	3-1 0-0		1-0	3-0	1-0 1-1 2-0 2-0 2-1 2-0	2-2	2-1 0-2	1-0	1-2 2-1		
Partizani Tiranë	33	17	6	10	44	25	57	0-2	2-0 0-0 0-1			2-1	0-0 2-1 0-1 1-0 1-0 4-1	0-3	2-0 5-0	3-1	3-2 2-0		
Dinamo Tiranë	33	14	5	14	40	38	47	1-2	1-3	0-0 1-2 0-0 0-2			3-1	2-1 1-1 2-0 2-0	1-0	2-1 5-0	4-1	2-1 2-1	
Besa Kavajë ‡	33	11	8	14	35	38	41	1-2 0-1 1-1 0-1	1-1	0-2	0-0 2-0			2-2	0-0 3-0 2-0	2-1	3-1 1-2 2-1 2-1		
KF Elbasani	33	10	10	13	34	39	40	2-2 1-2 0-1 0-0	0-1	0-2	1-0 1-0 3-0				1-0 2-1 1-1	2-0	1-0 4-4	2-0	
Kastrioti Krujë	33	9	10	14	32	47	37	2-1 1-1 1-1 1-2	1-1	2-2	0-1	2-2 1-1 1-0 1-1				1-0	0-0 1-0 1-0	1-1	
Flamurtari Vlorë	33	9	7	17	34	40	34	3-2	1-2	1-1 0-2 1-0 0-2 2-0 2-3	1-2	0-2	2-0 0-0				1-1 2-0	1-0	4-0
Shkumbini Peqin	33	10	4	19	36	53	34	1-2 2-1 0-2 0-1	3-1	0-2	0-1 0-1 3-1 3-0 4-2 0-2 2-1	2-1						1-0	0-1
Luftëtari Gjirokastër	33	9	6	18	28	44	33	0-2	2-1	2-3 0-1 0-0 3-1 2-0 0-2	1-0	0-0	2-0	0-0	2-0	0-0 2-1 1-0 1-3			1-0
Apolonia Fier	33	7	5	21	32	59	26	0-2	2-2	1-4	0-2	1-0	0-1	2-2 1-2 2-3 1-2 0-2 1-0 3-2 3-1 0-0 2-1					

26/08/2006 - 19/05/2007 • † Qualified for the UEFA Champions League • ‡ Qualified for the UEFA Cup
Top scorers: Vioresin SINANI, SK Tirana 23; Daniel XHAFA, Teuta 20; Sebino PLAKU, Apolonia 15; Hamdi SALIHI, Tirana 13

ALBANIA 2006-07
KATEGORIA E PARE (2)

	Pl	W	D	L	F	A	Pts
Skënderbeu Korçë	24	17	5	2	46	18	56
Besëlidhja Lezhë	24	16	6	2	46	13	54
Turbina Cërrik	24	14	3	7	26	20	45
KS Lushnja	24	13	3	8	47	24	42
Laçi	24	10	8	6	34	20	38
Erzeni Shijak	24	10	2	12	35	45	32
Pogradeci	24	10	0	14	23	31	30
Minatori Tepelenë	24	8	5	11	29	30	29
Gramshi	24	9	1	14	27	37	28
Sopoti Librazhd	24	7	5	12	27	35	26
Bilisht Sport §3	24	8	3	13	24	38	24
Ada Velipojë	24	6	3	15	20	49	21
Tomori Berat	24	5	2	17	17	41	17
Burreli				Excluded after 10 matches			

8/09/2006 - 12/05/2007 • § = points deducted

KUPA E SHQIPERISE 2006-07

Round of 16		Quarter-finals		Semi-finals		Final	
Besa Kavaje	0 4						
Kastrioti Krujë *	3 0	Besa Kavajë *	1 2				
Skënderbeu Korçë *	2 0	Dinamo Tiranë	2 0				
Dinamo Tiranë	3 1			Besa Kavaje	3 1		
Turbina Cërrik *	2 0			Shkumbini Peqin *	3 1		
KF Elbasani	0 0	Turbina Cërrik	0 1				
Flamurtari Vlorë *	1 0	Shkumbini Peqin *	4 2				
Shkumbini Peqin	4 1						
Partizani Tiranë	1 1					Besa Kavajë ‡	3
KS Lushnja *	0 0	Partizani Tiranë	1 0			Teuta Durrës	2
Luftëtari Gjirokastër	1 0	Vllaznia Shkodër *	1 0				
Vllaznia Shkodër	1 3						
SK Tirana	2 2			Partizani Tiranë	0 1		
Erzeni Shijak *	1 0	SK Tirana	1 2	Teuta Durrës *	0 1		
Apollonia Fier *	1 0	Teuta Durrës *	2 2				
Teuta Durrës	2 0	* Home team in the first leg • ‡ Qualified for the UEFA Cup					

CUP FINAL
Qemal Stafa, Tirana
16-05-2007
Scorers - Xhihani 3, Belisha 42, Veliaj 70 for Besa;
Xhafa.D 9, Grizha OG 88 f or Teuta

ALG – ALGERIA

NATIONAL TEAM RECORD
JULY 10TH 2006 TO JULY 12TH 2010

PL	W	D	L	F	A	%
9	3	2	4	11	13	44.4

FIFA/COCA-COLA WORLD RANKING

1993	1994	1995	1996	1997	1998	1999	2000	2001	2002	2003	2004	2005	2006	High		Low	
35	57	48	49	59	71	86	82	75	68	62	73	80	80	**30**	09/93	**89**	08/06

2006–2007											
08/06	09/06	10/06	11/06	12/06	01/07	02/07	03/07	04/07	05/07	06/07	07/07
89	83	73	79	80	78	80	78	64	65	67	77

Algerian football continued to suffer setbacks at both club and country level. JS Kabylie qualified for the group phase of the 2006 African Champions League but finished bottom in their group while the national team were faced with the possibility of missing out on the African Nations Cup finals for a second tournament in a row. Having led for most of the campaign, a 2-0 home defeat by Guinea in June saw the 'Fennecs' hand the top place in the standings to their opponents with just one round left to play. It left Algeria a long way off the heady heights of the 1980s, when they twice participated at the FIFA World Cup finals. French coach Jean Michel Cavalli continued to

INTERNATIONAL HONOURS
Qualified for the FIFA World Cup™ finals 1982 1986 **CAF African Cup of Nations** 1990
CAF Youth Cup 1979 **All Africa Games** 1978 **African Champions League** Mouloudia Alger 1976, JS Kabylie 1981 1990

battle with the same problems that beset his predecessors, merging the growing number of French-born players with locals in the national side. Entente Setif celebrated double success at the end of the season, winning the title by two points from JSK and also taking the Arab Champions League in a dramatic away victory over Jordan's Al Faysali in the second leg of the final. Mouloudia Alger, coached by the Italian Enrico Fabbro, won the Cup for a second successive year by beating USM Alger, a goal from international midfielder Fodil Hadjadj settling the encounter.

THE FIFA BIG COUNT OF 2006

	Male	Female		Total
Number of players	1 719 100	71 100	Referees and Assistant Referees	1 700
Professionals	300		Admin, Coaches, Technical, Medical	22 800
Amateurs 18+	138 800		Number of clubs	2 090
Youth under 18	64 800		Number of teams	2 560
Unregistered	248 300		Clubs with women's teams	0
Total players	1 790 200		Players as % of population	5.44%

Fédération Algérienne de Football (FAF)
Chemin Ahmed Ouaked, Case Postale 39, Dely-Ibrahim, Alger, Algeria
Tel +213 21 372929   Fax +213 21 367266
faffoot@yahoo.fr   www.faf.org.dz
President: HADDADJ Hamid   General Secretary: BOUCHEMLA Mourad
Vice-President: KHELAIFIA Mohamed   Treasurer: MECHRARA Mohamed   Media Officer: HADDADJ Hamid
Men's Coach: CAVALLI Jean-Michel   Women's Coach: CHIH Azzedine
FAF formed: 1962   CAF: 1964   FIFA: 1963
Green shirts, White shorts, Green socks or White shirts, Green shorts, White socks

RECENT INTERNATIONALS PLAYED BY ALGERIA

2003	Opponents	Score		Venue	Comp	Scorers	Att	Referee
4-09	Qatar	W	1-0	Dinard	Fr	Cherrad [26]	400	
24-09	Gabon	D	2-2	Algiers	Fr	Fellahi [51], Achiou [59]. W 4-3p	2 000	Zekrini ALG
26-09	Burkina Faso	D	0-0	Algiers	Fr	W 4-3p	1 500	Benouza ALG
11-10	Niger	W	1-0	Niamey	WCq	Boutabout [63]	20 126	Coulibaly MLI
14-11	Niger	W	6-0	Algiers	WCq	Cherrad 2 [16 22], Boutabout 2 [42 70], Mamouni [45], Akrour [82]	50 000	El-Arjoun MOR
2004								
15-01	Mali	L	0-2	Algiers	Fr		7 000	Zehmoun TUN
25-01	Cameroon	D	1-1	Sousse	CNr1	Zafour [51]	20 000	Codjia BEN
29-01	Egypt	W	2-1	Sousse	CNr1	Mamouni [13], Achiou [85]	15 000	Hamer LUX
3-02	Zimbabwe	L	1 2	Sousse	CNr1	Achiou [72]	10 000	Maillet SEY
8-02	Morocco	L	1-3	Sfax	CNqf	Cherrad [83]	20 000	Shelmani LBY
28-04	China PR	L	0-1	Clermont-Ferrand	Fr		1 600	Poulat FRA
30-05	Jordan	D	1-1	Annaba	Fr	Cherrad [60]	20 000	Zahmoul TUN
5-06	Angola	D	0-0	Annaba	WCq		55 000	Daami TUN
20-06	Zimbabwe	D	1-1	Harare	WCq	Cherrad [3]	65 000	Ntambidila COD
3-07	Nigeria	L	0-1	Abuja	WCq		35 000	Hisseine CHA
17-08	Burkina Faso	D	2-2	Blida	Fr	Tahraoui [33], Arrache [54]	15 000	Tahri MAR
5-09	Gabon	L	0-3	Annaba	WCq		51 000	Ndoye SEN
9-10	Rwanda	D	1-1	Kigali	WCq	Bourahli [14]	20 000	Abdel Rahmen SUD
17-11	Senegal	L	1-2	Toulon	Fr	Daoud [77]	4 000	Bata FRA
2005								
9-02	Burkina Faso	W	3-0	Algiers	Fr	Saifi 2 [29 42], Sofiane [72]	5 000	Benaissa ALG
27-03	Rwanda	W	1-0	Oran	WCq	Boutabout [48]	20 000	Abd El Fatah EGY
5-06	Angola	L	1-2	Luanda	WCq	Boutabout [63]	27 000	Hicuburundi BDI
12-06	Mali	L	0-3	Arles	Fr			Derrien FRA
19-06	Zimbabwe	D	2-2	Oran	WCq	Yahia [17], Daoud [48]	15 000	Pare BFA
4-09	Nigeria	L	2-5	Oran	WCq	Yacef [48], Boutabout [58]	11 000	Shelmani LBY
8-10	Gabon	D	0-0	Port-Gentil	WCq		37 000	Diouf SEN
2006								
28-02	Burkina Faso	D	0-0	Rouen	Fr		2 000	Duhamel FRA
4-06	Sudan	W	1-0	Algiers	Fr	Deham [47]		El Harzi TUN
15-08	Gabon	L	0-2	Aix-en-Provence	Fr			Mezouar
3-09	Guinea	D	0-0	Conakry	CNq			Coulibaly MLI
7-10	Gambia	W	1-0	Algiers	CNq	Ziani [75p]	48 000	Auda EGY
15-11	Burkina Faso	L	1-2	Aix-en-Provence	Fr	Saifi [88p]	700	Falcone FRA
2007								
7-02	Libya	W	2-1	Algiers	Fr	Saifi [63], Meniri [68]		El Harzi TUN
24-03	Cape Verde Islands	W	2-0	Algiers	CNq	Deham [60], Meniri [89]		Abd El Fatah EGY
2-06	Cape Verde Islands	D	2-2	Praia	CNq	Bougherra [33], Saifi [84]		Aboubacar CIV
5-06	Argentina	L	3-4	Barcelona	Fr	Yahia [9], Belhadj 2 [42 77]		Izquierdo ESP
16-06	Guinea	L	0-2	Algiers	CNq		80 000	Guezzaz MAR

Fr = Friendly match • CN = CAF African Cup of Nations • WC = FIFA World Cup • q = qualifier • r1 = first round group • qf = quarter-final

ALGERIA NATIONAL TEAM RECORDS AND RECORD SEQUENCES

Records			Sequence records					
Victory	15-1	YEM 1973	Wins	10	1957-1963	Clean sheets	4	Five times
Defeat	0-5	BFA 1975, GDR 1976	Defeats	5	1974	Goals scored	16	2000-2001
Player Caps	n/a		Undefeated	15	1989-1991	Without goal	5	1989
Player Goals	n/a		Without win	11	2004	Goals against	9	2000-2001

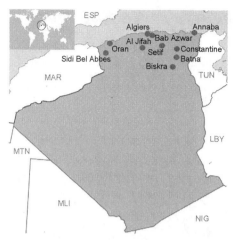

MAJOR CITIES/TOWNS

		Population '000
1	Algiers	2 029
2	Oran	642
3	Constantine	446
4	Bab Azwar	295
5	Batna	286
6	Setif	227
7	Djelfa	223
8	Annaba	204
9	Biskra	199
10	Sidi bel Abbès	193
11	Tibissah	186
12	Tiyaret	180
13	El Bouni	177
14	Béjaïa	166
15	Bordj Bou Arreridj	162
16	Blida	162
17	Chlef	157
18	Ouargla	155
19	Tizi-Ouzou	146
20	Béchar	144
21	Saïda	129
22	Tlemcen	120
23	Oum El Bouaghi	104
24	Mascara	87

AL JAZA'IR; PEOPLE'S DEMOCRATIC REPUBLIC OF ALGERIA

Capital	Algiers	Language	Arabic, French, Berber dialects	Independence	1962		
Population	32 930 091	Area	2 381 740 km²	Density per km²		% in cities	56%
GDP per cap	$6 000	Dailling code	+213	Internet .dz		GMT +/-	+1

MEDALS TABLE

			Overall			League			Cup			Africa			City	Stadium	Cap'ty	DoF
			G	S	B	G	S	B	G	S	B	G	S	B				
1	JS Kabylie	JSK	23	13	5	13	9	3	4	4		6		2	Tizi-Ouzou	1er Novembre	25 000	1946
2	USM Alger	USMA	12	13	3	5	4	1	7	9				2	Algiers	Omar Hammadi	10 000	1937
3	MC Alger	MCA	13	2	4	6	2	4	6		1				Algiers	5 Juillet	70 000	1921
4	CR Belouizdad	CRB	11	5	3	6	3	2	5	2				1	Algiers	20 Août	15 000	1962
5	ES Sétif	ESS	10	2	4	3	2	3	6			1		1	Sétif	8 Mai	30 000	1958
6	MC Oran	MCO	8	12	4	4	9	3	4	2		1	1		Oran	Ahmed Zabana	50 000	1946
7	USM El Harrach	USMH	3	2		1	2		2						Algiers	1er Novembre	5 000	1931
8	NA Hussein Dey	NAHD	2	8	5	1	4	4	1	3		1	1		Algiers	Frères Zioui	7 000	1945
9	WA Tlemcem	WAT	2	2	3				3	2		2			Tlemcen	Frères Zerga	6 000	1962
10	USM Annaba	USMAn	2			1			1						Annaba	19 Mai	70 000	1937
11	MO Constantine	MOC	1	4	2	1	1	2		3					Constantine	Chahid Hamlaoui	40 000	1939
12	RC Kouba	RCK	1	3	2	1	2	2		1					Algiers	Omar Benhaddad	10 000	1942
13	CS Constantine	CSC	1	2		1	1			1					Constantine	Chahid Hamlaoui	40 000	1926
14	ASO Chlef	ASO	1	1	3			3	1	1					Chlef	Boumezrag Mohamed	15 000	1947
15	USM Bel Abbès	USMBA	1		2			2	1						Sidi Bel Abbés	24 Février	50 000	1933

ABBREVIATIONS CR = Chabab Riadhi • CS = Club Sportif • ES = Entente Sportive • GC = Ghali Club • JS = Jeunesse Sportive • MC = Mouloudia Chaabia (Alger) • MC = Mouloudia Club (Oran) • NA = Nasr Athletic • USM = Union Sportive Madinet • WA = Widad Athletic

RECENT LEAGUE AND CUP RECORD

		Championship						Cup		
Year	Champions	Pts	Runners-up	Pts	Third	Pts		Winners	Score	Runners-up
1995	JS Kabylie	40	MC Oran	35	USM Blida	33		CR Belouizdad	2-1	OM Médéa
1996	USM Algiers	60	MC Oran	58	WA Tlemcen	51		MC Oran	1-0	Ittihad Blida
1997	CS Constantine	56	MC Oran	55	USM Algiers	49		USM Algiers	1-0	CA Batna
1998	USM El Harrach	3-2	USM Algiers					WA Tlemcen	1-0	MC Oran
1999	MC Alger	1-0	JS Kabylie					USM Alger	2-0	JS Kabylie
2000	CR Belouizdad	47	MC Oran	38	MC Constantine	38		MC Ouargla	2-1	WA Tlemcen
2001	CR Belouizdad	62	USM Algiers	55	JS Kabylie	52		USM Alger	1-0	CR Méchria
2002	USM Alger	57	JS Kabylie	52	WA Tlemcen	51		WA Tlemcen	1-0	MC Oran
2003	USM Alger	58	USM Blida	51	NA Hussein Dey	51		USM Alger	2-1	CR Belouizdad
2004	JS Kabylie	61	USM Alger	58	NA Hussein Dey	49		USM Alger	0-0 5-4p	JS Kabylie
2005	USM Alger	67	JS Kabylie	54	MC Alger	49		ASO Chlef	1-0	USM Sétif
2006	JS Kabylie	58	USM Alger	57	ASO Chlef	52		MC Alger	2-1	USM Alger
2007	ES Sétif	54	JS Kabylie	52	JSM Béjaïa	49		MC Alger	1-0	USM Alger

ALGERIA 2006-07

PREMIERE DIVISION

	Pl	W	D	L	F	A	Pts	ESS	JSK	JSMB	USMA	ASO	MCO	NAHC	CABBA	USMB	CRB	MCA	WAT	OMR	PAC	ASMO	CAB
ES Sétif †	30	15	9	6	32	19	54		0-0	0-0	2-0	0-0	1-0	1-0	2-1	1-0	0-1	2-0	2-1	0-0	3-1	1-1	2-0
JS Kabylie †	30	14	10	6	33	20	52	2-3		1-0	1-0	2-1	2-1	1-1	2-0	3-0	1-0	1-0	1-0	4-2	0-0	1-1	1-0
JSM Béjaïa	30	13	10	7	30	19	49	1-0	1-0		1-0	0-0	2-0	2-0	2-1	0-0	1-1	1-1	0-0	0-0	2-1	1-0	1-0
USM Alger	30	13	8	9	32	25	47	0-0	1-0	2-1		2-0	2-0	0-1	2-1	0-0	2-1	2-2	3-0	0-0	0-0	3-2	2-0
ASO Chlef	30	12	10	8	29	22	46	2-1	0-0	2-1	0-1		1-0	4-1	2-0	1-1	3-1	0-0	0-0	1-0	2-1	1-1	1-0
MC Oran	30	12	6	12	28	25	42	0-2	1-0	1-0	2-1	1-0		4-0	1-0	2-0	0-0	1-2	1-0	3-0	0-0	2-0	0-0
NA Hussein Dey	30	11	8	11	27	33	41	0-0	0-0	0-0	0-1	2-0	0-1		3-2	2-0	0-4	1-1	1-1	2-1	3-2	2-0	1-0
CA Bordj Bou Arréridj	30	12	4	14	24	38	40	0-0	1-0	1-0	1-0	2-1	0-0	1-0		2-1	1-0	2-1	1-0	0-1	1-1	3-1	1-0
USM Blida	30	9	12	9	33	28	39	2-1	0-1	2-2	2-0	0-0	0-0	4-0	1-0		0-0	2-2	1-0	2-1	2-1	1-1	4-0
CR Bélouizdad	30	11	6	13	34	37	39	1-2	3-2	2-0	2-2	1-0	2-1	0-1	2-0	1-0		0-2	0-1	1-0	0-3	3-1	3-1
MC Alger ‡	30	8	14	8	34	30	38	1-1	0-0	0-1	0-0	1-0	1-1	1-1	3-1	2-1	4-3		0-1	1-1	1-0	1-1	3-0
WA Tlemcen	30	10	8	12	24	32	38	1-0	2-2	1-6	1-1	1-2	0-0	1-0	0-0	1-1	2-0	1-0		2-0	1-0	2-1	0-0
OMR El Anasser	30	9	9	12	33	35	36	3-0	0-0	2-1	2-3	2-1	1-0	0-1	4-0	3-1	1-1	1-1	1-2		0-1	2-1	2-0
Paradou AC	30	8	10	12	31	32	34	0-2	1-2	0-0	0-1	0-0	2-0	2-0	3-1	0-0	0-2	2-2	4-1	0-0		1-0	6-3
ASM Oran	30	5	12	13	28	38	27	0-1	0-2	1-2	1-1	1-1	1-0	0-1	1-1	2-1	1-0	1-1	1-1	1-1	1-1		2-1
CA Batna	30	7	6	17	28	47	27	1-2	1-1	0-1	0-2	0-1	3-2	1-1	3-2	1-1	2-1	1-0	2-1	4-1	3-0	1-1	

10/08/2006 - 11/06/2007 • † Qualified for the CAF Champions League ‡ Qualified for the CAF Confederation Cup • Top scorer: Cheïkh Omar DABO, JSK 17

ALGERIA 2006-07 SECONDE DIVISION (2)

	Pl	W	D	L	F	A	Pts
USM Annaba	34	24	5	5	65	19	77
AS Khroub	34	19	8	7	41	31	65
MC Saïda	34	19	4	11	50	33	61
MC El Eulma	34	18	6	10	46	28	60
CS Constantine	34	15	9	10	36	30	54
MO Constantine	34	12	9	13	47	39	45
MO Béjaïa	34	11	11	12	27	33	44
US Biskra	34	13	5	16	40	52	44
RC Kouba	34	10	13	11	30	27	43
USM El Harrach	34	12	7	15	26	32	43
UMS Dréan	34	10	11	13	37	39	41
Bou Saada	34	11	8	15	33	46	41
MSP Batna	34	10	10	14	41	44	40
SA Mohamadia	34	11	7	16	28	42	40
NARB Réghaïa	34	12	4	18	35	53	40
USM Bel Abbès	34	11	6	17	28	30	39
WA Boufarik	34	10	8	16	24	37	38
JSM Tiaret	34	11	3	20	30	49	36

17/08/2006 - 7/06/2007

COUPE D'ALGERIE 2006-07

Round of 16

MC Alger	2
WR Bentalha	0
RC Kouba	1
ASO Chlef	2
CR Bélouizdad	3
UMS Dréan	1
JSM Béjaïa	0
USM Blida	1
JS Kabylie	4
AS Khroub	2
MC Mekhadma	0
MC Oran	1
ES Sétif	1
CS Constantine	0
ES Mostaganem	2
USM Alger	3

Quarter-finals

MC Alger	1
ASO Chlef	0
CR Bélouizdad	0
USM Blida	2
JS Kabylie	2 6p
MC Oran	2 5p
ES Sétif	0
USM Alger	1

Semi-finals

MC Alger	0 7p
USM Blida	0 6p
JS Kabylie	1
USM Alger	4

Final

MC Alger ‡	1
USM Alger	0

CUP FINAL

Stade du 5 Juillet, Algiers
28-06-2007, Att: 80 000, Ref: Zekrini

Scorer - Fodil Hadjadj 70

‡ Qualified for the CAF Confederation Cup

AND – ANDORRA

NATIONAL TEAM RECORD
JULY 10TH 2006 TO JULY 12TH 2010

PL	W	D	L	F	A	%
9	0	1	8	1	31	5.5

FIFA/COCA-COLA WORLD RANKING

1993	1994	1995	1996	1997	1998	1999	2000	2001	2002	2003	2004	2005	2006	High	Low
-	-	-	187	185	171	145	145	140	137	147	138	125	164	**125** 12/05	**188** 06/97

2005–2006											
08/06	09/06	10/06	11/06	12/06	01/07	02/07	03/07	04/07	05/07	06/07	07/07
132	160	164	166	164	165	161	163	161	161	157	157

Something quite out of the ordinary happened during the course of the 2006-07 season in Andorra, something that took everyone by surprise - there was an outbreak of hooliganism at a match between Principat and Lusitans which saw the match at the Aixovall stadium abandoned. Nothing like it had ever happened before in this tiny and usually tranquil principality in the Pyrenees. Perhaps the often bruising defending of the players of the national team and their ongoing battle to avoid heavy defeats is spreading to the crowds! Proof that the players are not afraid of getting stuck in came in the Cup Final where Santa Coloma finished with eight players but still managed to force

INTERNATIONAL HONOURS
None

an equaliser against Sant Julià. They then went on to win the penalty shoot-out to win the Cup for a fifth season in a row. For Sant Julià it was the fifth defeat in the final of the Copa Constitucio in seven seasons. The Cup win was consolation for Santa Coloma who threw away a winning position in the league, which was won for the second season by Rangers, under new coach Jesús Lucendo. The title earned Rangers the right to become the first Andorran club to take part in the UEFA Champions League. The prospects don't look good, however. In ten years of playing in the UEFA Cup to the end of the 2006-07 season, Andorran clubs had lost all 20 matches played.

THE FIFA BIG COUNT OF 2006

	Male	Female		Total
Number of players	4 681	356	Referees and Assistant Referees	52
Professionals	0		Admin, Coaches, Technical, Medical	116
Amateurs 18+	804		Number of clubs	26
Youth under 18	1366		Number of teams	34
Unregistered	700		Clubs with women's teams	1
Total players	5 037		Players as % of population	7.07%

Federació Andorrana de Fútbol (FAF)

Avinguda Carlemany 67, 3° pis, Apartado postal 65 AD, Escaldes-Engordany, Principat d'Andorra

Tel +376 805830   Fax +376 862006

administracio@fedanfut.com   www.fedanfut.com

President: AMAT ESCOBAR Francesc   General Secretary: GEA Tomas

Vice-President: MORALES Antonio   Treasurer: GARCIA Josep   Media Officer: GEA Tomas

Men's Coach: RODRIGO David   Women's Coach: RODRIGO David

FAF formed: 1994   UEFA: 1996   FIFA: 1996

Blue shirts with yellow and red trimmings, Blue shorts, Blue socks or Red shirts with yellow and black trimmings, Blue shorts, Blue socks

RECENT INTERNATIONALS PLAYED BY ANDORRA

2002 Opponents		Score	Venue	Comp	Scorers	Att	Referee
21-08 Iceland	L	0-3	Rejkjavik	Fr		2 900	Isaksen FRO
12-10 Belgium	L	0-1	Andorra la Vella	ECq		700	Nalbandyan ARM
16-10 Bulgaria	L	1-2	Sofia	ECq	Lima.A [80]	42 000	Richards WAL
2003							
2-04 Croatia	L	0-2	Varazdin	ECq		8 500	Salomir ROM
30-04 Estonia	L	0-2	Andorra la Vella	ECq		500	Aydin TUR
7-06 Estonia	L	0-2	Tallinn	ECq		3 500	Juhos HUN
11-06 Belgium	L	0-3	Gent	ECq		12 000	Shmolik BLR
13-06 Gabon	L	0-2	Andorra la Vella	Fr			
6-09 Croatia	L	0-3	Andorra la Vella	ECq		800	Liba CZE
10-09 Bulgaria	L	0-3	Andorra la Vella	ECq		1 000	Mikulski POL
2004							
14-04 China PR	D	0-0	Peralada	Fr			
28-05 France	L	0-4	Montpellier	Fr		27 750	Daami TUN
5-06 Spain	L	0-4	Getafe	Fr		14 000	Trefolini ITA
4-09 Finland	L	0-3	Tampere	WCq		7 437	Siric CRO
8-09 Romania	L	1-5	Andorra la Vella	WCq	Pujol [26p]	1 100	Kircher GER
13-10 FYR Macedonia	W	1-0	Andorra la Vella	WCq	Bernaus [60]	350	Podeschi SMR
17-11 Netherlands	L	0-3	Andorra la Vella	WCq		2 000	Yefet ISR
2005							
9-02 FYR Macedonia	D	0-0	Skopje	WCq		5 000	Verbist BEL
26-03 Armenia	L	1-2	Yerevan	WCq	Silva [56]	2 100	Attard MLT
30-03 Czech Republic	L	0-4	Andorra la Vella	WCq		900	Messner AUT
4-06 Czech Republic	L	1-8	Liberec	WCq	Riera [36]	9 520	Dereli TUR
17-08 Romania	L	0-2	Constanta	WCq		8 200	Jakov ISR
3-09 Finland	D	0-0	Andorra la Vella	WCq		860	Ver Eecke BEL
7-09 Netherlands	L	0-4	Eindhoven	WCq		34 000	Hanacsek HUN
12-10 Armenia	L	0-3	Andorra la Vella	WCq		430	Stokes IRL
2006							
16-08 Belarus	L	0-3	Minsk	Fr			
2-09 England	L	0-5	Manchester	ECq		56 290	Brugger AUT
6-09 Israel	L	1-4	Nijmegan	ECq	Fernández [84]	400	Zrnic BIH
7-10 Croatia	L	0-7	Zagreb	ECq		17 618	Zammit MLT
11-10 FYR Macedonia	L	0-3	Andorra la Vella	ECq		300	Silagava GEO
2007							
7-02 Armenia	D	0-0	Andorra la Vella	Fr			
28-03 England	L	0-3	Barcelona	ECq		12 800	Duarte Paixao POR
2-06 Russia	L	0-4	St Petersburg	ECq		21 520	Skjerven NOR
6-06 Israel	L	0-2	Andorra la Vella	ECq		680	Stokes IRL

Fr = Friendly match • EC = UEFA EURO 2004/2008 • WC = FIFA World Cup • q = qualifier

ANDORRA NATIONAL TEAM RECORDS AND RECORD SEQUENCES

Records			Sequence records				
Victory	2-0	BLR 2000, ALB 2002	Wins	1		Clean sheets	2	2000
Defeat	1-8	CZE 2005	Defeats	11	2002-2003	Goals scored	2	Three times
Player Caps	63	SONEJEE Oscar	Undefeated	3	2000	Without goal	11	2003-2004
Player Goals	3	LIMA I, LUCENDO	Without win	23	1996-2000	Goals against	11	2000-02, 2002-03

ANDORRA COUNTRY INFORMATION

Capital	Andorra la Vella	Independence	1278		GDP per Capita	$19 000
Population	69 865	Status	Principality		GNP Ranking	150
Area km²	468	Language	Catalan (official), French		Dialling code	+376
Population density	149 per km²	Literacy rate	99%		Internet code	.ad
% in urban areas	63%	Main religion	Christian 94%		GMT + / −	+1
Towns/Cities ('000)	Andorra la Vella 22; Les Escaldes 13; Encamp 9					
Neighbours (km)	France 56; Spain 63					
Main stadia	Comunal – Andorra la Vella 1 140					

ANDORRA 2006–07

LLIGA ANDORRANA PRIMERA DIVISIO	Pl	W	D	L	F	A	Pts	Ranger's	S. Coloma	Sant Julià	Lusitans	Inter	Principat	Encamp	Athlètic
Rangers FC †	20	17	2	1	60	11	53		1-2 1-0	2-1 1-1	3-0 7-2	4-0	4-0	4-0	2-0
Santa Coloma ‡	20	14	2	4	41	17	44	0-0 0-1		1-0 1-4	3-0 1-1	4-2	2-0	2-1	2-0
Sant Julià	20	10	4	6	38	17	34	2-4 0-1	3-1 0-2		0-0 3-0	2-0	7-0	3-1	4-1
Lusitans	20	6	3	11	22	41	21	1-2 0-7	1-3 0-2	1-5 0-1		3-1	2-1	5-0	0-0
Inter Escaldes	20	7	3	10	20	32	24	0-1	0-4	0-0	1-0		2-3 1-0	2-1 0-1	2-1 1-0
CE Principat	20	5	4	11	21	43	19	0-4	0-3	1-0	0-2	1-1 3-1		2-0 2-2	3-1 0-2
FC Encamp	20	4	5	11	19	34	17	0-3	2-3	0-0	1-2	1-1 0-1	1-1 2-0		1-1 0-1
Athlètic Escaldes	20	4	3	13	18	44	15	2-8	0-5	0-2	0-1	3-2 0-2	3-3 2-1	1-4 0-1	

24/09/2006 - 6/05/2007 • † Qualified for the UEFA Champions League • ‡ Qualified for the UEFA Cup • Relegation play-off: Engorday 2-1 3-3 Encamp

ANDORRA 2006–07 SEGONA DIVISIO (2)

	Pl	W	D	L	F	A	Pts
Benfica	14	10	3	1	25	12	33
Santa Coloma B	14	8	4	2	38	18	28
Engordany ‡	14	7	4	3	29	19	25
CE Principat B	14	6	4	4	35	27	22
UE Extremenya	14	4	3	7	30	29	15
Sporting Escaldes	14	4	1	9	19	38	14
Lusitans B	14	3	3	8	26	41	12
Ranger's B	14	3	0	11	17	35	9

23/09/2006 - 7/05/2007 • ‡ Qualified for play-off

COPA CONSTITUCIO 2006–07

Quarter–finals		Semi–finals		Final	
Santa Coloma	3				
Athlètic Escaldes	0	Santa Coloma	3		
Encamp	6	Lusitans	2		
Lusitans	7			Santa Coloma	2 2p
Rangers	4			Sant Julià	2 0p
Inter Escaldes	0	Rangers	1	19-05-2007	
Principat	1	Sant Julià	3	Scorers - Roger Costa ³, Ayala ¹²⁰ for Santa Coloma	
Sant Julià	3				

RECENT LEAGUE AND CUP RECORD

	Championship						Cup		
Year	Champions	Pts	Runners-up	Pts	Third	Pts	Winners	Score	Runners-up
1997	Principat	61	Veterans d'Andorra	59	Encamp	41	Principat	7-0	Sant Julia
1998	Principat	56	Santa Coloma	55	Encamp	38	Principat	4-3	Santa Coloma
1999	Principat	62	Santa Coloma	54	Encamp	43	Principat	3-1	Santa Coloma
2000	Constelació	64	Santa Coloma	28	Inter d'Escaldes	20	Constelació	6-0	Encamp
2001	Santa Coloma	24	Sant Julia	22	Inter d'Escaldes	12	Santa Coloma	2-0	Sant Julià
2002	Encamp	44	Sant Julià	43	Santa Coloma	42	Lusitans	2-0	Inter d'Escaldes
2003	Santa Coloma	49	Encamp	48	Sant Julià	38	Santa Coloma	5-3	Sant Julià
2004	Santa Coloma	45	Sant Julià	43	Rangers	34	Santa Coloma	1-0	Sant Julià
2005	Sant Julià	54	Rangers	51	Santa Coloma	37	Santa Coloma	2-1	Sant Julià
2006	Rangers	51	Sant Julià	39	Santa Coloma	36	Santa Coloma	1-1 5-3p	Rangers
2007	Rangers	53	Santa Coloma	44	Sant Julià	34	Santa Coloma	2-2 2-0p	Sant Julià

ANG – ANGOLA

NATIONAL TEAM RECORD
JULY 10TH 2006 TO JULY 12TH 2010

PL	W	D	L	F	A	%
11	6	4	1	20	7	72.7

FIFA/COCA-COLA WORLD RANKING

1993	1994	1995	1996	1997	1998	1999	2000	2001	2002	2003	2004	2005	2006	High	Low
102	106	80	70	58	50	52	55	55	76	83	72	61	55	**45** 07/00	**124** 06/94

	2006–2007										
08/06	09/06	10/06	11/06	12/06	01/07	02/07	03/07	04/07	05/07	06/07	07/07
53	52	52	54	55	55	58	57	57	56	54	55

Angola's elevation to the top ranks of African footballing nations continued with easy qualification for the 2008 African Nations Cup finals. The southern African country, who will host the 2010 tournament, romped through a relatively easy group with the swagger of a side full of self-confidence, built on the back of their first-ever FIFA World Cup finals appearance in 2006. Coach Luis Oliveira Goncalves, despite losing his talisman Akwa, continued with much of the squad that had done duty in Germany. Angola reached the final of the 2006 COSAFA Castle Cup with a home-based team in October but were beaten 2-0 by hosts Zambia and suffered a surprisingly early elimination in the

INTERNATIONAL HONOURS
Qualified for the FIFA World Cup™ 2006   CAF Youth Championship 2001   COSAFA Cup 1999 2001 2004

2007 edition when they lost on penalties to Botswana. Army club Primeiro Agosto did the League and Cup double, winning their first GiraBola title since 1999 under the tutelage of Dutch coach Jan Brouwer with a multi-national side comprising Zambians, Congolese and Namibian imports. They also won the cup, albeit on post-match penalties against Benfica Luanda. But both Primeiro Agosto and Petro Atlético were surprisingly eliminated in the early stages of the 2007 African Champions League while Benfica Luanda were kicked out of the Confederation Cup by the CAF for using a player who should have been suspended after an earlier red card in the tournament.

THE FIFA BIG COUNT OF 2006

	Male	Female		Total
Number of players	634 090	30 600	Referees and Assistant Referees	259
Professionals	0		Admin, Coaches, Technical, Medical	1 800
Amateurs 18+	5 240		Number of clubs	100
Youth under 18	10 800		Number of teams	500
Unregistered	36 250		Clubs with women's teams	3
Total players	664 690		Players as % of population	5.48

Federaçao Angolana de Futebol (FAF)
Compl. da Cidadela Desportiva, Luanda - 3449, Angola
Tel +244 2 264948   Fax +244 2 260566
fafutebol@ebonet.net   www.fafutebol-angola.og.ao
President: FERNANDES Justino Dr   General Secretary: PEREIRA DA SILVA Augusto
Vice-President: MANGUEIRA Antonio   Treasurer: GOMES FURTADO Antonio   Media Officer: MACEDO Arlindo
Men's Coach: DE OLIVEIRA GONCALVES Luis   Women's Coach: NZUZI Andre
FAF formed: 1979   CAF: 1996   FIFA: 1980
Red shirts with black trimmings, Black shorts, Red socks

RECENT INTERNATIONALS PLAYED BY ANGOLA

2004	Opponents	Score		Venue	Comp	Scorers	Att	Referee
5-06	Algeria	D	0-0	Annaba	WCq		55 000	Daami TUN
20-06	Nigeria	W	1-0	Luanda	WCq	Akwa 84	40 000	Nkole ZAM
3-07	Gabon	D	2-2	Libreville	WCq	Akwa 19, Marco Paulo 81	20 000	Louzaya CGO
18-07	Botswana	D	1-1	Luanda	CCqf	Flavio 3, W 5-3p	6 000	Phomane LES
5-09	Rwanda	W	1-0	Luanda	WCq	Freddy 52	30 000	Damon RSA
19-09	Mozambique	W	1-0	Maputo	CCsf	Flavio 68	50 000	Jovinala MWI
10-10	Zimbabwe	W	1-0	Luanda	WCq	Flavio 53	17 000	Lwanja MWI
20-11	Zambia	D	0-0	Lusaka	CCf	W 5-4p		Lwanja MWI
2005								
22-02	Congo	W	2-0	Brazzaville	Fr			
27-03	Zimbabwe	L	0-2	Harare	WCq			Codjia BEN
27-05	Tunisia	L	1-4	Tunis	Fr	Flavio 77p	4 000	
3-06	Algeria	W	2-1	Luanda	WCq	Flavio 50, Akwa 58	27 000	Hicuburundi BDI
17-06	Nigeria	D	1-1	Kano	WCq	Figueiredo 60	17 000	Abd El Fatah EGY
9-08	Botswana	D	0-0	Johannesburg	Fr			
10-08	Botswana	D	0-0	Johannesburg	Fr			
13-08	Zimbabwe	L	1-2	Mmabatho	CCsf	Love 52		Kapanga MWI
17-08	Cape Verde Islands	W	2-1	Lisbon	Fr	Mantorras 46, Love 86		
4-09	Gabon	W	3-0	Luanda	WCq	OG 25, Mantorras 44, Ze Kalanga 89	35 000	Coulibaly MLI
8-10	Rwanda	W	1-0	Kigali	WCq	Akwa 79	25 000	Guezzaz MAR
16-11	Japan	L	0-1	Tokyo	Fr		52 406	
2006								
17-01	Morocco	D	2-2	Marrakech	Fr	Akwa 41 Mantorras 74p		
21-01	Cameroon	L	1-3	Cairo	CNr1	Flavio 31p	8 000	Guezzaz MAR
25-01	Congo DR	D	0-0	Cairo	CNr1		2 000	Diatta SEN
29-01	Togo	W	3-2	Cairo	CNr1	Flavio 2 9 39, Maurito 86	4 000	El Arjoun MAR
1-03	Korea Republic	L	0-1	Seoul	Fr		63 255	Supian MAS
29-04	Mauritius	W	5-1	Maseru	CCr1	Akwa 3 3 28 55, Mateus 59, Love 89		Moeketsi LES
30-04	Lesotho	W	3-1	Maseru	CCr2	Mateus 47, Ze Kalanga 2 50 61		Mlangeni SWZ
30-05	Argentina	L	0-2	Salerno	Fr		7 000	Farina ITA
2-06	Turkey	L	2-3	Arnhem	Fr	Akwa 32, Love 83	1 200	Wegereef NED
11-06	Portugal	L	0-1	Cologne	WCr1		45 000	Larrionda URU
16-06	Mexico	D	0-0	Hanover	WCr1		43 000	Maidin SIN
21-06	Iran	D	1-1	Leipzig	WCr1	Flavio 60	38 000	Shield AUS
3-09	Swaziland	W	2-0	Mbabane	CNq	Gumbi OG 21, Loco 80		Maillet SEY
17-09	Zimbabwe	W	2-1	Harare	CCsf	Gazeta 43, Love 75		Kaoma ZAM
8-10	Kenya	W	3-1	Luanda	CNq	Flavio 2 37 68, Mateus 60		Lwanja MWI
21-10	Zambia	L	0-2	Lusaka	CCf			Raolimanana MAD
18-11	Tanzania	D	1-1	Dar es Salaam	Fr	Manucho 83		
2007								
25-03	Eritrea	W	6-1	Luanda	CNq	Flavio 2 28 69, Mantorras 36p, Ze Kalanga 43, Mendonca 47, Figueiredo 84		Evehe CMR
4-04	Congo	D	0-0	Cabinda	Fr			
2-06	Eritrea	D	1-1	Asmara	CNq	Maurito 62		Marange ZIM
17-06	Swaziland	W	3-0	Luanda	CNq	Figueiredo 18, Love 30, Flavio 57p		
28-07	Lesotho	W	2-0	Gaborone	CCr1	Manucho 40, Santana 83		Disang BOT
29-07	Botswana	D	0-0	Gaborone	CCr1	L 1-3p		

Fr = Friendly match • CN = CAF African Cup of Nations • CC = COSAFA Castle Cup • WC = FIFA World Cup
q = qualifier • r1 = first round group • qf = quarter-final • sf = semi-final • f = final

ANGOLA NATIONAL TEAM RECORDS AND RECORD SEQUENCES

Records			Sequence records				
Victory	7-1	SWZ 2000	Wins	3	Seven times	Clean sheets	5	2004-2005
Defeat	0-6	POR 1989	Defeats	6	1989-1990	Goals scored	11	2001
Player Caps	80	AKWA	Undefeated	12	2004-2005	Without goal	3	1980-1981
Player Goals	36	AKWA	Without win	13	1980-1982	Goals against	8	1989-90, 1998-91

REPUBLICA DE ANGOLA; REPUBLIC OF ANGOLA

Capital	Luanda	Language	Portuguese	Independence	1975
Population	12 127 071	Area	1 246 700 km²	Density	9 per km²	% in cities	32
GDP per cap	$1 900	Dailling code	+244	Internet	.ao	GMT +/-	+1

MAJOR CITIES/TOWNS

Population '000

1	Luanda	2 875
2	Huambo	233
3	Lobito	213
4	Benguela	155
5	Kuito	114
6	Lubango	102
7	Malanje	87
8	Namibe	82
9	Soyo	74
10	Cabinda	67
11	Uige	60
12	Saurimo	40
13	Sumbe	33
14	Caluquembe	30
15	Caxito	28
16	M'banza-Kongo	25
17	Longonjo	24
18	Caála	21
19	Luena	21
20	N'dalatando	21
21	Lucapa	20
22	N'zeto	19
23	Camacupa	19
24	Catobola	

MEDALS TABLE

		Overall			League			Cup			Africa			City	Stadium	Cap'ty	DoF
		G	S	B	G	S	B	G	S	B	G	S	B				
1	Petro Atlético	21	5	4	13	3	4	8	2					Luanda	Coqueiros	12 000	1980
2	Primeiro de Agosto	13	5	3	9	1	3	4	4					Luanda	Coqueiros	12 000	1977
3	Atlético Sport Aviação	5	7	1	3	5	1	2	2					Luanda	Joaquim Dinis	10 000	1953
4	Primeiro de Maio	4	6		2	4		2	2					Benguela	Municipal	15 000	1955
5	Sagrada Esperança	3	3		1	2		2	1					Dundo	Quintalão	3 000	
6	Inter Clube	2	5	4		1	4	2	4					Luanda	22 de Junho	10 000	1953
7	Ferroviário Huila	2	1	1			1	2	1					Lubango	Ferroviario	5 000	
8	Atlético Petróleas Namibe	2						2						Namibe	Joaquim Morais	5 000	
9	Progresso Sambiganza	1						1						Luanda	Campo de São Paulo	4 000	
10	Petro Huambo		2	3		1	3			1				Huambo	Ferrovia	17 000	1955
11	Independente		2	1			1		2					Tombwa	Tombwa	7 000	
12	Nacional Benguela		1	1		1	1							Benguela	Arregaca	8 000	
13	11 de Novembro		1						1					Kuando Kubango			
14	Academica Lobito		1			1								Lobito	Electro Clube	3 000	
15	SL Benfica Luanda		1						1					Luanda	Cidadela	60 000	

Atlético Petróleas Namibe were known as Sonangol until 2005

RECENT LEAGUE AND CUP RECORD

	Championship						Cup		
Year	Champions	Pts	Runners-up	Pts	Third	Pts	Winners	Score	Runners-up
1995	Petro Atlético						Atlético Aviação	3-1	Independente
1996	Primeiro de Agosto						Prog. Sambizanga	1-0	Primeiro de Maio
1997	Petro Atlético						Petro Atlético	2-1	Primeiro de Agosto
1998	Primeiro de Agosto	62	Petro Atlético	58	Atlético Aviação	50	Petro Atlético	4-1	Primeiro de Agosto
1999	Primeiro de Agosto	59	Académica Lobito	51	Inter Clube	49	Sagrada Esperança	1-0	Atlético Aviação
2000	Petro Atlético	63	Atlético Aviação	44	Petro Huambo	42	Petro Atlético	1-0	Inter Clube
2001	Petro Atlético	57	Atlético Aviação	50	Petro Huambo	42	Sonangol	3-2	Sporting Cabinda
2002	Atlético Aviação	57	Primeiro de Agosto	53	Petro Atlético	51	Petro Atlético	3-0	Desportivo Huíla
2003	Atlético Aviação	53	Petro Atlético	52	Petro Huambo	46	Inter Clube	1-0	Sagrada Esperança
2004	Atlético Aviação	56	Sagrada Esperança	53	Inter Clube	51	Sonangol	2-0	Primeiro de Agosto
2005	Sagrada Esperança	51	Atlético Aviação	50	Petro Atlético	48	Atlético Aviação	1-0	Inter Clube
2006	Primeiro de Agosto	56	Petro Atlético	46	Inter Clube	44	Primeiro de Agosto	1-1 4-3p	Benfica Luanda

ANGOLA 2006

CAMPEONATO NACIONAL XXVII GIRABOLA 1° DIVISAO

	PI	W	D	L	F	A	Pts	1° Agosto	Petro At.	Inter Clube	Benfica Lb	ASA	Sagrada	Huilá	Acad. Soyo	Benfica Ln	1° Maio	At. Namibie	Onze Br.	Progresso	Cabinda
Primeiro de Agosto †	26	16	8	2	34	15	56		1-0	2-1	2-0	3-1	0-0	2-1	0-0	1-0	0-0	1-0	0-0	2-0	2-0
Petro Atlético †	26	12	10	4	32	17	46	0-0		0-1	2-2	1-0	2-0	1-1	1-1	1-0	2-1	1-1	2-1	2-1	0-0
Inter Clube ‡	26	12	8	6	36	21	44	0-1	0-1		0-3	3-0	3-1	1-0	5-0	2-1	3-0	2-2	0-0	2-1	3-1
Benfica Lubango	26	11	6	9	31	28	39	2-1	1-1	0-0		0-1	1-1	0-0	2-0	0-3	1-2	2-0	3-0	1-1	**3-0**
Atlético Aviação	26	10	6	10	31	26	36	3-1	1-2	2-1	3-4		0-0	4-0	5-1	0-1	1-0	1-2	0-1	1-1	3-1
Sagrada Esperança	26	9	9	8	17	16	36	0-1	1-1	0-0	2-0	0-1		1-0	1-0	1-0	1-0	2-1	3-0	1-0	0-0
Desportivo Huíla	26	10	6	10	24	24	36	0-1	0-1	1-0	2-0	0-1	1-0		1-0	2-1	1-1	2-0	1-0	2-0	2-0
Académica Soyo	26	8	8	10	19	27	32	2-2	1-0	1-1	1-0	0-2	0-0	1-0		1-2	2-1	0-1	0-0	1-0	1-0
Benfica Luanda ‡	26	10	2	14	23	28	32	0-1	0-3	2-2	0-2	3-1	2-0	1-0	0-3		0-1	2-0	1-0	0-1	1-0
Primeiro de Maio	26	7	10	9	22	23	31	1-3	1-1	0-0	4-0	0-0	0-1	2-0	1-0	1-0		1-1	2-2	0-0	2-0
At. Petróleos Namibe	26	6	13	7	22	25	31	0-0	0-1	0-0	0-1	0-0	1-0	1-1	2-0	2-0	1-1		0-0	1-1	2-1
Onze Bravos Maqui	26	6	12	8	14	21	30	0-0	0-0	0-1	2-1	1-0	0-0	1-1	0-0	1-0	0-0	2-2		0-1	0-0
Progresso Sambizanga	26	5	9	12	20	31	24	0-2	0-5	1-2	0-1	0-0	1-1	2-2	0-0	2-3	2-0	1-1	0-1		1-0
Sporting Cabinda	26	3	7	16	15	38	16	2-1	2-1	1-3	0-1	0-0	1-0	2-3	0-3	0-0	1-0	1-1	1-2	0-2	

25/02/2006 - 26/11/2006 • † Qualified for CAF Champions League • ‡ Qualified for CAF Confederation Cup
Top scorers: Manucho GONCALVES, Petro Atlético 16; SERGE, Benfica Luanda 10; GAZETA, 1° Agosto 8

ANGOLA 2006 2° DIVISAO

Zona A	PI	W	D	L	F	A	Pts
Santos	8	7	1	0	24	5	22
Belenenses Samba	7	5	1	1	11	6	16
Kabuscorp Palanca	7	4	0	3	17	8	12
FC Uíge	8	0	2	6	3	16	2
Dom Afonso Nteka	8	0	2	6	4	24	2

Zona B	PI	W	D	L	F	A	Pts
Petro Huambo	11	8	2	1	14	4	26
Recreativo Libolo	11	6	2	3	6	5	20
Académica Pet. Lobito	11	5	3	3	10	5	18
Recreativo Cála	11	5	1	5	14	11	16
Benfica Huambo	11	4	4	3	6	6	16
Desportivo Chibia	11	2	1	8	4	11	7
Desportivo Kakuvas	10	1	1	8	3	14	4

9/07/2005 - 23/10/2005

Zona C	PI	W	D	L	F	A	Pts
Juventude do Moxico	8	6	2	0	9	4	20
Ritondo Malanje	8	4	2	2	9	8	14
Heróis da Baixa	7	1	3	3	11	10	6
28 de Fevereiro	6	1	3	2	7	6	6
Aguias Saurimo	7	0	2	5	9	17	2

TAÇA NACIONAL 2006

Round of 16

Primeiro de Agosto * 2
Académica Soyo 1

Atlético Aviação 1
Sporting Cabinda * 2

Santos 2 4p
Progresso Sambizanga* 2 3p

Juventude do Moxico * 0
Sagrada Esperança 1

Petro Atlético 2
Inter Clube * 1

Onze Bravos Maqui 0
Atlético Pet. Namibe * 1

Primeiro de Maio 0 4p
Desportivo Huilá 0 2p

Benfica Lubango * 1 1p
Benfica Luanda 1 4p

Quarter-finals

Primeiro de Agosto 2
Sporting Cabinda * 0

Santos 0
Sagrada Esperança * 3

Petro Atlético * 2
Atlético Pet. Namibe 1

Primeiro de Maio * 1
Benfica Luanda 2

Semi-finals

Primeiro de Agosto 1 4p
Sagrada Esperança 1 2p

Petro Atlético 1 2p
Benfica Luanda 1 4p

Final

Primeiro de Agosto 1 4p
Benfica Luanda ‡ 1 3p

CUP FINAL
Cidadela, Luanda
11-11-2006, Att: 10 000, Ref: Dos Santos

Scorers: Gazeta 46+ for 1° Agosto; Vado 62 for Benfica

* Home team • ‡ Qualified for CAF Confederation Cup

ANT – NETHERLANDS ANTILLES

NATIONAL TEAM RECORD
JULY 10TH 2006 TO JULY 12TH 2010

PL	W	D	L	F	A	%
3	0	1	2	1	7	8.3

FIFA/COCA-COLA WORLD RANKING

1993	1994	1995	1996	1997	1998	1999	2000	2001	2002	2003	2004	2005	2006	High		Low	
128	152	125	142	156	156	167	175	183	177	188	163	168	177	**118**	07/95	**188**	12/03

2006–2007											
08/06	09/06	10/06	11/06	12/06	01/07	02/07	03/07	04/07	05/07	06/07	07/07
182	171	172	177	177	172	172	172	170	174	173	174

The national team made a welcome return to international competition after an absence of over two years but despite hosting a four team tournament in the first qualifying round of the Digicel Caribbean Cup qualifiers, there was not much joy on the field. A goal in the first minute of the first match against Grenada was the only one the Netherlands Antilles scored in all three matches as they finished in a disappointing last place in the group. The under 20 team had a better time in the CONCACAF U–20 Tournament where they finished top of their first round group in Paramaribo, Surinam. A satisfying 2-1 win over their hosts in the final match sealed their place in the second

INTERNATIONAL HONOURS
None

round, but the adventure ended there in a tough group dominated by Haiti and Jamaica. In domestic football Centro Barber were once again the dominant side, winning the Curacão championship for the fifth time in six years by beating Jong Colombia 2-1 in the final. Centro Barber also took part in the CONCACAF Champions' Cup and were one match away from reaching the semi-finals of the Caribbean Championship. Having beaten Positive Vibes from the US Virgin Islands and Aigle Noir from Haiti they then lost to hosts Harbour View from Jamaica to finish second in their first round group.

THE FIFA BIG COUNT OF 2006

	Male	Female		Total
Number of players	3 940	280	Referees and Assistant Referees	42
Professionals	0		Admin, Coaches, Technical, Medical	320
Amateurs 18+	780		Number of clubs	40
Youth under 18	980		Number of teams	75
Unregistered	2 400		Clubs with women's teams	1
Total players	4 220		Players as % of population	1.90%

Nederlands Antilliaanse Voetbal Unie (NAVU)
Bonamweg 49, Curaçao
Tel +599 97365040   Fax +599 97365047
navusoccer@interneeds.net   www.navusoccer.com
President: FRANCISCA Rignaal   General Secretary: ISENIA Hubert
Vice-President: TBD   Treasurer: MARIA Nelson   Media Officer: None
Men's Coach: TBD   Women's Coach: None
NAVU formed: 1921   CONCACAF: 1961   FIFA: 1932
White shirts with blue trimmings, Blue shorts, Red socks or Blue shirts, White shorts, Blue socks

RECENT INTERNATIONALS PLAYED BY NETHERLANDS ANTILLES

2002	Opponents		Score	Venue	Comp	Scorers	Att	Referee
28-07	Guyana	L	1-2	Georgetown	CCq	Muzo [14]		
11-08	Guyana	W	1-0	Willemstad	CCq	Martis [43]. W 3-2p		Villar Polo ARU
20-11	Antigua and Barbuda	D	1-1	Port-au-Prince	CCq	Forbuis [88]		Bowen CAY
22-11	Haiti	L	0-3	Port-au-Prince	CCq			Bowen CAY
2003								
No international matches played in 2003								
2004								
10-01	Surinam	D	1-1	Paramaribo	Fr	Forbuis [38]		Jol NED
17-01	Surinam	W	2-0	Willemstad	Fr	Silberie, Christina		
28-01	Aruba	W	6-1	Willemstad	Fr			
18-02	Antigua and Barbuda	L	0-2	St John's	WCq		1 500	Navarro CAN
31-03	Antigua and Barbuda	W	3-0	Willemstad	WCq	Siberie [27], Martha [46], Hose [48]	9 000	Piper TRI
27-04	Dominican Republic	W	3-1	Willemstad	Fr	Bernardus 2 [6 32], Cicilia [7]		Faneite ANT
12-06	Honduras	L	1-2	Willemstad	WCq	Hose [75]	12 000	McArthur GUY
19-06	Honduras	L	0-4	San Pedro Sula	WCq		30 000	Alcala MEX
2005								
No international matches played in 2005								
2006								
6-09	Grenada	D	1-1	Willemstad	CCq	Maria [1]		
8-09	Guyana	L	0-5	Willemstad	CCq			
10-09	Surinam	L	0-1	Willemstad	CCq			Suazo DOM

No international matches played in 2007 before August

Fr = Friendly match • CC = Digicel Caribbean Cup • WC = FIFA World Cup • q = qualifier

NETHERLANDS ANTILLES NATIONAL TEAM RECORDS AND RECORD SEQUENCES

Records			Sequence records					
Victory	15-0	PUR 1959	Wins	5	Three times	Clean sheets	3	1961-1962, 1966
Defeat	0-8	NED 1962, MEX 1973	Defeats	6	1973-1980	Goals scored	30	1926-1948
Player Caps	n/a		Undefeated	9	1959-1961	Without goal	3	Four time
Player Goals	n/a		Without win	17	1969-1980	Goals against	19	1968-1980

RECENT LEAGUE AND CUP RECORD

	Kopa Antiano			Curacao Champions			Bonaire Champions		
Year	Winners	Score	Runners-up	Winners	Score	Runners-up	Winners	Score	Runners-up
2000	No tournament held			Jong Colombia	2-1	Centro Barber	Estrellas	4-1	Uruguay
2001	Jong Colombia	3-0	Juventus		-		Estrellas	2-0	Real Rincon
2002	Centro Barber	1-0	SUBT	Centro Barber	2-1	SUBT	Estrellas	1-0	Real Rincon
2003	Centro Barber	2-1	Jong Colombia	Centro Barber	1-0	Jong Colombia	Real Rincon	3-0	Juventus
2004	No tournament held			Centro Barber	1-0	Victory Boys	Real Rincon	0-0 1-0	Estrellas
2005	Centro Barber	2-1	Victory Boys	Centro Barber	4-1	Victory Boys	Juventus	1-0	Estrellas
2006				Undeba	1-0	Centro Barber	No tournament held		
2007				Centro Barber	2-1	Jong Colombia			

NETHERLANDS ANTILLES COUNTRY INFORMATION

Capital	Willemstad	Independence		Part of the Netherlands with	GDP per Capita	$11 400	
Population	218 126	Status		autonomy in internal affairs	GNP Ranking	n/a	
Area km²	960	Language	Dutch		Dialling code	+599	
Population density	227 per km²	Literacy rate	96%		Internet code	.an	
% in urban areas	n/a	Main religion	Christian		GMT +/–	-4	
Towns/Cities ('000)	Willemstad (Curaçao) 97; Princess Quarter (Sint Maarten) 13; Kraleendijk (Bonaire) 3;						
Neighbours (km)	Netherlands Antilles is a group of Caribbean islands consisting of Bonaire, Curaçao, Saba, Sint Eustatius & Sint Maarten						
Main stadia	Ergilio Hato – Willemstad 15 000; Municipal – Kralendijk 3 000						

ARG – ARGENTINA

NATIONAL TEAM RECORD

JULY 10TH 2006 TO JULY 12TH 2010

PL	W	D	L	F	A	%
12	7	2	3	23	15	66.6

Over the years the Copa América has helped create many a hero in Argentine football and legendary teams, the most famous of which is perhaps the 'angels with dirty faces' side that won the 1957 tournament in Peru. At the 2007 Copa in Venezuela, Argentina came very close to being regarded in the same light. Not for a long time has a team so thoroughly dominated a tournament. On the way to the final they scored 16 goals in five straight wins by playing some of the best football the Copa América has ever seen. And then in the final it all went horribly wrong as they were shut down by a pedestrian and functional Brazil team - their 3-0 defeat was the third time in a row that they have lost to the Brazilians by three clear goals. A month earlier Boca Juniors had beaten Grêmio 5-0 on aggregate in the final of the Copa Libertadores to deny Brazilian teams a hat-trick of titles in the tournament. It was Argentina's first success since Boca won the 2003 tournament and they now have six titles to their name - just one short of the record held by Independiente. There can be little doubt that Boca deserve the accolade as the best South American team of the decade as four of those six titles have come since the start of 2000. The hero of their latest triumph

was Juan Roman Riquelme who scored three of the five goals in the final. In a season yet again dominated by the vexed issue of hooliganism and the gang culture, the championship produced two surprising winners in Estudiantes and San Lorenzo who revived memories of former glories for their fans. Boca Juniors lost coach Alfio Basile at the start of the season when he replaced Jose Pekerman as national team coach and although Boca lead the Apertura right to the end, new coach Ricardo La Volpe struggled to maintain the consistency of his predecessor. Crucially, they lost their last two matches which let Estudiantes, on the back of a run of 11 wins in their last 12 matches, finish level with them on points. Coached by Diego Simeone and bolstered by the return of Juan Sebastian Verón to the club, Estudiantes won a championship play-off against Boca to win their first title since 1983. Financially stricken San Lorenzo won the Clausura thanks largely to the inspirational coaching of Ramón Diaz and a string of close fought victories. Indeed, of their first 12 victories in the campaign, 11 of them were by a margin of a single goal.

Asociación del Fútbol Argentino (AFA)

Viamonte 1366/76, Buenos Aires - 1053

Tel +54 11 43727900   Fax +54 11 43754410

gerencia@afa.org.ar   www.afa.org.ar

President: GRONDONA Julio H.   General Secretary: MEISZNER Jose Luis

Vice-President: AGUILAR Jose Maria   Treasurer: PORTELL Carlos   Media Officer: TBD

Men's Coach: BASILE Alfio   Women's Coach: BORRELO Jose Carlos

AFA formed: 1893   CONMEBOL: 1916   FIFA: 1912

Light blue and white striped shirts, Black shorts, White socks or Dark blue shirts, Black shorts, White socks

RECENT INTERNATIONAL MATCHES PLAYED BY ARGENTINA

2004	Opponents	Score		Venue	Comp	Scorers	Att	Referee
18-08	Japan	W	2-1	Shizuoka	Fr	Galletti [4], Santana [40]	45 000	Lu CHN
4-09	Peru	W	3-1	Lima	WCq	Rosales [14], Coloccini [66], Sorin [92]	28 000	Simon BRA
9-10	Uruguay	W	4-2	Buenos Aires	WCq	Gonzalez.L [6], Figueroa 2 [32 54], Zanetti [44]	50 000	Souza BRA
13-10	Chile	D	0-0	Santiago	WCq		57 671	Amarilla PAR
16-11	Venezuela	W	3-2	Buenos Aires	WCq	Rey OG [3], Riquelme [45+], Saviola [65]	30 000	Hidalgo PER
2005								
9-02	Germany	D	2-2	Dusseldorf	Fr	Crespo 2 [40p 81]	52 000	Farina ITA
9-03	Mexico	D	1-1	Los Angeles	Fr	Zarate [67]	51 345	Hall USA
26-03	Bolivia	W	2-1	La Paz	WCq	Figueroa [57], Galletti [63]	25 000	Larrionda URU
30-03	Colombia	W	1-0	Buenos Aires	WCq	Crespo [65]	40 000	Amarilla PAR
4-06	Ecuador	L	0-2	Quito	WCq		37 583	Selman CHI
8-06	Brazil	W	3-1	Buenos Aires	WCq	Crespo 2 [3 40], Riquelme [18]	49 497	Mendez URU
15-06	Tunisia	W	2-1	Köln	CCr1	Riquelme [33p], Saviola [57]	28 033	Rosetti ITA
18-06	Australia	W	4-2	Nürnberg	CCr1	Figueroa 3 [12 53 89], Riquelme [31p]	25 618	Maidin SIN
21-06	Germany	D	2-2	Nürnberg	CCr1	Riquelme [33], Cambiasso [74]	42 088	Michel SVK
26-06	Mexico	D	1-1	Hanover	CCsf	Figueroa [110]	40 718	Rosetti ITA
29-06	Brazil	L	1-4	Frankfurt	CCf	Aimar [65]	45 591	Michel SVK
17-08	Hungary	W	2-1	Budapest	Fr	Rodriguez.M [19], Heinze [62]	27 000	Merk GER
3-09	Paraguay	L	0-1	Asuncion	WCq		32 000	Simon BRA
9-10	Peru	W	2-0	Buenos Aires	WCq	Riquelme [81p], OG [90]	36 977	Torres PAR
12-10	Uruguay	L	0-1	Montevideo	WCq		55 000	Souza BRA
12-11	England	L	2-3	Geneva	Fr	Crespo [34], Samuel [54]	29 000	Leuba SUI
16-11	Qatar	W	3-0	Doha	Fr	Riquelme [70], Cruz [72], Ayala [73]		Al Fadhli KUW
2006								
1-03	Croatia	L	2-3	Basel	Fr	Tevez [4], Messi [6]	13 138	Nobs SUI
30-05	Angola	W	2-0	Salerno	Fr	Rodriguez.M [28], Sorin [36]	7 000	Farina ITA
10-06	Côte D'Ivoire	W	2-1	Hamburg	WCr1	Crespo [24], Saviola [38]	49 480	De Bleeckere BEL
16-06	Serbia & Montenegro	W	6-0	Gelsenkirchen	WCr1	Rodriguez.M 2 [6 41], Cambiasso [31], Crespo [78] Tevez [84], Messi [88]	52 000	Rosetti ITA
21-06	Netherlands	D	0-0	Frankfurt	WCr1		48 000	Medina Cantalejo ESP
24-06	Mexico	W	2-1	Leipzig	WCr2	Crespo [10], Rodriguez.M [98]	43 000	Busacca SUI
30-06	Germany	D	1-1	Berlin	WCqf	Ayala [49]. L 2-4p	72 000	Michel SVK
3-09	Brazil	L	0-3	London	Fr		59 032	Bennett ENG
11-10	Spain	L	1-2	Murcia	Fr	Bilos [34]	31 000	Duhamel FRA
2007								
7-02	France	W	1-0	Paris	Fr	Saviola [15]	79 862	Skomina SVN
18-04	Chile	D	0-0	Mendoza	Fr		38 000	Vazquez URU
2-06	Switzerland	D	1-1	Basel	Fr	Tevez [49]	29 000	Messina ITA
5-06	Algeria	W	4-3	Barcelona	Fr	Tevez [1], Messi 2 [54 73], Cambiasso [56]		Izquierdo ESP
28-06	USA	W	4-1	Maracaibo	CAr1	Crespo 2 [11 60], Aimar [76], Tevez [84]	34 500	Chandia CHI
2-07	Colombia	W	4-2	Maracaibo	CAr1	Crespo [20p], Riquelme 2 [34 45], Milito.D [91+]	35 000	Simon BRA
5-07	Paraguay	W	1-0	Barquisimeto	CAr1	Mascherano [79]	37 000	Larrionda URU
8-07	Peru	W	4-0	Barquisimeto	CAqf	Riquelme 2 [47 85], Messi [61], Mascherano [75]	37 000	Simon BRA
11-07	Mexico	W	3-0	Puerto Ordaz	CAsf	Heinze [44], Messi [61], Riquelme [66p]	40 000	Chandia CHI
15-07	Brazil	L	0-3	Maracaibo	CAf		42 000	Amarilla PAR

Fr = Friendly match • KC = Kirin Cup • CA = Copa América • CC = FIFA Confederations Cup • WC = FIFA World Cup
q = qualifier • r1 = 1st round • qf = quarter-final • sf = semi-final • f = final

ARGENTINA NATIONAL TEAM RECORDS AND RECORD SEQUENCES

Records			Sequence records					
Victory	12-0	ECU 1942	Wins	9	1941-1942	Clean sheets	8	1998
Defeat	1-6	CZE 1958	Defeats	4	1911-1912	Goals scored	42	1942-1954
Player Caps	115	AYALA Roberto	Undefeated	31	1991-1993	Without goal	8	1989-1990
Player Goals	56	BATISTUTA Gabriel	Without win	10	1989-1990	Goals against	13	1906-1910

MAJOR CITIES/TOWNS

Population '000

1	Buenos Aires	11 612
2	Córdoba	1 457
3	Rosario	1 178
4	Mendoza	890
5	Tucumán	803
6	La Plata	699
7	Mar del Plata	558
8	Salta	535
9	Santa Fé	476
10	San Juan	460
11	Resistencia	401
12	Santiago del Estero	368
13	Corrientes	351
14	Posadas	328
15	Jujuy	320
16	Bahía Blanca	278
17	Paraná	269
18	Neuquén	250
19	Tandil	105
20	Rafaela	91
21	Zárate	89
22	Junín	86
23	San Martín	84
24	Tres Arroyos	47

ARGENTINE REPUBLIC; REPUBLICA ARGENTINA

Capital	Buenos Aires	Language	Spanish			Independence	1816
Population	40 301 927	Area	2 766 890 km²	Density	14 per km²	% in cities	88%
GDP per cap	$11 200	Dailling code	+54	Internet	.ar	GMT + / -	-3

MEDALS TABLE

		Overall			League			Sth Am			City	Stadium	Cap'ty	DoF
		G	S	B	G	S	B	G	S	B				
1	Boca Juniors	37	24	20	28	20	17	9	4	3	Buenos Aires	La Bombonera	57 395	1905
2	River Plate	36	34	29	33	30	15	3	4	14	Buenos Aires	Monumental	65 645	1901
3	Independiente	25	17	14	16	16	9	9	1	5	Buenos Aires	Doble Visera	52 823	1905
4	Racing Club	18	8	14	16	7	12	2	1	2	Buenos Aires	El Cilindro	64 161	1903
5	San Lorenzo	15	13	21	13	13	15	2		6	Buenos Aires	Nuevo Gasometro	43 480	1908
6	Alumni	10	2		10	2					Buenos Aires			1891-1911
7	Vélez Sarsfield	8	8	10	6	8	8	2		2	Buenos Aires	José Amalfitani	49 540	1910
8	Estudiantes La Plata	8	7	10	5	6	8	3	1	2	La Plata	Luis Jorge Hirsch	20 000	1905
9	Huracán	5	5	8	5	5	7			1	Buenos Aires	Tomás Adolfo Ducó	48 314	1908
10	Rosario Central	5	5	5	4	4	2	1	1	3	Rosario	Gigante de Arroyito	41 654	1889
11	Newell's Old Boys	5	4	3	5	2	3		2		Rosario	El Coloso del Parque	42 000	1903
12	Lomas Athletic Club	5	2	3	5	2	3				Buenos Aires			1891
13	Belgrano Athletic Club	3	3	3	3	3	3				Buenos Aires			1896
14	Argentinos Juniors	3	2	3	2	2	1	1		2	Buenos Aires	Diego Maradona	24 800	1904
15	Ferro Carril Oeste	2	3	1	2	3	1				Buenos Aires	Ricardo Etcheverry	34 268	1904

RECENT LEAGUE RECORD

	Torneo Clausura					Torneo Apertura				
Year	Champions	Pts	Runners-up	Pts	Third	Pts	Champions	Pts	Runners-up	Pts	Third	Pts

Year	Champions	Pts	Runners-up	Pts	Third	Pts	Champions	Pts	Runners-up	Pts	Third	Pts
1996	Vélez Sarsfield	40	Gimnasia LP	39	Lanús	34	River Plate	46	Independiente	37	Lanús	37
1997	River Plate	41	Colón Santa Fé	35	Newell's Old Boys	35	River Plate	45	Boca Juniors	44	Rosario Central	35
1998	Vélez Sarsfield	46	Lanús	40	Gimnasia LP	37	Boca Juniors	45	Gimnasia LP	36	Racing Club	33
1999	Boca Juniors	44	River Plate	37	San Lorenzo	36	River Plate	44	Rosario Central	43	Boca Juniors	41
2000	River Plate	42	Independiente	36	Colón Santa Fé	36	Boca Juniors	41	River Plate	37	Gimnasia LP	37
2001	San Lorenzo	47	River Plate	41	Boca Juniors	30	Racing Club	42	River Plate	41	Boca Juniors	33
2002	River Plate	43	Gimnasia LP	37	Boca Juniors	35	Independiente	43	Boca Juniors	40	River Plate	36
2003	River Plate	43	Boca Juniors	39	Vélez Sarsfield	38	Boca Juniors	39	San Lorenzo	36	Banfield	32
2004	River Plate	40	Boca Juniors	36	Talleres Cordoba	35	Newell's Old Boys	36	Vélez Sarsfield	34	River Plate	33
2005	Vélez Sarsfield	39	Banfield	33	Racing Club	32	Boca Juniors	40	Gimnasia LP	37	Vélez Sarsfield	33
2006	Boca Juniors	43	Lanús	35	River Plate	34	Estudiantes LP	44	Boca Juniors	44	River Plate	38
2007	San Lorenzo	45	Boca Juniors	39	Estudiantes LP	37						

ARGENTINA 2006–07
PRIMERA A DIVISION APERTURA

	Pl	W	D	L	F	A	Pts
Estudiantes LP	19	14	2	3	41	17	44
Boca Juniors	19	14	2	3	35	12	44
River Plate	19	11	5	3	33	17	38
Independiente	19	10	2	7	33	24	32
Arsenal	19	9	5	5	26	22	32
Lanús	19	9	4	6	26	24	31
Vélez Sarsfield	19	8	6	5	25	18	30
Rosario Central	19	8	4	7	28	22	28
San Lorenzo	19	8	4	7	30	33	28
Racing Club	19	7	5	7	22	19	26
Gimnasia y Esgrima Jy	19	8	2	9	19	19	26
Belgrano Córdoba	19	6	5	8	18	24	23
Gimnasia y Esgrima LP	19	7	2	10	21	40	23
Nueva Chicago	19	6	4	9	20	32	22
Banfield	19	4	8	7	21	26	20
Argentinos Juniors	19	5	5	9	22	28	20
Colón Santa Fe	19	5	3	11	20	34	18
Godoy Cruz	19	3	8	8	19	26	17
Newell's Old Boys	19	3	7	9	21	28	16
Quilmes	19	2	3	14	23	38	9

4/08/2006 - 9/12/2006 • Top scorers: Rodrigo PALACIO, Boca 12;
Mauro ZARATE, Vélez 12; Oscar CARDOZO, Newell's 11; Martin
PALERMO, Boca 11; Mariano PAVONE, Estudiantes 11

ARGENTINA 2006–07
PRIMERA A DIVISION CLAUSURA

	Pl	W	D	L	F	A	Pts
San Lorenzo	19	14	3	2	34	17	45
Boca Juniors	19	11	6	2	38	20	39
Estudiantes LP	19	10	7	2	28	17	37
River Plate	19	9	6	4	26	16	33
Arsenal	19	8	6	5	31	24	30
Lanús	19	7	7	5	24	19	28
Colón Santa Fe	19	7	7	5	28	24	28
Argentinos Juniors	19	6	8	5	21	17	26
Vélez Sarsfield	19	7	5	7	22	26	26
Godoy Cruz	19	7	4	8	24	22	25
Independiente	19	6	7	6	23	24	25
Rosario Central	19	7	3	9	17	21	24
Racing Club	19	5	8	6	28	30	23
Newell's Old Boys	19	6	4	9	21	30	22
Nueva Chicago	19	5	6	8	19	28	21
Banfield	19	5	4	10	22	30	19
Belgrano Córdoba	19	4	6	9	24	27	18
Gimnasia y Esgrima LP	19	4	5	10	19	28	17
Gimnasia y Esgrima Jy	19	4	5	10	11	22	17
Quilmes	19	3	3	13	18	36	12

9/02/2007 - 18/06/2007 • Top scorers: Martin PALERMO, Boca 11;
Oscar CARDOZO, Newell's 10; Gaston FERNANDEZ, San Lorenzo 9;
Dario CVITANICH, Banfield 8; Facundo SAVA, Racing Club 8

Apertura Play-off: Estudiates LP 2-1 Boca Juniors (José Amaltfitani, 13-12-2006, Att: 30 000, Ref: Pezzotta, Scorers: Sosa [64], Pavone [80] for Estudiantes;
Palermo [4] for Boca. Sent off: Ledesma, Boca & Alvarez, Estudiantes after 38 minutes.)

ARGENTINA 2006–07

PRIMERA A DIVISION TORNEO APERTURA AND CLAUSURA GILLETTE PRESTOBARA EXCEL RESULTS

	Pl	W	D	L	F	A	Pts	RA	Boca Juniors	Estudiantes	San Lorenzo	River Plate	Arsenal	Lanús	Independiente	Vélez	Rosario Central	Racing Club	Arg. Juniors	Colón	Gim. Jujuy	Nueva Chicago	Godoy Cruz	Belgrano	GELP	Banfield	Newell's	Quilmes
Boca Juniors † ‡	38	25	8	5	79	37	83	1.877		2-0	0-3	1-1	1-1	1-2	1-0	3-2	1-1	2-2	2-1	4-1	3-1	2-0	0-0	1-0	5-1	3-0	3-1	3-1
Estudiantes LP † ‡	38	24	9	5	63	29	81	1.702	1-3		2-1	3-1	2-0	0-0	2-1	1-1	3-0	2-0	2-0	2-2	1-0	2-1	1-0	1-2	7-0	0-0	4-4	2-0
San Lorenzo † ‡	38	22	7	9	64	50	73	1.588	1-7	0-1		0-0	4-2	1-0	4-3	2-2	3-1	3-0	0-0	5-0	2-1	3-2	3-0	1-0	1-0	2-1	2-1	2-4
River Plate † ‡	38	20	11	7	59	33	71	1.693	3-1	0-1	5-0		2-1	1-0	1-1	3-2	2-0	4-2	2-0	1-0	1-1	0-1	1-2	0-1	1-1	2-0	2-1	3-3	2-1
Arsenal † ‡	38	17	11	10	57	46	62	1.404	1-2	1-1	2-2	0-2		1-1	0-1	3-1	1-0	3-2	0-2	2-1	1-0	2-0	2-1	4-3	3-1	2-2	3-2	3-1
Lanús ‡	38	16	11	11	50	43	59	1.500	0-0	0-3	2-0	0-2	0-0		2-4	2-0	1-2	2-1	3-0	1-1	0-3	3-1	0-1	2-1	3-2	3-1		
Independiente	38	16	9	13	56	48	57	1.412	1-3	0-0	0-1	0-2	1-1	1-0		1-0	2-0	2-0	1-1	1-3	1-2	3-2	0-2	3-1	3-0	2-1	1-1	4-1
Vélez Sarsfield	38	15	11	12	47	44	56	1.640	1-3	0-1	2-1	1-1	0-0	1-1	2-1		0-2	0-0	0-2	1-1	2-0	2-1	2-0	2-0	0-0	2-2	2-0	1-0
Rosario Central	38	15	7	16	45	43	52	1.386	1-3	0-1	2-0	0-2	2-3	2-2	1-2		1-0	2-1	3-0	2-0	3-0	1-1	1-0	1-0	1-1	4-1	4-2	
Racing Club	38	12	13	13	50	49	49	1.325	0-0	2-0	0-1	3-1	2-2	0-1	1-1	2-1		2-3	2-1	0-1	2-0	4-2	3-3	3-1	1-1	0-1	1-0	
Argentinos Juniors	38	11	13	14	43	45	46	1.219	3-3	2-2	1-1	2-1	1-2	1-2	1-3	2-0	0-1	0-0	1-0		1-1	2-1	3-0	1-0	2-1	0-0	1-0	0-0	1-1
Colón Santa Fe	38	12	10	16	48	58	46	1.272	2-1	0-2	1-1	0-0	1-1	1-3	1-4	1-0	3-1	1-1	3-1		3-1	1-2	2-0	2-0	1-2	3-0	1-1	0-0
Gimnasia Jujuy	38	12	7	19	30	41	43	1.237	1-2	0-0	0-1	1-2	0-0	2-0	1-3	0-1	1-0	0-3	0-0	2-0		3-0	2-1	0-0	3-1	0-1	1-0	1-2	2-1
Nueva Chicago	38	11	10	17	39	60	43	1.132	0-1	1-2	2-1	2-0	4-2	1-0	0-1	0-3	1-1	3-2	1-0	0-0		0-0	2-0	2-2	2-1	2-1	2-1
Godoy Cruz	38	10	12	16	43	48	42	**1.105**	0-1	1-3	1-2	0-1	2-1	2-2	3-1	0-2	2-1	0-0	2-0	2-0	0-0	4-0		1-1	2-1	1-3	1-1	3-0
Belgrano Córdoba	38	10	11	17	42	51	41	**1.079**	1-0	1-2	2-2	1-1	0-1	1-1	0-0	3-0	1-0	0-1	0-2	1-3	0-1	1-1	3-2		1-0	3-0	0-2	3-0
Gimnasia La Plata	38	11	7	20	40	68	40	1.430	1-4	1-2	3-2	0-3	0-2	0-1	4-1	0-3	0-1	1-2	1-0	3-2	2-0	2-2	2-1	2-2		0-1	2-1	3-2
Banfield	38	9	12	17	43	56	39	1.377	0-4	1-2	0-1	1-2	1-1	2-1	1-3	1-1	2-3	1-1	3-2	2-1	0-1	3-0	0-1	1-0	1-0		4-0	2-3
Newell's Old Boys	38	9	11	18	42	58	35	1.281	1-2	1-2	0-1	1-2	2-2	0-1	0-1	3-0	0-0	1-0	1-3	1-0	0-2	2-2	0-1	0-1	0-0			2-2
Quilmes	38	5	6	27	41	74	21	**0.912**	1-2	0-1	1-2	0-1	0-1	1-2	1-3	0-3	0-1	2-3	2-2	2-1	2-0	1-0	0-0	2-3	2-2	1-2	2-3	

† Qualified for the Copa Libertadores • ‡ Qualified for the Copa Sudamericana • Apertura results are in the shaded boxes
RA = Relegation average based on the average number of points per game over the past three seasons. Belgrano and Quilmes had the lowest and
so were relegated automatically. Nueva Chicago and Godoy Cruz had the next lowest average and so entered a play-off with Nacional B teams
Relegation play-offs: **Huracán BA** 2-0 3-2 Godoy Cruz; **Tigre** 1-0 2-1 Nueva Chicago • Huracan and Tigre promoted

ARGENTINA 2006-07 NACIONAL B (2) APERTURA

	Pl	W	D	L	F	A	Pts
Olímpo Bahía Blanco †	19	12	4	3	36	17	40
Platense	19	11	5	3	31	14	38
Tigre	19	10	5	4	23	17	35
San Martín San Juan	19	9	7	3	25	18	34
Chacarita Juniors	19	8	9	2	22	14	33
Huracán BA	19	9	6	4	29	26	33
Atlético Rafaela	19	9	5	5	24	14	32
Unión Santa Fé	19	8	4	7	28	17	28
San Martín Tucumán	19	6	7	6	21	20	25
Aldosivi	19	6	6	7	25	32	24
CAI	19	6	5	8	26	27	23
Ferro Carril Oeste	19	6	5	8	19	23	23
Instituto Córboba	19	5	5	9	22	29	20
Talleres Córdoba	19	4	7	8	19	23	19
Tiro Federal	19	4	7	8	23	28	19
Defensa y Justicia	19	4	7	8	11	19	19
Almagro	19	4	7	8	18	31	19
Villa Mitre	19	3	8	8	22	27	17
Huracán Tres Arroyos	19	3	7	9	17	33	16
Ben Hur Rafaela	19	3	4	12	22	34	13

3/08/2006 - 11/12/2006 • † Qualified for the championship play-off

ARGENTINA 2006-07 NACIONAL B (2) CLAUSURA

	Pl	W	D	L	F	A	Pts
Olímpo Bahía Blanco †	19	11	5	3	29	14	38
Defensa y Justicia	19	11	5	3	28	16	38
Huracán BA ‡	19	10	6	3	33	20	36
Atlético Rafaela ‡	19	10	6	3	27	17	36
San Martín San Juan ‡	19	9	8	2	26	12	35
Tigre ‡	19	8	8	3	25	15	32
Almagro	19	8	6	5	26	24	30
Unión Santa Fé	19	7	8	4	17	16	29
Chacarita Juniors ‡	19	8	4	7	21	16	28
Platense ‡	19	7	2	10	19	25	23
Instituto Córdoba	19	7	2	10	16	23	23
Ben Hur Rafaela	19	7	2	10	19	28	23
CAI	19	5	7	7	17	16	22
Huracán Tres Arroyos	19	6	4	9	19	23	22
Aldosivi	19	6	3	10	19	25	21
Tiro Federal	19	4	8	7	12	15	20
San Martín Tucumán	19	4	7	8	17	29	19
Ferro Carril Oeste	19	3	7	9	8	18	16
Villa Mitre	19	4	4	11	18	30	16
Talleres Córdoba	19	1	6	12	15	29	9

26/01/2007 - 2/06/2007 • † Qualified for the championship play-off • ‡ Qualified for play-offs on season record

NACIONAL B CHAMPIONSHIP Olímpo Bahía Blanca are automatic champions and are promoted

Second Promotion Place Play-off: Huracán BA 1-0 1-3 **San Martín** • San Martin promoted • Huracan BA play-off against Godoy Cruz.
The four teams with the next best season records play-off in the Reducido for the right to meet Nueva Chicago.
Reducido semi-finals: Platense 1-0 2-2 Atlético Rafaela; Chacarita Juniors 3-2 0-1 Tigre • Reducido final: Platense 0-0 0-2 Tigre. Tigre meet Nueva Chicago

ARGENTINA 2006-07 PRIMERA B (3) APERTURA

	Pl	W	D	L	F	A	Pts
Estudiantes BA †	21	12	6	3	35	14	42
Deportivo Morón	21	12	6	3	31	16	42
Almirante Brown	21	12	5	4	27	16	41
Deportivo Merlo	21	9	8	4	25	21	35
Central Córdoba	21	9	7	5	36	22	34
Deportivo Armenio	21	9	6	6	22	15	33
Tristán Suarez	21	7	10	4	32	24	31
Social Español	21	8	7	6	17	13	31
All Boys	21	9	4	8	29	27	31
San Telmo	21	8	6	7	25	28	30
Brown Adrogué	21	7	8	6	26	27	29
Temperley	21	8	5	8	23	27	29
Sarmiento Junín	21	7	4	10	23	32	25
Sportivo Italiano	21	5	9	7	23	28	24
Defensores Cambaceres	21	5	9	7	22	28	24
Los Andes	21	6	5	10	25	29	23
Comunicaciones	21	6	5	10	20	26	23
Talleres	21	5	7	9	20	29	22
Flandria	21	6	4	11	21	32	22
Defensores de Belgrano	21	4	8	9	25	36	20
Atlanta	21	4	6	11	21	25	18
El Porvenir	21	2	7	12	15	28	13

28/07/2006 - 9/12/2006 • † Qualified for the championship play-off

ARGENTINA 2006-07 PRIMERA B (3) CLAUSURA

	Pl	W	D	L	F	A	Pts
Almirante Brown †	21	14	5	2	32	11	47
Tristán Suarez ‡	21	14	2	5	43	25	44
Sarmiento Junín ‡	21	9	8	4	36	25	35
Deportivo Merlo ‡	21	9	6	6	22	22	33
Los Andes	21	8	8	5	34	28	32
Deportivo Morón ‡	21	9	4	8	25	23	31
Central Córdoba ‡	21	9	3	9	30	23	30
Defensores de Belgrano	21	8	6	7	22	25	30
Estudiantes BA	21	8	5	8	26	24	29
All Boys ‡	21	7	7	7	22	28	28
Comunicaciones	21	7	6	8	26	27	27
Social Español	21	8	3	10	24	26	27
El Porvenir	21	7	6	8	25	30	27
San Telmo	21	6	8	7	25	25	26
Talleres	21	7	4	10	25	27	25
Temperley	21	6	7	8	21	23	25
Defensores Cambaceres	21	6	6	9	25	28	24
Flandria	21	6	6	9	13	19	24
Brown Adrogué	21	5	8	8	31	36	23
Atlanta	21	5	7	9	26	36	22
Deportivo Armenio	21	4	9	8	18	30	21
Sportivo Italiano	21	4	6	11	21	30	18

27/01/2007 - 21/05/2007 • † Qualified for the championship play-off • ‡ Qualified for play-offs on season record

PRIMERA B CHAMPIONSHIP Estudiantes BA 0-0 0-1 **Almirante Brown**

Play-off first round: Tristán Suarez 1-3 **All Boys**; **Deportivo Morón** 2-0 Central Córdoba; Deportivo Merlo 1-1 3-5p **Sarmiento**
Play-off semi-finals: **Deportivo Morón** 0-0 3-1p Sarmiento; **Estudiantes BA** 2-0 All Boys
Play-off final: **Estdiantes BA** 2-0 Deportivo Morón • Promotion Play-off: Estudiantes BA 0-0 1-1 **Ferro Carril Oeste**. FC Oeste remain in Primera B

BOCA JUNIORS 2006-07

Date	Opponents	Score		Comp	Scorers
6-08-2006	Banfield	W 3-0	H	TAP	Palermo 2 [57 75], Battaglia [66]
12-08-2006	Rosario Central	W 2-1	A	TAP	Krupoviesa [60], Díaz [83]
19-08-2006	Independiente	W 1-0	H	TAP	Silvestre [36]
27-08-2006	San Lorenzo	W 7-1	A	TAP	Palacio 2 [22 48], Palermo 3 [27 32 87], Cardozo [53], Franzoia [86]
3-09-2006	Estudiantes La Plata	W 2-0	H	TAP	Palacio [11], Palermo [70]
10-09-2006	Gimnasia y Esgrima La Plata		A	TAP	Abandoned at half-time. Second half played on 8-11-2006
17-09-2006	Godoy Cruz Mendoza	D 0-0	H	TAP	
24-09-2006	Nueva Chicago	W 1-0	A	TAP	Cardozo [11]
28-09-2006	Nacional - URU	L 1-2	A	CSr2	Palacio [45]
1-10-2006	Vélez Sarsfield	W 3-2	H	TAP	Gago [69], Palacio 2 [75 88]
8-10-2006	River Plate	L 1-3	A	TAP	Palacio [31]
12-10-2006	Nacional - URU	W 2-1	H	CSr2	Palacio [55], Bertolo [83]. L 1-3p
15-10-2006	Newell's Old Boys	W 3-1	H	TAP	Barros Schelotto.G [31], Días [76], Bertolo [81]
29-10-2006	Argentinos Juniors	W 2-1	H	TAP	Krupoviesa [40], Boselli [72]
1-11-2006	Racing Club	D 0-0	A	TAP	
5-11-2006	Arsenal	W 2-1	A	TAP	Boselli [69], Palacio [77]
8-11-2006	Gimnasia y Esgrima La Plata	W 4-1	H	TAP	Palermo [46], Palacio 2 [49 86], Marino [72]
12-11-2006	Quilmes	W 3-1	H	TAP	Palermo 2 [20 77], Palacio [50]
19-11-2006	Gimnasia y Esgrima Jujuy	W 2-1	A	TAP	Cardozo [27], Díaz [63]
26-11-2006	Colón Santa Fe	W 4-1	H	TAP	Cardozo [17], Marino [51], Palacio 2 [61 90]
3-12-2006	Belgrano Córdoba	L 0-1	A	TAP	
10-12-2006	Lanús	L 1-2	H	TAP	Palermo [30p]
13-12-2006	Estudiantes La Plata	L 1-2	N	TAPpo	Palermo [4]
10-02-2007	Banfield	W 4-0	A	TCL	Cardozo [8], Morel [21], Orteman [36], Galván [70]
14-02-2007	Bolívar - BOL	D 0-0	A	CLg7	
18-02-2007	Rosario Central	D 1-1	H	TCL	Palacio [55]
24-02-2007	Independiente	W 3-1	A	TCL	Cardozo [42], Palacio [43], Palermo [93+]
1-03-2007	Cienciano - PER	W 1-0	H	CLg7	Ibarra [81]
3-03-2007	San Lorenzo	L 0-3	H	TCL	
10-03-2007	Estudiantes La Plata	W 3-0	A	TCL	Palermo 3 [39 43 63]
14-03-2007	Toluca - MEX	L 0-2	A	CLg7	
18-03-2007	Gimnasia y Esgrima La Plata	W 5-1	H	TCL	Cardozo [2], Palermo 4 [6 10 15 72]
22-03-2007	Toluca - MEX	W 3-0	H	CLg7	Maidana [15], Riquelme [23], Boselli [82]
25-03-2007	Godoy Cruz Mendoza	W 1-0	A	TCL	Boselli [83]
31-03-2007	Nueva Chicago	W 2-0	H	TCL	Rodríguez.C [55], Cardozo [64]
4-04-2007	Cienciano - PER	L 0-3	A	CLg7	
8-04-2007	Vélez Sarsfield	W 3-1	A	TCL	Cardozo [2], Palacio 2 [26 79]
15-04-2007	River Plate	D 1-1	H	TCL	Ledesma [1]
22-04-2007	Newell's Old Boys	W 2-1	A	TCL	Palermo [62p], Palacio [81]
26-04-2007	Bolívar - BOL	W 7-0	H	CLg7	Palacio 2 [32 45], Palermo [37p], OG [51], Datolo [57], Marioni 2 [64 85]
29-04-2007	Racing Club	D 2-2	H	TCL	Riquelme [10], Palermo [14]
2-05-2007	Vélez Sarsfield - ARG	W 3-0	H	CLr2	Riquelme [9], Palermo [60], Rodríguez [89]
6-05-2007	Argentinos Juniors	D 3-3	A	TCL	Cardozo [32], Palermo [58], Ibarra [65]
9-05-2007	Vélez Sarsfield - ARG	L 1-3	A	CLr2	Riquelme [32]
13-05-2007	Arsenal	D 1-1	H	TCL	Riquelme [76]
17-05-2007	Libertad - PAR	D 1-1	H	CLqf	Palermo [90]
20-05-2007	Quilmes	W 2-1	A	TCL	Dátolo [25], Palacio [31]
24-05-2007	Libertad - PAR	W 2-0	A	CLqf	Riquelme [61], Palacio [71]
27-05-2007	Gimnasia y Esgrima Jujuy	W 3-1	H	TCL	Palacio [52], Bataglia [73], Rodríguez [82]
31-05-2007	Cúcuta Deportivo - COL	L 1-3	A	CLsf	Ledesma [27]
3-06-2007	Colón Santa Fe	L 1-2	A	TCL	Boselli [44]
7-06-2007	Cúcuta Deportivo - COL	W 3-0	H	CLsf	Riquelme [44], Palermo [61], Battaglia [90]
10-06-2007	Belgrano Córdoba	W 1-0	H	TCL	Marioni [10]
13-06-2007	Grêmio - BRA	W 3-0	H	CLf	Palacio [18], Riquelme [73], Patricio OG [89]
17-06-2007	Lanús	D 0-0	A	TCL	
20-06-2007	Grêmio - BRA	W 2-0	A	CLf	Riquelme 2 [68 80]

TAP = Torneo Apertura • CS = Copa Sudamericana • TCL = Torneo Clausura • CL = Copa Libertadores
g7 = Group 7 • r2 = second round • qf = quarter-final • sf = semi-final • f = final
H = Ernesto Martearena, Salta • N = José Amalfitani, Buenos Aires

ESTUDIANTES DE LA PLATA 2006-07

Date	Opponents	Score		Comp	Scorers
6-08-2006	Quilmes	W 1-0	A	TAP	Pavone [34]
13-08-2006	Gimnasia y Esgrima Jujuy	W 1-0	H	TAP	Calderón [25]
20-08-2006	Colón Sante Fe	W 2-0	A	TAP	Pavone 2 [26p 80]
27-08-2006	Belgrano Córdoba	L 1-2	H	TAP	Verón [33]
3-09-2006	Boca Juniors	L 0-2	A	TAP	
8-09-2006	Banfield	D 0-0	H	TAP	
17-09-2006	Rosario Central	L 0-1	A	TAP	
22-09-2006	Independiente	W 2-1	H	TAP	Calderón [41], Alayes [50]
30-09-2006	San Lorenzo	W 1-0	A	TAP	Alvarez [37]
7-10-2006	Lanús	W 3-0	A	TAP	Pavone 2 [48 60], Cominges [78]
15-10-2006	Gimnasia y Esgrima La Plata	W 7-0	H	TAP	Galván 2 [3 50], Calderón 3 [23 72 84], Pavone [35], Lugüercio [77]
22-10-2006	Godoy Cruz Mendoza	W 3-1	A	TAP	Alayes [1], Sosa [30], Pavone [34]
28-10-2006	Nueva Chicago	W 2-1	H	TAP	Pavone [17], González OG [32]
4-11-2006	Vélez Sarsfield	W 1-0	A	TAP	Alayes [8]
11-11-2006	River Plate	W 3-1	H	TAP	Alayes [16], Benítez [65], Lussenhoff OG [80]
18-11-2006	Newell's Old Boys	W 2-1	A	TAP	Calderón [85], Piatti [88]
25-11-2006	Racing Club	W 2-0	H	TAP	Galván [16], Saucedo [76]
3-12-2006	Argentinos Juniors	D 2-2	A	TAP	Pavone [77], Verón [86]
10-12-2006	Arsenal	W 2-0	H	TAP	Alayes [85], Pavone [89]
13-12-2006	Boca Juniors	W 2-1	N	TAPpo	Sosa 64, Pavone [80]
12-02-2007	Quilmes	W 2-0	H	TCL	Pavone [55p], Calderón [62]
17-02-2007	Gimnasia y Esgrima Jujuy	D 0-0	A	TCL	
23-02-2007	Colón Sante Fe	D 2-2	H	TCL	Calderón [12], Pavone [69]
3-03-2007	Belgrano Córdoba	W 2-1	A	TCL	Piatti [37], Calderón [92+]
10-03-2007	Boca Juniors	L 0-3	H	TCL	
16-03-2007	Banfield	W 2-0	A	TCL	Mosquera [18], Pavone [60]
24-03-2007	Rosario Central	W 3-0	H	TCL	Piatti [43], Lugüercio 2 [77 86]
1-04-2007	Independiente	D 0-0	A	TCL	
7-04-2007	San Lorenzo	W 4-1	H	TCL	Silva [20], Leguizamón 2 [54 56], Leal [59]
15-04-2007	Lanús	D 0-0	H	TCL	
22-04-2007	Gimnasia y Esgrima La Plata	W 2-1	A	TCL	Pavone 2 [40p 63]
27-04-2007	Godoy Cruz Mendoza	W 1-0	H	TCL	Lugüercio [72]
4-05-2007	Nueva Chicago	W 2-1	A	TCL	Lugüercio 2 [20 26]
12-05-2007	Vélez Sarsfield	D 1-1	H	TCL	Lugüercio [63]
20-05-2007	River Plate	W 1-0	A	TCL	Maggiolo [94+]
26-05-2007	Newell's Old Boys	D 4-4	H	TCL	Pavone 2 [10 48], Calderón [20], Piatti [52]
3-06-2007	Racing Club	L 0-2	A	TCL	
10-06-2007	Argentinos Juniors	W 2-0	H	TCL	Benítez [15], Angeleri [94+]
17-06-2007	Arsenal	D 1-1	A	TCL	Benítez [10]

TAP = Torneo Apertura • CS = Copa Sudamericana • TCL = Torneo Clausura
r2 = second round • qf = quarter-final • sf = semi-final • f = final • H = Salta

FIFA/COCA-COLA WORLD RANKING

1993	1994	1995	1996	1997	1998	1999	2000	2001	2002	2003	2004	2005	2006	High	Low
8	10	7	22	17	5	6	3	2	5	5	3	4	3	1 03/07	24 08/96

2006–2007											
08/06	09/06	10/06	11/06	12/06	01/07	02/07	03/07	04/07	05/07	06/07	07/07
3	3	4	3	3	3	3	1	2	3	5	2

SAN LORENZO 2006-07

Date	Opponents	Score		Comp	Scorers
6-08-2006	Gimnasia y Esgrima Jujuy	W 1-0	A	TAP	Bottinelli.J [3]
12-08-2006	Colón Santa Fe	W 5-0	H	TAP	Ferreyra 2 [20] [84], Jiménez 2 [27] [83], Lavezzi [52]
18-08-2006	Belgrano Córdoba	D 2-2	A	TAP	Quatrocchi [9], Lavezzi [16]
22-08-2006	Banfield - ARG	W 2-1	H	CSr1	Jiménez [24], González.A [33p]
27-08-2006	Boca Juniors	L 1-7	H	TAP	Hirsig [15]
2-09-2006	Banfield	W 2-1	A	TAP	Silvera 2 [32] [49]
8-09-2006	Rosario Central	W 3-1	H	TAP	Bottinelli.D [48], Silvera 2 [75] [88]
12-09-2006	Banfield - ARG	D 0-0	A	CSr1	
17-09-2006	Independiente	W 1-0	A	TAP	Silvera [51]
23-09-2006	Lanús	L 0-2	A	TAP	
27-09-2006	Santos - BRA	W 3-0	H	CSr2	González.A [7], Jiménez [52], Lavezzi [66]
30-09-2006	Estudiantes La Plata	L 0-1	H	TAP	
6-10-2006	Gimnasia y Esgrima La Plata	L 2-3	A	TAP	Silvera [52], Rivero [92+]
11-10-2006	Santos - BRA	L 0-1	A	CSr2	
15-10-2006	Godoy Cruz Mendoza	W 3-0	H	TAP	Silvera [10], Lavezzi [58], Tula [78]
20-10-2006	Nueva Chicago	L 1-2	A	TAP	Bottinelli.J [24]
25-10-2006	Toluca - MEX	W 3-1	H	CSqf	Quatrocchi [17], Silvera 2 [51] [56]
28-10-2006	Vélez Sarsfield	D 2-2	H	TAP	Ferreyra [89], Jiménez [92+]
1-11-2006	Toluca - MEX	L 0-2	A	CSqf	
5-11-2006	River Plate	L 0-5	A	TAP	
12-11-2006	Newell's Old Boys	W 2-1	H	TAP	Jiménez 2 [6] [14]
24-11-2006	Argentinos Juniors	D 0-0	H	TAP	
2-12-2006	Arsenal	D 2-2	A	TAP	Quatrocchi [4], Silvera [42]
8-12-2006	Quilmes	L 2-4	H	TAP	González.A 2 [2p] [11p]
11-02-2007	Gimnasia y Esgrima Jujuy	W 2-1	H	TCL	Bottinelli.J [24], Ferreyra [26]
17-02-2007	Colón Santa Fe	D 1-1	A	TCL	Ledesma [85]
21-02-2007	Racing Club	W 1-0	A	TAP	Jiménez [75]
25-02-2007	Belgrano Córdoba	W 1-0	H	TCL	Jiménez [41]
4-03-2007	Boca Juniors	W 3-0	A	TCL	Lavezzi [20], Fernández.G [66], Silvera [71]
11-03-2007	Banfield	W 2-1	H	TCL	Fernández.G 2 [35p] [66]
17-03-2007	Rosario Central	W 1-0	H	TCL	Fernández.G [51]
25-03-2007	Independiente	W 4-3	H	TCL	Silvera 2 [9] [63], Fernández.G [44], Bottinelli.J [76]
1-04-2007	Lanús	W 1-0	H	TCL	Silvera [17]
7-04-2007	Estudiantes La Plata	L 1-2	A	TCL	Lavezzi [93+]
14-04-2007	Gimnasia y Esgrima La Plata	W 1-0	H	TCL	Fernández.G [17]
22-04-2007	Godoy Cruz Mendoza	W 2-1	H	TCL	Silvera 2 [14] [74]
29-04-2007	Nueva Chicago	W 3-2	H	TCL	González.A 2 [27] [42], Lavezzi [45]
5-05-2007	Vélez Sarsfield	L 1-2	A	TCL	Tula [72]
13-05-2007	River Plate	D 0-0	H	TCL	
19-05-2007	Newell's Old Boys	W 1-0	H	TCL	Méndez [82]
27-05-2007	Racing Club	W 3-0	H	TCL	Fernández.G [7], Tula [38], Hirsig [73]
1-06-2007	Argentinos Juniors	D 1-1	A	TCL	Tula [24]
10-06-2007	Arsenal	W 4-1	H	TCL	Tula [6], Lavezzi [17], Fernández.G 2 [46] [50p]
16-06-2007	Quilmes	W 2-1	A	TCL	Ferreyra [17], Silvera [85]

TAP = Torneo Apertura • CS = Copa Sudamericana • TCL = Torneo Clausura
r1 = first round • r2 = second round • qf = quarter-final

THE FIFA BIG COUNT OF 2006

	Male	Female		Total
Number of players	2 349 811	30 900	Referees and Assistant Referees	3 340
Professionals	3 530		Admin, Coaches, Technical, Medical	33 821
Amateurs 18+	88 090		Number of clubs	3 348
Youth under 18	231 196		Number of teams	23 623
Unregistered	1 225 000		Clubs with women's teams	29
Total players	2 658 811		Players as % of population	6.66%

ARM – ARMENIA

NATIONAL TEAM RECORD
JULY 10TH 2006 TO JULY 12TH 2010

PL	W	D	L	F	A	%
9	2	3	4	4	8	38.8

FIFA/COCA-COLA WORLD RANKING

1993	1994	1995	1996	1997	1998	1999	2000	2001	2002	2003	2004	2005	2006	High	Low
-	141	113	106	105	100	85	90	95	107	113	119	108	123	**79** 07/07	**159** 07/94

2006–2007											
08/06	09/06	10/06	11/06	12/06	01/07	02/07	03/07	04/07	05/07	06/07	07/07
104	112	119	124	123	123	119	119	127	128	80	79

The 2006 Armenian championship proved to be another stroll in the park for an invincible Pyunik team that easily won a sixth straight title, with the championship clinched in typical fashion courtesy of a 12-1 thrashing of poor Kilikia. Pyunik, who lost just one game all season, boasted a team made up almost exclusively of Armenian players but there are fears for the overall standard of football in the country with investment in the game at a record low. Runners-up Banants Yerevan won their first Cup for 15 years when they beat Ararat Yerevan in the final 3-1 after extra-time. Dominance at home for Pyunik did not translate into success in Europe with a first preliminary round defeat at

INTERNATIONAL HONOURS
None

the hands of Moldova's Sheriff Tiraspol in the UEFA Champions League. Armenia's UEFA Euro 2008 qualifying campaign never really got off the ground, despite the appointment of veteran Scot Ian Porterfield as coach. The national team went the whole of 2006 without scoring a goal and it was only a penalty in a friendly against Panama that halted a record-equalling run of seven games without a goal. There was a real danger that the season would end with Armenia beating their record of ten games without a win but Porterfield's side signed off the season with impressive back to back wins over Kazakhstan and then group leaders Poland.

THE FIFA BIG COUNT OF 2006

	Male	Female		Total
Number of players	136 212	15 141	Referees and Assistant Referees	134
Professionals	656		Admin, Coaches, Technical, Medical	4 810
Amateurs 18+	37 228		Number of clubs	80
Youth under 18	2 915		Number of teams	178
Unregistered	37 900		Clubs with women's teams	3
Total players	151 353		Players as % of population	5.09%

Football Federation of Armenia (FFA)
Khanjyan str. 27, Yerevan 375 010, Armenia
Tel +374 1 568 883   Fax +374 1 539 517
ffarm@arminco.com   www.ffa.am
President: HAYRAPETYAN Ruben   General Secretary: MINASYAN Armen
Vice-President: TBD   Treasurer: PAPIKYAN Gevorg   Media Officer: TBD
Men's Coach: PORTERFIELD Ian   Women's Coach: MIKAYELYAN Mher
FFA formed: 1992   UEFA: 1993   FIFA: 1992
Red shirts with white trimmings, Blue shorts, Orange socks or White shirts with blue trimmings, Blue shorts, White socks

RECENT INTERNATIONALS PLAYED BY ARMENIA

2002	Opponents	Score		Venue	Comp	Scorers	Att	Referee
7-09	Ukraine	D	2-2	Yerevan	ECq	Petrosyan.Art 73, Sargsyan 90p	9 000	Vuorela FIN
16-10	Greece	L	0-2	Athens	ECq		6 000	Ceferin SVN
2003								
12-02	Israel	L	0-2	Tel Aviv	Fr		8 000	Trentlange ITA
29-03	Northern Ireland	W	1-0	Yerevan	ECq	Petrosyan.Art 86	10 321	Beck LIE
2-04	Spain	L	0-3	Leon	ECq		13 500	Yefet ISR
7-06	Ukraine	L	3-4	Lviv	ECq	Sargsyan 2 14p 52, Petrosyan.Art 74	35 000	Albrecht GER
6-09	Greece	L	0-1	Yerevan	ECq		6 500	Temmink NED
10-09	Northern Ireland	W	1-0	Belfast	ECq	Karamyan.Arm 29	8 616	Stredak SVK
11-10	Spain	L	0-4	Yerevan	ECq		15 000	Meier SUI
2004								
18-02	Hungary	L	0-2	Paphos	Fr		400	Gerasimou CYP
19-02	Kazakhstan	D	3-3	Paphos	Fr	Petrosyan.G 52, Karamyan.Art 2 73 80 L 2-3p	100	
21-02	Georgia	W	2-0	Nicosia	Fr	Karamyan.Arm 42, Karamyan.Art 52		
28-04	Turkmenistan	W	1-0	Yerevan	Fr	Ara Hakobyan 68	7 500	
18-08	FYR Macedonia	L	0-3	Skopje	WCq		4 375	Guenov BUL
8-09	Finland	L	0-2	Yerevan	WCq		2 864	Malzinskas LTU
9-10	Finland	L	1-3	Tampere	WCq	Shahgeldyan 32	7 894	Fandel GER
13-10	Czech Republic	L	0-3	Yerevan	WCq		3 205	Granat POL
17-11	Romania	D	1-1	Yerevan	WCq	Dokhoyan 62	1 403	De Bleeckere BEL
2005								
18-03	Kuwait	L	1-3	Al Ain	Fr	Mkhitaryan 87p		
26-03	Andorra	W	2-1	Yerevan	WCq	Ara Hakobyan 30, Khachatryan.R 73	2 100	Attard MLT
30-03	Netherlands	L	0-2	Eindhoven	WCq		35 000	Trefoloni ITA
4-06	FYR Macedonia	L	1-2	Yerevan	WCq	Manucharyan 55	2 870	Mikulski POL
8-06	Romania	L	0-3	Constanta	WCq		5 146	Briakos GRE
17-08	Jordan	D	0-0	Amman	Fr		1 747	Dougal SCO
3-09	Netherlands	L	0-1	Yerevan	WCq		12 015	Hansson SWE
7-09	Czech Republic	L	1-4	Olomouc	WCq	Ara Hakobyan 85	430	Stoks IRL
12-10	Andorra	W	3-0	Andorra la Vella	WCq	OG 40, Aram Hakobyan 52, Ara Hakobyan 62		
2006								
28-02	Romania	L	0-2	Nicosia	Fr		1 000	Tsacheilidis GRE
1-03	Cyprus	L	0-2	Limassol	Fr			
6-09	Belgium	L	0-1	Yerevan	ECq		4 122	Lehner AUT
7-10	Finland	D	0-0	Yerevan	ECq		2 800	Skomina SVN
11-10	Serbia	L	0-3	Belgrade	ECq		10 987	Kasnaferis GRE
15-11	Finland	L	0-1	Lahti	ECq		9 445	Thomson SCO
2007								
14-01	Panama	D	1-1	Monterey Park	Fr	Ara Hakopyan p		
7-02	Andorra	D	0-0	Andorra la Vella	Fr			
28-03	Poland	L	0-1	Kielce	ECq		13 450	Undiano ESP
2-06	Kazakhstan	W	2-1	Almaty	ECq	Arzumanyan 31, Hovsepyan 39p	17 100	Kralovec CZE
6-06	Poland	W	1-0	Yerevan	ECq	Mkhitaryan 66	9 800	Balaj ROU

Fr = Friendly match • EC = UEFA EURO 2004/2008 • WC = FIFA World Cup • q = qualifier

ARMENIA NATIONAL TEAM RECORDS AND RECORD SEQUENCES

Records			Sequence records					
Victory	3-0	ALB 1997, AND x2	Wins	2	2004, 2007	Clean sheets	2	2004
Defeat	0-7	CHI 1997, GEO 1997	Defeats	5	1995-1996	Goals scored	6	1999-2000
Player Caps	78	HOVSEPYAN Sargis	Undefeated	3	Four times	Without goal	7	1999
Player Goals	11	PETROSYAN Artur	Without win	10	1996-1997	Goals against	13	1994-1996

REPUBLIC OF ARMENIA; HAYASTANI HANRAPETUT'YUN

Capital	Yerevan	Language	Armenian	Independence	1991
Population	2 976 372	Area km²	29 800	Density 100 per km²	% in cities 69
GDP per cap	$3 500	Dailling code	+374	Internet .am	GMT + / - +4

MEDALS TABLE

		Overall			League			Cup			Europe			City	Stadium	Cap'ty	DoF
		G	S	B	G	S	B	G	S	B	G	S	B				
1	Pyunik Yerevan	12	4		9	1		3	3					Yerevan	Hanrapetakan (Republican)	14 968	1992
2	Ararat Yerevan	5	5	1	1	3	1	4	2					Yerevan	Razdan	48 250	1935
3	Mika Ashtarak	5	2	1		2	1	5						Ashtarak	Vardanank	12 000	1985
4	Shirak Gyumri	3	8	2	3	5	2		3					Gyumri	City Stadium	7 000	1958
5	Tsement Yerevan	3		1	1		1	2						Yerevan			
6	Banants Yerevan	2	4	3		2	3	2	2					Yerevan	Banants	10 000	1992
7	FK Yerevan	1	1	3	1		3		1					Yerevan			1995
8	Araks Ararat	1			1									Ararat			
9	Zvartnots Yerevan		3			1			2					Yerevan			
10	Kotayk Abovyan		2	2			2		2					Abovyan	Kotayk	5 500	1955
11	Kilikia Yerevan		1						1					Yerevan	Razdan	48 250	1992
12	Homenmen Yerevan			1		1								Yerevan			
	Spartak Yerevan			1		1								Yerevan			
14	Gandzasar													Kapan	Lernagorts	3 500	2004
	Lernayin Artsakh													Yerevan	Nayri	6 800	
	Kilikia													Yerevan	Razdan	48 250	
	Ulysses													Yerevan	Hanrapetakan (Republican)	15 000	2004

RECENT LEAGUE AND CUP RECORD

	Championship							Cup		
Year	Champions	Pts	Runners-up	Pts	Third	Pts		Winners	Score	Runners-up
1998	Tsement Ararat	64	Shirak Gyumri	61	FK Yerevan	48		Tsement Ararat	3-1	FK Yerevan
1999	Shirak Gyumri	73	Ararat Yerevan	72	Tsement Ararat	71		Tsement Ararat	3-2	Shirak Yerevan
2000	Araks Ararat	61	Ararat Yerevan	59	Shirak Gyumri	58		Mika Ashtarak	2-1	Zvarnots Yerevan
2001	Pyunik Yerevan	53	Zvarnots Yerevan	48	Spartak Yerevan	48		Mika Ashtarak	1-1 4-3p	Ararat Yerevan
2002	Pyunik Yerevan	59	Shirak Gyumri	51	Banants Yerevan	50		Pyunik Yerevan	2-0	Zvarnots Yerevan
2003	Pyunik Yerevan	74	Banants Yerevan	66	Shirak Gyumri	53		Mika Ashtarak	1-0	Banants Yerevan
2004	Pyunik Yerevan	71	Mika Ashtarak	55	Banants Yerevan	43		Pyunik Yerevan	0-0 6-5p	Banants Yerevan
2005	Pyunik Yerevan	39	Mika Ashtarak	35	Banants Yerevan	33		Mika Ashtarak	2-0	Kilikia Yerevan
2006	Pyunik Yerevan	73	Banants Yerevan	57	Mika Ashtarak	57		Mika Ashtarak	1-0	Pyunik Yerevan
2007								Banants Yerevan	3-1	Ararat Yerevan

ARMENIA 2006

PREMIER LEAGUE

	Pl	W	D	L	F	A	Pts	Pyunik	Banants	Mika	Ararat	Gandzasar	Kilikia	Shirak	Ulysses
Pyunik Yerevan †	28	23	4	1	86	23	73		3-0 1-2	3-1 1-1	1-0 2-0	3-0 5-1	4-2 12-1	7-0 3-1	2-1 4-1
Banants Yerevan ‡	28	18	3	7	67	26	57	2-4 1-2		2-1 1-0	2-1 3-1	0-0 4-1	1-0 2-1	6-0 3-0	2-0 0-0
Mika Ashtarak ‡	28	17	6	5	45	21	57	0-3 0-0	1-0 1-0		2-0 2-3	3-0 2-0	2-0 4-1	4-0 1-1	1-1 3-2
Ararat Yerevan	28	15	4	9	48	35	49	0-5 1-1	1-0 3-0	0-2 0-1		3-1 1-0	3-2 1-0	1-1 4-1	1-0 2-0
Gandzasar Kapan	28	7	3	18	28	60	24	0-1 0-1	1-7 1-5	0-1 0-2	2-1 1-3		4-2 2-0	2-2 1-0	1-0 2-3
Kilikia Yerevan	28	6	5	17	38	69	23	2-2 0-3	1-5 1-1	1-2 0-3	1-1 0-6	3-0 2-2		1-0 0-1	1-2 6-2
Shirak Gyumri	28	4	7	17	21	64	19	1-2 1-2	0-5 1-2	0-0 0-0	1-1 2-6	2-1 2-1	1-1 0-4		0-1 1-3
Ulysses Yerevan	28	5	2	21	31	66	17	1-3 3-6	0-4 0-7	2-3 0-2	2-3 0-1	1-2 1-2	1-2 2-3	1-2 1-0	

14/04/2006 - 9/11/2006 • † Qualified for the UEFA Champions League • ‡ Qualified for the UEFA Cup
Relegation play-off: Ulysses 4-2 Dinamo

ARMENIA 2006
SECOND DIVISION

	Pl	W	D	L	F	A	Pts
Pyunik-2 Yerevan	18	14	3	1	80	11	45
Lernayin Artsakh	18	12	3	3	57	32	39
Banants-2 Yerevan	18	11	3	4	40	16	36
Ararat-2 Yerevan	18	11	1	6	46	24	34
Dinamo Yerevan	18	9	4	5	36	34	31
Patani	18	6	3	9	43	49	21
Gandzasar Kapan	18	5	4	9	33	36	19
Mika-2 Ashtarak	18	4	5	9	20	24	17
Hay Ari Yerevan	18	3	2	13	22	60	11
Yezerq Noyemberian	18	1	0	17	12	103	3

1/05/2006 - 24/10/2006

FFA CUP 2007

First round

Banants Yerevan *	5	3
Dinamo Yerevan	0	1
Banants-2 Yerevan	2	2
Kilikia Yerevan *	3	4
Shirak Gyumri *	2	1
Mika-2 Ashtarak	0	0
Mika Ashtarak	Bye	
Pyunik Yerevan	Bye	
Gandzasar Kapan *	1	0
Bentonit Ijevan	0	2
Ulysses Yerevan	2	2
Ararat-2 Yerevan *	0	0
Pyunik-2 Yerevan *	0	0
Ararat Yerevan	2	1

Quarter–finals

Banants Yerevan *	5	6
Kilikia Yerevan	1	1
Shirak Gyumri	1	1
Mika Ashtarak *	4	1
Pyunik Yerevan *	4	4
Bentonit Ijevan	0	1
Ulysses Yerevan	0	1
Ararat Yerevan *	2	2

Semi–finals

Banants Yerevan *	1	1
Mika Ashtarak	0	1
Pyunik Yerevan	0	1
Ararat Yerevan *	1	1

Final

Banants Yerevan ‡	3
Ararat Yerevan	1

CUP FINAL

Hanrapetakan, Yerevan
9-05-2007
Scorers - Muradyan 2 [78,115],
Bareghamyan [108] for Banants;
Pizeli 32 for Ararat [32]

* Home team in the first leg • ‡ Qualified for the UEFA Cup

ARU – ARUBA

NATIONAL TEAM RECORD
JULY 10TH 2006 TO JULY 12TH 2010

PL	W	D	L	F	A	%
0	0	0	0	0	0	0

FIFA/COCA-COLA WORLD RANKING

1993	1994	1995	1996	1997	1998	1999	2000	2001	2002	2003	2004	2005	2006	High		Low	
165	173	171	181	177	180	191	184	185	189	195	198	200	198	**164**	02/94	**201**	04/06

2006–2007												
08/06	09/06	10/06	11/06	12/06	01/07	02/07	03/07	04/07	05/07	06/07	07/07	
197	198	198	198	198	199	199	199	199	199	199	199	

The decision not to enter the Digicel Caribbean Cup meant that there was no escape for the Aruban national team right at the bottom of the FIFA/Coca-Cola World Ranking, a place they share with eight other nations. The national team hasn't been in action since March 2004, which has left the youth teams as Aruba's only representatives at international level. Both the under 17 and under 20 teams entered the CONCACAF tournaments used as qualification for the FIFA tournaments at both age groups, but both finished bottom of their respective first round groups. Britannia carried the flag abroad in club football when they travelled to St Thomas in the US Virgin Islands for a first

INTERNATIONAL HONOURS
None

round group in the Caribbean section of the CONCACAF Champions' Cup. They managed a draw with hosts New Vibes but then lost 8-0 against Trinidad's San Juan Jabloteh and 7-1 against Antigua's SAP. The championship in Aruba - the Division di Honor - does, however, remain very competitive and Britannia won the ten team first stage comfortably clear of Racing Club Aruba, Nacional and Fama. Unfortunately for them, first round records count for nothing in the four team play-off to determine the two finalists. A draw against Nacional in their final match meant Nacional qualified instead to meet Racing, whom they beat over three legs.

THE FIFA BIG COUNT OF 2006

	Male	Female		Total
Number of players	9 900	800	Referees and Assistant Referees	26
Professionals	0		Admin, Coaches, Technical, Medical	100
Amateurs 18+	2 400		Number of clubs	60
Youth under 18	3 500		Number of teams	140
Unregistered	1 000		Clubs with women's teams	2
Total players	10 700		Players as % of population	14.88%

Arubaanse Voetbal Bond (AVB)
Ferguson Street Z/N, PO Box 376, Oranjestad, Aruba
Tel +297 829550   Fax +297 829550
avbaruba@setarnet.aw   www.avbaruba.aw
President: KELLY Rufo   General Secretary: LACLE Egbert
Vice-President: FARO Bernardo   Treasurer: CROES Adrian   Media Officer: CROES Adrian
Men's Coach: MUNOZ Marcelo   Women's Coach: ENGELBRECHT Gregory
AVB formed: 1932   CONCACAF: 1961   FIFA: 1988
Yellow shirts, Blue shorts, Yellow and Blue socks

RECENT INTERNATIONALS PLAYED BY ARUBA

2002	Opponents	Score		Venue	Comp	Scorers	Att	Referee
28-07	Surinam	L	0-2	Oranjestad	CCq			Faneijte ANT
11-08	Surinam	L	0-6	Paramaribo	CCq		2 500	Mercera ANT
2003								
No international matches played in 2003								
2004								
28-01	Netherlands Antilles	L	1-6	Willemstad	Fr			
28-02	Surinam	L	1-2	Oranjestad	WCq	Escalona.M [89]	2 108	Moreno PAN
27-03	Surinam	L	1-8	Paramaribo	WCq	Escalona.M [24]	4 000	Prendergast JAM
2005								
No international matches played in 2005								
2006								
No international matches played in 2006								
2007								
No international matches played in 2007								

Fr = Friendly match • CC = Digicel Caribbean Cup • WCq = FIFA World Cup • q = qualifier

ARUBA NATIONAL TEAM RECORDS AND RECORD SEQUENCES

Records			Sequence records					
Victory	4-1	CUB 1953	Wins	1		Clean sheets	1	
Defeat	1-8	SUR 2004	Defeats	11	1953-1996	Goals scored	9	1944-1953
Player Caps	n/a		Undefeated	3	1944-1953	Without goal	5	1991-1992
Player Goals	n/a		Without win	12	1953-1996	Goals against	24	1934-1997

ARUBA 2006-07 DIVISION DI HONOR

FIRST ROUND

	Pl	W	D	L	F	A	Pts
Britannia †	18	15	2	1	65	20	47
Racing Club Aruba †	18	13	3	2	41	5	42
Nacional †	18	9	5	4	53	17	32
La Fama †	18	8	7	3	49	18	31
Dakota	18	7	4	7	44	29	25
Estrella	18	7	4	7	39	38	25
Independiente Caravel	18	4	4	10	31	40	16
Jong Aruba	18	5	1	12	20	70	16
Caiquetio	18	3	3	12	27	63	12
Juventud T'ki Leendert	18	2	1	15	16	85	7

† Qualified for the play-offs

PLAY-OFFS

	Pl	W	D	L	F	A	Pts
Racing Club Aruba ‡	6	3	2	1	8	3	11
Nacional ‡	6	3	2	1	6	4	11
Britannia	6	2	3	1	12	7	9
La Fama	6	0	1	5	2	14	1

‡ Qualified for the final

FINAL

Nacional 1-0 0-4 1-0 Racing Club Aruba
15/09/2006 - 9/06/2007

RECENT LEAGUE AND CUP RECORD

	Championship		
Year	Champions	Score	Runners-up
1998	Estrella	2-1	Dakota
1999	Estrella	2-1	Nacional
2000	Nacional	1-1 1-1 1-0	Dakota
2001	Nacional	3-1 1-0	Racing Club
2002	Racing Club	†	Nacional
2003	Nacional	1-0 2-1	Estrella
2004	No tournament due to season readjustment		
2005	Britannia	2-1 1-0	Racing Club
2006	Estrella	1-0 1-4 2-1	Britannia
2007	Nacional	1-0 0-4 1-0	Racing Club

† Played on a league basis

ARUBA COUNTRY INFORMATION

Capital	Oranjestad	Independence	Part of the Netherlands with	GDP per Capita	$28 000
Population	71 218	Status	autonomy in internal affairs	GNP Ranking	n/a
Area km²	193	Language	Dutch	Dialling code	+297
Population density	369 per km²	Literacy rate	97%	Internet code	.aw
% in urban areas	n/a	Main religion	Christian 90%	GMT + / –	-5
Towns/Cities ('000)	Oranjestad 29; Sint Nicolaas 17; Druif; Santa Cruz; Barcadera;				
Neighbours (km)	Caribbean Sea 68				
Main stadia	Guillermo Trinidad – Oranjestad 5 500				

ASA – AMERICAN SAMOA

NATIONAL TEAM RECORD
JULY 10TH 2006 TO JULY 12TH 2010

PL	W	D	L	F	A	%
0	0	0	0	0	0	0

FIFA/COCA-COLA WORLD RANKING

1993	1994	1995	1996	1997	1998	1999	2000	2001	2002	2003	2004	2005	2006	High	Low
-	-	-	-	-	193	199	203	201	201	202	204	205	198	**192** 10/98	**205** 12/05

2006–2007											
08/06	09/06	10/06	11/06	12/06	01/07	02/07	03/07	04/07	05/07	06/07	07/07
197	198	198	198	198	199	199	199	199	199	199	199

Rarely have the football activities of a nation relied so heavily on the benefits brought about by the FIFA Goal program but without the construction of Pago Park, the game in American Samoa would have been left in the wilderness. Football had all but ground to a halt in the country, but with the completion of Pago Park in mid 2007 the country now has a first class facility to improve the standard of the game. The Football Association relocated from their temporary office in Tafuna to Pago Park and they will oversee a number of training and development courses to be held at the new technical centre at Pago Park. Perhaps more importantly, American Samoa now has its first

INTERNATIONAL HONOURS
None

dedicated football field. The lack of a suitable pitch has meant there has been no championship for the past three years but the plans for the future include the staging of the Youth Summer League as the first event, followed by the National League club competition for both men's and women's teams. Equally important will be the ability to develop national teams at all levels to try and avoid the heavy defeats handed out at international competitions in the past. Phase two of the project will involve the refurbishment of the grandstand at Pago Park and the extension of the technical centre to include accommodation for players.

THE FIFA BIG COUNT OF 2006

	Male	Female		Total
Number of players	2 406	842	Referees and Assistant Referees	102
Professionals	0		Admin, Coaches, Technical, Medical	135
Amateurs 18+	810		Number of clubs	27
Youth under 18	1 000		Number of teams	33
Unregistered	410		Clubs with women's teams	6
Total players	3 248		Players as % of population	5.62%

American Samoa Football Association (ASFA)
ASFA Normalisation Committee, PO Box 999413, Pago Pago, American Samoa
Tel +684 6998160   Fax +689 6998161
asfa@blueskynet.as   www.asfa.as
President: SUPAPO Pou   General Secretary: TBC
Vice-President: TBC   Treasurer: TBC   Media Officer: None
Men's Coach: None   Women's Coach: None
ASFA formed: 1984   OFC: 1994   FIFA: 1998
Navy blue shirts, White shorts, Red socks

RECENT INTERNATIONALS PLAYED BY AMERICAN SAMOA

2002	Opponents	Score	Venue	Comp	Scorers	Att	Referee
No international matches played in 2002							
2003							
No international matches played in 2003							
2004							
10-05	Samoa	L 0-4	Apia	WCq		500	Afu SOL
12-05	Vanuatu	L 1-9	Apia	WCq	Natia 39	400	Fox NZL
15-05	Fiji	L 0-11	Apia	WCq		300	Fox NZL
17-05	Papua New Guinea	L 0-10	Apia	WCq		150	Afu SOL
2005							
No international matches played in 2005							
2006							
No international matches played in 2006							
No international matches played in 2007 before August							

WC = FIFA World Cup • q = qualifier

AMERICAN SAMOA NATIONAL TEAM RECORDS AND RECORD SEQUENCES

Records			Sequence records					
Victory	3-0	Wallis/Futuna 1983	Wins	1		Clean sheets	1	
Defeat	0-31	AUS 2001	Defeats	28	1983-	Goals scored	3	1983, 1994
Player Caps	n/a		Undefeated	1		Without goal	5	2001-2002
Player Goals	n/a		Without win	28	1983-	Goals against	28	1983-

RECENT LEAGUE AND CUP RECORD

	Championship	Cup
Year	Champions	Winners
1996	No tournament held	No tournament held
1997	Fat Boys	No tournament held
1998	No tournament held	No tournament held
1999	Konica Machine	No tournament held
2000	PanSa & Wild Wild West	No tournament held
2001	PanSa	No tournament held
2002	PanSa	No tournament held
2003	No tournament held	No tournament held
2004	PanSa	No tournament held
2005	No tournament held	No tournament held
2006	No tournament held	No tournament held
2007	No tournament held	No tournament held

AMERICAN SAMOA COUNTRY INFORMATION

Capital	Pago Pago	Independence	Unincorporated territory of the USA	GDP per Capita	$8 000
Population	57 902	Status		GNP Ranking	n/a
Area km²	199	Language	Samoan	Dialling code	+684
Population density	291 per km²	Literacy rate	97%	Internet code	.as
% in urban areas	n/a	Main religion	Christian	GMT +/−	-10
Towns/Cities ('000)	Tafuna 11; Nu'uuli 5; Pago Pago 4; Leone 4; Faleniu 3; Ili'ili 3				
Neighbours (km)	South Pacific Ocean 116				
Main stadia	Veterans Memorial – Pago Pago 10 000				

ATG – ANTIGUA AND BARBUDA

NATIONAL TEAM RECORD
JULY 10TH 2006 TO JULY 12TH 2010

PL	W	D	L	F	A	%
10	4	2	4	13	20	50

FIFA/COCA-COLA WORLD RANKING

1993	1994	1995	1996	1997	1998	1999	2000	2001	2002	2003	2004	2005	2006	High	Low
117	136	137	145	159	137	147	144	157	155	170	153	154	132	**109** 10/06	**170** 01/04

					2006–2007						
08/06	09/06	10/06	11/06	12/06	01/07	02/07	03/07	04/07	05/07	06/07	07/07
146	127	109	126	132	137	138	130	125	126	129	131

An unusually busy season for football in Antigua saw the national team competing in the Digicel Caribbean Cup and both Sap and Hoppers taking part in the Caribbean Championship. Having been knocked out in the first round group of the 2005 Caribbean Cup, Antigua went one stage further in the 2007 tournament, finishing second behind Barbados in the qualifying group that they hosted. The goals of 'Big Pete' Byers played a part in the upturn in fortunes, but there was nothing former Northern Ireland manager Bryan Hamilton, drafted in as a Technical Director to the ABFA, could do to help the side in the second round group at the end of 2006 as Antigua came away from

INTERNATIONAL HONOURS
None

Guyana without a point. The overall record for the season was encouraging, however, and the three straight wins at the start of the season equalled their record, whilst the run of scoring in nine consecutive matches set a new record. At home, Bassa were unrivalled in the League, winning 15 of their 18 matches and ending the season unbeaten with striker Ranjae Christian topping the scoring charts with 15 goals. 2006 Champions Sap won two games in their Caribbean Championship first round group in St Thomas, but they finished second behind Trinidad's San Juan Jabloteh and were knocked out. Hoppers finished bottom of their first round group in Puerto Rico.

THE FIFA BIG COUNT OF 2006

	Male	Female		Total
Number of players	6 000	600	Referees and Assistant Referees	33
Professionals	0		Admin, Coaches, Technical, Medical	100
Amateurs 18+	1 100		Number of clubs	20
Youth under 18	1 100		Number of teams	60
Unregistered	800		Clubs with women's teams	1
Total players	6 600		Players as % of population	9.55%

Antigua and Barbuda Football Association (ABFA)
Suite 19, Vendors Mall, PO Box 773, St John's, Antigua
Tel +1 268 5626012   Fax +1 268 5626016
abfa@candw.ag   www.antiguafootball.org
President: RICHARDS Mervyn   General Secretary: DERRICK Gordon
Vice-President: GATESWORTH James   Treasurer: GARDNER Dwight   Media Officer: RAYNE Joel
Men's Coach: EDWARDS Derrick   Women's Coach: BROWN Chesley
ABFA formed: 1928   CONCACAF: 1980   FIFA: 1970
Red shirts with black, yellow and white trimmings, Black shorts, Black socks

RECENT INTERNATIONALS PLAYED BY ANTIGUA AND BARBUDA

2004	Opponents	Score	Venue	Comp	Scorers	Att	Referee
2-11	Montserrat	W 5-4	Basseterre	CCq	OG [30], Frederick [53], Gonsalves [67 82], Thomas [72]		Phillip GRN
4-11	St Kitts and Nevis	L 0-2	Basseterre	CCq			Phillip GRN
6-11	St Lucia	L 1-2	Basseterre	CCq	Dublin [65]		Bedeau GRN
2005							
12-01	Trinidad and Tobago	W 2-1	St John's	Fr	Byers [48], Isaac [57]	2 000	
6-02	Barbados	L 2-3	Bridgetown	Fr	Thomas [2], Byers [74]	4 000	
18-12	Hungary	L 0-3	Fort Lauderdale	Fr			
2006							
24-02	Guyana	L 1-2	Linden	Fr	Skepples [77]		James GUY
26-02	Guyana	L 1-4	Georgetown	Fr	Julian [76]		Lancaster GUY
27-08	St Vincent/Grenadines	W 1-0	St John's	Fr	Thomas.T [18]		Willett ATG
3-09	Dominica	W 1-0	St John's	Fr	Byers.P [50]		Willett ATG
20-09	Anguilla	W 5-3	St John's	CCq	Byers.P 3 [8p 16 71], Thomas.T [29], Thomas.J [90]	300	Wijngaarde SUR
22-09	Barbados	L 1-3	St John's	CCq	Byers.P [16]	2 500	Frederick VIR
24-09	St Kitts and Nevis	W 1-0	St John's	CCq	Gregory [77]	2 800	Wijngaarde SUR
3-11	Grenada	D 1-1	Kingstown	Fr	Simon.T		
5-11	St Vincent/Grenadines	D 2-2	Kingstown	Fr	Byers.P 2 [8 21p]		
24-11	Guyana	L 0-6	Georgetown	CCq		5 000	
26-11	Dominican Republic	L 0-2	Georgetown	CCq			
28-11	Guadeloupe	L 1-3	Georgetown	CCq	Gregory [45]		Davis TRI
2007							

No international matches played in 2007 before July

Fr = Friendly match • CC = Digicel Caribbean Cup • WC = FIFA World Cup • q = qualifier

ANTIGUA AND BARBUDA NATIONAL TEAM RECORDS AND RECORD SEQUENCES

Records			Sequence records					
Victory	8-0	MSR 1994	Wins	3	Four times	Clean sheets	3	1992, 1999
Defeat	1-11	TRI 1972	Defeats	7	1972-1984	Goals scored	9	2006
Player Caps	n/a		Undefeated	6	2000	Without goal	3	1990, 2003
Player Goals	n/a		Without win	8	2002-2003	Goals against	12	2000-2001

ANTIGUA AND BARBUDA 2006-07 PREMIER LEAGUE

	Pl	W	D	L	F	A	Pts
Bassa	18	15	3	0	42	12	48
Sap	18	9	5	4	35	20	32
Hoppers	18	7	5	6	18	17	26
Freemansville	18	6	7	5	22	20	25
Villa Lions	18	6	5	7	18	18	23
Parham	18	6	4	8	25	24	22
Liberta	18	6	4	8	19	29	22
Empire	18	6	3	9	21	30	21
Sea View Farm	18	3	7	8	17	27	16
Old Road	18	3	3	12	17	37	12

29/09/2006 - 25/02/2007

RECENT LEAGUE RECORD

	Championship					
Year	Champions	Pts	Runners-up	Pts	Third	Pts
1998	Empire	32	English Harbour	29	Sap	29
1999	Empire		Parham			
2000	Empire	2-0	English Harbour			
2001	Empire	58	Bassa	37	Sap	33
2002	Parham	57	Empire	53	Sap	37
2003	Parham	38	Sap	37	Hoppers	35
2004	Bassa	34	Sap	28	Parham	23
2005	Bassa	43	Hoppers	43	Empire	39
2006	Sap	42	Hoppers	35	Bassa	34
2007	Bassa	48	Sap	32	Hoppers	26

ANTIGUA AND BARBUDA COUNTRY INFORMATION

Capital	St John's	Independence	1981	GDP per Capita	$11 000
Population	68 320	Status	Commonwealth	GNP Ranking	164
Area km²	443	Language	English	Dialling code	+1 268
Population density	154 per km²	Literacy rate	95%	Internet code	.ag
% in urban areas	36%	Main religion	Christian 96%	GMT +/–	-4.5
Towns/Cities ('000)	St John's 25; All Saints 2; Liberta 1; Potters Village 1				
Neighbours (km)	Caribbean Sea & North Atlantic Ocean 153				
Main stadia	Recreation Ground – St John's 18 000; Police Ground – St George's 3 000				

AUS – AUSTRALIA

AUSTRALIA NATIONAL TEAM RECORD
JULY 10TH 2006 TO JULY 12TH 2010

PL	W	D	L	F	A	%
13	5	4	4	20	14	53.8

In the aftermath of a successful FIFA World Cup, it was always likely to be a good year for football in Australia and so it proved to be. Most encouraging was the progress of the Hyundai A-League which has managed to establish itself into the mainstream of Australian sport in just two years. Twice in the 2006-07 season, Melbourne Victory beat the attendance record for domestic football in Australia - in round 16 the first crowd of over 50,000 turned up at the Telstra Dome to watch the match against Sydney, whilst 55,436 turned up at the same venue for the Grand Final against Adelaide United. Having won 11 of their first 13 games, Victory were always going to be the team to beat and they proved that in emphatic fashion with a 6-0 thrashing of Adelaide in the final. Archie Thompson, who once scored 13 goals in a FIFA World Cup qualifier against American Samoa, scored five times as the season ended in spectacular fashion. The Grand Final was headline news in Australia even while the cricket team was in the grip of an Ashes series against England and the Australian Open tennis was taking place in Melbourne, a testament to the growing popularity of football in the country. With Australia now settled into the Asian Football

INTERNATIONAL HONOURS
Qualified for the FIFA World Cup 1974 2006
Oceania Nations Cup 1980 1996 2000 2004   **Oceania Women's Championship** 1995 1998 2003
Oceania Youth Cup 1978 1982 1985 1987 1988 1990 1994 1996 1998 2001 2003
Oceania U-17 1983 1986 1989 1991 1993 1995 1999 2001 2003
Oceania Champions Cup Adelaide City 1987, South Melbourne 1999, Wollongong Wolves 2001, Sydney FC 2005

Confederation, Adelaide United had to pick themselves up from their humiliation in the final to take part, along with Sydney FC, in the Asian Champions League. Both teams had qualified a whole year earlier and had Victory taken part there may have been more success to boast about after both failed to get past the group stage. Sydney came closest but could not beat Japan's Urawa Reds on the final day and had to settle for second place. The national team also made its debut in Asian football by qualifying for the AFC Asian Cup finals ahead of Bahrain and Kuwait in their qualifying group. Based in Bangkok for the finals, the Socceroos with their team of European based stars were clearly taken by surprise in their first two matches. It took a last gasp goal from Tim Cahill to secure a draw against Oman in their opening match whilst they were soundly beaten by Iraq in their second. That left a win-at-all-costs match against hosts Thailand and thanks to three goals in the last ten minutes - two from Mark Viduka and one from Harry Kewell, Australia managed to avoid the embarrassment of a first round exit. Their campaign ended in the quarter-finals, however, when after drawing with defending champions Japan, they lost 4-2 on penalties.

Football Federation Australia Limited (FFA)
Suite 701 Level 7, 26 College Street, Locked Bag A4071, Sydney South, NSW 2000 1235, Australia
Tel +61 2 83545555   Fax +61 2 83545590
info@footballaustralia.com.au   www.footballaustralia.com.au
President: LOWY Frank   General Secretary: BUCKLEY Ben
Vice-President: SCHWARTZ Brian   Treasurer: TBD   Media Officers: HODGE Stuart
Men's Coach: ARNOLD Graham   Women's Coach: TBD
FFA formed: 1961   OFC: 1966-72 & 1978-2005   AFC: 2006   FIFA: 1963
Yellow shirts with green trimmings, Green shorts, Yellow socks

RECENT INTERNATIONALS PLAYED BY AUSTRALIA

2004 Opponents	Score	Venue	Comp	Scorers	Att	Referee
9-10 Solomon Islands	W 5-1	Honaria	OCf	Skoko 2 [5 28], Milicic [19], Emerton [44], Elrich [79]	21 000	O'Leary NZL
12-10 Solomon Islands	W 6-0	Sydney	OCf	Milicic [5], Kewell [9], Vidmar.T [60], Thompson [79] Elrich [80], Emerton [89]	19 208	Rakaroi FIJ
16-11 Norway	D 2-2	London	Fr	Cahill [45], Skoko [58]	7 364	Styles ENG
2005						
9-02 South Africa	D 1-1	Durban	Fr	Chipperfield [70]	25 000	Lim Kee Chong MRI
26-03 Iraq	W 2-1	Sydney	Fr	Bresciano [22], Elrich [72]	30 258	O'Leary NZL
29-03 Indonesia	W 3-0	Perth	Fr	Milicic 2 [25 57], Zdrilic [85]	13 719	Yamanishi JPN
9-06 New Zealand	W 1-0	London	Fr	Colosimo [86]	9 023	Dean ENG
15-06 Germany	L 3-4	Frankfurt	CCr1	Skoko [21], Aloisi 2 [31 92+]	46 466	Amarilla PAR
18-06 Argentina	L 2-4	Nürnberg	CCr1	Aloisi 2 [61p 70]	25 618	Maidin SIN
21-06 Tunisia	L 0-2	Leipzig	CCr1		23 952	Chandia CHI
3-09 Solomon Islands	W 7-0	Sydney	WCq	Culina [20], Viduka 2 [36 43], Cahill [57], Chipperfield [64], Thompson [68], Emerton [89]	16 000	Mohd Salleh MAS
6-09 Solomon Islands	W 2-1	Honiara	WCq	Thompson [19], Emerton [58]	16 000	Maidin SIN
9-10 Jamaica	W 5-0	London	Fr	Bresciano [2], Thompson [27], Viduka [47], Aloisi [59], Griffiths [84]	6 570	Riley ENG
12-11 Uruguay	L 0-1	Montevideo	WCpo		55 000	Larsen DEN
16-11 Uruguay	W 1-0	Sydney	WCpo	Bresciano [35], W 4-2p	82 698	Medina Cantalejo ESP
2006						
22-02 Bahrain	W 3-1	Manama	ACq	Thompson [53], Skoko [79], Elrich [87p]	2 500	Mohd Salleh MAS
25-05 Greece	W 1-0	Melbourne	Fr	Skoko [16]	95 103	Riley ENG
4-06 Netherlands	D 1-1	Rotterdam	Fr	Cahill [41]	49 000	Dean ENG
7-06 Liechtenstein	W 3-1	Ulm	Fr	Sterjovski [19], Kennedy [74], Aloisi [82]	5 872	Star GER
12-06 Japan	W 3-1	Kaiserslautern	WCr1	Cahill 2 [84 89], Aloisi [92+]	46 000	Abd El Fatah EGY
18-06 Brazil	L 0-2	Munich	WCr1		66 000	Merk GER
22-06 Croatia	D 2-2	Stuttgart	WCr1	Moore [38p], Kewell [79]	52 000	Poll ENG
26-06 Italy	L 0-1	Kaiserslautern	WCr2		46 000	Medina Cantalejo ESP
16-08 Kuwait	W 2-0	Sydney	ACq	Dodd [75], Petrovski [86]	32 000	Huang Junje CHN
6-09 Kuwait	L 0-2	Kuwait City	ACq		8 000	Kamikawa JPN
7-10 Paraguay	D 1-1	Brisbane	Fr	Popovic [88]	47 609	Kashihara JPN
11-10 Bahrain	W 2-0	Sydney	ACq	Aloisi [17], Bresciano [23]	37 000	Al Marzouqi UAE
14-11 Ghana	D 1-1	London	Fr	Aloisi [25p]	14 379	Clattenburg ENG
2007						
6-02 Denmark	L 1-3	London	Fr	Emerton [85]	12 476	Styles ENG
24-03 China PR	W 2-0	Guangzhou	Fr	Holman [8], Bresciano [27]	20 000	Wu Chaojue HKG
2-06 Uruguay	L 1-2	Sydney	Fr	Sterjovski [6]	61 795	Rosetti ITA
30-06 Singapore	W 3-0	Singapore	Fr	Viduka 2 [52 89], Kewell [77]		Iemoto JPN
8-07 Oman	D 1-1	Bangkok	ACr1	Cahill [90]	5 000	Mailett SEY
13-07 Iraq	L 1-3	Bangkok	ACr1	Viduka [47]	7 884	Karim BHR
16-07 Thailand	W 4-0	Bangkok	ACr1	Beauchamp [21], Viduka 2 [80 83], Kewell [90]	46 000	Kwon Jong Chul KOR
21-07 Japan	D 1-1	Hanoi	ACqf	Aloisi [69]	25 000	Al Fadhli KUW

Fr = Friendly match • OC = OFC Oceania Nations Cup • CC = FIFA Confederations Cup • AC = AFC Asian Cup • WC = FIFA World Cup
q = qualifier • r1 = first round group • sf = semi-final • f = final

AUSTRALIA NATIONAL TEAM RECORDS AND RECORD SEQUENCES

Records			Sequence records					
Victory	31-0	ASA 2001	Wins	14	1996-1997	Clean sheets	6	2000, 2001
Defeat	0-8	RSA 1955	Defeats	5	1955	Goals scored	31	1924-1954
Player Caps	87	TOBIN Alex	Undefeated	20	1996-1997	Without goal	4	Three times
Player Goals	29	MORI Damian	Without win	6	Five times	Goals against	11	1936-1947

COMMONWEALTH OF AUSTRALIA

Capital	Canberra	Language	English	Independence	1901
Population	20 264 082	Area	7 686 850	% in cities	85%
GDP per cap	$29 000	Dailling code	+61	Density	2 per km²
			Internet	.au	GMT + / -	+10

MAJOR CITIES/TOWNS

		Population '000
1	Sydney	4 444
2	Melbourne	3 780
3	Brisbane	1 891
4	Perth	1 472
5	Adelaide	1 076
6	Gold Coast	523
7	Newcastle	500
8	Sunshine Coast	332
9	Canberra	324
10	Wollongong	261
11	Hobart	206
12	Cairns	161
13	Geelong	151
14	Townsville	141
15	Albury	109
16	Shoalhaven	97
17	Toowoomba	93
18	Darwin	93
19	Ballarat	85
20	Bendigo	82
21	Mandurah	79
22	Mackay	77
23	Launceston	73
24	Rockhampton	66

MEDALS TABLE

A-League teams in bold • ST = State Championship

		Overall			League			Cup		CL	ST	City	Stadium	Cap'ty	DoF
		G	S	B	G	S	B	G	S	G	G				
1	Sydney City	7	4	1	4	3	1	3	1		5	Sydney	Sydney Athletic Field	15 000	1939
2	South Melbourne	7	3	2	4	2	2	2	1	1	7	Melbourne	Bob Jane Stadium	14 000	1959
3	Adelaide City	7	3		3	2		3	1	1	12	Adelaide	Ram Park	3 000	1946
4	Marconi Stallions	5	6		4	3		1	3			Sydney	Marconi Stadium	11 500	1956
5	Sydney Olympic	4	6		2	4		2	2			Sydney	Belmore Sports Ground	11 500	1957
6	APIA Leichhardt Tigers	4	3		1			3	3		4	Sydney	Lambert Park	7 000	1954
7	Melbourne Knights	3	4		2	3		1	1		1	Melbourne	Somers Street	15 000	1953
8	Wollongong City Wolves	3		1	2		1				1	Wollongong	WIN Stadium	18 500	1980
9	Heidelberg United	2	6	1		2	1	2	4		1	Melbourne	Olympic Village	10 000	1958
10	**Perth Glory**	2	2		2	2						Perth	Members Equity Stadium	18 450	1996
11	Parramatta Eagles	2	1					2	1			Sydney	Melita Stadium	10 000	1956
12	Brisbane City	2		1			1	2				Brisbane	Spencer Park	3 000	1952
13	**Sydney FC**	2			1						1	Sydney	Aussie Stadium	41 159	2004
14	Sydney United	1	4			3		1	1			Sydney	King Tom	12 000	1957
15	St George Saints	1	3	1	1	1	1		2		3	Sydney	St George Stadium	2 500	1957
16	West Adelaide	1	2		1				2		7	Adelaide	Hindmarsh	16 500	1961-99
17	Brunswick	1	1		1				1		7	Melbourne			1948
	Newcastle Jets	1	1					1	1			Newcastle	Energy Australia Stadium	26 164	2000
19	Brisbane Lions	1						1				Brisbane			
	Brisbane Strikers	1			1							Brisbane	Perry Park	10 000	
	George Cross	1						1				Melbourne			
	Melbourne HSC	1						1				Melbourne			
	Melbourne Victory	1			1							Melbourne	Telstra Dome	53 355	2004
	Slavia Melbourne	1						1				Melbourne			
	SSC Yugal	1						1				Sydney			
26	Preston Lions		3	1		1	1	2				Melbourne	BT Connor Reserve	8 000	1947
27	**Adelaide United**		1			1						Adelaide	Hindmarsh Stadium	16 500	2003
	Central Coast Mariners		1			1						Gosford	Central Coast Stadium	20 059	2004
29	**Queensland Roar**											Brisbane	Suncorp Stadium	52 579	2005

RECENT LEAGUE RECORD

A–League Regular Season						Grand Final		
Year First	Pts	Second	Pts	Third	Pts	Champions	Score	Runners-up
2006 Adelaide United	43	Sydney FC	36	Central Coast Mar's	32	Sydney FC	1-0	Central Coast Mar's
2007 Melbourne Victory	45	Adelaide United	33	Newcastle Utd Jets	30	Melbourne Victory	6-0	Adelaide United

AUSTRALIA 2005–06

HYUNDAI A-LEAGUE

	Pl	W	D	L	F	A	Pts	Victory	Adelaide	Jets	Sydney	Roar	Mariners	Glory	Knights
Melbourne Victory †	21	14	3	4	41	20	45		2-0 0-1	0-1	3-2 0-0	4-1 1-2	1-0 3-3	1-0	4-0
Adelaide United †	21	10	3	8	32	27	33	1-3		5-1 3-2	1-4 1-0	0-1	3-1	3-0 3-2	4-2 1-1
Newcastle United Jets ‡	21	8	6	7	32	30	30	0-2 4-0	2-1		1-1 0-2	2-3	3-1 1-0	0-3	3-0
Sydney FC §3 ‡	21	8	8	5	29	19	29	1-2	2-1	2-2		1-1 3-0	1-0	1-1 1-0	4-0 0-1
Queensland Roar	21	8	5	8	25	27	29	0-2	0-0 0-1	0-1 0-3	1-1		1-1	3-0 1-0	5-0
Central Coast Mariners	21	6	6	9	22	26	24	1-2	2-0 1-3	1-1	3-1 0-0	0-0 2-3		2-1 1-0	0-0
Perth Glory	21	5	5	11	24	30	20	1-2 2-2	0-0	2-1 3-3	1-1	1-2	2-0		1-0 4-1
New Zealand Knights	21	5	4	12	13	39	19	0-3 0-4	1-0	0-0 1-1	0-1	1-0 3-1	0-1 0-2	2-0	

25/08/2006 - 21/01/2007 • † Qualified for the Major Semi-final • ‡ Qualified for the Minor Semi-final • § = points deducted

A-LEAGUE PLAY-OFFS

Major Semi-final

Melbourne Victory	0	2
Adelaide United	0	1

Grand Final

Melbourne Victory	6
Adelaide United	0

Preliminary Final

Newcastle Jets	1 3p
Adelaide United	1 4p

Minor Semi-final

Sydney FC	2	0
Newcastle Jets	1	2

26/01/2007 - 18/02/2007 • The loser of the Major Semi-final meets the winner of the Minor Semi-final in the Preliminary Final

GRAND FINAL 2007

Telstra Dome, Melbourne, 18-02-2007, 18.00, Att: 55 436, Ref: Shield

Melbourne Victory   6   Thompson 5 [21 29 40 56 73], Sarkies [91+]

Adelaide United   0

Victory - Michael THEOKLITOS - Steve PANTELIDIS, Rodrigo VARGAS, Adrian LEIJER - Simon STOREY, Kevin MUSCAT, Grant BREBNER (Leigh BROXHAM 59), FRED•, Adrian CACERES (James ROBINSON 62) - Danny ALLSOPP, Archie THOMPSON (Kristian SARKIES 90). Tr: Ernie MERRICK
United - Daniel BELTRAME - Richie ALAGICH (Jason Spagnulo 70), Michael VALKANIS•, Carl VEART• - Travis DODD, Angelo COSTANZO•, Diego WALSH, Ross ALOISI••●34, FERNANDO (Bruce DJITE 59) - Greg OWENS (Aaron GOULDING 46), Nathan BURNS. Tr: John KOSMINA

FIFA/COCA-COLA WORLD RANKING

1993	1994	1995	1996	1997	1998	1999	2000	2001	2002	2003	2004	2005	2006	High		Low	
49	58	51	50	35	39	89	73	48	50	82	58	48	39	31	07/97	92	06/00

	2006–2007											
08/06	09/06	10/06	11/06	12/06	01/07	02/07	03/07	04/07	05/07	06/07	07/07	
37	38	37	39	39	39	39	40	43	42	48	49	

THE FIFA BIG COUNT OF 2006

	Male	Female		Total
Number of players	781 246	189482	Referees and Assistant Referees	8 650
Professionals	200		Admin, Coaches, Technical, Medical	58 982
Amateurs 18+	107 013		Number of clubs	2 316
Youth under 18	299 775		Number of teams	20 018
Unregistered	338 000		Clubs with women's teams	1 552
Total players	970 728		Players as % of population	4.79%

MELBOURNE VICTORY 2006–07

Date	Opponents		Score		Comp	Scorers	
25-08-2006	Adelaide United	W	2-0	H	HAL	Muscat [29p], Claudinho [78]	15 781
2-09-2006	Sydney FC	W	3-2	H	HAL	Allsopp 2 [8 51], Muscat [11p]	39 730
10-09-2006	New Zealand Knights	W	3-0	A	HAL	Allsopp [9], Thompson [22], Muscat [35]	2 107
17-09-2007	Central Coast Mariners	W	1-0	H	HAL	Thompson [51]	17 617
24-09-2007	Perth Glory	W	2-1	A	HAL	Caceres [55], Muscat [72p]	7 983
1-10-2006	Queensland Roar	W	4-1	H	HAL	Fred [11], Muscat 2 [22p 57p], McCloughan OG [82]	25 921
8-10-2006	Newcastle Jets	W	2-0	A	HAL	Allsopp 2 [69 90]	4 635
15-10-2006	Adelaide United	L	0-1	H	HAL		32 368
21-10-2006	Sydney FC	W	2-1	A	HAL	Thompson 2 [50 73]	20 881
27-10-2006	New Zealand Knights	W	4-0	A	HAL	Fred [8], Thompson [57], Caceres [59], Allsopp [72]	2 357
3-11-2006	Central Coast Mariners	D	3-3	H	HAL	Allsopp 2 [4 86], Thompson [10]	28 118
9-11-2006	Perth Glory	W	1-0	H	HAL	Brebner [88]	22 890
17-11-2006	Queensland Roar	W	2-0	A	HAL	Packer OG [18], Thompson [46]	14 797
26-11-2006	Newcastle Jets	L	0-1	H	HAL		27 753
1-12-2006	Adelaide United	W	3-1	A	HAL	Muscat [16p], Allsopp [61], Fred [86]	16 378
8-12-2006	Sydney FC	D	0-0	H	HAL		50 333
17-12-2006	New Zealand Knights	W	4-0	H	HAL	Allsopp 2 [35 45], Caceres [39], Thompson [48+]	15 563
31-12-2006	Central Coast Mariners	W	2-1	A	HAL	Fred [23], Thompson [26]	15 404
7-01-2007	Perth Glory	D	2-2	H	HAL	Sarkies 2 [58 76]	6 462
12-01-2007	Queensland Roar	L	1-2	H	HAL	Thompson [79]	28 937
19-01-2007	Newcastle Jets	L	0-4	A	HAL		19 601
28-01-2007	Adelaide United	D	0-0	A	HALsf		15 575
4-02-2007	Adelaide United	W	2-1	H	HALsf	Allsopp [48], Robinson [92+]	47 413
18-02-2007	Adelaide United	W	6-0	H	HALf	Thompson 5 [20 29 39 56 72], Sarkies [93+]	55 436

HAL = Hyundai A-League • sf = semi-final • f = final

ADELAIDE UNITED 2006–07

Date	Opponents		Score		Comp	Scorers	
25-08-2006	Melbourne Victory	L	0-2	A	HAL		15 781
2-09-2006	New Zealand Knights	L	0-1	A	HAL		4 100
8-09-2006	Newcastle Jets	W	5-1	H	HAL	Fernando 2 [8 73], Cornthwaite [19], Qu [27], Durante OG [65]	8 785
16-09-2006	Perth Glory	W	3-0	H	HAL	Fernando [14], Dodd [34], Coyne OG [50]	11 474
22-09-2006	Queensland Roar	D	0-0	A	HAL		16 143
2-10-2006	Sydney FC	L	1-4	H	HAL	Burns [54]	15 119
6-10-2006	Central Coast Mariners	W	3-1	A	HAL	Veart [25], Rees [58], Burns [91+]	10 493
15-10-2006	Melbourne Victory	W	1-0	A	HAL	Owens [82]	32 368
22-10-2006	New Zealand Knights	W	4-2	H	HAL	Burns [23], Veart [35], Petta [56], Dodd [84]	11 600
27-10-2006	Newcastle Jets	L	1-2	A	HAL	Veart [37p]	10 895
5-11-2006	Perth Glory	W	3-2	A	HAL	Veart [16p], Owens [24], Kemp [57]	11 032
11-11-2006	Queensland Roar	W	1-0	H	HAL	Dodd [62]	14 154
19-11-2006	Sydney FC	L	1-2	A	HAL	Aloisi.R [9]	14 308
25-11-2006	Central Coast Mariners	L	0-2	A	HAL		13 119
1-12-2006	Melbourne Victory	L	1-3	H	HAL	Fernando [42]	16 378
10-12-2006	New Zealand Knights	D	1-1	H	HAL	Owens [72]	11 548
15-12-2006	Newcastle Jets	W	3-2	H	HAL	Romario [15], Fernando [60], Owens [78]	12 214
28-12-2006	Perth Glory	D	0-0	A	HAL		8 226
4-01-2007	Queensland Roar	L	0-1	H	HAL		10 435
14-01-2007	Sydney FC	W	1-0	H	HAL	Fernando [89]	14 704
21-01-2007	Central Coast Mariners	W	3-1	A	HAL	Burns 3 [10 49 66]	8 128
28-01-2007	Melbourne Victory	D	0-0	H	HALsf		15 575
4-02-2007	Melbourne Victory	L	1-2	A	HALsf	Dodd [4]	47 413
11-02-2007	Newcastle Jets	D	1-1	H	HALpf	Veart [57]. W 4-3 on pens	13 798
18-02-2007	Melbourne Victory	L	0-6	A	HALf		55 436
7-03-2007	Shandong Luneng - CHN	L	0-1	H	CLgG		7 645
21-03-2007	Gach Dong Tam Long An - VIE	W	2-0	A	CLgG	Fernando [18], Dodd [30]	10 460
11-04-2007	Seongnam Ilhwa Chunma - KOR	D	2-2	H	CLgG	Fernando [48], Djite [55]	9 093
25-04-2007	Seongnam Ilhwa Chunma - KOR	L	0-1	A	CLgG		30 000
9-05-2007	Shandong Luneng - CHN	D	2-2	A	CLgG	Fernando [36p], Burns [48]	30 000
23-05-2007	Gach Dong Tam Long An - VIE	W	3-0	H	CLgG	Dodd 3 [7 22 48]	6 917

HAL = Hyundai A-League • CL = AFC Champions League • gG = group G • sf = semi-final • pf = preliminary final • f = final

AUT – AUSTRIA

NATIONAL TEAM RECORD
JULY 10TH 2006 TO JULY 12TH 2010

PL	W	D	L	F	A	%
11	3	4	4	13	13	45.4

FIFA/COCA-COLA WORLD RANKING

1993	1994	1995	1996	1997	1998	1999	2000	2001	2002	2003	2004	2005	2006	High		Low	
36	49	39	34	25	22	28	44	56	65	67	83	69	65	17	05/99	90	09/04

2006–2007											
08/06	09/06	10/06	11/06	12/06	01/07	02/07	03/07	04/07	05/07	06/07	07/07
57	70	74	63	65	65	61	63	75	77	83	82

After failing to win the championship in the first year after buying Austria Salzburg, drinks magnate Dieter Mateschitz replaced coach Kurt Jara with the veteran Giovanni Trapattoni and Lothar Matthäus, a move that paid handsome dividends with a first championship in 10 years for the renamed Red Bull Salzburg. With internationals from around the world, Salzburg were a class above the rest and won the title with five games to spare. The insolvency of both Sturm Graz and Grazer AK, both champions in recent seasons, was a vivid illustration of how other teams will struggle to match Salzburg in the future if Mateschitz maintains his involvement. Both Salzburg

INTERNATIONAL HONOURS
Qualified for the FIFA World Cup™ 1934 1954 1958 1978 1982 1990 1998 International Cup 1932
FIFA Junior Tournament 1950 UEFA Junior Tournament 1957 Mitropa Cup SK Rapid 1930, First Vienna 1931, FK Austria 1933 1936

and the Salzburg amateur team made it to semi-finals of the Cup, but it was FK Austria Wien who won it - for the third year running - in a repeat of the previous year's final, against Mattersburg. The national team continued its preparations for the Euro 2008 finals with a series of friendly matches, but apart from a win over co-hosts Switzerland, there was very little for coach Josef Hickersberger to cheer about. Austrian fans will be hoping for a kind draw and vociferous home support to take them further than the group stage and if there was one ray of hope it was in the performance of the under 20 side that reached the semi-finals of the FIFA U–20 World Cup in Canada in July 2007.

THE FIFA BIG COUNT OF 2006

	Male	Female		Total
Number of players	912 580	54 701	Referees and Assistant Referees	2 302
Professionals	906		Admin, Coaches, Technical, Medical	390 500
Amateurs 18+	370 828		Number of clubs	2 211
Youth under 18	221 547		Number of teams	9 685
Unregistered	260 000		Clubs with women's teams	100
Total players	967 281		Players as % of population	11.81%

Osterreichischer Fussball-Bund (OFB)
Ernst Happel Stadion, Sektor A/F, Postfach 340, Meiereistrasse 7, Wien 1021, Austria
Tel +43 1 727180   Fax +43 1 7281632
office@oefb.at   www.oefb.at
President: STICKLER Friedrich   General Secretary: LUDWIG Alfred
Vice-President: EHRENBERGER Kurt   Treasurer: TALOS Rudolf   Media Officer: KLINGMUELLER Peter
Men's Coach: HICKERSBERGER Josef   Women's Coach: WEBER Ernst
OFB formed: 1904   UEFA: 1954   FIFA: 1907
Red shirts, White shorts, Red socks or White shirts, Black shorts, White socks

RECENT INTERNATIONALS PLAYED BY AUSTRIA

2002	Opponents	Score		Venue	Comp	Scorers	Att	Referee
21-08	Switzerland	L	2-3	Basle	Fr	Wallner 2 [11 81]	23 500	Rosetti ITA
7-09	Moldova	W	2-0	Vienna	ECq	Herzog 2 [4p 30p]	18 300	Dougal SCO
12-10	Belarus	W	2-0	Minsk	ECq	Schopp [57], Akagunduz [90]	15 000	Poulat FRA
16-10	Netherlands	L	0-3	Vienna	ECq		46 300	Collina ITA
20-11	Norway	L	0-1	Vienna	Fr		15 800	Abraham HUN
2003								
26-03	Greece	D	2-2	Graz	Fr	Schopp [52], Haas [81]	8 500	Ovrebo NOR
2-04	Czech Republic	L	0-4	Prague	ECq		20 000	Nieto ESP
30-04	Scotland	W	2-0	Glasgow	Fr	Kirchler [28], Haas [34]	12 189	Vollquartz DEN
7-06	Moldova	L	0-1	Tiraspol	ECq		10 000	Silva POR
11-06	Belarus	W	5-0	Innsbruck	ECq	Aufhauser [33], Haas [47], Kirchler [52], Wallner [62], Cerny [70]	8 100	Frojdfeldt SWE
20-08	Costa Rica	W	2-0	Vienna	Fr	Glieder [34p], Wallner [70]	16 000	Hamer LUX
6-09	Netherlands	L	1-3	Rotterdam	ECq	Pogatetz [34]	47 000	Poulat FRA
11-10	Czech Republic	L	2-3	Vienna	ECq	Haas [51], Ivanschitz [77]	32 350	Kasnaferis GRE
2004								
31-03	Slovakia	D	1-1	Bratislava	Fr	Kollmann [90]	4 500	Vidlak CZE
28-04	Luxembourg	W	4-1	Innsbruck	Fr	Kirchler [5], Kiesenebner [9], Haas [85], Kollmann [88]	9 400	Skomina SVN
25-05	Russia	D	0-0	Graz	Fr		9 600	Vuorela FIN
18-08	Germany	L	1-3	Vienna	Fr	Amerhauser [10]	37 900	Collina ITA
4-09	England	D	2-2	Vienna	WCq	Kollmann [71], Ivanschitz [72]	48 000	Lubos SVK
8-09	Azerbaijan	W	2-0	Vienna	WCq	Stranzl [23], Kollmann [44]	26 400	Sammut MLT
9-10	Poland	L	1-3	Vienna	WCq	Schopp [30]	46 100	Batista POR
13-10	Northern Ireland	D	3-3	Belfast	WCq	Schopp 2 [14 72], Mayrleb [59]	11 810	Shield AUS
2005								
8-02	Cyprus	D	1-1	Limassol	Fr	Kirchler [43]. L 4-5p	300	Hyytia FIN
9-02	Latvia	D	1-1	Limassol	Fr	Sariyar [41]	50	Theodotou CYP
26-03	Wales	W	2-0	Cardiff	WCq	Vastic [81], Stranzl [85]	47 760	Allaerts BEL
30-03	Wales	W	1-0	Vienna	WCq	Aufhauser [87]	29 500	Mejuto Gonzalez ESP
17-08	Scotland	D	2-2	Graz	Fr	Ibertsberger [83], Standfest [87]	13 800	Dereli TUR
3-09	Poland	L	2-3	Chorzow	WCq	Linz 2 [61 80]	40 000	De Santis ITA
7-09	Azerbaijan	D	0-0	Baku	WCq		2 800	Verbist BEL
8-10	England	L	0-1	Manchester	WCq		64 822	Medina Cantalejo ESP
12-10	Northern Ireland	W	2-0	Vienna	WCq	Aufhauser 2 [44 90]	12 500	Briakos GRE
2006								
1-03	Canada	L	0-2	Vienna	Fr		9 000	Van Egmond NED
23-05	Croatia	L	1-4	Vienna	Fr	Ivanschitz [14]	22 000	Fandel GER
16-08	Hungary	L	1-2	Graz	Fr	Kuljic [74]	11 000	Havrilla SVK
2-09	Costa Rica	D	2-2	Geneva	Fr	Linz 2 [36p 60]	300	Circhetta SUI
6-09	Venezuela	L	0-1	Basel	Fr		1 453	Bartolini SUI
6-10	Liechtenstein	W	2-1	Vaduz	Fr	Garics [77], Prager [84]	3 750	Rogalla SUI
11-10	Switzerland	W	2-1	Innsbruck	Fr	Linz [24p], Kuljic [36]	11 000	Svendsen DEN
15-11	Trinidad and Tobago	W	4-1	Vienna	Fr	Aufhauser 3 [14 25 44], Feldhofer [80]	13 100	Matejek CZE
2007								
7-02	Malta	D	1-1	Ta'Qali	Fr	Ivanschitz [48]	3 000	Bartolini SUI
24-03	Ghana	D	1-1	Graz	Fr	Aufhauser [55]	10 608	Verbist BEL
28-03	France	L	0-1	Paris	Fr		68 403	Briakos GRE
30-05	Scotland	L	0-1	Vienna	Fr		13 200	Szabo HUN
2-06	Paraguay	D	0-0	Vienna	Fr		12 700	Bebek CRO

Fr = Friendly match • EC = UEFA EURO 2004 • WC = FIFA World Cup • q = qualifier

AUSTRIA NATIONAL TEAM RECORDS AND RECORD SEQUENCES

Records			Sequence records					
Victory	9-0	MLT 1977	Wins	7	1933-1934	Clean sheets	5	1931, 1996
Defeat	1-11	ENG 1908	Defeats	6	1946-1947	Goals scored	28	1931-1934
Player Caps	103	HERZOG Andreas	Undefeated	14	1931-1932	Without goal	3	
Player Goals	44	POLSTER Toni	Without win	9	1973-1974	Goals against	17	1919-22, 1954-56

MAJOR CITIES/TOWNS

Population '000

1	Vienna	1 570
2	Graz	221
3	Linz	179
4	Salzburg	145
5	Innsbruck	112
6	Klagenfurt	90
7	Villach	59
8	Wels	58
9	Sankt Polten	48
10	Dornbirn	43
11	Steyr	39
12	Wiener Neustadt	38
13	Feldkirch	29
14	Bregenz	26
15	Leoben	24
16	Krems	24
17	Kapfenberg	21
18	Modling	20
19	Lustenau	20
20	Reid	11
21	Altach	6
22	Gratkorn	6
23	Mattersburg	6
24	Pasching	6

REPUBLIC OF AUSTRIA; REPUBLIK OESTERREICH

Capital	Vienna/Wien	Language	German	Independence	1918
Population	8 192 880	Area	83 870 km²	Density	97 per km²	% in cities	56%
GDP per cap	$30 000	Dailling code	+43	Internet	.at	GMT +/-	+1

MEDALS TABLE

		Overall			League			Cup		Europe			City	Stadium	Cap'ty	DoF
		G	S	B	G	S	B	G	S	G	S	B				
1	FK Austria Wien	51	27	15	23	17	11	26	9	2	1	4	Vienna	Franz-Horr-Stadion	11 800	1911
2	SK Rapid Wien	46	38	21	31	22	19	14	12	1	4	2	Vienna	Gerhard-Hanappi-Stadion	19 600	1899
3	FC Wacker Tirol	17	11	7	10	5	6	7	6			1	Innsbruck	Tivoli Neu	17 400	1914
4	Admira Wien	13	6	6	8	5	5	5	0		1	1	Vienna	Südstadt		1905-71
5	First Vienna FC	10	12	13	6	6	11	3	6	1		2	Vienna	Hohe Warte	6 000	1894
6	SK Sturm Graz	5	9	4	2	5	4	3	4				Graz	Graz-Liebenau	15 428	1909
7	Grazer AK	5	4	6	1	2	6	4	2				Graz	Graz-Liebenau	15 428	1902
8	Wiener Sport-Club	4	14	5	3	7	5	1	7				Vienna	Sport-Club Platz	8 700	1883
9	RB Austria Salzburg	4	9	1	4	4	1		4		1		Salzburg	Wals-Siezenheim	18 686	1933
10	Wiener AC	4	5	6	1	1	6	3	3		1		Vienna	WAC Platz		1896
11	Wacker Wien	2	8	3	1	7	3	1	1				Vienna	Maidlinger Platz		1908-71
12	Linzer ASK	2	5	4	1	1	4	1	4				Linz	Linzer Stadion	21 328	1908
13	Wiener AF	2	2	3	1	2	3	1					Vienna	Meldenorm Stadion		1912-35
14	FC Linz	1	4	1	1	2	1		2				Linz	Linzer Stadion		1949-97
15	Floridsdorfer AC	1	3	1	1	3	1						Vienna	FAC-Platz		1904

European medals include those won in the Mitropa Cup 1927-1939

RECENT LEAGUE AND CUP RECORD

	Championship						Cup		
Year	Champions	Pts	Runners-up	Pts	Third	Pts	Winners	Score	Runners-up
1995	SV Austria Salzburg	47	SK Sturm Graz	47	SK Rapid Wien	46	SK Rapid Wien	1-0	DSV Leoben
1996	SK Rapid Wien	73	SK Sturm Graz	67	FC Tirol Innsbruck	62	SK Sturm Graz	3-1	Admira-Wacker
1997	SV Austria Salzburg	69	SK Rapid Wien	66	SK Sturm Graz	55	SK Sturm Graz	2-1	First Vienna FC
1998	SK Sturm Graz	81	SK Rapid Wien	62	Grazer AK	61	SV Ried	3-1	SK Sturm Graz
1999	SK Sturm Graz	73	SK Rapid Wien	70	Grazer AK	65	SK Sturm Graz	1-1 4-2	LASK Linz
2000	FC Tirol Innsbruck	74	SK Sturm Graz	74	SK Rapid Wien	66	Grazer AK	2-2 4-3p	SV Austria Salzburg
2001	FC Tirol Innsbruck	68	SK Rapid Wien	60	Grazer AK	57	FC Kärnten	2-1	FC Tirol Innsbruck
2002	FC Tirol Innsbruck	75	SK Sturm Graz	65	Grazer AK	63	Grazer AK	3-2	SK Sturm Graz
2003	FK Austria Wien	70	Grazer AK	57	SV Austria Salzburg	56	FK Austria Wien	3-0	FC Kärnten
2004	Grazer AK	72	FK Austria Wien	71	SV Pasching	63	Grazer AK	3-3 5-4p	FK Austria Wien
2005	SK Rapid Wien	71	Grazer AK	70	FK Austria Wien	69	FK Austria Wien	3-1	SK Rapid Wien
2006	FK Austria Wien	67	SV Austria Salzburg	63	SV Pasching	58	FK Austria Wien	3-0	SV Mattersburg
2007	SV Austria Salzburg	75	SC Ried	56	SV Mattersburg	55	FK Austria Wien	2-1	SV Mattersburg

AUSTRIA 2006–07

T-MOBILE BUNDESLIGA

Team	Pl	W	D	L	F	A	Pts	Salzburg	Ried	Mattersburg	Rapid	Pasching	FK Austria	Sturm Graz	Altach	Wacker Tirol	GAK
RB Austria Salzburg †	36	22	9	5	72	25	75		1-1 2-0	1-1 4-0	3-1 3-0	2-3 4-0	2-2 2-0	3-1 3-0	1-1 4-0	3-0 4-1	2-1
SV Ried †	36	15	11	10	47	42	56	0-3 0-1		6-2 1-0	1-0 1-2	1-1 2-1	1-0 1-0	2-1 2-1	1-2 2-0	0-1 2-1	1-1 3-1
SV Mattersburg ‡	36	16	7	13	61	58	55	2-1 2-1	0-0 1-2		1-0 1-0	0-2 2-4	1-0 3-1	1-4 1-0	6-3 2-1	1-1 6-1	2-1 5-1
SK Rapid Wien	36	14	10	12	55	49	52	1-1 2-2	2-2 5-2	4-1 2-2		1-1 2-0	1-3 0-4	1-3 0-0	3-2 2-1	1-1 2-1	1-4 1-0
SV Pasching	36	14	10	12	47	41	52	1-1 0-1	0-0 3-1	1-2 2-0	1-0 0-1		2-0 2-1	1-0 1-1	4-2 1-1	0-2 3-1	1-0 3-0
FK Austria Wien ‡	36	11	12	13	43	43	45	1-1 0-2	1-1 2-1	3-1 1-1	0-0 2-1	1-1 2-0		1-1 0-1	2-0 3-0	4-1 4-1	0-0 2-2
SK Sturm Graz §13	36	16	6	14	40	40	41	2-1 0-2	1-0 1-1	0-0 3-1	2-0 1-0	0-0 2-1	1-0 0-1		2-0 1-0	2-3 2-0	0-2 1-0
SC Rheindorf Altach	36	11	5	20	45	64	38	2-1 0-2	1-2 0-0	2-1 1-3	2-2 2-3	0-0 0-0	1-1 2-2	2-0 0-2		0-1 1-1	4-1 3-1
FC Wacker Tirol	36	8	10	18	40	64	34	2-1 0-2	1-2 0-0	2-1 1-1	3-2 2-3	0-0 0-0	1-1 2-2	2-0 0-2	0-1 1-1		1-1 5-1
Grazer AK §28	36	8	10	18	43	67	6	0-2 0-0	2-2 2-3	0-2 3-3	1-1 0-2	2-1 2-1	1-3 2-1	0-0 0-2	0-1 1-1	2-1 3-2	

18/07/2006 – 20/05/2007 • † Qualified for the UEFA Champions League • ‡ Qualified for the UEFA Cup • § = points deducted
Top scorers: Alexander ZICKLER, RB Salzburg 22; LEONARDO, Altach 14; Christian MAYRLEB, Pasching 11; Mate BILIC, Rapid 11

AUSTRIA 2006–07

ERSTE LIGA (2)

Team	Pl	W	D	L	F	A	Pts	LASK	Schwanen.	Leoben	Austria	Gratkorn	Lustenau	Kärnten	FK Austria	Parndorf	VfB Admira	Kapfenberg	Hartberg
LASK Linz	33	24	4	5	74	34	76		2-1	4-0	0-3 3-2	2-0	2-4	2-1 2-0	2-1 0-2	3-1 3-1	6-1 1-0	1-0 0-2	4-0
SC Schwanenstadt	33	19	6	8	59	41	63	1-3 1-5		3-0	2-3 2-0	1-0 1-3	1-2 2-2	2-1 0-3	1-1	1-0	5-3	1-0	2-1
DSV Leoben	33	14	13	6	55	36	55	1-1 1-1	2-1 0		6-2	0-1 3-0	1-3 3-1	4-0	4-0	2-0 1-0	1-1	3-3	4-1 2-2
SC Austria Lustenau	33	13	11	9	57	50	50	0-0	4-1	1-1 1-0		2-4	3-0	0-0 0-0	0-2 0-2	1-2 2-4	2-2 2-3	0-2 1-2	3-1
FC Gratkorn	33	13	8	12	45	41	47	0-2 2-3	0-0	0-0 3-1	4-2		2-1	3-0 2-0	2-0	3-1 1-3	1-1 1-1	5-1 1-2	3-0
FC Lustenau	33	12	11	10	54	51	47	3-1 0-1	1-0	1-0	1-1	3-3 0-0 1-2 0		1-3 0-0	0-2	1-0 0-1 1-0	3-2	1-2 1-3	
FC Kärnten	33	11	9	13	41	41	42	1-2	1-3	2-3 1-1	2-1	2-0	1-1		3-1 1-1	0-1	3-0 3-2	3-1 2-0	4-1 1-1
FK Austria Amateure	33	10	8	15	42	52	38	1-4	0-3 3-1 0-0 0-0	2-2	2-1 2-1	3-2 2-2	1-2			2-1 2-4	2-2	3-0	0-1 2-1
SC/ESV Parndorf	33	9	8	16	41	47	35	0-1	1-1 2-3	0-1	0-0	0-1	2-2 0-2 1-0 0-0	2-1			3-0	3-1 5-1 1-1 1-0	
VfB Admira Wacker	33	8	9	16	45	67	33	1-3	1-5 0-2 1-4 1-2	0-2	1-1	0-2 3-1	1-1	2-1 1-1 2-0 1-1	0-3	2-4		4-0 3-0	
SV Kapfenberg	33	8	8	17	41	60	32	2-2	0-2 0-0 1-1 1-1	3-0	0-0	1-3	1-0	0-1 1-0	3-2	1-2 1-3			1-1 2-0
TSV Hartberg	33	7	5	21	31	65	26	1-4 0-4 0-1 2-3	1-2	1-2 2-1 0-0 1-0	1-2 1-3 1-0	0-3	3-1	1-0	1-2	2-0			

18/07/2006 – 20/05/2007 • Top scorers: Ivica VASTIC, LASK 23; Lukas MOSSNER, Schwanenstadt 22

OFB STIEGL-CUP 2006–07

Round of sixteen		Quarter-finals		Semi-finals		Final	
FK Austria Wien *	1 4p						
SV Pasching	1 2p	FK Austria Wien	3				
SK Sankt Andrä *	1	SV Ried *	0				
SV Ried	3			FK Austria Wien	1 3p		
SV Horn	3			RB Salzburg Amateure	1 1p		
SK Voitsberg *	0	SV Horn *	1				
LASK Linz	0	RB Salzburg Amateure	3				
RB Salzburg Amateure*	2					FK Austria Wien ‡	2
RB Austria Salzburg	2					SV Mattersburg	1
Grazer AK *	0	RB Austria Salzburg	3				
SC Schwanenstadt	1	FC Kärnten *	0				
FC Kärnten *	3			RB Austria Salzburg	2		
FC Lustenau	0 5p			SV Mattersburg	3		
First Vienna FC *	0 3p	FC Lustenau *	1				
Wiener Sport-Club *	0	SV Mattersburg	3				
SV Mattersburg	2						

* Home team • ‡ Qualified for the UEFA Cup

CUP FINAL
Gerhard-Hanappi-Stadion, Vienna
1-05-2007, Att: 15 000
Scorers – Lafata [54], Lasnik [56] for FK Austria; Schmidt [23] for Mattersburg

AZE – AZERBAIJAN

NATIONAL TEAM RECORD
JULY 10TH 2006 TO JULY 12TH 2010

PL	W	D	L	F	A	%
13	3	3	7	6	24	34.6

FIFA/COCA-COLA WORLD RANKING

1993	1994	1995	1996	1997	1998	1999	2000	2001	2002	2003	2004	2005	2006	High		Low	
-	147	141	125	123	99	97	115	113	113	119	113	114	125	97	06/99	170	07/94

2006–2007											
08/06	09/06	10/06	11/06	12/06	01/07	02/07	03/07	04/07	05/07	06/07	07/07
106	117	128	123	125	127	130	123	103	103	109	109

It took 28 attempts over the course of just under three years but Sahin Diniyev's Azeri national team finally won an match when they beat Uzbekistan in a friendly tournament in Kazakhstan in March 2007. Two months later, they followed that up with a win over Finland in the UEFA Euro 2008 qualifiers - only their third win since first entering the European Championship. It was not without controversy, however, thanks to the policy of using naturalised players such as Andre Ladaga from Brazil and Branimir Subasic from Serbia, both of whom scored for Azerbaijan during the season. In an effort to deflect criticism, Diniyev pointed out that Germany often use 'foreigners'

INTERNATIONAL HONOURS
None

in their national team but the whole issue was a matter of huge debate, also at League level where initial attempts to restrict the numbers in the League were relaxed. Khazar Lenkoran, under coach Agasalim Mirdjavadov, lived up to their billing as the wealthiest team in the country thanks to their links with the Palmali shipping firm. They played with a core of South American players and duly won their first trophies by completing the double, although it took a last minute goal by Rashad Kerimov to secure the Cup. In Europe, Karvan became the first Azeri team to progress through a round in the UEFA Cup when they beat Slovakia's Spartak Trnava home and away.

THE FIFA BIG COUNT OF 2006

	Male	Female		Total
Number of players	267 900	38 470	Referees and Assistant Referees	100
Professionals	400		Admin, Coaches, Technical, Medical	12 900
Amateurs 18+	3 150		Number of clubs	80
Youth under 18	14 120		Number of teams	320
Unregistered	82 700		Clubs with women's teams	3
Total players	306 370		Players as % of population	3.85%

Association of Football Federations of Azerbaijan (AFFA)
Nobel prospekti, 2208,, Baku AZ 1025, Azerbaijan
Tel +994 12 908308　　　Fax +994 12 4908722
info@affa.za　　　www.affa.za
President: MIRZAYEV Ramiz　　　General Secretary: MAMMADOV Elkhan
Vice-President: ALIYEV Rauf　　　Treasurer: JAFAROV Lativ　　　Media Officer: HASANOV Natiq
Men's Coach: DINIYEV Sahin　　　Women's Coach: TIBILOV Boris
AFFA formed: 1992　　　UEFA: 1994　　　FIFA: 1994
White shirts, Blue shorts, White socks or Blue shirts, White shorts, Blue socks

RECENT INTERNATIONALS PLAYED BY AZERBAIJAN

2003 Opponents	Score	Venue	Comp	Scorers	Att	Referee
6-09 Finland	L 1-2	Baku	ECq	Ismailov [89]	7 500	Hrinak SVK
11-10 Italy	L 0-4	Reggio Calabria	ECq		30 000	Dougal SCO
14-12 United Arab Emirates	D 3-3	Dubai	Fr	Nabiyev 2 [35 90], Kerimov [85]		Mohamed UAE
18-12 Oman	L 0-1	Muscat	Fr			
20-12 Saudi Arabia	L 0-1	Riyadh	Fr			
2004						
18-02 Israel	L 0-6	Tel Aviv	Fr		13 250	Paraty POR
31-03 Moldova	L 1-2	Chisinau	Fr	Gurbanov.G [20]	5 500	Godulyan UKR
28-04 Kazakhstan	W 3-2	Almaty	Fr	Nabiyev [31], Guliev [57], Sadigov [80]	20 000	Chynybekov KGZ
28-05 Uzbekistan	W 3-1	Baku	Fr	Gurbanov.G [31], Gurbanov.I [64], Guliev [75]	12 000	
6-06 Latvia	D 2-2	Riga	Fr	Guliev [55], Gurbanov.G [74p]	8 000	Maisonlahti FIN
18-08 Jordan	D 1-1	Amman	Fr	Ponomarev [23]	4 000	
4-09 Wales	D 1-1	Baku	WCq	Sadigov [55]	8 000	Trivkovic CRO
8-09 Austria	L 0-2	Vienna	WCq		26 400	Sammut MLT
9-10 Northern Ireland	D 0-0	Baku	WCq		6 460	Hanacsek HUN
13-10 England	L 0-1	Baku	WCq		17 000	Hamer LUX
17-11 Bulgaria	D 0-0	Baku	Fr		10 000	Sipailo LVA
2005						
21-01 Trinidad and Tobago	L 0-1	Port of Spain	Fr		500	
23-01 Trinidad and Tobago	L 0-2	Marabella	Fr		1 000	Gordon TRI
9-02 Moldova	D 0-0	Baku	Fr		3 000	
26-03 Poland	L 0-8	Warsaw	WCq		9 000	Vollquartz DEN
30-03 England	L 0-2	Newcastle	WCq		49 046	Costa POR
29-05 Iran	L 1-2	Tehran	Fr	Gurbanov.G [67]		
4-06 Poland	L 0-3	Baku	WCq		10 458	Undiano Mallenco ESP
17-08 Albania	L 1-2	Tirana	Fr	Tagizade [2]	7 300	
3-09 Northern Ireland	L 0-2	Belfast	WCq		12 000	Stanisic SCG
7-09 Austria	D 0-0	Baku	WCq		2 800	Verbist BEL
12-10 Wales	L 0-2	Cardiff	WCq		32 628	Hansson SWE
2006						
28-02 Ukraine	D 0-0	Baku	Fr			Sipailo LVA
12-04 Turkey	D 1-1	Baku	Fr	Sadygov.RF [64p]		Paniashvili GEO
18-05 Moldova	D 0-0	Chisinau	Fr			
15-08 Ukraine	L 0-6	Kyiv	Fr		6 000	Sukhina RUS
2-09 Serbia	L 0-1	Belgrade	ECq		BCD	Kircher GER
6-09 Kazakhstan	D 1-1	Baku	ECq	Ladaga [16]	8 500	Szabo HUN
7-10 Portugal	L 0-3	Porto	ECq		14 000	Halsey ENG
11-10 Belgium	L 0-3	Brussels	ECq		11 917	Lajuks LVA
2007						
7-02 Uzbekistan	D 0-0	Karshi	Fr			
7-03 Uzbekistan	W 1-0	Shymkent	Fr	Subasic [55]		
9-03 Kazakhstan	L 0-1	Shymkent	Fr			
11-03 Kyrgyzstan	W 1-0	Shymkent	Fr	Dzavadov [17]		
24-03 Poland	L 0-5	Warsaw	ECq		13 000	Jakobsson ISL
28-03 Finland	W 1-0	Baku	ECq	Imamaliev [82]	14 500	Messina ITA
2-06 Poland	L 1-3	Baku	ECq	Subasic [6]	25 800	Kapitanis CYP
6-06 Kazakhstan	D 1-1	Almaty	ECq	Nadyrov [30]	11 800	Toussaint LUX

Fr = Friendly match • EC = UEFA EURO 2004/2008 • WCq = FIFA World Cup • q = qualifier • BCD = Behind closed doors

AZERBAIJAN NATIONAL TEAM RECORDS AND RECORD SEQUENCES

Records			Sequence records				
Victory	4-0	LIE 1999	Wins	2	1998, 2004	Clean sheets	2
Defeat	0-10	FRA 1995	Defeats	11	1994-1995	Goals scored	6	2004
Player Caps	73	AKHMEDOV Tarlan	Undefeated	4	2002	Without goal	9	1999-2000, 2004-05
Player Goals	12	GURBANOV Gurban	Without win	27	2004-2007	Goals against	19	2002-2004

1	Baku	1856
2	Gäncä	305
3	Sumqayit	293
4	Mingäçevir	96
5	Qaraçuxur	73
6	Ali Bayramli	70
7	Bakikhanov	67
8	Naxçivan	64
9	Säki	62
10	Yevlakh	54
11	Xankändi	52
12	Lenkoran	49
13	Räsulzadä	45
14	Biläcäri	42
15	Mastaga	40
16	Agdam	40
17	Shamkir	35
18	Imisli	31
19	Sabirabad	28
20	Buzovna	24
21	Quba	22
22	Khusar	16
23	Tovuz	12
24	Masali	9

REPUBLIC OF AZERBAIJAN; AZARBAYCAN RESPUBLIKASI

Capital	Baku	Language	Azeri	Independence	1991
Population	7 961 619	Area	86 600 km²	% in cities	56%
GDP per cap	$3 400	Dailling code	+994	Internet	.az	GMT +/-	+5

MEDALS TABLE

		Overall			League			Cup		Europe			City	Stadium	Cap'ty	DoF
		G	S	B	G	S	B	G	S	G	S	B				
1	Neftchi Baku	10	3	3	5	2	3	5	1				Baku	Tofik Bakhramov	29 858	1937
2	FK Gança	7	1	2	3	1	2	4					Gança	Sahar	9 300	1959
3	Karabakh Agdam	3	6	1	1	3	1	2	3				Baku	Tofik Ismailov	9 300	1950
4	FK Shamkir	2	4	1	2	1	1		3				Shamkir	Sähär	11 500	
5	Khazar Lenkoran	2	2		1	1		1	1				Lenkoran	Rasim Kara	15 000	1975
6	FK Baku	2		1	1		1	1					Baku	Tofik Bakhramov	29 858	1997
7	Turan Tovuz	1	1	1	1	1	1						Tovuz	Shehar	5 000	1954
8	Inshaatchi Baku	1					1						Baku			
	Shafa Baku	1					1						Baku	Shafa	7 852	
10	Karvan Yevlakh		2	1		1	1		1				Yevlakh	Yevlakh	5 000	2004
	Khazri Buznova		2	1		1	1		1				Buznova	Genclik	5 000	
12	Khazar Sumqayit		2			2							Sumqayit	Mehdi Huseyinzade	16 000	
	Kur-Nur Mingäçevir		2						2				Mingäçevir	Shehar	16 000	
14	Dinamo Baku	1	1		1	1							Baku	Tofik Bakhramov	29 858	
15	Inshaatchi Sabirabad	1					1						Baku			
	Inter Baku	1					1						Baku	Zabrat	3 000	1995
	MTK-Araz Imishli	1					1						Imishli	Habio Halilov	8 500	1995

RECENT LEAGUE AND CUP RECORD

	Championship						Cup		
Year	Champions	Pts	Runners-up	Pts	Third	Pts	Winners	Score	Runners-up
1995	Kapaz Gança	42	Turan Tovuz	40	Neftchi Baku	38	Neftchi Baku	1-0	Kur-Nur
1996	Neftchi Baku	36	Khazri Buzovna	33	Kapaz Gança	32	Neftchi Baku	3-0	Karabakh Agdam
1997	Neftchi Baku	74	Karabakh Agdam	71	Khazri Buzovna	66	Kapaz Gança	1-0	Khazri Buzovna
1998	Kapaz Gança	70	Dinamo Baku	54	Shamkir	54	Kapaz Gança	2-0	Karabakh Agdam
1999	Kapaz Gança	58	Karabakh Agdam	54	Dinamo Baku	52	Neftchi Baku	0-0 5-4p	Shamkir
2000	Shamkir	55	Kapaz Gança	44	Neftchi Baku	43	Kapaz Gança	2-1	Karabakh Agdam
2001	Shamkir	51	Neftchi Baku	51	Vilash Masalli	38	Shafa Baku	2-1	Neftchi Baku
2002	Championship abandoned with eight rounds to play						Neftchi Baku	W-0	Shamkir
2003	No championship played						No tournament played		
2004	Neftchi Baku	69	Shamkir	64	Karabakh Agdam	60	Neftchi Baku	1-0	Shamkir
2005	Neftchi Baku	78	Khazar Lenkoran	78	Karvan Yevlakh	76	FK Baku	2-1	Inter Baku
2006	FK Baku	58	Karvan Yevlakh	57	Neftchi Baku	54	Karabakh Agdam	2-1	Karvan Yevlakh
2007	Khazar Lenkoran	56	Neftchi Baku	54	FK Baku	48	Khazar Lenkoran	1-0	MTK-Araz Imishli

AZERBAIJAN 2006-07

YUKSAK LIGA (1)

	Pl	W	D	L	F	A	Pts	Khazar	Neftchi	FK Baku	Inter Baku	MTK-Araz	Olimpik	Karvan	Karabakh	Simurq	Turan	Gilan	Gen'birliyi	Shahdag	FK Gança
Khazar Lenkoran †	24	17	5	2	50	16	56		2-1	1-0	0-0	4-1	3-2	3-1	2-0	1-1	0-0	4-0	3-1	3-1	
Neftchi Baku ‡	24	17	3	4	47	15	54	1-0		1-0	1-0	3-0	3-0	3-1	0-0	1-0	4-2	4-1	6-1	5-0	
FK Baku	24	14	6	4	25	10	48	0-0	0-1		2-0	1-0	1-0	2-0	0-0	3-2	2-0	1-0	3-0	3-1	
Inter Baku	24	13	6	5	36	12	45	0-0	1-0	0-1		0-1	0-0	1-1	1-0	2-0	1-0	2-0	4-1	2-0	
MTK-Araz Imishli ‡	24	12	5	7	23	18	41	0-2	1-1	2-0	0-2		0-0	1-0	1-1	1-1	1-0	4-1	5-1	1-0	
Olimpik Baku	24	11	8	5	28	17	41	1-2	2-1	0-0	1-0	1-0		1-0	0-0	3-0	1-0	3-1	2-0	3-1	
Karvan Yevlakh	24	10	5	9	36	30	35	2-1	0-1	1-2	1-1	0-1	1-0		2-0	3-0	2-1	3-3	3-2	3-1	
Karabakh Agdam	24	6	9	9	20	27	27	1-4	0-2	1-1	0-1	1-0	1-1	1-1		1-1	1-1	3-2	3-0	3-1	
Simurq Zaqatala	24	6	7	11	27	33	25	0-1	0-1	0-0	1-2	0-1	2-2	1-1	3-0		0-0	3-1	1-0	3-0	
Turan Tovuz	24	5	5	14	24	38	20	2-3	2-1	0-1	1-7	0-1	0-1	2-4	3-1	3-1			0-0	4-1	1-1
Gilan Khanlar	24	4	4	16	17	47	16	0-3	1-4	0-1	0-0	1-0	0-3	1-4	0-2	1-2	1-0		2-0	0-0	
Genclerbirliyi Sumgayit	24	3	3	18	16	54	12	0-3	0-1	0-1	0-4	0-0	1-1	1-0	1-0	4-2	2-0	0-1			1-1
Shahdag Khusar	24	1	8	15	15	47	11	1-5	1-1	0-0	1-5	0-0	0-0	0-2	0-0	1-3	1-2	0-1	**3-0**		

FK Gança   Excluded

5/08/2006 - 23/05/2007 • † Qualified for the UEFA Champions League • ‡ Qualified for the UEFA Cup • Match in bold awarded 3-0
Top scorers: Zaur RAMAZANOV, Khazar 20; Huseyn MAMMADOV, Olimpik 13

AZERBAIJAN 2006-07
BIRINCI DASTA (2)

	Pl	W	D	L	F	A	Pts
FK Masalli	10	7	1	2	17	7	22
Standard Baku	10	7	0	3	24	16	21
Geyazan Gazakh	10	5	1	4	15	13	16
ABN Barda	10	4	3	3	14	16	15
ANSAD-Petrol Neftçala	10	2	2	6	17	21	8
Bakili Baku	10	1	1	8	8	22	4

17/05/2007 - 11/06/2007

FFA CUP 2006-07

Round of 16			Quarter–finals			Semi–finals			Final		
Khazar Lenkoran *	4	3									
Bakili Baku	0	0	Khazar Lenkoran	2	0						
Gilan Khanlar *	0	0	FK Baku *	0	1						
FK Baku	2	1				Khazar Lenkoran	1	1			
Gen'birliyi Sumgayit	2	8				Inter Baku *	0	0			
MTK-Araz Imishli-2 *	1	2	Gen'birliyi Sumgayit *	0	2						
Shahdag Khusar *	1	0	Inter Baku	2	3						
Inter Baku	2	4							Khazar Lenkoran		1
Neftchi Baku	2	0							MTK-Araz Imishli ‡		0
Karabakh Agdam *	1	1	Neftchi Baku *	7	1						
Olimpik Baku	0	1	Turan Tovuz	2	0						
Turan Tovuz	2	0				Neftchi Baku	0	1			
Karvan Yevlakh	1	1				MTK-Araz Imishli *	0	1			
Simurq Zaqatala *	1	0	Karvan Yevlakh	2	0						
Vilash Masalli *	0	0	MTK-Araz Imishli *	2	1						
MTK-Araz Imishli	1	1									

* Home team in the first leg • ‡ Qualified for the UEFA Cup

CUP FINAL

Tofik Bakhramov, Baku
28-05-2007

Scorer - Rashad Kerimov [30] for Khazar

BAH – BAHAMAS

NATIONAL TEAM RECORD
JULY 10TH 2006 TO JULY 12TH 2010

PL	W	D	L	F	A	%
6	2	0	4	9	18	33.3

FIFA/COCA-COLA WORLD RANKING

1993	1994	1995	1996	1997	1998	1999	2000	2001	2002	2003	2004	2005	2006	High		Low	
167	-	-	-	-	-	189	178	184	187	193	192	193	146	**138**	09/06	**197**	03/99

2006–2007											
08/06	09/06	10/06	11/06	12/06	01/07	02/07	03/07	04/07	05/07	06/07	07/07
193	138	146	143	146	147	148	150	149	150	148	148

There was a welcome return to international football for the Bahamas national team after an absence of two and a half years and their return was capped by some spirited performances in the Digicel Caribbean Cup. Grouped in the first round with Cuba, the Cayman Islands and the Turks and Caicos Islands, Bahamas travelled to Havana and finished second in the group behind Cuba. The 6-0 defeat at the hands of the hosts may have been expected, but the victories over their other two opponents were the first by the national team for over seven years and qualified the Bahamas for a second round group in Barbados. There the lack of experience was evident with three straight

INTERNATIONAL HONOURS
None

defeats at the hands of the hosts, Bermuda and St Vincent but hopes will have been raised that the team can cause an upset in the upcoming FIFA World Cup qualifiers. The CONCACAF youth tournaments brought mixed results for Bahamas - a 10-0 trashing at the hands of Cuba for the under 17 team, but a 15-0 win against the British Virgin Islands for the under 20s. In domestic football Bears FC won their first title since 2004 when they beat defending champions Caledonia Celtic 6-1 on the final day of the New Providence League season in a winner takes all tie. A week later Bears then beat United FC 2-1 in the New Providence Cup Final to secure the double.

THE FIFA BIG COUNT OF 2006

	Male	Female		Total
Number of players	14 536	3 408	Referees and Assistant Referees	36
Professionals	0		Admin, Coaches, Technical, Medical	230
Amateurs 18+	820		Number of clubs	34
Youth under 18	1 652		Number of teams	111
Unregistered	2 400		Clubs with women's teams	7
Total players	17 944		Players as % of population	5.91%

Bahamas Football Association (BFA)
Plaza on the Way, West Bay Street, PO Box N-8434, Nassau, NP, Bahamas
Tel +1 242 3225897   Fax +1 242 3225898
lehaven@bahamas.net.bs   www.bahamasfootballassoc.com
President: SEALEY Anton   General Secretary: HAVEN Lionel E.
Vice-President: LUNN Fred   Treasurer: LAFLEUR Pierre   Media Officer: HAVEN Lionel E.
Men's Coach: DOS SANTOS Neider   Women's Coach: BETHEL Vandyke
BFA formed: 1967   CONCACAF: 1981   FIFA: 1968
Yellow shirts with sky blue trimmings, Black shorts, Yellow socks

RECENT INTERNATIONAL MATCHES PLAYED BY BAHAMAS

2002	Opponents	Score	Venue	Comp	Scorers	Att	Referee
No international matches played in 2002							
2003							
27-12	Haiti	L 0-6	Miami	Fr			
2004							
26-03	Dominica	D 1-1	Nassau	WCq	Casimir 88	800	Forde BRB
28-03	Dominica	L 1-3	Nassau	WCq	Jean 67	900	Pineda HON
2005							
No international matches played in 2005							
2006							
2-09	Cayman Islands	W 3-1	Havana	CCq	OG 5, Moseley 36, Thompson 86		Stewart JAM
4-09	Cuba	L 0-6	Havana	CCq		100	
6-09	Turks & Caicos Isl	W 3-2	Havana	CCq	Nassies 59, Hall 63, Jean 87	120	Campbell JAM
19-11	Barbados	L 1-2	Bridgetown	CCq	Jean 76p	4 500	
21-11	Bermuda	L 0-4	Bridgetown	CCq			
23-11	St Vincent/Grenadines	L 2-3	Bridgetown	CCq	Christie 55, Moseley 65		
2007							
No international matches played in 2007 before July							

Fr = Friendly match • CC = Digicel Caribbean Cup • WC = FIFA World Cup • q = qualifier

BAHAMAS NATIONAL TEAM RECORDS AND RECORD SEQUENCES

Records			Sequence records					
Victory	3-0	TCA 1999	Wins	2	2000	Clean sheets	2	1999
Defeat	0-9	HAI 2000	Defeats	4	1999, 2000-2003	Goals scored	2	2000, 2004
Player Caps	n/a		Undefeated	2	1999, 2000	Without goal	4	2000-2003
Player Goals	n/a		Without win	6	2000-present	Goals against	12	1999-present

RECENT LEAGUE RECORD

	New Providence Championship					Grand Bahama	New Prov. Cup	National
Year	Champions	Pts	Runners-up	Pts	3rd Place	Pts	Champions	Winners	Winners
2000	Cavalier FC						Abacom United	Cavalier FC	Abacom United
2001	Cavalier FC	42	Gunite Pool Sharks	33	Team Toyota	33	Abacom United	Cavalier FC	Cavalier FC
2002	Bears FC	19	Team Toyota	18	United FC	15	Abacom United	Khaki Superstars	Not played
2003	Bears FC	23	United FC	22	Team Toyota	19	Abacom United	Bears FC	Bears FC
2004	Bears FC	29	United FC	26	Caledonia Celtic	23	Haitian Superstars	Bears FC	Not played
2005	Caledonia Celtic	27	RCA Racing Blue	21	Bears FC	18	Not played	Bears FC	
2006	Caledonia Celtic	29	Bears FC	26	Gunite Pool Sharks	17	Brita Red Bulls	Bears FC	
2007	Bears FC	31	Caledonia Celtic	26	United FC	20	Not played	Bears FC	

The National Championship is played between the champions of New Providence and the champions of Grand Bahama

BAHAMAS COUNTRY INFORMATION

Capital	Nassau	Independence	1973	GDP per Capita	$16 700
Population	299 697	Status	Commonwealth	GNP Ranking	117
Area km2	13 940	Language	English	Dialling code	+1 242
Population density	21 per km2	Literacy rate	96%	Internet code	.bs
% in urban areas	87%	Main religion	Christian 94%	GMT +/−	-5
Towns/Cities ('000)	Nassau 227; Freeport 46; Coppers Town 8; Marsh Harbour 5; Freetown 4; High Rock 3				
Neighbours (km)	North Atlantic Ocean 3 542				
Main stadia	Thomas A. Robinson – Nassau 9 100; Grand Bahama – Freeport 3 100				

BAN – BANGLADESH

NATIONAL TEAM RECORD
JULY 10TH 2006 TO JULY 12TH 2010

PL	W	D	L	F	A	%
4	0	0	4	1	13	0

FIFA/COCA-COLA WORLD RANKING

1993	1994	1995	1996	1997	1998	1999	2000	2001	2002	2003	2004	2005	2006	High		Low	
116	130	138	136	141	157	130	151	146	159	151	167	160	144	**110**	04/96	**176**	05/07

2006–2007											
08/06	09/06	10/06	11/06	12/06	01/07	02/07	03/07	04/07	05/07	06/07	07/07
145	152	155	158	144	151	154	155	176	176	172	172

In 2004, AFC President Mohammed Bin Hammam singled out Bangladesh to take part in a pilot project to develop football in the country. The first major step of the AFC's Vision Bangladesh programme was the launch of the Bangladesh Professional Football League in March 2007 with a match between Abahani and Muktijodha. It is hoped that the B.League will be the launchpad for a new era in which football can exploit the widespread support that exists for the game around the country. Bengal was historically the one area of India in which football thrived, with Calcutta, just across the border from Bangladesh, the epicentre of the game. It is no coincidence that East Bengal,

INTERNATIONAL HONOURS
Qualified for AFC Asian Cup Finals 1980   Represented in the Football Tournament of the Asian Games 1978 1982 1986 1990
South Asian Federation Games 1999   South Asian Football Federation Cup 2003

named after the area that comprises Bangladesh, are the most popular club in India. Vision Bangladesh aims to give the football authorities help on a number of different levels to build a sustainable infrastructure for football and to make it a formidable force at the international level. However, the performance of the national team at the AFC Asian Cup qualifiers in which Bangladesh lost all six matches, shows the size of the task ahead. In the meantime Abahani were crowned as the first B.League champions when the tournament finished in early August.

THE FIFA BIG COUNT OF 2006

	Male	Female		Total
Number of players	6 070 200	210 100	Referees and Assistant Referees	4 304
Professionals	0		Admin, Coaches, Technical, Medical	71 300
Amateurs 18+	98 980		Number of clubs	4 100
Youth under 18	172 320		Number of teams	8 200
Unregistered	5 815 000		Clubs with women's teams	0
Total players	6 280 300		Players as % of population	4.26%

Bangladesh Football Federation (BFF)
BFF House, Motijheel, Dhaka 1000, Bangladesh
Tel +880 2 7161582   Fax +880 2 7160270
bffbd@citechco.net   www.bffonline.com
President: SULTAN S.A.   General Secretary: HUQ Anwarul
Vice-President: AHMED Monir   Treasurer: ALAM CHOWDHURY Shah   Media Officer: AL FATAH Ahmed Sayed
Men's Coach: HASANUZZAMAN Bablu   Women's Coach: ABU Yusef
BFF formed: 1972   AFC: 1974   FIFA: 1974
Green with black and red trimmings, Green shorts, Red socks or White shirts with black and red trimmings, White shirts, White socks

RECENT INTERNATIONAL MATCHES PLAYED BY BANGLADESH

2002 Opponents	Score	Venue	Comp	Scorers	Att	Referee
No international matches played in 2002						
2003						
11-01 Nepal	W 1-0	Dhaka	SAr1	Ahmed Alfaz [30]		Kunsuta THA
13-01 Maldives	W 1-0	Dhaka	SAr1	Arif Khan [89]		Vidanagamage SRI
15-01 Bhutan	W 3-0	Dhaka	SAr1	Ariful Kabir Farhad 2 [4 54], Rukunuzzaman Kanchan [79]		Balu IND
18-01 India	W 2-1	Dhaka	SAsf	Rukunuzzaman Kanchan [78], Matiur Munna [98 GG]		Kunsuta THA
20-01 Maldives	D 1-1	Dhaka	SAf	Rukunuzzaman Kanchan [14] W 5-3p		Vidanagamage SRI
27-03 Laos	L 1-2	Hong Kong	ACq	Ariful Kabir Farhad [90]		Liu Sung Ho TPE
30-03 Hong Kong	D 2-2	Hong Kong	ACq	Mahmud Hossein Titu [66], Hossein Monwar [78]		
26-11 Tajikistan	L 0-2	Dhaka	WCq		6 000	Khanthachai THA
30-11 Tajikistan	L 0-2	Dushanbe	WCq		12 000	Pereira IND
2004						
No international matches played in 2004						
2005						
8-12 Bhutan	W 3-0	Karachi	SAr1	Ariful Kabir Farhad 2 [42 58], Zahid Hasan Ameli [85]		
10-12 Nepal	W 2-0	Karachi	SAr1	Rokonuzzaman Kanchan 2 [27 87]		
12-12 India	D 1-1	Karachi	SAr1	Zahid Hasan Ameli [77]		
14-12 Pakistan	W 1-0	Karachi	SAsf	Mohammad Sujan [44p]		
17-12 India	L 0-2	Karachi	SAf			
22-12 Pakistan	D 0-0	Dhaka	ACq			
26-12 Pakistan	W 1-0	Karachi	ACq	Firaj Mahmud Hossain [84]		
2006						
22-02 Uzbekistan	L 0-5	Uzbekistan	ACq		12 000	Ebrahim BHR
1-03 Hong Kong	L 0-1	Dhaka	ACq		1 000	Sarkar IND
1-04 Cambodia	W 2-1	Dhaka	CCr1	Alfaz Ahmed [31], Hasan Ameli [64]	35 000	Tan Hai CHN
3-04 Guam	W 3-0	Dhaka	CCr1	Hasan Ameli [49], Abdul Hossain 2 [83 85]	18 000	U Ein Cho MYA
5-04 Palestine	D 1-1	Dhaka	CCr1	Mahadi Tapu [55]	22 000	Mombini IRN
10-04 Tajikistan	L 1-6	Dhaka	CCqf	Alfaz Ahmed [17]	15 000	AK Nema IRQ
16-08 Qatar	L 1-4	Chittagong	ACq	Mohamad Arman [23]	7 000	Al Yarimi YEM
6-09 Qatar	L 0-3	Doha	ACq		500	Najm LIB
11-10 Uzbekistan	L 0-4	Dhaka	ACq		120	Tan Hai CHN
15-11 Hong Kong	L 0-2	Hong Kong	ACq		1 273	Kim Dong Jin KOR
2007						
No international matches played in 2007 before August						

SA = South Asian Football Federation Cup • AC = AFC Asian Cup • CC = AFC Challenge Cup • WCq = FIFA World Cup
q = qualifier • r1 = first round group • sf = semi-final • f = final • GG = Golden Goal

BANGLADESH NATIONAL TEAM RECORDS AND RECORD SEQUENCES

Records			Sequence records					
Victory	8-0	MDV 1985	Wins	4	2003	Clean sheets	3	1984, 1999, 2003
Defeat	0-9	KOR 1979	Defeats	7	1979-1981	Goals scored	8	1984, 2001-2003
Player Caps	n/a		Undefeated	6	2001-2003	Without goal	5	1980-82, 2000-01
Player Goals	n/a		Without win	19	1973-1979	Goals against	34	1973-1983

BANGLADESH COUNTRY INFORMATION

Capital	Dhaka	Independence	1971	GDP per Capita	$1 900
Population	141 340 476	Status	Republic	GNP Ranking	51
Area km²	144 000	Language	Bengali	Dialling code	+880
Population density	98 per km²	Literacy rate	40%	Internet code	.bd
% in urban areas	18%	Main religion	Muslim 87%	GMT +/–	+6
Towns/Cities ('000)	Dhaka 6 493; Chittagong 3 672; Khulna 1 342; Rajshahi 700; Comilla 389; Tungi 337; Mymensingh 330; Sylhet 326; Rangpur 285; Narsinghdi 281; Barisal 280;				
Neighbours (km)	India 4 053; Burma 193; Bay of Bengal 580				
Main stadia	Bangabandhu – Dkaka 36 000; Sher-e-Bangla Mirpur – Dhaka 30 000				

BANGLADESH 2007

B. LEAGUE	Pl	W	D	L	F	A	Pts	Abahani D	Mohammedan	Muktijoddha	Sheikh Russell	Brothers Union	Arambagh	Mohammed. C	Farashganj	Abahani K	Abahani C	Rahmatganj
Abahani Dhaka	20	14	5	1	36	8	47		0-0	1-0	0-0	1-0	3-0	0-0	3-1	1-2	2-1	1-0
Mohammedan	20	11	7	2	40	13	40	0-1		1-1	1-1	1-0	1-1	7-0	3-1	6-1	2-1	7-1
Muktijoddha Sangsad	20	9	6	5	29	19	33	0-0	1-0		0-3	2-0	1-0	2-1	0-0	4-2	4-0	3-1
Sheikh Russell	20	8	9	3	23	13	33	0-2	0-0	2-1		1-1	0-0	2-1	0-0	2-0	4-3	2-0
Brothers Union	20	8	5	7	32	19	29	0-0	0-1	0-1	0-0		3-0	1-2	1-1	2-4	3-0	2-1
Arambagh	20	8	3	9	22	23	27	0-2	0-1	2-1	1-0	1-3		4-2	0-1	2-0	2-0	1-2
Mohammedan Ch'gong	20	7	5	8	20	26	26	1-2	0-0	1-0	1-1	0-1	2-0		0-1	3-0	1-0	1-1
Farashganj	20	5	7	8	17	22	22	2-3	1-2	2-2	0-1	0-0	0-2	3-0		2-1	0-1	0-0
Abahani Khulna	20	4	4	12	21	16	16	1-5	1-1	1-1	1-1	0-5	1-3	0-1	0-1		1-1	2-0
Abahani Chittagong	20	4	3	13	18	15	15	0-2	1-3	1-1	0-3	1-4	0-3	1-1	2-0	2-0		1-2
Rahmatganj	20	3	4	13	15	13	13	0-7	1-3	1-4	1-0	2-6	0-0	0-2	1-1	0-3	1-2	

2/03/2007 - 23/07/2007

RECENT LEAGUE RECORD

Dhaka League

Year	Champions	Pts	Runners-up	Pts	Third	Pts
1992	Abahani	37	Mohammedan	33	Brothers Union	27
1993	Mohammedan	30	Abahani	29	Brothers Union	23
1994	Abahani	28	Muktijoddha	25	Mohammedan	25
1995	Abahani	43	Mohammedan	42	Muktijoddha	33
1996	Mohammedan	48	Abahani	43	Muktijoddah	33
1997	No championship due to a readjustment in the timings of the season					
1998	Muktijoddha	52	Mohammedan	50	Abahani	42
1999	Mohammedan	40	Abahani	37	Muktijoddha	34
2000	Muktijoddha	40	Abahani	37	Mohammedan	33
2001	Abahani	41	Mohammedan	27	Rahmatganj	18
2002	Mohammedan	33	Abahani	31	Muktijoddha	29
2003	No championship due to a readjustment in the timings of the season					
2004	Brothers Union	40	Sheikh Russell	38	Abahani	33
2005	Brothers Union ‡	39	Mohammedan	39	Abahani	38

† played on a league system • ‡ Play-off in 2005: Brothers Union 1-0 Mohammedan

B.League

Year	Champions	Pts	Runners-up	Pts	Third	Pts
2007	Abahani	47	Mohammedan	40	Muktijoddha	33

National Championship

Winners	Score	Runners-up
Abahani	†	Mohammedan
	Not played	
Mohammedan	0-0 6-5p	Abahani
Muktijoddha	1-1 3-2p	Mohammedan
Brothers Union	0-0 4-2p	Muktijoddha
Mohammedan	2-0	Abahani

BDI – BURUNDI

NATIONAL TEAM RECORD
JULY 10TH 2006 TO JULY 12TH 2010

PL	W	D	L	F	A	%
7	3	0	4	8	10	42.8

FIFA/COCA-COLA WORLD RANKING

1993	1994	1995	1996	1997	1998	1999	2000	2001	2002	2003	2004	2005	2006	High		Low	
101	126	146	137	152	141	133	126	139	135	145	152	147	117	96	08/93	160	07/98

2006–2007											
08/06	09/06	10/06	11/06	12/06	01/07	02/07	03/07	04/07	05/07	06/07	07/07
156	159	133	128	117	120	117	117	120	121	111	116

Burundi were hoping to scale previously unclimbed heights in the 2008 African Nations Cup qualifiers after two wins from their first four qualifiers kept them in contention for a place in the finals in Ghana. The installation of artificial turf at the Prince Louis Rugasore stadium in Bujumbura caused all sorts of problems in their campaign, however. They had to play their June 2007 qualifier against Botswana in Kigali, Rwanda whilst the home match against Egypt in the same month was postponed until October. The tiny east African country has come close to qualifying for the finals once before when they were beaten in a play-off match in 1993 by Guinea

INTERNATIONAL HONOURS
None

on post-match penalties in a bid for the place in the 1994 finals in Tunisia. Solid form in the Nations Cup qualifiers, under their new Egyptian coach Lotfi Nassem, contrasted with their failure to get past the first phase of the East and Central African Senior Challenge Cup played in Addis Ababa in November and December. At club level, too, Burundian teams were disappointing in the African competitions with 2006 champions Vital'O hammered by Egyptian giants Zamalek in the first round of the 2007 African Champions League while Prince Louis lost to Atraco from neighbouring Rwanda in the African Confederation Cup.

THE FIFA BIG COUNT OF 2006

	Male	Female		Total
Number of players	335 284	17 050	Referees and Assistant Referees	412
Professionals	3		Admin, Coaches, Technical, Medical	9 220
Amateurs 18+	5 612		Number of clubs	165
Youth under 18	6 289		Number of teams	189
Unregistered	17 400		Clubs with women's teams	0
Total players	352 334		Players as % of population	4.36%

Fédération de Football du Burundi (FFB)
Building Nyogozi, Boulevard de l'Uprona, Case postale 3426, Bujumbura, Burundi
Tel +257 928762   Fax +257 242892
lydiansekera@yahoo.fr   www.none
President: NSEKERA Lydia   General Secretary: TBD
Vice-President: SAMUGABO Mustapha   Treasurer: NDEBERI Robert   Media Officer: None
Men's Coach: NASSEM Lotfi   Women's Coach: HAKIZIMANA Kebe
FFB formed: 1948   CAF: 1972   FIFA: 1972
Red shirts with white trimmings, White shorts, Green socks

RECENT INTERNATIONAL MATCHES PLAYED BY BURUNDI

2004	Opponents	Score		Venue	Comp	Scorers	Att	Referee
11-12	Ethiopia	L	1-2	Addis Abeba	CCrl	Hakizimana 75p		
13-12	Rwanda	W	3-1	Addis Abeba	CCrl	Hakizimana 51p, Ntibazonkizia 54, Nzohabonayo 83		
15-12	Tanzania	W	2-0	Addis Abeba	CCrl	Kubis 2 46 90		
17-12	Zanzibar †	W	2-1	Addis Abeba	CCrl	Nahimana 43, Hakizimana 78p		
22-12	Sudan	W	2-1	Addis Abeba	CCsf	Ntibazonkizia 22, Kubis 75		
25-12	Ethiopia	L	0-3	Addis Abeba	CCf			
2005								
28-11	Tanzania	L	1-2	Kigali	CCrl			
30-11	Zanzibar †	L	1-2	Kigali	CCrl	Ndahimana 61		
2-12	Eritrea	D	0-0	Kigali	CCrl			
4-12	Rwanda	L	0-2	Kigali	CCrl			
2006								
2-09	Egypt	L	1-4	Alexandria	CNq	Ndikumana 78p		Haimoudi ALG
8-10	Mauritania	W	3-1	Bujumbura	CNq	Ndikumana 2 2 30, Mbuzumutima 44		Abdelrahman SUD
26-11	Zambia	W	3-2	Addis Abeba	CCrl	Ndizeye 8, Nzohabonayo 17, Ndikumana 46		
29-11	Zanzibar †	D	0-0	Addis Abeba	CCrl			
6-12	Sudan	L	0-1	Addis Abeba	CCqf			
2007								
25-03	Botswana	L	0-1	Gaborone	CNq			Marange ZIM
27-05	Rwanda	L	0-1	Kigali	Fr			
3-06	Botswana	W	1-0	Kigali	CNq	Hakizimana 85		

Fr = Friendly match • CN = CAF African Cup of Nations qualifier • CC = CECAFA Cup • WCq = FIFA World Cup
q = qualifier • rl = 1st round • † Not a full international

BURUNDI NATIONAL TEAM RECORDS AND RECORD SEQUENCES

Records			Sequence records					
Victory	6-2	RWA 1976	Wins	5	1996-1998	Clean sheets	6	1993-1998
Defeat	1-6	CIV 2003	Defeats	4	1999	Goals scored	9	1982-1992
Player Caps	n/a		Undefeated	8	1993-1998	Without goal	4	2006-2007
Player Goals	n/a		Without win	14	2001-2004	Goals against	10	1975-1981

RECENT LEAGUE AND CUP RECORD

Year	Champions	Cup Winners
1996	Fantastique	Vital'O
1997	Maniema	Vital'O
1998	Vital'O	Elite
1999	Vital'O	Vital'O
2000	Vital'O	Atletico Olympique
2001	Prince Louis	
2002	Muzinga	
2003	Championship abandoned	
2004	Atletico Olympique	Bafalo Muramvya
2005	Inter Stars	
2006	Vital'O	

BURUNDI COUNTRY INFORMATION

Capital	Bujumbura	Independence	1962	GDP per Capita	$600
Population	6 231 221	Status	Republic	GNP Ranking	161
Area km²	27 830	Language	Kirundi/French	Dialling code	+257
Population density	224 per km²	Literacy rate	45%	Internet code	.bi
% in urban areas	8%	Main religion	Muslim 43%	GMT +/−	+2
Towns/Cities ('000)	Bujumbura 330; Muyinga 71; Ruyigi 38; Gitega 23; Ngozi 21; Rutana 20; Bururi 19;				
Neighbours (km)	Rwanda 290, Tanzania 451, Congo DR 233. Burundi also borders Lake Tanganyika				
Main stadia	Prince Louis Rwagasore – Bujumbura 22 000				

BEL – BELGIUM

NATIONAL TEAM RECORD
JULY 10TH 2006 TO JULY 12TH 2010

PL	W	D	L	F	A	%
9	2	1	6	5	12	22.2

FIFA/COCA-COLA WORLD RANKING

1993	1994	1995	1996	1997	1998	1999	2000	2001	2002	2003	2004	2005	2006	High		Low	
25	24	24	42	41	35	33	27	20	17	16	45	55	53	16	01/03	71	06/07

2006–2007											
08/06	09/06	10/06	11/06	12/06	01/07	02/07	03/07	04/07	05/07	06/07	07/07
55	50	47	53	53	53	52	55	59	62	71	70

After the problems of the previous season there was a return to normality in the Jupiler League and for much of the campaign it looked as if a third title was on the cards for Racing Club Genk. Coached by Hugo Broos, they led the table until mid March but then a 6-0 defeat by Anderlecht in the Cup and a 5-0 defeat to Mons in the league saw them lose their nerve and they finished second. That let in defending champions Anderlecht. Frankie Vercauteren's side, bolstered by the summer signings of Mohammed Tchiti and 2006 Belgian player of the year Mbark Boussoufa, stormed through at the end scoring 19 goals in their final three games to clinch the title. A last minute goal

INTERNATIONAL HONOURS
Qualified for the FIFA World Cup™ finals 1930 1934 1938 1954 1970 1982 1986 1990 1994 1998 2002 **Olympic Gold** 1920

in the final game by St Truiden's Jeroen Simaeys sent Beveren down, whilst Lierse, the only club other than Anderlecht, Club Brugge and Genk to win the title since 1990, joined them. Brugge had their worst league campaign in a number of years but they did salvage their season and claim a place in Europe by winning the Cup, beating Standard 1-0 in the final. Zulte-Waregem were the only success story in Europe, qualifying from the UEFA Cup group stage before losing to Newcastle, but internationally Belgium's stock is at a very low ebb with the national team likely to miss out on their third consecutive finals after a terrible start to their UEFA Euro 2008 campaign.

THE FIFA BIG COUNT OF 2006

	Male	Female		Total
Number of players	745 269	71 314	Referees and Assistant Referees	6 898
Professionals	1 399		Admin, Coaches, Technical, Medical	72 747
Amateurs 18+	212 009		Number of clubs	1 869
Youth under 18	208 551		Number of teams	17 960
Unregistered	128 200		Clubs with women's teams	189
Total players	816 583		Players as % of population	7.87%

Union Royale Belge des Sociétés de Football Association / Koninklijke Belgische Voetbalbond (URBSFA/KBVB)
145 Avenue Houba de Strooper, Bruxelles 1020, Belgium
Tel +32 2 4771211   Fax +32 2 4782391
urbsfa.kbvb@footbel.com   www.footbel.com
President: DE KEERSMAECKER Francois   General Secretary: HOUBEN Jean-Paul
Vice-President: TBD   Treasurer: LANDSHEERE Germain   Media Officer: CORNU Nicolas
Men's Coach: VANDEREYCKEN Rene   Women's Coach: NOE-HAESENDONCK Anne
URBSFA/KBVB formed: 1895   UEFA: 1954   FIFA: 1904
Red shirts with black trimmings, Red shorts, Red socks or Black shirts with red trimmings, Black shorts, Black socks

RECENT INTERNATIONAL MATCHES PLAYED BY BELGIUM

2002	Opponents	Score		Venue	Comp	Scorers	Att	Referee
21-08	Poland	D	1-1	Szczecin	Fr	Sonck [42]	19 000	Ingvarsson SWE
7-09	Bulgaria	L	0-2	Brussels	ECq		20 000	Hauge NOR
12-10	Andorra	W	1-0	Andorra La Vella	ECq	Sonck [61]	700	Nalbandyan ARM
16-10	Estonia	W	1-0	Tallinn	ECq	Sonck [2]	2 500	Riley ENG
2003								
12-02	Algeria	W	3-1	Annaba	Fr	Mpenza.E 2 [2 57], Sonck [7]	40 000	Baraket TUN
29-03	Croatia	L	0-4	Zagreb	ECq		25 000	Fandel GER
30-04	Poland	W	3-1	Brussels	Fr	Sonck [28], Buffel [56], Soetaers [86]	27 000	McDonald SCO
7-06	Bulgaria	D	2-2	Sofia	ECq	OG [31], Clement [56]	42 000	Collina ITA
11-06	Andorra	W	3-0	Gent	ECq	Goor 2 [20 68], Sonck [44]	12 000	Shmolik BLR
20-08	Netherlands	D	1-1	Brussels	Fr	Sonck [39]	38 000	Fandel GER
10-09	Croatia	W	2-1	Brussels	ECq	Sonck 2 [34 42]	35 000	Poll ENG
11-10	Estonia	W	2-0	Liege	ECq	OG [45], Buffel [61]	26 000	Busacca SUI
2004								
18-02	France	L	0-2	Brussels	Fr		43 160	Halsey ENG
31-03	Germany	L	0-3	Cologne	Fr		46 500	Wegereef NED
28-04	Turkey	L	2-3	Brussels	Fr	Sonck [33], Dufer [85]	25 000	Van Egmond NED
29-05	Netherlands	W	1-0	Eindhoven	Fr	Goor [77p]	32 500	Colombo FRA
18-08	Norway	D	2-2	Oslo	Fr	Buffel 2 [25 34]	16 669	Stupik POL
4-09	Lithuania	D	1-1	Charleroi	WCq	Sonck [61]	19 218	Loizou CYP
9-10	Spain	L	0-2	Santander	WCq		17 000	Nielsen DEN
17-11	Serbia & Montenegro	L	0-2	Brussels	WCq		28 350	Frojdfeldt SWE
2005								
9-02	Egypt	L	0-4	Cairo	Fr		5 000	Beltagi EGY
26-03	Bosnia-Herzegovina	W	4-1	Brussels	WCq	Mpenza.E 2 [15 54], Daerden [44], Buffel [77]	36 700	Hrinak SVK
30-03	San Marino	W	2-1	Serravalle	WCq	Simons [18p], Van Buyten [65]	871	Kasnaferis GRE
4-06	Serbia & Montenegro	D	0-0	Belgrade	WCq		16 662	Ivanov.V RUS
17-08	Greece	W	2-0	Brussels	Fr	Mpenza.E [19], Mpenza.M [24]	20 000	Berntsen NOR
3-09	Bosnia-Herzegovina	L	0-1	Zenica	WCq		12 000	Benquerenca POR
7-09	San Marino	W	8-0	Antwerp	WCq	Simons [34p], Daerden 2 [39 67], Buffel [44], Mpenza.M 2 [52 71], Vandenbergh [53], Van Buyten [83]	8 207	Stokes IRL
8-10	Spain	L	0-2	Brussels	WCq		40 300	Michel SVK
12-10	Lithuania	D	1-1	Vilnius	WCq	Garaerts [20]	1 500	Riley ENG
2006								
1-03	Luxembourg	W	2-0	Luxembourg	Fr	Vandenbergh [42], Pieroni [61]. Abandoned 65 mins		Einwaller AUT
11-05	Saudi Arabia	W	2-1	Sittard	Fr	Caluwe [3], Vanden Borre [55]		Bossen NED
20-05	Slovakia	D	1-1	Trnava	Fr	Geraerts [76]	4 174	Kassai HUN
24-05	Turkey	D	3-3	Genk	Fr	OG [28], Sonck [43], Hoefkens [90]	15 000	Stuchlik AUT
16-08	Kazakhstan	D	0-0	Brussels	ECq		15 495	Courtney NIR
6-09	Armenia	W	1-0	Yerevan	ECq	Van Buyten [41]	4 122	Lehner AUT
7-10	Serbia	L	0-1	Belgrade	ECq		16 901	Messina ITA
11-10	Azerbaijan	W	3-0	Brussels	ECq	Simons [24p], Vandenbergh [47], Dembélé [82]	11 917	Lajuks LVA
15-11	Poland	L	0-1	Brussels	ECq		37 928	Dougal SCO
2007								
7-02	Czech Republic	L	0-2	Brussels	Fr		12 000	Granat POL
24-03	Portugal	L	0-4	Lisbon	ECq		47 009	Vassaras GRE
2-06	Portugal	L	1-2	Brussels	ECq	Fellaini [55]	45 383	Hansson SWE
6-06	Finland	L	0-2	Helsinki	ECq		34 818	Riley ENG

Fr = Friendly match • EC = UEFA EURO 2004/2008 • WCq = FIFA World Cup • q = qualifier

BELGIUM NATIONAL TEAM RECORDS AND RECORD SEQUENCES

Records				Sequence records				
Victory	10-1	SMR 2001	Wins	7	1979-1980	Clean sheets	5	1972-1973, 1989
Defeat	2-11	ENG 1909	Defeats	7	1927-1928	Goals scored	21	1937-1945
Player Caps	96	CEULEMANS Jan	Undefeated	11	1988-1989	Without goal	5	1999
Player Goals	30	VOORHOOF & VAN HIMST	Without win	13	1933-1935	Goals against	38	1928-1933

KONINKRIJK BELGIE; ROYAUME DE BELGIQUE; KINGDOM OF BELGIUM

Capital	Brussels	Language	Flemish 60%, French 40%	Independence	1830
Population	10 379 067	Area	30 528 km²	Density 339 per km²	% in cities 97%
GDP per cap	$29 100	Dailling code	+32	Internet .be	GMT +/- +1

MEDALS TABLE

		Overall			League			Cup		Europe						
		G	S	B	G	S	B	G	S	G	S	B	City	Stadium	Cap'ty	DoF
1	RSC Anderlecht	40	25	9	29	18	7	8	3	3	4	2	Brussels	Vanden Stock	28 063	1908
2	Club Brugge	23	25	12	13	17	10	10	6		2	2	Bruges	Jan Breydel	29 042	1891
3	Standard Liège	13	20	21	8	10	19	5	9		1	2	Liège	Sclessin	30 035	1898
4	Union St Gilloise	13	8	8	11	8	7	2				1	Brussels	Joseph Marien	8 000	1897
5	Beerschot VAV	9	8	5	7	7	5	2	1				Antwerp	Kielstadion		1899-1999
6	Racing CB	7	5	3	6	5	3	1					Brussels	Ganzenvijver/Fallon		1891-1973
7	Royal Antwerp	6	14	7	4	12	7	2	1		1		Antwerp	Bosuil	16 649	1880
8	KV Mechelen	6	8	4	4	5	3	1	3	1		1	Mechelen	Scarletstadion	14 145	1904
9	Royal FC Liègeois	6	4	5	5	3	4	1	1			1	Liège	Ans		1892
10	Lierse SK	6	3	2	4	2	2	2	1				Lier	Herman Vanderpoorten	14 538	1906
11	Daring CB	5	5	4	5	4	4		1				Brussels	Edmond Machtens		1895-1973
12	Cercle Brugge	5	3	6	3		6	2	3				Bruges	Jan Breydel	29 268	1899
13	SK Beveren	4	3	1	2			2	3			1	Beveren-Waas	Freethiel	13 290	1934
14	KRC Genk	4	2		2	2		2					Genk	Feniksstadion	24 738	1988
15	KAA Gent	2	1	6		1	6	2					Gent	Jules Ottenstadion	13 265	1898
16	Waterschei Thor	2	1	2			1	2	1			1	Genk	Andre Dumont		1925-1988

RECENT LEAGUE AND CUP RECORD

	Championship						Cup		
Year	Champions	Pts	Runners-up	Pts	Third	Pts	Winners	Score	Runners-up
1995	RSC Anderlecht	52	Standard Liège	51	Club Brugge	49	Club Brugge	3-1	Germinal Ekeren
1996	Club Brugge	81	RSC Anderlecht	71	Germinal Ekeren	53	Club Brugge	2-1	Cercle Brugge
1997	Lierse SK	73	Club Brugge	71	Excelsior Mouscron	61	Germinal Ekeren	4-2	RSC Anderlecht
1998	Club Brugge	84	KRC Genk	66	Germinal Ekeren	58	KRC Genk	4-0	Club Brugge
1999	KRC Genk	73	Club Brugge	71	RSC Anderlecht	70	Lierse SK	3-1	Standard Liège
2000	RSC Anderlecht	75	Club Brugge	67	KAA Gent	63	KRC Genk	4-1	Standard Liège
2001	RSC Anderlecht	83	Club Brugge	78	Standard Liège	60	KVC Westerlo	1-0	KFC Lommelse
2002	KRC Genk	72	Club Brugge	72	RSC Anderlecht	66	Club Brugge	3-1	Excelsior Mouscron
2003	Club Brugge	79	RSC Anderlecht	71	KSC Lokeren	60	La Louvière	3-1	Sint-Truidense
2004	RSC Anderlecht	81	Club Brugge	72	Standard Liège	65	Club Brugge	4-2	KSK Beveren
2005	Club Brugge	79	RSC Anderlecht	76	Standard Liège	70	Germinal Beerschot	2-1	Club Brugge
2006	RSC Anderlecht	70	Standard Liège	65	Club Brugge	64	Zulte Waregem	2-1	Excelsior Mouscron
2007	RSC Anderlecht	77	KRC Genk	72	Standard Liège	64	Club Brugge	1-0	Standard Liège

BELGIUM 2006-07

LIGUE JUPILER

	Pl	W	D	L	F	A	Pts	Anderlecht	Genk	Standard	Gent	Charleroi	Brugge	Beerschot	Westerlo	Mons	Mouscron	Roeselare	Cercle	Brussels	Waregem	St-Truiden	Lokeren	Lierse	Beveren
RSC Anderlecht †	34	23	8	3	75	30	77		1-4	1-0	1-0	3-2	1-0	1-0	1-0	4-1	2-1	3-2	2-0	6-0	0-0	2-0	2-0	2-0	8-1
KRC Genk †	34	22	6	6	71	37	72	1-1		1-1	3-1	0-2	0-0	4-0	3-1	5-1	3-2	3-0	3-0	3-1	3-1	2-0	1-0	3-0	1-0
Standard Club Liège ‡	34	19	7	8	62	38	64	0-0	2-1		0-1	1-2	1-0	2-2	3-0	1-0	2-0	2-1	1-0	2-1	1-1	1-2	3-1	3-2	0-0
KAA Gent	34	18	6	10	56	40	60	2-1	1-3	2-1		2-1	0-0	1-2	2-0	4-1	1-3	2-0	2-1	1-1	3-1	3-1	3-1	4-0	2-1
RSC Charleroi	34	17	9	8	51	40	60	1-1	4-1	2-5	1-0		1-1	3-3	1-2	1-0	1-0	2-1	2-1	1-0	2-1	2-1	4-3	0-0	2-1
Club Brugge ‡	34	14	9	11	58	40	51	2-2	0-1	4-4	5-0	2-0		1-0	2-0	0-0	5-1	0-1	3-3	4-1	4-1	1-0	2-2	4-0	2-0
Germinal Beerschot	34	14	9	11	52	46	51	1-3	2-1	1-3	0-3	1-1	4-0		0-0	2-1	6-2	3-0	1-0	3-0	1-1	3-2	1-2	2-3	1-0
KVC Westerlo	34	12	10	12	41	44	46	3-4	0-1	1-1	1-1	0-1	1-2	1-1		2-1	1-0	2-1	0-0	1-1	4-2	1-0	4-1	2-0	2-0
RAEC Mons	34	12	8	14	41	41	44	3-1	5-0	2-3	0-1	1-2	1-0	2-1	1-1		1-0	6-1	1-0	1-0	0-0	2-0	1-0	1-1	1-0
Excelsior Mouscron	34	10	12	12	51	55	42	1-1	2-2	2-0	0-3	2-1	2-1	1-0	4-0	2-2		2-2	2-1	2-2	3-0	1-0	1-1	2-2	4-2
KSV Roeselare	34	10	9	15	50	72	39	0-5	3-3	2-3	1-3	1-3	3-2	1-1	2-0	2-1	2-1		1-0	1-1	3-1	3-2	2-2	2-0	2-1
Cercle Brugge	34	10	8	16	31	36	38	0-1	0-1	0-2	0-1	0-0	1-0	1-2	4-1	3-0	2-1	1-1		1-0	2-0	0-1	0-0	2-1	2-2
FC Brussels	34	8	14	12	39	50	38	0-1	3-1	0-3	1-1	0-2	1-1	1-2	0-1	1-0	1-1	6-2	0-0		2-0	2-2	0-0	2-1	2-0
Zulte-Waregem	34	9	10	15	40	54	37	0-4	2-2	3-1	3-2	1-0	2-1	0-2	2-2	1-2	0-0	4-2	1-2	0-1		3-0	1-1	2-1	2-1
Sint-Truiden VV	34	9	8	17	39	52	35	2-4	1-2	0-3	0-1	1-1	2-3	2-0	0-2	1-0	1-1	1-1	2-0	2-2	2-2		1-0	4-0	3-2
KSC Lokeren	34	5	15	14	32	48	30	1-1	0-1	2-1	1-0	0-0	3-2	0-0	1-1	0-2	1-1	1-1	2-0	0-0	0-2	1-1		1-4	2-0
Lierse SK ‡‡	34	6	8	20	33	66	26	1-4	0-3	1-3	1-4	2-1	1-2	2-3	1-1	0-0	3-3	3-1	0-2	0-1	1-0	0-0	1-0		0-1
KSK Beveren	34	5	10	19	31	64	25	1-1	0-5	0-3	1-0	2-2	0-2	1-1	0-3	0-0	3-1	2-2	1-1	2-2	1-0	1-2	3-2	1-1	

28/07/2006 - 19/05/2007 • † Qualified for the UEFA Champions League • ‡ Qualified for the UEFA Cup • ‡‡ Relegation play-off

Top scorers: François STERCHELE, Beerschot 21; Patrick OGUNSOTO, Westerlo 20; Mohammed TCHITE, Anderlecht 20; Adnan CUSTOVIC, Mouscron 18; Bosko BALABAN, Club Brugge 16

BELGIUM 2006-07
TWEEDE CLASSE (2)

	Pl	W	D	L	F	A	Pts
Verbroedering Dender	34	25	2	7	73	28	77
KV Mechelen ‡	34	21	7	6	64	36	70
KV Kortrijk ‡	34	19	10	5	69	36	67
Royal Antwerp ‡	34	17	9	8	63	37	60
Oud-Heverlee Leuven	34	16	8	10	55	49	56
KMSK Deinze	34	15	5	14	50	54	50
AS Eupen	34	12	12	10	50	47	48
Union St Gilloise	34	13	7	14	48	44	46
AFC Tubize	34	13	7	14	36	34	46
KVK Tienen	34	12	9	13	50	57	45
Excelsior Virton	34	11	8	15	38	55	41
VW Hamme	34	9	12	13	38	43	39
KV Oostende	34	9	12	13	51	60	39
Red Star Waasland	34	9	12	13	43	56	39
KVSK United	34	9	9	16	39	50	36
Dessel Sport	34	10	4	20	45	58	34
KRC Waregem	34	7	8	19	34	58	29
KSK Ronse	34	4	9	21	28	72	21

23/08/2006 - 20/05/2007 • ‡ Qualified for play-offs

BELGIUM 2006-07
TWEEDE CLASSE PLAY-OFFS

	Pl	W	D	L	F	A	Pts	Mechelen	Antwerp	Lierse	Kortrijk
KV Mechelen	6	5	1	0	11	3	16		1-0	2-0	3-0
Royal Antwerp	6	3	1	2	7	4	10	0-0		2-1	3-0
Lierse SK	6	3	0	3	10	8	9	1-2	2-0		5-2
KV Kortrijk	6	0	0	6	4	17	0	2-3	0-2	0-1	

27/05/2007 - 14/06/2007

COUPE DE BELGIQUE 2006-07

Round of 16		Quarter–finals		Semi–finals		Final	
Club Brugge *	1						
KVC Westerlo	0	Club Brugge *	2 1				
Sint-Truiden VV	2	KV Kortrijk	1 1				
KV Kortrijk *	4			Club Brugge	1 2		
KV Mechelen *	1			KAA Gent *	3 0		
Zulte-Waregem	0	KV Mechelen	1 0				
KSV Roeselare	2	KAA Gent *	2 1			Club Brugge ‡	1
KAA Gent	3					Standard Club Liège	0
RSC Anderlecht *	5						
Verbroedering Dender	2	RSC Anderlecht	1 6				
Excelsior Mouscron	0	KRC Genk *	0 0				
KRC Genk *	1			RSC Anderlecht *	0 1		
Royal Antwerp	4			Standard Club Liège	1 2		
Lierse SK *	1	Royal Antwerp *	0 0				
VW Hamme	0	Standard Club Liège	1 4				
Standard Club Liège *	5						

CUP FINAL
Stade Roi Baudouin, Brussels
26-05-2007, Att: 45 380
Scorer - Ishiaku [17] for Club Brugge

* Home team/home team in 1st leg • ‡ Qualified for the UEFA Cup

BEN – BENIN

NATIONAL TEAM RECORD
JULY 10TH 2006 TO JULY 12TH 2010

PL	W	D	L	F	A	%
7	2	2	3	9	7	42.8

FIFA/COCA-COLA WORLD RANKING

1993	1994	1995	1996	1997	1998	1999	2000	2001	2002	2003	2004	2005	2006	High		Low	
130	143	161	143	137	127	140	148	152	146	121	122	113	114	85	07/07	165	07/96

2006–2007											
08/06	09/06	10/06	11/06	12/06	01/07	02/07	03/07	04/07	05/07	06/07	07/07
105	101	109	111	114	115	116	118	107	107	103	85

Benin again proved competitive in the qualifiers of the 2008 African Nations Cup finals but missed out on a place at the finals tournament, although much of that disappointment will have been dissipated by a thumping 4-1 win over neighbours and fierce rivals Togo in June 2007. It was a win which catapulted the country to an all-time high of 85 in the FIFA/Coca-Cola World Ranking. Benin's participation in the 2004 Nations Cup finals is now fading into the distant memory but the players who took the country to the FIFA World U-20 Championship in the Netherlands in 2005 are now beginning to progress through to the senior national side. There was a change in coaching

INTERNATIONAL HONOURS
None

personnel in January when Codjo Edme resigned, leaving Waby Gomez to take over at the helm of Les Ecureuils. Champions Mogas '90 lost both home and away to Libya's Al Ittihad in the first round of the 2007 African Champions League while Dragons l'Oueme also failed to score as they went out in the first round of the African Confederation Cup to Nigeria's Kwara United. But there was individual glory for Benin international Muri Ogunbiyi, who starred for Tunisian side Etoile du Sahel team when they won the 2006 African Confederation Cup in November. He had previously won the CAF Champions League with Nigeria's Enyimba.

THE FIFA BIG COUNT OF 2006

	Male	Female		Total
Number of players	320 600	0	Referees and Assistant Referees	200
Professionals	0		Admin, Coaches, Technical, Medical	1 500
Amateurs 18+	5 000		Number of clubs	110
Youth under 18	2 800		Number of teams	440
Unregistered	33 800		Clubs with women's teams	0
Total players	320 600		Players as % of population	4.08%

Fédération Béninoise de Football (FBF)
Stade René Pleven d'Akpakpa, Case Postale 965, Cotonou 01, Benin
Tel +229 330537   Fax +229 330537
www.none
President: ANJORIN Moucharafou   General Secretary: DIDAVI Bruno Arthur
Vice-President: AKPLOGAN Firmin   Treasurer: AHOUANVOEBLA Augustin   Media Officer: None
Men's Coach: GOMEZ Waby   Women's Coach: None
FBF formed: 1962   CAF: 1969   FIFA: 1962
Green shirts with yellow and red trimmings, Yellow shorts, Red socks

RECENT INTERNATIONAL MATCHES PLAYED BY BENIN

2004	Opponents	Score	Venue	Comp	Scorers	Att	Referee
20-05	Togo	L 0-1	Cotonou	Fr			
23-05	Togo	D 1-1	Lome	Fr	Amoussou [9]		
26-05	Burkina Faso	W 1-0	Cotonou	Fr	Maiga [75]		
6-06	Cameroon	L 1-2	Yaoundé	WCq	Tchomogo.S [11]	40 000	Mbera GAB
13-06	Burkina Faso	L 2-4	Ouagadougou	Fr	Amoussou [33], Adjamonsi [44p]		
20-06	Sudan	D 1-1	Cotonou	WCq	Ogunbiyi [30]	20 000	Guezzaz MAR
4-07	Egypt	D 3-3	Cotonou	WCq	Tchomogo.O [8p], Ahoueya [46], Ogunbiyi [58]	15 000	Chukwujekwu NGA
3-09	Libya	L 1-4	Tripoli	WCq	Osseni [12]	30 000	Kidane Tesfu ERI
3-10	Gabon	L 0-2	Libreville	Fr			
10-10	Côte d'Ivoire	L 0-1	Cotonou	WCq		25 000	Sowe GAM
2005							
27-03	Côte d'Ivoire	L 0-3	Abidjan	WCq		35 000	Guirat TUN
4-06	Cameroon	L 1-4	Cotonou	WCq	Agbessi [81]	20 000	El Arjoun MAR
17-08	Sudan	L 0-1	Omdurman	WCq		12 000	Maillet SEY
4-09	Egypt	L 1-4	Cairo	WCq	Sessegnon [60]	5 000	Buenkadila COD
23-09	United Arab Emirates	D 0-0	Dubai	Fr			
9-10	Libya	W 1-0	Cotonou	WCq	Chitou [60]	1 880	Mususa ZIM
2006							
26-02	Equatorial Guinea	L 0-1	Cotonou	Fr			
29-03	Equatorial Guinea	L 0-2	Bata	Fr			
3-09	Togo	L 1-2	Lome	CNq	Tchomogo [86]		Louzaya CGO
8-10	Sierra Leone	W 2-0	Cotonou	CNq	Chitou [22p], Ogunbiyi [82]		Sowe GAM
2007							
7-02	Senegal	L 1-2	Rouen	Fr	Omotoyossi [79]		Lannoy FRA
22-02	Chad	L 0-1	Cotonou	Fr			
25-03	Mali	D 1-1	Bamako	CNq	Ogunbiyi [44]		Doue CIV
3-06	Mali	D 0-0	Cotonou	CNq			
16-06	Togo	W 4-1	Cotonou	CNq	Omotoyossi 2 [45 53], Sessegnon [48], Ogonbiyi [58]		

Fr = Friendly match • CN = CAF African Cup of Nations • WCq = FIFA World Cup • q = qualifier • r1 = first round group

BENIN NATIONAL TEAM RECORDS AND RECORD SEQUENCES

Records			Sequence records					
Victory	6-2	CHA 1963	Wins	3	2003	Clean sheets	3	2003
Defeat	1-10	NGA 1959	Defeats	9	1991-1993	Goals scored	7	1963-1965, 2004
Player Caps	n/a		Undefeated	7	1963-1965	Without goal	5	1988-1990, 1991
Player Goals	n/a		Without win	24	1984-1991	Goals against	14	1963-1969

RECENT LEAGUE AND CUP RECORD

	Championship						Coupe de l'Independence		
Year	Champions	Pts	Runners-up	Pts	Third	Pts	Winners	Score	Runners-up
2001	No championship held						Buffles Borgou	1-0	Dragons
2002	Dragons	15	Requins	15	Postel	13	Jeunesse Pobe	0-0 1-1 4-3p	Mogas 90
2003	Dragons	21	Buffles Borgou	19	Postel	14	Mogas 90	1-0	Soleil
2004	Championship unfinished						Mogas 90	1-0	Requins
2005	No championship held						No competition		
2006	Mogas 90	34	Dragons	33	Buffles Borgou	32	Dragons	0-0 2-0	Mogas 90

BENIN COUNTRY INFORMATION

Capital	Porto-Novo	Independence	1960	GDP per Capita	$1 100
Population	7 250 033	Status	Republic	GNP Ranking	135
Area km²	112 620	Language	French, Fon, Yoruba	Dialling code	+229
Population density	64 per km²	Literacy rate	40%	Internet code	.bj
% in urban areas	31%	Main religion	Indigenous 50%	GMT +/−	+1
Towns/Cities ('000)	Cotonou 690; Abomey 385; Porto Novo 234; Djougou 202; Parakou 163; Bohicon 125				
Neighbours (km)	Niger 226; Nigeria 773; Togo 644; Burkina Faso 306; Atlantic Ocean (Bight of Benin) 121				
Main stadia	Stade de l'Amitié – Cotonou 35 000; Stade Municipale – Porto Novo 20 000				

BER – BERMUDA

NATIONAL TEAM RECORD
JULY 10TH 2006 TO JULY 12TH 2010

PL	W	D	L	F	A	%
8	3	1	4	14	13	43.7

FIFA/COCA-COLA WORLD RANKING

1993	1994	1995	1996	1997	1998	1999	2000	2001	2002	2003	2004	2005	2006	High	Low
84	102	140	167	176	185	163	153	166	172	183	157	161	107	**78** 08/93	**185** 12/98

						2006–2007						
08/06	09/06	10/06	11/06	12/06	01/07	02/07	03/07	04/07	05/07	06/07	07/07
160	163	122	121	107	121	118	116	123	123	127	130

Bermuda came within a whisker of a first ever appearance in the Digicel Caribbean Cup, just missing out on the finals in Trinidad at the last hurdle. The team actually travelled to Trinidad, along with the other finalists, but they had to play-off against Haiti to determine the last place available and lost 5-0 on aggregate. Bermuda had advanced through two qualifying groups scoring 15 goals in five games with Kwame Steede the top scorer with four and it proved that the national team is improving and is now capable of competing at a level just below the top Caribbean nations such as Trinidad, Jamaica, Haiti and Cuba. The domestic setup certainly provides a good foundation for the game and

INTERNATIONAL HONOURS
None

once again the League was very competitive. It was won for the second time in three seasons by Devonshire Cougars, who finished two points ahead of a North Village team that finished trophyless for the first season since 1998. With four cup tournaments, there is certainly a lot to play for and there were surprise winners of the FA Cup in Devonshire Colts. The three other Cups saw a double for Somerset Trojans in the Friendship trophy and the Dudley Eve Trophy - both against Devonshire Cougars whilst Cougars won the other remaining tournament of the season, the Martonmere Cup, to complete a double of their own.

THE FIFA BIG COUNT OF 2006

	Male	Female		Total
Number of players	6 205	950	Referees and Assistant Referees	35
Professionals	5		Admin, Coaches, Technical, Medical	220
Amateurs 18+	2 250		Number of clubs	50
Youth under 18	1 600		Number of teams	100
Unregistered	800		Clubs with women's teams	8
Total players	7 155		Players as % of population	10.88

Bermuda Football Association (BFA)
48 Cedar Avenue, Hamilton, HM 12, Bermuda
Tel +1 441 2952199   Fax +1 441 2950773
bfa@northrock.bm   www.bfa.bm
President: MUSSENDEN Larry   General Secretary: SABIR David
Vice-President: BLANKENDAL Calvin   Treasurer: GRIFFITH Andrew   Media Officer: None
Men's Coach: LIGHTBOURNE Kyle   Women's Coach: BROWN Vance
BFA formed: 1928   CONCACAF: 1966   FIFA: 1966
Blue shirts with red and white trimmings, Blue shorts, Blue socks

RECENT INTERNATIONAL MATCHES PLAYED BY BERMUDA

2002	Opponents	Score	Venue	Comp	Scorers	Att	Referee
No international matches played in 2002							
2003							
26-12	Barbados	L 1-2	Hamilton	Fr	Nusum [79]		Mouchette BER
2004							
1-01	Barbados	L 0-4	Hamilton	Fr			Raynor BER
10-02	Trinidad and Tobago	L 0-1	Hamilton	Fr		3 000	Raynor BER
12-02	Trinidad and Tobago	D 2-2	Hamilton	Fr	Smith.C [36], Simons [76]		Crockwell BER
29-02	Montserrat	W 13-0	Hamilton	WCq	Ming 3 [5 20 50], Nusum 3 [15 54 60], Smith.K [36], Bean.R 2 [41 52], Steede [43], Wade [77], Simons [83], Burgess [87]	3 000	Kennedy USA
21-03	Montserrat	W 7-0	Plymouth	WCq	Hill [15], Nusum 2 [21 44], Bean.R [39], Smith.K 2 [45 46], Ming [76]	250	Charles DOM
31-03	Nicaragua	W 3-0	Hamilton	Fr	Goater 2 [33 65p], Simons [90]		Crockwell BER
2-04	Nicaragua	W 2-1	Hamilton	Fr	Nusum 2 [47 67]		Raynor BER
28-04	Panama	L 1-4	Panama City	Fr	Ashwood [14]		
30-04	Nicaragua	L 0-2	Diriamba	Fr		800	
2-05	Nicaragua	L 0-2	Esteli	Fr			
13-06	El Salvador	L 1-2	San Salvador	WCq	Nusum [30]	12 000	Campos NCA
20-06	El Salvador	D 2-2	Hamilton	WCq	Burgess [5p], Nusum [21]	4 000	Whittaker CAY
24-11	Cayman Islands	W 2-1	Kingstown	CCq	Smith.K [4], Hill [34]	200	Mathews SKN
26-11	St Vincent/Grenadines	D 3-3	Kingstown	CCq	Smith.K [42], Lowe [82], Ming [90p]		
28-11	British Virgin Islands	L 0-2	Kingstown	CCq		400	Mathews SKN
2005							
25-05	Trinidad and Tobago	L 0-4	Port of Spain	Fr		400	
27-05	Trinidad and Tobago	L 0-1	Marabella	Fr			
2006							
27-09	US Virgin Islands	W 6-0	Charlotte Amalie	CCq	Steede 2 [1 36], Cordington 2 [31 54], Nusum [38], Jennings [90]	150	Small BRB
29-09	Dominican Republic	W 3-1	Charlotte Amalie	CCq	Zuill [25], Cox [48], Steede [53]	300	Martis ANT
19-11	St Vincent/Grenadines	L 0-3	Bridgetown	CCq			
21-11	Bahamas	W 4-0	Bridgetown	CCq	Smith.K 2 [6 28], Barry [17], Steede [87]		
23-11	Barbados	D 1-1	Bridgetown	CCq	Nusum [42]		
2007							
7-01	Haiti	L 0-2	Couva	CCq			Brizan TRI
9-01	Haiti	L 0-3	Couva	CCq			Davis TRI
25-03	Canada	L 0-3	Hamilton	Fr			

Fr = Friendly match • CC = Digicel Caribbean Cup • WC = FIFA World Cup • q = qualifier

BERMUDA NATIONAL TEAM RECORDS AND RECORD SEQUENCES

Records			Sequence records				
Victory	13-0	MSR 2004	Wins	4	2004	Clean sheets	3	2004
Defeat	0-6	DEN 1969, CAN 1983	Defeats	6	1968-1969	Goals scored	17	1990-1992
Player Caps	n/a		Undefeated	7	1990-1991	Without goal	3	2004-2005, 2007
Player Goals	n/a		Without win	10	1964-1969	Goals against	12	1968-1971

BERMUDA COUNTRY INFORMATION

Capital	Hamilton	Independence	British Crown Colony	GDP per Capita	$36 000
Population	64 935	Status		GNP Ranking	n/a
Area km²	53.3	Language	English	Dialling code	+1 441
Population density	1 218 per km²	Literacy rate	99%	Internet code	.bm
% in urban areas	100%	Main religion	Christian	GMT + / –	-4
Towns/Cities ('000)	Hamilton 1; St George 1				
Neighbours (km)	North Atlantic Ocean				
Main stadia	National Stadium – Hamilton 8 500; White Hill – Sandys				

BERMUDA 2006–07

PREMIER DIVISION

	Pl	W	D	L	F	A	Pts	Cougars	North Village	Blazers	Dandy Town	Trojans	Zebras	Lions	St David's
Devonshire Cougars	14	9	3	2	37	15	30		3-0	2-1	1-1	0-2	2-1	5-1	4-1
North Village	14	8	4	2	40	18	28	3-3		2-0	4-2	3-0	3-1	7-1	5-2
Boulevard Blazers	14	7	4	3	31	18	25	2-1	1-0		1-3	1-1	2-2	1-1	2-1
Dandy Town	14	5	6	3	35	16	21	1-1	0-0	2-2		3-0	1-2	11-0	2-0
Somerset Trojans	14	5	4	5	19	23	19	1-3	0-5	1-2	1-0		2-1	3-1	1-1
PHC Zebras	14	4	4	6	21	25	16	1-4	2-2	0-3	2-2	1-1		1-0	4-0
Paget Lions	14	2	2	10	15	66	8	0-5	3-3	1-9	0-5	1-5	3-2		2-1
St David's	14	1	3	10	18	35	6	0-3	0-3	1-4	2-2	1-1	0-1	8-1	

1/10/2006 - 27/03/2007 • Top scorers: Ralph BEAN, North Village 13; Kwame STEEDE, Cougars 9

FRIENDSHIP TROPHY 2006–07

Semi–finals		Final	
Somserset Trojans	3		
Boulevard Blazers	2		
		Somserset Trojans	4
		Devonshire Cougars	0
Paget Lions	0		1-04-2007
Devonshire Cougars	2		

MARTONMERE CUP 2006

Semi–finals		Final	
Devonshire Cougars	5		
Dandy Town	0		
		Devonshire Cougars	2
		PHC Zebras	0
Somset Trojans	0		11-11-2006
PHC Zebras	1		

FA CUP 2006–07

Round of sixteen		Quarter–finals		Semi–finals		Final	
Devonshire Colts	4						
St David's	2	Devonshire Colts	4				
Valley	1	Prospect United	1				
Prospect United	2			Devonshire Colts	2		
North Village	2			St George's Colts	0		
Crossroads	0	North Village	1				
Paget Lions	2 1	St George's Colts	3				
St George's Colts	2 3					Devonshire Colts	2
Somerset Trojans	5					Boulevard Blazers	0
Ireland Rangers	1	Somerset Trojans	3 1				
Southampton Rangers	0	Devonshire Cougars	3 0			CUP FINAL	
Devonshire Cougars	5			Somerset Trojans	0		
PHC Zebras	2			Boulevard Blazers	1	22-04-2007, Ref: Raynor	
Key West Rangers	0	PHC Zebras	0			Scorers - Ming & Zuill for Colts	
Somset Eagles	0	Boulevard Blazers	3				
Boulevard Blazers	3						

RECENT LEAGUE AND CUP RECORD

			Championship						FA Cup		
Year	Champions	Pts	Runners-up	Pts	Third	Pts		Winners	Score	Runners-up	
1997	Devonshire Colts	41	Vasco da Gama	34	Dandy Town	31		Boulevard Blazers	3-2	Wolves	
1998	Vasco da Gama		Dandy Town		Boulevard Blazers			Vasco da Gama	2-1	Devonshire Colts	
1999	Vasco da Gama	41	Dandy Town	33	North Village	32		Devonshire Colts	1-0	Dandy Town	
2000	PHC Zebras	39	North Village	37	Dandy Town	32		North Village	2-1	Devonshire Colts	
2001	Dandy Town	29	North Village	28	Devonshire Colts	26		Devonshire Colts	3-1	North Village	
2002	North Village	27	Dandy Town	23	Devonshire Cougars	22		North Village	3-0	Dandy Town	
2003	North Village	29	Devonshire Cougars	23	Boulevard Blazers	20		North Village	5-1	Prospect	
2004	Dandy Town	31	Devonshire Cougars	30	Boulevard Blazers	25		Dandy Town	3-3 2-1	Devonshire Cougars	
2005	Devonshire Cougars	32	Dandy Town	30	PHC Zebras	26		North Village	2-0	Hamilton Parish	
2006	North Village	35	Somerset Trojans	28	Dandy Town	28		North Village	4-1	Dandy Town	
2007	Devonshire Cougars	30	North Village	28	Boulevard Blazers	25		Devonshire Colts	2-0	Boulevard Blazers	

BFA – BURKINA FASO

NATIONAL TEAM RECORD
JULY 10TH 2006 TO JULY 12TH 2010

PL	W	D	L	F	A	%
10	2	3	5	7	11	35

FIFA/COCA-COLA WORLD RANKING

1993	1994	1995	1996	1997	1998	1999	2000	2001	2002	2003	2004	2005	2006	High	Low
127	97	101	107	106	75	71	69	78	75	78	84	87	61	**54** 05/07	**127** 12/93

2006–2007											
08/06	09/06	10/06	11/06	12/06	01/07	02/07	03/07	04/07	05/07	06/07	07/07
71	97	64	62	61	62	57	56	55	54	59	84

Burkina Faso's national team crashed badly in the African Nations Cup qualifiers, even after they brought back French coach Didier Notheaux to resurrect their chances. 'Les Etalons' had high hopes of reaching the finals in neighbouring Ghana in 2008, after bringing back Idrissa 'Saboteur' Traore to the helm in a bid to replicate his success of a decade earlier when he took an unfancied Burkinabe team to the 1996 Nations Cup finals. More than 10 years on, Traore was able to call upon a much better-heeled squad of players, the vast majority playing in Europe, but he was fired after securing just four points from their first 12 in the qualifying campaign. Notheaux did not fare

much better, however, as Burkina Faso crashed to defeat against Mozambique and Tanzania and out of the race. Commune FC Ouagadougou won the national championship, snatching a first-ever title by one point from Etoile Filante. CFO won their last game of the season against Santos FC, although there was much controversy and an attack on the match referee when Santos were not awarded a last minute penalty. The capital city club, coached by Seydou Zerbo, denied Etoile their first title in six years. In the 21st Coupe du Faso final a week later, Racing Club from Bobo-Dioulasso beat USO from Ouagadougou 2-1, to win the trophy for the first time since 1987.

THE FIFA BIG COUNT OF 2006

	Male	Female		Total
Number of players	576 800	28 300	Referees and Assistant Referees	700
Professionals	0		Admin, Coaches, Technical, Medical	2 400
Amateurs 18+	13 000		Number of clubs	100
Youth under 18	10 200		Number of teams	850
Unregistered	45 900		Clubs with women's teams	0
Total players	605 100		Players as % of population	4.35

Fédération Burkinabé de Foot-Ball (FBF)

Centre Technique National, Ouaga 2000, 01 Casa Postale 57, Ouagadougou 01, Burkina Faso
Tel +226 50 396864   Fax +226 50 396866
febefoo@fasonet.bf   www.fasofoot.com
President: DIAKITE Seydou   General Secretary: ZANGREYANOGHO Joseph
Vice-President: KABORE Salif   Treasurer: TRAORE SOME Clemence   Media Officer: BARRY Alpha
Men's Coach: NOTHEAUX Didier   Women's Coach: None
FBF formed: 1960   CAF: 1964   FIFA: 1964
Green shirts with red and white trimmings, Green shorts, Green socks

RECENT INTERNATIONAL MATCHES PLAYED BY BURKINA FASO

2004	Opponents	Score		Venue	Comp	Scorers	Att	Referee
17-01	Egypt	D	1-1	Port Said	Fr	Dagano 35	8 000	
20-01	Guinea	L	0-1	Sainte-Maxime	Fr			
26-01	Senegal	D	0-0	Tunis	CNr1		2 000	Guezzaz MAR
30-01	Mali	L	1-3	Tunis	CNr1	Minoungou 50	1 500	Shelmani LBY
2-02	Kenya	L	0-3	Bizerte	CNr1		4 550	Sowe GAM
26-05	Benin	L	0-1	Cotonou	Fr			
30-05	Libya	W	3-2	Ouagadougou	Fr	Kone.Y 11, Kabore.I 34, Diabate 70		
5-06	Ghana	W	1-0	Ouagadougou	WCq	Zongo 79	25 000	Chukwujekwu NGA
13-06	Benin	W	4-2	Ouagadougou	Fr	Toure.A 41, Coulibaly.A 55, Dagano 89, Ouedraogo.A 90		
20-06	Congo DR	L	2-3	Kinshasa	WCq	Toure.A 26, Dagano 85	75 000	Djaoupe TOG
3-07	South Africa	L	0-2	Johannesburg	WCq		25 000	Ramanampamony MAD
17-08	Algeria	D	2-2	Blida	Fr	Zongo 50p, Ouedraogo.H 67	15 000	Tahri MAR
4-09	Uganda	W	2-0	Ouagadougou	WCq	Dagano 34, Nikiema 79	30 000	Lemghambodj MTN
9-10	Cape Verde Islands	L	0-1	Praia	WCq		6 000	Aziaka TOG
17-11	Morocco	L	0-4	Rabat	Fr		5 000	Keita.M MLI
2005								
9-02	Algeria	L	0-3	Algiers	Fr		3 000	Benaissa ALG
20-03	Korea Republic	L	0-1	Dubai	Fr			
26-03	Cape Verde Islands	L	1-2	Ouagadougou	WCq	Dagano 71	27 500	Evehe CMR
29-05	Togo	L	0-1	Lome	Fr			
5-06	Ghana	L	1-2	Kumasi	WCq	Dagano 30	11 920	Abd El Fatah EGY
18-06	Congo DR	W	2-0	Ouagadougou	WCq	Panandetiguiri 3, Dagano 68	25 000	Shelmani LBY
3-09	South Africa	W	3-1	Ouagadougou	WCq	Abdoulaye Cisse 2 32 47, Kebe 39	25 000	Codjia BEN
8-10	Uganda	D	2-2	Kampala	WCq	Kebe 15, Rouamba 75	1 433	Benouza ALG
2006								
28-02	Algeria	D	0-0	Rouen	Fr		2 000	Duhamel FRA
16-08	Morocco	L	0-1	Rabat	Fr			
29-08	Uganda	D	0-0	Kampala	Fr			
2-09	Tanzania	L	1-2	Dar es Salaam	CNq	Abdoulaye Cisse 39		Ndinya KEN
7-10	Senegal	W	1-0	Ouagadougou	CNq	Yameogo 59p		Guezzaz MAR
15-11	Algeria	W	2-1	Aix-en-Provence	Fr	Yameogo 60p, Koffi 82	700	Falcone FRA
2007								
24-03	Mozambique	D	1-1	Ouagadougou	CNq	Pitroipa 26		Imiere NGA
29-05	Zimbabwe	D	1-1	Masvingo	Fr	Kabore 71	12 000	
3-06	Mozambique	L	1-3	Maputo	CNq	Sanou 33		
9-06	Mali	L	0-1	Ouagadougou	Fr			
16-06	Tanzania	L	0-1	Ouagadougou	CNq			

Fr = Friendly match • CN = CAF African Cup of Nations • WC = FIFA World Cup • q = qualifier, r1 = first round group

BURKINA FASO NATIONAL TEAM RECORDS AND RECORD SEQUENCES

Records			Sequence records					
Victory	4-0	MOZ 2003	Wins	6	1988	Clean sheets	6	2003
Defeat	0-7	ALG 1981	Defeats	10	1976-1981	Goals scored	24	1998-2000
Player Caps	n/a		Undefeated	7	1999	Without goal	4	Three times
Player Goals	n/a		Without win	13	1976-82, 1994-96	Goals against	13	1960-1967

BURKINA FASO COUNTRY INFORMATION

Capital	Ouagadougou	Independence	1960	GDP per Capita	$1 100
Population	13 574 820	Status	Republic	GNP Ranking	133
Area km²	274 200	Language	French	Dialling code	+226
Population density	49 per km²	Literacy rate	26%	Internet code	.bf
% in urban areas	27%	Main religion	Muslim 50%	GMT +/–	0
Towns/Cities ('000)	Ouagadougou 1 031; Bobo-Dioulasso 370; Koudougou 86; Banfora 63; Ouahigouya 61				
Neighbours (km)	Mali 1,000; Niger 628; Benin 306; Togo 126; Ghana 549; Côte d'Ivoire 584				
Main stadia	Stade du 4 Août – Ouagadougou 40 000; Stade Municipal – Bobo-Dioulasso 30 000				

BURKINA FASO 2005-06

PREMIERE DIVISION

	Pl	W	D	L	F	A	Pts	CFO	EFO	USFA	USO	RCB	SONABEL	ASFA/Y	RCK	ASFB	Santos	USY	USCO	Bobo Sport	ASECK
Commune FC †	26	13	10	3	23	13	49		3-0	0-0	**0-1**	1-1	1-0	0-1	1-0	0-0	2-1	0-4	1-1	1-1	1-0
Etoile Filante	26	13	9	4	29	17	48	0-0		2-1	2-2	1-0	1-0	0-1	0-0	2-0	1-1	0-0	1-0	0-0	2-1
US Forces Armées	26	10	12	4	30	15	42	0-1	0-0		2-0	2-1	2-0	0-3	1-1	0-0	0-0	2-0	1-1	3-0	1-1
US Ouagadougou	26	10	11	5	29	20	41	2-2	3-1	2-2		1-1	1-1	1-0	0-2	1-1	1-1	1-0	2-0	0-0	2-0
Racing Club B-D	26	9	13	4	22	13	40	0-0	0-1	0-0	1-0		0-0	1-0	0-0	2-0	0-0	2-0	2-0	2-2	2-0
AS SONABEL	26	9	9	8	22	22	36	0-0	0-3	0-5	1-0	1-1		0-0	2-1	3-2	0-1	0-1	3-0	2-0	0-0
ASFA/Yennenga	26	9	8	9	22	14	35	0-1	1-1	0-0	0-0	0-1	0-2		0-0	4-0	0-0	0-2	2-0	1-0	3-0
Rail Club Kadiogo	26	8	11	7	21	14	35	0-1	1-2	0-0	1-1	1-0	0-1	1-0		4-0	1-0	1-0	3-0	1-1	2-0
ASF Bobo-Dioulasso	26	9	7	10	25	29	34	0-1	0-4	0-3	1-0	0-1	1-2	1-0	1-0		0-0	3-0	3-0	5-0	2-0
Santos	26	7	12	7	22	17	33	0-2	1-1	0-1	1-1	1-1	0-0	1-0	2-0	1-1		2-0	4-0	1-0	1-2
US Yatenga	26	7	9	10	16	19	30	0-1	2-0	1-0	0-1	0-1	0-0	1-1	1-1	0-2	0-0		0-0	0-0	2-0
US Comoé	26	4	10	12	10	31	22	1-1	0-2	0-1	0-2	0-0	1-0	0-0	0-0	0-0	1-0	0-1		1-0	0-0
Bobo Sport	26	2	12	12	14	33	18	0-1	0-1	2-2	0-2	2-2	1-1	1-2	0-0	0-1	0-2	0-0	2-2		1-0
ASEC Koudougou	26	2	7	17	8	36	13	0-1	0-1	0-1	0-2	0-0	**0-3**	**0-3**	0-0	1-1	2-1	1-1	0-2	0-1	

20/01/2007 - 28/07/2007 • † Qualified for the CAF Champions League • Matches in bold were awarded

COUPE NATIONALE DU FASO 2006-07

Round of 16		Quarter-finals		Semi-finals		Final	
Racing Club B-D *	2						
BPFC Koudougou	1	Racing Club B-D * †	0				
AS SONABEL	0	Rail Club Kadiogo	1				
Rail Club Kadiogo *	1			Racing Club B-D	1		
Commune FC *	2			US Yatenga *	0		
Santos	0	Commune FC	1				
US Forces Armées *	1 7p	US Yatenga *	2				
US Yatenga	1 8p					Racing Club B-D ‡	2
ASFA/Yennenga *	2					US Ouagadougou	1
ASEC Koudougou	0	ASFA/Yennenga	2				
USFRAN B-D *	0 2p	Etoile Filante *	1				
Etoile Filante	0 3p			ASFA/Yennenga *	0		
AS Koupèla	2 4p			US Ouagadougou	2		
Futuro Club Ouaga *	2 3p	AS Koupèla	0				
ASF Bobo-Dioulasso *	0	US Ouagadougou *	2			* Home team	
US Ouagadougou	1	† Match awarded to RCBD • ‡ Qualified for the CAF Confederation Cup					

CUP FINAL

Stade du 4 août, Ouagadougou
5-08-2007

Scorers - Oumarou Nébié 2 63 79 for RCBD; Simplice Yameogo 8 for USO

RECENT LEAGUE AND CUP RECORD

	Championship						Cup		
Year	Champions	Pts	Runners-up	Pts	Third	Pts	Winners	Score	Runners-up
1990	Etoile Filante	64	ASFA Yennega	61	Rail Club Kadiogo	61	Etoile Filante	2-1	ASFA Yennenga
1991	Etoile Filante	60	US Cheminots	52	Rail Club Kadiogo	51	ASFA Yennenga		
1992	Etoile Filante	53	ASFA Yennega	53	AS Fonctionnaire	49	Etoile Filante	2-1	Rail Club Kadiogo
1993	Etoile Filante	55	Racing Club B-D	54	Rail Club Kadiogo	49	Etoile Filante	2-0	ASF Bobo-Dioulasso
1994	Etoile Filante						Rail Club Kadiogo	1-0	Racing Club B-D
1995	ASFA Yennega						Etoile Filante		
1996	Racing Club B-D								
1997	Racing Club B-D						ASF Bobo-Dioulasso		
1998	US Forces Armées						ASF Bobo-Dioulasso	0-0 7-6p	US Forces Armées
1999	ASFA Yennega	53	Etoile Filante	47	US Forces Armées	43	Etoile Filante	3-2	US Forces Armées
2000	US Forces Armées	44	Etoile Filante	41	ASFA Yennega	39	Etoile Filante	3-1	US Ouagadougou
2001	Etoile Filante	51	ASFA Yennenga	49	US Forces Armées	41	Etoile Filante	3-1	ASF Bobo-Dioulasso
2002	ASFA Yennega	49	US Forces Armées	44	Etoile Filante	39	US Forces Armées	2-0	ASF Bobo-Dioulasso
2003	ASFA Yennega	51	US Ouagadougou	47	Etoile Filante	45	Etoile Filante	0-0 5-4p	ASFA Yennega
2004	ASFA Yennega	43	US Ouagadougou	40	Etoile Filante	39	ASF Bobo-Dioulasso	0-0 3-2p	US Forces Armées
2005	Rail Club Kadiogo	57	US Ouagadougou	50	US Forces Armées	50	US Ouagadougou	2-0	ASF Bobo-Dioulasso
2006	ASFA Yennega	53	Rail Club Kadiogo	52	US Ouagadougou	50	Etoile Filante	3-2	Racing Club B-D
2007	Commune FC	49	Etoile Filante	48	US Forces Armées	41	Racing Club B-D	2-1	US Ouagadougou

BHR – BAHRAIN

BAHRAIN NATIONAL TEAM RECORD
JULY 10TH 2006 TO JULY 12TH 2010

PL	W	D	L	F	A	%
15	4	3	8	19	26	36.6

FIFA/COCA-COLA WORLD RANKING

1993	1994	1995	1996	1997	1998	1999	2000	2001	2002	2003	2004	2005	2006	High	Low
78	73	99	118	121	119	136	138	110	105	64	49	52	97	**44** 09/04	138 12/00

				2006–2007							
08/06	09/06	10/06	11/06	12/06	01/07	02/07	03/07	04/07	05/07	06/07	07/07
93	98	108	97	97	97	98	96	100	101	100	88

Bahrain qualified for successive AFC Asian Cup finals for the first time when they beat Kuwait on the final day of the qualifiers to claim second place in their group behind Australia. Remarkably that one was their only victory of the campaign but it proved to be enough after the withdrawal of Lebanon had reduced the group to just three teams. Based in Jakarta for the finals, Bahrain lost to hosts Indonesia in their opening match but Milan Macala's team revived their hopes with an impressive 2-1 victory over South Korea in their next match. That left Bahrain needing a draw against Saudi to qualify, but a 4-0 defeat saw them finish bottom of the group. In club football

INTERNATIONAL HONOURS
Qualified for the AFC Asian Cup finals 1988 2004 2007 Represented at the Asian Games 1974 1978 1986 1994 2002

champions Muharraq were the team of the season. In the League they finished 12 points ahead of their nearest rivals Riffa to win their 29th championship and they also retained the Crown Prince Cup by beating Al Najma 1-0 in the final. Muharraq also underlined their pedigree by becoming the first club from Bahrain to appear in a continental final for 15 years - against Jordan's Al Faysali in the AFC Cup. Having lost the first leg 3-0 in Amman, they staged a spirited comeback in Manama but eventually lost 5-4 on aggregate. In the Kings Cup Al Najma beat Al Hala 2-0 whilst in the less prestigious FA Cup they lost on penalties in the final to Al Ahli.

THE FIFA BIG COUNT OF 2006

	Male	Female		Total
Number of players	16 828	1 450	Referees and Assistant Referees	90
Professionals	66		Admin, Coaches, Technical, Medical	620
Amateurs 18+	730		Number of clubs	48
Youth under 18	2 800		Number of teams	150
Unregistered	2 400		Clubs with women's teams	4
Total players	18 278		Players as % of population	2.62%

Bahrain Football Association (BFA)
Bahrain National Stadium, PO Box 5464, Manama, Bahrain
Tel +973 17 689569   Fax +973 17 781188
bhrfa@batelco.com.bh   www.bahrainfootball.org
President: AL-KHALIFA Sheik Salman Bin Ibrahim   General Secretary: JASSEM Ahmed Mohammed
Vice-President: AL-KHALIFA Sheik Ali Bin Khalifa   Treasurer: AL NA'AMI Ahmed Abdulla⁻   Media Officer: AL BASHA Ali Abdullah
Men's Coach: MACALA Milan   Women's Coach: AL HARBAN Khaled
BFA formed: 1957   AFC: 1970   FIFA: 1966
Red shirts with white trimmings, Red shorts, Red socks or White shirts with red trimmings, White shorts, White socks

RECENT INTERNATIONAL MATCHES PLAYED BY BAHRAIN

2004	Opponents	Score		Venue	Comp	Scorers	Att	Referee
11-12	Yemen	D	1-1	Doha	GCr1	Talal Yusuf 25		
14-12	Kuwait	D	1-1	Doha	GCr1	Hussain Ali 45		
17-12	Saudi Arabia	W	3-0	Doha	GCr1	Al Marzouki 64, Salman Issa 78, Talal Yusuf 90		
20-12	Oman	L	2-3	Doha	GCsf	Jalal 51, Duaij 77		
23-12	Kuwait	W	3-1	Doha	GC3p	Nada OG 31, Hubail.A 56, Duaij 90		
2005	Opponents							
25-01	Norway	L	0-1	Manama	Fr			
2-02	Lebanon	W	2-1	Doha	Fr	Salem, Hussain Ali		
9-02	Iran	D	0-0	Manama	WCq		25 000	Mohd Salleh MAS
25-03	Korea DPR	W	2-1	Pyongyang	WCq	Hussain Ali 2 7 58	50 000	Rungklay THA
30-03	Japan	L	0-1	Saitama	WCq		67 549	Irmatov UZB
27-05	Saudi Arabia	D	1-1	Riyadh	Fr	Mahfoodh 18p		
3-06	Japan	L	0-1	Manama	WCq		32 000	Mohd Salleh MAS
8-06	Iran	L	0-1	Tehran	WCq		80 000	Kwon Jong Chul KOR
3-08	Turkmenistan	W	5-0	Manama	Fr	Al Marzooki 7, Mahfoodh 35, Hussain Ali 63, Farhan 82p, Al Dakeel 84		
7-08	Iraq	D	2-2	Manama	Fr	Mahfoodh 27, Hussain Ali 86		
17-08	Korea DPR	L	2-3	Manama	WCq	Salman Isa 49, Hussain Ali 54	3 000	Maidin SIN
8-10	Uzbekistan	D	1-1	Tashkent	WCpo	Mohamed.T 17	55 000	Busacca SUI
12-10	Uzbekistan	D	0-0	Manama	WCpo		25 000	Poll ENG
27-10	Panama	W	5-0	Manama	Fr	Al Dakeel 44, Al Hejeri 82, Abbas 83, Al Marzooki 88, Mubarak 89		
12-11	Trinidad and Tobago	D	1-1	Port of Spain	WCpo	Salman Issa 72	24 991	Shield AUS
16-11	Trinidad and Tobago	L	0-1	Manama	WCpo		35 000	Ruiz COL
2006								
30-01	Syria	D	1-1	Manama	Fr	Fawzi Ayesh 60		
16-02	Palestine	L	0-2	Muharraq	Fr			
22-02	Australia	L	1-3	Manama	ACq	Hussain Ali 35	2 500	Mohd Salleh MAS
1-03	Kuwait	D	0-0	Kuwait City	ACq		16 000	Moradi IRN
9-08	Saudi Arabia	L	0-1	Dammam	Fr			
2-09	Jordan	L	0-2	Manama	Fr			
11-10	Australia	L	0-2	Sydney	ACq		37 000	Al Marzouqi UAE
8-11	Oman	D	1-1	Muscat	Fr	Hubail.A 18		
15-11	Kuwait	W	2-1	Manama	ACq	Talal Yusuf 34, Salman Isa 43	20 000	Kwon Jong Chul KOR
2007								
12-01	Yemen	W	4-0	Dubai	Fr	Al Marzooki 2 22 62, Maki Habib 31, Talal Yusuf 45		
18-01	Saudi Arabia	L	1-2	Abu Dhabi	GCr1	Talal Yusuf 14p		
21-01	Iraq	D	1-1	Abu Dhabi	GCr1	Al Marzouki 8		
24-01	Qatar	W	2-1	Abu Dhabi	GCr1	Hubail.A 2 45 91+		
27-01	Oman	L	0-1	Abu Dhabi	GCr1			
27-06	UAE	D	2-2	Kuala Lumpur	Fr	Sayed Mahmoud Jalal 7, Jaycee John 88		
30-06	Vietnam	L	3-5	Hanoi	Fr	Abdul Rahman 3, A'ala Hubail 62, Jaycee John 72		
10-07	Indonesia	L	1-2	Jakarta	ACr1	Sayed Mahmoud Jalal 27	60 000	Nishimura JPN
15-07	Korea Republic	W	2-1	Jakarta	ACr1	Salman Isa 43, Ismael Abdullatif 85	9 000	Sun Baojie CHN
18-07	Saudi Arabia	L	0-4	Palembang	ACr1		500	Nishimura JPN

Fr = Friendly match • AC = AFC Asian Cup • GC = Gulf Cup • WC = FIFA World Cup
q = qualifier • r1 = first round group • qf = quarter-final • sf = semi-final • f = final • 3p = third place play-off • po = play-off

BAHRAIN NATIONAL TEAM RECORDS AND RECORD SEQUENCES

Records			Sequence records					
Victory	6-0	SRI 1991	Wins	5	2001	Clean sheets	5	1988
Defeat	1-10	IRQ 1966	Defeats	9	1974-1975	Goals scored	11	2004
Player Caps	n/a		Undefeated	6	1993, 2001	Without goal	7	1988-1990
Player Goals	n/a		Without win	12	1988-1990	Goals against	12	1974-1976

BAHRAIN COUNTRY INFORMATION

Capital	Manama	Independence	1971	GDP per Capita	$16 900
Population	677 886	Status	Kingdom	GNP Ranking	101
Area km²	665	Language	Arabic	Dialling code	+973
Population density	1 019 per km²	Literacy rate	89%	Internet code	.bh
% in urban areas	90%	Main religion	Muslim 100%	GMT + / −	+3
Towns/Cities ('000)	Manama 147; Al-Muharraq 97; Al-Riffa 94; Madinat 65; Al-Wusta 51; Ali 55; Issa 38				
Neighbours (km)	Persian Gulf 161				
Main stadia	National Stadium – Manama 30 000; Issa Town – Issa 20 000; Al Muharraq – Muharraq 10 000				

BAHRAIN 2006–07

FIRST DIVISION	Pl	W	D	L	F	A	Pts	Muharraq	Riffa	Al Najma	Busaiteen	Bahrain	Al Hala	Al Shabab	Al Ahli	East Riffa	Manama	Malikiya	Setra
Muharraq †	22	17	2	3	56	17	53		1-0	0-1	3-2	3-1	4-0	1-1	5-1	1-1	3-0	1-0	2-0
Riffa	22	12	5	5	34	16	41	0-3		3-0	1-0	0-1	4-1	3-1	3-1	1-0	0-0	1-1	1-0
Al Najma †	22	11	5	6	32	23	38	1-2	1-0		2-2	2-1	0-1	3-0	1-0	1-1	2-0	0-0	2-0
Busaiteen	22	9	6	7	35	27	33	0-1	2-1	1-2		0-0	0-5	1-1	1-0	1-2	1-0	3-0	6-0
Bahrain Club	22	7	8	7	27	32	29	0-6	0-1	2-2	1-1		0-1	2-2	0-0	2-3	2-1	2-1	1-1
Al Hala	22	8	4	10	42	44	28	6-3	1-1	2-3	1-3	3-4		0-3	0-2	2-2	1-2	2-2	7-4
Al Shabab	22	6	9	7	30	29	27	0-4	1-1	1-0	0-2	0-0	1-2		1-1	0-1	1-2	1-1	1-0
Al Ahli	22	6	9	7	29	30	27	1-0	1-1	3-3	1-1	2-2	3-1	1-1		0-3	2-1	0-1	5-1
East Riffa	22	6	9	7	27	32	27	1-5	0-2	1-4	1-1	0-1	0-3	0-1	1-1		1-1	2-2	1-0
Manama	22	6	4	12	23	38	22	0-2	1-3	1-2	2-1	1-2	1-0	2-6	1-0	2-2		1-3	2-0
Malikiya	22	4	10	8	22	30	22	1-2	0-2	1-0	2-3	0-2	1-1	1-1	0-2	1-1	2-2		1-1
Setra	22	3	3	16	17	56	12	0-4	0-5	1-0	1-3	2-1	1-2	1-6	2-2	0-3	2-0	0-1	

4/11/2006 - 13/05/2007 • † Qualified for the AFC Cup • Match in bold awarded • Relegation play-off: Malikiya 0-1 Manama. Malikiya relegated

KINGS CUP 2007

Quarter–finals		Semi–finals		Final	
Al Najma	3				
Malikiya	1	Al Najma	2		
Al Shabab	0	Muharraq	1		
Muharraq	5			Al Najma	2
Riffa	2			Al Hala	0
Setra	0	Riffa	2	9-06-2007	
Manama	0	Al Hala	3	Scorer - Rashid Jamal 2 [80] [90p]	
Al Hala	2				

CROWN PRINCE CUP 2007

Semi–finals		Final	
Muharraq	1		
Busaiteen	0	Muharraq	1
Riffa	0	Al Najma	0
Al Najma	2	31-05-2007	

Played between the top four in the League

FA CUP 2007

Semi–finals		Final	
Al Ahli	1		
East Riffa	0	Al Ahli	1 4p
Busaiteen	0	Al Najma	1 3p
Al Najma	1	16-01-2007	

The first round had four groups with 19 teams in total

RECENT LEAGUE AND CUP RECORD

	Championship						King's Cup		
Year	Champions	Pts	Runners-up	Pts	Third	Pts	Winners	Score	Runners-up
1999	Muharraq	39	Al Ahli	30	West Riffa	28	East Riffa	1-0	Al-Hala
2000	West Riffa	4-0	East Riffa				East Riffa	3-1	Qadisiya
2001	Muharraq	52	Besaiteen	45	West Riffa	40	Al Ahli	1-0	Essa Town
2002	Muharraq	46	Al Ahli	46	Riffa	36	Muharraq	0-0 4-2p	Al Ahli
2003	Riffa	40	Muharraq	34	Al Ahli	32	Al Ahli	2-1	Muharraq
2004	Muharraq	48	Riffa	36	Al Ahli	30	Al Shabab	2-1	Busaiteen
2005	Riffa	40	Muharraq	36	Al Ahli	33	Muharraq	1-0	Al Shabab
2006	Muharraq	38	Al Ahli	37	Riffa	33	Al Najma	1-0	Al Ahli
2007	Muharraq	53	Riffa	41	Al Najma	38	Al Najma	2-0	Al Hala

BHU – BHUTAN

NATIONAL TEAM RECORD
JULY 10TH 2006 TO JULY 12TH 2010

PL	W	D	L	F	A	%
0	0	0	0	0	0	0

FIFA/COCA-COLA WORLD RANKING

1993	1994	1995	1996	1997	1998	1999	2000	2001	2002	2003	2004	2005	2006	High	Low
-	-	-	-	-	-	-	201	202	199	187	187	190	192	**187** 08/06	**202** 05/01

					2006–2007							
08/06	09/06	10/06	11/06	12/06	01/07	02/07	03/07	04/07	05/07	06/07	07/07
187	189	192	194	192	191	192	192	193	196	196	196

Bhutan may not be bottom of the FIFA/Coca-Cola World Ranking, courtesy of the draw achieved at the 2006 AFC Challenge Cup against Brunei Darussalam, but it may not be long before they join fellow AFC members East Timor and Guam on the lowest rung of the ladder. Bhutan were one of just four countries that did not apply to enter the 2010 FIFA World Cup qualifiers and although that number is likely to grow as other countries withdraw, Bhutan's football chiefs do not believe the national team or any of the youth selections are at a level where they can compete in the major world or Asian tournaments. Hence the absence of the U-17 and U-19 teams from the AFC

INTERNATIONAL HONOURS
None

tournaments for their respective age groups. One team in Bhutan that is determined to forge an international profile, however, is Transport United, who in 2006 completed a hat-trick of domestic titles. That qualified them for a third successive appearance in the AFC President's Cup, which was due to have taken place in Pakistan in May 2007. Grouped with Pakistan Army, Ratnam SC of Sri Lanka and Regar TadAZ of Tajikistan, Transport were hoping for a repeat of the 1-0 victory over Pakistan Army in the 2006 tournament - their only points to date - but due to problems obtaining visas for the participants, the tournament was delayed until September.

THE FIFA BIG COUNT OF 2006

	Male	Female		Total
Number of players	17 100	0	Referees and Assistant Referees	100
Professionals	0		Admin, Coaches, Technical, Medical	100
Amateurs 18+	600		Number of clubs	10
Youth under 18	600		Number of teams	70
Unregistered	2 900		Clubs with women's teams	0
Total players	17 100		Players as % of population	0.75%

Bhutan Football Federation (BFF)
PO Box 365, Thimphu, Bhutan
Tel +975 2 322350   Fax +975 2 321131
bff@druknet.net.bt   www.none
President: WANGCHUK Lyonpo Khandu HE   General Secretary: WANGCHUK Ugyen
Vice-President: TSHERING Dasho Gyom   Treasurer: DORJI B.T.   Media Officer: None
Men's Coach: BASNET Khare   Women's Coach: None
BFF formed: 1983   AFC: 1993   FIFA: 2000
Yellow shirts with red trimmings, Yellow shorts, Yellow socks or Red shirts with yellow trimmings, Red shorts, Red socks

RECENT INTERNATIONAL MATCHES PLAYED BY BHUTAN

2002	Opponents	Score	Venue	Comp	Scorers	Att	Referee
No international matches played in 2002 after June							
2003							
11-01	Maldives	L 0-6	Dhaka	SAr1			Vidanagamage SRI
13-01	Nepal	L 0-2	Dhaka	SAr1		25 000	Magheshwaran IND
15-01	Bangladesh	L 0-3	Dhaka	SAr1		15 000	Magheshwaran IND
23-04	Guam	W 6-0	Thimphu	ACq	Wangyel Dorji 2 31 33, Dinesh Chetri 59, Passang Tshering 76p, Pema Chophel 88 Yeshey Nedup 89		
27-04	Mongolia	D 0-0	Thimphu	ACq			
6-10	Indonesia	L 0-2	Jeddah	ACq			
8-10	Saudi Arabia	L 0-6	Jeddah	ACq			
10-10	Yemen	L 0-8	Jeddah	ACq			
13-10	Indonesia	L 0-2	Jeddah	ACq			
15-10	Saudi Arabia	L 0-4	Jeddah	ACq			
17-10	Yemen	L 0-4	Jeddah	ACq			
2004							
No international matches played in 2004							
2005							
8-12	Bangladesh	L 0-3	Karachi	SAr1			
10-12	India	L 0-3	Karachi	SAr1			
12-12	Nepal	L 1-3	Karachi	SAr1	Pradhan 47		
2006							
2-04	Nepal	L 0-2	Chittagong	CCr1		3 500	Gosh BAN
4-04	Sri Lanka	L 0-1	Chittagong	CCr1			Saidov UZB
6-04	Brunei Darussalam	D 0-0	Chittagong	CCr1		2 000	Al Ghatrifi OMA
2007							
No international matches played in 2007 before August							

SA = South Asian Football Federation Cup • AC = AFC Asian Cup • CC = AFC Challenge Cup • q = qualifier • r1 = first round group

BHUTAN NATIONAL TEAM RECORDS AND RECORD SEQUENCES

Records			Sequence records				
Victory	6-0	GUM 2003	Wins	1		Clean sheets	2	2003
Defeat	0-20	KUW 2000	Defeats	15	1984-2001	Goals scored	3	2000-2002
Player Caps	n/a		Undefeated	2	2003	Without goal	9	2003-2005
Player Goals	5	WANGYEL DORJI	Without win	15	1984-2001	Goals against	15	1984-2001

RECENT LEAGUE AND CUP RECORD

	Championship		Cup
Year	Champions		Winners
2001	Druk Pol		No tournament played
2002	Druk Star		No tournament played
2003	Druk Pol		No tournament played
2004	Transport United		Druk Pol
2005	Transport United		Druk Pol
2006	Transport United		

BHUTAN COUNTRY INFORMATION

Capital	Thimphu	Independence	1949	GDP per Capita	$1 300
Population	2 185 569	Status	Kingdom	GNP Ranking	170
Area km²	47 000	Language	Dzongkha	Dialling code	+975
Population density	46 per km²	Literacy rate	44%	Internet code	.bt
% in urban areas	6%	Main religion	Buddhist 70%	GMT +/−	+6
Towns/Cities ('000)	Thimphu 66; Phuntsholing 65; Punakha 18; Samdrup Jongkhar 14; Geylegphug 7; Jakar 4				
Neighbours (km)	China 470; India 605				
Main stadia	Changlimithang – Thimphu 15 000; PSA Phuntsholing – Phuntsholing 6 000				

BIH – BOSNIA-HERZEGOVINA

NATIONAL TEAM RECORD
JULY 10TH 2006 TO JULY 12TH 2010

PL	W	D	L	F	A	%
8	4	1	3	15	16	56.2

FIFA/COCA-COLA WORLD RANKING

1993	1994	1995	1996	1997	1998	1999	2000	2001	2002	2003	2004	2005	2006	High		Low	
-	-	-	152	99	96	75	78	69	87	59	79	65	59	27	07/07	173	09/96

2006–2007											
08/06	09/06	10/06	11/06	12/06	01/07	02/07	03/07	04/07	05/07	06/07	07/07
42	54	58	59	59	58	55	58	47	48	28	27

'Referees are sold out as whores, journalists write what they are told and betting offices rule our football.' Those were the rather harsh words spoken by former national team coach Blaz Sliskovic after he ordered his Zrinjski team off the field after 83 minutes of a match against Orasje, complaining of biased refereeing. Zrinjski finished the campaign as runners-up to Sarajevo in a three way fight at the top, but the extraordinary thing about the final table was that just six points separated fourth placed Siroki Brijeg and relegated Borac Banja Luka. There were just 24 away wins all season - less than one a week - whilst the top 10 teams lost just nine home games between

INTERNATIONAL HONOURS
None

them! On the surface football appeared to be in rude health with the national team having only just missed out on qualifying for the 2006 FIFA World Cup and for Euro 2004. A terrible start to the UEFA Euro 2008 campaign, however, saw Sliskovic relinquish the national team reigns to concentrate on his club post after the defeat to Greece. He was replaced by Fuad Muzurovic who was immediately faced with a player boycott aimed at forcing changes at the federation. With a number of new players and the talents of Bochum's Zvjezdan Misimovic and Parma's Zlatan Muslimovic, Bosnia remarkably won their next three matches to put themselves back in contention.

THE FIFA BIG COUNT OF 2006

	Male	Female		Total
Number of players	181 640	18 600	Referees and Assistant Referees	1 720
Professionals	430		Admin, Coaches, Technical, Medical	10 100
Amateurs 18+	40 370		Number of clubs	763
Youth under 18	26 570		Number of teams	1 000
Unregistered	36 200		Clubs with women's teams	10
Total players	200 240		Players as % of population	4.45%

Football Federation of Bosnia–Herzegovina (FFBH/NSBiH)

Nogometni/Fudbalski Savez Bosne i Hercegovine, Ferhadija 30, Sarajevo - 71000, Bosnia-Herzegovina
Tel +387 33 276660   Fax +387 33 444332
nsbih@bih.net.ba   www.nfsbih.ba
President: JELIC Milan   General Secretary: USANOVIC Munib
Vice-President: DOMINKOVIC Iljo   Treasurer: KURES Miodrag   Media Officer: PECIKOZA Slavica
Men's Coach: MUZUROVIC Fuad   Women's Coach: BAJRIC Ismet
FFBH formed: 1992   UEFA: 1996   FIFA: 1996
White shirts with blue trimmings, Blue shorts, White socks or Blue shirts with white trimmings, White shorts, Blue socks

RECENT INTERNATIONAL MATCHES PLAYED BY BOSNIA–HERZEGOVINA

2002	Opponents	Score		Venue	Comp	Scorers	Att	Referee
21-08	Yugoslavia	L	0-2	Sarajevo	Fr		9 000	Siric CRO
7-09	Romania	L	0-3	Sarajevo	ECq		4 000	Batista POR
11-10	Germany	D	1-1	Sarajevo	Fr	Baljic [21]	5 000	De Santis ITA
16-10	Norway	L	0-2	Oslo	ECq		24 169	Benes CZE
2003								
12-02	Wales	D	2-2	Cardiff	Fr	Baljic [5], Barbarez [64]	25 000	Malcolm NIR
29-03	Luxembourg	W	2-0	Zenica	ECq	Bolic [53], Barbarez [79]	10 000	Hyytia FIN
2-04	Denmark	W	2-0	Copenhagen	ECq	Barbarez [23], Baljic [29]	30 845	Stredak SVK
7-06	Romania	L	0-2	Craiova	ECq		36 000	Bossen NED
6-09	Norway	W	1-0	Zenica	ECq	Bajramovic [86]	18 000	Bre FRA
10-09	Luxembourg	W	1-0	Luxembourg	ECq	Barbarez [36]	3 500	Kapitanis CYP
11-10	Denmark	D	1-1	Sarajevo	ECq	Bolic [39]	35 500	Barber ENG
2004								
18-02	Macedonia FYR	L	0-1	Skopje	Fr		8 000	Vrajkov BUL
31-03	Luxembourg	W	2-1	Luxembourg	Fr	Misimovic [63], Bolic [71]	2 000	Rogalla SUI
28-04	Finland	W	1-0	Zenica	Fr	Misimovic [88]	20 000	Bozinovski MKD
18-08	France	D	1-1	Rennes	Fr	Grlic [37]	26 527	McDonald SCO
8-09	Spain	D	1-1	Zenica	WCq	Bolic [79]	14 380	De Santis ITA
9-10	Serbia & Montenegro	D	0-0	Sarajevo	WCq		22 440	Veissiere FRA
2005								
2-02	Iran	L	1-2	Tehran	Fr	Bolic [17]	15 000	
26-03	Belgium	L	1-4	Brussels	WCq	Bolic [1]	36 700	Hrinak SVK
30-03	Lithuania	D	1-1	Sarajevo	WCq	Misimovic [21]	6 000	Baskakov RUS
4-06	San Marino	W	3-1	Serravalle	WCq	Salihamidzic 2 [17 38], Barbarez [75]	750	Demirlek TUR
8-06	Spain	D	1-1	Valencia	WCq	Misimovic [39]	38 041	Bennett ENG
17-08	Estonia	L	0-1	Tallinn	Fr		4 000	Fojdfeldt SWE
3-09	Belgium	W	1-0	Zenica	WCq	Barbarez [62]	12 000	Benquerenca POR
7-09	Lithuania	W	1-0	Vilnius	WCq	Barbarez [28]	4 000	Kassai HUN
8-10	San Marino	W	3-0	Zenica	WCq	Bolic 3 [46 75 82]	8 500	Hamer LUX
12-10	Serbia & Montenegro	L	0-1	Belgrade	WCq		46 305	Vassaras GRE
2006								
28-02	Japan	D	2-2	Dortmund	Fr	Misimovic [56p], Spahic [67]	10 000	Wack GER
26-05	Korea Republic	L	0-2	Seoul	Fr		64 836	Cheung Yim Yau HKG
31-05	Iran	L	2-5	Tehran	Fr	Misimovic [4], Barbarez [17]		Mohd Salleh MAS
16-08	France	L	1-2	Sarajevo	Fr	Barbarez [16]	35 000	Wack GER
2-09	Malta	W	5-2	Ta'Qali	ECq	Barbarez [4], Hrgovic [10], Bartolovic [46+], Muslimovic [48], Misimovic [51]	2 000	Vejlgaard DEN
6-09	Hungary	L	1-3	Zenica	ECq	Misimovic [64]	11 800	Kapitanis CYP
7-10	Moldova	D	2-2	Chisinau	ECq	Misimovic [62], Grlic [68]	7 114	Piccirillo FRA
11-10	Greece	L	0-4	Zenica	ECq		8 000	Baskakov RUS
2007								
24-03	Norway	W	2-1	Oslo	ECq	Misimovic [18], Muslimovic [33]	16 987	Riley ENG
2-06	Turkey	W	3-2	Sarajevo	ECq	Muslimovic [27], Dzeko [47], Custovic [90]	13 800	Fröjdfeldt SWE
6-06	Malta	W	1-0	Sarajevo	ECq	Muslimovic [6]	15 000	Richards WAL

Fr = Friendly match • EC = UEFA EURO 2004/2008 • WC = FIFA World Cup • q = qualifier

BOSNIA–HERZEGOVINA NATIONAL TEAM RECORDS AND RECORD SEQUENCES

Records			Sequence records					
Victory	5-0	LIE 2001	Wins	3	Four times	Clean sheets	3	2005
Defeat	0-5	ARG 1998	Defeats	3	Five times	Goals scored	10	1998-1999
Player Caps	52	BOLIC Elvir	Undefeated	4	1997, 2004	Without goal	3	Three times
Player Goals	24	BOLIC Elvir	Without win	7	2002-2003	Goals against	7	2002-2003

BOSNIA AND HERCEGOVINA; BOSNIA I HERCEGOVINA

Capital	Sarajevo	Language	Bosnian, Croatian, Serbian	Independence	1992
Population	4 498 976	Area	51 129 km²	Density	78 per km²	% in cities	49%
GDP per cap	$6 100	Dailling code	+387	Internet	.ba	GMT +/-	+1

MEDALS TABLE

		Overall G	S	B	League G	S	B	Cup G	S	B	Europe G	S	B	City	Stadium	Cap'ty	DoF
1	Zeljeznicar Sarajevo	6	5	1	3	3		3	2					Sarajevo	Grbavica	15 000	1921
2	FK Sarajevo	5	6	3	1	4	3	4	2					Sarajevo	Olimpijski Kosevo	37 500	1946
3	Celik Zenica	5			3			2						Zenica	Bilino Polje	16 000	1945
4	NK Siroki Brijeg	3	3	1	2	1	1	1	2					Siroki Brijeg	Pecara	6 000	1948
5	Brotnjo Citluk	1	1	1	1	1	1							Citluk	Bare	4 800	1955
	Zrinjski Mostar	1	1	1	1	1	1							Mostar	Bijeli brijeg	10 000	1912
7	Leotar Trebinje	1	1		1				1					Trebinje	Police	8 500	1925
8	Bosna Visoko	1		2				2	1					Visoko	Luke	3 500	1953
9	FK Modrica Maxima	1							1					Modrica	Modrica	2 500	1974
	NK Orasje	1							1					Orasje	Goal	3 000	1996
11	Sloboda Tuzla		3	1			1		3					Tuzla	Tusanj	7 000	1919
12	Slavija Sarajevo	1	1			1	1		1					Sarajevo-Lukavica	Slavija Lukavica	5 000	1908
13	Buducnost Banovici	1			1				1					Banovici	Gradski	5 000	1947
	Borac Banja Luka	1							1					Banja Luka	Gradski	15 000	1926
	Radniki Lukavac	1			1									Lukavac			1923

BOSNIAN CLUBS IN YUGOSLAV FOOTBALL

		Overall G	S	B	League G	S	B	Cup G	S	B	Europe G	S	B
7	Velez Mostar	2	5	4		3	4	2	2				
9	FK Sarajevo	2	4		2	2			2				
13	Zeljeznicar Sarajevo	1	2	2	1	1	2		1			1	
14	Borac Banja Luka	1	1					1	1				

RECENT LEAGUE AND CUP RECORD

	Championship						Cup		
Year	Champions	Pts	Runners-up	Pts	Third	Pts	Winners	Score	Runners-up
2001	Zeljeznicar	91	Brotnjo Citluk	84	Sarajevo	81	Zeljeznicar	3-2	Sarajevo
2002	Zeljeznicar	62	Siroki Brijeg	51	Brotnjo Citluk	47	Sarajevo	2-1	Zeljeznicar
2003	Leotar Trebinje	85	Zeljeznicar	82	Sarajevo	69	Zeljeznicar	0-0 2-0	Leotar Trebinje
2004	Siroki Brijeg	61	Zeljeznicar	59	Sarajevo	56	Modrica Maksima	1-1 4-2p	Borac Banja Luka
2005	Zrinjski Mostar	61	Zeljeznicar	51	Siroki Brijeg	45	Sarajevo	1-0 1-1	Siroki Brijeg
2006	Siroki Brijeg	63	Sarajevo	60	Zrinjski Mostar	54	Orasje	0-0 3-0	Siroki Brijeg
2007	Sarajevo	57	Zrinjski Mostar	54	Slavija Sarajevo	53	Siroki Brijeg	1-1 1-0	Slavija Sarajevo

BOSNIA-HERZEGOVINA 2006-07

PREMIJER LIGA

	Pl	W	D	L	F	A	Pts	Sarajevo	Zrinjski	Slavija	Siroki	Zeljeznicar	Modrica	Leotar	Velez	Jedinstvo	Zepce	Posusje	Sloboda	Orasje	Celik	Borac	Radnik
Sarajevo †	30	17	6	7	44	26	57		1-0	1-0	2-0	2-1	4-0	1-0	2-1	2-0	2-0	2-1	1-1	2-0	3-1	3-1	5-0
Zrinjski Mostar §1 ‡	30	17	4	9	67	40	54	1-1		2-1	2-4	2-1	3-0	4-3	2-1	6-1	5-2	3-0	3-0	4-1	1-0	2-0	1-0
Slavija Sarajevo	30	17	2	11	41	35	53	1-1	2-1		2-0	2-1	2-1	3-1	2-0	2-1	1-0	2-0	2-0	1-0	1-0	3-2	3-1
Siroki Brijeg ‡	30	13	6	11	39	32	45	1-0	0-2	0-1		2-1	1-1	0-0	0-0	3-1	1-1	0-0	2-0	2-0	4-1	2-0	
Zeljeznicar Sarajevo	30	13	5	12	51	40	44	0-1	2-1	5-2	3-2		5-2	3-0	1-1	3-0	1-1	7-1	1-0	0-0	3-0	3-1	1-0
Modrica Maksima	30	13	5	12	42	42	44	3-1	1-3	2-1	1-1	4-1		3-1	4-0	2-1	1-0	1-1	2-0	1-1	1-0	2-1	2-1
Leotar Trebinje	30	14	1	15	47	48	43	4-0	3-4	1-0	2-1	3-0	2-1		2-0	5-3	4-0	0-2	3-1	2-0	3-2	3-2	1-0
Velez Mostar	30	12	7	11	41	42	43	1-1	2-1	1-1	2-0	2-0	2-1	2-0		1-1	1-0	3-0	2-0	1-0	2-1	4-3	1-0
Jedinstvo Bihac	30	13	4	13	46	57	43	1-1	2-2	1-0	2-1	2-0	1-1	3-1	2-1		1-0	2-1	3-1	2-1	2-0	3-2	
Zepce Limorad	30	12	4	14	30	37	40	2-3	1-0	2-0	1-2	2-0	2-0	2-0	2-2	1-0		1-0	1-0	1-0	0-0	1-0	3-0
Posusje	30	12	4	14	42	51	40	2-0	2-2	3-0	0-2	0-0	2-1	3-0	3-2	4-3	4-0		3-2	2-2	1-0	4-1	1-0
Sloboda Tuzla	30	12	4	14	36	45	40	1-0	0-6	3-1	2-1	2-2	2-1	3-1	2-0	2-1	2-1	5-1		1-2	1-0	1-0	3-1
Orasje	30	11	6	13	39	35	39	0-1	**3-0**	2-1	1-1	1-3	2-1	1-0	1-1	4-0	2-0	4-1	2-2		4-0	2-0	2-0
Celik Zenica	30	12	3	15	29	34	39	0-0	2-1	1-0	2-1	1-0	0-1	3-1	3-2	2-0	0-0	1-0	2-0	2-1		3-0	2-0
Borac Banja Luka	30	13	0	17	42	47	39	2-1	1-0	1-2	2-1	2-1	0-1	1-0	4-1	5-0	1-2	3-0	1-0	1-0	1-0		3-0
Radnik Bijeljina	30	8	1	21	25	50	25	1-0	2-2	1-2	0-1	1-2	1-0	0-1	3-2	2-4	2-1	1-0	2-0	1-0	2-0	1-2	

5/08/2006 - 23/05/2007 • † Qualified for the UEFA Champions League • ‡ Qualified for the UEFA Cup • Match in bold awarded • § = Points deducted

BOSNIA 2006-07 PRVA LIGA FBIH (2)

	Pl	W	D	L	F	A	Pts
Travnik	30	18	2	10	45	35	56
Rudar Kakanj	30	17	4	9	48	23	55
Zvijezda Gradacac	30	16	4	10	45	28	52
Napredak Sarajevo	30	16	1	13	36	32	49
Troglav Livno	30	14	4	12	43	35	46
GOSK Gabela	30	14	3	13	38	42	45
Gradina Srebrenik	30	13	4	13	37	33	43
Buducnost Banovici	30	12	7	11	30	28	43
Igman Konjic	30	13	3	14	48	42	42
Bosna Visoko	30	13	2	15	35	42	41
Brotnjo Citluk	30	13	2	15	35	43	41
Radnicki Lukavac	30	12	5	13	30	38	41
MIS Kresevo	30	12	3	15	40	46	39
Krajina Cazin	30	11	5	14	27	32	38
Mramor	30	10	2	18	36	54	32
TOSK Tesanj	30	8	5	17	30	50	29

12/08/2007 - 10/06/2007

BOSNIA 2006-07 PRVA LIGA FBIH (2)

	Pl	W	D	L	F	A	Pts
Laktasi	30	17	8	5	45	21	59
Borac Samac	30	16	7	7	61	32	55
Rudar Ugljevik	30	13	8	9	35	24	47
Drina Visegrad	30	14	2	14	42	36	44
Ljubic Prnjavor	30	13	2	15	29	37	44
Sloboda Novi Grad	30	13	4	13	49	43	43
Kozara Gradiska	30	13	4	13	41	38	43
Famos Vojkovici	30	13	4	13	37	36	43
Mladost Gacko	30	13	3	14	41	41	42
Crni Djordje Banja Luka	30	11	9	10	32	33	42
Sloga Doboj	30	12	6	11	30	34	42
Jedinstvo Brcko	30	12	6	12	27	34	42
Drina Zvornik §6	30	13	7	9	41	20	40
Rudar Prijedor	30	13	1	16	36	41	40
Glasinac Sokolac §6	30	13	2	14	33	35	35
Omladinac Banja Luka	30	1	1	28	20	94	4

12/08/2007 - 10/06/2007 • § = points deducted

KUP BIH 2006-07

Round of sixteen

Siroki Brijeg	2 1
Velez Mostar *	2 0
Leotar Trebinje	0 2
Modrica Maxima *	2 3
Borac Banja Luka	2 1
Nektar Banja Luka *	0 1
Ljubic Prnjavor *	1 0
Celik Zenica	0 2
Sarajevo	3 3
Posusje *	3 0
Zvijezda Gradacac	0 2
Zeljeznicar Sarajevo *	1 1
Mrkaljevic Celik	1 2 1p
Gorazde †	2 1 4p
Orasje	0 1
Slavija Sarajevo *	3 2

Quarter-finals

Siroki Brijeg *	0 2 5p
Modrica Maxima	2 0 4p
Borac Banja Luka	0 0
Celik Zenica *	2 1
Sarajevo	0 3
Zeljeznicar Sarajevo *	0 2
Mrkaljevic Celik	
Slavija Sarajevo	

Semi-finals

Siroki Brijeg	0 2 5p
Celik Zenica *	2 0 4p
Sarajevo *	1 1
Slavija Sarajevo	1 2

Final

Siroki Brijeg ‡	1 1
Slavija Sarajevo	1 0

* Home team in the 1st leg • † Expelled • ‡ Qualified for the UEFA Cup

CUP FINAL
1st leg. Pecara, Siroki Brijeg
9-05-2007, Att: 1000, Ref: Radic
Scorers - Selson [23] for Siroki Brijeg; Simic [4] for Slavija
2nd leg. Slavija Lukavica, Sarajevo
26-05-2007, Att: 3000, Ref: Buljan
Scorer - Kovacic [71] for Siroki Brijeg

BLR – BELARUS

NATIONAL TEAM RECORD
JULY 10TH 2006 TO JULY 12TH 2010

PL	W	D	L	F	A	%
10	3	2	5	16	19	40

FIFA/COCA-COLA WORLD RANKING

1993	1994	1995	1996	1997	1998	1999	2000	2001	2002	2003	2004	2005	2006	High		Low	
137	121	88	90	110	104	95	96	85	74	90	69	61	70	**59**	11/05	**142**	07/94

2006–2007											
08/06	09/06	10/06	11/06	12/06	01/07	02/07	03/07	04/07	05/07	06/07	07/07
69	65	61	71	70	70	69	66	63	64	72	71

BATE Borisov won their third championship after a close race involving Dinamo Minsk, Shakhter Soligorsk and the Vladimir Romanov owned MTZ-RIPO, a race that went down to the last weekend. Having lost their last match, BATE had a nervous two hour wait for Dinamo's snow delayed match away to Dinamo Brest. Needing a win to take the title, Dinamo Minsk were held to a draw and have now won the League just once in the past eight seasons. Dinamo Brest were not in such a giving mood six months later when they met BATE in the Cup Final. BATE were on for a hat-trick of trophies having also won the Cup the previous year, but after a goalless draw they lost in a penalty

INTERNATIONAL HONOURS
None

shoot out. It was a first trophy for Dinamo, from the southwest of the country on the border with Poland. There were also first time winners in the newly created Belarus Football Federation Cup - a pre-season tournament that received mixed reviews - which was won by Naftan Novopolotsk. There was little to cheer on the international front with none of the clubs making it past the preliminary rounds of the UEFA Champions League or the UEFA Cup, whilst the national team struggled to make an impact in a UEFA Euro 2008 qualifying group dominated by Bulgaria, Romania and the Netherlands which resulted in the appointment of Bernd Stange as coach.

THE FIFA BIG COUNT OF 2006

	Male	Female		Total
Number of players	326 390	47 420	Referees and Assistant Referees	527
Professionals	1 370		Admin, Coaches, Technical, Medical	948
Amateurs 18+	4 530		Number of clubs	155
Youth under 18	18 760		Number of teams	270
Unregistered	113 000		Clubs with women's teams	5
Total players	373 810		Players as % of population	3.63%

Belarus Football Federation (BFF)
Prospekt Pobeditelei 20/3 Minsk 222 020, Belarus
Tel +375 172 545600   Fax +375 172 544483
info@bff.by   www.bff.by
President: NEVYGLAS Gennady   General Secretary: DMITRANITSA Leonid
Vice-President: NOVIKOV Victor   Treasurer: KOLTOVICH Valentina   Media Officer: NOVYSH Siarhei
Men's Coach: STANGE Bernd   Women's Coach: VOLOKH Oleg
BFF formed: 1989   UEFA: 1993   FIFA: 1992
Red shirts with green trimmings, Green shorts, Red socks or White shirts, White shorts, White socks

RECENT INTERNATIONAL MATCHES PLAYED BY BELARUS

2003	Opponents	Score	Venue	Comp	Scorers	Att	Referee
20-08	Iran	W 2-1	Minsk	Fr	Romaschenko.Ma [10p], Shtanyuk [41]	10 000	Ivanov.N RUS
6-09	Czech Republic	L 1-3	Minsk	ECq	Bulyga [14]	11 000	McCurry SCO
10-09	Moldova	L 1-2	Tiraspol	ECq	Vasilyuk [89p]	7 000	Selevic SCM
2004							
14-02	Estonia	L 1-2	Valletta	Fr	Tarasenko [89]	200	Casha MLT
16-02	Moldova	W 1-0	Valletta	Fr	Hleb.V [39]	40	Attard MLT
18-02	Malta	W 4-0	Valletta	Fr	Kornilenko [12], Tsygalko [30], Biahanski [71], Lashankou [85]		Kaldma EST
18-02	Cyprus	W 2-0	Achnas	Fr	Romaschenko.Ma 2 [56 70]	500	Kalis CYP
21-02	Latvia	W 4-1	Limassol	Fr	Bulyga [20], Romaschenko.Ma 3 [73p 87p 90]	100	
28-04	Lithuania	W 1-0	Minsk	Fr	Blizniuk [75]	8 000	Ivanov RUS
18-08	Turkey	W 2-1	Denizli	Fr	Hleb.V [67], Kouba [90]	18 000	Mrkovic BIH
8-09	Norway	D 1-1	Oslo	WCq	Kutuzov [77]	25 272	Gomes Costa POR
9-10	Moldova	W 4-0	Minsk	WCq	Omelyanchuk [45], Kutuzov [65], Bulyga [75], Romaschenko.Ma [90]	21 000	Dereli TUR
13-10	Italy	L 3-4	Parma	WCq	Romaschenko 2 [52 88], Bulyga [76]	19 833	Megia Davila ESP
22-11	United Arab Emirates	W 3-2	Dubai	Fr	Shkabara [44], Kovel [60], Kulchy [90]	600	Al Delawar BHR
2005							
9-02	Poland	W 3-1	Warsaw	Fr	Hleb.A [8], Hleb.V [84], Lavrik [92+]	6 000	Zuta LTU
30-03	Slovenia	D 1-1	Celje	WCq	Kulchy [49]	6 450	Al Ghamdi KSA
4-06	Slovenia	D 1-1	Minsk	WCq	Belkevich [18]	29 042	Hansson SWE
8-06	Scotland	D 0-0	Minsk	WCq		28 287	Benquerenca POR
17-08	Lithuania	L 0-1	Vilnius	Fr		2 500	Sipailo LVA
3-09	Moldova	L 0-2	Chisinau	WCq		5 000	Duhamel FRA
7-09	Italy	L 1-4	Minsk	WCq	Kutuzov [4]	30 299	Temmink NED
8-10	Scotland	W 1-0	Glasgow	WCq	Kutuzov [5]	51 105	Szabo HUN
12-10	Norway	L 0-1	Minsk	WCq		13 222	Plautz AUT
12-11	Latvia	W 3-1	Minsk	Fr	Kortyko [26], Kornilenko 2 [52 90]	8 300	Egorov RUS
2006							
28-02	Greece	L 0-1	Limassol	Fr		3 000	Salomir ROU
1-03	Finland	D 2-2	Larnaca	Fr	Kornilenko [34], Shkabara [53]. L 4-5p	120	Krajnic SVN
30-05	Tunisia	L 0-3	Radès/Tunis	Fr			
2-06	Libya	D 1-1	Radès/Tunis	Fr	Shtanyuk [13]. L 1-3p		
16-08	Andorra	W 3-0	Minsk	Fr	Hleb.A [36], Bulyga [77], Kornilenko [85]		
2-09	Albania	D 2-2	Minsk	ECq	Kalachev [2], Romashchenko [24]	23 000	Asumaa FIN
6-09	Netherlands	L 0-3	Eindhoven	ECq		30 089	Webb ENG
7-10	Romania	L 1-3	Bucharest	ECq	Kornilenko [20]	12 000	Undiano ESP
11-10	Slovenia	W 4-2	Minsk	ECq	Kovba [18], Kornilenko 2 [52 60], Korythko [85]	21 150	Kassai HUN
15-11	Estonia	L 1-2	Tallinn	Fr	Hleb.V [63p]	3 000	Hermansen DEN
2007							
7-02	Iran	D 2-2	Tehran	Fr	Hleb.V 2 [53 59]	15 000	Al Fadhli KUW
24-03	Luxembourg	W 2-1	Luxembourg	ECq	Kalachev [25], Kutuzov [54]	2 021	Whitby WAL
2-06	Bulgaria	L 0-2	Minsk	ECq		29 000	Jara CZE
6-06	Bulgaria	L 1-2	Sofia	ECq	Vasilyuk [5p]	10 501	Jakobsson ISL

Fr = Friendly match • EC = UEFA EURO 2004/2008 • WC = FIFA World Cup • q = qualifier

BELARUS NATIONAL TEAM RECORDS AND RECORD SEQUENCES

Records			Sequence records					
Victory	5-0	LTU 1998	Wins	6	2004	Clean sheets	3	1998, 2004
Defeat	0-5	AUT 2003	Defeats	8	1997	Goals scored	17	2003-2005
Player Caps	78	GURENKO Sergei	Undefeated	8	2004	Without goal	3	Four times
Player Goals	13	ROMASHCHENKO Maxym	Without win	14	1998-2000	Goals against	13	2002-2004

MAJOR CITIES/TOWNS
Population '000

1	Minsk	1 747
2	Gomel	480
3	Mogilev	366
4	Vitebsk	342
5	Grodno	320
6	Brest	303
7	Bobruisk	220
8	Baranovici	169
9	Borisov	150
10	Pinsk	131
11	Orsja	125
12	Mozyr	112
13	Soligorsk	101
14	Novopolotsk	100
15	Molodechno	98
16	Lida	97
17	Polotsk	81
18	Zhlobin	73
19	Svetlogorsk	70
20	Rechitsa	64
21	Slutsk	62
22	Zhodino	61
23	Slonim	51
24	Kobrin	50

REPUBLIC OF BELARUS; RESPUBLIKA BYELARUS

Capital	Minsk	Language	Belarusian, Russian	Independence	1991
Population	10 293 011	Area	207 600km²	% in cities	71%
GDP per cap	$6 100	Dailling code	+375	Internet	.by	GMT +/-	+2

MEDALS TABLE

		Overall			League			Cup			Europe			City	Stadium	Cap'ty	DoF
		G	S	B	G	S	B	G	S	B	G	S	B				
1	Dinamo Minsk	10	7	2	7	5	2	3	2					Minsk	Dinamo	42 375	1927
2	BATE Borisov	5	7	1	4	4	1	1	3					Borisov	City	5 500	1996
3	Slavija Mozyr	4	4		2	2		2	2					Mozyr	Traktor	17 600	1987
4	Belshina Bobruisk	4	2	2	1	1	2	3	1					Bobruisk	Spartak	3 700	1977
5	Shakhter Soligorsk	2	1	4		1	4	1	1					Soligorsk	Stroitel	5 000	1963
6	FC Gomel	2	1	1	1		1	1	1					Gomel	Centralnyi	15 000	1995
7	Dinamo-93 Minsk	1	2	2		1	2	1	1					Minsk	Dinamo		1993-98
	Lokomotiv Vitebsk	1	2	2		2	2	1						Vitebsk	Central Sport Komplex	8 350	1960
9	Dnepr-Transmash	1	2		1	1		1						Mogilev	Spartak	6 800	1960
10	Neman Grodno	1	1		1			1						Grodno	Neman	6 300	1964
11	Dinamo Brest	1		1	1		1							Brest	Sportkomplex Brestskiy	10 080	1960
	MTZ-RIPO Minsk	1		1	1		1							Minsk	Traktor	17 600	1947
13	Lokomtiv Minsk	1						1						Minsk	Lokomotiv	2 000	2000
	Torpedo Mogilev	1						1						Mogilev	Torpedo	7 000	1974
	Torpedo-SKA Minsk	1						1						Minsk	Torpedo	5 000	1947
	Vedrich Rechitsa	1						1						Rechitsa	Rechitsadrev	5 500	1952

BELARUS CLUBS IN THE SOVIET LEAGUE AND CUP

14	Dynamo Minsk	1	1	3	1	1	3	1			

RECENT LEAGUE AND CUP RECORD

	Championship					Cup		
Year	Champions	Pts	Runners-up	Pts	Third	Pts	Winners	Score	Runners-up
1995	Dinamo Minsk	48	Dvina Minsk	45	Dinamo-93 Minsk	42	Dinamo-93 Minsk	1-1 7-6p	Torpedo Mogilev
1995	Dinamo Minsk	38	MPKC Mozyr	36	Dinamo-93 Minsk	32		-	
1996	MPKC Mozyr	76	Dinamo Minsk	75	Belshina Bobruisk	63	MPKC Mozyr	4-1	Dinamo Minsk
1997	Dinamo Minsk	70	Belshina Bobruisk	66	Lokomotiv Vitebsk	59	Belshina Bobruisk	2-0	Dinamo-93 Minsk
1998	Dnepr-Transmash	67	BATE Borisov	58	Belshina Bobruisk	57	Lokomotiv Vitebsk	2-1	Dinamo Minsk
1999	BATE Borisov	77	Slavija Mozyr	65	FC Gomel	63	Belshina Bobruisk	1-1 4-2p	Slavija Mozyr
2000	Slavija Mozyr	74	BATE Borisov	64	Dinamo Minsk	62	Slavija Mozyr	2-1	Torpedo-SKA Minsk
2001	Belshina Bobruisk	56	Dinamo Minsk	53	BATE Borisov	51	Belshina Bobruisk	1-0	Slavija Mozyr
2002	BATE Borisov	56	Neman Grodno	56	Shakhtyor Soligorsk	51	FC Gomel	2-0	BATE Borisov
2003	FC Gomel	74	BATE Borisov	66	Dinamo Minsk	64	Dinamo Minsk	2-0	Lokomotiv Minsk
2004	Dinamo Minsk	75	BATE Borisov	70	Shakhtyor Soligorsk	65	Shakhtyor Soligorsk	1-0	FC Gomel
2005	Shakhtyor Soligorsk	63	Dinamo Minsk	50	MTZ-RIPO Minsk	49	MTZ-RIPO Minsk	2-1	BATE Borisov
2006	BATE Borisov	54	Dinamo Minsk	52	Shakhtyor Soligorsk	51	BATE Borisov	3-1	Shakhtyor Soligorsk
2007							Dinamo Brest	0-0 4-3p	BATE Borisov

BELARUS 2006

VYSSHAYA LIGA

	Pl	W	D	L	F	A	Pts	BATE	Dinamo	Shakhter	MTZ-RIPO	Gomel	Lokomotiv	Naftan	Darida	Dinamo	Neman	Torpedo	Dnepr	Lokomotiv	Belshina
BATE Borisov †	26	16	6	4	47	27	54		2-2	2-1	1-3	1-1	2-2	2-1	1-0	3-0	2-0	1-0	3-0	4-2	1-0
Dinamo Minsk ‡	26	15	7	4	44	22	52	4-2		0-2	1-3	4-1	3-1	2-2	1-2	1-1	0-2	2-0	0-0	4-2	2-0
Shakhter Soligorsk	26	16	3	7	50	31	51	3-2	0-2		2-0	3-0	3-1	5-2	1-3	1-0	5-3	1-1	4-1	3-3	3-1
MTZ-RIPO Minsk	26	16	3	7	54	24	51	0-0	0-0	3-1		0-2	0-0	2-1	1-0	3-0	0-2	0-1	3-1	7-1	2-0
FC Gomel	26	12	6	8	33	32	42	0-1	0-3	2-0	2-8		2-0	1-3	0-0	0-0	0-0	3-0	1-1	2-0	1-0
Lokomotiv Vitebsk	26	9	11	6	21	18	38	1-1	0-2	0-0	1-0	0-1		1-2	1-0	1-0	0-0	2-2	0-0	2-0	1-0
Naftan Novopolotsk	26	11	4	11	45	42	37	0-2	0-2	0-2	2-1	2-3	0-0		2-0	3-0	2-0	1-1	4-3	0-3	2-1
Darida Mikashevichi	26	10	7	9	23	21	37	3-1	0-0	0-2	0-1	1-0	0-0	2-1		1-2	2-1	0-0	3-2	0-1	1-0
Dinamo Brest ‡	26	8	7	11	17	31	31	0-2	0-0	3-1	0-2	0-3	0-0	0-4	0-0		1-0	2-0	1-0	2-1	0-1
Neman Grodno	26	8	6	12	24	30	30	1-2	0-1	0-1	0-3	1-1	0-2	2-3	1-0	0-0		2-0	2-1	1-0	1-1
Torpedo Zhodino	26	7	9	10	21	27	30	1-1	0-1	1-0	0-1	2-0	0-2	2-0	1-1	1-1	2-1		1-2	1-0	1-1
Dnepr-Transmash	26	6	5	15	29	47	23	0-3	0-2	0-2	5-3	0-2	0-2	2-1	1-2	0-1	0-1	0-0		2-1	3-3
Lokomotiv Minsk	26	5	4	17	26	52	19	1-3	1-2	0-1	0-4	0-1	0-0	3-3	0-2	3-2	1-3	1-0	1-3		1-0
Belshina Bobruisk	26	1	6	19	16	46	9	1-2	1-3	1-3	1-4	1-3	0-1	0-4	0-0	0-1	0-0	1-3	1-2	0-0	

18/04/2006 - 4/11/2006 • † Qualified for the UEFA Champions League • ‡ Qualified for the UEFA Cup

Top scorers: Alexandr KLIMENKO, Shakhter 17; Roman VASILYUK, Gomel 14; Vyacheslav HLEB, MTZ-RIPO 13; Artem KONTSEVOI, MTZ-RIPO 12

BELARUS 2006 SECOND DIVISION

	Pl	W	D	L	F	A	Pts
FC Minsk	26	17	5	4	44	13	56
FC Smorgon	26	16	7	3	57	27	55
Khimik Svetiogorsk	26	14	7	5	48	30	49
FC Moazyr-ZLIN	26	11	10	5	44	24	43
FC Mikashevichi	26	12	4	10	38	33	40
FC Polatsak	26	11	4	11	36	41	37
Vedrich-97 Rechitsa	26	10	6	10	31	32	36
Khvalya Pinsk	26	10	4	12	47	48	34
Veras Nesvizh	26	9	5	12	27	33	32
FC Baranovichi	26	8	8	10	27	42	32
Kommunalnik Slonim	26	7	5	14	32	44	26
Zorka-BDU Minsk	26	5	10	11	32	39	25
FC Lida	26	6	5	15	23	45	23
FC Bereza	26	3	6	17	23	58	15

22/04/2006 - 28/10/2006

BFF CUP 2006–07

Round of sixteen			Quarter–finals			Semi–finals			Final		
Dinamo Brest *	4	3									
Lokomotiv Minsk	1	1	Dinamo Brest	2	4						
Lokomotiv Vitebsk *	1	1	Shakhter Soligorsk *	0	1						
Shakhter Soligorsk	1	4				Dinamo Brest *	2	2			
Dinamo Minsk	4	3				Neman Grodno	2	1			
Vedrich-97 Rechitsa *	0	0	Dinamo Minsk	2	0						
FC Gomel *	0	1	Neman Grodno *	1	3						
Neman Grodno	2	3							Dinamo Brest ‡	0	4p
FC Minsk *	5	0							BATE Borisov	0	3p
Dnepr-Transmash	1	1	FC Minsk *	1	1						
FC Polatsak *	1	0	Torpedo Zhodino	1	0						
Torpedo Zhodino	0	2				FC Minsk *	0	0			
MTZ-RIPO Minsk	3	3				BATE Borisov	1	1			
Spartak Shklou *	1	0	MTZ-RIPO Minsk *	1	0						
Darida Mikashevichi *	1	0	BATE Borisov	2	1						
BATE Borisov	0	4									

CUP FINAL

Dinamo Stadium, Minsk
27-05-2007, Att: 9500, Ref: Chabykin

* Home team in the 1st leg • ‡ Qualified for the UEFA Cup

BLZ – BELIZE

NATIONAL TEAM RECORD
JULY 10TH 2006 TO JULY 12TH 2010

PL	W	D	L	F	A	%
3	0	0	3	3	7	0

FIFA/COCA-COLA WORLD RANKING

1993	1994	1995	1996	1997	1998	1999	2000	2001	2002	2003	2004	2005	2006	High	Low
-	-	173	182	179	186	190	186	167	158	174	181	180	198	157 05/02	199 07/07

	2006–2007											
08/06	09/06	10/06	11/06	12/06	01/07	02/07	03/07	04/07	05/07	06/07	07/07	
197	198	198	198	198	199	199	199	199	199	199	199	

There has been a huge increase in the profile of football in Belize, by far the smallest country in the Central American region. There is now a unified League that is going from strength to strength, a new cup competition - the FFB Cup - while the national team was back in action after a two year break. Two editions of the RGF Insurance League were played over the course of the 2006-07 season, both of which were won by FC Belize. A six-team competition took place in the second half of 2006 with the top four qualifying for the play-offs. Unbeaten Wagiya looked odds-on for the title but lost for the first time in the first leg of the final, which was enough to give the title to FC Belize.

INTERNATIONAL HONOURS
None

An expanded 12 team tournament kicked off in February 2007 from which the top four in both groups of six qualified for the play-offs. This time FC Belize were unbeaten in the group stage and they went on to beat Revolutionary Conquerors in the final. Just before the start of the League, Conquerors had beaten Sugar Boys Juventus in the first FFB Cup Final. Competition at continental level, however, was not so positive with both Hankook Verdes and Wagiya knocked out in the first round of the Torneo Interclubes de UNCAF and the national team lost all three of their UNCAF Cup ties and they have now lost a record eight matches on the trot.

THE FIFA BIG COUNT OF 2006

	Male	Female		Total
Number of players	14 800	3 000	Referees and Assistant Referees	45
Professionals	150		Admin, Coaches, Technical, Medical	625
Amateurs 18+	1 700		Number of clubs	32
Youth under 18	1 300		Number of teams	140
Unregistered	3 650		Clubs with women's teams	10
Total players	17 800		Players as % of population	6.19%

Football Federation of Belize (FFB)
26 Hummingbird Highway, Belmopan, PO Box 1742, Belize City
Tel +501 822 3410   Fax +501 822 3377
info@belizefootball.bz   www.belizefootball.bz
President: CHIMILIO Bertie Dr   General Secretary: HULSE Marguerite
Vice-President: PECH Bernaldino   Treasurer: BAXTER Matthews   Media Officer: None
Men's Coach: VIEIRA Carlos   Women's Coach: TBD
FFB formed: 1980   CONCACAF: 1986   FIFA: 1986
Red shirts with white and blue trimmings, Red shorts, Red socks

RECENT INTERNATIONAL MATCHES PLAYED BY BELIZE

2002	Opponents	Score	Venue	Comp	Scorers	Att	Referee
No international matches played in 2002 after June							
2003							
No international matches played in 2003							
2004							
13-06	Canada	L 0-4	Kingston, Ontario	WCq		8 245	Batres GUA
16-06	Canada	L 0-4	Kingston, Ontario	WCq		5 124	Gordon TRI
2005							
19-02	Guatemala	L 0-2	Guatemala City	UCr1		10 000	Quesada CRC
21-02	Honduras	L 0-4	Guatemala City	UCr1		3 000	Campos NCA
23-02	Nicaragua	L 0-1	Guatemala City	UCr1		3 000	Campos NCA
2006							
No international matches played in 2006							
2007							
8-02	El Salvador	L 1-2	San Salvador	UCr1	Benavides 61		Quesada CRC
10-02	Guatemala	L 0-1	San Salvador	UCr1			Vidal PAN
12-02	Nicaragua	L 2-4	San Salvador	UCr1	McCauley 2 25 34		Quesada CRC

UC = UNCAF Cup • WC = FIFA World Cup • q = qualifier

BELIZE NATIONAL TEAM RECORDS AND RECORD SEQUENCES

Records			Sequence records					
Victory	7-1	NCA 2002	Wins	3	2001-2002	Clean sheets	2	2000-2001
Defeat	0-7	CRC 1999	Defeats	8	2004-	Goals scored	5	2001-2002
Player Caps	n/a		Undefeated	3	2000-01, 2001-02	Without goal	5	2004-2005
Player Goals	n/a		Without win	12	1995-2000	Goals against	15	2001-

RECENT LEAGUE RECORD

Year	Winners	Score	Runners-up
2005	New Site Erei	0-0 1-1 5-4p	Boca FC
2006	New Site Erei	1-0 2-0	Hankook Verdes
2006	FC Belize	2-1 1-1	Wagiya
2007	FC Belize	1-0 1-0	Conquerors

BELIZE 2007 RFG INSURANCE LEAGUE

Group A	Pl	W	D	L	F	A	Pts
FC Belize ‡	10	7	3	0	21	5	24
Tex Mar Boys ‡	10	7	1	2	15	7	22
Wagiya ‡	10	4	1	5	14	10	13
Hankook Verdes Utd ‡	10	3	3	4	15	13	12
Belmopan Bandits	10	3	1	6	6	26	10
Toledo United	10	0	3	7	5	15	3
Group B							
Revolut'ry Conquerors‡	10	6	2	2	26	11	20
Sugar Boys Juventus ‡	10	5	3	2	18	13	18
Santel's ‡	10	5	2	3	14	11	17
Costa Del Sol Nairi's ‡	10	4	2	4	18	15	14
Alpha Glitters	10	3	5	2	10	12	14
Pickstock Lake	10	0	0	10	5	29	0

25/02/2007 - 29/04/2007 • ‡ Qualified for the play-offs

BELIZE 2006 RFG INSURANCE LEAGUE

Semi-finals		Final	
FC Belize *	0 0		
Hankook Verdes	0 0	FC Belize *	2 1
Belmopan Bandits	1 2	Wagiya	1 1
Wagiya *	3 5		

The first round had one group with 6 teams. The top four qualified

BELIZE 2007 RFG INSURANCE LEAGUE PLAY-OFFS

Quarter-finals		Semi-finals		Final	
FC Belize *	2 0				
Costa Del Sol	0 1	FC Belize *	1 1		
Santel's	1 0	Tex Mar Boys	0 2		
Tex Mar Boys *	2 1			FC Belize *	1 1
Wagiya	6 4			R. Conquerors	0 0
SB Juventus *	2 1	Wagiya	0 2		
Hankook Verdes	0 1	R. Conquerors *	3 0	3-06-2007 & 10-06-2007	
R. Conquerors *	0 1			* Home team in the first leg	

BELIZE COUNTRY INFORMATION

Capital	Belmopan	Independence	1981	GDP per Capita	$4 900
Population	272 945	Status	Commonwealth	GNP Ranking	159
Area km²	22 966	Language	English	Dialling code	+501
Population density	11 per km²	Literacy rate	75%	Internet code	.bz
% in urban areas	47%	Main religion	Christian 77%	GMT +/–	-6
Towns/Cities ('000)	Belize City 61; San Ignacio 16; Orange Walk 15; Belmopan 13; Dangriga 10; Corozal 8				
Neighbours (km)	Mexico 250; Guatemala 266; Caribbean Sea 386				
Main stadia	People's Stadium – Orange Walk 3 000; MCC Grounds – Belize City 2 500				

BOL – BOLIVIA

NATIONAL TEAM RECORD
JULY 10TH 2006 TO JULY 12TH 2010

PL	W	D	L	F	A	%
7	2	4	1	11	7	57.1

FIFA/COCA-COLA WORLD RANKING

1993	1994	1995	1996	1997	1998	1999	2000	2001	2002	2003	2004	2005	2006	High	Low
58	44	53	39	24	61	61	65	70	92	99	94	96	101	18 07/97	114 08/03

2006–2007											
08/06	09/06	10/06	11/06	12/06	01/07	02/07	03/07	04/07	05/07	06/07	07/07
82	79	107	101	101	101	101	101	97	97	92	68

The news that FIFA had introduced a ban on international matches being staged above an altitude of 2,500 meters caused huge uproar in Bolivia where the capital La Paz stands at 3,600 meters. President Evo Morales, a big football fan, personally led the campaign to get the ban overturned, questioning the medical evidence on which the decision had been taken. A Copa Libertadores match between Real Potosí and Brazilian club Flamengo played in freezing rain at an altitude of 4,000 meters, conditions which the Brazilians had described as inhumane, prompted FIFA to act but La Paz was made an exception in time for the start of the 2010 FIFA World Cup qualifying

INTERNATIONAL HONOURS
Qualified for the FIFA World Cup™ finals 1930 1950 1994   Copa América 1963

campaign. In the meantime, Bolivia didn't have much luck at the Copa America with a defeat against Uruguay - their only one of the season - and draws against Venezuela and Peru meaning that they finished bottom of their first round group. Bolivia's two most successful clubs, Bolívar and Jorge Wilstermann, shared the honours in the 2006 season. Bolívar won the Apertura ahead of Real Potosí, who then also finished second in the Clausura behind Wilstermann. Potosi met Wilstermann in a winner takes all match on the final day of the season in Cochabamba, a game Wilstermann won 2-1 with a late goal from Horacio Chiorazzo.

THE FIFA BIG COUNT OF 2006

	Male	Female		Total
Number of players	504 700	74 100	Referees and Assistant Referees	500
Professionals	400		Admin, Coaches, Technical, Medical	2 800
Amateurs 18+	16 400		Number of clubs	890
Youth under 18	33 300		Number of teams	1 100
Unregistered	236 600		Clubs with women's teams	7
Total players	578 800		Players as % of population	6.44%

Federación Boliviana de Fútbol (FBF)
Av. Libertador Bolivar 1168, Cochabamba, Bolivia
Tel +591 4 4244982   Fax +591 4 4282132
fbfcba@hotmail.com   www.fbf.com.bo
President: CHAVES Carlos   General Secretary: ZAMBRANO Jose Pedro
Vice-President: SANCHEZ Erwin   Treasurer: PACHECO Jorge   Media Officer: SILVER Javier
Men's Coach: MESA Ovidio   Women's Coach: MELGAR Herman
FBF formed: 1925   CONMEBOL: 1926   FIFA: 1926
Green shirts, White shorts, Green socks

RECENT INTERNATIONAL MATCHES PLAYED BY BOLIVIA

2002	Opponents	Score	Venue	Comp	Scorers	Att	Referee
21-08	Venezuela	L 0-2	Caracas	Fr		25 000	Ibarra VEN
2003							
19-03	Mexico	L 0-2	Dallas	Fr		40 000	Terry USA
10-06	Portugal	L 0-4	Lisbon	Fr		10 000	Kenan ISR
31-08	Panama	W 3-0	La Paz	Fr	Mendez [21], Ricaldi [51], Gutierrez.L [84]	8 000	Ortube BOL
7-09	Uruguay	L 0-5	Montevideo	WCq		45 000	Hidalgo PER
10-09	Colombia	W 4-0	La Paz	WCq	Baldivieso [12p], Botero 3 [27 48 58]	30 000	Oliveira BRA
11-10	Honduras	W 1-0	Washington	Fr	Pena.JM [89]	20 000	Kennedy USA
15-11	Argentina	L 0-3	Buenos Aires	WCq		30 042	Hidalgo PER
18-11	Venezuela	L 1-2	Maracaibo	WCq	Botero [60]	25 000	Reinoso ECU
2004							
30-03	Chile	L 0-2	La Paz	WCq		42 000	Martin ARG
1-06	Paraguay	W 2-1	La Paz	WCq	Cristaldo [8], Suarez.R [72]	23 013	Rezende BRA
5-06	Ecuador	L 2-3	Quito	WCq	Gutierrez.L [58], Castillo [75]	30 020	Brand VEN
6-07	Peru	D 2-2	Lima	CAr1	Botero [36], Alvarez [57]	45 000	Baldassi ARG
9-07	Colombia	L 0-1	Lima	CAr1		35 000	Ramos ECU
12-07	Venezuela	D 1-1	Trujillo	CAr1	Galindo [32]	25 000	Mattus CRC
5-09	Brazil	L 1-3	Sao Paulo	WCq	Cristaldo [48]	60 000	Baldassi ARG
9-10	Peru	W 1-0	La Paz	WCq	Botero [56]	23 729	Reinoso ECU
12-10	Uruguay	D 0-0	La Paz	WCq		24 349	Rezende BRA
13-11	Guatemala	L 0-1	Washington DC	Fr		22 000	Prus USA
17-11	Colombia	L 0-1	Barranquilla	WCq		25 000	Torres PAR
2005							
26-03	Argentina	L 1-2	La Paz	WCq	Castillo [49]	25 000	Larrionda URU
29-03	Venezuela	W 3-1	La Paz	WCq	Cichero OG [2], Castillo [25], Vaca [84]	7 908	Lecca PER
4-06	Chile	L 1-3	Santiago	WCq	Castillo [83p]	46 729	Rezende BRA
8-06	Paraguay	L 1-4	Asuncion	WCq	Galindo [30]	5 534	Brand VEN
3-09	Ecuador	L 1-2	La Paz	WCq	Vaca [41]	8 434	Baldassi ARG
9-10	Brazil	D 1-1	La Paz	WCq	Castillo [49]	22 725	Larrionda URU
12-10	Peru	L 1-4	Tacna	WCq	Gutierrez.L [66]	14 774	Sequeira ARG
2006							
15-11	El Salvador	W 5-1	La Paz	Fr	Sossa [29], Arce [33], Sanchez.O [41], Reyes [82], Peña.D [90]	25 000	
2007							
28-03	South Africa	W 1-0	Johannesburg	Fr	Vaca [19]	5 000	Ramocha BOT
26-05	Republic of Ireland	D 1-1	Boston	Fr	Hoyos [14]		
20-06	Paraguay	D 0-0	Santa Cruz	Fr		35 000	Antequera BOL
26-06	Venezuela	D 2-2	San Cristobal	CAr1	Moreno [38], Arce [84]	42 000	Reinoso ECU
30-08	Uruguay	L 0-1	San Cristobal	CAr1		18 000	Toledo USA
3-07	Peru	D 2-2	Merida	CAr1	Moreno [24], Campos [45]	35 000	Chandia CHI

Fr = Friendly match • CA = Copa América • WC = FIFA World Cup • q = qualifier • r1 = first round group

BOLIVIA NATIONAL TEAM RECORDS AND RECORD SEQUENCES

Records			Sequence records				
Victory	9-2	HAI 2000	Wins	5	1963, 1993, 1998	Clean sheets	3	1998, 1999
Defeat	1-10	BRA 1949	Defeats	9	1926-1930	Goals scored	15	1995-1996
Player Caps	93	SANDY Marco	Undefeated	9	1997	Without goal	7	1994
Player Goals	16	UGARTE Víctor	Without win	19	1945-1948	Goals against	18	1977-1980

MAJOR CITIES/TOWNS

Population '000

1	Santa Cruz	1 404
2	Cochabamba	932
3	El Alto	872
4	La Paz	817
5	Sucre	232
6	Oruro	210
7	Tarija	165
8	Potosí	143
9	Montero	91
10	Yacuíba	88
11	Trinidad	86
12	Riberalta	76
13	Guayaramerín	36
14	Villazón	30
15	Bermejo	28
16	Cobija	28
17	Camiri	28
18	Llallagua	27
19	San Ignacio	24
20	Warnes	23
21	Tupiza	22
22	San Borja	20
23	Villamontes	19
24	Cotoca	19

REPUBLIC OF BOLIVIA; REPUBLICA DE BOLIVIA

Capital	Sucre; La Paz	Language	Spanish	Independence	1825
Population	8 989 046	Area	1 098 580 km²	Density	8 per km²	% in cities	61%
GDP per cap	$2 400	Dailling code	+591	Internet	.bo	GMT + / -	-4

MEDALS TABLE

		Overall			Pro			Nat			LL			Sth Am			City	Stadium	Cap'ty	DoF
		G	S	B	G	S	B	G	S	G	S		G	S	B					
1	Bolívar	20	8	2	16	5		4	2	12	11			1	2	La Paz	Libertador Bolívar	25 000	1925
2	Jorge Wilstermann	9	7	1	4	5		5	2	12	3				1	Cochabamba	Felix Capriles	35 000	1949
3	The Strongest	7	8		6	6		1	2	18	10					La Paz	Rafael Castellón	15 000	1908
4	Oriente Petrolero	5	11		4	9		1	2	7	3					Santa Cruz	Tahuichi	40 000	1955
5	Blooming	4	2	1	4	2				1	2				1	Santa Cruz	Tahuichi	40 000	1946
6	San José	2	2		1	2		1		9	2					Oruro	Jesus Bermudez	28 000	1942
7	Deportivo Municipal	1	4					1	4	4	3					La Paz	Luís Lastra	10 000	1944
8	Always Ready	1	2					1	2	2	5					La Paz	Rafael Castellón	15 000	
9	Guabirá	1	2		1		1	1	1	1	1					Montero	Gilberto Parada	18 000	1962
10	Chaco Petrolero	1	1					1	1		1					La Paz	Hernando Siles	55 000	1942
11	Litoral	1						1		4	1					La Paz	Rafael Castellón	15 000	
12	Universitario	1						1		1	4					La Paz	Hernando Siles	55 000	
13	Real Potosí		4		4												Potosi	Mario Guzman	15 000	1941
14	Aurora		1		1					3	8						Cochabamba	Felix Capriles	35 000	1935
15	31 de Octubre		1					1	1	1	2					La Paz			
16	Deportivo Chaco		1					1	1								La Paz			
17	Destroyers									2	1						Santa Cruz	Tahuichi	40 000	1948

Pro = the Professional League played since 1977 • Nat = the various national competitions played between 1954 and 1976 • LL = the local leagues played throughout the country until 1976 • The totals for the local leagues are not included in the overall totals

RECENT LEAGUE RECORD

	Championship Play-off		
Year	Champions	Score	Runners-up
2000	Jorge Wilsterman	4-1 0-4 2-2 4-3p	Oriente Petrolero
2001	Oriente Petrolero	1-4 4-3 2-0	Bolívar
2002	Bolívar	†	

	Torneo Apertura			
Year	Champions	Pts	Runners-up	Pts
2003	The Strongest	46	Bolívar	45
2004	Bolívar	53	Aurora	38
2005	Bolívar	44	The Strongest	43
2006	Bolívar	48	Real Potosí	45

Torneo Clausura			
Champions	Pts	Runners-up	Pts
The Strongest	13	Jorge Wilsterman	10
The Strongest	27	Oriente Petrolero	27
Blooming	19	Bolívar	14
Jorge Wilsterman	21	Real Potosí	18

† Won both stages so no play-off

BOLIVIA 2006

TORNEO APERTURA

	Pl	W	D	L	F	A	Pts	Bolívar	Real Potosí	Universitario	San José	Blooming	Oriente	Wilstermann	Strongest	Unión	Destroyers	Aurora	La Paz
Bolívar †	22	14	6	2	40	17	48		1-1	5-1	1-1	2-1	1-1	2-1	2-0	3-0	3-0	2-0	2-0
Real Potosí	22	13	6	3	54	25	45	4-2		3-1	2-1	4-0	3-0	3-3	3-1	5-1	5-0	2-0	1-0
Universitario Sucre	22	12	6	4	38	30	42	1-1	1-1		1-2	2-1	3-2	2-2	2-2	1-0	3-0	2-1	3-2
San José	22	10	8	4	34	20	38	0-0	2-1	0-1		4-1	1-2	3-2	2-0	1-1	2-0	5-0	0-0
Blooming	22	10	5	7	36	31	35	0-1	1-1	1-1	0-0		1-1	1-0	3-0	3-1	4-0	3-1	1-1
Oriente Petrolero	22	7	8	7	30	41	29	1-0	1-4	0-0	1-1	1-4		3-3	1-0	2-3	2-1	1-1	2-0
Jorge Wilstermann	22	6	8	8	38	35	26	2-2	1-1	1-2	2-2	0-1	5-1		2-0	1-0	4-1	2-1	1-1
The Strongest	22	7	4	11	32	36	25	0-2	3-2	0-2	0-2	6-1	5-1	2-1		4-2	0-0	1-1	2-0
Unión Central	22	6	3	13	28	39	21	0-1	2-1	0-1	0-1	2-3	1-2	3-1	1-1		1-0	3-1	2-0
Destroyers	22	6	2	14	30	50	20	0-1	1-3	3-2	3-1	1-4	2-3	1-1	3-2	3-2		2-0	6-0
Aurora	22	3	8	11	22	40	17	2-4	2-2	2-4	1-1	0-1	1-1	2-1	1-0	0-0	3-1		1-1
La Paz FC	22	3	6	13	24	42	15	1-2	1-2	1-2	1-2	2-1	1-1	1-2	2-3	4-3	4-2	1-1	

11/02/2006 - 4/06/2006 • † Qualified for the Copa Libertadores
Top scorers: Cristino JARA, Real Potosí 16; Eduardo MONTEIRO, Real Potosí 13; José CASTILLO, Oriente Petrolero 11; José MENACHO, Bolívar 10

BOLIVIA 2006

TORNEO CLAUSURA 1ST STAGE

Serie A

	Pl	W	D	L	F	A	Pts	Wilstermann	Real Potosí	Blooming	Destroyers	Strongest	La Paz	Bolívar	Oriente	Universitario	San José	Aurora	Unión
Jorge Wilstermann ‡	12	8	3	1	24	9	27		2-1	2-1	3-1	4-0	2-1					1-1	
Real Potosí ‡	12	5	3	4	20	20	18	1-1		3-2	2-0	1-1	2-1			4-3			
Blooming ‡	12	4	3	5	15	18	15	1-2	4-3		1-1	1-0	1-0		1-1				
Destroyers	12	4	1	7	13	19	13	1-0	1-0	1-2		2-3	3-1						2-1
The Strongest	12	3	4	5	10	17	13	0-3	1-1	1-0	2-1		1-1	0-1					
La Paz FC	12	3	3	6	11	15	12	0-3	0-1	0-0	3-0	1-0					2-1		

Serie B

	Pl	W	D	L	F	A	Pts	Wilstermann	Real Potosí	Blooming	Destroyers	Strongest	La Paz	Bolívar	Oriente	Universitario	San José	Aurora	Unión
Bolívar ‡	12	7	2	3	21	12	23					1-1			0-0	1-0	2-0	4-1	6-0
Oriente Petrolero ‡	12	6	4	2	23	9	22		4-1					6-0		1-0	2-2	4-0	0-0
Universitario Sucre ‡	12	6	2	4	19	15	20		4-1					2-1	3-2		1-1	1-0	2-0
San José	12	3	5	4	12	14	14						1-1	2-1	2-0	0-1		0-0	1-1
Aurora	12	3	3	6	11	19	12	1-1						0-2	0-2	3-1	3-1		1-0
Unión Central	12	2	3	7	6	18	9					1-0		0-2	0-1	1-1	0-1	2-1	

29/07/2006 - 1/10/2006 • ‡ Qualified for the 2nd stage with the group winners taking one bonus point each

TORNEO CLAUSURA 2ND STAGE

	Pl	W	D	L	F	A	Pts	Wilstermann	Real Potosí	Oriente	Universitario	Blooming	Bolívar
Jorge Wilsterman	10	6	2	2	16	8	21		2-1	3-1	2-0	2-0	2-0
Real Potosí †	10	5	2	3	20	15	17	2-1		2-2	3-2	2-1	4-2
Oriente Petrolero	10	3	4	3	13	21	13	2-1	0-3		2-1	1-1	1-1
Universitario Sucre	10	3	3	4	12	13	12	0-0	1-0	1-2		2-2	2-0
Blooming †	10	2	5	3	14	15	11	1-2	2-1	1-1	2-2		3-0
Bolívar	10	1	4	5	15	18	8	1-1	2-2	7-1	0-1	2-2	

7/10/2006 - 3/12/2006 • † Qualified for the Copa Libertadores • ‡ Qualified for the Copa Sudamericana
Top scorers: Cristino JARA, Potosí 19; Pablo ZEBALLOS, Oriente 15; Carlos MONTEIRO, Potosí 10; Daniel JUAREZ, Wilstermann 9
Unión Central relegated on overall season record over 2005 and 2006 • Copa Simon Bolivar winners: Municipal Real Mamoré. Municipal promoted to the top level • Runners-up, Ciclón, entered a play-off against Destroyers: Destroyers 1-1 2-1 Ciclón. Destroyers remain at the top level.

BOT – BOTSWANA

NATIONAL TEAM RECORD
JULY 10TH 2006 TO JULY 12TH 2010

PL	W	D	L	F	A	%
14	6	5	3	7	7	60.7

FIFA/COCA-COLA WORLD RANKING

1993	1994	1995	1996	1997	1998	1999	2000	2001	2002	2003	2004	2005	2006	High		Low	
140	145	155	161	162	155	165	150	153	136	112	102	101	108	96	09/05	165	02/00

					2006–2007						
08/06	09/06	10/06	11/06	12/06	01/07	02/07	03/07	04/07	05/07	06/07	07/07
102	104	105	104	108	107	105	105	101	102	105	101

The formbook in domestic football was turned on its head with a first-ever league triumph for ECCO City Green, who ended five points clear of Mochudi Centre Chiefs. It was also the first title for a club from the northern town of Francistown, Botswana's second city, which for decades has had to play second fiddle to clubs from the capital Gaborone and the more populous south. Zimbabwean-born coach Barry Daka led his unfashionable side to their surprise triumph, on the back of the goal scoring form of Malepa 'Chippa' Bolelang. Botswana also continued to create surprises in the international forum, notably with the country's under-23 team eliminating Tunisia

INTERNATIONAL HONOURS
None

to qualify for the group phase of the 2008 Olympic Games qualifiers. Many of the side then quickly won a berth in the senior side under English coach Colwyn Rowe, who has turned the normally porous Zebras defence into one of the most formidable in the region. Botswana remain unbeaten at home since October 2005 conceding just one goal at the National Stadium in that time. The only blip on their record was 4-0 defeat at the start of their 2008 African Nations Cup qualifying campaign in Mauritania, which set them back in their bid to reach the finals for the first time. A growing exodus of top talent to clubs in South Africa has helped boost the form of the side.

THE FIFA BIG COUNT OF 2006

	Male	Female		Total
Number of players	93 712	4 920	Referees and Assistant Referees	208
Professionals	12		Admin, Coaches, Technical, Medical	2 370
Amateurs 18+	10 440		Number of clubs	63
Youth under 18	4 000		Number of teams	348
Unregistered	12 180		Clubs with women's teams	0
Total players	98 632		Players as % of population	6.01%

Botswana Football Association (BFA)
PO Box 1396, Gaborone, Botswana
Tel +267 3900279   Fax +267 3900280
bfa@info.bw   www.none
President: MAKGALEMELE Philip   General Secretary: NTSHINOGANG Thabo
Vice-President: RAMOTLHWA Segolame   Treasurer: KANDJII David   Media Officer: MOOKI Utlwang Ishmael
Men's Coach: ROWE Colwyn   Women's Coach: None
BFA formed: 1970   CAF: 1976   FIFA: 1978
Blue shirts with white and black stripes, Blue shorts, Blue socks

RECENT INTERNATIONAL MATCHES PLAYED BY BOTSWANA

2004	Opponents		Score	Venue	Comp	Scorers	Att	Referee
29-02	Lesotho	D	0-0	Maseru	CCr1	W 11-10p	10 000	Mufeti NAM
28-04	Namibia	D	0-0	Windhoek	Fr		1 500	
26-05	Mozambique	D	0-0	Maputo	Fr		2 000	
5-06	Tunisia	L	1-4	Tunis	WCq	Selolwane [65]	2 844	Abdel Rahman SUD
19-06	Malawi	W	2-0	Gaborone	WCq	Selolwane [7], Gabolwelwe [25]	15 000	Awuye UGA
3-07	Morocco	L	0-1	Gaborone	WCq		22 000	Dlamini SWZ
18-07	Angola	D	1-1	Luanda	CCqf	Motlhabankwe [25]. L 3-5p	6 000	Phomane LES
18-08	Zimbabwe	L	0-2	Bulawayo	Fr		5 000	
5-09	Guinea	L	0-4	Conakry	WCq		25 000	Agbenyega GHA
9-10	Kenya	W	2-1	Gaborone	WCq	Molwantwa [51], Selolwane [58]	16 500	Colembi ANG
15-12	Lesotho	D	1-1	Maseru	Fr			
2005								
26-02	Zambia	D	0-0	Gaborone	Fr			
16-03	Zimbabwe	D	1-1	Harare	Fr	Moathiaping [72]	3 000	
26-03	Kenya	L	0-1	Nairobi	WCq		15 000	Buenkadila COD
16-04	Namibia	D	1-1	Windhoek	CCr1	Moathiaping [90]		Sentso LES
17-04	Zimbabwe	L	0-2	Windhoek	CCr1			Mavunza ANG
4-06	Tunisia	L	1-3	Gaborone	WCq	Gabonamong [13]	20 000	Mana NGA
18-06	Malawi	W	3-1	Blantyre	WCq	Molwantwa [10], Selolwane [40], Motlhabankwe [87]	20 000	Evehe CMR
1-07	Congo DR	D	0-0	Gaborone	Fr			
9-08	Angola	D	0-0	Johannesburg	Fr			
10-08	Angola	D	0-0	Johannesburg	Fr			
3-09	Morocco	L	0-1	Rabat	WCq		25 000	Benouza ALG
8-10	Guinea	L	1-2	Gaborone	WCq	Molwantwa [35]	16 800	Sowe GAM
2006								
14-05	Zambia	D	0-0	Gaborone	Fr	W 5-4p		
20-05	Madagascar	W	2-0	Gaborone	CCr1	Moathiaping [66], Mothibane [68]		Colembi ANG
21-05	South Africa	D	0-0	Gaborone	CCr1	W 6-5p		Infante MOZ
6-07	Malawi	L	1-2	Lilongwe	Fr	Moloi.P [38]		
8-07	Malawi	D	0-0	Blantyre	Fr			
5-08	Uganda	D	0-0	Kampala	Fr	L 1-3p		
19-08	Zambia	L	0-1	Lusaka	CCsf			Mnkantjo ZIM
3-09	Mauritania	L	0-4	Nouakchott	CNq			Djaoupe TOG
3-10	Lesotho	W	1-0	Gaborone	Fr	Moathiaping [60]		
7-10	Egypt	D	0-0	Gaborone	CNq			Bennett RSA
15-11	Swaziland	W	1-0	Gaborone	Fr	Ramatlhakwane [19]		
2007								
6-02	Namibia	W	1-0	Gaborone	Fr	Moloi.P [60]		
25-03	Burundi	W	1-0	Gaborone	CNq	Siska [64]		Marange ZIM
27-05	Libya	D	0-0	Gaborone	Fr			
3-06	Burundi	L	0-1	Kigali	CNq			
16-06	Mauritania	W	2-1	Gaborone	CNq	Marumo [19], Selolwane [40]		
21-07	Zambia	D	0-0	Orapa	Fr	W 3-2p		
28-07	Namibia	W	1-0	Gaborone	CCr1	Mogaladi [19]		Lwanja MWI
29-07	Angola	D	0-0	Gaborone	CCr1	W 3-1p		

Fr = Friendly match • CN = CAF African Cup of Nations • CC = COSAFA Cup • WC = FIFA World Cup
q = qualifier • r1 = first round group • qf = quarter-final • sf = semi-final

BOTSWANA NATIONAL TEAM RECORDS AND RECORD SEQUENCES

Records			Sequence records				
Victory	6-2	SWZ 2002	Wins	4	2001-2002	Clean sheets	6	2006-2007
Defeat	1-8	MWI 1968	Defeats	8	1968-1986	Goals scored	4	Three times
Player Caps	n/a		Undefeated	6	2006-2007	Without goal	6	1990-91, 2002
Player Goals	n/a		Without win	24	1994-1999	Goals against	14	1983-1995

BOTSWANA COUNTRY INFORMATION

Capital	Gaborone	Independence	1966	GDP per Capita	$9000
Population	1 561 973	Status	Republic	GDP Ranking	
Area km²	600 370	Language	English, Setswana	Dialling code	+267
Population density	2 per km²	Literacy rate	74%	Internet code	.bw
% in urban areas	28%	Main religion	Indigenous 85%	GMT + / –	+2
Towns/Cities ('000)	Gaborone 208; Francistown 89; Molepolole 63; Selibe Phikwe 53; Maun 49; Serowe 47
Neighbours (km)	Zimbabwe 813; South Africa 1,840; Namibia 1,360
Main stadia	National Stadium – Gaborone 22,500

BOTSWANA 2006–07 PREMIER LEAGUE

	Pl	W	D	L	F	A	Pts
ECCO City Green †	30	21	4	5	65	37	67
Centre Chiefs	30	19	5	6	72	36	62
Defence Force	30	16	9	5	43	25	57
Police	30	12	10	8	47	42	46
Gaborone United	30	14	6	10	41	43	48
Bot. Meat Commission	30	11	11	8	32	26	44
Notwane FC	30	11	9	10	49	36	42
Township Rollers	30	11	9	10	43	36	42
TAFIC	30	10	8	12	40	45	38
Nico United	30	8	11	11	38	46	35
Uniao Flamengo Santos	30	10	5	15	37	47	35
TASC	30	9	7	14	37	45	34
Lobtrans Gunners	30	7	10	13	31	40	31
Jwaneng Comets	30	7	10	13	28	40	31
Prisons	30	5	9	16	27	47	24
FC Satmos	30	4	7	19	25	64	19

16/09/2006 - 10/06/2007

† Qualified for the CAF Champions League
Top scorers: Pontsho MOLOI, Centre Chiefs 22; Tshepiso MOLWANTWA, Notwane 21

COCA-COLA CUP 2006

Round of 16		Quarter–finals		Semi–finals		Final	
Notwane	3						
Mosquito	0	Notwane					
Red Sparks	1	ECCO City Greens					
ECCO City Greens	2			Notwane	2		
Mogoditshane Fighters	1 5p			TASC	0		
Un. Flamengo Santos	1 3p	Mogoditshane Fighters	0				
Nico United	4 4p	TASC	2				
TASC	4 5p					Notwane ‡	2
Township Rollers	5					Defence Force	1
Police	1	Township Rollers	1				
Gaborone United	0 2 2p	Mochudi Chiefs	0				
Mochudi Chiefs	0 2 4p			Township Rollers †	3		
Bot. Meat Commission	0 4p			Defence Force	0		
FC Satmos	0 3p	Bot. Meat Commission	0				
Boteti Young Fighters	0	Defence Force	1	† Rollers disqualified			
Defence Force	1			* Home Team • ‡ Qualified for the CAF Confederation Cup			

CUP FINAL

9-09-2006, National Stadium, Gaborone

Scorers - Dirang Moloi [36], Keoagile Radipotsane [65] for Notwane; Mpho Mabogo [90] for BDF

RECENT LEAGUE AND CUP RECORD

	Championship						Cup		
Year	Champions	Pts	Runners-up	Pts	Third	Pts	Winners	Score	Runners-up
1999	Mogoditshane	25	Defence Force	21	Centre Chiefs	21	Mogodishane	3-0	Satmos
2000	Mogoditshane	42	Centre Chiefs	40	Defence Force	37	Mogodishane	1-1 5-4p	Gaborone United
2001	Mogoditshane	45	Defence Force	44	Police	43	TASC	2-0	Extension Gunners
2002	Defence Force	47	Mogoditshane	38	Centre Chiefs	36	TAFIC	0-0 6-5p	TASC
2003	Mogoditshane	2-1	Police				Mogoditshane	1-0	Township Rollers
2004	Defence Force		Police		TASC	39	Defence Force	2-1	Mogoditshane
2005	Township Rollers	52	Police	51	Centre Chiefs	45	Township Rollers	3-1	Defence Force
2006	Police	66	Defence Force	51	Meat Commission	51	Notwane	2-1	Defence Force
2007	ECCO City Green	67	Centre Chiefs	62	Defence Force	57			

BRA – BRAZIL

NATIONAL TEAM RECORD
JULY 10TH 2006 TO JULY 12TH 2010

PL	W	D	L	F	A	%
16	10	4	2	31	11	75

Brazil's record in the Copa América has never made happy reading; before 1989 they had won the title just three times in the 33 tournaments played. The traditional view has been that the tournament isn't regarded as that important by Brazilians but this is now increasingly being challenged, especially in the light of their latest success in the 2007 Copa América in Venezuela. With both Kaká and Ronaldinho asking to be excused after tough seasons with their clubs, Brazil sent a second-string side to Venezuela, in direct contrast to overwhelming favourites Argentina, and yet they still managed to beat the Argentines convincingly in the final. It was Brazil's fifth title since 1989 and their fourth in the last five tournaments. It also brought some welcome relief for coach Dunga after a difficult first year in charge during which he was accused of placing more emphasis on workrate than flair, and nowhere was that more evident than in the final against Argentina. There was also surprising international success for Internacional of Porto Alegre in the 2006 FIFA Club World Cup in Japan. The South American champions beat African champions Al Ahly 2-1 in the semi-finals and then European champions Barcelona 1-0 in the final. A goal eight minutes from

INTERNATIONAL HONOURS
FIFA World Cup™ 1958 1962 1970 1994 2002   **FIFA Confederations Cup** 1997 2005
FIFA World Youth Championship 1983 1985 1993 2003   **FIFA U-17 World Championship** 1997 1999 2003
Copa América 1919 1922 1949 1989 1997 1999 2004 2007   **South American Women's Championship** 1991 1995 1998 2003
FIFA Club World Championship Corínthians 2000 São Paulo FC 2005 International 2006
Copa Toyota Libertadores Santos 1962 1963 Cruzeiro 1976 1997 Flamengo 1981 Grêmio 1983 1995
São Paulo 1992 1993 2005 Vasco da Gama 1998 Palmeiras 1999 Internacional 2006

time by Adriano won the title for Inter, sealing a remarkable hat-trick for Brazilian clubs in the first three editions of the tournament. Inter's cross town rivals Grêmio came close to qualifying for the 2007 tournament but in the final of the Copa Libertadores they lost 5-0 on aggregate to Argentina's Boca Juniors. In domestic competition São Paulo FC won the Championship for the first time since 1991, reaping the rewards of a successful youth system that, with the sale of players like Kaká, has left the club in a stable situation financially. Remarkably goalkeeper Rogerio Ceni finished as the club's joint top scorer with eight goals from free-kicks. 2007 saw some welcome success for football in Rio de Janeiro with Fluminense winning the Copa do Brasil for the first time after beating Figueirense 2-1 on aggregate in the final. Attention now turns to Brazil's bid to host the 2014 FIFA World Cup and the job of convincing FIFA they are capable of rising to the challenge after Colombia withdrew their rival bid. With the backing of President Lula, at least the political will to succeed is there.

Confederação Brasileira de Futebol (CBF)
Rua Victor Civita 66, Bloco 1 - Edificio 5 - 5 Andar, Barra da Tijuca, Rio de Janeiro 22.775-040, Brazil
Tel +55 21 35359610   Fax +55 21 35359611
CBF@cbffutebol.com.br   www.cbfnews.com.br
President: TEIXEIRA Ricardo Terra   General Secretary: TEIXEIRA Marco Antonio
Vice-President: BASTOS Jose Sebastiao   Treasurer: OSORIO LOPES DA COSTA Antonio   Media Officer: PAIVA Rodrigo
Men's Coach: DUNGA Carlos   Women's Coach: FERREIRA Luiz
CBF formed: 1914   CONMEBOL: 1916   FIFA: 1923
Yellow shirts with green trimmings, Blue shorts, White socks or Blue shirts with white trimmings, White shorts, White socks

RECENT INTERNATIONAL MATCHES PLAYED BY BRAZIL

2004	Opponents	Score		Venue	Comp	Scorers	Att	Referee
13-10	Colombia	D	0-0	Maceio	WCq		20 000	Larrionda URU
16-11	Ecuador	L	0-1	Quito	WCq		38 308	Ruiz COL
2005								
9-02	Hong Kong	W	7-1	Hong Kong	Fr	Lucio 19, Roberto Carlos 30, Ricardo Oliveira 2 45 57, Ronaldinho 49, Robinho 77, Alex 79p	23 425	Zhou Weixin CHN
27-03	Peru	W	1-0	Goiania	WCq	Kaka 74	49 163	Amarilla PAR
30-03	Uruguay	D	1-1	Montevideo	WCq	Emerson 67	60 000	Baldassi ARG
27-04	Guatemala	W	3-0	Sao Paulo	Fr	Anderson 4, Romario 16, Grafite 65	36 235	Vazquez URU
5-06	Paraguay	W	4-1	Porto Alegre	WCq	Ronaldinho 2 32p 41p, Ze Roberto 70, Robinho 82	45 000	Vazquez URU
8-06	Argentina	L	1-3	Buenos Aires	WCq	Roberto Carlos 71	49 497	Mendez URU
16-06	Greece	W	3-0	Leipzig	CCr1	Adriano 41, Robinho 46, Juninho Pernambuco 81	42 507	Michel SVK
19-06	Mexico	L	0-1	Hanover	CCr1		43 677	Rosetti ITA
22-06	Japan	D	2-2	Köln	CCr1	Robinho 10, Ronaldinho 32	44 922	Daami TUN
26-06	Germany	W	3-2	Nürnberg	CCsf	Adriano 2 21 76, Ronaldinho 43p	42 187	Breeze AUS
29-06	Argentina	W	4-1	Frankfurt	CCf	Adriano 2 11 63, Kaka 16, Ronaldinho 47	45 591	Michel SVK
17-08	Croatia	D	1-1	Split	Fr	Ricardinho 41	30 000	Meyer GER
4-09	Chile	W	5-0	Brasilia	WCq	Juan 11, Robinho 21, Adriano 3 27 29 92+	39 000	Amarilla PAR
9-10	Bolivia	D	1-1	La Paz	WCq	Juninho Pernambuco 25	22 725	Larrionda URU
12-10	Venezuela	W	3-0	Belem	WCq	Adriano 28, Ronaldo 51, Roberto Carlos 61	47 000	Baldassi ARG
12-11	United Arab Emirates	W	8-0	Abu Dhabi	Fr	Kaka 20, Adriano 52, Fred 2 57 84, Lucio 64, Juninho Pernambuco 2 70 79, Cicinho 90	50 000	Abd El Fatah EGY
2006								
1-03	Russia	W	1-0	Moscow	Fr	Ronaldo 15	19 000	Busacca SUI
4-06	New Zealand	W	4-0	Geneva	Fr	Ronaldo 43, Adriano 51, Kaká 86, Juninho P'buco 90	32 000	Laperriere SUI
13-06	Croatia	W	1-0	Berlin	WCr1	Kaká 44	72 000	Archundia MEX
18-06	Australia	W	2-0	Munich	WCr1	Adriano 49, Fred 90	66 000	Merk GER
22-06	Japan	W	4-1	Dortmund	WCr1	Ronaldo 2 46+ 81, Juninho P'buco 53, Gilberto 59	65 000	Poulat FRA
27-06	Ghana	W	3-0	Dortmund	WCr2	Ronaldo 5, Adriano 46+, Ze Roberto 84	65 000	Michel SVK
1-07	France	L	0-1	Frankfurt	WCqf		48 000	Medina Cantalejo ESP
16-08	Norway	D	1-1	Oslo	Fr	Daniel Carvalho 62	25 062	Dougal SCO
3-09	Argentina	W	3-0	London	Fr	Elano Blumer 2 3 67, Kaka 89	59 032	Bennett ENG
5-09	Wales	W	2-0	London	Fr	Marcelo 61, Vágner Love 74	22 008	Riley ENG
10-10	Ecuador	W	2-1	Stockholm	Fr	Fred 44, Kaka 75	34 592	Johannesson SWE
15-11	Switzerland	W	2-1	Basel	Fr	Luisão 23, Kaka 35	39 000	Merk GER
2007								
6-02	Portugal	L	0-2	London	Fr		59 793	Atkinson ENG
24-03	Chile	W	4-0	Gothenburg	Fr	Ronaldinho 2 16p 49, Kaka 31, Juan 60	30 122	Berntsen NOR
27-03	Ghana	W	1-0	Stockholm	Fr	Vágner Love 17	20 104	Fröjdfeldt SWE
1-06	England	D	1-1	London	Fr	Diego 92+	88 745	Merk GER
5-06	Turkey	D	0-0	Dortmund	Fr		26 700	Meyer GER
27-06	Mexico	L	0-2	Puerto Ordaz	CCr1		40 000	Pezzotta ARG
1-07	Chile	W	3-0	Maturin	CCr1	Robinho 3 36p 84 87	42 000	Torres PAR
4-07	Ecuador	W	1-0	Puerto La Cruz	CCr1	Robinho 56p	34 000	Pezzotta ARG
7-07	Chile	W	6-1	Puerto La Cruz	CCqf	Juan 16, Baptista 23, Robinho 2 27 50, Josué 68, Vágner Love 85	25 000	Larrionda URU
10-07	Uruguay	D	2-2	Maracaibo	CCsf	Maicon 13, Julio Baptista 45. W 5-4p	40 000	Ruiz COL
15-07	Argentina	W	3-0	Maracaibo	CCf	Julio Baptista 4, Ayala OG 40, Daniel Alves 69	42 000	Amarilla PAR

Fr = Friendly match • CC = FIFA Confederations Cup • CA = Copa America • WC = FIFA World Cup
FIFA = FIFA Centennial celebration match • q = qualifier • r1 = 1st round • r2 = second round • qf = quarter-final • sf = semi-final • f = final

BRAZIL NATIONAL TEAM RECORDS AND RECORD SEQUENCES

Records			Sequence records					
Victory	10-1	BOL 1949	Wins	14	1997	Clean sheets	8	1989
Defeat	0-6	URU 1920	Defeats	4	2001	Goals scored	47	1994-1997
Player Caps	142	CAFU	Undefeated	45	1993-1997	Without goal	5	1990
Player Goals	77	PELE	Without win	7	1983-84, 1990-91	Goals against	24	1937-1944

MAJOR CITIES/TOWNS

Population '000

1	São Paulo	10 059
2	Rio de Janeiro	6 055
3	Salvador	2 762
4	Belo Horizonte	2 399
5	Fortaleza	2 349
6	Brasilia	2 260
7	Curitiba	1 746
8	Manaus	1 642
9	Recife	1 489
10	Belém	1 436
11	Porto Alegre	1 380
12	Guarulhos	1 198
13	Goiânia	1 188
14	Campinas	1 047
15	Nova Iguaçu	1 019
16	Maceió	989
17	São Gonçalo	949
18	São Luis	935
19	Duque de Caxias	829
20	Natal	774
21	Teresina	758
22	São Bernardo	756
23	Campo Grande	745
24	Jaboatão	729

FEDERATIVE REPUBLIC OF BRAZIL; REPUBLICA FEDERATIVA DO BRASIL

Capital Brasilia	Language Portuguese		Independence 1822
Population 188 078 227	Area 8 511 965 km²	Density 21 per km²	% in cities 78%
GDP per cap $7 600	Dailling code +55	Internet .br	GMT + / - -3

MEDALS TABLE

	Overall			Nat		Cup		SL	Sth Am			City	Stadium	Cap'ty	DoF
	G	S	B	G	S	G	S		G	S	B				
1 Cruzeiro	10	8	4	1	3	5	1	33	4	4	4	Belo Horizonte	Mineirão	81 987	1921
2 Santos	10	6	4	2	3	5	2	16 8	3	1	4	Santos	Vila Belmiro	25 120	1912
3 São Paulo FC	9	10	4	4	5		1	21 17	5	4	4	São Paulo	Morumbi	80 000	1935
4 Palmeiras	9	8	2	4	2	3	1	21 23	2	5	2	São Paulo	Parque Antartica	29 650	1914
5 Flamengo	9	7	3	5		2	4	28 25	2	3	3	Rio de Janeiro	Arena Petrobrás	30 000	1895
6 Grêmio	8	5	4	2	1	4	2	34	2	2	4	Porto Alegre	Olímpico	51 081	1903
7 Corinthians	6	4	3	4	3	2	1	25 18			3	São Paulo	Pacaembu	37 180	1910
8 Vasco da Gama	6	4	1	4	2		2	22 21	2		1	Rio de Janeiro	São Januário	35 000	1898
9 Internacional	5	6	3	3	4	1	1	37	1	1	3	Porto Alegre	Beira Rio	58 306	1909
10 Atlético Mineiro	3	4	4	1	3			38	2	1	4	Belo Horizonte	Mineirão	81 987	1908
11 Botafogo	3	4	2	1	2	1	2	17 12	1		2	Rio de Janeiro	Arena Petrobrás	30 000	1904
12 EC Bahia	2	2		1		1	2	45				Salvador	Fonte Nova	66 080	1931
Fluminense	2	2		1		1	2	30 20				Rio de Janeiro	Raulino de Oliveira	20 000	1902
14 Guarani	1	2	1	1	2			1			1	Campinas	Brinco de Ouro	30 988	1911
Atlético Paranaense	1	2	1	1	1			20		1	1	Curitiba	Arena da Baixada	32 000	1924

Nat = the national championship played since 1971 • Cup = the Copa do Brasil played between 1959-68 and since 1989 • SL = the state leagues
played throughout the country • The totals for the state leagues are not included in the overall totals •

RECENT LEAGUE AND CUP RECORD

National Championship					Cup		
Year	Champions	Score/Runners-up	Runners-up/Third		Winners	Score	Runners-up
1995	Botafogo	2-1 1-1	Santos		Corinthians	2-1 1-0	Grêmio
1996	Grêmio	0-2 2-0	Portuguesa		Cruzeiro	1-1 2-1	Palmeiras
1997	Vasco da Gama	0-0 0-0	Palmeiras		Grêmio	0-0 2-2	Flamengo
1998	Corinthians	2-2 1-1 2-0	Cruzeiro		Palmeiras	0-1 2-0	Cruzeiro
1999	Corinthians	2-3 2-0 0-0	Atlético Mineiro		Juventude	2-1 0-0	Botafogo
2000	Vasco da Gama	1-1 3-1	São Caetano		Cruzeiro	0-0 2-1	São Paulo FC
2001	Atlético Paranaense	4-2 1-0	São Caetano		Grêmio	2-2 3-1	Corinthians
2002	Santos	2-0 3-2	Corinthians		Corinthians	2-1 1-1	Brasiliense
2003	Cruzeiro	100	Santos	87	São Paulo FC	78	Cruzeiro	1-1 3-1	Flamengo
2004	Santos	89	Atlético Paranaense	86	São Paulo FC	82	Santo André	2-2 2-0	Flamengo
2005	Corinthians	81	Internacional	78	Goiás	74	Paulista	2-0 0-0	Fluminense
2006	São Paulo FC	78	Internacional	69	Grêmio	67	Flamengo	2-0 1-0	Vasco da Gama
2007					Fluminense	1-1 1-0	Figueirense

BRAZIL 2006

SERIE A

	Pl	W	D	L	F	A	Pts	São Paulo	Inter	Grêmio	Santos	Paraná	Vasco	Figueirense	Goiás	Corinthians	Cruzeiro	Flamengo	Botafogo	Atlético PR	Juventude	Fluminense	Palmeiras	Ponte Preta	Fortaleza	S. Caetano	Santa Cruz
São Paulo FC †	38	22	12	4	66	32	**78**		2-0	2-1	0-4	3-2	5-1	2-1	2-1	0-0	2-0	1-0	3-0	1-1	5-0	1-0	4-1	1-1	1-1	1-0	4-0
Internacional †	38	20	9	9	52	36	**69**	3-1		0-0	0-0	3-2	1-2	2-4	1-4	1-1	1-1	1-0	0-0	2-0	1-0	2-0	1-1	2-0	3-0	1-0	1-0
Grêmio †	38	20	7	11	64	45	**67**	1-1	0-1		1-0	2-1	1-2	1-2	2-0	2-0	2-1	3-0	4-0	2-0	1-0	4-4	2-1	4-0	4-1	1-1	3-1
Santos †	38	18	10	10	58	36	**64**	0-1	2-1	1-0		1-0	0-2	2-1	2-1	2-0	2-0	3-0	0-0	2-0	3-2	1-1	5-1	3-1	2-0	1-0	3-1
Paraná ‡	38	18	6	14	56	49	**60**	0-0	1-0	5-2	1-1		2-1	0-0	1-0	1-2	1-0	0-2	0-0	2-1	0-1	1-0	4-2	2-1	2-0	1-0	3-0
Vasco da Gama ‡	38	15	14	9	57	50	**59**	1-1	1-1	1-1	1-1	3-1		3-1	0-0	2-4	1-0	3-1	0-0	2-1	1-1	1-1	3-0	2-2	2-0	1-2	2-1
Figueirense ‡	38	15	12	11	52	44	**57**	0-2	1-0	2-0	2-1	0-1	0-0		2-2	0-0	0-2	1-1	1-0	3-3	1-0	1-0	6-1	2-1	0-0	1-1	2-0
Goiás ‡	38	15	10	13	63	49	**55**	0-2	2-2	4-0	0-0	1-2	2-0	2-1		3-1	2-3	0-1	2-2	2-2	2-0	3-1	1-3	3-0	1-1	2-1	5-3
Corinthians ‡	38	15	8	15	41	46	**53**	1-3	0-1	0-2	0-3	1-0	1-1	1-3	0-1		1-0	0-2	1-0	2-1	5-3	1-1	1-0	1-0	2-2	3-0	1-0
Cruzeiro ‡	38	14	11	13	52	45	**53**	2-2	2-1	3-1	1-1	2-2	2-1	2-2	0-0	2-0		2-1	3-1	1-1	2-0	2-3	1-0	5-1	0-0	1-0	3-3
Flamengo †	38	15	7	16	44	48	**52**	1-1	1-2	1-0	2-2	1-4	0-1	0-2	1-0	3-0	1-0		1-0	1-0	3-1	4-1	2-1	0-0	0-0	4-1	1-1
Botafogo	38	13	12	13	52	50	**51**	1-1	0-1	2-2	4-3	4-0	4-1	2-3	2-2	0-0	1-0	0-2		0-4	2-1	2-1	1-3	4-1	1-0	2-1	3-0
Atlético Paranaense	38	13	9	16	61	62	**48**	0-0	1-2	2-3	2-1	4-0	6-4	1-4	2-3	1-2	1-1	1-0	0-5		1-0	1-2	2-0	3-0	0-0	3-1	2-1
Juventude	38	13	8	17	44	54	**47**	1-1	2-0	1-2	3-2	1-0	0-0	1-0	1-1	0-0	2-0	1-0	1-0	3-2		1-1	3-2	0-1	2-2	1-0	4-1
Fluminense	38	11	12	15	48	58	**45**	1-2	2-3	1-2	1-0	2-1	1-1	2-0	1-0	1-2	1-0	1-0	1-1	1-2	3-2		1-1	0-0	1-3	2-2	1-1
Palmeiras	38	12	8	18	58	70	**44**	3-1	1-4	0-1	1-2	4-2	4-2	1-1	1-3	1-0	1-1	3-1	2-1	2-2	1-1	3-0		2-3	3-0	3-1	2-1
Ponte Preta	38	10	9	19	45	65	**39**	1-3	0-2	1-1	1-0	2-5	1-2	3-0	3-2	3-2	0-1	3-0	1-2	1-1	3-1	3-0	1-1		1-3	1-2	2-0
Fortaleza	38	8	14	16	39	62	**38**	1-0	1-2	1-0	1-1	1-1	1-1	1-1	0-3	0-4	0-2	3-4	2-3	3-4	4-1	2-5	0-0	1-0		2-1	1-4
São Caetano	38	9	9	20	37	53	**36**	0-1	1-1	0-2	2-0	0-2	0-1	3-1	1-2	0-1	2-1	2-2	1-1	2-1	0-2	1-1	2-0	1-1	0-0		2-0
Santa Cruz	38	7	7	24	41	76	**28**	1-3	0-2	2-4	1-1	1-3	0-4	0-0	2-1	1-0	4-1	3-0	1-1	1-2	1-0	1-2	3-2	1-1	0-1	0-3	

15/04/2006 - 3/12/2006 • † Qualified for the Copa Libertadores • ‡ Qualified for the Copa Sudamericana

BRAZIL 2006

SERIE B

	Pl	W	D	L	F	A	Pts	Atlético MG	Sport	Náutico	América RN	Paulista	Coritiba	S. André	Brasiliense	Marília	Ituano	Gama	Remo	Avaí	Portuguesa	Ceará	CRB	Paysandu	Guarani	Raimundo	Vila Nova
Atlético Mineiro	38	20	11	7	70	39	**71**		2-0	3-1	2-2	2-0	2-1	1-1	1-0	2-0	1-2	4-2	3-1	4-1	2-1	3-0	5-0	3-0	4-1	4-0	1-1
Sport Recife	38	18	10	10	57	36	**64**	0-0		2-0	2-0	1-2	2-0	0-0	3-0	1-1	2-0	3-0	3-1	2-0	2-3	1-0	1-2	4-2	8-1	1-0	3-0
Náutico	38	18	10	10	64	48	**64**	3-0	2-1		1-0	3-3	2-2	2-0	3-2	2-1	2-0	1-0	2-0	4-1	2-0	2-1	3-2	3-2	4-1	5-1	2-3
América Natal	38	19	4	15	59	51	**61**	3-2	2-0	3-1		1-0	0-0	1-2	2-1	1-0	1-2	5-1	3-0	3-0	2-0	3-1	2-1	0-1	3-1	2-1	2-0
Paulista	38	17	10	11	72	51	**61**	1-1	2-0	1-0	0-1		2-0	1-0	1-1	1-1	2-2	4-3	3-1	0-1	0-2	4-0	2-2	9-0	2-1	1-0	5-1
Coritiba	38	16	11	11	64	51	**59**	2-3	1-1	1-1	5-1	2-1		0-0	0-2	6-2	3-1	2-1	3-2	4-2	3-0	1-1	2-1	1-0	1-1	0-0	2-1
Santo André	38	14	14	10	47	45	**56**	1-2	0-1	1-1	1-0	2-0	2-1		1-0	1-1	2-1	1-0	3-0	3-1	0-0	1-1	2-1	1-1	1-0	3-1	2-2
Brasiliense	38	15	8	15	66	51	**53**	1-0	2-0	1-0	2-4	3-4	4-1	6-1		1-0	2-0	0-2	2-0	2-0	1-1	1-1	4-1	4-0	1-0	4-1	4-1
Marília	38	13	11	14	58	58	**50**	1-1	2-2	4-0	2-1	0-3	1-0	2-0	1-1		0-1	2-0	2-0	0-0	4-0	3-3	2-1	4-1	1-0	3-2	2-1
Ituano	38	12	14	12	49	48	**50**	1-2	1-1	1-1	0-1	1-1	2-1	0-0	3-2	2-2		1-0	1-1	0-0	1-1	4-1	0-1	1-1	2-2	1-2	1-1
Gama	38	14	6	18	52	61	**48**	2-1	0-1	1-3	2-1	1-1	1-1	3-3	3-2	3-0	1-0		4-3	3-1	1-0	1-2	3-2	3-1	2-2	1-0	2-0
Remo	38	13	7	18	50	60	**46**	2-1	2-0	0-0	2-0	2-2	1-2	1-1	2-2	3-1	0-5	3-1		2-0	1-2	1-1	1-0	0-2	2-0	3-0	4-1
Avaí	38	12	10	16	36	51	**46**	2-0	1-2	1-1	3-2	1-0	1-2	1-0	1-1	2-0	2-0	1-0	1-0		1-1	0-0	1-2	2-1	2-1	0-1	1-0
Portuguesa	38	11	12	15	47	58	**45**	1-1	1-1	1-0	4-0	2-4	2-2	2-3	1-1	2-1	1-2	0-0	3-1	0-0		2-4	1-0	2-6	0-1	1-1	2-0
Ceará	38	10	15	13	47	56	**45**	0-1	2-2	2-1	4-2	0-2	2-0	1-1	2-1	1-1	2-2	2-1	1-1	3-2	1-2		0-0	2-1	0-0	1-0	1-2
CRB	38	12	8	18	61	67	**44**	0-1	1-1	1-2	4-2	3-4	2-2	3-0	4-3	2-2	3-4	1-0	2-1	2-0	1-0	1-1		2-1	1-1	5-1	2-3
Paysandu	38	12	8	16	51	70	**44**	2-2	0-1	1-0	1-0	1-1	1-3	3-1	1-0	4-1	2-1	3-1	1-3	1-1	1-3	1-2	0-2		2-2	1-0	2-1
Guarani §3	38	11	14	13	53	61	**44**	0-0	2-0	2-2	1-2	3-1	1-0	0-0	2-2	1-4	1-1	3-1	0-1	2-2	3-1	2-1	3-2	1-1		3-1	2-1
São Raimundo	38	11	10	17	42	59	**43**	2-2	0-1	2-2	1-1	4-1	1-2	3-2	1-0	4-3	0-1	2-0	1-0	0-0	2-0	1-0	2-0	1-1	1-1		1-1
Vila Nova	38	11	9	18	45	68	**42**	1-1	1-1	1-0	0-0	2-1	1-5	1-3	2-0	2-1	0-1	0-1	1-2	2-0	2-2	2-1	3-1	2-1	1-5	1-1	

15/04/2006 - 25/11/2006 • § = Points deducted

BRAZIL 2006

SERIE C FINAL ROUND

	Pl	W	D	L	F	A	Pts	Criciúma	Vitória	Ipatinga	Grêmio	Ferroviário	Bahia	Brasil	Treze
Criciúma	14	9	4	1	27	11	31		6-0	1-2	2-2	4-0	1-0	1-0	1-0
Vitória	14	8	1	5	23	18	25	0-0		3-0	1-2	4-0	1-2	2-0	2-0
Ipatinga	14	7	3	4	21	15	24	0-0	2-1		2-2	1-0	3-1	5-1	0-0
Grêmio Barueri	14	7	2	5	27	22	23	1-2	0-1	0-3		3-0	2-0	5-2	3-2
Ferroviário	14	6	1	7	21	26	19	1-2	3-1	3-1	1-0		7-2	3-0	2-1
Bahia	14	4	2	8	21	30	14	2-2	1-2	0-2	4-3	4-1		2-2	3-1
Brasil	14	4	1	9	16	25	13	1-2	0-1	1-0	0-1	3-0	1-0		4-0
Treze	14	3	2	9	17	26	11	2-3	2-4	2-0	2-3	0-0	2-0	3-1	

8/10/2006 - 29/11/2006 • Serie C consisted of 64 teams divided into 16 groups of four in the first round. The top two from each group qualified for the second round where the 32 teams were divided into eight groups of four. Once again the top two from each group progressed with the third round consisting of four groups of four. The top two from these four groups then qualified for the final round

BRAZIL STATE CHAMPIONSHIPS 2007

CAMPEONATO CARIOCA 2007 RESULTS

	Flamengo	Botafogo	Madureira	Vasco	Volta	Friburgense	América	Fluminense	Cabofriense	Americano	Boavista	Nova Iguaçu
Flamengo							4-1		2-0		1-0	2-1
Botafogo	3-3		2-2	2-0	2-1	7-0	1-0		3-0			
Madureira	4-1			0-1	3-1	1-0			1-0	1-1		
Vasco da Gama	3-0		4-1		6-1				0-0		2-0	
Volta Redonda	2-1						3-2	1-3	2-1			2-1
Friburguense	1-2		1-4	1-0					1-0	3-2		3-2
América		2-1	1-3	2-1	1-1	3-4		0-2				
Fluminense	2-1				4-4	1-0	0-2		3-1		4-3	
Cabofriense		0-1	0-1	2-1	1-2						3-3	4-1
Americano	1-2					0-1	1-0	2-1			1-0	
Boavista		3-2		2-6	1-5	3-1			1-1			4-4
Nova Iguaçu			2-6	0-3			1-2	1-1			4-4	

Clubs listed according to overall position • Taça Guanabara results in shaded boxes • Taça Rio results in unshaded boxes

TAÇA GUANABARA

Group A	Pl	W	D	L	F	A	Pts
Madureira †	5	3	2	0	9	4	11
Flamengo †	5	3	1	1	9	8	10
Botafogo	5	2	2	1	11	8	8
Boavista	5	1	3	1	8	8	6
Americano	5	1	1	3	4	8	4
Cabofriense	5	0	1	4	4	9	1

Group B	Pl	W	D	L	F	A	Pts
Vasco da Gama †	5	3	1	1	17	8	10
América †	5	3	1	1	10	7	10
Friburgense	5	3	0	2	9	10	9
Volta Redonda	5	2	1	2	7	11	7
Fluminense	5	1	2	2	8	10	5
Nova Iguçu	5	0	1	4	5	10	1

24/01/2007 - 17/02/2007 • † Qualified for the semis
Semi-finals: Madureira 2-1 América; Vasco 1-1 1-3p
Flamengo • Final: **Flamengo** 0-1 4-1 Madureira

CARIOCA FINAL

(Played between the winners of the Taça Guanabara and Taça Rio)

Flamengo 2-2 Botafogo
1st leg. Maracana, Rio de Janeiro
29-04-2007, Att: 46 422
Scorers - Renato 62, Souza 78 for Flamengo;
Dodô 32, Lucio Flavio 41 for Botafogo

Botafogo 2-2 2-4p **Flamengo**
2nd leg. Maracana, Rio de Janeiro
6-05-2007, Att: 63 614
Scorers - Juninho 57, Dodô 61 for Botafogo;
Souza 52, Renato Augusto 72 for Flamengo

Flamengo are 2007 champions

TAÇA RIO

Group A	Pl	W	D	L	F	A	Pts
Botafogo †	6	5	0	1	19	5	15
Cabofriense †	6	4	0	2	13	8	12
Madureira	6	4	0	2	11	7	12
Flamengo	6	3	0	3	10	10	9
Americano	6	2	1	3	3	4	7
Boavista	6	1	1	4	15	23	4

Group B	Pl	W	D	L	F	A	Pts
Volta Redonda †	6	4	0	2	12	8	12
Vasco da Gama †	6	3	1	2	14	7	10
Fluminense	6	3	0	3	9	8	9
Friburgense	6	3	0	3	8	15	9
América	6	2	0	4	6	13	6
Nova Iguaçu	6	0	1	5	8	20	1

10/03/2007 - 8/04/2007 • † Qualified for the semis
Semi-finals: Botafogo 4-4 4-1 Vasco; Volta 1-1 5-6p
Cabofriense • Final: Botafogo 2-2 3-1 Cabofriense

2007 STATE CHAMPIONSHIPS

State	Winners	Score	Runners-up
Acre	Rio Branco	‡	
Alagoas	Coruripe	‡	
Amapá	Trem	2-2 1-0	Cristal
Amazonas	Nacional	1-1 2-2	Fast
Bahia	Vitória	†	Bahia
Ceará	Fortaleza	2-2 1-0	Icasa
Distrito Federal	Brasiliense	†	Esportivo
Espírito Santo	Linhares	1-0 0-0	Jaguaré
Goiás	Atlético Goiânia	2-2 2-1	Goias
Maranhão	Sampaio Corrêa	0-0 0-0	Imperatriz
Mato Grosso	Cacerense	1-0 2-0	Jaciara
Mato Grosso Sul	Cacerense	1-0 2-0	Jaciara
Minas Gerais	Atlético Mineiro	4-0 0-2	Cruzeiro
Pará			

2007 STATE CHAMPIONSHIPS

State	Winners	Score	Runners-up
Paraíba	Nacional	1-2 3-0	Atlético Cajazeiras
Paraná	Paranavaí	1-0 0-0	Paraná
Pernambuco			
Piauí	Ríver	4-1 3-1	Barras
Rio de Janeiro	Flamengo	2-2 2-2 4-2p	Botafogo
Rio Grande Nor.	ABC	1-1 5-2	América Natal
Rio Grande Sul	Grêmio	3-3 4-1	Juventude
Rondônia	Ulbra	0-1 3-2	Jaruense
Roraima	Atlético Roraima	‡	
Santa Catarina	Chapecoense	1-0 2-2	Criciúma
São Paulo	Santos	2-0 0-2	São Caetano
Sergipe	América	†	
Tocantins	Palmas	1-0 1-1	Araguaína

‡ Won both stages so no final needed. † Played on a league basis

BRAZIL STATE CHAMPIONSHIPS 2007

CAMPEONATO PAULISTA SERIE A1

	Pl	W	D	L	F	A	Pts	Santos	São Paulo	S. Caetano	Bragantino	Palmeiras	Paulista	Noroeste	Ponte Preta	Corinthians	Guaragueta	Ituano	Rio Claro	Juventus	Marília	Barueri	Sertãozinho	América	São Bento	Rio Branco	Santo André
Santos ‡	19	16	2	1	45	19	50		1-1	3-0		2-1			2-1	2-0								4-1	4-1	0-2	
São Paulo FC ‡	19	13	5	1	41	14	44	1-0		3-0		1-0	3-1	2-1	1-0				2-2						3-0	4-0	1-1
São Caetano ‡	19	11	3	5	32	22	36	1-0			1-2		2-1		2-0	4-1				2-0	0-0				2-2	2-0	2-1
Bragantino ‡	19	10	5	4	35	17	35	2-3	1-0			4-1	2-1		1-2			3-0		2-1					3-0		3-0
Palmeiras	19	10	5	4	39	25	35	3-3	1-1					4-2	1-2		2-2		1-1	4-1	3-2	1-1			1-0		
Paulista	19	9	4	6	34	31	31				2-2	2-2				3-2	2-0	1-0	2-3		1-0				3-1	2-1	
Noroeste	19	9	3	7	38	30	30	1-4	1-1	5-2			1-2			2-3			4-0	3-1					1-1	4-2	1-0
Ponte Preta	19	9	3	7	29	24	30	2-4				0-0	2-1	3-1					2-0					0-0	3-2	2-2	3-1
Corinthians	19	8	5	6	35	27	29					0-1		0-3			2-1	3-1		1-2	5-0		0-0	2-2	2-0		1-1
Guaratinguetá	19	7	4	8	29	26	25						0-0					2-4	1-0	2-3		0-0	3-2	3-1	3-1		1-0
Ituano	19	7	4	8	22	25	25	1-2					1-1	1-0		1-0	1-2			1-1			0-1	3-1		1-0	4-2
Rio Claro	19	5	7	7	23	31	22		0-2	0-1	1-1											1-0	2-1	2-2	1-0	3-3	4-0
Juventus	19	6	2	11	18	31	20		0-2				2-1	1-0	1-4		2-0					2-2	0-1	1-0	0-1		3-0
Marília	19	5	5	9	29	30	20	0-1			1-4					0-3	1-1	0-2	1-1				3-0			3-0	3-0
Barueri	19	5	5	9	21	31	20	1-2	0-5	1-3					2-3	2-1		0-2		4-2				1-1			2-1
Sertãozinho	19	4	7	8	22	33	19	1-3					1-0	2-4	1-1	1-0			2-1	2-3	0-0						3-2
América	19	4	5	10	22	36	17	2-4					2-4	0-2	2-2		1-1	2-2		1-0	2-1	2-0				1-1	
São Bento	19	4	4	11	27	48	16	0-3	1-2				2-4	1-6	2-0			1-1	1-6	0-1	2-1						
Rio Branco	19	3	4	12	18	40	13	0-3			3-2	1-3	1-2			0-2	2-1					0-0	2-2	4-1	2-3		
Santo André	19	2	4	13	21	40	10	1-2		0-3			2-3			1-1				1-1	1-2			2-1	4-3	1-1	

17/01/2007 - 5/07/2007 • ‡ Qualified for the semi-finals • Semi-finals: Bragantino 0-0 0-0 **Santos**; **São Caetano** 1-1 4-1 São Paulo FC
Final: São Caetano 2-0 0-2 Santos. **Santos** are champions. Tied matches are awarded to the team with the better record in the league stage

FIFA/COCA-COLA WORLD RANKING

1993	1994	1995	1996	1997	1998	1999	2000	2001	2002	2003	2004	2005	2006	High	Low
3	1	1	1	1	1	1	1	3	1	1	1	1	1	1	8 08/93

2006–2007											
08/06	09/06	10/06	11/06	12/06	01/07	02/07	03/07	04/07	05/07	06/07	07/07
1	1	1	1	1	1	2	3	3	2	3	1

THE FIFA BIG COUNT OF 2006

	Male	Female		Total
Number of players	11 752 783	1 444 950	Referees and Assistant Referees	16 000
Professionals	16 200		Admin, Coaches, Technical, Medical	45 000
Amateurs 18+	472 165		Number of clubs	28 970
Youth under 18	1 347 100		Number of teams	86 910
Unregistered	6 080 000		Clubs with women's teams	238
Total players	13 197 733		Players as % of population	7.02%

COPA DO BRASIL 2007

First Round

Team	Score
Fluminense	2 6
Adesg *	1 0
Baré *	0 0
América Natal	1 2
Goiás	3
Moto Clube *	1
Itabaiana *	1 1
Bahia	2 0
Atlético Goiânia *	2 0
Guarani	1 0
Sampaio Corrêa *	1
Fortaleza	3
Vitória (BA)	1 1 3p
Baraúnas * ‡	1 1 5p
Coxim *	0
Atlético Paranaense	5
Ipatinga	0 3
Vitória (ES)	1 1
Operário *	0
Palmeiras	5
Ananindeua *	2 0
São Raimundo	0 1
Campinense *	1 0
Sport Recife	1 3
Cruzeiro	0 1
Veranópolis *	0 0
SER Chapadão *	0
Portuguesa	2
Juventude	1 2
Ferroviária *	3 0
Barra do Garças *	1
Brasiliense	4
Botafogo	1 5
CSA *	1 2
Barras *	1 0
Ceará	0 2
Ulbra Ji-Paraná *	2 2
Santa Cruz	0 1
Caxias *	2 1
Coritiba	1 4
Avaí	1 0
Rio Branco * ‡	1 1
Ponte Preta	0 2
Villa Nova *	1 3
América Rio de Janeiro	1 3
Coruripe *	1 1
Colo Colo *	1
Atlético Mineiro	3
Náutico	2 6
Parnahyba *	1 0
São José *	0 2
Paysandu	1 2
Treze	0 3
Vilavelhense *	1 1
Olímpico Pirambu *	1 0
Corinthians	1 3
Gama	3
Araguaína *	1
Fast Clube *	1 0
Vasco da Gama	2 6
Noroeste	4
ADAP Galo Maringá *	1
Madureira *	2 0
Figueirense	3 2

Second Round

Team	Score
Fluminense	2 0
América Natal *	1 1
Goiás	1 3
Bahia *	1 3
Atlético Goiânia *	2 3 5p
Fortaleza	3 2 3p
Vitória	4 0
Atlético Paranaense	1 3
Ipatinga *	2 0 4p
Palmeiras	0 2 3p
Ananindeua *	0
Sport Recife	5
Cruzeiro	0 2
Portuguesa *	0 1
Juventude	0 2
Brasiliense *	0 3
Botafogo	2 2
Ceará *	1 0
Ulbra Ji-Paraná *	2 0
Coritiba	2 1
Avaí	0 3
Villa Nova *	0 2
América Rio de Janeiro *	1 1
Atlético Mineiro	1 2
Náutico	0 5
Paysandu *	1 0
Treze *	0
Corinthians	2
Gama *	2 2
Vasco da Gama	2 1
Noroeste *	0 1
Figueirense	0 4

Third Round

Team	Score
Fluminense *	1 2
Bahia	1 2
Atlético Goiânia *	3 0
Atlético Paranaense	1 2
Ipatinga *	1 1 4p
Sport Recife	1 1 2p
Cruzeiro *	0 1
Brasiliense	1 1
Botafogo	1 3
Coritiba *	0 3
Avaí *	0 0
Atlético Mineiro	2 1
Náutico *	2 2
Corinthians	2 0
Gama *	2 1
Figueirense	4 2

If the away team wins the first leg by two goals in the first or second round no second leg is played

COPA DO BRASIL 2007

Quarter-finals	Semi-finals	Final

Fluminense * 1 1
Atlético Paranaense 1 0

Fluminense * 4 1
Brasiliense 2 1

Ipatinga 2 0
Brasiliense * 2 1

Fluminense * † 1 1
Figueirense 1 0

Botafogo 0 2
Atlético Mineiro * 0 1

Botafogo 0 3
Figueirense * 2 1

COPA DO BRASIL FINAL

First leg. Maracanã, Rio de Janeiro, 30-05-2007, 21:45, Att: 63 557, Ref: Seneme

FLUMINENSE 1 Adriano Magrão [88]
FIGUERENSE 1 Henrique [83]

Flu - Fernando Henrique - Carlinhos, Thiago Silva, Luiz Alberto (Roger), Ivan - Fabinho (David), Arouco, Cícero (Thiago Neves), Carlos Alberto - Alex Dias, Adriano Magrão. Tr: Renato Gaúcho
Figuerense - Wilson - Vinícius, Felipe Santana, Edson, Chicão - Diogo, Henrique, Ruy, Claiton Xavier - Andre Santos, Victor Simões (Ramon). Tr: Mário Sérgio

Náutico * 2 0
Figueirense 2 1

Second leg. Orlando Scarpelli, Florianópolis, 6-06-2007, 21:45, Att: 17 415, Ref: Lopez

FIGUERENSE 0
FLUMINENSE 1 Roger [2]

Figuerense - Wilson - Anderson Luiz (Fernandes), Felipe Santana, Chicão, Vinícius (Edson) - André Santos, Henrique, Claiton Xavier, Diogo (Ramon) - Ruy, Victor Simões. Tr: Mário Sérgio
Flu - Fernando Henrique - Carlinhos, Thiago Silva, Roger, Junior Cesar - Fabinho, Arouco, Cícero, Carlos Alberto (Thiago Neves) - Alex Dias (Rafael Moura), Adriano Magrão (David). Tr: Renato Gaúcho

† Qualified for the Copa Libertadores
* Home team in the first leg
‡ Baraúnas and Rio Branco disqualified

SAO PAULO FC 2006

Date	Opponents	Score		Comp	Scorers
16-04-2006	Flamengo	W 1-0	H	SA	Rogério Ceni [31p]
20-04-2006	Caracas FC - VEN	W 2-0	H	CLg1	Danilo [57], Rogério Ceni [92+p]
23-04-2006	Fortaleza	L 0-1	A	SA	
26-04-2006	Palmeiras - BRA	D 1-1	A	CLr2	Aloísio [23]
29-04-2006	Santa Cruz	W 4-0	H	SA	Danilo [48], Leandro [51], Mineiro [61], Rogério Ceni [75]
3-05-2006	Palmeiras - BRA	W 2-1	H	CLr2	Aloísio [13], Rogério Ceni [86p]
7-05-2006	Corinthians	W 3-1	A	SA	Souza [39], Alex Dias [69], Lenílson [73]
10-05-2006	Estudiantes LP - ARG	L 0-1	A	CLqf	
14-05-2006	Internacional	L 1-3	A	SA	Aloísio [47]
20-05-2006	São Caetano	W 1-0	H	SA	Alex Dias [37]
24-05-2006	Palmeiras	W 4-1	H	SA	OG [5], Ricardo Oliveira 2 [52 56], Alex Dias [82]
28-05-2006	Vasco da Gama	D 1-1	A	SA	Alex Dias [11]
31-05-2006	Fluminense	W 1-0	H	SA	Souza [45]
4-06-2006	Juventude	D 1-1	A	SA	Júnior [89]
12-07-2006	Grêmio	W 2-1	H	SA	Ricardo Oliveira 2 [18 55]
15-07-2006	Figueirense	W 2-1	H	SA	Ricardo Oliveira [2], André Dias [91+]
19-07-2006	Estudiantes LP - ARG	W 1-0	H	CLqf	Edcarlos [44p]. W 4-3p
23-07-2006	Ponte Preta	W 3-1	A	SA	Lenílson 2 [41 72], Alex Silva [52]
26-07-2006	Chivas Guadalajara	W 1-0	A	CLsf	Rogério Ceni [84p]
30-07-2006	Santos	L 0-4	H	SA	
2-08-2006	Chivas Guadalajara	W 3-0	H	CLsf	Leandro [32], Mineiro [39], Ricardo Oliveira [47]
6-08-2006	Botafogo	D 1-1	A	SA	Thiago [50]
9-08-2006	Interacnional - BRA	L 1-2	H	CLf	Edcarlos [75]
13-08-2006	Goiás	W 2-1	H	SA	Lenílson 2 [18 73]
16-08-2006	Internacional - BRA	D 2-2	A	CLf	Fabão [50], Leníson [85]
20-08-2006	Cruzeiro	D 2-2	A	SA	Rogério Ceni 2 [42 60]
24-08-2006	Paraná	W 3-2	H	SA	Aloísio [6], Leandro [21], Alex Silva [76]
27-08-2006	Flamengo	D 1-1	A	SA	Lenílson [66]
31-08-2006	Fortaleza	D 1-1	H	SA	Lenílson [88]
3-09-2006	Santa Cruz	W 3-1	A	SA	Rogério Ceni [25], Thiago 2 [79 84]
7-09-2006	Boca Juniors - ARG	L 1-2	A	RC	Thiago [30]
10-09-2006	Corinthians	D 0-0	H	SA	
14-09-2006	Boca Juniors - ARG	D 2-2	H	RC	Júnior [34], OG [85]
17-09-2006	Internacional	W 2-0	H	SA	Lenílson [8], Júnior [71]
20-09-2006	São Caetano	W 1-0	A	SA	Richarlyson [48]
24-09-2006	Palmeiras	L 1-3	A	SA	Souza [21]
30-09-2006	Atlético Paranaense	D 0-0	A	SA	
4-10-2006	Vasco da Gama	W 5-1	H	SA	OG [7], Danilo [15], Fabão, Miranda [48], Rogério Ceni [63]
7-10-2006	Fluminense	W 2-1	A	SA	Aloísio [18], Leandro [35]
14-10-2006	Juventude	W 5-0	H	SA	Alex Silva [78], Aloísio [87], Danilo [37], Ilsinho [41], Leandro [44]
22-10-2006	Grêmio	D 1-1	A	SA	Danilo 1 (50")
28-10-2006	Figueirense	W 2-0	H	SA	Aloísio [21], Ilsinho [45]
2-11-2006	Ponte Preta	D 1-1	H	SA	Rogério Ceni [75]
5-11-2006	Santos	W 1-0	H	SA	Mineiro [29]
9-11-2006	Botafogo	W 3-0	H	SA	Leandro 2 [45 93+], Souza [71]
12-11-2006	Goiás	W 2-0	A	SA	Mineiro [9], Fabão [17],
19-11-2006	Atlético Paranaense	D 1-1	H	SA	Fabão [25]
26-11-2006	Cruzeiro	W 2-0	H	SA	Rogério Ceni [57], Fabão [81]
3-12-2006	Paraná	D 0-0	A	SA	

SA = Serie A • CL = Copa Libertadores • RC = Recopa
g1 = group 1 • r2 = second round • qf = quarter-final • sf = semi-final • f = final

BRB – BARBADOS

NATIONAL TEAM RECORD
JULY 10TH 2006 TO JULY 12TH 2010

PL	W	D	L	F	A	%
14	5	6	3	28	15	57.1

FIFA/COCA-COLA WORLD RANKING

1993	1994	1995	1996	1997	1998	1999	2000	2001	2002	2003	2004	2005	2006	High		Low	
114	107	103	110	113	121	113	104	107	99	124	121	115	98	93	06/00	152	07/06

2006–2007											
08/06	09/06	10/06	11/06	12/06	01/07	02/07	03/07	04/07	05/07	06/07	07/07
150	152	100	109	98	99	108	109	113	113	116	118

Barbados may not exactly be minnows in Caribbean terms but the national team has always struggled to match the achievements of their larger neighbours Jamaica and Trinidad. In a bid to close the gap, the football association has looked more and more to players in England with Bajan roots, and both Paul Ifill of Crystal Palace and Mark McCammon of Doncaster Rovers made significant contributions as Barbados qualified for the Digicel Caribbean Cup finals in Trinidad. They scored four goals each as Barbados made it through from a first round group in Antigua, with both scoring hat-tricks in a record 7-1 victory over Anguilla. Barbados then hosted a second round

INTERNATIONAL HONOURS
None

group, and with two more goals from Ifill they finished ahead of St Vincent, Bermuda and the Bahamas to qualify for the finals. With a place in the CONCACAF Gold Cup finals on offer for the semi-finalists, Barbados looked in good shape with a draw against Trinidad in the opening match but that was followed by defeat against Haiti and Martinique as they finished bottom of the group. A close race in the 2007 Premier Division in Barbados saw Defence Force win their final game of the season 5-0 against defending champions Youth Milan to win the title for the first time in 12 years. Gall Hill, the Cup winners in 2006, finished two points behind.

THE FIFA BIG COUNT OF 2006

	Male	Female		Total
Number of players	33 590	3 960	Referees and Assistant Referees	86
Professionals	0		Admin, Coaches, Technical, Medical	1240
Amateurs 18+	7 095		Number of clubs	130
Youth under 18	8 505		Number of teams	240
Unregistered	18 710		Clubs with women's teams	4
Total players	37 550		Players as % of population	13.41%

Barbados Football Association (BFA)
Richmond Welches, PO Box 1362, Bridgetown, St Michael, BB 11000, Barbados
Tel +1 246 2281707   Fax +1 246 2286484
bdosfootball@caribsurf.com   www.barbadossoccer.com
President: JONES Ronald   General Secretary: TBD
Vice-President: BARROW Keith   Treasurer: HUNTE Curtis   Media Officer: FONES Ronald
Men's Coach: SEALY Eyre   Women's Coach: SMITH Edward
BFA formed: 1910   CONCACAF: 1968   FIFA: 1968
Royal blue shirts with gold trimmings, Gold shorts, White socks

RECENT INTERNATIONAL MATCHES PLAYED BY BARBADOS

2002	Opponents	Score		Venue	Comp	Scorers	Att	Referee
25-07	Trinidad & Barbados	D	0-0	Basseterre	Fr		700	
27-07	St Kitts & Nevis	L	0-3	Basseterre	Fr			
6-10	St Lucia	W	3-2	Bridgetown	Fr	Valencius, Xavier, Forde.M		
9-11	Jamaica	D	1-1	St George's	CCq	Goodridge [88]	3 000	Murray TRI
11-11	Grenada	W	2-0	St George's	CCq	Lucas [66], Goodridge [90]	2 500	Murray TRI
13-11	Guadeloupe	L	0-1	St George's	CCq		3 250	Brizan TRI
2003								
12-01	Jamaica	W	1-0	Bridgetown	Fr	Williams [61]	7 500	
26-01	Finland	D	0-0	Bridgetown	Fr			Bynoe TRI
12-02	Martinique	D	3-3	Bridgetown	Fr	Lucas [5], Williams [9], Straker [48]		
23-03	Jamaica	L	1-2	Kingston	Fr	Cox [59]		Bowen CAY
26-12	Bermuda	W	2-1	Hamilton	Fr	Lovell 2 [39 43]		Mouchette BER
2004								
1-01	Bermuda	W	4-0	Hamilton	Fr	Parris [6], Riley [51], Goodridge 2 [74 76]		Raynor BER
11-01	Grenada	W	2-0	Bridgetown	Fr	Forde.N [35], Riley [58]	2 000	Small BRB
18-01	Canada	L	0-1	Bridgetown	Fr			Forde BRB
31-01	Grenada	W	1-0	St George's	Fr	Riley [70]		
15-02	Guyana	L	0-2	Bridgetown	Fr		1 200	Small BRB
12-03	Dominica	W	2-1	Bridgetown	Fr	OG [28], Burrowes [85]	46	
30-05	Northern Ireland	D	1-1	Bridgetown	Fr	Skinner [40]	8 000	Brizan TRI
13-06	St Kitts & Nevis	L	0-2	Bridgetown	WCq		3 700	Alfaro SLV
19-06	St Kitts & Nevis	L	2-3	Basseterre	WCq	Skinner [33], Goodridge [45]	3 500	Pineda HON
2005								
23-01	Guyana	W	3-0	Bridgetown	Fr	Forde.M [41], OG [53], Goodridge [58],		
30-01	St Vincent/Grenadines	W	3-1	Bridgetown	Fr	Riley 2 [47 82], Goodridge [80]	3 000	
6-02	Antigua & Barbuda	W	3-2	Bridgetown	Fr	Forde.M [10], Stanford [40], Goodridge [57]	4 000	
13-02	Guyana	D	3-3	Bridgetown	Fr	Forde.N [5], Lucas [29], James [56]	6 000	Callender BRB
20-02	Cuba	L	0-3	Bridgetown	CC		5 000	Prendergast JAM
22-02	Jamaica	L	0-1	Bridgetown	CC			Brizan TRI
24-02	Trinidad & Tobago	L	2-3	Bridgetown	CC	Forde.N [32], Lucas [86]	3 000	Prendergast JAM
2006								
2-09	Guyana	L	0-1	Bridgetown	Fr		2 000	Forde BRB
10-09	St Vincent/Grenadines	D	1-1	Bridgetown	Fr	Parris [51]		Small BRB
17-09	Dominica	W	5-0	Roseau	Fr	Lovell 2 [27 57], Goodridge [42p], Williams [75], Marshall [80]		
20-09	St Kitts and Nevis	D	1-1	St John's	CCq	Ifill [42]	300	Campbell JAM
22-09	Antigua & Barbuda	W	3-1	St John's	CCq	Williams [44], McCammon [58], Lovell [90]	2 500	Frederick VIR
24-09	Anguilla	W	7-1	St John's	CCq	McCammon 3 [35 44 76], Ifill 3 [40 58 83], Niblett [75]		Campbell JAM
5-11	Grenada	D	2-2	Black Rock	Fr	Parris [28], Goodridge [67p]		
19-11	Bahamas	W	2-1	Bridgetown	CCq	Forde.N [38], Skinner [44]		
21-11	St Vincent/Grenadines	W	3-0	Bridgetown	CCq	James [16], Forde.N [34], Ifill [60p]		
23-11	Bermuda	D	1-1	Bridgetown	CCq	Ifill [4]		
2007								
12-01	Trinidad and Tobago	D	1-1	Port of Spain	CCr1	Harvey [66]		Moreno PAN
15-01	Haiti	L	0-2	Port of Spain	CCr1			Jauregua ANT
17-01	Martinique	L	2-3	Port of Spain	CCr1	Harvey [27], Soares [42]		Jauregua ANT
25-03	Guatemala	D	0-0	Bridgetown	Fr			

Fr = Friendly match • CC = Digicel Caribbean Cup • WC = FIFA World Cup • q = qualifier • r1 = first round group

BARBADOS NATIONAL TEAM RECORDS AND RECORD SEQUENCES

Records			Sequence records					
Victory	7-1	AIA 2006	Wins	3	Five times	Clean sheets	3	1990, 1996
Defeat	0-7	USA 2000	Defeats	5	2000	Goals scored	10	2006-2007
Player Caps	n/a		Undefeated	10	2006-2007	Without goal	3	Three times
Player Goals	n/a		Without win	10	1976-1988	Goals against	15	2000-01

BARBADOS COUNTRY INFORMATION

Capital	Bridgetown	Independence	1966 from the UK	GDP per Capita	$15 700
Population	278 289	Status	Commonwealth	GNP Ranking	132
Area km²	431	Language	English	Dialling code	+1 246
Population density	645 per km²	Literacy rate	98%	Internet code	.bb
% in urban areas	47%	Main religion	Christian 71%	GMT + / –	-4
Towns/Cities ('000)	Bridgetown 98; Speightstown 3; Oistins 2, Bathsheba 1; Holetown 1; Bulkeley 1; Crane 1				
Neighbours (km)	Barbados is an island bordered by the Caribbean Sea and the Atlantic Ocean				
Main stadia	Waterford National Stadium – Bridgetown 15 000				

BARBADOS 2007

PREMIER DIVISION

	Pl	W	D	L	F	A	Pts	BDF	Gall Hill	Brittons Hill	Silver Sands	Notre Dame	Youth Milan	Technico	Tudor Bridge	Haggatt Hall	Eden Stars
Bar'dos Defence Force	18	11	1	6	44	24	34		2-3	0-1	2-0	2-6	5-0	0-1	0-1	3-0	4-0
Pride of Gall Hill	18	10	2	6	31	25	32	1-2		1-0	3-1	0-2	1-3	1-0	3-0	4-0	2-1
Brittons Hill	18	8	7	3	33	14	31	2-2	2-2		0-1	0-0	1-1	0-0	4-0	1-1	1-1
Silver Sands	18	9	3	6	34	24	30	2-3	2-1	0-2		1-1	0-1	3-2	3-1	5-0	3-0
Notre Dame	18	8	5	5	39	21	29	1-2	0-0	0-2	1-2		5-1	3-0	5-1	3-0	3-1
Youth Milan	18	9	1	8	38	43	28	2-3	6-0	0-9	0-2	3-1		0-2	1-1	0-3	6-2
Technico	18	7	5	6	24	20	26	1-0	1-2	1-2	2-0	2-2	2-4		3-0	3-1	2-0
Tudor Bridge	18	5	4	9	17	40	19	0-6	0-4	1-2	2-2	3-3	1-0	1-1		2-1	2-1
Haggatt Hall	17	4	3	10	16	37	15	1-4	2-1	0-0	1-5	1-0	2-3	1-1	1-0		1-2
Eden Stars	17	1	3	13	17	45	6	2-4	1-2	1-4	2-2	0-3	3-5	0-0	0-1	0-2†	

18/02/2007 - 22/07/2007 • † Match abandoned • Top scorers: Dwayne McCLEAN, BDF 16; John PARRIS, Notre Dame 12

FA CUP 2006

Round of 16		Quarter–finals		Semi–finals		Final	
Gall Hill	3						
Belfield	2	Gall Hill	5p				
Clarkes Hill	0	Brittons Hill	4p				
Brittons Hill	2			Gall Hill			
BDF	3			Silver Sands			
Technico	1	BDF	2				
St. John Sonnets	0	Silver Sands	3				
Silver Sands	4					Gall Hill	1
Notre Dame	4					Paradise	0
Hillaby	0	Notre Dame	5				
Youth Milan	1	Weymouth Wales	1				
Weymouth Wales	2			Notre Dame			
Villa United	4			Paradise			
UWI	1	Villa United	0				
Tudor Bridge	0	Paradise	3				
Paradise	2						

CUP FINAL

27-08-2006

Scorer - Andrew Butcher [111] for Gall Hill

RECENT LEAGUE AND CUP RECORD

	Championship									Cup		
Year	Champions	Pts	Runners-up	Pts	Third	Pts				Winners	Score	Runners-up
1997	Notre Dame									Notre Dame	1-0	Paradise
1998	Notre Dame	39	Budg-Buy	38	Bayer Pride					Bayer Pride	1-0	Notre Dame
1999	Notre Dame									Gall Hill	2-1	Paradise
2000	Notre Dame	35	Paradise	31	Youth Milan					Paradise	2-1	Notre Dame
2001	Paradise	43	Youth Milan	41	Notre Dame	35				Notre Dame	1-0	Youth Milan
2002	Notre Dame	44	Paradise	32	Youth Milan	30				Youth Milan	2-1	Notre Dame
2003	Paradise	*	BDF							Paradise	1-0	Weymouth Wales
2004	Notre Dame	52	Beverly Hills	42	Youth Milan	40				Notre Dame	3-2	Silver Sands
2005	Notre Dame	41	BDF	33	Silver Sands	32				Paradise	3-1	BDF
2006	Youth Milan	37	Notre Dame	36	Silver Sands	30				Gall Hill	1-0	Paradise
2007	BDF	34	Gall Hill	32	Brittons Hill	31						

* Paradise beat Barbados Defence Force 4-1 on penalties in the Championship final

BRU – BRUNEI DARUSSALAM

NATIONAL TEAM RECORD
JULY 10TH 2006 TO JULY 12TH 2010

PL	W	D	L	F	A	%
4	1	1	2	6	11	37.5

FIFA/COCA-COLA WORLD RANKING

1993	1994	1995	1996	1997	1998	1999	2000	2001	2002	2003	2004	2005	2006	High	Low
151	165	167	170	178	183	185	193	189	194	194	199	199	175	145 08/93	199 12/04

2006–2007											
08/06	09/06	10/06	11/06	12/06	01/07	02/07	03/07	04/07	05/07	06/07	07/07
178	179	180	167	175	174	174	174	173	173	170	171

Brunei is one of just four countries that didn't enter the 2010 FIFA World Cup and of all the countries in the world it is hard to find a nation in which the national team has such a low profile. It was surprising therefore that Brunei played seven internationals in 2006 - in the AFC Challenge Cup and in the qualifying tournament for the ASEAN Football Federation Championship. Of those seven, only three were lost and the team managed to set a new record of four games undefeated. Competition does remain restricted to the minor and regional Asian tournaments. For many supporters, DPMM Brunei have become the focus for national pride. Not only do they represent

INTERNATIONAL HONOURS
None

Brunei in the Malaysia Cup, but promotion in 2006 saw them compete at the highest level in the Malaysian Super League, finishing a creditable third in the 2007 season. The B-League in Brunei has inevitably suffered with the departure of DPMM in 2005 and there was a gap of over a year before the 2007 edition kicked-off. In the interim, attention was focused on the League Cup which was won by the Armed Forces, who beat QAF 3-2 in an exciting final won in the last minute of extra-time. A new competition called the Hyundai Cup was also launched. Played in April and May 2007, it too was won by the Armed Forces, this time against Wijaya.

THE FIFA BIG COUNT OF 2006

	Male	Female		Total
Number of players	7 300	200	Referees and Assistant Referees	33
Professionals	0		Admin, Coaches, Technical, Medical	100
Amateurs 18+	300		Number of clubs	20
Youth under 18	600		Number of teams	40
Unregistered	1 100		Clubs with women's teams	0
Total players	7 500		Players as % of population	1.98%

The Football Association of Brunei Darussalam (BAFA)
Stadium Negara Hassanal Bolkiah, PO Box 2010, Bandar Seri Begawan, BB 4313, Brunei Darussalam
Tel +673 2 382761   Fax +673 2 382760
bruneifasg@yahoo.com   www.bafa.org.bn
President: HUSSAIN YUSSOFF Pehin Dato Haji   General Secretary: MATUSIN MATASAN Pengiran Haji
Vice-President: HASSAN ABAS Pengiran Haji   Treasurer: PANG Jeffery   Media Officer: None
Men's Coach: BUKETA Ranko   Women's Coach: None
BAFA formed: 1959   AFC: 1970   FIFA: 1969
Yellow shirts, Black shorts, Black socks

RECENT INTERNATIONAL MATCHES PLAYED BY BRUNEI DARUSSALAM

2006	Opponents		Score	Venue	Comp	Scorers	Att	Referee
2-04	Sri Lanka	L	0-1	Chittagong	CCr1		2 000	Saidov UZB
4-04	Nepal	W	2-1	Chittagong	CCr1	Safari [47], Sallehuddin [70]	2 500	Al Ghatrifi OMA
6-04	Bhutan	D	0-0	Chittagong	CCr1		2 000	Al Ghatrifi OMA
12-11	Timor Leste	W	3-2	Bacolod	AFq	Adie Mohammed Salleh 2 [11 70], Mardi Bujang [66]		
16-11	Cambodia	D	1-1	Bacolod	AFq	Mardi Bujang [90]		
18-11	Laos	L	1-4	Bacolod	AFq	Riwandi Wahit [20]		
20-11	Philippines	L	1-4	Bacolod	AFq	Kamarul Ariffin Ramlee [81]		
2007								

No international matches played in 2007 before August

CC = AFC Challenge Cup • AF = ASEAN Championship • q = qualifier • r1 = first round group

BRUNEI DARUSSALAM NATIONAL TEAM RECORDS AND RECORD SEQUENCES

Records			Sequence records					
Victory	2-0	PHI 1980, PHI 1989	Wins	2	1980	Clean sheets	1	
Defeat	0-12	UAE 2001	Defeats	12	1972-80, 1999-01	Goals scored	4	1998-1999, 2006
Player Caps	n/a		Undefeated	4	2006	Without goal	11	1999-2001
Player Goals	n/a		Without win	23	1999-2006	Goals against	26	1982-1987

BRUNEI CUP 2006

Round of 16		Quarter–finals		Semi–finals		Final	
ABDB Armed Forces	2						
Brunei Shell	1	ABDB Armed Forces	5				
Kamudi	0	March United	0				
March United	2			ABDB Armed Forces	2		
Kasuka	4			AH United	0		
Sengkurong	1	Kasuka	0				
AM Gunners	2	AH United	10				
AH United	3					ABDB Armed Forces	3
Wijaya	2					QAF	2
Bandaran	1	Wijaya	3				
NBT	1 5p	Kota Ranger	0				
Kota Ranger	1 6p			Wijaya	1		
Majra	3			QAF	3		
Jerudong	1	Majra	1				
Perkasa	0	QAF	4				
QAF	3						

CUP FINAL

National Stadium, Bandar Seri Bagawan
24-01-2007

Scorers - Mattyassin [34], Sulaiman [64p],
Saini [118] for ABDB;
Ambun [7], Bayong [24] for QAF

RECENT LEAGUE AND CUP RECORD

	Championship						Cup		
Year	Champions	Pts	Runners-up	Pts	Third	Pts	Winners	Score	Runners-up
2002	DPMM	19	ABDB Armed Forces	16	Kasuka	9	Wijaya	1-0	ABDB Armed Forces
2003	Wijaya	25	DPMM	22	ABDB Armed Forces	21	ABDB Armed Forces	3-0	Kota Ranger
2004	DPMM	52	AH United	42	ABDB Armed Forces	37	DPMM	0-0 3-1p	ABDB Armed Forces
2005	QAF	41	ABDB Armed Forces	39	AH United	38	AH United	2-2 4-3p	ABDB Armed Forces
2006	No tournament played						ABDB Armed Forces	3-2	QAF

BRUNEI DARUSSALAM COUNTRY INFORMATION

Capital	Bandar Seri Begawan	Independence	1984 from the UK	GDP per Capita	$18 600
Population	365 251	Status	Sultanate	GNP Ranking	97
Area km²	5 770	Language	Malay	Dialling code	+673
Population density	63 per km²	Literacy rate	90%	Internet code	.bn
% in urban areas	70%	Main religion	Muslim 67%	GMT + / –	+8
Towns/Cities ('000)	Bandar Seri Begawan 64; Kuala Belait 31; Pekan Seria 30; Tutong 19; Bangar 3				
Neighbours (km)	Malaysia 381; South China Sea 161				
Main stadia	Sultan Hassal Bolkiah – Bandar Ser Begawan 30 000				

BUL – BULGARIA

NATIONAL TEAM RECORD
JULY 10TH 2006 TO JULY 12TH 2010

PL	W	D	L	F	A	%
11	6	4	1	17	7	72.7

FIFA/COCA-COLA WORLD RANKING

1993	1994	1995	1996	1997	1998	1999	2000	2001	2002	2003	2004	2005	2006	High		Low	
31	16	17	15	36	49	37	53	51	42	34	37	39	43	**8**	06/95	**58**	08/02

2006–2007											
08/06	09/06	10/06	11/06	12/06	01/07	02/07	03/07	04/07	05/07	06/07	07/07
36	37	38	43	43	42	37	39	38	36	33	30

Bulgaria were unbeaten in their opening seven UEFA Euro 2008 qualifying matches but were hit by the departure of coach Hristo Stoitchkov to Celta Vigo in April 2007, although his temporary replacement Stanimir Stoilov impressed in the two matches against Belarus at the end of the season. Stoilov had just led Levski Sofia to the 13th double in their history, finishing ahead of city rivals Lokomotiv Sofia and CSKA Sofia in the League and beating Litex Lovech in the Cup Final. CSKA had been bought during the season by Indian steel magnate Pramod Mittal, but with just one defeat all season, Levski finished 10 points clear of them, clinching the title on the penultimate weekend

INTERNATIONAL HONOURS
European Youth Tournament 1959 1969 1974, Balkan Cup 1932 1935 1976

with a 5-3 victory away to Lokomotiv. Spare a thought, however, for Chernomorets who picked up just one point all season but were then docked three to finish on minus two. In an entertaining Cup Final, Frenchman Cédric Bardon scored the only goal in Levski's win over Litex, although Litex had missed a golden chance when Brazilian Beto shot wide at the end of normal time with the scores level. In Europe, Bulgarian clubs found it hard to follow the success of the previous season, although Levski did become the first Bulgarian club to qualify for the Champions League group stage. Their misfortune, though, was to be drawn with Barcelona, Werder and Chelsea in the toughest group.

THE FIFA BIG COUNT OF 2006

	Male	Female		Total
Number of players	289 348	37 685	Referees and Assistant Referees	1 411
Professionals	1 060		Admin, Coaches, Technical, Medical	1 160
Amateurs 18+	31 324		Number of clubs	559
Youth under 18	17 389		Number of teams	1 301
Unregistered	90 400		Clubs with women's teams	20
Total players	327 033		Players as % of population	4.43%

Bulgarian Football Union (BFU)
Bulgarski Futbolen Soius, 26 Tzar Ivan Assen II Str., Sofia - 1124, Bulgaria
Tel +359 2 9426253   Fax +359 2 9426200
bfu@bfunion.bg   www.bfunion.bg
President: MIHAILOV Borislav   General Secretary: POPOV Borislav
Vice-President: LECHKOV Yordan   Treasurer: PEEV Todor   Media Officer: KONSTANTINOV Borislav
Men's Coach: STOILOV Stanimir   Women's Coach: ATANASSOV Emil
BFU formed: 1923   UEFA: 1954   FIFA: 1924
White shirts with green trimmings, Green shorts, White socks or Red shirts, Green, White

RECENT INTERNATIONAL MATCHES PLAYED BY BULGARIA

2003	Opponents	Score		Venue	Comp	Scorers	Att	Referee
20-08	Lithuania	W	3-0	Sofia	Fr	Dimitrov 2 25p 45, Berbatov 33	2 000	Bolognino ITA
6-09	Estonia	W	2-0	Sofia	ECq	Petrov.M 16, Berbatov 67	25 128	Wack GER
10-09	Andorra	W	3-0	Andorra la Vella	ECq	Berbatov 2 10 23, Hristov 58	1 000	Mikulski POL
11-10	Croatia	L	0-1	Zagreb	ECq		37 000	Veissiere FRA
18-11	Korea Republic	W	1-0	Seoul	Fr	Manchev 19	38 257	Saleh MAS
2004								
18-02	Greece	L	0-2	Athens	Fr		6 000	Poll ENG
31-03	Russia	D	2-2	Sofia	Fr	Berbatov 2 15 66	14 938	Garcia POR
28-04	Cameroon	W	3-0	Sofia	Fr	Berbatov 2 7 54p, Lazarov 56	13 987	Verbist BEL
2-06	Czech Republic	L	1-3	Prague	Fr	Petkov.M 90	6 627	Stredak SVK
14-06	Sweden	L	0-5	Lisbon	ECr1		31 652	Riley ENG
18-06	Denmark	L	0-2	Braga	ECr1		22 000	Cortez Batista POR
22-06	Italy	L	1-2	Guimaraes	ECr1	Petrov.M 45p	16 002	Ivanov RUS
18-08	Republic of Ireland	D	1-1	Dublin	Fr	Bojinov 70	31 887	Brines SCO
4-09	Iceland	W	3-1	Reykjavik	WCq	Berbatov 35 49, Yanev 62	5 014	Hamer LUX
9-10	Croatia	D	2-2	Zagreb	WCq	Petrov.M 77, Berbatov 86	31 565	Collina ITA
13-10	Malta	W	4-1	Sofia	WCq	Berbatov 2 43 55, Yanev 47, Yankov 88	16 800	Richards WAL
17-11	Azerbaijan	D	0-0	Baku	Fr		3 000	Sipailo LVA
29-11	Egypt	D	1-1	Cairo	Fr	Gargorov 90		
2005								
9-02	Serbia & Montenegro	D	0-0	Sofia	Fr		2 957	Genov BUL
26-03	Sweden	L	0-3	Sofia	WCq		42 530	Fandel GER
30-03	Hungary	D	1-1	Budapest	WCq	Petrov.S 51	11 586	Wegereef NED
4-06	Croatia	L	1-3	Sofia	WCq	Petrov.M 72	35 000	Nielsen DEN
17-08	Turkey	W	3-1	Sofia	Fr	Berbatov 2 24 43, Petrov.M 38	25 000	Zografos GRE
3-09	Sweden	L	0-3	Stockholm	WCq		35 000	De Bleeckere BEL
7-09	Iceland	W	3-2	Sofia	WCq	Berbatov 21, Iliev.G 69, Petrov.M 86	18 000	Demirlek TUR
8-10	Hungary	W	2-0	Sofia	WCq	Berbatov 29, Lazarov 55	4 652	Delevic SCG
12-10	Malta	D	1-1	Ta'Qali	WCq	Yankov 67	2 844	Godulyan UKR
12-11	Georgia	W	6-2	Sofia	Fr	Yankov 2 2 28, Berbatov 2 35 47, Todorov 2 63 90p		
16-11	Mexico	W	3-0	Phoenix	Fr	Valkanov 4, Bojinov 34, Berbatov 80	35 526	Hall USA
2006								
1-03	FYR Macedonia	W	1-0	Skopje	Fr	Petrov.M 38	8 000	
9-05	Japan	W	2-1	Osaka	Fr	Todorov.S 1, Yanev 90	44 851	Megia Davila ESP
11-05	Scotland	L	1-5	Kobe	Fr	Todorov.Y 26	5 780	Kamikawa JPN
15-08	Wales	D	0-0	Swansea	Fr		8 200	Attard MLT
2-09	Romania	D	2-2	Constanta	ECq	Petrov.M 2 82 84	12 620	Farina ITA
6-09	Slovenia	W	3-0	Sofia	ECq	Bozhinov 58, Petrov.M 72, Telkiyski 81	14 491	Bo Larsen DEN
7-10	Netherlands	D	1-1	Sofia	ECq	Petrov.M 12	30 547	Ovrebø NOR
11-10	Luxembourg	W	1-0	Luxembourg	ECq	Tunchev 26	3 156	Panic BIH
15-11	Slovakia	L	1-3	Zilina	Fr	Karadzinov 80	4 823	Granat POL
2007								
6-02	Latvia	W	2-0	Larnaca	Fr	Surnins OG 14, Yovov 29	500	Andronikou CYP
7-02	Cyprus	W	3-0	Nicosia	Fr	Berbatov 2 44p 87, Georgiev 68	2 000	
28-03	Albania	D	0-0	Sofia	ECq		19 800	Eriksson SWE
2-06	Belarus	W	2-0	Minsk	ECq	Berbatov 2 28 46	29 000	Jara CZE
6-06	Belarus	W	2-1	Sofia	ECq	Petrov.M 10, Yankov 40	10 501	Jakobsson ISL

Fr = Friendly match • EC = UEFA EURO 2004/2008 • WC = FIFA World Cup • q = qualifier • r1 = first round group

BULGARIA NATIONAL TEAM RECORDS AND RECORD SEQUENCES

Records			Sequence records					
Victory	7-0	NOR 1957, MLT 1982	Wins	5	1983 & 1987	Clean sheets	4	1963, 2007
Defeat	0-13	ESP 1933	Defeats	7	1924-1927	Goals scored	18	1934-1938
Player Caps	102	MIKHAILOV Borislav	Undefeated	11	1972-1973	Without goal	4	1984 & 1998
Player Goals	47	BONEV Hristo	Without win	16	1977-1978	Goals against	24	1924-1932

REPUBLIC OF BULGARIA; REPUBLIKA BALGARIYA

Capital	Sofia	Language	Bulgarian			Independence	1908
Population	7 385 367	Area	110 910 km²	Density	67 per km²	% in cities	71%
GDP per cap	$7 600	Dailling code	+359	Internet	.bg	GMT +/-	+2

MEDALS TABLE

		Overall			League			Cup		SAC		Europe			City	Stadium	Cap'ty	DoF
		G	S	B	G	S	B	G	S	G	S	G	S	B				
1	Levski Sofia	54	38	7	25	29	7	13	5	16	4				Sofia	Georgi Asparukhov	29 698	1914
2	CSKA Sofia	53	31	6	30	18	3	10	7	13	6			3	Sofia	Bulgarska Armia	24 000	1948
3	Slavia Sofia	14	11	13	7	9	12	1		6	2			1	Sofia	Slavia	28 000	1913
4	Lokomotiv Sofia	8	9	8	4	6	8	1		3	3				Sofia	Lokomotiv	25 000	1929
5	Botev Plovdiv	4	11	11	2	2	11		4	2	5				Plovdiv	Hristo Botev	21 000	1912
6	Cherno More Varna	4	9	2	4	6	2		1		2	°			Varna	Ticha	12 000	1913
7	Litexs Lovech	4	4	2	2	1	2	2	3						Lovech	Lovech	7 000	1921
8	Spartak Sofia	3	4			2			2	1	2				Sofia	Rakovski		1907-69
9	Lokomotiv Plovdiv	2	5	4	1	1	4			1	4				Plovdiv	Lokomotiv	20 000	1936
10	Spartak Plovdiv	2	3		1	1				1	2				Plovdiv	9 Septemvri		1947
11	AC 23 Sofia	2			1			1							Sofia	Atletic Park		1923
12	Beroe Stara Zagora	1	4	1	1		1				4				Stara Zagora	Beroe	22 300	1916
	Spartak Varna	1	4	1	1	2	1		1		1				Varna	Spartak	7 500	1918
14	SC Sofia	1	1		1	1									Sofia	Sport Club		1919

SAC = Soviet Army Cup (main cup competition 1946-81)

RECENT LEAGUE AND CUP RECORD

	Championship						Cup		
Year	Champions	Pts	Runners-up	Pts	Third	Pts	Winners	Score	Runners-up
1995	Levski Sofia	79	Lokomotiv Sofia	68	Botev Plovdiv	60	Lokomotiv Sofia	4-2	Botev Plovdiv
1996	Slavia Sofia	67	Levski Sofia	62	Lokomotiv Sofia	58	Slavia Sofia	1-0	Levski Sofia
1997	CSKA Sofia	71	Neftohimik Burgas	67	Slavia Sofia	57	CSKA Sofia	3-1	Levski Sofia
1998	Liteks Lovech	69	Levski Sofia	64	CSKA Sofia	61	Levski Sofia	5-0	CSKA Sofia
1999	Liteks Lovech	73	Levski Sofia	71	Levski Kjustendil	57	CSKA Sofia	1-0	Litex Lovech
2000	Levski Sofia	74	CSKA Sofia	64	Velbazhd	55	Levski Sofia	2-0	Neftohimik Burgas
2001	Levski Sofia	69	CSKA Sofia	62	Velbazhd	57	Litex Lovech	1-0	Velbazhd
2002	Levski Sofia	65	Litex Lovech	55	Lokomotiv Plovdiv	53	Levski Sofia	3-1	CSKA Sofia
2003	CSKA Sofia	66	Levski Sofia	60	Litex Lovech	55	Levski Sofia	2-1	Litex Lovech
2004	Lokomotiv Plovdiv	75	Levski Sofia	72	CSKA Sofia	65	Litex Lovech	2-2 4-3p	CSKA Sofia
2005	CSKA Sofia	79	Levski Sofia	76	Lokomotiv Plovdiv	58	Levski Sofia	2-1	CSKA Sofia
2006	Levski Sofia	68	CSKA Sofia	65	Litex Lovech	60	CSKA Sofia	3-1	Cherno More Varna
2007	Levski Sofia	77	CSKA Sofia	72	Lokomotiv Sofia	72	Levski Sofia	1-0	Litex Lovech

BULGARIA 2006-07

'A' PFG

	Pl	W	D	L	F	A	Pts	Levski	CSKA	Lokomotiv S	Litex	Slavia	Cherno More	Lokomotiv P	Belasitsa	Vihren	Botev	Beroe	Marek	Spartak	Rilski sportist	Rodopa	Chernomorets
Levski Sofia †	30	24	5	1	96	13	77		1-0	3-0	6-2	2-0	5-0	6-1	1-0	4-0	3-0	3-0	8-0	3-0	5-0	3-0	10-0
CSKA Sofia ‡	30	23	3	4	68	13	72	0-1		4-1	2-0	6-1	0-0	3-0	2-1	5-0	2-0	2-0	4-0	3-0	1-0	6-0	
Lokomotiv Sofia ‡	30	23	3	4	70	28	72	3-5	1-1		1-0	2-1	2-0	2-0	1-0	1-0	3-1	1-0	1-0	2-0	2-0	5-0	7-0
Litex Lovech ‡	30	19	5	6	65	29	62	0-0	0-1	2-1		2-0	0-0	5-1	7-1	1-0	2-0	2-0	4-1	1-0	3-1	2-1	11-0
Slavia Sofia	30	14	7	9	47	35	49	0-3	0-1	1-1	2-2		0-0	1-0	2-1	3-1	2-0	2-1	1-0	1-1	0-1	4-1	8-0
Cherno More Varna	30	14	5	11	35	29	47	1-1	0-2	2-3	1-0	0-1		1-0	1-0	1-2	4-0	1-0	1-0	3-0	2-1	2-1	3-1
Lokomotiv Plovdiv	30	13	4	13	48	43	43	1-3	1-1	2-4	1-1	0-0	2-0		1-0	2-0	2-0	1-0	1-1	4-0	1-0	5-0	6-0
Belasitsa Petrich	30	11	5	14	38	43	38	0-1	1-3	1-2	2-3	1-3	1-0	3-0		2-1	2-1	1-0	2-2	2-0	4-1	1-0	2-0
Vihren Sandanski	30	11	4	15	27	39	37	0-0	0-2	0-2	0-1	3-2	0-2	3-2	1-1		1-0	2-0	1-2	2-0	1-2	0-0	2-0
Botev Plovdiv	30	11	4	15	41	45	37	2-2	1-0	1-2	1-2	1-0	2-0	3-2	3-1	1-2		1-0	3-0	5-1	1-0	2-1	5-1
Beroe Stara Zagora	30	10	6	14	34	33	36	0-0	0-1	2-2	2-1	1-2	2-1	0-5	0-0	2-0	2-0		1-1	1-0	1-0	2-1	6-0
Marek Dupnitsa	30	9	7	14	39	58	34	0-8	1-0	1-2	1-2	2-2	0-1	3-1	1-1	0-1	2-2	1-1		3-1	3-2	4-2	4-1
Spartak Varna	30	10	3	17	27	52	33	1-2	1-3	0-2	1-3	1-0	2-0	2-1	3-3	0-0	1-0	2-1	1-0		3-1	1-0	2-1
Rilski sportist Samokov	30	10	0	20	31	53	30	2-1	1-3	1-3	1-3	0-1	1-2	1-3	1-2	1-0	3-1	0-1	3-0	1-0		1-0	3-1
Rodopa Smolyan	30	5	4	21	22	52	19	0-3	1-2	0-2	1-3	0-1	0-0	0-1	1-0	0-1	1-1	0-0	1-2	3-0	3-1		1-0
Chernomorets Sofia §3	30	0	1	29	8	131	-2	0-3	0-6	0-9	0-0	0-4	0-6	0-1	1-2	0-3	1-0	0-8	1-4	0-3	0-1	1-2	

4/08/2006 - 27/05/2007 • † Qualified for the UEFA Champions League • ‡ Qualified for the UEFA Cup • § = Points deducted
Top scorers: Tsvetan GENKOV, Lokomotiv Sofia 27; Todor KOLEV, Slavia Sofia 25; Enyo KRASTOVCHEV, Marek 16; Eugen TRICA, CSKA 16

BULGARIA 2006-07 WESTERN 'B' PFG (2)

	Pl	W	D	L	F	A	Pts
Pirin Blagoevgrad	26	18	6	2	41	11	60
Vidima-Rakovski †	26	15	8	3	50	24	53
Pirin Gotse Delchev	26	13	3	10	38	30	42
Vihar Sofia	26	10	10	6	33	27	40
Spartak Pleven	26	10	8	8	32	27	38
Etar Veliko Tarnovo	26	10	5	11	36	34	35
Chavdar Byala Slatina	26	9	5	12	28	32	32
Minyor Pernik	26	8	8	10	30	32	32
Velbazhd Kyustendil	26	9	5	12	37	44	32
Montana	26	8	8	10	30	33	32
Belite orli Pleven	26	9	4	13	27	30	31
Lokomotiv Mezdra	26	7	8	11	27	42	29
Hebar Pazardzhik	26	7	4	15	22	41	25
Minyor Bobov dol	26	5	6	15	18	42	21

12/08/2006 - 26/05/2007 • † Play-off
Promotion play-off: Naftex 0-1 Vidima-Rakovski

BULGARIA 2006-07 EASTERN 'B' PFG (2)

	Pl	W	D	L	F	A	Pts
Chernomorets Burgas	26	19	6	1	57	20	63
Naftex Burgas †	26	17	9	0	51	10	60
Haskovo	26	12	7	7	38	27	43
Nesebar	26	12	4	10	40	32	40
Dunav Ruse	26	10	9	7	46	35	39
Spartak Plovdiv	26	11	5	10	32	28	38
Shumen 2001	26	10	7	9	29	36	37
Kaliakra Kavarna	26	10	6	10	25	31	36
Svetkavitsa Targovishte	26	10	4	12	36	41	34
Maritsa Plovdiv	26	9	5	12	35	36	32
Minyor Radnevo	26	7	4	15	34	45	25
Sliven 2000	26	4	11	11	32	52	23
Dobrudzha Dobrich	26	5	5	16	25	51	20
Lokomotiv Stara Zagora	26	3	4	19	22	58	13

12/08/2006 - 26/05/2007 • † Play-off

BFU CUP 2006-07

Round of 16		Quarter-finals		Semi-finals		Final	
Levski Sofia	1						
Chernomorets Burgas*	0	Levski Sofia	0 4p				
Lokomotiv Sofia	2 3p	Pirin Blagoevgrad*	0 2p				
Pirin Blagoevgrad*	2 4p			Levski Sofia	3		
Vihren Sandanski*	0 4p			Lokomotiv Plovdiv	0		
Cherno More Varna	0 3p	Vihren Sandanski	0				
Dunav Ruse*	1	Lokomotiv Plovdiv*	1			Levski Sofia	1
Lokomotiv Plovdiv	4					Litex Lovech ‡	0
Beroe Stara Zagora	2						
Sliven 2000*	1	Beroe Stara Zagora*	1				
Montana*	1	CSKA Sofia	0				
CSKA Sofia	2			Beroe Stara Zagora	0		
Slavia Sofia*	3			Litex Lovech	1		
Botev Plovdiv	1	Slavia Sofia	1				
Rilski sportist	0	Litex Lovech*	2				
Litex Lovech*	4						

CUP FINAL
Beroe, Stara Zagora
24-05-2007
Scorer - Cedric Bardon 11 1p for Levski

* Home team • ‡ Qualified for the UEFA Cup

CAM – CAMBODIA

NATIONAL TEAM RECORD
JULY 10TH 2006 TO JULY 12TH 2010

PL	W	D	L	F	A	%
5	1	2	2	7	11	40

FIFA/COCA-COLA WORLD RANKING

1993	1994	1995	1996	1997	1998	1999	2000	2001	2002	2003	2004	2005	2006	High	Low
-	-	180	186	170	162	168	169	169	176	178	184	188	174	156 07/98	188 03/06

2006–2007											
08/06	09/06	10/06	11/06	12/06	01/07	02/07	03/07	04/07	05/07	06/07	07/07
184	185	185	178	174	176	176	176	170	171	169	170

While neighbours Thailand and Vietnam were hosting the AFC Asian Cup, the continent's showpiece football event, Cambodia was left looking in from the outside having not even been able to take part in the qualifiers. The national team did provide Malaysia with one warm-up game but their 6-0 defeat gives a good indication of their standing in the region at present. Of the five games played during the 2006-07 season, however, just one other was lost. Indeed, for the first time in its history, the national team went more than a single game without losing. Following on from the victory over Guam in the last match of the 2006 AFC Challenge Cup, Cambodia then drew their first two

INTERNATIONAL HONOURS
None

matches of the qualifying tournament for the ASEAN Football Federation Championship, setting a new record of three games without defeat! There was also a 4-2 victory over East Timor to celebrate but thanks to a 1-0 reverse against the Philippines, qualification for the final tournament was just out of reach. In domestic football, Khemera remain the dominant force. Their 2006 title qualified them to take part again in the AFC President's Cup although there was a delay in taking part with the 2007 tournament postponed until September. In May 2007, Khemera won the Samdech Hun Sen Cup defeating Naga Corp on 4-2 on penalties in the final after a 1-1 draw.

THE FIFA BIG COUNT OF 2006

	Male	Female		Total
Number of players	229 411	100	Referees and Assistant Referees	70
Professionals	11		Admin, Coaches, Technical, Medical	160
Amateurs 18+	1 600		Number of clubs	65
Youth under 18	3 900		Number of teams	420
Unregistered	6 000		Clubs with women's teams	0
Total players	229 511		Players as % of population	1.65%

Cambodian Football Federation (CFF)
National Football Centre, Road Kabsrov, Sangkat Samrong Krom, Khan Dangkor, Phnom Penh, Cambodia
Tel +855 23 364889   Fax +855 23 223537
ffc.cam@gmail.com   www.aseanfootball.org
President: SAO Sokha   General Secretary: CHHEANG Yean
Vice-President: KHEK Ravy   Treasurer: PHUONG-BOPHA Saradeth   Media Officer: None
Men's Coach: O'DONELL Scott   Women's Coach: None
CFF formed: 1933   AFC: 1957   FIFA: 1953
Blue shirts, Blue shorts, Blue socks

RECENT INTERNATIONAL MATCHES PLAYED BY CAMBODIA

2002	Opponents	Score		Venue	Comp	Scorers	Att	Referee
11-12	Malaysia	L	0-5	Kuala Lumpur	Fr			
15-12	Vietnam SR	L	2-9	Jakarta	TCr1	Hok Sochetra [27], Ung Kanyanith [53]	5 000	Nagalingham SIN
17-12	Indonesia	L	2-4	Jakarta	TCr1	Hok Sochetra 2 [10 44]	20 000	Khantachai THA
19-12	Myanmar	L	0-5	Jakarta	TCr1		2 000	Ebrahim BHR
21-12	Philippines	W	1-0	Jakarta	TCr1	Ung Kanyanith [90]	2 500	Napitupulu IDN
2003								
No international matches played in 2003								
2004								
9-12	Vietnam SR	L	1-9	Ho Chi Minh City	TCr1	Hang Sokunthea [44]	8 000	Supian MAS
11-12	Laos	L	1-2	Ho Chi Minh City	TCr1	Hing Darith [27]	20 000	Kwon Jong Chul KOR
13-12	Indonesia	L	0-8	Ho Chi Minh City	TCr1		17 000	Sun Baojie CHN
15-12	Singapore	L	0-3	Ho Chi Minh City	TCr1		2 000	Ebrahim BHR
2005								
11-10	Singapore	L	0-2	Phnom Penh	Fr			
2006								
1-04	Bangladesh	L	1-2	Dhaka	CCr1	Chan Rithy [68]	35 000	Tan Hai CHN
3-04	Palestine	L	0-4	Dhaka	CCr1		2 500	AK Nema IRQ
6-04	Guam	W	3-0	Dhaka	CCr1	Sok Buntheang [37], Keo Kosal [40], Kouch Sokumpheak [63]	500	U Win Cho MYA
14-11	Laos	D	2-2	Bacolod	TCq	Teab Vadhanak [50], Hem Samchay [75]		
16-11	Brunei Darussalam	D	1-1	Bacolod	TCq	Samel Nasa [79]		
18-11	Philippines	L	0-1	Bacolod	TCq			
20-11	Timor Leste	W	4-1	Bacolod	TCq	Hem Samchay [37], Teab Vadhanak [58], Chan Rithy 2 [82 86]		
2007								
18-06	Malaysia	L	0-6	Kuala Lumpur	Fr			

Fr = Friendly match • TC = ASEAN Football Federation Cup/Tiger Cup • CC = AFC Challenge Cup • r1 = first round group

CAMBODIA NATIONAL TEAM RECORDS AND RECORD SEQUENCES

Records			Sequence records				
Victory	11-0	YEM 1966	Wins	1		Clean sheets	1	
Defeat	0-10	IDN 1995	Defeats	10	1995-1997	Goals scored	3	1997
Player Caps	n/a		Undefeated	3	2006	Without goal	5	1996-1997
Player Goals	n/a		Without win	17	1998-2002	Goals against	20	1997-2000

RECENT LEAGUE RECORD

Year	Champions
1996	Body Guards Club
1997	Body Guards Club
1998	Royal Dolphins
1999	Royal Dolphins
2000	National Police
2001	No tournament played
2002	Samart United
2003	No tournament played
2004	No tournament played
2005	Khemera
2006	Khemera

CAMBODIA COUNTRY INFORMATION

Capital	Phnom Penh	Independence	1953	GDP per Capita	$1 900
Population	13 363 421	Status	Kingdom	GNP Ranking	127
Area km²	181 040	Language	Khmer	Dialling code	+855
Population density	73 per km²	Literacy rate	66%	Internet code	.kh
% in urban areas	21%	Main religion	Buddhist 95%	GMT +/-	+7
Towns/Cities ('000)	Phnom Penh 1 573; Preah Sihanouk 157; Bat Dambang 150; Siem Reab 148				
Neighbours (km)	Laos 541; Vietnam 1,228; Thailand 803; Gulf of Thailand 443				
Main stadia	National Olympic – Phnom Penh 50 000				

CAN – CANADA

NATIONAL TEAM RECORD
JULY 10TH 2006 TO JULY 12TH 2010

PL	W	D	L	F	A	%
9	5	1	3	15	8	61.1

FIFA/COCA-COLA WORLD RANKING

1993	1994	1995	1996	1997	1998	1999	2000	2001	2002	2003	2004	2005	2006	High	Low
44	63	65	40	66	101	81	63	92	70	87	90	84	82	**40** 12/96	**103** 03/07

2006–2007											
08/06	09/06	10/06	11/06	12/06	01/07	02/07	03/07	04/07	05/07	06/07	07/07
82	71	71	82	82	81	87	103	94	94	56	52

It's not often that Canada manages to grab a share of the limelight where football is concerned but 2007 was a busy year for the country, a year that culminated in the hosting of the FIFA U–20 World Cup. In late 2006 Vancouver Whitecaps got the celebratory mood in swing when they won the A-League in the USA. April 2007 saw Toronto FC made its much anticipated debut in America's MLS although fans had to wait until the fifth week for the team's first goal and win - Danny Dichio opening the scoring in a 3-1 victory over Chicago Fire. The national team was then in action in June in the CONCACAF Gold Cup in the USA and with victories over Costa Rica and Haiti,

INTERNATIONAL HONOURS
Qualified for the FIFA World Cup™ 1986   Qualified for the FIFA Women's World Cup 1995 1999 2003   Olympic Gold 1904 (Unofficial)
CONCACAF Gold Cup 2000   CONCACAF Women's Gold Cup 1998   CONCACAF U-20 Championship 1986 1996

Canada topped their first round group in Miami. They then went on to comfortably beat Guatemala 3-0 in the quarter-finals setting up a semi-final clash with America which the hosts won 2-1 although Canada were controversially denied a last minute equaliser when Atiba Hutchinson's goal was disallowed for offside. In July world attention was focused on the country for the FIFA U–20 World Cup and although the host team fared badly, losing all three matches, the tournament was a major success with most of the games being played before capacity crowds.

THE FIFA BIG COUNT OF 2006

	Male	Female		Total
Number of players	1 800 378	895 334	Referees and Assistant Referees	19 624
Professionals	150		Admin, Coaches, Technical, Medical	170 000
Amateurs 18+	129 725		Number of clubs	7 000
Youth under 18	715837		Number of teams	55 000
Unregistered	800 000		Clubs with women's teams	3 000
Total players	2 695 712		Players as % of population	8.14%

The Canadian Soccer Association (CSA)
Place Soccer Canada, 237 Metcalfe Street, Ottawa, Ontario, K2P 1R2, Canada
Tel +1 613 2377678   Fax +1 613 2371516
info@soccercan.ca   www.canadasoccer.com
President: LINFORD Colin   General Secretary: NYKAMP Fred
Vice-President: MONTAGLIANI Victor   Treasurer: URSINI Vincent   Media Officer: SCOTT Richard
Men's Coach: MITCHELL Dale   Women's Coach: PELLERUD Even
CSA formed: 1912   CONCACAF: 1978   FIFA: 1912-28, 1946
Red shirts with white trimmings, Red shorts, Red socks or White shirts with red trimmings, White shorts, White socks

RECENT INTERNATIONAL MATCHES PLAYED BY CAMBODIA

2002	Opponents	Score		Venue	Comp	Scorers	Att	Referee
15-10	Scotland	L	1-3	Edinburgh	Fr	De Rosario [9p]	16 207	Huyghe BEL
2003								
18-01	USA	L	0-4	Fort Lauderdale	Fr		6 549	Sibrian SLV
12-02	Libya	W	4-2	Tripoli	Fr	McKenna [18], Brennan [34], Stalteri [47], Canizalez [81]	45 000	
29-03	Estonia	L	1-2	Tallinn	Fr	Stalteri [47]	2 500	Hansson SWE
1-06	Germany	L	1-4	Wolfsburg	Fr	McKenna [20]	24 000	Poulat FRA
12-07	Costa Rica	W	1-0	Foxboro	GCr1	Stalteri [59]	33 652	Piper TRI
14-07	Cuba	L	0-2	Foxboro	GCr1		8 780	Prendergast JAM
11-10	Finland	L	2-3	Tampere	Fr	Radzinski [75], De Rosario [85]	5 350	
15-11	Czech Republic	L	1-5	Teplice	Fr	Radzinski [89]	8 343	Sundell SWE
18-11	Republic of Ireland	L	0-3	Dublin	Fr		23 000	Whitby WAL
2004								
18-01	Barbados	W	1-0	Bridgetown	Fr	Corazzin [10]		Ford BRB
30-05	Wales	L	0-1	Wrexham	Fr		10 805	McKeon IRE
13-06	Belize	W	4-0	Kingston	WCq	Peschisolido [39], Radzinski [55], McKenna [75], Brennan [83]	8 245	Batres GUA
16-06	Belize	W	4-0	Kingston	WCq	Radzinski [45], De Rosario 2 [63 73], Brennan [85]	5 124	Gordon TRI
18-08	Guatemala	L	0-2	Vancouver	WCq		6 725	Sibrian SLV
4-09	Honduras	D	1-1	Edmonton	WCq	De Vos [82]	9 654	Archundia MEX
8-09	Costa Rica	L	0-1	San Jose	WCq		13 000	Ramdhan TRI
9-10	Honduras	D	1-1	San Pedro Sula	WCq	Hutchinson [73]	42 000	Stott USA
13-10	Costa Rica	L	1-3	Vancouver	WCq	De Rosario [12]	4 728	Prendergast JAM
17-11	Guatemala	W	1-0	Guatemala City	WCq	De Rosario [57]	18 000	Rodriguez MEX
2005								
9-02	Northern Ireland	W	1-0	Belfast	Fr	Occean [31]	11 156	Attard MLT
26-03	Portugal	L	1-4	Barcelos	Fr	McKenna [85]	13 000	Ishchenko UKR
2-07	Honduras	L	1-2	Vancouver	Fr	McKenna [70]	4 105	Valenzuela USA
7-07	Costa Rica	L	0-1	Seattle	GCr1		15 831	Prendergast JAM
9-07	USA	L	0-2	Seattle	GCr1		15 109	Brizan TRI
12-07	Cuba	W	2-1	Foxboro	GCr1	Gerba [69], Hutchinson [87]	15 211	Moreno PAN
3-09	Spain	L	1-2	Santander	Fr	Grande [73]	11 978	Colombo FRA
16-11	Luxembourg	W	1-0	Hesperange	Fr	Hume [69]		Gomes Costa POR
2006								
22-01	USA	D	0-0	San Diego	Fr		6 077	Archundia MEX
1-03	Austria	W	2-0	Vienna	Fr	Brennan [65], Reda [71]	9 000	Van Egmond NED
4-09	Jamaica	W	1-0	Montreal	Fr	Friend [41]	6 526	Quesada CRC
8-10	Jamaica	L	1-2	Kingston	Fr	Radzinski [8]	5 000	Brizan TRI
15-11	Hungary	L	0-1	Szekesfehervar	Fr		6 000	Weiner GER
2007								
25-03	Bermuda	W	3-0	Hamilton	Fr	Hutchinson [25], Radzinski [30], Stalteri [44]		
1-06	Venezuela	D	2-2	Maracaibo	Fr	De Rosario [5], Gerba [85]		Lopez COL
6-06	Costa Rica	W	2-1	Miami	GCr1	Deguzman 2 [57 73]	17 420	Wingaarde SUR
9-06	Guadeloupe †	L	1-2	Miami	GCr1	Gerba [35]	22 529	Brizan TRI
11-06	Haiti	W	2-0	Miami	GCr1	De Rosario 2 [32 35p]	15 892	
16-06	Guatemala	W	3-0	Foxboro	GCqf	De Rosario [17], Gerba 2 [33 44]	22 412	Campbell JAM
21-06	USA	L	1-2	Chicago	GCsf	Hume [76]	50 760	Archundia MEX

Fr = Friendly match • GC = CONCACAF Gold Cup • WC = FIFA World Cup • † Not a full international
q = qualifier • r1 = first round group • qf = quarter-final • sf = semi-final

CANADA NATIONAL TEAM RECORDS AND RECORD SEQUENCES

Records			Sequence records					
Victory	7-0	USA 1904	Wins	6	2000	Clean sheets	5	1996
Defeat	0-8	MEX 1993	Defeats	9	1974-1976	Goals scored	10	1980-1983 & 1985
Player Caps	82	SAMUEL Randy	Undefeated	15	1999-2000	Without goal	5	1986 & 2000
Player Goals	19	CATLIFF & MITCHELL	Without win	12	1974-1976	Goals against	17	1988-1992

MAJOR CITIES/TOWNS

		Population '000
1	Toronto	4 670
2	Montreal	3 280
3	Vancouver	1 839
4	Calgary	991
5	Ottawa	885
6	Edmonton	831
7	Hamilton	661
8	Quebec	647
9	Winnipeg	632
10	Kitchener	414
11	London	348
12	St Catherines	320
13	Victoria	289
14	Windsor	281
15	Halifax	263
16	Oshawa	251
17	Saskatoon	199
18	Barrie	198
19	Regina	175
20	Abbotsford	157
21	Sherbrooke	129
22	Kelowna	129
23	Trois-Rivières	120
24	Guelph	117

CANADA

Capital	Ottawa	Language	English & French	Independence	1867
Population	33 098 932	Area	9 984 670 km²	Density 3 per km²	% in cities 77%
GDP per cap	$29 800	Dailling code	+1	Internet .ca	GMT + / - -3.5 / -8

CLUB DIRECTORY

Club	Town/City	Stadium	Capacity	www.	League
Montreal Impact	Montreal	Claude Robillard	14 000	impactmontreal.com	USL A-League
Toronto FC	Toronto	BMO Field	20 000	toronto.fc.mlsnet.com	MLS
Vancouver Whitecaps	Vancouver	Swangard, Burnaby	6 100	whitecapsfc.com	USL A-League

USA 2006
USL FIRST DIVISION (2)

	Pl	W	D	L	F	A	Pts
Montreal Impact ‡	28	14	9	5	31	15	51
Rochester Rhinos ‡	28	13	11	4	34	21	50
Charleston Battery ‡	28	13	7	8	33	25	46
Vancouver Whitecaps ‡	28	12	10	6	40	28	46
Miami FC ‡	28	11	6	11	47	44	39
Puerto Rico Islanders ‡	28	10	8	10	38	36	38
Seattle Sounders	28	11	4	13	42	48	37
Atlanta Silverbacks	28	10	5	13	36	42	35
Virginia Beach M'ners	28	8	8	12	26	37	32
Toronto Lynx	28	8	8	12	30	36	32
Portland Timbers	28	7	6	15	25	39	27
Minnesota Thunder	28	7	6	15	34	45	27

‡ Qualified for the play-offs

USL FIRST DIVISION PLAY-OFFS

Quarter–finals			Semi–finals			Final
Vancouver Whitecaps *	4	2				
Miami FC	1	0	**Vancouver Whitecaps ***	0	2	
			Montreal Impact	0	0	
Montral Impact	Bye					**Vancouver Whitecaps**
Charleston Battery *	2	1				Rochester Raging Rhinos *
Puerto Rico Islanders	2	0	Charleston Battery	0	0	PAETEC Park, Rochester
			Rochester Raging Rhinos *	1	0	30-09-2006, Att: 9547, Ref: Chapin
Rochester Raging Rhinos	Bye					Scorers - OG [45], Donatelli [55], Matondo [86] for Whitecaps

* Home team/home team in the first leg

CAY – CAYMAN ISLANDS

NATIONAL TEAM RECORD
JULY 10TH 2006 TO JULY 12TH 2010

PL	W	D	L	F	A	%
3	0	0	3	1	12	0

FIFA/COCA-COLA WORLD RANKING

1993	1994	1995	1996	1997	1998	1999	2000	2001	2002	2003	2004	2005	2006	High	Low
154	150	131	148	164	153	148	159	165	164	181	176	181	189	**127** 11/95	**191** 03/07

					2006–2007						
08/06	09/06	10/06	11/06	12/06	01/07	02/07	03/07	04/07	05/07	06/07	07/07
176	177	178	180	189	190	191	191	189	186	184	185

Not since 1998 has the Cayman Islands' national team qualified for the finals of the Caribbean Cup and there was no danger of that changing in the latest edition of the tournament. Drawn against Cuba, the Turks and Caicos Islands and the Bahamas, their first round qualifying group in Havana offered possibilities but all three matches were lost. In the 1990s the Caymans qualified for the finals four times and hosted the event in 1995, but on present form hosting the tournament again looks to be about the only feasible route back. This is a rich island which has the eighth highest GDP per capita in the world due the successful tourism industry and its position as one of the

INTERNATIONAL HONOURS
None

world's leading off-shore banking centres, but despite the efforts of the football association to improve standards, football is not high on the list of priorities. The Fosters League was won by Scholars International for the fourth time in seven seasons. They won the Western Zone of the regular season ahead of Latinos and both went on to win their semi-finals against the Eastern Zone winners George Town and East End United. It took penalties for Scholars to win the final against Latinos after the match had finished level at 2-2. Scholars had earlier beaten Tigers in the final of the Digicel Cup but it was Latinos who won the CIFA Cup at the end of the season.

THE FIFA BIG COUNT OF 2006

	Male	Female		Total
Number of players	3 400	300	Referees and Assistant Referees	100
Professionals	0		Admin, Coaches, Technical, Medical	200
Amateurs 18+	700		Number of clubs	10
Youth under 18	600		Number of teams	50
Unregistered	1 100		Clubs with women's teams	0
Total players	3 700		Players as % of population	8.14%

Cayman Islands Football Association (CIFA)
Truman Bodden Sports Complex, Olympic Way, Off Walkers Road, PO Box 178, GT, Grand Cayman, Cayman Islands
Tel +1 345 9495775   Fax +1 345 9457673
cifa@candw.ky   www.caymanfootball.ky
President: WEBB Jeffrey   General Secretary: BLAKE Bruce
Vice-President: FREDERICK David   Treasurer: WATSON Canover   Media Officer: MORGAN Kenisha
Men's Coach: TBD   Women's Coach: CUNHA Thiago
CIFA formed: 1966   CONCACAF: 1993   FIFA: 1992
Red shirts, Blue shorts, White socks or White shirts, White shorts, Red socks

RECENT INTERNATIONAL MATCHES PLAYED BY THE CAYMAN ISLANDS

2002	Opponents	Score		Venue		Scorers	Att.	Referee
17-11	Nicaragua	L	0-1	Grand Cayman	Fr			
27-11	Cuba	L	0-5	Grand Cayman	CCq			Prendergast JAM
29-11	Dominican Republic	W	1-0	Grand Cayman	CCq	Forbes [27]		Grant HAI
1-12	Martinique	L	0-3	Grand Cayman	CCq			Prendergast JAM
2003								
No international matches played in 2003								
2004								
22-02	Cuba	L	1-2	Grand Cayman	WCq	Elliot [72]	1 789	Sibrian SLV
27-03	Cuba	L	0-3	Havana	WCq		3 500	Rodriguez MEX
24-11	Bermuda	L	1-2	Kingstown	CCq	Berry [48]	200	Matthew SKN
26-11	British Virgin Islands	W	1-0	Kingstown	CCq	Whittaker [49]		
28-11	St Vincent/Grenadines	L	0-4	Kingstown	CCq		850	Prendergast JAM
2005								
No international matches played in 2005								
2006								
2-09	Bahamas	L	1-3	Havana	CCq	Whittaker [76]		Stewart JAM
4-09	Turks & Caicos Isl	L	0-2	Havana	CCq		100	Stennett JAM
6-09	Cuba	L	0-7	Havana	CCq		120	Stewart JAM
2007								
No international matches played in 2007 before August								

Fr = Friendly match • CC = Digicel Caribbean Cup • WC = FIFA World Cup • q = qualifier

CAYMAN ISLANDS NATIONAL TEAM RECORDS AND RECORD SEQUENCES

Records			Sequence records					
Victory	5-0	VGB 1994	Wins	3	1994	Clean sheets	2	1994, 1995
Defeat	2-9	TRI 1995	Defeats	8	1991-1993	Goals scored	5	1993-94, 2000
Player Caps	n/a		Undefeated	4	1994-1995	Without goal	5	2000
Player Goals	n/a		Without win	9	1991-93, 1995-98	Goals against	10	1991-1993

RECENT LEAGUE AND CUP RECORD

	Championship				Cup		
Year	Champions	Score	Runners-up		Winners	Score	Runners-up
2001	Scholars International	†	George Town		Bodden Town		
2002	George Town	2-1	Future		George Town	4-0	Scholars International
2003	Scholars International	3-1	Sunset		Scholars International	2-1	Bodden Town
2004	Latinos	3-2	Scholars International		Latinos	2-1	George Town
2005	Western Union	0-0 3-2p	Scholars International		Western Union	2-0	Scholars International
2006	Scholars International	2-1	George Town		Scholars International	2-0	Money Express
2007	Scholars International	2-2 6-5p	Latinos		Latinos	3-0	Elite

† Played on a league system

CAYMAN ISLANDS COUNTRY INFORMATION

Capital	George Town	Independence		GDP per Capita	$35 000
Population	43 103	Status	British Crown Colony	GNP Ranking	n/a
Area km²	262	Language	English	Dialling code	+1 345
Population density	164 per km²	Literacy rate	98%	Internet code	.ky
% in urban areas	%	Main religion	Christian	GMT +/–	-5
Towns/Cities ('000)	George Town 27; West Bay 10; Bodden Town 6; East End 1; North Side 1				
Neighbours (km)	The Cayman Islands consist of three islands in the Caribbean Sea				
Main stadia	Truman Boden – George Town 7 000; ED Bush – West Bay 2 500				

CGO – CONGO

NATIONAL TEAM RECORD
JULY 10TH 2006 TO JULY 12TH 2010

PL	W	D	L	F	A	%
12	5	5	2	15	11	62.5

FIFA/COCA-COLA WORLD RANKING

1993	1994	1995	1996	1997	1998	1999	2000	2001	2002	2003	2004	2005	2006	High		Low	
103	114	119	100	101	112	94	86	94	97	108	117	110	89	79	04/07	139	04/96

2006–2007											
08/06	09/06	10/06	11/06	12/06	01/07	02/07	03/07	04/07	05/07	06/07	07/07
109	100	92	91	89	89	93	93	79	81	87	96

Congo's focus over the last 12 months has been at junior level, with the country hosting and winning the African youth championship and then participating at the FIFA U–20 World Cup in Canada. Under French coach Eddie Hudanski, and with the assistance of French club AJ Auxerre, Congo's under–20 side spent over a year in residential camp, traveling widely to countries like France and South Africa in preparation for the tournament in March 2007. Despite the pressure of high expectation, the team dramatically marched through the tournament, overcoming an early loss to Gambia, to win a first-ever continental title at junior level with a 1-0 triumph over Nigeria in the

INTERNATIONAL HONOURS
CAF African Cup of Nations 1972   African Games 1965   African Youth Championship 2007   CAF Champions League CARA Brazzaville 1974

final. Scorer Francel Ibara was the hero of the side and was quickly snapped up by Auxerre. Hudanski's team made it past the first stage in Canada but then ran into Mexico in the round of 16 and were eliminated 3-0. At senior level, the 'Diables Noires' made a positive start to their 2008 African Nations Cup qualifying campaign but coach Noel Tosi quit in March 2007, citing overt interference from officials. That saw Gaston Tchiangana return at the helm but he was replaced by veteran Frenchman Robert Corfu, for their qualifier at home to South Africa in June. That ended in a draw and effectively put paid to their hopes of making it to the finals in Ghana.

THE FIFA BIG COUNT OF 2006

	Male	Female		Total
Number of players	191 600	8 610	Referees and Assistant Referees	504
Professionals	0		Admin, Coaches, Technical, Medical	595
Amateurs 18+	5 410		Number of clubs	90
Youth under 18	3 650		Number of teams	320
Unregistered	35 150		Clubs with women's teams	0
Total players	200 210		Players as % of population	5.41%

Fédération Congolaise de Football (FECOFOOT)
80 Rue Eugene Etienne, Centre Ville Brazzaville, Case postale 11, Brazzaville, Congo
Tel +242 811563   Fax +242 812524
fecofoot@yahoo.fr   www.none
President: IBOVI Antoine   General Secretary: YOULOU Bakith
Vice-President: BAKALA Thomas   Treasurer: NDENGUET Lylian   Media Officer: BAKANDILA Joseph
Men's Coach: CORFU Robert   Women's Coach: KAYA Gilbert
FECOFOOT formed: 1962   CAF: 1966   FIFA: 1962
Green shirts, Yellow shorts, Red socks

RECENT INTERNATIONAL MATCHES PLAYED BY CONGO

2002	Opponents		Score	Venue	Comp	Scorers	Att	Referee
8-09	Burkina Faso	D	0-0	Brazzaville	CNq		60 000	Itur KEN
13-10	Mozambique	W	3-0	Maputo	CNq	Tsoumou [49], Nguie [70], Bakouma [73]		Lwanja MWI
2003								
9-03	Congo DR	L	0-3	Kinshasa	Fr			
4-05	Central African Rep.	W	2-1	Brazzaville	CNq	Embingou [6], Owolo [52]		
8-06	Central African Rep.	D	0-0	Bangui	CNq			Hissene CHA
21-06	Burkina Faso	L	0-3	Ouagadougou	CNq		36 000	Mana NGA
6-07	Mozambique	D	0-0	Brazzaville	CNq			
12-10	Sierra Leone	W	1-0	Brazzaville	WCq	Mvoubi [89p]	4 800	Mana NGA
16-11	Sierra Leone	D	1-1	Freetown	WCq	Nguie [67]	20 000	Monteiro Lopez CPV
5-12	Gabon	W	3-2	Brazzaville	CMr1	Ayessa [25], Ndey [56], Beaulia [67]		Tchoumba CMR
9-12	Gabon	D	1-1	Brazzaville	CMr1	Ayessa [56]		
10-12	Cameroon	L	0-2	Brazzaville	CMsf			Mbera GAB
13-12	Gabon	W	1-0	Brazzaville	CM3p			
2004								
5-06	Senegal	L	0-2	Dakar	WCq		18 000	Benouza ALG
20-06	Liberia	W	3-0	Brazzaville	WCq	Bouanga [52], Mamouna-Ossila [55], Batota [66]	25 000	Lemghambodj MTN
4-07	Mali	W	1-0	Brazzaville	WCq	Mamouna-Ossila [30]	20 000	Evehe CMR
5-09	Togo	L	0-2	Lome	WCq		20 000	Mbera GAB
10-10	Zambia	L	2-3	Brazzaville	WCq	Bouanga [75], Mamouna-Ossila [81]	20 000	Yacoubi TUN
2005								
5-02	Central African Rep.	W	1-0	Libreville	CMr1	Bhebey [10]		
8-02	Gabon	L	0-1	Libreville	CMr1			
12-02	Gabon	L	1-2	Libreville	CM3p	Lakou [35]		
22-02	Angola	L	0-2	Brazzaville	Fr			
19-03	Gabon	D	0-0	Libreville	Fr			
26-03	Zambia	L	0-2	Chililabombwe	WCq		20 000	Maillet SEY
5-06	Senegal	D	0-0	Brazzaville	WCq		40 000	Damon RSA
19-06	Liberia	W	2-0	Paynesville	WCq	Bhebey 2 [3 73]	5 000	Sillah GAM
3-09	Mali	L	0-2	Bamako	WCq		10 000	Mbera GAB
8-10	Togo	L	2-3	Brazzaville	WCq	Bouity [26], Mamouna-Ossila [56]	20 000	Shelmany LBY
2006								
4-03	Equatorial Guinea	L	1-2	Bata	CMr1			
8-03	Chad	D	0-0	Bata	CMr1			
2-09	South Africa	D	0-0	Joheannesburg	CNq			Aboubacar CIV
8-10	Chad	W	3-1	Brazzaville	CNq	Abdoulaye Bruce [17], Malonga [30], Nguessi [46]		Djaoupe TOG
14-11	Mali	L	0-1	La Courneuve	Fr			
2007								
5-03	Equatorial Guinea	W	2-1	N'Djamena	CMr1	Likibi [81], Ngoua [94+]		
7-03	Gabon	D	2-2	N'Djamena	CMr1	Lepaye 2 [27 44]		
12-03	Central African Rep	W	4-1	N'Djamena	CMsf	Lepaye [4], Likibi 2 [28 84], Beaulia [47]		
16-03	Gabon	W	1-0	N'Djamena	CMf	Papou [59]		
25-03	Zambia	D	0-0	Brazzaville	CNq			Coulibaly MLI
4-04	Angola	D	0-0	Cabinda	Fr			
28-05	Congo DR	W	2-1	Brazzaville	Fr	Minga [35], De Bouisson [55p]		
2-06	Zambia	L	0-3	Chililabombwe	CNq			
17-06	South Africa	D	1-1	Pointe-Noire	CNq	Bantsimba [64]		

Fr = Friendly match • CN = African Cup of Nations • CM = CEMAC Cup • WC = FIFA World Cup
q = qualifier • r1 = first round group • sf = semi-final • 3p = third place play-off

CONGO NATIONAL TEAM RECORDS AND RECORD SEQUENCES

Records			Sequence records					
Victory	11-0	STP 1976	Wins	5	1983	Clean sheets	4	1983, 1998-1999
Defeat	1-8	MAD 1960	Defeats	5	1968, 1973, 1993	Goals scored	11	1975-1977
Player Caps	n/a		Undefeated	8	1963-1965	Without goal	7	1992-1993
Player Goals	n/a		Without win	9	2001-2002	Goals against	14	1965-1968

CONGO COUNTRY INFORMATION

Capital	Brazzaville	Independence	1960 from France	GDP per Capita	$700
Population	2 998 040	Status	Republic	GNP Ranking	137
Area km²	342 000	Language	French	Dialling code	+242
Population density	8 per km²	Literacy rate	77%	Internet code	.cg
% in urban areas	59%	Main religion	Christian 50%	GMT + / –	+1
Towns/Cities ('000)	Brazzaville 1 115; Pointe-Noire 628; Loubomo 70; Nkayi 70; Loandjili 26; Madingou 22				
Neighbours (km)	Central African Republic 467; Congo DR 2 410; Angola 201; Gabon 1 903; Cameroon 523; Atlantic Ocean 169				
Main stadia	Stade de la Révolution – Brazzaville 50 000				

CHAMPIONNAT NATIONALE 2006

Quarter–finals		Semi–finals		Final	
Etoile du Congo	2				
CARA Brazzaville	1	**Etoile du Congo**	3		
		JS Bougainvillées	1		
JS Bougainvillées				**Etoile du Congo**	1
Patronage St Anne	3			La Mancha	0
JS Talangaï	0	Patronage St Anne	1		
Diables Noirs	1 1p	**La Mancha**	3	Massamba-Débat, Brazzaville
La Mancha	1 3p			12-09-2006
				Scorer - Eder Lébali [18] for Etoile	

COUPE DU CONGO 2006

Quarter–finals		Semi–finals		Final	
Etoile du Congo	1 5				
Inter Club	2 0	**Etoile du Congo**	1 1		
Jambon	1 1	St Michel Ouenzé	1 0		
St Michel Ouenzé	4 3			**Etoile du Congo**	2
Abeilles	0 1 4p			JS Talangaï	1
Diables Noirs	1 0 2p	Abeilles	1 0		
Vita Club Pointe-Noire	1 0	**JS Talangaï**	0 4	Dolisie
JS Talangaï	0 2			15-08-2006	

RECENT LEAGUE AND CUP RECORD

	Championship				Cup		
Year	Champions	Score	Runners-up		Winners	Score	Runners-up
1994	Etoile du Congo	2-0	Inter Club		EPB Pointe Noire		Inter Club
1995	AS Cheminots	1-0	Patronage Sainte Anne		Etoile du Congo	1-0	Inter Club
1996	Munisport				Vita Club Mokanda		
1997	Munisport				Tournament not played		
1998	Vita Club Mokanda	1-0	Etoile du Congo		Tournament not played		
1999	Vita Club Mokanda				Tournament not played		
2000	Etoile du Congo	†			Etoile du Congo	5-1	Vita Club Mokanda
2001	Etoile du Congo	1-0	La Mancha		AS Police	1-0	Etoile du Congo
2002	AS Police	2-1	Etoile du Congo		Etoile du Congo	2-1	FC Abeilles
2003	St Michel Ouenzé	0-0	La Mancha		Diables Noirs	0-0 3-2p	Vita Club Mokanda
2004	Diables Noirs	2-1	AS Police		Munisport	0-0 3-0p	Vita Club Mokanda
2005	Final abandoned. Neither St Michel nor Diables Noirs awarded title				Diables Noirs	1-1 4-2p	Patronage Sainte Anne
2006	Etoile du Congo	1-0	La Mancha		Etoile du Congo	2-1	JS Talangaï

† Played on a league system

CHA – CHAD

NATIONAL TEAM RECORD
JULY 10TH 2006 TO JULY 12TH 2010

PL	W	D	L	F	A	%
10	4	1	5	12	18	45

FIFA/COCA-COLA WORLD RANKING

1993	1994	1995	1996	1997	1998	1999	2000	2001	2002	2003	2004	2005	2006	High		Low	
166	175	180	188	184	178	166	163	176	173	152	168	159	142	**128**	07/06	190	09/97

2006–2007											
08/06	09/06	10/06	11/06	12/06	01/07	02/07	03/07	04/07	05/07	06/07	07/07
130	132	142	140	142	141	144	135	134	133	141	139

At first sight, Chad's record of four defeats in their first five qualifying matches for the 2008 African Nations Cup might seem disastrous but the point they picked-up in Zambia in June 2007 was their first ever away from home in the Nations Cup. Chad's 'Sao', the name carried by the national team in honour of the country's ancient inhabitants, hadn't won a point on the road in a FIFA World Cup qualifier either so the 1-1 draw in Chililabombwe, on Zambia's northern Copper Belt, represented an historic first. The reality remains, however, that the country is still one of the few whipping boys left in African football and they lost all their other qualifying games, finishing

INTERNATIONAL HONOURS
None

bottom of their group. The international experience will have come as a boost to a team who are little more than well meaning amateurs although by their standards, they did have a busy international year. In March 2007, Chad's capital N'Djamena hosted the regional CEMAC Cup for the first time and after beating Cameroon and Benin, Chad made it through to the semi-finals before losing to Gabon. The Central African Republic were beaten in a play-off as the team took third place for the second year in a row. There was a notable success in club competition when AS Coton Tchad beat Libyan opposition to get past the opening round of the African Confederation Cup.

THE FIFA BIG COUNT OF 2006

	Male	Female		Total
Number of players	408 740	21 010	Referees and Assistant Referees	427
Professionals	0		Admin, Coaches, Technical, Medical	1 855
Amateurs 18+	3 610		Number of clubs	50
Youth under 18	2 140		Number of teams	148
Unregistered	53 000		Clubs with women's teams	0
Total players	429 750		Players as % of population	4.32

Fédération Tchadienne de Football (FTF)
Case postale 886, N'Djamena, Chad
Tel +235 518740   Fax +235 523806
ftfa@intnet.td   www.none
President: MAHAMAT Saleh Issa   General Secretary: RAMADANE Daouda
Vice-President: BANAYE Hisseine   Treasurer: RAMADANE Daouda   Media Officer: ZOUTANE DABA Martin
Men's Coach: NATOLTIGA Okalan   Women's Coach: None
FTF formed: 1962   CAF: 1962   FIFA: 1988
Blue shirts, Yellow shorts, Red socks

RECENT INTERNATIONAL MATCHES PLAYED BY CHAD

2003	Opponents	Score		Venue	Comp	Scorers	Att	Referee
12-10	Angola	W	3-1	N'Djamena	WCq	Oumar 3 [53 74 83]	30 000	Nahi CIV
16-11	Angola	L	0-2	Luanda	WCq		30 000	Buenkadila COD
2004								
No international matches played in 2004								
2005								
8-02	Equatorial Guinea	D	0-0	Libreville	CMr1			
10-02	Gabon	W	3-2	Libreville	CMsf	Djenet [3], Doumbé [8], Nguembaye [56]		
22-05	Sudan	L	1-4	Khartoum	Fr			
27-05	Sudan	D	1-1	Khartoum	Fr			
2006								
6-03	Equatorial Guinea	D	1-1	Bata	CMr1			
8-03	Congo	D	0-0	Bata	CMr1			
11-03	Cameroon †	L	0-1	Bata	CMsf			
14-03	Gabon	D	2-2	Bata	CM3p	Mahamat [20p], Doumbé [52]		
3-09	Zambia	L	0-2	N'Djamena	CNq			Shelmani LBY
8-10	Congo	L	1-3	Brazzaville	CNq	Missdongarle Betolinga [89]		Djaoupe TOG
2007								
22-02	Benin	W	1-0	Cotonou	Fr	Mahamat [53]		
4-03	Cameroon	W	2-1	N'Djamena	CMr1			
6-03	Central African Rep	W	3-2	N'Djamena	CMr1	Ndouassel [60p], Missdongarle Betolinga [61], Mahamat [89]		
11-03	Gabon	L	1-2	N'Djamena	CMsf	Kedigui [70]		
16-03	Central African Rep	W	1-0	N'Djamena	CM3p	Medego [95]		
24-03	South Africa	L	0-3	N'Djamena	CNq			Aguidissou BEN
2-06	South Africa	L	0-4	Durban	CNq			
16-06	Zambia	D	1-1	Chililabombwe	CNq	Kedigui [13]		

Fr = Friendly match • CN = African Cup of Nations • CM = CEMAC Cup • WC = FIFA World Cup
q = qualifier • r1 = first round group • sf = semi-final • 3p = third place play-off • † Not an official international

CHAD NATIONAL TEAM RECORDS AND RECORD SEQUENCES

Records			Sequence records					
Victory	5-0	STP 1976	Wins	3	1999, 2007	Clean sheets	2	1986, 1999
Defeat	2-6	BEN 1963	Defeats	7	1991-1997	Goals scored	6	2006-2007
Player Caps	n/a		Undefeated	4	1984-85, 2005-06	Without goal	5	1992-1997
Player Goals	n/a		Without win	12	1976-86, 1991-99	Goals against	9	1978-86, 1991-98

RECENT LEAGUE RECORD

Year	Champions
1996	AS Coton Chad
1997	Tourbillon
1998	AS Coton Chad
1999	Renaissance
2000	Tourbillon
2001	Tourbillon
2002	No tournament
2003	No tournament
2004	Renaissance
2005	Renaissance
2006	Renaissance

CHAD COUNTRY INFORMATION

Capital	N'Djamena	Independence	1960 from France	GDP per Capita	$1 200
Population	9 538 544	Status	Republic	GNP Ranking	145
Area km²	1 284 000	Language	French, Arabic	Dialling code	+235
Population density	7 per km²	Literacy rate	47%	Internet code	.td
% in urban areas	21%	Main religion	Muslim 51%, Christian 35%	GMT +/−	+1
Towns/Cities ('000)	N'Djamena 721; Moundou 135; Sarh 102; Abeche 74; Kelo 42; Koumra 36; Pala 35				
Neighbours (km)	Libya 1 055; Sudan 1 360; Central African Republic 1 197; Cameroon 1 094; Nigeria 87; Niger 1 175				
Main stadia	Stade National – N'Djamena 30 000				

CHI – CHILE

NATIONAL TEAM RECORD
JULY 10TH 2006 TO JULY 12TH 2010

PL	W	D	L	F	A	%
17	8	4	5	20	24	58.8

FIFA/COCA-COLA WORLD RANKING

1993	1994	1995	1996	1997	1998	1999	2000	2001	2002	2003	2004	2005	2006	High		Low	
55	47	36	26	16	16	23	19	39	84	80	74	64	41	**8**	04/98	**84**	12/02

					2006–2007						
08/06	09/06	10/06	11/06	12/06	01/07	02/07	03/07	04/07	05/07	06/07	07/07
44	45	44	42	41	40	34	32	37	43	53	47

After missing out on the past two World Cups, confidence is growing in Chile that the national team can once again become a potent force on the continent. Much of this hope is based on the talented crop of youngsters coming through the ranks and that was shown at the FIFA U–20 World Cup in Canada where Chile finished in third place, their joint-highest finish in a FIFA tournament. At the 2007 Copa América in Venezuela, the senior team started well by beating Ecuador but that was the only game they won. They did make it through to the quarter-finals, however, courtesy of a 0-0 draw against Mexico where they faced Brazil who had already beaten them 3-0. This time

INTERNATIONAL HONOURS
Qualified for the FIFA World Cup™ 1930 1950 1962 1966 1974 1982 1998   **Copa Libertadores** Colo Colo 1991

the score was 6-1. At home Colo Colo powered to a hat-trick of League titles, inspired by South American footballer of the year Matias Fernandez. His form earned him a move to Villarreal at the end of the Clausura in which Colo Colo beat Audax Italiano 6-2 on aggregate in the final. Colo Colo also reached the final of the 2006 Copa Sudamericana - the first club from Chile to reach a South American final for 13 years - but having done the hard work by drawing with Pachuca away from home in Mexico, they then surprisingly lost 2-1 at home. Coached by Argentina's Claudio Borghi, Colo Colo completed their League hat-trick by winning the 2007 Apertura.

THE FIFA BIG COUNT OF 2006

	Male	Female		Total
Number of players	2 469 837	138 500	Referees and Assistant Referees	5 204
Professionals	637		Admin, Coaches, Technical, Medical	21 170
Amateurs 18+	138 200		Number of clubs	5 715
Youth under 18	326 500		Number of teams	31 228
Unregistered	2 010 000		Clubs with women's teams	47
Total players	2 608 337		Players as % of population	16.17%

Federación de Fútbol de Chile (FFCH)
Avenida Quilin No. 5635, Comuna Peñalolén, Casilla No. 3733, Central de Casillas, Santiago de Chile, Chile
Tel +56 2 8101800   Fax +56 2 2843510
ffch@anfpchile.cl   www.anfp.cl
President: MAYNE-NICHOLLS Harold   General Secretary: CONTADOR Jorge
Vice-President: JELVEZ Sergio   Treasurer: OLIVARES Claudio   Media Officer: OLMEDO Claudio
Men's Coach: ACOSTA Nelson   Women's Coach: RUBIO Nibaldo
FFCH formed: 1895   CONMEBOL: 1916   FIFA: 1913
Red shirts with blue and white trimmings, Blue shorts, White socks or White shirts, White shorts, Blue socks

RECENT INTERNATIONAL MATCHES PLAYED BY CHILE

2004 Opponents	Score	Venue	Comp	Scorers	Att	Referee
18-02 Mexico	D 1-1	Carson	Fr	Navia [46]	20 173	Cruz USA
30-03 Bolivia	W 2-0	La Paz	WCq	Villarroel [38], Gonzalez.M [60]	42 000	Martin ARG
28-04 Peru	D 1-1	Antofagasta	Fr	Fuentes [56]	23 000	Amarilla PAR
1-06 Venezuela	W 1-0	San Cristobal	WCq	Pinilla [84]	30 000	Torres PAR
6-06 Brazil	D 1-1	Santiago	WCq	Navia [89p]	65 000	Elizondo ARG
8-07 Brazil	L 0-1	Arequipa	CАr1		35 000	Rodriguez MEX
11-07 Paraguay	D 1-1	Arequipa	CАr1	Gonzalez.S [71]	35 000	Mendez URU
14-07 Costa Rica	L 1-2	Tacna	CАr1	Olarra [40]	20 000	Ortube BOL
5-09 Colombia	D 0-0	Santiago	WCq		62 523	Souza BRA
10-10 Ecuador	L 0-2	Quito	WCq		27 956	Ortube BOL
13-10 Argentina	D 0-0	Santiago	WCq		57 671	Amarilla PAR
17-11 Peru	L 1-2	Lima	WCq	Gonzalez.S [91+]	39 752	Baldassi ARG
2005						
9-02 Ecuador	W 3-0	Vina del Mar	Fr	Maldonado [25], Gonzalez.M [35], Pinilla [83]	15 000	Favale ARG
26-03 Uruguay	D 1-1	Santiago	WCq	Mirosevic [47]	55 000	Ruiz COL
30-03 Paraguay	L 1-2	Asuncion	WCq	Pinilla [72]	10 000	Elizondo ARG
4-06 Bolivia	W 3-1	Santiago	WCq	Fuentes 2 [8 34], Salas [66]	46 729	Rezende BRA
8-06 Venezuela	W 2-1	Santiago	WCq	Jimenez 2 [31 60]	35 506	Torres PAR
17-08 Peru	L 1-3	Tachna	Fr	Fuentes [37]		Ortube BOL
4-09 Brazil	L 0-5	Brasilia	WCq		39 000	Amarilla PAR
8-10 Colombia	D 1-1	Barranquilla	WCq	Rojas [64]	22 380	Souza BRA
12-10 Ecuador	D 0-0	Santiago	WCq		49 350	Elizondo ARG
2006						
25-04 New Zealand	W 4-1	Rancagua	Fr	Suazo [36], OG [39], Roco [61], Rubio [67]	8 000	Osorio CHI
27-04 New Zealand	W 1-0	La Calera	Fr	Rubio [35]		Acosta CHI
24-05 Republic of Ireland	W 1-0	Dublin	Fr	Iturra [49]	41 200	Ingvarsson SWE
30-05 Côte d'Ivoire	D 1-1	Vittel	Fr	Suazo [77p]		Lamarre FRA
2-06 Sweden	D 1-1	Stockholm	Fr	Suazo [51]	34 735	Stark GER
16-08 Colombia	L 1-2	Santiago	Fr	Suazo [82p]	15 000	Larrionda URU
7-10 Peru	W 3-2	Viña del Mar	Fr	Fernandez.M 2 [28 49], Navia [70]		Vieira URU
11-10 Peru	W 1-0	Tacna	Fr	Navia [24]	12 000	Haro ECU
15-11 Paraguay	W 3-2	Viña del Mar	Fr	Ponce [39], Valdivia [50], Figueroa [62p]	9 000	Baldassi ARG
2007						
7-02 Venezuela	W 1-0	Maracaibo	Fr	Fernandez.M [43]	9 000	Buitrago COL
24-03 Brazil	L 0-4	Gothenburg	Fr		30 122	Berntsen NOR
28-03 Costa Rica	D 1-1	Talca	Fr	Fonseca [60]	8 000	Ortube BOL
18-04 Argentina	D 0-0	Mendoza	Fr		38 000	Vazquez URU
9-05 Cuba	W 3-0	Osorno	Fr	Gutierrez.R [5], Rojas.J [27], Flores.L [89]	1 800	Cabrera URU
16-05 Cuba	W 2-0	Temuco	Fr	Gutierrez.R [40], Gonzalez.D [71]	3 500	Grance PAR
23-05 Haiti	D 0-0	Port-au-Prince	Fr		12 000	Edouard HAI
2-06 Costa Rica	L 0-2	San Jose	Fr		25 000	Glower MEX
5-06 Jamaica	W 1-0	Kingston	Fr	Lorca [19]	15 000	Guerrero NCA
27-06 Ecuador	W 3-2	Puerto Ordaz	CАr1	Suazo 2 [20 80], Villanueva [86]	35 000	Ruiz COL
1-07 Brazil	L 0-3	Maturin	CАr1		42 000	Torres PAR
4-07 Mexico	D 0-0	Puerto La Cruz	CАr1		30 000	Amarilla PAR
7-07 Brazil	L 1-6	Puerto La Cruz	CАqf	Suazo [76]	25 000	Larrionda URU

Fr = Friendly match • CA = Copa América • WC = FIFA World Cup • q = qualifier • r1 = first round group

CHILE NATIONAL TEAM RECORDS AND RECORD SEQUENCES

Records			Sequence records					
Victory	7-0	VEN 1979	Wins	5	1950-1952	Clean sheets	8	1983-1985
Defeat	0-7	BRA 1959	Defeats	10	1922-1924	Goals scored	18	1995-1997
Player Caps	84	SANCHEZ Leonel	Undefeated	10	1995-1996	Without goal	4	Three times
Player Goals	35	SALAS Marcelo	Without win	33	1910-1924	Goals against	41	1910-1928

REPUBLIC OF CHILE; REPUBLICA DE CHILE

Capital	Santiago	Language	Spanish			Independence	1818
Population	16 134 219	Area	756 950 km²	Density	20 per km²	% in cities	84%
GDP per cap	$9 900	Dailling code	+56	Internet	.cl	GMT + / -	-4

MEDALS TABLE

		Overall			League			Cup		Sth Am			City	Stadium	Cap'ty	DoF
		G	S	B	G	S	B	G	S	G	S	B				
1	Colo Colo	37	21	20	26	15	15	10	4	1	2	5	Santiago	Monumental	62 500	1925
2	Universidad de Chile	15	8	16	12	8	13	3				3	Santiago	Nacional	77 000	1911
3	Universidad Catolica	12	23	9	9	15	4	3	7	1		5	Santiago	San Carlos	20 000	1937
4	Cobreloa	9	12	6	8	7	5	1	3	2		1	Calama	Municipal	20 180	1977
5	Union Española	8	10	6	6	7	5	2	2	1		1	Santiago	Santa Laura	25 000	1909
6	Santiago Wanderers	5	5	2	3	3	2	2	2				Valparaíso	Playa Ancha	19 000	1892
7	Audax Italiano	4	10	8	4	8	8		2				Santiago	Municipal La Florida	8 500	1910
8	Palestino	4	4	3	2	3	2	2	1			1	Santiago	La Cisterna	12 000	1920
9	Magallanes	4	4	2	4	4	2						Santiago	Santiago Bueras	8 000	1897
10	Everton	4	2		3	2		1					Viña del Mar	Sausalito	18 037	1909
11	Santiago Morning	1	3	1	1	2	1		1			1	Santiago	Santiago Bueras	8 000	1936
12	Cobresal	1	2		2			1					El Salvador	El Cobre	20 752	1979
13	Deportes La Serena	1	1	2		2		1	1				La Serena	La Portada	18 000	1955
14	Temuco	1	2		1	2							Temuco	Municipal	28 000	1916
15	Huachipato	1		1	1		1						Talcahuano	Las Higueras	10 000	1947
	Deportes Iquique	1		1		1	1						Iquique	Terra de Campeones	10 000	1978

RECENT LEAGUE AND CUP RECORD (2000–2001)

	Championship								Cup		
Year	Champions	Pts	Runners-up	Pts	Third	Pts		Winners	Score	Runners-up	
2000	Univ. de Chile	61	Cobreloa	52	Colo Colo	49		Univ. de Chile	2-1	Santiago Morning	
2001	Santiago Wanderers	66	Univ. Católica	60	Univ. de Chile	57		Tournament discontinued			

RECENT LEAGUE RECORD (2002-2006)

	Apertura				Clausura		
Year	Champions	Score	Runners-up		Winners	Score	Runners-up
2002	Univ. Católica	1-1 4-0	Rangers		Colo Colo	2-0 3-2	Univ. Católica
2003	Cobreloa	0-0 4-0	Colo Colo		Cobreloa	2-2 2-1	Colo Colo
2004	Univ. de Chile	0-0 1-1 4-2p	Cobreloa		Cobreloa	3-1 0-0	Unión Española
2005	Unión Española	1-0 3-2	Coquimbo Unido		Univ. Católica	1-0 1-2 5-4p	Univ. de Chile
2006	Colo Colo	2-1 0-1 4-2p	Univ. de Chile		Colo Colo	3-0 3-2	Audax Italiano

RECENT LEAGUE AND CUP RECORD (FROM 2007)

	Apertura						Clausura				
Year	Champions	Pts	Runners-up	Pts	Third	Pts	Champions	Pts	Runners-up	Pts	Third	Pts
2007	Colo Colo	47	Univ. Católica	46	Audax Italiano	44					

CHILE 2006
PRIMERA DIVISION CLAUSURA

Grupo 1	Pl	W	D	L	F	A	Pts
Cobreloa †	18	11	4	3	40	24	37
Colo Colo †	18	8	5	5	37	31	29
Santiago Wanderers †	18	8	4	6	22	21	28
Palestino	18	5	5	8	16	25	20
Cobresal	18	5	3	10	20	28	18

Grupo 2	Pl	W	D	L	F	A	Pts
O'Higgins †	18	10	5	3	31	20	35
Coquimbo Unido †	18	8	5	5	23	22	29
Rangers	18	6	6	6	22	24	24
Huachipato	18	6	2	10	29	32	20
Unión Española	18	3	5	10	20	34	14

Grupo 3	Pl	W	D	L	F	A	Pts
Puerto Montt †	18	10	3	5	26	21	33
Audax Italiano †	18	9	2	7	32	24	29
Univ. Concepción	18	7	4	7	34	30	25
La Serena	18	4	6	8	32	39	18
Santiago Morning	18	4	5	9	22	32	17

Grupo 4	Pl	W	D	L	F	A	Pts
Univ. Católica †	18	9	4	5	24	18	31
Univ. de Chile †	18	7	2	9	24	25	23
Antofagasta	18	5	6	7	25	25	21
Everton	18	5	6	7	23	27	21
Dep. Concepción				Withdrew			

† Qualified for the play-offs • † Qualified for the repechaje

See *Almanack of World Football 2007* for tables and play-off
results for the 2006 Apertura

CLAUSURA PLAY-OFFS 2006

Repechaje

Santiago Wand.   0-1   **Univ. de Chile**

Quarter–finals	Semi–finals	Final
Colo Colo *	1 4				
Puerto Montt	0 0	**Colo Colo ***	3 3		
Univ. de Chile *	1 1	Cobreloa	0 3		
Cobreloa	0 3			**Colo Colo ***	3 3
O'Higgins	0 2			Audax Italiano	0 2
Coquimbo Unido*	0 1	O'Higgins	1 4		
Univ. Católica	0 0	**Audax Italiano ***	4 2		
Audax Italiano *	1 3				

* At home in the first leg • Colo Colo won the Apertura and qualified for the
Copa Libertadores 2007 • Audax Italiano and Cobreloa also qualified. Audax had
a better overall record than Univ. de Chile, the Apertura runners-up, while
Cobreloa had the best regular season record in the Clausura
Top Apertura scorers: Leonardo MONJE, Univ. Concepción 17; Humberto SUAZO,
Colo Colo 15; Matías FERNANDEZ, Colo Colo 15; Carlos VILLANEUVA, Audax 12;
Lucas BARRIOS, Cobreloa 12

RELEGATION PLAY-OFFS 2006

Home team first leg	Scores	Home team second leg
Fernández Vial	1-3 0-1	**Palestino**
Rangers	2-1 1-2 3-4p	**Lota Schwager**

Santiago Morning and Deportes Concepción were automatically relegat-
ed with the worst overall record in 2006. Deportes Melipilla and
Nublense were promoted automatically. Rangers, Palestino, Lota
Schwager and Fernández Vial entered the play-offs

CHILE 2006
PRIMERA DIVISION AGGREGATE TABLE

	Pl	W	D	L	F	A	Pts	Colo Colo	Cobreloa	U. Católica	Audax	U. Concepción	U. de Chile	Huachipato	O'Higgins	Puerto Montt	Coquimbo	Wanderers	Antofagasta	Un. Española	Everton	La Serena	Cobresal	Rangers	Palestino	Santiago M.	D. Concepción
Colo Colo	36	21	6	9	91	53	69		2-0	2-3	2-3	4-2	4-2	0-2	4-1	4-1	5-1	5-0	3-0	1-0	5-3	4-4	3-0	7-2	1-3	2-2
Cobreloa	36	20	7	9	72	48	67	2-2		2-3	0-1	1-0	2-1	1-1	3-1	2-1	3-1	3-1	3-1	1-0	3-0	2-2	3-1	5-1	1-0	2-1
Universidad Católica	36	18	9	9	51	38	63	0-1	1-0		5-1	0-2	0-2	3-1	0-1	1-1	0-0	0-2	5-2	2-1	2-1	2-0	2-0	2-1	1-0	1-0
Audax Italiano	36	18	7	11	64	46	61	1-3	5-3	0-0		1-2	0-1	2-1	3-0	1-1	2-0	2-0	1-1	1-1	3-0	3-2	5-0	1-1	2-2	1-2
Univ. de Concepción	36	16	10	10	65	53	58	3-2	1-0	1-1	1-0		2-2	2-2	0-0	2-3	2-1	2-2	4-2	5-1	4-1	2-1	1-3	3-2	1-0	
Universidad de Chile	36	17	7	12	51	45	58	1-3	1-1	1-0	2-2	1-1		1-2	2-2	1-1	2-2	1-1	2-0	1-0	1-0	1-2	2-1	2-0	4-0	2-1	2-0
Huachipato	36	17	5	14	61	51	56	1-2	4-2	1-2	1-3	2-3	2-0		0-0	3-2	0-1	2-3	2-0	1-0	2-0	2-0	1-1	1-3	1-0	3-1
O'Higgins	36	15	11	10	51	45	56	1-3	0-3	2-2	1-0	0-2	2-0	3-2		1-1	3-0	1-0	3-1	1-3	2-0	3-2	0-1	2-0	0-0	4-2
Puerto Montt	36	14	8	14	59	53	50	0-1	4-1	3-1	0-3	1-0	3-0	1-1		0-1	4-0	3-3	0-1	1-1	2-3	2-0	4-1	2-1	3-1
Coquimbo Unido	36	11	13	12	39	48	46	1-4	1-1	1-1	1-0	0-2	2-2	1-0	1-1		2-0	0-0	1-1	0-0	4-3	1-0	0-0	3-0	1-1
Santiago Wanderers	36	13	6	17	38	51	45	1-0	3-0	1-1	1-2	1-4	0-1	1-0	0-0	3-0	2-1		1-0	2-2	1-1	2-0	0-1	1-2	2-0	2-0
Antofagasta	36	10	12	14	51	56	42	1-1	1-1	1-2	1-1	3-2	0-1	2-0	1-2	3-1	0-1	2-1		3-0	0-0	3-2	3-1	1-1	3-1	1-1
Unión Española	36	11	9	16	44	55	42	1-0	0-3	1-1	0-1	1-0	2-6	1-0	0-2	3-1	1-1	3-3		3-3	1-3	0-0	0-2	3-1
Everton	36	10	12	14	43	54	42	3-0	0-2	1-0	4-3	1-2	1-1	1-3	0-2	1-2	1-0	2-0	2-0	1-2		1-1	2-0	3-0	1-1	1-1
Deportes La Serena	36	9	13	14	64	70	40	3-3	3-6	2-3	2-1	1-1	3-0	1-2	4-4	0-0	2-2	2-1	3-1	3-0	2-2		1-1	1-2	1-1	1-0
Cobresal	36	11	7	18	46	60	40	4-1	2-4	1-2	2-4	4-1	3-3	1-2	2-1	3-2	2-0	2-1	1-0	2-4	0-0	1-1		0-0	4-0	2-0
Rangers	36	10	10	16	48	64	40	0-0	1-3	1-1	3-0	2-1	1-2	1-3	1-1	1-1	1-2	3-1	2-2	1-3	2-0	1-0	1-2		3-1	3-1
Palestino	36	9	9	18	38	60	36	1-4	0-2	0-1	0-3	2-2	1-0	2-4	0-0	1-5	3-1	3-0	1-1	1-0	1-1	1-2	1-1	2-2		1-0
Santiago Morning	36	6	11	19	37	63	29	0-3	1-1	1-0	1-2	1-1	1-0	3-4	0-3	2-0	2-1	1-1	4-0	0-1	2-2	1-1	4-3	0-1	
Deportes Concepción				Withdrew			

Matches in the shaded boxes were played in the Apertura

CHILE 2006
PRIMERA B (2)

	Pl	W	D	L	F	A	Pts
Deportes Melipilla	36	17	12	7	53	29	63
Nublense	36	18	9	9	57	38	63
Lota Schwager §1	36	17	8	11	55	43	58
Fernández Vial	36	15	8	13	53	49	53
San Luis	36	12	15	9	45	40	52
Curicó Unido	36	11	19	6	40	36	52
Unión San Felipe	36	10	16	10	48	47	46
Unión La Calera	36	10	12	14	45	51	42
Deportes Copiapó	28	8	11	9	39	41	35
Deportes Temuco §3	28	8	6	14	29	37	27
Provincial Osorno	28	4	12	12	36	50	24
Magallanes	28	2	8	18	14	53	14

4/03/2006 - 5/11/2006 • § = points deducted • After 22 games the teams were split into a championship group and into a relegation group • Top scorer: Patrico MORALES, Lota 18

CHILE 2007
PRIMERA DIVISION APERTURA

	Pl	W	D	L	F	A	Pts	Colo Colo	U. Católica	Audax	Huachipato	Cobreloa	Cobresal	Nublense	Melipilla	Un. Española	O'Higgins	La Serena	Everton	Univ. de Chile	Palestino	D. Concepción	Antofagasta	U. Concepción	Puerto Montt	Coquimbo	Wanderers	Lota Schwager
Colo Colo	20	14	5	1	47	16	47		2-1			4-2				2-1	6-2				1-0	4-0	3-0		3-0		3-1	2-2
Universidad Católica	20	14	4	2	36	14	46					2-0	2-1			4-1	1-0	4-1			0-0	2-0		0-0			1-0	2-0
Audax Italiano	20	13	5	2	39	20	44	1-0	1-3			1-0	2-0					2-1	4-2			2-0	0-0	0-0				3-2
Huachipato	20	12	4	4	35	21	40	2-2					1-0	1-1		2-1				2-1	3-0	3-0	3-1		3-1	1-0		
Cobreloa	20	10	5	5	44	23	35	2-2						3-1		1-2		5-0			3-2	3-0	7-1		2-0	5-1		2-1
Cobresal	20	9	5	6	31	21	32							1-1	1-3		1-0		2-0	2-1		4-1			1-0	3-0	3-1	6-0
Nublense	20	8	8	4	31	31	32	0-2	3-3	3-2			1-1			1-1					1-0	2-3		2-0		2-1	2-1	
Deportes Melipilla	20	8	4	8	35	34	28	1-2				1-3	2-4	2-1		2-0		2-1	2-0			1-1			3-2	2-1		
Unión Española	20	8	4	8	29	25	28					2-2		1-1	1-0		2-2	1-0	1-0	2-1	1-1						1-2	4-0
O'Higgins	20	8	3	9	30	38	27	1-2	0-0				0-1			3-0				1-0	4-1		4-2	2-1			3-2	3-3
Deportes La Serena	20	7	5	8	31	30	26	1-1	1-2			2-4		6-2	2-1		2-1			1-1			1-0	3-0		2-1		
Everton	20	6	8	6	24	27	26	0-3	1-0			1-1	0-0	1-2	2-2			2-0			1-1			2-1			1-1	
Universidad de Chile	20	6	7	7	20	21	25	0-0				2-2	1-0	0-1		1-1	3-0					0-0	2-4		1-0	2-0		
Palestino	20	5	8	7	27	30	23	0-2	1-1				1-1			1-1		3-2		1-1			2-0	4-1		1-2	3-2	
Deportes Concepción	20	6	5	9	20	34	23	0-1							1-1		3-2	1-2	1-1	1-1	1-0				2-1	1-0	3-2	
Antofagasta	20	5	7	8	24	34	22							0-1	3-1	2-1	0-1	1-1	1-4	1-1	1-1				3-1		3-2	
Univ. de Concepción	20	4	5	11	25	33	17	0-2	2-4			2-3	1-1	3-1			0-2					0-0	0-0			0-0	3-1	
Puerto Montt	20	4	2	14	19	40	14	0-1	0-4						1-1		2-5				1-3	2-0	3-1	3-1		1-3		0-1
Coquimbo Unido	20	4	2	14	18	40	14	0-3	0-2	1-1	1-3				1-2		3-2	1-0		0-2	1-2		2-1	2-0				
Santiago Wanderers §3	20	4	4	12	24	33	13		1-2				1-1		3-2	1-0		0-2	1-2			0-0		1-1	3-1			5-2
Lota Schwager	20	2	6	12	28	52	12		1-2				1-1	1-4		2-2	2-0	1-2	3-3		1-1	2-4			1-3			

27/01/2007 - 17/06/2007 • § = Points deducted • No play-offs were held for the Apertura • Deportes Concepción reinstated at the start of the season
Top scorers: Humberto SUAZO, Colo Colo, 17; José Luis DIAZ, Cobreloa 15; Lucas BARRIOS, Cobreloa 14

CHN – CHINA PR

NATIONAL TEAM RECORD
JULY 10TH 2006 TO JULY 12TH 2010

PL	W	D	L	F	A	%
13	6	3	4	21	16	57.7

These are not great times for Chinese football. The 2006 domestic season set few pulses racing whilst the national team faced derision at home after they were embarrassingly knocked out of the 2007 AFC Asian Championship in the first round. China had qualified for the finals easily enough although they were never impressive, losing to Iraq and only beating Singapore in Tianjin with a penalty deep into injury time. No-one, however, could have expected the catastrophe in the finals which saw the team fail to progress from the group stage for the first time since 1980. Having beaten hosts Malaysia, the Chinese then drew with Iran which left a winner-takes-all tie against Uzbekistan. Three goals in the last 18 minutes by the Uzbeks saw the Chinese crash out of the tournament. Much attention during the season had been paid to the Olympic squad's progress in the hope of winning gold at the 2008 games in Beijing. The team certainly impressed in spells at the Asian Games, eventually going down to Iran on penalties in the quarter-finals but not long afterwards they ended up in hot water. A six week tour through France and England had been intended to aid player bonding, but, after a busy season, it came to a head when a friendly against

INTERNATIONAL HONOURS
Qualified for the FIFA World Cup™ 2002
AFC Asian Women's Championship 1986 1989 1991 1993 1995 1997 1999
Asian U-19 Championship 1985   Asian U-17 Championship 1992 2004
AFC Asian Champions League Liaoning 1990

Queens Park Rangers was abandoned after a massive brawl, which left defender Zheng Tao with a broken jaw. On the domestic front, Shandong Luneng were so superior to the rest that they clinched the title with six matches still to play. Veteran centre-forward Li Jinyu broke all domestic scoring records with 26 strikes, whilst his team-mate Zheng Zhi was the player of the tournament earning himself a move to England's Charlton Athletic. Shandong completed their second double with a 2-0 Cup Final win over Dalian. Shanghai Shenhua finished second, a full 17 points adrift of Shandong, but from 2007 they have China's largest city to themselves. A few weeks before the start of the season, Zhu Jun, owner of cross-town rivals Shanghai United, bought them out merged the clubs under the Shenhua banner. The 2007 Asian Champions League proved to be a big disappointment for Chinese clubs with Shanghai Shenhua finishing bottom of their group whilst Shandong lost out on goal difference to Seongnam Ilhwa Chunma after losing 3-0 to their Korean opponents in the final round of matches. Finally, one of China's football landmarks, the Wulihe Stadium in Shenyang was demolished in early 2007. Long used as a base for the national team, the challenge will be for the current players to do justice to the new stadium that has been built for the Olympics.

Football Association of the People's Republic of China (CFA)
Building A, Dongjiudasha, Xizhaosi Street, Chongwen District, Beijing 100061, China PR
Tel +86 10 59291031   Fax +86 10 59290309
li_chen@fa.org.cn   www.fa.org.cn
President: YUAN Weimin   General Secretary: YALONG Xie
Vice-President: YALONG Xie   Treasurer: NAN Yong   Media Officer: CHENG Wei
Men's Coach: ZHU Guanghu   Women's Coach: DOMANSKI-LYFORS Marika
CFA formed: 1924   AFC: 1974   FIFA: 1931-58 & 1974
White shirts with red trimmings, White shorts, White socks or Red shirts with white trimmings, Red shorts, Red socks

RECENT INTERNATIONAL MATCHES PLAYED BY CHINA PR

2004	Opponents	Score		Venue	Comp	Scorers	Att	Referee
9-06	Malaysia	W	4-0	Tianjin	WCq	Hao Haidong [43], Sun Jihai [62], Li Xiaopeng 2 [66 76]	35 000	Park Sang Gu KOR
3-07	Lebanon	W	6-0	Chongqing	Fr	Li Jinyu 2 [15 50], Yan Song [61], Li Ming [69], Zhang Shuo [79], Li Yi [86]		
10-07	United Arab Emirates	D	2-2	Hohhot	Fr	Zheng Zhi 2 [63 90p]		
17-07	Bahrain	D	2-2	Beijing	ACr1	Zheng Zhi [58], Li Jinyu [66p]	40 000	Subkhiddin MAS
21-07	Indonesia	W	5-0	Beijing	ACr1	Shao Jiayi 2 [24 65], Hao Haidong [39], Li Ming [51], Li Yi [80]		Talaat LIB
25-07	Qatar	W	1-0	Beijing	ACr1	Xu Yunlong [78]	60 000	Moradi IRN
30-07	Iraq	W	3-0	Beijing	ACqf	Hao Haidong [8], Zheng Zhi 2 [79p 90p]	60 000	Maidin SIN
3-08	Iran	D	1-1	Beijing	ACsf	Shao Jiayi [19] W 4-3p	51 000	Talaat LIB
7-08	Japan	L	1-3	Beijing	ACf	Li Ming [31]	62 000	Al Fadhi KUW
8-09	Malaysia	W	1-0	Penang	WCq	Li Jinyu [67]	14 000	Karim BHR
13-10	Kuwait	L	0-1	Kuwait City	WCq		10 000	Kunsuta THA
17-11	Hong Kong	W	7-0	Guangzhou	WCq	Li Jinyu 2 [8 47], Shao Jiayi 2 [42 44], Xu Yunlong [49], Yu Genwei [88], Li Weifeng [90+2]	20 300	Lee Jong Kuk KOR
2005								
26-03	Spain	L	0-3	Salamanca	Fr		17 000	Batista POR
29-03	Republic of Ireland	L	0-1	Dublin	Fr		35 222	Casha MLT
19-06	Costa Rica	D	2-2	Changsa	Fr	Zhang Yaokun [27], Sun Xiang [79]	20 000	Lee Gi Young KOR
22-06	Costa Rica	W	2-0	Guangzhou	Fr	Zheng Zhi [44p], Xie Hui [54]	15 000	Yu Byung Seob KOR
31-07	Korea Republic	D	1-1	Daejon	EAC	Sun Xiang [52]	25 374	Nishimura JPN
3-08	Japan	D	2-2	Daejon	EAC	Li Jinyu [37], Zhang Yonghai [43]	1 827	
7-08	Korea DPR	W	2-0	Daegu	EAC	Li Yan [14], Xie Hui [67]		
12-10	Germany	L	0-1	Hamburg	Fr		48 734	Batista POR
13-11	Serbia & Montenegro	L	0-2	Nanjing	Fr		30 000	
2006								
12-02	Honduras	L	0-1	Guangzhou	Fr		20 000	Supian MAS
22-02	Palestine	W	2-0	Guangzhou	ACq	Du Wei [23], Li Weifeng [62]	16 500	Kwon Jong Chul KOR
1-03	Iraq	L	1-2	Al Ain	ACq	Tao Wei [54]	7 700	Al Saeedi UAE
3-06	Switzerland	L	1-4	Zurich	Fr	Dong Fangzhuo [91+]	16 000	Stokes IRL
7-06	France	L	1-3	St Etienne	Fr	Zheng Zhi [69p]	34 147	Davila ESP
10-08	Thailand	W	4-0	Qinhuangdao	Fr			
16-08	Singapore	W	1-0	Tianjin	ACq	Shao Jiayi [93+p]	27 000	Ebrahim BHR
6-09	Singapore	D	0-0	Singapore	ACq		38 824	Shamsuzzaman BAN
11-10	Palestine	W	2-0	Amman	ACq	Mao Jianqing [27], Sun Xiang [64]	3 000	Al Fadhli KUW
15-11	Iraq	D	1-1	Changsha	ACq	Han Peng [40]		Mohd Salleh MAS
2007								
7-02	Kazakhstan	W	2-1	Suzhou	Fr	Han Peng [30], Li Jinyu [48]		
24-03	Australia	L	0-2	Guangzhou	Fr		20 000	Wu Chaojue HKG
27-03	Uzbekistan	W	3-1	Macau	Fr	Han Peng 2 [6 41], Karaev OG [65]		
16-05	Thailand	L	0-1	Bangkok	Fr			
2-06	USA	L	1-4	San Jose	Fr	Zhang Yaokun [15]	20 821	Guajardo MEX
10-07	Malaysia	W	5-1	Kuala Lumpur	ACr1	Han Peng 2 [15 55], Shao Jiayi [36], Wang Dong 2 [51 93+]	20 000	Basma SYR
15-07	Iran	D	2-2	Kuala Lumpur	ACr1	Shao Jiayi [6], Mao Jianqing [33]	5 938	Al Ghamdi KSA
18-07	Uzbekistan	L	0-3	Kuala Lumpur	ACr1		2 200	Al Fadhli KUW

Fr = Friendly match • EAC = East Asian Championship • AC = AFC Asian Cup • WC = FIFA World Cup
q = qualifier • r1 = first round group • qf = quarter-final • sf = semi-final • f = final

CHINA PR NATIONAL TEAM RECORDS AND RECORD SEQUENCES

Records			Sequence records					
Victory	19-0	GUM 2000	Wins	10	1919-1930	Clean sheets	8	1998-2000
Defeat	0-5	USA 1992	Defeats	5	1982, 2002	Goals scored	20	1915-1934
Player Caps	115	HAO Haidong	Undefeated	19	2003-2004	Without goal	5	2002
Player Goals	41	HAO Haidong	Without win	7	1996, 2000-2001	Goals against	9	1934-57, 2006-07

Includes records dating back to the Far-Eastern Games of 1913-1934

PEOPLE'S REPUBLIC OF CHINA; ZHONGHUA RENMIN GONGHEGUO

Capital	Beijing	Language	Mandarin, Cantonese, Shanghaiese	Independence	221BC
Population	1313973713	Area	9 596 960 km²	Density	135 per km²	% in cities	30%
GDP per cap	$5 000	Dailling code	+86	Internet	.cn	GMT +/-	+8

MEDALS TABLE

		Overall			League			Cup			Asia			City	Stadium	Cap'ty
		G	S	B	G	S	B	G	S	B	G	S	B			
1	Liaoning	11	9	5	8	6	4	2	2		1	1	1	Anshan & Fushun	City & Lei Feng	30 000
2	Dalian Shide	11	6	6	8		5	3	4		2	1		Dalian	Jinzhou	31 000
3	Beijing Guoan	9	5	12	5	2	11	4	3				1	Beijing	Fengtai	33 000
4	Shanghai Shenhua	7	12	4	4	10	4	3	2					Shanghai	Hongkou	35 000
5	August 1st (now defunct)	6	6	5	5	6	5	1						Beijing		
6	Shandong Luneng	6	5	1	2	3	1	4	2					Ji'nan	Provincial	43 700
7	Tianjin Teda	3	6	4	2	5	4	1	1					Tianjin	Teda	36 000
9	Guangdong Hongyuan	1	5	1	1	1	1		4					Guangzhou	Provincial	30 000
10	Shenzhen Kingway	1	1	1	1	1							1	Shenzhen	City	33 000
11	Chongqing Lifan	1						1						Chongqing	Yanghe	58 680
	Qingdao Zhongneng	1						1						Qingdao	Yizhong	60 000
19	Guangzhou Yiyao		3	1		2	1		1					Guangzhou	Yuexiushan	35 000
20	Sichuan Guancheng (now defunct)		1	2					2					Chengdu	Sichuan	40 000
22	Xi'an Chanba	1	1		1	1								Xi'an	Coca-Cola	30 000
23	Shenyang Ginde	1			1									Changsha	Wulihe	65 000

The table only includes teams that have been active in recent years. Teams such as North East China, who won two championships in the 1950s, have not been included

RECENT LEAGUE AND CUP RECORD

	Championship							FA Cup		
Year	Champions	Pts	Runners-up	Pts	Third	Pts		Winners	Score	Runners-up
1994	Dalian	33	Guangzhou	27	Shanghai Shenhua	26		No Tournament		
1995	Shanghai Shenhua	46	Beijing	42	Dalian	42		Jinan	2-0	Shanghai Shenhua
1996	Dalian	46	Shanghai Shenhua	39	August 1st	35		Beijing	4-1	Jinan
1997	Dalian	51	Shanghai Shenhua	40	Beijing	34		Beijing	2-1	Shanghai Shenhua
1998	Dalian	62	Shanghai Shenhua	45	Beijing	43		Shanghai Shenhua	2-1 2-1	Liaoning
1999	Shandong	48	Liaoning	47	Sichuan	45		Shandong	2-1 2-1	Dalian
2000	Dalian	56	Shanghai Shenhua	50	Sichuan	44		Chongqing	0-1 4-1	Beijing
2001	Dalian	53	Shanghai Shenhua	48	Liaoning	48		Dalian	1-0 2-1	Beijing
2002	Dalian	57	Shenzhen	52	Beijing	52		Qingdao	1-3 2-0	Liaoning
2003	Shanghai Shenhua	55	Shanghai Int'l	54	Dalian	53		Beijing	3-0	Dalian
2004	Shenzhen	42	Shandong	36	Shanghai Int'l	32		Shandong	2-1	Sichuan
2005	Dalian	65	Shanghai Shenhua	53	Shandong	52		Dalian	1-0	Shandong
2006	Shandong	69	Shanghai Shenhua	52	Beijing Hyundai	49		Shandong	2-0	Dalian Shide

CHINA PR 2006

CSL (CHINESE SUPER LEAGUE)

	Pl	W	D	L	F	A	Pts	Shandong	Shanghai S	Beijing	Changchun	Dalian	Tianjin	Shanghai U	Xiamen	Xi'an	Wuhan	Shenzhen	Shenyang	Liaoning	Qingdao	Chongqing
Shandong Luneng T. †	28	22	3	3	74	26	69		2-1	1-0	2-0	0-0	2-1	3-1	2-0	5-1	5-1	2-0	3-1	3-1	3-1	4-0
Shanghai Shenhua †	28	14	10	4	37	19	52	2-1		0-0	0-0	1-1	1-0	0-0	2-2	1-1	3-1	1-0	0-0	3-0	2-0	2-0
Beijing Hyundai	28	13	10	5	27	16	49	0-0	0-1		1-0	1-0	1-1	1-2	1-0	3-1	1-1	2-0	1-0	1-0	1-0	1-0
Changchun Yatai	28	13	7	8	41	26	46	3-2	0-1	4-1		2-1	3-1	2-0	3-0	1-1	2-0	3-0	0-0	2-0	2-1	3-1
Dalian Shide	28	13	6	9	43	29	45	1-4	1-2	0-0	3-2		2-1	1-1	1-0	2-0	5-0	3-1	2-0	3-1	6-0	
Tianjin Teda	28	10	10	8	40	38	40	0-3	1-1	0-0	1-1	0-0		3-1	3-2	2-2	3-0	2-0	4-2	1-1	1-0	
Shanghai United	28	9	12	7	32	25	39	5-1	1-1	0-0	2-1	1-1	3-0		1-1	1-1	0-0	0-0	1-1	1-1	1-0	3-0
Xiamen Lanshi	28	9	11	8	28	27	38	1-3	0-0	2-0	0-0	1-0	3-1	0-0		0-1	2-0	0-0	1-2	0-0	0-0	3-2
Xi'an Chanba	28	8	12	8	33	34	36	0-2	0-0	0-2	1-1	4-2	1-1	1-1	0-2		3-0	0-0	3-0	2-1	2-1	2-0
Wuhan Guanggu	28	8	7	13	28	42	31	1-2	0-2	1-1	4-2	0-1	3-4	1-1	1-1	1-0		2-1	2-0	1-1	2-1	2-1
Shenzhen Kingway	28	8	6	14	22	42	30	0-3	1-0	0-4	1-0	1-2	2-3	0-2	3-2	2-2	1-0		2-0	2-2	1-0	0-0
Shenyang Ginde	28	6	8	14	22	43	26	2-7	1-0	0-1	0-2	3-2	0-0	1-3	0-0	2-1	0-1			1-0	2-2	1-1
Liaoning	28	6	8	14	24	42	26	0-5	1-2	1-2	1-1	2-1	0-1	2-0	0-0	1-1	2-1	2-1	1-1		0-0	1-1
Qingdao Zhongneng	28	6	7	15	25	36	25	1-2	1-2	0-0	0-1	0-1	3-2	1-0	0-1	0-1	0-0	2-1	2-1	2-0		1-1
Chongqing Lifan	28	3	7	18	20	51	16	2-2	2-5	1-1	1-0	1-0	1-1	0-1	1-1	1-1	0-2	0-1	0-1	2-1	3-4	

11/03/2006 - 22/10/2006 • † Qualified for the AFC Champions League • Top scorers: Li Jinyu, Shandong 26; Zheng Zhi, Shandong 21; Luis RAMIREZ (HON), Shanghai Shenhua 13; VICENTE (BRA), Xi'an 11; Han Peng, Shandong 10; Zoran JANKOVIC (BUL), Dalian 10; Zou Yougen, Xiamen 10

CHINA PR 2006

CHINA LEAGUE (2)

	Pl	W	D	L	F	A	Pts	Henan	Zhejiang	Guangzhou	Chengdu	Nanjing	Jiangsu	Qingdao	Yanbian	Shanxi	Shanghai	Nanchang	Beijing	Hunan
Henan Jianye	24	18	5	1	38	13	59		1-1	1-0	2-1	3-2	3-3	2-0	1-0	4-1	2-0	2-0	1-0	1-0
Zhejiang Lucheng	24	17	4	3	41	18	55	1-0		2-1	2-1	1-0	3-1	2-0	2-2	3-1	3-0	1-0	3-0	2-0
Guangzhou Yiyao	24	15	3	6	45	25	48	1-3	3-2		2-0	0-1	2-1	3-1	1-0	5-1	5-1	2-1	5-1	2-1
Chengdu Blades	24	11	5	8	27	18	38	0-0	0-2	0-1		1-0	3-1	1-0	2-0	2-0	3-0	2-0	3-0	1-0
Nanjing Yoyo	24	10	5	9	24	20	35	0-0	1-2	1-0	2-0		0-1	1-1	1-2	1-0	2-0	0-1	2-1	1-0
Jiangsu Shuntian	24	9	6	9	37	21	33	0-1	1-3	2-3	0-0	1-1		1-1	0-3	1-2	2-0	4-0	2-0	4-1
Qingdao Hisense	24	8	7	9	25	32	31	0-0	2-0	1-1	0-1	0-2	2-1		2-1	3-0	0-2	1-1	2-1	1-1
Yanbian	24	8	5	11	28	22	29	1-2	0-1	2-3	1-1	1-0	0-1	4-0		1-0	6-0	1-1	0-0	1-0
Shanxi Luhu	24	7	5	12	32	41	26	0-1	1-2	2-0	0-0	1-1	1-4	5-3	1-0		2-2	3-0	4-1	1-1
Shanghai Qunying	24	5	7	12	15	37	22	1-2	0-0	1-2	1-0	1-0	1-3	1-2	1-0	1-0		0-0	2-2	0-0
Nanchang August 1st	24	4	8	12	11	27	20	0-1	0-1	0-0	1-1	0-0	0-2	0-1	0-0	2-1	0-0		0-0	1-0
Beijing Hongdeng	24	4	7	13	18	40	19	1-3	1-1	0-3	3-1	0-1	0-0	1-1	1-0	1-3	1-0	1-2		0-0
Hunan Xiangjun	24	2	9	13	16	33	15	0-2	2-1	0-0	0-3	3-4	1-1	0-1	1-1	2-2	0-0	2-1	1-2	

25/03/2006 - 28/10/2006 • Top scorer: TICO (BRA), Zhejiang 15 • Dalian Changbo relocated and renamed as Shanxi Luhu

CHINA PR 2006
YIJIDUI (3)

Northern Group

	PI	W	D	L	F	A	Pts
Beijing IT †	16	10	5	1	32	9	35
Harbin Yiteng †	16	9	5	2	23	10	32
Tianjin Locomotive †	16	7	6	3	25	14	27
Hebei Xuechi †	16	6	6	4	13	13	24
Beijing Bus	16	5	7	4	19	13	22
Xinjiang Ticai	16	6	4	6	17	16	22
Tianjin Dongli	16	3	5	8	9	18	15
Qingdao Liming	16	3	2	11	11	35	11
Liaoning Zhongba	16	3	0	13	12	33	9

Southern Group

	PI	W	D	L	F	A	Pts
Anhui Jiufang †	16	12	1	3	24	11	37
Lijiang Dongba †	16	11	1	4	30	14	34
Wuhan Yaqi †	16	8	4	4	23	16	28
Ningbo Huaao †	16	8	3	5	25	17	27
Sichuan	16	7	5	4	20	19	26
Guangxi Tianji	16	5	3	8	20	27	18
Shanghai Dongya	16	3	5	8	26	29	14
Suzhou Qupushi	16	4	1	11	16	32	13
Ningbo Zhongbao	16	0	5	11	4	23	5

6/05/2006 - 7/10/2006 • † Qualified for the play-offs

CHINA PR 2006
YIJIDUI PLAY-OFFS

Quarter–finals		Semi–finals		Final	
Beijing IT	6 1				
Ningbo Huaao	0 1	Beijing IT	1 2 6p		
Lijiang Dongba	0 0	Tianjin Loco'tive	1 2 5p		
Tianjin Loco'tive	0 1			Beijing IT	3
Tianjin Loco'tive	0 0			Harbin Yiteng	0
Hebei Xuechi	0 1	Anhui Jiufang	1 0 1p		
Anhui Jiufang	3 1				
Wuhan Yaqi	1 1 4p	Harbin Yiteng	1 0 3p		
Harbin Yiteng	0 2 5p				

Beijing Institute of Technology and Harbin Yiteng promoted

LANDI FA CUP 2006

First Round

Team	Score
Shandong Luneng	Bye
Chengdu Blades	0
Qingdao Hisense *	1
Henan Jianye †	2
Chongqing Lifan *	2
Yanbian	0
Shanghai Shenhua * †	3
Xiamen Lanshi	Bye
Nanchang August 1st	0
Guangzhou Yiyao *	1
Shanghai United	1
Wuhan Guanggu *	0
Beijing Hongdeng	2
Xi'an Chanba *	0
Zhejiang Lucheng *	2
Qingdao Zhongneng	1
Beijing Hyundai	Bye
Nanjing Yoyo ‡	3
Hunan Xiangjun *	0
Shanghai Qunying	0
Shenzhen Kingway *	2
Tianjin Teda	1
Shanxi Luhua *	0
Liaoning *	1
Shenyang Ginde *	2
Jiangsu Shuntian *	5
Changchun Yatai	0
Dalian Shide	Bye

Round of 16

Team	Score
Shandong Luneng *	5
Qingdao Hisense	0
Henan Jianye	1
Shanghai Shenhua *	5
Xiamen Lanshi *	2
Guangzhou Yiyao	1
Shanghai United	1
Xi'an Chanba *	2
Zhejiang Lucheng	2
Beijing Hyundai *	0
Nanjing Yoyo	1
Shenzhen Kingway *	6
Tianjin Teda	1 4p
Shenyang Ginde *	1 3p
Jiangsu Shuntian	1
Dalian Shide *	4

Quarter-finals

Team	Score
Shandong Luneng	2 1
Shanghai Shenhua *	1 0
Xiamen Lanshi	0 0
Xi'an Chanba *	3 2
Zhejiang Lucheng	1 2
Shenzhen Kingway *	2 0
Tianjin Teda *	1 0
Dalian Shide	2 1

Semi-finals

Team	Score
Shandong Luneng	3 1
Xi'an Chanba *	1 0
Zhejiang Lucheng *	1 4
Dalian Shide	3 3

Final

Team	Score
Shandong Luneng	2
Dalian Shide	0

CUP FINAL

He Long Stadium, Changsha
18-11-2006

Scorers - Li Jinyu [34], Han Peng [73] for Shandong

* Home team/home team in the first leg • † Henan qualified due to scoring the first goal in extra-time • ‡ Walk-over

SHANDONG LUNENG TAISHAN 2006

Date	Opponents		Score		Comp	Scorers
12-03-2006	Xiamen Lanshi	W	3-1	A	CSL	Li Jinyu 2 [24 85], Zheng Zhi [76]
19-03-2006	Qingdao Zhongneng	W	3-1	H	CSL	Zheng Zhi [15], Zhou Haibin [34], Zivkovic [70]
26-03-2006	Shanghai United	L	1-5	A	CSL	Li Jinyu [37]
29-03-2006	Shenzhen Kingway	W	2-0	H	CSL	Zheng Zhi 2 [1 14]
1-04-2006	Wuhan Guanggu	W	2-1	A	CSL	Zivkovic [76], Han Peng [84]
5-04-2006	Qingdao Hisense	W	5-0	H	FACr2	Glusevic 3 [10 17 90], Han Peng 2 [30 54]
8-04-2006	Shenyang Ginde	W	3-1	H	CSL	Li Jinyu [52], Ri Ke Fu [58], Lu Zheng [83]
16-04-2006	Tianjin Teda	W	3-0	A	CSL	Han Peng [22], Zheng Zhi [24], Li Jinyu [76]
19-04-2006	Xi'an Chanba	W	5-1	H	CSL	Li Jinyu [18], OG [23], Zheng Zhi 2 [38 85], Han Peng [42]
22-04-2006	Beijing Hyundai	D	0-0	A	CSL	
7-05-2006	Shanghai Shenhua	W	2-1	H	CSL	Li Jinyu 2 [10 13]
10-05-2006	Chongqing Lifan	D	2-2	A	CSL	Cui Peng [26], Zheng Zhi [59]
13-05-2006	Dalian Shide	D	0-0	H	CSL	
21-05-2006	Liaoning	W	5-0	A	CSL	Li Jinyu 4 [18 44 49 52], Gao Yao [55]
24-05-2006	Changchun Yatai	W	2-0	H	CSL	Shu Chang [29], Han Peng [42]
28-05-2006	Xiamen Lanshi	W	2-0	H	CSL	Zhou Haibin [70], Li Jinyu [79]
29-06-2006	Shanghai Shenhua	W	2-1	A	FACqf	Gao Yao [53], Han Peng [58]
8-07-2006	Shanghai Shenhua	W	1-0	H	FACqf	Zheng Zhi [23]
12-07-2006	Qingdao Zhongneng	W	2-1	A	CSL	Zheng Zhi [13], Zhou Haibin [31]
15-07-2006	Shanghai United	W	3-1	H	CSL	Zheng Zhi [4p], Li Jinyu 2 [8 15]
22-07-2006	Shenzhen Kingway	W	3-0	A	CSL	Li Jinyu 2 [37 89], OG [63]
26-07-2006	Wuhan Guanggu	W	5-1	H	CSL	Pazin 2 [17 67], Zheng Zhi [22p], Li Jinyu [49], Han Peng [59]
29-07-2006	Shenyang Ginde	W	7-2	A	CSL	Li Jinyu 3 [18 52 54], Han Peng 2 [20 37], Glusevic [81], Zheng Zhi [86]
12-08-2006	Xi'an Chanba	W	3-1	A	FACsf	Li Jinyu [54], Han Peng [61], Pazin [78]
19-08-2006	Tianjin Teda	W	2-1	H	CSL	Zheng Zhi 2 [52 65]
23-08-2006	Xi'an Chanba	W	2-0	A	CSL	Li Jinyu [7], Zheng Zhi [38]
27-08-2006	Beijing Hyundai	W	1-0	H	CSL	Han Peng [1]
1-09-2006	Xi'an Chanba	W	1-0	H	FACsf	Zivkovic [53]
23-09-2006	Chongqing Lifan	W	4-0	H	CSL	Han Peng [3], Li Jinyu [32], Zheng Zhi 2 [55 90]
30-09-2006	Dalian Shide	W	4-1	A	CSL	Zheng Zhi 2 [9 33], Li Jinyu [85], Han Peng [86]
5-10-2006	Shanghai Shenhua	L	1-2	A	CSL	Lu Zheng [3]
15-10-2006	Liaoning	W	3-1	H	CSL	Li Jinyu [19], Pazin [27], Zheng Zhi [58]
22-10-2006	Changchun Yatai	L	2-3	A	CSL	Zheng Zhi [16], Li Jinyu [83]
18-11-2006	Dalian Shide	W	2-0	N	FACf	Li Jinyu [34], Han Peng [73]

FAC = FA Cup • CSL = Chinese Super League

r1 = first round • r2 = second round • qf = quarter-final • sf = semi-final • f = final

FIFA/COCA-COLA WORLD RANKING

1993	1994	1995	1996	1997	1998	1999	2000	2001	2002	2003	2004	2005	2006	High	Low
53	40	66	76	55	37	88	75	54	63	86	54	72	84	**37** 12/98	**103** 08/06

2006–2007											
08/06	09/06	10/06	11/06	12/06	01/07	02/07	03/07	04/07	05/07	06/07	07/07
103	91	87	84	84	83	79	75	72	73	76	73

THE FIFA BIG COUNT OF 2006

	Male	Female		Total
Number of players	24 266 330	1 900 000	Referees and Assistant Referees	21 657
Professionals	2 239		Admin, Coaches, Technical, Medical	107 400
Amateurs 18+	325 992		Number of clubs	1 621
Youth under 18	382 762		Number of teams	11 347
Unregistered	5 045 100		Clubs with women's teams	600
Total players	26 166 335		Players as % of population	1.99%

CIV – COTE D'IVOIRE

NATIONAL TEAM RECORD
JULY 10TH 2006 TO JULY 12TH 2010

PL	W	D	L	F	A	%
7	6	0	1	18	1	85.7

FIFA/COCA-COLA WORLD RANKING

1993	1994	1995	1996	1997	1998	1999	2000	2001	2002	2003	2004	2005	2006	High	Low
33	25	20	51	52	44	53	51	44	64	70	40	42	18	18 12/06	75 05/04

2006–2007											
08/06	09/06	10/06	11/06	12/06	01/07	02/07	03/07	04/07	05/07	06/07	07/07
18	19	18	18	18	18	21	20	25	25	20	31

Didier Drogba's election as African Footballer of the Year in March 2007 was the icing on the cake following a highly successful period for the Ivorian 'Elephants', who have rapidly developed into African football's form side. The goals scored for Chelsea in the English Premier League and in the UEFA Champions League has handed superstar status to the striker, and he was feted as a national hero when he narrowly pipped Samuel Eto'o in the polling. Drogba was quick to try and help cement the national unity process after the cessation of fighting between the government-controlled south and rebel forces in the north of the country. He went to the northern city of Bouake to display his trophy

INTERNATIONAL HONOURS
Qualified for the FIFA World Cup finals 2006   **African Cup of Nations** 1992   **CAF African Champions League** ASEC Mimosas 1998

and was back again in June when the national team played a highly symbolic game in a previously no-go area, beating Madagascar 5-0 in the 2008 African Nations Cup qualifiers. Drogba's individual success has been matched by the national side, who since former German international Uli Stielike took over as coach, have racked up six successive wins, all of them without conceding a goal. The Ligue 1 title race ended in a yet another triumph for ASEC Abidjan and their French coach Patrick Liewig. ASEC also made it to the semifinals of the 2006 African Champions League and qualified for the 2007 group phase for a record-equalling eighth time in the last 11 years.

THE FIFA BIG COUNT OF 2006

	Male	Female		Total
Number of players	801 700	0	Referees and Assistant Referees	600
Professionals	100		Admin, Coaches, Technical, Medical	3 900
Amateurs 18+	12 100		Number of clubs	220
Youth under 18	11 000		Number of teams	1 320
Unregistered	82 500		Clubs with women's teams	0
Total players	801 700		Players as % of population	4.54%

Fédération Ivoirienne de Football (FIF)
01 Case postale 1202, Abidjan 01, Côte d'Ivoire
Tel +225 21240027   Fax +225 21259552
fifci@aviso.ci   www.fif.ci
President: ANOUMA Jacques   General Secretary: OUATTARA Hego
Vice-President: KESSE Feh Lambert   Treasurer: ABINAN Pascal   Media Officer: None
Men's Coach: STIELIKE Uli   Women's Coach: None
FIF formed: 1960   CAF: 1960   FIFA: 1960
Orange shirts with white trimmings, White shorts, Green socks

RECENT INTERNATIONAL MATCHES PLAYED BY COTE D'IVOIRE

2002 Opponents	Score	Venue	Comp	Scorers	Att	Referee
10-09 Tunisia	L 2-3	Tunis	Fr	Dindane [88], Kalou [90p]	17 000	Djaballah ALG
15-11 Senegal	L 0-1	Dakar	Fr		50 000	Daami TUN
2004						
31-03 Tunisia	W 2-0	Tunis	Fr	Drogba 2 [34 65]	10 000	Haimoudi ALG
28-04 Guinea	W 4-2	Aix-les-Bains	Fr	Drogba [8], Toure [32], Kalou [45], Bakari [68]	2 000	
6-06 Libya	W 2-0	Abidjan	WCq	Dindane [35], Drogba [63p]	40 827	Colembi ANG
20-06 Egypt	W 2-1	Alexandria	WCq	Dindane [22], Drogba [75]	13 000	Guirat TUN
4-07 Cameroon	L 0-2	Yaounde	WCq		80 000	Guezzaz MAR
18-08 Senegal	W 2-1	Avignon	Fr	Boka [32], Dindane [68]	5 000	
5-09 Sudan	W 5-0	Abidjan	WCq	Drogba [12p], Dindane 2 [15 64], Yapi [25], Bakary Kone [56]	20 000	Mana NGA
10-10 Benin	W 1-0	Cotonou	WCq	Dindane [48]	25 000	Sowe GAM
2005						
8-02 Congo DR	D 2-2	Rouen	Fr	Dindane [39], Kalou [88p]	4 000	Duhamel FRA
27-03 Benin	W 3-0	Abidjan	WCq	Kalou [7], Drogba 2 [19 59]	35 000	Guirat TUN
3-06 Libya	D 0-0	Tripoli	WCq		45 000	Lim Kee Chong MRI
19-06 Egypt	W 2-0	Abidjan	WCq	Drogba 2 [41 49]	30 000	Damon RSA
17-08 France	L 0-3	Montpellier	Fr		31 457	Bertini ITA
4-09 Cameroon	L 2-3	Abidjan	WCq	Drogba 2 [38 47]	34 500	Daami TUN
8-10 Sudan	W 3-1	Omdurman	WCq	Akale [22], Dindane 2 [51 73]	20 000	Damon RSA
12-11 Romania	W 2-1	Le Mans	Fr	Arouna Kone [48], Bakary Kone [91+]	5 377	Fautrel FRA
16-11 Italy	D 1-1	Geneva	Fr	Drogba [71]	18 500	Bertolini SUI
2006						
17-01 Jordan	W 2-0	Abu Dhabi	Fr	Drogba [30], Akale [80]		
21-01 Morocco	W 1-0	Cairo	CNr1	Drogba [38]	8 000	Damon RSA
24-01 Libya	W 2-1	Cairo	CNr1	Drogba [10], Yaya Toure [74]	42 000	Maidin SIN
28-01 Egypt	L 1-3	Cairo	CNr1	Arouna Kone [43]	74 000	Maillet SEY
4-02 Cameroon	D 1-1	Cairo	CNqf	Bakary Kone [91]. W 12-11p	4 000	Sowe GAM
7-02 Nigeria	W 1-0	Alexandria	CNsf	Drogba [47]	20 000	Damon RSA
10-02 Egypt	D 0-0	Cairo	CNf	L 2-4p	74 000	Daami TUN
1-03 Spain	L 2-3	Valladolid	Fr	Akale [12], Kalou [47]	30 000	Rodomonti ITA
27-05 Switzerland	D 1-1	Basel	Fr	Fae [47]	22 000	Vuorela FIN
30-05 Chile	D 1-1	Vittel	Fr	Dindane [71p]		Lamarre FRA
4-06 Slovenia	W 3-0	Every-Bondoufle	Fr	Drogba 2 [35 36], Akale [70]	8 000	
10-06 Argentina	L 1-2	Hamburg	WCr1	Drogba [82]	49 480	De Bleeckere BEL
16-06 Netherlands	L 1-2	Stuttgart	WCr1	Bakary Kone [38]	52 000	Ruiz COL
21-06 Serbia & Montenegro	W 3-2	Munich	WCr1	Dindane 2 [37p 67], Kalou [86p]	66 000	Rodriguez MEX
16-08 Senegal	L 0-1	Tours	Fr		4 000	Husset FRA
8-10 Gabon	W 5-0	Abidjan	CNq	Kolo Toure [11], Kone 3 [23 56 68], Dindane [32]		Buenkadila COD
15-11 Sweden	W 1-0	Le Mans	Fr	Drogba [37]	3 844	Fautrel FRA
2007						
6-02 Guinea	W 1-0	Rouen	Fr	Drogba [77]		
21-03 Mauritius	W 3-0	Bellevue	Fr	Kalou.S [60], Gohouri 2 [76 90]		
25-03 Madagascar	W 3-0	Antananarivo	CNq	Gohouri [29], Dindane [35], Diane [81]		Maillet SEY
3-06 Madagascar	W 5-0	Bouake	CNq	Kalou.S [18], Kone 2 [37 82], Toure.Y [48], Drogba [87]		

Fr = Friendly match • CN = African Cup of Nations • WC = FIFA World Cup
q = qualifier • r1 = first round group • qf = quarter-final • sf = semi-final • f = final

COTE D'IVOIRE NATIONAL TEAM RECORDS AND RECORD SEQUENCES

Records			Sequence records					
Victory	6-0	Four times	Wins	7	1984	Clean sheets	9	1991
Defeat	2-6	GHA 1971	Defeats	6	1977-1979	Goals scored	15	1983-1984
Player Caps	n/a		Undefeated	16	1987-1989	Without goal	3	1985, 1989
Player Goals	n/a		Without win	7	1985	Goals against	11	1980-1983

REPUBLIC OF CÔTE D'IVOIRE; REPUBLIQUE DE CÔTE D'IVOIRE

Capital	Yamoussoukro	Language	French	Independence	1960
Population	17 654 843	Area	322 460 km²	Density 53 per km²	% in cities 44%
GDP per cap	$1 400	Dailling code	+225	Internet .ci	GMT + / - 0

MAJOR CITIES/TOWNS
Population '000

1	Abidjan	3 796
2	Bouaké	582
3	Daloa	221
4	San Pedro	207
5	Yamoussoukro	200
6	Korhogo	170
7	Man	142
8	Divo	131
9	Gagnoa	125
10	Abengourou	106
11	Anyama	103
12	Agboville	84
13	Grand Bassam	75
14	Dabou	71
15	Dimbokro	69
16	Ferkessedougou	63
17	Adzopé	63
18	Bouaflé	62
19	Sinfra	61
20	Bingerville	52
21	Issia	51
22	Odienné	51
23	Lakota	39
24	Bouna	24

MEDALS TABLE

		Overall			Lge	Cup			Africa				City	Stadium	Cap'ty	DoF
		G	S	B	G	G	S		G	S	B					
1	ASEC Mimosas	37	4	6	22	14	3		1	1	6		Abidjan	Houphouët-Boigny	45 000	1948
2	Africa Sports National	29	10	2	14	13	7		2	3	2		Abidjan	Houphouët-Boigny	45 000	1936
3	Stade d'Abidjan	11	7	1	5	5	7		1		1		Abidjan	Municipal	9 000	1936
4	Stella Club d'Adjamé	6	6		3	2	5		1	1			Abidjan	Parc des Sports	10 000	1936
5	Onze Freres	2			2								Grand-Bassam	Leon Robert	10 000	
6	Sporting Club de Gagnoa	1	7		1		7						Gagnoa	Victor-Biaka-Boda	12 000	
7	ASC Bouaké	1	2			1	2						Bouaké	Bouaké	15 000	
8	SCR Alliance Bouaké	1	1			1	1						Bouaké	Bouaké	15 000	
	Réveil Club de Daloa	1	1			1	1						Daloa	Municipal	4 000	
	Société Omnisport de l'Armée	1	1			1	1						Abidjan	Robert-Champroux	20 000	
11	ASI Abengourou	1				1							Abengourou	Abengourou	12 000	
	CO Bouaflé	1				1							Bouaflé	Bouaflé	4 000	
	ASC Espoir de Man	1				1							Man	Leon Robert	10 000	
	Issia Wazi FC	1				1							Gagnoa	Victor-Biaka-Boda	12 000	
	Jeunesse Club d'Abidjan	1				1							Abidjan	Robert-Champroux	20 000	
16	Séwé Sport de San Pedro		2				2						San Pedro	Auguste-Demise	8 000	

RECENT LEAGUE AND CUP RECORD

	Championship							Cup		
Year	Champions	Pts	Runners-up	Pts	Third	Pts		Winners	Score	Runners-up
1995	ASEC Mimosas	23	SO Armée	18	Africa Sports	15		ASEC Mimosas	2-0	Stade Abidjan
1996	Africa Sports							SO Armée	0-0 10-9p	Africa Sports
1997	ASEC Mimosas	26	SO Armée	15	Africa Sports	12		ASEC Mimosas	4-0	Africa Sports
1998	ASEC Mimosas	24	FC Man	16	Africa Sports	13		Africa Sports	3-0	Stade Abidjan
1999	Africa Sports	28	ASEC Mimosas	23	Stade Abidjan	16		ASEC Mimosas	5-0	Séwé San Pedro
2000	ASEC Mimosas	21	Sabé Bouna	16	Africa Sports	16		Stade Abidjan	2-1	ASEC Mimosas
2001	ASEC Mimosas	55	Satellite FC	45	Africa Sports	41		Alliance Bouaké	2-0	ASC Bouaké
2002	ASEC Mimosas	22	Jeunesse Abidjan	18	Satellite FC	16		Africa Sports	2-0	Renaissance
2003	ASEC Mimosas	21	Africa Sports	19	Stella Adjamé	15		ASEC Mimosas	1-1 4-2p	Africa Sports
2004	ASEC Mimosas	68	Africa Sport	48	Stella Adjamé	43		CO Bouaflé	2-1	Stade Abidjan
2005	ASEC Mimosas	66	Africa Sport	55	Jeunesse Abidjan	45		ASEC Mimosas	1-0	Séwé San Pedro
2006	ASEC Mimosas	56	Séwé San Pedro	49	Denguélé Odienné	44		Issia Wazi	1-0	SO Armée

COTE D'IVOIRE 2006

LIGUE 1

	Pl	W	D	L	F	A	Pts	ASEC	Séwé	Denguélé	Bingerville	Sabé	Stade	Issia	Africa Sp.	Gagnoa	Stella	JCA	Daloa	EFYM	Lakota
ASEC Mimosas †	26	17	5	4	42	16	56		1-1	3-1	3-0	4-0	4-0	2-1	1-1	2-0	3-1	1-1	0-1	1-0	2-0
Séwé San Pedro †	26	14	7	5	29	16	49	0-1		1-0	1-2	0-1	1-0	1-1	1-1	2-1	1-0	2-1	1-0	1-0	1-0
Denguélé Odienné ‡	26	12	8	6	29	19	44	2-1	1-0		0-0	0-1	1-3	2-0	0-1	1-0	1-1	3-0	0-0	0-0	0-0
Entente Bingerville	26	10	9	7	25	21	39	1-1	0-0	0-1		1-2	1-1	1-3	0-0	2-0	2-0	2-0	0-0	1-0	2-1
Sabé Sports Bouna	26	9	11	6	21	22	38	1-2	1-1	0-2	0-0		0-1	1-1	0-0	1-0	1-1	1-1	1-0	3-1	1-0
Stade Abidjan	26	10	7	9	23	26	37	0-1	1-2	0-1	0-2	0-0		1-0	2-2	1-0	1-0	2-2	0-1	0-2	2-0
Issia Wazi	26	9	9	8	21	19	36	1-0	0-1	1-1	1-0	3-1	0-0		0-0	0-1	1-1	2-0	1-0	1-0	0-0
Africa Sports	26	8	11	7	19	22	35	0-1	0-0	0-2	1-0	1-1	2-2	2-0		0-1	**0-3**	2-3	1-0	0-0	3-1
Sporting Gagnoa	26	8	5	13	23	31	29	2-4	1-2	4-3	1-3	0-1	0-2	0-0	1-1		0-0	1-0	1-0	2-0	1-2
Stella Adjamé	26	5	12	9	22	24	27	0-0	1-2	0-2	1-2	1-1	0-1	0-0	0-1	1-1		3-0	2-0	0-0	3-2
Jeunesse Abidjan	26	6	9	11	25	33	27	1-0	0-0	2-3	3-1	1-1	3-0	2-1	1-2	0-1	1-1		1-0	0-0	1-1
Réveil Daloa	26	7	6	13	15	25	27	2-0	1-5	1-1	1-1	1-0	0-1	1-2	1-0	2-1	0-0	2-1		0-1	1-1
Ecole Yéo Martial	26	5	7	14	13	22	22	0-1	1-1	0-1	0-1	0-1	1-2	0-1	1-0	3-1	1-2	2-0			2-0
Lakota	26	4	10	12	13	29	22	0-2	0-2	0-0	0-0	0-0	0-0	1-0	0-3	1-3	0-0	0-0	1-0	2-0	

29/01/2006 - 6/10/2006 • † Qualified for the CAF Champions League • ‡ Qualified for the CAF Confederation Cup • Match in bold was awarded and Africa Sports were deducted five goals

COTE D'IVOIRE 2006 — 2ÈME DIVISION (2) – POULE A

	Pl	W	D	L	F	A	Pts
Lagoké FC †	10	7	2	1	12	7	23
ASC Ouragahio	10	3	4	3	13	11	13
FC Hiré	10	2	6	2	14	9	12
Ban Danané	10	3	3	4	10	11	12
AC Sinfra	10	3	2	5	5	13	11
Sempa San Pedro	10	2	3	5	9	12	9

25/03/2006 - 22/06/2006 • † Qualified for play-off

COTE D'IVOIRE 2006 — 2ÈME DIVISION (2) – POULE B

	Pl	W	D	L	F	A	Pts
RC Koumassi †	10	6	4	0	14	6	22
USC Bassam	10	5	3	2	13	10	18
US Koumassi	10	4	2	4	9	10	14
Oryx Yopougon	10	1	7	2	8	7	10
Espoir Koumassi	10	2	2	6	6	13	8
Satellite FC	10	1	4	5	5	9	7

25/03/2006 - 22/06/2006 • † Qualified for play-off

COTE D'IVOIRE 2006 — 2ÈME DIVISION (2) – POULE C

	Pl	W	D	L	F	A	Pts
SO Armée †	10	8	2	0	21	6	26
Renaissance Bettié	10	4	3	3	9	8	15
Sacraboutou Bondoukou	10	4	3	3	10	10	15
ASI Abengourou	10	3	2	5	5	8	11
FC Adzopé	10	3	0	7	14	17	9
Anéby Agboville	10	3	0	7	5	15	9

25/03/2006 - 22/06/2006 • † Qualified for play-off

COTE D'IVOIRE 2006 — 2ÈME DIVISION (2) – POULE D

	Pl	W	D	L	F	A	Pts
CO Bouaflé †	10	6	2	2	16	13	20
US Yamassoukro	10	5	3	2	24	13	18
CO Korhogo	10	4	4	2	13	8	16
Man FC	10	4	4	2	13	8	16
VAC Bouaké	10	2	2	6	13	16	8
Toumodi FC	10	1	1	8	5	23	4

25/03/2006 - 22/06/2006 • † Qualified for play-off

Play-offs: CO Bouaflé 0-2 **SO Armée**; **Lagoké FC** 1-0 RC Koumassi • SO Armée and Lagoké promoted

COUPE NATIONALE 2006

Round of sixteen

Issia Wazi	0	5p
JAC Zuénoula	0	4p
Santa Cruz Alépé	1	
FC Hiré	2	
Jeunesse Abidjan	Bye	
ASEC Mimosas	0	
Séwé San Pedro	1	
Stade Abidjan	4	
COSAP San Pedro	1	
Entente Bingerville	2	1p
Ecole Yéo Martial	2	3p
Lagoké FC	1	2p
SO Armée	1	4p

Quarter–finals

Issia Wazi	2	
FC Hiré	0	
Jeunesse Abidjan	1	2p
Séwé San Pedro	1	3p
Stade Abidjan	1	
Ecole Yéo Martial	0	
SO Armée	Bye	

Semi–finals

Issia Wazi	1	4p
Séwé San Pedro	1	3p
Stade Abidjan	1	2p
SO Armée	1	3p

Final

Issia Wazi	1
SO Armée	0

CUP FINAL

Stade Houphouët-Boigny, Abidjan
6-08-2006, Att: 10 000. Ref: Lacina

Scorer - Victorien Djédjé [47]

Issia - Zogbo; Ehounou (Diomandé.I 72), Doumbia, Diomandé.L, Largaton, Yapo Atsin, Kouakou, N'Guessan, Cissé, N'Zue (Zohi 76), Djédjé, Boni (Gundina 65)
SOA - Diomandé.M; Aubert, Kouassi, Yoro, Anékoré Gohousou, Yobouet Kouadio, Konan Kouakou (Takoré 71), N'Da (Ahou 84), M'Boua, Tanoh (Biland 58), Tiecoura Sea

‡ Qualified for the CAF Confederation Cup

CMR – CAMEROON

NATIONAL TEAM RECORD
JULY 10TH 2006 TO JULY 12TH 2010

PL	W	D	L	F	A	%
7	5	2	0	16	6	85.7

FIFA/COCA-COLA WORLD RANKING

1993	1994	1995	1996	1997	1998	1999	2000	2001	2002	2003	2004	2005	2006	High		Low	
23	31	37	56	53	41	58	39	38	16	14	23	23	11	11	12/06	62	04/97

					2006–2007						
08/06	09/06	10/06	11/06	12/06	01/07	02/07	03/07	04/07	05/07	06/07	07/07
12	12	12	11	11	11	17	18	13	13	14	15

Cameroon breezed through the African Nations Cup qualifiers as expected, securing a berth at the 2008 finals in Ghana in their penultimate group game, keeping up a 100 percent record through their first five matches. But that did not provide any security of tenure for coach Jules Nyongha who was told that he was to be replaced in time for the finals by yet another expatriate coach. Despite a ringing endorsement from Samuel Eto'o and other leading players, Nyongha is set to revert back to the supplementary role with the national team that he has held for more than a decade. Cameroon's latest foreign coach, Arie Haan, quit in frustration in February 2007, blaming

INTERNATIONAL HONOURS
Qualified for the FIFA World Cup™ finals 1982 1990 1994 1998 2002 **African Cup of Nations** 1984 1988 2000 2002 **African Games** 1991 1999 2003 **African Youth** 1995 **African U-17** 2003 **CAF African Champions League** Oryx Doula 1965, Canon Yaounde 1971 1978 1980, Union Douala 1979

poor organisation. Success at national team level, where the squad is exclusively made up of European-based players, contrasts with the country's inability to find any continental success at club level, at least not for the past two and a half decades. Cotonsport, from the town of Garoua in the far north of the country, continued their remarkable domestic dominance by winning their seventh title in the past ten seasons, but they again failed to qualify for the group phase of the 2007 African Champions League. However, unfancied Astres Douala, rookies in African club competition, did qualify for the last eight of the 2007 African Confederation Cup.

THE FIFA BIG COUNT OF 2006

	Male	Female		Total
Number of players	749 576	35 939	Referees and Assistant Referees	2 260
Professionals	540		Admin, Coaches, Technical, Medical	5 516
Amateurs 18+	10 975		Number of clubs	220
Youth under 18	10 110		Number of teams	1 100
Unregistered	45 470		Clubs with women's teams	3
Total players	785 515		Players as % of population	4.53%

Fédération Camerounaise de Football (FECAFOOT)
Avenue du 27 aout 1940, Tsinga-Yaoundé, Case Postale 1116, Yaoundé, Cameroon
Tel +237 22210012   Fax +237 22216662
fecafoot@fecafootonline.com   www.fecafootonline.com
President: IYA Mohammed   General Secretary: TBD
Vice-President: ATANGANA Jean Rene   Treasurer: EPACKA Henri   Media Officer: ABDOURAMAN M.
Men's Coach: NYONGHA Jules   Women's Coach: KAMDEM Charles
FECAFOOT formed: 1959   CAF: 1963   FIFA: 1962
Green shirts with yellow trimmings, Red shorts, Yellow socks or Red shirts, Green shorts, Yellow socks

RECENT INTERNATIONAL MATCHES PLAYED BY CAMEROON

2003	Opponents	Score		Venue	Comp	Scorers	Att	Referee
19-06	Brazil	W	1-0	Paris	CCr1	Eto'o [83]	46 719	Ivanov RUS
21-06	Turkey	W	1-0	Paris	CCr1	Geremi [90p]	43 743	Amarilla PAR
23-06	United States	D	0-0	Lyon	CCr1		19 206	Shield AUS
26-06	Colombia	W	1-0	Lyon	CCsf	N'Diefi [9]	12 352	Merk GER
29-06	France	L	0-1	Paris	CCf		51 985	Ivanov RUS
19-11	Japan	D	0-0	Oita	Fr		38 627	Lu CHN
7-12	Central African Rep	D	2-2	Brazzaville	CM r1	Mokake [60]		
9-12	Central African Rep	L	0-1	Brazzaville	CMr1			
10-12	Congo	W	2-0	Brazzaville	CMsf	Ambassa [45], Abada [90]		Youssouf GAB
13-12	Central African Rep	W	3-2	Brazzaville	CMf	Mevengue [16p], Mokake.M [69], Mokake.E [78]		Bantsimba CGO
2004								
25-01	Algeria	D	1-1	Sousse	CNr1	Mboma [44]	20 000	Codjia BEN
29-01	Zimbabwe	W	5-3	Sfax	CNr1	Mboma 3 [31 44 64], Mbami 2 [39 66]	15 000	Aboubacar CIV
3-02	Egypt	D	0-0	Monastir	CNr1		20 000	Bujsaim UAE
8-02	Nigeria	L	1-2	Monastir	CNqf	Eto'o [42]	18 000	Guezzaz MAR
28-04	Bulgaria	L	0-3	Sofia	Fr		13 987	Verbist BEL
6-06	Benin	W	2-1	Yaoundé	WCq	Eto'o [42], Song [45]	40 000	Mbera GAB
18-06	Libya	D	0-0	Misurata	WCq		7 000	Lim Kee Chong MRI
4-07	Côte d'Ivoire	W	2-0	Yaoundé	WCq	Eto'o [80], Feutchine [82]	80 000	Guezzaz MAR
5-09	Egypt	L	2-3	Cairo	WCq	Tchato [88], Eto'o [90]	25 000	Lim Kee Chong MRI
9-10	Sudan	D	1-1	Omdurman	WCq	Job [90+2]	30 000	Buenkadila COD
17-11	Germany	L	0-3	Leipzig	Fr		4 200	De Santis ITA
2005								
9-02	Senegal	W	1-0	Creteil	Fr	Geremi [87]	8 000	Lhermite FRA
27-03	Sudan	W	2-1	Yaoundé	WCq	Geremi [34], Webo [90]	30 000	Diatta SEN
4-06	Benin	W	4-1	Cotonou	WCq	Song [19], Webo [51], Geremi [64], Eto'o [69]	20 000	El Arjoun MAR
19-06	Libya	W	1-0	Yaoundé	WCq	Webo [37]	36 000	Coulibaly MLI
4-09	Côte d'Ivoire	W	3-2	Abidjan	WCq	Webo 3 [30 47 85]	34 500	Daami TUN
8-10	Egypt	D	1-1	Yaounde	WCq	Douala [20]	38 750	Coulibaly MLI
15-11	Morocco	D	0-0	Clairefontaine	Fr			
2006								
21-01	Angola	W	3-1	Cairo	CNr1	Eto'o 3 [21 39 78]	8 000	Guezzaz MAR
25-01	Togo	W	2-0	Cairo	CNr1	Eto'o [68], Meyong Ze [86]	3 000	Sowe GAM
29-01	Congo DR	W	2-0	Cairo	CNr1	Geremi [31], Eto'o [33]	5 000	Coulibaly MLI
4-02	Côte d'Ivoire	D	1-1	Cairo	CNqf	Meyong Ze [96], L 11-12p	4 000	Sowe GAM
27-05	Netherlands	L	0-1	Rotterdam	Fr		46 228	Plautz AUT
16-08	Guinea	D	1-1	Rouen	Fr	Webo [90]		Duhamel FRA
3-09	Rwanda	W	3-0	Kigali	CNq	Feutchine [56], Geremi [62], Nguemo [85]		Ssegonga UGA
7-10	Equatorial Guinea	W	3-0	Yaoundé	CNq	Idrissou 2 [72 89], Webo [79]		Daami TUN
2007								
7-02	Togo	D	2-2	Lome	Fr	Boya [65], Ngom Kome [90]		
24-03	Liberia	W	3-1	Yaoundé	CNq	Webo 2 [12 24], Idrissou [85]		Djaoupe TOG
3-06	Liberia	W	2-1	Monrovia	CNq	Mbia [12], Eto'o		
17-06	Rwanda	W	2-1	Garoua	CNq	Idrissou [33], Geremi [48]		Sowe GAM

Fr = Friendly match • CC = FIFA Confederations Cup • CN = African Cup of Nations • CM = CEMAC Championship • WC = FIFA World Cup
q = qualifier • r1 = 1st round • qf = quarter-final • sf = semi-final • f = final

CAMEROON NATIONAL TEAM RECORDS AND RECORD SEQUENCES

Records			Sequence records					
Victory	9-2	SOM 1960	Wins	7	2002	Clean sheets	7	2002
Defeat	1-6	NOR 1990, RUS 1994	Defeats	3	Five times	Goals scored	24	1967-1972
Player Caps	109	SONG Rigobert	Undefeated	16	1981-1983	Without goal	4	1981, 2001
Player Goals	33	MBOMA Patrick	Without win	9	1994-1995	Goals against	11	1969-1972

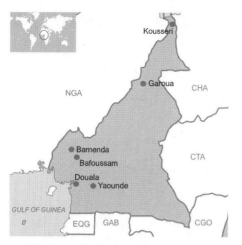

Kousséri

NGA

Garoua

CHA

Bamenda

CTA

Bafoussam

Douala

Yaounde

GULF OF GUINEA

EQG | GAB | CGO

REPUBLIC OF CAMEROON; REPUBLIQUE DU CAMEROUN

Capital	Yaoundé	Language French, English		Independence	1960
Population	17 340 702	Area 475 440 km²	Density 33 per km²	% in cities	45%
GDP per cap	$1 800	Dailling code +237	Internet .cm	GMT +/-	+1

MAJOR CITIES/TOWNS

Population '000

1	Douala	1 371
2	Yaoundé	1 344
3	Kousséri	476
4	Garoua	461
5	Bamenda	419
6	Maroua	335
7	Bafoussam	305
8	Mokolo	298
9	Ngaoundéré	244
10	Bertoua	234
11	Edéa	218
12	Loum	188
13	Kumba	149
14	Nkongsamba	118
15	Mbouda	118
16	Djang	101
17	Guider	88
18	Bafang	83
19	Limbe	73
20	Bangangté	69
21	Buéa	66
22	Baham	-
23	Batie	-
24	Ngoumou	4

MEDALS TABLE

		Overall			Lge	Cup		Africa			City	Stadium	Cap'ty	DoF
		G	S	B	G	G	S	G	S	B				
1	Canon Sportif Yaoundé	26	8	4	10	12	5	4	3	4	Yaoundé	Stade Ahmadou Ahidjo	80 000	1930
2	Union Sportive Douala	13	6	1	4	7	6	2		1	Douala	Stade de la Reunification	30 000	1957
3	Tonnerre Kalara Club Yaoundé	11	5	1	5	5	3	1	2	1	Yaoundé	Stade Ahmadou Ahidjo	80 000	1938
4	Oryx Douala	10	1	1	5	4	1	1		1	Douala	Akwa	12 000	
5	Cotonsport Garoua	9	2	1	7	2	1		1	1	Garoua	Omnisport Poumpoum Rey	22 000	
6	Racing Club Bafoussam	5	3		4	1	3				Bafoussam	Municipal de Bamendzi	5 000	
7	Diamant Yaoundé	4	4	1		3	4			1	Yaoundé	Stade Ahmadou Ahidjo	80 000	
8	Caïman Douala	4	3		3	1	3				Douala	Stade de la Reunification	30 000	
9	Lion Club Yaoundé	4				4					Yaoundé	Militaire	20 000	
10	Dynamo Douala	3			3						Douala	Akwa	12 000	
11	Léopards Douala	2	3	1	2		3			1	Douala	Akwa	12 000	
12	Aigle Royal Nkongsamba	2	2		2		2				Nkongsamba	Omnisports	6 000	
13	Fovu Club Baham	2	1		1	1	1				Baham	Stade Municipal	7 000	
14	Olympique Mvolyé	2				2					Mvolyé	Mvolyé	11 000	
15	Sable Batié	1	2		1		2				Batié	Batié	5 000	
	Unisport Bafang	1	2		1		2				Bafang	Stade Municipal	5 000	
17	Dihep Nkam Yabassi	1	1			1	1				Yabassi	Yabassi	8 000	
18	Kumbo Strikers	1		1		1				1	Kumbo	Municipal	10 000	

RECENT LEAGUE AND CUP RECORD

	Championship							Cup		
Year	Champions	Pts	Runners-up	Pts	Third	Pts		Winners	Score	Runners-up
1995	Racing Bafoussam	52	Léopard Douala	48	Unisport Bafang	48		Canon Yaoundé	1-0	Océan Kribi
1996	Unisport Bafang	56	Cotonsport Garoua	47	Canon Yaoundé	47		Racing Bafoussam	1-0	Stade Banjoun
1997	Cotonsport Garoua	62	Stade Bandjoun	60	Union Douala	55		Union Douala	2-1	Ports FC Douala
1998	Cotonsport Garoua	54	Canon Yaoundé	53	Tonnerre Yaoundé	51		Dynamo Douala	1-0	Canon Yaoundé
1999	Sable Batié	58	Cotonsport Garoua	56	Racing Bafoussam	49		Canon Yaoundé	2-1	Cotonsport Garoua
2000	Fovu Baham	59	Cotonsport Garoua	53	Union Douala	51		Kumbo Strikers	1-0	Unisport Bafang
2001	Cotonsport Garoua	58	Tonnerre Yaoundé	53	Fovu Baham	50		Fovu Baham	3-2	Cintra Yaoundé
2002	Canon Yaoundé	55	Cotonsport Garoua	53	Bamboutos Mbouda	50		Mt Cameroun	2-1	Sable Batié
2003	Cotonsport Garoua	62	Canon Yaoundé	51	PWD Bamenda	51		Cotonsport Garoua	2-1	Sable Batié
2004	Cotonsport Garoua	30	Racing Bafoussam	28	Union Douala	26		Cotonsport Garoua	1-0	Union Douala
2005	Cotonsport Garoua	71	Aigle Royal Menoua	53	Astres Douala	51		Impôts Yaoundé	1-0	Unisport Bafang
2006	Cotonsport Garoua	53	Canon Yaoundé	49	Astres Douala	47		Union Douala	1-0	Fovu Baham

CAMEROON 2006

PREMIERE DIVISION

	Pl	W	D	L	F	A	Pts	Cotonsport	Canon	Astres	Fovu	Espérance	Aigle	Foudre	Sable	Sahel	Bamboutos	Mt Cameroon	Union	Fédéral	Impôts	Racing	KSA
Cotonsport Garoua †	30	14	11	5	50	22	53		1-1	4-0	0-0	1-0	7-0	4-0	2-0	2-0	2-0	0-0	1-1	5-2	3-0	1-0	2-0
Canon Yaoundé	30	12	13	5	36	21	49	2-1		3-1	2-1	1-0	4-0	2-0	3-2	0-0	0-0	0-1	0-0	0-0	1-2	1-0	4-0
Les Astres Douala ‡	30	11	14	5	36	24	47	2-1	0-0		1-1	0-0	1-1	3-1	1-0	3-2	1-1	1-1	0-0	10-2	1-0	0-0	1-1
Fovu Baham	30	10	15	5	29	17	45	2-1	0-1	0-0		1-1	0-0	1-1	0-1	0-0	1-1	1-0	1-0	2-1	**3-0**	0-1	1-1
Espérance Guider	30	11	8	11	28	30	41	0-1	1-0	1-1	0-0		1-0	0-0	3-1	1-1	3-1	0-0	2-0	2-0	1-0	1-0	3-1
Aigle Royal Dschang	30	9	13	8	28	35	40	1-2	1-1	1-0	0-1	1-0		2-0	1-3	4-0	1-0	0-0	1-0	0-0	2-2	3-1	1-0
Foudre Akonolinga	30	9	12	9	27	29	39	2-0	0-0	0-0	0-0	2-0	1-2		1-1	1-0	0-0	0-0	1-0	1-0	2-0	2-0	1-0
Sable Batie	30	8	14	8	27	26	38	1-1	1-1	0-1	0-1	3-0	1-1	2-0		0-0	0-0	1-0	1-0	2-2	1-1	1-1	0-0
Sahel Maroua	30	9	11	10	34	39	38	1-2	2-2	0-0	0-0	3-1	3-1	2-1	0-0		3-1	1-0	3-1	3-0	2-3	1-0	1-0
Bamboutos Mbouda	30	8	14	8	26	28	38	1-1	0-1	2-1	0-2	1-1	1-1	2-0	0-1	2-1		0-0	0-0	0-0	0-0	2-1	3-1
Mount Cameroon	30	7	17	6	28	32	38	1-1	2-1	2-2	1-5	2-1	1-1	1-1	1-1	0-0	2-3		1-1	2-2	1-0	1-1	2-1
Union Douala ‡	30	8	13	9	23	22	37	1-1	2-1	1-0	1-0	4-1	1-1	2-2	0-1	1-0	0-0	2-2		2-0	0-0	0-0	1-0
Fédéral Noun	30	8	13	9	29	39	37	0-0	1-1	0-1	0-0	1-0	1-0	2-0	0-0	3-1	1-1	1-1	1-0		1-1	4-1	2-0
Impôts Yaoundé §1	30	·9	9	12	36	36	35	1-0	0-0	0-1	2-2	0-1	4-1	1-2	2-0	4-1	2-3	4-1	1-0	1-1		3-1	1-2
Racing Bafoussam	30	5	12	13	23	32	27	1-1	1-2	0-0	1-3	1-2	0-0	1-1	1-1	5-1	1-0	0-1	0-0	1-0	1-1		0-0
Kadji Sports Douala	30	4	7	19	16	44	19	2-2	1-1	0-3	0-1	3-1	0-0	0-2	2-1	1-1	0-1	0-1	0-2	0-1	1-0	0-2	

28/01/2006 - 3/09/2006 • † Qualified for the CAF Champions League • ‡ Qualified for the Confederation Cup • §1 = One point deducted • Match in bold was awarded 3-0 • Top scorer: Francis LITSINGI, Cotonsport 15

CAMEROON 2006
TOURNOI INTER POULES (2)

Pool A - in Garoua	Pl	W	D	L	F	A	Pts
International Lion NE	4	3	0	1	9	7	9
Cetef Bonabéri	4	3	0	1	7	4	9
Tonnerre Kalara	4	2	1	1	7	3	7
Panthère Bangangté	4	1	0	3	4	9	3
Kohi Maroua	4	0	1	3	8	12	1

Pool B - in Buea	Pl	W	D	L	F	A	Pts
Univ. Ngaoundéré	4	2	2	0	5	1	8
CPS Abong-Mbang	4	2	1	1	5	5	7
Tiko United	4	2	1	1	6	4	7
Pilote Garoua	4	1	1	2	6	7	4
Bali United	4	0	1	3	2	7	1

Promotion play-off: Cetef Bonabéri 1-0 CPS Abong-Mbang

COUPE DE CAMEROUN 2006

Round of 16

Union Douala *	5	0
Mbalmayo FC	0	0
Espérance Guider *	1	0
Impôts Yaoundé	0	2
Bandja FC *	1	1
Mount Cameroon	0	0
Douala AC 2000	0	1
Cotonsport Garoua *	6	1
Sable Batié	1	0
International Lion NE*	1	0
Kadji Sports Douala *	1	1
Acada Sport Limbe	2	1
Bamboutos Mbouda	0	2
Sahel Maroua *	0	0
Aigle Royal Menoua *	0	1
Fovu Baham	1	2

Quarter–finals

Union Douala *	1	1
Impôts Yaoundé	1	0
Bandja FC *	0	0
Cotonsport Garoua	3	3
Sable Batié *	2	2
Acada Sport Limbe	0	0
Bamboutos Mbouda *	1	1
Fovu Baham	1	2

Semi–finals

Union Douala	1	0
Cotonsport Garoua *	1	0
Sable Batié	1	1
Fovu Baham *	5	0

Final

Union Douala ‡	1
Fovu Baham	0

CUP FINAL

Stade Ahmadou Ahidjo, Yaoundé
3-12-2005, Att: 45 000

Scorer - Samuel Inogue 70

* Home team in the first leg • ‡ Qualified for the CAF Confederation Cup

COD – CONGO DR

NATIONAL TEAM RECORD
JULY 10TH 2006 TO JULY 12TH 2010

PL	W	D	L	F	A	%
7	2	2	3	8	9	42.8

FIFA/COCA-COLA WORLD RANKING

1993	1994	1995	1996	1997	1998	1999	2000	2001	2002	2003	2004	2005	2006	High		Low	
71	68	68	66	76	62	59	70	77	65	56	78	77	66	51	09/03	84	04/07

					2006–2007						
08/06	09/06	10/06	11/06	12/06	01/07	02/07	03/07	04/07	05/07	06/07	07/07
63	64	66	65	66	60	82	83	84	61	65	72

Congo DR were well on course to qualify for a ninth successive appearance at the African Nations Cup finals, needing a home win in their last qualifying game to ensure a trip to Ghana. The competent performance of the 'Leopards', the nickname of the team having being restored after several years as the 'Simbas', came as a symbol of the potential of the massive country, for decades embroiled in civil strife and steady degradation. It also came despite ongoing administrative problems which saw the national team's new Belgian coach Henri Depireux threaten to resign on several occasions as his wages had not been paid. He also had to battle with maintaining a consistent team selection

INTERNATIONAL HONOURS
Qualified for the FIFA World Cup finals 1974

African Cup of Nations 1968 1974 CAF Champions League TP Mazembe 1967 1968 AS Vita Club 1973

as foreign-based players responded with occasional apathy to call-ups. Captain Shabani Nonda kept up his self-imposed exile from the team but after a meeting with authorities in mid-2007 promised to make a return. At club level the rivalry of the major teams in Kinshasa and Lubumbashi continued with TP Mazembe Engelbert winning the LINAFOOT play-offs from fellow Lubumbashi-based club FC St Eloi Lupopo. Mazembe's striker Tresor Mputu scored nine goals in three rounds of the 2007 African Champions League but still saw his side eliminated.

THE FIFA BIG COUNT OF 2006

	Male	Female		Total
Number of players	2 515 600	0	Referees and Assistant Referees	2 900
Professionals	0		Admin, Coaches, Technical, Medical	7 700
Amateurs 18+	55 600		Number of clubs	770
Youth under 18	22 000		Number of teams	3 300
Unregistered	165 000		Clubs with women's teams	0
Total players	2 515 600		Players as % of population	4.01%

Fédération Congolaise de Football-Association (FECOFA)
31 Avenue de la Justice, c/Gombe, Case postale 1284, Kinshasa 1, Congo DR
Tel +243 81 9049788   Fax +243 81 3013527
nzilafanan@hotmail.com   www.none
President: SELEMANI Omari   General Secretary: BADI Gregoire
Vice-President: TSHIMANGA Donatien   Treasurer: BONDEMBE Bokanyanga   Media Officer: NZILA Fanan
Men's Coach: DEPIREUX Henri   Women's Coach: BONGANYA Polycarpe
FECOFA formed: 1919   CAF: 1973   FIFA: 1962
Blue shirts with yellow trimmings, Blue shorts, Blue socks or Yellow shirts with blue trimmings, Blue shorts, Yellow socks

RECENT INTERNATIONAL MATCHES PLAYED BY CONGO DR

2003	Opponents	Score	Venue	Comp	Scorers	Att	Referee
30-03	Swaziland	D 1-1	Mbabane	CNq	Musasa [65]		Katjimune NAM
8-06	Swaziland	W 2-0	Kinshasa	CNq	Mpiana [18], Musasa [71]	60 000	Ravelotslam MRI
22-06	Libya	W 2-1	Kinshasa	CNq	Masudi [29], Mpiana [83]		
5-07	Botswana	D 0-0	Gaborone	CNq			
20-08	Angola	W 2-0	Luanda	Fr	Massaro [46], Mbotale [52]		
2004							
14-01	Egypt	D 2-2	Port Said	Fr	Dinzey [52], Mbala [70]	10 000	Kamal EGY
25-01	Guinea	L 1-2	Tunis	CNr1	Masudi [30]	3 000	Aboubacar CIV
28-01	Tunisia	L 0-3	Tunis	CNr1		20 000	Damon RSA
1-02	Rwanda	L 0-1	Bizerte	CNr1		700	Ndoye SEN
23-05	Angola	L 1-3	Kinshasa	Fr	Kalulika [30p]	60 000	Ntambidila COD
6-06	Uganda	L 0-1	Kampala	WCq		45 000	Maillet SEY
20-06	Burkina Faso	W 3-2	Kinshasa	WCq	Mbajo [12], Mbala [75], Bageta [88p]	75 000	Djaoupe TOG
3-07	Cape Verde Islands	D 1-1	Praia	WCq	Kaluyitu [1]	3 800	Nahi CIV
18-08	Mali	L 0-3	Paris	Fr			Derrien FRA
5-09	South Africa	W 1-0	Kinshasa	WCq	Kabamba [86]	85 000	Hicuburundi BDI
10-10	Ghana	D 0-0	Kumasi	WCq		30 000	Coulibaly MLI
2005							
8-02	Côte d'Ivoire	D 2-2	Rouen	Fr	Makondele [44], Nonda [92+p]	4 000	Duhamel FRA
27-03	Ghana	D 1-1	Kinshasa	WCq	Nonda [50]	80 000	Sowe GAM
5-06	Uganda	W 4-0	Kinshasa	WCq	Nonda 2 [2 69p], Ilongo [58], Matumona [78]	80 000	Daami TUN
18-06	Burkina Faso	L 0-2	Ouagadougou	WCq		25 000	Shelmani LBY
1-07	Botswana	D 0-0	Gaborone	Fr			
16-08	Guinea	W 3-1	Paris	Fr	Mbala [37], LuaLua [62], Mputu [79]		
4-09	Cape Verde Islands	W 2-1	Kinshasa	WCq	Mubiala [21], Mputu [49]	75 000	Guezzaz MAR
25-09	Zambia	D 2-2	Chililabombwe	Fr	Bokese [54], Matumona [65]		
27-09	Zambia	D 0-0	Lubumbashi	Fr			
8-10	South Africa	D 2-2	Durban	WCq	Mputu [11], Nonda [44]	35 000	Mbera GAB
11-11	Tunisia	D 2-2	Paris	Fr	Mputu [16], Lutula [57]		Garibian FRA
16-11	Libya	L 1-2	Paris	Fr	Mbokane [47]		
11-12	Zambia	D 1-1	Lubumbashi	Fr	OG [28]		
14-12	Zambia	L 1-4	Chingola	Fr	Ilingo [55]		
2006							
9-01	Morocco	L 0-3	Rabat	Fr			
14-01	Senegal	D 0-0	Dakar	Fr			Sowe GAM
21-01	Togo	W 2-0	Cairo	CNr1	Mputu [42], LuaLua [61]	6 000	Daami TUN
25-01	Angola	D 0-0	Cairo	CNr1		2 000	Diatta SEN
29-01	Cameroon	L 0-2	Cairo	CNr1		5 000	Coulibaly MLI
3-02	Egypt	L 1-4	Cairo	CNqf	OG [45]	74 000	Sowe GAM
12-05	Mexico	L 1-2	Mexico City	Fr	Mbokani [51]	75 000	Flores MEX
3-09	Namibia	W 3-2	Kinshasa	CNq	Mbele [32], Kalulika [63], Kinkela [80]		Evehe CMR
8-10	Libya	D 1-1	Tripoli	CNq	Bageta [37]		Pare BFA
9-12	Tanzania	L 0-2	Dar es Salaam	Fr			
2007							
29-04	Ethiopia	W 2-0	Kinshasa	CNq	Mbungu [25], Lua Lua [57p]		
28-05	Congo	L 1-2	Brazzaville	Fr	Miala [72]		
1-06	Ethiopia	L 0-1	Addis Abeba	CNq			
16-06	Namibia	D 1-1	Windhoek	CNq	Matumona [27]		

Fr = Friendly match • CN = CAF African Cup of Nations • WC = FIFA World Cup • q = qualifier • r1 = first round group • qf = quarter-final

CONGO DR NATIONAL TEAM RECORDS AND RECORD SEQUENCES

Records			Sequence records				
Victory	10-1	ZAM 1969	Wins	5	1973-1974	Clean sheets	4	Four times
Defeat	0-9	YUG 1974	Defeats	5	2004	Goals scored	38	1976-1985
Player Caps	n/a		Undefeated	12	2002-2004	Without goal	4	1990
Player Goals	n/a		Without win	9	2005-2006	Goals against	13	1964-1966

CONGO DR COUNTRY INFORMATION

Capital	Kinshasa	Independence	1960 from Belgium	GDP per Capita	$700
Population	58 317 930	Status	Republic	GNP Ranking	120
Area km²	2 345 410	Language	French	Dialling code	+243
Population density	24 per km²	Literacy rate	65%	Internet code	.zr
% in urban areas	29%	Main religion	Christian 70%	GMT + / –	+1
Towns/Cities ('000)	Kinshasa 7 787; Lubumbashi 1 374; Kolwezi 910; Mbuji-Mayi 874; Kisangani 539; Kananga 463; Likasi 422; Boma 344; Tshikapa 267; Bukavu 225; Mwene-Ditu 189; Kikwit 186				
Neighbours (km)	Congo 2 410; Central African Republic 1 577; Sudan 628; Uganda 765; Rwanda 217; Burundi 233; Tanzania 459; Zambia 1 930; Angola 2 511; Atlantic Ocean 37				
Main stadia	Stade des Martyrs – Kinshasa 80 000; Stade Municipal – Lubumbashi 35 000; Stade Municipal – Kinshasa 20 000; Stade de Virunga – Goma 8 000				

CONGO DR 2006

LIGUE NATIONAL DE FOOTBALL XI FINAL ROUND	Pl	W	D	L	F	A	Pts	Mazembe	St Eloi	Bukavu	Cilu	Inter	Vita Club
TP Mazembe †	10	8	1	1	19	8	25		1-0	3-2	1-0	3-0	3-2
St Eloi Lupopo †	10	4	4	2	16	10	16	0-2		1-1	1-1	4-1	3-1
Bukavu Dawa ‡	10	3	4	3	11	11	13	1-1	1-1		2-3	1-0	1-0
Cilu Lukala	10	2	4	4	8	11	10	0-2	1-1	0-1		0-1	2-1
SC Inter Kinshasa	10	3	1	6	8	10	10	2-1	1-3	1-0	1-1		0-2
AS Vita Club Kinshasa	10	2	2	6	11	15	8	1-2	0-2	1-1	0-0	3-1	

30/04/2006 - 16/09/2006 • † Qualified for the CAF Champions League • ‡ Qualified for the CAF Confederation Cup

CONGO DR 2006
KINSHASA LEAGUE (EPFKIN)

	Pl	W	D	L	F	A	Pts
DC Motema Pembe	30	21	5	4	51	20	68
AS Vita Club Kinshasa	30	17	10	3	44	19	61
SC Inter Kinshasa	30	15	9	6	38	21	54
FC Les Stars	30	13	8	9	32	27	47
AS Dragons	30	13	6	11	41	28	45
AC Okinawa	30	11	11	8	29	25	44
BC Att Sport	30	11	11	8	30	30	44
AC Bel'Or	30	12	7	11	32	29	43
SC Kintainers	30	8	12	10	23	28	36
Olympic Club	30	9	9	12	34	34	36
SC Malaïka	30	11	2	17	35	46	35
Style du Congo	30	8	10	12	26	32	34
AS Le Blue	30	8	10	12	33	45	34
AS St Herman	30	6	9	15	29	41	27
TP Authidon	30	6	5	19	24	52	23
AJ Vainqueurs	30	4	10	16	23	48	22

10/12/2005 - 2/08/2006

CONGO DR 2006
COUPE DU CONGO (XXIII) FINAL ROUND

Poule A

	Pl	W	D	L	F	A	Pts	SB	MB
DC Motema Pembe †	2	2	0	0	5	0	6	2-0*	3-0
Sanga Balende	2	1	0	1	2	3	3		2-1
Muungano Bukavu	2	0	0	2	1	5	0		

Poule B

	Pl	W	D	L	F	A	Pts	KG	TK
AS Dragons Kinshasa †	2	1	1	0	3	1	4	1-1	2-0
AS Kabasha Goma	2	1	1	0	3	1	4		2-0
Tshinkunku Kananga	2	0	0	2	0	4	0		

* Dragons won 4-1p

† Qualified for the final • Played in Kinshasa

Final: **DC Motema Pembe** 4-1 AS Dragons (13-08-2006 in Kinshasa). Scorers - Ebong 3 55 73 82, Bokungu 62 for Motema Pembe; Bayenga 40 for Dragons • Motema Pembe qualify for the CAF Confederation Cup

RECENT LEAGUE AND CUP RECORD

	Championship						Cup		
Year	Champions	Pts	Runners-up	Pts	Third	Pts	Winners	Score	Runners-up
1997	AS Vita Club	†	DC Motema Pembe				AS Dragons	2-1	AS Vita Club
1998	DC Motema Pembe	13	AS Vita Club	8	SM Sanga Balende	6	AS Dragons	1-0	AS Sucrière
1999	DC Motema Pembe		TP Mazembe		AS Vita Club		AS Dragons	3-2	AS Paulino
2000	TP Mazembe	16	SM Sanga Balende	8	AS Vita Club	5	TP Mazembe	2-0	AS St-Luc Kananga
2001	TP Mazembe	†	FC St-Eloi Lupopo				AS Vita Club	3-0	AS Veti Matadi
2002	FC St-Eloi Lupopo	25	TP Mazembe	23	AS Vita Club	18	US Kenya	2-1	SM Sanga Balende
2003	AS Vita Club	27	SC Cilu	18	FC St-Eloi Lupopo	17	DC Motema Pembe	2-0	TP Mazembe
2004	DC Motema Pembe	14	TP Mazembe	11	FC St-Eloi Lupopo	6	CS Cilu Lukala	1-0	AS St Luc Kananga
2005	DC Motema Pembe	19	FC St-Eloi Lupopo	18	TP Mazembe	17	AS Vita Kabasha	1-1 4-2p	CS Cilu Lukala
2006	TP Mazembe	25	FC St-Eloi Lupopo	16	Bukava Dawa	13	DC Motema Pembe	4-1	AS Dragons

† Knock-out format • Toute Puissant Mazembe beat FC Saint-Eloi Lupopo 1-1 3-1 in the 2001 final

COK – COOK ISLANDS

NATIONAL TEAM RECORD
JULY 10TH 2006 TO JULY 12TH 2010

PL	W	D	L	F	A	%
0	0	0	0	0	0	0

FIFA/COCA-COLA WORLD RANKING

1993	1994	1995	1996	1997	1998	1999	2000	2001	2002	2003	2004	2005	2006	High		Low	
-	-	-	188	192	173	182	170	179	182	190	190	194		169	07/00	198	07/07

	2006–2007										
08/06	09/06	10/06	11/06	12/06	01/07	02/07	03/07	04/07	05/07	06/07	07/07
195	197	197	197	197	198	198	198	198	198	198	198

Their isolation in the middle of the South Pacific, 3000 miles away from New Zealand, and their tiny population of just over 21,000 makes any sort of international activity very difficult for teams from the Cook Islands. With the effective exclusion of their club sides from the OFC's new O-League, the qualifiers for the FIFA World Cup are now the only international competition that the country takes part in. Even at youth level the Cook Islands didn't enter a team in any of the Oceania qualifiers whilst the women were also absent from their Oceania qualifiers at senior and youth level. The men's national team will, however, help to get the 2010 FIFA World Cup underway

INTERNATIONAL HONOURS
None

when they take part in the 13th South Pacific Games in Samoa. The games are acting as an OFC preliminary round with the top three qualifying to join New Zealand in the final round. In club football Nikao Sokattack completed a hat trick of League titles but they lost in the final of the Cup to Takuvaine on penalties after a 0-0 draw. It was only the second time Takuvaine had won the tournament, following on from their initial success in 1991. Nikao Sokattack were initially included in the preliminary phase of the 2008 OFC O–League in a group with the champions from Vanuatu, New Caledonia and Papua New Guinea but they withdrew before the kick-off.

THE FIFA BIG COUNT OF 2006

	Male	Female		Total
Number of players	2 200	0	Referees and Assistant Referees	100
Professionals	0		Admin, Coaches, Technical, Medical	100
Amateurs 18+	800		Number of clubs	40
Youth under 18	1 000		Number of teams	120
Unregistered	200		Clubs with women's teams	2
Total players	2 200		Players as % of population	10.29%

Cook Islands Football Association (CIFA)
Matavora Main Road, PO Box 29, Tupapa, Rarotonga, Cook Islands
Tel +682 28980   Fax +682 28981
cifa@cisoccer.org.ck   www.none
President: HARMON Lee   General Secretary: PIRI Mii
Vice-President: PARKER Allen   Treasurer: NUMANGA Jake   Media Officer: TBD
Men's Coach: JERKS Tim   Women's Coach: JERKS Tim
CIFA formed: 1971   OFC: 1994   FIFA: 1994
Green shirts with white sleeves, Green shorts, White socks

RECENT INTERNATIONAL MATCHES PLAYED BY COOK ISLANDS

2002	Opponents	Score		Venue	Comp	Scorers	Att	Referee
No international matches played in 2002								
2003								
No international matches played in 2003								
2004								
5-05	Samoa	D	0-0	Auckland	Fr			
10-05	Tahiti	L	0-2	Honiara	WCq		12 000	Singh FIJ
12-05	Solomon Islands	L	0-5	Honiara	WCq		14 000	Fred VAN
15-05	Tonga	L	1-2	Honiara	WCq	Pareanga 59	15 000	Sosongan PNG
17-05	New Caledonia	L	0-8	Honiara	WCq		400	Singh FIJ
2005								
No international matches played in 2005								
2006								
No international matches played in 2006								
2007								
No international matches played in 2007 before August								

Fr = Friendly match • WC = FIFA World Cup • q = qualifier

COOK ISLANDS NATIONAL TEAM RECORDS AND RECORD SEQUENCES

Records			Sequence records					
Victory	3-0	ASA 2000	Wins	2	1998, 2000	Clean sheets	1	
Defeat	0-30	TAH 1971	Defeats	6	1971-85, 2000-01	Goals scored	4	1996-1998
Player Caps	n/a		Undefeated	3	1998	Without goal	5	2001-2004
Player Goals	n/a		Without win	11	2000-	Goals against	16	1971-2000

RECENT LEAGUE AND CUP RECORD

	Championship		Cup		
Year	Champions	Winners	Score	Runners-up
1996	Avatiu FC	Avatiu FC		
1997	Avatiu FC	Avatiu FC		
1998	No Tournament	Teau-o-Tonga		
1999	Tupapa FC	Tupapa FC		Avatiu FC
1999	Avatiu FC	Avatiu FC	3-1	Tupapa FC
2000	Nikao Sokattacck	Avatiu FC	3-1	Nikao Sokattack
2001	Tupapa FC	Tupapa FC	5-1	Avatiu FC
2002	Tupapa FC	Nikao Sokattack	3-2	Tupapa FC
2003	Tupapa FC	Nikao Sokattack	3-1	Tupapa FC
2004	Nikao Sokattack	Tupapa FC	3-3 3-1p	Nikao Sokattack
2005	Nikao Sokattack	Nikao Sokattack		
2006	Nikao Sokattack	Takuvaine	0-0 4-1p	Nikao Sokattack

COOK ISLANDS COUNTRY INFORMATION

Capital	Avarua	Independence	Self-governing in free asso-	GDP per Capita	$5 000
Population	21 200	Status	ciation with New Zealand	GNP Ranking	n/a
Area km²	240	Language	English, Maori	Dialling code	+682
Population density	88 per km²	Literacy rate	95%	Internet code	.ck
% in urban areas	n/a	Main religion	Christian	GMT + / –	-10
Towns/Cities ('000)	Avarua 13; Mangaia; Amuri; Omoka; Atiu; Mauke				
Neighbours (km)	South Pacific Ocean 120				
Main stadia	National Stadium – Avarua 3 000				

COL – COLOMBIA

NATIONAL TEAM RECORD
JULY 10TH 2006 TO JULY 12TH 2010

PL	W	D	L	F	A	%
11	7	1	3	19	15	68.1

FIFA/COCA-COLA WORLD RANKING

1993	1994	1995	1996	1997	1998	1999	2000	2001	2002	2003	2004	2005	2006	High	Low
21	17	15	4	10	34	25	15	5	37	39	26	24	34	4 12/96	41 03/04

						2006–2007					
08/06	09/06	10/06	11/06	12/06	01/07	02/07	03/07	04/07	05/07	06/07	07/07
29	20	35	34	34	34	31	31	26	26	31	32

Colombia went into the 2007 Copa América in Venezuela as one of the form teams. Under new coach Jorge Luis Pinto they had won five of the seven games played in the build up to the finals, but in their opening match against Paraguay, the 2001 champions suffered a humiliating 5-0 thrashing and that set the tone for the tournament. In their next match the Colombians lost 4-2 to Argentina and although they beat the USA 1-0 in their final match they were the only third placed team not to qualify for the quarter-finals. Pinto had always said that his main focus was on making sure Colombia qualified for the FIFA World Cup finals for the first time since 1998 but there was

INTERNATIONAL HONOURS
Qualified for the FIFA World Cup finals 1962 1990 1994 1998 Copa América 2001 Juventud de América 1987 2005 South America U-17 1993
Copa Toyota Libertadores Atlético Nacional Medellin 1989 Once Caldas 2004

no hiding the disappointment at his teams' performance. Pinto had earlier led Deportivo Cúcuta to their first title when they beat Tolima 2-1 on aggregate in the 2006 Clausura final. Cúcuta then had an excellent Copa Libertadores campaign where they reached the semi-finals before being knocked out by eventual winners Boca Juniors, this despite winning the first leg 3-1 at home. The opening tournament of the 2007 season was won by Atlético Nacional Medellin who beat debut finalists Atlético Huila 3-1 on aggregate to clinch their ninth League title.

THE FIFA BIG COUNT OF 2006

	Male	Female		Total
Number of players	2 670 029	364 200	Referees and Assistant Referees	2 200
Professionals	929		Admin, Coaches, Technical, Medical	13 600
Amateurs 18+	89 000		Number of clubs	2 750
Youth under 18	166 000		Number of teams	7 700
Unregistered	1 440 000		Clubs with women's teams	23
Total players	3 043 229		Players as % of population	6.98%

Federación Colombiana de Fútbol (COLFUTBOL)
Avenida 32, No. 16-22 Piso 4°, Apdo Aéreo 17602, Bogotá, Colombia
Tel +57 1 2889838   Fax +57 1 2889559
info@colfutbol.org   www.colfutbol.org
President: BEDOYA Luis   General Secretary: SIERRA Celina
Vice-President: JESURUN Ramon   Treasurer: TBD   Media Officer: ROSAS Victor
Men's Coach: PINTO Jorge   Women's Coach: AGUDELO John
COLFUTBOL formed: 1924   CONMEBOL: 1940   FIFA: 1936
Yellow shirts with blue and red trimmings, Blue shorts, Red socks or Blue shirts,

RECENT INTERNATIONAL MATCHES PLAYED BY COLOMBIA

2004	Opponents	Score	Venue	Comp	Scorers	Att	Referee
6-07	Venezuela	W 1-0	Lima	CAr1	Moreno [22p]	45 000	Rezende BRA
9-07	Bolivia	W 1-0	Lima	CAr1	Perea [90]	35 000	Ramos ECU
12-07	Peru	D 2-2	Trujillo	CAr1	Congo [34], Aguilar [52]	25 000	Rodriguez MEX
17-07	Costa Rica	W 2-0	Trujillo	CAqf	Aguilar [41], Moreno [45p]	18 000	Mendez URU
20-07	Argentina	L 0-3	Lima	CAsf		22 000	Hidalgo PER
24-07	Uruguay	L 1-2	Cusco	CA3p	Herrera [70]	35 000	Ortube BOL
5-09	Chile	D 0-0	Santiago	WCq		62 523	Souza BRA
9-10	Paraguay	D 1-1	Barranquilla	WCq	Grisales [17]	25 000	Elizondo ARG
13-10	Brazil	D 0-0	Maceio	WCq		20 000	Larrionda ARG
17-11	Bolivia	W 1-0	Barranquilla	WCq	Yepes [18]	25 000	Torres PAR
2005							
15-01	Korea Republic	W 2-1	Los Angeles	Fr	Castillo [41p], Perea [75]	20 000	Fris
17-01	Guatemala	D 1-1	Los Angeles	Fr	Hurtado [80]	15 000	Vaughn USA
23-02	Mexico	D 1-1	Culiacan	Fr	Perea [58]	10 000	Gasso MEX
9-03	USA	L 0-3	Fullerton	Fr		7 086	Moreno MEX
26-03	Venezuela	D 0-0	Maracaibo	WCq		18 000	Simon BRA
30-03	Argentina	L 0-1	Buenos Aires	WCq		40 000	Amarilla PAR
31-05	England	L 2-3	New Jersey	Fr	Yepes [45], Ramirez.A [78]	58 000	Hall USA
4-06	Peru	W 5-0	Barranquilla	WCq	Rey [29], Soto [55], Angel [58], Restrepo [75], Perea [78]	15 000	Torres PAR
8-06	Ecuador	W 3-0	Barranquilla	WCq	Moreno [2 5 9], Arzuaga [70]	20 402	Simon BRA
6-07	Panama	L 0-1	Miami	GCr1		10 311	Batres GUA
10-07	Honduras	L 1-2	Miami	GCr1	Moreno [30p]	17 292	Hall USA
12-07	Trinidad and Tobago	W 2-0	Miami	GCr1	Aguilar [77], Hurtado [79]	11 000	Rodriguez MEX
17-07	Mexico	W 2-1	Houston	GCqf	Castrillón [58], Aguilar [74]	60 050	Sibrian SLV
21-07	Panama	L 2-3	New Jersey	GCsf	Patiño [2 62 88]	41 721	Sibrian SLV
4-09	Uruguay	L 2-3	Montevideo	WCq	Soto [79], Angel [82]	60 000	Elizondo ARG
8-10	Chile	D 1-1	Barranquilla	WCq	Rey [24]	22 380	Souza BRA
12-10	Paraguay	W 1-0	Asuncion	WCq	Rey [7]	12 374	Rezende BRA
2006							
1-03	Venezuela	D 1-1	Maracaibo	Fr	Soto [70]	15 000	Carpio ECU
24-05	Ecuador	D 1-1	East Rutherford	Fr	Soto [54]	52 425	Vaughn USA
27-05	Romania	D 0-0	Chicago	Fr		15 000	Hall USA
30-05	Poland	W 2-1	Chorzow	Fr	Murillo [19], Martinez [64]	40 000	Szabo HUN
2-06	Germany	L 0-3	Mönchengladbach	Fr		45 600	Hauge NOR
4-06	Morocco	W 2-0	Barcelona	Fr	Rodallega [41p], Soto [86]	11 000	Segura Garcia ESP
16-08	Chile	W 2-1	Santiago	Fr	Preciado [68], Soto [88]	15 000	Larrionda URU
2007							
7-02	Uruguay	L 1-3	Cucuta	Fr	Rodallega [80]	26 000	Hoyos COL
25-03	Switzerland	W 3-1	Miami	Fr	Perea [5], Viafara [57], Chitiva [85]	16 000	Vaughn USA
28-03	Paraguay	W 2-0	Bogota	Fr	Mosquera [32], Dominguez [86]	32 000	
9-05	Panama	W 4-0	Panama City	Fr	Mendoza [20], Valoyes [58], Rodallega [63], Anchico [67]	4 000	Archundia MEX
3-06	Montenegro	W 1-0	Matsumoto	Fr	Falcao [33]	10 070	Ogiya JPN
5-06	Japan	D 0-0	Saitama	Fr		45 091	Vollquartz DEN
23-06	Ecuador	W 3-1	Barranquilla	Fr	Rodallega [16], Yepes [30], Perea [79]	35 000	Gomes VEN
28-06	Paraguay	L 0-5	Maracaibo	CAr1		30 000	Larrionda URU
2-07	Argentina	L 2-4	Maracaibo	CAr1	Perea [10], Castrillón [76]	35 000	Simon BRA
5-07	USA	W 1-0	Barquisimeto	CAr1	Castrillón [15]	37 000	Andarcia VEN

Fr = Friendly match • CC = FIFA Confederations Cup • GC = CONCACAF Gold Cup • CA = Copa América • WC = FIFA World Cup
q = qualifier • r1 = first round group • qf = quarter-final • sf = semi-final • 3p = third place play-off

COLOMBIA NATIONAL TEAM RECORDS AND RECORD SEQUENCES

Records			Sequence records				
Victory	5-0	ARG 93, URU 04, PER 05	Wins	7	1988-1989	Clean sheets	6	2001
Defeat	0-9	BRA 1957	Defeats	7	1947-1949	Goals scored	15	1995-1997
Player Caps	111	VALDERRAMA Carlos	Undefeated	27	1992-1994	Without goal	6	2002-2003
Player Goals	25	IGUARAN Arnoldo	Without win	15	1947-1957	Goals against	14	1938-46, 1961-63

REPUBLIC OF COLOMBIA; REPUBLICA DE COLOMBIA

Capital	Bogotá	Language	Spanish			Independence	1810
Population	43 593 035	Area	1 138 910 km²	Density	37 per km²	% in cities	73%
GDP per cap	$6 300	Dailling code	+57	Internet	.co	GMT + / -	-5

MAJOR CITIES/TOWNS

Population '000

1	Bogotá	7 363
2	Cali	2 498
3	Medellín	2 042
4	Barranquilla	1 429
5	Cartagena	1 001
6	Cúcuta	760
7	Bucaramanga	591
8	Pereira	460
9	Santa Marta	459
10	Ibagué	430
11	Bello	413
12	Pasto	400
13	Neiva	370
14	Manizales	362
15	Soledad	360
16	Villavicencio	338
17	Soacha	332
18	Armenia	326
19	Valledupar	324
20	Itagüí	300
21	Montería	281
22	Sincelejo	275
23	Envigado	172
24	Tuluá	170

MEDALS TABLE

		Overall G S B	League G S B	Sth Am G S B	City	Stadium	Cap'ty	Formed
1	Millonarios	14 10 12	13 9 8	1 1 4	Bogotá	El Campin	48 600	1946
2	América Cali	13 10 12	12 6 5	1 4 7	Cali	Pascual Guerrero	45 000	1927
3	Atlético Nacional Medellín	12 11 10	9 9 5	3 2 5	Medellin	Atanasio Girardot	52 700	1942
4	Deportivo Cali	8 15 8	8 12 6	3 2	Cali	Pascual Guerrero	45 000	1908
5	Independiente Santa Fe	6 5 5	6 3 4	2 1	Bogotá	El Campin	48 600	1941
6	Atlético Junior	5 5 3	5 5 2	1	Barranquilla	Metropolitano	58 000	1924
7	Independiente Medellín	4 6 4	4 6 3	1	Medellin	Atanasio Girardot	52 700	1913
8	Once Caldas	3 1 1	2 1 1	1	Manizales	Palogrande	33 000	1930
9	Deportes Tolima	1 4 2	1 4 1	1	Ibagué	Manuel Toro	19 000	1954
10	Deportes Quindío	1 2 1	1 2 1		Armenia	Centenario	29 000	1951
11	Cúcuta Deportivo	1 1 3	1 1 2	1	Cúcuta	General Santander	25 000	1949
12	Deportivo Pasto	1 1	1 1		Pasto	Libertad	14 000	1919
13	Union Magdalena	1 1	1 1		Santa Marta	Eduardo Santos	23 000	1950
14	Boca Junior	2 2	2 2		Cali			
15	Atlético Bucaramanga	1 3	1 3		Bucaramanga	Alfonso Lopez	33 000	1949
16	Atlético Huila	1	1		Neiva	Guillermo Alcid	15 000	1990
	Real Cartagena	1	1		Cartagena	Olimpico	14 000	1971

RECENT LEAGUE AND CUP RECORD

Championship Play-off/Apertura from 2002				Clausura		
Year	Champions	Score	Runners-up	Winners	Score	Runners-up
1997	América Cali	1-0 2-0	Atlético Bucaramanga			
1998	Deportivo Cali	4-0 0-0	Once Caldas			
1999	Atlético Nacional	1-1 0-0 4-2p	América Cali			
2000	América Cali	‡	Atlético Junior			
2001	América Cali	1-0 2-0	Independiente Medellín			
2002	América Cali	2-1 1-0	Independiente Medellín	Independiente Medellín	2-0 1-1	Deportivo Pasto
2003	Once Caldas	0-0 1-0	Atlético Junior	Deportes Tolima	2-0 1-3 4-2p	Deportivo Cali
2004	Independiente Medellin	2-1 0-0	Atlético Nacional	Atlético Junior	3-0 2-5 5-4p	Atlético Nacional
2005	Atlético Nacional	0-0 2-0	Independiente Santa Fe	Deportivo Cali	2-0 1-0	Real Cartagena
2006	Deportivo Pasto	1-0 1-1	Deportivo Cali	Cúcuta Deportivo	1-0 1-1	Deportes Tolima
2007	Atlético Nacional	1-0 2-1	Atlético Huila			

Colombia adopted the format of two Championships per year in 2002 • ‡ Final tournament played as a league

COLOMBIA 2006 DIMAYOR TORNEO CLAUSURA

	Pl	W	D	L	F	A	Pts
Deportes Tolima †	18	10	4	4	31	19	34
Independ. Medellín †	18	10	2	6	29	22	32
Boyacá Chicó †	18	10	2	6	22	15	32
Atlético Huila †	18	9	4	5	25	17	31
At. Nacional Medellín †	18	9	4	5	20	15	31
Cúcuta Deportivo †	18	9	4	5	22	18	31
Deportivo Pasto †	18	9	3	6	23	15	30
Millonarios †	18	8	3	7	23	19	27
Deportes Quindío	18	8	3	7	24	25	27
Deportivo Cali	18	6	7	5	23	21	25
Real Cartagena	18	7	4	7	17	17	25
Independ. Santa Fe	18	6	6	6	34	30	24
Deportes Pereira	18	6	4	8	23	24	22
Atlético Junior	18	5	5	8	19	29	20
Once Caldas	18	5	4	9	23	31	19
Atlético Bucaramanga	18	4	4	10	22	32	16
América Cali	18	3	4	11	20	33	13
Envigado	18	3	3	12	14	32	12

15/07/2006 - 12/11/2006 • † Qualified for the second stage

TORNEO CLAUSURA SECOND STAGE

Group A	Pl	W	D	L	F	A	Pts	DT	AN	DP	BC
Deportes Tolima †	6	4	0	2	10	5	12		1-0	4-0	2-0
At. Nacional Medellín	6	2	2	2	6	5	8	1-2		2-1	2-0
Deportivo Pasto	6	2	2	2	8	11	8	2-1	0-0		1-1
Boyacá Chicó	6	1	2	3	7	10	5	2-0	1-1	3-4	

Group B	Pl	W	D	L	F	A	Pts	CD	IM	Mi	AH
Cúcuta Deportivo †	6	3	1	2	6	4	10		2-1	2-0	0-0
Independ. Medellín	6	3	0	3	12	7	9	2-1		4-0	3-0
Millonarios	6	3	0	3	6	10	9	1-0	1-0		2-1
Atlético Huila	6	2	1	3	7	10	7	0-1	3-2	3-2	

18/11/2006 - 13/12/2006 • † Qualified for the final

TORNEO CLAUSURA FINAL

Home team first leg	Score	Home team second leg
Cúcuta Deportivo	1-0 1-1	Deportes Tolima

See *Almanack of World Football 2007* for the 2006 Apertura tables

COLOMBIA 2006 LIGA DIMAYOR REGULAR SEASON RESULTS

PRIMERA A	América	Bucaramanga	Cali	Cartagena	Chicó	Cúcuta	Envigado	Huila	Junior	Medellin	Millonarios	Nacional	Once Caldas	Pasto	Pereira	Quindío	Santa Fe	Tolima
América Cali		1-2	0-3 1-3	2-1	0-1	0-1	2-1	2-1	1-0	3-2	1-0	0-2	0-0	1-1	0-2	0-1	2-2	1-0
Atlético Bucaramanga	1-0		2-2	0-1	1-0	2-1 0-1	3-1	1-0	2-0	0-2	2-3	0-2	1-2	3-3	1-0	2-1	1-1	
Deportivo Cali	1-1 2-1	4-1		1-2	1-3	0-2	0-1	0-0	0-0	1-0	0-1	1-1	1-2	1-0	1-1	1-0	3-2	2-1
Real Cartagena	2-1	2-0	0-1		1-1	0-1	0-1	0-1	1-2 1-0	2-2	1-0	0-1	1-2	0-3	0-1	1-2	1-0	1-2
Boyacá Chicó	1-0	2-1	1-1	4-2		1-0	0-0	1-0	1-1	1-0	0-2	0-1	3-0	0-0 1-0	3-0	1-2	2-0	0-1
Cúcuta Deportivo	2-0	1-1 3-2	1-1	1-1	1-1		1-0	4-0	2-0	1-0	2-1	3-2	1-1	3-1	0-1	3-0	2-0	1-0
Envigado	1-4	0-0	0-3	1-0	1-2	1-2		2-0	1-3	0-0	0-1	1-0	1-1	0-1	2-0	2-0 3-3	0-0	3-7
Atlético Huila	2-0	2-1	3-1	1-3	3-1	1-1	1-0		3-0	1-1	1-1	1-0	3-2	1-0	0-3	4-1	2-1	1-4 3-2
Atlético Junior	1-2	2-2	0-0	2-0 2-1	2-0	0-1	3-2	3-0		2-2	4-4	2-1	0-0	1-0	1-1	0-1	3-3	1-2
Indep. Medellin	2-3	2-0	3-1	1-0	1-2	2-0	2-1	0-1	3-1		1-0	1-1 0-1	3-2	2-2	1-0	2-0	0-1	4-1
Millonarios	1-0	2-0	0-1	2-1	2-1	1-0	1-1	1-1	3-1	3-0		2-0	1-1	1-0	2-3	1-0	3-3 2-2	0-3
At. Nacional Medellín	6-0	3-0	2-0	1-0	1-0	2-1	0-0	1-0	2-2	2-1 0-1	2-0		3-1	1-1	2-0	2-1	2-1	1-1
Once Caldas	4-1	1-0	0-2	1-1	2-2	2-2	1-0	1-0	2-0	6-0	2-2	1-0		4-2	2-1 1-0	3-2	0-2	1-3
Deportivo Pasto	2-1	2-1	1-0	0-2	1-1 1-0	2-1	5-0	4-1	2-0	3-0	1-0	0-0	2-1		1-1	2-3	4-1	1-0
Deportivo Pereira	2-2	3-2	2-0	0-0	1-1	0-1	2-3	0-1	1-0	3-1	1-1	2-1	0-0 0-0	2-1		1-0	1-1	1-2
Deportes Quindío	2-2	1-0	0-1	1-0	3-1	0-1	1-1 1-0	2-0	3-0	2-0	1-1	1-0	1-3	2-1	2-0		1-1	2-1
Indep. Santa Fe	1-3	4-2	2-1	2-1	1-1	4-1	3-3	1-1	4-2	3-2	1-3 3-2	4-0	3-1	0-1	1-4	0-0		0-2
Deportes Tolima	2-0	0-0	1-1	4-1	3-1	2-2	1-0	2-0 3-2	4-0	0-0	1-0	5-1	1-3	1-1	0-0	2-0	2-0	

Apertura 2006 results are shown in the shaded boxes • Local rivals play each other four times in the regular season. In this instance the Apertura results are listed first • Envigado had the worst record over three seasons and were relegated. Atlético Huila, with the second worst record, entered a play-off against the Primera B runners-up Valledupar • Relegation play-off: Valledupar 0-1 0-2 Atlético Huila

COLOMBIA 2006
PRIMERA B (2) APERTURA

Group A	Pl	W	D	L	F	A	Pts
Unión Magdalena †	18	12	4	2	27	9	40
Valledupar †	18	8	6	4	17	18	30
Bajo Cauca	18	8	3	7	17	19	27
Córdoba Montería	18	5	8	5	19	22	23
Alianza Petrolera	18	6	4	8	19	17	22
Expreso Rojo	18	5	7	6	18	19	22
Deportivo Rionegro	18	5	4	9	14	21	19
Atlético Bello	18	3	7	8	13	23	16
Barranquilla FC	18	3	6	9	17	21	15

Group B	Pl	W	D	L	F	A	Pts
CD La Equidad †	18	11	3	4	24	15	36
Academia Bogotá †	18	10	4	4	29	13	34
Depor Jamundí	18	9	3	6	23	19	30
Patriotas·Tunja	18	7	8	3	28	17	29
Corporación Tuluá	18	7	8	3	26	23	29
Centauros Villavicencio	18	5	6	7	12	15	21
Girardot FC	18	4	5	9	21	28	17
Bogotá FC	18	3	5	10	12	26	14
Los Pumas de Casanare	18	2	7	9	22	33	13

11/02/2006 - 20/05/2006 • † Qualified for the second stage

COLOMBIA 2006
PRIMERA B (2) CLAUSURA

Group A	Pl	W	D	L	F	A	Pts
Centauros Villavicencio†	18	9	7	2	28	17	34
Deportivo Rionegro †	18	8	5	5	24	17	29
Valledupar	18	8	4	6	23	18	28
Academia Bogotá	18	6	7	5	22	21	25
Bajo Cauca	18	6	5	7	28	25	23
Unión Magdalena	18	6	5	7	23	29	23
Depor Jamundí	18	6	3	9	17	25	21
Bogotá FC	18	5	5	8	22	26	20
Girardot FC	18	3	9	6	25	25	18

Group B	Pl	W	D	L	F	A	Pts
Corporación Tuluá †	18	12	4	2	31	14	40
CD La Equidad †	18	10	5	3	30	19	35
Barranquilla FC	18	10	3	5	39	26	33
Los Pumas de Casanare	18	8	5	5	28	22	29
Patriotas Tunja	18	5	6	7	21	21	21
Alianza Petrolera	18	5	4	9	16	26	19
Córdoba Montería	18	5	4	9	16	33	19
Atlético Bello	18	3	4	11	19	35	13
Expreso Rojo	18	2	5	11	16	29	11

15/07/2006 - 7/10/2006 • † Qualified for the second stage

PRIMERA B APERTURA CUADRANGULAR FINAL

	Pl	W	D	L	F	A	Pts
CD La Equidad †	6	3	3	0	6	3	12
Valledupar	6	2	2	2	9	9	8
Academia Bogotá	6	2	1	3	6	5	7
Unión Magdalena	6	1	2	3	4	8	5

31/05/2006 - 17/06/2006 • † Qualified for season final

PRIMERA B CLAUSURA CUADRANGULAR FINAL

	Pl	W	D	L	F	A	Pts
CD La Equidad †	6	3	2	1	12	6	11
Corporación Tuluá	6	3	1	2	6	6	10
Centauros Villavicencio	6	2	2	2	5	9	8
Deportivo Rionegro	6	1	1	4	7	9	4

14/10/2006 - 4/11/2006 • † Qualified for season final

CD La Equidad won both the Apertura and Clausura and so were promoted automatically • Second place play-off: Valledupar 3-2 0-0 CorTuluá. Valledupar qualified to meet Atlético Huila in a promotion/relegation play-off.

COLOMBIA 2007
DIMAYOR TORNEO APERTURA

	Pl	W	D	L	F	A	Pts
Deportivo Cali †	18	9	7	2	33	20	34
Cúcuta Deportivo †	18	10	3	5	28	17	33
At. Nacional Medellín†	18	9	5	4	32	20	32
Millonarios †	18	8	6	4	26	17	30
Boyacá Chicó †	18	9	3	6	20	16	30
Indep. Medellín †	18	8	5	5	33	31	29
Indep. Santa Fe †	18	8	5	5	23	21	29
Atlético Huila †	18	9	1	8	24	23	28
Atlético Bucaramanga	18	7	6	5	23	21	27
Deportivo Pasto	18	6	5	7	19	21	23
Atlético Junior	18	5	8	5	22	26	23
Deportes Tolima	18	6	2	10	26	28	20
América Cali	18	4	7	7	24	35	19
Once Caldas	18	4	6	8	18	25	18
Deportes Quindío	18	4	6	8	14	22	18
Real Cartagena	18	3	8	7	14	22	17
Deportes Pereira	18	3	6	9	14	21	15
La Equidad Bogotá	18	2	7	9	21	28	13

3/02/2007 - 12/05/2007 • † Qualified for the second stage

TORNEO APERTURA SECOND STAGE

Group A	Pl	W	D	L	F	A	Pts	NM	DC	BC	SF
At. Nacional Medellín†	6	4	1	1	12	4	13		3-0	3-0	3-1
Deportivo Cali	6	3	2	1	8	6	11	0-0		3-1	2-0
Boyacá Chicó	6	2	0	4	10	12	6	2-3	1-2		5-1
Indep. Santa Fe	6	1	1	4	4	12	4	1-0	1-1	0-1	

Group B	Pl	W	D	L	F	A	Pts	AH	CD	Mi	IM
Atlético Huila †	6	3	2	1	8	8	11		1-1	2-0	1-0
Cúcuta Deportivo	6	2	3	1	9	5	9	4-0		3-1	1-1
Millonarios	6	2	3	1	8	9	9	0-1	2-0		1-0
Indep. Medellín	6	0	3	3	6	9	3	3-3	0-0	2-3	

16/05/2007 - 10/06/2007 • † Qualified for the final

TORNEO APERTURA FINAL

Home team first leg	Score	Home team second leg
Atlético Huila	0-1 1-2	**Atlético Nacional Medellín**

The results of the 2007 Apertura along with details of the 2007 Clausura will appear in next year's *Almanack of World Football*

COM – COMOROS

NATIONAL TEAM RECORD
JULY 10TH 2006 TO JULY 12TH 2010

PL	W	D	L	F	A	%
2	1	0	1	4	4	50

FIFA/COCA-COLA WORLD RANKING

1993	1994	1995	1996	1997	1998	1999	2000	2001	2002	2003	2004	2005	2006	High		Low	
-	-	-	-	-	-	-	-	-	-	-	-	-	207	**180**	06/07	**187**	03/07

2006–2007											
08/06	09/06	10/06	11/06	12/06	01/07	02/07	03/07	04/07	05/07	06/07	07/07
207	207	207	207	207	187	187	187	184	182	180	182

The Comoros Islands, among the newest members of FIFA, celebrated their arrival on the world stage with participation in two Arab Nations Cup qualifiers in Yemen in December 2006. The first game against the host country was lost but Comoros overcame Djibouti 4-2 in their second match to register a first-ever official win. Previously the country's only international participation had been at the Indian Ocean Island Games but matches were not recognised because the island archipelago had yet to join the ranks of FIFA. For the second year running, Comoros entered teams in African club competition in 2007 with Champions League representatives AJSM Mutsamudu

INTERNATIONAL HONOURS
None

forced to play a single tie away from home because the stadium in the Comoros capital Moroni had not been passed fit for use in international games. The result was 5-1 thumping away in Dar-es-Salaam at the hands of Tanzania's Young Africans. Elan Club played against Mozambique's Ferroviario Beira, losing 2-0 in the first round of the Confederation Cup. The sandy surface of the Moroni stadium has now been upgraded to an artificial pitch by FIFA. In the 2006 Coupe des Comoros final, Chirazienne beat Gombess Sports 4-1 at home in Domoni on penalties and they will represent the island nation in the 2007/2008 Arab Champions League for the first time.

THE FIFA BIG COUNT OF 2006

	Male	Female		Total
Number of players	27 100	0	Referees and Assistant Referees	0
Professionals	0		Admin, Coaches, Technical, Medical	100
Amateurs 18+	600		Number of clubs	10
Youth under 18	500		Number of teams	30
Unregistered	0		Clubs with women's teams	0
Total players	27 100		Players as % of population	3.92

Fédération Comorienne de Football (FFC)
Case Postale 798, Moroni, Comoros
Tel +269 733179   Fax +269 733236
dhl@snpt.km   www.none
President: SALIM Tourqui   General Secretary: ABDOU CHAKOUR Mariyatta
Vice-President: TOURQUI Salim   Treasurer: TBD   Media Officer: None
Men's Coach: none   Women's Coach: none
FFC formed: 1979   CAF: 1986   FIFA: 2005
Green shirts, Green shorts, Green Socks

RECENT INTERNATIONAL MATCHES PLAYED BY COMOROS

2002 Opponents	Score	Venue	Comp	Scorers	Att	Referee
No international matches played in 2002						
2003						
30-08 Reunion †	L 0-1	Flacq	IOr1		103	Labrosse SEY
2-09 Reunion †	L 0-4	Flacq	IOr1			
4-09 Mauritius †	L 0-5	Curepipe	IOsf		4 500	Labrosse SEY
6-09 Seychelles †	L 0-2	Curepipe	IO3p			
2004						
No international matches played in 2004						
2005						
No international matches played in 2005						
2006						
14-12 Yemen	L 0-2	Sana'a	ARq			
17-12 Djibouti	W 4-2	Sana'a	ARq	Meknesh Bin Daoud [5], Ahmed Seif 2 [33 75], Mohamed Moni [70]		
2007						
No international matches played in 2007 before August						

IO = Indian Ocean Games • AR = Arab Cup • q = qualifier • r1 = first round group • sf = semi-final • 3p = third place play-off
† Not regarded as a full international because Comoros was not yet a member of FIFA

COMOROS NATIONAL TEAM RECORDS AND RECORD SEQUENCES

Records			Sequence records		
Victory	2-1	REU 1979	Wins	1	1979, 1990
Defeat	1-6	REU 1979	Defeats	10	1990-
Player Caps	n/a		Undefeated	1	1979, 1985, 1990
Player Goals	n/a		Without win	10	1990

Clean sheets	1	1990
Goals scored	3	1979
Without goal	8	1993-
Goals against	10	1990-

Comoros joined FIFA in 2005 and have yet to play an official international. The above data relates to games played in the Indian Ocean Games

RECENT LEAGUE AND CUP RECORD

	Comoros	Grande Comore	Anjouan	Mwali	Cup
Year	Champions	Champions	Champions	Champions	Winners
2003		Volcan Club		Belle Lumière	Coin Nord
2004		Elan Club	Etoile d'Or	Belle Lumière	
2005	Coin Nord	Coin Nord	Chirazienne	Belle Lumière	Volcan Club
2006	AJSM Mutsamudu				Chirazienne
2007					

COMOROS COUNTRY INFORMATION

Capital	Moroni	Independence	1975 from France	GDP per Capita	$700
Population	671 247	Status	Republic	GNP Ranking	155
Area km²	2 170	Language	Arabic, French, Shikomoro	Dialling code	+269
Population density	309 per km²	Literacy rate	56.5%	Internet code	.km
% in urban areas	34%	Main religion	Muslim 98%	GMT +/–	+3
Towns/Cities ('000)	Moroni 42 (Grande Comore/Njazidja); Mutsamudu 14 (Anjouan/Nzwani); Fomboni 14 (Moheli/Mwali)				
Neighbours (km)	Indian Ocean 340				
Main stadia	Stade de Beaumer, Moroni				

CPV – CAPE VERDE ISLANDS

NATIONAL TEAM RECORD
JULY 10TH 2006 TO JULY 12TH 2010

PL	W	D	L	F	A	%
5	1	2	2	3	6	40

FIFA/COCA-COLA WORLD RANKING

1993	1994	1995	1996	1997	1998	1999	2000	2001	2002	2003	2004	2005	2006	High		Low	
147	161	144	155	171	167	177	156	159	154	143	129	118	78	**68**	07/07	**182**	04/00

					2006–2007						
08/06	09/06	10/06	11/06	12/06	01/07	02/07	03/07	04/07	05/07	06/07	07/07
101	113	83	78	78	78	78	79	88	88	77	68

The Portuguese-speaking island continued its remarkable surge up the FIFA/Coca-Cola World Ranking, reaching a high of 68 in July 2007, a climb of some 120 places over just seven years. The island archipelago is among the smallest and least populous in Africa yet is reaping the benefits of its massive migrant population, who have been settling coastal communities around the world for over a century. The Cape Verdian community on the east coast of the USA is bigger, for example, than the Cape Verde's entire population, estimated at just over 400,000. Similarly there are more Cape Verdians in the former colonial power Portugal and it is from this community that the island's

INTERNATIONAL HONOURS
Copa Amilcar Cabral 2000

national team has been able to thrive. The latest is the striker Dady of Belenenses, who was among the top scorers in the league last season. While Cape Verde have not yet been able to qualify for the finals of a major competition, they were strong contenders for a berth at the 2006 FIFA World Cup finals and were competitive throughout the 2008 African Nations Cup qualifiers. Sporting Praia retained their League title, beating Academica Mindelo on away goals in the final. The first leg was a goalless draw in Praia and Academica looked to be on their way to the title after a 70th minute goal from striker Kelly before conceding a penalty in the last minute which Sporting's Dario converted.

THE FIFA BIG COUNT OF 2006

	Male	Female		Total
Number of players	33 500	1 600	Referees and Assistant Referees	256
Professionals	0		Admin, Coaches, Technical, Medical	500
Amateurs 18+	7 000		Number of clubs	82
Youth under 18	4 500		Number of teams	180
Unregistered	4 200		Clubs with women's teams	0
Total players	35 100		Players as % of population	8.34%

Federação Caboverdiana de Futebol (FCF)
Praia Cabo Verde, FCF CX, Case postale 234, Praia, Cape Verde Islands
Tel +238 2 611362   Fax +238 2 611362
fcf@cvtelecom.cv   www.fcf.cv
President: SEMEDO Mario   General Secretary: REZENDE Jose João
Vice-President: ALMEIDA Fernando   Treasurer: REZENDE Jose João   Media Officer: None
Men's Coach: RICARDO ROCHA   Women's Coach: none
FCF formed: 1982   CAF: 1986   FIFA: 1986
Blue shirts, Blue shorts, Blue socks or White shirts, White shorts, Red socks

RECENT INTERNATIONAL MATCHES PLAYED BY THE CAPE VERDE ISLANDS

2002 Opponents		Score	Venue	Comp	Scorers	Att	Referee
8-06 Togo	L	2-5	Lome	CNq	Lito [7], Calo [27]		Pare BFA
21-06 Mauritania *	W	3-0	Praia	CNq	Lito [58], Calo 2 [72p 73]		
5-07 Kenya	L	0-1	Nairobi	CNq		35 000	
12-10 Swaziland	D	1-1	Mbabane	WCq	Calo [59]	5 000	Teshome ERI
16-11 Swaziland	W	3-0	Praia	WCq	Cafu 2 [51 65], Calo [89]	6 000	Aboubacar CIV
2004							
5-06 South Africa	L	1-2	Bloemfontein	WCq	Janicio [78]	30 000	Tessema ETH
13-06 Senegal	L	1-3	Praia	Fr	Gabei [76]	10 000	
19-06 Uganda	W	1-0	Praia	WCq	Cafu [42]	5 000	Coulibaly MLI
3-07 Congo DR	D	1-1	Praia	WCq	Modeste [26]	3 800	NAHI CIV
5-09 Ghana	L	0-2	Kumasi	WCq		35 000	Tamuni LBY
9-10 Burkina Faso	W	1-0	Praia	WCq	Cafu [2]	6 000	Aziaka TOG
2005							
26-03 Burkina Faso	W	2-1	Ouagadougou	WCq	Calo 2 [48 87]	27 500	Evehe CMR
4-06 South Africa	L	1-2	Praia	WCq	Gomes [77]	6 000	Benouza ALG
18-06 Uganda	L	0-1	Kampala	WCq		5 000	Kidane ERI
17-08 Angola	L	1-2	Lisbon	Fr	Lito [26]		
4-09 Congo DR	L	1-2	Kinshasa	WCq	Cafu [24]	75 000	Guezzaz MAR
8-10 Ghana	L	0-4	Praia	WCq		6 500	Daami TUN
2006							
27-05 Portugal	L	1-4	Evora	Fr	OG [21]		
3-09 Gambia	L	0-2	Bakau	CNq			Pare BFA
7-10 Guinea	W	1-0	Praia	CNq	Lito [52]		Diatta SEN
2007							
24-03 Algeria	L	0-2	Algiers	CNq			Abd El Fatah EGY
2-06 Algeria	D	2-2	Praia	CNq	Marco Soares [58], Hernani [92+]		Aboubacar CIV
16-06 Gambia	D	0-0	Praia	CNq			

r = Friendly match • CN = CAF African Cup of Nations • WC = FIFA World Cup
q = qualifier • * Abandoned after 85 minutes when Mauritania were reduced to six players - the result stood

CAPE VERDE ISLANDS NATIONAL TEAM RECORDS AND RECORD SEQUENCES

Records			Sequence records				
Victory	3-0	GNB 81, MTN 03, SWZ 03	Wins	3	2000	Clean sheets	3	2000
Defeat	2-5	SEN 1981	Defeats	7	2005-2006	Goals scored	7	2000
Player Caps	n/a		Undefeated	7	2000	Without goal	5	1985-87, 1998-2000
Player Goals	n/a		Without win	9	1997-2000	Goals against	9	1988-1989

RECENT LEAGUE RECORD

	Championship						Championship Play-off		
Year	Champions	Pts	Runners-up	Pts	Third	Pts	Champions	Score	Runners-up
2001	Onze Unidos	14	Académica do Sal	13	Botafogo	11			
2002	Sporting da Praia	19	Batuque		Académica Fogo	16			
2003	Académico do Sal						Académico do Sal	3-1 3-2	FC Ultramarina
2004	Sal-Rei SC						Sal-Rei SC	2-0 1-2	Académica Praia
2005	Derby São Vicente						Derby São Vicente	1-1 4-3	Sporting da Praia
2006	Sporting da Praia						Sporting da Praia	1-0 2-2	Académica do Sal
2007	Sporting da Praia						Sporting da Praia	0-0 1-1	Académica Mindelo

CAPE VERDE ISLANDS COUNTRY INFORMATION

Capital	Praia	Independence	1975 from Portugal	GDP per Capita	$1 400
Population	415 294	Status	Republic	GNP Ranking	166
Area km²	4 033	Language	Portuguese	Dialling code	+238
Population density	102 per km²	Literacy rate	76%	Internet code	.cv
% in urban areas	54%	Main religion	Christian	GMT +/–	-1
Towns/Cities ('000)	Praia 111; Mindelo 69; Santa Maria 16; Pedra Badejo 9; São Filipe 8; Assomada 7				
Neighbours (km)	Cape Verde consists of a group of 13 islands in the North Atlantic Ocean				
Main stadia	Estadio da Varzea – Praia 8 000; Estadio Municipal Adérito Sena – Midelo 5 000				

CRC – COSTA RICA

NATIONAL TEAM RECORD
JULY 10TH 2006 TO JULY 12TH 2010

PL	W	D	L	F	A	%
14	6	4	4	22	12	57.1

FIFA/COCA-COLA WORLD RANKING

1993	1994	1995	1996	1997	1998	1999	2000	2001	2002	2003	2004	2005	2006	High		Low	
42	65	78	72	51	67	64	60	30	21	17	27	21	68	17	05/03	93	07/96

					2006–2007						
08/06	09/06	10/06	11/06	12/06	01/07	02/07	03/07	04/07	05/07	06/07	07/07
47	53	68	68	68	66	54	50	52	52	46	50

Deportivo Saprissa, one of three clubs owned by Mexican film producer Jorge Vergara (along with Guadalajara and Chivas USA) continued their recent revival as they defended their League title, winning both the Apertura and Clausura for the second year running. However, their limelight was stolen in the UNCAF club championship with Municipal Puntarenas winning the title for the first time, but they got no further than the quarter-finals of the CONCACAF Champions Cup leaving Costa Rica without a representative in the semi-finals for the first time since 2003. Liga Deportiva

INTERNATIONAL HONOURS
Qualified for the FIFA World Cup finals 1990 2002 2006 **Central American Championship** 1941 1946 1948 1953 1955 1960 1961 1963
UNCAF Championship 1991 1997 1999 2003 2005 **CONCACAF U-20 Championship** 1954 1960 1988 **CONCACAF U-17 Championship** 1994
CONCACAF Club Championship LD Alajuelense 1986 2004 Deportivo Saprissa 1993 1995 2005 CS Cartiginés 1995

Alajuelense took part in the 2006 Copa Sudamericana but the gap with their South American opponents was noticeable as they lost 11-2 on aggregate to Colo Colo of Chile. Under new coach Hernan Medford the national team won the UNCAF Cup, beating Panama on penalties in the final and that qualified Los Ticos for the Gold Cup in the USA at the end of the season. Having struggled to qualify from what should have been a straightforward group containing Canada, Haiti and Guadeloupe, Costa Rica were then drawn with Mexico in the quarter-finals and lost 1-0.

THE FIFA BIG COUNT OF 2006

	Male	Female		Total
Number of players	1 050 120	34 468	Referees and Assistant Referees	630
Professionals	1 025		Admin, Coaches, Technical, Medical	4 236
Amateurs 18+	17 500		Number of clubs	248
Youth under 18	31 208		Number of teams	1 391
Unregistered	1 005 000		Clubs with women's teams	6
Total players	1 084 588		Players as % of population	26.61%

Federación Costarricense de Fútbol (FEDEFUTBOL)
Costado Norte Estatua, León Cortés, Sabana Este, San José 670-1000, Costa Rica
Tel +506 2221544   Fax +506 2552674
ejecutivo@fedefutbol.com   www.fedefutbol.com
President: LI Eduardo   General Secretary: ORTEGA Jorge
Vice-President: CHACON Miguel   Treasurer: ROJAS ULLOA Rafael Angel   Media Officer: HIDALGO Marvin
Men's Coach: MEDFORD Hernan   Women's Coach: QUESADA Juan Diego
FEDEFUTBOL formed: 1921   CONMEBOL: 1962   FIFA: 1927
Red shirts, Blue shorts, White socks or White shirts, White shorts, Red socks

RECENT INTERNATIONAL MATCHES PLAYED BY COSTA RICA

2005	Opponents	Score	Venue	Comp	Scorers	Att	Referee
12-01	Haiti	D 3-3	San Jose	Fr	Centeno [2], Scott [10], Herron [13p]		Porras CRC
9-02	Mexico	L 1-2	San Jose	WCq	Wanchope [38]	22 000	Batres GUA
16-02	Ecuador	L 1-2	Heredia	Fr	Alfaro [46]	1 000	Duran CRC
21-02	El Salvador	W 2-1	Guatemala City	UCr1	Wilson [75], Myrie [90]	3 000	Batres GUA
23-02	Panama	W 1-0	Guatemala City	UCr1	Myrie [83]	3 000	Archundia MEX
25-02	Guatemala	W 4-0	Guatemala City	UCsf	Segura [9], Sequeira [22], Wilson [41], Scott [61]	11 159	Archundia MEX
27-02	Honduras	D 1-1	Guatemala City	UCf	Wilson [68], W 7-6p	1 491	Batres GUA
26-03	Panama	W 2-1	San Jose	WCq	Wilson [40p], Myre [91+]	8 000	Rodriguez MEX
30-03	Trinidad and Tobago	D 0-0	Port of Spain	WCq		8 000	Navarro CAN
24-05	Norway	L 0-1	Oslo	Fr		21 251	Van Egmond NED
4-06	USA	L 0-3	Salt Lake City	WCq		40 586	Batres GUA
8-06	Guatemala	W 3-2	San Jose	WCq	Hernandez.C [34], Gomez [65], Wanchope [92+]	BCD	Archundia MEX
19-06	China PR	D 2-2	Changsha	Fr	Solis [57], Gomez [75]	20 000	Lee Gi Young KOR
22-06	China PR	L 0-2	Guangzhou	Fr		15 000	Yu Byung Seob KOR
7-07	Canada	W 1-0	Seattle	GCr1	Soto.J [30p]	15 831	Prendergast JAM
9-07	Cuba	W 3-1	Seattle	GCr1	Brenes 2 [61 85p], Soto.J [81p]	15 109	Archundia MEX
12-07	USA	D 0-0	Foxboro	GCr1		15 211	Archundia MEX
16-07	Honduras	L 2-3	Foxboro	GCqf	Bolaños [39], Ruíz [81]	22 108	Archundia MEX
17-08	Mexico	L 0-2	Mexico City	WCq		27 000	Pineda HON
3-09	Panama	W 3-1	Panama City	WCq	Saborio [44], Centeno [51], Gomez [73]	21 000	Stott USA
7-09	Trinidad and Tobago	W 2-0	San Jose	WCq	Saborio [15], Centeno [50]	17 000	Batres GUA
8-10	USA	W 3-0	San Jose	WCq	Wanchope [34], Hernandez.C 2 [60 88]	18 000	Archundia MEX
12-10	Guatemala	L 1-3	Guatemala City	WCq	Myre [60]	23 912	Hall USA
9-11	France	L 2-3	Fort-de-France	Fr	Saborio [14], Fonseca [41]	16 216	Pineda MEX
2006							
11-02	Korea Republic	W 1-0	Oakland	Fr	Saborio [40p]		Vaughn USA
1-03	Iran	L 2-3	Tehran	Fr	Hernandez.C [43], Fonseca [60]	25 000	Al Marzouqi UAE
28-05	Ukraine	L 0-4	Kyiv	Fr		25 000	Ivanov.N RUS
30-05	Czech Republic	L 0-1	Jablonec	Fr		14 500	Bede HUN
9-06	Germany	L 2-4	Munich	WCr1	Wanchope 2 [12 73]	66 000	Elizondo ARG
15-06	Ecuador	L 0-3	Hamburg	WCr1		50 000	Codjia BEN
20-06	Poland	L 1-2	Hanover	WCr1	Gomez [25]	43 000	Maidin SIN
2-09	Austria	D 2-2	Geneva	Fr	Saborio 2 [16p 40]		Circhetta SUI
6-09	Switzerland	L 0-2	Geneva	Fr		12 000	Van Egmond NED
2007							
4-02	Trinidad & Tobago	W 4-0	Alajuela	Fr	Wallace [28], Solis 2 [43 52], Fonseca [57]		Porras CRC
9-02	Honduras	W 3-1	San Salvador	UCr1	Fonseca 2 [4 70], Gonzalez.L [46]	*	Archundia MEX
13-02	Panama	L 0-1	San Salvador	UCr1			Batres GUA
16-02	El Salvador	W 2-0	San Salvador	UCsf	Wallace [10], Fonseca [12]		Archindia MEX
18-02	Panama	D 1-1	San Salvador	UCf	Bernard [85], W 4-1p		Batres GUA
24-03	New Zealand	W 4-0	San Jose	Fr	Saborio 2 [7 79p], Solis [18], Ruiz [57]	15 000	Rodriguez CRC
28-03	Chile	D 1-1	Talca	Fr	Fonseca [60]	8 000	Ortube BOL
2-06	Chile	W 2-0	San Jose	Fr	Badilla [28], Ruiz [59]	25 000	Glower MEX
6-06	Canada	L 1-2	Miami	GCr1	Centeno [56]	17 420	Wingaarde SUR
9-06	Haiti	D 1-1	Miami	GCr1	Centeno [61]	22 529	Campbell JAM
11-06	Guadeloupe	W 1-0	Miami	GCr1	Centeno [14]	15 892	Wingaarde SUR
17-06	Mexico	L 0-1	Houston	GCqf		70 092	Vaughn USA

Fr = Friendly match • UC = UNCAF Cup • GC = CONCACAF Gold Cup • CA = Copa América • WC = FIFA World Cup
q = qualifier • r1 = first round group • qf = quarter-finals • BCD = behind closed doors

COSTA RICA NATIONAL TEAM RECORDS AND RECORD SEQUENCES

Records			Sequence records				
Victory	12-0	PUR 1946	Wins	11	1960-1961	Clean sheets	5	1961, 2001-2002
Defeat	0-7	MEX 1975	Defeats	6	2006	Goals scored	28	1935-1946
Player Caps	123	MARIN Luis	Undefeated	12	1965	Without goal	4	1980-1983
Player Goals	45	WANCHOPE Paulo	Without win	8	1997, 2006	Goals against	12	Three times

MAJOR CITIES/TOWNS
Population '000

1	San José	343
2	Limón	65
3	San Francisco	63
4	Liberia	50
5	Alajuela	49
6	Paraíso	44
7	Desamparados	40
8	San Isidro	37
9	Puntarenas	36
10	Curridabat	36
11	San Vicente	35
12	San José (Alajuela)	32
13	Purral	31
14	Turrialba	30
15	San Miguel	30
16	Aguacaliente	29
17	San Rafael Abajo	29
18	Mercedes	28
19	Quesada	28
20	San Rafael	28
21	San Pedro	27
22	Cartago	27
23	Heredia	22
24	Guápiles	20

REPUBLIC OF COSTA RICA; REPUBLICA DE COSTA RICA

Capital	San José	Language	Spanish	Independence	1821
Population	4 075 261	Area	51 100 km²	% in cities	50%
GDP per cap	$9100	Dailling code	+506	Density 77 per km² · Internet .cr	GMT +/- -6

MEDALS TABLE

		Overall			League			CON'CAF			City	Stadium	Cap'ty	DoF
		G	S	B	G	S	B	G	S	B				
1	Deportivo Saprissa	28	16	7	25	15	1	3	1	6	San José	Ricardo Saprissa	21 260	1935
2	Liga Deportiva Alajuelense	26	22	13	24	19	9	2	3	4	Alajuela	Alejandro Morera Soto	22 500	1919
3	CS Herediano	21	11	11	21	11	10			1	Heredia	Eladio Rosabal Cordero	8 144	1921
4	CS La Libertad	6	6	4	6	6	4				San José			
5	CS Cartaginés	4	9	7	3	9	7	1			Cartago	Fello Meza	18 000	1906
6	Orión FC	2	7	7	2	7	7							
7	Municipal Puntarenas	1	3	1	1	3	1				Puntarenas			
8	Universidad de Costa Rica	1		3	1		3				San José			
9	CS Uruguay	1			1						Coronado			
10	SG Española		7	5		7	5							
11	Alajuela Junior		2			2					Alajuela			
12	AD Limonense		1			1					Limón	Juan Goban	3 000	1961
	AD Barrio Mexico		1			1								
	AD Pérez Zeledón		1			1					San Isidro	Municipal	5 500	1991
	Puntarenas FC		1			1					Puntarenas	Lito Pérez	8 700	2004
	AD Santos		1			1					Guápiles	Ebal Rodrigues	3 000	

RECENT LEAGUE RECORD

Year	Winners	Score	Runners-up
1995	Deportivo Saprissa	3-1 0-1	Liga Deportiva Alajuelense
1996	Liga Deportiva Alajuelense	3-1 1-1	CS Cartaginés
1997	Liga Deportiva Alajuelense	3-2 1-1	Deportivo Saprissa
1998	Deportivo Saprissa	0-1 2-0	Liga Deportiva Alajuelense
1999	Deportivo Saprissa	†	Liga Deportiva Alajuelense
2000	Liga Deportiva Alajuelense	†	Deportivo Saprissa
2001	Liga Deportiva Alajuelense	0-1 3-0	CS Herediano
2002	Liga Deportiva Alajuelense	2-2 4-0	Santos de Guápiles
2003	Liga Deportiva Alajuelense	†	CS Herediano
2004	Deportivo Saprissa	1-1 2-1	CS Herediano
2005	Liga Deportiva Alajuelense	3-1 1-0	AD Pérez Zeledón
2006	Deportivo Saprissa	†	Liga Deportiva Alajuelense

† Won both Apertura and Clausura so automatic champions

COSTA RICA 2006–07
TORNEO APERTURA

Group A	Pl	W	D	L	F	A	Pts
LD Alajuelense †	16	10	2	4	28	15	32
Puntarenas FC †	16	8	3	5	29	19	27
CS Herediano †	16	6	5	5	21	12	23
San Carlos †	16	5	5	6	17	20	20
Municipal Liberia	16	3	3	10	15	38	12
Santacruceña	16	1	3	12	9	30	6

Group B	Pl	W	D	L	F	A	Pts
Deportivo Saprissa †	16	8	5	3	29	17	29
Pérez Zeledón †	16	8	4	4	20	15	28
CS Cartaginés †	16	7	3	6	22	25	24
Brujas Escazú † §5	16	8	4	4	20	13	23
AD Carmelita	16	4	6	6	21	20	18
SD Santos	16	4	5	7	15	22	17

5/08/2006 - 19/11/2006 • † Qualified for the play-offs •
§ = points deducted

COSTA RICA 2006–07
TORNEO CLAUSURA

Group A	Pl	W	D	L	F	A	Pts
Deportivo Saprissa †	16	9	5	2	28	12	32
Puntarenas FC †	16	8	5	3	23	16	29
CS Herediano †	16	7	5	4	22	12	26
San Carlos †	16	4	4	8	19	29	16
Municipal Liberia	16	3	5	8	14	22	14
Santacruceña	16	2	4	10	13	28	10

Group B	Pl	W	D	L	F	A	Pts
LD Alajuelense †	16	8	6	2	22	14	30
CS Cartaginés †	16	7	4	5	14	14	25
Pérez Zeledón †	16	6	6	4	21	17	24
Brujas Escazú †	16	6	5	5	18	16	23
SD Santos	16	6	3	7	24	20	21
AD Carmelita	16	3	2	11	15	33	11

13/01/2007 - 22/04/2007 • † Qualified for the play-offs

APERTURA PLAY-OFFS

Quarter-finals

Dep. Saprissa 3 1
San Carlos * 0 2

Cartaginés * 0 0
Puntarenas 1 1

Pérez Zeledón 0 4 7p
Herediano * 3 1 6p

Brujas Escazú * 0 0
LD Alajuelense 1 4

Semi-finals

Dep. Saprissa 0 2

Puntarenas * 1 0

Pérez Zeledón * 0 1
LD Alajuelense 2 0

* at home in the first leg

Final

Dep. Saprissa * 2 2
LD Alajuelense 0 0

Final 1st leg, 20-12-2006, San José; Scorers - Alonso Solís 59p, Allan Aleman 91+ for Saprissa • 2nd leg, 23-12-2006, Alajuela; Scorers - Alonso Solís 2 39 73 for Saprissa

CLAUSURA PLAY-OFFS

Quarter-finals

Dep. Saprissa 0 1
Brujas Escazú* 0 0

Cartaginés 3 0
CS Herediano * 4 0

Puntarenas 0 2
Pérez Zeledón * 0 0

San Carlos * 0 0
LD Alajuelense 3 1

Semi-finals

Dep. Saprissa 0 2 4p

CS Herediano * 2 0 2p

Puntarenas * 2 0
LD Alajuelense 2 1

* at home in the first leg

Final

Dep. Saprissa 1 3
LD Alajuelense* 1 2

Final 1st leg, 10-05-2007, Alajuela; Scorers - Carlos Hernandez 39 for LDA; Victor Cordero 89 for Saprissa • 2nd leg, San José; Scorers - Cristian Bolaños 60, Gabriel Badilla 2 89 82 for Saprissa; Pablo Herrera 13, Victor Núñez 64 for LDA

COSTA RICA 2006–07
PRIMERA DIVISION CHAMPIONSHIP FINAL

Home team first leg   Score   Home team second leg

Deportivo Saprissa are automatically champions having won both the Apertura and Clausura

COSTA RICA 2006–07 — AGGREGATE TABLE

	Pl	W	D	L	F	A	Pts	LDA	Saprissa	Puntarenas	Pérez Zeledón	Herediano	Cartaginés	Brujas	Santos	San Carlos	Carmelita	Liberia	Santa'ceña
LD Alajuelense	32	18	8	6	50	29	62		0-1	0-3 1-1	0-2	1-0	1-0 2-1	1-1	1-1	2-0 3-1	1-0 1-1	1-0	2-0
Deportivo Saprissa	32	17	10	5	57	29	61	3-0		5-2 1-0	0-0	1-1 0-0	3-0 1-2	1-1	1-1 3-1	1-0 6-1	0-4	1-1	1-0
Puntarenas FC	32	16	8	8	52	35	56	2-2 0-0	3-1		2-1	1-1 2-1	2-2	0-1	2-0	1-0 1-1	1-2	8-1 1-0	2-0 3-1
AD Pérez Zeledón	32	14	10	8	41	32	52	0-0	2-1 1-1	0-1		1-0	1-2 3-2	2-2 2-2	1-0 2-0	1-0	2-1 1-0	1-2	1-0
CS Herediano	32	13	10	9	43	24	49	1-2 3-0	0-0	1-2 2-0	3-2		0-1	0-0	3-0 1-0	2-1 1-1	5-1 0-0	3-0	3-1
CS Cartaginés	32	14	7	11	36	39	49	0-3 0-4	1-0	4-0	3-1 1-1	1-1		2-1 2-0	1-0 1-0	1-1 2-1	2-0	1-0	0-0
Brujas Escazú FC §5	32	14	9	9	38	29	46	0-1	2-0 0-1	4-2	1-2 1-0	1-3	1-0 0-0		3-1 0-0	3-1	1-1 2-0	2-0	2-0
Santos de Guápiles	32	10	8	14	39	42	38	2-1 0-2	1-3	0-2	1-0 1-2	2-1	2-1 2-0	1-2 1-1		4-2	2-0 2-3	1-1	3-0
San Carlos	32	9	9	14	36	49	36	0-4 1-1	1-1	2-1 2-0	0-1	1-0 1-0	2-0 2-0	2-2	1-0		0-1 2-1	2-2	1-2
AD Carmelita	32	7	8	17	36	53	29	2-3	2-2 1-2	1-3	2-2 0-2	1-1	2-1 0-1	1-1 1-1	3-0	2-1		1-4	0-2
Municipal Liberia	32	6	8	18	29	60	26	3-6	0-2 1-3	1-2 0-1	1-1	1-0 1-1	1-2	0-1	0-4	2-2 2-1	1-2		0-2 2-0
Santacruceña	32	3	7	22	22	58	16	0-3	0-4 0-3	0-2 1-1	1-1	0-1 0-2	1-3	0-1	0-0	2-3 1-2	1-1	1-2 2-2	

Clausura matches listed in bold • § = points deducted

CRO – CROATIA

NATIONAL TEAM RECORD
JULY 10TH 2006 TO JULY 12TH 2010

PL	W	D	L	F	A	%
9	7	2	0	20	5	88.8%

FIFA/COCA-COLA WORLD RANKING

1993	1994	1995	1996	1997	1998	1999	2000	2001	2002	2003	2004	2005	2006	High	Low
122	62	41	24	19	4	9	18	19	32	20	23	20		3 01/99	125 03/94

2006–2007											
08/06	09/06	10/06	11/06	12/06	01/07	02/07	03/07	04/07	05/07	06/07	07/07
21	24	19	15	15	15	12	12	12	12	11	7

The season in Croatia got off to a great start when the national team, under new coach Slaven Bilic, beat newly crowned world champions Italy, and they remained unbeaten for the rest of the season. Croatia's Brazilian born striker Eduardo da Silva was an important factor in the team's winning start, scoring six goals in the UEFA Euro 2008 qualifiers, including a crucial strike in the 2-0 home victory over key group rivals England. There was disappointment, however, that a joint bid with Hungary to stage the European Championship in 2012 was passed over in favour of another by Poland and the Ukraine. Da Silva was also a key feature in Dinamo Zagreb's extraordinary double

INTERNATIONAL HONOURS
Qualified for the FIFA World Cup finals 1998 2002 2006

winning team, scoring a record 34 goals in the League campaign. Rarely has a team so dominated a domestic season. Defeat at the hands of Arsenal in the UEFA Champions League and Auxerre in the UEFA Cup saw Dinamo eventually sack coach Josip Kuze in early November. His replacement, the former Iran coach Branko Ivankovic, then guided Dinamo to victory in all 20 League games after joining as his side comfortably drew away from rivals Hajduk Split. The two met in the semi-finals of the Cup but Dinamo qualified to meet Slaven in what turned out to be a close final over two legs - a last-minute goal from Gordon Schildenfeld securing the double for Dinamo.

THE FIFA BIG COUNT OF 2006

	Male	Female		Total
Number of players	339 882	22 632	Referees and Assistant Referees	2 380
Professionals	321		Admin, Coaches, Technical, Medical	15 108
Amateurs 18+	42 219		Number of clubs	1 463
Youth under 18	64 495		Number of teams	3 353
Unregistered	232 715		Clubs with women's teams	1
Total players	362 514		Players as % of population	8.07%

Croatian Football Federation (HNS)
Hrvatski nogometni savez, Rusanova 13, Zagreb 10 000, Croatia
Tel +385 1 2361555   Fax +385 1 2441501
info@hns-cff.hr   www.hns-cff.hr
President: MARKOVIC Vlatko   General Secretary: SREBRIC Zorislav
Vice-President: ZEC Vlado   Treasurer: BAJRIC Ruzica   Media Officer: SUDAC Ivancica
Men's Coach: BILIC Slaven   Women's Coach: RUHEK Damir
HNS formed: 1912   UEFA: 1993   FIFA: 1992
Red and white chequered shirts, White shorts, Blue socks or Blue shirts, Blue shorts, Blue socks

RECENT INTERNATIONAL MATCHES PLAYED BY CROATIA

2004	Opponents	Score	Venue	Comp	Scorers	Att	Referee
18-02	Germany	L 1-2	Split	Fr	Neretljak 86	15 000	Frojdfeldt SWE
31-03	Turkey	D 2-2	Zagreb	Fr	Sokota 2, Srna 76	12 000	Ferreira POR
28-04	FYR Macedonia	W 1-0	Skopje	Fr	Klasnic 33	15 000	Arzuman TUR
29-05	Slovakia	W 1-0	Rijeka	Fr	Olic 29	5 000	Kassai HUN
5-06	Denmark	W 2-1	Copenhagen	Fr	Sokota 27, Olic 39	30 843	Stuchlik AUT
13-06	Switzerland	D 0-0	Leiria	ECr1		24 000	Cortez Batista POR
17-06	France	D 2-2	Leiria	ECr1	Rapajic 48p, Prso 52	28 000	Milton Nielsen DEN
21-06	England	L 2-4	Lisbon	ECr1	Kovac.N 5, Tudor 73	62 000	Collina ITA
18-08	Israel	W 1-0	Zagreb	Fr	Simunic 29	10 000	Granat POL
4-09	Hungary	W 3-0	Zagreb	WCq	Prso 2 31 54, Gyepes OG 80	20 853	Riley ENG
8-09	Sweden	W 1-0	Gothenburg	WCq	Srna 64	40 023	Dauden Ibanez ESP
9-10	Bulgaria	D 2-2	Zagreb	WCq	Srna 2 15 31	31 565	Collina ITA
16-11	Republic of Ireland	L 0-1	Dublin	Fr		33 200	Orrason ISL
2005							
9-02	Israel	D 3-3	Jerusalem	Fr	Klasnic 2 15 78, Srna 55p	4 000	Kailis CYP
26-03	Iceland	W 4-0	Zagreb	WCq	Kovac.N 2 38 75, Simunic 70, Prso 91+	17 912	Damon RSA
30-03	Malta	W 3-0	Zagreb	WCq	Prso 2 22 35, Tudor 79	15 510	Kapitanis CYP
4-06	Bulgaria	W 3-1	Sofia	WCq	Babic 19, Tudor 57, Kranjcar 80	35 000	Nielsen DEN
17-08	Brazil	D 1-1	Split	Fr	Kranjcar 32	30 000	Meyer GER
3-09	Iceland	W 3-1	Reykjavik	WCq	Balaban 2 56 61, Srna 82	5 520	Stark GER
7-09	Malta	D 1-1	Ta'Qali	WCq	Kranjcar 19	916	Briakos GRE
8-10	Sweden	W 1-0	Zagreb	WCq	Srna 55	34 015	De Santis ITA
12-10	Hungary	D 0-0	Budapest	WCq		6 979	Larsen DEN
12-11	Portugal	L 0-2	Coimbra	Fr		15 000	Nielsen DEN
2006							
29-01	Korea Republic	L 0-2	Hong Kong	Fr		16 841	Fong Yau Fat HKG
1-02	Hong Kong	W 4-0	Hong Kong	Fr	Knezevic 16, OG 30, Eduardo 64, Bosnjak 72	13 971	Iemoto JPN
1-03	Argentina	W 3-2	Basel	Fr	Klasnic 3, Srna 52, Simic 92+	13 138	Nobs SUI
23-05	Austria	W 4-1	Vienna	Fr	Klasnic 2 11 35, Babic 54, Balaban 69	22 000	Fandel GER
28-05	Iran	D 2-2	Osijek	Fr	Prso 31, Babic 97+	19 500	Siric CRO
3-06	Poland	L 0-1	Wolfsburg	Fr		8 000	Meyer GER
7-06	Spain	L 1-2	Geneva	Fr	OG 14	15 000	Lannoy FRA
13-06	Brazil	L 0-1	Berlin	WCr1		72 000	Archundia MEX
18-06	Japan	D 0-0	Nuremberg	WCr1		41 000	De Bleeckere BEL
22-06	Australia	D 2-2	Stuttgart	WCr1	Srna 2, Kovac.N 56	52 000	Poll ENG
16-08	Italy	W 2-0	Livorno	Fr	Eduardo 27, Modric 43	16 150	Kircher GER
6-09	Russia	D 0-0	Moscow	ECq		27 500	Mejuto Gonzalez ESP
7-10	Andorra	W 7-0	Zagreb	ECq	Petric 4 12 37 48 50, Klasnic 58, Balaban 62, Modric 83	17 618	Zammit MLT
11-10	England	W 2-0	Zagreb	ECq	Eduardo 61, Neville.G OG 69	31 991	Rosetti ENG
15-11	Israel	W 4-3	Tel Aviv	ECq	Srna 35p, Eduardo 3 39 54 72	35 000	Iturralde Gonzalez ESP
2007							
7-02	Norway	W 2-1	Rijeka	Fr	Petric 26, Modric 38	8 000	Kalt FRA
24-03	FYR Macedonia	W 2-1	Zagreb	ECq	Srna 58, Eduardo 88	29 969	Plautz AUT
2-06	Estonia	W 1-0	Tallinn	ECq	Eduardo 32	8 651	Kassai HUN
6-06	Russia	D 0-0	Zagreb	ECq		36 194	Michel SVK

Fr = Friendly match • EC = UEFA EURO 2004/2008 • WC = FIFA World Cup
q = qualifier • po = play-off • r1 = first round group

CROATIA NATIONAL TEAM RECORDS AND RECORD SEQUENCES

Records			Sequence records					
Victory	7-0	AUS 1998	Wins	6	2006-2007	Clean sheets	4	1994, 2002
Defeat	1-5	GER 1941, GER 1942	Defeats	3	2006	Goals scored	21	1996-1998
Player Caps	82	SIMIC Dario	Undefeated	12	2000-2001	Without goal	3	2005-2006
Player Goals	45	SUKER Davor	Without win	6	1999, 2006	Goals against	8	1996-1997

REPUBLIC OF CROATIA; REPUBLIKA HRVATSKA

Capital	Zagreb	Language	Croatian	Independence	1991
Population	4 494 749	Area	56 542 km²	Density 79 per km²	% in cities 64%
GDP per cap	$10 600	Dailling code	+385	Internet .hr	GMT +/- +1

MAJOR CITIES/TOWNS

Population '000

1	Zagreb	702
2	Split	176
3	Rijeka	139
4	Osijek	86
5	Zadar	72
6	Slavonski Brod	61
7	Pula	59
8	Sesvete	56
9	Karlovac	47
10	Varazdin	41
11	Sibenik	37
12	Velika Gorica	35
13	Sisak	35
14	Vinkovci	33
15	Vukovar	29
16	Bjelovar	28
17	Dubrovnik	27
18	Koprivnica	25
19	Dakovo	21
20	Pozega	21
21	Zapresic	17
22	Solin	15
23	Cakovec	15
24	Velika	2

MEDALS TABLE

		Overall G	S	B	League G	S	B	Cup G	S	Europe G	S	B	City	Stadium	Cap'ty	DoF
1	Dinamo Zagreb	17	7	2	9	3	2	8	4				Zagreb	Maksimir	38 923	1945
2	Hajduk Split	10	10	1	6	8	1	4	2				Split	Poljud	39 941	1911
3	NK Rijeka	2	3	1		2	1	2	1				Rijeka	Kantrida	10 275	1946
4	NK Zagreb	1	3	3	1	2	3	1					Zagreb	Kranjceviceva	12 000	1903
5	Inter Zapresic	1	1			1		1					Zapresic	Inter	8 000	1929
6	NK Osijek	1	5			5	1						Osijek	Gradski Vrt	19 500	1946
7	Varteks Varazdin		5	3		3			5				Varazdin	Varteksa	9 300	1931
8	Cibalia Vinkovci	1						1					Vinkovci	Cibalia	12 000	1947
	NK Pula	1						1					Pula	Gradski	7 000	2003
	Slaven Belupo	1						1					Koprivnica	Gradski	3 054	1912
11	Dragovoljac Zagreb		1			1							Zagreb	Siget	6 000	1975

CROATIAN CLUBS IN YUGOSLAV FOOTBALL

3	Hajduk Split	19	16	11	9	10	10	9	5	1	1	1	
4	Dinamo Zagreb	12	20	8	4	12	6	8	8			2	
6	Gradanski Zagreb	5	2	3	5	2	3						
11	Concordia Zagreb	2	1		2	1							
	NK Rijeka	2	1		2	1							

RECENT LEAGUE AND CUP RECORD

	Championship						Cup		
Year	Champions	Pts	Runners-up	Pts	Third	Pts	Winners	Score	Runners-up
1995	Hajduk Split	65	Croatia Zagreb	64	NK Osijek	59	Hajduk Split	3-2 1-0	Croatia Zagreb
1996	Croatia Zagreb	26	Hajduk Split	26	Varteks Varazdin	24	Croatia Zagreb	2-0 1-0	Varteks Varazdin
1997	Croatia Zagreb	81	Hajduk Split	60	Dragovoljac Zagreb	49	Croatia Zagreb	2-1	NK Zagreb
1998	Croatia Zagreb	49	Hajduk Split	36	NK Osijek	32	Croatia Zagreb	1-0 2-1	Varteks Varazdin
1999	Croatia Zagreb	45	NK Rijeka	44	Hajduk Split	39	NK Osijek	2-1	Cibalia Vinkovci
2000	Dinamo Zagreb	75	Hajduk Split	61	NK Osijek	53	Hajduk Split	2-0 0-1	Dinamo Zagreb
2001	Hajduk Split	66	Dinamo Zagreb	65	NK Osijek	57	Dinamo Zagreb	2-0 1-0	Hajduk Split
2002	NK Zagreb	67	Hajduk Split	65	Dinamo Zagreb	59	Dinamo Zagreb	1-1 1-0	Varteks Varazdin
2003	Dinamo Zagreb	78	Hajduk Split	70	Varteks Varazdin	57	Hajduk Spit	1-0 4-0	Uljanik Pula
2004	Hajduk Split	78	Dinamo Zagreb	76	NK Rijeka	42	Dinamo Zagreb	1-1 0-0†	Varteks Varazdin
2005	Hajduk Split	56	Inter Zapresic	54	NK Zagreb	50	Rijeka	2-1 1-0	Hajduk Split
2006	Dinamo Zagreb	76	NK Rijeka	65	Varteks Varazdin	47	Rijeka	4-0 1-5	Varteks Varazdin
2007	Dinamo Zagreb	92	Hajduk Split	72	NK Zagreb	58	Dinamo Zagreb	1-0 1-1	Slaven Koprivnica

Dinamo Zagreb previously known as HASK Gradjanski and then as Croatia Zagreb • † Dinamo won on away goals

CROATIA 2006-07

PRVA HNL OZUJSKO (1)

	Pl	W	D	L	F	A	Pts	Dinamo	Hajduk	Zagreb	Sibenik	Slaven	Osijek	Rijeka	Varteks	Medimurje	Cibalia	Pula	Kamen
Dinamo Zagreb †	33	30	2	1	84	22	92		2-1	2-1	4-3 3-0	1-0	1-0 1-0	1-0 1-0	4-1	4-1 4-0	4-0 4-0	5-1	2-0
Hajduk Split ‡	33	22	6	5	60	25	72	2-2		2-0 3-1	3-0	2-0 1-1	3-0	3-0 2-2 3-1	2-0	2-0	2-0	2-0 0-1	4-0 4-0
NK Zagreb	33	18	4	11	57	40	58	0-3 0-4	3-0		3-0 3-1	3-0	2-0 2-1 1-0 1-3	3-0	4-0 1-1	3-0 1-1	0-3	2-1	
NK Sibenik	33	14	7	12	50	47	49	2-1	1-2 2-2	1-0		2-1 0-0	1-2	2-2 3-1 2-0 3-4	3-0	1-0	1-0 1-0	4-1 3-1	
Slaven B. Koprivnica ‡	33	14	7	12	40	37	49	1-1 0-3	0-1	0-1 4-2	1-1		1-0 0-1 3-2 3-0	3-2	1-0 2-0 2-0 1-0	1-0	2-1		
NK Osijek	33	11	10	12	42	45	43	0-4	1-0 1-2	1-1	1-1	1-1		1-0	4-1 1-0 1-6 1-3 1-2-2	0-0	2-1		
NK Rijeka	33	12	6	15	51	53	42	2-3	0-1	2-1	1-3	2-0 2-2 0-2		2-2 3-0	1-3	4-1 1-2-2 0-1-1	4-2		
Varteks Varazdin	33	12	6	15	49	62	42	1-3 2-3	0-1	1-3	2-1 0-0 4-3	3-1	2-1		3-1	1-0	0-0 2-2 3-0 3-2		
Medimurje Cakovec	33	11	4	18	40	60	37	2-3 0-2 2-4	2-0	2-1 0-1	0-3	2-0	1-2 1-1 5-1 1-1-2		3-1	1-0 1-0 2-0 1-1			
Cibalia Vinkovci	33	9	5	19	33	53	32	0-1	0-0 0-1	0-1	0-1 2-1	2-0	3-0	3-4	1-2 1-0	0-3		3-1 1-0	1-3
Pula Staro cesko	33	6	11	16	28	40	29	0-2 1-2	0-0	0-2 2-3	1-1	2-1	2-2 3-1	2-3	1-1	3-0	0-0		2-0 0-0
Kamen Ingrad Velika	33	3	4	26	27	77	13	0-2 0-1	2-3	1-3 0-6	3-1	1-3 1-2 1-1 0-2	0-1	1-4	0-2	2-2 1-3	1-0		

29/07/2006 - 19/05/2007 • † Qualified for the UEFA Champions League • ‡ Qualified for the UEFA Cup
Play-off: Zadar 3-0 3-2 Pula Staro cesko • Top scorer: Eduardo Da Silva, Dinamo Zagreb 34

CROATIA 2006-07
DRUGA HNL (2)

	Pl	W	D	L	F	A	Pts
Inter Zapresic	30	21	5	4	60	28	68
NK Zadar	30	20	5	5	55	25	62
Croatia Sesvete	30	18	5	7	67	38	59
Hrvatski dragovoljac	30	18	4	8	60	25	58
NK Solin	30	16	5	9	58	33	53
NK Imotski	30	12	8	10	41	44	4
NK Belisce	30	11	9	10	46	40	42
Pomorac Kostrena	30	11	9	10	53	51	42
HNK Vukovar '91	30	9	8	13	40	42	35
HASK Naftas Zagreb	30	8	11	11	44	49	35
Mosor Zrnovnica	30	9	8	13	37	46	35
Marsonia Slav'ski Brod	30	9	7	14	38	50	34
Moslavina Kutina	30	9	6	15	44	57	33
NK Koprivnica	30	7	8	15	42	66	26
NK Bjelovar	30	4	6	20	25	66	18
NK Cakovec	30	4	4	22	37	87	16

19/08/2006 - 20/05/2007

HRVATSKOG NOGOMETNOG KUPA 2006-07

Round of sixteen		Quarter–finals		Semi–finals		Final	
Dinamo Zagreb *	3						
NK Sibenik	0	Dinamo Zagreb	2 2				
NK Osijek	1	Inter Zapresic *	1 1				
Inter Zapresic *	3			Dinamo Zagreb *	0 2		
Cibalia Vinkovci *	2			Hajduk Split	1 2		
HNK Vukovar	0	Cibalia Vinkovci *	2 2				
Belisce	2	Hajduk Split	3 3				
Hajduk Split *	5					Dinamo Zagreb *	1 1
NK Rijeka	0 5p					Slaven B. Koprivnica ‡	0 1
Hrvatski dragovoljac	0 3p	NK Rijeka *	3 1				
Segesta Sisak	0	Konavljanin Cilipi	1 2				
Konavljanin Cilipi *	2			NK Rijeka *	0 2		
NK Zagreb *	1 5p			Slaven B. Koprivnica	0 3		
Kamen Ingrad Velika	1 3p	NK Zagreb	0 2				
NK Hrvace	2	Slaven B. Koprivnica *	6 3				
Slaven B. Koprivnica *	4	* Home team/home team in the first leg • ‡ Qualified for the UEFA Cup					

CUP FINAL

1st leg, Zagreb, 9-05-2007
Scorer - Eduardo [76p]

2nd leg, Koprivnica, 26-05-2007
Scorers - Schildenfeld [89] for Dinamo;
Mumlek [68p] for Slaven

CTA – CENTRAL AFRICAN REPUBLIC

NATIONAL TEAM RECORD
JULY 10TH 2006 TO JULY 12TH 2010

PL	W	D	L	F	A	%
4	0	1	3	3	8	12.5

FIFA/COCA-COLA WORLD RANKING

1993	1994	1995	1996	1997	1998	1999	2000	2001	2002	2003	2004	2005	2006	High	Low
157	174	180	183	188	192	175	176	182	179	177	180	183	179	153 08/93	197 10/99

2006–2007											
08/06	09/06	10/06	11/06	12/06	01/07	02/07	03/07	04/07	05/07	06/07	07/07
173	178	179	181	179	180	182	183	180	180	184	185

The Central African Republic again failed to enter in the qualifiers for the African Nations Cup but still gave some international exposure to their national side in regional competition. The 'Fauves de Bazou Bangui' competed in neighbouring Chad in March 2007 in the CEMAC Cup where they lost to the hosts in the third and fourth place play-off game. The Central African Republic were among just a handful of teams who did not participate in the Nations Cup preliminaries, having also balked at entering the last FIFA World Cup qualifiers. But they have put their name into the hat for the draw for 2010 FIFA World Cup preliminaries. Their four matches at the 2007 CEMAC Cup did not produce

INTERNATIONAL HONOURS
None

any wins but there was an eye-catching draw against a Cameroonian A team in Ndjamena. It means that the team has now gone nine matches since they last tasted success at full international level, when they beat Gabon in the same tournament in 2003 en route to a surprise final appearance. Local league football was suspended last September by the country's government after accusations of poor administration in the football federation. FIFA have had to step in to alleviate a crisis, extending the mandate of its leadership until September, when new elections are scheduled. FIFA have also installed artificial turf at the Barthélemy Boganda stadium in Bangui.

THE FIFA BIG COUNT OF 2006

	Male	Female		Total
Number of players	183 004	9 400	Referees and Assistant Referees	360
Professionals	4		Admin, Coaches, Technical, Medical	3 250
Amateurs 18+	5 200		Number of clubs	80
Youth under 18	3 200		Number of teams	400
Unregistered	13 000		Clubs with women's teams	60
Total players	192 404		Players as % of population	4.47%

Fédération Centrafricaine de Football (RCA)
Avenue de Martyrs, Case Postale 344, Bangui, Central African Republic
Tel +236 619545   Fax +236 615660
fedefoot60@yahoo.fr   www.none
President: KAMACH Thierry   General Secretary: GBATE Jeremie
Vice-President: SAKILA Jean-Marie   Treasurer: MABOGNA Patrick   Media Officer: NDOTAH Christian
Men's Coach: NGATO Sebastien   Women's Coach: NGBANGANDIMBO Camille
RCA formed: 1961   CAF: 1965   FIFA: 1963
Blue shirts, White shorts, Blue socks

RECENT INTERNATIONAL MATCHES PLAYED BY THE CENTRAL AFRICAN REPUBLIC

2002 Opponents	Score		Venue	Comp	Scorers	Att	Referee
9-09 Mozambique	D	1-1	Bangui	CNq	Tamboula [72]		Ndong EQG
12-10 Burkina Faso	L	1-2	Ouagadougou	CNq	Ouefio [38]	25 000	Camara GUI
2003							
4-05 Congo	L	1-2	Brazzaville	CNq	Makita [84]		
8-06 Congo	D	0-0	Bangui	CNq			Hissene CHA
22-06 Mozambique	L	0-1	Maputo	CNq		15 000	
6-07 Burkina Faso	L	0-3	Bangui	CNq			
7-12 Cameroon	D	2-2	Brazzaville	CMr1	Oroko [10], Sandjo [30]		Mbera GAB
9-12 Cameroon	W	1-0	Brazzaville	CMr1	Sandjo [85]		Mandioukouta CGO
11-12 Gabon	W	2-0	Brazzaville	CMsf			
13-12 Cameroon	L	2-3	Brazzaville	CMf	Oroko [63], Destin [74]		Bansimba CGO
2004							
No international matches played in 2004							
2005							
3-02 Gabon	L	0-4	Libreville	CMr1			
5-02 Congo	L	0-1	Libreville	CMr1			
2006							
6-03 Cameroon	L	0-2	Malabo	CMr1			
8-03 Gabon	D	2-2	Malabo	CMr1			
2007							
6-03 Chad	L	2-3	N'Djamena	CMr1	Hilaire [14], Fiacre [34]		
8-03 Cameroon	D	0-0	N'Djamena	CMr1			
12-03 Congo	L	1-4	N'Djamena	CMsf	Romaric [15]		
16-03 Chad	L	0-1	N'Djamena	CM3p			

CN = CAF African Cup of Nations • CM = CEMAC Cup
q = qualifier • r1 = first round group • sf = semi-final • 3p = third place play-off • f = final

CENTRAL AFRICAN REPUBLIC NATIONAL TEAM RECORDS AND RECORD SEQUENCES

Records			Sequence records				
Victory	4-0	CHA 1999	Wins	2	1976, 1999, 2003	Clean sheets	2	2003
Defeat	1-7	CMR 1984	Defeats	9	1985-1987	Goals scored	7	1990-1999
Player Caps	n/a		Undefeated	3	2003	Without goal	4	1988-1989
Player Goals	n/a		Without win	16	1976-1987	Goals against	19	1976-1988

RECENT LEAGUE AND CUP RECORD

	League		Cup		
Year	Champions		Winners	Score	Runners-up
1996	Tempête Mocaf				
1997	Tempête Mocaf		USCA de Bangui	2-0	Anges de Fatima
1998	Championship not finished		Anges de Fatima	3-0	AS Petroca
1999	Tempête Mocaf		Olympique Réal		
2000	Olympique Réal		Anges de Fatima	2-1	Olympique Réal
2001	Olympique Réal		Stade Centrafricain	2-1	Tempête Mocaf
2002	Championship annulled				
2003	Tempête Mocaf		Tempête Mocaf	8-0	Ouham Pendé
2004	Olympique Réal		Tempête Mocaf	2-0	SCAF
2005	Anges de Fatima		USCA de Bangui		Lobaye

CENTRAL AFRICAN REPUBLIC COUNTRY INFORMATION

Capital	Bangui	Independence	1960 from France	GDP per Capita	$1100
Population	3 742 482	Status	Republic	GNP Ranking	154
Area km²	622 984	Language	French	Dialling code	+236
Population density	6 per km²	Literacy rate	42%	Internet code	.cf
% in urban areas	39%	Main religion	Christian 50%	GMT +/–	+1
Towns/Cities ('000)	Bangui 684; Carnot 83; Kaga-Bandoro 82; Mbaiki 76; Berbérati 59; Bouar 55; Bouar 55				
Neighbours (km)	Sudan 1 165; Congo DR 1 577; Congo 467; Cameroon 797; Chad 1 197				
Main stadia	Barthelemy Boganda – Bangui 35 000				

CUB – CUBA

NATIONAL TEAM RECORD
JULY 10TH 2006 TO JULY 12TH 2010

PL	W	D	L	F	A	%
19	8	4	7	36	25	52.6

FIFA/COCA-COLA WORLD RANKING

1993	1994	1995	1996	1997	1998	1999	2000	2001	2002	2003	2004	2005	2006	High	Low
159	175	96	68	88	107	77	77	76	71	75	76	75	46	46 12/06	175 12/94

2006–2007											
08/06	09/06	10/06	11/06	12/06	01/07	02/07	03/07	04/07	05/07	06/07	07/07
100	69	68	46	46	48	51	59	65	71	78	90

Football remains at the fringes of popular sporting culture in Cuba, but there can be little doubt that the game is beginning to make more of an impact and it now has a much higher profile than 10 years ago. Since then the national team has built a reputation in Caribbean football that continues to grow and by qualifying for the CONCACAF Gold Cup for the fourth time in a row, Cuba established a new record for the region. Small steps maybe, but significant ones. Haiti's triumph in the Digicel Caribbean Cup, in which Cuba finished third, has shown that both Trinidad and Jamaica are not invincible at the summit of the Caribbean game. At home the 2006 Cuban

INTERNATIONAL HONOURS
Qualified for the FIFA World Cup™ finals 1938
CONCACAF U-17 Championship 1988 Central American and Caribbean Games 1930 1974 1978 1986

championship was full of surprises and ended with a grandstand finish. Defending champions Holguín failed to even qualify for the ten team final round after finishing bottom of their preliminary group. After a slow start Villa Clara had a fine run in the second half of the season but lost out on the final day to Pinar del Río who won their first title since 2001. Having ended Cienfuegos' challenge in the penultimate round Pinar del Río went into the final game level against Villa Clara level on points with their opponents, and it was a first half Reinier Alcantara goal that won them the title.

THE FIFA BIG COUNT OF 2006

	Male	Female		Total
Number of players	1 045 900	95 925	Referees and Assistant Referees	225
Professionals	100		Admin, Coaches, Technical, Medical	5 030
Amateurs 18+	27 375		Number of clubs	338
Youth under 18	12 650		Number of teams	1 500
Unregistered	1 012 400		Clubs with women's teams	15
Total players	1 141 825		Players as % of population	10.03%

Asociación de Fútbol de Cuba (AFC)
Calle 41 No. 4109 e/ 44 y 46, La Habana, Cuba
Tel +53 7 2076440   Fax +53 7 2043563
futbol@inder.co.cu   www.none
President: HERNANDEZ Luis   General Secretary: GARCES Antonio
Vice-President: ARAGON Victor   Treasurer: CAMINO Otto   Media Officer: PEREIRA Jesus
Men's Coach: GONZALEZ Raul   Women's Coach: SOTOLONGO Rufino
AFC formed: 1924   CONCACAF: 1961   FIFA: 1932
Red shirts with white trimmings, Red shorts, Red socks or White shirts, White shorts, White socks

RECENT INTERNATIONAL MATCHES PLAYED BY CUBA

2004	Opponents	Score		Venue	Comp	Scorers	Att	Referee
22-02	Cayman Islands	W	2-1	Grand Cayman	WCq	Moré [53], Marten [89]	1 789	Sibrian SLV
16-03	Panama	D	1-1	Havana	Fr	Moré [33]		Rojas Corbeas CUB
18-03	Panama	W	3-0	Havana	Fr	Colome [36], Galindo [49], Moré [55]		Yero Rodriguez CUB
27-03	Cayman Islands	W	3-0	Havana	WCq	Moré 3 [7 50 66]	3 500	Rodriguez MEX
20-05	Grenada	D	2-2	Havana	Fr	Galindo [15], Faife [23]		
12-06	Costa Rica	D	2-2	Havana	WCq	Moré 2 [24 75]	18 500	Archundia MEX
20-06	Costa Rica	D	1-1	Alajuela	WCq	Cervantes [46+]	12 000	Prendergast JAM
2005								
9-01	Haiti	W	1-0	Port-au-Prince	GCq	Galindo [51]	15 000	Minyetti DOM
16-01	Haiti	D	1-1	Havana	GCq	Marquez [112]		Brizan TRI
20-02	Barbados	W	3-0	Bridgetown	GCq	Moré 2 [24 71], Galindo [90]	7 000	Prendergast JAM
22-02	Trinidad and Tobago	W	2-1	Bridgetown	GCq	Moré 2 [23 48]	2 100	Lancaster GUY
24-02	Jamaica	L	0-1	Bridgetown	GCq		3 000	Brizan TRI
7-07	USA	L	1-4	Seattle	GCr1	Moré [18]	15 831	Pineda HON
9-07	Costa Rica	L	1-3	Seattle	GCr1	Galindo [72]	15 109	Archundia MEX
12-07	Canada	L	1-2	Foxboro	GCr1	Cervantes [90]	15 211	Moreno PAN
2006								
2-09	Turks & Caicos Isl	W	6-0	Havana	CCq	Alonso [4], Arencibia [18], Alcantara 3 [20 58 71], Ocaña [83]		Campbell JAM
4-09	Bahamas	W	6-0	Havana	CCq	Alcantara 3 [22 50 64], Colome [30], Ocaña [40], Martinez [42]	100	Prendergast JAM
6-09	Cayman Islands	W	7-0	Havana	CCq	Alcantara [5], Ocaña 2 [10 34], Martinez 2 [45 58], Colome [83], Muñoz [85]	120	Campbell JAM
17-10	Haiti	D	0-0	Port-au-Prince	Fr			
19-10	Haiti	W	1-0	Cap Haitien	Fr	Villaurrutia [8p]		
8-11	Haiti	W	2-1	Fort-de-France	CCq	Marquez [21], Moré [79]		
10-11	Suriname	W	3-1	Fort-de-France	CCq	Alvarez 2 [4 26], Colome [41]		
12-11	Martinique	D	0-0	Fort-de-France	CCq			
2007								
14-01	Guadeloupe	L	1-2	Marabella	CCr1	Alonso [69]		Brizan TRI
16-01	St Vincent/Grenadines	W	3-0	Marabella	CCr1	Moré 2 [27 59], Duarte [90]		
18-01	Guyana	D	0-0	Marabella	CCr1			Moreno PAN
20-01	Trinidad and Tobago	L	1-3	Port of Spain	CCsf	Duarte [75]		Campbell JAM
23-01	Guadeloupe	W	2-1	Port of Spain	CC3p	Cervantes 2 [24 48]		Brizan TRI
24-03	Venezuela	L	1-3	Merida	Fr	Alcantara [47]	12 000	Andarcia VEN
9-05	Chile	L	0-3	Osorno	Fr		1 800	Cabrera VEN
16-05	Chile	L	0-2	Temuco	Fr		3 500	Grance PAR
8-06	Mexico	L	1-2	New Jersey	GCr1	Alcantara [22]	20 230	Aguilar SLV
10-06	Panama	D	2-2	New Jersey	GCr1	Colome [29], Alcantara [78]	68 123	
13-06	Honduras	L	0-5	Houston	GCr1		68 417	

Fr = Friendly match • GC = CONCACAF Gold Cup • WC = FIFA World Cup • q = qualifier • r1 = first round group

CUBA NATIONAL TEAM RECORDS AND RECORD SEQUENCES

Records			Sequence records					
Victory	9-0	PUR 1995	Wins	7	1998-1999	Clean sheets	7	1996
Defeat	0-8	SWE 1938	Defeats	18	1949-1960	Goals scored	12	2003-2005
Player Caps	n/a		Undefeated	11	1981-83, 2004-05	Without goal	4	1957, 1983, 2002
Player Goals	n/a		Without win	20	1949-1960	Goals against	26	1949-1961

CUBA COUNTRY INFORMATION

Capital	Havana	Independence	1902 from Spain	GDP per Capita	$2 900
Population	11 308 764	Status	Republic	GNP Ranking	69
Area km²	110 860	Language	Spanish	Dialling code	+53
Population density	102 per km²	Literacy rate	97%	Internet code	.cu
% in urban areas	76%	Main religion	None	GMT +/–	-5
Towns/Cities ('000)	Havana 2 163; Santiago 555; Camagüey 347; Holguín 319; Guantánamo 272; Santa Clara 250				
Neighbours (km)	North Atlantic Ocean, Caribbean Sea and the Gulf of Mexico 3 735				
Main stadia	Estadio Panamericano – Havana 34 000; Pedro Marrero – Havana 28 000				

CUBA 2006
CAMPEONATO NACIONAL FIRST ROUND

Group A	Pl	W	D	L	F	A	Pts
Pinar del Río †	8	5	1	2	14	7	16
Ciudad de La Habana †	8	5	1	2	13	6	16
La Habana †	8	4	0	4	10	8	12
Matanzas †	8	4	0	4	14	13	12
Isla de la Juventud	8	1	0	7	5	22	3

Group B	Pl	W	D	L	F	A	Pts
Villa Clara †	8	6	1	1	12	5	19
Camagüey †	8	5	0	3	9	12	15
Cienfuegos †	8	4	2	2	9	5	14
Sancti Spíritus	8	1	2	5	7	10	5
Ciego de Avila	8	1	1	6	5	10	4

9/09/2006 - 14/10/2006 • † Clubs qualifying for the Second Round

CUBA 2006
CAMPEONATO NACIONAL FIRST ROUND

Group C	Pl	W	D	L	F	A	Pts
Las Tunas †	8	4	1	3	4	8	13
Guantánamo †	8	4	0	4	15	9	12
Granma †	8	4	0	4	13	11	12
Santiago de Cuba †	8	3	2	3	10	11	11
Holguín	8	3	1	4	11	14	10

9/09/2006 - 14/10/2006 • † Clubs qualifying for the Second Round

CUBA 2006
CAMPEONATO NACIONAL SECOND ROUND

	Pl	W	D	L	F	A	Pts	Pinar del Río	Villa Clara	Cienfuegos	Guantánamo	Matanzas	Ciudad LH	La Habana	Camagüey	Las Tunas	Granma
Pinar del Río	18	11	5	2	26	7	38		1-0	1-0	4-1	2-0	0-1	2-0	1-0	0-0	1-0
Villa Clara	18	10	5	3	27	10	35	1-1		2-0	1-0	2-0	0-1	6-0	0-0	2-0	2-1
Cienfuegos	18	9	5	4	25	15	32	0-0	1-1		2-0	2-0	2-0	2-1	2-1	2-0	1-1
Guantánamo	18	6	7	5	19	21	25	0-0	1-1	3-2		2-0	1-1	2-2	2-2	2-2	0-0
Matanzas	18	7	3	8	16	18	24	1-2	1-1	1-0	1-0		3-1	0-0	2-2	1-0	1-0
Ciudad de La Habana	18	6	5	7	16	19	23	1-4	0-1	1-1	4-0	1-0		0-0	0-2	0-1	0-2
La Habana	18	5	7	6	15	22	22	0-0	1-2	1-1	0-1	1-0	0-2		3-1	1-0	2-1
Camagüey	18	3	8	7	19	24	17	1-3	0-1	2-4	0-0	0-2	0-0	1-1		1-1	3-0
Las Tunas	18	4	4	10	10	25	16	0-4	1-4	0-1	0-2	1-0	1-1	1-1	1-2		2-1
Granma	18	3	3	12	12	24	12	1-0	1-0	0-2	1-2	1-3	1-2	0-1	1-1	0-1	

21/10/2006 - 27/12/2006 • Top scorers: Alexei ZUAZNABAR, Guantánamo 15; Yordanis TIELVES, Matanzas 13; Armando CORONEAUX, Camagüey 11

CLUB DIRECTORY

Club	Town/City	Stadium	Lge
Camagüey	Camagüey	Terreno de Futbol de Florida	0
Ciego de Avila	Ciego de Avila	CVD Deportivo	3
Cienfuegos	Cienfuegos		2
Ciudad de La Habana	Havana	Pedro Marrero	6
Granma	Bayamo	Conrado Benítez	0
Holguín	Holguín	Turcio Lima	1
Industriales	Havana	Campo Armada	4
Las Tunas	Victoria de Las Tunas	Ovidio Torres	0
Matanzas	Matanzas	Terreno de Futbol de Colon	0
Pinar del Río	Pinar del Río	La Bombonera	6
Santiago de Cuba	Santiago de Cuba	Antonio Maceo	0
Villa Clara	Santa Clara	Camilo Cienfuegos	10

RECENT LEAGUE RECORD

Year	Winners	Score	Runners-up
1996	Villa Clara	2-3 4-0	Cienfuegos
1997	Villa Clara	1-2 2-0	Pinar del Río
1998	Ciudad de La Habana	2-1 1-0	Villa Clara
1999	No championship due to season readjustment		
2000	Pinar del Río	0-1 2-1†	Ciudad de La Habana
2001	Ciudad de La Habana	2-1 0-0	Villa Clara
2002	Ciego de Avila	1-0 0-0	Granma Bayamo
2003	Villa Clara	1-0 2-0	Ciudad de La Habana
2003	Ciego de Avila	1-1 2-0	Villa Clara
2004	Villa Clara	0-1 3-0	Pinar del Río
2005	Holguín	‡	Ciudad de La Habana

† Won on away goals • ‡ Played on a league basis

CYP – CYPRUS

NATIONAL TEAM RECORD
JULY 10TH 2006 TO JULY 12TH 2010

PL	W	D	L	F	A	%
9	2	1	6	11	22	27.7

FIFA/COCA-COLA WORLD RANKING

1993	1994	1995	1996	1997	1998	1999	2000	2001	2002	2003	2004	2005	2006	High	Low
72	67	73	78	82	78	63	62	79	80	97	108	96	73	**58** 02/99	**113** 03/05

2006–2007											
08/06	09/06	10/06	11/06	12/06	01/07	02/07	03/07	04/07	05/07	06/07	07/07
90	103	80	73	73	74	73	68	80	80	81	81

While the national team still often finds itself on the end of heavy defeats away from home, back in Cyprus they are capable of giving anyone a run for their money, and that was borne out in the UEFA Euro 2008 qualifiers. They started their campaign with a 6-1 drubbing at the hands of Slovakia in Bratislava but picked themselves up and thumped the Republic of Ireland 5-2 in Nicosia in the next match. Even more impressive perhaps was the 1-1 draw with Germany a month later, and there can be little doubt that the influx of foreign players into the Cypriot League is having a positive effect on the national team. Those foreigners may not be at the peak of their game but they have helped make

INTERNATIONAL HONOURS
None

the League much more competitive. APOEL had a number of foreigners in their championship winning side, notably Esteban Solari, brother of Inter's Santiago Solari, who was the League's top scorer with 20 goals. APOEL's success saw them match Omonia's 19 titles and it owed much to coach Marinos Ouzounides who was in his first season in charge. Both Omonia and Anorthosis Famagusta kept the championship alive as they chased APOEL but in the end both had to be content with a place in the Cup Final. They produced a five-goal thriller won by Anorthosis to give Timuri Ketsbaia his second trophy as coach of the club.

THE FIFA BIG COUNT OF 2006

	Male	Female		Total
Number of players	47 768	4 635	Referees and Assistant Referees	200
Professionals	800		Admin, Coaches, Technical, Medical	2 000
Amateurs 18+	10 091		Number of clubs	100
Youth under 18	6 644		Number of teams	328
Unregistered	20 200		Clubs with women's teams	8
Total players	52 403		Players as % of population	6.68%

Cyprus Football Association (CFA)
10 Achaion Street, 2413 Engomi, Nicosia, Cyprus
Tel +357 22 352341   Fax +357 22 590544
info@cfa.com.cy   www.none
President: KOUTSOKOUMNIS Costakis   General Secretary: GEORGIADES Chris
Vice-President: KATSIKIDES Tassos   Treasurer: MARANGOS Spyros   Media Officer: GIORGALIS Kyriakos
Men's Coach: ANASTASIADIS Angelos   Women's Coach: IAKOVOU Pepis
CFA formed: 1934   UEFA: 1962   FIFA: 1948
Blue shirts with white trimmings, White shorts, Blue socks or White shirts with blue trimmings, White shorts, White socks

RECENT INTERNATIONAL MATCHES PLAYED BY CYPRUS

2002	Opponents	Score	Venue	Comp	Scorers	Att	Referee
7-09	France	L 1-2	Nicosia	ECq	Okkas [15]	10 000	Fandel GER
20-11	Malta	W 2-1	Nicosia	ECq	Rauffmann [50], Okkas [74]	5 000	Guenov BUL
2003							
29-01	Greece	L 1-2	Larnaca	Fr	Konstantinou.M [28p]	2 000	Loizou CYP
12-02	Russia	L 0-1	Limassol	Fr		300	Efthimiadis GRE
13-02	Slovakia	L 1-3	Larnaca	Fr	Rauffmann [40]	250	Kapitanis CYP
29-03	Israel	D 1-1	Limassol	ECq	Rauffmann [61]	8 500	McCurry SCO
2-04	Slovenia	L 1-4	Ljubljana	ECq	Konstantinou.M [10]	5 000	Costa POR
30-04	Israel	L 0-2	Palermo	ECq		1 000	Benes CZE
7-06	Malta	W 2-1	Ta'Qali	ECq	Konstantinou.M 2 [22p 53]	3 000	Brugger AUT
6-09	France	L 0-5	Paris	ECq		55 000	Irvine NIR
11-10	Slovenia	D 2-2	Limassol	ECq	Georgiou.S [74], Yiasoumi [84]	2 346	Ovrebo NOR
2004							
18-02	Belarus	L 0-2	Achnas	Fr		500	Kailis CYP
19-02	Georgia	W 3-1	Nicosia	Fr	Charalampidis 2 [44 55], Ilia [73]	200	Kapitanis CYP
21-02	Kazakhstan	W 2-1	Larnaca	Fr	Charalampidis [3], Michail.C [8]	300	Lajuks LVA
19-05	Jordan	D 0-0	Nicosia	Fr		2 500	Loizou CYP
18-08	Albania	W 2-1	Nicosia	Fr	Konstantinou.M 2 [13p 48]	200	Kapitanis CYP
4-09	Republic of Ireland	L 0-3	Dublin	WCq		36 000	Paniashvili GEO
8-09	Israel	L 1-2	Tel Aviv	WCq	Konstantinou.M [59]	21 872	Shmolik BLR
9-10	Faroe Islands	D 2-2	Nicosia	WCq	Konstantinou.M [15], Okkas [81]	1 400	Gadiyev AZE
13-10	France	L 0-2	Nicosia	WCq		3 319	Larsen DEN
17-11	Israel	L 1-2	Nicosia	WCq	Okkas [45]	1 624	Kaldma EST
2005							
8-02	Austria	D 1-1	Limassol	Fr	Charalampidis [90]. W 5-4p	300	Hyytia FIN
9-02	Finland	L 1-2	Nicosia	Fr	Michail.C [24]	300	Lajuks LVA
26-03	Jordan	W 2-1	Larnaca	Fr	Charalampidis [9], Okkas [28]	200	Kapitanis CYP
30-03	Switzerland	L 0-1	Zurich	WCq		16 066	Dougal SCO
13-08	Iraq	W 2-1	Limassol	Fr	Yiasoumi 2 [63 79]	500	
17-08	Faroe Islands	W 3-0	Toftir	WCq	Konstantinou.M 2 [39 77], Krassas [95+]	2 720	Johannesson SWE
7-09	Switzerland	L 1-3	Nicosia	WCq	Aloneftis [35]	2 561	Ivanov.N RUS
8-10	Republic of Ireland	L 0-1	Nicosia	WCq		13 546	Kassai HUN
12-10	France	L 0-4	Paris	WCq		78 864	Stark GER
16-11	Wales	W 1-0	Limassol	Fr	Michail.C [43p]	1 000	Jakov ISR
2006							
28-02	Slovenia	L 0-1	Larnaca	Fr		1 000	Tsacheilidis GRE
1-03	Armenia	W 2-0	Limassol	Fr	Okkas [18], Michail.C [61]		
16-08	Romania	L 0-2	Constanta	Fr		10 000	Corpodean ROU
2-09	Slovakia	L 1-6	Bratislava	ECq	Yiasoumis [90]	4 723	Orekhov UKR
7-10	Republic of Ireland	W 5-2	Nicosia	ECq	Konstantinou.M 2 [10 50p], Garpozis [16], Charalambides 2 [60 75]	5 000	Batista OR
11-10	Wales	L 1-3	Cardiff	ECq	Okkas [83]	20 456	Granat POL
15-11	Germany	D 1-1	Nicosia	ECq	Okkas [43]	12 300	Fröjdfeldt SWE
2007							
6-02	Hungary	W 2-1	Limassol	Fr	Yiasoumis [18], Okkas [72]	500	Gerasimou CYP
7-02	Bulgaria	L 0-3	Nicosia	Fr		2 000	
24-03	Slovakia	L 1-3	Nicosia	ECq	Aloneftis [43]	2 696	Lehner AUT
28-03	Czech Republic	L 0-1	Liberec	ECq		9 310	Bebek CRO

Fr = Friendly match • EC = UEFA EURO 2004/2008 • WC = FIFA World Cup • q = qualifier

CYPRUS NATIONAL TEAM RECORDS AND RECORD SEQUENCES

Records			Sequence records					
Victory	5-0	AND 2000	Wins	3	1992, 1998, 2000	Clean sheets	2	1992-93, 1994,1996
Defeat	0-12	GER 1969	Defeats	19	1973-1978	Goals scored	7	1997-1998
Player Caps	82	PITTAS Pambos	Undefeated	6	1997-1998	Without goal	6	1975, 1987-1988
Player Goals	24	KONSTANTINOU Michalis	Without win	39	1984-1992	Goals against	36	1973-1981

REPUBLIC OF CYPRUS; KYPRIAKI DIMOKRATIA

Capital	Nicosia	Language	Greek, Turkish, English	Independence	1960
Population	784 301	Area	9 250 km²	Density 83 per km²	% in cities	54%
GDP per cap	$19 200	Dailling code	+357	Internet .cy	GMT + / -	+2

MEDALS TABLE

		Overall			League			Cup			Europe			City	Stadium	Cap'ty	DoF
		G	S	B	G	S	B	G	S	B	G	S	B				
1	APOEL Nicosia	37	25	15	19	17	15	18	8					Nicosia	Pancypria	23 400	1926
2	Omonia Nicosia	31	19	7	19	13	7	12	6					Nicosia	Pancypria	23 400	1948
3	Anorthosis Famagusta	20	15	5	12	10	5	8	5					Larnaca	Andonis Papadopoulos	9 500	1911
4	AEL Limassol	12	6	6	6	1	6	6	5					Limassol	Tsirion	13 152	1930
5	Apollon Limassol	8	10	4	3	4	4	5	6					Limassol	Tsirion	13 152	1954
6	EPA Larnaca	7	9	4	2	6	4	5	3					Larnaca	Zenon		1932-94
7	Olympiakos Nicosia	4	7	2	3	4	2	1	3					Nicosia	Pancypria	23 400	1931
8	Trust AC	4	3		1	2		3	1					Larnaca	Old Gymnastica		1896-44
9	Pezoporikos Larnaca	3	15	14	2	8	14	1	7					Larnaca	Old Gymnastica		1927-94
10	Chetin Kaya	3	4	3	1	1	3	2	3					Nicosia	GSP		1916
11	NEA Salamina	1	2	4			4	1	2					Larnaca	Ammochostos	8 000	1948
12	AEK Larnaca	1	2					1	2					Larnaca	Zenon	13 032	1994
13	Union Paralimni (ENP)		5	2		1	2		4					Paralimni	Municipal	8 000	1936
14	Alki Larnaca		5	1			1		5					Larnaca	Zenon	13 032	1948
15	Digenis Morphou		2			1			1					Nicosia	Makarion	20 000	1931
16	Aris Limassol	1	1				1		1					Limassol	Tsirion	13 152	1930
17	Ethnikos Achnas	1						1						Achna	Dasaki	4 000	1968

RECENT LEAGUE AND CUP RECORD

	Championship						Cup		
Year	Champions	Pts	Runners-up	Pts	Third	Pts	Winners	Score	Runners-up
1995	Anorthosis F'gusta	73	Omonia Nicosia	67	NEA Salamina	57	APOEL Nicosia	4-2	Apollon Limassol
1996	APOEL Nicosia	64	Anorthosis F'gusta	55	Omonia Nicosia	53	APOEL Nicosia	2-0	AEK Larnaca
1997	Anorthosis F'gusta	65	Apollon Limassol	52	Omonia Nicosia	46	APOEL Nicosia	2-0	Omonia Nicosia
1998	Anorthosis F'gusta	66	Omonia Nicosia	62	Apollon Limassol	55	Anothosis F'gusta	3-1	Apollon Limassol
1999	Anorthosis F'gusta	67	Omonia Nicosia	67	APOEL Nicosia	59	APOEL Nicosia	2-0	Anorthosis F'gusta
2000	Anorthosis F'gusta	65	Omonia Nicosia	59	APOEL Nicosia	46	Omonia Nicosia	4-2	APOEL Nicosia
2001	Omonia Nicosia	57	Olympiakos	54	AEL Limassol	52	Apollon Limassol	1-0	NEA Salamina
2002	APOEL Nicosia	59	Anorthosis F'gusta	58	AEL Limassol	54	Anorthosis F'gusta	1-0	Ethnikos Achnas
2003	Omonia Nicosia	60	Anorthosis F'gusta	59	APOEL Nicosia	55	Anorthosis F'gusta	0-0 5-3p	AEL Limassol
2004	APOEL Nicosia	65	Omonia Nicosia	62	Apollon Limassol	49	AEK Larnaca	2-1	AEL Limassol
2005	Anorthosis F'gusta	62	APOEL Nicosia	58	Omonia Nicosia	47	Omonia Nicosia	2-0	Digenis Morfu
2006	Apollon Limassol	64	Omonia Nicosia	63	APOEL Nicosia	62	APOEL Nicosia	3-2	AEK Larnaca
2007	APOEL Nicosia	64	Omonia Nicosia	57	Anorthosis F'gusta	53	Anorthosis F'gusta	3-2	Omonia Nicosia

CYPRUS 2006-07

DIVISION A

	Pl	W	D	L	F	A	Pts	APOEL	Omonia	Anorthosis	Ethnikos	ENP	Apollon	AEK	Aris	Nea S'mina	AEL	Olympiakos	Digenis	Ayia Napa	AEP
APOEL Nicosia †	26	20	4	2	59	22	64		2-2	1-0	2-1	3-2	1-0	2-1	5-0	1-0	2-1	5-0	4-0	3-0	2-1
Omonia Nicosia ‡	26	18	3	5	62	22	57	1-2		2-0	3-0	1-3	3-0	3-0	4-1	4-0	2-0	3-1	6-0	1-1	3-0
Anorthosis Famagusta‡	26	16	5	5	42	20	53	1-1	0-2		3-2	1-0	2-1	1-1	2-0	4-1	1-0	2-1	2-1	1-1	4-0
Ethnikos Achnas	26	10	7	9	38	33	37	3-1	1-3	2-3		0-0	3-1	2-0	5-1	0-1	3-1	0-0	0-0	2-2	1-1
ENP Paralimni	26	10	5	11	31	27	35	0-0	2-0	0-2	1-0		1-0	2-3	2-0	0-0	3-0	1-1	2-0	0-0	0-1
Apollon Limassol	26	10	5	11	35	36	35	2-1	1-2	1-1	3-1	1-3		1-1	1-0	1-1	2-4	0-3	3-0	1-0	1-2
AEK Larnaca	26	8	10	8	33	32	34	0-1	1-2	0-3	0-2	1-1	0-0		7-1	1-0	1-1	1-2	1-1	2-0	2-1
Aris Limassol	26	9	5	12	39	58	32	2-3	0-5	2-1	4-2	3-1	1-2	1-1		5-2	1-2	2-0	2-2	2-1	2-0
Nea Salamina	26	7	9	10	32	41	30	0-3	0-2	1-0	0-1	0-1	3-1	0-1	3-3		0-3	5-1	3-1	1-1	3-1
AEL Limassol	26	8	6	12	31	42	30	0-4	0-2	0-2	1-3	2-1	1-1	0-1	3-3	2-2		0-2	1-2	2-1	3-2
Olympiakos Nicosia	26	6	10	10	24	36	28	1-2	2-1	0-0	0-1	1-0	1-3	0-2	1-1	3-3	0-2		1-1	2-0	1-1
Digenis Morfu	26	5	10	11	23	41	25	1-3	1-2	0-2	1-1	1-2	1-0	1-1	1-2	1-1	0-0	0-0		2-0	1-1
Ayia Napa	26	4	8	14	26	41	20	2-2	2-1	0-2	1-1	2-1	2-3	0-1	4-1	1-2	0-1	0-0	1-3		3-1
AEP Paphos	26	3	9	14	21	45	18	1-3	2-2	0-2	0-1	1-0	1-5	1-1	1-2	0-0	1-1	0-0	0-1	1-1	

12/08/2006 - 6/05/2007 • † Qualified for the UEFA Champions League • ‡ Qualified for the UEFA Cup
Top scorers: Esteban SOLARI, APOEL 20; Adrian MIHALCEA, Aris 16; Giorgos VAKOUFTSIS, Omonia 14; Kyriakos CHAILIS, Nea Salamina 12

CYPRUS 2006-07
DIVISION B

	Pl	W	D	L	F	A	Pts
APOP	26	18	4	4	65	22	58
Alki Larnaca	26	17	5	4	46	16	56
Doxa Katokopia	26	15	5	6	36	20	50
THOI Lakatamia	26	13	10	3	54	36	49
ASIL	26	13	8	5	48	26	47
Anagennisi Yermasoyia	26	8	12	6	30	27	36
Omonia Aradippou	26	10	5	11	38	31	35
MEAP Nisou	26	9	8	9	33	40	35
Onisilos Sotiras	26	9	6	11	39	31	33
APEP	26	9	4	13	38	43	31
Akritas Chloraka	26	8	6	12	33	41	30
Halkanoras Dhaliou	26	6	8	12	36	47	26
Iraklis Yerolakkou	26	3	4	19	25	62	13
AEM Mesogis	26	0	3	23	25	104	3

23/09/2006 - 6/05/2007

COCA-COLA CUP 2006-07

Round of 16

Anorthosis Famagusta*	3	2
AEP Paphos	0	1
Ahironas Liopetriou	0	0
ENP Paralimni *	3	2
Apollon Limassol	1	1
Ayia Napa *	0	1
Digenis Morfu	0	0
AEK Larnaca *	0	2
APOEL Nicosia *	2	2
Aris Limassol	1	0
Nea Salamina	0	2
Ethnikos Achnas *	2	1
AEL Limassol *	3	2
MEAP Nisou	0	3
Onisilos Sotiras *	0	1
Omonia Nicosia	3	6

Quarter-finals

Group A	Pts
APOEL Nicosia	10
Anorthosis Famagusta	9
ENP Paralimni	8
Apollon Limassol	4

Group B	Pts
Omonia Nicosia	10
AEK Larnaca	9
Ethnikos Achnas	8
AEL Limassol	4

Semi-finals

Anorthosis Famagusta	1	2
AEK Larnaca *	1	1

APOEL Nicosia	1	1
Omonia Nicosia *	1	2

Final

Anorthosis Famagusta ‡	3
Omonia Nicosia	2

CUP FINAL
GSP, Nicosia
12-05-2007
Scorers - Nikos Frousos [25], Alexandre Soares [60], Nikos Nicolaou [75] for Anorthosis; Guilherme [20], Georgios Constantinou [50p] for Omonia

* Home team in the first leg • ‡ Qualified for the UEFA Cup

CZE – CZECH REPUBLIC

NATIONAL TEAM RECORD
JULY 10TH 2006 TO JULY 12TH 2010

PL	W	D	L	F	A	%
10	5	3	2	19	8	65

FIFA/COCA-COLA WORLD RANKING

1993	1994	1995	1996	1997	1998	1999	2000	2001	2002	2003	2004	2005	2006	High	Low
-	34	14	5	3	8	2	5	14	15	6	4	2	10	2	67 03/94

2006–2007											
08/06	09/06	10/06	11/06	12/06	01/07	02/07	03/07	04/07	05/07	06/07	07/07
10	7	8	10	10	10	9	9	10	10	10	11

Karel Bruckner survived the now traditional post World Cup cull of coaches but the retirement from international football of both Karel Poborsky and Pavel Nedved didn't make his job any easier. Nor did the indiscipline of some of the players after a crucial defeat at home to Germany which ceded the advantage in their UEFA Euro 2008 qualifying group to their opponents. That left the Czech Republic facing a battle with the Republic of Ireland for the second qualifying spot in their quest to qualify for a fourth successive appearance at the finals. In domestic football, Sparta's season got off to a poor start leading to the appointment of Michal Bilek as coach and by the end of the

INTERNATIONAL HONOURS
Qualified for the FIFA World Cup™ finals 2006   UEFA U-21 Championship 2002

season he had led them to the first League and Cup double achieved in Czech football since the split with Slovakia. The League went down to the final day with defending champions Slovan Liberec one point behind Sparta. Sparta went on to beat Siad Most 5-0 to clinch the title while Slovan lost to Mladá, ending up fourth and out of Europe. Four days earlier Sparta had completed the first leg of the double by beating FK Jablonec 2-1 in the Cup Final. In Europe Sparta failed to make it three qualifications in a row for the UEFA Champions League group stage, but they did qualify for the UEFA Cup groups along with Mladá and Slovan. None of them made it any further.

THE FIFA BIG COUNT OF 2006

	Male	Female		Total
Number of players	976 355	64 002	Referees and Assistant Referees	4 351
Professionals	1 558		Admin, Coaches, Technical, Medical	8 530
Amateurs 18+	435 605		Number of clubs	3 968
Youth under 18	208 451		Number of teams	15 463
Unregistered	103 100		Clubs with women's teams	140
Total players	1 040 357		Players as % of population	10.16

Football Association of Czech Republic (CMFS)
Ceskomoravsky Fotbalovy Svaz, Diskarska 100, PO Box 11, Praha 6 - 16900, Czech Republic
Tel +420 2 33029111   Fax +420 2 33353107
cmfs@fotbal.cz   www.fotbal.cz
President: MOKRY Pavel   General Secretary: REPKA Rudolf
Vice-President: KOSTAL Vlastimil   Treasurer: FISCHER Jiri   Media Officer: TUCEK Lukas
Men's Coach: BRUCKNER Karel   Women's Coach: ZOVINEC Dusan
CMFS formed: 1901   UEFA: 1954   FIFA: 1907 & 1994
Red shirts with blue and white trimmings, White shorts, Blue socks or White shirts, White shorts, White socks

RECENT INTERNATIONAL MATCHES PLAYED BY THE CZECH REPUBLIC

2004	Opponents		Score	Venue	Comp	Scorers	Att	Referee
15-06	Latvia	W	2-1	Aveiro	ECr1	Baros [73], Heinz [85]	21 744	Veissiere FRA
19-06	Netherlands	W	3-2	Aveiro	ECr1	Koller [23], Baros [71], Smicer [88]	29 935	Gonzalez ESP
23-06	Germany	W	2-1	Lisbon	ECr1	Heinz [30], Baros [77]	46 849	Hauge NOR
27-06	Denmark	W	3-0	Porto	ECqf	Koller [49], Baros 2 [63 65]	41 092	Ivanov RUS
1-07	Greece	L	0-1	Porto	ECsf		42 449	Collina ITA
18-08	Greece	D	0-0	Prague	Fr		15 050	Dougal SCO
8-09	Netherlands	L	0-2	Amsterdam	WCq		48 488	Merk GER
9-10	Romania	W	1-0	Prague	WCq	Koller [36]	16 028	Rosetti ITA
13-10	Armenia	W	3-0	Yerevan	WCq	Koller 2 [3 75]	3 205	Granat POL
17-11	FYR Macedonia	W	2-0	Skopje	WCq	Lokvenc [88], Koller [90]	7 000	Meier SUI
2005								
9-02	Slovenia	W	3-0	Celje	Fr	Koller [10], Jun [47], Polak [79]	4 000	Strahonja CRO
26-03	Finland	W	4-3	Teplice	WCq	Baros [7], Rosicky [34], Polak [58], Lokvenc [87]	16 200	Larsen DEN
30-03	Andorra	W	4-0	Andorra la Vella	WCq	Jankulovski [31p], Baros [40], Lokvenc [53], Rosicky [92+p]	900	Messner AUT
4-06	Andorra	W	8-1	Liberec	WCq	Lokvenc 2 [12 92], Koller [30], Smicer [37], Galasek [52], Baros [79], Rosicky [84], Polak [86]	9 520	Dereli TUR
8-06	FYR Macedonia	W	6-1	Teplice	WCq	Koller 4 [41 45 48 52], Rosicky [73p], Baros [87]	14 150	Dauden Ibanez ESP
17-08	Sweden	L	1-2	Gothenburg	Fr	Koller [22p]	23 117	Bennett ENG
3-09	Romania	L	0-2	Constanta	WCq		7 000	Hauge NOR
7-09	Armenia	W	4-1	Olomouc	WCq	Heinz [47], Polak 2 [52 76], Baros [58]	12 015	Hansson SWE
8-10	Netherlands	L	0-2	Prague	WCq		17 478	Sars FRA
12-10	Finland	W	3-0	Helsinki	WCq	Jun [6], Rosicky [51], Heinz [58]	11 234	Mejuto Gonzalez ESP
12-11	Norway	W	1-0	Oslo	WCpo	Smicer [31]	24 264	Busacca SUI
16-11	Norway	W	1-0	Prague	WCpo	Rosicky [35]	17 464	Poll ENG
2006								
1-03	Turkey	D	2-2	Izmir	Fr	Poborsky [21p], Stajner [63]	58 000	Meyer GER
26-05	Saudi Arabia	W	2-0	Innsbruck	Fr	Baros [15], Jankulovski [90p]	4 000	Einwaller AUT
30-05	Costa Rica	W	1-0	Jablonec	Fr	Lokvenc [82]	14 500	Bede HUN
3-06	Trinidad and Tobago	W	3-0	Prague	Fr	Koller 2 [6 40], Nedved [22]	15 910	Johansson SWE
12-06	USA	W	3-0	Gelsenkirchen	WCr1	Koller [5], Rosicky 2 [36 76]	52 000	Amarilla PAR
17-06	Ghana	L	0-2	Cologne	WCr1		45 000	Elizondo ARG
22-06	Italy	L	0-2	Hamburg	WCr1		50 000	Archundia MEX
16-08	Serbia	L	1-3	Uherske Hradiste	Fr	Stajner [3]	8 047	Drabek AUT
2-09	Wales	W	2-1	Teplice	ECq	Lafata 2 [76 89]	16 200	Eriksson SWE
6-09	Slovakia	W	3-0	Bratislava	ECq	Sionko 2 [10 21], Koller [57]	27 684	Bennett ENG
7-10	San Marino	W	7-0	Liberec	ECq	Kulic [15], Polak [22], Baros 2 [28 68], Koller 2 [43 52], Jaroléim [49]	9 514	Aliyev AZE
11-10	Republic of Ireland	D	1-1	Dublin	ECq	Koller [64]	35 500	Layec FRA
15-11	Denmark	D	1-1	Prague	Fr	Baros [93+]	6 852	Skomina SVN
2007								
7-02	Belgium	W	2-0	Brussels	Fr	Koller [6], Kulic [74]	12 000	Granat POL
24-03	Germany	L	1-2	Prague	ECq	Baros [77]	17 821	Rosetti ITA
28-03	Cyprus	W	1-0	Liberec	ECq	Kovác [22]	9 310	Bebek CRO
2-06	Wales	D	0-0	Cardiff	ECq		30 174	Allaerts BEL

Fr = Friendly match • EC = UEFA EURO 2004/2008 • WC = FIFA World Cup
q = qualifier • r1 = first round group • qf = quarter-final • sf = semi-final • po = play-off

CZECH REPUBLIC NATIONAL TEAM RECORDS AND RECORD SEQUENCES

Records			Sequence records					
Victory	8-1	AND 2005	Wins	8	2004-2005	Clean sheets	4	Three times
Defeat	0-3	SUI 1994	Defeats	3	2000, 2006	Goals scored	17	2002-2004
Player Caps	118	POBORSKY Karel	Undefeated	20	2002-2004	Without goal	3	2004
Player Goals	48	KOLLER Jan	Without win	3	Five times	Goals against	8	1999-2000, 2003-04

MAJOR CITIES/TOWNS

Population '000

1	Prague	1 168
2	Brno	363
3	Ostrava	309
4	Plzen	163
5	Olomouc	100
6	Liberec	97
7	Hradec Králové	93
8	Ceske Budejovice	93
9	Usti nad Labem	93
10	Pardubice	87
11	Havirov	84
12	Zlin	77
13	Kladno	69
14	Most	67
15	Karvina	62
16	Frydek-Mistek	59
17	Opava	59
18	Decin	51
19	Teplice	51
20	Prostejov	46
21	Jablonec nad Nisou	44
22	Mladá Boleslav	43
23	Pribram	36
24	Uhersky Hradiste	26

CZECH REPUBLIC; CESKA REPUBLIKA

Capital	Prague (Praha)	Language	Czech			Independence	1993
Population	10 235 455	Area	78 866	Density	129 per km²	% in cities	65%
GDP per cap	$15 700	Dailling code	+420	Internet	.cz	GMT + / -	+1

CZECH REPUBLIC MEDALS TABLE POST 1993

		Overall			League			Cup		Europe			City	Stadium	Cap'ty	DoF
		G	S	B	G	S	B	G	S	G	S	B				
1	Sparta Praha	14	5		10	2		4	3				Prague	Strahov (Toyota Arena)	20 565	1893
2	Slavia Praha	4	9	2	1	9	2	3					Prague	Evzena Rosickeho	19 336	1893
3	Slovan Liberec	3	1		2			1	1				Liberec	U Nisy	9 900	1958
4	Baník Ostrava	2	2	1		1		1	2				Ostrava	Bazaly	17 372	1922
5	Viktoria Zizkov	2	1	2		2		2	1				Prague	Viktoria	4 898	1903
6	FK Jablonec 97	1	2	2		2		1	2				Jablonec nad Nisou	Strelnice	6 246	1945
7	FK Teplice	1	1	1		1	1	1					Teplice	Na Stinadlech	18 221	1945
8	FC Hradec Králové	1						1					Hradec Králové	Vsesportovni	17 000	1905

CLUBS IN CZECHOSLOVAKIAN FOOTBALL 1925–1993

		G	S	B	G	S	B	G	S		G	S	B
1	Sparta Praha	27	21	8	19	16	7	8	5				1
2	Dukla Praha	19	9	5	11	7	3	8	2				2
4	Slavia Praha	9	11	8	9	9	7		2				1
6	Baník Ostrava	6	7	2	3	6	1	3	1				1
10	Bohemians Praha	1	2	12	1	1	11		1				1

CLUBS IN CZECH FOOTBALL 1896–1946

		Overall			League			Cup	
		G	S	B	G	S	B	G	S
1	Sparta Praha	25	15		11	3		14	12
2	Slavia Praha	25	13		10	7		15	6
3	Viktoria Zizkov	7	4	3	1	2		7	3

RECENT LEAGUE AND CUP RECORD

	Championship						Cup		
Year	Champions	Pts	Runners-up	Pts	Third	Pts	Winners	Score	Runners-up
1995	Sparta Praha	70	Slavia Praha	64	Boby Brno	54	SK Hradec Kralové	0-0 3-1p	Viktoria Zizkov
1996	Slavia Praha	70	Sigma Olomouc	61	Jablonec nad Nisou	53	Sparta Praha	4-0	Petra Drnovice
1997	Sparta Praha	65	Slavia Praha	61	Jablonec nad Nisou	56	Slavia Praha	1-0	Dukla Praha
1998	Sparta Praha	71	Slavia Praha	59	Sigma Olomouc	55	FK Jablonec	2-1	Petra Drnovice
1999	Sparta Praha	60	FK Teplice	55	Slavia Praha	55	Slavia Praha	1-0	Slovan Liberec
2000	Sparta Praha	76	Slavia Praha	68	FK Drnovice	48	Slovan Liberec	2-1	Baník Ratiskovice
2001	Sparta Praha	68	Slavia Praha	52	Sigma Olomouc	52	Viktoria Zizkov	2-1	Sparta Praha
2002	Slovan Liberec	64	Sparta Praha	63	Viktoria Zizkov	63	Slavia Praha	2-1	Sparta Praha
2003	Sparta Praha	65	Slavia Praha	64	Viktoria Zizkov	50	FK Teplice	1-0	FK Jablonec
2004	Baník Ostrava	63	Sparta Praha	58	Sigma Olomouc	55	Sparta Praha	2-1	Baník Ostrava
2005	Sparta Praha	64	Slavia Praha	53	FK Teplice	53	Baník Ostrava	2-1	1.FC Slovácko
2006	Slovan Liberec	59	Mladá Boleslav	54	Slavia Praha	54	Sparta Praha	0-0 4-2p	Baník Ostrava
2007	Sparta Praha	62	Slavia Praha	58	Mladá Boleslav	58	Sparta Praha	2-1	FK Jablonec

CZECH REPUBLIC 2006-07

I. GAMBRINUS LIGA

	Pl	W	D	L	F	A	Pts	Sparta	Slavia	M. Boleslav	Liberec	1.FC Brno	Plzen	Baník	Teplice	Jablonec	Ceské B	Kladno	Siad Most	Tescoma	Sigma	Marila	Slovácko
Sparta Praha †	30	18	8	4	44	20	62		1-0	4-1	1-1	2-0	1-0	3-0	2-1	0-3	3-0	0-0	5-0	2-0	1-0	2-1	3-1
Slavia Praha †	30	17	7	6	44	23	58	0-0		1-1	0-2	2-1	0-1	2-1	3-2	2-2	2-0	0-0	3-0	2-1	3-0	1-1	0-0
Mladá Boleslav ‡	30	17	7	6	48	27	58	3-0	1-3		4-0	2-0	0-0	2-0	2-0	2-0	4-2	2-0	2-1	2-0	2-1	2-1	2-2
Slovan Liberec	30	16	10	4	44	22	58	0-0	0-1	1-1		0-0	4-1	2-0	2-0	3-1	2-0	4-1	3-0	2-2	4-1	3-0	2-1
1.FC Brno	30	13	7	10	34	32	46	1-2	1-0	2-0	1-2		1-2	2-1	2-2	3-2	5-0	1-0	1-1	1-0	2-1	2-0	1-0
Viktoria Plzen	30	12	10	8	35	29	46	0-1	0-4	0-0	0-1	1-1		0-1	2-0	1-0	2-2	1-1	1-1	2-0	2-0	2-0	2-0
Baník Ostrava	30	12	10	8	43	33	46	2-2	0-2	2-0	1-1	1-2	1-1		1-1	3-0	5-1	5-1	1-0	1-0	3-1	1-1	1-0
FK Teplice	30	11	9	10	44	39	42	1-1	2-4	2-0	3-0	0-0	1-2	1-2		1-0	1-3	2-0	2-2	1-0	2-2	1-0	3-2
FK Jablonec 97 ‡	30	9	11	10	31	32	38	0-0	1-0	0-2	1-1	0-1	2-1	1-1	2-1		0-0	3-0	2-2	1-1	2-0	0-0	3-1
Ceské Budejovice	30	9	7	14	28	46	34	2-0	1-2	0-3	0-2	0-0	2-1	2-2	1-2	1-0		0-2	0-0	1-1	2-0	2-1	1-0
SK Kladno	30	7	10	13	23	37	31	0-2	0-1	0-0	0-1	3-0	1-1	1-1	0-2	0-1	2-1		2-2	0-0	3-2	0-0	2-1
Siad Most	30	5	16	9	31	41	31	1-1	2-0	1-1	0-0	4-2	1-1	2-1	0-0	3-1	1-2	1-3		0-0	1-1	1-1	2-0
Tescoma Zlin	30	5	12	13	21	34	27	2-0	1-2	0-2	0-0	3-0	1-2	0-0	1-4	0-0	2-1	0-0	2-1		1-1	1-0	1-1
Sigma Olomouc	30	6	8	16	29	43	26	0-2	1-2	3-1	0-1	1-0	1-3	1-3	1-1	1-1	0-0	2-0	1-0	1-0		1-1	0-1
Marila Pribram	30	3	12	15	15	37	21	0-2	0-2	1-2	1-0	0-1	1-1	0-0	0-3	0-1	1-0	1-0	0-0	1-1	1-1		1-1
1.FC Slovácko	30	3	10	17	20	39	19	0-1	0-0	0-2	0-1	0-0	0-2	1-2	2-2	1-1	0-1	0-1	1-1	0-0	1-0	2-0	

20/07/2006 - 28/05/2007 • † Qualified for the UEFA Champions League • ‡ Qualified for the UEFA Cup • Top scorer: Lubos PECKA, Mladá 16

CZECH REPUBLIC 2006-07
DRUHA LIGA (2)

	Pl	W	D	L	F	A	Pts
Viktoria Zizkov	30	19	7	4	55	23	64
Bohemians Praha	30	18	6	6	47	21	60
HFK Olomouc	30	16	5	9	40	28	53
Slezsky Opava	30	15	8	7	47	28	53
Vysocina Jihlava	30	14	9	7	49	26	51
Baník Sokolov	30	12	10	8	36	33	46
Hradec Králové	30	11	10	9	41	34	43
Chmel Blsany	30	11	5	14	27	33	38
MFK Usti nad Labem	30	10	7	13	41	44	37
Zenit Cáslav	30	11	4	15	34	48	37
Jacubcovice	30	10	7	13	35	44	37
Trinec	30	10	2	18	21	42	32
Vitkovice	30	8	8	14	31	50	32
Hlucin	30	6	11	13	24	34	29
Sigma Olomouc B	30	8	5	17	27	43	29
Dosta Bystrc Kninicky	30	7	4	19	22	46	25

4/08/2006 - 16/06/2007

POHAR CMFS 2006-07

Round of 16

Round of 16		Quarter-finals		Semi-finals		Final	
Sparta Praha	2						
Breclav *	0	Sparta Praha	2				
Viktoria Zizkov *	1 2p	Marila Pribram *	1				
Marila Pribram	1 4p			Sparta Praha	2		
Mladá Boleslav	4			Tescoma Zlin	1		
Hradec Králové	1	Mladá Boleslav	1				
Banik Ostrava	0	Tescoma Zlin *	2				
Tescoma Zlin *	1					Sparta Praha	2
Ceske Budejovice	2					FK Jablonec 97 ‡	1
Slovan Liberec *	1	Ceske Budejovice *	2				
Slezsky Opava *	0	1.FC Slovácko	0				
1.FC Slovácko	1			Ceske Budejovice	0 2p		
Viktoria Plzen *	0 4p			FK Jablonec 97	0 4p		
FK Teplice	0 3p	Viktoria Plzen *	0				
Siad Most *	0	FK Jablonec 97	3				
FK Jablonec 97	2						

CUP FINAL
Strahov, Prague
24-05-2007
Scorers - Marek Kulic [45], Pavel Horvath [69p] for Sparta; Jan Svátek [6] for Jablonec

* Home team • ‡ Qualified for the UEFA Cup

DEN – DENMARK

NATIONAL TEAM RECORD
JULY 10TH 2006 TO JULY 12TH 2010

PL	W	D	L	F	A	%
11	7	2	2	23	9	72.7

FIFA/COCA-COLA WORLD RANKING

1993	1994	1995	1996	1997	1998	1999	2000	2001	2002	2003	2004	2005	2006	High		Low	
6	14	9	6	8	19	11	22	18	12	13	14	13	21	3	05/97	27	06/07

2006–2007											
08/06	09/06	10/06	11/06	12/06	01/07	02/07	03/07	04/07	05/07	06/07	07/07
17	16	22	21	21	23	18	22	22	23	27	26

The moment that Denmark's Christian Poulsen punched Sweden's Markus Rosenborg in a UEFA Euro 2008 qualifier, the possibility that Denmark might miss out on the finals of a tournament that they won in 1992 and have qualified for ever since, became very real. They had pulled back from 3-0 down to level the match at 3-3 before Poulsen saw red. The German referee Herbert Fandel had awarded Sweden a penalty but it was never taken as a spectator ran onto the pitch prompting Fandel to abandoned the match which was then awarded 3-0 to Sweden. Having lost earlier in the year to Spain, the task of qualifying was never going to be easy but the Sweden match is one that

INTERNATIONAL HONOURS
Qualified for the FIFA World Cup™ finals 1986 1998 2002 Qualified for the FIFA Women's World Cup finals 1991 1995 1999
UEFA European Championship 1992

Danes will quickly want to forget. In club football, FC København continued to dominate winning a very one-sided title race. For Stale Solbakken's team it was their fifth success in the past seven seasons and they even made a first foray into the UEFA Champions League group stage, finishing last in a group won by Manchester United. København missed out on Denmark's very own version of the treble when they lost two Cup Finals in early 2007. In March they lost to Brøndby in the final of the Royal League and then in May to OB Odense in the Danish Cup Final.

THE FIFA BIG COUNT OF 2006

	Male	Female		Total
Number of players	420 258	91 075	Referees and Assistant Referees	2 992
Professionals	852		Admin, Coaches, Technical, Medical	54 000
Amateurs 18+	111 757		Number of clubs	1 615
Youth under 18	188 724		Number of teams	17 365
Unregistered	100 000		Clubs with women's teams	768
Total players	511 333		Players as % of population	9.38%

Dansk Boldspil-Union (DBU)
DBU Allé 1, Brøndby 2605, Denmark
Tel +45 43 262222   Fax +45 43 262245
dbu@dbu.dk   www.dbu.dk
President: HANSEN Allan   General Secretary: HANSEN Jim
Vice-President: MOLLER Jesper   Treasurer: MOGENSEN Torben   Media Officer: BERENDT Lars
Men's Coach: OLSEN Morten   Women's Coach: HEINER-MOLLER Kenneth
DBU formed: 1889   UEFA: 1954   FIFA: 1904
Red shirts with white trimmings, White shorts, Red socks or White shirts with red trimmings, Red shorts, White socks

RECENT INTERNATIONAL MATCHES PLAYED BY DENMARK

2004	Opponents	Score		Venue	Comp	Scorers	Att	Referee
14-06	Italy	D	0-0	Guimaraes	ECr1		19 595	Gonzalez ESP
18-06	Bulgaria	W	2-0	Braga	ECr1	Tomasson [44], Gronkjaer [90]	24 131	Baptista POR
22-06	Sweden	D	2-2	Porto	ECr1	Tomasson 2 [28 66]	26 115	Merk GER
27-06	Czech Republic	L	0-3	Porto	ECqf		41 092	Ivanov RUS
18-08	Poland	W	5-1	Poznan	Fr	Madsen 3 [23 30 90], Gaardsoe [51], Jensen.C [86]	4 500	Bebek CRO
4-09	Ukraine	D	1-1	Copenhagen	WCq	Jorgensen.M [9]	36 335	Meier SUI
9-10	Albania	W	2-0	Tirana	WCq	Jorgensen.M [52], Tomasson [72]	14 500	Baskakov RUS
13-10	Turkey	D	1-1	Copenhagen	WCq	Tomasson [27p]	41 331	De Santis ITA
17-11	Georgia	D	2-2	Tbilisi	WCq	Tomasson 2 [7 64]	20 000	Ceferin SVN
2005								
9-02	Greece	L	1-2	Athens	WCq	Rommedahl [46+]	32 430	Collina ITA
26-03	Kazakhstan	W	3-0	Copenhagen	WCq	Moller.P 2 [10 48], Poulsen [33]	20 980	Gilewski POL
30-03	Ukraine	L	0-1	Kyiv	WCq		60 000	Michel SVK
2-06	Finland	W	1-0	Tampere	Fr	Silberhauser [90]	9 238	Wegereef NED
8-06	Albania	W	3-1	Copenhagen	WCq	Larsen.S 2 [5 47], Jorgensen.M [55]	26 366	Frojdfeldt SWE
17-08	England	W	4-1	Copenhagen	Fr	Rommedahl [60], Tomasson [63], Gravgaard [67], Larsen [92+]	41 438	Ovrebro NOR
3-09	Turkey	D	2-2	Istanbul	WCq	Jensen [40], Larsen [93+]	29 721	Mejuto Gonzalez ESP
7-09	Georgia	W	6-1	Copenhagen	WCq	Jensen [10], Poulsen [30], Agger [43], Tomasson [55], Larsen 2 [80 84]	27 177	Bozinovski MKD
8-10	Greece	W	1-0	Copenhagen	WCq	Gravgaard [40]	42 099	De Bleeckere BEL
12-10	Kazakhstan	W	2-1	Almaty	WCq	Gravgaard [46], Tomasson [49]	8 050	Trivkovic CRO
2006								
26-01	Singapore	W	2-1	Singapore	Fr	Bech 2 [58 67]	10 392	Srinivasan IND
29-01	Hong Kong	W	3-0	Hong Kong	Fr	Berg [19], Augustinussen [39], Due [51]	16 841	Iemoto JPN
1-02	Korea Republic	W	3-1	Hong Kong	Fr	Jacobsen [43], Bech [65], Silberbauer [88]	13 971	Fong Yau Fat HKG
1-03	Israel	W	2-0	Tel Aviv	Fr	Perez [3], Skoubo [18]	15 762	Sippel GER
27-05	Paraguay	D	1-1	Aarhus	Fr	Tomasson [51]	20 047	Bennett ENG
31-05	France	L	0-2	Lens	Fr		39 000	Kelly IRL
16-08	Poland	W	2-0	Odense	Fr	Bendtner [33], Rommedahl [63]	11 088	Asumaa FIN
1-09	Portugal	W	4-2	Copenhagen	Fr	Tomasson [14], Kahlenberg [21], Jorgensen [77], Bendtner [92+]	13 186	Kelly IRL
6-09	Iceland	W	2-0	Reykjavík	ECq	Rommedahl [5], Tomasson [33]	10 007	Ivanov.N RUS
7-10	Northern Ireland	D	0-0	Copenhagen	ECq		41 482	Plautz AUT
11-10	Liechtenstein	W	4-0	Vaduz	ECq	Jensen.D [29], Gravgaard [32], Tomasson 2 [51 64]	2 665	Richards WAL
15-11	Czech Republic	D	1-1	Prague	Fr	Løvenkrands [28]	6 852	Skomina SVN
2007								
6-02	Australia	W	3-1	London	Fr	Tomasson 2 [4 37], Jensen.D [27]	12 476	Styles END
24-03	Spain	L	1-2	Madrid	ECq	Gravgaard [49]	73 575	Busacca SUI
28-03	Germany	W	1-0	Duisberg	Fr	Bendtner [81]	31 500	Webb ENG
2-06	Sweden	D	3-3	Copenhagen	ECq	Agger [34], Tomasson [62], Andreason [75]. Abandoned after 89 minutes. Match awarded 3-0 to Sweden	42 083	Fandel GER
6-06	Latvia	W	2-0	Riga	ECq	Rommedahl 2 [15 17]	7 500	Trefoloni ITA

Fr = Friendly match • EC = UEFA EURO 2004/2008 • WC = FIFA World Cup • q = qualifier • r1 = first round group • qf = quarter-final

DENMARK NATIONAL TEAM RECORDS AND RECORD SEQUENCES

Records			Sequence records				
Victory	17-1	FRA 1908	Wins	11	1912-1916	Clean sheets	4	1993, 1995
Defeat	0-8	GER 1937	Defeats	7	1970-1971	Goals scored	26	1942-1948
Player Caps	129	SCHMEICHEL Peter	Undefeated	12	1992-93, 2005-06	Without goal	7	1970-1971
Player Goals	52	NIELSEN Poul 'Tist'	Without win	14	1969-1971	Goals against	21	1939-1946

KINGDOM OF DENMARK; KONGERIGET DANMARK

Capital	Copenhagen	Language	Danish		Independence	950
Population	5 468 120	Area	43 094 km^2	Density	125 per km^2	% in cities 85
GDP per cap	$31 100	Dailling code	+45	Internet	.dk	GMT + / - +1

MAJOR CITIES/TOWNS

Population '000

1	Copenhagen	1 093
2	Aarhus	230
3	Odense	146
4	Aalborg	123
5	Esbjerg	71
6	Kolding	56
7	Randers	55
8	Vejle	52
9	Horsens	50
10	Roskilde	44
11	Greve Strand	41
12	Næstved	41
13	Silkeborg	39
14	Hørsholm	37
15	Fredericia	37
16	Helsingør	35
17	Viborg	34
18	Køge	34
19	Herning	30
20	Holbæk	24
21	Fredrikshavn	23
22	Nykøbing	16
23	Ikast	14
24	Farum	11

MEDALS TABLE

		Overall			League			Cup		Europe			City	Stadium	Cap'ty	DoF
		G	S	B	G	S	B	G	S	G	S	B				
1	KB København	16	19	8	15	15	8	1	4				Copenhagen	Parken		1876-1992
2	Brøndby IF	15	11	3	10	9	2	5	2		1		Copenhagen	Brøndby	29 000	1964
3	AGF Aarhus	14	8	11	5	5	11	9	3				Aarhus	Aarhus Idrætspark	21 000	1880
4	B 93 København	11	5	9	10	5	9	1					Copenhagen	Østerbro	7 000	1893
5	Vejle BK	11	4	2	5	3	2	6	1				Vejle	Vejle	15 000	1891
6	Akademisk København	10	14	11	9	11	11	1	3				Copenhagen	Gladsaxe	13 200	1889
7	B 1903 København	9	10	8	7	8	8	2	2				Copenhagen	Gentofte		1903-1992
8	FC Københvn	9	6	1	6	3	1	3	3				Copenhagen	Parken	42 305	1992
9	Frem København	8	15	9	6	12	9	2	3				Copenhagen	Valby Idrætspark	12 000	1886
10	OB Odense	8	4	5	3	3	5	5	1				Odense	Odense	15 633	1887
11	Esbjerg FB	7	8	2	5	3	2	2	5				Esbjerg	Esbjerg Idrætspark	13 282	1924
12	Lyngby BK	5	5	3	2	3	3	3	2				Lyngby	Lyngby	12 000	1921
13	AaB Aalborg	4	7	3	2		3	2	7				Aalborg	Aalborg	16 000	1885
14	B 1909 Odense	4	1	1	2		1	2	1				Odense	Atletikstadion	8 000	1909-2006
	Hvidovre IF	4	1	1	3	1	1	1					Copenhagen	Hvidovre	15 000	1925
16	Randers FC	4	1			1		4					Randers	Essex Park	12 000	2002

RECENT LEAGUE AND CUP RECORD

	Championship						Cup		
Year	Champions	Pts	Runners-up	Pts	Third	Pts	Winners	Score	Runners-up
1995	AaB Aalborg	31	Brøndby IF	29	Silkeborg IF	24	FC København	5-0	Akademisk
1996	Brøndby IF	67	AGF Aarhus	66	OB Odense	60	AGF Aarhus	2-0	Brøndby IF
1997	Brøndby IF	68	Vejle BK	54	AGF Aarhus	52	FC København	2-0	Ikast FS
1998	Brøndby IF	76	Silkeborg IF	63	FC København	61	Brøndby IF	4-1	FC København
1999	AaB Aalborg	64	Brøndby IF	61	Akademisk	56	Akademisk	2-1	AaB Aalborg
2000	Herfølge BK	56	Brøndby IF	54	Akademisk	52	Viborg FF	1-0	AaB Aalborg
2001	FC København	63	Brøndby IF	58	Silkeborg IF	56	Silkeborg IF	4-1	Akademisk
2002	Brøndby IF	69	FC København	69	FC Midtjylland	57	OB Odense	2-1	FC København
2003	FC København	61	Brøndby IF	56	Farum BK	51	Brøndby IF	3-0	FC Midtjylland
2004	FC København	68	Brøndby IF	67	Esbjerg FB	62	FC København	1-0	AaB Aalborg
2005	Brøndby IF	69	FC København	57	FC Midtjylland	57	Brøndby IF	3-2	FC Midtjylland
2006	FC København	73	Brøndby IF	67	OB Odense	58	Randers FC	1-0	Esbjerg FB
2007	FC København	76	FC Midtjylland	63	AaB Aalborg	61	OB Odense	2-1	FC København

DENMARK 2006-07

SAS LIGAEN

	Pl	W	D	L	F	A	Pts	København	Midtjylland	AaB Aalborg	OB Odense	Nordsjælland	Brøndby	Esbjerg	Randers	Viborg	Horsens	Vejle	Silkeborg
FC København †	33	23	7	3	60	23	76		2-1 2-2	0-2	1-2 1-1	4-2	1-0 1-1	1-0	3-1 1-2	2-1	1-0 3-0	3-1	3-0 3-1
FC Midtjylland ‡	33	18	9	6	58	39	63	1-4		1-0 2-1	3-0	2-2 1-1	1-1	1-1 3-1	2-1	2-1 3-1	1-2	1-0 2-2	3-1
AaB Aalborg	33	18	7	8	55	35	61	0-1	0-2		0-1 3-1	0-3	1-1 1-1	3-2	2-0 2-1	0-4	3-1 0-2	4-0	4-0 2-0 1-0
OB Odense ‡	33	17	7	9	46	36	58	0-0	1-1 1-0	1-1		2-1	0-1 2-2	1-0	0-2 0-0	1-1 2-2	0-2 2-3	2-0	3-2 2-0
FC Nordsjælland	33	16	9	8	67	39	57	0-1	1-4	1-1	2-1		3-3	1-1 5-0	4-2 2-0	4-1 0-0	4-0 1-0	3-0	1-0 5-1
Brøndby IF	33	13	10	10	50	38	49	0-1	1-3	1-2	1-0	2-1 2-0		2-0 2-1	3-0 3-0	3-1 3-0	2-0	2-1 4-0	1-1 3-1
Esbjerg FB	33	10	10	13	46	51	40	2-2	0-0 4-2	3-0 1-2	0-2	1-2	3-5 1-0		1-1	3-1	2-2	0-1	3-3 1-0 2-1 1-2
Randers FC	33	10	8	15	41	53	38	0-2	0-0	1-1	1-2	1-6	1-1 2-0 3-1 3-2			3-2	1-0 2-1	2-1 0-1 0-0	1-1
Viborg FF	33	8	5	20	34	64	29	1-3 0-1 0-1 0-1	0-2	0-2	1-2	1-1 0-4	1-1 3-2 1-1		1-0	1-0 2-1 2-3 2-1			
AC Horsens	33	6	10	17	29	53	28	0-1 1-3	2-2	0-0 1-4	0-2 1-2	2-3	0-0 1-1 1-1	2-1 2-2 3-1				1-2	2-1
Vejle BK	33	6	7	20	35	64	25	0-4	0-0 2-5	1-2	1-1 1-3 1-2	3-2	3-0 3-0	0-2	2-0 2-0 2-0	0-0	1-2		2-4 0-2
Silkeborg IF	33	5	7	21	34	60	22	1-4 0-1 0-2 0-1 0-2	4-6	0-1 1-3	1-1	2-1	1-2 0-0	1-2	0-2 1-1	1-1			

19/07/2006 - 27/05/2007 • † Qualified for the UEFA Champions League • ‡ Qualified for the UEFA Cup
Top scorers: Rade PRICA, AaB Aalborg 19; Morten NORDSTRAND, Nordsjælland 18; Morten RASMUSSEN, Brøndby 15

DENMARK 2006-07
VIASAT SPORT DIVISION (2)

	Pl	W	D	L	F	A	Pts
Lyngby BK	30	19	7	4	71	43	64
AGF Aarhus	30	18	5	7	58	38	59
SønderjyskE	30	16	5	9	57	34	53
FC Fredericia	30	16	5	9	50	37	53
Frem København	30	14	8	8	48	43	50
Kolding FC	30	14	7	9	58	53	49
Køge BK §3	30	14	5	11	57	54	44
Næstved BK	30	12	7	11	54	35	43
Herfølge BK	30	12	7	11	54	41	43
Akademisk Boldclub	30	8	9	13	36	53	33
Aarhus Fremad	30	8	7	15	33	45	31
Ølstykke	30	8	6	16	36	41	30
Hellerup IK	30	6	11	13	33	49	29
Braband	30	6	10	14	30	43	28
Thisted FC	30	4	13	13	41	64	25
Fremad Amager	30	6	6	18	35	78	24

29/07/2006 - 24/06/2007 • § = points deducted

DBU LANDSPOKAL 2006-07

Round of 16		Quarter-finals		Semi-finals		Final	
OB Odense *	1	OB Odense *	1				
Brøndby IF	0	Randers FC	0				
AGF Aarhus *	1			OB Odense *	1 2		
Randers FC	2			Viborg FF	2 0		
Holbæk BK *	4	Holbæk BK *	1				
SønderjyskE	2	Viborg FF	6			OB Odense ‡	2
Glostrup FK *	2					FC København	1
Viborg FF	3						
Lyngby BK *	5	Lyngby BK *	1				
Kolding FC	1	AC Horsens	0				
FC Fredericia *	1			Lyngby BK *	2 0		
AC Horsens	2			FC København	3 4		
FC Midtjylland	2						
Frederikshavn *	0	FC Midtjylland *	2				
Esbjerg FB	1	FC København	3				
FC København *	3						

CUP FINAL
Parken, Copenhagen
17-05-2007, Att: 30 013, Ref: Hermansen

Scorers - Martin Borre [36], Bechara [48] for OB; Hutchinson [15] for København

* Home team/home team in the first leg • ‡ Qualified for the UEFA Cup

DJI – DJIBOUTI

NATIONAL TEAM RECORD

JULY 10TH 2006 TO JULY 12TH 2010

PL	W	D	L	F	A	%
5	0	0	5	3	18	0

FIFA/COCA-COLA WORLD RANKING

1993	1994	1995	1996	1997	1998	1999	2000	2001	2002	2003	2004	2005	2006	High		Low	
-	169	177	185	189	191	195	189	193	195	197	201	200	198	169	12/94	201	12/04

2006–2007											
08/06	09/06	10/06	11/06	12/06	01/07	02/07	03/07	04/07	05/07	06/07	07/07
197	198	198	198	198	199	199	199	199	199	199	199

The installation of a new artificial pitch at Djibouti's national stadium offers the opportunity for the tiny Red Sea state to take a more active role in international competition. The pitch forms part of the FIFA 'Win in Africa with Africa' programme which will see a similar surface installed in each of 52 African countries in the build-up to the 2010 FIFA World Cup finals. Poor facilities in the former French colony meant that Djibouti were forced to withdraw from the 2008 African Nations Cup qualifiers meaning there has not been an international in Djibouti since June 2000 when the country's national team lost to Burundi. Previously only the Democratic Republic of

INTERNATIONAL HONOURS

None

Congo and Kenya had also played full intentional matches at the venue. Djibouti's national team did compete in 2006, losing three games at the East and Central African Senior Challenge Cup tournament in Addis Ababa and also in the Arab Nations Cup qualifiers in Yemen, where they were opponents for the first international match ever played by the Comoros Islands. CDE Djibouti won back the league title they ceded to Societe Immobiliere Djibouti last season but lost the Cup Final to their vice-champions, who finished the match down to nine men. Societe Immobiliere Djibouti also won the Super Cup in May 2007 with a 4-0 thumping of AS Ali Sabieh.

THE FIFA BIG COUNT OF 2006

	Male	Female		Total
Number of players	34 480	1 840	Referees and Assistant Referees	75
Professionals	0		Admin, Coaches, Technical, Medical	405
Amateurs 18+	1 800		Number of clubs	6
Youth under 18	720		Number of teams	84
Unregistered	2 800		Clubs with women's teams	2
Total players	36 320		Players as % of population	7.47%

Fédération Djiboutienne de Football (FDF)

Centre Technique National, Case postale 2694, Djibouti

Tel +253 353599   Fax +253 353588

fdf-1979@yahoo.fr   www.none

President: DABAR Houssein Fadoul   General Secretary: KAMIL Hasan

Vice-President: YONIS Mohamed Yacin   Treasurer: HASSAN Ziad Moussa   Media Officer: None

Men's Coach: OMAR Mohamed   Women's Coach: TBD

FDF formed: 1979   CAF: 1986   FIFA: 1994

Green shirts, White shorts, Blue socks

RECENT INTERNATIONAL MATCHES PLAYED BY DJIBOUTI

2002 Opponents	Score	Venue	Comp	Scorers	Att	Referee
No international matches played in 2002						
2003						
No international matches played in 2003						
2004						
No international matches played in 2004						
2005						
27-11 Somalia	L 1-2	Kigali	CCr1	Abdoul Rahman Okishi		
30-11 Uganda	L 1-6	Kigali	CCr1	Abdirahman Okieh		
3-12 Ethiopia	L 0-6	Kigali	CCr1			
5-12 Sudan	L 0-4	Kigali	CCr1			
2006						
26-11 Malawi	L 0-3	Addis Abeba	CCr1			
28-11 Ethiopia	L 0-4	Addis Abeba	CCr1			
1-12 Tanzania	L 0-3	Addis Abeba	CCr1			
17-12 Comoros	L 2-4	Sana'a	ARq	Khaliff Hassan [45], Abdoul Rahman Okishi [92+]		
20-12 Yemen	L 1-4	Sana'a	ARq	Abdoul Rahman Okishi [7]		
2007						
No international matches played in 2007 before August						

CC = CECAFA Cup • AR = Arab Cup • q = qualifier • r1 = First round group

DJIBOUTI NATIONAL TEAM RECORDS AND RECORD SEQUENCES

Records			Sequence records					
Victory	4-1	YEM 1988	Wins	1		Clean sheets	1	
Defeat	1-10	UGA 2001	Defeats	9	2005-2006	Goals scored	6	1998-2000
Player Caps	n/a		Undefeated	1		Without goal	5	2005-2006
Player Goals	n/a		Without win	22	1994-2006	Goals against	20	1983-2000

RECENT LEAGUE AND CUP RECORD

	League		Cup		
Year	Champions	Winners	Score	Runners-up
1996	Force Nationale de Police	Balbala		
1997	Force Nationale de Police	Force Nationale de Police		
1998	Force Nationale de Police	Force Nationale de Police		
1999	Force Nationale de Police	Balbala		
2000	CDE Djibouti			
2001	Force Nationale de Police	Chemin de Fer		
2002	AS Borreh	Jeunesse Espoir		Chemin de Fer
2003	Gendarmerie Nationale	AS Borreh	1-1 5-4p	AS Ali-Sabieh
2004	Gendarmerie Nationale	Chemin de Fer	6-2	AS Borreh
2005	CDE Djibouti	Poste de Djibouti	2-0	AS Port
2006	Société Immobiliere Djibouti	AS Ali Sabieh	3-0	Gendarmerie Nationale
2007	CDE Djibouti	Société Immobiliere Djibouti	1-1 4-3p	CDE Djibouti

Poste de Djibouti renamed Société Immobiliere Djibouti in 2005

DJIBOUTI COUNTRY INFORMATION

Capital	Djibouti	Independence	1977 from France	GDP per Capita	$1 300
Population	768 200	Status	Republic	GNP Ranking	167
Area km²	23 000	Language	Arabic, French	Dialling code	+253
Population density	20 per km²	Literacy rate	49%	Internet code	.dj
% in urban areas	83%	Main religion	Muslim 94%	GMT +/-	+3
Towns/Cities ('000)	Djibouti 623; Ali Sabieh 40; Tadjoura 22; Obock 17; Dikhil 12				
Neighbours (km)	Somalia 58; Ethiopia 349; Eritrea 109; Red Sea & Gulf of Aden 314				
Main stadia	Stade du Ville – Djibouti 10 000				

DMA – DOMINICA

NATIONAL TEAM RECORD
JULY 10TH 2006 TO JULY 12TH 2010

PL	W	D	L	F	A	%
2	0	0	2	0	6	0

FIFA/COCA-COLA WORLD RANKING

1993	1994	1995	1996	1997	1998	1999	2000	2001	2002	2003	2004	2005	2006	High	Low
-	-	158	138	139	133	149	152	161	174	185	165	172	181	**129** 7/98	**185** 11/06

2006–2007											
08/06	09/06	10/06	11/06	12/06	01/07	02/07	03/07	04/07	05/07	06/07	07/07
184	185	185	185	181	181	180	181	181	181	179	184

Dominica's national team set two records in 2006, neither of which they will be happy with. You have to go back to March 2004 for the last time Dominica scored in an official international and since then the team has gone six games without scoring, all of them lost. If you add in matches played against non FIFA members, the losing streak grows to 11 and the games without goals to nine. In the 2006 Digicel Caribbean Cup, Dominica were drawn with Martinique, Saint Martin and hosts Guadeloupe, and as all of them are associate members of CONCACAF and not members of FIFA, none of the results are full internationals. That was perhaps a good thing as Martinique won

INTERNATIONAL HONOURS
None

4-0 and Guadeloupe, inspired by the 41-year-old Jocelyn Angloma, won 1-0. The final match against Saint Martin did at least bring the relief of a draw, but unfortunately no goals. It is hoped that the decision to build an international standard stadium at Geneva in Grand Bay will help the national improve in the future. In domestic football there was a first ever championship for Sagicor South East who finished two points ahead of Fone Shack Bombers. Bombers had missed out on the chance to secure the title by losing to Grand Bazaar Dublanc in the last round of games and the following day South East beat 4D Agri Centre Bath Estate 3-2 in Grand Bay to secure the title.

THE FIFA BIG COUNT OF 2006

	Male	Female		Total
Number of players	3 900	600	Referees and Assistant Referees	39
Professionals	0		Admin, Coaches, Technical, Medical	100
Amateurs 18+	500		Number of clubs	20
Youth under 18	700		Number of teams	20
Unregistered	600		Clubs with women's teams	1
Total players	4 500		Players as % of population	6.53%

Dominica Football Association (DFA)
Patrick John Football House, Bath Estate, PO Box 372, Roseau, Dominica
Tel +1 767 4487577   Fax +1 767 4487587
domfootball@cwdom.dm   www.none
President: FRANCIS Dexter   General Secretary: WALSH Regina
Vice-President: PANDENQUE Mervin   Treasurer: GREENAWAY Walter   Media Officer: GEORGE Gerald
Men's Coach: LEOGAL Don   Women's Coach: ROBERTSON Hypolite
DFA formed: 1970   CONMEBOL: 1994   FIFA: 1994
Emerald shirts, Black shorts, Green socks

RECENT INTERNATIONAL MATCHES PLAYED BY DOMINICA

2004	Opponents	Score		Venue	Comp	Scorers	Att	Referee
28-01	British Virgin Islands	W	1-0	Tortola	Fr	Cuffy [34]		Matthew SKN
31-01	US Virgin Islands	W	5-0	St Thomas	Fr	OG [12], Marshall [42], Dangler [68], Casimir [87], George [90]		Matthew SKN
1-02	British Virgin Islands	W	2-1	Tortola	Fr	Marshall [44], Peters [70]		Charles DMA
12-03	Barbados	L	1-2	Bridgetown	Fr	Peters [88]	46	
26-03	Bahamas	D	1-1	Nassau	WCq	Casimir [88]	800	Forde BRB
28-03	Bahamas	W	3-1	Nassau	WCq	Casimir 2 [39 86], Peters [85]	900	Pineda HON
19-06	Mexico	L	0-10	San Antonio, USA	WCq		36 451	Callender BRB
27-06	Mexico	L	0-8	Aguascalientes	WCq		17 000	Stott USA
10-11	Martinique †	L	1-5	Fort de France	CCq	Peltier [42]		Arthur LCA
12-11	Guadeloupe †	L	0-7	Rivière-Pilote	CCq			Arthur LCA
14-11	French Guyana †	L	0-4	Fort de France	CCq		5 800	Fenus LCA
2005								
30-09	Guyana	L	0-3	Linden	Fr			Lancaster GUY
2-10	Guyana	L	0-3	Georgetown	Fr			Kia SUR
2006								
3-09	Antigua and Barbuda	L	0-1	St John's	Fr			Willett ATG
17-09	Barbados	L	0-5	Roseau	Fr			
20-09	Martinique †	L	0-4	Abymes	CCq		1 000	Fanus LCA
22-09	Guadeloupe †	L	0-1	Abymes	CCq		1 100	Willett ATG
24-09	Saint Martin †	D	0-0	Abymes	CCq			
2007								

No international matches played in 2007 before August

Fr = Friendly match • CC = Digicel Caribbean Cup • WC = FIFA World Cup • q = qualifier • † Not a full international

DOMINICA NATIONAL TEAM RECORDS AND RECORD SEQUENCES

Records			Sequence records					
Victory	6-1	VGB 1997	Wins	3	1997, 1999, 2004	Clean sheets	2	1997 2004
Defeat	0-10	MEX 2004	Defeats	6	2004-2006	Goals scored	8	1999-2000
Player Caps	n/a		Undefeated	4	1998	Without goal	6	2004-2006
Player Goals	n/a		Without win	8	2001-2002	Goals against	17	1997-1999

RECENT LEAGUE AND CUP RECORD

	Championship						Cup		
Year	Champions	Pts	Runners-up	Pts	Third	Pts	Winners	Score	Runners-up
1997	Harlem United	22	Black Rocks	19	Pointe Michel	12	Harlem Bombers	1-0	Black Rocks
1998	Pointe Michel						Pointe Michel	1-0	ACS Zebians
1999	Harlem United	46	Superwoods United						
2000	Harlem United	13	Dublanc Strikers	13					
2001	Harlem United	22	Dublanc Strikers	22	South East	19			
2002	St Joseph	12	ACS Zebians	12	Harlem Bombers	10	South East	1-0	Antilles Kensbro
2003	Harlem United	†	ACS Zebians				Harlem United		
2004	Harlem United						Harlem United	3-0	ACS Zebians
2005	Dublanc Strikers	31	Pointe Michel	29	South East	29	South East	2-0	Harlem United
2006	Harlem United	29	River Bombers	28					
2007	Sagicor South East	31	Fone Shack Bombers	29					

† Harlem United beat Zebians in the final

DOMINICA COUNTRY INFORMATION

Capital	Roseau	Independence	1978 from the UK	GDP per Capita	$5 400
Population	69 278	Status	Republic/Commonwealth	GNP Ranking	181
Area km²	754	Language	English	Dialling code	+1767
Population density	91 per km²	Literacy rate	94%	Internet code	.dm
% in urban areas	69%	Main religion	Christian 92%	GMT +/−	-4
Towns/Cities ('000)	Roseau 16; Berekua 3; Portsmouth 3; Marigot 2; Atkinson 2; La Plaine 2; Mahaut 2				
Neighbours (km)	Caribbean Sea and the North Atlantic 148				
Main stadia	Windsor Park – Roseau 6 000				

DOM – DOMINICAN REPUBLIC

NATIONAL TEAM RECORD
JULY 10TH 2006 TO JULY 12TH 2010

PL	W	D	L	F	A	%
7	2	0	5	11	16	28.5

FIFA/COCA-COLA WORLD RANKING

1993	1994	1995	1996	1997	1998	1999	2000	2001	2002	2003	2004	2005	2006	High	Low
153	164	159	130	144	152	155	157	160	149	171	170	174		116 05/96	186 07/06

2006–2007											
08/06	09/06	10/06	11/06	12/06	01/07	02/07	03/07	04/07	05/07	06/07	07/07
171	188	160	159	136	136	135	135	139	138	140	140

The Dominican Republic made a rare foray into international competition with entry into the 2006 Digicel Caribbean Cup and they managed to proceed through two rounds. Indeed they were just a play-off away from qualifying for the finals for the first time in 16 years. In the first qualifying round a 6-1 victory over the US Virgin Islands ensured they made it through to a second round group played in Guyana. Despite defeats against Guadeloupe and the hosts, a victory over Antigua and Barbuda saw the Dominican Republic finish third in the group and that meant a play-off against Bermuda and Haiti for a place in the finals. The games were scheduled to be played in

INTERNATIONAL HONOURS
None

Trinidad just before the tournament kicked-off there - but the week before they were due to travel, the Dominican Republic pulled out citing lack of funds. There can be no clearer indication as to the state of the game in a country that is so dominated by baseball and other sports. The lack of regular domestic competition is also a problem. When the Liga Mayor was set up in 2001 it was supposed to have provided the foundation for the development of club football. Instead, the competition was not held in 2004 and 2006 and when the 2007 tournament kicked off in May, only four of the eight teams had taken part in the 2005 edition.

THE FIFA BIG COUNT OF 2006

	Male	Female		Total
Number of players	417 804	83 200	Referees and Assistant Referees	1 420
Professionals	4		Admin, Coaches, Technical, Medical	190
Amateurs 18+	35 000		Number of clubs	250
Youth under 18	12 000		Number of teams	600
Unregistered	106 000		Clubs with women's teams	100
Total players	501 004		Players as % of population	5.46%

Federación Dominicana de Fútbol (FEDOFUTBOL)
Centro Olimpico Juan Pablo Duarte, Ensanche Miraflores, Apartado postal 1953, Santo Domingo, Dominican Republic
Tel +1 809 5426923   Fax +1 809 3812734
fedofutbol.f@verizon.net.do   www.fedofutbol.org
President: GUZMAN Osiris   General Secretary: MIRANDA Angel
Vice-President: QUISPE MENDOZA Fortunato   Treasurer: LEDESMA Felix   Media Officer: SANCHEZ Angel
Men's Coach: CRNOKRAK Ljubomir   Women's Coach: ELEJALDE G. Jose
FEDOFUTBOL formed: 1953   CONCACAF: 1964   FIFA: 1958
Navy blue shirts, White shorts, Red socks

RECENT INTERNATIONAL MATCHES PLAYED BY THE DOMINICAN REPUBLIC

2004	Opponents	Score		Venue	Comp	Scorers	Att	Referee
19-03	Anguilla	D	0-0	Santo Domingo	WCq		400	Mattus CRC
21-03	Anguilla	W	6-0	Santo Domingo	WCq	Zapata [15], Severino 2 [38 61], Contrera 2 [57 90], Casquez [77]	850	Porras CRC
27-04	Netherlands Antilles	L	1-3	Willemstad	Fr	Zapata [9]		Faneijte ANT
13-06	Trinidad and Tobago	L	0-2	Santo Domingo	WCq		2 500	Moreno PAN
20-06	Trinidad and Tobago	L	0-4	Marabella	WCq		5 500	Pinas SUR
2005								
No international matches played in 2005								
2006								
15-09	Haiti	L	1-3	Saint-Marc	Fr	Perez.M [22]		
17-09	Haiti	L	1-2	Port-au-Prince	Fr	Perez.M [30p]		
29-09	Bermuda	L	1-3	Charlotte Amalie	CCq	Faña [85]	300	Martis ANT
1-10	US Virgin Islands	W	6-1	Charlotte Amalie	CCq	Corporan [14], Faña 4 [25 55 82 89], Rodriguez.K [87]	250	Davis TRI
24-11	Guadeloupe	L	0-3	Georgetown	CCq		5 000	
26-11	Antigua and Barbuda	W	2-0	Georgetown	CCq	Severino [70p], Batista [81]	5 000	
28-11	Guyana	L	0-4	Georgetown	CCq		4 000	
2007								
No international matches played in 2007 before August								

Fr = Friendly match • CC = Digicel Caribbean Cup • WC = FIFA World Cup • q = qualifier

DOMINICAN REPUBLIC NATIONAL TEAM RECORDS AND RECORD SEQUENCES

Records			Sequence records					
Victory	6-0	AIA 2004	Wins	4	1999-2000	Clean sheets	3	1999-2000
Defeat	0-8	HAI 1967, TRI 1996	Defeats	6	2004-2006	Goals scored	5	1987-91, 1991-93
Player Caps	n/a		Undefeated	4	1999-2000	Without goal	3	Three times
Player Goals	n/a		Without win	16	1987-1992	Goals against	15	1991-1996

RECENT LEAGUE AND CUP RECORD

	Championship						Cup		
Year	Champions	Pts	Runners-up	Pts	Third	Pts	Winners	Score	Runners-up
1997	San Cristóbal	21	Moca	17	Bancredicard	15			
1998	No tournament played								
1999	FC Don Bosco								
2000	No tournament played								
2001	CD Pantoja	21	Baninter Jarabacoa	19	Bancredicard	13	Domingo Savio	2-2 5-4p	CD Pantoja
2002	Baninter Jarabacoa	25	Moca	19	Bancredicard	14	Bancredicard	1-0	Cañabrava
2003	Baninter Jarabacoa	31	Bancredicard	26	Moca	23			
2004	No tournament played								
2005	Deportivo Pantoja	40	Barcelona	39	Don Bosco	39			
2006	No tournament played								
2007									

Bancredicard renamed Barcelona

DOMINICAN REPUBLIC COUNTRY INFORMATION

Capital	Santo Domingo	Independence	1865	GDP per Capita	$6 000
Population	8 833 634	Status	Republic	GNP Ranking	67
Area km²	48 730	Language	Spanish	Dialling code	+1 809
Population density	181 per km²	Literacy rate	84%	Internet code	.do
% in urban areas	65%	Main religion	Christian 95%	GMT +/−	-4
Towns/Cities ('000)	Santo Domingo 2 240; Santiago 505; La Romana 171; San Pedro de Macorís 152; Puerto Plata 135				
Neighbours (km)	Haiti 360; Atlantic Ocean & Caribbean Sea 1 288				
Main stadia	Olimpico – Santo Domingo 35 000; Quisqueya – Santo Domingo 30 000				

ECU – ECUADOR

NATIONAL TEAM RECORD
JULY 10TH 2006 TO JULY 12TH 2010

PL	W	D	L	F	A	%
12	2	3	7	15	21	29.1

FIFA/COCA-COLA WORLD RANKING

1993	1994	1995	1996	1997	1998	1999	2000	2001	2002	2003	2004	2005	2006	High		Low	
48	55	55	33	28	63	65	54	37	31	37	39	37	30	24	03/07	76	06/95

	2006–2007										
	08/06	09/06	10/06	11/06	12/06	01/07	02/07	03/07	04/07	05/07	06/07	07/07
	27	30	34	30	30	29	25	24	30	30	44	53

Of the coaches of the four South American nations that qualified for the 2006 FIFA World Cup in Germany, only Ecuador's Luis Suarez was still in his job going into the Copa América finals in Venezuela a year later. Desperate to maintain the momentum that had seen them qualify for the second round in Germany, Ecuador lost all three games they played in Venezuela, each of them by a single goal in what was a tough group containing Brazil, Mexico and Chile. The federation is convinced that stability is the key to maintaining a strong presence in South American football although it will take a herculean effort for the national team to make it through to a third successive

INTERNATIONAL HONOURS
Qualified for the FIFA World Cup™ finals 2002 2006

World Cup finals. They will be buoyed, however, by FIFA's decision to increase the altitude at which the qualifiers can be played from 2,500 to 3,000 meters above sea-level as Quito lies at 2,800 meters. The army club El Nacional, fielding Ecuadorian players only, won the 2006 championship by finishing two points ahead of Emelec in the end-of-season hexagonal tournament. The tournament was marred, however, by a fierce brawl between LDU and Barcelona on the final day of the season which saw four Barcelona players in hospital and seven LDU players banned for between two and 12 months, notably Ecuador's best-known player Agustin Delgado.

THE FIFA BIG COUNT OF 2006

	Male	Female		Total
Number of players	918 800	110 855	Referees and Assistant Referees	405
Professionals	700		Admin, Coaches, Technical, Medical	4 050
Amateurs 18+	12 855		Number of clubs	199
Youth under 18	9 800		Number of teams	416
Unregistered	811 800		Clubs with women's teams	2
Total players	1 029 655		Players as % of population	7.60%

Federación Ecuatoriana de Fútbol (FEF)
Avenida las Aguas y Calle, Alianza, PO Box 09-01-7447, Guayaquil 593, Ecuador
Tel +593 42 880610   Fax +593 42 880615
fef@gye.satnet.net   www.ecuafutbol.org
President: CHIRIBOGA Luis   General Secretary: ACOSTA Francisco
Vice-President: VILLACIS Carlos   Treasurer: MORA Hugo   Media Officer: MESTANZA Victor
Men's Coach: SUAREZ Luis   Women's Coach: ESTUPINAN Garis
FEF formed: 1925   CONMEBOL: 1930   FIFA: 1926
Yellow shirts with blue and red trimmings, Blue shorts, Red socks

RECENT INTERNATIONAL MATCHES PLAYED BY ECUADOR

2004	Opponents	Score		Venue	Comp	Scorers	Att	Referee
5-09	Uruguay	L	0-1	Montevideo	WCq		28 000	Hidalgo PER
10-10	Chile	W	2-0	Quito	WCq	Kaviedes [49], Mendez.E [64]	27 956	Ortube BOL
14-10	Venezuela	L	1-3	San Cristobal	WCq	Ayovi.M [41p]	13 800	Lecca PER
20-10	Jordan	L	0-3	Tripoli	Fr			
22-10	Nigeria	D	2-2	Tripoli	Fr	Poroso [65], W 5-4p		
27-10	Mexico	L	1-2	New Jersey	Fr	Calle [80]		Prus USA
17-11	Brazil	W	1-0	Quito	WCq	Mendez.E [77]	38 308	Ruiz COL
2005								
26-01	Panama	W	2-0	Ambato	Fr	Tenorio.O [88 91+]	5 000	Vasco ECU
29-01	Panama	W	2-0	Babahoyo	Fr	Kaviedes [45], Tenorio.O [56]		
9-02	Chile	L	0-3	Vina del Mar	Fr		15 000	Favale ARG
16-02	Costa Rica	W	2-1	Heredia	Fr	Ayovi [60p], Guagua [86]	1 000	Duran CRC
27-03	Paraguay	W	5-2	Quito	WCq	Valencia 2 [32 49], Mendez 2 [47+ 47], Ayovi [77p]	32 449	Mendez URU
30-03	Peru	D	2-2	Lima	WCq	De la Cruz [4], Valencia [45]	40 000	Chandia CHI
4-05	Paraguay	W	1-0	East Rutherford	Fr	Mendez [51]	26 491	
4-06	Argentina	W	2-0	Quito	WCq	Lara [53], Delgado [89]	37 583	Selman CHI
8-06	Colombia	L	0-3	Barranquilla	WCq		20 402	Simon BRA
11-06	Italy	D	1-1	East Rutherford	Fr	Ayovi [18p]	27 583	Vaughn USA
17-08	Venezuela	W	3-1	Loja	Fr	Borja [7], Lara 2 [40 67]	10 000	Vasco ECU
3-09	Bolivia	W	2-1	La Paz	WCq	Delgado 2 [8 49]	8 434	Baldassi ARG
8-10	Uruguay	D	0-0	Quito	WCq		37 270	Rezende BRA
12-10	Chile	D	0-0	Santiago	WCq		49 530	Elizondo ARG
13-11	Poland	L	0-3	Barcelona	Fr		6 000	Delgado ESP
29-12	Uganda	L	1-2	Cairo	Fr	Kaviedes [1]		
2006								
25-01	Honduras	W	1-0	Guayaquil	Fr	Caicedo [67]	10 000	Ramos ECU
1-03	Netherlands	L	0-1	Amsterdam	Fr		35 000	Benquerenca POR
30-03	Japan	L	0-1	Oita	Fr		36 507	Maidin ECU
24-05	Colombia	D	1-1	East Rutherford	Fr	Castillo [51]	52 425	Vaughn USA
28-05	FYR Macedonia	L	1-2	Madrid	Fr	Tenorio.C [25]	4 000	
9-06	Poland	W	2-0	Gelsenkirchen	WCr1	Tenorio.C [24]	52 000	Kamikawa JPN
15-06	Costa Rica	W	3-0	Hamburg	WCr1	Tenorio.C [8], Delgado [54], Kaviedes [92+]	50 000	Codjia BEN
20-06	Germany	L	0-3	Berlin	WCr1		72 000	Ivanov.V RUS
25-06	England	L	0-1	Stuttgart	WCr2		52 000	De Bleeckere BEL
6-09	Peru	D	1-1	New Jersey	Fr	Benitez.C [14]	20 000	
10-10	Brazil	L	1-2	Stockholm	Fr	Borja [23]	34 592	Johannesson SWE
2007								
18-01	Sweden	W	2-1	Cuenca	Fr	Vaca [16], Tenorio [25]	20 000	Carrillo PER
21-01	Sweden	D	1-1	Quito	Fr	Zura [82]	18 000	Garay PER
25-03	USA	L	1-3	Tampa	Fr	Caicedo [11]	31 547	Petrescu CAN
28-03	Mexico	L	2-4	Oakland	Fr	Tenorio.C [44], Espinoza OG [57]	47 416	Toledo USA
23-05	Republic of Ireland	D	1-1	New Jersey	Fr	Benitez.C [13]	20 823	
3-06	Peru	L	1-2	Madrid	Fr	Tenorio.C [10p]	25 000	Puerta ESP
6-06	Peru	W	2-0	Barcelona	Fr	Benitez.C [85], De la Cruz [94+]	20 000	Crespo ESP
27-06	Chile	L	2-3	Puerto Ordaz	CAr1	Valencia [16], Benítez [23]	35 000	Ruiz COL
1-07	Mexico	L	1-2	Maturin	CAr1	Méndez [84]	42 000	Ortube BOL
4-07	Brazil	L	0-1	Puerto La Cruz	CAr1		34 000	Pezzotta ARG

Fr = Friendly match • CA = Copa América • WC = FIFA World Cup • q = qualifier • r1 = first round group

ECUADOR NATIONAL TEAM RECORDS AND RECORD SEQUENCES

Records			Sequence records					
Victory	6-0	PER 1975	Wins	6	1996	Clean sheets	3	Five times
Defeat	0-12	ARG 1942	Defeats	18	1938-1945	Goals scored	16	1991-1993
Player Caps	141	HURTADO Iván	Undefeated	8	1996, 2000-2001	Without goal	5	1985-1987
Player Goals	31	DELGADO Augustín	Without win	34	1938-1949	Goals against	28	1953-1963

Population '000

1	Guayaquil	1 952
2	Quito	1 399
3	Cuenca	276
4	Santo Domingo	200
5	Machala	198
6	Manta	183
7	Portoviejo	170
8	Eloy Alfaro	167
9	Ambato	154
10	Riobamba	124
11	Quevedo	119
12	Loja	117
13	Milagro	110
14	Ibarra	108
15	Esmeraldas	95
16	Babahoyo	76
17	La Libertad	75
18	El Carmen	66
19	Daule	52
20	Latacunga	51
21	Velasco Ibarra	50
22	Ventanas	48
23	Tulcán	47
24	Salinas	45

REPUBLIC OF ECUADOR; REPUBLICA DEL ECUADOR

Capital Quito	Language Spanish		Independence 1822
Population 13 547 510	Area 283 560 km²	Density 46 per km²	% in cities 58%
GDP per cap $3300	Dailling code +593	Internet .ec	GMT + / - -5

MEDALS TABLE

		Overall			League			Sth Am			City	Stadium	Cap'ty	DoF
		G	S	B	G	S	B	G	S	B				
1	El Nacional	15	7	7	15	7	4			3	Quito	Olimpico Atahualpa	40 948	1964
2	Barcelona	13	13	10	13	11	5		2	5	Guayaquil	Monumental	59 283	1925
3	Emelec	10	11	12	10	10	10		1	2	Guayaquil	George Capwell	18 222	1929
4	Liga Deportiva Universitaria (LDU)	7	3	9	7	3	6			3	Quito	Casa Blanca	41 596	1930
5	Deportivo Quito	2	3	3	2	3	3				Quito	Olimpico Atahualpa	40 948	1940
6	Deportivo Cuenca	1	3		1	3					Cuenca	Alejandro Aguilar	18 830	1971
7	Olmedo	1	1	1	1	1	1				Riobamba	Olimpico Riobamba	18 936	1919
8	Everest	1		1	1		1				Guayaquil			1931
9	Universidad Católica		2	2		2	2				Quito	Olimpico Atahualpa	40 948	1961
10	América Quito		2	1		2	1				Quito			1939
	9 de Octubre		2	1		2	1				Guayaquil			1926
	Tecnico Universitario		2	1		2	1				Ambato	Bellavista	20 000	1971
13	Filanbanco		1	1		1	1				Guayaquil			1979-91
	Patria Guayaquil		1	1		1	1				Guayaquil			
15	Espoli			1			1				Quito	Guillermo Albornoz		1986
	Valdez			1			1				Milagro			1991

RECENT LEAGUE RECORD

	Championship						Championship Play-off		
Year	Champions	Pts	Runners-up	Pts	Third	Pts	Champions	Score	Runners-up
1995	Barcelona						Barcelona	2-0 1-0	Espoli
1996	El Nacional						El Nacional	2-1 2-0	Emelec
1997	Barcelona	19	Deportivo Quito	19	Emelec	15			
1998	LDU Quito						LDU Quito	0-1 7-0	Emelec
1999	El Nacional	20	LDU Quito	19	Emelec	18			
2000	Olmedo	23	El Nacional	20	Emelec	20			
2001	Emelec	22	El Nacional	21	Olmedo	20			
2002	Emelec	20	Barcelona	19	El Nacional	18			
2003	LDU Quito	26	Barcelona	23	El Nacional	20			
2004	Deportivo Cuenca	19.5	Olmedo	19	LDU Quito	18			
2005	LDU Quito						LDU Quito	0-1 3-0	Barcelona
2005	El Nacional	25	Deportivo Cuenca	20	LDU Quito	17			
2006	El Nacional	19	Emelec	17	LDU Quito	16			

ECUADOR 2006
SERIE A — TORNEO APERTURA

	PI	W	D	L	F	A	Pts	LDU Quito	Nacional	Olmedo	Emelec	Dep. Quito	Barcelona	Aucas	Cuenca	Macará	Espoli
LDU Quito † ‡	18	11	3	4	37	24	36		3-2	3-0	3-1	3-2	2-1	4-2	1-2	3-2	3-2
El Nacional †	18	9	4	5	35	26	31	2-2		2-0	2-2	0-3	2-0	4-0	4-1	2-0	5-2
Olmedo †	18	9	2	7	19	21	29	1-0	1-3		2-0	1-0	1-0	3-1	1-0	1-0	1-1
Emelec	18	8	4	6	30	21	28	1-1	0-2	2-1		0-0	3-2	1-0	3-0	6-0	4-1
Deportivo Quito	18	7	4	7	22	23	25	1-2	1-1	2-1	2-1		2-1	1-2	1-0	0-2	0-3
Barcelona	18	8	0	10	26	24	24	1-0	6-0	1-0	0-3	3-2		4-1	1-0	1-2	1-0
Aucas	18	6	4	8	25	35	22	0-2	2-1	3-3	0-0	1-2	1-0		2-1	0-0	2-2
Deportivo Cuenca	18	7	0	11	18	26	21	1-3	2-0	0-1	2-0	1-2	1-0	3-2		2-1	1-0
Macará	18	6	3	9	17	28	21	1-0	0-2	0-1	3-2	0-0	2-1	1-2	1-0		1-4
Espoli	18	4	6	8	31	32	18	2-2	1-1	3-0	0-1	1-1	2-3	3-4	3-1	1-1	

28/01/2006 - 14/05/2006 • † Qualified for the Hexagonal final • ‡ Qualified for the Copa Sudamericana

ECUADOR 2006
SERIE A — TORNEO CLAUSURA

	PI	W	D	L	F	A	Pts	Nacional	Emelec	Barcelona	Olmedo	Dep. Quito	LDU Quito	Cuenca	Macará	Azogues	Aucas
El Nacional † ‡	18	8	7	3	31	16	31		2-0	6-1	2-1	0-0	0-1	0-0	4-2	3-1	2-2
Emelec †	18	8	7	3	29	19	31	2-2		1-1	2-3	4-1	3-0	0-0	1-0	2-2	3-2
Barcelona †	18	9	4	5	27	20	31	0-2	1-2		2-0	2-0	3-0	1-0	3-2	1-2	3-1
Olmedo	18	8	7	3	24	18	31	1-0	1-0	1-1		1-1	1-0	1-1	2-2	0-0	1-0
Deportivo Quito †	18	6	4	8	21	25	22	0-3	1-2	0-0	0-0		5-1	2-1	3-1	3-1	1-2
LDU Quito	18	6	3	9	21	32	21	1-0	3-3	1-1	1-2	2-1		1-0	1-3	0-1	4-3
Deportivo Cuenca	18	4	8	6	16	14	20	0-1	0-0	1-3	2-1	2-0	1-1		1-1	3-0	3-0
Macará	18	5	5	8	28	29	20	1-1	0-0	0-3	2-4	1-2	1-3	0-0		1-0	6-0
Deportivo Azogues	18	5	4	9	16	28	19	0-0	0-3	0-1	0-2	2-0	2-0	1-1	1-4		3-2
Aucas	18	5	3	10	23	35	18	3-3	0-1	1-0	2-2	0-1	2-1	1-0	0-1	2-0	

7/07/2006 - 22/10/2006 • † Qualified for the Hexagonal final. As El Nacional had already qualified from the Apertura, the sixth place went to Deportivo Quito due to their overall record in both the Apertura and Clausura • ‡ Qualified for the Copa Sudamericana

ECUADOR 2006
SERIE A — HEXAGONAL FINAL

	PI	W	D	L	F	A	Pts	Nacional	Emelec	LDU Quito	Olmedo	Barcelona	Dep. Quito
El Nacional §5	10	3	5	2	16	11	19		2-2	0-3	1-1	4-0	2-1
Emelec §2	10	4	3	3	20	17	17	3-2		2-1	3-1	1-1	4-0
LDU Quito §3	10	3	4	3	17	13	16	0-0	3-2		1-1	1-1	4-1
Olmedo §1	10	3	5	2	14	12	15	0-0	3-0	1-1		2-2	2-0
Barcelona §1	10	3	4	3	10	15	14	0-0	2-1	1-0	2-3		1-0
Deportivo Quito	10	3	1	6	14	23	10	1-5	2-2	4-3	2-0	3-0	

28/10/2006 - 17/12/2006 • † Qualified for the Copa Libertadores • § = Bonus points from the first two stages • Top scorers: Luis Miguel ESCALADA, Emelec 29; Hernán Barcos, Olmedo 18; Wilson SEGURA, Aucas 17; Evelio ORDONEZ, El Nacional 17; Derlis FLORENTIN, Barcelona 17; Christian BENITEZ, El Nacional 16

ECUADOR 2006 — SERIE B APERTURA

	PI	W	D	L	F	A	Pts
Deportivo Azogues	18	10	5	3	45	23	35
Universidad Católica	18	8	7	3	25	18	31
Manta	18	8	5	5	38	29	29
Técnico Universitario	18	9	2	7	26	27	29
LDU de Loja	18	6	7	5	20	18	25
Imbabura	18	6	6	6	29	27	24
Delfín	18	6	3	9	21	25	21
LDU Portoviejo	18	3	10	5	20	25	19
Deportivo Quevedo	18	2	9	8	19	34	12
Esmeraldas Petrolero	18	3	6	9	16	33	11

10/02/2006 - 3/06/2006 • § = four points deducted

ECUADOR 2006 — SERIE B CLAUSURA

	PI	W	D	L	F	A	Pts
Imbabura	18	11	4	3	27	20	37
Universidad Católica	18	11	3	4	29	16	36
Técnico Universitario	18	8	3	7	22	16	27
LDU de Loja	18	6	8	4	23	22	26
Espoli	18	6	6	6	30	21	24
Esmeraldas Petrolero ‡	18	6	4	8	21	27	22
LDU Portoviejo	18	5	6	7	28	32	21
Delfín	18	5	6	7	24	30	21
Manta	18	5	5	8	21	22	20
Deportivo Quevedo ‡	18	2	5	11	12	31	11

14/07/2006 - 11/11/2006 • ‡ relegated on season record

EGY – EGYPT

NATIONAL TEAM RECORD
JULY 10TH 2006 TO JULY 12TH 2010

PL	W	D	L	F	A	%
8	4	3	1	12	5	68.7

Egypt ended the year where they started it off, at the top of the African footballing tree. Cairo giants Al Ahly retained the African Champions League title to confirm their pre-eminent role in the continent's club football. Having finished runners-up to the Tunisian club CS Sfaxien in the group phase, Al Ahly battled with injury to key players as they sought a successful defence of their title. They overcame a tough challenge from ASEC Abidjan of Cote d'Ivoire in the semifinals before setting up a return meeting with the Tunisian upstarts in the final of the continent's top club competition. Al Ahly started as overwhelming favourites but were held to a surprise 1-1 draw in the first leg in the Egyptian capital, showing chinks in their normally impenetrable armour. The return match at Rades in Tunisia saw the Egyptians hit the woodwork but seemingly on their way to defeat on the away goals rule with the score pegged at 0-0 as the match moved into referee's added time at the end of the 90 minutes. But then Mohamed Aboutrika, later to be named the best Champions League player, hammered home a volley from the edge of the penalty area for a dramatic goal that handed Al Ahly a record-equaling fifth win. They followed up December's

INTERNATIONAL HONOURS
Qualified for the FIFA World Cup finals 1934 1990
CAF African Cup of Nations 1957 1959 1986 1998 2006   African Games 1987 1991
CAF African Youth Championship 1981 1991 2003 CAF African U-17 Championship 1997
CAF African Champions League Ismaili 1969, Al Ahly 1982 1987 2001 2005 2006, Zamalek 1984 1986 1993 1996 2002

triumph by winning their African Super Cup against Tunisia's Etoile Sahel in February 2007 and then by doing the double in Egypt. A record breaking 32nd league title in the club's centenary year was wrapped up early although their 30-month unbeaten record in domestic football came to an end in January when Ismaili shocked them 3-0 away. Al Ahly lost to the same club again plus arch rivals Zamalek at the end of the Premier League season but only after sending the bulk of their first team on early vacation in a note of haughty arrogance. The drama of the Champions League final was repeated in the Egyptian Cup final as Al Ahly came from behind three times to beat Zamalek 4-3 in extra time with the last two goals scored by substitute Osama Hosni. Egypt's national team, winners of the 2006 Nations Cup, began the defence their title in the qualifiers with a 4-1 thumping of Burundi in September 2006 but then suffered an embarrassing away draw at lowly Botswana with a full strength side although wins over South Africa and Sweden in friendly matches stretched their unbeaten run over the last 12 months to seven matches. Coach Hassan Shehata's side will turn their focus in the coming months to their plans to hold onto their title at what should be a highly competitive 2008 Nations Cup tournament in Ghana.

Egyptian Football Association (EFA)
5 Gabalaya Street, Gezira, El Borg Post Office, Cairo, Egypt
Tel +20 2 7351793   Fax +20 2 7367817
www.efa.com.eg
President: ZAHER Samir   General Secretary: HOSNY Salah
Vice-President: SHOUBEIR Ahmed   Treasurer: ABDEL HAMID SHAHIN Ahmed Shaker   Media Officer: TBD
Men's Coach: SHEHATA Hassan   Women's Coach: None
EFA formed: 1921   CAF: 1957   FIFA: 1923
Red shirts with white trimmings, White shorts, White socks

RECENT INTERNATIONAL MATCHES PLAYED BY EGYPT

2004	Opponents	Score		Venue	Comp	Scorers	Att	Referee
6-06	Sudan	W	3-0	Khartoum	WCq	Abdelhalim Ali [6], Aboutraika [53], Abdel Wahab [88]	10 000	Kidane Tesfu ERI
20-06	Côte d'Ivoire	L	1-2	Alexandria	WCq	Aboutraika [55]	13 000	Guirat TUN
4-07	Benin	D	3-3	Cotonou	WCq	Ahmed Hassan [66], Aboutraika [75], Moustafa.H [80]	15 000	Chukwujekwu NGA
5-09	Cameroon	W	3-2	Cairo	WCq	Shawky [45], Ahmed Hassan [74p], El Sayed [86]	25 000	Lim Kee Chong MRI
8-10	Libya	L	1-2	Tripoli	WCq	Zaki [57]	40 000	Haimoudi ALG
29-11	Bulgaria	D	1-1	Cairo	Fr	Moteab [85]		
2005								
8-01	Uganda	W	3-0	Cairo	Fr	Zaki 2 [38 67p], Shawky [63]		
4-02	Korea Republic	W	1-0	Seoul	Fr	Moteab [14]	16 054	
9-02	Belgium	W	4-0	Cairo	Fr	Moteab 2 [39 50], Abdelmalk [52], Hosni [80]	5 000	El Beltagy EGY
14-03	Saudi Arabia	W	1-0	Dammam	Fr	Moteab [64]		
27-03	Libya	W	4-1	Cairo	WCq	Hossam Mido [55] Moteab 2 [56 80], Ahmed Hassan [76]	30 000	Poulat FRA
27-05	Kuwait	W	1-0	Kuwait City	Fr	Ahmed Hassan [52]		
5-06	Sudan	W	6-1	Cairo	WCq	Abdelhalim Ali 2 [8 31], Zaki 2 [28 50], El Sayed [62], Abdelmalk [71]	20 000	Mususa ZIM
19-06	Côte d'Ivoire	L	0-2	Abidjan	WCq		30 000	Damon RSA
29-07	Qatar	W	5-0	Geneva	Fr	Aboutraika 2 [59 84], Hosni [66], Zaki 2 [70 88]		
31-07	United Arab Emirates	D	0-0	Geneva	Fr	W 5-4p		
17-08	Portugal	L	0-2	Ponta Delgada	Fr		20 000	Granat POL
4-09	Benin	W	4-1	Cairo	WCq	Zaki 3 [12 15 84], Hossam Mido [71]	5 000	Buenkadila COD
8-10	Cameroon	D	1-1	Yaounde	WCq	Shawky [79]	38 750	Coulibaly MLI
16-11	Tunisia	L	1-2	Cairo	Fr	Hossam Mido [49]		
27-12	Uganda	W	2-0	Cairo	Fr	Amr Zaki 2 [45 66]		
2006								
5-01	Zimbabwe	W	2-0	Alexandria	Fr	Abdelhalim Ali 2 [33 78]		
14-01	South Africa	L	1-2	Cairo	Fr	Zaki [24p]		
20-01	Libya	W	3-0	Cairo	CNr1	Hossam Mido [18], Aboutraika [22], Ahmed Hassan [78]	65 000	Pare BFA
24-01	Morocco	D	0-0	Cairo	CNr1		75 000	Codjia BEN
28-01	Côte d'Ivoire	W	3-1	Cairo	CNr1	Moteab 2 [8 69], Aboutraika [61]	74 000	Mailett SEY
3-02	Congo DR	W	4-1	Cairo	CNqf	Ahmed Hassan 2 [33p 89], Hossam Hassan [41], Moteab [58]	74 000	Sowe GAM
7-02	Senegal	W	2-1	Cairo	CNsf	Ahmed Hassan [36p], Zaki [80]	74 000	Evehe CMR
10-02	Côte d'Ivoire	D	0-0	Cairo	CNf	W 4-2p	74 000	Daami TUN
3-06	Spain	L	0-2	Elche	Fr		38 000	Farina ITA
16-08	Uruguay	L	0-2	Alexandria	Fr		10 000	Benouza ALG
2-09	Burundi	W	4-1	Alexandria	CNq	Zidan [5], Abd Rabou [29], Aboutraika [39], Ahmed Hassan [53p]		Haimoudi ALG
7-10	Botswana	D	0-0	Gaborone	CNq			Bennett RSA
15-11	South Africa	W	1-0	London	Fr	Moteab [3]	2 000	Styles ENG
2007								
7-02	Sweden	W	2-0	Cairo	Fr	Zaki [44], Ahmed Fathi [87]	40 000	Abdalla LBY
25-03	Mauritania	W	3-0	Cairo	CNq	Zidan [20], Sidibe OG [23], Ghali [66]		Benouza ALG
3-06	Mauritania	D	1-1	Nouakchott	CNq	Ahmed Hassan [11]		
12-06	Kuwait	D	1-1	Kuwait City	Fr	Abd El Razak [56]		

Fr = Friendly match • CN = CAF African Cup of Nations • WC = FIFA World Cup • q = qualifier • r1 = first round group

EGYPT NATIONAL TEAM RECORDS AND RECORD SEQUENCES

Records			Sequence records					
Victory	15-0	LAO 1963	Wins	9	2003-2004	Clean sheets	10	1989
Defeat	3-11	ITA 1928	Defeats	4	1990	Goals scored	22	1963-1964
Player Caps	170	HASSAN Hossam	Undefeated	15	1963-64, 2000-01	Without goal	4	1985, 1990
Player Goals	69	HASSAN Hossam	Without win	9	1981-1983	Goals against	13	1972-1973

ARAB REPUBLIC OF EGYPT; JUMHURIYAT MISR AL ARABIYAH

Capital	Cairo	Language	Arabic	Independence	1936
Population	76 117 421	Area	1 001 450 km²	Density	76 per km²	% in cities	45%
GDP per cap	$4000	Dailling code	+20	Internet	.eg	GMT +/-	+2

MAJOR CITIES/TOWNS
Population '000

1	Cairo	7 933
2	Alexandria	4 368
3	Giza	2 491
4	Shubra	1 019
5	Port Said	554
6	Suez	506
7	Assiout	438
8	Mehalla Al Kubra	437
9	Luxor	437
10	Mansoura	431
11	Tanta	411
12	El Faiyum	316
13	Ismailya	291
14	El Zagazig	288
15	Kafr el Dauwar	275
16	Qena	251
17	Aswan	245
18	Menia	232
19	Damanhoor	231
20	Sohag	218
21	Beni Suef	193
22	Shebin El Kom	189
23	Edfo	188
24	Talkha	175

MEDALS TABLE

		Overall			League			Cup		Africa			City	Stadium	Cap'ty	DoF
		G	S	B	G	S	B	G	S	G	S	B				
1	Al Ahly	76	20	4	32	10	2	35	9	9	1	2	Cairo	Cairo Stadium	74 100	1907
2	Zamalek	37	39	9	11	28	5	20	10	6	1	4	Cairo	Cairo Stadium	74 100	1911
3	Al Tersana	7	8	7	1	4	7	6	4				Cairo	Mit Okba	15 000	1920
4	Mokawloon	7	3	2	1		1	3	3	3		1	Cairo	Osman Ahmed Osman	60 000	1962
5	Ismaily	6	10	18	3	4	14	2	4	1	2	4	Ismailya	Ismailiya Stadium	16 500	1920
6	Al Ittihad	6	4	3		2		6	4			1	Alexandria	Alexandria Stadium	20 000	1914
7	Olympic	3	3	1	1		1	2	3				Cairo			1905
8	Al Masry	1	9	7		5		1	9			2	Port Said	Port Said Stadium	22 000	1920
9	Ghazl Al Mehalla	1	7	6	1	5		6			1	1	Al Mehalla	Al Mehalla	20 000	1946
10	Suez	1	3	1		1	1	3								
11	ENPPI	1	1	1	1	1		1					Cairo	Osman Ahmed Osman	60 000	1985
12	Al Teram	1				1										
13	Sekka		6					6					Cairo			
14	Mansoura		1	2	1		1	1		1						
15	Aswan		1					1								
	Baladeyet Mehalla		1					1								
	Shroeders		1					1								
18	Sawahel			1	1								Alexandria	Harras El-Hedoud	22 000	

RECENT LEAGUE AND CUP RECORD

	Championship						Cup		
Year	Champions	Pts	Runners-up	Pts	Third	Pts	Winners	Score	Runners-up
1995	Al Ahly	58	Zamalek	50	Ismaili	43	Mokawloon	2-0	Ghazl Al Mehalla
1996	Al Ahly	70	Zamalek	66	Ismaili	52	Al Ahly	3-1	Mansoura
1997	Al Ahly	69	Zamalek	60	Mansoura	49	Ismaily	1-0	Al Ahly
1998	Al Ahly	68	Zamalek	62	Mokawloon	54	Al Masry	4-3	Mokawloon
1999	Al Ahly	68	Zamalek	41	Ismaily	40	Zamalek	3-1	Ismaily
2000	Al Ahly	60	Ismaily	54	Zamalek	52	Ismaily	4-0	Mokawloon
2001	Zamalek	65	Al Ahly	57	Al Masry	46	Al Ahly	2-0	Ghazl Al Mehalla
2002	Ismaily	66	Al Ahly	64	Zamalek	53	Zamalek	1-0	Baladeyet Mehalla
2003	Zamalek	67	Al Ahly	66	Ismaily	46	Al Ahly	1-1 4-3p	Ismaily
2004	Zamalek	68	Al Ahly	59	Ismaily	51	Mokawloon	2-1	Al Ahly
2005	Al Ahly	74	ENPPI	43	Sawahel	39	ENPPI	1-0	Ittihad
2006	Al Ahly	72	Zamalek	58	ENPPI	46	Al Ahly	3-0	Zamalek
2007	Al Ahly	73	Zamalek	68	Ismaily	67	Al Ahly	4-3	Zamalek

EGYPT 2006-07

PREMIER LEAGUE

	Pl	W	D	L	F	A	Pts	Al Ahly	Zamalek	Ismaily	Al Jaish	Sawahel	Ghazl	Petrojet	Mokawloon	ENPPI	Al Masry	Suez Cem't	Al Tersana	Ittihad	Tanta	Assiout	Olympic
Al Ahly †	30	23	4	3	64	17	73		0-2	0-3	2-0	4-0	2-0	4-0	0-0	2-0	2-0	3-1	1-1	4-0	2-0	1-0	5-1
Zamalek †	30	21	5	4	58	23	68	1-2		2-2	3-0	3-2	0-1	2-0	4-2	2-0	3-0	3-1	0-0	1-0	4-0	1-1	1-1
Ismaily ‡	30	20	7	3	64	23	67	1-0	0-1		3-1	4-2	3-2	2-1	0-0	1-1	3-0	1-0	1-0	5-0	3-0	4-0	6-0
Al Jaish ‡	30	11	11	8	31	29	44	0-4	2-0	2-2		2-2	1-0	2-3	0-0	2-0	1-0	1-1	0-0	1-0	1-1	2-0	1-0
Sawahel	30	12	8	10	36	39	44	0-2	0-3	2-2	1-0		1-0	2-2	0-0	1-2	1-0	1-1	1-0	2-1	2-1	1-0	2-1
Ghazl Al Mehalla	30	12	6	12	33	28	42	0-0	0-0	0-1	1-2	1-0		1-1	0-1	1-0	3-0	2-0	2-1	3-1	2-1	0-2	1-0
Petrojet	30	9	13	8	36	39	40	2-2	1-2	1-2	1-0	0-0	2-2		0-0	2-1	2-0	1-2	1-0	1-1	0-0	2-2	3-1
Mokawloon	30	9	10	11	21	30	37	1-5	0-2	0-1	0-3	0-2	0-0	0-0		2-1	1-0	1-0	1-0	1-1	2-1	1-1	0-1
ENPPI	30	8	11	11	21	26	35	1-2	0-3	1-0	1-1	2-0	1-1	0-1	1-0		0-0	1-0	0-0	1-0	0-0	4-1	1-2
Al Masry	30	9	8	13	23	33	35	0-2	2-0	1-1	0-0	1-1	1-0	4-1	1-0	1-1		0-0	1-0	3-1	3-1	1-1	3-0
Suez Cement	30	9	6	15	25	39	33	0-2	1-2	1-3	0-1	1-2	1-0	1-0	3-4	1-0	1-0		2-1	1-1	2-1	0-1	2-0
Al Tersana	30	6	13	11	26	28	31	2-3	1-4	1-1	1-1	1-0	3-1	3-3	1-0	0-0	2-0	4-0		0-1	1-0	0-0	0-0
Ittihad	30	7	10	13	27	40	31	0-1	1-2	1-2	1-0	3-2	1-0	0-0	0-0	0-0	4-0	0-0	2-1		1-2	2-1	1-1
Tanta	30	5	11	14	20	37	26	0-1	0-2	2-1	0-0	0-0	1-3	1-2	2-1	0-0	0-0	3-1	0-0	2-2		0-1	1-0
Assiout Petrol	30	4	10	16	21	44	22	1-3	3-4	0-3	0-0	0-2	0-3	2-3	0-1	0-1	1-0	0-1	1-1	0-0	0-0		1-2
Olympic	30	5	7	18	22	53	22	0-3	0-1	1-3	2-4	2-4	1-3	0-0	0-2	0-1	0-1	0-0	1-1	3-1	0-0	2-1	

3/08/2006 - 25/05/2007 • † Qualified for the CAF Champions League • ‡ Qualified for the CAF Confederation Cup

CUP 2006-07

Round of 16		Quarter–finals		Semi–finals		Final	
Al Ahly *	1						
Petrojet	0	Al Ahly *	3				
Al Tersana *	2	Al Jaish	1				
Al Jaish	3			Al Ahly	2		
Sawahel *	3			Ismaily	0		
Olympic	1	Sawahel	0 2p				
Al Masry *	1	Ismaily *	0 4p				
Ismaily	3					Al Ahly	4
Assiout Petrol	5					Zamalek	3
Tanta *	1	Assiout Petrol	2				
Suez Cement *	1	ENPPI *	1				
ENPPI	4			Assiout Petrol	0		
Mansoura *	3			Zamalek	1		
Mokawloon	1	Mansoura	0				
Telephonat Beni Suez	0	Zamalek *	3				
Zamalek *	9						

CUP FINAL

Cairo, 2-07-2007

Scorers - Emad Moteab [57], Mohamed Aboutrika [88], Osama Hosni 2 [106] [107] for Ahly; Amr Zaki [50], Mahmoud Abdel Razak [65], Gamal Hamza [100] for Zamalek

* Home team

FIFA/COCA-COLA WORLD RANKING

1993	1994	1995	1996	1997	1998	1999	2000	2001	2002	2003	2004	2005	2006	High		Low	
26	22	23	28	32	28	38	33	41	39	32	34	32	27	17	05/98	44	05/03

				2006–2007							
08/06	09/06	10/06	11/06	12/06	01/07	02/07	03/07	04/07	05/07	06/07	07/07
24	27	25	26	27	19	42	41	39	38	39	42

THE FIFA BIG COUNT OF 2006

	Male	Female		Total
Number of players	3 137 420	690	Referees and Assistant Referees	2 270
Professionals	48		Admin, Coaches, Technical, Medical	16 000
Amateurs 18+	20 135		Number of clubs	590
Youth under 18	30 777		Number of teams	6 495
Unregistered	260 000		Clubs with women's teams	18
Total players	3 138 110		Players as % of population	3.98%

AL AHLY 2005–06

Date	Opponents		Score		Comp	Scorers
15-07-2006	CS Sfaxien - TUN	L	0-1	A	CLgA	
29-07-2006	Jeunesse Kabylie - ALG	W	2-0	H	CLgA	Sedik [35], Hosni [44]
3-08-2006	Tanta	W	2-0	H	Lge	Moteab [38], Gomaa [84]
7-08-2006	Mokawloon	D	0-0	H	Lge	
13-08-2006	Asante Kotoko - GHA	D	0-0	A	CLgA	
21-08-2006	Assiout Petrol	W	3-1	A	Lge	Flavio 2 [5 76], Wael Riad [43]
26-08-2006	Asante Kotoko - GHA	W	4-0	H	CLgA	Aboutrika [9], Hosni [12], Shawky [17], Flavio [20]
9-09-2006	CS Sfaxien - TUN	W	2-1	A	CLgA	Aboutrika [29], Flavio [39]
17-09-2006	Jeunesse Kabylie	D	2-2	A	CLgA	
21-09-2006	Ittihad	W	4-0	H	Lge	Sedik [10], Hosni [39], Flavio 2 [47 91]
25-09-2006	Al Tersana	D	1-1	H	Lge	Moteab [18]
1-10-2006	ASEC Mimosas - CIV	W	2-0	H	CLsf	Aboutrika [25], Moteab [38]
15-10-2006	ASEC Mimosas - CIV	L	1-2	A	CLsf	Flavio [38]
19-10-2006	Ghazl Al Mehalla	W	2-0	H	Lge	Flavio [5], Aboutrika [33]
29-10-2006	CS Sfaxien - TUN	D	1-1	H	CLf	Aboutrika [27]
2-11-2006	Al Masry	W	2-0	A	Lge	Aboutrika [33], Moteab [93+]
11-11-2006	CS Sfaxien	W	1-0	A	CLf	Aboutrika [92+]
19-11-2006	Petrojet	W	4-0	H	Lge	Sedik [19], Moteab [20], Flavio 2 [46 59]
23-11-2006	Al Jaish	W	4-0	A	Lge	Flavio [50], Aboutrika 2 [54 68], Moteab [66]
27-11-2006	Suez Cement	W	3-1	H	Lge	Shawky [50+], Aboutrika [52], Moteab [76]
1-12-2006	Olympic	W	5-1	H	Lge	Moteab [2], Shady Mohamed [33p], Shawky [45], Hosni [64], Flavio [77]
10-12-2006	Auckland City - NZL	W	2-0	N	CWCr1	Flavio [51], Aboutrika [73]
13-12-2006	Internacional - BRA	L	1-2	N	CWCsf	Flavio [54]
17-12-2006	América - MEX	W	2-1	N	CWC3p	Aboutrika 2 [42 79]
22-12-2006	Sawahel	W	2-0	A	Lge	Moteab 2 [38 68]
26-12-2006	ENPPI	W	2-1	A	Lge	Flavio [19], Moteab [93+]
30-12-2006	Zamalek	W	2-1	A	Lge	Flavio 2 [30 41]
3-01-2007	Tanta	W	1-0	A	Lge	Ahmed Hassan [70]
7-01-2007	Ismaily	L	0-3	H	Lge	
11-01-2007	Mokawloon	W	5-1	A	Lge	Hosni [15], Aboutrika [34], Moteab 2 [53 87], Flavio [91+]
15-01-2007	Assiout Petrol	W	1-0	H	Lge	Hassan Mostafa [54]
19-01-2007	Suez Cement	W	2-0	A	Lge	Moteab 2 [62 74p]
27-01-2007	Talka Electricity	W	3-0	H	ECr1	Ahmed Galal 3 [53 74 87]
2-02-2007	Sawahel	W	4-0	H	Lge	Abdel Hassan [1], Moteab [22], Shawky [67], Flavio [81]
12-02-2007	Ittihad	W	1-0	A	Lge	Moteab [92+]
23-02-2007	Al Tersana	W	3-2	A	Lge	Flavio 2 [16 67], El Nahhas [84p]
4-03-2007	Highlanders - ZIM	D	0-0	A	CLr2	
14-03-2007	Al Masry	W	2-0	H	Lge	El Shater [4], Flavio [82]
18-03-2007	Highlanders - ZIM	W	2-0	H	CLr2	Shady Mohammed [14], Flavio [60]
29-03-2007	Ghazl Al Mehalla	D	0-0	A	Lge	
7-04-2007	Mamelodi Sundowns - RSA	D	2-2	A	CLr3	Barakat [27], Flavio [54]
13-04-2007	ENPPI	W	2-0	H	Lge	Shady Mohamed 2p, Barakat [57]
20-04-2007	Mamelodi Sundowns - RSA	W	2-0	H	CLr3	Shady Mohamed [69], Aboutrika [81]
30-04-2007	Petrojet	D	2-2	A	Lge	Aboutrika 2p, Hosni [95+]
5-05-2007	Petrojet	W	1-0	H	ECr2	Flavio [24]
13-05-2007	Al Jaish	W	2-0	H	Lge	Shady Mohamed [23p], El Nahhas [80]
17-05-2007	Olympic	W	3-0	A	Lge	Belal [9], Hosni [52], Sedik [79]
21-05-2007	Zamalek	L	0-2	H	Lge	
25-05-2007	Ismaily	L	0-1	A	Lge	
8-06-2007	Al Jaish	W	3-1	H	ECqf	Aboutrika 2 [43 50], Flavio [60]
28-06-2007	Ismaily	W	2-0	H	ECsf	Shady Mohamed [6p], Aboutrika [51]
2-07-2007	Zamalek	W	4-3	N	ECf	Moteab [57], Aboutrika [88], Hosni 2 [106 107]

Lge = Egyptian League • EC = Egyptian Cup • CL = CAF Champions League • CWC = FIFA Club World Championship
r1 = first round • r2 = second round • r3 = third round • 5p = fifth place play-off
N = Toyota Stadium, Toyota • *N* = National Stadium, Tokyo • N = Yokohama International Stadium

ENG – ENGLAND

NATIONAL TEAM RECORD
JULY 10TH 2006 TO JULY 12TH 2010

PL	W	D	L	F	A	%
11	5	4	2	18	5	63.6

The Chelsea bandwagon may not have exactly come off the rails - a cup double, runners-up in the League and the semi-finals of the Champions League would be a sensational season for most - but the Abramovich revolution looked to be on shaky grounds at times with all manner of speculation filling the newspapers, particularly surrounding the position of manager Jose Mourinho. On the field it was reinvigorated Manchester United who grabbed most of the headlines as they stormed to the title in some style, with player of the year Ronaldo in sparkling form throughout. They were in charge right from the start, leaving Chelsea chasing their tail on the way to a sixteenth championship and their first since 2003. The two also met in the first FA Cup Final at the magnificent new Wembley Stadium although the game never lived up to the occasion and was settled by a Didier Drogba goal four minutes from the end of extra-time. On the face of it English club football appears to be in rude health - over 40,000 fans attended the conference play-off final, in what was in effect a fifth division match - but grave concerns are being voiced within the game at the harm the domination of the big four clubs is doing. Just once in the past 16 years has the FA Cup been

INTERNATIONAL HONOURS
FIFA World Cup 1966

Qualified for the FIFA World Cup 1950 1954 1958 1962 1966 1970 1982 1986 1990 1998 2002 2006 **Qualified for the FIFA Women's World Cup** 1995

European U-21 Championship 1982 1984   **European Junior Championship** 1948 1963 1964 1971 1972 1973 1975 1980 1993

UEFA Champions League Manchester United 1968 1999 Liverpool 1977 1978 1981 1984 2005 Nottingham Forest 1979 1980 Aston Villa 1982

prised out of their hands and that has not only critically damaged the appeal of the tournament but crushed the ambitions of teams that in the past would have expected to do well. Even in the League Cup, the big four can put out experimental youth teams and still beat all-comers and Arsenal reached the final doing just that. Once there, however, they lost 2-1 against Chelsea with Didier Drogba once again the match winner with both goals. All four English representatives in the Champions League topped their groups while Chelsea, Liverpool and Manchester United all made it to the semi-finals. United's 7-1 thrashing of Roma in the quarter-finals will go down as one of the all-time great European displays but it was Liverpool who made it to the final although there was no repeat of heroics of Istanbul of two years earlier as they lost 2-1 to Milan. The post World Cup hangover cast a shadow over the England national team's season although it was Steve McClaren's decision to drop David Beckham that hogged the headlines. Without him England lost to Croatia and drew with Macedonia and Israel, leaving the team with an uphill struggle to qualify for the Euro 2008 finals in Austria and Switzerland. That left McClaren with little choice but to recall Beckham, with many calling for him to resign after less than a year in the job.

The Football Association (The FA)
25 Soho Square, London W1D 4FA, United Kingdom
Tel +44 20 77454545   Fax +44 20 77454546
info@TheFA.com   www.TheFA.com
President: THOMPSON Geoffrey   General Secretary: BARWICK Brian
Vice-President: DEIN David   Treasurer: WILLIAMS Steve   Media Officer: BEVINGTON Adrian
Men's Coach: McCLAREN Steve   Women's Coach: POWELL Hope
The FA formed: 1863   UEFA: 1954   FIFA: 1905-20 & 1945
White shirts with red trimmings, Navy blue shorts, White socks or Red shirts with white trimmings, White shorts, Red socks

RECENT INTERNATIONAL MATCHES PLAYED BY ENGLAND

2004	Opponents	Score		Venue	Comp	Scorers	Att	Referee
1-06	Japan	D	1-1	Manchester	Fr	Owen [22]	38 581	Rosetti ITA
5-06	Iceland	W	6-1	Manchester	Fr	Lampard [25], Rooney 2 [27 38], Vassell 2 [57 77], Bridge [68]	43 500	Wegereef NED
13-06	France	L	1-2	Lisbon	ECr1	Lampard [38]	62 487	Merk GER
17-06	Switzerland	W	3-0	Coimbra	ECr1	Rooney 2 [23 75], Gerrard [82]	28 214	Ivanov RUS
21-06	Croatia	W	4-2	Lisbon	ECr1	Scholes [40], Rooney 2 [45 68], Lampard [79]	57 047	Collina ITA
24-06	Portugal	D	2-2	Lisbon	ECqf	Owen [3], Lampard [115]. L 5-6p	62 564	Meier SUI
18-08	Ukraine	W	3-0	Newcastle	Fr	Beckham [28], Owen [50], Wright-Phillips [70]	35 387	McCurry SCO
4-09	Austria	D	2-2	Vienna	WCq	Lampard [24], Gerrard [63]	48 500	Lubos SVK
8-09	Poland	W	2-1	Chorzow	WCq	Defoe [37], Glowacki OG [58]	38 000	Farina ITA
9-10	Wales	W	2-0	Manchester	WCq	Lampard [4], Beckham [76]	65 224	Hauge NOR
13-10	Azerbaijan	W	1-0	Baku	WCq	Owen [22]	15 000	Hamer LUX
17-11	Spain	L	0-1	Madrid	Fr		48 000	Kasnaferis GRE
2005								
9-02	Netherlands	D	0-0	Birmingham	Fr		40 705	Frojdfeldt SWE
26-03	Northern Ireland	W	4-0	Manchester	WCq	Cole.J [47], Owen 2 [52], Baird OG [54], Lampard [62]	62 239	Stark GER
30-03	Azerbaijan	W	2-0	Newcastle	WCq	Gerrard [51], Beckham [62]	49 046	Costa POR
28-05	USA	W	2-1	Chicago	Fr	Richardson 2 [4 44]	47 637	Archundia MEX
31-05	Colombia	W	3-2	New Jersey	Fr	Owen 3 [35 44 58]	58 000	Hall USA
17-08	Denmark	L	1-4	Copenhagen	Fr	Rooney [87]	41 438	Ovrebro NOR
3-09	Wales	W	1-0	Cardiff	WCq	Cole.J [53]	70 795	Ivanov.V RUS
7-09	Northern Ireland	L	0-1	Belfast	WCq		14 069	Busacca SUI
8-10	Austria	W	1-0	Manchester	WCq	Lampard [25p]	64 822	Medina ESP
12-10	Poland	W	2-1	Manchester	WCq	Owen [43], Lampard [80]	65 467	Nielsen DEN
12-11	Argentina	W	3-2	Geneva	Fr	Rooney [38], Owen 2 [87 90]	29 000	Leuba SUI
2006								
1-03	Uruguay	W	2-1	Liverpool	Fr	Crouch [75], Cole.J [93+]	40 013	Farina ITA
30-05	Hungary	W	3-1	Manchester	Fr	Gerrard [47], Terry [51], Crouch [83]	56 323	Vink NED
3-06	Jamaica	W	6-0	Manchester	Fr	Lampard [11], Taylor OG [17], Crouch 3 [29 65 89], Owen [32]	70 373	Plautz AUT
10-06	Paraguay	W	1-0	Frankfurt	WCr1	Gamarra OG [3]	48 000	Rodriguez MEX
15-06	Trinidad and Tobago	W	2-0	Nuremburg	WCr1	Crouch [83], Gerrard [91+]	41 000	Kamikawa JPN
20-06	Sweden	D	2-2	Cologne	WCr1	Cole.J [34], Gerrard [85]	45 000	Busacca SUI
25-06	Ecuador	W	1-0	Stuttgart	WCr2	Beckham [60]	52 000	De Bleeckere BEL
1-07	Portugal	D	0-0	Gelsenkirchen	WCqf	L 1-3p	52 000	Elizondo ARG
16-08	Greece	W	4-0	Manchester	Fr	Terry [14], Lampard [30], Crouch 2 [36 42]	45 864	Stark GER
2-09	Andorra	W	5-0	Manchester	ECq	Crouch 2 [5 67], Gerrard [13], Defoe 2 [38 47]	56 290	Brugger AUT
6-09	Macedonia	W	1-0	Skopje	ECq	Crouch [46]	16 500	Layec FRA
7-10	Macedonia	D	0-0	Manchester	ECq		72 062	Merk GER
11-10	Croatia	L	0-2	Zagreb	ECq		38 000	Rosetti ITA
15-11	Netherlands	D	1-1	Amsterdam	Fr	Rooney [37]	44 000	Michel SVK
2007								
7-02	Spain	L	0-1	Manchester	Fr		58 247	Weiner GER
24-03	Israel	D	0-0	Tel Aviv	ECq		38 000	Ovrebo NOR
28-03	Andorra	W	3-0	Barcelona	ECq	Gerrard 2 [54 76], Nugent [92+]	12 800	Paixao POR
1-06	Brazil	D	1-1	London	Fr	Terry [68]	88 745	Merk GER
6-06	Estonia	W	3-0	Tallinn	ECq	Cole.J [37], Crouch [54], Owen [62]	11 000	Gilewski POL

Fr = Friendly match • EC = UEFA EURO 2004/2008 • WC = FIFA World Cup • q = qualifier • r1 = first round group • qf = quarter-final

ENGLAND NATIONAL TEAM RECORDS AND RECORD SEQUENCES

Records			Sequence records				
Victory	13-0	IRL 1882	Wins	10	1908-1909	Clean sheets	7	1908-1909
Defeat	1-7	HUN 1954	Defeats	3	Six times	Goals scored	52	1884-1902
Player Caps	125	SHILTON Peter	Undefeated	20	1890-1896	Without goal	4	1981
Player Goals	49	CHARLTON Bobby	Without win	7	1958	Goals against	13	1873-81, 1959-60

The England Amateur team beat France 15-0 in 1906. The FA do not regard it as a full international although the match is part of the official French records • The England Amateurs won a world record 17 consecutive matches from 1906 to 1909 • Vivian Woodward scored a combined 73 goals for the England team and the England amateur team

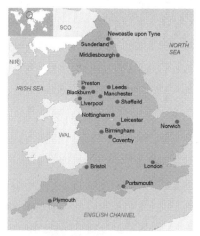

MAJOR CITIES/TOWNS

		Population '000
1	London	7 172
2	West Midlands	2 555
3	Greater Manchester	2 482
4	West Yorkshire	2 079
5	Merseyside	1 362
6	South Yorkshire	1 266
7	Tyne & Wear	1 075
8	Bristol	380
9	Leicester	279
10	Nottingham	266
11	Hull	243
12	Stoke-on-Trent	240
13	Plymouth	240
14	Derby	221
15	Southampton	217
16	Portsmouth	186
17	Luton	184
18	Reading	143
19	Blackpool	142
20	Blackburn	137
21	Middlesbrough	134
22	Preston	129
23	Norwich	121
24	Ipswich	117

ENGLAND (PART OF THE UNITED KINGDOM)

Capital	London	Language	English	Independence	n/a
Population	49 138 831	Area	130 439 km²	Density	380 per km²	% in cities	89%
GDP per cap	$29 600	Dailling code	+44	Internet	.uk	GMT +/-	0

West Midlands is made up of Birmingham, Coventry, Dudley, Sandwell (West Bromwich), Solihull, Walsall and Wolverhampton • **Greater Manchester** is made up of Bolton, Bury, Manchester, Oldham, Rochdale, Salford, Stockport, Tameside, Trafford and Wigan • **West Yorkshire** is made up of Bradford, Calderdale, Kirklees (Huddersfield), Leeds and Wakefield • **Merseyside** is made up of Liverpool, Knowsley, St Helens, Sefton and Wirral • **South Yorkshire** is made up of Barnsley, Doncaster, Rotherham and Sheffield • **Tyne & Wear** is made up of Newcastle upon Tyne, Gateshead, North Tyneside, South Tyneside and Sunderland

MEDALS TABLE

		Overall			League			Cup			LC			Europe			Stadium	Cap'ty	DoF
		G	S	B	G	S	B	G	S	B	G	S	B	G	S	B			
1	Liverpool	40	23	22	18	11	7	7	6	9	7	3	3	8	3	3	Anfield	45 362	1892
2	Manchester United	32	24	27	16	13	6	11	7	7	2	4	4	3		9	Old Trafford	76 212	1878
3	Arsenal	27	23	19	13	8	5	10	7	8	2	4	6	2	4		The Emirates	60 000	1886
4	Aston Villa	20	15	16	7	10	2	7	3	9	5	2	5	1			Villa Park	42 551	1874
5	Tottenham Hotspur	16	8	26	2	4	9	8	1	8	3	2	6	3	1	3	White Hart Lane	36 237	1882
6	Everton	15	16	19	9	7	7	5	7	11		2	1	1			Goodison Park	40 394	1878
7	Chelsea	13	7	23	3	2	4	4	4	9	4	1	4	2		6	Stamford Bridge	42 294	1905
8	Newcastle United	11	10	8	4	2	4	6	7	3		1		1		1	St James' Park	52 387	1881
9	Blackburn Rovers	10	3	17	3	1	3	6	2	10	1		4				Ewood Park	31 154	1875
10	Wolverhampton Wanderers	9	10	14	3	5	6	4	4	6	2		1		1	1	Molineux	29 277	1877
11	Manchester City	9	8	4	2	3	3	4	4	2	2	1	2	1		1	City of Manchester	47 500	1887
12	Nottingham Forest	9	5	14	1	2	4	2	1	9	4	2		2		1	City Ground	30 602	1865
13	Sunderland	8	8	18	6	5	8	2	2	8		1	2				Stadium of Light	49 000	1879
14	Sheffield Wednesday	8	5	19	4	1	7	3	3	10	1	1	2				Hillsborough	39 812	1867
15	Leeds United	7	12	13	3	5	2	1	3	4	1	1	3	2	3	4	Elland Road	39 460	1919
16	West Bromwich Albion	7	9	11	1	2	1	5	5	9	1	2	1				The Hawthorns	28 000	1878
17	Sheffield United	5	4	8	1	2		4	2	7			1				Bramall Lane	30 864	1889
18	The Wanderers	5						5											
19	Preston North End	4	11	5	2	6	2	2	5	3							Deepdale	20 600	1881
20	Huddersfield Town	4	7	6	3	3	3	1	4	2			1				The Galpharm	24 590	1908
21	Bolton Wanderers	4	5	11			3	4	3	6		2	2				The Reebok	28 101	1874
22	West Ham United	4	5	9			1	3	2	2		2	5	1	1	1	Upton Park	35 303	1895
23	Leicester City	3	7	5		1	1		4	4	3	2					The Walkers	32 312	1884
24	Derby County	3	6	15	2	3	4	1	3	9			1			1	Pride Park	33 597	1884
25	Burnley	3	4	13	2	2	5	1	2	5			3				Turf Moor	22 610	1882
26	Ipswich Town	3	2	8	1	2	3	1		2			3	1			Portman Road	30 311	1878
27	Portsmouth	3	2	3	2		1	1	2	2							Fratton Park	20 328	1898
28	Old Etonians	2	4					2	4										
29	Norwich City	2	2	5			1			3	2	2	1				Carrow Road	26 034	1902
30	Bury	2		1				2					1				Gigg Lane	11 669	1885

MEDALS TABLE (CONT'D)

#	Team	Overall			League			Cup			LC			Europe			Stadium	Cap'ty	DoF
		G	S	B	G	S	B	G	S	B	G	S	B	G	S	B			
31	Birmingham City	1	5	10					2	7	1	1	2		2	1	St Andrews	30 007	1875
32	Southampton	1	5	8		1		1	3	7		1	1				St Mary's	32 689	1885
33	Middlesbrough	1	4	4		1			1	1	1	2	2			1	The Riverside	35 041	1876
34	Blackpool	1	3	2		1	1	1	2				1				Bloomfield Road	9 612	1887
	Oxford University	1	3	2				1	3	2									
36	Queens Park Rangers	1	3	1		1					1	1	1				Loftus Road	18 769	1885
37	Royal Engineers	1	3					1	3										
38	Cardiff City	1	2	3		1		1	1	1			1			1	Ninian Park	21 432	1899
	Luton Town	1	2	3					1	3	1	1					Kenilworth Road	10 260	1885
40	Charlton Athletic	1	2	1		1	1	1	1								The Valley	27 113	1905
41	Notts County	1	1	5			2	1	1	3							Meadow Lane	20 300	1862
42	Stoke City	1	1	3						3	1	1					The Brittania	28 218	1868
43	Clapham Rovers	1	1	1				1	1	1									
44	Barnsley	1	1					1	1								Oakwell	23 186	1887
45	Swindon Town	1		4						2	1		2				County Ground	14 255	1881
46	Wimbledon/MK Dons	1		3				1		1			2				National Hockey	8 836	1889
47	Old Carthusians	1		2				1		2									
	Coventry City	1		2				1					2				Ricoh Arena	32 000	1883
49	Blackburn Olympic	1		1				1		1									
	Oxford United	1		1							1		1				The Kassam	12 500	1893
51	Bradford City	1			1												Valley Parade	25 136	1903
52	Watford		2	6		1			1	4			2				Vicarage Road	19 920	1881
53	Bristol City		2	3		1			1	1			2				Ashton Gate	21 497	1894
	Oldham Athletic		2	3		1				3		1					Boundary Park	13 624	1895
55	Queens Park Glasgow		2	2					2	2									
56	Crystal Palace		1	6			1		1	2			3				Selhurst Park	26 225	1905
57	Fulham		1	5					1	5							Craven Cottage	22 602	1879
58	Millwall		1	3					1	3							The Den	20 146	1885
59	Tranmere Rovers		1	1								1	1				Prenton Park	16 567	1884
60	Brighton & Hove Albion		1						1								Withdean	8 850	1901
	London Select XI		1												1				
	Rochdale		1									1					Spotland	10 208	1907
	Rotherham United		1									1					Millmoor	8 200	1870
	Wigan Athletic		1									1					The JJB	25 138	1932
65	Plymouth Argyle			3						1			2				Home Park	20 922	1886
	The Swifts			3						3									
67	Grimsby Town			2						2							Blundell Park	9 106	1878
	Swansea City			2						2							The Liberty	20 520	1912
	Wycombe Wanderers			2						2							Adams Park	10 000	1887
70	Cambridge University			1						1									
	Carlisle United			1									1				Brunton Park	16 065	1903
	Chester City			1									1				Saunders Honda	6 012	1885
	Chesterfield			1						1							Recreation Ground	8 502	1866
	Crewe Alexandra			1						1							Gresty Road	10 046	1877
	Crystal Palace (am)			1						1									
	Darwen			1						1									
	Derby Junction			1						1									
	Glasgow Rangers			1						1									
	Hull City			1						1							Kingston Comm'cations	25 404	1904
	Leyton Orient			1						1							Brisbane Road	7 872	1881
	Marlow			1						1									
	Old Harrovians			1						1									
	Peterborough United			1									1				London Road	15 460	1934
	Port Vale			1						1							Vale Park	18 892	1876
	Reading			1						1							The Madejski	24 225	1871
	Shrewsbury Town			1									1				Gay Meadow	8 000	1886
	Shropshire W			1						1									
	Stockport County			1									1				Edgeley Park	10 641	1883
	Walsall			1									1				Bescot	11 126	1888
	York City			1						1							KitKat Crescent	9 459	1922
		309	298	457	108	108	108	126	126	242	47	47	93	28	17	33			

ENGLAND 2006-07

BARCLAYS PREMIERSHIP

	Pl	W	D	L	F	A	Pts	Man United	Chelsea	Liverpool	Arsenal	Spurs	Everton	Bolton	Reading	Portsmouth	Blackburn	Aston Villa	Midd'bro	Newcastle	Man City	West Ham	Fulham	Wigan	Sheff Utd	Charlton	Watford
Manchester United †	38	28	5	5	83	27	89		1-1	2-0	0-1	1-0	3-0	4-1	3-2	3-0	4-1	3-1	1-1	2-0	3-1	0-1	5-1	3-1	2-0	2-0	4-0
Chelsea †	38	24	11	3	64	24	83	0-0		1-0	1-1	1-0	1-1	2-2	2-2	2-1	3-0	1-1	3-0	1-0	2-2	4-0	3-0	2-1	4-0
Liverpool †	38	20	8	10	57	27	68	0-1	2-0		4-1	3-0	0-0	3-0	2-0	0-0	1-1	3-1	2-0	2-0	1-0	2-1	4-0	2-0	4-0	2-2	2-0
Arsenal †	38	19	11	8	63	35	68	2-1	1-1	3-0		3-0	1-1	2-1	2-1	2-2	6-2	1-1	1-1	1-1	3-1	0-1	3-1	2-1	3-0	4-0	3-0
Tottenham Hotspur ‡	38	17	9	12	57	54	60	0-4	2-1	0-1	2-2		0-2	4-1	1-0	2-1	1-1	2-1	2-3	2-1	1-0	0-0	3-1	2-0	5-1	3-1
Everton ‡	38	15	13	10	52	36	58	2-4	2-3	3-0	1-0	1-2		1-0	1-1	3-0	1-0	0-0	3-0	1-1	2-0	4-1	2-2	2-0	2-1	2-1
Bolton Wanderers ‡	38	16	8	14	47	52	56	0-4	0-1	2-0	3-1	2-0	1-1		1-3	3-2	1-2	2-2	0-0	2-1	0-0	4-0	2-1	0-1	1-0	1-1	1-0
Reading	38	16	7	15	52	47	55	1-1	0-1	1-2	0-4	3-1	0-2	1-0		0-0	1-2	2-0	3-2	1-0	1-0	6-0	1-0	3-2	3-1	2-0	0-2
Portsmouth	38	14	12	12	45	42	54	2-1	0-2	2-1	0-0	1-1	2-0	0-1	3-1		3-0	2-2	0-0	2-1	2-1	2-0	1-1	1-0	3-1	0-1	2-1
Blackburn Rovers	38	15	7	16	52	54	52	0-1	0-2	1-0	0-2	1-1	1-1	1-0	3-3	3-0		1-2	2-1	1-3	4-2	1-2	2-0	2-1	2-1	4-1	3-1
Aston Villa	38	11	17	10	43	41	50	0-3	0-0	0-0	0-1	1-1	1-0	1-2	1-0	0-2	0-0		1-1	2-0	1-3	1-0	1-1	1-1	3-0	2-0	2-0
Middlesbrough	38	12	10	16	44	49	46	1-2	2-1	0-0	1-1	2-3	2-1	5-1	2-1	0-4	0-1	1-3		1-0	0-1	0-3	1-1	3-1	2-0	4-1
Newcastle United	38	11	10	17	38	47	43	2-2	0-0	2-1	0-0	3-1	1-1	1-2	3-2	1-0	0-2	3-1	0-0		0-1	2-2	1-2	2-1	0-1	0-0	2-1
Manchester City	38	11	9	18	29	44	42	0-1	0-1	0-0	0-1	2-1	2-0	0-2	0-0	0-3	0-2	1-0	0-0		2-0	3-1	1-0	0-0	0-0	0-0
West Ham United	38	12	5	21	35	59	41	1-0	1-4	1-2	1-0	3-4	1-0	3-1	0-1	1-2	2-1	1-1	2-0	0-2	0-1		3-3	0-2	1-0	3-1	0-1
Fulham	38	8	15	15	38	60	39	1-2	0-2	1-0	2-1	1-1	1-0	1-1	0-1	1-1	1-1	1-2	1-2	1-1	1-3	0-0		0-1	1-0	2-1	0-0
Wigan Athletic	38	10	8	20	37	59	38	1-3	2-3	0-4	0-1	3-3	0-2	1-3	1-0	1-0	0-3	0-0	0-1	1-0	4-0	0-3	0-0		0-1	3-2	1-1
Sheffield United	38	10	8	20	32	55	38	2-2	0-1	1-1	0-3	2-1	1-1	2-2	1-2	1-1	1-0	0-2	2-2	2-1	1-2	0-1	3-0	2-0	1-2		2-1	1-0
Charlton Athletic	38	8	10	20	34	60	34	0-3	0-1	0-3	1-2	0-2	1-1	2-0	0-0	0-1	1-2	0-1	1-3	2-0	1-0	4-0	2-2	1-0	1-1		0-0
Watford	38	5	13	20	29	59	28	1-2	0-1	0-3	1-2	0-0	0-3	0-1	0-0	4-2	2-1	0-0	2-0	1-1	1-1	1-1	1-3	3-1	1-0	1-2	2-2

19/08/2006 - 13/05/2007 • † Qualified for the UEFA Champions League • ‡ Qualified for the UEFA Cup
Top scorers: Didier DROGBA, Chelsea 20; Benni McCARTHY, Blackburn Rovers 18; Cristiano RONALDO, Manchester Utd 17; Wayne ROONEY, Manchester Utd 14; Mark VIDUKA, Middlesbrough 14; Darren BENT, Charlton Ath 13; Kevin DOYLE, Reading 13

ENGLAND 2006-07

COCA-COLA FOOTBALL LEAGUE CHAMPIONSHIP (2)

	Pl	W	D	L	F	A	Pts	Sunderland	B'ham City	Derby	WBA	Wolves	South'ton	PNE	Stoke	Sheff Wed	Colchester	Plymouth	Palace	Cardiff	Ipswich	Burnley	Norwich	Coventry	QPR	Leicester	Barnsley	Hull	Southend	Luton	Leeds
Sunderland	46	27	7	12	76	47	88		0-1	2-1	2-0	2-1	1-1	0-1	2-1	0-3	1-2	3-0	0-1	0-3	2-1	0-2	0-2	1-1	2-0	2-0	4-0	1-0	2-0
Birmingham City	46	26	8	12	67	42	86	1-1		1-0	2-0	1-1	2-1	3-1	1-1	0-2	0-2	1-3	0-2	2-1	1-0	2-0	1-0	1-3	0-2	1-1	2-0	1-0	1-3	2-2	1-0
Derby County ‡	46	25	9	12	62	46	84	1-2	0-1		2-1	0-2	2-2	1-0	2-1	0-5	1-1	0-1	0-3	1-2	1-1	0-0	0-1	1-1	1-0	2-1	2-3	0-1	0-2	0
West Bromwich Alb ‡	46	22	10	14	81	55	76	1-2	1-1	0-1		3-0	1-1	4-2	1-3	0-1	2-1	2-1	1-0	2-1	0-3	3-0	0-5	0-3	3-2	0-7	0-2	0-1	1-3	2-4	2
Wolverhampton W ‡	46	22	10	14	59	56	76	1-1	2-3	0-1	1-0		0-6	1-3	2-0	2-2	1-0	2-2	1-1	1-2	0-1	2-2	0-1	2-2	0-3	1-3	1-1	1-0	1-0
Southampton ‡	46	21	12	13	77	53	75	1-2	4-3	0-1	0-2	0-0		1-1	1-0	2-1	1-2	1-1	1-2	2-1	1-0	0-0	2-1	0-2	1-2	0-5	2-0	0-4	1-2	1-1	0
Preston North End	46	22	8	16	64	53	74	4-1	1-0	1-2	1-0	0-1	3-1		3-2	0-0	1-0	3-0	0-0	0-2	1-1	0-2	0-2	1-1	1-1	1-0	1-1	0-2	1-2	3-3	0-4	1
Stoke City	46	19	16	11	62	41	73	2-1	0-0	2-0	1-0	1-2	1-1	1-1		1-2	3-1	1-1	2-1	3-0	0-0	0-0	1-5	0-1	0-1	0-4	2-0	1-1	1-1	1-1	0-3	1
Sheffield Wed'day	46	20	11	15	70	66	71	2-4	0-3	1-2	3-1	2-2	3-1	3-1	1-1		2-0	1-1	3-2	0-0	2-0	1-1	3-2	2-1	2-1	1-2	3-0	2-1	0-1	1
Colchester United	46	20	9	17	70	56	69	3-1	1-1	4-3	1-2	2-1	2-0	1-0	3-0	4-0		0-1	0-2	3-1	1-0	0-0	0-3	0-0	2-1	1-1	1-1	2-5	1-3	0-4	1
Plymouth Argyle	46	17	16	13	63	62	67	0-2	0-1	3-1	2-2	1-1	1-1	2-0	1-1	2-3	0		1-0	3-3	1-0	0-3	1-3	2-1	1-3	0-2	4-1	2-0	2-1	1-0	1-2
Crystal Palace	46	18	11	17	59	51	65	1-0	0-1	2-0	0-2	2-2	0-3	0-0	1-1	2-1	3-0	1		1-2	2-0	2-2	3-1	1-0	3-0	2-0	2-0	1-1	3-1	2-1	1-0
Cardiff City	46	13	16	17	53	53	64	1-2	0-2	2-1	1-4	0-1	0-4	1-1	1-1	2-0	0-2	2-0	0		2-1	1-0	1-0	0-0	1-4	1-1	0-0	1-4	1-1
Ipswich Town	46	18	8	20	64	59	62	3-1	1-0	2-1	1-5	0-1	2-1	2-3	0-1	0-3	2-3	0-1	2-3	1		1-1	3-1	2-1	2-1	0-2	5-1	0-0	0-2	5-0	1-0
Burnley	46	15	12	19	52	49	57	2-2	1-2	0-0	3-2	0-1	2-3	3-2	0-1	1-1	1-1	2-4	0-1	1-2	1-0		3-0	1-2	2-0	0-0	1-4	2-2	0-0	0-0	0-2	1
Norwich City	46	16	9	21	56	71	57	1-0	1-0	1-2	1-2	0-1	0-2	1-0	1-0	1-2	1-1	1-3	0	1-1	0-1	1-1	4		1-1	1-0	3-1	5-1	1-1	1-0	0-3	2-2	1
Coventry City	46	16	8	22	47	62	56	2-1	0-1	1-2	0-1	2-1	0-4	0-0	3-1	2-1	4-2	2-1	2-1	0-3	0		0-1	0-4	4-2	0-1	0-1	4-1	1-1	0-1	1-0
Queens Park Rang	46	14	11	21	54	68	53	1-2	0-2	1-2	0-1	0-1	0-1	1-1	0-1	1-1	4-1	0-1	3-3	1-3	3-3	0-1		1-1	1-0	2-0	2-3	2-2
Leicester City	46	13	14	19	49	64	53	0-2	1-2	1-1	1-1	4-3	2-0	1-2	1-1	4-0	0-2	2-1	1-0	0-3	1-0	1-1	2-3	0-1	3		2-0	0-1	1-0	1-1	1-1
Barnsley	46	15	5	26	53	85	50	0-2	1-0	1-2	1-1	1-1	0-2	2-0	1-2	1-2	2-0	0-3	2-2	2-0	1-2	1-0	0-1	0-1	2-3		3-0	2-0	1-2	3-2
Hull City	46	13	10	23	51	67	49	0-1	2-0	1-2	0-2	4-2	0-0	2-1	1-1	1-1	1-4	1-2	5-2	0-1	2-0	1-2	1-1	2-2	3		4-0	0-1	2
Southend United	46	10	12	24	47	80	42	3-1	0-4	0-1	3-1	0-1	2-0	0-1	0-0	0-3	1-1	0-1	1-3	0-3	1-3	0-3	2-3	5-0	2-2	1-3	2-3		1-3	1-1
Luton Town	46	10	10	26	53	81	40	0-5	3-2	0-2	2-2	3-0	2-2	0-2	2-2	2-3	2-1	1-1	2-2	1-0	0-0	0-2	2-2	3-3	1-2	3-2	0-0	2-1	2-0		5-1
Leeds United §10	46	13	7	26	46	72	36	0-3	3-2	0-1	2-3	0-1	0-3	2-1	0-4	2-3	3-0	2-1	2-1	0-1	1-1	1-1	0-1	0-2	1-0	0-1	2-2	0-2	0-2	0-1	0	

5/08/2006 - 6/05/2007 • ‡ Qualified for the play-offs • § = points deducted • Top scorers: Jamie CURETON, Colchester 23; Michael CHOPRA, Cardiff 22
Play-off semi-finals: Southampton 1-2 3-2 3-4p **Derby County**; Wolverhampton Wanderers 2-3 0-1 **West Bromwich Albion**
Play-off final: **Derby County** 1-0 West Bromwich Albion (Wembley, 28-05-2007. Att: 74 993. Scorer - Pearson [61])

ENGLAND 2006–07

COCA-COLA FOOTBALL LEAGUE ONE (3)

	Pl	W	D	L	F	A	Pts	Results (vs Scunthorpe, Bristol City, Blackpool, Nottm For, Yeovil, Oldham, Swansea, Carlisle, Tranmere, Millwall, Doncaster, Port Vale, Crewe, Northants, Hud'field, Gillingham, Cheltenham, Brighton, B'mouth, Orient, Chesterfield, Bradford, Rotherham, Brentford)
Scunthorpe United	46	26	13	7	73	35	91	1-0 1-3 1-1 0-1 1-2 2-3 0-1 1-3 0-2 0-3 0-2 2-1 0-2 0-3 1-1 0-1 2-3 2-3 1-1 0-2 1-0 1-0 1-1
Bristol City	46	25	10	11	63	39	85	1-0 2-4 1-1 2-0 0-0 0-1 0-3 2-1 0-1 0-2 1-2 1-1 0-1 1-3 1-0 1-1 0-2 2-2 1-3 2-3 1-1-0
Blackpool ‡	46	24	11	11	76	49	83	3-1 0-1 0-2 1-2 2-1 2-2 1-1 3-2 0-1 3-1 2-1 2-1 4-1 3-1 1-1 2-1 0-2 0-3 0-1 4-1 0-1 0-1-3
Nottingham Forest ‡	46	23	13	10	65	41	82	0-4 1-0 1-1 1-0 0-2 3-1 0-0 1-3 1-0 1-3 0-0 0-1 0-5 1-1 0-3 0-2 1-3 0-1 3-4 0-1 0-1 1-2-0
Yeovil Town ‡	46	23	10	13	55	39	79	0-2 2-1 0-1 0-1 1-0 1-0 2-1 0-2 0-1 1-0 1-0 2-0 0-0 3-1 2-0 0-1 2-0 0-0 2-1 1-0 0-1 0-1-0
Oldham Athletic ‡	46	21	12	13	69	47	75	1-0 0-3 0-1 5-0 1-0 1-0 0-1 0-1 2-4 0-0 1-1 0-3 2-1 1-1-2 3-3 1-0 2-0 2-1-3-0
Swansea City	46	20	12	14	69	53	72	2-0 0-3 6-0 0-1 1-0 1 5-0 0-0 2-0 3-0 2-2 1-2 1-1 2-2 0-1 2-2 1-4 2-0 0-2 0-1 0-1-1-2-0
Carlisle United	46	19	11	16	54	55	68	0-2 1-3 2-0 1-0 1-4 1-1 1-2 1-0 1-2 3-2 0-2 2-1 1-1 5-0 2-0 3-1 3-1-3 1-0 0-1 0-1-1-2-0
Tranmere Rovers	46	18	13	15	58	53	67	0-2 1-0 2-0 0-2 1-1 0-0 2-0 2 3-1 1-0 1-2 1-0 1-1-2 2-2 3-2 2-1 1-0 3-0 2-0 1-1 2-1 3-1
Millwall	46	19	9	18	59	62	66	0-1 1-0 0-0 1-1 1-0 2-0 2-0 2-2 2-2 1-1 2-2 0-1 0-0 4-1 2-0 1-0 2-5 2-1 2-0 4-0 1-1
Doncaster Rovers	46	16	15	15	52	47	63	2-2 0-1 0-0 1-0 0-0 1-1 2-2 1-2 0-0 1-2 1-0 3-1 2-3 0-1 2-0 2-1 0-1 1-0 0-1 0-3 3-3 2-3-0
Port Vale	46	18	6	22	64	65	60	0-0 0-2 2-1 1-1 4-2 3-0 0-2 0-2 2-3 0-1 2 3-0 1-0 1-2 2-0 1-2 0-1 2-0 1-0 1-0 1-0 3-0 3-2 0-3 2-0 1-3-1-0
Crewe Alexandra	46	17	9	20	66	72	60	1-3 0-1 1-2 1-4 2-3 2-1 1-3 5-1 1-1 1-0 2-1 2-1 2-2 0-4 3-3 1-1 2-0 0-4 2-0 3-1 0-3-1
Northampton Town	46	15	14	17	48	51	59	2-1 1-3 1-1 0-1 1-1-2 3-1 0-3 2-1 3-3 0-0 2-2 1-1 1-1 2-0 0-2 3-1 0-1 1-0 0-0 3-0-0 1
Huddersfield Town	46	14	17	15	60	69	59	1-1 2-1 0-2 1-1 2-3 0-3 3-2 2-1 2-2 4-2 0-0 2-2 1-2 1 3-1 2-0 0-3 2-2 3-1 1-1 2-0 3-0 0-2
Gillingham	46	17	8	21	56	77	59	0-2 1-0 2-0 1-0 0-3 3-1 2-0 2-0 2-0 1-2 3-2 1-0 0-1 2-1 2-1 0-1 1-1-2 1-2-1 2-1 1-1-0 1-0-2-1
Cheltenham Town	46	15	9	22	49	61	54	1-1 2-1 2-0 2-1 2-1 2-2 1-1 2-1 0-3 2-0 2-0 1-1 1-0 2-2 1-1 1 1-1 0-2 1-0 0-1 2-2 0-2-0
Brighton & Hove Alb	46	14	11	21	49	58	53	1-1 0-2 0-3 2-1 1-3 1-2 3-2 1-2 0-1 0-1 0-2 0-0 1-4 1-0 0-1 0-2-1 2-2 4-1-1-2 0-1-0 0-2
Bournemouth	46	13	13	20	50	64	52	1-1 0-1 1-3 2-0 0-3 2-2 2-0 1-2 0-0-4 0-0 0-0 1-2 1-2 1-1-0 5-0 0-3-1 1-3 1-0
Leyton Orient	46	12	15	19	61	77	51	2-2 1-1 0-1 1-3 0-0 2-2 0-1 1-1 3-1 2-0 1-1 2-1 1-1 0-2 1-0-3 3-2 0-1 4-3-2 0-0-1-2-2-3-1
Chesterfield	46	12	11	23	45	53	47	0-1 1-3 2-0 0-1 1-1-2 1-2 3-0 0-0 2-5 1-1 1-3 0-2 1-0-0-0-0-0 1-1-0-0-1-0-1 3-0-2-1-3-1
Bradford City	46	11	14	21	47	65	47	0-1 2-1 1-3 2-2 0-2 1-2 2-1 1-2 0-2 2-0 1-2 0-0 1-1-2-0-1-4 2-2-2-2 3-0-0-0-2 1-0 1-1-1
Rotherham Utd §10	46	13	9	24	58	75	38	2-1 1-1 1-0 1-1 3-2 1-0 2-0 2-0-0 1-5-5 1-1-2-2 3-3-2-2-4 0-1-0-2-2-2-0-1-4 2-0
Brentford	46	8	13	25	40	79	37	2-1-1-1-0 2-4 1-2 2-2-0-2-0-0-1-1-4 0-4 4-3-0-4-0-1-2-2-2-2-0-2-1-0-0-0-2-2-1-2-1-0-1

5/08/2006 - 5/05/2007 • ‡ Qualified for the play-offs • § = points deducted • Top scorers: Billy SHARP, Scunthorpe 30; Leon CONSTANTINE, Port Vale 22
Play-off semi-finals: Oldham Athletic 1-2 1-3 **Blackpool**; Yeovil Town 0-2 5-2 Nottingham Forest
Play-off final: Blackpool 2-0 Yeovil Town (Wembley, 27-05-2007. Att: 59 313. Scorers – Williams [43], Parker [52])

ENGLAND 2006–07

COCA-COLA FOOTBALL LEAGUE TWO (4)

	Pl	W	D	L	F	A	Pts	Results (vs Walsall, Hartlepool, Swindon, MK Dons, Lincoln, Bristol Rov, Shrewsbury, Stockport, Rochdale, Peter'bro, Darlington, Wycombe, Notts Co, Barnet, Grimsby, Hereford, Mansfield, Chester, Wrexham, Accrington, Bury, Macc'field, Boston, Torquay)
Walsall	46	25	14	7	66	34	89	2-0 0-2 0-0 1-2 2-2 1-0 2-0 1-1 5-0 1-0 0-2 0-2 1-4 1-2 0-1 0-4 0-1 0-1-0 3-2 0-1 2-0 1-1-1-0
Hartlepool	46	26	10	10	65	40	88	3-1 0-1 1-0 1-1 1-2 0-3 1-1 1-0 1-0 0-0 1-0 1-2 0-3 0-2 0-3 0-3 0-1 0-2 0-3 2-2 1-1
Swindon Town	46	25	10	11	58	38	85	1-1 0-1 2-1 0-1 2-1 2-0 0-0 1-1 1-2 1-1 1-2 1-3 0-1 2-2 0-1 0-2-2 2-0-2-1 2-0-1-1-2-1
Milton Keynes Dons‡	46	25	9	12	76	58	84	1-1 0-0 0-1 2-2 2-0 2-0 2-0 1-0 2-1 0-3 3-2 3-1 1-1-2-1 3-1 1-1-2-1 3-1 2-1 3-3-2-3-2
Lincoln City ‡	46	21	11	14	70	59	74	2-2 2-0 2-3 1-0 1-1 0-0 7-1 1-0 3-1 0-1 0-1 0-2 0-1 4-1 2-2 0-0 3-3 1-0 2-2 1-2 1-1-0
Bristol Rovers ‡	46	20	12	14	49	42	72	1-2 0-2 1-0 1-1-0 1-0 2-1 0-0 3-2 1-2 2-2 0-2 0-1 0-2 1-1 0-0 0-1 1-4 0-2 0-0 0-1 0-1-0
Shrewsbury Town ‡	46	18	17	11	68	46	71	1-1 1-1 2-2 1-0 1-0 0-1 4-2 3-0 2-1 2-2 0-2 0-2 1-0 2-1 2-3 0-2-2 1-0 2-1 1-3-2 1-5-0 1-0
Stockport County	46	21	8	17	65	54	71	1-0 3-3 0-1 2-2 0-2 1-0-3 2-7 0-1 5-2 2-0-2 0-3 0-0-2 1-0-2 0-5-2 1-0 1-0-1-2 0-1-0
Rochdale	46	12	16	12	70	50	66	0-1 2-0 0-0 5-0 2-0 0-1 1-1-3 0-1 0-0-0 2-0-1-0 2-1 1-2-0-0-0-2-4 2-1-3-5-0-4-0-2-0
Peterborough Utd	46	18	11	17	70	61	65	0-2 3-5 1-1 4-0 1-2 4-1 2-1 0-3 3-3 1 1-3 3-3-2 0-1-1-2-2-3-0-2-0-0-2-3-0-4-2-0-1-3-1 1-1-5-2
Darlington	46	17	14	15	52	56	65	0-0 0-3 1-2 1-0 1-1 1-1-2-0 5-0-5-3-1 3-2-0-1-2-0-2-1-0-0-1-2-1-1-1-4-0-2-0-1
Wycombe Wanderers	46	14	16	16	52	47	62	1-1 0-1-1-0-2-1-3-0-1-1-2-1-0-2-1-0 0-0-1-1-1-0-0-1-0-0-1-1-1-3-0-3-0-0-0-2-0
Notts County	46	16	14	16	55	53	62	1-2 0-1-1-2-2-3-1-1-2-1-1-0-1-2-0-0-0-1-1-0 1-1-2-0-0-1-0-0-1-2-2-1-3-2-0-1-1-2-2-0-5-2
Barnet	46	16	11	19	55	70	59	1-1-2-1-1-0-3-3-0-5-1-0-0-3-1-3-2-1-0-2-1-2-1-3 0-1-3-0-2-1-1-0-1-1-2-1-2-2-1-1-0-3-3-0-1
Grimsby Town	46	17	8	21	57	73	59	2-1-1-4-1-0-1-3-0-4-3-2-1-0-1-0-4-0-0-1-2-2-0-2-5-0 2-1-1-1-0-2-2-1-0-2-0-2-1-1-3-2-2-0
Hereford United	46	14	13	19	45	53	55	0-1-3-1-0-0-0-1-2-0-0-0-1-2-0-0-0-0-1-1-2-3-2-2-0-0-1 1-3-2-0-2-0-1-0-1-0-1-0-3-0-1-1
Mansfield Town	46	14	12	20	58	63	54	2-1-0-1-2-0-2-1-2-4-0-1-1-1-1-1-1-2-0-2-1-0-3-2-2-2-2-1-1-2-4-1 2-1-3-0-2-2-0-2-1-2-1-2-5-0
Chester City	46	13	14	19	40	48	53	0-0-2-1-0-2-0-3-4-1-2-0-0-0-1-1-1-1-1-1-1-0-1-1-0-1-0-0-2-0-0-2 - 1-1 1-2-2-0-1-0-0-3-3-1-1-1
Wrexham	46	13	12	21	43	65	51	1-1-1-2-1-1-2-2-1-2-0-1-3-0-1-1-2-0-0-0-2-0-1-1-1-3-0-1-0-0-0-0 1-3-1-1-0-0-3-1-1-0
Accrington Stanley	46	13	11	22	70	81	50	1-2-1-2-1-3-4-2-2-1-1-3-3-0-1-1-1-3-2-0-2-2-1-1-2-2-1-4-1-2-0-3-2-0-1-5-0 1-1-3-2-2-1-1-0
Bury	46	13	11	22	46	61	50	1-2-0-1-0-1-0-2-2-2-0-2-1-2-2-0-0-1-0-3-1-1-0-4-0-1-2-3-0-2-2-1-1-1-3-1-0-2-2 1-1-2-1-0-1
Macclesfield Town	46	12	12	22	55	77	48	0-2-0-0-2-1-1-2-2-2-0-1-0-2-1-1-0-2-1-1-0-2-1-2-3-2-0-3-1-1-2-0-3-3-2-3 2-3-3-3
Boston United	46	12	10	24	51	80	46	1-1-0-1-1-3-0-1-1-0-2-1-0-3-2-1-0-3-0-1-4-1-0-1-3-3-2-1-0-6-1-1-1-1-0-4-0-1-0-0-1-4-1 1-1
Torquay United	46	7	14	25	36	63	35	1-2-0-1-0-1-0-2-1-2-0-0-0-0-1-0-1-0-1-1-0-1-3-0-0-1-1-4-1-0-0-1-0-1-0-2-2-1-1-0-2-2-0-1-0-1

5/08/2006 - 5/05/2007 • ‡ Qualified for the play-offs • Top scorers: Richard BARKER, Hartlepool 21; Izale McLEOD, MK Dons 21
Play-off semi-finals: Bristol Rovers 2-1 5-3 Lincoln City; **Shrewsbury Town** 0-0 2-1 Milton Keynes Dons;
Play-off final: **Bristol Rovers** 3-1 Shrewsbury Town (Wembley, 26-05-2007. Att: 61 589. Scorers – Walker 2 [21] [35], Igoe [90] for Rovers; Drummond [3] for Town)

ENGLAND 2006–07

NATIONWIDE CONFERENCE (5)

	Pl	W	D	L	F	A	Pts																			
								Dag & Red	Oxford	Morecombe	York	Exeter	Burton	Gravesend	Stevenage	Aldershot	Kidderm'ster	Weymouth	Rusden & D	Northwich	Forest G.	Woking	Halifax	Cambridge	Crawley	Grays	Stafford R	Altrincham	Tamworth	Southport	St Albans
Dagenham & Red.	46	28	11	7	93	48	95		0-1	2-1	2-1	4-1	3-0	2-1	2-0	2-1	1-3	4-1	1-2	5-0	1-1	3-2	1-0	2-0	2-1	0-0	1-4	1-4	0-0	0-4-2
Oxford United ‡	46	22	15	9	66	33	81	2-2		0-0	2-0	1-0	0-0	1-0	2-0	2-0	0-1	4-1	0-1	5-1	0-2	0-2	0-1	1-1	1-1	1-2	0-1	1-2	1-2	2-2-1
Morecombe ‡	46	23	12	11	64	46	81	1-1	0-3		1-3	2-2	0-1	1-0	3-3	2-1	0-1	2-0	1-0	2-1	0-2	1-1	2-1	0-1	0-1	0-0	1-0	0-0	0-0	2-0
York City ‡	46	23	11	12	65	45	80	2-3	1-0	2-3		0-0	3-2	0-2	0-1	1-0	1-0	1-0	1-4-1		1-0	0-0	1-2	0-1	2-5	0-2	2-0	0-1	0-0	2-2	2-0-0
Exeter City ‡	46	22	12	12	67	48	78	3-2	2-1	1-0	1-1		3-0	1-3	1-1	0-0	1-1	4-0	0-0	1-1	1-0	1-0	4-1	2-0	1-1	2-1	1-2	1-1	2-2	1-1	0-2-1	4-2
Burton Albion	46	22	9	15	52	47	75	0-2	1-2	2-1	1-2	1-0		0-1	2-1	1-3	1-1	1-1	1-1	2-2	0-1	0-2	1-1	0-2	1-2	1-2	1-3	0-0	0-2	1-1	0-0	1-1-0
Gravesend & N'fleet	46	21	11	14	63	56	74	0-0	1-0	2-1	0-2	2-0	0-0		1-1	1-1	1-3	1-3	1-0	3-0	1-1	1-0	2-0	2-0	1-0	2-0	1-0	2-0	1-4	3-1	4-1	0-4-3-2
Stevenage Borough	46	20	10	16	76	66	70	1-2	2-2	3-3	1-3	1-0	0-0	2-1		3-0	3-2	1-2	1-0	1-0	0-2	3-3	3-2	2-1	4-1	2-3	1-0	6-0	0-1	3-0	3-1	1-2
Aldershot	46	18	11	17	64	62	65	1-1	1-1	0-1	0-2	3-2	3-2	3-2	4-0		4-2	1-0	2-2	1-3	2-1	2-2	1-0	0-1	0-2	1-0	4-2	0-0	3-3	2-2	2-0
Kidderminster Har.	46	17	12	17	43	50	63	1-4	0-0	1-0	2-1	0-2	0-0	1-2	1-2	0-0		0-1	0-0	1-2	2-0	1-1	0-1	0-1	0-0	1-2	1-2	0-3	2-0	2-2	0-1-3
Weymouth	46	18	9	19	56	73	63	1-1	1-1	2-1	1-2	1-1	1-2	1-0	1-0	1-1	1-0		1-1	1-1	0-2	3-1	0-2	3-2	3-2	1-2	1-2	3-1	2-0	2-1
Rushden & D'monds	46	17	11	18	58	54	62	2-3	1-0	2-2	0-1	3-0	1-2	0-0	2-2	0-1	0-1	4-1		1-0	2-0	2-0	0-1	3-1	1-1	1-1	3-2	1-3	0-1	1-2	3-1
Northwich Victoria	46	18	4	24	51	69	58		1-0	0-1	2-1	0-0	3-3	1-2	0-1	3-0	1-0	1-4	1		2-0	0-2	3-2	0-4	2-1	0-4	0-1	0-3	1-0	1-0	1-3	1-0-3
Forest Green	46	13	18	15	59	64	57	0-1	1-5	1-3	0-1	2-1	1-0	0-1	4-4	3-0	2-1	3-2	0-2	1		2-3	2-0	1-1	1-0	0-0	2-1	2-2	0-1	1-2	2-2
Woking	46	15	12	19	56	61	57	2-2	1-0	1-1	1-2	0-2	0-0	2-2	0-1	2-0	3-0	4-0	3-0	3-0	3-2	3-3		2-2	0-1	1-2	1-0	1-1	2-0	0-2	1-1	1-2
Halifax Town	46	15	10	21	55	62	55	3-1	1-1	1-1	1-2	1-1	2-1	1-2	1-2	0-2	0-4	1-0	0-0	2-2	3-3	0		1-0	2-1	0-2	3-1	1-1	3-1	1-1	1-4	1
Cambridge United	46	15	10	21	57	66	55	4-2	0-3	1-3	0-5	1-3	1-2	3-0	1-0	2-0	1-1	7-0	0-1	0-1	1-1	3-0	1-2		1-2	2-0	1-2	2-1	0-2	2-0-2
Crawley Town	46	17	12	17	52	52	53	0-0	0-1	4-0	3-0	0-3	1-0	1-3	0-1	2-0	0-0	3-1	0-0	2-3	1-0	0-2	0-1	1		0-1	1-2	1-1	1-0	2-1	2-1
Grays Athletic	46	13	13	20	56	55	52	0-1	2-0	1-0	0-2	2-0	1-0	2-0	1-2	2-3	0-2	2-3	1-1	0-1	1-0	0-1	0-0		1-1	1-1	0-4	0-2-1
Stafford Rangers	46	14	10	22	49	71	52	1-2	0-1	1-3	0-0	0-1	1-1	3-1	1-3	0-3	1-2	2-0	1-1	2-0-0	1-1	0-2	3-1	2-0	1-4-2		1-0	0-4	1-0-2-2
Altrincham	46	13	12	21	53	67	51	0-5	0-3	0-2	0-4	1-2	2-3	0-2	2-1	0-0	0-1	0-0	2-1	3-0	2-2	3-1	0-5	0-1	1-1	0-0	1		2-0-2-1-2-0
Tamworth	46	13	9	24	43	61	48	0-2	1-3	0-1	2-2	1-0	0-1	2-1	2-1	2-0	0-0	1-3	1-4	0-1	1-1	3-1	1-0	0-1	0-0	1-0		1-1-1
Southport	46	11	14	21	57	67	47	1-4	0-1	1-2	0-1	0-1	3-1	2-2	1-2	1-0	0-1	0-1	2-1	2-1	2-0	0-1	1-1	2-3	1-5	1-2-1	1-0		1-1
St Albans	46	10	10	26	57	89	40	1-2	0-2	0-2	4-2	1-2	0-1	2-3	2-3-3	5-1	1-1	0-3	2-1	3-0	0-0	1-3	2-0	0-2	2-0	6-0	3-1	5-1	0-2-2	

12/08/2006 – 28/04/2007 • ‡ Qualified for the play-offs • Top scorers: Paul BENSON, Dag & Red 28; Charlie MACDONALD, Gravesend 27
Play-off semi-finals: York City 0-0 1-2 **Morecambe**; **Exeter City** 0-1 2-1 4-3p Oxford United
Play-off final: **Morecambe** 2-1 Exeter City (Wembley, 20-05-2007. Att: 40 043. Scorers - Thompson [42], Carlton [82] for Morecambe; Phillips [8] for Exeter)

RECENT LEAGUE AND CUP RECORD

	Championship						Cup		
Year	Champions	Pts	Runners-up	Pts	Third	Pts	Winners	Score	Runners-up
1995	Blackburn Rovers	89	Manchester United	88	Nottingham Forest	77	Everton	1-0	Manchester United
1996	Manchester United	82	Newcastle United	78	Liverpool	71	Manchester United	1-0	Liverpool
1997	Manchester United	75	Newcastle United	68	Arsenal	68	Chelsea	2-0	Middlesbrough
1998	Arsenal	78	Manchester United	77	Liverpool	65	Arsenal	2-0	Newcastle United
1999	Manchester United	79	Arsenal	78	Chelsea	75	Manchester United	2-0	Newcastle United
2000	Manchester United	91	Arsenal	73	Leeds United	69	Chelsea	1-0	Aston Villa
2001	Manchester United	80	Arsenal	70	Liverpool	69	Liverpool	2-1	Arsenal
2002	Arsenal	87	Liverpool	80	Manchester United	77	Arsenal	2-0	Chelsea
2003	Manchester United	83	Arsenal	78	Newcastle United	69	Arsenal	1-0	Southampton
2004	Arsenal	90	Chelsea	79	Manchester United	75	Manchester United	3-0	Millwall
2005	Chelsea	95	Arsenal	83	Manchester United	77	Arsenal	0-0 5-4p	Manchester United
2006	Chelsea	91	Manchester United	83	Liverpool	82	Liverpool	3-3 3-1p	West Ham United
2007	Manchester United	89	Chelsea	83	Liverpool	68	Chelsea	1-0	Manchester United

FIFA/COCA-COLA WORLD RANKING

1993	1994	1995	1996	1997	1998	1999	2000	2001	2002	2003	2004	2005	2006	High		Low	
11	18	21	12	4	9	12	17	10	7	8	8	9	5	**4**	09/06	**27**	02/96

2006–2007											
08/06	09/06	10/06	11/06	12/06	01/07	02/07	03/07	04/07	05/07	06/07	07/07
5	4	5	5	5	6	6	6	8	8	8	12

THE FIFA BIG COUNT OF 2006

	Male	Female		Total
Number of players	3 829 000	335 110	Referees and Assistant Referees	33 186
Professionals	6 110		Admin, Coaches, Technical, Medical	135 000
Amateurs 18+	656 800		Number of clubs	40 000
Youth under 18	820 000		Number of teams	119 000
Unregistered	2 415 000		Clubs with women's teams	2 490
Total players	4 164 110		Players as % of population	8.47%

FA CUP (SPONSORED BY E.ON) 2006–07

Third Round			Fourth Round			Fifth Round		
Chelsea *	6							
Macclesfield Town	1		Chelsea *	3				
Charlton Athletic	0		Nottingham Forest	0				
Nottingham Forest *	2					Chelsea *	4	
Blackpool *	4					Norwich City	0	
Aldershot Town	2		Blackpool *	1	2			
Tamworth *	1		Norwich City	1	3			
Norwich City	4							
Fulham	2	4						
Leicester City *	2	3	Fulham *	3				
Millwall	0		Stoke City	0				
Stoke City *	2					Fulham *	0	
Southend United *	1	2				Tottenham Hotspur	4	
Barnsley	1	0	Southend United	1				
Cardiff City *	0	0	Tottenham Hotspur *	3				
Tottenham Hotspur	0	4						
Manchester City	1	2						
Sheffield Wednesday *	1	1	Manchester City *	3				
Torquay United *	0		Southampton	1				
Southampton	2					Manchester City	3	
Crystal Palace *	2					Preston North End *	1	
Swindon Town	1		Crystal Palace *	0				
Sunderland	0		Preston North End	2				
Preston North End *	1							
Arsenal	3							
Liverpool *	1		Arsenal *	1	3			
Doncaster United *	0		Bolton Wanderers	1	1			
Bolton Wanderers	4					Arsenal *	0	0
Luton Town	2	1				Blackburn Rovers	0	1
Queens Park Rangers *	2	0	Luton Town *	0				
Everton *	1		Blackburn Rovers	4				
Blackburn Rovers	4							
Watford *	4							
Stockport County	1		Watford	1				
Brighton & Hove Albion	0		West Ham United *	0				
West Ham United *	3					Watford *	1	
Swansea City	3					Ipswich Town	0	
Sheffield United *	0		Swansea City	0				
Chester City *	0	0	Ipswich Town *	1				
Ipswich Town	0	1						
Derby County *	3							
Wrexham	1		Derby County *	1				
Hereford United	0		Bristol Rovers	0				
Bristol Rovers *	1					Derby County	0	
Barnet *	2					Plymouth Argyle *	2	
Colchester United	1		Barnet *	0				
Peterborough United *	1	1	Plymouth Argyle	2				
Plymouth Argyle	1	2						
Middlesbrough	1	4						
Hull City *	1	3	Middlesbrough	2	2 5p			
Coventry City	3	0	Bristol City *	2	2 4p			
Bristol City *	3	2				Middlesbrough *	2	1 5p
Wolverhampton Wanderers *	2	2				West Bromwich Albion	2	1 4p
Oldham Athletic	2	0	Wolverhampton Wanderers *	0				
Leeds United	1		West Bromwich Albion	3				
West Bromwich Albion *	3							
Reading *	3							
Burnley	2		Reading	3				
Newcastle United	2	1	Birmingham City *	2				
Birmingham City *	2	5				Reading	1	2
Portsmouth *	2					Manchester United *	1	3
Wigan Athletic	1		Portsmouth	1				
Aston Villa	1		Manchester United *	2				
Manchester United *	2							

* Home team

FA CUP (SPONSORED BY E.ON) 2006–07

Quarter–finals	Semi–finals	Final

Chelsea *	3	2
Tottenham Hotspur	3	1

Chelsea †	2
Blackburn Rovers	1

Manchester City	0
Blackburn Rovers *	2

Chelsea	1
Manchester United	0

Watford	1
Plymouth Argyle *	0

Watford	1
Manchester United ‡	4

Middlesbrough *	2	0
Manchester United	2	1

† Played at Old Trafford, Manchester
‡ Played at Villa Park, Birmingham

FA CUP FINAL 2007

Wembley Stadium, London, 19-05-2007, 15:00, Att: 89 826, Ref: Bennett

Chelsea	1	Drogba [116]
Manchester United	0	

Chelsea - Petr CECH - Paulo FERREIRA●, Michael ESSIEN, John TERRY, Wayne BRIDGE - John MIKEL, Claude MAKELELE●, Frank LAMPARD, Shaun WRIGHT-PHILLIPS (Salomon KALOU● 93), Joe COLE (Arjen ROBBEN 46) (Ashley COLE● 108) - Didier DROGBA. Tr: José MOURINHO

Manchester United - Edwin VAN DER SAR - Wes BROWN, Rio FERDINAND, Nemanja VIDIC●, Gabriel HEINZE - Darren FLETCHER (Alan SMITH● 92), Paul SCHOLES●, Michael CARRICK (John O'SHEA 112), CRISTIANO RONALDO, Ryan GIGGS (Ole Gunnar SOLSKJÆR 112) - Wayne ROONEY. Tr: Alex FERGUSON

CARLING LEAGUE CUP 2006-07

Second Round

Chelsea	Bye
Blackburn Rovers	Bye
Leicester City	3
Hereford United *	1
Scunthorpe United *	1
Aston Villa	2
Watford *	0 6p
Accrington Stanley	0 5p
Hartlepool	0 2p
Hull City *	0 3p
Portsmouth	2
Mansfield Town *	1
Newcastle United	Bye
Charlton Athletic *	1
Carlisle United	0
Walsall *	1
Bolton Wanderers	3
West Ham United	Bye
Manchester City	1
Chesterfield *	2
Notts County	1
Middlesbrough *	0
Millwall *	0
Southampton	4
Doncaster Rovers *	3 8p
Derby County	3 7p
Fulham *	1
Wycombe Wanderers	2
Tottenham Hotspur	Bye
Barnsley *	1
Milton Keynes Dons	2
Norwich City	4
Rotherham United *	2
Queens Park Rangers	2
Port Vale *	3
Manchester United	Bye
Wigan Athletic	0
Crewe Alexandra *	2
Leeds United *	3
Barnet	1
Brighton & Hove Albion	2
Southend United *	3
Liverpool	Bye
Darlington	3 2p
Reading *	3 4p
Sheffield United *	1
Bury	0
Wrexham	1
Birmingham City *	4
Everton	2
Peterborough United *	1
Brentford *	0
Luton Town	3
West Bromwich Albion *	3
Cheltenham Town	1
Arsenal	Bye

Third Round

Chelsea	2
Blackburn Rovers *	0
Leicester City *	2
Aston Villa	3
Watford *	2
Hull City	1
Portsmouth	0
Newcastle United *	3
Charlton Athletic *	1
Bolton Wanderers	0
West Ham United	1
Chesterfield *	2
Notts County *	2
Southampton	0
Doncaster Rovers	2 2p
Wycombe Wanderers *	2 3p
Tottenham Hotspur	5
Milton Keynes Dons *	0
Norwich City	0 2p
Port Vale *	0 3p
Manchester United	2
Crewe Alexandra *	1
Leeds United *	1
Southend United	3
Liverpool *	4
Reading	3
Sheffield United *	2
Birmingham City	4
Everton *	4
Luton Town	0
West Bromwich Albion *	0
Arsenal	2

Fourth Round

Chelsea *	4
Aston Villa	0
Watford *	2 4p
Newcastle United	2 5p
Charlton Athletic	3 4p
Chesterfield *	3 3p
Notts County *	0
Wycombe Wanderers	1
Tottenham Hotspur *	3
Port Vale	1
Manchester United	0
Southend United *	1
Liverpool	1
Birmingham City *	0
Everton *	0
Arsenal	1

* Home team

CARLING LEAGUE CUP 2006–07

Quarter–finals	Semi–finals	Final

Chelsea	1
Newcastle United *	0

Chelsea	1	4
Wycombe Wanderers *	1	0

Charlton Athletic *	0
Wycombe Wanderers	1

Chelsea	2
Arsenal	1

Tottenham Hotspur *	1
Southend United	0

Tottenham Hotspur *	2	1
Arsenal	2	3

CARLING CUP FINAL 2007

Millennium Stadium, Cardiff, 25-02-2007, Att: 70 073, Ref: Webb

Liverpool *	3
Arsenal	6

Chelsea	2	Drogba 2 [20] [84]
Arsenal	1	Walcott [12]

Chelsea - Petr CECH - Lassana DIARRA•, John TERRY (John MIKEL 63•96+), Ricardo CARVALHO•, Wayne BRIDGE - Claude MAKELELE (Arjen ROBBEN 45), Frank LAMPARD•, Michael BALLACK, Michael ESSIEN• - Andriy SHEVCHENKO (Salomon KALOU 99+), Didier DROGBA. Tr: José MOURINHO

Arsenal - Manuel ALMUNIA - Justin HOYTE, Kolo TOURE•96+, Philippe SENDEROS, Armand TRAORE (Emmanuel EBOUE 66), Theo WALCOTT, Cesc FABREGAS, DENILSON, Abou DIABY (Alexander HLEB 68) - Jérémie ALIADIERE (Emmanuel ADEBAYOR 80•96+), Júlio BAPTISTA. Tr: Arsène WENGER

‡ Qualified for the UEFA Cup

MANCHESTER UNITED 2006–07

Date	Opponents	Score				Scorers	Att
20-08-2006	Fulham	W	5-1	H	PL	Saha [7], Pearce OG [15], Rooney 2 [16 64], Ronaldo [19]	75 115
23-08-2006	Charlton Athletic	W	3-0	A	PL	Fletcher [49], Saha [80], Solskjaer [90]	25 422
26-08-2006	Watford	W	2-1	A	PL	Silvestre [12], Giggs [52]	19 453
9-09-2006	Tottenham Hotspur	W	1-0	H	PL	Giggs [9]	75 433
13-09-2006	Celtic - SCO	W	3-2	H	CLgF	Saha 2 [30p 40], Solskjaer [47]	74 031
17-09-2006	Arsenal	L	0-1	H	PL		75 595
23-09-2006	Reading	D	1-1	A	PL	Ronaldo [73]	24 098
26-09-2006	Benfica - POR	W	1-0	A	CLgF	Saha [60]	53 000
1-10-2006	Newcastle United	W	2-0	H	PL	Solskjaer 2 [41 49]	75 664
14-10-2006	Wigan Athletic	W	3-1	A	PL	Vidic [62], Saha [66], Solskjaer [93+]	20 631
17-10-2006	FC København - DEN	W	3-0	H	CLgF	Scholes [39], O'Shea [46], Richardson [83]	72 020
22-10-2006	Liverpool	W	2-0	H	PL	Scholes [39], Ferdinand [66]	75 828
25-10-2006	Crewe Alexandra	W	2-1	A	LCr3	Solskjaer [26], Lee [119]	10 046
28-10-2006	Bolton Wanderers	W	4-0	A	PL	Rooney 3 [10 16 89], Ronaldo [82]	27 229
1-11-2006	FC København - DEN	L	0-1	A	CLgF		40 308
4-11-2006	Portsmouth	W	3-0	H	PL	Saha [3], Ronaldo [10], Vidic [66]	76 004
7-11-2006	Southend United	L	0-1	A	LCr4		11 532
11-11-2006	Blackburn Rovers	W	1-0	A	PL	Saha [64]	26 162
18-11-2006	Sheffield United	W	2-1	A	PL	Rooney 2 [30 75]	32 584
21-11-2006	Celtic - SCO	L	0-1	A	CLgF		59 179
26-11-2006	Chelsea	D	1-1	H	PL	Saha [29]	75 948
29-11-2006	Everton	W	3-0	H	PL	Ronaldo [39], Evra [36], O'Shea [89]	75 723
2-12-2006	Middlesbrough	W	2-1	A	PL	Saha [19], Fletcher [68]	31 238
6-12-2006	Benfica - POR	W	3-1	H	CLgF	Vidic [46+], Giggs [61], Saha [75]	74 955
9-12-2006	Manchester City	W	3-1	H	PL	Rooney [6], Saha [45], Ronaldo [84]	75 858
17-12-2006	West Ham United	L	0-1	H	PL		34 966
23-12-2006	Aston Villa	W	3-0	A	PL	Ronaldo 2 [58 85], Scholes [64]	42 551
26-12-2006	Wigan Athletic	W	3-1	H	PL	Ronaldo 2 [47 51], Solskjaer [59]	76 018
30-12-2006	Reading	W	3-2	H	PL	Solskjaer [33], Ronaldo 2 [59 77]	75 910
1-01-2007	Newcastle United	D	2-2	A	PL	Scholes 2 [40 46]	52 302
7-01-2007	Aston Villa	W	2-1	H	FACr3	Larsson [54], Solskjaer [90]	74 924
13-01-2007	Aston Villa	W	3-1	A	PL	Park [11], Carrick [13], Ronaldo [35]	76 078
21-01-2007	Arsenal	L	1-2	A	PL	Rooney [53]	60 128
27-01-2007	Portsmouth	W	2-1	H	FACr4	Rooney 2 [76 82]	71 173
31-01-2007	Watford	W	4-0	H	PL	Ronaldo [20], Doyley OG [61], Larsson [70], Rooney [71]	76 032
4-02-2007	Tottenham Hotspur	W	4-0	H	PL	Ronaldo [45], Vidic [48], Scholes [54], Giggs [77]	36 146
10-02-2007	Charlton Athletic	W	2-0	H	PL	Park [24], Fletcher [82]	75 883
17-02-2007	Reading	D	1-1	H	FACr5	Carrick [45]	70 608
20-02-2007	Lille OSC - FRA	W	1-0	**A**	CLr2	Giggs [83]	40 725
24-02-2007	Fulham	W	2-1	A	PL	Giggs [29], Ronaldo [88]	24 459
27-02-2007	Reading	W	3-2	A	FACr5	Heinze [1], Saha [3], Solskjaer [5]	23 821
3-03-2007	Liverpool	W	1-0	A	PL	O'Shea [91+]	44 403
7-03-2007	Lille OSC - FRA	W	1-0	H	CLr2	Larsson [72]	75 182
10-03-2007	Middlesbrough	D	2-2	A	FACqf	Rooney [22], Ronaldo [67p]	33 308
17-03-2007	Bolton Wanderers	W	4-1	H	PL	Park 2 [14 25], Rooney 2 [17 74]	76 058
19-03-2007	Middlesbrough	W	1-0	H	FACqf	Ronaldo [75p]	71 325
31-03-2007	Blackburn Rovers	W	4-1	H	PL	Scholes [61], Carrick [73], Park [83], Solskjaer [90]	76 098
4-04-2007	Roma - ITA	L	1-2	A	CLqf	Rooney [60]	68 389
7-04-2007	Portsmouth	L	1-2	A	PL	O'Shea [90]	20 223
10-04-2007	Roma - ITA	W	7-1	H	CLqf	Carrick 2 [11 60], Smith [17], Rooney [19], Ronaldo 2 [44 49], Evra [81]	74 476
14-04-2007	Watford	W	4-1	N	FACsf	Rooney 2 [6 65], Ronaldo [27], Richardson [81]	37 425
17-04-2007	Sheffield United	W	2-0	H	PL	Carrick [4], Rooney [50]	75 540
21-04-2007	Middlesbrough	D	1-1	H	PL	Richardson [3]	75 967
24-04-2007	Milan - ITA	W	3-2	H	CLsf	Ronaldo [5], Rooney 2 [59 91+]	73 820
28-04-2007	Everton	W	4-2	A	PL	O'Shea [61], Neville.P OG [68], Rooney [79], Eagles [93+]	39 682
2-05-2007	Milan	L	0-3	A	CLsf		67 500
5-05-2007	Manchester City	W	1-0	H	PL	Ronaldo [34p]	47 244
9-05-2007	Chelsea	D	0-0	A	PL		41 794
13-05-2007	West Ham United	L	0-1	H	PL		75 927
19-05-2007	Chelsea	L	0-1	**N**	FACf		89 826

PL = FA Premier League (Barclays Premiership) • CL = UEFA Champions League • FAC = FA Cup • LC = Carling League Cup
gF = Group F • r3 = 3rd round • r4 = 4th round • r5 = 5th round • qf = quarter-final • sf = semi-final • f = final
A = Stade Félix-Bollaert, Lens • N = Villa Park • **N** = Wembley

CHELSEA 2006-07

Date	Opponents	Score		Comp	Scorers	Att
13-08-2006	Liverpool	L	1-2	N	CS	Shevchenko [43]	56 275
20-08-2006	Manchester City	W	3-0	H	PL	Terry [11], Lampard [26], Drogba [78]	41 953
23-08-2006	Middlesbrough	L	1-2	A	PL	Shevchenko [16]	29 198
27-08-2006	Blackburn Rovers	W	2-0	A	PL	Lampard [50], Drogba [81]	19 398
9-09-2006	Charlton Athletic	W	2-1	H	PL	Drogba [6], Carvalho [63]	41 194
12-09-2006	Werder Bremen - GER	W	2-0	H	CLgA	Essien [24], Ballack [68p]	32 135
17-09-2006	Liverpool	W	1-0	H	PL	Drogba [42]	41 882
23-09-2006	Fulham	W	2-0	A	PL	Lampard 2 [73 80]	24 290
27-09-2006	Levski Sofia - BUL	W	3-1	A	CLgA	Drogba 3 [39 52 68]	42 226
30-09-2006	Aston Villa	D	1-1	H	PL	Drogba [3]	41 951
14-10-2006	Reading	W	1-0	A	PL	Ingimarson OG [48+]	24 025
18-10-2006	Barcelona - ESP	W	1-0	H	CLgA	Drogba [47]	40 599
21-10-2006	Portsmouth	W	2-1	H	PL	Shevchenko [55], Ballack [57]	41 838
25-10-2006	Blackburn Rovers	W	2-0	A	LCr3	Cole.J [53], Kalou [81]	14 732
28-10-2006	Sheffield United	W	2-0	H	PL	Lampard [43], Ballack [49]	32 321
31-10-2006	Barcelona - ESP	D	2-2	A	CLgA	Lampard [52], Drogba [93+]	90 166
5-11-2006	Tottenham Hotspur	L	1-2	A	PL	Makelele [15]	36 070
8-11-2006	Aston Villa	W	4-0	H	LCr4	Lampard [32], Shevchenko [65], Essien [82], Drogba [84]	41 516
11-11-2006	Watford	W	4-0	H	PL	Drogba 3 [27 36 69], Shevchenko [52]	41 936
18-11-2006	West Ham United	W	1-0	H	PL	Geremi [22]	41 916
22-11-2006	Werder Bremen - GER	L	0-1	H	CLgA		36 908
26-11-2006	Manchester United	D	1-1	A	PL	Carvalho [69]	75 948
29-11-2006	Bolton Wanderers	W	1-0	A	PL	Ballack [48+]	23 559
5-12-2006	Levski Sofia - BUL	W	2-0	H	CLgA	Shevchenko [27], Wright-Phillips [83]	33 358
10-12-2006	Arsenal	D	1-1	H	PL	Essien [84]	41 917
13-12-2006	Newcastle United	W	1-0	H	PL	Drogba [74]	41 945
17-12-2006	Everton	W	3-2	H	PL	Ballack [49], Lampard [81], Drogba [87]	33 970
20-12-2006	Newcastle United	W	1-0	A	LCqf	Drogba [79]	37 406
23-12-2006	Wigan Athletic	W	3-2	A	PL	Lampard [13], Kalou [31], Robben [93+]	22 077
26-12-2006	Reading	D	2-2	H	PL	Drogba 2 [38 72]	41 885
30-12-2006	Fulham	D	2-2	H	PL	Rosenior OG [35], Drogba [62]	41 926
2-01-2007	Aston Villa	D	0-0	A	PL		41 006
6-01-2007	Macclesfield Town	W	6-1	H	FACr3	Lampard 3 [16 40 50p], Wright-Phillips [67], Mikel [81], Carvalho [85]	41 434
10-01-2007	Wycombe Wanderers	D	1-1	A	LCsf	Bridge [36]	5 771
13-01-2007	Wigan Athletic	W	4-0	H	PL	Lampard [13], Robben [63], Kirkland OG [70], Drogba [92+]	40 846
20-01-2007	Liverpool	L	0-2	A	PL		44 245
23-01-2007	Wycombe Wanderers	W	4-0	H	LCsf	Shevchenko 2 [22 43], Lampard 2 [69 90]	41 591
28-01-2007	Nottingham Forest	W	3-0	H	FACr4	Shevchenko [8], Drogba [17], Mikel [45]	41 516
31-01-2007	Blackburn Rovers	W	3-0	H	PL	Drogba [6], Lampard [67], Kalou [91+]	38 000
3-02-2007	Charlton Athletic	W	1-0	A	PL	Lampard [18]	27 111
10-02-2007	Middlesbrough	W	3-0	H	PL	Drogba 2 [47+ 83], Xavier OG [66]	41 699
17-02-2007	Norwich City	W	4-0	H	FACr5	Wright-Phillips [38], Drogba [51], Essien [90], Shevchenko [90]	41 537
21-02-2007	FC Porto - POR	D	1-1	A	CLr2	Shevchenko [16]	50 216
25-02-2007	Arsenal	W	2-1	N	LCf	Drogba 2 [20 84]	70 073
3-03-2007	Portsmouth	W	2-0	A	PL	Drogba [33], Kalou [82]	20 219
6-03-2007	FC Porto - POR	W	2-1	H	CLr2	Robben [48], Ballack [79]	39 113
11-03-2007	Tottenham Hotspur	D	3-3	H	FACqf	Lampard 2 [21 70], Kalou [85]	41 471
14-03-2007	Manchester City	W	1-0	H	PL	Lampard [28p]	39 429
17-03-2007	Sheffield United	W	3-0	H	PL	Shevchenko [4], Kalou [17], Ballack [58]	41 897
19-03-2007	Tottenham Hotspur	W	2-1	A	FACqf	Shevchenko [54], Wright-Phillips [60]	34 400
31-03-2007	Watford	W	1-0	H	PL	Kalou [92+]	19 793
4-04-2007	Valencia -ESP	D	1-1	H	CLqf	Drogba [53]	38 065
7-04-2007	Tottenham Hotspur	W	1-0	H	PL	Carvalho [52]	41 864
10-04-2007	Valencia - ESP	W	2-1	A	CLqf	Shevchenko [52], Essien [90]	47 280
15-04-2007	Blackburn Rovers	W	2-1	N	FACsf	Lampard [15], Ballack [108]	50 559
18-04-2007	West Ham United	W	4-1	H	PL	Wright-Phillips 2 [31 36], Kalou [52], Drogba [62]	34 966
22-04-2007	Newcastle United	D	0-0	A	PL		52 056
25-04-2007	Liverpool - ENG	W	1-0	H	CLsf	Cole.J [29]	39 483
28-04-2007	Bolton Wanderers	D	2-2	H	PL	Kalou [22], Jaaskelainen OG [34]	41 105
1-05-2007	Liverpool - ENG	L	0-1	A	CLsf	L 1-4 on pens	42 554
5-05-2007	Arsenal	D	1-1	A	PL	Essien [70]	60 102
9-05-2007	Manchester United	D	0-0	H	PL		41 794
13-05-2007	Everton	D	1-1	H	PL	Drogba [57]	41 746
19-05-2007	Manchester United	W	1-0	N	FACf	Drogba [116]	89 826

CS = Community Shield • PL = FA Premier League (Barclays Premiership) • CL = UEFA Champions League • FAC = FA Cup • LC = Carling League Cup
gA = Group A • r3 = 3rd round • r4 = 4th round • r5 = 5th round • qf = quarter-final • sf = semi-final • f = final
N = Millennium Stadium • *N* = Old Trafford • N = Wembley

LIVERPOOL 2006–07

Date	Opponents		Score			Scorers	Att
9-08-2006	Maccabi Haifa - ISR	W	2-1	H	CLpr3	Bellamy [32], Gonzalez [87]	40 058
13-08-2006	Chelsea	W	2-1	N	CS	Riise [9], Crouch [80]	56 275
19-08-2006	Sheffield United	D	1-1	A	PL	Fowler [70]	31 726
22-08-2006	Maccabi Haifa - ISR	D	1-1	N	CLpr3	Crouch [54]	15 000
26-08-2006	West Ham United	W	2-1	H	PL	Agger [42], Crouch [45]	43 965
9-09-2006	Everton	L	0-3	A	PL		40 004
12-09-2006	PSV Eindhoven - NED	D	0-0	A	CLgC		32 000
17-09-2006	Chelsea	L	0-1	A	PL		41 882
20-09-2006	Newcastle United	W	2-0	H	PL	Kuyt [29], Alonso [79]	43 754
23-09-2006	Tottenham Hotspur	W	3-0	H	PL	Gonzalez [63], Kuijt [73], Riise [89]	44 330
27-09-2007	Galatasaray - TUR	W	3-2	H	CLgC	Crouch 2 [9 52], Luis Garcia [14]	41 976
30-09-2006	Bolton Wanderers	L	0-2	A	PL		25 061
14-10-2006	Blackburn Rovers	D	1-1	H	PL	Bellamy [64]	44 206
18-10-2006	Girondins Bordeaux - FRA	W	1-0	A	CLgC	Crouch [58]	31 471
22-10-2006	Manchester United	L	0-2	A	PL		75 828
25-10-2006	Reading	W	4-3	H	LCr3	Fowler [44], Riise [45], Paletta [49], Crouch [77]	42 445
28-10-2006	Aston Villa	W	3-1	H	PL	Kuijt [31], Crouch [38], Luis Garcia [44]	44 117
31-10-2006	Girondins Bordeaux - FRA	W	3-0	H	CLgC	Luis Garcia 2 [23 76], Gerrard [72]	41 978
4-11-2006	Reading	W	2-0	H	PL	Kuijt 2 [14 73]	43 741
8-11-2006	Birmingham City	W	1-0	A	LCr4	Agger [45]	23 061
12-11-2006	Arsenal	L	0-3	A	PL		60 110
18-11-2006	Middlesbrough	D	0-0	A	PL		31 424
22-11-2006	PSV Eindhoven - NED	W	2-0	H	CLgC	Gerrard [65], Crouch [89]	41 948
25-11-2006	Manchester City	W	1-0	H	PL	Gerrard [67]	44 081
29-11-2006	Portsmouth	D	0-0	H	PL		42 467
2-12-2006	Wigan Athletic	W	4-0	A	PL	Bellamy 2 [9 26], Kuijt [40], McCulloch OG [45]	22 089
5-12-2006	Galatasaray - TUR	L	2-3	A	CLgC	Fowler 2 [22 90]	22 434
9-12-2006	Fulham	W	4-0	H	PL	Gerrard [54], Carragher [61], Luis Garcia [66], Gonzalez [93+]	43 189
16-12-2006	Charlton Athletic	W	3-0	A	PL	Alonso [3], Bellamy [82], Gerrard [88]	27 111
23-12-2006	Watford	W	2-0	H	PL	Bellamy [47], Alonso [88]	42 807
26-12-2006	Blackburn Rovers	L	0-1	A	PL		29 342
30-12-2006	Tottenham Hotspur	W	1-0	A	PL	Luis Garcia [46+]	36 170
1-01-2007	Bolton Wanderers	W	3-0	H	PL	Crouch [61], Gerrard [63], Kuijt [83]	41 370
6-01-2007	Arsenal	L	1-3	H	FACr3	Kuijt [71]	43 619
9-01-2007	Arsenal	L	3-6	H	LCqf	Fowler [32], Gerrard [68], Hyypia [80]	42 614
13-01-2007	Watford	W	3-0	A	PL	Bellamy [34], Crouch 2 [40 48]	19 746
20-01-2007	Chelsea	W	2-0	H	PL	Kuijt [4], Pennant [18]	44 245
30-01-2007	West Ham United	W	2-1	A	PL	Kuijt [46], Crouch [53]	34 966
3-02-2007	Everton	D	0-0	H	PL		44 234
10-02-2007	Newcastle United	L	1-2	H	PL	Bellamy [6]	52 305
21-02-2007	Barcelona	W	2-1	A	CLr2	Bellamy [43], Riise [74]	93 641
24-02-2007	Sheffield United	W	4-0	H	PL	Fowler 2 [20p 25p], Hyypia [70], Gerrard [73]	44 198
3-03-2007	Manchester United	L	0-1	A	PL		44 403
6-03-2007	Barcelona - ESP	L	0-1	H	CLr2		42 579
18-03-2007	Aston Villa	D	0-0	A	PL		42 551
31-03-2007	Arsenal	W	4-1	H	PL	Crouch 3 [4 35 81], Agger [60]	43 958
3-04-2007	PSV Eindhoven - NED	W	3-0	A	CLqf	Gerrard [27], Riise [49], Crouch [63]	35 100
7-04-2007	Reading	W	2-1	A	PL	Arbeloa [15], Kuijt [86]	24 121
11-04-2007	PSV Eindhoven - NED	W	1-0	H	CLqf	Crouch [67]	41 447
14-04-2007	Manchester City	D	0-0	A	PL		45 883
18-04-2007	Middlesbrough	W	2-0	H	PL	Gerrard 2 [58 65]	41 458
21-04-2007	Wigan Athletic	W	2-0	H	PL	Kuijt 2 [30 68]	44 003
25-04-2007	Chelsea - ENG	L	0-1	A	CLsf		39 483
28-04-2007	Portsmouth	L	1-2	A	PL	Hyypia [59]	20 201
1-05-2007	Chelsea - ENG	W	1-0	H	CLsf	Agger [22], W 4-1 on pens	42 554
5-05-2007	Fulham	L	0-1	A	PL		24 554
13-05-2007	Charlton Athletic	D	2-2	H	PL	Alonso [62], Kewell [90p]	43 134
23-05-2007	Milan - ITA	L	1-2	N	CLf	Kuijt [89]	63 800

CS = Community Shield • PL = FA Premier League (Barclays Premiership) • CL = UEFA Champions League • FAC = FA Cup • LC = Carling League Cup
pr3 = third preliminary round • gC = Group C • r3 = 3rd round • r4 = 4th round • qf = quarter-final • sf = semi-final • f = final
N = Millennium Stadium • N = Kiev • N = Olympic Stadium, Athens

ARSENAL 2006–07

Date	Opponents		Score			Scorers	Att
8-08-2006	Dinamo Zagreb - CRO	W	3-0	A	CLpr3	Fabregas 2 [63 78], Van Persie [64]	31 120
19-08-2006	Aston Villa	D	1-1	H	PL	Gilberto [84]	60 023
23-08-2006	Dinamo Zagreb - CRO	W	2-1	H	CLpr3	Ljungberg [77], Flamini [91+]	52 498
26-08-2006	Manchester City	L	0-1	A	PL		40 699
9-09-2006	Middlesbrough	D	1-1	H	PL	Henry [67]	60 007
13-09-2006	Hamburger SV - GER	W	2-1	A	CLgG	Gilberto [12p], Rosicky [53]	50 389
17-09-2006	Manchester united	W	1-0	H	PL	Adebayor [86]	75 595
23-09-2006	Sheffield United	W	3-0	H	PL	Gallas [65], Jagielka OG [69], Henry [80]	59 912
26-09-2007	FC Porto - POR	W	2-0	H	CLgG	Henry [38], Hleb [48]	59 861
30-09-2006	Charlton Athletic	W	2-1	A	PL	Van Persie 2 [32 49]	26 770
14-10-2006	Watford	W	3-0	H	PL	Stewart OG [33], Henry [43], Adebayor [67]	60 018
17-10-2006	CSKA Moskva - RUS	L	0-1	A	CLgG		28 800
22-10-2006	Reading	W	4-0	H	PL	Henry 2 [1 70], Hleb [39], Van Persie [50]	24 004
24-10-2006	West Bromwich Albion	W	2-0	A	LCr3	Aliadiere 2 [34 49]	21 566
28-10-2006	Everton	D	1-1	H	PL	Van Persie [71]	60 047
1-11-2006	CSKA Moskva - RUS	D	0-0	H	CLgG		60 003
5-11-2006	West Ham United	L	0-1	A	PL		34 969
8-11-2006	Everton	W	1-0	A	LCr4	Adebayor [85]	31 045
12-11-2006	Liverpool	W	3-0	H	PL	Flamini [41], Touré [56], Gallas [80]	60 110
18-11-2006	Newcastle United	D	1-1	H	PL	Henry [70]	60 058
21-11-2006	Hamburger SV - GER	W	3-1	H	CLgG	Van Persie [52], Eboué [83], Baptista [88]	59 962
25-11-2006	Bolton Wanderers	L	1-3	A	PL	Gilberto [49+]	24 409
29-11-2006	Fulham	L	1-2	A	PL	Van Persie [36]	24 510
2-12-2006	Tottenham Hotspur	W	3-0	H	PL	Adebayor [20], Gilberto 2 [42 72]	60 115
6-12-2006	FC Porto - POR	D	0-0	A	CLgG		45 609
10-12-2006	Chelsea	D	1-1	A	PL	Flamini [78]	41 917
13-12-2006	Wigan Athletic	W	1-0	A	PL	Adebayor [88]	15 311
16-12-2006	Portsmouth	D	2-2	H	PL	Adebayor [58], Gilberto [60]	60 037
23-12-2006	Blackburn Rovers	W	6-2	H	PL	Gilberto [10], Hleb [23], Adebayor [27], Van Persie 2 [85 88], Flamini [93+]	59 913
26-12-2006	Watford	W	2-1	A	PL	Gilberto [19], Van Persie [83]	19 750
30-12-2006	Sheffield United	L	0-1	A	PL		32 086
2-01-2007	Charlton Athletic	W	4-0	H	PL	Henry [30], Hoyte [46+], Van Persie 2 [76 90]	60 057
6-01-2007	Liverpool	W	3-1	A	FACr3	Rosicky 2 [36 44], Henry [83]	43 619
9-01-2007	Liverpool	W	6-3	H	LCqf	Aliadiere [27], Baptista 4 [40 51+ 60 84], Song [47+]	42 614
13-01-2007	Blackburn Rovers	W	2-0	A	PL	Touré [37], Henry [71]	21 852
21-01-2007	Manchester United	W	2-1	H	PL	Van Persie [83], Henry [93+]	60 128
24-01-2007	Tottenham Hotspur	D	2-2	A	LCsf	Baptista 2 [64 77]	35 485
28-01-2007	Bolton Wanderers	D	1-1	H	FACr4	Touré [77]	59 778
31-01-2007	Tottenham Hotspur	W	3-1	H	LCsf	Adebayor [77], Aliadiere [105], Chimbonda OG [113]	55 872
3-02-2007	Middlesbrough	D	1-1	A	PL	Henry [77]	31 122
11-02-2007	Wigan Athletic	W	2-1	H	PL	Hall OG [81], Rosicky [85]	60 049
14-02-2007	Bolton Wanderers	W	3-1	A	FACr4	Adebayor 2 [12 120], Ljungberg [107]	21 088
17-02-2007	Blackburn Rovers	D	0-0	H	FACr5		56 761
20-02-2007	PSV Eindhoven - NED	L	0-1	A	CLr2		35 100
25-02-2007	Chelsea	L	1-2	N	LCf	Walcott [12]	70 073
28-02-2007	Blackburn Rovers	L	0-1	A	FACr5		18 882
3-03-2007	Reading	W	2-1	H	PL	Silva [51], Baptista [62]	60 132
7-03-2007	PSV Eindhoven - NED	D	1-1	H	CLr2	Alex OG [58]	50 073
14-03-2007	Aston Villa	W	1-0	A	PL	Diaby [10]	39 968
18-03-2007	Everton	L	0-1	A	PL		37 162
31-03-2007	Liverpool	L	1-4	H	PL	Gallas [73]	43 958
7-04-2007	West Ham United	L	0-1	H	PL		60 098
9-04-2007	Newcastle United	D	0-0	A	PL		52 293
14-04-2007	Bolton Wanderers	W	2-1	H	PL	Rosicky [31], Fabregas [46]	60 101
21-04-2007	Tottenham Hotspur	D	2-2	H	PL	Touré [64], Adebayor [78]	36 050
29-04-2007	Fulham	W	3-1	H	PL	Baptista [4], Adebayor [84], Silva [87]	60 043
6-05-2007	Chelsea	D	1-1	H	PL	Silva [43]	60 102
13-05-2007	Portsmouth	D	0-0	A	PL		20 188

PL = FA Premier League (Barclays Premiership) • CL = UEFA Champions League • FAC = FA Cup • LC = Carling League Cup
pr3 = 3rd preliminary round • gG = Group G • r2 = 2nd round • r3 = 3rd round • r4 = 4th round • r5 = 5th round • qf = quarter-final •
sf = semi-final • f = final • N = Millennium Stadium, Cardiff

EQG - EQUATORIAL GUINEA

NATIONAL TEAM RECORD
JULY 10TH 2006 TO JULY 12TH 2010

PL	W	D	L	F	A	%
7	2	2	3	7	10	42.8

FIFA/COCA-COLA WORLD RANKING

1993	1994	1995	1996	1997	1998	1999	2000	2001	2002	2003	2004	2005	2006	High		Low	
-	-	-	-	-	195	188	187	190	192	160	171	171	109	**86**	05/07	**195**	12/98

2006–2007											
08/06	09/06	10/06	11/06	12/06	01/07	02/07	03/07	04/07	05/07	06/07	07/07
92	90	102	107	109	108	107	107	87	86	102	104

The dramatic rise of Equatorial Guinea up the ranks of African football's hierarchy has seen the tiny central African country break into the top 100 of the FIFA/Coca-Cola World Ranking. They reached a high of 86th in May 2007 on the back of solid results at home in the 2008 African Nations Cup qualifiers, where the Nzalang Boys beat both Liberia and Rwanda. Much of this has to do with a vastly expanded player pool as the team actively recruits players with family connections in Spain, the former colonial power. The likes of Benjamín Zarandona at Betis, Rodolfo Bodipo at Deportivo, Juvenal Edjogo at Tenerife, Juan Epitié at Alavés and Javier Balboa at Santander have

INTERNATIONAL HONOURS
CEMAC Cup 2006

all become an integral part of the side. They are complemented by players born in Brazil, Cameroon, Liberia and Senegal, who have been naturalised after playing for clubs in Equatorial Guinea over the last 12 months. The side went through several coaches though after the departure last year of Antonio Dumas, who was followed by Quique Setien of Spain and Brazilian Djordan de Freitas. Home-based players made up the bulk of the side that tried to defend their CEMAC Cup title in Chad in March, but a defeat by eventual winners Congo and a draw with Gabon saw Equatorial Guinea fail to advance past the first round of the annual regional tournament.

THE FIFA BIG COUNT OF 2006

	Male	Female		Total
Number of players	25 240	350	Referees and Assistant Referees	50
Professionals	230		Admin, Coaches, Technical, Medical	65
Amateurs 18+	1 400		Number of clubs	18
Youth under 18	600		Number of teams	48
Unregistered	3 300		Clubs with women's teams	4
Total players	25 590		Players as % of population	4.74%

Federación Ecuatoguineana de Fútbol (FEGUIFUT)
Apartado de correo numero 1017, Malabo, Equatorial Guinea
Tel +240 9 1874   Fax +240 9 6565
feguifut@orange.gq   www.feguifut.net
President: MANGA OBIANG Bonifacio   General Secretary: MARTIN PEDRO Ndong
Vice-President: ESONO MELCHOR Edjo   Treasurer: MANUEL Nsi Nguema   Media Officer: BORABOFA Clemente
Men's Coach: DE FREITAS Djordan   Women's Coach: EKANG Jose Davio
FEGUIFUT formed: 1960   CAF: 1986   FIFA: 1986
Red shirts, Red shorts, Red socks

RECENT INTERNATIONAL MATCHES PLAYED BY EQUATORIAL GUINEA

2003	Opponents	Score		Venue	Comp	Scorers	Att	Referee
22-06	Sierra Leone	L	0-2	Freetown	CNq			
6-07	Morocco	L	0-1	Malabo	CNq			
11-10	Togo	W	1-0	Bata	WCq	Barila 25p	25 000	Evehe CMR
12-11	São Tomé e Príncipe	W	3-1	Malabo	Fr			
16-11	Togo	L	0-2	Lome	WCq		12 000	Mandzioukouta CGO
2004								
No international matches played in 2004								
2005								
5-02	Cameroon †	L	0-3	Libreville	CMr1			
8-02	Chad	D	0-0	Libreville	CMr1			
2006								
26-02	Benin	W	1-0	Cotonou	Fr	Daniel Sahino 9		
4-03	Congo	W	2-1	Bata	CMr1			
6-03	Chad	D	1-1	Bata	CMr1			
11-03	Gabon	D	0-0	Bata	CMsf	W 4-2p		
14-03	Cameroon †	D	1-1	Bata	CMf	W 4-2p		
29-03	Benin	W	2-0	Bata	Fr	Ivan Zarandona 18, Armando Justice 44		
3-09	Liberia	W	2-1	Malabo	CNq	Juan Epitie 24, Rodolfo Bodipo 88		Agbenyega GHA
7-10	Cameroon	L	0-3	Yaounde	CNq			Daami TUN
2007								
5-03	Congo	L	1-2	N'Djamena	CMr1	Desire Pierre 18		
9-03	Gabon	D	1-1	N'Djamena	CMr1	Ibrahima Toure 44p		
25-03	Rwanda	W	3-1	Malabo	CNq	Andre Moreira 29, Juvenal Edjo 75, Juan Epitie 81		Louzaya CGO
2-06	Rwanda	L	0-2	Kigali	CNq			
17-06	Liberia	D	0-0	Monrovia	CNq			

Fr = Friendly match • CN = CAF African Cup of Nations • CM = CEMAC Cup • WC = FIFA World Cup
q = qualifier • r1 = first round group • sf = semi-final • f = final • † Not a full international

EQUATORIAL GUINEA NATIONAL TEAM RECORDS AND RECORD SEQUENCES

Records			Sequence records					
Victory	4-2	CAR 1999	Wins	2	2003, 2006x2	Clean sheets	2	2005-2006
Defeat	0-6	CGO 1990	Defeats	9	1999-2003	Goals scored	3	2006, 2007
Player Caps	n/a		Undefeated	7	2005-2006	Without goal	2	Five times
Player Goals	n/a		Without win	22	1984-1999	Goals against	22	1988-2003

RECENT LEAGUE AND CUP RECORD

Year	Champions	Cup Winners
1997	Deportivo Mongomo	Union Vesper
1998	CD Ela Nguema	Union Vesper
1999	FC Akonangui	CD Unidad
2000	CD Ela Nguema	CD Unidad
2001	FC Akonangui	Atlético Malabo
2002	CD Ela Nguema	FC Akonangui
2003	Atlético Malabo	Deportivo Mongomo
2004	Renacimiento	CD Ela Nguema
2005	Renacimiento	
2006	Renacimiento	

EQUATORIAL GUINEA COUNTRY INFORMATION

Capital	Malabo	Independence	1968 from Spain	GDP per Capita	$2 700
Population	523 051	Status	Republic	GNP Ranking	175
Area km²	28 051	Language	Spanish	Dialling code	+240
Population density	18 per km²	Literacy rate	80%	Internet code	.gq
% in urban areas	42%	Main religion	Christian	GMT +/−	+1
Towns/Cities ('000)	Malabo 101; Bata 82; Ebebiyin 13; Mbini 12; Luba 7				
Neighbours (km)	Cameroon 189; Gabon 350; Bight of Biafra 296. Malabo is on the island of Bioko in the Atlantic				
Main stadia	Internacional – Malabo 6 000				

ERI – ERITREA

NATIONAL TEAM RECORD
JULY 10TH 2006 TO JULY 12TH 2010

PL	W	D	L	F	A	%
8	3	3	2	8	13	56.2

FIFA/COCA-COLA WORLD RANKING

1993	1994	1995	1996	1997	1998	1999	2000	2001	2002	2003	2004	2005	2006	High		Low	
-	-	-	-	-	189	169	158	171	157	155	169	169	140	123	07/07	189	12/98

2006–2007											
08/06	09/06	10/06	11/06	12/06	01/07	02/07	03/07	04/07	05/07	06/07	07/07
177	135	138	135	140	139	140	142	140	139	125	123

Eritrea won away from home in a competitive international for the first time at the start of their 2008 African Nations Cup qualifying campaign, beating Kenya in sensational circumstances in Nairobi, to begin a run of some success for the small Red Sea state. The 2-1 triumph, set up by a horrendous Kenyan own goal early in the game, was the perfect start to their qualifying campaign under Romanian coach Dorian Marian and following a home win against Kenya in June 2007, the Eritreans had won a remarkable eight points to give themselves an outside chance of qualifying for the finals. There was also major success at under–17 level where Eritrea beat Egypt on the way to

INTERNATIONAL HONOURS
None

qualifying for an African championship for the first time. Although Eritrea's juniors conceded 17 goals without scoring and lost all three matches at the tournament in Togo in March, their progress to the finals was a major boost for the game. A week later, however, the senior side received a reality check when they lost heavily against Angola in the Nations Cup, with six players deserting the team to seek political asylum. Eritrea missed out on the annual CECAFA Cup in Ethiopia at the end of 2006, electing to stay away because of the political tension between the two countries, while the 2006 champions, Adulis Club from Asmara, didn't enter the 2007 African Champions League.

THE FIFA BIG COUNT OF 2006

	Male	Female		Total
Number of players	307 799	73 419	Referees and Assistant Referees	239
Professionals	0		Admin, Coaches, Technical, Medical	1 314
Amateurs 18+	6 524		Number of clubs	24
Youth under 18	21		Number of teams	258
Unregistered	694		Clubs with women's teams	2
Total players	381 218		Players as % of population	7.96%

Eritrean National Football Federation (ENFF)
Sematat Avenue 29-31, PO Box 3665, Asmara, Eritrea
Tel +291 1 120335   Fax +291 1 126821
enff@tse.co.er   www.none
President: GEBREYESUS Tesfaye   General Secretary: GHEBREMARIAM Yemane
Vice-President: TBD   Treasurer: GUISH Tuccu   Media Officer: LIJAM Amamel
Men's Coach: MARIN Dorian   Women's Coach: TBD
ENFF formed: 1996   CAF: 1998   FIFA: 1998
Blue shirts, Red shorts, Green socks

RECENT INTERNATIONAL MATCHES PLAYED BY ERITREA

2003	Opponents	Score		Venue	Comp	Scorers	Att	Referee
30-03	Mali	L	0-2	Asmara	CNq			
7-06	Mali	L	0-1	Bamoko	CNq			
21-06	Seychelles	W	1-0	Asmara	CNq	Yonnas Fessehaye [62]		
5-07	Zimbabwe	L	0-2	Harare	CNq			
12-10	Sudan	L	0-3	Khartoum	WCq		18 000	Tamuni LBY
16-11	Sudan	D	0-0	Asmara	WCq		12 000	Abdulle Ahmed SOM
30-11	Uganda	L	1-2	Kassala	CCr1	Ghirmay Shinash [70]		
2-12	Kenya	L	2-3	Kassala	CCr1	Tesfaldet Goitom 2 [30 48]		
2004								
No international matches played in 2004								
2005								
28-11	Zanzibar †	L	0-3	Kigali	CCr1			
30-11	Rwanda	L	2-3	Kigali	CCr1	Suleiman Muhamoul 2		
2-12	Burundi	D	0-0	Kigali	CCr1			
4-12	Tanzania	L	0-1	Kigali	CCr1			
2006								
2-09	Kenya	W	2-1	Nairobi	CNq	Origi OG [15], Shimangus Yidnekachew [67]		Lwanja MWI
7-10	Swaziland	D	0-0	Asmara	CNq			Gasingwa RWA
2007								
7-01	Yemen	L	1-4	Sana'a	Fr			
25-03	Angola	L	1-6	Luanda	CNq	Misgina Besirat [73]		Evehe CMR
21-05	Sudan	W	1-0	Asmara	Fr	Shimangus Yidnekachew [46]		
26-05	Sudan	D	1-1	Asmara	Fr			
2-06	Angola	D	1-1	Asmara	CNq	Elias Ali Abubeker [15]		
16-06	Kenya	W	1-0	Asmara	CNq	Berhane Aregay [80]		

CN = CAF African Cup of Nations • CC = CECAFA Cup • WC = FIFA World Cup • q = qualifier • r1 = first round group • † Not a full international

ERITREA NATIONAL TEAM RECORDS AND RECORD SEQUENCES

Records			Sequence records					
Victory	2-0	KEN 1994	Wins	2	1994	Clean sheets	3	1994
Defeat	1-6	ANG 2007	Defeats	3	Three times	Goals scored	6	2007
Player Caps	n/a		Undefeated	4	2007	Without goal	6	1999-2000
Player Goals	n/a		Without win	10	2000-2002	Goals against	9	2001-2003

RECENT LEAGUE AND CUP RECORD

Year	Champions	Cup Winners
1998	Red Sea FC Asmara	Hintsa Asmara
1999	Red Sea FC Asmara	
2000	Red Sea FC Asmara	
2001	Hintsa Asmara	
2002	Red Sea FC Asmara	
2003	Anseba Sports Club Keren	
2004	Adulis Club Asmara	
2005	Red Sea FC Asmara	
2006	Adulis Club Asmara	
2007		

ERITREA COUNTRY INFORMATION

Capital	Asmara	Independence	1993	GDP per Capita	$700
Population	4 447 307	Status	Transitional	GNP Ranking	162
Area km²	121 320	Language	Tigrinya, Arabic	Dialling code	+291
Population density	36 per km²	Literacy rate	80%	Internet code	.er
% in urban areas	17%	Main religion	Christian, Muslim	GMT +/−	+3
Towns/Cities ('000)	Asmara 563; Assab 78; Keren 58; Mitsiwa 39; Addi Ugri 17; Barentu 15; Addi Keyih 13				
Neighbours (km)	Djibouti 109; Ethiopia 912; Sudan 605; Red Sea 2 234				
Main stadia	ChicChero – Asmara 12 000				

ESP – SPAIN

NATIONAL TEAM RECORD
JULY 10TH 2006 TO JULY 12TH 2010

PL	W	D	L	F	A	%
11	7	1	3	16	8	68.1

It may have not been a vintage year for Spanish football but the season was never without interest. It began in terrible fashion for the national team with an embarrassing defeat in Belfast to Northern Ireland in the qualifiers for UEFA Euro 2008 and that was then followed by defeat away to Sweden, leaving Spain's ambitions for the tournament looking decidely shaky. Coach Luis Aragonés remained at the helm despite widespread criticism and from the start of 2007 results improved with five straight wins, to put Spain back in contention for the finals. There was also a mixed season in European club football with both defending champions Barcelona and Real Madrid knocked out of the Champions League in the first knock-out round. Valencia went one round further but they were undone by a last-minute goal at home to Chelsea and Spain were left without a representative in the last four for only the third time in the past decade. Spanish clubs did, however, occupy three of the semi-finals berths in the UEFA Cup. The city of Glasgow turned Spanish for the day of the final between Sevilla and Espanyol and both clubs contributed to the spectacle with an entertaining match. In the end Sevilla retained the title on penalties after a 2-2 draw. The Andalusian club had

INTERNATIONAL HONOURS
Qualified for the FIFA World Cup™ finals 1934 1950 1962 1966 1978 1982 (hosts) 1986 1990 1994 1998 2002 2006
Olympic Gold 1992   **FIFA Futsal World Championship** 2000 2004
FIFA World Youth Championship 1999   **FIFA Junior Tournament** 1952 1954
UEFA U-21 Championship 1986 1998 **UEFA U-19 Championship** 1995 2002 2004 2006 **UEFA U-17 Championship** 1986 1988 1991 1997 1999 2001
UEFA Champions League Real Madrid 1956 1957 1958 1959 1960 1966 1998 2000 2002 Barcelona 1992 2006

a fantastic season, also winning the Copa del Rey and leading the championship for much of the campaign. Indeed, they were still in with a chance of winning it on the final day. In the event, it was won by Real Madrid who finished level on points with Barcelona but with a better head-to-head record. Real's achievement was extraordinary given the crisis the club endured mid-season. Successive defeats against Recreativo and Deportivo, along with two lacklustre performances, almost saw coach Fabio Capello on his way out. Real were accused of playing dull and defensive football but thanks largely to the goals of Ruud Van Nistelrooij, players like David Beckham rediscovering their form, and their uncanny knack of winning games at the death, Real won 10 of their last 12 matches to lift their first trophy in four years. For Barcelona it was a disappointing season but for those in the Camp Nou for the Copa de Rey semi-final against Getafe, they will always be able to say that they were there when Lionel Messi scored the goal of the season and perhaps one of the greatest goals of all-time - better even, some said, than the Maradona goal in 1986 against England to which it bore a remarkable resemblance.

Real Federación Española de Fútbol (RFEF)
Ramon y Cajal s/n, Apartado postale 385, Las Rozas 28230, Madrid, Spain
Tel +34 91 4959800   Fax +34 91 4959801
rfef@rfef.es   www.rfef.es
President: VILLAR LLONA Angel Maria   General Secretary: PEREZ Jorge
Vice-President: PADRON Juan   Treasurer: LARREA Juan   Media Officer: ANTORANZ Paloma
Men's Coach: ARAGONES Luis   Women's Coach: QUEREDA Ignacio
RFEF formed: 1913   UEFA: 1954   FIFA: 1904
Red shirts with yellow trimmings, Blue shorts, Blue socks or White shirts with red trimmings, White shorts, White socks

RECENT INTERNATIONAL MATCHES PLAYED BY SPAIN

2004 Opponents	Score	Venue	Comp	Scorers	Att	Referee
18-02 Peru	W 2-1	Barcelona	Fr	Etxeberria [30], Baraja [32]	23 580	Layec FRA
31-03 Denmark	W 2-0	Gijon	Fr	Morientes [22], Raúl [60]	18 600	Almeida Costa POR
28-04 Italy	D 1-1	Genoa	Fr	Torres [53]	30 300	Poll ENG
5-06 Andorra	W 4-0	Getafe	Fr	Morientes [25], Baraja [45], Cesar [65], Valeron [89]	14 000	Trefolini ITA
12-06 Russia	W 1-0	Faro-Loule	ECr1	Valeron [60]	28 100	Meier SUI
16-06 Greece	D 1-1	Porto	ECr1	Morientes [28]	25 444	Michel SVK
20-06 Portugal	L 0-1	Lisbon	ECr1		52 000	Frisk SWE
18-08 Venezuela	W 3-2	Las Palmas	Fr	Morientes [40], Tamudo 2 [56 67]	32 500	Rodomonti ITA
3-09 Scotland	D 1-1	Valencia	Fr	Raúl [56p]. Abandoned 59' after floodlight failure	11 000	Bre FRA
8-09 Bosnia-Herzegovina	D 1-1	Zenica	WCq	Vicente [65]	14 380	De Santis ITA
9-10 Belgium	W 2-0	Santander	WCq	Luque [60], Raúl [65]	17 000	Nielsen DEN
13-10 Lithuania	D 0-0	Vilnius	WCq		9 114	Pouat FRA
17-11 England	W 1-0	Madrid	Fr	Del Horno [9]	70 000	Kasnaferis GRE
2005						
9-02 San Marino	W 5-0	Almeria	WCq	Joaquin [15], Torres [32], Raúl [42], Guti [61], Del Horno [75]	12 580	Clark SCO
26-03 China	W 3-0	Salamanca	Fr	Torres [3p], Xavi [32], Joaquin [53]	17 000	Cortes POR
30-03 Serbia & Montenegro	D 0-0	Belgrade	WCq		48 910	Busacca SUI
4-06 Lithuania	W 1-0	Valencia	WCq	Luque [68]	25 000	Farina ITA
8-06 Bosnia-Herzegovina	D 1-1	Valencia	WCq	Marchena [96+]	38 041	Bennett ENG
17-08 Uruguay	W 2-0	Gijon	Fr	OG [24], Vicente [38p]	23 348	Benquerenca POR
3-09 Canada	W 2-1	Santander	Fr	Tamudo [7], Morientes [69]	11 978	Colombo FRA
7-09 Serbia & Montenegro	D 1-1	Madrid	WCq	Raul [19]	51 491	Poll ENG
8-10 Belgium	W 2-0	Brussels	WCq	Fernando Torres 2 [56 66]	40 300	Michel SVK
12-10 San Marino	W 6-0	Serravalle	WCq	Antonio Lopez [1], Fernando Torres 3 [11 78 89p], Sergio Ramos 2 [31 48]	3 426	Meyer GER
12-11 Slovakia	W 5-1	Madrid	WCpo	Luis Garcia 3 [10 18 75], Fernando Torres [65], Morientes [79]	47 210	De Santis ITA
16-11 Slovakia	D 1-1	Bratislava	WCpo	Villa [71]	23 587	Merk GER
2006						
1-03 Côte d'Ivoire	W 3-2	Valladolid	Fr	Villa [22], Reyes [74], Juanito [85]	30 000	Rodomonti ITA
27-05 Russia	D 0-0	Albacete	Fr		15 000	Ferreira POR
3-06 Egypt	W 2-0	Elche	Fr	Raul [14], Reyes [57]	38 000	Farina ITA
7-06 Croatia	W 2-1	Geneva	Fr	Pernia [62], Fernando Torres [92+]	15 000	Lannoy FRA
14-06 Ukraine	W 4-0	Leipzig	WCr1	Xabi Alonso [13], Villa 2 [17 48p], Fernando Torres [81]	43 000	Busacca SUI
19-06 Tunisia	W 3-1	Stuttgart	WCr1	Raul [71], Fernando Torres 2 [76 91+]	52 000	Simon BRA
23-06 Saudi Arabia	W 1-0	Kaiserslautern	WCr1	Juanito [36]	46 000	Codjia BEN
27-06 France	L 1-3	Hanover	WCr2	Villa [28p]	43 000	Rosetti ITA
15-08 Iceland	D 0-0	Reykjavik	Fr		12 327	Stokes IRL
2-09 Liechtenstein	W 4-0	Badajoz	ECq	Torres [20], Villa 2 [45 62], Luis Garcia [66]	13 876	Bozinovski MKD
6-09 Northern Ireland	L 2-3	Belfast	ECq	Xavi [14], Villa [52]	13 885	De Bleeckere BEL
7-10 Sweden	L 0-2	Stockholm	ECq		41 482	Bennett ENG
11-10 Argentina	W 2-1	Murcia	Fr	Xavi [33], Villa [64p]	31 000	Duhamel FRA
15-11 Romania	L 0-1	Cadiz	Fr		15 000	Messina ITA
2007						
7-02 England	W 1-0	Manchester	Fr	Iniesta [63]	58 247	Weiner GER
24-03 Denmark	W 2-1	Madrid	ECq	Morientes [34], Villa [46+]	73 575	Busacca SUI
28-03 Iceland	W 1-0	Palma	ECq	Iniesta [81]	18 326	Duhamel FRA
2-06 Latvia	W 2-0	Riga	ECq	Villa [45], Xavi [60]	10 000	Thomson SCO
6-06 Liechtenstein	W 2-0	Vaduz	ECq	Villa 2 [8 14]	5 739	Ivanov.N RUS

Fr = Friendly match • EC = UEFA EURO 2004/2008 • WC = FIFA World Cup • q = qualifier • po = play-off • r1 = first round group • r2 = second round

SPAIN NATIONAL TEAM RECORDS AND RECORD SEQUENCES

Records			Sequence records		
Victory	13-0	BUL 1933	Wins	9	1924-1927
Defeat	1-7	ITA 1928, ENG 1931	Defeats	3	Five times
Player Caps	126	ZUBIZARRETA Andoni	Undefeated	30	1994-1997
Player Goals	44	Raúl	Without win	10	1980
			Clean sheets	7	1992
			Goals scored	20	1947-1951
			Without goal	3	1985, 1992
			Goals against	11	1952 1955

MAJOR CITIES/TOWNS
Population '000

1	Madrid	6 097
2	Barcelona	4 853
3	Valencia	1 759
4	Sevilla	1 293
5	Bilbao	1 132
6	Málaga	851
7	Las Palmas	684
8	Zaragoza	683
9	Murcia	626
10	Palma	481
11	Granada	467
12	Alicante	460
13	Oviedo	432
14	Tenerife	427
15	Vigo	407
16	Donostia †	400
17	Cádiz	398
18	Valladolid	379
19	La Coruña	375
20	Pamplona	300
21	Gijón	283
22	Vitoria	227
23	Santander	183
24	Huelva	144

KINGDOM OF SPAIN; REINO DE ESPANA

Capital Madrid	Language Spanish, Catalan, Galician, Basque	Independence 1492
Population 40 397 842	Area 504 782 km² Density 79 per km²	% in cities 76%
GDP per cap $22 000	Dailling code +34 Internet .es	GMT +/- +1

The population totals for the Spanish cities above are for the metropolitan areas where relevant. † Official name is Donostia-San Sebastián

MEDALS TABLE

	Overall G S B	League G S B	Cup G S	Europe G S B	City	Stadium	Cap'ty	DoF
1 Real Madrid	58 41 17	30 17 7	17 19	11 5 10	Madrid	Santiago Bernabeu	80 000	1902
2 Barcelona	51 37 19	18 22 11	24 8	9 6 8	Barcelona	Camp Nou	98 260	1899
3 Athletic Bilbao	31 19 10	8 7 10	23 11	1	Bilbao	San Mamés	39 750	1898
4 Atlético Madrid	19 19 19	9 8 12	9 8	1 3 7	Madrid	Vicente Calderón	54 851	1903
5 Valencia	16 18 7	6 6 7	6 9	4 3	Valencia	Mestalla	55 000	1919
6 Real Zaragoza	8 7 6	1 4	6 5	2 1 2	Zaragoza	La Romareda	34 596	1932
7 Sevilla	7 6 3	1 4 3	4 2	2	Sevilla	Sánchez Pizjuán	43 000	1905
8 Real Sociedad	4 7 3	2 3 2	2 4	1	San Sebastián	Anoeta	32 082	1909
9 RCD Espanyol	4 7 4	4	4 5	2	Barcelona	Olímpic de Montjuïc	55 000	1900
10 Deportivo La Coruña	3 5 6	1 5 4	2	2	La Coruña	Riazor	34 178	1906
11 Real Betis Balompié	3 2 2	1	2	2 2	Sevilla	Ruiz de Lopera	52 500	1907
12 Real Union Irún	3 1		3 1		Irún	Gal	5 000	1915
13 RCD Mallorca	1 3 2	2	1 2	1	Palma	Son Moix	24 142	1916
14 Arenas Guecho Bilbao	1 3 1	1	1 3		Bilbao	Gobela	1 200	1909
15 Racing Irún	1		1		Irún			1908-15

RECENT LEAGUE AND CUP RECORD

	Championship						Cup		
Year	Champions	Pts	Runners-up	Pts	Third	Pts	Winners	Score	Runners-up
1995	Real Madrid	55	Deportivo	51	Real Betis	46	Deportivo	2-1	Valencia
1996	Atlético Madrid	87	Valencia	83	Barcelona	80	Atlético Madrid	1-0	Barcelona
1997	Real Madrid	92	Barcelona	90	Deportivo	77	Barcelona	3-2	Real Betis
1998	Barcelona	74	Athletic Bilbao	65	Real Sociedad	63	Barcelona	1-1 4-3p	Mallorca
1999	Barcelona	79	Real Madrid	68	Mallorca	66	Valencia	3-0	Atlético Madrid
2000	Deportivo	69	Barcelona	64	Valencia	64	Espanyol	2-1	Atlético Madrid
2001	Real Madrid	80	Deportivo	73	Mallorca	71	Real Zaragoza	3-1	Celta Vigo
2002	Valencia	75	Deportivo	68	Real Madrid	66	Deportivo	2-1	Real Madrid
2003	Real Madrid	78	Real Sociedad	76	Deportivo	72	Mallorca	3-0	Recreativo Huelva
2004	Valencia	77	Barcelona	72	Deportivo	71	Real Zaragoza	3-2	Real Madrid
2005	Barcelona	84	Real Madrid	80	Villarreal	65	Real Betis	2-1	Osasuna
2006	Barcelona	82	Real Madrid	70	Valencia	69	Espanyol	4-1	Real Zaragoza
2007	Real Madrid	76	Barcelona	76	Sevilla	71	Sevilla	1-0	Getafe

SPAIN 2006-07

PRIMERA DIVISION

Team	Pl	W	D	L	F	A	Pts
Real Madrid †	38	23	7	8	66	40	76
Barcelona †	38	22	10	6	78	33	76
Sevilla †	38	21	8	9	64	35	71
Valencia †	38	20	6	12	57	42	66
Villarreal ‡	38	18	8	12	48	44	62
Real Zaragoza ‡	38	16	12	10	55	43	60
Atlético Madrid	38	17	9	12	46	39	60
Recreativo Huelva	38	15	9	14	54	52	54
Getafe ‡	38	14	11	13	40	33	53
Racing Santander	38	12	14	12	42	48	50
RCD Espanyol	38	12	13	13	46	53	49
RCD Mallorca	38	14	7	17	41	47	49
Deportivo La Coruña	38	12	11	15	32	45	47
Osasuna	38	13	7	18	51	49	46
Levante	38	10	12	16	37	53	42
Real Betis	38	8	16	14	36	49	40
Athletic Bilbao	38	10	10	18	44	62	40
Celta Vigo	38	10	9	19	40	59	39
Real Sociedad	38	8	11	19	32	47	35
Gimnàstic Tarragona	38	6	8	24	34	70	26

Results grid (home team in rows vs columns: Real Madrid, Barcelona, Sevilla, Valencia, Villarreal, Zaragoza, At. Madrid, Recreativo, Getafe, Racing, Espanyol, Mallorca, Deportivo, Osasuna, Levante, Real Betis, Athletic, Celta, Sociedad, Gimnàstic):

	RMA	BAR	SEV	VAL	VIL	ZAR	ATM	REC	GET	RAC	ESP	MAL	DEP	OSA	LEV	BET	ATH	CEL	SOC	GIM
Real Madrid	–	2-0	3-2	2-1	0-0	1-0	1-1	0-3	1-1	3-1	4-3	3-1	3-1	2-0	0-1	0-0	2-1	1-2	2-0	2-0
Barcelona	3-3	–	3-1	1-1	4-0	3-1	1-1	3-0	1-0	2-0	2-2	1-0	2-1	3-0	1-0	1-1	3-0	3-1	1-0	3-0
Sevilla	2-1	2-1	–	3-0	0-1	3-1	3-1	2-1	1-0	0-0	3-1	1-2	4-0	2-0	4-0	3-2	4-1	2-0	0-0	2-1
Valencia	0-1	2-1	2-0	–	2-3	2-0	3-1	2-0	2-0	0-2	3-2	3-1	4-0	1-0	3-0	2-1	1-1	1-0	3-3	4-0
Villarreal	1-0	2-0	0-0	0-1	–	3-2	0-1	1-0	2-1	0-0	2-1	0-2	1-0	2-1	4-1	1-1	3-2	3-1	1-0	2-0
Real Zaragoza	2-2	1-0	2-1	0-1	1-0	–	1-0	0-0	3-0	1-0	0-3	0-2	0-1	1-1	2-2	2-2	1-4	3-2	3-2	3-0
Atlético Madrid	1-1	0-6	2-1	0-1	3-1	0-1	–	2-1	1-0	1-1	1-2	1-1	2-0	1-0	0-0	1-0	0-1	0-2	3-1	3-0
Recreativo Huelva	2-3	0-4	1-3	2-0	2-1	1-1	1-0	–	1-2	4-2	0-1	1-1	1-1	2-0	0-1	2-0	0-0	4-2	1-0	2-1
Getafe	1-0	1-1	0-0	3-0	3-0	2-2	1-4	1-1	–	1-0	0-1	1-0	2-0	2-0	0-0	1-1	0-0	1-0	0-1	0-0
Racing Santander	2-1	0-3	0-0	1-0	2-1	0-2	0-1	4-3	1-0	–	1-1	0-2	0-0	1-0	2-3	0-2	5-4	1-1	1-0	4-1
RCD Espanyol	0-1	3-1	2-1	1-1	1-1	2-1	0-1	1-5	2-2	3-1	–	1-3	0-0	1-1	2-2	3-2	2-1	1-0	0-1	1-0
RCD Mallorca	0-1	1-4	0-0	0-1	1-2	2-1	0-0	2-1	0-1	2-1	0-0	–	0-0	3-1	3-1	2-0	1-3	2-2	0-0	1-0
Deportivo La Coruña	2-0	1-1	1-2	1-2	2-0	3-2	1-0	2-5	1-0	0-0	0-0	1-0	–	1-0	0-0	0-1	0-2	0-1	2-0	1-0
Osasuna	1-4	0-0	0-0	1-1	1-4	2-2	1-2	1-1	0-2	0-1	0-2	3-0	4-1	–	2-1	5-1	1-1	0-1	2-0	2-0
Levante	1-4	1-1	2-4	4-2	0-2	0-0	0-3	2-1	1-1	2-0	0-0	0-1	2-0	1-4	–	1-1	0-0	1-1	2-0	2-0
Real Betis	0-1	1-0	0-2	1-3	3-1	1-0	1-0	0-0	2-1	1-1	1-0	1-1	0-5	2-1	3-0	–	1-0	0-1	1-1	1-0
Athletic Bilbao	1-4	1-3	1-3	1-0	0-1	0-0	1-4	4-2	2-0	0-0	2-1	1-0	1-1	0-3	2-0	1-2	–	0-1	1-1	0-2
Celta Vigo	1-2	2-3	1-2	3-2	1-1	1-1	1-3	1-2	2-1	2-2	0-2	0-3	1-0	0-2	1-2	2-1	1-1	–	0-0	1-1
Real Sociedad	1-2	0-2	1-3	0-1	0-1	1-3	2-0	2-3	0-0	0-1	3-1	0-1	2-1	1-0	0-0	0-2	3-1	3-2	–	3-2
Gimnàstic Tarragona	1-3	1-5	1-0	1-0	3-1	0-0	3-1	1-1	3-2	4-0	2-3	0-0	2-3	2-1	0-1	2-3	1-2	1-3	2-0	–

26/08/2006 - 17/06/2007 • † Qualified for the UEFA Champions League • ‡ Qualified for the UEFA Cup
Top scorers: Ruud VAN NISTELROOY, Real Madrid 21; Diego MILITO, Real Zaragoza 20; Frederic KANOUTE, Sevilla 20; RONALDINHO, Barcelona 19; Diego FORLAN, Villarreal 15; David VILLA, Valencia 13

SPAIN 2006-07

SEGUNDA DIVISION A (2)

Team	Pl	W	D	L	F	A	Pts
Real Valladolid	42	26	10	6	70	35	88
Almería	42	24	8	10	73	48	80
Real Murcia	42	21	13	8	62	45	76
Ciudad de Murcia	42	18	9	15	52	44	63
Cádiz	42	15	16	11	53	45	61
Albacete	42	16	12	14	49	48	60
Tenerife	42	15	6	18	48	51	60
Numancia	42	15	13	14	48	44	58
Xerez	42	16	10	16	47	42	58
Elche	42	16	10	16	46	46	58
Polideportivo Ejido	42	16	10	16	52	50	58
Salamanca	42	15	12	15	53	50	57
Sporting Gijón	42	16	8	18	53	53	56
Castellón	42	15	11	16	48	41	56
Málaga	42	14	13	15	49	50	55
Hércules	42	14	12	16	48	52	54
Deportivo Alavés	42	13	13	16	51	60	52
Las Palmas	42	13	12	17	51	59	51
Castilla	42	13	10	19	55	67	49
Ponferradina	42	11	13	18	45	61	46
Lorca Deportiva	42	9	10	23	37	60	37
Vecindario	42	9	7	26	42	81	34

Results grid (columns: Valladolid, Almería, Real Murcia, C. Murcia, Cádiz, Albacete, Tenerife, Numancia, Xerez, Elche, Ejido, Salamanca, Sporting, Castellón, Málaga, Hércules, Alavés, Las Palmas, Castilla, Ponferradina, Lorca, Vecindario):

	VLL	ALM	RMU	CMU	CAD	ALB	TEN	NUM	XER	ELC	EJI	SAL	SPG	CAS	MAL	HER	ALA	LPA	CST	PON	LOR	VEC
Real Valladolid	–	2-2	1-1	0-2	2-4	2-1	0-2	0-1	1-1	0-0	1-2	3-1	0-1	0-1	0-0	1-1	0-2	0-4	0-1	0-1	0-3	3-0
Almería	3-2	–	2-1	3-1	2-1	2-1	0-1	3-0	1-1	2-0	3-1	3-1	2-0	2-1	2-2	3-0	2-2	2-2	1-1	0-3	1-4	0-3
Real Murcia	1-4	3-2	–	2-1	1-0	1-1	4-3	0-3	0-0	2-0	1-0	1-3	2-3	1-1	0-3	2-1	1-1	2-0	4-3			
Ciudad de Murcia	1-0	0-1	1-1	–	1-1	2-1	2-1	1-0	1-0	1-3	0-1	0-3	1-1	1-2	0-2	1-5	1-4	2-0	0-1	1-2	1-2	2-0
Cádiz	0-0	2-2	1-1	2-0	–	1-2	1-0	1-0	1-2	3-1	0-0	2-0	1-0	1-2	0-1	1-1	1-0	0-3	3-0	0-0	0-3	0-0
Albacete	0-2	1-1	0-0	2-2	4-1	–	2-0	1-3	0-0	0-0	1-1	1-2	1-0	1-2	1-0	1-2	2-1	1-1	0-2	0-1	0-3	2-...
Tenerife	0-2	2-1	1-1	0-0	1-1	0-0	–	1-0	0-2	2-0	0-1	0-0	4-2	0-1	2-3	2-1	2-3	1-3	2-0	1-1	1-0	
Numancia	1-2	1-1	1-0	1-0	1-0	1-0	1-3	–	2-3	1-0	0-2	0-2	1-0	2-0	2-2	1-2	0-2	1-3	0-0	1-1	0-0	
Xerez	1-1	3-0	1-2	0-1	4-0	1-1	2-1	2-1	–	2-1	2-1	5-0	3-1	1-0	1-0	0-2	0-2	0-0	3-1	3-1	1-0	
Elche	0-1	1-2	1-1	2-1	1-1	2-0	1-1	2-1	2-0	–	1-1	1-0	1-0	2-1	2-0	1-0	2-1	2-1	1-0	0-2	2-1	
Polideportivo Ejido	2-3	1-2	0-2	2-0	0-0	1-0	4-2	0-0	0-2	2-1	–	1-0	4-1	0-2	3-2	0-5	2-1	0-0	1-0	0-1	1-1	1-0
Salamanca	1-1	2-0	3-2	1-0	2-0	4-0	0-4	1-1	1-0	2-0	0-0	–	0-1	1-1	2-0	2-0	3-0	2-3	2-3	3-2	1-2	3-...
Sporting Gijón	1-3	1-2	0-1	4-3	5-4	0-1	1-1	1-0	2-1	0-0	0-1	2-1	–	2-2	1-3	1-0	1-1	2-0	0-1	1-0	0-1	1-1
Castellón	2-1	1-1	0-2	2-0	2-0	0-0	2-1	3-1	1-0	2-0	0-1	0-2	0-3	–	0-1	0-0	2-0	2-0	1-1	4-0	2-1	0-0
Málaga	0-1	2-1	1-2	0-0	1-0	3-1	0-1	2-0	2-0	1-1	0-1	1-1	0-0	0-0	–	1-3	3-1	3-1	1-4	0-3	2-...	
Hércules	2-2	0-0	1-1	1-0	1-0	4-8	2-5	2-1	1-1	1-2	3-6	2-0	2-0	2-0	2-0	–	3-1	1-1	3-3	1-0	3-2	
Deportivo Alavés	1-2	1-0	1-0	1-1	1-0	0-2	2-1	0-1	1-2	1-0	2-0	0-2	0-0	0-0	1-2	3-...	–	1-2	3-1	1-2	3-1	5-1
Las Palmas	2-2	3-1	1-0	0-1	0-3	0-1	0-0	1-1	0-1	2-2	0-2	2-2	3-1	1-1	0-2	1-3	1-6	–	2-1	0-0	2-1	3-1
Castilla	1-3	3-1	0-2	1-0	1-2	1-2	3-0	0-1	1-0	2-4	1-2	1-0	3-1	2-1	0-3	1-1	0-3	1-0	–	3-1	2-0	3-2
Ponferradina	2-2	0-1	1-1	1-0	1-3	4-3	1-0	2-0	1-1	1-1	2-0	2-0	2-4	1-0	2-3	0-0	0-3	2-1	3-3	–	2-1	3-3
Lorca Deportiva	0-2	3-1	1-1	1-1	0-3	2-0	3-1	1-2	1-2	0-1	3-0	2-0	2-0	4-2	2-0	1-1	2-0	1-2	0-1	0-0	–	1-1
Vecindario	1-2	0-1	1-1	0-1	1-2	1-0	2-1	1-5	2-1	1-4	0-4	0-3	0-2	4-2	1-1	1-0	1-1	0-1	1-1	0-1	1-1	–

26/08/2006 - 17/06/2007

COPA DEL REY 2006–07

Third Round			Fourth Round			Round of Sixteen		
			Sevilla	1	3			
Burgos *	2	5p	Gimnastica Segoviana *	0	0			
Gimnastica Segoviana	2	6p				**Sevilla**	0	3
						Rayo Vallecano *	0	1
			Espanyol	1	0			
Puertollano	0	4p	**Rayo Vallecano** *	1	1			
Rayo Vallecano	0	5p						
			Real Madrid	1	5			
Eibar	0	4p	Ecija *	1	1			
Ecija *	0	5p				Real Madrid	0	1
						Real Betis *	0	1
			Recreativo Huelva *	0	0			
			Real Betis	0	2			
Real Valladolid	1							
Elche *	0		**Real Valladolid** *	1	3			
			Gimnàstic Tarragona	0	1			
						Real Valladolid *	2	1
Castellón *	1					Villarreal	1	0
Cádiz	0		Castellón *	0	0			
			Villarreal	2	2			
			Mallorca	1	2			
			Athletic Bilbao *	1	1			
						Mallorca *	1	1
						Deportivo La Coruña	2	1
			Racing Santander	0	1 1p			
			Deportivo La Coruña *	1	0 3p			
			Barcelona	2	4			
Universidad LPCG	1	6p	Badalona *	1	0			
Badalona *	1	7p				**Barcelona**	2	3
						Alavés *	0	2
			Celta Vigo	0	0			
Poli Ejido	1	4p	**Alavés** *	0	1			
Alavés	1	5p						
Málaga	0	5p						
Almería	0	4p	**Málaga** *	4	1			
			Real Sociedad	1	2			
						Málaga *	0	1
Hércules	2					**Real Zaragoza**	3	0
Las Palmas	0		Hércules *	1	0			
			Real Zaragoza	1	2			
			Osasuna	0	4			
Alcoyano	0		Peña Sport *	0	0			
Peña Sport	2					**Osasuna**	1	2
						Atlético Madrid *	1	0
			Levante	1	0 3p			
			Atlético Madrid *	0	1 4p			
			Valencia	2	2			
Linares	0		Portuense *	1	0			
Portuense *	1					Valencia	1	2
						Getafe *	1	4
			Xerez *	0	2			
			Getafe	2	1			

* Home team/home team in the first leg

COPA DEL REY 2006–07

Quarter–finals	Semi–finals	Final

| Sevilla * | 0 1 |
| Real Betis | 0 0 |

| Sevilla | 3 2 |
| Deportivo La Coruña * | 0 0 |

| Real Valladolid | 1 1 |
| Deportivo La Coruña * | 4 1 |

| Sevilla | 1 |
| Getafe | 0 |

| Barcelona * | 0 2 |
| Real Zaragoza | 1 1 |

| Barcelona * | 5 0 |
| Getafe | 2 4 |

| Osasuna | 0 1 |
| Getafe * | 3 0 |

COPA DEL REY FINAL 2007

Bernabeu, Madrid, 23-06-2007, Att: 80 000, Ref: Rodriguez Santiago

| Sevilla | 1 | Kanoute [11] |
| Getafe | 0 | |

Sevilla - Andrés PALOP - DANIEL ALVES, Ivica DRAGUTINOVIC, Julien ESCUDE, JAVI NAVARRO - Christian POULSEN, Antonio PUERTA (Sergio DUDA∘ 75), RENATO∘ (José Luis MARTI 79), Jesús NAVAS - Frédéric KANOUTE●88, LUIS FABIANO (Alexander KERZHAKOV 48). Tr: Juande RAMOS
Getafe - LUIS GARCIA - David BELENGUER∘, Cosmin CONTRA (Valentin PACHON 84), Javier PAREDES∘, Ruben PULIDO∘ - Javi CASQUERO, Fabio CELESTINI∘, Mario COTELO, Perez NACHO∘ (Angel VIVAR DORADO 70) - Daniel GUIZA∘, MANU DEL MORAL (Maris VERPAKOVSKIS 76). Tr: Bernd SCHUSTER

‡ Qualified for the UEFA Cup

SPAIN 2006–07
SEGUNDA DIVISION B (3)

Grupo 1	Pl	W	D	L	F	A	Pts
Pontevedra ‡	38	21	10	7	59	27	73
Rayo Vallecano ‡	38	18	13	7	47	29	67
Racing Ferrol ‡	38	17	15	6	49	25	66
Universidad LPCG ‡	38	19	8	11	55	25	65
Talavera	38	18	10	10	50	43	64
San Sebastian Reyes	38	16	15	7	48	38	63
Puertollano	38	17	11	10	52	40	62
Leganés	38	14	11	13	42	38	53
Lugo	38	14	10	14	47	45	52
Fuenlabrada	38	14	9	15	42	52	51
Alcorcón	38	12	12	14	39	40	48
Lanzarote	38	11	14	13	57	55	47
Celta B	38	11	11	16	46	65	44
Atlético Madrid B	38	12	8	18	51	54	44
Ourense	38	13	5	20	43	60	44
Pájara Playas Jandía‡	38	10	13	15	43	48	43
Gimnástica	38	10	12	16	36	51	42
Cobeña	38	10	9	19	50	61	39
Orientación Marítima	38	8	10	20	42	73	34
Racing Santander B	38	8	8	22	33	62	32

27/08/2006 - 27/05/2007 • ‡ Qualified for play-offs

SPAIN 2006–07
SEGUNDA DIVISION B (3)

Grupo 2	Pl	W	D	L	F	A	Pts
Eibar ‡	38	21	8	9	51	26	71
Burgos ‡	38	20	9	9	51	24	69
Palencia ‡	38	17	14	7	38	29	65
Real Unión ‡	38	19	8	11	43	26	65
Sestao River	38	18	11	9	42	29	65
Barakaldo	38	16	15	7	45	26	63
Real Sociedad B	38	17	10	11	54	39	61
Lemona	38	15	15	8	40	28	60
Zamora	38	12	16	10	44	36	52
Logroñes CF	38	12	15	11	36	38	51
Cultural Leonesa	38	14	9	15	37	40	51
Guijuelo	38	14	8	16	41	33	50
Marino	38	13	10	15	31	31	49
CD Logroñes	38	12	10	16	36	49	46
Bilbao Athletic	38	11	12	15	39	49	45
Real Valladolid B ‡	38	12	7	19	31	47	43
Alfaro	38	11	8	19	41	55	41
Universidad Oviedo	38	10	6	22	34	68	36
Real Oviedo	38	7	11	20	27	47	32
Amurrio	38	3	10	25	19	60	19

27/08/2006 - 27/05/2007 • ‡ Qualified for play-offs

SPAIN 2006–07
SEGUNDA DIVISION B (3)

Grupo 3	Pl	W	D	L	F	A	Pts
Alicante ‡	38	20	5	13	51	36	65
Huesca ‡	38	18	8	12	44	33	62
Alcoyano ‡	38	18	8	12	45	34	62
L'Hospitalet ‡	38	16	13	9	43	36	61
Badalona	38	16	12	10	47	28	60
Terrassa	38	16	11	11	46	34	59
Orihuela	38	14	14	10	46	33	56
Villajoyosa	38	14	12	12	39	40	54
Benidorm	38	14	10	14	51	53	52
Levante B	38	13	13	12	33	35	52
Atlético Gramanet	38	14	10	14	39	41	52
Figueres	38	13	10	15	37	43	49
Espanyol B	38	13	10	15	45	47	49
Lleida	38	12	13	13	44	38	49
Atlético Osasuna B	38	12	9	17	34	43	45
Valencia Mestalla ‡	38	11	12	15	32	46	45
Sant Abreu	38	12	9	17	35	43	45
Eldense	38	9	15	14	32	44	42
Barcelona B	38	7	16	15	33	47	37
Barbastro	38	7	12	19	31	53	33

27/08/2006 - 27/05/2007 • ‡ Qualified for play-offs

SPAIN 2006–07
SEGUNDA DIVISION B (3)

Grupo 4	Pl	W	D	L	F	A	Pts
Sevilla Atlético ‡	38	22	10	6	54	22	76
Linares ‡	38	20	13	5	64	38	73
Racing Portuense ‡	38	21	8	9	60	36	71
Córdoba ‡	38	20	9	9	73	46	69
Cartagena	38	19	10	9	63	41	67
Real Jaén	38	16	14	8	49	40	62
Marbella	38	15	11	12	40	34	56
Aguilas	38	15	9	14	48	42	54
Ecija	38	13	13	12	52	47	52
Ceuta	38	13	13	12	38	33	52
Melilla	38	13	13	12	47	47	52
Baza	38	13	13	12	51	46	52
Granada	38	14	9	15	39	36	51
Alcalá	38	13	10	15	45	47	49
Mérida	38	14	6	18	34	44	48
Extremadura ‡	38	12	9	17	39	59	45
Cerro Reyes Atlético	38	11	8	19	31	59	41
Villanueva	38	9	8	21	41	55	35
Villanovense	38	5	7	26	39	76	22
Málaga B	38	3	5	30	21	80	14

27/08/2006 - 27/05/2007 • ‡ Qualified for play-offs

SEGUNDA DIVISION B (3) PLAY-OFFS

Grupo A • Semi-finals: Universidad LPGC 1-0 0-4 **Sevilla Atlético**; Alcoyano 0-0 0-0 4-5p **Burgos** • Final: Burgos 0-0 0-1 **Sevilla Atlético**

Grupo B • Semi-finals: **Córdoba** 1-1 2-2 Pontevedra; Palencia 0-0 1-2 **Huesca** • Final: **Córdoba** 2-0 1-1 Huesca

Grupo C • Semi-finals: Real Unión 1-0 0-2 **Alicante**; Racing Ferrol 2-0 0-2 4-3p Linares • Final: **Racing Ferrol** 2-0 0-1 Alicante

Grupo D • Semi-finals: L'Hospitalet 0-0 0-2 **Eibar**; Portuense 0-2 2-2 Rayo Vallecano • Final: Rayo Vallecano 1-0 0-2 **Eibar**

Relegation play-offs: **Pájara Playas Jandía** 3-0 1-1 Extremadura; **Real Valladolid B** 2-1 1-1 Valencia Mestalla • Extremadura & Valencia relegated

THE FIFA BIG COUNT OF 2006

	Male	Female		Total
Number of players	2 536 103	298 087	Referees and Assistant Referees	9 573
Professionals	1 331		Admin, Coaches, Technical, Medical	53 000
Amateurs 18+	136 132		Number of clubs	18 092
Youth under 18	419 485		Number of teams	39 811
Unregistered	1 915 000		Clubs with women's teams	98
Total players	2 834 190		Players as % of population	7.02%

REAL MADRID 2006-07

Date	Opponents	Score		Comp	Scorers	Att
27-08-2006	Villarreal	D 0-0	H	PD		65 000
10-09-2006	Levante	W 4-1	A	PD	Van Nistelrooij 3 [17 56 90], Cassano [26]	18 677
13-09-2006	Olympique Lyonnais - FRA	L 0-2	A	CLgA		40 013
17-09-2006	Real Sociedad	W 2-0	H	PD	Reyes [69], Beckham [90]	60 000
23-09-2006	Real Betis	W 1-0	A	PD	Diarra [6]	45 000
27-09-2006	Dynamo Kyiv - UKR	W 5-1	H	CLgA	Van Nistelrooij 2 [20 70p], Raul 2 [27 61], Reyes [46+]	68 105
1-10-2006	Atlético Madrid	D 1-1	H	PD	Raul	78 000
14-10-2006	Getafe	L 0-1	A	PD		13 000
17-10-2006	Steaua Bucuresti - ROU	W 4-1	H	CLgA	Sergio Ramos [9], Raúl [34], Robinho [56], Van Nistelrooij [76]	24 123
22-10-2006	Barcelona	W 2-0	H	PD	Raul [3], Van Nistelrooij [51]	78 000
25-10-2006	Ecija Balompie	D 1-1	A	CDRr4	Cassano [66]	9 000
28-10-2006	Gimnastic Tarragona	W 3-1	A	PD	Roberto Carlos [43], Helguera [49], Robinho [85]	14 500
1-11-2006	Steaua Bucuresti - ROU	W 1-0	H	CLgA	Nicolita OG [70]	69 105
5-11-2006	Celta Vigo	L 1-2	H	PD	Emerson [43]	75 000
8-11-2006	Ecija Balompie	W 5-1	H	CDRr4	Beckham [49], Ronaldo [67], Van Nistelrooij 2 [73p 79], De la Red [87]	47 000
12-11-2006	Osasuna	W 4-1	A	PD	Van Nistelrooij 4 [11 26 44 83]	22 230
18-11-2006	Racing Santander	W 3-0	H	PD	Sergio Ramos [5], Reyes [58], Diarra [70]	78 000
21-11-2006	Olympique Lyonnais - FRA	D 2-2	H	CLgA	Diarra [39], Van Nistelrooij [83]	69 906
26-11-2006	Valencia	W 1-0	A	PD	Raul [51]	50 000
3-12-2006	Athletic Bilbao	W 2-1	H	PD	Ronaldo [64], Roberto Carlos [81]	78 000
6-12-2006	Dynamo Kyiv - UKR	D 2-2	A	CLgA	Ronaldo 2 [86 88p]	32 000
9-12-2006	Sevilla	L 1-2	A	PD	Beckham [12]	45 500
17-12-2006	Espanyol	W 1-0	H	PD	Van Nistelrooij [49]	33 502
20-12-2007	Recreativo Huelva	L 0-3	H	PD		50 000
7-01-2007	Deportivo La Coruña	L 0-2	A	PD		30 000
10-01-2007	Real Betis	D 0-0	A	CDRr5		30 000
14-01-2007	Real Zaragoza	W 1-0	H	PD	Van Nistelrooij [41]	65 000
17-01-2007	Real Betis	D 1-1	H	CDRr5	Robinho [5]	70 000
21-01-2007	Mallorca	W 1-0	A	PD	Reyes [77]	18 000
27-01-2007	Villarreal	L 0-1	A	PD		22 000
4-02-2007	Levante	L 0-1	H	PD		65 000
10-02-2007	Real Sociedad	W 2-1	A	PD	Beckham [37], Van Nistelrooij [48]	23 408
17-02-2007	Real Betis	D 0-0	H	PD		75 000
20-02-2007	Bayern München - GER	W 3-2	H	CLr2	Raúl 2 [10 28], Van Nistelrooij [34]	70 928
24-02-2007	Atlético Madrid	D 1-1	A	PD	Higuain [62]	56 000
3-03-2007	Getafe	D 1-1	H	PD	Van Nistelrooij [44p]	75 000
7-03-2007	Bayern München - GER	L 1-2	A	CLr2	Van Nistelrooij [83p]	66 000
10-03-2007	Barcelona	D 3-3	A	PD	Van Nistelrooij 2 [5 13p], Sergio Ramos [58]	97 823
18-03-2007	Gimnastic Tarragona	W 2-0	H	PD	Robinho [55], David Garcia OG [80]	75 000
1-04-2007	Celta Vigo	W 2-1	A	PD	Van Nistelrooij [26p], Robinho [82]	22 000
8-04-2007	Osasuna	W 2-0	H	PD	Raul [23], Robinho [79]	72 000
14-04-2007	Racing Santander	L 1-2	A	PD	Raul [32]	21 741
21-04-2007	Valencia	W 2-1	H	PD	Van Nistelrooij [18], Sergio Ramos [73]	75 000
29-04-2007	Athletic Bilbao	W 4-1	A	PD	Sergio Ramos [13], Van Nistelrooij 2 [34 49], Guti [84]	27 000
6-05-2007	Sevilla	W 3-2	H	PD	Van Nistelrooij 2 [63 86], Robinho [77]	75 000
12-05-2007	Espanyol	W 4-3	H	PD	Van Nistelrooij [30], Raul 48, Reyes [57], Higuain [89]	75 000
20-05-2007	Recreativo Huelva	W 3-2	H	PD	Robinho [9], Van Nistelrooij [55p], Roberto Carlos [90]	20 092
26-05-2007	Deportivo La Coruna	W 3-1	H	PD	Sergio Ramos [29], Raul [57], Van Nistelrooij [74]	45 000
9-06-2007	Real Zaragoza	D 2-2	A	PD	Van Nistelrooij 2 [43 88]	35 000
17-06-2007	Mallorca	W 3-1	H	PD	Reyes 2 [68 84], Diarra [81]	80 000

PD = Primera División • CL = UEFA Champions League • CDR = Copa del Rey
gA = Group A • r2 = second round • r4 = fourth round • r5 = fifth round

FIFA/COCA-COLA WORLD RANKING

1993	1994	1995	1996	1997	1998	1999	2000	2001	2002	2003	2004	2005	2006	High		Low	
5	2	4	8	11	15	4	7	7	3	3	5	5	12	2	12/94	25	03/98

2006-2007											
08/06	09/06	10/06	11/06	12/06	01/07	02/07	03/07	04/07	05/07	06/07	07/07
7	10	10	12	12	12	10	10	9	9	7	9

BARCELONA 2006–07

Date	Opponents	Score		Comp	Scorers	Att
17-08-2006	Espanyol	W 1-0	A	SC	Giuly [44]	22 560
20-08-2006	Espanyol	W 3-0	H	SC	Xavi [3], Deco 2 [12 62]	57 000
25-08-2006	Sevilla	L 0-3	N	ESC		18 500
28-08-2006	Celta Vigo	W 3-2	A	PD	Eto'o [55], Messi [59], Gudjohnsen [87]	25 000
9-09-2006	Osasuna	W 3-0	H	PD	Eto'o 2 [2 27], Messi [36]	63 720
12-09-2006	Levski Sofia - BUL	W 5-0	H	CLgA	Iniesta [5], Giuly [39], Puyol [49], Eto'o [58], Ronaldinho [93+]	62 839
17-09-2006	Racing Santander	W 3-0	A	PD	Eto'o [15], Giuly [84], Ronaldinho [90p]	19 241
24-09-2006	Valencia	D 1-1	H	PD	Iniesta [49]	83 331
27-09-2006	Werder Bremen - GER	D 1-1	A	CLgA	Messi [89]	37 000
30-09-2006	Athletic Bilbao	W 3-1	A	PD	Ustaritz OG [45], Gudjohnsen [61]	39 000
15-10-2006	Sevilla	W 3-1	H	PD	Ronaldinho 2 [28p 39], Messi [81]	91 220
18-10-2006	Chelsea - ENG	L 0-1	A	CLgA		40 599
22-10-2006	Real Madrid	L 0-2	A	PD		78 000
25-10-2006	Badalona	W 2-1	A	CDRr4	Gudjohnsen 2 [63 77]	7 500
28-10-2006	Recreativo Huelva	W 3-0	H	PD	Ronaldinho 2 [28p 56], Xavi [59]	72 630
31-10-2006	Chelsea - ENG	D 2-2	H	CLgA	Deco [3], Gudjohnsen [58]	90 166
4-11-2006	Deportivo La Coruña	D 1-1	A	PD	Ronaldinho [40p]	34 600
8-11-2006	Badalona	W 4-0	H	CDRr4	Van Bronkhorst [24], Ezquerro [40], Saviola 2 [79 83]	12 916
12-11-2006	Real Zaragoza	W 3-1	H	PD	Ronaldinho 2 [31 86], Saviola [90]	73 201
19-11-2006	Real Mallorca	W 4-1	A	PD	Gudjohnsen 2 [42 58], Iniesta [85], Ezquerro [90]	21 000
22-11-2006	Levski Sofia - BUL	W 2-0	A	CLgA	Giuly [5], Iniesta [65]	41 423
25-11-2006	Villarreal	W 4-0	H	PD	Ronaldinho 2 [35p 88], Gudjohnsen [55], Iniesta [70]	78 417
2-12-2006	Levante	D 1-1	A	PD	Deco [41]	21 004
5-12-2006	Werder Bremen - GER	W 2-0	H	CLgA	Ronaldinho [13], Gudjohnsen [18]	95 824
9-12-2006	Real Sociedad	W 1-0	H	PD	Ronaldinho [60]	69 093
14-12-2006	Club América - MEX	W 4-0	N	CWCsf	Gudjohnsen [11], Marquez [30], Ronaldinho [65], Deco [85]	62 316
17-12-2006	Internacional - BRA	L 0-1	N	CWCf		67 128
21-12-2006	Atlético Madrid	D 1-1	H	PD	Ronaldinho [40]	53 685
7-01-2007	Getafe	D 1-1	A	PD	Xavi [70]	14 000
10-01-2007	Alavés	W 2-0	A	CDRr5	Saviola 2 [57 80]	6 027
13-01-2007	Espanyol	L 1-3	A	PD	Saviola [60]	31 450
17-01-2007	Alavés	W 3-2	H	CDRr5	Saviola 3 [16 21 63]	39 723
21-01-2007	Gimnastic Tarragona	W 3-0	H	PD	Saviola [18], Giuly [67], Iniesta [80]	74 343
24-01-2007	Real Betis	D 1-1	A	PD	Marquez [60]	45 000
28-01-2007	Celta Vigo	W 3-1	H	PD	Saviola [34], Ronaldinho [78p], Giuly [86]	68 549
31-01-2007	Real Zaragoza	L 0-1	H	CDRqf		31 015
4-02-2007	Osasuna	D 0-0	A	PD		17 982
11-02-2007	Racing Santander	W 2-0	H	PD	Ronaldinho 2 [51 67]	75 631
18-02-2007	Valencia	L 1-2	A	PD	Ronaldinho [90]	50 000
21-02-2007	Liverpool - ENG	L 1-2	H	CLr2	Deco [14]	93 641
25-02-2007	Athletic Bilbao	W 3-0	H	PD	Amorebieta OG [23], Xavi [30], Eto'o [42]	64 804
28-02-2007	Real Zaragoza	W 2-1	A	CDRqf	Xavi [19], Iniesta [26]	28 000
3-03-2007	Sevilla	L 1-2	A	PD	Ronaldinho [13]	45 500
6-03-2007	Liverpool - ENG	W 1-0	A	CLr2	Gudjohnsen [75]	42 579
10-03-2007	Real Madrid	D 3-3	H	PD	Messi 3 [11 28 90]	97 823
17-03-2007	Recreativo Huelva	W 4-0	A	PD	Eto'o 2 [3 42], Zambrotta [40], Messi [86]	19 000
31-03-2007	Deportivo La Coruña	W 2-1	H	PD	Messi [45], Eto'o [52]	63 827
7-04-2007	Real Zaragoza	L 0-1	A	PD		29 000
15-04-2007	Real Mallorca	W 1-0	H	PD	Fernando Navarro OG [88]	70 441
18-04-2007	Getafe	W 5-2	H	CDRsf	Xavi [19], Messi 2 [29 45], Gudjohnsen [63], Eto'o [74]	53 599
22-04-2007	Villarreal	L 0-2	A	PD		25 000
29-04-2007	Levante	W 1-0	H	PD	Eto'o [28]	73 863
5-05-2007	Real Sociedad	W 2-0	A	PD	Iniesta [46], Eto'o [88]	29 777
10-05-2007	Getafe	L 0-4	A	CDRsf		15 000
13-05-2007	Real Betis	D 1-1	H	PD	Ronaldinho [5p]	77 748
20-05-2007	Atlético Madrid	W 6-0	H	PD	Messi 2 [39 80], Zambrotta [44], Eto'o [45], Ronaldinho [58], Iniesta [90]	50 000
26-05-2007	Getafe	W 1-0	H	PD	Ronaldinho [3]	64 574
10-06-2007	Espanyol	D 2-2	H	PD	Messi 2 [43 57]	90 695
17-06-2007	Gimnastic Tarragona	W 5-1	A	PD	Puyol [20], Messi 2 [34 49], Ronaldinho [37], Zambrotta [90]	14 600

SC = Supercopa • ESC = UEFA Super Cup • PD = Primera División • CL = UEFA Champions League • CDR = Copa del Rey • CWC = FIFA Club World Cup
gA = Group A • r2 = second round • r4 = fourth round • r5 = fifth round • qf = quarter-final • sf = semi-final • f = final
N = Stade Louis II, Monaco • **N** = Yokohama International

SEVILLA 2006-07

Date	Opponents	Score		Comp	Scorers	Att
25-08-2006	Barcelona	W 3-0	N	ESC	Renato [7], Kanouté [45], Maresca [90p]	18 500
29-08-2006	Levante	W 4-0	H	PD	Kanouté [7], Kepa 3 [28 50 88]	45 000
10-09-2006	Real Sociedad	W 3-1	A	PD	Renato [6], Kanouté 76, Dragutinovic 90	20 983
14-09-2006	Atromitas - GRE	W 2-1	A	UCr1	Kepa [16], Valente [43]	3 500
17-09-2006	Real Betis	W 3-2	H	PD	Kanouté 2 [26 58], Renato [85]	45 000
24-09-2006	Atlético Madrid	L 1-2	A	PD	Renato [39]	55 000
28-09-2006	Atromitas - GRE	W 4-0	H	UCr1	Luis Fabiano 2 [2 29], Ionnoy OG [10], Kepa [86]	30 644
1-10-2006	Getafe	W 1-0	H	PD	Luis Fabiano [31]	40 000
15-10-2006	Barcelona	L 1-3	A	PD	Kanouté [37]	91 220
19-10-2006	Slovan Liberec - CZE	D 0-0	A	UCgC		7 023
22-10-2006	Gimnastic Tarragona	W 2-1	H	PD	Kanouté 2 [22 28]	40 000
25-10-2006	Gimnástic Segoviana	W 1-0	A	CDRr4	Kepa [36]	
29-10-2006	Celta Vigo	W 2-1	A	PD	Poulsen [30], Adriano Correa [78]	17 000
5-11-2006	Osasuna	W 2-0	H	PD	Kanouté [50p], Adriano Correa [87]	43 000
8-11-2006	Gimnástic Segoviana	W 3-0	H	CDRr4	Maresca [26p], Ocio [45], Duda [65]	
12-11-2006	Racing Santander	D 0-0	A	PD		15 961
18-11-2006	Valencia	W 3-0	H	PD	Escude [19], Luis Fabiano [55], Kanouté [71]	45 000
23-11-2006	Sporting Braga - POR	W 2-0	H	UCgC	Luis Fabiano [40], Chevantón [76]	28 225
26-11-2006	Athletic Bilbao	W 3-1	A	PD	Luis Fabiano 2 [4 90], Marti [10]	35 000
29-11-2006	Grasshopper-Club - SUI	W 4-0	A	UCgC	Daniel 2 [12 53], Chevantón [62], Kepa [84]	7 300
3-12-2006	Espanyol	L 1-2	A	PD	Kanouté [22p]	22 230
9-12-2006	Real Madrid	W 2-1	H	PD	Kanouté [16], Chevanton [76]	45 500
14-12-2006	AZ Alkmaar - NED	L 1-2	H	UCgC	Chevantón [52p]	29 373
17-12-2006	Recreativo Huelva	W 3-1	A	PD	Luis Fabiano [10p], Kanouté [34], Jesus Navas [53]	20 096
20-12-2006	Deportivo La Coruña	W 4-0	H	PD	Kanouté 2 [29 63p], Luis Fabiano [65], Daniel Alves [73]	45 000
6-01-2007	Real Zaragoza	L 1-2	A	PD	Luis Fabiano [70]	28 000
10-01-2007	Rayo Vallecano	D 0-0	A	CDRr5		10 000
14-01-2007	Mallorca	L 1-2	H	PD	Kanouté [22p]	45 000
17-01-2007	Rayo Vallecano	W 3-1	H	CDRr5	Alfaro 2 [17 85], Kanouté [71]	35 000
20-01-2007	Villarreal	D 0-0	A	PD		20 000
28-01-2007	Levante	W 4-2	A	PD	Kanouté [34], Kerzhakov [55], Tommasi OG [63], Alfaro [77]	12 707
1-02-2007	Real Betis	D 0-0	H	CDRqf		45 000
4-02-2007	Real Sociedad	D 0-0	H	PD		40 000
10-02-2007	Real Betis	D 0-0	A	PD		45 000
15-02-2006	Steaua Bucuresti - ROU	W 2-0	A	UCr2	Poulsen [41], Kanouté [77p]	23 927
18-02-2007	Atlético Madrid	W 3-1	H	PD	Kanouté 2 [14 73], Daniel Alves [21]	42 000
22-02-2007	Steaua Bucuresti - ROU	W 1-0	H	UCr2	Kerzhakov [48+]	19 336
25-02-2007	Getafe	D 0-0	H	PD		12 000
28-02-2007	Real Betis	- -	H	CDRqf	Kanouté [56]. Abandoned after 56 minutes due to crowd trouble	
3-03-2007	Barcelona	W 2-1	H	PD	Kerzhakov [38], Daniel Alves [60]	45 500
8-03-2007	Shakhter Donetsk - UKR	D 2-2	H	UCr3	Martí [8p], Maresca [88p]	25 599
11-03-2007	Gimnastic Tarragona	L 0-1	A	PD		14 500
18-03-2007	Celta Vigo	W 2-0	H	PD	Kanouté [52p], Kerzhakov [90]	45 000
20-03-2007	Real Betis	W 1-0	N	CDRqf	Kanouté [56]. Remaining 23 minutes played from 28-02-2007	BCD
25-03-2007	Shakhter Donetsk - UKR	W 3-2	A	UCr3	Maresca [53], Palop [94+], Chevantón [105]	25 500
1-04-2007	Osasuna	D 0-0	A	PD		16 673
5-04-2007	Tottenham Hotspur - ENG	W 2-1	H	UCqf	Kanouté [19p], Kerzhakov [36]	32 738
8-04-2007	Racing Santander	D 0-0	H	PD		45 000
12-04-2007	Tottenham Hotspur - ENG	D 2-2	A	UCqf	Malbranque OG [3], Kanouté [8]	35 234
15-04-2007	Valencia	L 0-2	A	PD		45 000
19-04-2007	Deportivo La Couriña	W 3-0	A	CDRsf	Kanouté [11], Navas [14], Luis Fabiano [93p]	20 000
22-04-2007	Athletic Bilbao	W 4-1	H	PD	Kerzhakov [49], Puerta [54], Chevantón [69], Luis Fabiano [82]	43 000
26-04-2007	Osasuna - ESP	L 0-1	H	UCsf		18 134
29-04-2007	Espanyol	W 3-1	H	PD	Puerta [51], Chevantón [53], Marti [74]	45 000
3-05-2007	Osasuna - ESP	W 2-0	H	CDRsf	Luis Fabiano [37], Renato [53]	38 497
6-05-2007	Real Madrid	L 2-3	A	PD	Maresca [42], Chevantón [90]	75 000
9-05-2007	Deportivo La Coruña	W 2-0	H	CDRsf	Duda [3], Chevantón [33]	40 000
12-05-2007	Recreativo Huelva	W 2-1	H	PD	Maresca [13], Luis Fabiano [81p]	45 000
16-05-2007	Espanyol - ESP	D 2-2	N	UCf	Riera [28], Jônatas [115]. W 3-1 on penalties	47 602
20-05-2007	Deportivo La Coruña	W 2-1	A	PD	Renato [76], Kanouté [83]	12 000
27-05-2007	Real Zaragoza	W 3-1	H	PD	Luis Fabiano [26], Kerzhakov [82], Kanouté [90]	45 000
9-06-2007	Mallorca	D 0-0	A	PD		18 000
17-06-2007	Villarreal	L 0-1	H	PD		45 000
23-06-2006	Getafe	W 1-0	N	CDRf	Kanouté [11]	80 000

ESC = UEFA Super Cup • PD = Primera División • CDR = Copa del Rey • UC = UEFA Cup
r1 = first round • gC = group C • r2 = second round • r3 = third round • r4 = fourth round • r5 = fifth round • qf = quarter-final •
sf = semi-final • f = final • N = Stade Louis II, Monaco • N = Getafe • N = Hampden Park, Glasgow • N = Bernabeu

EST – ESTONIA

NATIONAL TEAM RECORD
JULY 10TH 2006 TO JULY 12TH 2010

PL	W	D	L	F	A	%
10	1	0	9	2	20	10

FIFA/COCA-COLA WORLD RANKING

1993	1994	1995	1996	1997	1998	1999	2000	2001	2002	2003	2004	2005	2006	High	Low
109	119	129	102	100	90	70	67	83	60	68	81	76	106	**60** 12/02	**135** 02/96

2006–2007											
08/06	09/06	10/06	11/06	12/06	01/07	02/07	03/07	04/07	05/07	06/07	07/07
78	102	112	105	106	106	106	106	110	110	121	124

The Estonian national team managed to score just two goals during the course of the season - both in a friendly against Belarus - and unsurprisingly they found themselves at the bottom of Group E in the UEFA Euro 2008 qualifiers. In defence of Jelle Goes and his team, it was one of the toughest groups, but after their commendable World Cup qualifying campaign, no-one expected Estonia to be involved with Andorra in a battle to avoid the wooden spoon. There was much better news on the international front in the UEFA Cup where Levadia Tallinn sensationally beat Dutch side Twente Enschede in the second preliminary round, having already overcome Finland's Haka

INTERNATIONAL HONOURS
Baltic Cup 1929 1931 1938

Valkeakoski, which meant a first appearance for an Estonian team in the first round. There they met Newcastle United who beat them 3-1 on aggregate. In the Estonian championship the big four of Levadia, Trans Narva, Flora and TVMK were once again streets ahead of the rest. Between them they lost just three games all season against the other six clubs in the division. Levadia emerged as champions, 11 points ahead of Trans Narva, having won 30 of their 36 games, gone unbeaten for 25 matches and having scored 114 goals in the process. It was to no great surprise when Levadia completed the double six months later by beating Trans Narva 3-0 in the Cup Final.

THE FIFA BIG COUNT OF 2006

	Male	Female		Total
Number of players	49 725	7 299	Referees and Assistant Referees	182
Professionals	140		Admin, Coaches, Technical, Medical	480
Amateurs 18+	3 922		Number of clubs	138
Youth under 18	5 042		Number of teams	671
Unregistered	15 700		Clubs with women's teams	14
Total players	57 024		Players as % of population	4.31%

Estonian Football Association (EFA)
Eesti Jalgpalli Liit, A.Le Coq Arena, Asula 4c, Tallinn 11312, Estonia
Tel +372 6 279960   Fax +372 6 279969
efa@jalgpall.ee   www.jalgpall.ee
President: POHLAK Aivar   General Secretary: SIREL Tonu
Vice-President: SEDIN Pjotr   Treasurer: TBD   Media Officer: UIBOLEHT Mihkel
Men's Coach: GOES Jelle   Women's Coach: SAAR Juri
EFA formed: 1921   UEFA: 1992   FIFA: 1923-43 & 1992
Blue shirts with white trimmings, Black shorts, White socks or White shirts with black trimmings, Black shorts, Blue socks

RECENT INTERNATIONAL MATCHES PLAYED BY ESTONIA

2003	Opponents	Score		Venue	Comp	Scorers	Att	Referee
17-12	Saudi Arabia	D	1-1	Dammam	Fr	Zahhovaiko [40]	1 500	Al-Mehannah KSA
20-12	Oman	L	1-3	Muscat	Fr	Zelinski [45]	1 000	Al-Harrassi OMA
2004								
14-02	Belarus	W	2-1	Ta'Qali	Fr	Rooba.M [13], Lemsalu [45]	200	Casha MLT
16-02	Malta	L	2-5	Ta'Qali	Fr	Zahhovaiko [16], Piiroja [44]		Orlic MDA
18-02	Moldova	W	1-0	Ta'Qali	Fr	Lindpere [58]	100	Sammut MLT
31-03	Northern Ireland	L	0-1	Tallinn	Fr		2 900	Petteri FIN
28-04	Albania	D	1-1	Tallinn	Fr	Viikmäe [80]	1 500	Sipailo LVA
27-05	Scotland	L	0-1	Tallinn	Fr		4 000	Poulsen DEN
30-05	Denmark	D	2-2	Tallinn	Fr	Viikmäe [77], Lindpere [90]	3 000	Bossen NED
6-06	Czech Republic	L	0-2	Teplice	Fr		11 873	Brugger AUT
11-06	Macedonia FYR	L	2-4	Tallinn	Fr	Zahhovaiko [54], Teever [65]	2 200	Frojdfeldt SWE
18-08	Liechtenstein	W	2-1	Vaduz	WCq	Viikmäe [34], Lindpere [80]	912	Bozinovski MKD
4-09	Luxembourg	W	4-0	Tallinn	WCq	Teever [7], Schauls OG [41], Oper [61], Viikmäe [67]	3 000	Kelly IRL
8-09	Portugal	L	0-4	Leiria	WCq		27 214	Demirlek TUR
13-10	Latvia	D	2-2	Riga	WCq	Oper [72], Teever [79]	8 500	Meyer GER
17-11	Russia	L	0-4	Krasnodar	WCq		29 000	Busacca SUI
30-11	Thailand	D	0-0	Bangkok	Fr	L 3-4p	35 000	Mat Amin MAS
2-12	Hungary	L	0-5	Bangkok	Fr		800	Tongkhan THA
2005								
9-02	Venezuela	L	0-3	Maracaibo	Fr		8 000	Vasco Villacis ECU
26-03	Slovakia	L	1-2	Tallinn	WCq	Oper [57]	3 051	Frojdfeldt SWE
30-03	Russia	D	1-1	Tallinn	WCq	Terekhov [63]	8 850	Paparesta ITA
20-04	Norway	L	1-2	Tallinn	Fr	Saharov [81]	2 500	Vink NED
4-06	Liechtenstein	W	2-0	Tallinn	WCq	Stepanov [27], Oper [57]	3 000	Whitby WAL
8-06	Portugal	L	0-1	Tallinn	WCq		10 280	Riley ENG
17-08	Bosnia-Herzegovina	W	1-0	Tallinn	Fr	Viikmäe 35	4 000	Frojdfeldt SWE
3-09	Latvia	W	2-1	Tallinn	WCq	Oper [11], Smirnov [71]	8 970	Undiano Mallenco ESP
8-10	Slovakia	L	0-1	Bratislava	WCq		12 800	Allaerts BEL
12-10	Luxembourg	W	2-0	Luxembourg	WCq	Oper 2 [7 78]	2 010	Dereli TUR
12-11	Finland	D	2-2	Helsinki	Fr	Kruglov [62p], Lindpere [85]	1 900	Gilewski POL
16-11	Poland	L	1-3	Ostrowiec	Fr	Teever [68]	8 500	Hyytia FIN
2006								
1-03	Northern Ireland	L	0-1	Belfast	Fr		13 600	Vink NED
28-05	Turkey	D	1-1	Hamburg	Fr	Neemelo [87]	6 000	Weiner GER
31-05	New Zealand	D	1-1	Tallinn	Fr	Klavan [3]	3 500	Rasmussen DEN
16-08	FYR Macedonia	L	0-1	Tallinn	ECq		7 500	Jakbsson ISL
2-09	Israel	L	0-1	Tallinn	ECq		7 800	Verbist BEL
11-10	Russia	L	0-2	St Petersburg	ECq		21 517	Braamhaar NED
15-11	Belarus	W	2-1	Tallinn	Fr	Oper 2 [17 66]	3 000	Hermansen DEN
2007								
3-02	Poland	L	0-4	Jerez	Fr		100	Ruiz-Herrera ESP
7-02	Slovenia	L	0-1	Domzale	Fr		3 000	Ledentu FRA
24-03	Russia	L	0-2	Tallinn	ECq		8 212	Ceferin SVN
28-03	Israel	L	0-4	Tel Aviv	ECq		21 000	Cüneyt Cakir TUR
2-06	Croatia	L	0-1	Tallinn	ECq		8 651	Kassai HUN
6-06	England	L	0-3	Tallinn	ECq		9 635	Gilewski POL

Fr = Friendly match • EC = UEFA EURO 2004/2008 • BC = Baltic Cup • WC = FIFA World Cup • q = qualifier

ESTONIA NATIONAL TEAM RECORDS AND RECORD SEQUENCES

Records			Sequence records					
Victory	6-0	LTU 1928	Wins	3	2000	Clean sheets	3	1999, 2000, 2003
Defeat	2-10	FIN 1922	Defeats	13	1994-1995	Goals scored	13	1928-30, 1999-00
Player Caps	150	REIM Martin	Undefeated	6	Three times	Without goal	11	1994-1995
Player Goals	32	OPER Andreas	Without win	34	1993-1996	Goals against	19	1934-1937

MAJOR CITIES/TOWNS

Population '000

1	Tallinn	390
2	Tartu	100
3	Narva	66
4	Kohtla-Järve	45
5	Pärnu	43
6	Viljandi	20
7	Maardu	16
8	Rakvere	16
9	Sillamäe	16
10	Kuressaare	14
11	Voru	14
12	Valga	13
13	Haapsalu	11
14	Jõhvi	11
15	Paide	9
16	Keila	9
17	Kivioli	6
18	Polva	6
19	Tapa	6
20	Jogeva	6
21	Türi	6
22	Elva	5
23	Rapla	5
24	Saue	5

REPUBLIC OF ESTONIA; EESTI VABARIIK

Capital	Tallinn	Language	Estonian, Russian
Population	1 324 333	Area	45 226 km²
GDP per cap	$12 300	Dailling code	+372

Density	3 per km²	Independence	1991
Internet	.ee	% in cities	73%
		GMT +/-	+2

MEDALS TABLE

		Overall			League			Cup			Europe			City	Stadium	Cap'ty	DoF
		G	S	B	G	S	B	G	S	B	G	S	B				
1	Flora Tallinn	9	7	3	7	4	3	2	3					Tallinn	A. Le Coq Arena	9 300	1990
2	Levadia Tallinn	9	3	2	4	2	2	5	1					Tallinn	Kadriorg Staadion	4 700	1999
3	TVMK Tallinn	3	5	3	1	3	3	2	2					Tallinn	Kadriorg Staadion	4 700	1951
4	Lantana Tallinn	3	4	5	2	1	5	1	3					Tallinn			1994-99
5	Norma Tallinn	3	2		2	1		1	1					Tallinn			1990-97
6	Tallinna Sadam	2	2	1		2	1	2						Tallinn			1991-99
7	Trans Narva	1	3	2		1	2	1	2					Narva	Kreenholmi Staadion	3 000	1979
8	Tulevik Viljandi		3			1			2					Viljandi	Linnastaadion	2 506	1992
9	EP Jõhvi		2			1			1					Jõhvi	Kaevur	2 000	1974
10	Ajax Lasnamäe													Lasnamäe	Ajax	500	1993
	Maag Tartu													Tartu	Tamme Stadion	700	1990
	Tammeka Tartu													Tartu	Tamme Stadion	700	1989
	Vaprus Pärnu													Pärnu	Pärnu Kalevi Staadion	1 900	1999
	Warrior Valga													Valga	Valga Keskstaadion	2 500	1997

RECENT LEAGUE AND CUP RECORD

	Championship						Cup			
Year	Champions	Pts	Runners-up	Pts	Third	Pts		Winners	Score	Runners-up
1995	Flora Tallinn	41	Lantana-Marlekor	40	Trans Narva	26		Flora Tallinn	2-0	Lantana-Marlekor
1996	Lantana Tallinn	37	Flora Tallinn	31	Tevalte-Marlekor	31		Tallinna Sadam	2-0	EP Jõhvi
1997	Lantana Tallinn	41	Flora Tallinn	38	Tallinna Sadam	24		Tallinna Sadam	3-2	Lantana Tallinn
1998	Flora Tallinn	42	Tallinna Sadam	32	Lantana Tallinn	25		Flora Tallinn	3-2	Lantana Tallinn
1998	Flora Tallinn	35	Tallinna Sadam	34	Lantana Tallinn	25				
1999	Levadia Maardu	73	Tulevik Viljandi	53	Flora Tallinn	47		Levadia Maardu	3-2	Tulevik Viljandi
2000	Levadia Maardu	74	Flora Tallinn	55	TVMK Tallinn	48		Levadia Maardu	2-0	Tulevik Viljandi
2001	Flora Tallinn	68	TVMK Tallinn	56	Levadia Maardu	55		Trans Narva	1-0	Flora Tallinn
2002	Flora Tallinn	64	Levadia Maardu	62	TVMK Tallinn	53		Levadia Tallinn	2-0	Levadia Maardu
2003	Flora Tallinn	76	TVMK Tallinn	65	Levadia Maardu	49		TVMK Tallinn	2-2 4-1p	Flora Tallinn
2004	Levadia Tallinn	69	TVMK Tallinn	63	Flora Tallinn	58		Levadia Tallinn	3-0	TVMK Tallinn
2005	TVMK Tallinn	95	Levadia Tallinn	89	Trans Narva	75		Levadia Tallinn	1-0	TVMK Tallinn
2006	Levadia Tallinn	94	Trans Narva	83	Flora Tallinn	82		TVMK Tallinn	1-0	Flora Tallinn
2007								Levadia Tallinn	3-0	Trans Narva

ESTONIA 2006

MEISTRILIIGA

	Pl	W	D	L	F	A	Pts	Levadia	Trans Narva	Flora	TVMK	Maag	Tammeka	Vaprus	Ajax	Tulevik	Warrior
Levadia Tallinn †	36	30	4	2	114	29	94		1-1 1-1	4-1 2-2	2-1 3-1	2-0 2-1	4-1 2-0	4-1 3-1	8-0 11-3	2-0 3-0	5-0 7-1
Trans Narva ‡	36	25	8	3	106	36	83	1-1 2-3		2-2 2-1	1-0 3-2	2-2 6-1	3-2 2-0	6-3 5-1	2-0 2-0	6-1 3-0	4-0 4-0
Flora Tallinn ‡	36	26	4	6	93	34	82	0-1 1-0	2-1 3-2		1-4 1-1	1-1 2-0	3-0 5-2	4-0 2-0	6-0 6-0	3-0 2-0	2-0 6-0
TVMK Tallinn	36	22	6	8	83	37	72	0-2 2-3	1-1 1-1	1-0 3-2		5-0 3-0	1-2 1-1	7-1 3-1	8-0 1-0	2-1 3-1	4-1 1-0
Maag Tartu	36	13	9	14	65	68	48	1-2 4-2	2-2 2-6	1-2 2-3	2-0 1-1		0-2 1-1	0-3 4-3	3-1 2-2	0-0 4-3	6-0 4-1
Tammeka Tartu	36	12	7	17	45	57	43	0-5 0-3	0-3 2-4	0-1 1-3	0-1 1-2	1-2 0-0		2-0 1-1	4-1 2-1	0-0 1-0	3-0 5-0
Vaprus Pärnu	36	10	4	22	49	86	34	1-2 1-3	1-4 0-3	2-4 1-4	1-0 0-3	2-3 1-4	0-2 1-1		1-0 0-0	3-0 1-2	2-0 5-2
Ajax Lasnanäe	36	6	7	23	35	104	25	0-3 0-8	0-3 0-5	1-4 0-2	1-2 2-2	3-3 3-2	1-2 2-0	3-1 1-2		1-0 1-1	2-0 1-2
Tulevik Viljandi	36	5	5	26	29	74	20	1-3 0-2	0-3 1-2	0-3 0-2	1-2 1-4	0-3 0-2	0-2 1-2	1-1 1-2	5-2 0-0		3-0 1-0
Warrior Valga	36	3	2	31	16	110	11	0-4 0-1	0-5 0-3	0-2 0-5	0-5 0-3	0-2 1-0	1-1 0-2	1-3 1-2	1-3 0-0	3-0 1-4	

22/03/2006 - 5/11/2006 • † Qualified for the UEFA Champions League • ‡ Qualified for the UEFA Cup
Relegation play-off: Tallinna Kalev 3-0 3-0 Tulevik Viljandi. Both legs awarded after Tulevik fielded an ineligible player. Tulevik remained in the Meistriliiga after the merger of Maag and Tammeka • Top scorers: Maksim GRUZNOV, Trans 31; Dmitriy LIPARTOV, Trans 27; Vjatseslav ZAHOVAIKO, Flora 25; Indrek ZELINSKI, Levadia 21; Aleksandr DUBOKIN, Trans 19; Vitali GUSSEV, Maag 18; Vladislav GUSSEV, TVMK 18; Konstantin Vassiljev, Levadia 18

ESTONIA 2006
ESILIIGA (2)

	Pl	W	D	L	F	A	Pts
Levadia Tallinn II	36	28	4	4	132	24	88
Kuressaare	36	22	5	9	64	44	71
Tallinna Kalev	36	20	6	10	84	63	66
Flora Tallinn II	36	19	3	14	81	56	60
Nomme Kalju	36	18	5	13	76	80	59
TVMK Tallinn II	36	17	4	15	66	63	55
Tulevik Viljandi II	36	9	11	16	52	51	38
Lootus Kohtla-Järve	36	10	3	23	46	99	33
Dünamo Tallinn	36	7	8	21	44	85	29
Elva	36	4	3	29	20	100	15

11/03/2006 - 4/11/2006 • Levadia ineligible for promotion

EFA CUP 2006-07

Round of sixteen

Levadia Tallinn	2 5p
FC Kuressare *	2 4p
Trans II Narva	1
Maag Tartu *	5
Vaprus Pärnu	2
Rakvere *	1
Toompea Tallinn	0
TVMK Tallinn *	9
Tulevik II Viljandi	2
Nomme United *	0
Püsivus Kohila	
Välk 494 Tartu *	w-o
Ajax Lasnamäe *	3
Ararat Tallinn	0
Nomme Kalju *	2
Trans Narva	5

Quarter-finals

Levadia Tallinn	1
Maag Tammeka Tartu *	0
Vaprus Pärnu	0
TVMK Tallinn *	5
Tulevik II Viljandi	1
Välk 494 Tartu *	0
Ajax Lasnamäe *	0
Trans Narva	6

Semi-finals

Levadia Tallinn	1
TVMK Tallinn	0
Tulevik II Viljandi	0
Trans Narva	4

Final

| Levadia Tallinn | 3 |
| Trans Narva ‡ | 0 |

CUP FINAL
Kadriorg, Tallinn
15-05-2007

Scorers - Konstantin Nahk 2 [26p 46+p], Tarmo Kink [49] for Levadia

* Home team • ‡ Qualified for the UEFA Cup

ETH – ETHIOPIA

NATIONAL TEAM RECORD
JULY 10TH 2006 TO JULY 12TH 2010

PL	W	D	L	F	A	%
12	7	0	5	12	9	58.3

FIFA/COCA-COLA WORLD RANKING

1993	1994	1995	1996	1997	1998	1999	2000	2001	2002	2003	2004	2005	2006	High		Low	
96	115	105	108	126	145	142	133	155	138	130	151	112	92	**86**	06/07	**155**	12/01

2006–2007											
08/06	09/06	10/06	11/06	12/06	01/07	02/07	03/07	04/07	05/07	06/07	07/07
96	86	97	100	92	91	91	87	95	99	86	91

Ethiopians had high hopes for their national team going into the 2006-07 season having put together a record run of nine consecutive wins, and they did achieve their ambition of returning to the top 100 in the FIFA/Coca-Cola World Ranking, but they were left disappointed by failure in the annual East and Central African Senior Challenge Cup and in the qualifiers for the 2008 African Nations Cup finals. Ethiopia were seeking a third successive title in the regional championship and were firm favourites as the host nation but only got as far as the quarter-finals, losing 1-0 to Zambia in a match that officials tried to have replayed because the referee was alleged to have blown the final

INTERNATIONAL HONOURS
CAF African Cup of Nations 1962   CECAFA Cup 1987 2001 2004 2005

whistle three minutes short of full time. Disappointment for home fans was compounded by indifferent results in the Nations Cup qualifiers, dropping points at home to Congo DR and losing away in Namibia and Libya, where their chances were effectively ended in June 2007. The Premier League ended in disarray as provincial club Awasa Kenema were declared champions, but 10 of the 16 clubs boycotted the last five rounds of the season in a spat over control of the country's football. It left Awasa Kenema, Harar Brewery, Trans Ethiopia, Mugher Cement, Air Force and Defence Force to finish the campaign, with the newly crowned champions finishing on 44 points.

THE FIFA BIG COUNT OF 2006

	Male	Female		Total
Number of players	3 309 020	165 225	Referees and Assistant Referees	10 100
Professionals	20		Admin, Coaches, Technical, Medical	300 500
Amateurs 18+	21 225		Number of clubs	1 000
Youth under 18	35 000		Number of teams	3 000
Unregistered	520 000		Clubs with women's teams	4
Total players	3 474 245		Players as % of population	4.65%

Ethiopian Football Federation (EFF)
Addis Abeba Stadium, PO Box 1080, Addis Abeba, Ethiopia
Tel +251 115 514321   Fax +251 115 515899
eff@telecom.net.et   www.none
President: WOLDEGIORGIS Ashebir Dr   General Secretary: EJIGU Ashenafi
Vice-President: BEKELE Horpdfa   Treasurer: YADEITA Abu   Media Officer: None
Men's Coach: ABATE Seydoum   Women's Coach: MELESE Shale
EFF formed: 1943   CAF: 1957   FIFA: 1953
Green shirts, Yellow shorts, Red socks

RECENT INTERNATIONAL MATCHES PLAYED BY ETHIOPIA

2005	Opponents	Score	Venue	Comp	Scorers	Att	Referee
12-03	Sudan	L 1-3	Khartoum	Fr			
24-11	Sudan	W 5-1	Khartoum	Fr	Fikru Teffera [22], Tafesse Tesfaye [45], Sebsebe Shegere [56], Behailu Demeke [90], Anteneh Feleke [91+]		
27-11	Uganda	D 0-0	Kigali	CCr1			
1-12	Sudan	W 3-1	Kigali	CCr1	Anteneh Alamrew [40], Sebsebe Shegere 2 [67 75]		
3-12	Djibouti	W 6-0	Kigali	CCr1	Dawit Mebratu [12], Fikru Teffera 2 [39 58], Andualem Negussie [58], Adugna Deyus [78p], Ashenafi Girma [91+]		
5-12	Somalia	W 3-1	Kigali	CCr1			
8-12	Zanzibar †	W 4-0	Kigali	CCsf	Ashenafi Girma [14], Fikru Teffera 3 [46 48 82]		
10-12	Rwanda	W 1-0	Kigali	CCf	Andualem Negussie [59]		
2006							
17-07	Yemen	W 1-0	Addis Abeba	Fr	Andre Lomani [72]		
11-08	Kenya	W 1-0	Addis Abeba	Fr			
13-08	Kenya	W 1-0	Addis Abeba	Fr			
3-09	Libya	W 1-0	Addis Abeba	CNq	Dawit Mebratu [15]		Abd El Fatah EGY
7-10	Namibia	L 0-1	Katutura	CNq			Moeketsi LES
25-11	Tanzania	L 1-2	Addis Abeba	CCr1	Binyam Assefa [24]		
28-11	Djibouti	W 4-0	Addis Abeba	CCr1	Dawit Mebratu [27p], Tafesse Tesfaye [45], Behailu Demeke [57p], Bizuneh Worku [64]		
1-12	Malawi	W 1-0	Addis Abeba	CCr1	Dawit Mebratu [42]		
5-12	Zambia	L 0-1	Addis Abeba	CCqf			
2007							
29-04	Congo DR	L 0-2	Kinshasa	CNq			
1-06	Congo DR	W 1-0	Addis Abeba	CNq	Salahdin Seid [31]		
17-06	Libya	L 1-3	Tripoli	CNq	Fikru Tefera [58]		

Fr = Friendly match • CN = CAF African Cup of Nations • CC = CECAFA Cup • WC = FIFA World Cup
q = qualifier • r1 = first round group • sf = semi-final • f = final • † Not an official International

ETHIOPIA NATIONAL TEAM RECORDS AND RECORD SEQUENCES

Records			Sequence records				
Victory	8-1	DJI 1983	Wins	9	2005-2006	Clean sheets	6	2005-2006
Defeat	0-13	IRQ 1992	Defeats	4	Five times	Goals scored	10	1995-97, 2000-02
Player Caps	n/a		Undefeated	11	1984-88, 2005-06	Without goal	5	1995
Player Goals	n/a		Without win	9	1996-1999	Goals against	18	1956-1962

RECENT LEAGUE AND CUP RECORD

	Championship						Cup		
Year	Champions	Pts	Runners-up	Pts	Third	Pts	Winners	Score	Runners-up
2000	St George	46	EEPCO Mebrat Hail	39	Ethiopian Coffee	38	Ethiopian Coffee	2-1	Awassa City
2001	EEPCO Mebrat Hail	59	St George	49	Ethiopian Coffee	48	EEPCO Mebrat Hail	2-1	Guna Trading
2002	St George	61	Ethiopian Coffee	50	EEPCO Mebrat Hail	45	Medhin	6-3p	EEPCO Mebrat Hail
2003	St George	56	Arba Minch Textile	55	Ethiopian Coffee	44	Ethiopian Coffee	2-0	EEPCO Mebrat Hail
2004	Awassa City	48	Ethiopian Coffee	46	Trans Ethiopia	45	Banks	1-0	Ethiopian Coffee
2005	St George	64	Trans Ethiopia	46	Awassa City	44	Awassa City	2-2 wop	Muger Cement
2006	St George	56	Ethiopian Coffee	52	EEPCO Mebrat Hail		Mekelakeya	1-0	Ethiopian Coffee

ETHIOPIA COUNTRY INFORMATION

Capital	Addis Abeba	Independence	Occupied by Italy 1936-41	GDP per Capita	$700
Population	67 851 281	Status	Republic	GNP Ranking	103
Area km²	1 127 127	Language	Amharic	Dialling code	+251
Population density	60 per km²	Literacy rate	42%	Internet code	.et
% in urban areas	13%	Main religion	Muslim 45%, Christian 40%	GMT +/-	+3
Towns/Cities ('000)	Addis Abeba 2 757; Dire Dawa 252; Nazret 214; Bahir Dar 168; Gondar 153; Mek'ele 151; Dese 136; Awassa 133; Jimma 128; Debre Zeyit 104; Kembolcha 93; Harer 90				
Neighbours (km)	Eritrea 912; Djibouti 349; Somalia 1 600; Kenya 861; Sudan 1 606				
Main stadia	Addis Abeba Stadium – Addis Abeba 35 000; Awassa Kenema – Awassa 25 000				

FIJ – FIJI

NATIONAL TEAM RECORD
JULY 10TH 2006 TO JULY 12TH 2010

PL	W	D	L	F	A	%
0	0	0	0	0	0	0

FIFA/COCA-COLA WORLD RANKING

1993	1994	1995	1996	1997	1998	1999	2000	2001	2002	2003	2004	2005	2006	High	Low
107	120	139	157	146	124	135	141	123	140	149	135	135	150	**94** 07/94	**165** 07/07

2006–2007											
08/06	09/06	10/06	11/06	12/06	01/07	02/07	03/07	04/07	05/07	06/07	07/07
149	149	153	153	150	154	153	153	152	148	164	165

Ba continued their dominance of football in Fiji by winning every major title on offer over the course of 2006 and 2007. Having won the Super Cup in April 2006, the Fiji Bitter FA Cup the following month, thanks to a 3-0 victory over Labassa, Ba then followed up with a 2-1 victory over Suva in August 2006 to win the Battle of the Giants. September saw them crowned Pepsi Football League champions, finishing the season 11 points ahead of Nadi, and they ended the year with a 3-0 victory over Suva in the final of the Inter-District Soccer Tournament to complete the clean sweep of all five trophies. 2007 began with a 7-3 aggregate victory over Suva in the Champions versus

INTERNATIONAL HONOURS
Melanesian Cup 1988 1989 1992 1998 2000 **South Pacific Games** 1991 2003

Champion Super Cup in April, followed by a 1-0 victory over Labasa in the FA Cup final and a 2-1 victory over Nadi in the Battle of the Giants in June to take to eight the number of consecutive tournaments won. Ba almost added a ninth when they came within a whisker of winning the inaugural OFC O-League. Having won their first round group ahead of Tahiti's Temanava and Marist from the Solomon Islands, they met New Zealand's Waitakere United in the final. A 2-1 victory at home in the first leg was followed by a 1-0 defeat in Auckland which meant they lost on away goals, and missed out on a trip to the FIFA Club World Cup in Japan.

THE FIFA BIG COUNT OF 2006

	Male	Female		Total
Number of players	46 338	3 350	Referees and Assistant Referees	117
Professionals	0		Admin, Coaches, Technical, Medical	2 929
Amateurs 18+	11 188		Number of clubs	400
Youth under 18	17 300		Number of teams	2 000
Unregistered	8 200		Clubs with women's teams	10
Total players	49 688		Players as % of population	5.48%

Fiji Football Association (FFA)
73 Knolly Street, PO Box 2514, Suva, Fiji
Tel +679 3300453   Fax +679 3304642
bobkumar@fijifootball.com.fj   www.fijifootball.com
President: SAHU KHAN Muhammad   General Secretary: KUMAR Bob Sant
Vice-President: YUSUF Mohammed   Treasurer: TBD   Media Officer: None
Men's Coach: BUZZETTI Juan   Women's Coach: FAROUK Janeman
FFA formed: 1938   OFC: 1966   FIFA: 1963
White shirts, Black shorts, Black socks

RECENT INTERNATIONAL MATCHES PLAYED BY FIJI

2003	Opponents	Score		Venue	Comp	Scorers	Att	Referee
30-06	Vanuatu	D	0-0	Suva	SPr1			Taga VAN
7-07	Solomon Islands	W	2-1	Lautoka	SPr1	Veresa Toma [4], Esala Masi [13]	6 000	Ariiotima TAH
9-07	Tahiti	W	2-1	Lautoka	SPsf	Waqa [9], Veresa Toma [106]	8 000	Attison VAN
11-07	New Caledonia	W	2-0	Suva	SPf	Manoa Masi [30], Esala Masi [63]	10 000	Attison VAN
2004								
12-05	Papua New Guinea	W	4-2	Apia	WCq	Rabo [24], Veresa Toma [48+], Gataurua [78], Rokotakala [90]	400	Diomis AUS
15-05	American Samoa	W	11-0	Apia	WCq	Veresa Toma 3 [7 11 16], Vulivulu [24], Rokotakala 2 [32 38], Sabutu 2 [46+ 81], Esala Masi [60], Gataurua 2 [75 77]	300	Fox NZL
17-05	Samoa	W	4-0	Apia	WCq	Veresa Toma [17], Sabutu [52], Esala Masi [82], Rokotakala [84]	450	Diomis AUS
19-05	Vanuatu	L	0-3	Apia	WCq		200	Breeze AUS
29-05	Tahiti	D	0-0	Adelaide	WCq		3 000	Farina ITA
31-05	Vanuatu	W	1-0	Adelaide	WCq	Veresa Toma [73]	500	Ariiotima TAH
2-06	Australia	L	1-6	Adelaide	WCq	Gataurua [19]	2 200	Iturralde González ESP
4-06	Solomon Islands	L	1-2	Adelaide	WCq	Veresa Toma [21]	1 500	Attison VAN
6-06	New Zealand	L	0-2	Adelaide	WCq		300	Larsen DEN
2005								
12-08	India	W	1-0	Lautoka	Fr	Esala Masi [14p]	10 000	Fox NZL
14-08	India	W	2-1	Suva	Fr	Luke Vidovi [25], Esala Masi [61]	11 000	O'Leary NZL
2006								

No international matches played in 2006
2007

No international matches played in 2007 before August

OC = Oceania Nations Cup • SP = South Pacific Games • WC = FIFA World Cup • q = qualifier • r1 = first round group • sf = semi-final • f = final

FIJI NATIONAL TEAM RECORDS AND RECORD SEQUENCES

Records			Sequence records					
Victory	15-1	GUM 1991, COK 1971	Wins	6	2003-2004	Clean sheets	4	1992, 1989-90
Defeat	0-13	NZL 1981	Defeats	8	1985-1986	Goals scored	15	1985-1989
Player Caps	n/a		Undefeated	13	1989-1991	Without goal	5	1985
Player Goals	n/a		Without win	12	1983-1988	Goals against	13	1983-1988

RECENT LEAGUE AND CUP RECORD

	League	Inter-District Competition			Battle of the Giants			FA Cup		
Year	Winners	Winners	Score	Finalist	Winners	Score	Finalist	Winners	Score	Finalist
1997	Suva	Ba	2-0	Nadi	Labasa	1-0	Nadi	Labasa	0-0	Ba
1998	Nadi	Nadi	3-1	Lautoka	Ba	3-0	Nadi	Ba	3-0	Nadi
1999	Ba	Nadi	1-0	Ba	Ba	1-0	Tavua	Labasa	2-1	Lautoka
2000	Nadi	Ba	1-0	Nadi	Ba	2-0	Labasa	Lautoka	2-0	Nadroga
2001	Ba	Rewa	1-0	Ba	Ba	2-0	Lautoka	Nadroga	1-1 7-6p	Labasa
2002	Ba	Nadi	1-1 4-2p	Rewa	Nadroga	2-1	Labasa	Lautoka	1-1 3-2p	Nasinu
2003	Ba	Ba	1-0	Nadi	Rewa	1-0	Ba	Navua	1-0	Rewa
2004	Ba	Ba	3-0	Rewa	Rewa	2-0	Nadi	Ba	2-0	Suva
2005	Ba	Lautoka	2-0	Ba	Navua	1-0	Rewa	Ba	1-0	Nadi
2006	Ba	Ba	3-0	Suva	Ba	2-1	Suva	Ba	3-0	Labasa
2007		Ba	2-1	Nadi	Ba	2-1	Nadi	Ba	1-0	Labasa

FIJI COUNTRY INFORMATION

Capital	Suva	Independence	1970 from the UK	GDP per Capita	$5 800
Population	880 874	Status	Republic	GNP Ranking	141
Area km²	18 270	Language	English, Fijian	Dialling code	+679
Population density	48 per km²	Literacy rate	93%	Internet code	.fj
% in urban areas	41%	Main religion	Christian 52%, Hindu 38%	GMT +/−	+12
Towns/Cities ('000)	Suva 199; Nadi 53; Lautoka 49; Labasa 33; Nausori 32; Lami 21; Ba 20; Sigatoka 12				
Neighbours (km)	Fiji consists of two large islands, Viti Levu and Vanua Levu, along with 880 islets in the South Pacific				
Main stadia	National Stadium – Suva 5 000; Govind Park – Ba 4 000; Churchill Park – Lautoka 2 000				

FIN – FINLAND

NATIONAL TEAM RECORD
JULY 10TH 2006 TO JULY 12TH 2010

PL	W	D	L	F	A	%
9	4	2	3	10	7	55.5

FIFA/COCA-COLA WORLD RANKING

1993	1994	1995	1996	1997	1998	1999	2000	2001	2002	2003	2004	2005	2006	High		Low	
45	38	44	79	60	55	56	59	46	43	40	43	46	52	33	03/07	79	12/96

					2006–2007							
	08/06	09/06	10/06	11/06	12/06	01/07	02/07	03/07	04/07	05/07	06/07	07/07
	67	61	56	52	52	52	48	33	45	45	42	41

Roy Hodgson's appointment as Finland national team coach eventually brought results as a 10 match winless run was brought to an end with an impressive 3-1 away victory over Poland in their opening UEFA Euro 2008 qualifier. Other wins followed - notably over Belgium - but inconsistency undermined their chances of qualifying for the finals in Austria and Switzerland, despite heading the group in the early stages. The experience of older players like Jari Litmanen has helped Hodgson create a settled side and his goals in the qualifiers have taken his overall tally to a record 28. Although most of the players in the national team continue to play abroad, the League in

INTERNATIONAL HONOURS
None

Finland is improving, helped by the emergence of ambitious clubs like Honka from Espoo, the second largest city in the country. They led the table in their first season in the top flight and although they finished fourth, they did qualify for Europe. The championship went down to the final day with the top two, Tampere United and HJK Helsinki playing each other. On the back of an unbeaten run of 13 matches, HJK needed to win to overtake Tampere, but they lost 3-0 handing the title to their opponents. There was consolation for HJK the following week when they beat KPV Kokkola in the Cup Final, Algerian Farid Ghazi scoring the only goal of the game.

THE FIFA BIG COUNT OF 2006

	Male	Female		Total
Number of players	304 398	58 251	Referees and Assistant Referees	2 655
Professionals	360		Admin, Coaches, Technical, Medical	14 300
Amateurs 18+	26 555		Number of clubs	990
Youth under 18	101 334		Number of teams	4 258
Unregistered	120 000		Clubs with women's teams	270
Total players	362 469		Players as % of population	6.93%

Suomen Palloliitto (SPL/FBF)
Urheilukatu 5, PO Box 191, Helsinki 00251, Finland
Tel +358 9 742151   Fax +358 9 74215200
firstname.lastname@palloliitto.fi   www.palloliitto.fi
President: HAMALAINEN Pekka   General Secretary: HOLOPAINEN Teuvo
Vice-President: LEHTOLA Markku   Treasurer: HOLOPAINEN Teuvo   Media Officer: TERAVA Sami
Men's Coach: HODGSON Roy   Women's Coach: KALD Michael
SPL/FBF formed: 1907   UEFA: 1954   FIFA: 1908
White shirts with blue trimmings, Blue shorts, White socks or Blue shirts with white trimmings, White shorts, Red socks

RECENT INTERNATIONAL MATCHES PLAYED BY FINLAND

2004	Opponents	Score		Venue	Comp	Scorers	Att	Referee
3-02	China	L	1-2	Guangzhou	Fr	Eremenko [51]	15 000	Lee Gi Young KOR
7-02	China	L	1-2	Shenzhen	Fr	Kopteff [37]	18 000	Bae Jae Young KOR
31-03	Malta	W	2-1	Ta'Qali	Fr	Eremenko [51], Litmanen [86]	1 100	Trefoloni ITA
28-04	Bosnia-Herzegovina	L	0-1	Zenica	Fr		20 000	Bozinovski MKD
28-05	Sweden	L	1-3	Tammerfors	Fr	Litmanen [8p]	16 500	Undiano Mallenco ESP
18-08	Romania	L	1-2	Bucharest	WCq	Eremenko [90+3]	17 500	Gilewski POL
4-09	Andorra	W	3-0	Tampere	WCq	Eremenko 2 [42 64], Riihhilahti [58]	7 437	Siric CRO
8-09	Armenia	W	2-0	Yerevan	WCq	Forssell [24], Eremenko [67]	2 864	Malzinskas LTU
9-10	Armenia	W	3-1	Tampere	WCq	Kuqi 2 [9 87], Eremenko [28]	7 894	Fandel GER
13-10	Netherlands	L	1-3	Amsterdam	WCq	Tainio [13]	50 000	Bennett ENG
17-11	Italy	L	0-1	Messina	Fr		7 043	Tudor ROU
1-12	Bahrain	W	2-1	Manama	Fr	Pohja [9], Huusko [67]	10 000	Najm LIB
3-12	Oman	D	0-0	Manama	Fr	L 3-4p	3 000	Masoudi IRN
2005								
8-02	Latvia	W	2-1	Nicosia	Fr	Johansson J [31], Huusko [72]	102	Kailis CYP
9-02	Cyprus	W	2-1	Nicosia	Fr	Roiha 2 [66 70]	1 502	Romans LVA
12-03	Kuwait	W	1-0	Kuwait City	Fr	Kuqi.N [16]	1 500	Al Shatti KUW
18-03	Saudi Arabia	W	4-1	Dammam	Fr	Kuivasto [4], Kuqi.N 2 [71 78], Nurmela [76]	8 000	Al Amri KSA
26-03	Czech Republic	L	3-4	Teplice	WCq	Litmanen [46], Riihilahti [73], Johansson J [79]	16 200	Larsen DEN
2-06	Denmark	L	0-1	Tampere	Fr		9 238	Wegereef NED
8-06	Netherlands	L	0-4	Helsinki	WCq		37 786	Hamer LUX
17-08	FYR Macedonia	W	3-0	Skopje	WCq	Eremenko 2 [8 45], Roiha [87]	6 800	Messias ENG
3-09	Andorra	D	0-0	Andorra la Vella	WCq		860	Van Eecke BEL
7-09	FYR Macedonia	W	5-1	Tampere	WCq	Forssell 3 [10 12 61], Tihinen [41], Eremenko [54]	6 467	Jakobsson ISL
8-10	Romania	L	0-1	Helsinki	WCq		11 500	Guenov BUL
12-10	Czech Republic	L	0-3	Helsinki	WCq		11 234	Mejuto Gonzalez ESP
12-11	Estonia	D	2-2	Helsinki	Fr	Sjolund [7], Arkivuo [59]	1 900	Gilewski POL
2006								
21-01	Saudi Arabia	D	1-1	Riyadh	Fr	Roiha [87]	3 000	Al Anzi KUW
25-01	Korea Republic	L	0-1	Riyadh	Fr		800	Al Jerman KSA
18-02	Japan	L	0-2	Shizuoka	Fr		40 702	Lee Gi Young KOR
28-02	Kazakhstan	D	0-0	Larnaca	Fr	L 1-3p	100	Trattos CYP
1-03	Belarus	D	2-2	Larnaca	Fr	Riihilahti [82], Forssell [90]. W 5-4p	120	Krajnic SVN
25-05	Sweden	D	0-0	Gothenburg	Fr		25 754	Gilewski POL
16-08	Northern Ireland	L	1-2	Helsinki	Fr	Väyrynen [74]	12 500	Svendsen DEN
2-09	Poland	W	3-1	Bydgoszcz	ECq	Litmanen 2 [54 76p], Väyrynen [84]	13 000	Duhamel FRA
6-09	Portugal	D	1-1	Helsinki	ECq	Johansson [22]	38 010	Plautz AUT
7-10	Armenia	D	0-0	Yerevan	ECq		2 800	Skomina SVN
11-10	Kazakhstan	W	2-0	Almaty	ECq	Litmanen [27], Hyypiä [65]	17 863	Briakos GRE
15-11	Armenia	W	1-0	Helsinki	ECq	Nurmela [10]	9 445	Thomson SCO
2007								
28-03	Azerbaijan	L	0-1	Baku	ECq		14 500	Messina ITA
2-06	Serbia	L	0-2	Helsinki	ECq		33 615	Mejuto Gonzalez ESP
6-06	Belgium	W	2-0	Helsinki	ECq	Johansson [27], Eremenko Jr [71]	34 818	Riley ENG

Fr = Friendly match • EC = UEFA EURO 2004/2008 • WC = FIFA World Cup • q = qualifier

FINLAND NATIONAL TEAM RECORDS AND RECORD SEQUENCES

Records			Sequence records					
Victory	10-2	EST 1922	Wins	4	2005	Clean sheets	3	1924, 1993
Defeat	0-13	GER 1940	Defeats	14	1967-1969	Goals scored	14	1925-1927
Player Caps	107	LITMANEN Jari	Undefeated	10	2001-2002	Without goal	5	1937, 1971-1972
Player Goals	28	LITMANEN Jari	Without win	27	1939-1949	Goals against	44	1936-1949

MAJOR CITIES/TOWNS
Population '000

1	Helsinki	558
2	Espoo	235
3	Tampere	204
4	Vantaa	192
5	Turku	176
6	Oulu	131
7	Lahti	99
8	Kuopio	89
9	Jyväskylä	87
10	Pori	77
11	Lappeenranta	59
12	Vaasa	57
13	Kotka	54
14	Joensuu	54
15	Porvoo	48
16	Hämeenlinna	47
17	Mikkeli	46
18	Hyvinkää	43
19	Kokkola	35
20	Rovaniemi	34
21	Kouvola	30
22	Valkeakoski	20
23	Pietarsaari	19
24	Anjalankoski	16

REPUBLIC OF FINLAND; SUOMEN TASAVALTA

Capital	Helsinki	Language	Finnish	Independence	1917
Population	5 231 372	Area	338 145 km^2	Density 15 per km^2	% in cities 63%
GDP per cap	$27 000	Dailling code	+358	Internet .fi	GMT + / - +2

MEDALS TABLE

	Overall			League			Cup			Europe			City	Stadium	Cap'ty	DoF
	G	S	B	G	S	B	G	S	B	G	S	B				
1 HJK Helsinki	30	17	11	21	13	11	9	4					Helsinki	Finnair Stadion	10 770	1907
2 Haka Valkeakoski	21	9	10	9	6	10	12	3					Valkeakoski	Tehtaan kenttä	6 400	1934
3 TPS Turku	10	17	6	8	12	6	2	5					Turku	Veritas Stadion	9 000	1922
4 Reipas Lahti	10	9	3	3	6	3	7	3					Lahti			1891
5 HPS Helsinki	10	7	2	9	6	2	1	1					Helsinki			1917
6 HIFK Helsinki	7	8	4	7	7	4		1					Helsinki			1897
7 KuPS Kuopio	7	8	1	5	8	1	2						Kuopio	Magnum Arena	2 700	1923
8 FC Lahti	7	8		5	4		2	4					Lahti	Lahden Stadion	14 500	1996
9 Tampere United	6	3	3	4	1	3	2	2					Tampere	Ratina Stadion	16 850	1998
10 KTP Kotka	6	3	2	2		2	4	3					Kotka			1927-2001
11 MyPa-47	4	5	3	1	5	3	3						Anjalankoski	Jalkapallokenttä	4 067	1947
12 Abo IFK Turku	4	5	1	3	5	1	1						Turku			1908
13 Kronshagen IF Helsinki	4	2	3	4	1	3						1	Helsinki			1908
14 IFK Vaasa	3	2	2	3	2	2							Vaasa			1900
15 VPS Vaasa	2	6	1	2	5	1		1					Vaasa	Hietalahti	4 300	1924

RECENT LEAGUE AND CUP RECORD

	Championship						Cup		
Year	Champions	Pts	Runners-up	Pts	Third	Pts	Winners	Score	Runners-up
1995	Haka Valkeakoski	59	MyPa-47	53	HJK Helsinki	52	MyPa-47	1-0	FC Jazz Pori
1996	FC Jazz Pori	47	MyPa-47	45	TPS Turku	44	HJK Helsinki	0-0 4-3p	TPS Turku
1997	HJK Helsinki	58	VPS Vaasa	48	FinnPa Helsinki	39	Haka Valkeakoski	2-1	TPS Turku
1998	Haka Valkeakoski	48	VPS Vaasa	45	PK-35 Helsinki	44	HJK Helsinki	3-2	PK-35 Helsinki
1999	Haka Valkeakoski	67	HJK Helsinki	65	MyPa-47	47	Jokerit Helsinki	2-1	FF Jaro Pietarsaari
2000	Haka Valkeakoski	66	Jokerit Helsinki	62	MyPa-47	61	HJK Helsinki	1-0	KTP Kotka
2001	Tampere United	68	HJK Helsinki	67	MyPa-47	62	Atlantis Helsinki	1-0	Tampere United
2002	HJK Helsinki	65	MyPa-47	60	Haka Valkeakoski	52	Haka Valkeakoski	4-1	FC Lahti
2003	HJK Helsinki	57	Haka Valkeakoski	53	Tampere United	47	HJK Helsinki	2-1	Allianssi Vantaa
2004	Haka Valkeakoski	59	Allianssi Vantaa	48	Tampere United	47	MyPa-47	2-1	Hämeenlinna
2005	MyPa-47	56	HJK Helsinki	52	Tampere United	51	Haka Valkeakoski	4-1	TPS Turku
2006	Tampere United	51	HJK Helsinki	45	Haka Valkeakoski		HJK Helsinki	1-0	KPV Kokkola

FINLAND 2006

VEIKKAUSLIIGA (1)

	Pl	W	D	L	F	A	Pts	Tampere	HJK	Haka	Honka	IFK	MyPa-47	TPS	Lahti	VPS	Inter	KooTeePee	Jaro	KuPS
Tampere United †	24	16	3	5	39	18	51		0-2	1-0	2-1	2-2	1-1	4-2	3-1	2-3	3-1	1-0	0-0	1-0
HJK Helsinki ‡	24	13	6	5	45	18	45	0-3		1-2	3-0	0-0	4-1	3-2	0-1	3-0	5-0	5-0	4-0	1-0
Haka Valkeakoski ‡	24	13	5	6	37	24	44	0-3	2-2		2-0	1-0	1-2	0-1	1-1	4-1	0-0	3-1	3-1	2-1
Honka Espoo	24	13	3	8	50	32	42	1-3	0-0	0-2		2-1	2-2	0-1	5-0	2-1	6-0	4-1	3-2	4-0
IFK Mariehamn	24	10	7	7	31	22	37	1-0	0-0	2-1	1-2		1-0	0-1	1-1	0-1	0-1	4-1	0-0	2-0
MyPa-47 Anjalankoski ‡	24	10	4	10	25	26	34	0-2	0-0	0-1	2-1	0-2		1-3	1-0	1-2	1-0	2-0	2-0	3-0
TPS Turku	24	9	4	11	35	38	31	0-1	1-4	1-2	0-2	0-4	0-0		1-0	2-1	2-2	7-0	0-3	1-2
FC Lahti	24	9	4	11	26	34	31	0-2	0-2	2-2	1-3	3-0	0-2	3-1		1-0	1-2	0-4	3-1	2-0
VPS Vaasa	24	8	5	11	26	36	29	1-0	2-2	2-1	1-2	2-2	3-0	1-1	0-2		0-2	2-1	0-0	0-2
Inter Turku	24	7	7	10	25	35	28	0-1	0-1	1-3	2-1	1-1	1-0	0-0	0-1	2-0		0-0	2-2	1-1
KooTeePee Kotka	24	8	3	13	26	44	27	1-0	2-1	0-2	1-2	1-2	0-1	0-3	2-1	2-0	3-1		2-1	3-1
Jaro Pietarsaari	24	4	7	13	27	42	19	1-2	2-0	0-0	2-5	1-3	1-3	5-0	1-2	1-1	1-5	0-0		1-0
KuPS Kuopio	24	5	4	15	18	41	19	0-2	0-2	1-2	2-2	1-2	1-0	0-5	0-0	1-2	2-1	1-1	2-1	

19/04/2006 - 29/10/2006 • † Qualified for the UEFA Champions League • ‡ Qualified for the UEFA Cup • Top scorers: Hermanni VUORINEN, Honka 16; RAFAEL, Lahti 13; Farid GHAZI, HJK 12; Antti POHJA, HJK 11; Mikko PAATELAINEN, Jaro 11; Ville LEHTINEN, Tampere 11

FINLAND 2006
YKKONEN (2)

	Pl	W	D	L	F	A	Pts
Viikingit Helsinki	26	17	5	4	65	25	56
AC Oulu	26	15	7	4	53	25	52
Atlantis Helsinki	26	13	8	5	49	34	47
TP-47 Tornio	26	12	5	9	35	25	41
JIPPO Joensuu	26	11	8	7	33	34	41
Klubi-04 Helsinki	26	11	5	10	49	27	38
RoPS Rovaniemi	26	10	8	8	40	35	38
VIFK Vaasa	26	9	8	9	45	46	35
KPV Kokkola	26	8	9	9	42	47	33
PK-35 Helsinki	26	6	12	8	33	39	30
FC Hämeenlinna	26	6	10	10	35	35	28
PP-70 Tampere	26	6	7	13	28	51	25
MP Mikkeli	26	7	3	16	30	54	24
Rakuunat Lappeenranta	26	2	3	21	14	74	9

29/04/2006 - 21/10/2006

SUOMEN CUP 2006

Round of 16		Quarter–finals		Semi–finals		Final	
HJK Helsinki	1						
Viikingit Helsinki *	0	HJK Helsinki *	2				
OLS *	0	FC Lahti	1				
FC Lahti	3			HJK Helsinki	2		
Inter Turku	1 11p			Tampere United	1		
Honka Espoo *	1 10p	Inter Turku *	0				
Kultsu FC *	0	Tampere United	2				
Tampere United	1					HJK Helsinki ‡	1
TPS Turku *	3					KPV Kokkola	0
PoPa	2	TPS Turku *	1				
PP-70 Tampere	1	KuPS Kuopio	0				
KuPS Kuopio *	2			TPS Turku	0		
PS Kemi *	3			KPV Kokkola	1		
TP-Seinäjoki	0	PS Kemi	0				
IFK Mariehamn	1	KPV Kokkola *	3				
KPV Kokkola *	2						

CUP FINAL

Finnair Stadium, Helsinki
4-11-2006

Goals - Farid Ghazi [63] for HJK

* Home team • ‡ Qualified for the UEFA Cup

FRA – FRANCE

NATIONAL TEAM RECORD

JULY 10TH 2006 TO JULY 12TH 2010

PL	W	D	L	F	A	%
11	9	0	2	19	4	81.8

To think that at the start of the decade French football fans were asking if Lyon would ever fulfil their potential and win the French League. Now the question being asked is how long will it be before someone else wins the title again. By winning their sixth successive Championship Lyon eclipsed the great Marseille team of the Tapie era that won five in a row. Gerard Houllier arrived to replace Paul Le Guen at the start of the season and the change of coach seemed to spur the team on. By the end of the year Lyon were 15 points clear of Lens and in an almost unassailable position. A dip in form in the new year barely affected their position and they finished 17 points ahead of Marseille in second place. However, the loss of form did scupper their UEFA Champions League hopes as they meekly bowed out to an inferior Roma side in the first knock-out round. Lyon also lost to Marseille in the Cup and despite winning six consecutive titles they have yet to do the double. Marseille, under the relative unknown Albert Emon, were the surprise of the season but had to settle for the runners-up spot in the Cup as well as the League. In a Cup tournament dominated by the exploits of small giantkilling clubs - notably fourth level Montceau who beat

INTERNATIONAL HONOURS

FIFA World Cup™ 1998   Qualified for the FIFA Women's World Cup finals 2003

Qualified for the FIFA World Cup™ finals 1930 1934 1938 1954 1958 1966 1978 1982 1986 1998 2002 2006

FIFA Junior Tournament 1949   FIFA U-17 World Championship 2001   UEFA European Championship 1984 2000

UEFA U-21 Championship 1988 UEFA U-19 Championship 1983 1996 1997 2000 UEFA U-17 Championship 2004

UEFA Champions League Olympique Marseille 1993

Bordeaux and Lens on the way to the semi-finals - it was unfancied Ligue 1 side Sochaux who won the tournament. They twice came from behind against Marseille in the final with Anthony Le Tallec equalising four minutes from the end of extra-time to force a penalty shoot-out. With the scores at 4-4, goalkeeper Teddy Richert saved from Ronald Zubar to win the Cup for Sochaux for the first time since 1937. The other trophy winners in the season were Bordeaux, who won the League Cup after beating Lyon 1-0 in the final. The season was marred by a rise in crowd trouble with a fireman losing two fingers after picking up an explosive device thrown onto the pitch by Marseille fans, whilst a PSG fan was shot dead by a policeman trying to protect a Hapoel Tel Aviv fan after a UEFA Cup match between the two. Continuity was the name of the game as far as the national team was concerned with Raymond Domenech continuing as coach after the World Cup. With six wins in their first seven UEFA Euro 2008 qualifiers, including a 3-1 triumph in a rematch of the World Cup final over Italy, the French looked to be comfortably on course for the finals in Austria and Switzerland.

Fédération Française de Football (FFF)

87, Boulevard de Grenelle, Paris 75738, France

Tel +33 1 44317300   Fax +33 1 44317373

webmaster@fff.fr   www.fff.fr

President: ESCALETTES Jean-Pierre   General Secretary: LAMBERT Jacques

Vice-President: THIRIEZ Frederic   Treasurer: DESUMER Bernard   Media Officer: LE GUILLARD Yann

Men's Coach: DOMENECH Raymond   Women's Coach: BINI Bruno

FFF formed: 1919   UEFA: 1954   FIFA: 1904

Blue shirts with white trimmings, White shorts, Red socks or White shirts with blue trimmings, Blue shorts, Red socks

RECENT INTERNATIONAL MATCHES PLAYED BY FRANCE

2003	Opponents	Score	Venue	Comp	Scorers	Att	Referee
13-06	England	W 2-1	Lisbon	ECr1	Zidane 2 [90 90+3]	65 272	Merk GER
17-06	Croatia	D 2-2	Leiria	ECr1	Tudor OG [22], Trezeguet [64]	29 160	Nielsen DEN
21-06	Switzerland	W 3-1	Coimbra	ECr1	Zidane [20], Henry 2 [76 84]	28 111	Michel SVK
25-06	Greece	L 0-1	Lisbon	ECqf		45 390	Frisk SWE
18-08	Bosnia-Herzegovina	D 1-1	Rennes	Fr	Luyindula [7]	26 527	McDonald SCO
4-09	Israel	D 0-0	Paris	WCq		43 527	Temmink NED
8-09	Faroe Islands	W 2-0	Tórshavn	WCq	Giuly [32], Cisse [73]	5 917	Thomson SCO
9-10	Ireland Republic	D 0-0	Paris	WCq		78 863	Dauden Ibañez ESP
13-10	Cyprus	W 2-0	Nicosia	WCq	Wiltord [38], Henry [72]	3 319	Larsen DEN
17-11	Poland	D 0-0	Paris	Fr		50 480	Benquerença POR
2005							
9-02	Sweden	D 1-1	Paris	Fr	Trezeguet [35]	56 923	Rodriguez Santiago ESP
26-03	Switzerland	D 0-0	Paris	WCq		79 373	De Santis ITA
30-03	Israel	D 1-1	Tel Aviv	WCq	Trezeguet [50]	32 150	Merk GER
31-05	Hungary	W 2-1	Metz	Fr	Cisse [10], Malouda [35]	26 000	Allaerts BEL
17-08	Côte d'Ivoire	W 3-0	Montpellier	Fr	Gallas [28], Zidane [62], Henry [66]	31 457	Bertini ITA
3-09	Faroe Islands	W 3-0	Lens	WCq	Cisse 2 [14 76], Olsen OG [18]	40 126	Jara CZE
7-09	Republic of Ireland	W 1-0	Dublin	WCq	Henry [68]	36 000	Fandel GER
8-10	Switzerland	D 1-1	Berne	WCq	Cisse [53]	31 400	Hauge NOR
12-10	Cyprus	W 4-0	Paris	WCq	Zidane [29], Wiltord [32], Dhorasoo [44], Giuly [84]	78 864	Stark GER
9-11	Costa Rica	W 3-2	Fort-de-France	Fr	Anelka [49], Cisse [80], Henry [87]	16 000	Alcala MEX
12-11	Germany	D 0-0	Paris	Fr		58 889	Bennett ENG
2006							
1-03	Slovakia	L 1-2	Paris	Fr	Wiltord [75p]	55 000	Thomson FRA
27-05	Mexico	W 1-0	Paris	Fr	Malouda [45]	80 000	Daami TUN
31-05	Denmark	W 2-0	Lens	Fr	Henry [13], Wiltord [76p]	39 000	Kelly IRL
7-06	China PR	W 3-1	St Etienne	Fr	Trezeguet [30], OG [89], Henry [92+]	34 147	Megia Davila ESP
13-06	Switzerland	D 0-0	Stuttgart	WCr1		52 000	Ivanov RUS
18-06	Korea Republic	D 1-1	Leipzig	WCr1	Henry [9]	43 000	Archundia MEX
23-06	Togo	W 2-0	Cologne	WCr1	Vieira [55], Henry [61]	45 000	Larrionda URU
27-06	Spain	W 3-1	Hanover	WCr2	Ribery [41], Vieira [83], Zidane [92+]	43 000	Rosetti ITA
1-07	Brazil	W 1-0	Frankfurt	WCqf	Henry [57]	48 000	Medina Cantalejo ESP
5-07	Portugal	W 1-0	Munich	WCsf	Zidane [33p]	66 000	Larrionda URU
9-07	Italy	D 1-1	Berlin	WCf	Zidane [7p]. L 3-5p	69 000	Elizondo ARG
16-08	Bosnia-Herzegovina	W 2-1	Sarajevo	Fr	Gallas [41], Faubert [90]	35 000	Wack GER
2-09	Georgia	W 3-0	Tbilisi	ECq	Malouda [7], Saha [16], Asatiani OG [47]	54 000	Wegereef NED
6-09	Italy	W 3-1	Paris	ECq	Govou 2 [2 55], Henry [18]	78 831	Fandel GER
7-10	Scotland	L 0-1	Glasgow	ECq		50 456	Busacca SUI
11-10	Faroe Islands	W 5-0	Sochaux	ECq	Saha [1], Henry [22], Anelka [77], Trezeguet 2 [78 84]	19 314	Corpodean ROU
15-11	Greece	W 1-0	Paris	Fr	Henry [27]	63 680	Wack GER/Wezel GER
2007							
7-02	Argentina	L 0-1	Paris	Fr		79 862	Skomina SVN
24-03	Lithuania	W 1-0	Kaunas	ECq	Anelka [73]	8 740	Webb ENG
28-03	Austria	W 1-0	Paris	Fr	Benzema [53]	65 000	Briakos GRE
2-06	Ukraine	W 2-0	Paris	ECq	Ribery [57], Anelka [71]	79 000	Medina Cantalejo ESP
6-06	Georgia	W 1-0	Auxerre	ECq	Nasri [33]	19 345	Batista POR

Fr = Friendly match • EC = UEFA EURO 2004/2008 • FIFA = FIFA Centennial match • WC = FIFA World Cup
q = qualifier • r1 = first round group • r2 = second round • qf = quarter-final • sf = semi-final • f = final

FRANCE NATIONAL TEAM RECORDS AND RECORD SEQUENCES

Records			Sequence records		
Victory	10-0	AZE 1995	Wins	14	2003-2004
Defeat	1-17	DEN 1908	Defeats	12	1908-1911
Player Caps	121	THURAM Lilian	Undefeated	30	1994-1996
Player Goals	41	PLATINI Michel	Without win	15	1908-1911

Clean sheets	11	2003-2004
Goals scored	17	1999-2000
Without goal	4	1924-1925, 1986
Goals against	24	1905-1912

FRENCH REPUBLIC; REPUBLIQUE FRANCAISE

Capital	Paris	Language	French	Unified state	486
Population	60 876136	Area	547 030 km²	Density 110 per km²	% in cities	73%
GDP per cap	$27 600	Dailling code	+33	Internet .fr	GMT + / -	+1

MEDALS TABLE

		Overall			League			Cup		LC		Europe			Stadium	Cap'ty	DoF
		G	S	B	G	S	B	G	S	G	S	G	S	B			
1	Olympique Marseille	19	19	6	8	8	4	10	8			1	3	2	Stade Velodrome	60 013	1899
2	AS Saint-Etienne	16	7	3	10	3	2	6	3			1	1		Geoffroy-Guichard	35 616	1920
3	AS Monaco	13	11	14	7	5	10	5	3	1	1	2	4		Stade Louis II	18 521	1924
4	Paris Saint-Germain	12	10	6	2	6	3	7	2	2	1	1	1	3	Parc des Princes	48 527	1970
5	FC Nantes Atlantique	11	13	4	8	7	2	3	5		1			2	Stade Beaujoire	38 373	1943
6	Girondins Bordeaux	10	17	6	5	8	4	3	6	2	2	1	2		Chaban-Delmas	34 198	1881
7	Olympique Lyonnais	10	6	5	6	2	4	3	3	1	1		1		Stade Gerland	41 044	1950
8	Lille OSC	8	11	3	3	7	3	5	4						Métropole	18 086	1944
9	Stade de Reims	8	6	4	6	3	4	2	1			2			Auguste-Delaune	7 000	1931
10	OGC Nice	7	5		4	3		3	1	1					Stade du Ray	18 696	1904
11	Racing Club Paris	6	4	5	1	2	5	5	2						Colombes	7 000	1897
12	Racing Club Strasbourg	6	4	3	1	1	3	3	3	2					Stade de la Meinau	29 000	1906
13	FC Sochaux-Montbéliard	5	7	5	2	3	4	2	3	1	1		1		Stade Bonal	20 005	1930
14	AJ Auxerre	5	1	5	1		4	4	1				1		Abbé-Deschamps	23 493	1905
15	Red Star 93 Paris	5	1					5	1						Stade de Marville	10 003	1897
16	FC Sète	4	4	1	2		1	2	4						Louis-Michel	1 200	1914
17	FC Metz	3	3	1	1	1		2	1	1	1				Saint-Symphorien	26 304	1932
18	Racing Club Lens	2	7	3	1	4	2		3	1			1		Félix-Bollaert	41 233	1906

RECENT LEAGUE AND CUP RECORD

	Championship						Cup		
Year	Champions	Pts	Runners-up	Pts	Third	Pts	Winners	Score	Runners-up
1995	FC Nantes	79	Olympique Lyonnais	69	Paris St-Germain	67	Paris St-Germain	1-0	RC Strasbourg
1996	AJ Auxerre	72	Paris St-Germain	68	AS Monaco	68	AJ Auxerre	2-1	Nîmes Olympique
1997	AS Monaco	79	Paris St-Germain	67	FC Nantes	64	OGC Nice	1-1 4-3p	Guingamp
1998	Racing Club Lens	68	FC Metz	68	AS Monaco	59	Paris St-Germain	2-1	Racing Club Lens
1999	Girondins Bordeaux	72	Olympique Marseille	71	Olympique Lyonnais	63	FC Nantes	1-0	CS Sedan Ardennes
2000	AS Monaco	65	Paris St-Germain	58	Olympique Lyonnais	56	FC Nantes	2-1	Calais
2001	FC Nantes	68	Olympique Lyonnais	64	Lille OSC	59	RC Strasbourg	0-0 5-4p	Amiens SC
2002	Olympique Lyonnais	66	Racing Club Lens	64	AJ Auxerre	59	FC Lorient	1-0	SC Bastia
2003	Olympique Lyonnais	68	AS Monaco	67	Olympique Marseille	65	AJ Auxerre	2-1	Paris St-Germain
2004	Olympique Lyonnais	79	Paris St-Germain	76	AS Monaco	75	Paris St-Germain	1-0	Châteauroux
2005	Olympique Lyonnais	79	Lille OSC	67	AS Monaco	63	AJ Auxerre	2-1	CS Sedan
2006	Olympique Lyonnais	84	Girondins Bordeaux	69	Lille OSC	62	Paris St-Germain	2-1	Olympique Marseille
2007	Olympique Lyonnais	81	Olympique Marseille	64	Toulouse FC	58	Sochaux	2-2 5-4p	Olympique Marseille

FRANCE 2006–07

LIGUE 1 ORANGE

	Pl	W	D	L	F	A	Pts	Lyon	Marseille	Toulouse	Rennes	Lens	Bordeaux	Sochaux	Auxerre	Monaco	Lille	St-Etienne	Le Mans	Nancy	Lorient	PSG	Nice	Val'ciennes	Troyes	Sedan	Nantes
Olympique Lyonnais †	38	24	9	5	64	27	81	—	1-1	1-1	0-0	3-0	1-2	3-3	1-0	0-0	4-1	2-1	2-1	1-0	1-0	3-1	1-1	2-1	2-0	1-0	3-1
Olympique Marseille †	38	19	7	12	53	38	64	1-4	—	3-0	2-0	0-1	2-1	4-2	3-1	2-1	4-1	2-1	2-0	2-1	0-1	1-1	3-0	1-0	2-1	1-0	0-0
Toulouse FC †	38	17	7	14	44	43	58	2-0	3-0	—	1-0	0-1	3-1	1-2	2-0	1-1	1-0	1-0	0-1	2-2	0-0	1-3	1-0	3-0	1-1	3-1	0-4
Stade Rennais ‡	38	14	15	9	38	30	57	1-0	0-2	3-2	—	1-0	0-2	3-1	1-1	1-2	0-1	1-1	4-1	1-0	1-0	1-0	1-0	1-0	2-2		
Racing Club Lens	38	15	12	11	47	41	57	0-4	1-1	2-0	0-0	—	3-0	3-1	1-0	1-0	1-1	3-3	2-0	2-2	1-1	1-2	0-0	3-0	1-0	0-1	1-2
Girondins Bordeaux ‡	38	16	9	13	39	35	57	1-2	1-0	2-0	1-2	1-0	—	2-0	0-0	1-0	0-1	1-0	1-0	3-0	1-0	0-0	3-2	2-1	2-1	3-1	0-1
Sochaux-Montbéliard ‡	38	15	12	11	46	48	57	0-1	1-0	4-2	0-0	0-3	2-1	—	1-1	2-1	0-0	1-0	2-0	2-1	1-1	3-2	1-1	1-0	1-0	1-1	1-2
AJ Auxerre	38	13	15	10	41	41	54	0-0	0-3	1-0	1-0	0-0	1-0		—	2-1	2-1	1-2	0-3	2-1	0-0	0-0	1-1	1-0	2-2	1-0	
AS Monaco	38	13	12	13	45	38	51	1-0	1-2	1-3	0-2	0-0	0-0	3-0	2-1	—	3-1	1-2	2-1	2-0	2-2	1-2	0-0	3-0	0-0	2-1	2-1
Lille OSC	38	13	11	14	45	43	50	1-2	1-0	1-3	1-1	4-0	3-0	2-0	1-1	1-1	—	2-2	0-2	0-1	1-0	1-0	1-0	0-2	4-0	2-1	0-0
AS Saint-Etienne	38	14	7	17	52	50	49	1-3	1-2	3-0	1-3	3-2	0-2	1-2	2-3	0-1	2-1	—	2-0	1-0	2-0	1-0	2-1	3-0	3-1	1-2	2-1
Le Mans UC 72	38	11	16	11	45	46	49	0-1	2-0	2-0	0-0	1-1	1-2	2-2	2-0	2-1	2-1		—	0-0	1-1	1-1	3-0	1-2	2-0	3-2	1-1
AS Nancy-Lorraine	38	13	10	15	37	44	49	0-3	2-0	2-1	0-0	2-1	2-1	5-2	1-0	1-0	1-3	0-2	1-1	—		0-1	0-3	3-0	1-0	1-0	1-1
FC Lorient	38	12	13	13	33	40	49	1-3	2-1	0-1	0-0	1-0	0-1	1-3	2-1	0-0	0-0	0-0	2-1	2-0	—		0-1	0-0	1-0	0-0	2-0	3-1
Paris Saint-Germain	38	12	12	14	42	42	48	1-1	1-3	0-0	1-0	1-3	0-2	0-0	0-1	4-2	1-0	0-2	2-1	0-0	2-3	—		0-0	1-2	2-1	4-2	4-0
OGC Nice	38	9	16	13	34	40	43	1-4	2-1	0-1	1-1	1-2	2-1	0-0	0-0	1-2	1-1	3-3	0-0	3-0	1-0		—	2-0	3-0	2-2		
Valenciennes FC	38	11	10	17	36	48	43	0-0	0-0	0-0	3-1	1-3	2-0	0-0	1-3	2-2	0-3	1-0	1-1	0-0	0-0	0-1		—	3-1	2-1	1-0
ES Troyes FC	38	9	12	17	39	54	39	1-0	1-1	1-2	2-2	3-0	1-0	0-1	3-3	0-4	1-1	3-1	2-2	0-0	0-0	1-1	1-2	0-1	—	3-2	1-0
CS Sedan Ardennes	38	7	14	17	46	58	35	0-1	0-0	0-2	1-0	2-2	1-1	1-1	2-2	0-1	2-0	2-2	1-2	2-2	3-1	2-0	1-1	1-1	1-2	—	1-1
FC Nantes	38	7	13	18	29	49	34	1-3	2-1	0-0	0-2	0-0	0-0	0-2	1-1	1-0	1-1	2-2	0-0	2-1	0-2	1-1	1-0	2-5	1-1	0-1	—

4/08/2006 - 26/05/2007 • † Qualified for the UEFA Champions League • ‡ Qualified for the UEFA Cup

Top scorers: PAULETA, PSG 15; Steve SAVIDAN, Valenciennes 13; Mamadou NIANG, Marseille 12; GRAFITE, Le Mans 12; Ismael BANGOURA, Le Mans 12

FRANCE 2006–07

LIGUE 2 ORANGE

	Pl	W	D	L	F	A	Pts	Metz	Caen	Strasbourg	Amiens	Grenoble	Le Havre	Châteauroux	Dijon	Bastia	Gueugnon	Reims	Ajaccio	Guingamp	Brest	Montpellier	Niort	Libourne	Créteil	Istres	Tours
FC Metz	38	22	10	6	54	22	76	—	2-0	4-1	1-0	1-2	1-0	2-0	5-0	2-1	1-2	2-2	2-0	1-0	0-0	2-1	0-0	1-0	2-0	3-0	2-1
SM Caen	38	19	14	5	65	40	71	0-0	—	2-2	3-1	0-1	1-1	1-0	3-2	2-0	1-1	2-1	4-0	1-1	1-0	0-0	4-0	2-1	1-0	4-0	1-0
RC Strasbourg	38	19	13	6	47	33	70	2-1	3-2	—	1-0	1-0	1-1	2-0	0-0	1-1	2-1	1-0	0-0	2-0	1-0	2-0	1-0	2-1	1-0	2-0	2-1
Amiens SFC	38	21	6	11	57	42	69	0-2	2-2	1-0	—	0-1	2-0	3-1	0-4	1-0	2-0	2-1	1-3	1-2	2-0	4-1	1-0	1-1	1-0	1-2	1-3 0-0
Grenoble Foot 38	38	15	14	9	51	39	59	1-1	1-1	1-1	0-1	—	1-1	2-1	0-1	2-1	1-1	2-2	5-1	2-0	1-0	0-0	3-2	4-1	2-1	1-3	1-3 0-2
Le Havre AC	38	15	11	12	52	38	56	1-1	2-2	0-1	1-3	1-1	—	1-0	1-2	2-0	6-1	0-4	1-2	0-0	3-0	2-2	2-2	0-2	1-1	0-3	0-0
LB Châteauroux	38	15	9	14	42	44	54	0-1	1-1	1-1	3-1	2-2	2-2	—	2-1	1-2	2-1	1-1	2-1	1-0	1-0	0-1	0-0	1-1	1-0	0-0	3-1
Dijon FCO	38	14	12	12	44	47	54	0-3	0-2	3-1	1-2	1-1	2-1	2-0	—	0-0	1-0	1-0	2-2	2-1	1-1	1-1	2-1	0-1	1-1	1-0	2-1
SC Bastia	38	14	11	13	52	49	53	1-0	2-0	1-2	2-0	0-1	1-1	2-1	1-1	—	0-1	1-0	4-1	0-0	4-2	1-0	4-1	3-2	1-2	4-1	2-0
FC Gueugnon	38	13	9	16	47	52	48	0-1	0-1	0-1	2-1	0-0	2-1	3-0	0-2	4-2	—	0-0	1-0	2-0	4-2	3-0	0-1	1-3	1-3	3-3	2-1
Stade de Reims	38	12	11	15	43	46	47	2-0	2-2	2-0	1-0	0-1	3-2	0-2	1-0	1-1	1-0	—	4-1	1-0	2-0	4-1	2-1	3-1	1-0	0-1	2-2 1-1
AC Ajaccio	38	12	11	15	44	50	47	2-1	0-0	2-2	3-1	3-1	0-0	2-3	3-0	0-1	1-1	2-1	—	0-0	2-1	0-2	1-1	1-0	5-0	2-0	0-1
En Avant Guingamp	38	11	13	14	45	44	46	0-2	1-3	1-1	2-3	2-2	1-2	1-2	2-4	6-1	1-0	1-1	—	1-1	1-0	1-0	2-1	2-1	1-3	0-3	1-1
Stade Brestois	38	10	15	13	40	40	45	0-1	2-2	1-1	1-1	1-0	2-0	0-0	0-0	3-1	2-1	3-0	0-1	2-3	—	0-0	1-0	2-2	4-1	0-0	1-1
Montpellier-Hérault	38	11	11	16	41	48	44	1-1	1-2	0-0	1-2	1-0	2-1	1-3	3-0	4-0	0-3	2-0	1-2	1-1	0-0	—	2-1	0-1	1-1	4-0	1-0
Chamois Niortais	38	10	14	14	36	44	44	1-1	2-2	2-2	2-0	2-1	0-0	2-0	2-1	0-0	1-1	0-3	0-0	1-1	1-0	1-1	—	2-0	2-1	0-0	0-0
Libourne St-Seurin	38	12	8	18	43	52	44	0-2	1-2	1-0	1-1	2-1	0-0	0-1	0-1	2-4	2-1	2-3	1-0	1-1	3-2	2-2	3-1	—	0-2	1-2	1-0
US Créteil-Lusitanos	38	9	13	16	33	50	40	1-1	4-3	0-2	0-2	1-1	1-3	1-1	1-0	0-0	1-0	0-0	0-0	1-0	3-1	1-0	—	1-0	4-3		
FC Istres	38	8	11	19	35	63	35	0-0	1-2	3-2	1-3	3-0	0-1	3-1	2-2	2-2	0-1	2-2	1-4	1-0	1-1	1-2	1-0	2-2	0-0	—	2-1
Tours	38	6	8	24	30	58	26	0-1	2-3	0-0	0-2	1-1	0-2	2-1	0-1	0-3	2-1	0-0	1-0	1-1	1-2	1-1	1-1	0-0	1-2	1-1 2-0	—

28/07/2006 - 25/05/2007 • Top scorers: Jean-Michel LESAGE, Le Havre 18; Kandia TRAORE, Le Havre 18; Babacar GUEYE, Metz 16

COUPE DE FRANCE 2006–07

Round of 64		
Sochaux-Montbéliard	3	
AS Saint-Etienne *	1	
Entente SSG	0	
Lyon-Duchère *	1	
Toulouse FC	1	4p
Châtellerault *	1	3p
Quevilly *	0	
AS Monaco	2	
Valenciennes FC *	2	
SM Caen	1	
Stade Rennais *	1	
Romorantin	3	
FC Gueugnon *	3	
Louhans-Cuiseaux	1	
Nîmes Olympique	0	
Paris Saint-Germain *	3	
Racing Club Lens	3	9p
AS Nancy-Lorraine *	3	8p
Moulins	1	
Orléans *	2	
Rodez *	3	
Angoulême	1	
Dunkerque	1	
Clermont Foot *	3	
Girondins Bordeaux *	2	
SC Bastia	0	
AJ Auxerre *	2	4p
Chamois Niortais	2	5p
Pontivy *	1	
Vitré	0	
Feignies *	1	
Montceau-les-Mines	2	
FC Nantes *	1	
En Avant Guingamp	0	
Grenoble	0	
Amiens SFC *	3	
RC Strasbourg	2	
GFCO Ajaccio *	1	
FC Metz *	0	
Lille OSC	2	
Libourne Saint-Seurin *	4	
ES Troyes FC	2	
Amnéville	0	
Jarville *	1	
Calais *	2	
Lorient	0	
Pont de Chéruy *	0	
CS Sedan Ardennes	1	
Vannes Olympique Club *	3	
Concarneau	2	
Châteaubriant	1	
Bois-Guillaume * §	0	
OGC Nice	2	
US Créteil-Lusitanos *	1	
Saint-Lô	1	
Montpellier-Hérault *	4	
Olympique Lyonnais	2	
Bayonne *	1	
Palaiseau *	0	
Laon	4	
Le Mans	3	
Pluvigner Keriolets *	0	
Cambrai *	1	
Olympique Marseille	4	

Round of 32		
Sochaux-Montbéliard *	2	
Lyon-Duchère	1	
Toulouse FC	0	
AS Monaco *	2	
Valenciennes FC	2	
Romorantin *	1	
FC Gueugnon	0	
Paris Saint-Germain *	1	
Racing Club Lens	3	
Orléans *	1	
Rodez	0	
Clermont Foot *	1	
Girondins Bordeaux *	3	5p
Chamois Niortais	3	4p
Pontivy *	0	
Montceau-les-Mines	2	
FC Nantes	3	
Amiens SFC *	1	
RC Strasbourg *	2	
Lille OSC	3	
Libourne Saint-Seurin	5	
Jarville *	3	
Calais *	1	
CS Sedan Ardennes	2	
Vannes Olympique Club	1	6p
Bois Guillaume *	1	5p
OGC Nice	1	2p
Montpellier-Hérault *	1	4p
Olympique Lyonnais	3	
Laon *	1	
Le Mans *	0	
Olympique Marseille	1	

Round of 16		
Sochaux-Montbéliard	2	
AS Monaco *	0	
Valenciennes FC	0	
Paris Saint-Germain *	1	
Racing Club Lens	4	
Clermont Foot *	1	
Girondins Bordeaux	2	4p
Montceau-les-Mines *	2	5p
FC Nantes *	1	
Lille OSC	0	
Libourne Saint-Seurin *	1	
CS Sedan Ardennes	2	
Vannes Olympique Club	2	
Montpellier-Hérault *	0	
Olympique Lyonnais	1	
Olympique Marseille *	2	

* Home team • § Awarded to Bois-Guillaume

COUPE DE FRANCE 2006–07

Quarter–finals	Semi–finals	Final

Sochaux-Montbéliard — 2
Paris Saint-Germain — 1

Sochaux-Montbéliard — 2
Montceau-les-Mines * † — 0

Racing Club Lens — 0
Montceau-les-Mines * † — 1

Sochaux-Montbéliard ‡ — 2 5p
Olympique Marseille — 2 4p

FC Nantes — 1 5p
CS Sedan Ardennes — 1 4p

FC Nantes — 0
Olympique Marseille * — 3

COUPE DE FRANCE FINAL 2007

Stade de France, Paris, 12-05-2007, Att: 79 797, Ref: Eric Poulat

Sochaux-Montbéliard — 2 5p — Dagano [67], Le Tallec [116]
Olympique Marseille — 2 4p — Cissé 2 [5 98]

Sochaux - Teddy RICHERT - Stephane PICHOT, Rabiu AFOLABI, Jeremie BRECHET, Dusko TOSIC - Karim ZIANI, Romain PITAU (Philippe BRUNEL 106), Guiranne N'DAW, Jerome LEROY• - Sebastien GRAX (Walter BIRSA 74), Moumouni DAGANO (Anthony LE TALLEC 104). Tr: Alain PERRIN

Marseille - Cédric CARRASSO - Habib BEYE, Julien RODRIGUEZ•, Ronald ZUBAR, Taye Ismailia TAIWO - Modeste M'BAMI (Toifilou MAOULIDA 94), Lorik CANA - Franck RIBERY, Samir NASRI, Mamadou NIANG (Wilson ORUMA• 74) - Djibril CISSE. Tr: Albert EMON

Vannes Olympique Club — 0
Olympique Marseille — 5

PENALTY SHOOT-OUT (SOCHAUX WON 5-4)

Ziani ✓; Taiwo ✓; Birsa ✓; Maoulida ✗; Le Tallec ✓; Cana ✓;
Leroy ✓; Nasri ✗; Bréchet ✗; Zubar ✗; Brunel ✓

‡ Qualified for the UEFA Cup
† Played in Gueugnon

COUPE DE LA LIGUE 2006-07

Third Round

Girondins Bordeaux	Bye
RC Strasbourg	0
AJ Auxerre*	2
Olympique Marseille	2
Montpellier-Hérault*	1
FC Sète	1
AS Saint-Etienne*	4
Stade Rennais*	2
Libourne St-Seurin	0
FC Istres*	0
Lille OSC	1
AS Monaco	0 5p
Valenciennes*	0 4p
Clermont Foot	1
Stade de Reims*	3
Le Mans	2
ES Troyes FC*	1
US Créteil-Lusitanos*	1
Racing Club Lens	4
Dijon FCO*	2
Amiens SFC	1
Sedan-Ardennes*	0
Sochaux-Montbéliard	1
AS Nancy-Lorraine*	1
OGC Nice	0
FC Nantes*	0
Toulouse FC	2
Paris Saint-Germain*	3
FC Lorient	1
Olympique Lyonnais	Bye

Fourth Round

Girondins Bordeaux	1
AJ Auxerre*	0
Olympique Marseille	1
AS Saint-Etienne*	4
Stade Rennais	2
Lille OSC*	0
AS Monaco	0 3p
Stade de Reims*	0 4p
Le Mans*	3
Racing Club Lens	1
Dijon FCO	0
Sochaux-Montbéliard*	5
AS Nancy-Lorraine*	2
Toulouse FC	1
Paris Saint-Germain	1
Olympique Lyonnais*	2

Quarter-finals

Girondins Bordeaux*	1
AS Saint-Etienne	0
Stade Rennais*	0
Stade de Reims	1
Le Mans	2
Sochaux-Montbéliard*	1
AS Nancy-Lorraine	1
Olympique Lyonnais*	3

Semi-finals

Girondins Bordeaux	2
Stade de Reims*	1
Le Mans	0
Olympique Lyonnais*	1

Final

Girondins Bordeaux ‡	1
Olympique Lyonnais	0

* Home team • Ligue 1 clubs enter in the third round • ‡ Qualified for the UEFA Cup

LEAGUE CUP FINAL

Stade de France, St-Denis, Paris
31-03-2007, Att: 79 072, Ref: Piccirillo

Scorer - Carlos Henrique 89 for Bordeaux

Bordeaux - Ramé - Carlos Henrique, Jurietti*, Faubert, Planus - Menegazzo, Micoud*, Wendell (Jussiê 68), Mavuba - Darcheville, Chamakh* (Marange 46). Tr: Ricardo Gomes

Lyon - Vercoutre - Clerc* Cris, Abidal, Squillaci - Juninho (Källström 68), Malouda, Tiago - Juninho (Wiltord 91+), Toulalan - Fred* (Baros* 72), Govou. Tr: Gérard Houllier

OLYMPIQUE LYONNAIS 2006–07

Date	Opponents	Score			Scorers	Att
30-07-2006	Paris Saint-Germain	D 1-1	H	SC	Benzema [70p], W 5-4p	30 529
4-08-2006	Nantes	W 3-1	A	Lge	Benzema [5], Squillaci [63], Fred [87]	35 828
12-08-2006	Toulouse	D 1-1	H	Lge	Malouda [83]	39 280
20-08-2006	Girondins Bordeaux	W 2-1	A	Lge	Fred [28], Wiltord [86]	32 008
26-08-2006	OGC Nice	W 4-1	A	Lge	Malouda [49], Benzema 2 [69 91+p], Tiago [74]	13 814
9-09-2006	Troyes	W 2-0	H	Lge	Cris [16], Juninho [86]	37 391
13-09-2006	Real Madrid - ESP	W 2-0	H	CLgE	Fred [11], Tiago [31]	40 013
16-09-2006	Lorient	W 3-1	A	Lge	Tiago [6], Fred [62], Malouda [65]	15 230
23-09-2006	Lille OSC	W 4-1	H	Lge	Malouda [6], Juninho [52], Fred 2 [64 70]	40 165
26-09-2006	Steaua Bucuresti - ROU	W 3-0	A	CLgE	Fred [43], Tiago [55], Benzema [89]	26 169
30-09-2006	Sochaux	W 1-0	A	Lge	Wiltord [78]	18 788
14-10-2006	Saint Etienne	W 2-1	H	Lge	Tiago [65], Juninho [88]	39 218
17-10-2006	Dynamo Kyiv - UKR	W 3-0	H	CLgE	Juninho [31], Källström [38], Malouda [50]	35 500
22-10-2006	Olympique Marseille	W 4-1	A	Lge	Juninho 2 [20 78], Benzema [48], Källström [87]	57 376
25-10-2006	Paris Saint-Germain	W 2-1	H	LCr4	Wiltord 2 [88 90]	35 816
29-10-2006	Nancy-Lorraine	W 1-0	H	Lge	Carew [13]	40 298
1-11-2006	Dynamo Kyiv - UKR	W 1-0	H	CLgE	Benzema [14]	40 520
4-11-2006	Stade Rennais	L 0-1	A	Lge		28 499
10-11-2006	Valenciennes	W 2-1	H	Lge	Cris [84], Squillaci [86]	39 833
18-11-2006	Sedan Ardennes	W 1-0	A	Lge	Abdou OG [79]	21 025
21-11-2006	Real Madrid - ESP	D 2-2	A	CLgE	Carew [11], Malouda [31]	69 906
26-11-2006	Auxerre	W 1-0	H	Lge	Malouda [25]	39 576
2-12-2006	Le Mans	W 1-0	A	Lge	Wiltord [57]	14 432
6-12-2006	Steaua Bucuresti - ROU	D 1-1	H	CLgE	Diarra [12]	39 351
10-12-2006	Paris Saint-Germain	W 3-1	H	Lge	Wiltord [45], Cris [87], Malouda [88]	36 072
17-12-2006	RC Lens	W 4-0	A	Lge	Juninho 2 [23 62], Malouda [34], Cris [51]	40 038
20-12-2006	Nancy-Lorraine	W 3-1	H	LCqf	Malouda [53], Govou [78], Diarra [90]	26 757
23-12-2006	Monaco	D 0-0	H	Lge		38 225
7-01-2007	Bayonne	W 2-1	A	CDFr9	Degoul OG [10], Juninho [75]	33 940
13-01-2007	Toulouse	L 0-2	A	Lge		33 940
17-01-2007	Le Mans	W 1-0	H	LCsf	Abidal [22]	27 541
20-01-2007	Laon	W 3-1	A	CDFr10	Clerc [27], Govou [70], Fred [85]	
24-01-2007	Girondins Bordeaux	L 1-2	H	Lge	Fred [64]	35 305
27-01-2007	OGC Nice	D 1-1	H	Lge	Baros [69]	33 971
31-01-2007	Olympique Marseille	L 1-2	A	CDFr11	Cris [23]	57 000
4-02-2007	Troyes	L 0-1	A	Lge		14 009
10-02-2007	Lorient	W 1-0	H	Lge	Fred [6]	37 976
16-02-2007	Lille OSC	W 2-1	A	Lge	Fred [83], Squillaci [89]	17 092
21-02-2007	Roma - ITA	D 0-0	A	CLr2		60 053
24-02-2007	Sochaux	D 3-3	H	Lge	Baros [40], Wiltord [90], Juninho [93+p]	40 363
3-03-2007	Saint Etienne	W 3-1	A	Lge	Källström [28], Tiago [37], Fred [47]	35 201
6-03-2007	Roma - ITA	L 0-2	H	CLr2		39 260
11-03-2007	Olympique Marseille	D 1-1	H	Lge	Baros [19]	38 930
17-03-2007	Nancy-Lorraine	W 3-0	A	Lge	Baros [36], Källström [76], Fred [81]	19 919
31-03-2007	Girondins Bordeaux	L 0-1	N	LCf		79 072
7-04-2007	Valenciennes	D 0-0	A	Lge		15 999
15-04-2007	Sedan Ardennes	W 1-0	H	Lge	Ben Arfa [44]	37 539
18-04-2007	Stade Rennais	D 0-0	H	Lge		39 848
22-04-2007	Auxerre	D 0-0	A	Lge		16 141
28-04-2007	Le Mans	W 2-1	H	Lge	Fred [39], Malouda [68]	40 226
5-05-2007	Paris Saint-Germain	D 1-1	A	Lge	Juninho [94+]	41 577
9-05-2007	RC Lens	W 3-0	H	Lge	Govou [21], Juninho [38], Diarra [45p]	38 213
19-05-2007	Monaco	L 0-1	A	Lge		13 145
26-05-2007	Nantes	W 3-1	H	Lge	Malouda 2 [22 66], Benzema [83]	40 149

SC = Trophée des champions • Lge = Ligue 1 • CDF = Coupe de France • LC = Coupe de la Ligue • CL = UEFA Champions League
gE = Group E • r4 = fourth round • r9 = ninth round • r10 = tenth round • qf = quarter-final • sf = semi-final • f = final • N = Stade de France

FIFA/COCA-COLA WORLD RANKING

1993	1994	1995	1996	1997	1998	1999	2000	2001	2002	2003	2004	2005	2006	High	Low
15	19	8	3	6	2	3	2	1	2	2	2	5	4	1 05/01	25 04/98

2006–2007											
08/06	09/06	10/06	11/06	12/06	01/07	02/07	03/07	04/07	05/07	06/07	07/07
4	2	3	4	4	4	4	4	4	4	2	4

FC SOCHAUX MONTEBELIARD 2006–07

Date	Opponents		Score			Scorers	Att
5-08-2006	Saint-Etienne	W	2-1	A	Lge	Leroy [22], Ziani [75]	32 786
12-08-2006	Auxerre	D	1-1	H	Lge	Birsa [52]	14 759
19-08-2006	Sedan Ardennes	D	1-1	A	Lge	Quercia [16]	11 227
26-08-2006	Paris Saint-Germain	W	3-2	H	Lge	Ziani 2 [30 82p], Sène [36]	16 317
9-09-2006	Stade Rennais	L	1-2	A	Lge	Santos [56]	21 326
17-09-2006	RC Lens	L	0-3	H	Lge		12 361
20-09-2006	Sedan Ardennes	W	1-0	A	LCr3	N'Daw [21]	5 000
23-09-2006	Le Mans	D	2-2	A	Lge	Quercia [2], Sène [71]	9 452
30-09-2006	Olympique Lyonnais	L	0-1	H	Lge		18 788
14-10-2006	Nantes	W	2-0	A	Lge	Afolabi [27], Santos [49p]	26 904
21-10-2006	Girondins Bordeaux	W	2-1	H	Lge	Santos [4], Birsa [69]	13 475
24-10-2006	Dijon FCO	W	5-0	H	LCr4	Sène 2 [6 36], Isabey [26], Ziani [70], Mézague [90]	11 648
28-10-2006	Toulouse	W	2-1	A	Lge	Santos [32], Ziani [88]	20 846
4-11-2006	Troyes	W	1-0	H	Lge	N'Daw [67]	16 740
11-11-2006	OGC Nice	D	0-0	A	Lge		10 688
18-11-2006	Lille OSC	D	0-0	H	Lge		12 397
25-11-2006	Lorient	W	3-1	A	Lge	Le Tallec 2 [23 26], Ziani [45p]	12 513
3-12-2006	Olympique Marseille	W	1-0	H	Lge	Afolabi [76]	19 990
9-12-2006	Valenciennes	D	0-0	A	Lge		12 889
16-12-2006	Monaco	L	0-3	A	Lge		11 292
20-12-2006	Le Mans	L	1-2	H	LCqf	Isabey [74]	17 437
23-12-2006	Nancy-Lorraine	W	2-1	H	Lge	Ziani 2 [61 65p]	17 700
6-01-2007	Saint-Etienne	W	3-1	A	CDFr9	Quercia [21], Alvaro [23], Le Tallec [90]	17 063
13-01-2007	Auxerre	L	0-1	A	Lge		7 046
20-01-2007	Lyon Duchère	W	2-1	H	CDFr10	Pitau [77], Alvaro [90p]	9 103
24-01-2007	Sedan Ardennes	D	1-1	H	Lge	Santos [62]	9 930
27-01-2007	Paris Saint-Germain	D	0-0	A	Lge		33 119
30-01-2007	Monaco	W	2-0	A	CDFr11	Pitau [28], Le Tallec [64]	
3-02-2007	Stade Rennais	D	0-0	H	Lge		10 477
11-02-2007	RC Lens	L	1-3	A	Lge	Tosic [85]	31 122
17-02-2007	Le Mans	W	2-0	H	Lge	Santos [13p], Yebda OG [79]	9 996
24-02-2007	Olympique Lyonnais	D	3-3	A	Lge	Santos [9], Ziani [29p], Grax [86]	40 363
28-02-2007	Paris Saint-Germain	W	2-1	H	CDFqf	Isabey [24], Dagano [39]	18 054
4-03-2007	Nantes	L	1-2	H	Lge	Santos [34p]	14 664
10-03-2007	Girondins Bordeaux	L	0-2	A	Lge		25 128
17-03-2007	Toulouse	W	4-2	H	Lge	Grax 2 [22 54], Leroy [32], Isabey [63]	11 485
1-04-2007	Troyes	W	1-0	A	Lge	Pitau [33]	11 554
7-04-2007	OGC Nice	D	1-1	H	Lge	Dagano [71]	16 759
14-04-2007	Lille OSC	L	0-2	A	Lge		15 454
17-04-2007	Montceau-les-Mines	W	2-0	A	CDFsf	Grax [96], Leroy [113]	12 900
21-04-2007	Lorient	D	1-1	H	Lge	Grax [73]	13 952
29-04-2007	Olympique Marseille	L	2-4	A	Lge	Leroy [5], Rodriguez OG [92+]	54 702
5-05-2007	Valenciennes	W	1-0	H	Lge	Le Tallec [88]	15 657
9-05-2007	Monaco	W	2-1	H	Lge	Toure OG [29], Grax [80]	13 451
12-05-2007	Olympique Marseille	D	2-2	N	CDFf	Dagano [67], Le Tallec [116]	79 797
19-05-2007	Nancy-Lorraine	L	2-5	A	Lge	Birsa [44], Dagano [89]	19 503
26-05-2007	Saint-Etienne	W	1-0	H	Lge	Le Tallec [19]	19 938

Lge = Ligue 1 • CDF = Coupe de France • LC = Coupe de la Ligue
r3 = third round • r4 = fourth round • r9 = ninth round • r10 = tenth round • r11 = eleventh round • qf = quarter-final • sf = semi-final • f = final
N = Stade de France

THE FIFA BIG COUNT OF 2006

	Male	Female		Total
Number of players	3 851 161	338 879	Referees and Assistant Referees	27 782
Professionals	1 825		Admin, Coaches, Technical, Medical	257 941
Amateurs 18+	753 244		Number of clubs	18 823
Youth under 18	1 034 046		Number of teams	111 760
Unregistered	1 233 100		Clubs with women's teams	1 239
Total players	4 190 040		Players as % of population	6.88%

FRO – FAROE ISLANDS

NATIONAL TEAM RECORD
JULY 10TH 2006 TO JULY 12TH 2010

PL	W	D	L	F	A	%
8	0	0	8	2	27	0

FIFA/COCA-COLA WORLD RANKING

1993	1994	1995	1996	1997	1998	1999	2000	2001	2002	2003	2004	2005	2006	High		Low	
115	133	120	135	117	125	112	117	117	114	126	131	132		104	07/99	188	07/07

2006–2007											
08/06	09/06	10/06	11/06	12/06	01/07	02/07	03/07	04/07	05/07	06/07	07/07
169	179	185	185	181	181	183	182	179	185	186	188

The Faroes arrived on the international scene with a bang in 1990 thanks to a 1-0 victory over Austria in their first competitive international. The hope was that similar giantkilling feats would follow but that hasn't happened and by mid 2007 the national team had chalked up an embarrassing run of 16 consecutive defeats dating back to 2004. The irony is that the team hasn't been playing badly, causing both Italy and Scotland problems in their final two UEFA Euro 2008 qualifying matches before the summer break. One area where there has been an improvement is in club football and in the 2006-07 UEFA Champions League, B'36 Tórshavn became the first club from

INTERNATIONAL HONOURS
None

the Faroes to progress beyond the first preliminary round of the tournament. They beat Malta's Birkirkara to set up a second preliminary round tie against Fenerbahçe to whom they lost 9-0 on aggregate. At home there was a fifth Cup triumph for B'36 when they beat KI Klaksvik 2-1 in the delayed 2006 Cup Final, but the real drama came in the Championship. A close race saw long time leaders EB/Streymur knocked off the top of the League in the last minute of the last match by HB Tórshavn. Needing just a draw, they lost to KI whilst an 89th minute winner by Vagnur Mortensen gave HB the three points they needed to leapfrog EB to win the title by one point.

THE FIFA BIG COUNT OF 2006

	Male	Female		Total
Number of players	6 290	1 804	Referees and Assistant Referees	60
Professionals	0		Admin, Coaches, Technical, Medical	990
Amateurs 18+	1 654		Number of clubs	23
Youth under 18	4 040		Number of teams	303
Unregistered	2 000		Clubs with women's teams	17
Total players	8 094		Players as % of population	17.13%

The Faroe Islands' Football Association (FSF)

Gundadalur, PO Box 3028, Tórshavn 110, Faroe Islands
Tel +298 351979   Fax +298 319079
fsf@football.fo   www.football.fo
President: HOLM Oli   General Secretary: MIKLADAL Isak
Vice-President: A LIDARENDA Niklas   Treasurer: TBD   Media Officer: MIKLADAL Isak
Men's Coach: OLSEN Jogvan   Women's Coach: HANSEN Alvur
FSF formed: 1979   UEFA: 1988   FIFA: 1988
White shirts with blue trimmings, Blue shorts, White socks or Blue shirts with white trimmings, White shorts, White socks

RECENT INTERNATIONAL MATCHES PLAYED BY THE FAROE ISLANDS

2002 Opponents		Score	Venue	Comp	Scorers	Att	Referee
21-08 Liechtenstein	W	3-1	Tórshavn	Fr	Jacobsen.JR [70], Benjaminsen [75], Johnsson.J [84]	3 200	Orrason ISL
7-09 Scotland	D	2-2	Toftir	ECq	Petersen.J 2 [7 13]	4 000	Granat POL
12-10 Lithuania	L	0-2	Kaunas	ECq		2 500	Delevic YUG
16-10 Germany	L	1-2	Hannover	ECq	Friedrich OG [45]	36 628	Koren ISR
2003							
27-04 Kazakhstan	W	3-2	Toftir	Fr	Borg [17p], Petersen.J [45], Lakjuni [49]	420	Jakobsson ISL
29-04 Kazakhstan	W	2-1	Tórshavn	Fr	Flotum [65], Johnsson.J [75]	800	Bergmann ISL
7-06 Iceland	L	1-2	Reykjavik	ECq	Rógvi Jacobsen [62]	6 038	Liba CZE
11-06 Germany	L	0-2	Tórshavn	ECq		6 130	Wegereef NED
20-08 Iceland	L	1-2	Toftir	ECq	Rógvi Jacobsen [65]	3 416	Iturralde Gonzalez ESP
6-09 Scotland	L	1-3	Glasgow	ECq	Johnsson.J [35]	40 901	Ceferin SVN
10-09 Lithuania	L	1-3	Toftir	ECq	Olsen [43]	2 175	Trivkovic CRO
2004							
21-02 Poland	L	0-6	San Fernando	Fr		100	Cascales ESP
1-06 Netherlands	L	0-3	Lausanne	Fr		3 200	Leuba SUI
18-08 Malta	W	3-2	Toftir	Fr	Borg [20], Petersen.J [35], Benjaminsen [77]	1 932	Laursen DEN
4-09 Switzerland	L	0-6	Basel	WCq		11 880	Tudor ROU
8-09 France	L	0-2	Tórshavn	WCq		5 917	Thomson SCO
9-10 Cyprus	D	2-2	Nicosia	WCq	Jorgensen.CB [21], Rógvi Jacobsen [43]	1 400	Gadiyev AZE
13-10 Ireland Republic	L	0-2	Dublin	WCq		36 000	Lajuks LVA
2005							
4-06 Switzerland	L	1-3	Toftir	WCq	Rógvi Jacobsen [70]	2 047	Gumienny BEL
8-06 Ireland Republic	L	0-2	Tórshavn	WCq		5 180	Guenov BUL
17-08 Cyprus	L	0-3	Toftir	WCq		2 720	Johannesson SWE
3-09 France	L	0-3	Lens	WCq		40 126	Jara CZE
7-09 Israel	L	0-2	Tórshavn	WCq		2 240	Vink NED
8-10 Israel	L	1-2	Tel Aviv	WCq	Samuelsen [93+]	31 857	Brugger AUT
2006							
14-05 Poland	L	0-4	Wronki	Fr		4 000	Prus USA
16-08 Georgia	L	0-6	Toftir	ECq		2 114	Ross NIR
2-09 Scotland	L	0-6	Glasgow	ECq		50 059	Egorov RUS
7-10 Lithuania	L	0-1	Tórshavn	ECq		1 982	Buttimer IRL
11-10 France	L	0-5	Sochaux	ECq		19 314	Corpodean ROU
2007							
24-03 Ukraine	L	0-2	Toftir	ECq		717	Skomina SVN
28-03 Georgia	L	1-3	Tbilisi	ECq	Rógvi Jacobsen [57]	12 000	Saliy KAZ
2-06 Italy	L	1-2	Tórshavn	ECq	Rógvi Jacobsen [77]	5 800	Malek POL
6-06 Scotland	L	0-2	Toftir	ECq		4 100	Kasnaferis GRE

Fr = Friendly match • EC = UEFA EURO 2004/2008 • WC = FIFA World Cup • q = qualifier

FAROE ISLANDS NATIONAL TEAM RECORDS AND RECORD SEQUENCES

Records			Sequence records				
Victory	3-0	SMR 1995	Wins	2	1997, 2002, 2003	Clean sheets	1	
Defeat	0-9	ISL 1985	Defeats	16	2004-	Goals scored	5	1986
Player Caps	77	JOHANNESEN Oli	Undefeated	3	2002	Without goal	7	1991-1992
Player Goals	9	JONSSON Todi	Without win	26	1990-1995	Goals against	33	2002-2007

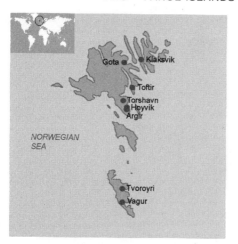

FAROE ISLANDS; FOROYAR

Capital	Tórshavn	Language	Faroese, Danish			Independence	n/a
Population	47 246	Area	1 399 km^2	Density	33 per km^2	% in cities	n/a
GDP per cap	$22 000	Dailling code	+298	Internet	.fo	GMT + / -	0

MAJOR CITIES/TOWNS

		Population
1	Tórshavn	13 392
2	Klaksvík	4 618
3	Hoyvík	2 817
4	Argir	1 898
5	Fuglafjarð	1 659
6	Vágur	1 627
7	Vestmanna	1 298
8	Tvøroyri	1 237
9	Sørvag	1 123
10	Kollafjarð	1 076
11	Kollafjørður	1 064
12	Miðvágur	1 063
13	Leirvík	1 011
14	Strendur	867
15	Toftir	867
16	Saltangará	811
17	Sandavágur	805
18	Hvalba	677
19	Eiði	667
20	Skáli	630
21	Sandur	621
22	Norðragøta	582
23	Runavik	511
24	Skopun	450

MEDALS TABLE

		Overall			League			Cup		Europe			City	Stadium	Cap'ty	DoF
		G	S	B	G	S	B	G	S	G	S	B				
1	HB Tórshavn	45	23	4	19	13	4	26	10				Tórshavn	Gundadalur	6 000	1904
2	KI Klaksvík	22	10	8	17	2	8	5	8				Klaksvik	Klaksvik	4 000	1904
3	B'36 Tórshavn	13	13	4	8	4	4	5	9				Tórshavn	Gundadalur	6 000	1936
4	TB Tvøroyri	12	10		7	5		5	5				Tvøroyri	Sevmyri	3 000	1892
5	GI Gøtu	12	6	4	6	3	4	6	3				Gøtu	Serpugerdi	3 000	1926
6	B'68 Toftir	3	2	6	3	1	6		1				Toftir	Svangaskard	8 020	1962
7	NSI Runavík	2	5			1		2	4				Runavik	Runavik	2 000	1957
8	VB Vágur/Sumba	2	3	2	1		2	1	3				Vágur	Vestri a Eidinum	3 000	2006
9	B'71 Sandur	2	2	1	1	1		1	2				Sandur	Sandur	2 000	1970
10	IF Fuglafjørdur	1	4		1				4				Fuglafjurdur	Fuglafjørdur	3 000	1946
11	SI Sørvagur	1			1								Sørvag	Sørvágur	2 000	1905
12	Skála		1	1		1	1						Skali	Skali	1 000	1965
13	EB/Streymur		1			1							Oyrabakki	Molini	1 000	1993
	LIF Leirvik		1						1				Leirvik	Leirvik	2 000	1928
	Royn Valba		1						1				Valba	Hvalba	2 000	1923
16	MB Midvágur			1		1							Miðvágur	Miðvágur	1 000	1905

RECENT LEAGUE AND CUP RECORD

	Championship						Cup		
Year	Champions	Pts	Runners-up	Pts	Third	Pts	Winners	Score	Runners-up
1995	GI Gøtu	41	HB Tórshavn	33	B'68 Tórshavn	30	HB Tórshavn	3-1	B'68 Toftir
1996	GI Gøtu	39	KI Klaksvík	39	HB Tórshavn	32	GI Gøtu	2-2 5-3	HB Tórshavn
1997	B'36 Tórshavn	48	HB Tórshavn	41	GI Gøtu	35	GI Gøtu	6-0	VB Vágur
1998	HB Tórshavn	45	KI Klaksvík	38	B'36 Tórshavn	37	HB Tórshavn	2-0	KI Klaksvík
1999	KI Klaksvík	41	GI Gøtu	39	B'36 Tórshavn	38	KI Klaksvík	3-1	B'36 Tórshavn
2000	VB Vágur	40	HB Tórshavn	38	B'68 Toftir	31	GI Gøtu	1-0	HB Tórshavn
2001	B'36 Tórshavn	46	GI Gøtu	42	B'68 Toftir	31	B'36 Tórshavn	1-0	KI Klaksvík
2002	HB Tórshavn	41	NSI Runavík	36	KI Klaksvík	33	NSI Runavík	2-1	HB Tórshavn
2003	HB Tórshavn	41	B'36 Tórshavn	37	B'68 Toftir	35	B'36 Tórshavn	3-1	GI Gøtu
2004	HB Tórshavn	41	B'36 Tórshavn	34	Skála	30	HB Tórshavn	3-1	NSI Runavík
2005	B'36 Tórshavn	54	Skála	50	HB Tórshavn	50	GI Gøtu	4-1	IF Fuglafyørdur
2006	HB Tórshavn	55	EB Streymur Eidi	54	B'36 Tórshavn	47	B'36 Tórshavn	2-1	KI Klaksvík

FAROE ISLANDS 2006

FORMULADEILDIN

	Pl	W	D	L	F	A	Pts	HB	EB	B'36	KI	NSI	GI	Skála	VB	B'68	IF
HB Tórshavn †	27	16	7	4	61	36	55		2-3 2-2	2-0 2-1	5-1	4-0 2-1	1-2	1-1	4-1 2-0	3-2	5-1 2-0
EB/Streymur Eidi ‡	27	16	6	5	63	30	54	1-1		2-1	1-1 0-1	4-1	2-1 2-3	2-0 2-0	4-0	2-1 8-2	2-0
B'36 Tórshavn ‡	27	13	8	6	45	32	47	6-0	2-2 2-1		1-1 1-5	1-1 1-5	0-0 1-1	2-2	2-2	2-1 3-1	4-1
KI Klaksvík	27	12	9	6	54	39	45	2-2 3-3	1-4 1-4	0-1		2-1	1-1 1-4	2-2 2-1	3-0 0-1	1-3	3-0
NSI Runavík	27	12	6	9	50	39	42	1-3	2-0 3-2	1-1	0-1 1-1		4-2	2-1 2-0	2-1	1-1 2-0	6-1 3-0
GI Gøtu	27	10	11	6	39	34	40	3-2 1-4	0-2	1-2	1-1 1-1			0-0	3-0 2-0	1-1	3-1 1-1
Skála	27	7	10	10	33	29	31	1-1 0-1	1-1	0-1 1-0	1-1	2-0	1-2 0-0		5-0 1-1	1-0	1-2 1-1
VB Vagur/Sumba	27	5	5	17	24	73	20	1-1	0-5 1-4	1-2 3-2	1-7	2-5 2-0	0-0	0-4		3-2 1-1	1-4
B'68 Toftir	27	4	6	17	34	58	18	1-2 0-1	1-1	0-1	0-4 2-3	1-5	1-1 0-1	1-0 2-4	6-1		1-1
IF Fuglafjørdur	27	4	4	19	29	62	16	1-3	1-2	1-3 2-1	2-3 0-0	1-3	1-3 1-3	0-2	1-2 1-2	3-0 2-3	

2/04/2006 - 21/10/2006 • † Qualified for the UEFA Champions League • ‡ Qualified for the UEFA Cup

---

FAROE ISLANDS 2006 — 1. DEILD (2)

	Pl	W	D	L	F	A	Pts
B'71 Sandur	21	15	4	2	72	26	50
AB Argir	21	15	2	4	54	27	47
LIF Leirvík	21	11	4	6	39	25	37
TB Tvøroyri	21	9	3	9	33	32	30
HB Tórshavn 2	21	7	3	11	42	49	24
FS Vágar	21	7	1	13	28	37	22
KI Klaksvík 2	21	6	3	12	36	70	21
SI Sorvágur	21	3	2	16	36	74	11
VB Vagur/Sumba 2							Withdrew
Royn Hvalba							Withdrew

1/04/2006 - 14/10/2006 • VB and Royn withdrew in September and their results were annulled

FAROE ISLANDS 2006 — 2. DEILD (3)

	Pl	W	D	L	F	A	Pts
NSI Runavík 2	18	14	2	2	60	22	44
B'36 Tórshavn 2	18	12	3	3	49	19	39
EB/Streymur Eidi 2	18	10	2	6	50	42	31
MB Midvágur	18	9	4	5	36	32	31
GI Gøtu 2	18	7	2	9	35	46	23
Skála 2	18	6	3	9	41	49	21
IF Fuglafjørdur 2	18	6	3	9	45	55	21
B'68 Toftir 2	18	5	2	11	27	38	17
Fram Tórshavn	18	3	4	11	42	65	15
KI Klaksvík 3	18	4	2	12	46	63	14

23/04/2006 - 30/09/2006

FFA CUP 2006

Round of 16		Quarter-finals		Semi-finals		Final	
B'36 Tórshavn	5						
TB Tvøroyri	0	B'36 Tórshavn	1				
IF Fuglafjørdur	1 3p	B'68 Toftir	0				
B'68 Toftir	1 4p			B'36 Tórshavn	0 1 5p		
HB Tórshavn	4			EB/Streymur Eidi	1 0 4p		
VB Vagur/Sumba	1	HB Tórshavn	2				
B'71 Sandur	2	EB/Streymur Eidi	6				
EB/Streymur Eidi	3					B'36 Tórshavn ‡	2
Skála	2					KI Klaksvík	1
AB Argir	1	Skála	1				
SI Sorvágur	1	NSI Runavík	0				
NSI Runavík	4			Skála	0 0		
GI Gøtu	4			KI Klaksvík	3 2		
LIF Lervík	1	GI Gøtu	2				
Fram Tórshavn		KI Klaksvík	4				
KI Klaksvík	w-o						

CUP FINAL

Tórsvøllur, Tórshavn, 14-10-2006

Scorers - Frodi Benjaminsen 45p, Ahmed Sylla 83 for B'36 Tóorshavn; Atli Danielsen 46 for KI Klaksvík

‡ Qualified for the UEFA Cup

First round: **TB Tvøroyri** 3-1 Royn Hvalba; **Fram Tórshavn** 4-1 NIF; FS Vagar 1-2 **AB Argir**; **SI Sorvágur** 1-0 MB Midvágur

GAB – GABON

NATIONAL TEAM RECORD
JULY 10TH 2006 TO JULY 12TH 2010

PL	W	D	L	F	A	%
9	4	2	3	13	16	55.5

FIFA/COCA-COLA WORLD RANKING

1993	1994	1995	1996	1997	1998	1999	2000	2001	2002	2003	2004	2005	2006	High		Low	
60	64	67	46	63	82	74	89	102	121	111	109	104	95	**45**	01/96	**125**	05/03

2006–2007											
08/06	09/06	10/06	11/06	12/06	01/07	02/07	03/07	04/07	05/07	06/07	07/07
93	84	96	97	95	96	99	98	105	104	104	108

Gabon had the misfortune to be drawn with the Côte d'Ivoire in their African Nations Cup qualifying group and then suffered an even bigger blow when Djibouti withdrew from the contest. That left the Gabonese in a three team group with only a top place finish enough to secure a ticket to the 2008 tournament in Ghana. Had Djibouti participated, Gabon would have been well placed to take one of the three spots in the finals, reserved for the best group runners-up. When the Ivorians beat Gabon 5-0 in Abidjan in October 2006 it effectively ended their campaign before it had a chance to get off the ground. Gabon did win both home and away over Madagascar, the other team in

INTERNATIONAL HONOURS
None

group, but they were meaningless affairs. The central African country had ambitious plans following the hiring of coach Alain Giresse, but the former French international was left fighting for honours in the regional CEMAC Cup. At the tournament in Chad in March 2007, he saw his home-based team reach the final, only to lose to Congo. A four point advantage gave MangaSport a hat-trick of League titles as they finished ahead of army club FC105 Libreville. In the 2007 African Champions League, they eliminated Angolan champions Primeiro Agosto in the first round but were then narrowly beaten 4-3 by JS Kabylie of Algeria at the next stage of the competition.

THE FIFA BIG COUNT OF 2006

	Male	Female		Total
Number of players	69 800	0	Referees and Assistant Referees	100
Professionals	0		Admin, Coaches, Technical, Medical	900
Amateurs 18+	5 500		Number of clubs	60
Youth under 18	2 800		Number of teams	220
Unregistered	5 500		Clubs with women's teams	0
Total players	69 800		Players as % of population	4.90%

Fédération Gabonaise de Football (FGF)
Case postale 181, Libreville, Gabon
Tel +241 774862   Fax +241 564199
fegafoot@internetgabon.com   www.none
President: ABABE Leon   General Secretary: BOUASSA MOUSSADJI Barthelemy
Vice-President: OSSAMY NDJOUBI Alain   Treasurer: NZE NGUEMA Jean   Media Officer: SALA Ngouahbeaud
Men's Coach: GIRESSE Alain   Women's Coach: None
FGF formed: 1962   CAF: 1967   FIFA: 1963
Green shirts, Blue shorts, White socks or Yellow shirts, Yellow shorts, White socks

RECENT INTERNATIONAL MATCHES PLAYED BY GABON

2003	Opponents	Score	Venue	Comp	Scorers	Att	Referee
8-06	Equatorial Guinea	L 1-2	Malabo	CNq	Dissikadie [43]		Buenkadila COD
13-06	Andorra	W 2-0	Andorra la Vella	Fr			Ledentu FRA
20-06	Morocco	L 0-2	Rabat	CNq		15 000	Shelmani LBY
6-07	Sierra Leone	W 2-0	Libreville	CNq	Mbanangoye [33], Mintsa		
24-09	Algeria	D 2-2	Algiers	Fr	Nguéma [21], Moubamba [83], L 3-4p	2 000	Zekkini ALG
26-09	Benin	W 4-0	Algiers	Fr	Mockom [17], Mintsa [44], Nguéma 2 [65 74]		
12-10	Burundi	D 0-0	Bujumbura	WCq		10 000	Itur KEN
8-11	Burkina Faso	D 0-0	Moanda	Fr			
15-11	Burundi	W 4-1	Libreville	WCq	Nzigou [2], Mwinyi OG [16], Nguéma 2 [38 80]	15 000	Ndoye SEN
5-12	Congo	L 2-3	Brazzaville	CMrl	Nguéma [40], Edou [63]		Tchoumba CMR
9-12	Congo	D 1-1	Brazzaville	CMrl			
11-12	Central African Rep	L 0-2	Brazzaville	CMsf			
13-12	Congo	L 0-1	Brazzaville	CM3p			
2004							
29-05	Egypt	L 0-2	Cairo	Fr		15 000	Auda EGY
5-06	Zimbabwe	D 1-1	Libreville	WCq	Zue [52]	25 000	Quartey GHA
19-06	Rwanda	L 1-3	Kigali	WCq	Zue [20]	16 325	Abdulkadir TAN
3-07	Angola	D 2-2	Libreville	WCq	Issiemou [44], Zue [49]	20 000	Louzaya CGO
5-09	Algeria	W 3-0	Annaba	WCq	Aubame [56], Akiremy [73], Bito'o [84]	51 000	Ndoye SEN
3-10	Benin	W 2-0	Libreville	Fr	Djissikadie, Nguéma		
9-10	Nigeria	D 1-1	Libreville	WCq	Issiemou [29]	26 000	Yameogo BFA
2005							
3-02	Central African Rep	W 4-0	Libreville	CMrl	Akoué [32p], Nguéma [42], Yinda 2 [52 82]		
8-02	Congo	W 1-0	Libreville	CMrl	Poaty [38]		
10-02	Chad	L 2-3	Libreville	CMsf	Akoué [58p], Mabiala [69]		
12-02	Congo	W 2-1	Libreville	CM3p	Yembi, Akoué		
19-03	Congo	D 0-0	Libreville	Fr			
26-03	Nigeria	L 0-2	Port Harcourt	WCq		16 489	Hicuburundi BDI
5-06	Zimbabwe	L 0-1	Harare	WCq		55 000	Ssegonga UGA
18-06	Rwanda	W 3-0	Libreville	WCq	Djissikadie [10], Londo [55], Zue [60]	10 000	El Arjoun MAR
4-09	Angola	L 0-3	Luanda	WCq			
8-10	Algeria	D 0-0	Port-Gentil	WCq			
2006							
4-03	Cameroon	D 0-0	Malabo	CMrl			
8-03	Central African Rep	D 2-2	Malabo	CMrl	Bito'o [26], Tamboulas OG [58]		
11-03	Equatorial Guinea	D 0-0	Bata	CMsf	L 2-4p		
14-03	Chad	D 2-2	Bata	CM3p	Akiremy 2 [63 73], W 7-6p		
15-08	Algeria	W 2-0	Aix-en-Provence	Fr	Mouloungui [65], Djissikadie [67]		Mezouar
2-09	Madagascar	W 4-0	Libreville	CNq	Nchouet [37], Cousin [70p], Nzigou 2 [76 82]		Diatta SEN
8-10	Côte d'Ivoire	L 0-5	Abidjan	CNq			Buenkadila COD
15-11	Morocco	L 0-6	Rabat	Fr		5 000	Ousmane Sidebe MLI
2007							
7-03	Congo	D 2-2	N'Djamena	CMrl	Ambourouet [62], Akiremy [89]		
9-03	Equatorial Guinea	D 1-1	N'Djamena	CMrl	Akiremy [15]		
11-03	Chad	W 2-1	N'Djamena	CMsf	Akiremy 2 [44 56]		
16-03	Congo	L 0-1	N'Djamena	CMf			
17-06	Madagascar	W 2-0	Antananarivo	CNq	Akiremy [20], Kedi [89]		

Fr = Friendly match • CN = CAF African Cup of Nations • CM = CEMAC Cup • WC = FIFA World Cup
q = qualifier • r1 = first round group • sf = semi-final • 3p = third place play-off • f = final

GABON NATIONAL TEAM RECORDS AND RECORD SEQUENCES

Records			Sequence records				
Victory	7-0	BEN 1995	Wins	4	1985, 1992	Clean sheets	5	1986-87, 1988
Defeat	0-6	MAR 2006	Defeats	5	1967-1971	Goals scored	14	1998-1999
Player Caps	n/a		Undefeated	11	1996	Without goal	4	2002
Player Goals	n/a		Without win	20	1977-1984	Goals against	11	1996-1997

GABON COUNTRY INFORMATION

Capital	Libreville	Independence	1960 from France	GDP per Capita	5 500
Population	1 355 246	Status	Republic	GNP Ranking	121
Area km²	267 667	Language	French	Dialling code	+241
Population density	5 per km²	Literacy rate	63%	Internet code	.ga
% in urban areas	%	Main religion	Christian 75%	GMT + / –	+1
Towns/Cities ('000)	Libreville 578; Port-Gentil 109; Masuku 42; Oyem 30; Moanda 30; Mouila 22; Lambaréné 20				
Neighbours (km)	Equatorial Guinea 350; Cameroon 298; Congo 1 903				
Main stadia	Stade Omar Bongo – Libreville 40 000				

GABON 2006

CHAMPIONNAT NATIONAL DE D1

	Pl	W	D	L	F	A	Pts	Mangasport	FC 105	US Bitam	Mandji	US Oyem	Munadji 76	Wongosport	Missiles	Téléstar	Franceville	Sogéa	CMS	Akébe	Jeunesse
Mangasport Moanda †	26	20	6	0	53	12	66		1-0	0-0	4-1	4-0	2-0	3-0	2-1	2-0	3-0	1-0	1-0	4-0	4-2
FC 105 Libreville	26	20	2	4	59	19	62	0-1		3-2	2-0	2-1	2-1	2-1	3-0	0-0	2-0	2-1	3-0	3-2	9-0
US Bitam	26	16	5	5	44	19	53	1-2	0-1		1-1	1-0	1-0	3-2		0-0	2-1	2-0	2-0	2-0	**3-0**
AS Stade Mandji	25	12	6	7	31	26	42	1-1	1-1	1-0		2-1	0-2	1-0	1-0	0-1	2-0	1-0	1-1	4-0	3-1
US Oyem	25	11	5	9	27	25	38	0-0	**0-3**	0-3	1-0		2-0	0-2	3-0	1-0	3-0	1-0	0-1	1-0	3-0
Munadji 76 Tchibanga	25	9	4	12	26	34	31	0-3	2-0	0-0	0-0			3-0	0-0	1-2	2-1	1-3	2-2	0-1	1-0
Wongosport	24	8	6	10	24	28	30	1-1	3-2	1-1	1-1	2-0	4-2		0-1	1-0	0-1		1-3		0-1
Missiles Libreville	26	8	7	11	26	32	31	3-3	1-2	3-5	4-1	1-1	1-2	0-0		1-0	0-1	1-2	1-2	1-0	2-1
Delta Téléstar ‡	26	7	8	11	19	23	29	0-1	0-2	1-2	1-2	0-0	2-1	0-0	0-2		1-2	2-0	0-0	3-0	2-1
Franceville FC	26	8	5	13	27	36	29	1-1	1-3	0-2	3-0	1-1	**3-0**	0-1	0-0	2-1		0-1	2-1	0-0	0-1
Sogéa FC	25	8	4	13	23	31	28	0-1	1-4	2-4	0-2	1-1	3-1		0-0	0-0	1-1		1-0	0-1	2-1
Cercle Mbéri Sportif	26	8	3	15	23	34	27	0-1	0-4	1-2	2-0	0-1	0-1	1-0	2-3	0-1	2-0	1-3		1-2	1-3
Stade d'Akébe	26	5	5	16	17	46	20	0-3	0-2	0-4	0-2	0-1	1-2	1-1	0-0	2-2	2-4	1-0	0-2		1-3
JS Libreville	26	5	2	19	24	58	17	1-4	0-2	0-1	0-3	2-5	1-2	1-2	1-0	0-0	3-4	1-2	0-2	0-0	

5/02/2006 - 2/08/2006 • † Qualified for the CAF Champions League • ‡ Qualified for the CAF Confederation Cup • Munadji 76 relegated
Matches in bold were awarded 3-0

COUPE DU GABON INTERCLUBS 2006

Round of 16		Quarter–finals		Semi–finals		Final	
Delta Télestar	4						
Cercle Mbéri Sportif	0	Delta Télestar	4				
Wongosport	0						
Sogéa	1	Sogéa	0	Delta Télestar	3		
Mangasport	1			Missiles	0		
US Bitam	0	Mangasport	0 2p				
USTM Franceville	0	Missiles	0 4p				
Missiles	1					Delta Télestar ‡	3
Franceville FC	4					FC 105	2
USM Libreville	1	Franceville FC	2				
Temple Mouila	1						
Moukona Koulamoutou	2	Moukona Koulamoutou	0				
Ana Mbombet Mouila	w-0			Franceville FC	1		
AS Santé	0	Ana Mbombet Mouila	0	FC 105	2		
Lambasport	1	FC 105	6				
FC 105 †	0						

† FC 105 awarded tie • ‡ Qualified for the CAF Confederation Cup

CUP FINAL

Stade Augustin Monedan de Sibang, Libreville, 6-08-2006

Scorers - Lukuni Moussavou [4], Claude Mvé Mintsa [52], Barro Seydou [71], Kota Pitchou [56], Ndong Ella [75]

RECENT LEAGUE AND CUP RECORD

Championship							Cup		
Year	Champions	Pts	Runners-up	Pts	Third	Pts	Winners	Score	Runners-up
2000	Mangasport	30	AO Evizo	30	FC 105	22	AO Evizo		
2001	FC 105	62	Mangasport	59	TP Akwembé	59	Mangasport	1-0	TP Akwembé
2002	USM Libreville	54	FC 105	49	Mangasport	39	USM Libreville	1-1 4-2p	Jeunesse
2003	US Bitam	45	FC 105	45	Wongosport	37	US Bitam	1-1 4-3p	USM Libreville
2004	Mangasport	32	Téléstar	31	US Bitam	26	FC 105	3-2	Mangasport
2005	Mangasport	23	US Bitam	20	Sogéa	13	Mangasport	2-0	Sogéa
2006	Mangasport	66	FC 105	62	US Bitam	53	Delta Téléstar	3-2	FC 105

GAM – GAMBIA

NATIONAL TEAM RECORD
JULY 10TH 2006 TO JULY 12TH 2010

PL	W	D	L	F	A	%
7	1	2	4	5	10	28.5

FIFA/COCA-COLA WORLD RANKING

1993	1994	1995	1996	1997	1998	1999	2000	2001	2002	2003	2004	2005	2006	High		Low	
125	117	112	128	132	135	151	155	148	143	138	154	164	134	**101**	09/94	**166**	05/06

2006–2007											
08/06	09/06	10/06	11/06	12/06	01/07	02/07	03/07	04/07	05/07	06/07	07/07
157	119	137	134	134	135	134	134	133	132	131	129

Gambia missed out on qualification for the 2008 African Nations Cup finals but for the first time proved to be tough opponents to overcome. The Scorpions were let down by a change in coaching personnel during a campaign which saw German coach Antonie Hey depart after a handful of games in frustration at a lack of resources and monetary support. José Martinez of Spain was brought in but by then qualification for the finals in Ghana was out of reach. The number of Gambians now playing in Europe continues to grow, and that has added vital experience to the small playing pool Martinez has to choose from. The side that won the 2005 African under-17

INTERNATIONAL HONOURS
CAF African U-17 Championship 2005

championship graduated to under-20 level and finished third at the African youth championship in Congo in April 2007, qualifying for the FIFA U-20 World Cup in Canada, where they made it into the last 16. Real Banjul won their first league title since 2000 by pipping Wallidan to the championship on goal difference with a margin of just three goals. Real scrambled a dramatic goal seven minutes from time in their last league match to draw against Bakau United while Wallidan were winning their final match to level the title race on points. Defending champions Gambia Ports Authority also had a chance to win on the final day but lost and ended fourth.

THE FIFA BIG COUNT OF 2006

	Male	Female		Total
Number of players	67 400	630	Referees and Assistant Referees	100
Professionals	0		Admin, Coaches, Technical, Medical	600
Amateurs 18+	3 080		Number of clubs	50
Youth under 18	1 450		Number of teams	200
Unregistered	2 500		Clubs with women's teams	1
Total players	68 030		Players as % of population	4.14%

Gambia Football Association (GFA)
Independence Stadium, Bakau, PO Box 523, Banjul, The Gambia
Tel +220 4496980   Fax +220 4494802
info@gambiafa.org   www.gambiafa.org
President: KINTEH Seedy   General Secretary: BOJANG Jammeh
Vice-President: TAMBA Lang Tombong Lt Col   Treasurer: CEESSAY Kemo   Media Officer: SAINE Pape
Men's Coach: MARTINEZ Jose   Women's Coach: PASUWAREH Faye
GFA formed: 1952   CAF: 1962   FIFA: 1966
Red shirts, Red shorts, Red socks or Blue shirts, Blue shorts, Blue socks

RECENT INTERNATIONAL MATCHES PLAYED BY GAMBIA

2002	Opponents	Score		Venue	Comp	Scorers	Att	Referee
25-08	Sierra Leone	W	1-0	Banjul	Fr	Samba 58		
1-09	Guinea	W	1-0	Banjul	Fr	Assan Jatta 70		
12-10	Lesotho	W	6-0	Banjul	CNq	Nyang 2 7 40, Sarr 45, Jatto Ceesay 2 55 88, Soli	25 000	Ba MTN
2003								
16-02	Nigeria	L	0-1	Banjul	Fr		30 000	
30-03	Senegal	D	0-0	Banjul	CNq		30 000	Djingarey NIG
31-05	Mauritania	W	4-1	Banjul	Fr			
7-06	Senegal	L	1-3	Dakar	CNq	Sillah 63		Guirat TUN
6-07	Lesotho	L	0-1	Maseru	CNq		10 000	
12-10	Liberia	W	2-0	Bakau	WCq	Njie 64, Sonko 79	20 000	Codjia BEN
16-11	Liberia	L	0-3	Monrovia	WCq		10 000	Coulibaly MLI
2004								
No international matches played in 2004								
2005								
12-06	Sierra Leone	L	0-1	Freetown	Fr			
2006								
3-09	Cape Verde Islands	W	2-0	Bakau	CNq	Jatto Ceesay 8p, Assan Jatta 89		Pare BFA
7-10	Algeria	L	0-1	Algiers	CNq			Auda EGY
2007								
8-01	Saudi Arabia	L	0-3	Dammam	Fr			
7-02	Luxembourg	L	1-2	Hesperange	Fr	Jarjue 15	520	Circhetta SUI
24-03	Guinea	L	0-2	Bakau	CNq			Kotey GHA
3-06	Guinea	D	2-2	Conakry	CNq	Sonko 51, Jagne 71		
16-06	Cape Verde Islands	D	0-0	Praia	CNq			

Fr = Friendly match • CN = CAF African Cup of Nations • WC = FIFA World Cup • q = qualifier

GAMBIA NATIONAL TEAM RECORDS AND RECORD SEQUENCES

Records			Sequence records					
Victory	6-0	LES 2002	Wins	3	2002	Clean sheets	3	1991, 2002
Defeat	0-8	GUI 1972	Defeats	9	1968-1977	Goals scored	7	1962-1971
Player Caps	n/a		Undefeated	4	Four times	Without goal	7	1998-2000
Player Goals	n/a		Without win	17	1997-2001	Goals against	16	1962-1979

RECENT LEAGUE AND CUP RECORD

Championship		Cup				GAMBIA 2007 GFA LEAGUE 1ST DIVISION					
Year	Champions	Winners	Score	Runners-up			Pl	W	D	L	Pts
1997	Real Banjul	Real Banjul	1-0	Banjul Hawks		Real Banjul	18	9	6	3	33
1998	Real Banjul	Wallidan	1-1 4-3p	Ports Authority		Wallidan	18	9	6	3	33
1999	Ports Authority	Wallidan	1-1 4-3p	Mass Sosseh		GAMTEL	18	9	5	4	32
2000	Real Banjul	Steve Biko	1-1 4-2p	Wallidan		Ports Authority	18	8	7	3	31
2001	Wallidan	Wallidan	3-0	Blackpool		Hawks	18	6	5	7	23
2002	Wallidan	Wallidan	1-0	Real Banjul		Armed Forces	18	6	5	7	23
2003	Armed Forces	Wallidan	1-0	Banjul Hawks		Sait Matty	18	4	6	8	18
2004	Wallidan	Wallidan	1-1 9-8p	Armed Forces		Bakau United	18	3	7	8	16
2005	Wallidan	Bakau United	4-1	Wallidan		Sea View	18	4	4	10	16
2006	Ports Authority	Hawks	3-0	Steve Biko		Steve Bilko	18	2	9	7	15
2007	Real Banjul					14/03/2007 - 24/05/2007					

GAMBIA COUNTRY INFORMATION

Capital	Banjul	Independence	1965 from the UK	GDP per Capita	$1 700
Population	1 546 848	Status	Republic	GNP Ranking	172
Area km²	11 300	Language	English	Dialling code	+220
Population density	136 per km²	Literacy rate	33%	Internet code	.gm
% in urban areas	26%	Main religion	Muslim 90%	GMT +/ –	0
Towns/Cities ('000)	Serekunda 218; Brikama 101; Bakau 47; Farafenni 36; Banjul 34; Lamin 16; Sukuta 15				
Neighbours (km)	Senegal 740; Atlantic Ocean 80				
Main stadia	Independence Stadium – Bakau 20 000; Brikama – Banjul 15 000				

GEO – GEORGIA

NATIONAL TEAM RECORD
JULY 10TH 2006 TO JULY 12TH 2010

PL	W	D	L	F	A	%
11	4	0	7	16	16	36.3

FIFA/COCA-COLA WORLD RANKING

1993	1994	1995	1996	1997	1998	1999	2000	2001	2002	2003	2004	2005	2006	High	Low
-	92	79	95	69	52	66	66	58	90	93	104	104	94	**42** 09/98	**156** 04/94

2006–2007											
08/06	09/06	10/06	11/06	12/06	01/07	02/07	03/07	04/07	05/07	06/07	07/07
84	93	98	95	94	95	86	85	85	92	97	95

For the second year running, Dinamo Tbilisi, the traditional giants of Georgian football, finished the season empty-handed. Instead, there was a first championship for Olimpi from the town of Rustavi, 30 kilometres to the south east of the capital. Formed at the beginning of the season through a merger of FC Tbilisi and FC Rustavi, Olimpi were coached to the title by former national team boss Revaz Dzodzuashvili, pipping Dinamo to the title on the final day of the season thanks to a 4-2 win over Torpedo Kutaisi. At the other end of the table, hapless Kakheti Telavi picked up just two points all season. In the Cup there was a repeat of the 2006 final with Ameri Tbilisi

INTERNATIONAL HONOURS
None

consigning FC Zestafoni to a third consecutive defeat in the final. Formed in 2003 it was a second trophy in just four years for Ameri. The UEFA Euro 2008 qualifiers saw Georgia drawn in the most difficult group, with three teams - Italy, France and the Ukraine - that had reached the quarter-finals of the FIFA World Cup. Add to the fact that Scotland were also ranked with the other trio in the top 15 of the FIFA rankings, and the task facing Klaus Toppmöller's team was never going to be an easy one. And so it proved to be, as they failed to pick up a single point against their main rivals during the season.

THE FIFA BIG COUNT OF 2006

	Male	Female		Total
Number of players	200 246	21 940	Referees and Assistant Referees	123
Professionals	1 279		Admin, Coaches, Technical, Medical	1 110
Amateurs 18+	1 137		Number of clubs	202
Youth under 18	23 990		Number of teams	522
Unregistered	122 400		Clubs with women's teams	7
Total players	222 186		Players as % of population	4.77%

Georgian Football Federation (GFF)

76a Chavchavadze Avenue, Tbilisi 0162, Georgia

Tel +995 32 912680   Fax +995 32 001128

gff@gff.ge   www.gff.ge

President: AKHALKATSI Nodar   General Secretary: UGULAVA Ucha

Vice-President: KAVTARADZE Gogi   Treasurer: CHKHIKVADZE Nargiza   Media Officer: TZONBILADZE Alexander

Men's Coach: TOPPMOLLER Klaus   Women's Coach: JAPARIDZE Maia

GFF formed: 1990   UEFA: 1992   FIFA: 1992

White shirts with red trimmings, White shorts, White socks or Red shirts with white trimmings, Red shorts, Red socks

RECENT INTERNATIONAL MATCHES PLAYED BY GEORGIA

2003	Opponents	Score		Venue	Comp	Scorers	Att	Referee
6-09	Albania	W	3-0	Tbilisi	ECq	Arveladze.S 2 [9 44], Ashvetia [18]	18 000	Vollquartz DEN
10-09	Albania	L	1-3	Tirana	ECq	Arveladze.S [63]	10 500	Salomir ROU
11-10	Russia	L	1-3	Moscow	ECq	Iashvili [5]	30 000	Plautz AUT
2004								
18-02	Romania	L	0-3	Larnaca	Fr		200	Lajuks LVA
19-02	Cyprus	L	1-3	Nicosia	Fr	Gabidauri [56]		Kapitanis CYP
21-02	Armenia	L	0-2	Nicosia	Fr		200	Loizou CYP
27-05	Israel	L	0-1	Tbilisi	Fr		24 000	Oriekhov UKR
18-08	Moldova	L	0-1	Tiraspol	Fr		8 000	Godulyan UKR
4-09	Turkey	D	1-1	Trabzon	WCq	Asatiani [85]	10 169	Medina Cantalejpo ESP
8-09	Albania	W	2-0	Tbilisi	WCq	Iashvili [15], Demetradze [90+1]	20 000	Courtney NIR
13-10	Ukraine	L	0-2	Lviv	WCq		28 000	Stark GER
17-11	Denmark	D	2-2	Tbilisi	WCq	Demetradze [33], Asatiani [76]	20 000	Ceferin SVN
2005								
9-02	Lithuania	W	1-0	Tbilisi	Fr	Ashvetia [57]	1 000	Gadiyev AZE
26-03	Greece	L	1-3	Tbilisi	WCq	Asatiani [22]	23 000	Rosetti ITA
30-03	Turkey	L	2-5	Tbilisi	WCq	Amisulashvili [13], Iashvili [40]	10 000	Hauge NOR
4-06	Albania	L	2-3	Tirana	WCq	Burduli [85], Kobiashvili [94+]	BCD	Tudor ROU
17-08	Kazakhstan	W	2-1	Almaty	WCq	Demetradze 2 [50 82]	9 000	Havrilla SVK
3-09	Ukraine	D	1-1	Tbilisi	WCq	Gakhokidze [89]	BCD	Ovrebo NOR
7-09	Denmark	L	1-6	Copenhagen	WCq	Demetradze [37]	27 177	Bozinovski MKD
8-10	Kazakhstan	D	0-0	Tbilisi	WCq		BCD	Hyytia FIN
12-10	Greece	L	0-1	Athens	WCq		28 186	Trefoloni ITA
12-11	Bulgaria	L	2-6	Sofia	Fr	Jakobia [83], Gogua [90]		
16-11	Jordan	W	3-2	Tbilisi	Fr	Demetradze 2 [3 64], Arveladze.S [73]		
2006								
27-02	Moldova	L	1-5	Ta'Qali	Fr	Tskitishvili [18p]	330	Casha MLT
1-03	Malta	W	2-0	Ta'Qali	Fr	Martsvaladze [8], Kankava [18]	1 100	Banari MDV
22-03	Albania	D	0-0	Tirana	Fr			Dondarini ITA
27-05	New Zealand	L	1-3	Altenkirchen	Fr	Arveladze.S [41]	1 000	
31-05	Paraguay	L	0-1	Dornbirn	Fr		2 000	Gangle AUT
16-08	Faroe Islands	W	6-0	Toftir	ECq	Mujiri [16], Iashvili [18], Arveladze 3 [37 62 82], Kobiashvili [51p]	2 114	Ross NIR
2-09	France	L	0-3	Tbilisi	ECq		54 000	Wegereef NED
6-09	Ukraine	L	2-3	Kyiv	ECq	Arveladze [38], Demetradze [61]	35 000	Jara CZE
7-10	Germany	L	0-2	Rostock	Fr		28 000	Lehner AUT
11-10	Italy	L	1-3	Tbilisi	ECq	Shashiashvili [26]	48 000	Riley ENG
15-11	Uruguay	W	2-0	Tbilisi	Fr	Kobiashvili 2 [38p 60]	12 000	Godulyan UKR
2007								
7-02	Turkey	W	1-0	Tbilisi	Fr	Siradze [76]	53 000	Lajuks LVA
24-03	Scotland	L	1-2	Glasgow	ECq	Arveladze [41]	52 063	Vollquartz DEN
28-03	Faroe Islands	W	3-1	Tbilisi	ECq	Siradze 26, Iashvili 2 [46+ 92+]	12 000	Saliy KAZ
2-06	Lithuania	L	0-1	Kaunas	ECq		6 400	Circhetta SUI
6-06	France	L	0-1	Auxerre	ECq		19 345	Batista POR

Fr = Friendly match • EC = UEFA EURO 2004/2008 • WC = FIFA World Cup • q = qualifier • BCD = Behind closed doors

GEORGIA NATIONAL TEAM RECORDS AND RECORD SEQUENCES

Records			Sequence records					
Victory	7-0	ARM 1997	Wins	5	1997-1998	Clean sheets	3	1997
Defeat	0-5	ROM 1996	Defeats	7	2003-2004	Goals scored	10	2001-2002
Player Caps	69	NEMSADZE Giorgi	Undefeated	8	1997-1998	Without goal	3	Four times
Player Goals	20	ARVELADZE Shota	Without win	8	1999, 2003-2004	Goals against	11	1998-1999

GEORGIA; SAKARTVELO

Capital	Tbilisi	Language	Geirgian, Russian, Armenian, Azeri	Independence	1991
Population	4 661 473	Area	69 700 km²	% in cities	58%
GDP per cap	$2500	Dailling code	+995	Internet	.ge	GMT + / -	+4

MEDALS TABLE

		Overall			League			Cup			Europe			City	Stadium	Cap'ty	DoF
		G	S	B	G	S	B	G	S	G	S	B					
1	Dinamo Tbilisi	20	2	5	12	1	5	8	1				Tbilisi	Boris Paichadze	20 500	1925
2	Torpedo Kutaisi	5	6	2	3	3	2	2	3				Kutaisi	Torpedo	19 400	1949
3	Lokomotivi Tbilisi	3	3	1		2	1	3	1				Tbilisi	Lokomotivi	24 500	1936
4	Ameri Tbilisi	2		1		1	2						Tbilisi	Ameri	1 000	2003
5	Dinamo Batumi	1	5	1		1	1	1	4				Batumi	Central	19 600	1923
6	WIT Georgia	1	2	1	1	2	1						Tbilisi	Mtskheta Central	2 000	1968
7	Sioni Bolnisi	1	2		1	1			1				Bolnisi	Temur Stapania	3 000	1936
	Guria Lanchkhuti	1	2			2		1					Lanchkhuti	Central	22 000	1952
9	Olimpi Rustavi	1		1	1		1						Rustavi	Poladi	6 000	1991
10	FC Zestafoni		3						3				Zestafoni	Central	5 000	2004
	Tskhumi Sukhumi		3			1			2				Sukhumi			
12	Kolkheti-1913	2	3		2	3							Poti	Phazisi	6 000	1913
13	Gorda Rustavi	1	2			2			1				Rustavi	Poladi	6 000	1948
14	Margveti Zestafoni	1			1								Zestafoni	Central	5 000	1938
	Samgurali	1							1				Tskhaltubo	Central	12 000	1945
	Samtredia	1			1								Samtredia	Erosi Manjgaladze	15 000	1936
	Shevardeni 1906	1			1								Tbilisi	Shevardeni	2 500	1906
18	Alazani Gurdzhaani			1					1				Gurdzhaani			

GEORGIAN CLUBS IN THE SOVIET UNION

6	Dinamo Tbilisi	4	11	13	2	5	13	2	6	1		1

RECENT LEAGUE AND CUP RECORD

	Championship						Cup		
Year	Champions	Pts	Runners-up	Pts	Third	Pts	Winners	Score	Runners-up
1996	Dinamo Tbilisi	79	Margveti Zestafoni	68	Kolkheti 1913 Poti	68	Dinamo Tbilisi	1-0	Dinamo Batumi
1997	Dinamo Tbilisi	81	Kolkheti 1913 Poti	64	Dinamo Batumi	62	Dinamo Tbilisi	1-0	Dinamo Batumi
1998	Dinamo Tbilisi	71	Dinamo Batumi	61	Kolkheti 1913 Poti	57	Dinamo Batumi	2-1	Dinamo Tbilisi
1999	Dinamo Tbilisi	77	Torpedo Kutaisi	67	Lokomotivi Tbilisi	64	Torpedo Kutaisi	0-0 4-2p	Samgurali
2000	Torpedo Kutaisi	46	WIT Georgia Tbilisi	41	Dinamo Tbilisi	41	Lokomotivi Tbilisi	0-0 4-2p	Torpedo Kutaisi
2001	Torpedo Kutaisi	44	Lokomotivi Tbilisi	41	Dinamo Tbilisi	38	Torpedo Kutaisi	0-0 4-3p	Lokomotivi Tbilisi
2002	Torpedo Kutaisi	48	Lokomotivi Tbilisi	47	Dinamo Tbilisi	44	Lokomotivi Tbilisi	2-0	Torpedo Kutaisi
2003	Dinamo Tbilisi	48	Torpedo Kutaisi	46	WIT Georgia Tbilisi	41	Dinamo Tbilisi	3-1	Sioni Bolnisi
2004	WIT Georgia Tbilisi	41	Sioni Bolnisi	41	Dinamo Tbilisi	40	Dinamo Tbilisi	2-1	Torpedo Kutaisi
2005	Dinamo Tbilisi	75	Torpedo Kutaisi	70	FC Tbilisi	69	Lokomotivi Tbilisi	2-0	FC Zestafoni
2006	Sioni Bolnisi	73	WIT Georgia Tbilisi	68	Dinamo Tbilisi	64	Ameri Tbilisi	2-2 4-3p	FC Zestafoni
2007	Olimpi Rustavi	63	Dinamo Tbilisi	62	Ameri Tbilisi	57	Ameri Tbilisi	1-0	FC Zestafoni

GEORGIA 2006–07

UMAGLESI LIGA

	Pl	W	D	L	F	A	Pts	Olimpi	Dinamo T.	Zestafoni	Ameri	WIT Georgia	Sioni	Torpedo	Borjomi	Lokomotivi	Dinamo B.	Merani	Chikhura	Dila Gori	Kakheti
Olimpi Rustavi †	26	19	6	1	57	9	63		0-0	0-0	1-1	4-0	3-0	1-0	2-0	1-0	2-1	1-0	5-0	5-1	7-0
Dinamo Tbilisi ‡	26	20	2	4	56	19	62	1-0		2-1	2-2	1-0	1-0	0-1	3-0	1-0	4-2	3-0	3-1	6-1	2-1
Ameri Tbilisi ‡	26	17	6	3	53	14	57	2-2	2-0	1-1		3-0	1-0	1-0	2-0	3-0	0-0	6-0	2-0	2-1	3-0
FC Zestafoni	26	16	9	1	55	11	57	0-0	1-0		0-0	5-0	3-0	2-0	4-0	2-0	4-0	1-1	2-0	4-1	7-0
WIT Georgia Tbilisi	26	12	9	5	40	28	45	0-0	2-1	4-3	3-0		3-2	0-0	0-0	3-0	0-0	0-0	3-2	1-1	5-1
Sioni Bolnisi	26	12	4	10	29	25	40	0-1	0-1	1-1	0-0	1-0		1-0	2-1	0-3	2-0	3-0			5-0
Torpedo Kutaisi	26	9	4	13	24	35	31	2-4	0-5	0-1	0-1	0-0	0-0		2-1	1-3	2-1	3-1	2-0	2-0	2-1
FC Borjomi	26	8	6	12	29	35	30	0-4	0-2	1-0	1-2	2-2	2-0	5-1		1-1	0-0	3-4	3-1	1-0	4-1
Lokomotivi Tbilisi	26	8	6	12	25	34	30	0-1	0-3	0-1	1-4	0-3	3-1	0-3	0-0		1-0	3-1	0-0	3-0	1-0
Dinamo Batumi	26	7	6	13	26	31	27	1-2	1-3	0-1	0-0	0-1	1-2	2-0	1-0	0-1		3-0	3-0	2-1	3-2
Merani Tiflis	26	6	8	12	20	40	26	0-1	1-2	0-4	0-3	0-0	0-3	2-0	0-0	1-1	1-1		0-0	0-0	3-1
Chikhura Sachkhere	26	5	6	15	13	46	21	0-4	0-5	0-2	0-0	0-1	0-1	0-0	1-1	1-0	1-0			1-1	3-1
Dila Gori	26	3	6	17	21	56	15	0-1	1-2	1-4	0-4	0-6	0-1	1-0	0-3	1-1	0-0	0-1	5-0		3-1
Kakheti Telavi	26	0	2	24	21	86	2	0-5	2-3	1-7	0-2	2-3	1-1	2-3	0-2	1-5	1-3	0-1	0-1	2-2	

29/07/2006 - 20/05/2007 • † Qualified for the UEFA Champions League • ‡ Qualified for the UEFA Cup
Play-off: Chikhura Sachkhere 2-1 FC Gagra. Chikhura remain in the Umaglesi Liga

GEORGIA 2006–07 PIRVELI LIGA (2)

	Pl	W	D	L	F	A	Pts
Mglebi Zugdidi	34	24	4	6	58	24	76
Meskheti Akhaltsikhe	34	22	6	6	69	19	72
FC Gagra	34	18	6	10	52	36	60
WIT Georgia-2 Tbilisi	34	17	7	10	60	29	58
Magharoeli Chiatura	34	16	9	9	49	32	57
Ameri-2 Tbilisi	34	15	12	7	58	36	57
Meshakre Agara	34	15	10	9	45	36	55
Norchi Dinamoeli	34	16	4	14	50	49	52
Meshakhte Tqibuli	34	15	6	13	53	40	51
Olimpi Tbilisi	34	14	8	12	52	47	50
FC Samtredia	34	13	8	13	35	43	47
FC Zestafoni-2	34	10	10	14	34	40	40
Racha Ambrolauri	34	9	12	13	41	49	39
Dinamo-2 Tbilisi	34	9	9	16	49	40	36
Guria Lanchkhuti	34	8	7	19	36	76	31
Chikhura-2 Sachkhere	34	8	5	21	28	67	29
Spartaki Tbilisi	34	7	6	21	19	51	27
Mertskhali Ozurgeti	34	3	5	26	21	95	14

14/08/2006 - 23/05/2007

GEORGIAN CUP 2006–07

Group Stage

Group A	Pts
FC Zestafoni	13
Ameri Tbilisi	13
Kakheti Telavi	7
Spartaki Tbilisi	1

Group B	Pts
Torpedo Kutaisi	11
FC Borjomi	8
WIT Georgia Tbilisi	6
Meskheti Akhaltsikhe	6

Group C	Pts
Dinamo Tbilisi	12
Chikhura Sachkhere	11
Olimpi Rustavi	6
Norchi Dinamoeli	4

Group D	Pts
Sioni Bolnisi	16
Dinamo Batumi	11
Merani Tbilisi	4
Meshakre Agara	3

Quarter-finals

Ameri Tbilisi *	2	0
Dinamo Tbilisi	1	0
Chikhura Sachkhere *	2	1
Sioni Bolnisi	3	0
Dinamo Batumi *	0	3
Torpedo Kutaisi	0	0
FC Borjomi *	1	1
FC Zestafoni	2	1

Semi-finals

Ameri Tbilisi *	3	1
Sioni Bolnisi	0	4
Dinamo Batumi	0	0
FC Zestafoni *	4	1

Final

Ameri Tbilisi ‡	1
FC Zestafoni	0

CUP FINAL
26-05-2007
Scorer - Dimitri Tatanashvili [61]

* Home team in the first leg • ‡ Qualified for the UEFA Cup

GER – GERMANY

NATIONAL TEAM RECORD
JULY 10TH 2006 TO JULY 12TH 2010

PL	W	D	L	F	A	%
11	9	1	1	37	6	86.3

The post FIFA World Cup euphoria lasted well into the following season in Germany as fans were treated to a hugely entertaining season in both the Bundesliga and the Cup. Attendances were up to a record 12,239,304 for the top flight and with an average of 39,998 a game, the Bundesliga remained well ahead of the rest as the best supported League in the world, with over twice as many fans as Italy's Serie A. Ticket prices remain relatively affordable compared to many other European Leagues and with standing areas still allowed in many grounds, the Bundesliga retains much of the traditional atmosphere and spirit, something which has been lost in other, more corporate Leagues. It has come at a price, however, as German clubs have been unable to compete on a level playing field in Europe with the richer clubs in England, Spain and Italy. The record numbers attending matches in the Bundesliga were no doubt encouraged by the open competition, with back to back double winners Bayern Munich never challenging for honours. Even the return of their talismanic former coach Ottmar Hitzfeld could not rescue a season that saw Bayern fail to qualify for the UEFA Champions League for the first time since 1996. That left a three way fight for the title

INTERNATIONAL HONOURS

FIFA World Cup 1954 1974 1990   **FIFA Women's World Cup** 2003

Olympic Gold 1976 (GDR)   **FIFA World Youth Championship** 1981   **FIFA Women's U-19 Championship** 2004

UEFA European Championship 1972 1980 1996   **UEFA Women's European Championship** 1989 1991 1995 1997 2001 2005

UEFA U-19 Championship 1981 1986 (GDR)   **UEFA U-17 Championship** 1984 1992   **UEFA Women's U-19 Championship** 2000 2001 2002 2006

UEFA Champions League Bayern München 1974 1975 1976 2001, Hamburger SV 1983, Borussia Dortmund 1997

between VfB Stuttgart, Schalke and Werder Bremen which went down to the final day of the season. With memories of 2001 still fresh, long time leaders Schalke choked at the death once again, losing their penultimate match to neighbours VfL Bochum. That gave Stuttgart, who finished with eight straight wins, the lead for the first time, a lead they held on to by beating Cottbus on the final day. The previous four seasons had seen the champions go on to complete the double by winning the DFB Pokal and Stuttgart had the chance to extend that sequence, but they lost to 1.FC Nürnberg in Berlin in the final. For 1.FC Nürnberg it was a first trophy since winning the Bundesliga in 1968 whilst Hans Meyer became the first coach win the Cup in both Germany and the old East Germany, having won three with Carl Zeiss Jena in the 1970s. The German national team got off to a good start under new coach Joachim Loew, losing just one match all season, to Denmark in a friendly. Their 13-0 thrashing of San Marino was a European Championship record and although they dropped two points against Cyprus, victories against both the Republic of Ireland and the Czech Republic saw the team well placed to qualify for the finals.

Deutscher Fussball-Bund (DFB)

Otto-Fleck-Schneise 6, Postfach 71 02 65, Frankfurt 60528, Germany
Tel +49 69 67880   Fax +49 69 6788266
info@dfb.de   www.dfb.de
President: ZWANZIGER Theo   General Secretary: SCHMIDT Horst R.
Vice-President: NELLE Engelbert   Treasurer: SCHMIDHUBER Heinrich   Media Officer: STENGER Harald
Men's Coach: LOEW Joachim   Women's Coach: NEID Silvia
DFB formed: 1900   UEFA: 1954   FIFA: 1904
White shirts with black trimmings, Black shorts, White socks or Red shirts with black trimmings, White shorts, White socks

RECENT INTERNATIONAL MATCHES PLAYED BY GERMANY

2005	Opponents	Score		Venue	Comp	Scorers	Att	Referee
9-02	Argentina	D	2-2	Dusseldorf	Fr	Frings [28p], Kuranyi [45]	52 000	Farina ITA
26-03	Slovenia	W	1-0	Celje	Fr	Podolski [27]	8 500	Poll ENG
4-06	Northern Ireland	W	4-1	Belfast	Fr	Asamoah [17], Ballack 2 [62 66p], Podolski [81]	14 000	Richmond SCO
8-06	Russia	D	2-2	Mönchengladbach	Fr	Schweinsteiger 2 [30 69]	46 228	Plautz AUT
15-06	Australia	W	4-3	Frankfurt/Main	CCr1	Kuranyi [17], Mertesacker [23], Ballack [60p], Podolski [88]	46 466	Amarilla PAR
18-06	Tunisia	W	3-0	Cologne	CCr1	Ballack [74p], Schweinsteiger [80], Hanke [88]	44 377	Prendergast JAM
21-06	Argentina	D	2-2	Nuremberg	CCr1	Kuranyi [29], Asamoah [51]	42 088	Michel SVK
25-06	Brazil	L	2-3	Nuremberg	CCsf	Podolski [23], Ballack [48+p]	42 187	Chandia CHI
29-06	Mexico	W	4-3	Leipzig	CC3p	Podolski [37], Schweinsteiger [41], Huth [79], Ballack [97]	43 335	Breeze AUS
17-08	Netherlands	D	2-2	Rotterdam	Fr	Ballack [49], Asamoah [81]	41 000	Hauge NOR
3-09	Slovakia	L	0-2	Bratislava	Fr		9 276	Braamhaar NED
7-09	South Africa	W	4-2	Bremen	Fr	Podolski 3 [12 48 55], Borowski [47]	28 100	Gilewski POL
8-10	Turkey	L	1-2	Istanbul	Fr	Neuivlle [90]	25 000	Messina ITA
12-10	China PR	W	1-0	Hamburg	Fr	Frings [51p]	48 734	Batista POR
12-11	France	D	0-0	Paris	Fr		58 889	Bennett ENG
2006								
1-03	Italy	L	1-4	Florence	Fr	Huth [82]	28 317	Iturralde ESP
22-03	USA	W	4-1	Dortmund	Fr	Schweinsteiger [46], Neuville [73], Klose [75], Ballack [79]	64 500	Fröjdfeldt SWE
27-05	Luxembourg	W	7-0	Freiburg	Fr	Klose 2 [5 59], Frings [19p], Podolski 2 [36 65p], Neuville 2 [90 90]	23 000	Rogallo SUI
30-05	Japan	D	2-2	Leverkusen	Fr	Klose [75], Schweinsteiger [80]	22 500	Vassaras GRE
2-06	Colombia	W	3-0	Mönchengladbach	Fr	Ballack [20], Schweinsteiger [37], Borowski [69]	45 000	Hauge NOR
9-06	Costa Rica	W	4-2	Munich	WCr1	Lahm [6], Klose 2 [17 61], Frings [87]	66 000	Elizondo ARG
14-06	Poland	W	1-0	Dortmund	WCr1	Neuville [91+]	65 000	Medina Cantalejo ESP
20-06	Ecuador	W	3-0	Berlin	WCr1	Klose 2 [4 44], Podolski [57]	72 000	Ivanov RUS
24-06	Sweden	W	2-0	Munich	WCr2	Podolski 2 [4 12]	66 000	Simon BRA
30-06	Argentina	D	1-1	Berlin	WCqf	Klose [80]	72 000	Michel SVK
4-07	Italy	L	0-2	Dortmund	WCsf		65 000	Archundia MEX
8-07	Portugal	W	3-1	Stuttgart	WC3p	Schweinsteiger 2 [56 78], Petit OG [60]	52 000	Kamikawa JPN
16-08	Sweden	W	3-0	Gelsenkirchen	Fr	Schneider [4], Klose 2 [8 44]	53 000	Farina ITA
2-09	Republic of Ireland	W	1-0	Stuttgart	ECq	Podolski [57]	53 198	Medina Cantalejo ESP
6-09	San Marino	W	13-0	Serravalle	ECq	Podolski 4 [11 43 64 72], Schweinsteiger 2 [28 47], Klose 2 [30 46+], Ballack [35], Hitzlsperger 2 [66 73], Friedrich.M [87], Schneider [90p]	5 090	Dereli TUR
7-10	Georgia	W	2-0	Rostock	Fr	Schweinsteiger [24], Ballack [67]	28 000	Lehner AUT
11-10	Slovakia	W	4-1	Bratislava	ECq	Podolski 2 [13 72], Ballack [25], Schweinsteiger [36]	27 580	Hauge NOR
15-11	Cyprus	D	1-1	Nicosia	ECq	Ballack [16]	12 300	Fröjdfeldt SWE
2007								
7-02	Switzerland	W	3-1	Dusseldorf	Fr	Kuranyi [7], Gomez [30], Frings [66]	51 333	Bossen NED
24-03	Czech Republic	W	2-1	Prague	ECq	Kuranyi 2 [42 62]	17 821	Rosetti ITA
28-03	Denmark	L	0-1	Duisburg	Fr		31 500	Webb ENG
2-06	San Marino	W	6-0	Nuremberg	ECq	Kuranyi [45], Jansen [52], Frings [56p], Gómez 2 [63 65], Fritz [67]	43 967	Asumaa FIN
6-06	Slovakia	W	2-1	Hamburg	ECq	Durica OG [10], Hitzlsperger [43]	51 600	Benquerença POR

Fr = Friendly match • EC = UEFA EURO 2004/2008 • CC = FIFA Confederations Cup • WC = FIFA World Cup
q = qualifier • r1 = first round group • r2 = second round • qf = quarter-final • sf = semi-final • 3p = third place play-off

GERMANY NATIONAL TEAM RECORDS AND RECORD SEQUENCES

Records			Sequence records			
Victory	16-0	RUS 1912	Wins	12	1979-1980	Clean sheets	6	1966
Defeat	0-9	ENG 1909	Defeats	7	1912-1913	Goals scored	33	1940-1952
Player Caps	150	MATTHAUS Lothar	Undefeated	23	1978-1980	Without goal	3	1985
Player Goals	68	MULLER Gerd	Without win	10	1912-1920	Goals against	15	1910-1912

MAJOR CITIES/TOWNS
Population '000

1	Berlin	3 370
2	Hamburg	1 748
3	Munich/München	1 281
4	Cologne/Köln	958
5	Frankfurt	642
6	Essen	598
7	Stuttgart	590
8	Dortmund	585
9	Düsseldorf	573
10	Bremen	548
11	Hanover	513
12	Leipzig	504
13	Duisburg	500
14	Nuremberg	493
15	Dresden	492
16	Bochum	382
17	Bielefeld	337
18	Bonn	317
19	Karlsruhe	285
20	Aachen	280
21	Gelsenkirchen	265
22	Mönchengladbach	260
23	Leverkusen	164
24	Wolfsburg	123

FEDERAL REPUBLIC OF GERMANY; BUNDESREPUBLIK DEUTSCHLAND

Capital Berlin	Language German		Independence 1871	
Population 82 422 299	Area 357 021 km²	Density 230 per km²	% in cities 85%	
GDP per cap $27 600	Dailling code +49		Internet .de	GMT +/- +1

The major metropolitan areas are: Rhein-Ruhr 11 805; Berlin 4 025; Hamburg 3 279; Rhein-Mann 3 123; Stuttgart 2 344; München 2 324; Alma 2 128; Rhein-Neckar 1 515; Bielefeld 1 448; Halle-Leipzig 1 395; Nürnberg 1 182; Bremen 1 180; Chemnitz-Zwickau 1 167; Hannover 1 108; Saarbrücken-Forbach 1 104; Dresden 1 076; Karlsruhe 625; Kassel 324;

MEDALS TABLE FOR THE FORMER GERMAN DEMOCRATIC REPUBLIC

		Overall			League			Cup		Europe			City	Stadium	Cap'ty	DoF
		G	S	B	G	S	B	G	S	G	S	B				
1	Dynamo Dresden	15	12	8	8	8	6	7	4			1	Dresden	Rudolf-Harbig-Stadion	18 808	1953
2	Dynamo Berlin	13	10	4	10	4	3	3	6			1	Berlin	Sportforum Berlin	10 000	1953
3	1.FC Magdeburg	11	2	6	3	2	6	7		1			Magdeburg	Stadion Magdeburg	27 250	1965
4	Viktoria 91 Frankfurt	8	7	1	6	4	1	2	3				Frankfurt/Oder	Stadion der Freundschaft	12 000	1951
5	Carl Zeiss Jena	7	13	6	3	9	5	4	3	1	1		Jena	Ernst-Abbe-Sportfeld	12 000	1903
6	Sachsenring Zwickau	5	1	4	2		3	3	1		1		Zwickau	Westsachsenstadion	14 000	1912
7	Lokomotive Leipzig	4	8	9		3	8	4	4	1	1		Leipzig	Bruno-Plache-Stadion	15 600	1893
8	Wismut Aue	4	3		3	2		1	1				Aue	Erzgebirgestadion	16 500	1945
9	Chemie Leipzig	4	2	4	2	1	4	2	1				Leipzig	Zentralstadion	44 193	1899
10	Chemie Halle	4	1	1	2	1	1	2					Halle	Kurt-Wabbel Stadion	24 000	1946
11	Hansa Rostock	2	9		1	4		1	5				Rostock	Ostseestadion	30 000	1965

RECENT LEAGUE AND CUP RECORD

	Championship						Cup		
Year	Champions	Pts	Runners-up	Pts	Third	Pts	Winners	Score	Runners-up
1995	Borussia Dortmund	49	Werder Bremen	48	SC Freiburg	46	B. Mönchengladbach	3-0	VfL Wolfsburg
1996	Borussia Dortmund	68	Bayern München	62	Schalke 04	56	1.FC Kaiserslautern	1-0	Karlsruher SC
1997	Bayern München	71	Bayer Leverkusen	69	Borussia Dortmund	63	VfB Stuttgart	2-0	Energie Cottbus
1998	1.FC Kaiserslautern	68	Bayern München	66	Bayer Leverkusen	55	Bayern München	2-1	MSV Duisburg
1999	Bayern München	78	Bayer Leverkusen	63	Hertha BSC Berlin	62	Werder Bremen	1-1 5-4p	Bayern München
2000	Bayern München	73	Bayer Leverkusen	73	Hamburger SV	59	Bayern München	3-0	Werder Bremen
2001	Bayern München	63	Schalke 04	62	Borussia Dortmund	58	Schalke 04	2-0	1.FC Union Berlin
2002	Borussia Dortmund	70	Bayer Leverkusen	69	Bayern München	68	Schalke 04	4-2	Bayer Leverkusen
2003	Bayern München	75	VfB Stuttgart	59	Borussia Dortmund	58	Bayern München	3-1	1.FC Kaiserslautern
2004	Werder Bremen	74	Bayern München	68	Bayer Leverkusen	65	Werder Bremen	3-2	Alemannia Aachen
2005	Bayern München	77	Schalke 04	63	Werder Bremen	59	Bayern München	2-1	Schalke 04
2006	Bayern München	75	Werder Bremen	70	Hamburger SV	68	Bayern München	1-0	Eintracht Frankfurt
2007	VfB Stuttgart	70	Schalke 04	68	Werder Bremen	66	1.FC Nürnberg	3-2	VfB Stuttgart

MEDALS TABLE

Rank	Club	Overall			League			Cup		Europe			City	Stadium	Cap'ty	DoF
		G	S	B	G	S	B	G	S	G	S	B				
1	Bayern München	39	12	14	20	7	4	13	2	6	3	10	Munich	Allianz-Arena	69 901	1900
2	1.FC Nürnberg	14	5	1	9	3		5	2			1	Nuremburg	Frankenstadion	46 780	1900
3	Schalke 04	12	16	3	7	9	1	4	7	1		2	Gelsenkirchen	Veltins Arena	61 524	1904
4	Hamburger SV	11	15	4	6	8	2	3	4	2	3	2	Hamburg	AOL Arena	55 000	1887
5	Werder Bremen	10	9	9	4	6	5	5	3	1		4	Bremen	Weserstadion	42 466	1899
6	Borussia Dortmund	10	7	8	6	4	5	2	1	2	2	3	Dortmund	Signal Iduna Park	80 700	1909
	B. Mönchengladbach	10	7	8	5	2	5	3	2	2	3	3	Mönchengladbach	Borussia-Park	54 019	1900
8	VfB Stuttgart	9	9	5	6	4	3	3	3		2	2	Stuttgart	Gottlieb-Daimler	55 875	1893
9	1.FC Köln	7	15	9	3	8	2	4	6		1	7	Cologne	Rhein Energy Stadion	50 997	1948
10	1.FC Kaiserslautern	6	9	4	4	4	2	2	5			2	Kaiserslautern	Fritz-Walter-Stadion	48 500	1900
11	Eintracht Frankfurt	6	4	7	1	1	5	4	2	1	1	2	Frankfurt	Commerzbank-Arena	51 052	1899
12	Lokomotive Leipzig (VfB)	4	2		3	2		1					Leipzig	Bruno-Plache-Stadion	15 600	1893
13	Dresdner SC	4	1		2	1		2					Dresden	Heinz-Steyer-Stadion	24 000	1898-1950
14	Fortuna Düsseldorf	3	7	2	1	1	2	2	5		1		Düsseldorf	LTU Arena	51 500	1895
15	Karlsruher SC	3	3	1	1	1		2	2			1	Karlsruhe	Wildparstadion	33 800	1894
16	TSV München 1860	3	3		1	2		2	1				Munich	Allianz-Arena	69 901	1860
17	SpVgg Fürth	3	1		3	1							Fürth	Playmobil Stadion	15 500	1903
18	Hannover 96	3			2			1					Hanover	AWD Arena	49 000	1896
19	Hertha BSC Berlin	2	7	5	2	5	4		2			1	Berlin	Olympiastadion	74 400	1892
20	Bayer 04 Leverkusen	2	6	4		4	3	1	1	1	1	1	Leverkusen	BayArena	22 500	1904
21	Viktoria 89 Berlin	2	2		2	2							Berlin	Friedrich-Ebert-Stadion	5 000	1889
22	Rot-Weiss Essen	2	1		1			1	1				Essen	Georg Melches Stadion	25 250	1907
23	SK Rapid Wien	2			1			1					Vienna - AUT			
24	Holstein Kiel	1	2		1	2							Kiel	Holstein-Stadion	13 000	1900
	Karlsruher FV	1	2		1	2							Karlsruhe	Telegrafenkaserne		1891-2004
	Kickers Offenbach	1	2			2		1					Offenbach	Bieberer Berg	31 500	1901
27	Blau-Weiß Berlin	1	1		1	1							Berlin	Rathausstrasse	1 000	1890
	First Vienna	1	1		1				1				Vienna - AUT			
29	KFC Uerdingen 05	1					2	1				1	Krefeld	Grotenburg-Stadion	34 500	1905
30	Eint. Braunschweig	1	1		1	1							Braunschweig	Hamberger Straße	25 000	1895
31	Freiburger FC	1			1								Freiburg	Schönbergstadion	3 000	1897
	Schwarz-Weiss Essen	1						1					Essen	Ulhenkrug	25 000	1881
	VfR Mannheim	1			1								Mannheim	Rhein-Neckar-Stadion	12 000	1896
34	MSV Duisburg		5	1		2			3			1	Duisburg	MSV-Arena	31 500	1902
35	TSV Alemania Aachen		4			1			3				Aachen	Tivoli Stadion	24 816	1900
36	1.FC Saarbrücken		2			2							Saarbrücken	Ludwigsparkstadion	35 286	1903
	FSV Frankfurt		2			1			1				Frankfurt	Bornheimer Hang	32 000	1899
	Stuttgarter Kickers		2			1			1				Stuttgart	Waldau-Stadion	11 544	1899
	VfL Bochum		2						2				Bochum	Ruhrstadion	31 328	1848
	1.FC Union Berlin		2			1			1				Berlin	Alte Försterei	18 000	1966
41	Admira Wien		1			1							Vienna - AUT			
	Borussia Neunkirchen		1						1				Neunkirchen	Ellenfeld	29 200	1905
	DFC Prag		1			1							Prague - CZE			
	Energie Cottbus		1						1				Cottbus	Stadion der Freundschaft	22 450	1966
	Fortuna Köln		1						1				Cologne	Bezirkssportanlage	12 000	1948
	Hertha BSC Berlin am		1						1				Berlin			
	1.FC Phorzheim		1			1							Pforzheim	Brötzinger Tal	10 000	1896
	LSV Groß Hamburg		1			1							Hamburg			1942-1945
	Preußen Münster		1			1							Münster	Preußenstadion	15 050	1906
	Waldhof Mannheim		1						1				Mannheim	Carl-Benz-Stadion	27 000	1907
	VfL Wolfsburg		1						1				Wolfsburg	Volkswagen-Arena	30 000	1945
52	SC Freiburg			1			1						Freiburg	Badenova-stadion	25 000	1904
53	Arminia Bielefeld												Bielefeld	Schüco Arena	26 601	1905
	FC Augsburg												Augsburg	Rosenaustadion	32 400	1907
	TuS Koblenz												Koblenz	Stadion Oberwerth	17 000	1911
	1.FSV Mainz 05												Mainz	Stadion am Bruchweg	20 300	1905
	VfL Osnabrück												Osnabrück	OSNAtel Arena	18 415	1899
	SC Paderborn 07												Paderborn	Herman Löns Stadion	10 222	1907
	FC St Pauli												Hamburg	Millerntor-Stadion	19 400	1910
	SpVgg Unterhaching												Munich	Generali Sportpark	15 053	1925
	Wacker Burghausen												Burghausen	Wacker Arena	8 400	1930
	Wuppertaler SV												Wuppertal	Zoo-Stadion	28 000	1954
		177	179	89	96	96	46	65	65	16	18	43				

GERMANY 2006-07

1. BUNDESLIGA

	Pl	W	D	L	F	A	Pts	VfB Stuttgart	Schalke 04	Werder Bremen	Bayern	Leverkusen	1.FC Nürnberg	Hamburger SV	VfL Bochum	Bor. Dortmund	Hertha Berlin	Hannover 96	Arm. Bielefeld	Energie Cottbus	Eint. Frankfurt	VfL Wolfsburg	1.FSV Mainz	Alemannia	Gladbach
VfB Stuttgart †	34	21	7	6	61	37	70		3-0	4-1	2-0	3-0	0-3	2-0	1-0	1-3	0-0	2-1	3-2	2-1	1-1	0-0	2-0	3-1	1-0
Schalke 04 †	34	21	5	8	53	32	68	1-0		2-0	2-2	0-1	1-0	0-2	3-1	2-0	2-1	2-1	2-0	1-1	2-0	4-0	2-1	2-0	—
Werder Bremen †	34	20	6	8	76	40	66	2-3	0-2		3-1	2-1	1-0	0-2	3-0	1-3	3-1	3-0	3-0	1-1	1-2	2-1	2-0	3-1	3-0
Bayern München ‡	34	18	6	10	55	40	60	2-1	2-0	1-1		2-1	0-0	1-2	0-0	2-0	4-2	0-1	1-0	2-1	2-0	2-1	5-2	2-1	1-1
Bayer Leverkusen ‡	34	15	6	13	54	49	51	3-1	3-1	0-2	2-3		2-0	1-2	1-4	2-1	2-1	0-1	1-2	3-1	2-2	1-1	1-1	3-0	1-0
1.FC Nürnberg ‡	34	11	15	8	43	32	48	4-1	0-0	1-2	3-0	3-2		0-2	1-1	1-1	2-1	3-1	1-1	1-0	2-2	1-1	1-1	1-0	1-0
Hamburger SV	34	10	15	9	43	37	45	2-4	1-2	1-1	1-2	0-0	0-0		0-3	3-0	1-1	0-0	1-1	1-1	3-1	1-0	2-2	4-0	1-1
VfL Bochum	34	13	6	15	49	50	45	2-3	2-1	0-6	1-2	1-3	0-2	2-1		2-0	1-3	2-0	2-1	0-1	4-3	0-1	0-1	2-2	2-0
Borussia Dortmund	34	12	8	14	41	43	44	0-1	2-0	0-2	3-2	1-2	0-0	1-0	1-1		1-2	2-2	1-1	2-3	2-0	1-0	1-1	0-0	1-0
Hertha BSC Berlin	34	12	8	14	50	55	44	2-2	2-0	1-4	2-3	2-3	2-1	2-1	3-3	0-1		4-0	1-1	0-1	1-0	2-1	1-2	1-2	2-1
Hannover 96	34	12	8	14	41	50	44	1-2	1-1	2-4	1-2	1-1	0-3	0-0	0-2	4-2	5-0		1-1	2-0	1-1	2-2	1-0	0-3	1-0
Arminia Bielefeld	34	11	9	14	47	49	42	2-3	0-1	3-2	2-1	0-0	3-2	1-1	1-3	1-0	2-2	3-1		3-1	2-4	0-0	1-0	5-1	0-2
Energie Cottbus	34	11	8	15	38	49	41	0-0	2-4	0-0	0-3	2-1	1-1	2-2	0-0	2-3	2-0	0-1	2-1		0-1	3-2	2-0	0-2	3-1
Eintracht Frankfurt	34	9	13	12	46	58	40	0-4	1-3	2-6	1-0	3-1	2-2	2-2	0-3	1-1	1-2	2-0	0-3	1-3		0-0	0-0	4-0	1-0
VfL Wolfsburg	34	8	13	13	37	45	37	1-1	2-2	0-2	1-0	3-2	1-1	1-0	3-1	0-2	0-0	1-2	2-3	0-0	2-2		3-2	1-2	1-0
1.FSV Mainz	34	8	10	16	34	57	34	0-0	0-3	1-6	0-4	1-3	2-1	0-0	2-1	1-0	1-1	1-2	1-0	4-1	1-1	1-2		1-3	3-0
Alemannia Aachen	34	9	7	18	46	70	34	2-4	0-1	2-2	1-0	2-3	1-1	3-3	2-1	1-4	0-4	1-4	2-0	1-2	2-3	2-2	2-1		4-2
Bor. Mönchengladbach	34	6	8	20	23	44	26	0-1	0-2	2-2	1-1	0-2	0-0	0-1	0-2	1-0	3-1	0-1	1-0	2-0	1-1	3-1	1-1	0-0	

11/08/2006 - 19/05/2007 • † Qualified for the UEFA Champions League • ‡ Qualified for the UEFA Cup
Top scorers: Theofanis GEKAS, VfL Bochum 20; Roy MAKAAY, Bayern München 16; Alexander FREI, Borussia Dortmund 16; Kevin KURANYI, Schalke 15

GERMANY 2006-07

2. BUNDESLIGA (2)

	Pl	W	D	L	F	A	Pts	Karlsruher SC	Hansa Rostock	MSV Duisburg	SC Freiburg	Greuther Fürth	Kaiserslautern	FC Augsburg	1860 München	1.FC Köln	Erzgebirge Aue	SC Paderborn	TuS Koblenz	Carl Zeiss Jena	Kick. Offenbach	Rot-Weiss Essen	Unterhaching	Burghausen	Braunschweig
Karlsruher SC	34	21	7	6	69	41	70		4-4	3-3	0-3	2-0	2-0	3-2	4-1	2-1	0-1	3-0	3-1	4-1	2-1	1-3	1-0	2-1	2-0
Hansa Rostock	34	16	14	4	49	30	62	1-2		1-0	0-1	1-0	2-0	2-2	1-1	1-1	1-0	2-0	0-3	1-1	2-1	2-0	3-1	0-0	4-0
MSV Duisburg	34	16	12	6	66	40	60	2-1	1-2		1-1	0-2	1-1	3-0	0-0	1-3	4-2	1-1	2-1	4-0	4-0	3-0	4-2	3-4	0-0
SC Freiburg	34	17	9	8	55	39	60	0-4	0-0	2-1		3-3	4-1	2-0	3-0	0-0	5-4	0-1	2-0	1-3	1-3	3-1	1-1	2-0	1-0
SpVgg Greuther Fürth	34	16	6	12	53	40	54	1-3	1-3	3-5	0-0		2-2	2-1	1-1	1-2	2-1	3-0	0-0	2-0	0-2	2-1	0-0	4-1	3-0
1.FC Kaiserslautern	34	13	14	7	48	34	53	1-1	1-1	0-3	1-3	3-0		0-0	3-1	2-2	4-0	2-0	4-3	0-0	4-0	1-0	4-0	4-0	1-1
FC Augsburg	34	14	10	10	43	32	52	3-1	1-1	1-2	2-0	1-0	3-2		3-0	0-2	3-0	0-1	2-0	1-2	1-1	0-0	2-1	1-0	0-0
TSV 1860 München	34	14	6	14	47	49	48	2-0	1-2	2-2	1-1	0-3	0-1	0-3		3-1	4-0	1-0	2-1	2-0	3-0	2-0	1-0	5-1	2-0
1.FC Köln	34	12	10	12	49	50	46	1-1	2-1	1-3	0-2	2-1	1-2	1-2	1-1		0-1	1-1	3-1	1-2	1-0	4-1	5-1	4-1	2-0
Erzgebirge Aue	34	13	6	15	46	48	45	2-2	3-0	0-1	3-1	0-3	1-0	1-1	2-2	0-1		1-0	4-1	5-1	2-1	0-0	1-0	3-0	3-0
SC Paderborn	34	11	9	14	32	41	42	1-2	0-2	0-3	1-1	0-0	0-1	1-0	3-0	2-0	1-0		1-2	0-1	2-1	3-2	2-0	1-1	0-0
TuS Koblenz	34	11	8	15	36	45	41	1-1	0-3	1-1	0-1	1-0	0-0	1-1	2-1	3-1	2-1	3-1		0-0	1-1	0-1	0-0	1-2	1-0
Carl Zeiss Jena	34	9	9	16	42	59	36	1-1	1-3	1-2	3-3	2-1	1-1	1-1	0-2	3-2	2-1	1-1	2-0		2-3	0-0	0-2	0-0	1-0
Kickers Offenbach	34	9	9	16	42	59	36	0-1	1-1	0-0	2-3	1-2	0-1	3-2	2-1	2-0	3-1	0-2	2-3	2-2		1-0	1-1	2-1	1-1
Rot-Weiss Essen	34	8	11	15	34	40	35	1-2	0-0	1-2	2-0	1-0	0-0	0-0	0-2	5-0	0-1	2-2	0-1	4-4	2-2		1-1	1-1	2-0
SpVgg Unterhaching	34	9	8	17	33	49	35	0-1	0-0	0-1	0-2	2-1	1-1	0-1	5-1	0-0	1-1	0-3	1-0	2-0	2-0	2-1		0-2	3-2
Wacker Burghausen	34	7	11	16	42	63	32	0-4	0-1	1-1	2-2	3-4	0-0	0-2	0-2	1-3	1-1	5-1	0-0	1-1	4-1	1-1	4-1		1-1
Eint. Braunschweig	34	4	11	19	20	48	23	2-2	1-1	1-0	2-0	0-1	0-1	1-0	0-0	0-2	1-0	1-2	0-1	2-3	3-1	1-2	0-1	2-3	

11/08/2006 - 20/05/2007 • Top scorers: FEDERICO, Karlsruher 19; KAPLLANI, Karlsruher 17; LAWAREE, Augsburg 15

GERMANY 2006-07

REGIONALLIGA NORD (3)

	Pl	W	D	L	F	A	Pts	St Pauli	VfL Osnabrück	1.FC Magdeburg	Kickers Emden	Wuppertaler DV	HSV-2	Dyn'mo Dresden	Werder-2	VfB Lübeck	Fortuna	Rot-Weiß Erfurt	Union Berlin	Rot-Weiß Ahlen	B. Dortmund-2	Holstein Kiel	Gladbach-2	B. Leverkusen-2	Hertha-2	Wilhelmshaven
FC St Pauli	36	17	12	7	52	32	63		2-2	2-0	2-0	1-1	0-0	2-2	2-1	2-0	2-0	1-1	0-0	3-0	2-1	2-0	1-0	2-0	3-0	2-0
VfL Osnabrück	36	17	10	9	59	43	61	0-0		1-1	2-2	1-1	5-1	3-1	0-0	3-2	1-0	4-0	1-0	2-1	1-1	3-2	1-0	3-3	2-0	2-0
1.FC Magdeburg	36	16	12	8	52	41	60	1-1	2-0		1-1	1-0	0-0	1-0	2-0	0-2	2-2	1-0	3-1	0-2	2-2	0-0	3-0	1-1	2-0	3-0
BSV Kickers Emden	36	16	11	9	50	41	59	1-1	1-1	4-2		3-1	2-0	1-0	4-2	0-1	1-0	1-0	2-1	3-0	3-2	0-0	1-1	3-1	1-0	1-3
Wuppertaler DV	36	16	9	11	59	49	57	3-1	3-1	1-3	2-4		0-3	3-1	2-0	1-1	1-1	3-1	2-1	3-0	2-1	1-1	0-3	2-0	1-3	5-2
Hamburger SV-2	36	15	11	10	56	46	56	0-0	4-2	1-1	1-0	1-4		1-0	0-3	1-0	1-0	0-0	0-0	3-4	2-0	0-0	1-2	4-1	4-1	3-1
1.FC Dynamo Dresden	36	16	7	13	54	45	55	3-0	0-1	2-1	3-0	1-1	2-4		1-4	2-0	0-0	2-1	2-0	2-1	2-1	4-1	1-0	4-1	0-1	2-1
Werder Bremen-2	36	15	7	14	53	47	52	0-2	3-1	2-2	2-1	1-2	3-1	1-1		2-0	2-0	0-1	3-2	0-2	0-1	2-3	2-0	1-0	0-1	2-1
VfB Lübeck	36	15	6	15	53	43	51	1-0	2-0	0-1	4-1	5-0	1-4	1-0	0-2		2-3	0-2	0-1	2-1	1-3	1-1	4-2	1-0	4-0	6-0
Fortuna Düsseldorf	36	13	12	11	50	47	51	2-0	2-0	3-1	1-1	1-3	3-2	1-1	2-2	2-1		3-2	2-1	0-3	4-0	2-0	4-1	1-1	0-2	1-1
Rot-Weiß Erfurt	36	13	11	12	41	44	50	0-3	1-2	2-2	1-1	0-0	0-3	0-2	1-1	2-0	1-1		1-0	1-1	0-1	0-1	1-0	2-3	2-1	1-0
1.FC Union Berlin	36	13	9	14	45	39	48	2-0	2-2	1-2	1-0	0-3	0-1	2-1	0-2	1-1	1-0	2-4		1-1	2-0	0-2	3-1	4-0	2-2	2-0
Rot-Weiß Ahlen	36	13	9	14	48	52	48	1-1	0-3	2-1	1-1	1-1	1-2	3-0	2-0	1-3	4-1	2-2	0-1		0-2	1-0	0-3	1-1	1-1	1-0
Borussia Dortmund-2	36	14	6	16	42	47	48	0-1	1-0	1-3	0-0	1-0	1-2	2-3	1-0	1-1	0-0	1-1	1-1	1-2		2-0	2-1	2-0	1-1	2-1
KSV Holstein Kiel	36	13	9	14	42	52	48	1-2	2-0	5-0	0-0	1-1	1-0	1-0	2-2	1-0	2-0	0-2	0-4	2-1	5-1		2-3	0-3	1-0	3-1
B. Mönchengladbach-2	36	9	8	19	45	62	35	1-5	0-4	1-2	2-3	2-1	1-1	1-2	2-3	1-1	1-1	1-0	0-3	2-2	2-1	6-1		1-1	1-0	0-0
Bayer Leverkusen-2	36	8	10	18	40	58	34	2-1	1-2	1-1	0-1	0-3	2-1	3-2	3-3	0-1	1-3	0-0	0-0	0-1	2-0	4-0	2-0		2-1	1-1
Hertha BSC Berlin-2	36	8	8	20	31	55	32	3-0	1-3	0-2	0-1	0-1	1-1	1-1	0-1	1-0	1-2	1-1	0-3	0-3	0-3	3-0	0-2	2-0		2-2
SV Wilhelmshaven	36	7	9	20	40	69	30	3-3	1-0	0-2	2-1	2-1	3-3	1-1	2-1	1-3	1-1	3-5	0-0	4-1	0-2	0-1	1-2	2-1	0-1	

4/08/2006 – 2/06/2007

GERMANY 2006-07

REGIONALLIGA SUD (3)

	Pl	W	D	L	F	A	Pts	SV Wehen	TSG Hoffenheim	VfB Stuttgart-2	St'gart Kickers	FC Ingolstadt	VfR Aalen	SC Pfullendorf	Bayern-2	SV Elversberg	Hessen Kassel	SSV Reutlingen	SF Siegen	TSV 1860-2	Karlsruher SC-2	Saarbrücken	SV Darmstadt	FK Prmasens	Kaiserslautern-2
SV Wehen	34	21	9	4	58	25	72		2-1	0-0	1-0	2-3	1-1	3-0	1-0	4-2	2-1	0-0	2-1	2-0	1-0	1-0	3-1	5-0	2-1
TSG Hoffenheim	34	20	8	6	62	31	68	2-1		1-1	1-1	0-0	1-1	3-1	2-2	1-1	3-1	2-0	4-0	2-2	3-2	4-0	4-2	2-1	2-0
VfB Stuttgart-2	34	15	8	11	47	42	53	1-0	0-3		1-0	0-1	0-3	2-1	4-0	3-1	2-0	0-1	2-1	0-0	0-0	2-0	1-2	2-1	3-2
Stuttgarter Kickers	34	14	9	11	51	41	51	0-3	4-1	1-1		1-1	4-1	1-2	1-1	2-0	1-3	0-0	0-3	1-0	2-1	1-1	3-0	0-0	3-0
FC Ingolstadt 04	34	13	12	9	45	39	51	1-0	0-1	2-2	2-4		1-1	1-1	0-0	2-0	1-2	0-2	3-0	1-0	3-2	1-0	0-3	2-3	4-0
VfR Aalen	34	12	13	9	51	46	49	1-1	0-1	5-2	2-5	0-1		0-1	2-1	1-0	0-2	1-1	3-2	2-2	2-2	2-0	0-0	5-2	2-1
SC Pfullendorf	34	13	8	13	45	46	47	1-0	0-1	1-0	1-2	2-2	1-2		0-1	1-1	1-2	0-2	1-1	1-1	3-1	2-2	5-2	2-0	3-2
Bayern München-2	34	11	13	10	41	37	46	0-1	1-0	4-1	1-0	2-1	2-2	1-0		4-4	0-2	3-0	0-1	1-1	1-1	0-0	2-0	1-2	0-0
SV Elversberg	34	12	10	12	51	54	46	0-1	1-0	0-1	1-2	0-1	2-3	2-1	2-2		2-3	1-1	2-0	1-3	0-1	1-0	3-2	2-1	2-1
KSV Hessen Kassel	34	13	7	14	45	56	46	0-3	1-0	1-3	2-1	0-5	0-0	0-1	1-1	0-2		0-0	3-3	3-8	3-1	3-0	0-3	2-0	2-0
SSV Reutlingen	34	10	15	9	31	37	45	0-0	0-2	1-1	0-1	0-1	2-0	0-0	2-2	1-1	2-1		2-0	2-2	3-1	2-1	2-1	0-0	2-0
SF Siegen	34	12	8	14	53	49	44	1-3	1-2	1-2	4-1	0-1	4-3	2-0	0-0	2-2	1-2	3-0		1-2	2-2	2-1	1-2	1-1	2-1
TSV 1860 München-2	34	9	16	9	54	47	43	2-2	1-1	1-4	1-1	1-1	1-1	2-0	1-1	2-3	3-0	0-0	3-0		1-1	3-1	2-0	3-2	2-0
Karlsruher SC-2	34	10	13	11	44	43	43	2-1	1-1	0-0	3-0	0-1	1-1	4-2	4-0	1-4	4-2	0-1	1-1	0-3		0-0	3-2	2-2	0-0
1.FC Saarbrücken	34	10	12	12	52	50	42	2-2	1-3	3-2	3-3	6-0	4-2	2-0	1-0	1-1	2-2	4-0	1-1	5-2	1-0		0-1	4-1	0-0
SV Darmstadt 98	34	11	6	17	47	59	39	1-2	2-0	2-1	1-3	2-2	0-1	0-1	2-2	1-3	2-1	2-2	2-1	1-0	1-5	4-0		1-2	4-0
FK 03 Pirmasens	34	8	7	19	31	61	31	0-2	0-3	0-1	2-1	0-1	0-2	1-3	0-2	1-0	2-0	1-1	0-3	0-2	2-2	1-0	3-1		2-0
1.FC Kaiserslautern-2	34	0	10	24	19	63	10	0-0	1-2	0-2	0-2	0-2	1-1	0-3	2-3	1-4	0-1	1-1	0-2	1-1	0-1	0-0	0-0	1-1	

4/08/2006 – 2/06/2007

DFB POKAL 2006-07

First Round

Team	Score
1.FC Nürnberg	1
BV Cloppenburg *	0
1.FC Magdeburg *	1 6p
SC Paderborn 07	1 7p
FK Pirmasens *	1 4p
Werder Bremen	1 2p
SSVg Velbert *	0
SpVgg Unterhaching	3
MSV Duisburg	2
Rot-Weiß Ahlen *	1
TuS Koblenz *	2 1p
Bayer Leverkusen	2 3p
Borussia Dortmund	3
TSG Thannhausen *	0
Dynamo Dresden *	2
Hannover 96	3
Kickers Offenbach	2
SpVgg Bayreuth *	0
Arminia Bielefeld	1
SC Pfullendorf *	2
VfB Lübeck *	1
TSV 1860 München	0
FC Augsburg *	3
Wacker Burghausen	4
1.FC Köln	2
Carl Zeiss Jena *	1
Hansa Rostock II *	1
Schalke 04	9
Rot-Weiss Essen *	1
Energie Cottbus	0
Sportfreunde Siegen *	0
Eintracht Frankfurt	2
VfL Wolfsburg	3
FC Bremerhaven *	1
Delbrücker SC	2
SC Freiburg	4
1.FC Saarbrücken *	1
FSV Mainz 05	0
SV Sandhausen *	0
SpVgg Greuther Fürth	2
Bayern München	2
FC Sankt Pauli *	1
1.FC Gera 03 *	0
1.FC Kaiserslautern	2
Erzgebirge Aue	2
SC Westfalia Herne *	1
Chemnitzer FC *	0
Alemannia Aachen	2
Hertha BSC Berlin	1
SV Darmstadt 98 *	0
Hamburger SV	3
Stuttgarter Kickers *	4
Borussia Mönchengladbach	4
SV Rossbach *	1
Eintracht Braunschweig	1
VfL Osnabrück *	3
VfL Bochum	2
FC 08 Homburg *	1
Tennis Borussia Berlin *	1
Karlsruher SC	3
SV Babelsberg 03 *	2
Hansa Rostock	1
Alemannia Aachen II *	0
VfB Stuttgart	4

Second Round

Team	Score
1.FC Nürnberg	2
SC Paderborn 07 *	1
FK Pirmasens *	0
SpVgg Unterhaching	3
MSV Duisburg *	3
Bayer Leverkusen	2
Borussia Dortmund *	0
Hannover 96	1
Kickers Offenbach	2
SC Pfullendorf *	0
VfB Lübeck *	0 4p
Wacker Burghausen	0 5p
1.FC Köln *	4
Schalke 04	2
Rot-Weiss Essen *	1
Eintracht Frankfurt	2
VfL Wolfsburg *	1
SC Freiburg	0
1.FC Saarbrücken *	0
SpVgg Greuther Fürth	2
Bayern München *	1
1.FC Kaiserslautern	0
Erzgebirge Aue	2
Alemannia Aachen *	4
Hertha BSC Berlin	2
Stuttgarter Kickers *	0
Borussia Mönchengladbach	1
VfL Osnabrück *	2
VfL Bochum *	3
Karlsruher SC	2
SV Babelsberg 03 *	2
VfB Stuttgart	4

Third Round

Team	Score
1.FC Nürnberg *	0 2p
SpVgg Unterhaching	0 1p
MSV Duisburg	0
Hannover 96 *	1
Kickers Offenbach *	2
Wacker Burghausen	1
1.FC Köln	1
Eintracht Frankfurt *	3
VfL Wolfsburg	3
SpVgg Greuther Fürth *	1
Bayern München	2
Alemannia Aachen *	4
Hertha BSC Berlin	3
VfL Osnabrück *	0
VfL Bochum *	1
VfB Stuttgart	4

DFB POKAL 2006–07

Quarter–finals	Semi–finals	Final

1.FC Nürnberg *	0 4p
Hannover 96	0 2p

1.FC Nürnberg *	4
Eintracht Frankfurt	0

Kickers Offenbach *	0
Eintracht Frankfurt	3

1.FC Nürnberg ‡	3
VfB Stuttgart	2

VfL Wolfsburg *	2
Alemannia Aachen	0

VfL Wolfsburg *	0
VfB Stuttgart	1

Hertha BSC Berlin	0
VfB Stuttgart *	2

DFB POKAL FINAL 2007

Olimpiastadion, Berlin, 26-05-2007, 20:00, Att: 74 220, Ref: Weiner

1.FC Nürnberg	3	Mintal [27], Engelhardt [47], Kristiansen [109]
VfB Stuttgart	2	Cacau [20], Pardo [80p]

Nürnberg - Raphael SCHAFER - Dominik REINHARDT, Andreas WOLF, Marek NIKL• (Matthew SPIRANOVIC• 73), Javier PINOLA (Ivica BANOVIC 115) - Jan KRISTIANSEN, Tomas GALASEK•, Marco ENGELHARDT - Marek MINTAL (Jan POLAK 35) - Markus SCHROTH•, Ivan SAJENKO. Tr: Hans MEYER
Stuttgart - Timo HILDEBRAND - Ricardo OSORIO• (Arthur BOKA 68), Freitas Fernando MEIRA•, Mathieu DELPIERRE, Ludovic MAGNIN - Pavel PARDO - Sami KHEDIRA• (Serdar TASCI 101), Thomas HITZLSPERGER - Roberto HILBERT, Antonio DA SILVA (Mario GOMEZ• 46), Jerónimo CACAU•31. Tr: Armin VEH

* Home team • ‡ Qualified for the UEFA Cup

VFB STUTTGART 2006-07

Date	Opponents	Score		Comp	Scorers	Att
12-08-2006	1.FC Nürnberg	L 0-3	H	BL		39 000
20-08-2006	Arminia Bielefeld	W 3-2	A	BL	Fernando Meira [39], Cacau 2 [73 82]	22 095
25-08-2006	Borussia Dortmund	L 1-3	H	BL	Tasci [30]	44 000
9-09-2006	Alemannia Aachen II	W 4-0	A	DPr1	Bierofka [11], Tomasson [50p], Hilbert [70], Cacau [73]	4 897
16-09-2006	Werder Bremen	W 3-2	A	BL	Hilbert [38], Pardo [58], Gomez [88]	39 654
23-09-2006	Eintracht Frankfurt	D 1-1	H	BL	Gomez [73]	41 000
1-10-2006	Hertha BSC Berlin	D 2-2	A	BL	Gomez [4], Cacau [57]	48 637
14-10-2006	Bayer Leverkusen	W 3-0	H	BL	Gomez [22], Boka [48], Hitzlsperger [76]	35 000
21-10-2006	VfL Wolfsburg	D 1-1	A	BL	Gomez [30]	21 927
24-10-2006	SV Babelsberg 03	W 4-2	A	DPr2	Hilbert [14], Delpierre [53], Gomez [61], Cacau [80]	7 120
29-10-2006	Schalke 04	W 3-0	H	BL	Khedira 2 [32 46], Tasci [75]	53 000
4-11-2006	Alemannia Aachen	W 4-2	A	BL	Gomez [24], Hitzlsperger [26], Streller 2 [46 63]	20 300
7-11-2006	Hamburger SV	W 2-0	H	BL	Gomez [80], Hitzlsperger [85]	37 000
12-11-2006	Hannover 96	W 2-1	A	BL	Hitzlsperger [49], Cacau [54]	28 847
18-11-2006	Bayern München	L 1-2	A	BL	Gomez [7]	69 000
26-11-2006	Borussia Mönchengladbach	W 1-0	H	BL	Cacau [6]	53 000
1-12-2006	1.FSV Mainz	D 0-0	A	BL		20 300
9-12-2006	VfL Bochum	W 1-0	H	BL	Streller [87]	48 000
16-12-2006	Energie Cottbus	D 0-0	A	BL		13 650
19-12-2006	VfL Bochum	W 4-1	A	DPr3	Gomez [34], Hitzlsperger 2 [49 58], Cacau [90]	18 650
27-01-2007	1.FC Nürnberg	L 1-4	A	BL	Cacau [33]	35 082
30-01-2007	Arminia Bielefeld	W 3-2	H	BL	Gomez 2 [9 59], Cacau [52]	23 000
4-02-2007	Borussia Dortmund	W 1-0	A	BL	Gomez [59]	63 600
10-02-2007	Werder Bremen	W 4-1	H	BL	Hilbert [3], Gomez [15], Magnin [33], Streller [86]	56 500
16-02-2007	Eintracht Frankfurt	W 4-0	H	BL	Hilbert [2], Gomez [16], Osorio [44], Hitzlsperger [78]	46 000
23-02-2007	Hertha BSC Berlin	D 0-0	H	BL		45 000
28-02-2007	Hertha BSC Berlin	W 2-0	H	DPqf	Cacau [38], Hitzlsperger [77]	32 000
3-03-2007	Bayer Leverkusen	L 1-3	A	BL	Cacau [73]	22 500
10-03-2007	VfL Wolfsburg	D 0-0	A	BL		44 000
17-03-2007	Schalke 04	L 0-1	A	BL		61 482
31-03-2007	Alemannia Aachen	W 3-1	H	BL	Streller [29], Lauth [75], Cacau [84]	43 000
7-04-2007	Hamburger SV	W 4-2	A	BL	Cacau [10], Khedira [13], Hilbert [27], Fernando Meira [50]	57 000
14-04-2007	Hannover 96	W 2-1	H	BL	Hilbert [2], Zuraw OG [74]	53 000
18-04-2007	VfL Wolfsburg	W 1-0	A	DPsf	Da Silva [16]	30 000
21-04-2007	Bayern München	W 2-0	H	BL	Cacau 2 [23 25]	56 000
28-04-2007	Borussia Mönchengladbach	W 1-0	A	BL	Hilbert [53]	48 014
5-05-2007	1.FSV Mainz	W 2-0	H	BL	Fernando Meira [26], Hilbert [64]	56 000
12-05-2007	VfL Bochum	W 3-2	A	BL	Hitzlsperger [24], Gomez [61], Cacau [72]	31 328
19-05-2007	Energie Cottbus	W 2-1	H	BL	Hitzlsperger [27], Khedira [63]	56 000
26-05-2007	1.FC Nürnberg	L 2-3	N	DPf	Cacau [20], Pardo [80p]	74 220

BL = Bundesliga • DP = DFB Pokal
r1 = first round • r2 = second round • r3 = third round • qf = quarter-final • sf = semi-final • f = final • N = Olimpiastadion, Berlin

THE FIFA BIG COUNT OF 2006

	Male	Female		Total
Number of players	14 438 313	1 870 633	Referees and Assistant Referees	81 372
Professionals	864		Admin, Coaches, Technical, Medical	77 800
Amateurs 18+	4 221 170		Number of clubs	25 922
Youth under 18	2 081 912		Number of teams	170 480
Unregistered	10 000 000		Clubs with women's teams	915
Total players	16 308 946		Players as % of population	19.79%

FC SCHALKE 04 2006–07

Date	Opponents		Score		Comp	Scorers	Att
29-07-2006	Bayer Leverkusen	·	D 1-1	N	LPqf	Bordon [37]	23 000
2-08-2006	Bayern München		L 1-4	A	LPsf	Løvenkrands [88]	
12-08-2006	Eintracht Frankfurt		D 1-1	H	BL	Halil Altintop [30]	61 482
19-08-2006	Alemannia Aachen		W 1-0	A	BL	Rodriguez [53]	21 300
25-08-2006	Werder Bremen		W 2-0	H	BL	Kuranyi [7], Hamit Altintop [74]	61 482
9-09-2006	Hansa Rostock II		W 9-1	A	DPr1	Kuranyi 2 [12 31], Asamoah 2 [15 35], Lincoln 2 [21 73], Bordon [56], Halil Altintop [63], Varela [83]	3 500
14-09-2006	AS Nancy-Lorraine - FRA		W 1-0	H	UCr1	Larsen [86]	45 878
17-09-2006	Hertha BSC Berlin		L 0-2	H	BL		60 547
23-09-2006	VfL Wolfsburg		W 2-0	H	BL	Kuranyi [57], Lincoln [89]	60 404
28-09-2006	AS Nancy-Lorraine - FRA		L 1-3	A	UCr1	Bordon [77]	18 029
1-10-2006	Bayer Leverkusen		L 1-3	A	BL	Bordon [6]	22 500
14-10-2006	Hamburger SV		W 2-1	A	BL	Halil Altintop [16], Bordon [53]	57 000
21-10-2006	Hannover 96		W 2-1	H	BL	Bajramovic [17], Kobiashvili [27]	61 031
24-10-2006	1.FC Köln		L 2-4	A	DPr2	Løvenkrands [55], Rodriguez [75]	50 000
29-10-2006	VfB Stuttgart		L 0-3	H	BL		52 000
5-11-2006	Bayern München		D 2-2	H	BL	Løvenkrands [13], Kobiashvili [20]	61 482
8-11-2006	Borussia Mönchengladbach		W 2-0	A	BL	Ze Antonio OG [11], Varela [31]	52 018
11-11-2006	1.FSV Mainz		W 4-0	H	BL	Kuranyi 2 [13 32], Halil Altintop 2 [21 67]	61 482
18-11-2006	Energie Cottbus		W 4-2	A	BL	Hamit Altintop [4], Kuranyi [15], Pander [52], Kobiashvili [84]	17 210
24-11-2006	VfL Bochum		W 2-1	H	BL	Rafinha [19], Løvenkrands [27]	61 482
3-12-2006	1.FC Nürnberg		D 0-0	A	BL		43 242
10-12-2006	Borussia Dortmund		W 3-1	H	BL	Pander [14], Kuranyi [25], Løvenkrands [47]	61 482
16-12-2006	Arminia Bielefeld		W 1-0	A	BL	Bajramovic [82]	26 601
27-01-2007	Eintracht Frankfurt		W 3-1	A	BL	Varela [16], Kuranyi 2 [70 90]	51 500
31-01-2007	Alemannia Aachen		W 2-1	H	BL	Rafinha [23p], Sichone OG [74]	61 482
4-02-2007	Werder Bremen		W 2-0	A	BL	Løvenkrands 2 [20 73]	42 100
10-02-2007	Hertha BSC Berlin		W 2-0	H	BL	Kuranyi [64], Løvenkrands [75]	61 482
17-02-2007	VfL Wolfsburg		D 2-2	A	BL	Kuranyi 2 [10 29]	28 346
25-02-2007	Bayer Leverkusen		L 0-1	H	BL		61 482
2-03-2007	Hamburger SV		L 0-2	H	BL		61 482
10-03-2007	Hannover 96		D 1-1	A	BL	Halil Altintop [2]	49 000
17-03-2007	VfB Stuttgart		W 1-0	H	BL	Krstajic [76]	61 482
31-03-2007	Bayern München		L 0-2	A	BL		69 000
7-04-2007	Borussia Mönchengladbach		W 2-0	H	BL	Asamoah [57], Kuranyi [71]	61 482
14-04-2007	1.FSV Mainz		W 3-0	A	BL	Kuranyi [10], Asamoah [34], Lincoln [71]	20 300
21-04-2007	Energie Cottbus		W 2-0	H	BL	Rost OG [60], Bordon [64]	61 481
27-04-2007	VfL Bochum		L 1-2	A	BL	Kuranyi [8]	31 328
5-05-2007	1.FC Nürnberg		W 1-0	H	BL	Kuranyi [74]	61 482
12-05-2007	Borussia Dortmund		L 0-2	A	BL		80 708
19-05-2007	Arminia Bielefeld		W 2-1	H	BL	Lincoln [12], Halil Altintop [16]	61 482

LP = Liga-Pokal (Super Cup) • BL = Bundesliga • UC = UEFA Cup • DP = DFB Pokal
r1 = first round • r2 = second round • N = Düsseldorf

FIFA/COCA-COLA WORLD RANKING

1993	1994	1995	1996	1997	1998	1999	2000	2001	2002	2003	2004	2005	2006	High		Low	
1	5	2	2	2	3	5	11	12	4	12	19	16	6	**1**	08/93	**22**	03/06

2006–2007											
08/06	09/06	10/06	11/06	12/06	01/07	02/07	03/07	04/07	05/07	06/07	07/07
9	8	6	6	6	5	5	5	5	5	4	5

1.FC NURNBERG 2006–07

Date	Opponents	Score		Comp	Scorers	Att
12-08-2006	VfB Stuttgart	W 3-0	A	BL	Vittek [37], Schroth [45], Saenko [78]	39 000
18-08-2006	Borussia Mönchengladbach	W 1-0	H	BL	Schroth [5]	47 000
26-08-2006	Bayern München	D 0-0	A	BL		69 000
9-09-2006	BV Cloppenburg	W 1-0	A	DPr1	Banovic [58]	7 000
16-09-2006	VfL Bochum	D 1-1	H	BL	Polak [30]	40 240
24-09-2006	Energie Cottbus	D 1-1	A	BL	Mnari [10]	16 900
30-09-2006	1.FSV Mainz	D 1-1	H	BL	Polak [24]	38 004
15-10-2006	Arminia Bielefeld	D 1-1	H	BL	Polak [39]	39 788
22-10-2006	Eintracht Frankfurt	D 2-2	A	BL	Saenko [5], Pinola [51]	50 300
25-10-2006	SC Paderborn 07	W 2-1	A	DPr2	Mintal [82], Vittek [92]	7 028
28-10-2006	Borussia Dortmund	D 1-1	H	BL	Mnari [59p]	46 229
4-11-2006	Hertha BSC Berlin	L 1-2	A	BL	Banovic [47]	41 162
7-11-2006	Werder Bremen	L 1-2	H	BL	Banovic [90p]	37 174
12-11-2006	Alemannia Aachen	D 1-1	A	BL	Galasek [29]	20 800
18-11-2006	Bayer Leverkusen	W 3-2	H	BL	Vittek [12], Schroth [48], Saenko [85]	37 143
25-11-2006	VfL Wolfsburg	D 1-1	A	BL	Saenko [7]	16 397
3-12-2006	Schalke 04	D 0-0	H	BL		43 242
9-12-2006	Hamburger SV	D 0-0	A	BL		54 628
16-12-2006	Hannover 96	W 3-1	H	BL	Banovic [32], Schroth [56], Mnari [90p]	28 683
19-12-2006	SpVgg Unterhaching	D 0-0	H	DPr3	W 2-1 on pens	16 676
27-01-2007	VfB Stuttgart	W 4-1	H	BL	Saenko [25], Gresko [50], Schroth [70], Magnin OG [77]	35 082
30-01-2007	Borussia Mönchengladbach	D 0-0	A	BL		33 116
2-02-2007	Bayern München	W 3-0	H	BL	Saenko [13], Schroth [71], Vittek [86]	47 000
11-02-2007	VfL Bochum	W 2-0	A	BL	Saenko 2 [88] [90]	18 110
17-02-2007	Energie Cottbus	W 1-0	H	BL	Beauchamp [73]	40 580
24-02-2007	1.FSV Mainz	L 1-2	A	BL	Saenko [64]	20 300
27-02-2007	Hannover 96	D 0-0	H	DPqf	W 4-2 on pens	31 500
3-03-2007	Arminia Bielefeld	L 2-3	A	BL	Banovic [16], Engelhardt [83]	18 444
9-03-2007	Eintracht Frankfurt	D 2-2	H	BL	Spycher OG [81], Vittek [87]	44 055
17-03-2007	Borussia Dortmund	D 0-0	A	BL		80 100
31-03-2007	Hertha BSC Berlin	W 2-1	H	BL	Galasek [4], Engelhardt [60]	45 649
8-04-2007	Werder Bremen	L 0-1	A	BL		40 000
14-04-2007	Alemannia Aachen	W 1-0	H	BL	Pagenburg [12]	22 298
17-04-2007	Eintracht Frankfurt	W 4-0	H	DPsf	Engelhardt [2], Saenko [25], Galasek [54], Pagenburg [89]	47 000
21-04-2007	Bayer Leverkusen	L 0-2	A	BL		22 500
28-04-2007	VfL Wolfsburg	D 1-1	H	BL	Wolf [23]	46 200
5-05-2007	Schalke 04	L 0-1	A	BL		61 482
12-05-2007	Hamburger SV	L 0-2	H	BL		47 000
19-05-2007	Hannover 96	W 3-0	A	BL	Mintal [54], Engelhardt [62], Banovic [90]	49 000
26-05-2007	VfB Stuttgart	W 3-2	N	DPf	Mintal [27], Engelhardt [47], Kristiansen [109]	74 220

BL = Bundesliga • DP = DFB Pokal
r1 = first round • r2 = second round • r3 = third round • qf = quarter-final • sf = semi-final • f = final • N = Olimpiastadion, Berlin

GHA – GHANA

NATIONAL TEAM RECORD
JULY 10TH 2006 TO JULY 12TH 2010

PL	W	D	L	F	A	%
7	4	2	1	12	5	71.4

Once the power house of African football, Ghana's Black Stars are beginning to shine with the same brightness as the 1960s when they strode unchallenged across Africa. Ominous signs of their potential have been shown over the last 12 months as the country prepares for the hosting of the 2008 African Nations Cup finals. Buoyed by their debut performance at the 2006 FIFA World Cup finals, the team have won morale boosting victories in Japan and South Korea and an impressive win over arch foes Nigeria in a friendly in London. That 4-1 win was followed a month later by a competent showing against Brazil, who only beat Ghana 1-0 in a friendly international in Stockholm, Sweden. Ghana's new French coach Claude LeRoy enthuses over the quality at his disposal, led by the Turkish-based midfielder Stephen Appiah and Chelsea's Michael Essien. The veteran trainer, who has already coached at a record number of Nations Cup tournaments, reckons it is potentially the best side he has ever been in charge of. Recent evidence has also been provided by the surge in form of Sulley Muntari and Asamoah Gyan, both of who saw regular action in Italy's Serie A in the 2006-07 season. Domestically, the battle between Hearts of Oak and Asante

INTERNATIONAL HONOURS
FIFA World U-17 Championship 1991 1995

Qualified for the FIFA World Cup finals™ 2006   Qualified for the FIFA Women's World Cup finals 1999 2003

CAF African Cup of Nations 1963 1965 1978 1982

CAF African Youth Championship 1993 1999   CAF African U-17 Championship 1995 1999

CAF Champions League Asante Kotoko 1970 1983 Hearts of Oak 2000

Kotoko continued in the Premier League before a late season setback for Kotoko allowed Hearts to go on and reclaim their title with some ease. Kotoko's dramatic slump at the finish of the campaign allowed AshantiGold to finish second in the standings. In the 2007 CAF Champions League, Kotoko suffered an embarrassing defeat in the first round, losing on penalties after a 1-1 aggregate tie with Gambia Port Authority whilst AshantiGold were also eliminated in the knockout phase. Hearts had refused to compete in the African Confederation Cup after disputing the way in which the representatives for the 2007 African club competition campaigns were decided by the Ghana Football Association, who had set a cut off point in the league campaign in November to determine which clubs participated in the Champions League and the Confederation Cup. The league season in Ghana has been changed from its traditional run through a calendar year to match those of Europe from August to May. In the African junior events, the Black Starlets failed to qualify for the U–20 African championship but the U–17s did qualify for the FIFA U-17 World Cup in South Korea after finishing third at the African championship in Togo.

Ghana Football Association (GFA)
General Secretariat, South East Ridge, PO Box AN 19338, Accra, Ghana

Tel +233 21 910170   Fax +233 21 668590

info@ghanafa.org   www.ghanafa.org

President: NYANTAKYI Kwesi   General Secretary: NSIAH Kofi

Vice-President: TBD   Treasurer: TBD   Media Officer: RANSFORD Abbey

Men's Coach: LEROY Claude   Women's Coach: PAHA Isaac

GFA formed: 1957   CAF: 1958   FIFA: 1958

Yellow shirts with black trimmings, Yellow shorts, Yellow socks

RECENT INTERNATIONAL MATCHES PLAYED BY GHANA

2003 Opponents	Score		Venue	Comp	Scorers	Att	Referee
27-03 Tunisia	D	2-2	Tunis	Fr	Amoah.C 2 [45 48]. L 7-8p	30 000	
30-03 Madagascar	D	3-3	Tunis	Fr	Appiah [5], Amoah.C [32], Gyan [60]. W 10-9p		
30-05 Nigeria	L	1-3	Abuja	Fr	Agyema [2]	60 000	
13-06 Kenya	L	1-3	Accra	Fr	Appiah [60]		
22-06 Uganda	D	1-1	Kumasi	CNq	Amoah.C [84]		
6-07 Rwanda	L	0-1	Kigali	CNq		40 000	
16-11 Somalia	W	5-0	Accra	WCq	Arhin Duah 2 [25 56], Boakye 2 [69 89], Gyan [82]	19 447	Bebou TOG
19-11 Somalia	W	2-0	Kumasi	WCq	Appiah [27], Adjei [90]	12 000	Chaibou NIG
2004							
28-04 Angola	D	1-1	Accra	Fr	Morgan [90]		Kotey GHA
5-06 Burkina Faso	L	0-1	Ouagadougou-	WCq		25 000	Chukwujekwu NGA
14-06 Togo	D	0-0	Kumasi	Fr			
20-06 South Africa	W	3-0	Kumasi	WCq	Muntari [13], Appiah 2 [55 78]	32 000	Diatta SEN
25-06 Mozambique	W	1-0	Maputo	Fr	Gyan [72]		
3-07 Uganda	D	1-1	Kampala	WCq	Gyan [88]	20 000	El Beltagy EGY
5-09 Cape Verde Islands	W	2-0	Kumasi	WCq	Essien [24p], Veiga OG [62]	35 000	Tamuni LBY
10-10 Congo DR	D	0-0	Kumasi	WCq		30 000	Coulibaly MLI
2005							
23-03 Kenya	D	2-2	Nairobi	Fr	Gyan [23], Amoah [89]		
27-03 Congo DR	D	1-1	Kinshasa	WCq	Gyan [30]	80 000	Sowe GAM
5-06 Burkina Faso	W	2-1	Kumasi	WCq	Appiah [66p], Amoah [83]	11 920	Abd el Fatah EGY
18-06 South Africa	W	2-0	Johannesburg	WCq	Amoah [59], Essien [91+]	50 000	Guezzaz MAR
17-08 Senegal	D	0-0	London	Fr			
4-09 Uganda	W	2-0	Kumasi	WCq	Essien [10], Amoah [15]	45 000	Hicuburundi BDI
8-10 Cape Verde Islands	W	4-0	Praia	WCq	Asamoah [5], Muntari [35], Gyan [75], Attram [87]	6 500	Daami TUN
14-11 Saudi Arabia	W	3-1	Jeddah	Fr	Muntari [41], Gyan 2 [45 72]		
2006							
11-01 Togo	L	0-1	Monastir	Fr		2 500	Piccirillo FRA
15-01 Tunisia	L	0-2	Rades/Tunis	Fr		25 000	Walid Salah
23-01 Nigeria	L	0-1	Port Said	CNr1		20 000	Abd El Fatah EGY
27-01 Senegal	W	1-0	Port Said	CNr1	Amoah [13]	20 000	El Arjoun MAR
31-01 Zimbabwe	L	1-2	Ismailia	CNr1	Armando [93+]	14 000	Liuzaya CGO
1-03 Mexico	L	0-1	Frisco	Fr		19 513	Hall USA
26-05 Turkey	D	1-1	Bochum	Fr	Amoah [60]	9 738	Meier GER
29-05 Jamaica	W	4-1	Leicester	Fr	Muntari [5], OG [19], Appiah [66], Amoah [68]	11 163	Halsey ENG
4-06 Korea Republic	W	3-1	Edinburgh	Fr	Gyan [37p], Muntari [63], Essien [81]	15 000	McDonald SCO
12-06 Italy	L	0-2	Hanover	WCr1		43 000	Simon BRA
17-06 Czech Republic	W	2-0	Cologne	WCr1	Gyan [2], Muntari [82]	45 000	Elizondo ARG
22-06 USA	W	2-1	Nuremberg	WCr1	Draman [22], Appiah [47+p]	41 000	Merk GER
27-06 Brazil	L	0-3	Dortmund	WCr2		65 000	Michel SVK
15-08 Togo	W	2-0	London	Fr	Pimpong [75], Tachie-Mensah [85]		Dean ENG
4-10 Japan	W	1-0	Yokohama	Fr	Dramani [73]	52 437	Yu Byung Seob KOR
8-10 Korea Republic	W	3-1	Seoul	Fr	Gyan 2 [48 83], Essien [58]	36 515	Takayama JPN
14-11 Australia	D	1-1	London	Fr	Agogo [74]	14 379	Clattenburg ENG
2007							
6-02 Nigeria	W	4-1	London	Fr	Kingston [50], Muntari [53], Agogo [60], Frimpong [74]		
24-03 Austria	D	1-1	Graz	Fr	Muntari [87]	10 608	Verbist BEL
27-03 Brazil	L	0-1	Stockholm	Fr		20 104	Fröjdfeldt SWE

Fr = Friendly match • CN = CAF African Cup of Nations • WC = FIFA World Cup • q = qualifier • r1 = first round group • r2 = second round

GHANA NATIONAL TEAM RECORDS AND RECORD SEQUENCES

Records			Sequence records					
Victory	9-1	NIG 1969	Wins	8	1965-1967	Clean sheets	6	1990-1991
Defeat	2-8	BRA 1996	Defeats	6	1996	Goals scored	29	1963-1967
Player Caps	n/a		Undefeated	21	1981-1983	Without goal	5	1985
Player Goals	n/a		Without win	9	1996-1997	Goals against	15	1967-1968

REPUBLIC OF GHANA

Capital	Accra	Language	English	Independence	1957
Population	22 409 572	Area	239 460 km²	Density	86 per km²	% in cities	36%
GDP per cap	$2200	Dailling code	+233	Internet	.gh	GMT +/-	0

The Accra metropolitan area includes Accra 2 096; Ashiaman 228; Tema 161; Teshie 154; Madina 112; Nungua 75; Tema New Town 74; Dome 56; Lashibi 54; Gbawe 52, Taifa 48 and Adenta East 39

MEDALS TABLE

		Overall			League			Cup		Europe			City	Stadium	Cap'ty	DoF
		G	S	B	G	S	B	G	S	G	S	B				
1	Asante Kotoko	29	22	6	19	13	3	8	2	2	7	3	Kumasi	Kumasi Sports Stadium	51 500	1935
2	Hearts of Oak	29	17	7	18	11	5	9	4	2	2	2	Accra	Ohene Djan	35 000	1911
3	Great Olympics	5	3	6	2	2	5	3	1			1	Accra	Accra Sports Stadium	40 000	1954
4	Real Republicans	5		1	1			4				1	Accra			1962-66
5	Ashanti Gold	4	5	3	3	3	3	1	1	1		1	Obuasi	Len Clay	30 000	1978
6	Eleven Wise	2	5	3	1	3	3	1	2				Sekondi	Gyandu Park	15 000	1919
7	Sekondi Hasaacas	2	4	2	1	3	1	1	1			1	Sekondi	Gyandu Park	15 000	1931
8	Cape Coast Dwarfs	2	3	4	1	1	4	1	2				Cape Coast	Sudu Park	10 000	1968
9	Cornerstones	1	7			4		1	3				Kumasi	Kumasi Sports Stadium	51 500	1931
10	Okwahu United	1	3	2		1	2	1	2				Nkawkaw	Nkawkaw Sports Stadium	15 000	
11	Ghapoha Tema	1	1					1	1				Tema	Tema Sports Stadium	10 000	
12	Voradep Ho	1						1					Ho	Ho Sports Stadium	8 000	
13	Real Tamale United		5	3		2	3		3				Tamale	Kaladan Park	10 000	1976
14	Brong-Ahofu United		2	3		1	3		1				Sunyani	Coronation Park	10 000	
15	Bofoakwa Tano		2	2		1	2		1				Sunyani	Coronation Park	10 000	

RECENT LEAGUE AND CUP RECORD

	Championship						Cup		
Year	Champions	Pts	Runners-up	Pts	Third	Pts	Winners	Score	Runners-up
1995	Goldfields Obuasi	33	Real Tamale United	36	Asante Kotoko	33	Great Olympics		Hearts of Oak
1996	Goldfields Obuasi	51	Asante Kotoko	50	Okwahu United	46	Hearts of Oak	1-0	Ghapoha Tema
1997	Hearts of Oak	54	Real Tamale United	51	Goldfields Obuasi	48	Ghapoha Tema	1-0	Okwahu United
1998	Hearts of Oak	52	Asante Kotoko	48	Great Olympics	39	Asante Kotoko	1-0	Real Tamale United
1999	Hearts of Oak	62	Cape Coast Dwarfs	53	Real Tamale United	52	Hearts of Oak	3-1	Great Olympics
2000	Hearts of Oak	57	Goldfields Obuasi	52	King Faisal Babies	46	Hearts of Oak	2-0	Okwahu United
2001	Hearts of Oak	64	Asante Kotoko	55	Goldfields Obuasi	45	Asante Kotoko	1-0	King Faisal Babies
2002	Hearts of Oak	78	Asante Kotoko	73	Liberty Professionals	48	Not played		
2003	Asante Kotoko	75	Hearts of Oak	66	King Faisal Babies	54	Not played		
2004	Hearts of Oak	1-0	Asante Kotoko				Real Tamale United	1-2 1-0	Asante Kotoko
2005	Asante Kotoko	63	Hearts of Oak	56	King Faisal Babies	50	Not played		
2006	Season readjustment						Not played		
2007	Hearts of Oak	58	AshantiGold	53	Asante Kotoko	51	Not played		

GHANA 2006-07

ONE TOUCH PREMIER LEAGUE

	Pl	W	D	L	F	A	Pts	Hearts of Oak	AshantiGold	Kotoko	Heart of Lions	Arsenal	Real Sp. Tema	Olympics	Liberty Pros	Tema Youth	Hasaacas	RTU	All Blacks	King Faisal	Tano Bofoakwa	Feyenoord	Power FC
Hearts of Oak	30	16	10	4	33	15	58		0-0	3-1	2-0	1-0	1-2	2-1	1-1	0-1	2-1	0-0	1-0	0-0	1-0	2-1	**3-0**
AshantiGold †	30	15	8	7	35	24	53	0-1		1-0	5-2	2-0	1-2	2-1	0-0	2-1	0-0	2-1	2-1	1-0	4-1	3-1	
Asante Kotoko †	30	15	6	9	35	24	51	0-1	1-0		1-0	0-1	3-0	2-1	5-3	1-1	2-0	1-2	0-1	1-0	0-0	2-1	2-1
Heart of Lions	30	13	8	9	40	27	47	1-2	3-0	1-1		2-1	1-1	1-1	0-0	4-1	4-0	1-0	3-0	1-1	2-1	1-0	3-0
Arsenal Berekum §3	30	14	4	12	37	36	43	1-0	2-0	2-0	3-1		2-1	3-1	1-0	0-0	3-0	2-0	1-0	1-0	**0-3**	1-0	4-2
Real Sportive Tema	30	11	10	9	22	22	43	0-0	0-0	0-0	2-1	2-1		1-0	0-2	0-0	1-0	1-0	2-0	1-0	0-0	1-0	1-1
Great Olympics	30	12	6	12	35	34	42	1-1	0-1	0-0	0-0	2-1	1-0		1-0	0-0	2-0	2-1	2-0	1-3	1-0	4-2	
Liberty Professionals	30	10	10	10	27	25	40	0-0	0-1	1-2	2-1	1-0	0-0	0-1		1-0	0-1	0-0	3-1	1-1	0-0	1-0	2-0
Tema Youth ‡	30	9	13	8	23	23	40	0-1	0-0	1-0	0-1	0-1	1-1	1-0	0-0		1-0	1-1	1-1	2-0	2-0	2-1	2-1
Hasaacas Sekondi	30	11	5	14	29	37	38	1-3	3-2	0-1	2-4	1-1	1-0	2-1	3-1	1-2		1-0	1-1	1-0	2-0	0-1	2-0
Real Tamale United	30	8	12	10	23	23	36	0-0	1-1	1-1	2-0	1-1	2-0	1-2	1-1	1-0	1-0		0-0	2-1	2-0	0-0	3-0
Gamba All Blacks	30	9	9	12	22	29	36	2-1	0-0	0-1	1-0	1-1	2-0	1-0	2-1	1-1	0-0	0-0		0-0	2-1	2-0	1-0
King Faisal Babies §3	30	9	10	11	27	31	34	1-1	2-1	1-3	1-1	2-0	0-1	2-1	2-3	2-1	1-0	2-1	2-0		**0-3**	1-0	3-1
Tano Bofoakwa §3	30	9	8	13	24	29	32	0-0	0-1	0-1	1-1	3-2	0-0	1-0	1-2	1-1	1-1	1-0	2-0	0-0		1-0	1-0
Feyenoord Academy §3	30	9	5	16	24	32	32	0-2	0-1	1-0	0-2	0-1	3-0	0-2	1-1	2-1	1-1	2-1	1-1	0-1	**3-0**		2-1
Power FC Koforidua §3	30	5	6	19	26	51	18	0-1	1-1	0-2	0-1	3-0	0-2	1-1	2-1	1-1	0-1	3-2	1-0	1-1	2-0	1-1	

19/08/2006 - 29/04/2007 • † Qualified for the CAF Champions League • ‡ Qualified for the Confederation Cup (teams qualified not on their position at the end of the season but on their position at the end of November • § = points deducted • Matches in bold were awarded

FIFA/COCA-COLA WORLD RANKING

1993	1994	1995	1996	1997	1998	1999	2000	2001	2002	2003	2004	2005	2006	High		Low	
37	26	29	25	57	48	48	57	59	61	78	77	50	28	**15**	04/96	**89**	06/04

2006–2007											
08/06	09/06	10/06	11/06	12/06	01/07	02/07	03/07	04/07	05/07	06/07	07/07
25	23	24	28	28	28	22	19	28	28	19	37

THE FIFA BIG COUNT OF 2006

	Male	Female		Total
Number of players	987 500	0	Referees and Assistant Referees	800
Professionals	0		Admin, Coaches, Technical, Medical	4 400
Amateurs 18+	16 500		Number of clubs	280
Youth under 18	11 000		Number of teams	1 650
Unregistered	110 000		Clubs with women's teams	0
Total players	987 500		Players as % of population	4.41%

GNB – GUINEA-BISSAU

NATIONAL TEAM RECORD
JULY 10TH 2006 TO JULY 12TH 2010

PL	W	D	L	F	A	%
0	0	0	0	0	0	0

FIFA/COCA-COLA WORLD RANKING

1993	1994	1995	1996	1997	1998	1999	2000	2001	2002	2003	2004	2005	2006	High	Low
131	122	118	133	148	165	173	177	174	183	186	190	186	191	**115** 07/94	**193** 03/07

					2006–2007						
08/06	09/06	10/06	11/06	12/06	01/07	02/07	03/07	04/07	05/07	06/07	07/07
179	181	181	192	191	192	193	193	190	187	186	188

Guinea Bissau extended their self imposed international exile after financial considerations saw them fail to enter the qualifiers for the 2008 African Nations Cup finals. The country's last official international was played in the 2005 Amilcar Cabral Cup, the regional tournament for west African countries that Guinea Bissau hopes to host again in November 2007. As a result, the country has crashed down the FIFA/Coca-Cola World Ranking, standing at 188th in July 2007. The only work for their Brazilian national coach José António Nogueira over the last year has been taking charge of the country's under-23 side who lost to Guinea in an All-Africa Games qualifying tie. More

INTERNATIONAL HONOURS
None

activity came off the field with a former president of the Guinea Bissau Football Federation Hipólito José Mendes jailed for four years for fraud after being found to have embezzled funds destined for the country's GOAL project. Atletico Bissau appointed a woman to coach their side in the top flight, with former club cook Helena Domigues taking charge towards the end of the season. 2006 champions OS Balantas, participated in the African Champions League but never had any real chances after being drawn with former continental champions JS Kabylie in the first round. Sporting Bissau won the league under the tutelage of former national coach Baciro Cande.

THE FIFA BIG COUNT OF 2006

	Male	Female		Total
Number of players	71 900	0	Referees and Assistant Referees	100
Professionals	0		Admin, Coaches, Technical, Medical	300
Amateurs 18+	1 100		Number of clubs	40
Youth under 18	1 200		Number of teams	110
Unregistered	7 500		Clubs with women's teams	0
Total players	71 900		Players as % of population	4.99%

Federação de Futebol da Guiné-Bissau (FFGB)
Alto Bandim (Nova Sede), Case Postale 375, Bissau 1035, Guinea-Bissau
Tel +245 201918   Fax +245 211414
federacaofutebol@hotmail.com   www.none
President: LOBATO Jose   General Secretary: CASSAMA Infali
Vice-President: GOMES VAZ Alberto   Treasurer: DAVYES Lolita Francisca Maria   Media Officer: TCHAGO Jorge
Men's Coach: NOGUEIRA José António   Women's Coach: CASSAMA Lassana
FFGB formed: 1974   CAF: 1986   FIFA: 1986
Red shirts, Green shorts, Red socks

RECENT INTERNATIONAL MATCHES PLAYED BY GUINEA-BISSAU

2002 Opponents	Score	Venue	Comp	Scorers	Att	Referee
No international matches played after June 2002						
2003						
10-10 Mali	L 1-2	Bissau	WCq	Dionisio Fernandes 50	22 000	Sowe GAM
14-11 Mali	L 0-2	Bamako	WCq		13 251	Seydou MTN
2004						
No International matches played in 2004						
2005						
18-11 Guinea	D 2-2	Conakry	ACr1	Manuel Fernandes 2 35p 49		
20-11 Sierra Leone	D 1-1	Conakry	ACr1	Agostino Soares 62		
25-11 Senegal †	D 1-1	Conakry	ACsf			
27-11 Mali †	L 0-1	Conakry	AC3p			
2006						
No international matches played in 2006						
2007						
No international matches played in 2007 before August						

AC = Amilcar Cabral Cup • WC = FIFA World Cup
q = qualifier • r1 = first round group • sf = semi-final • 3p = third place play-off • † Not a full international

GUINEA-BISSAU NATIONAL TEAM RECORDS AND RECORD SEQUENCES

Records			Sequence records					
Victory	7-2	BEN 2001	Wins	3	1990-1991	Clean sheets	5	1987-1988
Defeat	1-6	MLI 1997	Defeats	5	1980-1981	Goals scored	6	1989-1991
Player Caps	n/a		Undefeated	11	1987-1989	Without goal	3	1985, 1997-2000
Player Goals	n/a		Without win	8	1979-1981	Goals against	13	1994-1997

RECENT LEAGUE AND CUP RECORD

	Championship						Cup		
Year	Champions	Pts	Runners-up	Pts	Third	Pts	Winners	Score	Runners-up
1997	Sporting Bissau						No tournament		
1998	Sporting Bissau						No tournament		
1999	No competition held						No tournament		
2000	Sporting Bissau	38	Benfica	36	União Bissau	36	Portas Bissau	2-1	Mavegro FC
2001	No competition held						No tournament		
2002	Sporting Bissau	39	Portas Bissau	37	União Bissau	32	Mavegro FC	3-1	Sporting Bafatá
2003	União Bissau	47	Sporting Bissau	44	Sporting Bafatá	43	Tournament not finished		
2004	Sporting Bissau	39	Benfica	28	Mavegro FC	28	Mavegro FC	1-0	Sporting Bissau
2005	Sporting Bissau	45	Atlético Bissorã	38	Mavegro FC	37	Sporting Bissau	4-2	Atlético Bissorã
2006	Os Balantas	50	Mavegro FC	47	Desportivo Mansabá	33	Portas Bissau	2-1	Benfica
2007	Sporting Bissau	47	Os Balantas	46					

GUINEA-BISSAU COUNTRY INFORMATION

Capital	Bissau	Independence	1973 from Portugal	GDP per Capita	$800
Population	1 388 363	Status	Republic	GNP Ranking	184
Area km²	36 120	Language	Portuguese	Dialling code	+245
Population density	38 per km²	Literacy rate	34%	Internet code	.gw
% in urban areas	22%	Main religion	Indigenous 50%, Muslim 45%	GMT +/–	0
Towns/Cities ('000)	Bissau 388; Bafatá 22; Gabú 14; Bissorã 12; Bolama 10; Cacheu 10; Bubaque 9				
Neighbours (km)	Senegal 338; Guinea 386; Atlantic Ocean 350				
Main stadia	24 de Setembro – Bissau 20 000; Lino Correia – Bissau 12 000				

GRE – GREECE

NATIONAL TEAM RECORD
JULY 10TH 2006 TO JULY 12TH 2010

PL	W	D	L	F	A	%
10	6	0	4	12	11	60

FIFA/COCA-COLA WORLD RANKING

1993	1994	1995	1996	1997	1998	1999	2000	2001	2002	2003	2004	2005	2006	High	Low
34	28	34	35	42	53	34	42	57	48	30	18	16	16	**13** 03/07	**66** 09/98

2006–2007											
08/06	09/06	10/06	11/06	12/06	01/07	02/07	03/07	04/07	05/07	06/07	07/07
32	22	14	16	16	16	13	13	15	16	15	16

Greece won six and lost four of their ten internationals during the 2006-07 season but fortunately their hopes of retaining their European Championship title were not damaged as all six of the wins came in the qualifiers for UEFA Euro 2008 while three of the defeats were in friendlies. That left Otto Rehhagel's team in pole position going into the finals stages of the qualifying group, although their one defeat, a 4-1 thrashing at home to Turkey was deeply embarrassing. In the UEFA Champions League both Olympiacos and AEK, failed once again to make it past the group stage and not since Panathinaikos in 2002 has a Greek club made it to the knock-out round, despite having

INTERNATIONAL HONOURS
UEFA European Championship 2004   Qualified for the FIFA World Cup™ 1994

two clubs in the group stage every year. At home in the League, however, Olympiacos were in imperious form once again and although Panathinaikos scored a rare double over them, winning 1-0 home and away, Olympiacos finished a massive 17 points ahead of their rivals and nine ahead of second placed AEK. Olympiacos did fail in their bid to win what would have been an historic third consecutive League and Cup double. They were surprisingly beaten by second division PAS Giannina in the quarter-finals. Instead the Cup was won by Larisa, 2-1 victors over Panathinaikos in the final, the first club outside of Athens or Salonica to win a trophy for 19 years.

THE FIFA BIG COUNT OF 2006

	Male	Female		Total
Number of players	705 164	55 457	Referees and Assistant Referees	3 230
Professionals	1 818		Admin, Coaches, Technical, Medical	10 100
Amateurs 18+	268 570		Number of clubs	5 571
Youth under 18	86 779		Number of teams	5 899
Unregistered	145 400		Clubs with women's teams	197
Total players	760 621		Players as % of population	7.12%

Hellenic Football Federation (HFF)
137 Singrou Avenue, Nea Smirni, Athens 17121, Greece
Tel +30 210 9306000   Fax +30 210 9359666
epo@epo.gr   www.epo.gr
President: GAGATSIS Vassilis   General Secretary: ECONOMIDES Ioannis Dr
Vice-President: KOKKALIS Petros   Treasurer: GIRTZIKIS George   Media Officer: TSAPIDIS Michael
Men's Coach: REHHAGEL Otto   Women's Coach: BATSILAS Dimitrios
HFF formed: 1926   UEFA: 1954   FIFA: 1927
Blue shirts with white trimmings, Blue shorts, Blue socks or White shirts with blue trimmings, White shirts, White socks

RECENT INTERNATIONAL MATCHES PLAYED BY GREECE

2004	Opponents	Score		Venue	Comp	Scorers	Att	Referee
31-03	Switzerland	W	1-0	Irákleio	Fr	Tsartas [55]	33 000	Temmink NED
28-04	Netherlands	L	0-4	Eindhoven	Fr		25 000	Bolognino ITA
29-05	Poland	L	0-1	Szczecin	Fr		17 000	Kari FIN
3-06	Liechtenstein	W	2-0	Vaduz	Fr	Vryzas [24], Charisteas [88]	2 000	Petignat SUI
12-06	Portugal	W	2-1	Porto	ECr1	Katagounis [7], Basinas [51p]	48 761	Collina ITA
16-06	Spain	D	1-1	Porto	ECr1	Charisteas [66]	25 444	Michel SVK
20-06	Russia	L	1-2	Faro-Loule	ECr1	Vryzas [43]	24 000	Veissiere FRA
25-06	France	W	1-0	Lisbon	ECqf	Charisteas [65]	45 390	Frisk SWE
1-07	Czech Republic	W	1-0	Porto	ECsf	Dellas [105 SG]	42 449	Collina ITA
4-07	Portugal	W	1-0	Lisbon	ECf	Charisteas [57]	62 865	Merk GER
18-08	Czech Republic	D	0-0	Prague	Fr		15 050	Dougal SCO
4-09	Albania	L	1-2	Tirana	WCq	Giannakopoulos [38]	15 800	Iturralde Gonzalez ESP
8-09	Turkey	D	0-0	Piraeus	WCq		32 182	Frisk SWE
9-10	Ukraine	D	1-1	Kyiv	WCq	Tsartas [83]	56 000	Mejuto Gonzalez ESP
17-11	Kazakhstan	W	3-1	Piraeus	WCq	Charisteas 2 [24 46+], Katsouranis [85]	31 838	Kostadinov BUL
2005								
9-02	Denmark	W	2-1	Piraeus	WCq	Zagorakis [25], Basinas [32p]	32 430	Collina ITA
26-03	Georgia	W	3-1	Tbilisi	WCq	Kapsis [43], Vryzas [44], Giannakopoulos [53]	23 000	Rosetti ITA
30-03	Albania	W	2-0	Piraeus	WCq	Charisteas [33], Karagounis [84]	31 700	Layec FRA
4-06	Turkey	D	0-0	Istanbul	WCq		26 700	Merk GER
8-06	Ukraine	L	0-1	Piraeus	WCq		33 500	Temmink NED
16-06	Brazil	L	0-3	Leipzig	CCr1		42 507	Michel SVK
19-06	Japan	L	0-1	Frankfurt	CCr1		34 314	Fandel GER
22-06	Mexico	D	0-0	Frankfurt	CCr1		31 285	Amarilla PAR
17-08	Belgium	L	0-2	Brussels	Fr		20 000	Berntsen NOR
7-09	Kazakhstan	W	2-1	Almaty	WCq	Giannakopoulos [78], Lymperopoulos [94+]	18 000	Tudor ROU
8-10	Denmark	L	0-1	Copenhagen	WCq		42 099	De Bleeckere BEL
12-10	Georgia	W	1-0	Athens	WCq	Papadopoulos [17]	28 186	Trefoloni ITA
16-11	Hungary	W	2-1	Piraeus	Fr	Giannakopoulos [31], Kafes [91+]	12 500	Vink NED
2006								
21-01	Korea Republic	D	1-1	Riyadh	Fr	Zagorakis [10]		Al Shehri KSA
25-01	Saudi Arabia	D	1-1	Riyadh	Fr	Zagorakis [59p]	2 900	Mohammoud BHR
28-02	Belarus	W	1-0	Limassol	Fr	Samaras [15]	3 000	Salomir ROU
1-03	Kazakhstan	W	2-0	Nicosia	Fr	Samaras [68], Giannakopoulos [90]	2 000	Kailis CYP
25-05	Australia	L	0-1	Melbourne	Fr		95 103	Riley ENG
16-08	England	L	0-4	Manchester	Fr		45 864	Stark GER
2-09	Moldova	W	1-0	Chisinau	ECq	Liberopoulos [77]	10 500	Trefoloni ITA
7-10	Norway	W	1-0	Piraeus	ECq	Katsouranis [33]	21 189	Michel SVK
11-10	Bosnia-Hercegovina	W	4-0	Zenica	ECq	Charisteas [8p], Patsatzoglou [82], Samaras [85], Katsouranis [94+]	8 000	Baskakov RUS
15-11	France	L	0-1	Paris	Fr		63 680	Wack GER/Wezel GER
2007								
6-02	Korea Republic	L	0-1	London	Fr		9 242	Dean ENG
24-03	Turkey	L	1-4	Piraeus	ECq	Kyrgiakos [5]	31 405	Stark GER
28-03	Malta	W	1-0	Ta'Qali	ECq	Basinas [66p]	8 700	Garcia POR
2-06	Hungary	W	2-0	Irákleio	ECq	Gekas [16], Seitaridis [29]	17 244	Larsen DEN
6-06	Moldova	W	2-1	Irákleio	ECq	Charisteas [30], Liberopoulos [95+]	22 000	Wegereef NED

Fr = Friendly match • EC = UEFA EURO 2004 • WC = FIFA World Cup • CC = FIFA Confederations Cup
q = qualifier • r1 = First round group • qf = quarter-final • sf = semi-final • f = final • SG = Silver goal

GREECE NATIONAL TEAM RECORDS AND RECORD SEQUENCES

Records			Sequence records				
Victory	8-0	SYR 1949	Wins	6	1994-1994	Clean sheets	4	Five times
Defeat	1-11	HUN 1938	Defeats	10	1931-1933	Goals scored	17	1934-1949
Player Caps	118	ZAGORAKIS Theodoros	Undefeated	15	2002-2004	Without goal	6	2005
Player Goals	29	ANASTOPOULOS Nikos	Without win	12	1954-1960	Goals against	21	1957-1964

1	Athens	3 799
2	Thessaloníki	966
3	Pátra	164
4	Irákleio	140
5	Lárisa	130
6	Volos	85
7	Ioánnina	65
8	Kavála	59
9	Ródos	58
10	Sérrai	56
11	Alexandroúpoli	55
12	Khaniá	55
13	Khalkís	54
14	Kateríni	54
15	Kalamáta	52
16	Trikala	50
17	Xánthi	49
18	Lamía	47
19	Komotiní	46
20	Véroia	45
21	Dráma	45
22	Agrínion	44
23	Kozáni	37
24	Kérkira	26

HELLENIC REPUBLIC; ELLINIKI DHIMOKRATIA

Capital	Athens	Language	Greek	Independence	1829
Population	10 688 058	Area	131 940 km²	% in cities	65%
GDP per cap	$20 000	Dailling code	+30	Internet	.gr	GMT +/-	+2

Density 80 per km²

The Athens metropolitan population figure includes: Piraeus 170; Peristéri 137; Kallithéa 106; Níkaia 95; Glifáda 92; Akharnaí 86; Néa Smírni 76; Egaleo 71 • The Thessaloníki metropolitan figure includes: Kalamariá 93

MEDALS TABLE

		Overall			League			Cup			Europe			City	Stadium	Cap'ty	DoF
		G	S	B	G	S	B	G	S	G	S	B					
1	Olympiacos	57	27	10	35	16	10	22	11				Piraeus	Karaiskaki	33 500	1925
2	Panathinaikos	35	30	17	19	19	15	16	10		1	2	Athens	Apostolos Nikolaidis	16 620	1908
3	AEK	23	24	15	11	18	14	12	6			1	Athens	Olympic Stadium	72 000	1924
4	PAOK	6	16	8	2	4	8	4	12				Thessaloníki	Toumba	28 701	1926
5	Aris	4	9	8	3	3	8	1	6				Thessaloníki	Harilaou	18 308	1914
6	Panionios	2	6	3		2	3	2	4				Athens	Nea Smyrni	11 700	1890
7	Larissa	3	3		1	1		2	2				Larissa	Alkazar	13 108	1964
8	Iraklis	1	7	2		3	2	1	4				Thessaloníki	Kaftanzoglio	28 028	1908
9	OFI Crete	1	2	2		1	2	1	1				Irákleio	Pankritio	33 240	1925
10	Ethnikos	1	2			2		1					Piraeus	Georgios Kamaras	14 200	1925
11	Kastoria	1						1					Kastoria	Kastoria	8 000	1963
12	Apollon Smyrnis		3	5		2	5		1				Athens	Georgios Kamaras	14 200	1891
13	Doxa Dramas		3						3				Drama	Doxa Dramas	7 000	1918
14	Athinaikos		1						1				Athens	Vyrona	4 340	1917
	Ionikos		1						1				Piraeus	Neapolis Public	7 026	1965
	Pierikos Kateríni		1						1				Kateríni			1961
17	Atromitos-Chalkidona			1			1						Peristéri	Peristeri	8 939	1923

RECENT LEAGUE AND CUP RECORD

	Championship						Cup		
Year	Champions	Pts	Runners-up	Pts	Third	Pts	Winners	Score	Runners-up
1995	Panathinaikos	83	Olympiacos	67	PAOK	65	Panathinaikos	1-0	AEK
1996	Panathinaikos	83	AEK	81	Olympiacos	65	AEK	7-1	Apollon
1997	Olympiacos	84	AEK	72	OFI Crete	66	AEK	0-0 5-3p	Panathinaikos
1998	Olympiacos	88	Panathinaikos	85	AEK	74	Panionios	1-0	Panathinaikos
1999	Olympiacos	85	AEK	75	Panathinaikos	74	Olympiacos	2-0	Panathinaikos
2000	Olympiacos	92	Panathinaikos	88	AEK	66	AEK	2-0	Ionikos
2001	Olympiacos	78	Panathinaikos	66	AEK	61	PAOK	4-2	Olympiacos
2002	Olympiacos	58	AEK	58	Panathinaikos	55	AEK	2-1	Olympiacos
2003	Olympiacos	70	Panathinaikos	70	AEK	68	PAOK	1-0	Aris
2004	Panathinaikos	77	Olympiacos	75	PAOK	60	Panathinaikos	3-1	Olympiacos
2005	Olympiacos	65	Panathinaikos	64	AEK	62	Olympiacos	3-0	Aris
2006	Olympiacos	70	AEK	67	Panathinaikos	67	Olympiacos	3-0	AEK
2007	Olympiacos	71	AEK	62	Panathinaikos	54	Larisa	2-1	Panathinaikos

GREECE 2006–07
SUPEREAGUE

	Pl	W	D	L	F	A	Pts	Olympiacos	AEK	Panath'kos	Aris	Panionios	PAOK	OFI	Atromitos	Ergotelis	Larisa	Xánthi	Apollon	Iraklis	Kérkira	Egaleo	Ionikos
Olympiacos †	30	22	5	3	62	23	71		1-0	0-1	0-0	1-0	2-0	4-1	4-1	1-0	4-0	2-1	5-0	2-0	3-1	3-2	3-0
AEK Athens †	30	18	8	4	60	27	62	3-3		1-4	3-1	4-0	0-0	3-1	3-0	3-1	5-0	0-0	1-0	3-0	4-1	5-2	2-0
Panathinaikos ‡	30	16	6	8	47	28	54	1-0	1-2		0-1	2-0	2-1	2-2	1-2	0-1	1-0	1-0	3-2	1-0	2-2	1-0	0-2
Aris Thessaloniki ‡	30	11	13	6	32	26	46	2-3	1-3	1-0		2-2	0-0	3-1	1-2	2-0	1-1	1-0	3-2	1-0	0-0	3-1	1-0
Panionios	30	12	9	9	33	31	45	0-3	3-1	0-1	0-0		3-1	1-0	0-0	2-0	2-1	0-2	3-1	2-1	3-1	0-0	2-0
PAOK Thessaloniki	30	13	6	11	32	29	45	2-3	2-0	2-1	1-0	1-1		1-0	0-3	1-0	1-3	1-0	1-1	3-1	1-0	2-0	3-0
OFI Crete	30	12	6	12	41	45	42	1-2	1-1	3-3	1-0	3-1	1-0		4-1	1-3	0-1	0-2	2-0	1-0	3-4	1-0	2-1
Atromitos/Chalkidonia	30	10	10	10	40	44	40	1-0	1-1	0-4	1-1	0-1	2-1	2-2		2-1	2-2	3-3	1-1	2-2	4-2	1-1	1-0
Ergotelis	30	11	6	13	30	32	39	1-2	0-0	0-1	0-1	2-1	0-0	2-0	1-0		2-0	3-1	0-1	2-1	1-1	3-0	1-1
Larisa ‡	30	9	9	12	30	38	36	0-0	0-1	1-1	1-1	1-0	1-2	1-2	2-1	2-1		1-0	0-1	0-1	2-2	2-2	3-0
Xánthi	30	8	12	10	24	22	36	0-0	0-0	0-0	0-0	1-1	1-1	1-0	4-1	1-0	0-0		0-0	1-2	1-1	0-0	2-0
Apollon Kalamarias	30	9	8	13	27	36	35	1-2	1-2	1-1	1-1	1-1	3-1	1-0	1-0	0-0	1-2	2-0		2-1	1-0	0-1	1-0
Iraklis Thessaloniki	30	10	5	15	25	34	35	0-1	1-1	0-1	0-0	0-0	1-0	2-3	2-3	0-1	1-0	1-0	0-1		1-0	2-1	1-0
Kérkira	30	8	11	11	34	36	35	0-2	0-1	3-1	1-1	0-1	0-0	1-0	1-0	5-1	0-0	0-0	2-1	0-0		3-0	2-0
Egaleo	30	7	7	16	27	45	28	1-1	1-2	1-4	1-1	0-2	0-2	1-2	0-0	2-0	1-2	1-0	2-0	0-1	2-1		3-1
Ionikos §5	30	2	3	25	14	62	4	3-5	1-5	0-4	0-1	1-1	0-2	0-2	1-4	1-3	1-2	0-2	1-0	0-3	0-0	0-1	

19/08/2006 - 13/05/2007 • † Qualified for the UEFA Champions League • ‡ Qualified for the UEFA Cup • § = points deducted

GREECE 2006–07
BETA ETHNIKI (2)

	Pl	W	D	L	F	A	Pts
Asteras Tripolis	34	20	9	5	56	25	69
Levadiakos	34	21	5	8	49	33	68
Veria	34	16	11	7	46	26	59
Kastoria	34	16	9	9	55	40	57
PAS Giannina	34	14	11	9	49	34	53
Ethnikos Piraeus	34	15	4	15	35	33	49
Kallithea	34	13	8	13	45	42	47
Thrasivoulos	34	13	8	13	37	48	47
Agrotikos Asteras	34	11	11	12	35	38	44
Kalamata	34	11	10	13	36	40	43
Panthrakikos	34	12	6	16	40	44	42
Ilisiakos	34	11	9	14	44	49	42
Chaidari	34	12	6	16	37	43	42
Ethnikos Asteras	34	11	8	15	29	38	41
Panserraikos	34	10	9	15	41	46	39
Proodeftiki	34	9	9	16	20	38	36
Messiniakos	34	9	7	18	34	50	34
Niki Volos	34	8	8	18	23	44	32

10/09/2006 - 3/06/2007

HELLENIC CUP 2006–07

Round of 16

Larisa	1	3
OFI Crete *	1	1
Ionikos	0	1
Kérkira *	0	2
Olympiacos	3	0
Chaidari *	1	0
Iraklis Thessaloniki *	1	0
PAS Giannina	1	2
Xánthi	1	0
Panionios *	0	0
Niki Volou *	0	0
Ilisiakos	1	0
PAOK Thessaloniki *	1	0
Ergoteis	0	0
Apollon Kalamarias	0 1 3p	
Panathinaikos *	0 1 4p	

Quarter-finals

Larisa	0	2
Kérkira *	0	0
Olympiacos	0	2
PAS Giannina *	2	1
Xánthi	2	1
Ilisiakos *	0	0
PAOK Thessaloniki *	2	1
Panathinaikos	1	3

Semi-finals

Larisa *	2	2
PAS Giannina	0	0
Xánthi	0	0
Panathinaikos *	0	1

Final

Larisa ‡	2
Panathinaikos	1

CUP FINAL

5-05-2007

Scorers -

* Home team/home team in the first leg • ‡ Qualified for the UEFA Cup

GRN – GRENADA

NATIONAL TEAM RECORD
JULY 10TH 2006 TO JULY 12TH 2010

PL	W	D	L	F	A	%
6	0	3	3	5	10	25

FIFA/COCA-COLA WORLD RANKING

1993	1994	1995	1996	1997	1998	1999	2000	2001	2002	2003	2004	2005	2006	High	Low
143	142	141	127	111	117	121	143	133	131	154	144	151	163	**105** 08/97	**165** 02/07

2006–2007											
08/06	09/06	10/06	11/06	12/06	01/07	02/07	03/07	04/07	05/07	06/07	07/07
159	157	157	145	163	163	165	160	158	156	155	156

2006 was not a vintage year for the Spice Boyz of Grenada as they were knocked out of the Digicel Caribbean Cup in the first qualifying round. They managed to pick up just one point in their group in Willemstad, against hosts Netherlands Antilles, and you have to go back to November 2004 for the last time that Grenada won a match. Failure to win their next one will mean that the Spice Boyz will have matched their worst ever run of 10 games without a win. Qualification for their first finals of the Caribbean Cup since 1999 does not look to be on the cards in the near future unless they can persuade the island's most-high profile player, Jason Roberts of Blackburn Rovers, to turn out for

INTERNATIONAL HONOURS
None

the team on a regular basis. Playing in the Caribbean Cup is just not practicable for Roberts but in a bid to improve standards, he is starting an academy on the island as part of his charitable foundation, the main goal of which is to work on a grassroots level to help disadvantaged kids. In the Digicel Premier League there was a second title in four years for Carib Hurricanes who finished a point ahead of Queen's Park Rangers from the capital St George's. Rangers, the most successful club on the island, were denied a first championship in five years when Hurricanes beat GBSS on the final day of the season to secure the title.

THE FIFA BIG COUNT OF 2006

	Male	Female		Total
Number of players	705 164	55 457	Referees and Assistant Referees	3 230
Professionals	1 818		Admin, Coaches, Technical, Medical	10 100
Amateurs 18+	268 570		Number of clubs	5 571
Youth under 18	86 779		Number of teams	5 899
Unregistered	145 400		Clubs with women's teams	197
Total players	760 621		Players as % of population	7.12%

Grenada Football Association (GFA)

Deco Building, PO Box 326, St George's, Grenada
Tel +1 473 4409903   Fax +1 473 4409973
gfa@caribsurf.com   www.grenadafootball.com
President: FOLKES Ashley Ram   General Secretary: DANIEL Victor
Vice-President: CHENEY Joseph   Treasurer: DANIEL Victor   Media Officer: BASCOMBE Michael
Men's Coach: DEBELLOTTE Alister   Women's Coach: DEAN Jules
GFA formed: 1924   CONCACAF: 1969   FIFA: 1978
Green and yellow striped shirts, Red shorts, Yellow socks

RECENT INTERNATIONAL MATCHES PLAYED BY GRENADA

2004	Opponents	Score		Venue	Comp	Scorers	Att	Referee
14-03	Guyana	W	3-1	Blairmont	WCq	Charles [15], Roberts [69], Bubb [87]	1 200	Quesada Cordero CRC
8-05	St Vincent/Grenadines	D	1-1	Kingstown	Fr			
20-05	Cuba	D	2-2	Havana	Fr	Roberts [47], Bishop [75]		
2-06	St Lucia	W	2-0	St George's	Fr	Roberts [7], Bain.K [65]	2 500	
13-06	USA	L	0-3	Columbus	WCq		10 000	Navarro CAN
20-06	USA	L	2-3	St George's	WCq	Roberts [12], Charles [77]	10 000	Brizan TRI
17-10	St Lucia	L	1-3	Castries	Fr			
13-11	St Vincent/Grenadines	L	2-6	Kingstown	Fr	Rennie [42], Bishop [81]		
20-11	St Vincent/Grenadines	W	3-2	Gouyave	Fr	Modeste.A [6], Charles 2 [13 88]	3 000	Bedeau GRN
24-11	Surinam	D	2-2	Tunapuna	CCq	Charles [46], Bishop [50]	2 000	Forde BRB
26-11	Trinidad and Tobago	L	0-2	Tunapuna	CCq			Callender BRB
28-11	Puerto Rico	W	5-2	Tunapuna	CCq	OG [1], Charles [3], Rennie [58], Williams [68], Langiagne [75]		Callender BRB
12-12	St Vincent/Grenadines	L	1-3	Kingstown	CCq	Rennie [59]		Fanus LCA
19-12	St Vincent/Grenadines	L	0-1	St George's	CCq			Small BRB
2005								
23-01	Barbados	L	0-3	Bridgetown	Fr			
2006								
6-09	Netherlands Antilles	D	1-1	Willemstad	CCq	Rennie [52]		
8-09	Surinam	L	0-1	Willemstad	CCq			
10-09	Guyana	L	0-1	Willemstad	CCq			Angela ARU
1-11	St Vincent/Grenadines	L	1-4	Kingstown	Fr			
3-11	Antigua and Barbuda	D	1-1	Kingstown	Fr			
5-11	Barbados	D	2-2	Black Rock	Fr	Redhead 2 [7 45]		
2007								

No international matches played in 2007 before August

Fr = Friendly match • CC = Digicel Caribbean Cup • WC = FIFA World Cup • q = qualifier

GRENADA NATIONAL TEAM RECORDS AND RECORD SEQUENCES

Records			Sequence records		
Victory	14-1	AIA 1998	Wins	3	1996
			Clean sheets	2	1989, 1994
Defeat	0-7	TRI 1999	Defeats	5	2002-2004
			Goals scored	15	2001-2002
Player Caps	n/a		Undefeated	5	1997, 2004
			Without goal	3	1990
Player Goals	n/a		Without win	10	1990-1994
			Goals against	17	1996-1999

RECENT LEAGUE AND CUP RECORD

	Championship						Cup		
Year	Champions	Pts	Runners-up	Pts	Third	Pts	Winners	Score	Runners-up
1998	Fontenoy United	3-2	Saint Andrews FL						
1999	Cable Vision SAFL	30	Fontenoy United	28	GBSS	27	Queens Park Rangers		
2000	GBSS	29	Saint John's Sports	27	Fontenoy United	20	Hurricane FC	3-1	GBSS
2001	GBSS	34	Hurricane FC	22	Saint Andrews FL	22	Hurricane FC		GBSS
2002	Queens Park Rangers								
2003	Hurricane FC	45	Paradise	39	Fontenoy United	31	Hurricane FC	1-0	GBSS
2004	Abandoned due to Hurricane Ivan						Police SC	2-1	Paradise
2005	ASOMS Paradise	37	Fontenoy United	36	Hurricane	35	St John's Sports		Fontenoy United
2006	Hurricane FC		Queens Park Rang's						

GRENADA COUNTRY INFORMATION

Capital	Saint George's	Independence	1974 from the UK	GDP per Capita	$5 500
Population	89 357	Status	Commonwealth	GNP Ranking	174
Area km²	344	Language	English	Dialling code	+1 473
Population density	259 per km²	Literacy rate	98%	Internet code	.gd
% in urban areas	37%	Main religion	Christian	GMT +/-	-4
Towns/Cities ('000)	Saint George's 4; Gouyave 3; Grenville 2; Victoria 2				
Neighbours (km)	Atlantic Ocean and the Caribbean Sea 121				
Main stadia	National Stadium – Saint George's 9 000				

GUA – GUATEMALA

NATIONAL TEAM RECORD
JULY 1OTH 2006 TO JULY 12TH 2010

PL	W	D	L	F	A	%
16	4	5	7	11	17	40.6

FIFA/COCA-COLA WORLD RANKING

1993	1994	1995	1996	1997	1998	1999	2000	2001	2002	2003	2004	2005	2006	High	Low
120	149	145	105	83	73	73	56	67	78	77	71	56	105	**50** 08/06	**163** 11/95

	2006–2007										
08/06	09/06	10/06	11/06	12/06	01/07	02/07	03/07	04/07	05/07	06/07	07/07
50	66	101	102	105	105	87	90	90	87	81	75

A place in the quarter-finals of the CONCACAF Gold Cup and third place in the UNCAF Cup was very much in line with what was expected of the Guatemala national team, but coach Hernán Dario Gomez will be disappointed with a return of just four wins in 16 games over the course of the season. In the UNCAF Cup, Guatemala were knocked out in the semi-finals by an ever improving Panama side while in the Gold Cup they were comprehensively beaten 3-0 by Canada, having made heavy work of progressing from the group stage. It was not ideal preparation for Guatemala as they seek to qualify for the World Cup for the first time. At club level Deportivo Marquense finished third

INTERNATIONAL HONOURS
CONCACAF Championship 1967 UNCAF Championship 2001 CONCACAF Club Championship Municipal 1974, Comunicaciones 1978

in the UNCAF club championship to qualify for the quarter-finals of the CONCACAF Champions Cup but they were drawn against the eventual winners Pachuca and lost 3-0 on aggregate. At home Municipal won the Apertura to complete a run of five successive titles going back to their Apertura win in 2004. However, it took away goals to beat eternal rivals Communications in the final and they then failed to make it six in a row when they lost to Xelajú in the Clausura semi-finals. Marquense looked set for their first ever title when they beat Xelajú away in the first leg of the final but they then lost 4-1 at home to hand Xelajú their first title in ten years.

THE FIFA BIG COUNT OF 2006

	Male	Female		Total
Number of players	1 847 811	158 838	Referees and Assistant Referees	373
Professionals	600		Admin, Coaches, Technical, Medical	5 030
Amateurs 18+	60 008		Number of clubs	138
Youth under 18	93 709		Number of teams	225
Unregistered	1 805 000		Clubs with women's teams	1
Total players	2 006 649		Players as % of population	16.32%

Federación Nacional de Fútbol de Guatemala (FNFG)
2a. Calle 15-57, Zona 15, Boulevard Vista Hermosa, Guatemala City 01015, Guatemala
Tel +502 24227777   Fax +502 24227780
info@fedefutguate.com   www.fedefut.org
President: ARROYO Oscar   General Secretary: MONGE Carlos Eduardo
Vice-President: TBD   Treasurer: DE TORREBIARTE Adela   Media Officer: None
Men's Coach: GOMEZ Hernan   Women's Coach: GARCIA Antonio
FNFG formed: 1919   CONCACAF: 1961   FIFA: 1946
Blue shirts, White shorts, Blue socks

RECENT INTERNATIONAL MATCHES PLAYED BY GUATEMALA

2004	Opponents	Score		Venue	Comp	Scorers	Att	Referee
13-11	Bolivia	W	1-0	Washington DC	Fr	Ruiz [21]	22 000	Prus USA
17-11	Canada	L	0-1	Guatemala City	WCq		18 000	Rodriguez MEX
21-12	Venezuela	W	1-0	Caracas	Fr	Ruiz [89]	5 000	Solorzano VEN
2005								
17-01	Colombia	D	1-1	Los Angeles	Fr	Ruiz [3]	15 000	Vaughn USA
23-01	Paraguay	L	1-2	Los Angeles	Fr	Rivera [36]		
9-02	Panama	D	0-0	Panama City	WCq		20 000	Prendergast JAM
13-02	Haiti	W	2-1	Fort Lauderdale	Fr	Villatoro [18], Castillo [70]	10 000	Salazar USA
19-02	Belize	W	2-0	Guatemala City	UCr1	Villatoro [35], Plata [72p]	10 000	Quesada CRC
21-02	Nicaragua	W	4-0	Guatemala City	UCr1	Plata [11], Sandoval 2 [30 77], Villatoro [66]	8 000	Sibrian SLV
23-02	Honduras	D	1-1	Guatemala City	UCr1	Romero [22]	3 000	Moreno PAN
25-02	Costa Rica	L	0-4	Guatemala City	UCsf		11 159	Archundia MEX
27-02	Panama	W	3-0	Panama City	UC3p	Villatoro [7], Plata 2 [41 49]	1 491	Quesada CRC
26-03	Trinidad and Tobago	W	5-1	Guatemala City	WCq	Ramirez [17], Ruiz 2 [30 38], Pezzarossi 2 [78 87]	22 506	Stott USA
30-03	USA	L	0-2	Birmingham	WCq		31 624	Ramdhan TRI
20-04	Jamaica	L	0-1	Atlanta	Fr		7 000	Prus USA
27-04	Brazil	L	0-3	Sao Paulo	Fr		38 000	Vazquez URU
4-06	Mexico	L	0-2	Guatemala City	WCq		26 723	Hall USA
8-06	Costa Rica	L	2-3	San Jose	WCq	Villatoro [74], Rodriguez [77]	BCD	Archundia MEX
8-07	Jamaica	L	3-4	Carson	GCr1	Ruiz 3 [11p 48+ 87]	27 000	Hall USA
10-07	Mexico	L	0-4	Los Angeles	GCr1		30 710	Ruiz COL
13-07	South Africa	D	1-1	Houston	Fr	Romero [37]	45 311	Stott USA
17-08	Panama	W	2-1	Guatemala City	WCq	Baloy OG [70], Romero [93+]	24 000	Sibrian SLV
3-09	Trinidad and Tobago	L	2-3	Port of Spain	WCq	Andrews OG [3], Romero [61]	15 000	Archundia MEX
7-09	USA	D	0-0	Guatemala City	WCq		27 000	Rodriguez MEX
1-10	Jamaica	L	1-2	Fort Lauderdale	Fr			
8-10	Mexico	L	2-5	San Luis Potosi	WCq	Ruiz [1], Poniciano [53]	30 000	Prendergast JAM
12-10	Costa Rica	W	3-1	Guatemala City	WCq	Poniciano [2], Garcia [16], Ruiz [30]	23 912	Hall USA
2006								
19-02	USA	L	0-4	Frisco	Fr		14 453	Navarro CAN
16-08	Haiti	D	1-1	Miami	Fr	Rodriguez.M [58]	15 000	
6-09	Panama	L	1-2	Guatemala City	Fr	Sandoval [80]		
7-10	Honduras	L	2-3	Fort Lauderdale	Fr	Pezzarossi [27], Avila [32]	19 173	Vaughn USA
10-10	Honduras	L	1-2	Atlanta	Fr	Ruiz [69p]		Prus USA
15-11	Venezuela	L	1-2	Caracas	Fr	Martinez [73]	9 000	Andarcia VEN
2007								
8-02	Nicaragua	W	1-0	San Salvador	UCr1	Quiñónez [29]		Pineda HON
10-02	Belize	W	1-0	San Salvador	UCr1	Cabrera [8]		Vidal PAN
12-02	El Salvador	D	0-0	San Salvador	UCr1			Archundia MEX
16-02	Panama	L	0-2	San Salvador	UCsf			Arredondo MEX
18-02	El Salvador	W	1-0	San Salvador	UC3p	Albizuris [81]		Quesada CRC
25-03	Barbados	D	0-0	Bridgetown	Fr			
28-03	USA	D	0-0	Frisco	Fr		10 932	Archundia MEX
7-06	USA	L	0-1	Los Angeles	GCr1		21 344	Pineda NON
9-06	El Salvador	W	1-0	Los Angeles	GCr1	Contreras [68]	27 000	Jauregui ANT
12-06	Trinidad and Tobago	D	1-1	Foxboro	GCr1	Ruiz [84]	26 523	Pineda HON
16-06	Canada	L	0-3	Foxboro	GCqf		22 412	

Fr = Friendly match • UC = UNCAF Cup • GC = CONCACAF Gold Cup • WC = FIFA World Cup
q = qualifier • r1 = first round group • qf = quarter-final • sf = semi-final • 3p = third place play-off • BCD = Behind closed doors

GUATEMALA NATIONAL TEAM RECORDS AND RECORD SEQUENCES

Records			Sequence records					
Victory	9-0	HON 1921	Wins	6	1967	Clean sheets	4	1984-1985
Defeat	1-9	CRC 1955	Defeats	7	2005	Goals scored	16	1957-1965
Player Caps	n/a		Undefeated	13	1996-1997	Without goal	8	1989-1991
Player Goals	n/a		Without win	14	1989-1991	Goals against	13	1953-1961

MAJOR CITIES/TOWNS

Population '000

1	Guatemala City	3 122
2	Quetzaltenango	140
3	Chichicastenango	119
4	Escuintla	116
5	Huehuetenango	99
6	Chimaltenango	98
7	Totonicapán	94
8	San Francisco	77
9	Cotzumalguapa	72
10	Puerto Barrios	62
11	Sololá	59
12	Cobán	57
13	Jalapa	50
14	Coatepeque	48
15	San Pedro	46
16	Mazatenango	46
17	Antigua	45
18	Chiquimula	44
19	Jacaltenango	44
20	Zacapa	40
21	Retalhuleu	38
22	San Marcos	29
23	Asunción Mita	16
24	Morales	23

REPUBLIC OF GUATEMALA; REPUBLICA DE GUATEMALA

Capital	Guatemala City	Language	Spanish	Independence	1821
Population	12 293 545	Area	108 890 km²	% in cities	41%
GDP per cap	$4100	Dailling code	+502	Internet .gt	GMT + / - -6

The Guatemala City metropolitan area includes: Guatemala City 1 024; Mixco 540; Villa Nueva 499; San Juan Sacatepéquez 200; Petapa 189; Villa Canales 174; Chinaulta 112; Santa Caterina Pinula 91, Amatitlán 80; San Pedro Ayampuc 65; San José Pinula 63; Fraijanes 37 and Palencia 22

MEDALS TABLE

		Overall			League			Cup		Cent Am			City	Stadium	Cap'ty	DoF
		G	S	B	G	S	B	G	S	G	S	B				
1	Deportivo Municipal	33	16	7	25	13	6	7	2	1	1	1	Guatemala City	Mateo Flores	30 000	1936
2	Comunicaciones	26	19	10	21	18	7	4		1	2	3	Guatemala City	Mateo Flores	30 000	1949
3	Aurora	10	9	6	8	8	5	2	1			1	Guatemala City	Del Ej		1945
4	Xelajú	5	5	2	4	3	1	1	2			1	Quetzaltenango	Mario Camposeco	11 000	1928
5	Suchitepéquez	3	5	2	1	4	1	2	1			1	Mazatenango	Carlos Salazar Hijo	12 000	1960
6	Deportivo Jalapa	3	1					3	1				Jalapa	Las Flores	10 000	1973
	Tip Nac	3	1		3	1							Guatemala City			1924
8	Cobán Imperial	1	6	2	1	3	2		3				Cobán	Verapáz	15 000	1924
9	Juventud Retalteca	1	3	2	2	2		1	1				Retalhuleu	Oscar Monterroso Izaguirre	8 000	
10	IRCA	1		2		2		1								
11	Hospicio	1	1		1	1										
	Amatitlan	1	1		1	1							Amatitlán	Municipal	12 000	
13	Deportivo Marquense		2			2							San Marcos	Marquesa de la Ensenada	10 000	1958
14	Universidad		1	4	1	4							Guatemala City	Campo de Marte		1922
15	Antigua		1	1	1	1							Antigua	Pensativo	9 000	

RECENT LEAGUE AND CUP RECORD

Championship/Clausura from 2000				Apertura			Cup		
Year	Winners	Score	Runners-up	Winners	Score	Runners-up	Winners	Score	Runners-up
1995	Comunicaciones	1-0	Municipal				Municipal	3-0	Suchitepéquez
1996	Xelajú MC	1-0 1-1	Comunicaciones				Municipal	1-1 1-0	Xelajú MC
1997	Comunicaciones	2-0 3-1	Aurora				Amatitlan	1-1 4-3	Municipal
1998	Comunicaciones	†					Suchitepéquez	3-1	Cobán Imperial
1999	Comunicaciones	†		Comunicaciones	1-1 2-1	Municipal	Municipal		Aurora
2000	Municipal	0-1 2-0	Comunicaciones	Municipal	0-0 1-1	Comunicaciones	No tournament		
2001	Comunicaciones	4-0 2-3	Antigua GFC	Municipal	3-0 0-3	Cobán Imperial	No tournament		
2002	Municipal	1-2 2-0	Comunicaciones	Comunicaciones	2-1 1-1	Municipal	Deportivo Jalapa	5-2	Cobán Imperial
2003	Comunicaciones	0-0 3-2	Cobán Imperial	Municipal	3-2 0-0	Comunicaciones	Municipal	2-1 1-0	Cobán Imperial
2004	Cobán Imperial	3-2 2-2	Municipal	Municipal	5-1 4-1	Comunicaciones	Municipal	1-0 4-2	Deportivo Jalapa
2005	Municipal	1-0 4-2	Suchitepéquez	Municipal	0-0 2-0	Comunicaciones	Deportivo Jalapa	3-0 0-2	Xelajú MC
2006	Municipal	2-0 2-1	Marquense	Municipal	0-0 1-1	Comunicaciones	Deportivo Jalapa	1-1 1-0	Municipal
2007	Xelajú	0-1 4-1	Marquense						

† Automatic champions as winners of both the regular season and the play-offs

GUATEMALA 2006–07

TORNEO APERTURA

	Pl	W	D	L	F	A	Pts	Com'ciones	Xelajú	Municipal	Jalapa	Marquense	Zacapa	Petapa	Heredia	Suchit'quez	Mictlán
Comunicaciones †	18	12	4	2	31	13	40		1-0	1-0	2-0	0-0	2-1	3-2	4-0	2-1	2-1
Xelajú †	18	10	2	6	35	16	32	1-2		2-1	3-0	0-0	4-1	2-0	6-0	2-0	5-0
Municipal †	18	8	5	5	30	22	29	1-3	0-0		1-1	2-0	4-2	2-1	3-0	3-0	2-1
Deportivo Jalapa †	18	8	3	7	26	23	27	1-0	2-1	4-2		3-1	4-0	1-1	4-1	1-2	0-0
Deportivo Marquense †	18	7	4	7	26	20	25	0-3	1-2	4-1	3-0		6-2	4-2	0-0	0-1	4-0
Deportivo Zacapa †	18	7	3	8	20	32	24	2-0	2-1	1-1	1-0	1-0		0-2	2-1	1-0	2-0
Petapa	18	6	5	7	31	30	23	2-2	1-0	0-0	2-1	0-1	5-1		4-1	2-2	1-0
Deportivo Heredia	18	5	4	9	24	36	19	1-1	4-3	1-1	1-2	2-0	1-0	3-3		3-0	5-1
Suchitepéquez	18	5	3	10	17	29	18	0-3	1-2	0-2	0-2	0-1	1-1	5-2	1-0		3-2
Mictlán	18	3	5	10	12	31	14	0-0	0-1	1-4	2-0	1-1	0-0	2-1	1-0	0-0	

29/07/2006 - 26/11/2006 • † Qualified for the play-offs • Top two receive a bye to the semi-finals

APERTURA PLAY-OFFS

Quarter–finals			Semi–finals			Final		
Municipal	1	2						
Deportivo Zacapa *	0	0	**Municipal ***	3	0			
			Xelajú	0	1			
						Municipal * ‡	0	1
						Comunicaciones	0	1
Deportivo Jalapa	2	2						
Deportivo Marquense*	3	0	Deportivo Jalapa *	1	1			
			Comunicaciones	2	3			

* Home team in first leg • ‡ won on away goals

GUATEMALA 2006–07

TORNEO CLAUSURA

	Pl	W	D	L	F	A	Pts	Municipal	Petapa	Marquense	Xelajú	Heredia	Suchit'quez	Zacapa	Com'ciones	Jalapa	Mictlán
Municipal †	18	9	5	4	43	21	32		4-4	3-1	2-1	3-2	4-0	4-0	1-1	7-0	4-0
Petapa †	18	9	4	5	31	23	31	1-1		1-0	0-2	4-2	2-1	4-0	3-2	1-0	5-2
Deportivo Marquense †	18	8	5	5	35	26	29	2-0	2-1		2-2	1-0	5-2	4-4	4-0	2-1	6-1
Xelajú †	18	7	5	6	24	20	26	2-0	0-1	2-1		2-1	1-0	2-0	1-2	1-1	2-1
Deportivo Heredia †	18	7	4	7	26	28	25	2-1	1-3	2-0	2-1		1-1	4-3	1-1	1-0	3-2
Suchitepéquez †	18	6	5	7	21	25	23	1-1	3-0	1-2	1-1	1-0		0-0	1-0	4-2	1-0
Deportivo Zacapa	18	5	6	7	25	35	21	1-4	1-0	4-1	3-2	2-4	1-1		1-1	0-0	3-2
Comunicaciones	18	4	8	6	17	21	20	0-2	1-1	0-0	1-0	0-0	3-1	0-1		0-1	1-1
Deportivo Jalapa	18	5	5	8	19	27	20	2-1	1-0	1-1	2-2	0-0	0-1	1-0	1-3		5-1
Mictlán	18	3	7	8	21	36	16	1-1	0-0	1-1	0-0	3-0	2-1	1-1	1-1	2-1	

13/01/2007 - 6/05/2007 • † Qualified for the play-offs • Top two receive a bye to the semi-finals • Mictlán were relegated due to having the worst overall season record • Suchitepéquez and Heredia entered a relegation play-off: Cobán 1-0 0-2 **Suchitepéquez**; Sacachispas 1-1 0-1 **Heredia**

CLAUSURA PLAY-OFFS

Quarter–finals			Semi–finals			Final		
			Xelajú *	3	1			
Xelajú	1	3	Municipal	1	1			
Deportivo Heredia *	2	0						
						Xelajú *	0	4
Suchitepéquez *	1	1				Deportivo Marquense	1	1
Deportivo Marquense	2	0	Petapa	0	0			
			Deportivo Marquense*	3	0			

* Home team in first leg

GUI – GUINEA

NATIONAL TEAM RECORD
JULY 10TH 2006 TO JULY 12TH 2010

PL	W	D	L	F	A	%
7	2	3	2	7	5	50

FIFA/COCA-COLA WORLD RANKING

1993	1994	1995	1996	1997	1998	1999	2000	2001	2002	2003	2004	2005	2006	High	Low
63	66	63	73	65	79	91	80	108	120	101	86	79	23	22 01/07	123 05/03

2006–2007											
08/06	09/06	10/06	11/06	12/06	01/07	02/07	03/07	04/07	05/07	06/07	07/07
22	26	31	27	23	22	62	62	50	50	50	43

In the qualifiers for the Africa Cup of Nations finals in Ghana, the 'Syli Nationale' looked to be in desperate straits after picking up a single point in their first two matches in October 2006. It precipitated the sacking of French coach Patrice Neveu, who less than nine months earlier had earned himself hero status by taking the side to the quarter-finals of the 2006 Nations Cup finals in Egypt. Veteran French coach Robert Nouzaret, who had two previous spells in charge of nearby Cote d'Ivoire, came in at the start of 2007 and set about salvaging the campaign, lifting the team from last to first in the course of three matches. Confidence from the national team's performance

INTERNATIONAL HONOURS
Copa Amilcar Cabral 1981 1982 1987 1988 2005   **CAF Champions League** Hafia Conakry 1972 1975 1977

permeated down to the under-23 team, who made it to the gold medal match at the All-Africa Games in Algiers, but had to settle for silver when Cameroon beat them 1-0. 2006 champions Fello Star Labé got a walkover into the second round of the 2007 African Champions League but were drawn against fancied Tunisian side Etoile du Sahel, who swiftly dispatched them 5-1 on aggregate. Satellite Conakry, who have close links with Belgian club Lokeren, lost 7-1 on aggregate in their meeting with Tunisian opposition in the African Confederation Cup. CS Sfaxien easily eliminated them in the second round of the competition.

THE FIFA BIG COUNT OF 2006

	Male	Female		Total
Number of players	406 600	3 500	Referees and Assistant Referees	433
Professionals	0		Admin, Coaches, Technical, Medical	2 400
Amateurs 18+	10 100		Number of clubs	150
Youth under 18	8 000		Number of teams	700
Unregistered	90 000		Clubs with women's teams	0
Total players	410 100		Players as % of population	4.23%

Fédération Guinéenne de Football (FGF)
PO Box 3645, Conakry, Guinea
Tel +224 455878   Fax +224 455879
guineefoot59@yahoo.fr   www.none
President: BANGOURA Aboubacar Bruno   General Secretary: CAMARA Fode Capi
Vice-President: CONTE Sory   Treasurer: DIALLO Mamadou   Media Officer: None
Men's Coach: NOUZARET Robert   Women's Coach: CAMARA Fabert
FGF formed: 1960   CAF: 1962   FIFA: 1962
Red shirts, Yellow shorts, Green socks

RECENT INTERNATIONAL MATCHES PLAYED BY GUINEA

2003 Opponents	Score	Venue	Comp	Scorers	Att	Referee
12-02 Mali	L 0-1	Toulon	Fr			
30-03 Niger	W 2-0	Conakry	CNq	Mansare [40p], Sylla.A [90]		Monteiro Duatre CPV
7-06 Niger	L 0-1	Niamey	CNq			Wellington GHA
21-06 Liberia	W 2-1	Accra	CNq	Soulemane 2 [11 50]		
6-07 Ethiopia	W 3-0	Conakry	CNq	Youla 2 [32 72], Feindouno [55]		
20-08 Tunisia	D 0-0	Radès/Tunis	Fr		20 000	
12-10 Mozambique	W 1-0	Conakry	WCq	Sambegou Bangoura [70]	13 400	Ndoye SEN
16-11 Mozambique	W 4-3	Maputo	WCq	Youla [14], Sambegou Bangoura 3 [21 35 54]	50 000	Mochubela RSA
2004						
20-01 Burkina Faso	W 1-0	Saint-Maxime	Fr	Camara.T [72]		
25-01 Congo DR	W 2-1	Tunis	CNr1	Camara.T [68], Feindouno [81]	3 000	Aboubacar CIV
28-01 Rwanda	D 1-1	Bizerte	CNr1	Camara.T [48]	4 000	Sowe GAM
1-02 Tunisia	D 1-1	Radès/Tunis	CNr1	Camara.T [84]	18 000	Tessema ETH
7-02 Mali	L 1-2	Bizerte	CNqf	Feindouno [15]	1 450	El Fatah EGY
28-04 Côte d'Ivoire	L 2-4	Aix-les-Bains	Fr	Feidouno [12], Oulare [39]	2 000	
29-05 Senegal	D 1-1	Paris	Fr	Diawara [24p]	2 000	Garibian FRA
20-06 Tunisia	W 2-1	Conakry	WCq	Diawara 2 [12 46]	15 300	Codjia BEN
3-07 Malawi	D 1-1	Lilongwe	WCq	Diawara [80]	11 383	Abdulkadir TAN
5-09 Botswana	W 4-0	Conakry	WCq	Feindouno [44], Youla [54], Diawara [60], Mansare [82]	25 000	Agbenyega GHA
10-10 Morocco	D 1-1	Conakry	WCq	Mansare [50]	25 000	Monteiro Duatre CPV
17-11 Kenya	L 1-2	Nairobi	WCq	Feindouno [19p]	16 000	Abd El Fatah EGY
2005						
9-02 Mali	D 2-2	Paris	Fr	Thiam [6], Feindouno [55]		
26-03 Morocco	L 0-1	Rabat	WCq		70 000	Coulibaly MLI
5-06 Kenya	W 1-0	Conakry	WCq	Sambegou Bangoura [68]	21 000	Mbera GAB
11-06 Tunisia	L 0-2	Tunis	WCq		30 000	Lim Kee Chong MRI
16-08 Congo DR	L 1-3	Paris	Fr	Ibrahima Bangoura [70]	2 000	Piccirillo FRA
4-09 Malawi	W 3-1	Conakry	WCq	Feindouno [12], Diawara [36], Sambegou Bangoura [67]	2 518	Mana NGA
8-10 Botswana	W 2-1	Gaborone	WCq	Ousmane Bangoura 2 [73 76]	16 800	Sowe GAM
18-11 Guinea-Bissau	D 2-2	Conakry	ACr1	Soumah [7], Camara.O [75]		
22-11 Sierra Leone	W 1-0	Conakry	ACr1	Diawara [19]		
25-11 Mali	D 0-0	Conakry	ACsf	W 6-5p		
27-11 Senegal †	W 1-0	Conakry	ACf	Barujakis [5]	30 000	
2006						
7-01 Togo	W 1-0	Viry-Chatillon	Fr	Bangoura.O [65p]	2 500	Piccirillo FRA
22-01 South Africa	W 2-0	Alexandria	CNr1	Sambegou Bangoura [76], Ousmane Bangoura [87]	10 000	Benouza ALG
26-01 Zambia	W 2-1	Alexandria	CNr1	Feindouno 2 [74p 90]	24 000	Imeire NGA
30-01 Tunisia	W 3-0	Alexandria	CNr1	Ousmane Bangoura [16], Feindouno [69], Diawara [90]	18 000	Maidin SIN
3-02 Senegal	L 2-3	Alexandria	CNqf	Diawara [24], Feindouno [95+]	17 000	Codjia BEN
16-08 Cameroon	D 1-1	Rouen	Fr	Mansare [70p]		Duhamel FRA
3-09 Algeria	D 0-0	Conakry	CNq			Coulibaly MLI
7-10 Cape Verde Islands	L 0-1	Praia	CNq			Diatta SEN
2007						
6-02 Côte d'Ivoire	L 0-1	Rouen	Fr			
24-03 Gambia	W 2-0	Bakau	CNq	Diawara [57], Feindouno [69]		Kotey GHA
3-06 Gambia	D 2-2	Conakry	CNq	Jabi [10], Mansare [53]		
16-06 Algeria	W 2-0	Algiers	CNq	Mansare [43], Feindouno [84]		

Fr = Friendly match • CN = CAF African Cup of Nations • AC = Amilcar Cabral Cup • WC = FIFA World Cup
q = qualifier • r1 = first round group • sf = semi-final • f = final • † = not a full international

GUINEA NATIONAL TEAM RECORDS AND RECORD SEQUENCES

Records			Sequence records				
Victory	14-0	MTN 1972	Wins	7	1972-1973	Clean sheets	7	1986-1987
Defeat	2-6	GHA 1975	Defeats	4	1984, 1998-1999	Goals scored	29	1973-1977
Player Caps	n/a		Undefeated	13	1980-1981	Without goal	6	1991
Player Goals	n/a		Without win	14	1983-1984	Goals against	14	1967-1969

REPUBLIC OF GUINEA; REPUBLIQUE DE GUINEE

Capital	Conakry	Language	French	Independence	1958
Population	9 690 222	Area	245 857 km²	% in cities	30%
GDP per cap	$2100	Dailling code	+224	Density	37 per km²
		Internet	.gn	GMT +/-	0

MAJOR CITIES/TOWNS
Population '000

1	Conakry	2 064
2	Nzérékoré	138
3	Kindia	122
4	Kankan	117
5	Kamsar	100
6	Kissidougou	46
7	Labé	44
8	Macenta	43
9	Siguiri	43
10	Mamou	41
11	Télimélé	30
12	Tougué	25
13	Pita	19
14	Boké	15
15	Kouroussa	14
16	Beyla	13
17	Koundara	13
18	Dabola	12
19	Dalaba	12
20	Tondon	12
21	Forécariah	12
22	Dubréka	10
23	Mandiana	10
24	Koubia	9

MEDALS TABLE

		Overall			L	C	Africa			
		G	S	B	G	G	G	S	B	City
1	Hafia Conakry	18	2		12	3	3	2		Conakry
2	Kaloum Star	16	1	2	11	5		1	2	Conakry
3	Horoya Conakry	14	2		9	4	1		2	Conakry
4	ASFAG Conakry	4			1	3				Conakry
5	Conakry II Kakimbo	3	1		3				1	Conakry
6	Fello Star Labé	3			1	2				Labé
	Satellite Conakry	3			2	1				Conakry
8	Olympique Kakandé	2				2				Boké
9	Etoile du Guinée	1				1				Conakry
	Mankona	1			1					

RECENT LEAGUE AND CUP RECORD

	Championship				Cup		
Year	Champions	Score	Runners-up		Winners	Score	Runners-up
2000	Hafia Conakry	†			Fello Stars Labé	2-1	Horoya Conakry
2001	Horoya Conakry	3-1	Satellite Conakry		Kaloum Stars		
2002	Satellite Conakry	3-2	Kaloum Star		Hafia Conakry	5-3	Satellite Conakry
2003	ASFAG Conakry	†			Etoile de Guinée		Etoile de Coléah
2004	No championship played				Fello Star Labé	2-2 5-4p	CIK Kamsar
2005	Satellite Conakry	†	Fello Star Labé		Kaloum Stars	0-0 5-4p	Gangan Kindia
2006	Fello Star Labé	†	Kaloum Star				

† Championship played on a league system

GUINEA 2006
CHAMPIONNAT NATIONAL FINAL STAGE

	Pl	W	D	L	F	A	Pts	FSL	KS	AC	HC	SC	AGB
Fello Star Labé	10	7	1	2	19	8	**22**		1-1	1-0	3-0	3-1	5-2
Kaloum Star	10	7	1	2	16	8	**22**	1-0		**3-0**	1-0	4-2	1-0
Athlético Coléah	9	4	1	4	8	9	**13**	2-1	0-1		1-2	2-1	2-0
Hafia Conakry	10	3	2	5	7	14	**11**	1-3	1-0	0-0		0-2	1-0
Satellite Conakry	10	2	2	6	11	16	**8**	0-1	2-3	0-1	1-1		2-1
Ashanti Golden Boys	9	2	1	6	8	14	**7**	0-1	2-1		3-1	0-0	

12/10/2006 - 2411/2006 • † Qualified for the CAF Champions League • Match in bold awarded 3-0

GUM – GUAM

NATIONAL TEAM RECORD
JULY 10TH 2006 TO JULY 12TH 2010

PL	W	D	L	F	A	%
3	0	0	0	3	30	0

FIFA/COCA-COLA WORLD RANKING

1993	1994	1995	1996	1997	1998	1999	2000	2001	2002	2003	2004	2005	2006	High		Low	
-	-	-	188	191	198	200	199	199	200	201	2005	204	198	182	08/96	205	12/04

2006–2007											
08/06	09/06	10/06	11/06	12/06	01/07	02/07	03/07	04/07	05/07	06/07	07/07
197	198	198	198	198	199	199	199	199	199	199	199

Guam have never won a full international match and there was never any danger of that changing at the qualifiers for the East Asian Championship played in Macau in June 2007. Chinese Taipei put ten past the Pacific Islanders, Hong Kong piled in with a massive 15 and even lowly Mongolia managed to find the back of the net five times. Guam did score three goals, however, scoring in consecutive matches for the first time ever, and there was the huge satisfaction of beating near neighbours Northern Marianas home and away in a preliminary round. A 3-2 win away in Saipan was followed by an impressive 9-0 win in Hagatna, a match that saw Guam play at home for only the

INTERNATIONAL HONOURS
None

fifth time in the 32 years since their first international. Remarkably this wasn't a record win for Guam. In 1998 they beat the Micronesian island of Yap 15-0, but as neither Micronesia or Northern Marianas are members of FIFA, the matches do not go down in the official record. In domestic competition Guam Shipyard won their fourth championship in five years. Having won the Spring League at the start of 2006, they were declared automatic champions after winning the Fall League too. In a shortened Spring League at the start of 2007, Guam Shipyard finished third behind winners Quality Distributers and the under-19 national team.

THE FIFA BIG COUNT OF 2006

	Male	Female		Total
Number of players	4 172	1 288	Referees and Assistant Referees	21
Professionals	0		Admin, Coaches, Technical, Medical	135
Amateurs 18+	457		Number of clubs	13
Youth under 18	1 943		Number of teams	195
Unregistered	675		Clubs with women's teams	7
Total players	5 460		Players as % of population	3.19%

Guam Football Association (GFA)
PO Box 5093, Hagatna, Guam 96932
Tel +1 671 6374321   Fax +1 671 6374323
info@guamfootball.com   www.guamfootball.com
President: LAI Richard   General Secretary: SAN GIL Valentino
Vice-President: ARTERO Pascual   Treasurer: LAI George   Media Officer: CEPEDA Joseph
Men's Coach: TSUKITATE Norio   Women's Coach: KIM Sang Hoon
GFA formed: 1975   AFC: 1996   FIFA: 1996
Blue shirts, White shorts, Blue socks

RECENT INTERNATIONAL MATCHES PLAYED BY GUAM

2003	Opponents	Score		Venue	Comp	Scorers	Att	Referee
24-02	Mongolia	L	0-2	Hong Kong	EACq		1 602	Huang Junjie CHN
26-02	Macao	L	0-2	Hong Kong	EACq		672	Cheung Yim Yau HKG
28-02	Chinese Taipei	L	0-7	Hong Kong	EACq		1 814	
2-03	Hong Kong	L	0-11	Hong Kong	EACq		6 862	Huang Junjie CHN
23-04	Bhutan	L	0-6	Thimphu	ACq			
25-04	Mongolia	L	0-5	Thimphu	ACq			
2004								
No international matches played in 2004								
2005								
5-03	Chinese Taipei	L	0-9	Taipei	EACq			
7-03	Hong Kong	L	0-15	Taipei	EACq			
9-03	Mongolia	L	1-4	Taipei	EACq	Pangelinan [69]		
11-03	Korea DPR	L	0-21	Taipei	EACq			
2006								
1-04	Palestine	L	0-11	Dhaka	CCr1		3 000	AK Nema IRQ
3-04	Bangladesh	L	0-3	Dhaka	CCr1		18 000	U Win Cho MYA
6-04	Cambodia	L	0-3	Dhaka	CCr1		500	U Win Cho MYA
2007								
25-03	Northern Marianas †	W	3-2	Saipan	EACq	Jamison [9], Pangelinan 2 [65 78]		
1-04	Northern Marianas †	W	9-0	Hagatna	EACq	Pangelinan 5 [6 21 42 54 61], Mendoza [56], Merfalen [57], Jamison [85], Calvo [90]	1 324	
17-06	Chinese Taipei	L	0-10	Macau	EACq			
21-06	Hong Kong	L	1-15	Macau	EACq			
23-06	Mongolia	L	2-5	Macau	EACq			

EAC = East Asian Championship • AC = AFC Asian Cup • CC = AFC Challenge Cup
q = qualifier • r1 = first round group • † Not an official international

GUAM NATIONAL TEAM RECORDS AND RECORD SEQUENCES

Records			Sequence records					
Victory	-	Yet to win a match	Wins	0		Clean sheets	0	
Defeat	0-21	PRK 2005	Defeats	37	1975-	Goals scored	1	
Player Caps	n/a		Undefeated	0		Without goal	15	1996-2005
Player Goals	n/a		Without win	37	1975-	Goals against	32	1975-2006

RECENT LEAGUE AND CUP RECORD

Overall Champions				Spring League				Fall League		
Year	Winners	Score	Runners-up	Winners	Score	Runners-up		Winners	Score	Runners-up
1999	Silver Bullets			Carpet One				Silver Bullets		
2000	Silver Bullets	4-2	Navy	Silver Bullets				Navy	4-3	Anderson
2001				Silver Bullets	4-1	Lai National		Staywell Zoom	2-1	Guam Insurance
2002	Guam Shipyard	‡		Guam Shipyard	2-0	Guam Insurance		Guam Shipyard	4-2	IT&E Pumas
2003	Guam Shipyard	‡		Guam Shipyard	2-1	Quality Distrib's		Guam Shipyard	†	
2004	Under-18	‡		Under-18	5-0	IT&E Pumas		Under-18	4-0	Guam Shipyard
2005	Guam Shipyard	‡		Guam Shipyard	6-0	Quality Distrib's		Guam Shipyard	4-3	Crushers
2006	Guam Shipyard	‡		Guam Shipyard	6-1	Quality Distrib's		Guam Shipyard	†	Under-17
2007				Quality Distrib's	†	Under-19				

‡ Won both stages so automatic champions • † Played on a league system • Guam Shipyard previously known as Silver Bullets

GUAM COUNTRY INFORMATION

Capital	Hagatna	Independence	Unincorporated territory of the USA	GDP per Capita	$21 000
Population	166 090	Status		GNP Ranking	n/a
Area km²	549	Language	English	Dialling code	+1 671
Population density	302 per km²	Literacy rate	99%	Internet code	.GU
% in urban areas	n/a	Main religion	Christian 99%	GMT +/-	+10
Towns/Cities ('000)	Tamuning 11; Mangilao 8; Yigo 8; Astumbo 5; Barrigada 4; Agat 4; Ordot 4				
Neighbours (km)	North Pacific Ocean 125				
Main stadia	Wettengel Rugby Field – Hagatna				

GUY – GUYANA

NATIONAL TEAM RECORD
JULY 10TH 2006 TO JULY 12TH 2010

PL	W	D	L	F	A	%
12	10	1	1	34	9	87.5

FIFA/COCA-COLA WORLD RANKING

1993	1994	1995	1996	1997	1998	1999	2000	2001	2002	2003	2004	2005	2006	High		Low	
136	154	162	153	168	161	171	183	178	169	182	182	167	100	95	03/07	185	02/04

2006–2007											
08/06	09/06	10/06	11/06	12/06	01/07	02/07	03/07	04/07	05/07	06/07	07/07
120	120	106	105	100	100	104	95	99	98	98	100

Simply stunning. That has to be the verdict on Guyana's 13-match winning run that started in September 2005 and carried on until the end of 2006. Had they managed to beat St Vincent in the first round of the Digicel Caribbean Cup finals in January 2007, Guyana would have equalled the world record of 14 consecutive wins held by Australia, Brazil and France. In all, Guyana went 14 matches unbeaten spanning the whole of 2005 and 2006. 'The sleeping giant of Caribbean football which is about to awake' is how coach Jamaal Shabazz described his team. At the Digicel Caribbean Cup finals in Trinidad the defeat against St Vincent was followed by a good win over

INTERNATIONAL HONOURS
None

CONCACAF Gold Cup semi-finalists Guadeloupe and a draw with Cuba but they finished third on goal difference with Cuba progressing to the semi-finals and also to the Gold Cup finals. It was a sad end to two extraordinary years for the likes of Gregory Richardson, Nigel Codrington and Randolph Jerome, who between them had contributed 27 goals to Guyana's cause. In domestic football, Alpha United won the Georgetown League in 2006, finishing 10 points ahead of Pele FC in second place. Pele FC did win two Cup tournaments - the Fruta Challenge and Mayor's Cup whilst Joe Public of Trinidad won the Kashif and Shanghai Cup.

THE FIFA BIG COUNT OF 2006

	Male	Female		Total
Number of players	43 000	7 740	Referees and Assistant Referees	95
Professionals		0	Admin, Coaches, Technical, Medical	650
Amateurs 18+		3 240	Number of clubs	90
Youth under 18		4 600	Number of teams	270
Unregistered		12 800	Clubs with women's teams	8
Total players		50 740	Players as % of population	6.61%

Guyana Football Federation (GFF)
Lot 17 Dadanawa Street, Section K, Campbellville, PO Box 10727, Georgetown, Guyana
Tel +592 2 278758   Fax +592 2 262641
gff@networksgy.com   www.guyanaff.com
President: KLASS Colin   General Secretary: RUTHERFORD George
Vice-President: CALLENDER Winston   Treasurer: HENRY Aubrey   Media Officer: GRANGER Frederick
Men's Coach: SHABAZZ Jamaal   Women's Coach: SHABAZZ Jamaal
GFF formed: 1902   CONCACAF: 1969   FIFA: 1968
Green shirts, Green shorts, Yellow socks

RECENT INTERNATIONAL MATCHES PLAYED BY GUYANA

2002 Opponents	Score	Venue	Comp	Scorers	Att	Referee
28-07 Netherlands Antilles	W 2-1	Georgetown	CCq	Cole [6], Forbes [56]		
11-08 Netherlands Antilles	L 0-1	Willemstad	CCq	L 2-3p		Villar-Polo ARU
2003						
No international matches played in 2003						
2004						
15-02 Barbados	W 2-0	Bridgetown	Fr	Hernandez [59], Richardson [86]	1 200	Small BRB
28-02 Grenada	L 0-5	St George's	WCq		7 000	Archundia MEX
2-03 Trinidad and Tobago	L 0-1	Tunapuna	Fr			Randham TRI
14-03 Grenada	L 1-3	Blairmont	WCq	Harris [29]	1 200	Quesada Cordero CRC
2005						
13-02 Barbados	D 3-3	Bridgetown	Fr	Richardson [21], Cadogan [36], Abrams [71]	6 000	Callender BRB
30-09 Dominica	W 3-0	Linden	Fr	Abrams [10], Parks [60], Manning [81]		Lancaster GUY
2-10 Dominica	W 3-0	Georgetown	Fr	McKinnon 2 [19 42], Codrington [85]		Kia SUR
2006						
24-02 Antigua and Barbuda	W 2-1	Linden	Fr	Abrams [3], Codrington [61]		James GUY
26-02 Antigua and Barbuda	W 4-1	Linden	Fr	Pollard [34], Abrams [37], Beveney 2 [40 66]		Lancaster GUY
28-07 St Lucia	W 3-2	Linden	Fr	Jerome [5], Hernandez [29], McKinnon [91+]		Lancaster GUY
30-07 St Lucia	W 2-0	Georgetown	Fr	Pollard [74], Codrington [80p]		James GUY
2-09 Barbados	W 1-0	Bridgetown	Fr	Jerome [44p]	2 000	Forde BRB
6-09 Surinam	W 5-0	Willemstad	CCq	Richardson [4], Codrington 2 [15 73], Jerome [42], Abrams [89]		
8-09 Netherlands Antilles	W 5-0	Willemstad	CCq	Richardson [35], Codrington [58], Bishop [65], Abrams [84], Jerome [89]		
10-09 Grenada	W 1-0	Willemstad	CCq	Bishop [46]		Angela ARU
24-11 Antigua and Barbuda	W 6-0	Georgetown	CCq	Richardson 2 [3 12], Jerome 2 [35 54], Codrington [75], McKinnon [77]	5 000	
26-11 Guadeloupe	W 3-2	Georgetown	CCq	Codrington 2 [22 66], Richardson [24]	5 000	
28-11 Dominican Republic	W 4-0	Georgetown	CCq	Richardson [45], Jerome [49], Codrington [57p], Hercules [79]		
2007						
14-01 St Vincent/Grenadines	L 0-2	Marabella	CCr1			
16-01 Guadeloupe	W 4-3	Marabella	CCr1	Codrington 3 [23p 60 81], Lowe [66]		
18-01 Cuba	D 0-0	Marabella	CCr1			

Fr = Friendly match • GC = CONCACAF Gold Cup • WC = FIFA World Cup • q = qualifier

GUYANA NATIONAL TEAM RECORDS AND RECORD SEQUENCES

Records			Sequence records				
Victory	14-0	AIA 1998	Wins	13	2005-2006	Clean sheets	6	2005-2006
Defeat	0-9	MEX 1987	Defeats	8	1987-1990	Goals scored	15	2004-2006
Player Caps	n/a		Undefeated	14	2005-2006	Without goal	7	1987-1990
Player Goals	n/a		Without win	10	1987-1990	Goals against	13	1992-1996

GUYANA COUNTRY INFORMATION

Capital	Georgetown	Independence	1966 from the UK	GDP per Capita	$4 000
Population	705 803	Status	Republic within Commonwealth	GNP Ranking	163
Area km²	214 970	Language	English	Dialling code	+592
Population density	3 per km²	Literacy rate	98%	Internet code	.gy
% in urban areas	36%	Main religion	Christian 50%, Hindu 35%	GMT +/–	-4
Towns/Cities ('000)	Georgetown 235; Linden 44; New Amsterdam 35; Corriverton 12; Bartica 11				
Neighbours (km)	Surinam 600; Brazil 1 119; Venezuela 743; Caribbean Sea 459				
Main stadia	Georgetown Football Stadium – Georgetown 2 000				

FRUTA FESTIVAL 2006

First round		Quarter-finals		Semi-finals		Final	
Pele	2						
Ann's Grove United	0	Pele	1				
GDF	0	Mocha Champs	0				
Mocha Champs	1			Pele	1		
Timehri Panthers	2			Pouderoyen	0		
Fruta Conquerors	1	Timehri Panthers	1				
Beacon	0	Pouderoyen	1				
Pouderoyen	2					Pele	1
Alpha United	6					Western Tigers	0
Buxton United	3	Alpha United	3				
Amelia's Ward	0	Santos	0				
Santos	2			Alpha United	1		
Campdown	5			Western Tigers	2		
Grove Hi-Tech	0	Campdown	0				
Young Achievers	1	Western Tigers	2				
Western Tigers	5						

CUP FINAL
4-11-2006
Scorer - Shawn Bishop for Pele

Third place: Alpha United 2-1 Pouderoyen

KASHIF & SHANGHAI CUP 2006-07

First round		Quarter-finals		Semi-finals		Final	
Joe Public	4						
Blueberry Hill	0	Joe Public	3				
Victoria Kings	2	Pele	0				
Pele	3			Joe Public	2		
Santos	1			Alpha United	0		
Pouderoyen	0	Santos	1				
Rusal FC	0	Alpha United	2				
Alpha United	2					Joe Public	1
Western Tigers						Topp XX	0
Mabouya Valley		Western Tigers	1				
Den Amstel	0	Team Guyana USA	0				
Team Guyana USA	4			Western Tigers	0		
Camptown	2			Topp XX	2		
Silver Shattas	0	Camptown	0				
BV Triumph United	0	Topp XX	1				
Topp XX	2						

CUP FINAL
McKenzie Sports Club, Linden
1-01-2007
Scorer - Gary Glasgow [41] for Joe Public

Third place: Alpha United 6-0 Western Tigers

MAYOR'S CUP 2007

First round		Quarter-finals		Semi-finals		Final	
Pele	0						
Den Amstel	0	Pele	5				
Pouderoyen	0	Campdown	0				
Campdown	2			Pele	7		
Western Tigers	1 3p			Victoria Kings	0		
Uprising	1 2p	Western Tigers	1				
Police	0	Victoria Kings	2				
Victoria Kings	1					Pele	2
Topp XX						Fruta Conquerors	1
GDF		Topp XX	4				
BV Triumph United	0	Alpha United	3				
Alpha United	4			Topp XX	1		
Santos	2			Fruta Conquerors	2		
Mocha Champs	0	Santos	0 3p				
Uitvlugt	0	Fruta Conquerors	0 5p				
Fruta Conquerors	4						

CUP FINAL
25-02-2007
Scorer - Shawn Bishop for Pele

Third place: Topp XX 3-0 Victoria Kings

HAI – HAITI

NATIONAL TEAM RECORD
JULY 10TH 2006 TO JULY 12TH 2010

PL	W	D	L	F	A	%
27	14	6	7	45	22	62.9

FIFA/COCA-COLA WORLD RANKING

1993	1994	1995	1996	1997	1998	1999	2000	2001	2002	2003	2004	2005	2006	High	Low
145	132	153	114	125	109	99	84	82	72	96	95	98	102	72 12/02	155 04/96

				2006–2007							
08/06	09/06	10/06	11/06	12/06	01/07	02/07	03/07	04/07	05/07	06/07	07/07
123	118	83	92	102	92	92	88	86	85	95	92

For 14 years Jamaica and Trinidad had held an iron grip on the Caribbean Championship, but that all changed in January 2007 when, against the odds, Haiti won the Digicel Caribbean Cup after beating Trinidad 2-1 in the final in Port of Spain. It was an historic victory and on their return home the team was greeted by over 50,000 ecstatic fans at the airport. Alexandre Boucicaut and Fucien Brunel were the heroes for Haiti, scoring the goals in the final, but after Trinidad pulled the score back to 2-1, it took a steadfast rearguard action to secure the title, as well as qualification for the CONCACAF Gold Cup. There was to be no repeat of the heroics in America, however, as Luis

INTERNATIONAL HONOURS
Qualified for the FIFA World Cup finals 1974

CCCF Championship 1957   **CFU Caribbean Championship** 2007   **CONCACAF Champions Cup** Racing Club 1963 Violette 1984

Amelia Garcia's team bowed out meekly in the first round. At home, a change to the timings of the season saw the usual opening and closing championship abandoned for a 45 match three stage tournament held over the course of 12 months in which the eight clubs with the highest aggregate number of points qualified for the play-offs. Baltimore St Marc continued their recent fine run by beating Racing Club on penalties in the final and they then won the restored opening championship in the first half of 2007 to make it four titles in a row.

THE FIFA BIG COUNT OF 2006

	Male	Female		Total
Number of players	376 278	75 446	Referees and Assistant Referees	234
Professionals	100		Admin, Coaches, Technical, Medical	2 090
Amateurs 18+	7 664		Number of clubs	310
Youth under 18	15 844		Number of teams	1 200
Unregistered	83 300		Clubs with women's teams	30
Total players	451 724		Players as % of population	5.44%

Fédération Haïtienne de Football (FHF)
128 Avenue Christiophe, Case postale 2258, Port-au-Prince, Haiti
Tel +509 2440115   Fax +509 2440117
jbyves@yahoo.com   www.haitifoot.com
President: JEAN-BART Yves Dr   General Secretary: DESIR Lionel
Vice-President: JEAN MARIE Georges   Treasurer: BERTIN Eddy   Media Officer: CHARLES M. Louis
Men's Coach: GARCIA Luis   Women's Coach: LAMARRE Wilnea
FHF formed: 1904   CONCACAF: 1961   FIFA: 1933
Blue shirts, Red shorts, Blue socks

RECENT INTERNATIONAL MATCHES PLAYED BY HAITI

2004	Opponents	Score		Venue	Comp	Scorers	Att	Referee
12-06	Jamaica	D	1-1	Miami	WCq	Peguero [50]	30 000	Stott USA
20-06	Jamaica	L	0-3	Kingston	WCq			Sibrian SLV
18-08	Brazil	L	0-6	Port-au-Prince	Fr		15 000	Oliveira BRA
24-11	US Virgin Islands	W	11-0	Kingston	CCq	Mesidor 3 [13 30 48], Ulcena 2 [15 78], Saint-Preux [33], Chery 2 [40 90], Lormera [57], Germain [64], Thelamour [87]	250	Piper TRI
26-11	Saint-Martin †	W	2-0	Montego Bay	CCq	Bruny [25], Thelamour [67]	500	Brizan TRI
28-11	Jamaica	L	1-3	Kingston	CCq	Ulcena [41]	4 000	Piper TRI
12-12	St Kitts and Nevis	W	1-0	Fort Lauderdale	CCq	Cadet [62]		McNab BAH
15-12	St Kitts and Nevis	W	2-0	Basseterre	CCq	Cadet [16], Dorcelus [70]		Bhimull TRI
2005								
9-01	Cuba	L	0-1	Port-au-Prince	CCq		15 000	Minyetti DOM
12-01	Costa Rica	D	3-3	San Jose	Fr	Cadet 2 [18 39], Germain [90]		Porras CRC
16-01	Cuba	D	1-1	Havana	CCq	Cadet [59]		Brizan TRI
1-02	Trinidad and Tobago	L	0-1	Port of Spain	Fr			
3-02	Trinidad and Tobago	L	1-2	Port of Spain	Fr	Romulus [47]		
6-02	Trinidad and Tobago	W	1-0	Scarborough	Fr	Germain [19p]		
13-02	Guatemala	L	1-2	Fort Lauderdale	Fr	Cadet [61]	10 000	Salazar USA
2006								
16-08	Guatemala	D	1-1	Miami	Fr	Dorcelus [60]	15 000	
15-09	Dominican Republic	W	3-1	Saint-Marc	Fr	Francois [13], Saint-Cyr [66], Cadet [92+]		
17-09	Dominican Republic	W	2-1	Port-au-Prince	Fr	Fritzson [26], Saint-Jean [79p]		
27-09	St Vincent/Grenadines	W	4-0	Kingston	CCq	Mayard [18], Ftitzson [54], Jean-Jacques [79], Gracien [90]	3 000	Forde BRB
29-09	St Lucia	W	7-1	Kingston	CCq	Jamil 2 [4 13], Fritzson 2 [17 83], Chéry [42], Neol [64], Mayard [81]	3 000	Callendar BRB
1-10	Jamaica	L	0-2	Kingston	CCq		3 000	Brizan TRI
17-10	Cuba	D	0-0	Port-au-Prince	Fr			
19-10	Cuba	L	0-1	Cap-Haitien	Fr			
8-11	Cuba	L	1-2	Fort-de-France	CCq	Fritzson [88]		
10-11	Martinique	L	0-1	Fort-de-France	CCq			
12-11	Surinam	D	1-1	Fort-de-France	CCq	Jamil [78p]		
2007								
7-01	Bermuda	W	2-0	Couva	CCq	Cadet [9], Lormera [72]		Brizan TRI
9-01	Bermuda	W	3-0	Couva	CCq	Cadet 2 [25 90], Boucicaut [63]		Davis TRI
12-01	Martinique	W	1-0	Port of Spain	CCr1	Brunel [12]		
15-01	Barbados	W	2-0	Port of Spain	CCr1	Boucicaut [55], Lormera [91+]		
17-01	Trinidad and Tobago	L	1-3	Port of Spain	CCr1	Brunel [54]		
20-01	Guadeloupe	W	3-1	Port of Spain	CCsf	Cadet [56], Brunel [65], Fritzson [76]		
23-01	Trinidad and Tobago	W	2-1	Port of Spain	CCf	Boucicaut [23], Brunel [52]		Moreno PAN
24-03	Panama	W	3-0	Miami	Fr	Cadet [28], Brunel [53], Saint-Jean [86]	12 000	
17-04	El Salvador	W	1-0	San Salvador	Fr	Noncent [92+]		
19-04	Honduras	W	3-1	La Ceiba	Fr	Boucicaut [40], Cadet [69], Germain [77]		Soriano HON
23-05	Chile	D	0-0	Port-au-Prince	Fr			
28-05	Trinidad and Tobago	L	0-1	Port of Spain	Fr			
30-05	St Vincent/Grenadines	W	3-0	Port of Spain	Fr	Alcenat 2 [38 59], Pierre-Louis [67]		
6-06	Guadeloupe	D	1-1	Miami	GCr1	Chery [35p]	17 420	Vaughn USA
9-06	Costa Rica	D	1-1	Miami	GCr1	Boucicaut [71]	22 529	Campbell JAM
11-06	Canada	L	0-2	Miami	GCr1		15 892	

Fr = Friendly match • CC = Digicel Caribbean Cup • GC = CONCACAF Gold Cup • WC = FIFA World Cup
q = qualifier • † Not a full international

HAITI NATIONAL TEAM RECORDS AND RECORD SEQUENCES

Records			Sequence records					
Victory	12-1	VIR 2001	Wins	8	1979	Clean sheets	5	1997-1998
Defeat	1-9	BRA 1959	Defeats	6	1974-75, 1984-89	Goals scored	12	1997-1999
Player Caps	n/a		Undefeated	18	1977-1980	Without goal	6	1973-1974
Player Goals	n/a		Without win	12	1973-1975	Goals against	9	1974-1975

HAITI COUNTRY INFORMATION

Capital	Port-au-Prince	Independence	1804 from France	GDP per Capita	$1 600
Population	7 656 166	Status	Republic	GNP Ranking	122
Area km²	27 750	Language	French	Dialling code	+509
Population density	275 per km²	Literacy rate	52%	Internet code	.ht
% in urban areas	32%	Main religion	Christian 96%	GMT +/–	-5
Towns/Cities ('000)	Port-au-Prince 1 234; Carrefour 439; Delmas 377; Cap-Haïtien 134; Pétionville 108				
Neighbours (km)	Dominican Republic 360; Atlantic Ocean & Caribbean Sea 1 771				
Main stadia	Stade Sylvio Cator – Port-au-Prince 10 500; Park St Victor – Cap-Haïtien 7 500				

HAITI 2006 DIVISION 1

	Pl	W	D	L	F	A	Pts
Don Bosco †	45	22	12	11	56	31	78
Aigle Noir †	45	23	9	13	62	39	78
Baltimore St Marc †	45	19	15	11	40	28	72
Cavaly Léogâne †	45	17	18	10	47	34	69
Racing Club Haïtien †	45	16	18	11	36	25	66
AS Mirebalais †	45	17	13	15	43	32	64
Zénith Cap Haïtien †	45	15	19	11	40	34	64
Victory FC †	45	17	12	16	47	39	63
Racing Gônaïves	45	15	15	15	45	40	60
Violette AC	45	15	15	15	45	40	60
Tempête St Marc	45	16	12	17	35	39	60
Roulado Gônaïves	45	13	17	15	43	56	56
AS Capoise	45	14	13	18	48	56	55
AS Carrefour	45	11	11	23	36	53	44
Dynamite St Marc	45	7	19	19	28	68	40
US Frères Pétion-Ville	45	7	14	24	27	64	35

4/11/2005 - 26/11/2006 • † Qualified for Super Huit play-offs

HAITI 2006 SUPER HUIT PLAY-OFFS

Quarter–finals		Semi–finals		Final	
Baltimore *	1 2				
Mirebalais	2 0	Baltimore	3 1		
Aigle Noir *	1 0	Zénith *	1 1		
Zénith	2 1			Baltimore	1 5p
Victory	1 1			Racing Club	1 4p
Don Bosco *	0 1	Victory	0 1 1p		
Cavaly	1 0	Racing Club *	1 0 4p	23-12-2006	
Racing Club *	0 2	* Home team in first leg			

HAITI 2007 DIVISION 1 OUVERTURE

	Pl	W	D	L	F	A	Pts
Baltimore St Marc	15	9	5	1	19	7	32
Cavaly Léogâne	15	6	8	1	14	5	26
AS Mirebalais	15	6	6	3	12	7	24
Zénith Cap Haïtien	15	6	5	4	16	15	23
Violette AC	15	5	7	3	13	7	22
Tempête St Marc	15	5	7	3	14	13	22
AS Capoise	15	5	7	3	12	12	22
AS Carrefour	15	5	6	4	15	14	21
Don Bosco	15	6	3	6	14	14	21
Racing Gônaïves	15	5	6	4	11	13	21
Victory FC	15	5	5	5	15	11	20
Aigle Noir	15	5	4	6	13	11	19
Racing Club Haïtien	15	4	5	6	11	14	17
AS Rive Artibonitienne	15	3	3	9	9	19	12
Roulado Gônaïves	15	2	4	9	13	21	10
AS Grand Goâve	15	0	5	10	5	23	5

24/02/2007 - 13/05/2007

RECENT LEAGUE RECORD

Championnat Fermature/Ouverture from 2007				Championnat Ouverture/Fermature from 2007			
Year Champions	Pts	Runners-up	Pts	Champions	Pts	Runners-up	Pts
2001				Roulado Gônaïves	33	Aigle Noir	26
2002 Racing Club	31	Aigle Noir	29	Don Bosco †	30	Cavaly Léogâne	30
2003 Roulado Gônaïves	27	Victory FC	27	Championship cancelled ‡			
2004 Championship cancelled ‡				AS Mirebalais	32	Racing Club	31
2005 Baltimore St Marc	31	Zénith Cap Haïtien	26	Baltimore St Marc	32	Racing Gônaïves	31
2006 Baltimore St Marc	††	Racing Club					
2007 Baltimore St Marc	32	Cavaly Léogâne	26				

† Play-off: Don Bosco 2-0 1-0 Cavaly Léogâne • ‡ Don Bosco and Roulado played in a match of champions in October 2004 with Roulado winning 5-4 on penalties after a 0-0 draw • †† Baltimore 1-1 5-4p Racing Club Haïtiene

HKG – HONG KONG

NATIONAL TEAM RECORD
JULY 10TH 2006 TO JULY 12TH 2010

PL	W	D	L	F	A	%
10	3	3	4	23	13	45

FIFA/COCA-COLA WORLD RANKING

1993	1994	1995	1996	1997	1998	1999	2000	2001	2002	2003	2004	2005	2006	High		Low	
112	98	111	124	129	136	122	123	137	150	142	133	117	117	90	02/96	154	02/03

2006–2007											
08/06	09/06	10/06	11/06	12/06	01/07	02/07	03/07	04/07	05/07	06/07	07/07
120	109	120	117	117	117	111	108	109	109	115	128

In April 2006, South China, Hong Kong's oldest and most famous club, seemed destined to be relegated for the first time ever, but an expansion of the League from eight to ten clubs saved the Caroliners and they made the most of their reprieve by winning the treble in 2007. South China won two of the three knockout tournaments played and then clinched the League with a last day win against Lanwa. This match was played at Dongguan in China, home of Lanwa, the latest of a number of Chinese clubs to try their luck in Hong Kong competition. It was South China's 28th title and came largely thanks to their Brazilian strike partnership of Detinho and Tales Schutz who,

INTERNATIONAL HONOURS
None

with 17 goals, was the League's top scorer. Pity poor Kitchee, though, who having finished level on points with South China missed out on what would have been their first championship since 1964 due to a worse head-to-head record. In the Asian Championship qualifiers, Hong Kong had a better than expected campaign, beating Bangladesh home and away and drawing twice against Uzbekistan, but it was not enough to see them into the finals. In the East Asian Championship preliminaries in Macau, Hong Kong managed a huge 15-1 win over Guam, but they then fell to a late goal against North Korea in the final to lose out on the only qualifying place.

THE FIFA BIG COUNT OF 2006

	Male	Female		Total
Number of players	139 960	9 996	Referees and Assistant Referees	149
Professionals	211		Admin, Coaches, Technical, Medical	910
Amateurs 18+	2 203		Number of clubs	82
Youth under 18	1 762		Number of teams	582
Unregistered	50 780		Clubs with women's teams	2
Total players	149 956		Players as % of population	2.16%

The Hong Kong Football Association Ltd (HKFA)
55 Fat Kwong Street, Homantin, Kowloon, Hong Kong
Tel +852 27129122   Fax +852 27604303
hkfa@hkfa.com   www.hkfa.com
President: FOK Timothy Tsun Ting   General Secretary: LAM Martin
Vice-President: HONG Martin   Treasurer: LI Sonny   Media Officer: TBD
Men's Coach: LEE Kin Woo   Women's Coach: TBD
HKFA formed: 1914   AFC: 1954   FIFA: 1954
Red shirts, Red shorts, Red socks

RECENT INTERNATIONAL MATCHES PLAYED BY HONG KONG

2003	Opponents		Score	Venue	Comp	Scorers	Att	Referee
6-11	Uzbekistan	L	1-4	Tashkent	ACq	Law Chun Bong [45]		
8-11	Tajikistan	D	0-0	Tashkent	ACq			
10-11	Thailand	W	2-1	Tashkent	ACq	Siang Sai Ho [28], Wong Sun Liu [69]		
17-11	Thailand	L	0-4	Bangkok	ACq			
19-11	Uzbekistan	L	0-1	Bangkok	ACq			
21-11	Tajikistan	L	0-1	Bangkok	ACq			
4-12	Korea Republic	L	1-3	Tokyo	EAC	Akandu [34]	14 895	Napitupulu IDN
7-12	Japan	L	0-1	Saitama	EAC		45 145	Piromya THA
10-12	China PR	L	1-3	Yokohama	EAC	Lo Chi Kwan [75]	17 400	Piromya THA
2004								
18-02	Malaysia	W	3-1	Kuantan	WCq	Ng Wai Chiu [17], Chu Siu Kei [84], Kwok Yue Hung [93+]	12 000	Nagalingham SIN
31-03	China PR	L	0-1	Hong Kong	WCq		9 000	Rungklay THA
9-06	Kuwait	L	0-4	Kuwait City	WCq		9 000	Najm LIB
8-09	Kuwait	L	0-2	Hong Kong	WCq		1 500	Busurmankulov KGZ
13-10	Malaysia	W	2-0	Hong Kong	WCq	Chu Siu Kei [5], Wong Chun Yue [51]	2 425	Ahamd Rakhil MAS
17-11	China PR	L	0-7	Guangzhou	WCq		20 300	Lee Jong Kuk KOR
30-11	Singapore	D	0-0	Singapore	Fr	W 6-5p	3 359	
2-12	Myanmar	D	2-2	Singapore	Fr	Feng Ji Zhi, Law Chun Bong	2 000	
2005								
9-02	Brazil	L	1-7	Hong Kong	Fr	Lee Sze Ming [85]	23 425	Zhou Weixin CHN
5-03	Mongolia	W	6-0	Taipei	EACq	Chu Siu Kei [30p], Law Chun Bong [48], Wong Chun Yue [50], Lam Ka Wai [73], Chan Yiu Lun 2 [92 93]		
7-03	Guam	W	15-0	Taipei	EACq	Chan Wai Ho [1], Chan Siu Ki 7 [8 18 28 30 36 42 87], Chan Yiu Lun 2 [16 31], Wong Chun Yue 3 [24 43 45], Chu Siu Kei [67], Poon Man Tik [89]		
11-03	Chinese Taipei	W	5-0	Taipei	EACq	Chan Yiu Lun 2 [7 45], Lam Ka Wai [20], Poon Yiu Cheuk [58p], Cheung Sai Ho [60]		
13-03	Korea DPR	L	0-2	Taipei	EACq			
29-05	Macao	W	8-1	Hong Kong	Fr	Chan Siu Ki 3, Lee Chi Ho, Lam Ka Wei, Leung Sze Chung, Cheng Lai Hin		
2006								
29-01	Denmark	L	0-3	Hong Kong	Fr		16 841	Iemoto JPN
1-02	Croatia	L	0-4	Hong Kong	Fr		13 971	Iemoto JPN
15-02	Singapore	D	1-1	Hong Kong	Fr	Ambassa Guy [65]	610	Ong Kim Heng MAS
18-02	India	D	2-2	Hong Kong	Fr	Ambassa Guy [3], Law Chun Bong [17]	3 672	Jae Yong Bae KOR
22-02	Qatar	L	0-3	Hong Kong	ACq		1 806	Nishimura JPN
1-03	Bangladesh	W	1-0	Dhaka	ACq	Chan Siu Ki [82]	1 000	Sarkar IND
3-06	Macao	D	0-0	Macao	Fr			
12-08	Singapore	L	1-2	Hong Kong	Fr	Lee Sze Ming [68]		
16-08	Uzbekistan	D	2-2	Tashkent	ACq	Sham Kwok Keung 2 [66 87]	15 000	Shaban KUW
6-09	Uzbekistan	D	0-0	Hong Kong	ACq		7 608	Lee Gi Young KOR
11-10	Qatar	L	0-2	Doha	ACq		1 000	Kousa SYR
15-11	Bangladesh	W	2-0	Hong Kong	ACq	Ambassa Guy 2 [43 74p]	1 273	Kim Dong Jin KOR
2007								
1-06	Indonesia	L	0-3	Jakarta	Fr			
10-06	Macau	W	2-1	Hong Kong	Fr	Chan Siu Ki 2 [24 66]		
19-06	Chinese Taipei	D	1-1	Macau	EACq	Lo Chi Kwan [56]		
21-06	Guam	W	15-1	Macau	EACq			
24-06	Dorea DPR	L	0-1	Macau	EACq			

Fr = Friendly match • EAC = East Asian Championship • AC = AFC Asian Cup • WC = FIFA World Cup • q = qualifier

HONG KONG NATIONAL TEAM RECORDS AND RECORD SEQUENCES

Records			Sequence records					
Victory	15-0	GUM 2005	Wins	7	1985	Clean sheets	4	2003
Defeat	0-7	CHN 1980 2004	Defeats	9	1977-1979	Goals scored	24	1949-1958
Player Caps	n/a		Undefeated	10	1984-1985	Without goal	7	1988-1989
Player Goals	n/a		Without win	13	1967-1968	Goals against	23	1992-1995

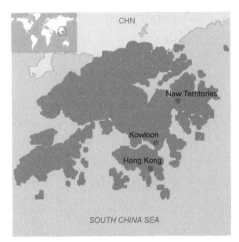

MAJOR CITIES/TOWNS

Population '000

1	Sha Tin, NT	628
2	Eastern, HKI	616
3	Kwun Tong, Kowloon	562
4	Tuen Mun, NT	488
5	Kwai Tsing, NT	477
6	Yuen Long, NT	449
7	Wong Tai Sin, Kowloon	444
8	Kowloon City	381
9	Sham Shui Po, Kowloon	353
10	Sai Kung, NT	327
11	Tai Po, NT	310
12	North, NT	298
13	Southern, HKI	290
14	Yau Tsim Mong, Kowloon	282
15	Tsuen Wan, NT	275
16	Central & Western, HKI	261
17	Wan Chai, HKI	167
18	Islands, NT	86

NT = New Territories
HKI = Hong Kong Island

HONG KONG SPECIAL ADMINISTRATIVE REGION; XIANGGANG TEBIE XINGZHENGQU

Capital	Victoria	Language	Cantonese, English			Independence	n/a
Population	6 980 412	Area	1 092 km^2	Density	6 277 per km^2	% in cities	100%
GDP per cap	$28 800	Dailling code	+852	Internet	.hn	GMT +/-	+8

MEDALS TABLE

		Overall		Lge		FAC		Shield		VC		LC		Asia		
		G	S	G	B	G	B	G	B	G	B	G	B	G	S	DoF
1	South China	66	37	28	15	9	4	20	10	8	7	1			1	1910
2	Seiko	29	8	9	3	6	1	8	2	6	2					1970-86
3	Happy Valley	15	38	6	16	2	5	5	9	1	3	1	5			1950
4	Eastern	15	10	4	3	3	1	6	2	2	4					
5	Kitchee	10	9	3	5		1	5	3			2				1931
6	Sun Hei	10	7	3	2	3	1	1	3			3	1			1986
7	Rangers	9	8	1		2	3	4	2	2	2	1				1958
	Sing Tao	9	8	1	4		1	6	2	2	1					1940-99
9	Instant-Dict (Double Flower)	6	11	2	2	3	2		4	1	3					
10	Bulova	5	4		2	2	1	1	1	2	1					1977-85
11	Kowloon Motor Bus Co.	3	9	2	5			1	4							1947-81
12	Lai Sun	3	4			1	2		1	2	1					
13	Jardines	3	1	1	1			1		1						
	Yuen Long	3	1	1		1		1	1							1959
15	Ernest Borel	2	1			1	1			1						1990-93
16	Caroline Hill	1	3		1					1	2					
17	Orient & Yee Hope Union	1	1				1	1								
18	Kwong Wah	1					1									
	Royal Air Force	1		1												
	Royal Navy B	1							1							

Lge = League • FAC = FA Cup • Shield = Senior Shield • VC = Viceroy Cup • LC = League Cup

RECENT LEAGUE AND CUP RECORD

	League				FA Cup				Challenge Shield		
Year	Champions	Score	Runners-up		Winners	Score	Runners-up		Winners	Score	Runners-up
2001	Happy Valley	1-0	Instant-Dict		Instant-Dict	2-1	South China		O & YH Union	1-0	Instant-Dict
2002	Sun Hei	†	Happy Valley		South China	1-0	Sun Hei		South China	3-2	Sun Hei
2003	Happy Valley	†	Sun Hei		Sun Hei	2-1	Buler Rangers		South China	2-1	Happy Valley
2004	Sun Hei	†	Kitchee		Happy Valley	3-1	Kitchee		Happy Valley	3-0	Sun Hei
2005	Sun Hei	†	Happy Valley		Sun Hei	2-1	Happy Valley		Sun Hei	4-2	Happy Valley
2006	Happy Valley	†	Sun Hei		Sun Hei	1-0	Happy Valley		Kitchee	3-0	Happy Valley
2007	South China	†	Kitchee		South China	3-1	Happy Valley		South China	2-1	Sun Hei

† Played on a league basis - in 2002 the Championship reverted to a single stage round robin format

HONG KONG 2006-07

COOLPOINT VENTILATION FIRST DIVISION

	Pl	W	D	L	F	A	Pts	South China	Kitchee	Sun Hei	Rangers	Lanwa	H. Valley	Tai Po	Citizen	HKFC	HK 08
South China †	18	13	3	2	47	18	42		1-1	2-2	0-3	2-0	2-0	4-1	5-2	2-0	3-1
Kitchee †	18	13	3	2	51	19	42	0-2		2-0	3-2	3-2	5-0	1-2	3-2	4-0	4-1
Sun Hei	18	9	4	5	33	18	31	0-1	3-3		1-1	1-2	0-2	2-1	2-0	3-0	5-0
Rangers	18	7	7	4	23	19	28	0-3	1-1	2-4		2-1	1-1	1-0	3-0	3-1	0-0
Lanwa	18	8	3	8	37	26	26	0-1	0-1	3-0			2-4	6-0	3-2	6-0	2-0
Happy Valley	18	7	4	7	27	29	25	1-3	0-3	1-1	0-0	1-1		4-2	1-2	0-1	1-0
Tai Po	18	7	2	8	28	35	24	2-3	1-6	1-0	0-2	2-0	4-3		1-1	1-1	4-1
Citizen	18	5	4	9	26	32	19	1-1	2-3	0-3	0-1	2-2	0-1	0-0		4-1	5-1
HKFC	18	3	2	13	12	46	11	3-2	0-4	0-3	0-0	1-3	1-4	0-3	0-1		1-2
Hong Kong 08	18	1	2	15	11	53	5	0-8	0-4	0-2	1-1	1-3	1-3	0-3	1-2	1-2	

2/09/2006 - 29/04/2007 • † Qualified for the AFC Cup

HONG KONG 2006-07 SECOND DIVISION

	Pl	W	D	L	F	A	Pts
Tung Po	20	15	3	2	47	8	48
Shek Kip Mei	20	14	4	2	68	18	46
Fukien	20	9	5	6	39	28	32
Double Flower	20	8	4	8	27	35	28
New Fair Kui Tan	20	9	4	7	18	28	31
Kwai Tsing	20	7	5	8	23	33	26
Lucky Mile	20	8	2	10	28	31	26
Mutual	20	5	8	7	22	25	23
Kwok Keung	20	7	1	12	17	31	22
Eastern	20	5	4	11	28	45	19
Yau Tsim Mong	20	1	4	15	16	51	7

10/10/2006 - 15/04/2007

SENIOR SHIELD 2006-07

Quarter-finals		Semi-finals		Final	
South China	3 3p				
Happey Valley	3 5p	South China	4		
Tai Po	0	Lanwa	1		
Lanwa	1			South China	2
Kitchee	1			Sun Hei	1
Hong Kong FC	0	Kitchee	0		
Citizen	1	Sun Hei	1		
Sun Hei	2				

Prelim round: **HKFC** 2-1 Hong Kong 08
Prelim round: **South China** 1-0 Rangers

CUP FINAL
Hong Kong Stadium,
21-01-2007, Att: 4980
Scorers - Wong Chun Yue [68],
Schutz [90p] for South China;
Lo Chi Kwan [39] for Sun Hei

FA CUP 2006-07

Quarter-finals		Semi-finals		Final	
South China	2				
Sun Hei	1	South China	4		
Hong Kong 08	0	Kitchee	2		
Kitchee	2			South China	3
Rangers	1			Happy Valley	1
HKFC	0	Rangers	0		
Lanwa	0	Happy Valley	4		
Happy Valley	4				

Prelim round: **Lanwa** 4-2 Citizen
Prelim round: **South China** 3-0 Tai Po

CUP FINAL
Hong Kong Stadium, 19-05-2007,
Att 6427, Ref: Riley ENG
Scorers - Detinho [22p], Chan Chi
Hong [27], Cheng Siu Wai [85] for SC;
Poon Yiu Cheuk [85] for HV;

LEAGUE CUP 2006-07

Round of 16

Group A	Pts	SH	TP	La	HK
Kitchee	10	1-1	2-1	2-1	2-0
Sun Hei	8		1-1	3-0	3-0
Tai Po	4			2-0	0-1
Lanwa	3				2-0
Hong Kong 08	3				

Group B	Pts	SC	Ci	Ra	HK
Happy Valley	7	2-1	0-0	1-2	5-2
South China	7		0-0	2-0	2-0
Citizen	6			2-2	3-1
Rangers	5				1-1
HKFC	1				

Semi-finals		Final	
Kitchee	2		
South China	1	Kitchee	2
		Happy Valley	1
Sun Hei	2 2p		
Happy Valley	2 4p		

CUP FINAL
Mongkok Stadium, 17-03-2007
Att: 1500
Scorers - Darko Rakocevic 2 [72 76] for
Kitchee; Poon Yiu Cheuk [57p] for
Happy Valley

HON – HONDURAS

NATIONAL TEAM RECORD
JULY 10TH 2006 TO JULY 12TH 2010

PL	W	D	L	F	A	%
16	9	2	5	37	20	62.5

FIFA/COCA-COLA WORLD RANKING

1993	1994	1995	1996	1997	1998	1999	2000	2001	2002	2003	2004	2005	2006	High	Low
40	53	49	45	73	91	69	46	27	40	49	59	41	56	**20** 09/01	**98** 11/98

2006–2007											
08/06	09/06	10/06	11/06	12/06	01/07	02/07	03/07	04/07	05/07	06/07	07/07
81	81	55	56	56	56	59	52	52	55	55	63

Despite setting a new national record after scoring in 15 consecutive internationals, the Honduras national team, under new coach Reinaldo Rueda, ended the season on a low, bowing out of the CONCACAF Gold Cup in the quarter-finals to tiny Guadeloupe. Having beaten Mexico and then thrashed Cuba, the Hondurans were hoping to qualify for successive Gold Cup semi-finals, but Guadeloupe, with Jocelyn Angloma and other European professionals, had other ideas. One consolation was that Real España's Carlos Pavón finished the tournament as top scorer with five goals. Earlier in the year Honduras had had a very disappointing UNCAF Cup, finishing fifth,

INTERNATIONAL HONOURS
Qualified for the FIFA World Cup finals 1982 UNCAF Cup 1993 1995 CONCACAF Club Championship Olimpia 1972 1988

although they did beat Nicaragua 9-1 to secure their place in the Gold Cup. In continental club competition, Olimpia progressed to the quarter-finals of the CONCACAF Champions Cup before losing to DC United 7-3 on aggregate. Earlier they had been denied a first UNCAF club championship title since 2000 after losing on penalties to Costa Rica's Municipal Puntarenas in the final. Olimpia also ended the season trophyless at home, despite having the highest overall points total for the season. In the final of the Apertura they lost 4-2 on aggregate to Motagua, while in the Clausura they lost in the semi-finals to Marathon who then lost in the final to Real España.

THE FIFA BIG COUNT OF 2006

	Male	Female		Total
Number of players	360 800	59 800	Referees and Assistant Referees	1 100
Professionals	100		Admin, Coaches, Technical, Medical	5 700
Amateurs 18+	27 700		Number of clubs	220
Youth under 18	32 800		Number of teams	1 100
Unregistered	79 300		Clubs with women's teams	7
Total players	420 600		Players as % of population	5.74%

Federación Nacional Autónoma de Fútbol de Honduras (FENAFUTH)
Colonia Florencia Norte, Ave. Roble, Edificio Plaza América, Ave. Roble, 1 y 2 Nivel, Tegucigalpa, Honduras
Tel +504 2311436   Fax +504 2398826
fenafuth@fenafuth.com   www.fenafuth.com
President: CALLEJAS Rafael   General Secretary: HAWIT BANEGAS Alfredo
Vice-President: ATALA Javier   Treasurer: WILLIAMS Vicente   Media Officer: BANEGAS Martin
Men's Coach: RUEDA Reinaldo   Women's Coach: GUITIERREZ ALVAREZ Cesar Efrain
FENAFUTH formed: 1951   CONCACAF: 1961   FIFA: 1951
Blue shirts, Blue shorts, Blue socks

RECENT INTERNATIONAL MATCHES PLAYED BY HONDURAS

2004	Opponents	Score		Venue	Comp	Scorers	Att	Referee
2-06	USA	L	0-4	Foxboro	Fr		11 533	Sibrian SLV
12-06	Netherlands Antilles	W	2-1	Willemstad	WCq	Suazo 2 [9 68]	12 000	McArthur GUY
19-06	Netherlands Antilles	W	4-0	San Pedro Sula	WCq	Guevara [7], Suazo [22], Alvarez [50], Pavon [70]	30 000	Alcala MEX
28-07	Panama	D	0-0	Tegucigalpa	Fr		5 000	Zelaya HON
3-08	El Salvador	W	4-0	San Salvador	Fr	Izaguirre [4], Palacios.J 3 [5 71 75]		Aguilar SLV
18-08	Costa Rica	W	5-2	Alajuela	WCq	Suazo [22], Leon [35], Guevara 2 [77 87], Martinez.S [89]	14 000	Rodriguez MEX
4-09	Canada	D	1-1	Edmonton	WCq	Guevara [88p]	8 000	Archundia MEX
8-09	Guatemala	D	2-2	San Pedro Sula	WCq	Guevara [51], Suazo [65]	40 000	Prendergast JAM
9-10	Canada	D	1-1	San Pedro Sula	WCq	Turcios [92+]	42 000	Stott USA
13-10	Guatemala	L	0-1	Guatemala City	WCq		26 000	Brizan TRI
17-11	Costa Rica	D	0-0	San Pedro Sula	WCq		18 000	Sibrian SLV
2005								
19-02	Nicaragua	W	5-1	Guatemala City	UCr1	Núñez 2 [19 84], Velásquez 3 [42 51 73]	5 306	Moreno PAN
21-02	Belize	W	4-0	Guatemala City	UCr1	Velásquez [7], Núñez 2 [33 80], Palacios.W [88]	3 000	Campos NCA
23-02	Guatemala	D	1-1	Guatemala City	UCr1	Velásquez [72]	3 000	Moreno PAN
25-02	Panama	W	1-0	Guatemala City	UCsf	Velásquez [72]	11 159	Sibrian SLV
27-02	Costa Rica	D	1-1	Guatemala City	UCf	Núñez [58]. L 6-7p	1 491	Batres GUA
19-03	USA	L	0-1	Albuquerque	Fr		9 222	Navarro CAN
4-06	Jamaica	D	0-0	Atlanta	Fr		6 500	Valenzuela USA
2-07	Canada	W	2-1	Vancouver	Fr	Ramirez.F [52], Velásquez [56]	4 105	Valenzuela USA
6-07	Trinidad and Tobago	D	1-1	Miami	GCr1	Figueroa [43]	10 311	Navarro CAN
10-07	Colombia	W	2-1	Miami	GCr1	Velásquez 2 [79 82]	17 292	Rodriguez MEX
12-07	Panama	W	1-0	Miami	GCr1	Caballero [81]	11 000	Wyngaarde SUR
16-07	Costa Rica	W	3-2	Foxboro	GCqf	Velásquez [6], Turcios [27], Núñez [29]	22 108	Archundia MEX
21-07	USA	L	1-2	New Jersey	GCsf	Guerrero [30]	41 721	Prendergast JAM
7-09	Japan	L	4-5	Miyagi	Fr	Velásquez 3 [8 27 50], Martinez.S [45]	45 198	
2006								
25-01	Ecuador	L	0-1	Guayaquil	Fr		10 000	Ramos ECU
12-02	China PR	W	1-0	Guangzhou	Fr	Oliva [54]	20 000	Supian MAS
16-08	Venezuela	D	0-0	Maracay	Fr		9 000	Brandt VEN
6-09	El Salvador	W	2-0	Tegucigalpa	Fr	Bernardez [32], Palacios [81]	7 000	Zelaya HON
7-10	Guatemala	W	3-2	Fort Lauderdale	Fr	Núñez [52p], De Leon [69], Suazo [87p]	19 173	Vaughn USA
10-10	Guatemala	W	2-1	Atlanta	Fr	Figueroa [4], Martinez.W [49]	7 000	Prus USA
2007								
9-02	Costa Rica	L	1-3	San Salvador	UCr1	Martinez.E [59]		Archundia MEX
11-02	Panama	D	1-1	San Salvador	UCr1	Guardia OG [25]		Aguilar SLV
15-02	Nicaragua	W	9-1	San Salvador	UC5p	Martinez.J [4], Velásquez 4 [6 27 38 39p], Martinez.S 3 [69 81 86], Mejía [77]		Aguilar SLV
24-03	El Salvador	W	2-0	Fort Lauderdale	Fr	Oliva 2 [25 66]	17 095	Marrufo USA
27-03	El Salvador	W	2-0	Cary	Fr	Martinez.J 2 [1 57]	8 365	
19-04	Haiti	L	1-3	La Ceiba	Fr	Pavon [6p]		Soriano HON
25-05	Venezuela	L	1-2	Merida	Fr	Pavon [44]	42 000	Gomez VEN
2-06	Trinidad and Tobago	W	3-1	San Pedro Sula	Fr	Izaguirre [49], Guevara [52p], Costly [84]	1 907	Soriano HON
8-06	Panama	L	2-3	New Jersey	GCr1	Guevara [40], Costly [90]	20 230	Navarro CAN
10-06	Mexico	W	2-1	New Jersey	GCr1	Costly 2 [60 90]	68 123	
13-06	Cuba	W	5-0	Houston	GCr1	Pavon 4 [3 12 43 53], Guevara [90]	68 417	
17-06	Guadeloupe	L	1-2	Houston	GCqf	Pavon [71]	70 092	Navarro CAN

Fr = Friendly match • UC = UNCAF Cup • GC = CONCACAF Gold Cup • WC = FIFA World Cup
q = qualifier • r1 = first round group • qf = quarter-final • sf = semi-final • f = final

HONDURAS NATIONAL TEAM RECORDS AND RECORD SEQUENCES

Records			Sequence records					
Victory	10-0	NCA 1946	Wins	6	1980-81, 1985-86	Clean sheets	6	1992
Defeat	1-10	GUA 1921	Defeats	6	1963-1965	Goals scored	15	2006-2007
Player Caps	n/a		Undefeated	14	1991-1992	Without goal	5	1988
Player Goals	n/a		Without win	14	1987-1991	Goals against	13	1993-1995

Population '000

1	Tegucigalpa	1 765
2	San Pedro Sula	735
3	La Ceiba	138
4	El Progreso	106
5	Choluteca	78
6	Comayagua	61
7	Puerto Cortés	50
8	Danli	46
9	Siguatepeque	45
10	Juticalpa	35
11	Catacamas	35
12	Villanueva	33
13	Tocoa	33
14	Tela	29
15	Santa Rosa Copán	28
16	Olanchito	27
17	San Lorenzo	23
18	Cofradía	21
19	El Paraíso	19
20	La Paz	18
21	Potrerillos	16
22	Yoro	16
23	Santa Bárbara	15
24	La Entrada	15

REPUBLIC OF HONDURAS; REPUBLICA DE HONDURAS

Capital	Tegucigalpa	Language	Spanish			Independence	1821
Population	7 326 496	Area	112 090 km²	Density	60 per km²	% in cities	44%
GDP per cap	$2 600	Dailling code	+504	Internet	.hn	GMT + / -	-6

MEDALS TABLE

		Overall			Lge			Cent Am			City	Stadium	Cap'ty	DoF
		G	S	B	G	B		G	S	B				
1	Olimpia	22	16	1	20	14		2	2	1	Tegucigalpa	Tiburcio Carias Andino	35 000	1912
2	Motagua	11	7		11	7					Tegucigalpa	Tiburcio Carias Andino	35 000	1928
3	Real España	9	8	1	9	8				1	San Pedro Sula	Francisco Morazán	20 000	1929
4	Marathón	5	10	1	5	10				1	San Pedro Sula	Olímpico Metropolitano	40 000	1925
5	Platense	2	3		2	3					Puerto Cortés	Excelsior	10 000	1960
	Vida	2	3		2	3					La Ceiba	Nilmo Edwards	15 000	1940
7	Victoria	1	1		1	1					La Ceiba	Nilmo Edwards	15 000	1935
8	Universidad National - UNAH		3			2			1		Choluteca	Fausto Flores Lagos	5 000	1965
9	Atlético Morazán		1			1								
10	Atlético Olanchano										Catacamas	Rubén Guifarro	5 000	1988
	Hispano										Comayagua	Carlos Miranda	10 000	1945

RECENT LEAGUE RECORD

Championship/Torneo Clausura from 1998				Torneo Apertura		
Year	Champions	Score	Runners-up	Champions	Score	Runners-up
1995	Victoria	0-0 1-1	Olimpia			
1996	Olimpia	3-0 0-0	Real España			
1997	Olimpia	1-1 3-0	Platense	Motagua	3-0 2-1	Real España
1998	Motagua	0-0 1-0	Olimpia	Olimpia	0-0 1-0	Real España
1999	Season readjustment			Motagua	0-0 0-0 6-5p	Olimpia
2000	Motagua	1-1 1-1 3-2p	Olimpia	Olimpia	1-0 1-1	Platense
2001	Platense	1-0 1-1	Olimpia	Motagua	0-1 3-2	Marathón
2002	Marathón	4-1 0-1	Olimpia	Olimpia	1-1 2-1	Platense
2003	Marathón	1-0 3-1	Motagua	Real España	2-2 2-0	Olimpia
2004	Olimpia	1-1 1-0	Marathón	Marathón	3-2 2-1	Olimpia
2005	Olimpia	1-1 2-1	Marathón	Olimpia	1-2 2-0	Marathón
2006	Olimpia	3-3 1-0	Victoria Ceiba	Motagua	1-1 3-1	Olimpia
2007	Real España	1-2 3-1	Marathón			

HONDURAS 2006-07

TORNEO APERTURA

	Pl	W	D	L	F	A	Pts	Olimpia	Motagua	Hispano	Marathón	Platense	Olanchano	España	Victoria	UNAH	Vida
Olimpia †	18	10	5	3	26	14	35		2-1	1-1	0-0	0-2	1-0	1-0	1-2	1-1	1-0
Motagua †	18	9	4	5	27	22	31	2-2		2-0	3-0	1-3	1-0	2-0	2-1	1-0	2-0
Hispano †	18	7	9	2	25	14	30	0-2	0-0		2-0	0-0	0-0	2-1	5-0	3-1	3-1
Marathón †	18	8	6	4	30	20	30	2-3	4-0	1-1		4-1	0-1	0-0	2-2	2-1	1-0
Platense	18	7	8	3	32	29	29	0-3	2-1	2-2	2-2		2-2	3-2	1-0	4-3	3-1
Atlético Olanchano	18	6	5	7	24	25	23	0-2	3-0	1-1	0-3	2-2		3-2	2-2	2-1	3-1
Real España	18	5	6	7	18	20	21	0-0	1-1	0-0	2-2	2-2	1-0		2-1	1-0	2-0
Victoria	18	5	4	9	21	28	19	1-2	1-1	1-2	0-1	2-1	2-1	0-1		1-2	2-0
Universidad	18	3	5	10	17	26	14	1-0	3-5	0-0	0-1	0-0	1-2	1-0	1-1		1-1
Vida	18	3	2	13	17	39	11	1-4	0-2	1-3	2-5	2-2	3-2	2-1	1-2	1-0	

12/08/2006 - 26/11/2006 • † Qualified for the play-offs

APERTURA PLAY-OFFS

Semi–finals			Final		
Motagua	1	5			
Hispano *	2	0	**Motagua ***	1	3
Marathón *	2	0	Olimpia	1	1
Olimpia	1	2			

* Home team in the first leg

10-12-2006 & 17-12-2006

HONDURAS 2006-07

TORNEO CLAUSURA

	Pl	W	D	L	F	A	Pts	España	Marathón	Olimpia	Motagua	Platense	Vida	Hispano	Olanchano	Victoria	UNAH
Real España †	18	12	4	2	29	8	40		1-0	0-1	2-1	3-0	2-2	1-0	1-0	2-0	5-0
Marathón †	18	11	3	4	32	16	36	1-1		2-0	0-1	2-0	3-0	2-0	2-0	4-2	3-1
Olimpia †	18	11	3	4	26	12	36	0-2	0-1		1-2	2-1	2-1	1-1	1-0	2-1	4-0
Motagua †	18	10	1	7	31	26	31	0-1	3-4	0-4		2-2	3-2	0-1	5-1	1-0	1-0
Platense	17	7	2	8	17	22	23	1-0	3-2	0-1	0-3		1-2	2-0	2-1	2-1	n/p
Vida	18	6	4	8	21	23	22	0-2	1-2	0-1	1-2	1-0		1-0	0-0	2-1	3-0
Hispano	18	5	5	8	19	21	20	1-3	1-1	1-1	3-1	0-1	1-1		2-0	2-1	5-1
Atlético Olanchano	17	5	3	9	16	23	18	0-0	1-0	**0-2**	1-2	2-1	1-3	2-0		2-0	5-2
Victoria	17	3	5	9	14	22	14	1-1	0-0	0-0	2-0	0-1	2-1	2-1	n/p		1-1
Universidad	17	0	6	11	7	39	6	0-2	1-3	0-3	1-4	0-0	0-0	0-0	0-0	0-0	

13/01/2007 - 29/04/2007 • † Qualified for the play-offs • Match in bold was awarded • Top scorer: Carlos PAVON, Real España 15

CLAUSURA PLAY-OFFS

Semi–finals			Final		
Real España	3	1			
Motagua *	1	0	**Real España**	1	3
Olimpia *	2 0	0p	Marathón *	2	1
Marathón	0 2	3p			

* Home team in the first leg

12-05-2007 & 19-05-2007

AGGREGATE RELEGATION TABLE

	Pl	W	D	L	F	A	Pts
Olimpia	36	21	8	7	52	26	69
Marathón	36	19	9	8	62	36	66
Motagua	36	19	5	12	58	48	62
Real España	36	17	10	9	47	28	61
Platense	35	14	10	11	49	51	52
Hispano	36	12	14	10	44	35	50
Atlético Olanchano	35	11	8	16	40	48	39
Victoria	35	8	9	18	35	50	33
Vida	36	9	6	21	38	62	33
Universidad	35	3	11	21	24	65	20

HUN - HUNGARY

NATIONAL TEAM RECORD
JULY 10TH 2006 TO JULY 12TH 2010

PL	W	D	L	F	A	%
11	5	0	6	13	17	45.4

FIFA/COCA-COLA WORLD RANKING

1993	1994	1995	1996	1997	1998	1999	2000	2001	2002	2003	2004	2005	2006	High	Low
50	61	62	75	77	46	45	47	66	56	72	64	74	62	**42** 08/93	**87** 07/96

2006–2007											
08/06	09/06	10/06	11/06	12/06	01/07	02/07	03/07	04/07	05/07	06/07	07/07
80	59	76	67	62	61	64	64	58	57	66	65

2006 was the year in which Hungary said goodbye to its most famous son - Ferenc Puskás - and how fans there must pine for a return to the days when the national team was the most feared on the planet. In the qualifiers for UEFA Euro 2008, Hungary suffered the embarrassment of defeat at the hands of Malta as the team fumbled its way through a season which also saw defeats by Norway, Turkey and Greece in the qualifiers and against Cyprus in a friendly. In the UEFA Champions League, Debreceni VSC were humbled by Macedonia's Rabotnicki Skopje in the second preliminary round whilst Ujpesti suffered the indignity of losing 4-0 at home to Liechtenstein's

INTERNATIONAL HONOURS
Qualified for the FIFA World Cup finals 1934 1938 1954 1958 1962 1966 1978 1982 1986   **Olympic Gold** 1952 1964 1968

FC Vaduz in the UEFA Cup. Rarely has the stock of Hungarian football been so low. For the third year running it was provincial outfit Debreceni VSC who won the championship - the first time a club from outside of the capital has ever won a hat-trick of titles. After the defeat against Rabotnicki, Debrecen appointed Czech coach Miroslav Beránek to replace Attila Supka and he took them to within a whisker of becoming the first provincial team to secure a double. In the Cup Final they faced a Budapest Honvéd side coached by Supka, but after a 2-2 draw Debrecen lost the penalty shoot-out 3-1 to give the club Puskás once graced their first trophy since 1996.

THE FIFA BIG COUNT OF 2006

	Male	Female		Total
Number of players	477 368	49 958	Referees and Assistant Referees	3 615
Professionals	468		Admin, Coaches, Technical, Medical	7 150
Amateurs 18+	61 208		Number of clubs	2 748
Youth under 18	63 744		Number of teams	4 631
Unregistered	203 100		Clubs with women's teams	30
Total players	527 326		Players as % of population	5.28%

Hungarian Football Federation (MLSZ)
Magyar Labdarúgó Szövetség, Koerberek-Tovaros, Kanai u. 314/24.hrsz, Budapest 1112, Hungary
Tel +36 1 5779500   Fax +36 1 5779503
mlsz@mlsz.hu   www.mlsz.hu
President: KISTELEKI Istvan   General Secretary: FUEZESI Zsolt
Vice-President: TBD   Treasurer: KRIZSO Ibolya   Media Officer: DINNYES Marton
Men's Coach: BOZSIK Peter   Women's Coach: BACSO Istvan
MLSZ formed: 1901   UEFA: 1954   FIFA: 1906
Red shirts with white trimmings, White shirts, Green socks or White shirts with red trimmings, White shorts, White socks

RECENT INTERNATIONAL MATCHES PLAYED BY HUNGARY

2003	Opponents	Score		Venue	Comp	Scorers	Att	Referee
20-08	Slovenia	L	1-2	Murska Sobota	Fr	Fehér.M [90]	5 000	Sowa AUT
10-09	Latvia	L	1-3	Riga	ECq	Lisztes [53]	7 500	Larsen DEN
11-10	Poland	L	1-2	Budapest	ECq	Szabics [49]	15 500	Mejuto Gonzalez ESP
19-11	Estonia	L	0-1	Budapest	Fr		1 000	Sedivy CZE
2004								
18-02	Armenia	W	2-0	Paphos	Fr	Szabics [63], Lisztes [75]	400	Gerasimou CYP
19-02	Latvia	W	2-1	Limassol	Fr	Tököli [82], Kenesei [85]	500	Kailis CYP
31-03	Wales	L	1-2	Budapest	Fr	Kenesei [17p]	10 000	Meyer GER
25-04	Japan	W	3-2	Zalaegerszeg	Fr	Kuttor [53], Juhasz [67], Huszti [90p]	7 000	Trivkovic CRO
28-04	Brazil	L	1-4	Budapest	Fr	Torghelle [56]	45 000	De Santis ITA
1-06	China PR	L	1-2	Beijing	Fr	Kenesei [4p]	18 000	Chiu HKG
6-06	Germany	W	2-0	Kaiserslautern	Fr	Torghelle 2 [7 31]	36 590	Bennett ENG
18-08	Scotland	W	3-0	Glasgow	Fr	Huszti 2 [45p 53], Marshall OG [73]	15 933	Duhamel FRA
4-09	Croatia	L	0-3	Zagreb	WCq		20 853	Riley ENG
8-09	Iceland	W	3-2	Budapest	WCq	Gera [62], Torghelle [75], Szabics [79]	5 461	Ovrebo NOR
9-10	Sweden	L	0-3	Stockholm	WCq		32 288	Dougal SCO
17-11	Malta	W	2-0	Ta'Qali	WCq	Gera [39], Kovacs.P [93+]	14 500	Asumaa FIN
30-11	Slovakia	L	0-1	Bangkok	Fr		750	Veerapool THA
2-12	Estonia	W	5-0	Bangkok	Fr	Rosa [12], Waltner [14], Kerekes [19], Rajczi [24], Pollak [63]	800	Tongkhan THA
2005								
2-02	Saudi Arabia	D	0-0	Istanbul	Fr		100	Dereli TUR
9-02	Wales	L	0-2	Cardiff	Fr		16 672	Richmond SCO
30-03	Bulgaria	D	1-1	Budapest	WCq	Rajczi [90]	11 586	Wegereef NED
31-05	France	L	1-2	Metz	Fr	Kerekes [78]	26 000	Allaerts BEL
4-06	Iceland	W	3-2	Reykjavik	WCq	Gera 2 [45p 56p], Huszti 73	4 613	Cardoso Batista POR
17-08	Argentina	L	1-2	Budapest	Fr	Torghelle [29]	27 000	Merk GER
3-09	Malta	W	4-0	Budapest	WCq	Torghelle 34, OG 55, Takacs 64, Rajczi 85	5 900	Godulyan UKR
7-09	Sweden	L	0-1	Budapest	WCq		20 161	Farina ITA
8-10	Bulgaria	L	0-2	Sofia	WCq		4 652	Delevic SCG
12-10	Croatia	D	0-0	Budapest	WCq		6 979	Larsen DEN
16-11	Greece	L	1-2	Piraeus	Fr	Kenesei [77]	12 500	Vink NED
14-12	Mexico	L	0-2	Phoenix	Fr		32 466	Valenzuela USA
18-12	Antigua and Barbuda	W	3-0	Fort Lauderdale	Fr	Vadocz [10], Feczesin 2 [32 80]	250	Rutty USA
2006								
24-05	New Zealand	W	2-0	Budapest	Fr	Huszti [48], Szabics [81]	5 000	Hrinak SVK
30-05	England	L	1-3	Manchester	Fr	Dardai [55]	56 323	Vink NED
16-08	Austria	W	2-1	Graz	Fr	Gera [11], Horvath [37]	12 000	Havrilla SVK
2-09	Norway	L	1-4	Budapest	ECq	Gera [90p]	12 283	Braamhaar NED
6-09	Bosnia-Herzogovina	W	3-1	Zenica	ECq	Huszti [36p], Gera [46], Dárdai [49]	11 800	Kapitanis CYP
7-10	Turkey	L	0-1	Budapest	ECq		6 800	Hamer LUX
11-10	Malta	L	1-2	Ta'Qali	ECq	Torghelle [19]	3 600	Ver Eecke BEL
15-11	Canada	W	1-0	Székesfehérvár	Fr	Priskin [36]	6 000	Weiner GER
2007								
6-02	Cyprus	L	1-2	Limassol	Fr	Priskin [88]	500	Gerasimou CYP
7-02	Latvia	W	2-0	Limassol	Fr	Priskin 2 [31 53]	400	Kailisz CYP
28-03	Moldova	W	2-0	Budapest	ECq	Priskin [9], Gera [63]	6 150	Ingvarsson SWE
2-06	Greece	L	0-2	Irákleio	ECq		17 244	Larsen DEN
6-06	Norway	L	0-4	Oslo	ECq		19 198	Iturralde Gonzalez ESP

Fr = Friendly match • EC = UEFA EURO 2004/2008 • WC = FIFA World Cup • q = qualifier • † Not a full international

HUNGARY NATIONAL TEAM RECORDS AND RECORD SEQUENCES

Records				Sequence records			
Victory	13-1	FRA 1927	Wins	11	1951-1952	Clean sheets	4	Five times
Defeat	0-7	ENG 1908, GER 1941	Defeats	6	1978	Goals scored	74	1949-1957
Player Caps	101	BOZSIK József	Undefeated	30	1950-1954	Without goal	4	1993
Player Goals	84	PUSKAS Ferenc	Without win	12	1994	Goals against	19	Three times

MAJOR CITIES/TOWNS
Population '000

1	Budapest	2 571
2	Debrecen	203
3	Miskolc	177
4	Szeged	159
5	Pécs	155
6	Györ	128
7	Nyíregyháza	116
8	Kecskemét	105
9	Székesfehérvár	103
10	Szombathely	79
11	Szolnok	75
12	Tatabánya	71
13	Kaposvár	66
14	Békéscsaba	65
15	Zalaegerszeg	60
16	Veszprém	59
17	Eger	55
18	Sopron	55
19	Dunaújváros	53
20	Hódmezövásárhely	47
21	Salgótarján	43
22	Cegléd	40
23	Ozd	38
24	Pápa	32

REPUBLIC OF HUNGARY; MAGYAR KOZTARSASAG

Capital	Budapest	Language	Hungarian	Unification	1001
Population	9 981 334	Area	93 030 km²	% in cities	65%
GDP per cap	$13 900	Dailling code	+36	Internet .hu	GMT + / - +1

MEDALS TABLE

		Overall		League			Cup		Europe				City	Stadium	Cap'ty	DoF
	G	S	B	G	S	B	G	S	G	S	B					
1 Ferencvárosi TC	49	45	22	28	34	20	20	9	1	2	2	Budapest	Ullöi út	18 100	1899
2 MTK Hungária FC	34	23	16	22	20	15	12	2		1	1	Budapest	Hidegkuti Nandor	7 702	1888
3 Ujpest FC	28	27	20	20	20	18	8	6		1	2	Budapest	Szusza Ferenc	13 501	1885
4 Budapest-Honvéd FC	19	21	5	13	12	5	6	9				Budapest	Bozsik József	13 500	1909
5 Vasas SC	10	5	14	6	2	13	4	3			1	Budapest	Illovsky Rudolf	18 000	1911
6 Györi ETO FC	7	4	4	3	2	3	4	2			1	Györ	Stadion ETO	22 000	1904
7 Debreceni VSC	5	2	3	3		3	2	2				Debrecen	Oláh Gábor út	10 200	1902
8 Csepel SC	4		2	4		2						Budapest	Béke téri	10 000	1912
9 Diósgyöri VTK	2	3	1			1	2	3				Miskolc	DVTK	17 000	1910
10 Budapest TC	2	2	3	2	1	3		1				Budapest	Fehér út		1885
11 Dunakanyar-Vac FC	1	5		1	2						3	Vác	Városi	12 000	1899
12 Videoton FC Fehérvár	1	4	3		1	3	1	2			1	Székesfehervár	Sóstói	19 000	1941
13 Pécsi MFC	1	3	1		1	1	1	2				Pécs	PMFC	7 160	1973
14 Dunaferr	1	1		1	1							Dunaújváros	Dunaferr	11 600	1951
Nagyváradi AC	1	1		1	1							Oradea - ROU	Varosi		1911

RECENT LEAGUE AND CUP RECORD

	Championship							Cup		
Year	Champions	Pts	Runners-up	Pts	Third	Pts		Winners	Score	Runners-up
1995	Ferencvárosi TC	59	Ujpesti TE	52	Debreceni VSC	49		Ferencvárosi TC	2-0 3-4	Vac FC
1996	Ferencvárosi TC	66	BVSC	61	Ujpesti TE	48		Kispest-Honvéd	0-1 2-0	BVSC
1997	MTK-Hungária	85	Ujpesti TE	76	Ferencvárosi TC	74		MTK-Hungária	6-0 2-0	BVSC
1998	Ujpesti TE	73	Ferencvárosi TC	67	Vasas SC	64		MTK-Hungária	1-0	Ujpesti TE
1999	MTK-Hungária	83	Ferencvárosi TC	64	Ujpesti TE	63		Debreceni VSC	2-0	LFC Tatabánya
2000	Dunaferr FC	79	MTK-Hungária	63	Vasas SC	61		MTK-Hungária	3-1	Vasas SC
2001	Ferencvárosi TC	48	Dunaferr FC	46	Vasas SC	40		Debreceni VSC	5-2	Videoton Fehérvar
2002	Zalaegerszegi TE	71	Ferencvárosi TC	69	MTK-Hungária	59		Ujpesti TE	2-1	Haladás
2003	MTK-Hungária	66	Ferencvárosi TC	64	Debreceni VSC	53		Ferencvárosi TC	2-1	Debreceni VSC
2004	Ferencvárosi TC	57	Ujpesti TE	56	Debreceni VSC	56		Ferencvárosi TC	3-1	Honvéd FC
2005	Debreceni VSC	62	Ferencvárosi TC	56	MTK-Hungária	56		Mátav FC Sopron	5-1	Ferencvárosi TC
2006	Debreceni VSC	68	Ujpesti TE	65	Fehérvár FC	64		Fehérvár	2-2 6-5p	Vasas SC
2007	Debreceni VSC	69	MTK-Hungária	61	Zalaegerszegi TE	55		Honvéd FC	2-2 3-1p	Debreceni VSC

HUNGARY 2006–07

BORSODI LIGA NB I

	Pl	W	D	L	F	A	Pts	Debrecen	MTK	ZTE	Ujpest	Vasas	Fehérvár	Kaposvár	Honvéd	Diósgyör	Sopron	Paksi	Tatabánya	Györ	REAC	Pécs	Dunakanyar
Debreceni VSC †	30	22	3	5	63	21	69		3-0	3-1	0-2	3-0	3-1	1-0	2-1	1-1	2-1	1-0	2-0	3-0	4-1	2-1	4-0
MTK-Hungária ‡	30	19	4	7	61	33	61	1-0		2-0	2-0	2-2	0-1	2-0	2-2	4-2	4-1	1-0	4-0	1-0	4-0	0-0	3-0
Zalaegerszegi TE	30	17	4	9	54	38	55	0-1	1-0		2-0	1-0	2-1	2-1	3-2	2-2	1-3	4-0	1-0	2-2	3-0	4-1	1-1
Ujpesti TE §3	30	15	4	11	39	32	46	2-0	2-3	0-1		2-0	0-2	0-0	4-2	0-3	1-0	3-2	2-0	2-0	0-0	1-0	1-0
Vasas SC	30	13	6	11	43	41	45	0-1	1-5	4-0	1-2		2-2	1-0	3-1	2-2	0-0	0-1	2-0	3-2	1-0	3-3	2-2
FC Fehérvár	30	13	5	12	45	43	44	0-4	5-3	2-3	3-1	2-0		1-2	1-0	2-0	3-1	1-1	2-0	2-1	2-2	2-2	1-0
Kaposvári Rákóczi	30	12	5	13	40	36	41	1-2	1-0	3-1	1-0	0-1	1-0		1-2	1-2	2-2	1-1	4-0	2-1	3-1	1-2	3-0
Honvéd ‡	30	11	8	11	48	43	41	2-1	2-1	1-2	1-1	0-1	1-1	2-2		1-1	2-0	0-0	2-0	4-1	2-1	0-1	6-0
Diósgyöri VTK	30	11	5	14	40	52	38	1-5	0-1	1-4	1-0	1-2	2-1	1-1	2-1		0-2	2-1	3-1	4-3	1-0	1-3	1-0
FC Sopron	30	11	4	15	33	46	37	1-6	0-3	1-2	0-2	1-0	1-1	1-0				1-3	1-0	0-1	2-3	3-1	3-1
Paksi SE	30	10	7	13	34	38	37	0-0	3-1	2-0	1-1	4-2	0-2	1-0	1-2	2-1	1-0		0-1	2-2	1-1	0-1	0-0
Tatabánya FC	30	11	3	16	46	58	36	2-1	2-4	0-3	3-2	1-3	3-2	4-2	1-2	5-3	2-0	3-0		2-1	2-3	4-0	1-0
Györi ETO	30	9	8	13	37	43	35	0-0	3-4	2-1	0-3	0-2	2-0	3-1	2-0	4-0	2-0	2-1	0-0		2-2	0-0	1-0
Rákospalotai EAC	30	9	7	14	42	55	34	1-3	0-0	2-1	1-2	1-3	2-0	1-1	3-4	0-2	1-3	4-3	2-4	2-0		1-0	4-0
Pécsi MFC	30	7	12	11	31	41	33	0-2	0-1	1-1	0-1	2-1	2-0	2-3	1-1	0-0	0-2	3-3	0-0	2-2			1-1
Dunakanyar-Vác	30	4	7	19	21	57	19	1-3	2-3	0-5	3-1	0-1	0-2	0-1	3-1	1-0	1-2	0-2	2-2	0-0	0-1	1-1	

28/07/2006 - 25/05/2007 • † Qualified for the UEFA Champions League • ‡ Qualified for the UEFA Cup • § = Points deducted
Top scorers: Peter BAJZAT Györi ETO 18; Ibrahima SIDIBE, DVSC 17; József KANTA, MTK 16; Gábor TORMA, REAC 15

HUNGARY 2006–07 NB II NYUGATI (WEST)

	Pl	W	D	L	F	A	Pts
Bodajk FC Siófok	30	19	5	6	59	24	62
Szombathelyi Haladás §8	30	21	5	4	66	25	60
Felcsút SE	30	18	6	6	53	25	60
Barcsi FC	30	18	5	7	49	30	59
Pápa TFC	30	14	9	7	42	24	51
Dunaújvárosi Kohász	30	15	1	14	51	46	46
Gyirmót SE §9	30	16	5	9	58	40	44
Mosonmagyaróvári TE	30	12	4	14	45	64	40
Soroksári SC	30	11	6	13	35	30	39
Kaposvölgye-Nagyberki	30	11	6	13	37	48	39
Integrál-DAC Györ	30	10	9	11	53	48	39
BKV Elöre	30	10	8	12	41	48	38
Budaörs	30	7	7	16	29	52	28
Celldömölki VSE	30	6	6	19	22	57	21
Hévíz FC	30	5	3	22	23	49	18
Balatonlelle SE	30	3	5	22	25	78	14

12/08/2006 - 16/06/2007 • § = Points deducted

HUNGARY 2006–07 NB II KELETI (EAST)

	Pl	W	D	L	F	A	Pts
Nyíregyházi	30	20	9	1	67	24	69
Ferencvárosi TC	30	18	11	1	70	21	65
Orosháza FC	30	16	7	7	58	40	55
Szolnoki MAV	30	13	10	7	45	35	49
Bocsi KSC	30	12	10	8	37	37	46
Tuzsér	30	13	6	11	40	47	45
Vecsés FC	30	11	9	10	49	43	42
Kecskeméti TE	30	10	10	10	46	46	40
Karcagi SE	30	9	10	11	31	39	37
Baktalóránrgáza VSE	30	8	9	13	33	44	33
Kazincbarcika SC	30	6	14	10	41	45	32
Makó FC	30	9	8	13	30	45	31
Jászberény	30	9	2	19	40	55	29
Békéscsabai Elore FC	30	8	4	18	33	48	28
Jászapáti VSE	30	7	6	17	26	48	27
Budafoki LC	30	6	5	19	31	60	23

12/08/2006 - 16/06/2007 • § = Points deducted

MAGYAR KUPA 2006–07

Round of 16			Quarter–finals			Semi–finals			Final		
Honvéd *	1	4									
Kaposvári Rákóczi	1	0	Honvéd	2	2						
Györi ETO *	1	0	MTK-Hungária *	2	1						
MTK-Hungária	3	5				Honvéd *	0	2			
Ferencvárosi TC *	1	3				Vasas SC	0	1			
Gyirmót SE	0	1	Ferencvárosi TC *	0	3						
Dunakanyar-Vác	1	1	Vasas SC	2	2						
Vasas SC *	2	1							Honvéd ‡	2	3p
Diósgyöri VTK	2	4							Debreceni VSC	2	1p
FC Sopron *	1	1	Diósgyöri VTK *	2	3						
Rákospalotai EAC	0	4	Zalaegerszegi TE	1	3						
Zalaegerszegi TE *	1	3				Diósgyöri VTK *	0	2			
Ujpesti TE	2	4				Debreceni VSC	1	2			
Pápa TFC *	0	2	Ujpesti TE	0	1						
Dunaújvárosi Kohász *	0	0	Debreceni VSC	0	3						
Debreceni VSC	1	3									

CUP FINAL
Ferenc Szusza Stadion, Budapest
9-05-2007
Scorers - Gellért Ivancsics [28], Tibor Szabó [104p] for Honvéd; Robert Zsolnai [69], Ibrahima Sidibe [97p] for DVSC

* Home team in the first leg • ‡ Qualified for the UEFA Cup

IDN – INDONESIA

INDONESIA NATIONAL TEAM RECORD
JULY 10TH 2006 TO JULY 12TH 2010

PL	W	D	L	F	A	%
14	5	4	5	17	14	50

FIFA/COCA-COLA WORLD RANKING

1993	1994	1995	1996	1997	1998	1999	2000	2001	2002	2003	2004	2005	2006	High	Low
106	134	130	119	91	87	90	97	87	110	91	91	109	153	**76** 09/98	**153** 12/06

2006–2007											
08/06	09/06	10/06	11/06	12/06	01/07	02/07	03/07	04/07	05/07	06/07	07/07
146	139	144	144	153	149	146	146	148	149	143	127

With both Saudi Arabia and South Korea in their group, it was never going to be an easy job for Ivan Kolev's Indonesian team to make it through to the quarter-finals of the 2007 AFC Asian Cup which they were co-hosting, but buoyed by the biggest crowds of the tournament they very nearly made it. Their campaign started well with a 2-1 win in a potentially tricky match against Bahrain, the winner coming from star forward Bambang Pamungkas, and against Saudi the Indonesians were moments away from potential qualification only to concede a goal three minutes into injury-time to lose the match 2-1. That meant they needed a win against the Koreans to be sure of

INTERNATIONAL HONOURS
AFC Youth Championship 1961

progressing, but in another close fought match, played before just under 90,000 fans in Jakarta, Indonesia lost 1-0 and were out. The disappointment was palpable. No-one had expected them to qualify given the disappointing form earlier in the year in the ASEAN Championship, but with Kolev replacing Peter Withe, the team was re-invigorated and deserved more. In the Liga Indonesia, Persik Kediri claimed their second League title in July 2006, beating PSIS Semarang 2-1 in the final whilst Arema Malang won the Cup, beating Persipura 2-0. There then followed a five month delay until the new League season kicked-off with the 2007 final scheduled for December.

THE FIFA BIG COUNT OF 2006

	Male	Female		Total
Number of players	7 094 260	0	Referees and Assistant Referees	669
Professionals	800		Admin, Coaches, Technical, Medical	400
Amateurs 18+	2 560		Number of clubs	73
Youth under 18	62 600		Number of teams	73
Unregistered	6 982 300		Clubs with women's teams	10
Total players	7 094 260		Players as % of population	2.89%

Football Association of Indonesia (PSSI)
Gelora Bung Karno, Pintu X-XI, Senayan, PO Box 2305, Jakarta 10023, Indonesia
Tel +62 21 5704762   Fax +62 21 5734386
pssi@pssi-football.com   www.pssi-football.com
President: HALID Nurdin   General Secretary: BESOES Nugraha
Vice-President: NIRWAN Bakire   Treasurer: YANDHU Hamka   Media Officer: HALMAHERA John
Men's Coach: KOLEV Ivan   Women's Coach: none
PSSI formed: 1930   AFC: 1954   FIFA: 1952
Red shirts with white trimmings, White shirts, Red socks

RECENT INTERNATIONAL MATCHES PLAYED BY INDONESIA

2003	Opponents	Score		Venue	Comp	Scorers	Att	Referee
26-09	Malaysia	D	1-1	Kuala Lumpur	Fr	Elie Aiboy [62]		
6-10	Bhutan	W	2-0	Jeddah	ACq	Arif 2 [19 50]		
8-10	Yemen	W	3-0	Jeddah	ACq	Uston 2 [51 90], Arif [62]		
10-10	Saudi Arabia	L	0-5	Jeddah	ACq			
13-10	Bhutan	W	2-0	Jeddah	ACq	Edwarar [19], Arif [33]		
15-10	Yemen	D	2-2	Jeddah	ACq	Edwarar [12p], Donald [38]		
17-10	Saudi Arabia	L	0-6	Jeddah	ACq			
2004								
12-02	Jordan	L	1-2	Amman	Fr	Bambang Pamungkas [15]		
18-02	Saudi Arabia	L	0-3	Riyadh	WCq		1 000	Al Ghafary JOR
17-03	Malaysia	D	0-0	Johor Bahru	Fr		8 000	Kim Heng MAS
31-03	Turkmenistan	L	1-3	Ashgabat	WCq	Budi [30]	5 000	Sahib Shakir IRQ
3-06	India	D	1-1	Jakarta	Fr	Ponyaro [33]		
9-06	Sri Lanka	W	1-0	Jakarta	WCq	Elie Aiboy [30]	30 000	Nesar BAN
18-07	Qatar	W	2-1	Beijing	ACr1	Budi [26], Ponaryo [48]	5 000	Moradi IRN
21-07	China PR	L	0-5	Beijing	ACr1			Najm LIB
25-07	Bahrain	L	1-3	Jinan	ACr1	Elie Aiboy [75]	20 000	Codjia BEN
4-09	Singapore	L	0-2	Singapore	Fr			
8-09	Sri Lanka	D	2-2	Colombo	WCq	Jaya [8], Sofyan [51]	4 000	Marshoud JOR
12-10	Saudi Arabia	L	1-3	Jakarta	WCq	Jaya [50]	30 000	Mohd Salleh MAS
17-11	Turkmenistan	W	3-1	Jakarta	WCq	Jaya 3 [20 47 59]	15 000	Shaban KUW
7-12	Laos	W	6-0	Ho Chi Minh City	TCr1	Boas [26], Jaya 2 [29 34], OG [53], Aiboy [60], Kurniawan [87]		Rungklay THA
9-12	Singapore	D	0-0	Ho Chi Minh City	TCr1		4 000	Kwong Jong Chul KOR
11-12	Vietnam	W	3-0	Hanoi	TCr1	Lessy [18], Boas [21], Jaya [45]	40 000	Ebrahim BHR
13-12	Cambodia	W	8-0	Hanoi	TCr1	Jaya 3 [9 48 57], Aiboy 2 [30 55], Kurniawan 2 [72 74], Ortisan [82]	17 000	Sun Baojie CHN
28-12	Malaysia	L	1-2	Jakarta	TCsf	Kurniawan [7]	100 000	Irmatov UZB
2005								
3-01	Malaysia	W	4-1	Kuala Lumpur	TCsf	Kurniawan [59], Yulianto [74], Jaya [77], Boas [84]	70 000	Kunsuta THA
8-01	Singapore	L	1-3	Jakarta	TCf	Mahyadi [90+3]	120 000	Kwong Jong Chul KOR
16-01	Singapore	L	1-2	Singapore	TCf	Elie Aiboy [76]	55 000	Al Ghamdi KSA
29-03	Australia	L	0-3	Perth	Fr		14 000	Yamanishi JPN
2006								
23-08	Malaysia	D	1-1	Kuala Lumpur	Fr	Bambang Pamungkas [16]	20 000	Zhang Lei CHN
25-08	Myanmar	D	0-0	Kuala Lumpur	Fr			Shahrul MAS
27-08	Thailand	W	1-0	Kuala Lumpur	Fr	Baya Sutha [26]	8 000	Lee Jong Kuk KOR
29-08	Myanmar	L	1-2	Kuala Lumpur	Fr	Zaenal Arif [87]	30 000	Shahrul MAS
2007								
13-01	Laos	W	3-1	Singapore	TCr1	Atep 2 [51 75], Saktiawan Sinaga [67]		
15-01	Vietnam	D	1-1	Singapore	TCr1	Saktiawan Sinaga [90]	4 500	Shahbuddin
17-01	Singapore	D	2-2	Singapore	TCr1	Ilham Jaya Kesuma [27], Zaenal Arif [56]	13 819	Sananwai THA
1-06	Hong Kong	W	3-0	Jakarta	Fr	Bambang Pamungkas [16], OG [62], Zaenal Arif [78p]		
3-06	Singapore	L	0-1	Jakarta	Fr			
21-06	Jamaica	W	2-1	Jakarta	Fr	Bambang Pamungkas 2 [58 90]		
24-06	Oman	L	0-1	Jakarta	Fr			
10-07	Bahrain	W	2-1	Jakarta	ACr1	Budi Sunarsoni [14], Bambang Pamungkas [64]	60 000	Nishimura JPN
14-07	Saudi Arabia	L	1-2	Jakarta	ACr1	Elie Aiboy [17]	87 000	Al Badwawi UAE
18-07	Korea Republic	L	0-1	Jakarta	ACr1		87 000	Shield AUS

Fr = Friendly match • TC = ASEAN Tiger Cup/ASEAN Football Federation Championship • AC = AFC Asian Cup • WC = FIFA World Cup
q = qualifier • r1 = first round group • sf = semi-final • f = final

INDONESIA NATIONAL TEAM RECORDS AND RECORD SEQUENCES

Records			Sequence records			
Victory	12-0	PHI 1972	Wins	10	1968-1969	Clean sheets	4	1987, 2004
Defeat	0-9	DEN 1974	Defeats	7	1996	Goals scored	24	1967-1969
Player Caps	59	KURNIAWAN Dwi Julianto	Undefeated	10	Three times	Without goal	5	Three times
Player Goals	33	KURNIAWAN Dwi Julianto	Without win	18	1985-1986	Goals against	19	1985-1986

REPUBLIC OF INDONESIA; REPUBLIK INDONESIA

Capital	Jakarta	Language	Bahasa Indonesia			Independence	1945
Population	245 452 739	Area	1 919 440 km²	Density	124 per km²	% in cities	35%
GDP per cap	$3200	Dailling code	+62	Internet	.id	GMT + / -	+7

MAJOR CITIES/TOWNS

Population '000

1	Jakarta	8 568
2	Surabaya	2 358
3	Medan	1 763
4	Bandung	1 651
5	Palembang	1 619
6	Tangerang	1 433
7	Makassar	1 380
8	Depok	1 315
9	Semarang	1 286
10	Palembang	1 257
11	Padang	899
12	Bandar Lampung	857
13	Bogor	801
14	Malang	752
15	Pekan Baru	705
16	Yogyakarta	669
17	Banjarmasin	590
18	Surakarta/Solo	559
19	Balikpapan	447
20	Banda Aceh	268
21	Purwakarta	239
22	Kediri	233
23	Sidoarjo	151
24	Jayapura	140

MEDALS TABLE

		Overall			Lge		Cup		Asia				City	Stadium	Cap'ty	DoF
		G	S	B	G	S	G	S	G	S	B					
1	Persija Jakarta	11	6		11	5		1				Jakarta	Lebak Bulus	12 000	1928
2	Persis Solo	8	1		8	1						Solo	Manahan	15 000	1923
3	Persebaya Surabaya	7	11		7	11						Surabaya	Gelora	30 000	1927
4	Tiga Berlian	7	1	1	4	1	3				1	Palembang			
5	Persib Bandung	6	8		6	8						Bandung	Siliwangi	20 000	1933
	PSM Makasar	6	8		6	8						Makassar	Mattoangin	30 000	1915
7	PSMS Medan	6	6		6	6						Medan	Teladan	15 000	1930
8	Pelita Jaya	3	5		3	2	3					Purwakarta	Punawarman	10 000	1980
9	Mitra Kukar	3	2		3	1		1				Tenggarong	Rondong Demang	20 000	2003
10	Arema Malang	3	1		1		2	1				Malang	Gajayana	20 000	1982
11	Persipura Jayapura	2	2		2	1		1				Jayapura	Mandala	15 000	1950
12	Arseto	2	1		1	1	1					Solo			
	PSIS Semarang	2	1		2	1						Semarang	Jatidiri	21 000	1932
14	Persik Kediri	2			2							Kediri	Brawijaya	10 000	1950
15	PSIM Yogyakarta	1	5		1	5						Yogyakarta	Mandala Krida	25 000	
16	Petrokimia / Gresik United	1	1		1	1						Gresik	Tri Dharma	25 000	1986

RECENT LEAGUE RECORD

	Championship				Cup		
Year	Champions	Score	Runners-up		Champions	Score	Runners-up
1995	Persib	1-0	Petrokimia Putra		No Cup competition		
1996	Bandung Raya	2-0	PSM		No Cup competition		
1997	Persebaya	3-1	Bandung Raya		No Cup competition		
1998	Season not finished due to political unrest				No Cup competition		
1999	PSIS	1-0	Persebaya		No Cup competition		
2000	PSM	3-2	Pupuk Kaltim		No Cup competition		
2001	Persija	3-2	PSM		No Cup competition		
2002	Petrokimia Putra	2-1	Persita		No Cup competition		
2003	Persik	†	PSM		No Cup competition		
2004	Persebaya	†	PSM		No Cup competition		
2005	Persipura	3-2	Persija		Arema Malang	4-3	Persija
2006	Persik	1-0	PSIS Semarang		Arema Malang	2-0	Persipura

† Championship played on a league system

INDONESIA 2006

LIGA INDONESIA DIVISI UTAMA WILAYA BARAT (WEST)

	Pl	W	D	L	F	A	Pts	Arema	Persija	PSIS	Persek pas	PSMS	Sriwijaya	Persikota	Persitara	Persijap	Persita	Semen	Persib	PSDS	PSIM
Arema Malang †	26	13	8	5	39	17	47		0-0	1-0	3-0	1-1	1-1	4-1	3-0	3-0	2-0	1-0	3-1	3-0	**3-0**
Persija Jakarta †	26	13	8	5	26	16	47	1-0		0-1	2-0	1-0	2-1	1-0	1-1	1-0	3-0	0-1	0-0	1-0	0-0
PSIS Semarang †	26	13	8	5	33	27	44	1-1	1-0		0-1	1-0	2-1	2-0	5-0	2-0	2-0	0-0	1-1	3-1	2-1
Persekabpas †	26	12	6	8	35	27	42	1-2	1-0	2-0		3-1	3-2	1-1	2-0	1-0	1-1	1-0	1-0	3-0	**3-0**
PSMS Medan	26	12	3	11	31	27	39	2-1	2-0	2-0	0-0		2-2	1-0	0-1	0-1	3-1	1-0	2-1	3-1	5-2
Sriwijaya Palembang	26	8	10	8	29	24	34	1-1	0-1	1-1	2-2	2-0		1-0	1-0	3-1	1-0	1-0	0-0	2-0	**3-0**
Persikota Tangerang	26	9	7	10	34	37	34	2-1	3-3	1-1	2-1	2-0	1-0		3-2	2-1	0-1	1-0	0-0	6-0	4-3
Persitara Jakarta Utara	26	10	4	12	29	34	34	1-1	1-2	2-1	1-3	2-1	1-0	0-1		1-1	2-1	2-1	3-1	3-0	1-2
Persijap Jepara	26	8	9	9	25	27	33	1-1	2-2	1-1	0-0	0-1	0-0	6-1	1-0		1-0	1-0	1-1	2-1	1-0
Persita Tangerang	26	8	8	10	25	30	32	0-0	0-1	3-2	1-1	1-0	1-1	0-0	1-0	2-2		3-0	2-1	2-1	1-1
Semen Padang	26	8	6	12	20	24	30	1-2	0-0	1-0	2-1	2-0	1-1	3-1	1-0	1-0	1-1		0-1	1-1	**3-0**
Persib Bandung	26	7	8	11	23	30	29	1-0	1-1	1-2	3-2	0-2	0-0	2-1	0-1	0-1	2-0	1-0		1-2	1-1
PSDS Lubuk Pakam	26	8	5	13	32	41	29	1-1	0-1	6-0	2-1	0-1	3-2	0-0	1-1	3-1	2-0	2-0	4-1		1-1
PSIM Yogyakarta	26	7	5	14	23	43	26	0-1	**0-3**	1-2	2-0	2-1	1-0	2-1	**0-3**	0-0	**0-3**	2-0	**0-3**	0-2	1-0

LIGA INDONESIA DIVISI UTAMA WILAYA TIMUR (EAST)

	Pl	W	D	L	F	A	Pts	Persmin	Persik	PSM	Persiba	Persiwa	Persela	Persema	Persipura	Persiter	PKT	Persibom	Deltras	PSS	Persegi
Persmin Minahasa †	26	16	2	8	37	26	50		2-1	1-0	2-0	3-1	2-0	1-0	2-1	1-0	1-0	3-1	2-0	2-0	1-0
Persik Kediri †	26	14	5	7	53	24	47	5-1		6-0	2-0	0-0	2-0	4-2	1-1	1-1	3-0	2-0	2-1	**3-0**	7-1
PSM Makassar †	26	12	6	8	44	32	42	3-1	3-1		1-0	0-0	3-1	4-1	1-1	1-1	2-0	5-1	1-1	1-0	2-0
Persiba Balikpapan †	26	12	5	9	35	28	41	0-0	1-0	0-0		5-1	4-0	2-1	2-1	1-0	1-0	3-1	2-1	1-0	4-0
Persiwa Wamena	26	11	7	8	34	34	40	2-1	1-1	2-1	0-0		1-0	2-1	1-2	2-0	3-0	2-0	3-1	1-0	3-0
Persela Lamongan	26	10	8	8	23	23	38	1-0	0-1	1-0	2-2	1-1		0-1	0-0	1-0	3-0	2-0	1-0	**3-0**	1-0
Persema Malang	26	11	3	12	39	37	36	1-0	0-1	3-2	0-1	0-1	0-1		0-2	4-0	4-2	4-0	2-2	0-0	0-0
Persipura Jayapura	26	9	8	9	27	23	35	3-2	0-3	1-0	2-0	0-1	0-0	5-0		2-0	2-0	0-0	2-0	0-0	0-0
Persiter Ternate	26	10	5	11	33	34	35	0-1	1-0	1-3	2-1	4-1	1-1	2-2	3-0		3-1	0-1	1-0	2-0	1-0
PKT Bontang	26	10	5	11	33	42	35	1-1	2-1	2-2	2-3	2-1	2-0	2-1	1-0	3-1		4-2	3-2	2-1	1-1
Persibom Kotamobagu	26	9	6	11	35	46	33	1-2	3-0	1-0	3-1	2-2	1-1	2-1	2-2	2-0			1-0	2-2	3-0
Delta Putra Sidoarjo	26	9	5	12	35	32	32	2-1	1-1	4-2	2-1	3-0	1-1	2-0	2-0	4-0	0-1	1-1		1-0	2-0
PSS Sleman	26	6	5	15	18	40	23	1-0	2-1	**0-3**	1-1	4-1	0-0	**0-3**	1-0	**0-3**	1-1	2-1	3-2		**0-3**
Persegi Mojokerto	26	5	6	15	24	49	21	2-4	1-2	2-4	2-0	1-1	1-2	0-3	1-1	1-4	1-1	4-2	1-0	2-0	

14/01/2006 - 24/06/2006 • † Qualified for the play-offs • Matches in bold awarded 3-0 after PSIM and PSS withrew following an earthquake in Central Java • No relegation due to the expansion of the league to 36 clubs

SUPERLIGA BABAK 8 BESAR

West	Pl	W	D	L	F	A	Pts	PS	AM	PB
Persik Kediri †	3	2	1	0	4	1	7	3-1	1-0	0-0
PSIS Semarang†	3	2	0	1	3	3	6		1-0	1-0
Arema Malang	3	1	0	2	3	2	3			3-0
Persiba Balikpapan	3	0	1	2	0	4	1			

East	Pl	W	D	L	F	A	Pts	PM	PJ	PM
Persekabpas †	3	2	1	0	10	4	7	2-2	3-1	5-1
Persmin Minahasa†	3	0	3	0	4	4	3		0-0	2-2
Persija Jakarta	3	0	2	1	1	3	2	0-0		
PSM Makassar	3	0	2	1	3	7	2			

17/07/2006 - 24/07/2006 • † Qualified for the semi-finals

PLAY-OFFS

Semi-finals		Finals	
Persik Kediri	3		
Persmin Minahasa	1		
		Persik Kediri	1
		PSIS Semarang	0
Persekabpas	0		
PSIS Semarang	1		

Third place play-off:

LIGA INDONESIA FINAL

Stadion Manahan, Solo, 30-07-2006, Att: 25 000, Ref: Napitupulu

Persik Kediri 1   Christian Gonzales 109
PSIS Semarang 0

Persik - Wahyudi - Suroso, Aris Indarto, Leonardo Gutierrez - Harianto, Danilo Fernando, Jefry Dwi Hadi (Suswanto 55), Ebi Sukore, Khusnul Yulu - Christian Gonzales, Budi Sudarsono (Bertha Yuwana 116). Tr: Daniel Roekito
PSIS - Komang Putra - Maman Abdurrahman, Foffe Kamara, Zoubairou Garba (Deni Rumba 113) - Ridwan, Ortiz, Suwita Patha, Indriyanto Nugroho (Miguel Angel Dominguez 54), Harry Salisburi - Emanuel de Porras, Imral Usman (Khusnul Yakin 64). Tr: Bonggo Pribadi

PIALA INDONESIA 2006

Second Round

Arema Malang*	2	0	
Persekaba Badung	0	1	
Persipasi Bekasi	0	1	
Persipur Purwodadi*	0	1	
PKT Bontang	0	1	
Persibom Kotamobagu*	0	0	
Persela Lamongan	0	1	
Persebaya Surabaya*	2	0	
Persma Mando	w-o		
Persmin Minhasa			
Persikad Depok			
Persiku Kudus	w-o		
Persik Kediri*	4	1	
Persibo Bojonegoro	2	2	
Persita Tangerang*	2	1	3p
PSMS Medan	1	2	4p
Persija Jakarta	1	1	
PSIS Semarang*	0	0	
PSP Padang	0	2	
PSSB Bireuen*	1	1	
Periswa Wamena*	3	2	
PSM Makassar	1	3	
PSPS Pekanbaru	0	2	
Semen Padang*	2	1	
Delta Putra Sidoarjo*	1	0	
Persema Malang*	1	0	
Persitara Jakarta Utara*	0	2	
Persikota Tangerang	1	2	
Persikab Bandung*	2	1	
Pelita Jaya	1	1	
Persiba Balikpapan	0	2	
Persipura Jayapura*	4	0	

Round of 16

Arema Malang*	4	2
Persipur Purwodadi	0	0
PKT Bontang*	3	0
Persebaya Surabaya	2	5
Persma Mando	2	4
Persiku Kudus*	1	2
Persik Kediri*	2	1
PSMS Medan	1	4
Persija Jakarta	1	3
PSSB Bireuen*	0	1
Periswa Wamena*	2	0
Semen Padang	1	1
Delta Putra Sidoarjo*	0	1 3p
Persikota Tangerang	1	0 2p
Persikab Bandung	0	0
Persipura Jayapura*	2	1

Quarter-finals

Arema Malang*	1	0
Persebaya Surabaya	0	0
Persma Mando*	0	1
PSMS Medan	3	4
Persija Jakarta	2	1
Semen Padang*	1	0
Delta Putra Sidoarjo	1	1
Persipura Jayapura*	2	1

Semi-finals

Arema Malang	1	4
PSMS Medan*	1	2
Persija Jakarta	1	0
Persipura Jayapura	1	2

Final

Arema Malang	2
Persipura Jayapura	0

PIALA INDONESIA FINAL

Stadion Gelora Delta, Sidoarjo
16-09-2006, Att: 20 000, Ref: Napitupulu
Scorers - Prasetyo 51p, Ballah 58

Arema - Kurniawan - Soputan, Pulalo, De Marie (Wasidi 75), Ballah (Quintao 87) - Prasetyo, Iba, Gede, Tao (Utina 79) - Ngongue, Sutaji

Persipura - Pitoy - Carrasco (Mahuse 13), Worabay, Darocha, Ivakldalam – Komboy, Fingkreuw, Lessy, Raymond (Yves 71) – Salampessy, Igbonefo

* Home team in the first leg • Third place play-off: Persija 2-0 PSMS

IND – INDIA

NATIONAL TEAM RECORD
JULY 10TH 2006 TO JULY 12TH 2010

PL	W	D	L	F	A	%
4	0	0	4	2	15	0

FIFA/COCA-COLA WORLD RANKING

1993	1994	1995	1996	1997	1998	1999	2000	2001	2002	2003	2004	2005	2006	High		Low	
100	109	121	120	112	110	106	122	121	127	127	132	127	157	94	02/96	165	05/07

2006–2007											
08/06	09/06	10/06	11/06	12/06	01/07	02/07	03/07	04/07	05/07	06/07	07/07
128	136	143	148	157	157	157	165	165	165	161	162

On a visit to India in April 2007 to open the new headquarters of the All India Football Federation, FIFA president Sepp Blatter referred to India as a sleeping giant, and with backing from the AFC Vision Asia programme there are plans to radically develop the game in the country. National team coach Bob Houghton, who saw his team outplayed in their AFC Asian Cup qualification group, is under no illusions as to the size of the task ahead. Just finding players with the physical stature to match those of countries like Iran, Saudi, Japan, Korea or Australia will be a massive challenge. Motivating the business community to back local football is another major task, but already the

INTERNATIONAL HONOURS
Asian Games 1951 1962 South Asian Federation Games 1985 1987 1995 South Asian Football Federation Cup 1995

signs are positive. Houghton compares football in India to where China was in the mid 1990s when professional league football was in its infancy, but India has a huge advantage in that club football is well established and has deep roots. Extending the National League from its current five month duration and cutting down on the number of smaller tournaments is likely to be one of the central strategies as India moves forward. It proved to be a good year for Dempo SC from Goa who won the National Football League for the second time in three years, along with winning the Durand Cup. Calcutta's Mohun Bagan won the Federation Cup for a record twelfth time.

THE FIFA BIG COUNT OF 2006

	Male	Female		Total
Number of players	19 020 900	1 567 000	Referees and Assistant Referees	17 640
Professionals	400		Admin, Coaches, Technical, Medical	21 000
Amateurs 18+	71 000		Number of clubs	6 500
Youth under 18	313 500		Number of teams	12 000
Unregistered	2 212 000		Clubs with women's teams	40
Total players	20 587 900		Players as % of population	1.88%

All India Football Federation (AIFF)
Football House, Sector 19, Dwarka, New Dehli 110075, India
Tel +91 11 28041430   Fax +91 11 28041434
alb@sancharnet.in   www.the-aiff.com
President: DAS MUNSI Priya Ranjan   General Secretary: COLACO Alberto
Vice-President: PATEL Praful   Treasurer: SALGAOCAR Shivanand   Media Officer: None
Men's Coach: HOUGHTON Bob   Women's Coach: SINGH Moirangthem
AIFF formed: 1937   AFC: 1954   FIFA: 1948
Sky blue shirts, Navy blue shorts, Sky blue and navy blue socks

RECENT INTERNATIONAL MATCHES PLAYED BY INDIA

2003	Opponents		Score	Venue	Comp	Scorers	Att	Referee
24-03	Korea DPR	L	0-2	Pyongyang	ACq			
30-03	Korea DPR	D	1-1	Margao	ACq	Vijayan [29]		
16-10	Thailand	L	0-2	Bangkok	Fr			
22-10	Rwanda	W	3-1	Hyderabad	AAr1	Vijayan [13], Suresh [54], Biswas [79]		
24-10	Malaysia	W	2-0	Hyderabad	AAr1	Bisht [50], Vijayan [64]		
29-10	Zimbabwe	W	5-3	Hyderabad	AAsf	Vijayan 2 [25 33], Bhutia 2 [41 83p], Singh.R [58]		
31-10	Uzbekistan	L	0-1	Hyderabad	AAf			Lu Jun CHN
2004								
18-02	Singapore	W	1-0	Margao	WCq	Singh.R [50]	28 000	Yasrebi IRN
31-03	Oman	L	1-5	Kochin	WCq	Singh.R [18]	48 000	Kim Heng MAS
3-06	Indonesia	D	1-1	Jakarta	Fr	Ancheri [89p]		
9-06	Japan	L	0-7	Saitama	WCq		63 000	Huang Junjie CHN
22-08	Myanmar	W	2-1	Ho Chi Minh City	Fr	Prakash 2 [42 83]		
24-08	Vietnam	L	1-2	Ho Chi Minh City	Fr	Lawrence [87]		
8-09	Japan	L	0-4	Calcutta	WCq		90 000	Hajjar SYR
13-10	Singapore	L	0-2	Singapore	WCq		3 609	Husain BHR
5-11	Kuwait	W	3-2	Kuwait City	Fr	Singh.T [48], Zirsanga [64], Yadav [75]		
17-11	Oman	D	0-0	Muscat	WCq		2 000	Nurilddin Salman IRQ
2005								
12-06	Pakistan	D	1-1	Quetta	Fr	Chetri [65]	20 000	Khan PAK
16-06	Pakistan	W	1-0	Peshawar	Fr	Abdul Hakim [67]	15 000	Imtiaz PAK
18-06	Pakistan	L	0-3	Lahore	Fr			Asif PAK
12-08	Fiji	L	0-1	Lautoka	Fr		10 000	Fox NZL
14-08	Fiji	L	1-2	Suva	Fr	Singh.I [10]	11 000	O'Leary NZL
8-12	Nepal	W	2-1	Karachi	SAr1	Mehtab Hossain 2 [6 28]		
10-12	Bhutan	W	3-0	Karachi	SAr1	Bhutia [45], Gawli [51], Abdul Hakim [64]		
12-12	Bangladesh	D	1-1	Karachi	SAr1	Lawrence [17]		
14-12	Maldives	W	1-0	Karachi	SAsf	Shivananju [38]		
17-12	Bangladesh	W	2-0	Karachi	SAf	Din Wadoo [33], Bhutia [81]		
2006								
18-02	Hong Kong	D	2-2	Hong Kong	Fr	Nabi [61], Bhutia [68p]	3 672	Jae Yong Bae
22-02	Japan	L	0-6	Yokohama	ACq		38 025	Huang CHN
1-03	Yemen	L	0-3	New Dehli	ACq		8 000	Torky IRN
1-04	Afghanistan	W	2-0	Chittagong	CCr1	Pariyar 2 [35 60]	2 500	Al Ghatrifi OMA
3-04	Philippines	D	1-1	Chittagong	CCr1	Pariyar [8]	2 000	Mujghef JOR
5-04	Chinese Taipei	D	0-0	Chittagong	CCr1		2 000	Gosh BAN
9-04	Nepal	L	0-3	Chittagong	CCqf		3 000	Gosh BAN
16-08	Saudi Arabia	L	0-3	Calcutta	ACq		10 000	Tongkhan THA
6-09	Saudi Arabia	L	1-7	Jeddah	ACq	Nanjangud [22]	3 000	Al Saeedi UAE
11-10	Japan	L	0-3	Bangalore	ACq		5 000	Chan Siu Kee HKG
15-11	Yemen	L	1-2	Sana'a	ACq	Pradeep [54]	5 500	Marshoud JOR
2007								

No international matches played in 2007 before August

Fr = Friendly match • SA = South Asian Football Federation Cup • CC - AFC Confederation Cup • AC = AFC Asian Cup • AA = Afro-Asian Games •
WC = FIFA World Cup
q = qualifier • r1 = first round group • qf = quarter-final • sf = semi-final • f = final

INDIA NATIONAL TEAM RECORDS AND RECORD SEQUENCES

Records			Sequence records				
Victory	7-1	SRI 1963	Wins	7	1962-1964	Clean sheets	4	1966
Defeat	1-11	URS 1955	Defeats	8	1978-1980	Goals scored	21	1958-1961
Player Caps	n/a		Undefeated	7	1962-64, 1999	Without goal	6	1984-1985
Player Goals	n/a		Without win	11	1986-92, 1993	Goals against	15	1952-58, 1973-76

REPUBLIC OF INDIA; BHARATIYA GANARAJYA

Capital	New Dehli	Language Hindi, English, 14 other official languages	Independence 1947
Population	1 095 351 995	Area 3 287 590 km²	Density 324 per km²	% in cities 27%
GDP per cap	$2900	Dailling code +91	Internet .in	GMT +/- +5.5

MEDALS TABLE

		Overall			League			F Cup		D Cup		St	Asia			City	Stadium	Cap'ty	DoF
		G	S	B	G	S	B	G S	G S		G S		G S B						
1	Mohun Bagan	31	14	2	3	1	1	12 4	16 19	26		1			Calcutta	Saltlake	120 000	1889
2	East Bengal FC	22	20	2	3	3	2	4 7	15 10	31					Calcutta	Saltlake	120 000	1920
3	JCT Mills	8	7		1	1		2	5 6	9					Phagwara	Guru Gobind Singh	12 000	1971
4	Border Security Force	8	3					1 1	7 2	3					Jalandhar			
5	Salgoacar SC	6	4	2	1	1	2	3 3	2	18					Vasco, Goa	Fatorda, Madgaon	35 000	1955
6	Mahindra United	5	4	2	1		2	2 2	2 2	12					Mumbai	The Cooperage	12 000	1962
7	Mohammedan Sporting	3	6					2 3	1 3	11					Calcutta	Mohammedan	7 000	1892
8	Dempo Sports Club	4	3		2	1		1 2	1	10					Panaji, Goa	Fatorda, Madgaon	35 000	1968

FC = Federation Cup • D Cup = Durand Cup • St = State championship (not included in overall total)

RECENT LEAGUE AND CUP RECORD

	National Football League						Federation Cup		
Year	Champions	Pts	Runners-up	Pts	Third	Pts	Winners	Score	Runners-up
2000	Mohun Bagan	47	Churchill Brothers	41	Salgaocar	39	Not played		
2001	East Bengal	46	Mohun Bagan	45	Churchill Brothers	36	Mohun Bagan	2-0	Dempo
2002	Mohun Bagan	44	Churchill Brothers	42	Vasco	40	Not played		
2003	East Bengal	49	Salgaocar	44	Vasco	43	Mahindra United	1-0	Mohammedan Sporting
2004	East Bengal	49	Dempo	45	Mahindra United	41	Dempo	2-0	Mohun Bagan
2005	Dempo	47	Sporting Clube Goa	45	East Bengal	43	Mahindra United	2-1	Sporting Clube Goa
2006	Mahindra United	36	East Bengal	31	Mohun Bagan	30	Mohun Bagan	1-1 3-1p	Sporting Clube Goa
2007	Dempo	36	JCT Mills	31	Mahindra United	30			

DURAND CUP 2006

Quarter–final groups		Semi–finals		Final	
Group A	Pts				
Mohun Bagan	7	**Dempo Sports Club**	2		
Sporting Club Goa	6	Mohun Bagan	0		
Mahindra United	4				
Air India	0			**Dempo Sports Club**	1
Group B				JCT Mills	0
JCT Mills	5				
Dempo Sports Club	5	Sporting Clube Goa	0		
Army XI	4	**JCT Mills**	1		
East Bengal	1	6/11/2006 - 27/11/2006 in Dehli with three stages prior to the semis			

INDIA 2007

11TH NATIONAL FOOTBALL LEAGUE

	Pl	W	D	L	F	A	Pts	Dempo	JCT Mills	Mahindra	Churchill	East Bengal	Sporting	Air India	Mohun B.	Moham'dan	Hindustan
Dempo Sports Club †	18	11	3	4	37	21	36		2-3	0-1	3-1	5-3	3-2	2-1	1-0	5-0	2-1
JCT Mills †	18	9	4	5	31	19	31	0-0		1-0	0-0	1-2	1-1	3-0	2-0	1-2	3-0
Mahindra United	18	8	6	4	29	14	30	2-1	3-2		1-1	2-2	0-1	1-0	4-1	9-0	1-0
Churchill Brothers	18	7	8	3	30	23	29	0-2	4-3	0-0		3-2	2-0	4-1	2-2	3-1	1-0
East Bengal	18	7	5	6	29	29	26	0-0	2-3	2-1	2-2		0-2	1-1	1-0	2-1	3-2
Sporting Clube Goa	18	6	7	5	23	19	25	0-2	2-0	1-3	1-1	1-1		1-1	0-0	0-0	4-0
Air India	18	4	9	5	20	23	21	2-2	0-0	0-0	2-0	1-0	1-1		0-0	2-2	3-1
Mohun Bagan	18	5	6	7	15	21	21	1-2	1-3	1-1	1-1	2-1	1-2	2-1		1-0	1-0
Mohammedan Sporting	18	2	6	10	17	42	12	3-2	0-2	0-0	1-4	1-2	1-3	3-3	0-1		0-0
Hindustan Aeronautics	18	2	4	12	12	32	10	1-3	0-3	1-0	1-1	1-3	2-1	0-1	0-0	2-2	

5/01/2007 - 19/05/2007 • † Qualified for the AFC Cup

28TH FEDERATION CUP 2006

First round		Quarter–finals		Semi–finals		Final	
Mohun Bagan	4						
Viva Kerala	1	Mohun Bagan	2 3p				
Air India	0	Churchill Brothers	2 1p				
Churchill Brothers	3			Mohun Bagan	2 5p		
East Bengal	2			Dempo Sports Club	2 4p		
State Bank of Trv'core	0	East Bengal	0				
HAL SC	0	Dempo Sports Club	1				
Dempo Sports Club	1					Mohun Bagan	1 3p
Mahindra United	1					Sporting Clube Goa	1 1p
United Sports Club	0	Mahindra United	2				
Vasco Sports Club	0	Mohemmedan Sporting	1				
Mohammedan Sporting	1			Mahindra United	0		
Salgoacar Sports Club	1			Sporting Clube Goa	1		
JCT Mills	0	Salgoacar Sports Club	0				
Army XI	0	Sporting Clube Goa	1				
Sporting Clube Goa	4						

CUP FINAL
30-12-2006

Scorers - Fabio Cortez Vidal [28] for Mohun; Harmanjot Singh Khabra [5] for Sporting

18/12/2006 - 30/12/2006 in Calcutta • ‡ Qualified for the AFC Cup

INDIA 2007
NATIONAL LEAGUE 2ND DIVISION

	Pl	W	D	L	F	A	Pts
Salgaocar SC	5	3	2	0	8	5	11
Viva Kerala	5	3	1	1	14	9	10
Chirag United SC	5	2	1	2	6	5	7
Vasco Sports Club	5	1	2	2	5	8	5
Army XI	5	0	3	2	6	9	3
ONGC Mumbai	5	0	3	2	5	8	3

25/03/2007 - 8/04/2007

INDIA 2006
PUNJAB SUPER LEAGUE

	Pl	W	D	L	F	A	Pts
JCT Mills	12	9	2	1	22	5	29
Border Security	12	8	3	1	23	3	27
Punjab Police	12	5	2	5	14	11	17
JCT Academy	12	4	4	4	15	17	16
Rail Coach Factory	12	3	5	4	11	13	14
Punjab Electricity	12	3	1	8	7	24	10
Bassi FC	12	0	3	9	9	28	3

26/07/2006 - 27/08/2006

INDIA 2006
CALCUTTA SUPER DIVISION

	Pl	W	D	L	F	A	Pts
East Bengal	14	10	2	2	20	5	32
Mohun Bagan	14	9	3	2	21	8	30
Mohammedan Sporting	14	6	6	2	15	8	24
EverReady SA	14	5	2	7	11	20	17
Calcutta Port Trust	14	3	5	6	11	16	14
Eastern Railway	14	4	2	8	9	16	14
George Telegraph	14	2	7	5	7	9	13
Railway FC	14	1	5	8	4	16	8

21/07/2006 - 9/11/2006

INDIA 2006
9TH GOAN PRO LEAGUE

	Pl	W	D	L	F	A	Pts
Sporting Clube Goa	14	12	1	1	30	7	37
Churchill Brothers	14	9	4	1	36	14	31
Salgoacar Sports Club	14	6	4	4	23	13	22
Dempo Sports Club	14	6	2	6	31	20	20
Vasco Sports Club	14	4	4	6	13	21	16
Raia Sporting Club	14	5	1	8	17	24	15
Velsao Pale Sports Club	14	3	2	9	7	38	11
Corps of Signals	14	1	2	12	5	26	5

15/08/2006 - 3/12/2006

IRL – REPUBLIC OF IRELAND

NATIONAL TEAM RECORD
JULY 10TH 2006 TO JULY 12TH 2010

PL	W	D	L	F	A	%
10	4	3	3	14	14	55

FIFA/COCA-COLA WORLD RANKING

1993	1994	1995	1996	1997	1998	1999	2000	2001	2002	2003	2004	2005	2006	High	Low
10	9	28	36	47	56	35	31	17	14	14	12	24	49	**6** 08/93	**57** 11/98

	2006–2007										
08/06	09/06	10/06	11/06	12/06	01/07	02/07	03/07	04/07	05/07	06/07	07/07
38	43	49	49	49	49	46	51	31	32	38	39

A late, late winner by Stephen Ireland four minutes into injury-time against San Marino in Serravalle not only saved manager Steve Staunton his job but it spared Irish blushes and kicked started their campaign to qualify for the finals of UEFA Euro 2008. That victory was followed by two more, against Wales and Slovakia, before huge and enthusiastic crowds as the national team played their first ever matches at the impressive Croke Park. However, earlier defeats against Germany and Cyprus meant it was always going to be an uphill battle to qualify for the finals. In domestic football there were dramatic developments when newly crowned league champions

INTERNATIONAL HONOURS
Qualified for the FIFA World Cup finals 1990 1994 2002 UEFA U-17 Championship 1998

Shelbourne were sensationally relegated to the second division because of debts totalling €4m. The club had won the championship three times in four seasons under talismanic manager Pat Fenlon but the decision led to a mass exodus from the club. Their title had been secured on the last day of the season, a 2-1 victory over Bohemians ensuring that they finished ahead of Derry City on goal difference. Derry had earlier beaten Shelbourne on penalties in the final of the League Cup and they completed at Cup double at the end of the season with a late comeback against St Patrick's Athletic in the Cup Final, winning 4-3 after extra-time.

THE FIFA BIG COUNT OF 2006

	Male	Female		Total
Number of players	390 444	31 200	Referees and Assistant Referees	1 020
Professionals	476		Admin, Coaches, Technical, Medical	6 310
Amateurs 18+	77 870		Number of clubs	5 629
Youth under 18	174 498		Number of teams	15 025
Unregistered	98 800		Clubs with women's teams	199
Total players	421 644		Players as % of population	10.38%

The Football Association of Ireland (FAI)
80 Merrion Square South, Dublin 2
Tel +353 1 7037500   Fax +353 1 6610931
info@fai.ie   www.fai.ie
President: BLOOD David   General Secretary: DELANEY John
Vice-President: FLEMING Maurice   Treasurer: MURRAY Edward   Media Officer: McDermott Gerry
Men's Coach: STAUNTON Steve   Women's Coach: KING Noel
FAI formed: 1921   UEFA: 1954   FIFA: 1923
Green shirts with white trimmings, White shirts, Green socks or White shirts with green trimmings, Green shorts, White socks

RECENT INTERNATIONAL MATCHES PLAYED BY THE REPUBLIC OF IRELAND

2003	Opponents		Score	Venue	Comp	Scorers	Att	Referee
19-08	Australia	W	2-1	Dublin	Fr	O'Shea [74], Morrison [81]	37 200	Vidlak CZE
6-09	Russia	D	1-1	Dublin	ECq	Duff [35]	36 000	Michel SVK
9-09	Turkey	D	2-2	Dublin	Fr	Connolly [35], Dunne [90]	27 000	Wegereef NED
11-10	Switzerland	L	0-2	Basel	ECq		31 006	Frisk SWE
18-11	Canada	W	3-0	Dublin	Fr	Duff [24], Keane.Rb 2 [60 84]	23 000	Whitby WAL
2004								
18-02	Brazil	D	0-0	Dublin	Fr		44 000	Frisk SWE
31-03	Czech Republic	W	2-1	Dublin	Fr	Harte [52], Keane.Rb [90]	42 000	Fisker DEN
28-04	Poland	D	0-0	Bydgoszcz	Fr		15 500	Shebek UKR
27-05	Romania	W	1-0	Dublin	Fr	Holland [85]	42 356	Jara CZE
29-05	Nigeria	L	0-3	London	Fr		7 438	D'Urso ENG
2-06	Jamaica	W	1-0	London	Fr	Barrett [26]	6 155	Styles ENG
5-06	Netherlands	W	1-0	Amsterdam	Fr	Keane.Rb [45]	42 000	Dean ENG
18-08	Bulgaria	D	1-1	Dublin	Fr	Reid [15]	31 887	Brines SCO
4-09	Cyprus	W	3-0	Dublin	WCq	Morrison [33], Reid [38], Keane.Rb [54]	36 000	Paniashvili GEO
8-09	Switzerland	D	1-1	Basel	WCq	Morrison [8]	28 000	Vassaras GRE
9-10	France	D	0-0	Paris	WCq		78 863	Dauden Ibanez ESP
13-10	Faroe Islands	W	2-0	Dublin	WCq	Keane.Rb 2 [14p 32]	36 000	Lajuks LVA
16-11	Croatia	W	1-0	Dublin	Fr	Keane.Rb [24]	33 200	Orrason ISL
2005								
9-02	Portugal	W	1-0	Dublin	Fr	O'Brien [21]	44 100	Messias ENG
26-03	Israel	D	1-1	Tel Aviv	WCq	Morrison [43]	32 150	Ivanov.V RUS
29-03	China PR	W	1-0	Dublin	Fr	Morrison [82]	35 222	Casha MLT
4-06	Israel	D	2-2	Dublin	WCq	Harte [5], Keane.Rb [11]	36 000	Vassaras GRE
8-06	Faroe Islands	W	2-0	Torshavn	WCq	Harte [51p], Kilbane [59]	5 180	Guenov BUL
17-08	Italy	L	1-2	Dublin	Fr	Reid.A [32]	44 000	Gomes Costa POR
7-09	France	L	0-1	Dublin	WCq		36 000	Fandel GER
8-10	Cyprus	W	1-0	Nicosia	WCq	Elliott [6]	13 546	Kassai HUN
12-10	Switzerland	D	0-0	Dublin	WCq		35 944	Merk GER
2006								
1-03	Sweden	W	3-0	Dublin	Fr	Duff [36], Keane.Rb [48], Miller [71]	44 109	Ledentu FRA
24-05	Chile	L	0-1	Dublin	Fr		41 200	Ingvarsson SWE
16-08	Netherlands	L	0-4	Dublin	Fr		42 400	Ovrebo NOR
2-09	Germany	L	0-1	Stuttgart	ECq		53 198	Medina Cantalejo ESP
7-10	Cyprus	L	2-5	Nicosia	ECq	Ireland [8], Dunne [44]	5 000	Batista POR
11-10	Czech Republic	D	1-1	Dublin	ECq	Kilbane [62]	35 500	Layec FRA
15-11	San Marino	W	5-0	Dublin	ECq	Reid [7], Doyle [24], Keane.Rb 3 [31 58p 85]	34 018	Isaksen FRO
2007								
7-02	San Marino	W	2-1	Serravalle	ECq	Kilbane [49], Ireland [94+]	3 294	Rasmussen DEN
24-03	Wales	W	1-0	Dublin	ECq	Ireland [39]	73 000	Hauge NOR
28-03	Slovakia	W	1-0	Dublin	ECq	Doyle [13]	71 257	Baskakov RUS
23-05	Ecuador	D	1-1	New Jersey	Fr	Doyle [44]	20 823	
26-05	Bolivia	D	1-1	Foxboro	Fr	Long [13]	13 156	

Fr = Friendly match • EC = UEFA EURO 2004/2008 • WC = FIFA World Cup • q = qualifier

REPUBLIC OF IRELAND NATIONAL TEAM RECORDS AND RECORD SEQUENCES

Records			Sequence records					
Victory	8-0	MLT 1983	Wins	8	1987-1988	Clean sheets	5	1989, 1996-1997
Defeat	0-7	BRA 1982	Defeats	5	Six times	Goals scored	17	1954-59, 2000-01
Player Caps	102	STAUNTON Stephen	Undefeated	17	1989-1990	Without goal	5	1995-1996
Player Goals	26	KEANE Robbie	Without win	20	1968-1971	Goals against	35	1966-1973

MAJOR CITIES/TOWNS

		Population '000
1	Dublin	1 036
2	Cork	190
3	Limerick	92
4	Galway	73
5	Waterford	48
6	Drogheda	35
7	Dundalk	34
8	Bray	33
9	Navan	28
10	Ennis	26
11	Tralee	23
12	Naas	22
13	Kilkenny	22
14	Carlow	21
15	Sligo	20
16	Newbridge	20
17	Celbridge	19
18	Mullingar	18
19	Letterkenny	18
20	Wexford	18
21	Clonmel	17
22	Athlone	15
23	Longford	7
24	Ballybofey	4

IRELAND; EIRE

Capital	Dublin	Language	English, Irish (Gaelic or Gaeilge)	Independence	1921
Population	4 062 235	Area	70 280 km²	Density	56 per km²	% in cities	58%
GDP per cap	$29 600	Dailling code	+353	Internet	.ie	GMT + / -	0

MEDALS TABLE

		Overall			League			Cup			LC			Europe				Stadium	Cap'ty	DoF
		G	S	B	G	S	B	G	S	B	G	S	B	G	S	B				
1	Shamrock Rovers	40	26	12	15	13	12	24	8		1	5					Dublin	Tolka Park	9 681	1901
2	Shelbourne	21	24	11	13	11	11	7	10		1	3					Dublin	Tolka Park	9 681	1895
3	Dundalk	21	19	6	9	10	6	8	5		4	4					Dundalk	Oriel Park	11 000	1903
4	Bohemian FC	17	22	13	9	13	13	6	7		2	2					Dublin	Dalymount Park	8 200	1890
5	Derry City	13	9	1	2	4	1	4	3		7	2					Londonderry	Brandywell	7 700	1928
6	Cork Athletic	12	8	2	7	2	2	5	6								Cork	Ballinlough Road		1912-57
7	St. Patrick's Athletic	11	11	2	7	2	2	2	7		2	2					Dublin	Richmond Park	5 500	1929
8	Waterford United	10	11	8	6	4	8	2	7		2						Waterford	RSC	8 200	1930
9	Drumcondra	10	9	4	5	5	4	5	4								Dublin	Tolka Park		1924-72
10	Limerick	7	6	3	2	2	3	2	3		3	1					Limerick	Hogan Park	10 000	1937
11	Cork City	6	9	4	2	5	4	1	3		3	1					Cork	Turner's Cross	8 000	1984
12	Athlone Town	6	3	3	2	1	3	1			3	2					Athlone	Lissywoollen	6 000	1887
13	Sligo Rovers	5	10	5	2	2	5	2	5		1	3					Sligo	Showgrounds	5 500	1928
14	St. James' Gate	4	3		2	1		2	2								Dublin	Iveagh Grounds		1913
15	Cork Hibernians	3	3	3	1	1	3	2	2								Cork	Flower Lodge		1957-76
16	Galway United	3	3	1		1	1	1	1		2	1					Galway	Terryland Park	3 000	1937
17	Longford Town	3	2					2	1		1	1					Longford	Flancare Park	6 000	1924
18	Drogheda United	2	3	4		1	4	1	2		1						Drogheda	United Park	5 400	1919

RECENT LEAGUE AND CUP RECORD

	Championship						Cup		
Year	Champions	Pts	Runners-up	Pts	Third	Pts	Winners	Score	Runners-up
1995	Dundalk	59	Derry City	58	Shelbourne	57	Derry City	2-1	Shelbourne
1996	St Patrick's Ath	67	Bohemians	62	Sligo Rovers	55	Shelbourne	1-1 2-1	St Patrick's Ath
1997	Derry City	67	Bohemians	57	Shelbourne	54	Shelbourne	2-0	Derry City
1998	St Patrick's Ath	68	Shelbourne	67	Cork City	53	Cork City	0-0 1-0	Shelbourne
1999	St Patrick's Ath	73	Cork City	70	Shelbourne	47	Bray Wanderers	0-0 2-2 2-1	Finn Harps
2000	Shelbourne	69	Cork City	58	Bohemians	57	Shelbourne	0-0 1-0	Bohemians
2001	Bohemians	62	Shelbourne	60	Cork City	56	Bohemians	1-0	Longford Town
2002	Shelbourne	63	Shamrock Rovers	57	St Patrick's Ath	53	Dundalk	2-1	Bohemians
2003	Bohemians	54	Shelbourne	49	Shamrock Rovers	43	Derry City	1-0	Shamrock Rovers
2003	Shelbourne	69	Bohemians	64	Cork City	53	Longford Town	2-0	St Patrick's Ath
2004	Shelbourne	68	Cork City	65	Bohemians	60	Longford Town	2-1	Waterford United
2005	Cork City	74	Derry City	72	Shelbourne	67	Drogheda United	2-0	Cork City
2006	Shelbourne	62	Derry City	62	Drogheda United	58	Derry City	4-3	St Patrick's Ath

REPUBLIC OF IRELAND 2006

EIRCOM LEAGUE OF IRELAND PREMIER DIVISION

	Pl	W	D	L	F	A	Pts	Shelbourne	Derry	Drogheda	Cork	Sligo	UCD	St Pats	Longford	Bohemians	Bray	Waterford	Dublin City
Shelbourne	30	18	8	4	60	27	62		1-0	2-2	1-2 2-2	2-2	3-0	6-0	3-0	0-0 2-0	2-0 2-1	4-1	5-1 1-0
Derry City †	30	18	8	4	46	20	62	2-0		1-2 0-0	2-0 1-0	3-1	4-0 2-0 0-0	3-1	1-0	1-0 1-1	3-0 0-0	4-0	3-0
Drogheda United ‡	30	16	10	4	37	23	58	1-3	3-1		0-0 0-0	2-2	1-0 1-0	2-1	1-0 2-0	1-0	1-0 1-1	4-0 1-0	2-2
Cork City	30	15	11	4	37	15	56	2-1 1-0	1-1	1-0		2-0 2-0	1-0	0-0	2-1 1-1 1-0	1-0	6-0	2-0 4-1	1-0
Sligo Rovers	30	11	7	12	33	42	40	1-1 0-2	3-1	0-0 2-3	0-3		0-1	1-1 3-2	3-1	1-0 1-0	2-0	3-1 0-0	2-0
University College	30	9	11	10	26	26	38	1-2 0-2	0-0	0-0	0-0 1-1 3-0 1-0			0-1 0-0 2-2 3-1	0-1	4-1 4-0	2-1		
St Patrick's Athletic ‡	30	9	11	10	32	29	37	2-2 1-3	1-0	1-0	1-3	2-0 0-0	3-1		0-0	0-1	3-0 5-1 0-0 0-1		
Longford Town	30	8	10	12	23	27	34	0-0 0-1 0-2	0-0	0-2 0-0 0-2	0-0 2-0 0-0		3-1 3-0 1-0			3-1 3-0 1-0	3-0		1-1
Bohemians §3	30	9	5	16	29	34	29	2-1	1-2	0-1 2-2	0-0	0-2	2-1 0-1 0-0 0-1	0-1			3-0 1-1 4-2 3-1		
Bray Wanderers	30	3	8	19	22	64	17	2-2 2-3	2-3	0-1	0-0 2-1 1-2 1-1	1-1	1-2	1-0 0-2	0-3			3-1	0-2
Waterford United	30	2	6	22	20	58	12	0-1 0-1 1-2 0-1	2-3	0-0	1-2	0-1 0-0	1-3	0-0 1-2	1-3	1-1 3-0			0-1
Dublin City			Withdrew					1-2	1-0	0-1	0-4	0-0	2-1	0-2	0-2	1-2			

10/03/2006 - 17/11/2006 • † Qualified for the UEFA Champions League • ‡ Qualified for the UEFA Cup • §3 = three points deducted • Dublin City withdrew after 17 rounds. All games involving them were annulled • Top scorers: Jason BYRNE, Shelbourne 17; Glen CROWE, Shelbourne 12; Roy O'DONOVAN, Cork 11; Mark FARREN, Derry 9; Cairan MARTIN, Derry 8; Gary O'NEILL, Shelbourne 8 • Champions Shelbourne were refused a license for the 2007 season and were relegated. Waterford escaped relegation as a result

REPUBLIC OF IRELAND 2006 FIRST DIVISION

	Pl	W	D	L	F	A	Pts
Shamrock Rovers §3	36	21	12	3	53	13	72
Dundalk	36	22	5	9	57	33	71
Galway United	36	19	12	5	57	25	69
Cobh Ramblers	36	16	10	10	50	33	58
Limerick	36	14	5	17	38	48	47
Finn Harps	36	12	10	14	49	45	46
Kildare County	36	11	10	15	38	55	43
Athlone Town	36	11	9	16	29	47	42
Monaghan United	36	6	9	21	32	64	27
Kilkenny City	36	3	8	25	25	65	17

10/03/2006 - 19/11/2006 • §3 = three points deducted
Galway United were promoted following the restructuring of the league • Limerick were refused a license and replaced by a new club called Limerick 37

IRELAND LEAGUE CUP 2006

Quarter-finals		Semi-finals		Final	
Derry City	4				
Drogheda Utd	0	Derry City	3		
Shamrock Rov	0	Limerick	0		
Limerick	1			Derry City	0 3p
Bohemians	1			Shelbourne	0 0p
Cobh Ramblers	0	Bohemians	0		
Finn Harps	1	Shelbourne	1	Brandywell, Londonderry 18-09-2006	
Shelbourne	4	* Home team			

FA OF IRELAND CUP 2006

Round of 16		Quarter-finals		Semi-finals		Final	
Derry City	1						
Shelbourne *	0	Derry City *	2				
Limerick	1	University College	0				
University College *	3			Derry City	0 5		
Killester United	w-o			Sligo Rovers	0 0		
Dublin City		Killester United	0 3				
Bray Wanderers	1	Sligo Rovers *	0 4			Derry City	4
Sligo Rovers *	2					St Patrick's Athletic ‡	3
Shamrock Rovers *	1 2						
Bohemians	1 0	Shamrock Rovers	2				
Finn Harps *	0 2	Athlone Town *	1				
Athlone Town	0 3			Shamrock Rovers	0		
Longford Town	1 1			St Patrick's Athletic	2		
Waterford United *	1 0	Longford Town	1				
Dundalk	0	St Patrick's Athletic *	4				
St Patrick's Athletic *	2	* Home team • ‡ Qualified for the UEFA Cup					

CUP FINAL
Lansdowne Road, Dublin, 3-12-2006
Scorers - Forde [25], Delany [85], Hutton [107], Brennan OG [110] for Derry, Mulcahy [20], Molloy [75], O'Connor [103] for St Patrick's

IRN – IRAN

NATIONAL TEAM RECORD
JULY 10TH 2006 TO JULY 12TH 2010

PL	W	D	L	F	A	%
21	13	7	1	35	13	78.5

FIFA/COCA-COLA WORLD RANKING

1993	1994	1995	1996	1997	1998	1999	2000	2001	2002	2003	2004	2005	2006	High	Low
59	75	108	83	46	27	49	37	29	33	28	20	19	38	15 07/05	122 05/96

2006–2007											
08/06	09/06	10/06	11/06	12/06	01/07	02/07	03/07	04/07	05/07	06/07	07/07
45	43	43	38	38	37	32	34	42	41	47	46

The last time Iran reached the final of the AFC Asian Cup, the Shah was still ruling the country - but going into the 2007 tournament hopes were high with Iran the form team on the continent. In the aftermath of the 2006 World Cup in Germany, Team Melli lost just once in 17 games, and by the end of the Asian Cup that figure was just one defeat in 21 games, but alas there was still no sign of a first final in 29 years. Iran won their first round group with relative ease but then came up against South Korea in the quarter-finals for the fourth tournament running. The tie finished goalless

INTERNATIONAL HONOURS
Qualified for the FIFA World Cup finals 1978 1998 2006 **AFC Asian Cup** 1968 1972 1976 **Asian Games** 1974 1990 1998 2002
AFC Asian U-19 Championship 1973 1974 1975 1976 **AFC Champions League** Esteghlal 1970 1991

with an under-strength Korean team then winning the penalty shoot-out - the third time in four tournaments that the Iranians had gone out on penalties. In club football the season started with Sepahan winning the delayed 2006 Cup Final on penalties against Pirouzi. The season also ended with Sepahan winning a Cup Final, this time against Baba Battery in the 2007 final. In between the League campaign saw Saipa win the title for a third time after a close fought battle between the top five. Other news included the demise of the police team Pas, who sold their licence, and the expulsion of Esteghlal from the AFC Champions League for failing to register their players on time.

THE FIFA BIG COUNT OF 2006

	Male	Female		Total
Number of players	1 696 548	109 996	Referees and Assistant Referees	7 300
Professionals	560		Admin, Coaches, Technical, Medical	18 500
Amateurs 18+	286 800		Number of clubs	100
Youth under 18	158 496		Number of teams	270
Unregistered	345 900		Clubs with women's teams	20
Total players	1 806 544		Players as % of population	2.63%

IR Iran Football Federation (IRIFF)
No. 2/2 Third St., Seoul Ave., 19958-73591 Tehran, Iran
Tel +98 21 88213308   Fax +98 21 8213302
info@iriff   www.iriff.ir
President: SAFAEI FARAHANI Mohsen   General Secretary: MOHAMMAD NABI Mehdi
Vice-President: HASHEMI Qumars   Treasurer: KAHAZAEI Mohammad Taghi   Media Officer: SHAHABI Azhdar
Men's Coach: GHALENOEI Amir   Women's Coach: XINFENG Zhou
IRIFF formed: 1920   AFC: 1958   FIFA: 1945
White shirts with green timmings, White shorts, White socks

RECENT INTERNATIONAL MATCHES PLAYED BY IRAN

2004	Opponents	Score	Venue	Comp	Scorers	Att	Referee
17-11	Laos	W 7-0	Tehran	WCq	Daei 4 [8 20 28 58], Nekounam 2 [63 72], Borhani [69]	30 000	Mamedov TKM
18-12	Panama	W 1-0	Tehran	Fr	Daei [38p]	8 000	Esfahanian IRN
2005							
2-02	Bosnia-Herzegovina	W 2-1	Tehran	Fr	Daei [41], Borhani [73]	15 000	
9-02	Bahrain	D 0-0	Manama	WCq		25 000	Mohd Salleh MAS
25-03	Japan	W 2-1	Tehran	WCq	Hashemian 2 [13 66]	110 000	Maidin SIN
30-03	Korea DPR	W 2-0	Pyongyang	WCq	Mahdavikia [32], Nekounam [79]	55 000	Kousa SYR
29-05	Azerbaijan	W 2-1	Tehran	Fr	Zandi [9], Nekounam [29]	30 000	Al Fadhli KUW
3-06	Korea DPR	W 1-0	Tehran	WCq	Rezaei [45]	35 000	Al Ghamdi KSA
8-06	Bahrain	W 1-0	Tehran	WCq	Nosrati [47]	80 000	Kwon Jong Chul KOR
17-08	Japan	L 1-2	Yokohama	WCq	Daei [79]	66 098	Shaban KUW
24-08	Libya	W 4-0	Tehran	Fr	Alavi [7], Nekounam 2 [41 90], Daei [56]	15 000	Delawar BHR
12-10	Korea Republic	L 0-2	Seoul	Fr		61 457	Al Ghamdi KSA
13-11	Togo	W 2-0	Tehran	Fr	Daei [11p], Hashemian [58p]		
2006							
22-02	Chinese Taipei	W 4-0	Tehran	ACq	Timotian [35], Madanchi 2 [47 60], Daei [82]	5 000	AK Nema IRQ
1-03	Costa Rica	W 3-2	Tehran	Fr	Karimi [9], Daei [16], Hashemian [34]	25 000	Marzouqi UAE
28-05	Croatia	D 2-2	Osijek	Fr	Karimi [21], Borhani [81]	19 000	Siric CRO
31-05	Bosnia-Herzegovina	W 5-2	Tehran	Fr	Madanchi [25], Rezaei [45], Hashemian [45], Enayati [88], Khatibi [90]	40 000	Mohd Salleh MAS
11-06	Mexico	L 1-3	Nuremburg	WCr1	Golmohammadi [36]	41 000	Rosetti ITA
17-06	Portugal	L 0-2	Frankfurt	WCr1		48 000	Poulat FRA
21-06	Angola	D 1-1	Leipzig	WCr1	Bakhtiarizadeh [75]	38 000	Shield AUS
8-08	UAE	W 1-0	Tehran	Fr	Enayati [5]	4 000	
16-08	Syria	D 1-1	Tehran	ACq	Nekounam [72]	40 000	Irmatov UZB
2-09	Korea Republic	D 1-1	Seoul	ACq	Hashemian [93+]	63 113	Breeze AUS
6-09	Syria	W 2-0	Damascus	ACq	Nosrati [27], Nekounam [55]	10 000	Matsumura JPN
4-10	Iraq	W 2-0	Amman	Fr	Rezaei [25], Rajabzadeh [70]	5 000	
6-10	Jordan	D 0-0	Amman	Fr		500	Al Blooshi QAT
11-10	Chinese Taipei	W 2-0	Taipei	ACq	Karimi 2 [11 58]	2 000	Shamsuzzaman BAN
15-11	Korea Republic	W 2-0	Tehran	ACq	Enayati [48], Badamaki [91+]	30 000	Ebrahim BHR
2007							
12-01	UAE	W 2-0	Abu Dhabi	Fr	Khatibi [45p], Sadeghi [90]	9 000	Omar UAE
7-02	Belarus	D 2-2	Tehran	Fr	Khatibi [5], Rajabzadeh [88]	15 000	Al Fadhli KUW
24-03	Qatar	W 1-0	Doha	Fr	Vahedi-Nikbakht [7]	5 000	Al Khabbaz BHR
2-06	Mexico	L 0-4	San Luis Potosi	Fr		30 000	Silvera URU
16-06	Iraq	D 0-0	Amman	WАr1		5 000	Abbas SYR
20-06	Palestine	W 2-0	Amman	WАr1	Midavoodi [56], Rajabzadeh [85]	2 000	Abu Loum JOR
22-06	Jordan	W 1-0	Amman	WАsf	Rajabzadeh [32]	5 000	Won Lon Soon KOR
24-06	Iraq	W 2-1	Amman	WАf	Badamaki [9], Beikzadeh [21]	8 000	Ghandour LIB
2-07	Jamaica	W 8-1	Tehran	Fr	Nekounam 2 [1 17], Madanchi 2 [2 45], Hashemian [35], Khatibi 2 [81 88], Enayati [90]	15 000	Mombini IRN
11-07	Uzbekistan	W 2-1	Kuala Lumpur	ACr1	Hosseini [55], Kazemeyan [78]	1 863	Al Fadhli KUW
15-07	China PR	D 2-2	Kuala Lumpur	ACr1	Zandi [45], Nekounam [73]	5 938	Al Ghamdi KSA
18-07	Malaysia	W 2-0	Kuala Lumpur	ACr1	Nekounam [29p], Teymourian [77]	4 520	Basma SYR
22-07	Korea Republic	D 0-0	Kuala Lumpur	ACqf	L 2-4p	8 629	Al Badwawi UAE

Fr = Friendly match • WA = West Asian Federation Championship • AC = AFC Asian Cup • WC = FIFA World Cup
q = qualifier • r1 = first round group • sf = semi-final • f = final

IRAN NATIONAL TEAM RECORDS AND RECORD SEQUENCES

Records		Sequence records					
Victory	19-0 GUM 2000	Wins	8	1974, 1996	Clean sheets	7	1977
Defeat	1-6 TUR 1950	Defeats	3	1989-1990	Goals scored	20	2000-2001
Player Caps	149 DAEI Ali	Undefeated	15	1996-1997	Without goal	4	1951-1958, 1988
Player Goals	109 DAEI Ali	Without win	10	1997	Goals against	9	1959-1963

MAJOR CITIES/TOWNS

		Population '000
1	Tehran	12 486
2	Esfahan	2 961
3	Mashhad	2 463
4	Tabriz	1 496
5	Shiraz	1 307
6	Qom	1 081
7	Ahvaz	832
8	Kermanshah	765
9	Orumiyeh	644
10	Rasht	642
11	Kerman	636
12	Zahedan	589
13	Hamadan	542
14	Arak	538
15	Yazd	531
16	Abadan	465
17	Ardabil	431
18	Zanjan	377
19	Sanandaj	367
20	Qazvin	349
21	Khorramabad	348
22	Khorramshahr	345
23	Bandar-e Abbas	328
24	Sari	269

ISLAMIC REPUBLIC OF IRAN; JOMHURI-YE ESLAMI-YE IRAN

Capital	Tehran	Language	Persian, Turkic, Kurdish	Formation	1502
Population	68 688 433	Area	1648000 km²	Density 42 per km²	% in cities 59%
GDP per cap	$7000	Dailling code	+98	Internet .ir	GMT + / - +3.5

The figure for the Tehran metropolitan area also includes: Karaj 1 602; Eslamshahr 324; Qods 303; Qarchak 277; Nazarabad 250; Varamin 197

MEDALS TABLE

		Overall			League			Cup			Asia			City	Stadium	Cap'ty	DoF
		G	S	B	G	S	B	G	S	G	S	B					
1	Esteghlal (ex Taj)	12	9	5	6	4	2	4	3	2	2	3	Tehran	Azadi	110 000	1945
2	Pirouzi (aka Persopolis)	12	3	5	8	1	2	3	1	1	1	3	Tehran	Azadi	110 000	1963
3	Pas	6	3		5	3			1				Tehran	Dastgerdi	15 000	1963-07
4	Saipa Karaj	4		2	3		2	1					Karaj	Enghelab	30 000	1989
5	Sepahan Esfahan	4		2	1		2	3					Esfahan	Naghsh e Jahan	50 000	1967
6	Malavan Anzali	3	3					3	3				Bandar Anzali	Takhti	20 000	1969
7	Bahman Karaj	1	4			2		1	2				Karaj	Dr Shariati	20 000	1994
8	Fajr-Sepasi Shiraz	1	2	1			1	1	2				Shiraz	Hafezieh	20 000	1988
	Zob-Ahan Esfahan	1	2	1		1	1	1	1				Esfahan	Fooladshahr	25 000	1969
10	Bargh Shiraz	1	1					1	1				Shiraz	Hafezieh	20 000	1946
	Saba Battery	1	1					1	1				Tehran	Derakshan	12 000	2002
12	Foolad Ahvaz	1		2	1		2						Ahvaz	Takhti	30 000	1986
13	Shahin Ahvaz	1						1					Ahvaz	Takhti	30 000	

RECENT LEAGUE AND CUP RECORD

	Championship						Cup		
Year	Champions	Pts	Runners-up	Pts	Third	Pts	Winners	Score	Runners-up
1995	Pirouzi						Bahman	0-1 2-0	TraktorSazi
1996	Pirouzi	57	Bahman	51	Esteghlal	51	Esteghlal	3-1 2-0	Bargh
1997	Pirouzi	59	Bahman	53	Sepahan	50	Bargh	1-1 3-0p	Bahman
1998	Esteghlal	58	Pas	52	Zob Ahan	45		No tournament held	
1999	Pirouzi	65	Esteghlal	53	Sepahan	53	Pirouzi	2-1	Esteghlal
2000	Pirouzi	54	Esteghlal	47	Fajr Sepasi	44	Esteghlal	3-1	Bahman
2001	Esteghlal	50	Pirouzi	46	Saipa	33	Fajr Sepasi	1-0 2-1	Zob Ahan
2002	Esteghlal	49	Esteghlal	48	Foolad	45	Esteghlal	2-1 2-2	Fajr Sepasi
2003	Sepahan	52	Pas	45	Pirouzi	44	Zob Ahan	2-2 2-2 6-5p	Fajr Sepasi
2004	Pas	53	Esteghlal	51	Foolad	47	Sepahan	3-2 2-0	Esteghlal
2005	Foolad	64	Zob Ahan	58	Esteghlal	58	Saba Battery	1-1 2-2 4-2p	AbooMoslem
2006	Esteghlal	59	Pas	58	Saipa	52	Sepahan	1-1 1-1 4-2p	Pirouzi
2007	Saipa	56	Esteghlal Ahvaz	54	Pirouzi	53	Sepahan	1-0 3-0	Saba Battery

IRAN 2006–07

IRAN PRO LEAGUE

	Pl	W	D	L	F	A	Pts	Saipa	Esteghlal A	Pirouzi	Esteghlal T	Sepahan	AbooMoslem	Paykan	Zob Ahan	Mes	Fajr Sepasi	Pas	Bargh	Saba batry	Malavan	Foolad	Rah Ahan
Saipa †	30	15	11	4	45	31	56		0-1	2-2	3-1	4-2	2-1	2-1	2-1	2-0	1-0	1-1	1-1	1-1	1-1	2-2	3-1
Esteghlal Ahvaz †	30	16	6	8	33	28	54	2-0		1-0	0-1	2-1	2-1	1-0	1-1	1-1	1-0	3-1	0-0	2-0	0-0	0-0	1-0
Pirouzi	30	14	11	5	49	33	53	2-2	4-0		2-1	2-1	3-4	3-4	3-1	4-1	2-2	1-1	1-0	1-0	1-0	2-1	1-2
Esteghlal Tehran	30	14	10	6	39	30	52	1-2	1-1	1-1		2-1	1-0	0-1	2-1	0-0	3-2	2-1	3-0	1-1	2-1	3-2	1-1
Sepahan	30	14	7	9	41	28	49	1-0	4-0	0-0	1-0		1-0	2-1	2-0	1-1	1-2	1-0	3-1	3-2	2-0	2-1	1-0
AbooMoslem	30	11	10	9	40	36	43	1-1	3-4	3-2	1-1	2-0		2-1	4-1	1-1	1-0	3-2	1-0	2-0	3-2	1-0	1-3
Paykan	30	11	8	11	37	42	41	2-0	3-2	0-2	2-1	0-4	2-2		2-1	4-2	2-2	2-1	1-3	0-0	1-1	0-1	0-0
Zob Ahan	30	10	9	11	39	42	39	0-2	0-1	2-3	0-0	2-1	1-0	2-2		2-1	1-1	3-2	1-1	1-0	2-0	3-0	4-3
Mes	30	8	12	10	35	39	36	2-2	3-1	0-0	0-1	2-1	0-0	1-1	1-1		2-0	0-1	2-1	2-3	1-0	1-1	1-1
Fajr Sepasi	30	7	13	10	29	32	34	0-1	0-1	1-1	1-1	1-1	2-0	1-0	1-0	0-0		**0-3**	1-3	1-1	2-0	0-0	2-2
Pas §1	30	7	13	10	36	36	33	1-2	1-0	1-1	1-1	0-0	1-1	3-0	1-1	0-1	1-1		2-2	2-1	1-2	1-2	2-2
Bargh	30	8	9	13	35	45	33	1-2	1-0	1-2	1-2	2-1	1-1	2-1	2-0	1-4	1-1	1-0		0-0	0-1	2-4	3-1
Saba Battery	30	7	11	12	28	31	32	1-2	1-0	0-1	2-3	0-0	1-1	0-1	1-2	4-1	0-1	0-0	3-0		1-0	0-0	1-1
Malavan	30	7	11	12	21	30	32	0-0	0-1	0-0	0-1	0-2	0-0	0-0	1-0	2-1	1-0	2-2	2-1	2-3		1-1	2-1
Foolad	30	5	13	12	24	33	28	1-2	0-1	0-0	0-0	0-0	0-0	1-0	1-1	1-1	2-1	0-3	1-1	1-2	0-1		3-1
Rah Ahan	30	2	14	14	30	45	20	0-0	1-3	1-2	1-2	1-1	0-0	1-2	1-2	1-2	1-1	1-1	1-1	1-2	0-0	0-1	

9/09/2006 - 28/05/2007 • † Qualified for the AFC Champions League • Match in bold awarded • § = points deducted
Play-off semi-finals: Foolad 1-0 1-0 Teraktor-Sazi; Rah Ahan 2-0 3-0 Shahrdari; Final: Foolad 0-1 Rah Ahan

JAAM HAZFI 2005–06

Round of 16		Quarter–finals		Semi–finals		Final	
Sepahan	0 4p						
Pas Tehran	0 3p	Sepahan	1				
Maziran Sari	0	Teraktorsazi Tabriz	0				
Teraktorsazi Tabriz	1			Sepahan	3		
Sepahan 'B'	1			Saba Battery	1		
Payam Shiraz	0	Sepahan 'B'	1				
Sanay Arak	1	Saba Battery	2				
Saba Battery	2					Sepahan	1 1 4p
Nojan Sari	2					Pirouzi	1 1 2p
Zobahan Esfahan	1	Nojan Sari	w-0				
Shahin Boshehr †	-	Esteghlal Tehran †	-				
Esteghlal Tehran	w-0			Nojan Sari	2 6p		
Malavan Anzali	3			Pirouzi	2 7p		
Peykan Tehran	2	Malavan Anzali	1				
AbooMoslem Mashhad	2	Pirouzi	3				
Pirouzi	3			* Home team • † Teams withdrew			

CUP FINAL

1st leg. Azadi, Tehran
13-09-2007, Att: 80 000, Ref: Tourki
Scorers - V.Nikbakht [45]; Shafiei [73]
2nd leg. Naghsh e Jahan, Esfahan
22-09-2007, At: 35,000, Ref: Moradi
Scorers - Shafiei [63]; Asadi [55]

JAAM HAZFI 2006–07

Round of 16		Quarter–finals		Semi–finals		Final	
Sepahan *	2						
Saipa	0	Sepahan *	3				
Malavan	0	Tarbiat Yazd	2				
Tarbiat Yazd *	2			Sepahan	4		
Bargh Tehran *	0 5p			Pirouzi	1		
Damash Tehran	0 4p	Bargh Tehran *	2 3p				
Mersad Shiraz	0	Pirouzi	2 5p				
Pirouzi *	2					Sepahan	1 3
Paykan Tehran	2					Saba Battery	0 0
Mes *	1	Paykan Tehran *	2				
Pas *	1	Esteghlal Ahvaz	1				
Esteghlal Ahvaz	4			Paykan Tehran	1		
Naft Abadan *	1			Saba Battery	2		
Foolad	0	Naft Abadan *	0				
Bargh Shiraz	1	Saba Battery	1				
Saba Battery *	2			* Home team			

CUP FINAL

1st leg. Tehran, 10-06-2007
Scorer - Hadi Aghili [59p]

2nd leg. Esfahan, 16-06-2007
Scorers - Mahmoud Karimi [44], Ebrahim
Loveinian [50], Hosein Papi [88]

IRQ – IRAQ

NATIONAL TEAM RECORD
JULY 10TH 2006 TO JULY 12TH 2010

PL	W	D	L	F	A	%
26	11	9	6	32	23	59.6

FIFA/COCA-COLA WORLD RANKING

1993	1994	1995	1996	1997	1998	1999	2000	2001	2002	2003	2004	2005	2006	High	Low
65	88	110	98	68	94	78	79	72	53	43	44	54	83	**39** 10/04	**139** 07/96

	2006–2007										
08/06	09/06	10/06	11/06	12/06	01/07	02/07	03/07	04/07	05/07	06/07	07/07
87	92	89	88	83	82	81	82	78	79	84	80

The fact that football is still played in Iraq is testament to the place the sport has in Iraqi culture, but for the national team to not only qualify for the Asian Cup finals, but to then go on and win the tournament was nothing short of a miracle. The 1-0 win against Saudi Arabia in the the final once again saw Iraq make headline news around the world, but for once those headlines weren't about the near civil war in the country. Football may not change the world but if Iraq follows in the footsteps of Rwanda, where the national team has been used as a symbol of unity to help heal a divided society, then that can be no bad thing. The hopes of a nation rested on the

INTERNATIONAL HONOURS
Qualified for the FIFA World Cup finals 1986   AFC Asian Cup 2007
Asian Games 1982 AFC Youth Championship 1975 1977 1978 1988 2000 Gulf Cup 1979 1984 1988

shoulders of players from all sides of the divide, but that didn't appear to be a burden and it was Younis Mahmoud who was the hero of the day, heading the historic goal against the Saudis that sparked wild celebrations back home. A week before the Asian Cup, the 2007 League Championship was completed, with the final rounds held in Arbil and it was local side Arbil FC who won the title for the first time. By beating Al Quwa Al Jawia - the team of the Air Force - 1-0 in the final, they also became the first Kurdish club to qualify for the AFC Champions League.

THE FIFA BIG COUNT OF 2006

	Male	Female		Total
Number of players	500 100	39 900	Referees and Assistant Referees	600
Professionals	0		Admin, Coaches, Technical, Medical	2 300
Amateurs 18+	6 600		Number of clubs	110
Youth under 18	7 900		Number of teams	170
Unregistered	100 000		Clubs with women's teams	0
Total players	540 000		Players as % of population	2.02%

Iraqi Football Association (IFA)
Al Shaab Stadium, PO Box 484, Baghdad, Iraq
Tel +964 1 7743652   Fax +964 1 5372021
iraqfed@yahoo.com   www.iraqfootball.org
President: HUSSAIN Mohammed Saeed   General Secretary: AHMED A. Ibrahim
Vice-President: HUMOUD Najih   Treasurer: ABDUL KHALIQ Masounel Ahmed   Media Officer: WALID Tabra
Men's Coach: VIEIRA Jorvan   Women's Coach: AL MUMIN Husam Dr.
IFA formed: 1948   AFC: 1971   FIFA: 1950
White shirts, White shorts, White socks

RECENT INTERNATIONAL MATCHES PLAYED BY IRAQ

2005	Opponents	Score		Venue	Comp	Scorers	Att	Referee
26-03	Australia	L	1-2	Sydney	Fr	Mohammad Nassir [12]	30 258	O'Leary NZL
8-06	Jordan	W	1-0	Amman	Fr	Mahdi Kareem [15]		
7-08	Bahrain	D	2-2	Manama	Fr	Younis Mahmoud [52], Mohammed Nassir [75]		
13-08	Cyprus	L	1-2	Limassol	Fr	Mohammed Nassir [17]	500	
11-10	Qatar	D	0-0	Doha	Fr			
26-11	Kuwait	D	0-0	Kuwait City	Fr			
1-12	Palestine	W	4-0	Rayyan	WGr1	Razzaq Farhan [4], Hawar Mohammed Taher [56], Loay Salah [73], Ahmed Salah [86]		
5-12	Saudi Arabia	W	5-1	Rayyan	WGr1	Haidar Abdul Amir [8], Emad Mohammed [19], Nashat Akram [30], Younis Mahmoud 2 [51 78]		
8-12	Saudi Arabia	W	2-0	Doha	WGsf	Loay Saleh [33], Razzaq Farhan [85]		
10-12	Syria	D	2-2	Doha	WGf	Razzaq Farhan [45], Younis Mahmoud [78]. W 4-3p		
2006								
13-02	Oman	L	0-1	Wattayah	Fr		11 000	Shaban KUW
16-02	Thailand	L	3-4	Ayutthaya	Fr	Emad Mohammed 3 [8 44 90]	25 000	Waiyabot THA
22-02	Singapore	L	0-2	Singapore	ACq		10 221	Shield AUS
1-03	China PR	W	2-1	Al Ain	ACq	Mahdi Ajeel [16], Hawar Mohammed [67]	7 700	Al Saeedi UAE
15-03	Saudi Arabia	D	2-2	Jeddah	Fr	Mohammed Nassir [40], Haidar Abdul Amir [92+]		Al Hamdan KSA
15-07	Syria	W	3-1	Damascus	Fr	Emad Mohammed [33], Younis Mahmoud 2 [45 82p]		
21-07	Jordan	L	1-2	Amman	Fr	Younis Mahmoud [53]		
25-07	Syria	W	2-1	Damascus	Fr	Emad Mohammed [34], Saleh Sadir [60]		
9-08	Jordan	W	1-0	Amman	Fr	Younis Mahmoud [12]		
17-08	Palestine	W	3-0	Amman	ACq	Younis Mahmoud 2 [59 61], Mohammad Nasser [90]	5 000	Basma SYR
6-09	Palestine	D	2-2	Al Ain	ACq	Saleh Sadir [70], Hawar Taher [75]	1 000	Mujghef JOR
4-10	Iran	L	0-2	Amman	Fr			
11-10	Singapore	W	4-2	Al Ain	ACq	Younis Mahmoud 2 [35 68], Mahdi Kareem [60], Hawar Mohammed [93+]	3 000	Mamedov TKM
15-11	China PR	D	1-1	Changsha	ACq	Alwan Ahmad [65]		Mohd Salleh MAS
2007								
18-01	Qatar	W	1-0	Abu Dhabi	GCr1	Hawar Mohammed [40]		
21-01	Bahrain	D	1-1	Abu Dhabi	GCr1	Hawar Mohammed [11]		
24-01	Saudi Arabia	L	0-1	Abu Dhabi	GCr1			
8-06	Jordan	D	1-1	Amman	Fr	Ahmed Menajed [25]		
12-06	Jordan	D	0-0	Amman	Fr			
16-06	Iran	D	0-0	Amman	WAr1			
18-06	Palestine	W	1-0	Amman	WAr1	Hawar Mohammed [86]		
22-06	Syria	W	3-0	Amman	WAsf	Younis Mahmoud [10p], Ahmad Manajid [42], Saleh Sadir [85]		
24-06	Iran	L	1-2	Amman	WAf	Saleh Sadir [86p]		
29-06	Korea Republic	L	0-3	Jeju	Fr		32 642	Tojo JPN
2-07	Uzbekistan	L	0-2	Paju	Fr			
7-07	Thailand	D	1-1	Bangkok	ACr1	Younis Mahmoud [32]	30 000	Kwon Jong Chul
13-07	Australia	W	3-1	Bangkok	ACr1	Nashat Akram [22], Hawar Mohammed [60], Karrar Jassim [86]	7 884	Karim BHR
16-07	Oman	D	0-0	Bangkok	ACr1		500	Maillet SEY
21-07	Vietnam	W	2-0	Bangkok	ACqf	Younis Mahmoud 2 [2 65]	9 720	Nishimura JPN
25-07	Korea Republic	D	0-0	Kuala Lumpur	ACsf	W 4-3p	12 500	Al Fadhli KUW
29-07	Saudi Arabia	W	1-0	Jakarta	ACf	Younis Mahmoud [73]	60 000	Shield AUS

Fr = Friendly • WA = West Asian Federation Championship • WG = West Asian Games • AC = AFC Asian Cup • GC = Gulf Cup • WC = FIFA World Cup
q = qualifier • r1 = first round group • qf = quarter-final • sf = semi-final • f = final

IRAQ NATIONAL TEAM RECORDS AND RECORD SEQUENCES

Records			Sequence records				
Victory	10-1	BHR 1966	Wins	8	1985	Clean sheets	5	Four times
Defeat	1-7	TUR 1959	Defeats	5	1967-1969	Goals scored	21	1993-1996
Player Caps	126	HUSSAIN Saeed	Undefeated	17	1982-84, 1988-89	Without goal	3	2003-2004
Player Goals	63	HUSSAIN Saeed	Without win	9	1967-1971	Goals against	22	2004-2005

TUR
SYR
JOR
KSA
KUW
IRN
Mosul
Irbil
Sulaimaniya
Kirkuk
Baghdad
Karbala
Al Amarah
Nasiriyah
Najaf
Basra

REPUBLIC OF IRAQ; AL JUMHURIYAH AL IRAQIYAH

Capital	Baghdad	Language	Arabic, Kurdish		Independence	1932
Population	26 783 383	Area	437 072 km²	Density	58 per km²	% in cities 75%
GDP per cap	$1500	Dailling code	+964	Internet	.iq	GMT + / - +3

MAJOR CITIES/TOWNS

		Population '000
1	Baghdad	8 044
2	Basra	2 786
3	Mosul	2 220
4	Arbil	993
5	Sulamaniya	773
6	Kirkuk	620
7	Najaf	502
8	Karbala	449
9	Nasiriyah	414
10	Amara	336
11	Diwaniya	333
12	Al Kut	331
13	Al Hillah	289
14	Ramadi	282
15	Falluja	202
16	Tall Afar	193
17	Samarra	167
18	Samawah	163
19	Qubba	155
20	Dahuk	139
21	Al Kufah	136
22	Zubair	126
23	Shatt al Arab	122
24	Al Faw	119

MEDALS TABLE

		Overall			League			Cup			Asia			City	Stadium	Cap'ty	DoF
		G	S	B	G	S	B	G	S	B	G	S	B				
1	Al Zawra'a	25	7	1	11	5	1	14	1		1			Baghdad	Al Zawra'a Stadium	10 000	1969
2	Al Quwa Al Jawia	11	12	7	6	9	7	5	3					Baghdad	Al Quwa Al Jawia Stadium	10 000	1931
3	Al Talaba	7	13	4	5	6	4	2	6			1		Baghdad	Al Talaba Stadium	10 000	1977
4	Al Karkh (ex Rasheed)	5	3	1	3	2	1	2				1		Baghdad	Al Karkh Stadium	6 000	1963
5	Al Jaish	3	6		1	2		2	4					Baghdad	Al Jaish Stadium	6 000	1974
6	Al Shurta	2	9	8	2	3	8		5			1		Baghdad	Al Kashafa Stadium	12 000	1938
7	Al Mina'a	1	1	1	1	1	1							Basra	Al Mina'a Stadium	10 000	1931
8	Al Sina'a	1		2			2	1						Baghdad	Al Sina'a Stadium	6 000	1974
9	Arbil FC	1			1									Arbil	Franso Hariri	40 000	1958
	Salah al Deen	1			1									Tikrit			
11	Al Shabab		3	1			1		3					Baghdad			
12	Najaf FC		2	1	2	1								Najaf	Al Najaf Stadium	12 000	1961

RECENT LEAGUE AND CUP RECORD

	Championship						Cup		
Year	Champions	Pts	Runners-up	Pts	Third	Pts	Winners	Score	Runners-up
1995	Al Zawra'a	120	Al Quwa Al Jawia	107	Al Najaf	107	Al Zawra'a	3-0	Al Jaish
1996	Al Zawra'a	55	Al Najaf	38	Al Shurta	37	Al Zawra'a	2-1	Al Shurta
1997	Al Quwa Al Jawia	69	Al Zawra'a	67	Al Talaba	60	Al Quwa Al Jawia	1-1 8-7p	Al Shurta
1998	Al Shurta	73	Al Quwa Al Jawia	71	Al Zawra'a	70	Al Zawra'a	1-1 4-3p	Al Quwa Al Jawia
1999	Al Zawra'a	57	Al Talaba	53	Al Quwa Al Jawia	47	Al Zawra'a	1-0	Al Talaba
2000	Al Zawra'a	114	Al Quwa Al Jawia	110	Al Shurta	110	Al Zawra'a	0-0 4-3p	Al Quwa Al Jawia
2001	Al Zawra'a	70	Al Quwa Al Jawia	62	Al Shurta	60	No tournament held		
2002	Al Talaba	91	Al Quwa Al Jawia	85	Al Shurta	80	Al Talaba	1-0	Al Shurta
2003	Championship abandoned						Al Talaba	1-0	Al Shurta
2004	Championship abandoned						No tournament held		
2005	Al Quwa Al Jawia	2-0	Al Mina'a				No tournament held		
2006	Al Zawra'a	†	Al Quwa Al Jawia				No tournament held		
2007	Arbil	1-0	Al Quwa Al Jawia				No tournament held		

† Won 4-3 on penalties after a 0-0 draw

IRAQ 2006-07
FIRST ROUND GROUP 1 SOUTH

	Pl	W	D	L	F	A	Pts
Al Najaf †	12	10	1	1	24	9	31
Al Mina'a †	12	8	3	1	19	6	27
Karbala †	12	5	6	1	18	8	21
Nafir Al Janob	12	3	4	5	12	12	13
Maysan Umara	12	2	3	7	10	20	9
Shatra Dhi Qar	12	2	2	8	10	19	8
Furat	12	2	1	9	7	26	7

28/12/2006 - 7/05/2007 • † Qualified for the next round

IRAQ 2006-07
FIRST ROUND GROUP 2 NORTH

	Pl	W	D	L	F	A	Pts
Arbil †	12	8	3	1	21	8	27
Duhok †	12	6	4	2	12	11	22
Sirwan Sulamaniya †	12	5	5	2	12	9	20
Sulamaniya	12	4	4	4	13	13	16
Samara'a	12	2	5	5	11	16	11
Mosul	12	1	5	6	7	12	8
Kirkuk	12	2	2	8	7	14	8

22/12/2006 - 16/04/2007 • † Qualified for the next round

IRAQ 2006-07
FIRST ROUND GROUP 3A

	Pl	W	D	L	F	A	Pts
Al Zawra'a †	8	3	5	0	9	3	14
Al Talaba †	8	3	4	1	7	5	13
Al Nafit †	8	2	3	3	9	8	9
Kahrabaa	8	2	3	3	6	9	9
Al Adala	8	1	3	4	1	7	6

15/02/2007 - 4/04/2007 • † Qualified for the next round

IRAQ 2006-07
FIRST ROUND GROUP 3B

	Pl	W	D	L	F	A	Pts
Al Shurta †	6	6	0	0	12	1	18
Al Quwa Al Jawiya †	6	3	1	2	12	6	10
Al Sina'a	6	1	2	3	7	7	5
Al Jaish	6	0	1	5	1	14	1

15/02/2007 - 27/03/2007 • † Qualified for the next round

CHAMPIONSHIP PLAY-OFFS

Second round

Group 1 (played in Arbil)	Pl	W	D	L	F	A	Pts	AT	Ka	AM	AN	AS
Arbil †	5	4	0	1	10	3	12	0-1	2-1	2-1	2-0	4-0
Al Talaba †	5	2	2	1	3	2	8		1-1	0-1	0-0	1-0
Karbala	5	2	1	2	7	7	7			3-1	0-2	2-1
Al Mina'a	5	2	1	2	4	5	7				1-0	0-0
Al Nafit	5	1	1	3	2	4	4					0-1
Al Shurta	5	1	1	3	2	7	4					

Group 2 (played in Duhok)	Pl	W	D	L	F	A	Pts	AN	AS	AZ	Du	SS
Al Quwa Al Jawiya †	5	4	1	0	8	4	13	2-2	1-0	1-0	3-2	1-0
Al Najaf †	5	2	3	0	11	5	9		1-1	2-1	1-1	5-0
Al Sina'a	5	2	2	1	5	4	8			1-1	2-1	1-0
Al Zawra'a	5	1	2	2	8	8	5				4-2	2-2
Duhok	5	0	2	3	6	10	2					0-0
Sirwan Sulamaniya	5	0	2	3	2	9	2					

19/06/2007 - 6/07/2007 • † Qualified for the semi-finals

Semi-finals

Arbil	2
Najaf	0

Al Talaba	0
Al Quwa Al Jawiya	2

Final

Arbil	1
Al Quwa Al Jawiya	0

Third place play-off

Al Najaf	2
Al Talaba	1

ISL – ICELAND

NATIONAL TEAM RECORD
JULY 10TH 2006 TO JULY 12TH 2010

PL	W	D	L	F	A	%
8	1	2	5	5	15	25

FIFA/COCA-COLA WORLD RANKING

1993	1994	1995	1996	1997	1998	1999	2000	2001	2002	2003	2004	2005	2006	High	Low
47	39	50	60	72	64	43	50	52	58	58	93	94	93	**37** 09/94	**109** 07/07

					2006–2007						
08/06	09/06	10/06	11/06	12/06	01/07	02/07	03/07	04/07	05/07	06/07	07/07
106	87	95	93	93	93	95	86	97	96	109	109

After making a promising start to the UEFA Euro 2008 qualifying campaign with a 3-0 win over Northern Ireland in Belfast, Iceland saw their hopes of a first ever appearance in the finals disintegrate as the season went on. It ended with a draw at home to Liechtenstein and the prospect of finishing below their rivals in the table. What good news there was came from the women's game where there were record crowds for the senior team in their European Championship qualifying group and the successful hosting of the UEFA European Women's Under-19 Championship finals in July 2007. In domestic football, FH Hafnarfjördur completed a hat-trick of

INTERNATIONAL HONOURS
None

titles when they won the League in September 2006. Their success may not have been as emphatic as in the two previous seasons but they still finished six points ahead of nearest rivals KR Reykjavík. Remarkably, for all their dominance in the League, FH have still to win the Cup after losing early on in the competition to Vikingur. The final saw Keflavík win the trophy for the first time in ten years, their 2-0 victory consigning KR to a second runners-up spot in the season. 2006 also saw Icelandic business increase its role in English football as Eggert Magnusson, with the backing of Landsbanki chairman Bjorgolfur Gudmundsson, took control of West Ham United.

THE FIFA BIG COUNT OF 2006

	Male	Female		Total
Number of players	25 108	7 300	Referees and Assistant Referees	1 044
Professionals	408		Admin, Coaches, Technical, Medical	750
Amateurs 18+	5 100		Number of clubs	97
Youth under 18	16 000		Number of teams	870
Unregistered	5 100		Clubs with women's teams	48
Total players	32 408		Players as % of population	10.82%

Knattspyrnusamband Islands (KSI)
The Football Association of Iceland, Laugardal, Reykjavík 104, Iceland
Tel +354 5102900   Fax +354 5689793
ksi@ksi.is   www.ksi.is
President: THORNSTEINSSON Geir   General Secretary: HAKONARSON Thorir
Vice-President: JONSSON Halldor   Treasurer: SIVERTSEN Gudrun Inga   Media Officer: SAMARASON Omar
Men's Coach: SVERRISSON Eyjolfur   Women's Coach: EYJOLFSSON Siggi
KSI formed: 1947   UEFA: 1954   FIFA: 1947
Blue shirts with red and white trimmings, Blue shorts, Blue socks or White shirts with blue trimmings, Blue shirts, White socks

RECENT INTERNATIONAL MATCHES PLAYED BY ICELAND

2002	Opponents	Score	Venue	Comp	Scorers	Att	Referee
21-08	Andorra	W 3-0	Reykjavík	Fr	Gudjohnsen.E [19], Dadason 2 [26 43]	2 900	Isaksen FRO
7-09	Hungary	L 0-2	Reykjavík	Fr		3 190	Maisonlahti FIN
12-10	Scotland	L 0-2	Reykjavík	ECq		7 065	Sars FRA
16-10	Lithuania	W 3-0	Reykjavík	ECq	Helguson [49], Gudjohnsen.E 2 [61 73]	3 513	Gilewski POL
20-11	Estonia	L 0-2	Tallinn	Fr		478	Haverkort NED
2003							
29-03	Scotland	L 1-2	Glasgow	ECq	Gudjohnsen.E [48]	37 548	Temmink NED
30-04	Finland	L 0-3	Vantaa	Fr		4 005	Frojdfeldt SWE
7-06	Faroe Islands	W 2-1	Reykjavík	ECq	Sigurdsson.H [49], Gudmundsson.T [88]	6 038	Liba CZE
11-06	Lithuania	W 3-0	Kaunas	ECq	Gudjónsson.Th [59], Gudjohnsen.E [72], Hreidarsson [90]	7 500	Corpodean ROU
20-08	Faroe Islands	W 2-1	Toftir	ECq	Gudjohnsen.E [55], Marteinsson [70]	3 416	Iturralde Gonzalez ESP
6-09	Germany	D 0-0	Reykjavík	ECq		7 035	Barber ENG
11-10	Germany	L 0-3	Hamburg	ECq		50 780	Ivanov RUS
19-11	Mexico	D 0-0	San Francisco	Fr		17 000	Saheli USA
2004							
31-03	Albania	L 1-2	Tirana	Fr	Gudjónsson.Th [66]	12 000	Bertini ITA
28-04	Latvia	D 0-0	Riga	Fr		6 500	Shmolik BLR
30-05	Japan	L 2-3	Manchester	Fr	Helguson 2 [5 50]	1 500	Riley ENG
5-06	England	L 1-6	Manchester	Fr	Helguson [42]	43 500	Wegereef NED
18-08	Italy	W 2-0	Reykjavík	Fr	Gudjohnsen.E [17], Einarsson [19]	20 204	Frojdfeldt SWE
4-09	Bulgaria	L 1-3	Reykjavík	WCq	Gudjohnsen.E [51p]	5 014	Hamer LUX
8-09	Hungary	L 2-3	Budapest	WCq	Gudjohnsen.E [39], Sigurdsson.I [78]	5 461	Ovrebo NOR
9-10	Malta	D 0-0	Ta'Qali	WCq		1 130	Corpodean ROU
13-10	Sweden	L 1-4	Reykjavík	WCq	Gudjohnsen.E [66]	7 037	Busacca SUI
2005							
26-03	Croatia	L 0-4	Zagreb	WCq		17 912	Damon RSA
30-03	Italy	D 0-0	Padova	Fr		16 697	Hamer LUX
4-06	Hungary	L 2-3	Reykjavík	WCq	Gudjohnsen.E [17], Sigurdsson.K [68]	4 613	Cardoso Batista POR
8-06	Malta	W 4-1	Reykjavík	WCq	Thorvaldsson.G [27], Gudjohnsen.E [33], Gudmundsson.T [74], Gunnarsson.V [84]	4 887	Skomina SVN
17-08	South Africa	W 4-1	Reykjavík	Fr	Steinsson [25], Vidarsson [42], Helguson [67], Gunnarsson.V [73]		
3-09	Croatia	L 1-3	Reykjavík	WCq	Gudjohnsen.E [24]	5 520	Stark GER
7-09	Bulgaria	L 2-3	Sofia	WCq	Steinsson [9], Hreidarsson [16]	18 000	Demirlek TUR
7-10	Poland	L 2-3	Warsaw	Fr	Sigurdsson.K [15], Sigurdsson.H [39]	7 500	Sukhina RUS
12-10	Sweden	L 1-3	Stockholm	WCq	Arnason [11]	33 716	Ivanov.V RUS
2006							
28-02	Trinidad and Tobago	L 0-2	London	Fr		7 890	
15-08	Spain	D 0-0	Reykjavík	Fr		12 327	Stokes IRL
2-09	Northern Ireland	W 3-0	Belfast	ECq	Thorvaldsson [13], Hreidarsson [20], Gudjohnsen.E [37]	13 522	Skjerven NOR
6-09	Denmark	L 0-2	Reykjavík	ECq		10 007	Ivanov.N RUS
7-10	Latvia	L 0-4	Riga	ECq		6 800	Kelly IRL
11-10	Sweden	L 1-2	Reykjavík	ECq	Vidarsson [6]	8 725	Gilewski POL
2007							
28-03	Spain	L 0-1	Palma	ECq		18 326	Duhamel FRA
2-06	Liechtenstein	D 1-1	Reykjavík	ECq	Gunnarsson.B [27]	5 139	Kaldma EST
6-06	Sweden	L 0-5	Stockholm	ECq		33 358	Hamer LUX

Fr = Friendly match • EC = UEFA EURO 2004/2008 • WC = FIFA World Cup • q = qualifier

ICELAND NATIONAL TEAM RECORDS AND RECORD SEQUENCES

Records			Sequence records					
Victory	9-0	FRO 1985	Wins	4	2000	Clean sheets	3	1984
Defeat	2-14	DEN 1967	Defeats	10	1978-1980	Goals scored	7	Three times
Player Caps	104	KRISTINSSON Rúnar	Undefeated	11	1998-1999	Without goal	6	1977-1978
Player Goals	17	JONSSON Rikhardur	Without win	17	1977-1980	Goals against	19	1978-1981

MAJOR CITIES/TOWNS
Population '000

1	Reykjaveik	115
2	Kópavogur	26
3	Hafnarfjörðor	23
4	Akureyri	17
5	Garðabær	9
6	Keflavík	7
7	Mosfellsbær	7
8	Selfoss	5
9	Akranes	5
10	Seltjarnarnes	4
11	Vestmannæyjar	4
12	Njarðvík	2
13	Sauðárkrókur	2
14	Grindavík	2
15	Isafjörður	2
16	Alftanes	2
17	Húsavik	2
18	Egilsstaðir	2
19	Hveragerði	1
20	Borgarnes	1
21	Höfn	1
22	Garður	1
23	Neskaupstaður	1
24	Sandgerði	1

REPUBLIC OF ICELAND; LYDVELDID ISLAND

Capital Reykjavik	Language Icelandic	Independence 1918
Population 299 388	Area 103 000 km²	Density 3 per km²	% in cities 92%
GDP per cap $30 900	Dailling code +354	Internet .is	GMT +/- 0

MEDALS TABLE

	Overall G S B	League G S B	Cup G S	Europe G S B	City	Stadium	Cap'ty	DoF
1 KR Reykjavík	34 30 12	24 26 12	10 4		Reykjavík	KR-Völlur	2 781	1899
2 Valur	28 20 18	19 17 18	9 3		Reykjavík	Hlidarendi	4 590	1911
3 IA Akranes	27 21 12	18 12 12	9 9		Akranes	Akranesvöllur	2 780	1946
4 Fram	25 26 15	18 17 15	7 9		Reykjavík	Laugardalsvöllur	7 176	1908
5 Keflavik IF	8 7 7	4 2 7	4 5		Keflavik	Keflavíkurvöllur	4 957	1929
6 IBV Vestmannæyjar	7 12 7	3 6 7	4 6		Vestmannæyjar	Hásteinsvöllur	2 384	1945
7 Víkingur	6 8 8	5 7 8	1 1		Reykjavík	Víkin	1 249	1908
8 FH Hafnarfjördur	3 7 1	3 4 1	3		Hafnarfjördur	Kaplakrikavöllur	6 738	1929
9 Fylkir	2 2	2	2		Reykjavík	Fylkisvöllur	2 872	1967
10 KA Akureyri	1 3	1	3		Akureyri	Akureyrarvöllur	2 000	1928
11 IBA Akureyri	1 4	4 1			Akureyri	Akureyrarvöllur	2 000	1928
12 Leiftur	1 3	3 1			Olafsfjördur	Olafsfjördurvöllur	1 000	1931
13 Grindavík	1 2	2 1			Grindavík	Grindavíkurvöllur	1 750	1935
14 Breiðablik Kópavogur	1 1	1 1			Kópavogur	Kópavogsvöllur	5 501	1950
15 Vídir Gardur	1	1			Gardi	Gardsvöllur	1 500	1936
16 Thór Akureyri	2	2			Akureyri	Akureyrarvöllur	2 000	1915
17 Thróttur					Reykjavík	Valbjarnarvöllur	2 500	1949

RECENT LEAGUE AND CUP RECORD

	Championship							Cup		
Year	Champions	Pts	Runners-up	Pts	Third	Pts		Winners	Score	Runners-up
1995	IA Akranes	49	KR Reykjavik	35	IBV Vestmannæyjar	31		KR Reykjavík	2-1	Fram Reykjavik
1996	IA Akranes	40	KR Reykjavik	37	Leiftur	29		IA Akranes	2-1	IBV Vestmannæyjar
1997	IBV Vestmannæyjar	40	IA Akranes	35	Leiftur	30		Keflavik	1-1 0-0 5-4p	IBV Vestmannæyjar
1998	IBV Vestmannæyjar	38	KR Reykjavik	33	IA Akranes	30		IBV Vestmannæyjar	2-0	Leiftur
1999	KR Reykjavik	45	IBV Vestmannæyjar	38	Leiftur	26		KR Reykjavik	3-1	IA Akranes
2000	KR Reykjavik	37	Fylkir Reykjavík	35	Grindavík	30		IA Akranes	2-1	IBV Vestmannæyjar
2001	IA Akranes	36	IBV Vestmannæyjar	36	FH Hafnarfjördur	32		Fylkir Reykjavik	2-2 5-4p	KA Akureyri
2002	KR Reykjavik	36	Fylkir Reykjavik	34	Grindavík	29		Fylkir Reykjavik	3-1	Fram Reykjavik
2003	KR Reykjavik	33	FH Hafnarfjördur	30	IA Akranes	30		IA Akranes	1-0	FH Hafnarfjördur
2004	FH Hafnarfjördur	37	IBV Vestmannæyjar	31	IA Akranes	31		Keflavik	3-0	KA Akureyri
2005	FH Hafnarfjördur	48	Valur Reykjavík	32	IA Akranes	32		Valur Reykjavik	1-0	Fram Reykjavik

ICELAND 2006

URVALSDEILD (1)

	Pl	W	D	L	F	A	Pts	FH	KR	Valur	Keflavík	Breiðablik	IA	Vikingur	Fylkir	Grindavík	IBV
FH Hafnarfjördur †	18	10	6	2	31	14	36		2-0	1-2	2-1	1-1	2-1	4-0	2-2	2-0	3-1
KR Reykjavík ‡	18	9	3	6	23	27	30	0-3		1-1	2-2	3-2	2-3	1-0	1-0	3-0	2-0
Valur Reykjavík	18	7	8	3	27	18	29	0-2	2-2		0-0	1-1	2-1	0-0	3-1	2-1	5-0
Keflavík ‡	18	6	6	6	30	20	24	2-1	3-0	1-1		5-0	0-1	2-1	1-1	2-0	6-2
Breiðablik	18	6	5	7	27	33	23	1-1	0-1	2-1	2-0		2-2	1-0	3-2	2-3	4-1
IA Akranes	18	6	4	8	27	30	22	0-1	1-2	1-1	1-0	2-1		1-4	0-1	2-1	4-2
Vikingur Reykjavík	18	5	6	7	21	18	21	0-0	0-1	3-1	1-1	4-1	1-1		0-2	0-0	5-0
Fylkir Reykjavík	18	5	6	7	22	25	21	1-2	1-2	0-1	2-1	1-1	3-3	1-0		2-1	1-1
Grindavík	18	4	7	7	24	26	19	1-1	5-0	1-1	1-1	4-2	3-2	1-1	1-1		0-0
IBV Vestmannæyjar	18	5	3	10	18	39	18	1-1	2-0	0-3	2-1	0-1	2-1	0-1	2-1	2-1	

14/05/2006 - 23/09/2006 • † Qualified for the UEFA Champions League • ‡ Qualified for the UEFA Cup
Top scorers: Marel Johann BALDVINSSON, Breiðablik 11; Johann THORHALLSSON, Grindavík 10; Bjorgolfur TAKEFUSA, KR 10

ICELAND 2006
1.DEILD (2)

	Pl	W	D	L	F	A	Pts
Fram Reykjavík	18	13	2	3	32	14	41
HK Kópavogur	18	10	2	6	30	18	32
Fjölnir Reykjavík	18	8	5	5	23	15	29
Thróttur Reykjavík	18	9	2	7	21	18	29
Stjarnan Garðabær	18	6	6	6	26	23	24
KA Akureyri	18	6	3	9	22	25	21
Vikingur Olafsvík	18	4	7	7	16	22	19
Thór Akureyri	18	5	4	9	16	38	19
Leiknir Reykjavík	18	4	6	8	21	25	18
Haukar Hafnarfjördur	18	4	5	9	20	29	17

14/05/2006 - 16/09/2006

ICELAND 2006
2.DEILD (3)

	Pl	W	D	L	F	A	Pts
Fjarðabyggð	18	14	2	2	39	12	44
Njarðvík	18	13	4	1	46	13	41
Reynir Sandgerði	18	9	5	4	37	18	32
Selfoss	18	7	6	5	26	18	27
IR Reykjavík	18	8	3	7	36	32	27
Völsungur Húsavík	18	6	4	8	24	32	22
Aftureiding Mosfellsbær	18	5	3	10	27	41	18
KS/Leiftur Siglufjörður	18	4	4	10	24	34	16
Sindri Hofn	18	3	3	12	19	60	12
Huginn Seyðisfjörður	18	2	4	12	25	43	10

14/05/2006 - 9/09/2006

BIKARKEPPNI 2006

Round of 16

Keflavík	3
Leiknir Reykjavík *	0
Fram Reykjavík *	2
IA Akranes	3
Valur Reykjavík	2
Fjarðabyggð *	0
FH Hafnarfjördur *	1
Vikingur Reykjavík	2
Thróttur Reykjavík *	2
Grindavík	1
Breiðablik	2
KA Akureyri *	3
IBV Vestmannæyjar	2
Fylkir Reykjavík *	1
Njarðvík *	0
KR Reykjavík	1

Quarter-finals

Keflavík	4
IA Akranes *	3
Valur Reykjavík *	1
Vikingur Reykjavík	2
Thróttur Reykjavík	5
KA Akureyri *	1
IBV Vestmannæyjar	1 2p
KR Reykjavík *	1 4p

Semi-finals

Keflavík	2
Vikingur Reykjavík	0
Thróttur Reykjavík	0
KR Reykjavík	1

Final

Keflavík ‡	2
KR Reykjavík	0

CUP FINAL
Laugardalsvøllur, Reykjavík
30-09-2006, Att: 4699, Ref: Valgeirsson

Scorers - Gudjon Arni Antoniusson [21], Baldur Sigurdsson [30]

* Home team • ‡ Qualified for the UEFA Cup

Semis played at Laugardalsvøllur

ISR – ISRAEL

NATIONAL TEAM RECORD
JULY 10TH 2006 TO JULY 12TH 2010

PL	W	D	L	F	A	%
10	5	4	1	19	9	70

FIFA/COCA-COLA WORLD RANKING

1993	1994	1995	1996	1997	1998	1999	2000	2001	2002	2003	2004	2005	2006	High		Low	
57	42	42	52	61	43	26	41	49	46	51	48	44	44	**22**	06/99	**71**	09/93

2006–2007											
08/06	09/06	10/06	11/06	12/06	01/07	02/07	03/07	04/07	05/07	06/07	07/07
51	36	36	44	44	44	40	38	33	34	34	33

Israeli teams had to contend with serious security concerns at the start of the season, concerns that saw the national team play its first home match in the UEFA Euro 2008 qualifiers in the Netherlands. The 4-1 victory over Andorra meant that no advantage had been lost in a very tough group. However, a 4-3 defeat at the hands of Croatia in Tel Aviv weakened their position, and despite five wins and a draw in seven matches, a first appearance at the finals looked like being a long shot. Israeli clubs also found themselves playing home matches outside of Israel at the start of the season, with Maccabi Haifa playing their match in the third preliminary round of the UEFA

INTERNATIONAL HONOURS
Qualified for the FIFA World Cup finals 1970   AFC Asian Cup 1964   AFC Champions League Hapoel Tel Aviv 1967 Maccabi Tel Aviv 1969 1971

Champions League against Liverpool in Kyiv. Having lost the first leg 2-1 in Liverpool they could only force a draw and were out although they did go on to reach the last 16 of the UEFA Cup. Maccabi had an unusually poor season at home, finishing fifth in the League and failing to win a fourth consecutive title. It was the first time since 1999 that Maccabi had finished outside of the top two. The title went instead to Beitar Jerusalem whose billionaire owner Arkady Gaydamak finally saw some return on his investment in the club. Hapoel Tel Aviv won the Cup but only after a penalty shoot-out against Hapoel Ashkelon who were later relegated to the third division.

THE FIFA BIG COUNT OF 2006

	Male	Female		Total
Number of players	251 516	32 350	Referees and Assistant Referees	1 350
Professionals	1 360		Admin, Coaches, Technical, Medical	10 800
Amateurs 18+	8 423		Number of clubs	280
Youth under 18	33 883		Number of teams	1 400
Unregistered	77 000		Clubs with women's teams	10
Total players	283 866		Players as % of population	4.47%

The Israel Football Association (IFA)
Ramat-Gan Stadium, 299 Aba Hilell Street, Ramat Gan 52134, Israel
Tel +972 3 6171500   Fax +972 3 5702044
r.dori@israel-football.org.il   www.israel-football.org.il
President: LUZON Avi   General Secretary: SHILO Ori
Vice-President: TBD   Treasurer: HALUBA Shtern   Media Officer: AIZENBERG Shaul
Men's Coach: KASHTAN Dror   Women's Coach: SCHRAIER Alon
IFA formed: 1928 & 1948   UEFA: 1992 (AFC 1956-1976)   FIFA: 1929
Blue shirts with white trimmings, White shorts, Blue socks or White shirts with blue trimmings, Blue shorts, White socks

RECENT INTERNATIONAL MATCHES PLAYED BY ISRAEL

2002	Opponents	Score	Venue	Comp	Scorers	Att	Referee
21-08	Lithuania	W 4-2	Kaunas	Fr	Afek 2 [20 64], Zandberg [47], Tal [74]	3 000	Chykun BLR
5-09	Luxembourg	W 5-0	Luxembourg	Fr	Udi 2 [1 68], Badeer [24], Keisi [79], Benayoun [85]	1 400	Allaerts BEL
12-10	Malta	W 2-0	Ta'Qali	ECq	Balili [56], Revivo [77]	5 200	Shebek UKR
20-11	FYR Macedonia	W 3-2	Skopje	Fr	Zandberg [19], Nimni [28], Biton [90]	5 000	Delevic YUG
2003							
12-02	Armenia	W 2-0	Tel Aviv	Fr	Nimni [19], Zandberg [62]	8 000	Trentlange ITA
5-03	Moldova	D 0-0	Tel Aviv	Fr		8 000	Bertini ITA
29-03	Cyprus	D 1-1	Limassol	ECq	Afek [1]	8 500	McCurry SCO
2-04	France	L 1-2	Palermo	ECq	Afek [2]	4 000	Barber ENG
30-04	Cyprus	W 2-0	Palermo	ECq	Badeer [88], Holtzman [90]	1 000	Benes CZE
7-06	Slovenia	D 0-0	Antalya	ECq		2 500	Busacca SUI
20-08	Russia	W 2-1	Moscow	Fr	Nimni [52], Balili [82]	5 000	Ishchenko UKR
6-09	Slovenia	L 1-3	Ljubljana	ECq	Revivo [69]	8 000	Fandel GER
10-09	Malta	D 2-2	Antalya	ECq	Revivo [16], Abuksis [78]	300	Blareau BEL
11-10	France	L 0-3	Paris	ECq		57 900	Bolognino ITA
2004							
18-02	Azerbaijan	W 6-0	Tel Aviv	Fr	Arbeitman 3 [9 65 69], Tal [24p], Katan 2 [45 61]	13 250	Gomes Paraty POR
30-03	Lithuania	W 2-1	Tel Aviv	Fr	Balili [34], Badeer [64]	9 872	Dougal SCO
28-04	Moldova	D 1-1	Tel Aviv	Fr	Covalenco OG [31]	4 500	Corpodean ROU
27-05	Georgia	W 1-0	Tbilisi	Fr	Badeer [33]	22 000	Oriekhov UKR
18-08	Croatia	L 0-1	Zagreb	Fr		10 000	Granat POL
4-09	France	D 0-0	Paris	WCq		43 527	Temmink NED
8-09	Cyprus	W 2-1	Tel Aviv	WCq	Benayoun [64], Badeer [75]	21 872	Shmolik BLR
9-10	Switzerland	D 2-2	Tel Aviv	WCq	Benayoun 2 [9 48]	37 976	Shield AUS
17-11	Cyprus	W 2-1	Nicosia	WCq	Keisi [17], Nimni [86]	1 624	Kaldma EST
2005							
9-02	Croatia	D 3-3	Jerusalem	Fr	Balili [38], Benayoun [74], Golan [84]	4 000	Kailis CYP
26-03	Republic of Ireland	D 1-1	Tel Aviv	WCq	Souan [90]	32 150	Ivanov.V RUS
30-03	France	D 1-1	Tel Aviv	WCq	Badeer [83]	32 150	Merk GER
4-06	Republic of Ireland	D 2-2	Dublin	WCq	Yemiel [39], Nimni [46+]	36 000	Vassaras GRE
15-08	Ukraine	D 0-0	Kyiv	Fr	W 5-3p		Mikullski POL
17-08	Poland	L 2-3	Kyiv	Fr	Badir [35], Katan [47]	2 000	Karadzic SCG
3-09	Switzerland	D 1-1	Basel	WCq	Keisi [20]	30 000	Rosetti ITA
7-09	Faroe Islands	W 2-0	Tórshavn	WCq	Nimni [54], Katan [79]	2 240	VINK NED
8-10	Faroe Islands	W 2-1	Tel Aviv	WCq	Benayoun [1], Zaudberg [91+]	31 857	Brugger AUT
2006							
1-03	Denmark	L 0-2	Tel Aviv	Fr		15 762	Sippel GER
15-08	Slovenia	D 1-1	Celje	Fr	Benayoun [81]	3 000	Kralovec CZE
2-09	Estonia	W 1-0	Tallinn	ECq	Colautti [8]	7 800	Verbist BEL
6-09	Andorra	W 4-1	Nijmegan	ECq	Benayoun [9], Ben Shushan [11], Gershon [43p], Tamuz [69]	400	Zrnic BIH
7-10	Russia	D 1-1	Moscow	ECq	Ben Shushan [84]	22 000	Meyer GER
15-11	Croatia	L 3-4	Tel Aviv	ECq	Colautti 2 [8 89], Benayoun [68]	35 000	Iturralde Gonzalez ESP
2007							
7-02	Ukraine	D 1-1	Tel Aviv	Fr	Badeer [38]	12 000	S. Rodriguez ESP
24-03	England	D 0-0	Tel Aviv	ECq		38 000	Ovrebø NOR
28-03	Estonia	W 4-0	Tel Aviv	ECq	Idan Tal [19], Colautti [29], Sahar 2 [77 80]	21 000	Cüneyt Cakir TUR
2-06	FYR Macedonia	W 2-1	Skopje	ECq	Itzhaki [11], Colautti [44]	12 000	Kircher GER
6-06	Andorra	W 2-0	Andorra-La-Vella	ECq	Tamuz [37], Colautti [53]	680	Stokes IRL

Fr = Friendly match • EC = UEFA EURO 2004/2008 • WC = FIFA World Cup • q = qualifier

ISRAEL NATIONAL TEAM RECORDS AND RECORD SEQUENCES

Records			Sequence records				
Victory	9-0	TPE 1988	Wins	7	1973-1974	Clean sheets	4	Four times
Defeat	1-7	EGY 1934, GER 2002	Defeats	8	1950-1956	Goals scored	9	1968-69, 2000-01
Player Caps	93	BENADO Arik	Undefeated	12	1971-1973	Without goal	5	1964-1965
Player Goals	26	SPIEGLER Mordechai	Without win	22	1985-1988	Goals against	22	1934-1958

STATE OF ISRAEL; MEDINAT YISRA'EL

Capital Jerusalem	Language Hebrew, Arabic, English		Independence 1948
Population 6 352 117	Area 20 770 km²	Density 298 per km²	% in cities 91%
GDP per cap $19 800	Dailling code +972	Internet .il	GMT +/- +2

MAJOR CITIES/TOWNS
Population '000

1	Jerusalem	743
2	Tel Aviv-Jaffa	388
3	Haifa	265
4	Rishon Letzion	228
5	Ashdod	214
6	Be'er Sheva	190
7	Petah Tikva	182
8	Netanya	176
9	Holon	165
10	Ben Beraq	148
11	Ramat Gan	128
12	Bat Yam	126
13	Ashkelon	108
14	Rehoboth	106
15	Hertzelia	83
16	Kfar Saba	82
17	Bet Shemesh	78
18	Hadera	77
19	Ra'anana	73
20	Lod	67
21	Nazerat	67
22	Ramla	64
23	Nahariyya	52
24	Qiryat Atta	49

MEDALS TABLE

		Overall			League			Cup			Asia/Eur			City	Stadium	Cap'ty	DoF
		G	S	B	G	S	B	G	S	B	G	S	B				
1	Maccabi Tel Aviv	42	20	7	18	9	7	22	11		2			Tel Aviv	Bloomfield	15 400	1906
2	Hapoel Tel Aviv	24	18	6	11	10	6	12	7		1	1		Tel Aviv	Bloomfield	15 400	1928
3	Maccabi Haifa	15	12	5	10	5	5	5	7					Haifa	Kiryat Eli'ezer	17 000	1913
4	Beitar Jerusalem	10	9	4	5	6	4	5	3					Jerusalem	Teddi Malcha	18 500	1939
5	Hapoel Petach Tikva	8	15	4	6	9	4	2	6					Petach Tikva	Petach Tikva	8 000	1935
6	Maccabi Netanya	6	5	4	5	3	4	1	2					Netanya	Maccabi Netanya	6 500	1942
7	Hapoel Haifa	4	7	8	1	2	8	3	5					Haifa	Kiryat Eli'ezer	17 000	1921
8	Hakoah Ramat Gan	4	1	1	2		1	2	1					Ramat Gan	Winter	8 000	1961
9	Hapoel Kfar Saba	4			1			3						Kfar Saba	Levita	4 500	1936
10	Bnei Yehuda Tel Aviv	3	6	2	1	3	2	2	3					Tel Aviv	Shchonat H'atikva	8 000	1935
11	Hapoel Beer Sheva	3	2	5	2		5	1	2					Beer Sheva	Artur Vasermil	13 000	1949
12	Maccabi Petach Tikva	2	5	1	3	1	2	2	2					Petach Tikva	Petach Tikva	8 000	1912
13	Beitar Tel Aviv	2	2	1			1	2	2					Tel Aviv	Bloomfield	15 400	1934-2000
14	British Police	2			1			1									
15	Hapoel Ramat Gan	2			1			1						Ramat Gan	HaMakhtesh	5 500	1927

RECENT LEAGUE AND CUP RECORD

	Championship						Cup		
Year	Champions	Pts	Runners-up	Pts	Third	Pts	Winners	Score	Runners-up
1995	Maccabi Tel Aviv	63	Maccabi Haifa	58	Hapoel Beer Sheva	50	Maccabi Haifa	2-0	Hapoel Haifa
1996	Maccabi Tel Aviv	74	Maccabi Haifa	66	Beitar Jerusalem	64	Maccabi Tel Aviv	4-1	Hapoel Ironi RL
1997	Beitar Jerusalem	69	Hapoel Petah Tikva	60	Hapoel Beer Sheva	60	Hapoel Beer Sheva	1-0	Maccabi Tel Aviv
1998	Beitar Jerusalem	69	Hapoel Tel Aviv	68	Hapoel Haifa	60	Maccabi Haifa	2-0	Hapoel Jerusalem
1999	Hapoel Haifa	71	Maccabi Tel Aviv	63	Maccabi Haifa	60	Hapoel Tel Aviv	1-1 3-1p	Beitar Jerusalem
2000	Hapoel Tel Aviv	85	Maccabi Haifa	76	Hapoel Petah Tikva	74	Hapoel Tel Aviv	2-2 4-2p	Beitar Jerusalem
2001	Maccabi Haifa	82	Hapoel Tel Aviv	75	Hapoel Haifa	71	Maccabi Tel Aviv	3-0	Maccabi Petah Tikva
2002	Maccabi Haifa	75	Hapoel Tel Aviv	67	Maccabi Tel Aviv	57	Maccabi Tel Aviv	0-0 5-4p	Maccabi Haifa
2003	Maccabi Tel Aviv	69	Maccabi Haifa	69	Hapoel Tel Aviv	67	Hapoel Ramat Gan	1-1 5-4p	Hapoel Beer Sheva
2004	Maccabi Haifa	63	Maccabi Tel Aviv	57	Maccabi Petach Tikva	56	Hapoel Bnei Sakhnin	4-1	Hapoel Haifa
2005	Maccabi Haifa	71	Maccabi Petah Tikva	60	Ashdod	50	Maccabi Tel Aviv	2-2 5-3p	Maccabi Herzliya
2006	Maccabi Haifa	75	Hapoel Tel Aviv	59	Beitar Jerusalem	58	Hapoel Tel Aviv	1-0	Bnei Yehuda
2007	Beitar Jerusalem	67	Maccabi Netanya	54	Maccabi Tel Aviv	54	Hapoel Tel Aviv	1-1 5-4p	Hapoel Ashkelon

ISRAEL 2006-07

LIGAT HA'AL

	Pl	W	D	L	F	A	Pts	Beitar	Netanya	M. Tel Aviv	H. Tel Aviv	M. Haifa	Maccabi PT	Ashdod	H. Kfar Saba	Bnei Yehuda	M. Hertzelia	H. Ramat Gan	Hapoel PT
Beitar Jerusalem †	33	19	10	4	52	24	67		0-0 0-1	0-0	2-1 2-1	1-1 4-1	0-0	2-0	2-0 2-1	0-0	3-0 2-2	0-0	2-0 2-0
Maccabi Netanya ‡	33	15	12	6	37	25	57	3-1		1-1	1-1 0-2	3-1	2-0 0-0	0-1 3-2	1-0	0-0 3-0	1-0	1-0 2-1	1-1 2-1
Maccabi Tel Aviv ‡ §2	33	15	11	7	42	28	54	1-2 0-1	0-0 2-1		0-0	1-1 0-1	1-0	1-0	0-2 2-2	4-0	2-1 3-0	1-0	1-0 2-2
Hapoel Tel Aviv ‡	33	15	9	9	53	40	54	1-1	2-1	1-3 3-0		2-0	0-1 2-2	1-0 2-1	1-1	3-1 0-0	2-0	4-1 1-2	2-0 5-1
Maccabi Haifa	33	14	9	10	45	39	51	0-3	1-0 0-0	0-0	3-2 4-0		1-0 0-1	1-0	3-3	2-0 2-0	0-4	3-3 1-2	2-1 6-1
Maccabi Petah Tikva	33	14	8	11	31	27	50	3-1 0-1	0-1	2-1 0-2	0-1	0-1		2-1 2-0	0-1 0-0	1-0	2-2 4-2	0-0	1-0
MS Ashdod	33	12	6	15	49	49	42	1-4 1-1	2-3	2-2 0-1	2-1	1-1 0-1	1-2		3-0	2-0 1-1	1-0 0-2	3-0	2-1 4-1
Hapoel Kfar Saba	33	8	16	9	41	40	40	2-3	1-1 0-0	1-1	0-1 1-1	1-1 1-0	1-1	3-0 2-2		1-2 1-1	2-1	1-3 0-0	4-1
Bnei Yehuda Tel Aviv	33	7	14	12	34	50	35	0-2 1-3	1-1	1-1 3-2	1-1	2-1	2-1 0-1	2-3 3-2	2-2		2-1 1-4	0-0	3-1
Maccabi Hertzelia	33	9	7	17	47	55	34	2-1	1-0 2-3	0-2	2-2 4-1	2-2	0-2	0-3	1-2	1-3 1-3		1-2 5-0	0-0
Hakoah Ramat Gan	33	6	10	17	32	54	28	0-2 1-1	0-1	0-1 0-2	3-4	1-0 0-0	0-1 0-1	4-4	0-0	3-2 2-2	1-2		0-3
Hapoel Petah Tikva §3	33	3	10	20	29	61	16	0-1	0-0	1-2	0-2	0-2	0-1 1-1	2-3	0-0 2-0	0-1 1-1	1-1 2-3	2-1 3-2 1-3	

26/08/2006 - 27/05/2007 • † Qualified for the UEFA Champions League • ‡ Qualified for the UEFA Cup • § = points deducted
Top scorer: Yaniv AZRAN, Ashdod, 15

ISRAEL 2006-07 LIGA LEUMIT (2)

	Pl	W	D	L	F	A	Pts
Ironi Kiriat Shmona	33	18	10	5	57	34	64
Hapoel Bnei Sakhnin	33	17	9	7	54	29	60
Hapoel Haifa	33	14	5	14	45	45	47
Hapoel Be'er Sheva §1	33	13	13	9	47	36	45
Hapoel Acre	33	12	8	13	39	47	44
Hapoel Ranana	33	10	12	11	34	31	42
Hapoel Upper Nazareth	33	10	12	11	34	38	42
Maccabi Akhi Nazareth	33	10	9	14	31	37	39
Ironi Ramat Hasharon	33	9	12	12	34	45	39
Bnei Lod	33	11	6	16	33	50	39
Hapoel Ashkelon	33	8	14	11	35	33	38
Hapoel Jerusalem §1	33	7	12	14	30	48	32

25/08/2006 - 26/05/2007 • § = points deducted

ISRAEL 2006-07 LIGA ARTZIT (3)

	Pl	W	D	L	F	A	Pts
Hapoel Ramat Gan	33	19	9	5	46	21	66
Ironi Rishon Letzion	33	18	7	8	53	34	61
Hapoel Bnei Timra	33	15	9	9	39	33	54
Sektzia Nes Tziona	33	13	13	7	46	31	52
Maccabi Tirat Carmel	33	12	9	12	43	46	45
Beitar/Shimshon TA	33	10	14	9	31	28	44
Maccabi HaShikma	33	11	9	13	33	33	42
Maccabi Kfar Kana	33	12	6	15	28	38	42
Hapoel Marmorek	33	10	11	12	37	38	41
MI Kiriat Ata	33	10	10	13	37	39	40
Hapoel Hertzelia	33	10	7	16	35	41	37
Maccabi Be'er Sheva	33	2	8	23	15	61	14

25/08/2006 - 26/05/2007

STATE CUP 2006-07

Round of 16

Hapoel Tel Aviv	1
Hapoel Marmurek *	0
Maccabi Tel Aviv	1
Hapoel Bnei Sakhnin*	2
Maccabi Petah Tikva*	1
Hapoel Hertzelia	0
Hapoel Nazrat Ilit *	0
MS Ashdod	1
Hapoel Ramat Gan	1 3p
Hapoel Kfar Saba *	1 2p
Hapoel Acre	1
Maccabi Haifa *	2
Hapoel Haifa *	2
Bnei Lod	1
Maccabi HaShikma *	0
Hapoel Ashkelon	2

Quarter-finals

Hapoel Tel Aviv *	3
Hapoel Bnei Sakhnin	0
Maccabi Petah Tikva *	0
MS Ashdod	4
Hapoel Ramat Gan *	1
Maccabi Haifa	0
Hapoel Haifa	0
Hapoel Ashkelon *	2

Semi-finals

Hapoel Tel Aviv	1
MS Ashdod	0
Hapoel Ramat Gan	0
Hapoel Ashkelon	1

Final

Hapoel Tel Aviv ‡	1 5p
Hapoel Ashkelon	1 4p

CUP FINAL
Ramat Gan, 16-05-2007
Scorers - Luciano de Bruno 75 for Hapoel TA; Nir Nahum 7 for Hapoel Ashkelon

* Home team • Semis played at Ramat Gan • ‡ Qualified for the UEFA Cup

ITA – ITALY

NATIONAL TEAM RECORD
JULY 10TH 2006 TO JULY 12TH 2010

PL	W	D	L	F	A	%
9	5	2	2	14	10	66.6

For the second year running there was a silver lining to the dark clouds that have gathered over Italian football. Just as the national team struck gold at the 2006 FIFA World Cup amidst the corruption scandal, Milan secured another notable triumph by winning the European Cup at the end of a season scarred by violence; violence which culminated in the murder of policeman Filippo Raciti at a match between Catania and Palermo in February 2007. Milan's triumph in the final in Athens against Liverpool may have failed to scale the heights of the classic final between the two in Istanbul two years previously, but it did provide a welcome distraction from the woes of Serie A, which is perhaps at the lowest ebb in its history. Crowds fell to an average of just over 18,000 a match - less than half that of the Bundesliga in Germany and roughly the same as the J.League in Japan, MLS in the USA and Holland's Eredivisie. The situation has drawn comparisons with the English League 20 years ago and the Italian Federation were hoping to follow the lead of England and use the staging of the European Championship to modernise both the game and the stadia in the country. In an extraordinary rebuff, however, Italy's bid to stage Euro 2012 was passed over by

INTERNATIONAL HONOURS
FIFA World Cup™ 1934 1938 1982 2006

Olympic Gold 1936

International Cup 1930 1935   UEFA European Championship 1968   UEFA Junior Tournament 1958 1966

UEFA U-21 Championship 1992 1994 1996 2000 2004   UEFA U-19 Championship 2003   UEFA U-17 Championship 1982 1987

UEFA Champions League Milan 1963 1969 1989 1990 1994 2003 2007, Internazionale 1964 1965, Juventus 1985 1996

UEFA in favour of Poland and the Ukraine. Aside from the violence and matches played behind closed doors, the season in Italy always had a surreal feel to it with five clubs starting the Serie A with substantial points deductions. By the end of December there was only ever going to be one winner - Inter. They retained the Scudetto by losing just one match all season, winning a record 17 consecutive League matches in the process and going 39 games unbeaten in all competitions. It's a shame then that the titles won by Inter in the past two seasons will always be judged in the light of the off-the-field problems that have tainted Serie A. Inter were denied consecutive doubles when they lost the Coppa Italia final to Roma and then to add insult to injury, rivals Milan stole their limelight by walking off with the European Cup. Milan's triumph was remarkable in many ways. UEFA were unhappy at their entry in the first place following their involvement in the bribery scandal and for parts of the season, the football they played was at best average. Vintage Milan they certainly were not but they proved that with team spirit, self belief in abundance and a little help from one of the best players in the world in Kaká, anything is possible.

Federazione Italiana Giuoco Calcio (FIGC)
Via Gregorio Allegri 14, Roma 00198, Italy
Tel +39 06 84912500   Fax +39 06 84912526
press@figc.it   www.figc.it
President: ABETE Giancarlo   General Secretary: DI SEBASTIANO Antonio
Vice-President: GUSSONI Cesare   Treasurer: DE CESARE Sergio   Media Officer: VALENTINI Antonio
Men's Coach: DONADONI Roberto   Women's Coach: GHEDIN Pietro
FIGC formed: 1898   UEFA: 1954   FIFA: 1905
Blue shirts with white trimmings, White shorts, Blue socks or White shirts with blue trimmings, Blue shorts, White socks

RECENT INTERNATIONAL MATCHES PLAYED BY ITALY

2004	Opponents	Score		Venue	Comp	Scorers	Att	Referee
14-06	Denmark	D	0-0	Guimaraes	ECr1		19 595	Mejuto Gonzalez ESP
18-06	Sweden	D	1-1	Porto	ECr1	Cassano 37	44 927	Meier SUI
22-06	Bulgaria	W	2-1	Guimaraes	ECr1	Perrotta 48, Cassano 90	16 002	Ivanov RUS
18-08	Iceland	L	0-2	Reykjavik	Fr		20 204	Frojdfeldt SWE
4-09	Norway	W	2-1	Palermo	WCq	De Rossi 4, Toni 80	21 463	Sars FRA
8-09	Moldova	W	1-0	Chisinau	WCq	Del Piero 32	5 200	Benes CZE
9-10	Slovenia	L	0-1	Celje	WCq		9 262	De Bleeckere BEL
13-10	Belarus	W	4-3	Parma	WCq	Totti 2 26p 74, De Rossi 32, Gilardino 86	19 833	Megia Davila ESP
17-11	Finland	W	1-0	Messina	Fr	Miccoli 33	7 043	Tudor ROU
2005								
9-02	Russia	W	2-0	Cagliari	Fr	Gilardino 56, Barone 62	15 700	Michel SVK
26-03	Scotland	W	2-0	Milan	WCq	Pirlo 2 35 85	45 000	Vassaras GRE
30-03	Iceland	D	0-0	Padova	Fr		16 697	Hamer LUX
4-06	Norway	D	0-0	Oslo	WCq		24 829	Mejuto Gonzalez ESP
8-06	Serbia & Montenegro	D	1-1	Toronto	Fr	Lucarelli 83	35 000	Depiero CAN
11-06	Ecuador	D	1-1	East Rutherford	Fr	Toni 6	27 583	Vaughn USA
17-08	Republic of Ireland	W	2-1	Dublin	Fr	Pirlo 10, Gilardino 31	44 000	Gomes Costa POR
3-09	Scotland	D	1-1	Glasgow	WCq	Grosso 75	50 185	Michel SVK
7-09	Belarus	W	4-1	Minsk	WCq	Toni 3 6 13 55, Camoranesi 45	30 299	Temmink NED
8-10	Slovenia	W	1-0	Palermo	WCq	Zaccardo 78	19 123	Poulat FRA
12-10	Moldova	W	2-1	Lecce	WCq	Viera 70, Gilardino 85	28 160	Benquerenca POR
12-11	Netherlands	W	3-1	Amsterdam	Fr	Gilardino 41, Vlaar OG 45, Toni 50	50 000	Ivanov RUS
16-11	Côte d'Ivoire	D	1-1	Geneva	Fr	Diana 86	18 500	Bertolini SUI
2006								
1-03	Germany	W	4-1	Florence	Fr	Gilardino 4, Toni 7, De Rossi 39, Del Piero 57	28 317	Iturralde Gonzalez ESP
31-05	Switzerland	D	1-1	Geneva	Fr	Gilardino 10	30 000	Sippel GER
2-06	Ukraine	D	0-0	Lausanne	Fr		10 000	Nobs SUI
12-06	Ghana	W	2-0	Hannover	WCr1	Pirlo 40, Iaquinta 83	43 000	Simon BRA
17-06	USA	D	1-1	Kaiserslautern	WCr1	Gilardino 22	46 000	Larrionda URU
22-06	Czech Republic	W	2-0	Hamburg	WCr1	Materazzi 26, Inzaghi 87	50 000	Archundia MEX
26-06	Australia	W	1-0	Kaiserslautern	WCr2	Totti 95+p	46 000	Medina Cantalejo ESP
30-06	Ukraine	W	3-0	Hamburg	WCqf	Zambrotta 6, Toni 2 59 69	50 000	De Bleeckere BEL
4-07	Germany	W	2-0	Dortmund	WCsf	Grosso 119, Del Piero 121+	65 000	Archundia MEX
9-07	France	D	1-1	Berlin	WCf	Materazzi 19. W 5-3p	69 000	Elizondo ARG
16-08	Croatia	L	0-2	Livorno	Fr		16 150	Kircher GER
2-09	Lithuania	D	1-1	Naples	ECq	Inzaghi 30	43 440	Hansson SWE
6-09	France	L	1-3	Paris	ECq	Gilardino 20	78 831	Fandel GER
7-10	Ukraine	W	2-0	Rome	ECq	Oddo 71p, Toni 79	49 149	Vassaras GRE
11-10	Georgia	W	3-1	Tbilisi	ECq	De Rossi 18, Camoranesi 63, Perrotta 71	48 000	Riley ENG
15-11	Turkey	D	1-1	Bergamo	Fr	Di Natale 39	24 386	Busacca SUI
2007								
28-03	Scotland	W	2-0	Bari	ECq	Toni 2 12 70	37 600	De Bleeckere BEL
2-06	Faroe Islands	W	2-1	Torshavn	ECq	Inzaghi 2 12 48	5 800	Malek POL
6-06	Lithuania	W	2-0	Kaunas	ECq	Quagliarella 2 31 45	7 800	Vink NED

Fr = Friendly match • EC = UEFA EURO 2004/2008 • WC = FIFA World Cup
q = qualifier • r1 = first round group • r2 = second round • qf = quarter-finals • sf = semi-finals • f = final

ITALY NATIONAL TEAM RECORDS AND RECORD SEQUENCES

Records			Sequence records					
Victory	9-0	USA 1948	Wins	9	1938-1939	Clean sheets	12	1972-1974
Defeat	1-7	HUN 1924	Defeats	3	Three times	Goals scored	43	1931-1937
Player Caps	126	MALDINI Paolo	Undefeated	30	1935-1939	Without goal	3	Three times
Player Goals	35	RIVA Luigi	Without win	8	1958-1959	Goals against	19	1927-1930

ITALIAN REPUBLIC; REPUBBLICA ITALIANA

Capital Rome	Language Italian		Formation 1870
Population 58 133 509	Area 301 230 km²	Density 193 per km²	% in cities 67%
GDP per cap $26 700	Dailling code +39	Internet .it	GMT +/- +1

MEDALS TABLE

		Overall			League			Cup		Europe			City	Stadium	Cap'ty	DoF
		G	S	B	G	S	B	G	S	G	S	B				
1	Juventus	42	31	18	27	19	12	9	4	6	8	6	Turin	Stadio delle Alpi	69 041	1897
2	Milan	31	24	20	17	13	16	5	6	9	5	4	Milan	Giuseppe Meazza (San Siro)	85 700	1899
3	Internazionale	25	21	22	15	13	14	5	5	5	3	8	Milan	Giuseppe Meazza (San Siro)	85 700	1908
4	Torino	13	17	7	8	9	6	5	7		1	1	Turin	Stadio delle Alpi	69 041	1906
5	Roma	12	17	7	3	9	5	8	6	1	2	2	Rome	Stadio Olimpico	82 307	1927
6	Genoa 1893	10	5	2	9	4	1	1	1			1	Genoa	Luigi Ferraris	40 117	1893
7	Fiorentina	9	11	6	2	5	5	6	3	1	3	1	Florence	Artemio Franchi	44 781	1926
8	Bologna	9	4	5	7	4	3	2				2	Bologna	Renato Dall'Ara	39 444	1909
9	Lazio	7	8	5	2	6	4	4	1	1	1	1	Rome	Stadio Olimpico	82 307	1900
10	Pro Vercelli	7	1		7	1							Vercelli	Silvio Piola	6 165	1892
11	Napoli	6	8	7	2	4	6	3	4	1		1	Naples	San Paolo	78 210	1904
12	Sampdoria	6	5	4	1	1	3	4	2	1	2	1	Genoa	Luigi Ferraris	40 117	1946
13	Parma	6	4	3		1	2	3	2	3	1	1	Parma	Ennio Tardini	28 783	1913
14	Hellas-Verona	1	3		1				3				Verona	Marc'Antonio Bentegodi	42 160	1903
15	Atalanta	1	2	1				1	2			1	Bergamo	Atleti Azzurri d'Italia	28 430	1907
	Venezia	1	2	1	1	1		1	1				Venice	Pierluigi Penzo	9 977	1907
	Vicenza	1	2	1		2		1				1	Vicenza	Romeo Menti	17 163	1902
18	Cagliari	1	1	1	1	1						1	Cagliari	Sant'Elia	24 000	1920

RECENT LEAGUE AND CUP RECORD

	Championship							Cup		
Year	Champions	Pts	Runners-up	Pts	Third	Pts		Winners	Score	Runners-up
1995	Juventus	73	Lazio	63	Parma	63		Juventus	1-0 2-0	Parma
1996	Milan	73	Juventus	65	Lazio	59		Fiorentina	1-0 2-0	Atalanta
1997	Juventus	65	Parma	64	Internazionale	59		Vicenza	0-1 3-0	Napoli
1998	Juventus	74	Internazionale	69	Udinese	64		Lazio	0-1 3-1	Milan
1999	Milan	70	Lazio	69	Fiorentina	56		Parma	1-1 2-2	Fiorentina
2000	Lazio	72	Juventus	71	Milan	61		Lazio	2-1 0-0	Internazionale
2001	Roma	75	Juventus	73	Lazio	69		Fiorentina	1-0 1-1	Parma
2002	Juventus	71	Roma	70	Internazionale	69		Parma	1-2 1-0	Juventus
2003	Juventus	72	Internazionale	65	Milan	61		Milan	4-1 2-2	Roma
2004	Milan	82	Roma	71	Juventus	69		Lazio	2-0 2-2	Juventus
2005	Juventus	86	Milan	79	Internazionale	72		Internazionale	2-0 1-0	Roma
2006	Internazionale	76	Roma	69	Milan	58		Internazionale	1-1 3-1	Roma
2007	Internazionale	97	Roma	75	Lazio	62		Roma	6-2 1-2	Internazionale

Juventus were stripped of the titles they won in 2005 and 2006

ITALY 2006-07

SERIE A

	Pl	W	D	L	F	A	Pts	Inter	Roma	Lazio	Milan	Palermo	Fiorentina	Empoli	Atalanta	Sampdoria	Udinese	Livorno	Parma	Catania	Reggina	Siena	Torino	Cagliari	Chievo Verona	Ascoli	Messina
Internazionale †	38	30	7	1	80	34	97		1-3	4-3	2-1	2-2	3-1	3-1	2-1	1-1	1-1	4-1	2-0	2-1	1-0	2-0	3-0	1-0	4-3	2-0	2-0
Roma †	38	22	9	7	74	34	75	0-1		0-0	1-1	4-0	3-1	1-0	2-1	4-0	3-1	2-0	3-0	7-0	3-0	1-0	0-1	2-0	1-1	2-2	4-3
Lazio §3 †	38	18	11	9	59	33	62	0-2	3-0		0-0	1-2	0-1	3-1	1-0	1-0	5-0	1-0	0-0	3-1	0-0	1-1	2-0	0-0	0-0	3-1	1-0
Milan §8 †	38	19	12	7	57	36	61	3-4	1-2	2-1		0-2	0-0	3-1	1-0	1-0	2-3	2-1	1-0	3-0	3-1	0-0	0-0	3-1	3-1	1-0	1-0
Palermo ‡	38	16	10	12	58	51	58	1-2	1-2	0-3	0-0		1-1	0-1	2-3	2-0	2-0	3-0	3-4	5-3	4-3	2-1	3-0	1-3	1-1	4-0	2-1
Fiorentina §15 ‡	38	21	10	7	62	31	58	2-3	0-0	1-0	2-2	2-3		2-0	3-1	5-1	2-0	2-1	1-0	3-0	3-0	1-0	5-1	1-0	1-0	4-0	4-0
Empoli ‡	38	14	12	12	42	43	54	0-3	1-0	1-1	1-0	0-2	0-1		2-0	2-0	1-1	2-2	2-0	2-1	3-3	1-0	0-0	1-1	1-4	1-3	1-2
Atalanta	38	12	14	12	56	54	50	1-1	2-1	0-0	2-0	1-1	2-2	0-0		3-2	1-2	5-1	1-1	1-1	1-1	3-1	0-2	3-3	1-0	3-1	3-2
Sampdoria	38	13	10	15	44	48	49	0-2	2-4	2-0	1-1	1-1	0-0	1-2	2-1		3-3	4-1	3-2	1-0	0-0	0-0	1-0	1-1	3-0	2-0	3-1
Udinese	38	12	10	16	49	55	46	0-0	0-1	2-4	0-3	1-2	1-0	0-1	2-3	1-0		4-0	3-3	0-1	1-1	3-0	2-0	3-1	2-1	0-0	1-0
Livorno	38	10	13	15	41	54	43	1-2	1-1	1-1	0-0	1-2	1-0	0-0	4-2	1-0	1-0		3-0	4-1	1-1	0-0	1-1	2-1	0-2	0-0	2-1
Parma	38	10	12	16	41	56	42	1-2	0-4	1-3	0-2	0-0	2-0	3-1	3-1	0-1	0-3	1-0		1-1	2-2	1-0	0-2	1-2	1-2	1-0	4-1
Catania	38	10	11	17	46	68	41	2-5	0-2	3-1	1-1	1-2	0-1	2-1	0-0	4-2	1-0	3-2	2-0		1-4	1-1	1-1	0-1	2-0	3-3	2-2
Reggina §11	38	12	15	11	52	50	40	0-0	1-0	2-3	2-0	0-0	1-1	4-1	1-1	0-1	1-1	2-2	3-2	0-1		0-1	1-1	2-1	1-1	2-1	3-1
Siena §1	38	9	14	15	35	45	40	1-2	1-3	2-1	3-4	1-1	1-1	2-0	1-1	0-2	2-2	0-0	2-1	1-1	0-1		1-0	0-0	2-1	0-1	3-1
Torino	38	10	10	18	27	47	40	1-3	1-2	0-4	0-1	0-0	0-1	0-1	2-1	0-2	3-0	0-1	1-1	0-1	1-2		1-0	1-0	1-0	1-1	
Cagliari	38	9	13	16	35	46	40	1-1	3-2	0-2	2-2	1-0	0-2	0-0	2-0	1-0	2-1	2-2	0-0	0-1	0-2	2-2	0-0		0-2	1-0	2-0
Chievo Verona	38	9	12	17	38	48	39	0-2	2-2	0-1	0-1	0-1	0-1	0-0	2-2	1-1	2-0	2-1	1-0	2-1	3-2	1-2	3-0	0-0		1-0	1-1
Ascoli	38	5	12	21	36	67	27	1-2	1-1	2-2	2-5	3-2	1-1	0-1	1-3	1-2	2-0	0-0	2-2	2-3	0-1	0-2	2-1	3-0			1-1
Messina	38	5	11	22	37	69	26	0-1	1-1	1-4	1-3	2-0	2-2	2-2	0-0	0-2	1-0	0-1	1-1	1-1	2-0	1-0	0-3	2-2	2-1	1-2	

9/09/2006 - 27/05/2007 • † Qualified for the UEFA Champions League • ‡ Qualified for the UEFA Cup • § = points deducted
Top scorers: Francesco TOTTI, Roma 26; Cristiano LUCCARELLI, Livorno 20; Christian RIGANO, Messina 19; Rolando BIANCHI, Reggina 18; Nicola AMORUSO, Reggina 17; Gionatha SPINESI, Catania 17

ITALY 2006-07

SERIE B

	Pl	W	D	L	F	A	Pts	Juventus	Napoli	Genoa	Piacenza	Rimini	Brescia	Bologna	Mantova	Lecce	Albinoleffe	Vicenza	Treviso	Bari	Frosinone	Modena	Cesena	Triestina	Hellas Verona	Spezia	Arezzo	Crotone	Pescara
Juventus §9	42	28	10	4	83	30	85		2-0	3-1	4-0	0-0	2-0	3-1	2-0	4-1	1-1	2-1	1-0	4-2	1-0	4-0	2-1	5-1	1-0	2-3	2-2	5-0	2-0
Napoli	42	21	16	5	52	29	79	1-1		1-1	1-0	1-0	3-1	1-0	0-1	0-1	0-0	0-4	2-1	1-1	1-1	1-2	0-1	1-1	1-0	3-1	2-2	1-0	1-0
Genoa	42	23	9	10	68	44	78	1-1	0-0		2-0	2-1	3-0	3-0	2-1	1-0	1-0	2-0	2-1	0-0	3-2	1-0	4-3	3-2	3-1	1-2	3-0	1-1	3-0
Piacenza	42	20	8	14	57	50	68	0-2	2-1	3-1		1-1	1-2	1-0	3-4	3-2	1-1	0-3	1-0	3-1	2-1	3-0	5-1	4-0	1-1	1-0	2-1	1-0	2-1	3-1
Rimini	42	17	16	9	55	38	67	1-1	1-1	0-2	0-0		2-0	0-0	2-1	1-0	1-1	2-1	1-1	0-1	2-1	1-1	1-0	1-1	0-3	1-2	0-1	2-0	1-2	3-1
Brescia	42	19	10	13	51	43	67	3-1	0-1	0-2	2-0	0-2		1-1	0-0	1-1	3-0	2-0	0-1	0-0	1-1	0-4	2-2	0-0	0-1	1-1	1-0	2-2	2-1
Bologna	42	18	11	13	52	43	65	0-1	2-3	3-1	0-2	1-3	0-1		1-1	3-1	1-0	2-1	0-2	0-1	0-2	0-1	1-0	0-2	0-2	1-1	0-2	1-2	1-2	1
Mantova	42	15	19	8	47	36	64	1-0	1-0	1-0	1-0	2-1	2-1	0-2		4-0	0-2	0-0	0-0	1-1	0-4	3-1	1-0	2-0	0-1	1-3	0-2	1
Lecce	42	17	7	18	56	53	58	1-3	1-3	2-1	1-0	2-1	1-2	2-1	2-0		3-1	1-2	1-1	3-5	0-1	0-2	0-2	2-2	0-1	1-0	0-1	1-4	1
Albinoleffe	42	11	20	11	46	48	53	1-1	1-1	1-2	0-0	0-2	3-2	5-2	1-0	0-0		0-3	1-2	3-1	1-0	0-0	3-2	1-1	1-0	0-0	2-1	0-0	2-1
Vicenza	42	12	14	16	42	43	50	2-2	1-1	2-1	2-1	1-1	3-1	1-0	0-1	3-0	1		2-2	3-0	1-2	2-0	1-3	0-0	1-0	2-1	1-0	2-0	1-0
Treviso	42	11	17	14	44	47	50	0-1	0-3	2-3	1-1	1-0	2-0	1-1	1-1	0-3	1-1		0-0	3-0	1-1	1-0	0-1	1-3	0-1	3-1	2-1	0
Bari	42	12	14	16	40	46	50	1-0	0-1	2-2	1-2	2-2	1-1	2-0	0-1	1-1	0-0	0-0	2-0		1-1	1-0	2-0	0-0	0-1	2-1	1-1	1-2
Frosinone	42	12	14	16	44	54	50	0-2	1-2	0-2	0-1	2-1	2-1	1-1	1-2	1-2	0-0	1-1	0		0-0	4-1	2-0	2-0	1-1	0-1	0-2
Modena	42	12	13	17	38	46	49	0-1	0-0	2-0	1-2	0-0	1-0	1-0	1-2	2-2	0-0	3-1	1-1	0-2	1-2	1		0-1	1-0	0-1	4-0	1-1	3-2	2-0
Cesena	42	12	13	17	51	66	49	2-2	1-2	1-2	1-1	1-1	1-2	1-1	4-1	1-0	0-2	2-1	2-0	0-1	0-2	1-1	0		0-1	0-1	1-0	2-0	3-1	3-3
Triestina §1	42	11	16	15	37	48	48	0-1	1-3	0-1	0-0	1-1	0-1	0-3	0-0	2-3	1-2	0-0	0-1	2-1	0-1	0-1	0-3	1		1-2	1-2	0-2	0-2	1
Hellas Verona	42	12	12	18	34	46	48	0-1	1-3	1-1	3-1	1-0	0-1	0-0	1-0	3-1	1-0	2-1	0-0	4-2	2-2	1-1	2-1	1-0		1-0	1-0	0-0	0-2	1
Spezia	42	11	13	18	50	61	46	1-1	0-1	1-2	3-3	3-4	1-3	2-0	1-0	2-3	1-1	0-1	2-1	2-1	1-0	1-1	1-2	2-1	0		3-1	2-1	2-2
Arezzo §6	42	12	15	15	42	46	45	1-5	0-0	0-0	1-0	4-1	0-2	1-1	1-0	1-2	1-2	1-1	2-0	1-0	0-0	0-3	0-0	1-3	1-1	1		0-0	4-1
Crotone	42	7	11	24	36	67	32	0-3	2-1	0-3	0-0	0-2	0-0	0-2	1-3	1-1	1-0	1-0	2-3	2-2	3-3	0-1	2-0	0-0	1-0	2-1	2-2		2-2
Pescara §1	42	5	10	27	36	77	24	0-1	0-1	2-1	0-2	0-5	1-3	0-1	0-0	2-0	2-0	1-0	2-2	1-2	2-6	1-0	0-0	0-2	1-2	2-3		

8/09/2006 - 10/06/2007 • § = points deducted • No promotion play-off as the gap between third and fourth place was greater than nine points
Relegation play-off (the gap between 18th and 19th place was less than six points): Spezia 2-1 0-0 Hellas Verona. Verona relegated
Top scorers: Alessandro DEL PIERO, Juventus 20; Claudio BELLUCCI, Bologna 19; N'Diaye PAPA WAIGO, Cesena 15; David TREZEGUET, Juventus 15

ITALY 2006–07
SERIE C1 GROUP A

	Pl	W	D	L	F	A	Pts
Grosseto	34	16	14	4	46	27	62
Sassuolo ‡	34	17	10	7	42	27	61
Pisa ‡	34	15	13	6	32	20	58
Venezia ‡	34	14	12	8	41	29	54
Monza Brianza ‡	34	13	15	6	42	32	54
Cittadella	34	13	15	6	38	26	54
Padova	34	14	8	12	34	24	50
Lucchese	34	10	15	9	44	32	45
Pistoiese	34	10	13	11	33	29	43
Pro Patria	34	10	11	13	34	44	41
Cremonese	34	10	11	13	33	43	41
Novara	34	10	11	13	32	37	41
Massese	34	9	14	11	32	39	41
Pro Sesto ‡	34	11	8	15	24	28	41
Sangiovannese ‡	34	9	9	16	41	51	36
Pizzighettone ‡	34	7	12	15	24	41	33
Ivrea ‡	34	7	10	17	25	43	31
Pavia	34	5	11	18	29	54	26

3/09/2006 - 13/05/2007 • ‡ Entered play-offs

ITALY 2006–07
SERIE C1 GROUP B

	Pl	W	D	L	F	A	Pts
Ravenna	34	21	6	7	50	30	69
Avellino §2 ‡	34	20	8	6	64	37	66
Cavese ‡	34	17	11	6	46	30	62
Foggia ‡	34	16	11	7	41	25	59
Taranto ‡	34	15	11	8	45	31	56
Perugia	34	15	9	10	40	29	54
Juve Stabia	34	13	14	7	34	27	53
Sambenedettese	34	14	7	13	45	45	49
Manfredonia	34	12	10	12	41	43	46
Salernitana	34	11	11	12	37	41	44
Gallipoli	34	12	8	14	42	49	44
Ternana	34	9	12	13	30	36	39
Lanciano	34	9	12	13	26	33	39
Martina ‡	34	9	10	15	27	40	37
Teramo ‡	34	9	10	15	27	39	37
Ancona ‡	34	9	6	19	37	49	33
San Marino ‡	34	8	8	18	37	43	32
Giulianova	34	2	6	26	18	60	12

3/09/2006 - 13/05/2007 • ‡ Entered play-offs
§ Points deducted

SERIE C1 GROUP A PROMOTION PLAY-OFFS

Semi–finals			Final		
Pisa	1	3			
Venezia *	1	1	Pisa	0	2
Sassuolo	1	2	Monza Brianza *	1	0
Monza Brianza *	0	4			

* Home team in the first leg • Pisa promoted along with champions Grosseto

SERIE C1 GROUP A RELEGATION PLAY-OFFS

Ivrea 0-0 0-1 **Pro Sesto**

Pizzighettone 0-0 0-1 **Sangiovannese**

Ivrea and Pizzighettone relegated along with Pavia

SERIE C1 GROUP B PROMOTION PLAY-OFFS

Semi–finals			Final		
Avellino	0	1			
Taranto *	1	0	Avellino	0	3
Cavese	2	3	Foggia *	1	0
Foggia *	5	1			

* Home team in the first leg • Avellino promoted along with champions Ravenna

SERIE C1 GROUP B RELEGATION PLAY-OFFS

San Marino 0-2 1-1 **Martina**

Ancona 2-0 2-2 Sangiovannese

San Marino and Sangiovannese relegated along with Giulianova

FIFA/COCA-COLA WORLD RANKING

1993	1994	1995	1996	1997	1998	1999	2000	2001	2002	2003	2004	2005	2006	High		Low	
2	4	3	10	9	7	14	4	6	13	10	10	12		1	06/07	16	04/98

					2006–2007						
08/06	09/06	10/06	11/06	12/06	01/07	02/07	03/07	04/07	05/07	06/07	07/07
2	5	2	2	2	2	1	2	1	1	1	3

THE FIFA BIG COUNT OF 2006

	Male	Female		Total
Number of players	4 688 929	291 367	Referees and Assistant Referees	24 981
Professionals	3 541		Admin, Coaches, Technical, Medical	53 500
Amateurs 18+	877 602		Number of clubs	16 128
Youth under 18	557 453		Number of teams	80 864
Unregistered	3 207 700		Clubs with women's teams	569
Total players	4 980 296		Players as % of population	8.57%

COPPA ITALIA 2006-07

Second Round   **Third Round**   **Round of 16**

					Roma	2	2
Atalanta	3				Triestina *	1	0
Pescara *	0	Atalanta	2				
Siena	1	Triestina *	3				
Triestina *	2						
Napoli *	1						
Ascoli	0	Napoli *	3 8p				
Cesena *	1	Juventus	3 7p				
Juventus	2				Napoli *	1	1
					Parma	0	3

					Arezzo *	2	1
Udinese	2				Livorno	1	1
Albinoleffe *	1	Udinese	1 6p				
Venezia *	0	Arezzo	1 7p				
Arezzo	1						
Brescia	1						
Taranto *	0	Brescia *	1				
Hellas Verona *	1	Cagliari	0				
Cagliari	2				Brescia	2	1
					Milan *	4	2

					Sampdoria *	1	3
Bologna	2				Palermo	0	2
Cavese *	0	Bologna *	2				
Rimini *	1	Sampdoria	3				
Sampdoria	2						
Reggina	1						
Cremonese *	0	Reggina	1				
Torino	1	Crotone *	0				
Crotone *	2				Reggina *	2	1
					Chievo Verona	2	1

					Empoli *	1	1
Modena *	1 5p				Genoa	0	0
Mantova	1 4p	Modena	1				
Fiorentina	0	Genoa *	3				
Genoa *	1						
Messina *	2						
Piacenza	0	Messina *	4				
Monza *	1 3p	Lazio	3				
Lazio	1 4p				Messina *	0	0
					Internazionale	1	4

Serie A clubs playing in Europe join in at the round of 16

COPPA ITALIA 2006–07

Quarter–finals   Semi–finals   Final

Roma *	2	2
Parma	1	2

Roma	2	3
Milan *	2	1

Arezzo	0	1
Milan *	2	0

Roma	6	1
Internazionale	2	2

Sampdoria *	1	2
Chievo Verona	0	1

Sampdoria *	0	0
Internazionale	3	0

Empoli *	0	0
Internazionale	2	2

COPPA ITALIA FINAL

First leg. Stadio Olimpico, Rome, 9-05-2007, Att: 39 095, Ref: Saccani

Roma	6	Totti [1], De Rossi [5], Perrotta [16], Mancini [31], Panucci 2 [54 89]
Internazionale	2	Crespo 2 [20 56]

Roma - Doni - Chivu, Ferrari, Mexes (Cassetti 46), Panucci - De Rossi, Mancini, Perrotta, Pizarro (Tonetto• 86), Taddei (Aquilani 76) - Totti. Tr: Spalletti
Inter - Toldo - Cordoba•, Maicon•, Materazzi•, Maxwell (Grosso 67), Zanetti - Dacourt•, Figo (Vieira• 51), Stankovic - Crespo, Adriano (Recoba 56). Tr: Mancini

Second leg. San Siro, Milan, 17-05-2007, Att: 26 606 Ref: Morganti

Internazionale	2	Crespo [50], Cruz [56]
Roma	1	Perrotta [83]

Inter - Toldo - Burdisso, Cordoba•71, Maicon, Zanetti - Cambiasso•, Figo (Maxwell 82), Gonzalez (Recoba 54), Vieira (Cruz 27), Stankovic - Crespo. Tr: Mancini
Roma - Doni - Chivu•, Ferrari, Mexes, Panucci•90 - Aqualani• (Pizarro 58), De Rossi, Mancini (Tonetto 79), Perrotta•, Taddei - Totti. Tr: Spalletti

* Home team in the first leg

INTERNAZIONALE 2006–07

Date	Opponents	Score		Comp	Scorers	Att
26-08-2006	Roma	W 4-3	H	SC	Vieira 2 [44 74], Crespo [65], Figo [95]	45 528
9-09-2006	Fiorentina	W 3-2	A	SA	Cambiasso 2 [11 41], Ibrahimovic [61]	41 334
12-09-2006	Sporting CP - POR	L 0-1	A	CLgB		30 222
16-09-2006	Sampdoria	D 1-1	H	SA	Bonanni OG [81]	45 194
20-09-2006	Roma	W 1-0	A	SA	Crespo [44]	56 476
24-09-2006	Chievo Verona	W 4-3	H	SA	Crespo 2 [11 70], Samuel [58], Stankovic [64]	41 357
27-09-2006	Bayern München - GER	L 0-2	H	CLgB		36 460
1-10-2006	Cagliari	D 1-1	A	SA	Grosso [38]	20 185
14-10-2006	Catania	W 2-1	H	SA	Stankovic 2 [28 77]	47 505
18-10-2006	Spartak Moskva - RUS	W 2-1	H	CLgB	Cruz 2 [1 9]	21 945
22-10-2006	Udinese	D 0-0	A	SA		19 969
25-10-2006	Livorno	W 4-1	H	SA	Pfertzel OG [2], Materazzi [13], Ibrahimovic [71], Cruz [78]	39 057
28-10-2006	Milan	W 4-3	A	SA	Crespo [17], Stankovic [22], Ibrahimovic [47], Materazzi [69]	78 921
31-10-2006	Spartak Moskva - RUS	W 1-0	A	CLgB	Cruz [1]	45 000
5-11-2006	Ascoli	W 2-0	H	SA	Zanetti [41], Cudini OG [53]	43 372
9-11-2006	Messina	W 1-0	A	CUPr4	Cruz [40]	16 123
12-11-2006	Parma	W 2-1	A	SA	Ibrahimovic [15], Cruz [90]	20 488
19-11-2006	Reggina	W 1-0	H	SA	Crespo [4]	43 772
22-11-2006	Sporting CP - POR	W 1-0	H	CLgB	Crespo [36]	36 935
26-11-2006	Palermo	W 2-1	A	SA	Ibrahimovic [7], Vieira [61]	34 095
29-11-2006	Messina	W 4-0	H	CUPr4	Burdisso 2 [27 71], Gonzalez [37], Andreolli [61]	6 040
2-12-2006	Siena	W 2-0	H	SA	Burdisso [11], Crespo [54]	42 299
5-12-2006	Bayern München - GER	D 1-1	A	CLgB	Vieira [91+]	66 000
10-12-2006	Empoli	W 3-0	A	SA	Crespo [60], Ibrahimovic [78], Samuel [87]	11 471
17-12-2006	Messina	W 2-0	H	SA	Materazzi [49], Ibrahimovic [59]	41 683
20-12-2006	Lazio	W 2-0	A	SA	Cambiasso [39], Materazzi [85]	35 203
23-12-2006	Atalanta	W 2-1	H	SA	Adriano [65], Loria OG [75]	43 428
9-01-2007	Empoli	W 2-0	A	CUPqf	Adriano [71], Cordoba [91+]	3 544
13-01-2007	Torino	W 3-1	A	SA	Adriano [34], Ibrahimovic [60], Materazzi [85p]	25 126
17-01-2007	Empoli	W 2-0	H	CUPqf	Cambiasso [28], Grosso [77]	8 241
21-01-2007	Fiorentina	W 3-1	H	SA	Stankovic [19], Adriano [24], Ibrahimovic [71]	61 391
24-01-2007	Sampdoria	W 3-0	A	CUPsf	Burdisso [9], Crespo [24], Burdisso [56]	12 484
28-01-2007	Sampdoria	W 2-0	A	SA	Ibrahimovic [38], Maicon [75]	27 519
1-02-2007	Sampdoria	D 0-0	H	CUPsf		10 396
11-02-2007	Chievo Verona	W 2-0	A	SA	Adriano [1], Crespo [51]	BCD
17-02-2007	Cagliari	W 1-0	H	SA	Burdisso [11]	35 152
21-02-2007	Valencia - ESP	D 2-2	H	CLr2	Cambiasso [29], Maicon [76]	25 269
25-02-2007	Catania	W 5-2	A	SA	Samuel [45], Solari [49], Grosso [57], Ibrahimovic [67], Cruz [77]	BCD
28-02-2007	Udinese	D 1-1	H	SA	Crespo [67]	38 496
3-03-2007	Livorno	W 2-1	A	SA	Cruz [35], Ibrahimovic [66]	5 641
6-03-2007	Valencia - ESP	D 0-0	A	CLr2		48 109
11-03-2007	Milan	W 2-1	H	SA	Cruz [55], Ibrahimovic [75]	63 681
18-03-2007	Ascoli	W 2-1	A	SA	Ibrahimovic 2 [65 71]	4 787
1-04-2007	Parma	W 2-0	H	SA	Maxwell [56], Crespo [71]	38 888
7-04-2007	Reggina	D 0-0	A	SA		18 506
15-04-2007	Palermo	D 2-2	H	SA	Cruz [67], Adriano [74]	46 611
18-04-2007	Roma	L 1-3	H	SA	Materazzi [52p]	56 577
22-04-2007	Siena	W 2-1	A	SA	Materazzi 2 [18 61p]	14 027
29-04-2007	Empoli	W 3-1	H	SA	Cruz [27], Recoba [59], Stankovic [60]	60 534
6-05-2007	Messina	W 1-0	A	SA	Crespo [72]	13 410
9-05-2007	Roma	L 2-6	A	CUPf	Crespo 2 [20 56]	39 095
13-05-2007	Lazio	W 4-3	H	SA	Crespo 3 [20 35 81], Materazzi [85]	45 525
17-05-2007	Roma	W 2-1	H	CUPf	Crespo [50], Cruz [56]	26 606
20-05-2007	Atalanta	D 1-1	A	SA	Figo [48p]	22 099
27-05-2007	Torino	W 3-0	H	SA	Materazzi [12], Maicon [60], Figo [67p]	64 758

SC = Supercoppa Italia • SA = Serie A • CL = UEFA Champions League • CUP = Coppa Italia • A = Cesena
gB = group B • r2 = second round • r4 = fourth round • qf = quarter-final • sf = semi-final • f = final • BCD = behind closed doors

ROMA 2006-07

Date	Opponents	Score		Comp	Scorers	Att
26-08-2006	Internazionale	L 3-4	A	SC	Mancini [13], Aquilani 2 [24 34]	45 528
9-09-2006	Livorno	W 2-0	H	SA	De Rossi [45], Mancini [54]	38 529
12-09-2006	Shakhtar Donetsk - UKR	W 4-0	H	CLgD	Taddei [67], Totti [76], De Rossi [79], Pizarro [89]	34 035
17-09-2006	Siena	W 3-1	A	SA	Taddei [47], Pizarro [70], Okaka [90]	11 136
20-09-2006	Internazionale	L 0-1	H	SA		56 476
24-09-2006	Parma	W 4-0	A	SA	Montella [5], Perrotta [45], Rosi [54], Aquilani [90]	15 495
27-09-2006	Valencia - ESP	L 1-2	A	CLgD	Totti [18p]	40 593
1-10-2006	Empoli	W 1-0	H	SA	Montella [23]	35 197
14-10-2006	Reggina	L 0-1	H	SA		11 719
18-10-2006	Olympiacos - GRE	W 1-0	A	CLgD	Perrotta [76]	31 009
22-10-2006	Chievo Verona	D 1-1	H	SA	Totti [66]	34 272
25-10-2006	Ascoli	D 2-2	H	SA	Totti [50], Mexes [90]	32 187
28-10-2006	Udinese	W 1-0	A	SA	Ferrari [66]	16 466
31-10-2006	Olympiacos - GRE	D 1-1	H	CLgD	Totti [66]	28 828
5-11-2006	Fiorentina	W 3-1	H	SA	De Rossi [38], Taddei 2 [49 66]	37 585
8-11-2006	Triestina	W 2-1	A	CUPr4	Montella 2 [44 51]	6 500
11-11-2006	Milan	W 2-1	H	SA	Totti 2 [7 83]	55 322
19-11-2006	Catania	W 7-0	H	SA	Panucci 2 [12 48], Mancini [19], Perrotta 2 [24 40], Montella [60], Totti [75]	46 503
22-11-2006	Shakhtar Donetsk - UKR	L 0-1	A	CLgD		23 900
26-11-2006	Sampdoria	W 4-2	A	SA	Totti 2 [13 74], Perrotta [33], Panucci [44]	22 929
29-11-2006	Triestina	W 2-0	H	CUPr4	Virga [22], Montella [27]	5 190
2-12-2006	Atalanta	W 2-1	H	SA	Totti 2 [50p 64p]	33 755
5-12-2006	Valencia - ESP	W 1-0	H	CLgD	Panucci [13]	38 898
10-12-2006	Lazio	L 0-3	A	SA		60 815
17-12-2006	Palermo	W 4-0	H	SA	Mancini 2 [44 86], Totti [59p 90]	40 124
20-12-2006	Torino	W 2-1	A	SA	Totti [37], Mancini [80]	21 320
23-12-2006	Cagliari	W 2-0	H	SA	Taddei [5], Mancini [56]	35 122
9-01-2007	Parma	W 2-1	H	CUPqf	Mancini [19], Totti [67]	17 201
14-01-2007	Messina	D 1-1	A	SA	Mancini [39]	12 974
17-01-2007	Parma	D 2-2	A	CUPqf	De Rossi [30], Pizarro [86]	3 434
21-01-2007	Livorno	D 1-1	A	SA	Totti [73]	10 389
24-01-2007	Milan	D 2-2	A	CUPsf	Perrotta [29], Pizarro [38]	6 045
28-01-2007	Siena	W 1-0	H	SA	Vucinic [63]	30 824
1-02-2007	Milan	W 3-1	H	CUPsf	Mancini [8], Perrotta [23], Pizarro [48]	39 249
11-02-2007	Parma	W 3-0	H	SA	Totti [50], Perrotta [66], Taddei [90]	38 897
17-02-2007	Empoli	L 0-1	A	SA		BCD
21-02-2007	Olympique Lyonnais - FRA	D 0-0	H	CLr2		60 053
25-02-2007	Reggina	W 3-0	H	SA	Tavano [55], Mexes [65], Panucci [90]	45 650
28-02-2007	Chievo Verona	D 2-2	A	SA	Totti 2 [34 50]	4 221
3-03-2007	Ascoli	D 1-1	A	SA	Wilhelmsson [86]	4 787
6-03-2007	Olympique Lyonnais - FRA	W 2-0	A	CLr2	Totti [22], Mancini [44]	39 260
11-03-2007	Udinese	W 3-1	H	SA	Totti 2 [33 60], Perrotta [40]	30 817
18-03-2007	Fiorentina	D 0-0	A	SA		23 900
31-03-2007	Milan	D 1-1	H	SA	Mexes [4]	43 830
4-04-2007	Manchester United - ENG	W 2-1	H	CLqf	Taddei [44], Vucinic [66]	68 389
7-04-2007	Catania	W 2-0	A	SA	Tavano [37], Vucinic [84]	BCD
10-04-2007	Manchester United - ENG	L 1-7	A	CLqf	De Rossi [69]	74 476
15-04-2007	Sampdoria	W 4-0	H	SA	Totti 2 [21 68], Ferrari [73], Panucci [89]	31 875
18-04-2007	Internazionale	W 3-1	H	SA	Perrotta [44], Totti [89], Cassetti [90]	56 577
22-04-2007	Atalanta	L 1-2	A	SA	Perrotta [74]	12 258
29-04-2007	Lazio	D 0-0	H	SA		61 292
6-05-2007	Palermo	W 2-1	A	SA	Totti [17], Cassetti [36]	24 680
9-05-2007	Internazionale	W 6-2	H	CUPf	Totti [1], De Rossi [5], Perrotta [16], Mancini [31], Panucci 2 [54 89]	39 095
13-05-2007	Torino	L 0-1	H	SA		32 242
17-05-2007	Internazionale	L 1-2	A	CUPf	Perrotta [83]	26 606
20-05-2007	Cagliari	L 2-3	A	SA	Totti 2 [29p 85]	14 500
27-05-2007	Messina	W 4-3	H	SA	Totti 2 [10 73], Mancini [19], Rosi [84]	28 191

SC = Supercoppa Italia • SA = Serie A • CL = UEFA Champions League • CUP = Coppa Italia • **A** = Lecce
gD = group D • r2 = second round • r4 = fourth round • qf = quarter-final • sf = semi-final • f = final • BCD = behind closed doors

MILAN 2006–07

Date	Opponents	Score		Comp	Scorers	Att
9-08-2006	Crvena Zvezda Beograd - SRB	W 1-0	H	CLpr3	Inzaghi [22]	70 510
22-08-2006	Crvena Zvezda Beograd - SRB	W 2-1	A	CLpr3	Inzaghi [29], Seedorf [79]	49 604
10-09-2006	Lazio	W 2-1	H	SA	Inzaghi [27], Ricardo Oliveira [70]	44 770
13-09-2006	AEK Athens - GRE	W 3-0	H	CLgH	Inzaghi [17], Gourcuff [41], Kaká [76p]	31 836
17-09-2006	Parma	W 2-0	A	SA	Seedorf [25], Kaka [86p]	18 617
20-09-2006	Ascoli	W 1-0	H	SA	Jankulovski [68]	43 085
23-09-2006	Livorno	D 0-0	A	SA		13 456
26-09-2006	Lille OSC - FRA	D 0-0	A	CLgH		33 302
1-10-2006	Siena	D 0-0	H	SA		44 658
14-10-2006	Sampdoria	D 1-1	A	SA	Kaladze [74]	25 334
17-10-2006	RSC Anderlecht - BEL	W 1-0	A	CLgH	Kaká [58]	21 845
22-10-2006	Palermo	L 0-2	H	SA		50 028
25-10-2006	Chievo Verona	W 1-0	A	SA	Jankulovski [31]	12 343
28-10-2006	Internazionale	L 3-4	H	SA	Seedorf [50], Gilardino [76], Kaká [90]	78 921
1-11-2006	RSC Anderlecht - BEL	W 4-1	H	CLgH	Kaká 3 [6p 22 56], Gilardino [88]	37 768
5-11-2006	Atalanta	L 0-2	A	SA		23 799
8-11-2006	Brescia	W 4-1	H	CUPr4	Borriello 2 [60 86], Brocchi [64], Inzaghi [78]	1 833
11-11-2006	Roma	L 1-2	H	SA	Brocchi [56]	55 322
18-11-2006	Empoli	D 0-0	A	SA		7 317
21-11-2006	AEK Athens - GRE	L 0-1	A	CLgH		56 203
25-11-2006	Messina	W 1-0	H	SA	Maldini [13]	42 515
28-11-2006	Brescia	W 2-1	A	CUPr4	Ricardo Oliveira [15], Zoboli OG [19]	3 000
3-12-2006	Cagliari	D 2-2	A	SA	Gilardino [48], Borriello [70]	18 275
6-12-2006	Lille OSC - FRA	L 0-2	H	CLgH		27 067
10-12-2006	Torino	D 0-0	H	SA		50 422
16-12-2006	Fiorentina	D 2-2	A	SA	Gilardino 2 [4 89]	41 578
20-12-2006	Catania	W 3-0	H	SA	Kaká 2 [4 88], Gilardino [82]	41 232
23-12-2006	Udinese	W 3-0	A	SA	Kaká [31p], Gilardino [35], Ricardo Oliveira [76]	20 140
11-01-2007	Arezzo	W 2-0	H	CUPqf	Gilardino [35], Inzaghi [52]	3 822
14-01-2007	Reggina	W 3-1	H	SA	Pirlo [6], Seedorf [35], Gilardino [77]	43 996
18-01-2007	Arezzo	L 0-1	A	CUPqf		8 882
21-01-2007	Lazio	D 0-0	A	SA		28 948
25-01-2007	Roma	D 2-2	H	CUPsf	Ricardo Oliveira [4], Inzaghi [23]	6 045
28-01-2007	Parma	W 1-0	H	SA	Inzaghi [77]	41 752
31-01-2007	Roma	L 1-3	A	CUPsf	Gilardino [18]	39 249
11-02-2007	Livorno	W 2-1	H	SA	Gattuso [29], Jankulovski [68]	21 649
17-02-2007	Siena	W 4-3	A	SA	Ronaldo 2 [15 81], Ricardo Oliveira [28], Molinaro OG [90]	11 191
20-02-2007	Celtic - SCO	D 0-0	A	CLr2		58 785
25-02-2007	Sampdoria	W 1-0	H	SA	Ambrosini [90]	39 168
28-02-2007	Palermo	D 0-0	A	SA		25 361
3-03-2007	Chievo Verona	W 3-1	H	SA	Gilardino [33], Oddo [57], Seedorf [90]	41 072
7-03-2007	Celtic - SCO	W 1-0	H	CLr2	Kaká [93]	52 914
11-03-2007	Internazionale	L 1-2	A	SA	Ronaldo [40]	63 681
18-03-2007	Atalanta	W 1-0	H	SA	Ambrosini [40]	45 491
31-03-2007	Roma	D 1-1	A	SA	Gilardino [62]	43 830
3-04-2007	Bayern München - GER	D 2-2	H	CLqf	Pirlo [40], Kaká [84p]	67 500
7-04-2007	Empoli	W 3-1	H	SA	Ronaldo [12], Gilardino [44], Favalli [78]	45 566
11-04-2007	Bayern München - GER	W 2-0	A	CLqf	Seedorf [27], Inzaghi [31]	66 000
15-04-2007	Messina	W 3-1	A	SA	Kaká [14], Favalli [30], Ronaldo [86]	17 521
18-04-2007	Ascoli	W 5-1	H	SA	Gilardino 2 [3 27], Kaká 2 [25p 35], Seedorf [75]	15 004
21-04-2007	Cagliari	W 3-1	A	SA	Ronaldo 2 [14 69], Pirlo [80]	43 728
24-04-2007	Manchester United - ENG	L 2-3	A	CLsf	Kaká 2 [22 37]	73 820
28-04-2007	Torino	W 1-0	A	SA	Seedorf [26]	22 539
2-05-2007	Manchester United - ENG	W 3-0	H	CLsf	Kaká [11], Seedorf [30], Gilardino [78]	67 500
6-05-2007	Fiorentina	D 0-0	H	SA		55 078
13-05-2007	Catania	D 1-1	A	SA	Seedorf [6]	4 000
19-05-2007	Udinese	L 2-3	H	SA	Gourcuff [36], Costacurta [57p]	51 125
23-05-2007	Liverpool - ENG	W 2-1	N	CLf	Inzaghi 2 [45 82]	63 800
27-05-2007	Reggina	L 0-2	A	SA		20 835

SA = Serie A • CL = UEFA Champions League • CUP = Coppa Italia • **A** = Bologna • N = Olympic Stadium, Athens
pr3 = third preliminary round • gH = group H • r2 = second round • r4 = fourth round • qf = quarter-final • sf = semi-final • f = final

JAM – JAMAICA

NATIONAL TEAM RECORD
JULY 10TH 2006 TO JULY 12TH 2010

PL	W	D	L	F	A	%
13	4	2	7	15	22	38.4

FIFA/COCA-COLA WORLD RANKING

1993	1994	1995	1996	1997	1998	1999	2000	2001	2002	2003	2004	2005	2006	High		Low	
80	96	56	32	39	33	41	48	53	51	46	49	42	57	27	08/98	96	12/94

2006–2007											
08/06	09/06	10/06	11/06	12/06	01/07	02/07	03/07	04/07	05/07	06/07	07/07
74	77	57	58	57	57	56	61	68	69	68	93

The Reggae Boyz suffered a surprising setback at the end of September 2006 when they were knocked out of the Digicel Caribbean Cup in the first qualifying round. Only twice before - in 1989 and 1994 - had the Jamaicans failed to qualify for the finals, but what made it was all the more surprising was that it happened on home soil. A 2-1 defeat at the hands of St Vincent put paid to any hopes of qualifying for the finals in Trinidad and ultimately for a place at the CONCACAF Gold Cup 2007 in America. That left the team scrabbling around for friendlies which saw them embark on an end of season tour to South East Asia to provide warm up opposition for the AFC

INTERNATIONAL HONOURS
Qualified for the FIFA World Cup™ finals 1998 **Caribbean Cup** 1991 1998 2005

Asian Cup. There was also disappointment in the Caribbean club championship. Waterhouse were knocked out in a first round group played in Kingston by Haiti's Baltimore St Marc and although Harbour View won their first round group, they were beaten in the semi-finals by Williams Connection of Trinidad. At home there was a first championship in seven seasons for Harbour View while Portmore United beat Boys' Town in the first JFF Cup Final to be decided on penalties. Xavean Virgo of Boy's Town hit the crossbar as the shoot-out went to sudden death which left Eric Vernon to seal the win for Portmore.

THE FIFA BIG COUNT OF 2006

	Male	Female		Total
Number of players	144 884	23 610	Referees and Assistant Referees	312
Professionals	270		Admin, Coaches, Technical, Medical	4 725
Amateurs 18+	11 974		Number of clubs	270
Youth under 18	13 060		Number of teams	900
Unregistered	47 900		Clubs with women's teams	4
Total players	168 494		Players as % of population	6.11%

Jamaica Football Federation (JFF)
20 St Lucia Crescent, Kingston 5, Jamaica
Tel +1 876 9298036   Fax +1 876 9290438
jamff@hotmail.com   www.jamaicafootballfederation.com
President: BOXHILL Crenston   General Secretary: GIBSON Burchell
Vice-President: TBD   Treasurer: SPEID Rudolph   Media Officer: WILLIAMS Gareth
Men's Coach: MILUTINOVIC Bora   Women's Coach: EDWARDS Carlos
JFF formed: 1910   CONCACAF: 1961   FIFA: 1962
Gold shirts, Black shorts, Gold socks

RECENT INTERNATIONAL MATCHES PLAYED BY JAMAICA

2004	Opponents	Score		Venue	Comp	Scorers	Att	Referee
12-06	Haiti	D	1-1	Miami	WCq	King [39]	30 000	Stott USA
20-06	Haiti	W	3-0	Kingston	WCq	King 3 [4 14 31]	30 000	Sibrian SLV
18-08	USA	D	1-1	Kingston	WCq	Goodison [49]	30 000	Mattus CRC
4-09	Panama	L	1-2	Kingston	WCq	Ralph [77]	24 000	Batres GUA
8-09	El Salvador	W	3-0	San Salvador	WCq	King 2 [3 38], Hyde [40]	25 000	Alcala MEX
2-10	Guatemala	D	2-2	Fort Lauderdale	Fr	Hue [89], Jackson [90]	8 500	Vaughn USA
9-10	Panama	D	1-1	Panama City	WCq	Whitmore [75]	16 000	Pineda HON
13-10	El Salvador	D	0-0	Kingston	WCq		12 000	Quesada Cordero CRC
17-11	USA	D	1-1	Columbus	WCq	Williams.A [26]	9 088	Navarro CAN
24-11	Saint-Martin †	W	12-0	Kingston	CCq	Dean 3 [2 11 30], Hue [10], Shelton 4 [17 39 45 52], Stephenson [18], Scarlett 2 [20 85], West [54]	2 600	Brizan TRI
26-11	US Virgin Islands	W	11-1	Kingston	CCq	Shelton [8], Dean 2 [23 32], Hue 3 [35 53 56], Stephenson [40] Williams.A [50], Davis.F [64], Bennett [67], Priestly [68]	4 200	Piper TRI
28-11	Haiti	W	3-1	Kingston	CCq	Stephenson 20, Dean 22, Shelton 30	4 000	Piper TRI
12-12	St Lucia	D	1-1	Vieux Fort	CCq	Priestly [42]		Jeanvillier MTQ
19-12	St Lucia	W	2-1	Kingston	CCq	Dean [1], Hue [67]	2 500	Gutierrez CUB
2005								
20-02	Trinidad and Tobago	W	2-1	Bridgetown	CC	Shelton [13], Williams.A [35]	5 000	Callender BRB
22-02	Barbados	W	1-0	Bridgetown	CC	Williams.A [8]	2 100	Brizan TRI
24-02	Cuba	W	1-0	Bridgetown	CC	Shelton [48]	3 000	Brizan TRI
20-04	Guatemala	W	1-0	Atlanta	Fr	Shelton [14]	7 000	Prus USA
4-06	Honduras	D	0-0	Atlanta	Fr		6 500	Valenzuela USA
8-07	Guatemala	W	4-3	Carson	GCr1	Shelton [3], Fuller [5], Williams.A [46+p], Hue [57]	27 000	Hall USA
10-07	South Africa	D	3-3	Los Angeles	GCr1	Hue [35], Stewart [43], Bennett [80]	30 710	Stott USA
13-07	Mexico	L	0-1	Houston	GCr1		45 311	Quesada CRC
16-07	USA	L	1-3	Foxboro	GCqf	Fuller [88]	22 108	Batres GUA
1-10	Guatemala	W	2-1	Fort Lauderdale	Fr	Shelton [41], Crawford [70]	6 000	Rutty USA
9-10	Australia	L	0-5	London	Fr		6 570	Riley ENG
2006								
11-04	USA	D	1-1	Carey	Fr	Bennett [4]	8 093	Gasso MEX
29-05	Ghana	L	1-4	Leicester	Fr	Euell [58]	12 000	Halsey ENG
3-06	England	L	0-6	Manchester	Fr		70 373	Plautz AUT
4-09	Canada	L	0-1	Montreal	Fr		6 526	Quesada CRC
27-09	St Lucia	W	4-0	Kingston	CCq	Smith.W [3], Lemey 2 [22 36], Phillips [31]	4 000	Tamayo CUB
29-09	St Vincent/Grenadines	L	1-2	Kingston	CCq	Dean [72]	3 000	Brizan TRI
1-10	Haiti	W	2-0	Kingston	CCq	Smith.W [9], Dawkins [31]	3 000	Tamayo CUB
8-10	Canada	W	2-1	Kingston	Fr	Shelton [35], Phillips [38]	5 000	Brizan TRI
15-11	Peru	D	1-1	Kingston	Fr	Hue [78p]		
2007								
22-03	Switzerland	L	0-2	Fort Lauderdale	Fr		3 254	Prus USA
26-03	Panama	D	1-1	Kingston	Fr	Shelton [45]	16 554	Brizan TRI
5-06	Chile	L	0-1	Kingston	Fr		15 000	Guerrero NCA
21-06	Indonesia	L	1-2	Jakarta	Fr	Wolfe [72]		
24-06	Vietnam	L	0-3	Hanoi	Fr			
28-06	Malaysia	W	2-0	Kuala Lumpur	Fr	Harvey [44], Wolfe [45]		
2-07	Iran	L	1-8	Tehran	Fr			

Fr = Friendly match • CC = Digicel Caribbean Cup • GC = CONCACAF Gold Cup • WC = FIFA World Cup
q = qualifier • r1 = first round group • qf = quarter-final • † Not a full international

JAMAICA NATIONAL TEAM RECORDS AND RECORD SEQUENCES

Records			Sequence records					
Victory	12-0	BVI 1994	Wins	7	2000	Clean sheets	5	Three times
Defeat	0-9	CRC 1999	Defeats	7	1967-68, 2001-02	Goals scored	19	1997
Player Caps	105	WHITMORE Theodore	Undefeated	23	1997-1998	Without goal	7	2000
Player Goals	n/a		Without win	12	1975-79, 1988-90	Goals against	23	1966-1969

JAMAICA COUNTRY INFORMATION

Capital	Kingston	Independence	1962 from the UK	GDP per Capita	$3 900
Population	2 713 130	Status	Commonwealth	GNP Ranking	100
Area km²	10 991	Language	English	Dialling code	+1 876
Population density	247 per km²	Literacy rate	87%	Internet code	.jm
% in urban areas	54%	Main religion	Christian 61%	GMT +/–	-4
Towns/Cities ('000)	Kingston 584; Spanish Town 145; Portmore 102; Montego Bay 83; Mandeville 47				
Neighbours (km)	Caribbean Sea 1 022				
Main stadia	Independence Park – Kingston 35 000; Harbour View – Kingston 7 000				

JAMAICA 2006–07

WRAY AND NEPHEW PREMIER LEAGUE

	Pl	W	D	L	F	A	Pts	Harbour V.	Portmore	Reno	Waterhouse	Tivoli Gdns	August T.	Village Utd	Arnett Gdns	Boys' Town	Seba Utd	Wadadah	Naggo H.
Harbour View	33	22	8	3	67	30	74		1-0 1-1	2-1	3-1	0-0 2-0	2-0 1-2	3-0 0-0 4-0	1-1	4-1 5-0	3-2 4-0	4-3	
Portmore United	33	17	13	3	48	19	64	0-0		0-1 4-0	0-0	2-2 2-2	0-3-1 1-2-1	1-0	2-0	0-2 2-1	4-1 2-2	2-0	
Reno	33	16	8	9	51	37	56	2-1 1-2 0-0	1-1 2-1 1-0 1-1		2-1	5-0	2-1 2-2 3-1	2-1	1-0 1-1 3-1 5-1				
Waterhouse	33	13	13	7	55	29	52	2-2 0-0 0-1 1-1	1-0		2-1	2-0	0-1 4-2 0-0 1-1 3-0	4-1 3-0 9-2 3-0 0-1					
Tivoli Gardens	33	13	13	7	46	31	51	4-0 1-3	0-1	3-2 0-1 1-0	1-0		1-1 1-0 2-0 2-1 2-0	1-0 0-0 4-1 3-1 5-1					
August Town	33	12	8	13	38	41	44	2-3	0-0 0-2 1-0 2-3 3-2-1 1-0-0		1-1-3-1	1-4	0-0 0-1 1-0	2-1	1-1				
Village United	33	11	10	12	26	34	43	1-2	0-0 0-2 3-0-1-1-0-0-1-1-0-0 0-2		2-1	0-1 0-0 0-1	0-2 1-0 2-0						
Arnett Gardens	33	11	5	17	41	46	38	1-2	0-2 0-1 3-2 1-0	1-1	3-2	1-0 1-3 0-1	1-2		0-1	2-0 3-2 5-1 0-0	2-0		
Boys' Town	33	8	12	13	33	44	36	2-3 0-2 1-4 0-1	1-1	0-1	2-2 0-2 1-2	1-2	1-1 3-1		3-1	1-0	1-0 1-1		
Seba United	33	9	6	18	34	54	33	1-3	0-3	2-3 1-1 2-1 1-1 1-2 0	1-1	0-1 0-1	0-2 1-1 0-2			2-2	2-1		
Wadadah	33	6	8	19	34	69	26	0-1	1-3	0-0	0-3	1-2	0-2 3-2 0-0 1-0	3-1	1-2 2-2 1-0 0-3				0-1 3-4
Naggo Head	33	5	6	22	26	65	21	0-2 1-1 0-1 0-3	0-2	0-4	0-0 1-2 1-2	1-0	1-4 1-0	0-0	1-2 1-2	1-0	2-3 0-0	2-3	

10/09/2006 - 29/04/2007 • Top scorers: Irvino ENGLISH, Waterhouse 18; Kavin BRYAN, Harbour View 17

RED STRIPE CHAMPIONS CUP 2006–07

Round of 16		Quarter–finals		Semi–finals		Final		
Portmore United *	5 1							
Duhaney Park	0 1	**Portmore United** *	1 4					
Montpelier *	1 1	Wadadah	1 0					
Wadadah	2 1			**Portmore United**	2			
Harbour View *	4 6			Tivoli Gardens	1			
Downs	0 0	Harbour View	0 1					
Arnett Gardens *	0 0	**Tivoli Gardens** *	3 0			**Portmore United**	1	4p
Tivoli Gardens	2 2					Boys' Town	1	3p
August Town *	1 1							
Reno	0 2	**August Town** *	4 2					
Star Cosmos	0 0	Village United	0 2	August Town	0			
Village United *	2 1			**Boys' Town**	1			
Waterhouse *	2 1							
Sena United	1 1	Waterhouse *	0 1					
Naggo Head	2 1	**Boys' Town**	1 1					
Boys' Town *	2 3			* Home team in the first leg				

CUP FINAL

Harbour View Mini Stadium
8-04-2007

Scorers - Wolry Wolfe 59 for Portmore; Fabian Watkins 47 for Boy's Town

RECENT LEAGUE AND CUP RECORD

	Championship				Cup		
Year	Champions	Score	Runners-up		Winners	Score	Runners-up
1998	Waterhouse	0-0 2-1	Seba United		Harbour View	1-0	Waterhouse
1999	Tivoli Gardens	3-1 0-0	Harbour View		Tivoli Gardens	2-0	Violet Kickers
2000	Harbour View	0-0 2-1	Waterhouse		Hazard United	1-0	Wadadah
2001	Arnett Gardens	2-1 2-1	Waterhouse		Harbour View	3-0	Wadadah
2002	Arnett Gardens	1-1 2-1	Hazard United		Harbour View	2-1	Rivoli United
2003	Hazard United	1-1 3-2	Arnett Gardens		Hazard United	1-0	Harbour View
2004	Tivoli Gardens	4-1 1-2	Harbour View		Waterhouse	2-1	Village United
2005	Portmore United	1-1 1-0	Tivoli Gardens		Portmore United	3-1	Harbour View
2006	Waterhouse	†	Harbour View		Tivoli Gardens	3-2	Portmore United
2007	Harbour View	†	Portmore United		Portmore United	1-1 4-3p	Boys' Town

† Played on a League basis • Hazard United now known as Portmore United

JOR – JORDAN

NATIONAL TEAM RECORD
JULY 10TH 2006 TO JULY 12TH 2010

PL	W	D	L	F	A	%
15	6	4	5	19	10	53.3

FIFA/COCA-COLA WORLD RANKING

1993	1994	1995	1996	1997	1998	1999	2000	2001	2002	2003	2004	2005	2006	High		Low	
87	113	143	146	124	126	115	105	99	77	47	40	86	95	**37**	08/04	**152**	07/96

					2006–2007						
08/06	09/06	10/06	11/06	12/06	01/07	02/07	03/07	04/07	05/07	06/07	07/07
97	96	99	96	95	94	85	81	80	82	87	98

The disappointment of not qualifying for the 2007 AFC Asian Cup finals was tempered by the superb run enjoyed by Jordanian clubs in the AFC Cup as well as the under-20 team reaching the finals of the FIFA U–20 World Cup in Canada - Jordan's first appearance at a world finals. The 2007 AFC Cup saw Al Wihdat, Shabab Al Ordun and Al Faysali all qualify from their groups to give Jordan three teams in the quarter-final draw. This came on the back of Al Faysali's historic AFC Cup Final victory over Bahrain's Al Muharraq in November 2006 which saw them retain the title thanks to two goals from Almaharmeh in the first leg. In a sign of the growing reputation of

INTERNATIONAL HONOURS
AFC Cup Al Faysali 2005 2006

Jordanian clubs abroad, Al Faysali also became the first Jordanian club to reach the final of the Arab Champions League, knocking out ENPPI and Zamalek from Egypt before losing to Algeria's Entente Setif in the final. Faysali were not so dominant at home, however. Al Wihdat were unbeaten in the League for the second time in three seasons as they powered their way to a ninth title and they remained unbeaten in domestic competition after being knocked-out in the Cup only by penalties in the quarter-finals. The final of the Cup saw a repeat of the 2006 final between Shabab Al Ordon and Al Faysali and was won 2-0 by Shabab Al Ordon.

THE FIFA BIG COUNT OF 2006

	Male	Female		Total
Number of players	112 856	8 335	Referees and Assistant Referees	161
Professionals	21		Admin, Coaches, Technical, Medical	6 070
Amateurs 18+	3 637		Number of clubs	93
Youth under 18	1 163		Number of teams	146
Unregistered	40 250		Clubs with women's teams	9
Total players	121 191		Players as % of population	2.05%

Jordan Football Associatiom (JFA)

Al-Hussein Youth City, PO Box 962024, Amman 11196, Jordan
Tel +962 6 5657662   Fax +962 6 565 7660
jfa@nets.com.jo   www.jfa.com.jo
President: HRH Prince Ali AL-HUSSEIN   General Secretary: AL DAOUD Mohammad
Vice-President: AL-HADID Nidal   Treasurer: AL DAOUD Jamal   Media Officer: FAKHOURY Munem
Men's Coach: EL GOHARY Mahmoud   Women's Coach: AL Turk Issa
JFA formed: 1949   AFC: 1970   FIFA: 191958
White shirts with red trimmings, White shorts, White socks or Red shirts with with trimmings, Red shorts, Red socks

RECENT INTERNATIONAL MATCHES PLAYED BY JORDAN

2003	Opponents		Score	Venue	Comp	Scorers	Att	Referee
17-06	Palestine	D	1-1	Tehran	WFr1	Al Shboul [3]		
21-06	Iraq	W	2-0	Tehran	WFr1	Mansour [48], Shelbaieh [79]		
23-06	Syria	D	1-1	Tehran	WFsf	Amer Deeb [21], L 2-3p		
25-06	Iraq	W	3-1	Tehran	WF3p	Al Shagran 2 [27 47], Abu Alieh [76]		
8-07	Thailand	D	0-0	Bangkok	Fr			
19-07	Korea Rep	D	0-0	Jinan	ACr1		26 000	Maidin SIN
23-07	Kuwait	W	2-0	Jinan	ACr1	Sa'ed [90], Al Zboun [90]	28 000	Lu Jun CHN
27-07	United Arab Emirates	D	0-0	Beijing	ACr1		25 000	Talaat LIB
31-07	Japan	D	1-1	Chongqing	ACqf	Shelbaieh [11], L 3-4p	52 000	Salleh MAS
18-08	Azerbaijan	D	1-1	Amman	Fr	Aqel [21]	4 000	
31-08	Lebanon	D	2-2	Amman	Fr	Shelbaieh, Al Zboun		
8-09	Iran	L	0-2	Amman	WCq		20 000	Lu Jun CHN
8-10	Thailand	W	3-2	Bangkok	Fr	Al Maharmeh 2, Shehdeh		
13-10	Laos	W	3-2	Vientiane	WCq	Al Maharmeh [28], Al Shagran 2 [73 76]	3 000	Gosh BAN
20-10	Ecuador	W	3-0	Tripoli	Fr	Al Maltah [45], Shelbaieh [53], Suleiman [69]		
22-10	Libya	L	0-1	Tripoli	Fr			Bennaceur TUN
11-11	United Arab Emirates	L	0-1	Abu Dhabi	Fr			
17-11	Qatar	L	0-2	Doha	WCq		800	Yoshida JPN
2005								
28-01	Norway	D	0-0	Amman	Fr		8 000	Al Shoufi SYR
26-03	Cyprus	L	1-2	Larnaca	Fr	Ahmet [85]		
8-06	Iraq	L	0-1	Amman	Fr			
17-08	Armenia	D	0-0	Amman	Fr			
16-11	Georgia	L	2-3	Amman	Fr	Salimi [35], Saedi [59]		
2006								
17-01	Côte d'Ivoire	L	0-2	Abu Dhabi	Fr			
23-01	Sweden	D	0-0	Abu Dhabi	Fr			
1-02	Thailand	D	0-0	Ayutthaya	Fr			
7-02	Kuwait	L	1-2	Kuwait City	Fr	Abdulfattah		
14-02	Kazakhstan	W	2-0	Amman	Fr	Ali [13], Aqel [53]		
22-02	Pakistan	W	3-0	Amman	ACq	Aqel [30p], Shelbaieh [38], Al Shagran [41]		Basma SYR
1-03	Oman	L	0-3	Wattayah	ACq		11 000	Irmatov UZB
21-07	Iraq	W	2-1	Amman	Fr	Saleem Mansour [36], Rafat Ali [41]		
30-07	Syria	W	3-0	Amman	Fr	Rafat Ali 3		
9-08	Iraq	L	0-1	Amman	Fr			
16-08	UAE	L	1-2	Amman	ACq	Rafat Ali [88]	18 000	Al Hamdan KSA
2-09	Bahrain	W	2-0	Manama	Fr	Saleem Mansour [5], Siraj Al Tall [61]		
6-09	UAE	D	0-0	Dubai	ACq		9 000	Al Fadhli KUW
6-10	Iran	D	0-0	Amman	Fr			
11-10	Pakistan	W	3-0	Lahore	ACq	Al Maharmeh [16], Rafat Ali [37], Khaled Saed [85]	4 000	Orzuev TJK
8-11	Saudi Arabia	L	1-2	Riyadh	Fr	Hassouneh Qasem [31]		
15-11	Oman	W	3-0	Amman	ACq	Amer Deeb [80], Rafat Ali [83], Al Shiekh [87]	3 000	Najm LIB
2007								
8-06	Iraq	D	1-1	Amman	Fr	Awad Ragheb [10]		
12-06	Iraq	D	0-0	Amman	Fr			
18-06	Syria	L	0-1	Amman	WAr1			
20-06	Lebanon	W	3-0	Amman	WAr1	Awad Ragheb [28], Al Maltaah [53], Al Saify [58]		
22-06	Iran	L	0-2	Amman	WAr1			

Fr = Friendly match • WA = West Asian Federation Championship • AC = AFC Asian Cup • WC = FIFA World Cup
q = qualifier • r1 = first round group • qf = quarter-final • sf = semi-final • 3p = third place play-off

JORDAN NATIONAL TEAM RECORDS AND RECORD SEQUENCES

Records			Sequence records				
Victory	6-0	TPE 2001	Wins	5	1992, 2003-2004	Clean sheets	4	1988, 2004
Defeat	0-6	SYR, ALG, CHN	Defeats	6	Three times	Goals scored	9	1992
Player Caps	n/a		Undefeated	14	2004	Without goal	7	1996-1997
Player Goals	n/a		Without win	13	1957-1966	Goals against	13	1992-1993

JORDAN COUNTRY INFORMATION

Capital	Amman	Independence	1946 from the UK	GDP per Capita	$4 300
Population	5 611 202	Status	Kingdom	GNP Ranking	90
Area km²	92 300	Language	Arabic	Dialling code	+962
Population density	61	Literacy rate	91.3%	Internet code	.jo
% in urban areas	71%	Main religion	Muslim 92%, Christian 6%	GMT + / –	+2
Towns/Cities ('000)	Amman 2 201; Irbid 1 027; Al Zarqa 915; Al Balqa 378; Al Mafraq 273; Al Karak 231				
Neighbours (km)	Syria 375; Iraq 181; Saudi Arabia 744; Israel 238; West Bank 97				
Main stadia	Al-Qwaismeh (King Abdullah International) – Amman 18 000				

JORDAN 2006–07

FIRST DIVISION

	Pl	W	D	L	F	A	Pts	Wahdat	Faysali	Buq'aa	Shabab	Hussein	Jazeera	Arabi	Ramtha	Yarmouk	Ittihad
Al Wihdat ‡	18	13	5	0	40	11	44		2-0	0-0	1-1	0-0	2-0	2-1	1-0	1-0	1-0
Al Faysali	18	10	6	2	25	14	36	0-0		1-0	1-1	0-2	1-0	2-1	4-1	1-0	3-1
Al Buq'aa	18	10	4	4	25	17	34	1-4	0-0		0-1	1-0	1-3	3-1	3-1	1-0	2-1
Shabab Al Ordon	18	9	5	4	35	19	32	3-4	1-1	1-2		2-0	1-2	1-1	3-1	2-0	2-0
Al Hussein	18	7	5	6	26	18	26	1-1	2-2	0-1	1-3		2-1	1-2	4-0	1-1	4-1
Al Jazeera	18	7	5	6	22	19	26	0-2	1-1	1-2	2-2	0-0		1-1	1-0	0-0	4-1
Al Arabi	18	3	6	9	17	31	15	2-4	2-4	2-2	0-2	1-4	0-1		1-0	2-1	0-0
Al Ramtha	18	4	3	11	22	38	15	1-2	0-2	1-3	2-1	2-2	3-2	2-0		1-1	2-2
Al Yarmouk	18	3	5	10	15	28	14	1-6	0-1	1-1	1-6	1-0	0-2	0-0	5-1		3-1
Al Ittihad Al Ramtha	18	0	4	14	10	42	4	0-7	0-1	0-2	0-2	0-2	0-1	1-1	1-4	1-1	

22/09/2006 - 30/05/2007 • ‡ Qualified for the AFC Cup

JFA CUP 2006–07

Round of 16		Quarter–finals		Semi–finals		Final	
Shabab Al Ordun	7						
Al Badiah	0	**Shabab Al Ordun**	3				
Al Ittihad Ramtha *	1	Sareeh *	0				
Sareeh	3			**Shabab Al Ordun**	2		
Al Wihdat	2			Al Buq'aa	0		
Karmel *	0	Al Wihdat *	1 3p				
Al Jezeera	0	**Al Buq'aa**	1 4p				
Al Buq'aa *	1					**Shabab Al Ordun** ‡	2
Al Hussein	2					Al Faysali	0
Shabab Al Hussein *	0	**Al Hussein**	3				
Al Ramtha *	1	Al Arabi *	2				
Al Arabi	2			Al Hussein	0		
Al Yarmouk *	3			**Al Faysali**	2		
Al Ahli	0	Al Yarmouk *	0				
Al Rsaifa	0	**Al Faysali**	1				
Al Faysali	3						

CUP FINAL
Amman
14-06-2007

Scorers - Issam Abu Touq [7p],
Ahmed Omair [45]

* Home team • ‡ Qualified for the AFC Cup

RECENT LEAGUE AND CUP RECORD

	Championship						Cup		
Year	Champions	Pts	Runners-up	Pts	Third	Pts	Winners	Score	Runners-up
1997	Al Wihdat	41	Al Faysali	41	Al Ramtha	29	Al Wihdat	2-1	Al Ramtha
1997	Al Wihdat	47	Al Faysali	46	Al Hussein	30	No tournament due to season readjustment		
1998	Al Wihdat	34	Al Faysali	33	Al Ramtha	19	Al Faysali	2-1	Al Wihdat
1999	Al Faysali	57	Al Wihdat	49	Al Ramtha	48	Al Faysali	0-0 5-4p	Al Wihdat
2000	Al Faysali	52	Al Wihdat	44	Al Ahly	34	Al Wihdat	2-0	Al Faysali
2001	Al Faysali	48	Al Wihdat	44	Al Hussein	31	Al Faysali	2-0	Al Hussein
2002	No championship due to season readjustment						No tournament due to season readjustment		
2003	Al Faysali	48	Al Wihdat	45	Al Hussein	35	Al Faysali	2-0	Al Hussein
2004	Al Faysali	9	Al Hussein	4	Al Wihdat	4	Al Faysali	3-1	Al Hussein
2005	Al Wihdat	50	Al Hussein	36	Al Faysali	31	Al Faysali	3-0	Shabab Al Hussein
2006	Shabab Al Ordon	42	Al Faysali	40	Al Wahdat	35	Shabab Al Ordon	2-1	Al Faysali
2007	Al Wihdat	44	Al Faysali	36	Al Buq'aa	34	Shabab Al Ordon	2-0	Al Faysali

JPN – JAPAN

NATIONAL TEAM RECORD
JULY 10TH 2006 TO JULY 12TH 2010

PL	W	D	L	F	A	%
16	9	4	3	26	10	68.7

Japan has had a chequered history in the AFC Asian Cup. They didn't enter or failed to qualify for the first eight tournaments before making their first appearance at the finals in 1988. Four years later they were champions and so completely have they dominated the competition since then, that their failure to win a fourth title in 2007 was seen as a major disappointment. Having taken over from Zico after the World Cup finals in Germany, new coach Ivica Osim was straight in at the deep end as the Japanese first had to secure qualification for the finals - which they did with relative ease - and then prepare for the defence of the title that they won in China three years previously. Based in Hanoi for the tournament, Japan had a tricky tie against hosts Vietnam to secure a place in the quarter-finals, but showing the form of true champions they won 4-1 to set up a dream tie against Australia. The win over Vietnam proved to be their last of the tournament, although they did knock-out the Australians on penalties after a 1-1 draw. Japan's semi-final against Saudi Arabia was a classic, pitting against each other the two teams that had won all of the previous six tournaments. In a see-saw match it was the Saudis who emerged as 3-2 winners to end Japanese dreams of a

INTERNATIONAL HONOURS
Qualified for the FIFA World Cup™ 1998 2002 2006
Qualified for the FIFA Women's World Cup 1991 1995 1999 2003
Asian Cup 1992 2000 2004
AFC U-16 Championship 1994
AFC Champions League Furukawa 1987, Jubilo Iwata 1999

hat-trick of titles. In domestic football, winning the J.League had become something of an obsession for Urawa Reds, one of the best supported clubs in the world. Over three quarters of a million fans attended their home games in the 2006 season - an average of 45,573 - and they finally saw their dreams come true. The League went down to the final afternoon with Urawa at home to second placed Gamba Osaka, the defending champions. Gamba needed to win by three clear goals but that was never on the cards with Urawa's 3-2 victory clinching the long awaited title. Victory was certainly sweet for their German coach Guido Buchwald who had seen his Urawa side finish second in the previous two seasons and who was stepping down at the end of the year to return home. Before he went, however, he steered Urawa Reds to the Emperor's Cup Final where Gamba once again stood between them and silverware. Although Urawa were outplayed by Gamba for the whole game, Yuichiro Nagai scored a very late winner to clinch the double for Urawa - the first since 2000 and only the second since the J.League started in 1993. The other trophy on offer during the season - the J.League Cup - was won by JEF United Chiba.

Japan Football Association (JFA)
JFA House, Football Ave., Bunkyo-ku, Tokyo 113-8311, Japan
Tel +81 3 38302004   Fax +81 3 38302005
www.jfa.or.jp/e/index.html
President: KAWABUCHI Saburo   General Secretary: TASHIMA Kohzo
Vice-President: OGURA Jinji   Treasurer: SAITO Koji   Media Officer: TESHIMA Hideto
Men's Coach: OSIM Ivica   Women's Coach: OHASHI Hiroshi
JFA formed: 1921   AFC: 1954   FIFA: 1929-46 & 1950
Blue shirts with white trimmings, White shorts, Blue socks

RECENT INTERNATIONAL MATCHES PLAYED BY JAPAN

2005	Opponents	Score		Venue	Comp	Scorers	Att	Referee
22-05	Peru	L	0-1	Niigata	KC		39 856	Michel SVK
27-05	United Arab Emirates	L	0-1	Tokyo	KC		53 123	Michel SVK
3-06	Bahrain	W	1-0	Manama	WCq	Ogasawara [34]	32 000	Mohd Salleh MAS
8-06	Korea DPR	W	2-0	Manama	WCq	Yanagisawa [67], Oguro [89]	BCD	De Bleeckere BEL
16-06	Mexico	L	1-2	Hanover	CCr1	Yanagisawa [12]	24 036	Breeze AUS
19-06	Greece	W	1-0	Frankfurt	CCr1	Oguro [76]	34 314	Fandel GER
22-06	Brazil	D	2-2	Cologne	CCr1	Nakamura.S [27], Oguro [88]	44 922	Daami TUN
31-07	Korea DPR	L	0-1	Daejon	EAF		23 150	Tan Hai CHN
3-08	China PR	D	2-2	Daejon	EAF	Moniwa [59], Tanaka [87]	1 827	
7-08	Korea Republic	W	1-0	Daejon	EAF	Nakazawa [86]	42 753	Tan Hai CHN
17-08	Iran	W	2-1	Yokohama	WCq	Kaji [28], Oguro [76]	66 098	Shaban KUW
7-09	Honduras	W	5-4	Miyagi	Fr	Takahara [33], Yanagisawa 2 [48 70], Nakamura.S [55], Ogasawara [78]	45 198	
8-10	Latvia	D	2-2	Riga	Fr	Takahara [5], Nakamura.S [52]	6 500	Granatas POL
12-10	Ukraine	L	0-1	Kyiv	Fr			Lajuks LVA
16-11	Angola	W	1-0	Tokyo	Fr	Matsui [90]	52 406	
2006								
10-02	USA	L	2-3	San Francisco	Fr	Maki [62], Nakazawa [90]	37 365	Elizondo ARG
18-02	Finland	W	2-0	Shizuoka	Fr	Kubo [47], Ogasawara [57]	40 702	Lee Gi Young KOR
22-02	India	W	6-0	Yokohama	ACq	Ono [32], Maki [58], Fukunishi [68], Kubo 2 [78 90], Sato [82]	38 025	Huang CHN
28-02	Bosnia-Herzegovina	D	2-2	Dortmund	Fr	Takahara [45], Nakata.H [90]	8 120	Wack GER
30-03	Ecuador	W	1-0	Oita	Fr	Sato [85]	36 507	Maidin SIN
9-05	Bulgaria	L	1-2	Osaka	Fr	Maki [76]	44 851	Megia Davila ESP
13-05	Scotland	D	0-0	Saitama	Fr		58 648	Itturalde Gonzalez ESP
30-05	Germany	D	2-2	Leverkusen	Fr	Takahara 2 [57 65]	22 500	Vassaras GRE
4-06	Malta	W	1-0	Dusseldorf	Fr	Tamada [2]	10 800	Kircher GER
12-06	Australia	L	1-3	Kaiserslautern	WCr1	Nakamura.S [26]	46 000	Abd El Fatah EGY
18-06	Croatia	D	0-0	Nuremberg	WCr1		41 000	De Bleeckere BEL
22-06	Brazil	L	1-4	Dortmund	WCr1	Tamada [34]	65 000	Poulat FRA
9-08	Trinidad & Tobago	W	2-0	Tokyo	Fr	Santos 2 [17 22]	47 482	Sun Baojie CHN
16-08	Yemen	W	2-0	Niigata	ACq	Abe [70], Sato [91+]	40 913	Lee Gi Young KOR
3-09	Saudi Arabia	L	0-1	Jeddah	ACq		15 000	Maidin SIN
6-09	Yemen	W	1-0	Sana'a	ACq	Ganaha [91+]	7 000	Al Ghatrifi OMA
4-10	Ghana	L	0-1	Yokohama	Fr		52 437	Yu Byung Seob KOR
11-10	India	W	3-0	Bangalore	ACq	Bando 2 [22 43], Nakamura.K [81]	5 000	Chan Siu Kee HKG
15-11	Saudi Arabia	W	3-1	Sapporo	ACq	Tanaka.TM [20], Ganaha 2 [29 50]	40 965	Shield AUS
2007								
24-03	Peru	W	2-0	Yokohama	Fr	Maki [19], Takahara [54]	60 400	Nardi AUS
1-06	Montenegro	W	2-0	Shizuoka	KC	Nakazawa [23], Takahara [38]	28 635	Svendsen DEN
5-06	Colombia	D	0-0	Saitama	KC		45 091	Vollquartz DEN
9-07	Qatar	D	1-1	Hanoi	ACr1	Takahara [60]	5 000	Breeze AUS
13-07	UAE	W	3-1	Hanoi	ACr1	Takahara 2 [22 27], Nakamura.S [42p]	5 000	Tongkhan THA
16-07	Vietnam	W	4-1	Hanoi	ACr1	Maki 2 [12 59], Nakamura.S [52]	40 000	Breeze AUS
21-07	Australia	D	1-1	Hanoi	ACqf	Takahara [72], W 4-3p	25 000	Al Fadhli KUW
25-07	Saudi Arabia	L	2-3	Hanoi	ACsf	Nakazawa [37], Abe [53]	10 000	Breeze AUS
28-07	Korea Republic	D	0-0	Palembang	AC3p	W 6-5p	10 000	Al Badwawi UAE

Fr = Friendly match • KC = Kirin Cup • CC = FIFA Confederations Cup • EAF - East Asian Federation Cup • AC = AFC Asian Cup • WC = FIFA World Cup
q = qualifier • r1 = first round group • qf = quarter-final • sf = semi-final • 3p = third place play-off • BCD = behind closed doors

JAPAN NATIONAL TEAM RECORDS AND RECORD SEQUENCES

Records			Sequence records				
Victory	15-0	PHI 1966	Wins	8	Four times	Clean sheets	7	2003-2004
Defeat	2-15	PHI 1917	Defeats	9	1917-1927	Goals scored	14	1966-1968
Player Caps	123	IHARA Masami	Undefeated	12	2000, 2004	Without goal	6	1988, 1989-1990
Player Goals	82	KAMAMOTO Kunishige	Without win	11	1976-1977	Goals against	31	1960-1966

MAJOR CITIES/TOWNS

		Population '000
1	Tokyo	8 403
2	Yokohama	3 632
3	Osaka	2 588
4	Nagoya	2 197
5	Sapporo	1 908
6	Kobe	1 541
7	Kyoto	1 456
8	Fukuoka	1 412
9	Kawasaki	1 328
10	Hiroshima	1 150
11	Saitama	1 100
12	Sendai	1 050
13	Kitakyushu	991
14	Chiba	932
15	Sakai	778
16	Shizuoka	699
17	Niigata	506
18	Oita	453
19	Toyota	366
20	Kashiwa	345
21	Ichihara	286
22	Ibaraki	264
23	Hiratsuka	260
24	Kashima	67

JAPAN; NIPPON-KOKU

Capital	Tokyo	Language	Japanese	Formation	1600
Population	127 463 611	Area	377835 km²	Density	337 per km²	% in cities	78%
GDP per cap	$28 000	Dailling code	+81	Internet	.jp	GMT +/-	+9

The totals for the major metropolitan areas are: Tokyo 37 037; Osaka-Kobe-Kyoto 17 536; Nagoya 8 833; Fukuoka-Kitakyushu 4 288

MEDALS TABLE

	Overall			League			Cup		LC	Asia			City	Previously	Stadium	Cap'ty	DoF
	G	S	B	G	S	B	G	S		G	S	B					
1 Tokyo Verdy 1969	19	7	1	7	4		5	3	6	1		1	Tokyo	Yomiuri	Ajinomoto	50 000	1969
2 Yokohama F.Marinos	17	7	1	5	5		6	1	4	2	1	1	Yokohama	Nissan	International	72 370	1972
3 Urawa Reds	14	11	5	5	8	5	6	3	3				Saitama	Mitsubishi	Saitama 2002	63 700	1950
4 JEF United	11	3	4	2	1	4	4	2	5	1			Ichihara	Furukawa	Ichihara	16 933	1946
5 Cerezo Osaka	9	12	1	4	4	1	3	8	2				Osaka	Yanmar	Nagai	50 000	1957
6 Kashima Antlers	9	4	4	4	2	1	2	2	3			1	Ibaraki	Sumitomo	Kashima	39 026	1947
7 Sanfrecce Hiroshima	8	11	2	5	2	1	3	9				1	Hiroshima	Toyo Kogyo	Big Arch	50 000	1938
8 Jubilo Iwata	8	6	3	4	2	3	2	2	1	1	2		Iwata	Yamaha	Yamaha	16 893	1970
9 Shonan Bellmare	7	5	3	3	1	3	3	4		1			Hiratsuka	Fujita	Hiratsuka	18 500	1968
10 Kashiwa Reysol	5	3	5	1	1	5	2	2	2				Kashiwa	Hitachi	Hitachi Kashiwa	15 900	1940
11 Shimizu S-Pulse	3	4	1		1		1	3	1	1		1	Shimizu		Nihondaira	20 339	1991
12 Nippon Kokan	3	4		3			1	1	2								
13 Yokohama Flugels	3	2	3	1	2		2	1		1		1	Yokohama	All Nippon			
14 Nagoya Grampus Eight	2	2		1			2			1			Nagoya	Toyota	Mizuho-ku	17 000	
15 Gamba Osaka	2	1	1	1		1	1	1					Osaka	Matsushita	Expo'70	23 000	1980

RECENT LEAGUE AND CUP RECORD

	National Championship				Cup		
Year	Champions	Score/Runners-up	Runners-up/Third		Winners	Score	Runners-up
1995	Yokohama Marinos	1-0 1-0	Verdy Kawasaki		Nagoya G'pus Eight	3-0	S'frecce Hiroshima
1996	Kashima Antlers	‡	Nagoya Grampus Eight		Verdy Kawasaki	3-0	S'frecce Hiroshima
1997	Jubilo Iwata	3-2 1-0	Kashima Antlers		Kashima Antlers	3-0	Yokohama Flugels
1998	Kashima Antlers	2-1 2-1	Jubilo Iwata		Yokohama Flugels	2-1	Shimizu S-Pulse
1999	Jubilo Iwata	2-1 1-2 4-2p	Shimizu S-Pulse		Nagoya G'pus Eight	2-0	S'frecce Hiroshima
2000	Kashima Antlers	0-0 3-0	Yokohama F.Marinos		Kashima Antlers	3-2	Shimizu S-Pulse
2001	Kashima Antlers	2-2 1-0	Jubilo Iwata		Shimizu S-Pulse	3-2	Cerezo Osaka
2002	Jubilo Iwata	†			Kyoto Purple Sanga	2-1	Kashima Antlers
2003	Yokohama F.Marinos	†			Jubilo Iwata	1-0	Cerezo Osaka
2004	Yokohama F.Marinos	1-0 0-1 4-2p	Urawa Reds		Tokyo Verdy 1969	2-1	Jubilo Iwata

2005	Gamba Osaka	60	Urawa Reds	59	Kashima Antlers	59	Urawa Reds	2-1	Shimizu S-Pulse
2006	Urawa Reds	72	Kawasaki Frontale	67	Gamba Osaka	66	Urawa Reds	1-0	Gamba Osaka

† Both stages won by the same team so no play-off was required • ‡ Played on a single stage league system with no play-off

JAPAN 2006

J.LEAGUE DIVISION 1

Team	Pl	W	D	L	F	A	Pts	Urawa Reds	Kawasaki	Gamba	Shimizu	Jubilo	Antlers	Nagoya	Oita	Marinos	Sanfrecce	JEF United	Omiya	Tokyo	Albirex	Ventforet	Avispa	Cerezo	Kyoto
Urawa Reds ‡	34	22	6	6	67	28	72	—	2-2	3-2	1-0	3-1	4-0	0-0	1-0	1-0	2-1	2-0	2-0	4-0	3-1	3-0	2-1	3-0	3-0
Kawasaki Frontale ‡	34	20	7	7	84	55	67	0-2	—	3-2	2-2	3-4	3-2	4-2	2-1	1-1	3-3	2-2	3-1	2-2	6-0	2-0	2-1	1-0	2-0
Gamba Osaka	34	20	6	8	80	48	66	1-1	4-0	—	3-0	2-2	1-0	5-1	1-3	1-1	3-2	1-0	3-1	1-0	3-0	2-0	2-2	3-1	3-2
Shimizu S-Pulse	34	18	6	10	60	41	60	2-1	4-3	2-3	—	2-0	1-2	2-0	4-1	1-0	3-0	1-2	1-1	2-0	1-1	4-0	4-0	1-0	1-0
Jubilo Iwata	34	17	7	10	68	51	58	3-2	1-2	3-2	1-0	—	3-3	2-2	2-3	3-1	3-0	3-1	2-1	4-1	7-0	2-0	1-1	3-1	1-1
Kashima Antlers	34	18	4	12	62	53	58	2-2	2-4	3-1	3-1	3-0	—	2-1	0-1	0-3	0-2	0-4	2-1	3-2	5-1	3-1	4-1	2-0	1-0
Nagoya Grampus Eight	34	13	9	12	51	49	48	1-0	0-2	3-3	1-1	3-1	0-0	—	0-3	1-1	2-3	2-1	2-0	1-2	3-1	5-1	2-0	3-2	1-1
Oita Trinita	34	13	8	13	47	45	47	2-1	1-1	0-2	3-3	1-2	2-0	0-1	—	1-2	1-1	0-3	1-2	0-1	4-0	3-2	0-0	1-1	2-1
Yokohama F-Marinos	34	13	6	15	49	43	45	1-3	1-2	3-4	2-3	0-1	2-1	2-1	0-1	—	2-1	1-1	1-2	1-1	2-0	3-0	0-0	3-1	4-1
Sanfrecce Hiroshima	34	13	6	15	50	56	45	1-4	1-3	1-3	1-2	2-1	3-4	0-0	0-1	3-0	—	2-4	1-0	5-2	2-1	1-3	1-0	1-1	1-0
JEF United Chiba	34	13	5	16	57	58	44	2-0	1-2	1-2	1-3	0-0	0-1	2-3	2-1	0-2	0-1	—	1-3	3-4	1-3	2-2	2-2	2-1	2-0
Omiya Ardija	34	13	5	16	43	55	44	0-2	1-5	0-2	1-0	2-1	0-3	1-4	2-2	2-1	0-1	4-2	—	0-1	1-2	4-1	2-2	2-0	1-0
FC Tokyo	34	13	4	17	56	65	43	0-0	5-4	3-2	0-1	3-1	2-4	2-1	2-0	1-2	0-2	2-3	1-2	—	1-4	1-3	5-1	2-3	2-1
Albirex Niigata	34	12	6	16	46	65	42	2-1	2-1	1-0	4-2	0-2	0-1	2-1	3-3	1-0	1-1	1-2	1-2	2-0	—	3-0	0-1	2-2	1-1
Ventforet Kofu	34	12	6	16	42	64	42	1-1	1-0	3-2	0-2	1-1	2-1	2-1	2-0	1-0	1-0	2-3	3-2	1-3	0-4	—	1-1	0-1	3-1
Avispa Fukuoka	34	5	12	17	32	56	27	0-1	1-2	1-1	1-2	2-1	2-0	1-0	1-0	2-3	1-1	1-1	0-0	2-0	1-1	1-1	—	1-0	4-5
Cerezo Osaka	34	6	9	19	44	70	27	1-2	1-3	1-6	1-1	2-3	2-2	1-1	0-2	2-0	4-2	0-1	1-5	3-1	2-3	0-0	2-2	—	2-2
Kyoto Sanga	34	4	10	20	38	74	22	1-5	2-7	1-4	2-1	1-3	1-2	0-1	1-0	4-2	1-2	1-1	1-0	1-1	0-1	1-2	1-1	2-1	—

4/03/2006 - 2/12/2006 • ‡ Qualified for the AFC Champions League • Relegation play-off: **Vissel Kobe** 0-0 1-1 Avispa Fukuoka
Top scorers: WASHINGTON, Urawa Reds 26; MAGNO ALVES, Gamba Osaka 26; JUNINHO, Kawasaki 20; Hisato SATO, Sanfrecce 18; LUCAS, FC Tokyo 18; Kazuki GANAHA, Kawasaki 18; CHO Jae Jin, Shimizu 16; Ryuji BANDO, Gamba Osaka 16; UESLEI, Sanfrecce 16

FIFA/COCA-COLA WORLD RANKING

1993	1994	1995	1996	1997	1998	1999	2000	2001	2002	2003	2004	2005	2006	High		Low	
43	36	31	21	14	20	57	38	34	22	29	17	15	47	**9**	02/98	**62**	02/00

2006–2007											
08/06	09/06	10/06	11/06	12/06	01/07	02/07	03/07	04/07	05/07	06/07	07/07
48	47	46	47	47	46	41	42	46	44	40	36

JAPAN 2006

J.LEAGUE DIVISION 2

Team	Pl	W	D	L	F	A	Pts
Yokohama FC	48	26	15	7	61	32	93
Kashiwa Reysol	48	27	7	14	84	60	88
Vissel Kobe †	48	25	11	12	78	53	86
Sagan Tosu	48	22	13	13	64	49	79
Vegalta Sendai	48	21	14	13	75	43	77
Consadole Sapporo	48	20	12	16	77	67	72
Tokyo Verdy 1969	48	21	8	19	69	75	71
Montedio Yamagata	48	17	14	17	68	57	65
Ehime FC	48	14	11	23	51	63	53
Mito Hollyhock	48	14	9	25	48	69	51
Shonan Bellmare	48	13	10	25	61	87	49
Thespa Kusatsu	48	9	15	24	54	86	42
Tokushima Vortis	48	8	11	29	43	92	35

4/03/2006 - 2/12/2006 • † Qualified for play-off • No clubs relegated • Promotion play-off: **Vissel Kobe** 0-0 1-1 Avispa Fukuoka
Top scorers: BORGES, Vegalta 26; HULK, Consadole 25; LEANDRO, Montedio 23; Tatsunori ARAI, Sagan 23; DIEGO, Kashiwa 21; ALEMAO, Yokohama 18

JAPAN 2006

8TH JAPAN FOOTBALL LEAGUE (JFL) (3)	Pl	W	D	L	F	A	Pts	Honda	Sagawa T	Sagawa O	YKK	Rosso	Yokogawa	Tochigi	Alo's	Sony	Arte	Tottori	JEF Club	Kariya	Ryukyu	Sagawa P	Ryutsu	Mitsubishi	Honda Lock
Honda FC	34	26	5	3	77	36	83		0-3	2-3	2-2	2-1	1-0	2-0	1-0	0-0	4-1	3-3	4-1	2-0	1-0	3-0	4-1	2-0	2-1
Sagawa Express Tokyo	34	23	6	5	84	23	75	1-1		1-0	0-0	0-1	1-2	1-2	1-0	0-1	3-1	2-0	3-0	1-1	5-0	1-0	5-1	3-0	2-0
Sagawa Express Osaka	34	23	3	8	68	29	72	0-2	2-2		0-1	1-0	2-1	2-1	1-0	5-0	1-0	3-1	6-0	3-2	1-0	3-0	4-2	2-1	2-1
YKK AP	34	19	10	5	68	34	67	0-1	0-3	2-1		3-1	1-1	1-1	0-0	1-1	5-1	2-1	1-0	2-2	1-0	5-1	2-1	3-0	7-1
Rosso Kumamoto	34	20	6	8	64	39	66	1-2	2-3	1-0	2-1		2-2	0-1	2-1	3-1	3-2	1-1	1-0	3-1	3-1	0-0	0-0	4-0	2-0
Yokogawa Musashino	34	17	9	8	58	38	60	0-1	3-4	0-0	2-3	1-1		1-1	0-0	2-1	1-2	2-0	1-0	2-0	5-0	2-0	3-1	1-0	3-0
Tochigi SC	34	17	9	8	50	35	60	3-2	0-0	0-2	3-0	1-3	4-0		1-2	3-2	1-2	3-2	2-1	0-0	3-2	2-1	3-1	1-0	0-0
Alo's Hokuriku	34	16	9	9	53	30	57	1-2	3-3	0-2	2-1	1-2	2-2	2-1		4-2	0-1	0-0	1-0	2-0	0-0	3-1	1-1	4-0	4-1
Sony Sendai	34	10	7	17	48	65	37	2-3	0-1	2-1	0-3	2-1	0-2	0-4	0-0		2-1	0-0	2-4	1-1	1-0	1-1	0-2	4-0	2-3
Arte Takasaki	34	10	7	17	36	62	37	1-2	1-0	1-2	0-2	0-2	1-5	0-0	0-3	2-6		2-2	2-4	1-0	3-1	1-0	2-0	0-4	0-0
SC Tottori	34	7	15	12	61	62	36	3-4	0-3	0-0	2-2	2-2	1-3	1-1	1-1	2-1	1-1		3-4	3-4	1-1	2-1	4-1	3-0	7-0
JEF United Club	34	11	2	21	52	68	35	0-3	1-3	0-1	0-3	3-1	4-1	2-2	1-2	4-1	2-1	3-4		1-3	0-1	0-3	1-2	1-2	3-1
FC Kariya	34	8	8	18	46	63	32	1-2	0-6	0-1	1-3	2-3	0-1	0-2	1-0	2-3	1-1	1-3	2-1		2-1	2-2	5-1	2-3	3-2
FC Ryukyu	34	6	11	17	29	57	29	1-5	0-6	1-1	2-2	1-2	0-0	0-0	2-4	1-2	1-1	3-3	0-1	1-0		2-0	3-0	0-0	0-0
Sagawa Printing	34	7	8	19	32	61	29	1-4	1-3	0-4	1-1	2-4	1-1	2-0	0-1	0-0	0-2	3-1	1-2	0-0			1-0	1-1	1-3
Ryutsu Keizai Univ.	34	8	4	22	48	83	28	1-2	0-8	2-5	0-2	1-2	2-3	0-1	0-3	3-0	3-0	2-1	3-5	2-2	4-2	1-2		3-2	2-2
Mitsubishi Mizushima	34	7	6	21	32	74	27	0-0	0-5	0-6	0-4	0-3	0-2	1-2	0-1	4-2	0-1	2-2	1-1	3-2	0-0	3-1	0-4		4-2
Honda Lock	34	5	7	22	39	86	22	4-6	0-1	2-1	1-2	1-5	2-3	0-1	0-5	2-6	1-1	1-1	0-3	1-1	0-1	0-1	2-3	2-1	

19/03/2006 - 3/12/2006 • None of the top three clubs qualified for promotion • Relegation play-off: FC Gifu 4-0 1-4 Honda Lock • The two Sagawa Express clubs from Tokyo and Osaka merged for the 2007 season
Top scorers: Tetsuya OKUBO, Sagawa Tokyo 26; Junya NITTA, Honda FC 23; Yosuke KOBAYASHI, Yokogawa 23

J.LEAGUE YAMAZAKI NABISCO CUP 2006

Group Stage

Group A	Pts
Urawa Reds	16
Yokohama F.Marinos	10
Avispa Fukuoka	5
FC Tokyo	2

Group B	Pts
Kawasaki Frontale	15
Kashima Antlers	9
Oita Trinita	9
Kyoto Purple Sanga	3

Group C	Pts
JEF United Chiba	13
Shimizu S-Pulse	8
Albirex Niigata	6
Sanfrecce Hiroshima	5

Group D	Pts
Cerezo Osaka	12
Jubilo Iwata	10
Ventforet Kofu	8
Omiya Ardija	7
Nagoya Grampus Eight	3

Quarter-finals

JEF United Chiba	5	3
Cerezo Osaka *	2	2

Urawa Reds *	4	1
Kawasaki Frontale	3	2

Yokohama F.Marinos *	2	2
Jubilo Iwata	1	0

Gamba Osaka	0	0
Kashima Antlers *	0	2

Semi-finals

JEF United Chiba	2	2
Kawasaki Frontale *	2	3

Yokohama F.Marinos	0	2
Kashima Antlers *	1	1

Final

JEF United Chiba	2
Kashima Antlers	0

CUP FINAL
National Stadium, Tokyo
3-11-2006, Att: 44 704, Ref: Kamikawa
Scorers - Mizuno 80, Abe 82 for JEF Utd
JEF - Okamoto - Mizumoto, Nakajima, Saito - Mizuno, Abe, Sato, Yamagishi, Hanyu (Kudo 83) - Haas (Sakamoto 28), Maki. Tr: Osim
Kashima - Sogahata - Araiba, Iwamasa, Oiwa (Motoyama 85), Fabio Santos, Aoki, Masuda, Nozawa, Fukai (Koroki 85), Yanagisawa, Alex Mineiro (Tashiro 85). Tr: Paulo Autori

Gamba Osaka qualified directly for the knock-out stage due to AFC Champions League commitments • * Home team in the first leg

THE FIFA BIG COUNT OF 2006

	Male	Female		Total
Number of players	4 500 506	304 644	Referees and Assistant Referees	189 603
Professionals	976		Admin, Coaches, Technical, Medical	60 000
Amateurs 18+	292 562		Number of clubs	1 000
Youth under 18	629 140		Number of teams	29 132
Unregistered	3 000 000		Clubs with women's teams	1 000
Total players	4 805 150		Players as % of population	3.77%

EMPEROR'S CUP 2006

Third Round		Fourth Round		Fifth Round	
		Urawa Reds *	5		
Shizuoko FC	1	Shizuoka FC	0		
Mito Hollyhock *	0			**Urawa Reds ***	3
				Avispa Fukuoka	0
		Kyoto Sanga	1 3p		
		Avispa Fukuoka *	1 4p		
		Omiya Ardija *	2		
YKK AP	4	YKK AP	1		
Vissel Kobe *	2			Omiya Ardija *	0
				Jubilo Iwata	1
		Kashiwa Reysol	1 8p		
Kashiwa Reysol *	3	**Jubilo Iwata ***	1 9p		
Hosei University	0				
		Shimizu S-Pulse *	6		
Tochigi SC	1	Tochigi SC	4		
Tokyo Verdy 1969 *	0			**Shimizu S-Pulse ***	3
				FC Tokyo	2
		Banditonce Kobe	0		
Banditonce Kobe	1	**FC Tokyo ***	7		
Yokohama FC *	0				
		Nagoya Grampus Eight *	1		
Vegalta Sendai *	1	Vegalta Sendai	0		
Rosso Kumamoto	0			Nagoya Grampus Eight	1
				Kashima Antlers *	2
		Honda FC	0		
Honda FC *	1	**Kashima Antlers ***	4		
Kochi University	0				
		Consadole Sapporo	1		
Consadole Sapporo *	3	JEF United Ichihara/Chiba *	0		
Nippon Steel Oita	1			**Consadole Sapporo ***	2 8p
				Albirex Niigata	2 7p
		Tokushima Vortis	0		
Tokushima Vortis *	4	**Albirex Niigata ***	2		
Miyazaki S-K University	1				
		Kawasaki Frontale *	3		
Sagan Tosu *	4	Sagan Tosu	0		
Ritsumeikan University	3			Kawasaki Frontale *	2
				Ventforet Kofu	5
		Montedio Yamagata	2		
Montedio Yamagata *	6	**Ventforet Kofu ***	3		
Mitsubishi Mizushima	2				
		Yokohama F-Marinos *	1		
Ehime FC *	2	Ehime FC	0		
Biwako Seikei	0			**Yokohama F-Marinos**	1 4p
				Oita Trinita *	1 2p
		Thespa Kusatsu	1		
Thespa Kusatsu *	3	**Oita Trinita ***	4		
FC Gifu	0				
		Sanfrecce Hiroshima *	3		
		Cerezo Osaka	0		
				Sanfrecce Hiroshima	2
Shonan Bellmare *	4			**Gamba Osaka ***	4
Kansai University	1	Shonan Bellmare	1		
		Gamba Osaka *	2		

J.2 clubs join in the third round • J.League clubs join in the fourth round • * Home team

EMPEROR'S CUP 2006

Quarter–finals	Semi–finals	Final

Urawa Reds *	3 10p
Jubilo Iwata	3 9p

Urawa Reds	2
Kashima Antlers	1

Shimizu S-Pulse	2
Kashima Antlers *	3

Urawa Reds ‡	1
Gamba Osaka	0

Consadole Sapporo	2
Ventforet Kofu *	0

Consadole Sapporo	1
Gamba Osaka ††	2

Yokohama F-Marinos	1
Gamba Osaka *	3

EMPEROR'S CUP FINAL 2006
National Stadium, Tokyo, 1-01-2007, Att: 46 880

Urawa Reds	1	Yuichiro Nagai [88]
Gamba Osaka	0	

Urawa - Ryota TSUZUKI - Hajime HOSOGAI•, Hideki UCHIDATE, NENE•, Tadaaki HIRAKAWA (Makoto HASEBE 62) - Keita SUZUKI (Satoshi HORINOUCHI 88), Shinji ONO (Masayuki OKANO 76), Takahito SOMA - Nobuhisa YAMADA, Robson PONTE, Yuichiro NAGAI. Tr: BUCHWALD Guido
Gamba - Naoki MATSUYO - Noritada SANEYOSHI, Tsuneyasu MIYAMOTO, Satoru YAMAGUCHI, Akira KAJI• - Tomokazu MYOJIN, Yasuhito ENDO, Akihiro IENAGA•, Takahiro FUTAGAWA - Ryuji BANDO, MAGNO ALVES. Tr: Akira NISHINO

† Played at the National Stadium, Tokyo
†† Played at Ecopa Stadium, Shizuoka
‡ Qualified for the AFC Champions League

URAWA REDS 2006

Date	Opponents	Score			Comp	Scorers	Att
25-02-2006	Gamba Osaka	W	3-1	N	SC	Horinouchi [9], Washington [17], Ponte [51]	35 674
4-03-2006	Gamba Osaka	D	1-1	A	JL	Washington [2]	20 916
11-03-2006	Jubilo Iwata	W	3-1	H	JL	Tanaka.MT [33], Santos [42], Ponte [61]	56 512
18-03-2006	Sanfrecce Hiroshima	W	4-1	A	JL	Santos [28], Ponte [32], Suzuki [62], Washington [66]	16 742
21-03-2006	Cerezo Osaka	W	3-0	H	JL	Ono [47], Washington [57], Tanaka.MT [79]	43 815
25-03-2006	Yokohama F.Marinos	W	3-1	A	JL	Yamada [43], Washington [48], Hasebe [89]	50 572
29-03-2006	FC Tokyo	W	2-0	H	JLCgA	Escudero [62], Sakai [89]	16 065
2-04-2006	Nagoya Grampus Eight	D	0-0	H	JL		44 625
9-04-2006	Avispa Fukuoka	W	1-0	A	JL	Tanaka.MT [89]	21 545
15-04-2006	Kyoto Purple Sanga	W	3-0	H	JL	Hasebe [55], Washington 2 [72 84]	40 657
12-04-2006	Avispa Fukuoka	W	3-1	H	JLCgA	Horinouchi [25], Yamada [55], Tanaka.MT [83]	14 695
22-04-2006	Shimizu S-Pulse	L	1-2	A	JL	Washington [42]	23 406
26-04-2006	Avispa Fukuoka	W	3-1	A	JLCgA	Ono [18], Nagai [27], Hirakawa [38]	7 614
29-04-2006	Omiya Ardija	W	2-0	H	JL	Washington [32], Nagai [89]	54 774
3-05-2006	JEF United Chiba	L	0-2	A	JL		17 438
7-05-2006	Kashima Antlers	W	4-0	H	JL	Ono 2 [3 46], Washington 2 [17 87]	56 982
14-05-2006	Yokohama F.Marinos	W	2-1	A	JLCgA	Nagai [13], Washington [58]	34 310
17-05-2006	FC Tokyo	D	0-0	A	JLCgA		19 098
21-05-2006	Yokohama F.Marinos	W	4-2	H	JLCgA	Washington 3 [23 43 70], Soma [32]	43 129
3-06-2006	Kawasaki Frontale	W	4-3	H	JLCqf	Washington 4 [9 49 68 73]	19 292
7-06-2006	Kawasaki Frontale	L	1-2	A	JLCqf	Washington [31]	16 342
19-07-2006	Albitrex Niigata	L	1-2	A	JL	Yamada [85]	38 592
22-07-2006	Kawasaki Frontale	W	2-0	A	JL	Tanaka.T [30], Nagai [76]	23 005
26-07-2006	Oita Trinita	W	1-0	H	JL	Tanaka.T [78]	16 040
29-07-2006	Ventforet Kofu	D	1-1	A	JL	Santos [75]	17 000
12-08-2006	FC Tokyo	W	4-0	H	JL	Ono [5], Santos 2 [55 71], Tanaka.T [88]	50 195
19-08-2006	Kashima Antlers	D	2-2	A	JL	Ono [71], Washington [89]	34 236
23-08-2006	Albirex Niigata	W	3-1	H	JL	Washington 3 [22 35 89]	34 417
26-08-2006	Cerezo Osaka	W	2-1	A	JL	Horinouchi [16], Nagai [68]	23 386
30-08-2006	Oita Trinita	L	1-2	A	JL	Washington [76]	27 843
10-09-2006	Omiya Ardija	W	2-0	A	JL	Washington [44], Nagai [89]	35 059
16-09-2006	Sanfrecce Hiroshima	W	2-1	H	JL	Tanaka.MT [35], Yamada [86]	39 123
23-09-2006	Shimizu S-Pulse	W	1-0	H	JL	Washington [16]	48 378
30-09-2006	Kyoto Purple Sanga	W	5-1	A	JL	Tanaka.MT [14], Hirakawa [22], Tanaka.T [40], Yamada [46], Soma [83]	16 492
7-10-2006	JEF United Chiba	W	2-0	H	JL	Washington [16], Tanaka.MT [58]	48 952
15-10-2006	Avispa Fukuoka	W	2-1	H	JL	Tanaka.MT [20], Washington [45]	17 541
21-10-2006	Kawasaki Frontale	D	2-2	H	JL	Washington [19], Ponte [52]	50 134
28-10-2006	Jubilo Iwata	L	2-3	A	JL	Washington 2 [48 70]	16 162
4-11-2006	Shizuoka FC	W	5-0	H	ECr4	Tanaka.T 2 [5 58], Hasebe [23], Washington 2 [47 90]	13 636
11-11-2006	Yokohama F.Marinos	W	1-0	H	JL	Yamada [33]	52 582
18-11-2006	Nagoya Grampus Eight	L	0-1	A	JL		32 109
23-11-2006	Ventforet Kofu	W	3-0	H	JL	Washington 2 [46 68], Yamada [64]	57 781
26-11-2006	FC Tokyo	D	0-0	A	JL		41 528
2-12-2006	Gamba Osaka	W	3-2	H	JL	Ponte [27], Washington 2 [44 59]	62 241
16-12-2006	Avispa Fukuoka	W	3-0	H	ECr5	Ponte [94], Washington [109], Nagai [119]	17 675
23-12-2006	Jubilo Iwata	D	3-3	H	ECqf	Nagai [55], Ono 2 [64 81], W 10-9p	27 242
29-12-2006	Kashima Antlers	W	2-1	N	ECsf	Ono [41], Ponte [83]	35 782
1-01-2007	Gamba Osaka	W	1-0	N	ECf	Nagai [88]	46 880

SC = XEROX Super Cup • JL = J.League • JLC = J.League Cup • EC = Emperor's Cup
gA = Group A • r4 = fourth round • r5 = fifth round • qf = quarter-final • sf = semi-final • f = final
H = Saitama Stadium 2002, Saitama • **H** = Urawa Komaba, Saitama • **A** = Saitama Stadium 2002, Saitama • N = National Stadium, Tokyo

KAZ – KAZAKHSTAN

NATIONAL TEAM RECORD
JULY 10TH 2006 TO JULY 12TH 2010

PL	W	D	L	F	A	%
15	3	6	6	13	18	40

FIFA/COCA-COLA WORLD RANKING

1993	1994	1995	1996	1997	1998	1999	2000	2001	2002	2003	2004	2005	2006	High		Low	
-	153	163	156	107	102	123	120	98	117	136	147	137	135	98	12/01	166	05/96

2006–2007											
08/06	09/06	10/06	11/06	12/06	01/07	02/07	03/07	04/07	05/07	06/07	07/07
141	120	135	135	135	142	145	143	116	115	119	118

March 24, 2007 may well go down as a significant landmark in the development of football in Kazakhstan. The 2-1 victory over Serbia was the national team's first competitive victory since joining UEFA and concrete evidence of the improvements made since the move. That the victory came against one of the traditional powers of the European game - albeit in a reduced state from the old Yugoslavia - was even more satisfying for Arno Pijpers' team. The result was not a one-off either as the UEFA Euro 2008 qualifiers also saw Kazakhstan draw away in Belgium whilst Azerbaijan were held home and away. Kazakhstan also scored in nine consecutive matches

INTERNATIONAL HONOURS
None

between December 2006 and June 2007 - a new national team record. There were encouraging signs too at club level with Kairat managing to beat Hungary's Fehérvár in the UEFA Cup, although they were knocked out on away goals. FK Astana (previously Zhenis), also managed by Pijpers, won the 2006 championship thanks largely to an excellent youth programme that is also beginning to reap dividends for the national team. They just missed out on the double, however, losing to FK Almaty - a team created only in 2003 - in the Cup Final. Almaty's 3-1 victory, thanks to a Jafar Irismetov hat trick, meant a first trophy for the club from the capital.

THE FIFA BIG COUNT OF 2006

	Male	Female		Total
Number of players	437 820	72 600	Referees and Assistant Referees	210
Professionals	1 450		Admin, Coaches, Technical, Medical	2 950
Amateurs 18+	5 250		Number of clubs	43
Youth under 18	20 500		Number of teams	300
Unregistered	79 600		Clubs with women's teams	2
Total players	510 420		Players as % of population	3.35%

The Football Union of Kazakhstan (FSK)
Satpayev Street 29/3, Almaty 480 072, Kazakhstan
Fax +7 3272 921885
kfo@mail.online.kz   www.fsk.kz
President: AKPAYEV Tlekbek   General Secretary: AKHMETOV Askar
Vice-President: PIJPERS Arno   Treasurer: TBD   Media Officer: KAMASHEV Timur
Men's Coach: PIJPERS Arno   Women's Coach: JAMANTAYEV Aitpay
FSK formed: 1914   AFC: 1994-2002, UEFA: 2002   FIFA: 1994
Blue shirts with yellow trimmings, Blue shorts, Yellow socks or Yellow shirts with blue trimmings, Yellow shorts, Blue socks

RECENT INTERNATIONAL MATCHES PLAYED BY KAZAKHSTAN

2002	Opponents	Score		Venue	Comp	Scorers	Att	Referee
7-07	Estonia	D	1-1	Almaty	Fr	Litvinenko [38]	15 000	Kapanin KAZ
2003								
12-02	Malta	D	2-2	Ta'Qali	Fr	Zhumaskaliyev [72], Tarasov [83]	200	Rogalla SUI
27-04	Faroe Islands	L	2-3	Toftir	Fr	Lunev [56], Mumanov [76]	420	Jakobsson ISL
29-04	Faroe Islands	L	1-2	Tórshavn	Fr	Lovchev [6p]	800	Bergmann ISL
6-06	Poland	L	0-3	Poznan	Fr		6 000	Fisker DEN
20-08	Portugal	L	0-1	Chaves	Fr		8 000	Rodriguez Santiago ESP
2004								
18-02	Latvia	L	1-3	Larnaca	Fr	Aksenov [23]	500	Constantinou CYP
19-02	Armenia	D	3-3	Paphos	Fr	Zhumaskaliyev 2 [53 75], Finonchenko [76]. W 3-2p	100	Loizou CYP
21-02	Cyprus	L	1-2	Larnaca	Fr	Uzdenov [68]	300	Lajaks LVA
28-04	Azerbaijan	L	2-3	Almaty	Fr	Karpovich [55], Lunev [77]	20 000	Chynybekov KGZ
8-09	Ukraine	L	1-2	Almaty	WCq	Karpovich [34]	23 000	Alves Garcia POR
9-10	Turkey	L	0-4	Istanbul	WCq		39 900	Hrinak SVK
13-10	Albania	L	0-1	Almaty	WCq		12 300	Stuchlik AUT
17-11	Greece	L	1-3	Piraeus	WCq	Baltiyev [88]	31 838	Kostadinov BUL
2005								
29-01	Japan	L	0-4	Yokohama	Fr		46 941	
26-03	Denmark	L	0-3	Copenhagen	WCq		20 980	Gilewski POL
4-06	Ukraine	L	0-2	Kyiv	WCq		45 000	Lehner AUT
8-06	Turkey	L	0-6	Almaty	WCq		20 000	Kassai HUN
17-08	Georgia	L	1-2	Almaty	WCq	Kenzhekhanov [23]	9 000	Havrilla SVK
3-09	Albania	L	1-2	Tirana	WCq	Nizovtsev [62]	3 000	Slupik POL
7-09	Greece	L	1-2	Almaty	WCq	Zhalmagambetov [53]	18 000	Tudor ROU
8-10	Georgia	D	0-0	Tbilisi	WCq		BCD	Hyytia FIN
12-10	Denmark	L	1-2	Almaty	WCq	Kuchma [86]	8 050	Trivkovic CRO
2006								
14-02	Jordan	D	0-0	Amman	Fr			
28-02	Finland	D	0-0	Larnaca	Fr	W 3-1p		
1-03	Greece	L	0-2	Nicosia	Fr		2 000	Kailis CYP
2-07	Tajikistan	W	4-1	Almaty	Fr	Zhumaskaliev [22], Familtsev [40], Kuchma [63], Tleshev [90]		
5-07	Kyrgyzstan	W	1-0	Almaty	Fr	Baltiev [20p]		
16-08	Belgium	D	0-0	Brussels	ECq		15 495	Courtney NIR
6-09	Azerbaijan	D	1-1	Baku	ECq	Byakov [36]	8 500	Szabó HUN
7-10	Poland	L	0-1	Almaty	ECq		22 000	Trivkovic CRO
11-10	Finland	L	0-2	Almaty	ECq		17 863	Briakos GRE
15-11	Portugal	L	0-3	Coimbra	ECq		29 500	Rogalla SUI
24-12	Singapore	D	0-0	Bangkok	Fr			
26-12	Vietnam	L	1-2	Bangkok	Fr	Finonchenko [57]		
28-12	Thailand	D	2-2	Bangkok	Fr	Rodionov [66], Ashirbekov [70]		
2007								
7-02	China PR	L	1-2	Suzhou	Fr	Suyumagambetov [14]		
7-03	Kyrgyzstan	W	2-0	Shymkent	Fr	Byakov [3], Chichulin [68]		
9-03	Azerbaijan	W	1-0	Shymkent	Fr	Finonchenko [80]		
11-03	Uzbekistan	D	1-1	Shymkent	Fr	Suyumagambetov [13]		
24-03	Serbia	W	2-1	Almaty	ECq	Ashirbekov [47], Zhumaskaliyev [61]	19 600	Hrinák SVK
2-06	Armenia	L	1-2	Almaty	ECq	Baltiev [88p]	17 100	Kralovec CZE
6-06	Azerbaijan	D	1-1	Almaty	ECq	Baltiev [53]	11 800	Toussaint LUX

Fr = Friendly match • EC = UEFA EURO 2008 • WC = FIFA World Cup • q = qualifier • BCD = behind closed doors

KAZAKHSTAN NATIONAL TEAM RECORDS AND RECORD SEQUENCES

Records			Sequence records					
Victory	7-0	PAK 1997	Wins	4	1997	Clean sheets	3	1994-1995
Defeat	0-6	TUR 2005	Defeats	13	2004-2005	Goals scored	9	2006-2007
Player Caps	34	BALTIYEV Ruslan	Undefeated	7	2001-2003	Without goal	5	1994-1995
Player Goals	12	ZUBAREV Viktor	Without win	29	2001-2006	Goals against	16	2002-

RUS

Uralsk
Petropavlovsk
Aktobe
Astana • Pavlodar
Karagandy • Oskamen •
UZB
TKM Shymkent • Taraz Almaty
KGZ
CHN
TJK

REPUBLIC OF KAZAKHSTAN; QAZAQSTAN RESPUBLIKASY

Capital	Astana	Language	Kazakh, Russian		Independence	1991
Population	15 233 244	Area	2 717 300 km²	Density 5 per km²	% in cities	60%
GDP per cap	$6300	Dailling code	+7	Internet .kz	GMT +/-	+4

MAJOR CITIES/TOWNS

Population '000

1	Almaty	1 227
2	Shymkent	420
3	Karagandy	404
4	Taraz	366
5	Astana	356
6	Pavlodar	330
7	Oskemen	320
8	Semey	291
9	Aktobe	264
10	Uralsk	235
11	Kostanay	231
12	Petropavl	194
13	Temirtau	169
14	Akmechet	169
15	Aktau	167
16	Atyrau	147
17	Ekibastuz	145
18	Kokshetau	123
19	Rudni	117
20	Taldykorgan	107
21	Zhezkazgan	104
22	Turkistan	100
23	Balkhash	81
24	Sarkand	76

MEDALS TABLE

		Overall			League			Cup			Asia/Eur			City	Stadium	Cap'ty	DoF
		G	S	B	G	S	B	G	S	B	G	S	B				
1	Kairat Almaty	7	2	3	2		3	5	2					Almaty	Almaty Centralny	26 400	1952
2	Irtysh Pavlodar	6	5	3	5	3	3	1	2					Pavlodar	Centralny	12 000	1965
3	FK Astana (Ex Zhenis)	6	2	1	3		1	3	2					Astana	Kazhimukan Munaitpasov	12 343	1964
4	FK Semey	4		1	3		1	1						Semey	Spartak	11 000	
5	FK Taraz	2	4		1	2		1	2					Taraz	Centralny	12 000	1961
6	Vostock Oskemen	1	2					1	2					Oskemen	Vostock	12 000	1963
	FK Aktobe	1	2		1	1			1					Aktobe	Centralny	13 200	1967
8	Kaisar Kyzylorda	1	1					1	1					Kyzylorda	Gany Muratbayeva	7 000	1968
9	FK Almaty	1							1					Almaty	Almaty Centralny	26 400	2003
	Dostyk Almaty	1						1						Almaty			
11	Tobol Kostanay		3	3		2	3		1					Kostanay	Centralny	5 800	1967
12	Yesil-Bogatyr Petropavl		3	1		2	1		1					Petropavl	Avangard	12 000	1968
13	FK Atyrau		2			2								Atyrau	Munayshy	9 000	1980
	Ekibastuzetc		2			2								Ekibastuz	Shakhtyor	6 300	1979
	Ordabasy Shymkent		2			1			1					Shymkent	Munaytpasova	30 000	1998

RECENT LEAGUE AND CUP RECORD

	Championship						Cup		
Year	Champions	Pts	Runners-up	Pts	Third	Pts	Winners	Score	Runners-up
1995	Yelimay Semey	67	Taraz Zhambul	62	Shakhtyor Karagandy	60	Yelimay Semipal'sk	1-0	Ordabasy Shymkent
1996	Taraz Zhambul	76	Irtysh Pavlodar	74	Yelimay Semey	74	Kairat Almaty	2-0	Vostock Oskemen
1997	Irtysh Pavlodar	56	FC Taraz	56	Kairat Almaty	53	Not played due to season readjustment		
1998	Yelimay Semey	63	Batyr Ekibastuz	59	Irtysh Pavlodar	57	Irtysk Pavlodar	2-1	Kaysar Kzyl-Orda
1999	Irtysh Pavlodar	76	Yesil Petropavlovsk	72	Kairat Almaty	64	Kaysar Kzyl-Orda	1-1 2-0p	Vostock Oskemen
2000	Zhenis Astana	74	Yesil Petropavlovsk	74	Irtysh Pavlodar	60	Kairat Almaty	5-0	Yesil Petropavlovsk
2001							Zhenis Astana	1-1 5-4p	Irtysh Pavlodar
2001	Zhenis Astana	81	FK Atyrau	70	Yesil Petropavlovsk	69	Kairat Almaty	3-1	Zhenis Astana
2002	Irtysh Pavlodar	71	FK Atyrau	63	Tobol Kostanay	52	Zhenis Astana	1-0	Irtysh Pavlodar
2003	Irtysh Pavlodar	78	Tobol Kostanay	76	Zhenis Astana	64	Kairat Almaty	3-1	Tobol Kostanai
2004	Kairat Almaty	83	Irtysh Pavlodar	79	Tobol Kostanay	77	FC Taraz	1-0	Kairat Almaty
2005	Aktobe Lento	70	Tobol Kostanay	69	Kairat Almaty	62	Zhenis Astana	2-1	Kairat Almaty
2006	FK Astana	64	FK Aktobe	60	Tobol Kostanay	56	FK Almaty	3-1	FK Astana

Irtysh beat Taraz 1-0 in a play-off in 1997 • Zhenis beat Petropavlovsk 2-0 in a play-off in 2000 • Two cup competitions were held in 2001

KAZAKHSTAN 2006

SUPER LEAGUE

	Pl	W	D	L	F	A	Pts	Astana	Aktobe	Tobol	Shakhter	Almaty	Irtysh	Kairat	Ekibast'ts	Vostock	Taraz	Okzhetpes	Yesil	Ordabasy	Atyrau	Kaisar	Energetik
FK Astana †	30	19	7	4	45	23	64		1-0	0-2	4-1	1-0	0-0	2-1	0-0	3-1	0-1	0-0	3-1	2-0	3-2	2-3	3-1
FK Aktobe ‡	30	18	6	6	48	21	60	2-2		2-0	0-0	3-0	3-0	2-1	1-0	2-0	2-0	1-0	2-0	3-0	3-0	5-0	1-0
Tobol Kostanay	30	16	8	6	43	22	56	1-0	2-1		3-1	1-1	0-1	3-0	0-0	1-1	1-0	1-0	1-0	4-1	1-0	5-1	3-0
Shakhter Karagandy	30	15	5	10	35	24	50	0-1	0-0	1-0		1-0	1-2	1-1	1-0	3-0	2-1	5-0	2-0	3-2	3-1	2-1	1-0
FK Almaty ‡	30	13	9	8	36	29	48	1-3	4-2	0-0	1-0		1-0	**3-0**	2-1	1-0	2-1	0-0	1-1	1-0	1-0	3-0	0-1
Irtysh Pavlodar	30	13	8	9	34	24	47	0-1	1-2	1-0	1-0	3-2		0-0	1-0	2-2	3-0	1-0	5-0	1-1	0-0	2-0	0-1
Kairat Almaty	30	12	10	8	39	30	46	1-2	1-2	0-0	1-0	3-2	1-1		3-1	0-0	0-0	2-0	4-0	1-0	2-1	2-3	3-1
Ekibastuzetc	30	12	6	12	29	28	42	0-0	1-0	2-1	0-1	1-1	1-0	0-0		2-1	1-0	2-0	1-0	3-1	4-1	1-2	1-0
Vostock Oskemen	30	9	8	13	33	40	35	2-3	1-2	1-1	1-2	1-1	1-0	1-1	1-0		2-1	3-2	1-0	2-0	1-1	2-1	3-1
FK Taraz	30	9	6	15	32	34	33	1-2	1-1	2-3	1-0	1-2	1-1	1-2	2-0	2-2		1-0	3-0	3-2	3-0	3-0	2-1
Okzhetpes Kokshetau	30	8	9	13	23	36	33	1-1	0-0	1-1	0-0	0-1	0-2	1-4	2-1	1-0	1-0		2-0	1-1	1-0	2-1	3-1
Yesil-Bogatyr Petropavl	30	8	9	13	20	37	33	1-1	0-1	1-2	2-1	1-1	1-0	1-1	2-1	1-0	2-1	1-1		1-0	0-1	1-0	2-0
Ordabasy Shymkent	30	8	8	14	29	36	32	0-1	2-0	0-2	0-0	0-0	3-1	0-0	0-1	0-0	2-1	0-0	0-0		3-0	3-0	5-1
FK Atyrau	30	8	5	17	25	47	29	0-1	3-2	2-1	0-2	2-1	0-2	0-1	3-1	3-2	1-0	1-2	0-0	0-0		2-0	1-1
Kaisar Kyzylorda	30	8	4	18	29	53	28	0-1	0-2	1-1	0-1	1-2	0-0	2-1	0-1	3-1	1-0	3-1	1-1	1-2	1-1		2-1
Energetik Pavlodar	30	6	10	16	28	44	26	0-2	1-1	1-2	1-0	1-1	2-3	0-2	2-2	0-0	0-0	0-0	0-0	**3-0**	5-0	2-1	

8/04/2006 - 4/11/2006 • † Qualified for the UEFA Champions League • ‡ Qualified for the UEFA Cup • Matches in bold awarded 3-0
Top scorers: Jafar IRISMETOV, FK Almaty 17; Andrey FINONCHENKO, Shakhter 16; Sergiu ROGACIOV, Aktobe 16

KAZAKHSTAN 2006 — CONFERENCE NORTH-EAST (2)

	Pl	W	D	L	F	A	Pts
Avangard Petropavl	24	16	3	5	39	19	51
Asbest Jitikara	24	15	5	4	37	17	50
Bolat Temirtau	24	12	8	4	25	12	44
FK Semey	24	12	7	5	46	25	43
Kazakmis Satpayev	24	12	5	7	36	35	41
Shakhter-Yunost	24	11	5	8	41	25	38
Aksu Stepnogorsk	24	10	6	8	32	28	36
Irtysh-2 Pavlodar	24	10	4	10	38	28	34
Rahat Astana	24	9	6	9	27	26	33
Vostock-2 Oskemen	24	9	5	10	33	37	32
Tobol-2 Kostanay	24	4	4	16	20	41	16
Energetik-2 Pavlodar	24	4	2	18	17	47	14
Batyr Ekibastuz	24	2	0	22	13	64	6

4/05/2006 - 8/10/2006

KAZAKHSTAN 2006 — CONFERENCE SOUTH-WEST (2)

	Pl	W	D	L	F	A	Pts
Zhetysu Taldykorgan	26	25	1	0	119	14	76
Kaspiy Aktau	26	19	3	4	63	20	60
Gornyak Khromtau	26	17	1	8	40	25	52
Cesna Almaty	26	16	4	6	64	30	52
Temirzholshy Almaty	26	15	5	6	39	25	50
Zhayik Uralsk	26	16	1	9	56	31	49
Zhambil Taraz	26	9	8	9	35	30	35
Aktobe-Zhas	26	10	3	13	43	50	33
Munayli Atyrau	26	6	7	13	25	48	25
Ordabasy-2 Shymkent	26	7	3	16	34	65	24
Koksu Taldykorgan	26	6	2	18	32	59	20
Universitet Turkistan	26	5	4	17	29	57	19
Kaisar-Jas Kyzylorda	26	4	3	19	23	71	15
Zhastar Uralsk	26	3	3	20	12	89	12

4/05/2006 - 8/10/2006

FOOTBALL CUP OF KAZAKHSTAN 2006

Second round

FK Almaty *	3
FK Taraz	2
FK Atyrau *	0
Tobol Kostanay	2
Energetik Pavlodar	3 4p
Kairat Almaty *	3 3p
Yesil-Bogatyr Petropavl	0
Irtysh Pavlodar *	1
Shakhter Karagandy *	4
Zhetysu Taldykorgan	1
Ordabasy Shymkent	1
FK Aktobe *	5
Okzhetpes Kokshetau	3
Ekibastuzetc *	1
Vostock-2 Oskemen	0
FK Astana *	3

Quarter-finals

FK Almaty	2	1
Tobol Kostanay *	2	0
Energetik Pavlodar *	0	1
Irtysh Pavlodar	2	0
Shakhter Karagandy	1	1
FK Aktobe *	2	0
Okzhetpes Kokshetau *	0	0
FK Astana	0	1

Semi-finals

FK Almaty	1	2
Irtysh Pavlodar *	3	0
Shakhter Karagandy *	2	1
FK Astana	2	1

Final

FK Almaty	3
FK Astana	1

CUP FINAL
Centralny, Almaty
8-11-2006, Att: 4 700, Ref: Hrinák (SVK)
Scorers - Irismetov 3 [45] [103] [108] for Almaty; Jalmaghambetov [85] for Astana

* Home team in first leg • ‡ Qualified for the UEFA Cup

KEN – KENYA

NATIONAL TEAM RECORD
JULY 10TH 2006 TO JULY 12TH 2010

PL	W	D	L	F	A	%
10	2	2	6	6	9	30

FIFA/COCA-COLA WORLD RANKING

1993	1994	1995	1996	1997	1998	1999	2000	2001	2002	2003	2004	2005	2006	High		Low	
74	83	107	112	89	93	103	108	104	81	72	74	89	127	70	02/04	137	07/07

2006–2007											
08/06	09/06	10/06	11/06	12/06	01/07	02/07	03/07	04/07	05/07	06/07	07/07
117	127	129	132	127	128	127	128	122	124	126	137

Kenya had their suspension by FIFA lifted in March 2007, just in time to continue what has turned out to be a fruitless campaign in the 2008 African Nations Cup qualifiers. The country had been suspended by FIFA in October after failure to fulfill an agreement to bring the country's football structure back to normality, but with sufficient progress six months later, the suspension was rescinded. FIFA had first taken action against Kenya 2004 because of government interference in football activities and the past three years have seen little but chaos in the game. The latest FIFA action cost Kenya their place in the annual East and Central Senior Challenge Cup, a tournament

INTERNATIONAL HONOURS

Gossage Cup 1926 1931 1941 1942 1944 1946 1953 1958 1959 1960 1961 1966 **Challenge Cup** 1967 1971 **CECAFA Cup** 1975 1981 1982 1983 2002
CECAFA Club Championship Luo Union 1976 1977, AFC Leopards 1979 1982 1983 1984 1997, Gor Mahia 1985, Tusker 1988 1989 2000 2001

they last won in 2002. Kenyan clubs were also barred from playing in the 2007 African club competitions. Perhaps most embarrassing was the home defeat against Eritrea in the first of their African Nations Cup qualifiers, a result that precipitated the departure of Bernard Lama as coach in September. His successor Tom Olaba lasted just one match before Kenya called back Jacob Mulee for his third stint at the helm of the Harambee Stars. In June 2007, however, Kenya lost again to Eritrea as football in the country reached an all-time low.

THE FIFA BIG COUNT OF 2006

	Male	Female		Total
Number of players	1 952 326	88 776	Referees and Assistant Referees	3 700
Professionals	55		Admin, Coaches, Technical, Medical	48 310
Amateurs 18+	25 906		Number of clubs	690
Youth under 18	49 141		Number of teams	3 450
Unregistered	1 003 000		Clubs with women's teams	21
Total players	2 041 102		Players as % of population	5.88%

Kenya Football Federation (KFF)
Nyayo Stadium, PO Box 40234, Nairobi, Kenya
Tel +254 2 602310   Fax +254 2 602294
kffkenya@kff.co.ke   www.kff.co.ke
President: HATIMY Mohammed   General Secretary: OBINGO Sammy
Vice-President: KASUVE Titus Mutuku   Treasurer: TBD   Media Officer: GAITHO Francis
Men's Coach: MULEE Jacob   Women's Coach: None
KFF formed: 1960   CAF: 1968   FIFA: 1960
Red shirts with black trimmings, Red shorts, Red socks

RECENT INTERNATIONAL MATCHES PLAYED BY KENYA

2003	Opponents	Score		Venue	Comp	Scorers	Att	Referee
2-12	Eritrea	W	3-2	Kassala	CCr1	Omondi [27], Mathenge [91+], Mulama [93+]		
4-12	Uganda	D	1-1	Kassala	CCr1	Sunguti [93+]		
8-12	Rwanda	D	1-1	Khartoum	CCsf	Omondi [44]. L 3-4p		
10-12	Sudan	W	2-1	Khartoum	CC3p	Sunguti [24], Omondi [35]		
12-12	Egypt	L	0-1	Manama	Fr			
15-12	Iraq	L	0-2	Manama	Fr			
18-12	Bahrain	L	1-2	Manama	Fr	Omondi [65]		
21-12	United Arab Emirates	D	2-2	Abu Dhabi	Fr	Omolisi [86], Juma [90]		
2004								
16-01	Libya	L	0-2	Zawyan	Fr			
19-01	Libya	L	0-2	Tripoli	Fr			
26-01	Mali	L	1-3	Bizerte	CNr1	Mulama [58]	6 000	Tessema ETH
30-01	Senegal	L	0-3	Bizerte	CNr1		13 500	Abd El Fatah EGY
2-02	Burkina Faso	W	3-0	Bizerte	CNr1	Ake [50], Oliech [63], Baraza [83]	4 550	Sowe GAM
7-08	Uganda	D	1-1	Kampala	Fr	Obua [27p]	25 000	
18-08	Uganda	W	4-1	Nairobi	Fr	Baraza 2 [11 33], Sirengo [65], Omondi [85]	5 000	
4-09	Malawi	W	3-2	Nairobi	WCq	Barasa 2 [21 29], Oliech [25]	13 000	Mwanza ZAM
9-10	Botswana	L	1-2	Gaborone	WCq	Oliech [5]	16 500	Colembi ANG
17-11	Guinea	W	2-1	Nairobi	WCq	Oliech [10], Mukenya [61]	16 000	Abd El Fatah EGY
12-12	Sudan	D	2-2	Addis Abeba	CCr1	Simiyu [37], Baraza [73]		
14-12	Somalia	W	1-0	Addis Abeba	CCr1	Baraza [7]		
18-12	Uganda	D	1-1	Addis Abeba	CCr1	Obua [77p]		
22-12	Ethiopia	D	2-2	Addis Abeba	CCsf	Mururi [66], Baraza [85]. L 4-5p	50 000	Ssegonga UGA
25-12	Sudan	L	1-2	Addis Abeba	CC3p	Baraza [82]		
2005								
9-02	Morocco	L	1-5	Rabat	WCq	Otieno [93+]	40 000	Tamuni LBY
12-03	Rwanda	D	1-1	Nairobi	Fr	Mkenya [25]		
23-03	Ghana	D	2-2	Nairobi	Fr	Baraza [44], Sunguti [87]		
26-03	Botswana	W	1-0	Nairobi	WCq	Oliech [44]	15 000	Buenkadila COD
5-06	Guinea	L	0-1	Conakry	WCq		21 000	Mbera GAB
18-06	Morocco	D	0-0	Nairobi	WCq		50 000	Diatta SEN
17-08	Tunisia	L	0-1	Rades	WCq		60 000	Evehe CMR
3-09	Tunisia	L	0-2	Nairobi	WCq			Sowe GAM
8-10	Malawi	L	0-3	Blantyre	WCq		12 000	Codjia BEN
2006								
11-08	Ethiopia	L	0-1	Addis Abeba	Fr			
13-08	Ethiopia	L	0-1	Addis Abeba	Fr			
2-09	Eritrea	L	1-2	Nairobi	CNq	Mambo [64]		Lwanja MWI
30-09	Tanzania	D	0-0	Dar es Salaam	Fr			
8-10	Angola	L	1-3	Luanda	CNq	Ambani [81]		Lwanja MWI
2007								
25-03	Swaziland	W	2-0	Nairobi	CNq	Mariga [51], Oboya [75]		Seechurn MRI
27-05	Nigeria	L	0-1	Nairobi	Fr			
3-06	Swaziland	D	0-0	Mbabane	CNq			
10-06	Rwanda	W	2-0	Nairobi	Fr	Mulinge [10p], Ambani [20]		
16-06	Eritrea	L	0-1	Asmara	CNq			

Fr = Friendly match • CN = CAF African Cup of Nations • CC = CECAFA Cup • WC = FIFA World Cup
q = qualifier • r1 = first round group • sf = semi-final • 3p = third place play-off • f = final

KENYA NATIONAL TEAM RECORDS AND RECORD SEQUENCES

Records			Sequence records					
Victory	9-0	TAN 1956	Wins	5	1993	Clean sheets	7	1983
Defeat	0-13	GHA 1965	Defeats	7	1932-1940	Goals scored	16	1931-1948
Player Caps	n/a		Undefeated	10	1997-1998	Without goal	7	2005-2006
Player Goals	n/a		Without win	10	1984-85, 2005-06	Goals against	16	1931-1948

KENYA COUNTRY INFORMATION

Capital	Nairobi	Independence	1963 from the UK	GDP per Capita	$1 000
Population	32 021 586	Status	Republic	GNP Ranking	84
Area km²	582 650	Language	Kiswahili, English	Dialling code	+254
Population density	55 per km²	Literacy rate	90%	Internet code	.ke
% in urban areas	28%	Main religion	Christian 78%, Muslim 10%	GMT + / –	+3
Towns/Cities ('000)	Nairobi 2 750; Mombasa 799; Nakuru 260; Eldoret 218; Kisumu 216; Ruiru 114; Thika 99				
Neighbours (km)	Ethiopia 861; Somalia 682; Tanzania 769; Uganda 933; Sudan 232; Indian Ocean 536				
Main stadia	Kasarani – Nairobi 60 000; Nyayo – Nairobi 20 000				

PRESIDENT'S CUP 2007

Quarter–finals		Semi–finals		Final	
Sofapaka	4				
Kenyatta N. Hospital	0	Sofapaka	1		
Sacramento	1	Nakuru Police	0		
Nakuru Police	2			Sofapaka	2
Gor Mahia	0 2			Homegrown	0
Kenya Revenue	0 1	Gor Mahia	1		
Green Berets	0	Homegrown	2		
Homegrown	1				

Nyayp, Nairobi
1-07-2007
Scorer - James Kiarie 2 [53] [61]

RECENT LEAGUE AND CUP RECORD

	Championship						Cup		
Year	Champions	Pts	Runners-up	Pts	Third	Pts	Winners	Score	Runners-up
1996	Kenya Breweries	71	AFC Leopards	65	Eldoret KCC	63	Mumias Sugar	1-0	Reli
1997	Utalii	66	Gor Mahia	64	Mumias Sugar	62	Eldoret KCC	4-1	AFC Leopards
1998	AFC Leopards	69	Mumias Sugar	66	Gor Mahia	60	Mathare United	2-1	Eldoret KCC
1999	Tusker						Mumias Sugar	3-2	Coast Stars
2000	Tusker	6	Oserian Fastac	4	Mumias Sugar	4	Mathare United	2-1	AFC Leopards
2001	Oserian Fastac	88	Mathare United	81	Mumias Sugar	68	AFC Leopards	2-0	Mathare United
2002	Oserian Fastac	†	Nzoia Sugar				Pipeline	1-0	Mumias Sugar
2003	Ulinzi Stars	†	Coast Stars				Chemelil	1-0	AFC Leopards
2004	Ulinzi Stars	†	Tusker				KCB	1-0	Thika United
2005	Ulinzi Stars	†	Tusker				World Hope	2-1	Tusker
2006	Sony Sugar	75	Tusker	74	Thika United				
2007							Sofapaka	2-0	Homegrown

† Championship play-offs • 2002: Oserian Fastac 2-2 1-0 Nzoia Sugar • 2003: Ulinzi Stars 3-3 4-2p Coast Stars • 2004: Ulinzi Stars 2-2 4-3p Tusker • 2005: Ulinzi Stars 0-0 4-2p Tusker • The original final in 2003 was won by Nzoia Sugar, who beat Tusker 2-1. It was declared void by the KFF after a number of clubs broke away. The 2003 Moi Golden Cup was also disrupted with Utalii beating Gor Mahia 2-1 in an alternative final. The dispute between the KFF, the breakaway clubs and the Kenyan Sports Ministry saw the 2004 season badly affected which lead to the intervention of FIFA and the creation of Stake-holders Transition Committee (STC). Two separate championships had been played but a play-off for all the leading clubs was organised to qualify for CAF competitions

KGZ – KYRGYZSTAN

NATIONAL TEAM RECORD
JULY 10TH 2006 TO JULY 12TH 2010

PL	W	D	L	F	A	%
3	0	0	3	0	9	0

FIFA/COCA-COLA WORLD RANKING

1993	1994	1995	1996	1997	1998	1999	2000	2001	2002	2003	2004	2005	2006	High	Low
-	166	172	168	140	151	159	174	164	171	157	150	157	139	**119** 08/06	**175** 11/03

2006–2007											
08/06	09/06	10/06	11/06	12/06	01/07	02/07	03/07	04/07	05/07	06/07	07/07
119	125	134	142	139	138	139	145	151	153	149	152

There was a certain inevitability to the 2006 season in Kyrgyzstan and sure enough Dordoy-Dinamo walked off with the double for the third year running. They lost just once all season in the league - against Muras-Sport in the first stage - although they did need a play-off victory against Abdish-Ata to secure the title after both clubs finished level on points in the final stage of the campaign. In the play-off an Andrey Krasnov goal secured the title for Dordoy-Dinamo in a 1-0 victory. The League defeat against Muras-Sport was Dordoy-Dinamo's only reverse all season as they made their way to an all to predictable Cup Final meeting with Zhashtyk, who were appearing

INTERNATIONAL HONOURS
None

in their sixth consecutive final. Zhashtyk had lost the first three of those to SKA-PVO Bishkek and their 4-0 defeat in the 2006 final meant a third straight defeat in the final at the hands of Dordoy-Dinamo and a new world record of six consecutive Cup Final defeats. Previously Zhashtyk had held the record jointly with USM Alger and Jordan's Al Ramtha. The only national team action of the season came in the Alma TV Cup held in Shymkent, Kazakhstan - but defeats against the hosts, Uzbekistan and Azerbaijan left Kyrgyzstan rooted firmly to the bottom of the table and on a run of five consecutive defeats without scoring.

THE FIFA BIG COUNT OF 2006

	Male	Female		Total
Number of players	116 605	7 872	Referees and Assistant Referees	69
Professionals	0		Admin, Coaches, Technical, Medical	1 425
Amateurs 18+	7 985		Number of clubs	100
Youth under 18	460		Number of teams	500
Unregistered	50 500		Clubs with women's teams	0
Total players	124 477		Players as % of population	2.39%

Football Federation of Kyrgyz Republic (FFKR)

Kurenkeeva Street 195, PO Box 1484, Bishkek 720 040, Kyrgyzstan
Tel +996 312 670573   Fax +996 312 670573
media@ffkr.kg   www.ffkr.kg
President: MURALIEV Amangeldi   General Secretary: BERDYBEKOV Klichbek
Vice-President: KUTUEV Omurbek   Treasurer: DJAMANGULOVA Raiham   Media Officer: TOKABAEV Kemel
Men's Coach: PODKORYTOV Boris   Women's Coach: UMATALIEVA Gulbara
FFKR formed: 1992   AFC: 1994   FIFA: 1994
Red shirts, Red shorts, Red socks

RECENT INTERNATIONAL MATCHES PLAYED BY KYRGYZSTAN

2002	Opponents	Score		Venue	Comp	Scorers	Att	Referee
No international matches played in 2002								
2003								
16-03	Afghanistan	L	1-2	Kathmandu	ACq	Gulov [60]		
20-03	Nepal	W	2-0	Kathmandu	ACq	Nikov 2 [27 47]		
29-11	Pakistan	W	2-0	Karachi	WCq	Boldygin [36], Chikishev [59]	10 000	Nesar BAN
3-12	Pakistan	W	4-0	Bishkek	WCq	Chikishev [18], Chertkov [28], Boldygin [67], Krasnov [9]	12 000	Mamedov TKM
2004								
18-02	Tajikistan	L	1-2	Bishkek	WCq	Berezovsky [12]	14 000	Lutfullin UZB
31-03	Syria	D	1-1	Bishkek	WCq	Ishenbaev.A [55]	17 000	Bose IND
5-06	Qatar	D	0-0	Doha	Fr			
9-06	Bahrain	L	0-5	Al Muharraq	WCq		2 800	Al Saeedi UAE
8-09	Bahrain	L	1-2	Bishkek	WCq	Kenjisariev [86]	10 000	Rungklay THA
13-10	Tajikistan	L	1-2	Dushanbe	WCq	Chikishev [84]	11 000	El Enezi KUW
10-11	Kuwait	L	0-3	Kuwait City	Fr			
17-11	Syria	W	1-0	Damascus	WCq	Amin [47]	1 000	Tongkhan THA
2005								
No international matches played in 2005								
2006								
2-04	Pakistan	L	0-1	Dhaka	CCr1		2 500	Shamsuzzaman BAN
6-04	Tajikistan	W	1-0	Dhaka	CCr1	Krasnov [22]	2 000	AK Nema IRQ
7-04	Macao	W	2-0	Dhaka	CCr1	Ablakimov [35], Ishenbaev.A [58]	1 000	Tan Hai CHN
9-04	Palestine	W	1-0	Dhaka	CCqf	Djamshidov [91]	150	U Win Cho MYA
13-04	Tajikistan	L	0-2	Dhaka	CCsf		2 000	Tan Hai CHN
5-07	Kazakhstan	L	0-1	Almaty	Fr			
2007								
7-03	Kazakhstan	L	0-2	Shymkent	Fr			
9-03	Uzbekistan	L	0-6	Shymkent	Fr			
11-03	Azerbaijan	L	0-1	Shymkent	Fr			

Fr = Friendly match • AC = AFC Asian Cup • CC = AFC Challenge Cup • WC = FIFA World Cup
q = qualifier • r1 = first round group • qf = quarter-final • sf = semi-final

KYRGYZSTAN NATIONAL TEAM RECORDS AND RECORD SEQUENCES

Records			Sequence records				
Victory	6-0	MDV 1997	Wins	3	2003, 2006	Clean sheets	3	2003, 2006
Defeat	0-7	IRN 1997	Defeats	8	1999-2001	Goals scored	7	2001-2004
Player Caps	30	SALO Vladimir	Undefeated	3	2003, 2006	Without goal	6	1994-1996
Player Goals	3	Four players	Without win	8	1999-2001	Goals against	8	1991-2001

KYRGYZSTAN COUNTRY INFORMATION

Capital	Bishkek	Independence	1991 from Soviet Union	GDP per Capita	$1 600
Population	5 081 429	Status	Republic	GNP Ranking	148
Area km²	198 500	Language	Kyrgyz, Russian	Dialling code	+996
Population density	25 per km²	Literacy rate	97%	Internet code	.kg
% in urban areas	39%	Main religion	Muslim 75%, Orthodox 20%	GMT +/−	+6
Towns/Cities ('000)	Bishkek 896; Os 230; Celabad 77; Karakol 70; Tokmak 63; Karabalta 63; Balikici 45				
Neighbours (km)	Kazakhstan 1 051; China 858; Tajikistan 870; Uzbekistan 1 099				
Main stadia	Spartak – Bishkek 23 000; Dynamo – Bishkek 10 000				

KYRGYZSTAN 2006

FIRST DIVISION FIRST ROUND GROUP A

	Pl	W	D	L	F	A	Pts	Dordoy	Abdish	Muras	Sher-Ak	U-17
Dordoy-Dinamo †	16	13	2	1	42	11	41		1-1 3-1	2-0 1-2	1-0 2-1	6-1 7-0
Abdish-Ata Kant †	16	7	6	3	45	23	27	1-1 2-3		5-0 4-1	2-2 1-1	9-3 4-1
Muras-Sport Bishkek †	16	7	1	8	26	31	22	0-3 0-1	3-3 2-1		0-1 2-1	5-0 4-1
Sher-Ak Dan Bisjkek †	16	6	3	7	24	22	21	0-1 0-1	2-2 0-2	4-1 2-4		3-0 2-1
Kyrgyzstan U-17	16	1	0	15	13	63	3	1-5 1-4	0-4 0-3	0-2 2-0	1-3 1-2	

21/04/2006 - 5/08/2006 • † Qualified for the final round • Sher-Ak qualified after Shakhtyor withdrew

KYRGYZSTAN 2006

FIRST DIVISION FIRST ROUND GROUP B

	Pl	W	D	L	F	A	Pts	Zhashtyk	Alay	Shakhtyor	Ak-Bura	Dinamo	Dostuk
Zhashtyk Kara-Su †	10	8	1	1	44	8	25		2-1	6-1	3-0	8-0	11-0
Alay Osh †	10	6	1	3	37	8	19	0-0		4-0	3-0	9-0	6-0
Shakhtyor Kizil-Kiya †	10	6	0	4	32	23	18	4-3	3-2		4-0	5-2	9-1
Ak-Bura Osh	10	3	1	6	11	26	10	0-4	1-7	2-1		2-0	5-2
Dinamo Aravan	10	3	1	6	11	36	10	1-3	1-0	3-2	0-0		3-2
Dostuk Ozgön	10	2	0	8	14	48	6	1-4	1-5	0-3	2-1	5-1	

22/04/2006 - 1/07/2006 • † Qualified for the final round • Shakhtyor withdrew before the final round

KYRGYZSTAN 2006

FIRST DIVISION FINAL STAGE

	Pl	W	D	L	F	A	Pts	Dordoy	Abdish	Zhashtyk	Muras	Alay	Sher-Ak
Dordoy-Dinamo Naryn	10	7	3	0	29	1	24		0-0	5-0	6-0	3-0	5-0
Abdish-Ata Kant	10	7	3	0	16	2	24	0-0		1-1	1-0	2-0	2-0
Zhashtyk Kara-Su	10	5	3	2	17	13	18	0-0	1-3		4-1	2-1	1-0
Muras-Sport Bishkek	10	2	1	7	10	29	7	1-2	0-4	0-5		2-2	4-1
Alay Osh	10	1	3	6	8	16	6	0-2	0-2	0-0	3-0		1-1
Sher-Ak Dan Bishkek	10	1	1	8	7	26	4	0-6	0-1	2-3	1-2	2-1	

3/09/2006 - 21/10/2006 • Play-off: Bishkek, 25-10-2006, Dordoy-Dinamo 1-0 Abdish-Ata (Andrey Krasnov [15])
Top scorers (overall): Vycheslav PRYANISHNIKOV, Abdish-Ata 24; Yevgeniy BOLDYGIN, Zhashtyk 21

KYRGYZSTAN CUP 2006

Second round		Quarter–finals		Semi–finals		Final	
Dordoy-Dinamo Naryn	6						
Kyrgyzstan U-17 *	0	Dordoy-Dinamo Naryn*	2 1				
Ala-Too Naryn *	0	Abdysh-Ata Kant	0 1				
Abdysh-Ata Kant	6			Dordoy-Dinamo Naryn	2 4		
Tekhnolog Talas	2			Sher-Ak-Dan Bishkek*	0 1		
Egrisi-Bereket Bishkek*	1	Tekhnolog Talas	1 0				
Isik-Kol Karakol *	1	Sher-Ak-Dan Bishkek*	2 1				
Sher-Ak-Dan Bishkek	2					Dordoy-Dinamo Naryn	4
Alay Osh	w-0					Zhashtyk Kara-Su	0
Kurbanov-100		Alay Osh *	1 3				
Dinamo Aravan	0	Shakhtyor Kizil-Kiya	0 3				
Shakhtyor Kizil-Kiya *	5			Alay Osh	0 1		
Ak-Bura Osh	w-0			Zhashtyk Kara-Su *	0 2		
FK Nooken		Ak-Bura Osh *	1 0				
FK Jalalabat *	2	Zhashtyk Kara-Su	4 5				
Zhashtyk Kara-Su *	3			* Home team in first leg			

CUP FINAL

Spartak Stadium, Bishkek, 31-08-2006
Att: 10 000, Ref: Busurmankulov

Scorers - Malikov OG [26], Kasimov [33], Kudrenko [65], Krasnov [85] for Dordoy-Dinamo

KOR – KOREA REPUBLIC

NATIONAL TEAM RECORD
JULY 10TH 2006 TO JULY 12TH 2010

PL	W	D	L	F	A	%
17	6	6	5	22	14	52.9

For a nation that has so utterly dominated the FIFA World Cup qualifying competitions in Asia for the past twenty years, it is extraordinary that you have to go back to 1988 for the last time that South Korea appeared in the AFC Asian Cup Final, and you have to go way back to 1960 for the last time that they actually won it. The task facing Pim Verbeek on taking over as national team coach after the World Cup was to re-write the history books, but yet again the Koreans failed to live up to the lofty expectations of their fans. Based in Jakarta for the first round, a weakened team without English based stars Park Ji Sung, Seol Ki Hyeon and Lee Young Po as well as playmaker Kim Nam Il, very nearly didn't make it past the first stage after suffering an embarrassing defeat at the hands of Bahrain, although a 1-0 win against the hosts did see them squeeze through to the knock-out stage. They were then involved in three penalty shoot-outs after three successive 0-0 draws. The first of them, in the quarter-finals against Iran, went their way but their luck ran out in the semi-finals when they lost to Iraq. The third shoot-out, this time against Japan saw them seal third place in the tournament but that was little consolation for once again missing out on the main

INTERNATIONAL HONOURS

Qualified for the FIFA World Cup finals 1954 1986 1990 1994 1998 2002 2006 Qualified for the FIFA Women's World Cup finals 2003

AFC Asian Cup 1956 1960 Asian Games Football Tournament 1970 (shared) 1978 (shared) 1986 East Asian Championship 2003

AFC Youth Championship 1959 1960 1963 1978 1980 1982 1990 1996 1998 2002 2004 AFC U-17 Championship 1986 2002

AFC Champions League Daewoo Royals 1986, Ilhwa Chunma 1996, Pohang Steelers 1997 1998, Suwon Samsung Bluewings 2001 2002

prize. In the 2006 AFC Champions League unfancied Jeonbuk Motors won a strong first round group ahead of Dalian and Gamba Osaka and then beat Shanghai Shenhua and fellow Koreans Ulsan Hyundai Horang-i on the way to a final against Al Karama from Syria. Their victory in the final came courtesy of two Brazilians - Botti who scored in the last minute of the first leg to give Jeonbuk a 2-0 victory, and Ze Carlo whose 86th minute goal in the second leg gave the Koreans a 3-2 aggregate win. The 2006 domestic season saw three different clubs get their hands on the three trophies up for grabs. In the K-League, the most successful team in the country - if not the most popular - were back to their winning ways as Seongnam Ilhwa Chunma claimed their seventh title after beating Suwon Samsung Bluewings - the best supported club - in the final. After looking a good bet to win the first League and FA Cup double in Korean football, Bluewings had a miserable end to the season as they also lost in the FA Cup final against Chunnam Dragons, who claimed the trophy for the second time. FC Seoul were the season's other winners, finishing top of the Samsung Hauzen Cup table ahead of Seongnam Ilhwa Chunma. It was their first trophy since the controversial move away from Anyang to the capital in 2004 caused such an uproar.

Korea Football Association (KFA)
1-131 Sinmunno, 2-ga, Jongno-Gu, Seoul 110-062, Korea Republic
Tel +82 2 7336764   Fax +82 2 7352755
fantasista@kfa.or.kr   www.kfa.or.kr
President: CHUNG Mong Joon Dr   General Secretary: KA Sam Hyun
Vice-President: KIM Ho Kon   Treasurer: CHUNG Dong Hwan   Media Officer: SONG Ki Ryong
Men's Coach: VERBEEK Pim   Women's Coach: AN Jong Goan
KFA formed: 1928   AFC: 1954   FIFA: 1948
Red shirts with blue trimmings, Blue shorts, Red socks

RECENT INTERNATIONAL MATCHES PLAYED BY KOREA REPUBLIC

2004	Opponents	Score		Venue	Comp	Scorers	Att	Referee
31-07	China PR	D	1-1	Daejon	EAC	Kim Jin Kyu [74]	25 374	Nishimura JPN
4-08	Korea DPR	D	0-0	Jeonju	EAC		27 455	Ghahremani IRN
7-08	Japan	L	0-1	Daejon	EAC		42 753	Tan Hai CHN
14-08	Korea DPR	W	3-0	Seoul	Fr	Chung Kyung Ho [34], Kim Jin Ryong [36], Park Chu Young [68]		
17-08	Saudi Arabia	L	0-1	Seoul	WCq		61 586	Kunsuta THA
12-10	Iran	W	2-0	Seoul	Fr	Cho Won Hee [1], Kim Jin Kyu [90]	61 457	Al Ghamdi KSA
12-11	Sweden	D	2-2	Seoul	Fr	Ahn Jung Hwan [7], Kim Young Chul [51]	59 113	Wan Daxue CHN
16-11	Serbia & Montenegro	W	2-0	Seoul	Fr	Choi Jin Cheul [4], Lee Dong Gook [66]	40 127	
2006								
18-01	United Arab Emirates	L	0-1	Dubai	Fr			Al Hilali OMA
21-01	Greece	D	1-1	Riyadh	Fr	Park Chu Young [24]		Al Shehri KSA
25-01	Finland	W	1-0	Riyadh	Fr	Park Chu Young [46]	800	Al Jerman KSA
29-01	Croatia	W	2-0	Hong Kong	Fr	Kim Dong Jin [35], Lee Chin Soo [49]	16 841	Fong Yau Fat HKG
1-02	Denmark	L	1-3	Hong Kong	Fr	Cho Jae Jin [13]	13 971	Fong Yau Fat HKG
11-02	Costa Rica	L	0-1	Oakland	Fr			Vaughn USA
15-02	Mexico	W	1-0	Los Angeles	Fr	Lee Dong Gook [14]	64 128	Salazar USA
22-02	Syria	W	2-1	Aleppo	ACq	Kim D Heon [5], Lee Chin Soo [50]	35 000	Maidin SIN
1-03	Angola	W	1-0	Seoul	Fr	Park Chu Young [22]	63 255	Supian MAS
23-05	Senegal	D	1-1	Seoul	Fr	Kim Do Heon [74]	64 836	
26-05	Bosnia-Herzegovina	W	2-0	Seoul	Fr	Seol Ki Hyeon [50], Cho Jae Jin [92+]	64 835	Cheung Yim Yau HKG
1-06	Norway	D	0-0	Oslo	Fr		15 487	Verbist BEL
4-06	Ghana	L	1-3	Edinburgh	Fr	Lee Eul Yong [50]	15 000	McDonald SCO
13-06	Togo	W	2-1	Frankfurt	WCr1	Lee Chun Soo [54], Ahn Jung Hwan [72]	48 000	Poll ENG
18-06	France	D	1-1	Leipzig	WCr1	Park Ji Sung [81]	43 000	Archundia MEX
23-06	Switzerland	L	0-2	Hannover	WCr1		43 000	Elizondo ARG
16-08	Chinese Taipei	W	3-0	Taipei	ACq	Ahn Jung Hwan [32], Jung Jo Gook [55], Kim Do Heon [81]	1 300	Sarkar IND
2-09	Iran	D	1-1	Seoul	ACq	Seol Ki Hyeon [46]	63 113	Breeze AUS
6-09	Chinese Taipei	W	8-0	Suwon	ACq	Seol Ki Hyeon 2 [4 43], Jung Jo Gook 3 [5 46+ 88], Cho Jae Jin 2 [64 83p], Kim Do Heon [78]	21 053	Arambakade SRI
8-10	Ghana	L	1-3	Seoul	Fr	Kim Dong Hun [63]	36 515	Takayama JPN
11-10	Syria	D	1-1	Seoul	ACq	Cho Jae Jin [9]	24 140	Kunsuta THA
15-11	Iran	L	0-2	Tehran	ACq		30 000	Ebrahim BHR
2007								
6-02	Greece	W	1-0	London	Fr	Lee Chun Soo	9 242	Dean ENG
24-03	Uruguay	L	0-2	Seoul	Fr		42 159	Ogiya JPN
2-06	Netherlands	L	0-2	Seoul	Fr		62 884	Ramachandran MAS
29-06	Iraq	W	3-0	Jeju	Fr	Yeom Ki Hun [5], Lee Chun Soo [34], Lee Keun Ho [40]	32 642	Tojo JPN
5-07	Uzbekistan	W	2-1	Seoul	Fr	Cho Jae Jin 2 [5 19]	21 019	Prayoon THA
11-07	Saudi Arabia	D	1-1	Jakarta	ACr1	Choi Sung Kuk [65]	15 000	Shield AUS
15-07	Bahrain	L	0-1	Jakarta	ACr1		9 000	Sun Baojie CHN
18-07	Indonesia	W	1-0	Jakarta	ACr1	Kim Jung Woo [34]	87 000	Shield AUS
22-07	Iran	D	0-0	Kuala Lumpur	ACqf	W 4-2p	68 629	Al Badwawi UAE
25-07	Iraq	D	0-0	Kuala Lumpur	ACsf	L 3-4p	12 500	Al Fadhli KUW
28-07	Japan	D	0-0	Palembang	AC3p		10 000	Al Badwawi UAE

Fr = Friendly match • AC = AFC Asian Cup • EAC = East Asian Championship • WC = FIFA World Cup
q = qualifier • r1 = first round group • qf = quarter-final • sf = semi-final • 3p = third place play-off

KOREA REPUBLIC NATIONAL TEAM RECORDS AND RECORD SEQUENCES

Records			Sequence records					
Victory	16-0	NEP 2003	Wins	11	1975, 1978	Clean sheets	9	1970, 1988-1989
Defeat	0-12	SWE 1948	Defeats	3	Seven times	Goals scored	23	1975-76, 1977-78
Player Caps	136	HONG Myung Bo	Undefeated	28	1977-1978	Without goal	3	Four times
Player Goals	55	CHA Bum Kun	Without win	8	1981-1982	Goals against	11	1948-1953

REPUBLIC OF KOREA; TAEHAN-MIN'GUK

Capital Seoul	Language Korean		Independence 1945
Population 48 846 823	Area 98 480 km²	Density 493 per km²	% in cities 81%
GDP per cap $17 800	Dailling code +82	Internet .kr	GMT + / - +9

MAJOR CITIES/TOWNS

		Population '000
1	Seoul	10 451
2	Busan	3 663
3	Incheon	2 657
4	Daegu	2 591
5	Daejeon	1 515
6	Gwangju	1 442
7	Goyang	1 413
8	Suwon	1 368
9	Seongnam	1 072
10	Ulsan	1 002
11	Bucheon	852
12	Shiheung	796
13	Jeonju	747
14	Anyang	653
15	Changwon	545
16	Uijongbu	534
17	Kimhae	407
18	Jeju	347
19	Pohang	298
20	Gangneung	229
21	Gimpo	203
22	Icheon	190
23	Gwangyang	138
24	Seogwipo	98

MEDALS TABLE

		Overall			League			Cup			LC			Asia			City	Stadium	Cap'ty	DoF
		G	S	B	G	S	B	G	S	B	G	S	B	G	S	B				
1	Seongnam Ilhwa Chunma	11	8		7	1			2	3	3			1	2		Seongnam	Seongnam	27 000	1989
2	Suwon Samsung Bluewings	11	5	3	3	2	3	1	2	5				2	1		Suwon	World Cup	44 047	1996
3	Busan I'Park	9	5	7	4	3	2	1		3	2	4		1		1	Busan	Asiad Main	55 982	1983
4	Pohang Steelers	7	8	4	3	4	3	1	2	1	2	1	2				Pohang	Steel Yard	25 000	1973
5	Ulsan Hyundai Horang-i	5	8	7	3	4	4		1	2	3	1				2	Ulsan	Big Crown	43 550	1983
6	FC Seoul	5	8	1	3	4		1			3	1		1	1		Seoul	World Cup	64 677	1983
7	Jeju United	4	7	4	1	4	4		1	3	2						Seogwipo	World Cup	42 256	1982
8	Jeonbuk Hyundai Motors	4	1	2				3				1	1	1	1		Jeonju	World Cup	42 477	1993
9	Chunnam Dragons	2	5	1		1	1	2	1		2			1			Gwangyang	Gwangyang	14 284	1997
10	Daejeon Citizen	1	1					1			1						Daejeon	World Cup	42 176	1997
11	Gimpo Halleluyah	1			1												Gimpo	Gimpo	10 000	1980
12	Incheon United		1			1											Incheon	Munhak	51 179	2003
	Ulsan Mipo Dockyard	1							1								Ulsan	Mipo	2 500	1988
14	Gyeongnam FC			1							1						Changwon	Changwon	27 085	2005
15	Daegu FC																Daegu	World Cup	68 014	2002
	Gwangju Sangmu Phoenix																Gwangju	Guus Hidink	42 880	1985

NAME CHANGES Ilhwa Chunma → Seongnam Ilhwa Chunma • Daewoo Royals → Pusan Daewoo Royals → Pusan Icons → Busan I-Park • POSCO Dolphins → POSCO Atoms → Pohang Atoms → Pohang Steelers • Lucky Goldstar → Anyang LG Cheetahs → FC Seoul • Yukong Elephants → Puchong Yukong → Puchong SK → Bucheon SK→ Jeju United • All clubs adopted the revised official Korean spellings in 2000

RECENT LEAGUE AND CUP RECORD

	National Championship				Cup		
Year	Champions	Score/Runners-up	Runners-up/Third		Winners	Score	Runners-up
1997	Pusan Royals	37 Chunnam Dragons 36	Ulsan Horang-i 30		Pohang Steelers	0-0 7-6p	Suwon Bluewings
1998	Suwon Bluewings	1-0 0-0	Ulsan Horang-i		Chunnam Dragons	1-0	Ilhwa Chunma
1999	Suwon Bluewings	59 Bucheon SK 47	Chunnam Dragons 38		Anyang Cheetahs	2-1	Ulsan Horang-i
2000	Anyang Cheetahs	4-1 1-1 (4-2p)	Bucheon SK		Chonbuk Hyundai	2-0	Ilhwa Chunma
2001	Ilhwa Chunma	45 Anyang Cheetahs 43	Suwon Bluewings 41		Daejeon Citizen	1-0	Pohang Steelers
2002	Ilhwa Chunma	49 Ulsan Horang-i 47	Suwon Bluewings 45		Suwon Bluewings	1-0	Pohang Steelers
2003	Ilhwa Chunma	91 Ulsan Horang-i 73	Suwon Bluewings 72		Chonbuk Hyundai	2-2 4-2p	Chunnam Dragons
2004	Suwon Bluewings	0-0 0-0 4-3p	Pohang Steelers		Busan Icons	1-1 4-3p	Bucheon SK
2005	Ulsan Horang-i	5-1 1-2	Incheon United		Chonbuk Hyundai	1-0	Ulsan Dockyard
2006	Ilhwa Chunma	1-0 2-1	Suwon Bluewings		Chunnam Dragons	2-0	Suwon Bluewings

KOREA REPUBLIC 2006
K-LEAGUE FIRST STAGE

	Pl	W	D	L	F	A	Pts
Seongnam Ilhwa Chunma	13	10	2	1	21	9	32
Pohang Steelers	13	6	4	3	21	15	22
Daejeon Citizen	13	4	7	2	13	10	19
FC Seoul	13	3	7	3	13	10	16
Chunnam Dragons	13	2	10	1	14	12	16
Busan I'Park	13	4	4	5	24	25	16
Jeonbuk Hyundai Motors	13	3	7	3	13	14	16
Suwon Samsung Bluewings	13	3	7	3	11	13	16
Ulsan Hyundai Horang-i	13	3	6	4	9	13	15
Incheon United	13	2	8	3	11	13	14
Daegu FC	13	2	7	4	14	16	13
Gwangju Sangmu Phoenix	13	2	7	4	10	13	13
Gyeongnam FC	13	3	4	6	10	15	13
Jeju United	13	1	6	6	8	14	9

12/03/2006 - 10/05/2006

KOREA REPUBLIC 2006
K-LEAGUE SECOND STAGE

	Pl	W	D	L	F	A	Pts
Suwon Samsung Bluewings	13	8	3	2	18	9	27
Pohang Steelers	13	7	4	2	21	13	25
FC Seoul	13	6	5	2	18	12	23
Daegu FC	13	6	3	4	18	14	21
Ulsan Hyundai Horang-i	13	5	5	3	12	9	20
Incheon United	13	5	4	4	13	14	19
Chunnam Dragons	13	5	3	5	14	13	18
Busan I'Park	13	5	3	5	16	17	18
Seongnam Ilhwa Chunma	13	4	5	4	21	16	17
Jeju United	13	4	4	5	15	16	16
Gyeongnam FC	13	4	1	8	12	20	13
Daejeon Citizen	13	3	3	7	15	22	12
Jeonbuk Hyundai Motors	13	2	4	7	11	20	10
Gwangju Sangmu Phoenix	13	3	1	9	7	16	10

23/08/2006 - 15/117/2006

KOREA REPUBLIC 2006
K-LEAGUE OVERALL

	Pl	W	D	L	F	A	Pts	Ilhwa	Pohang	Suwon	Seoul	Ulsan	Chunnam	Daegu	Busan	Incheon	Daejeon	Jeonbuk	Gyeongnam	Jeju	Gwangju
Seongnam Ilhwa Chunma †	26	14	7	5	42	25	49		2-1	0-1	2-0	0-1	0-0	2-1	4-3	0-0	4-0	3-3	3-0	3-3	2-0
Pohang Steelers ‡	26	13	8	5	42	28	47	3-2		2-0	0-1	0-0	2-1	0-0	4-1	2-2	5-4	3-1	2-0	1-0	2-1
Suwon Samsung Bluewings †	26	11	10	5	29	22	43	3-0	1-2		1-1	1-0	1-1	0-0	1-4	1-0	1-1	2-2	2-0	2-1	1-0
FC Seoul ‡	26	9	12	5	31	22	39	2-2	3-1	1-1		2-2	0-0	1-2	5-2	0-0	1-1	1-1	1-0	1-0	0-0
Ulsan Hyundai Horang-i	26	8	11	7	21	22	35	1-3	0-1	1-2	0-0		1-0	1-0	1-1	2-2	3-1	0-0	1-0	2-2	1-0
Chunnam Dragons	26	7	13	6	28	25	34	1-1	2-2	1-0	0-2	1-0		1-1	1-3	3-0	2-2	0-0	1-1	2-2	2-1
Daegu FC	26	8	10	8	32	30	34	0-2	2-1	1-2	2-0	0-1	2-2		4-4	3-2	1-1	0-1	0-1	2-2	2-0
Busan I'Park	26	9	7	10	40	42	34	0-2	2-1	0-2	1-1	1-1	1-1	1-3		1-2	4-2	3-1	3-2	0-0	2-0
Incheon United	26	7	12	7	24	27	33	1-1	1-1	1-2	1-0	1-0	0-2	0-0	0-0		1-0	0-0	3-1	0-0	1-1
Daejeon Citizen	26	7	10	9	28	32	31	0-1	2-1	0-0	0-0	0-0	2-0	0-1	1-0	1-0		0-1	3-1	0-1	3-1
Jeonbuk Hyundai Motors	26	5	11	10	34	35	26	0-1	1-1	1-1	1-2	1-1	1-1	0-3	3-2	1-0	2-2		2-0	0-0	1-1
Gyeongnam FC	26	7	5	14	22	35	26	0-1	0-1	2-1	2-1	0-1	0-2	3-2	1-0	2-2	0-0	3-0		0-0	1-1
Jeju United	26	5	10	11	23	30	25	0-1	0-0	0-0	0-3	3-0	2-2	0-0	0-1	2-3	0-1	2-1	2-1		1-0
Gwangju Sangmu Phoenix	26	5	8	13	17	29	23	1-0	0-3	0-0	0-2	0-0	0-0	0-1	2-0	2-0	2-2	2-1	0-1	2-0	

† Qualified for the play-offs as stage winners • ‡ Qualified for play-offs thanks to overall record • Matches in bold played in the first stage

K-LEAGUE PLAY-OFFS 2006

Semi–finals

Seongnam Ilhwa Chunma	2
FC Seoul *	1

Pohang Steelers	0
Suwon Samsung Bluewings *	2

Finals

Seongnam Ilhwa Chunma †	1	2
Suwon Samsung Bluewings	0	1

* At home as stage winners
† Qualified for the 2006 AFC Champions Cup

K-LEAGUE PLAY-OFF 2006 1ST LEG
Incheon Munhak, Incheon, 27-11-2005

Ilhwa Chunma	1	Woo Sung Yong 88
Suwon Bluewings	0	

K-LEAGUE PLAY-OFF 2006 2ND LEG
Ulsan Big Crown, Ulsan, 4-12-2005

Suwon Bluewings	1	Silva 75
Ilhwa Chunma	2	Motta 2 25 65

KOREA REPUBLIC 2005 — N-LEAGUE (2) FIRST STAGE

	Pl	W	D	L	F	A	Pts
Goyang Kookmin Bank	10	8	2	0	26	8	26
Changwon City Office	10	7	0	3	20	13	21
Busan Kyotong	10	5	4	1	21	14	19
Ulsan Mipo Dockyard	10	6	1	3	23	17	19
Suwon City Office	10	4	4	2	14	11	16
Incheon Korail	10	4	3	3	14	13	15
Gimpo Halleluyah	10	3	3	4	11	12	12
Seosan Citizen	10	2	3	5	7	14	9
Daejeon Hydro & Nuclear	10	1	3	6	8	15	6
Icheon Hummel Korea	10	0	4	6	6	17	4
Gangneung City Office	10	1	1	8	5	21	4

7/04/2006 - 8/07/2006
Goyang qualified to meet second stage winners for the title

KOREA REPUBLIC 2005 — N-LEAGUE (2) SECOND STAGE

	Pl	W	D	L	F	A	Pts
Gimpo Halleluyah	10	7	2	1	16	8	23
Ulsan Mipo Dockyard	10	7	1	2	25	13	22
Suwon City Office	10	5	4	1	17	10	19
Incheon Korail	10	5	3	2	16	8	18
Gangneung City Office	10	4	4	2	14	11	16
Goyang Kookmin Bank	10	4	2	4	12	10	14
Busan Kyotong	10	3	4	3	13	11	13
Icheon Hummel Korea	10	2	3	5	13	18	9
Daejeon Hydro & Nuclear	10	2	2	6	10	22	8
Changwon City Office	10	1	3	6	11	22	6
Seosan Citizen	10	0	2	8	6	20	2

2/09/2006 - 18/11/2006
Championship play-off: Halleluyah 0-0 1-2 **Goyang Kookmin Bank**

KOREA REPUBLIC 2006 — SAMSUNG HAUZEN CUP

	Pl	W	D	L	F	A	Pts	Seoul	Ilhwa	Gyeongnam	Daejeon	Ulsan	Jeonbuk	Chunnam	Jeju	Pohang	Busan	Gwangju	Suwon	Daegu	Incheon
FC Seoul	13	8	3	2	20	11	27						4-1	1-2	1-0	3-4		1-0			1-0
Seongnam Ilhwa Chunma	13	6	4	3	16	12	22	1-1					2-2	1-0	0-1			2-1	0-1		2-1
Gyeongnam FC	13	7	1	5	16	14	22	1-2	1-3			1-2	1-2		1-0	2-0					
Daejeon Citizen	13	5	6	2	15	9	21	0-1	0-0				2-2		0-1		4-2		0-0		
Ulsan Hyundai Horang-i	13	6	3	4	17	12	21	0-1					0-1			2-0	1-0			3-0	1-3
Jeonbuk Hyundai Motors	13	6	2	5	15	13	20							0-1	0-2		0-1	2-0	1-0		3-0
Chunnam Dragons	13	6	2	5	14	13	20				0-2	0-0			1-1	1-2	0-1	2-0			3-4
Jeju United	13	6	2	5	12	12	20					2-1		2-1			0-1	1-0	2-0	1-1	2-0
Pohang Steelers	13	6	1	6	17	19	19	1-2	0-2	2-2	0-2						2-0		0-2		3-2
Busan I'Park	13	4	2	7	14	17	14	1-3		0-1		0-2						1-1	5-1	0-0	
Gwangju Sangmu Phoenix	13	4	2	7	9	14	14			0-1	0-0	1-2			2-1	1-0			1-1		3-2
Suwon Samsung Bluewings	13	2	6	5	9	14	12	1-1	1-1	1-1		0-1			0-1			0-1			2-0
Daegu FC	13	2	6	5	14	21	12	0-0		2-0	0-0				3-3			0-1	1-2		
Incheon United	13	1	4	8	11	18	7		0-1	2-3	0-1		0-0	1-2					1-1	0-0	

14/05/2006 - 29/07/2006 • Match in bold awarded 2-0

FIFA/COCA-COLA WORLD RANKING

1993	1994	1995	1996	1997	1998	1999	2000	2001	2002	2003	2004	2005	2006	High		Low	
41	35	46	44	27	17	51	40	42	20	22	22	29	51	**17**	12/98	**62**	02/96

2006–2007											
08/06	09/06	10/06	11/06	12/06	01/07	02/07	03/07	04/07	05/07	06/07	07/07
52	49	48	51	51	51	44	48	51	51	51	58

THE FIFA BIG COUNT OF 2006

	Male	Female		Total
Number of players	1 021 677	72 550	Referees and Assistant Referees	948
Professionals	550		Admin, Coaches, Technical, Medical	3 700
Amateurs 18+	12 372		Number of clubs	96
Youth under 18	18 205		Number of teams	864
Unregistered	423 100		Clubs with women's teams	4
Total players	1 094 227		Players as % of population	2.24%

HANA BANK KOREAN FA CUP 2006

First Round

Chunnam Dragons	2	
Hannam University	1	
Daejeon HNP	0	
Busan I'Park	1	
Joongang University	1	4p
Seongnam Ilhwa Chunma	1	2p
Daegu University	1	
Daegu FC	2	
Honam University	2	3p
Jeju United	2	1p
Gangneung	1	
Ulsan Mipo Dockyard	2	
Jeonbuk Hyundai Motors	2	
Gimpo Halleluyah	0	
Icheon Hummel	0	
Incheon United	2	
Goyang Kookmin Bank	0	3p
Ulsan Hyundai Horang-i	0	2p
Dongkuk University	0	
Gwangju Sangmu Phoenix	1	
Incheon Korail	2	5p
Suwon City	2	4p
Bongshin Club	1	
Gyeongnam FC	2	
FC Seoul	4	
Hongik University	0	
Changwon City	1	
Pohang Steelers	2	
Daejeon Citizen	4	
Seosan	1	
Soongsil University	0	
Suwon Samsung Bluewings	2	

Second Round

Chunnam Dragons	1	
Busan I'Park	0	
Joongang University	0	
Daegu FC	6	
Honam University	2	
Ulsan Mipo Dockyard	1	
Jeonbuk Hyundai Motors	0	3p
Incheon United	0	4p
Goyang Kookmin Bank	0	3p
Gwangju Sangmu Phoenix	0	1p
Incheon Korail	1	
Gyeongnam FC	2	
FC Seoul	3	
Pohang Steelers	1	
Daejeon Citizen	1	2p
Suwon Samsung Bluewings	1	4p

Quarter-finals

Chunnam Dragons	2	
Daegu FC	0	
Honam University	1	
Incheon United	2	
Goyang Kookmin Bank	1	5p
Gyeongnam FC	1	3p
FC Seoul	2	5p
Suwon Samsung Bluewings	2	6p

Semi-finals

Chunnam Dragons	0	4p
Incheon United	0	3p
Goyang Kookmin Bank	0	
Suwon Samsung Bluewings	2	

Final

Chunnam Dragons †	2
Suwon Samsung Bluewings	0

CUP FINAL

World Cup Stadium, Seoul
3-12-2005
Scorers - Song Jung Hyun 56, Kim Tae Soo 85

† Qualified for the AFC Champions Cup

KSA – SAUDI ARABIA

NATIONAL TEAM RECORD
JULY 10TH 2006 TO JULY 12TH 2010

PL	W	D	L	F	A	%
24	17	4	3	48	18	79.1

Job security is a concept alien to all but a few coaches around the world but in Saudi Arabia the lack of job security is often taken to extremes. National team coach Paqueta saw his Saudi side win 11 out of 14 games at the start of the 2006–07 season but was fired in March 2007 because the Saudi federation was unhappy with his preparations for the AFC Asian Cup. The first round exit at the 2006 FIFA World Cup hadn't helped his cause but the final straw came when Saudi were knocked out in the semi-finals of the Gulf Cup played in the UAE in February. He was replaced by fellow Brazilian Helio dos Anjos and although it was three months before Helio took charge of an international, he hardly put a foot wrong as Saudi made it through to the final of the AFC Asian Cup for the sixth time in seven tournaments. Based in Jakarta for the first round, the Saudis drew their first match against South Korea, but then went on to win their next four games, including an impressive 3-2 victory against defending champions Japan in the semi-final. Between the two of them, they had won all of the previous six tournaments so the winners were expected to walk the final against Iraq. The Iraqis, however, weren't going to be easily beaten and their 1-0

INTERNATIONAL HONOURS
Qualified for the FIFA World Cup finals 1994 1998 2002 2006
FIFA U-17 World Championship 1989
AFC Asian Cup 1984 1988 1996   AFC Asian Youth Cup 1986 1992   AFC Asian U-17 1985 1988
AFC Champions League Al Hilal 1992 2000, Al Ittihad 2004 2005

victory over the Saudis made headline news around the world. In Asian club competitions Saudi clubs failed to scale the heights of the previous two years with Al Ittihad failing to win an unprecedented hat-trick of titles in the AFC Champions League. They were surprisingly knocked out in the quarter-finals of the 2006 tournament by surprise package Al Karama of Syria whilst Saudi champions Al Shabab fell at the same stage to Korea's Ulsan Horang-i. Shabab also failed to get past the group stage of the 2007 tournament, finishing second behind Iran's Sepahan leaving Saudi hopes resting with Al Hilal. Hilal were the form team of the domestic season but they still felt the need to sack coach Jose Bisero, replacing him with Toniho Cerezo. They were winners of the regular season in the championship, finishing comfortably ahead of Al Ittihad, Al Wahda and Al Shabab, but in Saudi that is not the end of the story. The top four enter a play-off and although Hilal were seeded through to the final, they lost that final to Ittihad. Leading 1-0 with 15 minutes to go, they conceded and equaliser and then an injury-time winner by Ittihad's Hamad Al Montashari. Victory was sweet for Ittihad who had lost against Jeddah rivals Al Ahli in the final of both the Prince Faisal bin Fahd Cup for under 23s and in the final of the Crown Prince Cup.

Saudi Arabian Football Federation (SAFF)
Al Mather Quarter, Prince Faisal Bin Fahad Street, PO Box 5844, Riyadh 11432, Saudi Arabia
Tel +966 1 4822240   Fax +966 1 4821215
www.saff.com.sa
President: HRH Prince Sultan bin Fahad BIN ABDULAZIZ   General Secretary: AL-ABDULHADI Faisal
Vice-President: HRH Prince Nawaf Bin Faisal B.F. BIN ABDULAZIZ   Treasurer: AL-ATHEL Abdullah
Men's Coach: HELIO DOS ANJOS   Women's Coach: None
SAFF formed: 1959   AFC: 1972   FIFA: 1959
White shirts with green trimmings, Green shorts, White socks

RECENT INTERNATIONAL MATCHES PLAYED BY SAUDI ARABIA

2005 Opponents	Score	Venue	Comp	Scorers	Att	Referee
3-12 Palestine	W 2-0	Rayyan	WGr1	Al Sawailh [18], Al Mahyani [22]		
5-12 Iraq	L 1-5	Rayyan	WGr1	Al Qadhi [53]		
8-12 Iraq	L 0-2	Rayyan	WGsf			
2006						
18-01 Sweden	D 1-1	Riyadh	Fr	Haidar [70]		
21-01 Finland	D 1-1	Riyadh	Fr	Al Shlhoub [58]	3 000	Al Anzi KUW
25-01 Greece	D 1-1	Riyadh	Fr	Khaled Aziz [89]	60 000	Jassim Mohamed BHR
27-01 Lebanon	L 1-2	Riyadh	Fr	Al Mahyani [42]		
14-02 Syria	D 1-1	Jeddah	Fr	Al Khatani [40]		
22-02 Yemen	W 4-0	Sana'a	ACq	Al Sawailh 2 [14 89], Al Shlhoub 2 [77 92+]	55 000	Al Fadhli KUW
1-03 Portugal	L 0-3	Dusseldorf	Fr		8 430	Stark GER
15-03 Iraq	D 2-2	Jeddah	Fr	Al Temyat [19], Al Jaber [59]		Al Hamdan KSA
28-03 Poland	L 1-2	Riyadh	Fr	Redha Tukar [27]	2 000	Al Mutlaq KSA
11-05 Belgium	L 1-1	Sittard	Fr	OG [35]	3 283	Bossen NED
14-05 Togo	W 1-0	Sittard	Fr	Malek Maaz [85]	400	Braamhaar NED
26-05 Czech Republic	L 0-2	Innsbruck	Fr		4 000	
31-05 Turkey	L 0-1	Offenbach	Fr		9 000	Fleischer GER
14-06 Tunisia	D 2-2	Munich	WCr1	Al Khatani [57], Al Jaber [84]	66 000	Shield AUS
19-06 Ukraine	L 0-4	Hamburg	WCr1		50 000	Poll ENG
23-06 Spain	L 0-1	Kaiserslautern	WCr1		46 000	Codjia BEN
9-08 Bahrain	W 1-0	Dammam	Fr	Al Khatani [16]		
16-08 India	W 3-0	Calcutta	ACq	Sulaimani [2], Al Khatani 2 [18 52]	10 000	Tongkhan THA
27-08 UAE	W 1-0	Jeddah	Fr	Saleh Al Dosari [9]		
3-09 Japan	W 1-0	Jeddah	ACq	Saleh Al Dosari [73]	15 000	Maidin SIN
6-09 India	W 7-1	Jeddah	ACq	Saleh Al Dosari 2 [31 45], Al Mahyani [34], Haidar [57], Al Hagbani [62], Al Suwailh 2 [79 86]	3 000	Al Saeedi UAE
11-10 Yemen	W 5-0	Jeddah	ACq	Saleh Al Dosari [22], Haidar [27], Fallatah [66], Al Mahyani 2 [68 92+]	1 500	Nema IRQ
8-11 Jordan	W 2-1	Riyadh	Fr	Al Suwailh 2 [74 90]		
15-11 Japan	L 1-3	Sapporo	ACq	Al Khatani [33p]	40 965	Shield AUS
2007						
8-01 Gambia	W 3-0	Dammam	Fr	Al Montasheri [20], Al Khatani 2 [31 50]		
11-01 Syria	W 2-1	Dammam	Fr	Hagbani [79p], Saleh Al Dosari [88]		
18-01 Bahrain	W 2-1	Abu Dhabi	GCr1	Saleh Al Dosari 2 [25 88]		
21-01 Qatar	D 1-1	Abu Dhabi	GCr1	Malek Maaz [71]		
24-01 Iraq	W 1-0	Abu Dhabi	GCr1	Al Khatani [12p]		
27-01 UAE	L 0-1	Abu Dhabi	GCsf			
24-06 UAE	W 2-0	Singapore	Fr	Al Harthi [49], Malek Maaz [59]		
27-06 Singapore	W 2-1	Singapore	Fr	Abdulrahman Al Khatani [26], Al Jassam [34]		
1-07 Oman	D 1-1	Singapore	Fr	Al Shlhoub [56]. W 3-1p		
4-07 Korea DPR	D 1-1	Singapore	Fr	Malek Maaz [64]		
11-07 Korea Republic	D 1-1	Jakarta	ACr1	Yasser Al Khatani [77p]	15 000	Shield AUS
14-07 Indonesia	W 2-1	Jakarta	ACr1	Yasser Al Khatani [12], Al Harthi [89]	87 000	Al Badwawi UAE
18-07 Bahrain	W 4-0	Palembang	ACr1	Al Mousa [18], Al Khatani.A [45], Al Jassam 2 [68 79]	500	Nishimura JPN
22-07 Uzbekistan	W 2-1	Jakarta	ACqf	Yasser Al Khatani [2], Al Mousa [75]	12 000	Kwon Jong Chul KOR
25-07 Japan	W 3-2	Hanoi	ACsf	Yasser Al Khatani [35], Malek Maaz 2 [47 57]	10 000	Breeze AUS
29-07 Iraq	L 0-1	Jakarta	ACf		60 000	Shield AUS

Fr = Friendly match • AC = AFC Asian Cup • GC = Gulf Cup • WG = West Asian Games • WC = FIFA World Cup
q = qualifier • r1 = first round group • sf = semi-final • f = final

SAUDI ARABIA NATIONAL TEAM RECORDS AND RECORD SEQUENCES

Records			Sequence records					
Victory	8-0	MAC 1993	Wins	11	2001	Clean sheets	9	2001
Defeat	0-13	EGY 1961	Defeats	6	1995	Goals scored	15	2001
Player Caps	181	Mohamed AL DAEYEA	Undefeated	19	2003-2004	Without goal	5	1998
Player Goals	67	Majed ABDULLAH	Without win	10	1988	Goals against	10	1981-1982

KINGDOM OF SAUDI ARABIA; AL MAMLAKAH AL ARABIYAH AS SUUDIYAH

Capital	Riyadh	Language	Arabic	Formation	1932
Population	27 019 731	Area	1 960 582 km²	Density	13 per km²	% in cities	80%
GDP per cap	$11 800	Dialling code	+966	Internet	.sa	GMT +/-	+3

MAJOR CITIES/TOWNS
Population '000

1	Riyadh	4 453
2	Jeddah	3 002
3	Mecca	1 383
4	Medina	1 004
5	Dammam	819
6	Taif	550
7	Tabuk	484
8	Khamis Mushayt	418
9	Beraida	418
10	Al Hufuf	303
11	Al Mubarraz	302
12	Ha'il	291
13	Najran	283
14	Al Jubayl	270
15	Hafar al Batin	260
16	Abha	229
17	Yanbu	225
18	Al Kharj	215
19	Taqbah	210
20	Khobar	171
21	Ara'ar	155
22	Al Rass	120
23	Saihat	67
24	Al Majma'ah	42

MEDALS TABLE

		Overall			Lge		Cup		Asia			City	Stadium	Cap'ty	DoF
		G	S	B	G	S	G	S	G	S	B				
1	Al Ittihad	20	10	2	7	2	10	8	3		2	Jeddah	Prince Abdullah Al Faisal	24 000	1928
2	Al Hilal	14	10		6	2	7	6	1	2		Riyadh	Prince Faisal bin Fahd	27 000	1957
3	Al Ahli	15	11		2	4	13	6		1		Jeddah	Prince Sultan bin Fahd	15 000	1937
4	Al Nasr	14	9		6	1	7	6	1	2		Riyadh	Prince Faisal bin Fahd	27 000	1955
5	Al Shabab	9	8		5	2	3	5	1	1		Riyadh	Prince Faisal bin Fahd	27 000	1947
6	Al Ittifaq	4	6		2	1	2	5				Dammam	Prince Mohamed bin Fahd	35 000	1944
7	Al Wahda	2	5				2	5				Mecca	King Abdul Aziz	33 500	1945
8	Al Qadisiya	2	1				1	1	1			Khobar	Prince Saud bin Jalawi	10 000	1967
9	Al Riyadh	1	5		1		1	4				Riyadh	Prince Faisal bin Fahd	27 000	1954
10	Al Ta'ee		1					1				Ha'il	Prince Abdul Aziz bin Musa'ed	10 000	1937

RECENT LEAGUE AND CUP RECORD

	Championship				Cup		
Year	Champions	Score	Runners-up		Winners	Score	Runners-up
1995	Al Nasr	3-1	Al Hilal		Al Hilal	1-0	Al Riyadh
1996	Al Hilal	2-1	Al Ahli		Al Shabab	3-0	Al Nasr
1997	Al Ittihad	2-0	Al Hilal		Al Ittihad	2-0	Al Ta'ee
1998	Al Hilal	3-2	Al Shabab		Al Ahli	3-2	Al Riyadh
1999	Al Ittihad	1-0	Al Ahli		Al Shabab	1-0	Al Hilal
2000	Al Ittihad	2-1	Al Ahli		Al Hilal	3-0	Al Shabab
2001	Al Ittihad	1-0	Al Nasr		Al Ittihad	3-0	Al Ittifaq
2002	Al Hilal	2-1	Al Ittihad		Al Ahli	2-1	Al Ittihad
2003	Al Ittihad	3-2	Al Ahli		Al Hilal	1-0	Al Ahli
2004	Al Shabab	1-0	Al Ittihad		Al Ittihad	1-0	Al Ahli
2005	Al Hilal	1-0	Al Shabab		Al Hilal	2-1	Al Qadisiya
2006	Al Shabab	3-0	Al Hilal		Al Hilal	1-0	Al Ahli
2007	Al Ittihad	2-1	Al Hilal		Al Ahli	2-1	Al Ittihad

SAUDI ARABIA 2006-07

THE CUSTODIAN OF THE TWO HOLY MOSQUES LEAGUE CUP

	Pl	W	D	L	F	A	Pts	Hilal	Ittihad	Wahda	Shabab	Ahli	Ittifaq	Ta'ee	Hazm	Nasr	Qadisiya	Faysali	Khaleej
Al Hilal †	22	17	2	3	38	15	53		2-1	0-0	4-0	3-0	2-1	3-2	1-0	2-1	3-0	2-0	3-0
Al Ittihad †‡	22	15	3	4	52	25	48	1-2		1-0	2-1	3-0	1-1	3-2	2-0	3-0	2-1	5-2	2-0
Al Wahda ‡	22	14	5	3	41	25	47	2-1	2-2		1-0	1-0	2-1	1-0	5-2	2-0	2-2	1-1	4-3
Al Shabab ‡	22	14	2	6	45	27	44	3-1	3-1	3-1		0-2	2-0	1-1	2-1	2-0	3-0	2-1	3-1
Al Ahli	22	7	8	7	29	33	29	2-3	1-1	2-0	1-5		1-1	3-2	3-2	1-1	1-0	0-0	1-1
Al Ittifaq	22	6	7	9	34	34	25	0-1	2-3	0-1	3-3	2-2		2-2	0-3	2-1	0-0	4-2	2-0
Al Ta'ee	22	6	5	11	32	37	23	0-2	0-1	1-4	4-2	4-2	1-0		2-2	0-2	3-3	1-1	0-1
Al Hazm	22	6	3	13	28	38	21	2-0	1-2	2-2	1-3	2-1	0-1	2-1		2-1	2-3	0-1	1-0
Al Nasr	22	5	6	11	24	37	21	0-1	1-3	2-3	0-3	0-3	3-3	1-0	3-1		2-1	1-1	0-0
Al Qadisiya	22	5	5	12	22	36	20	0-1	1-0	1-3	1-3	0-1	2-1	0-2	0-0	1-2		1-3	1-2
Al Faysali	22	4	6	12	23	42	18	0-1	1-5	1-2	1-0	1-1	0-3	0-2	4-2	2-2	0-2		1-4
Al Khaleej	22	4	6	12	21	40	18	0-0	2-8	0-2	0-1	1-1	2-5	1-2	1-0	1-1	1-2	1-0	

5/09/2006 - 10/05/2007 • † Qualified for the play-off final • †‡ Qualified for the play-off semi-final • ‡ Qualified for the play-off first round

CHAMPIONSHIP PLAY-OFFS 2006-07

First round	Semi-final	Final
	Al Ittihad 3	
Al Shabab 1	Al Wahda 2	
Al Wahda 2		Al Ittihad 2
		Al Hilal 1

CHAMPIONSHIP FINAL

‡ Qualified for the AFC Champions League

Riyadh, 1-06-2007, Scorers - Al Mowallad 75, Al Montashari 90 for Ittihad; Al Ghamdi 22 for Hilal

SAUDI ARABIA 2006-07

FIRST DIVISION (2)

	Pl	W	D	L	F	A	Pts	Watani	Najran	Dhemk	Hajr	Faiha'a	Taawun	Fat'h	Riyadh	Ansar	Abha	Sudoos	Jabalain	Sho'ala	Nahda
Al Watani	26	15	10	1	40	18	55		0-0	0-0	1-1	3-1	0-0	1-0	3-1	1-0	2-0	0-0	3-2	2-0	2-0
Najran	26	13	9	4	48	32	48	3-2		2-2	2-1	4-1	3-1	0-1	2-2	3-3	2-2	2-1	3-1	3-0	5-1
Dhemk	26	10	10	6	35	27	40	0-1	1-1		2-2	1-1	0-1	0-1	0-0	1-1	3-2	1-0	3-0	1-1	1-0
Hajr	26	10	8	8	32	30	38	1-2	1-1	1-2		1-0	0-0	2-1	1-0	2-0	1-1	0-1	1-0	2-1	3-1
Faiha'a	26	9	8	9	32	31	35	1-1	1-2	0-1	1-0		1-1	3-0	0-0	1-2	2-2	1-0	1-2	1-0	1-0
Al Taawun	26	8	10	8	33	31	34	2-3	2-2	3-2	0-1	2-3		1-0	0-1	2-2	1-0	4-1	0-1	1-0	1-1
Al Fat'h	26	11	1	14	31	36	34	2-3	1-3	1-0	1-2	3-1	0-0		1-3	2-1	3-0	3-2	2-0	1-2	1-4
Al Riyadh §6	26	9	10	7	34	31	31	1-2	2-0	0-3	1-1	1-3	2-2	2-1		2-1	1-1	1-0	2-0	0-0	0-1
Al Ansar	26	7	10	9	40	40	31	1-1	0-1	2-2	4-1	3-1	4-3	1-0	2-1		4-3	1-2	1-2	0-0	0-0
Abha	26	8	7	11	35	46	31	1-5	0-2	0-2	3-2	1-1	0-1	2-0	2-2	4-3		3-1	1-0	1-0	3-1
Sudoos	26	7	9	10	33	34	30	1-1	2-0	1-1	1-1	0-1	1-1	1-0	2-3	1-1	4-1		0-0	3-0	2-3
Al Jabalain	26	6	8	12	24	34	26	0-0	1-2	2-3	1-2	1-1	1-0	1-2	2-2	2-1	2-0	1-1		0-1	1-1
Al Sho'ala	26	5	9	12	21	32	24	0-1	3-0	1-2	1-1	0-4	1-1	0-1	1-1	0-0	1-2	3-3	0-0		3-1
Al Nahda	26	5	9	12	25	41	24	0-0	0-0	3-1	2-1	0-0	1-3	1-3	0-3	2-2	0-0	1-2	1-1	0-2	

2/11/2006 - 3/05/2007 • § = points deducted

SAUDI ARABIA 2006-07
SECOND DIVISION (3)

	Pl	W	D	L	F	A	Pts
Al Ra'ed	22	16	4	2	50	21	52
Ohod	22	12	4	6	38	20	40
Al Urooba	22	11	5	6	27	27	38
Hamada	22	9	6	7	44	34	33
Al Najma	22	8	6	8	24	25	30
Al Qoth	22	6	8	8	25	27	26
Al Babi'a	22	7	5	10	23	28	26
Ukhdood	22	6	7	9	29	31	25
Al Adala	22	4	13	5	23	27	25
Tahami	22	5	8	9	21	28	23
Al Uyoon	22	3	10	9	26	45	19
Al Noor	22	4	6	12	15	32	18

2/11/2006 - 2/05/2007

CROWN PRINCE CUP 2006-07

First Round		Quarter-finals		Semi-finals		Final	
Al Ahli	3						
Al Riyadh *	0	Al Ahli *	1				
Al Nasr *	1 4p	Al Faysali	0				
Al Faysali	1 5p			Al Ahli *	2 1		
Al Hazm *	2			Al Hilal	0 1		
Al Jabalain	1	Al Hazm	0				
Al Wahda	1	Al Hilal *	2				
Al Hilal *	2					Al Ahli ‡	2
Al Ittifaq	2					Al Ittihad	1
Al Khaleej	1	Al Ittifaq	1				
Rabi'a	0	Al Shabab *	0				
Al Shabab *	5			Al Ittifaq *	1 1		
Najran *	2			Al Ittihad	0 4		
Al Qadisiya	1	Najran	0				
Al Ta'ee	1	Al Ittihad *	10				
Al Ittihad *	6						

* Home team in the first leg • ‡ Qualified for the AFC Champions League

CUP FINAL
Riyadh
27-04-2007

Scorers - Tayseer Al Jassem [80],
Malik Moad [87] for Al Ahli;
Al Hassane Keita [88] for Ittihad

FIFA/COCA-COLA WORLD RANKING

1993	1994	1995	1996	1997	1998	1999	2000	2001	2002	2003	2004	2005	2006	High		Low	
38	27	54	37	33	30	39	36	31	38	26	28	33	64	21	07/04	81	07/06

2006-2007											
08/06	09/06	10/06	11/06	12/06	01/07	02/07	03/07	04/07	05/07	06/07	07/07
75	68	62	64	64	64	63	64	62	63	62	61

THE FIFA BIG COUNT OF 2006

	Male	Female		Total
Number of players	438 644	0	Referees and Assistant Referees	642
Professionals	488		Admin, Coaches, Technical, Medical	650
Amateurs 18+	9 390		Number of clubs	153
Youth under 18	5 266		Number of teams	780
Unregistered	92 500		Clubs with women's teams	0
Total players	438 644		Players as % of population	1.62%

KUW – KUWAIT

NATIONAL TEAM RECORD
JULY 10TH 2006 TO JULY 12TH 2010

PL	W	D	L	F	A	%
10	3	3	4	20	12	45

FIFA/COCA-COLA WORLD RANKING

1993	1994	1995	1996	1997	1998	1999	2000	2001	2002	2003	2004	2005	2006	High	Low
64	54	84	62	44	24	82	74	74	83	48	54	72	78	**24** 12/98	**100** 07/06

2006–2007											
08/06	09/06	10/06	11/06	12/06	01/07	02/07	03/07	04/07	05/07	06/07	07/07
95	71	67	80	78	76	84	84	96	95	93	94

It proved to be a disappointing season for Kuwaiti football with the national team missing out on qualification for the AFC Asian Cup finals, followed by a poor performance at the Gulf Cup, a tournament that Kuwait has traditionally dominated. Mihai Stoichita lost his job after the Asian Cup debacle but there was little that veteran Kuwaiti coach Salah Zakaria could do to improve performances at the Gulf Cup. So disgruntled were the government that the Public Authority for Sports and Youth Affairs dissolved the KFA board, a move that brought it into conflict with FIFA. There was better news on the club front with Al Qadisiya's bid to become the first Kuwaiti club to

INTERNATIONAL HONOURS
Qualified for the FIFA World Cup finals 1982   Asian Cup 1980   Gulf Cup 1970 1972 1974 1976 1982 1986 1990 1996 1998

appear in the AFC Champions League Final but that came to an end after a tight semi-final clash with Syria's Al Karama. At home, a League that had been reduced from 14 teams to eight was won by Al Kuwait who beat Kazma in a play-off after the two had finished level on points. With a season of just 14 games, however, there was plenty of interest in the various Cup competitions. Kazma won two of them - against Al Qadisiya in the Hasawy Cup and Al Kuwait in the Al Khuraifi Cup, but they lost in the final of the Crown Prince Cup to Al Arabi while Al Qadisiya beat Salmiya to win the Emir Cup, the main Cup competition.

THE FIFA BIG COUNT OF 2006

	Male	Female		Total
Number of players	45 800	0	Referees and Assistant Referees	100
Professionals	0		Admin, Coaches, Technical, Medical	300
Amateurs 18+	1 100		Number of clubs	40
Youth under 18	1 100		Number of teams	110
Unregistered	6 600		Clubs with women's teams	0
Total players	45 800		Players as % of population	1.89%

Kuwait Football Association (KFA)
Udailiya, Block 4, Al-Ittihad Street, PO Box 2029, Safat 13021, Kuwait
Tel +965 2555851   Fax +965 2549955
info@kfa.org.kw   www.kfa.org.kw
President: AL-SABAH Shk. Ahmad   General Secretary: AL HABASHI Wael
Vice-President: AL-SABAH Shk. Khaled Fahad A.   Treasurer: AL-MUTAIRY Haiyef Hussain   Media Officer: None
Men's Coach: ZAKARIA Saleh   Women's Coach: None
KFA formed: 1952   AFC: 1962   FIFA: 1962
Blue shirts with white trimmings, Blue shorts, Blue socks

RECENT INTERNATIONAL MATCHES PLAYED BY KUWAIT

2004	Opponents	Score		Venue	Comp	Scorers	Att	Referee
13-10	China PR	W	1-0	Kuwait City	WCq	Jumah [47]	10 000	Kunsuta THA
5-11	India	L	2-3	Kuwait City	Fr	Al Fahed [35], Bashar [54]		
10-11	Kyrgyzstan	W	3-0	Kuwait City	Fr			
17-11	Malaysia	W	6-1	Kuwait City	WCq	Al Mutwa [17], Bashar 2 [60 70], Saeed 2 [75 85], Al Hamad [82]	15 000	Lutfullin UZB
27-11	United Arab Emirates	W	1-0	Abu Dhabi	Fr	Al Harbi [50]		
3-12	United Arab Emirates	D	1-1	Dubai	Fr	Al Fahad [80]		
6-12	Tajikistan	W	3-0	Kuwait City	Fr	Bashar [19], Laheeb [90], Al Humaidan [90]		
11-12	Saudi Arabia	W	2-1	Doha	GCr1	Al Enezi [75], Al Mutwa [86]		
14-12	Bahrain	D	1-1	Doha	GCr1	Jarragh [16]		
17-12	Yemen	W	3-0	Doha	GCr1	Bashar 2 [18 90], Al Mutwa [82]		
20-12	Qatar	L	0-2	Doha	GCsf			
23-12	Bahrain	L	1-3	Doha	GC3p	Khodeir [35]		
2005								
22-01	Norway	D	1-1	Kuwait City	Fr	Bashar [27]	200	Shaban KUW
26-01	Syria	W	3-2	Kuwait City	Fr	OG [8], Mussa [70], Al Humaidan [83]		
2-02	Korea DPR	D	0-0	Beijing	Fr			
9-02	Korea Republic	L	0-2	Seoul	WCq		53 287	Maidin SIN
12-03	Finland	L	0-1	Kuwait City	Fr		10 000	
18-03	Armenia	W	3-1	Al Ain	Fr	Abdulreda [70], Al Mutwa [79], Al Subaih [90]		
25-03	Uzbekistan	W	2-1	Kuwait City	WCq	Bashar 2 [7 62]	12 000	Sun Baojie CHN
30-03	Saudi Arabia	D	0-0	Kuwait City	WCq		25 000	Moradi IRN
27-05	Egypt	L	0-1	Kuwait City	Fr			
3-06	Saudi Arabia	L	0-3	Riyadh	WCq		72 000	Kamikawa JPN
8-06	Korea Republic	L	0-4	Kuwait City	WCq		15 000	Khanthama THA
29-07	United Arab Emirates	D	1-1	Geneva	Fr	Al Mutawa [43], L 6-7p		
31-07	Qatar	L	0-1	Geneva	Fr			
17-08	Uzbekistan	L	2-3	Tashkent	WCq	Al Mutwa [15], Abdulaziz [30]	40 000	Mohd Salleh MAS
26-11	Iraq	D	0-0	Kuwait City	Fr			
2006								
3-02	Singapore	D	2-2	Kuwait City	Fr	Jarragh [8], Al Mutawa [30]		
7-02	Jordan	W	2-1	Kuwait City	Fr	Salama [6], Ali [16]		
22-02	Lebanon	D	1-1	Beirut	ACq	Al Hamad [25]	8 000	Mujghef JOR
1-03	Bahrain	D	0-0	Kuwait City	ACq		16 000	Moradi IRN
16-08	Australia	L	0-2	Sydney	ACq		32 000	Huang Junjie CHN
6-09	Australia	W	2-0	Kuwait City	ACq	Khalaf Al Mutairi [55], Al Mutwa [60]	8 000	Kamikawa JPN
11-10	Lithuania	W	1-0	Kuwait City	Fr	Al Hamad [11]		Abo QAT
9-11	Chinese Taipei	W	10-0	Al Ain	Fr	Hakem [7], Faraj Laheeb 3 [25 35 46], Al Shaikh [27], Al Otaibi [42], Al Rashidi 2 [62 85], Al Mutwa [73], Khalaf Al Mutairi [75]		
15-11	Bahrain	L	1-2	Manama	ACq	Faraj Laheeb [70]	20 000	Kwon Jong Chul KOR
2007								
17-01	Yemen	D	1-1	Abu Dhabi	GCr1	Al Mutwa [73p]		
20-01	Oman	L	1-2	Abu Dhabi	GCr1	Al Rashidi [81]		
23-01	UAE	L	2-3	Abu Dhabi	GCr1	Al Mutwa [31], Al Hamad [35]		
5-06	Portugal	D	1-1	Kuwait City	Fr	Faraj Laheeb [87]	10 000	Al Marquozi UAE
12-06	Egypt	D	1-1	Kuwait City	Fr	Bashar [10]		

Fr = Friendly match • AC = AFC Asian Cup • GC = Gulf Cup • WC = FIFA World Cup
q = qualifier • r1 = first round group • sf = semi-final • 3p = third place play-off

KUWAIT NATIONAL TEAM RECORDS AND RECORD SEQUENCES

Records				Sequence records					
Victory	20-0	BHU 2000		Wins	7	1974	Clean sheets	7	1988
Defeat	0-8	EGY 1961, POR 2003		Defeats	5	1964-1965	Goals scored	17	1986-1987
Player Caps	132	Bashar ABDULLAH		Undefeated	21	1985-1987	Without goal	5	1988
Player Goals	74	Bashar ABDULLAH		Without win	12	1988	Goals against	18	1964-1971

IRQ

Bubian Island

Al Jahra   Kuwait City

The Gulf

Al Wafra

KSA

STATE OF KUWAIT; DAWLAT AL KUWAYT

Capital	Kuwait City	Language	Arabic	Independence	1961
Population	2 418 393	Area	17 820 km²	% in cities	97%
GDP per cap	$19 000	Dailling code	+965	Internet	.kw	GMT +/-	+3

MAJOR CITIES/TOWNS
Population '000

1	Jaleeb al Shuyukh	177
2	Subbah al Salem	162
3	Salmiya	153
4	Al Qurayn	150
5	Hawalli	97
6	Farwaniya	92
7	Sulaibiah	84
8	Fahaheel	74
9	Tayma	73
10	Al Fardaws	70
11	Al Kuwayt	67
12	Al Qasr	61
13	Ardiya	58
14	Reqa	56
15	Abrak Khitan	50
16	Zahar	44
17	Salwa	42
18	Mangaf	42
19	Doha	42
20	Al Ahmadi	41
21	Sulaibkhat	36
22	Abu Hlaifa	31
23	Kaifan	30
24	Meshref	19

All of the towns listed fall within the Al Kuwayt (Kuwait City) metropolitan area

MEDALS TABLE

		Overall			League			Cup			LC			Asia			City	Stadium	Cap'ty	DoF
		G	S	B	G	S	B	G	S	B	G	S	B	G	S	B				
1	Al Arabi	35	14	3	16	3	3	14	10		5	1					Kuwait City	Sabah Al Salem	22 000	1960
2	Al Qadisiya	28	13	5	11	6	4	12	7		5				1		Kuwait City	Mohammed Al Hamad	20 000	1960
3	Al Kuwait	19	13	2	9	3	2	8	7		2	3					Kaifan	Al Kuwait SC	18 000	1960
4	Kazma	11	12	5	4	3	5	6	8		1	1					Kuwait City	Al Sadaqua Walsalam	21 500	1964
5	Salmiya	7	10	4	4	5	4	2	5	1							Salmiya	Thamer	14 000	1964
6	Al Yarmouk	2	2			1		2	1								Meshref	Meshref	12 000	1965
7	Al Jahra	1	2		1				2								Al Jahra			1966
8	Al Fahaheel	1						1									Fahaheel	Al Fahaheel	1 000	1964
9	Al Tadamon		5			1			4								Farwaniya	Al Farwaniya	14 000	1965
10	Al Nasr		1			1											Jaleeb al Shuyukh	Jaleeb al Shuyukh	15 000	1965
	Al Sahel		1						1								Abu Hlaifa	Abu Halayfah	2 000	1967
12	Khitan																Abrak Khitan	Abraq Khitan	3 000	1965
	Al Shabab																Al Ahmadi	Al Ahmadi	18 000	1963
	Sulaibikhat																Kuwait City			1972

RECENT LEAGUE AND CUP RECORD

	Championship						Cup		
Year	Champions	Pts	Runners-up	Pts	Third	Pts	Winners	Score	Runners-up
1996	Kazma	24	Salmiya	22	Al Qadisiya	15	Al Arabi	2-1	Jahra
1997	Al Arabi						Kazma	2-0	Al Qadisiya
1998	Salmiya	64	Kazma	55	Al Qadisiya	50	Kazma	3-1	Al Arabi
1999	Al Qadisiya	1-0	Al Tadamon				Al Arabi	2-1	Al Sahel
2000	Salmiya	23	Al Qadisiya	20	Al Kuwait SC	15	Al Arabi	2-1	Al Tadamon
2001	Al Kuwait SC	28	Al Qadisiya	24	Al Arabi	24	Salmiya	3-1	Kazma
2002	Al Arabi	26	Al Qadisiya	25	Salmiya	23	Al Kuwait SC	1-0	Jahra
2003	Al Qadisiya	28	Al Arabi	26	Kazma	24	Al Qadisiya	2-2 4-1p	Al Salimiya
2004	Al Qadisiya	2-1	Salmiya				Al Qadisiya	2-0	Al Kuwait SC
2005	Al Qadisiya	9	Al Kuwait SC	8	Al Arabi	6	Al Arabi	1-1 6-5p	Kazma
2006	Al Kuwait SC	66	Al Qadisiya	62	Salmiya	58	Al Arabi	2-2 3-2p	Al Qadisiya
2007	Al Kuwait SC	32	Kazma	32	Salmiya	31	Al Qadisiya	5-0	Al Salimiya

KUWAIT 2006–07

PREMIER LEAGUE

	Pl	W	D	L	F	A	Pts	Kuwait	Kazma	Salmiya	Qadisiya	Sahel	Arabi	Tadamon	Fehayheel
Al Kuwait SC †	14	10	2	2	24	12	32		1-0	2-1	0-3	3-0	2-2	1-0	2-1
Kazma	14	10	2	2	23	8	32	1-2		1-0	3-2	2-1	3-0	1-1	2-0
Salmiya	14	10	1	3	33	15	31	1-0	0-2		2-1	4-0	0-0	3-0	3-2
Al Qadisiya	14	8	1	5	27	19	25	2-3	0-2	3-4		2-1	2-1	1-0	3-0
Al Sahel	14	3	3	8	14	31	12	0-2	1-1	1-6	1-1		2-1	2-2	2-1
Al Arabi	14	1	6	7	11	21	9	0-0	0-1	2-4	1-3	0-1		3-2	0-0
Al Tadamon	14	2	3	9	15	28	9	1-3	0-3	1-4	1-2	4-2	1-1		1-0
Fehayheel	14	2	2	10	8	21	8	0-3	0-1	0-1	0-2	2-0	0-0	2-1	

23/11/2006 - 14/04/2006 • † Qualified for the AFC Champions League • Play-off: Kuwait 2-0 Kazma (21-04-2007. Scorers - Macanga [39], Jumah [58])

KUWAIT 2006–07 FIRST DIVISION (2)

	Pl	W	D	L	F	A	Pts
Al Nasr	12	8	4	0	21	9	28
Jahra	12	8	2	2	24	14	26
Khitan	12	5	1	6	20	17	16
Al Yarmouk	12	2	4	6	11	20	10
Al Shabab	12	1	1	10	11	27	4

18/11/2006 - 10/04/2007 • Sulaibkhat withdrew after five games

CROWN PRINCE CUP 2006–07 GROUP A

	Pl	W	D	L	F	A	Pts
Al Arabi †	6	4	2	0	12	4	14
Kazma †	6	4	2	0	10	2	14
Salmiya	6	4	0	2	15	6	12
Al Kuwait SC	6	3	1	2	12	5	10
Al Yarmouk	6	2	0	4	4	16	6
Khitan	6	1	0	5	7	16	3
Al Sahel	6	0	1	5	3	14	1

28/04/2007 - 30/05/2007 • † Qualified for the semi-finals

CROWN PRINCE CUP 2006–07 GROUP B

	Pl	W	D	L	F	A	Pts
Al Qadisiya †	6	4	1	1	14	5	13
Al Tadamon †	6	4	1	1	11	9	13
Fehayheel	6	4	0	2	10	4	12
Jahra	6	3	0	3	11	7	9
Al Shabab	6	3	0	3	9	10	9
Solaybeekhat	6	1	1	4	6	20	4
Al Nasr	6	0	1	5	5	11	1

29/04/2007 - 30/05/2007

CROWN PRINCE CUP 2006–07 FINAL ROUNDS

Semi-finals

Al Arabi	3
Al Tadamon	1
Al Qadisiya	0
Kazma	2

Final

Al Arabi	1
Kazma	0

11-06-2007

EMIR CUP 2006–07

First Round

Al Qadisiya	2
Fehayheel	1
Khitan	2
Solaybeekhat	3
Al Shabab	2 4p
Jahra	2 1p
Al Kuwait SC	Bye
Al Arabi	Bye
Al Sahel	1
Al Tadamon	5
Kazma	3
Al Nasr	0
Al Yarmouk	1 2p
Salmiya	1 4p

Quarter-finals

Al Qadisiya	5
Solaybeekhat	0
Al Shabab	0
Al Kuwait SC	5
Al Arabi	2
Al Tadamon	1
Kazma	4 2p
Salmiya	4 4p

Semi-finals

Al Qadisiya	1
Al Kuwait SC	0
Al Arabi	2
Salmiya	3

Final

Al Qadisiya †	5
Salmiya	0

† Qualified for the AFC Champions League

CUP FINAL

Kuwait City
25-06-2007

LAO – LAOS

NATIONAL TEAM RECORD
JULY 10TH 2006 TO JULY 12TH 2010

PL	W	D	L	F	A	%
7	3	1	3	12	29	50

FIFA/COCA-COLA WORLD RANKING

1993	1994	1995	1996	1997	1998	1999	2000	2001	2002	2003	2004	2005	2006	High		Low	
146	160	152	147	143	144	156	165	162	170	167	162	170	151	**134**	09/98	**184**	09/06

2006–2007											
08/06	09/06	10/06	11/06	12/06	01/07	02/07	03/07	04/07	05/07	06/07	07/07
182	184	183	157	151	150	157	161	165	165	162	163

The decision by the Laos Football Federation not to enter the 2010 FIFA World Cup - one of only four federations to do so - means that the country looks set to confine its international schedule to the ASEAN Football Federation Championship that is held every two years. In the 2006-07 edition, the national team excelled in the qualifying round, winning a five team group to secure a place in the finals in Singapore. But if the wins against the Philippines, Bhutan and Brunei had raised hopes of a good performance the finals, those hopes were dashed in dramatic fashion. A respectable 3-1 defeat at the hands of Indonesia in the opening match was followed by an 11-0

INTERNATIONAL HONOURS
None

thrashing by the hosts in the next. One more goal and the result would have equalled their worst ever. A miserable week for Laos was then completed by a 9-0 hammering by Vietnam. Earlier Laos had been suspended by the AFC for fielding an over-age player in a youth tournament which meant that the under–17 team, after having sensationally knocked out Australia in the qualifiers, was barred from taking part in the AFC U–17 Championship in Singapore in September 2006. At home there was a first League title for the Laos-American College who finished ahead of defending champions Vientiane.

THE FIFA BIG COUNT OF 2006

	Male	Female		Total
Number of players	108 550	50	Referees and Assistant Referees	70
Professionals	0		Admin, Coaches, Technical, Medical	350
Amateurs 18+	1 400		Number of clubs	50
Youth under 18	1 200		Number of teams	150
Unregistered	23 000		Clubs with women's teams	0
Total players	108 600		Players as % of population	1.71%

Laos Football Federation (LFF)

National Stadium, Konboulom Street, PO Box 3777, Vientiane 856-21, Laos

Tel +856 21 251593   Fax +856 21 213460

laosff@laotel.com   www.none

President: INTHARA Kasem   General Secretary: THANAVADY Phothone

Vice-President: SIRIPANYA Boualane   Treasurer: KEOMANY Khammoui   Media Officer: VILAYSAK Sisay

Men's Coach: SAVATDY Xaysana   Women's Coach: SIVISAY Veunsavanh

LFF formed: 1951   AFC: 1980   FIFA: 1952

Red shirts, Red shorts, Red socks

RECENT INTERNATIONAL MATCHES PLAYED BY LAOS

2003	Opponents	Score	Venue	Comp	Scorers	Att	Referee
25-03	Hong Kong	L 1-5	Hong Kong	ACq	Phaphouvanin [66]		
27-03	Bangladesh	W 2-1	Hong Kong	ACq	Phonephachan [30], Phaphouvanin [38]		
29-11	Sri Lanka	D 0-0	Vientiane	WCq		4 500	Luong VIE
3-12	Sri Lanka	L 0-3	Colombo	WCq		6 000	Saleem MDV
2004							
18-02	Jordan	L 0-5	Amman	WCq		5 000	Al Mozahmi OMA
31-03	Iran	L 0-7	Vientiane	WCq		7 000	Yang Mu Sheng TPE
9-06	Qatar	L 0-5	Doha	WCq		500	Abu Armana PAL
8-09	Qatar	L 1-6	Vientiane	WCq	Chanthalome [88]	2 900	Napitupulu IDN
13-10	Jordan	L 2-3	Vientiane	WCq	Phaphouvanin [13], Thongphachan [53]	3 000	Gosh BAN
17-11	Iran	L 0-7	Tehran	WCq		30 000	Mamedov TKM
7-12	Indonesia	L 0-6	Ho Chi Minh City	TCr1			Mongkol THA
11-12	Cambodia	W 2-1	Hanoi	TCr1	Chalana 2 [63 73]	20 000	Kwong Jong Chul KOR
13-12	Singapore	L 2-6	Hanoi	TCr1	Phaphouvanin [22], Chalana [72p]	17 000	Supian MAS
15-12	Vietnam	L 0-3	Hanoi	TCr1		20 000	Mongkul THA
2005							
No international matches played in 2005.							
2006							
12-11	Philippines	W 2-1	Bacolod	TCq	Sisomephone [47], Phaphouvanin [49]		
14-11	Cambodia	D 2-2	Bacolod	TCq	Soukhavong [30], Sisomephone [35]		
16-11	Timor Leste	W 3-2	Bacolod	TCq	Saysongkham [34], Phothilath [61], Saynakhonevieng [91+]		
18-11	Brunei Darussalam	W 4-1	Bacolod	TCq	Saysongkham [6], Phaphouvanin [17], Leupvisay [43], Phothilath [55]		
2007							
13-01	Indonesia	L 1-3	Singapore	TCr1	Xaysongkham [13]		
15-01	Singapore	L 0-11	Singapore	TCr1		5 224	U Hla Tint MYA
17-01	Vietnam	L 0-9	Singapore	TCr1		1 005	

TC = Tiger Cup • AC = AFC Asian Cup 2004 • WC = FIFA World Cup • q = qualifier • r1 = first round group

LAOS NATIONAL TEAM RECORDS AND RECORD SEQUENCES

Records			Sequence records					
Victory	4-1	PHI	Wins	3	1993-1995	Clean sheets	3	1995
Defeat	0-12	OMA 2001	Defeats	11	1970-1974	Goals scored	9	1996-1998
Player Caps	n/a		Undefeated	4	1993-1995, 2006	Without goal	8	2000-2001
Player Goals	n/a		Without win	19	1970-1993	Goals against	14	1961-1969

RECENT LEAGUE AND CUP RECORD

Championship		Cup
Year	Champions	Winners
2000	Vientiane Municipality	
2001		
2002	MCPTC	
2003	MCPTC	MCPTC
2004	MCPTC	Vientiane FC
2005	Vientiane FC	
2006	Vientiane FC	
2007	Laos-American College	

LAOS COUNTRY INFORMATION

Capital	Vientiane	Independence	1953 from France	GDP per Capita	$1 700
Population	6 068 117	Status	Republic	GNP Ranking	143
Area km²	236 800	Language	Lao	Dialling code	+856
Population density	25.5 per km²	Literacy rate	66%	Internet code	.la
% in urban areas	22%	Main religion	Buddhist 60%	GMT +/−	+7
Towns/Cities ('000)	Vientiane 196; Pakxe 88; Savannakhet 66; Luang Prabang 47; Xam Nua 39; Xaignabury 31				
Neighbours (km)	China 423; Vietnam 2 130; Cambodia 541; Thailand 1 754; Burma 235				
Main stadia	National Stadium – Vientiane 18 000				

LBR – LIBERIA

NATIONAL TEAM RECORD
JULY 10TH 2006 TO JULY 12TH 2010

PL	W	D	L	F	A	%
5	1	1	3	6	9	30

FIFA/COCA-COLA WORLD RANKING

1993	1994	1995	1996	1997	1998	1999	2000	2001	2002	2003	2004	2005	2006	High		Low	
123	127	87	94	94	108	105	95	73	88	110	123	135	115	**66**	07/01	**143**	09/06

2006–2007											
08/06	09/06	10/06	11/06	12/06	01/07	02/07	03/07	04/07	05/07	06/07	07/07
135	143	112	112	115	112	112	114	118	119	128	121

With just one win in their last 15 internationals it has been a slippery downhill slope for the Liberian national team, who can no longer rely on the massive influence of George Weah. The one-time FIFA World Footballer of the Year has turned his hand to politics and business, leaving a new generation to take up the mantle. Liberia are finding it hard, however, to match playing resources of the Weah generation who qualified for the 1996 Nations Cup finals in South Africa. The dire financial situation of the country has also inhibited any chance for the national team to develop, with most of the foreign-based players having to pay their own travel costs when on

INTERNATIONAL HONOURS
None

international duty. Liberian footballers are spread all over world, with a large contingent playing for clubs in Indonesia and Malaysia but also throughout Europe and the USA. Their 2008 African Nations Cup qualifying campaign produced just a single win for coach Frank Jericho Nagbe's charges, against Rwanda in October 2006, as they battled to avoid the wooden spoon in the group. In the 2007 African Champions League, Liberia's representatives Mighty Barolle did not get past the first round, eliminated by Sewe Sport of Cote d'Ivoire while in the African Confederation Cup, NPA Anchors lost both home and away to Senegal's US Goree in their first round tie.

THE FIFA BIG COUNT OF 2006

	Male	Female		Total
Number of players	162 667	600	Referees and Assistant Referees	206
Professionals	27		Admin, Coaches, Technical, Medical	450
Amateurs 18+	6 210		Number of clubs	45
Youth under 18	3 030		Number of teams	125
Unregistered	11 000		Clubs with women's teams	2
Total players	163 267		Players as % of population	5.37%

Liberia Football Association (FLFA)
Antoinette Tubman Stadium (ATS), PO Box 10-1066, Monrovia 1000, Liberia
Tel +231 77314463   Fax +231 227223
gwilliams@liberiafa.com   www.liberiafa.com
President: WESLEY Sombo   General Secretary: WILLIAMS George
Vice-President: BESTMAN Pennoh   Treasurer: KOON Joseph S.   Media Officer: None
Men's Coach: NAGBE Frank   Women's Coach: TOGBA Lucretius
FLFA formed: 1936   CAF: 1962   FIFA: 1962
Blue shirts, White shorts, Red socks

RECENT INTERNATIONAL MATCHES PLAYED BY LIBERIA

2002	Opponents	Score		Venue	Comp	Scorers	Att	Referee
8-09	Guinea	L	0-3	Conakry	CNq		35 000	Diouf.AS SEN
13-10	Niger	W	1-0	Monrovia	CNq	Daye [80]	40 000	
2003								
30-03	Ethiopia	L	0-1	Addis Ababa	CNq		40 000	Ali Mohamed DJI
8-06	Ethiopia	W	1-0	Monrovia	CNq	Mennoh [57]	14 000	Aguidissou BEN
21-06	Guinea	L	1-2	Accra	CNq	Daye [20]		Sowe GAM
5-07	Niger	L	0-1	Niamey	CNq			
12-10	Gambia	L	0-2	Bakau	WCq		20 000	Codjia BEN
16-11	Gambia	W	3-0	Monrovia	WCq	Roberts [10], Tondo 2 [76 83]	10 000	Coulibaly MLI
2004								
6-06	Mali	W	1-0	Monrovia	WCq	Kieh [85]	30 000	Codjia BEN
20-06	Congo	L	0-3	Brazzaville	WCq		25 000	Lemghambodj MTN
4-07	Togo	D	0-0	Monrovia	WCq		30 000	Soumah GUI
4-09	Zambia	L	0-1	Lusaka	WCq		30 000	Nchengwa BOT
10-10	Senegal	L	0-3	Monrovia	WCq		26 000	Aboubacar CIV
2005								
26-03	Senegal	L	1-6	Dakar	WCq	Tondo [86]	50 000	Shelmani LBY
5-06	Mali	L	1-4	Segou	WCq	Toe [54]	11 000	Pare BFA
10-06	Sierra Leone	L	0-2	Freetown	Fr			
19-06	Congo	L	0-2	Paynesville	WCq		5 000	Sillah GAM
4-09	Togo	L	0-3	Lome	WCq		28 000	Abdel Rahman SUD
1-10	Zambia	L	0-5	Monrovia	WCq		0	Evehe CMR
2006								
3-09	Equatorial Guinea	L	1-2	Malabo	CNq	Krangar [35]		Agbenyega GHA
8-10	Rwanda	W	3-2	Monrovia	CNq	Doe [27], Makor [68], Williams [76]		Olatunde NGA
2007								
24-03	Cameroon	L	1-3	Yaoundé	CNq	Doe [39]		Djaoupe TOG
3-06	Cameroon	L	1-2	Monrovia	CNq	Mennoh [71]		
17-06	Equatorial Guinea	D	0-0	Monrovia	CNq			

CN = CAF African Cup of Nations • WC = FIFA World Cup • q = qualifier

LIBERIA NATIONAL TEAM RECORDS AND RECORD SEQUENCES

Records			Sequence records			
Victory	4-0	GAM 1996, MRI 2000	Wins	4	2001	Clean sheets	4	1987-1995
Defeat	2-7	TUN 2001	Defeats	9	2004-2006	Goals scored	8	2001, 2001-02
Player Caps	n/a		Undefeated	11	1994-1995	Without goal	4	Six times
Player Goals	n/a		Without win	17	1971-1980	Goals against	13	1984-1986

RECENT LEAGUE AND CUP RECORD

Championship		Cup
Year	Champions	Winners
2000	Mighty Barolle	LPRC Oilers
2001	Mighty Barolle	
2002	LPRC Oilers	Mighty Blue Angels
2003	Not finished	
2004	Mighty Barolle	LISCR FC
2005	LPRC Oilers	LPRC Oilers
2006	Mighty Barolle	NPA Anchors

LIBERIA COUNTRY INFORMATION

Capital	Monrovia	Independence	1847	GDP per Capita	$1 000
Population	3 390 635	Status	Republic	GNP Ranking	171
Area km²	111 370	Language	English	Dialling code	+231
Population density	30 per km²	Literacy rate	57%	Internet code	.lr
% in urban areas	45%	Main religion	Christian & Indigenous 40%	GMT +/−	0
Cities/Towns ('000)	Monrovia 935; Gbarnga 45; Bensonville 33; Harper 33; Buchanan 26; Zwedru 26				
Neighbours (km)	Guinea 563; Côte d'Ivoire 716; Sierra Leone 306; Atlantic Ocean 579				
Main stadia	Samuel Doe Sports Complex – Monrovia 35 000; Antoinette Tubman – Monrovia 10 000				

LBY – LIBYA

NATIONAL TEAM RECORD
JULY 10TH 2006 TO JULY 12TH 2010

PL	W	D	L	F	A	%
14	5	4	5	14	14	50

FIFA/COCA-COLA WORLD RANKING

1993	1994	1995	1996	1997	1998	1999	2000	2001	2002	2003	2004	2005	2006	High	Low
152	167	175	184	147	147	131	116	116	104	83	61	80	99	61 12/04	187 07/97

2006–2007											
08/06	09/06	10/06	11/06	12/06	01/07	02/07	03/07	04/07	05/07	06/07	07/07
77	89	93	97	99	98	97	97	93	89	95	87

Tripoli club Al Ittihad broke new ground for Libyan football by reaching the last eight of the 2007 African Champions League, the first time a club from the north African country had got through to the lucrative group stage of Africa's top club competition. Al Ittihad have dominated domestic tournaments, with five league titles in the last six campaigns, but had never previously been able to turn that into success abroad. Under Serbian coach Branko Smiljanic they eliminated Etoile du Congo in the last knockout round to continue the recent revival in Libyan football. Qualification for the 2006 African Nations Cup tournament in Egypt, the first time the national team had been

INTERNATIONAL HONOURS
None

at the finals since they hosted the event in 1982, has given a huge boost to the game in the country. However, in the 2008 Nations Cup qualifiers, the Libyans were always struggling after losing their first match away at Ethiopia and after the home draw with the Democratic Republic of Congo coach Mohsen Salah was fired. Three matches later his successor, Mohamed El Khemsy, was also shown the door as their chances of reaching the finals disappeared. In July 2007, Libya announced the appointment of Faouzi Benzarti, former coach of Etoile Sahel and Esperance in Tunisia. He has a contract through to the end of the 2010 FIFA World Cup qualifiers.

THE FIFA BIG COUNT OF 2006

	Male	Female		Total
Number of players	263 800	0	Referees and Assistant Referees	300
Professionals	0		Admin, Coaches, Technical, Medical	2 100
Amateurs 18+	5 500		Number of clubs	110
Youth under 18	2 800		Number of teams	550
Unregistered	22 000		Clubs with women's teams	0
Total players	263 800		Players as % of population	4.47%

Libyan Football Federation (LFF)
General Sports Federations Building, Sports City, Gorji, PO Box 5137, Tripoli, Libya
Tel +218 21 4782001   Fax +218 21 4782006
libyaff@hotmail.com   www.lff.org.ly
President: EL JAAFRI Jamal Saleh   General Secretary: AL SAEDY Ahmed Abdulmagid
Vice-President: KHATABI Abdulrazag Al Tayb   Treasurer: EL MUGHRBI Abdulmula   Media Officer: BEN TAHIA Mohamad
Men's Coach: BENZARTI Faouzi   Women's Coach: None
LFF formed: 1962   CAF: 1965   FIFA: 1963
Green shirts with white trimmings, Green shorts, Green socks or White shirts with green trimmings, White shorts, White socks

RECENT INTERNATIONAL MATCHES PLAYED BY LIBYA

2003	Opponents	Score		Venue	Comp	Scorers	Att	Referee
20-10	Nigeria	W	2-1	Tripoli	Fr	Kara 2 [23 44]		
22-10	Jordan	W	1-0	Tripoli	Fr	Kara [59p]		
2005								
27-03	Egypt	L	1-4	Cairo	WCq	Ferjani [50]	30 000	Poulat FRA
27-05	Malawi	D	1-1	Tripoli	Fr			
3-06	Côte d'Ivoire	D	0-0	Tripoli	WCq		45 000	Lim Kee Chong MRI
19-06	Cameroon	L	0-1	Yaoundé	WCq		36 000	Coulibaly MLI
17-08	Nigeria	L	0-1	Tripoli	Fr			
24-08	Iran	L	0-4	Tehran	Fr			
2-09	Sudan	D	0-0	Tripoli	WCq			
9-10	Benin	L	0-1	Cotonou	WCq			
16-11	Congo DR	W	2-1	Paris	Fr	Shebani [25], Erwani [76]		
2-12	United Arab Emirates	D	1-1	Sharjah	Fr	Dawood [39]		
2006								
2-01	Qatar	L	0-2	Doha	Fr			
12-01	Tunisia	L	0-1	Radès/Tunis	Fr			
20-01	Egypt	L	0-3	Cairo	CNr1		65 000	Pare BFA
24-01	Côte d'Ivoire	L	1-2	Cairo	CNr1	Khamis [41]	42 000	Maidin SIN
28-01	Morocco	D	0-0	Cairo	CNr1		5 000	Daami TUN
30-05	Uruguay	L	1-2	Radès/Tunis	Fr	Tarek Tayeb [61]		
2-06	Belarus	D	1-1	Radès/Tunis	Fr	Osman [90], W 3-1p		
5-06	Ukraine	L	0-3	Gossau	Fr		2 500	Wilzhaber SUI
5-08	Sryia	L	1-2	Damascus	Fr	Osman [61]		
16-08	Uganda	W	3-2	Tripoli	Fr	Tarek Tayeb [59], Osman [72], Khaled Hussain [90]		
26-08	Yemen	W	1-0	Sana'a	Fr	Kara [16]		
29-08	Yemen	D	1-1	Sana'a	Fr			
3-09	Ethiopia	L	0-1	Addis Abeba	CNq			Abd El Fatah EGY
1-10	Sudan	W	1-0	Tripoli	Fr	El Masli [24]		
8-10	Congo DR	D	1-1	Tripoli	CNq	Khaled Hussain [75]		Pare BFA
15-11	Tunisia	L	0-2	Radès/Tunis	Fr			
2007								
7-02	Algeria	L	1-2	Algiers	Fr	Al Shaibani [48]		
20-03	Mauritania	D	0-0	Tripoli	Fr			
25-03	Namibia	W	2-1	Tripoli	CNq	Salem Rewane [12], Tarek Tayeb [61]		
27-05	Botswana	D	0-0	Gaborone	Fr			
2-06	Namibia	L	0-1	Windhoek	CNq			
17-06	Ethiopia	W	3-1	Tripoli	CNq	Alzowi 2 [11 48], Salem Rewane [23]		

Fr = Friendly match • CN = CAF African Cup of Nations • WC = FIFA World Cup • q = qualifier • r1 = first round

LIBYA NATIONAL TEAM RECORDS AND RECORD SEQUENCES

Records			Sequence records					
Victory	21-0	OMA 1966	Wins	5	2003-04, 2004	Clean sheets	4	1996, 2003-04
Defeat	2-10	EGY 1953	Defeats	5	1953-1960	Goals scored	15	1998-1999
Player Caps	n/a		Undefeated	7	1982-1983	Without goal	6	2005
Player Goals	n/a		Without win	10	2005-2006	Goals against	16	1953-65, 1992-99

LIBYA COUNTRY INFORMATION

Capital	Tripoli	Independence	1951 from Italy	GDP per Capita	$6 400	
Population	5 631 585	Status	Republic	GNP Ranking	59	
Area km²	1 759 540	Language	Arabic	Dialling code	+218	
Population density	3 per km²	Literacy rate	82%	Internet code	.ly	
% in urban areas	86%	Main religion	Muslim	GMT + / −	+1	
Towns/Cities ('000)	Tripoli 1 150; Benghazi 650; Misurata 386; Al Aziziyah 287; Tarhunah 210; Al-Hums 201; Az-Zawiyah 186; Zuwarah 180; Ajdabiya 134; Surt 128; Sabha 126; Tubruq 121					
Neighbours (km)	Egypt 1 115 km; Sudan 383; Chad 1 055; Niger 354; Algeria 982; Tunisia 459; Mediterranean 1 770					
Main stadia	11 June Stadium – Tripoli 80 000; 28 March Stadium – Benghazi 60 000					

LIBYA 2006–07

FIRST DIVISION

	Pl	W	D	L	F	A	Pts	Ittihad	Ahly T	Medina	Akhdar	Ahly B	Nasr	Khaleej	Olympique	Soukour	Shat	Tahaddi	Hilal	Rafik	Charara
Al Ittihad Tripoli †	24	16	7	1	32	6	55		1-0	1-0	3-0	1-0	3-0	1-0	3-0	2-1	0-0	1-0	1-0	2-0	1-1
Al Ahly Tripoli	24	16	1	7	41	16	49	0-2		2-0	2-1	2-1	0-1	4-0	2-0	3-1	3-0	4-1	2-0	2-0	
Al Medina Tripoli	24	12	7	5	35	21	43	1-1	2-1		2-3	1-0	0-1	0-0	1-0	3-3	1-0	2-2	1-0	2-1	1-0
Al Akhdar Darnah	24	12	4	8	40	32	40	1-1	1-0	1-0		3-2	1-0	6-1	4-2	2-1	1-2	0-2	2-1	4-1	
Al Ahly Benghazi	24	8	11	5	26	19	35	0-0	1-0	2-2	2-0		1-1	1-0	2-0	1-1	3-0	3-3	0-0	0-0	
Al Nasr Benghazi §1	24	7	11	6	26	29	31	0-2	1-2	0-3	2-1	1-1		2-2	0-0	0-0	3-0	1-0	1-1	2-2	3-2
Khaleej Saart	24	7	7	10	21	31	28	1-0	2-4	0-0	2-0	0-1	2-2		1-0	2-0	1-3	1-3	2-0	1-2	
Olympique Az-Zwiyah	24	5	9	10	9	22	24	0-0	0-0	0-2	1-1	0-0	0-0	0-0		3-0	1-0	0-1	1-0	0-0	2-1
Al Soukour	24	6	6	12	27	33	24	1-3	1-0	0-1	2-3	1-2	4-0	1-1	0-1		1-0	1-0	2-0	2-2	
Al Shat Tripoli	24	6	6	12	15	30	24	0-2	0-3	0-0	1-0	0-2	0-0	0-1	1-2	2-1		1-0	1-2	1-1	1-0
Al Tahaddi Benghazi	24	4	10	10	18	26	22	0-0	0-1	0-4	0-0	0-0	0-1	0-1	2-0	0-0	0-0		2-2	1-1	
Al Hilal Benghazi	24	5	7	12	19	28	22	1-1	0-1	0-2	1-1	0-0	2-3	1-0	2-0	4-2	1-0	0-1		1-1	1-0
Rafik Sorman	24	4	10	10	23	39	20	0-1	0-3	3-5	1-4	3-1	1-4	0-0	0-0	0-1	2-2	1-0	1-0		
Al Charara		Excluded after 12 matches						0-2		0-1	1-1					2-0			1-1		1-1

14/09/2006 – 29/05/2007 • † Qualified for the CAF Champions League • § = points deducted • All matches played by Al Charara were annulled

AL FATIH CUP 2006–07

Round of 16			Quarter–finals			Semi–finals			Final	
Al Ittihad Tripoli *	2	1								
Al Tahaddi Benghazi	0	0	Al Ittihad Tripoli	0	3					
Al Wahda *	0	0	Olympique Az-Zwiyah*	0	2					
Olympique Az-Zwiyah	1	0				Al Ittihad Tripoli *	2	0		
						Al Medina Tripoli	0	1		
Al Ahly Benghazi *	0	1								
Al Jazeera	2	2	Al Ahly Benghazi *	1	3					
Al Soukour *	2	0	Al Medina Tripoli	2	3					
Al Medina Tripoli	2	2							Al Ittihad Tripoli	1
Al Nasr Benghazi	1	4							Al Akhdar Darnah ‡	0
Al Uruba *	1	0	Al Nasr Benghazi *	2	2					
Rafik Sorman	1	0	Al Shat Tripoli	1	2					
Al Shat Tripoli *	1	1				Al Nasr *	0	1		
Al Ahly Tripoli	1	1				Al Akhdar Darnah	2	1		
Al Hilal Benghazi *	0	1	Al Ahly Tripoli	1	1					
Al Slam	1	0	Al Akhdar Darnah *	3	0					
Al Akhdar Darnah *	1	3								

* Home team in the first leg • ‡ Qualified for the CAF Confederation Cup

CUP FINAL

Tripoli
15-07-2007

Scorer - Coulibaly 52

RECENT LEAGUE AND CUP RECORD

	Championship							Cup		
Year	Champions	Pts	Runners-up	Pts	Third	Pts		Winners	Score	Runners-up
1997	Al Tahaddi Benghazi	54	Al Ahly Tripoli	53	Al Ittihad Tripoli	51		Al Nasr Benghazi	1-1 4-3p	Al Yarmouk
1998	Al Mahalah Tripoli							Al Shaat Tripoli	1-1 4-2p	Al Hilal Benghazi
1999	Al Mahalah Tripoli	30	Al Shat Tripoli	23	Al Hilal Benghazi	21		Al Ittihad Ytipoli	2-0	Al Tahaddi Benghazi
2000	Al Ahly Tripoli	1-0	Al Hilal Benghazi					Al Ahly Tripoli	2-0	Al Shawehly Misurata
2001	Al Medina Tripoli	1-1	Al Tahaddi Benghazi							
2002	Al Ittihad Tripoli	67	Al Nasr Benghazi	67	Al Hilal Benghazi	52				
2003	Al Ittihad Tripoli	65	Al Nasr Benghazi	52	Al Hilal Benghazi	43				
2004	Olympique Az-Zwiyah	57	Al Ittihad Tripoli	52	Al Ahly Tripoli	51		Al Ittihad Tripoli	0-0 8-7p	Al Hilal
2005	Al Ittihad Tripoli	51	Al Uruba	43	Olympique Az-Zwiyah	42		Al Ittihad Tripoli	3-0	Al Akhdar Darnah
2006	Al Ittihad Tripoli	27	Al Ahly Tripoli	27	Al Akhdar Darnah	10		Al Ahly Tripoli	2-1	Olympique Az-Zwiyah
2007	Al Ittihad Tripoli	55	Al Ahly Tripoli	49	Al Medina Tripoli	43		Al Ittihad Tripoli	1-0	Al Akhdar Darnah

Al Medina won the 2001 Championship on penalties after a 1-1 draw

LCA – ST LUCIA

NATIONAL TEAM RECORD
JULY 10TH 2006 TO JULY 12TH 2010

PL	W	D	L	F	A	%
5	0	0	5	3	24	0

FIFA/COCA-COLA WORLD RANKING

1993	1994	1995	1996	1997	1998	1999	2000	2001	2002	2003	2004	2005	2006	High		Low	
139	157	114	134	142	139	152	135	130	112	130	114	128	160	**108**	04/03	**164**	04/07

2006–2007											
08/06	09/06	10/06	11/06	12/06	01/07	02/07	03/07	04/07	05/07	06/07	07/07
115	115	116	155	160	164	161	157	164	163	160	157

St Lucia played five international matches in 2006 and by losing all five of them the national team set a new record of six consecutive defeats. In preparation for the Caribbean Cup qualifiers, St Lucia played two matches against in-form Guyana and although Guyana needed an injury-time goal to beat them in the first of those games, things got progressively worse, especially in their Caribbean Cup group. Admittedly St Lucia were up against strong opposition but Emanuel Belase's team had a wretched time in Jamaica, losing 4-0 to the hosts, 7-1 to the eventual champions Haiti and then to cap it all they were on the end of an 8-0 thrashing by their smaller neighbours St Vincent.

INTERNATIONAL HONOURS
None

The football association in St Lucia have voiced their ambitions to follow in the footsteps of Jamaica and Trinidad by becoming the third English speaking island in the Caribbean to qualify for the World Cup, but just implementing a development plan that would see them qualify for the finals of the Caribbean Cup would be a big achievement. In club football the 2007 National Football Championship final was an all Soufrière affair with Anse Chastanet GYSO beating Elite Challengers 2-1 in Vieux-Fort in February. Having trailed 1-0 for most of the match, GYSO scored twice through Luke Julian and Immanuel Marchand in the last two minutes to clinch the title.

THE FIFA BIG COUNT OF 2006

	Male	Female		Total
Number of players	9 560	1 463	Referees and Assistant Referees	66
Professionals	0		Admin, Coaches, Technical, Medical	324
Amateurs 18+	2 413		Number of clubs	40
Youth under 18	650		Number of teams	125
Unregistered	1 960		Clubs with women's teams	1
Total players	11 023		Players as % of population	6.54%

St Lucia Football Association (SLFA)
La Clery, PO Box 255, Castries, St Lucia
Tel +1 758 4530687   Fax +1 758 4560510
slfa@candw.lc   www.none
President: LARCHER Oswald W.   General Secretary: BOXIL Brian
Vice-President: SEALEY John   Treasurer: BOXIL Brian   Media Officer: PIERRE Michel
Men's Coach: MILLAR Carson   Women's Coach: KIRTON Sean
SLFA formed: 1979   CONCACAF: 1988   FIFA: 1988
Colours: White with yellow/blue/black stripe, White with yellow/blue/black stripe, White/blue/yellow

RECENT INTERNATIONAL MATCHES PLAYED BY ST LUCIA

2003	Opponents	Score		Venue	Comp	Scorers	Att	Referee
26-03	Jamaica	L	0-5	Kingston	CCq		22 000	Brizan TRI
28-03	Haiti	W	2-1	Kingston	CCq	Emmanuel [45], Flavius [90]	14 500	Lee ATG
30-03	Martinique	L	4-5	Kingston	CCq	Elva [21], Mark [38], Jean [52], Joseph.V [56]	7 200	Lee ATG
2004								
1-02	Guadeloupe †	L	0-2		Fr			
8-02	St Vincent/Grenadines	L	1-2	Castries	Fr			
22-02	British Virgin Islands	W	1-0	Tortola	WCq	Elva [55]	800	Stewart JAM
21-03	St Vincent/Grenadines	D	1-1	Kingstown	Fr	Elva [15]		
28-03	British Virgin Islands	W	9-0	Vieux Fort	WCq	Emmanuel 2 [13p 66], Joseph.E [26], Jean 2 [28 52] Skeete 2 [49 55], Elva [69], Baptiste [90]	665	Corrivault CAN
2-06	Grenada	L	0-2	St George's	Fr		2 500	
13-06	Panama	L	0-4	Panama City	WCq		15 000	Phillip GRN
20-06	Panama	L	0-3	Vieux Fort	WCq		400	Gurley VIN
17-10	Grenada	W	3-1	Castries	Fr	Gilbert 3		
2-11	St Kitts and Nevis	D	1-1	Basseterre	CCq	Gilbert [67]		Bedeau GRN
4-11	Montserrat	W	3-0	Basseterre	CCq	St Lucia awarded match 3-0		
6-11	Antigua and Barbuda	W	2-1	Basseterre	CCq	Elva [22], Gilbert [27]		Bedeau GRN
12-12	Jamaica	D	1-1	Vieux Fort	CCq	Joseph.E [23]		Jeanvillier MTQ
19-12	Jamaica	L	1-2	Kingston	CCq	Elva [23]	2 500	Gutierrez CUB
2005								
No international matches played in 2005								
2006								
28-07	Guyana	L	2-3	Linden	Fr	Elva [62], Gilbert Levi [70]		Lancaster GUY
30-07	Guyana	L	0-2	Georgetown	Fr			James GUY
27-09	Jamaica	L	0-4	Kingston	CCq		4 000	Tamayo CUB
29-09	Haiti	L	1-7	Kingston	CCq	Valcin [90]	3 000	Callendar BRB
1-10	St Vincent/Grenadines	L	0-8	Kingston	CCq		3 000	Tamayo CUB
2007								
No international matches played in 2007 before August								

Fr = Friendly match • CC = Digicel Caribbean Cup • WC = FIFA World Cup • q = qualifier • † Not a full international

NATIONAL TEAM RECORDS AND RECORD SEQUENCES

Records			Sequence records					
Victory	14-1	VIR 2001	Wins	5	2000	Clean sheets	5	1990-1991
Defeat	0-8	VIN 2006	Defeats	6	2004-2006	Goals scored	14	1999-2000
Player Caps	n/a		Undefeated	7	1982-1983	Without goal	3	2004
Player Goals	n/a		Without win	7	2004-2006	Goals against	12	2001-02

RECENT LEAGUE AND CUP RECORD

Championship		Cup	
Year	Champions		Winners
2001	VSADC		VSADC
2002	VSADC		VSADC
2003	season readjustment		18 Plus
2004	Roots Alley Ballers		Northern United
2005	Northern United		No tournament played
2006	Canaries		Elite Challengers
2007	Anse Chastanet GYSO		

ST LUCIA COUNTRY INFORMATION

Capital	Castries	Independence	1979 from the UK	GDP per Capita	$5 400
Population	164 213	Status	Parliamentary democracy	GNP Ranking	165
Area km²	616	Language	English	Dialling code	+1758
Population density	266 per km²	Literacy rate	67%	Internet code	.lc
% in urban areas	48%	Main religion	Christian	GMT +/–	-4
Towns/Cities ('000)	Castries 13; Vieux Fort 4; Micoud 3; Dennery 3; Soufrière 3; Gros Islet 2				
Neighbours (km)	Atlantic Ocean & Carribbean Sea 158				
Main stadia	Bones Park – Castries 20 000; National Stadium – Vieux Fort				

LES – LESOTHO

NATIONAL TEAM RECORD
JULY 10TH 2006 TO JULY 12TH 2010

PL	W	D	L	F	A	%
12	2	2	8	8	18	25

FIFA/COCA-COLA WORLD RANKING

1993	1994	1995	1996	1997	1998	1999	2000	2001	2002	2003	2004	2005	2006	High		Low	
138	135	149	162	149	140	154	136	126	132	120	144	145	160	**120**	12/03	**166**	03/07

2006–2007											
08/06	09/06	10/06	11/06	12/06	01/07	02/07	03/07	04/07	05/07	06/07	07/07
133	144	158	160	160	160	161	166	147	146	146	143

Lesotho is one of just three countries in the world completely surrounded by a single country, but as that country is South Africa, it feels very much like Lesotho is hosting the 2010 World Cup too! The World Cup has certainly opened up all sorts of associated opportunities for the tiny mountain kingdom and has galvanised the game in the country. Coach Motheo Mohapi has taken the bulk of the under-20 side, who were surprise qualifiers for the 2005 African Youth Championship in Benin, and promoted them up to senior duty, with the view of building a team that might stand a chance of qualifying for the finals. While many reckon that to be a long shot, Lesotho have grand ambitions.

INTERNATIONAL HONOURS
None

The young side were thrown in at the deep end in October 2007 when the mighty Nigeria came to play in a 2008 African Nations Cup qualifier and 'Likuena' (the crocodiles) did well to only lose by only a single goal. Wins over Swaziland and Niger in 2007 and draws with Uganda and Zimbabwe seem to indicate potential for Mohapi and his teenage campaigners. But with a population of less than two million Lesotho are always going to be handicapped by the lack of a decent playing pool. Club football is also relatively undeveloped although 2006 champions LCS Maseru only narrowly lost to Zambia's Zanaco in the first round of the 2007 Champions League.

THE FIFA BIG COUNT OF 2006

	Male	Female		Total
Number of players	109 900	100	Referees and Assistant Referees	100
Professionals	0		Admin, Coaches, Technical, Medical	2 200
Amateurs 18+	27 200		Number of clubs	110
Youth under 18	2 300		Number of teams	1 000
Unregistered	5 500		Clubs with women's teams	0
Total players	110 000		Players as % of population	5.44%

Lesotho Football Association (LEFA)
Old Polo Ground, PO Box 1879, Maseru-100, Lesotho
Tel +266 22311879   Fax +266 22310586
lefa@leo.co.ls   www.lesothofa.com
President: PHAFANE Salemane   General Secretary: SEMATLANE Mafole
Vice-President: MOSOTHOANE Pitso   Treasurer: TBD   Media Officer: MONNE Tslu
Men's Coach: MOHAPI Motheo   Women's Coach: MASIMONA Lethoia
LEFA formed: 1932   CAF: 1964   FIFA: 1964
Blue shirts, Green shorts, White socks

RECENT INTERNATIONAL MATCHES PLAYED BY LESOTHO

2004	Opponents	Score		Venue	Comp	Scorers	Att	Referee
29-02	Botswana	D	0-0	Maseru	CCr1	L 10-11p	10 000	Mufeti NAM
15-12	Botswana	D	1-1	Maseru	Fr			
2005								
19-03	Namibia	L	1-2	Maseru	Fr			
1-06	Swaziland	L	3-4	Somhlolo	Fr			
11-06	Malawi	L	1-2	Lusaka	CCr1	Potse [46]		Mpanisi ZAM
26-06	Mozambique	L	0-1	Maputo	Fr			
2006								
14-04	Swaziland	W	5-0	Maseru	Fr	Ramafole [27], Mothoane [38], Shale 2 [64 74], Muso [85]		
16-04	Swaziland	D	2-2	Maseru	Fr	Seema [83], Shale [88]		
29-04	Mozambique	D	0-0	Maseru	CCr1	W 5-4p		Jovinala MWI
30-04	Angola	L	1-3	Maseru	CCr1	Moletsane [89]		Mlangeni SWZ
10-05	South Africa	D	0-0	Maseru	Fr			
26-08	Swaziland	L	1-3	Mbabane	Fr	Ranchobe [9]		
2-09	Uganda	L	0-3	Kampala	CNq			Abdelrahman SUD
3-10	Botswana	L	0-1	Gaborone	Fr			
8-10	Nigeria	L	0-1	Maseru	CNq			Marange ZIM
2007								
13-02	Swaziland	L	0-1	Maseru	Fr			
18-03	Swaziland	W	1-0	Lobamba	Fr	Potse [75]		
25-03	Niger	W	3-1	Maseru	CNq	Potse 2 [18 47], Marai [81]		Lwanja MWI
25-05	Zimbabwe	D	1-1	Masvingo	Fr	Ranchobe [58]		
3-06	Niger	L	0-2	Niamey	CNq			
19-06	Uganda	D	0-0	Maseru	CNq			
28-07	Angola	L	0-2	Gaborone	CCr1			Disang BOT
29-07	Namibia	L	2-3	Gaborone	CCr1			

Fr = Friendly match • CN = CAF African Cup of Nations • CC = COSAFA Castle Cup • WC = FIFA World Cup • q = qualifier • r1 = first round group

LESOTHO NATIONAL TEAM RECORDS AND RECORD SEQUENCES

Records			Sequence records					
Victory	5-0	SWZ 2006	Wins	3	1979	Clean sheets	3	1992
Defeat	0-7	COD 1993	Defeats	6	1995-1997	Goals scored	6	1992
Player Caps	n/a		Undefeated	7	1992	Without goal	4	2006-2007
Player Goals	n/a		Without win	11	1981-1992	Goals against	12	2000-2001

RECENT LEAGUE AND CUP RECORD

Championship		Cup	
Year	Champions		Winners
2000	LPS Maseru		RLDF Maseru
2001	RLDF Maseru		
2002	LPS Maseru		
2003	Matlama FC Maseru		
2004	RLDF Maseru		
2005	Likhopo Maseru		
2006	Likhopo Maseru		
2007	LCS Maseru		

LESOTHO COUNTRY INFORMATION

Capital	Maseru	Independence	1966 from the UK	GDP per Capita	3 000
Population	1 865 040	Status	Constutional Monarchy	GNP Ranking	153
Area km²	30 355	Language	Sesotho, English	Dialling code	+266
Population density	61 per km²	Literacy rate	84%	Internet code	.ls
% in urban areas	23%	Main religion	Christian 80%	GMT + / –	+2
Towns/Cities ('000)	Maseru 194; Hlotse 46; Mafeteng 40; Maputsoa 31; Teyateyaneng 25; Mohale's Hoek 22				
Neighbours (km)	South Africa 909				
Main stadia	National Stadium – Maseru 20 000				

LIB – LEBANON

NATIONAL TEAM RECORD
JULY 10TH 2006 TO JULY 12TH 2010

PL	W	D	L	F	A	%
5	1	2	2	4	4	40

FIFA/COCA-COLA WORLD RANKING

1993	1994	1995	1996	1997	1998	1999	2000	2001	2002	2003	2004	2005	2006	High		Low	
108	129	134	97	90	85	111	110	93	119	115	105	125	126	85	12/98	145	11/95

2006–2007											
08/06	09/06	10/06	11/06	12/06	01/07	02/07	03/07	04/07	05/07	06/07	07/07
111	108	126	127	126	110	124	132	130	130	135	135

The 2006-07 season in Lebanon was played out against the backdrop of an increasingly unstable political situation in the country. In June 2007 a bomb blast in Beirut killed two Al Nijmah players, Hussein Dokmak and Hussein Neim, both of whom were looking forward to taking part in the latter stages of the AFC Cup having helped Al Nijmah qualify from the group stage. The fighting between Israel and Hezbollah in August 2006 caused widespread chaos in the country and the start of the League was delayed until mid December. Once underway, defending champions Al Ansar won their first ten matches and didn't lose until the 18th round when they were almost assured of

INTERNATIONAL HONOURS
None

the title. Unlike Nijmah, however, Ansar failed to make it past the first round group stage of the AFC Cup finishing third in a very close group. Nijmeh will be hoping to make it to the final having been knocked out in the semi-finals in both 2005 and 2006. The political problems took their toll on the Lebanese national team which was forced to withdraw from the AFC Asian Cup qualifiers. That left a preliminary qualifying group for the forthcoming Arab Cup to play for, which was won, along with the West Asian Championship held in June 2007 in Amman. Originally scheduled to take place in Beirut in 2006, Lebanon lost to both Syria and the new hosts to crash out in the first round.

THE FIFA BIG COUNT OF 2006

	Male	Female		Total
Number of players	318 385	100	Referees and Assistant Referees	184
Professionals	50		Admin, Coaches, Technical, Medical	3 311
Amateurs 18+	12 240		Number of clubs	178
Youth under 18	6 130		Number of teams	877
Unregistered	300 000		Clubs with women's teams	0
Total players	318 485		Players as % of population	8.22%

Lebanese Football Association (FLFA)
Verdun Street - Bristol, Radwan Center, PO Box 4732, Beirut, Lebanon
Tel +961 1 745745   Fax +961 1 349529
libanfa@cyberia.net.lb   www.lebanesefa.com
President: HAYDAR Hachem   General Secretary: ALAMEH Rahif
Vice-President: KAMAR EDDINE Ahmad   Treasurer: AL RABA'A Mahmoud   Media Officer: ALAMEH Rahif
Men's Coach: MEKDACHE Adnan   Women's Coach: SAKRISSIAN Vathe
FLFA formed: 1933   AFC: 1964   FIFA: 1935
Red shirts, White shorts, Red socks

RECENT INTERNATIONAL MATCHES PLAYED BY LEBANON

2002 Opponents	Score		Venue	Comp	Scorers	Att	Referee
1-09 Jordan	L	0-1	Damascus	WAr1			
3-09 Iran	L	0-2	Damascus	WAr1		2 000	Haj Khader SYR
19-12 Saudi Arabia	L	0-1	Kuwait City	ARr1		700	El Beltagy EGY
21-12 Syria	L	1-4	Kuwait City	ARr1	Kassas 54	1 000	Guezzaz MAR
24-12 Yemen	W	4-2	Kuwait City	ARr1	Antar.R 3 11 51 60, Hojeij 62	1 000	Hamza KUW
26-12 Bahrain	D	0-0	Kuwait City	ARr1		1 000	Guirat TUN
2003							
15-08 Syria	D	0-0	Damascus	Fr	Abandoned at half-time		
22-08 Syria	W	1-0	Beirut	Fr	Ali Atwi 57		
4-09 Korea DPR	W	1-0	Pyongyang	ACq	Farah 56		
19-09 Bahrain	L	3-4	Manama	Fr	Kassas 53, Mohammed 69, Al Jamal 86		
17-10 Jordan	L	0-1	Amman	ACq			
3-11 Korea DPR	D	1-1	Beirut	ACq	Hamieh 58	25 000	
12-11 Jordan	L	0-2	Beirut	ACq		15 000	
19-11 Iran	L	0-3	Beirut	ACq			Al Marzouqi UAE
28-11 Iran	L	0-1	Tehran	ACq			Rungklay THA
16-12 Kuwait	L	0-2	Larnaca	Fr			
18-12 Kuwait	D	0-0	Larnaca	Fr			
2004							
8-02 Bahrain	W	2-1	Beirut	Fr	Chahoud 90, Al Jamal 90		
18-02 Korea Republic	L	0-2	Suwon	WCq		22 000	Al Dosari KSA
23-03 Syria	L	0-1	Jounieh	Fr			
31-03 Vietnam	W	2-0	Nam Dinh	WCq	Antar.R 83, Hamieh 88	25 000	Irmatov UZB
26-05 Bahrain	D	2-2	Beirut	Fr	Ali Atwi 70, Balout 81		
9-06 Maldives	W	3-0	Beirut	WCq	Zein 21, Antar.R 87, Nasseredine 93+	18 000	Nurilddin Salman IRQ
17-06 Iran	L	0-4	Tehran	WAr1			
19-06 Syria	L	1-3	Tehran	WAr1	Zein 65		
3-07 China PR	L	0-6	Chongqing	Fr			
31-08 Jordan	D	2-2	Amman	Fr			
8-09 Maldives	W	5-2	Male	WCq	Nasseredine 2 4 58, Antar.F 44, Chahoud 63, Antar.R 75	12 000	Al Ajmi OMA
3-10 Kuwait	L	1-3	Tripoli	Fr	Chahoud 64		
6-10 Kuwait	D	1-1	Beirut	Fr	Chahoud 45		
13-10 Korea Republic	D	1-1	Beirut	WCq	Nasseredine 27	38 000	Irmatov UZB
17-11 Vietnam	D	0-0	Beirut	WCq		1 000	Ebrahim BHR
1-12 Qatar	L	1-4	Doha	Fr	Nasseredine		
2005							
2-02 Bahrain	L	1-2	Doha	Fr	Ali Atwi		
2006							
27-01 Saudi Arabia	W	2-1	Riyadh	Fr	Ghaddar 14, Nasseredine 70		
22-02 Kuwait	D	1-1	Beirut	ACq	Nasseredine 67	8 000	Mujghef JOR
21-12 Mauritania	D	0-0	Beirut	ARq			Al Khabbaz BHR
24-12 Somalia	W	4-0	Beirut	ARq	Ghaddar 2 4 28, Nasseredine 72, Rustom 83		Hazem Hussain IRQ
27-12 Sudan	D	0-0	Beirut	ARq			
2007							
16-06 Syria	L	0-1	Amman	WAr1			
20-06 Jordan	L	0-3	Amman	WAr1			

Fr = Friendly match • WA = West Asian Federation Cup • AR = Arab Cup • AC = AFC Asian Cup • WC = FIFA World Cup
q = qualifier • r1 = first round group

LEBANON NATIONAL TEAM RECORDS AND RECORD SEQUENCES

Records			Sequence records				
Victory	11-1	PHI 1967	Wins	6	1995-1996	Clean sheets	4	1997, 2002-2003
Defeat	0-8	IRQ 1959	Defeats	5	1979-1985	Goals scored	10	1993-1996
Player Caps	n/a		Undefeated	9	1993-96, 1996-97	Without goal	11	1974-1988
Player Goals	n/a		Without win	11	1998	Goals against	11	1997-1998

LEBANON COUNTRY INFORMATION

Capital	Beirut	Independence	1944 from France	GDP per Capita	$4 800
Population	3 777 218	Status	Republic	GNP Ranking	70
Area km²	10 400	Language	Arabic	Dialling code	+961
Population density	363 per km²	Literacy rate	87%	Internet code	.lb
% in urban areas	87%	Main religion	Muslim 60%, Christian 39%	GMT + / −	+2
Towns/Cities ('000)	Beirut 1 252; Tripoli 229; Sidon 163; Sour 135; Nabatiye 98; Jounieh 96; Zahlah 78				
Neighbours (km)	Syria 375; Israel 79; Mediterranean Sea 225				
Main stadia	Camille Chamoun – Beirut 57 000; International Olympic – Tripoli 22 400				

LEBANON 2006–07

PREMIER LEAGUE

	Pl	W	D	L	F	A	Pts	Ansar	Safa	Mabarra	Nijmeh	Ahed	Hikma	Ahly	Sahel	Tadamon	Tripoli	Rayyan	Salam
Al Ansar †	22	15	4	3	42	24	49		2-0	3-0	0-1	1-0	1-0	3-2	2-1	4-1	3-1	2-1	2-0
Safa	22	13	6	3	47	16	45	4-2		0-2	1-	0-0	3-2	3-1	2-0	3-0	1-0	1-1	9-0
Al Mabarra	22	12	3	7	31	17	39	4-1	0-1		2-1	0-2	1-0	0-1	3-0	0-0	2-0	4-0	
Al Nijmeh	22	10	6	6	51	22	36	1-2	1-2	3-1		0-0	2-3	4-1	3-0	2-2	0-1	1-0	4-0
Al Ahed	22	9	9	4	43	23	36	3-4	0-0	0-1	3-2		4-3	1-0	2-2	1-1	0-0	1-1	0-0
Al Hikma	22	10	5	7	39	32	35	1-1	1-0	2-1	2-2	3-2		5-3	2-1	2-2	3-2	1-1	**2-0**
Al Ahly Saida	22	5	9	8	25	27	24	0-0	1-1	0-0	0-1	1-1	2-0		2-2	1-1	1-1	3-0	2-0
Shabab Al Sahel	22	6	6	10	24	37	24	0-0	0-3	1-2	0-0	0-5	1-1	2-1		0-0	0-1	1-3	2-1
Al Tadamon Tyre	22	5	9	8	20	34	24	0-2	1-3	0-2	0-0	1-4	1-0	0-0	2-4		1-0	1-1	2-0
Tripoli SC	22	5	7	10	27	33	22	0-1	1-1	1-1	2-6	1-3	2-0	1-1	2-4	2-3		0-2	7-1
Al Rayyan	22	5	7	10	21	45	22	2-2	0-6	0-1	0-9	2-10	0-1	1-0	2-0	0-1	0-0		1-1
Salam Zgharta §6	22	0	3	19	8	68	-3	2-4	0-4	0-7	0-1	0-5	**0-2**	1-2	0-0	1-2	1-3		

15/12/2006 - 3/06/2007 • † Qualified for AFC Cup • § = points deducted • Matches in bold were awarded

FA CUP 2006–07

Round of 16		Quarter–finals		Semi–finals		Final	
Al Ansar *	2						
Al Tadamon Tyre	0	**Al Ansar** *	6				
Riyadi Abbassieh	0	Al Rayyan	1				
Al Rayyan *	4			**Al Ansar**	3		
Mawadda Tripoli *	2			Al Mabarra	2		
Shabab Al Sahel	1	Mawadda Tripoli *	0				
Safa	0	**Al Mabarra**	1				
Al Mabarra *	1					**Al Ansar**	3
Al Ahly Saida *	4					Al Ahed	1
Bourj	0	**Al Ahly Saida**	2				
Tripoli SC	0	**Al Nijmah** *	0				
Al Nijmah *	2			Al Ahly Saida	0		
Al Hikma	2			**Al Ahed**	3		
Salam Zgharta *	1	Al Hikma	2				
Al Ahly Nabatiye	1	**Al Ahed** *	3				
Al Ahed *	6			* Home team			

CUP FINAL

Al Ansar 3 – Al Ahed 1

Beirut
1-07-2007

RECENT LEAGUE AND CUP RECORD

	Championship						Cup		
Year	Champions	Pts	Runners-up	Pts	Third	Pts	Winners	Score	Runners-up
1997	Al Ansar	65	Al Nijmeh	58	Homenetmen	49	Al Nijmeh	2-0	Al Ansar
1998	Al Ansar	63	Al Nijmeh	53	Al Tadamon	43	Al Nijmeh	2-1	Homenmen
1999	Al Ansar	48	Safa	38	Al Tadamon	36	Al Ansar	2-1	Homenmen
2000	Al Njmeh	47	Al Ansar	44	Al Akha 'a-Ahly	33	Shabab Al Sahel	1-1 5-4p	Safa
2001	Championship cancelled due to match fixing scandal						Al Tadamon	2-1	Al Ansar
2002	Al Nijmeh	61	La Sagesse	60	Al Tadamon	59	Al Ansar	2-0	Al Ahed
2003	Olympic Beirut	54	Al Nijmeh	53	Al Ahed	50	Olympic Beirut	3-2	Al Nijmeh
2004	Al Nijmeh	54	Al Ahed	47	Olympic Beirut	35	Al Ahed	2-1	Al Nijmeh
2005	Al Nijmeh	44	Al Ansar	44	Al Ahed	36	Al Ahed	2-1	Olympic Beirut
2006	Al Ansar	47	Al Nijmeh	44	Safa	32	Al Ansar	3-1	Al Hikma
2007	Al Ansar	49	Safa	45	Al Mabarra	39	Al Ansar	3-1	Al Ahed

LIE – LIECHTENSTEIN

NATIONAL TEAM RECORD
JULY 10TH 2006 TO JULY 12TH 2010

PL	W	D	L	F	A	%
10	1	1	8	5	27	15

FIFA/COCA-COLA WORLD RANKING

1993	1994	1995	1996	1997	1998	1999	2000	2001	2002	2003	2004	2005	2006	High	Low
160	156	157	154	158	159	125	147	150	147	148	142	122	158	**122** 12/05	**165** 09/98

2006–2007											
08/06	09/06	10/06	11/06	12/06	01/07	02/07	03/07	04/07	05/07	06/07	07/07
124	155	161	160	158	159	160	162	131	134	133	133

Liechtenstein may lose a lot of international matches but that just makes the victories even sweeter, and the highlight of the season was the 1-0 win over Euro 2004 finalists Latvia at the redeveloped Rheinpark Stadion in Vaduz. That was then followed by an equally impressive 1-1 draw with Iceland in Reykjavík which meant that going into the summer break, Liechtenstein were above both of their rivals in their UEFA Euro 2008 qualifying group. There were also triumphs for Liechtenstein to celebrate in European club football with FC Vaduz easily beating Hungary's Ujpesti in the first preliminary round of the UEFA Cup. In the next round they also beat

INTERNATIONAL HONOURS
None

Switzerland's FC Basel, winning 2-1 in Vaduz, but having lost 1-0 in Basel, Vaduz were knocked out on away goals. Playing in the UEFA Cup is almost a guaranteed annual attraction for Vaduz and by beating FC Ruggell 8-0 in the Cup Final they qualified for the 2007-08 tournament. As the only top level team in the country they have little trouble winning the Cup and the victory over Ruggell was their tenth in a row. Liechtenstein is the only country in Europe without a League so Vaduz play in Switzerland where they have established themselves as one of the leading second division sides, although they only managed to finish a disappointing ninth the 2006-07 season.

THE FIFA BIG COUNT OF 2006

	Male	Female		Total
Number of players	2 990	325	Referees and Assistant Referees	34
Professionals	10		Admin, Coaches, Technical, Medical	240
Amateurs 18+	795		Number of clubs	7
Youth under 18	1 400		Number of teams	95
Unregistered	310		Clubs with women's teams	3
Total players	3 315		Players as % of population	9.75%

Liechtensteiner Fussballverband (LFV)
Landstrasse 149, 9494 Schaan, Postfach 165, 9490 Vaduz, Liechtenstein
Tel +423 2374747   Fax +423 2374748
info@lfv.li   www.lfv.li
President: WALSER Reinhard   General Secretary: OSPELT Roland
Vice-President: HILTI Fredi   Treasurer: GERNER Urs   Media Officer: FROMMELT Judith
Men's Coach: ZAUGG Hanspeter   Women's Coach: None
LFV formed: 1934   UEFA: 1992   FIFA: 1974
Blue shirts with white trimmings, Red shorts, Blue socks or Red shirts with white trimmings, Blue shorts, Red Socks

RECENT INTERNATIONAL MATCHES PLAYED BY LIECHTENSTEIN

2002	Opponents	Score		Venue	Comp	Scorers	Att	Referee
21-08	Faroe Islands	L	1-3	Tórshavn	Fr	Hetta [40p]	3 200	Orrason ISL
8-09	Macedonia FYR	D	1-1	Vaduz	ECq	Stocklasa.Mk [90]	2 300	Godulyan UKR
16-10	Turkey	L	0-5	Istanbul	ECq		8 000	Baskakov RUS
2003								
29-03	England	L	0-2	Vaduz	ECq		3 548	Kasnaferis GRE
2-04	Slovakia	L	0-4	Trnava	ECq			Ceferin SVN
30-04	Saudi Arabia	W	1-0	Vaduz	Fr	Burgmeier.F [22]	1 200	Rogalla SUI
7-06	Macedonia FYR	L	1-3	Skopje	ECq	Beck.R [18]	6 000	Jara CZE
20-08	San Marino	D	2-2	Vaduz	Fr	Frick.M [16], Burgmeier.F [23]	850	Wildhaber SUI
6-09	Turkey	L	0-3	Vaduz	ECq		3 548	Van Egmond NED
10-09	England	L	0-2	Manchester	ECq		64 931	Fisker DEN
11-10	Slovakia	L	0-2	Vaduz	ECq		800	Hyytia FIN
2004								
28-04	San Marino	L	0-1	Serravalle	Fr		700	Sammut MLT
3-06	Greece	L	0-2	Vaduz	Fr		2 000	Petignat SUI
6-06	Switzerland	L	0-1	Zürich	Fr		10 200	Drabek AUT
18-08	Estonia	L	1-2	Vaduz	WCq	D'Elia [49]	912	Bozinovski MKD
3-09	Netherlands	L	0-3	Utrecht	Fr		15 000	Brines SCO
8-09	Slovakia	L	0-7	Bratislava	WCq		5 620	Delevic SCG
9-10	Portugal	D	2-2	Vaduz	WCq	Burgmeier.F [48], Beck.T [76]	3 548	Panic BIH
13-10	Luxembourg	W	4-0	Luxembourg	WCq	Stocklasa.Mt [41], Burgmeier.F 2 [44 85], Frick.M [57p]	3 748	Jara CZE
17-11	Latvia	L	1-3	Vaduz	WCq	Frick.M [32]	1 460	Szabo HUN
2005								
26-03	Russia	L	1-2	Vaduz	WCq	Beck.T [40]	2 400	Bernsten NOR
4-06	Estonia	L	0-2	Tallinn	WCq		3 000	Whitby WAL
8-06	Latvia	L	0-1	Riga	WCq		8 000	Eriksson SWE
17-08	Slovakia	D	0-0	Vaduz	WCq		1 150	Layec FRA
3-09	Russia	L	0-2	Moscow	WCq		18 123	Hyytia FIN
7-09	Luxembourg	W	3-0	Vaduz	WCq	Frick.M [38], Fischer [77], Beck [92+]	2 300	Skomina SVN
8-10	Portugal	L	1-2	Aveiro	WCq	Fischer [32]	29 000	Gilewski POL
12-11	FYR Macedonia	L	1-2	Vaduz	Fr	D'Elia [35]	1 350	Nobs SUI
2006								
2-06	Togo	L	0-1	Vaduz	Fr		2 700	Schorgenhofer AUT
7-06	Australia	L	1-3	Ulm	Fr	OG [8]	5 872	Stark GER
16-08	Switzerland	L	0-3	Vaduz	Fr		4 837	Brugger AUT
2-09	Spain	L	0-4	Badajoz	ECq		13 876	Bozinovski MKD
6-09	Sweden	L	1-3	Gothenburg	ECq	Frick.M [27]	17 735	Banari MDA
6-10	Austria	L	1-2	Vaduz	Fr	Frick.M [69]	3 750	Rogalla SUI
11-10	Denmark	L	0-4	Vaduz	ECq		2 665	Richards WAL
14-11	Wales	L	0-4	Wrexham	Fr		8 752	Wilmes LUX
2007								
24-03	Northern Ireland	L	1-4	Vaduz	ECq	Burgmeier.F [91+]	4 340	Oriekhov UKR
28-03	Latvia	W	1-0	Vaduz	ECq	Frick.M [17]	1 680	Gumienny BEL
2-06	Iceland	D	1-1	Reykjavík	ECq	Rohrer [69]	5 139	Kaldma EST
6-06	Spain	L	0-2	Vaduz	ECq		5 739	Ivanov.N RUS

Fr = Friendly match • EC = UEFA EURO 2004/2008 • WC = FIFA World Cup • q = qualifier

LIECHTENSTEIN NATIONAL TEAM RECORDS AND RECORD SEQUENCES

Records				Sequence records			
Victory	4-0	LUX 2004	Wins	3	1981-1982	Clean sheets	2	1981-82, 1999
Defeat	1-11	MKD 1996	Defeats	21	1983-1995	Goals scored	4	2004-2005
Player Caps	75	HASLER Daniel	Undefeated	3	1981-1982	Without goal	11	1994-96, 2000-02
Player Goals	11	FRICK Mario	Without win	29	1984-1998	Goals against	22	1995-1999

PRINCIPALITY OF LIECHTENSTEIN; FUERSTENTUM LIECHTENSTEIN

Capital	Vaduz	Language	German		Formation 1719
Population	33 987	Area	160 km²	Density 208 per km²	% in cities 21%
GDP per cap	$25 000	Dailling code	+423	Internet .li	GMT + / - +1

MEDALS TABLE

		Overall			Cup			Europe			Town	Stadium	Cap'ty	DoF
		G	S	B	G	S	B	G	S	B				
1	FC Vaduz	36	12		36	12					Vaduz	Rheinpark Stadion	6 127	1932
2	FC Balzers	11	12		11	12					Balzers	Sportplatz Rheinau Stadion	1 000	1932
3	FC Triesen	8	10		8	10					Triesen	Blumenau Stadion	2 100	1932
4	USV Eschen/Mauren	4	12		4	12					Eschen/Mauren	Sportpark Eschen/Mauren	6 000	1963
5	FC Schaan	3	10		3	10					Schaan	Rheinwiese Stadion	1 000	1949
6	FC Ruggell	5			5						Ruggell	Freizeitpark Widau	1 000	1958
7	FC Triesenberg										Triesenberg	Sportanlage Leitawis Stadion	1 000	1972

LIECHTENSTEINER CUP 2006–07

Second Preliminary round		Quarter–finals		Semi–finals		Final	
FC Vaduz	Bye						
		FC Vaduz	6				
FC Triesen	1	FC Schaan	0				
FC Schaan	4			FC Vaduz	3		
FC Balzers	Bye			USV Eschen/Mauren	1		
		FC Balzers	2				
		USV Eschen/Mauren	3				
USV Eschen/Mauren	Bye					FC Vaduz ‡	8
USV Eschen/Mauren-2	7p					FC Ruggell	0
FC Balzers-2	6p	USV Eschen/Mauren-2	1				
FC Vaduz-2	1	FC Triesenberg-2	0				
FC Triesenberg-2	2			USV Eschen/Mauren-2	0		
FC Schaan-2	2			FC Ruggell	2		
FC Triesen-2	1	FC Schaan-2	2				
		FC Ruggell	3				
FC Ruggell	Bye						

* Home team in the first leg • ‡ Qualified for the UEFA Cup

CUP FINAL

Rheinparkstadion, Vaduz
1-05-2007, Att: 950
Scorers - Fischer [2], Pape Faye 2 [43 52],
Oehri OG [53], Langlet 2 [63 92+], Polverino [67],
Bern [86]

LTU – LITHUANIA

NATIONAL TEAM RECORD
JULY 10TH 2006 TO JULY 12TH 2010

PL	W	D	L	F	A	%
11	3	1	7	11	15	31.8

FIFA/COCA-COLA WORLD RANKING

1993	1994	1995	1996	1997	1998	1999	2000	2001	2002	2003	2004	2005	2006	High	Low
85	59	43	48	45	54	50	85	97	100	101	100	100	69	42 08/97	118 09/04

2006–2007											
08/06	09/06	10/06	11/06	12/06	01/07	02/07	03/07	04/07	05/07	06/07	07/07
65	67	70	70	69	68	72	76	89	92	79	78

The draw for the UEFA Euro 2008 qualifiers ensured that it was always going to be tough work for Lithuania, and despite holding Italy to a draw in Naples in the opening game, the team has struggled in a group containing three of the nations that finished in the last eight of the FIFA World Cup in Germany. There was some success in international competition when FBK Kaunas won the inaugural Baltic Champions Cup. They beat Estonian champions TVMK 6-4 and then drew with Latvia's Metalurgs Leipaja to finish top of the group. It certainly made a change from the usual first round exits in the UEFA Champions League and in the UEFA Cup. There was a big influx of

INTERNATIONAL HONOURS
None

foreigners into the Lithuanian League and for the first time the top scorer was not a local, that honour going to Vetra's Ukrainian striker Serhiy Kuznetsov, although his contribution wasn't enough to win a first title for the club. Having lost out to Ekranas in the 2005 season, FBK Kaunas bounced back to win their seventh championship in eight years giving owner Vladimir Romanov something to smile about after his other clubs Hearts and MTZ-RIPO ended up trophyless. Kaunas failed to complete a hat-trick of Cup wins, however. They lost in the quarter-finals of a tournament won by Suduva Marijampole, who beat Ekranas in the final to claim their first trophy.

THE FIFA BIG COUNT OF 2006

	Male	Female		Total
Number of players	119 020	16 854	Referees and Assistant Referees	195
Professionals	340		Admin, Coaches, Technical, Medical	1 370
Amateurs 18+	3 510		Number of clubs	64
Youth under 18	9 764		Number of teams	367
Unregistered	38 100		Clubs with women's teams	1
Total players	135 874		Players as % of population	3.79%

Lithuanian Football Federation (LFF)

Seimyniskiu 15, 2005 Vilnius, Lithuania

Tel +370 52638741   Fax +370 52638740

info@futbolas.lt   www.futbolas.lt

President: VARANAVICIUS Liutauras   General Secretary: KVEDARAS Julius

Vice-President: BABRAVICIUS Gintautas   Treasurer: ZYGELIENR Dalia   Media Officer: ZIZAITE Vaiva

Men's Coach: LIUBINSKAS Algimantas   Women's Coach: VIKTORAVICIUS Rimas

LFF formed: 1922   UEFA: 1992   FIFA: 1923-1943 & 1992

Yellow shirts with green trimmings, Green shorts, Yellow socks or Green shirts with yellow trimming, Green shorts, Green socks

RECENT INTERNATIONAL MATCHES PLAYED BY LITHUANIA

2003	Opponents	Score	Venue	Comp	Scorers	Att	Referee
12-02	Latvia	L 1-2	Antalya	Fr	OG [34]	700	
29-03	Germany	D 1-1	Nuremberg	ECq	Razanauskas [73]	40 754	Esquinas Torres ESP
2-04	Scotland	W 1-0	Kaunas	ECq	Razanauskas [75p]	8 000	Stuchlik AUT
30-04	Romania	L 0-1	Kaunas	Fr		5 000	Sipailo LVA
11-06	Iceland	L 0-3	Kaunas	ECq		7 500	Corpodean ROU
3-07	Estonia	W 5-1	Valga	BC	Morinas [39], Cesnauskis.D [45], Velicka [72] Bezykornovas [84], Cesnauskas.E [90]	800	Ingvarsson SWE
4-07	Latvia	L 1-2	Valga	BC	Tamosauskas [73]	500	Frojdfeldt SWE
20-08	Bulgaria	L 0-3	Sofia	Fr		2 000	Bolognino ITA
10-09	Faroe Islands	W 3-1	Toftir	ECq	Morinas 2 [23 57], Vencevicius [88]	2 175	Trivcovic CRO
11-10	Scotland	L 0-1	Glasgow	ECq		50 343	Colombo FRA
14-12	Poland	L 1-3	Ta'Qali	Fr	Butrimavicius [5]	100	Attard MLT
2004							
30-03	Israel	L 1-2	Tel Aviv	Fr	OG [43]	9 782	Dougal SCO
28-04	Belarus	L 0-1	Minsk	Fr		8 000	Ivanov RUS
5-06	Portugal	L 1-4	Alcochete	Fr	Vencevicius [74p]	25 000	Wilmes LUX
18-08	Russia	L 3-4	Moscow	Fr	Danilevicius [40], Poskus [83], Barasa [89]	3 500	Mikulski POL
4-09	Belgium	D 1-1	Charleroi	WCq	Jankauskas [73]	19 218	Loizou CYP
8-09	San Marino	W 4-0	Kaunas	WCq	Jankauskas 2 [18 50], Danilevicius [65], Gedgaudas [92+]	4 000	Jareci ALB
13-10	Spain	D 0-0	Vilnius	WCq		9 114	Poulat FRA
17-11	San Marino	W 1-0	Serravalle	WCq	Cesnauskis.D [41]	1 457	Nalbandyan ARM
2005							
9-02	Georgia	L 0-1	Tbilisi	Fr		1 000	Gadiyev AZE
30-03	Bosnia-Herzegovina	D 1-1	Sarajevo	WCq	Stankevicius [60]	6 000	Baskakov RUS
21-05	Latvia	W 2-0	Kaunas	BC	Morinas 2 [25 81]		
4-06	Spain	L 0-1	Valencia	WCq		25 000	Farina ITA
17-08	Belarus	W 1-0	Vilnius	Fr	Cesnauskis.D [45]	2 500	Sipailo LVA
3-09	Serbia & Montenegro	L 0-2	Belgrade	WCq		20 203	Nielsen DEN
7-09	Bosnia-Herzegovina	L 0-1	Vilnius	WCq		4 000	Kassai HUN
8-10	Serbia & Montenegro	L 0-2	Vilnius	WCq		1 500	Wegereef NED
12-10	Belgium	D 1-1	Vilnius	WCq	OG [82]	1 500	Riley ENG
2006							
1-03	Albania	W 2-1	Tirana	Fr	Savenas [34], Danilevicius [41]		Pieri ITA
2-05	Poland	W 1-0	Belchatow	Fr	Gedgaudas [14]	3 200	Bozinovski MKD
16-08	Moldova	L 2-3	Chisinau	Fr	Poskus [14], Danilevicius [38]		Godulyan UKR
2-09	Italy	D 1-1	Naples	ECq	Danilevicius [21]	43 440	Hansson SWE
6-09	Scotland	L 1-2	Kaunas	ECq	Miceika [85]	8 000	Hrinák SVK
7-10	Faroe Islands	W 1-0	Tórshavn	ECq	Skerla [89]	1 982	Buttimer IRL
11-10	Kuwait	L 0-1	Kuwait City	Fr			Abo QAT
15-11	Malta	W 4-1	Ta'Qali	Fr	Danilevicius 2 [37 66], Radzinevicius [58], Kavaliauskus [90]		Lawlor WAL
2007							
6-02	Mali	L 1-3	La Courneuve	Fr	Jankauskas [28]		Piccirillo FRA
24-03	France	L 0-1	Kaunas	ECq		8 740	Webb ENG
28-03	Ukraine	L 0-1	Odessa	ECq		33 600	Meyer GER
2-06	Georgia	W 1-0	Kaunas	ECq	Mikoliunas [78]	6 400	Circhetta SUI
6-06	Italy	L 0-2	Kaunas	ECq		7 800	Vink NED

Fr = Friendly match • EC = UEFA EURO 2004/2008 • BC = Baltic Cup • WC = FIFA World Cup • q = qualifier

LITHUANIA NATIONAL TEAM RECORDS AND RECORD SEQUENCES

Records			Sequence records				
Victory	7-0	EST 1995	Wins	3	1992	Clean sheets	3	2004
Defeat	0-10	EGY 1924	Defeats	10	1936-1938	Goals scored	15	1934-1937
Player Caps	65	SKARBALIUS Aurelijus	Undefeated	5	1935, 1992	Without goal	4	1993, 1997
Player Goals	13	LINGIS Antanas	Without win	13	1936-1939	Goals against	18	1923-1936

MAJOR CITIES/TOWNS
Population '000

1	Vilnius	541
2	Kaunas	372
3	Klaipeda	191
4	Siauliai	128
5	Panevézys	116
6	Alytus	70
7	Marijampolé	47
8	Mazeikiai	40
9	Jonava	35
10	Utena	32
11	Kédainiai	31
12	Telsiai	29
13	Ukmerge	28
14	Visaginas	27
15	Tauragé	26
16	Plungé	23
17	Kretinga	22
18	Siluté	21
19	Radviliskis	19
20	Palanga	17
21	Druskininkai	17
22	Gargzdai	16
23	Rokiskis	16
24	Birzai	14

REPUBLIC OF LITHUANIA; LIETUVOS RESPUBLIKA

Capital	Vilnius	Language	Lithuanian, Russian, Polish	Independence	1991
Population	3 585 906	Area	65 200 km²	Density	55 per km²	% in cities	72%
GDP per cap	$11 400	Dailling code	+370	Internet	.lt	GMT + / -	+2

MEDALS TABLE

		Overall			League			Cup		Europe			City	Stadium	Cap'ty	DoF
		G	S	B	G	S	B	G	S	G	S	B				
1	FBK Kaunas	10	3	1	7	1	1	3	2				Kaunas	S. Darius & S. Girenas	7 262	1960
2	Zalgiris Vilnius	8	13	2	3	8	2	5	5				Vilnius	Zalgiris	15 030	1947
3	Ekranas Panevezys	4	6	3	2	3	3	2	3				Panevezys	Aukstaitijos	3 000	1964
4	Kareda Siauliai	4	2		2	2		2					Siauliai	Siauliai	5 000	1954
5	Inkaras Kaunas	3	2	1	2		1	1	2				Kaunas	Inkaras	2 000	1937
6	Atlantas Klaipeda	2	3	3		2	3	2	1				Klaipeda	Klaipeda Central	10 000	1960
7	Sirijus Klaipeda	2	1	1	1		1	1	1				Klaipeda	Zalgiris	15 030	1973
8	Suduva Marijampole	1	1	1		1		1	1				Marijampole	Suduvos	4 000	1942
9	Neris Vilnius	1	1			1		1					Vilnius			1966
10	ROMAR Mazeikiai	1		1	1		1						Mazeikiai	Mazeikiai	8 000	1947
11	Vetra Vilnius		2	2			2		2				Vilnius	Vetra	5 300	1996
12	Panerys Vilnius	1	1		1	1							Vilnius	Panerys	2 000	1975-98
13	Tauras Siauliai	1							1				Siauliai			

RECENT LEAGUE AND CUP RECORD

	Championship						Cup		
Year	Champions	Pts	Runners-up	Pts	Third	Pts	Winners	Score	Runners-up
1995	Inkaras Kaunas	36	Zalgiris Vilnius	36	ROMAR Mazeikiai	34	Inkaras Kaunas	2-1	Zalgiris Vilnius
1996	Inkaras Kaunas	56	Kareda Siauliai	52	Zalgiris Vilnius	50	Kareda Siauliai	1-0	Inkaras Kaunas
1997	Kareda Siauliai	64	Zalgiris Vilnius	56	Inkaras Kaunas	53	Zalgiris Vilnius	1-0	Inkaras Kaunas
1998	Kareda Siauliai	79	Zalgiris Vilnius	77	Ekranas Panevezys	68	Ekranas Panevezys	1-0	FBK Kaunas
1999	Zalgiris Vilnius	59	Kareda Siauliai	58	FBK Kaunas	57	Kareda Siauliai	3-0	FBK Kaunas
1999	FBK Kaunas	41	Zalgiris Vilnius	36	Atlantas Klaipeda	33			
2000	FBK Kaunas	86	Zalgiris Vilnius	83	Atlantas Klaipeda	67	Ekranas Panevezys	1-0	Zalgiris Vilnius
2001	FBK Kaunas	85	Atlantas Klaipeda	69	Zalgiris Vilnius	69	Atlantas Klaipeda	1-0	Zalgiris Vilnius
2002	FBK Kaunas	78	Atlantas Klaipeda	67	Ekranas Panevezys	55	FBK Kaunas	3-1	Sūduva Marijampole
2003							Atlantas Klaipeda	1-1 3-1p	Vetra Rudiskes
2003	FBK Kaunas	68	Ekranas Panevezys	62	Vetra	47	Zalgiris Vilnius	3-1	Ekranas Panevezys
2004	FBK Kaunas	65	Ekranas Panevezys	62	Atlantas Klaipeda	50	FBK Kaunas	0-0 2-1p	Atlantas Klaipeda
2005	Ekranas Panevezys	92	FBK Kaunas	82	Sūduva Marijampole	59	FBK Kaunas	2-0	Vetra Vilnius
2006	FBK Kaunas	88	Ekranas Panevezys	67	Vetra Vilnius	61	Suduva Marijampolé	1-0	Ekranas Panevezys

LITHUANIA 2006

A LYGA

	Pl	W	D	L	F	A	Pts	Kaunas	Ekranas	Vetra	Zalgiris	Suduva	Atlantas	Vilnius	Siauliai	Silute	Nevezis
FBK Kaunas †	36	28	4	4	85	30	88		0-1 4-0	4-0 1-2	2-1 2-2	2-0 2-0	2-1 1-1	3-2 2-1	3-0 2-0	6-1 4-0	2-0 1-1
Ekranas Panevezys ‡	36	20	7	9	63	39	67	1-2 0-1		4-1 1-0	1-0 4-3	0-0 0-1	0-0 3-1	1-1 2-0	2-0 2-0	0-0 3-1	4-1 1-1
Vetra Vilnius	36	17	10	9	49	35	61	1-4 0-1	2-0 2-0		0-1 0-1	1-0 2-1	2-2 2-1	1-0 1-0	1-1 2-1	1-1 5-1	2-0 1-0
Zalgiris Vilnius	36	14	12	10	52	39	54	1-2 0-1	0-2 2-2	1-1 1-1		0-0 0-0	0-1 3-1	1-1 1-1	2-3 2-1	0-1 2-0	2-1 3-2
Suduva Marijampole ‡	36	15	8	13	48	44	53	1-3 0-3	1-4 1-3	1-1 1-2	3-1 2-3		1-0 3-1	1-1 2-1	1-1 2-0	1-0 2-0	3-0 2-0
Atlantas Klaipeda	36	14	10	12	46	41	52	1-2 2-1	2-0 1-3	2-1 0-0	0-0 2-2	3-0 0-1		0-0 1-2	1-0 1-1	2-1 4-1	1-1 2-0
FK Vilnius	36	11	14	11	46	40	47	2-2 1-3	0-0 2-0	0-0 0-0	0-3 0-0	0-0 5-3	1-4 0-1		0-1 1-1	2-1 1-0	2-0 5-0
KFK Siauliai	36	10	11	15	42	46	41	1-2 3-0	4-1 1-3	0-0 0-4	0-0 0-2	2-1 1-1	3-1 0-0	1-1 0-2		0-1 2-1	5-0 0-0
FK Silute	36	5	3	28	25	77	18	0-3 0-3	1-3 0-1	0-4 1-2	0-1 0-2	0-3 1-4	1-2 1-0	0-1 1-3	1-1 1-0		1-2 1-2
Nevezis Kedainiai	36	4	5	27	35	100	17	1-3 2-6	0-4 3-6	3-2 0-2	1-5 1-4	0-2 1-3	2-3 0-1	1-5 2-2	0-3 2-5	2-1 3-4	

15/04/2006 - 12/11/2006 • † Qualified for the UEFA Champions League • ‡ Qualified for the UEFA Cup • Top scorers: Serhiy KUZNETSOV, Vetra 18; Mantas SAVENAS, Ekranas, 16; Illya HALYUZA, Siauliai 16; Ricardas BENIUSIS, FBK Kaunas, 14; Andrius VELICKA, FBK Kaunas, 14
Relegation play-off: Interas 1-1 1-1 4-3p FK Silute. Silute retained their place after Alytis withdrew before the start of the 2007 season

LITHUANIA 2006
LFF 1 LYGA (2)

	Pl	W	D	L	F	A	Pts
Kauno Jegeriai	34	23	7	4	75	28	76
Alytis Alytus	34	22	7	5	69	23	73
Atlantas-2 Klaipeda	34	19	8	7	70	35	65
Kruoja Pakruojis	34	17	9	8	71	36	60
Rodiklis Kaunas	34	17	7	10	70	44	58
Vetra-2 Vilnius	34	15	7	12	64	40	52
Interas Visaginas	34	15	7	12	59	47	52
LKKA Teledema Kaunas	34	15	7	12	50	53	52
Zalgiris-2 Vilnius	34	13	7	14	42	42	46
FC Vilnius-2	34	10	12	12	51	51	42
Suduva-2 Marijampole	34	12	5	17	44	65	41
Banga Gargzdai	34	9	12	13	44	49	39
KFK Siauliai-2	34	11	6	17	51	69	39
Vilkmerge Ukmerge	34	10	8	16	40	51	38
Lietava Jonava	34	9	11	14	43	56	38
Atletas Kaunas	34	8	10	16	39	47	34
Gelezinis Vilkas Vilnius	34	7	10	17	37	55	31
Babrungas Plunge	34	3	2	29	24	152	11

7/04/2006 - 29/10/2006

LFF TAURE 2006

First round

Suduva Marijampole *	4	0
Alytis Alytus	1	0
FK Silute *	1	2
Nevezis Kedainiai	3	1
FBK Kaunas *	3	3
KFK Siauliai	0	1
Zalgiris-2 Vilnius	0	2
Atlantas Klaipeda *	2	1
FC Vilnius *	0	2
Vetra-2 Vilnius	0	0
Kauno Jegeriai	0	0
Zalgiris Vilnius *	2	2
Vetra Vilnius *	3	6
Lietava Jonava	0	0
Kruoja Pakruojis	0	0
Ekranas Panevezys *	7	2

Quarter-finals

Suduva Marijampole *	7	1
Nevezis Kedainiai	1	2
FBK Kaunas	0	0
Atlantas Klaipeda *	2	1
FC Vilnius	1	0
Zalgiris Vilnius *	1	0
Vetra Vilnius *	1	0
Ekranas Panevezys	1	1

Semi-finals

Suduva Marijampole *	1	1
Atlantas Klaipeda	1	0
FC Vilnius *	2	0
Ekranas Panevezys	2	1

Final

Suduva Marijampole ‡	1
Ekranas Panevezys	0

CUP FINAL
Darius & Girenas, Kaunas
21-10-2006, Ref: Chileckis
Scorer - Darius Maciulevicius [1]

* Home team in the first leg • ‡ Qualified for the UEFA Cup

LUX – LUXEMBOURG

NATIONAL TEAM RECORD
JULY 10TH 2006 TO JULY 12TH 2010

PL	W	D	L	F	A	%

FIFA/COCA-COLA WORLD RANKING

1993	1994	1995	1996	1997	1998	1999	2000	2001	2002	2003	2004	2005	2006	High	Low
111	128	100	123	138	143	124	139	142	148	153	155	150	186	**93** 04/96	**195** 08/06

2006–2007											
08/06	09/06	10/06	11/06	12/06	01/07	02/07	03/07	04/07	05/07	06/07	07/07
195	193	193	189	186	186	181	178	177	178	174	174

Chris Sagramola should be the toast of Luxembourg. His late goal against Gambia in February 2007 brought to an end the longest run without a win in the history of international football, covering 12 years and 83 games. Luxembourg had last won a match on September 6, 1995 when they beat Malta in a European Championship qualifier and when they lost to Bulgaria in the qualifiers of UEFA Euro 2008, they beat the old record of 80 matches, which they also happened to hold. Earlier in the campaign their draw against Latvia in Hesperange had brought to a halt a run of 25 consecutive defeats and brought the team their first point in a competitive match since the victory over Malta. Full

INTERNATIONAL HONOURS
None

marks for effort but the stark facts are that in World Cup and European Championship matches since 1934, Luxembourg have won just six times - with three of those in 1995 alone! In club football F'91 Dudelange continued their domination of the League with a sixth title since the start of the decade. They also completed the double for the second year running when they beat Grevenmacher 2-1 in the Cup Final, their third Cup triumph in four seasons. Formed in 1991 through a merger of three local clubs, Dudelange come from the third largest town in the country and have been coached for the past two years by Michel Leflochmoan who has a team largely made up of French players.

THE FIFA BIG COUNT OF 2006

	Male	Female		Total
Number of players	44 626	2 954	Referees and Assistant Referees	264
Professionals	300		Admin, Coaches, Technical, Medical	1 050
Amateurs 18+	15 806		Number of clubs	111
Youth under 18	11 874		Number of teams	746
Unregistered	4 100		Clubs with women's teams	24
Total players	47 580		Players as % of population	10.03%

Fédération Luxembourgeoise de Football (FLF)
PO Box 5, Monderange 3901, Luxembourg
Tel +352 4886651   Fax +352 48866582
flf@football.lu   www.football.lu
President: PHILIPP Paul   General Secretary: WOLFF Joel
Vice-President: SCHAACK Charles   Treasurer: DECKER Erny   Media Officer: DIEDERICH Marc
Men's Coach: HELLERS Guy   Women's Coach: JEAN Romain
FLF formed: 1908   UEFA: 1954   FIFA: 1910
Red shirts with white trimmings, Red shorts, Red socks or White shirts with blue trimmings, White shorts, White socks

RECENT INTERNATIONAL MATCHES PLAYED BY LUXEMBOURG

2002	Opponents		Score	Venue	Comp	Scorers	Att	Referee
12-10	Denmark	L	0-2	Copenhagen	ECq		40 259	Bede HUN
16-10	Romania	L	0-7	Luxembourg	ECq		2 000	Lajuks LVA
20-11	Cape Verde Islands	D	0-0	Hesperange	Fr			
2003								
29-03	Bosnia-Herzegovina	L	0-2	Zenica	ECq		10 000	Hyytia FIN
2-04	Norway	L	0-2	Luxembourg	ECq		3 000	Dobrinov BUL
30-04	Hungary	L	1-5	Budapest	Fr	Strasser [25]	1 205	Skomina SVN
11-06	Denmark	L	0-2	Luxembourg	ECq		6 869	Baskakov RUS
19-08	Malta	D	1-1	Luxembourg	Fr	Strasser [53p]		Lehner AUT
6-09	Romania	L	0-4	Ploiesti	ECq		4 500	Yefet ISR
10-09	Bosnia-Herzegovina	L	0-1	Luxembourg	ECq		3 500	Kapitanis CYP
11-10	Norway	L	0-1	Oslo	ECq		22 255	Szabo HUN
20-11	Moldova	L	1-2	Hesperange	Fr	Schauls [77]	623	
2004								
31-03	Bosnia-Herzegovina	L	1-2	Luxembourg	Fr	Huss [87]	2 000	Rogalla SUI
28-04	Austria	L	1-4	Innsbruck	Fr	Huss [63]	9 400	Skomina SVN
29-05	Portugal	L	0-3	Agueda	Fr		9 000	Styles ENG
18-08	Slovakia	L	1-3	Bratislava	WCq	Strasser [2]	5 016	Kassai HUN
4-09	Estonia	L	0-4	Tallinn	WCq		3 000	Kelly IRL
8-09	Latvia	L	3-4	Luxembourg	WCq	Braun [11], Leweck [55], Cardoni [62]	2 125	Kasnaferis GRE
9-10	Russia	L	0-4	Luxembourg	WCq		3 670	Braamhaar NED
13-10	Liechtenstein	L	0-4	Luxembourg	WCq		3 478	Jara CZE
17-11	Portugal	L	0-5	Luxembourg	WCq		8 045	Godulyan UKR
2005								
30-03	Latvia	L	0-4	Riga	WCq		8 203	Kovacic CRO
8-06	Slovakia	L	0-4	Luxembourg	WCq		2 108	Styles ENG
3-09	Portugal	L	0-6	Faro-Loule	WCq		25 300	Van Egmond NEd
7-09	Liechtenstein	L	0-3	Vaduz	WCq		2 300	Skomina SVN
8-10	Russia	L	1-5	Moscow	WCq	Reiter [51]	20 000	Tudor ROU
12-10	Estonia	L	0-2	Luxembourg	WCq		2 010	Dereli TUR
16-11	Canada	L	0-1	Hesperange	Fr			Gomes Costa POR
2006								
1-03	Belgium	L	0-2	Luxembourg	Fr	Abandoned after 65 minutes due to snow		Einwaller AUT
27-05	Germany	L	0-7	Freiburg	Fr		23 000	Rogalla SUI
3-06	Portugal	L	0-3	Metz	Fr		19 157	Duhamel FRA
8-06	Ukraine	L	0-3	Luxembourg	Fr			Vervecken BEL
16-08	Turkey	L	0-1	Luxembourg	Fr		3 353	Weiner GER
2-09	Netherlands	L	0-1	Luxembourg	ECq		8 055	Lopes Ferreira POR
6-09	Latvia	D	0-0	Hesperange	Fr		1 755	Bozinovski MKD
7-10	Slovenia	L	0-2	Celje	ECq		3 800	Kailis CYP
11-10	Bulgaria	L	0-1	Luxembourg	ECq		3 156	Panic BIH
15-11	Togo	D	0-0	Luxembourg	Fr		1 417	Richards WAL
2007								
7-02	Gambia	W	2-1	Hesperange	Fr	Joachim [65], Sagramola [83]	520	Circhetta SUI
24-03	Belarus	L	1-2	Luxembourg	ECq	Sagramola [68]	2 021	Whitby WAL
28-03	Romania	L	0-3	Piatra-Neamt	ECq		9 120	Lajuks LVA
2-06	Albania	L	0-2	Tirana	ECq		3 000	Silgava GEO
6-06	Albania	L	0-3	Luxembourg	ECq		4 325	Malzinskas LTU

Fr = Friendly match • EC = UEFA EURO 2004/2008 • WC = FIFA World Cup • q = qualifier

LUXEMBOURG NATIONAL TEAM RECORDS AND RECORD SEQUENCES

Records			Sequence records				
Victory	6-0	AFG 1948	Wins	3	1939-1943	Clean sheets	3	1995
Defeat	0-12	ITA 'B' 1932	Defeats	34	1980-1985	Goals scored	7	1948-1951
Player Caps	87	WEIS Carlo	Undefeated	4	1963	Without goal	11	2005-2006
Player Goals	16	MART Léon	Without win	83	1995-2006	Goals against	31	1987-95

MAJOR CITIES/TOWNS
Population '000

1	Luxembourg	76
2	Esch-sur-Alzette	28
3	Dudelange	18
4	Schifflange	8
5	Bettembourg	7
6	Pétange	7
7	Ettelbruck	6
8	Diekirch	6
9	Strassen	6
10	Bertrange	5
11	Differdange	5
12	Wiltz	4
13	Bascharage	4
14	Rodange	4
15	Rumelange	4
16	Grevenmacher	4
17	Mondercange	3
18	Niedercorn	3
19	Tétange	2
20	Hesperange	1
21	Eischen	1
22	Frisange	1
23	Walferdange	1
24	Rosport	1

GRAND DUCHY OF LUXEMBOURG; GRAND DUCHE DE LUXEMBOURG

Capital	Luxembourg	Language	Luxembourgish, German, French	Independence	1839		
Population	474 413	Area	2 586 km²	Density	179 per km²	% in cities	89%
GDP per cap	$55 100	Dailling code	+352	Internet	.lu	GMT +/-	+1

MEDALS TABLE

		Overall			League			Cup			Europe			City	Stadium	Cap'ty	DoF
		G	S	B	G	S	B	G	S	B	G	S	B				
1	Jeunesse Esch/Alzette	39	23	14	27	12	14	12	11					Esch-sur-Alzette	Stade de la Frontière	7 500	1907
2	Red Boys Differdange	21	19	14	6	10	14	15	9					Differdange	Thillenberg		1907-2003
3	AC Spora Luxembourg	19	18	10	11	10	10	8	8					Luxembourg	Municipal		1923-2005
4	Union Luxembourg	16	18	12	6	8	12	10	10					Luxembourg	Achille Hammerel		1925-2005
5	Stade Dudeldange	14	13	6	10	6	6	4	7					Dudelange	Alois Mayer		1913-91
6	Avenir Beggen	13	9	3	6	5	3	7	4					Beggen	Henri Dunant	5 500	1915
7	F'91 Dudelange	9	6		6	3		3	3					Dudelange	Jos Nosbaum	5 000	1991
8	Fola Esch/Alzette	8	8	4	5	7	4	3	1					Esch-sur-Alzette	Emile Mayrisch	3 900	1906
9	Progres Niedercorn	7	8	8	3	5	8	4	3					Niedercorn	Jos Haupert	4 000	1919
10	US Hollerich	5	3	2	5	3	2							Luxembourg	Stade Hollerich		1908-25
11	CS Grevenmacher	4	11	2	1	7	2	3	4					Grevenmacher	Op Flohr	4 500	1909
12	Aris Bonnevoie	4	6	2	3	1	2	1	5					Luxembourg	Camille Polfer		1922-2001
13	US Rumelange	2	5	1		3	1	2	2					Rumelange	Municipal	2 950	1908
14	Sporting Club Luxembourg	2	3	2	2	3	2							Luxembourg	Municipal		1908-23
15	The National Schifflange	2	3		1	2		1	1					Schifflange	Stade National		1912
16	Alliance Dudelange	2	2			1		2	1					Dudelange	Amadeo Barozzi		1916-91
17	Racing Club Luxembourg	2		3	1		3	1						Luxembourg	Municipal		1907-23

RECENT LEAGUE AND CUP RECORD

	Championship						Cup		
Year	Champions	Pts	Runners-up	Pts	Third	Pts	Winners	Score	Runners-up
1995	Jeunesse d'Esch	35	CS Grevenmacher	35	Avenir Beggen	30	CS Grevenmacher	1-1 3-2	Jeunesse d'Esch
1996	Jeunesse d'Esch	48	CS Grevenmacher	47	Union Luxembourg	42	Union Luxembourg	3-1	Jeunesse d'Esch
1997	Jeunesse d'Esch	56	CS Grevenmacher	50	Union Luxembourg	38	Jeunesse d'Esch	2-0	Union Luxembourg
1998	Jeunesse d'Esch	54	Union Luxembourg	53	CS Grevenmacher	43	CS Grevenmacher	2-0	Avenir Beggen
1999	Jeunesse d'Esch	51	F'91 Dudelange	47	Avenir Beggen	45	Jeunesse d'Esch	3-0	FC Mondercange
2000	F'91 Dudelange	57	CS Grevenmacher	46	Jeunesse d'Esch	46	Jeunesse d'Esch	4-1	FC Mondercange
2001	F'91 Dudelange	63	CS Grevenmacher	59	CS Hobscheid	46	Etzella Ettelbruck	5-3	FC Wiltz
2002	F'91 Dudelange	62	CS Grevenmacher	58	Union Luxembourg	47	Avenir Beggen	1-0	F'91 Dudelange
2003	CS Grevenmacher	59	F'91 Dudelange	52	Jeunesse d'Esch	48	CS Grevenmacher	1-0	Etzella Ettelbruck
2004	Jeunesse d'Esch	68	F'91 Dudelange	59	Etzella Ettelbruck	48	F'91 Dudelange	3-1	Etzella Ettelbruck
2005	F'91 Dudelange	70	Etzella Ettelbruck	64	Jeunesse d'Esch	45	CS Petange	5-0	Cebra
2006	F'91 Dudelange	64	Jeunesse d'Esch	53	Etzella Ettelbruck	49	F'91 Dudelange	3-2	Jeunesse d'Esch
2007	F'91 Dudelange	65	Etzella Ettelbruck	52	FC Differdange 03	48	F'91 Dudelange	2-1	UN Käerjéng 97

LUXEMBOURG 2006–07

DIVISION NATIONALE

	Pl	W	D	L	F	A	Pts	Dudelange	Etzella	Differdange	Racing Un.	Swift	Grev'cher	Niedercorn	Käerjeng	Jeunesse	Pétange	Wiltz	Victoria	Mond'cange	Mamer
F91 Dudelange †	26	21	2	3	71	20	65		4-1	3-0	2-2	2-0	2-1	7-2	3-0	1-0	4-1	7-1	5-0	3-0	5-1
Etzella Ettelbruck ‡	26	16	4	6	60	30	52	2-0		5-1	2-0	1-0	1-2	6-0	1-2	2-0	2-1	3-1	3-0	2-0	2-0
FC Differdange 03	26	14	6	6	71	41	48	1-2	2-2		1-1	2-1	2-2	4-3	7-1	4-1	0-1	3-0	3-0	4-0	5-1
Racing Union	26	11	8	7	52	35	41	1-0	2-1	1-1		2-2	0-1	1-3	2-0	1-3	3-0	3-0	0-0	7-2	1-0
Swift Hesperange	26	11	8	7	40	28	41	0-2	1-1	1-1	4-1		2-2	0-1	2-0	0-0	0-1	2-0	2-0	3-0	3-2
CS Grevenmacher	26	11	8	7	43	34	41	0-0	0-3	2-0	4-0	1-1		2-4	0-2	2-1	1-0	0-2	0-3	0-0	4-1
Progrès Niedercorn	26	10	5	11	53	61	35	1-3	2-4	5-4	2-2	2-2	4-8		4-0	0-1	0-0	0-2	3-2	2-0	5-1
UN Käerjeng ‡	26	10	4	12	38	51	34	2-5	3-1	3-4	3-2	3-2	2-2	0-2		2-4	0-0	1-0	0-0	1-0	4-0
Jeunesse d'Esch	26	9	5	12	29	34	32	0-2	3-3	1-2	1-1	0-1	1-1	0-3	2-0		2-0	0-2	2-0	0-2	2-1
CS Pétange	26	8	8	10	29	38	32	0-2	1-1	2-3	0-5	2-2	1-1	1-0	2-2	1-0		2-1	2-1	1-1	4-0
FC Wiltz 71	26	9	4	13	31	38	31	0-2	3-2	1-3	1-1	0-1	0-1	4-0	3-0	1-3	2-1		1-1	0-0	1-0
Victoria Rosport	26	7	6	13	28	47	27	3-0	1-2	0-4	1-6	0-2	2-0	2-2	2-1	1-0	2-0	1-0		2-3	3-3
FC Mondercange	26	4	6	16	23	59	18	1-3	1-3	2-2	1-4	0-3	0-4	3-1	1-3	1-1	1-3	1-5	2-0		0-1
FC Mamer 32	26	1	6	19	19	71	9	0-2	0-4	0-8	0-3	2-3	0-2	2-2	0-3	0-1	2-2	0-0	1-1	1-1	

5/08/2006 - 20/05/2006 • † Qualified for the UEFA Champions League • ‡ Qualified for the UEFA Cup
Top scorers: Daniel DA MOTA, Etzella 24; Pierre Olivier PISKOR, Differdange 23; Joris DI GREGORIO, Dudelange 22

LUXEMBOURG 2006–07 EHRENPROMOTION (2)

	Pl	W	D	L	F	A	Pts
RM Hamm	26	17	6	3	59	23	57
Avenir Beggen	26	15	5	6	52	23	50
Fola Esch/Alzette	26	13	6	7	38	29	45
US Rumelange	26	13	4	9	49	37	43
Un. Mertet/Wasserbillig	26	14	3	9	42	31	43
Sporting Steinfort	26	13	3	10	43	39	42
CS Obercorn	26	11	7	7	44	38	40
FC 72 Erpeldange	26	11	3	12	47	51	36
Sporting Mertzig	26	10	5	11	42	41	35
Jeunesse Canach	26	10	5	11	34	50	35
Koeppchen W'dange	26	10	3	13	40	53	30
FC Cessange	26	7	5	14	36	47	26
US Hostert	26	5	3	18	38	59	18
Jeunesse Schieren	26	4	1	21	26	69	13

8/09/2005 - 26/05/2006 • ‡ qualified for play-offs
Play-offs: Victoria Rosport 2-0 Fola Esch
Koeppchen 0-2 Blue Boys; Cessange 2-0 FC Kehlen

COUPE DE LUXEMBOURG 2006–07

Round of 16

F91 Dudelange *	5
FC Wiltz 71	3
FC Mondercange *	2
Etzella Ettelbruck	3
Avenir Beggen *	3
Progrès Niedercorn	2
FC Differdange 03 *	1
CS Grevenmacher	3
Swift Hesperange	1
Racing Union *	0
Victoria Rosport	0
CS Pétange *	2
Jeunesse Biwer *	1
CS Obercorn	0
Koeppchen W'dange *	0
UN Käerjeng	3

Quarter–finals

F91 Dudelange *	2
Etzella Ettelbruck	0
Avenir Beggen	1
CS Grevenmacher *	3
Swift Hesperange *	2 4p
CS Pétange	2 2p
Jeunesse Biwer *	0 3p
UN Käerjeng	0 5p

Semi–finals

F91 Dudelange	2
CS Grevenmacher	1
Swift Hesperange	0
UN Käerjeng	1

Final

F91 Dudelange	2
UN Käerjeng ‡	1

CUP FINAL

Stade Josy Barthel, Luxembourg
26-05-2007

Scorers - Joris Di Gregorio [33], Thomas Gruszczynski [41] for Dudelange; Carlo Pace [80] for Käerjeng

* Home team • ‡ Qualified for the UEFA Cup

LVA – LATVIA

NATIONAL TEAM RECORD
JULY 10TH 2006 TO JULY 12TH 2010

PL	W	D	L	F	A	%
10	1	1	8	4	12	15

FIFA/COCA-COLA WORLD RANKING

1993	1994	1995	1996	1997	1998	1999	2000	2001	2002	2003	2004	2005	2006	High		Low	
86	69	60	82	75	77	62	92	106	79	51	65	69	90	**51**	12/03	**111**	07/07

2006–2007											
08/06	09/06	10/06	11/06	12/06	01/07	02/07	03/07	04/07	05/07	06/07	07/07
78	94	90	89	90	90	96	98	104	104	107	111

Latvia's qualification for the finals of Euro 2004 must have seemed a world away for the national team players as they languished below Liechtenstein midway through their UEFA Euro 2008 qualifying group. The 2-0 defeat at the hands of Denmark in June 2007 not only set a new record of six consecutive defeats for the team but was also their sixth game without a goal - another record. Indeed, of the 10 games played in the 2006-07 season, Latvia failed to score in nine of them. The 1-0 defeat by Liechtenstein in March 2007 was the final straw for the federation who replaced Jurjis Andrejevs with Aleksandrs Starkovs, the man who led Latvia to the Euro 2004

INTERNATIONAL HONOURS
Baltic Cup 1928 1932 1933 1936 1937 1993 1995 2001 2003

finals. In domestic football times are bad for the previously invincible Skonto Riga. Their failure to beat FK Ventspils in any of the four games they played each other in the League cost the 14 times champions dearly, but it did mean that Ventspils were able to become only the third team to win the title. In the Cup, Skonto had made up for their poor form against Ventspils with a victory over them in the semi-finals, but then lost to Metalurgs in a final that was decided by an extra-time Kristaps Grebis goal. It was Metalurg's first triumph in the Cup, capping a great season for the western port towns of Liepaja and Ventspils and leaving Skonto trophyless for a second year.

THE FIFA BIG COUNT OF 2006

	Male	Female		Total
Number of players	73 885	11 400	Referees and Assistant Referees	225
Professionals	265		Admin, Coaches, Technical, Medical	430
Amateurs 18+	1 450		Number of clubs	68
Youth under 18	6 550		Number of teams	420
Unregistered	17 900		Clubs with women's teams	29
Total players	85 285		Players as % of population	3.75%

Latvian Football Federation (LFF)

Latvijas Futbola Federacija, Augsiela 1, Riga LV1009, Latvia
Tel +371 7292988   Fax +371 67315604
futbols@lff.lv   www.lff.lv
President: INDRIKSONS Guntis   General Secretary: MEZECKIS Janis
Vice-President: GORKSS Juris   Treasurer: BAHAREVA Nina   Media Officer: HARTMANIS Martins
Men's Coach: STARKOVS Aleksandrs   Women's Coach: BANDOLIS Agris
LFF formed: 1921   UEFA: 1992   FIFA: 1923-43, 1992
Carmine red shirts with white trimmings, Carmine red shorts, Carmine red socks or White shirts, White shorts, White socks

RECENT INTERNATIONAL MATCHES PLAYED BY LATVIA

2004	Opponents	Score		Venue	Comp	Scorers	Att	Referee
18-02	Kazakhstan	W	3-1	Larnaca	Fr	Pahars [40], Laizans 2 [45 56]	500	Constantinou CYP
19-02	Hungary	L	1-2	Limassol	Fr	Stepanovs [64]	100	Kailis CYP
21-02	Belarus	L	1-4	Limassol	Fr	Zemlinskis [37p]	100	Theodotou CYP
31-03	Slovenia	W	1-0	Celje	Fr	Verpakovskis [36]	1 500	Stredak SVK
28-04	Iceland	D	0-0	Riga	Fr		6 500	Shmolik BLR
6-06	Azerbaijan	D	2-2	Riga	Fr	Verpakovskis [53], Zemlinskis [82p]	8 000	Maisonlahti FIN
15-06	Czech Republic	L	1-2	Aveiro	ECr1	Verpakovskis [45]	21 744	Veissiere FRA
19-06	Germany	D	0-0	Porto	ECr1		22 344	Riley ENG
23-06	Netherlands	L	0-3	Braga	ECr1		27 904	Milton Nielsen DEN
18-08	Wales	L	0-2	Riga	Fr		6 500	Ivanov RUS
4-09	Portugal	L	0-2	Riga	WCq		9 500	Poll ENG
8-09	Luxembourg	W	4-3	Luxembourg	WCq	Verpakovskis [4], Zemlinskis [40p], OG [65], Prohorenkovs [67]	2 125	Kasnaferis GRE
9-10	Slovakia	L	1-4	Bratislava	WCq	Verpakovskis [3]	13 025	Farina ITA
13-10	Estonia	D	2-2	Riga	WCq	Astafjevs [65], Laizans [82]	8 500	Meyer GER
17-11	Liechtenstein	W	3-1	Vaduz	WCq	Verpakovskis [7], Zemlinskis [57], Prohorenkovs [89]	1 460	Szabo HUN
1-12	Oman	L	2-3	Manama	Fr	Rimkus [56], Rubins [68]		Al Hilali OMA
3-12	Bahrain	D	2-2	Manama	Fr	Kolesnicenko [22p], Zakresevskis [35]. L 2-4p	2 000	Al Hilali OMA
2005								
8-02	Finland	L	1-2	Nicosia	Fr	Zemlinskis [62p]	102	Kailis CYP
9-02	Austria	D	1-1	Limassol	Fr	Visnakovs [70]. W 5-3p	50	Theodotou CYP
30-03	Luxembourg	W	4-0	Riga	WCq	Bleidelis [32], Laizans [38p], Verpakovskis 2 [73 90]	8 203	Kovacic CRO
21-05	Lithuania	L	0-2	Kaunas	BC			
4-06	Russia	L	0-3	St Pertersburg	WCq		21 575	Poulat FRA
8-06	Liechtenstein	W	1-0	Riga	WCq	Bleidelis [17]	8 000	Eriksson SWE
17-08	Russia	D	1-1	Riga	WCq	Astafjevs [6]	10 000	Poll ENG
3-09	Estonia	L	1-2	Tallinn	WCq	Laizans [90]	8 970	Undiano Mallenco ESP
7-09	Slovakia	D	1-1	Riga	WCq	Laizans [74]	8 800	Plautz AUT
8-10	Japan	D	2-2	Riga	Fr	Rimkus [67], Rubins [89]	6 500	Granatas POL
12-10	Portugal	L	0-3	Porto	WCq		35 000	Frojdfeldt SWE
12-11	Belarus	L	1-3	Minsk	Fr	Visnakovs [24]	8 300	Egorov RUS
24-12	Thailand	D	1-1	Phang Nga	Fr	Solonicins [19]		
26-12	Korea DPR	D	1-1	Phuket	Fr	Karlsons [65]		
30-12	Korea DPR	W	2-1	Phuket	Fr	Karlsons [38], Prohorenkovs [40]		
2006								
28-05	USA	L	0-1	Hartford	Fr		24 636	Dipiero CAN
16-08	Russia	L	0-1	Moscow	Fr		25 600	Gilewski POL
2-09	Sweden	L	0-1	Riga	ECq		7 500	Ceferin SVN
6-09	Luxembourg	D	0-0	Hesperange	Fr			
7-10	Iceland	W	4-0	Riga	ECq	Karlsons.G [14], Verpakovskis 2 [15 25], Visnakovs [52]	6 800	Kelly IRL
11-10	Northern Ireland	L	0-1	Belfast	ECq		13 500	Fleischer GER
2007								
6-02	Bulgaria	L	0-2	Larnaca	Fr		500	Andronikou CYP
7-02	Hungary	L	0-2	Limassol	Fr		400	Kailisz CYP
28-03	Liechtenstein	L	0-1	Vaduz	ECq		1 680	Gumienny BEL
2-06	Spain	L	0-2	Riga	ECq		10 000	Thomson SCO
6-06	Denmark	L	0-2	Riga	ECq		7 500	Trefoloni ITA

Fr = Friendly match • EC = UEFA EURO 2004/2008 • BC = Baltic Cup • WC = FIFA World Cup
q = qualifier • po = play-off • r1 = first round group

LATVIA NATIONAL TEAM RECORDS AND RECORD SEQUENCES

Records			Sequence records					
Victory	8-1	EST 1942	Wins	4	1936	Clean sheets	2	
Defeat	0-12	SWE 1927	Defeats	6	2006-2007	Goals scored	10	Three times
Player Caps	133	ASTAFJEVS Vitalijs	Undefeated	6	1937, 1938	Without goal	6	2006-2007
Player Goals	24	PETERSONS Eriks	Without win	10	1995-1997	Goals against	21	1933-1937

REPUBLIC OF LATVIA; LATVIJAS REPUBLIKA

Capital	Riga	Language	Latvian, Russian			Independence	1991
Population	2 274 735	Area	64 589 km²	Density	35 per km²	% in cities	73%
GDP per cap	$10 200	Dailling code	+371	Internet	.lv	GMT + / -	+2

MAJOR CITIES/TOWNS
Population '000

1	Riga	733
2	Daugavpils	110
3	Liepaja	83
4	Jelgava	61
5	Jurmala	53
6	Ventspils	42
7	Rezekne	37
8	Jekabspils	26
9	Valmiera	26
10	Ogre	25
11	Tukums	18
12	Cesis	17
13	Salaspils	17
14	Kuldiga	13
15	Olaine	12
16	Saldus	12
17	Talsi	11
18	Dobele	11
19	Kraslava	10
20	Bauska	10
21	Ludza	10
22	Sigulda	10
23	Livani	9
24	Gulbene	9

MEDALS TABLE

		Overall			League			Cup			Europe			City	Stadium	Cap'ty	DoF
		G	S	B	G	S	B	G	S	B	G	S	B				
1	Skonto Riga	21	7	1	14	1	1	7	6					Riga	Stadions Skonto	8 500	1991
2	FK Ventspils	4	3	5	1	3	5	3						Ventspils	Olimpiska Centra	3 200	1997
3	Liepajas Metalurgs	2	9	3	1	5	3	1	4					Liepaja	Daugavas Stadions	5 083	1996
4	RAF Jelgava	2	2	2		2	2	2						Jelgava			1988-97
5	Dinaburg Daugavpils	1	3	2		1	2	1	2					Daugavpils	Celtnieka Stadions	4 070	1990
6	Olimpija Riga	1	1			1		1						Riga			
7	FK Riga	1						1						Riga	Latvijas Universitates	5 000	1999
8	Daugava Riga		5			3			2					Riga	Daugava Stadions	5 000	1995
9	VEF/DAG/Olimpija/FK		2	3			2		2					Riga/Liepaja			
10	FK Jurmala													Jurmala	Sloka	1 500	2003
	Olimps Riga													Riga	Stadions Skonto	9 300	2005
	Venta Kuldiga													Ventspils	Olimpiska Centra	3 200	2004-06
	Daugava Daugavpils													Daugavpils	Celtnieka Stadions	4 070	2007
	Dizvanagi Rezekne													Rezekne	Rezekne	500	2000

RECENT LEAGUE AND CUP RECORD

	Championship						Cup		
Year	Champions	Pts	Runners-up	Pts	Third	Pts	Winners	Score	Runners-up
1995	Skonto Riga	78	Vilan-D Daugavpils	51	RAF Jelgava	48	Skonto Riga	3-0	DAG Liepaja
1996	Skonto Riga	73	Daugava Riga	61	Dinaburg Daugavpils	47	RAF Jelgava	2-1	Skonto Riga
1997	Skonto Riga	64	Daugava Riga	43	Dinaburg Daugavpils	42	Skonto Riga	2-1	Dinaburg Daugavpils
1998	Skonto Riga	67	Liepajas Metalurgs	57	FK Ventspils	54	Skonto Riga	1-0	Liepajas Metalurgs
1999	Skonto Riga	69	Liepajas Metalurgs	60	FK Ventspils	56	FK Riga	1-1 6-5p	Skonto Riga
2000	Skonto Riga	75	FK Ventspils	65	Liepajas Metalurgs	55	Skonto Riga	4-1	Liepajas Metalurgs
2001	Skonto Riga	68	FK Ventspils	67	Liepajas Metalurgs	64	Skonto Riga	2-0	Dinaburg Daugavpils
2002	Skonto Riga	73	FK Ventspils	71	Liepajas Metalurgs	51	Skonto Riga	3-0	Liepajas Metalurgs
2003	Skonto Riga	73	Liepajas Metalurgs	68	FK Ventspils	61	FK Ventspils	4-0	Skonto Riga
2004	Skonto Riga	69	Liepajas Metalurgs	66	FK Ventspils	55	FK Ventspils	2-1	Skonto Riga
2005	Liepajas Metalurgs	71	Skonto Riga	58	FK Ventspils	55	FK Ventspils	2-1	Liepajas Metalurgs
2006	FK Ventspils	62	Liepajas Metalurgs	60	Skonto Riga	54	Liepajas Metalurgs	2-1	Skonto Riga

LATVIA 2006

VIRSLIGA

	Pl	W	D	L	F	A	Pts	Ventspils	Metalurgs	Skonto	Dinaburg	Ditton	Jurmala	Riga	Dizvanagi
FK Ventspils †	28	19	5	4	48	23	62		1-1 1-2	1-0 1-0	3-2 3-0	2-1 1-1	1-0 0-2	1-0 4-0	7-1 1-0
Liepajas Metalurgs ‡	28	18	6	4	66	20	60	0-1 4-0		2-1 3-1	1-1 2-0	0-0 2-1	3-2 7-1	5-0 3-1	6-1 6-0
Skonto Riga ‡	28	16	6	6	55	21	54	1-1 0-1	0-0 2-1		0-2 2-0	0-0 2-2	2-0 3-1	5-1 1-1	6-0 6-0
Dinaburg Daugavpils	28	12	5	11	33	38	41	2-1 3-3	0-2 1-2	0-2 0-6		1-3 1-0	1-1 0-1	1-0 2-0	2-1 2-0
Ditton Daugavpils	28	10	8	10	33	31	38	0-1 0-1	1-2 2-0	1-1 0-2	1-1 2-4		2-1 0-0	3-1 0-1	1-0 2-1
FK Jurmala	28	11	4	13	36	36	37	1-1 1-2	1-1 1-0	0-1 1-2	1-0 0-1	0-1 6-1		3-0 2-1	2-1 3-0
FK Riga	28	6	4	18	21	57	22	0-1 0-2	0-4 0-5	1-4 1-2	0-0 0-1	0-0 0-4	2-1 2-0		1-0 3-1
Dizvanagi Rezekne	28	0	2	26	11	77	2	0-3 1-3	0-0 0-2	0-2 0-1	1-3 0-2	0-3 0-1	0-1 1-3	0-0 2-5	

8/04/2006 - 5/11/2006 • † Qualified for the UEFA Champions League • ‡ Qualified for the UEFA Cup
Relegation/promotion play-off: FK Riga 3-0 2-0 FK Valmiera • Top scorers: Mihail MIHOLAPS, Skonto 15; Girts KARLSONS, Metalurgs 14

LATVIA 2006
PIRMALIGA (2)

	Pl	W	D	L	F	A	Pts
Olimps Riga	30	26	2	2	111	15	80
Ditton-2 Daugavspils	30	21	7	2	88	24	70
Skonto-2 Riga	30	20	5	5	78	23	65
FK Ventspils-2	30	20	4	6	108	25	64
FK Riga-2	30	17	3	10	74	44	54
Dinaburg/Zemessardze	30	16	3	11	61	51	51
FK Valmiera	30	13	7	10	50	53	46
Liepajas Metalurgs-2	30	13	6	11	68	48	45
FK Jelgava	30	12	6	12	53	49	42
Eirobaltija Riga	30	11	7	12	50	40	40
FK Jurmala-2	30	10	5	15	86	74	35
Tranzits Ventspils	30	8	4	18	37	88	28
Multibank Riga	30	7	6	17	34	58	27
Auda Riga	30	5	2	23	28	79	17
Alberts Riga	30	4	4	22	32	114	16
Abuls Smiltene	30	1	1	28	18	191	4

21/04/2006 - 4/11/2006 • Second teams ineligible for promotion

LATVIJAS KAUSS 2006

Fourth Round		Quarter-finals		Semi-finals		Final	
Liepajas Metalurgs	3						
Olimps Riga *	1	Liepajas Metalurgs	2				
FK Jelgava *	0	Dinaburg Daugavpils *	1				
Dinaburg Daugavpils	5			Liepajas Metalurgs *	6		
FK Jurmala	8			Dizvanagi Rezekne	1		
Viesulis Riga *	0	FK Jurmala	1				
FK Valmiera *	1	Dizvanagi Rezekne *	3			Liepajas Metalurgs	2
Dizvanagi Rezekne	2					Skonto Riga	1
FK Ventspils	5						
Tranzits Ventspils *	0	FK Ventspils	3				
Eirobaltija Riga *	0	FK Riga *	2				
FK Riga	2			FK Ventspils *	1		
Ditton Daugavpils	5			Skonto Riga	2		
Melna Roze Riga *	1	Ditton Daugavpils	0				
Jekabpils SC *	0	Skonto Riga *	3				
Skonto Riga	8						

CUP FINAL
Skonto, Riga
24-09-2006, Att: 6 000, Ref: Lajuks

Scorers - Girts Karlsons [56]
Kristaps Grebis [99] for Metalurgs;
Andrejs Stolcers [20p] for Skonto

* Home teams • ‡ Qualified for the UEFA Cup

MAC – MACAU

NATIONAL TEAM RECORD
JULY 10TH 2006 TO JULY 12TH 2010

PL	W	D	L	F	A	%
5	0	1	4	4	17	10

FIFA/COCA-COLA WORLD RANKING

1993	1994	1995	1996	1997	1998	1999	2000	2001	2002	2003	2004	2005	2006	High	Low
166	175	180	172	157	174	176	180	180	188	184	188	192	185	**156** 09/97	**192** 06/07

2006–2007											
08/06	09/06	10/06	11/06	12/06	01/07	02/07	03/07	04/07	05/07	06/07	07/07
184	185	185	185	185	185	186	188	190	187	192	185

Macau's failure to win an international match during the season meant that by the end of the East Asian Championship qualifiers in June 2007, their record run without a win had increased to 15 games. The East Asian qualifiers usually provide Macau with an opportunity to win games, but despite hosting the tournament, they lost heavily to Chinese Taipei and North Korea and could only manage a draw with Mongolia. At the start of the season Macau had been unlucky to lose to Chinese Taipei in a friendly and also gave Hong Kong a good match in the annual Interport Cup, so the performance in the East Asian qualifiers was particularly disappointing for Japanese coach

INTERNATIONAL HONOURS
None

Masanaga Kageyama. In October 2006 Macau hosted the first Jogos da Lusofonia, a multisport games for the Portuguese-speaking nations of the world. The under 21 selection came bottom of their first round group containing the Cape Verde Islands and a Goa XI whilst Portugal emerged as winners of the nine team tournament, beating Angola 2-0 in the final. At home Lam Pak successfully defended their League title in a close race with Va Luen and newly promoted Vong Chiu. Keong Sai finished with no points after being thrown out of the competition midway through for turning up to a match with only seven players one week and with six the next.

THE FIFA BIG COUNT OF 2006

	Male	Female		Total
Number of players	13 423	700	Referees and Assistant Referees	51
Professionals	1		Admin, Coaches, Technical, Medical	703
Amateurs 18+	4 130		Number of clubs	96
Youth under 18	592		Number of teams	120
Unregistered	1 750		Clubs with women's teams	0
Total players	14 123		Players as % of population	3.12%

Macau Football Association (AFM)
Avenida Wai Leong Taipa, University of Science and Technology, Football Field, Block I, Taipa, Macau
Tel +853 830287   Fax +853 830409
futebol@macau.ctm.net   www.macaufa.com
President: CHEUNG Vitor Lup Kwan   General Secretary: CHOI Kam Vai
Vice-President: CHONG Coc Veng   Treasurer: CHIO Kam Vai   Media Officer: None
Men's Coach: KAGEYAMA Masanaga   Women's Coach: None
AFM formed: 1939   AFC: 1976   FIFA: 1976
Green shirts, Green shorts, Green socks

RECENT INTERNATIONAL MATCHES PLAYED BY MACAU

2003	Opponents	Score		Venue	Comp	Scorers	Att	Referee
22-02	Mongolia	W	2-0	Hong Kong	EAq	Che Chi Man [34p], Chan Man Hei [82]	6 055	Matsumura JPN
24-02	Hong Kong	L	0-3	Hong Kong	EAq		1 602	Park Sang Gu KOR
26-02	Guam	W	2-0	Hong Kong	EAq	De Sousa 2 [37 77]	672	Cheung Yim Yau HKG
2-03	Chinese Taipei	L	1-2	Hong Kong	EAq	Hoi Man Io [35]	6 862	
21-03	Pakistan	L	0-3	Singapore	ACq			
23-03	Singapore	L	0-2	Singapore	ACq			
23-11	Chinese Taipei	L	0-3	Taipei	WCq		2 000	Napitupulu IDN
29-11	Chinese Taipei	L	1-3	Macau	WCq	Lei Fu Weng [87]	250	Zhou Weixin CHN
2004								
No international matches played in 2004								
2005								
21-05	Hong Kong	L	1-8	Hong Kong	Fr	Chung Koon Kan [86]		
2006								
2-04	Tajikistan	L	0-4	Dhaka	CCr1		2 000	Mombini IRN
6-04	Pakistan	D	2-2	Dhaka	CCr1	Chan Kin Seng 2 [16 52]	1 000	Shamsuzzaman BAN
7-04	Kyrgyzstan	L	0-2	Dhaka	CCr1		1 000	Tan Hai CHN
3-06	Hong Kong	D	0-0	Macau	Fr			
9-08	Chinese Taipei	L	0-1	Macau	Fr			
2007								
10-06	Hong Kong	L	1-2	Hong Kong	Fr	Chan Kin Seng [29]		
17-06	Mongolia	D	0-0	Macau	EAq			
21-06	Korea DPR	L	1-7	Macau	EAq			
24-06	Chinese Taipei	L	2-7	Macau	EAq	De Sousa [48], Leong Chong In [78]		

Fr = Friendly match • EA = East Asian Championship • AC = AFC Asian Cup • CC = AFC Challenge Cup • WC = FIFA World Cup
q = qualifier • r1 = first round group

MACAU NATIONAL TEAM RECORDS AND RECORD SEQUENCES

Records			Sequence records					
Victory	5-1	PHI	Wins	2	1997-1990	Clean sheets	1	Seven times
Defeat	0-10	JPN 1997 (Twice)	Defeats	9	2000-2001	Goals scored	5	1975-1978
Player Caps	n/a		Undefeated	2	Three times	Without goal	5	1985-1987
Player Goals	n/a		Without win	15	2003-2007	Goals against	15	1992-1997

MACAU 2006 CAMPEONATO 1° DIVISAO

	Pl	W	D	L	F	A	Pts
Lam Pak	18	15	1	2	63	10	46
Monte Carlo	18	14	3	1	82	19	45
Va Luen	18	13	1	4	45	21	40
Kin Chong	18	11	3	4	56	24	36
Heng Tai	18	7	2	9	29	36	23
Kuan Tai	18	6	4	8	25	24	22
Polícia	18	7	0	11	31	35	21
Hoi Fan	18	6	1	11	39	66	19
Alfândega	18	3	1	14	24	74	10
Macao U–18	18	0	0	18	4	89	0

3/02/2006 - 21/06/2006

LEAGUE RECORD

Year	Champs
1996	Artilheiros
1997	Lam Pak
1998	Lam Pak
1999	Lam Pak
2000	Polícia
2001	Lam Pak
2002	Monte Carlo
2003	Monte Carlo
2004	Monte Carlo
2005	Polícia
2006	Lam Pak
2007	Lam Pak

MACAU 2007 CAMPEONATO 1° DIVISAO

	Pl	W	D	L	F	A	Pts
Lam Pak	18	15	1	2	63	10	46
Vong Chiu	18	14	3	1	82	19	45
Va Luen	18	13	1	4	45	21	40
Monte Carlo	18	11	3	4	56	24	36
Heng Tai	18	7	2	9	29	36	23
Polícia	18	6	4	8	25	24	22
Macao U–19	18	7	0	11	31	35	21
Kin Chong	18	6	1	11	39	66	19
Kuan Tai	18	3	1	14	24	74	10
Keong Sai	18	0	0	18	4	89	0

27/01/2007 - 21/04/2007

MACAU COUNTRY INFORMATION

Capital	Macau	Status	Special administrative region of China	GDP per Capita	$19 400
Population	445 286			GNP Ranking	n/a
Area km²	25.4 per km²	Language	Portuguese, Cantonese	Dialling code	+853
Population density	17 530	Literacy rate	94%	Internet code	.mo
% in urban areas	100%	Main religion	Buddhist 50%, Christian 15%	GMT +/–	+8
Towns/Cities ('000)	Macao 445				
Neighbours (km)	China 0.34; South China Sea 41				
Main stadia	Campo Desportivo – Macau 15 000				

MAD – MADAGASCAR

NATIONAL TEAM RECORD
JULY 10TH 2006 TO JULY 12TH 2010

PL	W	D	L	F	A	%
6	1	0	5	5	15	16.6

FIFA/COCA-COLA WORLD RANKING

1993	1994	1995	1996	1997	1998	1999	2000	2001	2002	2003	2004	2005	2006	High		Low	
89	111	132	140	163	150	134	114	122	101	118	147	149	184	**81**	08/93	**188**	11/06

					2006–2007						
08/06	09/06	10/06	11/06	12/06	01/07	02/07	03/07	04/07	05/07	06/07	07/07
154	168	174	188	184	184	185	184	182	171	167	167

A win over the Seychelles in the COSAFA Castle Cup in April 2007 was only Madagascar's second international victory since 2003, during which time they have played 23 matches. The Indian Ocean islanders, who have changed the nickname of the national team from the 'Scorpions' to 'Barea', were among the first sides eliminated from the 2008 African Nations Cup qualifiers and have been through a host of coaches as they prepare to stage the Indian Ocean Island Games in August 2007. Jean Francois Debon was removed after a 4-0 defeat at the hands of Gabon at the start of the qualifiers, but his French successor Jean Paul Rossignol lasted just one game, fired after a home

INTERNATIONAL HONOURS
Indian Ocean Games 1990 1993

loss to Côte d'Ivoire. Former international Herve Arsene, who was Madagascar's first high profile export to France in his playing days, stepped in as caretaker for the COSAFA Cup mini tournament in Mozambique although German coach Gunter Zittel has also been working with the team on a short assignment sponsored by a German development agency. AS Adema won the League at the end of 2006 in the post-season play-offs, pipping Academie Ny Antsika by one point to the title. The academy, set up by Frenchman Jean Marc Guillou, founder of the ASEC academy in the Côte d'Ivoire, is already starting to produce players for the Malagasy junior national teams.

THE FIFA BIG COUNT OF 2006

	Male	Female		Total
Number of players	787 470	38 950	Referees and Assistant Referees	680
Professionals	0		Admin, Coaches, Technical, Medical	4 108
Amateurs 18+	16 650		Number of clubs	220
Youth under 18	13 700		Number of teams	880
Unregistered	27 000		Clubs with women's teams	0
Total players	826 420		Players as % of population	4.44%

Fédération Malagasy de Football (FMF)
26 rue de Russie, Isoraka, PO Box 4409, Tananarive 101, Madagascar
Tel +261 20 2268374   Fax +261 20 2268373
fmf@blueline.mg   www.none
President: AHMAD   General Secretary: RABIBISOA Anselme
Vice-President: RAZAFINDKIAKA Sylvain   Treasurer: ZAFINANDRO René   Media Officer: RANJALAHY Sylvain
Men's Coach: ARSENE Herve   Women's Coach: ANDRIANTANASASOA Herihaja
FMF formed: 1961   CAF: 19   FIFA: 1962
Red shirts with green trimmings, White shorts, Green socks

RECENT INTERNATIONAL MATCHES PLAYED BY MADAGASCAR

2002	Opponents	Score		Venue	Comp	Scorers	Att	Referee
21-07	South Africa	D	0-0	Port Elizabeth	CCqf	L 1-4p	8 000	Colembi ANG
8-09	Egypt	W	1-0	Antananarivo	CNq	Menakely [73]		Nkole ZAM
12-10	Mauritius	W	1-0	Port Louis	CNq	Menakely [18]	1 819	Maillet SEY
2003								
22-02	Mauritius	W	2-1	Antananarivo	CCr1	Menakely [16p], Radonamahafalison [33]	25 000	Motau RSA
27-03	Cameroon	L	0-2	Tunis	Fr		14 000	Zahmoul TUN
29-03	South Africa	L	0-2	Johannesburg	Fr		5 000	Shikapande ZAM
30-03	Ghana	D	3-3	Tunis	Fr	OG [47], Rasonaivo [82], Randriandelison [88]. L 9-10p		
24-04	Algeria	L	1-3	Amiens	Fr	Menakely [78p]	1 295	Garibian FRA
27-04	Mali	L	0-2	Paris	Fr			
20-06	Egypt	L	0-6	Port Said	CNq			
6-07	Mauritius	L	0-2	Antananarivo	CNq			
13-07	Swaziland	L	0-2	Mbabane	CCqf		8 000	Mpofu BOT
28-08	Seychelles	D	1-1	Curepipe	IOG	Menakely [32]	1 000	Lim Kee Chong MRI
30-08	Mauritius	L	1-3	Curepipe	IOG	Ralaitafika [54]	4 500	Ramsamy REU
11-10	Benin	D	1-1	Antananarivo	WCq	Edmond [28]	5 131	Maillet SEY
16-11	Benin	L	2-3	Cotonou	WCq	Radonamahafalison [15], Rakotondramanana [23]	20 000	Imiere NGA
2004								
18-04	Mozambique	L	0-2	Maputo	CCr1		28 000	Damon RSA
2005								
26-02	Mauritius	L	0-2	Curepipe	CCq			Fakude SWZ
23-10	Mauritius	W	2-0	Antananarivo	Fr	Randriamalala [16p], Andriatsima [80]		
2006								
20-05	Botswana	L	0-2	Gaborone	CCr1			Colembi ANG
21-05	Swaziland	L	0-2	Gaborone	CCr1			Malepa BOT
2-09	Gabon	L	0-4	Libreville	CNq			Diatta SEN
2007								
25-03	Côte d'Ivoire	L	0-3	Antananarivo	CNq			Maillet SEY
28-04	Zimbabwe	L	0-1	Maputo	CCr1			Faduco MOZ
29-04	Seychelles	W	5-0	Maputo	CCr1	Voavy 3 [11 14 69], Ramiadamanana [62], Andriatsima [84]		Mpopo LES
3-06	Côte d'Ivoire	L	0-5	Bouaké	CNq			
17-06	Gabon	L	0-2	Antananarivo	CNq			

Fr = Friendly match • CN = CAF African Cup of Nations • CC = COSAFA Cup • IOG = Indian Ocean Games • WC = FIFA World Cup
q = qualifier • r1 = first round group • qf = quarter-final

MADAGASCAR NATIONAL TEAM RECORDS AND RECORD SEQUENCES

Records			Sequence records				
Victory	8-1	CGO 1960	Wins	8	1957-1963	Clean sheets	4	1990, 1992-93
Defeat	0-7	MRI 1952	Defeats	8	2001	Goals scored	14	1957-1965
Player Caps	n/a		Undefeated	10	1979-1980	Without goal	6	2001
Player Goals	n/a		Without win	14	2003-2005	Goals against	17	1971-1980

MADAGASCAR COUNTRY INFORMATION

Capital	Antananarivo	Independence	1960 from France	GDP per Capita	$800
Population	17 501 871	Status	Republic	GNP Ranking	119
Area km²	587 040	Language	French, Malagasy	Dialling code	+261
Population density	29 per km²	Literacy rate	68%	Internet code	.mg
% in urban areas	27%	Main religion	Indigenous 52%, Christian 41%	GMT +/-	+3
Towns/Cities ('000)	Antananarivo 1 391; Toamasina 206; Antsirabé 183; Fianarantsoa 167; Mahajanga 155; Toliary 115; Antsiranana 82; Antanifotsy 70; Ambovombe 66; Amparafaravola 51				
Neighbours (km)	Indian Ocean 4 828				
Main stadia	Mahamasina – Antananarivo 22 000				

MADAGASCAR 2006 NATIONAL CHAMPIONSHIP SECOND STAGE

Group A - Fianarantsoa

	Pl	W	D	L	F	A	Pts
ASCUM Mahajanga ‡	3	2	1	0	5	1	7
Fortior Toamasina ‡	3	2	0	1	10	2	6
Ajesaia Antananarivo	3	1	1	1	2	3	4
Espoir Ambovombe	3	0	0	3	0	11	0

Group B - Toliara

	Pl	W	D	L	F	A	Pts
USCAFOOT	3	2	0	1	5	2	6
MTM Maintirano	3	2	0	1	3	3	6
Bazarico	3	1	0	2	2	3	3
Boeny Mahajanga	3	1	0	2	2	4	3

Group C - Mahajanga

	Pl	W	D	L	F	A	Pts
Fanilo Actuels ‡	3	3	0	0	7	2	9
Jirama Fianarantsoa ‡	3	1	1	1	5	4	4
Cospn Antananarivo	3	1	1	1	4	5	4
3FB Ambatondrazaka	3	0	0	3	3	8	0

Group D - Toamasina

	Pl	W	D	L	F	A	Pts
Adema Antananarivo ‡	3	3	0	0	12	0	9
Académie Ny Antsika ‡	3	2	0	1	6	1	6
Fort Dauphin	3	1	0	2	2	8	3
Jirama Sava	3	0	0	3	1	12	0

4/10/2006 - 8/10/2006 • ‡ Qualified for the third stage

MADAGASCAR 2006 NATIONAL CHAMPIONSHIP THIRD & FOURTH STAGES

Group A - Toamasina

	Pl	W	D	L	F	A	Pts
ASCUM Mahajanga ‡	3	2	0	1	4	1	6
Académie Ny Antsika ‡	3	2	0	1	4	2	6
USCAFOOT	3	2	0	1	4	3	6
Jirama Fianarantsoa	3	0	0	3	2	0	0

Group B - Mahajanga

	Pl	W	D	L	F	A	Pts
Adema Antananarivo ‡	3	1	2	0	5	2	5
Fortior Toamasina ‡	3	1	2	0	2	1	5
Fanilo Actuels	3	1	1	1	9	3	4
MTM Maintirano	3	0	1	2	1	11	1

Final Stage - Mahamasina

	Pl	W	D	L	F	A	Pts
Adema Antananarivo †	3	2	1	0	2	0	7
Académie Ny Antsika	3	2	0	1	7	4	6
ASCUM Mahajanja	3	0	2	1	5	7	2
Fortior Toamasina	3	0	1	2	6	9	1

22/10/2006 - 26/11/2006 • ‡ Qualified for the final stage •
† Qualified for the CAF Champions League

COUPE DE MADAGASCAR 2006

Round of 16

Ajesaia Antananarivo	3
CONC	1
Faniry Atsinanana	1
Fomela Ambositra	3
Boeny Mahajanga	1
Cospn Antananarivo	0
FCM Ilakaka	1
ASCUM Mahajanga	3
Adema Antananarivo	5
ASAM	1
SUCA Ambalavao	0
Jirama Toamasina	3
Tiko Antsirabe	1
Fanilo Actuel	0
US EPN	0
USCAFOOT	5

Quarter-finals

Ajesaia Antananarivo	2
Fomela Ambositra	0
Boeny Mahajanga	2 1
ASCUM Mahajanga	2 2
Adema Antananarivo	4
Jirama Toamasina	0
Tiko Antsirabe	0
USCAFOOT	1

Semi-finals

Ajesaia Antananarivo	2 4p
ASCUM Mahajanga	2 2p
Adema Antananarivo	0
USCAFOOT	1

Final

Ajesaia Antananarivo ‡	1
USCAFOOT	0

CUP FINAL

Mahamasina, Antananarivo
5-11-2006

Scorer - Njaka Harimalala
Razafimahatratra 77

‡ Qualified for the CAF Confederation Cup

RECENT LEAGUE AND CUP RECORD

	Championship		Cup		
Year	Champions	Winners	Score	Runners-up
1998	DSA Antananarivo	FC Djivan Farafangana	2-0	Fortior Club Mahajanga
1999	Fortior Toamasina	FC Djivan Farafangana	3-0	Akon'Ambatomena
2000	Fortior Toamasina	FC Djivan Farafangana	1-0	FC Jirama Antsirabe
2001	Stade Olympique Antananarivo (SOE)	US Transfoot Toamasina	1-0	Fortior Toamasina
2002	Adema Antananarivo	Fortior Toamasina	3-0	US Transfoot Toamasina
2003	Eco Redipharm Tamatave	Léopards Transfoot	1-0	SOE Antananarivo
2004	USJF/Ravinala	USJF/Ravinala	2-1	USCAFOOT Antananarivo
2005	USCAFOOT Antananarivo	USCAFOOT Antananarivo	2-1	USJF/Ravinala
2006	Adema Antananarivo	Ajesaia Antananarivo	1-0	USCAFOOT Antananarivo

MAR – MOROCCO

NATIONAL TEAM RECORD
JULY 10TH 2006 TO JULY 12TH 2010

PL	W	D	L	F	A	%
7	5	2	0	14	2	85.7

FIFA/COCA-COLA WORLD RANKING

1993	1994	1995	1996	1997	1998	1999	2000	2001	2002	2003	2004	2005	2006	High		Low	
30	33	38	27	15	13	24	28	36	35	38	33	36	39	10	04/98	48	04/07

2006–2007											
08/06	09/06	10/06	11/06	12/06	01/07	02/07	03/07	04/07	05/07	06/07	07/07
39	41	40	39	39	42	43	44	48	47	35	34

Morocco qualified with ease for the 2008 African Nations Cup finals in Ghana after proving far too strong for opponents Malawi and Zimbabwe. The only points dropped were in a draw in Harare but the other games in their three team group were won. Qualification quelled much of the talk over the future of coach Mohamed Fakhir, who has had to wade through a constant stream of speculation about the imminent arrival of a foreign coach to take charge of the side. The Morocco federation have given him a vote of confidence and Fakhir looks likely to take the side to a second successive Nations Cup tournament. In club football, Olympique Khouribga won a first league title having earlier in the

INTERNATIONAL HONOURS
Qualified for the FIFA World Cup finals 1970 1986 1994 1998 CAF African Cup of Nations 1976
African Youth Championship 1997 CAF Champions League FAR Rabat 1985, Raja Casablanca 1989 1997 1999, Wydad Casablanca 1992

season won the delayed 2006 Cup Final. Olympique had a comfortable lead through most of the League campaign and only lost for the first time as they were on the brink of securing the championship. They then struggled with an attack of nerves for several more matches before finally wrapping up the title. Royal Armed Forces were League runners-up and they also lost in the final of the Confederation Cup, beaten on the away goals rule by Tunisia's Etoile du Sahel. The soldiers had a late goal disallowed, setting off attacks on the match officials but no action was taken by the CAF.

THE FIFA BIG COUNT OF 2006

	Male	Female		Total
Number of players	1 553 748	74 268	Referees and Assistant Referees	2 007
Professionals	601		Admin, Coaches, Technical, Medical	6 644
Amateurs 18+	40 010		Number of clubs	563
Youth under 18	123 647		Number of teams	2 815
Unregistered	165 000		Clubs with women's teams	36
Total players	1 628 016		Players as % of population	4.90%

Fédération Royale Marocaine de Football (FRMF)
51 Bis Avenue Ibn Sina, Agdal, Case Postale 51, Rabat 10 000, Morocco
Tel +212 37 672706   Fax +212 37 671070
contact@fedefoot.ma   www.frmf.ma
President: BENSLIMANE Housni   General Secretary: BENCHEIKH Larci
Vice-President: AOUZAL Mohamed   Treasurer: EL AOUFIR Larbi   Media Officer: MOUFID Mohamed
Men's Coach: FAKHIR Mohammed   Women's Coach: ALAOUI Slimani
FRMF formed: 1955   CAF: 1966   FIFA: 1960
Green shirts with red trimmings, Green shorts, Green socks or Red shirts with green trimmings, Red shorts, Red socks

RECENT INTERNATIONAL MATCHES PLAYED BY MOROCCO

2002	Opponents	Score		Venue	Comp	Scorers	Att	Referee
15-11	Burkina Faso	W	1-0	Meknés	Fr	Ouaddou [24]	25 000	Boukhtir TUN
18-11	Mali	L	0-1	Casablanca	Fr		6 000	Shelmani LBY
19-11	Mali	L	0-1	Meknés	Fr			
2004								
27-01	Nigeria	W	1-0	Monastir	CNr1	Youssef Hadji [77]	15 000	Ndoye SEN
31-01	Benin	W	4-0	Sfax	CNr1	Chamakh [15], Mokhtari [73], Ouaddou [75], El Karkouri [80]	20 000	Maillet SEY
4-02	South Africa	D	1-1	Sousse	CNr1	Safri [38p]	6 000	Guirat TUN
8-02	Algeria	W	3-1	Sfax	CNqf	Chamakh [90], Youssef Hadji [113], Zairi [120]	22 000	Shelmani LBY
11-02	Mali	W	4-0	Sousse	CNsf	Mokhtari 2 [14 58], Youssef Hadji [80], Baha [90]	15 000	Sharaf CIV
14-02	Tunisia	L	1-2	Tunis	CNf	Mokhtari [38]	60 000	Ndoye SEN
18-02	Switzerland	W	2-1	Rabat	Fr	Adjou [78], Iajour [82]	1 700	Berber ALG
31-03	Angola	W	3-1	Casablanca	Fr	Baha 2 [67 74], Zairi [77]	7 000	Risha EGY
28-04	Argentina	L	0-1	Casablanca	Fr		65 000	Ndoye SEN
28-05	Mali	D	0-0	Bamako	Fr		35 000	Sidibe MLI
5-06	Malawi	D	1-1	Blantyre	WCq	Safri [25]	30 040	Mususa ZIM
3-07	Botswana	W	1-0	Gaborone	WCq	Mokhtari [30]	22 000	Dlamini SWZ
4-09	Tunisia	D	1-1	Rabat	WCq	El Karkouri [74]	45 000	Auda EGY
10-10	Guinea	D	1-1	Conakry	WCq	Chamakh [5]	25 000	Monteiro Duarte CPV
17-11	Burkina Faso	W	4-0	Rabat	Fr	Oulmers [52], Boukhari [68], Sarssar [78], Abdessadki [82]	5 000	Keita MLI
2005								
9-02	Kenya	W	5-1	Rabat	WCq	Zairi 3 [12 39 90], Diane [46], Youssef Hadji [81]	40 000	Tamuni LBY
26-03	Guinea	W	1-0	Rabat	WCq	Youssef Hadji [62]	70 000	Coulibaly MLI
4-06	Malawi	W	4-1	Rabat	WCq	Chamakh [16], Youssef Hadji 2 [21 75], Kharja [72]	48 000	Buenkadila COD
18-06	Kenya	D	0-0	Nairobi	WCq		50 000	Diatta SEN
17-08	Togo	L	0-1	Rouen	Fr			
3-09	Botswana	W	1-0	Rabat	WCq	El Karkouri [56]	25 000	Benouza ALG
8-10	Tunisia	D	2-2	Tunis/Rades	WCq	Chamakh [3], El Karkouri [42]	60 000	Abd El Fatah EGY
15-11	Cameroon	D	0-0	Clairfontaine	Fr			
2006								
9-01	Congo DR	W	3-0	Rabat	Fr	Chamakh [32], Aboucherouane [52], Armoumen [67]		
14-01	Zimbabwe	W	1-0	Marrakech	Fr	Armoumen [89]		
17-01	Angola	D	2-2	Marrakech	Fr	Chamakh [6], Youssef Hadji [8]		
21-01	Côte d'Ivoire	L	0-1	Cairo	CNr1		8 000	Damon RSA
24-01	Egypt	D	0-0	Cairo	CNr1		75 000	Codjia BEN
28-01	Libya	D	0-0	Cairo	CNr1		5 000	Daami TUN
23-05	USA	W	1-0	Nashville	Fr	Madihi [90]	26 141	Navarro CAN
28-05	Mali	L	0-1	Paris	Fr			Garibian FRA
4-06	Colombia	L	0-2	Barcelona	Fr		11 000	Segura Garcia ESP
16-08	Burkina Faso	W	1-0	Rabat	Fr	Youssef Hadji [44]		
3-09	Malawi	W	2-0	Rabat	CNq	Chammakh [50], Boussoufa [72]		Codjia BEN
15-11	Gabon	W	6-0	Rabat	Fr	El Moubarki 2 [40 64], Ouaddouch [61], Boukhari [68], Al Mahdoufi [71], Souari [90]	5 000	Sidebe MLI
2007								
7-02	Tunisia	D	1-1	Casablanca	Fr	Chammakh [29]		
25-03	Zimbabwe	D	1-1	Harare	CNq	Youssef Hadji [7]		Damon RSA
2-06	Zimbabwe	W	2-0	Casablanca	CNq	Chamakh [3], Youssef Hadji [26]		
16-06	Malawi	W	1-0	Blantyre	CNq	El Moubarki [9]		

Fr = Friendly match • AR = Arab Cup • CN = CAF African Cup of Nations • WC = FIFA World Cup
q = qualifier • r1 = first round group • qf = quarter-final • sf = semi-final • f = final

MOROCCO NATIONAL TEAM RECORDS AND RECORD SEQUENCES

Records			Sequence records				
Victory	7-0	TOG 1979	Wins	8	1997	Clean sheets	9	1997
Defeat	0-6	HUN 1964	Defeats	4	1994	Goals scored	12	1975-1976
Player Caps	115	NAYBET Noureddine	Undefeated	15	1983-84, 1996-97	Without goal	6	1983
Player Goals	n/a		Without win	7	1988	Goals against	9	1959-1961

MAJOR CITIES/TOWNS

Population '000

1	Casablanca	3 209
2	Rabat	1 721
3	Fez	1 001
4	Marrakesh	872
5	Agadir	739
6	Tangier	726
7	Meknes	564
8	Oujda	414
9	Kenitra	381
10	Tetouan	337
11	Safi	294
12	Laâyoune	217
13	Mohammedia	196
14	Beni Mellal	172
15	Khouribga	170
16	El Jadida	153
17	Taza	146
18	Nador	135
19	Settat	124
20	Larache	113
21	Ksar El Kebir	111
22	Khemisset	110
23	Guelmim	103
24	Berrechid	102

KINGDOM OF MOROCCO; AL MAMLAKAH AL MAGHRIBIYAH

Capital Rabat	Language Arabic, Berber, French	Independence 1956
Population 33 241 259	Area 446 550 km² Density 72 per km²	% in cities 48%
GDP per cap $4 000	Dailling code +212 Internet .ma	GMT + / - 0

MEDALS TABLE

			Overall			League			Cup			Africa			City	Stadium	Cap'ty	DoF
			G	S	B	G	S	B	G	S	B	G	S	B				
1	Wydad Casablanca	WAC	22	14	9	11	7	7	9	6		2	1	2	Casablanca	Stade Mohammed V	67 000	1937
2	FAR Rabat	FAR	21	11	6	11	5	4	8	4		2	2	2	Rabat	Moulay Abdallah	52 000	1958
3	Raja Casablanca	RCA	18	11	9	8	6	8	6	4		4	1	1	Casablanca	Stade Mohammed V	67 000	1949
4	Kawkab Marrakech	KACM	9	8	3	2	6	3	6	2		1			Marrakech	El Harti	25 000	1947
5	Maghreb Fès	MAS	6	8	2	4	2	2	2	6					Fès	Complexe Hassan II	45 000	1946
6	KAC Kénitra	KAC	5	5	1	4	2	1	1	3					Kénitra	Stade Municipal	15 000	1938
7	Mouloudia Oujda	MCO	5	2	3	1	1	3	4	1					Oujda	Stade d'Honneur	35 000	1946
8	FUS Rabat	FUS	4	3	1		2	1	4	1					Rabat	Ahmed Choude	10 000	1946
9	Olympic Casablanca	OC	3	1		1	1		2						Casablanca	Derejega	15 000	to 1995
10	Olympique Khouribga	OCK	2	6	3	1	2	3	1	4					Khouribga	Complexe OCP	10 000	1923
11	Rennaisance Settat	RSS	2	5	3	1	2	3	1	3					Settat	Stade Municipal	16 000	1946
12	Chabab Mohammedia	SCCM	2	2	1	1		1	1	2					Mohammedia	El Bachir	5 000	1946
13	Hassania Agadir	HUSA	2	2		2				2					Agadir	Al Inbiaâte	15 000	1946
14	COD Meknès	CODM	2	1	1	1		1	1	1					Meknès	Stade d'Honneur	20 000	1962
15	Racing Casablanca	RAC	1	2			2		1						Casablanca	Père Jégo	12 000	

RECENT LEAGUE AND CUP RECORD

	Championship							Cup		
Year	Champions	Pts	Runners-up	Pts	Third	Pts		Winners	Score	Runners-up
1995	COD Meknès	66	Olympic Casablanca	65	Kawkab Marrakech	65		FUS Rabat	2-0	Olympic Khouribga
1996	Raja Casablanca	57	Olympic Khouribga	48	Wydad Casablanca	47		Raja Casablanca	1-0	FAR Rabat
1997	Raja Casablanca	55	Wydad Casablanca	53	Renaissance Settat	53		Wydad Casablanca	1-0	Kawkab Marrakech
1998	Raja Casablanca	67	Kawkab Marrakech	53	Wydad Casablanca	51		Wydad Casablanca	2-1	FAR Rabat
1999	Raja Casablanca	62	Kawkab Marrakech	58	Olympic Khouribga	54		FAR Rabat	1-0	Chabab Mohammedia
2000	Raja Casablanca	59	Wydad Casablanca	54	Maghreb Fès	53		Majd Casablanca	1-1 8-7p	Renaissance Settat
2001	Raja Casablanca	64	FUS Rabat	55	Maghreb Fès	48		Wydad Casablanca	1-0	Maghreb Fès
2002	Hassania Agadir	65	Wydad Casablanca	62	Raja Casablanca	55		Raja Casablanca	2-0	Maghreb Fès
2003	Hassania Agadir	54	Raja Casablanca	52	Wydad Casablanca	52		FAR Rabat	1-0	Wydad Casablanca
2004	Raja Casablanca	56	FAR Rabat	56	AS Salé	51		FAR Rabat	0-0 3-0p	Wydad Casablanca
2005	FAR Rabat	62	Raja Casablanca	60	Wydad Casablanca	50		Raja Casablanca	0-0 5-4p	Olympic Khouribga
2006	Wydad Casablanca	61	FAR Rabat	58	Olympic Khouribga	53		Olympic Khouribga	1-0	Hassania Agadir
2007	Olympic Khouribga	62	FAR Rabat	55	MA Tétouan	54				

MOROCCO 2006–07

CHAMPIONNAT DU GNFE1

	Pl	W	D	L	F	A	Pts	OCK	FAR	MAT	WAC	DHJ	KACM	IZK	JSM	HUSA	MCO	RCA	OCS	CODM	MAS	IRT	ASS
Olympique Khouribga†	30	17	11	2	38	16	62		2-0	2-1	2-0	1-0	1-2	1-0	0-1	1-0	2-1	1-0	3-0	2-0	1-0	3-1	1-0
FAR Rabat†	30	16	7	7	31	17	55	1-0		1-0	0-1	2-1	2-0	0-0	1-1	1-0	1-0	1-0	1-0	1-0	4-1	1-0	2-0
MA Tétouan‡	30	15	9	6	37	31	54	1-2	1-0		4-2	0-4	1-0	1-0	1-0	1-0	2-1	1-1	4-3	1-0		3-1	
Wydad Casablanca	30	11	14	5	30	20	47	0-0	1-0	3-0		1-1	1-1	3-1	2-1	1-1	2-1	1-1	0-1	1-0	2-0	1-2	1-1
Diffa El Jadida	30	9	15	6	29	19	42	1-1	1-1	1-1	0-0		1-1	2-0	1-0	0-0	0-0	1-1	1-0	2-0	3-0	1-1	3-1
Kawkab Marrakech	30	10	12	8	23	17	42	0-0	0-2	2-0	0-0	0-1		1-0	0-0	0-0	0-1	1-1	0-0	1-1	1-0	1-0	4-0
IZ Khemisset	30	10	12	8	24	23	42	0-0	1-1	1-1	0-0	0-1	1-0		1-0	2-0	0-0	0-0	1-0	2-0	0-0	1-0	2-1
JS Massira	30	8	13	9	21	21	37	1-1	0-0	1-1	1-0	2-1	0-0	1-1		1-1	4-1	1-0	1-0	1-0	0-0	1-0	1-1
HUS Agadir	30	8	12	10	22	23	36	1-1	2-1	2-2	1-2	0-0	0-0	3-1	2-0		1-0	1-0	0-0	0-1	2-0	2-1	1-0
Mouloudia Oujda	30	8	12	10	25	35	36	1-1	2-1	3-3	0-0	2-1	1-0	0-0	0-0	1-0		0-0	2-1	0-1	1-0	1-1	2-2
Raja Casablanca	30	7	14	9	23	20	35	0-0	0-0	0-0	0-1	0-0	1-1	1-1	1-0	1-1	5-1		2-1	3-1	3-0	1-0	1-0
Olympique Safi	30	7	11	12	22	31	32	1-1	0-1	1-2	1-1	1-0	0-3	0-2	1-0	2-0	2-2	0-0		1-1	1-0	1-1	1-2
COD Meknès	30	6	13	11	17	24	31	1-1	0-0	0-0	0-0	0-0	0-1	3-1	1-1	1-0	2-0	1-0	2-2		0-1	0-0	1-1
Maghreb Fès	30	7	8	15	19	34	29	1-2	1-2	0-1	0-0	0-0	1-0	0-0	1-0	1-0	1-2	2-0	0-1	1-0		2-1	0-0
IR Tanger	30	5	11	14	21	30	26	0-0	0-2	0-0	0-0	2-0	1-2	2-3	1-0	0-0	3-0	1-0	0-1	0-0	2-2		1-1
AS Salé	30	3	12	15	21	42	21	1-3	0-1	0-2	0-3	1-1	0-1	1-2	1-2	1-1	0-0	1-0	1-1	0-0	1-1	2-0	

16/09/2006 - 27/05/2007 • † Qualified for the CAF Champions League • ‡ Qualified for the CAF Confederation Cup

MOROCCO 2006–07
CHAMPIONNAT DU GNFE2

	Pl	W	D	L	F	A	Pts
FUS Rabat	30	14	13	3	31	13	55
Kénitra AC	30	14	11	5	38	22	53
Chabab Houara	30	12	11	7	26	18	47
US Touarga	30	12	7	11	26	20	43
Rachad Bernoussi	30	8	17	5	22	14	41
US Sidi Kacem	30	10	10	10	25	26	40
RS Settat	30	9	12	9	27	30	39
Chabab Mohammedia	30	9	11	10	20	25	38
TUS Temara	30	8	13	9	30	27	37
Racing Casablanca	30	8	13	9	27	27	37
US Mohammedia	30	9	10	11	20	24	37
CAY Berrechid	30	8	11	11	18	23	35
WW Sidi Othmane	30	9	6	15	26	37	33
Hilal Nador §1	30	7	12	11	19	29	32
Stade Marocain	30	5	16	9	18	27	31
RS Berkane	30	5	13	12	21	32	28

16/09/2006 - 27/05/2007 • § = points deducted

COUPE DU TRONE 2006

Round of 16
- Olympique Khouribga — 0 4p
- Jeunesse Ben Guérir — 0 3p
- US Mohammedia — 0 2p
- Rachad Bernoussi — 0 4p
- IZ Khemisset — 1 9p
- Kénitra AC — 1 8p
- Etoile Tanger — 1
- IR Tanger — 2
- COD Meknès — 1
- MA Tétouan — 0
- FAR Rabat — 0
- AS Salé — 2
- Raja Casablanca — 1
- NR Marrakech — 0
- Wydad Casablanca — 0
- Hassania Agadir — 1

Quarter-finals
- Olympique Khouribga — 2
- Rachad Bernoussi — 0
- IZ Khemisset — 1 2p
- IR Tanger — 1 4p
- COD Meknès — 1
- AS Salé — 0
- Raja Casablanca
- Hassania Agadir — W-0

Semi-finals
- Olympique Khouribga — 4
- IR Tanger — 0
- COD Meknès — 0
- Hassania Agadir — 1

Final
- Olympique Khouribga — 1
- Hassania Agadir‡ — 0

CUP FINAL
Moulay Abdallah, Rabat
5-11-2006

Scorer - Mohamed Morsadi [15] for OCK

* Home team • ‡ Qualified for the CAF Confederation Cup

MAS – MALAYSIA

NATIONAL TEAM RECORD
JULY 10TH 2006 TO JULY 12TH 2010

PL	W	D	L	F	A	%
16	4	4	8	23	27	37.5

FIFA/COCA-COLA WORLD RANKING

1993	1994	1995	1996	1997	1998	1999	2000	2001	2002	2003	2004	2005	2006	High		Low	
79	89	106	96	87	113	117	107	111	128	116	120	123	152	**75**	08/93	**157**	01/07

2006–2007											
08/06	09/06	10/06	11/06	12/06	01/07	02/07	03/07	04/07	05/07	06/07	07/07
148	148	153	153	152	157	156	154	154	156	149	154

The hosting of the 2007 AFC Asian Cup should have been a cause for celebration, but even during the tournament you could be forgiven for thinking that Malaysians weren't even aware that it was taking place in their country. Just over 62,000 fans turned up to watch the eight matches played in Malaysia - well under 10,000 per game in the huge Bukit Jalil stadium that boasts a capacity of over 100,000. It didn't help that the Malaysian national team were simply awful, and of the four co-hosts, Malaysia will feel this was a missed opportunity to increase the profile of the game in the country. The tournament started off in disastrous fashion for the national team with a

INTERNATIONAL HONOURS
Southeast Asian Games 1961 1977 1979 1989

5-1 drubbing at the hands of China but it got worse in the second match when Uzbekistan put another five past them, this time without reply. Iran then completed the misery with a 2-0 win to seal the worst performance by a host nation in the history of the tournament. The Malaysian Super League took a six week break for the duration of the finals and was completed shortly afterwards with Kedah winning the title. Having won the FA Cup just before the break, they completed an historic double - the first since the creation of the FA Cup in 1990. The other major trophy on offer, the Malaysia Cup, was won by Perlis who beat Negeri Sembilan 2-1 in the final.

THE FIFA BIG COUNT OF 2006

	Male	Female		Total
Number of players	549 300	36 430	Referees and Assistant Referees	1 810
Professionals	600		Admin, Coaches, Technical, Medical	10 000
Amateurs 18+	1 430		Number of clubs	110
Youth under 18	7 300		Number of teams	550
Unregistered	259 800		Clubs with women's teams	0
Total players	585 730		Players as % of population	2.40%

Football Association of Malaysia (FAM)

3rd Floor Wisma FAM, Jalan SS5A/9, Kelana Jaya, Selangor Darul Ehsan 47301, Malaysia
Tel +60 3 78733100   Fax +60 3 78757984
gensec@fam.org.my   www.fam.org.my
President: HRH Sultan AHMAD SHAH   General Secretary: SAAD Dato Seri
Vice-President: HRH Abdullah AHMED SHAH   Treasurer: KEAP TAI Cheong   Media Officer: KHAWARI Ahmad
Men's Coach: BAKAR Norizan   Women's Coach: SINGH Macky
FAM formed: 1933   AFC: 1954   FIFA: 1956
Yellow shirts with black trimmings, Yellow shorts, Yellow socks

RECENT INTERNATIONAL MATCHES PLAYED BY MALAYSIA

2004 Opponents		Score	Venue	Comp	Scorers	Att	Referee
7-02	Japan	L 0-4	Ibaraki	Fr		29 530	Moradi IRN
18-02	Hong Kong	L 1-3	Kuantan	WCq	Talib [39p]	12 000	Nagalimgam SIN
17-03	Indonesia	D 0-0	Johor Bahru	Fr		8 000	Kim Heng MAS
31-03	Kuwait	L 0-2	Kuantan	WCq		9 327	Matsumura JPN
9-06	China PR	L 0-4	Tianjin	WCq		35 000	Park Sang Gu KOR
12-07	Singapore	W 2-0	Kuala Lumpur	Fr			
19-08	Thailand	W 2-1	Bangkok	Fr	Kit Hong [8], Vellu [57]		
8-09	China PR	L 0-1	Penang	WCq		14 000	Karim BHR
13-10	Hong Kong	L 0-2	Hong Kong	WCq		2 425	Ghandour LIB
1-11	Singapore	W 2-1	Singapore	Fr	Bin Jamlus [68], Amri [90]	3 293	Luong The Tai VIE
17-11	Kuwait	L 1-6	Kuwait City	WCq	Mohd [19]	15 000	Lutfullin UZB
8-12	East Timor †	W 5-0	Kuala Lumpur	TCr1	Kit Kong [27], Amri 2 [47 83], Saari [67], Adan [85]	6 000	Lazar SIN
10-12	Philippines	W 4-1	Kuala Lumpur	TCr1	Kit Kong [17], Bin Jamlus 2 [67 77p], Hussein [74]		Napitupulu IDN
12-12	Myanmar	L 0-1	Kuala Lumpur	TCr1		10 000	Hsu Chao Lo TPE
14-12	Thailand	W 2-1	Kuala Lumpur	TCr1	Bin Jamlus 2 [63 65]	10 000	Moradi IRN
28-12	Indonesia	W 2-1	Jakarta	TCsf	Kit Kong 2 [28 47]	100 000	Irmatov UZB
2005							
3-01	Indonesia	L 1-4	Kuala Lumpur	TCsf	Bin Jamlus [26]	70 000	Kunsuta THA
15-01	Myanmar	W 2-1	Singapore	TC3p	Bin Jamlus [15], Nor [56]	2 000	Vo Minh Tri VIE
4-06	Singapore	L 0-2	Singapore	Fr		18 000	Kunsuta THA
8-06	Singapore	L 1-2	Penang	Fr	Ayob [25]	10 000	Napitupulu IDN
2006							
19-02	New Zealand	L 0-1	Christchurch	Fr		10 100	O'Leary NZL
23-02	New Zealand	L 1-2	Albany	Fr	Safee Sali [24]	8 702	Fox NZL
31-05	Singapore	D 0-0	Singapore	Fr	L 4-5p	18 604	Li Yuhong CHN
3-06	Singapore	D 0-0	Paroi	Fr	L 7-8p		
23-08	Indonesia	D 1-1	Kuala Lumpur	Fr	Ridwan OG [77]	20 000	Zhang Lei CHN
25-08	Thailand	W 2-1	Kuala Lumpur	Fr	Indra Putra 2 [39 77]		Lee Jong Kuk KOR
27-08	Myanmar	L 1-2	Kuala Lumpur	Fr	Indra Putra [12p]		Zhang Lei CHN
2007							
12-01	Philippines	W 4-0	Bangkok	TCr1	Hairuddin Omar 2 [9 80], Niaruddin Yusof [16], OG [69]	5 000	Daud SIN
14-01	Myanmar	D 0-0	Bangkok	TCr1		28 000	Tri Minh Vo VIE
16-01	Thailand	L 0-1	Bangkok	TCr1		25 000	Matsuo JPN
23-01	Singapore	D 1-1	Kuala Lumpur	TCsf	Hardi Jaafar [57]	40 000	Wan Daxue CHN
27-01	Singapore	D 1-1	Singapore	TCsf	Helmi Manan [57]. L 4-5p	55 000	Cheung Yim Yau HKG
24-03	Sri Lanka	W 4-1	Colombo	Fr	Hardi Jaafar [5], Fadzli Saari [12], Azlan Ismail [45], Norhafiz Zamani Misbah [65]		
26-03	Sri Lanka	L 1-2	Colombo	Fr	Kaironnisam Sahabuddin Hussain [16]		Da Silva SRI
18-06	Cambodia	W 6-0	Kuala Lumpur	Fr	Rosdi Talib [23], Mohd Ivan Yusof [47], Hairuddin Omar [58], Helmi Manan 2 [61 88], Aidil Zafuan [90]		
21-06	UAE	L 1-3	Kelana Jaya	Fr	Akmal Rizal Rakhli [88]		
28-06	Jamaica	L 0-2	Kuala Lumpur	Fr			
10-07	China PR	L 1-5	Kuala Lumpur	ACr1	Indra Putra [72]	20 000	Basma SYR
14-07	Uzbekistan	L 0-5	Kuala Lumpur	ACr1		7 137	Abdou QAT
18-07	Iran	L 0-2	Kuala Lumpur	ACr1		4 520	Basma SYR

Fr = Friendly match • TC = ASEAN Tiger Cup • AC = AFC Asian Cup • AAG = Afro-Asian Games • WC = FIFA World Cup
q = qualifier • r1 = first round group • sf = semi-final • 3p = third place play-off • † not a full international

MALAYSIA NATIONAL TEAM RECORDS AND RECORD SEQUENCES

Records			Sequence records				
Victory	15-1	PHI 1962	Wins	6	1975, 1989	Clean sheets	5	1979
Defeat	2-8	NZL 1967	Defeats	7	1980-81, 2003-04	Goals scored	14	1999-2000
Player Caps	n/a		Undefeated	10	1961-1962, 1971	Without goal	5	1997-1998
Player Goals	n/a		Without win	12	2003-2004	Goals against	15	1970-1971

MALAYSIA

Capital	Kuala Lumpur	Language	Malay, English, Chinese	Independence	1963
Population	24 385 858	Area	329 750 km²	Density	71 per km²	% in cities	54%
GDP per cap	$9 000	Dailling code	+60	Internet	.my	GMT +/-	+8

MAJOR CITIES/TOWNS
Population '000

1	Kuala Lumpur	1 509
2	Subang Jaya	1 091
3	Klang	995
4	Johor Bahru	876
5	Ampang Jaya	721
6	Ipoh	710
7	Kuching	634
8	Shah Alam	563
9	Petaling Jaya	550
10	Kota Kinabalu	532
11	Sandakan	448
12	Batu Sembilan Cheras	430
13	Seremban	408
14	Kuantan	399
15	Kajang-Sungai Chua	386
16	Tawau	349
17	Kuala Terengganu	295
18	Kota Bahru	287
19	Miri	256
20	Selayang Baru	251
21	Alor Setar	227
22	Melaka	193
23	George Town	174
24	Kangar	66

MEDALS TABLE

		Overall			League			M Cup		FAC		Asia			City	Stadium	Cap'ty	DoF
		G	S	B	G	S	B	G	S		G	S	B					
1	Selangor	40	18		4	2		32	14	4 1	1			Selangor	Shah Alam	80 000	1936
2	FA of Singapore	26	19		2			24	19					Singapore			1892
3	Perak	11	14	3	2	1	3	7	10	2 3				Ipoh	Perak Stadium	40 000	1921
4	Penang	8	13		3	2		4	9	1 2				George Town	Negeri Pulau Pinang	40 000	
5	Pahang	8	7		5	2		2	4	1 1				Kuantan	Darulmakmur	40 000	
6	Kuala Lumpur	8	2		2			3	1	3 1				Kuala Lumpur	KLFA Stadium	18 000	1974
7	Kedah	6	9		2	3		2	6	2				Alor Setar	Darul Aman	40 000	1935
8	Johor	4	1		1			2	1	1				Johor Bahru	Hassan Yunos	30 000	
9	Perlis	3	4	2	1	2		2	1	3				Kangar	Utama	20 000	
10	Negri Sembilan	3	2	3	1	3		1	2	1				Seremban	Abdul Rahman	30 000	
11	Terengganu	2	7			2		1	3	1 2				Kuala Terengganu	Nasiruddin Shah	25 000	1972
12	Sabah	2	6	2	1	2			3	1 3				Kota Kinabalu	Likas	20 000	
13	Sarawak	2	3	1	1	1		1		1 2				Kuching	Sarawak Stadium	40 000	1974
14	Brunei D'salam	1	1		1	1								Bandar Seri Beg.			1956
15	Malacca	1			1									Melaka	Bandar Melaka	15 000	
	Selangor MPPJ	1						1						Petaling Jaya	MPPJ	25 000	

RECENT LEAGUE AND CUP RECORD

	Championship							FA Cup		
Year	Champions	Pts	Runners-up	Pts	Third	Pts		Winners	Score	Runners-up
1995	Pahang	65	Selangor	54	Sarawak	54		Sabah	3-1	Pahang
1996	Sabah	58	Kedah	57	Negri Sembilan	57		Kedah	1-0	Sarawak
1997	Sarawak	54	Kedah	50	Sabah	49		Selangor	1-0	Penang
1998	Penang	41	Pahang	40	Brunei	35		Johor	1-0	Sabah
1999	Pahang	34	Penang	31	Negri Sembilan	29		Kuala Lumpur	0-0 5-3p	Terengganu
2000	Selangor	45	Penang	43	Perak	41		Terengganu	1-1 4-3p	Penang
2001	Penang	50	Terengganu	41	Kelantan	38		Selangor	1-0	Sarawak
2002	Perak	60	Selangor	56	Sabah	47		Penang	1-0	Perak
2003	Perak	47	Kedah	45	Perlis	45		Negri Sembilan	2-1	Perlis
2004	Pahang	47	Selangor Public Bank	38	Perlis	36		Perak	3-0	Terengganu
2005	Perlis	45	Pahang	35	Perak	30		Selangor	4-2	Perak
2006	Negri Sembilan	40	Melaka Telekom	33	Perak	30		Pahang	0-0 4-2p	Perlis
2007	Kedah	55	Perak	53	DPMM Brunei	44		Kedah	0-0 4-2p	Perlis

MALAYSIA 2006-07

MALAYSIAN SUPER LEAGUE (MSL)

	Pl	W	D	L	F	A	Pts	Kedah	Perak	DPMM	Terengganu	Perlis	Johor	Telekom	Selangor	Pahang	P. Pinang	Negeri S.	Sarawak	Melaka
Kedah †	24	17	4	3	54	21	55		4-3	1-2	3-0	1-0	1-0	4-1	2-1	4-1	2-0	7-0	4-2	4-2
Perak	24	16	5	3	58	22	53	1-0		3-0	1-1	2-0	0-0	2-1	2-0	3-1	0-0	5-1	2-1	2-0
DPMM FC	24	13	5	6	46	29	44	0-1	4-3		1-0	2-2	3-1	1-1	2-0	1-3	1-1	5-1	4-0	4-0
Terengganu	24	13	5	6	41	29	44	3-2	0-0	2-0		2-0	1-2	1-1	1-0	1-1	3-0	2-0	5-1	4-0
Perlis	24	13	4	7	47	25	43	1-1	0-1	3-2	4-1		2-1	0-1	2-0	2-1	0-1	3-0	5-1	6-0
Johor FC	24	11	6	7	35	26	39	1-2	1-0	0-0	0-2	3-1		0-1	0-0	2-1	2-0	0-0	3-1	4-0
Telekom FC	24	10	6	8	35	35	36	0-0	0-3	1-4	4-2	0-1	0-2		2-1	1-2	2-1	3-1	2-1	3-2
Selangor	24	8	4	12	28	35	28	0-2	2-4	2-1	1-2	0-1	2-3	3-1		2-0	1-1	2-1	2-1	1-0
Pahang	24	7	6	11	32	41	27	0-0	1-2	1-1	0-1	1-5	2-3	0-3	1-1		2-0	2-2	3-1	5-1
Pinang	24	6	6	12	25	36	24	1-4	1-4	1-3	0-1	0-2	3-2	0-0	1-2	1-1		1-0	5-0	1-0
Negeri Sembilan	24	6	6	12	29	46	24	0-1	2-2	0-1	4-0	2-2	1-1	0-0	3-1	0-1	2-1		3-1	3-1
Sarawak	24	2	4	18	28	65	10	1-1	2-4	0-1	3-3	2-2	1-2	2-5	1-1	3-0	**0-3**	3-0		0-2
Melaka	24	2	3	19	24	72	9	1-3	0-9	2-3	1-3	0-3	2-2	2-2	1-3	1-2	2-2	1-3	3-0	

16/12/2006 - 4/08/2007 • † Qualified for the AFC Cup • Match in bold awarded

MALAYSIA 2006-07 PREMIER LEAGUE (2)

	Pl	W	D	L	F	A	Pts
PDRM	20	14	2	4	40	24	44
UPB/My Team Melaka	20	12	5	3	36	22	41
Selangor PKNS	20	9	5	6	29	28	32
Johor Pasing Gudang	20	8	6	6	33	22	30
Pahang Shahzan Muda	20	7	7	6	28	24	28
Sabah	20	6	9	5	26	21	27
Kuala Lumpur	20	6	6	8	22	28	24
Kelantan	20	4	8	8	23	33	20
ATM Lumut	20	5	4	11	23	36	19
Kuala Muda	20	4	6	10	19	26	18
KL Plus FC	20	4	4	12	26	41	16

22/12/2006 - 31/07/2007

MALAYSIA CUP 2006

Quarter-finals		Semi-finals		Final	
Perlis	3 1				
Terengganu	2 1	**Perlis**	0 2		
Pulau Pinang	0 2	Perak	0 1		
Perak	3 2				
Melaka Telecom	3 2			**Perlis**	2
Selangor MPPJ	0 0	Melaka Telecom	1 0	Negeri Sembilan	1
Sarawak	114p	**Negeri Sembilan**	1 2		
Negeri Sembilan	115p				

First round played in four groups of four

Bukit Jalil, 16-09-2006
Chepita 4, Simikonda 77 for Perlis; Bekamenga 82 for NG

See page 1045 for details of the 2006 FA Cup which was missing from the previous edition of the *Almanack of World Football*

FA CUP 2007

Second Round		Quarter-finals		Semi-finals		Final	
Kedah *	1						
Perak	0	**Kedah**	4 3				
Negeri Sembilan	1	UPB FC *	1 0				
UPB FC *	3			**Kedah** *	2 1		
PKNS Selangor	1 5p			Selangor	0 1		
Pahang *	1 4p	PKNS Selangor	1 1				
ATM *	1	**Selangor** *	2 1				
Selangor	4					**Kedah** †	0 4p
Johor Pasir Gudang *	2 5p					Perlis	0 2p
Kelantan	2 4p	**Johor Pasir Gudang** *	2 2				
Shahzan Muda	1	Kuala Muda Naza	0 1				
Kuala Muda Naza	5			Johor Pasir Gudang *	2 0		
Sabah	4			**Perlis**	1 1		
Johor FC *	3	Sabah *	2 0				
Melaka Telekom *	0	**Perlis**	2 3				
Perlis	3						

CUP FINAL

Negeri Pulau Pinang Stadium, Batu Kawan, 30-06-2007, Att: 40 000

* Home team/home team in the first leg • † Qualified for the AFC Cup

MDA – MOLDOVA

NATIONAL TEAM RECORD
JULY 10TH 2006 TO JULY 12TH 2010

PL	W	D	L	F	A	%
9	1	2	6	7	19	22.2

FIFA/COCA-COLA WORLD RANKING

1993	1994	1995	1996	1997	1998	1999	2000	2001	2002	2003	2004	2005	2006	High		Low	
-	118	109	117	131	116	93	94	103	111	106	114	107	86	73	08/06	149	07/94

2006–2007											
08/06	09/06	10/06	11/06	12/06	01/07	02/07	03/07	04/07	05/07	06/07	07/07
73	85	86	85	86	85	83	94	92	90	101	102

Sheriff Tiraspol were relentless in their search for a seventh consecutive League title and in the process they became the first team from Moldova to go through the season unbeaten. They finished a massive 21 points ahead of Zimbru who have had to get used to being second best after dominating the Moldovan League in the 1990s. If Sheriff win the title in 2008 they will equal Zimbru's total of eight championships and they will perhaps have one eye on the world record held by Skonto Riga which stands at 14 consecutive titles. It may be a bit early to be talking in such terms and Zimbru are certainly not to be taken for granted. The two met in the semi-final of the Cup and in

INTERNATIONAL HONOURS
None

the first leg Zimbru beat Sheriff 2-1, a result that was enough to take them through to the final where they beat Nistru thanks to a last minute goal by Andrei Cojocaru. In the qualifiers for UEFA Euro 2008, Moldova had a wretched start to their campaign picking up just two points from their first seven matches. They were always going to be involved in a dog fight with Malta to avoid the wooden spoon in a very tough group, but going into the 2007 summer break they found themselves ensconced at the bottom of the table much to the disappointment of new coach Igor Dobrovolsky who had replaced Anatoly Teslev in December 2006.

THE FIFA BIG COUNT OF 2006

	Male	Female		Total
Number of players	147 430	21 140	Referees and Assistant Referees	151
Professionals	543		Admin, Coaches, Technical, Medical	560
Amateurs 18+	6 629		Number of clubs	86
Youth under 18	2 603		Number of teams	2 036
Unregistered	66 150		Clubs with women's teams	3
Total players	168 570		Players as % of population	3.77%

Football Association of Moldova (FMF)
Federatia Moldoveneasca de Fotbal, Str. Tricolorului nr. 39, Chisinau MD-2012, Moldova
Tel +373 22 210413   Fax +373 22 210432
fmf@mfotbal.mldnet.com   www.fmf.md
President: CEBANU Pavel   General Secretary: CEBOTARI Nicolai
Vice-President: ANGHEL Mihai   Treasurer: SOROCEAN Victor   Media Officer: DAGHI Victor
Men's Coach: DOBROVOLSKY Igor   Women's Coach: PUSICOV Evgheni
FMF formed: 1990   UEFA: 1992   FIFA: 1994
Red shirts, Blue shirts, Red socks or Blue shirts, Red shorts, Blue socks

RECENT INTERNATIONAL MATCHES PLAYED BY MOLDOVA

2002	Opponents	Score		Venue	Comp	Scorers	Att	Referee
21-08	Estonia	L	0-1	Tallinn	Fr		1 500	Kaldma EST
7-09	Austria	L	0-2	Vienna	ECq		18 300	Dougal SCO
12-10	Czech Republic	L	0-2	Chisinau	ECq		4 000	Irvine NIR
20-11	Hungary	D	1-1	Budapest	Fr	Patula [16]	6 000	Sowa AUT
2003								
12-02	Georgia	D	2-2	Tbilisi	Fr	Golban [75], Dadu [84p]	7 000	Hovanisyan ARM
5-03	Israel	D	0-0	Tel Aviv	Fr		8 000	Bertini ITA
29-03	Belarus	L	1-2	Minsk	ECq	Cebotari [14]	7 500	Verbist BEL
2-04	Netherlands	L	1-2	Tiraspol	ECq	Boret [16]	12 000	Sars FRA
7-06	Austria	W	1-0	Tiraspol	ECq	Frunza [60]	10 000	Paraty Silva POR
11-06	Czech Republic	L	0-5	Olomouc	ECq		12 907	Jakobsson ISL
20-08	Turkey	L	0-2	Ankara	Fr		15 300	Plautz AUT
10-09	Belarus	W	2-1	Tiraspol	ECq	Dadu [23], Covaliciuc [88]	7 000	Delevic SCG
11-10	Netherlands	L	0-5	Eindhoven	ECq		30 995	Siric CRO
20-11	Luxembourg	W	2-1	Hesperange	Fr	Golban [19], Dadu [90]	623	Duhamel FRA
2004								
14-02	Malta	D	0-0	Ta'Qali	Fr		600	Vialichka BLR
16-02	Belarus	L	0-1	Ta'Qali	Fr		40	Attard MLT
18-02	Estonia	L	0-1	Ta'Qali	Fr		100	Sammut MLT
31-03	Azerbaijan	W	2-1	Chisinau	Fr	Dadu 2 [42p 84]	5 500	Godulyan UKR
28-04	Israel	D	1-1	Tel Aviv	Fr	Rogaciov [71]	4 500	Corpodean ROU
18-08	Georgia	W	1-0	Tiraspol	Fr	Miterev [68]	8 000	Godulyan UKR
4-09	Slovenia	L	0-3	Celje	WCq		3 620	Hyytia FIN
8-09	Italy	L	0-1	Chisinau	WCq		5 200	Benes CZE
9-10	Belarus	L	0-4	Minsk	WCq		21 000	Dereli TUR
13-10	Scotland	D	1-1	Chisinau	WCq	Dadu [28]	7 000	Jakobsson ISL
2005								
9-02	Azerbaijan	D	0-0	Baku	Fr		1 500	
30-03	Norway	D	0-0	Chisinau	WCq		5 000	Meyer GER
4-06	Scotland	L	0-2	Glasgow	WCq		45 317	Braamhaar NED
3-09	Belarus	W	2-0	Chisinau	WCq	Rogaciov 2 [17 49]	5 000	Duhamel FRA
7-09	Slovenia	L	1-2	Chisinau	WCq	Rogaciov [31]	7 200	Baskakov RUS
8-10	Norway	L	0-1	Oslo	WCq		23 409	Bennett RSA
12-10	Italy	L	1-2	Lecce	WCq	Gatcan [76]	28 160	Benquerenca POR
2006								
25-02	Malta	W	2-0	Ta'Qali	Fr	Namasco 46, Bugaiov 73	1 125	Silagava GEO
27-02	Georgia	W	5-1	Ta'Qali	Fr	Zislis 2 [5 13], Alexeev [48], Namasco [55p], Golovatenco [72]	330	Casha MLT
18-05	Azerbaijan	D	0-0	Chisinau	Fr			
16-08	Lithuania	W	3-2	Chisinau	Fr	Dadu [15p] Iepureanu [56], Clescenco [87p]		Godulyan UKR
2-09	Greece	L	0-1	Chisinau	ECq		10 500	Trefoloni ITA
6-09	Norway	L	0-2	Oslo	ECq		23 848	Ristoskov BUL
7-10	Bosnia-Herzegovina	D	2-2	Chisinau	ECq	Rogaciov 2 [13 32p]	7 114	Piccirillo FRA
11-10	Turkey	L	0-5	Frankfurt	ECq		BCD	Vollquartz DEN
2007								
7-02	Romania	L	0-2	Bucharest	Fr		8 000	Deaconu ROU
24-03	Malta	D	1-1	Chisinau	ECq	Epureanu [85]	8 033	Aliyev AZE
28-03	Hungary	L	0-2	Budapest	ECq		6 150	Ingvarsson SWE
6-06	Greece	L	1-2	Irákleio	ECq	Frunza [80]	22 000	Wegereef NED

Fr = Friendly match • EC = UEFA EURO 2004/2008 • WC = FIFA World Cup • q = qualifier

MOLDOVA NATIONAL TEAM RECORDS AND RECORD SEQUENCES

Records			Sequence records					
Victory	5-1	GEO 2006	Wins	3	1994	Clean sheets	2	2000, 2005
Defeat	0-6	SWE 2001	Defeats	9	1996-1998	Goals scored	7	1998-1999
Player Caps	69	CLESCENKO Serghei	Undefeated	4	2006	Without goal	7	1997-98, 2000-01
Player Goals	11	CLESCENKO Serghei	Without win	10	1996-98, 2002-03	Goals against	25	1994-1998

MAJOR CITIES/TOWNS

		Population '000
1	Chisinau	610
2	Tiraspol	152
3	Balti	109
4	Tighina	103
5	Ribnita	52
6	Ungheni	32
7	Cahul	32
8	Soroca	25
9	Orhei	23
10	Edinet	22
11	Comrat	21
12	Dubasari	21
13	Causeni	21
14	Ocnita	18
15	Ciadir Lunga	18
16	Straseni	18
17	Floresti	16
18	Drochia	15
19	Singerei	14
20	Ialoveni	14
21	Slobozia	14
22	Leova	14
23	Briceni	13
24	Hincesti	13

REPUBLIC OF MOLDOVA; REPUBLICA MOLDOVA

Capital	Chisinau	Language	Moldovan, Russian			Independence	1991
Population	4 466 706	Area	33 843 km²	Density	131 per km²	% in cities	52%
GDP per cap	$1800	Dailling code	+373	Internet	.md	GMT + / -	+2

MEDALS TABLE

		Overall			League			Cup			Europe			City	Stadium	Cap'ty	DoF
		G	S	B	G	S	B	G	S	B	G	S	B				
1	Zimbru Chisinau	13	7	2	8	5	2	5	2					Chisinau	Baza CSF Zimbru	10 500	1947
2	Sheriff Tiraspol	11	2		7	1		4	1					Tiraspol	Complex Sheriff	14 300	1997
3	Tiligul-Tiras	3	8	3		6	3	3	2					Tiraspol	Municipal	3 525	1938
4	FC Tiraspol	3	3	4	1	1	4	2	2					Tiraspol	Municipal	3 525	1993
5	Nistru Otaci	1	10	2		3	2	1	7					Otaci	Calarasauca	3 000	1953
6	Bugeac Comrat	1		1		1	1							Comrat	Bugeac		
7	Dacia Chisnau		1	1		1			1					Chisinau	Republican	8 100	2000
8	Dinamo Chisinau		1						1					Chisinau			
9	Codru Calarasi			1		1								Calarasi	Codru		
	Moldova Boroseni			1		1								Boroseni			
	Olimpia Balti			1		1								Balti	Municipal	5 000	1984
12	Dinamo Bender													Tighina	Selkovic	1 000	1950
	Iscra-Stali Ribnita													Ribnita	Municipal	3 000	
	Floreni Anenii Noi																
	Politehnica Chisinau													Chisinau	Dinamo	2 900	1964
	Rapid Ghidghici													Ghidghici			

RECENT LEAGUE AND CUP RECORD

	Championship							Cup		
Year	Champions	Pts	Runners-up	Pts	Third	Pts		Winners	Score	Runners-up
1995	Zimbru Chisinau	67	Tiligul Tiraspol	66	Olimpia Balti	57		Tiligul Tiraspol	1-0	Zimbru Chisinau
1996	Zimbru Chisinau	81	Tiligul Tiraspol	74	Constructorul	74		Constructorul	2-1	Tiligul Tiraspol
1997	Constructorul	81	Zimbru Chisinau	70	Tiligul Tiraspol	68		Zimbru Chisinau	0-0 7-6p	Nistru Otaci
1998	Zimbru Chisinau	69	Tiligul Tiraspol	59	Constructorul	54		Zimbru Chisinau	1-0	Constructorul
1999	Zimbru Chisinau	61	Constructorul	51	Tiligul Tiraspol	39		Sheriff Tiraspol	2-1	Constructorul
2000	Zimbru Chisinau	82	Sheriff Tiraspol	81	Constructorul	65		Constructorul	1-0	Zimbru Chisinau
2001	Sheriff Tiraspol	67	Zimbru Chisinau	66	Tiligul Tiraspol	41		Sheriff Tiraspol	0-0 5-4p	Nistru Otaci
2002	Sheriff Tiraspol	67	Nistru Otaci	52	Zimbru Chisinau	46		Sheriff Tiraspol	3-2	Nistru Otaci
2003	Sheriff Tiraspol	60	Zimbru Chisinau	50	Nistru Otaci	42		Zimbru Chisinau	0-0 4-2p	Nistru Otaci
2004	Sheriff Tiraspol	65	Nistru Otaci	57	Zimbru Chisinau	49		Zimbru Chisinau	2-1	Sheriff Tiraspol
2005	Sheriff Tiraspol	70	Nistru Otaci	54	Dacia Chisinau	45		Nistru Otaci	1-0	Dacia Chisinau
2006	Sheriff Tiraspol	71	Zimbru Chisinau	53	FC Tiraspol	37		Sheriff Tiraspol	2-0	Nistru Otaci
2007	Sheriff Tiraspol	92	Zimbru Chisinau	71	Nistru Otaci	57		Zimbru Chisinau	1-0	Nistru Otaci

MOLDOVA 2006-07

DIVIZIA NATIONALA

	Pl	W	D	L	F	A	Pts	Sheriff	Zimbru	Nistru	Dacia	Tiraspol	Olimpia	Politehnica	Tiligul-Tiras	Iscra-Stali	Dinamo
Sheriff Tiraspol †	36	28	8	0	70	7	92		0-0 2-0	2-1 3-0	1-0 1-0	3-0 2-1	4-0 2-0	2-1 3-0	0-0 4-2	4-0 0-0	4-0 5-0
Zimbru Chisinau ‡	36	21	8	7	63	23	71	0-0 1-2		2-0 3-1	1-1 4-0	0-0 0-1	5-0 2-1	2-0 4-1	4-0 2-0	1-1 3-0	2-1 6-0
Nistru Otaci ‡	36	16	9	11	44	36	57	0-5 0-1	2-0 2-1		1-1 1-2	3-2 3-2	3-2 2-1	2-1 1-0	0-0 1-1	2-1 1-0	1-1 4-0
Dacia Chisinau	36	13	16	7	36	30	55	0-0 0-0	1-1 1-2	2-2 0-2		0-0 0-0	1-0 1-2	1-0 0-0	1-0 0-1	1-1 1-0	0-0 2-2
FC Tiraspol	36	10	16	10	37	32	46	0-3 0-2	0-1 0-0	0-0 1-1	1-1 1-1		2-1 0-1	5-0 2-0	1-1 0-0	1-1 0-0	4-0 3-1
Olimpia Balti	36	12	6	18	38	50	42	1-3 0-1	3-4 1-0	3-1 0-0	1-3 0-1	0-2 0-0		0-0 1-0	5-3 1-0	0-1 0-2	2-2 1-0
Politehnica Chisinau	36	7	12	17	29	47	33	0-3 0-0	0-1 0-2	2-1 0-1	0-2 3-4	3-1 0-0	1-1 0-1		1-1 0-0	1-1 2-1	2-0 4-0
Tiligul-Tiras Tiraspol	36	6	15	15	23	46	33	0-2 0-0	1-1 0-3	0-2 1-0	0-2 1-3	0-1 0-0	0-1 1-0	0-2 1-1		1-1 2-1	2-1 1-1
Iscra-Stali Ribnita	36	6	13	17	22	43	31	0-3 0-1	0-2 1-0	0-3 2-1	0-0 0-1	1-3 1-1	1-0 0-2	0-0 1-1	2-0 0-0		1-1 1-1
Dinamo Bender	36	3	13	20	24	72	22	0-3 0-3	0-1 0-2	0-0 0-1	0-0 1-2	2-1 2-2	2-2 0-4	0-1 2-2	2-0 1-0	1-0 1-0	

2/07/2006 - 30/05/2007 • † Qualified for the UEFA Champions League • ‡ Qualified for the UEFA Cup
Top scorers: Alexei KUCKIUK, Sheriff 17; Vladimir TARANU, Nistru 16; Aleksej ZDANOV, Zimbru 14; Sergiu CHIRILOV, Zimbru 12

MOLDOVA 2006-07
DIVIZIA A (2)

	Pl	W	D	L	F	A	Pts
Zimbru-2 Chisinau	26	17	6	3	62	22	57
Rapid Ghidighici	26	17	5	4	57	19	56
CSCA Chisinau	26	15	10	1	52	17	55
Dinamo-2 Bender	26	15	5	6	61	29	50
Floreni Anenii Noi	26	12	9	5	46	28	45
Olimpia-2 Balti	26	11	8	7	36	33	41
Intersport	26	10	7	9	25	29	37
Dacia-2 Chisinau	26	9	9	8	39	36	36
Sheriff-2 Tiraspol	26	9	6	11	48	35	33
Academia Chisinau	26	9	5	12	38	47	32
Energetic Dubasari	26	5	6	15	17	38	21
Izvoras 67 Ratus	26	5	4	17	26	65	19
Moldova 03 Ungheni	26	3	4	19	21	81	13
Gagauziya Comrat	26	1	4	21	15	64	7

12/08/2006 - 26/05/2007 • Zimbru ineligible for promotion

CUPA MOLDOVEI 2006-07

Round of sixteen		Quarter–finals		Semi–finals		Final	
Zimbru Chisinau *	2						
Rapid Ghidighici	0	**Zimbru Chisinau ***	4 0				
Podis Inesti *	0	Politehnica Chisinau	0 0				
Politehnica Chisinau	3			**Zimbru Chisinau ***	2 1		
Tiligul-Tiras Tiraspol *	12			Sheriff Tiraspol	1 1		
Flacara	0	Tiligul-Tiras Tiraspol *	0 0				
Viisoara	1	**Sheriff Tiraspol**	0 4				
Sheriff Tiraspol *	11					**Zimbru Chisinau ‡**	1
FC Tiraspol	2					Nistru Otaci	0
FC Cahul 2005 *	0	**FC Tiraspol ***	1 2				
Floreni Anenii Noi *	2 3p	Dinamo Bender	1 2				
Dinamo Bender	2 4p			FC Tiraspol	0 1		
Dacia Chisinau	2			**Nistru Otaci ***	1 2		
Kolos Copceac *	1	Dacia Chisinau *	3 0				
Olimpia Balti *	0	**Nistru Otaci**	1 2				
Nistru Otaci	3						

* Home team in the first leg • ‡ Qualified for the UEFA Cup

CUP FINAL
Municipal, Chisinau
9-05-2007

Scorer - Andrei Cojocaru [89]

MDV – MALDIVES

NATIONAL TEAM RECORD
JULY 10TH 2006 TO JULY 12TH 2010

PL	W	D	L	F	A	%
0	0	0	0	0	0	0

FIFA/COCA-COLA WORLD RANKING

1993	1994	1995	1996	1997	1998	1999	2000	2001	2002	2003	2004	2005	2006	High		Low	
148	162	169	176	160	166	143	154	147	152	141	139	133	158	126	08/06	183	09/97

2006–2007											
08/06	09/06	10/06	11/06	12/06	01/07	02/07	03/07	04/07	05/07	06/07	07/07
126	129	149	146	158	160	157	158	159	159	157	157

After achieving increased success and a higher profile in recent years, football in the Maldives suffered a letdown in 2006. Just four internationals have been played since the Christmas Eve Tsunami which caused such widespread damage in December 2004, and as all four of those matches were at the 2005 edition of the South Asian Football Federation Cup, there was no international football throughout the whole of 2006 or in the first half of 2007. The under–23 team did take part in the South Asian Games in Sri Lanka in August 2006, but despite winning two of their three games were knocked-out in the first round on goal difference. Club football has always had a

INTERNATIONAL HONOURS
None

passionate and long-standing following in the Maldives, with Victory and New Radiant the two most popular clubs. Both qualified for the 2007 AFC Cup but it wasn't a vintage year as both failed to get past the first round group stage. New Radiant, semi-finalists in 2005, had an especially torrid time finishing bottom of their group and losing all six matches. In local tournaments the National Championship was won by Victory after a penalty shoot-out in the final against Valencia. Valencia then beat New Radiant 3-1 in the final of the 2007 Cup Winners Cup, whilst the FA Cup was won in turn by New Radiant who beat Valencia 2-0 for the third year running in the final.

THE FIFA BIG COUNT OF 2006

	Male	Female		Total
Number of players	18 976	1 310	Referees and Assistant Referees	134
Professionals	120		Admin, Coaches, Technical, Medical	44
Amateurs 18+	3 250		Number of clubs	60
Youth under 18	1 616		Number of teams	367
Unregistered	14 800		Clubs with women's teams	0
Total players	20 286		Players as % of population	5.65%

Football Association of Maldives (FAM)
Ujaalaa Hin'gun, Maafannu, Male 20388, Maldives
Tel +960 317006   Fax +960 317005
famaldvs@dhivehinet.net.mv   www.famaldives.gov.mv
President: SHAKOOR Abdul   General Secretary: ABDUL GHAFOOR Abdul Hameed
Vice-President: TBD   Treasurer: ZARIYANDH Ismail   Media Officer: TBD
Men's Coach: IODAN Ivanov   Women's Coach: ATHIF Mohamed
FAM formed: 1982   AFC: 1986   FIFA: 1986
Red shirts, Green shorts, White socks

RECENT INTERNATIONAL MATCHES PLAYED BY THE MALDIVES

2002	Opponents	Score		Venue	Comp	Scorers	Att	Referee
No international matches played in 2002 after June								
2003								
11-01	Bhutan	W	6-0	Dhaka	SAFr1	Nizam [2], Luthfy [11], Shiham 3 [24 25 67], Umar [80]		Vidanagamage SRI
13-01	Bangladesh	L	0-1	Dhaka	SAFr1		20 000	Vidanagamage SRI
15-01	Nepal	W	3-2	Dhaka	SAFr1	Nizam [63], Luthfy [75], Umar [85]	15 000	Kunsuta THA
18-01	Pakistan	W	1-0	Dhaka	SAFsf	Fazeel [12]		Gurung NEP
20-01	Bangladesh	D	1-1	Dhaka	SAFf	Umar [58]. L 3-5p	46 000	Vidanagamage SRI
4-03	Singapore	L	1-4	Singapore	Fr	Umar [44]		Abdul Bashir SIN
21-03	Brunei Darussalam	D	1-1	Malé	ACq	Umar [42]		
25-03	Myanmar	L	0-2	Malé	ACq			
29-11	Mongolia	W	1-0	Ulaan-Baatar	WCq	Nizam [24]	2 000	Yang Zhiqiang CHN
3-12	Mongolia	W	12-0	Malé	WCq	Ashfaq 4 [4 61 63 68], Nizam [42], Fazeel 2 [46+ 49+], Ghani [65], Thariq [74], OG [75], Nazeeh [80]	9 000	Arambekade SRI
2004								
18-02	Vietnam	L	0-4	Hanoi	WCq		25 000	Fong KKG
31-03	Korea Republic	D	0-0	Malé	WCq		12 000	Vidanagamage SRI
31-05	Oman	L	0-3	Muscat	Fr			
3-06	Oman	L	1-4	Muscat	Fr			
9-06	Lebanon	L	0-3	Beirut	WCq		18 000	Nurilddin Salman IRQ
31-08	Oman	L	0-1	Malé	Fr			
3-09	Oman	L	1-2	Malé	Fr			
8-09	Lebanon	L	2-5	Malé	WCq	Fazeel [79], Umar [88]	12 000	Al Ajmi OMA
13-10	Vietnam	W	3-0	Malé	WCq	Thariq [29], Ashfaq 2 [68 85]	10 000	Haq IND
17-11	Korea Republic	L	0-2	Seoul	WCq		64 000	Lazar SIN
18-12	Sri Lanka	D	0-0	Malé	Fr			
2005								
7-12	Afghanistan	W	9-1	Karachi	SAFr1	Umar [11], Fazeel 3 [27 45 69], Ashfaq 2 [32 88], Thariq 3 [45 46 86]		
9-12	Sri Lanka	W	2-0	Karachi	SAFr1	Ashfaq [15], Umar [82p]		
11-12	Pakistan	D	0-0	Karachi	SAFr1			
14-12	India	L	0-1	Karachi	SAFsf			
2006								
No international matches played in 2006								
2007								
No international matches played in 2007 before August								

Fr = Friendly match • SAF = South Asian Football Federation Cup • AC = AFC Asian Cup • WC = FIFA World Cup
q = qualifier • r1 = first round group • sf = semi-final • f = final

MALDIVES NATIONAL TEAM RECORDS AND RECORD SEQUENCES

Records			Sequence records					
Victory	6-0	CAM 2001	Wins	3	1999	Clean sheets	2	1993, 1999, 2003
Defeat	0-17	IRN 1997	Defeats	12	1996-1997	Goals scored	7	1999
Player Caps	n/a		Undefeated	4	2000	Without goal	6	1997
Player Goals	n/a		Without win	23	1985-1997	Goals against	14	1996-1997

MALDIVES COUNTRY INFORMATION

Capital	Malé	Independence	1965 from the UK	GDP per Capita	$3 900
Population	339 330	Status	Republic	GNP Ranking	168
Area km²	300	Language	Maldivian Dhiveti	Dialling code	+960
Population density	1 131 per km²	Literacy rate	97%	Internet code	.mv
% in urban areas	27%	Main religion	Muslim	GMT +/−	+5
Towns/Cities ('000)	Malé 85; Hithadoo 9; Fuvammulah 8; Kulhudhuffushi 8; Thinadhoo 5; Naifaru 4				
Neighbours (km)	Indian Ocean 644				
Main stadia	Galolhu National Stadium – Male				

MALDIVES 2006

MALE LEAGUE

	Pl	W	D	L	F	A	Pts	Victory	IFC	Valencia	Radiant	G'aidhoo	Maziya	Hurriyya	Eagles
Victory	7	4	3	0	19	4	15		2-2	1-0	0-0	4-0	6-1	1-1	5-0
Island FC	7	4	1	2	12	7	13	1-2		0-1	1-0	4-1	1-0		3-1
Valencia	7	4	1	2	11	7	13				2-0	1-1	2-3	2-1	2-0
New Radiant	7	3	2	2	13	10	11					2-3	2-2	5-2	3-1
Guraidhoo ZJ	7	2	2	3	6	12	8						0-3	0-0	2-1
Maziya SR	7	2	2	3	12	19	8							0-3	2-2
Hurriyya	7	1	3	3	8	10	6								1-1
Eagles	7	0	2	5	6	18	2								

19/04/2006 - 12/06/2006 • Top six qualify for the Dhivehi League

MALDIVES 2006

DHIVEHI LEAGUE

	Pl	W	D	L	F	A	Pts	Radiant	Victory	Valencia	IFC	Maziya	G'aidhoo	F'aidhoo	M'adhoo
New Radiant †	12	9	1	2	29	16	28		1-0	1-3	5-4	3-0	1-0	1-0	7-1
Victory	12	8	3	1	33	7	27	1-1		4-1	1-1	3-0	4-0	2-0	8-0
Valencia	12	8	2	2	31	13	26	3-1	2-2		1-0	1-0	0-2	1-1	8-0
Island FC	12	4	3	5	22	22	15	1-2	0-1	0-5		1-0	5-2	1-1	5-1
Maziya SR	12	2	3	7	8	19	9	1-2	0-2	1-3	2-2		0-0	1-1	2-1
Guraidhoo ZJ	12	2	1	9	16	29	7	2-4	1-5	1-3	1-2	0-1		4-0	3-4
Foakaidhoo EJ	7	0	4	3	4	11	4								1-1
Mahibadhoo ZJ	7	1	1	5	8	34	4								

4/07/2006 - 19/09/2006 • Top four qualify for the National Championship play-offs • † Qualified for the AFC Cup

NATIONAL CHAMPIONSHIP 2006

Preliminary round

Major Semi–final

Victory	2
New Radiant	0

Second semi-final

New Radiant	1
Island FC	2
Valencia	3

Valencia | 2 (Second semi-final)

Final

Victory †	0 3p
Valencia	0 1p

18-10-2006

† Qualified for AFC Cup

CUP WINNERS CUP 2007

	Pl	W	D	L	F	A	Pts
New Radiant	4	2	2	0	7	2	8
Valencia	4	2	0	2	7	6	6
Victory	4	0	2	2	1	7	2

Final: Valencia 3-1 New Radiant • 29-03-2007; Scorers: Wahid [26], Wadheeu [48], Azim [87] for Valencia; Akram [80] for New Radiant

FA CUP 2007

Quarter–finals

New Radiant	2
Vyansa	1

Guraidhoo	1
Victory	7

VB Sports	7
Maziya	0

Eagles	1
Valencia	2

Semi–finals

New Radiant	1
Victory	0

VB Sports	1
Valencia	2

† Qualified for AFC Cup

Final

New Radiant †	2
Valencia	0

30-04-2007

Scorers - Idris [61], Ali Ashfaq [81]

RECENT LEAGUE AND CUP RECORD

National Championship

Year	Winners	Score	Runners-up
1998	Valencia	1-1 2-0	Victory
1999	Valencia	2-1	Hurriyya
2000	Victory		
2001	Victory	2-1	Valencia
2002	Victory	4-2	Valencia
2003	Victory	2-1	Valencia
2004	New Radiant	1-1 6-5p	Valencia
2005	Victory	1-0	New Radiant
2006	Victory	0-0 3-1p	Valencia
2007			

FA Cup

Winners	Score	Runners-up
New Radiant	1-0	Hurriyya
Valencia	2-2 2-1	New Radiant
Victory	3-0	Hurriyya
New Radiant	1-1 2-0	Valencia
IFC	2-0	New Radiant
IFC	1-0	Valencia
Valencia	2-0	Victory
New Radiant	2-0	Valencia
New Radiant	2-0	Valencia
New Radiant	2-0	Valencia

Cup Winners Cup

Winners	Score	Runners-up
Valencia	2-0	New Radiant
New Radiant	3-1	Victory
New Radiant		
Victory	1-1 5-4p	Valencia
Victory	4-3	Valencia
New Radiant	1-1 3-1p	Valencia
Valencia	1-0	IFC
Valencia	2-1	Victory
Victory	3-3 2-1p	New Radiant
Valencia	3-1	New Radiant

MEX – MEXICO

NATIONAL TEAM RECORD
JULY 10TH 2006 TO JULY 12TH 2010

PL	W	D	L	F	A	%
18	12	1	5	33	16	69.4

Mexico is fast developing into a major player on football's world stage as both the national team and club sides continue to make good progress. In the past, Europeans have tended to be very dismissive of Mexico, claiming that they only qualified for major tournaments because they played in the CONCACAF region. But no longer. With players like Rafael Marquez making a huge impact at Barcelona, and Ricardo Osorio and Pavel Pardo helping Stuttgart to the Bundesliga title in Germany, Mexicans are now in high demand, although very few of them leave for Europe because of the high wages and good working conditions in the Mexican league. In a sign of the growing status of the League, Pachuca made history in December 2006 when they won the Copa Sudamericana - the first Mexican team to win a South American trophy. Formed in 1901 by Cornish miners, Pachuca are the best run club in the country and by beating the country's richest club América to win the closing championship in May 2007, they claimed their fifth domestic title since 1999. They also won the CONCACAF Champions' Cup for the second time to qualify for the the 2007 FIFA Club World Cup in Japan by beating fellow Mexicans Guadalajara on penalties

INTERNATIONAL HONOURS
Qualified for the FIFA World Cup finals 1930 1950 1954 1958 1962 1966 1970 (hosts) 1978 1986 (hosts) 1994 1998 2002 2006

FIFA Confederations Cup 1999   Qualified for the FIFA Women's World Cup finals 1999

North American Championship 1947 1949   CONCACAF Championship 1965 1971   CONCACAF Gold Cup 1993 1996 1998 2003

CONCACAF U-20 1962 1970 1973 1976 1978 1980 1984 1990 1992   CONCACAF U-17 1985 1987 1991 1996

CONCACAF Club Championship Guadalajara 1962 Toluca 1968 2003 Cruz Azul 1969 1970 1971 1996 1997 America 1977 1990 1992 2006

UAG Tecos 1978 UNAM Pumas 1980 1982 1989 Atlante 1983 Puebla 1991 Necaxa 1999 Pachuca 2002 2007

in the final. Earlier in the season Guadalajara, Mexico's most popular club, had won their first title since 1997 when they beat Toluca in the final of the opening championship bringing flamboyant owner Jorge Vergara his first trophy since buying the club for £70m in 2002. Vergara's aim is to turn Guadalajara into the biggest club in Latin America although sceptics say he will eventually have to relax the no foreign players rule at the club to achieve that. After the departure of Ricardo La Volpe as national team coach, the federation eventually turned to the outspoken Hugo Sánchez as his replacement. Sanchez was quickly into two major competitions. At the CONCACAF Gold Cup the Mexicans were below par but still managed to reach the final where they lost 2-1 to the USA despite dominating the game. At the Copa América, they were much better, beating Brazil with a youthful team on their way to a semi-final against their current nemesis Argentina. Once again the Argentines triumphed, just as they had done at the World Cup and the FIFA Confederations Cup.

Federación Mexicana de Fútbol Asociación, A.C. (FMF)
Colima No. 373, Colonia Roma, Mexico D.F. 06700, Mexico

Tel +52 55 52410166   Fax +52 55 52410191

ddemaria@femexfut.org.mx   www.femexfut.org.mx

President: COMPEAN Justino   General Secretary: DE MARIA Decio

Vice-President: TBD   Treasurer: LEON-PAEZ Luis   Media Officer: KOCHEN Juan Jose

Men's Coach: SANCHEZ Hugo   Women's Coach: CUELLAR Leonardo

FMF formed: 1927   CONCACAF: 1961   FIFA: 1929

Green shirts with white trimmings, White shorts, Red socks or White shirts with green trimmings, Green shorts, White socks

RECENT INTERNATIONAL MATCHES PLAYED BY MEXICO

2005	Opponents	Score		Venue	Comp	Scorers	Att	Referee
8-07	South Africa	L	1-2	Carson	GCr1	Rodriguez.F [83]	27 000	Quesada CRC
10-07	Guatemala	W	4-0	Los Angeles	GCr1	Borgetti 2 [5 14], Galindo [54], Bravo [65]	30 710	Ruiz COL
13-07	Jamaica	W	1-0	Houston	GCr1	Medina [19]	45 311	Quesada CRC
17-07	Colombia	L	1-2	Houston	GCqf	Pineda [65]	60 050	Sibrian SLV
17-08	Costa Rica	W	2-0	Mexico City	WCq	Borgetti [63], Fonseca [86]	27 000	Pineda HON
3-09	USA	L	0-2	Columbus	WCq		24 685	Batres GUA
7-09	Panama	W	5-0	Mexico City	WCq	Perez.L [31], Márquez [54], Borgetti [59], Fonseca [75], Pardo [76]	40 000	Hall USA
8-10	Guatemala	W	5-2	San Luis Potosi	WCq	Franco 19, Fonseca 4 [48 51 62 66]	30 000	Prendergast JAM
12-10	Trinidad and Tobago	L	1-2	Port of Spain	WCq	Lozano [38]	23 000	Pineda HON
26-10	Uruguay	W	3-1	Guadalajara	Fr	Salcido [16], Martinez [47p], Perez.L [53]	45 000	Guajardo MEX
16-11	Bulgaria	L	0-3	Phoenix	Fr		35 526	Hall USA
14-12	Hungary	W	2-0	Phoenix	Fr		32 466	Valenzuela USA
2006								
25-01	Norway	W	2-1	San Francisco	Fr	Fonseca [36], Perez.L [87]	44 729	Vaughn USA
15-02	Korea Republic	L	0-1	Los Angeles	Fr		64 128	Salazar USA
1-03	Ghana	W	1-0	Frisco	Fr	Franco [75]	19 513	Hall USA
29-03	Paraguay	W	2-1	Chicago	Fr	Bravo 2 [30p 81]	46 510	Kennedy USA
5-05	Venezuela	W	1-0	Pasadena	Fr	Bravo [57p]	58 147	Vaughn USA
12-05	Congo DR	W	2-1	Mexico City	Fr	Fonseca 2 [3 41]	75 000	Flores MEX
27-05	France	L	0-1	Paris	Fr		80 000	Daami TUN
1-06	Netherlands	L	1-2	Eindhoven	Fr	Borgetti [19]	35 000	Frojdfeldt SWE
11-06	Iran	W	3-1	Nuremberg	WCr1	Bravo 2 [28 76], Zinha [79]	41 000	Rosetti ITA
16-06	Angola	D	0-0	Hanover	WCr1		43 000	Maidin SIN
21-06	Portugal	L	1-2	Gelsenkirchen	WCr1	Fonseca [29]	52 000	Michel SVK
24-06	Argentina	L	1-2	Leipzig	WCr2	Márquez [6]	43 000	Busacca SUI
2007								
7-02	USA	L	0-2	Glendale	Fr		62 462	Navarro CAN
28-02	Venezuela	W	3-1	San Diego	Fr	Guardado [25], Arce [34], Blanco [47p]	63 328	Stott USA
25-03	Paraguay	W	2-1	San Nicolas	Fr	Borgetti 2 [79 82]		Pineda HON
28-03	Ecuador	W	4-1	Oakland	Fr	Palencia [1], Márquez [72], Bravo [83], Bautista [87]	47 416	Toledo USA
2-06	Iran	W	4-0	San Luis Potosi	Fr	Borgetti [2], Lozano [27], Fonseca [81], Torrado [84]	30 000	Silvera URU
5-06	Paraguay	L	0-1	Mexico City	Fr		60 000	Larrionda URU
8-06	Cuba	W	2-1	New Jersey	GCr1	Borgetti [37], Castillo [55]	20 230	Aguilar SLV
10-06	Honduras	L	1-2	New Jersey	GCr1	Blanco [23p]	68 123	Quezada CRC
13-06	Panama	W	1-0	Houston	GCr1	Salcido [60]	68 417	Batres GUA
17-06	Costa Rica	W	1-0	Houston	GCqf	Borgetti [97]	70 092	Vaughn USA
21-06	Guadeloupe	W	1-0	Chicago	GCsf	Pardo [70]	50 790	Moreno PAN
24-06	USA	L	1-2	Chicago	GCf	Guardado [44]	60 000	Batres GUA
27-06	Brazil	W	2-0	Puerto Ordaz	CAr1	Castillo [23], Morales [28]	40 000	Pezzotta ARG
1-07	Ecuador	W	2-1	Maturín	CAr1	Méndez [84]	42 000	Ortube BOL
4-07	Chile	D	0-0	Puerto la Cruz	CAr1		30 000	Amarilla PAR
8-07	Paraguay	W	6-0	Maturín	CAqf	Castillo 2 [5p 38], Torrado [27], Arce [79], Blanco [87p], Bravo [91+]	50 000	Pezzotta ARG
11-07	Argentina	L	0-3	Puerto Ordaz	CAsf		40 000	Chandia CHI
14-07	Uruguay	W	3-1	Caracas	CA3p	Blanco [38p], Bravo [68], Guardado [76]	30 000	Reinoso ECU

Fr = Friendly match • GC = CONCACAF Gold Cup • CA = Copa America • CC = FIFA Confederations Cup • WC = FIFA World Cup
q = qualifier • r1 = first round group • r2 = second round • qf = quarter-final • sf = semi-final • f = final

MEXICO NATIONAL TEAM RECORDS AND RECORD SEQUENCES

Records			Sequence records					
Victory	11-0	VIN 1992	Wins	8	1947-49, 2004	Clean sheets	6	1965-1966
Defeat	0-8	ENG 1961	Defeats	7	1950-1952	Goals scored	22	1930-1950
Player Caps	179	SUAREZ Claudio	Undefeated	21	2004-2005	Without goal	5	1975-1976
Player Goals	42	BORGETTI Jared	Without win	11	1971	Goals against	12	1957-1960

MEXICO

Capital	Mexico City	Language	Spanish	Independence	1836
Population	107 449 525	Area	1 972 550 km²	% in cities	75%
GDP per cap	$9 000	Dailling code	+52	Internet .mx	GMT + / - -6

The whole Mexico City conurbation totals some 22 million people and includes Ecatepec, Nezahualcóyotl, Naucalpan, Tlalnepantla and Toluca, along with others. The Guadalajara courbation totals just over 4 million and includes Zapopan amongst others

See page 1046 for Mexico's FIFA/Coca-Cola World Ranking statistics and for their details in the 2006 FIFA Big Count

MEDALS TABLE

		Overall G S B	League G S B	Cup G S	CON'CAF G S B	City	Stadium	Cap'ty	DoF
1	Club América	25 13 8	14 10 5	6 3	5 3	Mexico City	Azteca	101 000	1916
2	Real Club España	20 5 4	15 5 4	5					
3	Club Necaxa	15 8 9	7 7 7	7	1 1 2	Aguascalientes	Victoria	20 000	1923
4	Cruz Azul	15 9	8 6	2 2	5 1	Mexico City	Azul	35 161	1927
5	CD Guadalajara	14 16 8	11 9 4	2 5	1 2 4	Guadalajara	Jalisco	56 713	1906
6	CD Toluca	12 8 4	8 5 2	2 1	2 2 2	Toluca	La Bombonera	27 000	1917
7	CF Pachuca	12 5 6	7 5 5	2	3 1	Pachuca	Hidalgo	25 000	1901
8	Asturias	11 4 3	3 4 3	8					
9	Club León	10 10 6	5 5 4	5 4	1 2	León	Estadio León	40 338	1944
10	UNAM Pumas	9 7	5 5	1	3 2	Mexico City	Olimpico	63 186	1954
11	CF Atlante	8 13 3	4 8 3	3 4	1 1	Mexico City	Azteca	101 000	1916
12	Reforma	8 3 2	6 3 2	2					
13	Puebla FC	7 4 3	2 2 3	4 2	1	Puebla	Cuauhtémoc	42 649	1904
14	CF Atlas	5 4 4	1 3 4	4 1		Guadalajara	Jalisco	56 713	1916
15	Tigres UANL	4 4 1	2 3	2 1	1	Monterrey	Universitario	43 000	1960
16	CD Zacatepec	4 3 1	2 1 1	2 2		Zacatepec	Agustin Diaz		

RECENT LEAGUE RECORD

	Clausura				Apertura		
Year	Champions	Score	Runners-up		Winners	Score	Runners-up
1996					Santos Laguna	0-1 4-2	Necaxa
1997	Guadalajara	1-1 6-1	Neza		Cruz Azul	1-0 1-1	Leon
1998	Toluca	1-2 5-2	Necaxa		Necaxa	0-0 2-0	Guadalajara
1999	Toluca	3-3 2-2 5-4p	Atlas		Pachuca	2-2 1-0	Cruz Azul
2000	Toluca	2-0 5-1	Santos Laguna		Monarcas Morelia	3-1 0-2 5-4p	Toluca
2001	Santos Laguna	1-2 3-1	Pachuca		Pachuca	2-0 1-1	Tigres UANL
2002	América	0-2 3-0	Necaxa		Toluca	0-1 4-1	Monarcas Morelia
2003	Monterrey	3-1 0-0	Monarcas Morelia		Pachuca	3-1 0-1	Tigres UANL
2004	UNAM Pumas	1-1 0-0 5-4p	Guadalajara		UNAM Pumas	2-1 1-0	Monterrey
2005	América	1-1 6-3	UAG Tecos		Toluca	3-3 3-0	Monterrey
2006	Pachuca	0-0 1-0	San Luis		Guadalajara	1-1 2-1	Toluca
2007	Pachuca	2-1 1-1	América				

MEXICO 2006-07

PRIMERA DIVISION NACIONAL (APERTURA)

Group 1

	Pl	W	D	L	F	A	Pts	Cruz Azul	Atlas	Guadalajara	Jaguares	Querétaro	Necaxa	Monterrey	Pachuca	Veracruz	Atlante	San Luis	Tecos	Pumas	América	Toluca	Morelia	Tigres	Santos
Cruz Azul †	17	9	3	5	27	20	30		2-1		1-0			1-2	2-0		2-1	0-1		0-1	1-2	·			1-0
Atlas †	17	7	6	4	25	19	27							2-1	2-1	1-1	3-1	0-1			1-0	3-0	0-0		
Guadalajara †	17	7	5	5	26	18	26	2-3	3-1		1-0	4-0					1-1	1-0			0-0	2-0			3-1
Jaguares	17	6	5	6	19	16	23	4-0						1-0	1-0	0-1			1-1		0-1	2-0	1-1		
Querétaro §3	17	5	6	6	20	25	18	2-1	1-1	1-1	1-2					1-2	2-2			1-1	1-0				2-1
Necaxa	17	4	5	8	18	26	17					1-2			1-1	3-1	1-2	0-0		2-1		0-2	1-3	1-0	

Group 2

	Pl	W	D	L	F	A	Pts	Cruz Azul	Atlas	Guadalajara	Jaguares	Querétaro	Necaxa	Monterrey	Pachuca	Veracruz	Atlante	San Luis	Tecos	Pumas	América	Toluca	Morelia	Tigres	Santos
Monterrey †	17	7	6	4	27	21	27			1-1	2-2					3-1	3-0	3-0	3-2		2-1	2-0	2-1		
Pachuca †	17	7	5	5	32	22	26	2-3		1-2	0-0					0-0	2-2		5-2	3-1	2-0	5-0			
Veracruz	17	8	2	7	26	31	26	0-2		3-2	3-1	3-0							1-1			1-0	2-1	5-1	
Atlante	17	6	5	6	19	20	23		0-2		0-1							2-0	1-0		0-0	2-2	2-0	2-0	2-3
San Luis §3	17	6	5	6	14	12	20							1-1	1-0	0-3	4-0				0-1	0-1	1-0	2-0	
UAG Tecos	17	3	4	10	22	35	13	1-1	1-6	2-1	2-3	0-2					3-1	0-0			0-0				4-2

Group 3

	Pl	W	D	L	F	A	Pts	Cruz Azul	Atlas	Guadalajara	Jaguares	Querétaro	Necaxa	Monterrey	Pachuca	Veracruz	Atlante	San Luis	Tecos	Pumas	América	Toluca	Morelia	Tigres	Santos
Pumas UNAM †	17	8	6	4	21	11	29							1-1	3-0	1-3	3-1	0-1			2-0	0-0	1-0	5-0	
América †	17	8	5	4	21	15	29							2-1	1-1	3-1	5-1					2-0	1-1	2-1	1-1
Toluca †	17	7	2	4	27	16	27	1-1			1-0	3-0								2-3	2-1		2-1	7-0	1-0
Morelia	17	7	5	8	24	26	23	4-4	1-1	3-2	2-1	2-0								1-0	2-1				3-2
Tigres UANL	17	3	5	9	14	37	14	0-2	1-1	0-0	1-1	3-2									2-1		2-1		2-2
Santos Laguna	17	1	8	8	19	31	11					1-1					0-0			2-2	2-2	1-1	0-0	1-0	

5/08/2006 - 12/11/2006 • † Qualified for the play-offs • Repechaje: Veracruz 1-2 0-4 **Guadalajara**; Jaguares 1-0 0-2 **Toluca**
Top scorers (inc play-offs): Bruno MARIONI, Toluca 15; Omar BRAVO, Guadalajara 11; Miguel SABAH, Cruz Azul 10; KLEBER Boas, Necaxa 9

MEXICO 2006-07

PRIMERA DIVISION NACIONAL (CLAUSURA)

Group 1

	Pl	W	D	L	F	A	Pts	Guadalajara	Cruz Azul	Atlas	Querétaro	Jaguares	Necaxa	Pachuca	Tecos	San Luis	Atlante	Monterrey	Veracruz	América	Tigres	Santos	Morelia	Pumas	Toluca
Guadalajara †	17	9	4	4	27	14	31				2-0			0-1	2-2		1-1		4-0			1-0		2-1	1-1
Cruz Azul †	17	8	4	5	22	17	28	1-2				0-0		3-2	1-0			4-2		3-0				3-2	0-0
Atlas †	17	7	4	6	20	17	25	0-2	1-0			2-0	0-1		4-1		1-1			2-0	3-3	2-0			
Querétaro	17	4	7	6	15	20	19							2-0	0-0	2-2	2-1		0-0	2-1		3-1			0-0
Jaguares	17	5	4	8	16	26	19	1-0	2-2		2-0				1-1		2-1		0-2	2-3	1-1	2-1			
Necaxa	17	4	6	7	19	26	18	2-4	0-2		2-1			3-1		1-2					1-2	1-0		1-1	

Group 2

	Pl	W	D	L	F	A	Pts	Guadalajara	Cruz Azul	Atlas	Querétaro	Jaguares	Necaxa	Pachuca	Tecos	San Luis	Atlante	Monterrey	Veracruz	América	Tigres	Santos	Morelia	Pumas	Toluca
Pachuca †	17	12	3	2	36	12	36				4-2	3-0	1-1				3-0	4-0		1-0	1-0			0-0	
UAG Tecos †	17	6	7	4	30	23	25							2-1		3-4	2-0	3-0		2-1		4-0	2-2	0-0	
San Luis †	17	7	3	7	21	23	24	1-0		2-0	1-0	1-0	1-0	0-2			3-0				2-3	1-2			
Atlante	17	6	3	8	21	27	21	0-3	1-0			3-1		3-0				1-4	2-2	2-0				1-1	
Monterrey	17	5	4	8	17	23	19	1-2	2-0			2-0		2-2					3-2			1-0	1-0	0-1	
Veracruz	17	3	3	11	11	33	12			0-1				1-1	0-5		0-1	2-1		0-0	2-4	1-0		2-1	0-1

Group 3

	Pl	W	D	L	F	A	Pts	Guadalajara	Cruz Azul	Atlas	Querétaro	Jaguares	Necaxa	Pachuca	Tecos	San Luis	Atlante	Monterrey	Veracruz	América	Tigres	Santos	Morelia	Pumas	Toluca
América †	17	9	3	5	26	15	30	1-0	0-0			0-1	2-0	4-1		2-1	4-1	1-0				2-0			
Tigres UANL †	17	6	5	6	17	20	23					1-1	2-0	1-1		1-0	3-3	1-0		1-0				1-1	0-2
Santos Laguna †	17	6	4	7	21	20	22	2-3	2-0		0-0			1-1			3-0	1-0		0-1	2-1				2-1
Morelia †	17	7	1	9	23	25	22							0-1	0-1		3-1	1-0	5-0	2-1		0-0		2-1	2-1
Pumas UNAM	17	3	11	3	19	18	20	0-0	0-1		0-0	3-3	2-0			1-1					1-1	2-1			
Toluca	17	3	10	4	19	17	19							0-0	0-1	1-0			2-4	1-0	1-1	2-1		2-2	

19/01/2007 - 29/04/2007 • † Qualified for the play-offs • Repechaje: **Santos** 0-1 2-0 San Luis; Morelia 1-1 0-0 **Atlas**
Top scorers (inc play-offs): Omar BRAVO, Guadalajara 11; Juan Carlos CACHO, Pachuca 11; Javier CAMPORA, Jaguares 10

APERTURA PLAY-OFFS

Quarter-finals		Semi-finals		Final	
Guadalajara	2 2				
Cruz Azul	0 2	Guadalajara	2 0		
Atlas	1 3	América	0 0		
América	3 3			Guadalajara	1 2
Pachuca	1 1			Toluca	1 1
UNAM	1 0	Pachuca	1 0		
Monterrey	0 1	Toluca	1 1		
Toluca	0 2	* Home team in the first leg			

APERTURA FINAL

First leg. Jalisco, Guadalajara, 7-12-2006

Guadalajara	1	Bravo [44]
Toluca	1	Marioni [75]

Second leg. La Bombonera, Toluca, 10-12-2006

Toluca	1	Marioni [18]
Guadalajara	2	Rodríguez.F [52], Bautista [70]

MEXICO 2006-07
PRIMERA A (2) APERTURA

Group 1	Pl	W	D	L	F	A	Pts
Petroleros Salamanca †	17	8	7	2	28	16	31
Tijuana †	17	9	4	4	21	16	31
Durango †	17	6	9	2	17	14	27
León †	17	8	1	8	26	30	25
Pegaso Real de Colima	17	6	5	6	20	15	23
Santos Laguna	17	6	5	6	25	26	23
UAG Tecos Zapopan	17	5	5	7	24	24	20
Académicos	17	5	5	7	21	23	20
Tapatío Guadalajara	17	5	5	7	22	31	20
Dorados	17	4	7	6	17	21	19
Tigres Los Mochis	17	4	4	9	12	22	16
Monarcas Morelia	17	2	2	13	12	34	8

Group B	Pl	W	D	L	F	A	Pts
Puebla †	17	9	6	2	30	17	33
Cruz Azul Hidalgo †	17	9	6	2	23	15	33
Indios Ciudad Juarez †	17	9	2	6	30	21	29
Tiburones Rojas †	17	7	5	5	27	22	26
Lobos BUAP Puebla	17	7	4	6	27	26	25
Correcaminos	17	7	4	6	24	26	25
Pumas Morelos	17	7	2	8	25	22	23
Zacatepec	17	7	1	9	21	22	22
Rayados Monterrey	17	6	3	8	24	27	21
Tampico Madero	17	5	5	7	20	20	20
Tabasco Villahermosa	17	5	5	7	24	26	20
Atlético Mexiquense	17	3	8	6	20	24	17

5/08/2006 - 26/11/2006 • † Qualified for the play-offs

APERTURA PLAY-OFFS

Quarter-finals		Semi-finals		Final	
Puebla	2 3				
Tiburones	2 1	Puebla ‡	0 2		
Durango	1 1	Cruz Azul	2 0		
Cruz Azul	1 2			Puebla	1 2 6p
Tijuana ‡	1 1			Petroleros	1 2 5p
Indios	1 1	Tijuana	0 0		
León	1 0	Petroleros	0 1		
Petroleros	2 2	‡ Qualified on overall season record			

CLAUSURA PLAY-OFFS

Quarter-finals		Semi-finals		Final	
Pachuca	1 1				
Santos *	1 1	Pachuca	3		
UAG Tecos *	0 0	Cruz Azul *	1		
Cruz Azul	1 1			Pachuca	2 1
Guadalajara	3 3			América *	1 1
Tigres UANL*	1 2	Guadalajara	0 0		
Atlas *	3 1	América *	1 1		
América	3 4	* Home team in the first leg			

CLAUSURA FINAL

First leg. Azteca, Mexico City, 25-05-2007, Ref: Ovalle

América	1	Blanco [82p]
Pachuca	2	Cacho 2 [53 75]

Second leg. Hidalgo, Pachuca, 27-05-2007, Ref: Moreno

Pachuca	1	Cacho [82]
América	1	Blanco [68p]

MEXICO 2006-07
PRIMERA A (2) APERTURA

Group 1	Pl	W	D	L	F	A	Pts
Dorados †	17	13	1	3	33	10	40
Celaya (ex Tijuana) †	17	10	5	2	27	13	35
León †	17	10	3	4	18	16	33
Pegaso Real Colima †	17	8	5	4	30	21	29
Petroleros Salamanca	17	6	9	2	21	15	27
Monarcas Morelia	17	7	2	8	26	31	23
Tapatío Guadalajara	17	5	5	7	18	20	20
Tigres Los Mochis	17	4	7	6	15	22	19
Santos Laguna	17	4	4	9	22	30	16
Durango	17	3	6	8	16	20	15
UAG Tecos Zapopan	17	3	5	9	16	28	14
Académicos	17	2	4	11	12	39	10

Group B	Pl	W	D	L	F	A	Pts
Puebla †	17	11	3	3	42	16	36
Cruz Azul Hidalgo †	17	11	1	5	34	22	34
Pumas Morelos †	17	8	5	4	20	14	29
Tiburones Rojas †	17	8	4	5	25	21	28
Aguila (ex Zacatepec)	17	7	5	5	24	21	26
Tijuana (ex Tabasco)	17	8	1	8	26	30	25
Indios Ciudad Juarez	17	6	5	6	25	21	23
Rayados Monterrey	17	5	5	7	17	22	20
Correcaminos	17	5	3	9	20	23	18
Lobos BUAP Puebla	17	5	2	10	23	34	17
Tampico Madero	17	3	5	9	20	30	14
Atlético Mexiquense	17	3	3	11	12	23	12

12/01/2007 - 29/04/2007 • † Qualified for the play-offs

CLAUSURA PLAY-OFFS

Quarter-finals		Semi-finals		Final	
Dorados ‡	1 1				
Tiburones *	0 2	Dorados	0 1		
Celaya	0	Pegaso *	0 0		
Pegaso *	2			Dorados	1 4
Puebla	3 1			León	3 1
Pumas *	2 1	Puebla	0 3		
Cruz Azul	3 0	León *	2 3		
León *	1 3	* Home team in the first leg			

PRIMERA A PLAY-OFF   Dorados   1-1 2-3   Puebla   Puebla replace Querétaro in the Primera Division

PACHUCA 2006-07

Date	Opponents		Score		Comp	Scorers
6-08-2006	Cruz Azul	L	2-3	H	TA	Mosquera [43], Aguilar [56]
12-08-2006	Monterrey	L	1-3	A	TA	Chitiva [27]
20-08-2006	Chivas Guadalajara	L	1-2	H	TA	Salazar [39]
26-08-2006	Necaxa	L	1-3	A	TA	Giménez.C [56]
30-08-2006	Querétaro	D	0-0	H	TA	
3-09-2006	Pumas UNAM	W	3-2	A	TA	Alvarez [42], Mosquera [54], Cacho [77]
9-09-2006	UAG Tecos	W	5-2	H	TA	Cacho [10], Salazar [38], Giménez.C 2 [69 82], Correa [90]
13-09-2006	América	L	1-3	A	TA	Caballero [12]
16-06-2006	Monarcas Morelia	W	2-0	H	TA	Aguilar [16], Cacho [70]
23-09-2006	San Luis	W	3-0	A	TA	López.L [30], Salazar [53], Cacho [71]
26-09-2006	Deportes Tolima - COL	L	1-2	A	CSr2	Caballero [34]
30-09-2006	Tigres UANL	W	5-0	H	TA	Caballero 2 [7 64], Alvarez [21], Cacho [28], Mosquera [52]
7-10-2006	Atlas	D	1-1	H	TA	Alvarez [56]
10-10-2006	Deportes Tolima - COL	W	5-1	H	CSr2	Aguilar [10], Cacho [46], Mosquera [62], Chitiva [78], Cabrera [83]
14-10-2006	Veracruz	D	0-0	H	TA	
18-10-2006	Lanús - ARG	W	3-0	A	CSqf	Cacho 2 [16 89], Giménez.C [79]
22-10-2006	Jaguares	W	1-0	A	TA	Cacho [70]
28-10-2006	Toluca	W	3-1	H	TA	Cacho [34], Alvarez [62], Landín [92+]
31-10-2006	Lanús - ARG	W	2-0	H	CSqf	Giménez.C [58], Alvarez [93+]
5-11-2006	Santos Laguna	D	1-1	A	TA	Cacho [49]
11-11-2006	Atlante	D	2-2	H	TA	Chitiva 2 [35 44]
15-11-2006	Atlético Paranaense - BRA	W	1-0	A	CSsf	Alvarez [86]
22-11-2006	Atlético Paranaense - BRA	W	4-1	H	CSsf	Giménez.C 2 [57 63], Alvarez [75], Cacho [80]
24-11-2006	Pumas UNAM	D	1-1	H	TAqf	De la Barrera [60]
26-11-2006	Pumas UNAM	W	1-0	A	TAqf	Caballero [52]
29-11-2006	Toluca	D	1-1	H	TAsf	Landín [70]
30-11-2006	Colo Colo - CHI	D	1-1	H	CSf	Chitiva [27]
3-12-2006	Toluca	L	0-1	A	TAsf	
13-12-2006	Colo Colo - CHI	W	2-1	A	CSf	Caballero [53], Giménez.C [72]
20-01-2007	Cruz Azul	L	2-3	A	TC	Giménez.C [27], Alvarez [50]
27-01-2007	Monterrey	W	4-0	H	TC	Cacho 2 [55 74], Salazar [65], Caballero [80]
3-02-2007	Chivas Guadalajara	W	1-0	A	TC	Landín [92+]
10-02-2007	Necaxa	D	1-1	H	TC	Mosquera [89]
14-02-2007	Querétaro	D	0-0	A	TC	
17-02-2007	Pumas UNAM	D	0-0	H	TC	
22-02-2007	Deportivo Marquense - GUA	W	2-0	H	CLqf	Alvarez [12], Caballero [57]
25-02-2007	UAG Tecos	W	4-3	A	TC	Rodríguez.C [21], Cacho [75], Landín 2 [86 90]
28-02-2007	Deportivo Marquense - GUA	W	1-0	A	CLqf	Landín [16]
4-03-2007	América	W	1-0	H	TC	Cacho [5]
10-03-2007	Monarcas Morelia	W	1-0	A	TC	Giménez.C [76]
15-03-2007	Houston Dynamo - USA	L	0-2	A	CLsf	
21-03-2007	San Luis	W	3-0	H	TC	Cacho 2 [63 69], Chitiva [71]
25-03-2007	Atlas	W	4-2	H	TC	Giménez.C 3 [20 35 37], Alvarez [71]
31-03-2007	Veracruz	W	5-0	A	TC	Giménez.C 2 [27 73], Montes [39], Landín [48], Alvarez [70]
5-04-2007	Houston Dynamo - USA	W	5-2	H	CLsf	Caballero 2 [3 85], Giménez.C 3 [15 58 104]
8-04-2007	Jaguares	W	3-0	H	TC	Riverón [1], Salazar [15], Brambila [53]
11-04-2007	Tigres UANL	L	0-2	A	TC	
15-04-2007	Toluca	W	2-0	H	TC	Riverón [42], Alvarez [71]
18-04-2007	Chivas Guadalajara - MEX	D	2-2	H	CLf	Cacho [21], Cabrera [82]
21-04-2007	Santos Laguna	W	1-0	H	TC	Mosquera [23]
25-04-2007	Chivas Guadalajara - MEX	D	0-0	H	CLf	W 7-6p
28-04-2007	Atlante	W	4-1	A	TC	Landín [59], Cacho 2 [71 88], Correa [75]
10-05-2007	Santos Laguna	D	1-1	A	TCqf	Caballero [9]
13-05-2007	Santos Laguna	D	1-1	H	TCqf	Salazar [62]
17-05-2007	Cruz Azul	W	3-1	A	TCsf	Caballero [20], Giménez.C [34p 62]
20-05-2007	Cruz Azul	-	-	H	TCsf	Tie awarded to Pachuca after Cruz Azul fielded ineligible player
25-05-2007	América	W	2-1	A	TCf	Cacho 2 [53 75]
27-05-2007	América	D	1-1	H	TCf	Cacho [82]
31-05-2007	Internacional - BRA	W	2-1	H	RS	Giménez.C 2 [15 79]
7-06-2007	Internacional - BRA	L	0-4	A	RS	

TA = Toneo Apertura • CS = Copa Suamericana • TC = Torneo Clausura • CL = CONCACAF Champions Cup • RS = Recopa Sudamericana
r2 = second round • qf = quarter-final • sf = semi-final • f = final

MGL – MONGOLIA

NATIONAL TEAM RECORD
JULY 10TH 2006 TO JULY 12TH 2010

PL	W	D	L	F	A	%
3	1	1	1	5	9	50

FIFA/COCA-COLA WORLD RANKING

1993	1994	1995	1996	1997	1998	1999	2000	2001	2002	2003	2004	2005	2006	High	Low
-	-	-	-	-	196	198	196	187	193	179	185	179	181	**173** 07/07	**200** 02/00

2006–2007											
08/06	09/06	10/06	11/06	12/06	01/07	02/07	03/07	04/07	05/07	06/07	07/07
181	183	183	183	181	181	183	184	182	193	193	173

"Thank goodness for Guam" ought to be the motto of the Mongolian national team, because without their opponents from the Pacific island, Mongolia would be on a winless run stretching back to their debut in 1942! Mongolia have won four international matches against Guam - twice in 2003, once in 2005 and most recently, in 2007, in the qualifiers for the East Asian Championship. In those qualifiers, Mongolia finished bottom of group A after drawing with hosts Macau and losing to North Korea, with their win against Guam coming in the fifth place play-off. Since joining FIFA in 1998, Mongolia have managed to score a respectable 19 goals in 27 matches, but

INTERNATIONAL HONOURS
None

of those 19 goals only three have come against opponents other than Guam. In domestic football, 12 clubs from six towns and cities took part in the 2006 Championship with the teams divided into three groups of four in the first round. From those the top eight teams qualified for two groups of four in the second round. Defending champions Khoromkhon from Ulaan-Baatar topped their second round group to make it to their third consecutive final where they met Khasin Khultood, also from Ulaan-Baatar, who were making their first appearance. After a 2-2 draw and a 4-2 penalty shoot-out victory, Khasin were soon also celebrating their first title triumph.

THE FIFA BIG COUNT OF 2006

	Male	Female		Total
Number of players	51 200	20	Referees and Assistant Referees	30
Professionals	200		Admin, Coaches, Technical, Medical	73
Amateurs 18+	800		Number of clubs	10
Youth under 18	3 020		Number of teams	70
Unregistered	11 000		Clubs with women's teams	0
Total players	51 200		Players as % of population	1.81%

Mongolia Football Federation (MFF)

PO Box 259, Ulaan-Baatar 210646, Mongolia

Tel +976 11 345968   Fax +976 11 345966

ubmaya@yahoo.com   www.none

President: AMARJARGAL Renchinnyam   General Secretary: GANBOLD Buyannemekh

Vice-President: TBD   Treasurer: OYUNTSETSEG Davaa   Media Officer: BAYARTSOGT Ganjuur

Men's Coach: OTGONBAYAR Ishdorj   Women's Coach: TBD

MFF formed: 1959   AFC: 1998   FIFA: 1998

White shirts, Red shorts, White socks

RECENT INTERNATIONAL MATCHES PLAYED BY MONGOLIA

2002	Opponents	Score	Venue	Comp	Scorers	Att	Referee
No international matches played in 2002							
2003							
22-02	Macau	L 0-2	Hong Kong	EAq		6 055	Chan Siu Kee HKG
24-02	Guam	W 2-0	Hong Kong	EAq	Tugsbayar [52], Lumbengarav [59]	1 602	Huang Junjie CHN
26-02	Chinese Taipei	L 0-4	Hong Kong	EAq		672	Chan Siu Kee HKG
28-02	Hong Kong	L 0-10	Hong Kong	EAq		1 814	
25-04	Guam	W 5-0	Thimphu	ACq	Batyalat [20], Tugsbayer 3 [26 56 90], Lunmbengaran [61]		
27-04	Bhutan	D 0-0	Thimphu	ACq			
29-11	Maldives	L 0-1	Ulaan-Baatar	WCq		2 000	Yang Zhiqiang CHN
3-12	Maldives	L 0-12	Malé	WCq		9 000	Arambekade SRI
2004							
No international matches played in 2004							
2005							
5-03	Hong Kong	L 0-6	Taipei	EAq			
7-03	Korea DPR	L 0-6	Taipei	EAq			
9-03	Guam	W 4-1	Taipei	EAq	Tugsbayer 2 [31 34], Bayarzorig [46], Buman-Uchral [81]		
13-03	Chinese Taipei	D 0-0	Taipei	EAq			
2006							
No international matches played in 2006							
2007							
17-06	Macau	D 0-0	Macau	EAq			
19-06	Korea DPR	L 0-7	Macau	EAq			
23-06	Guam	W 5-2	Macau	EAq			

EA = EAFF East Asian Championship • AC = AFC Asian Cup • WC = FIFA World Cup • q = qualifier

MONGOLIA NATIONAL TEAM RECORDS AND RECORD SEQUENCES

Records			Sequence records				
Victory	5-0	GUM 2003	Wins	1		Clean sheets	2	2003
Defeat	0-15	UZB 1998	Defeats	15	1942-2001	Goals scored	1	
Player Caps	n/a		Undefeated	3	2005-2007	Without goal	5	2001, 2003-2005
Player Goals	n/a		Without win	17	1942-2003	Goals against	13	1998-2003

RECENT LEAGUE RECORD

	Championship		
Year	Champions	Score	Runners-up
1997	Delger	2-1	Erchim
1998	Erchim		Delger
1999	ITI Bank Bars		Erchim
2000	Erchim		Sonor
2001	Khangarid		Mon Uran
2002	Erchim		Khangarid
2003	Khangarid	2-1	Mon Uran
2004	Khangarid	1-0	Khoromkon
2005	Khoromkhon	1-0	Khangarid
2006	Khasin Khultood	2-2 4-2p	Khoromkhon

MONGOLIA COUNTRY INFORMATION

Capital	Ulaan-Baatar	Independence	1921 from China	GDP per Capita	$1 800
Population	2 751 314	Status	Republic	GNP Ranking	156
Area km²	1 564 116	Language	Khalkha Mongol	Dialling code	+976
Population density	2 per km²	Literacy rate	97%	Internet code	.mn
% in urban areas	61%	Main religion	Buddhist 50%, None 40%	GMT +/−	+8
Towns/Cities ('000)	Ulaan-Baatar 844; Ërdènèt 76; Darhan 72; Cojbalsan 44; Ölgij 30; Sahnsand 28; Ulaangom 28				
Neighbours (km)	China 4 677; Russia 3 543				
Main stadia	National Sports Stadium – Ulaan-Baatar 20 000				

MKD – FYR MACEDONIA

NATIONAL TEAM RECORD
JULY 10TH 2006 TO JULY 12TH 2010

PL	W	D	L	F	A	%
8	3	1	4	7	7	43.7

FIFA/COCA-COLA WORLD RANKING

1993	1994	1995	1996	1997	1998	1999	2000	2001	2002	2003	2004	2005	2006	High		Low	
-	90	94	86	92	59	68	76	89	85	92	92	87		49	03/07	147	05/94

2006–2007											
08/06	09/06	10/06	11/06	12/06	01/07	02/07	03/07	04/07	05/07	06/07	07/07
67	51	50	55	54	54	53	49	54	53	61	60

The magic that Srecko Katanec weaved to take his native Slovenia to the Euro 2000 finals and the FIFA World Cup in 2002 hasn't quite returned yet with Macedonia, but he has steadied the ship after a very poor spell that included a defeat against Andorra. There was no danger of a repeat of that result in the UEFA Euro 2008 qualifiers as the Andorrans were comfortably dispatched. Indeed, the Macedonians proved to be tricky opponents, even holding England to a draw in Manchester. All of the big home games, however - against England, Russia and Israel as well as Croatia away - were lost, leaving them stuck in no-man's-land in their group, comfortably clear of Andorra and Estonia at

INTERNATIONAL HONOURS
None

the bottom but well behind the group leaders. In club football Rabatnicki Skopje made it through two rounds of the UEFA Champions League before falling to Lille in the third preliminary round, but the defence of their title at home did not go according to plan. In a tight championship race they finished second behind Pobeda Prilep, who won 13 of their final 14 games. Pobeda fell just short of achieving the double, however, when three days before securing the Championship, they lost lost 2-1 to Vardar in the Cup Final. The one black cloud on the horizon came with the threatened suspension of Macedonia by FIFA and UEFA after internal disputes within the federation.

THE FIFA BIG COUNT OF 2006

	Male	Female		Total
Number of players	82 546	11 350	Referees and Assistant Referees	740
Professionals	356		Admin, Coaches, Technical, Medical	1 125
Amateurs 18+	14 530		Number of clubs	456
Youth under 18	7 760		Number of teams	615
Unregistered	19 000		Clubs with women's teams	16
Total players	93 896		Players as % of population	4.58%

Football Federation of Macedonia (FFM)
8-ma Udarna brigada 31-a, Skopje 1000, FYR Macedonia
Tel +389 23 222603   Fax +389 23 165448
fsm@fsm.org.mk   www.ffm.com.mk
President: HADZI-RISTESKI Haralampie   General Secretary: ATANASOVSKI Ilija
Vice-President: BEDZETI Redzep   Treasurer: MITROVSKI Lazar   Media Officer: NIKOLOVSKI Zoran
Men's Coach: KATANEC Srecko   Women's Coach: DIMOVSKI Dobre
FFM formed: 1908   UEFA: 1994   FIFA: 1994
Red shirts with white trimmings, Red shorts, Red socks or White shirts with red trimmings, White shorts, White socks

RECENT INTERNATIONAL MATCHES PLAYED BY FYR MACEDONIA

2002 Opponents	Score	Venue	Comp	Scorers	Att	Referee
16-10 England	D 2-2	Southampton	ECq	Sakiri [10], Trajanov [24]	32 095	Dauden Ibanez ESP
20-11 Israel	L 2-3	Skopje	Fr	Vasoski [63], Sedloski [89]	5 000	Delevic SCG
2003						
9-02 Croatia	D 2-2	Sibenik	Fr	Sedloski [10p], Toleski [60]	4 000	Zrnic BIH
14-02 Poland	L 0-3	Split	Fr		500	Trivkovic POL
29-03 Slovakia	L 0-2	Skopje	ECq		11 000	Duhamel FRA
2-04 Portugal	L 0-1	Lausanne	Fr		14 258	Nobs SUI
7-06 Liechtenstein	W 3-1	Skopje	ECq	Sedloski [39p], Krstev [51], Stojkov [82]	6 000	Jara CZE
11-06 Turkey	L 2-3	Istanbul	ECq	Grozdanovski [24], Sakiri [28]	23 000	Rosetti ITA
20-08 Albania	W 3-1	Prilep	Fr	Naumoski [9], Pandev [36], Dimitrovski [77]	3 000	Mihajlevic SCG
6-09 England	L 1-2	Skopje	ECq	Hristov [28]	20 500	De Bleeckere BEL
10-09 Slovakia	D 1-1	Zilina	ECq	Dimitrovski [62]	2 286	Sundell SWE
11-10 Ukraine	D 0-0	Kyiv	Fr		13 000	Orlic MDA
2004						
27-01 China PR	D 0-0	Shanghai	Fr		25 000	Lee Yu CHN
29-01 China PR	L 0-1	Shanghai	Fr		17 500	Zhig Yang CHN
18-02 Bosnia-Herzegovina	W 1-0	Skopje	Fr	Pandev [20]	8 000	Vrajkov BUL
31-03 Ukraine	W 1-0	Skopje	Fr	Stavrevski [26]	16 000	Karagic SCG
28-04 Croatia	L 0-1	Skopje	Fr		15 000	Arzuman TUR
11-06 Estonia	W 4-2	Tallinn	Fr	Sedloski [11], Popov [15], Pandev [31], Grozdanovski [65]	1 500	Fröjfeldt SWE
18-08 Armenia	W 3-0	Skopje	WCq	Pandev [5], Sakiri [37], Sumolikoski [90]	4 375	Guenov BUL
4-09 Romania	L 1-2	Craiova	WCq	Vasoski [70]	14 500	Plautz AUT
9-10 Netherlands	D 2-2	Skopje	WCq	Pandev [45], Stojkov [71]	15 000	Frojdfeldt SWE
13-10 Andorra	L 0-1	Andorra La Vella	WCq		350	Podeschi SMR
17-11 Czech Republic	L 0-2	Skopje	WCq		7 000	Meier SUI
2005						
9-02 Andorra	D 0-0	Skopje	WCq		5 000	Verbist BEL
30-03 Romania	L 1-2	Skopje	WCq	Maznov [31]	15 000	Ovrebo NOR
4-06 Armenia	W 2-1	Yerevan	WCq	Pandev 2 [29p 47]	2 870	Mikulski POL
8-06 Czech Republic	L 1-6	Teplice	WCq	Pandev [13]	14 150	Dauden Ibanez ESP
17-08 Finland	L 0-3	Skopje	WCq		6 800	Messias ENG
7-09 Finland	L 1-5	Tampere	WCq	Maznov [48]	6 467	Jakobsson ISL
12-10 Netherlands	D 0-0	Amsterdam	WCq		50 000	Farina ITA
12-11 Liechtenstein	W 2-1	Vaduz	Fr	Ilijoski [82], Nuhiji [90]	1 350	Nobs SUI
2006						
1-03 Bulgaria	L 0-1	Skopje	Fr		8 000	
28-05 Ecuador	W 2-1	Madrid	Fr	Maznov [28], Mitreski [73p]	4 000	
4-06 Turkey	W 1-0	Krefeld	Fr	Maznov [82]	7 000	
16-08 Estonia	W 1-0	Tallinn	ECq	Sedloski [73]	7 500	Jakobsson ISL
6-09 England	L 0-1	Skopje	ECq		15 000	Layec FRA
7-10 England	D 0-0	Manchester	ECq		72 060	Merk GER
11-10 Andorra	W 3-0	Andorra la Vella	ECq	Pandev [13], Noveski [16], Naumoski [31]	300	Silagava GEO
15-11 Russia	L 0-2	Skopje	ECq		13 000	Allaerts BEL
2007						
7-02 Albania	W 1-0	Tirana	Fr	Ristic [33]	8 000	Bertini ITA
24-03 Croatia	L 1-2	Zagreb	ECq	Sedloski [38]	29 969	Plautz AUT
2-06 Israel	L 1-2	Skopje	ECq	Stojkov [13]	12 000	Kircher GER

Fr = Friendly match • EC = UEFA EURO 2004/2008 • WC = FIFA World Cup • q = qualifier

FYR MACEDONIA NATIONAL TEAM RECORDS AND RECORD SEQUENCES

Records			Sequence records				
Victory	11-1	LIE 1996	Wins	4	1993-1994	Clean sheets	2	
Defeat	1-6	CZE 2005	Defeats	3	Five times	Goals scored	8	2002-2003
Player Caps	75	SEDLOSKI Goce	Undefeated	8	1998	Without goal	4	2001-2002
Player Goals	16	HRISTOV Gjorgji	Without win	19	2000-2002	Goals against	13	2001-2002

MAJOR CITIES/TOWNS

Population '000

1	Skopje	480
2	Kumanovo	111
3	Bitola	86
4	Tetovo	74
5	Prilep	74
6	Veles	58
7	Ohrid	55
8	Gostivar	51
9	Stip	48
10	Strumica	45
11	Kavadarci	39
12	Struga	37
13	Kocani	34
14	Kicevo	31
15	Lipkovo	28
16	Saraj	26
17	Zelino	26
18	Radovis	25
19	Tearce	23
20	Gevgelija	20
21	Kriva Palanka	20
22	Negotino	19
23	Studenicani	18
24	Kratovo	10

REPUBLIC OF MACEDONIA; REPUBLIKA MAKEDONIJA

Capital	Skopje	Language	Macedonian, Albanian	Independence	1991
Population	2 050 554	Area	25 333 km^2	% in cities	60%
GDP per cap	$6 700	Dailling code	+389		
		Density	82 per km^2		
		Internet	.mk	GMT + / -	+1

MEDALS TABLE

		Overall			League			Cup			Europe			City	Stadium	Cap'ty	DoF
		G	S	B	G	S	B	G	S	B	G	S	B				
1	Vardar Skopje	10	3	3	5	2	3	5	1					Skopje	Gradski	22 000	1947
2	Sloga Jugomagnat	6	7	2	3	2	2	3	5					Skopje	Cair	4 500	1927
3	Sileks Kratovo	5	6		3	5		2	1					Kratovo	Sileks	3 000	1965
4	Pobeda Prilep	3	4	4	2	2	4	1	2					Prilep	Goce Delcev	15 000	1941
5	Rabotnicki Kometal	2	1	1	2	1	1							Skopje	Gradski	22 000	1937
6	Pelister Bitola	1	2					1	2					Bitola	Pod Timbe Kafe	9 000	1945
7	Cementarnica Skopje	1	1	1		1		1	1					Skopje	Cementarnica	2 000	1955
	Makedonija Skopje	1	1	2	1	2		1						Skopje	Gorce Petrov	3 000	1934
9	Baskimi Kumanovo	1						1						Kumanovo	Gradski Arena	7 000	1947
10	Belasica Strumica		2			2								Strumica	Mladost	6 370	1922
11	Madzari Skopje		1					1						Skopje			
	Napredok Kicevo		1					1						Kicevo	Gradski	5 000	1924
	Shkendija Tetovo		1					1						Tetovo	Gradski	20 500	1960
14	Balkan Skopje			1		1								Skopje			
	Balkan Stokokomerc			1		1								Skopje			

RECENT LEAGUE AND CUP RECORD

	Championship						Cup		
Year	Champions	Pts	Runners-up	Pts	Third	Pts	Winners	Score	Runners-up
1995	Vardar Skopje	76	Sileks Kratovo	60	Sloga Jugomagnat	58	Vardar Skopje	2-1	Sileks Kratovo
1996	Sileks Kratovo	70	Sloga Jugomagnat	58	Vardar Skopje	57	Sloga Jugomagnat	0-0 5-3p	Vardar Skopje
1997	Sileks Kratovo	62	Pobeda Prilep	54	Sloga Jugomagnat	42	Sileks Kratovo	4-2	Sloga Jugomagnat
1998	Sileks Kratovo	48	Sloga Jugomagnat	43	Makedonija Skopje	42	Vardar Skopje	2-0	Sloga Jugomagnat
1999	Sloga Jugomagnat	60	Sileks Kratovo	57	Pobeda Prilep	53	Vardar Skopje	2-0	Sloga Jugomagnat
2000	Sloga Jugomagnat	61	Pobeda Prilep	52	Rabotnicki Skopje	50	Sloga Jugomagnat	6-0	Pobeda Prilep
2001	Sloga Jugomagnat	63	Vardar Skopje	63	Pobeda Prilep	56	Pelister Bitola	2-1	Sloga Jugomagnat
2002	Vardar Skopje	37	Belasica Strumica	36	Cementarnica	27	Pobeda Prilep	3-1	Cementarnica
2003	Vardar Skopje	72	Belasica Strumica	69	Pobeda Prilep	65	Cementarnica	4-4 3-2p	Sloga Jugomagnat
2004	Pobeda Prilep	71	Sileks Kratovo	66	Vardar Skopje	60	Sloga Jugomagnat	1-0	Napredok Kicevo
2005	Rabotnicki Skopje	78	Vardar Skopje	72	Pobeda Prilep	55	Baskimi Kumanovo	2-1	Madzari Skopje
2006	Rabotnicki Skopje	72	Makedonija Skopje	69	Vardar Skopje	64	Makedonije Skopje	3-2	Shkendija Tetovo
2007	Pobeda Prilep	71	Rabotnicki Skopje	67	Makedonija Skopje	64	Vardar Skopje	2-1	Pobeda Prilep

FYR MACEDONIA 2006-07

PRVA LIGA

	Pl	W	D	L	F	A	Pts	Pobeda	Rabotnicki	Makedonija	Vardar	Renova	Pelister	Napredok	Baskimi	Sileks	Shkendija	Bregalnica	Vlazrimi
Pobeda Prilep †	33	21	8	4	73	42	71		1-1	1-1 1-0	3-2	1-0	2-1	3-1 3-2	4-0 3-2	5-1 1-0	3-2 4-2	3-1 4-1	3-0
Rabotnicki Skopje ‡	33	19	10	4	75	25	67	2-0 1-2		3-2 3-3	1-1	3-0 1-1	1-0	4-0 0-0	3-2	6-2	5-1 3-0	8-0	5-0 5-0
Makedonija Skopje	33	18	10	5	65	29	64	0-0	3-0		0-2 1-1	1-1	2-0 2-0	2-1 2-1	1-1	3-0 3-1	2-0 2-0	3-0 4-0	3-0
Vardar Skopje ‡	33	17	8	8	63	34	59	2-1 2-3	0-2 0-0	2-2		1-1 0-1	2-1	5-1 2-0	3-0	0-1	0-0 1-0	1-1	3-0 10-0
Renova Cepciste	33	17	8	8	54	31	59	2-3 4-3	1-1	0-2 2-0	3-0		1-0	0-0 2-0	2-2 2-0	3-0 2-1	1-2	3-0 4-0	3-0
Pelister Bitola	33	14	3	16	37	32	45	1-0	2-0 0-2	0-1	1-2 1-2	1-2 0-1		2-2 2-0	2-0	2-0	3-0 2-1	3-0	1-0 2-0
Napredok Kicevo	33	12	9	12	50	47	45	2-2	0-0	1-0	1-3	1-1	0-0		1-0 4-0	2-0 2-0	2-2 2-1	7-0 2-0	1-0 3-1
Baskimi Kumanovo	33	12	6	15	54	60	42	2-2	1-3 0-0	2-2	0-3 4-1	0-3	1-2 1-0	2-1		1-0 1-4	6-1	8-1 2-1	2-0
Sileks Kratovo	33	12	5	16	54	50	41	2-2	2-1 0-1	1-2	3-2 2-2	3-0	2-0 2-1	3-3	0-1 0-0		6-0	4-0 3-0	1-1
Shkendija Tetovo	33	10	8	15	39	63	38	1-1 0-2	1-1	2-2 1-1	0-2	1-5 2-1	0-1	2-1	2-0 1-1	2-1		3-1	2-0 4-2
Bregalnica Stip	33	3	4	26	19	97	13	1-1	0-3 0-3	2-3	0-3 0-2	1-0	0-4 0-0	1-2	0-5	0-2	0-3 1-2		5-1 2-1
Vlazrimi Kicevo	33	2	3	28	22	95	9	2-4 1-2	0-3	0-5 0-5	0-1	1-1 0-1	0-1	1-3	2-3 2-3	2-1 2-5	3-0	0-0	

6/08/2006 - 27/05/2007 • † Qualified for the UEFA Champions League • ‡ Qualified for the UEFA Cup

FYR MACEDONIA 2006-07
VTORA LIGA (2)

	Pl	W	D	L	F	A	Pts
Milano Kumanovo	33	21	6	6	74	31	69
Cementarnica Skopje	33	16	11	6	53	24	59
Teteks Tetovo	33	16	6	11	48	32	54
Skopje	33	13	10	10	32	21	49
Turnovo	33	12	9	12	36	41	45
Sloga Jugomagnat	33	12	7	14	48	46	43
Metalurg Skopje	33	10	13	10	38	37	43
Madzari Solidarnost	33	10	12	11	35	33	42
Belasica Strumica	33	11	7	15	36	59	40
Karaorman Struga	33	12	3	18	37	50	39
Vardar Dekamen	33	9	6	18	26	56	33
Ilinden Skopje §6	33	5	12	16	30	63	21

5/08/2006 - 26/05/2007 • § = points deducted

MAKEDONSKI CUP 2006-07

Round of sixteen

Vardar Skopje *	4	1
Metalurg Skopje	1	0
Makedonija Skopje *	0	0
Meridian FCU	2	0
Renova Cepciste	4	2
Gostivar *	1	2
Madzari Solidarnost *	2	0
Pelister Bitola	2	2
Milano Kumanovo *	2	2
Bashkimi Kumanovo	1	2
Ilinden Skopje	0	1
Rabotnicki Skopje *	4	4
Drita *	3	1
Bregalnica Stip	0	2
Shkendija Tetovo	0	0
Pobeda Prilep *	2	1

Quarter-finals

Vardar Skopje *	4	0
Meridian FCU	1	1
Renova Cepciste	1	1
Pelister Bitola *	0	2
Milano Kumanovo	1	1
Rabotnicki Skopje *	1	0
Drita *	2	1
Pobeda Prilep	1	6

Semi-finals

Vardar Skopje *	2	1
Pelister Bitola	1	1
Milano Kumanovo	1	0
Pobeda Prilep *	2	1

Final

Vardar Skopje ‡	2
Pobeda Prilep	1

CUP FINAL

24-05-2007
Skopje

Scorers - Hristijan Kirovski [22], Wandeir [27] for Vardar; Marjan Nacev [72] for Pobeda

* Home team in the first leg • ‡ Qualified for the UEFA Cup

MLI – MALI

NATIONAL TEAM RECORD
JULY 10TH 2006 TO JULY 12TH 2010

PL	W	D	L	F	A	%
9	6	3	0	14	2	83.3

FIFA/COCA-COLA WORLD RANKING

1993	1994	1995	1996	1997	1998	1999	2000	2001	2002	2003	2004	2005	2006	High		Low	
70	52	52	67	80	70	72	98	112	73	54	51	63	36	**43**	09/04	**117**	10/01

2006–2007											
08/06	09/06	10/06	11/06	12/06	01/07	02/07	03/07	04/07	05/07	06/07	07/07
60	60	41	36	36	36	35	35	40	40	49	48

With an increasing list of high quality players, Mali have the potential to develop into one of the continent's top footballing powers. But their elevation has been slow and they were embroiled in a tough battle for African Nations Cup qualification with group rivals Togo, after drawing three of their first four matches. Mali also did not qualify for the last Nations Cup finals in Egypt in 2006 but since the end of 2005 have racked up a run of 10 matches without defeat. Key to potential success is a midfield led by Mahamadou Diarra, who was out of national team action for almost a year after a CAF suspension, and Seydou Keita, who captained Racing Lens in France. Both now

INTERNATIONAL HONOURS
None

play in Spain, Diarra at champions Real Madrid and Keita a new signing at Sevilla, where he will be alongside his compatriot Frédéric Kanouté, another vital part of Mali's attack. Kanoute scored some 20 goals in Spain last season, and won a UEFA Cup winners' medal, but for Mali his tally over the last two years is just three goals. With much of Mali's talent exported, their representatives in continental club football have made no impression in the African Champions League or the African Confederation Cup. Stade Malien won the League and Cup double, edging Djoliba in the championship and AS Bamako in the Cup Final.

THE FIFA BIG COUNT OF 2006

	Male	Female		Total
Number of players	1 363 775	27 850	Referees and Assistant Referees	575
Professionals	0		Admin, Coaches, Technical, Medical	5 503
Amateurs 18+	5 100		Number of clubs	140
Youth under 18	9 075		Number of teams	700
Unregistered	1 352 450		Clubs with women's teams	0
Total players	1 391 625		Players as % of population	11.88%

Fédération Malienne de Football (FMF)
Avenue du Mali, Hamdallaye ACI 2000, PO Box 1020, Bamako 12582, Mali
Tel +223 2238844   Fax +223 2224254
malifoot@afribone.net.ml   www.none
President: KEITA Salif   General Secretary: TRAORE Jacouba
Vice-President: KEITA Karounga   Treasurer: TRAORE Brehima   Media Officer: KALOGA Mamadou
Men's Coach: JODAR Jean-Francois   Women's Coach: DIAKITE Aly
FMF formed: 1960   CAF: 1963   FIFA: 1962
Green shirts, Yellow shorts, Red socks

RECENT INTERNATIONAL MATCHES PLAYED BY MALI

2003	Opponents	Score	Venue	Comp	Scorers	Att	Referee
12-02	Guinea	W 1-0	Toulon	Fr	Doukantie [20]		
30-03	Eritrea	W 2-0	Asmara	CNq	Thiam [54], Coulibaly.Dr [90]		Abdulkadir TAN
27-04	Madagascar	W 2-0	Paris	Fr	Toure.B [25], Bagayoko [73]		
7-06	Eritrea	W 1-0	Bamako	CNq	Coulibaly.S [20]		Aboubacar CIV
22-06	Zimbabwe	D 0-0	Bamako	CNq			
5-07	Seychelles	W 2-0	Victoria	CNq	Traore.D [60], Bagayoko [90]	5 000	Lim Kee Chong MRI
10-10	Guinea-Bissau	W 2-1	Bissau	WCq	Keita.S [8], Coulibaly.S [69]	22 000	Sowe GAM
14-11	Guinea-Bissau	W 2-0	Bamako	WCq	Coulibaly.S [15], Sidibe.D [84p]	13 251	Seydou MTN
19-11	Morocco	W 1-0	Meknes	Fr	Coulibaly.Dv [35]	6 000	Shelmani LBY
2004							
15-01	Algeria	W 2-0	Algiers	Fr	Traore.D [4], Toure.B [57]	7 000	Zehmoun TUN
26-01	Kenya	W 3-1	Bizerte	CNr1	Sissoko [27], Kanoute 2 [63 82]	6 000	Tessema ETH
30-01	Burkina Faso	W 3-1	Tunis	CNr1	Kanoute [33], Diarra.M [37], Coulibaly.S [78]	1 500	Shelmani LBY
2-02	Senegal	D 1-1	Tunis	CNr1	Traore.D [33]	7 550	Evehe CAM
7-02	Guinea	W 2-1	Bizerte	CNqf	Kanoute [45], Diarra.M [90]	1 450	Abd El Fatah EGY
11-02	Morocco	L 0-4	Sousse	CNsf		15 000	Aboubacar CIV
13-02	Nigeria	L 1-2	Monastir	CN3p	Abouta [70]	2 500	Sowe GAM
28-04	Tunisia	L 0-1	Sfax	Fr		8 000	Shelmani LBY
28-05	Morocco	D 0-0	Bamako	Fr		35 000	
6-06	Liberia	L 0-1	Monrovia	WCq		30 000	Codjia BEN
19-06	Zambia	D 1-1	Bamako	WCq	Kanoute [80]	19 000	Sowe GAM
4-07	Congo	L 0-1	Brazzaville	WCq		20 000	Evehe CMR
18-08	Congo DR	W 3-0	Paris	Fr	Keita.S 2 [2 21], Kanoute [81]		Bruno FRA
5-09	Senegal	D 2-2	Bamako	WCq	Diallo.M [4], Kanoute [54]	45 000	Guezzaz MAR
10-10	Togo	L 0-1	Lome	WCq		45 000	Njike CMR
2005							
9-02	Guinea	D 2-2	Paris	Fr	Traore.D [8], Diao [51]	2 000	
27-03	Togo	L 1-2	Bamako	WCq	Coulibaly.S [12]	45 000	Agbenyega GHA
5-06	Liberia	W 4-1	Liberia	WCq	Coulibaly.D 2 [7p 34], Diamoutene [48p], Diarra.M [75]	11 000	Pare BFA
12-06	Algeria	W 3-0	Arles	Fr	Coulibaly.D [33], Dissa 2 [58 79]	2 000	Derrien FRA
17-06	Zambia	L 1-2	Chililabombwe	WCq	Coulibaly.S [73]	29 000	Colembi ANG
3-09	Congo	W 2-0	Bamako	WCq	Demba [48], Sissoko [51]	10 000	Mbera GAB
8-10	Senegal	L 0-3	Dakar	WCq		30 000	Maillet SEY
2006							
28-05	Morocco	W 1-0	Paris	Fr	Kanoute [70]		Garibian FRA
16-08	Tunisia	W 1-0	Narbonne	Fr	Kanoute [39p]		
3-09	Sierra Leone	D 0-0	Freetown	CNq			Mbera GAB
8-10	Togo	W 1-0	Bamako	CNq	Traore.D [89]		Benouza ALG
14-11	Congo	W 1-0	La Corneuve	Fr	Kante [90]		
2007							
6-02	Lithuania	W 3-1	La Corneuve	Fr	Tamboura [25], Diarra.M [31], Diallo.M [43]		Piccirillo FRA
25-03	Benin	D 1-1	Bamako	CNq	Kanoute [53p]		Doue CIV
3-06	Benin	D 0-0	Cotonou	CNq			
9-06	Burkina Faso	W 1-0	Ouagadougou	Fr	Diallo.M [57]		
17-06	Sierra Leone	W 6-0	Bamako	CNq	Sidibe [20p], Keita.S 2 [68 88], Diallo.M [76], Diallo.L [90], Toure.B [93+]		

Fr = Friendly match • CN = CAF African Cup of Nations • WC = FIFA World Cup
q = qualifier • r1 = first round group • qf = quarter-final • sf = semi-final • 3p = third place play-off

MALI NATIONAL TEAM RECORDS AND RECORD SEQUENCES

Records			Sequence records				
Victory	6-0	MTN 1975, SLE 2007	Wins	8	2002-2003	Clean sheets	6	2003
Defeat	1-8	KUW 1997	Defeats	5	1997	Goals scored	11	1971-1972
Player Caps	n/a		Undefeated	18	2002-2004	Without goal	4	Three times
Player Goals	n/a		Without win	8	1989-90, 1995-96	Goals against	12	1987-1988

MAJOR CITIES/TOWNS

Population '000

1	Bamako	1 388
2	Sikasso	154
3	Mopti	112
4	Koutiala	106
5	Kayes	103
6	Ségou	92
7	Nioro	75
8	Markala	59
9	Kolokani	54
10	Kati	43
11	Gao	39
12	Bougouni	37
13	Niono	34
14	Banamba	33
15	Timbuktu	32
16	Bafoulabé	30
17	Nara	30
18	Koulikoro	24
19	San	24
20	Djenné	23
21	Kangaba	17
22	Yorosso	17
23	Kidal	11
24	Diré	10

REPUBLIC OF MALI; REPUBLIQUE DE MALI

Capital	Bamako	Language	French, Bambara	Independence	1960
Population	11 716 829	Area	1 240 000 km²	Density 10 per km²	% in cities 27%
GDP per cap	$900	Dailling code	+223	Internet .ml	GMT + / - 0

MEDALS TABLE

		Overall G	S	B	Lge G	Cup G	S	Africa G	S	B	City	Stadium	Cap'ty	DoF
1	Doliba AC	35	10	3	19	16	10			3	Bamako	Complex Sportif Hérémakono	5 000	1960
2	Stade Malien	30	9		14	16	8	1			Bamako	Stade 26 mars	50 000	1960
3	Real Bamako	15	8		6	9	7	1			Bamako	Stade Mobido Keita	35 000	
4	Cercle Olympique	2	1			2	1				Bamako	Stade 26 mars	50 000	
5	AS Bamako	1	1			1	1				Bamako	Stade Municipal	5 000	
	USFAS Bamako	1	1			1	1				Bamako	Stade Municipal de USFAS	5 000	
7	AS Sigui Kayes	1				1					Kayes	Stade Abdoulaye Nakoro Cissoko	15 000	
8	Avenir Ségou		4				4				Ségou			
9	AS Nianan Koulikoro		3				3				Koulikoro	Stade Municipal de Koulikoro	8 000	
10	Kayésienne		2				2				Kayes			
11	Africa Sports Gao		1				1				Gao			
	AS Biton Ségou		1				1				Ségou	Stade Amari Daou	15 000	1960
	Jeunesse Sportive		1				1				Ségou	Stade Amari Daou	15 000	
	Mamahira AC Kati		1				1				Kati			
	AS Mandé Bamako		1				1				Bamako	Stade de Mandé	7 000	
	US Sevaré		1				1				Sevaré			
	AS Tata National		1				1				Sikasso	Stade Omnisports	20 000	
	Tibo Club de Mopti		1				1				Mopti	Stade Taïkiri	6 000	
	Sonni Gao		1				1				Gao			
20	AS Commune II										Bamako	Stade Municipal de Commune II	3 000	
	Baoulé Club										Dioila			
	JS Centre Salif Keita										Bamako	Stade Centre Salif Keita	4 000	1995
	AS Bakaridjan										Baraouéli			

RECENT LEAGUE AND CUP RECORD

	Championship						Cup		
Year	Champions	Pts	Runners-up	Pts	Third	Pts	Winners	Score	Runners-up
1999	Djoliba	54	USFAS Bamoko	53	Centre Salif Keita		Stade Malien	1-0	Nianan
2000	Stade Malien	52	Djoliba	47	Centre Salif Keita	40	Cercle Olympique	1-0	Stade Malien
2001	Stade Malien	66	Djoliba	54	Cercle Olympique	45	Stade Malien	5-0	Mamahira Kati
2002	Stade Malien	68	Djoliba	61	Centre Salif Keita	54	Cercle Olympique	2-1	Stade Malien
2003	Stade Malien	62	Djoliba	60	Cercle Olympique	53	Djoliba	2-1	Tata National
2004	Djoliba	63	Stade Malien	58	Centre Salif Keita	58	Djoliba	2-0	Nianan
2005	Stade Malien	64	Cercle Olympique	55	Réal Bamako	47	AS Bamako	1-1 5-4p	Djoliba
2006	Stade Malien	62	Djoliba	60	Cercle Olympique	50	Stade Malien	2-1	AS Bamoko

MALI 2006

PREMIERE DIVISION

	Pl	W	D	L	F	A	Pts	Stade	Djoliba	COB	CSK	AS Bamako	USFAS	Réal	Comune II	Nianan	Sigui	Stade Sik.	Bakaridjan	Tata	Biton
Stade Malien †	26	19	5	2	54	18	62		0-0	1-2	2-0	2-2	1-1	3-2	3-1	3-2	2-0	4-0	3-0	3-0	3-1
Djoliba	26	18	6	2	62	21	60	3-1		0-1	0-3	5-1	2-0	2-2	1-1	1-1	3-0	2-1	2-0		4-1
Cercle Olympique	26	15	5	6	32	20	50	0-3	1-2		1-0	2-0	1-0	1-3	1-3	2-2	3-0	4-0	**2-0**	2-1	1-0
Centre Salif Keita	26	14	5	7	41	19	47	1-2	1-2	0-0		1-1	2-0	1-0	1-2	1-1	4-0	1-0	3-1	3-0	2-1
AS Bamako ‡	26	10	7	9	33	25	37	1-2	0-2	0-1	0-4		0-0	2-0	2-1	2-0	0-0	3-0	3-1	0-0	4-0
USFAS Bamako	26	9	10	7	24	26	37	0-2	1-3	0-0	1-3	2-1		1-1	1-0	0-0	0-0	2-2	1-0	2-0	1-0
Réal Barnako	26	10	6	10	38	34	36	0-3	1-2	3-0	1-0	0-1	1-1		2-2	1-1	0-0	2-1	2-0	1-2	1-0
Comune II Bamako	26	9	8	9	33	36	35	1-1	1-5	0-2	1-1	0-0	0-2	4-2		2-1	1-0	4-1	1-1	0-1	1-1
Nianan Koulikoro	26	7	7	12	26	33	28	0-1	1-3	1-0	1-2	1-0	1-3	2-1	**0-2**		0-1	2-1	0-1	1-1	3-0
Sigui Kayes	26	6	8	12	14	30	26	0-1	1-5	0-0	0-0	0-5	0-1	2-0	3-0	0-2		1-0	0-0	4-0	0-2
Stade Sikasso	26	7	5	14	17	35	26	0-0	1-1	0-1	1-0	0-1	0-1	0-2	2-1	1-0	1-0		2-1	2-0	0-0
Bakaridjan Ségou	26	4	9	13	18	34	21	1-3	1-1	1-2	1-2	0-0	1-1	0-2	1-2	2-0	0-0	1-0		0-0	2-1
Tata National Sikasso	26	4	9	13	11	30	21	0-1	0-2	0-0	0-1	0-1	3-0	0-2	0-0	1-1	0-0	0-0	0-0		2-0
Biton Ségou	26	3	4	19	19	61	13	0-4	0-7	0-2	0-4	0-4	2-2	3-6	1-2	1-2	**0-2**	2-1	1-1	2-0	

5/12/2005 - 27/08/2006 • † Qualified for the CAF Champions League • ‡ Qualified for the CAF Confederation Cup • Matches in bold were awarded

COUPE BDM-SA 2006

Quarter-finals		Semi-finals		Final	
Djoliba					
USFAS Bamako		Djoliba	2		
AS Commune II		Real Bamako	0		
Real Bamako				Djoliba	1
Centre Salif Keita				Stade Malien	0
Cercle Olympique		Centre Salif Keita	0 7p	Stade Modibo Keita, Bamako	
AS Bamako		Stade Malien	0 8p	7-05-2006, Ref: Keita	
Stade Malien				Scorer - Adama Tamboura [90]	

COUPE INPS 2006

Quarter-finals		Semi-finals		Final	
Cercle Olympique	2 4p				
Comunne II	2 3p	Cercle Olympique	1 5p		
Real Bamako	1	Centre Salif Keita	1 3p		
Centre Salif Keita	4			Cercle Olympique	1
Djoliba	3			Stade Malien	0
AS Bamako	0	Djoliba	0	Stade Modibo Keita, Bamako	
USFAS Bamako	1	Stade Malien	2	30-04-2006, Ref: Karembe	
Stade Malien	4			Scorer - Jean Koupaki [49]	

COUPE DU MALI 2006

Round of 16		Quarter-finals		Semi-finals		Final	
Stade Malien	3						
Sonni Gao	0	Stade Malien					
Biton Ségou	0	Tata National Sikasso					
Tata National Sikasso	2			Stade Malien	1 4p		
Bakaridjan Ségou	2			Centre Salif Keita	1 2p		
Stade Sikasso	1	Bakaridjan Ségou					
Racing Timbuktu	0	Centre Salif Keita					
Centre Salif Keita	6					Stade Malien	2
Cercle Olympique	9					AS Bamako ‡	1
Haïré Douentza	1	Cercle Olympique					
Debo Mopti	0	Nianan Koulikoro					
Nianan Koulikoro	2			Cercle Olympique	1 2p		
Sigui Kayes	1			AS Bamako	1 4p		
Moribabougou	0	Sigui Kayes					
Atar Kidal		AS Bamako					
AS Bamako	w-0						

CUP FINAL

Omnisports, Bamako
30-07-2006, Att: 25 000, Ref: Koman
Scorers - Lassana Diallo [33], Amado Diallo [61] for Stade Malien; Ousmane Bagayoko [35] for AS Bamako

‡ Qualified for the CAF Confederation Cup

MLT – MALTA

NATIONAL TEAM RECORD
JULY 10TH 2006 TO JULY 12TH 2010

PL	W	D	L	F	A	%
10	1	2	7	7	23	20

FIFA/COCA-COLA WORLD RANKING

1993	1994	1995	1996	1997	1998	1999	2000	2001	2002	2003	2004	2005	2006	High		Low	
83	78	90	122	133	130	116	119	131	122	129	134	118	119	66	09/94	144	09/06

2006–2007											
08/06	09/06	10/06	11/06	12/06	01/07	02/07	03/07	04/07	05/07	06/07	07/07
122	144	111	115	119	118	114	111	110	112	117	120

A 2-1 victory over Hungary wouldn't usually be the cause for wild celebrations but that's exactly what happened when Malta beat the Hungarians in October 2006. As Malta hadn't won a match in the European Championship for nearly a quarter of a century the celebrations were perhaps justified. It was also Malta's first win in any competitive match since beating Estonia in the 1994 World Cup qualifiers and brought to an end a run of 22 games without a win in all matches played. The hero of the day was Andre Schembri who scored both goals, but there is little doubt that coach Dusan Fitzel has helped improve the game in Malta. By the end of the season Malta were even above

INTERNATIONAL HONOURS
None

Moldova in the table after a draw in Chisinau. Schembri also helped unfancied Marsaxlokk to a first ever trophy. Coached by Brian Talbot, they ran away with the League title, finishing 12 points ahead of Sliema Wanderers. After beating Sliema in the last match of the season, the players brought the trophy back to the southern seaside town on a boat. Daniel Bogdanovic was the top scorer in the League with 31 goals - just one short of the all-time record held by Danilo Doncic. There was drama in the Cup final after a goal deep into injury-time drew Hibernians level with Sliema and they went on to win the Cup on penalties.

THE FIFA BIG COUNT OF 2006

	Male	Female		Total
Number of players	22 451	2 402	Referees and Assistant Referees	99
Professionals	430		Admin, Coaches, Technical, Medical	2 105
Amateurs 18+	7 000		Number of clubs	51
Youth under 18	2 773		Number of teams	325
Unregistered	3 100		Clubs with women's teams	10
Total players	24 853		Players as % of population	6.21%

Malta Football Association (MFA)
Millenium Stand, Floor 2, National Stadium, Ta'Qali, ATD 400, Malta
Tel +356 21 232581   Fax +356 21 245136
info@mfa.com.mt   www.mfa.com.mt
President: MIFSUD Joseph Dr   General Secretary: GAUCHI Joseph
Vice-President: BARTOLO Carmelo   Treasurer: MANFRE Alex   Media Officer: VELLA Alex
Men's Coach: FITZEL Dusan   Women's Coach: BRINCAT Pierre
MFA formed: 1900   UEFA: 1960   FIFA: 1959
Red shirts with white trimmings, White shorts, Red socks or White shirts with red trimmings, Red shorts, White socks

RECENT INTERNATIONAL MATCHES PLAYED BY MALTA

2002	Opponents		Score	Venue	Comp	Scorers	Att	Referee
21-08	FYR Macedonia	L	0-5	Skopje	Fr		4 000	Supraha CRO
7-09	Slovenia	L	0-3	Ljubljana	ECq		7 000	Borovilos GRE
12-10	Israel	L	0-2	Ta'Qali	ECq		5 200	Shebek UKR
16-10	France	L	0-4	Ta'Qali	ECq		10 000	Tudor ROU
20-11	Cyprus	L	1-2	Nicosia	ECq	Mifsud.Mc [90]	5 000	Guenov BUL
2003								
12-02	Kazakhstan	D	2-2	Ta'Qali	Fr	Bogdanovic [15], Nwoko [61]	200	Rogalla SUI
29-03	France	L	0-6	Lens	ECq		40 775	Bozinovski MKD
30-04	Slovenia	L	1-3	Ta'Qali	ECq	Mifsud.Mc [90]	5 000	Hanacsek HUN
7-06	Cyprus	L	1-2	Ta'Qali	ECq	Dimech [72]	3 000	Brugger AUT
19-08	Luxembourg	D	1-1	Luxembourg	Fr	Giglio [55]	2 000	Lehner AUT
10-09	Israel	D	2-2	Antalya	ECq	Mifsud.Mc [51p], Carabott [52]	300	Blareau BEL
11-12	Poland	L	0-4	Larnaca	Fr		300	Kasnaferis GRE
2004								
14-02	Moldova	D	0-0	Ta'Qali	Fr		600	Vialichka BLR
16-02	Estonia	W	5-2	Ta'Qali	Fr	Barbara 2 [12 60], Said [28], Turner [57], Zahra [87]		Orlic MDA
18-02	Belarus	L	0-4	Ta'Qali	Fr			Kaldma EST
31-03	Finland	L	1-2	Ta'Qali	Fr	Mifsud.Mc [90]		Trefoloni ITA
27-05	Germany	L	0-7	Freiburg	Fr		22 000	Stredak SVK
18-08	Faroe Islands	L	2-3	Toftir	Fr	Giglio [50], Mifsud.Mc [65]	1 932	Laursen DEN
4-09	Sweden	L	0-7	Ta'Qali	WCq		4 200	Jakov ISR
9-10	Iceland	D	0-0	Ta'Qali	WCq		1 130	Corpodean ROU
13-10	Bulgaria	L	1-4	Sofia	WCq	Mifsud.Mc [11]	16 800	Richards WAL
17-11	Hungary	L	0-2	Ta'Qali	WCq		14 500	Asumaa FIN
2005								
9-02	Norway	L	0-3	Ta'Qali	Fr		1 000	Malcolm NIR
30-03	Croatia	L	0-3	Zagreb	WCq		15 510	Kapitanis CYP
4-06	Sweden	L	0-6	Gothenburg	WCq		35 593	Ivanov.N RUS
8-06	Iceland	L	1-4	Reykjavik	WCq	Said [58]	4 887	Skomina SVN
17-08	Northern Ireland	D	1-1	Ta'Qali	Fr	Woods [35]	1 850	Riley ENG
3-09	Hungary	L	0-4	Budapest	WCq		5 900	Godulyan UKR
7-09	Croatia	D	1-1	Ta'Qali	WCq	Wellman [74]	916	Briakos GRE
12-10	Bulgaria	D	1-1	Ta'Qali	WCq	Zahra [79]	2 844	Godulyan UKR
2006								
25-02	Moldova	L	0-2	Ta'Qali	Fr		1 125	Silagava GEO
1-03	Georgia	L	0-2	Ta'Qali	Fr		1 100	Banari MDA
4-06	Japan	L	0-1	Dusseldorf	Fr		10 800	Kircher GER
15-08	Slovakia	L	0-3	Bratislava	Fr		2 437	Lajuks LVA
2-09	Bosnia-Herzegovina	L	2-5	Ta'Qali	ECq	Pace [6], Mifsud [85]	2 000	Vejlgaard DEN
6-09	Turkey	L	0-2	Frankfurt	ECq		BCD	Vázquez ESP
11-10	Hungary	W	2-1	Ta'Qali	ECq	Schembri 2 [14 53]	3 600	Ver Eecke BEL
15-11	Lithuania	L	1-4	Paola	Fr	Agius [85]		Lawlor WAL
2007								
7-02	Austria	D	1-1	Ta'Qali	Fr	Agius [8]	3 000	Bartolini SUI
24-03	Moldova	D	1-1	Chisinau	ECq	Mallia [73]	8 033	Aliyev AZE
28-03	Greece	L	0-1	Ta'Qali	ECq		8 700	Garcia POR
2-06	Norway	L	0-4	Oslo	ECq		16 364	Granat POL
6-06	Bosnia-Herzegovina	L	0-1	Sarajevo	ECq		10 500	Richards WAL

Fr = Friendly match • EC = UEFA EURO 2004/2008 • WC = FIFA World Cup • q = qualifier

MALTA NATIONAL TEAM RECORDS AND RECORD SEQUENCES

Records			Sequence records				
Victory	5-0	AZE 1994	Wins	3	1981, 1999-2000	Clean sheets	4	1999-2000
Defeat	1-12	ESP 1983	Defeats	16	1982-1985	Goals scored	7	1991-1992
Player Caps	122	CARABOTT David	Undefeated	6	2001-2002	Without goal	8	2000-2001
Player Goals	23	BUSUTTIL Carmel	Without win	34	1994-1998	Goals against	29	1996-19999

REPUBLIC OF MALTA; REPUBBLIKA TA' MALTA

Capital	Valletta	Language	Maltese, English	Independence	1964
Population	400 214	Area	316 km²	Density 1255 per km²	% in cities 89%
GDP per cap	$17 700	Dailling code	+356	Internet .mt	GMT +/- +1

MEDALS TABLE

		Overall			League			Cup		Europe			City	Stadium	Cap'ty	DoF
		G	S	B	G	S	B	G	S	G	S	B				
1	Sliema Wanderers	45	50	19	26	31	19	19	19				Sliema	Ta'Qali	17 797	1909
2	Floriana	43	23	13	25	11	13	18	12				Floriana	Ta'Qali	17 797	1894
3	Valletta	29	25	20	18	14	20	11	11				Valletta	Ta'Qali	17 797	1943
4	Hibernians	17	19	9	9	9	9	8	10				Paola	Hibernians Ground	8 000	1922
5	Hamrun Spartans	13	12	13	7	10	13	6	2				Hamrun	Ta'Qali	17 797	1907
6	Birkirkara	5	9	3	2	6	3	3	3				Birkirkara	Infetti	2 500	1950
7	Rabat Ajax	3	2	1	2	1	1	1	1				Rabat	Ta'Qali	17 797	1930
8	St. Georges	1	6	5	1	4	5		2				Cospicua			1890
9	Zurrieq	1	2	2			2	1	2				Zurrieq	Ta'Qali	17 797	1949
10	Melita St. Julians	1	2	1		1	1	1	1				Melita	Ta'Qali	17 797	1906
11	Marsaxlokk	1	1	1	1		1		1				Marsaxlokk	Ta'Qali	17 797	1949
12	Gzira United	1		1			1	1					Gzira	Ta'Qali	17 797	1950
13	KOMR Militia	1			1											
14	Birkana United		3			1			2							
15	Marsa		2			2							Marsa	Ta'Qali	17 797	1920
16	Msida St Joseph	1	1					1					Msida	Ta'Qali	17 797	1906

RECENT LEAGUE AND CUP RECORD

	Championship						Cup		
Year	Champions	Pts	Runners-up	Pts	Third	Pts	Winners	Score	Runners-up
1995	Hibernians	43	Sliema Wanderers	39	Valletta	37	Valletta	1-0	Hamrun Spartans
1996	Sliema Wanderers	46	Valletta	42	Floriana	37	Valletta	0-0 1-0	Sliema Wanderers
1997	Valletta	67	Birkirkara	60	Floriana	53	Valletta	2-0	Hibernians
1998	Valletta	65	Birkirkara	63	Sliema Wanderers	56	Hibernians	2-1	Valletta
1999	Valletta	70	Birkirkara	68	Sliema Wanderers	47	Valletta	1-0	Birkirkara
2000	Birkirkara	46	Sliema Wanderers	39	Valletta	36	Sliema Wanderers	4-1	Birkirkara
2001	Valletta	46	Sliema Wanderers	40	Birkirkara	36	Valletta	3-0	Birkirkara
2002	Hibernians	43	Sliema Wanderers	36	Birkirkara	31	Birkirkara	1-0	Sliema Wanderers
2003	Sliema Wanderers	42	Birkirkara	37	Valletta	35	Birkirkara	1-0	Sliema Wanderers
2004	Sliema Wanderers	43	Birkirkara	39	Hibernians	35	Sliema Wanderers	2-0	Marsaxlokk
2005	Sliema Wanderers	40	Birkirkara	38	Hibernians	35	Birkirkara	2-1	Msida St Joseph
2006	Birkirkara	42	Sliema Wanderers	37	Marsaxlokk	36	Hibernians	1-0	Floriana
2007	Marsaxlokk	47	Sliema Wanderers	35	Birkirkara	34	Hibernians	1-1 3-0p	Sliema Wanderers

MALTA 2006-07

PREMIER LEAGUE

	Pl	W	D	L	F	A	Pts	Marsaxlokk	Sliema W.	Birkirkara	Valletta	Hibernians	Msida SJ	Floriana	Pietà Hot.	St George's	Marsa
Marsaxlokk (22) †	28	22	3	3	74	28	47		3-2 1-4	2-2 3-2	1-0 0-1	2-1 3-1	3-0 2-0	4-2	5-0	1-1	4-0
Sliema Wanderers (17) ‡	28	15	7	6	50	34	35	1-3 1-4		1-0 1-1	1-0 2-0	3-1 2-1	3-0 3-2	2-0	4-1	1-0	2-0
Birkirkara (15)	28	15	4	9	48	44	34	1-0 1-6	3-3 2-1		1-3 1-0	3-2 2-1	1-3 2-1	1-0	2-1	4-0	3-0
Valletta (16)	28	13	7	8	55	31	29	1-2 1-3	1-0 1-1	1-0 3-0		1-2 3-1	1-1 1-1	2-2	6-0	4-1	6-1
Hibernians (12) ‡	28	10	3	15	45	52	21	2-2 2-3	2-1 1-1	3-2 0-2	3-1 2-2		0-4 2-0	1-2	0-1	1-2	4-0
Msida St Joseph (16)	28	9	8	11	40	40	19	0-1 0-4	1-1 1-3	5-1 1-3	2-2 2-2	3-0 1-3		1-0	3-1	2-0	1-1
Floriana (12)	24	9	7	8	41	30	22	0-1	1-1	1-1	1-2	4-1	1-1		4-0 1-0	3-0 3-2	4-1 2-2
Pietà Hotspurs (5)	24	6	5	13	29	56	18	0-1	2-2	1-4	0-5	1-2	0-3	1-1 3-1		0-0 4-5	1-1 2-1
St George's (6)	24	3	7	14	23	52	10	1-5	2-3	0-1	0-2	0-3	1-1	0-0 2-6	1-1 1-2		0-0 1-1
Marsa (1)	24	2	5	17	20	58	10	1-5	1-2	1-2	0-3	1-3	0-1	0-2 1-0	3-5 0-2	1-2 3-1	

19/08/2006 - 13/05/2007 • † Qualified for the UEFA Champions League • ‡ Qualified for the UEFA Cup • Points taken forward for the final round in brackets • Top scorer: Daniel BOGDANOVIC, Marsaxlokk 31

MALTA 2006-07 FIRST DIVISION (2)

	Pl	W	D	L	F	A	Pts
Hamrun Spartans	18	12	3	3	34	11	39
Mqabba	18	10	4	4	33	25	34
Tarxien Rainbows	18	7	7	4	30	25	28
St Patrick	18	8	3	7	31	23	27
Senglea Athletic	18	6	9	3	27	22	27
Qormi	18	6	7	5	32	26	25
Vittoriosa Stars	18	5	7	6	27	27	22
Mosta	18	6	4	8	26	32	22
San Gwann	18	2	5	11	20	39	11
Naxxar Lions	18	2	3	13	20	50	9

3/09/2006 - 13/05/2007

MALTA 2006-07 SECOND DIVISION (3)

	Pl	W	D	L	F	A	Pts
Dingli Swallows	22	14	5	3	47	15	47
Mellieha	22	12	6	4	38	25	42
Rabat Ajax	22	11	6	5	36	24	39
Birzebbuga St Peter's	22	10	5	7	31	25	35
Balzan Youth	22	10	4	8	38	25	34
Melita	22	10	4	8	38	28	34
Lija Athletic	22	8	6	8	27	25	30
Lightenings	22	9	3	10	27	32	30
St Andrews	22	7	5	10	21	28	26
Zebbug Rangers	22	5	8	9	18	29	23
Gudja United	22	4	3	15	17	50	15
Gozo	22	2	5	15	20	52	11

23/09/2006 - 6/05/2007

FA TROPHY 2006-07

Round of 16		Quarter-finals		Semi-finals		Final	
Hibernians	Bye						
		Hibernians	4				
Tarxien Rainbows	3 4p	Marsa	0				
Marsa	3 2p			Hibernians	2		
				Valletta	1		
Marsaxlokk	Bye						
		Marsaxlokk	0 3p				
Mqabba	2	Valletta	0 4p				
Valletta	3					Hibernians ‡	1 3p
						Sliema Wanderers	1 0p
Msida St Joseph	5						
Mosta	1	Msida St Joseph	1				
St Patrick	2	Pietà Hotspurs	0				
Pietà Hotspurs	3			Msida St Joseph	0		
				Sliema Wanderers	3		
Birkirkara	Bye						
		Birkirkara	1				
		Sliema Wanderers	2				
Sliema Wanderers	Bye						

‡ Qualified for the UEFA Cup

CUP FINAL

Ta'Qali, 25-05-2007, Ref: Attard

Scorers - Da Silva [92+] for Hibernians; Ian Ciantar [70] for Sliema Wanderers

MNE – MONTENEGRO

NATIONAL TEAM RECORD
JULY 10TH 2006 TO JULY 12TH 2010

PL	W	D	L	F	A	%
3	1	0	2	2	4	33.3

FIFA/COCA-COLA WORLD RANKING

1993	1994	1995	1996	1997	1998	1999	2000	2001	2002	2003	2004	2005	2006	High		Low	
-	-	-	-	-	-	-	-	-	-	-	-	-	-	199	06/07	199	07/07

2006–2007											
08/06	09/06	10/06	11/06	12/06	01/07	02/07	03/07	04/07	05/07	06/07	07/07
-	-	-	-	-	-	-	-	-	-	199	199

Montenegro may be the latest addition to the FIFA family, but they do come with a fair amount of history and tradition, personified by the president of the federation, Dejan Savicevic, who was one of the finest footballers of the 1990s - a Champions League winner with Red Star in 1991 and Milan in 1994, with whom he also won three Serie A titles. Another famous name to emerge from the country was Predrag Mijatovic, the current director of football at Real Madrid, who in 1998 scored the winning goal for Real in the Champions League final against Juventus. Having voted for independence in June 2006, the federation took just two months to launch a championship with

INTERNATIONAL HONOURS
None

Zeta Golubovci, Buducnost Podgorica and Jedinstvo Bijelo Polje all withdrawing from the top division in Serbia. As expected both Zeta and Buducnost dominated the new League, finishing well ahead of the rest in a very tight race won by Zeta. Neither reached the first Cup Final, however, that honour going to winners Rudar who beat Sutjeska 2-1. The national team made its international debut with a 2-1 victory over Hungary in Podgorica with Roma based captain Mirko Vucinic scoring the first goal in the history of his nation. Montenegro's competitive debut will come in the qualifiers for the 2010 FIFA World Cup in South Africa.

THE FIFA BIG COUNT OF 2006

	Male	Female		Total
Number of players	n/a	n/a	Referees and Assistant Referees	n/a
Professionals	n/a		Admin, Coaches, Technical, Medical	n/a
Amateurs 18+	n/a		Number of clubs	n/a
Youth under 18	n/a		Number of teams	n/a
Unregistered	n/a		Clubs with women's teams	n/a
Total players	n/a		Players as % of population	n/a

Football Association of Montenegro (FAM)
Fudbalski savez Crne Gore, Ulica Mirka Banjevica 29, 81000 Podgorica, Montenegro
Tel +381 81 650663   Fax +381 81 650663
fscgmontenegro@cg.yu   www.fscg.cg.yu
President: SAVICEVIC Dejan   General Secretary: DURDEVAC Momir
Vice-President: LAZOVIC Boro   Treasurer: TBD   Media Officer: RADOVIC Aleksandar
Men's Coach: FILIPOVIC Zoran   Women's Coach: TBD
FAM formed: 1931   UEFA: 2007   FIFA: 2007
Red shirts with gold trimmings, Red shorts, Red socks

MAJOR CITIES/TOWNS

Population '000

1	Podgorica	163
2	Niksic	67
3	Pljevlja	27
4	Bijelo Polje	15
5	Cetinje	15
6	Bar	13
7	Herceg Novi	12
8	Berane	11
9	Budva	10
10	Ulcinj	10
11	Tivat	9
12	Rozaje	9
13	Dobrota	8
14	Kotor	5
15	Danilovgrad	5
16	Mojkovac	4
17	Igalo	3
18	Plav	3
19	Tuzi	3
20	Bijela	3
21	Burtaisi	3
22	Kolasin	2
23	Zablejak	2
24	Pluzine	1

REPUBLIC OF MONTENEGRO; REPUBLIKA CRNA GORA

Capital	Podgorica	Language	Serbian, Bosnian, Albanian, Croatian	Independence	2006
Population	630 548	Area	14 026 km²	% in cities	57%
GDP per cap	$3800	Dailling code	+381	Internet .me	GMT +/- +1

RECENT INTERNATIONAL MATCHES PLAYED BY MONTENEGRO

2007	Opponents	Score		Venue	Comp	Scorers	Att	Referee
24-03	Hungary	W	2-1	Podgorica	Fr	Vucinic [64p], Burzanovic [82p]	11 000	Kranjc SVN
1-06	Japan	L	0-2	Shizuoka	Fr		28 635	Svendsen DEN
3-06	Colombia	L	0-1	Matsumoto	Fr		10 070	Ogiya JPN

Fr = Friendly match

MONTENEGRO NATIONAL TEAM RECORDS AND RECORD SEQUENCES

Records			Sequence records					
Victory	2-1	HUN 2007	Wins	1	2007	Clean sheets	0	
Defeat	0-2	JPN 2007	Defeats	2	2007	Goals scored	1	2007
Player Caps	-		Undefeated	1	2007	Without goal	2	2007
Player Goals	-		Without win	2	2007	Goals against	3	2007

MEDALS TABLE

		Overall			League			Cup		Europe			City	Stadium	Cap'ty	DoF
		G	S	B	G	S	B	G	S	G	S	B				
1	Rudar Pljevlja	1						1					Pljevlja	Gradski	7 000	1920
	Zeta Golubovci	1			1								Golubovci, Podgorica	Tresnjica	3 000	1927
3	Buducnost Podgorica		1			1							Podgorica	Pod Goricom	18 000	1925
	Sutjeska Niksic		1						1				Niksic	Gradski	10 800	1927
5	Grbalj Radanovici			1		1							Radanovici, Kotor	u Radanovicima	1 500	1970
6	Bokelj Kotor												Kotor	Pod Vrmcem	5 000	
	Decic Tuzi												Tuzi	Tusko Polje	1 000	1926
	Kom Podgorica												Podgorica	Zlatica	3 000	1958
	Lovcen Cetinje												Cetinje	Obilica Poljana	5 000	1913
	Mladost Podgorica												Podgorica	Cvijetni Brijeg	1 500	1950
	Mogren Budva												Budva	Lugovi	4 000	1920
	OFK Petrovac												Petrovac	Pod Malim Brdom	5 000	
		2	2	1	1	1	1	1	1							

RECENT LEAGUE AND CUP RECORD

Championship						Cup		
Year	Champions	Pts	Runners-up	Pts	Third	Pts	Winners	Score	Runners-up
2007	Zeta Golubovci	78	Buducnost Podg'ica	76	Grbalj Radanovici	49	Rudar Pljevlja	2-1	Sutjeska Niksic

MONTENEGRO 2006–07

PRVA CRNOGORSKA LIGA

	Pl	W	D	L	F	A	Pts	Zeta	Buducnost	Grbalj	Rudar	Mogren	OFK Petrovac	Kom	Sutjeska	Mladost	Decic	Jedinstvo	Berane
Zeta Golubovci §1 †	33	25	4	4	65	18	78		0-3	1-0	2-0 1-0	4-0 1-0	2-1 4-0	1-0	1-0 2-0	3-0	2-0 2-0	4-2 5-1	2-1
Buducnost Podgorica ‡	33	22	10	1	58	12	76	0-0 1-0		0-0 5-1	1-0	1-0	3-0	2-0 2-0	1-0	4-3 2-0	3-2	4-0 1-1	4-0 3-0
Grbalj Radanovici	33	14	7	12	37	30	49	2-1 2-3	1-2		3-0	1-0 0-1	0-2 0-0	1-0 0-2	1-3	2-1 3-1	3-0	2-1 3-0	1-0 0-1
Rudar Pljevlja ‡	33	14	5	14	37	32	47	1-2	0-2 0-0	1-0 0-2		1-0	2-1	2-1 3-0	2-0	4-0 3-1	3-0	3-0 2-1	1-0 1-1
Mogren Budva	33	10	12	11	27	27	42	1-1	1-0 0-0	1-1	3-1 1-2		1-2 2-0 1-0 2-0	1-0	0-0	1-1	1-1	2-0 0-0	
OFK Petrovac	33	10	10	13	24	37	40	1-0	1-1 0-2	0-2	1-0 2-0	0-2		0-0 2-3	1-0	2-1 0-0	0-1	3-2 2-0	1-0 2-1
Kom Podgorica	33	9	11	13	27	31	38	0-1 0-0	1-1	1-0 2-2	1-0	0-0	3-1		1-0 0-1 1-2 2-0 0-1 1-0		4-1		1-1
Sutjeska Niksic	33	10	8	15	24	33	38	0-2	0-0 1-1	0-0	1-0 2-1 1-0 1-2 1-1 1-0	0-0		3-5		1-0		1-0	1-0 2-0
Mladost Podgorica	33	9	11	13	34	49	38	1-1 0-4	0-3	2-0 2-0	1-0	0-0 2-2	0-0	0-0 0-1 1-1			0-0 2-4	3-0 1-1	2-1
Decic Tuzi	33	8	10	15	29	46	34	0-4	0-3 0-1	1-1	1-3 0-0 0-2 0-0 0-1-1		2-2	1-0 2-1	3-0			1-1	2-2
Jedinstvo Bijelo Polje	33	6	13	14	27	51	31	0-3	0-0	0-3	1-1	1-1 1-0	0-0	1-0 0-0 2-2 2-2	0-0	1-0 3-0			1-2 2-0
FK Berane	33	7	7	19	25	48	28	1-4 0-2	0-2	2-0 1-3	0-0	2-0	0-0	1-1 1-0	1-0	3-1 1-3	2-0 1-2	0-1	

11/08/2006 - 26/05/2007 • † Qualified for the UEFA Champions League • ‡ Qualified for the UEFA Cup • Match in bold awarded • § = points deducted • Relegation play-offs: Jedinstvo 1-4 1-0 Bokelj; Ibar 2-2 0-1 Decic • Top scorers: Damir CAKAR, Rudar 16; Zarko KORAC, Zeta 16

MONTENEGRO 2006–07 II LIGA (2)

	Pl	W	D	L	F	A	Pts
Lovcen Cetinje	33	21	6	6	50	21	69
Bokelj Kotor	33	20	6	7	57	24	66
Ibar Rozaje	33	19	6	8	42	25	63
Zabjelo Podgorica	33	14	8	11	50	40	50
Arsenal Tivat	33	11	10	12	40	38	43
Gusinje	33	10	10	13	32	43	40
Bratstvo Cijevna	33	10	9	14	35	41	39
Crvena stijena	33	10	9	14	29	37	39
Jezero Plav	33	11	5	17	27	42	38
Celik Niksic §1	33	10	6	17	31	47	35
Mornar Bar	33	9	8	16	27	40	35
Zora Spuz §1	33	9	5	19	30	52	31

13/08/2006 - 27/05/2007 • § = points deducted

KUPA CRNE GORE 2006–07

Round of 16

Rudar Pljevlja	2 1
FK Berane *	0 1
Otrant *	2 0
Mladost Podgorica	2 3
Crvena stijena *	1 0
Bratstvo Cijevna	0 0
Kom Podgorica	0 2
Grbalj Radanovici *	5 3
Zeta Golubovci	0 3
Buducnost Podgorica *	2 0
Komovi *	1 0
Zora Spuz	5 0
Decic Tuzi	1 3
OFK Petrovac *	1 1
Bokelj Kotor	1 0 3p
Sutjeska Niksic *	0 1 4p

Quarter–finals

Rudar Pljevlja *	2 0
Mladost Podgorica	0 0
Crvena stijena *	1 0
Grbalj Radanovici	1 1
Zeta Golubovci	1 1
Zora Spuz *	1 0
Decic Tuzi	0 1
Sutjeska Niksic *	0 1

Semi–finals

Rudar Pljevlja	2 0
Grbalj Radanovici *	0 0
Zeta Golubovci *	3 0
Sutjeska Niksic	2 1

Final

Rudar Pljevlja ‡	2
Sutjeska Niksic	1

CUP FINAL

Stadion pod Goricom
30-05-2007, Att: 4500, Ref: Kaluderovic

Scorers - Milos Vranes [31], Ramiz Lukovac [35] for Rudar; Drazen Mededovic [54] for Sutjeska

* Home team in the first leg • ‡ Qualified for the UEFA Cup

MOZ – MOZAMBIQUE

NATIONAL TEAM RECORD
JULY 10TH 2006 TO JULY 12TH 2010

PL	W	D	L	F	A	%
7	2	4	1	6	4	57.1

FIFA/COCA-COLA WORLD RANKING

1993	1994	1995	1996	1997	1998	1999	2000	2001	2002	2003	2004	2005	2006	High	Low
104	94	76	85	67	80	101	112	128	125	127	126	130	128	**66** 11/97	**134** 09/06

2006–2007											
08/06	09/06	10/06	11/06	12/06	01/07	02/07	03/07	04/07	05/07	06/07	07/07
127	134	132	128	128	129	131	131	126	118	99	86

The arrival of new coach Mart Nooij injected a fillip of potential into a national team locked in the doldrums for several years. The Dutchman, who had been at the helm of Burkina Faso's team when they competed at the 2003 FIFA U-20 World Cup in the UAE, took his new charges back to his former employer in March 2007 and forced a 1-1 draw that handed renewed vigour to Mozambique's bid to qualify for the 2008 African Nations Cup finals in Ghana. Four more points in the campaign left the Mambas with an outside chance of a surprise qualification for the first time since the tournament in 1998, ironically also in Burkina Faso. Nooij also saw his side through to

INTERNATIONAL HONOURS
None

the semi-final of the COSAFA Castle Cup, matching Mozambique's previous best in the annual regional event. Increased sponsorship and professionalism also ensured a boost to the domestic MocamBola, with clubs now sponsored to travel long distances by plane for their league matches. Desportivo Maputo won the 2006 title and beat Textil Punge 1-0 in the Taca Mocambique final to claim the double. Former European Cup winner Mario Coluna, one-time captain of both Benfica and Portugal, came to the end of his second term at the helm of the Mozambique football federation and was replaced as president by Feizal Sedat, a long-serving committee member.

THE FIFA BIG COUNT OF 2006

	Male	Female		Total
Number of players	885 600	100	Referees and Assistant Referees	1 000
Professionals	400		Admin, Coaches, Technical, Medical	5 100
Amateurs 18+	19 500		Number of clubs	170
Youth under 18	14 800		Number of teams	850
Unregistered	55 000		Clubs with women's teams	0
Total players	885 700		Players as % of population	4.50%

Federação Moçambicana de Futebol (FMF)
Av. Samora Machel, Número 11-2 Andar, Maputo 1467, Mozambique
Tel +258 1 300366   Fax +258 1 300367
fmfbol@tvcabo.co.mz   www.fmf.org.mz
President: SEDAT Feizal   General Secretary: JOHANE Filipe Lucas
Vice-President: NHANCOLO Luis   Treasurer: NHANCOLO Luis   Media Officer: MONTEIRO Manuel
Men's Coach: NOOIJ Mart   Women's Coach: MACUACUA Chadreque
FMF formed: 1976   CAF: 1978   FIFA: 1980
Red shirts with black trimmings, Black shorts, Red socks

RECENT INTERNATIONAL MATCHES PLAYED BY MOZAMBIQUE

2003	Opponents	Score	Venue	Comp	Scorers	Att	Referee
22-03	Lesotho	D 0-0	Maputo	CCr1	W 5-4p		Lwanja MWI
30-03	Burkina Faso	W 1-0	Maputo	CNq	Dario Monteiro [89]		Nunkoo MRI
7-06	Burkina Faso	L 0-4	Ouagadougou	CNq		25 000	Ould Mohamed MTN
22-06	Central African Rep.	W 1-0	Maputo	CNq	Jossias [73p]	15 000	
6-07	Congo	D 0-0	Brazzaville	CNq			
27-07	Zambia	L 2-4	Lusaka	CCqf	To [44], Tico-Tico [60]	10 000	Katjimune NAM
12-10	Guinea	L 0-1	Conakry	WCq		13 400	Ndoye SEN
9-11	Swaziland	W 2-0	Maputo	Fr			
16-11	Guinea	L 3-4	Maputo	WCq	Dario Monteiro 3 [75 80 89]	50 000	Mochubela RSA
2004							
11-04	Swaziland	W 2-0	Maputo	Fr	Nando [42], Amilcar [72]		
18-04	Madagascar	W 2-0	Maputo	CCr1	Tico-Tico [64], Fala-Fala [89]	28 000	Damon RSA
26-05	Botswana	D 0-0	Maputo	Fr		2 000	
31-05	Swaziland	D 1-1	Maputo	Fr	Nelinho [43]	5 000	
13-06	Malawi	W 2-0	Maputo	CCqf	Mabedi OG [42], To [62]	30 000	Kaoma ZAM
25-06	Ghana	L 0-1	Maputo	Fr			
19-09	Angola	L 0-1	Maputo	CCsf		50 000	Jovinala MWI
2005							
16-04	Zimbabwe	L 0-3	Windhoek	CCr1			Mufeti NAM
26-06	Lesotho	W 1-0	Maputo	Fr			
28-08	Zimbabwe	D 0-0	Mutare	Fr			
2006							
29-04	Lesotho	D 0-0	Maseru	CCr1	L 4-5p		Jovinala MWI
30-04	Mauritius	D 0-0	Maseru	CCr1			Moeketsi LES
24-06	Swaziland	W 4-0	Maputo	Fr	Macamo [12], Butoana [22], Manoso [60], Massima [79]		
25-06	Malawi	L 1-2	Maputo	Fr	Lomba Da Costa		
2-09	Senegal	L 0-2	Dakar	CNq			Sule NGA
8-10	Tanzania	D 0-0	Maputo	CNq			Kaoma ZAM
2007							
24-03	Burkina Faso	D 1-1	Ouagadougou	CNq	Mano [2]		Imiere NGA
28-04	Seychelles	W 2-0	Maputo	CCr1	Bino 2 [51 77]		Mpopo LES
29-04	Zimbabwe	D 0-0	Maputo	CCr1	W 5-4p		Seechun MRI
3-06	Burkina Faso	W 3-1	Maputo	CNq	Dario Monteiro [4p], Tico-Tico 2 [42 48]		
17-06	Senegal	D 0-0	Maputo	CNq			

Fr = Friendly match • CN = CAF African Cup of Nations • CC = COSAFA Cup • WC = FIFA World Cup • q = qualifier

MOZAMBIQUE NATIONAL TEAM RECORDS AND RECORD SEQUENCES

Records			Sequence records				
Victory	6-1	LES 1980	Wins	5	1989-1990	Clean sheets	4	Four times
Defeat	0-6	ZIM 1979, ZIM 1980	Defeats	7	1998	Goals scored	15	1980-1982
Player Caps	n/a		Undefeated	7	1995	Without goal	3	1986, 1989, 1991
Player Goals	n/a		Without win	18	1985-1989	Goals against	17	1985-1989

MOZAMBIQUE COUNTRY INFORMATION

Capital	Maputo	Independence	1975 from Portugal	GDP per Capita	$1 200
Population	18 811 731	Status	Republic	GNP Ranking	123
Area km²	801 590	Language	Portuguese, Makhuwa, Tsonga	Dialling code	+258
Population density	23 per km²	Literacy rate	47%	Internet code	.mz
% in urban areas	34%	Main religion	Indigenous 50%, Christian 30%	GMT +/−	+2
Towns/Cities ('000)	Maputo 1 191; Matola 544; Beira 531; Nampula 388; Chomoio 257; Nacala 225; Quelimane 188				
Neighbours (km)	South Africa 491; Swaziland 105; Zimbabwe 1 231; Zambia 419; Malawi 1 569; Tanzania 756; Indian Ocean 2 470				
Main stadia	Estádio da Machava – Maputo 6 000; Estádio do Ferroviário – Beira 7 000				

MOZAMBIQUE 2006

CAMPEONATO NACIONAL DA 1ª DIVISAO

	Pl	W	D	L	F	A	Pts	GD Maputo	Ferro M.	Costa	Ferro B.	Academ'ca	Têxtil	Chingale	Ferro N.	Maxaquene	Benfica	Red Star	Sporting
Desportivo Maputo †	22	14	5	3	33	8	47		0-1	1-0	1-0	2-0	2-0	2-1	3-1	1-0	5-0	4-0	2-0
Ferroviário Maputo	22	11	5	6	22	14	38	1-3		0-1	1-2	2-0	2-0	0-2	1-1	1-0	2-0	2-0	0-0
Costa do Sol	22	9	8	5	17	9	35	0-0	0-1		1-0	1-1	0-0	1-0	1-0	2-0	1-1	0-0	2-0
Ferroviário Beira	22	8	8	6	16	12	32	1-0	0-0	1-0		0-1	1-1	1-2	0-0	2-0	1-0	2-0	2-1
Académica Maputo	22	7	9	6	17	19	30	0-2	1-1	0-2	1-1		0-0	1-1	0-0	2-1	1-1	1-0	1-0
Têxtil Púnguè	22	7	8	7	14	17	29	0-1	1-2	0-3	0-0	0-0		2-1	1-0	0-0	1-0	1-0	3-0
Chingale Tete	22	7	8	7	13	13	29	0-0	1-0	0-1	0-0	0-1	1-1		0-0	1-0	1-0	0-0	1-0
Ferroviário Nampula	22	6	9	7	16	17	27	1-0	1-0	2-0	0-0	2-1	2-0	0-0		0-1	2-0	1-2	0-0
Maxaquene	22	6	8	8	14	14	26	1-1	0-1	0-0	1-1	2-1	2-0	0-0			0-1	1-0	0-0
Benfica Quelimane	22	6	7	9	12	21	25	0-0	0-0	1-1	1-0	0-0	0-2	1-0	3-1	0-0		0-1	2-1
Estrela Vermelha	22	6	6	10	13	24	24	0-2	0-2	0-0	1-0	1-1	0-1	2-0	2-2	0-2	1-0		2-2
Sporting Nampula	22	1	7	14	7	26	10	1-1	1-2	1-0	0-1	0-1	0-0	0-1	0-0	0-3	0-1	0-1	

11/03/2006 - 12/11/2006 • † Qualified for the CAF Champions League • Estrela Vermelha won a four way relegation play-off to retain their place

TACA NACIONAL 2006

Round of 16		Quarter–finals		Semi–finals		Final	
Desportivo Maputo	6						
Vilankulo	1	Desportivo Maputo	3				
Muçulmano Matola	0	Ferroviário Maputo	0				
Ferroviário Maputo	3			Desportivo Maputo	w-0		
Chingale Tete	2			Benfica Quelimane			
Desportivo Chingussura	0	Chingale Tete	0				
Leões de Vumba	0	Benfica Quelimane	1				
Benfica Quelimane	3					Desportivo Maputo	1
Liga Muçulmana	2					Têxtil Púnguè ‡	0
Gaza Xai-Xai	1	Liga Muçulmana	2				
Sporting Nampula	0	Desportiva Pemba	0				
Desportiva Pemba	3			Liga Muçulmana	0		
Costa do Sol	1			Têxtil Púnguè	1		
Maxaquene	0	Costa do Sol	1 3p				
Desportivo Chimoio	0	Têxtil Púnguè	1 4p				
Têxtil Púnguè	3						

CUP FINAL
Machava, Maputo
26-11-2006, Ref: Massango

Scorer - Abílio 19

‡ Qualified for the CAF Confederation Cup

CLUB DIRECTORY

Club	City/Town	Stadium	Capacity	Lge	Cup
Costa do Sol	Maputo	Costa do Sol	10 000	8	9
Desportivo	Maputo	Desportivo	4 000	5	1
Ferroviário	Beira	Ferroviário	7 000	0	2
Ferroviário	Maputo	Machava	60 000	7	4
Ferroviário	Nampula	Nampula	4 000	1	1
Lichinga	Lichinga	Lichinga	3 000	0	0
Matchedje	Maputo	Costa do Sol	10 000	2	0
Maxaquene	Maputo	Maxaquene	15 000	4	6
Têxtil Púnguè	Beira	Chiveve	5 000	1	0

RECENT LEAGUE AND CUP RECORD

	Championship						Cup		
Year	Champions	Pts	Runners-up	Pts	Third	Pts	Winners	Score	Runners-up
1999	Ferroviário Maputo	23	Costa do Sol	23	Chingale Tete	14	Costa do Sol	5-0	Sporting Nampula
2000	Costa do Sol	51	Ferroviário Maputo	47	Matchadje	38	Costa do Sol	1-0	Matchadje
2001	Costa do Sol	45	Ferroviário Maputo	38	Maxaquene	33	Maxaquene	3-1	Textáfrica Chimoio
2002	Ferroviário Maputo	50	Maxaquene	46	Costa do Sol	43	Costa do Sol	2-0	Académica Maputo
2003	Maxaquene	47	Costa do Sol	43	Desportivo Maputo	40	Ferroviário Nampula	1-1 5-4p	Ferroviário Maputo
2004	Ferroviário Nampula	44	Desportivo Maputo	42	Ferroviário Maputo	35	Ferroviário Maputo	5-1	Textáfrica Chimoio
2005	Ferroviário Maputo	46	Costa do Sol	41	Desportivo Maputo	41	Ferroviário Beira	1-0	Costa do Sol
2006	Desportivo Maputo	47	Ferroviário Maputo	38	Costa do Sol	35	Desportivo Maputo	1-0	Têxtil Púnguè

MRI – MAURITIUS

NATIONAL TEAM RECORD
JULY 10TH 2006 TO JULY 12TH 2010

PL	W	D	L	F	A	%
8	0	2	6	2	14	12.5%

FIFA/COCA-COLA WORLD RANKING

1993	1994	1995	1996	1997	1998	1999	2000	2001	2002	2003	2004	2005	2006	High		Low	
133	146	154	150	151	148	118	118	124	126	123	140	143	138	116	08/00	158	05/96

2006–2007											
08/06	09/06	10/06	11/06	12/06	01/07	02/07	03/07	04/07	05/07	06/07	07/07
139	126	139	139	138	144	142	144	145	142	145	144

The Mauritius national team continued to have a familiar look about it despite the furious efforts of coach Sarjoo Gowreesunkur to unearth new talent. With a limited pool of players on the Indian Ocean Island, the coach turned to Mauritius communities in Australia and Europe for new playing personnel but without much success. Such was his desperation that he even gave an international cap to two players from the amateur leagues in Victoria, Australia, but both Thierry Boi and Chris Driver looked hopelessly out of their depth in the brief time they were given on the pitch. The reason for the need for new talent is the island's record run of 14 games since their last win in an

INTERNATIONAL HONOURS
None

international – a 2-0 triumph over nearby Madagascar in a friendly played in early 2005. It is even a year further back since Mauritius last won a competitive game, beating a full strength South Africa in the first round of the COSAFA Castle Cup in January, 2004. Curepipe Starlight won their first-ever league title with a runaway triumph in the Premier League, finishing 12 points ahead of second-placed Pamplemousse, who were the defending champions. The previous month Starlight had won the Republic Cup, but the main cup tournament the Skylight MFA Cup was won by Petite Rivière Noire, who beat AS Port-Louis in the final at the end of the season.

THE FIFA BIG COUNT OF 2006

	Male	Female		Total
Number of players	73 600	3 200	Referees and Assistant Referees	100
Professionals	0		Admin, Coaches, Technical, Medical	4 400
Amateurs 18+	12 500		Number of clubs	70
Youth under 18	4 600		Number of teams	700
Unregistered	6 700		Clubs with women's teams	0
Total players	76 800		Players as % of population	6.19%

Mauritius Football Association (MFA)
Football House, Trianon, Mauritius
Tel +230 4652200   Fax +230 4547909
mfaho@intnet.mu   www.mauritiusfootball.com
President: JODHA Premlall   General Secretary: VUDDAMALAY Ananda
Vice-President: ELAHEE Mohammed Anwar   Treasurer: BOWUD A.H. Nazir   Media Officer: ARNASSALON Manen
Men's Coach: GOWREESUNKUR Sarjoo   Women's Coach: JULES Alain
MFA formed: 1952   CAF: 1962   FIFA: 1962
Red shirts, Red shorts, Red socks

RECENT INTERNATIONAL MATCHES PLAYED BY MAURITIUS

2002	Opponents	Score		Venue	Comp	Scorers	Att	Referee
1-08	Swaziland	W	1-0	Mbabane	Fr	Zuel [2]		
3-08	Swaziland	D	0-0	Big Bend	Fr			Sitriongomyane SWZ
26-09	Seychelles	W	1-0	Port Louis	Fr	Laboiteuse [70]	166	Roopnah MRI
12-10	Madagascar	L	0-1	Port Louis	CNq		1 819	Maillet SEY
2003								
22-02	Madagascar	L	1-2	Antananarivo	CCr1	Appou [50]	25 000	Motau RSA
29-03	Egypt	L	0-1	Port Louis	CNq		800	
8-06	Egypt	L	0-7	Cairo	CNq		40 000	Abdalla LBY
6-07	Madagascar	W	2-0	Antananarivo	CNq	Perle [13], Appou [30p]		
30-08	Madagascar	W	3-1	Curepipe	IOr1	Appou 2 [11p 56], Perle [15]	4 500	Ramsamy REU
2-09	Seychelles	D	0-0	Curepipe	IOr1			
4-09	Comoros †	W	5-0	Curepipe	IOsf	Perle 2 [8 87], Appou 2 [42p 70], Cundasamy [49]	4 500	Labrosse SEY
6-09	Reunion	W	2-1	Curepipe	IOf	Cundasamy [41], Ithier [83]	10 000	Labrosse SEY
11-10	Uganda	L	0-3	Kampala	WCq		6 800	Tangawarima ZIM
16-11	Uganda	W	3-1	Curepipe	WCq	Naboth [37], Mourgine [70], Louis [82]	2 465	Maillet SEY
2004								
10-01	South Africa	W	2-0	Curepipe	CCr1	Lekgetho OG [53], Perle [81]	5 230	Raolimanana MAD
31-07	Zambia	L	1-3	Lusaka	CCqf	Appou [70]		Manuel ZIM
2005								
26-02	Madagascar	W	2-0	Curepipe	CCr1	Appou [44], Louis [48]		Fakude SWZ
27-02	South Africa	L	0-1	Curepipe	CCr1			Mnkantjo ZIM
23-10	Madagascar	L	0-2	Antananarivo	Fr			
2006								
29-04	Angola	L	1-5	Maseru	CCr1	Louis [2]		Moeketsi LES
30-04	Mozambique	D	0-0	Maseru	CCr1	L 4-5p		Jovinala MWI
26-06	Tanzania	L	1-2	Victoria	Fr	Godon [17]		
28-06	Seychelles	L	1-2	Victoria	Fr	Mourgine [90]		
3-09	Tunisia	D	0-0	Curepipe	CNq			Ncobo RSA
7-10	Seychelles	L	1-2	Roche Caiman	CNq	Godon [53]		Raolimanana MAD
2007								
21-03	Côte d'Ivoire	L	0-3	Bellevue	Fr			
25-03	Sudan	L	1-2	Curepipe	CNq	Naboth [61]		Mwanza ZAM
26-05	Swaziland	D	0-0	Mbabane	CCr1	W 6-5p		Labrosse SEY
27-05	South Africa	L	0-2	Mbabane	CCr1			Mufeti NAM
2-06	Sudan	L	0-3	Omdurman	CNq			
16-10	Tunisia	L	0-2	Rades/Tunis	CNq			

Fr = Friendly match • CN = CAF African Cup of Nations • CC = COSAFA Cup • IO = Indian Ocean Games • WC = FIFA World Cup
q = qualifier • r1 = first round group • qf = quarter-final • sf = semi-final • f = final • † not a full international

MAURITIUS NATIONAL TEAM RECORDS AND RECORD SEQUENCES

Records			Sequence records					
Victory	15-0	REU 1950	Wins	17	1947-1955	Clean sheets	4	1957-1958
Defeat	0-7	EGY 2003	Defeats	6	1974-1975	Goals scored	25	1947-1958
Player Caps	n/a		Undefeated	17	1947-1955	Without goal	6	1994-1995
Player Goals	n/a		Without win	14	2005-2007	Goals against	10	1999-2000

MAURITIUS COUNTRY INFORMATION

Capital	Port Louis	Independence	1968 from the UK	GDP per Capita	$11 400
Population	1 220 481	Status	Republic	GNP Ranking	116
Area km²	2 040	Language	French, English	Dialling code	+230
Population density	598 per km²	Literacy rate	85%	Internet code	.mu
% in urban areas	41%	Main religion	Hindu 52%, Christian 28%	GMT +/–	+4
Towns/Cities ('000)	Port Louis 155; Beau Bassin-Rose Hill 110; Vascoas-Pheinix 107; Curepipe 84; Quatre Bras 80				
Neighbours (km)	Indian Ocean 2 740				
Main stadia	George V Stadium – Curepipe 10 000; Auguste Vollaire – Port Louis				

MAURITIUS 2006-07

PREMIER LEAGUE

	Pl	W	D	L	F	A	Pts	Starlight	Pampl'ses	Savanne	ASPL 2000	PAS Mates	ASVP	BB/RH	Olympique	Rempart	PR Noire	Faucon	Grand Port
Curepipe Starlight †	22	17	3	2	48	16	54		2-1	1-1	0-1	3-2	1-0	0-2	3-2	5-1	3-0	5-1	1-0
Pamplemousses SC	22	13	3	6	42	23	42	1-3		1-3	0-0	3-2	2-0	1-0	3-0	2-0	1-0	0-2	1-0
Savanne SC	22	12	5	5	43	25	41	1-3	1-0		1-0	0-0	1-1	4-2	0-3	2-3	5-0	1-0	3-1
AS Port-Louis 2000	22	10	8	4	38	16	38	2-2	1-5	1-0		0-0	1-1	0-1	0-0	0-0	0-1	5-0	6-0
Pointe-aux-Sables	22	10	4	8	29	23	34	1-1	0-1	1-5	1-3		2-0	3-1	2-1	5-0	2-1	1-0	3-0
AS Vacoas-Phoenix	22	9	4	9	24	20	31	0-1	2-1	2-0	1-1	0-2		0-0	1-0	2-0	0-2	1-0	3-0
Beau-Basin/Rose Hill	22	8	6	8	26	28	30	1-2	2-2	1-1	1-2	1-0	2-1		1-1	0-1	0-1	3-2	2-1
Olympique Moka	22	8	5	9	41	30	29	0-3	2-2	2-2	0-1	0-1	2-0	4-1		3-1	4-1	4-0	4-0
AS Rivière Rempart	22	6	6	10	22	47	24	0-2	1-5	1-3	0-7	2-0	0-3	0-0	2-2		3-2	2-1	3-1
Petite Rivière Noire	22	6	4	12	27	44	22	0-1	0-1	2-5	0-4	0-0	1-3	2-2	5-4	1-1		1-0	3-0
Faucon Flacq SC	22	5	3	14	15	36	18	0-2	1-2	0-3	0-1	1-0	1-0	0-1	1-0	0-0	2-1		2-2
Grand Port United	22	0	5	17	13	60	5	0-5	1-7	0-1	2-2	0-1	0-3	0-2	0-3	1-1	3-3	1-1	

24/09/2006 - 29/04/2007 • † Qualified for the CAF Champions League • Top scorer: Praxis RABEMANANJARA, Pamplemousses 19

REPUBLIC CUP 2007

First round		Quarter–finals		Semi–finals		Final	
AS Vacoas-Phoenix	1	Curepipe Starlight	3				
Faucon Flacq SC	0	AS Vacoas-Phoenix	0	Curepipe Starlight	1		
Petite Rivière Noire	0	US Beau-Basin/RH	0 4p	AS Port Louis 2000	0		
AS Port Louis 2000	2	AS Port Louis 2000	0 5p			Curepipe Starlight	1
Rivière du Rempart	w-o	Rivière du Rempart	1 4p			Savanne SC	0
Grand Port United		Pamplemousses SC	1 2p	Rivière du Rempart	0	Stade George V, Curepipe
PAS Mates	1 2p	Olympique de Moka	0	Savanne SC	2	11-03-2007, Att: 6000, Ref: Parahoo
Savanne SC	1 4p	Savanne SC	5			Scorer: Kersley Appou [29]

SKYLINE MFA CUP 2006-07

Round of 16		Quarter–finals		Semi–finals		Final	
Petite Rivière Noire	4						
Belin SC	0	Petite Rivière Noire	3				
Entente BR/RM	1	Bolton City	1				
Bolton City	2			Petite Rivière Noire	1		
US Highlands	1 4p			Olympique Moka	0		
Faucon Flacq SC	1 1p	US Highlands	0				
Case Noyale	0	Olympique Moka	4				
Olympique Moka	5					Petite Rivière Noire ‡	2
Curepipe Starlight SC	5					AS Port-Louis 2000	0
AS Rivière Rempart	0	Curepipe Starlight SC	2				
St Etienne	0	Pointe-aux-Sables	0			CUP FINAL	
Pointe-aux-Sables	2			Curepipe Starlight SC	0	Stade George V, Curepipe
Pamplemousses SC	1			AS Port-Louis 2000	1	13-05-2007, Att: 2000, Ref: Simisse
Beau-Basin/Rose Hill	0	Pamplemousses SC	1			Scorers - Daniel Dig-Dig [24], Dany Février [72]
Cercle Joachim	0	AS Port-Louis 2000	2			for PR Noire
AS Port-Louis 2000	2			‡ Qualified for the CAF Confederation Cup			

RECENT LEAGUE AND CUP RECORD

	Championship							Cup		
Year	Champions	Pts	Runners-up	Pts	Third	Pts		Winners	Score	Runners-up
2001	Olympique Moka	57	AS Port Louis 2000	44	US Beau-Basin/RH			US Beau-Basin/RH	2-1	Olympique Moka
2002	AS Port Louis 2000	58	US Beau-Basin/RH	52	Faucon Flacq	40		AS Port Louis 2000	3-0	Olympique Moka
2003	AS Port Louis 2000	26	Faucon Flacq SC	21	US Beau-Basin/RH	21		Savanne SC	1-1 4-2p	AS Port Louis 2000
2004	AS Port Louis 2000	56	Pamplemousses SC	43	Savanne SC	37		Savanne SC	3-2	Faucon Flacq SC
2005	AS Port Louis 2000	31	Savanne SC	26	US Beau-Basin/RH	23		AS Port Louis 2000	2-0	PAS Mates
2006	Pamplemousses SC	28	AS Vacoas-Phoenix	23	Curepipe Starlight	20		Curepipe Starlight	0-0 9-8p	Savanne SC
2007	Curepipe Starlight	54	Pamplemousses SC	42	Savanne SC	41		Petite Rivière Noire	2-0	AS Port Louis 2000

MSR – MONTSERRAT

NATIONAL TEAM RECORD
JULY 10TH 2006 TO JULY 12TH 2010

PL	W	D	L	F	A	%
0	0	0	0	0	0	0

FIFA/COCA-COLA WORLD RANKING

1993	1994	1995	1996	1997	1998	1999	2000	2001	2002	2003	2004	2005	2006	High	Low
-	-	-	-	-	-	201	202	203	203	204	202	202	198	**196** 07/06	**205** 10/04

	2006–2007										
08/06	09/06	10/06	11/06	12/06	01/07	02/07	03/07	04/07	05/07	06/07	07/07
197	198	198	198	198	199	199	199	199	199	199	199

The decision by the Montserrat Football Association not to enter the Digicel Caribbean Cup - one of only four Caribbean nations not to do so - means that the national team has not played a game since October 2004. It wasn't for lack of trying but it is becoming increasingly difficult to put a team together given the association's meagre resources. There just aren't enough players on the island to support a national team, let alone a League. Wigan's Titus Bramble and his brother Tesfaye, who plays for Stockport County in England, qualify to play for Montserrat through their parents and there are others like Notts County's Junior Mendes and Wayne Dyer, who now plays in non League

INTERNATIONAL HONOURS
None

football, but since the flurry of activity in 2004 when Ruel Fox was coach, there has been little success in rekindling that pioneering spirit. The test will come with the qualifiers for the 2010 FIFA World Cup, which Montserrat have entered. With the capital Plymouth lying abandoned due to the devastation caused by the volcanic eruptions of Mount Soufriere, FIFA approved a second Goal project in December 2006 aimed at improving facilities at the training centre in Blakes. This included the installation of seating and the construction of dressing rooms and offices for the association at a cost of nearly US$500,000.

THE FIFA BIG COUNT OF 2006

	Male	Female		Total
Number of players	600	100	Referees and Assistant Referees	6
Professionals	0		Admin, Coaches, Technical, Medical	0
Amateurs 18+	100		Number of clubs	0
Youth under 18	100		Number of teams	10
Unregistered	100		Clubs with women's teams	0
Total players	700		Players as % of population	7.42%

Montserrat Football Association Inc. (MFA)
PO Box 505, Woodlands, Montserrat
Tel +1 664 4918744   Fax +1 664 4918801
monfa@candw.ms   www.montserrat-football.com
President: CASSELL Vincent   General Secretary: TBD
Vice-President: POLLIDORE Clement   Treasurer: TBD   Media Officer: None
Men's Coach: LABORDE Ottley   Women's Coach: LAKE Cecil
MFA formed: 1994   CONCACAF: 1996   FIFA: 1996
Green shirts with black and white stripes, Green shorts, Green socks

RECENT INTERNATIONAL MATCHES PLAYED BY MONTSERRAT

2002	Opponents	Score	Venue	Comp	Scorers	Att	Referee
No international matches played in 2002 after June							
2003							
No international matches played in 2003							
2004							
29-02	Bermuda	L 0-13	Hamilton	WCq		3 000	Kennedy USA
21-03	Bermuda	L 0-7	Plymouth	WCq		250	Charles DMA
31-10	St Kitts and Nevis	L 1-6	Basseterre	CCq	Adams [81]		Bedeau GRN
2-11	Antigua and Barbuda	L 4-5	Basseterre	CCq	Tesfaye Bramble [36], Fox [41], Mendes [50], Farrel [61]		Phillip GRN
4-11	St Lucia	L 0-3	Basseterre	CCq	Not played. St Lucia awarded the match 3-0		
2005							
No international matches played in 2005							
2006							
No international matches played in 2006							
2007							
No international matches played in 2007 before August							

Fr = Friendly match • CC = Digicel Caribbean Cup • WC = FIFA World Cup • q = qualifier

MONTSERRAT NATIONAL TEAM RECORDS AND RECORD SEQUENCES

Records			Sequence records					
Victory	3-2	AIA 1995	Wins	2	1995	Clean sheets	1	1995
Defeat	0-13	BER 2004	Defeats	16	1995-2004	Goals scored	3	1996-99, 2000-01
Player Caps	n/a		Undefeated	2	1995	Without goal	4	2004-2004
Player Goals	n/a		Without win	16	1995-2004	Goals against		

RECENT LEAGUE RECORD

	Championship
Year	Champions
1996	Royal Montserrat Police Force
1997	Abandoned
1998	Not held
1999	Not Held
2000	Royal Montserrat Police Force
2001	Royal Montserrat Police Force
2002	Not held due to season readjustment
2003	Royal Montserrat Police Force
2004	Ideal SC
2005	Not held
2006	Not held

MONTSERRAT COUNTRY INFORMATION

Capital	Plymouth	Status	UK Dependent Territory	GDP per Capita	$3 400
Population	9 245			GNP Ranking	n/a
Area km²	102	Language	English	Dialling code	+1 664
Population density	91 per km²	Literacy rate	97%	Internet code	.ms
% in urban areas	n/a	Main religion	Christian	GMT + / –	-4
Towns/Cities	Cork Hill 732; Salem 680; Saints Johns 627; Bransby Point 550; Davy Hill 366; Geralds 314				
Neighbours (km)	Caribbean Sea 40				
Main stadia	Blakes Estate Football Ground – Plymouth				

MTN – MAURITANIA

MAURITANIA NATIONAL TEAM RECORD
JULY 10TH 2006 TO JULY 12TH 2010

PL	W	D	L	F	A	%
9	2	3	4	15	13	38.8

FIFA/COCA-COLA WORLD RANKING

1993	1994	1995	1996	1997	1998	1999	2000	2001	2002	2003	2004	2005	2006	High	Low
144	137	85	113	135	142	160	161	177	180	165	175	178	133	**85** 12/95	**182** 05/03

	2006–2007										
08/06	09/06	10/06	11/06	12/06	01/07	02/07	03/07	04/07	05/07	06/07	07/07
166	124	127	133	133	122	121	122	129	129	124	136

Mauritania won a rare competitive match at the start of the 2008 African Nations Cup qualifiers but their achievement remained clouded by opposition protests over the use of players previously 'imported' from France. Striker Yoann Langlet, scorer of three goals in the Nations Cup preliminaries, was one of a trio of players offered Mauritanian nationality in 2003 by former club coach Noel Tosi to play for the country in the 2006 FIFA World Cup qualifying campaign. Surprisingly, even after the departure of Tosi, Langlet continued to be part of 'Mourabitounes' squad for the Nations Cup Group Two matches, including scoring in the 4-0 win over Botswana in

INTERNATIONAL HONOURS
None

September 2006, which got their campaign off to the best possible start. Mauritania also brought in Algerian coach Ali Fergani, a veteran of the African scene, in an effort to take their fortunes to a higher level. Subsequent results, however, saw them drop out of the race. There was also a record 8-2 win over Somalia in an Arab Nations Cup qualifier in Lebanon at the end of 2006. In the league, NASR Sebkha won the championship in the board room after ASC Concorde were docked six points after being found to have used an unregistered player in three matches towards the end of the League campaign, two of which were won.

THE FIFA BIG COUNT OF 2006

	Male	Female		Total
Number of players	137 920	0	Referees and Assistant Referees	177
Professionals	0		Admin, Coaches, Technical, Medical	700
Amateurs 18+	3 520		Number of clubs	68
Youth under 18	1 600		Number of teams	250
Unregistered	14 300		Clubs with women's teams	0
Total players	137 920		Players as % of population	4.34%

Fédération de Foot-Ball de la République Islamique de Mauritanie (FFM)
Case postale 566, Nouakchott, Mauritania
Tel +222 5 241860   Fax +222 5 241861
ffrim@mauritel.mr   www.none
President: OULD BOUKHREIS Mohemed Salem   General Secretary: OULD MOHAMEDEN Gleiguem
Vice-President: OULD MOHAMED VALL Adallahi   Treasurer: OULD MAOULOUD Cheik   Media Officer: None
Men's Coach: FERGANI Ali   Women's Coach: FALL Rey
FFM formed: 1961   CAF: 1968   FIFA: 1964
Green shirts with yellow trimmings, Yellow shorts, Green socks

RECENT INTERNATIONAL MATCHES PLAYED BY MAURITANIA

2003	Opponents	Score		Venue	Comp	Scorers	Att	Referee
29-03	Kenya	L	0-4	Nairobi	CNq		30 000	Berhane ERI
31-05	Gambia	L	1-4	Banjul	Fr	Mouhamed Khouma		
6-06	Kenya	D	0-0	Nouakchott	CNq		6 000	Keita GUI
21-06	Cape Verde Islands	L	0-3	Praia	CNq			
5-07	Togo	D	0-0	Nouakchott	CNq		2 000	Djingarey NIG
12-10	Zimbabwe	L	0-3	Harare	WCq		55 000	Damon RSA
14-11	Zimbabwe	W	2-1	Nouakchott	WCq	Yoann Langlet [3], Sidibe.A [10]	3 000	Keita GUI
2004								
No international matches played in 2004								
2005								
No international matches played in 2005								
2006								
3-09	Botswana	W	4-0	Nouakchott	CNq	Seydou Mbodji [3], Moussa Karamoko 2 [8] [23], Yohan Langlet [83]		Djaoupe TOG
8-10	Burundi	L	1-3	Bujumbura	CNq	Mohamed Benyachou [51]		Abdelrahman SUD
21-12	Lebanon	D	0-0	Beirut	ARr1			Al Jannaz BHR
24-12	Sudan	L	0-2	Beirut	ARr1			Ebel KUW
27-12	Somalia	W	8-2	Beirut	ARr1			
2007								
20-03	Libya	D	0-0	Tripoli	Fr			
25-03	Egypt	L	0-3	Cairo	CNq			Benouza ALG
3-06	Egypt	D	1-1	Nouakchott	CNq	Yohan Langlet [72]		
16-06	Botswana	L	1-2	Gaborone	CNq	Yohan Langlet [75]		

Fr = Friendly match • CN = CAF African Cup of Nations • AR = Arab Cup • WC = FIFA World Cup • q = qualifier • r1 = first round group

MAURITANIA NATIONAL TEAM RECORDS AND RECORD SEQUENCES

Records			Sequence records				
Victory	8-2	SOM 2006	Wins	2	Three times	Clean sheets	4	1994-95, 1995-96
Defeat	0-14	GUI 1972	Defeats	11	1976-1979	Goals scored	9	1979-1980
Player Caps	n/a		Undefeated	7	1994-95, 1995-96	Without goal	5	1983-1984
Player Goals	n/a		Without win	34	1995-2003	Goals against	25	1963-1979

RECENT LEAGUE AND CUP RECORD

	Championship		Cup		
Year	Champions	Winners	Score	Runners-up
1997	Not held	ASC Sonalec	2-0	Garde Nationale
1998	Garde Nationale	ASC Sonalec	3-2	SDPA Trarza
1999	SDPA Rosso	ASC Police	2-1	Garde Nationale
2000	ASC Mauritel	Air Mauritanie	4-0	ASC Gendrim
2001	FC Nouadhibou	Garde Nationale		
2002	FC Nouadhibou	No tournament held		
2003	NASR Sebkha	Entente Sebkha	1-0	ACS Ksar
2004	ACS Ksar	FC Nouadhibou	1-0	ACS Ksar
2005	NASR Sebkha	Entente Sebkha	2-1	ASC Socogim
2006	ASC Mauritel	NASR Sebkha	1-0	Trarza Rosso
2007	NASR Sebkha			

MAURITANIA 2006-07 CHAMPIONNAT NATIONAL

	Pl	W	D	L	F	A	Pts
NASR Sebkha	22	10	11	1	30	13	41
SNIM Nouadhibou	22	12	5	5	27	15	41
Mauritel	22	10	9	3	32	13	39
ACS Ksar	22	10	8	4	44	18	38
Concorde	22	11	4	5	34	17	37
Trarza Rosso	22	7	9	6	27	28	30
ASC Police	22	8	5	9	20	32	29
Garde Nationale	22	5	10	7	21	23	25
El Ahmedi Sebkha	22	5	6	11	26	30	21
ASC Armée	22	4	7	11	14	26	19
AMSME Sebkha	22	5	2	15	16	51	17
Entente Sebkha	22	3	8	11	14	39	17

19/08/2006 - 29/04/2007

MAURITANIA COUNTRY INFORMATION

Capital	Nouakchott	Independence	1960 from France	GDP per Capita	$1 800
Population	2 998 563	Status	Republic	GNP Ranking	154
Area km²	1 030 700	Language	Arabic, French, Pulaar	Dialling code	+222
Population density	3 per km²	Literacy rate	47%	Internet code	.mr
% in urban areas	54%	Main religion	Muslim	GMT +/-	0
Towns/Cities ('000)	Nouakchott 709; Nouadhibou 80; Kifah 68; Kayhaydi 51; Zuwarat 44; an-Na'mah 36				
Neighbours (km)	Western Sahara 1 561; Algeria 463; Mali 2 237; Senegal 813; North Atlantic 754				
Main stadia	Stade National – Nouakchott 40 000				

MWI – MALAWI

NATIONAL TEAM RECORD
JULY 10TH 2006 TO JULY 12TH 2010

PL	W	D	L	F	A	%
13	2	2	9	11	18	23.1

FIFA/COCA-COLA WORLD RANKING

1993	1994	1995	1996	1997	1998	1999	2000	2001	2002	2003	2004	2005	2006	High		Low	
67	82	89	88	97	89	114	113	120	95	105	109	106	104	67	12/93	124	06/01

2006–2007											
08/06	09/06	10/06	11/06	12/06	01/07	02/07	03/07	04/07	05/07	06/07	07/07
91	95	94	94	104	103	103	104	107	107	108	112

Malawi crashed out of African Nations Cup contention and found themselves in a downward spiral, stretching their winless streak to eight games by mid-2007. This run of form came despite the hiring of English coach Steve Constantine, who had previously worked in India and at English league club Millwall. He took over in April 2007 from former international Kinnah Phiri, who had been holding the fort subsequent to the departure of the controversial German Burkhard Ziese, who had been fired after the Flames lost their opening 2008 Nations Cup qualifier in Morocco. Phiri took the team to the East and Central African Senior Challenge Cup tournament in Ethiopia at the

INTERNATIONAL HONOURS
None

end of 2006, where Malawi were one of two guest competitors. Despite missing all of their key foreign-based players the Flames made it to the quarter-finals, where they lost on a penalty shoot-out to Uganda after a 0-0 draw. Malawi continued to export the majority of their top players to South Africa, whose league has featured top Malawian talent for some three decades. The latest is midfielder Joseph Kamwendo, who has signed for Orlando Pirates. Blantyre's Wanderers won the Super League after a close battle with Silver Strikers from the country's capital Lilongwe. It was the only competition played after the Cup tournament was cancelled.

THE FIFA BIG COUNT OF 2006

	Male	Female		Total
Number of players	515 600	200	Referees and Assistant Referees	600
Professionals	0		Admin, Coaches, Technical, Medical	1 800
Amateurs 18+	11 400		Number of clubs	70
Youth under 18	8 700		Number of teams	120
Unregistered	29 700		Clubs with women's teams	0
Total players	515 800		Players as % of population	3.96%

Football Association of Malawi (FAM)
Mpira House, Old Chileka Road, PO Box 865, Blantyre, Malawi
Tel +265 1 623197   Fax +265 1 623204
gensec@fam.mw   www.fam.mw
President: NYAMILANDU MANDA Walter   General Secretary: OSMAN Yasin
Vice-President: ANDERSON Zimba   Treasurer: TBD   Media Officer: JANGALE Casper
Men's Coach: CONSTANTINE Steve   Women's Coach: MBOLEMBOLE Stuart
FAM formed: 1966   CAF: 1968   FIFA: 1967
Red shirts, White shorts, Red socks

RECENT INTERNATIONAL MATCHES PLAYED BY MALAWI

2003	Opponents	Score		Venue	Comp	Scorers	Att	Referee
25-05	Botswana	D	1-1	Gaborone	CCqf	Chavula [86], W 3-1p	25 000	Infante MOZ
7-06	Nigeria	L	1-4	Lagos	CNq	Kanyenda [7]		Ndoye SEN
6-07	Angola	L	1-5	Luanda	CNq	Mgangira [78]	10 000	
16-08	Zambia	D	1-1	Blantyre	CCsf	Mwafulirwa [35]		Mnkantjo ZIM
27-09	Zimbabwe	L	1-2	Blantyre	CCf	Mwafulirwa [83]	60 000	Bennett RSA
5-10	Zimbabwe	L	0-2	Harare	CCf		25 000	Nkole ZAM
12-10	Ethiopia	W	3-1	Addis Abeba	WCq	Kanyenda 2 [39 55], Mgangira [88]	20 000	Abd El Fatah EGY
15-11	Ethiopia	D	0-0	Lilongwe	WCq		20 000	Abdel Rahman SUD
2004								
22-05	Zambia	W	2-0	Kitwe	Fr	Mwakasungula [15], Munthali [70]	20 000	Nkole ZAM
5-06	Morocco	D	1-1	Blantyre	WCq	Munthali [35]	30 040	Mususa ZIM
13-06	Mozambique	L	0-2	Maputo	CCqf		30 000	Kaoma ZAM
19-06	Botswana	L	0-2	Gaborone	WCq		15 000	Awuye UGA
3-07	Guinea	D	1-1	Lilongwe	WCq	Mpinganjira [71]	11 383	Abdulkadir TAN
6-07	Swaziland	L	1-2	Blantyre	Fr			
8-07	Swaziland	D	1-1	Lilongwe	Fr			
4-09	Kenya	L	2-3	Nairobi	WCq	Munthali [41], Mabedi [90p]	13 000	Mwanza ZAM
9-10	Tunisia	D	2-2	Blantyre	WCq	Mwafulirwa [19], Chipatala [37]	20 000	Awuye UGA
2005								
27-02	Zimbabwe	W	2-1	Blantyre	Fr	Tambala [45], Phiri.V [51]		
26-03	Tunisia	L	0-7	Tunis	WCq		30 000	Abdel Rahman SUD
27-05	Libya	D	1-1	Tripoli	Fr			
4-06	Morocco	L	1-4	Rabat	WCq	Chipatala [10]	48 000	Buenkadila COD
11-06	Lesotho	W	2-1	Lusaka	CCr1	Chitsulo [54], Zakazaka [73]		Mpanisi ZAM
12-06	Zambia	L	1-2	Lusaka	CCr1	Maduka [55]		Nhlapo RSA
18-06	Botswana	L	1-3	Blantyre	WCq	Mwafulirwa [48]	20 000	Gabonamong BOT
4-09	Guinea	L	1-3	Conakry	WCq	Mkandwire [36]	2 518	Mana NGA
8-10	Kenya	W	3-0	Blantyre	WCq	Zakazaka [6], Mkandwire 2 [49 61]	12 000	Codjia BEN
2006								
24-06	Zimbabwe	D	1-1	Maputo	Fr	Chipatala [6], W 2-1p		
25-06	Mozambique	W	2-0	Maputo	Fr	Wadabwa [29], Kamwendo		
6-07	Botswana	W	2-1	Lilongwe	Fr	Zakazaka [57], Wadabwa [49]		
8-07	Botswana	D	0-0	Blantyre	Fr	L 2-3p		
22-07	Zambia	L	1-3	Katutura	CCr1	Mkhandawire [16]		Katjimune NAM
23-07	Namibia	L	2-3	Katutura	CCr1	Chavula [19], Chilapondwa [85]		Simisse MRI
3-09	Morocco	L	0-2	Rabat	CNq			Codji BEN
7-10	Zimbabwe	W	1-0	Blantyre	CNq	Chavula [78]		Seechurn MRI
26-11	Djibouti	W	3-0	Addis Abeba	CFr1	Wadabwa [6], Mkhandawire [52], Munthali [82]		
28-11	Tanzania	L	1-2	Addis Abeba	CFr1	Wadabwa [15]		
1-12	Ethiopia	L	0-1	Addis Abeba	CFr1			
6-12	Uganda	D	0-0	Addis Abeba	CFqf	L 2-4p		
2007								
26-05	South Africa	D	0-0	Mbabane	CCr1	L 4-5p		Dlamini SWZ
27-05	Swaziland	L	0-1	Mbabane	CCr1			Labrosse SEY
10-06	Senegal	L	2-3	Blantyre	Fr	Mwafulirwa [75], Mkhandawire [78]		
16-06	Morocco	L	0-1	Blantyre	CNq			
6-07	Namibia	L	1-2	Blantyre	Fr	Kafoteka [48]		

Fr = Friendly match • CN = CAF African Cup of Nations • CC = COSAFA Cup • CF = CECAFA Cup • WC = FIFA World Cup
q = qualifier • r1 = first round group • qf = quarter-final • sf = semi-final • f = final

MALAWI NATIONAL TEAM RECORDS AND RECORD SEQUENCES

Records			Sequence records				
Victory	8-1	BOT 1968	Wins	8	1984	Clean sheets	5	1989
Defeat	0-7	ZAM 1969, TUN 2005	Defeats	9	1962-1968	Goals scored	13	1986-1987
Player Caps	n/a		Undefeated	15	1989-1990	Without goal	5	Three times
Player Goals	n/a		Without win	14	1998-2000	Goals against	18	1971-1975

MALAWI COUNTRY INFORMATION

Capital	Lilongwe	Independence	1964 from the UK	GDP per Capita	$600
Population	11 906 855	Status	Republic	GNP Ranking	
Area km²	118 480	Language	English, Chichewa	Dialling code	+265
Population density	100 per km²	Literacy rate	62%	Internet code	.mw
% in urban areas	14%	Main religion	Christian 75%, Muslim 20%	GMT + / –	+2
Towns/Cities ('000)	Lilongwe 647; Blantyre 585; Mzuzu 128; Zomba 81; Kasungu 42; Mangochi 40; Karonga 34				
Neighbours (km)	Mozambique 1 569; Zambia 837; Tanzania 475				
Main stadia	Chichiri – Blantyre 60 000; Chivo – Lilongwe 40 000				

MALAWI 2006 SUPER LEAGUE

	Pl	W	D	L	F	A	Pts
MTL Wanderers	28	19	5	4	52	17	**62**
Silver Strikers	28	18	6	4	43	19	**60**
Big Bullets	28	15	10	3	26	13	**55**
Super ESCOM	28	13	11	4	38	14	**50**
ADMARC Tigers	28	13	6	9	39	32	**45**
Blue Eagles	28	12	7	9	27	22	**43**
Red Lions	28	10	9	9	31	26	**39**
CIVO United	28	6	13	9	21	25	**31**
Eagle Beaks	28	9	3	16	31	44	**30**
Moyale Barracks	28	5	12	11	17	26	**27**
Dwangwa United	28	6	9	13	25	38	**27**
Nchalo United	28	7	6	15	30	44	**27**
Mzuzu Cent. Hospital	28	7	6	15	21	40	**27**
Sammy's United	28	6	8	14	24	45	**26**
Cobbe Barracks	28	6	5	17	32	53	23

30/04/2006 - 23/12/2006

RECENT LEAGUE AND CUP RECORD

	Championship						Cup		
Year	Champions	Pts	Runners-up	Pts	Third	Pts	Winners	Score	Runners-up
1996	Telecom Wanderers								
1997	Telecom Wanderers								
1998	Telecom Wanderers								
1999	Bata Bullets	62	Telecom Wanderers	60	Red Lions	44	Bata Bullets	3-0	MDC United
2000	Bata Bullets	44	MDC United	41	Silver Strikers	40	Telecom Wanderers	2-1	Bata Bullets
2001	Total Big Bullets	69	MTL Wanderers	66	MDC United	44	Moyale Barracks	1-0	Super ESCOM
2002	Total Big Bullets	62	Silver Strikers	50	MDC United	45	Total Big Bullets	1-0	MTL Wanderers
2003	Bakili Bullets	70	MTL Wanderers	69	MDC United	60	Final between Wanderers and Bullets abandoned		
2004	Bakili Bullets		MTL Wanderers		Silver Strikers		No competition		
2005	Big Bullets	55	MTL Wanderers	54	Silver Strikers	53	ADMARC Tigers	1-1 5-4p	MTL Wanderers
2006	MTL Wanderers	62	Silver Strikers	60	Big Bullets	55	No competition		

Bakili Bullets previously known as Bata Bullets and Total Big Bullets • MTL Wanderers previously known as Limbe Leaf Wanderers and Telecom Wanderers

MYA – MYANMAR

NATIONAL TEAM RECORD
JULY 10TH 2006 TO JULY 12TH 2010

PL	W	D	L	F	A	%
7	2	5	0	7	5	64.2

FIFA/COCA-COLA WORLD RANKING

1993	1994	1995	1996	1997	1998	1999	2000	2001	2002	2003	2004	2005	2006	High		Low	
110	124	115	104	114	115	126	124	151	162	140	144	147	154	97	04/96	164	08/06

2006–2007											
08/06	09/06	10/06	11/06	12/06	01/07	02/07	03/07	04/07	05/07	06/07	07/07
164	139	148	150	154	145	149	151	154	156	153	151

With their ASEAN neighbours Indonesia, Malaysia, Thailand and Vietnam all enjoying a spell in the limelight by hosting the AFC Asian Cup in mid 2007, Myanmar did all it could to remind onlookers that it was once the most powerful nation in the region by going the whole season unbeaten. In the run up to the finals, one of Asia's most famous tournaments, the Merdeka Cup in Malaysia, was revived after an absence of five years and in an echo of times past Myanmar won the tournament for a fourth time. In front of 30,000 fans in the Shah Alam stadium in Kuala Lumpur they beat Indonesia 2-1 in the final having earlier also surprisingly beaten hosts Malaysia.

INTERNATIONAL HONOURS
Asian Games 1966 1970   SEA Games 1965 1967 1969 1971   AFC Youth Championship 1961 1963 1964 1966 1968 1969 1970

In the ASEAN Football Federation Championship in Bangkok five months later, Myanmar were also unbeaten against Thailand, Malaysia and the Philippines, drawing all three matches. Had they beaten the Philippines in their third group match as they were strongly expected to do, Myanmar would have qualified for the semi-finals but instead it was Malaysia who went through. The federation is looking into the possibility of Myanmar hosting one of the groups in the 2009 ASEAN Football Federation Championship as this secretive and closed nation seeks to return to the mainstream of Asian football once again.

THE FIFA BIG COUNT OF 2006

	Male	Female		Total
Number of players	1 043 159	78 880	Referees and Assistant Referees	830
Professionals	0		Admin, Coaches, Technical, Medical	2 920
Amateurs 18+	104 405		Number of clubs	598
Youth under 18	24 990		Number of teams	4 200
Unregistered	214 380		Clubs with women's teams	7
Total players	1 122 039		Players as % of population	2.37%

Myanmar Football Federation (MFF)

National Football Training Centre, Thuwunna Thingankyun, Township, Yangon, Myanmar
Tel +951 577366   Fax +951 570000
mff@myanmar.com.mm   www.myanmarfootball.org
President: ZAW Zaw   General Secretary: AUNG Tin
Vice-President: NAING Zaw Win   Treasurer: ZAW Than   Media Officer: NAING Tun Tun
Men's Coach: FALOPA Marcos   Women's Coach: AYE Maung
MFF formed: 1947   AFC: 1954   FIFA: 1957
Red shirts, White shorts, Red socks

RECENT INTERNATIONAL MATCHES PLAYED BY MYANMAR

2003	Opponents	Score		Venue	Comp	Scorers	Att	Referee
8-10	Malaysia	L	0-4	Kuala Lumpur	ACq		4 500	Yang Zhiqiang CHN
10-10	Bahrain	L	1-3	Kuala Lumpur	ACq	Soe Myat Min [77]	500	Naglingham SIN
12-10	Iraq	L	0-3	Kuala Lumpur	ACq		500	Yang Zhiqiang CHN
20-10	Bahrain	L	0-4	Manama	ACq		15 000	Al Harrassi OMA
22-10	Iraq	L	1-3	Manama	ACq	Zaw Zaw [45]	300	Yasrebi IRN
24-10	Malaysia	W	2-1	Isa Town	ACq	Soe Myat Min [25], Fadzli OG [43]	200	Al Harrassi OMA
2004								
17-03	China PR	L	0-2	Guangzhou	Fr			
20-08	Vietnam	L	0-5	Ho Chi Minh	Fr			
22-08	India	L	1-2	Ho Chi Minh	Fr	Win Nawng [81]		
27-11	Singapore	L	0-1	Singapore	Fr			
2-12	Hong Kong	D	2-2	Singapore	Fr	Yan Paing 2 [28 84]		
8-12	Philippines	W	1-0	Kuala Lumpur	TCr1	San Day Thien [92+]	1 000	Vo Minh Tri VIE
10-12	Thailand	D	1-1	Kuala Lumpur	TCr1	Zaw Lynn Tun [89]		Moradi IRN
12-12	Malaysia	W	1-0	Kuala Lumpur	TCr1	Soe Myat Min [20]	10 000	Hsu Chao Lo TPE
16-12	East Timor †	W	3-1	Kuala Lumpur	TCr1	Soe Myat Min [4], San Day Thien [43], Myo Hlaing Win [51]	1 000	Hsu Chao Lo TPE
29-12	Singapore	L	3-4	Kuala Lumpur	TCsf	Soe Myat Min 2 [34 90], Min Thu [36]	12 000	Rungklay THA
2005								
2-01	Singapore	L	2-4	Singapore	TCsf	Soe Myat Min [15], Aung Kyaw Moe [50]	30 000	Kamikawa JPN
15-01	Malaysia	L	1-2	Singapore	TC3p	Soe Myat Min [52]	2 000	Vo Minh Tri VIE
2006								
23-08	Thailand	D	2-2	Kuala Lumpur	Fr	Si Thu Win 2 [35 70]	8 000	Heng MAS
25-08	Indonesia	D	0-0	Kuala Lumpur	Fr			Sharul MAS
27-08	Malaysia	W	2-1	Kuala Lumpur	Fr	Kyaw Thu Ra [52], Soe Myat Min [59]		Zhang Lei CHN
29-08	Indonesia	W	2-1	Kuala Lumpur	Fr	Kyaw Thu Ra [61], Soe Myat Min [85]	30 000	Shahrul MAS
2007								
12-01	Thailand	D	1-1	Bangkok	TCr1	Si Thu Win [25]	15 000	Matsuo JPN
14-01	Malaysia	D	0-0	Bangkok	TCr1		28 000	Tri Minh Vo VIE
16-01	Philippines	D	0-0	Bangkok	TCr1		500	Daud SIN

Fr = Friendly match • TC = Tiger Cup/ASEAN Football Federation Championship • AC = AFC Asian Cup
q = qualifier • r1 = 1st round • sf = semi-final • 3p = 3rd place play-off • † Not a full international

MYANMAR NATIONAL TEAM RECORDS AND RECORD SEQUENCES

Records			Sequence records					
Victory	9-0	SIN 1969	Wins	8	1971-1972	Clean sheets	7	1966-1967
Defeat	1-9	MAS 1977	Defeats	7	1957-1961	Goals scored	14	1964-1966
Player Caps	n/a		Undefeated	14	1970-1971	Without goal	4	1987-1991
Player Goals	n/a		Without win	9	1987-1993	Goals against	11	2003-2004

MYANMAR RECENT LEAGUE RECORD

Championship		Interstate Championship		
Year	Champions	Winners	Score	Runners-up
2002	Finance & Revenue Yangon	Mandalay		Sagaing
2003	Finance & Revenue Yangon	Shan State	2-0	Kayin State
2004	Finance & Revenue Yangon			
2005	Finance & Revenue Yangon			
2006	Finance & Revenue Yangon	Ayerwady	1-1 5-3p	Shan State

MYANMAR COUNTRY INFORMATION

Capital	Yangon (Rangoon)	Independence	1948 from the UK	GDP per Capita	$1 800
Population	42 720 196	Status	Republic	GNP Ranking	52
Area km²	678 500	Language	Burmese	Dialling code	+95
Population density	63 per km²	Literacy rate	85%	Internet code	.mm
% in urban areas	29%	Main religion	Buddhist 90%	GMT +/–	+6.5
Towns/Cities ('000)	Yangon 4 477; Mandalay 1 208; Mawlamyine 439; Bago 244; Pathein 237; Monywa 182				
Neighbours (km)	China 2 185; Laos 235; Thailand 1 800; Bangladesh 193; India 1 463; Indian Ocean 1 930				
Main stadia	Bogyoke Aung San – Yangon 40 000; Thuwanna YTC – Yangon 30 000				

NAM – NAMIBIA

NATIONAL TEAM RECORD
JULY 10TH 2006 TO JULY 12TH 2010

PL	W	D	L	F	A	%
14	5	2	7	18	20	42.8

FIFA/COCA-COLA WORLD RANKING

1993	1994	1995	1996	1997	1998	1999	2000	2001	2002	2003	2004	2005	2006	High	Low
156	123	116	103	86	69	80	87	101	123	144	158	161	116	**68** 11/98	**161** 07/94

					2006–2007						
08/06	09/06	10/06	11/06	12/06	01/07	02/07	03/07	04/07	05/07	06/07	07/07
137	139	104	113	116	115	122	123	128	131	123	126

Namibia brought in a new football association president and coach in an attempt to lift the country's results out of a downward spiral that has seen the southern Africa country plummet down the down the FIFA/Coca-Cola World Ranking from a high of 68 in late 1998 to 139 in September 2006. John Muinjo, a former referee has taken over at the helm of the game while the Zambian coach Ben Bamchufile has able to improve matters on the pitch. The Brave Warriors had a sudden spurt of international activity, highlighted by two wins over Ethiopia and Libya in their 2008 African Nations Cup qualifiers and a vastly increased schedule of friendly encounters, seriously

INTERNATIONAL HONOURS
None

lacking in preceeding years. Qualification for the Nations Cup finals in Ghana remained a possibility going into the final round of fixtures but the Namibians again flopped in the regional COSAFA Cup, losing with a weakened side to Botswana in the mini tournament in Gaborone in July 2007. Civics were again crowned champions, runaway winners in the Premier League ahead of Oshakati City and Windhoek-based Ramblers. Civics, also from the capital, have now won three successive titles but were unable to reproduce their heroics of 2006 in the African Champions League. In 2007, they were narrowly beaten in the first round by Angola's Petro Atletico.

THE FIFA BIG COUNT OF 2006

	Male	Female		Total
Number of players	130 960	6 000	Referees and Assistant Referees	230
Professionals	0		Admin, Coaches, Technical, Medical	1 415
Amateurs 18+	6 260		Number of clubs	100
Youth under 18	34 000		Number of teams	250
Unregistered	10 500		Clubs with women's teams	1
Total players	136 960		Players as % of population	6.70%

Namibia Football Association (NFA)
Richard Kamumuka Street, Soccer House, Katutura, PO Box 1345, Windhoek 9000, Namibia
Tel +264 61 265691   Fax +264 61 265693
nfass@iafrica.com.na   www.none
President: MUINJO John   General Secretary: RUKORO Barry
Vice-President: AMUTENYA Korbinian   Treasurer: KAPENDA Cornelius   Media Officer: BEU Kauta
Men's Coach: BAMFUCHILE Ben   Women's Coach: FREYER Gabriel
NFA formed: 1990   CAF: 1990   FIFA: 1992
Red shirts, Red shorts, Red socks

RECENT INTERNATIONAL MATCHES PLAYED BY NAMIBIA

2002 Opponents	Score	Venue	Comp	Scorers	Att	Referee
7-09 Algeria	L 0-1	Windhoek	CNq		13 000	Tangawarima ZIM
2003						
16-03 Botswana	L 0-1	Windhoek	CCr1			Kakudze SWA
30-03 Chad	L 0-2	N'Djamena	CNq			Dimanche CTA
7-06 Chad	W 2-1	Windhoek	CNq	Diergaardt [24], Hummel [76p]	5 000	Bernardo Colembi ANG
20-06 Algeria	L 0-1	Blida	CNq		30 000	Auda EGY
7-09 Angola	L 0-2	Luanda	Fr		5 000	Antonio De Sousa ANG
20-09 Angola	L 1-3	Windhoek	Fr	Hindjou [4]		
12-10 Rwanda	L 0-3	Kigali	WCq		22 000	Abdulkadir TAN
15-11 Rwanda	D 1-1	Windhoek	WCq	Shipanga [39]	9 000	Mbera GAB
2004						
28-04 Botswana	D 0-0	Windhoek	Fr		1 500	
9-05 Angola	L 1-2	Luanda	CCr1	Petrus [70]	4 000	Ngcamphalala SWA
2005						
19-03 Lesotho	W 2-1	Maseru	Fr	Guriras, Malgas		
16-04 Botswana	D 1-1	Windhoek	CCr1	Botes [35]. L 4-5p		Sentso LES
2006						
22-07 Seychelles	D 1-1	Katutura	CCr1	Khaiseb [18]. L 2-4p		Simisse MRI
23-07 Malawi	W 3-2	Katutura	CCr1	Iasaacks [44], Bester [47], Botes [66p]		Simisse MRI
16-08 South Africa	L 0-1	Katutura	Fr			
3-09 Congo DR	L 2-3	Kinshasa	CNq	Plaatjies 2 [34 60]		Evehe CMR
7-10 Ethiopia	W 1-0	Katutura	CNq	Jacobs [20p]		Moeketsi LES
15-11 Zimbabwe	L 2-3	Harare	Fr	Helu [36], Khaiseb [55p]		
2007						
6-02 Botswana	L 0-1	Gaborone	Fr			
25-03 Libya	L 1-2	Tripoli	CNq	Benjamin [85]		
26-05 Zambia	L 1-2	Windhoek	Fr	Shatimuene [89]		
2-06 Libya	W 1-0	Windhoek	CNq	Benjamin [9]		
16-06 Congo DR	D 1-1	Windhoek	CNq	Pienaar [40]		
6-07 Malawi	W 2-1	Blantyre	Fr	Katjatenja [23], Bester [65]		
28-07 Botswana	L 0-1	Gaborone	CCr1			Lwanja MWI
29-07 Lesotho	W 3-2	Gaborone	CCr1			

Fr = Friendly match • CN = CAF African Cup of Nations • CC = COSAFA Cup • WC = FIFA World Cup • q = qualifier • r1 = first round group

NAMIBIA NATIONAL TEAM RECORDS AND RECORD SEQUENCES

Records			Sequence records				
Victory	8-2	BEN 2000	Wins	3	1997	Clean sheets	3	1995-1996, 1996
Defeat	2-8	EGY 2001	Defeats	7	2001-03	Goals scored	15	1997-1998
Player Caps	69	HINDJOU Johannes	Undefeated	8	1995-1996	Without goal	5	1992-1993, 2001
Player Goals	12	KHOB Gervatius Uri	Without win	8	1998	Goals against	25	1997-1998

NAMIBIA COUNTRY INFORMATION

Capital	Windhoek	Independence	1990 from South Africa	GDP per Capita	$7 200
Population	1 954 033	Status	Republic	GNP Ranking	125
Area km²	825 415	Language	English, Afrikaans, Oshivambo	Dialling code	+264
Population density	2 per km²	Literacy rate	84%	Internet code	.na
% in urban areas	37%	Main religion	Christian 80%	GMT +/-	+2
Towns/Cities ('000)	Windhoek 268; Rundu 58; Walvis Bay 52; Oshakati 34; Swakopmund 25; Katima Mulilo 25				
Neighbours (km)	Angola 1 376; Zambia 233; Botswana 1 360; South Africa 967; South Atlantic 1 572				
Main stadia	Independence Stadium – Windhoek 25 000				

NAMIBIA 2006–07

TAFEL LAGER PREMIER LEAGUE

	Pl	W	D	L	F	A	Pts	Civics	Oshakati City	Ramblers	Windhoek	Eleven Arrows	African Stars	Pirates	Black Africa	Tigers	Blue Waters	Friends	Golden Bees
Civics †	22	15	5	2	53	11	50		4-1	3-0	3-0	2-0	1-0	2-0	2-0	3-1	0-0	12-1	4-0
Oshakati City	22	12	4	6	37	25	40	1-2		1-1	2-1	2-1	2-1	3-0	1-0	1-2	3-1	6-2	4-1
Ramblers	22	10	8	4	33	24	38	1-1	1-0		2-0	2-1	1-0	2-1	1-0	1-1	4-2	4-2	2-0
SK Windhoek	22	8	7	7	24	22	31	1-1	1-1	0-0		3-1	0-0	2-1	1-2	2-0	3-2	1-0	1-1
Eleven Arrows	22	9	3	10	38	33	30	0-4	0-0	2-1	2-1		2-1	1-2	1-1	3-0	1-2	7-0	4-2
African Stars	22	8	5	9	24	17	29	2-0	0-1	0-0	0-1	3-2		0-1	1-1	1-1	0-0	8-1	2-0
Orlando Pirates	22	9	2	11	25	30	29	1-1	0-1	1-3	1-0	1-0	0-1		0-1	1-2	4-2	1-0	2-4
Black Africa	22	8	3	11	23	31	27	1-0	0-1	3-2	0-3	0-1	1-0	1-2		2-3	3-2	1-0	1-0
United Africa Tigers	22	7	6	9	25	37	27	0-4	1-2	2-2	1-1	0-4	1-0	2-4	2-0		1-0	1-1	3-2
Blue Waters	22	6	7	9	27	34	25	0-2	2-1	1-1	1-0	2-2	0-1	1-0	0-0	2-1		2-1	2-2
Friends	22	5	5	12	26	58	20	1-1	2-1	1-0	0-1	4-2	0-1	1-1	3-2	0-0	3-2		1-1
Golden Bees	22	4	7	11	29	42	19	0-1	2-2	2-2	1-1	0-1	1-2	0-1	5-3	1-0	1-1	3-2	

11/11/2006 – 13/05/2007 • † Qualified for the CAF Champions League • Top scorers: William CHILUFYA, Civics 17; Rudolph BESTER, Arrows 16

MTL NFA CUP 2006–07

Round of 16		Quarter-finals		Semi-finals †		Final		
African Stars	1 5p							
Oshakati City	1 4p	African Stars	2					
PC Blue Boys	0	SK Windhoek	1					
SK Windhoek	4			African Stars	1			
Black Africa	5			Mighty Gunners	0			
Major Power	1	Black Africa	1					
Volcano	1	Mighty Gunners	2					
Mighty Gunners	5					African Stars ‡	0 5p	
Ramblers	1 5p					Orlando Pirates	0 3p	
Invincible United	1 3p	Ramblers	4					
Civics	1	Eleven Arrows	0			CUP FINAL		
Eleven Arrows	3			Ramblers	1			
Eleven Brothers	3			Orlando Pirates	2	Independence Stadium, Windhoek		
Rundu Chiefs	1	Eleven Brothers	2			19-05-2007		
Tough Guys	0	Orlando Pirates	4	Semi-finals played in Walvis Bay				
Orlando Pirates	9			‡ Qualified for the CAF Confederation Cup				

CLUB DIRECTORY

Club	Town/City	Lge	Cup
African Stars	Windhoek	0	1
Black Africans	Windhoek	5	3
Blue Waters	Walvis Bay	4	1
Chief Santos	Tsumeb	2	4
Civics	Windhoek	3	1
Eleven Arrows	Walvis Bay	1	0
Orlando Pirates	Walvis Bay	1	1
Ramblers	Windhoek	1	1
Tigers	Windhoek	0	2

RECENT LEAGUE AND CUP RECORD

	Championship						Cup		
Year	Champions	Pts	Runners-up	Pts	Third	Pts	Winners	Score	Runners-up
1998	Black Africans	46	Civics	39	Chief Santos	37	Chief Santos	1-0	Tigers
1999	Black Africans	56	Life Fighters	43	Blue Waters	40	Chief Santos	1-0	Tigers
2000	Blue Waters	54	Black Africans	45	Nashua Young Ones	40	Chief Santos	4-2	Life Fighters
2001	No Championship due to season readjustment						Not held due to season readjustment		
2002	Liverpool	57	Blue Waters	56	Chief Santos	56	Orlando Pirates	2-1	Tigers
2003	Chief Santos						Civics	4-2	Tigers
2004	Blue Waters	72	Civics	69	Orlando Pirates	62	Black Africans	2-0	Life Fighters
2005	Civics	71	Blue Waters	69	Ramblers	61	Ramblers	2-2 5-4p	Black Africa
2006	Civics	53	Ramblers	44	Blue Waters	40	Orlando Pirates	1-0	SK Windhoek
2007	Civics	50	Oshakati City	40	Ramblers	38	African Stars	0-0 5-3p	Orlando Pirates

NCA – NICARAGUA

NATIONAL TEAM RECORD
JULY 10TH 2006 TO JULY 12TH 2010

PL	W	D	L	F	A	%
4	1	0	3	6	14	25

FIFA/COCA-COLA WORLD RANKING

1993	1994	1995	1996	1997	1998	1999	2000	2001	2002	2003	2004	2005	2006	High	Low
155	168	174	179	182	188	193	191	188	186	173	158	152	168	**150** 08/93	**193** 05/01

2006–2007											
08/06	09/06	10/06	11/06	12/06	01/07	02/07	03/07	04/07	05/07	06/07	07/07
162	165	165	169	168	168	167	156	154	154	151	153

The 2007 edition of the UNCAF Cup proved to be a big disappointment for the Nicaraguan national team. They started with two close defeats at the hands of Guatemala and hosts El Salvador, but by beating Belize in their third game, did manage to qualify for a fifth place play-off against Honduras with the prize of a berth in the CONCACAF Gold Cup on offer for the winners. However, any hopes of making a first appearance in the finals were crushed in dramatic fashion with a 9-1 defeat by Honduras. The four matches in the UNCAF Cup were the only matches played during the season and were the first for two years. In the UNCAF club championship there were predictable

INTERNATIONAL HONOURS
None

first round exits for both Diriangen and Real Estelí although Estelí did manage to hold Costa Rica's Saprissa at home and only narrowly lost to them in the return. Estelí were also the dominant team in Nicaragua losing just twice all season. In the Apertura they finished well ahead of Diriangen in the group stage and then beat Real Madriz 1-0 in both legs of the Apertura final. Both met again in the final of the Clausura with Estelí again winning both games which secured them the overall championship. With 32 goals, their Honduran striker Emer Mejía comfortably topped the scoring charts.

THE FIFA BIG COUNT OF 2006

	Male	Female		Total
Number of players	408 081	58 950	Referees and Assistant Referees	1 372
Professionals	0		Admin, Coaches, Technical, Medical	4 398
Amateurs 18+	22 050		Number of clubs	1 270
Youth under 18	94 377		Number of teams	4 221
Unregistered	190 354		Clubs with women's teams	11
Total players	467 031		Players as % of population	8.38%

Federación Nicaragüense de Fútbol (FENIFUT)
Hospital Bautista 1, Cuadra abajo, 1 cuadra al Sur y 1/2 cuadra abajo, Managua 976, Nicaragua
Tel +505 2227035   Fax +505 2227885
fenifut@tmx.com.ni   www.fenifut.org.ni
President: ROCHA LOPEZ Julio   General Secretary: LECHADO SARAVIA Douglas
Vice-President: LOPEZ SANDERS Rolando   Treasurer: TBD   Media Officer: ROSALES Marlon
Men's Coach: DE TORRO Carlos   Women's Coach: URROZ Edward
FENIFUT formed: 1931   CONCACAF: 1968   FIFA: 1950
Blue shirts, White shorts, Blue socks

RECENT INTERNATIONAL MATCHES PLAYED BY NICARAGUA

2002	Opponents	Score		Venue	Comp	Scorers	Att	Referee
17-11	Cayman Islands	W	1-0	Grand Cayman	Fr			
2003								
11-02	Honduras	L	0-2	Panama City	UC			Aguilar SLV
13-02	El Salvador	L	0-3	Panama City	UC			Moreno PAN
15-02	Costa Rica	L	0-1	Colon	UC			Aguilar SLV
18-02	Guatemala	L	0-5	Panama City	UC		5 000	Moreno PAN
21-02	Panama	W	1-0	Panama City	UC	Palacios [83]		Aguilar SLV
2004								
31-01	Haiti	D	1-1	West Palm Beach	Fr	Palacios [41]	53	
29-02	Haiti	D	1-1	Esteli	Fr	Calero [58]		
31-03	Bermuda	L	0-3	Hamilton	Fr			Crockwell BER
2-04	Bermuda	L	1-2	Hamilton	Fr	Palacios [72p]		Raynor BER
30-04	Bermuda	W	2-0	Diriamba	Fr	Solorzano [4], Palacios [30]	800	
2-05	Bermuda	W	2-0	Esteli	Fr	Rocha [8], Palacios [46]	4 000	Reyes NCA
4-06	Costa Rica	L	1-5	San Carlos	Fr	Lopez.F [1]	BCD	
13-06	St Vincent/Grenadines	D	2-2	Diriamba	WCq	Palacios [37], Calero [79]	7 500	Delgado CUB
20-06	St Vincent/Grenadines	L	1-4	Kingstown	WCq	Palacios [60]	5 000	Brohim DMA
2005								
19-02	Honduras	L	1-5	Guatemala City	UCr1	Bustos [54]	5 306	Moreno PAN
21-02	Guatemala	L	0-4	Guatemala City	UCr1		8 000	Sibrian SLV
23-02	Belize	W	1-0	Guatemala City	UCr1	Vilchez [85]	3 000	Quesada CRC
2006								
No international matches played in 2006								
2007								
8-02	Guatemala	L	0-1	San Salvador	UCr1			Pineda HON
10-02	El Salvador	L	1-2	San Salvador	UCr1	Wilson [53]		Arredondo MEX
12-02	Belize	W	4-2	San Salvador	UCr1	Palacios 3 [12 20 68], Bustos [28]		Quesada CRC
15-02	Honduras	L	1-9	San Salvador	UC5p	Wilson [31]		Aguilar SLV

Fr = Friendly match • UC = UNCAF Cup • WC = FIFA World Cup • q = qualifier • BCD = behind closed doors

NICARAGUA NATIONAL TEAM RECORDS AND RECORD SEQUENCES

Records			Sequence records					
Victory	4-2	BLZ 2007	Wins	2	2004	Clean sheets	2	2004
Defeat	1-11	ANT 1950	Defeats	25	1986-2001	Goals scored	7	2004-2005
Player Caps	n/a		Undefeated	3	2003-2004	Without goal	8	1999-2001
Player Goals	n/a		Without win	33	1975-2001	Goals against	55	1966-2002

NICARAGUA COUNTRY INFORMATION

Capital	Managua	Independence	1838 from Spain	GDP per Capita	$2 300
Population	5 359 759	Status	Republic	GNP Ranking	140
Area km²	129 494	Language	Spanish	Dialling code	+505
Population density	41 per km²	Literacy rate	67%	Internet code	.ni
% in urban areas	63%	Main religion	Christian 85%	GMT +/−	-6
Towns/Cities ('000)	Managua 1 140; Léon 150; Chinandega 128; Masaya 123; Granada 92; Esteli 92; Tipitapa 89				
Neighbours (km)	Costa Rica 309; Honduras 922; Caribbean Sea & Pacific Ocean 910				
Main stadia	Estadio Dennis Martinez – Managua 30 000; Cacique Diriangen – Diriamba				

NICARAGUA 2006–07

XXIV CAMPEONATO NACIONAL PRIMERA DIVISION TORNEO APERTURA

	PI	W	D	L	F	A	Pts	Real Estelí	Diriangén	Real Madriz	Masatepe	San Marcos	Scorpión	Jalapa	Walter Fer.	Bluefields	América
Real Estelí †	18	13	4	1	59	12	43		0-0	1-2	2-1	5-0	6-1	5-0	2-2	8-0	3-0
Diriangén †	18	11	2	5	43	19	35	1-2		1-0	3-0	2-3	6-1	5-1	2-0	**3-0**	6-0
Real Madriz †	18	10	4	4	43	18	34	1-1	3-2		0-2	3-1	0-0	1-3	8-0	10-0	2-0
Deportivo Masatepe †	18	9	4	5	34	25	31	2-2	0-6	1-1		2-2	4-1	4-0	4-1	6-0	2-1
San Marcos	18	5	6	7	28	37	21	0-6	1-1	1-2	0-1		2-2	3-3	2-0	5-2	2-2
Scorpión	18	6	2	10	26	37	20	0-3	4-1	0-1	3-1	2-0		2-0	1-2	2-1	1-3
Deportivo Jalapa	18	6	1	11	23	42	19	0-3	1-2	1-0	2-0	1-3	3-2		1-0	1-3	4-1
Dep. Walter Ferreti	18	4	5	9	23	34	17	1-2	0-1	2-2	0-1	1-2	**3-0**	3-1		3-0	2-2
Deportivo Bluefields	18	5	2	11	19	62	17	1-7	**3-0**	1-5	1-1	2-1	0-4	**3-0**	1-1		1-0
América	18	4	4	10	20	32	16	0-1	0-1	1-2	0-2	0-0	1-0	2-1	2-2	5-0	

22/07/2006 - 19/11/2006 • † Qualified for the Apertura play-offs • Matches in bold were awarded 3-0

NICARAGUA 2006–07

XXIV CAMPEONATO NACIONAL PRIMERA DIVISION TORNEO CLAUSURA STAGE ONE

	PI	W	D	L	F	A	Pts	Real Estelí	Diriangén	Real Madriz	América	Jalapa	Masatepe	Walter Fer.	San Marcos	Bluefields	Scorpión
Real Estelí †	9	5	3	1	31	5	18			2-0	1-1		8-0	7-0			8-0
Diriangén †	9	5	2	2	24	13	17	1-0			5-1		1-0	6-1	4-4		3-0
Real Madriz †	9	5	1	3	26	14	16		3-1		2-1	2-3			5-2	3-0	
América †	9	5	1	3	22	15	16						3-0	5-1	0-3		5-0
Deportivo Jalapa †	9	5	1	3	15	17	16	1-1	3-2						1-0	3-0	
Deportivo Masatepe †	9	4	1	4	18	22	13		2-1		6-0				2-2	4-2	
Dep. Walter Ferreti	9	3	2	4	18	23	11		1-1	2-3		1-0				2-1	8-1
San Marcos	9	2	4	3	19	21	10	1-3						3-3			3-0
Deportivo Bluefields	9	1	3	5	13	20	6	1-1	1-1			1-3	2-0		1-1		
Scorpión	9	1	0	8	11	47	3			2-9		1-4	2-3			5-4	

28/01/2007 - 25/03/2007 • † Qualified for the Clausura Hexagonal • Matches in bold were awarded 3-0

APERTURA PLAY-OFFS

Semi–finals

Real Estelí	2	1
Dep Masatepe	1	0

Diriangén	**0**	4
Real Madriz	**3**	1

Finals

Real Estelí	1	1
Real Madriz	0	0

10/12/2006 & 17/12/2006

CLAUSURA PLAY-OFFS

Semi–finals

Real Estelí	3	2
Dep Masatepe	1	0

Diriangén	1	0
Real Madriz	**3**	**0**

Finals

Real Estelí	2	2
Real Madriz	0	1

27/05/2007 & 3/06/2007

CHAMPIONSHIP FINAL

Real Estelí automatically won the championship having won both the Apertura and Clausura

CLAUSURA HEXAGONAL

	PI	W	D	L	F	A	Pts	RE	Di	RM	DM	Am	DJ
Real Estelí †	5	5	0	0	18	2	15		2-1		5-0	4-0	
Diriangén †	5	3	1	1	11	7	10			3-0		2-1	3-2
Real Madriz †	5	3	0	2	9	5	9	0-1				2-1	3-0
Deportivo Masatepe †	5	2	1	2	8	13	7			2-2		0-4	
América	5	1	0	4	6	12	3				1-3		3-1
Deportivo Jalapa	5	0	0	5	5	18	0	1-6			1-3		

1/04/2007 - 6/05/2007 • † Qualified for the Clausura play-offs

RECENT LEAGUE RECORD

	Championship/Clausura (2004–2005 only)			Apertura		
Year	Champions	Score	Runners-up	Winners	Score	Runners-up
2000	Diriangén	1-0	Deportivo Walter Ferreti			
2001	Deportivo Walter Ferreti	0-0 0-0 5-3p	Diriangén			
2002	Deportivo Jalapa	1-1 4-0	Deportivo Walter Ferreti			
2003	Real Estelí	0-1 3-0	Diriangén	Real Estelí	0-0 1-0	Diriangén
2004	Real Estelí	1-0 0-0	Diriangén	Diriangén	0-0 1-0	Real Estelí
2005	Diriangén	1-0 0-1 3-2p	Parmalat			
2006	Diriangén	2-1 0-1	Real Estelí			
2007	Real Estelí	‡	Real Madriz			

‡ No play-off as Real Estelí won both the Apertura and Clausura

NCL – NEW CALEDONIA

NEW CALEDONIA NATIONAL TEAM RECORD
JULY 10TH 2006 TO JULY 12TH 2010

PL	W	D	L	F	A	%
2	1	0	1	5	5	50

FIFA/COCA-COLA WORLD RANKING

1993	1994	1995	1996	1997	1998	1999	2000	2001	2002	2003	2004	2005	2006	High		Low	
-	-	-	-	-	-	-	-	-	-	-	186	187	176	**172**	08/06	**185**	06/05

2006–2007											
08/06	09/06	10/06	11/06	12/06	01/07	02/07	03/07	04/07	05/07	06/07	07/07
172	174	174	176	176	175	175	175	173	174	175	178

Like many of the other Pacific islands, New Caledonia suffers from a lack of regular competition and as one of the nations hoping to benefit most from the absence of Australia, this lack of progress is disappointing. After a three year gap, two matches were played against Vanuatu as the team prepared for the South Pacific games in August 2007, which were doubling up as the first round of World Cup qualification. At youth level the under–20 and under–17 teams entered the Oceania tournaments but with New Zealand progressing from both to the FIFA finals, the prospect of a first appearance on the world stage would still seem remote. It was the same story in the newly launched

INTERNATIONAL HONOURS
None

O-League. New Caledonian champions Monte Doré were grouped with New Zealand's Waitakere United and Auckland City in the first round and they lost all four matches they played. That meant the 2007 champions, JS Baco, had to pre qualify for the 2007-08 tournament, which they failed to do after finishing second behind Vanuatu's Tafea in a group held in June 2007. Baco had qualified after winning the National Championship but the other two trophies up for grabs during the season both went to AS Lössi. They won Grand Terre's Division d'Honneur ahead of Magenta and Baco and they also beat Mont-Dore 1-0 in the Cup Final.

THE FIFA BIG COUNT OF 2006

	Male	Female		Total
Number of players	9 150	650	Referees and Assistant Referees	100
Professionals	0		Admin, Coaches, Technical, Medical	200
Amateurs 18+	2 500		Number of clubs	100
Youth under 18	2 400		Number of teams	250
Unregistered	500		Clubs with women's teams	5
Total players	9 800		Players as % of population	4.47%

Fédération Calédonienne de Football (FCF)
7 bis, rue Suffren Quartien latin, BP 560, 99845 Nouméa CEDEX 99845, New Caledonia
Tel +687 272383   Fax +687 263249
fedcalfoot@canl.nc   www.fedcalfoot.com
President: FOURNIER Claude   General Secretary: SALVATORE Jean-Paul
Vice-President: TAVERGEUX Gilles   Treasurer: ELMOUR Eric   Media Officer: none
Men's Coach: CHAMBARON Didier   Women's Coach: DELANDE Stephane
FCF formed: 1928   OFC: 19   FIFA: 2004
Grey shirts, Red shorts, Grey socks

RECENT INTERNATIONAL MATCHES PLAYED BY NEW CALEDONIA

2002	Opponents	Score		Venue	Comp	Scorers	Att	Referee
6-07	Fiji	L	1-2	Auckland	OCr1	Sinedo [79]	1 000	Rugg NZL
8-07	Australia	L	0-11	Auckland	OCr1		200	Rugg NZL
10-07	Vanuatu	L	0-1	Auckland	OCr1		500	Ariiotima TAH
2003								
30-06	Papua New Guinea	W	2-0	Suva	SPr1	Djamali [69], Hmae.M [81]		Shah FIJ
1-07	Micronesia †	W	18-0	Suva	SPr1	Hmae.M 4 [3 41 49 53], Poatinda 6 [8 9 29 33 66 76] Wajoka 3 [15 62 85], Elmour [16], Joseph [71], Jacques [78] Theodore [80], Jacky [84]	3 000	Moli SOL
3-07	Tonga	W	4-0	Suva	SPr1	Djamali [10], Dokunengo [30], Cawa [54], Kabeu [74]	700	Shah FIJ
5-07	Tahiti	W	4-0	Nadi	SPr1	Lameu 2 [10 41], Djamali [31], Poatinda [88]	3 000	Shah FIJ
9-07	Vanuatu	D	1-1	Lautoka	SPsf	Kabeu [44]. W 4-3p	7 000	Shah FIJ
11-07	Fiji	L	0-2	Suva	SPf		10 000	Attison VAN
2004								
12-05	Tahiti	D	0-0	Honiara	WCq		14 000	Rakaroi FIJ
15-05	Solomon Islands	L	0-2	Honiara	WCq		20 000	Attison VAN
17-05	Cook Islands	W	8-0	Honiara	WCq	Wajoka [3], Hmae.M 5 [20 40 42 52 85], Hmae.J [35], Djamali [25]	400	Singh FIJ
19-05	Tonga	W	8-0	Honiara	WCq	HmaeJ [4], Poatinda 3 [26 42 79], Hmae.M [45], Wajoka 2 [54 58] Kaume [72]	14 000	Fred VAN
2005								
No international matches played in 2005								
2006								
No international matches played in 2006								
2007								
17-07	Vanuatu	W	5-3	Noumea	Fr	Mapou [40], Toto 2 [47 62], HmaeJ [56], Wajoka [69p]		
19-07	Vanuatu	L	0-2	Noumea	Fr			

Fr = Friendly match • OC = OFC Oceania Nations Cup • SP = South Pacific Games • WC = FIFA World Cup
q = qualifier • r1 = first round group • sf = semi-final • f = final • † Not a full international

NEW CALEDONIA NATIONAL TEAM RECORDS AND RECORD SEQUENCES

Records			Sequence records					
Victory	18-0	GUM 1991	Wins	6	1964-1966	Clean sheets	4	1987
Defeat	0-8	AUS 1980	Defeats	6	1995-1998	Goals scored	31	1951-1966
Player Caps	n/a		Undefeated	9	1969	Without goal	3	1988
Player Goals	n/a		Without win	6	1995-1998	Goals against	15	1969-1973

RECENT LEAGUE AND CUP RECORD

	Division d'Honneur				National Championship				Cup		
Year	Champions	Pts	Runners-up	Pts	Champions	Score	Runners-up		Winners	Score	Runners-up
1998					AS Poum	4-2	JS Traput Lifou		JS Traput Lifou	1-1 4-3p	CS Nékoué
1999					FC Gaïcha	2-2 4-3p	AS Auteuil		JS Traput Lifou	1-0	AS Auteuil
2000					JS Baco	1-0	JS Traput Lifou		AS Magenta	1-1 4-1p	JS Traput Lifou
2001					JS Baco	1-0	AS Mont-Doré		AS Magenta	4-3	AS Mont-Doré
2002	JS Baco	49	AS Magenta	42	AS Mont-Doré	2-2 4-3p	JS Baco		AS Magenta	5-2	JS Ouvéa
2003	AS Magenta	62	JS Baco	54	AS Magenta	5-3	JS Baco		AS Magenta	1-0	JS Baco
2004	AS Magenta	73	AS Mont-Doré	59	AS Magenta	3-1	AS Mont-Doré		AS Magenta	2-1	AS Mont-Doré
2005	AS Magenta	73	JS Baco	61	AS Magenta	3-2	AS Mont-Doré		AS Magenta	2-1	JS Baco
2006	AS Mont-Doré	49	JS Baco	42	Not played				AS Mont Dore	2-1	JS Baco
2007	AS Lossi	45	AS Magenta	41	JS Baco	League	AS Lossi		AS Lössi	1-0	AS Mont-Doré

NEW CALEDONIA COUNTRY INFORMATION

Capital	Nouméa	Status	French overseas territory		GDP per Capita	$15 000
Population	213 679				GNP Ranking	n/a
Area km²	19 060	Language	French		Dialling code	+687
Population density	11 per km²	Literacy rate	91%		Internet code	.nc
% in urban areas	n/a	Main religion	Christian 60%		GMT +/−	+11
Towns/Cities ('000)	Nouméa 93; Mont-Doré 26; Dumbéa 21; Wé 11; Paita 10; Tadine 8; Poindimié 5; Houailu 5					
Neighbours (km)	South Pacific Ocean 2 254					
Main stadia	Nouméa-Daly Magenta – Nouméa					

NED – NETHERLANDS

NATIONAL TEAM RECORD
JULY 10TH 2006 TO JULY 12TH 2010

PL	W	D	L	F	A	%
11	8	3	0	22	5	86.3

For the first time since 1981 it looked as if a team other than PSV, Ajax or Feyenoord would be crowned Dutch champions but breaking the grip of the big three requires nerves to handle the pressure and AZ Alkmaar lost theirs on the final day of what had been a dramatic and exciting season. Louis Van Gaal's young AZ team had been in sensational scoring form all season but after losing key games trailed Ronald Koeman's PSV for much of the campaign. However, a disastrous loss of form in March and April saw PSV's lead crumble and going into the final fixtures they were third behind AZ and Ajax on goal difference with all three clubs level of points. A win against lowly Excelsior was all AZ needed to win their first title since 1981 but remarkably they lost 3-2. Ajax, in second place, beat Willem II 2-0 but that was not enough thanks to PSV's 5-1 victory over Vitesse. PSV's fifth goal, scored by Phillip Cocu with 13 minutes to go, meant that they retained their title by the narrowest of margins - a goal difference of one. AZ's misery then continued after the end of the League campaign. Firstly, they lost the Cup Final to Ajax after a tense penalty shoot-out. With both teams having scored their first seven kicks, Ryan Donk missed AZ's eighth

INTERNATIONAL HONOURS
Qualified for the FIFA World Cup finals 1934 1938 1974 1978 1990 1994 1998 2006
UEFA European Championship 1988   **UEFA European U-21 Championship** 2006
UEFA Champions League Feyenoord 1970 Ajax 1971 1972 1973 1995 PSV Eindhoven 1988

which left Edgar Davids to score to win the Cup for Ajax. The season was then extended further thanks to the convoluted play-off system to determine European places. The chance to join PSV in the UEFA Champions League saw AZ and Ajax meet again, over two legs, and once more there was disappointment for AZ who had to settle for a place in the UEFA Cup. In Europe it was not a vintage year for Dutch clubs, especially for Feyenoord who were thrown out of the UEFA Cup after their fans went on the rampage in Nancy. AZ did reach the quarter-finals of the UEFA Cup and PSV made it to the quarter-finals of the UEFA Champions League, but despite having knocked-out Arsenal, PSV were abject in the manner of their defeat to Liverpool. In the Euro 2008 qualifiers, the national team made solid progress towards the finals, remaining undefeated in their first six group games, as well as in five other internationals. They did so without Mark van Bommel and Ruud van Nistelrooij who both refused to play under coach Marco van Basten. Van Nistelrooij had criticised the tendency not to pick players with strong personalities in order to limit disruption within the camp. With former coaches criticised for not doing enough to counter a trait that has cost the national team so dearly in the past, it was a case of damned if you do, dammed if you don't.

Koninklijke Nederlandse Voetbalbond (KNVB)
Woudenbergseweg 56-58, PO Box 515, Am Zeist 3700, Netherlands
Tel +31 343 499201   Fax +31 343 499189
concern@knvb.nl   www.knvb.nl
President: SPRENGERS Mathieu Dr   General Secretary: BEEN Hendrik
Vice-President: LESTERHUIS Hans   Treasurer: HOOGENDOORN Jan Willem   Media Officer: JANSMA Kees
Men's Coach: VAN BASTEN Marco   Women's Coach: PAUW Vera
KNVB formed: 1889   UEFA: 1954   FIFA: 1904
Orange shirts with white trimmings, White shorts, Orange socks or White shirts with orange trimmings, Orange shorts, White socks

RECENT INTERNATIONAL MATCHES PLAYED BY THE NETHERLANDS

2004	Opponents		Score	Venue	Comp	Scorers	Att	Referee
15-06	Germany	D	1-1	Porto	ECr1	Van Nistelrooij [81]	52 000	Frisk SWE
19-06	Czech Republic	L	2-3	Aveiro	ECr1	Bouma [4], Van Nistelrooij [19]	29 935	Mejuto Gonzalez ESP
23-06	Latvia	W	3-0	Braga	ECr1	Van Nistelrooij 2 [27p 35], Makaay [84]	27 904	Milton Nielsen DEN
26-06	Sweden	D	0-0	Faro-Loule	ECqf	W 5-4p	27 286	Michel SVK
30-06	Portugal	L	1-2	Lisbon	ECsf	Jorge Andrade OG [63]	46 679	Frisk SWE
18-08	Sweden	D	2-2	Stockholm	Fr	Sneijder [17], Van Bommel [43]	20 377	Styles ENG
3-09	Liechtenstein	W	3-0	Utrecht	Fr	Van Bommel [23], Ooijer [56], Landzaat [78]	15 000	Brines SCO
8-09	Czech Republic	W	2-0	Amsterdam	WCq	Van Hooijdonk 2 [34 84]	48 488	Merk GER
9-10	FYR Macedonia	D	2-2	Skopje	WCq	Bouma [42], Kuyt [65]	15 000	Frojdfeldt SWE
13-10	Finland	W	3-1	Amsterdam	WCq	Sneijder [39], Van Nistelrooij 2 [41 63]	50 000	Bennett ENG
17-11	Andorra	W	3-0	Barcelona	WCq	Cocu [21], Robben [31], Sneijder [78]	2 000	Yefet ISR
2005								
9-02	England	D	0-0	Birmingham	Fr		40 705	Frojdfeldt SWE
26-03	Romania	W	2-0	Bucharest	WCq	Cocu [1], Babel [84]	19 000	Medina Cantalejo ESP
30-03	Armenia	W	2-0	Eindhoven	WCq	Castelen [3], Van Nistelrooij [33]	35 000	Trefoloni ITA
4-06	Romania	W	2-0	Rotterdam	WCq	Robben [26], Kuyt [47]	47 000	De Santis ITA
8-06	Finland	W	4-0	Helsinki	WCq	Van Nistelrooij [36], Kuyt [76], Coco [85], Van Persie [87]	37 786	Hamer LUX
17-08	Germany	D	2-2	Rotterdam	Fr	Robben 2 [3 46]	45 500	Hauge NOR
3-09	Armenia	W	1-0	Yerevan	WCq	Van Nistelrooij [64]	1 747	Dougal SCO
7-09	Andorra	W	4-0	Eindhoven	WCq	Van der Vaart [23], Cocu [27], Van Nistelrooij 2 [43 89]	34 000	Hanacsek HUN
8-10	Czech Republic	W	2-0	Prague	WCq	Van der Vaart [31], Opdam [38]	17 478	Sars FRA
12-10	FYR Macedonia	D	0-0	Amsterdam	WCq		50 000	Farina ITA
12-11	Italy	L	1-3	Amsterdam	Fr	Babel [38]	50 000	Ivanov RUS
2006								
1-03	Ecuador	W	1-0	Amsterdam	Fr	Kuijt [48]	35 000	Benquerenca POR
27-05	Cameroon	W	1-0	Rotterdam	Fr	Van Nistelrooij [23]	46 228	Plautz AUT
1-06	Mexico	W	2-1	Eindhoven	Fr	Heitinga [53], Babel [57]	35 000	Frojdfeldt SWE
4-06	Australia	D	1-1	Rotterdam	Fr	Van Nistelrooij [9]	49 000	Dean ENG
11-06	Serbia & Montenegro	W	1-0	Leipzig	WCr1	Robben [18]	37 216	Merk GER
16-06	Côte d'Ivoire	W	2-1	Stuttgart	WCr1	Van Persie [23], Van Nistelrooij [27]	52 000	Ruiz COL
21-06	Argentina	D	0-0	Frankfurt	WCr1		48 000	Medina Cantalejo ESP
25-06	Portugal	L	0-1	Nuremberg	WCr2		41 000	Ivanov.V RUS
16-08	Republic of Ireland	W	4-0	Dublin	Fr	Huntelaar 2 [24 53], Robben [40], Van Persie [69]	42 400	Ovrebo NOR
2-09	Luxembourg	W	1-0	Luxembourg	ECq	Mathijsen [18]	8 055	Lopes Ferreira POR
6-09	Belarus	W	3-0	Eindhoven	ECq	Van Persie 2 [33 78], Kuyt [92+]	30 089	Webb ENG
7-10	Bulgaria	D	1-1	Sofia	ECq	Van Persie [62]	30 547	Ovrebø NOR
11-10	Albania	W	2-1	Amsterdam	ECq	Van Persie [15], Beqaj OG [42]	40 085	Yefet ISR
15-11	England	D	1-1	Amsterdam	Fr	Van der Vaart [86]	45 090	Michel SVK
2007								
7-02	Russia	W	4-1	Amsterdam	Fr	Babel [68], Sneijder [71], Mathijsen [79], Van der Vaart [89p]	24 589	Clattenburg ENG
24-03	Romania	D	0-0	Rotterdam	ECq		48 000	Merk GER
28-03	Slovenia	W	1-0	Celje	ECq	Van Bronckhorst [86]	10 000	Mejuto Gonzalez ESP
2-06	Korea Republic	W	2-0	Seoul	Fr	Van der Vaart 2 [31p 72]	62 884	Ramachandran MAS
6-06	Thailand	W	3-1	Bangkok	Fr	Van der Vaart [3], Heitinga [42], Hesselink [55]	20 000	Ganesan SIN

Fr = Friendly match • EC = UEFA EURO 2004/2008 • WC = FIFA World Cup • q = qualifier • r1 = first round group • qf = quarter-final

NETHERLANDS NATIONAL TEAM RECORDS AND RECORD SEQUENCES

Records			Sequence records					
Victory	9-0	FIN 1912, NOR 1972	Wins	7	1971-72, 2002-03	Clean sheets	6	1987, 2004-05
Defeat	2-12	ENG 1907	Defeats	8	1949-1950	Goals scored	23	1912-1920
Player Caps	113	VAN DER SAR Edwin	Undefeated	17	2001-2003	Without goal	3	1949-50, 1968
Player Goals	40	KLUIVERT Patrick	Without win	12	1951-1953	Goals against	24	1938-1948

KINGDOM OF THE NETHERLANDS; KONINKRIJK DER NEDERLANDEN

Capital	The Hague	Language	Dutch	Formation	1579
Population	16 491 461	Area	41 526 km²	Density 393 per km²	% in cities 89%
GDP per cap	$28 600	Dailling code	+31	Internet .nl	GMT +/- +1

MEDALS TABLE

		Overall			League			Cup			Europe			City	Stadium	Cap'ty	DoF
		G	S	B	G	S	B	G	S	G	S	B					
1	Ajax	51	27	13	29	19	10	16	5	6	3	3	Amsterdam	Amsterdam ArenA	51 859	1900
2	PSV Eindhoven	30	19	16	20	13	12	8	6	2		4	Eindhoven	Philips Stadion	36 500	1913
3	Feyenoord	27	22	16	14	19	12	10	3	3		4	Rotterdam	Feijenoord Stadion -De Kuip	51 180	1908
4	HVV Den Haag	9	3		8			1	3				The Hague			1883
5	Sparta Rotterdam	9	2	5	6		5	3	2				Rotterdam	Sparta - Het Kasteel	11 500	1888
6	HBS Den Haag	5	5		3			2	5				The Hague			1893
7	Willem II Tilburg	5	2	5	3	1	5	2	1				Tilburg	Willem II	14 700	1896
8	Quick Den Haag	5			1			4					The Hague			1896
9	ADO Den Haag	4	6	4	2		4	2	6				The Hague	Zuiderpark	11 000	1905
	Go Ahead Eagles	4	6	4	4	5	4		1				Deventer	Adelaarshorst	6 400	1902
11	AZ Alkmaar	4	4	6	1	2	5	3	1	1	1		Alkmaar	DSB Stadion	17 023	1967
12	FC Utrecht	4	3	2	1	1	2	3	2				Utrecht	Nieuw Galgenwaard	18 500	1970
13	RCH Heemstede	4			2			2					Haarlem			
14	Twente Enschede	3	7	13	1	2	11	2	4	1	2		Enschede	Arke Stadion	13 500	1965
15	Roda JC Kerkrade	3	5		1	2		2	3				Kerkrade	Parkstad Limburg	19 200	1962

RECENT LEAGUE AND CUP RECORD

	Championship						Cup		
Year	Champions	Pts	Runners-up	Pts	Third	Pts	Winners	Score	Runners-up
1995	Ajax	61	Roda JC Kerkrade	54	PSV Eindhoven	47	Feyenoord	2-1	FC Volendam
1996	Ajax	83	PSV Eindhoven	77	Feyenoord	63	PSV Eindhoven	5-2	Sparta Rotterdam
1997	PSV Eindhoven	77	Feyenoord	73	Twente Enschede	65	Roda JC Kerkrade	4-2	SC Heerenveen
1998	Ajax	89	PSV Eindhoven	72	Vitesse Arnhem	70	SC Heerenveen	3-1	Twente Enschede
1999	Feyenoord	80	Willem II Tilburg	65	PSV Eindhoven	61	Ajax	2-0	Fortuna Sittard
2000	PSV Eindhoven	84	SC Heerenveen	68	Feyenoord	64	Roda JC Kerkrade	2-0	NEC Nijmegan
2001	PSV Eindhoven	83	Feyenoord	66	Ajax	61	Twente Enschede	0-0 4-3p	PSV Eindhoven
2002	Ajax	73	PSV Eindhoven	68	Feyenoord	64	Ajax	3-2	FC Utrecht
2003	PSV Eindhoven	84	Ajax	83	Feyenoord	80	FC Utrecht	4-1	Feyenoord
2004	Ajax	80	PSV Eindhoven	74	Feyenoord	68	FC Utrecht	1-0	Twente Enschede
2005	PSV Eindhoven	87	Ajax	77	AZ Alkmaar	64	PSV Eindhoven	4-0	Willem II Tilburg
2006	PSV Eindhoven	84	AZ Alkmaar	74	Feyenoord	71	Ajax	2-1	PSV Eindhoven
2007	PSV Eindhoven	75	Ajax	75	AZ Alkmaar	72	Ajax	1-1 8-7p	AZ Alkmaar

KNVB BEKER 2006–07

Second Round

Team	Score
Ajax	5
Jong RKC Waalwijk *	2
Türkiyemspor *	1
ADO Den Haag	6
FC Den Bosch	4
HSC '21/Brein *	3
Sparta Nijkerk *	1
Haarlem	6
De Graafschap *	3
VVV Venlo	1
FC Zwolle	0
FC Emmen *	1
Be Quick '28 *	4
VVOG	1
Flevo Boys *	0
Willem II Tilburg	2
Roda JC Kerkrade	2
SC Heerenveen *	0
Cambuur Leeuwarden	2
ASWH *	4
SC Genemuiden *	3
FC Omniworld	2
ONS Sneek *	0
Jong AZ	2
Sparta Rotterdam	6
De Treffers/Kegro *	2
FC Volendam	0 3p
Achilles '29 *	0 4p
Feyenoord	3
BV Veendam *	2
FC Dordrecht	2
RKC Waalwijk *	3
NAC Breda	4
Ijselmeervogels *	2
Top Oss	1
FC Groningen *	2
NEC Nijmegan	2
EVV *	0
DOTO *	1
FC Twente Enschede	7
Go Ahead Eagles	1
Excelsior '31 *	0
RKSV Schijndel *	0
Excelsior	1
Vitesse Arnhem	3
Argon *	1
Kozakken Boys *	0
PSV Eindhoven	2
FC Utrecht *	3
AGOVV Apeldoorn	1
Fortuna Sittard	0
Rijnsburgse Boys *	1
FC Eindhoven *	3
Heracles Almelo	2
Helmond Sport	1
RBC Roosendaal *	3
MVV Maastricht	4
HHC *	1
Ter Leede *	1
Stormvogels/Telstar Velsen	2
Meerssen *	6
WHC	3
Bennekom/Tecpool *	0
AZ Alkmaar	10

Third Round

Team	Score
Ajax *	2
ADO Den Haag	0
FC Den Bosch	0
Haarlem *	1
De Graafschap *	1
FC Emmen	0
Be Quick '28 *	2
Willem II Tilburg	5
Roda JC Kerkrade *	5
ASWH	0
SC Genemuiden	1
Jong AZ *	8
Sparta Rotterdam	4
Achilles '29 *	0
Feyenoord	2
RKC Waalwijk *	3
NAC Breda	3
FC Groningen *	1
NEC Nijmegan	1
FC Twente Enschede *	3
Go Ahead Eagles *	2
Excelsior	0
Vitesse Arnhem *	0
PSV Eindhoven	4
FC Utrecht *	5
Rijnsburgse Boys	0
FC Eindhoven	0
RBC Roosendaal *	4
MVV Maastricht *	3
Stormvogels/Telstar Velsen	1
Meerssen	1
AZ Alkmaar *	10

Fourth Round

Team	Score
Ajax *	4
Haarlem	0
De Graafschap	2
Willem II Tilburg *	4
Roda JC Kerkrade *	2
Jong AZ	1
Sparta Rotterdam *	2
RKC Waalwijk	3
NAC Breda	2
FC Twente Enschede *	1
Go Ahead Eagles	2
PSV Eindhoven *	3
FC Utrecht *	1
RBC Roosendaal	0
MVV Maastricht	0
AZ Alkmaar *	5

* Home team • Professional clubs join in the second round

KNVB BEKER 2006–07

Quarter–finals	Semi–finals	Final

Ajax	2
Willem II Tilburg *	0

Ajax *	3
RKC Waalwijk	1

Roda JC Kerkrade	0
RKC Waalwijk *	1

Ajax	1 8p
AZ Alkmaar	1 7p

NAC Breda *	3
PSV Eindhoven	0

NAC Breda	0
AZ Alkmaar *	6

FC Utrecht *	1
AZ Alkmaar	2

CUP FINAL 2007

De Kuip, Rotterdam, 6-05-2007, Att: 42 200 Ref: Van Egmond

Ajax	1 8p	Huntelaar [51]
AZ Alkmaar	1 7p	Dembélé [4]

Ajax - Maarten STEKELENBURG - Johnny HEITINGA, Jaap STAM, Thomas VERMAELEN, Urby EMANUELSON (Tom DE MUL 76), Ryan BABEL (Olaf LINDENBERGH 120), Klaas Jan HUNTELAAR◦, Wesley SNEIJDER◦ (Kenneth PEREZ 87), Edgar DAVIDS, GABRI•89, George OGARARU. Tr:

AZ - Khalid SINOUH - Grétar STEINSSON, Kew JALIENS, Ryan DONK, Tim DE CLER, Julian JENNER, Demy DE ZEEUW (Rogier MOLHOEK 101), Simon CZIOMMER (Danny KOEVERMANS 70), Maarten MARTENS (Nourdin BOUKHARI 66), Moussa DEMBELE, Shota ARVELADZE. Tr: Louis VAN GAAL

Penalties: AZ first: Arveladze ✓; Perez ✓; Boukhari ✓; Huntelaar ✓; Steinsson ✓; Vermaelen ✓; De Cler ✓; Lindbergh ✓; Jenner ✓; Heitinga ✓; Dembélé ✓; De Mul ✓; Molhoek ✓; Ogararu ✓; Donk ✘; Davids ✓

NETHERLANDS 2006-07

EREDIVISIE

Team	Pl	W	D	L	F	A	Pts	PSV	Ajax	AZ	FC Twente	Heerenveen	Roda JC	Fetenoord	Groningen	Utrecht	NEC	NAC	Vitesse	Sparta	Heracles	Willem II	Excelsior	RKC	ADO
PSV Eindhoven †	34	23	6	5	75	25	75		1-5	2-3	2-0	3-1	4-1	2-1	1-0	5-0	3-1	3-0	5-1	7-0	3-0	4-0	4-0	2-0	2-1
Ajax †	34	23	6	5	84	35	75	0-1		2-2	1-1	0-1	2-0	4-1	3-2	2-0	2-0	2-0	3-0	5-2	3-0	6-0	2-2	5-0	2-0
AZ Alkmaar ‡	34	21	9	4	83	31	72	1-3	1-1		2-2	3-1	2-2	0-0	2-0	5-1	0-0	8-1	1-0	3-0	5-0	2-0	5-0	2-0	2-2
FC Twente Enschede ‡	34	19	9	6	67	37	66	1-0	1-4	3-0		5-1	2-2	3-0	7-1	3-0	4-0	2-1	2-0	2-0	1-1	0-0	4-1	4-3	3-1
SC Heerenveen ‡	34	16	7	11	60	43	55	0-0	0-2	1-3	1-2		1-0	5-1	4-2	0-0	3-0	4-2	0-0	2-0	5-1	5-0	2-0	1-0	1-1
Roda JC Kerkrade	34	15	9	10	47	36	54	2-0	2-0	0-2	2-0	1-0		1-2	0-1	0-0	1-0	3-2	2-4	2-1	7-0	2-1	2-0	1-1	1-0
Feyenoord	34	15	8	11	56	66	53	1-1	0-4	3-2	2-1	4-3	1-1		0-4	2-0	1-1	3-2	3-2	0-0	0-0	1-0		3-1	3-1
FC Groningen ‡	34	15	6	13	54	54	51	0-2	2-3	1-1	1-1	1-1	2-1	3-0		0-2	4-1	3-1	4-3	0-1	2-1	4-1	2-1	1-1	2-5
FC Utrecht	34	13	9	12	41	44	48	1-1	2-3	0-4	0-0	1-0	2-0	2-1	3-0		3-0	1-0	2-0	2-2	0-0	3-0	1-0	5-0	2-0
NEC Nijmegen	34	12	8	14	36	44	44	2-1	2-2	0-2	0-3	0-2	0-0	4-1	1-1	2-0		2-1	1-0	1-2	2-0	1-2	0-1	1-0	3-2
NAC Breda	34	12	7	15	43	54	43	1-1	1-2	1-4	0-0	1-0	0-2	4-1	0-0	2-1	0-2		2-1	3-1	1-1	0-0	2-1	2-1	2-2
Vitesse Arnhem	34	10	8	16	50	55	38	0-1	4-2	1-3	1-1	1-3	0-0	0-1	3-2	4-2	1-1	0-1		3-0	4-0	1-0	2-3	3-1	2-2
Sparta Rotterdam	34	10	7	17	40	66	37	1-1	3-0	0-2	3-0	2-2	2-2	1-4	0-1	1-1	0-4	0-3	1-2		0-0	1-0	2-1	1-0	2-1
Heracles Almelo	34	7	11	16	32	64	32	0-2	0-3	0-0	3-1	1-0	1-1	4-1	0-1	3-0	0-0	2-0	2-2	2-3		2-2	3-2	1-1	3-1
Willem II Tilburg	34	8	7	19	31	64	31	1-3	0-2	0-4	1-3	1-3	0-1	3-5	3-0	2-1	1-0	0-2	0-0	2-0			2-1	3-1	2-1
Excelsior Rotterdam ‡‡	34	8	6	20	43	65	30	0-0	1-3	3-2	1-2	3-1	0-1	1-3	0-2	0-1	1-1	0-2	2-2	3-1	6-1	3-2		0-3	3-1
RKC Waalwijk ‡‡	34	6	9	19	33	60	27	0-3	2-2	0-2	1-0	0-2	3-2	2-2	0-2	1-1	0-1	0-1	3-1	2-1	2-0	1-1	1-1		1-0
ADO Den Haag	34	3	8	23	40	72	17	0-2	1-2	1-3	1-2	1-3	2-3	0-2	3-3	1-3	1-1	0-2	0-4	2-4	2-0	2-1	2-2	1-1	

18/08/2006 - 29/04/2007 • † Qualified for the UEFA Champions League • ‡ Qualified for the UEFA Cup • ‡‡ relegation play-off
Champions League play-off semi-finals: Heerenveen 1-0 0-4 **Ajax**; FC Twente 1-1 0-2 **AZ**; Final: AZ 2-1 0-3 **Ajax**;
Ajax qualify for the UEFA Champions League whilst AZ, FC Twente and Heerenveen qualify for the UEFA Cup
UEFA Cup play-off semi-finals: **FC Utrecht** 0-0 1-1 Roda JC; **FC Groningen** 2-1 1-1 Feyenoord; Final: FC Utrecht 0-2 1-2 **FC Groningen**;
FC Groningen qualified for the UEFA Cup
Top scorers: Alfonso AVES, Heerenveen 34; Danny KOEVERMANS, AZ 22; Blaise N'KUFO, FC Twente 22; Jefferson FARFAN, PSV 21; Klaas-Jan HUNTELAAR, Ajax 21; Danko LAZAVIC, Vitesse 19; Wesley SNEIJDER, Ajax 18; Kennedy BAKIRCIOGLU, FC Twente 15; Shota ARVELADZE, AZ 14

NETHERLANDS 2006-07

EERSTE DIVISIE

Team	Pl	W	D	L	F	A	Pts	Graafschap	VVV	RBC	Volendam	Den Bosch	Dordrecht	Go Ahead	Veendam	Zwolle	Stormvogels	Emmen	Cambuur	MVV	Haarlem	Fortuna	Omniworld	TOP Oss	Helmond	Eindhoven	AGOVV
De Graafschap	38	25	8	5	88	41	83			4-2	0-1	4-2	3-1	2-0	0-1	1-0	2-1		3-3	3-3	4-1	6-1	2-0	3-1		1-3	3-1
VVV Venlo †	38	21	8	9	64	44	71	1-2			3-1	0-0	2-1	1-3	2-1	2-2	2-1	1-0	3-2	0-0	1-0	3-1	3-1	2-1	6-2	1-1	0-0
RBC Roosendaal †	38	20	10	8	82	44	70	1-3	3-1		1-1	2-0	3-2	3-3	1-1	3-0	3-1	5-0	2-0	4-1	2-0	2-0	2-0	3-1	5-0	0-2	5-1
FC Volendam †	38	19	11	8	65	40	68	2-1	1-0	1-1		2-1	1-3	3-0	1-1	1-0	4-1	6-3	0-1	3-1	3-1	2-0	0-0	4-1	3-0	1-3	1-0
FC Den Bosch †	38	20	8	10	65	43	68	0-4	0-1	2-1	3-0		1-0	1-1	1-1	2-2	2-0	3-0	3-1	2-1	4-1	2-0	3-0	1-0	3-0	1-2	2-3
FC Dordrecht †	38	20	7	11	76	49	67	1-3	2-0	0-4	1-0	0-0		1-2	1-1	0-4	2-2	0-0	1-4	0-1	3-0	4-1	3-0	4-1	2-2	1-4	1-0
Go Ahead Eagles †	38	16	9	13	56	51	57	3-1	0-1	1-1	1-2	1-1	0-3		0-0	1-1	1-2	2-0	1-0	2-0	3-1	3-1	2-1	5-0	1-2	2-0	1-2
BV Veendam †	38	14	13	11	57	50	55	1-4	2-1	1-1	0-4	0-2	2-1	2-0		3-1	2-1	1-1	0-1	2-1	2-2	1-1	0-2	2-0	3-0	2-2	4-0
FC Zwolle †	38	14	11	13	66	51	53	2-2	1-2	1-1	0-1	1-1	3-0	1-3			2-1	3-0	2-3	0-1	2-0	1-0	0-1	2-2	5-0	4-1	0-0
Stormvogels/Telstar	38	14	6	18	61	61	48	0-0	3-1	2-4	5-3	3-1	0-0	2-2	1-2	1-2		1-2	0-1	1-0	1-1	0-3	2-0	4-1	2-1	2-3	3-2
FC Emmen	38	13	9	16	59	65	48	0-3	1-2	2-2	2-2	3-0	1-1	1-1	4-0	3-3	0-1		0-1	0-0	1-1	0-2	2-1	1-1	2-1	3-2	3-2
Cambuur-Leeuwarden	38	13	8	17	44	57	47	1-1	2-1	2-1	0-1	1-2	4-2	3-1	0-0	0-4	1-4	0-2		1-1	1-0	2-1	4-1	2-1	0-0	0-0	1-1
MVV Maastricht	38	11	13	14	49	51	46	1-3	0-0	2-1	1-0	1-1	1-4	1-3	4-1	1-0	1-3	1-3	0-0		2-1	1-1	1-0	1-0	2-2	2-5	0-0
Haarlem	38	10	13	15	43	57	43	0-3	0-1	1-1	1-1	1-1	1-2	1-0	1-0	3-1	2-0	1-1	1-3	1-2		1-1	1-0	2-1	1-2	1-1	1-2
Fortuna Sittard	38	12	7	19	38	57	43	0-2	0-2	2-2	1-3	0-0	0-4	0-2	0-2	0-0	2-1	0-4	2-1	0-0	2-0		1-2	2-1	0-1	2-1	2-1
FC Omniworld Almere	38	11	8	19	55	82	41	0-1	2-3	1-4	0-0	1-4	2-5	0-1	3-1	2-7	2-5	5-3	2-2	3-1	2-0	1-1		3-2	1-1	1-1	2-0
TOP Oss	38	11	7	20	59	78	40	4-2	1-4	2-0	0-2	0-3	2-2	4-0	0-3	3-1	3-3	4-0	3-1	3-0	1-6	2-1	4-5		1-3	0-0	5-2
Helmond Sport	38	8	12	18	40	76	36	0-0	1-1	2-0	1-1	3-3	2-4	3-1	7-1	2-1	0-5	0-0	1-1	1-0	0-1	1-2	0-0	2-2		2-2	2-2
FC Eindhoven §3	38	7	12	19	47	80	30	1-2	0-5	2-3	1-0	2-1	1-7	0-4	1-2	1-2	2-1	1-4	0-2	1-6	1-0	2-2	1-1	0-2	1-1		4-1
AGOVV Apeldoorn	38	7	8	23	42	79	29	4-4	1-1	0-3	0-1	3-0	1-0	1-2	2-1	1-2	0-2	0-3	3-1	2-0	3-1	2-1	1-3	0-2	1-1	2-0	

11/08/2006 - 27/04/2007 • † Qualified for the play-offs • § = points deducted
Promotion play-off first round: Zwolle 0-1 1-1 **Dordrecht**; **Veendam** 5-1 0-2 Go Ahead
Second round: Den Bosch 1-2 1-0 0-1 **VVV**; Volendam 3-5 0-1 **RBC**; Veendam 1-0 0-3 **Excelsior Rotterdam**; Dordrecht 2-0 0-2 0-3 **RKC Waalwijk**
Third round: **VVV** 2-0 0-1 3-0 RKC Waalwijk; RBC 1-1 0-1 **Excelsior Rotterdam** • VVV promoted, RKC relegated

PSV EINDHOVEN 2006–07

Date	Opponents	Score		Comp	Scorers	Att
13-08-2006	Ajax	L 1-3	A	SC	Cocu [49]	35 000
20-08-2006	NEC Nijmegan	W 3-1	H	ED	Cocu [44], Alex [45], Hesselink [57]	33 400
27-08-2006	Twente Enschede	L 0-1	A	ED		13 000
9-09-2006	Willem II Tilburg	W 3-1	A	ED	Méndez 2 [14 21], Farfan [45p]	13 900
12-09-2006	Liverpool - ENG	D 0-0	H	CLgC		32 000
17-09-2006	Feyenoord	W 2-1	H	ED	Farfan [7], Alex [42]	35 000
20-09-2006	Kozakken Boys	W 2-0	A	KBr2	Arouna Koné [73], Simons [83p]	
23-09-2006	ADO Den Haag	W 2-0	A	ED	Diego Tardelli [57], Méndez [85]	7 133
27-09-2006	Girondins Bordeaux - FRA	W 1-0	A	CLgC	Väyrynen [65]	23 587
1-10-2006	SC Heerenveen	D 0-0	A	ED		25 400
15-10-2006	Roda JC Kerkrade	W 4-1	H	ED	Farfan [75], Alex [77], Aissati [90], Beerens [90]	12 755
18-10-2006	Galatasaray - TUR	W 2-1	A	CLgC	Kromkamp [59], Arouna Koné [72]	50 389
22-10-2006	AZ Alkmaar	W 3-1	A	ED	Da Costa [12], Méndez [45], Arouna Koné [45]	17 000
25-10-2006	Sparta Rotterdam	W 7-0	H	ED	Arouna Koné 2 [4 40], Farfan 3 [21p 28 81], Reiziger [78], Simons [90p]	33 800
28-10-2006	RKC Waalwijk	W 3-0	A	ED	Afellay [52], Arouna Koné 2 [59 90]	7 000
31-10-2006	Galatasaray - TUR	W 2-0	H	CLgC	Simons [59], Arouna Koné [84]	34 500
4-11-2006	NAC Breda	W 3-0	H	ED	Farfan 2 [27 85], Cocu [42]	33 800
8-11-2006	Vitesse Arnhem	W 4-0	A	KBr3	Arouna Koné [18], Culina [25], Farfan [78], Simons [84p]	
12-11-2006	Ajax	W 1-0	A	ED	Simons [63]	50 496
18-11-2006	Excelsior Rotterdam	W 4-0	H	ED	Arouna Koné [29], Alex [44], Farfan [80], Salcido [85]	33 120
22-11-2006	Liverpool - ENG	L 0-2	A	CLgC		41 948
25-11-2006	FC Utrecht	W 5-0	H	ED	OG [9], Afellay [28], Farfan 2 [39 76], Arouna Koné [54]	33 114
2-12-2006	Vitesse Arnhem	W 1-0	A	ED	Méndez [22]	18 900
5-12-2006	Girondins Bordeaux - FRA	L 1-3	H	CLgC	Alex [87]	30 000
9-12-2006	FC Groningen	W 2-0	A	ED	Afellay [61], Arouna Koné [88]	19 254
15-12-2006	Heracles Almelo	W 3-0	H	ED	Simons [25p], Cocu [51], Kluivert [64]	33 403
23-12-2006	Willem II Tilburg	W 4-0	H	ED	Afellay [4], Arouna Koné [16], Simons [22], Diego Tardelli [71]	33 100
26-12-2006	Feyenoord	D 1-1	A	ED	Cocu [24]	45 000
30-12-2006	ADO Den Haag	W 2-1	H	ED	Kluivert [33], Farfan [48]	32 800
20-01-2007	SC Heerenveen	W 3-1	H	ED	Simons [14p], Arouna Koné [22], Farfan [35p]	33 212
25-01-2007	Go Ahead Eagles	W 3-2	H	KBr4	Simons [58], Farfan [74], Arouna Koné [79]	
28-01-2007	Roda JC Kerkrade	L 0-2	A	ED		16 233
3-02-2007	AZ Alkmaar	L 2-3	H	ED	Farfan [20], Cocu [65]	33 300
11-02-2007	Sparta Rotterdam	D 1-1	A	ED	Culina [46]	10 350
17-02-2007	Heracles Almelo	W 2-0	A	ED	Farfan [74], Diego Tardelli [90]	8 500
20-02-2007	Arsenal - ENG	W 1-0	H	CLr2	Méndez [61]	35 100
24-02-2007	FC Groningen	W 1-0	H	ED	Alex [85]	33 400
28-02-2007	NAC Breda	L 0-3	A	KBqf		
3-03-2007	RKC Waalwijk	W 2-0	H	ED	Farfan [3], Alcides [19]	33 300
7-03-2007	Arsenal - ENG	D 1-1	A	CLr2	Alex [83]	50 073
11-03-2007	Excelsior Rotterdam	D 0-0	A	ED		3 300
18-03-2007	Ajax	L 1-5	H	ED	Kluivert [68]	35 100
31-03-2007	NAC Breda	D 1-1	A	ED	Farfan [74]	16 580
3-04-2007	Liverpool - ENG	L 0-3	H	CLqf		35 100
7-04-2007	NEC Nijmegan	L 1-2	A	ED	Cocu [61]	12 500
11-04-2007	Liverpool - ENG	L 0-1	A	CLqf		41 447
14-04-2007	Twente Enschede	W 2-0	H	ED	Farfan 2 [19 20]	33 600
22-04-2007	FC Utrecht	D 1-1	A	ED	Afellay [11]	23 000
29-04-2007	Vitesse Arnhem	W 5-1	H	ED	Alex [8], Farfan 2 [10 66], Afellay [59], Cocu [77]	33 500

SC = Johan Cruijff Super Cup • ED = Eredivisie • KB = KNVB Cup • CL = UEFA Champions League
gC = Group C • r2 = second round • r3 = third round • r4 = fourth round • qf = quarter-final

THE FIFA BIG COUNT OF 2006

	Male	Female		Total
Number of players	1 585 604	160 256	Referees and Assistant Referees	6 830
Professionals	1 000		Admin, Coaches, Technical, Medical	4 408
Amateurs 18+	562 260		Number of clubs	3 656
Youth under 18	510 091		Number of teams	55 060
Unregistered	250 000		Clubs with women's teams	1 200
Total players	1 745 860		Players as % of population	10.59%

AJAX 2006-07

Date	Opponents	Score		Comp	Scorers	Att
9-08-2006	FC København - DEN	W	2-1	A	CLpr3	Huntelaar 2 [37 84]	40 000
13-08-2006	PSV Eindhoven	W	3-1	H	SC	Rosales [7], Perez [69], Sneijder [82]	35 000
20-08-2006	RKC Waalwijk	W	5-0	H	ED	Babel [33], Sneijder 2 [44 69], Heitinga [52], Rosales [89]	46 668
23-08-2006	FC København - DEN	L	0-2	H	CLpr3		35 617
27-08-2006	NAC Breda	W	2-1	A	ED	Sneijder 2 [73 84]	15 432
10-09-2006	Vitesse Arnhem	W	3-0	H	ED	Huntelaar 2 [32 55], Roger [45]	46 100
14-09-2006	Start Kristiansand - NOR	W	5-2	A	UCr1	Huntelaar 2 [17 87], Rosenberg [42], Sneijder [63], Roger Garcia [67]	1 840
17-09-2006	Roda JC Kerkrade	L	0-2	A	ED		17 000
20-09-2006	Jong RKC Waalwijk	W	5-2	A	KBr2	Rosenberg 2 [20 85], Maduro [29], Perez [48], Huntelaar [58]	2 000
24-09-2006	NEC Nijmegan	W	2-0	H	ED	Perez 2 [60 82]	46 810
28-09-2006	Start Kristiansand - NOR	W	4-0	H	UCr1	Rosenberg 2 [6 26], Grygera [43], Babel [68]	24 000
1-10-2006	FC Utrecht	W	3-2	A	ED	Gabri [7], Heitinga [45], Perez [87]	24 000
14-10-2006	FC Groningen	W	3-2	H	ED	Babel 2 [51 75], Emanuelson [80]	49 782
22-10-2006	Feyenoord	W	4-0	A	ED	Huntelaar 2 [12 38], Perez 2 [50p 62]	41 000
25-10-2006	ADO Den Haag	W	4-0	H	ED	Gabri [30], Sneijder [32]	45 757
28-10-2006	SC Heerenveen	W	2-0	A	ED	De Mul [17], Sneijder [76]	26 000
2-11-2006	FK Austria - AUT	W	3-0	H	UCgF	Huntelaar 2 [35 68], Manucharyan [65]	32 285
5-11-2006	Heracles Almelo	W	3-0	A	ED	Perez 2 [39 82p], Sneijder [87]	8 500
9-11-2006	ADO Den Haag	W	2-0	H	KBr3	Stam [8], Huntelaar [65]	
12-11-2006	PSV Eindhoven	L	0-1	H	ED		50 496
19-11-2006	Twente Enschede	D	1-1	H	ED	Sneijder [48]	49 364
23-11-2006	Sparta Praha - CZE	D	0-0	A	UCgF		12 230
26-11-2006	Sparta Rotterdam	L	0-3	A	ED		10 800
30-11-2006	Espanyol - ESP	L	0-2	H	UCgF		42 000
3-12-2006	Willem II Tilburg	W	6-0	H	ED	Grygera [4], Emanuelson [9], Mitea [19], Huntelaar 2 [22 45], De Mul [78]	46 695
10-12-2006	AZ Alkmaar	D	2-2	H	ED	Heitinga [35], Huntelaar [57]	50 649
13-12-2006	Zulte Waregem - BEL	W	3-0	A	UCgF	Huntelaar 2 [4 57], Heitinga [83]	11 603
17-12-2006	Excelsior Rotterdam	W	3-1	A	ED	Huntelaar 3 [24 48 74]	3 500
24-12-2006	Vitesse Arnhem	L	2-4	H	ED	Grygera [4], De Mul [35]	24 250
27-12-2006	Roda JC Kerkrade	W	2-0	H	ED	Sneijder [15], Grygera [42]	50 334
30-12-2006	NEC Nijmegan	D	2-2	A	ED	Perez [62], Gabri [80]	12 500
21-01-2007	FC Utrecht	W	2-0	H	ED	Heitinga [11], Sneijder [21]	44 940
24-01-2007	Haarlem	W	4-0	H	KBr4	OG [8], Leonardo [34], Perez 2 [40 90]	22 000
28-01-2007	FC Groningen	W	3-2	A	ED	Stam [52], Heitinga [82], Leonardo [90]	19 777
4-02-2007	Feyenoord	W	4-1	H	ED	Sneijder 3 [20 32 87], De Mul [34]	50 490
11-02-2007	ADO Den Haag	W	2-1	A	ED	Heitinga [58], Huntelaar [69]	8 276
14-02-2007	Werder Bremen	L	0-3	A	UCr3		37 500
18-02-2007	Excelsior Rotterdam	D	2-2	H	ED	Davids [19], Huntelaar [38]	47 905
22-02-2007	Werder Bremen	W	3-1	H	UCr3	Leonardo [4], Huntelaar [60], Babel [74]	35 227
25-02-2007	AZ Alkmaar	D	1-1	A	ED	Perez [65]	16 458
28-02-2007	Willem II Tilburg	W	2-0	A	KBqf	Huntelaar [14], Heitinga [80]	11 000
4-03-2007	SC Heerenveen	L	0-1	H	ED		50 174
11-03-2007	Twente Enschede	W	4-1	H	ED	Huntelaar 3 [21 30 75], Babel [45]	13 250
18-03-2007	PSV Eindhoven	W	5-1	H	ED	Huntelaar 2 [17 72], Sneijder [44], Gabri [73], Perez [89]	35 100
1-04-2007	Heracles Almelo	W	3-0	H	ED	Sneijder [11], Huntelaar 2 [49 52]	50 109
8-04-2007	RKC Waalwijk	D	2-2	H	ED	Gabri [8], Sneijder [20]	5 000
13-04-2007	NAC Breda	W	2-0	H	ED	Perez [18], Babel [64]	49 737
18-04-2007	RKC Waalwijk	W	3-1	H	KBsf	Huntelaar [11], Gabri [67], Mitea [88]	34 600
22-04-2007	Sparta Rotterdam	W	5-2	H	ED	Sneijder 2 [9 18], Huntelaar [21], Perez [76p], Mitea [82]	50 364
29-04-2007	Willem II Tilburg	W	2-0	A	ED	Emanuelson [18], Huntelaar [68]	14 700
6-05-2007	AZ Alkmaar	D	1-1	N	KBf	Huntelaar [51], W 8-7p	42 200
9-05-2007	SC Heerenveen	L	0-1	A	EDpo		25 000
13-05-2007	SC Heerenveen	W	4-0	H	EDpo	Huntelaar 2 [22 61], Babel [23], Perez [86]	29 241
20-05-2007	AZ Alkmaar	L	1-2	A	EDpo	Sneijder [12]	15 993
27-05-2007	AZ Alkmaar	W	3-0	H	EDpo	Heitinga [56], Donk OG [58], Gabri [90]	50 201

SC = Super Cup • ED = Eredivisie • KB = KNVB Cup • CL = UEFA Champions League • UC = UEFA Cup • pr3 = third preliminary round • gF = Group F • r2 = second round • r4 = fourth round • qf = quarter-final • sf = semi-final • f = final • po = European play-off • N = De Kuip, Rotterdam

FIFA/COCA-COLA WORLD RANKING

1993	1994	1995	1996	1997	1998	1999	2000	2001	2002	2003	2004	2005	2006	High		Low	
7	6	6	9	22	11	19	8	8	6	4	6	3	7	2	11/93	25	05/98

2006-2007											
08/06	09/06	10/06	11/06	12/06	01/07	02/07	03/07	04/07	05/07	06/07	07/07
6	6	7	7	7	7	7	7	6	6	9	6

AZ ALKMAAR 2006–07

Date	Opponents	Score		Comp	Scorers	Att
19-08-2006	NAC Breda	W 8-1	H	ED	Koevermans 2 [33 71], Cziommer 3 [41 56 80], Mathijsen [54], Schaars [58], De Cler [64]	17 023
26-08-2006	Vitesse Arnhem	W 3-1	A	ED	Koevermans [20], Schaars [57], De Zeeuw [92+]	19 890
10-09-2006	NEC Nijmegan	W 2-0	A	ED	Arveladze [31], Schaars [80]	11 800
14-09-2006	Kayserispor - TUR	W 3-2	H	UCr1	Koevermans [6p], Molhoek [32], Arveladze [64]	12 200
17-09-2006	FC Twente Enschede	D 2-2	H	ED	Arveladze [57], Dembélé [88]	15 899
21-09-2006	Bennekom	W 10-0	A	KBr2	De Zeeuw [18], Martens 2 [29 64], Cziommer 3 [33 52 55], Dembélé 2 [36 41], Mendes da Silva [44], Schaars [63]	
24-09-2006	Roda JC Kerkrade	W 2-0	A	ED	Arveladze [69], Dembélé [78]	15 000
28-09-2006	Kayserispor - TUR	D 1-1	A	UCr1	Dembélé [54]	16 332
1-10-2006	ADO Den Haag	D 2-2	H	ED	Koevermans [10], Jaliens [69]	15 478
14-10-2006	Sparta Rotterdam	W 2-0	A	ED	Steinnson [55], Koevermans [78]	10 000
19-10-2006	Sporting Braga - POR	W 3-0	H	UCgC	Arveladze [37], Koevermans [75], Schaars [82]	13 534
22-10-2006	PSV Eindhoven	L 1-3	A	ED	De Zeeuw [71]	17 000
26-10-2006	Willem II Tilburg	W 4-0	H	ED	De Zeeuw [13], Martens [53], Dembélé [63], Koevermans [84]	12 200
29-10-2006	FC Utrecht	W 5-1	H	ED	Schaars [23], Arveladze [49], Mendes da Silva 2 [53 73], Martens [88]	15 297
2-11-2006	Grasshopper-Club	W 5-2	A	UCgC	Arveladze [48], De Zeeuw [56], Dembélé 2 [78 95+], Martens [93+]	5 500
5-11-2006	RKC Waalwijk	W 2-0	A	ED	Dembélé [6], Koevermans [31]	5 400
8-11-2006	SV Meerssen	W 10-1	H	KBr3	Martens 2 [12 86], Schaars 2 [17 64], De Cler [33], Cziommer [43], Andriën [53], Jenner [76], Koevermans 2 [80p 83], De Zeeuw [88]	
11-11-2006	Heracles Almelo	W 5-0	H	ED	Schaars [2], De Zeeuw [23], Arveladze 2 [81 89], Koevermans [90]	15 485
18-11-2006	Feyenoord	L 2-3	A	ED	De Zeeuw [32], Koevermans [73]	50 000
26-11-2006	SC Heerenveen	W 3-1	A	ED	Arveladze [27], Koevermans [81], Martens [85]	25 600
29-11-2006	Slovan Liberec - CZE	D 2-2	H	UCgC	Steinnson [70], Jenner [89]	16 000
3-12-2006	Excelsior Rotterdam	W 5-0	H	ED	Arveladze 2 [11 56], Koevermans 2 [27 42], Cziommer [77]	15 101
10-12-2006	Ajax	D 2-2	A	ED	Arveladze [51], Mendes da Silva [57]	50 649
14-12-2006	Sevilla - ESP	W 2-1	A	UCgC	Arveladze 2 [62 93+]	29 373
17-12-2006	FC Groningen	W 2-0	H	ED	Luirink [26], Koevermans [40p]	15 493
24-12-2006	NEC Nijmegan	D 0-0	H	ED		16 000
27-12-2006	FC Twente Enschede	L 0-3	A	ED		13 250
31-12-2006	Roda JC Kerkrade	D 2-2	H	ED	Opdam [65], Koevermans [84]	15 042
19-01-2007	ADO Den Haag	W 3-1	A	ED	Mendes da Silva [45p], Koevermans [57], Martens [83]	7 405
23-01-2007	MVV Maastricht	W 5-0	H	KBr4	Mendes da Silva 3 [21 43 60], Dembélé [24], Cziommer [45]	5 796
27-01-2007	Sparta Rotterdam	W 3-0	H	ED	Arveladze [21], Olfers OG [46], Martens [52]	15 873
3-02-2007	PSV Eindhoven	W 3-2	H	ED	Dembélé [50], Jenner [62], Koevermans [88]	33 300
10-02-2007	Willem II Tilburg	W 2-0	H	ED	Koevermans [15], Martens [72]	15 978
14-02-2007	Fenerbahçe - TUR	D 3-3	A	UCr3	De Zeeuw [15], Boukhari [62], Jenner [63]	38 711
18-02-2007	FC Groningen	D 1-1	A	ED	Koevermans [26]	19 000
22-02-2007	Fenerbahçe - TUR	D 2-2	H	UCr3	Martens [63], Opdam [86]	16 118
25-02-2007	Ajax	D 1-1	H	ED	Martens [80]	16 458
28-02-2007	FC Utrecht	W 3-0		KBqf	Boukhari 2 [28 33], Loval [56]	
4-03-2007	FC Utrecht	W 4-0	H	ED	Martens [18], Arveladze [22], Dembélé [68], Koevermans [87]	19 000
8-03-2007	Newcastle United - ENG	L 2-4	A	UCr4	Arveladze [31], Koevermans [73]	28 452
11-03-2007	Feyenoord	D 0-0	H	ED		16 529
15-03-2007	Newcastle United - ENG	W 2-0	H	UCr4	Arveladze [14], Koevermans [56]	16 100
18-03-2007	Heracles Almelo	D 0-0	A	ED		8 419
31-03-2007	RKC Waalwijk	W 2-0	H	ED	Arveladze [24], Jenner [76]	16 181
5-04-2007	Werder Bremen - GER	D 0-0	H	UCqf		16 800
8-04-2007	NAC Breda	W 4-1	A	ED	Koevermans 2 [27 80], Boukhari [54], Martens [69p]	14 780
12-04-2007	Werder Bremen - GER	L 1-4	A	UCqf	Dembélé [32]	35 000
15-04-2007	Vitesse Arnhem	W 1-0	H	ED	Arveladze [23p]	16 088
19-04-2007	NAC Breda	W 6-0	H	KBsf	Cziommer 2 [41 59], Arveladze [51p], Martens 2 [60 64], Steinnson [82]	14 198
22-04-2007	SC Heerenveen	W 3-1	H	ED	Cziommer [14], Martens [39], Cziommer [89]	16 272
29-04-2007	Excelsior Rotterdam	L 2-3	A	ED	Cziommer [25], Koevermans [70]	3 527
6-05-2007	Ajax	D 1-1	N	KBf	Dembélé [4]	42 200
9-05-2007	FC Twente Enschede	D 1-1	A	EDpo	Cziommer [12]	
13-05-2007	FC Twente Enschede	W 2-0	H	EDpo	De Cler [71], Lens [89]	13 232
20-05-2007	Ajax	W 2-1	H	EDpo	Cziommer 2, Arveladze [89]	15 993
27-05-2007	Ajax	L 0-3	A	EDpo		50 201

SC = Super Cup • ED = Eredivisie • KB = KNVB Cup • UC = UEFA Cup • N = De Kuip, Rotterdam
gC = Group C • r2 = second round • r3 = third round • r4 = fourth round • qf = quarter-final • sf = semi-final • f = final • po = European play-off

NEP – NEPAL

NATIONAL TEAM RECORD
JULY 10TH 2006 TO JULY 12TH 2010

PL	W	D	L	F	A	%
0	0	0	0	0	0	0

FIFA/COCA-COLA WORLD RANKING

1993	1994	1995	1996	1997	1998	1999	2000	2001	2002	2003	2004	2005	2006	High	Low
124	138	147	151	155	176	157	166	156	165	165	177	175	170	124 12/93	186 04/07

2006–2007											
08/06	09/06	10/06	11/06	12/06	01/07	02/07	03/07	04/07	05/07	06/07	07/07
165	169	170	172	170	170	171	170	186	184	182	183

With the national team out of action for over a year after taking part in the AFC Challenge Cup in April 2006, attention was focused on what turned out to be the most exciting League campaign in years. The prize of a place in the AFC President's Cup for the winners has made the League in Nepal ever more competitive and there was a four way race for the title between Tribhuvan Army Club, Mahendra Police Club, defending champions Manang Marsyangdi and the 2005 AFC President's Cup semi-finalists Three Star. It went down to the final day with Mahendra Police Club holding a two point lead over Tribhuvan Army club as the two met in the Dashrath Stadium in

INTERNATIONAL HONOURS
South Asian Games 1984 1993

Kathmandu. Ramesh Budhathoki and Jumanu Rai were the heroes for Mahendra as they won 2-0 to secure a first title for the club. There was some international activity with the under–17 team taking part in the Asian finals in Singapore were they finished bottom of their first round group, while the under–23 team took part in the South Asian Federations Games in Colombo, losing 2-1 to Pakistan in the semis before winning the bronze medal. In a bid to help develop women's football the association relaunched the All-Nepal Ladies Football Championship which was won by Armed Police Force and the intention is to organise regional tournaments to increase standards.

THE FIFA BIG COUNT OF 2006

	Male	Female		Total
Number of players	477 800	0	Referees and Assistant Referees	200
Professionals	0		Admin, Coaches, Technical, Medical	2 100
Amateurs 18+	6 300		Number of clubs	110
Youth under 18	7 200		Number of teams	440
Unregistered	110 000		Clubs with women's teams	0
Total players	477 800		Players as % of population	1.69%

All-Nepal Football Association (ANFA)
ANFA House, Ward No.4, Bishalnagar, PO Box 12582, Kathmandu, Nepal
Tel +977 1 5201060   Fax +977 1 4424314
ganesht@ntc.net.np   www.none
President: THAPA Ganesh   General Secretary: SHRESTHA Narendra
Vice-President: BISTA Mahesh   Treasurer: SHAH Birat Jun   Media Officer: None
Men's Coach: THAPA Shyam   Women's Coach: KISHOR K.C.
ANFA formed: 1951   AFC: 1971   FIFA: 1970
Red shirts, Red shorts, Red socks

RECENT INTERNATIONAL MATCHES PLAYED BY NEPAL

2003	Opponents	Score		Venue	Comp	Scorers	Att	Referee
25-09	Oman	L	0-7	Incheon	ACq			
27-09	Vietnam	L	0-5	Incheon	ACq			
29-09	Korea Republic	L	0-16	Incheon	ACq			
19-10	Oman	L	0-6	Muscat	ACq			Al Ghafary JOR
21-10	Vietnam	L	0-2	Muscat	ACq			
24-10	Korea Republic	L	0-7	Muscat	ACq			
2004								
No international matches played in 2004								
2005								
8-12	India	L	1-2	Karachi	SAFr1	Basanta Thapa 35		
10-12	Bangladesh	L	0-2	Karachi	SAFr1			
12-12	Bhutan	W	3-1	Karachi	SAFr1	Surendra Tamang 10, Basanta Thapa 16, Bijay Gurung 29		
2006								
2-04	Bhutan	W	2-0	Chittagong	CCr1	Pradeep Maharjan 2 52 68	3 500	Gosh BAN
4-04	Brunei Darussalam	L	1-2	Chittagong	CCr1	Tashi Tsering 60	2 500	Al Ghatrifi OMA
6-04	Sri Lanka	D	1-1	Chittagong	CCr1	Pradeep Maharjan 75p	2 500	Lee Gi Young KOR
9-04	India	W	3-0	Chittagong	CCqf	Pradeep Maharjan 2 16 26, Basanta Thapa 28	3 000	Gosh BAN
12-04	Sri Lanka	D	1-1	Chittagong	CCsf	Basanta Thapa 82, L 3-5p	2 500	Lee Gi Young KOR
2007								
No international matches played in 2007 before August								

Fr = Friendly match • SAF = South Asian Football Federation Cup • CC = AFC Challenge Cup • AC = AFC Asian Cup
q = qualifier • r1 = first round group • qf = quarter-final • sf = semi-final

NEPAL NATIONAL TEAM RECORDS AND RECORD SEQUENCES

Records			Sequence records					
Victory	7-0	BHU 1999	Wins	3	1982	Clean sheets	2	Four times
Defeat	0-16	KOR 2003	Defeats	10	1997-1998	Goals scored	6	2005-2006
Player Caps	n/a		Undefeated	3	1982, 1993, 2006	Without goal	13	1987-1989
Player Goals	n/a		Without win	20	1987-93, 1995-98	Goals against	21	1996-1999

RECENT LEAGUE AND CUP RECORD

Championship		Cup
Year	Champions	Winners
1995	New Road Team	
1996	No Tournament	
1997	Three Star Club	Tribhuvan Army Club
1998	Three Star Club	Mahendra Police
1999	No tournament	Mahendra Police
2000	Manang Marsyangdi	
2001	No tournament	
2002	No tournament	Mahendra Police
2003	Manang Marsyangdi	Manang Marsyangdi
2004	Three Star Club	Mahendra Police
2005	Season readjustment	
2006	Manang Marsyangdi	
2007	Mahendra Police Club	

The Cup from 1997 to 1999 refers to the National League Cup, in 2002 to the Tribhuvan Challenge Shield and for 2003 and 2004 to the Khukuri Gold Cup

NEPAL 2006-07 ANFA A DIVISION

	Pl	W	D	L	F	A	Pts
Mahendra Police Club	26	20	5	1	47	17	65
Tribhuvan Army Club	26	20	3	3	63	21	63
Three Star Club	26	18	3	5	57	27	57
Manang Marsyangdi	26	17	4	5	75	21	55
Armed Police Force	26	15	1	10	58	29	46
Machhindra FC	26	12	3	11	41	38	39
Friends Club	26	10	6	10	40	30	36
New Road Team	26	10	5	11	31	36	35
Sankata Boys Sp. Club	26	8	7	11	34	35	31
Ranipokhari Corner	26	7	6	13	38	51	27
Jawalakhel Youth Club	26	5	5	16	25	50	20
Boys Union Club	26	5	3	18	29	66	18
Saraswoti Youth Club	26	3	5	18	24	81	14
Brigade Boys Club	26	2	4	20	26	86	10

1/11/2006 - 8/03/2007

NEPAL COUNTRY INFORMATION

Capital	Kathmandu	Formation	1769	GDP per Capita	$1 400
Population	27 070 666	Status	Constitutional Monarchy	GNP Ranking	107
Area km²	140 800	Language	Nepali	Dialling code	+977
Population density	19 per km²	Literacy rate	45%	Internet code	.np
% in urban areas	14%	Main religion	Hindu 86%, Buddhism 8%	GMT +/-	5.75
Towns/Cities ('000)	Kathmandu 790; Pokhara 186; Laltipur 183; Biratnagar 183; Birganj 133; Bharatpur 107				
Neighbours (km)	China 1 236; India 1 690				
Main stadia	Dasarath Rangasala – Kathmandu 25 000				

NGA – NIGERIA

NATIONAL TEAM RECORD
JULY 10TH 2006 TO JULY 12TH 2010

PL	W	D	L	F	A	%
7	5	0	2	9	6	71.4

Securing qualification for the 2008 African Nations Cup finals in Ghana means Nigeria keep up a leading role in African football but the last 12 months have been far from happy for the Super Eagles or for club football in this populous country. First Nigeria had to sit on the sidelines as five other African nations competed at the 2006 FIFA World Cup finals, a privilege the Super Eagles has taken almost as a right over the last decade. Then came the ousting of Austin Eguavoen as coach, even after he had taken the team to the semi-finals of the last African Nations Cup tournament in Egypt. He was replaced as coach by the German Berti Vogts, whose appointment in January 2007 garnered a mixed reaction. Vogts took over with Nigeria already having won the opening two matches of their qualifying campaign for Ghana and his first experience with the side saw Nigeria lose 4-1 to arch rivals Ghana in a friendly and then battle through two controversial qualifiers against Uganda before finally making sure of top place in Group Three with an away win in Niger. Vogts also had to get used to the perennial problems of players reporting late for national team call-ups, of botched logistical arrangements and the constant din of intrigue among the board members

INTERNATIONAL HONOURS

Qualified for the FIFA World Cup finals 1994 1998 2002   Qualified for the FIFA Women's World Cup finals 1991 1995 1999 2003
Olympic Games Gold 1996   FIFA U-17 World Championship 1985 1993
CAF African Cup of Nations 1980 1994   African Women's Championship 1991 1995 1998 2000 2002 2004
African Youth Championship 1983 1985 1987 1989 2005 2007 African U-17 Championship 2001 African Women's U-19 Championship 2002 2004
CAF Champions League Enyimba 2003 2004

of the Nigerian FA. There was a blow to Nigerian prestige in continental club competition when champions 2006 Ocean Boys and runners-up Nasarawa United both failed to get into the group phase of the 2007 African Champions League. Nigerians will be hoping for a stronger performance in the 2008 tournament when Enyimba return to continental competition after they won back their Premier League title. At junior level, Nigeria missed out on qualification for the All-Africa Games but did make it through to the business end of the preliminaries for the 2008 Olympic Games. Nigeria's under-20 side did best among the four African teams at the FIFA U-20 World Cup in Canada in June, reaching the quarter-finals where they lost a heated game against Chile, conceding four extra time goals. In February, the under-20 side had lost 1-0 to hosts Congo in the final of the Africa Youth Championship. At under-17 level Nigeria went one better by winning the African championship in Togo in March, beating their hosts 1-0 in the final after extra time. The women's side won gold at the All-Africa Games and qualified for both the Beijing Olympics and the FIFA Women's World Cup, keeping up their number one status on the continent.

Nigeria Football Association (NFA)
Plot 2033, Olusegun Obasanjo Way, Zone 7, Wuse Abuja, PO Box 5101 Garki, Abuja, Nigeria
Tel +234 9 5237326   Fax +234 9 5237327
info@nigeriafa.com   www.nigeriafa.com
President: ABDULLAHI Sani   General Secretary: OJO-OBA Bolaji
Vice-President: UCHEGBULAM Amanzee   Treasurer: OJO-OBA Bolaji   Media Officer: OLAJIRE Ademola
Men's Coach: VOGTS Bertie   Women's Coach: EFFIOM Ntiero
NFA formed: 1945   CAF: 1959   FIFA: 1959
Green shirts with white trimmings, Green shorts, Green socks

RECENT INTERNATIONAL MATCHES PLAYED BY NIGERIA

2003	Opponents	Score		Venue	Comp	Scorers	Att	Referee
30-05	Ghana	W	3-1	Abuja	Fr	Aiyegbeni 2 [49p 71], Enakhire [82]	8 000	
7-06	Malawi	W	4-1	Lagos	CNq	Aiyegbeni 2 [10 17], Kanu 2 [22 35]	40 000	Ndoye SEN
11-06	Brazil	L	0-3	Abuja	Fr		30 000	Quartey GHA
21-06	Angola	D	2-2	Benin City	CNq	Uche [56], Odemwigie [62p]	15 000	
26-07	Venezuela	W	1-0	Watford	Fr	Okocha [8]	1 000	
20-08	Japan	L	0-3	Tokyo	Fr		54 860	Kim Tae Young KOR
2004								
27-01	Morocco	L	0-1	Monastir	CNr1		15 000	Ndoye SEN
31-01	South Africa	W	4-0	Monastir	CNr1	Yobo [4], Okocha [64p], Odemwingie 2 [81 83]	15 000	Bujsaim UAE
4-02	Benin	W	2-1	Sfax	CNr1	Lawal [35], Utaka [76]	15 000	Abd el Fatah EGY
8-02	Cameroon	W	2-1	Monastir	CNqf	Okocha [45], Utaka [73]	14 750	Guezzaz MAR
11-02	Tunisia	D	1-1	Tunis	CNsf	Okocha [67p]. L 3-5p	56 000	Coffi BEN
13-02	Mali	W	2-1	Monastir	CN3p	Okocha [16], Odemwingie [47]	2 500	Sowe GAM
28-04	Jordan	W	2-0	Lagos	Fr	Akueme [16], Nworgu [82]	40 000	
29-05	Republic of Ireland	W	3-0	London	Fr	Ogbeche 2 [36 69], Martins [49]	7 438	D'Urso ENG
31-05	Jamaica	W	2-0	London	Fr	Utaka [17], Ogbeche [55]	15 000	Bennett ENG
5-06	Rwanda	W	2-0	Abuja	WCq	Martins 2 [55 88]	35 000	Pare BFA
20-06	Angola	L	0-1	Luanda	WCq		40 000	Nkole ZAM
3-07	Algeria	W	1-0	Abuja	WCq	Yobo [84]	35 000	Hisseine CHA
5-09	Zimbabwe	W	3-0	Harare	WCq	Aghahowa [3], Enakahire [28], Aiyegbeni [48p]	60 000	Mandzioukouta CGO
9-10	Gabon	D	1-1	Libreville	WCq	Aiyegbeni [50]	26 000	Yameogo BFA
20-10	Libya	L	1-2	Tripoli	Fr	Ezeji [17]	50 000	Guirat TUN
22-10	Ecuador	D	2-2	Tripoli	Fr	Ademola, Ezeji [78]. L 3-4p	50 000	
17-11	South Africa	L	1-2	Johannesburg	Fr	Makinwa [62]	39 817	Marange ZIM
2005								
26-03	Gabon	W	2-0	Port Harcourt	WCq	Aghahowa [79], Kanu [81]	16 489	Hicuburundi BDI
5-06	Rwanda	D	1-1	Kigali	WCq	Martins [78]	30 000	Kidane ERI
18-06	Angola	D	1-1	Kano	WCq	Okocha [5]	17 000	Abd el Fatah EGY
17-08	Libya	W	1-0	Tripoli	Fr	Martins [20]		
4-09	Algeria	W	5-2	Oran	WCq	Martins 3 [20p 88 90], Utaka [42], Obodo [81]	11 000	Shelmani LBY
8-10	Zimbabwe	W	5-1	Abuja	WCq	Martins 2 [35 75p], Ayila [62], Kanu [80p], Odemwingie [89]	45 000	Pare BFA
16-11	Romania	L	0-3	Bucharest	Fr		500	Banari MDA
2006								
23-01	Ghana	W	1-0	Port Said	CNr1	Taiwo [86]	20 000	Abd El Fatah EGY
27-01	Zimbabwe	W	2-0	Port Said	CNr1	Obodo [57], Mikel [61]	10 000	Coulibaly MLI
31-01	Senegal	W	2-1	Port Said	CNr1	Martins 2 [79 88]	5 000	Damon RSA
4-02	Tunisia	D	1-1	Port Said	CNqf	Nsofor [5]. W 6-5p	15 000	Maillet SEY
7-02	Côte d'Ivoire	L	0-1	Alexandria	CNsf		20 000	Damon RSA
9-02	Senegal	W	1-0	Cairo	CN3p	Lawal [79]	11 354	Coulibaly MLI
2-09	Niger	W	2-0	Abuja	CNq	Aiyegbeni [27], Obodo [60]		Sowe GAM
8-10	Lesotho	W	1-0	Maseru	CNq	Aiyegbeni [48]		Marange ZIM
2007								
6-02	Ghana	L	1-4	London	Fr	Taiwo [65]		
24-03	Uganda	W	1-0	Abeokuta	CNq	Kanu [73]		Diatta SEN
27-05	Kenya	W	1-0	Niarobi	Fr	Akabueze [38]		
2-06	Uganda	L	0-1	Kampala	CNq			
17-06	Niger	W	3-1	Niamey	CNq	Kanu [41], Taiwo [70p], Aiyegbeni [89]		

Fr = Friendly match • CN = CAF African Cup of Nations • WC = FIFA World Cup
q = qualifier • r1 = first round group • qf = quarter-final • sf = semi-final • 3p = third place play-off

NIGERIA NATIONAL TEAM RECORDS AND RECORD SEQUENCES

Records			Sequence records					
Victory	8-1	UGA 1991	Wins	5	Four times	Clean sheets	6	1992-1993
Defeat	0-7	GHA 1955	Defeats	5	1963-1964	Goals scored	26	1972-1976
Player Caps	86	LAWAL Muda	Undefeated	12	1993-94, 1999-00	Without goal	4	Three times
Player Goals	37	YEKINI Rashidi	Without win	9	1985-1987	Goals against	11	1965-1967

FEDERAL REPUBLIC OF NIGERIA

Capital	Abuja	Language	English, Hausa, Yoruba, Igbo	Independence	1960
Population	135 031 164	Area	923 768 km²	% in cities	39%
GDP per cap	$900	Dailling code	+234	Internet	.ng	GMT + / -	+1

MEDALS TABLE

		Overall			Lge	Cup		Africa			City	Stadium	Cap'ty	DoF
		G	S	B	G	G	S	G	S	B				
1	Shooting Stars	15	4	1	5	8	2	2	2	1	Ibadan	Lekan Salami	18 000	1963
2	Enugu Rangers	11	7	4	5	5	6	1	1	4	Enugu	Nnamdi Azikiwe	25 000	
3	Enyimba	8			5	1		2			Aba	Enyimba International	10 000	1976
4	Lagos Railways	7	1			7	1				Lagos			
5	Iwuanyanwu Nationale	6	3	3	5	1	2		1	3	Owerri	Dan Anyiam	10 000	
6	Bendel Insurance	6	3	2	2	3	2	1	1	2	Benin City	Samuel Ogbemudia	20 000	1973
7	BCC Lions	6	2		1	4	1	1	1		Gboko			
8	Stationery Stores	5	3	1	1	4	2		1	1	Lagos			1958
9	Dolphin	5	1		2	3			1		Port Harcourt	Liberation Stadium	25 000	
10	Julius Berger	4	3		2	2	1	2			Lagos	Kashimawo Abiola	15 000	1972
11	Port Harcourt FC	3	3			3	3				Port Harcourt			
12	Leventis United	3	1		1	2		1			Ibadan	Liberty Stadium	35 000	to 1987
13	Lagos ECN	3				3					Lagos	Onikan	5 000	
14	Abiola Babes	2	2	1		2	2			1	Mashood			to 1989
15	El Kanemi Warriors	2	1	1		2	1			1	Maiduguri	El Kanemi Stadium	10 000	
16	Lobi Stars	2	1		1	1	1				Makurdi	Aper Aku	15 000	
17	Nigerian Ports Authority	2				2					Warri	Warri Township Stadium	20 000	
18	Plateau United	1	10			1	10				Jos	Rwang Pam	15 000	
19	Kano Pillars	1	2			1	2				Kano	Sani Abacha	25 000	
20	Mighty Jets	1	2		1		2				Jos	Rwang Pam	15 000	

RECENT LEAGUE AND CUP RECORD

	Championship					Cup		
Year	Champions	Pts	Runners-up	Pts	Third	Pts	Winners	Score	Runners-up
1996	Udoji United	58	Jasper United	58	Sharks	58	Julius Berger	1-0	Katsina United
1997	Eagle Cement	59	Jasper United	58	Shooting Stars	51	BCC Lions	1-0	Katsina United
1998	Shooting Stars	57	Kwara United	53	Enugu Rangers	53	Wikki Tourists	0-0 3-2	Plateau United
1999	Lobi Stars	5	Iwuanyanwu Nat.	5	Plateau United	4	Plateau United	1-0	Iwuanyanwu Nat.
2000	Julius Berger	7	Katsina United	6	Lobi Stars	3	Niger Tornados	1-0	Enugu Rangers
2001	Enyimba	9	Ports Authority	4	Gombe United	3	Dolphin	2-0	El Kanemi Warriors
2002	Enyimba	61	Enugu Rangers	57	Kano Pillars	56	Julius Berger	3-0	Yobe Stars
2003	Enyimba	63	Julius Berger	58	Enugu Rangers	58	Lobi Stars	2-0	Sharks
2004	Dolphin	62	Enyimba	60	Bendel Insurance	56	Dolphin	1-0	Enugu Rangers
2005	Enyimba	72	Enugu Rangers	67	Iwuanyanwu Nat.	65	Enyimba	1-1 6-5p	Lobi Stars
2006	Ocean Boys	7	Nasarawa United	6	Kwara United	2	Dolphin	2-2 4-2p	Bendel Insurance
2007	Enyimba	7	Gombe United	4	Wikki Tourists	3			

COCA-COLA FA CUP 2006

First National Round

Dolphin	2	
Akwa United	0	
Prime FC	0	
Julius Berger	2	
Gombe United †	3	
Yobe Stars	0	
Kano Pillars	1	
Shooting Stars	2	
Jigawa Stars	0	5p
Heartland	0	4p
Kwara United	0	
Sharks	1	
El Kanemi Warriors	1	
Enyimba	0	
Makwada	0	
Niger Tornadoes	2	
Kaduna United	2	
El Cruzeiro	1	
FC Abuja		
Offa United	3	
Nasarawa United †	3	
Ranchers Bees	0	
Lobi Stars	0	3p
Wikki Tourists	0	5p
Bayelsa United	0	5p
Gateway	0	4p
Univ. of Nigeria Enugu	2	
University Hospital	2	
Enugu Rangers	2	
Fountain FC	0	
Ocean Boys	1	
Bendel Insurance	2	

Second National Round

Dolphin	1	
Julius Berger	0	
Gombe United	0	
Shooting Stars	1	
Jigawa Stars	1	4p
Sharks	1	1p
El Kanemi Warriors	0	
Niger Tornadoes	1	
Kaduna United	1	
Offa United	0	
Nasarawa United	0	4p
Wikki Tourists	0	5p
Bayelsa United	1	
University Hospital	0	
Enugu Rangers	0	
Bendel Insurance	1	

Quarter-finals

Dolphin	3	
Shooting Stars	2	
Jigawa Stars	0	
Niger Tornadoes	3	
Kaduna United	1	4p
Wikki Tourists	1	1p
Bayelsa United	0	
Bendel Insurance	2	

Semi-finals

Dolphin	1	
Niger Tornadoes	0	
Kaduna United	1	
Bendel Insurance	2	

Final

Dolphin ‡	2	4p
Bendel Insurance	2	2p

CUP FINAL

MKO Abiola Stadium, Abeokuta, 29-10-2006

Scorers - Victor Ezeji, Ibrahim Ajani for Dolphin, Edwin Eziyodawe, John George for Bendel Insurance

Third Place Play-off

Niger Tornadoes	2
Kaduna United	1

† Match awarded 3-0 • ‡ Qualified for the CAF Confederation Cup

NIGERIA 2006

PREMIER LEAGUE GROUP A

	Pl	W	D	L	F	A	Pts	Kwara Utd	Wikki T	Dolphin	Pillars	Bayelsa	Rangers	El Kanemi	Insurance	Bees	J. Berger
Kwara United †	18	10	4	4	20	14	34		1-0	1-0	2-1	0-0	2-1	1-0	3-1	2-1	2-0
Wikki Tourists †	18	10	1	7	18	16	31	1-0		1-0	1-0	1-0	1-0	2-1	3-0	2-0	3-0
Dolphin	18	9	2	7	24	17	29	2-0	2-0		3-0	1-1	2-1	5-0	1-0	2-1	2-0
Kano Pillars	18	9	2	7	26	22	29	2-0	4-0	2-0		1-0	0-0	3-2	3-1	1-0	1-0
Bayelsa United	18	7	4	7	18	15	25	0-0	1-0	2-4	4-0		2-0	3-1	1-0	2-0	2-0
Enugu Rangers	18	7	4	7	19	19	25	2-2	2-0	2-0	3-2	2-0		2-0	0-0	1-1	1-0
El Kanemi Warriors	18	8	1	9	22	24	25	2-1	0-0	2-0	3-2	2-0	3-0		2-0	1-0	1-0
Bendel Insurance	18	6	5	7	16	20	23	1-1	2-1	0-0	2-0	0-0	2-0	2-1		2-0	2-0
Ranchers Bees	18	6	2	10	16	21	20	0-1	1-2	2-0	**0-3**	2-0	1-0	2-1	3-0		1-0
Julius Berger	18	4	3	11	10	21	15	0-1	2-0	2-0	1-1	1-0	1-2	1-0	1-1	1-1	

15/04/2006 - 13/08/2006 • † Qualified for the Super League • Match in bold awarded

NIGERIA 2006

PREMIER LEAGUE GROUP B

	Pl	W	D	L	F	A	Pts	Nasarawa	Ocean Boys	Enyimba	Heartland	Kaduna Utd	Tornadoes	Gombe Utd	Lobi Stars	Shooting St	Sharks
Nasarawa United †	18	9	3	6	18	15	30		1-0	0-0	2-1	3-1	2-1	1-0	2-2	2-0	2-1
Ocean Boys †	18	10	0	8	16	16	30	1-0		2-1	1-0	1-0	1-0	1-0	1-0	1-0	1-0
Enyimba	18	8	4	6	25	17	28	0-1	2-1		3-0	4-1	2-1	2-1	4-1	1-0	2-0
Heartland	18	8	2	8	14	14	26	1-0	1-0	0-0		1-0	2-0	1-0	4-0	1-0	1-0
Kaduna United	18	8	1	9	19	20	25	2-0	3-0	2-0	2-0		0-0	2-0	1-0	1-0	2-0
Niger Tornadoes	18	7	4	7	11	15	25	0-0	1-0	1-0	1-0	1-0		2-0	0-0	1-0	2-1
Gombe United	18	8	0	10	18	17	24	0-1	3-1	1-0	1-0	2-0	2-0		3-1	2-0	2-0
Lobi Stars	18	6	6	6	22	22	24	2-1	2-1	0-0	0-0	4-0	3-0	2-0		1-1	2-1
Shooting Stars	18	7	3	8	16	18	24	1-0	1-0	3-3	2-1	2-1	2-0	1-0	1-1		2-1
Sharks	18	7	1	10	18	23	22	2-0	1-3	2-1	2-0	2-1	0-0	2-1	2-1	1-0	

16/04/2006 - 27/08/2006 • † Qualified for the Super League

NIGERIA 2006
SUPER LEAGUE

	Pl	W	D	L	F	A	Pts	OB	NU	KU	WT
Ocean Boys †	3	2	1	0	3	0	7		2-0	0-0	1-0
Nasarawa United †	3	2	0	1	3	2	6			1-0	2-0
Kwara United	3	0	2	1	2	3	2				2-2
Wikki Tourists	3	0	1	2	2	5	1	All matches played in Abuja			

6/09/2006 - 10/09/2006 • † Qualified for the CAF Champions League

THE FIFA BIG COUNT OF 2006

	Male	Female		Total
Number of players	6 344 600	309 110	Referees and Assistant Referees	522
Professionals	2 440		Admin, Coaches, Technical, Medical	32 600
Amateurs 18+	26 170		Number of clubs	522
Youth under 18	30 000		Number of teams	52
Unregistered	565 000		Clubs with women's teams	1 320
Total players	6 653 710		Players as % of population	5.05%

NIGERIA 2007

PREMIER LEAGUE GROUP A

	Pl	W	D	L	F	A	Pts	Wikki T	Rangers	Heartland	Kwara Utd	Kano Pillars	Prime	Ocean Boys	Tornadoes	Kaduna Utd	Adamawa
Wikki Tourists †	18	10	3	5	20	13	33		1-2	2-1	1-0	1-0	3-0	2-0	0-0	2-1	2-1
Enugu Rangers †	18	9	3	6	20	11	30	2-0		1-1	1-0	2-0	2-0	2-0	2-2	1-0	3-0
Heartland	18	7	8	3	17	13	29	0-0	1-0		3-1	0-0	2-1	3-0	1-0	1-1	1-0
Kwara United	18	8	4	6	16	18	28	1-1	1-0	2-0		2-0	3-1	1-1	0-0	4-1	2-1
Kano Pillars	18	8	4	6	20	14	28	1-0	1-0	1-1	2-1		3-0	1-0	3-1	3-1	4-0
Prime	18	7	3	8	19	23	24	1-0	1-0	3-0	2-2	1-0		2-0	1-0	0-0	1-0
Ocean Boys	18	7	3	8	15	21	24	1-0	1-2	1-2	2-1	1-0	2-1		1-1	2-0	1-0
Niger Tornadoes	18	5	6	7	10	15	21	0-1	1-0	0-0	**0-3**	1-0	1-0	0-1		1-0	1-0
Kaduna United	18	3	7	8	15	23	16	1-2	1-0	0-0	1-2	0-0	3-3	1-1	1-0		3-1
Adamawa United	18	3	5	10	11	22	14	1-2	0-0	0-0	1-0	1-1	2-0	2-0	1-1	0-0	

6/01/2007 - 16/05/2007 • † Qualified for the Super League • Match in bold awarded

NIGERIA 2007

PREMIER LEAGUE GROUP B

	Pl	W	D	L	F	A	Pts	Enyimba	Gombe Utd	Insurance	Lobi Stars	Bayelsa Utd	Zamfara Utd	Nasarawa Utd	Akwa Utd	Dolphin	El Kanemi
Enyimba †	18	9	5	4	19	6	32		2-0	2-0	1-0	3-0	2-0	1-0	3-0	0-0	**3-0**
Gombe United †	18	8	2	8	19	16	26	1-0		2-0	0-0	3-0	4-1	2-1	1-0	2-0	1-0
Bendel Insurance	18	7	5	6	20	18	26	2-0	2-0		3-0	2-1	2-1	2-0	0-0	0-0	1-0
Lobi Stars	18	7	5	6	13	11	26	0-0	1-0	1-1		1-0	1-0	1-0	3-1	2-0	2-0
Bayelsa United	18	7	4	7	17	20	25	0-0	3-2	1-0	1-0		0-0	2-1	3-1	2-1	2-0
Zamfara United	18	7	4	7	15	18	25	0-1	1-0	2-1	1-0	2-0		2-2	2-1	1-0	1-0
Nasarawa United	18	7	3	8	17	18	24	2-1	1-0	3-1	1-0	1-1	2-0		1-0	1-0	0-0
Akwa United	18	6	5	7	15	19	23	0-0	2-0	1-1	2-1	1-0	1-1	1-0		0-1	1-0
Dolphin	18	4	9	5	13	11	21	0-0	0-0	2-0	0-0	1-1	0-0	2-1	1-1		5-0
El Kanemi Warriors	18	5	4	9	10	21	19	1-0	2-1	2-2	0-0	1-0	1-0	2-0	1-2	0-0	

6/01/2007 - 16/05/2007 • † Qualified for the Super League • Match in bold awarded

NIGERIA 2007 SUPER LEAGUE

	Pl	W	D	L	F	A	Pts	En	GU	WT	ER
Enyimba †	3	2	1	0	5	2	7		1-1	2-1	2-0
Gombe United †	3	1	1	1	2	2	4			1-0	0-1
Wikki Tourists	3	1	0	2	3	4	3				2-1
Enugu Rangers	3	1	0	2	2	4	3	All matches played in Lagos

6/06/2007 - 10/06/2007 • † Qualified for the CAF Champions League

FIFA/COCA-COLA WORLD RANKING

1993	1994	1995	1996	1997	1998	1999	2000	2001	2002	2003	2004	2005	2006	High	Low
18	12	27	63	71	65	76	52	40	29	35	21	24	9	5 04/94	82 11/99

	2006–2007											
08/06	09/06	10/06	11/06	12/06	01/07	02/07	03/07	04/07	05/07	06/07	07/07
11	11	11	9	9	9	36	36	27	27	32	25

NIG – NIGER

NATIONAL TEAM RECORD
JULY 10TH 2006 TO JULY 12TH 2010

PL	W	D	L	F	A	%
6	1	2	3	5	9	33.3

FIFA/COCA-COLA WORLD RANKING

1993	1994	1995	1996	1997	1998	1999	2000	2001	2002	2003	2004	2005	2006	High		Low	
81	70	93	129	150	154	164	182	191	184	164	173	177	147	**68**	11/94	**196**	08/02

2006–2007											
08/06	09/06	10/06	11/06	12/06	01/07	02/07	03/07	04/07	05/07	06/07	07/07
169	167	149	148	147	148	149	148	144	145	134	146

Niger ended a long hiatus from international football with participation in the 2008 African Nations Cup qualifiers but with just one win in their first five matches, they never stood a chance of making an impact. A 2-0 home win over Lesotho represented the only points haul for the arid Saharan country, whose earlier meeting with the Basotho in Maseru in March 2007 had been clouded in controversy. Protests over a goal for the home team saw Niger's coach Tchanille Bana order his players off the field, causing a lengthy delay. For his outburst and actions, the Togolese-born Bana was later banned by the CAF for three matches and subsequently fired by Niger. His replacement

INTERNATIONAL HONOURS
None

was Amadou Hamèye. In the 2007 African Champions League, AS FNIS caused a major upset by knocking out Algeria's USM Alger in the first round, albeit on the away goals rule, but they then crashed out 5-1 on aggregate to Al Ittihad of Libya in the next round. In the African Confederation Cup, Sahel SC were narrowly beaten on the away goals rule in their first round tie against Etoile Filante of Burkina Faso but did go on to win the domestic championship. Niger's one bright light on the international arena was the form of striker Kamilou Daouda, whose Cameroonian club Cotonsport won a league championship in 2006.

THE FIFA BIG COUNT OF 2006

	Male	Female		Total
Number of players	542 681	30	Referees and Assistant Referees	704
Professionals	20		Admin, Coaches, Technical, Medical	634
Amateurs 18+	6 357		Number of clubs	120
Youth under 18	1 054		Number of teams	1 010
Unregistered	30 000		Clubs with women's teams	0
Total players	542 711		Players as % of population	4.33%

Fédération Nigerienne de Football (FENIFOOT)
Avenue Francois Mitterand, Case postale 10299, Niamey, Niger, Niger
Tel +227 20725127   Fax +227 20725127
fenifoot@intnet.ne   www.none
President: DIALLO Amadou   General Secretary: ABDOU Sani
Vice-President: DIAMBEIDOU Oumarou   Treasurer: HASSANE DIABRI Ounteini   Media Officer: None
Men's Coach: BANA Tchanille   Women's Coach: ACOSTA Frederic
FENIFOOT formed: 1967   CAF: 1967   FIFA: 1967
Orange shirts, White shorts, Green socks

RECENT INTERNATIONAL MATCHES PLAYED BY NIGER

2002	Opponents	Score		Venue	Comp	Scorers	Att	Referee
7-09	Ethiopia	W	3-1	Niamey	CNq	Tankary 2 [55 61], Abdoulaye [80]	35 000	Pare BFA
3-10	Morocco	L	1-6	Rabat	Fr	Hamidou	4 300	Rouaissi MAR
13-10	Liberia	L	0-1	Monrovia	CNq		40 000	
2003								
7-03	Benin	D	1-1	Cotonou	Fr	L 1-3p		
30-03	Guinea	L	0-2	Conakry	CNq		25 000	Monteiro Duarte CPV
7-06	Guinea	W	1-0	Niamey	CNq	Tankary [69]	50 000	Wellington GHA
22-06	Ethiopia	L	0-2	Addis Abeba	CNq		25 000	
5-07	Liberia	W	1-0	Niamey	CNq	Alhassan [90p]		
11-10	Algeria	L	0-1	Niamey	WCq		20 126	Coulibaly MLI
14-11	Algeria	L	0-6	Algiers	WCq		50 000	El Arjoun MAR
2004								
No international matches played in 2004								
2005								
No international matches played in 2005								
2006								
29-08	Togo	D	1-1	Lomé	Fr	Fankele [90]		
2-09	Nigeria	L	0-2	Abuja	CNq			Sowe GAM
8-10	Uganda	D	0-0	Niamey	CNq			Abdou Diouf SEN
2007								
25-03	Lesotho	L	1-3	Maseru	CNq	Kamilou Daouda [41]		Lwanja MWI
3-06	Lesotho	W	2-0	Niamey	CNq	Djibou Hamidou [10], Souleymane Sacko [30]		
17-06	Nigeria	L	1-3	Niamey	CNq	Kamilou Daouda [68]		

Fr = Friendly match • CN = CAF African Cup of Nations • WC = FIFA World Cup • q = qualifier

NIGER NATIONAL TEAM RECORDS AND RECORD SEQUENCES

Records			Sequence records					
Victory	7-1	MTN 1990	Wins	2	1981	Clean sheets	2	1983
Defeat	1-9	GHA 1969	Defeats	9	1969-1972	Goals scored	5	1994-1995
Player Caps	n/a		Undefeated	4	Three times	Without goal	5	1987-1988
Player Goals	n/a		Without win	23	1963-1976	Goals against	25	1963-1980

RECENT LEAGUE AND CUP RECORD

	Championship		Cup		
Year	Champions		Winners	Score	Runners-up
1998	Olympic FC Niamey		JS Ténéré Niamey	4-0	Liberté FC Niamey
1999	Olympic FC Niamey		JS Ténéré Niamey	2-0	Sahel SC Niamey
2000	JS Ténéré Niamey		JS Ténéré Niamey	3-1	Olympic FC Niamey
2001	JS Ténéré Niamey		Akokana Agadez	1-1 5-4p	Jangorzo Maradi
2002	No competition held		Tournament not held		
2003	Sahel SC Niamey		Olympic FC Niamey	4-1	Alkali Nassara Zinder
2004	Sahel SC Niamey		Sahel SC Niamey	2-1	Akokana Agadez
2005	AS-FNIS Niamey				
2006	AS-FNIS Niamey		Sahel SC Niamey		
2007	Sahel SC Niamey				

NIGER COUNTRY INFORMATION

Capital	Niamey	Independence	1960 from France	GDP per Capita	$800
Population	11 360 538	Status	Republic	GNP Ranking	138
Area km²	1 267 000	Language	French, Hausa, Djerma	Dialling code	+227
Population density	9 per km²	Literacy rate	17%	Internet code	.ne
% in urban areas	17%	Main religion	Muslim 80%	GMT +/−	+1
Towns/Cities ('000)	Niamey 774; Zinder 191; Maradi 163; Agadez 88; Arlit 83; Tahoua 80; Dosso 49				
Neighbours (km)	Chad 1 175; Nigeria 1 497; Benin 266; Burkina Faso 628; Mali 821; Algeria 956; Libya 354				
Main stadia	General Seyni Kountche – Niamey 30 000; Municipal – Zinder 10 000; Municipal – Maradi 10 000				

NIR – NORTHERN IRELAND

NATIONAL TEAM RECORD
JULY 10TH 2006 TO JULY 12TH 2010

PL	W	D	L	F	A	%
8	5	2	1	12	8	75

FIFA/COCA-COLA WORLD RANKING

1993	1994	1995	1996	1997	1998	1999	2000	2001	2002	2003	2004	2005	2006	High		Low	
39	45	45	64	93	86	84	93	88	103	122	107	103	48	28	07/07	124	03/04

2006–2007											
08/06	09/06	10/06	11/06	12/06	01/07	02/07	03/07	04/07	05/07	06/07	07/07
72	58	45	48	48	47	49	47	33	33	29	28

How the Northern Irish must be ruing the 3-0 home defeat at the hands of Iceland at the start of their UEFA Euro 2008 qualifying campaign. The Irish, it was said, had had their moment of glory by beating England in the World Cup qualifiers and now it was business as usual. However, what happened next was completely off the script as they went the rest of the season unbeaten. In their next match the Irish sensationally beat Spain in Belfast with David Healy, England's conqueror, scoring a hat-trick. Healy, who couldn't buy a goal for his club Leeds United, went on to score six more in the campaign. The architect of this fine run, which also included a home win over Sweden,

INTERNATIONAL HONOURS
Qualified for the FIFA World Cup finals 1958 1982 1986   British International Championship 1903 1914 1956 1958 1959 1964 1980 1984

was coach Lawrie Sanchez, but he was tempted back into club football by Fulham and was replaced by Nigel Worthington. The question of a new home for the national team caused widespread debate especially with the the safety of Windsor Park being called into question. In club football, Linfield lost 3-0 at home on the first day of the season to arch rivals Cliftonville but then went the rest of the season unbeaten to win their 47th League title, just four shy of the world record held by Rangers. Linfield do hold the world record for Cup wins, however. Their victory over Swifts on penalties was their 38th and it secured a 19th double - another world record.

THE FIFA BIG COUNT OF 2006

	Male	Female		Total
Number of players	83 220	9 100	Referees and Assistant Referees	553
Professionals	220		Admin, Coaches, Technical, Medical	11 557
Amateurs 18+	22 600		Number of clubs	820
Youth under 18	16 000		Number of teams	1 570
Unregistered	10 500		Clubs with women's teams	9
Total players	92 320		Players as % of population	4.84%

Irish Football Association (IFA)
20 Windsor Avenue, Belfast, BT9 6EG, United Kingdom
Tel +44 28 90669458   Fax +44 28 90667620
enquiries@irishfa.com   www.irishfa.com
President: KENNEDY Raymond   General Secretary: WELLS Howard J C
Vice-President: MARTIN David   Treasurer: JARDINE Neil   Media Officer: HARRISON Sueann
Men's Coach: WORTHINGTON Nigel   Women's Coach: WYLIE Alfie
IFA formed: 1880   UEFA: 1954   FIFA: 1911-20, 1924-28, 1946
Green shirts with blue trimmings, White shorts, Green socks or White shirts with green trimmings, Green shorts, White socks

RECENT INTERNATIONAL MATCHES PLAYED BY NORTHERN IRELAND

2002	Opponents	Score		Venue	Comp	Scorers	Att	Referee
21-08	Cyprus	D	0-0	Belfast	Fr		6 922	Jones WAL
12-10	Spain	L	0-3	Albacete	ECq		16 000	Michel SVK
16-10	Ukraine	D	0-0	Belfast	ECq		9 288	Bolognino ITA
2003								
12-02	Finland	L	0-1	Belfast	Fr		6 137	McDonald SCO
29-03	Armenia	L	0-1	Yerevan	ECq		10 321	Beck LIE
2-04	Greece	L	0-2	Belfast	ECq		7 196	Gilewski POL
3-06	Italy	L	0-2	Campobasso	Fr		18 270	Cortez Batista POR
11-06	Spain	D	0-0	Belfast	ECq		11 365	Larsen DEN
6-09	Ukraine	D	0-0	Donetsk	ECq		24 000	Stark GER
10-09	Armenia	L	0-1	Belfast	ECq		8 616	Stredak SVK
11-10	Greece	L	0-1	Athens	ECq		15 500	Cortez Batista POR
2004								
18-02	Norway	L	1-4	Belfast	Fr	Healy [56]	11 288	Thomson SCO
31-03	Estonia	W	1-0	Tallinn	Fr	Healy [45]	2 900	Petteri FIN
28-04	Serbia & Montenegro	D	1-1	Belfast	Fr	Quinn [18]	9 690	Richards WAL
30-05	Barbados	D	1-1	Bridgetown	Fr	Healy [71]	8 000	Brizan TRI
2-06	St Kitts and Nevis	W	2-0	Basseterre	Fr	Healy [78], Jones [82]	5 000	Matthew SKN
6-06	Trinidad and Tobago	W	3-0	Port of Spain	Fr	Healy 2 [4 65], Elliott [41]	5 500	Callender BRB
18-08	Switzerland	D	0-0	Zurich	Fr		4 000	Vollquartz DEN
4-09	Poland	L	0-3	Belfast	WCq		12 487	Wegereef NED
8-09	Wales	D	2-2	Cardiff	WCq	Whitley [10], Healy [21]	63 500	Messina ITA
9-10	Azerbaijan	D	0-0	Baku	WCq		6 460	Hanacsek HUN
13-10	Austria	D	3-3	Belfast	WCq	Healy [36], Murdock [58], Elliott [93+]	11 810	Shield AUS
2005								
9-02	Canada	L	0-1	Belfast	Fr		11 156	Attard MLT
26-03	England	L	0-4	Manchester	WCq		62 239	Stark GER
30-03	Poland	L	0-1	Warsaw	WCq		13 515	Frojdfeldt SWE
4-06	Germany	L	1-4	Belfast	Fr	Healy [15p]	14 000	Richmond SCO
17-08	Malta	D	1-1	Ta'Qali	Fr	Healy [9]	1 850	Riley ENG
3-09	Azerbaijan	W	2-0	Belfast	WCq	Elliott [60], Feeney [84]	12 000	Stanisic SCG
7-09	England	W	1-0	Belfast	WCq	Healy [73]	14 069	Busacca SUI
8-10	Wales	L	2-3	Belfast	WCq	Duff [47], Davis [50]	13 451	Bossen NED
12-10	Austria	L	0-2	Vienna	WCq		12 500	Briakos GRE
15-11	Portugal	D	1-1	Belfast	Fr	Feeney [53]	20 000	Webb ENG
2006								
1-03	Estonia	W	1-0	Belfast	Fr	Sproule [2]	13 600	Vink NED
21-05	Uruguay	L	0-1	New Jersey	Fr		4 152	
26-05	Romania	L	0-2	Chicago	Fr		15 000	Kennedy USA
16-08	Finland	W	2-1	Helsinki	Fr	Healy [32], Lafferty [64]	12 500	Svendsen DEN
2-09	Iceland	L	0-3	Belfast	ECq		13 522	Skjerven NOR
6-09	Spain	W	3-2	Belfast	ECq	Healy 3 [20 64 80]	13 885	De Bleeckere BEL
7-10	Denmark	D	0-0	Copenhagen	ECq		41 482	Plautz AUT
11-10	Latvia	W	1-0	Belfast	ECq	Healy [35]	13 500	Fleischer GER
2007								
6-02	Wales	D	0-0	Belfast	Fr		13 500	Richmond SCO
24-03	Liechtenstein	W	4-1	Vaduz	ECq	Healy 3 [52 75 83], McCann [92+]	4 340	Oriekhov UKR
28-03	Sweden	W	2-1	Belfast	ECq	Healy 2 [31 58]	13 500	Braamhaar NED

Fr = Friendly match • EC = UEFA EURO 2004/2008 • WC = FIFA World Cup • q = qualifier

NORTHERN IRELAND NATIONAL TEAM RECORDS AND RECORD SEQUENCES

Records			Sequence records				
Victory	7-0	WAL 1930	Wins	3	1968, 1984	Clean sheets	6	1985-1986
Defeat	0-13	ENG 1882	Defeats	11	1884-87, 1959-61	Goals scored	13	1933-1938
Player Caps	119	JENNINGS Pat	Undefeated	9	1979-80, 1985-86	Without goal	13	2002-2003
Player Goals	29	HEALY David	Without win	21	1947-1953	Goals against	46	1882-1897

NORTHERN IRELAND (PART OF THE UNITED KINGDOM)

Capital	Belfast	Language	English	Independence	n/a
Population	1 716 942	Area	14 120 km²	Density	121 per km²	% in cities	89%
GDP per cap	$27 700	Dialling code	+44	Internet	.uk	GMT +/-	0

MAJOR CITIES/TOWNS

Population '000

1	Belfast	274
2	Londonderry	89
3	Lisburn	81
4	Newtonabbey	64
5	Bangor	61
6	Craigavon	60
7	Castlereagh	57
8	Carrickfergus	30
9	Newtonards	30
10	Ballymena	29
11	Newry	27
12	Coleraine	26
13	Portadown	24
14	Omagh	21
15	Antrim	19
16	Larne	18
17	Banbridge	17
18	Enniskillen	14
19	Armagh	14
20	Strabane	14
21	Holywood	13
22	Limavady	13
23	Dungannon	12
24	Cookstown	11

MEDALS TABLE

		Overall			League			Cup			LC			Europe				Stadium	Cap'ty	DoF
		G	S	B	G	S	B	G	S	B	G	S	B	G	S	B				
1	Linfield	93	42	14	47	19	14	38	20		8	3					Belfast	Windsor Park	20 332	1886
2	Glentoran	48	47	23	22	23	23	20	19		6	5					Belfast	The Oval	15 000	1882
3	Belfast Celtic	22	8	8	14	4	8	8	4								Belfast	Paradise		1891
4	Lisburn Distillery	18	15	9	6	8	9	12	7								Lisburn	New Grosvenor	8 000	1880
5	Cliftonville	12	15	5	3	5	5	8	10		1	2					Belfast	Solitude	6 000	1879
6	Glenavon	9	21	6	3	10	6	5	10		1	1					Lurgan	Mourneview Park	5 000	1889
7	Portadown	8	16	7	4	9	7	3	6		1	1					Portadown	Shamrock Park	8 000	1924
8	Coleraine	7	17	9	1	9	9	5	5		1	3					Coleraine	The Showgrounds	6 500	1927
9	Crusaders	7	5	3	4	2	3	2	1		1	2					Belfast	Seaview	6 500	1898
10	Ballymena United	6	10	5		2	5	6	8								Ballymena	The Showgrounds	8 000	1928
11	Ards	6	4	8	1	1	8	4	2		1	1					Newtownards	Clandeboye Park	4 000	1902
12	Derry City	4	10	3	1	7	3	3	3								Londonderry			
13	Shelbourne Dublin	3	4	1		1	1	3	3								Dublin			
14	Queen's Island	3	3		1	3		2												
15	Bangor	2	3	2		1	2	1	2		1						Bangor	Clandeboye Park	4 000	1918
16	Bohemians Dublin	1	5					1	5								Dublin			

RECENT LEAGUE AND CUP RECORD

	Championship							Cup		
Year	Champions	Pts	Runners-up	Pts	Third	Pts		Winners	Score	Runners-up
1995	Crusaders	67	Glenavon	60	Portadown	50		Linfield	3-1	Carrick Rangers
1996	Portadown	56	Crusaders	52	Glentoran	46		Glentoran	1-0	Glenavon
1997	Crusaders	46	Coleraine	43	Glentoran	41		Glenavon	1-0	Cliftonville
1998	Cliftonville	68	Linfield	64	Portadown	60		Glenavon	1-0	Glenavon
1999	Glentoran	78	Linfield	70	Crusaders	62		Portadown	w/o	Cliftonville
2000	Linfield	79	Coleraine	61	Glenavon	61		Glentoran	1-0	Portadown
2001	Linfield	75	Glenavon	62	Glentoran	57		Glentoran	1-0	Linfield
2002	Portadown	75	Glentoran	74	Linfield	62		Linfield	2-1	Portadown
2003	Glentoran	90	Portadown	80	Coleraine	73		Coleraine	1-0	Glentoran
2004	Linfield	73	Portadown	70	Lisburn Distillery	55		Glentoran	1-0	Coleraine
2005	Glentoran	74	Linfield	72	Portadown	58		Portadown	5-1	Larne
2006	Linfield	75	Glentoran	63	Portadown	54		Linfield	2-1	Glentoran
2007	Linfield	71	Glentoran	63	Cliftonville	61		Linfield	2-2 3-2p	Dungannon Swifts

NORTHERN IRELAND 2006-07

IRISH PREMIER LEAGUE

	Pl	W	D	L	F	A	Pts	Linfield	Glentoran	Cliftonville	Portadown	Distillery	Crusaders	Coleraine	Swifts	Ballymena	Limavady	Armagh	Newry	Donegal	Larne	Glenavon	Loughgall
Linfield †	30	21	8	1	73	19	71		1-1	0-3	0-0	3-0	1-0	2-1	0-0	2-0	3-2	5-3	2-0	3-0	5-0	0-0	7-0
Glentoran ‡	30	20	3	7	76	33	63	1-2		4-1	2-3	3-1	1-0	3-2	0-1	2-0	3-0	8-0	2-0	1-1	6-3	2-2	4-0
Cliftonville	30	18	7	5	47	26	61	0-0	1-2		0-0	3-1	4-2	2-1	1-0	2-1	0-1	1-0	2-1	0-0	0-0	0-0	2-0
Portadown	30	17	7	6	49	26	58	1-2	2-0	2-2		1-1	1-2	0-0	0-2	2-1	3-0	3-0	2-0	2-0	1-1	2-1	0-1
Lisburn Distillery	30	14	6	10	50	39	48	0-4	3-1	0-4	2-0		1-1	2-0	1-0	3-1	0-1	0-1	1-1	2-0	1-3	4-0	3-0
Crusaders	30	14	5	11	50	42	47	2-3	1-3	1-2	0-3	1-1		0-3	2-1	2-2	0-3	6-2	1-0	4-1	3-1	1-1	2-1
Coleraine	30	13	6	11	55	50	45	2-2	1-2	2-1	1-1	2-1	1-3		2-1	0-1	2-4	2-0	2-1	3-1	4-3	1-3	4-2
Dungannon Swifts ‡	30	13	5	12	41	41	44	1-5	2-4	3-2	0-1	2-3	1-2	1-1		1-0	2-1	4-2	3-2	1-2	2-1	1-1	3-1
Ballymena United	30	12	7	11	46	40	43	0-0	3-2	0-1	2-0	0-1	2-1	2-3	2-1		0-0	2-2	1-1	1-0	3-0	4-2	4-1
Limavady United	30	10	5	15	39	54	35	0-4	1-2	1-1	1-2	0-5	0-1	2-1	0-1	1-1		0-3	2-3	1-1	2-1	3-2	4-1
Armagh City	30	11	2	17	42	68	35	0-2	0-3	1-3	2-3	1-2	1-3	4-3	0-1	0-3	4-2		1-3	1-0	2-1	1-2	1-0
Newry City	30	8	7	15	39	52	31	0-4	0-4	1-2	0-2	0-0	2-1	1-1	2-3	1-3	3-1	2-3		1-1	2-3	3-2	1-0
Donegal Celtic	30	6	9	15	33	51	27	0-1	1-0	0-1	2-4	2-1	0-2	1-3	0-0	3-2	2-1	1-2	1-1		3-0	2-3	1-1
Larne	30	7	5	18	33	60	26	0-0	0-4	1-3	0-1	1-5	0-0	0-1	1-0	0-1	2-3	0-1	0-4	2-1		3-0	3-0
Glenavon	30	5	10	15	40	58	25	2-4	0-3	0-1	1-4	1-1	0-1	3-3	1-2	3-1	0-1	2-3	1-2	3-3	1-1		2-0
Loughgall	30	1	8	21	23	77	10	0-6	1-3	1-2	0-3	1-2	0-5	1-3	1-1	3-3	1-1	1-1	1-1	2-2	1-2	1-1	

23/09/2006 - 28/04/2007 • † Qualified for the UEFA Champions League • ‡ Qualified for the UEFA Cup
Play-off: Bangor 0-1 1-0 2-4p Glenavon

NORTHERN IRELAND 2006-07 FIRST DIVISION (2)

	Pl	W	D	L	F	A	Pts
Institute	22	17	3	2	50	14	54
Bangor	22	14	5	3	49	23	47
Banbridge Town	22	13	4	5	45	31	43
Carrick Rangers	22	12	6	4	38	27	42
Ards	22	11	5	6	42	25	38
Dundela	22	8	5	9	33	35	29
HW Welders	22	8	3	11	30	36	27
Coagh United	22	6	6	10	32	41	24
Tobermore United	22	5	5	12	39	54	20
Portstewart	22	6	2	14	29	44	20
Ballinamallard United	22	4	3	15	14	42	15
Moyola Park	22	4	1	17	24	53	13

9/09/2006 - 12/05/2007

CIS INSURANCE LEAGUE CUP 2006-07

Quarter-finals		Semi-finals		Final	
Glentoran *	1 5p				
Portadown	1 4p	Glentoran ‡	0 4p		
Swifts	0	Linfield	0 3p		
Linfield *	2			Glentoran	1
Crusaders *	8			Cliftonville	0
Newry City	0	Crusaders	0	Windsor Park, 2-12-2006
Distillery	1	Cliftonville †	1	Scorer - Gary Hamilton [31]
Cliftonville *	3			

* Home team • † At The Oval • ‡ At Windsor Park

IRISH CUP 2006-07

Round of 16		Quarter-finals		Semi-finals		Final	
Linfield	5						
Ards *	0	Linfield	1 4				
Comber	0	Ballymena United *	1 2				
Ballymena United *	1			Linfield	4		
Crusaders	5			Lisburn Distillery	1		
Limavady United *	0	Crusaders	1				
Glenavon	1	Lisburn Distillery *	4				
Lisburn Distillery *	4					Linfield	2 3p
Cliftonville *	2					Dungannon Swifts ‡	2 2p
Denegal Celtic	0	Cliftonville *	3				
Glentoran *	2	Portadown	1			CUP FINAL	
Portadown	2			Cliftonville	0 4p		
Armagh City	3			Dungannon Swifts	0 5p	Windsor Park, Belfast	
Loughgall *	1	Armagh City	0			5-05-2007	
Newry County	1	Dungannon Swifts *	2				
Dungannon Swifts *	2						

* Home team • † At The Oval • ‡ Qualified for the UEFA Cup

NOR – NORWAY

NATIONAL TEAM RECORD
JULY 10TH 2006 TO JULY 12TH 2010

PL	W	D	L	F	A	%
10	4	3	3	20	10	55

FIFA/COCA-COLA WORLD RANKING

1993	1994	1995	1996	1997	1998	1999	2000	2001	2002	2003	2004	2005	2006	High		Low	
4	8	10	14	13	14	7	14	26	26	42	35	38	50	2	10/93	52	07/06

2006–2007											
08/06	09/06	10/06	11/06	12/06	01/07	02/07	03/07	04/07	05/07	06/07	07/07
49	40	51	50	50	50	47	43	49	49	36	35

It was back to business as usual in Norway with Rosenborg regaining the championship they had lost in 2005 to Vålerenga. Long time leaders Brann, looking for a first title in 41 years, had led the table by ten points going into the break for the World Cup in Germany, but a poor run and the sensational form of Rosenborg, under stand-in coach Knut Torum, saw the Trondheim club secure the title by a margin of seven points. For midfielder Roar Strand it was a 14th title, just two short of Alfred Schäffer's world record. Before the relentless rise of Rosenborg, Fredrikstad had been Norway's most successful club with their glory years coming in the 1930s and 1950s and there was

INTERNATIONAL HONOURS
Qualified for the FIFA World Cup finals 1938 1994 1998
FIFA Women's World Cup 1995   Women's Olympic Gold 2000   European Women's Championship 1987 1993

an unexpected return to their winning ways when they beat Sandefjord 3-0 in the Cup Final - their first trophy since 1984 and only their second since 1966. In Scandinavia's Royal League, Norwegian clubs failed to wrest the title from Danish hands, despite Lillestrøm and Valerenga finishing top of their first round groups. Neither they or Brann made it past the quarter-finals. The national team were involved in a close UEFA Euro 2008 qualifying group but a 2-1 defeat at home to Bosnia-Herzegovina could prove to be costly for Age Hareide's men.

THE FIFA BIG COUNT OF 2006

	Male	Female		Total
Number of players	409 007	134 158	Referees and Assistant Referees	2 201
Professionals	1 000		Admin, Coaches, Technical, Medical	5 000
Amateurs 18+	78 207		Number of clubs	1 818
Youth under 18	272 958		Number of teams	19 841
Unregistered	110 000		Clubs with women's teams	1 400
Total players	543 165		Players as % of population	11.78%

Norges Fotballforbund (NFF)
Ullevaal Stadion, Sognsveien 75J, Serviceboks 1 Ullevaal Stadion, Oslo 0840, Norway
Tel +47 21029300   Fax +47 21029301
nff@fotball.no   www.fotball.no
President: KAAFJORD Sondre   General Secretary: ESPELUND Karen
Vice-President: HAMMERSLAND Mette   Treasurer: RIBERG Rune   Media Officer: SOLHEIM Roger
Men's Coach: HAREIDE Age   Women's Coach: BERNTSEN Bjarne
NFF formed: 1902   UEFA: 1954   FIFA: 1908
Red shirts with white and blue trimmings, White shorts, Blue socks or White shirts with blue trimmings, White shorts, White socks

RECENT INTERNATIONAL MATCHES PLAYED BY NORWAY

2004 Opponents	Score		Venue	Comp	Scorers	Att	Referee
22-01 Sweden	W	3-0	Hong Kong	Fr	Johnsen.F [44], Flo.H 2 [54] [63]	10 000	Fong HKG
25-01 Honduras	W	3-1	Hong Kong	Fr	Brattbakk [27], Johnsen.F [39], Hoseth [86]	14 603	Chan HKG
28-01 Singapore	W	5-2	Singapore	Fr	Stadheim [18], Aas [42], Flo.H 2 [59] [70], Brattbakk [67]	5 000	Supian MAS
18-02 Northern Ireland	W	4-1	Belfast	Fr	Gamst Pedersen 3 [17] [35], Iversen [43], OG [57]	11 288	Thomson SCO
31-03 Serbia & Montenegro	W	1-0	Belgrade	Fr	Andresen [76]p	8 000	Panic BIH
28-04 Russia	W	3-2	Oslo	Fr	Andresen [25], Rushfeldt [43], Solli [62]	11 435	Wegereef NED
27-05 Wales	D	0-0	Oslo	Fr		14 137	Hansson SWE
18-08 Belgium	D	2-2	Oslo	Fr	Johnsen.F [32], Riseth [59]	16 669	Slupik POL
4-09 Italy	L	1-2	Palermo	WCq	Carew [1]	21 463	Sars FRA
8-09 Belarus	D	1-1	Oslo	WCq	Riseth [39]	25 272	Costa POR
9-10 Scotland	W	1-0	Glasgow	WCq	Iversen [54]p	51 000	Allaerts BEL
13-10 Slovenia	W	3-0	Oslo	WCq	Carew [7], Pedersen.M [60], Odegaard [89]	24 907	Ivanov RUS
16-11 Australia	D	2-2	London	Fr	Iversen [42], Gamst Pedersen [72]	7 364	Styles ENG
2005							
22-01 Kuwait	D	1-1	Kuwait City	Fr	Kvisvik [49]	200	Shaban KUW
25-01 Bahrain	W	1-0	Manama	Fr	Kvisvik [49]	4 000	Al Bannai UAE
28-01 Jordan	D	0-0	Amman	Fr		8 000	Al Shoufi SYR
9-02 Malta	W	3-0	Ta'Qali	Fr	Rushfeldt 2 [71] [80], Riise [82]	1 000	Malcolm NIR
30-03 Moldova	D	0-0	Chisinau	WCq		5 000	Meyer GER
20-04 Estonia	W	2-1	Tallinn	Fr	Johnsen.F [24], Braaten [54]	2 500	Vink NED
24-05 Costa Rica	W	1-0	Oslo	Fr	Johnsen.F [77]	21 251	Van Egmond NED
4-06 Italy	D	0-0	Oslo	WCq		24 829	Mejuto Gonzalez ESP
8-06 Sweden	W	3-2	Stockholm	Fr	Riise [60], Helstad [64], Iversen [65]	15 345	Jara CZE
17-08 Switzerland	L	0-2	Oslo	Fr		19 623	Vollquartz DEN
3-09 Slovenia	W	3-2	Celje	WCq	Carew [3], Lundekvam [23], Pedersen [92+]	10 055	Medina Cantalejo ESP
7-09 Scotland	L	1-2	Oslo	WCq	Arst [89]	24 904	Hamer LUX
8-10 Moldova	W	1-0	Oslo	WCq	Rushfeldt [50]	23 409	Bennett RSA
12-10 Belarus	W	1-0	Minsk	WCq	Helstad [70]	13 222	Plautz AUT
12-11 Czech Republic	L	0-1	Oslo	WCpo		24 264	Busacca SUI
16-11 Czech Republic	L	0-1	Prague	WCpo		17 464	Poll ENG
2006							
25-01 Mexico	L	1-2	San Francisco	Fr	Vaagen Moen [9]	44 729	Vaughn USA
29-01 USA	L	0-5	Carson	Fr		16 366	Acosta COL
1-03 Senegal	L	1-2	Dakar	Fr	Hagen [41]	45 000	Pare BFA
24-05 Paraguay	D	2-2	Oslo	Fr	Johnsen.F 2 [22] [61]	10 227	Olsiak SVK
1-06 Korea Republic	D	0-0	Oslo	Fr		15 487	Verbist BEL
16-08 Brazil	D	1-1	Oslo	Fr	Pedersen [51]	25 062	Dougal SCO
2-09 Hungary	W	4-1	Budapest	ECq	Solskjær 2 [15] [54], Strømstad [32], Pedersen [41]	12 283	Braamhaar NED
6-09 Moldova	W	2-0	Oslo	ECq	Strømstad [73], Iversen [79]	23 848	Ristoskov BUL
7-10 Greece	L	0-1	Piraeus	ECq		21 189	Michel SVK
15-11 Serbia	D	1-1	Belgrade	Fr	Carew [22]	15 000	Kasnaferis GRE
2007							
7-02 Croatia	L	1-2	Rijeka	Fr	Moen [86]	8 000	Kalt FRA
24-03 Bosnia-Herzegovina	L	1-2	Oslo	ECq	Carew [50]p	16 987	Riley ENG
28-03 Turkey	D	2-2	Frankfurt	ECq	Brenne [31], Andresen [40]	BCD	Farina ITA
2-06 Malta	W	4-0	Oslo	ECq	Hæsted [31], Helstad [73], Iversen [79], Riise [91+]	16 364	Granat POL
6-06 Hungary	W	4-0	Oslo	ECq	Iversen [22], Braaten [57], Carew 2 [60] [78]	19 198	Iturralde Gonzalez ESP

Fr = Friendly match • EC = UEFA EURO 2004/2008 • WC = FIFA World Cup • q = qualifier • po = qualifying play-off

NORWAY NATIONAL TEAM RECORDS AND RECORD SEQUENCES

Records			Sequence records				
Victory	12-0	FIN 1946	Wins	9	1999	Clean sheets	6	Three times
Defeat	0-12	DEN 1917	Defeats	9	1908-1913	Goals scored	21	1929-1933
Player Caps	104	SVENSSEN Thorbjørn	Undefeated	17	1997-98	Without goal	7	1975-1976
Player Goals	33	JUVE Jørgen	Without win	27	1908-18	Goals against	20	1908-1916

MAJOR CITIES/TOWNS
Population '000

1	Oslo	830
2	Bergen	215
3	Stavanger	176
4	Trondheim	149
5	Drammen	92
6	Skien	85
7	Fredrikstad	70
8	Kristiansand	64
9	Tromsø	53
10	Sarpsborg	50
11	Tønsberg	45
12	Alesund	44
13	Haugesund	40
14	Sandefjord	40
15	Bodø	35
16	Moss	34
17	Arendal	31
18	Hamar	29
19	Horten	24
20	Larvik	23
21	Halden	22
22	Harstad	19
23	Lillehammer	19
24	Molde	18

KINGDOM OF NORWAY; KONGERIKET NORGE

Capital Oslo	Language Norwegian		Independence 1905
Population 4 627 926	Area 324 220 km²	Density 14 per km²	% in cities 73%
GDP per cap $37 800	Dailling code +47	Internet .no	GMT +/- +1

MEDALS TABLE

		Overall			League			Cup		Europe			City	Stadium	Cap'ty	DoF
		G	S	B	G	S	B	G	S	G	S	B				
1	Rosenborg BK	29	10	1	20	5	1	9	5				Trondheim	Lerkendal	21 166	1917
2	Fredrikstad FK	20	15	1	9	8	1	11	7				Fredrikstad	Nye Fredrikstad Stadion	12 500	1903
3	Viking SK Stavanger	13	7	7	8	2	7	5	5				Stavanger	Viking Stadion	15 300	1899
4	Odd Grenland	12	10			2		12	8				Skien	Odd Stadion	9 008	1894
5	SFK Lyn Oslo	10	10	4	2	4	4	8	6				Oslo	Ullevaal	25 572	1896
6	Lilleström SK	9	16	3	5	8	3	4	8				Lillestrøm	Aråsen	12 250	1917
7	FK Skeid Oslo	9	8	1	1	5	1	8	3				Oslo	Bislett	15 400	1915
8	SK Brann Bergen	8	12	3	2	5	3	6	7				Bergen	Brann Stadion	17 600	1908
9	Vålerenga IF	8	4	3	5	2	3	3	2				Oslo	Ullevaal	25 572	1913
10	FK Sarpsborg	6	6	2		2		6	6				Sarpsborg	Sarpsborg	5 500	1903
11	IF Stromsgodset	5	2	3	1		3	4	2				Drammen	Marienlyst	8 500	1907
12	Örn FK Horten	4	4					4	4				Horten			
13	Mjøndalen IF	3	7			2		3	5				Mjøndalen			1910
14	Frigg SK Oslo	3	3					3	3				Oslo			
15	Larvik Turn IF	3	1		3				1				Larvik	Lovisenlund		1906
16	Molde FK	2	7	3		5	3	2	2				Molde	Molde Stadion	11 167	1911
17	FK Bodö-Glimt	2	6			3		2	3				Bodø	Aspmyra	6 100	1916
18	FK Moss	2	2		1	1		1	1				Moss	Melløs	10 000	1906
19	IK Start Kristiansand	2	1	8	2	1	8						Kristiansand	Kristiansand Stadion	12 000	1905
20	Tromsö IL	2	1	1		1	1	2					Tromsø	Alfheim	9 362	1920

RECENT LEAGUE AND CUP RECORD

	Championship						Cup		
Year	Champions	Pts	Runners-up	Pts	Third	Pts	Winners	Score	Runners-up
1995	Rosenborg BK	62	Molde FK	47	FK Bodø/Glimt	43	Rosenborg BK	1-1 3-1	SK Brann
1996	Rosenborg BK	59	Lillestrøm	46	Viking SK	43	Tromsø IL	2-1	FK Bodø/Glimt
1997	Rosenborg BK	61	SK Brann	50	Strømsgodset	46	Vålerenga IF	4-2	Strømsgodset
1998	Rosenborg BK	63	Molde FK	54	Stabæk	53	Stabæk	3-1	Rosenborg BK
1999	Rosenborg BK	56	Molde FK	50	SK Brann	49	Rosenborg BK	2-0	SK Brann
2000	Rosenborg BK	54	SK Brann	47	Viking SK	45	Odd Grenland	2-1	Viking SK
2001	Rosenborg BK	57	Lillestrøm	56	Viking SK	49	Viking SK	3-0	Bryne FK
2002	Rosenborg BK	56	Molde FK	50	Lyn Oslo	47	Vålerenga	1-0	Odd Grenland
2003	Rosenborg BK	61	FK Bodø/Glimt	47	Stabæk	42	Rosenborg BK	3-1	FK Bodø/Glimt
2004	Rosenborg BK	48	Vålerenga IF	48	SK Brann	40	SK Brann	4-1	Lyn Oslo
2005	Vålerenga IF	46	IK Start	45	Lyn Oslo	44	Molde FK	4-2	Lillestrøm
2006	Rosenborg BK	53	SK Brann	46	Vålerenga IF	44	Fredrikstad FK	3-0	Sandefjord Fotball

NORWAY 2006

TIPPELIGAEN

	Pl	W	D	L	F	A	Pts	Rosenborg	Brann	Vålerenga	Lillestrøm	Stabæk	Start	Lyn	Fredrikstad	Sandefjord	Tromsø	Viking	Odd	HamKam	Molde
Rosenborg BK †	26	15	8	3	47	24	53		0-0	3-2	3-1	1-0	3-0	2-1	1-0	3-1	2-1	4-1	1-1	0-3	0-1
SK Brann ‡	26	14	4	8	39	36	46	1-3		3-1	1-1	2-2	0-1	2-0	3-1	5-3	2-1	2-0	1-0	2-1	2-1
Vålerenga IF ‡	26	13	5	8	43	28	44	0-0	2-1		0-1	3-1	1-0	1-2	5-1	4-1	3-1	1-0	0-0	0-0	2-0
Lillestrøm SK ‡	26	12	8	6	44	33	44	3-3	2-0	2-1		2-2	2-1	2-0	1-1	1-2	1-2	3-1	2-2	3-1	3-0
Stabæk Fotball	26	10	9	7	53	36	39	1-1	1-2	2-2	2-2		2-2	3-2	3-2	0-0	3-1	1-1	1-1	4-0	8-0
IK Start	26	10	7	9	29	32	37	2-1	0-1	1-2	2-0	1-0		0-0	0-0	0-2	1-1	3-1	2-1	2-0	3-2
FC Lyn Oslo	26	10	5	11	33	36	35	1-2	2-0	2-1	3-3	1-4	1-2		1-2	2-0	1-3	0-0	1-1	1-0	2-0
Fredrikstad FK ‡	26	8	8	10	38	46	32	1-1	1-1	2-1	0-1	2-1	4-0	1-2		2-1	5-3	2-1	2-1	2-2	1-1
Sandefjord Fotball	26	9	5	12	37	47	32	0-2	0-2	0-2	1-1	3-1	1-1	2-2	2-0		1-0	3-2	1-3	2-1	5-2
Tromsø IL	26	8	5	13	33	39	29	1-1	3-1	0-1	1-0	0-1	1-0	1-2	3-1	2-2		0-0	0-0	2-0	2-0
Viking FK	26	8	5	13	31	37	29	1-3	5-0	1-2	1-2	3-1	1-2	1-2	1-1	1-0	1-0		1-0	2-1	3-1
Odd Grenland	26	7	8	11	30	38	29	0-4	1-3	3-2	0-3	0-1	2-0	2-1	3-3	3-1	3-2	0-1		3-0	0-0
Hamarkameratene	26	7	7	12	35	39	28	1-1	4-0	1-1	1-2	1-5	2-2	1-0	3-1	3-0	2-3	0-0	3-0		1-2
Molde FK	26	7	4	15	29	50	25	0-2	0-2	0-3	2-0	1-3	1-1	0-1	4-0	2-3	3-1	3-1	2-0	1-1	

9/04/2006 - 5/11/2006 • † Qualified for the UEFA Champions League • ‡ Qualified for the UEFA Cup • Play-off: Odd Grenland 3-0 7-1 Bryne
Top scorer: Daniel NANNSKOG, Stabæk 19

NORWAY 2006
ADECCOLIGAEN (2)

	Pl	W	D	L	F	A	Pts
IF Strømgodset	30	20	5	5	68	36	64
Aalesunds SK	30	17	9	4	71	35	60
Bryne FK	30	14	10	6	52	44	52
Hønefoss BK	30	15	6	9	64	47	51
FK Bodø-Glimt	30	14	7	9	65	49	49
Sogndal IL	30	11	11	8	43	41	44
Kongsvinger IL	30	11	10	9	39	42	43
FK Moss	30	11	7	12	61	46	40
SK Haugesund	30	11	5	14	40	37	38
Sparta Sarpsborg §2	30	11	6	13	44	56	37
Løv-Ham Bergen	30	8	11	11	37	39	35
Tromsdalen UIL	30	8	11	11	48	52	35
Pors Grenland	30	10	5	15	51	65	35
Manglerud Star Oslo	30	7	7	16	47	79	28
Follo Fotball Ski	30	6	7	17	46	76	25
IL Hødd Ulsteivik	30	4	7	19	29	61	19

9/04/2006 - 5/11/2006 • § = points deducted

NM SAS BRAATHENS CUPEN 2006

Round of 16

Fredrikstad FK *	2 4p
Bryne FK	2 2p
Aalesunds FK	1
Vålerenga IF *	2
Lillestrøm SK *	2
FC Lyn Oslo	1
SK Brann	1
IK Start *	3
Rosenborg BK *	1
Mandalskameratene	0
FK Bodø-Glimt	0
Viking FK *	5
Follo Fotball Ski	2
Sogndal IL *	1
Hamarkameratene *	2
Sandefjord Fotball	3

Quarter-finals

Fredrikstad FK	3
Vålerenga IF *	0
Lillestrøm SK	2
IK Start *	3
Rosenborg BK	3
Viking FK *	1
Follo *	0
Sandefjord Fotball	1

Semi-finals

Fredrikstad FK *	3
IK Start	2
Rosenborg BK *	2
Sandefjord Fotball	5

Final

Fredrikstad FK ‡	3
Sandefjord Fotball	0

CUP FINAL

Ullevål, Oslo, 12-11-2006

Scorers - Hans Erik Ramberg [5], Raio Piiroja 2 [37 43] for Fredrikstad

* Home team • ‡ Qualified for the UEFA Cup

NZL – NEW ZEALAND

NATIONAL TEAM RECORD
JULY 10TH 2006 TO JULY 12TH 2010

PL	W	D	L	F	A	%
4	0	2	2	2	11	25

FIFA/COCA-COLA WORLD RANKING

1993	1994	1995	1996	1997	1998	1999	2000	2001	2002	2003	2004	2005	2006	High		Low	
77	99	102	132	120	103	100	91	84	49	88	95	120	131	47	08/02	154	06/07

2006–2007											
08/06	09/06	10/06	11/06	12/06	01/07	02/07	03/07	04/07	05/07	06/07	07/07
128	131	136	131	131	131	133	129	132	127	154	148

The Kiwis can barely believe their luck. Without Australia to cramp their style, these are unexpectedly positive times for the game in New Zealand. The under–17 team overcame their Oceania opponents with relative ease to qualify for the FIFA U-17 World Cup in South Korea while the under–20 team made it to the FIFA U-20 World Cup in Canada. That they lost all three games there was beside the point. Qualifying for the finals and getting vital experience is the aim as football seeks to raise its profile in this rugby-mad country. In club football, Auckland City and Waitakere United enjoyed a growing rivalry in the New Zealand Football Championship with

INTERNATIONAL HONOURS
Qualified for the FIFA World Cup finals 1982   Oceania Nations Cup 1973 1998 2002   Oceania Women's Championship 1983 1991
Oceania Youth Championship 1980 1992   Oceania U-17 Championship 1997

Auckland beating Waitakere 3-2 in the Grand Final to win the title for the third year running. There was revenge for Waitakere when they knocked Auckland out of the OFC O-League and then went on to beat Fiji's Ba in the final. That saw them qualify for the FIFA Club World Cup in Japan, matching Auckland who had taken part in the 2006 tournament where they lost to both Al Ahly and Jeonbuk. Continued poor results and low crowds saw Auckland's New Zealand Knights lose their license in Australia's Hyundai A-League. They were replaced by a new club, Wellington Phoenix.

THE FIFA BIG COUNT OF 2006

	Male	Female		Total
Number of players	164 667	34 090	Referees and Assistant Referees	800
Professionals	25		Admin, Coaches, Technical, Medical	19 000
Amateurs 18+	12 067		Number of clubs	325
Youth under 18	79 565		Number of teams	7 524
Unregistered	49 500		Clubs with women's teams	17
Total players	198 757		Players as % of population	4.88%

New Zealand Soccer Inc (NZS)
Albany, PO Box 301 043, Auckland, New Zealand
Tel +64 9 4140175   Fax +64 9 4140176
tracy.brady@nzfootball.co.nz   www.nzfootball.co.nz
President: MORRIS John   General Secretary: SEATTER Graham
Vice-President: TBD   Treasurer: ELDERKIN Peter   Media Officer: GRAY Kent
Men's Coach: HERBERT Ricki   Women's Coach: JONES Allan
NZS formed: 1891   OFC: 1966   FIFA: 1948
White shirts with black trimmings, White shorts, White socks

RECENT INTERNATIONAL MATCHES PLAYED BY NEW ZEALAND

2002	Opponents	Score	Venue	Comp	Scorers	Att	Referee
5-07	Tahiti	W 4-0	Auckland	OCr1	Nelsen [30], Vicelich [49], Urlovic [80], Campbell [88]	1 000	Atisson VAN
7-07	Papua New Guinea	W 9-1	Auckland	OCr1	Killen 4 [9 10 28 51], Campbell 2 [27 85], Nelson [54] Burton [87], De Gregorio [90]	2 200	Rakaroi FIJ
9-07	Solomon Islands	W 6-1	Auckland	OCr1	Vicelich 2 [28 45], Urlovic [42], Campbell 2 [50 75], Burton [88]	300	Atisson VAN
12-07	Vanuatu	W 3-0	Auckland	OCsf	Burton 2 [13 65], Killen [23]	1 000	Breeze AUS
14-07	Australia	W 1-0	Auckland	OCf	Nelsen [78]	4 000	Ariiotima TAH
12-10	Estonia	L 2-3	Tallinn	Fr	Hickey [41], Lines [45]	800	Pedersen NOR
16-10	Poland	L 0-2	Ostrowiec	Fr		8 000	Layec FRA
2003							
27-05	Scotland	D 1-1	Edinburgh	Fr	Nelsen [47]	10 016	Ingvarsson SWE
8-06	USA	L 1-2	Richmond	Fr	Coveny [23]	9 116	Liu CAN
18-06	Japan	L 0-3	Paris	CCr1		36 038	Codjia BEN
20-06	Colombia	L 1-3	Lyon	CCr1	De Gregorio [27]	22 811	Batres GUA
22-06	France	L 0-5	Paris	CCr1		36 842	Moradi IRN
12-10	Iran	L 0-3	Tehran	AO		40 000	Kousa SYR
2004							
29-05	Australia	L 0-1	Adelaide	WCq		12 100	Larsen DEN
31-05	Solomon Islands	W 3-0	Adelaide	WCq	Fisher [36], Oughton [81], Lines [90]	217	Iturralde Gonzalez ESP
2-06	Vanuatu	L 2-4	Adelaide	WCq	Coveny 2 [61 75]	356	Farina ITA
4-06	Tahiti	W 10-0	Adelaide	WCq	Coveny 3 [6 38 46+], Fisher 3 [16 22 63], Jones [72] Oughton [74], Nelsen 2 [82 87]	200	Shield AUS
6-06	Fiji	W 2-0	Adelaide	WCq	Bunce [8], Coveny [56]	300	Larsen DEN
2005							
9-06	Australia	L 0-1	London	Fr		9 023	Dean ENG
2006							
19-02	Malaysia	W 1-0	Christchurch	Fr	Old [87]	10 100	O'Leary NZL
23-02	Malaysia	W 2-1	Albany	Fr	Banks [18], Barron [88]	8 702	Fox NZL
25-04	Chile	L 1-4	Rancagua	Fr	Smeltz [14]	8 000	Osorio CHI
27-04	Chile	L 0-1	La Calera	Fr			Acosta CHI
24-05	Hungary	L 0-2	Budapest	Fr		5 000	Hrinak SVK
27-05	Georgia	W 3-1	Altenkirchen	Fr	Coveny 2 [35 53], Killen [37]	1 000	
31-05	Estonia	D 1-1	Tallinn	Fr	Hay [27]	3 000	Rasmussen DEN
4-06	Brazil	L 0-4	Geneva	Fr		32 000	Laperriere SUI
2007							
7-02	Tahiti	D 0-0	Auckland	Fr			Hester NZL
24-03	Costa Rica	L 0-4	San Jose	Fr		15 000	Rodriguez CRC
28-03	Venezuela	L 0-5	Maracaibo	Fr		12 000	
26-05	Wales	D 2-2	Wrexham	Fr	Smeltz 2 [2 24]	7 819	Skjerven DEN

Fr = Friendly match • OC = OFC Oceania Nations Cup • CC = FIFA Confederations Cup • AO = Asia/Oceania Challenge • WC = FIFA World Cup
q = qualifier • r1 = first round group • sf = semi-final • f = final

NEW ZEALAND NATIONAL TEAM RECORDS AND RECORD SEQUENCES

Records			Sequence records				
Victory	13-0	FIJ 1981	Wins	9	1951-1954	Clean sheets	10	1981
Defeat	0-10	AUS 1936	Defeats	16	1927-1951	Goals scored	22	1951-1967
Player Caps	64	COVENY Vaughan	Undefeated	11	1981	Without goal	5	1997-1998
Player Goals	28	COVENY/NEWALL	Without win	16	1927-1951	Goals against	19	1927-1951

NEW ZEALAND COUNTRY INFORMATION

Capital	Wellington	Independence	1907 from the UK	GDP per Capita	$21 600
Population	3 993 817	Status	Commonnwealth	GNP Ranking	48
Area km²	268 680	Language	English, Maori	Dialling code	+64
Population density	15 per km²	Literacy rate	99%	Internet code	.nz
% in urban areas	86%	Main religion	Christian	GMT + / –	+12
Towns/Cities ('000)	Aukland 417; Manukau 383; Christchurch 364; North Shore 207; Wellington 179; Waitakere 166; Hamilton 152; Dunedin 114; Tauranga 110; Lower Hutt 101; Palmerston North 75; Hastings 61				
Neighbours (km)	South Pacific Ocean 15 134				
Main stadia	Ericsson Stadium – Auckland 50 000; North Harbour Stadium – Albany, Auckland 25 000				

NEW ZEALAND 2006–07

NEW ZEALAND FOOTBALL CHAMPIONSHIP (NZFC)

	Pl	W	D	L	F	A	Pts	Waitakere	Manawatu	Auckland	Canterbury	Wellington	Hawkes Bay	Waikato	Otago Utd
Waitakere United	21	15	2	4	47	23	47		2-0 3-1	0-1‡	2-1	1-0 4-2	2-1	1-0 4-2	5-1 8-0
YoungHeart Manawatu	21	14	3	4	58	30	45	0-1		1-0	6-2	1-1 5-0	3-2 4-3	5-2 2-0	4-1
Auckland City	21	12	6	3	50	30	42	4-3 1-1	2-2 5-3		2-0 0-3	1-0	6-2	3-2	2-2
Canterbury United	21	9	4	8	33	30	31	1-0 2-1	1-3 2-3	1-1		4-1 1-2	2-1	1-1	1-0 2-2
Team Wellington	21	7	6	8	37	34	27	1-1	1-2	2-6 2-3	0-0		3-2 7-0	0-0 2-0	2-1
Hawkes Bay United	21	4	4	13	29	49	16	1-3 3-0	1-1	1-2 2-2	1-2 2-1	0-0		2-1	0-2
Waikato	21	3	5	13	19	45	14	1-3	1-6	1-1 0-2	0-4 0-1	0-5	2-0 4-2		0-0 1-0
Otago United	21	2	6	13	19	51	12	1-2	0-5 0-1	1-5 1-2	2-1	1-5 1-1	1-1 1-2	1-1	

14/10/2006 - 10/03/2007 • Top three qualified for the play-offs • † Qualified for the OFC Champions Cup • ‡ Awarded as a 0-0 win for Waitakere
Semi-final: Manawatu 1-3 Auckland; Grand Final: Waitakere Utd 2-3 Auckland City (North Harbour, Albany, Auckland, 16-04-2007, Ref: O'Leary.
Scorers: Liam Mulrooney 16, Paul Urlovic 51, Neil Sykes 78 for Auckland; Commins Menapi 21, Jeff Campbell 93+ for Waitakere)
Top scorers: Benjamin TOTORI, Manawatu 24; Graham LITTLE, Wellington 12; Commins MENAPI, Waitakere 12

CHATHAM CUP 2006

Round of sixteen		Quarter–finals		Semi–finals		Final	
Western Suburbs *	2						
Stop Out	1	Western Suburbs *	1				
Palmerston N. Marist	0	Roslyn Wakari	0				
Roslyn Wakari *	6			Western Suburbs *	4		
Wellington Olympic	2			Caversham	0		
Waterside Karori *	1	Wellington Olympic	1				
Nomads *	2	Caversham *	2				
Caversham	3					Western Suburbs	0 3p
Central United	2					Eastern Suburbs	0 0p
Mangere United *	1	Central United	2				
Glenfield Rovers	0	East Coast Bays *	0			CUP FINAL	
East Coast Bays *	1			Central United *	3 3p		
Tauranga City United *	1 5p			Eastern Suburbs	3 5p	North Harbour Stadium, Albany 2-09-2005, Ref: O'Leary	
Three Kings United	1 4p	Tauranga City United	0				
Hamilton Wanderers	0	Eastern Suburbs *	4				
Eastern Suburbs *	1				* Home team		

RECENT LEAGUE AND CUP RECORD

Championship				Chatham Cup			
Year	Champions	Score	Runners-up	Winners	Score	Runners-up	
1998	Napier City Rovers	5-2	Central United	Central United	5-0	Dunedin Technical	
1999	Central United	3-1	Dunedin Technical	Dunedin Technical	4-0	Waitakere City	
2000	Napier City Rovers	0-0 4-2p	University Mt Wellington	Napier City Rovers	4-1	Central United	
2001	Central United	3-2	Miramar Rangers	University Mt Wellington	3-3 5-4p	Central United	
2002	Miramar Rangers	3-1	Napier City Rovers	Napier City Rovers	2-0	Tauranga City United	
2003	Miramar Rangers	3-2	East Auckland	University Mt Wellington	3-1	Melville United	
2004	No tournament held			Miramar Rangers	1-0	Waitakere City	
2005	Auckland City	3-2	Waitakere United	Central United	2-1	Palmerston North Marist	
2006	Auckland City	3-3 4-3	Canterbury United	Western Suburbs	0-0 3-0p	Eastern Suburbs	
2007	Auckland City	3-2	Waitakere United				

OMA – OMAN

NATIONAL TEAM RECORD
JULY 10TH 2006 TO JULY 12TH 2010

PL	W	D	L	F	A	%
18	9	6	3	28	17	66.6

FIFA/COCA-COLA WORLD RANKING

1993	1994	1995	1996	1997	1998	1999	2000	2001	2002	2003	2004	2005	2006	High		Low	
97	71	98	91	81	58	92	106	91	96	62	56	91	72	**50**	08/04	**117**	07/03

2006–2007											
08/06	09/06	10/06	11/06	12/06	01/07	02/07	03/07	04/07	05/07	06/07	07/07
85	81	63	69	72	84	76	73	72	74	74	76

Having lost out on the last day of the 2006 season, Al Nahda made no mistake in securing their first title. Once again it went down to the final round of matches but a 1-0 victory over Majees saw Nahda maintain their two point lead over Al Urooba. The Oman Premier League is one of a number of Asian Leagues earmarked for development by the AFC Professional League Committee as it seeks to help help raise standards to a level where future participation in the AFC Champions League is a possibility. At present Omani clubs enter the AFC Cup where they have had limited success. Al Nasr made it to the quarter-finals of the 2006 edition but neither Dhofar or Muscat

INTERNATIONAL HONOURS
AFC U-17 Championship 1996 2000

made it past the group stage of the 2007 tournament. There is undoubted potential in Oman which was demonstrated by the national team who qualified for the AFC Asian Cup finals for the second time in a row having never qualified before that. Oman were beaten just twice in the 15 matches leading up to the finals, one of which was in the final of the Gulf Cup to hosts UAE, a defeat that surprisingly cost coach Milan Macala his job. His replacement was ex-Saudi coach Gabriel Calderón, but despite almost pulling off a shock victory against Australia in their first match in the finals, he couldn't lead his team past the first round.

THE FIFA BIG COUNT OF 2006

	Male	Female		Total
Number of players	57 610	0	Referees and Assistant Referees	105
Professionals	0		Admin, Coaches, Technical, Medical	500
Amateurs 18+	3 010		Number of clubs	43
Youth under 18	5 600		Number of teams	129
Unregistered	11 000		Clubs with women's teams	0
Total players	57 610		Players as % of population	1.86%

Oman Football Association (OFA)
Al Farahidy Street, PO Box 3462, Ruwi 112, Oman
Tel +968 24 787636   Fax +968 24 787632
omanfa@omantel.net.om   www.none
President: TBD   General Secretary: TBD
Vice-President: TBD   Treasurer: TBD   Media Officer: AL RAWAHI Aiman
Men's Coach: CALDERON Gabriel   Women's Coach: None
OFA formed: 1978   AFC: 1979   FIFA: 1980
White shirts, White shorts, White socks

RECENT INTERNATIONAL MATCHES PLAYED BY OMAN

2004	Opponents	Score		Venue	Comp	Scorers	Att	Referee
20-07	Japan	L	0-1	Chongqing	ACr1		35 000	Shield AUS
24-07	Iran	D	2-2	Chongqing	ACr1	Amad Ali 2 [32 41]	35 000	Al Delawar BHR
28-07	Thailand	W	2-0	Chengdu	ACr1	OG [11], Amad Ali [49]	13 000	Lu Jun CHN
31-08	Maldives	W	1-0	Malé	Fr			
3-09	Maldives	W	2-1	Malé	Fr			
8-09	Singapore	W	2-0	Singapore	WCq	Yousef Shaaban [3], Amad Ali [82]	4 000	Arambekade SRI
7-10	Iraq	W	1-0	Muscat	Fr			
13-10	Japan	L	0-1	Muscat	WCq		35 000	Lu Jun CHN
17-11	India	D	0-0	Muscat	WCq		2 000	Nurilddin Salman IRQ
1-12	Latvia	W	3-2	Manama	Fr	Ahmed Mubarak [39], Khalifa Ayil [62], Kamouna [90]		
3-12	Finland	D	0-0	Manama	Fr	W 4-3p		
10-12	Iraq	W	3-1	Doha	GCr1	Amad Ali 2 [29 46], Khalifa Ayil [53]		
13-12	United Arab Emirates	W	2-1	Doha	GCr1	Mudhafir [74], Al Maimani [85]		
16-12	Qatar	L	1-2	Doha	GCr1	Kamouna [26]		
20-12	Bahrain	W	3-2	Doha	GCsf	Amad Ali 2 [44 83], Al Maimani [50]		
24-12	Qatar	D	2-2	Doha	GCf	Al Maimani [26]. L 4-5p		
2005								
11-10	United Arab Emirates	D	2-2	Al Ain	Fr	Saleh 2 [60 85]		
25-10	Syria	D	0-0	Muscat	Fr			
3-12	Syria	L	1-3	Al Gharrafa	WGr1	Al Maghni [35]		
2006								
6-02	Singapore	W	1-0	Doha	Fr	Salah [90]		
13-02	Iraq	W	1-0	Wattayah	Fr	Khalifa Ayel [77]	11 000	Shaban KUW
22-02	United Arab Emirates	L	0-1	Dubai	ACq		15 000	Al Ghamdi KSA
1-03	Jordan	W	3-0	Wattayah	ACq	Saleh [7], Sulaiman [18], Al Maghni [54]	11 000	Irmatov UZB
16-08	Pakistan	W	4-1	Quetta	ACq	Bader Mubarak 2 [15p 35], Amad Ali [27], Al Ajmi [90]	4 000	Torky IRN
1-09	Syria	W	3-0	Muscat	Fr	Al Ajmi [41], Al Touqi [59], Sulaiman [65]		
6-09	Pakistan	W	5-0	Muscat	ACq	Amad Ali [7], Fawzi Bashir 2 [36 58], Al Ajmi [47+], Al Touqi [88]	10 000	Nema IRQ
11-10	UAE	W	2-1	Muscat	ACq	Hassan Yousuf [24], Al Ajmi [28]	28 000	Huang Junjie CHN
8-11	Bahrain	D	1-1	Muscat	Fr	Al Touqi [52]		
15-11	Jordan	L	0-3	Amman	ACq		3 000	Najm LIB
2007								
13-01	Qatar	D	1-1	Doha	Fr	Sulaiman [26]		
17-01	UAE	W	2-1	Abu Dhabi	GCr1	Fawzi Bashir [36], Sulaiman [50]		
20-01	Kuwait	W	2-1	Abu Dhabi	GCr1	Sulaiman [8], Hashim Saleh [84]		
23-01	Yemen	W	2-1	Abu Dhabi	GCr1	Al Touqi [1], Al Bufasi [88]		
27-01	Bahrain	W	1-0	Abu Dhabi	GCsf	Al Maimani [54]		
30-01	UAE	L	0-1	Abu Dhabi	GCf			
24-06	Indonesia	W	1-0	Jakarta	Fr	Ahmed Hadid [57]		
28-06	Korea DPR	D	2-2	Singapore	Fr	Ahmed Mubarak [48], Al Ajmi [52]. W 4-3p		
1-07	Saudi Arabia	D	1-1	Singapore	Fr	Fawzi Bashir [56]. W 3-1p		
8-07	Australia	D	1-1	Bangkok	ACr1	Badar Mubarak [32]	5 000	Maillet SEY
12-07	Thailand	L	0-2	Bangkok	ACr1		19 000	LI Gi Young KOR
16-07	Iraq	D	0-0	Bangkok	ACr1		500	Maillet SEY

Fr = Friendly match • GC = Gulf Cup • WG = West Asian Games • AC = AFC Asian Cup • WC = FIFA World Cup
q = qualifier • r1 = first round group • sf = semi-final • f = final

OMAN NATIONAL TEAM RECORDS AND RECORD SEQUENCES

Records			Sequence records					
Victory	12-0	LAO 2001	Wins	7	2003	Clean sheets	5	2001
Defeat	0-21	LBY 1966	Defeats	17	1976-1984	Goals scored	11	1994, 2001
Player Caps	n/a		Undefeated	10	2003	Without goal	8	1965-1976
Player Goals	n/a		Without win	29	1965-1984	Goals against	28	1965-1984

OMAN COUNTRY INFORMATION

Capital	Muscat	Independence	1650 Portuguese Expulsion	GDP per Capita	$13 100
Population	2 903 165	Status	Monarchy	GNP Ranking	75
Area km²	212 460	Language	Arabic	Dialling code	+968
Population density	13 per km²	Literacy rate	75%	Internet code	.om
% in urban areas	13%	Main religion	Muslim	GMT +/−	+4
Towns/Cities ('000)	Muscat 871; Salalah 178; Suhar 138; 'Ibri 88; Nizwa 86; as-Suwaiq 86; Sur 77, Saham 76				
Neighbours (km)	Saudi Arabia 676; UAE 410; Yemen 288; Arabian Sea & Persian Gulf 2 092				
Main stadia	Sultan Qaboos – Muscat 39 000, Nizwa Complex – Nizwa 11 000				

OMAN 2006-07

PREMIER LEAGUE

	Pl	W	D	L	F	A	Pts	Nahda	Urooba	Dhofar	Nasr	Muscat	Tali'aa	Seeb	Sur	Bahla	Khaboora	Majees	Salam
Al Nahda ‡	22	12	7	3	35	20	43		0-1	2-2	4-2	1-1	0-0	2-2	0-2	1-0	2-0	2-3	3-0
Al Urooba Sur	22	12	5	5	28	18	41	1-2		1-0	1-2	1-1	0-1	1-0	1-1	1-0	3-1	1-0	3-1
Dhofar Salalah	22	9	9	4	31	22	36	1-1	3-1		0-1	2-0	0-0	1-1	2-1	3-2	1-1	1-0	2-1
Al Nasr Salalah	22	9	8	5	28	19	35	1-1	0-2	3-3		1-1	1-0	0-0	0-2	0-0	3-0	0-0	2-1
Muscat	22	9	5	8	26	18	32	0-1	2-1	1-0	0-1		2-0	3-0	0-1	3-0	0-0	2-0	4-0
Al Tali'aa	22	8	8	6	19	17	32	1-2	0-2	1-1	1-0	1-0		0-1	2-0	2-2	0-0	3-1	2-1
Seeb	22	8	6	8	31	29	30	1-2	1-2	2-1	0-4	2-2	1-0		1-3	2-1	2-1	5-1	6-1
Sur	22	8	5	9	24	25	29	**0-2**	0-0	1-2	1-1	1-0	1-1	1-1		2-1	2-1	3-0	0-2
Bahla	22	6	4	12	24	32	22	0-3	2-2	0-1	0-2	0-1	1-1	1-0	2-0		3-0	4-3	3-2
Khaboora	22	5	7	10	15	26	22	0-1	0-1	0-0	1-1	3-1	0-1	1-1	2-1	1-0		1-0	1-0
Majees	22	5	5	12	16	32	20	0-1	0-0	1-4	1-0	1-0	0-1	1-0	2-0	0-2	0-0		0-0
Al Salam	22	4	5	13	24	43	17	2-2	1-2	1-1	0-3	1-2	1-1	0-2	2-1	2-0	3-1	2-2	

13/10/2006 - 3/05/2007 • ‡ Qualified for the AFC Cup • Match in bold awarded

SULTAN QABOOS CUP 2006-07

Round of 16		Quarter-finals		Semi-finals		Final	
Dhofar Salalah	4						
Suwaiq	3	Dhofar Salalah †	1				
Muscat	1	Khaboora	1				
Khaboora	2			Dhofar Salalah	3		
Fanja	2			Bahla	0		
Tali'aa	1	Fanja	0 1				
Wahda	1	**Bahla**	1 1				
Bahla	3					Dhofar Salalah ‡	2
Seeb	3					Sur	1
Al Nasr Salalah	1	Seeb	1 1				
Salam	1	Al Urooba Sur	0 1				
Al Urooba Sur	2			Seeb	1		
Al Nahda	2			Sur	2		
Majees	0	Al Nahda	1 2				
Oman	1	Sur	1 2				
Sur	3						

† tie awarded to Dhofar • ‡ Qualified for the AFC Cup

CUP FINAL

20-11-2006

Scorers - Hisham Al Noobi [5], Hani Al Thabit [45] for Dhofar; Yaqoub Saleem [2] for Sur

RECENT LEAGUE AND CUP RECORD

	Championship						Cup		
Year	Champions	Pts	Runners-up	Pts	Third	Pts	Winners	Score	Runners-up
2000	Al Urooba	42	Al Nasr	36	Seeb	31	Al Nasr	2-1	Al Urooba
2001	Dhofar	41	Al Urooba	36	Seeb	36	Al Urooba	1-0	Al Nasr
2002	Al Urooba	38	Sur	37	Seeb	30	Al Nasr	2-1	Dhofar
2003	Rowi	65	Dhofar	63	Al Nasr	55	Rowi	2-0	Seeb
2004	Al Nasr	46	Muscat	45	Al Urooba	41	Dhofar	1-0	Muscat
2005	Dhofar	46	Al Urooba	44	Muscat	40	Al Nasr	3-1	Seeb
2006	Muscat	45	Al Nahda	43	Al Tali'aa	43	Dhofar	2-1	Sur
2007	Al Nahda	43	Al Urooba	41	Dhofar	36			

Muscat were formed by the merger of Rowi and Bustan

PAK – PAKISTAN

NATIONAL TEAM RECORD

JULY 10TH 2006 TO JULY 12TH 2010

PL	W	D	L	F	A	%
4	0	0	4	3	15	0

FIFA/COCA-COLA WORLD RANKING

1993	1994	1995	1996	1997	1998	1999	2000	2001	2002	2003	2004	2005	2006	High		Low	
142	158	160	173	153	168	179	190	181	178	168	177	158	164	**141**	02/94	**192**	05/01

2006–2007											
08/06	09/06	10/06	11/06	12/06	01/07	02/07	03/07	04/07	05/07	06/07	07/07
153	160	162	165	164	171	169	170	184	182	178	176

When Pakistan Army took to the field against Navy for their last league match of the season, they had gone unbeaten in all their previous games and had let in just two goals. During this run goalkeeper Jaffar Khan had set a new Pakistani record of 1260 minutes unbeaten between the posts, but Army went down 1-0 to an early Nomi Martin Gill goal. Despite their watertight defence, it had not been plain sailing for Army as both WAPDA and Khan Research Labs doggedly persued them all season with both finishing just four points behind. Army qualified for the AFC President's Cup which Pakistan was due to host in May 2007, but after a mix up involving visas, the

INTERNATIONAL HONOURS

South Asian Federation Games 1989 1991 2004

tournament was postponed until September. AFC President Mohamed Bin Hammam had predicted that hosting the tournament would help "expoilt the untapped potential of the game in the country" but potential is all that there is at present. In the AFC Asian Cup qualifiers, the national team demonstrated just how far it lags behind even the smaller Middle East nations by losing all six matches - some heavily - in a group containing Oman, Jordan and the UAE. In the South Asian Federation Games held in Colombo in August 2006, however, the under–23 team did manage to win gold by beating Sri Lanka 1-0 in the final.

THE FIFA BIG COUNT OF 2006

	Male	Female		Total
Number of players	2 975 400	0	Referees and Assistant Referees	2 500
Professionals	0		Admin, Coaches, Technical, Medical	7 400
Amateurs 18+	40 700		Number of clubs	720
Youth under 18	22 000		Number of teams	2 830
Unregistered	880 000		Clubs with women's teams	0
Total players	2 975 400		Players as % of population	1.79%

Pakistan Football Federation (PFF)

Opposite Punjab Football Stadium, Ferozepur Road, Lahore, Pakistan

Tel +92 42 9230821   Fax +92 42 9230823

mail@pff.com.pk   www.pff.com.pk

President: SALEH HAYAT Makhdoom Syed   General Secretary: KHAN LODHI Ahmed Yar

Vice-President: ALI SHA Syed Zahir   Treasurer: HAYAT Ali Khan   Media Officer: ALI WAHIDI Syed Akber

Men's Coach: SHAREEDA Salman Ahmed   Women's Coach: None

PFF formed: 1948   AFC: 1954   FIFA: 1948

Green shirts, Green shorts, Green socks

RECENT INTERNATIONAL MATCHES PLAYED BY PAKISTAN

2002	Opponents	Score	Venue	Comp	Scorers	Att	Referee
No international matches played in 2002 after June							
2003							
10-01	India	W 1-0	Dhaka	SAFr1	Sarfraz Rasool 50		Hossain BAN
12-01	Sri Lanka	W 2-1	Dhaka	SAFr1	Zahid Niaz 50, Sarfraz Rasool 86		Ghosh BAN
14-01	Afghanistan	W 1-0	Dhaka	SAFr1	Sarfraz Rasool 9		Ghosh BAN
18-01	Maldives	L 0-1	Dhaka	SAFsf			Gurung NEP
20-01	India	L 1-2	Dhaka	SAF3p	Sarfraz Rasool 66		Hassan BAN
21-03	Macao	W 3-0	Singapore	ACq	Qadeer Ahmed 2 27 65, Sarfraz Rasool 51		
25-03	Singapore	L 0-3	Singapore	ACq			
29-11	Kyrgyzstan	L 0-2	Karachi	WCq		10 000	Nesar BAN
3-12	Kyrgyzstan	L 0-4	Bishkek	WCq		12 000	Mamedov TKM
2004							
No international matches played in 2004							
2005							
12-06	India	D 1-1	Quetta	Fr	Essa 81	20 000	Khan PAK
16-06	India	L 0-1	Peshawar	Fr		15 000	Imtiaz PAK
18-06	India	W 3-0	Lahore	Fr	Essa 2, Tanveer Ahmed 45+, Arif Mehmood 46		Asif PAK
7-12	Sri Lanka	W 1-0	Karachi	SAFr1	Imran Hussain 38		
9-12	Afghanistan	W 1-0	Karachi	SAFr1	Muhammad Essa 55		
11-12	Maldives	D 0-0	Karachi	SAFr1			
14-12	Bangladesh	L 0-1	Karachi	SAFsf			
22-12	Bangladesh	D 0-0	Dhaka	ACq			
26-12	Bangladesh	L 0-1	Karachi	ACq			
2006							
18-02	Palestine	L 0-3	Manama	Fr			
22-02	Jordan	L 0-3	Amman	ACq			Basma SYR
1-03	United Arab Emirates	L 1-4	Karachi	ACq	Muhammad Essa 60	10 000	Tongkhan THA
2-04	Kyrgyzstan	W 1-0	Dhaka	CCr1	Muhammad Essa 59	2 500	Shamsuzzaman BAN
4-04	Tajikistan	L 0-2	Dhaka	CCr1		5 000	Tan Hai CHN
6-04	Macau	D 2-2	Dhaka	CCr1	Adeel 12, Muhammad Essa 43	1 000	Shamsuzzaman BAN
16-08	Oman	L 1-4	Quetta	ACq	Muhammad Essa 79p	4 000	Torky IRN
6-09	Oman	L 0-5	Muscat	ACq		10 000	Nema IRQ
11-10	Jordan	L 0-3	Lahore	ACq		4 000	Orzuev TJK
15-11	UAE	L 2-3	Abu Dhabi	ACq	Naveed Akram 22, Tanveer Ahmed 67	6 000	Sarkar IND
2007							
No international matches played in 2007 before August							

Fr = Friendly match • SA = South Asian Federation Cup • AC = AFC Asian Cup • CC = AFC Challenge Cup • WC = FIFA World Cup
q = qualifier • r1 = first round group • sf = semi-final • 3p = third place play-off

PAKISTAN NATIONAL TEAM RECORDS AND RECORD SEQUENCES

Records			Sequence records				
Victory	7-0	THA 1960	Wins	3	2003	Clean sheets	5	1952-1953
Defeat	1-9	IRN 1969	Defeats	14	1992-1993	Goals scored	13	1953-1959
Player Caps	n/a		Undefeated	5	1952-1953	Without goal	6	Three times
Player Goals	n/a		Without win	19	1992-1993	Goals against	21	1965-1981

PAKISTAN COUNTRY INFORMATION

Capital	Islamabad	Independence	1947 from the UK	GDP per Capita	$2 100
Population	159 196 336	Status	Republic	GNP Ranking	44
Area km²	803 940	Language	Punjabi 48%, English	Dialling code	+92
Population density	198 per km²	Literacy rate	45%	Internet code	.pk
% in urban areas	35%	Main religion	Muslim	GMT +/-	+5
Towns/Cities ('000)	Karachi 11 627; Lahore 6 312; Faisalabad 2 507; Rawalpindi 1 743; Multan 1 437; Hyderabad 1 386; Gujranwala 1 384; Peshawar 1 219; Islamabad 756; Quetta 733; Bahawalpur 552				
Neighbours (km)	China 523; India 2 912; Iran 909; Afghanistan 2 430; Arabian Sea 1 046				
Main stadia	Jinnah Sport Stadium – Islamabad 48 200; National Stadium – Karachi 34 228				

PAKISTAN 2006–07

NATIONAL FOOTBALL LEAGUE A DIVISION

	Pl	W	D	L	F	A	Pts	Army	WAPDA	KRL	KPT	NBP	KESC	Navy	Railways	Afghan FC	Wohaib FC	HBL
Pakistan Army	20	15	4	1	27	3	49		0-0	2-0	2-0	1-0	2-0	1-0	3-0	2-0	1-0	1-0
WAPDA	20	13	5	2	41	10	44	0-1		0-0	6-0	6-0	2-1	2-0	4-0	1-0	1-0	1-0
Khan Research Labs	20	13	5	2	26	12	44	0-0	1-0		0-1	2-2	1-0	1-0	2-0	1-0	3-0	1-0
Karachi Port Trust	20	7	7	6	28	29	28	0-3	1-1	1-1		0-0	1-2	3-2	2-1	1-1	4-2	2-1
Nat. Bank of Pakistan	20	7	6	7	24	28	27	1-3	2-2	1-2	2-1		1-2	2-1	0-2	1-2	2-0	1-1
Karachi Electric SC	20	6	6	8	23	25	24	0-0	2-4	0-0	0-0	1-3		1-0	3-0	0-1	1-2	1-0
Pakistan Navy	20	6	5	9	19	21	23	1-0	0-0	2-3	2-1	0-2	1-1		2-1	0-1	0-0	1-0
Pakistan Railways	20	4	7	9	18	32	19	1-1	1-4	2-3	0-0	1-1	1-1	2-2		1-0	1-0	0-0
Afghan FC	20	4	5	11	17	27	17	0-1	1-3	1-2	2-2	1-1	1-4	0-2	1-2		0-0	1-2
Wohaib FC	20	3	4	13	10	33	13	0-1	0-1	0-2	0-6	0-1	3-1	0-3	2-1	1-1		0-0
Habib Bank Ltd	20	2	6	12	11	24	12	0-2	0-3	0-1	1-2	0-1	2-2	0-0	1-1	0-3	3-0	

10/09/2006 - 1/02/2007 • † Qualified for the AFC Presidents Cup

PFF SOCCER CUP 2006

Second Round Groups — **Semi–finals** — **Final**

Group A	Pl	W	D	L	F	A	Pts	PM	MB	BN
Sui Southern Gas	3	2	1	0	4	2	7	1-1	1-0	2-1
Punjab Medical College	3	1	2	0	4	2	5	1-1	2-0	
Mauripur Baloch	3	1	1	1	3	3	4			
Baloch Noshki	3	0	0	3	2	6	0			

Semi–finals:

2-1 **Pakistan Television** 1
Sui Southern Gas 0

Final

Pakistan Television 4
Punjab Medical College 0

Group B	Pl	W	D	L	F	A	Pts	PT	BQ	DE
Bannu Red	3	2	0	1	6	5	6	0-4	3-1	3-0
Pakistan Television	3	1	2	0	5	1	5	0-0	1-1	
Baloch Quetta	3	0	2	1	2	4	2	1-1		
Dera Eleven	3	0	2	1	2	5	2			

Semi–finals:

Bannu Red 0
1 **Punjab Medical College**

CUP FINAL
2-08-2006

Played in Faisalabad • Punjab Television and Punjab Medical College promoted to A Division

30TH NATIONAL GAMES 2007 FINAL ROUNDS

Semi–finals

Pakistan Army	2
Punjab	1
WAPDA	0
Sindh	1

Final

Pakistan Army	0 7p
Sindh	0 6p

13-04-2007

RECENT LEAGUE AND CUP RECORD

	Championship			Cup		
Year	Champions	Score	Runners-up	Winners	Score	Runners-up
1990	Punjub Red		Pakistan Int. Airlines	Karachi Port Trust		HBFC
1991	WAPDA		Habib Bank	Marker Club		Karachi Port Trust
1992	Pakistan Int. Airlines	†	Pakistan Army	Crescent Textile Mills		Marker Club
1993	Pakistan Army	†	WAPDA	National Bank		Pakistan Steel
1994	Crescent Textile Mills	1-0	WAPDA	Frontier Constabulary		Pakistan Air Force
1995	Pakistan Army	1-0	Allied Bank	No tournament held		
1996	No tournament held			Allied Bank	3-1	Pakistan Army
1997	Allied Bank	0-0 3-0p	Pakistan Int. Airlines	No tournament held		
1998	Pakistan Int. Airlines	1-1 3-1p	Allied Bank	Allied Bank	1-0	Karachi Port Trust
1999	Allied Bank	0-0 4-3p	Pakistan Navy	Allied Bank	1-1 5-4p	Khan Research Labs
2000	Allied Bank	1-0	Habib Bank	Pakistan Army	1-0	Allied Bank
2001	WAPDA	1-1 4-3p	Khan Research Labs	Pakistan Army		Khan Research Labs
2002	No tournament held			Allied Bank	1-1 4-2p	WAPDA
2003	WAPDA	0-0 4-2p	Pakistan Army	Pakistan Telecoms	1-1 ‡	Karachi Port Trust
2004	WAPDA	†	Pakistan Army	No tournament held		
2005	Pakistan Army	†	WAPDA	Pakistan Telecoms	2-1	WAPDA
2006	Pakistan Army	†	WAPDA			

† Played on a league basis • ‡ Won on the toss of a coin • The PFF does not recognise the National Championships in 1992, 1993 and 1994 as official tournaments

PAN – PANAMA

NATIONAL TEAM RECORD
JULY 10TH 2006 TO JULY 12TH 2010

PL	W	D	L	F	A	%
19	7	6	6	22	24	52.6

FIFA/COCA-COLA WORLD RANKING

1993	1994	1995	1996	1997	1998	1999	2000	2001	2002	2003	2004	2005	2006	High	Low
132	140	126	101	119	131	138	121	109	129	125	100	78	81	**52** 06/07	**150** 10/95

2006–2007											
08/06	09/06	10/06	11/06	12/06	01/07	02/07	03/07	04/07	05/07	06/07	07/07
98	74	74	72	81	80	74	54	56	60	52	57

Five minutes... that was all that separated Panama from a first ever title. Having taken the lead in the 2007 UNCAF Cup final after 36 minutes through star man Luis Tejada, Panama defended stoutly until the 85th minute when Costa Rica's Kurt Bernard equalised to take the final to penalties. Both Felipe Baloy and Victor Herrera had their spot kicks saved, after which there was no way back for Panama as they lost 4-1. It was the second major final in two years that the Panamanians had lost on penalties, following the Gold Cup in 2005 against the USA. If there was consolation in defeat, it was the fact that even five years ago no-one would have dared to predict

INTERNATIONAL HONOURS
None

that Panama would ever qualify for a final, such has been the dramatic progress of football in the country. The 2007 CONCACAF Gold Cup didn't provide the same fairy-tale as two years previously but Panama did qualify for the quarter-finals where they lost 2-1 to the Americans. Club football still has some catching-up to do and in the UNCAF club championship both Plaza Amador and San Francisco were knocked out in the first round. San Francisco won the 2006 Championship at home when they beat Tauro 1-0 in the final in December. They had beaten Plaza Amada 3-0 to win the Apertura whilst Tauro had beaten Arabe Unido 2-0 to win the Clausura.

THE FIFA BIG COUNT OF 2006

	Male	Female		Total
Number of players	176 000	27 400	Referees and Assistant Referees	300
Professionals	300		Admin, Coaches, Technical, Medical	1 700
Amateurs 18+	28 800		Number of clubs	570
Youth under 18	23 200		Number of teams	950
Unregistered	30 800		Clubs with women's teams	18
Total players	203 400		Players as % of population	6.37%

Federación Panameña de Fútbol (FEPAFUT)
Estadio Rommel Fernández, Puerta 24, Ave. Jose Aeustin Araneo, Apartado postal 8-391 Zona 8, Panama
Tel +507 2333896   Fax +507 2330582
fepafut@sinfo.net   www.fepafut.com
President: ALVARADO Ariel   General Secretary: UCROS Eric
Vice-President: ARCE Fernando   Treasurer: POUSA Juan   Media Officer: BOLVARAN Arturo
Men's Coach: GUIMARAES Alexandre   Women's Coach: PEREZ Gaspar
FEPAFUT formed: 1937   CONCACAF: 1961   FIFA: 1938
Red shirts, Red shorts, Red socks

RECENT INTERNATIONAL MATCHES PLAYED BY PANAMA

2005	Opponents		Score	Venue	Comp	Scorers	Att	Referee
26-01	Ecuador	L	0-2	Ambato	Fr		5 000	Vasco ECU
29-01	Ecuador	L	0-2	Babahoyo	Fr			
9-02	Guatemala	D	0-0	Panama City	WCq		20 000	Prendergast JAM
19-02	El Salvador	W	1-0	Guatemala City	UCr1	Solis 77	10 000	Archundia MEX
23-02	Costa Rica	L	0-1	Guatemala City	UCr1		3 000	Archundia MEX
25-02	Honduras	L	0-1	Guatemala City	UCsf		11 159	Sibrian SLV
27-02	Guatemala	L	0-3	Guatemala City	UC3p		1 491	Quesada CRC
26-03	Costa Rica	L	1-2	San Jose	WCq	Brown 58p	8 000	Rodriguez MEX
30-03	Mexico	D	1-1	Panama City	WCq	Tejada 75	13 000	Pineda HON
25-05	Venezuela	D	1-1	Caracas	Fr	Brown 34	15 000	Brand VEN
4-06	Trinidad and Tobago	L	0-2	Port of Spain	WCq		18 000	Prendergast JAM
8-06	USA	L	0-3	Panama City	WCq		15 000	Navarro CAN
6-07	Colombia	W	1-0	Miami	GCr1	Tejada 70	10 311	Batres GUA
10-07	Trinidad and Tobago	D	2-2	Miami	GCr1	Tejada 2 24 90	17 292	Wyngaarde SUR
12-07	Honduras	L	0-1	Miami	GCr1		11 000	Wyngaarde SUR
17-07	South Africa	D	1-1	Houston	GCqf	Jorge Dely Valdes 48 W 5-3p	60 050	Prendergast JAM
21-07	Colombia	W	3-2	New Jersey	GCsf	Phillips 2 11 72, Jorge Dely Valdes 26	41 721	Sibrian SLV
24-07	USA	D	0-0	New Jersey	GCf	L 1-3p	31 018	Batres GUA
17-08	Guatemala	L	1-2	Guatemala City	WCq	Jorge Dely Valdes 19	24 000	Sibrian SLV
3-09	Costa Rica	L	1-3	Panama City	WCq	Tejada 90	21 000	Stott USA
7-09	Mexico	L	0-5	Mexico City	WCq		40 000	Hall USA
8-10	Trinidad and Tobago	L	0-1	Panama City	WCq		1 000	Navarro CAN
12-10	USA	L	0-2	Boston	WCq		2 500	Alcala MEX
27-10	Bahrain	L	0-5	Manama	Fr			
2006								
16-08	Peru	W	2-0	Lima	Fr	Phillips 20, Gomez.G 86	1 000	Garay PER
6-09	Guatemala	W	2-1	Guatemala City	Fr	Torres 2, Perez.B 32		
7-10	El Salvador	W	1-0	Panama City	Fr	Tejada 65		Moreno PAN
11-10	Trinidad & Tobago	L	1-2	Port of Spain	Fr	Canales 44		
19-11	Peru	L	1-2	Panama City	Fr	Tejada 38p	2 000	Vidal PAN
29-11	El Salvador	D	0-0	San Salvador	Fr			
2007								
14-01	Armenia	D	1-1	Los Angeles	Fr	Tejada		
31-01	Trinidad & Tobago	W	2-1	Panama City	Fr	Canales 29, Aguilar 82	5 000	Vidal PAN
11-02	Honduras	D	1-1	San Salvador	UCr1	Rivera 78		Aguilar SLV
13-02	Costa Rica	W	1-0	San Salvador	UCr1	Blanco 86		Batres GUA
16-02	Guatemala	W	2-0	San Salvador	UCsf	Phillips 50, Baloy 92+		Arredondo MEX
18-02	Panama	D	1-1	San Salvador	UCf	Tejada 36, L 1-4p		Batres GUA
24-03	Haiti	L	0-3	Miami	Fr		12 000	
26-03	Jamaica	D	1-1	Kingston	Fr	Garces 3	16 554	Brizan TRI
9-05	Colombia	L	0-4	Panama City	Fr		4 000	Archundia MEX
8-06	Honduras	W	3-2	New Jersey	GCr1	Rivera 33, Perez.B 42, Garces 82	20 230	Navarro CAN
10-06	Cuba	D	2-2	New Jersey	GCr1	Garces 16, Perez.B 47	68 123	
13-06	Mexico	L	0-1	Houston	GCr1		68 417	
16-06	USA	L	1-2	Foxboro	GCqf	Perez.B 84	22 412	Brizan TRI

Fr = Friendly match • UC = UNCAF Cup • GC = CONCACAF Gold Cup • WC = FIFA World Cup
q = qualifier • r1 = first round group • qf = quarter-final • sf = semi-final • 3p = third place play-off • f = final

PANAMA NATIONAL TEAM RECORDS AND RECORD SEQUENCES

Records			Sequence records					
Victory	12-0	PUR 1946	Wins	4	2001, 2003	Clean sheets	3	2000
Defeat	0-11	CRC 1938	Defeats	9	1976-1977	Goals scored	11	1946-50, 1974-75
Player Caps	n/a		Undefeated	7	Three times	Without goal	6	1984-1985
Player Goals	n/a		Without win	13	1950-1963	Goals against	17	1975-1979

PANAMA COUNTRY INFORMATION

Capital	Panamá	Independence	1903	GDP per Capita	$6 300
Population	3 000 463	Status	Republic	GNP Ranking	87
Area km²	78 200	Language	Spanish	Dialling code	+507
Population density	38 per km²	Literacy rate	92%	Internet code	.pa
% in urban areas	53%	Main religion	Christian	GMT +/−	-5
Towns/Cities ('000)	Panamá 408; San Miguelito 321; Tocumen 88; David 82; Arraiján 77; Colón 76; Las Cumbres 69				
Neighbours (km)	Colombia 225; Costa Rica 330; Caribbean and North Pacific 2 490				
Main stadia	Rommel Fernandez – Panamá 25 000; Armando Dely Valdez – Colón 3 000				

PANAMA 2006

ANAPROF PRIMERA PROFESIONAL APERTURA

	Pl	W	D	L	F	A	Pts	Tauro	Plaza	Sporting	San Fran.	Chorillo	Alianza	Veraguense	Arabe Un.	Chiriqui	Policía
Tauro †	18	10	5	3	25	14	35		3-1	1-3	1-0	0-0	1-0	0-0	2-1	1-0	1-0
Plaza Amador †	18	9	4	5	30	18	31	1-2		1-0	1-2	1-1	1-0	3-2	1-0	6-1	5-1
Sporting 89 †	18	8	6	4	19	13	30	0-0	1-1		1-0	1-1	2-1	1-2	1-1	0-0	1-0
San Francisco †	18	7	8	3	20	11	29	2-2	1-0	1-0		1-1	1-0	3-0	0-0	1-0	0-0
Municipal Chorrillo	18	5	9	4	20	17	24	0-2	0-0	0-1	1-1		3-0	1-3	2-0	3-1	2-0
Alianza	18	7	3	8	22	22	24	2-1	0-2	1-2	1-0	1-2		1-1	0-0	4-2	4-1
Atlético Veragüense	18	6	6	6	25	27	24	1-4	1-2	0-2	1-1	2-0	1-2		2-1	3-3	1-0
Arabe Unido	18	3	10	5	15	18	19	1-1	1-1	2-1	1-1	0-0	0-0	2-2		1-2	1-0
Atlético Chiriquí	18	4	6	8	18	29	18	1-0	2-1	1-2	0-0	1-1	2-3	0-2	0-0		2-1
Policía Nacional	18	0	5	13	10	35	5	1-3	0-2	0-0	1-5	2-2	0-2	1-1	2-3	0-0	

3/02/2006 - 26/04/2006 • † Qualified for the Apertura play-offs • Match in bold awarded • Play-offs: Semi-finals - **San Francisco** 0-0 2-1 Tauro; **Plaza Amador** 2-0 2-1 Sporting; Final - **San Francisco** 3-0 Plaza Amador. San Francisco won the Apertura

PANAMA 2006

ANAPROF PRIMERA PROFESIONAL CLAUSURA

	Pl	W	D	L	F	A	Pts	Tauro	San Fran.	Arabe Un.	Veraguense	Plaza	Alianza	Chorillo	Sporting	Chiriqui	Policía
Tauro †	18	10	7	1	31	17	37		1-1	1-1	0-1	0-0	1-1	1-1	3-0	3-1	2-0
San Francisco †	18	11	2	5	40	25	35	4-5		2-1	1-2	3-1	4-0	1-0	3-0	2-0	3-1
Arabe Unido †	18	10	3	5	30	20	33	2-3	3-1		0-1	3-0	3-2	0-0	3-1	1-0	3-1
Atlético Veragüense †	18	9	6	3	22	16	33	0-1	2-2	1-0		2-1	0-0	3-2	1-2	0-0	1-0
Plaza Amador	18	9	4	5	25	17	31	1-2	4-1	2-1	0-0		4-1	2-0	2-1	0-1	2-0
Alianza	18	8	2	8	29	31	26	0-1	3-2	1-2	2-1	0-2		4-3	1-2	3-1	2-0
Municipal Chorillo	18	6	6	6	24	23	24	2-2	1-2	1-1	0-0	0-0	1-2		1-0	3-2	3-0
Sporting 89	18	4	1	13	17	31	13	0-2	0-1	0-1	2-3	1-2	3-2	0-1		4-2	0-0
Atlético Chiriquí	18	2	4	12	14	30	10	1-1	0-2	1-2	1-1	0-0	1-2	1-2	1-0		1-3
Policía Nacional	18	3	1	14	17	39	10	1-2	1-5	2-3	2-3	1-2	0-3	2-3	2-1	1-0	

28/07/2006 - 9/11/2006 • † Qualified for the Clausura play-offs • Play-offs: Semi-finals - **Arabe Unido** 1-2 3-1 San Francisco; Atlético Veragüense 1-1 0-2 **Tauro**; Final - **Tauro** 2-0 Arabe Unido. Tauro won the Clausura
Overall championship final: **SAN FRANCISCO** 1-0 Tauro (Rommel Fernandez, Panama City, 3-12-2006, Ref: Vidal. Scorer: Alberto Zapata [73])

CLUB DIRECTORY

Club	Town/City	Lge	CL
Alianza		0	0
Deportivo Arabe Unido	Colón	3	0
Atlético Chiriquí	San Cristobal	0	0
Atlético Veraguense	Veraguas	0	0
Colón River	Colón	0	0
El Chorrillo	Balboa	0	0
Plaza Amador	Panama City	5	0
Sporting 89	San Miguelito	0	0
San Francisco	La Chorrera	2	0
Tauro	Panama City	6	0

RECENT LEAGUE RECORD

Year	Championship		
	Winners	Score	Runners-up
1997	Tauro	1-0	Euro Kickers
1998	Tauro	1-0	Deportivo Arabe Unido
1999	Deportivo Arabe Unido	3-0	Tauro
2000	Tauro	2-0	Plaza Amador
2001	Panama Viejo	4-3	Tauro
2001	Deportivo Arabe Unido	†	
2002	Plaza Amador	2-0	Deportivo Arabe Unido
2003	Tauro	†	
2004	Deportivo Arabe Unido	†	
2005	Plaza Amador	2-0	San Francisco
2006	San Francisco	2-0	Tauro

† Won both Apertura and Clausura so automatic champions

PAR – PARAGUAY

NATIONAL TEAM RECORD
JULY 10TH 2006 TO JULY 12TH 2010

PL	W	D	L	F	A	%
11	3	3	5	13	16	40.9

FIFA/COCA-COLA WORLD RANKING

1993	1994	1995	1996	1997	1998	1999	2000	2001	2002	2003	2004	2005	2006	High	Low
61	87	64	38	29	25	17	10	13	18	22	30	30	35	8 03/01	103 05/95

2006–2007											
08/06	09/06	10/06	11/06	12/06	01/07	02/07	03/07	04/07	05/07	06/07	07/07
19	21	29	35	35	35	30	29	35	35	37	29

Without a win for almost a year after the World Cup in Germany, Paraguay surprised everyone in their opening match of the Copa América by thrashing Colombia 5-0, which they followed with 3-1 victory over the USA to qualify for the quarter-finals. Carlos Gamarra and José Cardozo may have disappeared from the scene but there is still plenty of talent for new coach Gerardo Martino to work with as Paraguay set out to qualify for a fourth consecutive World Cup. However, the manner of their defeat against Mexico in the quarter-finals will be a cause for concern as they crashed to

INTERNATIONAL HONOURS
Qualified for the FIFA World Cup finals 1930 1950 1958 1986 1998 2002 2006 Copa America 1953 1979
South America U-23 1992 Juventud de America 1971 South America U-16 2004 Copa Libertadores Olimpia 1979 1990 2002

a 6-0 defeat. Martino had been appointed in February after leading both Libertad and Cerro Porteno to the title in recent years. In the 2006 Championship he was in charge of Libertad as they won the championship for the 11th time in their history, regaining the title from Cerro Porteño, whom they beat in the final. Cerro had gone through their Clausura campaign unbeaten to qualify for the final but after a 0-0 draw in the first match they lost the return 2-1 to hand the title to Libertad. Sportivo Luqueño were surprise winners of the 2007 Apertura and will be out to win a first title since 1953 when they meet the Clausura winners at the end of the year.

THE FIFA BIG COUNT OF 2006

	Male	Female		Total
Number of players	886 966	150 469	Referees and Assistant Referees	802
Professionals	590		Admin, Coaches, Technical, Medical	3 200
Amateurs 18+	53 667		Number of clubs	1 696
Youth under 18	29 984		Number of teams	3 500
Unregistered	950 000		Clubs with women's teams	13
Total players	1 037 435		Players as % of population	15.94%

Asociación Paraguaya de Fútbol (APF)
Estadio de los Defensores del Chaco, Calle Mayor Martinez 1393, Asuncion, Paraguay
Tel +595 21 480120   Fax +595 21 480124
apf@telesurf.com.py   www.apf.org.py
President: NAPOUT juan Angel   General Secretary: FILARTIGA Arturo
Vice-President: DAHER Ramon Gonzalez   Treasurer: ACOSTA Federico   Media Officer: ARRUA Gilda
Men's Coach: MARTINO Gerardo   Women's Coach: CABRERA Agustin
APF formed: 1906   CONMEBOL: 1921   FIFA: 1925
Red and white striped shirts, Blue shorts, Blue socks

RECENT INTERNATIONAL MATCHES PLAYED BY PARAGUAY

2004	Opponents	Score		Venue	Comp	Scorers	Att	Referee
31-03	Brazil	D	0-0	Asuncion	WCq		40 000	Ruiz COL
28-04	Korea Republic	D	0-0	Incheon	Fr		26 237	Kamikawa JPN
1-06	Bolivia	L	1-2	La Paz	WCq	Cardozo [33]	23 013	Rezende BRA
6-06	Argentina	D	0-0	Buenos Aires	WCq		37 000	Simon BRA
8-07	Costa Rica	W	1-0	Arequipa	CAr1	Dos Santos [85p]	30 000	Ruiz COL
11-07	Chile	D	1-1	Arequipa	CAr1	Cristaldo [79]	15 000	Mendez URU
14-07	Brazil	W	2-1	Arequipa	CAr1	González.J [29], Bareiro [71]	8 000	Hidalgo PER
18-07	Uruguay	L	1-3	Tacna	CAqf	Gamarra [16]	20 000	Baldassi ARG
5-09	Venezuela	W	1-0	Asuncion	WCq	Gamarra [52]	30 000	Mendez URU
9-10	Colombia	D	1-1	Barranquilla	WCq	Gavilan [77]	25 000	Elizondo ARG
13-10	Peru	D	1-1	Asuncion	WCq	Paredes [13]	30 000	Ruiz COL
17-11	Uruguay	L	0-1	Montevideo	WCq		35 000	Simon BRA
2005								
19-01	Korea Republic	D	1-1	Los Angeles	Fr	Cardozo [45p]	10 000	Hall USA
23-01	Guatemala	W	2-1	Los Angeles	Fr	Cuevas [14], Dos Santos [74]		
27-03	Ecuador	L	2-5	Quito	WCq	Cardozo [10p], Cabanas [14]	32 449	Mendez URU
30-03	Chile	W	2-1	Asuncion	WCq	Morinigo [37], Cardozo [59]	10 000	Elizondo ARG
5-06	Brazil	L	1-4	Porto Alegre	WCq	Santa Cruz [72]	45 000	Vazquez URU
7-06	Bolivia	W	4-1	Asuncion	WCq	Gamarra [17], Santa Cruz [46+], Caceres [54], Nunez [68]	5 534	Brand VEN
17-08	El Salvador	W	3-0	Ciudad del Este	Fr	Barreto [22], Valdez [45], Dos Santos [75]	12 000	
3-09	Argentina	W	1-0	Asuncion	WCq	Santa Cruz [14]	32 000	Simon BRA
8-10	Venezuela	W	1-0	Maracaibo	WCq	Valdez [64]	13 272	Elizondo ARG
12-10	Colombia	L	0-1	Asuncion	WCq		12 374	Rezende BRA
11-11	Togo	W	4-2	Tehran	Fr	Lopez.D 2 [13 51], Bonet [56], Dos Santos [67]		
2006								
1-03	Wales	D	0-0	Cardiff	Fr		12 324	McDonald SCO
29-03	Mexico	L	1-2	Chicago	Fr	Cuevas [2]	46 510	Kennedy USA
24-05	Norway	D	2-2	Oslo	Fr	Gamarra [48], Valdez [54]	10 227	Olsiak SVK
27-05	Denmark	D	1-1	Aarhus	Fr	Cardozo [20]	20 047	Bennett ENG
31-05	Georgia	W	1-0	Dornbirn	Fr	Valdez [40]	2 000	Gangle AUT
10-06	England	L	0-1	Frankfurt	WCr1		48 000	Rodriguez MEX
15-06	Sweden	L	0-1	Berlin	WCr1		72 000	Michel SVK
20-06	Trinidad and Tobago	W	2-0	Kaiserslautern	WCr1	OG [25], Cuevas [86]	46 000	Rosetti ITA
7-10	Australia	D	1-1	Brisbane	Fr	Beauchamp OG [92+]	47 609	Kashihara JPN
15-11	Chile	L	2-3	Viña de Mar	Fr	Jimenez.E [57], Riveros [68]	9 000	Baldassi ARG
2007								
25-03	Mexico	L	1-2	San Nicolas	Fr	Santa Cruz [92+]		Pineda HON
28-03	Colombia	L	0-2	Bogota	Fr		32 000	
2-06	Austria	D	0-0	Vienna	Fr		12 700	Bebek CRO
5-06	Mexico	W	1-0	Mexico City	Fr	Cardozo [88]	60 000	Larrionda URU
20-06	Bolivia	D	0-0	Santa Cruz	Fr		35 000	Antequera BOL
28-06	Colombia	W	5-0	Maracaibo	CAr1	Santa Cruz 3 [30 46 80], Cabañas 2 [84 88]	30 000	Larrionda URU
2-07	USA	W	3-1	Barinas	CAr1	Barreto [29], Cardozo [56], Cabañas [92+]	23 000	Rivera PER
5-07	Argentina	L	0-1	Barquisimeto	CAr1		37 000	Larrionda URU
8-07	Mexico	L	0-6	Maturin	CAqf		50 000	Pezzotta ARG

Fr = Friendly match • CA = Copa América • WC = FIFA World Cup • q = qualifier • r1 = 1st round • qf = quarter-final

PARAGUAY NATIONAL TEAM RECORDS AND RECORD SEQUENCES

Records			Sequence records					
Victory	7-0	BOL 1949	Wins	8	1947-1949	Clean sheets	5	1947-49, 1988
Defeat	0-8	ARG 1926	Defeats	8	1959-1961	Goals scored	15	1958-1960
Player Caps	110	GAMARRA Carlos	Undefeated	14	1985-1986	Without goal	4	1981-83, 1993
Player Goals	25	CARDOZO José	Without win	20	1959-1962	Goals against	20	1931-1942

MAJOR CITIES/TOWNS
Population '000

1	Asunción	506
2	Ciudad del Este	287
3	San Lorenzo	245
4	Luque	239
5	Capiatá	232
6	Lambaré	130
7	Fernando de la Mora	123
8	Limpio	116
9	Nemby	113
10	Itauguá	80
11	Encarnación	78
12	Mariano Roque Alonso	77
13	San Antonio	73
14	Villa Elisa	72
15	Pedro Juan Caballero	69
16	Hernandaríaz	61
17	Presidente Franco	58
18	Caaguazú	57
19	Coronel Oviedo	53
20	Concepción	50
21	Villarrica	43
22	Pilar	26
23	Caacupé	23
24	Minga Guazú	19

REPUBLIC OF PARAGUAY; REPUBLICA DEL PARAGUAY

Capital	Asunción	Language	Spanish, Guarani			Independence	1811
Population	6 669 086	Area	406 750 km²	Density	15 per km²	% in cities	53%
GDP per cap	$4 700	Dailling code	+595	Internet	.py	GMT +/-	-4

San Lorenzo, Luque, Capiatá, Lambaré, Fernando de la Mora, Limpio, Nemby, Itaguá, San Antonio and Vila Elisa are part of the Greater Asunción metropolitan area which has a population of 1 944 000 • Ciudad del Este, Hernandaríaz, Presidente Franco and Minga Guazú are part of the Foz do Iguaçu metropolitan area which has a population of 713 000

MEDALS TABLE

		Overall			Lge		Sth Am			City	Stadium	Cap'ty	DoF
		G	S	B	G	S	G	S	B				
1	Olimpia	42	23	8	38	19	4	4	8	Asunción	Manuel Ferreira	20 000	1902
2	Cerro Porteño	27	25	5	27	25			5	Asunción	General Pablo Rojas 'La Olla'	25 000	1912
3	Libertad	11	18	2	11	18			2	Asunción	Dr. Nicolás Leoz	16 000	1905
4	Guaraní	9	11	1	9	11			1	Asunción	Rogelio Livieres	10 000	1903
5	Nacional	6	8		6	8				Asunción	Arsenio Erico	4 500	1904
6	Sol de América	2	12		2	12				Vila Elisa	Luis Alfonso Giagni	5 000	1909
7	Sportivo Luqueño	2	3		2	3				Luque	Feliciano Cáceres	24 000	1921
8	Presidente Hayes	1			1					Tacumbu	Kiko Reyes	5 000	1907
9	Atlántida		3			3				Asunción	Flaviano Díaz	1 000	1906
	River Plate		3			3				Asunción	River Plate	5 000	1911
11	12 de Octubre		1			1				Itaugua	Juan Canuto Pettengill	8 000	1914
12	Atlético Colegiales			1					1	Asunción	Luciano Zacarías	4 500	1977
13	3 de Febrero									Ciudad del Este	Antonio Oddone Sarubbi	25 000	1970
	General Caballero									Zeballos Cue	General Caballero	5 000	1918
	2 de Mayo									Pedro Juan Caballero	Monumental Río Parapití	25 000	1935

RECENT LEAGUE RECORD

	Championship		
Year	Winners	Score	Runners-up
1995	Olimpia	2-1 0-1 8-7p	Cerro Porteño
1996	Cerro Porteño	1-2 5-1	Guaraní
1997	Olimpia	1-0 1-1	Cerro Porteño
1998	Olimpia	2-2 3-1	Cerro Porteño
1999	Olimpia	1-0 3-2	Cerro Porteño
2000	Olimpia	†	Guaraní
2001	Cerro Porteño	†	Sportivo Luqueño
2002	Libertad	2-1 4-1	12 de Octubre
2003	Libertad	†	Guaraní
2004	Cerro Porteño	†	Libertad
2005	Cerro Porteño	†	Libertad
2006	Libertad	0-0 2-1	Cerro Porteño

† Won both Apertura and Clausura so automatic champions

PARAGUAY 2006
DIVISION PROFESIONAL CLAUSURA

	Pl	W	D	L	F	A	Pts	Cerro	Libertad	2 de Mayo	Tacuary	Nacional	Olimpia	Luqueño	Guaraní	3 Febrero	12 Octubre	FdlM
Cerro Porteño † ‡	20	16	4	0	35	10	52		1-0	3-1	1-1	1-0	1-0	3-1	5-1	1-0	1-0	3-1
Libertad †	20	12	5	3	35	20	41	1-4		2-2	2-0	2-1	0-0	4-0	1-1	2-1	4-0	2-1
2 de Mayo	20	9	6	5	27	21	33	0-1	2-2		2-2	0-0	2-1	1-2	1-0	1-0	3-2	0-1
Tacuary † ‡	20	8	8	4	25	19	32	1-2	1-1	0-1		2-1	2-2	1-0	1-0	1-0	1-1	1-2
Nacional	20	8	5	7	29	21	29	0-1	2-1	0-3	3-3		1-0	0-0	2-0	0-1	1-1	3-1
Olimpia	20	5	8	7	22	22	23	1-1	0-1	1-1	0-2	1-0		4-2	1-1	1-1	0-2	5-1
Sportivo Luqueño	20	5	8	7	20	30	23	0-0	2-3	0-0	0-0	0-4	1-1		3-1	0-0	2-1	1-0
Guaraní	20	4	9	7	21	26	21	0-1	1-2	2-0	1-1	2-2	0-0	1-1		1-0	1-1	3-1
3 de Febrero	20	4	5	11	17	26	17	1-1	0-1	1-2	0-2	0-3	1-0	4-2	3-3		1-0	1-2
12 de Octubre	20	3	5	12	21	35	14	0-1	1-2	1-3	0-1	1-4	2-3	2-3	0-0	3-2		2-2
Fernando de la Mora	20	3	3	14	14	36	12	1-3	0-2	0-2	0-2	1-2	0-1	0-0	0-2	0-0	0-1	

14/07/2006 - 3/12/2006 • Cerro qualified to meet Apertura champions Libertad for the title • † Qualified for the Copa Libertadores • ‡ Qualified for the Copa Sudamericana • Copa Sudamericana play-offs: Semi-finals Tacuary 1-1 2 de Mayo (qualified due to better season record); Cerro Porteño 2-0 Sportivo Luqueño; Final: Tacuary 3-2 Cerro Porteño. Tacuary qualified along with champions Libertad

CHAMPIONSHIP FINAL
First leg. La Olla, Asunción, 6-12-2006

Cerro Porteño   0
Libertad   0

Second leg. Dr. Nicolás Leoz, Asunción, 10-12-2006

Libertad   2   Hernan López 24, Sergio Aquino 28
Cerro Porteño   1   Alejandro da Silva 60

PARAGUAY 2006
DIVISION INTERMEDIA (2)

	Pl	W	D	L	F	A	Pts
Sol de América	18	12	2	4	34	16	38
Sportivo Trinidense	18	9	6	3	24	17	33
Rubio Ñu	18	7	7	4	27	24	28
Silvio Pettirossi	18	7	6	5	24	22	27
Sportivo Iteño	18	6	8	4	26	26	26
Choré Central	18	6	4	8	20	24	22
Cerro Porteño	18	5	6	7	21	27	21
General Caballero	18	5	4	9	26	29	19
Sport Colombia	18	5	3	10	18	21	18
Universal	18	2	6	10	20	34	12

23/04/2006 - 20/08/2006

PARAGUAY 2006
PRIMERO DE ASCENSO (3)

	Pl	W	D	L	F	A	Pts
Presidente Hayes	26	15	9	2	48	15	54
General Díaz	26	12	10	4	39	29	46
Sportivo San Lorenzo	26	12	9	5	37	27	45
3 de Noviembre	26	9	10	7	35	37	37
Atlético Tembetary	26	9	9	8	35	30	36
River Plate	26	10	6	10	41	37	36
29 de Setiembre	26	9	7	10	55	51	34
Atlético Colegiales	26	8	10	8	45	41	34
Resistencia	26	9	7	10	40	45	34
Independiente	26	7	10	9	29	32	31
1° de Marzo	26	8	6	12	32	41	30
Pilcomayo	26	7	8	11	35	39	29
Cerro Corá	26	6	10	10	48	49	28
Humaitá	26	4	3	19	30	76	15

11/03/2006 - 2/09/2006

PARAGUAY 2007
DIVISION PROFESIONAL APERTURA

	Pl	W	D	L	F	A	Pts	Luqueño	Cerro	Libertad	Olimpia	3 Febrero	Nacional	Tacuary	Trindense	Sol América	12 Octubre	2 Mayo	Guaraní
Sportivo Luqueño	22	14	5	3	45	22	47		3-2	0-1	2-2	2-0	2-1	2-0	4-3	1-2	4-1	2-0	3-0
Cerro Porteño	22	13	4	5	42	18	43	1-0		1-2	0-0	3-1	3-1	6-1	1-0	0-0	0-2	1-2	2-1
Libertad	22	11	7	4	30	16	40	0-2	0-1		2-2	2-1	1-1	2-0	4-0	0-0	3-1	2-0	0-0
Olimpia	22	10	8	4	29	21	38	0-0	0-1	0-1		2-2	1-1	2-2	3-1	1-0	3-2	3-1	3-1
3 de Febrero	22	8	6	8	23	25	30	1-1	1-0	1-0	0-1		1-0	4-1	0-1	1-0	1-2	0-0	2-1
Nacional	22	6	8	8	25	23	26	2-2	1-1	0-1	0-1	0-1		1-2	2-1	1-0	1-0	2-2	0-0
Tacuary	22	6	7	9	22	32	25	2-0	0-1	1-4	2-1	0-1	2-0		1-0	1-1	1-3	1-0	0-0
Sportivo Trindense	22	6	6	10	24	39	24	0-4	0-3	0-1	1-0	2-2	2-2	0-2		1-1	1-0	1-0	3-2
Sol de América	22	5	8	9	19	29	23	2-4	0-6	0-2	0-1	0-0	0-0	1-1	3-3		3-0	1-1	0-2
12 de Octubre	22	6	5	11	27	38	23	1-2	0-2	3-3	0-0	4-2	0-2	1-1	1-1	2-1		1-1	2-1
2 de Mayo	22	4	9	9	24	32	21	1-2	0-0	0-0	3-1	0-0	1-4	0-1	3-0	1-2	2-1		3-3
Guaraní	22	3	7	12	26	39	16	2-2	2-4	1-1	1-2	1-2	0-3	1-0	0-2	1-2	3-0	3-3	

16/02/2007 - 7/06/2007 • Sportivo Luqueño won the Apertura and qualified to meet the 2007 Clausura champions for the title

PER – PERU

NATIONAL TEAM RECORD
JULY 10TH 2006 TO JULY 12TH 2010

PL	W	D	L	F	A	%
13	3	3	7	14	22	34.6

FIFA/COCA-COLA WORLD RANKING

1993	1994	1995	1996	1997	1998	1999	2000	2001	2002	2003	2004	2005	2006	High		Low	
73	72	69	54	38	72	42	45	43	82	74	66	66	70	**34**	09/97	**86**	02/03

					2006–2007						
08/06	09/06	10/06	11/06	12/06	01/07	02/07	03/07	04/07	05/07	06/07	07/07
41	46	79	81	70	70	67	70	70	71	64	50

Should Peru fail to qualify for the World Cup in South Africa, it will mean that the national team will have been absent from seven consecutive tournaments, equalling their run from 1934 to 1966. In an attempt to prevent that, the federation turned to Julio Cesar Uribe, who was a player when Peru last appeared, in Spain in 1982. It was Uribe's second spell in charge but he didn't survive long in the job after Peru's indifferent performance at the Copa América in Venezuela. There is talent in the team - Chelsea's Claudio Pizarro, PSV's Jefferson Farfan and Hamburg's Paolo Guerrero - but what is lacking is depth and consistency and that was exposed at the Copa América. An opening

INTERNATIONAL HONOURS
Qualified for the FIFA World Cup finals 1930 1970 1978 1982   Copa America 1939 1975

3-0 win over Uruguay was followed by defeat to Venezuela and a draw against Bolivia, which was enough to see the team through to the quarter-finals - but for the fourth tournament running that's where their campaign ended as they were outclassed by Argentina. As coach of Cienciano, Uribe had led his team to the final of the 2006 Championship after winning the Clausura title in a play-off against Universitario. Three days later they beat Alianza 1-0 at altitude in their home town of Cusco in the first leg of the final, but back at sea level in Lima they lost the return 3-1 to miss out on a first League title. For Alianza, it was their 20th.

THE FIFA BIG COUNT OF 2006

	Male	Female		Total
Number of players	1 656 556	235 234	Referees and Assistant Referees	2 663
Professionals	799		Admin, Coaches, Technical, Medical	1 519
Amateurs 18+	70 050		Number of clubs	1 800
Youth under 18	166 140		Number of teams	3 000
Unregistered	835 000		Clubs with women's teams	300
Total players	1 891 790		Players as % of population	6.68%

Federación Peruana de Fútbol (FPF)
Av. Aviación 2085, San Luis, Lima 30, Peru
Tel +51 1 2258236   Fax +51 1 2258240
fepefutbol@fpf.org.pe   www.fpf.com.pe
President: BURGA Manuel Dr   General Secretary: QUINTANA Javier
Vice-President: PASTOR Julio   Treasurer: ALEMAN Lander   Media Officer: DEL AGUILA Wilmer
Men's Coach: DEL SOLAR José   Women's Coach: None
FPF formed: 1922   CONMEBOL: 1926   FIFA: 1926
White shirts with a red sash, White shorts, White socks

RECENT INTERNATIONAL MATCHES PLAYED BY PERU

2003	Opponents	Score		Venue	Comp	Scorers	Att	Referee
6-09	Paraguay	W	4-1	Lima	WCq	Solano [34], Mendoza [42], Soto.Jg [83], Farfan [90]	42 557	Baldassi ARG
9-09	Chile	L	1-2	Santiago	WCq	Mendoza [57]	54 303	Gimenez ARG
16-11	Brazil	D	1-1	Lima	WCq	Solano [50]	70 000	Ruiz COL
19-11	Ecuador	D	0-0	Quito	WCq		34 361	Gonzalez Chaves PAR
2004								
18-02	Spain	L	1-2	Barcelona	Fr	Solano [21]	23 580	Layec FRA
31-03	Colombia	L	0-2	Lima	WCq		29 325	Rezende BRA
28-04	Chile	D	1-1	Antofagasta	Fr	Zúñiga [91+]	23 000	Amarilla PAR
1-06	Uruguay	W	3-1	Montevideo	WCq	Solano [13], Pizarro [18], Farfan [61]	30 000	Selman CHI
6-06	Venezuela	D	0-0	Lima	WCq		40 000	Larrionda URU
30-06	Argentina	L	1-2	East Rutherford	Fr	Solano [36p]	41 013	Stott USA
6-07	Bolivia	D	2-2	Lima	CAr1	Pizarro [68p], Palacios [86]	45 000	Baldassi ARG
9-07	Venezuela	W	3-1	Lima	CAr1	Farfan [34], Solano [62], Acasiete [72]	43 000	Selman CHI
12-07	Colombia	D	2-2	Trujillo	CAr1	Solano [58], Maestri [60]	25 000	Rodriguez Moreno MEX
17-07	Argentina	L	0-1	Chiclayo	CAqf		25 000	Amarilla PAR
4-09	Argentina	L	1-3	Lima	WCq	Soto.Jg [62]	28 000	Simon BRA
9-10	Bolivia	L	0-1	La Paz	WCq		23 729	Reinoso ECU
13-10	Paraguay	D	1-1	Asuncion	WCq	Solano [74]	30 000	Ruiz COL
17-11	Chile	W	2-1	Lima	WCq	Farfan [56], Guerrero [85]	39 752	Baldassi ARG
2005								
27-03	Brazil	L	0-1	Goiania	WCq		49 163	Amarilla PAR
30-03	Ecuador	D	2-2	Lima	WCq	Guerrero [1], Farfan [58]	40 000	Chandia CHI
22-05	Japan	W	1-0	Niigata	Fr	Vassallo [94+]	39 856	Michel SVK
24-05	United Arab Emirates	D	0-0	Toyota	Fr		6 536	Nishimura JPN
4-06	Colombia	L	0-5	Barranquilla	WCq		15 000	Torres PAR
7-06	Uruguay	D	0-0	Lima	WCq		31 515	Baldassi ARG
17-08	Chile	W	3-1	Tacna	Fr	Vilchez [28], Guerrero [59], Villalta [64]		Ortube BOL
3-09	Venezuela	L	1-4	Maracaibo	WCq	Farfan [63]	6 000	Rezende BRA
9-10	Argentina	L	0-2	Buenos Aires	WCq		36 977	Torres PAR
12-10	Bolivia	W	4-1	Tacna	WCq	Vassallo [11], Acasiete [38], Farfan 2 [45 82]	14 774	Sequeira ARG
2006								
10-05	Trinidad and Tobago	D	1-1	Port of Spain	Fr	Vasallo [31]	20 000	Prendergast JAM
16-08	Panama	L	0-2	Lima	Fr		1 000	Garay PER
6-09	Ecuador	D	1-1	New Jersey	Fr	Guerrero [76]	20 000	
7-10	Chile	L	2-3	Viña del Mar	Fr	Guerrero [8], Pizarro [83]		Vieira URU
11-10	Chile	L	0-1	Tacna	Fr		12 000	Haro ECU
15-11	Jamaica	D	1-1	Kingston	Fr	Sanchez.A [64]		
19-11	Panama	W	2-1	Panama City	Fr	Mostto [41], Alva [80]	2 000	Vidal PAN
2007								
24-03	Japan	L	0-2	Yokohama	Fr		60 400	Nardi AUS
3-06	Ecuador	W	2-1	Madrid	Fr	Farfan [5], De la Cruz OG [51]	25 000	Puerta ESP
6-06	Ecuador	L	0-2	Barcelona	Fr		20 000	Crespo ESP
26-06	Uruguay	W	3-0	Merida	CAr1	Villalta [27], Mariño [70], Guerrero [89]		Amarilla PAR
30-06	Venezuela	L	0-2	San Cristobal	CAr1			Archundia MEX
3-07	Bolivia	D	2-2	Merida	CAr1	Pizarro 2 [34 85]		Chandia CHI
8-07	Argentina	L	0-4	Barquisimeto	CAqf			Simon BRA

Fr = Friendly match • CA = Copa América • WC = FIFA World Cup • q = qualifier • r1 = first round group • qf = quarter-final

PERU NATIONAL TEAM RECORDS AND RECORD SEQUENCES

Records			Sequence records					
Victory	9-1	ECU 1938	Wins	9	1937-1939	Clean sheets	4	1996
Defeat	0-7	BRA 1997	Defeats	9	1965-1968	Goals scored	12	1937-1941
Player Caps	120	PALACIOS Roberto	Undefeated	12	1937-1941	Without goal	3	Eight times
Player Goals	26	CUBILLAS Teófilo	Without win	15	1965-1969	Goals against	16	1959-1965

MAJOR CITIES/TOWNS

		Population '000
1	Lima	7 979
2	Arequipa	878
3	Trujillo	788
4	Chiclayo	607
5	Iquitos	468
6	Huancayo	398
7	Pucallpa	339
8	Piura	331
9	Chimbote	324
10	Cusco	322
11	Tacna	299
12	Juliaca	267
13	Ica	261
14	Sullana	162
15	Chincha Alta	160
16	Huánuco	154
17	Ayacucho	146
18	Cajamarca	139
19	Tarapoto	133
20	Puno	120
21	Tumbes	115
22	Talara	101
23	Chosica	90
24	Huaraz	89

REPUBLIC OF PERU; REPUBLICA DEL PERU

Capital	Lima	Language	Spanish, Quechua	Independence	1821
Population	28 674 757	Area	1 285 220 km²	Density	21 per km²	% in cities	72%
GDP per cap	$5 100	Dailling code	+51	Internet	.pe	GMT + / -	-5

MEDALS TABLE

		Overall			League			Sth Am			City	Stadium	Cap'ty	DoF
		G	S	B	G	S	B	G	S	B				
1	Universitario de Deportes	24	14	18	24	13	14	1		4	Lima	Teodoro Fernández	80 093	1924
2	Alianza Lima	20	17	12	20	17	9			3	Lima	Alejandro Villanueva	35 000	1901
3	Sporting Cristal	15	16	6	15	15	6		1		Lima	San Martin de Porres	18 000	1922
4	Sport Boys	6	7	5	6	7	5				Callao	Miguel Grau	15 000	1927
5	Deportivo Municipal	4	7	6	4	7	6				Lima	Municipal de Chorrillos	15 000	1935
6	Atlético Chalaco	2	5	4	2	5	4				Callao	Telmo Carbajo	8 000	1899
7	Mariscal Sucre	2	2	2	2	2	2							
8	Unión Huaral	2	1		2	1					Huaral	Julio Lores Colán	6 000	1947
9	Cienciano	1	3			3		1			Cusco	Inca Garcilaso de la Vega	42 056	1901
10	FBC Melgar	1	1	2	1	1	2				Arequipa	Mariano Melgar	20 000	1915
11	Defensor Lima	1		4	1		3			1	Lima			1931
12	Centro Iqueño	1		3	1		3				Chancay			1935-87
13	Colegio San Agustín	1			1						Lima			1982
	Sport Progreso	1			1						Lima			

RECENT LEAGUE RECORD

	Championship							Championship Play-off		
Year	Champions	Pts	Runners-up	Pts	Third	Pts		Winners	Score	Runners-up
1995	Sporting Cristal	96	Alianza Lima	84	Universitario	84				
1996	Sporting Cristal	69	Alianza Lima	60	Universitario	58				
1997								Alianza Lima	†	
1998								Universitario	2-1 1-2 4-2p	Sporting Cristal
1999								Universitario	3-0 0-1	Alianza Lima
2000								Universitario	†	
2001								Alianza Lima	3-2 0-1 4-2p	Cienciano
2002								Sporting Cristal	‡	
2003								Alianza Lima	2-1	Sporting Cristal
2004								Alianza Lima	0-0 5-4p	Sporting Cristal
2005								Sporting Cristal	1-0	Cienciano
2006								Alianza Lima	0-1 3-1	Cienciano

† Won both Apertura and Clausura so automatic champions. ‡ Apertura champions Universitario forfeited their place in the play-off by failing to finish in the top 4 of the Clausura

PERU 2006

PRIMERA DIVISION CLAUSURA

	Pl	W	D	L	F	A	Pts	Cienciano	Universitario	Bolognesi	Alianza	San Martin	Sp. Cristal	Melgar	Sport Boys	José Galvez	Ancash	Alianza At.	Unión Huaral
Cienciano †	22	13	2	7	40	31	41		3-3	3-1	2-1	0-1	2-1	2-0	1-0	1-0	1-3	4-1	5-1
Universitario ‡	22	12	5	5	34	24	41	2-1		1-2	3-2	3-0	0-0	2-1	1-3	1-0	4-1	3-1	3-0
Coronel Bolognesi ‡	22	12	3	7	32	20	39	1-2	4-1		1-1	1-2	0-1	2-0	3-0	2-1	3-0	1-0	1-0
Alianza Lima †	22	11	5	6	27	17	38	1-2	1-0	0-0		3-1	0-0	1-0	1-2	1-0	3-0	3-0	2-1
Univer'dad San Martin	22	10	4	8	24	21	34	4-1	0-1	2-0	0-1		0-2	0-0	2-1	0-1	2-0	2-1	0-1
Sporting Cristal †	22	9	4	9	24	15	31	1-0	0-1	1-2	0-1	0-2		2-0	0-1	3-0	3-0	3-1	4-0
FBC Melgar	22	8	7	7	23	22	31	1-2	1-1	1-0	3-2	2-0	2-1		4-1	2-0	1-1	2-1	2-1
Sport Boys	22	9	4	9	26	28	31	2-1	0-0	0-2	0-1	0-0	0-1	2-0		1-1	3-2	2-0	4-1
José Galvez	22	6	6	10	24	29	24	1-2	1-3	0-3	0-0	0-0	1-0	0-0	3-0		4-3	4-0	2-1
Sport Ancash	22	6	5	11	26	39	23	1-3	3-0	0-1	1-0	1-1	1-1	1-1	1-0	1-1		1-0	2-0
Alianza Atlético	22	5	6	11	29	40	21	4-1	0-0	4-2	1-1	2-3	0-0	0-0	2-2	3-3	4-2		2-0
Unión Huaral	22	4	3	15	15	38	15	1-1	0-1	0-0	0-1	0-2	1-0	0-0	1-2	2-1	3-1	1-2	

15/07/2006 - 17/12/2006 • Clausura play-off: Cienciano 2-1 Universitario (Estadio Mansiche, Trujillo, 20-12-2006. Scorers - Edinson Chará 71, Juan Marino 88 for Cienciano; Piero Alva 75p for Universitario). Cienciano qualified to meet Apertura winners Alianza in the championship decider
† Qualified for the Copa Libertadores • ‡ Qualified for the Copa Sudamericana • Match in bold was awarded
Top scorers: Miguel MOSTTO, Cienciano 17; Piero ALVA, Universitario 14; Sergio IBARRA, José Galvez 12; José HERRERA, Sport Boys 12

See *Almanack of World Football 2007* for Apertura details

Unión Huaral were relegated with the worst overall record in 2006 whilst José Galvez and Sport Boys were tied with the second worst record. In a play-off Sport Boys beat José Galvez 5-4 on penalties after a 0-0 draw

CHAMPIONSHIP FINAL

First leg. Inca Garcilaso de la Vega, Cusco, 23-12-2006

Cienciano	1	Miguel Mostto 37
Alianza	0	

Second leg. Alejandro Villanueva, Lima, 27-12-2006

Alianza	3	Ernesto Arakaki 22, OG 36, Flavio Maestri 52
Cienciano	1	Juan Carlos Mariño 49

PERU 2006 SEGUNDA DIVISION (2)

	Pl	W	D	L	F	A	Pts
Deportivo Municipal	22	12	9	1	35	15	45
Univ'dad San Marcos	22	11	8	3	28	11	41
Deportivo Aviación	22	10	7	5	29	19	37
Universidad Técnica	22	10	6	6	29	26	36
Atlético Minero	22	10	6	7	37	28	35
Alfonso Ugarte	22	9	5	8	31	36	32
América Cochahuayco	22	7	7	8	27	26	28
Olímpico Aurora	22	6	10	6	18	19	28
Univ'dad Cesar Vallejo	22	7	5	10	29	32	26
La Peña Sporting	22	5	5	12	29	36	20
Deportivo Curibamba	22	5	4	13	19	33	19
Defensor Villa del Mar	22	3	3	16	8	38	12

13/05/2006 - 22/10/2006

PERU 2007

PRIMERA DIVISION APERTURA

	Pl	W	D	L	F	A	Pts	San Martin	Cienciano	Ancash	Sport Boys	Universitario	Alianza	Melgar	Alianza At.	Municipal	Sp. Cristal	Total Clean	Bolognesi
Univer'dad San Martin	22	13	5	4	44	22	44		0-2	4-0	4-0	2-2	2-0	3-0	3-0	2-1	2-2	1-0	1-2
Cienciano	22	10	7	5	32	22	37	1-2		1-0	1-1	0-1	0-0	2-3	2-1	2-0	1-0	2-2	3-0
Sport Ancash	22	9	7	6	30	22	34	1-1	0-1		4-1	1-0	2-2	1-0	1-1	3-0	2-0	4-1	2-0
Sport Boys	22	9	5	8	33	29	34	2-0	0-1	1-0		1-1	2-1	4-4	0-1	2-0	0-1	2-1	1-0
Universitario	22	9	5	8	31	31	32	0-3	1-0	0-0	3-3		1-2	1-0	3-1	0-2	3-1	1-1	4-0
Alianza Lima §4	22	9	8	5	31	23	31	4-1	2-1	2-0	2-2	1-2		1-1	2-0	1-0	1-1	3-0	0-0
FBC Melgar	22	8	5	9	32	38	29	0-3	2-2	1-2	1-4	2-1	2-1		1-0	0-1	2-0	3-1	2-5
Alianza Atlético	22	6	10	6	23	23	28	2-2	2-2	2-2	0-0	3-0	0-1	0-0		2-1	0-0	1-0	2-0
Deportivo Municipal	22	6	6	10	25	30	24	0-1	1-1	1-1	1-1	2-1	2-2	1-2	1-1		1-2	3-0	1-0
Sporting Cristal	22	5	7	10	25	35	22	0-3	2-2	0-2	1-3	3-1	1-1	1-3	1-1	3-1		4-1	0-0
Total Clean Arequipa	22	6	2	14	28	45	20	2-3	0-2	3-2	2-1	1-2	1-2	3-2	0-2	1-3	2-1		3-0
Coronel Bolognesi	22	4	7	11	22	36	19	1-1	2-3	0-0	0-2	2-3	2-0	1-1	1-1	2-2	3-1	1-3	

3/02/2007 - 10/06/2007 • San Martin qualified to meet the winners of the 2007 Clausura in the Championship decider • § = points deducted
Match in bold was awarded

PHI – PHILIPPINES

NATIONAL TEAM RECORD
JULY 10TH 2006 TO JULY 12TH 2010

PL	W	D	L	F	A	%
8	3	1	4	14	15	43.7

FIFA/COCA-COLA WORLD RANKING

1993	1994	1995	1996	1997	1998	1999	2000	2001	2002	2003	2004	2005	2006	High	Low
163	171	166	166	175	175	181	179	175	181	189	188	191	171	**162** 08/93	**195** 10/06

2006–2007											
08/06	09/06	10/06	11/06	12/06	01/07	02/07	03/07	04/07	05/07	06/07	07/07
192	195	195	184	171	178	178	179	169	170	168	168

The Philippines will be the biggest country not represented in the 2010 FIFA World Cup qualifiers after the federation decided not to enter the tournament - one of just four nations to decline the invitation. As ever the ASEAN Football Federation Championship, known previously as the Tiger Cup, provided the national team with its staple diet of football, and fans in the Philippines were in for a treat when Bacolod hosted the preliminary qualifying round for the 2006-07 tournament. When the team took the field against Laos in the opening match, it was only the third time in 16 years that the Philippines had appeared at home. That match was lost but they went on to win the next three

INTERNATIONAL HONOURS
Far-Eastern Games 1913

- against East Timor, Cambodia and Brunei - to qualify for the final tournament in Bangkok. It was the first time that the national team had ever won three consecutive matches and by scoring in the next match, a friendly against Singapore, a new record of scoring in seven consecutive games was also established with Phil Younghusband finding the back of the net seven times in those seven games. The following week, however, it was business as usual in the finals with defeat against Malaysia and Thailand although Myanmar were held to a draw. In domestic football National Capital Region beat Negros Occidental 2-1 to win the National Men's Open Championship.

THE FIFA BIG COUNT OF 2006

	Male	Female		Total
Number of players	1 548 746	120 019	Referees and Assistant Referees	167
Professionals	0		Admin, Coaches, Technical, Medical	132
Amateurs 18+	20 910		Number of clubs	75
Youth under 18	8 123		Number of teams	229
Unregistered	340 090		Clubs with women's teams	10
Total players	1 668 765		Players as % of population	1.87%

Philippine Football Federation (PFF)
Room 405, Building B, Philsports Complex, Meralco Avenue, Pasig City, Metro Manila 1604, Philippines
Tel +63 2 6871594   Fax +63 2 6871598
domeka13@hotmail.com   www.philfootball.info
President: ROMUALDEZ Juan Miguel   General Secretary: ARANETA Pablito
Vice-President: ARANETA Pablito   Treasurer: MORAN Daniel   Media Officer: FORMOSO M. Eduardo
Men's Coach: CASLIB Jose Ariston   Women's Coach: MARO Marlon
PFF formed: 1907   AFC: 1954   FIFA: 1930
Blue shirts, Blue shorts, Blue socks or Red shirts, Red shorts, Red socks

RECENT INTERNATIONAL MATCHES PLAYED BY THE PHILIPPINES

2002 Opponents	Score	Venue	Comp	Scorers	Att	Referee
11-12 Singapore	L 0-2	Singapore	Fr			Nagalingham SIN
17-12 Myanmar	L 1-6	Jakarta	TCr1	Gonzales [81]		Mohd Salleh MAS
19-12 Vietnam	L 1-4	Jakarta	TCr1	Canedo [71]		Nagalingham SIN
21-12 Cambodia	L 0-1	Jakarta	TCr1			Napitupulu IDN
23-12 Indonesia	L 1-13	Jakarta	TCr1	Go [78]		Khanthachai THA
2003						
No international matches played in 2003						
2004						
8-12 Myanmar	L 0-1	Kuala Lumpur	TCr1		1 000	Napitupulu IDN
10-12 Malaysia	L 1-4	Kuala Lumpur	TCr1	Gould [93+]		Napitupulu IDN
14-12 Timor-Leste †	W 2-1	Kuala Lumpur	TCr1	Caligdong 2 [89 92+]	100	Napitupulu IDN
16-12 Thailand	L 1-3	Kuala Lumpur	TCr1	Caligdong [27]	300	Lazar SIN
2005						
No international matches played in 2005						
2006						
26-03 Thailand	L 0-5	Chonburi	Fr			
1-04 Chinese Taipei	L 0-1	Chittagong	CCr1		4 000	Lee Gi Young KOR
3-04 India	D 1-1	Chittagong	CCr1	Valeroso [19]	2 000	Mujghef JOR
5-04 Afghanistan	D 1-1	Chittagong	CCr1	Valeroso [59]	3 000	Mujghef JOR
12-11 Laos	L 1-2	Bacolod	TCq	Greatwich [62]		
14-11 Timor Leste	W 7-0	Bacolod	TCq	Younghusband 4 [22 25p 36 69], Greatwich [30], Zerrudo [51], Caligdong [82]		
18-11 Cambodia	W 1-0	Bacolod	TCq	Borromeo [81p]		
20-11 Brunei Darussalam	W 4-1	Bacolod	TCq	Del Rosario [25], Younghusband 2 [59 90], Caligdong [73]		
2007						
7-01 Singapore	L 1-4	Singapore	Fr	Younghusband [19p]	2 000	
12-01 Malaysia	L 0-4	Bangkok	TCr1		5 000	Daud SIN
14-01 Thailand	L 0-4	Bangkok	TCr1		30 000	
16-01 Myanmar	D 0-0	Bangkok	TCr1		500	Daud SIN

Fr = Friendly match • TC = ASEAN Tiger Cup/ASEAN Football Federation Championship • CC = AFC Challenge Cup
r1 = 1st round • † Not a full international

PHILIPPINES NATIONAL TEAM RECORDS AND RECORD SEQUENCES

Records			Sequence records					
Victory	15-2	JPN 1917	Wins	3	2006	Clean sheets	2	1972, 2006
Defeat	0-15	JPN 1967	Defeats	23	1958-1971	Goals scored	7	2006-2007
Player Caps	n/a		Undefeated	3	1972, 1991	Without goal	14	1980-1983
Player Goals	n/a		Without win	39	1977-1991	Goals against	33	1972-1982

RECENT LEAGUE AND CUP RECORD

National Men's Open Championship				ANG Liga			
Year	Champions	Pts	Runners-up	Winners	Score	Runners-up	
2003	National Capital Region	4-1	Laguna	San Beda College	1-0	University of Santo Tomas	
2004	National Capital Region	0-0 4-3p	Negros Occidental	San Beda College	2-1	University of Santo Tomas	
2005	Negros Occidental	2-1	National Capital Region	Saint Benilde	0-0 7-6p	San Beda College	
2006							
2007	National Capital Region	2-1	Negros Occidental				

PHILIPPINES COUNTRY INFORMATION

Capital	Manila	Independence	1946 from the USA	GDP per Capita	$4 600
Population	86 241 697	Status	Republic	GNP Ranking	41
Area km²	300 000	Language	Filipino, English	Dialling code	+63
Population density	274 per km²	Literacy rate	92%	Internet code	.ph
% in urban areas	54%	Main religion	Christian	GMT +/-	+8
Towns/Cities ('000)	Manila 10 443; Davao 1 212; Cebu 758; Antipolo 549; Zamboanga 460; Bacolod 454; Cagayan 445; Dasmariñas 441; Dadiangas 432; Iloilo 387; San Jose del Monte 357				
Neighbours (km)	Philippine Sea & South China Sea 36 289				
Main stadia	José Rizal Memorial Stadium – Manilla 30 000; Pana-ad Stadium – Bacolod 15 000				

PLE – PALESTINE

NATIONAL TEAM RECORD
JULY 10TH 2006 TO JULY 12TH 2010

PL	W	D	L	F	A	%
5	0	1	4	2	10	10

FIFA/COCA-COLA WORLD RANKING

1993	1994	1995	1996	1997	1998	1999	2000	2001	2002	2003	2004	2005	2006	High		Low	
-	-	-	-	-	184	170	171	145	151	139	126	137	128	**118**	08/06	**191**	08/99

2006–2007											
08/06	09/06	10/06	11/06	12/06	01/07	02/07	03/07	04/07	05/07	06/07	07/07
118	123	141	137	128	131	129	126	138	137	139	141

In its bid to qualify for the AFC Asian Cup finals, the Palestine national team based itself in the Jordanian capital Amman but played the last two qualifiers without coach Asmi Nasser as he battled cancer, a disease which eventually took his life in March 2007. The Palestinians finished bottom of their group but such was the chaos engulfing the Palestinian territories, especially the Gaza Strip, that the players couldn't travel to Singapore for the final match which was then cancelled. In June 2007 the players returned to Amman for the West Asian Championship but they didn't get past the first round after defeats by both Iraq and Iran. In August 2006 Saudi Arabia's King

INTERNATIONAL HONOURS
None

Abdullah bin Abdulaziz approved a grant of $1m for construction projects in Palestine related to football to complement money given by FIFA. With near civil war in the Gaza Strip, FIFA has concentrated on projects in Ram and El Bireh instead with the provision of artifical turf pitches. In Ram the pitch will have stands capable of accommodating up to 4,000 seats providing security guarantees can be met. In the meantime football is played on an ad hoc basis in the Gaza Strip and the West Bank, the two areas that make up the Palestinian territories, with Wadi Al Nes winning a Jericho tournament and Al Bireh winning the West Bank FA Cup.

THE FIFA BIG COUNT OF 2006

	Male	Female		Total
Number of players	87 060	5 100	Referees and Assistant Referees	301
Professionals	0		Admin, Coaches, Technical, Medical	494
Amateurs 18+	5 500		Number of clubs	40
Youth under 18	13 200		Number of teams	66
Unregistered	22 100		Clubs with women's teams	0
Total players	92 160		Players as % of population	2.43%

Palestine Football Association (PFA)
Al Yarmuk, Gaza
Tel +970 8 2834339   Fax +970 8 2825208
info@palfa.com   www.palfa.com
President: AFIFI Ahmed   General Secretary: NADI Mohammed
Vice-President: ALBEDD Georg   Treasurer: ZAQOUI Jamal   Media Officer: HASAN Khwalda
Men's Coach: TBD   Women's Coach: SHAHWAN Necola
PFA formed: 1928, 1962   AFC: 1998   FIFA: 1998
White shirts, Black shorts, White socks

RECENT INTERNATIONAL MATCHES PLAYED BY PALESTINE

2004	Opponents	Score		Venue	Comp	Scorers	Att	Referee
18-02	Chinese Taipei	W	8-0	Doha	WCq	Alkord [10], Habaib 2 [20 32], Atura [43], Beshe 2 [52 86] Amar [76], Keshkesh [82]	1 000	Al Yarimi YEM
26-03	Syria	D	1-1	Damascus	Fr			
31-03	Iraq	D	1-1	Doha	WCq	Beshe [72]	500	Al Shoufi SYR
9-06	Uzbekistan	L	0-3	Tashkent	WCq		35 000	Moradi IRN
17-06	Jordan	D	1-1	Tehran	WAr1	Alkord [12]		
19-06	Iraq	L	1-2	Tehran	WAr1	Alkord [40]		
2-09	Bahrain	L	0-1	Al Muharraq	Fr			
8-09	Uzbekistan	L	0-3	Rayyan	WCq		400	Maidin SIN
14-10	Chinese Taipei	W	1-0	Taipei	WCq	Amar [94+]	500	Rasheed MDV
16-11	Iraq	L	1-4	Doha	WCq	Zaatara [71]	500	Al Mutlaq KSA
2005								
1-12	Iraq	L	0-4	Al Rayyan	WGr1			
3-12	Saudi Arabia	L	0-2	Al Rayyan	WGr1			
2006								
7-02	Syria	L	0-3	Damascus	Fr			
16-02	Bahrain	W	2-0	Al Muharraq	Fr	Allam [26], Attal [88]		
18-02	Pakistan	W	3-0	Manama	Fr	Attal 2 [55 75], Salem [85]		
22-02	China PR	L	0-2	Guangzhou	ACq		16 500	Kwon Jong Chul KOR
1-03	Singapore	W	1-0	Amman	ACq	Attal [75]	1 000	Al Hilali OMA
1-04	Guam	W	11-0	Dhaka	CCr1	Keshkesh [6], Attal 6 [14 20 25 32 45 86], Atura [22], Al Amour [39], Al Kord 2 [59 67]	3 000	AK Nema IRQ
3-04	Cambodia	W	4-0	Dhaka	CCr1	Keshkesh [10], Al Sweirki 2 [12 75], Attal [30]	2 500	AK Nema IRQ
5-04	Bangladesh	D	1-1	Dhaka	CCr1	Attal [30]	22 000	Mombini IRN
9-04	Kyrgyzstan	L	0-1	Dhaka	CCqf		150	U Win Cho MYA
17-08	Iraq	L	0-3	Amman	ACq		5 000	Basma SYR
6-09	Iraq	D	2-2	Al Ain	ACq	Amar [13], Al Amour [78]	1 000	Mujghef JOR
11-10	China PR	L	0-2	Amman	ACq		3 000	Al Fadhli KUW
2007								
18-06	Iraq	L	0-1	Amman	WAr1			
20-06	Iran	L	0-2	Amman	WAr1			

Fr = Friendly match • AC = AFC Asian Cup • WA = West Asian Championship • WC = FIFA World Cup
q = qualifier • r1 = 1st round

PALESTINE NATIONAL TEAM RECORDS AND RECORD SEQUENCES

Records			Sequence records					
Victory	11-0	GUM 2006	Wins	3	2006	Clean sheets	3	1976-1992, 2006
Defeat	1-8	EGY 1953	Defeats	4	2001-02, 2003	Goals scored	8	1953-1965
Player Caps	n/a		Undefeated	4	1999, 2006	Without goal	3	2003
Player Goals	n/a		Without win	14	2001-2003	Goals against	13	2001-2003

The organisation of a Palestinian championship and cup tournament is sporadic and often haphazrad due to the political and geographical difficulties. Champions in the past have included Rafah Services club in 1996, Shabab Al Amari in 1997, Khadamat Rafah in 1998 and Al Aqsa in 2002

PALESTINE COUNTRY INFORMATION

Capital	Ramallah	Independence	1993	GDP per Capita	$600
Population	3 636 195	Status	Republic	GNP Ranking	n/a
Area km²	6 220	Language	Arabic	Dialling code	+972
Population density	584 per km²	Literacy rate	n/a	Internet code	.il
% in urban areas	n/a	Main religion	Muslim	GMT +/−	+2
Towns/Cities	Ramallah; Nablus; Jericho; Hebron; Gaza; Bethlehem				
Neighbours (km)	For the West Bank and Gaza: Israel 358; Jordan 97; Egypt 11; Mediterranean Sea 40				
Main stadia	None				

PNG – PAPUA NEW GUINEA

NATIONAL TEAM RECORD
JULY 10TH 2006 TO JULY 12TH 2010

PL	W	D	L	F	A	%
0	0	0	0	0	0	0

FIFA/COCA-COLA WORLD RANKING

1993	1994	1995	1996	1997	1998	1999	2000	2001	2002	2003	2004	2005	2006	High	Low
-	-	-	169	167	172	183	192	196	167	172	161	166	178	**160** 06/04	**197** 02/02

					2006–2007						
08/06	09/06	10/06	11/06	12/06	01/07	02/07	03/07	04/07	05/07	06/07	07/07
175	176	177	179	178	177	177	177	175	176	183	180

Papua New Guinea was the centre of attention for football in the Pacific region in January 2007 when Port Moresby hosted the OFC Congress with FIFA President Sepp Blatter in attendance. Blatter promised $1m to help develop facilities across the 22 provinces that make up the country as the football federation prepares the groundwork to help develop the game in what is now the most populous country in the OFC. With nearly five and a half million out of the twelve and a half million people in the OFC, Papua New Guinea could well rival New Zealand in the future, but much of the population lives in remote regions. Getting them involved will be the key task if

INTERNATIONAL HONOURS
South Pacific Mini Games 1989

football is to grow as a sport. The establishment of a semi-professional league to run alongside existing competitions remains a key factor in this development and the first winners of the new league were PRK Souths. They then met University, winners of the amateur National Championship for the right to take part in the 2007-08 O-League and it was the amateurs who surprisingly won the day. In June 2007 University had to take part in a qualifying group against JS Baco of New Caledonia and Vanuatu's Tafea and the gulf in class was apparent after losing both games and finishing bottom of the group.

THE FIFA BIG COUNT OF 2006

	Male	Female		Total
Number of players	188 900	8 000	Referees and Assistant Referees	1 200
Professionals	0		Admin, Coaches, Technical, Medical	5 200
Amateurs 18+	7 700		Number of clubs	440
Youth under 18	59 200		Number of teams	1 100
Unregistered	57 100		Clubs with women's teams	23
Total players	196 900		Players as % of population	3.47%

Papua New Guinea Football Association (PNGFA)
Lae 411, PO Box 957, Morobe Province, Papua New Guinea
Tel +675 4751359   Fax +675 4751399
pngsoka@datec.net.pg   www.pngfootball.com.pg
President: CHUNG David   General Secretary: DIMIRIT Mileng
Vice-President: DANIELS Seth   Treasurer: SATIMBU Lua   Media Officer: KAMBI Thomas
Men's Coach: GUSAMO Marcos   Women's Coach: TBD
PNGFA formed: 1962   OFC: 1966   FIFA: 1963
Red shirts with yellow trimmings, Black shorts, Yellow socks or Yellow shirts with red trimmings, Red shorts, Yellow socks

RECENT INTERNATIONAL MATCHES PLAYED BY PAPUA NEW GUINEA

2002	Opponents	Score		Venue	Comp	Scorers	Att	Referee
5-07	Solomon Islands	D	0-0	Auckland	OCr1		1 000	Breeze AUS
7-07	New Zealand	L	1-9	Auckland	OCr1	Aisa [35p]	1 000	Rakaroi FIJ
9-07	Tahiti	L	1-3	Auckland	OCr1	Davani [43]	800	Rakaroi FIJ
2003								
14-06	Solomon Islands	L	3-5	Port Moresby	Fr			
30-06	New Caledonia	L	0-2	Suva	SPr1			Shah FIJ
1-07	Tonga	D	2-2	Suva	SPr1	Sow [41], Habuka [76]	3 000	Singh FIJ
3-07	Tahiti	L	0-3	Suva	SPr1		1 000	Attison VAN
2004								
10-05	Vanuatu	D	1-1	Apia	WCq	Wasi [73]	500	Breeze AUS
12-05	Fiji	L	2-4	Apia	WCq	Davani [12], Komboi [44]	400	Diomis AUS
17-05	American Samoa	W	10-0	Apia	WCq	Davani 4 [23 24 40 79], Lepani 3 [26 28 64], Wasi [34] Komboi [37], Lohai [71]	150	Afu SOL
19-05	Samoa	W	4-1	Apia	WCq	Davani [16], Lepani 2 [37 55], Komeng [68]	300	Diomis AUS
2005								
No international matches played in 2005								
2006								
No international matches played in 2006								
2007								
No international matches played in 2007 before August								

Fr = Friendly match • OC = OFC Nations Cup • SP = South Pacific Games • WC = FIFA World Cup • q = qualifier • r1 = first round group

PAPUA NEW GUINEA NATIONAL TEAM RECORDS AND RECORD SEQUENCES

Records			Sequence records					
Victory	10-0	ASA 2004	Wins	4	2002	Clean sheets	2	2002
Defeat	2-11	AUS 1980	Defeats	6	1998-2000	Goals scored	7	2000-2002
Player Caps	n/a		Undefeated	5	1993-97, 2002	Without goal	4	1990-1993
Player Goals	n/a		Without win	10	1985-1986	Goals against	12	1980-1993

RECENT LEAGUE AND CUP RECORD

Year	National Championship			Port Moresby			Lae			Lahi		
	Winners	Score	Finalist	Winners	Score	Finalist	Winners	Score	Finalist	Winners	Score	Finalist
1997	ICF Univ'sity	2-0	Babaka							Guria		Sobou
1998	ICF Univ'sity	1-0	Blue Kumuls	ICF Univ'sity	2-1	Rapatona	Mopi	3-2	Bulolo Utd	Sobou	4-2	Guria
1999	Guria	2-1	Rapatona	Defence	1-1 4-2p	PS United	Bara	1-0	Buresong	Sobou	1-1 5-4p	Guria
2000	Unitech	3-2	Guria	PS United	1-0	Rapatona	Poro SC	1-1 4-3p	Blue Kumuls	Sobou	1-0	Unitech
2001	Sobou	3-1	ICF Univ'sity	ICF Univ'sity	1-0	PS United	Blue Kumuls	2-1	Goro	Unitech	2-0	Sobou
2002	Sobou	1-0	PS United	ICF Univ'sity	3-1	Rapatona	Tarangau	2-0	Poro SC	Sobou	w/o	Unitech
2003	Sobou	1-0	Unitech	Cosmos	2-1	ICF Univ'sity	Blue Kumuls		HC West	Unitech	2-0	Sobou
2004	Sobou	2-0	HC Water	Rapatona	1-0	PS Rutz	HC West	2-1	Tarangau	Sobou	3-0	Bismarck
2005	Sobou	4-2	Cosmos	PS Rutz	2-0	ICF Univ'sity	Blue Kumuls	2-1	HC West	Unitech	4-2	Sobou
2006	ICF Univ'sity	0-0 2-0p	Sobou	ICF Univ'sity	0-0 4-2p	Rapatona	Cosmos	3-2	Poro SC			

The National Championship is held over the course of a week with representatives from the regional leagues. The most successful of the regional leagues in the National Championship are Port Moresby, Lae and Lahi. Others include Alotau, East Sepik, Enga, Goroka, Kerema, Kompian, Kokopo, Madang, Manus, Mount Hagen, New Ireland, Popondetta, Sogeri, Tari, Wabag, Wau and Wewak

PAPUA NEW GUINEA COUNTRY INFORMATION

Capital	Port Moresby	Independence	1975 from Australia	GDP per Capita	$2 200
Population	5 420 280	Status	Constitutional Monarchy	GNP Ranking	131
Area km²	462 840	Language	Melanesian Pidgin, English	Dialling code	+675
Population density	12 per km²	Literacy rate	64%	Internet code	.pg
% in urban areas	16%	Main religion	Christian	GMT +/–	+10
Towns/Cities ('000)	Port Moresby 283; Lae 76; Arawa 40; Mount Hagen 33; Popondetta 28; Madang 27; Kokopo 26				
Neighbours (km)	Indonesia 820; South Pacific Ocean & Coral Sea 5 152				
Main stadia	Hubert Murray – Port Moresby 10 000				

POL – POLAND

NATIONAL TEAM RECORD
JULY 10TH 2006 TO JULY 12TH 2010

PL	W	D	L	F	A	%
13	8	2	3	25	12	69.2

FIFA/COCA-COLA WORLD RANKING

1993	1994	1995	1996	1997	1998	1999	2000	2001	2002	2003	2004	2005	2006	High		Low	
28	29	33	53	48	31	32	43	33	34	25	25	22	24	**18**	06/07	**61**	03/98

					2006–2007						
08/06	09/06	10/06	11/06	12/06	01/07	02/07	03/07	04/07	05/07	06/07	07/07
30	35	27	22	24	25	23	24	21	18	18	21

After the disappointing World Cup finals in Germany, the Polish Football Association turned to veteran Dutch coach Leo Beenhakker in an attempt to qualify for the European Championship finals for the first time. That looked to be just a pipe dream after Poland took one point from their first two games, both of which were at home. For the rest of the season, however, the Poles were in great form, rescuing their ambitions with six straight wins to head the group going into the 2007 summer recess. Had they beaten Armenia in the final game of the season, Poland would have had one foot in the finals, but their 1-0 defeat in Yerevan threw the group open once again. One thing

INTERNATIONAL HONOURS
Qualified for the FIFA World Cup Finals 1938 1974 1978 1982 1986 2002 2006

for sure, though, is that the Poles will be at the 2012 finals after UEFA chose their joint bid with Ukraine to stage the finals. It will be the first time that Poland will have hosted a major sporting event and should give the game there a massive boost. A first appearance in the UEFA Champions League group stages since 1995 would be a good start as once again there was little joy for Polish clubs in European competitions. Zaglebie Lubin were surprise champions in a close race with GKS Belchatow whilst Groclin Grodzisk Wielkopolski beat Korona Kielce 2-0 in the Cup Final to complete a miserable season for traditional giants Legia and Wisla.

THE FIFA BIG COUNT OF 2006

	Male	Female		Total
Number of players	1 817 819	182 445	Referees and Assistant Referees	11 658
Professionals	1 202		Admin, Coaches, Technical, Medical	60 100
Amateurs 18+	465 854		Number of clubs	5 690
Youth under 18	185 808		Number of teams	13 245
Unregistered	424 300		Clubs with women's teams	201
Total players	2 000 264		Players as % of population	5.19%

Polish Football Association (PZPN)
Polski Zwiazek Pilki Noznej, Miodowa 1, Warsaw 00-080, Poland
Tel +48 22 5512315   Fax +48 22 5512240
pzpn@pzpn.pl   www.pzpn.pl
President: LISTKIEWICZ Michal   General Secretary: KRECINA Zdzislaw
Vice-President: KOLATOR Eugeniusz   Treasurer: BIAKECKA Krystyna   Media Officer: KOCIEBA Michal
Men's Coach: BEENHAKKER Leo   Women's Coach: STEPCZAK Jan
PZPN formed: 1919   UEFA: 1954   FIFA: 1923
White shirts with red trimmings, Red shorts, White socks or Red shirts with white trimmings, Red shorts, Red socks

RECENT INTERNATIONAL MATCHES PLAYED BY POLAND

2004 Opponents	Score	Venue	Comp	Scorers	Att	Referee
18-08 Denmark	L 1-5	Poznan	Fr	Zurawski [76]	4 500	Bebek CRO
4-09 Northern Ireland	W 3-0	Belfast	WCq	Zurawski [4], Wlodarczyk [36], Krzynowek [56]	12 487	Wegereef NED
8-09 England	L 1-2	Chorzow	WCq	Zurawski [47]	30 000	Farina ITA
9-10 Austria	W 3-1	Vienna	WCq	Kaluzny [10], Krzynowek [78], Frankowski [90]	46 100	Cardoso Batista POR
13-10 Wales	W 3-2	Cardiff	WCq	Frankowski [72], Zurawski [81], Krzynowek [85]	56 685	Sars FRA
17-11 France	D 0-0	Paris	Fr		50 480	Benquerenca POR
2005						
9-02 Belarus	L 1-3	Warsaw	Fr	Zurawski [51]	6 000	Zuta LTU
26-03 Azerbaijan	W 8-0	Warsaw	WCq	Frankowski 3 [12 63 66], Hajiyev OG [16], Kosowski [40] Krzynowek [72], Saganowski 2 [84 90]	9 000	Vollquartz DEN
30-03 Northern Ireland	W 1-0	Warsaw	WCq	Zurawski [87]	13 515	Frojdfeldt SWE
27-04 Mexico	D 1-1	Chicago	Fr	Brozek [71]	54 427	Kennedy USA
29-05 Albania	W 1-0	Szczecin	Fr	Zurawski [1]	14 000	Weiner GER
4-06 Azerbaijan	W 3-0	Baku	WCq	Frankowski [28], Klos [57], Zurawski [81]	10 458	Undiano Mallenco ESP
15-08 Serbia & Montenegro	W 3-2	Kyiv	Fr	Frankowski 2 [30 42p], Rasiak [37]	2 000	Orekhov UKR
17-08 Israel	W 3-2	Kyiv	Fr	Szymkowiak [19], Rasiak 2 [77 89]	2 000	Karadzic SCG
3-09 Austria	W 3-2	Chorzow	WCq	Smolarek [13], Kosowski [22], Zurawski [67]	40 000	De Santis ITA
7-09 Wales	W 1-0	Warsaw	WCq	Zurawski [52]	13 500	Larsen DEN
7-10 Iceland	W 3-2	Warsaw	Fr	Krzynowek [25], Baszczynski [56], Smolarek [63]	7 500	Sukhina RUS
12-10 England	L 1-2	Manchester	WCq	Frankowski [45]	65 467	Nielsen DEN
13-11 Ecuador	W 3-0	Barcelona	Fr	Klos [2] Smolarek [58], Mila [90]	6 000	Moreno Delgado ESP
16-11 Estonia	W 3-1	Ostrowiec	Fr	Lewandowski [8], Mila [57], Piechna [87]	8 500	Hyytia FIN
2006						
1-03 USA	L 0-1	Kaiserslautern	Fr		13 395	Kinhofer GER
28-03 Saudi Arabia	W 2-1	Riyadh	Fr	Sosin 2 [7 63]	2 000	Al Mutlaq KSA
2-05 Lithuania	L 0-1	Belchatow	Fr		5 000	Bozinovski MKD
14-05 Faroe Islands	W 4-0	Wronki	Fr	Mila [15], Rasiak 2 [48 84], Saganowski [73]	4 000	Prus USA
30-05 Colombia	L 1-2	Chorzow	Fr	Jelen [91+]	40 000	Szabo HUN
3-06 Croatia	W 1-0	Wolfsburg	Fr	Smolarek [54]	10 000	Meyer GER
9-06 Ecuador	L 0-2	Gelsenkirchen	WCr1		52 000	Kamikawa JPN
14-06 Germany	L 0-1	Dortmund	WCr1		65 000	Medina Cantalejo ESP
20-06 Costa Rica	W 2-1	Hanover	WCr1	Bosacki 2 [33 66]	43 000	Maidin SIN
16-08 Denmark	L 0-2	Odense	Fr		11 008	Asumaa FIN
2-09 Finland	L 1-3	Bydgoszcz	ECq	Gargula [89]	13 000	Duhamel FRA
6-09 Serbia	D 1-1	Warsaw	ECq	Matusiak [30]	4 918	Poll ENG
7-10 Kazakhstan	W 1-0	Almaty	ECq	Smolarek [52]	22 000	Trivkovic CRO
11-10 Portugal	W 1-0	Chorzow	ECq	Smolarek 2 [9 18]	38 199	Stark GER
15-11 Belgium	W 1-0	Brussels	ECq	Matusiak [19]	37 928	Dougal SCO
6-12 UAE	W 5-2	Abu Dhabi	Fr	Grzelak 2 [8 50], Wasilewski [17], Magdon [87], Matusiak [94+]	1 000	Al Hilali OMA
2007						
3-02 Estonia	W 4-0	Jerez	Fr	Dudka [25], Kokoszka [32], Iwanski [70], Golanski [76]	100	Ruiz-Herrera ESP
7-02 Slovakia	D 2-2	Jerez	Fr	Zewlakow [48p], Matusiak [78]	200	Pacheco ESP
24-03 Azerbaijan	W 5-0	Warsaw	ECq	Bak [3], Dudka [6], Lobodzinski [34], Krzynówek [58], Kázmierczak [84]	13 000	Jakobsson ISL
28-03 Armenia	W 1-0	Kielce	ECq	Zurawski [26]	13 450	Undiano Mallenco ESP
2-06 Azerbaijan	W 3-1	Baku	ECq	Smolarek [63], Krzynówek 2 [66 90]	25 800	Kapitanis CYP
6-06 Armenia	L 0-1	Yerevan	ECq		9 800	Balaj ROU

Fr = Friendly match • EC = UEFA EURO 2004/2008 • WC = FIFA World Cup • q = qualifier • r1 = first round group

POLAND NATIONAL TEAM RECORDS AND RECORD SEQUENCES

Records			Sequence records					
Victory	9-0	NOR 1963	Wins	7	Four times	Clean sheets	4	1978, 1979, 2003
Defeat	0-8	DEN 1948	Defeats	6	1933-1934	Goals scored	28	1978-1980
Player Caps	100	LATO Grzegorz	Undefeated	13	2000-2001	Without goal	6	1999-2000
Player Goals	48	LUBANSKI Wlodzimeirz	Without win	13	1995-1996	Goals against	17	1957-1960

REPUBLIC OF POLAND; RZECZPOSPOLITA POLSKA

Capital	Warsaw	Language	Polish	Independence	1918
Population	38 518 241	Area	312 685 km²	Density	123 per km²	% in cities	65%
GDP per cap	$11 100	Dailling code	+48	Internet	.pl	GMT +/-	+1

MAJOR CITIES/TOWNS
Population '000

1	Warsaw	1 618
2	Lódz	756
3	Kraków	752
4	Wroclaw	631
5	Poznan	565
6	Gdánsk	462
7	Szczecin	413
8	Bydgoszcz	362
9	Lublin	362
10	Katowice	311
11	Bialystok	292
12	Gdynia	254
13	Sosnowiec	224
14	Kielce	206
15	Zabrze	190
16	Bytom	186
17	Rzeszow	157
18	Plock	127
19	Chorzów	111
20	Lubin	76
21	Belchatow	62
22	Mielec	60
23	Grod'sk Wielkopolski	14
24	Wronki	11

MEDALS TABLE

		Overall			League			Cup			Europe			City	Stadium	Cap'ty	DoF
		G	S	B	G	S	B	G	S	B	G	S	B				
1	Legia Warszawa	20	15	14	8	9	12	12	6				2	Warsaw	Wojska Polskiego	13 628	1916
2	Górnik Zabrze	20	12	7	14	4	7	6	7			1		Zabrze	Ernest Pohl	18 000	1948
3	Ruch Chorzów	16	9	7	13	5	7	3	4					Chorzów	Stadion Ruchu	13 000	1920
4	Wisla Kraków	15	16	9	11	11	9	4	5					Kraków	Stadion Wisly	15 850	1906
5	Lech Poznan	9	1	3	5		3	4	1					Poznan	Stadion Miejski	26 500	1922
6	Widzew Lódz	5	7	4	4	7	3	1					1	Lódz	Stadion Widzewa	9 892	1910
7	Cracovia	5	2		5	2								Kraków	Jana Pawla II	6 500	1906
8	Zaglebie Sosnowiec	4	5	2		4	2	4	1					Sosnowiec	Stadion Ludowy	7 500	1906
9	Pogon Lwow	4	3		4	3								Lvov – UKR	Marshal Rydz-Smigly	10 000	1904-39
	Polonia Warszawa	4	3		2	3		2						Warsaw	Stadion Polonii	7 000	1911
11	GKS Katowice	3	9	4		4	4	3	5					Katowice	Stadion GKS	25 568	1964
12	LKS Lódz	3	2	2	2	1	2	1	1					Lódz	Stadion LKS	25 000	1908
13	Slask Wroclaw	3	2	1	1	2	1	2						Wroclaw	Stadion Slaska	13 000	1947
14	Amica Wronki	3	1	2			2	3	1					Wronki	Stadion Amica	5 296	1992
15	Polonia Bytom	2	7	2	2	4	2		3					Bytom	Edwarda Szymkowiaka	1920	1920
16	Warta Poznan	2	5	6	2	5	6							Poznan	Stadion Warty	4 000	1912
17	Zaglebie Lubin	2	3	1	2	1	1			2				Lubin	Stadion Zaglebia	32 420	1945
18	Stal Mielec	2	2	3	2	1	3		1					Mielec	Stadion Stali Mielec	30 000	1939
19	Groclin Grodzisk	2	2			2		2						Grod'sk Wielkopolski	Stadion Dyskobolia	7 000	1922

RECENT LEAGUE AND CUP RECORD

	Championship						Cup		
Year	Champions	Pts	Runners-up	Pts	Third	Pts	Winners	Score	Runners-up
1995	Legia Warszawa	51	Widzew Lodz	45	GKS Katowice	42	Legia Warszawa	2-0	GKS Katowice
1996	Widzew Lódz	88	Legia Warszawa	85	Hutnik Kraków	52	Ruch Chorzów	1-0	GKS Belchatów
1997	Widzew Lódz	81	Legia Warszawa	77	Odra Wodzislaw	55	Legia Warszawa	2-0	GKS Katowice
1998	LKS Lódz	66	Polonia Warszawa	63	Wisla Kraków	61	Amica Wronki	5-3	Aluminium Konin
1999	Wisla Kraków	73	Widzew Lódz	56	Legia Warszawa	56	Amica Wronki	1-0	GKS Belchatów
2000	Polonia Warszawa	65	Wisla Kraków	56	Ruch Chorzów	55	Amica Wronki	2-2 3-0	Wisla Kraków
2001	Wisla Kraków	62	Pogon Szczecin	53	Legia Warszawa	50	Polonia Warszawa	2-1 2-2	Górnik Zabrze
2002	Legia Warszawa	42	Wisla Kraków	41	Amica Wronki	36	Wisla Kraków	4-2 4-0	Amica Wronki
2003	Wisla Kraków	68	Groclin Grodzisk	62	GKS Katowice	61	Wisla Kraków	0-1 3-0	Wisla Plock
2004	Wisla Kraków	65	Legia Warszawa	60	Amica Wronki	48	Lech Poznan	2-0 0-1	Legia Warszawa
2005	Wisla Kraków	62	Groclin Grodzisk	51	Legia Warszawa	47	Groclin Grodzisk	2-0 0-1	Zagliebie Lubin
2006	Legia Warszawa	66	Wisla Krakow	64	Zagliebie Lubin	49	Wisla Plock	3-2 3-1	Zagliebie Lubin
2007	Zagliebie Lubin	62	GKS Belchatow	61	Legia Warszawa	52	Groclin Grodzisk	2-0	Korona Kielce

POLAND 2006-07

LIGA POLSKA ORANGE EKSTRAKLASA

	Pl	W	D	L	F	A	Pts	Zaglebie	Belchatow	Legia	Cracovia	Groclin	Lech	Korona	Wisla	LKS	Odra	Arka	WWidzew	Leczna	Zabrze	Plock	Pogon
Zaglebie Lubin †	30	18	8	4	57	29	62		2-1	1-0	4-3	2-1	0-0	2-0	0-0	1-1	1-0	6-0	4-2	1-1	1-1	2-1	6-2
GKS Belchatow ‡	30	19	4	7	63	32	61	3-1		3-1	2-1	1-0	0-0	3-2	1-2	1-2	5-1	2-2	1-0	6-0	3-1	2-1	1-0
Legia Warszawa	30	16	4	10	53	33	52	1-2	1-2		3-1	0-1	3-2	3-0	1-1	2-1	2-0	3-0	2-0	5-0	3-2	5-0	3-1
Cracovia	30	14	7	9	48	41	49	2-4	2-1	0-0		1-1	3-0	1-0	0-0	1-1	1-0	1-1	2-1	5-0	3-1	2-2	1-0
Groclin Dy. Grodzisk ‡	30	11	15	4	40	26	48	0-0	1-1	1-1	0-0		1-0	1-0	2-2	2-0	1-1	2-1	0-0	1-1	2-0	1-1	3-1
Lech Poznan	30	12	11	7	53	36	47	0-2	1-1	3-1	3-4	2-2		3-0	3-3	4-0	0-0	1-1	6-1	1-0	2-0	3-2	3-0
Korona Kielce	30	14	5	11	41	34	47	1-2	5-3	3-1	1-2	2-0	2-2		0-0	1-0	0-1	1-0	3-0	2-0	4-2	0-0	2-1
Wisla Krakow	30	10	16	4	41	25	46	0-0	2-4	3-1	3-0	0-4	0-0	2-0		0-0	6-0	2-2	2-0	2-1	1-0	2-0	0-0
LKS Lodz	30	10	11	9	31	30	41	2-2	0-1	2-1	2-1	1-1	1-2	2-1	2-1		1-1	0-1	0-0	0-0	2-0	0-0	4-0
Odra Wodzislaw Slaski	30	10	10	10	29	36	40	1-0	1-0	1-2	0-1	0-0	0-0	1-2	2-1	1-2		1-1	3-0	2-1	0-0	1-0	2-2
Arka Gdynia	30	10	10	10	43	39	40	3-0	1-3	1-1	4-2	2-4	3-1	0-3	0-0	0-0	0-1		3-0	5-2	3-0	4-1	2-0
Widzew Lodz	30	7	7	16	27	48	28	0-2	0-3	0-1	1-3	2-1	3-2	0-1	0-0	2-1	1-2	1-1		3-0	2-1	0-0	0-1
Górnik Leczna	30	7	5	18	24	64	26	2-1	1-3	1-2	1-0	1-3	0-3	1-3	1-1	0-1	2-0	1-0	1-5		0-2	0-0	3-2
Górnik Zabrze	30	6	7	17	30	51	25	0-3	1-0	1-0	5-1	2-3	1-2	0-0	0-4	1-1	2-2	0-2	0-0	2-3		2-0	0-3
Wisla Plock	30	4	11	15	20	47	23	0-2	0-4	0-3	0-2	0-0	1-1	0-1	0-0	2-1	1-1	1-0	2-2	0-1	1-3		2-1
Pogon Szczecin	30	3	7	20	24	53	16	1-3	0-2	0-1	0-2	1-1	1-3	1-1	1-1	0-1	1-3	0-0	0-1	3-0	0-0	1-2	

28/07/2006 - 26/05/2007 • † Qualified for the UEFA Champions League • ‡ Qualified for the UEFA Cup •

POLAND 2006-07 II LIGA

	Pl	W	D	L	F	A	Pts
Ruch Chorzów	34	21	6	7	49	26	69
Jagiellonia Bialystok	34	18	9	7	49	28	63
Polonia Bytom §3	34	19	6	9	60	34	60
Zaglebie Sosnowiec	34	17	8	9	54	34	59
Lechia Gdansk	34	15	10	9	53	35	55
Polonia Warszawa	34	16	7	11	56	38	55
Górnik Polkowice	34	14	10	10	43	36	52
Piast Gliwice	34	13	6	15	42	35	45
Slask Wroclaw	34	12	9	13	31	33	45
Odra Opole	34	10	11	13	29	35	41
Ostrowiec	34	9	13	12	27	30	40
Podbeskidzie	34	11	6	17	26	46	39
LKS Lomza	34	9	12	13	38	49	39
Zawisza Bydgoszcz	34	12	2	20	30	64	38
Kmita Zabierzów	34	9	10	15	35	46	37
Stal Stalowa Wola	34	8	13	13	29	46	37
Unia Janikowo	34	9	9	16	38	52	36
Miedz Legnica	34	7	7	20	50	52	28

28/07/2006 - 9/06/2007 • § = points deducted

Arka Gdynia and Górnik Leczna from the Ekstraklasa, and Górnik Polkowice and Ostrowiec from the II Liga, were relegated due to their part in a major match-fixing case with Górnik Leczna relegated to the third level • Zawisza Bydgoszcz withdrew from the II Liga after 17 matches and their 17 remaining fixtures were awarded as 3-0 defeats • No otherteams were relegated from the II Liga

PUCHAR EKSTRAKLASY 2006-07

Quarter-finals		Semi-finals		Final	
Groclin Dy. G'sk	3 3				
Zaglebie Lubin *	3 0	Groclin Dy. G'sk	3 0		
Legia Warszawa	2 0	Górnik Leczna *	2 5		
Górnik Leczna *	2 2			Groclin Dy. G'sk	1
Wisla Krakow	2 3			GKS Belchatow	0
Lech Poznan *	2 2	Wisla Krakow *	0 0		
Korona Kielce	0 1	GKS Belchatow	1 2		
GKS Belchatow*	1 3	* Home team in first leg			

First round played in four groups of four

CUP FINAL
10-06-2007
Scorer - Blazej Telichowski [43]

PUCHAR POLSKI 2006-07

Round of sixteen		Quarter-finals		Semi-finals		Final	
Groclin Dy. Grodzisk	3						
Gornik Polkowice *	0	Groclin Dy. Grodzisk	1 3				
Wisla Krakow *	1	Ruch Chorzów *	0 1				
Ruch Chorzów	2			Groclin Dy. Grodzisk *	1 1		
Radomiak Radom	1			Cracovia	0 0		
LKS Lodz *	0	Radomiak Radom *	1 0				
Zaglebie Lubin	1	Cracovia	3 1				
Cracovia *	2					Groclin Dy. Grodzisk ‡	2
Wisla Plock *	2					Korona Kielce	0
Jagiellonia Bialystok	1	Wisla Plock * †	1				
Stal Sanok *	0	Arka Gdynia	1				
Arka Gdynia	1						
Lech Poznan *	2			Wisla Plock	2 1		
Pogon Szczecin	1	Lech Poznan	0 3	Korona Kielce *	3 1		
Gornik Zabrze *	0	Korona Kielce *	1 2	† Tie awarded to Wisla			
Korona Kielce	5	* Home team/home team in the first leg • ‡ Qualified for the UEFA Cup					

CUP FINAL
Stadion GKS, Belchatow
1-05-2007
Scorers - Radoslaw Majewski [16], Jaroslaw Lato [77]

POR – PORTUGAL

NATIONAL TEAM RECORD
JULY 10TH 2006 TO JULY 12TH 2010

PL	W	D	L	F	A	%
10	5	3	2	20	10	65

Despite a dip in form at the end of the season and a strong late challenge from Sporting, FC Porto managed to hang on to the lead at the top of the SuperLiga to win their third title in four years. The campaign had not got off to the best of starts when Co Adriaanse quit as coach just two weeks before the kick-off citing disagreements with club president Pinto da Costa over transfer policy. Adriaanse had led Porto to the double in 2006 but after the departure of Benni McCarthy he wasn't given funds for a replacement and was told to make it up with Helder Postiga with whom he had fallen out. In the event Postiga turned out to be a key player for new coach Jesualdo Ferreira as Porto stormed into a commanding lead, winning 11 of their first 13 matches. There had been controversy at the start of the season when Belenenses were reprieved from relegation after Gil Vicente were demoted having fielded the Angolan international Mateus during the 2006 season when he was ineligible. With Gil Vicente threatening to go through the civil courts to overturn the decision, the threat of a FIFA ban and the suspension of the national team and clubs from international competition was only just avoided. In the UEFA Champions League, Portugal had

INTERNATIONAL HONOURS
Qualified for FIFA World Cup finals 1966 1986 2002 2006
FIFA World Youth Championship 1989 1991
UEFA Youth Tournament 1961   **UEFA U-18 Championship** 1994 1999   **UEFA U-17 Championship** 1989 1995 1996 2000 2003
Intercontinental Cup FC Porto 1987 2004   **UEFA Champions League** Benfica 1961 1962, FC Porto 1987 2004

three representatives in the group stage for the first time but with mixed success. Despite beating Inter in their first match, Sporting finished bottom of their group whilst Benfica qualified for the UEFA Cup after finishing third behind Manchester United and Celtic in a close group. In the UEFA Cup they reached the quarter-finals before losing to Espanyol. Porto were the only one of the trio to make it through to the knock-out stage of the Champions League but were drawn against old boy Jose Mourinho's Chelsea who beat them 3-2 on aggregate. For Porto there was no repeat of the double celebrations of 2006 - they were ignominiously dumped out of the Portuguese Cup at home by third division side Atlético Clube Portugal. Instead it was Sporting, on their fine end-of-season run, who won the trophy, beating Belenenses 1-0 in the final, with Liedson scoring the winner five minutes from time. National team coach Luiz Felipe Scolari had the job of revitalizing his players after their semi-final defeat in the World Cup and although Portugal started their UEFA Euro 2008 qualifying campaign with a draw in Helsinki and then a defeat to Poland in the third match, they had all of their major opponents to play at home in the run-in and so qualification for the finals in Austria and Switzerland was very much in their own hands.

Federação Portuguesa de Futebol (FPF)
Rua Alexandre Herculano, no.58, Apartado 24013, Lisbon 1250-012, Portugal
Tel +351 21 3252700   Fax +351 21 3252780
secretario_geral@fpf.pt   www.fpf.pt
President: MADAIL Gilberto, Dr   General Secretary: BROU Angelo
Vice-President: LOUREIRO Helio   Treasurer: PACHECO LAMAS Carlos   Media Officers: COSTA Onofre
Men's Coach: SCOLARI Luiz Felipe   Women's Coach: AUGUSTO Jose
FPF formed: 1914   UEFA: 1954   FIFA: 1923
Red shirts with green trimmings, Green shorts, Red socks or White shirts with blue trimmings, Blue shorts, White socks

RECENT INTERNATIONAL MATCHES PLAYED BY PORTUGAL

2004	Opponents	Score	Venue	Comp	Scorers	Att	Referee
4-09	Latvia	W 2-0	Riga	WCq	Ronaldo [57], Pauleta [58]	9 500	Poll ENG
8-09	Estonia	W 4-0	Leiria	WCq	Ronaldo [75], Postiga 2 [83 91+], Pauleta [86]	27 214	Demirlek TUR
9-10	Liechtenstein	D 2-2	Vaduz	WCq	Pauleta [23], Hasler OG [39]	3 548	Panic BIH
13-10	Russia	W 7-1	Lisbon	WCq	Pauleta [26], Ronaldo 2 [39 69], Deco [45], Simão [82] Petit 2 [89 92+]	27 258	Vassaras GRE
17-11	Luxembourg	W 5-0	Luxembourg	WCq	Federspiel OG [11], Ronaldo [28], Maniche [52] Pauleta 2 [67 82]	8 045	Godulyan UKR
2005							
9-02	Republic of Ireland	L 0-1	Dublin	Fr		44 100	Messias ENG
26-03	Canada	W 4-1	Barcelos	Fr	Manuel Fernandes [2], Pauleta [11], Postiga [81] Nuno Gomes [90]	13 000	Ishchenko UKR
30-03	Slovakia	D 1-1	Bratislava	WCq	Postiga [62]	21 000	Sars FRA
4-06	Slovakia	W 2-0	Lisbon	WCq	Fernando Meira [21], Ronaldo [42]	64 000	Collina ITA
8-06	Estonia	W 1-0	Tallinn	WCq	Ronaldo [32]	10 280	Riley ENG
17-08	Egypt	W 2-0	Ponta Delgada	Fr	Fernando Meira [50], Postiga [69]	20 000	Granat POL
3-09	Luxembourg	W 6-0	Faro-Loule	WCq	Jorge [24], Carvalho [30], Pauleta 2 [38 57], Simão 2 [80 85]	25 300	Van Egmond NED
7-09	Russia	D 0-0	Moscow	WCq		28 800	Merk GER
8-10	Liechtenstein	W 2-1	Aveiro	WCq	Pauleta [48], Nuno Gomes [85]	29 000	Gilewski POL
12-10	Latvia	W 3-0	Porto	WCq	Pauleta 2 [20 22], Hugo Viana [86]	35 000	Frojdfeldt SWE
12-11	Croatia	W 2-0	Coimbra	Fr	Petit [32], Pauleta [65]	15 000	Nielsen DEN
15-11	Northern Ireland	D 1-1	Belfast	Fr	OG [40]	20 000	Webb ENG
2006							
1-03	Saudi Arabia	W 3-0	Dusseldorf	Fr	Ronaldo 2 [30 85], Maniche [45]	7 500	Stark GER
27-05	Cape Verde Islands	W 4-1	Evora	Fr	Pauleta 3 [1 38 83], Petit [60]	10 000	Van Egmond NED
3-06	Luxembourg	W 3-0	Metz	Fr	Simão 2 [47 72p], Figo [85]	19 157	Duhamel FRA
11-06	Angola	W 1-0	Cologne	WCr1	Pauleta [4]	45 000	Larrionda URU
17-06	Iran	W 2-0	Frankfurt	WCr1	Deco [63], Ronaldo [80p]	48 000	Poulat FRA
21-06	Mexico	W 2-1	Gelsenkirchen	WCr1	Maniche [6], Simão [24p]	52 000	Michel SVK
25-06	Netherlands	W 1-0	Nuremberg	WCr2	Maniche [23]	41 000	Ivanov.V RUS
1-07	England	D 0-0	Gelsenkirchen	WCqf	W 3-1p	52 000	Elizondo ARG
5-07	France	L 0-1	Munich	WCsf		66 000	Larrionda URU
8-07	Germany	L 1-3	Stuttgart	WC3p	Nuno Gomes [88]	52 000	Kamikawa JPN
1-09	Denmark	L 2-4	Copenhagen	Fr	Ricardo Carvalho [15], Nani [65]	13 186	Kelly IRL
6-09	Finland	D 1-1	Helsinki	ECq	Nuno Gomes [42]	38 010	Plautz AUT
7-10	Azerbaijan	W 3-0	Porto	ECq	Ronaldo 2 [25 63], Ricardo Carvalho [31]	14 000	Halsey ENG
11-10	Poland	L 1-2	Chorzow	ECq	Nuno Gomes [92+]	38 199	Stark GER
15-11	Kazakhstan	W 3-0	Coimbra	ECq	Simão 2 [8 86], Ronaldo [30]	29 500	Rogalla SUI
2007							
6-02	Brazil	W 2-0	London	Fr	Simão [82], Ricardo Carvalho [89]	60 000	Atkinson ENG
24-03	Belgium	W 4-0	Lisbon	ECq	Nuno Gomes [53], Ronaldo 2 [55 75], Quaresma [69]	47 009	Vassaras GRE
28-03	Serbia	D 1-1	Belgrade	ECq	Tiago [5]	46 810	Layec FRA
2-06	Belgium	W 2-1	Brussels	ECq	Nani [43], Postiga [64]	45 383	Hansson SWE
5-06	Kuwait	D 1-1	Kuwait City	Fr	João Tomas [72]	10 000	Al Marzouqi UAE

Fr = Friendly match • EC = UEFA EURO 2004/2008 • WC = FIFA World Cup
q = qualifier • r1 = first round group • r2 = second round • qf = quarter-final • sf = semi-final • 3p = third place play-off • f = final

PORTUGAL NATIONAL TEAM RECORDS AND RECORD SEQUENCES

Records			Sequence records					
Victory	8-0	LIE x2, KUW	Wins	9	1966	Clean sheets	8	1998-1999
Defeat	0-10	ENG 1947	Defeats	7	1957-59, 1961-62	Goals scored	16	1966-1967
Player Caps	127	FIGO	Undefeated	19	2005-2006	Without goal	4	1996-1997
Player Goals	47	PAULETA	Without win	13	1949-1953	Goals against	17	1949-1953

PORTUGUESE REPUBLIC; REPUBLICA PORTUGUESA

Capital Lisbon		Language Portuguese			Independence 1640	
Population 10 642 836		Area 92 391 km²	Density 114 per km²		% in cities 36%	
GDP per cap $18 000		Dailling code +351	Internet .pt		GMT + / - 0	

MAJOR CITIES/TOWNS
Population '000

1	Lisbon	498
2	Porto	242
3	Amadora	179
4	Braga	125
5	Setúbal	119
6	Queluz	111
7	Coimbra	108
8	Agualva-Cacém	100
9	Funchal	95
10	Algueirão	81
11	Vila Nova de Gaia	71
12	Loures	66
13	Rio de Mouro	59
14	Corroios	55
15	Aveiro	55
16	Odivelas	54
17	Amora	53
18	Rio Tinto	51
19	Barreiro	50
20	Leiria	47
21	Evora	46
22	Faro	41
23	Guimarães	41
24	Portimão	39

MEDALS TABLE

		Overall			League			Cup		Europe			City	Stadium	Cap'ty	DoF
		G	S	B	G	S	B	G	S	G	S	B				
1	SL Benfica	60	40	17	31	24	14	27	10	2	6	3	Lisbon	Estádio da Luz	65 647	1904
2	FC Porto	42	38	11	22	24	10	17	13	3	1	1	Porto	Estádio do Dragão	50 948	1893
3	Sporting Clube Portugal	37	34	27	18	17	25	18	16	1	1	2	Lisbon	José Alvalade XXI	52 000	1906
4	OS Belenenses	7	11	14	1	3	14	6	8				Lisbon	Estádio do Restelo	40 000	1919
5	Boavista FC	6	4	2	1	3	1	5	1			1	Porto	Estádio do Bessa	28 263	1903
6	Vitória FC Setúbal	3	9	3		1	3	3	8				Setúbal	Estádio do Bonfim	25 000	1910
7	Académica de Coimbra	1	5		1			1	4				Coimbra	Cidade de Coimbra	30 154	1887
8	Atlético Clube Portugal	1	3	2		2		1	3				Lisbon	Estádio Tapadinha	15 000	1942
9	Sporting Clube Braga	1	3					1	3				Braga	Municipal de Braga	30 359	1921
10	CS Marítimo	1	2					1	2				Funchal	Estádio dos Barreiros	14 000	1910
11	SC Olhanense	1	1					1	1				Olhão	José Arcanjo	21 530	1912
	Leixoes SC	1	1					1	1				Matosinhos	Estádio do Mar	25 035	1907
	SC Beira Mar	1	1					1	1				Aveiro	Municipal de Aveiro	31 498	1922
14	CF Estrella Amadora	1						1					Amadora	José Gomes	25 000	1932
15	Vitória SC Guimaraes		4	3			3		4				Guimarães	Afonso Henriques	29 865	1922
16	FC Barreirense		2						2				Barreiro	Manuel de Mello	10 500	1911

RECENT LEAGUE AND CUP RECORD

Championship						Cup		
Year	Champions	Pts	Runners-up	Pts	Third	Pts	Winners	Score	Runners-up

Year	Champions	Pts	Runners-up	Pts	Third	Pts
1995	FC Porto	62	Sporting CP	53	Benfica	49
1996	FC Porto	84	Benfica	73	Sporting CP	67
1997	FC Porto	85	Sporting CP	72	Benfica	58
1998	FC Porto	77	Benfica	68	Vitória Guimarães	59
1999	FC Porto	79	Boavista	71	Benfica	65
2000	Sporting CP	77	FC Porto	73	Benfica	69
2001	Boavista	77	FC Porto	76	Sporting CP	62
2002	Sporting CP	75	Boavista	70	FC Porto	68
2003	FC Porto	86	Benfica	75	Sporting CP	59
2004	FC Porto	82	Benfica	74	Sporting CP	73
2005	Benfica	65	FC Porto	62	Sporting CP	61
2006	FC Porto	79	Sporting CP	72	Benfica	67
2007	FC Porto	69	Sporting CP	68	Benfica	67

Winners	Score	Runners-up
Sporting CP	2-0	Marítimo
Benfica	3-1	Sporting CP
Boavista	3-2	Benfica
FC Porto	3-1	SC Braga
Beira-Mar	1-0	Campomaiorense
FC Porto	1-1 2-0	Sporting CP
FC Porto	2-0	Marítimo
Sporting CP	1-0	Leixões
FC Porto	1-0	União Leiria
Benfica	2-1	FC Porto
Vitória Setúbal	2-1	Benfica
FC Porto	1-0	Vitória Setúbal
Sporting CP	1-0	Os Belenenses

PORTUGAL 2006-07

SUPERLIGA

	Pl	W	D	L	F	A	Pts	Porto	Sporting	Benfica	Braga	Belenenses	P. Ferreira	Un. Leiria	Nacional	E. Amadora	Boavista	Marítimo	Naval	Académica	Vitória	Beira-Mar	Aves
FC Porto †	30	22	3	5	65	20	69		0-1	3-2	1-0	3-1	4-0	2-1	2-0	0-1	2-0	3-0	4-0	2-1	5-1	3-0	4-1
Sporting CP †	30	20	8	2	54	15	68	1-1		0-2	3-0	4-0	0-1	2-0	5-1	3-1	3-2	4-0	4-0	1-0	3-1	2-0	0-0
SL Benfica †	30	20	7	3	55	20	67	1-1	1-1		0-0	4-0	3-1	2-0	1-0	3-1	0-0	2-1	2-1	2-0	3-0	3-0	4-1
Sporting Braga ‡	30	14	8	8	35	30	50	2-1	0-1	3-1		2-1	2-1	0-1	1-1	2-1	2-2	1-4	2-1	4-2	0-0	0-0	1-0
Os Belenenses ‡	30	15	4	11	36	29	49	0-1	0-0	1-2	2-0		2-0	0-1	2-0	3-0	0-2	2-0	0-0	1-2	2-0	2-0	1-0
Paços de Ferreira ‡	30	10	12	8	31	36	42	1-1	1-1	1-1	3-2	0-2		0-0	2-1	1-1	2-0	2-1	1-1	1-1	1-0	1-0	2-0
União de Leiria	30	10	11	9	25	27	41	1-0	0-0	0-4	1-0	0-1	0-0		1-0	0-0	0-0	1-0	2-2	2-0	1-1	2-2	3-1
CD Nacional	30	11	6	13	41	38	39	1-2	0-1	0-2	0-0	2-1	5-1	2-1		1-0	2-0	3-2	1-1	4-0	1-0	3-0	3-4
Estrela Amadora	30	9	8	13	23	36	35	0-3	0-1	0-1	0-0	1-0	1-0	1-1	2-0		2-1	1-0	0-0	3-3	1-0	2-2	1-0
Boavista	30	8	11	11	32	34	35	2-1	1-1	3-0	0-1	0-0	3-1	1-1	0-4	1-1		1-1	0-1	2-2	1-1	3-0	2-1
CS Marítimo	30	8	8	14	30	44	32	1-2	0-1	0-3	1-2	1-4	1-1	2-1	1-0	2-1	1-2		1-1	0-0	1-0	2-1	0-0
Naval 1° de Maio	30	7	11	12	28	37	32	0-2	0-1	0-0	1-1	2-3	1-1	2-1	0-0	2-0	1-1	0-1		0-1	1-2	2-1	0-1
Académica Coimbra	30	6	8	16	28	46	26	1-2	0-2	0-2	0-1	1-1	0-2	0-0	1-3	2-0	0-2	1-2	1-2		0-1	3-1	2-0
Vitória FC Setúbal	30	5	9	16	21	45	24	0-3	0-3	0-1	1-2	0-1	1-1	1-2	1-1	2-0	1-0	1-1	0-3	1-1		1-3	1-1
SC Beira-Mar	30	4	11	15	28	55	23	0-5	3-3	2-2	0-3	1-2	1-1	1-0	1-1	2-0	1-0	2-2	1-3	0-1	1-1		2-2
Desportivo Aves	30	5	7	18	22	42	22	0-2	0-2	0-1	0-1	0-1	0-1	3-1	0-1	1-0	1-1	2-0	2-2	1-2	0-0		

25/08/2006 - 20/05/2007 • † Qualified for the UEFA Champions League • ‡ Qualified for the UEFA Cup
Top scorers: LIEDSON, Sporting CP 15; DADY, Belenenses 12; ADRIANO, FC Porto 11; SIMAO, Benfica 11

PORTUGAL 2006-07

LIGA DE HONRA (2)

	Pl	W	D	L	F	A	Pts	Leixões	Guimarães	Rio Ave	Santa Clara	Gondomar	Feirense	Varzim	Penafiel	Olhanense	Estoril	Trofense	Gil Vicente	Vizela	Port'nense	Olivais e M.	Chaves
Leixões	30	18	6	6	45	21	60		0-2	0-0	3-1	2-0	1-1	4-0	2-0	0-1	1-0	1-0	2-1	2-0	0-0	4-0	3-0
Vitória SC Guimarães	30	16	7	7	44	20	55	0-0		3-0	1-0	0-1	1-1	0-0	0-1	1-1	3-1	2-0	1-0	2-0	6-0	4-0	1-0
Rio Ave	30	15	8	7	44	37	53	1-2	5-3		2-0	1-3	2-1	0-0	1-0	1-1	1-0	2-1	1-0	2-1	1-2	2-1	3-2
GD Santa Clara	30	15	5	10	34	31	50	0-2	0-1	3-3		2-1	2-1	0-1	0-0	1-0	1-1	1-0	2-1	2-1	2-1	2-1	0-0
Gondomar SC	30	13	6	11	33	30	45	1-2	0-2	0-0	1-1		1-0	0-1	1-1	1-3	1-0	1-0	1-2	2-0	0-1	3-0	3-0
Feirense	30	11	11	8	38	26	44	1-1	0-0	4-1	3-0	0-0		2-2	0-0	3-0	1-0	1-2	1-2	0-2	2-0	1-0	1-0
Varzim SC	30	12	8	10	34	37	44	1-1	2-1	0-3	1-3	2-0	0-1		2-0	1-0	2-1	1-1	0-0	3-2	2-4	1-0	0-1
SC Penafiel	30	10	11	9	23	27	41	3-0	0-2	2-0	1-0	2-1	1-0	2-1		2-1	0-0	0-3	1-1	1-4	1-0	0-0	0-0
Olhanense	30	9	10	10	29	31	40	1-2	1-0	2-0	1-2	0-0	2-3	1-1	1-1		3-1	1-0	0-3	1-1	1-4	2-1	1-1
GD Estoril-Praia	30	10	7	13	30	35	37	1-0	1-1	1-2	0-1	2-1	2-2	2-1	2-1	1-2		1-2	**3-0**	2-0	1-0	1-1	1-1
Trofense	30	9	9	12	27	26	36	1-0	0-1	0-0	0-1	2-2	1-1	2-0	0-0	0-1	1-0		0-1	1-1	1-3	0-1	1-0
Gil Vicente §9	30	12	9	9	27	27	36	1-0	1-1	1-2	2-1	3-0	**0-3**	2-2	2-0	0-0	0-0	**0-3**		2-1	0-0	1-0	1-0
Vizela	30	9	7	14	29	32	34	2-3	2-0	1-1	2-0	0-1	1-2	0-0	1-0	1-0	1-2	0-0	0-1		1-0	1-2	1-0
Portimonense	30	7	9	14	28	42	30	1-4	1-3	1-3	0-1	1-2	0-0	1-2	1-1	1-0	0-1	1-1	1-1	0-0		1-1	1-0
Olivais e Moscavide	30	7	6	17	26	42	27	1-2	2-1	1-3	0-1	0-1	1-3	2-1	1-2	0-0	3-1	0-2	1-2	0-0	1-1		4-1
GD Chaves	30	3	7	20	16	43	16	0-1	0-1	1-1	0-4	2-3	1-1	1-3	0-0	0-1	0-1	2-1	0-1	1-1	1-2	1-0	

27/08/2006 - 20/05/2007 • § = points deducted • Matches in bold awarded 3-0

TAÇA DE PORTUGAL 2006-07

Fifth Round

Team	Score
Sporting CP *	2
Rio Ave	1
AD Camacha	0
CD Pinhalnovense *	2
Atlético Clube Portugal *	1
CD Santa Clara	0
Leixões *	1
Académica Coimbra	2
Boavista *	3
Penalva do Castelo	1
FC Penafiel	0 6p
CD Nacional *	0 7p
FC Maia *	1
Desportivo Aves	0
Louletano	2
SC Beira-Mar *	4
Sporting Braga *	2
AD Pontassolense	1
SL Benfica *	2
União Leiria	1
Sertanense FC	1
Varzim SC *	3
GD Bragança	Bye
Estrela Amadora *	0
Naval 1º de Maio	1
Odivelas *	3
CD Maffra	1
Gondomar SC *	0
Os Belenenses	4

Round of sixteen

Team	Score
Sporting CP	6
CD Pinhalnovense *	0
Atlético Clube Portugal *	0
Académica Coimbra	1
Boavista *	2
CD Nacional	0
FC Maia *	0
SC Beira-Mar	2
Sporting Braga	Bye
SL Benfica	1
Varzim SC *	2
GD Bragança	Bye
Naval 1º de Maio	0
Odivelas *	0
Os Belenenses	1

Quarter-finals

Team	Score
Sporting CP *	2
Académica Coimbra	1
Boavista	0
SC Beira-Mar *	2
Sporting Braga *	2
Varzim SC	0
GD Bragança *	1
Os Belenenses	2

Semi-finals

Team	Score
Sporting CP *	2
SC Beira-Mar	1
Sporting Braga	1
Os Belenenses *	2

Final

Team	Score
Sporting CP	1
Os Belenenses	0

CUP FINAL

Estádio Nacional, Lisbon
27-05-2007, Ref: Pedro Proença

Scorer - Liedson 85 for Sporting

Sporting - Ricardo - Abel, Carneira, Polga, Tello (Tonel 64) - Miguel Veloso, João Moutinho, Nani*, Romagnoli (Custódio 90) - Alecsandro (Yannick Djaló 65), Liedson. Tr: Paulo Bento

Belenenses - Costinha - Amaral (Carlitos 78), Rolando, Nivaldo, Rodrigo Alvim - Sandro Gaucho, Ruben Amorim (Fernando 66), José Pedro, Cândido Costa, Silas (Garcês 70), Dady. Tr: Jorge Jesus

* Home team ‡ Qualified for the UEFA Cup

FC PORTO 2006–07

Date	Opponents	Score		Comp	Scorers	
19-08-2006	Vitória FC Setúbal	W	3-0	N	SC	Adriano [54], Anderson [75], Vieirinha [89]	
25-08-2006	União Leiria	W	2-1	H	SL	Adriano [20], Quaresma [46]	40 728
10-09-2006	Estrela Amadora	W	3-0	A	SL	Rui Duarte OG [55], Raul Meireles [83], Lucho González [89]	5 000
13-09-2006	CSKA Moskva - RUS	D	0-0	H	CLgG		37 123
17-09-2006	Naval 1º de Maio	W	2-0	A	SL	Cech [19], Mario Sergio OG [25]	2 515
22-09-2006	SC Beira-Mar	W	3-0	H	SL	Helder Postiga [53], López [78], Sektioui [90]	31 423
26-09-2006	Arsenal - ENG	L	0-2	A	CLgG		59 861
2-10-2006	Sporting Braga	L	1-2	A	SL	Helder Postiga [42]	13 724
14-10-2006	SC Marítimo	W	3-0	H	SL	Helder Postiga 2 [34 84], Lucho González [60p]	33 023
17-10-2006	Hamburger SV - GER	W	4-1	H	CLgG	Lisandro López 2 [14 81], Lucho González [48+p], Helder Postiga [69]	31 109
22-10-2006	Sporting CP	D	1-1	A	SL	Quaresma [47]	37 136
28-10-2006	Benfica	W	3-2	H	SL	Lisandro López [12], Quaresma [20], Bruno Moraes [90]	50 223
1-11-2006	Hamburger SV - GER	W	3-1	A	CLgG	Lucho González [44], Lisandro López [61], Bruno Moraes [87]	51 000
6-11-2006	Vitória FC Setúbal	W	3-0	A	SL	Lisandro López [4], Helder Postiga [6], Quaresma [76]	5 000
18-11-2006	Académica Coimbra	W	2-1	H	SL	Helder Postiga [49], Ibson [82]	30 207
21-11-2006	CSKA Moskva - RUS	W	2-0	A	CLgG	Quaresma [2], Lucho González [61]	21 853
26-11-2006	Os Belenenses	W	1-0	A	SL	Helder Postiga [41]	7 000
2-12-2006	Boavista	W	2-0	H	SL	Quaresma [51], Helder Postiga [73]	38 729
6-12-2006	Arsenal - ENG	D	0-0	H	CLgG		45 609
11-12-2006	CD Nacional	W	2-1	A	SL	Bruno Moraes [74], Lucho González [89]	2 000
17-12-2006	Paços Ferreira	W	4-0	H	SL	Pepe 2 [24 68], Helder Postiga [42], Lucho González [86]	38 203
7-01-2007	Atlético Club Portugal	L	0-1	H	TPr4		
14-01-2007	Desportivo Aves	W	2-0	A	SL	Lucho González [9], Quaresma [90]	5 800
26-01-2007	União Leiria	L	0-1	A	SL		3 385
3-02-2007	Estrela Amadora	L	0-1	H	SL		26 309
16-02-2007	Naval 1º de Maio	W	4-0	H	SL	Lisandro López 2 [19 47], Lucho González [35], Adriano [90]	27 309
21-02-2007	Chelsea - ENG	D	1-1	H	CLr2	Raul Meireles [12]	50 216
25-02-2007	SC Beira-Mar	W	5-0	A	SL	Lisandro López [18], Lucho González [70], Raul Meireles [74], Alan [77], Adriano [87p]	14 540
3-03-2007	Sporting Braga	W	1-0	H	SL	Adriano [9]	41 228
6-03-2007	Chelsea - ENG	L	1-2	A	CLr2	Quaresma [15]	39 113
11-03-2007	SC Marítimo	W	2-1	A	SL	Adriano [17], Raul Meireles [27]	8 000
17-03-2007	Sporting CP	L	0-1	H	SL		49 429
1-04-2007	Benfica	D	1-1	A	SL	Pepe [40]	62 756
6-04-2007	Vitória FC Setúbal	W	5-1	H	SL	Jorginho [4], Adriano 2 [15 35], Helder Postiga [21], Anderson [76]	40 120
14-04-2007	Académica Coimbra	W	2-1	A	SL	Bruno Alves [42], Adriano [70]	16 115
22-04-2007	Os Belenenses	W	3-1	H	SL	Adriano [9], Lucho González [45p], Bruno Alves [85]	44 728
28-04-2007	Boavista	L	1-2	A	SL	Lucho González [72p]	14 127
5-05-2007	CD Nacional	W	2-0	H	SL	Anderson [66], Jorge Fucile [88]	39 628
13-05-2007	Paços Ferreira	D	1-1	A	SL	Adriano [76]	6 000
20-05-2007	Desportivo Aves	W	4-1	H	SL	Adriano [26], Lisandro López 2 [52 90], Jorge Ribeiro OG [59]	50 428

SC = Super Cup • SL = SuperLiga • TP = Taça de Portugal • CL = UEFA Champions League
gG = group G • r2 = second round • r4 = fourth round • N = Magalhães Pessoa, Leiria

THE FIFA BIG COUNT OF 2006

	Male	Female		Total
Number of players	488 787	58 947	Referees and Assistant Referees	4 471
Professionals	1 663		Admin, Coaches, Technical, Medical	34 000
Amateurs 18+	40 351		Number of clubs	2 284
Youth under 18	64 922		Number of teams	8 786
Unregistered	210 000		Clubs with women's teams	464
Total players	547 734		Players as % of population	5.16%

SPORTING CP 2006–07

Date	Opponents	Score		Comp	Scorers	
26-08-2006	Boavista	W	3-2	H	SL	Nani [63], Deivid 2 [66 89]	34 330
9-09-2006	CD Nacional	W	1-0	A	SL	Nani [11]	3 000
12-09-2006	Internazionale - ITA	W	1-0	H	CLgG	Caneira [64]	30 222
16-09-2006	Paços Ferreira	L	0-1	H	SL		35 116
23-09-2006	Desportivo Aves	W	2-0	A	SL	Alecsandro [14], Tonel [81]	3 500
27-09-2006	Spartak Moskva - RUS	D	1-1	A	CLgG	Nani [59]	36 000
2-10-2006	União Leiria	W	2-0	H	SL	Nani [33], Liedson [57p]	30 406
15-10-2006	Estrela Amadora	W	1-0	A	SL	Tonel [45]	5 000
18-10-2006	Bayern München - GER	L	0-1	H	CLgG		36 500
22-10-2006	FC Porto	D	1-1	H	SL	Yannick Djaló [43]	37 136
27-10-2006	SC Beira-Mar	D	3-3	A	SL	Alecsandro [56], Yannick Djaló [80], Liedson [89]	15 571
31-10-2006	Bayern München - GER	D	0-0	A	CLgG		66 000
6-11-2006	Sporting Braga	W	3-0	H	SL	Luís Filipe OG [12], Nem OG [33], Alecsandro [62]	29 511
19-11-2006	SC Marítimo	W	1-0	A	SL	Rodrigo Tello [62]	8 000
22-11-2006	Internazionale - ITA	L	0-1	A	CLgG		36 935
26-11-2006	Naval 1° de Maio	W	1-0	H	SL	Ronny [88]	2 577
1-12-2006	SL Benfica	L	0-2	H	SL		44 042
5-12-2006	Spartak Moskva - RUS	L	1-3	H	CLgG	Carlos Bueno [31]	17 000
9-12-2006	Vitória FC Setúbal	W	3-0	A	SL	Liedson 2 [3 53], Nani [19]	4 358
16-12-2006	Académica Coimbra	W	1-0	H	SL	Liedson [26]	41 411
21-12-2006	União da Madeira	W	3-1	H	TPr4	João Moutinho [2], Farnerud [9], Tello [40]	
13-01-2007	Os Belenenses	D	0-0	A	SL		7 000
21-01-2007	Rio Ave	W	2-1	H	TPr5	Ricardo Jorge OG [19], Liedson [28]	
28-01-2007	Boavista	D	1-1	A	SL	Liedson [49]	3 000
3-02-2007	CD Nacional	W	5-1	H	SL	Carlos Bueno 4 [74 77 80 90], Liedson [82]	28 459
10-02-2007	Pinhalnovense	W	6-0	H	TPr6	Liedson 2 [1 39], Custódio [12], Bueno 2 [27 85], Yannick Djaló [76]	
17-02-2007	Paços Ferreira	D	1-1	A	SL	Liedson [51]	6 000
23-02-2007	Desportivo Aves	D	0-0	H	SL		26 168
28-02-2007	Académica Coimbra	W	2-1	H	TPqf	Liedson 2 [5 10]	
4-03-2007	União Leiria	D	0-0	A	SL		6 829
10-03-2007	Estrela Amadora	W	3-1	H	SL	João Moutinho [38], Yannick Djaló 2 [47 49]	30 594
17-03-2007	FC Porto	W	1-0	A	SL	Rodrigo Tello [71]	49 429
2-04-2007	SC Beira-Mar	W	2-0	H	SL	Abel [14], Liedson [32]	29 309
7-04-2007	Sporting Braga	W	1-0	A	SL	Nani [52]	18 137
13-04-2007	SC Marítimo	W	4-0	H	SL	Liedson [11], Leandro Romagnoli [17], João Moutinho [79], Alecsandro [86]	31 466
18-04-2007	SC Beira-Mar	W	2-1	H	TPsf		
22-04-2007	Naval 1° de Maio	W	4-0	H	SL	Alecsandro 3 [11 13 80], João Moutinho [90p]	30 531
29-04-2007	SL Benfica	D	1-1	A	SL	Liedson [1]	54 370
6-05-2007	Vitória FC Setúbal	W	3-1	H	SL	N'Diaye OG [1], Liedson 2 [26 52], Amuneke [77]	31 207
13-05-2007	Académica Coimbra	W	2-0	A	SL	Liedson [4], João Moutinho [89]	16 000
20-05-2007	Os Belenenses	W	4-0	H	SL	Liedson [10], Alecsandro [19], Yannick Djaló [89], Bruno Pereirinha [90]	39 201
27-05-2007	Os Belenenses	W	1-0	N	TPf	Liedson [85]	

SL = SuperLiga • TP = Taça de Portugal • CL = UEFA Champions League
gB = group B • r4 = fourth round • r5 = fifth round • r6 = sixth round • qf = quarter-final • sf = semi-final • f = final • N = Estádio Nacional, Lisbon

FIFA/COCA-COLA WORLD RANKING

1993	1994	1995	1996	1997	1998	1999	2000	2001	2002	2003	2004	2005	2006	High	Low
20	20	16	13	30	36	15	6	4	11	17	9	10	8	4 03/01	43 08/98

2006–2007											
08/06	09/06	10/06	11/06	12/06	01/07	02/07	03/07	04/07	05/07	06/07	07/07
8	9	9	8	8	8	8	8	7	7	6	8

SL BENFICA 2006-07

Date	Opponents	Score		Comp	Scorers	
8-08-2006	FK Austria Wien - AUT	D 1-1	A	CLpr3	Nuno Gomes [16]	19 600
22-08-2006	FK Austria Wien - AUT	W 3-0	H	CLpr3	Rui Costa [21], Nuno Gomes [48+], Petit [57]	58 110
9-09-2006	Boavista	L 0-3	A	SL		8 000
13-09-2006	FC København - DEN	D 0-0	A	CLgF		40 085
17-09-2006	CD Nacional	W 1-0	H	SL	Luisão [28]	36 590
22-09-2006	Paços Ferreira	D 1-1	A	SL	Katsouranis [23]	4 500
26-09-2006	Manchester United - ENG	L 0-1	H	CLgF		53 000
1-10-2006	Desportivo Aves	W 4-1	H	SL	Paulo Jorge [19], Nuno Gomes [50], Simão [64], Karagounis [90]	32 079
14-10-2006	União Leiria	W 4-0	A	SL	Miccoli 2 [30 43], Nuno Gomes [62], Simão [67p]	11 433
17-10-2006	Celtic - SCO	L 0-3	A	CLgF		58 313
22-10-2006	Estrela Amadora	W 3-1	H	SL	Miccoli [31], Simão [54p], Karyaka [89]	26 084
28-10-2006	FC Porto	L 2-3	A	SL	Katsouranis [62], Nuno Gomes [81]	50 223
1-11-2006	Celtic - SCO	W 3-0	H	CLgF	Caldwell OG [10], Nuno Gomes [22], Karyaka [76]	47 574
5-11-2006	SC Beira-Mar	W 3-0	H	SL	Katsouranis [52], Petit [56], Ricardo OG [75]	37 056
18-11-2006	Sporting Braga	L 1-3	A	SL	Ricardo Rocha [30]	22 440
21-11-2006	FC København - DEN	W 3-1	H	CLgF	Léo [14], Miccoli 2 [26 37]	37 199
25-11-2006	SC Marítimo	W 2-1	H	SL	Von Schwedler OG [32], Katsouranis [66]	34 377
1-12-2006	Sporting CP	W 2-0	A	SL	Ricardo Rocha [2], Simão [35]	44 042
6-12-2006	Manchester United - ENG	L 1-3	A	CLgF	Nélson [27]	74 955
10-12-2006	Naval 1° de Maio	D 0-0	A	SL		5 120
16-12-2006	Vitória FC Setúbal	W 3-0	H	SL	Nuno Gomes [13], Simão [62], Nuno Assis [86]	30 767
21-12-2006	OS Belenenses	W 4-0	H	SL	Simão [19p], Karagounis [43], Fonseca [52], Katsouranis [79]	42 306
6-01-2007	Oliveira do Bairro	W 5-0	H	TPr4	Katsouranis [4], Nuno Gomes 2 [38 40], Kikin Fonseca 2 [52 59]	
15-01-2007	Académica Coimbra	W 2-0	A	SL	Ricardo Rocha [2], Léo [88]	19 464
21-01-2007	União Leiria	W 2-1	H	TPr5	Simão [80], Mantorras [85]	
27-01-2007	OS Belenenses	W 2-1	A	SL	Simão [13], Luisão [36]	42 306
2-02-2007	Boavista	D 0-0	H	SL		50 222
10-02-2007	Varzim SC	L 1-2	A	TPr6	Simão [30]	
14-02-2007	Dinamo Bucuresti - ROM	W 1-0	H	UCr2	Miccoli [90]	35 197
18-02-2007	CD Nacional	W 2-0	A	SL	Miccoli 2 [61 70]	2 500
22-02-2007	Dinamo Bucuresti - ROM	W 2-1	A	UCr2	Anderson [50], Katsouranis [64]	12 480
26-02-2007	Paços Ferreira	W 3-1	H	SL	Simão 2 [7 64], Nuno Gomes [32]	35 114
3-03-2007	Desportivo Aves	W 1-0	A	SL	Nuno Gomes [59]	5 000
8-03-2007	Paris Saint-Germain - FRA	L 1-2	A	UCr3	Simão [10]	33 962
12-03-2007	União Leiria	W 2-0	H	SL	Simão [16]	34 932
15-03-2007	Paris Saint-Germain - FRA	W 3-1	H	UCr3	Simão 2 [12 89p], Pauleta [32]	58 800
19-03-2007	Estrela Amadora	W 1-0	A	SL	Petit [81]	8 500
1-04-2007	FC Porto	D 1-1	H	SL	Lucho González OG [83]	62 756
5-04-2007	RCD Espanyol - ESP	L 2-3	A	UCqf	Nuno Gomes [63], Simão [65]	25 100
9-04-2007	SC Beira-Mar	D 2-2	A	SL	Mantorras [83], Simão [90p]	29 427
12-04-2007	RCD Espanyol - ESP	D 0-0	H	UCqf		51 100
16-04-2007	Sporting Braga	D 0-0	H	SL		36 259
21-04-2007	SC Marítimo	W 3-0	A	SL	Miccoli 2 [55 79], Katsouranis [90p]	8 500
29-04-2007	Sporting CP	D 1-1	H	SL	Miccoli [23]	54 370
5-05-2007	Naval 1° de Maio	W 2-1	H	SL	Petit [11], Miccoli [88]	29 240
13-05-2007	Vitória FC Setúbal	W 1-0	A	SL	Miccoli [79]	6 862
20-05-2007	Académica Coimbra	W 2-0	H	SL	Derlei [11], Mantorras [82]	42 994

SL = SuperLiga • TP = Taça de Portugal • CL = UEFA Champions League
pr3 = third preliminary round • gF = group F • r4 = fourth round • r5 = fifth round • r6 = round six • qf = quarter-final

PRK – KOREA DPR

NATIONAL TEAM RECORD
JULY 10TH 2006 TO JULY 12TH 2010

PL	W	D	L	F	A	%
7	3	2	2	19	7	57.1

FIFA/COCA-COLA WORLD RANKING

1993	1994	1995	1996	1997	1998	1999	2000	2001	2002	2003	2004	2005	2006	High		Low	
62	84	117	144	166	158	172	142	136	124	117	95	82	113	57	11/93	181	11/98

2006–2007											
08/06	09/06	10/06	11/06	12/06	01/07	02/07	03/07	04/07	05/07	06/07	07/07
86	111	117	110	113	133	137	140	142	141	136	115

1966 tends to be the year that springs to mind when you mention football in North Korea, thanks to the heroics of the national team at the World Cup in England, but forty years on 2006 also turned out to be a vintage year as the Koreans won a world title along with a continental title for good measure. Both triumphs were unexpected but then this still is one of the most secretive countries in the world. It all happened within the space of three months. At the FIFA Women's U–20 World Championship in Russia in August, the Koreans knocked out both France and Brazil on the way to a meeting with China in the final, whom they sensationally beat 5-0 to become only the second

INTERNATIONAL HONOURS
Qualified for the FIFA World Cup finals 1966   Qualified for the FIFA Women's World Cup finals 1999 2003
Asian Games 1978   Asian Women's Championship 2001 2003   Women's Asian Games 2002

nation from Asia to win a world title. In November the under–20 men's team then confounded onlookers by winning the AFC Youth Championship in India, beating Japan on penalties in the final. This extraordinary success at youth level continued into 2007 when the women's under–16 team won the Asian championship in Malaysia, beating Japan in the final having knocked out South Korea in the semi-finals. The main action for the men's senior team came in the East Asian Federation Championship where they managed to qualify for the finals in 2008.

THE FIFA BIG COUNT OF 2006

	Male	Female		Total
Number of players	436 956	65 956	Referees and Assistant Referees	360
Professionals	0		Admin, Coaches, Technical, Medical	1 498
Amateurs 18+	7 200		Number of clubs	170
Youth under 18	7 712		Number of teams	850
Unregistered	170 000		Clubs with women's teams	69
Total players	502 912		Players as % of population	2.18%

DPR Korea Football Association (PRK)
Kumsongdong, Kwangbok Street, Mangyongdae Dist., PO Box 56, Pyongyang, Korea DPR
Tel +850 2 182228164   Fax +850 2 3814403
noc-kp@co.chesin.com   www.none
President: CHOE Nam Gyun   General Secretary: KIM Jong Su
Vice-President: MUN Jang Hong   Treasurer: TBD   Media Officer: None
Men's Coach: HAN Hyong Yi   Women's Coach: KIM Kwang Min
PRK formed: 1945   AFC: 1974   FIFA: 1958
White shirts, White shorts, White socks

RECENT INTERNATIONAL MATCHES PLAYED BY KOREA DPR

2004	Opponents	Score	Venue	Comp	Scorers	Att	Referee
18-02	Yemen	D 1-1	Sana'a	WCq	Hong Yong Jo [85]	15 000	Husain BHR
31-03	United Arab Emirates	D 0-0	Pyongyang	WCq		20 000	Zhou Weixin CHN
9-06	Thailand	W 4-1	Bangkok	WCq	Kim Yong Su 2 [42 71], Sin Yong Nam [52], Hong Yong Jo [67]	30 000	Tseytlin UZB
8-09	Thailand	W 4-1	Pyongyang	WCq	An Yonh Hak 2 [49 73], Hong Yong Jo [55], Ri Hyok Chol [60]	20 000	Moradi IRN
13-10	Yemen	W 2-1	Pyongyang	WCq	Ri Han Ja [1], Hong Yong Jo [64]	15 000	Vo Minh Tri VIE
17-11	United Arab Emirates	L 0-1	Dubai	WCq		2 000	Abdul Hamid MAS
2005							
2-02	Kuwait	D 0-0	Beijing	Fr			
9-02	Japan	L 1-2	Saitama	WCq	Nam Song Chol [61]	60 000	Al Ghamdi KSA
7-03	Mongolia	W 6-0	Taipei	EAq	Kim Kwang Hyok 3 [18 39 66], Ri Hyok Chol 2 [22 30] Hong Yong Jo [64]		
9-03	Chinese Taipei	W 2-0	Taipei	EAq	Choe Chol Man 2 [13 14]		
11-03	Guam	W 21-0	Taipei	EAq	Hong Yong Jo 2 [6 17], Choe Chol Man 3 [10 37 54] Kim Kwang Hyok 7 [21 43 61 63 71 76 77], Park Nam Chol [83] Kim Yong Jun 3 [29 39 49], Kang Jin Hyok 5 [31 44 65 84 91+]		
13-03	Hong Kong	W 2-0	Taipei	EAq	Kang Jin Hyok [43], Ri Myong Sam [64]		
25-03	Bahrain	L 1-2	Pyongyang	WCq	Pak Song Gwan [63]	50 000	Rungklay THA
30-03	Iran	L 0-2	Pyongyang	WCq		55 000	Kousa SYR
3-06	Iran	L 0-1	Tehran	WCq		35 000	Al Ghamdi KSA
8-06	Japan	L 0-2	Bangkok	WCq		BCD	De Bleeckere BEL
31-07	Japan	W 1-0	Daejon	EA	Kim Yong Jun [25]	23 150	Tan Hai CHN
4-08	Korea Republic	D 0-0	Jeonju	EA		27 455	Ghahremani IRN
7-08	China PR	L 0-2	Daegu	EA			
14-08	Korea Republic	L 0-3	Seoul	Fr			
17-08	Bahrain	W 3-2	Manama	WCq	Choe Chol Man [28], Kim Chol Ho [43], An Chol Hyok [89]	3 000	Maidin SIN
26-12	Latvia	D 1-1	Phuket	Fr	An Chol Hyok [26]		
28-12	Thailand	W 2-0	Phuket	Fr	Kim Chol Ho [7], Hong Yong Jo [9]		
30-12	Latvia	L 1-2	Phuket	Fr	Hong Yong Jo [47]		
2006							
No international matches played in 2006							
2007							
19-06	Mongolia	W 7-0	Macau	EAq	Jong Tae Se 4		
21-06	Macau	W 7-1	Macau	EAq			
24-06	Hong Kong	W 1-0	Macau	EAq	Mun In Guk [82]		
24-06	Singapore	L 1-2	Singapore	Fr	An Chol Hyok [59]		
28-06	Oman	D 2-2	Singapore	Fr	Kang Jin Hyok [20], An Chol Hyok [45p]. L 3-4p		
1-07	UAE	L 0-1	Singapore	Fr			
4-07	Saudi Arabia	D 1-1	Singapore	Fr	Park Nam Chol [84]		

Fr = Friendly match • AC = AFC Asian Cup 2004 • EA = East Asian Championship • WC = FIFA World Cup • q = qualifier

KOREA DPR NATIONAL TEAM RECORDS AND RECORD SEQUENCES

Records			Sequence records		
Victory	21-0	GUM 2005	Wins	8	1993
Defeat	1-6	BUL 1974	Defeats	5	1993
Player Caps	n/a		Undefeated	13	1978-1980
Player Goals	n/a		Without win	15	1993-2000

Clean sheets	4	Four times	
Goals scored	18	1992-1993	
Without goal	4	1989-1990	
Goals against	12	1993-2000	

KOREA DPR COUNTRY INFORMATION

Capital	Pyongyang	Independence	1945 from Japan	GDP per Capita	$1 400
Population	22 912 177	Status	Communist Republic	GNP Ranking	68
Area km²	120 540	Language	Korean	Dialling code	+850
Population density	190 per km²	Literacy rate	99%	Internet code	.kp
% in urban areas	61%	Main religion	None	GMT +/−	+9
Towns/Cities ('000)	Pyongyang 2 787; Hamhung 840; Chongjin 689, Nampo 670; Sinuiju 385; Wonsan 355; Phyongsong 323; Sariwon 300; Haeju 271; Kanggye 264; Kimchaek 237; Hyesan 210				
Neighbours (km)	Korea Republic 238; China 1 416; Russia 19; Sea of Japan & Yellow Sea 2 495				
Main stadia	Kim Il-Sung Stadium – Pyongyang 70 000; Yanggakdo – Pyongyang 30 000				

PUR – PUERTO RICO

NATIONAL TEAM RECORD
JULY 10TH 2006 TO JULY 12TH 2010

PL	W	D	L	F	A	%
0	0	0	0	0	0	0

FIFA/COCA-COLA WORLD RANKING

1993	1994	1995	1996	1997	1998	1999	2000	2001	2002	2003	2004	2005	2006	High	Low
105	112	128	149	169	182	186	195	195	198	200	194	195	195	97 03/94	202 11/04

2006–2007											
08/06	09/06	10/06	11/06	12/06	01/07	02/07	03/07	04/07	05/07	06/07	07/07
190	192	191	193	195	196	195	195	195	193	193	194

The national team's absence from the 2006-07 Digicel Caribbean Cup qualifiers only reinforced the belief that of all of the Caribbean islands, Puerto Rico is the least interested in football. There are many countries around the world where football may not be the most popular sport, but in Puerto Rico it barely registers at all. Indeed, in a debate as to which country has the lowest profile in football, it would probably be a close-fought battle with perhaps Pakistan or the Philippines. But that might be about to change thanks to a team called the Puerto Rico Islanders. Founded in 2003 and based in Bayamon on the outskirts of San Juan, they compete in America's USL first division.

INTERNATIONAL HONOURS
None

Managed by Northern Ireland's Colin Clarke they qualified for the end-of-season play-offs in 2006 and regularly attract crowds of around 5,000 to the Estadio Juan Ramón Loubriel, formerly a baseball stadium. There is competitive football on the island apart from the Islanders with Fraigcomar winning the double of Liga Mayor and Torneo de Copa beating Academia de Quintana in the final of both. Puerto Rico have entered the qualifying tournament for the 2010 FIFA World Cup in South Africa after missing out on the 2006 qualifiers but you have to go back to 1993 for the last time that the national team actually won a match.

THE FIFA BIG COUNT OF 2006

	Male	Female		Total
Number of players	187 470	35 200	Referees and Assistant Referees	601
Professionals	45		Admin, Coaches, Technical, Medical	9 016
Amateurs 18+	9 400		Number of clubs	75
Youth under 18	13 700		Number of teams	350
Unregistered	43 900		Clubs with women's teams	2
Total players	222 670		Players as % of population	5.67%

Federación Puertorriquena de Fútbol (FPF)
392 Juan B. Rodriguez, Parque Central Hato Rey, PR 00918, San Juan 00918, Puerto Rico
Tel +1 787 7652895   Fax +1 787 7672288
jserralta@yahoo.com   www.fedefutbolpr.com
President: SERRALTA Joe   General Secretary: RODRIGUEZ Esteban
Vice-President: JIMENEZ Mickey   Treasurer: VILLEGAS Miguel   Media Officer: None
Men's Coach: AVEDISSIAN Garabet   Women's Coach: TBD
FPF formed: 1940   CONCACAF: 1962   FIFA: 1960
White shirts with red stripes and blue sleeves, White shorts, White socks

RECENT INTERNATIONAL MATCHES PLAYED BY PUERTO RICO

2002	Opponents	Score	Venue	Comp	Scorers	Att	Referee
7-07	Guadeloupe	L 0-4	Baie-Mahault	GCq			Ibrahim DMA
21-07	Guadeloupe	L 0-2	San Juan	GCq			Richard DMA
2003							
No international matches played in 2003							
2004							
24-11	Trinidad and Tobago	L 0-5	Tunapuna	GCq		2 000	Callender BRB
26-11	Surinam	D 1-1	Marabella	GCq	Ortiz 80		Forde BRB
28-11	Grenada	L 2-5	Malabar	GCq	Garcia 85, Nieves 86		Callender BRB
2005							
No international matches played in 2005							
2006							
No international matches played in 2006							
2007							
No international matches played in 2007 before August							

GC = CONCACAF Gold Cup • q = qualifier

PUERTO RICO NATIONAL TEAM RECORDS AND RECORD SEQUENCES

Records			Sequence records					
Victory	4-0	CAY 1993	Wins	4	1993	Clean sheets	4	1993
Defeat	0-9	CUB 1995	Defeats	15	1946-1962	Goals scored	6	1988-1992
Player Caps	n/a		Undefeated	4	1993	Without goal	6	1982-1988
Player Goals	n/a		Without win	37	1940-1970	Goals against	26	1949-1970

PUERTO RICO 2006 LIGA MAYOR

	Pl	W	D	L	F	A	Pts
Fraigcomar †	10	10	0	0	35	2	30
Academia Quintana †	10	5	1	4	27	13	16
Huracanes Caguas ‡	10	4	3	3	22	14	15
San Francisco ‡	10	4	2	4	17	14	14
Levittown ‡	10	3	0	7	13	39	9
Tornados Humacao ‡	10	0	2	8	7	39	2

17/06/2006 - 26/06/2006 • † Qualified for the semi-finals
‡ Qualified for the quarter-finals

LIGA MAYOR PLAY-OFFS

Quarter–finals		Semi–finals		Final	
		Fraigcomar	1		
Levittown		San Francisco	0		
San Francisco				Fraigcomar	2
Huracanes				Acad. Quintana	1
Tornados		Huracanes	0		
		Acad. Quintana	3	10-09-2006	

RECENT LEAGUE RECORD

	Championship		Liga Mayor		
Year	Champions	Winners	Score	Runners-up	
1997	Académicos Quintana	Leones Maunabo		Islanders San Juan	
1998	Académicos Quintana	Islanders San Juan	3-0	Brujos Guayama	
1999	CF Nacional Carolina	Islanders San Juan		Cardenales	
2000	Académicos Quintana	Vaqueros Bayamón	1-0	Gigantes Carolina	
2001	Académicos Quintana	Islanders San Juan	4-3	Brujos Guayama	
2002	Académicos Quintana	Vaqueros Bayamón	3-0	Islanders San Juan	
2003	Not held	Sporting Carolina	2-1	Vaqueros Bayamón	
2004	Not held	Sporting San Lorenzo	1-0	Huracanes Caguas	
2005	Fraigcomar	Real Quintana	2-1	Fraigcomar	
2006	Fraigcomar	Fraigcomar	4-1	Academia Quintana	

PUERTO RICO COUNTRY INFORMATION

Capital	San Juan	Status	Commonwealth associated with the US	GDP per Capita	$16 800
Population	3 897 960			GNP Ranking	n/a
Area km²	9 104	Language	Spanish, English	Dialling code	+1 787
Population density	428 per km²	Literacy rate	94%	Internet code	.pr
% in urban areas	71%	Main religion	Christian	GMT +/–	-5
Towns/Cities ('000)	San Juan 418; Bayamón 203; Carolina 170; Ponce 152; Caguas 86; Guaynabo 81; Mayagüez 76				
Neighbours (km)	Caribbean Sea & North Atlantic 501				
Main stadia	Estadio Sixto Escobar – San Juan 18 000; Country Club – San Juan 2 500				

QAT – QATAR

NATIONAL TEAM RECORD
JULY 10TH 2006 TO JULY 12TH 2010

PL	W	D	L	F	A	%
			·		·	

FIFA/COCA-COLA WORLD RANKING

1993	1994	1995	1996	1997	1998	1999	2000	2001	2002	2003	2004	2005	2006	High	Low
54	60	83	69	70	60	107	102	80	62	65	66	95	58	**51** 08/93	**107** 12/99

2006–2007											
08/06	09/06	10/06	11/06	12/06	01/07	02/07	03/07	04/07	05/07	06/07	07/07
64	63	53	57	58	59	77	80	83	83	85	83

For most of 2006 the Qatar national team looked unbeatable as they sailed through the AFC Asian Cup qualifiers, setting a new national record of seven consecutive victories, while the year ended in spectacular fashion when the under–23 team won gold at the Doha Asian Games. Qatar approached 2007 in high spirits as they looked forward to defending their title at the Gulf Cup and taking part in the Asian Cup finals, but inexplicably their form deserted them as they failed to get past the first round in either tournament - a crushing disappointment for Dzemaludin Musovic and his team. There was good news on the day before the Asian Cup final when Qatar was chosen to host the next

INTERNATIONAL HONOURS
Gulf Cup 1992 2004

tournament in 2011. In the Q–League Al Sadd could afford to lose five of their last seven matches and still win the title by a margin of 12 points, such was their dominance. Having won the League they then also won the Emir's Cup, although it took a penalty shoot-out in the final to secure the double, Khalifa Ayil scoring the vital penalty after Khor's Fernando had missed. Sadd also won the end of season Crown Prince Cup between the top four in the League to seal an unprecedented treble, but their form at home didn't stand them in good stead in the AFC Champions League as both they and Al Rayyan finished bottom of their respective first-round groups.

THE FIFA BIG COUNT OF 2006

	Male	Female		Total
Number of players	18 020	136	Referees and Assistant Referees	98
Professionals	0		Admin, Coaches, Technical, Medical	432
Amateurs 18+	2 236		Number of clubs	16
Youth under 18	4 320		Number of teams	160
Unregistered	2 600		Clubs with women's teams	0
Total players	18 156		Players as % of population	2.05%

Qatar Football Association (QFA)
7th Floor, QNOC Building, Cornich, PO Box 5333, Doha, Qatar
Tel +974 4944411   Fax +974 4944414
football@qatarolympics.org   www.qfa.com.qa
President: AL-THANI Shk. Hamad Bin Khalifa   General Secretary: AL-MOHANNADI Saud
Vice-President: TBD   Treasurer: AL BOANAIN Ahmed Abdulaziz   Media Officer: AL HUSAINI Khalifa
Men's Coach: MUSOVIC Dzemaludin   Women's Coach: None
QFA formed: 1960   AFC: 1972   FIFA: 1970
White shirts, White shorts, White socks

RECENT INTERNATIONAL MATCHES PLAYED BY QATAR

2004	Opponents	Score	Venue	Comp	Scorers	Att	Referee
13-02	Bahrain	W 2-0	Doha	Fr			
18-02	Iran	L 1-3	Tehran	WCq	Waleed Rasoul 70		Haj Khader SYR
26-03	Libya	L 0-1	Rome	Fr			
31-03	Jordan	L 0-1	Amman	WCq		15 000	Shaban KUW
31-05	Turkmenistan	W 5-0	Doha	Fr	Mijbel 2, Ali Bechir 3 15 60 88, Moussa 44		
5-06	Kyrgyzstan	D 0-0	Doha	Fr			
9-06	Laos	W 5-0	Doha	WCq	Fazli 2 17 37, Waleed Jassim 2 69 86, Ali Bechir 89	500	Abu Armana PAL
18-07	Indonesia	L 1-2	Beijing	ACr1	Magid 83	5 000	Moradi IRN
21-07	Bahrain	D 1-1	Beijing	ACr1	Wesam Rizak 58p		Toru JPN
25-07	China PR	L 0-1	Beijing	ACr1		60 000	Moradi IRN
8-09	Laos	W 6-1	Vientiane	WCq	Abdulmajid 36, Nasser Mubarak 42, Ali Bechir 50, Waleed Rasoul 70, Meshal Abdulla 86, Saad Al Shammari 89	2 900	Napitupulu IDN
8-10	Syria	L 1-2	Doha	Fr			
13-10	Iran	L 2-3	Doha	WCq	Bilal Rajab 18, Golmohammadi OG 75	8 000	Kwon Jong Chul KOR
17-11	Jordan	W 2-0	Doha	WCq	Salem Al Hamad 60, Nayef Al Khater 75	800	Yoshida JPN
1-12	Lebanon	W 4-1	Doha	Fr			
5-12	Yemen	W 3-0	Doha	Fr			
10-12	United Arab Emirates	D 2-2	Doha	GCr1	Waleed Jassim 90, Wisam Rizq 93+		
13-12	Iraq	D 3-3	Doha	GCr1	Bilal Mohammed 38, Waleed Jassim 2 43p 57		
16-12	Oman	W 2-1	Doha	GCr1	Sattam Al Shamari 10, Ali Bechir 27		
20-12	Kuwait	W 2-0	Doha	GCsf	Ali Bechir 39, Nasir Kamil 90p		
24-12	Oman	D 1-1	Doha	GCf	Wissam Rizq 4. W 5-4p		
2005							
29-07	Egypt	L 0-5	Geneva	Fr			
31-07	Kuwait	W 1-0	Geneva	Fr	Waleed Jassim 37		
11-10	Iraq	D 0-0	Doha	Fr			
16-11	Argentina	L 0-3	Doha	Fr			Al Fadhli KUW
2006							
2-01	Libya	W 2-0	Doha	Fr	Adel Lamy 2 55 61		
14-02	Tajikistan	W 2-0	Doha	Fr	Sayd Bechir, Waleed Jassim		
22-02	Hong Kong	W 3-0	Hong Kong	ACq	Abdulrahman 11, Sayd Bechir 44, Magid Hassan 95+	1 806	Nishimura JPN
1-03	Uzbekistan	W 2-1	Doha	ACq	Adel Lamy 45, Ali Naser 49	7 000	Sun Baoje CHN
16-08	Bangladesh	W 4-1	Dhaka	ACq	Wesam Rizik 7p, Adel Lamy 36, Khalfan Ibrahim 2 38 74	7 000	Al Yarimi YEM
6-09	Bangladesh	W 3-0	Doha	ACq	Hussain Yasser 25, Adel Lamy 30, Saad Al Shammari 52	500	Najm LIB
11-10	Hong Kong	W 2-0	Doha	ACq	Bilal Rajab 43, Hussain Yasser 53	1 000	Kousa SYR
15-11	Uzbekistan	L 0-2	Tashkent	ACq		14 000	Al Saeedi UAE
2007							
13-01	Oman	D 1-1	Doha	Fr	Majed Mohammed 66		
18-01	Iraq	L 0-1	Abu Dhabi	GCr1			
21-01	Saudi Arabia	D 1-1	Abu Dhabi	GCr1	Ali Nasser 10		
24-01	Bahrain	L 1-2	Abu Dhabi	GCr1	Khalfan Ibrahim 19		
24-03	Iran	L 0-1	Doha	Fr			
25-06	Turkmenistan	W 1-0	Doha	Fr	Waleed Jassim 64		
2-07	Thailand	L 0-2	Bangkok	Fr			
9-07	Japan	D 1-1	Hanoi	ACr1	Quintana 88	5 000	Breeze
12-07	Vietnam	D 1-1	Hanoi	ACr1	Quintana 79	40 000	Moradi IRN
16-07	UAE	L 1-2	Ho Chi Minh City	ACr1	Quintana 42	3 000	Moradi IRN

Fr = Friendly match • AC = AFC Asian Cup • GC = Gulf Cup • WC = FIFA World Cup
q = qualifier • r1 = first round group • sf = semi-final • f = final

QATAR NATIONAL TEAM RECORDS AND RECORD SEQUENCES

Records			Sequence records			
Victory	8-0	AFG 1984, LIB 1985	Wins	7	2006	Clean sheets	7	2003-2004
Defeat	0-9	KUW 1973	Defeats	8	1972-1974	Goals scored	12	1996
Player Caps	n/a		Undefeated	11	2001, 2003-04	Without goal	4	1998, 2003-04
Player Goals	n/a		Without win	11	1970-1974	Goals against	15	1994-1996

QATAR COUNTRY INFORMATION

Capital	Doha	Independence	1971 from the UK	GDP per Capita	$21 500
Population	840 290	Status	Monarchy	GNP Ranking	92
Area km²	11 437	Language	Arabic	Dialling code	+974
Population density	73 per km²	Literacy rate	82%	Internet code	.qa
% in urban areas	91%	Main religion	Muslim	GMT + / –	+3
Towns/Cities ('000)	Doha 344; Al Rayyan 272; Umm Salal 29; Al Wakra 26; Khor 19				
Neighbours (km)	Saudi Arabia 60; Persain Gulf 563				
Main stadia	Khalifa International – Doha 45 000				

QATAR 2006-07

Q-LEAGUE

	Pl	W	D	L	F	A	Pts	Sadd	Gharrafa	Umm Salal	Rayyan	Wakra	Qatar SC	Khor	Shamal	Arabi	Ahli
Al Sadd †	27	17	4	6	52	29	55		3-2	1-2 0-1	3-0 0-1	3-2 1-2	2-0	2-1 2-3	3-0	3-0	1-1
Al Gharrafa †	27	11	10	6	51	41	43	1-1 3-1		2-1	0-2	2-2 1-1	1-1 0-2	1-0	0-0 0-2	3-2	4-2
Umm Salal	27	11	6	10	35	28	39	1-2	0-1 2-4		1-0	1-1	1-2 1-0	3-0	2-2	2-1 1-2	2-0 1-2
Al Rayyan	27	9	10	8	40	42	37	3-3	1-3 2-2	0-2 0-2		0-1	2-1	3-1	1-1	1-1 1-1	4-2 1-1
Al Wakra	27	7	13	7	29	29	34	0-3	1-1	0-0 0-0	0-0 3-1		0-0	1-0	0-1	0-1 2-2	0-1 1-1
Qatar SC	27	10	4	13	35	36	34	0-1 0-4	3-1	1-0	2-3	0-2 2-1		2-1 3-2	3-0 0-1	1-2	2-3
Khor	27	9	6	12	35	40	33	2-3	1-5 0-0	1-1 2-0	2-2 2-3	1-0 2-2	1-0		0-2 1-1	1-0 2-1	2-0 3-1
Shamal	27	7	11	9	26	36	32	0-1 0-1	2-5	1-0 2-2	1-1 1-1	2-1 1-1	0-1	0-3		1-1	0-0
Al Arabi	27	8	6	13	35	41	30	0-2 1-2	2-2 2-2	1-2	4-2	2-3	2-1 0-3	2-1	3-0 0-1		0-1 0-1
Al Ahli	27	7	8	12	29	45	29	2-3 1-1	4-5 1-0	0-4	0-1	1-2	0-0 2-1	0-0	1-1 1-4	0-2	

7/09/2006 - 15/04/2007 • † Qualified for AFC Champions League

EMIR'S CUP 2006-07

Round of 16		Quarter–finals		Semi–finals		Final	
Al Sadd	Bye						
		Al Sadd	4				
Al Ahli	1	Qatar SC	1				
Qatar SC	2			Al Sadd	0 5p		
Al Wakra	2			Al Gharrafa	0 4p		
Siliya	1	Al Wakra	0				
		Al Gharrafa	3				
Al Gharrafa	Bye					Al Sadd	0 5p
Al Arabi	3					Khor	0 4p
Shamal	1	Al Arabi	2 5p				
		Al Rayyan	2 4p			**CUP FINAL**	
Al Rayyan	Bye			Al Arabi	0		
Umm Salal	Bye			Khor	1		
		Umm Salal	0			Doha, 26-05-2007	
Markheya	0	Khor	1				
Khor	2						

RECENT LEAGUE AND CUP RECORD

	Championship						Emir's Cup		
Year	Champions	Pts	Runners-up	Pts	Third	Pts	Winners	Score	Runners-up
1997	Al Arabi	34	Al Rayyan	32	Al Ittihad	29	Al Ittihad	1-1 3-2p	Al Rayyan
1998	Al Ittihad	32	Al Rayyan	29	Al Sadd	26	Al Ittihad	4-3	Al Ahli
1999	Al Wakra	39	Al Ittihad	34	Al Sadd	33	Al Rayyan	2-1	Al Ittihad
2000	Al Sadd	38	Al Rayyan	34	Al Arabi	26	Al Sadd	2-0	Al Rayyan
2001	Al Wakra	32	Al Arabi	29	Al Taawun	28	Qatar SC	3-2	Al Sadd
2002	Al Ittihad	41	Qatar SC	29	Al Rayyan	25	Al Ittihad	3-1	Al Sadd
2003	Qatar SC	34	Al Sadd	31	Khor	31	Al Sadd	2-1	Al Ahli
2004	Al Sadd	42	Qatar SC	34	Al Arabi	31	Al Rayyan	3-2	Qatar SC
2005	Al Gharrafa	66	Al Rayyan	52	Khor	48	Al Sadd	0-0 5-4p	Al Wakra
2006	Al Sadd	52	Qatar SC	49	Al Arabi	46	Al Rayyan	1-1 5-3p	Al Gharrafa
2007	Al Sadd	55	Al Gharrafa	43	Umm Salal	39	Al Sadd	0-0 5-4p	Khor

Name changes: Al Ittihad → Al Gharrafa; Al Taawun → Khor

ROU – ROMANIA

NATIONAL TEAM RECORD
JULY 10TH 2006 TO JULY 12TH 2010

PL	W	D	L	F	A	%
10	8	2	0	19	4	90

FIFA/COCA-COLA WORLD RANKING

1993	1994	1995	1996	1997	1998	1999	2000	2001	2002	2003	2004	2005	2006	High		Low	
13	11	11	16	7	12	8	13	15	24	27	29	27	19	3	09/97	35	08/04

2006–2007											
08/06	09/06	10/06	11/06	12/06	01/07	02/07	03/07	04/07	05/07	06/07	07/07
26	25	23	19	19	20	15	14	14	15	12	13

Eight wins and two draws in ten games was an excellent return for Victor Piturca's Romania and although the two draws came in UEFA Euro 2008 qualifiers, they still led the group going into the 2007 summer recess. However, with only two qualifying from the group, a place in the finals was in no way guaranteed despite such a fine run of form. Central to their campaign has been a resurgent Adrian Mutu, who was also in fine form for his club Fiorentina, helping them qualify for the UEFA Cup despite having started the season with a hefty points penalty. After the euphoria of the 2005-06 UEFA Cup campaign which saw Steaua make it all the way to the semi-finals, the

INTERNATIONAL HONOURS
Qualified for the FIFA World Cup finals 1930 1934 1938 1970 1990 1994 1998   **UEFA Champions League** Steaua Bucuresti 1986

2006-07 season saw Steaua reach the group stage of the UEFA Champions League for the first time in 10 years while both Rapid and Dinamo qualified for the group stage of the UEFA Cup. After finishing third behind Lyon and Real, Steaua found themselves back in the UEFA Cup but both they and Dinamo were eliminated in the first knock-out round. At home Dinamo prevented Steaua from winning a hat-trick of titles with a lot more to spare than the six points gap between themselves and Steaua suggests, while the Cup Final saw Politehnica Timisoara lose 2-0 in front of their own fans to Cup holders Rapid.

THE FIFA BIG COUNT OF 2006

	Male	Female		Total
Number of players	929 488	104 832	Referees and Assistant Referees	4 683
Professionals	1 139		Admin, Coaches, Technical, Medical	16 200
Amateurs 18+	54 158		Number of clubs	2 831
Youth under 18	48 010		Number of teams	4 319
Unregistered	556 700		Clubs with women's teams	1
Total players	1 034 320		Players as % of population	4.64%

Romanian Football Federation (FRF)
Federatia Romana de Fotbal, House of Football, Str. Serg. Serbanica Vasile 12, Bucharest 022186, Romania
Tel +40 21 3250678   Fax +40 21 3250679
frf@frf.ro   www.frf.ro
President: SANDU Mircea   General Secretary: KASSAI Adalbert
Vice-President: DRAGOMIR Dumitru   Treasurer: FILIMON Vasile   Media Officer: ZAHARIA Paul Daniel
Men's Coach: PITURCA Victor   Women's Coach: STAICU Gheorghe
FRF formed: 1909   UEFA: 1954   FIFA: 1923
Yellow shirts with red trimmings, Yellow shorts, Yellow socks or White shirts with red trimmings, White shorts, White socks

RECENT INTERNATIONAL MATCHES PLAYED BY ROMANIA

2003	Opponents	Score		Venue	Comp	Scorers	Att	Referee
30-04	Lithuania	W	1-0	Kaunas	Fr	Bratu [63]	5 000	Sipailo LVA
7-06	Bosnia-Herzegovina	W	2-0	Craiova	ECq	Mutu [46], Ganea [88]	36 000	Bossen NED
11-06	Norway	D	1-1	Oslo	ECq	Ganea [64]	24 890	Michel SVK
20-08	Ukraine	W	2-0	Donetsk	Fr	Mutu 2 [29p 57]	28 000	Yegorov RUS
6-09	Luxembourg	W	4-0	Ploiesti	ECq	Mutu [39], Pancu [42], Ganea [44], Bratu [77]	4 500	Yefet ISR
10-09	Denmark	D	2-2	Copenhagen	ECq	Mutu [61], Pancu [72]	42 049	Meier SUI
11-10	Japan	D	1-1	Bucharest	Fr	Mutu [17]	10 000	Carmona Mendez ESP
16-11	Italy	L	0-1	Ancona	Fr		11 700	Stark GER
2004								
18-02	Georgia	W	3-0	Larnaca	Fr	Mutu 2 [30 70], Cernat [87]	300	Lajuks LVA
31-03	Scotland	W	2-1	Glasgow	Fr	Chivu [37], Pancu [51]	20 433	Hyytia FIN
28-04	Germany	W	5-1	Bucharest	Fr	Plesan [21], Rat [23], Danciulescu 2 [35 43], Caramarin [85]	12 000	Rosetti ITA
27-05	Republic of Ireland	L	0-1	Dublin	Fr		42 356	Jara CZE
18-08	Finland	W	2-1	Bucharest	WCq	Mutu [50], Petre [90]	17 500	Gilewski POL
4-09	FYR Macedonia	W	2-1	Craiova	WCq	Pancu [15], Mutu [88]	14 500	Plautz AUT
8-09	Andorra	W	5-1	Andorra la Vella	WCq	Cernat 2 [1 17], Pancu 2 [5 83], Niculae [70]	1 100	Kircher GER
9-10	Czech Republic	L	0-1	Prague	WCq		16 028	Rosetti ITA
17-11	Armenia	D	1-1	Yerevan	WCq	Ciprian [29]	1 403	De Bleeckere BEL
2005								
9-02	Slovakia	D	2-2	Larnaca	Fr	Niculae [35], Ilie [87]	500	Kapitanis CYP
26-03	Netherlands	L	0-2	Bucharest	WCq		19 000	Medina Cantalejo ESP
30-03	FYR Macedonia	W	2-1	Skopje	WCq	Mitea 2 [18 58]	15 000	Ovrebo NOR
24-05	Moldova	W	2-0	Bacau	Fr	Niculescu [8], Dica [55]	6 000	Salomir ROU
4-06	Netherlands	L	0-2	Rotterdam	WCq		47 000	De Santis ITA
8-06	Armenia	W	3-0	Constanta	WCq	Petre [29], Bucur 2 [40 78]	5 146	Briakos GRE
17-08	Andorra	W	2-0	Constanta	WCq	Mutu 2 [29 41]	8 200	Jakov ISR
3-09	Czech Republic	W	2-0	Constanta	WCq	Mutu 2 [28 56]	7 000	Hauge NOR
8-10	Finland	W	1-0	Helsinki	WCq	Mutu [41p]	11 500	Guenov BUL
12-11	Côte d'Ivoire	L	1-2	Le Mans	Fr	Iencsi [52]	5 377	Fautrel FRA
16-11	Nigeria	W	3-0	Bucharest	Fr	Niculae [15], Petre [48], Rosu [90]	500	Banari MDA
2006								
28-02	Armenia	W	2-0	Nicosia	Fr	Maftei [72], Cocis [86]	1 000	Tsacheilidis GRE
1-03	Slovenia	W	2-0	Larnaca	Fr	Mazilu [22], OG [53]	300	Vialichka BLR
23-05	Uruguay	L	0-2	Los Angeles	Fr		10 000	Stott USA
26-05	Northern Ireland	W	2-0	Chicago	Fr	Buga [7], Niculae [11]	15 000	Kennedy USA
27-05	Colombia	D	0-0	Chicago	Fr		15 000	Hall USA
16-08	Cyprus	W	2-0	Constanta	Fr	Dica [4], Mutu [29]	10 000	Corpodean ROU
2-09	Bulgaria	D	2-2	Constanta	ECq	Rosu [40], Marica [44]	12 620	Farina ITA
6-09	Albania	W	2-0	Tirana	ECq	Dica [65], Mutu [75p]	12 000	Benquerença POR
7-10	Belarus	W	3-1	Bucharest	ECq	Mutu [7], Marica [10], Goian [76]	12 000	Undiano Mallenco ESP
15-11	Spain	W	1-0	Cadiz	Fr	Marica [59]	15 000	Messina ITA
2007								
7-02	Moldova	W	2-0	Bucharest	Fr	Mazilu [74], Mutu [87]	8 000	Deaconu ROU
24-03	Netherlands	D	0-0	Rotterdam	ECq		48 000	Merk GER
28-03	Luxembourg	W	3-0	Piatra-Neamt	ECq	Mutu [26], Contra [56], Marica [90]	9 120	Lajuks LVA
2-06	Slovenia	W	2-1	Celje	ECq	Tamas [52], Nicolita [69]	6 500	Dougal SCO
6-06	Slovenia	W	2-0	Timisoara	ECq	Mutu [40], Contra [70]	17 850	Yefet ISR

Fr = Friendly match • EC = UEFA EURO 2004/2008 • WC = FIFA World Cup • q = qualifier

ROMANIA NATIONAL TEAM RECORDS AND RECORD SEQUENCES

Records			Sequence records					
Victory	9-0	FIN 1973	Wins	8	1996-1997	Clean sheets	5	1996-97, 1999
Defeat	0-9	HUN 1948	Defeats	4	1924-25, 1979	Goals scored	16	1971-1972
Player Caps	131	MUNTEANU Dorinel	Undefeated	17	1989-1990	Without goal	4	1947-1948
Player Goals	35	HAGI Gheorghe	Without win	20	1968-1971	Goals against	21	1933-1937

MAJOR CITIES/TOWNS

		Population '000
1	Bucharest	1 848
2	Iasi	314
3	Cluj-Napoca	314
4	Timisoara	312
5	Craiova	304
6	Constanta	297
7	Galati	290
8	Brasov	270
9	Ploiesti	225
10	Braila	210
11	Oradea	201
12	Bacau	167
13	Arad	166
14	Pitesti	166
15	Sibiu	149
16	Târgu-Mures	144
17	Baia Mare	135
18	Buzau	129
19	Botosani	113
20	Satu Mare	110
21	Piatra Neamt	100
22	Bistrita	80
23	Resita	79
24	Petrosani	43

ROMANIA

Capital	Bucharest	Language	Romanian, Hungarian			Independence	1878
Population	22 276 056	Area	237 500 km²	Density	94 per km²	% in cities	55%
GDP per cap	$7 000	Dailling code	+40	Internet	.ro	GMT +/-	+2

MEDALS TABLE

		Overall			League			Cup		Europe			City	Stadium	Cap'ty	DoF
		G	S	B	G	S	B	G	S	G	S	B				
1	Steaua Bucuresti	45	20	9	23	12	7	21	7	1	1	2	Bucharest	Stadionul Ghencea	27 063	1947
2	Dinamo Bucuresti	31	31	10	19	20	8	12	11			2	Bucharest	Stadionul Dinamo	15 138	1948
3	Rapid Bucuresti	16	19	7	3	14	7	13	5				Bucharest	Stadionul Giulesti	19 100	1923
4	Universitatea Craiova	10	10	8	4	5	7	6	5			1	Craiova	Ion Oblemenco	27 915	1948
5	UT Arad	8	3	1	6	1	1	2	2				Arad	Stadionul UTA	12 000	1945
6	Venus Bucuresti	8	1	1	8		1		1				Bucharest	Venus		1915-49
7	Petrolul Ploiesti	6	4	2	4	3	2	2	1				Ploiesti	Stadionul Ilie Oana	18 000	1924
	Ripensia Timisoara	6	4	2	4	2	2	2	2				Timisoara	Electrica		1928-48
9	Chinezul Timisoara	6	1		6				1				Timisoara	Chinezul		1913-39
10	Politehnica Timisoara	2	5	5			5	2	5				Timisoara	Dan Paltinisanu	32 019	1921
11	FC Arges Pitesti	2	3	4	2	2	4		1				Pitesti	Nicolae Dobrin	15 170	1953
12	FC Bihor Oradea	2	3	1	1	2	1	1	1				Oradea	Municipal	18 000	1902
13	FCM Resita	2	1		1	1		1					Resita	Valea Domanului	12 000	1922
14	Colentina Bucuresti	2			2								Bucharest			
	Olimpia Bucuresti	2			2								Bucharest			
	Prahova Ploiesti	2			2								Ploiesti			

RECENT LEAGUE AND CUP RECORD

	Championship						Cup		
Year	Champions	Pts	Runners-up	Pts	Third	Pts	Winners	Score	Runners-up
1995	Steaua Bucuresti	77	Universit. Craiova	68	Dinamo Bucuresti	65	Petrolul Ploiesti	1-1 5-3p	Rapid Bucuresti
1996	Steaua Bucuresti	71	National Bucuresti	60	Rapid Bucuresti	59	Steaua Bucuresti	3-1	Gloria Bistrita
1997	Steaua Bucuresti	73	National Bucuresti	68	Dinamo Bucuresti	59	Steaua Bucuresti	4-2	National Bucuresti
1998	Steaua Bucuresti	80	Rapid Bucuresti	78	Arges Pitesti	65	Rapid Bucuresti	1-0	Universit. Craiova
1999	Rapid Bucuresti	89	Dinamo Bucuresti	82	Steaua Bucuresti	66	Steaua Bucuresti	2-2 4-2p	Rapid Bucuresti
2000	Dinamo Bucuresti	84	Rapid Bucuresti	72	Ceahlaul P. Neamt	57	Dinamo Bucuresti	2-0	Universit. Craiova
2001	Steaua Bucuresti	60	Dinamo Bucuresti	51	FC Brasov	50	Dinamo Bucuresti	4-2	Rocar Bucuresti
2002	Dinamo Bucuresti	60	National Bucuresti	58	Rapid Bucuresti	50	Rapid Bucuresti	2-1	Dinamo Bucuresti
2003	Rapid Bucuresti	63	Steaua Bucuresti	56	Gloria Bistrita	45	Dinamo Bucuresti	1-0	National Bucuresti
2004	Dinamo Bucuresti	70	Steaua Bucuresti	64	Rapid Bucuresti	55	Dinamo Bucuresti	2-0	Otelul Galati
2005	Steaua Bucuresti	63	Dinamo Bucuresti	62	Rapid Bucuresti	57	Dinamo Bucuresti	1-0	Farul Constanta
2006	Steaua Bucuresti	64	Rapid Bucuresti	59	Dinamo Bucuresti	56	Rapid Bucuresti	1-0	National Bucuresti
2007	Dinamo Bucuresti	77	Steaua Bucuresti	71	CFR 1907 Cluj	69	Rapid Bucuresti	2-0	Politehn. Timisoara

ROMANIA 2006–07

LIGA I BURGER

Team	Pl	W	D	L	F	A	Pts	Dinamo	Steaua	Cluj	Rapid	Otelul	Gloria	Politehnica	Vaslui	Criaova	Unirea	Pandurii	UTA	Politehnica	Farul	Ceahlaul	National	Arges	Jiul
Dinamo Bucuresti †	34	23	8	3	63	24	77		1-0	1-0	3-1	3-0	2-0	3-1	0-0	0-0	1-2	1-0	2-0	5-0	2-1	2-0	1-0	2-1	1-0
Steaua Bucuresti †	34	21	8	5	61	22	71	2-4		4-2	1-1	3-0	2-1	3-1	3-1	3-0	3-0	0-0	1-0	3-0	2-0	6-0	2-0	3-0	3-0
CFR 1907 Cluj ‡	34	21	6	7	59	32	69	2-1	1-2		3-2	2-1	2-1	2-1	2-2	5-1	4-0	1-0	5-0	2-1	1-0	1-1	1-0	2-0	1-1
Rapid Bucuresti ‡	34	16	11	7	63	39	59	1-4	2-3	3-1		3-3	4-0	2-0	2-0	1-1	1-0	1-1	4-0	3-0	3-2	4-1	2-1	2-1	1-0
Otelul Galati	34	17	5	12	60	56	56	2-1	2-1	1-3	0-7		1-1	1-0	2-0	4-1	3-2	2-0	2-1	3-1	0-0	3-1	5-2	5-1	2-1
Gloria Bistrita	34	16	6	12	42	35	54	0-1	2-0	3-2	3-3	1-2		1-1	3-0	4-1	0-0	2-0	1-0	1-0	3-2	2-1	2-0	3-1	0-0
Politehnica Timisoara	34	15	8	11	37	33	53	1-1	0-0	3-1	0-0	1-0	1-0		2-2	1-5	1-0	1-0	2-0	0-1	1-1	2-0	1-1	3-1	1-0
FC Vaslui	34	13	12	10	41	44	50	1-2	1-0	0-0	1-1	3-1	3-2	1-0		3-3	0-0	1-0	2-5	1-1	1-3	3-2	1-0	1-0	2-0
Universitatea Craiova	34	12	12	10	39	43	48	0-4	0-0	0-1	0-0	0-2	1-2	0-1	0-0		0-0	2-2	2-1	3-3	1-0	1-0	1-0	3-1	2-0
Unirea Val'm Urziceni	34	13	8	13	30	29	47	1-1	1-2	0-0	1-1	1-0	0-1	2-0	1-0	1-2		1-0	1-0	0-2	0-1	2-0	2-0	0-0	3-0
Pandurii Târgu Jiu	34	13	5	16	26	35	44	0-3	0-0	1-3	1-1	2-1	1-0	1-0	1-2	0-2	1-0		2-0	1-0	1-0	1-1	2-1	2-0	
UTA Arad	34	11	8	15	28	39	41	1-1	0-3	1-0	0-1	1-0	1-2	1-0	1-0	1-0	3-0		0-0	0-0	1-1	1-1	1-0	0-3	
Politehnica Iasi	34	10	10	14	34	41	40	1-1	1-1	0-1	0-0	1-1	0-1	0-0	2-0	1-1	1-3	2-1	1-0		0-2	1-0	1-1	1-0	4-0
Farul Constanta	34	8	13	13	31	35	37	1-1	1-1	1-0	1-2	0-2	1-3	0-1	0-0	1-3	1-1	0-0	0-1	2-0		0-1	1-1	1-1	0-0
Ceahlaul Piatra Neamt	34	8	7	19	27	53	31	2-2	0-0	1-3	0-3	4-3	1-0	1-2	3-2	0-2	2-1	1-0	2-1	0-4	0-0		1-1	1-1	1-0
National Bucuresti	34	6	6	22	27	52	24	1-2	0-3	0-1	4-0	1-3	1-0	0-2	0-1	1-2	0-2	0-1	1-2	2-1	2-0	2-0		0-2	0-0
Arges Pitesti	34	5	9	20	23	47	24	2-3	1-0	0-0	1-2	3-1	2-0	0-2	1-1	0-0	1-1	0-0	0-1	0-2	0-1	1-0	0-3		0-1
Jiul Petrosani	34	5	5	24	15	47	20	0-1	0-2	0-2	1-0	1-2	0-1	0-1	1-3	1-2	0-1	0-2	3-1	1-2	0-0	2-0	0-1	2-0	

28/06/2006 - 23/05/2007 • † Qualified for the UEFA Champions League • ‡ Qualified for the UEFA Cup

ROMANIA 2006–07 — LIGA II SERIE 1 (2)

Team	Pl	W	D	L	F	A	Pts
Delta Tulcea	34	19	7	8	71	40	64
Gloria Buzau	34	18	8	8	56	38	62
Petrolul Ploiesti	34	17	8	9	54	39	59
Forex Brasov	34	17	5	12	45	28	56
FCM Bacau	34	17	9	8	39	21	52
CS Otopeni	34	14	9	11	38	30	51
Dunarea Galati	34	14	9	11	34	33	51
Sportul Studentesc	34	13	11	10	45	49	50
Dunarea Giurgiu	34	13	10	11	47	35	49
FC Brasov	34	12	11	11	48	38	47
FC Botosani	34	13	7	14	37	38	46
Prefabricate Modelu	34	12	9	13	48	45	45
Precizia Sacele	34	11	10	13	34	43	43
Municipal Campina	34	11	9	14	33	32	42
FC Suceava	34	10	10	14	43	50	40
FC Snagov	34	8	5	21	29	75	29
Chimia Brazi	34	7	5	22	30	57	26
CF Braila	34	4	10	20	20	60	22

11/08/2006 - 9/06/2007 • Delta declined promotion

ROMANIA 2006–07 — LIGA II SERIE 2 (2)

Team	Pl	W	D	L	F	A	Pts
Universitatea Cluj	34	21	9	4	49	21	72
Dacia Mioveni	34	17	9	8	44	26	60
Râmnicu Vâlcea	34	18	5	11	40	31	59
Apulum Alba Iulia	34	15	9	10	34	28	54
Minerul Lupeni	34	16	4	14	39	37	52
Gaz Metan Medias	34	15	6	13	54	37	51
Corvinul Hunedoara	34	12	13	9	48	37	49
FC Caracal	34	15	4	15	40	33	49
Sârmei Câmpia Turzii	34	13	8	13	31	36	47
Politehnica Timisoara-2	34	12	10	12	45	37	46
CSM Resita	34	13	7	14	38	37	46
Bihor Oradea	34	12	10	12	40	42	46
FCM Târgoviste	34	12	10	12	29	31	46
CFR Timisoara	34	13	6	15	37	45	45
Vânju Mare	34	11	8	15	28	33	41
Baia Mare	34	9	8	17	27	54	35
Auxerre Trans Lugoj	34	5	10	19	24	44	25
Unirea Dej	34	6	6	22	28	66	24

12/08/2006 - 9/06/2007

CUPA ROMANIEI 2006–07

Round of 16		Quarter-finals		Semi-finals		Final	
Rapid Bucuresti	1						
Universitatea Craiova	0	Rapid Bucuresti	2				
UTA Arad	0	Arges Pitesti	0				
Arges Pitesti	2			Rapid Bucuresti	2		
National Bucuresti	3			Pandurii Târgu Jiu	0		
FC Caracal	2	National Bucuresti	2				
Dinamo Bucuresti	0	Pandurii Târgu Jiu	3				
Pandurii Târgu Jiu	1					Rapid Bucuresti ‡	2
Steaua Bucuresti	2					Politehnica Timisoara	0
Apulum Alba Iulia	1	Steaua Bucuresti	3 5p				
Unirea Val'm Urziceni	1	Otelul Galati	3 4p				
Otelul Galati	2			Steaua Bucuresti	0		
Politehnica Iasi	1			Politehnica Timisoara	1		
Farul Constanta	0	Politehnica Iasi	1				
CFR 1907 Cluj	0	Politehnica Timisoara	2				
Politehnica Timisoara	2	All matches played in neutral venues • ‡ Qualified for the UEFA Cup					

CUP FINAL
Dan Paltinisanu, Timisoara
26-05-2007, Att: 30 000
Scorers - Mugurel Buga [15], Ianis Zicu [48]

RSA – SOUTH AFRICA

NATIONAL TEAM RECORD
JULY 10TH 2006 TO JULY 12TH 2010

PL	W	D	L	F	A	%
10	5	3	2	12	3	65

South Africa continued to bask in the after glow of being awarded the right to host the 2010 FIFA World Cup, but moved from the celebratory phase onto the hard work. While it took a little prodding and pushing from FIFA president Sepp Blatter to get the cumbersome Local Organising Committee into action, firm plans for the construction or renovation of all 10 of the proposed stadiums for 2010 were set in motion by the end of 2006 and work begun in earnest a few months later. The organising committee, as well as FIFA's presence in the country, began to grow as the momentum increased. Plans to also make South Africa competitive on the pitch were finalised when the past FIFA World Cup winner Carlos Alberto Parreira of Brazil was hired as coach, taking up his position in January. Parreira visited several months earlier to get a preview of his new charges in action, in the first two matches of the 2008 African Nations Cup qualifiers, which produced vastly contrasting performances. In the first match, with caretaker coach Pitso Mosimane in charge, South Africa bumbled through a goalless draw at home against Congo where barely 6,000 spectators bothered to turn up to watch at the cavernous Soccer City, which has a capacity of 75,000. But then, facing the prospect of falling way behind in the preliminaries, Bafana Bafana bounced back with one of their best performances to date, beating Zambia 1-0 away in Lusaka with a first-ever

INTERNATIONAL HONOURS
Qualified for the FIFA World Cup finals 1998 2002
CAF African Cup of Nations 1996   CAF Champions League Orlando Pirates 1995

international goal from captain Aaron Mokoena. The momentum continued through the qualifying campaign with two wins over Chad and a draw away with Congo which left South Africa needing a single point from their last match in the qualifiers, at home to Zambia. Parreira's reputation added a new level of intensity to the national sides, which had been in a slump in previous years. There was also an added air of efficiency around the team and, at Parreira's insistence, a strong programme of friendlies in the next months to start building a team ahead of 2010. At club level, highly successful coach Gordon Igesund won a fourth championship in the last decade as Mamelodi Sundowns retained their League title. It was the seventh championship that the Pretoria club had won, but they did lose the Cup Final, 2-0 to Ajax Cape Town, the only team that consistently beat them through a season in which Sundowns had a spell of 17 wins and two draws in 19 games between January and April. Silver Stars were the surprise package, winning the League Cup with an emphatic 3-1 triumph over Ajax and finishing second in the League. Kaizer Chiefs, the country's most popular club, finished ninth, matching their previous worst-ever position, leading to the sacking of their German coach Ernst Middendorp.

South African Football Association (SAFA)
First National Bank Stadium, PO Box 910, Johannesburg 2000, South Africa
Tel +27 11 4943522   Fax +27 11 4943013
raymond.hack@safa.net   www.safa.net
President: OLIPHANT Molefi   General Secretary: HACK Raymond
Vice-President: KHOZA Irvin   Treasurer: HULYO Gronie   Media Officer: MARAWA Gugu
Men's Coach: PARREIRA Carlos Alberto   Women's Coach: MAKALAKALANE Augustine
SAFA formed: 1991   CAF: 1992   FIFA: 1992
White shirts with yellow stripes, White shorts, White socks

RECENT INTERNATIONAL MATCHES PLAYED BY SOUTH AFRICA

2004 Opponents	Score	Venue	Comp	Scorers	Att	Referee
27-01 Benin	W 2-0	Sfax	CNr1	Nomvete 2 [58 76]	12 000	Coulibaly MLI
31-01 Nigeria	L 0-4	Monastir	CNr1		15 000	Bujsaim UAE
4-02 Morocco	D 1-1	Sousse	CNr1	Mayo [29]	6 000	Guirat TUN
30-03 Australia	L 0-1	London	Fr		16 108	Halsey ENG
5-06 Cape Verde Islands	W 2-1	Bloemfontein	WCq	Mabizela 2 [40 68]	30 000	Tessema ETH
20-06 Ghana	L 0-3	Kumasi	WCq		32 000	Diatta SEN
3-07 Burkina Faso	W 2-0	Johannesburg	WCq	Pienaar [14], Bartlett [42]	25 000	Ramanampamonjy MAD
18-08 Tunisia	W 2-0	Tunis	Fr	McCarthy [2], Arsendse [82]	4 000	Zekrini ALG
5-09 Congo DR	L 0-1	Kinshasa	WCq		85 000	Hicuburundi BDI
10-10 Uganda	W 1-0	Kampala	WCq	McCarthy [68p]	50 000	Gasingwa RWA
17-11 Nigeria	W 2-1	Johannesburg	Fr	Bartlett [2], Vilakazi [60]	39 817	Marang ZIM
2005						
9-02 Australia	D 1-1	Durban	Fr	McCarthy [12]		Lim Kee Chong MRI
26-02 Seychelles	W 3-0	Curepipe	CCr1	Mphela 2 [12 16], Chabangu [44]	3 000	Roheemun MRI
27-02 Mauritius	W 1-0	Curepipe	CCr1	Mphela [36]	3 500	Mnkantjo ZIM
26-03 Uganda	W 2-1	Johannesburg	WCq	Fortune [21p], Pienaar [71]	20 000	Chukwujekwu NGA
4-06 Cape Verde Islands	W 2-1	Praia	WCq	McCarthy [10], Buckley [12]	6 000	Benouza ALG
18-06 Ghana	L 0-2	Johannesburg	WCq		50 000	Guezzaz MAR
8-07 Mexico	W 2-1	Carson	GCr1	Evans [28], Van Heerden [41]	27 000	Sibrian SLV
10-07 Jamaica	D 3-3	Los Angeles	GCr1	Raselemane [35], Ndela [41], Nomvete [56]	30 710	Stott USA
13-07 Guatemala	D 1-1	Houston	GCr1	Nkosi [45]	45 311	Sott USA
17-07 Panama	D 1-1	Houston	GCqf	Ndlela [68]	60 050	Prendergast JAM
13-08 Zambia	D 2-2	Mmabatho	CCsf	Ndela [53], Raselemane [68]. L 8-9p		Raolimanana MAD
17-08 Iceland	L 1-4	Rejklavík	Fr	Buckley [28]		
3-09 Burkina Faso	L 1-3	Ouagadougou	WCq	Zuma [75]	25 000	Codjia BEN
7-09 Germany	L 2-4	Bremen	Fr	Bartlett [28p], McCarthy [51]	28 100	Gilewski POL
8-10 Congo DR	D 2-2	Durban	WCq	Zuma 2 [5 52]	35 000	Mbera GAB
12-11 Senegal	L 2-3	Port Elizabeth	Fr	Zuma [9], Nomvete [68]		Ndoye SEN
2006						
14-01 Egypt	W 2-1	Cairo	Fr	OG [13], McCarthy [44]		
22-01 Guinea	L 0-2	Alexandria	CNr1		10 000	Benouza ALG
26-01 Tunisia	L 0-2	Alexandria	CNr1		10 000	Evehe CMR
30-01 Zambia	L 0-1	Alexandria	CNr1		4 000	Abd El Fatah EGY
10-05 Lesotho	D 0-0	Maseru	Fr		15 000	
20-05 Swaziland	W 1-0	Gaborone	CCr1	Mhlongo [13]		Malepa BOT
21-05 Botswana	D 0-0	Gaborone	CCr1	L 5-6p		Infante MOZ
16-08 Namibia	W 1-0	Katutura	Fr	Mashego [60]		
2-09 Congo	D 0-0	Johannesburg	CNq			Aboubacar CIV
8-10 Zambia	W 1-0	Lusaka	CNq	Mokoena [28]		Maillet SEY
15-11 Egypt	L 0-1	Brentford	Fr		2 000	Styles ENG
2007						
24-03 Chad	W 3-0	N'Djamena	CNq	Moriri [32], Buckley [44], Zuma [78]		Aguidissou BEN
28-03 Bolivia	L 0-1	Johannesburg	Fr		5 000	Ramocha BOT
26-05 Malawi	D 0-0	Mbabane	CCr1	W 5-4p		Dlamini SWZ
27-05 Mauritius	W 2-0	Mbabane	CCr1	Modise 2 [43p 65]		Mufeti NAM
2-06 Chad	W 4-0	Durban	CNq	Morris [13p], Zuma 2 [23 33], Nomvete [69]		
17-06 Congo	D 1-1	Pointe Noire	CNq	Zuma [47]		

Fr = Friendly match • CN = CAF African Cup of Nations • CC = COSAFA Cup • GC = CONCACAF Gold Cup • WC = FIFA World Cup
q = qualifier • r1 = first round group • qf = quarter-final • sf = semi-final • f = final

SOUTH AFRICA NATIONAL TEAM RECORDS AND RECORD SEQUENCES

Records			Sequence records					
Victory	8-0	AUS 1955	Wins	7	1947-50, 1954-92	Clean sheets	7	1997-1997, 2002
Defeat	1-5	AUS 1947	Defeats	3	Five times	Goals scored	12	1947-1950
Player Caps	74	BARTLETT Shaun	Undefeated	15	1994-1996	Without goal	4	2006
Player Goals	29	BARTLETT Shaun	Without win	9	1997-1998, 2005	Goals against	17	2005-2006

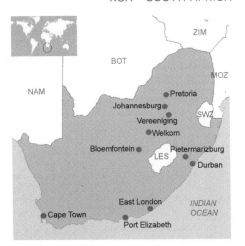

REPUBLIC OF SOUTH AFRICA

Capital	Pretoria	Language	Zulu, Xhosa, Afrikaans, Sepedi, English	Independence	1934
Population	43 997 828	Area	1 219 912 km²	Density	35 per km²	% in cities	51%
GDP per cap	$10 700	Dailling code	+27	Internet	.za	GMT + / -	+2

The Johannesburg metropolitan area has a total population of 7 372 000 and includes Johannesburg, Soweto, Pretoria, Benoni, Tembisa, Vereeniging, Boksburg, Krugersdorp, Brakpan, Verwoerdburg, Vanderbijlpark and Alberton

MEDALS TABLE

		Overall			League			Cup		T8		LCup		Africa			City	Stadium	Cap'ty	DoF
		G	S	B	G	S	B	G	S	G	S	G	S	G	S	B				
1	Kaiser Chiefs	46	19	2	10	6	2	12	5	13	5	10	3	1			Krugersdorp	Amakhosi - 2009	55 000	1970
2	Orlando Pirates	21	18	8	7	4	6	6	7	7	3		4	1		2	Johannesburg	Ellis Park	59 611	1937
3	Mamelodi Sundowns	14	13	3	7	2	3	2	4	2	4	2	2			1	Pretoria	Loftus Versfeld	51 762	1970
4	Moroka Swallows	6	7	1	1	1		4	1	2	3		2				Germiston	Germiston	18 000	1947
5	Jomo Cosmos	5	8	1	1	1		1	4	1	1	2	2			1	Katlehong	Huntersfield	45 000	1983
6	Wits University	5	5	2		2		1	1	2	3	2	1				Johannesburg	Bidvest	5 000	1921
7	Bush Bucks	4	2	1	1	1	1					3	1				Umtata	Independence	25 000	1957
8	Santos	4	1		1			2		1			1				Cape Town	Athlone	25 000	1982
9	SuperSport United	3	7	1		2	1	2	1	1	2		2				Pretoria	Loftus Versfeld	51 762	1994
10	AmaZulu	2	6	2	1	2		5		1	1						Durban	Princess Magogo	10 000	1932
11	Ajax Cape Town	2	4		1			1	1		1		1	1			Cape Town	Newlands	50 900	1999
12	Arcadia	2	2	1		1				1	2	1					Pretoria			1903
13	Witbank Aces	2	2					1	1	1	1						Witbank	Kwaguqa		1937
14	Cape Town Spurs	2	1		1	1		1									Cape Town	Greenpoint	18 000	1969
15	Bloemfontein Celtic	2		1			1	1		1							Bloemfontein	Seisa Ramabodu	20 000	1969

RECENT LEAGUE AND CUP RECORD

	Championship							Cup		
Year	Champions	Pts	Runners-up	Pts	Third	Pts		Winners	Score	Runners-up
1995	Cape Town Spurs	71	Mamelodi Sundowns	66	Orlando Pirates	60		Cape Town Spurs	3-2	Pretoria City
1996	Not played due to season adjustment							Orlando Pirates	1-0	Jomo Cosmos
1997	Manning Rangers	74	Kaiser Chiefs	66	Orlando Pirates	64		No tournament played		
1998	Mamelodi Sundowns	68	Kaiser Chiefs	63	Orlando Pirates	57		Mamelodi Sundowns	1-1 1-1 6-5p	Orlando Pirates
1999	Mamelodi Sundowns	75	Kaiser Chiefs	75	Orlando Pirates	60		SuperSport United	2-1	Kaiser Chiefs
2000	Mamelodi Sundowns	75	Orlando Pirates	64	Kaiser Chiefs	60		Kaiser Chiefs	1-0	Mamelodi Sundowns
2001	Orlando Pirates	61	Kaiser Chiefs	60	Mamelodi Sundowns	59		Santos Cape Town	1-0	Mamelodi Sundowns
2002	Santos Cape Town	64	SuperSport United	59	Orlando Pirates	57		No tournament played		
2003	Orlando Pirates	61	SuperSport United	55	Wits University	54		Santos Cape Town	2-0	Ajax Cape Town
2004	Kaiser Chiefs	63	Ajax Cape Town	57	SuperSport United	53		Moroka Swallows	3-1	Manning Rangers
2005	Kaiser Chiefs	62	Orlando Pirates	60	Mamelodi Sundowns	56		SuperSport United	1-0	Wits University
2006	Mamelodi Sundowns	57	Orlando Pirates	54	Kaiser Chiefs	50		Kaiser Chiefs	0-0 5-3p	Orlando Pirates
2007	Mamelodi Sundowns	61	Silver Stars	51	Moroka Swallows	51		Ajax Cape Town	2-0	Mamelodi Sundowns

SOUTH AFRICA 2006-07

PREMIER SOCCER LEAGUE

	Pl	W	D	L	F	A	Pts	Sundowns	Silver Stars	Swallows	Ajax	Pirates	SuperSport	Cosmos	Celtic	Chiefs	Santos	Leopards	Arrows	Wits	Benoni	AmaZulu	Maritzburg
Mamelodi Sundowns	30	18	7	5	45	17	**61**		0-0	1-0	1-2	2-1	1-0	0-0	0-0	2-1	2-1	3-0	3-0	2-0	5-2	4-0	2-1
Silver Stars	30	14	9	7	32	21	**51**	2-0		0-1	0-0	0-0	0-3	3-1	0-0	0-0	5-2	0-0	1-0	3-0	1-0	2-0	2-1
Moroka Swallows	30	14	9	7	32	24	**51**	0-1	1-0		2-0	2-2	0-0	1-2	0-0	1-1	2-0	2-2	1-0	0-4	1-0	0-0	3-2
Ajax Cape Town	30	13	8	9	34	26	**47**	2-1	1-2	1-2		2-1	0-2	3-0	2-0	0-0	1-1	0-1	2-2	1-0	2-1	1-0	2-0
Orlando Pirates	30	12	10	8	36	30	**46**	1-2	2-0	0-0	0-0		0-1	1-1	1-0	1-1	1-0	2-0	2-1	1-1	3-2	2-1	1-0
SuperSport United	30	11	11	8	38	22	**44**	0-2	1-2	1-0	0-0	0-1		1-1	2-2	2-2	1-1	0-1	5-1	1-0	5-0	2-0	3-0
Jomo Cosmos	30	12	8	10	38	34	**44**	1-0	0-1	1-1	3-0	1-2	0-0		1-0	2-1	2-1	2-1	1-2	1-1	0-1	2-0	2-1
Bloemfontein Celtic	30	12	8	10	32	32	**44**	1-3	2-1	1-3	2-1	3-1	1-2	2-0		2-0	2-2	3-2	1-0	1-0	1-0	1-0	1-1
Kaizer Chiefs	30	11	9	10	42	32	**42**	0-0	1-2	2-0	1-0	1-1	0-2	2-2	4-0		3-2	0-1	1-2	2-0	1-2	6-1	
Santos	30	9	10	11	34	40	**37**	0-0	2-0	0-3	0-2	2-3	2-1	1-0	1-0	3-1		2-1	1-1	0-0	2-0	0-0	3-0
Black Leopards	30	10	7	13	32	42	**37**	0-4	0-0	2-0	1-2	0-0	1-0	1-2	1-1	1-3	2-2		3-0	1-0	1-1	2-1	1-0
Golden Arrows	30	10	6	14	32	41	**36**	1-0	1-3	0-1	0-2	1-1	1-1	2-0	1-2	1-2	1-1	3-2		3-1	1-0	3-0	2-1
Wits University	30	9	8	13	29	34	**35**	0-2	1-1	0-2	1-1	3-2	1-0	0-4	1-0	0-1	1-2	4-0	1-0		0-0	2-1	3-0
Benoni United	30	6	10	14	22	37	**28**	0-0	0-0	0-0	1-1	2-1	0-0	0-0	0-0	4-0	1-2	0-1	2-1			2-1	0-2
AmaZulu	30	7	7	16	22	42	**28**	0-0	1-0	0-1	1-0	0-0	1-1	2-4	1-3	0-2	1-0	1-0	2-1	1-1	3-1		0-2
Maritzburg United	30	4	9	17	24	50	**21**	1-2	0-1	1-2	0-3	1-0	1-1	3-2	0-0	0-3	0-0	1-1	1-1	0-0	1-1	2-2	

23/08/2006 - 20/05/2007 • † Qualified for the CAF Champions League
Play-off semi-finals: **Pretoria University** 0-0 1-1 Winners Park; FC AZ 0-3 1-1 Amazulu • Final: Pretoria University 0-0 1-3 **AmaZulu**
Top scorers: Christopher KATONGO, Cosmos 15; Kaizer MOTAUNG Jnr, Kaizer Chiefs 12; Erwin ISAACS, Santos 11; Thembinkosi FANTENI, Ajax 11

SOUTH AFRICA 2006-07
MVELA GOLDEN LEAGUE (2)

	Pl	W	D	L	F	A	Pts
Free State Stars	30	22	4	4	74	26	**70**
Winners Park	30	13	13	4	51	34	**52**
Pretoria University	30	13	12	5	44	28	**51**
FC AK	30	14	6	10	42	30	**48**
City Pillars	30	13	10	7	53	39	**45**
Dynamos	30	13	6	11	45	36	**45**
Durban Stars	30	12	6	12	39	46	**42**
Witbank Spurs	30	12	5	13	39	44	**41**
Fidentia Rangers	30	12	4	14	43	42	**40**
Nathi Lions	30	10	8	12	33	37	**37**
Ga-Rankuwa United	30	8	11	11	35	38	**35**
Vasco da Gama	30	9	8	13	39	51	**35**
Bay United	30	7	12	11	32	43	**33**
PJ Stars Kings	30	8	8	14	32	48	**31**
Western Province Utd	30	6	7	17	35	60	**25**
OR Tambo District	30	6	4	20	29	63	**22**

12/08/2006 - 6/05/2007

ABSA CUP 2006-07

Second Round
- **Ajax Cape Town** 1
- Wits University 0
- Orlando Pirates 2 2p
- **Bloemfontein Celtic** 2 3p
- **Benoni United** 2
- Bay United 1
- AmaZulu 0
- **Santos** 2
- **Silver Stars** 1
- Ajax Cape Town-2 0
- Golden Arrows 0
- **SuperSport United** 1
- **Dynamos** 2
- Ga-Rankuwa United 1
- Maritzburg United 0
- **Mamelodi Sundowns** 1

Quarter-finals
- **Ajax Cape Town** 1
- Bloemfontein Celtic 0
- Benoni United 0
- **Santos** 1
- **Silver Stars** 0 7p
- SuperSport United 0 6p
- Dynamos 0
- **Mamelodi Sundowns** 1

Semi-finals
- **Ajax Cape Town** 1
- Santos 0
- Silver Stars 1 4p
- **Mamelodi Sundowns** 1 5p

Final
- **Ajax Cape Town** 2
- Mamelodi Sundowns 0

CUP FINAL
ABSA Stadium, Durban
26-05-2007

Scorers - Bryce Moon [16], Franklin Cale [79]

MAMELODI SUNDOWNS 2006–07

Date	Opponents	Score		Comp	Scorers
13-08-2006	Santos	W 4-1	H	SEqf	Torrealba 15, Ntwagae 18, Chabangu 38, Nyandoro 63p
9-09-2006	AmaZulu	D 0-0	A	PSL	
13-09-2006	Golden Arrows	L 0-1	A	PSL	
16-09-2006	Wits University	W 2-0	H	PSL	Torrealba 20, Moriri 74
20-09-2006	Moroka Swallows	W 1-0	A	PSL	Mabedi OG 54
23-09-2006	SuperSport United	L 0-2	A	SEsf	
30-09-2006	Bloemfontein Celtic	D 0-0	H	PSL	
14-10-2006	Kaizer Chiefs	D 0-0	A	PSL	
22-10-2006	Black Leopards	W 3-0	H	PSL	Sapula 33, Moriri 57, Ndlela 68
29-10-2006	AmaZulu	W 2-1	H	LCr1	Moriri 2 95+ 106
8-11-2006	Santos	D 0-0	A	PSL	
11-11-2006	SuperSport United	W 1-0	H	PSL	Sapula 65
18-11-2006	Black Leopards	W 3-1	H	LCqf	Kannemeyer 12, Moriri 45, Chabangu 72
26-11-2006	Maritzburg United	W 2-1	A	PSL	Mhlongo 42, Torrealba 54
3-12-2006	Ajax Cape Town	D 1-1	N	LCsf	Torrealba 38. L 3-5p
9-12-2006	Ajax Cape Town	L 1-2	H	PSL	Chabangu 73
13-12-2006	Benoni United	W 5-2	H	PSL	Sapula 3 24 41 58, Torrealba 2 67 76
20-12-2006	Silver Stars	D 0-0	H	PSL	
10-01-2007	Jomo Cosmos	L 0-1	A	PSL	
13-01-2007	AmaZulu	W 4-0	H	PSL	Torrealba 3, Chabangu 52, Ndlovu.P 78, Moriri 90
20-01-2007	Golden Arrows	W 3-0	H	PSL	Moriri 2 22 40, Dladla 47
27-01-2007	Royal Leopards - SWZ	W 4-2	H	CLr1	Torrealba 3 35 52 76, Moriri 72
3-02-2007	Kaizer Chiefs	W 2-1	H	PSL	Torrealba 10, Chabangu 51
11-02-2007	Royal Leopards - SWZ	W 2-0	A	CLr1	Chabangu 63, Ndlovu.P 84
14-02-2007	Orlando Pirates	W 2-1	H	PSL	Chabangu 22, Moriri 60p
17-02-2007	Moroka Swallows	W 1-0	H	PSL	Moriri 73
21-02-2007	Bloemfontein Celtic	W 3-1	A	PSL	Chabangu 12, Moriri 2 48 60
25-02-2007	YeboYes United	W 2-1	H	CUPr1	Torrealba 2 23 50
28-02-2007	Wits University	W 2-0	A	PSL	Torrealba 25, Chabangu 45
4-03-2007	GD Maputo - MOZ	D 1-1	A	CLr2	Moriri 13
7-03-2007	Black Leopards	W 4-0	A	PSL	Torrealba 16, Moriri 60, Sapula 2 82 93+
10-03-2007	Santos	W 2-1	H	PSL	Ntwagae 19, Sapula 65
14-03-2007	Maritzburg United	W 1-0	A	CUPr2	Apataki 89
17-03-2007	GD Maputo - MOZ	W 2-0	H	CLr2	Dladla 12, Moriri 88
31-03-2007	SuperSport United	W 2-0	A	PSL	Sapula 44, Sheppard 92+
7-04-2007	Al Ahly - EGY	D 2-2	H	CLr3	Ntwagae 78, Torrealba 88
11-04-2007	Maritzburg United	W 2-1	H	PSL	Dladla 8, Ndlovu.P 91+
14-04-2007	Dynamos	W 1-0	H	CUPqf	Moriri 70
20-04-2007	Al Ahly - EGY	L 0-2	A	CLr3	
25-04-2007	Silver Stars	L 0-2	A	PSL	
28-04-2007	Ajax Cape Town	L 1-2	A	PSL	Moriri 84p
2-05-2007	Silver Stars	D 1-1	N	CUPsf	Sheppard 78, W 5-4p
5-05-2007	EGS Gafsa - TUN	W 2-1	H	CCir	Chabangu 41, Sapula 57
9-05-2007	Orlando Pirates	W 2-1	A	PSL	Apataki 34, Mhlongo 60
13-05-2007	Benoni United	D 0-0	A	PSL	
16-05-2007	Jomo Cosmos	D 0-0	H	PSL	
19-05-2007	EGS Gafsa - TUN	D 1-1	A	CCir	Ndlovu 15
26-05-2007	Ajax Cape Town	L 0-2	N	CUPf	

PSL = Premier Soccer League • SE = SAA Supa8 Cup • LC = League Cup • CL = CAF Champions League • CUP = ABSA Cup
CC = CAF Confederation Cup • pr = preliminary round • r1 = first round • r2 = second round • qf = quarter-final • sf = semi-final • f = final
ir = intermediate round • H = Super Stadium • **H** = Loftus Stadium • *H* = Johannesburg Stadium • N = ABSA Stadium, Durban

SAA SUPA 8 CUP 2006

First Round		Semi-finals		Final	
Kaizer Chiefs	2				
Golden Arrows	0	**Kaizer Chiefs**	2		
Silver Stars	1	Moroka Swallows	1		
Moroka Swallows	2			**Kaizer Chiefs**	1
Mamelodi Sundowns	4			SuperSport United	0
Santos	1	Mamelodi Sundowns	1		
Orlando Pirates	1 6p	**SuperSport United**	2	21-10-2006	
SuperSport United	1 7p			Scorer - Rotson Kilambe 62	

AJAX CAPE TOWN 2006–07

Date	Opponents		Score		Comp	Scorers
27-08-2006	Benoni United	D	1-1	A	PSL	Shumana [43]
9-09-2006	Golden Arrows	D	2-2	H	PSL	Shumana [2], Tshinyama [65]
13-09-2006	Wits University	D	1-1	A	PSL	Moon [38]
17-09-2006	Kaizer Chiefs	D	0-0	H	PSL	
20-09-2006	Black Leopards	W	2-1	A	PSL	Cale 2 [4 83]
30-09-2006	Moroka Swallows	L	1-2	H	PSL	Fanteni [83]
15-10-2006	Bloemfontein Celtic	L	1-2	A	PSL	Evans [71]
21-10-2006	Santos	D	1-1	H	PSL	Mwafulirwa [56]
1-11-2006	Golden Arrows	D	1-1	H	LCr1	Siwahla [118]. W 4-2p
8-11-2006	SuperSport United	D	0-0	A	PSL	
11-11-2006	Maritzburg United	W	2-0	H	PSL	Fanteni 2 [4 25]
22-11-2006	Moroka Swallows	W	2-1	H	LCqf	Fanteni [25], Dikulu [51p]
26-11-2006	Silver Stars	D	0-0	A	PSL	
3-12-2006	Mamelodi Sundowns	D	1-1	N	LCsf	Fanteni [43]. W 5-3p
9-12-2006	Mamelodi Sundowns	W	2-1	A	PSL	Evans [84], Paulse [92+]
16-12-2006	Silver Stars	L	1-3	N	LCf	Bageta [85p]
20-12-2006	Orlando Pirates	W	2-1	H	PSL	Carelse [4], Fanteni [87]
5-01-2007	Benoni United	W	2-1	H	PSL	Mwafulirwa 2 [25 84]
10-01-2007	AmaZulu	L	0-1	A	PSL	
17-01-2007	Golden Arrows	W	2-0	A	PSL	Fanteni [27], Scott [39]
20-01-2007	Wits University	W	1-0	H	PSL	Carelse [15]
24-01-2007	Jomo Cosmos	W	3-0	H	PSL	Fanteni 2 [11 66], Scott [42]
27-01-2007	Kaizer Chiefs	L	0-1	A	PSL	
2-02-2007	Bloemfontein Celtic	W	2-0	H	PSL	Jagers [29], Fanteni [88]
11-02-2007	Moroka Swallows	L	0-2	A	PSL	
16-02-2007	Black Leopards	L	0-1	H	PSL	
25-02-2007	Fidentia Rangers	W	2-0	A	CUPr1	Paulse [19], Cale [83]
10-03-2007	SuperSport United	L	0-2	H	PSL	
17-03-2007	Wits University	W	1-0	H	CUPr2	
31-03-2007	Maritzburg United	W	3-0	A	PSL	Cale 2 [55 88], Fanteni [70]
7-04-2007	Silver Stars	L	1-2	H	PSL	Scott [52]
15-04-2007	Bloemfontein Celtic	W	1-0	A	CUPqf	Fanteni [2]
22-04-2007	Orlando Pirates	D	0-0	A	PSL	
28-04-2007	Mamelodi Sundowns	W	2-1	H	PSL	Moon [31], Ngobeni [55]
6-05-2007	Santos	W	1-0	N	CUPsf	Fanteni [2]
12-05-2007	Jomo Cosmos	L	0-3	A	PSL	
19-05-2007	AmaZulu	W	1-0	H	PSL	Fanteni [54]
26-05-2007	Mamelodi Sundowns	W	2-0	N	CUPf	Moon [16], Cale [79]

PSL = Premier Soccer League • SE = SAA Supa 8 Cup • LC = League Cup • CUP = ABSA Cup
r1 = first round • r2 = second round • qf = quarter–final • sf = semi–final • f = final
H = Green Point • H = Kimberley Stadium • H = Newlands • H = Athlone Stadium • N = ABSA Stadium, Durban

TELKOM KNOCK–OUT LEAGUE CUP 2006

First Round		Quarter–finals		Semi–finals		Final	
Silver Stars	1 4p						
Bloemfontein Celtic	1 3p	Silver Stars	2				
Wits University	1	Kaizer Chiefs	1				
Kaizer Chiefs	2			Silver Stars	4		
Olando Pirates	4			Santos	3		
Maritzburg United	2	Orlando Pirates	0				
Santos	0	Santos	1				
Santos	1					Silver Stars	3
Mamelodi Sundowns	2					Ajax Cape Town	1
AmaZulu	1	Mamelodi Sundowns	3				
SuperSport United	1	Black Leopards	1				
Black Leopards	2			Mamelodi Sundowns	1 3p		
Moroka Swallows	2			Ajax Cape Town	1 5p		
Benoni Premier Utd	1	Moroka Swallows	1				
Golden Arrows	1 2p	Ajax Cape Town	2				
Ajax Cape Town	1 4p						

CUP FINAL

Super Stadium, Pretoria, 16-12-2006

Scorers – Hareiapha Marumo 3 [9 34 40] for Silver Stars; Serge Bageta [85p] for Ajax

RUS – RUSSIA

NATIONAL TEAM RECORD
JULY 10TH 2006 TO JULY 12TH 2010

PL	W	D	L	F	A	%
9	5	3	1	13	5	72.2

FIFA/COCA-COLA WORLD RANKING

1993	1994	1995	1996	1997	1998	1999	2000	2001	2002	2003	2004	2005	2006	High		Low	
14	13	5	7	12	40	18	21	21	23	24	32	34	22	3	04/96	40	12/98

2006–2007											
08/06	09/06	10/06	11/06	12/06	01/07	02/07	03/07	04/07	05/07	06/07	07/07
33	39	33	23	22	24	27	23	16	17	24	23

The number of foreign players in the Russian League became a big issue during the season, prompting even president Putin to complain about the effect it was having on the national team. At the start of the 2006 season, over half of the players on the books of the 16 Premier League clubs were foreigners, a positive reflection on the growing status of the League perhaps, but for Guus Hiddink, the first foreigner to manage the national team, it made the job of qualifying for the Euro 2008 finals increasingly difficult with Russian players being overshadowed by glamourous imports. Four wins and three draws in the first seven games was not a bad start to the campaign

INTERNATIONAL HONOURS
Qualified for the FIFA World Cup finals 1994 2002 UEFA European Championship 1960 UEFA U-17 Championship 2006 UEFA Women's U-19 2005

but there was growing scepticism in the press as to the chances of making it to the finals. In this brave new era of Russian football, it's ironic that the most successful team is one that so vividly symbolises the old Soviet era - CSKA, the team of the army. CSKA won the League in 2006 for the third time in four seasons, but only just. They finished level on points with Spartak but won the title having won more games. Another of the old Soviet Stalwarts, Torpedo Moskva, experienced relegation for the first time since joining the top division in 1936. Lokomotiv Moskva won the Cup in May 2007 with Scotland's Gary O'Connor scoring the only goal in the victory over FK Moskva.

THE FIFA BIG COUNT OF 2006

	Male	Female		Total
Number of players	5 105 014	697 522	Referees and Assistant Referees	36 530
Professionals	3 724		Admin, Coaches, Technical, Medical	223 300
Amateurs 18+	582 383		Number of clubs	13 840
Youth under 18	196 170		Number of teams	55 350
Unregistered	1 443 800		Clubs with women's teams	489
Total players	5 802 536		Players as % of population	4.06%

Football Union of Russia (RFU)
8 Luzhnetskaya Naberezhnaja, Moscow 119 992, Russia
Tel +7 495 6372056   Fax +7 501 4867997
rfs@roc.ru   www.rfs.ru
President: MUTKO Vitaliy   General Secretary: KALAKOUTSKI Evgeny
Vice-President: SIMONIAN Nikita   Treasurer: MIRONOVA Svetlana   Media Officer: MALOSOLOV Andrey
Men's Coach: HIDDINK Guus   Women's Coach: BYSTRITSKIY Yury
RFU formed: 1912   UEFA: 1992   FIFA: 1992
White shirts with blue trimmings, White shorts, White socks or Blue shirts with white trimmings, Blue shorts, Blue socks

RECENT INTERNATIONAL MATCHES PLAYED BY RUSSIA

2003	Opponents	Score		Venue	Comp	Scorers	Att	Referee
12-02	Cyprus	W	1-0	Limassol	Fr	Khokhlov [43]	300	Efthimiadis GRE
29-03	Albania	L	1-3	Shkoder	ECq	Karyaka [77]	16 000	Allaerts BEL
30-04	Georgia	L	0-1	Tbilisi	ECq		11 000	Wack GER
7-06	Switzerland	D	2-2	Basel	ECq	Ignashevich 2 [24 67p]	30 500	Dauden Ibanez ESP
20-08	Israel	L	1-2	Moscow	Fr	Semak [86]	5 000	Ishchenko UKR
6-09	Republic of Ireland	D	1-1	Dublin	ECq	Ignashevich [42]	36 000	Michel SVK
10-09	Switzerland	W	4-1	Moscow	ECq	Bulykin 3 [20 33 59], Mostovoi [72]	29 000	Collina ITA
11-10	Georgia	W	3-1	Moscow	ECq	Bulykin [29], Titov [45], Sychev [73]	30 000	Plautz AUT
15-11	Wales	D	0-0	Moscow	ECpo		29 000	Cortez Batista POR
19-11	Wales	L	0-1	Cardiff	ECpo		73 062	Mejuto Gonzalez ESP
2004								
31-03	Bulgaria	D	2-2	Sofia	Fr	Sychev 2 [9 31]	14 938	Alves Garcia POR
28-04	Norway	L	2-3	Oslo	Fr	Radimov [85], Kirichenko [90]	11 435	Wegereef NED
25-05	Austria	D	0-0	Graz	Fr		9 600	Vuorela FIN
12-06	Spain	L	0-1	Faro-Loule	ECrl		28 182	Meier SUI
16-06	Portugal	L	0-2	Lisbon	ECrl		59 273	Hauge NOR
20-06	Greece	W	2-1	Faro-Loule	ECrl	Kirichenko [2], Bulykin [17]	24 347	Veissiere FRA
18-08	Lithuania	W	4-3	Moscow	Fr	Khokhlov [22], Karyaka [53], Bulykin [66], Sychev [88]	3 500	Mikulski POL
4-09	Slovakia	D	1-1	Moscow	WCq	Bulykin [14]	11 500	Mejuto Gonzalez ESP
9-10	Luxembourg	W	4-0	Luxembourg	WCq	Sychev 3 [56 69 86], Arshavin [62]	3 670	Braamhaar NED
13-10	Portugal	L	1-7	Lisbon	WCq	Arshavin [79]	27 258	Vassaras GRE
17-11	Estonia	W	4-0	Krasnodar	WCq	Karyaka [23], Izmailov [25], Sychev [32], Loskov [67p]	29 000	Busacca SUI
2005								
9-02	Italy	L	0-2	Cagliari	Fr		15 700	Michel SVK
26-03	Liechtenstein	W	2-1	Vaduz	WCq	Kerzhakov [23], Karyaka [37]	2 400	Berntsen NOR
30-03	Estonia	D	1-1	Tallinn	WCq	Arshavin [18]	8 850	Paparesta ITA
4-06	Latvia	W	2-0	Sankt Peterburg	WCq	Arshavin [56], Loskov [78p]	21 575	Poulat FRA
8-06	Germany	D	2-2	Mönchengladbach	Fr	Anyukov [26], Arshavin [91+]	46 228	Plautz AUT
17-08	Latvia	D	1-1	Riga	WCq	Arshavin [24]	10 000	Poll ENG
3-09	Liechtenstein	W	2-0	Moscow	WCq	Kerzhakov 2 [27 66]	18 123	Hyytia FIN
7-09	Portugal	D	0-0	Moscow	WCq		28 800	Merk GER
8-10	Luxembourg	W	5-1	Moscow	WCq	Izmailov [6], Kerzhakov [17], Pavluchenko [69], Kirichenko 2 [74 93+]	20 000	Tudor ROU
12-10	Slovakia	D	0-0	Bratislava	WCq		22 317	Rosetti ITA
2006								
1-03	Brazil	L	0-1	Moscow	Fr		19 000	Busacca SUI
27-05	Spain	D	0-0	Albacete	Fr		20 000	Ferreira POR
16-08	Latvia	W	1-0	Moscow	Fr	Pogrebnyak [93+]	25 600	Gilewski POL
6-09	Croatia	D	0-0	Moscow	ECq		27 500	Mejuto Gonzalez ESP
7-10	Israel	D	1-1	Moscow	ECq	Arshavin [5]	22 000	Meyer GER
11-10	Estonia	W	2-0	St Petersburg	ECq	Pogrebnyak [78], Sychev [91+]	21 517	Braamhaar NED
15-11	Macedonia FYR	W	2-0	Skopje	ECq	Bystrov [18], Arshavin [32]	13 000	Allaerts BEL
2007								
7-02	Netherland	L	1-4	Amsterdam	Fr	Bystrov [76]	24 589	Clattenburg ENG
24-03	Estonia	W	2-0	Tallinn	ECq	Kerzhakov.A 2 [66 78]	8 212	Ceferin SVN
2-06	Andorra	W	4-0	St Petersburg	ECq	Kerzhakov.A 3 [8 16 49], Sychev [71]	21 520	Skjerven NOR
6-06	Croatia	D	0-0	Zagreb	ECq		36 194	Michel SVK

Fr = Friendly match • EC = UEFA EURO 2004/2008 • WC = FIFA World Cup • q = qualifier • po = play-off • r1 = first round group

RUSSIA NATIONAL TEAM RECORDS AND RECORD SEQUENCES

Records			Sequence records				
Victory	7-0	SMR 1995	Wins	12	1995-1996	Clean sheets	4	1992-93, 2000
Defeat	0-16	GER 1912	Defeats	6	1998	Goals scored	23	1998-2001
Player Caps	109	ONOPKO Victor	Undefeated	17	1995-1996	Without goal	3	Three times
Player Goals	26	BESCHASTNYKH Vladimir	Without win	8	1912-1914, 1998	Goals against	8	Three times

RUSSIAN FEDERATION; ROSSIYSKAYA FEDERATSIYA

Capital	Moscow	Language	Russian	Independence	1991
Population	141 377 752	Area	17 075 200 km²	Density	8 per km²	% in cities	76%
GDP per cap	$8 900	Dailling code	+7	Internet	.ru	GMT + / -	+2/12

MEDALS TABLE

		Overall			League			Cup			Europe			City	Stadium	Cap'ty	DoF
		G	S	B	G	S	B	G	S		G	S	B					
1	Spartak Moskva	12	4	4	9	2	2	3	2				2	Moscow	Luzhniki	84 745	1922
2	CSKA Moskva	7	6	1	3	3	1	3	3		1			Moscow	Dinamo	36 540	1911
3	Lokomotiv Moskva	7	5	6	2	4	4	5	1				2	Moscow	Lokomotiv	30 979	1923
4	Dinamo Moskva	1	3	3		1	3	1	2					Moscow	Dinamo	36 540	1923
5	Zenit St Petersburg	1	2	1		1	1	1	1					Saint Petersburg	Petrovski	21 838	1925
6	Spartak Vladikavkaz	1	2		1	2								Vladikavkaz	Republican	32 464	1937
7	Topedo Moskva		1					1	1					Moscow	Luzhniki	84 745	1924
8	Terek Groznyi	1						1						Groznyi	Tsentralny (Pyatigorsk)	10 300	1946
9	Rotor Volgograd		3	1		2	1		1					Volgograd	Rotor	38 000	1929
10	Krylya Sovetov Samara		1	1				1	1					Samara	Metallurg	35 330	1942

RUSSIAN CLUBS IN SOVIET FOOTBALL

2	Spartak Moskva	22	17	10	12	12	9	10	5				1
3	Dinamo Moskva	17	17	7	11	11	5	6	5		1	2	
4	CSKA Moskva	12	7	6	7	4	6	5	3				
5	Torpedo Moskva	9	12	6	3	3	6	6	9				
10	Zenit Leningrad	2	3	1	1		1	1	3				

RECENT LEAGUE AND CUP RECORD

	Championship						Cup		
Year	Champions	Pts	Runners-up	Pts	Third	Pts	Winners	Score	Runners-up
1995	Spartak Vladikavkaz	71	Lokomotiv Moskva	65	Spartak Moskva	63	Dinamo Moskva	0-0 8-7p	Rotor Volograd
1996	Spartak Moskva	72	Alania Vladikavkaz	72	Rotor Volgograd	70	Lokomotiv Moskva	3-2	Spartak Moskva
1997	Spartak Moskva	73	Rotor Volgograd	68	Dinamo Moskva	68	Lokomotiv Moskva	2-0	Dinamo Moskva
1998	Spartak Moskva	59	CSKA Moskva	56	Lokomotiv Moskva	55	Spartak Moskva	1-0	Lokomotiv Moskva
1999	Spartak Moskva	72	Lokomotiv Moskva	65	CSKA Moskva	55	Zenit St-Peterburg	3-1	Dynamo Moskva
2000	Spartak Moskva	70	Lokomotiv Moskva	62	Torpedo Moskva	55	Lokomotiv Moskva	3-2	CSKA Moskva
2001	Spartak Moskva	60	Lokomotiv Moskva	56	Zenit St-Peterburg	56	Lokomotiv Moskva	2-1	Anzhi Makhachkala
2002	Lokomotiv Moskva	66	CSKA Moskva	66	Spartak Moskva	55	CSKA Moskva	2-0	Zenit St-Peterburg
2003	CSKA Moskva	59	Zenit St-Peterburg	56	Rubin Kazan	53	Spartak Moskva	1-0	FK Rostov
2004	Lokomotiv Moskva	61	CSKA Moskva	60	Krylya S. Samara	56	Terek Groznyi	1-0	Krylya S. Samara
2005	CSKA Moskva	62	Spartak Moskva	56	Lokomotiv Moskva	56	CSKA Moskva	1-0	FK Khimki
2006	CSKA Moskva	58	Spartak Moskva	58	Lokomotiv Moskva	53	CSKA Moskva	3-0	Spartak Moskva
2007							Lokomotiv Moskva	1-0	FK Moskva

RUSSIA 2006

PREMIER LEAGUE

	Pl	W	D	L	F	A	Pts	CSKA	Spartak	Lokomotiv	Zenit	Rubin	FK Moskva	Luch	Tomsk	Nalchik	Krylya	Saturn	Rostov	Amkar	Dinamo	Torpedo	Shinnik
CSKA Moskva †	30	17	7	6	47	28	58		2-2	1-2	1-0	2-1	2-1	2-1	2-0	2-1	1-1	1-0	1-2	2-0	1-2	2-0	5-1
Spartak Moskva †	30	15	13	2	60	36	58	1-1		2-1	1-0	3-0	3-3	1-1	3-1	1-0	3-2	1-1	5-2	4-1	3-2	2-0	3-1
Lokomotiv Moskva ‡	30	15	8	7	47	34	53	3-2	0-0		3-1	4-4	0-1	3-0	1-1	2-3	0-1	0-0	1-0	0-0	2-0	0-0	1-0
Zenit St Petersburg ‡	30	13	11	6	42	30	50	0-0	1-4	4-1		1-0	1-1	3-1	0-0	4-0	1-0	1-1	1-1	2-0	0-0	2-1	1-0
Rubin Kazan	30	13	7	10	43	37	46	1-0	2-0	2-4	3-0		2-0	1-0	2-0	0-0	2-1	0-3	2-1	1-0	0-1	1-1	0-0
FK Moskva	30	10	13	7	41	37	43	0-1	3-3	0-1	0-0	0-5		2-1	0-0	1-1	1-0	2-1	4-0	1-0	1-1	1-1	4-1
Luch Vladivostock	30	12	5	13	37	39	41	0-4	1-0	1-1	0-2	2-1	1-1		2-1	1-0	3-2	2-0	4-2	3-1	3-1	2-0	1-0
Tom Tomsk	30	11	8	11	35	33	41	0-1	2-2	3-1	2-2	4-0	1-0	2-1		1-0	2-1	0-0	3-1	1-3	1-0	0-0	3-1
Spartak Nalchik	30	11	8	11	33	32	41	0-1	2-2	0-1	1-1	3-1	2-2	0-0	1-0		1-1	2-0	3-1	2-1	1-0	0-0	2-1
Krylya Sovetov Samara	30	10	8	12	37	35	38	2-0	0-1	1-2	3-2	0-0	0-4	2-1	2-1	1-2		0-0	1-0	6-1	1-0	2-0	2-0
Saturn Ramenskoe	30	7	16	7	29	24	37	2-2	1-1	1-1	0-0	1-2	1-1	1-0	2-1	1-1	1-4		0-0	0-0	3-0	0-0	3-0
FK Rostov	30	10	6	14	42	48	36	1-2	3-4	1-2	1-3	2-1	4-0	1-0	2-1	2-1	2-2	0-2		1-1	2-1	1-1	0-0
Amkar Perm	30	8	11	11	22	36	35	0-0	1-3	1-3	1-3	0-0	2-2	0-0	0-0	1-0	1-0	1-0	1-0		3-2	1-0	1-0
Dinamo Moskva	30	8	10	12	31	40	34	2-3	0-0	2-0	2-2	2-2	1-1	2-1	2-1	1-0	1-1	1-1	0-1	0-0		2-1	1-1
Torpedo Moskva	30	3	13	14	22	40	22	2-2	1-1	1-4	1-2	1-2	0-2	2-1	1-2	2-0	1-1	0-3	0-2	0-0	3-0		1-1
Shinnik Yaroslavl	30	1	8	21	17	56	11	0-1	1-1	1-3	1-2	1-5	1-2	1-3	0-1	0-1	0-0	1-6	0-0	1-2	1-1		

17/03/2006 - 26/11/2006 • † Qualified for the UEFA Champions League • ‡ Qualified for the UEFA Cup
Top scorers: Roman PAVLYUCHENKO, Spartak Moskva 18; JO ALVES, CSKA 14; Alejandro DOMINGUEZ, Rubin 13; Dimitriy LOSKOV, Lokomotiv 13; Pavel POGREBNYAK, Tom 13

RUSSIA 2006

FIRST DIVISION (2)

	Pl	W	D	L	F	A	Pts	Khimki	Kuban	Ural	KamAZ	SKA	Sodovik	SIBIR	Terek	Dinamo Bry	Avangard	Volgar	Salyut	Mashuk	Baltika	Anzhi	Dinamo M.	Lada	Spartak NN	Fakel	Oryol	Metallurg	Angusht
FK Khimki	42	30	9	3	83	30	99		2-0	1-1	1-0	1-1	2-0	1-0	3-0	2-0	1-1	4-0	2-1	2-0	4-0	4-3	3-2	2-0	2-0	3-0	2-0	2-1	2-0
Kuban Krasnodar	42	30	7	5	92	25	97	1-1		0-0	2-0	1-1	1-0	0-0	3-1	3-0	1-0	2-1	3-0	7-0	2-0	1-0	5-2	1-0	4-2	5-0	2-1	4-0	6-0
Ural Yekaterinburg	42	27	9	6	67	23	90	2-1	1-0		2-1	2-1	1-1	3-1	2-0	2-1	5-0	2-1	2-0	1-0	0-0	2-0	0-0	2-0	0-2	2-1	1-0	4-0	3-0
KamAZ Chelny	42	22	11	9	54	26	77	1-1	1-1	1-0		4-1	1-1	0-1	2-0	2-0	2-0	1-0	0-1	0-0	0-0	0-1	1-2	1-2	1-1	1-0	5-0	3-0	2-1
SKA Khabarovsk	42	21	8	13	67	40	71	1-2	1-3	0-1	0-0		3-0	2-0	1-0	4-2	1-1	2-0	2-2	0-1	1-2	2-2	0-1	1-1	2-2	1-2	1-3	0-0	3-0
Sodovik Sterlitamak	42	18	15	9	59	35	69	2-2	2-0	1-0	0-1	0-0		3-1	1-1	1-0	3-2	0-3	0-1	0-4	0-1	3-0	3-0	0-0	0-0	1-3	0-0	5-2	
SIBIR Novosibirsk	42	19	8	15	67	45	65	1-0	1-3	1-2	1-1	3-1	0-0		0-1	0-1	1-1	1-0	3-1	3-1	2-0	4-0	4-0	0-1	2-1	2-0	4-1	4-1	8-0
Terek Groznyi	42	18	8	16	48	47	62	2-3	1-2	1-0	0-1	1-3	0-2	2-0		1-0	1-0	0-0	2-0	0-0	1-3	2-0	1-1	1-2	1-3	0-1	0-1	2-2	1-3
Dinamo Bryansk	42	17	10	15	42	38	61	4-1	1-0	1-0	0-1	0-0	2-1	1-0	0-0		1-1	1-1	1-3	2-0	0-1	1-1	1-0	0-0	1-0	1-0	1-0	1-0	1-2
Avangard Kursk	42	16	13	13	45	38	61	0-1	1-0	0-2	0-1	1-0	0-1	0-3	4-2	0-1		1-0	3-1	0-1	1-2	1-1	0-4	0-1	1-0	1-1			2-0
Volgar Astrakhan	42	17	9	16	45	47	60	2-1	0-1	1-0	0-1	0-0	1-0	0-0	0-3	1-7	1-1		2-1	2-1	0-0	2-3	1-0	2-1	3-0	5-0	2-1	2-0	1-0
Salyut Belgorod	42	15	11	16	46	58	56	1-2	0-3	1-0	0-3	1-0	1-1	1-1	0-0	0-0	1-2	2-2		2-1	3-2	1-0	3-1	2-1	1-1	0-0	0-0	0-4	2-1
Mashuk Pyatigorsk	42	16	7	19	41	56	55	1-4	0-1	1-3	1-0	1-4	0-1	1-2	0-1	1-1	0-3	1-3	0-0		3-1	3-2	1-1	2-1	3-1	1-0	1-0	0-0	0-4
Baltika Kaliningrad	42	14	13	15	41	56	55	2-4	0-0	2-2	2-1	0-2	1-3	1-1	1-2	0-0	1-2	1-1	1-0	1-1		0-1	2-1	2-0	1-0	0-0	2-1	1-0	2-1
Anzhi Makhachkala	42	15	8	19	57	66	53	0-2	1-3	0-2	1-2	2-1	1-1	2-3	0-0	1-3	0-3	3-2	0-1	2-3	1-1		1-2	3-0	1-0	0-2	2-1	2-1	2-1
Dinamo Makhachkala	42	13	12	17	56	54	51	2-3	2-1	1-1	1-2	0-1	1-0	3-2	0-1	1-0	0-1	2-3	1-0	0-0	0-2	3-1		0-0	2-1	1-0	1-1	4-0	2-0
Lada Togliatti	42	13	6	23	38	63	45	0-2	0-7	0-2	1-0	0-3	1-1	2-0	2-0	2-1	0-2	2-1	2-2	2-0	2-1	2-1	0-2		1-1	1-0	1-2	0-2	0-1
Sp. Nizhniy Novgorod	42	10	13	19	46	60	43	1-3	0-1	0-0	0-2	2-1	1-3	1-0	0-1	1-0	0-0	0-0	3-2	2-1	3-2	1-3	1-4	4-0		2-2	0-0	2-0	0-1
Fakel Voronezh	42	10	12	20	27	54	42	0-0	0-2	0-5	0-0	0-1	0-2	1-3	2-1	0-2	1-0	1-0	0-2	0-0	0-0	0-0	1-0	1-1	1-1		0-0	2-0	4-2
FK Oryol §6	42	8	11	23	35	72	29	0-3	1-2	0-2	1-4	0-3	1-3	2-1	1-1	0-3	0-1	1-0	1-1	2-1	2-2	1-2	2-1	1-2	7-1	0-2		2-1	1-0
Metallurg Krasnoyarsk	42	5	6	31	30	80	21	0-1	1-2	1-0	2-0	0-4	1-2	2-0	0-1	3-0	3-0	2-0	1-3	2-3	2-2	1-2	4-0	1-2	2-2	4-0	1-2		2-0
Angusht Nazran	42	3	4	35	32	105	13	1-1	0-3	1-3	0-1	1-4	1-2	2-4	2-2	1-4	2-2	4-2	3-3	2-0	2-3	1-1	3-1	1-0	1-0	2-0	3-1	0-1	

26/03/2006 - 5/11/2006 • Alania Vladikavkaz and Lokomotiv Chita relegated before the start of the season • § = points deducted
Top scorers: Yevgeniy ALKHIMOV, Ural 25; Dmitriy AKIMOV, Sibir 23; Robert ZEBELYAN, Kuban 23; Andrei TIKHONOV, Khimki 22

RUSSIAN CUP 2006-07

Fifth Round

Team	Leg 1	Leg 2
Lokomotiv Moskva *	4	1
Anzhi Makhachkala	2	1
Luch Vladivostock	0	3
Dinamo Makhachkala *	4	0
Tom Tomsk	4	2
Dinamo Kirov *	0	1
Sartak Nizhniy Novgorod*	1	0
Dinamo Moskva	3	2
Zenit St Petersburg	2	2
FK Chita *	1	1
Metallurg Krasnoyarsk	1	1
Saturn Ramenskoe *	4	2
SIBIR Novosibirsk	1	2
Spartak Nalchik *	1	0
Ural Yekaterinburg *	0	2
Spartak Moskva	1	2
Dinamo Bryansk *	2	1
Shinnik Yaroslavl	0	3
Fakel Voronezh *	0	1
Torpedo Moskva *	0	3
Rubin Kazan	3	2
Zenit St Petrsburg-2 *	0	0
FK Khimki *	0	1
FK Rostov	2	0
Krylya Sovetov Samara *	1	4
Kuban Krasnodar	1	1
Mordovia Saransk	0	1
CSKA Moskva *	4	0
Amkar Perm *	3	2
Angusht Nazran	0	1
Terek Grozny *	4	0
FK Moskva	1	4

Sixth Round

Team	Leg 1	Leg 2
Lokomotiv Moskva	w-o	
Dinamo Makhachkala		
Tom Tomsk	0	1
Dinamo Moskva *	2	0
Zenit St Petersburg *	1	1
Saturn Ramenskoe	0	1
SIBIR Novosibirsk	0	1
Spartak Moskva *	1	3
Dinamo Bryansk	1	0
Torpedo Moskva *	0	0
Rubin Kazan	1	0
FK Rostov *	3	1
Krylya Sovetov Samara	0	2
CSKA Moskva *	0	0
Amkar Perm	0	2
FK Moskva *	3	3

Quarter-finals

Team	Leg 1	Leg 2
Lokomotiv Moskva	0	4
Dinamo Moskva *	1	0
Zenit St Petersburg *	1	1
Spartak Moskva	2	1
Dinamo Bryansk	2	0
FK Rostov *	1	0
Krylya Sovetov Samara	2	0
FK Moskva *	3	2

Semi-finals

Team	Leg 1	Leg 2
Lokomotiv Moskva *	3	2
Spartak Moskva	0	1
Dinamo Bryansk *	1	0
FK Moskva	1	1

Final

Team	Score
Lokomotiv Moskva	1
FK Moskva	0

CUP FINAL

Luzhniki, Moscow
27-05-2007, Att: 50 000, Ref: Baskakov
Scorer - Gary O'Connor 102
Lokomotiv - Jakupovic - Ivanovic, Yefimov, Dantas, Spahic, Hurenka, Samedov (Fininho 110), Kontsedalov (O'Connor 62), Loskov, Bilyaletdinov, Sychov
FK Moskva - Zhaunou - Nababkin, Jop, Godunok, Kuzmin, Rebeja (Golubov 106), Barrientos, Semak (Ivanov 46), Bystrov,P. Adamov, Bracamonte (Cizek 76)

* Home team in the first leg

CSKA MOSKVA 2006

Date	Opponents	Score			Scorers	Crowd
5-03-2006	Spartak Kostroma	W 5-0	H	CUPr6	Jô Alves [10], Aldonin 2 [63 77], Zhirkov [66], Olic [85]	3 200
11-03-2006	Spartak Moskva	W 3-2	A	SC	Zhirkov [42], Odiah [72], Jô Alves [82]	35 000
15-03-2006	Spartak Kostroma	W 3-0	A	CUPr6	Salugin [35], Dudu Silva [69], Tikhonov [90]	3 000
22-03-2006	Rubin Kazan	D 1-1	A	CUPqf	Gusev [3]	14 100
18-03-2006	Spartak Nalchik	W 1-0	A	PL	Berezutskiy.V [92+]	14 400
26-03-2006	Shinnik Yaroslavl	W 5-1	H	PL	Ignashevich [11], Jô Alves 4 [49 58 80p 85], Khazov [31]	9 000
1-04-2006	Spartak Moskva	D 1-1	A	PL	Vágner Love [59]	55 000
8-04-2006	Tom Tomsk	W 2-0	H	PL	Jô Alves 2 [20 41p]	9 200
12-04-2006	Rubin Kazan	W 4-1	H	CUPqf	Jô Alves 2 [37 68], Vágner Love [42], Olic [90]	3 500
16-04-2006	Lokomotiv Moskva	L 2-3	A	PL	Gusev [27], Jô Alves [34]	23 723
22-04-2006	Saturn Ramenskoe	W 1-0	H	PL	Jô Alves [12]	10 000
29-04-2006	Rubin Kazan	L 0-1	A	PL		25 000
3-05-2006	Zenit St Petersburg	W 1-0	H	CUPsf	Daniel Carvalho [61]	6 500
6-05-2006	Amkar Perm	W 2-0	H	PL	Jô Alves 2 [12 75]	8 500
10-05-2006	Zenit St Petersburg	W 3-0	A	CUPsf	Vágner Love [9], Dudu Cearense [19], Ignashevich [29]	20 000
14-05-2006	FK Moskva	W 1-0	A	PL	Jô Alves [17]	12 500
20-05-2006	Spartak Moskva	W 3-0	A	CUPf	Jô Alves 2 [43 93+], Vágner Love [90]	67 000
2-07-2006	Mordovia Saransk	W 4-0	H	CUPr5	Daniel Carvalho [19], Jô Alves 2 [25p 62], Vágner Love [91+]	3 500
6-07-2006	Torpedo Moskva	W 2-0	H	PL	Jô Alves [7p], Olic [65p]	8 000
10-07-2006	FK Rostov	L 1-2	H	PL	Jô Alves [31p]	6 000
19-07-2006	Zenit St Petersburg	D 0-0	A	PL		21 500
23-07-2006	Krylya Sovetov Samara	D 1-1	H	PL	Krasic [90]	9 000
29-07-2006	Torpedo Moskva	D 2-2	A	PL	Krasic [31], Rahimic [83]	12 000
3-08-2006	Luch Vladivostock	W 2-1	H	PL	Krasic [16], Olic [69]	6 000
9-08-2006	MFK Ruzomberok - SVK	W 3-0	H	CLpr3	Olic 2 [58 65], Vágner Love [83]	9 947
13-08-2006	Dinamo Moskva	W 3-2	A	PL	Vágner Love 2 [40 68], Olic [48]	15 000
19-08-2006	Spartak Nalchik	W 2-1	H	PL	Jô Alves [79], Vágner Love [83]	7 000
23-08-2006	MFK Ruzomberok - SVK	W 2-0	A	CLpr3	Daniel Carvalho [8], Vágner Love [32]	4 715
27-08-2006	Shinnik Yaroslavl	W 1-0	A	PL	Olic [93+]	16 000
9-09-2006	Spartak Moskva	D 2-2	H	PL	Daniel Carvalho [27], Olic [63]	36 000
13-09-2006	FC Porto - POR	D 0-0	H	CLgG		37 123
17-09-2006	Tom Tomsk	W 1-0	H	PL	Olic [53]	15 000
20-09-2006	Mordovia Saransk	L 0-1	A	CUPr5		13 500
23-09-2006	Lokomotiv Moskva	L 1-2	H	PL	Dudu Cearense [36]	17 000
26-09-2006	Hamburger SV - GER	W 1-0	H	CLgG	Dudu Cearense [59]	23 000
1-10-2006	Saturn Ramenskoe	D 2-2	A	PL	Ignashevich [62], Daniel Carvalho [79p]	16 500
14-10-2006	Rubin Kazan	W 2-1	H	PL	Zhirkov [57], Dudu Cearense [71]	6 500
17-10-2006	Arsenal - ENG	W 1-0	H	CLgG	Daniel Carvalho [24]	28 800
21-10-2006	Amkar Perm	D 0-0	A	PL		16 500
25-10-2006	FK Moskva	W 2-1	H	PL	Vágner Love 2 [26 45]	6 500
28-10-2006	FK Rostov	W 2-1	A	PL	Olic 2 [54 85]	12 500
1-11-2006	Arsenal - ENG	D 0-0	A	CLgG		60 003
5-11-2006	Zenit St Petersburg	W 1-0	H	PL	Daniel Carvalho [58p]	19 000
8-11-2006	Krylya Sovetov Samara	L 0-2	A	PL		22 000
18-11-2006	Luch Vladivostok	W 4-0	A	PL	Daniel Carvalho [15], Vágner Love 3 [25 49 62]	10 200
21-11-2006	FC Porto - POR	L 0-2	H	CLgG		21 853
26-11-2006	Dinamo Moskva	L 1-2	H	PL	Olic [44]	15 000
6-12-2006	Hamburger SV - GER	L 2-3	A	CLgG	Olic [23p], Zhirkov [65]	49 649

SC = Super Cup • CUP = Russian Cup • PL = Premier League • CL = UEFA Champions League
pr3 = third preliminary round • r6 = sixth round • qf = quarter-final • sf = semi-final • f = final • gG = group G

RWA – RWANDA

NATIONAL TEAM RECORD
JULY 10TH 2006 TO JULY 12TH 2010

PL	W	D	L	F	A	%
15	4	3	8	13	18	36.6

FIFA/COCA-COLA WORLD RANKING

1993	1994	1995	1996	1997	1998	1999	2000	2001	2002	2003	2004	2005	2006	High		Low	
-	-	168	159	172	107	146	128	144	130	109	99	89	121	**89**	12/05	**178**	07/99

					2006–2007						
08/06	09/06	10/06	11/06	12/06	01/07	02/07	03/07	04/07	05/07	06/07	07/07
109	106	114	114	121	119	120	121	121	122	112	122

Rwanda's dreams of repeating their surprise qualification for the 2004 African Nations Cup finals flopped and they were out of contention long before the preliminaries ended thanks to three defeats in their first three matches. It was a disappointing run for their new German coach Michael Nees, consistently under pressure to match the past achievements of predecessor Radomir Dujkovic, now working in China. But Nees has moved quickly to change the focus to rebuilding the national side, using players promoted directly from the country's under-17 team. One of new young talents, Haruna Niyonzima, scored twice on his debut in June when Rwanda eventually garnered some

INTERNATIONAL HONOURS
CECAFA Cup 1999

Nations Cup qualifying points with a 2-0 home win over Equatorial Guinea. The high point for the national side was reaching the semifinals of the CECAFA Cup in Addis Ababa in December, where they lost to Zambia. But Rwanda then beat Uganda 4-2 on post-match penalties to take third place. APR FC won the league championship for the third time in four years by finishing one point ahead of ATRACO and they then won the Amahoro Cup with a 2-0 triumph over the league runners-up in July 2007. It was the seventh cup win for the army club, who in January hired former Democratic Republic of Congo national coach Andy Futila to handle their fortunes.

THE FIFA BIG COUNT OF 2006

	Male	Female		Total
Number of players	386 400	0	Referees and Assistant Referees	500
Professionals	0		Admin, Coaches, Technical, Medical	1 500
Amateurs 18+	4 400		Number of clubs	110
Youth under 18	6 500		Number of teams	550
Unregistered	27 500		Clubs with women's teams	0
Total players	386 400		Players as % of population	4.47%

Fédération Rwandaise de Football Amateur (FERWAFA)
Case Postale 2000, Kigali, Rwanda
Tel +250 518525   Fax +250 518523
ferwafa@yahoo.fr   www.none
President: KAZURA Jean-Bosco   General Secretary: KALISA Jules Cesar
Vice-President: NGOGA Martin Charles   Treasurer: ITANGISHAKA Bernard   Media Officer: None
Men's Coach: NEES Michael   Women's Coach: BEARD Kyle
FERWAFA formed: 1972   CAF: 1976   FIFA: 1978
Green shirts with red and yellow trimmings, Green shorts, Red socks

RECENT INTERNATIONAL MATCHES PLAYED BY RWANDA

2004	Opponents	Score	Venue	Comp	Scorers	Att	Referee
8-01	Egypt	L 1-5	Port Said	Fr	Said [87]	10 000	
24-01	Tunisia	L 1-2	Tunis	CNr1	Elias [31]	60 000	Evehe CMR
28-01	Guinea	D 1-1	Bizerte	CNr1	Kamanazi [90]	4 000	Sowe GAM
1-02	Congo DR	W 1-0	Bizerte	CNr1	Said [74]	700	N'Doye SEN
28-05	Uganda	D 1-1	Kigali	Fr	Kamanazi [5]		
5-06	Nigeria	L 0-2	Abuja	WCq		35 000	Pare BFA
19-06	Gabon	W 3-1	Kigali	WCq	Said 2 [4 64], Mulisa [27]	16 325	Abdulkadir TAN
3-07	Zimbabwe	L 0-2	Kigali	WCq			Chilinda MWI
14-08	Uganda	W 2-1	Kampala	Fr	Mulisa, Karekezi		
28-08	Zambia	L 1-2	Kitwe	Fr	Gaseruka [71]	15 000	Mwanza ZAM
5-09	Angola	L 0-1	Luanda	WCq		30 000	Damon RSA
9-10	Algeria	D 1-1	Kigali	WCq	Said [9]	20 000	Abdel Rahman SUD
11-12	Zanzibar †	W 4-2	Addis Abeba	CCr1	Lomani 3 [8 28 48], Karekezi [24]	20 000	
13-12	Burundi	L 1-3	Addis Abeba	CCr1	Gatete [59]		
15-12	Ethiopia	D 0-0	Addis Abeba	CCr1		20 000	
19-12	Tanzania	W 5-1	Addis Abeba	CCr1	Lomani 3, Karekezi, Sibomana		
2005							
12-03	Kenya	D 1-1	Niarobi	Fr	Bolla [10]		
27-03	Algeria	L 0-1	Oran	WCq		20 000	Abd El Fatah EGY
5-06	Nigeria	D 1-1	Kigali	WCq	Gatete [53]	30 000	Kidane ERI
18-06	Gabon	L 0-3	Libreville	WCq		10 000	El Arjoun MAR
4-09	Zimbabwe	L 1-3	Harare	WCq	OG [30]	55 000	Ssegona UGA
8-10	Angola	L 0-1	Kigali	WCq		25 000	Guezzaz MAR
26-11	Zanzibar †	L 0-1	Kigali	CCr1			
30-11	Eritrea	W 2-1	Kigali	CCr1	Gatete, Lomani 2		
4-12	Burundi	W 2-0	Kigali	CCr1			
6-12	Tanzania	W 3-1	Kigali	CCr1	Gatete [44p], Lomani 2 [58 61]		
8-12	Uganda	W 1-0	Kigali	CCsf	Karekezi [115]		
10-12	Ethiopia	L 0-1	Kigali	CCf			
2006							
26-07	Uganda	D 1-1	Kigali	Fr	Lomani [72]		
30-07	Tanzania	L 0-1	Dar es Salaam	Fr			
3-09	Cameroon	L 0-3	Kigali	CNq			Ssegonga UGA
8-10	Liberia	L 2-3	Monrovia	CNq	Karekezi [70], Mulenda [78]		Olatunde NGA
27-11	Somalia	W 3-0	Addis Abeba	CCr1	Kayihura [19], Ujeneza [70], Nyonzima [87]		
30-11	Uganda	L 0-1	Addis Abeba	CCr1			
3-12	Sudan	D 0-0	Addis Abeba	CCr1			
5-12	Tanzania	W 2-1	Addis Abeba	CCqf	Ujeneza [45], Witakenge [56p]		
8-12	Zambia	L 0-1	Addis Abeba	CCsf			
10-12	Uganda	D 0-0	Addis Abeba	CC3p	L 2-4p		
2007							
25-03	Equatorial Guinea	L 1-3	Malabo	CNq	Karekezi [73]		Louzaya CGO
27-05	Burundi	W 1-0	Kigali	Fr	Muhayimana [13]		
2-06	Equatorial Guinea	W 2-0	Kigali	CNq	Niyonzima 2 [55 71]		
10-06	Kenya	L 0-2	Nairobi	Fr			
17-06	Cameroon	L 1-2	Garoua	CNq	Gatete [78]		

Fr = Friendly match • CN = CAF African Cup of Nations • CC = CECAFA Cup • WC = FIFA World Cup
q = qualifier • r1 = first round group • sf = semi-final • f = final • † Not a full international

RWANDA NATIONAL TEAM RECORDS AND RECORD SEQUENCES

Records			Sequence records				
Victory	4-1	DJI 1999	Wins	4	2005	Clean sheets	4	1999
Defeat	1-6	COD 1976	Defeats	5	1976-77, 1983-86	Goals scored	14	2000-2001
Player Caps	n/a		Undefeated	10	1998-2000	Without goal	3	1983-1986
Player Goals	n/a		Without win	16	1983-1996	Goals against	11	2003-2004

RWANDA COUNTRY INFORMATION

Capital	Kigali	Independence	1962 from Belgium	GDP per Capita	$1 300
Population	7 954 013	Status	Repulblic	GNP Ranking	139
Area km²	26 338	Language	Kinyarwanda, English, French	Dialling code	+250
Population density	301 per km²	Literacy rate	70%	Internet code	.rw
% in urban areas	6%	Main religion	Christian	GMT + / -	+2
Towns/Cities ('000)	Kigali 745; Butare 89; Gitarama 87; Ruhengeri 86; Gisenyi 83; Byumba 70; Cyangugu 63				
Neighbours (km)	Tanzania 217; Burundi 290; Congo DR 217; Uganda 169				
Main stadia	Stade Amahoro - Kigali 15 000				

RWANDA 2006
CHAMPIONNAT NATIONAL

	Pl	W	D	L	F	A	Pts
APR FC	26	19	5	2	50	12	62
ATRACO	26	19	4	3	39	14	61
Rayon Sport	26	17	7	2	43	14	58
Kiyovu	26	11	11	4	33	18	44
Police	26	9	8	9	26	24	35
AS Kigali	26	8	10	8	27	26	34
Kibuye FC	26	7	11	8	21	28	32
Mukura VS	26	7	10	9	25	23	31
Marines FC	26	8	4	14	25	38	28
KIST FC	26	6	8	12	24	36	26
Zebres FC	26	6	5	15	14	35	23
La Jeunesse	26	4	10	12	20	30	22
Etincelles	26	6	4	16	19	38	22
Flash FC	26	4	5	17	18	48	17

7/01/2007 - 29/10/2006

COUPE AMAHORO 2007

Quarter-final groups	Semi-finals		Final	
Group A winners				
APR FC	APR FC	2 4		
Group B winners	AS Kigali	0 0		
ATRACO			APR FC	2
Group C winners			ATRACO	0
AS Kigali	Kibuye FC	1 0	4-07-2007	
Group D winners	ATRACO	2 1	Scorers - Joseph Bwalya [57],	
Kibuye FC			Jimmy Gatete [89]	

RECENT LEAGUE AND CUP RECORD

	Championship		Cup		
Year	Champions	Winners	Score	Runners-up
1995	APR FC Kigali	Rayon Sports Butare		
1996	APR FC Kigali	APR FC Kigali		
1997	Rayon Sports Butare	Rwanda FC		
1998	Rayon Sports Butare	Rayon Sports Butare	w-o	Kiyovu Sports
1999	APR FC Kigali	APR FC Kigali		
2000	APR FC Kigali	APR FC Kigali		
2001	APR FC Kigali	Citadins	0-0 6-5p	APR FC
2002	Rayon Sports Butare	APR FC Kigali	2-1	Rayon Sports Butare
2003	APR FC Kigali	No tournament held		
2004	Rayon Sports Butare	No tournament held		
2005	APR FC Kigali	Rayon Sports Butare	3-0	Mukura Victory
2006	APR FC Kigali	APR FC Kigali	1-0	ATRACO
2007		APR FC Kigali	2-0	ATRACO

SAM – SAMOA

NATIONAL TEAM RECORD
JULY 10TH 2006 TO JULY 12TH 2010

PL	W	D	L	F	A	%
0	0	0	0	0	0	0

FIFA/COCA-COLA WORLD RANKING

1993	1994	1995	1996	1997	1998	1999	2000	2001	2002	2003	2004	2005	2006	High	Low
-	-	-	177	183	164	180	173	172	163	176	179	182	187	**166** 03/02	**191** 07/07

2006–2007											
08/06	09/06	10/06	11/06	12/06	01/07	02/07	03/07	04/07	05/07	06/07	07/07
188	190	189	190	187	188	189	188	187	191	189	191

The FIFA World Cup has kicked off its qualifying campaign in some exotic places over the years and for the 2010 qualifiers it was no different. That special honour was given to Samoa, host of the 2007 South Pacific Games from which the top three from the ten-team tournament join New Zealand in the second round of qualifiers in the Oceania region. However, without a match since the last FIFA World Cup qualifying campaign in 2004, football in Samoa is struggling to keep up with the rest of the OFC, especially the likes of Fiji and the Solomon Islands. Nowhere was that more evident than in the inaugural O–League, from which Samoan clubs were excluded, and they

INTERNATIONAL HONOURS
None

weren't invited to the second edition either. In the Under–20 Oceania championship Samoa finished bottom without a point while the senior women's team also finished bottom in the 2007 Oceania Women's Championship held in Papua New Guinea. Football in Samoa does have one notable fan - Everton and Australia midfielder Tim Cahill. With a Samoan mother and an English father, Cahill once appeared for the Samoan U–13 side and his brother Chris is a member of the current Samoan team. Keen to promote the game in this rugby-mad country as well as to raise money for sports facilities in schools, Cahill helped with the draw for the South Pacific Games.

THE FIFA BIG COUNT OF 2006

	Male	Female		Total
Number of players	5 400	300	Referees and Assistant Referees	100
Professionals	0		Admin, Coaches, Technical, Medical	300
Amateurs 18+	1 100		Number of clubs	60
Youth under 18	1 100		Number of teams	220
Unregistered	1 100		Clubs with women's teams	3
Total players	5 700		Players as % of population	3.22%

Samoa Football Soccer Federation (SFSF)
Tuanaimato, PO Box 6172, Apia, Samoa
Tel +685 7783210   Fax +685 22855

www.soccersamoa.ws

President: ROEBECK Tautulu   General Secretary: SOLIA Tilomai
Vice-President: PAPALII Seiuli Poasa   Treasurer: LINO Maiava Visesio   Media Officer: SOLIA Tilomai
Men's Coach: BRAND David   Women's Coach: Brand David
SFSF formed: 1968   OFC: 1984   FIFA: 1986
Blue shirts, Blue shorts, Red socks

RECENT INTERNATIONAL MATCHES PLAYED BY SAMOA

2002	Opponents	Score	Venue	Comp	Scorers	Att	Referee
No international matches played in 2002 after June							
2003							
No international matches played in 2003							
2004							
5-05	Cook Islands	D 0-0	Auckland	Fr			
10-05	American Samoa	W 4-0	Apia	WCq	Bryce 12, Fasavalu 2 30 53, Michael 66	500	Afu SOL
15-05	Vanuatu	L 0-3	Apia	WCq		650	Breeze AUS
17-05	Fiji	L 0-4	Apia	WCq		450	Diomis AUS
19-05	Papua New Guinea	L 1-4	Apia	WCq	Michael 69	300	Diomis AUS
2005							
No international matches played in 2005							
2006							
No international matches played in 2006							
2007							
No international matches played in 2007 before August							

Fr = Friendly match • WC = FIFA World Cup • q = qualifier

SAMOA NATIONAL TEAM RECORDS AND RECORD SEQUENCES

Records			Sequence records				
Victory	5-0	ASA 2002	Wins	3	1998-2000	Clean sheets	2	2002, 2004
Defeat	0-13	TAH 1981	Defeats	8	1979-1981	Goals scored	8	1998-2000
Player Caps	n/a		Undefeated	3	1998-2000	Without goal	4	1983-1988
Player Goals	n/a		Without win	8	1979-1981	Goals against	22	1979-1998

RECENT LEAGUE AND CUP RECORD

Championship		Cup		
Year	Champions	Winners	Score	Runners-up
1997	Kiwi	Kiwi		Vaivase-tai
1998	Vaivase-tai	Togafuafua		
1999	Moata'a	Moaula		Moata'a
2000	Titavi	Gold Star	4-1	Faatoia
2001	Gold Star	Strickland Brothers	3-3 5-4p	Moata'a
2002	Strickland Brothers	Vaivase-tai		Hosanna
2003	Strickland Brothers	Strickland Brothers	5-2	Moata'a
2004	Strickland Brothers	Tunaimato Breeze	3-2	Central United
2005	Tunaimato Breeze			

SAMOA COUNTRY INFORMATION

Capital	Apia	Independence	1962 from New Zealand	GDP per Capita	$5 600
Population	177 714	Status	Constitutional Monarchy	GNP Ranking	178
Area km²	2 944	Language	Samoan, English	Dialling code	+685
Population density	60 per km²	Literacy rate	99%	Internet code	.ws
% in urban areas	21%	Main religion	Christian	GMT +/–	-11
Towns/Cities ('000)	Apia 40; Vaitele 5; Faleasiu 3; Vailele 3; Leauvaa 3; Faleula 2; Siusega 2; Malie 2; Fasitoouta 2				
Neighbours (km)	South Pacific Ocean 403				
Main stadia	Toleafoa J.S. Blatter Complex – Apia				

SCO – SCOTLAND

NATIONAL TEAM RECORD
JULY 10TH 2006 TO JULY 12TH 2010

PL	W	D	L	F	A	%
8	6	0	2	14	6	75

FIFA/COCA-COLA WORLD RANKING

1993	1994	1995	1996	1997	1998	1999	2000	2001	2002	2003	2004	2005	2006	High		Low	
24	32	26	29	37	38	20	25	50	59	54	86	60	25	14	05/07	88	03/05

2006–2007											
08/06	09/06	10/06	11/06	12/06	01/07	02/07	03/07	04/07	05/07	06/07	07/07
40	34	25	24	25	26	20	16	19	14	23	22

With five Championships and four Cups in the past seven years, the current generation of Celtic players is fast writing itself into club folklore. Bear in mind that Rangers had won 11 of the 12 League titles prior to that and it becomes apparent why the team created by Martin O'Neill and built upon by Gordon Strachan is so important in the history of the club. Celtic's title win was achieved with relative ease, helped in no small measure by the managerial changes at Rangers - Paul Le Guen lasted just seven months - and the circus at Hearts, where unrest in the dressing room led to the departure of captain Steven Pressley to Celtic. Rangers fans will be pinning their hopes on

INTERNATIONAL HONOURS
Qualified for the FIFA World Cup finals 1954 1958 1974 1978 1982 1986 1990   **UEFA Champions League** Celtic 1967

Walter Smith, who stood down as Scotland coach to return to the club with whom he won seven titles as manager. That was a big disappointment to Scotland fans of a non-Rangers persuasion, as he had given the national team a new sense of self-belief. Going into the new year Scotland topped their Euro 2008 qualifying group ahead of both France and Italy, having beaten the former 1-0 at Hampden Park. Qualification will prove difficult but at least the despondency has disappeared. There was also good news in the UEFA Champions League where Celtic qualified for the knock out stage for the first time; there they gave Milan a stern test before losing to an extra-time goal.

THE FIFA BIG COUNT OF 2006

	Male	Female		Total
Number of players	374 075	46 514	Referees and Assistant Referees	2 097
Professionals	4 132		Admin, Coaches, Technical, Medical	8 500
Amateurs 18+	39 234		Number of clubs	6 600
Youth under 18	67 123		Number of teams	8 200
Unregistered	302 500		Clubs with women's teams	127
Total players	420 589		Players as % of population	8.31%

The Scottish Football Association (SFA)
Hampden Park, Glasgow G42 9AY, United Kingdom
Tel +44 141 6166000   Fax +44 141 6166001
info@scottishfa.co.uk   www.scottishfa.co.uk
President: PEAT George   General Secretary: SMITH Gordon
Vice-President: OGILVIE Campbell   Treasurer: TBD   Media Officer: MITCHELL Andrew
Men's Coach: McLEISH Alex   Women's Coach: SIGNEUL Anna
SFA formed: 1873   UEFA: 1954   FIFA: 1910-20, 1924-28, 1946
Dark blue shirts with white trimmings, White shorts, Dark blue socks or yellow shirts with black trimmings, Back shorts, yellow socks

RECENT INTERNATIONAL MATCHES PLAYED BY SCOTLAND

2003	Opponents	Score		Venue	Comp	Scorers	Att	Referee
12-02	Republic of Ireland	L	0-2	Glasgow	Fr		33 337	Braamhaar NED
29-03	Iceland	W	2-1	Glasgow	ECq	Miller.K [12], Wilkie [70]	37 548	Temmink NED
2-04	Lithuania	L	0-1	Kaunas	ECq		8 000	Stuchlik AUT
30-04	Austria	L	0-2	Glasgow	Fr		12 189	Vollquartz DEN
27-05	New Zealand	D	1-1	Edinburgh	Fr	Crawford [10]	10 016	Ingvarsson SWE
7-06	Germany	D	1-1	Glasgow	ECq	Miller.K [69]	48 037	Messina ITA
20-08	Norway	D	0-0	Oslo	Fr		12 858	Vuorela FIN
6-09	Faroe Islands	W	3-1	Glasgow	ECq	McCann [7], Dickov [45], McFadden [74]	40 901	Ceferin SVN
10-09	Germany	L	1-2	Dortmund	ECq	McCann [60]	67 000	Frisk SWE
11-10	Lithuania	W	1-0	Glasgow	ECq	Fletcher [70]	50 343	Colombo FRA
15-11	Netherlands	W	1-0	Glasgow	ECpo	McFadden [22]	50 670	Hauge NOR
19-11	Netherlands	L	0-6	Amsterdam	ECpo		51 000	Michel SVK
2004								
18-02	Wales	L	0-4	Cardiff	Fr		47 124	Ross NIR
31-03	Romania	L	1-2	Glasgow	Fr	McFadden [57]	20 433	Hyytia FIN
28-04	Denmark	L	0-1	Copenhagen	Fr		22 485	Ingvarsson SWE
27-05	Estonia	W	1-0	Tallinn	Fr	McFadden [76]	4 000	Poulsen DEN
30-05	Trinidad and Tobago	W	4-1	Edinburgh	Fr	Fletcher [6], Holt [14], Caldwell.G [23], Quashie [34]	16 187	Vink NED
18-08	Hungary	L	0-3	Glasgow	Fr		15 933	Duhamel FRA
3-09	Spain	D	1-1	Valencia	Fr	McFadden [17]. Abandoned 59'	11 000	Bre FRA
8-09	Slovenia	D	0-0	Glasgow	WCq		38 279	Larsen DEN
9-10	Norway	L	0-1	Glasgow	WCq		51 000	Allaerts BEL
13-10	Moldova	D	1-1	Chisinau	WCq	Thompson [31]	7 000	Jakobsson ISL
17-11	Sweden	L	1-4	Edinburgh	Fr	McFadden [78p]	15 071	Jara CZE
2005								
26-03	Italy	L	0-2	Milan	WCq		45 000	Vassaras GRE
4-06	Moldova	W	2-0	Glasgow	WCq	Dailly [52], McFadden [88]	45 317	Braamhaar NED
8-06	Belarus	D	0-0	Minsk	WCq		28 287	Benquerenca POR
17-08	Austria	D	2-2	Graz	Fr	Miller.K [3], O'Connor [39]	13 800	Dereli TUR
3-09	Italy	D	1-1	Glasgow	WCq	Miller.K [13]	50 185	Michel SVK
7-09	Norway	W	2-1	Oslo	WCq	Miller.K 2 [20 30]	24 904	Hamer LUX
8-10	Belarus	L	0-1	Glasgow	WCq		51 105	Szabo HUN
12-10	Slovenia	W	3-0	Celje	WCq	Fletcher [4], McFadden [47], Hartley [84]	9 100	Temmink NED
12-11	USA	D	1-1	Glasgow	Fr	Webster [37]	26 708	Undiano Mallenco ESP
2006								
1-03	Switzerland	L	1-3	Glasgow	Fr	Miller.K [55]	20 952	Coue FRA
11-05	Bulgaria	W	5-1	Kobe	Fr	Boyd 2 [13 43], McFadden [69], Burke 2 [76 88]	5 780	Kamikawa JPN
13-05	Japan	D	0-0	Saitama	Fr		56 648	Iturralde Gonzalez ESP
2-09	Faroe Islands	W	6-0	Glasgow	ECq	Fletcher [7], McFadden [10], Boyd 2 [24p 38], Miller.K [30p], O'Connor [85]	50 059	Egorov RUS
6-09	Lithiania	W	2-1	Kaunas	ECq	Dailly [46], Miller.K [62]	8 000	Hrinák SVK
7-10	France	W	1-0	Glasgow	ECq	Caldwell.G [67]	50 456	Busacca SUI
11-10	Ukraine	L	0-2	Kyiv	ECq		50 000	Hansson SWE
2007								
24-03	Georgia	W	2-1	Glasgow	ECq	Boyd [11], Beattie [89]	52 063	Vollquartz DEN
28-03	Italy	L	0-2	Bari	ECq		37 600	De Bleeckere BEL
30-05	Austria	W	1-0	Vienna	Fr	O'Connor [59]	13 200	Szabo HUN
6-06	Faroe Islands	W	2-0	Toftir	ECq	Maloney [31], O'Connor [35]	4 100	Kasnaferis GRE

Fr = Friendly match • EC = UEFA EURO 2004/2008 • WC = FIFA World Cup • q = qualifier

SCOTLAND NATIONAL TEAM RECORDS AND RECORD SEQUENCES

Records			Sequence records					
Victory	11-0	NIR 1901	Wins	13	1879-1885	Clean sheets	7	1925-27,1996-97
Defeat	0-7	URU 1954	Defeats	5	2002	Goals scored	32	1873-1888
Player Caps	102	DALGLISH Kenny	Undefeated	22	1879-1887	Without goal	4	1971
Player Goals	30	LAW Denis/DALGLISH	Without win	9	1997-1998	Goals against	14	1957-1958

SCOTLAND (PART OF THE UNITED KINGDOM)

Capital	Edinburgh	Language	English		Independence	n/a
Population	5 057 400	Area	77 000 km²	Density	66 per km²	% in cities	89%
GDP per cap	$27 300	Dailling code	+44	Internet	.uk	GMT + / -	0

MAJOR CITIES/TOWNS
Population '000

1	Glasgow	604
2	Edinburgh	441
3	Aberdeen	184
4	Dundee	150
5	East Kilbride	74
6	Paisley	72
7	Livingston	55
8	Cumbernauld	49
9	Hamilton	47
10	Kirkcaldy	46
11	Ayr	45
12	Perth	43
13	Kilmarnock	42
14	Greenock	42
15	Inverness	40
16	Coatbridge	39
17	Dunfermline	39
18	Glenrothes	38
19	Airdrie	35
20	Stirling	33
21	Falkirk	32
22	Clydebank	30
23	Motherwell	29
24	Dumbarton	20

MEDALS TABLE

	Overall			League			Cup		LC		Europe			Town/City	Stadium	Cap'ty	DoF
	G	S	B	G	S	B	G	S	G	S	G	S	B				
1 Rangers	107	53	19	51	28	17	31	17	24	6	1	2	2	Glasgow	Ibrox	50 444	1873
2 Celtic	89	61	21	41	28	17	34	18	13	13	1	2	4	Glasgow	Celtic Park	60 554	1888
3 Aberdeen	17	28	9	4	13	8	7	8	5	7	1		1	Aberdeen	Pittodrie	21 487	1903
4 Heart of Midlothian	15	22	15	4	14	15	7	6	4	2				Edinburgh	Tynecastle	17 412	1874
5 Queen's Park	10	2					10	2						Glasgow	Hampden Park	52 000	1867
6 Hibernian	9	21	15	4	6	13	2	9	3	6			2	Edinburgh	Easter Road	17 400	1875
7 Dundee	5	11	3	1	4	1	1	4	3	3			2	Dundee	Dens Park	11 760	1893
8 Kilmarnock	4	14	4	1	4	3	3	5		5			1	Kilmarnock	Rugby Park	18 128	1869
9 Dundee United	4	11	8	1		7	1	7	2	3	1	1		Dundee	Tannadice Park	14 223	1909
10 Motherwell	4	11	6	1	5	6	2	4	1	2				Motherwell	Fir Park	13 742	1886
11 East Fife	4	2	2			2	1	2	3					Methil	Bayview	2 000	1903
12 Third Lanark	3	5	2	1		2	2	4		1				Glasgow	Cathkin Park		1872
13 Dumbarton	3	5		2			1	5						Dumbarton	Strathclyde Homes	2 050	1872
14 St. Mirren	3	4	2			2	3	3		1				Paisley	St Mirren Park	10 866	1877
15 Vale of Levan	3	4					3	4						Alexandria	Millburn Park		1872
16 Clyde	3	3	3			3	3	3						Cumbernauld	Broadwood	8 200	1877

RECENT LEAGUE AND CUP RECORD

	Championship						Cup		
Year	Champions	Pts	Runners-up	Pts	Third	Pts	Winners	Score	Runners-up
1995	Rangers	69	Motherwell	54	Hibernian	53	Celtic	1-0	Airdrieonians
1996	Rangers	87	Celtic	83	Aberdeen	55	Rangers	5-1	Heart of Midlothian
1997	Rangers	80	Celtic	75	Dundee United	60	Kilmarnock	1-0	Falkirk
1998	Celtic	74	Rangers	72	Heart of Midlothian	67	Heart of Midlothian	2-1	Rangers
1999	Rangers	77	Celtic	71	St. Johnstone	57	Rangers	1-0	Celtic
2000	Rangers	90	Celtic	69	Heart of Midlothian	54	Rangers	4-0	Aberdeen
2001	Celtic	97	Rangers	82	Hibernian	66	Celtic	3-0	Hibernian
2002	Celtic	103	Rangers	85	Livingston	58	Rangers	3-2	Celtic
2003	Rangers	97	Celtic	97	Heart of Midlothian	63	Rangers	1-0	Dundee
2004	Celtic	98	Rangers	81	Heart of Midlothian	68	Celtic	3-1	Dunfermline Ath.
2005	Rangers	93	Celtic	92	Hibernian	61	Celtic	1-0	Dundee United
2006	Celtic	85	Heart of Midlothian	65	Rangers	62	Heart of Midlothian	1-1 4-2p	Gretna
2007	Celtic	84	Rangers	72	Aberdeen	65	Celtic	1-0	Dunfermline Ath.

SCOTLAND 2006–07

BANK OF SCOTLAND PREMIER LEAGUE

	Pl	W	D	L	F	A	Pts	Celtic	Rangers	Aberdeen	Hearts	Kilmarnock	Hibs	Falkirk	ICT	Dundee U	Motherwell	St Mirren	D'fermline
Celtic †	38	26	6	6	65	34	84		2-0 0-1	1-0 2-1	2-1 1-3	4-1 2-0	2-1 1-0	1-0	1-0	3-0	2-2	2-1 1-0	2-0 5-1	1-0 2-1
Rangers †	38	21	9	8	61	32	72	1-1 2-0		1-0 3-0	2-0 0-0	3-0 0-1	3-0 3-3	4-0 2-1	0-1 1-1	1-2 2-5	0-1	1-1	1-1	2-0
Aberdeen ‡	38	19	8	11	55	38	65	0-1 1-2	1-2 2-0		1-3 1-0	3-1 3-0	2-1 2-0	2-1	1-1 1-1	3-1 2-4	2-1	2-0	1-0 3-0	
Heart of Midlothian	38	17	10	11	47	35	61	2-1 1-2	0-1 1-2	0-1 1-1		0-2 1-0	3-2 2-0	0-0 1-0	4-1 1-1	0-4 0-0	4-4 4-1	0-1 1-1	1-1
Kilmarnock	38	16	7	15	47	54	55	1-2 1-2	2-2 1-3	1-0 1-0	0-0		2-1 0-2	2-1	1-1 3-2	0-0 1-0	1-2	1-1	5-1
Hibernian	38	13	10	15	56	46	49	2-2 2-1	2-1 0-2	1-1 0-0	2-2 0-1	2-2 0-1		0-1 2-0	2-0	2-1	3-1 2-0	5-1	2-0
Falkirk	38	15	5	18	49	47	50	0-1 1-0	1-0	0-2 1-2	1-1	1-2 0-2	2-1		3-1 1-0	5-1 2-0	0-1 1-2	1-2 1-2	0-1 0-1
Inverness Caley Thistle	38	11	13	14	42	48	46	1-1 1-2	1-1	0-0	3-4	0-0 3-0	3-2 1-1		0-0 1-0	0-1 2-0	1-2 2-1	1-1 0-1	0-1 1-3
Dundee United	38	10	12	16	40	59	42	1-4 1-1	2-1	3-1	0-1	1-0	0-3 0-1	2-1 5-3	1-1		1-1 1-1	0-0 2-0	0-0 0-0
Motherwell	38	10	8	20	41	61	38	1-1	1-2 0-1	0-2 0-1	0-2 0-1	0-2 5-0	0-1	1-6	4-2 3-3	1-4 1-0		3-0	0-0 2-3 2-1 2-0
St Mirren	38	8	12	18	31	51	36	1-3	2-3 0-1	1-1 0-2	2-2	0-1 1-0	1-0	2-0 1-0	1-1	0-1 1-3	0-1 2-0		0-0 0-1
Dunfermline Athletic ‡	38	8	8	22	26	55	32	1-2	1-1 0-1	0-3	1-2 0-1	3-2 1-1	0-4 1-0	0-0 3-0	0-1 1-2	2-1 1-0	0-2 4-1	2-1 0-0	

29/07/2006 – 20/05/2007 • † Qualified for the UEFA Champions League • ‡ Qualified for the UEFA Cup • Matches in bold are away not home matches
Top scorers: Kris BOYD, Rangers 20; Scott McDONALD, Motherwell 15; Steven NAISMITH, Motherwell 15

SCOTLAND 2006–07

FIRST DIVISION (2)

	Pl	W	D	L	F	A	Pts	Gretna	St J'stone	Dundee	Hamilton	Clyde	Liv'ston	Partick	QOS	Airdrie	Ross C
Gretna	36	19	9	8	70	40	66		2-0 0-2	0-4 1-0	6-0 1-0	3-3 0-0	1-1 4-1	4-0 2-0	5-0 0-3	0-2 0-0	2-1 4-1
St Johnstone	36	19	8	9	65	42	65	3-3 2-1		2-1 2-0	0-0 4-2	0-0 2-1	1-2 1-2	2-0 2-0	5-0 3-0	1-0 4-3	3-1 2-1
Dundee	36	16	5	15	48	42	53	1-3 0-1	1-1 2-1		1-1 1-0	3-0 1-4	0-1 2-0	0-1 3-1	2-1 1-0	1-0 2-1	3-1 3-2
Hamilton Academical	36	14	11	11	46	47	53	3-1 0-0	2-2 3-4	1-0 1-0		3-1 1-1	1-3 0-1	2-2 1-1	1-2 2-1	3-0 0-0	1-0
Clyde	36	11	14	11	46	35	47	1-2 2-0	1-0 0-1	2-1 1-1	2-1 3-0		1-1 0-1	0-0 2-0	4-0 0-1	0-0 0-1	3-0 2-4
Livingston	36	11	12	13	41	46	45	1-2 1-1	1-3 2-2	3-1 3-1	0-1 1-1	2-1 1-0		2-2 0-1	2-0 0-1	3-0 3-0	0-1 1-1
Partick Thistle	36	12	9	15	47	63	45	0-6 2-2	1-5 2-0	3-1 2-1	3-1 0-2	1-0 4-2	3-0 0-0		1-1 0-0	4-2 0-1	3-2 1-1
Queen of the South	36	10	11	15	34	54	41	0-3 0-4	0-1 1-0	2-0 2-2	1-1 1-1	0-2 0-0	2-0 1-0	4-3		1-1 0-3	2-0 2-0
Airdrie United †	36	11	7	18	39	50	40	4-2 0-0	2-1 1-2	0-1 0-3	1-2 1-0	2-1 1-0	0-1 3-1	1-2 1-1	2-2 0-3		0-2 0-1
Ross County	36	9	10	17	40	57	37	0-1 2-3	2-2 1-1	1-0 0-0	0-1 4-1	1-1 2-2	0-3 0-2	2-5 2-1	1-0 1-0	2-1 1-1	

5/08/2006 – 28/04/2007 • † Play-off • Semis: Brechin 1-3 0-3 Airdrie; Raith 0-0 1-3 Stirling Albion • Final: Stirling Albion 2-2 3-2 Airdrie

SCOTLAND 2006–07

SECOND DIVISION (3)

	Pl	W	D	L	F	A	Pts	Morton	Stirling	Raith	Brechin	Ayr	C'beath	Alloa	P'head	Stranraer	Forfar
Greenock Morton	36	24	5	7	76	32	77		1-1 2-1	2-0 1-0	1-0 0-2	0-0 4-2	1-0 3-0	4-0 2-1	4-2 2-1	3-0 1-1	1-1 9-1
Stirling Albion †	36	21	6	9	67	39	69	2-1 2-1		1-1 0-1	2-1 0-1	1-3 4-2	1-0 1-0	5-0 4-0	2-0 2-1	3-3 0-2	3-0 4-0
Raith Rovers †	36	18	8	10	50	33	62	1-3 2-0	1-3 0-1		1-1 1-0	1-0 0-1	1-3 1-2	0-0 3-0	5-2 2-0	1-1 0-0	0-0 2-1
Brechin City †	36	18	6	12	61	45	60	2-3 0-1	0-1 1-4	1-0 1-2		0-2 2-0	4-2 1-0	2-0 2-3	1-0 3-1	3-0 1-1	4-2 2-2
Ayr United	36	14	8	14	46	47	50	0-1 1-0	0-0 3-2	1-0 0-2	1-2 1-1		0-4 0-2	0-1 4-3	1-2 0-0	0-2 1-0	5-0 3-1
Cowdenbeath	36	13	6	17	59	56	45	1-2 1-1	2-2 1-2	1-2 1-5	1-3 0-3	1-1 3-1		6-1 5-2	4-2 0-3	4-2 0-0	3-2 2-1
Alloa Athletic	36	11	9	16	47	70	42	3-2 0-3	1-2 1-1	1-2 2-3	2-2 2-3	0-1 1-1	2-1 0-0		1-1 2-4	1-1 1-0	2-0 2-0
Peterhead	36	11	8	17	60	62	41	0-4 1-2	2-3 2-1	1-0 1-0	0-1 1-4	3-1 2-1	2-0 0-2	1-2 1-0		5-2 5-0	8-0 2-2
Stranraer †	36	10	9	17	45	74	39	0-3 2-1	2-1 3-1	1-4 0-2	3-1 0-2	1-3 0-3	1-0 1-6	2-3 4-2	1-1		3-2 4-1
Forfar Athletic	36	4	7	25	37	90	19	1-3 0-4	0-2 0-2	1-1 1-2	1-2 3-2	0-1 1-1	1-1 2-0	0-2 0-2	2-3 1-2	2-1 5-0	

5/08/2006 – 28/04/2007 • † Play-off • Semis: Queen's Park 2-0 2-1 Arbroath; East Fife 4-1 0-1 Stranraer • Final: Queen's Park 4-2 3-0 East Fife

SCOTLAND 2006–07

SECOND DIVISION (3)

	Pl	W	D	L	F	A	Pts	Berwick	Arbroath	Q. Park	East Fife	D'barton	Albion	St'muir	Montrose	Elgin	E. S'ling
Berwick Rangers	36	24	3	9	51	29	75		3-2 1-0	1-0 0-2	2-1 2-0	3-0 2-1	1-3 0-1	2-1 1-2	1-3 1-0	3-1 0-0	2-2 0-0
Arbroath †	36	22	4	10	61	33	70	0-1 1-0		1-2 1-0	1-1 1-3	0-0 2-2	3-0 0-2	0-4 1-3	1-1 0-2	1-2 1-1	1-2 3-2
Queen's Park †	36	21	5	10	57	28	68	1-0 0-2	0-3 1-0		3-0 1-1	1-0 2-0	2-1 5-0	1-1 1-0	1-1 5-0	3-0 3-0	1-3 2-1
East Fife †	36	20	7	9	59	37	67	2-0 0-2	2-1 1-2	1-0 1-0		1-0 1-0	2-2 1-3	0-0 1-1	2-0 2-0	1-1 3-1	5-0 0-2
Dumbarton	36	18	5	13	52	37	59	2-0 1-2	0-2 0-1	0-0 1-2	2-1 0-2		3-1 3-1	4-0 1-1	2-0 2-1	3-1 1-0	2-0 2-1
Albion Rovers	36	14	6	16	56	61	48	0-1 0-1	1-3 0-1	3-1 1-2	1-0 1-0	3-2 1-0		2-5 2-1	3-1 2-3	1-6 2-4	0-2 1
Stenhousemuir	36	13	5	18	53	63	44	2-3 2-0	1-2 1-2	2-1 1-2	0-1 3-5	1-0 5-1	3-2 0-4		5-0 2-5	2-0 3-2	2-0 1-1
Montrose	36	11	4	21	42	62	37	0-1 1-2	0-1 1-0	0-2 1-0	3-3 1-1	0-5 2-1	2-3 0-1	1-3 2		2-0 0-1	1-0 4-0
Elgin City	36	9	2	25	39	69	29	1-2 2-1	0-4 0-1	1-2 0-3	1-2 2-3	0-2 0-1	0-3 2-0	2-0 2-1	3-2 0-2		5-0 2-1
East Stirling	36	6	3	27	27	78	21	0-1 0-3	0-2 1-5	2-1 0-2	0-4 0-2	0-2 1-5	0-1 0-0	5-0 0-0	0-3 0-2	2-1 0-2	

5/08/2006 – 28/04/2007 • † Play-off

TENNENTS SCOTTISH FA CUP 2006–07

Second Round		Third Round			Fourth Round		
		Celtic *	4				
Raith Rovers *	0	Dumbarton	0				
Dumbarton	1				**Celtic**	4	
					Livingston *	1	
		Hamilton Academical *	2				
		Livingston	4				
		Dundee United *	3				
		St Mirren	2				
					Dundee United	0	
Stirling Albion	1				**Inverness Caledonian Thistle** *	1	
Edinburgh City *	0	Stirling Albion *	1				
		Inverness Caledonian Thistle	6				
		Motherwell	1				
		Airdrie United *	0				
					Motherwell *	2	
					Greenock Morton	0	
		Kilmarnock	1				
Annan Athletic *	0	**Greenock Morton** *	3				
Greenock Morton	3						
		Falkirk	2				
Arbroath	0	Berwick Rangers *	0				
Berwick Rangers *	2				Falkirk *	0	
Ayr United	2				**St Johnstone**	3	
Peterhead *	0	Ayr United	0	1			
		St Johnstone *	0	2			
		Hibernian	2	4			
		Aberdeen *	2	1			
					Hibernian *	3	
					Gretna	1	
		Clyde *	0				
		Gretna	3				
Cowdenbeath *	5						
Edinburgh University	1	**Cowdenbeath** *	1	1			
Preston Athletic	1	Brechin City	1	0			
Brechin City *	2				Cowdenbeath	0	
					Queen of the South *	2	
		Dundee *	1 3 2p				
		Queen of the South	1 3 4p				
		Partick Thistle	1				
		Ross County *	0				
					Partick Thistle	1	
Elgin City *	1				Deveronvale *	0	
Buckie Thistle	0	Elgin City	4				
Fraserburgh	1	**Deveronvale** *	5				
Deveronvale *	2						
		Heart of Midlothian	4				
Forfar Athletic	1	Stranraer *	0				
Stranraer *	3				Heart of Midlothian	0	
					Dunfermline Athletic *	1	
		Rangers	2				
		Dunfermline Athletic *	3				

* Home team

TENNENTS SCOTTISH FA CUP 2006-07

Quarter–finals | **Semi–finals** | **Final**

Celtic — 2
Inverness Caledonian Thistle * — 1

Celtic — 2
St Johnstone — 1

Motherwell * — 1
St Johnstone — 2

Celtic — 1
Dunfermline Athletic — 0

Hibernian — 2
Queen of the South * — 1

Hibernian — 0 0
Dunfermline Athletic ‡ — 0 1

Partick Thistle — 0
Dunfermline Athletic * — 2

Both semi-finals played at Hampden Park
‡ Qualified for the UEFA Cup

SCOTTISH FA CUP FINAL 2007

Hampden Park, Glasgow, 26-05-2007, Att: 49 600, Ref: Clark

Celtic — 1 — Perrier Doumbe [84]
Dunfermline Athletic — 0

Celtic - Artur BORUC, Jean-Joël PERRIER DOUMBE•, Stephen MCMANUS, Steven PRESSLEY•, Lee NAYLOR, Shunsuke NAKAMURA, Neil LENNON (Gary CALDWELL 66), Paul HARTLEY, Aiden MCGEADY•, Kenny MILLER (Craig BEATTIE 56), Jan VENNEGOOR OF HESSELINK. Tr: Gordon STRACHAN

Dunfermline - Dorus DE VRIES, Greg SHIELDS, Scott WILSON, Souleymane BAMBA, Scott MUIRHEAD, Scott MORRISON (Stephen CRAWFORD 72), Darren YOUNG, Jamie MCCUNNIE, Adam HAMMILL, Mark BURCHILL• (Ian WILLIAMSON 89), Jim MCINTYRE (Jim HAMILTON 80). Tr: Stephen KENNY

CIS INSURANCE SCOTTISH LEAGUE CUP 2006-07

Second Round		Third Round	Quarter-finals		Semi-finals		Final	
Hibernian *	4	Hibernian *	Hibernian *	1	Hibernian ††	3	Hibernian	5
Peterhead	0	Gretna	Heart of Midlothian	0	St Johnstone	1	Kilmarnock	1
Gretna	Bye							
Alloa Athletic *	2	Alloa Athletic *						
Ross County	1	Heart of Midlothian						
Heart of Midlothian	Bye							
Rangers	Bye	Rangers	Rangers *	0				
Ayr United *	0 6p	Dunfermline Athletic *	St Johnstone	2				
Dunfermline Athletic	0 7p							
Dundee United *	1	Dundee United						
Airdrie United	0	St Johnstone *						
Elgin City	0							
St Johnstone *	4							
Falkirk	5	Falkirk	Falkirk	1 5p	Falkirk	0		
Cowdenbeath *	0	Inverness Caley Thistle *	Celtic *	1 4p	Kilmarnock †	3		
Dumbarton	1							
Inverness Caley Thistle *	3							
St Mirren *	3	St Mirren						
Stenhousemuir	1	Celtic *						
Celtic	Bye							
Motherwell	3	Motherwell	Motherwell	2				
Partick Thistle	2	Queen's Park *	Kilmarnock *	3				
Aberdeen	0 3p							
Queen's Park *	0 5p							
Livingston	3	Livingston						
Brechin City *	0	Kilmarnock *						
Queen of the South *	1							
Kilmarnock	2							

* Home team • † Played at Fir Park, Motherwell • †† Played at Tynecastle, Edinburgh

LEAGUE CUP FINAL

Hampden Park, Glasgow
18-03-2007. Ref: McDonald. Att: 52 000
Scorers - Jones 28 Benjelloun 2 59 85,
Fletcher 2 66 87 for Hibs; Greer 77 for Kilmarnock

Hibs - McNeil - Whittacker (Martis 90), Hogg
(McCann 90), Jones, Murphy, Beuzelin, Brown,
Stevenson, Fletcher, Benjelloun, Sproule
(Zemmama 79). Tr: John Collins

Kilmarnock - Combe - Ford, Greer, Wright,
Hay, Di Giacomo¯ (Locke 76), Johston, Fowler,
Leven (Wales 57), Nish, Naismith. Tr: Jim
Jefferies

CELTIC 2006–07

Date	Opponents	Score			Comp	Scorers	Att
29-07-2006	Kilmarnock	W	4-1	H	SPL	Zurawski 2 [25 90], Jarosik [38], Nakamura [75]	54 620
6-08-2006	Heart of Midlothian	L	1-2	A	SPL	Petrov [65]	16 822
12-08-2006	St Mirren	W	2-0	H	SPL	McManus [28], Petrov [65]	56 579
20-08-2006	Inverness Caledonian Thistle	D	1-1	A	SPL	Pearson [26]	7 332
26-08-2006	Hibernian	W	2-1	H	SPL	Zurawski [62], Vennegor of Hesselink [66]	58 078
9-09-2006	Aberdeen	W	1-0	A	SPL	Vennegor of Hesselink [78]	15 304
13-09-2006	Manchester United - ENG	L	2-3	A	CLgF	Vennegor of Hesselink [21], Nakamura [43]	74 031
16-09-2006	Dunfermline Athletic	W	1-0	H	SPL	McManus [31]	55 894
19-09-2006	St Mirren	W	2-0	H	LCr3	Beattie [75], Zurawski [85]	13 162
23-09-2006	Rangers	W	2-0	H	SPL	Gravesen [35], Miller [74]	59 341
26-09-2006	FC København - DEN	W	1-0	H	CLgF	Miller [36p]	58 000
1-10-2006	Falkirk	W	1-0	A	SPL	McGeady [84]	7 139
14-10-2006	Dundee United	W	4-1	H	SPL	Nakamura 3 [44 48 57], Vennegor of Hesselink [53]	10 504
17-10-2006	Benfica - POR	W	3-0	H	CLgF	Miller 2 [56 66], Pearson [90]	58 313
21-10-2006	Motherwell	W	2-1	H	SPL	Craigan OG [16], Zurawski [66]	57 742
29-10-2006	Kilmarnock	W	2-1	A	SPL	Nakamura [55], Miller [75]	10 083
1-11-2006	Benfica - POR	L	0-3	A	CLgF		47 574
4-11-2006	Heart of Midlothian	W	2-1	H	SPL	Jarosik [85], Gordon OG [94+]	58 971
7-11-2006	Falkirk	D	1-1	H	LCqf	Zurawski [98]. L 4-5p	19 316
12-11-2006	St Mirren	W	3-1	A	SPL	Gravesen 3 [2 21 68]	8 445
18-11-2006	Inverness Caledonian Thistle	W	3-0	H	SPL	Dodds OG [42], Vennegor of Hesselink [72], Jarosik [85]	56 637
21-11-2006	Manchester United - ENG	W	1-0	H	CLgF	Nakamura [81]	59 179
26-11-2006	Hibernian	D	2-2	A	SPL	Sno [70], McGeady [73]	16 747
2-12-2006	Aberdeen	W	1-0	H	SPL	Zurawski [72]	58 911
6-12-2006	FC København	L	1-3	A	CHgF	Jarosik [75]	38 647
10-12-2006	Dunfermline Athletic	W	2-1	A	SPL	McGeady [49], Zurawski [68]	7 080
17-12-2006	Rangers	D	1-1	A	SPL	Gravesen [38]	50 418
23-12-2006	Falkirk	W	1-0	H	SPL	Gravesen [24]	55 000
26-12-2006	Dundee United	D	2-2	H	SPL	O'Dea [78], Nakamura [80]	57 343
30-12-2006	Motherwell	D	1-1	A	SPL	Riordan [36]	9 769
2-01-2007	Kilmarnock	W	2-0	H	SPL	O'Dea [38], McGeady [90]	57 236
6-01-2007	Dumbarton	W	4-0	H	SCr3	Zurawski 2 [4 9], Vennegor of Hesselink [43], Riordan [69]	18 685
14-01-2007	Heart of Midlothian	W	2-1	A	SPL	Vennegor of Hesselink [59], Jarosik [81]	17 129
20-01-2007	St Mirren	W	5-1	H	SPL	Vennegor of Hesselink 3 [16 61p 75], McGeady [69], Miller [82]	58 382
28-01-2007	Inverness Caledonian Thistle	W	2-1	A	SPL	Riordan [37], Vennegor of Hesselink [90]	7 484
4-02-2007	Livingston	W	4-1	H	SCr4	O'Dea [30], Riordan 2 [45 59], Vennegor of Hesselink [61]	7 281
10-02-2007	Hibernian	W	1-0	H	SPL	Beattie [54]	59 659
17-02-2007	Aberdeen	W	2-1	A	SPL	Beattie [9], Nakamura [20]	16 711
20-02-2007	Milan - ITA	D	0-0	H	CLr2		58 785
25-02-2007	Inverness Caledonian Thistle	W	2-1	A	SCqf	Pressley [88], Miller [91+]	7 119
3-03-2007	Dunfermline Athletic	W	2-1	H	SPL	Miller [4], Vennegor of Hesselink [75]	59 131
7-03-2007	Milan - ITA	L	0-1	A	CLr2		52 914
11-03-2007	Rangers	L	0-1	A	SPL		59 425
18-03-2007	Falkirk	L	0-1	A	SPL		6 438
31-03-2007	Dundee United	D	1-1	A	SPL	Nakamura [48]	11 363
7-04-2007	Motherwell	W	1-0	H	SPL	Riordan [52]	58 654
14-04-2007	St Johnstone	W	2-1	N	SCsf	Vennegor of Hesselink 2 [13p 54]	28 339
22-04-2007	Kilmarnock	W	2-1	A	SPL	Vennegor of Hesselink [24], Nakamura [90]	13 673
29-04-2007	Heart of Midlothian	L	1-3	H	SPL	Pressley [63]	59 510
5-05-2007	Rangers	L	0-2	A	SPL		50 384
12-05-2007	Aberdeen	W	2-1	H	SPL	Vennegor of Hesselink 2 [33 49]	59 510
20-05-2007	Hibernian	L	1-2	A	SPL	Riordan [56]	13 855
26-05-2007	Dunfermline Athletic	W	1-0	N	SCf	Perrier-Doumbe [84]	49 600

SPL = Scottish Premier League • CL = UEFA Champions League • LC = League Cup • SC = Scottish FA Cup
gF = group F • r3 = third round • r4 = fourth round • qf = quarter-final • sf = semi-final • f = final • N = Hampden Park, Glasgow

RANGERS 2006-07

Date	Opponents	Score			Comp	Scorers	Att
30-07-2006	Motherwell	W	2-1	A	SPL	Sionko [8], Prso [65]	11 745
5-08-2006	Dundee United	D	2-2	H	SPL	Burke [57], Robb OG [79]	50 394
13-08-2006	Dunfermline Athletic	D	1-1	A	SPL	Buffel [63]	8 561
19-08-2006	Heart of Midlothian	W	2-0	H	SPL	Boyd 2 [47p 49]	50 239
27-08-2006	Kilmarnock	D	2-2	A	SPL	Boyd 2 [43 85]	13 506
9-09-2006	Falkirk	W	4-0	H	SPL	Bardsley [17], Prso [28], Boyd [68p], Buffel [78]	50 196
14-09-2006	Molde FK - NOR	D	0-0	A	UCr1		6 452
17-09-2006	Hibernian	L	1-2	A	SPL	Sebo [65]	16 450
20-09-2006	Dunfermline Athletic	W	2-0	H	LCr3	Bamba OG [65], Boyd [73]	5 702
23-09-2006	Celtic	L	0-2	A	SPL		59 341
28-09-2006	Molde FK - NOR	W	2-0	H	UCr1	Buffel [12], Ferguson [45]	44 624
1-10-2006	Aberdeen	W	1-0	H	SPL	Sebo [88]	50 488
14-10-2006	Inverness Caledonian Thistle	L	0-1	H	SPL		49 494
19-10-2006	Livorno	W	3-2	A	UCgA	Adam [27], Boyd [30p], Novo [35]	13 199
22-10-2006	St Mirren	W	3-2	A	SPL	Adam [18], Buffel [26], Novo [85]	8 384
28-10-2006	Motherwell	D	1-1	H	SPL	Boyd [36]	49 785
2-11-2006	Maccabi Haifa	W	2-0	H	UCgA	Novo [5], Adam [89p]	43 062
5-11-2006	Dundee United	L	1-2	A	SPL	Adam [50]	10 392
8-11-2006	St Johnstone	L	0-2	H	LCqf		31 074
11-11-2006	Dunfermline Athletic	W	2-0	H	SPL	Boyd [61], Smith [77]	48 218
19-11-2006	Heart of Midlothian	W	1-0	A	SPL	Novo [78]	17 040
23-11-2006	Auxerre - FRA	D	2-2	A	UCgA	Novo [62], Boyd [84]	8 305
26-11-2006	Kilmarnock	W	3-0	H	SPL	Adam [23], Boyd [28], Prso [58]	48 289
3-12-2006	Falkirk	L	0-1	A	SPL		7 245
9-12-2006	Hibernian	W	3-0	H	SPL	Prso [16], Sionko [32], Ferguson [36]	49 702
14-12-2006	Partizan Beograd	W	1-0	H	UCgA	Hutton [55]	43 129
17-12-2006	Celtic	D	1-1	H	SPL	Hemdani [88]	50 418
23-12-2006	Aberdeen	W	2-1	H	SPL	Novo [22], Sionko [24]	20 045
27-12-2006	Inverness Caledonian Thistle	L	1-2	A	SPL	Novo [22p]	7 522
30-12-2006	St Mirren	D	1-1	H	SPL	Boyd [19]	50 273
2-01-2007	Motherwell	W	1-0	H	SPL	Boyd [70p]	10 338
7-01-2007	Dunfermline Athletic	L	2-3	A	SCr3	Boyd 2 [54 68]	7 231
13-01-2007	Dundee United	W	5-0	H	SPL	Adam [23], Burke [36], Boyd 2 [59 68], Ferguson [88]	50 276
21-01-2007	Dunfermline Athletic	W	1-0	A	SPL	Adam [9]	7 868
27-01-2007	Heart of Midlothian	D	0-0	H	SPL		50 321
11-02-2007	Kilmarnock	W	3-1	A	SPL	Boyd 3 [9p 30 60p]	11 894
14-02-2007	Hapoel Tel Aviv - ISR	L	1-2	A	UCr2	Novo [53]	11 175
18-02-2007	Falkirk	W	2-1	H	SPL	Boyd [34], Ferguson [73]	49 850
22-02-2007	Hapoel Tel Aviv - ISR	W	4-0	H	UCr2	Ferguson 2 [24 73], Boyd [35], Adam [95+]	46 213
4-03-2007	Hibernian	W	2-0	A	SPL	Adam 2 [4 60]	16 265
8-03-2007	Osasuna - ESP	D	1-1	H	UCr3	Hemdani [92+]	50 290
11-03-2007	Celtic	W	1-0	H	SPL	Ehiogu [50]	59 425
14-03-2007	Osasuna	L	0-1	A	UCr3		19 126
17-03-2007	Aberdeen	W	3-0	H	SPL	Boyd 3 [8 25 31]	50 354
31-03-2007	Inverness Caledonian Thistle	D	1-1	H	SPL	Adam [15]	50 278
8-04-2007	St Mirren	W	1-0	A	SPL	Novo [4]	7 308
21-04-2007	Heart of Midlothian	W	2-1	H	SPL	Rae [52], Ferguson [79]	50 099
28-04-2007	Hibernian	D	3-3	A	SPL	Adam 2 [24 78], Hutton [54]	16 747
5-05-2007	Celtic	W	2-0	H	SPL	Boyd [34], Adam [55]	50 384
13-05-2007	Kilmarnock	L	0-1	H	SPL		50 085
20-05-2007	Aberdeen	L	0-2	A	SPL		20 010

SPL = Scottish Premier League • UC = UEFA Cup • LC = League Cup • SC = Scottish FA Cup
r1 = first round • gA = Group A • r1 = first round • r2 = second round • r3 = third round

HIBERNIAN 2006–07

Date	Opponents	Score		Comp	Scorers	Att
29-07-2006	Aberdeen	D 1-1	H	SPL	Shiels [31]	15 046
5-08-2006	Kilmarnock	L 1-2	A	SPL	Shiels [31]	6 299
13-08-2006	Inverness Caledonian Thistle	D 0-0	A	SPL		4 623
19-08-2006	Motherwell	W 3-1	H	SPL	Benjelloun [30], Brown.Sc [65], Jones [82]	13 274
22-08-2006	Peterhead	W 4-0	H	LCr2	Good OG [7], Benjelloun [32], Brown.Sc [52], McCluskey [66p]	7 834
26-08-2006	Celtic	L 1-2	A	SPL	Brown.Sc [8]	58 078
10-09-2006	Dundee United	W 3-0	A	SPL	Killen [52], Shiels [81], Sproule [90]	6 387
17-09-2006	Rangers	W 2-1	H	SPL	Killen 2 [8 81]	16 450
20-09-2006	Gretna	W 6-0	H	LCr3	Fletcher [11], Brown [18], Jones [20], Shiels 2 [24 63], Benjelloun [72]	11 075
23-09-2006	Falkirk	L 0-1	H	SPL		14 828
30-09-2006	St Mirren	L 0-1	A	SPL		6 008
15-10-2006	Heart of Midlothian	D 2-2	H	SPL	Zemmama [5], Killen [16]	16 623
23-10-2006	Dunfermline Athletic	W 4-0	A	SPL	Sproule [44], Killen 2 [62 90], Benjelloun [89]	6 057
30-10-2006	Aberdeen	L 1-2	A	SPL	Killen [47]	11 179
4-11-2006	Kilmarnock	D 2-2	H	SPL	Stewart [53], Fletcher [57]	13 510
8-11-2006	Heart of Midlothian	W 1-0	H	LCqf	Jones [31]	15 825
11-11-2006	Inverness Caledonian Thistle	W 2-0	H	SPL	Fletcher [65], Killen [83p]	12 868
18-11-2006	Motherwell	W 6-1	A	SPL	Brown.Sc [10], Killen [25], Sproule 2 [29 40], Jones [73], Shields [90]	6 190
26-11-2006	Celtic	D 2-2	H	SPL	Sproule [11], Thomson [64]	16 747
2-12-2006	Dundee United	W 2-1	H	SPL	Jones [45], Fletcher [73]	14 032
9-12-2006	Rangers	L 0-3	A	SPL		49 702
16-12-2006	Falkirk	L 1-2	A	SPL	Fletcher [56]	6 142
23-12-2006	St Mirren	W 5-1	H	SPL	Beuzelin [21], Killen [32], Shiels [58], Zemmama [65], Benjelloun [74]	13 053
26-12-2006	Heart of Midlothian	L 2-3	A	SPL	Killen [55], Shiels [61p]	17 369
30-12-2006	Dunfermline Athletic	W 2-0	H	SPL	Killen 2 [63 72p]	14 061
2-01-2007	Aberdeen	D 0-0	H	SPL		16 278
10-01-2007	Aberdeen	D 2-2	A	SCr3	Sproule [43], Killen [73]	7 905
15-01-2007	Kilmarnock	W 2-0	A	SPL	Sproule [51], Fletcher [87]	4 963
18-01-2007	Aberdeen	W 4-1	H	SCr3	Fletcher [13], Stewart [45], Benjelloun 2 [47 56]	11 375
21-01-2007	Inverness Caledonian Thistle	L 0-3	A	SPL		4 577
27-01-2007	Motherwell	W 2-0	H	SPL	Brown.Sc [66], Benjelloun [90]	14 280
31-01-2007	St Johnstone	W 3-1	N	LCsf	Fletcher [3], Murphy [92], Benjelloun [120]	16 112
3-02-2007	Gretna	W 3-1	H	SCr4	Jones [28], Fleming OG [54], Benjelloun [59]	14 075
10-02-2007	Celtic	L 0-1	H	SPL		59 659
18-02-2007	Dundee United	D 0-0	A	SPL		6 453
24-02-2007	Queen of the South	W 2-1	A	SCqf	Murphy [45], Sowunmi [51]	6 400
4-03-2007	Rangers	L 0-2	H	SPL		16 265
10-03-2007	Falkirk	W 2-0	H	SPL	Benjelloun 2 [52 74]	12 572
18-03-2007	Kilmarnock	W 5-1	N	LCf	Jones [28], Benjelloun 2 [59 85], Fletcher 2 [66 87]	52 000
1-04-2007	Heart of Midlothian	L 0-1	H	SPL		15 953
4-04-2007	St Mirren	D 1-1	A	SPL	Jones [20]	4 031
7-04-2007	Dunfermline Athletic	L 0-1	A	SPL		6 001
15-04-2007	Dunfermline Athletic	D 0-0	N	SCsf		25 336
21-04-2007	Aberdeen	D 2-2	A	SPL	Gray [19], Shiels [44]	9 753
24-04-2007	Dunfermline Athletic	L 0-1	N	SCsf		8 536
28-04-2007	Rangers	D 3-3	H	SPL	Fletcher [20], McCann [45], Whittaker [62]	16 747
5-05-2007	Kilmarnock	L 0-1	H	SPL		10 674
12-05-2007	Heart of Midlothian	L 0-2	A	SPL		17 349
20-05-2007	Celtic	W 2-1	H	SPL	Brown.Sc [60], Sproule [90]	13 855

SPL = Scottish Premier League • LC = League Cup • SC = Scottish FA Cup
r2 = second round • r3 = third round • r4 = fourth round • qf = quarter-final • sf = semi-final • f = final
N = Tynecastle, Edinburgh • N = Hampden Park, Glasgow

SEN – SENEGAL

NATIONAL TEAM RECORD
JULY 10TH 2006 TO JULY 12TH 2010

PL	W	D	L	F	A	%
8	5	2	1	13	5	75

FIFA/COCA-COLA WORLD RANKING

1993	1994	1995	1996	1997	1998	1999	2000	2001	2002	2003	2004	2005	2006	High		Low	
56	50	47	58	85	95	79	88	65	27	33	31	30	41	26	06/04	95	12/98

2006–2007											
08/06	09/06	10/06	11/06	12/06	01/07	02/07	03/07	04/07	05/07	06/07	07/07
35	33	39	41	41	41	38	45	40	39	43	44

The generation of players that helped catapult Senegal to world renown at the 2002 World Cup finals is now fast reaching the end of its shelf-life as the national team takes on a new look. It is, as yet, a far from polished outfit, and is hampered by constant comparisons to the 2002 team which also reached the final of the African Nations Cup in Mali. Coach Henryk Kasperczak, embarking on a new African adventure after past stints with Cote d'Ivoire, Tunisia and Morocco, has no shortage of talent on which to lay new foundations and while Senegal were involved in a tough tussle for qualification to the 2008 Nations Cup finals, they showed a potential to match, and maybe even

INTERNATIONAL HONOURS
Qualified for the FIFA World Cup finals 2002   Copa Amilcar Cabral 1979 1980 1983 1984 1985 1986 1991 2001

surpass in future, the achievements of 2002. At club level, the country continued to be allowed to enter two teams in the 2007 African Champions League but both Diaraf Dakar and Port Autonome failed at the first hurdle. Diaraf lost embarrassingly to Marantha Fiokpo of Togo while Douanes were disqualified for using an improperly registered player. They had won their first round tie against Malien opposition but were promptly kicked out of the competition by CAF. There was also chaos in the League with the suspension of eight clubs from the top division as the first stage of the season drew to a close. As a result the Championship play-offs were delayed.

THE FIFA BIG COUNT OF 2000

	Male	Female		Male	Female
Registered players	6 593	0	Referees	3 230	0
Non registered players	40 000	0	Officials	2 700	0
Youth players	146 689	0	Total involved	199 212	
Total players	193 282		Number of clubs	82	
Professional players	50	0	Number of teams	12 200	

Fédération Sénégalaise de Football (FSF)
VDN-Ouest-Foire en face du CICES, Case Postale 13021, Dakar, Senegal
Tel +221 8692828   Fax +221 8200592
fsf@senegalfoot.sn   www.senegalfoot.sn
President: NDOYE Mbaye   General Secretary: SENE Doudou
Vice-President: NDIAYE Momar   Treasurer: DIAGNE Blaise   Media Officer: SECK Mbacke
Men's Coach: KASPERCZAK Henryk   Women's Coach: DIABY Bassouare
FSF formed: 1960   CAF: 1963   FIFA: 1962
White shirts with yellow trimmings, White shorts, White socks or Green shirts with yellow trimmings, Green shorts, Green socks

RECENT INTERNATIONAL MATCHES PLAYED BY SENEGAL

2003	Opponents	Score		Venue	Comp	Scorers	Att	Referee
10-09	Japan	W	1-0	Niigata	Fr	Diop.PB [6]	40 000	Moradi IRN
10-10	Egypt	L	0-1	Cairo	Fr		20 000	
15-11	Côte d'Ivoire	W	1-0	Dakar	Fr	Diouf [89]	50 000	Daami TUN
2004								
18-01	South Africa	W	2-1	Dakar	Fr	Diop.PM [29], Mabizela OG [83]	50 000	El Achiri MAR
26-01	Burkina Faso	D	0-0	Tunis	CNr1		2 000	Guezzaz MAR
30-01	Kenya	W	3-0	Bizerte	CNr1	Niang 2 [4 31], Diop.PB [19]	13 500	Abd El Fatah EGY
2-02	Mali	D	1-1	Tunis	CNr1	Beye [45]	7 550	Evehe CMR
7-02	Tunisia	L	0-1	Tunis	CNqf		57 000	Bujsaim UAE
29-05	Guinea	D	1-1	Paris	Fr	Guaye [82]	2 000	Garibian FRA
5-06	Congo	W	2-0	Dakar	WCq	Diatta [59], Ndiaya [77]	18 000	Benouza ALG
13-06	Cape Verde Islands	W	3-1	Praia	Fr	Gueye [65], Kamara.D 2 [71 74]	10 000	
20-06	Togo	L	1-3	Lome	WCq	Diop.PB [81]	25 000	El Arjoun MAR
3-07	Zambia	W	1-0	Dakar	WCq	Gueye [21]	50 000	Monteiro Duarte CPV
18-08	Côte d'Ivoire	L	1-2	Avignon	Fr	Camara [12]	5 000	
5-09	Mali	D	2-2	Bamako	WCq	Camara.H [45], Dia [84]	45 000	Guezzaz MAR
10-10	Liberia	W	3-0	Monrovia	WCq	Diop.PB [41], Camara.H 2 [50 73]	26 000	Aboubacar CIV
17-11	Algeria	W	2-1	Toulon	Fr	Niang [35], Gueye [41]	4 000	Bata FRA
2005								
9-02	Cameroon	L	0-1	Creteil	Fr			
26-03	Liberia	W	6-1	Dakar	WCq	Fadiga [19], Diouf 2 [45p 84], Faye [56], Camara.H [72], Ndiaye [75]	50 000	Shelmani LBY
5-06	Congo	D	0-0	Brazzaville	WCq		40 000	Damon RSA
18-06	Togo	D	2-2	Dakar	WCq	Niang [15], Camara.H [30]	50 000	Guirat TUN
17-08	Ghana	D	0-0	London	Fr			
3-09	Zambia	W	1-0	Chililabombwe	WCq	Diouf [57]	20 000	Abd El Fatah EGY
8-10	Mali	W	3-0	Dakar	WCq	Camara.H 2 [18 65], Diouf [23]	30 000	Maillet SEY
12-11	South Africa	W	3-2	Port Elizabeth	Fr	Camara.S [3], Kamara [22], Momar N'Diaye [85]		N'Doye SEN
2006								
14-01	Congo DR	D	0-0	Dakar	Fr			
23-01	Zimbabwe	W	2-0	Port Said	CNr1	Camara.C [60], Issa Ba [80]	15 000	Abdel Rahman SUD
27-01	Ghana	L	0-1	Port Said	CNr1		20 000	El Arjoun MAR
31-01	Nigeria	L	1-2	Port Said	CNr1	Camara.S [59]	5 000	Damon RSA
3-02	Guinea	W	3-2	Alexandria	CNqf	Diop.PB [62], Niang [84], Camara.H [93+]	17 000	Codjia BEN
7-02	Egypt	L	1-2	Cairo	CNsf	Kamara [54]	74 000	Evehe CMR
9-02	Nigeria	L	0-1	Cairo	CN3p		11 354	Coulibaly MLI
1-03	Norway	W	2-1	Dakar	Fr	Moussa N'Diaye [20], Gueye [36]	45 000	Pare BFA
23-05	Korea Republic	D	1-1	Seoul	Fr	Moussa N'Diaye [80]	64 836	
16-08	Côte d'Ivoire	W	1-0	Tours	Fr	Niang [64]	4 000	Husset FRA
2-09	Mozambique	W	2-0	Dakar	CNq	Dario Khan OG [35], Ndaw [61]		Mana NGA
7-10	Burkina Faso	L	0-1	Ouagadougou	CNq			Guezzaz MAR
2007								
7-02	Benin	W	2-1	Rouen	Fr	Demba Toure [9], Papa N'Diaye [64]		Lannoy FRA
24-03	Tanzania	W	4-0	Dakar	CNq	Niang 3 [39 48 62], Diomansy Kamara [46]		Daami TUN
2-06	Tanzania	D	1-1	Mwanza	CNq	Demba Ba [71]		
10-06	Malawi	W	3-2	Blantyre	Fr	OG [22], Demba Toure 2 [44 85]		
17-06	Mozambique	D	0-0	Maputo	CNq			

Fr = Friendly match • CN = CAF African Cup of Nations • WC = FIFA World Cup • q = qualifier • r1 = first round group • qf = quarter-final

SENEGAL NATIONAL TEAM RECORDS AND RECORD SEQUENCES

Records			Sequence records					
Victory	6-0	MTN 1984	Wins	11	1985-1986	Clean sheets	6	1999-2000
Defeat	0-4	Seven times	Defeats	4	1969-1970	Goals scored	14	1999
Player Caps	n/a		Undefeated	12	1987-1989	Without goal	7	1987
Player Goals	n/a		Without win	12	2000-2001	Goals against	22	1965-1970

REPUBLIC OF SENEGAL; REPUBLIQUE DU SENEGAL

MAJOR CITIES/TOWNS	
	Population '000
1 Dakar	2 461
2 Thiès	261
3 Mbour	191
4 Kaolack	179
5 Rufisque	179
6 Saint-Louis	164
7 Ziguinchor	163
8 Diourbel	102
9 Louga	82
10 Tambacounda	77
11 Kolda	62
12 Mbacké	56
13 Tivaouane	53
14 Richard Toll	46
15 Joal-Fadiouth	39
16 Kaffrine	29
17 Dahra	28
18 Bignona	26
19 Fatick	24
20 Velingara	23
21 Bambey	22
22 Nioro	21
23 Sédhiou	20
24 Mékhé	20

Capital	Dakar	Language	French, Wolof, Pulaar, Jola, Mandinka	Independence	1960
Population	12 521 851	Area	196 190 km²	Density	55 per km²	% in cities	42%
GDP per cap	$1 600	Dailling code	+221	Internet	.sn	GMT +/-	0

MEDALS TABLE

		Overall			Lge	Cup		Africa				City	Stadium	Cap'ty	DoF
		G	S	B	G	G	S	G	S	B					
1	ASC Diaraf	22	6	1	10	12	6			1	Dakar	Stade de Diaraf	10 000	1969
2	Jeanne d'Arc	16	5	3	10	6	4		1	3	Dakar	Stade Leopold Sédar Senghor	60 000	1921
3	AS Douanes	9	1		3	6	1				Dakar	Stade Leopold Sédar Senghor	60 000	
4	US Gorée	7	5	2	3	4	5			2	Gorée, Dakar	Stade Demba Diop	15 000	
5	SUNEOR (ex Sonacos)	5	3		4	1	3				Diourbel	Stade Municipal	5 000	
6	ASF Police	4	3		1	3	3				Dakar	Stade Municipal de Police	5 000	
7	ASEC Ndiambour	4	2		3	1	2				Louga	Stade ASEC	15 000	
8	Port Autonome	4	1		3	1	1				Dakar	Stade Port Autonome	4 000	
9	ASC Linguère	3	3			3	3				Saint-Louis	Stade Julton	3 000	
10	ASFA Dakar	3	2		3		2				Dakar	Stade de ASFA	2 000	
11	US Ouakem	3				3					Dakar	Stade Demba Diop	15 000	
12	Olympique Thiès	2	2		2		2				Thiès	Stade Maniang Soumaré	8 000	
13	Espoir Saint-Louis	2			1	1					Saint-Louis	Stade Julton	3 000	
14	Casa Sports	1	1			1	1				Ziginchour	Stade Aline Sitoe Diatta	10 000	
	Saltigues	1	1			1	1				Rufisque	Stade Maniang Soumaré	8 000	

RECENT LEAGUE AND CUP RECORD

	Championship						Cup		
Year	Champions	Pts	Runners-up	Pts	Third	Pts	Winners	Score	Runners-up
1995	ASC Diaraf	2-1	ESO				ASC Diaraf	2-0	AS Douanes
1996	Sonacos	‡	Linguère				US Gorée	1-0	ASC Ndiambour
1997	ASC Douanes	46	Jeanne d'Arc	45	Linguère	43	AS Douanes	3-1	Linguère
1998	ASC Ndiambour	47	ASC Diaraf	46	AS Douanes	39	ASC Yeggo	1-0	US Gorée
1999	Jeanne d'Arc	53	ASC Ndiambour	46	CSS Richard-Toll	43	ASC Ndiambour	1-1 3-0p	Sonacos
2000	ASC Diaraf	37	Port Autoname	36	ASC Ndiambour	35	Port Autonome	4-0	AS Saloum
2001	Jeanne d'Arc	47	ASC Ndiambour	45	US Gorée	44	Sonacos	1-0	US Gorée
2002	Jeanne d'Arc	52	Sonacos	42	ASC Ndiambour	39	AS Douanes	1-1 4-1p	Sonacos
2003	Jeanne d'Arc	51	ASC Diaraf	47	AS Douanes	43	AS Douanes	1-0	ASC Thiès
2004	ASC Diaraf	72	AS Douanes	69	ASC Ndiambour	65	AS Douanes	2-1	ASC Diaraf
2005	Port Autonome	67	ASC Diaraf	54	CSS Richard-Toll	49	AS Douanes	1-0	DUC Dakar
2006	AS Douanes	14	ASC Diaraf	7	US Gorée	6	US Ouakem	1-0	ASC Médiour

‡ Sonacos 3-0 0-1 Linguère

SENEGAL 2006–07

CHAMPIONNAT NATIONAL 1ERE DIVISION POULE A

	Pl	W	D	L	F	A	Pts	Douanes	USO	Xam-Xam	Jeanne d'Arc	SUNEOR	Thiès	Ndiambour	Port	HLM
AS Douanes †	16	10	4	2	23	7	34		0-1	2-1	2-0	1-1	2-1	4-1	1-0	0-0
US Ouakem †	15	7	4	4	14	13	25	0-0		1-0	0-5	n/p	2-0	0-1	2-0	0-0
Xam-Xam †	16	6	5	5	18	16	23	1-3	1-0		1-1	2-1	1-2	0-0	1-0	1-1
Jeanne d'Arc	16	6	5	6	18	21	20	0-2	1-1	2-2		1-0	2-2	2-2	0-2	1-0
SUNEOR	14	4	6	4	9	7	18	0-0	0-1	1-0	0-1		1-1	0-0	0-0	0-0
ASC Thiès	15	4	5	6	18	20	17	0-2	2-2	1-2	2-0	n/p		0-1	0-1	1-1
ASEC Ndiambour	16	3	8	5	11	16	17	0-2	0-1	1-1	0-1	0-2	2-2		2-0	0-0
Port Autonome	16	5	2	9	10	17	17	1-0	0-2	0-2	3-1	0-1	0-2	1-1		1-0
ASC HLM Dakar	16	2	7	7	8	16	13	0-2	3-0	0-2	‡	0-2	1-2	0-0	2-1	

13/01/2007 - 8/07/2007 • † Qualified for the play-offs • Matches in bold awarded 2-0 • ‡ Awarded 2-0 against both sides • n/p = not played

SENEGAL 2006–07

CHAMPIONNAT NATIONAL 1ERE DIVISION POULE B

	Pl	W	D	L	F	A	Pts	Saloum	Stade Mbour	Casa	GFC	Diaraf	Gorée	Renaissance	Yakaar	DUC
AS Saloum Kaolack †	16	8	6	2	14	7	30		0-0	0-0	0-0	1-0	1-0	1-0	1-0	2-0
Stade Mbour †	16	7	7	2	18	10	28	0-0		2-1	2-1	1-1	2-0	2-0	3-1	1-1
Casa Sport †	16	7	7	2	17	9	28	2-1	2-0		2-0	2-1	1-1	2-0	1-0	1-0
Guédiawaye FC Dakar	16	4	7	5	11	10	19	1-1	1-1	0-0		2-0	1-0	0-0	0-1	0-0
ASC Diaraf	16	5	3	8	10	18	18	0-1	0-0	2-0	0-2		0-3	2-1	1-0	2-1
US Gorée	16	4	4	8	12	17	16	3-0	1-0	1-1	0-2	0-2		0-1	1-1	‡
Renaissance Dakar	16	2	4	10	5	19	10	1-1	0-2	0-0	1-0	0-1	1-1		‡	‡
ASC Yakaar	16	2	4	10	5	20	10	0-2	0-0	0-0	1-1	‡	‡	0-2		0-2
DUC Dakar	16	2	4	10	6	22	10	0-2	1-1	1-3	1-0	0-0	0-1	1-0	0-1	

13/01/2007 - 8/07/2007 • † Qualified for the play-offs • Matches in bold awarded 2-0 • ‡ Awarded 2-0 against both sides

COUPE NATIONALE 2006

Eighth-finals		Quarter-finals		Semi-finals		Final	
US Ouakem	0 4p						
CSS Richard-Toll	0 3p	US Ouakem	1				
AS Saloum Kaolack	0	ASC HLM Dakar	0				
ASC HLM Dakar	1			US Ouakem	2		
Jeanne d'Arc	2			Stade Mbour	1		
Casa Sports	1	Jeanne d'Arc	0				
Guédiawaye FC	0	Stade Mbour	1				
Stade Mbour	1					US Ouakem	1
US Gorée	1					ASC Médiour Rufisque	0
ASC Yakaar	0	US Gorée	3				
Port Autonome	1	Renaissance Dakar	1				
Renaissance Dakar	2			US Gorée	0		
Sonacos Diourbel	1			ASC Médiour Rufisque	1		
DUC Dakar	0	Sonacos Diourbel	0 p				
ASC Ndiatigué Louga	0	ASC Médiour Rufisque	0 p				
ASC Médiour Rufisque	2			‡ Qualified for the CAF Confederation Cup			

CUP FINAL

Stade Demba Diop, Dakar
29-07-2006, Att: 25 000, Ref: Fall

Scorer - Meissa Ndiaye [50]

SEY – SEYCHELLES

NATIONAL TEAM RECORD
JULY 10TH 2006 TO JULY 12TH 2010

PL	W	D	L	F	A	%
9	1	1	7	3	23	16.6

FIFA/COCA-COLA WORLD RANKING

1993	1994	1995	1996	1997	1998	1999	2000	2001	2002	2003	2004	2005	2006	High	Low
157	175	176	175	181	181	192	188	192	185	163	173	176	130	129 10/06	195 07/02

2006–2007											
08/06	09/06	10/06	11/06	12/06	01/07	02/07	03/07	04/07	05/07	06/07	07/07
136	146	129	130	130	130	132	132	136	143	152	150

After reaching an all-time high of 141 in the FIFA/Coca-Cola World Ranking in mid-2006, Seychelles looked to be going back on much of their progress as they lost five games in the first half of 2007. The defeats in African Nations Cup qualifiers and the regional COSAFA Castle Cup, came without the Seychellois being able to score once. In contrast, they conceded 16 goals in those five games and lost much of the momentum built up in 2006 when they won an unprecedented three matches in a single calendar year. Officials, however, remained buoyant about the future growth of football in Africa's smallest country where youth programmes are being steadily

INTERNATIONAL HONOURS
None

developed and facilities upgraded, with the help of FIFA's Goal project. National coach Raoul Shungu, originally from the Democratic Republic of Congo, was heavily involved in developmental work while at the same ensuring a more youthful edge to the national side, who are now known as the Pirates. Anse Reunion won a first championship after finishing two points clear in the standings of perennial challengers St Michel United who had to be content with winning the Cup. At the end of the 2006, Seychelles Football Federation president Suketu Patel won election to head the regional COSAFA body, replacing Ismail Bhamjee of Botswana.

THE FIFA BIG COUNT OF 2006

	Male	Female		Total
Number of players	5 675	185	Referees and Assistant Referees	70
Professionals	0		Admin, Coaches, Technical, Medical	320
Amateurs 18+	1 225		Number of clubs	20
Youth under 18	835		Number of teams	60
Unregistered	800		Clubs with women's teams	0
Total players	5 860		Players as % of population	7.19%

Seychelles Football Federation (SFF)
People's Stadium, PO Box 843, Victoria, Mahe, Seychelles
Tel +248 601160   Fax +248 601163
sff@seychelles.net   www.sff.sc
President: PATEL Suketu   General Secretary: NOURRICE Louis
Vice-President: ADAM Nicholas   Treasurer: MATHIOT Justin   Media Officer: LAURO Gian Carlo
Men's Coach: SHUNGU Rahoul   Women's Coach: none
SFF formed: 1979   CAF: 1986   FIFA: 1986
Red shirts, Red shorts, Red socks

RECENT INTERNATIONAL MATCHES PLAYED BY THE SEYCHELLES

2002	Opponents	Score		Venue	Comp	Scorers	Att	Referee
28-08	Madagascar	D	1-1	Curepipe	IOr1	Balde [87]	1 000	Lim Kee Chong MRI
2-09	Mauritius	D	0-0	Curepipe	IOr1			
4-09	Reunion	L	0-1	Curepipe	IOr1		1 000	
11-10	Zambia	L	0-4	Victoria	WCq		2 700	Lim Kee Chong MRI
15-11	Zambia	D	1-1	Lusaka	WCq	Suzette [69]	30 000	Abdulkadir TAN
2004								
No international matches played in 2004								
2005								
26-02	South Africa	L	0-3	Curepipe	CCr1			Roheemun MRI
2006								
28-06	Mauritius	W	2-1	Victoria	Fr	Brutus [47], Ladouche		
30-06	Tanzania	W	2-1	Victoria	Fr	Rose [23], Zialor [81]		
22-07	Namibia	D	1-1	Katutura	CCr1	Wilnes Brutus [18], W 4-2p		Simisse MRI
23-07	Zambia	L	0-2	Katutura	CCr1			Ngobo RSA
3-09	Sudan	L	0-3	Khartoum	CNq			Kidane ERI
7-10	Mauritius	W	2-1	Roche Caiman	CNq	Wilnes Brutus 2 [23 81]		Raolimanana MAD
2007								
24-03	Tunisia	L	0-3	Victoria	CNq			Ssegonga UGA
28-04	Mozambique	L	0-2	Maputo	CCr1			Mpopo LES
29-04	Madagascar	L	0-5	Maputo	CCr1			Mpopo LES
2-06	Tunisia	L	0-4	Rades/Tunis	CNq			
16-06	Sudan	L	0-2	Roche Caiman	CNq			

Fr = Friendly match • CN = CAN African Cup of Nations • IO = Indian Ocean Games • CC = COSAFA Castle Cup • WC = FIFA World Cup
q = qualifier • r1 = first round group

SEYCHELLES NATIONAL TEAM RECORDS AND RECORD SEQUENCES

Records			Sequence records					
Victory	9-0	MDV 1979	Wins	2	2006	Clean sheets	1	
Defeat	0-6	MAD 1990	Defeats	11	1992-1996	Goals scored	4	1979-1983
Player Caps	n/a		Undefeated	2	Four times	Without goal	5	2007
Player Goals	n/a		Without win	14	1992-1998	Goals against	17	1990-1998

SEYCHELLES 2006 FIRST DIVISION

	Pl	W	D	L	F	A	Pts
Anse Réunion	18	11	6	1	28	11	39
St Michel United	18	11	4	3	33	11	37
La Passe	18	8	5	5	28	16	29
Seychelles MB	18	7	6	5	30	26	27
St Louis	18	6	8	4	32	22	26
Northern Dynamo	18	8	2	8	22	23	26
Red Star	18	6	5	7	28	25	23
Light Stars	18	4	6	8	23	24	18
Sunshine	18	4	2	12	16	36	14
The Lions	18	2	2	14	14	60	8

15/04/2006 - 30/09/2006 • Play-off: Sunshine 2-1 At. Juniors

RECENT LEAGUE AND CUP RECORD

	Championship		Cup		
Year	Champions	Winners	Score	Runners-up	
1996	St Michel United	St Louis			
1997	St Michel United	St Michel			
1998	Red Star	St Michel United	4-0	Ascot	
1999	St Michel United	Red Star	2-1	Sunshine	
2000	St Michel United	Sunshine	1-1 4-2p	Red Star	
2001	Red Star	St Michel United	2-1	Sunshine	
2002	La Passe	Anse Reunion	2-1	Red Star	
2003	St Michel United	St Louis	2-1	Light Stars	
2004	La Passe	Red Star	1-0	Anse Réunion	
2005	La Passe	Seychelles MB	1-0	Anse Réunion	
2006	Anse Réunion	St Michel United	2-1	Red Star	

SEYCHELLES COUNTRY INFORMATION

Capital	Victoria	Independence	1976 from the UK	GDP per Capita	$7 800
Population	80 832	Status	Republic	GNP Ranking	169
Area km²	455	Language	English, French, Creole	Dialling code	+248
Population density	177 per km²	Literacy rate	58%	Internet code	.sc
% in urban areas	54%	Main religion	Christian	GMT +/−	+4
Towns/Cities	Victoria 26 361				
Neighbours (km)	Indian Ocean 491				
Main stadia	Stade Linité – Victoria 12 000				

SIN – SINGAPORE

NATIONAL TEAM RECORD
JULY 10TH 2006 TO JULY 12TH 2010

PL	W	D	L	F	A	%
18	5	7	6	30	22	47.2

FIFA/COCA-COLA WORLD RANKING

1993	1994	1995	1996	1997	1998	1999	2000	2001	2002	2003	2004	2005	2006	High	Low
75	95	104	92	103	81	104	101	115	118	106	112	92	111	**73** 08/93	**132** 07/07

2006–2007											
08/06	09/06	10/06	11/06	12/06	01/07	02/07	03/07	04/07	05/07	06/07	07/07
106	107	115	116	111	126	123	123	124	125	131	132

The 2007 AFC Asian Cup proved to be an awkward time for football fans in Singapore. The feeling of having not been invited to the party going on next door was compounded by the fact that the Singapore national team was actually playing better football than any of the four co-hosts. They proved that at the ASEAN Football Federation Championship in January, six months before the finals, where they got the better of all four of them on the way to retaining their title. Along the way they also set a new record score by beating Laos 11-0 with Noh Alam Shah scoring seven of them. Having beaten Malaysia on penalties in the semi-finals, Singapore then won the first leg of

INTERNATIONAL HONOURS
ASEAN Football Federation Championship 1998 2002 2005 2007

the final against Thailand 2-1 before a huge crowd at home in the National Stadium before securing the title when Khairul Amri equalised nine minutes from time in the second leg in Bangkok. Clubs from Singapore continued to be a force in the AFC Cup with Tampines Rovers reaching the quarter-finals of the 2006 edition, where they lost to Jordan's Al Wihdat. Both they and Singapore Armed Forces qualified for the 2007 edition after Singapore Armed Forces were crowned 2006 Singapore champions and Tampines Rovers won the Cup. They both won their respective groups in the 2007 AFC Cup to qualify for the knock-out stage.

THE FIFA BIG COUNT OF 2006

	Male	Female		Total
Number of players	188 626	8 377	Referees and Assistant Referees	171
Professionals	233		Admin, Coaches, Technical, Medical	1 345
Amateurs 18+	1 250		Number of clubs	41
Youth under 18	7 300		Number of teams	104
Unregistered	181 000		Clubs with women's teams	13
Total players	197 003		Players as % of population	4.39%

Football Association of Singapore (FAS)
100 Tyrwhitt Road, Singapore 207542
Tel +65 63483477   Fax +65 63921194
johnkoh@fas.org.sg   www.fas.org.sg
President: HO Peng Kee   General Secretary: YEO Steven
Vice-President: ZAINUDIN Nordin   Treasurer: PANTHRADIL Samuel   Media Officer: ONG Eric
Men's Coach: AVRAMOVIC Radojko   Women's Coach: NOOR Abdullah B.
FAS formed: 1892   AFC: 1954   FIFA: 1952
Red shirts with white trimmings, Red shorts, Red socks

RECENT INTERNATIONAL MATCHES PLAYED BY SINGAPORE

2004	Opponents	Score		Venue	Comp	Scorers	Att	Referee
8-10	United Arab Emirates	L	1-2	Singapore	Fr	Masturi [60]	2 809	Ong MAS
13-10	India	W	2-0	Singapore	WCq	Indra Sahdan Daud [73], Kairul Amri Mohd [76]	3 609	Husain BHR
1-11	Malaysia	L	1-2	Singapore	Fr	Dickson [21]	3 293	Luong VIE
17-11	Japan	L	0-1	Saitama	WCq		58 881	Torky IRN
27-11	Myanmar	W	1-0	Singapore	Fr	Noh Alam Shah [78]	4 881	Hadi IDN
30-11	Hong Kong	D	0-0	Singapore	Fr	L 5-6p	3 359	Phaengsupha THA
7-12	Vietnam	D	1-1	Ho Chi Minh City	TCr1	Indra Sahdan Daud [70]	20 000	Sun Baojie CHN
9-12	Indonesia	D	0-0	Ho Chi Minh City	TCr1		4 000	Kwon Jong Chul KOR
13-12	Laos	W	6-2	Hanoi	TCr1	Jailani [7], Indra Sahdan Daud 2 [19 74], OG [41], Casmir 2 [45 90p]	17 000	Supian MAS
15-12	Cambodia	W	3-0	Hanoi	TCr1	Dickson [21], Khaizan [27], Khairul Amri [54]	2 000	Ebrahim BHR
29-12	Myanmar	W	4-3	Kuala Lumpur	TCsf	Bennet [21], Casmir [39], Noh Alam Shah [64], Ishak [82]	12 000	Rungklay THA
2005								
2-01	Myanmar	W	4-2	Singapore	TCsf	Noh Alam Shah 3 [74 94 95], Casmir [110]	30 000	Kamikawa JPN
8-01	Indonesia	W	3-1	Jakarta	TCf	Bennett [5], Khairul Amri [39], Casmir [69]	120000	Kwon Jong Chul KOR
16-01	Indonesia	W	2-1	Singapore	TCf	Indra Sahdan Daud [5], Casmir [40p]	55 000	Al Ghamdi KSA
4-06	Malaysia	W	2-0	Singapore	Fr	Noh Alam Shah 2 [32 93+]	18 000	Kunsuta THA
8-06	Malaysia	W	2-1	Pinang	Fr	Noh Alam Shah [19], Bennett [66]	10 000	Napitupulu IDN
11-10	Cambodia	W	2-0	Phnom Penh	Fr	Shahril Ishak 2 [44 88]		
2006								
26-01	Denmark	L	1-2	Singapore	Fr	Indra Sahdan Daud [89]	10 392	Srinivasan IND
3-02	Kuwait	D	2-2	Kuwait City	Fr	Khairul Amri [73], Indra Sahdan Daud [90]		
6-02	Oman	L	0-1	Doha	Fr			
15-02	Hong Kong	D	1-1	Hong Kong	Fr	Noh Alam Shah [66p]	610	Heng MAS
22-02	Iraq	W	2-0	Singapore	ACq	Khairul Amri [24], Noh Alam Shah [83]	10 221	Shield AUS
1-03	Palestine	L	0-1	Amman	ACq		1 000	Al Hilali OMA
31-05	Malaysia	D	0-0	Singapore	Fr	W 5-4p	18 604	Li Yuhong CHN
3-06	Malaysia	D	0-0	Paroi	Fr	W 8-7p		
12-08	Hong Kong	W	2-1	Hong Kong	Fr	Noh Alam Shah [19], Dickson [76]		
16-08	China PR	L	0-1	Tianjin	ACq		27 000	Ebrahim BHR
6-09	China PR	D	0-0	Singapore	ACq		38 824	Shamsuzzaman BAN
11-10	Iraq	L	1-2	Al Ain	ACq	Goncalves [9], Khairul Amri [62]	3 000	Mamedov TKM
24-12	Kazakhstan	D	0-0	Bangkok	Fr			
26-12	Thailand	L	0-2	Bangkok	Fr			
28-12	Vietnam	L	2-3	Bangkok	Fr	Bennett [14], Fazrul [62]		
2007								
7-01	Philippines	W	4-1	Singapore	Fr	Bennet [12], Khairul Amri [26], Indra Sahdan Daud 2 [47 59]		
13-01	Vietnam	D	0-0	Singapore	TCr1		20 000	Sananwai THA
15-01	Laos	W	11-0	Singapore	TCr1	Ridhuan [10], Noh Alam Shah 7 [11 24 61 72 76 88 92+], Shahril Ishak [47], Khairul Amri Kamal [71], Dickson [79]	5 224	U Hla Tint MYA
17-01	Indonesia	D	2-2	Singapore	TCr1	Noh Alam Shah [10p], Indra Sahdan Daud [52]	13 819	Sananwai THA
23-01	Malaysia	D	1-1	Kuala Lumpur	TCsf	Noh Alam Shah [73]	40 000	Wan Daxue CHN
27-01	Malaysia	D	1-1	Singapore	TCsf	Ridhuan [74]. W 5-4p	55 000	Cheung Yim Yau
31-01	Thailand	W	2-1	Singapore	TCf	Noh Alam Shah [17], Fahrudin [90p]	55 000	Ravichandran MAS
4-02	Thailand	D	1-1	Bangkok	TCf	Khairul Amri [81]	30 000	Napitupulu IDN
24-06	Korea DPR	W	2-1	Singapore	Fr	Ridhuan [40], Indra Sahdan Daud [76]		
27-06	Saudi Arabia	L	1-2	Singapore	Fr	Ashrin Shariff [90]		
30-06	Australia	L	0-3	Singapore	Fr			

Fr = Friendly match • AC = AFC Asian Cup • TC = ASEAN Tiger Cup/ASEAN Football Federation Championship • WC = FIFA World Cup
q = qualifier • r1 = first round group • sf = semi-final • f = final

SINGAPORE NATIONAL TEAM RECORDS AND RECORD SEQUENCES

Records			Sequence records				
Victory	11-0	LAO 2007	Wins	9	2004-2005	Clean sheets	4	1985
Defeat	0-9	MYA 1969	Defeats	9	1977	Goals scored	14	1993-1995
Player Caps	105	ISKANDAR Aide	Undefeated	13	2004-2005	Without goal	5	1976-1977
Player Goals	n/a		Without win	19	1966-1968	Goals against	36	1966-1970

SINGAPORE COUNTRY INFORMATION

Capital	Singapore City	Independence	1965 from Malaysia	GDP per Capita	$23 700
Population	4 353 893	Status	Republic	GNP Ranking	38
Area km²	693	Language	Chinese, English, Malay	Dialling code	+65
Population density	6 282 per km²	Literacy rate	92%	Internet code	.sg
% in urban areas	100%	Main religion	Buddhist 54%, Muslim 15%	GMT + / –	+8
Towns/Cities ('000)	Singapore City 3 547				
Neighbours (km)	Strait of Singapore & Johore Strait 193				
Main stadia	Jalan Besar – Singapore 6 000; National Stadium – Singapore 55 000				

SINGAPORE 2006

S.LEAGUE

	Pl	W	D	L	F	A	Pts	SAF	Tampines	Young Lions	Home Utd	Woodlands	Albirex	Balestier	Gombak	Afrique	Geylang	Senkang
S'pore Armed Forces †	30	20	8	2	71	36	68		2-1 1-1	3-1	2-1 1-1	2-2 1-1	2-2 2-1	2-1	4-2	**2-0** 3-1	2-0	3-0
Tampines Rovers	30	16	9	5	70	42	57	1-1		2-3 3-2	1-1	0-2	2-2 1-0	3-2 1-1	2-1	4-2 4-2	6-1 1-0	3-2
Young Lions	30	15	7	8	67	43	52	2-0 0-1	0-0		2-3	4-2	1-1 3-0	2-0	1-0 3-1	2-2	5-0 4-0	1-2 5-3
Home United	30	15	6	9	49	40	51	0-2	3-1 3-2	3-2 0-1		2-2	1-2	2-1	2-1 2-2	1-1 2-1	3-1	2-0 1-0
Woodlands Wellington	30	13	8	9	60	45	47	2-2	1-3 1-3	2-0 2-3	3-2 1-2		2-1	0-1	0-1 0-3	1-0	0-2	4-1	3-0 1-1
Albirex Niigata	30	12	9	9	52	44	45	2-3	2-2	4-3	1-2 2-0	1-5 2-2		2-0 2-2	2-2	4-1 1-0	3-0	2-0 2-2
Balestier Khalsa	30	10	7	13	50	61	37	2-5 2-4	0-4	0-4 2-2	2-1 3-1	2-2 1-3	1-2		3-1	3-2 2-1	3-1	5-3
Gombak United	30	8	8	14	48	54	32	0-3 2-3	3-3 0-1	3-3	1-0	3-1	2-2 2-0	1-0 4-5		1-2	0-1 2-0	1-1
Sporting Afrique	30	5	9	16	36	58	24	0-4	3-3	2-2 0-3	0-2	2-1 0-2	0-2	0-0	2-2 2-4		1-1 0-1	2-0 1-1
Geylang United	30	6	5	19	22	62	23	1-4 3-2	0-2	1-1	1-3 0-2	1-3 0-2	0-3 1-0	2-2 0-0	2-0	1-1		1-0
Senkang Punggol	30	4	6	20	32	72	18	1-1 3-4	0-5 1-5	1-2	1-1	2-5	0-2	0-1 4-3	0-2 1-4	0-3	2-1 1-0	

1/03/2005 - 28/10/2005 • † Qualified for the AFC Cup • Match in bold awarded 2-0

SINGAPORE CUP 2006

First round		Quarter–finals		Semi–finals		Final	
Tampines Rovers *	1						
DPMM FC - BRU	0	Tampines Rovers	1 4				
Phnom Penh FC - CAM	1	S'pore Armed Forces *	1 2				
S'pore Armed Forces *	8			Tampines Rovers	1 7		
Young Lions	3			Woodlands Wellington*	2 2		
Sporting Afrique *	2	Young Lions *	1 1				
PEA Thailand - THA	0	Woodlands Wellington	1 3				
Woodlands Wellington*	1					Tampines Rovers †	3
Balestier Khalsa *	5					Chonburi FC	2
Malaysia U-23 - MAS	3	Balestier Khalsa	4 7				
Gombak United	0	Senkang Punggol *	4 1				
Senkang Punggol *	1			Balestier Khalsa	1 1 4p		
Albirex Niigata *	3			Chonburi FC *	2 0 5p		
Geylang United	2	Albirex Niigata	2 1				
Home United *	0	Chonburi FC *	2 2				
Chonburi FC - THA	4						

* Home Team in the first leg • † Qualified for the AFC Cup

CUP FINAL

26-11-2006

Scorers - Aliff Shafarin 2 [85] [120], Santi Chaiyaphuak [90] for Tampines; Pipob [74], Arthit Sunthornphit [76] for Chonburi

RECENT LEAGUE AND CUP RECORD

	Championship						Cup		
Year	Champions	Pts	Runners-up	Pts	Third	Pts	Winners	Score	Runners-up
1997	Sing. Armed Forces	37	Tanjong Pagar Utd	34	Woodlands Well'ton	33	Sing. Armed Forces	4-2	Woodlands Well'ton
1998	Sing. Armed Forces	46	Tanjong Pagar Utd	46	Geylang United	38	Tanjong Pagar Utd	2-0	Sing. Armed Forces
1999	Home United	51	Sing. Armed Forces	49	Tanjong Pagar Utd	41	Sing. Armed Forces	3-1	Jurong
2000	Sing. Armed Forces	52	Tanjong Pagar Utd	43	Geylang United	41	Home United	1-0	Sing. Armed Forces
2001	Geylang United	76	Sing. Armed Forces	74	Home United	72	Home United	8-0	Geylang United
2002	Sing. Armed Forces	84	Home United	64	Geylang United	59	Tampines Rovers	1-0	Jurong
2003	Home United	85	Geylang United	71	Sing. Armed Forces	69	Home United	2-1	Geylang United
2004	Tampines Rovers	63	Home United	53	Young Lions	47	Tampines Rovers	4-1	Home United
2005	Tampines Rovers	57	Sing. Armed Forces	52	Woodlands Well'ton	50	Home United	3-2	Woodlands Well'ton
2006	Sing. Armed Forces	68	Tampines Rovers	57	Young Lions	52	Tampines Rovers	3-2	Chonburi

SKN – ST KITTS AND NEVIS

NATIONAL TEAM RECORD
JULY 10TH 2006 TO JULY 12TH 2010

PL	W	D	L	F	A	%
3	1	1	1	7	3	50

FIFA/COCA-COLA WORLD RANKING

1993	1994	1995	1996	1997	1998	1999	2000	2001	2002	2003	2004	2005	2006	High	Low
166	175	150	121	127	132	137	146	129	109	134	118	129	143	**108** 07/04	**176** 11/94

2006–2007											
08/06	09/06	10/06	11/06	12/06	01/07	02/07	03/07	04/07	05/07	06/07	07/07
138	142	118	141	143	143	141	141	137	136	138	142

With increased expectations after a great 2004 in which the national team reached the second round of both the World Cup qualifiers and Digicel Caribbean Cup qualifiers, the failure to do well in the 2006-07 Caribbean Cup was a big disappointment to everyone involved with the game in the country. In their first round qualifying group in Antigua, St Kitts finished third behind Barbados and their hosts to crash out of the tournament at the first hurdle. Having not played a game at all in 2005, the three Caribbean Cup games were the only matches played in 2006, not exactly the ideal preparation for the 2010 World Cup qualifiers. The past ten years have been fantastic for St Kitts,

INTERNATIONAL HONOURS
None

starting with a runners-up spot in the 1997 Caribbean Cup, but the FIFA Goal project is helping to raise standards in the other islands, and St Kitts will have to work hard to maintain their advantage. In domestic football, Newtown United secured a League and Cup double, although it came in controversial circumstances. In the Cup Final in March, Village Superstars beat Newtown to win the trophy but the result was overturned after Superstars fielded an ineligible player. The two then met again in the final of the Championship which went to three matches - and, after losing the first, Newtown won the next two to secure the title and the double.

THE FIFA BIG COUNT OF 2006

	Male	Female		Total
Number of players	3 100	400	Referees and Assistant Referees	0
Professionals	0		Admin, Coaches, Technical, Medical	100
Amateurs 18+	900		Number of clubs	30
Youth under 18	600		Number of teams	40
Unregistered	600		Clubs with women's teams	1
Total players	3 500		Players as % of population	8.94%

St Kitts and Nevis Football Association (SKNFA)
Warner Park, PO Box 465, Basseterre, St Kitts and Nevis
Tel +1 869 4668502   Fax +1 869 4659033
info@sknfa.com   www.sknfa.com
President: JENKINS Peter   General Secretary: AMORY Spencer Leonard
Vice-President: FRASER Sylvester   Treasurer: AMORY Spencer Leonard   Media Officer: None
Men's Coach: TAYLOR Leonard   Women's Coach: McDOWELL Craig
SKNFA formed: 1932   CONCACAF: 1992   FIFA: 1992
Green shirts, Red shorts, Yellow socks

RECENT INTERNATIONAL MATCHES PLAYED BY ST KITTS AND NEVIS

2002	Opponents	Score		Venue	Comp	Scorers	Att	Referee
25-07	Chinese Taipei	W	3-0	Basseterre	Fr			
27-07	Barbados	W	3-0	Basseterre	Fr	Issac, Francis, Gumbs		
28-07	Trinidad and Tobago	W	2-1	Basseterre	Fr	Sargeant [49], Issac [75]	800	
29-10	Antigua and Barbuda	D	1-1	Basseterre	Fr			
13-11	St Lucia	W	2-1	Port of Spain	CCq	Isaac 2 [38 56]		Forde BRB
15-11	Trinidad and Tobago	L	0-2	Port of Spain	CCq		3 500	Faneijte ANT
2003								
29-07	Haiti	W	1-0	Basseterre	Fr	Isaac [3]		Matthew SKN
2-08	Trinidad and Tobago	L	1-2	Basseterre	Fr	Francis [50]		
2004								
1-02	Antigua and Barbuda	L	0-1	St John's	Fr			
18-02	US Virgin Islands	W	4-0	St Thomas	WCq	Huggins [26], Lake 2 [50 64], Isaac [62]	225	Brizan TRI
20-03	British Virgin Islands	W	4-0	Basseterre	Fr			
21-03	Antigua and Barbuda	L	2-3	Basseterre	Fr			
31-03	US Virgin Islands	W	7-0	Basseterre	WCq	Lake 5 [8 38 46 56 77], Isaac 2 [80 90]	800	Recinos SLV
23-05	St Vincent/Grenadines	W	3-2	Basseterre	Fr	Lake [9], Hodge [25], Willock [63]		Matthew SKN
2-06	Northern Ireland	L	0-2	Basseterre	Fr		5 000	Matthew SKN
13-06	Barbados	W	2-0	Bridgetown	WCq	Gumbs [78], Newton [88]	3 700	Alfaro SLV
19-06	Barbados	W	3-2	Basseterre	WCq	Gomez [16], Willock 2 [22 29]	3 500	Pineda HON
4-09	Trinidad and Tobago	L	1-2	Basseterre	WCq	Isaac [40]	2 800	Castillo GUA
10-09	St Vincent/Grenadines	L	0-1	Kingstown	WCq		4 000	Delgado CUB
10-10	Trinidad and Tobago	L	1-5	Marabella	WCq	Gumbs [43p]	7 000	Valenzuela USA
13-10	St Vincent/Grenadines	L	0-3	Basseterre	WCq		500	Whittaker CAY
31-10	Montserrat	W	6-1	Basseterre	CCq	Francis 3 [9 45 86], Connonier [36], Isaac [57], Hodge [83]		Bedeau GRN
2-11	St Lucia	D	1-1	Basseterre	CCq	Francis [14]		Bedeau GRN
4-11	Antigua and Barbuda	W	2-0	Basseterre	CCq	Sargeant [34], Isaac [45]		Phillip GRN
13-11	Mexico	L	0-5	Miami	WCq		18 312	Moreno PAN
17-11	Mexico	L	0-8	Monterrey	WCq		12 000	Stott USA
12-12	Haiti	L	0-1	Fort Lauderdale	CCq		2 500	McNab BAH
15-12	Haiti	L	0-2	Basseterre	CCq		1 000	Bhimull TRI
2005								
No international matches played in 2005								
2006								
20-09	Barbabdos	D	1-1	St John's	CCq	Harris [60]	300	Campbell JAM
22-09	Anguilla	W	6-1	St John's	CCq	Isaac 2 [14 68], Lake 3 [30 46 79], Francis [81]	500	Phillips GRN
24-09	Antigua and Barbuda	L	0-1	St John's	CCq		2 800	Wijngaarde SUR
2007								
No international matches played in 2007 before August								

Fr = Friendly match • CC = Digicel Caribbean Cup • WC = FIFA World Cup • q = qualifier

ST KITTS AND NEVIS NATIONAL TEAM RECORDS AND RECORD SEQUENCES

Records			Sequence records					
Victory	9-1	MSR 1994	Wins	4	1996, 2002	Clean sheets	3	1991-1992
Defeat	0-8	MEX 2004	Defeats	4	2004 (Twice)	Goals scored	10	1998-99, 2001
Player Caps	n/a		Undefeated	10	2001-2002	Without goal	4	2004
Player Goals	n/a		Without win	5	1996	Goals against	14	1998-2000

ST KITTS AND NEVIS COUNTRY INFORMATION

Capital	Basseterre	Independence	1983 from the UK	GDP per Capita	$8 800
Population	38 836	Status	Constitutional Monarchy	GNP Ranking	177
Area km²	261	Language	English	Dialling code	+1869
Population density	148 per km²	Literacy rate	97%	Internet code	.kn
% in urban areas	42%	Main religion	Christian	GMT +/-	-4
Towns/Cities	Basseterre 12 920; Charlestown 1 538; Saint Paul's 1 483; Sadlers 986; Middle Island 887				
Neighbours (km)	Caribbean Sea 135				
Main stadia	Warner Park – Basseterre 6 000				

ST KITTS 2006–07 PREMIER DIVISION

	Pl	W	D	L	F	A	Pts
Newtown United †	16	9	5	2	37	16	32
Garden Hotspurs †	16	10	2	4	30	21	32
Village Superstars †	16	10	1	5	39	19	31
St Peters †	16	9	2	5	33	23	29
St Pauls	16	7	7	2	17	8	28
Washington Archibald	15	5	3	7	23	28	18
Conaree	16	2	5	9	14	25	11
St Thomas Strikers	16	2	5	9	12	41	11
Cayon	15	0	4	11	8	32	4

21/11/2004 - 5/03/2005 • † Qualified for play-offs

ST KITTS 2006–07 PREMIER DIVISION SUPER FOUR

	Pl	W	D	L	F	A	Pts
Newtown United †	3	2	0	2	5	1	6
Village Superstars †	3	1	1	1	5	4	4
Garden Hotspurs	3	1	1	1	3	3	4
St Peters	3	1	0	2	1	6	3

28/04/2006 - 13/05/2006 • † Qualified for the final

ST KITTS AND NEVIS 2006–07 PREMIER DIVISION FINAL

Champions	Score	Runners-up
Newtown United	0-1 4-1 2-0	Village Superstars

RECENT LEAGUE AND CUP RECORD

	Championship				Cup		
Year	Champions	Score	Runners-up		Winners	Score	Runners-up
1997	Newtown United						
1998	Newtown United						
1999	St Paul's United	3-0 0-1 4-2	Garden Hotspurs				
2000	No tournament due to season adjustment						
2001	Garden Hotspurs	3-0 0-0 3-4p 1-0	Village Superstars				
2002	Cayon Rockets	0-0 3-2p 3-0	Garden Hotspurs		Cayon Rockets		
2003	Village Superstars	0-1 2-1 0-0 5-4p	Newtown United		Village Superstars	1-0	Newtown United
2004	Newtown United	0-1 1-0 2-0	Village Superstars		Village Superstars	3-1	Cayon Rockets
2005	Village Superstars	1-0 2-1	St Peter's				
2006	Village Superstars	3-1 3-0	St Paul's United				
2007	Newtown United	0-1 4-1 2-0	Village Superstars		Newtown United	0-1 †	Village Superstars

† Cup awarded to Newtown after Superstars fielded an ineligible player

SLE – SIERRA LEONE

NATIONAL TEAM RECORD
JULY 10TH 2006 TO JULY 12TH 2010

PL	W	D	L	F	A	%
5	0	1	4	1	12	10

FIFA/COCA-COLA WORLD RANKING

1993	1994	1995	1996	1997	1998	1999	2000	2001	2002	2003	2004	2005	2006	High	Low
76	76	58	84	84	111	120	129	138	133	146	160	163	148	**51** 01/96	**165** 05/06

					2006–2007						
08/06	09/06	10/06	11/06	12/06	01/07	02/07	03/07	04/07	05/07	06/07	07/07
154	133	147	151	148	151	151	152	153	155	156	161

Sierra Leone's lack of financial resources and damaged infrastructure, a legacy of the country's brutal civil strife, continued to hold back the 'Leone Stars'. Just a single point from the first five matches of their African Nations Cup qualifying campaign ensured a bottom place finish for the country in their qualifying group. This came despite an attempt to tap into the growing diaspora of Sierra Leone citizens around the world, including appointing former English league player Leroy Rosenoir as coach for two matches in June and inviting players of Sierra Leonean heritage from clubs throughout Europe to join their side. Sierra Leone lost to Togo at home and then suffered a

INTERNATIONAL HONOURS
Copa Amilcar Cabral 1993 1995

record 6-0 hiding at the hands of Mali, prompting a return to the coaching hot seat of Jebor Sherrington. A three match ban for captain Mohamed Kallon, the former Inter Milan and Monaco striker, also weakened the team throughout its qualifying campaign, but there was some success for Sierra Leone, notably in African club competition. FC Kallon, owned by the national team captain, made a spectacular debut in the African Champions League at the start of 2007, eliminating Nigeria's champions Ocean Boys in the first round before losing to ASEC Abidjan of Côte d'Ivoire. Port Authority also reached the second round of the African Confederation Cup.

THE FIFA BIG COUNT OF 2006

	Male	Female		Total
Number of players	247 240	12 390	Referees and Assistant Referees	263
Professionals	0		Admin, Coaches, Technical, Medical	2 200
Amateurs 18+	840		Number of clubs	24
Youth under 18	5 640		Number of teams	196
Unregistered	15 150		Clubs with women's teams	0
Total players	259 630		Players as % of population	4.32%

Sierra Leone Football Association (SLFA)
21 Battery Street, Kingtom, PO Box 672, Freetown, Sierra Leone
Tel +232 22 240071   Fax +232 22 241339
Starssierra@yahoo.com   www.slfa.tk
President: KHADI Nahim   General Secretary: BAH Alimu
Vice-President: BANGURA Bassie   Treasurer: TBD   Media Officer: none
Men's Coach: ROSENIOR Leroy   Women's Coach: MOSES
SLFA formed: 1967   CAF: 1967   FIFA: 1967
Green shirts, Green shorts, Green socks

RECENT INTERNATIONAL MATCHES PLAYED BY SIERRA LEONE

2002	Opponents	Score	Venue	Comp	Scorers	Att	Referee
25-08	Gambia	L 0-1	Banjul	Fr			
8-09	Equatorial Guinea	W 3-1	Malabo	CNq	Bah [38], Sesay [46], Mansaray [68]		Neto STP
12-10	Gabon	W 2-0	Freetown	CNq	Kpaka [45], Bah [52]		Ekoue TOG
19-10	Ghana	W 2-1	Freetown	Fr	Massaquoi [24], Kemokai Kallon [36]		Sanusie SLE
2003							
29-03	Morocco	D 0-0	Freetown	CNq			Kabu LBR
8-06	Morocco	L 0-1	Casablanca	CNq			Abd El Fatah EGY
22-06	Equatorial Guinea	W 2-0	Freetown	CNq	Mohanned Kallon [71], Kabbah [90]		
6-07	Gabon	L 0-2	Libreville	CNq			
12-10	Congo	L 0-1	Brazzaville	WCq		4 800	Mana NGA
16-11	Congo	D 1-1	Freetown	WCq	Koroma [58]	20 000	Monteiro Lopes CPV
2004							
No international matches played in 2004							
2005							
12-06	Gambia	W 1-0	Freetown	Fr	Kpaka [56]		
20-11	Guinea-Bissau	D 1-1	Conakry	ACr1	Moustapha Bangoura [49]		
22-11	Guinea	L 0-1	Conakry	ACr1			
2006							
3-09	Mali	D 0-0	Freetown	CNq			Mbera GAB
8-10	Benin	L 0-2	Cotonou	CNq			Sowe GAM
2007							
24-03	Togo	L 1-3	Lomé	CNq	Gibrilla Woobay [77]		Pare BFA
3-06	Togo	L 0-1	Freetown	CNq			
17-06	Mali	L 0-6	Bamako	CNq			

Fr = Friendly match • CN = CAF African Cup of Nations • AC = Amilcar Cabral Cup • WC = FIFA World Cup • q = qualifier

SIERRA LEONE NATIONAL TEAM RECORDS AND RECORD SEQUENCES

Records			Sequence records				
Victory	5-1	NIG 1976, NIG 1995	Wins	4	1986	Clean sheets	5	1984, 1991-92
Defeat	0-6	MLI 2007	Defeats	6	1982-83, 1996	Goals scored	11	1985-1987
Player Caps	n/a		Undefeated	14	1991-1993	Without goal	6	1982-83, 1996
Player Goals	n/a		Without win	9	1971-1973	Goals against	19	1976-1983

RECENT LEAGUE AND CUP RECORD

	Championship		Cup
Year	Champions		Winners
1995	Mighty Blackpool		
1996	Mighty Blackpool		
1997	East End Lions		
1998	Mighty Blackpool		
1999	East End Lions		
2000	Mighty Blackpool		Mighty Blackpool
2001	Mighty Blackpool		Old Edwardians
2002	No tournament		No tournament
2003	No tournament		
2004	No tournament		
2005	East End Lions		
2006	FC Kallon		

SIERRA LEONE COUNTRY INFORMATION

Capital	Freetown	Independence	1961 from UK	GDP per Capita	$500
Population	5 883 889	Status	Republic	GNP Ranking	160
Area km²	71 740	Language	English, Mende, Krio	Dialling code	+232
Population density	82 per km²	Literacy rate	31%	Internet code	.sl
% in urban areas	36%	Main religion	Muslim 60%	GMT +/-	0
Towns/Cities ('000)	Freetown 1 190; Koidu 111; Bo 80; Kenema 70; Makeni 54; Lunsar 21; Waterloo 21				
Neighbours (km)	Guinea 652; Liberia 306; North Atlantic Ocean 402				
Main stadia	National Stadium – Freetown 36 000				

SLV – EL SALVADOR

NATIONAL TEAM RECORD
JULY 10TH 2006 TO JULY 12TH 2010

PL	W	D	L	F	A	%
15	3	2	10	7	24	26.6

FIFA/COCA-COLA WORLD RANKING

1993	1994	1995	1996	1997	1998	1999	2000	2001	2002	2003	2004	2005	2006	High		Low	
66	80	82	65	64	92	96	83	86	94	95	106	124	156	60	10/93	169	11/06

2006–2007											
08/06	09/06	10/06	11/06	12/06	01/07	02/07	03/07	04/07	05/07	06/07	07/07
141	158	167	169	156	156	125	138	143	144	130	134

These are desperate times for football in El Salvador. The national team has never been at such a low ebb, while clubs from the country continue to struggle in Central American tournaments. In the 16 years that the UNCAF Cup for national teams has been running, El Salvador have failed to win, or even finish as runners-up, in any of the nine editions played. As hosts of the 2007 tournament they had hoped to change that and they started well, winning their first two games to bring to an end a record run of 12 games without a win. However, home advantage counted for little against Costa Rica in the semi-final as they lost 2-0, and they finished the tournament in fourth place after los-

INTERNATIONAL HONOURS
Qualified for the FIFA World Cup finals 1970 1982 **Central American Championship** 1943   **Central American and Caribbean Games** 1954 2002
CONCACAF Champions Cup   Alianza 1967   Aguila 1976   Deportivo FAS 1979

ing to Guatemala in a play-off. Of the 15 matches played during the season, just three were won - the third coming against Trinidad in the CONCACAF Gold Cup finals in America, but that wasn't enough for El Salvador to progress beyond the first round group stage. At home there were surprise winners of both the Apertura and the Clausura. Once Municipal won a Championship for the first time since 1949 by beating FAS 3-1 in the Apertura final while the Clausura provided a first title for Isidro-Metapán, 1-0 winners over LA Firpo in the final.

THE FIFA BIG COUNT OF 2006

	Male	Female		Total
Number of players	401 040	58 652	Referees and Assistant Referees	315
Professionals	200		Admin, Coaches, Technical, Medical	5 538
Amateurs 18+	21 404		Number of clubs	68
Youth under 18	24 108		Number of teams	2 828
Unregistered	225 900		Clubs with women's teams	2
Total players	459 692		Players as % of population	6.74%

Federacion Salvadorena de Futbol (FESFUT)
Avenida José Matias Delgado, Frente al Centro Español, Colonia Escalón, Zona 10, San Salvador CA 1029, El Salvador
Tel +503 22096200   Fax +503 22637528
rcalvo@fesfut.org.sv   www.fesfut.org.sv
President: CALVO Rodrigo   General Secretary: BERNAL Marvin
Vice-President: TORRES Jose Humberto   Treasurer: DIAZ Mario   Media Officer: LOPEZ Eduardo Alegria
Men's Coach: DE LOS COBOS Carlos   Women's Coach: HERRERA Jose
FESFUT formed: 1935   CONCACAF: 1961   FIFA: 1938
Blue shirts with white trimmings, Blue shorts, Blue socks

RECENT INTERNATIONAL MATCHES PLAYED BY EL SALVADOR

2003	Opponents	Score		Venue	Comp	Scorers	Att	Referee
29-06	Honduras	D	1-1	San Pedro Sula	Fr	Mejía [80]	5 000	Porras CRC
2-07	Paraguay	L	0-1	San Francisco	Fr			Valenzuela USA
6-07	Mexico	W	2-1	Carson	Fr	Mejía [30], Corrales [60]	19 271	Hall USA
8-07	Guatemala	L	1-2	Houston	Fr	Murgas [68]	21 047	Hall USA
12-07	USA	L	0-2	Boston	GCr1		33 652	Ramos MEX
16-07	Martinique	W	1-0	Boston	GCr1	González.M [76]	10 361	Batres GUA
19-07	Costa Rica	L	2-5	Boston	GCqf	Murgas [34p], Pacheco [53]	15 627	Ramos MEX
16-11	Jamaica	L	0-3	Kingston	Fr		12 000	Ramdhan TRI
2004								
28-01	Panama	D	1-1	San Salvador	Fr	Velasquez [36]		
31-03	Guatemala	L	0-3	San Salvador	Fr		5 047	Aguilar Chicas SLV
28-04	Colombia	L	0-2	Washington DC	Fr		23 000	Vaughn USA
12-05	Haiti	D	3-3	Houston	Fr	Góchez [29], Murgas [43p], Martínez.J [72]	4 000	Terry USA
13-06	Bermuda	W	2-1	San Salvador	WCq	Martínez.J [14], Velásquez [54]	12 000	Campos NCA
20-06	Bermuda	D	2-2	Hamilton	WCq	Pacheco 2 [20 41p]	4 000	Whittaker CAY
18-07	Guatemala	L	0-1	Los Angeles	Fr			Valenzuela USA
3-08	Honduras	L	0-4	San Salvador	Fr			Aguilar Chicas SLV
6-08	Guatemala	L	0-2	Washington DC	Fr		20 000	Valenzuela USA
18-08	Panama	W	2-1	San Salvador	WCq	Velásquez [7], Rodriguez.J [45]	11 400	Navarro CAN
4-09	USA	L	0-2	Boston	WCq		25 266	Brizan TRI
8-09	Jamaica	L	0-3	San Salvador	WCq		25 000	Alcala MEX
9-10	USA	L	0-2	San Salvador	WCq		20 000	Batres GUA
13-10	Jamaica	D	0-0	Kingston	WCq		12 000	Quesada Cordero CRC
17-11	Panama	L	0-3	Panama City	WCq		9 502	Archundia MEX
2005								
19-02	Panama	L	0-1	Guatemala City	UCr1		10 000	Archundia MEX
21-02	Costa Rica	L	1-2	Guatemala City	UCr1	Alas [40]	3 000	Batres GUA
17-08	Paraguay	L	0-3	Ciudad del Este	Fr		12 000	
2006								
6-09	Honduras	L	0-2	Tegucigalpa	Fr		7 000	Zelaya HON
7-10	Panama	L	0-1	Panama City	Fr			Moreno PAN
15-11	Bolivia	L	1-5	La Paz	Fr	Erazo [52]	25 000	
29-11	Panama	D	0-0	San Salvador	Fr			
2007								
8-02	Belize	W	2-1	San Salvador	UCr1	Díaz.J [25], Quintanilla [55]		Quesada CRC
10-02	Nicaragua	W	2-1	San Salvador	UCr1	Quintanilla 2 [16 64p]		Arredondo MEX
12-02	Guatemala	D	0-0	San Salvador	UCr1			Archundia MEX
16-02	Costa Rica	L	0-2	San Salvador	UCsf			Archundia MEX
18-02	Guatemala	L	0-1	San Salvador	UC3p			Quesada CRC
24-03	Honduras	L	0-2	Fort Lauderdale	Fr		17 095	Marrufo USA
27-03	Honduras	L	0-2	Cary	Fr		8 365	
17-04	Haiti	L	0-1	San Salvador	Fr			
7-06	Trinidad and Tobago	W	2-1	Carson	GCr1	Sánchez.R [38], Alas [81]	21 334	Arredondo MEX
9-06	Guatemala	L	0-1	Carson	GCr1		27 000	Jauregui ATG
12-06	USA	L	0-4	Foxboro	GCr1		26 523	Archundia MEX

Fr = Friendly match • UC = UNCAF Cup • GC = CONCACAF Gold Cup • WC = FIFA World Cup • q = qualifier

EL SALVADOR NATIONAL TEAM RECORDS AND RECORD SEQUENCES

Records			Sequence records					
Victory	9-0	NCA 1929	Wins	5	1967-1968	Clean sheets	5	1981-1982
Defeat	0-8	MEX 1988	Defeats	7	1989, 2004-06	Goals scored	11	1999-2000
Player Caps	n/a		Undefeated	10	1981-1982	Without goal	6	Three times
Player Goals	39	DIAZ ARCE Raúl	Without win	12	2004-2006	Goals against	18	1930-1941

EL SALVADOR COUNTRY INFORMATION

Capital	San Salvador	Independence	1841 from Spain	GDP per Capita	$4 800
Population	6 587 541	Status	Republic	GNP Ranking	80
Area km²	21 040	Language	Spanish	Dialling code	+503
Population density	313 per km²	Literacy rate	80%	Internet code	.sv
% in urban areas	45%	Main religion	Christian	GMT + / −	-6
Towns/Cities ('000)	San Salvador 526; Soyapango 329; Santa Ana 176; San Miguel 161; Mejicanos 160				
Neighbours (km)	Guatemala 203; Honduras 342; North Pacific Ocean 307				
Main stadia	Estadio Cuscatlán – San Salvador 39 000				

EL SALVADOR 2006-07

PRIMERA DIVISION PROFESIONAL TORNEO APERTURA

	Pl	W	D	L	F	A	Pts	FAS	Municipal	Aguila	Alianza	LA Firpo	S. Salvador	Ch'tenango	V. Hermosa	I-Metapán	Nacional
Deportivo FAS †	18	8	7	3	32	24	31		1-1	2-1	2-1	1-1	1-1	2-2	4-1	4-2	1-2
Once Municipal §1 †	18	7	8	3	17	12	28	0-0		2-2	1-0	1-0	1-1	0-0	1-1	1-0	1-0
CD Aguila †	18	8	3	7	35	22	27	3-3	1-0		1-0	3-0	2-3	2-0	5-3	4-1	8-0
Alianza †	18	6	8	4	25	21	26	3-1	0-0	1-0		1-2	3-0	2-1	0-0	0-2	2-0
Luis Angel Firpo	18	8	2	8	22	22	26	1-1	3-2	2-2	5-2		1-2	2-0	2-2	0-0	2-2
San Salvador	18	7	3	8	23	25	24	0-2	0-2	2-0	2-1	1-0		1-2	4-0	3-1	1-1
CD Chalatenango	18	6	5	7	17	20	23	0-1	1-1	1-0	1-2	0-0	2-1		0-1	0-0	2-0
Vista Hermosa	18	5	7	6	24	26	22	4-1	0-1	1-0	0-1	0-0	2-0	1-2		1-1	4-1
CD Isidro-Metapán	18	6	4	8	22	26	22	1-2	0-2	1-0	3-1	1-2	3-1	2-3	2-2		1-0
Indep. Nacional 1906	18	4	3	11	13	32	15	0-3	2-0	0-1	1-2	0-2	1-0	2-0	1-1	0-1	

12/08/2006 - 26/11/2006 • † Qualified for the play-offs (Alianza beat Firpo 3-1 in a play-off to determine 4th place) • §1 = one point deducted
Play-off semi-finals: Aguila 4-1 1-4 **Once Municipal** (Once qualified on season record); Alianza 2-1 0-3 **FAS**
Play-off final: FAS 1-3 Once Municipal • Once Municipal won the Apertura

EL SALVADOR 2006-07

PRIMERA DIVISION PROFESIONAL TORNEO CLAUSURA

	Pl	W	D	L	F	A	Pts	LA Firpo	I-Metapán	Municipal	Aguila	FAS	Ch'tenango	S. Salvador	V. Hermosa	Alianza	Nacional
Luis Angel Firpo †	18	9	6	3	27	19	33		1-0	1-1	2-3	1-1	2-1	0-0	2-0	2-1	1-1
CD Isidro-Metapán †	18	8	5	5	34	27	29	1-2		1-1	3-2	2-0	1-0	2-2	5-0	1-0	3-2
Once Municipal †	18	6	9	3	17	12	27	1-0	0-0		1-0	0-0	1-1	1-0	3-0	1-1	1-0
CD Aguila †	18	8	2	8	34	29	26	1-4	2-1	2-2		0-0	7-0	2-1	3-1	4-2	3-1
Deportivo FAS	18	6	6	6	21	21	24	2-2	4-5	1-1	1-0		2-0	2-1	1-0	0-1	0-1
CD Chalatenango	18	7	3	8	21	26	24	1-2	4-1	0-1	2-0	4-3		1-0	2-0	1-0	0-2
San Salvador	18	6	5	7	21	23	23	1-2	1-3	1-1	1-0	1-2	2-1		1-1	1-0	1-0
Vista Hermosa	18	6	4	8	23	28	22	3-1	5-4	1-0	3-1	0-0	1-1	2-3		0-1	3-0
Alianza	18	5	5	8	16	18	20	0-1	1-1	1-0	1-2	2-0	1-2	1-1	0-0		1-1
Indep. Nacional 1906	18	4	5	9	16	27	17	1-1	0-0	2-1	3-2	0-2	0-0	2-3	0-3	0-2	

24/02/2007 - 27/05/2007 • † Qualified for the play-offs
Play-off semi-finals: Once Municipal 2-1 1-4 **Isidro-Metapán**; Aguila 0-2 3-1 **LA Firpo** (LA Firpo qualified on season record)
Final: **Isidro-Metapán** 1-0 LA Firpo • Isidro-Metapán won the Clausura • Relegation play-off: • Atlético Balboa relegated, Nacional promoted

RECENT LEAGUE AND CUP RECORD

Championship/Clausura from 2000				Apertura		
Year	Champions	Score	Runners-up	Winners	Score	Runners-up
1998	Luis Angel Firpo	2-0	Deportivo FAS			
1999	Luis Angel Firpo	1-1 5-4p	Deportivo FAS	Aguila	1-0	Municipal Limeño
2000	Luis Angel Firpo	1-1 10-9p	AD El Tránsito	Aguila	3-2	Municipal Limeño
2001	Aguila	1-1 2-1	Deportivo FAS	Alianza	2-1	Luis Angel Firpo
2002	Deportivo FAS	4-0	Alianza	Deportivo FAS	3-1	San Salvador
2003	San Salvador	3-1	Luis Angel Firpo	Deportivo FAS	2-2 5-3p	Aguila
2004	Alianza	1-1 3-2p	Deportivo FAS	Deportivo FAS	0-0 4-3p	Atlético Balboa
2005	Deportivo FAS	3-1	Luis Angel Firpo	Vista Hermosa	2-0	Isidro-Metapán
2006	Aguila	4-2	Deportivo FAS	Once Municipal	3-1	Deportivo FAS
2007	Isidro-Metapán	1-0	LA Firpo			

SMR – SAN MARINO

NATIONAL TEAM RECORD
JULY 10TH 2006 TO JULY 12TH 2010

PL	W	D	L	F	A	%
7	0	0	7	1	39	0

FIFA/COCA-COLA WORLD RANKING

1993	1994	1995	1996	1997	1998	1999	2000	2001	2002	2003	2004	2005	2006	High	Low
121	131	951	165	173	179	150	168	158	160	162	164	155	194	**118** 09/03	**196** 04/07

2006–2007											
08/06	09/06	10/06	11/06	12/06	01/07	02/07	03/07	04/07	05/07	06/07	07/07
191	194	194	195	194	195	196	196	196	195	195	195

Without a single win in a competitive international since joining FIFA in 1988, San Marino's UEFA Euro 2008 qualifying group didn't offer much prospect of that unwelcome record changing, a record that involved 70 matches, the last 21 of which had all been lost. A 13-0 reverse in their opening match against Germany was a new record defeat not only for the San Marino national team but also for the European Championship itself, and over the rest of the season the goals against tally kept mounting - with one notable exception. In February 2007 San Marino were seconds away from a sensational draw with the Republic of Ireland. Trailing 1-0 with four minutes to go, Manuel

INTERNATIONAL HONOURS
None

Mariani looked to have earned San Marino a first point in 38 matches in the competition, but with just eight seconds of stoppage time left Stephen Ireland scored the winner for the Irish. The national team finished the season with a match away to Germany and the prospect of even more records being broken, but there was no repeat of the earlier humiliation as San Marino lost by a more respectable 6-0. At home Murata were the team of the season winning both the Campeonato Dilettanti and the Coppa Titano. They negotiated the fiendishly difficult-to-comprehend play-offs to beat Tre Fiori in the Championship Final having earlier beaten Libertas in the Cup Final.

THE FIFA BIG COUNT OF 2006

	Male	Female		Total
Number of players	2 421	415	Referees and Assistant Referees	35
Professionals	0		Admin, Coaches, Technical, Medical	225
Amateurs 18+	763		Number of clubs	16
Youth under 18	823		Number of teams	56
Unregistered	650		Clubs with women's teams	1
Total players	2 836		Players as % of population	9.70%

Federazione Sammarinese Giuoco Calcio (FSGC)
Viale Campo dei Giudei 14, Rep. San Marino 47890
Tel +378 054 9990515   Fax +378 054 9992348
fsgc@omniway.sm   www.fsgc.sm
President: CRESCENTINI Giorgio   General Secretary: CASADEI Luciano
Vice-President: CECCOLI Pier Luigi   Treasurer: GUIDI Joseph   Media Officer: ELISA Felici
Men's Coach: MAZZA Gianpaolo   Women's Coach: none
FSGC formed: 1931   UEFA: 1988   FIFA: 1988
Light blue shirts with white trimmings, Light blue shorts, Light blue socks or White shirts, White shorts, White socks

RECENT INTERNATIONAL MATCHES PLAYED BY SAN MARINO

2002 Opponents	Score	Venue	Comp	Scorers	Att	Referee
7-09 Poland	L 0-2	Serravalle	ECq		2 000	McKeon IRE
16-10 Hungary	L 0-3	Budapest	ECq		6 500	Orrason ISL
20-11 Latvia	L 0-1	Serravalle	ECq		600	Khudiev AZE
2003						
2-04 Poland	L 0-5	Ostrowiec	ECq		8 500	Loízou CYP
30-04 Latvia	L 0-3	Riga	ECq		7 500	Byrne IRE
7-06 Sweden	L 0-6	Serravalle	ECq		2 184	Delevic SCG
11-06 Hungary	L 0-5	Serravalle	ECq		1 410	Clark SCO
20-08 Liechtenstein	D 2-2	Vaduz	Fr	Alex Gasperoni [39], Nicola Ciacci [45]	850	Wildhaber SUI
6-09 Sweden	L 0-5	Gothenburg	ECq		31 098	Messner AUT
2004						
28-04 Liechtenstein	W 1-0	Serravalle	Fr	Andy Selva [5]	700	Sammut MLT
4-09 Serbia & Montenegro	L 0-3	Serravalle	WCq		1 137	Kholmatov KAZ
8-09 Lithuania	L 0-4	Kaunas	WCq		4 000	Jareci ALB
13-10 Serbia & Montenegro	L 0-5	Belgrade	WCq		4 000	Isaksen FRO
17-11 Lithuania	L 0-1	Serravalle	WCq		1 457	Nalbandyan ARM
2005						
9-02 Spain	L 0-5	Almeria	WCq		12 580	Clark SCO
30-03 Belgium	L 1-2	Serravalle	WCq	Andy Selva [41]	871	Kasnaferis GRE
4-06 Bosnia-Herzegovina	L 1-3	Serravalle	WCq	Andy Selva [39]	750	Demirlek TUR
7-09 Belgium	L 0-8	Antwerp	WCq		8 207	Stokes IRL
8-10 Bosnia-Herzegovina	L 0-3	Zenica	WCq		8 500	Hamer LUX
12-10 Spain	L 0-6	Serravalle	WCq		3 426	Meyer GER
2006						
16-08 Albania	L 0-3	Serravalle	Fr			
6-09 Germany	L 0-13	Serravalle	ECq		5 090	Dereli TUR
7-10 Czech Republic	L 0-7	Liberec	ECq		9 514	Aliyev AZE
15-11 Republic of Ireland	L 0-5	Dublin	ECq		34 018	Isaksen FRO
2007						
7-02 Republic of Ireland	L 1-2	Serravalle	ECq	Manuel Marani [86]	3 294	Rasmussen DEN
28-03 Wales	L 0-3	Cardiff	ECq		18 752	Tchagharyan ARM
2-06 Germany	L 0-6	Nuremberg	ECq		43 967	Asumaa FIN

Fr = Friendly match • EC = UEFA EURO 2004/2008 • WC = FIFA World Cup • q = qualifier

SAN MARINO NATIONAL TEAM RECORDS AND RECORD SEQUENCES

Records			Sequence records				
Victory	1-0	LIE 2004	Wins	1	2004	Clean sheets	1	1993, 2004
Defeat	0-13	GER 2006	Defeats	36	1993-2001	Goals scored	2	2005
Player Caps	48	GENNARI Mirco	Undefeated	1	Four times	Without goal	10	1995-1998
Player Goals	6	SELVA Andy	Without win	68	1986-2004	Goals against	50	1993-2003

SAN MARINO COUNTRY INFORMATION

Capital	San Marino	Formation	301	GDP per Capita	$34 600
Population	28 503	Status	Republic	GNP Ranking	185
Area km²	61	Language	Italian	Dialling code	+378
Population density	467 per km²	Literacy rate	96%	Internet code	.sm
% in urban areas	94%	Main religion	Christian	GMT +/−	+1
Towns/Cities	Serravalle 9 258; Borgo Maggiore 6 627; San Marino 4 598; Domagnano 2 724; Fiorentino 2 082				
Neighbours (km)	Italy 39				
Main stadia	Stadio Olimpico – Serravalle 2 210				

SAN MARINO 2006-07 CAMPIONATO DILETTANTI GIRONE A

	Pl	W	D	L	F	A	Pts
Tre Fiori †	20	16	1	3	45	17	49
La Fiorita †	20	11	3	6	38	23	36
Pennarossa †	20	10	4	6	30	24	34
Virtus	20	9	3	8	35	30	30
Tre Penne	20	9	3	8	30	26	30
Cosmos	20	6	4	10	34	42	22
Cailungo	20	2	6	12	19	42	12

16/09/2006 - 21/04/2007 • † Qualified for the play-offs

SAN MARINO 2006-07 CAMPIONATO DILETTANTI GIRONE B

	Pl	W	D	L	F	A	Pts
Libertas †	21	14	1	6	57	26	43
Domagnano †	21	12	6	3	42	20	42
Murata †	21	11	5	5	45	21	38
Folgore/Falciano	21	9	6	6	32	32	33
Faetano	21	7	3	11	27	46	24
Juvenes/Dogana	21	6	5	10	28	39	23
San Giovanni	21	4	1	16	27	61	13
Fiorentino	21	1	3	17	23	63	6

15/09/2006 - 22/04/2007 • † Qualified for the play-offs

CAMPIONATO DILETTANTI PLAY-OFFS

First round: Murata 4-0 La Fiorita; Domagnano 3-3 4-3p Pennarossa
Second round: Tre Fiori 3-0 Domagnano; Libertas 2-1 Murata
Third round: Domagnano 1-1 10-9p La Fiorita; Murata 3-0 Pennarossa
Fourth round: Tre Fiori 1-0 Libertas
Fifth round: Murata 4-0 Domagnano
Semi-final: Murata 5-0 Libertas

FINAL

Champions	Score	Runners-up
Murata	4-0	Tre Fiori

CLUB DIRECTORY

Club	Lge	Cup
Cailungo	0	1
Cosmos	1	3
Dogana	0	0
Domagnano	4	3
Faetano	3	1
Folgore	3	2
Fiorentino (ex Montevito)	1	0
La Fiorita	2	2
Libertas	1	4
Murata	2	1
Pennarossa	1	2
San Giovanni	0	0
Tre Fiori	4	2
Tre Penne	0	0
Virtus	0	1

COPPA TITANO 2006-07

Quarter-finals		Semi-finals		Final	
Murata	2				
Faetano	0	**Murata**	3		
Tre Fiori	2 1p	Juvenes/Dogana	0		
Juvenes/Dogana	2 4p			**Murata**	2
La Fiorita	3			Libertas	1
Cosmos	2	La Fiorita	0	Serravalle, 30-04-2007
Cailungo	1	**Libertas**	1	Scorers - Pasquale d'Orsi [39], Nicola Raschi [81] for Murata; Oscar Bianchi [78p] for Libertas
Libertas	3				

RECENT LEAGUE AND CUP RECORD

	Championship				Cup		
Year	Champions	Score	Runners-up		Winners	Score	Runners-up
1990	La Fiorita	1-0	Cosmos		Domagnano	2-0	Juvenes
1991	Faetano	1-0	Tre Fiori		Libertas	1-0	Faetano
1992	Montevito	4-2	Libertas		Domagnano	1-1 4-2p	Tre Fiori
1993	Tre Fiori	2-0	Domagnano		Faetano	1-0	Libertas
1994	Tre Fiori	2-0	La Fiorita		Faetano	3-1	Folgore
1995	Tre Fiori	1-0	La Fiorita		Cosmos	0-0 3-1p	Faetano
1996	Libertas	4-1	Cosmos		Domagnano	2-0	Cosmos
1997	Folgore Falciano	2-1	La Fiorita		Murata	2-0	Virtus
1998	Folgore Falciano	2-1	Tre Fiori		Faetano	4-1	Cosmos
1999	Faetano	1-0	Folgore Falciano		Cosmos	5-1	Domagnano
2000	Folgore Falciano	3-1	Domagnano		Tre Penne	3-1	Folgore
2001	Cosmos	3-1	Folgore Falciano		Domagnano	1-0	Tre Fiori
2002	Domagnano	1-0	Cailungo		Domagnano	6-1	Cailungo
2003	Domagnano	2-1	Pennarossa		Domagnano	1-0	Pennarossa
2004	Pennarossa	2-2 4-2p	Domanano		Pennarossa	3-0	Domagnano
2005	Domagnano	2-1	Murata		Pennarossa	4-1	Tre Penne
2006	Murata	1-0	Pennarossa		Libertas	4-1	Tre Penne
2007	Murata	4-0	Tre Fiori		Murata	2-1	Libertas

SOL – SOLOMON ISLANDS

NATIONAL TEAM RECORD
JULY 10TH 2006 TO JULY 12TH 2010

PL	W	D	L	F	A	%
1	1	0	0	2	1	100

FIFA/COCA-COLA WORLD RANKING

1993	1994	1995	1996	1997	1998	1999	2000	2001	2002	2003	2004	2005	2006	High	Low
149	163	170	171	130	128	144	130	134	142	156	130	140	160	124 10/98	177 08/96

2006–2007											
08/06	09/06	10/06	11/06	12/06	01/07	02/07	03/07	04/07	05/07	06/07	07/07
151	156	162	164	160	160	161	163	154	152	171	168

Recent successes have meant that football has grown steadily more popular in the Solomon Islands, one of the few South Pacific countries in which rugby is not the main sport, and for big matches at the Lawson Tama Stadium in Honiara demand for tickets is now often bigger than the 10,000 capacity allows. With the national team in hibernation before the qualifiers for the 2010 World Cup, the focus has been on domestic football, notably the revived League in Honiara. After a year in which it wasn't played, it was brought to life again in 2006 thanks to a sponsorship deal with DJ Graphics. Makuru won the title in the renamed DJ League which was played with 12 teams

INTERNATIONAL HONOURS
Melanesian Cup 1994

between July 2006 and May 2007. Normally Makuru would have played in the end of season National Championship to determine the Solomon's O–League representatives, but a failure to pay expenses saw Marist, Kossa and Koloale entered instead, all three of whom made it through from the group stage to the semi-finals. In the final Kossa beat Koloale to win the title for the first time in the four year history of the tournament to qualify for the O–League. They will be hoping to improve on Marist's performance in the inaugural tournament in 2007 which saw them finish bottom of a group containing Ba from Fiji and Temanava from Tahiti.

THE FIFA BIG COUNT OF 2006

	Male	Female		Total
Number of players	20 880	5 940	Referees and Assistant Referees	160
Professionals	0		Admin, Coaches, Technical, Medical	400
Amateurs 18+	3 000		Number of clubs	200
Youth under 18	5 500		Number of teams	500
Unregistered	15 000		Clubs with women's teams	12
Total players	26 820		Players as % of population	4.85%

Solomon Islands Football Federation (SIFF)
Lawson Tama, PO Box 854, Honiara, Solomon Islands
Tel +677 26496   Fax +677 26497
administration@siff.com.sb   www.siff.com.sb
President: ALUFURAI Martin   General Secretary: NGAVA Edward
Vice-President: RIQEO Robert   Treasurer: MAAHANUA Aloysio   Media Officer: PITUVAKA Francis
Men's Coach: ANDRIOLI Ayrton   Women's Coach: INIFIRI Timothy
SIFF formed: 1978   OFC: 1988   FIFA: 1988
Green shirts, Blue shorts, White socks

RECENT INTERNATIONAL MATCHES PLAYED BY THE SOLOMOM ISLANDS

2003	Opponents	Score		Venue	Comp	Scorers	Att	Referee
14-06	Papua New Guinea	W	5-3	Port Moresby	Fr	Samani [12], Menapi 2 [77 77p], Mehau [77], Suri [77p]		
1-07	Vanuatu	D	2-2	Suva	SPr1	Menapi 2 [49 57]		Shah FIJ
3-07	Kiribati †	W	7-0	Suva	SPr1	Waita [8], Menapi 5 [43 48 52 55 74], Mehau [78]	700	Ariiotima TAH
5-07	Tuvalu †	W	4-0	Nausori	SPr1	Maniadalo [16], Menapi 2 [27 87], Suri [80]	2 500	Bayung PNG
7-07	Fiji	L	1-2	Lautoka	SPr1	Menapi [68]	6 000	Ariiotima TAH
2004								
3-04	Vanuatu	W	2-1	Port Vila	Fr	Menapi 2 [52 71]	4 000	Lencie VAN
6-04	Vanuatu	W	2-1	Port Vila	Fr	Suri [34], Menapi [77]		
10-05	Tonga	W	6-0	Honiara	WCq	Faarodo 3 [12 30 77], Maemae 2 [62 76], Samani [79]	12 385	Attison VAN
12-05	Cook Islands	W	5-0	Honiara	WCq	Waita [21], Omokirio [27], Samani [45], Maemae [70], Leo [81]	14 000	Fred VAN
15-05	New Caledonia	W	2-0	Honiara	WCq	Omokirio [10], Suri [42]	20 000	Attison VAN
19-05	Tahiti	D	1-1	Honiara	WCq	Suri [80]	18 000	Rakaroi FIJ
29-05	Vanuatu	W	1-0	Adelaide	WCq	Suri [51p]	200	Shield AUS
31-05	New Zealand	L	0-3	Adelaide	WCq		217	Iturralde Gonzalez ESP
2-06	Tahiti	W	4-0	Adelaide	WCq	Faarodo [9], Menapi 2 [14 80], Suri [42]	50	Rakaroi FIJ
4-06	Fiji	W	2-1	Adelaide	WCq	Kakai [16], Houkarawa [82]	1 500	Attison VAN
6-06	Australia	D	2-2	Adelaide	WCq	Menapi 2 [43 75]	1 500	Iturralde Gonzalez ESP
9-10	Australia	L	1-5	Honiara	OCf	Suri [60]	21 000	O'Leary NZL
12-10	Australia	L	0-6	Sydney	OCf		19 208	Rakaroi FIJ
2005								
3-09	Australia	L	0-7	Sydney	WCq		16 000	Mohd Salleh MAS
6-09	Australia	L	1-2	Honiara	WCq	Faarodo [49]	16 000	Maidin SIN
2006								
No international matches played in 2006								
2007								
13-07	Papua New Guinea	W	2-1	Honiara	Fr	Iniga, Maemae		

Fr = Friendly match • OC = OFC Oceania Nations Cup • SP = South Pacific Games • WC = FIFA World Cup
q = qualifier • r1 = first round group • f = final • † Not a full international

SOLOMON ISLANDS NATIONAL TEAM RECORDS AND RECORD SEQUENCES

Records			Sequence records				
Victory	16-0	COK 1995	Wins	5	1994, 2004	Clean sheets	3	Three times
Defeat	0-8	NCL 1966	Defeats	5	1992-1993	Goals scored	14	2002-2004
Player Caps	n/a		Undefeated	7	2004	Without goal	4	1989-1990
Player Goals	n/a		Without win	9	1963-1975	Goals against	21	1997-2001

RECENT LEAGUE AND CUP RECORD

	National Club Championship			S.League	S.League Cup		Cup	Honiara League
Year	Winners		Finalist				Winners	Champions
2003	Koloale	4-0	Auki Kingz	Not played	Not played		Not played	Koloale
2004	Central Reales	w-o	Makuru	JP Su'uria	Wan Toks		Not played	Makuru
2005	Not played			JP Su'uria	JP Su'uria		Honiara Warriors	Not played
2006	Marist	1-0	Koloale					Not played
2007	Kossa	4-3	Koloale					Makuru

In the S.League Makuru are known as JP Su'uria, Marist as Systek Kingz and Uncles as Wan Toks

SOLOMON ISLANDS COUNTRY INFORMATION

Capital	Honiara	Independence	1978 from the UK	GDP per Capita	$1 700
Population	523 617	Status	Constitutional Monarchy	GNP Ranking	180
Area km²	28 450	Language	Melanesian, English	Dialling code	+677
Population density	18 per km²	Literacy rate	n/a	Internet code	.sb
% in urban areas	17%	Main religion	Christian	GMT +/−	+11
Towns/Cities ('000)	Honiara 56; Gizo 6; Auki 4; Buala 2; Tulagi 1; Kirakira 1				
Neighbours (km)	South Pacific Ocean 5 313				
Main stadia	Lawson Tama Stadium – Honiara 10 000				

SOM – SOMALIA

NATIONAL TEAM RECORD
JULY 10TH 2006 TO JULY 12TH 2010

PL	W	D	L	F	A	%
6	0	0	6	3	26	0

FIFA/COCA-COLA WORLD RANKING

1993	1994	1995	1996	1997	1998	1999	2000	2001	2002	2003	2004	2005	2006	High	Low
-	159	165	178	187	190	197	194	197	190	191	193	184	193	**158** 04/95	**199** 04/00

2006–2007											
08/06	09/06	10/06	11/06	12/06	01/07	02/07	03/07	04/07	05/07	06/07	07/07
179	181	181	182	193	194	194	194	194	192	190	192

Organised football continued to be an anomaly in war-torn Somalia where many of the country's stadiums are occupied by military forces, most recently by Ethiopian forces fighting Islamic militants. Reports of armed gangs extorting money from football teams before allowing them to play are common place and during last year's FIFA World Cup a ban was declared on the watching of matches from Germany by an Islamic government which has since been overthrown. In mid-July 2007 there were even reports of six children killed while playing football after a stray mortar landed on their village street. Somalia, nevertheless, still managed to put together a

INTERNATIONAL HONOURS
None

national side, travelling to both Ethiopia and Lebanon at the end of 2006 to participate, first, in the East and Central African Senior Challenge Cup and then in the Arab Nations Cup qualifying group. The Somalis failed to win a single one of the six matches played, scoring three times but conceding a hefty 26 goals in the process. The six defeats unsurprisingly contributed to the establishment of a new record run of nine consecutive defeats and it is a record that could well extend further. Despite the problems in the country, FIFA are planning to install an artificial pitch as part of the 'Win in Africa with Africa' programme.

THE FIFA BIG COUNT OF 2006

	Male	Female		Total
Number of players	522 433	23 835	Referees and Assistant Referees	1 300
Professionals	3		Admin, Coaches, Technical, Medical	6 030
Amateurs 18+	12 460		Number of clubs	48
Youth under 18	13 450		Number of teams	205
Unregistered	137 400		Clubs with women's teams	8
Total players	546 268		Players as % of population	6/16%

Somali Football Federation (SFF)
DHL Mogadishu, Mogadishu BN 03040, Somalia
Tel +252 1 216199   Fax +252 1 600000
sofofed@hotmail.com   www.somalifootballfederation.com
President: MOHAMUD Nor   General Secretary: ARAB Abdiqani Said
Vice-President: GULED Ali Said   Treasurer: TBD   Media Officer: MOHYADIN Shafici
Men's Coach: TBD   Women's Coach: HUSSEIN Ali Abdule
SFF formed: 1951   CAF: 1968   FIFA: 1960
Sky blue shirts, Sky blue shorts, White socks

RECENT INTERNATIONAL MATCHES PLAYED BY SOMALIA

2002	Opponents	Score		Venue	Comp	Scorers	Att	Referee
1-12	Uganda	L	0-2	Arusha	CCr1			Juma Ali TAN
3-12	Rwanda	L	0-1	Arusha	CCr1			
5-12	Zanzibar †	L	0-1	Arusha	CCr1			
7-12	Ethiopia	W	1-0	Arusha	CCr1			
2003								
16-11	Ghana	L	0-5	Accra	WCq		19 447	Bebou TOG
19-11	Ghana	L	0-2	Kumasi	WCq		12 000	Chaibou NIG
2004								
12-12	Uganda	L	0-2	Addis Abeba	CCr1			
14-12	Kenya	L	0-1	Addis Abeba	CCr1			
18-12	Sudan	L	0-4	Addis Abeba	CCr1			
2005								
27-11	Djibouti	W	2-1	Kigali	CCr1	Abdul Hakim [28], Mahmoud Sharki [87]		
29-11	Sudan	L	1-4	Kigali	CCr1	Abdullahi Sheikh Mohamed [37]		
1-12	Uganda	L	0-7	Kigali	CCr1			
5-12	Ethiopia	L	1-4	Kigali	CCr1			
2006								
27-11	Rwanda	L	0-3	Addis Abeba	CCr1			
30-11	Sudan	L	0-3	Addis Abeba	CCr1			
3-12	Uganda	L	0-2	Addis Abeba	CCr1			
21-12	Sudan	L	1-6	Beirut	ARr1	Mohammed Abdulaziz [93+]		
24-12	Lebanon	L	0-4	Beirut	ARr1			
27-12	Mauritania	L	2-8	Beirut	ARr1	Abdulaziz Ali 2 [26 67]		
2007								

No international matches played in 2007 before August

Fr = Friendly match • CC = CECAFA Cup • AR = Arab Cup • WC = FIFA World Cup
q = qualifier • r1 = first round group • † Not a full international

SOMALIA NATIONAL TEAM RECORDS AND RECORD SEQUENCES

Records			Sequence records					
Victory	5-2	MTN 1985	Wins	1		Clean sheets	1	
Defeat	2-9	CMR 1960	Defeats	9	2005-2006	Goals scored	4	Six times
Player Caps	n/a		Undefeated	4	1978-1980	Without goal	8	2000-2002
Player Goals	n/a		Without win	17	1995-2002	Goals against	10	1994-2000

RECENT LEAGUE RECORD

	Championship
Year	**Champions**
1998	Ports Authority
1999	No tournament
2000	Elman
2001	Elman
2002	Elman
2003	Elman
2004	
2005	
2006	Banaadir Telecom

SOMALIA COUNTRY INFORMATION

Capital	Mogadishu	Independence	1960	GDP per Capita	$500
Population	8 304 601	Status	Republic	GNP Ranking	151
Area km²	637 657	Language	Somali	Dialling code	+252
Population density	13 per km²	Literacy rate	37%	Internet code	.so
% in urban areas	26%	Main religion	Muslim	GMT +/−	+3
Towns/Cities ('000)	Mogadishu 2 590; Hargeysa 478; Marka 320; Berbera 242; Kismayo 234; Jamame 185				
Neighbours (km)	Kenya 682; Ethiopia 1 600; Djibouti 58; Gulf of Aden & Indian Ocean 3 025				
Main stadia	Mogadishu Stadium - Mogadishu 35 000				

SRB – SERBIA

NATIONAL TEAM RECORD
JULY 10TH 2006 TO JULY 12TH 2010

PL	W	D	L	F	A	%
9	5	3	1	14	6	72.2

FIFA/COCA-COLA WORLD RANKING

1993	1994	1995	1996	1997	1998	1999	2000	2001	2002	2003	2004	2005	2006	High	Low
-	-	-	-	-	-	-	-	-	19	41	46	47	33	**17** 07/07	**55** 10/04

2006–2007											
08/06	09/06	10/06	11/06	12/06	01/07	02/07	03/07	04/07	05/07	06/07	07/07
33	32	32	33	33	33	29	28	32	31	22	17

Serbia made a confident start to life without Montenegro with a 3-1 win over the Czech Republic in Uherske Hradiste and then won four of their first seven matches in the qualifiers for UEFA Euro 2008 to put themselves into a strong position to qualify for the finals, although they may come to regret the loss in Kazakhstan - their only defeat of the season. As Serbia is the successor state to Yugoslavia, it has inherited the history and the records of the old Yugoslavian team so technically the match against the Czech Republic didn't mark a new beginning. Serbia's biggest victory is still listed as the 10-0 victory over Venezuela in 1972 whilst their greatest international goalscorer is

INTERNATIONAL HONOURS
Qualified for the FIFA World Cup finals 2006   UEFA Champions League Crvena Zvezda 1991

Stjepan Bobek - a Croat. It all seems a touch incongruous and perhaps the time has come to treat the old Yugoslav side as a separate entity in its own right. Bobek's old side, Partizan Belgrade had a poor season in the new Serbian SuperLiga, finishing a distant second behind Red Star and they also lost to their eternal rivals in the semi-finals of the Cup. Red Star duly went on to beat Vojvodina 2-0 in the final to secure their third double in four seasons. Partizan did manage to go further in European club competition than Red Star, qualifying for the group stages of the UEFA Cup. Once there, however, they failed to win a game in a group won by Rangers.

THE FIFA BIG COUNT OF 2006

	Male	Female		Total
Number of players	400 800	40 882	Referees and Assistant Referees	4 284
Professionals	1 500		Admin, Coaches, Technical, Medical	9 800
Amateurs 18+	43 670		Number of clubs	2 076
Youth under 18	85 412		Number of teams	4 450
Unregistered	134 500		Clubs with women's teams	20
Total players	441 682		Players as % of population	4.70%

Football Association of Serbia (FSS)
Fudbalski savez Srbije, Terazije 35, PO Box 263, Belgrade 11000, Serbia
Tel +381 11 3234253   Fax +381 11 3233433
fsj@beotel.yu   www.fss.org.yu
President: TERZIC Zvezdan   General Secretary: LAKOVIC Zoran
Vice-President: TEOFILOVIC Predrag   Treasurer: BRDARIC   Media Officer: BOSKOVIC Aleksandar
Men's Coach: CLEMENTE Javier   Women's Coach: KRSTIC Perica
FSSCG formed: 1919   UEFA: 1954   FIFA: 1919
Blue shirts with white trimmings, White shorts, Red socks or White shirts with blue trimmings, White shorts, White socks

RECENT INTERNATIONAL MATCHES PLAYED BY SERBIA AND MONTENEGRO

2002	Opponents	Score		Venue	Comp	Scorers	Att	Referee
27-03	Bulgaria	L	1-2	Krusevac	Fr	Kovacevic.D [29]	10 000	Lazarevski MKD
30-04	Germany	L	0-1	Bremen	Fr		22 000	De Bleeckere BEL
3-06	England	L	1-2	Leicester	Fr	Jestrovic [45]	30 900	Allaerts BEL
7-06	Finland	L	0-3	Helsinki	ECq		17 343	Colombo FRA
11-06	Azerbaijan	L	1-2	Baku	ECq	Boskovic [27]	5 000	Fisker DEN
20-08	Wales	W	1-0	Belgrade	ECq	Mladenovic [73]	25 000	Frisk SWE
10-09	Italy	D	1-1	Belgrade	ECq	Ilic [82]	35 000	Hamer LUX
11-10	Wales	W	3-2	Cardiff	ECq	Vukic [4], Milosevic [82], Ljuboja [87]	72 514	Stuchlik AUT
16-11	Poland	L	3-4	Plock	Fr	Boskovic [70], Vukic [79], Iliev [89]	9 000	Weiner GER
2004								
31-03	Norway	L	0-1	Belgrade	Fr		8 000	Panic BIH
28-04	Northern Ireland	D	1-1	Belfast	Fr	Paunovic [7]	9 690	Richards WAL
11-07	Slovakia	W	2-0	Fukuoka	Fr	Milosevic [6], Jestrovic [90]	6 100	Yoshida JPN
13-07	Japan	L	0-1	Yokohama	Fr		57 616	Lennie AUS
18-08	Slovenia	D	1-1	Ljubljana	Fr	Jestrovic [49]	7 000	Ovrebo NOR
4-09	San Marino	W	3-0	Serravalle	WCq	Vukic [4], Jestrovic 2 [15 83]	1 137	Kholmatov KAZ
9-10	Bosnia-Herzegovina	D	0-0	Sarajevo	WCq		22 440	Veissiere FRA
13-10	San Marino	W	5-0	Belgrade	WCq	Milosevic [35], Stankovic 2 [45 50], Koroman [53], Vukic [69]	4 000	Isaksen FRO
17-11	Belgium	W	2-0	Brussels	WCq	Vukic [7], Kezman [60]	28 350	Frojdfeldt SWE
2005								
9-02	Bulgaria	D	0-0	Sofia	Fr		3 000	Guenov BUL
30-03	Spain	D	0-0	Belgrade	WCq		48 910	Busacca SUI
4-06	Belgium	D	0-0	Belgrade	WCq		16 662	Ivanov.V RUS
8-06	Italy	D	1-1	Toronto	Fr	Zigic [25]	35 000	Depiero CAN
15-08	Poland	L	2-3	Kyiv	Fr	Zigic [32], Vidic [59]	2 000	Orekhov UKR
17-08	Ukraine	L	1-2	Kyiv	Fr	Kezman [90]		
3-09	Lithuania	W	2-0	Belgrade	WCq	Kezman [18], Ilic [74]	20 203	Nielsen DEN
7-09	Spain	D	1-1	Madrid	WCq	Kezman [68]	51 491	Poll ENG
8-10	Lithuania	W	2-0	Vilnius	WCq	Kezman [44], Vukic [85]	1 500	Wegereef NED
12-10	Bosnia-Herzegovina	W	1-0	Belgrade	WCq	Kezman [7]	46 305	Vassaras GRE
13-11	China PR	W	2-0	Nanjing	Fr	Djordjevic [50], Zigic [64]	30 000	
16-11	Korea Republic	L	0-2	Seoul	Fr		40 127	
2006								
1-03	Tunisia	W	1-0	Rades/Tunis	Fr	Kezman [11]	6 000	Haimoudi ALG
27-05	Uruguay	D	1-1	Belgrade	Fr	Stankovic [17]	30 000	Kos SVN
11-06	Netherlands	L	0-1	Leipzig	WCr1		37 216	Merk GER
16-06	Argentina	L	0-6	Gelsenkirchen	WCr1		52 000	Rosetti ITA
21-06	Côte d'Ivoire	L	2-3	Munich	WCr1	Zigic [10], Ilic [20]	66 000	Rodriguez MEX
16-08	Czech Republic	W	3-1	Uherske Hradiste	Fr	Lazovic [41], Pantelic [54], Trisovic [72]	8 047	Drabek AUT
2-09	Azerbaijan	W	1-0	Belgrade	ECq	Zigic [72]	BDC	Kircher GER
6-09	Poland	D	1-1	Warsaw	ECq	Lazovic [71]	4 918	Poll ENG
7-10	Belgium	W	1-0	Belgrade	ECq	Zigic [54]	16 901	Messina ITA
11-10	Armenia	W	3-0	Belgrade	ECq	Stankovic [54p], Lazovic [62], Zigic [92+]	10 987	Kasnaferis GRE
15-11	Norway	D	1-1	Belgrade	Fr	Vidic [6]	15 000	Kasnaferis GRE
2007								
24-03	Kazakhstan	L	1-2	Almaty	ECq	Zigic [68]	19 600	Hrinák SVK
28-03	Portugal	D	1-1	Belgrade	ECq	Jankovic [37]	46 810	Layec FRA
2-06	Finland	W	2-0	Helsinki	ECq	Jankovic [3], Jovanovic [86]	33 615	Mejuto Gonzalez ESP

Fr = Friendly match • EC = UEFA EURO 2004/2008 • WC = FIFA World Cup • q = qualifier • BCD = Behind closed doors

SERBIA NATIONAL TEAM RECORDS AND RECORD SEQUENCES

Records			Sequence records					
Victory	10-0	VEN 1972	Wins	10	1978-1980	Clean sheets	7	2004-2005
Defeat	0-7	CZE, URU, CZE	Defeats	6	1931-1932	Goals scored	36	1959-1962
Player Caps	101	MILOSEVIC Savo	Undefeated	16	1996-1998	Without goal	4	1971-72, 1977-78
Player Goals	38	BOBEK Stjepan	Without win	7	2002-2003	Goals against	19	1920-1927

MAJOR CITIES/TOWNS

Population '000

1	Belgrade	1 111
2	Pristina	271
3	Novi Sad	196
4	Nis	173
5	Prizren	171
6	Kragujevac	151
7	Urosevac	101
8	Dakovica	100
9	Subotica	99
10	Pec	97
11	Gnjilane	94
12	Kosovska Mitrovica	88
13	Zrenjanin	79
14	Pancevo	77
15	Cacak	76
16	Leskovac	63
17	Smederevo	63
18	Valjevo	63
19	Krusevac	57
20	Vranje	56
21	Bor	39
22	Apatin	19
23	Kula	19
24	Banatski Dvor	1

REPUBLIC OF SERBIA; REPUBLIKA SRBIJA

Capital	Belgrade	Language	Serbian	Independence	2006
Population	10 150 265	Area	88 361 km²	Density	105 per km²	% in cities	57%
GDP per cap	$2 200	Dailling code	+381	Internet	.yu	GMT + / -	+1

MEDALS TABLE

	Overall G	S	B	League G	S	B	Cup G	S	Europe G	S	B	City	Stadium	Cap'ty	DoF
1 Crvena Zvedza (Red Star)	48	29	12	25	16	8	22	12	1	1	4	Belgrade	Crvena Zvezda	51 328	1945
2 Partizan Beograd	28	24	9	19	16	9	9	7		1		Belgrade	Partizana	30 887	1945
3 OFK Beograd	9	7	6	5	6	5	4	1			1	Belgrade	Omladinski	13 912	1911
4 Vojvodina Novi Sad	2	6	8	2	3	8		3				Novi Sad	Karadorde	12 754	1914
5 Yugoslavia Beograd	2	3	3	2	3	3						Belgrade	Jugoslavija		1919
6 Obilic Beograd	1	3	2	1	1	2		2				Belgrade	Milos Obilic	4 508	1924
7 FK Smederovo	1	1	1				1	1	1			Smederevo	Kraj Stare Zelezare	16 565	1924
8 Zeleznik Beograd	1		1				1	1				Belgrade			
9 Nasa Krila Zemun		2						2				Zemun, Belgrade	Gradski	10 000	1919
Spartak Subotica		2						2				Subotica	Gradski	25 000	1945
11 FK Radnicki	1	2					2	1				Belgrade	Radnicki		1920
12 FK Bor	1							1				Bor	Gradski		1919
Trepca Mitrovica	1							1				Kosovska Mitrovica	Kosovska Mitrovica	28 500	1932
Napredak Krusevac	1							1				Krusevac	Napredak	10 811	1946
Buducnost Dvor	1							1				Banatski Dvor	Mirko Vucurevic	2 400	

RECENT LEAGUE AND CUP RECORD

Championship						Cup		
Year	Champions	Pts	Runners-up	Pts	Third	Pts	Winners	Score	Runners-up
1995	Crvena Zvezda	42	Partizan Beograd	38	Vojvodina Novi Sad	37	Crvena Zvezda	4-0 0-0	FK Obilic
1996	Partizan Beograd	60	Crvena Zvezda	48	Vojvodina Novi Sad	43	Crvena Zvezda	3-0 3-1	Partizan Beograd
1997	Partizan Beograd	84	Crvena Zvezda	78	Vojvodina Novi Sad	53	Crvena Zvezda	0-0 1-0	Vojvodina Novi Sad
1998	FK Obilic	86	Crvena Zvezda	84	Partizan Beograd	70	Partizan Beograd	0-0 2-0	FK Obilic
1999	Partizan Beograd	66	FK Obilic	64	Crvena Zvezda	51	Crvena Zvezda	4-2	Partizan Beograd
2000	Crvena Zvezda	105	Partizan Beograd	101	FK Obilic	89	Crvena Zvezda	4-0	Napredak Krusevac
2001	Crvena Zvezda	88	Partizan Beograd	86	FK Obilic	63	Partizan Beograd	1-0	Crvena Zvezda
2002	Partizan Beograd	81	Crvena Zvezda	66	Sartid Smederevo	58	Crvena Zvezda	1-0	Sartid Smederevo
2003	Partizan Beograd	89	Crvena Zvezda	70	OFK Beograd	63	Sartid Smederevo	1-0	Crvena Zvezda
2004	Crvena Zvezda	74	Partizan Beograd	63	FK Zeleznik	58	Crvena Zvezda	1-0	Buducnost Dvor
2005	Partizan Beograd	80	Crvena Zvezda	74	Zeta Golubovci	59	Zeleznik Beograd	1-0	Crvena Zvezda
2006	Crvena Zvezda	78	Partizan Beograd	71	Vozdovac Beograd	51	Crvena Zvezda	4-2	OFK Beograd
2007	Crvena Zvezda	74	Partizan Beograd	57	Vojvodina Novi Sad		Crvena Zvezda	2-0	Vojvodina Novi Sad

SERBIA 2006-07

MERIDIAN SUPERLIGA

	Pl	W	D	L	F	A	Pts	Red Star	Partizan	Vojvodina	Bezanija	Hajduk	Mladost	OFK	Smederevo	Banat	Borac	Vozdovac	Zemun
Crvena Zvezda †	32	23	5	4	55	27	74		2-4 1-0	0-3 4-2	1-1 1-3	3-1 1-1	2-0 2-1	1-0	1-0	2-0	2-1	2-0	5-0
Partizan Beograd ‡	32	18	3	11	47	31	57	0-0 1-2		0-1 1-0	1-3 1-0	0-1 2-0	1-0 7-1	0-1	2-1	2-0	2-0	2-0	2-0
Vojvodina Novi Sad ‡	32	16	6	10	38	25	54	0-1 0-0	1-0 2-0		1-0 3-0	1-0 1-0	1-1 4-1	1-2	1-0	4-2	0-2	1-0	2-1
Bezanija Novi Beograd‡	32	12	12	8	36	31	48	1-1 2-4	3-4 2-1	0-0 3-2		1-0 1-0	2-0 1-0	0-0	2-2	0-0	1-1	1-2	2-0
Hajduk Kula	32	14	4	14	29	30	46	0-2 1-2	0-1 3-0	1-0 0-0	0-1 1-1		0-1 0-2	2-0	1-0	2-1	1-0	2-0	1-0
Mladost Apatin	32	11	8	13	25	33	41	0-1 0-1	1-0 0-2	2-0 0-1	1-1 1-1	0-1 0-1		0-0	3-0	1-1	1-0	1-0	2-0
OFK Beograd	32	14	8	10	49	29	50	0-1	1-1	0-1	1-1	5-1	2-0		0-0 4-0	3-0 2-1	0-0 4-1	6-2 2-3	3-0 2-0
FC Smederevo	32	12	7	13	33	40	43	1-2	2-2	0-0	2-0	1-1	1-2	2-1 3-2		0-1 3-2	1-0 1-0	3-1 2-1	2-1 0-4
Banat Zrenjanin	32	12	6	14	36	44	42	1-4	1-2	0-0	0-2	1-0	0-0	1-0 1-2	0-0 1-0		0-1 2-0	0-1 2-2	2-0 0-1
Borac Cacak	32	10	8	14	26	30	38	0-2	0-1	2-1	1-1	0-3	0-0	0-3 1-0	0-2 0-0	1-0 3-0		0-1 1-0	1-0 3-1
Vozdovac Beograd	32	10	7	15	33	45	37	2-0	1-3	1-0	0-1	1-2	0-0	1-1 1-0	3-0 4-1	1-3 1-4	0-0 1-0		1-1 3-2
FK Zemun	32	1	4	27	22	64	7	1-2	1-2	1-4	0-1	0-1	1-1	1-2 0-2	0-1 1-2	0-1 1-2	0-2 3-1	0-0 2-2	

4/08/2006 - 26/05/2007 • † Qualified for the UEFA Champions League • ‡ Qualified for the UEFA Cup • Relegation play-off: Napedak 0-0 0-1 Borac

II LIGA GRUPA SRBIJA (2)

	Pl	W	D	L	F	A	Pts
Mladost Lucani	38	24	10	4	49	19	82
Cukaricki Stankom	38	20	10	8	42	15	70
Napredak Krusevac †	38	19	8	11	52	38	65
BSK Borca †	38	16	14	8	55	35	62
Rad Beograd †	38	18	8	12	53	34	62
Radnicki Pirot †	38	17	8	13	52	36	59
Sevojno	38	17	8	13	47	42	59
CSK Pivara Celarevo	38	13	17	8	38	26	56
Vlasina Vlasotince	38	14	14	10	38	37	56
Mladenovac	38	15	10	13	55	44	55
Radnicki Nis	38	14	13	11	45	35	55
Habitpharm Javor	38	15	9	14	35	42	54
Novi Pazar	38	15	8	15	45	51	53
Srem Sremska Mitrovica	38	13	9	16	39	47	48
Indjija	38	11	13	14	42	51	46
Dinamo Vranje	38	10	15	13	33	37	45
Macva Sabac	38	10	11	17	26	49	41
BASK Beograd	38	8	11	19	32	46	35
Spartak Subotica	38	6	8	24	35	64	26
Obilic Beograd	38	0	6	32	16	81	6

12/08/2006 - 3/06/2007 • † play-offs
Semi-finals: Radnicki 0-0 0-2 Napredak; Rad 1-2 1-2 BSK
Final: BSK 2-1 0-2 Napredak

KUP 2006-07

Round of 16

Crvena Zvezda	2
Mokra Gora *	1
Vozdovac Beograd *	1
Cukaricki Stankom	2
Mladost Apatin *	2
OFK Beograd	0
Srem S'ska Mitrovica	0
Partizan Beograd *	2
Banat Zrenjanin *	1 8p
Napredak Krusevac	1 7p
Vlasina Vlasotince *	0 2p
Bezanija N. Beograd	0 4p
Radnicki Pirot *	3
Radnicki Nis	1
Mladenovac *	0
Vojvodina Novi Sad	1

Quarter-finals

Crvena Zvezda	0
Cukaricki Stankom *	2
Mladost Apatin *	0
Partizan Beograd	3
Banat Zrenjanin *	1
Bezanija N. Beograd	0
Radnicki Pirot *	1
Vojvodina Novi Sad	2

Semi-finals

Crvena Zvezda	1
Partizan Beograd	0
Banat Zrenjanin	0
Vojvodina Novi Sad	1

Final

Crvena Zvezda	2
Vojvodina Novi Sad ‡	0

CUP FINAL
Partizana, Belgrade
15-05-2007, Att: 17 000, Ref: Delevic
Scorers - Koroman 63, Djokic 85

* Home team • ‡ Qualified for the UEFA Cup

SRI – SRI LANKA

NATIONAL TEAM RECORD
JULY 10TH 2006 TO JULY 12TH 2010

PL	W	D	L	F	A	%
2	1	0	1	3	5	50

FIFA/COCA-COLA WORLD RANKING

1993	1994	1995	1996	1997	1998	1999	2000	2001	2002	2003	2004	2005	2006	High	Low
126	139	135	126	136	134	153	149	143	139	135	140	144	145	**122** 08/98	**164** 06/00

2006–2007											
08/06	09/06	10/06	11/06	12/06	01/07	02/07	03/07	04/07	05/07	06/07	07/07
139	147	156	156	145	145	147	147	160	161	159	160

Just two international matches were played during the 2006-07 season, both against a Malaysian team preparing to host the AFC Asian Cup, and so the focus was largely on domestic competition. In the League Ratnam Sports Club won their third title since the start of the decade, beating Blue Star 3-2 in the final. They had finished four points ahead of their rivals in the group stage to qualify for the knock-out stage where they beat New Young 6-2 in the semi-final. The final was played in Blue Stars home town of Kalutara but home advantage wasn't enough, as two goals from the Leagues's top scorer Kasum Jayasura clinched the title for Ratnam in a 3-2 victory and with it the

INTERNATIONAL HONOURS
None

first prize of 500,000 Sri Lankan rupees - approximately US$4600. That would have barely covered their expenses to take part in the AFC President's Cup in Pakistan in May 2007, but the event was postponed until September after the teams had trouble with visas applications. Ratnam were hoping to secure the double by winning the Holcim FA Cup but they lost in the semi-finals to Negombo Youth who then beat Saunders, the most successful team in the history of the Cup, to win it for the first time. In August 2006, Sri Lanka hosted the South Asian Games and in the football tournament the under–23 team reached the final before losing to Pakistan.

THE FIFA BIG COUNT OF 2006

	Male	Female		Total
Number of players	397 000	32 150	Referees and Assistant Referees	390
Professionals	0		Admin, Coaches, Technical, Medical	1 830
Amateurs 18+	23 200		Number of clubs	580
Youth under 18	26 800		Number of teams	1 100
Unregistered	68 000		Clubs with women's teams	3
Total players	429 150		Players as % of population	2.12%

Football Federation of Sri Lanka (FFSL)
100/9 Independence Avenue, Colombo 07, Sri Lanka
Tel +94 11 2686120   Fax +94 11 2682471
ffsl@srilankafootball.com   www.srilankafootball.com
President: SILVEIRA Hurley   General Secretary: MARIKAR Hafiz
Vice-President: WEERASKERA S.   Treasurer: HEWAPANNA Laxman   Media Officer: PERERA Rukmal
Men's Coach: BALANDERA Anthony   Women's Coach: DE SILVA Clement
FFSL formed: 1939   AFC: 1958   FIFA: 1950
White shirts, White shorts, White socks

RECENT INTERNATIONAL MATCHES PLAYED BY SRI LANKA

2002	Opponents	Score		DhakaVCCfenue	Comp	Scorers	Att	Referee
27-11	Vietnam	L	1-2	Colombo	Fr	Channa Edribandanage [78]		Deshapriya SRI
29-11	Vietnam	D	1-1	Colombo	Fr	Nazar [90]		Pingamage SRI
1-12	Vietnam	D	2-2	Colombo	Fr	Steinwall [??], Maduranga [??]		
2003								
10-01	Afghanistan	W	1-0	Dhaka	SAFr1	Steinwall [43]		Gurung NEP
12-01	Pakistan	L	1-2	Dhaka	SAFr1	Siyaguna [90]		Gosh BAN
14-01	India	D	1-1	Dhaka	SAFr1	Abeysekera [90]		Shamsuzzaman BAN
21-03	East Timor	W	3-2	Colombo	ACq	Kasun Weerarathna 2 [36 89], Channa Edribandanage [44]		
25-03	Chinese Taipei	W	2-1	Colombo	ACq	Kumara [13], Channa Edribandanage [79]		
15-10	Syria	L	0-5	Damascus	ACq			
18-10	Syria	L	0-8	Damascus	ACq			
9-11	Turkmenistan	L	0-1	Balkanabat	ACq			
12-11	Turkmenistan	L	0-3	Ashgabat	ACq			
18-11	United Arab Emirates	L	1-3	Dubai	ACq	Channa Edribandanage [31]		
22-11	United Arab Emirates	L	0-3	Dubai	ACq			
29-11	Laos	D	0-0	Vientiane	WCq		4 500	Luong The Tai VIE
3-12	Laos	W	3-0	Colombo	WCq	Channa Edribandanage [35], Kasun Weerarathna [59], Hameed [93+]	6 000	Saleem MDV
2004								
18-02	Turkmenistan	L	0-2	Ashgabat	WCq		11 000	Al Bannai UAE
31-03	Saudi Arabia	L	0-1	Colombo	WCq		6 000	Chynybekov KGZ
9-06	Indonesia	L	0-1	Jakarta	WCq		30 000	Nesar BAN
8-09	Indonesia	D	2-2	Colombo	WCq	Steinwall [81], Karunaratne [82]	4 000	Marshoud JOR
9-10	Turkmenistan	D	2-2	Colombo	WCq	Perera [47], Mudiyanselage [57]	4 000	Al Bannai UAE
17-11	Saudi Arabia	L	0-3	Dammam	WCq		2 000	Muflah OMA
18-12	Maldives	D	0-0	Male	Fr			
2005								
7-12	Pakistan	L	0-1	Karachi	SAFr1			
9-12	Maldives	L	0-2	Karachi	SAFr1			
11-12	Afghanistan	L	1-2	Karachi	SAFr1	Karunaratne [85]		
2006								
2-04	Brunei Darussalaam	W	1-0	Chittagong	CCr1	Kasun Weerarathna [74]	2 000	Saidov UZB
4-04	Bhutan	W	1-0	Chittagong	CCr1	Karu [45]		Saidov UZB
6-04	Nepal	D	1-1	Chittagong	CCr1	Izzadeen [19]	2 500	Lee Gi Young KOR
8-04	Chinese Taipei	W	3-0	Chittagong	CCqf	Izzadeen [44], Sanjaya [70], Ratnayaka [90]	2 500	Al Ghatrifi OMA
12-04	Nepal	D	1-1	Chittagong	CCsf	Kasun Weerarathna [65], W 5-3p	2 500	Lee Gi Young KOR
16-04	Tajikistan	L	0-4	Dhaka	CCf		2 000	Mombini IRN
2007								
24-03	Malaysia	L	1-4	Colombo	Fr	Kasun Weerarathna [75]		
26-03	Malaysia	W	2-1	Colombo	Fr	Fazal Fauzan [47], Azmeer Lathif [55]		

Fr = Friendly match • SAF = South Asian Federation Cup • AC = AFC Asian Cup • CC = AFC Challenge Cup • WC = FIFA World Cup
q = qualifier • r1 = first round group • qf = quarter-final • sf = semi-final • f = final

SRI LANKA NATIONAL TEAM RECORDS AND RECORD SEQUENCES

Records			Sequence records					
Victory	4-0	SIN, NEP, PAK	Wins	3	1996-97, 2002	Clean sheets	2	Five times
Defeat	0-8	IDN 1972, SYR 2003	Defeats	12	1972-79, 1979-84	Goals scored	12	2002-2003
Player Caps	n/a		Undefeated	7	2001-2002	Without goal	10	1991-1993
Player Goals	n/a		Without win	15	1954-72, 1984-93	Goals against	35	1952-1979

SRI LANKA COUNTRY INFORMATION

Capital	Colombo	Independence	1948 from UK	GDP per Capita	$3 700
Population	19 905 165	Status	Republic	GNP Ranking	73
Area km²	65 610	Language	Sinhala, Tamil, English	Dialling code	+94
Population density	303 per km²	Literacy rate	92.3%	Internet code	.lk
% in urban areas	22%	Main religion	Buddhist, Hindu	GMT + / –	+5.5
Towns/Cities ('000)	Colombo 648; Dehiwala-Mount Lavinia 215; Jaffna 169; Negombo 137; Chavakachcheri 121; Kotte 118; Kandy 111; Trincomalee 108; Kalmunai 100; Galle 93; Point Pedro 89				
Neighbours (km)	Indian Ocean 1 340				
Main stadia	Sugathadasa Stadium – Colombo 25 000				

SRI LANKA 2006–07 GROUP A

	Pl	W	D	L	F	A	Pts
Ratnam †	16	13	2	1	43	12	41
Blue Star †	16	12	1	3	26	20	37
Negombo Youth †	16	10	2	4	35	19	32
Saunders	16	8	2	6	22	16	26
Army	16	6	2	8	23	22	20
Renown	16	4	2	10	17	28	14
Air Force	16	3	4	9	17	32	13
Police	16	3	3	10	18	29	12
York	16	3	2	11	14	37	11

29/07/2006 - 20/01/2007 • † Qualified for play-offs
Play-off semi-finals: **Ratnams** 6-2 New Young;
Blue Star 3-0 Negombo Youth
Championship final: **Ratnams** 3-2 Blue Star (10-02-2007)

SRI LANKA 2006–07 GROUP B (2)

	Pl	W	D	L	F	A	Pts
New Young †	14	10	1	3	30	16	31
Jupiters	14	8	4	2	29	17	28
Old Bens	14	8	3	3	22	14	27
Red Sun	14	5	4	5	19	20	19
AJva Lane	14	5	3	6	24	16	18
Kalutara Park	14	3	3	8	18	29	12
Golden Star	14	2	4	8	8	22	10
Matara	14	1	6	7	18	34	9

29/07/2006 - 20/01/2007 • † Qualified for play-offs

HOLCIM FA CUP 2006–07

Round of 16		Quarter–finals		Semi–finals		Final	
Negombo Youth	8						
Youngsters	0	**Negombo Youth**	2				
Middle–X	0	Army	1				
Army	7			**Negombo Youth**	5		
Police	3			Ratnam	3		
Java Lane	1	Police	0				
Renown	2 4p	**Ratnam**	1				
Ratnam	2 5p					**Negombo Youth**	3
Air Force	1					Saunders	0
Don Bosco	0	**Air Force**	3 5p				
New Young	0	Blue Star	3 4p				
Blue Star	1			Air Force	0		
Cooray	0 5p			**Saunders**	1		
York	0 4p	Cooray	0				
Red Sun	0	**Saunders**	3				
Saunders	1						

CUP FINAL

1-07-2007

Scorers - Nimal Fernando, Chathura
Guneratne, Ratnayake

RECENT LEAGUE AND CUP RECORD

	Championship		Cup	
Year	Champions	Winners	Score	Runners-up
1997	Saunders	Saunders	1-0	Police
1998	Ratnam			
1999	Saunders	Saunders	3-2	Renown
2000	Ratnam	Ratnam	2-1	Saunders
2001	Saunders	Saunders	4-0	Negombo Youth
2002	Saunders			
2003	Negombo Youth	Renown	1-0	Air Force
2004	Blue Stars	Ratnam	2-2 4-2p	Renown
2005	Saunders	Ratnam	3-1	Saunders
2006	Negombo Youth	Ratnam	2-2 5-3p	Negombo Youth
2007	Ratnam	Negombo Youth	3-0	Saunders

CLUB DIRECTORY

Club	Town/City	Lge	Cup
Blue Stars	Kalutara	1	0
Jupiters	Colombo	0	0
Negombo Youth	Negombo	2	1
Old Bens	Colombo	1	1
Pettah United	Colombo	1	0
Ratnam SC	Kotahena	3	4
Renown	Colombo	3	5
Saunders	Colombo	12	6
York	Kandy	0	1

STP – SAO TOME E PRINCIPE

NATIONAL TEAM RECORD
JULY 10TH 2006 TO JULY 12TH 2010

PL	W	D	L	F	A	%
0	0	0	0	0	0	0

FIFA/COCA-COLA WORLD RANKING

1993	1994	1995	1996	1997	1998	1999	2000	2001	2002	2003	2004	2005	2006	High		Low	
-	-	-	-	-	194	187	181	186	191	192	195	197	198	179	08/00	199	07/07

2006–2007											
08/06	09/06	10/06	11/06	12/06	01/07	02/07	03/07	04/07	05/07	06/07	07/07
197	198	198	198	198	199	199	199	199	199	199	199

São Tomé e Príncipe didn't participate in the 2008 Africa Nations Cup qualifiers which has meant that this tiny two-island nation situated some 200 miles off the west coast of Africa has now gone almost four years without playing a single international match. The last game for the former Portuguese colony's national team was against Libya in November 2003 in the FIFA World Cup qualifying campaign and their next match is likely to be at the start of the preliminaries for the 2010 tournament. Neighbours Equatorial Guinea and Gabon would provide the most obvious opposition for friendly matches and although São Tomé is not a member of the CEMAC regional economic

INTERNATIONAL HONOURS
None

community, taking part in the CEMAC Cup would offer a good route back into mainstream football. No clubs from either São Tomé or Principe entered into African club competition either, further reinforcing the isolation. Local football is well organised, however, with the national championship split into two sections, with one on each of the islands. The bigger of the two is on the more populous São Tomé which was won by Sporting Club Praia Cruz who overtook their rivals Vitoria Riboque on the final day of the season thanks to a 2-1 victory over Agrosport while Vitória lost 1-0 to Santana. The winner on Príncipe was União Desportiva Aeroporto, Picão e Belo Monte.

THE FIFA BIG COUNT OF 2006

	Male	Female		Total
Number of players	8 400	0	Referees and Assistant Referees	22
Professionals	0		Admin, Coaches, Technical, Medical	100
Amateurs 18+	600		Number of clubs	10
Youth under 18	200		Number of teams	20
Unregistered	600		Clubs with women's teams	0
Total players	8 400		Players as % of population	4.34%

Federação Santomense de Futebol (FSF)
Rua Ex-João de Deus No QXXIII - 426/26, Casa postale 440, São Tomé, São Tomé e Príncipe
Tel +239 90 3672   Fax +239 2 21333
futebol@cstome.net   www.fsf.st
President: DENDE Manuel   General Secretary: BARROS Ricardino
Vice-President: DA GRACA ANDRADE Celestino   Treasurer: DA GRACA ANDRADE Celestino   Media Officer: none
Men's Coach: TBD   Women's Coach: TBD
FSF formed: 1975   CAF: 1986   FIFA: 1986
Green shirts, Yellow shorts, Green socks

RECENT INTERNATIONAL MATCHES PLAYED BY SAO TOME E PRINCIPE

2002	Opponents	Score	Venue	Comp	Scorers	Att	Referee
No international matches played in 2002 after June							
2003							
11-10	Libya	L 0-1	São Tomé	WCq		4 000	Yameogo JPN
12-11	Equatorial Guinea	L 1-3	Malabo	Fr			
16-11	Libya	L 0-8	Benghazi	WCq		20 000	Guirat TUN
2004							
No international matches played in 2004							
2005							
No international matches played in 2005							
2006							
No international matches played in 2006							
2007							
No international matches played in 2007 before August							

Fr = Friendly match • WC = FIFA World Cup • q = qualifier

SAO TOME E PRINCIPE NATIONAL TEAM RECORDS AND RECORD SEQUENCES

Records			Sequence records					
Victory	2-0	EQG 1999, SLE 2000	Wins	2	1999-2000	Clean sheets	2	1999-2000
Defeat	0-11	CGO 1976	Defeats	6	1998-1999	Goals scored	2	1999-2000, 2000
Player Caps	n/a		Undefeated	2	1999-2000	Without goal	3	1999
Player Goals	n/a		Without win	11	1976-1999	Goals against	11	1976-1999

RECENT LEAGUE AND CUP RECORD

	League	Cup			São Tomé	Príncipe
Year	Champions	Winners	Score	Finalist	Champions	Champions
1995	Inter Bom-Bom	Caixão Grande			Inter Bom-Bom	
1996	Caixão Grande	Aliança Nacional				
1997	No Tournament	No Tournament				
1998	Os Operários	Sporting Praia Cruz				
1999	Sporting Praia Cruz	Vitória Riboque	3-2	Os Operários	Sporting Praia Cruz	Os Operários
2000	Inter Bom-Bom	Sporting Praia Cruz	3-1	Caixão Grande	Inter Bom-Bom	GD Sundy
2001	Bairros Unidos	GD Sundy	4-3	Vitória Riboque	Bairros Unidos	GD Sundy
2002	No tournament	No Tournament				
2003	Inter Bom Bom	Os Operários	1-0	UDESCAI	Inter Bom-Bom	1º de Maio
2004	Os Operários	No Tournament			UDESCAI	Os Operários
2005	No Tournament	No Tournament			No Tournament	No Tournament
2006	No Tournament	No Tournament			No Tournament	No Tournament
2007					Sporting Praia Cruz	UDAPB

SAO TOME E PRINCIPE COUNTRY INFORMATION

Capital	Sao Tomé	Independence	1975 from Portugal	GDP per Capita	$1 200
Population	181 565	Status	Republic	GNP Ranking	190
Area km²	1 001	Language	Portuguese	Dialling code	+239
Population density	185 per km²	Literacy rate	79%	Internet code	.st
% in urban areas	46%	Main religion	Christian	GMT +/-	0
Towns/Cities ('000)	Sao Tomé 62; Santo Amaro 8; Neves 7; Santana 7; Trinidade 7; Sao José dos Agnolares 2				
Neighbours (km)	Atlantic Ocean/Gulf of Guinea 209				
Main stadia	Estadio Nacional 12 de Julho – São Tomé 6 500				

SUD – SUDAN

NATIONAL TEAM RECORD
JULY 10TH 2006 TO JULY 12TH 2010

PL	W	D	L	F	A	%
17	8	5	4	26	10	61.7

FIFA/COCA-COLA WORLD RANKING

1993	1994	1995	1996	1997	1998	1999	2000	2001	2002	2003	2004	2005	2006	High		Low	
119	116	86	74	108	114	132	132	118	106	103	114	92	120	74	12/96	137	04/00

2006–2007											
08/06	09/06	10/06	11/06	12/06	01/07	02/07	03/07	04/07	05/07	06/07	07/07
113	110	122	121	120	112	112	115	114	114	113	113

Sudan had arguably their best 12 month period since they were crowned African champions more than three decades ago. The national team qualified for the African Nations Cup finals for the first time since 1976, and were also declared winners of the CECAFA Cup. Added to the equation was Al Hilal's qualification for the group phase of the 2007 African Champions League, the first time since the current format was introduced in 1997 that a Sudanese side had managed to make it to the last eight. In the Nations Cup qualifiers, Sudan began with a 3-0 home win over Seychelles and then narrowly lost in a tough match in Tunisia, where they gifted their hosts an own goal from a

INTERNATIONAL HONOURS
CAF African Cup of Nations 1970 CECAFA Cup 1980

late corner. But subsequent wins over Mauritius and the Seychelles again, assured Sudan of a top two finish in the group and enough points to qualify for the tournament in Ghana, sparking off widespread celebrations across the country. In the CECAFA Cup, the Sudanese lost on post-match penalties in the final to Zambia but because Zambia were guest participants, the winners' trophy was handed to Sudan. Al Hilal were successful in their penalty shootout over Nigeria's Nasarawa United to win a place in the Champions League, whilst El Merreikh, who finished second in the Premier League, made the group phase of the 2007 African Confederation Cup.

THE FIFA BIG COUNT OF 2006

	Male	Female		Total
Number of players	1 567 300	0	Referees and Assistant Referees	1 100
Professionals	0		Admin, Coaches, Technical, Medical	7 700
Amateurs 18+	19 800		Number of clubs	440
Youth under 18	26 500		Number of teams	2 750
Unregistered	88 000		Clubs with women's teams	0
Total players	1 567 300		Players as % of population	3.80%

Sudan Football Association (SFA)
Bladia Street, Khartoum, Sudan
Tel +249 183 773495   Fax +249 183 776633
www.sudanfootball.com
President: SHADDAD Kamal, Dr   General Secretary: ABDELMAGEED Eldin
Vice-President: EL MAZZAL Ahmed Elhag   Treasurer: EL KHATEM Mustasim Gaffar Dr   Media Officer: none
Men's Coach: AHMED Mohamed   Women's Coach: None
SFA formed: 1936   CAF: 1957   FIFA: 1948
Red shirts, White shorts, Black socks

RECENT INTERNATIONAL MATCHES PLAYED BY SUDAN

2004	Opponents		Score	Venue	Comp	Scorers	Att	Referee
6-06	Egypt	L	0-3	Khartoum	WCq		10 000	Kidane Tesfu ERI
20-06	Benin	D	1-1	Cotonou	WCq	Abd Iaziz [47+]	20 000	Guezzaz MAR
3-07	Libya	L	0-1	Khartoum	WCq		10 000	Bennett RSA
5-09	Côte d'Ivoire	L	0-5	Abidjan	WCq		20 000	Mana NGA
9-10	Cameroon	D	1-1	Omdurman	WCq	Agab Sido [17]	30 000	Buenkadila COD
12-12	Kenya	D	2-2	Addis Abeba	CCr1	Mustafa Ali [45p], Kamal [79]		
14-12	Uganda	W	2-1	Addis Abeba	CCr1	Kamal [3], El Rasheed [75]		
18-12	Somalia	W	4-0	Addis Abeba	CCr1	Haitham Mostafa [46], Hameedama [63], Haitham Tambal [69], Omar Mohamed [90]		
22-12	Burundi	L	1-2	Addis Abeba	CCsf	Mustafa Haitham [54p]		
25-12	Kenya	W	2-1	Addis Abeba	CC3p	Kamal 2 [30 60]	30 000	
2005								
12-03	Ethiopia	W	3-1	Khartoum	Fr			
27-03	Cameroon	L	1-2	Yaoundé	WCq	Haitham Tambal [41]	30 000	Diatta SEN
22-05	Chad	W	4-1	Khartoum	Fr			
27-05	Chad	D	1-1	Khartoum	Fr			
5-06	Egypt	L	1-6	Cairo	WCq	Haitham Tambal [83]	20 000	Mususa ZIM
17-08	Benin	W	1-0	Omdurman	WCq	Haitham Tambal [20]	12 000	Maillet SEY
2-09	Libya	D	0-0	Tripoli	WCq		20 000	Pare BFA
8-10	Côte d'Ivoire	L	1-3	Omdurman	WCq	Haitham Tambal [89]	20 000	Damon RSA
24-11	Ethiopia	L	1-5	Khartoum	Fr			
29-11	Somalia	W	4-1	Kigali	CCr1	Galag El Dood 2, Faisal Agab, Haitham Tambal		
1-12	Ethiopia	L	1-3	Kigali	CCr1	Galag El Dood		
3-12	Uganda	L	0-3	Kigali	CCr1			
5-12	Djibouti	W	4-0	Kigali	CCr1	Haitham Tambal, Faisal Agab, Alaa Eldin		
2006								
4-06	Algeria	L	0-1	Algiers	Fr			
3-09	Seychelles	W	3-0	Khartoum	CNq	Galag El Dood [20], Haitham Tambal 2 [77 89p]		Kidane ERI
1-10	Libya	L	0-1	Tripoli	Fr			
7-10	Tunisia	L	0-1	Rades/Tunis	CNq			Coulibaly MLI
27-11	Uganda	L	1-2	Addis Abeba	CCr1	Ahmed Mugahid [45]		
30-11	Somalia	W	3-0	Addis Abeba	CCr1	Natali Gemi 2 [16 79], Zakariah Zuhar [69]		
3-12	Rwanda	D	0-0	Addis Abeba	CCr1			
6-12	Burundi	W	1-0	Addis Abeba	CCqf	Rtshard Lado [94p]		
8-12	Uganda	D	2-2	Addis Abeba	CCsf	Galag El Dood [3], Alaa Eldin [55], W 6-5p		
10-12	Zambia	D	0-0	Addis Abeba	CCf	L 10-11p		
21-12	Somalia	W	6-1	Beirut	ARr1	Al Tahir [8], Ali Mohamed 2 [16 18], Haitham Mostafa [21p], Faisal Agab [30], Natali Gemi [55]		
24-12	Mauritania	W	2-0	Beirut	ARr1	Faisal Agab [3], Haitham Tambal [90]		
27-12	Lebanon	D	0-0	Beirut	ARr1			
2007								
25-03	Mauritius	W	2-1	Curepipe	CNq	Faisal Agab 2 [42 77]		Mwanza ZAM
21-05	Eritrea	L	0-1	Asmara	Fr			
26-05	Eritrea	D	1-1	Asmara	Fr	Ahmed Mugahid [10]		
2-06	Mauritius	W	3-0	Omdurman	CNq	Rtshard Lado 2 [25p 65], Faisal Agab [44]		
16-06	Seychelles	W	2-0	Roche Caiman	CNq	Faisal Agab [44], Haitham Tambal [61]		

Fr = Friendly match • CN = CAF African Cup of Nations • CC = CECAFA Cup • AR = Arab Cup • WC = FIFA World Cup
q = qualifier • r1 = first round group • sf = semi-final • 3p = third place play-off • f = final

SUDAN NATIONAL TEAM RECORDS AND RECORD SEQUENCES

Records			Sequence records					
Victory	15-0	OMA 1965	Wins	5	1965	Clean sheets	5	2003
Defeat	0-8	KOR 1979	Defeats	5	2000-2001	Goals scored	12	1996-1998
Player Caps	n/a		Undefeated	9	1968-1969	Without goal	4	2000-2001
Player Goals	n/a		Without win	9	1980-1982	Goals against	15	1996-1998

SUDAN COUNTRY INFORMATION

Capital	Khartoum	Independence	1956 from Egypt and UK	GDP per Capita	$1 900
Population	39 148 162	Status	Republic	GNP Ranking	83
Area km²	2 505 810	Language	Arabic, English, Nubian	Dialling code	+249
Population density	15 per km²	Literacy rate	61%	Internet code	.sd
% in urban areas	25%	Main religion	Muslim	GMT + / –	+2
Towns/Cities ('000)	Omdurman 2 810; Khartoum 1 974; Khartoum North 1 530; Niyala 499; Port Sudan 459; Kassala 401; El Obeid 393; Kusti 345; Wad Madani 332; Gadaref 322, El Fasher 252				
Neighbours (km)	Eritrea 605; Ethiopia 1 606; Kenya 232; Uganda 435; Congo DR 628; Central African Republic 1 165; Chad 1 360; Libya 383; Egypt 1 273; Red Sea 853				
Main stadia	National Stadium – Khartoum 20 000; El Merriekh – Omdurman 30 000				

SUDAN 2006

PREMIER LEAGUE

	Pl	W	D	L	F	A	Pts	Hilal	Merreikh	Jazeerat	Mawrada	Ittihad	Hay Al Arab	Khartoum-3	Amal	Hilal PS	Merghani	Nil	Ahli
Al Hilal Omdurman †	22	18	3	1	66	11	57		1-1	6-0	6-0	2-0	3-1	3-0	4-0	2-2	4-0	2-0	7-1
Al Merreikh Omdurman‡	22	15	5	2	62	12	50	0-2		5-0	6-0	4-0	5-0	1-0	3-0	6-0	4-0	6-0	4-1
Jazeerat Al-Feel	22	9	6	7	31	36	33	0-0	2-1		0-5	0-1	1-1	3-2	3-0	3-0	3-1	3-0	4-2
Al Mawrada Omdurman	22	8	6	8	25	30	30	0-1	2-2	1-1		1-0	0-1	1-0	1-2	1-1	1-2	1-1	2-2
Al Ittihad Wad Medani	22	7	7	8	23	26	28	1-2	0-1	1-2	1-3		2-1	0-0	1-0	4-2	1-1	2-2	2-0
Hay Al Arab Pt. Sudan	22	6	9	7	20	25	27	2-1	1-1	1-1	0-1	1-3		0-0	0-0	0-1	1-0	1-1	1-0
Khartoum-3	22	6	7	9	21	25	25	2-4	1-2	1-1	1-0	0-0	1-0		3-0	2-2	2-3	3-1	1-0
Al Amal Atbara	22	6	6	10	18	30	24	0-2	1-1	2-0	1-0	0-1	1-1	1-2		0-1	0-0	1-0	2-0
Al Hilal Port Sudan	22	5	8	9	19	35	23	0-5	0-1	2-0	0-1	0-0	1-3	0-0	3-3		0-0	0-1	1-0
Al Merghani Kassala	22	4	10	8	21	34	22	1-4	0-2	2-3	1-1	2-2	2-2	2-0	1-1	1-0		0-0	1-1
Al Nil Wad Medani	22	4	8	10	16	36	20	0-3	1-1	2-1	0-1	1-1	0-2	0-0	2-1	2-3	1-0		1-1
Al Ahli Atbara	22	3	7	12	16	38	16	0-2	0-5	0-0	1-2	1-0	0-0	1-0	1-2	0-0	1-1	3-0	

24/02/2006 - 17/11/2006 • † Qualified for the CAF Champions League • ‡ Qualified for the CAF Confederations Cup • Al Ahli Wad Medani and Al Merreikh Al Thagher promoted

SUDAN CUP 2006

Quarter-finals		Semi-finals		Final	
Al Merreikh	6				
Al Amal Atbara	0	**Al Merreikh**	2		
Al Hilal El-Hasahisa	1	Al Hilal Port Sudan	0		
Al Hilal Port Sudan	6			**Al Merreikh**	2
Al Hilal Nyala	0 4p			Al Hilal Omdurman	0
Jazeerat Al-Feel	0 3p	Al Hilal Nyala	0	14-12-2006	
Al Mawrada	1	**Al Hilal Omdurman**	5	Scorers - Endurance Idahor [36], Faisal Al Ajab [80]	
Al Hilal Omdurman	3				

RECENT LEAGUE AND CUP RECORD

	Championship	Cup		
Year	Champions	Winners	Score	Runners-up
1998	Al Hilal	Al Hilal	2-0	Al Merreikh
1999	Al Hilal	Al Mawrada		
2000	Al Merreikh	Al Hilal	3-0	Al Ahly
2001	Al Merreikh	Al Merreikh	1-0	Al Mawrada
2002	Al Merreikh			
2003	Al Hilal			
2004	Al Hilal	Al Hilal	0-0 3-2p	Al Merreikh
2005	Al Hilal	Al Merreikh	0-0 4-2p	Al Hilal
2006	Al Hilal	Al Merreikh	2-0	Al Hilal

SUI – SWITZERLAND

NATIONAL TEAM RECORD
JULY 10TH 2006 TO JULY 12TH 2010

PL	W	D	L	F	A	%
9	4	1	4	13	11	50

FIFA/COCA-COLA WORLD RANKING

1993	1994	1995	1996	1997	1998	1999	2000	2001	2002	2003	2004	2005	2006	High	Low
12	7	18	47	62	83	47	58	63	44	44	51	35		3 08/93	83 12/98

2006–2007											
08/06	09/06	10/06	11/06	12/06	01/07	02/07	03/07	04/07	05/07	06/07	07/07
13	14	15	17	17	17	14	17	20	21	25	45

Despite the Swiss economy being set to prosper by up to some € 10 billion by hosting the Euro Championship finals in the summer of 2008, the good people of Berne needed some convincing as to the economic benefits, and only 52% of them voted in favour of releasing public funds to enable the city to host matches in the tournament - just enough to ensure matches will take place there. The optimism about Swiss chances took a knock during a season in which Kobi Kuhn's national team endured a run of four defeats in five games. More worrying perhaps were the reports of a rift in the camp between the German-speaking players led by Alexander Frei and French-speaking

INTERNATIONAL HONOURS
Qualified for the FIFA World Cup finals 1934 1938 1950 1954 1962 1966 1994 2006

players led by captain Johann Vogel. In a bid to quell the disquiet, Vogel was dropped but it seemed to do little to calm the situation. Once again the Swiss championship went right down to the wire with FC Zürich holding on despite a late surge by FC Basel. Having been 10 points behind at the winter break, Basel were just one point behind going into the final game, but were denied the title when Zürich beat Grasshoppers. A goal deep into injury-time gave Basel the Cup in a 1-0 win over Luzern, but it came courtesy of a controversial penalty awarded by referee Nicole Petignat after Scott Chipperfield was brought down in the area.

THE FIFA BIG COUNT OF 2006

	Male	Female		Total
Number of players	507 900	63 800	Referees and Assistant Referees	4 783
Professionals	550		Admin, Coaches, Technical, Medical	25 300
Amateurs 18+	103 700		Number of clubs	1 412
Youth under 18	127 700		Number of teams	13 005
Unregistered	240 000		Clubs with women's teams	394
Total players	571 700		Players as % of population	7.60%

Schweizerischer Fussball-Verband (SFV/ASF)
Worbstrasse 48, Postfach, Bern 15 3000, Switzerland
Tel +41 31 9508111   Fax +41 31 9508181
sfv.asf@football.ch   www.football.ch
President: ZLOCZOWER Ralph   General Secretary: GILLIERON Peter
Vice-President: SALADIN Urs   Treasurer: POMA Giuseppe   Media Officer: BENOIT Pierre
Men's Coach: KUHN Koebi   Women's Coach: VON SIEBENTHAL Beatrice
SFV/ASF formed: 1895   UEFA: 1954   FIFA: 1904
Red shirts with white trimmings, White shorts, Red socks or White shirts with red trimmings, Red shorts, White socks

RECENT INTERNATIONAL MATCHES PLAYED BY SWITZERLAND

2003	Opponents	Score		Venue	Comp	Scorers	Att	Referee
20-08	France	L	0-2	Geneva	Fr		30 000	Allaerts BEL
10-09	Russia	L	1-4	Moscow	ECq	Karyaka OG [12]	29 000	Collina ITA
11-10	Republic of Ireland	W	2-0	Basel	ECq	Yakin.H [6], Frei [60]	31 006	Frisk SWE
2004								
18-02	Morocco	L	1-2	Rabat	Fr	Frei [90]	3 000	Berber ALG
31-03	Greece	L	0-1	Heraklion	Fr		33 000	Temmink NED
28-04	Slovenia	W	2-1	Geneva	Fr	Celestini [66], Yakin.H [85]	7 500	Bossen NED
2-06	Germany	L	0-2	Basel	Fr		30 000	Messina ITA
6-06	Liechtenstein	W	1-0	Zurich	Fr	Gygax [90]	10 200	Drabek AUT
13-06	Croatia	D	0-0	Leiria	ECr1		24 090	Cortez Batista POR
17-06	England	L	0-3	Coimbra	ECr1		28 214	Ivanov.V RUS
21-06	France	L	1-3	Coimbra	ECr1	Vonlanthen [26]	28 111	Michel SVK
18-08	Northern Ireland	D	0-0	Zurich	Fr		4 000	Vollquartz DEN
4-09	Faroe Islands	W	6-0	Basel	WCq	Vonlanthen 3 [10 14 57], Rey 3 [29 44 55]	11 880	Tudor ROM
8-09	Republic of Ireland	D	1-1	Basel	WCq	Yakin.H [17]	28 000	Vassaras GRE
9-10	Israel	D	2-2	Tel Aviv	WCq	Frei [26], Vonlanthen [34]	37 976	Shield AUS
2005								
9-02	United Arab Emirates	W	2-1	Dubai	Fr	Gygax [9], Muller.P [79]	1 000	El Hilali OMA
26-03	France	D	0-0	Paris	WCq		79 373	De Santis ITA
30-03	Cyprus	W	1-0	Zurich	WCq	Frei [87]	16 066	Dougal SCO
4-06	Faroe Islands	W	3-1	Toftir	WCq	Wicky [25], Frei 2 [72 84]	2 047	Gumienny BEL
17-08	Norway	W	2-0	Oslo	Fr	Frei [50], OG [59]	19 623	Vollquartz DEN
3-09	Israel	D	1-1	Basel	WCq	Frei [6]	30 000	Rosetti ITA
7-09	Cyprus	W	3-1	Nicosia	WCq	Frei [15], Senderos [71], Gygax [84]	2 561	Ivanov.N RUS
8-10	France	D	1-1	Berne	WCq	Magnin [80]	31 400	Hauge NOR
12-10	Republic of Ireland	D	0-0	Dublin	WCq		35 944	Merk GER
12-11	Turkey	W	2-0	Berne	WCpo	Senderos [41], Behrami [86]	31 130	Michel SVK
16-11	Turkey	L	2-4	Istanbul	WCpo	Frei [2p], Streller [84]	42 000	De Bleeckere BEL
2006								
1-03	Scotland	W	3-1	Glasgow	Fr	Barnetta [21], Gygax [41], Cabanas [69]	20 952	Coue FRA
27-05	Côte d'Ivoire	D	1-1	Basel	Fr	Barnetta [32]	20 000	Vuorela FIN
31-05	Italy	D	1-1	Geneva	Fr	Gygax [32]	30 000	Sippel GER
3-06	China PR	W	4-1	Zurich	Fr	Frei 2 [40 49p], Streller 2 [47 73]	16 000	Stokes IRL
13-06	France	D	0-0	Stuttgart	WCr1		52 000	Ivanov.V RUS
19-06	Togo	W	2-0	Dortmund	WCr1	Frei [16], Barnetta [88]	65 000	Amarilla PAR
23-06	Korea Republic	W	2-0	Hanover	WCr1	Snderos [23], Frei [77]	43 000	Elizondo ARG
26-06	Ukraine	D	0-0	Cologne	WCr2	L 0-3p	45 000	Archundia MEX
16-08	Liechtenstein	W	3-0	Vaduz	Fr	Frei 2 [11 51p], Margairaz [65]	4 837	Brugger AUT
2-09	Venezuela	W	1-0	Basel	Fr	Frei [86]	12 500	Hamer LUX
6-09	Costa Rica	W	2-0	Geneva	Fr	Streller [12], Frei [39]	12 000	Van Egmond NED
11-10	Austria	L	1-2	Innsbruck	Fr	Streller [70]	11 000	Svendsen DEN
15-11	Brazil	L	1-2	Basel	Fr	Maicon OG [71]	39 000	Merk GER
2007								
7-02	Germany	L	1-3	Düsseldorf	Fr	Streller [71]	51 333	Bossen NED
22-03	Jamaica	W	2-0	Fort Lauderdale	Fr	Streller [7], Inler [12]	3 254	Prus USA
25-03	Colombia	L	1-3	Miami	Fr	Frei [39p]	16 000	Vaughn USA
2-06	Argentina	D	1-1	Basel	Fr	Streller [64]	29 000	Messina ITA

Fr = Friendly match • EC = UEFA EURO 2004/2008 • WC = FIFA World Cup • q = qualifier • po = play-off

SWITZERLAND NATIONAL TEAM RECORDS AND RECORD SEQUENCES

Records			Sequence records					
Victory	9-0	LTU 1924	Wins	5	1960-1961	Clean sheets	7	2006
Defeat	0-9	ENG 1909, HUN 1911	Defeats	11	1928-1930	Goals scored	22	1921-1924
Player Caps	117	HERMANN Heinz	Undefeated	14	2004-2005	Without goal	5	1985
Player Goals	34	ABEGGLEN/TURKYILMAZ	Without win	16	1928-1930	Goals against	45	1926-1932

MAJOR CITIES/TOWNS
Population '000

1	Zürich	1 024
2	Geneva	614
3	Basel	573
4	Bern	119
5	Lausanne	114
6	Winterthur	92
7	Rapperswil	71
8	St Gallen	69
9	Luzern	56
10	Biel	48
11	Thun	41
12	Köniz	37
13	La Chaux-de-Fonds	36
14	Schaffhausen	33
15	Chur	32
16	Fribourg	32
17	Neuchâtel	30
18	Sion	28
19	Emmen	26
20	Lugano	26
21	Kriens	24
22	Yverdon	23
23	Wil	16
24	Aarau	15

SWITZERLAND; SCHWEIZ; SUISSE; SVIZZERA

Capital	Bern	Language	German, French, Italian	Formation	1291
Population	7 554 661	Area	41 290 km²	Density	180 per km²	% in cities	61%
GDP per cap	$32 700	Dialling code	+41	Internet	.ch	GMT + / -	+1

MEDALS TABLE

		Overall			League			Cup			Europe			City	Stadium	Cap'ty	DoF
		G	S	B	G	S	B	G	S	G	S	B					
1	Grasshopper-Club	45	32	13	27	19	12	18	13			1	Zürich	Hardturm Stadion	17 666	1886
2	Servette FC	24	28	12	17	16	12	7	12				Geneva	Stade de Genève	30 084	1890
3	FC Basel	19	12	4	11	6	4	8	6				Basel	St Jakob Park	42 500	1893
4	FC Zürich	18	9	8	11	8	6	7	1			2	Zürich	Letzigrund	30 000	1896
5	BSC Young Boys Bern	17	19	10	11	13	9	6	6			1	Berne	Stade de Suisse Wankdorf	32 000	1898
6	Lausanne-Sport	16	15	9	7	8	8	9	7			1	Lausanne	Olympique de la Pontaise	16 000	1896
7	FC Sion	12	2	6	2	2	6	10					Sion	Stade Tourbillon	13 000	1909
8	FC La Chaux-de-Fonds	9	4	7	3	3	7	6	1				La Chaux-de-Fonds	Parc Charrière	13 000	1894
9	AC Lugano	6	9	10	3	5	10	3	4				Lugano	Stadio Cornaredo	15 000	1908
10	FC Aarau	4	3	3	3	1	3	1	2				Aarau	Brügglifeld Stadion	9 249	1902
11	Neuchâtel Xamax FC	3	8	9	3	3	9		5				Neuchâtel	Stade La Maladiere	22 100	1970
12	FC Luzern	3	4	1	1	1	1	2	3				Luzern	Stadion Allmend	18 400	1901
13	FC Winterthur	3	4	1	3	2	1		2				Wintherthur	Schützenwiese	15 000	1896
14	FC St Gallen	3	3	3	2		3	1	3				St Gallen	Espenmoos Stadion	11 300	1879
15	FC Grenchen	1	7	1		4	1	1	3				Grenchen	Bruehl Stadion		1906

RECENT LEAGUE AND CUP RECORD

	Championship						Cup		
Year	Champions	Pts	Runners-up	Pts	Third	Pts	Winners	Score	Runners-up
1995	Grasshopper-Club	37	FC Lugano	30	Neuchâtel Xamax	28	FC Sion	4-2	Grasshopper-Club
1996	Grasshopper-Club	52	FC Sion	47	Neuchâtel Xamax	43	FC Sion	3-2	Servette FC
1997	FC Sion	49	Neuchâtel Xamax	46	Grasshopper-Club	45	FC Sion	3-3 5-4p	FC Luzern
1998	Grasshopper-Club	57	Servette FC	41	Lausanne-Sports	40	Lausanne-Sports	2-2 4-3p	FC St. Gallen
1999	Servette FC	46	Grasshopper-Club	46	Lausanne-Sports	45	Lausanne-Sports	2-0	Grasshopper-Club
2000	FC St. Gallen	54	Lausanne-Sports	44	FC Basel	40	FC Zürich	2-2 3-0p	Lausanne-Sports
2001	Grasshopper-Club	46	FC Lugano	41	FC St. Gallen	40	Servette FC	3-0	Yverdon-Sports
2002	FC Basel	55	Grasshopper-Club	45	FC Lugano	42	FC Basel	2-1	Grasshopper-Club
2003	Grasshopper-Club	57	FC Basel	56	Neuchâtel Xamax	35	FC Basel	6-0	Neuchâtel Xamax
2004	FC Basel	85	BSC Young Boys	72	Servette FC	52	FC Wil	3-2	Grasshopper-Club
2005	FC Basel	70	FC Thun	60	Grasshopper-Club	50	FC Zürich	3-1	FC Luzern
2006	FC Zürich	78	FC Basel	78	BSC Young Boys	62	FC Sion	1-1 5-3p	BSC Young Boys
2007	FC Zürich	75	FC Basel	74	FC Sion	60	FC Basel	1-0	FC Luzern

SWITZERLAND 2006–07

AXPO SUPER LEAGUE

	Pl	W	D	L	F	A	Pts	Zürich	Basel	Sion	Young Boys	St Gallen	GC	Thun	Luzern	Aarau	S'haussen
FC Zürich †	36	23	6	7	67	32	75		3-2 0-1	2-1 2-1	3-1 1-0	2-1 3-0	2-1 2-0	5-0 0-0	2-1 2-0	3-0 2-2	0-1 0-0
FC Basel ‡	36	22	8	6	77	40	74	2-1 4-2		3-1 2-0	2-2 2-0	2-1 3-3	2-3 3-0	4-1 4-1	3-0 1-0	3-1 2-0	3-0 0-0
FC Sion ‡	36	17	9	10	57	42	60	2-2 1-2	4-2 0-0		1-0 2-0	4-0 0-0	2-2 1-1	3-0 2-1	3-2 2-0	2-1 1-1	2-2 3-0
BSC Young Boys ‡	36	17	8	11	52	42	59	2-0 2-3	1-1 0-3	2-1 2-0		3-0 1-1	1-3 1-0	5-0 3-1	3-2 3-1	2-1 1-1	3-2 2-0
FC St Gallen	36	14	13	9	47	44	55	3-1 2-2	3-2 0-0	5-1 0-3	2-1 1-1		0-0 0-0	1-2 2-0	1-0 0-0	1-0 1-0	3-1 1-1
Grasshopper-Club	36	13	11	12	54	41	50	0-1 0-0	1-2 1-5	0-0 0-0	1-2 1-2	4-1 1-1		4-1 0-3	2-0 5-0	3-1 1-0	5-0 1-2
FC Thun	36	10	7	19	30	58	37	0-2 0-1	1-1 0-2	0-1 1-3	0-0 0-1	0-3 0-1	0-1 0-2		1-1 2-1	2-1 1-0	1-0 2-0
FC Luzern	36	8	9	19	31	58	33	0-3 2-0	2-0 0-3	1-1 2-0	3-1 1-1	0-1 1-1	0-1 1-6	2-1 1-2		2-1 1-0	1-1 0-0
FC Aarau ††	36	6	8	22	28	55	26	0-4 0-3	2-3 0-1	1-3 0-2	0-1 1-1	0-3 1-1	1-0 0-0	1-1 0-0	0-1 4-1		1-0 3-2
FC Schaffhausen	36	4	13	19	27	58	25	0-2 0-4	4-2 2-2	1-3 0-1	1-0 0-1	1-1 0-1	3-3 1-1	0-0 1-2	1-1 0-0	0-0 1-0	

19/07/2006 - 24/05/2007 • † Qualified for the UEFA Champions League • ‡ Qualified for the UEFA Cup • †† Relegation play-off
Top scorers: Mladen PETRIC, Basel 19; Francisco AGUIRRE, St Gallen 16; Alberto SABORIO, Sion 14; Alexander TACHIE, St Gallen 14
Relegation play-off: AC Bellinzona 1-2 1-3 FC Aarau • Aarau remain in the Super League

SWITZERLAND 2006–07

CHALLENGE LEAGUE (2)

	Pl	W	D	L	F	A	Pts	Xamax	Bellinzona	Kriens	Chiasso	Concordia	Winterthur	Servette	Wil	Vaduz	C. de-Fonds	Yverdon-Sp	Lugano	Lausanne	Locarno	Delémont	Wohlen	Baulmes	Juventus
Neuchâtel Xamax	34	23	7	4	73	28	76		3-0	1-1	2-0	1-0	3-0	2-0	2-3	1-1	3-2	3-1	2-0	2-0	4-1	3-1	4-0	5-0	0-1
AC Bellinzona †	34	21	7	6	58	26	70	1-1		1-1	2-1	2-0	1-1	1-1	0-0	4-0	1-0	0-1	0-3	2-0	1-0	4-0	6-1	4-1	
SC Kriens	34	20	7	7	65	36	67	1-2	2-3		4-1	2-1	7-1	1-2	6-1	1-0	2-2	2-0	1-0	1-0	4-0	1-1	2-1	2-1	5-0
FC Chiasso	34	16	10	8	55	39	58	3-2	0-1	0-0		1-1	1-1	4-0	2-1	1-1	2-0	3-0	0-1	3-1	2-1	3-0	1-1	1-1	1-1
Concordia Basel	34	17	6	11	59	49	57	1-2	0-0	3-1	1-2		1-7	3-2	1-0	3-2	3-2	4-0	0-2	2-1	4-2	3-3	1-2	2-1	4-1
FC Winterthur	34	17	4	13	60	47	55	0-2	0-2	0-1	3-0	0-2		2-1	1-3	2-0	1-0	2-1	1-2	2-1	4-1	6-1	1-0	3-0	4-3
Servette FC	34	15	8	11	63	51	51	1-1	0-3	4-2	1-1	1-2	2-3		2-0	3-1	4-1	1-1	4-3	2-0	0-0	3-1	4-3		
FC Wil 1900	34	12	10	12	56	50	46	2-0	0-2	1-1	0-5	3-0	0-2	1-0		1-0	1-1	4-2	2-2	1-1	3-0	8-1	0-1	1-1	4-0
FC Vaduz	34	12	10	12	57	52	46	1-1	0-2	2-2	2-3	0-3	5-2	4-2	1-0		3-2	3-3	1-0	3-0	2-2	2-0	3-3	5-1	2-1
La Chaux-de-Fonds	34	13	7	14	51	47	46	1-2	1-3	3-0	4-1	1-2	0-0	1-2	1-1	1-0		2-0	2-1	2-3	1-1	1-0	2-2	0-1	1-2
Yverdon-Sport	34	12	6	16	45	60	42	1-2	0-1	0-1	3-2	2-1	1-1	2-3	4-2	0-3	1-0		1-1	1-1	3-2	0-0	1-1	1-0	
AC Lugano	34	11	8	15	42	46	41	1-3	3-1	0-1	1-3	1-1	1-0	3-3	2-2	2-1	1-2	1-1		4-1	2-0	2-0	1-1	1-0	2-2
Lausanne-Sport	34	10	9	15	44	51	39	1-3	3-3	0-2	1-1	1-1	2-2	1-0	2-1	1-0	0-1	0-1	4-0		2-1	0-3	1-0	0-0	3-0
FC Locarno	34	10	9	15	42	60	39	2-2	0-2	3-2	0-0	2-1	0-1	1-0	1-1	1-2	2-1	1-1	1-0	2-0		2-1	3-1	5-1	0-0
SR Delémont	34	9	6	19	39	63	33	2-3	0-2	0-1	2-1	0-2	3-2	1-1	1-3	0-1	1-0	2-4	1-1				1-2	1-0	3-0
FC Wohlen	34	7	10	17	39	64	31	0-2	1-2	1-2	2-2	2-3	2-1	1-5	1-2	2-2	2-2	1-0	0-2	0-2	4-2	0-1		2-2	2-2
FC Baulmes	34	7	9	18	30	63	30	0-0	1-0	1-2	0-1	0-2	0-4	1-0	0-2	0-3	0-1	2-4	2-1	2-1	2-2	1-1	2-0		1-1
Young Fellows Juventus	34	4	7	23	29	75	19	0-3	1-0	0-1	0-1	0-2	0-1	1-5	2-2	1-2	0-3	3-4	3-2	1-1	1-2	0-1	1-2	0-3	

21/07/2006 - 26/05/2007 • † Promotion play-off

SWISSCOM CUP 2006–07

Round of 16		Quarter–finals		Semi–finals		Final	
FC Basel	3						
FC Baulmes *	2	FC Basel *	1				
FC Winterthur *	1	FC Aarau	0				
FC Aarau	2			FC Basel	3		
BSC Young Boys *	3			FC Wil 1900	1		
FC Sion	0	BSC Young Boys	1				
FC Chiasso *	2 2p	FC Wil 1900 *	2				
FC Wil 1900	2 4p					FC Basel ‡	1
FC Zürich	5					FC Luzern	0
Yverdon-Sport *	2	FC Zürich *	1				
SR Delémont *	1	FC St Gallen	0				
FC St Gallen	3			FC Zürich	2		
Grasshopper-Club *	1			FC Luzern	3		
FC Thun	0	Grasshopper-Club	1				
FC Schaffhausen	0	FC Luzern *	3				
FC Luzern *	2						

SWISS CUP FINAL

Stade de Suisse, Berne
28-05-2007, Att: 30 000
Ref: Nicole Petignat

Scorer - Daniel Majstorovic 93+p

* Home team • ‡ Qualified for the UEFA Cup

SUR – SURINAM

NATIONAL TEAM RECORD
JULY 10TH 2006 TO JULY 12TH 2010

PL	W	D	L	F	A	%
5	2	1	2	4	9	50

FIFA/COCA-COLA WORLD RANKING

1993	1994	1995	1996	1997	1998	1999	2000	2001	2002	2003	2004	2005	2006	High		Low	
117	104	124	131	145	160	162	164	141	141	158	149	152	122	**92**	07/94	**168**	04/01

2006–2007											
08/06	09/06	10/06	11/06	12/06	01/07	02/07	03/07	04/07	05/07	06/07	07/07
160	163	122	108	122	114	114	113	115	115	120	125

For the third time running Surinam missed out on qualifying for the finals of the Digicel Caribbean Cup. Thrashed 5-0 by neighbours Guyana in the opening match of their first qualifying round group in the Netherlands Antilles, Kenneth Jaliens' side recovered well to beat Grenada and then the hosts, which saw them qualify for the next round. Drawn in a strong group containing Cuba, Haiti and hosts Martinique, Surinam struggled, losing their first two matches. Remarkably they still had a chance of qualifying for the finals through a third-place play-off as their final opponents Haiti had also lost their first two games. An inspired substitution by Jaliens saw

INTERNATIONAL HONOURS
CONCACAF Champions Cup Transvaal 1973 1981

Vangellino Sastrodimedjo give Surinam the lead from a magnificent free-kick but that lasted just three minutes and although they did hold on for a draw, Surinam were knocked out on goal difference. In the League there was a first title for Inter Moengotapoe. Based in the town of Moengo, 50 miles to the east of the capital Paramaribo, they are only major club not from the capital and by winning the championship they became the first provincial winners. Robinhood won the Cup for a record fifth time after beating Walking Bout Co on penalties in the final after the two had drawn 1-1. Surprisingly there were no Surinamese entrants in the Caribbean club championship.

THE FIFA BIG COUNT OF 2006

	Male	Female		Total
Number of players	31 950	3 300	Referees and Assistant Referees	100
Professionals	0		Admin, Coaches, Technical, Medical	275
Amateurs 18+	6 655		Number of clubs	30
Youth under 18	1 395		Number of teams	292
Unregistered	14 000		Clubs with women's teams	1
Total players	35 250		Players as % of population	8.03%

Surinaamse Voetbal Bond (SVB)
Letitia Vriesdelaan 7, PO Box 1223, Paramaribo, Surinam
Tel +597 473112   Fax +597 479718
svb@sr.net   www.svb.sr
President: GISKUS Louis   General Secretary: FELTER Harold
Vice-President: KOORNDIJK Ronald   Treasurer: GOBARDHAN Waldo   Media Officer: FELTER Harold
Men's Coach: JALIENS Kenneth   Women's Coach: BENZENSTEIN Arno
SVB formed: 1920   CONCACAF: 1964   FIFA: 1929
White shirts, Green shorts, Green socks

RECENT INTERNATIONAL MATCHES PLAYED BY SURINAM

2004	Opponents	Score	Venue	Comp	Scorers	Att	Referee
28-02	Aruba	W 2-1	Oranjestad	WCq	Felter 54p, Zinhagel 63	2 108	Moreno PAN
27-03	Aruba	W 8-1	Paramaribo	WCq	Kinsaini 2 6 49, Loswijk 14, Felter 3 18 65 66, Sandvliet 42, Zinhagel 90	4 000	Prendergast JAM
12-06	Guatemala	D 1-1	Paramaribo	WCq	Purperhart 14	5 500	Jimenez CRC
20-06	Guatemala	L 1-3	Guatemala City	WCq	Brandon 82	19 610	Rodriguez MEX
24-11	Grenada	D 2-2	Tunapuna	CCq	Modeste OG 27, Sandvliet 59	2 000	Forde BRB
26-11	Puerto Rico	D 1-1	Marabella	CCq	Sandvliet 45		Forde BRB
28-11	Trinidad and Tobago	L 0-1	Malabar	CCq			Forde BRB
2005							
No international matches played in 2005							
2006							
6-09	Guyana	L 0-5	Willemstad	CCq			
8-09	Grenada	W 1-0	Willemstad	CCq	Kinsaine 35		
10-09	Netherlands Antilles	W 1-0	Willemstad	CCq	Grootfaam 5		Suazo DOM
8-11	Martinique †	L 0-1	Fort de France	CCq			
10-11	Cuba	L 1-3	Fort de France	CCq	Aroepa 90		
12-11	Haiti	D 1-1	Fort de France	CCq	Sastrodimedjo 75		
2007							
No international matches played in 2007 before August							

Fr = Friendly match • GC = CONCACAF Gold Cup • WC = FIFA World Cup • q = qualifier • † Not a full international

SURINAM NATIONAL TEAM RECORDS AND RECORD SEQUENCES

Records			Sequence records					
Victory	8-1	ARU 2004	Wins	4	1992	Clean sheets	4	1980
Defeat	1-8	MEX 1977	Defeats	5	1997	Goals scored	9	1990-1992
Player Caps	n/a		Undefeated	9	1990-1992	Without goal	2	Six times
Player Goals	n/a		Without win	6	Four times	Goals against	22	1994-1999

SURINAM 2006-07 HOOFDKLASSE

	Pl	W	D	L	F	A	Pts
Inter Moengotapoe	24	17	4	3	55	29	55
Leo Victor	24	14	4	6	57	37	46
Walking Bout Co	24	14	4	6	55	32	46
Robinhood	24	12	7	5	55	38	43
Jai Hanuman	24	11	3	10	54	41	36
Transvaal	24	11	3	10	34	32	36
Super Red Eagles	24	10	5	9	40	42	35
FCS Nacional	24	9	5	10	33	35	32
Royal '95	24	8	7	9	36	38	31
Voorwarts	24	8	5	11	39	41	29
Boskamp	24	7	5	12	37	44	26
Takdier Boys	24	5	3	16	28	64	18
Cosmos	24	2	1	21	31	81	7

8/10/2006 - 30/05/2007
Second place play-off: Leo Victor 2-0 WBC
Relegation play-off: Boskamp 1-0 2-0 SNL

SVB CUP 2006-07

Quarter-finals		Semi-finals		Final	
Robinhood	2				
Excelsior	1	Robinhood	5		
Takdier Boys	0	Super R. Eagles	2		
Super R. Eagles	1			Robinhood	1 4p
Royal '95	2			Walking Bout Co	1 1p
FCS Nacional	0	Royal '95	0	Franklin Essed, Paramaribo	
Lavoco	2	Walking Bout Co	2	23-06-2007	
Walking Bout Co	3			Scorers - Doelbakir for Robinhood; Sandvliet for WBC	

RECENT LEAGUE RECORD

Year	Champions	Pts	Runners-up	Pts	Third	Pts
2003	FCS National	52	Robinhood	50	House of Billiards	43
2004	Walking Bout Co	55	Inter Moengotapoe	47	Transvaal	46
2005	Robinhood	62	Royal '95	54	Walking Bout Co	53
2006	Walking Bout Co	57	Robinhood	56	Inter Moengotapoe	48
2007	Inter Moengotapoe	55	Leo Victor	46	Walking Bout Co	46

SURINAM COUNTRY INFORMATION

Capital	Paramaribo	Independence	1975 from the Netherlands	GDP per Capita	$4 000
Population	436 935	Status	Republic	GNP Ranking	158
Area km²	163 270	Language	Dutch, English, Surinamese	Dialling code	+597
Population density	2.6 per km²	Literacy rate	93%	Internet code	.sr
% in urban areas	50%	Main religion	Christian, Hindu, Muslim,	GMT +/–	-3
Cities/Towns ('000)	Paramaribo 220; Lelydorp 17; Nieuw Nickerie 13; Moengo 7; Meerzorg 6; Nieuw Amsterdam 5				
Neighbours (km)	French Guiana 510; Brazil 597; Guyana 600; North Atlantic Ocean 386				
Main stadia	André Kamperveen Stadion – Paramaribo 18 000				

SVK – SLOVAKIA

NATIONAL TEAM RECORD
JULY 10TH 2006 TO JULY 12TH 2010

PL	W	D	L	F	A	%
11	6	1	4	26	17	59.1

FIFA/COCA-COLA WORLD RANKING

1993	1994	1995	1996	1997	1998	1999	2000	2001	2002	2003	2004	2005	2006	High		Low	
150	43	35	30	34	32	21	24	47	55	50	53	45	37	17	05/97	150	12/93

					2006–2007						
08/06	09/06	10/06	11/06	12/06	01/07	02/07	03/07	04/07	05/07	06/07	07/07
43	42	41	37	37	37	33	37	36	37	40	38

One of the stories of the season in Slovakia centered on ViOn Zlaté Moravce, a second division team from a town of just 13,000 inhabitants who against all the odds won the Slovakian Cup. Their victims on the way to the title included four top division teams including Artmedia Bratislava in the semi-finals. Only once before had a second division side won the Cup - FC Senec in 2002 - and ironically it was Senec that ViOn beat in the final. For owner Villiam Ondrejka, after whom the club are named, there was double joy as his team went on to win promotion to the top flight. The team of the season, however, were MSK Zilina who won the Championship with plenty to spare

INTERNATIONAL HONOURS
None

as they claimed a record-equalling fourth Slovakian title. Over the entire campaign Zilina scored 99 League goals in 36 matches and they beat their main rivals Artmedia by a resounding 6-1 in the run-in. The last time Zilina won the title in 2004, Marek Mintal was their star player and he had an excellent season with 1.FC Nürnberg in Germany, with whom he won a winners medal in the Cup, scoring a goal in the final. He was also on the mark four times for his country in their UEFA Euro 2008 qualifiers, although defeats by Germany, the Republic of Ireland and the Czech Republic have left hopes of qualifying for the finals in jeopardy.

THE FIFA BIG COUNT OF 2006

	Male	Female		Total
Number of players	596 135	26 533	Referees and Assistant Referees	2 437
Professionals	489		Admin, Coaches, Technical, Medical	16 300
Amateurs 18+	252 435		Number of clubs	2 417
Youth under 18	169 561		Number of teams	7 353
Unregistered	68 700		Clubs with women's teams	15
Total players	622 668		Players as % of population	11.45%

Slovak Football Association (SFZ)
Slovensky futbalovy zväz, Junácka 6, 832 80, Bratislava, Slovakia
Tel +421 2 49249151   Fax +421 2 49249595
international@futbalsfz.sk   www.futbalsfz.sk
President: LAURINEC Frantisek   General Secretary: TOMAS Milos
Vice-President: STRAPEK Stanislav   Treasurer: KOVAC Peter   Media Officer: ROMAN Zdeno
Men's Coach: KOCIAN Jan   Women's Coach: URVAY Frantisek
SFZ formed: 1993   UEFA: 1994   FIFA: 1907/1994
Blue shirts with white trimmings, Blue shorts, Blue socks or White shirts with blue trimmings, White shorts, White socks

RECENT INTERNATIONAL MATCHES PLAYED BY SLOVAKIA

2003	Opponents	Score		Venue	Comp	Scorers	Att	Referee
7-06	Turkey	L	0-1	Bratislava	ECq		15 000	Hauge NOR
11-06	England	L	1-2	Middlesbrough	ECq	Janocko [31]	35 000	Stark GER
20-08	Colombia	D	0-0	New Jersey	Fr		16 000	Stott USA
10-09	FYR Macedonia	D	1-1	Zilina	ECq	Nemeth.S [25]	2 286	Sundell SWE
11-10	Liechtenstein	W	2-0	Vaduz	ECq	Vittek 2 [40 56]	800	Hyytia FIN
10-12	Kuwait	W	2-0	Larnaca	Fr	Breska [53], Dovicovic [71]		
2004								
31-03	Austria	D	1-1	Bratislava	Fr	Mintal [72]	4 500	Vidlak CZE
28-04	Ukraine	D	1-1	Kyiv	Fr	Varga [65]	18 000	Ryszka POL
29-05	Croatia	L	0-1	Rijeka	Fr		10 000	Kassai HUN
9-07	Japan	L	1-3	Hiroshima	Fr	Babnic [65]	34 458	Breeze AUS
11-07	Serbia & Montenegro	L	0-2	Fukuoka	Fr		6 100	Yoshida JPN
18-08	Luxembourg	W	3-1	Bratislava	WCq	Vittek [26], Gresko [48], Demo [89]	5 016	Kassai HUN
4-09	Russia	D	1-1	Moscow	WCq	Vittek [87]	11 500	Mejuto Gonzalez ESP
8-09	Liechtenstein	W	7-0	Bratislava	WCq	Vittek 3 [15 59 81], Karhan [42], Nemeth.S [84], Mintal [85], Zabavnik [92+]	5 620	Delevic SCG
9-10	Latvia	W	4-1	Bratislava	WCq	Nemeth.S [36], Reiter [50], Karhan 2 [55 87]	13 025	Farina ITA
17-11	Slovenia	D	0-0	Trnava	Fr		5 482	Skjerven NOR
30-11	Hungary	W	1-0	Bangkok	Fr	Porazik [47]	750	Veerapool THA
2-12	Thailand	D	1-1	Bangkok	Fr	Durica [65p], W 5-4p	5 000	Chappanimutu MAS
2005								
9-02	Romania	D	2-2	Larnaca	Fr	Vittek [12], Karhan [44]	500	Kapitanis CYP
26-03	Estonia	W	2-1	Tallinn	WCq	Mintal [58], Reiter [65]	3 051	Frojdfeldt SWE
30-03	Portugal	D	1-1	Bratislava	WCq	Karhan [8]	21 000	Sars FRA
4-06	Portugal	L	0-2	Lisbon	WCq		64 000	Collina ITA
8-06	Luxembourg	W	4-0	Luxembourg	WCq	Nemeth [5], Mintal [15], Kisel [54], Reiter [60]	2 108	Styles ENG
17-08	Liechtenstein	D	0-0	Vaduz	WCq		1 150	Layec FRA
3-09	Germany	W	2-0	Bratislava	Fr	Karhan 2 [20p 38]	9 276	Braamahr NED
7-09	Latvia	D	1-1	Riga	WCq	Vittek [35]	8 800	Plautz AUT
8-10	Estonia	W	1-0	Bratislava	WCq	Hlinka [72]	12 800	Allaerts BEL
12-10	Russia	D	0-0	Bratislava	WCq		22 317	Rosetti ITA
12-11	Spain	L	1-5	Madrid	WCpo	Nemeth [49]	47 210	De Santis ITA
16-11	Spain	D	1-1	Bratislava	WCpo	Holosko [50]	23 587	Merk GER
2006								
1-03	France	W	2-1	Paris	Fr	Nemeth.S [62], Valachovic [82]	55 000	Thomson SCO
20-05	Belgium	D	1-1	Trnava	Fr	Holosko [64]	4 174	Kassai HUN
15-08	Malta	W	3-0	Bratislava	Fr	Sebo 3 [31 75 90]	2 437	Lajuks LVA
2-09	Cyprus	W	6-1	Bratislava	ECq	Skrtel [9], Mintal 2 [33 56], Sebo 2 [43 49], Karhan [52]	4 723	Orekhov UKR
6-09	Czech Republic	L	0-3	Bratislava	ECq		27 684	Bennett ENG
7-10	Wales	W	5-1	Cardiff	ECq	Svento [14], Mintal 2 [32 38], Karhan [51], Vittek [59]	28 415	Van Egmond NED
11-10	Germany	L	1-4	Bratislava	ECq	Varga [58]	27 580	Hauge NOR
15-11	Bulgaria	W	3-1	Zilina	Fr	Mintal [8], Sapara [53], Karhan [78]	4 823	Granat POL
10-12	UAE	W	2-1	Abu Dhabi	Fr	Jonas [50], Michalik [53]		Ibrahim QAT
2007								
7-02	Poland	D	2-2	Jerez	Fr	Jakubko [1], Skrtel [45]	200	Pacheco ESP
24-03	Cyprus	W	3-1	Nicosia	ECq	Vittek [54], Skrtel [67], Jakubko [77]	2 696	Lehner AUT
28-03	Republic of Ireland	L	0-1	Dublin	ECq		71 257	Baskakov RUS
6-06	Germany	L	1-2	Hamburg	ECq	Metzelder OG [20]	51 600	Benquerença POR

Fr = Friendly match • EC = UEFA EURO 2004/2008 • WC = FIFA World Cup • q = qualifier • po = play-off • BCD = Behind closed doors

SLOVAKIA NATIONAL TEAM RECORDS AND RECORD SEQUENCES

Records			Sequence records				
Victory	7-0	LIE 2004	Wins	3	Five times	Clean sheets	4	2000
Defeat	1-6	CRO 1942	Defeats	5	2001	Goals scored	8	1996-1997
Player Caps	84	KARHAN Miroslav	Undefeated	12	2000-2001	Without goal	4	2001
Player Goals	22	NEMETH Slizard	Without win	6	Four times	Goals against	11	2002-2003

MAJOR CITIES/TOWNS
Population '000

1	Bratislava	421
2	Kosice	236
3	Presov	95
4	Zilina	86
5	Nitra	85
6	Banská Bystrica	81
7	Trnava	69
8	Martin	61
9	Trencin	58
10	Poprad	58
11	Prievidza	52
12	Zvolen	44
13	Povazská Bystrica	44
14	Nové Zámky	41
15	Michalovce	40
16	Spisská Nová Ves	39
17	Humenné	35
18	Ruzomberok	31
19	Dubnica nad Váhom	26
20	Rimavská Sobota	25
21	Dunajská Streda	23
22	Púchov	18
23	Zlaté Moravce	15
24	Senec	14

SLOVAK REPUBLIC; SLOVENSKA REPUBLIKA

Capital	Bratislava	Language	Slovak, Hungarian		Independence	1993
Population	5 447 502	Area	48 845 km²	Density	111 per km²	% in cities	59%
GDP per cap	$13 300	Dailling code	+421	Internet	.sk	GMT + / -	+1

MEDALS TABLE

		Overall			League			Cup			Europe			City	Stadium	Cap'ty	DoF
		G	S	B	G	S	B	G	S	B	G	S	B				
1	Slovan Bratislava	7	2	3	4	1	3	3	1					Bratislava	Tehelné Pole	30 085	1919
2	Inter Bratislava	5	2	3	2	2	3	3						Bratislava	Pasienky Stadion	13 295	1945
3	MSK Zilina	4	1		4	1								Zilina	Pod Dubnon	6 233	1908
4	MFK Kosice	2	5	1	2	3	1		2					Kosice	Lokomotivy v Cermeli	9 600	1952
5	Artmedia Bratislava	2	4		1	3		1	1					Bratislava	Petrzalka Stadion	8 000	1898
6	MFK Ruzomberok	2	1	2	1		2	1	1					Ruzomberok	MFK Stadion	5 030	1906
7	Spartak Trnava	1	4	3		2	3	1	2					Trnava	Anton Malatinsky	18 448	1923
8	Dukla Banská Bystrica	1	2	1	1	1		1	1					Banská Bystrica	Stadion SNP	10 000	1965
9	Matador Púchov	1	2		1			1	1					Púchov	Matador	5 964	1920
10	FC Senec	1	1					1	1					Senec	NTC Stadion	3 264	2004
	1.HFC Humenné	1						1						Humenné	Stadion Humenné	5 000	1903
12	ViOn Zlaté Moravce	1												Zlaté Moravce	Stadion ViOn	4 000	1995

SLOVAK CLUBS IN CZECHOSLOVAKIAN FOOTBALL

3	Slovan Bratislava	14	16	3	8	10	3	5	6		1	
5	Spartak Trnava	9	2	2	5	1	1	4	1			1
7	Lokomotíva Kosice	2	1	2		2		2	1			
8	TJ Internacional	1	6	5	1	3	5		3			
9	1.FC Kosice	1	4	2		1	2	1	3			
14	DAC Dunajská Streda	1		1		1	1					

RECENT LEAGUE AND CUP RECORD

	Championship						Cup		
Year	Champions	Pts	Runners-up	Pts	Third	Pts	Winners	Score	Runners-up
1995	Slovan Bratislava	72	1.FC Kosice	52	Inter Bratislava	50	Inter Bratislava	1-1 3-1p	Dunajska Streda
1996	Slovan Bratislava	75	1.FC Kosice	65	Spartak Trnava	63	Chemlon Humenné	2-1	Spartak Trnava
1997	1.FC Kosice	70	Spartak Trnava	69	Slovan Bratislava	50	Slovan Bratislava	1-0	Tatran Presov
1998	1.FC Kosice	68	Spartak Trnava	66	Inter Bratislava	60	Spartak Trnava	2-0	1.FC Kosice
1999	Slovan Bratislava	70	Inter Bratislava	68	Spartak Trnava	64	Slovan Bratislava	3-0	Dukla B. Bystrica
2000	Inter Bratislava	70	1.FC Kosice	61	Slovan Bratislava	57	Inter Bratislava	1-1 4-2p	1.FC Kosice
2001	Inter Bratislava	80	Slovan Bratislava	71	SCP Ruzomberok	55	Inter Bratislava	1-0	SCP Ruzomberok
2002	MSK Zilina	69	Matador Puchov	62	Inter Bratislava	56	Koba Senec	1-1 4-2p	Matador Púchov
2003	MSK Zilina	70	Artmedia Bratislava	67	Slovan Bratislava	63	Matador Púchov	2-1	Slovan Bratislava
2004	MSK Zilina	64	Dukla B. Bystrica	64	SCP Ruzomberok	55	Artmedia Bratislava	2-0	Trans Licartovce
2005	Artmedia Bratislava	72	MSK Zilina	65	Dukla B. Bystrica	52	Dukla B. Bystrica	2-1	Artmedia Bratislava
2006	MFK Ruzomberok	80	Artmedia Bratislava	74	Spartak Trnava	68	MFK Ruzomberok	0-0 4-3p	Spartak Trnava
2007	MSK Zilina	69	Artmedia Bratislava	56	MFK Kosice	41	ViOn Zlaté Moravce	4-0	FC Senec

SLOVAKIA 2006-07

CORGON LIGA

	Pl	W	D	L	F	A	Pts	Zilina	Artmedia	Kosice	Ruzomberok	Dukla	Senec	Nitra	Slovan	Inter	Dubnica	Spartak	Trencín
MSK Zilina †	28	22	3	3	80	17	69		3-0	6-1	2-0	2-0	1-1	4-0	5-0	1-0	2-2	1-0	4-1
Artmedia Bratislava ‡	28	17	5	6	56	38	56	3-2		2-2	3-2	3-0	3-0	4-1	3-1	1-1	2-1	1-2	4-1
MFK Kosice	28	11	8	9	35	33	41	1-1	0-2		1-3	0-3	3-2	1-0	5-0	0-0	5-0	4-0	0-1
MFK Ruzomberok	28	10	7	11	25	29	37	0-1	1-4	0-3		0-2	1-0	2-0	0-0	0-0	1-0	3-2	2-0
Dukla Banska Bystrica	28	10	5	13	31	35	35	2-1	1-2	2-0	3-1		0-1	1-2	2-1	0-0	5-1	2-2	1-0
FC Senec	28	9	4	15	21	33	31	0-2	0-5	2-0	2-2	0-1		1-3	3-1	1-0	0-0	0-0	2-1
FC Nitra	28	7	6	15	24	46	25	0-2	0-2	2-1	1-1	0-0	1-0		1-1	1-3	1-3	2-0	2-1
Slovan Bratislava	28	3	8	17	22	63	17	0-3	3-2	1-2	3-1	0-0	1-1	2-1		2-1	1-0	2-0	1-0
Inter Bratislava	22	6	7	9	25	25	25	1-2	1-0	2-1	3-0	2-0	1-2	1-1	1-2		1-1	2-0	2-2
Dubnica nad Váham	22	6	7	9	24	35	25	1-5	0-1	2-1	1-0	0-1	0-3	1-1	1-1	5-2		1-0	0-0
Spartak Trnava	22	6	6	10	22	33	24	0-3	1-2	0-0	2-0	2-1	3-3	2-1	0-1	1-0	2-2		3-2
AS Trencín	22	3	5	14	18	33	14	1-1	4-0	0-2	0-0	0-1	0-2	1-2	0-1	2-1	0-1	0-0	

14/07/2006 - 30/05/2007 • † Qualified for the UEFA Champions League • ‡ Qualified for the UEFA Cup • The League split after 22 rounds with the top eight playing for the title and taking forward only their records against fellow qualifiers. The bottom four joined the top four of the II Liga to decide promotion and relegation • Top scorers: Tomás ORAVEC, Artmedia 16; Stanislav SESTAK, Zilina 15

SLOVAKIA 2006-07 II LIGA (2)

	Pl	W	D	L	F	A	Pts
Rimavska Sobota †	22	13	5	4	45	20	44
Slovan Duslo Sala †	22	12	7	3	36	20	43
ViOn Zlaté Moravce †	22	12	4	6	28	19	40
Eldus Mocenok †	22	11	6	5	39	30	39
Tatran Presov	22	8	9	5	28	19	33
LAFC Lucenec	22	8	5	9	25	23	29
MFK Kosice B	22	8	5	9	23	30	29
Sport Podbrezova	22	5	8	9	21	29	23
Zemplin Michalovce	22	4	10	8	25	31	22
DAC Dunajská Streda	22	5	7	10	21	32	22
HFC Humenné	22	5	7	10	23	38	22
SK Aqua Teplice	22	4	1	17	27	50	13

15/07/2006 - 25/11/2007 • † Qualified for play-offs

SLOVAKIA 2006-07 PROMOTION/RELEGATION

	Pl	W	D	L	F	A	Pts
Spartak Trnava	14	7	4	3	18	13	25
Dubnica nad Váhom	14	6	5	3	16	15	23
ViOn Zlaté Moravce	14	7	1	6	20	15	22
AS Trencin	14	5	6	3	20	17	21
Inter Bratislava	14	5	4	5	14	15	19
Eldus Mocenok	14	4	6	4	16	18	18
Rimavská Sobota	14	4	3	7	20	23	15
Slovan Duslo Sala	14	1	5	8	15	23	8

3/03/2007 - 30/05/2007

SLOVENSKY POHAR 2006-07

Round of 16

ViOn Zlaté Moravce	4		
Slovan Bratislava B	1		
Spisska Nova Ves	0 1p		
FC Nitra *	0 3p		
MSK Zilina	2		
Inter Bratislava *	0		
Rimavska Sobota	0		
Artmedia Bratislava *	3		
MFK Ruzomberok B *	1 2p		
Spartak Trnava	1 0p		
Zemplin Michalovce *	0		
Dukla Banska Bystrica	2		
Eldus Mocenok *	2		
FKS Nemsova	1		
Tatran Presov	1 3p		
FC Senec *	1 4p		

Quarter-finals

ViOn Zlaté Moravce	1
FC Nitra	0
MSK Zilina	0
Artmedia Bratislava *	3
MFK Ruzomberok B *	2
Dukla Banska Bystrica	1
Eldus Mocenok *	2 6p
FC Senec	2 7p

Semi-finals

ViOn Zlaté Moravce	0 4
Artmedia Bratislava *	1 2
MFK Ruzomberok B *	0 0 5p
FC Senec	0 0 6p

Final

ViOn Zlaté Moravce ‡	4
FC Senec	0

CUP FINAL

Pasienky, Bratislava, 8-05-2007

Scorers - Maros Choma 2 [38][49], Peter Cernak [88], Marek Plichta [90]

* Home team/home team in the first leg • ‡ Qualified for the UEFA Cup

SVN - SLOVENIA

NATIONAL TEAM RECORD
JULY 10TH 2006 TO JULY 12TH 2010

PL	W	D	L	F	A	%
9	2	2	5	7	13	33.3

FIFA/COCA-COLA WORLD RANKING

1993	1994	1995	1996	1997	1998	1999	2000	2001	2002	2003	2004	2005	2006	High	Low
134	81	71	77	95	88	40	35	25	36	31	42	68	77	**25** 12/01	**134** 02/94

2006-2007											
08/06	09/06	10/06	11/06	12/06	01/07	02/07	03/07	04/07	05/07	06/07	07/07
58	78	78	77	77	77	71	72	76	76	89	88

After the heartbreak of missing out on the Championship on the last day of the 2005-06 season, Domzale finally got their hands on the trophy for the first time in May 2007 after a season in which they were head and shoulders above the opposition. Defending champions Gorica sold five first team regulars at the start of the season and consequently finished 18 points behind Domzale, who went the first 27 games unbeaten before losing three games in four matches. A major trend in Slovenian football has been the success of clubs like Domzale from outside of the capital, and Ljubljana only just managed to maintain a presence in the top flight when Interblock beat Bonikika

INTERNATIONAL HONOURS
Qualified for the FIFA World Cup finals 2002

from Koper in a relegation play-off. Bought during the season by Joze Pececnic, one of Slovenia's richest men, there are high hopes that Interblock will become the first club from Ljubljana to win the title since 1995. FC Koper won the Slovenian Cup for the second year running when they beat Maribor 1-0 in the final making it the third season in a row that the once invincible Maribor ended up without a trophy. A poor start to the qualifiers for UEFA Euro 2008 saw national team coach Branko Oblak quit in November 2006. He was replaced by Matjaz Kek who started his reign with a 1-0 win over Estonia but he could do little to rescue Slovenia in the Euro qualifiers.

THE FIFA BIG COUNT OF 2006

	Male	Female		Total
Number of players	107 255	9 670	Referees and Assistant Referees	818
Professionals	284		Admin, Coaches, Technical, Medical	5 000
Amateurs 18+	9 410		Number of clubs	328
Youth under 18	20 831		Number of teams	1 060
Unregistered	55 200		Clubs with women's teams	12
Total players	116 925		Players as % of population	5.82%

Football Association of Slovenia (NZS)
Nogometna Zveza Slovenije, Cerinova 4, PO Box 3986, Ljubljana 1001, Slovenia
Tel +386 1 5300400   Fax +386 1 5300410
nzs@nzs.si   www.nzs.si
President: ZAVRL Rudi   General Secretary: JOST Dane
Vice-President: FRANTAR Anton   Treasurer: JOST Dane   Media Officer: STANIC Uros
Men's Coach: OBLAK Branko   Women's Coach: CIRKVENCIC Zoran
NZS formed: 1920   UEFA: 1992   FIFA: 1992
White shirts with green trimmings, White shorts, White socks or Green shirts with white trimmings, Green shorts, Green socks

RECENT INTERNATIONAL MATCHES PLAYED BY SLOVENIA

2002 Opponents	Score	Venue	Comp	Scorers	Att	Referee
21-08 Italy	W 1-0	Trieste	Fr	Cimirotic [32]	11 080	Brugger AUT
7-09 Malta	W 3-0	Ljubljana	ECq	OG [37], Siljak [59], Cimirotic [90]	7 000	Borovilos GRE
12-10 France	L 0-5	Paris	ECq		77 619	Milton Nielsen DEN
2003						
12-02 Switzerland	L 1-5	Nova Gorica	Fr	Rakovic [79]	3 500	Abraham HUN
2-04 Cyprus	W 4-1	Ljubljana	ECq	Siljak 2 [5 14], Zahovic [39p], Ceh.N [43]	5 000	Gomes Costa POR
30-04 Malta	W 3-1	Ta'Qali	ECq	Zahovic [15], Siljak 2 [37 57]	5 000	Hanacsek HUN
7-06 Israel	D 0-0	Antalya	ECq		2 500	Busacca SUI
20-08 Hungary	W 2-1	Murska Sobota	Fr	Sukalo [3], Cimirotic [75]	5 000	Sowa AUT
6-09 Israel	W 3-1	Ljubljana	ECq	Siljak [35], Knavs [37], Ceh.N [78]	8 000	Fandel GER
10-09 France	L 0-2	Ljubljana	ECq		8 000	Messina ITA
11-10 Cyprus	D 2-2	Limassol	ECq	Siljak 2 [12 42]	2 346	Ovrebo NOR
15-11 Croatia	D 1-1	Zagreb	ECpo	Siljak [22]	35 000	Merk GER
19-11 Croatia	L 0-1	Ljubljana	ECpo		9 000	Meier SUI
2004						
18-02 Poland	L 0-2	Cadiz	Fr		100	Barea Lopez ESP
31-03 Latvia	L 0-1	Celje	Fr		1 500	Stredak SVK
28-04 Switzerland	L 1-2	Geneva	Fr	Zahovic [45]	7 500	Bossen NED
18-08 Serbia & Montenegro	D 1-1	Ljubljana	Fr	Ceh.N [83]	8 000	Ovrebo NOR
4-09 Moldova	W 3-0	Celje	WCq	Acimovic 3 [5 27 48]	3 620	Hyytia FIN
8-09 Scotland	D 0-0	Glasgow	WCq		38 279	Larsen DEN
9-10 Italy	W 1-0	Celje	WCq	Cesar [82]	9 262	De Bleeckere BEL
13-10 Norway	L 0-3	Oslo	WCq		24 907	Ivanov.V RUS
17-11 Slovakia	D 0-0	Trnava	Fr		5 482	Skjerven NOR
2005						
9-02 Czech Republic	L 0-3	Celje	Fr		4 000	Strahonja CRO
26-03 Germany	L 0-1	Celje	Fr		9 000	Poll ENG
30-03 Belarus	D 1-1	Celje	WCq	Rodic [44]	6 450	Al Ghamdi KSA
4-06 Belarus	D 1-1	Minsk	WCq	Ceh.N [17]	29 042	Hansson SWE
17-08 Wales	D 0-0	Swansea	Fr		10 016	Stokes IRL
3-09 Norway	L 2-3	Celje	WCq	Cimirotic [4], Zlogar [83]	10 055	Medina Cantalejo ESP
7-09 Moldova	W 2-1	Chisinau	WCq	Lavric [47], Marvic [58]	7 200	Baskakov RUS
8-10 Italy	L 0-1	Palermo	WCq		19 123	Poulat FRA
12-10 Scotland	L 0-3	Celje	WCq		9 100	Temmink NED
2006						
28-02 Cyprus	W 1-0	Larnaca	Fr	Ljubijankic [84]		
1-03 Romania	L 0-2	Larnaca	Fr		300	Vialichka BLR
31-05 Trinidad and Tobago	W 3-1	Celje	Fr	Novakovic 3 [4 16 77]	2 500	Tanovic SCG
4-06 Côte d'Ivoire	L 0-3	Evry-Bondoufle	Fr		8 000	
15-08 Israel	D 1-1	Celje	Fr	Sukalo [83]	3 000	Kralovec CZE
6-09 Bulgaria	L 0-3	Sofia	ECq		14 491	Bo Larsen DEN
7-10 Luxembourg	W 2-0	Celje	ECq	Novakovic [30], Koren [44]	3 800	Kailis CYP
11-10 Belarus	L 2-4	Minsk	ECq	Cesar [19], Lavric [43]	21 150	Kassai HUN
2007						
7-02 Estonia	W 1-0	Domzale	Fr	Lavric [34p]	3 000	Ledentu FRA
24-03 Albania	D 0-0	Shkoder	ECq		7 000	Attard MLT
28-03 Netherlands	L 0-1	Celje	ECq		10 000	Mejuto Gonzalez ESP
2-06 Romania	L 1-2	Celje	ECq	Vrsic [94+]	6 500	Dougal SCO
6-06 Romania	L 0-2	Timisoara	ECq		17 850	Yefet ISR

Fr = Friendly match • EC = UEFA EURO 2004/2008 • WC = FIFA World Cup • q = qualifier • po = play-off

SLOVENIA NATIONAL TEAM RECORDS AND RECORD SEQUENCES

Records			Sequence records					
Victory	7-0	OMA 1999	Wins	4	1998	Clean sheets	4	2002
Defeat	0-5	FRA 1999, FRA 2002	Defeats	4	1997, 1998	Goals scored	9	2001-2002
Player Caps	80	ZAHOVIC Zlatko	Undefeated	8	2001	Without goal	4	2004-2005
Player Goals	35	ZAHOVIC Zlatko	Without win	8	2003-04, 2004-05	Goals against	13	1997-1998

MAJOR CITIES/TOWNS
Population '000

1	Ljubljana	253
2	Maribor	86
3	Celje	36
4	Kranj	34
5	Velenje	26
6	Koper	23
7	Novo Mesto	22
8	Ptuj	18
9	Trbovlje	15
10	Kamnik	12
11	Nova Gorica	12
12	Murska Sobota	12
13	Jesenice	11
14	Skofja Loka	11
15	Domzale	11
16	Izola	10
17	Kocevje	8
18	Postojna	8
19	Ajdovscina	6
20	Crnomelj	5
21	Prevalje	4
22	Lendava	3
23	Dravograd	3
24	Kidricevo	1

REPUBLIC OF SLOVENIA; REPUBLIKA SLOVENIJA

Capital	Ljubljana	Language	Slovenian, Serbo-Croat	Independence	1991
Population	2 009 245	Area	20 273 km²	% in cities	64%
GDP per cap	$19 000	Dailling code	+386	Internet .si	GMT +/- +1

MEDALS TABLE

		Overall G	S	B	League G	S	B	Cup G	S	B	Europe G	S	B	City	Stadium	Cap'ty	DoF
1	NK Maribor	12	4	3	7	3	3	5	1					Maribor	Ljudski vrt Stadion	10 210	1960
2	Olimpija Ljubljana	8	6	1	4	3	1	4	3					Ljubljana	Bezigrad Stadion	8 211	1911-2005
3	ND Gorica	6	4	3	4	3	3	2	1					Nova Gorica	Sportni Park	3 066	1947
4	FC Koper	2		2				2	2					Koper	SRC Bonifika Stadion	3 557	1955
5	NK Celje	1	5	1		1	1		1	4				Celje	Arena Petrol	12 350	1919
6	Mura Murska Sobota	1	3	2		2	2	1	1					Murska Sobota	Fazanerija Stadion	3 527	2005
7	NK Domzale	1	2		1	2								Domzale	Sportni Park	3 212	1921
8	Rudar Velenje	1		2				2	1					Velenje	Ob Jezeru	1 800	1948
9	Primorje Ajdovscina		5	1		2	1						3	Ajdovscina	Primorje Stadion	3 000	1924
10	Korotan Prevalje		1							1				Prevalje			
	Aluminij Kidricevo		1							1				Kidricevo			
	NK Dravograd		1							1				Dravograd			
13	Izola Belvedur			1		1								Izola			

RECENT LEAGUE AND CUP RECORD

Championship

Year	Champions	Pts	Runners-up	Pts	Third	Pts
1995	Olimpija Ljubljana	44	NK Maribor	42	ND Gorica	41
1996	ND Gorica	67	Olimpija Ljubljana	64	Mura Murska Sobota	58
1997	NK Maribor	71	Primorje Ajdovscina	66	ND Gorica	65
1998	NK Maribor	67	Mura Murska Sobota	67	ND Gorica	65
1999	NK Maribor	66	ND Gorica	62	Rudar Velenje	56
2000	NK Maribor	81	ND Gorica	62	Rudar Velenje	58
2001	NK Maribor	62	Olimpija Ljubljana	60	Primorje Ajdovscina	56
2002	NK Maribor	66	Primorje Ajdovscina	60	FC Koper	56
2003	NK Maribor	62	Publikum Celje	55	Olimpija Ljubljana	54
2004	ND Gorica	56	Olimpija Ljubljana	55	NK Maribor	54
2005	ND Gorica	65	Domzale	52	Publikum Celje	52
2006	ND Gorica	73	Domzale	71	FC Koper	57
2007	Domzale	76	ND Gorica	58	NK Maribor	57

Cup

Winners	Score	Runners-up
Mura Murska Sobota	1-1 1-0	Publikum Celje
Olimpija Ljubljana	1-0 1-1	Primorje Ajdovscina
NK Maribor	0-0 3-0	Primorje Ajdovscina
Rudar Velenje	1-2 3-0	Primorje Ajdovscina
NK Maribor	3-2 2-0	Olimpija Ljubljana
Olimpija Ljubljana	1-2 2-0	Korotan Prevalje
ND Gorica	0-1 4-2	Olimpija Ljubljana
ND Gorica	4-0 2-1	Aluminij Kidricevo
Olimpija Ljubljana	1-1 2-2	Publikum Celje
NK Maribor	4-0 3-4	Koroska Dravograd
Publikum Celje	1-0	ND Gorica
FC Koper	1-1 5-3p	Publikum Celje
FC Koper	1-0	NK Maribor

SLOVENIA 2006-07

SIMOBIL LIGA

	Pl	W	D	L	F	A	Pts	Domzale	Gorica	Maribor	Drava	Primorje	Koper	Celje	Nafta	Interblock	B. Krajina
Domzale †	36	21	12	3	64	29	76		1-0 4-0	3-1 3-0	1-1 2-0	3-1 1-1	3-2 2-1	0-0 0-0	6-2 3-0	1-0 3-0	1-0 1-0
ND Gorica ‡	36	17	7	12	66	63	58	0-0 6-1		1-4 4-1	3-2 2-1	3-1 1-3	1-0 1-7	2-0 1-3	2-0 2-1	5-0 3-2	1-4 3-2
NK Maribor	36	15	12	9	64	50	57	1-1 2-0	1-1 3-2		1-0 1-1	2-0 1-1	1-1 0-0	2-0 2-2	1-3 6-2	3-2 3-0	3-0 2-1
Drava Ptuj	36	15	10	11	61	52	55	1-1 1-2	3-1 6-4	1-1 1-1		0-2 1-1	2-1 2-1	2-2 3-1	3-0 3-1	0-2 3-0	4-2 1-6
Primorje Ajdovscina	36	15	10	11	52	47	55	0-2 0-4	3-3 1-2	3-2 3-1	1-0 1-3		0-0 2-1	2-0 2-3	1-0 3-0	3-1 3-2	2-0 2-1
FC Koper ‡	36	10	15	11	51	46	45	1-1 1-1	1-1 1-2	2-2 2-1	1-0 1-2	0-0 0-2		0-2 2-0	2-2 3-1	3-1 1-1	2-2 2-1
NK Celje	36	11	12	13	54	51	45	1-3 1-4	0-0 1-3	1-3 4-1	3-3 0-0	2-0 3-1	1-1 2-3		1-2 0-1	1-1 1-1	5-0 4-0
Nafta Lendava	36	12	9	15	45	59	45	1-2 0-0	2-0 1-1	0-4 1-1	1-3 2-0	1-1 1-1	1-1 1-0	2-1 1-1		2-2 3-1	1-0 1-2
Interblock Ljubljana	36	5	11	20	34	68	26	2-2 0-0	1-1 0-3	0-2 1-2	0-1 2-0	0-4 0-0	2-2 0-1	2-4 0-1	1-4 2-0		1-1 1-0
Bela Krajina	36	5	10	21	38	64	25	1-2 1-0	1-1 0-1	2-1 1-1	2-4 0-2	2-2 0-0	2-2 1-2	1-1 0-2	0-0 0-3	0-1 2-2	

29/07/2006 - 26/05/2007 • † Qualified for the UEFA Champions League • ‡ Qualified for the UEFA Cup
Play-off: Interblock Ljubljana 3-1 1-1 Bonifika. Interblock remain in the Simobil Liga

SLOVENIA 2006-07
2.SNL (2)

	Pl	W	D	L	F	A	Pts
Livar Ivanca Gorica	27	13	6	8	37	36	45
Bonifika Koper	27	12	6	9	46	39	42
Triglav Gorenjska Kranj	27	10	9	8	29	24	39
Krsko	27	11	6	10	38	43	39
Zagorje	27	9	10	8	37	30	37
Aluminij Kidricevo	27	10	7	10	29	29	37
Mura Murska Sobota	27	8	10	9	37	37	34
Rudar Velenje	27	9	7	11	44	41	34
Tinex Sencur	27	9	6	12	35	41	33
Dravinja Duol	27	9	3	15	26	38	30

13/08/2006 - 30/05/2007

POKAL HERVIS 2006-07

Round of 16		Quarter-finals		Semi-finals		Final	
FC Koper	3						
Zagorje *	1	FC Koper	1 5p				
Brda *	3	Rudar Velenje *	1 4p				
Rudar Velenje	5			FC Koper	3 4		
Nafta Lendava *	2			NK Celje *	1 1		
Interblock Ljubljana	1	Nafta Lendava	1				
Drava Ptuj	1	NK Celje *	3				
NK Celje *	2					FC Koper ‡	1
ND Gorica	3					NK Maribor	0
Bonifika Koper *	1	ND Gorica	2				
Bela Krajina *	1	Mura Murska Sobota *	0				
Mura Murska Sobota	2			ND Gorica *	2 1		
Primorje Ajdovscina	2			NK Maribor	4 1		
Domzale *	1	Primorje Ajdovscina	0				
Crensovci *	0	NK Maribor *	4				
NK Maribor	2						

CUP FINAL

22-05-2007

Scorer - Aleksandar Rajcevic 80

* Home team/home team in the first leg • ‡ Qualified for the UEFA Cup

SWE – SWEDEN

NATIONAL TEAM RECORD
JULY 10TH 2006 TO JULY 12TH 2010

PL	W	D	L	F	A	%
13	6	1	6	19	18	50

FIFA/COCA-COLA WORLD RANKING

1993	1994	1995	1996	1997	1998	1999	2000	2001	2002	2003	2004	2005	2006	High		Low	
9	3	13	17	18	18	16	23	16	25	19	13	14	14	2	11/94	31	08/98

2006–2007											
08/06	09/06	10/06	11/06	12/06	01/07	02/07	03/07	04/07	05/07	06/07	07/07
20	18	16	14	14	14	16	15	24	22	17	20

No-one will ever know if Sweden would have converted the infamous penalty that was never taken at the end of the Euro 2008 qualifier against Denmark. Having thrown away a 3-0 lead, the Swedes were handed the lifeline before Herbert Fandel abandoned the game after being assaulted by a spectator. With the game awarded 3-0 to Sweden, the much-criticised Lars Lagerbäck could take comfort from a commanding lead in the group with six wins in their first seven games, their only reverse coming against Northern Ireland in Belfast. In the Allsvenskan, Elfsborg were crowned champions for the first time since 1961 after beating defending champions Djurgårdens 1-0 on the

INTERNATIONAL HONOURS
Olympic Games Gold 1948   Qualified for the FIFA World Cup finals 1934 1938 1950 1958 (Hosts) 1970 1974 1978 1990 1994 2002 2006
Women's European Championship 1984   Qualified for the FIFA Women's World Cup 1991 1995 1999 2003

final day of the season. They finished one point ahead of AIK Stockholm who narrowly missed out on winning the Allsvenskan title just a year after winning the second division title. Henrik Larsson's Helsingborg won the Swedish Cup in November 2006 but with just 3,379 fans turning up to the Råsunda stadium in Stockholm for the final against Gefle, the profile of the tournament has never been lower. Michel Platini's idea to give a Champions League place to Cup winners may be exactly what is needed to revive the competition.

THE FIFA BIG COUNT OF 2006

	Male	Female		Total
Number of players	791 612	215 327	Referees and Assistant Referees	14 750
Professionals	2 001		Admin, Coaches, Technical, Medical	10 200
Amateurs 18+	231 399		Number of clubs	3 236
Youth under 18	319 599		Number of teams	31 000
Unregistered	375 000		Clubs with women's teams	1 000
Total players	1 006 939		Players as % of population	11.17%

Svenska Fotbollförbundet (SVFF)
PO Box 1216, Solna 17 123, Sweden
Tel +46 8 7350900   Fax +46 8 7350901
svff@svenskfotboll.se   www.svenskfotboll.se
President: LAGRELL Lars-Ake   General Secretary: HELLSTROMER Sune
Vice-President: AHLBERG Björn   Treasurer: SAHLSTROEM Kjell   Media Officer: SALTEG Thomas
Men's Coach: LAGERBACK Lars   Women's Coach: DENNERBY Thomas
SVFF formed: 1904   UEFA: 1954   FIFA: 1954
Yellow shirts with blue trimmings, Blue shorts, Yellow socks or Blue shirts with yellow trimmings, Blue shorts, Blue socks

RECENT INTERNATIONAL MATCHES PLAYED BY SWEDEN

2004	Opponents	Score	Venue	Comp	Scorers	Att	Referee
14-06	Bulgaria	W 5-0	Lisbon	ECr1	Ljungberg [32], Larsson 2 [57 58], Ibrahimovic [78p], Allback [90]	31 652	Riley ENG
18-06	Italy	D 1-1	Porto	ECr1	Ibrahimovic [85]	44 927	Meier SUI
22-06	Denmark	D 2-2	Porto	ECr1	Larsson [47p], Jonson.M [89]	26 115	Merk GER
26-06	Netherlands	D 0-0	Faro-Loule	ECqf		27 286	Michel SVK
18-08	Netherlands	D 2-2	Stockholm	Fr	Jonson.M [4], Ibrahimovic [69]	20 377	Styles ENG
4-09	Malta	W 7-0	Ta'Qali	WCq	Ibrahimovic 4 [4 11 14 71], Ljungberg 2 [46 74], Larsson [76]	4 200	Jakov ISR
8-09	Croatia	L 0-1	Gothenburg	WCq		40 023	Dauden Ibanez ESP
9-10	Hungary	W 3-0	Stockholm	WCq	Ljungberg [26], Larsson [50], Svensson.A [67]	32 288	Dougal SCO
13-10	Iceland	W 4-1	Reykjavík	WCq	Larsson 2 [24 39], Allback [27], Wilhelmsson [45]	7 037	Busacca SUI
17-11	Scotland	W 4-1	Edinburgh	Fr	Allback 2 [27 49], Elmander [72], Berglund [73]	15 071	Jara CZE
2005							
22-01	Korea Republic	D 1-1	Carson	Fr	Rosenberg [86]	9 941	Stott USA
26-01	Mexico	D 0-0	San Diego	Fr		35 521	Hall USA
9-02	France	D 1-1	Paris	Fr	Ljungberg [11]	59 923	Rodriguez Santiago ESP
26-03	Bulgaria	W 3-0	Sofia	WCq	Ljungberg 2 [17 92+p], Edman [74]	42 530	Fandel GER
4-06	Malta	W 6-0	Gothenburg	WCq	Jonson [6], Svensson.A [18], Wilhelmsson [29] Ibrahimovic [40], Ljungberg [57], Elmander [81]	35 593	Ivanov.N RUS
8-06	Norway	L 2-3	Stockholm	Fr	Kallstrom [16], Elmander [68]	15 345	Jara CZE
17-08	Czech Republic	W 2-1	Gothenburg	Fr	Larsson [19], Rosenberg [26]	23 117	Bennett ENG
3-09	Bulgaria	W 3-0	Stockholm	WCq	Ljungberg [60], Mellberg [75], Ibrahimovic [90]	35 000	De Bleeckere BEL
7-09	Hungary	W 1-0	Budapest	WCq	Ibrahimovic [91+]	20 161	Farina ITA
8-10	Croatia	L 0-1	Zagreb	WCq		34 015	De Santis ITA
12-10	Iceland	W 3-1	Stockholm	WCq	Ibrahimovic [29], Larsson [42], Kallstrom [91+]	33 176	Ivanov.V RUS
12-11	Korea Republic	D 2-2	Seoul	Fr	Elmander [9], Rosenberg [57]	59 113	Wan Daxue CHN
2006							
18-01	Saudi Arabia	D 1-1	Riyadh	Fr	Svensson.A [32]		Al Amri KSA
23-01	Jordan	D 0-0	Abu Dhabi	Fr		1 000	Almulla UAE
1-03	Republic of Ireland	L 0-3	Dublin	Fr		44 109	Ledentu FRA
25-05	Finland	D 0-0	Gothenburg	Fr		25 754	Gilewski POL
2-06	Chile	D 1-1	Stockholm	Fr	Larsson [32]	34 735	Stark GER
10-06	Trinidad and Tobago	D 0-0	Dortmund	WCr1		62 959	Maidin SIN
15-06	Paraguay	W 1-0	Berlin	WCr1	Ljungberg [89]	72 000	Michel SVK
20-06	England	D 2-2	Cologne	WCr1	Allback [51], Larsson [90]	45 000	Busacca SUI
24-06	Germany	L 0-2	Munich	WCr2		66 000	Simon BRA
16-08	Germany	L 0-3	Gelsenkirchen	Fr		53 000	Farina ITA
2-09	Latvia	W 1-0	Riga	ECq	Källström [38]	7 500	Ceferin SVN
6-09	Liechtenstein	W 3-1	Gothenburg	ECq	Allbäck 2 [2 69], Rosenberg [89]	17 735	Banari MDA
7-10	Spain	W 2-0	Stockholm	ECq	Elmander [10], Allbäck [82]	41 482	Bennett ENG
11-10	Iceland	W 2-1	Reykjavík	ECq	Källström [8], Wilhelmsson [59]	8 725	Gilewski POL
15-11	Côte d'Ivoire	L 0-1	Le Mans	Fr		3 844	Fautrel FRA
2007							
14-01	Venezuela	L 0-2	Maracaibo	Fr		14 000	Buitrago COL
18-01	Ecuador	L 1-2	Cuenca	Fr	Prica [91+]	20 000	Carrillo PER
21-01	Ecuador	D 1-1	Quito	Fr	Nannskog [69]	18 000	Garay PER
7-02	Egypt	L 0-2	Cairo	Fr		40 000	Abdalla LBY
28-03	Northern Ireland	L 1-2	Belfast	ECq	Elmander [26]	13 500	Braamhaar NED
2-06	Denmark	D 3-3	Copenhagen	ECq	Elmander 2 [7 26], Hansson [23]. Abandoned. Awarded 3-0	42 083	Fandel GER
6-06	Iceland	W 5-0	Stockholm	ECq	Allbäck 2 [11 51], Svensson.A [42], Mellberg [45], Rosenberg [50]	33 358	Hamer LUX

Fr = Friendly match • EC = UEFA EURO 2004/2008 • WC = FIFA World Cup • q = qualifier • r1 = first round group • r2 = second round • qf = quarter-final

SWEDEN NATIONAL TEAM RECORDS AND RECORD SEQUENCES

Records			Sequence records				
Victory	12-0	LVA 1927, KOR 1948	Wins	11	2001	Clean sheets	9	2001
Defeat	1-12	ENG 1908	Defeats	6	1908-1909	Goals scored	28	1958-1962
Player Caps	143	RAVELLI Thomas	Undefeated	23	2000-2002	Without goal	4	1998
Player Goals	49	RYDELL Sven	Without win	15	1920-1921	Goals against	17	1925-1927

MAJOR CITIES/TOWNS
Population '000

1	Stockolm	1 721
2	Göteborg	797
3	Malmö	266
4	Uppsala	129
5	Västeras	108
6	Örebro	99
7	Linköping	97
8	Helsingborg	92
9	Jönköping	83
10	Norrköping	82
11	Lund	77
12	Umeå	75
13	Gävle	68
14	Borås	63
15	Eskilstuna	59
16	Karlstad	58
17	Halmstad	56
18	Växjö	54
19	Sundsvall	48
20	Luleå	45
21	Ostersund	42
22	Borlänge	38
23	Kalmar	35
24	Landskrona	27

KINGDOM OF SWEDEN; KONUNGARIKET SVERIGE

Capital Stockholm	Language Swedish		Independence 1523
Population 9 031 088	Area 449 964 km²	Density 20 per km²	% in cities 83%
GDP per cap $26 800	Dailling code +46	Internet .se	GMT + / - +1

MEDALS TABLE

	Overall			League			Cup		Europe			City	Stadium	Cap'ty	DoF
	G	S	B	G	S	B	G	S	G	S	B				
1 Malmö FF	29	19	6	15	15	6	14	3		1		Malmö	Malmö Stadion	26 500	1910
2 IFK Göteborg	23	13	13	17	9	12	4	4	2		1	Gothenburg	Ullevi	43 000	1904
3 IFK Norrköping	18	14	4	12	10	4	6	4				Norrköping	Idrottsparken	19 400	1897
4 AIK Stockholm	17	19	9	10	12	9	7	7				Solna, Stockholm	Råsunda	36 608	1896
5 Djurgårdens IF	15	14	7	11	11	7	4	3				Stockholm	Stockholms Stadion	14 500	1891
6 Örgryte IS Göteborg	15	6	5	14	5	5	1	1				Gothenburg	Valhalla IP	3 500	1887
7 Helsingborgs IF	9	11	8	6	9	8	3	2				Helsingborg	Olympia Stadion	16 673	1907
8 IF Elfsborg Borås	7	8	3	5	5	3	2	3				Borås	Borås Arena	17 800	1904
9 GAIS Göteborg	7	5	3	6	4	3	1	1				Gothenburg	Ullevi	43 000	1894
10 Östers IF Växjö	5	7	4	4	3	4	1	4				Växjö	Värendsvallen	15 000	1930
11 Halmstads BK	5	2	2	4	2	2	1					Halmstad	Orjans Vall	15 500	1914
12 Åtvidabergs FF	4	6		2	2		2	4				Atvidaberg	Kopparvallen	7 200	1907
13 Kalmar FF	2	1	2			2	2	1				Kalmar	Fredriksskans	8 500	1910
14 Hammarby IF	1	5	2	1	3	2		2				Stockholm	Söderstadion	16 185	1897
15 IK Sleipner Norrköping	1	4	1	1	3	1		1				Norrköping			1903
Landskrona BoIS	1	4	1			1	1	4				Landskrona	Landskrona IP	12 000	1915

RECENT LEAGUE AND CUP RECORD

Championship						Cup		
Year	Champions	Pts	Runners-up	Pts	Third	Pts	Winners	Score	Runners-up
1995	IFK Göteborg	46	Helsingborgs IF	42	Halmstads BK	41	Halmstads BK	3-1	AIK Stockholm
1996	IFK Göteborg	56	Malmö FF	46	Helsingborgs IF	44	AIK Stockholm	1-0	Malmö FF
1997	Halmstads BK	52	IFK Göteborg	49	Malmö FF	46	AIK Stockholm	2-1	IF Elfsborg
1998	AIK Stockholm	46	Helsingborgs IF	44	Hammarby IF	42	Helsingborgs IF	1-1 1-1 3-0p	Orgryte IS
1999	Helsingborgs IF	54	AIK Stockholm	53	Halmstads BK	48	AIK Stockholm	1-0 0-0	IFK Göteborg
2000	Halmstads BK	52	Helsingborgs IF	46	AIK Stockholm	45	Orgryte IS	2-0 0-1	IFK Göteborg
2001	Hammarby IF	48	Djurgårdens IF	47	AIK Stockholm	45	IF Elfsborg	1-1 9-8p	AIK Stockholm
2002	Djurgårdens IF	52	Malmö FF	46	Orgryte IS	44	Djurgårdens IF	1-0	AIK Stockholm
2003	Djurgårdens IF	58	Hammarby IF	51	Malmö FF	48	IF Elfsborg	2-0	Assyriska
2004	Malmö FF	52	Halmstads BK	50	IFK Göteborg	47	Djurgårdens IF	3-1	IFK Göteborg
2005	Djurgårdens IF	53	IFK Göteborg	49	Kalmar FF	43	Djurgårdens IF	2-0	Atvidabergs FF
2006	Elfsborg IF	50	AIK Stockholm	49	Hammarby IF	43	Helsingborgs IF	2-0	Gefle IF

SWEDEN 2006

ALLSVENSKAN

	Pl	W	D	L	F	A	Pts	Elfsborg	AIK	Hammarby	Hels'borgs	Kalmar	Djurgårdens	Malmö	IFK	Gefle	GAIS	Halmstads	Hacken	Osters	Orgryte
Elfsborg IF †	26	13	11	2	41	19	50		1-1	3-0	0-0	1-0	1-0	4-2	1-1	0-1	1-0	3-0	2-2	0-0	2-0
AIK Stockholm ‡	26	13	10	3	46	23	49	2-2		0-2	2-2	1-0	3-1	3-0	4-0	2-2	2-0	3-0	1-0	5-1	2-1
Hammarby IF §3 ‡	26	13	7	6	40	31	43	1-0	2-0		4-2	1-2	0-3	2-2	3-3	1-0	5-2	0-0	3-0	2-0	0-1
Helsingborgs IF ‡	26	11	9	6	44	34	42	1-1	1-1	3-1		2-1	1-1	3-1	3-2	2-0	1-0	1-1	1-3	4-0	2-1
Kalmar FF	26	12	5	9	39	30	41	0-1	1-3	4-1	2-4		0-1	0-0	1-2	2-1	1-2	2-1	0-0	3-0	3-2
Djurgårdens IF	26	11	7	8	31	25	40	1-1	0-1	0-0	2-1	0-1		2-3	1-0	1-0	0-2	2-1	2-1	2-0	2-2
Malmö FF	26	10	8	8	43	39	38	1-1	3-1	1-2	3-1	2-2	0-1		2-1	2-2	2-0	1-0	1-1	2-0	4-2
IFK Göteborg	26	9	9	8	39	36	36	1-1	1-1	1-2	2-2	3-2	3-2	1-0		3-1	0-0	0-0	3-0	0-0	2-1
Gefle IF	26	8	7	11	28	39	31	1-1	1-1	0-1	1-0	2-2	2-0	4-3	1-0		2-2	0-2	0-4	1-0	2-0
GAIS Göteborg	26	5	12	9	25	33	27	0-3	0-0	2-2	0-2	2-2	1-1	0-0	1-2	1-0		1-1	2-2	1-1	2-0
Halmstads BK	26	5	12	9	22	30	27	0-1	2-2	0-0	1-1	0-1	0-0	2-2	1-4	3-0	0-0		2-2	1-0	1-0
BK Hacken Göteborg	26	4	10	12	29	41	22	1-4	0-1	0-0	3-0	0-2	0-2	1-3	1-4	4-1	0-2	0-0		0-1	2-2
Osters IF Växjö	26	4	7	15	19	46	19	3-4	0-4	1-2	0-3	0-1	0-3	2-1	1-1	1-2	2-2	3-1	1-1		0-0
Orgryte IS Göteborg	26	3	8	15	24	44	17	0-2	0-0	1-3	1-1	1-3	1-1	1-2	3-2	1-1	1-0	1-2	1-1	0-2	

1/04/2006 - 5/11/2006 • † Qualified for the UEFA Champions League • ‡ Qualified for the UEFA Cup • §3 = three points deducted
Relegation play-off: Brommapojkarna 2-0 2-1 BK Hacken

SWEDEN 2006 — SUPERETTAN (2)

	Pl	W	D	L	F	A	Pts
Trelleborgs IF	30	19	9	2	48	13	66
Orebro SK	30	17	7	6	56	28	58
IF Brommapojkarna	30	18	3	9	53	43	57
IFK Norrköping	30	15	9	6	55	30	54
Landskrona BoIS	30	15	5	10	53	39	50
Ljungskile SK	30	13	7	10	34	33	46
Mjällby AIF	30	11	10	9	51	49	43
GIF Sundsvall	30	11	7	12	42	33	40
Falkenbergs FF	30	10	10	10	43	40	40
Jönköpings Sodra	30	9	10	11	37	59	37
Degerfors IF	30	9	8	13	39	41	35
Atvidabergs FF	30	9	8	13	40	47	35
Assyriska FF	30	9	7	14	34	40	34
Väsby United	30	8	8	14	34	47	32
Qviding FF	30	4	6	20	31	63	18
Umeå FC	30	4	4	22	30	71	16

14/04/2006 - 21/10/2006 • Play-offs: Sirius 1-1 1-0 Väsby; Bunkeflo 0-0 1-1 Assyriska. Väsby and Assyriska relegated

SVENSKA CUPEN 2006

Fourth round

Helsingborgs IF *	3
Degerfors IF	0
Djurgårdens IF	1
IF Elfsborg *	2
Väsby United *	4
Falkenbergs FF *	3
Trelleborgs FF *	0
Osters IF Växjö	4
Kalmar FF	2
Visby IF Gute	1
Mjällby AIF	4
IFK Norrköping *	5
Landskrona BoIS	2
Västerås SK *	1
Halmstads BK *	0
Gefle IF	3

Quarter-finals

Helsingborgs IF *	4 5p
IF Elfsborg	4 3p
Väsby United	0
Osters IF Växjö *	2
Kalmar FF *	4
IFK Norrköping	2
Landskrona BoIS *	2
Gefle IF	3

Semi-finals

Helsingborgs IF	3
Osters IF Växjö	0
Kalmar FF	1 3p
Gefle IF	1 4p

Final

Helsingborgs IF ‡	2
Gefle IF	0

CUP FINAL
Råsunda, Stockholm
11-11-2006, Att: 3379, Ref: Johannesson
Scorers - Luton Shelton [28], Babis Stefanidis [53]

* Home team • ‡ Qualified for the UEFA Cup

SWZ – SWAZILAND

NATIONAL TEAM RECORD
JULY 10TH 2006 TO JULY 12TH 2010

PL	W	D	L	F	A	%
11	3	3	5	5	19	40.9

FIFA/COCA-COLA WORLD RANKING

1993	1994	1995	1996	1997	1998	1999	2000	2001	2002	2003	2004	2005	2006	High		Low	
99	125	148	160	165	149	127	137	132	116	114	126	134	148	92	10/93	174	10/97

2006–2007											
08/06	09/06	10/06	11/06	12/06	01/07	02/07	03/07	04/07	05/07	06/07	07/07
152	150	152	147	148	151	151	149	150	151	144	147

Swaziland continued to hover around the lower reaches of the FIFA/Coca-Cola World Ranking, winning just three of their 11 international matches played over the course of the 2006-07 season. Disappointingly for the kingdom, they failed to emerge from the COSAFA Cup mini tournament that they hosted at the Somhlolo stadium in May 2007, where they were eliminated by Mauritius in the semi-finals on post-match penalties. Swaziland were also unable to register a win in the first five of their six qualifying matches for the 2008 African Nations Cup finals, leaving 'Sihlangu', as the national team are known, out of contention long before the end of the preliminaries. Former

INTERNATIONAL HONOURS
None

Zambian international defender Manfred Chabinga was appointed the third national team coach inside the last 12 months, taking over from Gcina Dlamini and then the Egyptian Ayman Al Yamani, whose unhappy six month stint ended after the 2-0 defeat by Kenya in Nairobi in March. Police club Royal Leopards lost their first three league matches of the season but just one more to pip Green Mambas by a single point to the Premier League title. Green Mamba had led for most of the season only to see their chances slip in the closing stages. Royal Leopards were also Cup winners with a 1-0 triumph in the final over Manzini Sundowns.

THE FIFA BIG COUNT OF 2006

	Male	Female		Total
Number of players	54 900	0	Referees and Assistant Referees	100
Professionals	0		Admin, Coaches, Technical, Medical	800
Amateurs 18+	3 300		Number of clubs	60
Youth under 18	1 700		Number of teams	220
Unregistered	3 900		Clubs with women's teams	0
Total players	54 900		Players as % of population	4.83%

National Football Association of Swaziland (NFAS)
Sigwaca House, Plot 582, Sheffield Road, PO Box 641, Mbabane H100, Swaziland
Tel +268 4046852   Fax +268 4046206
nfas@swazi.net   www.nfas.org.sz
President: MTHETHWA Adam   General Secretary: MNGOMEZULU Frederick
Vice-President: SHONGWE Timothy   Treasurer: MNGOMEZULU Frederick   Media Officer: None
Men's Coach: CHABINGA Manfred   Women's Coach: THWALA Christian
NFAS formed: 1968   CAF: 1976   FIFA: 1978
Blue shirts, Gold shorts, Red socks

RECENT INTERNATIONAL MATCHES PLAYED BY SWAZILAND

2003	Opponents	Score	Venue	Comp	Scorers	Att	Referee
13-07	Madagascar	W 2-0	Mbabane	CCqf	Siza Dlamini [30], Mfanizle Dlamini [51]	8 000	Mpofu BOT
31-08	Zimbabwe	L 0-2	Harare	CCsf		25 000	Antonio De Souza ANG
6-09	Botswana	L 0-3	Mbabane	Fr			
4-10	Lesotho	L 2-5	Maseru	Fr			
12-10	Cape Verde Islands	D 1-1	Mbabane	WCq	Siza Dlamini [64]	5 000	Teshome ERI
9-11	Mozambique	L 0-2	Maputo	Fr			
16-11	Cape Verde Islands	L 0-3	Praia	WCq		6 000	Aboubacar CIV
2004							
11-04	Mozambique	L 0-2	Maputo	Fr			
31-05	Mozambique	D 1-1	Maputo	Fr	Lwazi Maziya [83p]	5 000	
27-06	Zimbabwe	L 0-5	Mbabane	CCqf			Infante MOZ
6-07	Malawi	W 2-1	Blantyre	Fr			
8-07	Malawi	D 1-1	Lilongwe	Fr			
2005							
1-06	Lesotho	W 4-3	Somhlolo	Fr	Jabulani Dlamini [21], Lwazi Maziya [63], Maxwell Zikalala [78], Mfanafuthi Bhembe [93+]		
11-06	Zambia	L 0-3	Lusaka	CCr1			Chidoda BOT
2006							
14-04	Lesotho	L 0-5	Maseru	Fr			
16-04	Lesotho	D 2-2	Maseru	Fr	Nkosingiphile Dlamini [5], Civil Matsebula [15]		
20-05	South Africa	L 0-1	Gaborone	CCr1			Malepa BOT
21-05	Madagascar	W 2-0	Gaborone	CCr1	Zweli Msibi [54], Mzwandile Mamba [82]		Malepa BOT
24-06	Mozambique	L 0-4	Maputo	Fr			
25-06	Zimbabwe	L 1-2	Maputo	Fr	Manqoba Kunene [6]		
26-08	Lesotho	W 3-1	Mbabane	Fr	Mduduzi Mdluli 2 [28 49], Salebona Jele [64]		
3-09	Angola	L 0-2	Mbabane	CNq			Maillet SEY
7-10	Eritrea	D 0-0	Asmara	CNq			Gasingwa RWA
15-11	Botswana	L 0-1	Gaborone	Fr			
2007							
13-02	Lesotho	W 1-0	Maseru	Fr	Bheki Msimango [5]		
18-03	Lesotho	L 0-1	Lobamba	Fr			
25-03	Kenya	L 0-2	Nairobi	CNq			Seechurn MRI
26-05	Mauritius	D 0-0	Mbabane	CCr1	L 5-6p		Labrosse SEY
27-05	Malawi	W 1-0	Mbabane	CCr1	Mphile Tsabedze [85]		Labrosse SEY
3-06	Kenya	D 0-0	Mbabane	CNq			
17-06	Angola	L 0-3	Luanda	CNq			

Fr = Friendly match • CN = CAF African Cup of Nations • CC = COSAFA Castle Cup • WC = FIFA World Cup
q = qualifier • r1 = first round group • qf = quarter-final • sf = semi-final

SWAZILAND NATIONAL TEAM RECORDS AND RECORD SEQUENCES

Records			Sequence records				
Victory	4-1	LES 1999	Wins	3	1999, 2001-2002	Clean sheets	3	2007
Defeat	1-9	ZAM 1978	Defeats	8	1969-1989	Goals scored	8	1998-1999
Player Caps	n/a		Undefeated	9	2001-2002	Without goal	6	1993-1997
Player Goals	n/a		Without win	18	1969-1990	Goals against	15	1981-1990

SWAZILAND COUNTRY INFORMATION

Capital	Mbabane	Independence	1968 from the UK	GDP per Capita	$4 900
Population	1 169 241	Status	Monarchy	GNP Ranking	147
Area km²	17 363	Language	English, siSwati	Dialling code	+46
Population density	67 per km²	Literacy rate	81%	Internet code	.sz
% in urban areas	31%	Main religion	Christian 60%	GMT +/−	+1
Towns/Cities ('000)	Manzini 110; Mbabane 76; Big Bend 10; Malkerns 9; Nhlangano 9; Mhlume 8; Hluti 6				
Neighbours (km)	Mozambique 105; South Africa 430				
Main stadia	Somholo National Stadium – Mbabane 30 000				

SWAZILAND 2006–07

MTN PREMIER LEAGUE

	Pl	W	D	L	F	A	Pts	Leopards	Mambas	Buffaloes	Wanderers	Sundowns	Swallows	Highlanders	Mbabane C	Rovers	XI Men	Chiefs	Hub S'wns
Royal Leopards †	22	11	7	4	36	18	40		2-3	1-1	2-0	1-0	1-1	5-0	2 1	2-0	3-0	3-2	4-1
Green Mamba	22	11	6	5	36	24	39	1-1		1-2	1-0	1-2	0-0	1-1	2-1	3-2	1-0	0-3	2-1
Young Buffaloes	22	8	10	4	26	24	34	1-1	1-0		0-3	2-2	1-1	0-2	1-3	2-2	2-1	0-0	1-0
Manzini Wanderers	22	7	10	5	26	18	31	0-0	2-1	1-1		0-1	0-1	1-0	1-1	1-1	2-1	4-0	1-2
Manzini Sundowns	22	7	10	5	23	18	31	1-0	2-1	0-1	1-1		0-0	0-0	0-1	1-1	2-2	3-1	2-2
Mbabane Swallows	22	6	11	5	24	19	29	1-1	1-2	0-0	1-2	**2-0**		1-0	1-1	0-0	1-0	1-1	2-1
Mbabane Highlanders	22	6	9	7	18	23	27	0-1	0-3	1-1	0-0	2-0	0-0		0-1	1-0	1-1	1-0	3-2
Midas Mbabane City	22	6	8	8	26	32	26	0-2	3-3	1-1	2-2	1-0	0-5	1-1		1-0	1-2	0-0	4-1
Mhlambanyatsi Rovers	22	6	7	9	26	32	25	1-2	0-4	1-3	1-2	1-1	4-1	2-1	2-0		0-0	2-1	2-2
Eleven Men in Flight	22	6	7	9	22	28	25	2-1	0-0	1-2	0-0	0-0	1-0	1-2	3-1	1-3		1-3	2-2
Malanti Chiefs	22	5	9	8	21	26	24	1-1	0-4	1-0	0-0	0-0	1-1	0-0	1-1	3-0	1-2		2-1
Hub Sundowns	22	4	4	14	23	45	16	1-0	0-1	1-3	0-3	0-3	1-5	2-2	2-1	0-1	0-1	1-0	

30/09/2006 - 20/05/2007 • † Qualified for the CAF Champions League

SWAZI BANK CUP 2006–07

Round of 16		Quarter-finals		Semi-finals		Final	
Royal Leopards	3						
JVP Junior Stars	1	**Royal Leopards**	1				
Bakers Pride Arsenal	0	Green Mamba	0				
Green Mamba	1			**Royal Leopards**	1		
Moneni City Stars	0 5p			Mbabane Highlanders	0		
Mbabane Swallows	0 4p	Moneni City Stars	0				
Illovo FC	2 2	**Mbabane Highlanders**	3				
Mbabane Highlanders	2 1					**Royal Leopards**	1
Young Buffaloes	4					Manzini Sundowns	0
RSSC United	1	**Young Buffaloes**	1				
Midas Mbane City	0 3p	Manzini Wanderers	0			CUP FINAL	
Manzini Wanderers	0 4p			Young Buffaloes	1 3p		
XI Men in Flight	0 4p	**Manzini Sundowns**	1 4p	Somhlolo, Mbabane			
Hub Sundowns	0 3p	XI Men in Flight	1			1-04-2007, Att: 8000, Ref: Fakudze	
Mhlambanyatsi Rovers	1 5p	**Manzini Sundowns**	2			Scorer - Bongani Sibandze [45]	
Manzini Sundowns	1 6p						

RECENT LEAGUE AND CUP RECORD

	Championship						Cup		
Year	Champions	Pts	Runners-up	Pts	Third	Pts	Winners	Score	Runners-up
1996	XI Men in Flight	69	Denver Sundowns	66	C&M Eagles	56			
1997	Mbabane High'ders	54	XI Men in Flight	52	Mbabane Swallows	52	Mbabane High'ders		
1998	No championship due to season readjustment								
1999	Manzini Wanderers	48	Mbabane High'ders	45	Mbabane Swallows	44	Mbabane High'ders		
2000	Mbabane High'ders	52	Green Mamba	45	Mbabane Swallows	37	Mhlume United		
2001	Mbabane High'ders	48	Manzini Wanderers	42	Mbabane Swallows	40	XI Men in Flight	1- 4-3p	Mbabane Swallows
2002	Manzini Wanderers	46	Mhlam'yatsi Rovers	43	Mbabane Swallows	43			
2003	Manzini Wanderers	45	Mhlam'yatsi Rovers	42	Mbabane Swallows	38			
2004	Mhlam'yatsi Rovers	50	Mbabane High'ders	45	Green Mamba	37	Green Mamba	5-1	Denver Sundowns
2005	Mbabane Swallows	43	Green Mamba	43	Royal Leopards	39	Hub Sundowns	2-0	Malanti Chiefs
2006	Royal Leopards	43	Young Buffaloes	40	Mbabane High'ders	37	Mbabane Swallows	1-0	Malanti Chiefs
2007	Royal Leopards	40	Green Mamba	39	Young Buffaloes	34	Royal Leopards	1-0	Manzini Sundowns

SYR – SYRIA

NATIONAL TEAM RECORD
JULY 10TH 2006 TO JULY 12TH 2010

PL	W	D	L	F	A	%
13	4	2	7	12	21	38.4

FIFA/COCA-COLA WORLD RANKING

1993	1994	1995	1996	1997	1998	1999	2000	2001	2002	2003	2004	2005	2006	High		Low	
82	105	136	115	98	84	109	100	90	91	85	85	98	112	**78**	08/03	**145**	05/96

2006–2007											
08/06	09/06	10/06	11/06	12/06	01/07	02/07	03/07	04/07	05/07	06/07	07/07
114	116	129	118	112	111	110	112	110	111	114	113

When Syrian clubs were invited to enter the AFC Champions League following the success of Al Jaish and Al Wahda in reaching the first AFC Cup final in 2004, most predicted that they would struggle at the higher level. Two years on and Al Karama nearly did the unthinkable, coming agonisingly close to being crowned Asian champions at the end of 2006. With four minutes left in the second leg against Korea's Jeonbuk Motors and the scores tied at 2-2 on aggregate, Brazilian striker Zé Carlo scored for Jeonbuk to break Syrian hearts. Defeat couldn't take the shine off what turned out to be a sensational year for Karama. They qualified for the knock-out stage of the 2007

INTERNATIONAL HONOURS
Asian Youth Championship 1994

AFC Champions League by winning their group whilst at home they were totally invincible, becoming the first team to go through both League and Cup campaigns undefeated as they powered their way to an historic double. In contrast, the national team had a poor season. In their AFC Asian Cup qualifying group, Syria finished third behind Iran and South Korea to miss out on the finals for the third tournament running. The season ended with the fourth West Asian Championship, but there was no first title for the Syrians. Having won their group comfortably ahead of Lebanon and hosts Jordan, they crashed out to Iraq in a one sided semi-final.

THE FIFA BIG COUNT OF 2006

	Male	Female		Total
Number of players	430 800	0	Referees and Assistant Referees	700
Professionals	0		Admin, Coaches, Technical, Medical	3 600
Amateurs 18+	4 700		Number of clubs	170
Youth under 18	29 700		Number of teams	760
Unregistered	214 200		Clubs with women's teams	0
Total players	430 800		Players as % of population	2.28%

Syrian Arab Federation for Football (FASF)

Maysaloon Street, PO Box 22296, Damascus, Syria
Tel +963 11 3335866   Fax +963 11 3331511
toufiksarhan@hotmail.com   www.syrian-soccer.com
President: AHMAD Jappan Dr   General Secretary: SARHAN Toufik
Vice-President: FARES Taj Addin   Treasurer: SELOU Aref   Media Officer: none
Men's Coach: RADINOVICH Milosaf   Women's Coach: None
FASF formed: 1936   AFC: 1970   FIFA: 1937
Red shirts, Red shorts, Red socks

RECENT INTERNATIONAL MATCHES PLAYED BY SYRIA

2004	Opponents	Score		Venue	Comp	Scorers	Att	Referee
26-08	Yemen	W	2-1	Sana'a	Fr			
28-08	Yemen	L	1-2	Sana'a	Fr			
8-09	Tajikistan	W	1-0	Dushanbe	WCq	Raja Rafe 35	18 000	Mohd Salleh MAS
29-09	Kuwait	D	1-1	Tripoli (LIB)	Fr			
6-10	Saudi Arabia	D	2-2	Riyadh	Fr	Raja Rafe 7, Rafat 90p		
8-10	Qatar	W	2-1	Doha	Fr			
13-10	Bahrain	D	2-2	Damascus	WCq	Shekh Eleshra 12, Jehad Al Houssain 18	35 000	Moradi IRN
17-11	Kyrgyzstan	L	0-1	Damascus	WCq		1 000	Tongkhan THA
2005								
26-01	Kuwait	L	2-3	Kuwait City	Fr	Amneh 39, Raja Rafe 74		
2-02	Japan	L	0-3	Saitama	Fr			
25-10	Oman	D	0-0	Muscat	Fr			
16-11	United Arab Emirates	L	0-3	Damascus	Fr			
3-12	Oman	W	3-1	Al Gharrafa	WGr1	Yhya Al Rachedd 41, Rafat 68, Alaya 81		
10-12	Iraq	D	2-2	Doha	WGf	Amena 19, Jehad Al Houssain 91+. L 3-4p		
2006								
30-01	Bahrain	D	1-1	Manama	Fr	Zyad Chaabo 6		
7-02	Palestine	W	3-0	Damascus	Fr			
14-02	Saudi Arabia	D	1-1	Jeddah	Fr	OG 45		
22-02	Korea Republic	L	1-2	Aleppo	ACq	Firas Al Khatib 49	35 000	Maidin SIN
1-03	Chinese Taipei	W	4-0	Taipei	ACq	Zyad Chaabo 2 29 58, Jehad Al Houssain 45, Firas Al Khatib 64	700	O Il Son PRK
2-05	United Arab Emirates	L	1-2	Dubai	Fr	Zyad Chaabo		
15-07	Iraq	L	1-3	Damascus	Fr	Zyad Chaabo 75		
25-07	Iraq	L	1-2	Damascus	Fr	Maher Al Sayed 61		
30-07	Jordan	L	0-3	Amman	Fr			
5-08	Libya	W	2-1	Damascus	Fr	Aatef Jenyat 23, Maher Al Sayad 35		
16-08	Iran	D	1-1	Tehran	ACq	Zyad Chaabo 88	40 000	Irmatov UZB
1-09	Oman	L	0-3	Muscat	Fr			
6-09	Iran	L	0-2	Damascus	ACq		10 000	Matsumura JPN
11-10	Korea Republic	D	1-1	Seoul	ACq	Maher Al Sayad 18	24 140	Kunsuta THA
15-11	Chinese Taipei	W	3-0	Damascus	ACq	Tarek Al Jabban 50, Firas Al Khatib 2 61 80	1 000	Al Hilali OMA
2007								
11-01	Saudi Arabia	L	1-2	Dammam	Fr	Majed Humssi 74		
16-06	Lebanon	W	1-0	Amman	WAr1	Zyad Chaabo 45		
18-06	Jordan	W	1-0	Amman	WAr1	Khaled Mansour 48		
22-06	Iraq	L	0-3	Amman	WAsf			

Fr = Friendly match • WA = West Asian Championship • WG = West Asian Games • AC = AFC Asian Cup • WC = FIFA World Cup
q = qualifier • r1 = first round group • sf = semi-final • 3p = third place play-off • f = final

SYRIA NATIONAL TEAM RECORDS AND RECORD SEQUENCES

Records			Sequence records					
Victory	13-0	OMA 1965	Wins	4	1998, 2001, 2004	Clean sheets	5	1985
Defeat	0-8	GRE 1949, EGY 1951	Defeats	9	1977-1978	Goals scored	14	2004
Player Caps	n/a		Undefeated	10	1987-1988	Without goal	4	Three times
Player Goals	n/a		Without win	13	1981-1983	Goals against	15	1981-1983

SYRIA COUNTRY INFORMATION

Capital	Damascus	Independence	1946 from France	GDP per Capita	$3 300	
Population	18 016 874	Status	Republic	GNP Ranking	72	
Area km2	185 180	Language	Arabic, Kurdish, Armenian	Dialling code	+963	
Population density	97 per km2	Literacy rate	76%	Internet code	.sy	
% in urban areas	52%	Main religion	Muslim	GMT +/ -	+2	
Towns/Cities ('000)	Aleppo 2 139; Damascus 1 576; Homs 736; Latakia 431; Hama 348; ar-Raqqah 261					
Neighbours (km)	Iraq 605; Jordan 375; Israel 76; Lebanon 375; Turkey 822; Mediterranean Sea 193					
Main stadia	Abbasiyyin – Damascus 45 000					

SYRIA 2006-07

FIRST DIVISION

	Pl	W	D	L	F	A	Pts	Karama	Ittihad	Taliya	Majd	Jaish	Teshrin	Foutoua	Wahda	Hottin	Shorta	Jabala	Horriya	Wathba	Qardaha
Al Karama Homs †	26	18	8	0	54	14	62		2-1	2-0	4-1	2-1	2-1	2-0	4-0	1-0	1-1	4-1	3-0	1-1	4-0
Al Ittihad Aleppo	26	17	4	5	44	20	55	0-1		1-0	3-2	2-0	3-0	2-0	0-1	2-1	2-0	1-0	2-0	5-1	1-0
Al Taliya Hama	26	14	7	5	35	22	49	1-1	4-3		2-1	2-3	1-0	2-1	0-2	2-0	1-0	1-1	3-1	1-0	2-1
Al Majd Damascus	26	9	9	8	33	29	36	1-1	2-1	1-1		2-0	1-1	0-1	1-0	3-0	1-4	2-0	1-0	1-2	4-0
Al Jaish Damascus	26	9	7	10	35	36	34	0-2	2-2	0-1	0-1		2-3	2-1	3-1	2-0	0-0	1-1	1-2	2-1	4-1
Teshrin Latakia	26	8	8	10	27	31	32	0-0	1-0	0-2	2-1	1-2		2-0	0-0	0-0	2-3	1-2	1-0	2-0	1-1
Al Foutoua Deir es-Zor	26	7	10	9	17	21	31	1-2	0-1	0-1	1-1	2-0	1-1		0-0	0-0	0-0	0-0	0-0	1-0	1-0
Al Wahda Damascus	26	5	14	7	27	34	29	2-2	1-1	0-3	0-0	2-5	0-0	2-2		1-1	2-0	0-1	2-0	3-1	3-0
Hottin Latakia	26	7	8	11	29	37	29	2-5	1-2	1-1	2-1	0-0	1-0	2-1	3-3		2-2	2-1	1-3	7-1	0-0
Al Shorta Damascus	26	5	13	8	27	31	28	0-3	0-2	0-0	0-0	2-2	3-2	0-0	0-0	3-0		0-2	2-3	2-0	0-0
Jabala	26	6	10	10	21	27	28	0-0	1-1	1-0	1-1	0-0	1-1	0-1	4-0	0-2	2-1		0-2	0-0	1-3
Al Horriya Aleppo	26	6	8	12	24	34	26	0-0	1-2	0-2	2-2	0-1	2-3	0-0	1-1	1-0	2-2	1-1		0-1	2-0
Al Wathba Homs	26	6	7	13	23	36	25	0-1	0-2	1-1	0-1	4-1	3-1	0-1	0-0	2-0	1-1	0-0	1-1		3-0
Al Qardaha	26	4	9	13	17	41	21	0-4	0-2	1-1	1-1	1-1	0-0	1-2	2-2	0-1	1-1	1-0	2-0	1-0	

22/09/2006 - 20/05/2007 • † Qualified for the AFC Champions League

FASF CUP 2006-07

Round of 16			Quarter-finals			Semi-finals			Final		
Al Karama	2	3									
Al Jaish *	1	0	**Al Karama ***		1 4						
Al Wathba *	1	3	Hottin		1 2						
Hottin	1	4				**Al Karama ***		3 2			
Efrin	1	1				Al Wahda		0 1			
Al Horriya *	0	0	Efrin		1 0						
Al Nwa'ir *	0	0	**Al Wahda ***		3 2						
Al Wahda	1	1							**Al Karama**		2
Al Majd	1	2							Al Taliya		1
Al Foutoua *	0	1	**Al Majd**		1 2						
Al Jihad *	0	0	Al Ittihad *		1 0						
Al Ittihad	3	3				Al Majd *		2 2 4p		CUP FINAL	
Teshrin	3	5				**Al Taliya**		2 2 5p			
Al Shabab *	1	1	Teshrin		1 3					1-07-2007	
Al Qardaha	0	0	**Al Taliya ***		4 1						
Al Taliya *	4	6				* Home team in the first leg					

RECENT LEAGUE AND CUP RECORD

		Championship						Cup		
Year	Champions	Pts	Runners-up	Pts	Third	Pts		Winners	Score	Runners-up
1990	Al Foutoua	43	Al Karama	43	Al Wathba	34		Al Foutoua	1-0	Al Karama
1991	Al Foutoua	44	Jabala	37	Al Shourta	34		Al Foutoua	1-0	Yaqaza
1992	Al Horriya	42	Jabala	41	Al Ittihad	38		Al Horriya	1-0	Al Ittihad
1993	Al Ittihad							Al Wahda	4-0	Hottin
1994	Al Horriya							Al Ittihad		
1995	Al Ittihad							Al Karama	3-0	Hottin
1996	Al Karama	62	Hottin	51	Teshrine	45		Al Karama	3-0	Jabala
1997	Teshrine	60	Al Jaish	57	Al Karama	49		Al Jaish	2-0	Jabala
1998	Al Jaish	62	Al Karama	48	Hottine	46		Al Jaish	5-2	Al Karama
1999	Al Jaish	58	Al Karama	55	Al Wahda	44		Jabala	2-2 3-0p	Hottin
2000	Jabala	51	Hottin	50	Teshrine	50		Al Jaish	4-1	Jabala
2001	Al Jaish	60	Al Karama	51	Al Ittihad	49		Hottin	1-0	Al Jaish
2002	Al Jaish	37	Al Ittihad	35	Al Wahda	29		Al Jaish	3-0	Jabala
2003	Al Jaish	57	Al Ittihad	54	Qardah	47		Al Wahda	5-2	Al Ittihad
2004	Al Wahda	60	Al Karama	58	Teshrine	54		Al Jaish	0-0 4-2p	Teshrine
2005	Al Ittihad	53	Al Karama	50	Al Wahda	44		Al Ittihad	3-1	Al Majd
2006	Al Karama	56	Al Jaish	53	Al Wahda	51		Al Ittihad	3-0	Teshrin
2007	Al Karama	62	Al Ittihad	55	Al Taliya	49		Al Karama	2-1	Al Taliya

TAH – TAHITI

NATIONAL TEAM RECORD
JULY 10TH 2006 TO JULY 12TH 2010

PL	W	D	L	F	A	%
0	0	0	0	0	0	0

FIFA/COCA-COLA WORLD RANKING

1993	1994	1995	1996	1997	1998	1999	2000	2001	2002	2003	2004	2005	2006	High		Low	
141	148	156	158	161	123	139	131	127	115	33	124	141	173	**111**	08/02	**181**	06/07

					2006–2007						
08/06	09/06	10/06	11/06	12/06	01/07	02/07	03/07	04/07	05/07	06/07	07/07
167	171	172	174	173	173	173	173	170	169	181	180

As one of the few Pacific islands in which football is very much the number one sport, Tahiti will be hoping for a strong performance in the 2010 FIFA World Cup qualifiers. Although both the Solomon Islands and Fiji can boast larger populations, Tahitians believe that they can cement their position as one of the select few nations able to challenge New Zealand for honours within the Oceania Confederation. With one of the best-developed leagues in the OFC, Tahiti were given an automatic berth in the inaugural OFC O–League, with the winners of the 2006 Coupe de Polynesie, AS Temanava, drawn against Ba from Fiji and Marist from the Solomon Islands in the group stage.

INTERNATIONAL HONOURS
South Pacific Games & Mini Games 1966 1975 1979 1981 1983 1985 1993 1995

Temanava, however, were unable to repeat the feats of Pirae who reached the 2006 OFC Cup final, with defeats away to both Ba and Marist ensuring that they finished well behind the Fijians, who qualified for the final. Despite winning the first stage of the Championship at home, Dragon failed to win a game in the second stage and it was Manu Ura who claimed the title, a point ahead of Tefana. Strictly speaking Tahiti is only one part of French Polynesia but the rest of the islands do get to take part in the Coupe de Polynesie and in the 2007 tournament Tefana made up for their disappointment in the Championship by beating Manu Ura on penalties in the final.

THE FIFA BIG COUNT OF 2006

	Male	Female		Total
Number of players	15 391	1 005	Referees and Assistant Referees	64
Professionals	0		Admin, Coaches, Technical, Medical	64
Amateurs 18+	4 429		Number of clubs	164
Youth under 18	5 367		Number of teams	650
Unregistered	4 500		Clubs with women's teams	7
Total players	16 396		Players as % of population	6.66%

Fédération Tahitienne de Football (FTF)
Rue Coppenrath, Stade de Fautaua, Case postale 50858, Pirae 98716, Tahiti, French Polynesia
Tel +689 540954   Fax +689 419629
contact@ftf.pf   www.ftf.pf
President: HAERERAAROA Eugene   General Secretary: TAVERE Victorine
Vice-President: ARIIOTIMA Henri Thierry   Treasurer: MARTIN Jean-François   Media Officer: LATEYRON Chrystele
Men's Coach: KAUTAI Gerard   Women's Coach: APUARII Ralph
FTF formed: 1989   OFC: 1990   FIFA: 1990
Red shirts, White shorts, Red socks

RECENT INTERNATIONAL MATCHES PLAYED BY TAHITI

2002	Opponents	Score	Venue	Comp	Scorers	Att	Referee
5-07	New Zealand	L 0-4	Auckland	OCr1		1 000	Attison VAN
7-07	Solomon Islands	W 3-2	Auckland	OCr1	Booene [42], Tagawa [57], Fatupua-Lecaill [90]	1 000	Breeze AUS
9-07	Papua New Guinea	W 3-1	Auckland	OCr1	Garcia [29], Tagawa 2 [49 64]	800	Rakaroi FIJ
12-07	Australia	L 1-2	Auckland	OCsf	Zaveroni [38]	400	Rugg NZL
14-07	Vanuatu	W 1-0	Auckland	OC3p	Auraa [65]	1 000	Rakaroi FIJ
2003							
30-06	Micronesia †	W 17-0	Suva	SPr1	Tagawa 4 [8 10 19 33], OG [17], Guyon 3 [32 41 56] Bennett 4 [48 70 76 86], Tchen [69], Papaaura [71] Senechal [72], Lecaill [78], Terevaura [81]		Rakaroi FIJ
3-07	Papua New Guinea	W 3-0	Suva	SPr1	Bennett 2 [13 69], Tagawa [62]	1 000	Attison VAN
5-07	New Caledonia	L 0-4	Nadi	SPr1		3 000	Shah FIJ
7-07	Tonga	W 4-0	Lautoka	SPr1	Tagawa 2 [2 27], Bennett 2 [81 83]	3 000	Shah FIJ
9-07	Fiji	L 1-2	Lautoka	SPsf	Papura [4]	8 000	Attison VAN
11-07	Vanuatu	L 0-1	Suva	SP3p		6 000	Rakaroi FIJ
2004							
10-05	Cook Islands	W 2-0	Honiara	WCq	Temataua [2], Moretta [80]	12 000	Singh FIJ
12-05	New Caledonia	D 0-0	Honiara	WCq		14 000	Rakaroi FIJ
17-05	Tonga	W 2-0	Honiara	WCq	Wajoka [1], Temataua [78]	400	Sosongan PNG
19-05	Solomon Islands	D 1-1	Honiara	WCq	Simon [30]	18 000	Rakaroi FIJ
29-05	Fiji	D 0-0	Adelaide	WCq		3 000	Farina ITA
31-05	Australia	L 0-9	Adelaide	WCq		1 200	Attison VAN
2-06	Solomon Islands	L 0-4	Adelaide	WCq		50	Rakaroi FIJ
4-06	New Zealand	L 0-10	Adelaide	WCq		200	Shield AUS
6-06	Vanuatu	W 2-1	Adelaide	WCq	Temataua [40], Wajoka [89]	300	Rakaroi FIJ
2005							
No international matches played in 2005							
2006							
No international matches played in 2006							
2007							
No international matches played in 2007 before August							

Fr = Friendly match • OC = OFC Oceania Cup • SP = South Pacific Games • WC = FIFA World Cup
q = qualifier • r1 = first roundgroup • sf = semi-final • 3p = third place play-off • † Not a full international

TAHITI NATIONAL TEAM RECORDS AND RECORD SEQUENCES

Records			Sequence records				
Victory	30-0	COK 1971	Wins	10	1978-1980	Clean sheets	5	1995
Defeat	0-10	NZL 2004	Defeats	5	1996-1997	Goals scored	17	1981-1983
Player Caps	n/a		Undefeated	17	1981-1983	Without goal	4	2004
Player Goals	n/a		Without win	17	1959-1963	Goals against	20	1953-1963

TAHITI COUNTRY INFORMATION

Capital	Papeete	Status	French Overseas Possession, part of French Polynesia	GDP per Capita	$17 920
Population	266 339			GNP Ranking	n/a
Area km²	4 167	Language	French, Tahitian	Dialling code	+689
Population density	62 per km²	Literacy rate	98%	Internet code	.pf
% in urban areas	n/a	Main religion	Christian	GMT + / −	-10
Towns/Cities ('000)	Faaa 29; Papeete 26; Punaauia 25; Pirae 14; Mahina 14; Paea 13; Papara 10; Arue 9				
Neighbours (km)	South Pacific Ocean 2 525				
Main stadia	Stade de Fautaua – Pirae; Stade Pater – Papeete 15 000				

TAHITI 2006–07

DIVISION FEDERALE STAGE 1

	Pl	W	D	L	F	A	Pts	Dragon	Tefana	Manu Ura	Pirae	Temanava	Tamarii	TAC	Vénus	Vairao
AS Dragon †	16	11	2	3	37	15	51		1-0	0-1	2-1	0-0	4-0	3-4	6-1	1-0
AS Tefana †	16	9	2	5	31	14	45	0-1		3-1	1-2	2-0	1-2	3-0	7-0	2-2
AS Manu Ura †	16	9	1	6	35	20	44	1-2	1-2		5-2	1-0	2-0	2-2	5-1	2-1
AS Pirae †	16	8	3	5	47	30	43	0-3	2-1	2-1		1-0	1-1	6-1	11-0	7-0
AS Temanava †	16	8	3	5	28	14	42	2-2	1-1	1-0	2-1		3-1	4-0	4-0	1-0
AS Tamarii Faa'a	16	8	1	7	30	33	41	3-1	0-3	0-6	4-1	**3-0**		5-1	3-2	4-2
AS Taravao AC	16	5	2	9	27	50	33	0-2	0-2	1-2	3-4	0-8	2-0		5-4	4-3
AS Vénus	16	5	1	10	23	55	32	0-3	0-1	3-2	4-4	2-0	2-1	0-2		3-1
AS Vairao	16	0	3	13	18	45	19	2-6	1-2	0-3	2-2	0-2	2-3	2-2	0-1	

31/08/2006 - 18/02/2007 • † Qualified for play-offs • Four points for a win, two points for a draw and one point for a defeat. Dragon took two bonus points forward as Stage 1 winners • Match in bold awarded

TAHITI 2006–07

DIVISION FEDERALE STAGE 1

	Pl	W	D	L	F	A	Pts	Manu Ura	Tefana	Temanava	Pirae	Dragon	Tamarii	TAC	Vairao	Vénus
AS Manu Ura	8	5	3	0	18	7	26		0-0	4-1	4-2	4-1				
AS Tefana	8	5	2	1	19	4	25	1-1		3-0	2-1	7-0				
AS Temanava	8	3	2	3	13	15	19	0-1	2-0		3-1	1-1				
AS Pirae	8	2	1	5	15	19	15	1-1	0-2	3-4		4-2				
AS Dragon	8	0	2	6	8	28	12	1-3	0-4	2-2	1-3					
AS Tamarii Faa'a	6	4	0	2	12	9	18							4-1	1-0	2-1
AS Taravao AC	6	3	0	3	12	11	15						4-0		4-2	2-0
AS Vairao	6	3	0	3	9	9	15						0-3	2-1		4-0
AS Vénus	6	2	0	4	7	11	12						3-2	3-0	0-1	

2/03/2007 - 1/06/2007 • † Qualified for the O–League • Top scorers: Naea BENNETT, Pirae 24; Samuel HNANYINE, Dragon 18

COUPE DE POLYNESIE 2006–07

Round of 16		Quarter–finals		Semi–finals		Final	
AS Tefana	3						
AS Roniu	0	**AS Tefana**	5 5				
AS Tamarii Faa'a	2	AS Pirae	1 0				
AS Pirae	3			**AS Tefana**	5 2		
AS Jeunes Tahitiens	1			AS Excelsior	1 1		
AS Temanava	0	AS Jeunes Tahitiens	1 1				
AS Dragon	1	**AS Excelsior**	2 1				
AS Excelsior	2					**AS Tefana**	1 1 4p
AS Vairao	2					AS Mana Ura	1 1 3p
AS Tohiea	0	**AS Vairao**	2 2				
AS Papenoo	1	AS Aorai	1 0				
AS Aorai	2			AS Vairao	1 0		
AS Vaiete	6			**AS Mana Ura**	5 4		
AS Mira	0	AS Vaiete	0 2				
AS Vénus	1	**AS Mana Ura**	5 6				
AS Mana Ura	2						

CUP FINAL
1st leg. Stade Punaruu 6-06-2007
2nd leg. Stade Punaruu 9-06-2007

RECENT LEAGUE AND CUP RECORD

Championship

Year	Champions
2000	AS Vénus
2001	AS Pirae
2002	AS Vénus
2003	AS Pirae
2004	AS Manu Ura
2005	AS Tefana
2006	AS Pirae
2007	AS Manu Ura

Cup

Winners	Score	Runners-up
AS Pirae		AS Vénus
AS Dragon	2-1	AS Vénus
AS Manu-Ura	0-0 4-3p	AS Pirae
AS Tefana	1-1 5-4p	AS Pirae
AS Manu-Ura	0-0 10-9p	AS Pirae
AS Tefana	2-0	AS Temariu

Polynesian Cup

Winners	Score	Runners-up
AS Pirae		
AS Vénus	6-0	Central Sport
AS Pirae	1-0	AS Vénus
AS Dragon	1-0	AS Manu Ura
AS Pirae	2-1	AS Manu Ura
AS Temanava	2-1	AS Dragon
AS Tefana	1-1 1-1 4-3p	AS Manu Ura

TAN – TANZANIA

NATIONAL TEAM RECORD
JULY 10TH 2006 TO JULY 12TH 2010

PL	W	D	L	F	A	%
15	7	6	2	18	13	66.6

FIFA/COCA-COLA WORLD RANKING

1993	1994	1995	1996	1997	1998	1999	2000	2001	2002	2003	2004	2005	2006	High		Low	
98	74	70	89	96	118	128	140	149	153	159	172	165	110	**65**	02/95	**175**	11/05

2006–2007											
08/06	09/06	10/06	11/06	12/06	01/07	02/07	03/07	04/07	05/07	06/07	07/07
134	105	121	120	110	109	109	110	116	117	118	105

The difference that active government support can make in the fortunes of football in an African county has been graphically illustrated in Tanzania where, for the first time in decades, the Taifa Stars stand on the brink of possible qualification for the 2008 African Nations Cup finals in Ghana. An away win in Burkina Faso in June 2007 represented a major breakthrough for the Tanzanians, normally tough to beat at home but a perennial walkover on the road. The election of the football loving Jakaya Kikwete as president of Tanzania in December 2005 has brought rich rewards for football, leading to investment by the government in a new Brazilian coach, Marco Maximo, the

INTERNATIONAL HONOURS
CECAFA Cup 1974 1994

bank rolling of extensive training camps in Europe and the staging of more regular friendlies and in a year and a half the national team has shot up over 60 places in the FIFA-Coca-Cola World Ranking. Maximo has developed an almost exclusively home-based squad into a competitive team that has pushed Senegal all the way in the battle for Nations Cup qualification. Tanzania's league title was won by Simba SC for the third time in four years but they needed a penalty shootout to overcome arch rivals Young Africans in the final of the end of the season play-off, which pits the top three teams in the mainland league with the top trio from the island of Zanzibar.

THE FIFA BIG COUNT OF 2006

	Male	Female		Total
Number of players	225 015	1 503	Referees and Assistant Referees	475
Professionals	18		Admin, Coaches, Technical, Medical	8 300
Amateurs 18+	13 500		Number of clubs	200
Youth under 18	12 800		Number of teams	5 000
Unregistered	200 200		Clubs with women's teams	4
Total players	226 518		Players as % of population	0.60%

The Football Association of Tanzania (FAT)
Karume Memorial Stadium, Uhuru/Shaurimoyo Street, PO Box 1574, Dar-es-Salaam, Tanzania
Tel +255 74 4264181   Fax +255 22 2861815
tfftz@yahoo.com   www.tfftanzania.com
President: TENGA Leodgar   General Secretary: MWAKALEBELA Frederik
Vice-President: MAGORI Crescentius   Treasurer: MWAKIBINGA Silas   Media Officer: KAIJAGE Florian
Men's Coach: MARCIO MAXIMO   Women's Coach: BAKARI Mohamed
FAT formed: 1930   CAF: 1960   FIFA: 1964
Green shirts, Black shorts, Green socks

RECENT INTERNATIONAL MATCHES PLAYED BY TANZANIA

2002	Opponents	Score		Venue	Comp	Scorers	Att	Referee
30-11	Kenya	W	1-0	Arusha	CCr1	Henry Morris [9]		
2-12	Sudan	D	1-1	Arusha	CCr1	Edward [81]		
5-12	Burundi	W	2-0	Arusha	CCr1	Machupa 2 [4 41]		
8-12	Eritrea	D	1-1	Arusha	CCr1	Mwakingwe [24]		
11-12	Rwanda	W	3-0	Arusha	CCsf	Mtiro [44], Edward [69], Machupa [83]		
14-12	Kenya	L	2-3	Arusha	CCf	Gabriel [28], Maxime [59p]		
2003								
12-03	Uganda	D	0-0	Arusha	Fr		30 000	
23-03	Kenya	L	0-4	Nairobi	Fr			
29-03	Zambia	L	0-1	Dar-es-Salaam	CNq		23 000	Haislemelk ETH
29-05	Uganda	L	1-3	Kampala	Fr	Kapirima [84p]		
31-05	Uganda	L	0-1	Kampala	Fr			
7-06	Zambia	L	0-2	Lusaka	CNq		30 000	Chilinda MWI
22-06	Benin	L	0-1	Dar-es-Salaam	CNq		20 000	
11-10	Kenya	D	0-0	Dar-es-Salaam	WCq		8 864	Tessema ETH
11-11	Uganda	L	1-2	Kampala	Fr	Abu Masula		
15-11	Kenya	L	0-3	Nairobi	WCq		14 000	El Beltagy EGY
2004								
13-12	Zanzibar †	L	2-4	Addis Abeba	CCr1	Maxime [23], Machupa [32]		
15-12	Burundi	L	0-2	Addis Abeba	CCr1			
17-12	Ethiopia	L	0-2	Addis Abeba	CCr1			
19-12	Rwanda	L	1-5	Addis Abeba	CCr1			
2005								
28-11	Burundi	W	2-1	Kigali	CCr1			
2-12	Zanzibar †	D	1-1	Kigali	CCr1			
4-12	Eritrea	W	1-0	Kigali	CCr1	Nurdin Bakari [38]		
6-12	Rwanda	L	1-3	Kigali	CCr1	Sammy Kessy		
2006								
26-06	Mauritius	W	2-1	Victoria	Fr	Abdi Kassim 2 [2p 19]		
30-06	Seychelles	L	1-2	Victoria	Fr	Salum Ussi [15]		
30-07	Rwanda	W	1-0	Dar es Salaam	Fr	Gaudence Mwaikimba [30]		
2-09	Burkina Faso	W	2-1	Dar es Salaam	CNq	OG [23], Nizar Khalfan [65]		Ndinya KEN
30-09	Kenya	D	0-0	Dar es Salaam	Fr			
8-10	Mozambique	D	0-0	Maputo	CNq			Kaoma ZAM
18-11	Angola	D	1-1	Dar es Salaam	Fr	Gaudence Mwaikimba [27]		
25-11	Ethiopia	W	2-1	Addis Abeba	CCr1	Amir Maftah [40], Bantu Adimin [60]		
28-11	Malawi	W	2-1	Addis Abeba	CCr1	Danny Mrwanda [5], Bantu Adimin [90]		
1-12	Djibouti	W	3-0	Addis Abeba	CCr1	Mrisho Ngassa [4], Hussein Swedi [44], Jerry Tegete [58]		
5-12	Rwanda	L	1-2	Addis Abeba	CCqf	Jerry Tegete [30]		
9-12	Congo DR	W	2-0	Dar es Salaam	Fr	Nizar Khalfan [36], Joseph Kaniki [86]		
2007								
24-03	Senegal	L	0-4	Dakar	CNq			Daami TUN
26-05	Uganda	D	1-1	Kampala	Fr	Nizar Khalfan [16]		
2-06	Senegal	D	1-1	Mwanza	CNq	Nizar Khalfan [18]		
9-06	Zambia	D	1-1	Morogoro	Fr	Danny Mrwanda [51]		
16-06	Burkina Faso	W	1-0	Ouagadougou	CNq	Henry Joseph [71]		

Fr = Friendly match • CN = CAF African Cup of Nations • CC = CECAFA Cup • WC = FIFA World Cup
q = qualifier • r1 = first round group • sf = semi-final • f = final • † Not a full international

TANZANIA NATIONAL TEAM RECORDS AND RECORD SEQUENCES

Records			Sequence records					
Victory	7-0	SOM 1995	Wins	5	1994	Clean sheets	5	1994
Defeat	0-9	KEN 1956	Defeats	6	Four times	Goals scored	11	1993-1994
Player Caps	n/a		Undefeated	9	1973-1975	Without goal	4	Four times
Player Goals	n/a		Without win	28	1984-1990	Goals against	12	2001-2002

TANZANIA COUNTRY INFORMATION

Capital	Dodoma	Independence	1964 from the UK	GDP per Capita	$600
Population	36 588 225	Status	Republic	GDP Ranking	88
Area km²	945 087	Language	Swahili, English	Dialling code	+255
Population density	38 per km²	Literacy rate	78%	Internet code	.tz
% in urban areas	24%	Main religion	Muslim 35%, Christian 30%	GMT + / –	+3
Towns/Cities ('000)	Dar es Salaam 2 698; Mwanza 436; Zanzibar 403; Arusha 341; Mbeya 291; Morogoro 250; Tanga 224; Dodoma 180; Kigoma 164; Moshi 156; Tabora 145; Songea 126, Musoma 121				
Neighbours (km)	Mozambique 756; Malawi 475; Zambia 338; Congo DR 459; Burundi 451; Rwanda 217; Uganda 396; Kenya 769; Indian Ocean 1 424				
Main stadia	National Stadium – Dar-es-Salaam 15 000; CCM Kirumba – Mwanza 30 000				

TANZANIA 2006 MAINLAND LEAGUE

	Pl	W	D	L	F	A	Pts
Young Africans	30	21	7	2	53	17	70
Simba SC	30	17	11	2	53	20	62
Mtibwa Sugar	30	17	7	6	58	29	58
Kagera Sugar	30	14	8	8	33	20	50
Moro United	30	12	8	10	37	34	44
Prisons	30	10	12	7	32	35	42
Polisi Morogoro	30	8	13	9	33	36	37
Ruvu Shooting Stars	30	10	7	13	29	43	37
Ashanti United	30	9	8	13	34	38	35
Twiga Sports	30	9	8	13	38	43	35
Arusha FC	30	10	4	16	30	36	34
Polisi Dodoma	30	8	9	13	28	33	33
JKT Ruvu Stars	30	8	9	13	27	31	33
Kahama United	30	9	6	15	33	51	33
Bandari	30	6	12	13	31	25	30
Transit Camp FC	30	5	5	20	21	48	20

25/02/2006 - 21/11/2006

TANZANIA 2007 STAGE 1

Group A - Arusha	Pl	W	D	L	F	A	Pts
Young Africans †	6	3	3	0	12	2	12
Polisi Morogoro †	6	3	2	1	8	4	11
Moro United	6	1	2	3	6	13	5
Arusha FC	6	1	1	4	6	13	4

Group B - Morogoro	Pl	W	D	L	F	A	Pts
Ashanti United †	6	4	1	1	6	2	13
Simba SC †	6	3	1	2	6	4	10
Prisons SC	6	1	2	3	5	8	5
Polisi Dodoma	6	1	2	3	4	7	5

Group C - Dodoma	Pl	W	D	L	F	A	Pts
Mtibwa Sugar †	7	3	3	1	8	4	12
JKT Ruvu Stars	7	3	2	2	8	5	11
Kagera Sugar	7	2	4	1	6	6	10
Ruvu Shooting Stars	7	2	2	3	5	7	8
Pan African	6	1	1	4	4	9	4

14/04/2007 - 4/05/2007 • † Qualified for the Super Six

TANZANIA 2007 STAGE 2

SUPER SIX

Group A - Arusha	Pl	W	D	L	F	A	Pts	YA	RS	MS
Young Africans	4	2	2	0	6	4	8		0-0	2-1
JKT Ruvu Stars	4	1	2	1	6	5	5	1-1		3-1
Mtibwa Sugar	4	1	0	3	7	10	3	2-3	3-2	

Group B - Morogoro	Pl	W	D	L	F	A	Pts	Si	PM	AU
Simba SC	4	3	1	0	7	1	10		0-0	2-0
Polisi Morogoro	4	2	1	1	3	3	7	0-3		1-0
Ashanti United	4	0	0	4	1	7	0	1-2	0-2	

FINAL

Jamhuri Stadium, Morogoro, 8-07-2007, Att: 9758, Ref: Mwandike
Simba SC 1-1 4-3p Young Africans
Scorers - Moses Odhiambo 2p for Simba; Said Maulid 56 for YANGA

RECENT LEAGUE AND CUP RECORD

	Tanzanian Mainland	Cup
Year	Champions	Winners
2000	Mtibwa Sugar	Simba SC Dar es Salaam
2001	Simba SC Dar es Salaam	Polisi Zanzibar
2002	Young Africans Dar es Salaam	Ruvu Stars
2003	Simba SC Dar es Salaam	
2004	Simba SC Dar es Salaam	
2005	Young Africans Dar es Salaam	
2007	Simba SC Dar es Salaam	

TCA – TURKS AND CAICOS ISLANDS

NATIONAL TEAM RECORD
JULY 10TH 2006 TO JULY 12TH 2010

PL	W	D	L	F	A	%
3	1	0	2	4	9	33.3

FIFA/COCA-COLA WORLD RANKING

1993	1994	1995	1996	1997	1998	1999	2000	2001	2002	2003	2004	2005	2006	High	Low
-	-	-	-	-	-	196	200	200	202	203	203	203	169	166 07/07	204 05/06

2006-2007											
08/06	09/06	10/06	11/06	12/06	01/07	02/07	03/07	04/07	05/07	06/07	07/07
197	170	168	171	169	169	169	168	168	168	166	166

2006 was an historic year in the annals of football in the Turks and Caicos Islands with the national team winning an international match for the first time. Only 100 people were inside Havana's Pedro Marrero stadium to witness the 2-0 victory over the Cayman Islands but that couldn't dampen the celebrations after the match. The team hadn't scored a goal for over seven years, so to score two was an added bonus. To then score two more in their next match two days later was beyond their wildest dreams. The Turks and Caicos team had travelled to Havana to take part in a first round qualifying group in the Digicel Caribbean Cup and they lost their first match against the

INTERNATIONAL HONOURS
None

hosts 6-0. In their final match they needed to beat the Bahamas to qualify for the next round and they took the lead in the second half and were still level at 2-2 with three minutes to go before Nesley Jean put an end to their dreams with a late winner for the Bahamas. With three of the four goals scored by the national team in Havana, striker Gavin Clinton now heads the all-time list having scored half of the six goals the Turks and Caicos have managed since playing their first international match in 1999. In March 2006 a new headquarters for the football association was approved by FIFA's Goal Bureau which will be integrated into the national training centre.

THE FIFA BIG COUNT OF 2006

	Male	Female		Total
Number of players	1 540	615	Referees and Assistant Referees	12
Professionals	0		Admin, Coaches, Technical, Medical	35
Amateurs 18+	165		Number of clubs	9
Youth under 18	450		Number of teams	9
Unregistered	1 000		Clubs with women's teams	0
Total players	2 155		Players as % of population	10.19%

Turks and Caicos Islands Football Association (TCIFA)
Tropicana Plaza, Leeward Highway, PO Box 626, Providenciales, Turks and Caicos Islands
Tel +1 649 9415532   Fax +1 649 9415554
tcifa@tciway.tc   www.football.tc
President: BRYAN Christopher   General Secretary: BIEN-AIME Sonia
Vice-President: SLATTERY James   Treasurer: DOUGLAS Jenny   Media Officer: None
Men's Coach: GREEN Matthew   Women's Coach: GREEN Matthew
TCIFA formed: 1996   CONCACAF: 1998   FIFA: 1998
White shirts, White shorts, White socks

RECENT INTERNATIONAL MATCHES PLAYED BY TURKS AND CAICOS

2002	Opponents	Score	Venue	Comp	Scorers	Att	Referee
No international matches played in 2002							
2003							
No international matches played in 2003							
2004							
18-02	Haiti	L 0-5	Miami †	WCq		3 000	Stott USA
21-02	Haiti	L 0-2	Hialeah †	WCq		3 000	Valenzuela USA
2005							
No international matches played in 2005							
2006							
2-09	Cuba	L 0-6	Havana	CCq			
4-09	Cayman Islands	W 2-0	Havana	CCq	Gavin Clinton 14, Maxime Fleuriot 72	100	Stennett JAM
6-09	Bahamas	L 2-3	Havana	CCq	Gavin Clinton 2 51 72	120	Campbell JAM
2007							
No international matches played in 2007 before August							

CC = Digicel Caribbean Cup • WC = FIFA World Cup • q = qualifier • † Both matches played in the USA

TURKS AND CAICOS ISLANDS NATIONAL TEAM RECORDS AND RECORD SEQUENCES

Records			Sequence records		
Victory	2-0	CAY 2006	Wins	1		Clean sheets	1	
Defeat	0-8	SKN 2000	Defeats	6	2000-2006	Goals scored	2	2006
Player Caps	n/a		Undefeated	1	1999, 2006	Without goal	6	2000-2006
Player Goals	3	Gavin CLINTON	Without win	8	1999-2006	Goals against	8	1999-2006

TURKS AND CAICOS ISLANDS 2006-07 MFL LEAGUE

	Pl	W	D	L	F	A	Pts
Beaches	10	8	2	0	39	11	**26**
Provo Haitian Stars	9	6	1	2	33	11	19
PWC Athletic	9	5	2	2	26	17	17
SWA Sharks	10	4	0	6	22	40	12
ProvoPool	10	2	0	8	24	43	6
Cost Right	10	1	1	8	12	34	4

7/10/2006 - 24/03/2007

RECENT LEAGUE AND CUP RECORD

	Championship						Cup		
Year	Champions	Pts	Runners-up	Pts	Third	Pts	Winners	Score	Runners-up
1999	Tropic All Stars	15	Fleches Rapides	13	Provo	7	No tournament		
2000	Masters	16	Beaches	10	Sans Complex	4	Masters	2-0	Beaches
2001	Sharks	1-0	Projetech				No tournament		
2002	Beaches †	2-2	Barefoot				No tournament		
2003	Caribbean All Stars	28	Master Hammer	25	KPMG United	13	Caribbean All Stars	2-1	Master Hammer
2004	KPMG United	27	Caribbean All Stars	22	Police	14	Police	4-3	KPMG United
2005	KPMG United	30	Caribbean All Stars	25	Cost Right	14			
2006	Beaches	19	Cost Right	18	Caribbean All Stars	17	Beaches	2-1	Provopool
2007	Beaches	26	Provo Haitian Stars	19	PWC Athletic	17			

† Final abandoned at 2-2. Beaches declared champions

TURKS AND CAICOS ISLANDS COUNTRY INFORMATION

Capital	Cockburn Town	Status	Overseas territory of the UK	GDP per Capita	$9 600
Population	19 956			GNP Ranking	n/a
Area km²	430	Language	English	Dialling code	+1649
Population density	46 per km²	Literacy rate	98%	Internet code	.tc
% in urban areas	n/a	Main religion	Christian	GMT +/–	-4
Towns/Cities	Cockburn Town 5 525; Cockburn Harbour 1 744				
Neighbours (km)	North Atlantic Ocean 389				
Main stadia	National Development Facility – Providenciales 1 500				

TGA – TONGA

NATIONAL TEAM RECORD
JULY 10TH 2006 TO JULY 12TH 2010

PL	W	D	L	F	A	%
0	0	0	0	0	0	0

FIFA/COCA-COLA WORLD RANKING

1993	1994	1995	1996	1997	1998	1999	2000	2001	2002	2003	2004	2005	2006	High	Low
-	-	-	164	174	163	178	185	173	175	180	183	185	188	163 10/98	192 07/07

2006–2007											
08/06	09/06	10/06	11/06	12/06	01/07	02/07	03/07	04/07	05/07	06/07	07/07
189	191	190	191	188	189	190	190	188	190	191	192

With the national team inactive since the World Cup qualifiers in May 2004, it was left to the women's national team to represent the country abroad as they took part in the Oceania championship in Papua New Guinea. The tournament doubled as a qualifying group for the 2007 Women's World Cup but after a 6-1 defeat at the hands of New Zealand in the opening match there was little chance of Tonga making it to the finals in China. With a number of players in the team who were runners-up at the Oceania U–19 Championship in 2006, Tonga recovered for the next two games, losing narrowly to Papua New Guinea and then holding Samoa to a 0-0 draw. The trip

INTERNATIONAL HONOURS
None

to Papua New Guinea was the only international action in the entire season after both the men's under–20 and under–17 teams didn't enter their respective OFC tournaments. The 2006 Tongan champions SC Lotoha'apai from the capital Nuku'alofa also failed to enter the inaugural OFC O–League at the start of 2007 and they were also absent from the qualifying group for the 2007-08 tournament. With King George Tupou V opening the second phase of the Goal project in March, Tonga has excellent football facilities at its disposal and it's now up to the players and administrators on the island to make the most of them.

THE FIFA BIG COUNT OF 2006

	Male	Female		Total
Number of players	4 600	400	Referees and Assistant Referees	100
Professionals	0		Admin, Coaches, Technical, Medical	100
Amateurs 18+	2 100		Number of clubs	100
Youth under 18	1 100		Number of teams	220
Unregistered	700		Clubs with women's teams	5
Total players	5 000		Players as % of population	4.36%

Tonga Football Association (FTF)
Loto Tonga Soko Center, Off Taufa'Ahau Road - 'Atele, PO Box 852, Nuku'alofa, Tonga
Tel +676 30233   Fax +676 30240
tfa@kalianet.to   www.tongafootball.com
President: VEEHALA Hon   General Secretary: FUSIMALOHI Ahongalu
Vice-President: FUSITUA Hon   Treasurer: AHO Lui   Media Officer: None
Men's Coach: JANKOVIC Milan   Women's Coach: UELE Kilifi
FTF formed: 1965   OFC: 1994   FIFA: 1994
Red shirts, White shorts, Red socks

RECENT INTERNATIONAL MATCHES PLAYED BY TONGA

2002	Opponents		Score	Venue	Comp	Scorers	Att	Referee
No international matches played in 2002 after June								
2003								
1-07	Papua New Guinea	D	2-2	Suva	SPr1		3 000	Singh FIJ
3-07	New Caledonia	L	0-4	Suva	SPr1		700	Shah FIJ
5-07	Micronesia †	W	7-0	Nausori	SPr1	Fonua [5], Tevi [15], Uhatahi 2 [22 36], Feao 2 [34 55], Uele [72]	1 000	Moli SOL
7-07	Tahiti	L	0-4	Lautoka	SPr1		3 000	Shah FIJ
2004								
10-05	Solomon Islands	L	0-6	Honiara	WCq		12 385	Attison VAN
15-05	Cook Islands	W	2-1	Honiara	WCq	Uhatahi [46], Vaitaki [61]	15 000	Sosongan PNG
17-05	Tahiti	L	0-2	Honiara	WCq		400	Sosongan PNG
19-05	New Caledonia	L	0-8	Honiara	WCq		14 000	Fred VAN
2005								
No international matches played in 2005								
2006								
No international matches played in 2006								
2007								
No international matches played in 2007 before August								

Fr = Friendly match • SP = South Pacific Games • WC = FIFA World Cup™ • q = qualifier • r1 = first round group • † Not a full international

TONGA NATIONAL TEAM RECORDS AND RECORD SEQUENCES

Records			Sequence records					
Victory	5-0	ASA 2001	Wins	3	1994-1996	Clean sheets	2	1996
Defeat	0-22	AUS 2001	Defeats	4	1998-2000	Goals scored	4	1994-96, 2000-01
Player Caps	n/a		Undefeated	4	1994-1996	Without goal	4	1993-1994
Player Goals	n/a		Without win	6	1983-1994	Goals against	12	2001-2004

TONGA CHAMPIONS

Year	Champions
1998	SC Lotoha'apai Nuku'alofa
1999	SC Lotoha'apai Nuku'alofa
2000	SC Lotoha'apai Nuku'alofa
2001	SC Lotoha'apai Nuku'alofa
2002	SC Lotoha'apai Nuku'alofa
2003	SC Lotoha'apai Nuku'alofa
2004	SC Lotoha'apai Nuku'alofa
2005	SC Lotoha'apai Nuku'alofa
2006	SC Lotoha'apai Nuku'alofa

TONGA COUNTRY INFORMATION

Capital	Nuku'alofa	Independence	1970 from the UK	GDP per Capita	$2 200
Population	110 237	Status	Constitutional Monarchy	GNP Ranking	186
Area km²	748	Language	Tongan, English	Dialling code	+676
Population density	147 per km²	Literacy rate	98%	Internet code	.to
% in urban areas	41%	Main religion	Christian	GMT + / −	+13
Towns/Cities ('000)	Nuku'alofa 23; Mu'a 5; Neiafu 4; Haveloloto 3; Vaini 3; Tofoa-Koloua 2; Pangai 2				
Neighbours (km)	South Pacific Ocean 419				
Main stadia	Mangweni Stadium – Nuku'alofa 3 000				

THA – THAILAND

NATIONAL TEAM RECORD
JULY 10TH 2006 TO JULY 12TH 2010

PL	W	D	L	F	A	%
18	9	5	4	26	20	63.8

FIFA/COCA-COLA WORLD RANKING

1993	1994	1995	1996	1997	1998	1999	2000	2001	2002	2003	2004	2005	2006	High	Low
69	85	77	57	54	45	60	61	61	66	60	79	111	137	43 09/98	137 12/06

2006–2007											
08/06	09/06	10/06	11/06	12/06	01/07	02/07	03/07	04/07	05/07	06/07	07/07
111	114	125	125	137	124	126	120	119	120	122	107

So near and yet so far. Thailand came within a whisker of making it through to the quarter-finals of the 2007 AFC Asian Cup which they were co-hosting, but after a 4-0 defeat against Australia in their final game, it wasn't to be. Before the tournament began, there was much speculation as to how the four co-hosts would get on and if any of them would get past the group stage, but the Thais settled their nerves by drawing with Iraq in the opening match of the tournament, which was played in heavy rain at the Rajamangala Stadium in Bangkok after the opening ceremony. They then won their next match against Oman before facing Australia. Thailand needed a draw to progress and

INTERNATIONAL HONOURS
SEA Games 1965 1975 1981 1983 1985 1993 1995 1997 1999 2001 2003 **Tiger Cup** 1996 2000 2002
AFC Champions League Thai Farmers Bank 1994 1995

although they dominated for much of the game after Australia had taken an early lead, three goals in the last ten minutes sealed their fate. Earlier in the season Chanwit Pholchivin's team had won the King's Cup played in Bangkok and had reached the final of the ASEAN Football Federation Championship before losing to Singapore. At club level the split that had marred the 2006 season was resolved as the two competing leagues joined forces with the new 16 team Thai League kicking off in March 2007.

THE FIFA BIG COUNT OF 2006

	Male	Female		Total
Number of players	1 207 500	90 500	Referees and Assistant Referees	1 100
Professionals	500		Admin, Coaches, Technical, Medical	5 500
Amateurs 18+	10 700		Number of clubs	150
Youth under 18	16 500		Number of teams	1 790
Unregistered	332 400		Clubs with women's teams	0
Total players	1 298 000		Players as % of population	2.01%

The Football Association of Thailand (FAT)
National Stadium, Gate 3, Rama 1 Road, Patumwan, Bangkok 10330, Thailand
Tel +66 2 2164691   Fax +66 2 2154494
www.fat.org.th
President: MAKUDI Worawi   General Secretary: KOSINKAR Ong-Arj
Vice-President: JANGJANKIT Rangsarit   Treasurer: CHANAWONGSE Kasom   Media Officer: None
Men's Coach: PHOLCHIVIN Chanwit   Women's Coach: YAPAPHA Suphon
FAT formed: 1916   AFC: 1957   FIFA: 1925
Red shirts, Red shorts, Red socks

RECENT INTERNATIONAL MATCHES PLAYED BY THAILAND

2004	Opponents	Score		Venue	Comp	Scorers	Att	Referee
5-07	Bahrain	L	0-2	Bangkok	Fr			
8-07	Jordan	D	0-0	Bangkok	Fr			
10-07	Trinidad and Tobago	W	3-2	Bangkok	Fr	Vachiraban [47], Suksomkit [53], Pichitpong [87]		
20-07	Iran	L	0-3	Chongqing	ACr1		37 000	Kousa SYR
24-07	Japan	L	1-4	Chongqing	ACr1	Suksomkit [11]	45 000	Al Marzouqi UAE
28-07	Oman	L	0-2	Chengdu	ACr1		13 000	Lu Jun CHN
19-08	Malaysia	L	1-2	Bangkok	Fr	Chaiman [90]		
8-09	Korea DPR	L	1-4	Pyongyang	WCq	Suksomkit [72]	20 000	Moradi IRN
8-10	Jordan	L	2-3	Bangkok	Fr			
13-10	United Arab Emirates	W	3-0	Bangkok	WCq	Jakapong [10], Nanok [30], Chaiman [67]	15 000	Nishimura JPN
17-11	Yemen	D	1-1	Bangkok	WCq	Siriwong [95+]	15 000	Baskar IND
30-11	Estonia	D	0-0	Bangkok	Fr	W 4-3p	35 000	Mat Amin MAS
2-12	Slovakia	D	1-1	Bangkok	Fr	Joemdee [15p]. L 4-5p	5 000	Chappanimutu MAS
10-12	Myanmar	D	1-1	Kuala Lumpur	TCr1	Chaiman [14]		Moradi IRN
12-12	East Timor †	W	8-0	Kuala Lumpur	TCr1	Yodyingyong [17], Domthaisong [41], Jitkuntod [53], Chaiman [59], Chaikamdee 3 [63 65 67], Konjan [84]		Vo Minh Try VIE
14-12	Malaysia	L	1-2	Kuala Lumpur	TCr1	Chaikamdee [45]	10 000	Moradi IRN
16-12	Philippines	W	3-1	Kuala Lumpur	TCr1	Poolsap [42], Sainui [56], Domthaisong [89]	300	Vo Minh Try VIE
21-12	Germany	L	1-5	Bangkok	Fr	Chaikamdee [57]	15 000	Maidin SIN
2005								
24-12	Latvia	D	1-1	Phang Nga	Fr	Teeratep [56]		
28-12	Korea DPR	L	0-2	Phuket	Fr			
2006								
1-02	Jordan	D	0-0	Ayutthaya	Fr			
16-02	Iraq	W	4-3	Ayutthaya	Fr	Prat 2 OG [10], Nirut [12], Apichate [55]		
26-03	Philippines	W	5-0	Chonburi	Fr	Bunkham [13], Teeratep 2 [20 44], Jaiharn [58], Phona [90]		
10-08	China PR	L	0-4	Qinhuangdao	Fr			
24-12	Vietnam	W	2-1	Bangkok	Fr	Sarayoot [36], Datsakorn [61]		
26-12	Singapore	W	2-0	Bangkok	Fr	Kiatsuk 2 [58 63]		
28-12	Kazakhstan	D	2-2	Bangkok	Fr	Suchao [41], Pipat [58]		
30-12	Vietnam	W	3-1	Bangkok	Fr	Sutee [38], Pipat [43], Suchao [69]		
2007								
12-01	Myanmar	D	1-1	Bangkok	TCr1	Suchao [94+]	15 000	Matsuo JPN
14-01	Philippines	W	4-0	Bangkok	TCr1	Sarayoot 2 [15 28], Pipat [21], Natthaphong [84]	30 000	
16-01	Malaysia	W	1-0	Bangkok	TCr1	Sarayoot [48]	25 000	Matsuo JPN
24-01	Vietnam	W	2-0	Hanoi	TCsf	Datsakorn [28], Pipat [81]	40 000	Napitupulu IDN
28-01	Vietnam	D	0-0	Bangkok	TCsf		35 000	Srinivasan IND
31-01	Singapore	L	1-2	Singapore	TCf	Pipat [50]	55 000	Ravichandran MAS
4-02	Singapore	D	1-1	Bangkok	TCf	Pipat [37]	30 000	Napitupulu IDN
16-05	China PR	W	1-0	Bangkok	Fr	Pipat [40]		
6-06	Netherlands	L	1-3	Bangkok	Fr	Tawan [65]	20 000	Ganesan SIN
2-07	Qatar	W	2-0	Bangkok	Fr	Tawan [8], Sutee [69p]		
7-07	Iraq	D	1-1	Bangkok	ACr1	Sutee [6p]	30 000	Kwon Jong Chul KOR
12-07	Oman	W	2-0	Bangkok	ACr1	Pipat 2 [70 78]	19 000	Lee Gi Young KOR
16-07	Australia	L	0-4	Bangkok	ACr1		46 000	Kwon Jong Chul KOR

Fr = Friendly match • TC = Tiger Cup/ASEAN Football Federation Championship • AC = AFC Asian Cup • WC = FIFA World Cup
q = qualifier • r1 = 1st round • sf = semi-final • f = final • † Not a full international

THAILAND NATIONAL TEAM RECORDS AND RECORD SEQUENCES

Records				Sequence records				
Victory	10-0	BRU 1970		Wins	8	1993	Clean sheets	4	Five times
Defeat	0-8	CZE 1968		Defeats	11	1959-1961	Goals scored	19	1960-1963
Player Caps	117	KIATISUK SENAMUANG		Undefeated	11	1995-1996	Without goal	9	1990-1991
Player Goals	64	KIATISUK SENAMUANG		Without win	23	1959-1963	Goals against	31	1959-1965

THAILAND COUNTRY INFORMATION

Capital	Bangkok	Foundation	1238	GDP per Capita	$7 400
Population	64 865 523	Status	Constitutional Monarchy	GNP Ranking	32
Area km²	514 000	Language	Thai	Dialling code	+66
Population density	126 per km²	Literacy rate	92%	Internet code	.th
% in urban areas	20%	Main religion	Buddhist	GMT + / −	+7

Towns/Cities ('000)	Bangkok 5 104; Samut Prakan 388; Nonthaburi 375; Udon Thani 247; Chon Buri 219; Nakhon Ratchasima 208; Chiang Mai 201; Hat Yai 191; Pak Kret 183; Si Racha 179
Neighbours (km)	Laos 1 754; Cambodia 803; Malaysia 506; Myanmar 1 800; Gulf of Thailand 3 219
Main stadia	Rajamangala – Bangkok 65 000; Suphachalasai – Bangkok 30 000

THAILAND 2006

PROFESSIONAL LEAGUE

Team	P	W	D	L	F	A	Pts	TOT	Port Authority	Nak. Pathom	Nak. Sawan	Narathiwat	Phitsanulok	Surat Thani	Chanthaburi	Bangkok	N. Ratchasima	Khon Kaen	Si Sa Ket	Sakon Nakhon	Chachoengsao	Satun	Chiang Mai
Telephone – TOT	30	19	10	1	72	22	67		0-2	1-1	0-0	2-1	1-1	2-2	3-1	2-0	5-1	3-0	5-3	0-0	7-0	2-2	3-1
Port Authority	30	20	6	4	55	23	66	1-1		0-0	1-0	3-0	4-4	1-0	1-2	3-3	2-0	1-0	2-0	1-1	1-1	1-0	2-1
Nakhon Pathom	30	17	11	2	42	15	62	0-1	1-0		0-0	2-0	1-0	2-0	3-1	0-0	1-1	1-0	0-2	3-2	2-0	1-0	4-0
Nakhon Sawan	30	14	9	7	42	28	51	1-1	0-1	0-1		0-0	2-2	3-1	5-0	0-1	2-1	1-1	3-0	1-0	1-0	1-0	2-0
Narathiwat	30	13	6	11	37	34	45	1-1	0-3	0-1	1-3		2-0	2-1	1-0	1-1	0-0	1-1	1-0	3-0	2-0	3-1	3-0
Phitsanulok	30	11	9	10	44	38	42	1-2	0-3	2-2	4-1	2-0		3-0	1-2	4-3	3-2	0-1	3-0	1-1	2-0	2-0	0-0
Surat Thani	30	11	8	11	44	46	41	0-2	2-3	0-3	1-0	1-1	1-0		3-3	2-1	1-2	2-4	2-1	6-1	1-0		4-1
Chanthaburi	30	11	7	12	52	45	40	1-1	2-1	1-2	6-1	0-1	3-2	0-1		0-1	2-2	0-1	3-2	1-0	3-0	5-0	5-0
Bangkok	30	9	12	9	31	34	39	0-2	0-2	0-0	0-1	2-1	0-0	1-1	0-1		0-1	0-0	2-0	2-1	2-2	1-0	0-0
Nakhon Ratchasima	30	8	12	10	37	43	36	0-2	1-3	1-3	1-1	2-1	0-0	1-2	2-1	1-2		2-1	1-1	1-1	2-1	2-1	1-1
Khon Kaen	30	9	8	13	32	35	35	0-2	0-1	1-3	1-1	2-1	2-0	1-2	2-0	3-2	2-1		3-0	1-0	0-1	3-3	1-0
Si Sa Ket	30	9	6	15	47	59	33	1-4	1-3	0-0	1-1	2-0	1-1	1-3	3-3	0-0	1-4	2-0		3-0	1-2	3-1	4-0
Sakon Nakhon	30	8	7	15	30	44	31	0-2	0-2	2-2	0-2	1-3	1-0	2-0	1-1	2-3	1-0	1-0	2-3		2-0	1-0	1-0
Chachoengsao	30	8	7	15	32	55	31	0-4	1-0	0-0	2-2	0-2	1-2	1-1	1-1	3-1	2-2	3-1	5-2	0-1		1-2	1-2
Satun	30	6	6	18	34	54	24	0-2	2-6	1-3	1-2	2-3	3-0	1-1	0-0	0-0	1-1	2-1	3-1	5-3	1-2		0-2
Chiang Mai	30	3	4	23	19	75	13	0-9	0-1	0-3	0-4	1-3	0-2	1-3	3-2	2-3	0-2	0-2	2-5	2-2	0-1	0-2	

14/01/2006 - 20/08/2006

RECENT LEAGUE RECORD

	Championship					
Year	Champions	Pts	Runners-up	Pts	Third	Pts
1997	Royal Thai Air Force	42	Sinthana	42	Bangkok Bank	38
1998	Sinthana	42	Royal Thai Air Force	40	BEC Tero Sasana	38
1999	Royal Thai Air Force	39	Port Authority	39	BEC Tero Sasana	39
2000	BEC Tero Sasana	49	Royal Thai Air Force	41	Thai Farmers Bank	37
2002	BEC Tero Sasana	50	Osotapa	44	Bangkok Bank	35
2003	Krung Thai Bank	36	BEC Tero Sasana	35	Port Authority	33
2004	Krung Thai Bank	38	BEC Tero Sasana	34	Osotapa	33
2005	Thailand Tobacco	34	Electical Authority	32	Osotapa	32
2006	Bangkok University	39	Osotspa	38	BEC Tero Sasana	36
2006	TOT	67	Port Authority	66	Nakhon Pathom	62

TJK – TAJIKISTAN

NATIONAL TEAM RECORD
JULY 10TH 2006 TO JULY 12TH 2010

PL	W	D	L	F	A	%
0	0	0	0	0	0	0

FIFA/COCA-COLA WORLD RANKING

1993	1994	1995	1996	1997	1998	1999	2000	2001	2002	2003	2004	2005	2006	High	Low
-	155	164	163	118	120	119	134	154	168	137	136	141	124	**114** 07/97	**180** 10/03

2006–2007											
08/06	09/06	10/06	11/06	12/06	01/07	02/07	03/07	04/07	05/07	06/07	07/07
116	122	140	119	124	125	127	127	145	147	147	145

Following on from success of the national team in winning the inaugural AFC Challenge Cup, both the under–20 and the under–17 teams took part in the finals of the AFC tournaments. The under–20s struggled in their first round group, failing to pick up a point but at the under–17 tournament in Singapore, Tajikistan not only won their first round group, but finished in third place. Iran, Iraq and Yemen were all dispatched at the group stage whilst South Korea were beaten 1-0 in the quarter-finals before a 3-0 defeat at the hands of North Korea put paid to any hopes of a third Asian title in the space of 18 months. By reaching the semi-finals, the Tajiks

INTERNATIONAL HONOURS
AFC Challenge Cup 2006   AFC President's Cup Regar TadAZ 2005

qualified for the 2007 FIFA U–17 World Cup in South Korea - an historic first appearance on the world stage for the country. In club football 2006 champions Regar TadAz were due to take part in the AFC President's Cup in May 2007 in Pakistan as they looked to regain the title they won in 2005 but the event was postponed until September due to visas problems in the host country. Regar had won the title in a close battle with Khima Dushanbe, a 7-5 victory over Tajiktelecom clinching their fifth title in six years, as well as the double. Two months earlier they had beaten Khima 2-1 in the Cup Final thanks to a winner from Tajik player of the year Khurshed Makmudov.

THE FIFA BIG COUNT OF 2006

	Male	Female		Total
Number of players	123 563	9 330	Referees and Assistant Referees	56
Professionals	428		Admin, Coaches, Technical, Medical	267
Amateurs 18+	980		Number of clubs	40
Youth under 18	2 135		Number of teams	260
Unregistered	32 150		Clubs with women's teams	10
Total players	132 893		Players as % of population	1.82%

Tajikistan Football Federation (TFF)
14/ Ainy Street, Dushanbe 734 025, Tajikistan
Tel +992 372 212447   Fax +992 372 510157
tff@tajikfootball.org   www.none
President: KOSIMOV Sukhrob   General Secretary: DAVLATOV Sherali
Vice-President: TURSUNOV Valery   Treasurer: KHOLOV Sherali   Media Officer: BURIEV Aloviddin
Men's Coach: KHABIBULLOEV Mahmad   Women's Coach: SATTOROV Shavkat
TFF formed: 1936   AFC: 1994   FIFA: 1994
White shirts, White shorts, White socks

RECENT INTERNATIONAL MATCHES PLAYED BY TAJIKISTAN

2002 Opponents	Score	Venue	Comp	Scorers	Att	Referee
No international matches played in 2002						
2003						
6-11 Thailand	W 1-0	Tashkent	ACq	Fuzailov [79]		
8-11 Hong Kong	D 0-0	Tashkent	ACq			
10-11 Uzbekistan	D 0-0	Tashkent	ACq			
17-11 Uzbekistan	L 1-4	Bangkok	ACq	Burkhanov [65]		
19-11 Thailand	L 0-1	Bangkok	ACq			
21-11 Hong Kong	W 1-0	Bangkok	ACq	Muhidinov [68]		
26-11 Bangladesh	W 2-0	Dhaka	WCq	Hamidov [11], Hakimov [51]	6 000	Khanthachai THA
30-11 Bangladesh	W 2-0	Dushanbe	WCq	Kholomatov [15], Rabiev [83]	12 000	Pereira IND
2004						
18-02 Kyrgyzstan	W 2-1	Bishkek	WCq	Burkhanon 2 [31 53]	14 000	Lutfullin UZB
31-03 Bahrain	D 0-0	Dushanbe	WCq		17 000	Maidin SIN
10-06 Syria	L 1-2	Homs	WCq	Kholomatov [35]	18 000	Al Fadhli KUW
8-09 Syria	L 0-1	Dushanbe	WCq		18 000	Mohd Salleh MAS
13-10 Kyrgyzstan	W 2-1	Dushanbe	WCq	Rabiev [19], Hakimov [37]	11 000	Naser Al Enezi KUW
17-11 Bahrain	L 0-4	Manama	WCq		15 000	Sun Baojie CHN
6-12 Kuwait	L 0-3	Kuwait City	Fr			
2005						
25-01 Saudi Arabia	L 0-3	Riyadh	Fr			
9-11 Afghanistan	W 4-0	Dushanbe	Fr	Hakimov 2 [28 31], Makhmudov [45], Ashurmamadov [67]		
2006						
14-02 Qatar	L 0-2	Doha	Fr			
2-04 Macau	W 4-0	Dhaka	CCr1	Makhmudov [9], Rabiev [13], Rabimov [56], Khojaev [77]	2 000	Mombini IRN
4-04 Pakistan	W 2-0	Dhaka	CCr1	Hakimov [14], Irgashev [20]	5 000	Tan Hai CHN
6-04 Kyrgyzstan	L 0-1	Dhaka	CCr1		2 000	AK Nema IRQ
10-04 Bangladesh	W 6-1	Dhaka	CCqf	Rabimov [2], Makhmudov [20], Muhidinov [31], Hakimov [51], Rabiev [65], Nematov [81]	15 000	AK Nema IRQ
13-04 Kyrgyzstan	W 2-0	Dhaka	CCsf	Rabiev 2 [51 92+]	2 000	Tan Hai CHN
16-04 Sri Lanka	W 4-0	Dhaka	CCf	Muhidinov 3 [1 61 71], Makhmudov [45]	2 000	Mombini IRN
2-07 Kazakhstan	L 1-4	Almaty	Fr	Saidov [75]		
2007						
No international matches played in 2007 before August						

Fr = Friendly match • AC = AFC Asian Cup • CC = AFC Challenge Cup • WC = FIFA World Cup
q = qualifier • r1 = first round group • qf = quarter-final • sf = semi-final • f = final

TAJIKISTAN NATIONAL TEAM RECORDS AND RECORD SEQUENCES

Records			Sequence records				
Victory	16-0	GUM 2000	Wins	4	2003-2004	Clean sheets	3	1997, 2003, 2003
Defeat	0-5	UZB 1996, IRN 1998	Defeats	3	Three times	Goals scored	5	1997-98, 1998-99
Player Caps	n/a		Undefeated	5	2003-2004	Without goal	3	1993-94, 2004-05
Player Goals	n/a		Without win	5	1998-1999	Goals against	7	1998-1999

TAJIKISTAN COUNTRY INFORMATION

Capital	Dushanbe	Independence	1991 from the USSR	GDP per Capita	$1 000
Population	7 011 556	Status	Republic	GNP Ranking	152
Area km²	143 100	Language	Tajik, Russian	Dialling code	+992
Population density	49 per km²	Literacy rate	99%	Internet code	.tj
% in urban areas	32%	Main religion	Muslim	GMT +/–	+5
Towns/Cities ('000)	Dushanbe 543; Khujand 144; Kulob 78; Qurgonteppa 60; Uroteppa 52; Konibodom 50				
Neighbours (km)	China 414; Afghanistan 1 206; Uzbekistan 1 161 Kyrgyzstan 870;				
Main stadia	National Stadium – Dushanbe 20 000				

TAJIKISTAN 2006 PREMIER DIVISION

	Pl	W	D	L	F	A	Pts
Regar TadAZ †	22	18	1	3	65	19	55
Khima Dushanbe	22	17	3	2	58	15	54
Vakhsh Qurghonteppa	22	15	2	5	41	18	47
Parvoz B. Gafurov	22	15	2	5	39	25	47
CSKA Dushanbe	22	11	2	9	38	31	35
TojikTelecom Qur'teppa	22	11	2	9	41	38	35
FK Hujand	22	9	3	10	27	33	30
SKA Pamir Dushanbe	22	5	5	12	24	39	20
Olimi Karimzod Mastchoh	22	5	4	13	22	39	19
Saroykamar Panj	22	5	2	15	27	50	17
Oriyono Dushanbe	22	3	4	15	25	53	13
Dinamo Dushanbe	22	0	6	16	12	59	6

23/04/2006 - 3/12/2006 • † Qualified for the AFC President's Cup

TAJIKISTAN CUP 2006

First round	Quarter–finals	Semi–finals	Final
Regar TadAZ			
	Regar TadAZ		
		Regar TadAZ 3 0	
		Parvoz B. Gafurov 0 2	
	Parvoz B. Gafurov		
Parvoz B. Gafurov			Regar TadAZ 2
Vakhsh Qurghonteppa			Khima Dushanbe 1
	Vakhsh Qurghonteppa		
		Vakhsh Qurghonteppa 1 1	
		Khima Dushanbe 2 1	
	Khima Dushanbe		
Khima Dushanbe		* Home team in the first leg	

CUP FINAL

National Stadium, Dushanbe
5-10-2006

Scorers - Ibraguim Rabimov, Khurshed Makmudov for Regar; Rakhmatullo Fuzaylov for Hima

RECENT LEAGUE AND CUP RECORD

		Championship						Cup		
Year	Champions	Pts	Runners-up	Pts	Third	Pts		Winners	Score	Runners-up
1992	Pamir Dushanbe	33	Regar TadAZ	26	Vakhsh Qur'teppa	24		Pamir Dushanbe	1-0	Regar TadAZ
1993	Sitora Dushanbe	55	Pamir Dushanbe	52	P'takor Proletarsk	42		Sitora Dushanbe	0-0 5-3p	Ravshan Kulyab
1994	Sitora Dushanbe	47	Pamir Dushanbe	45	P'takor Proletarsk	43		Ravshan Kulyab	2-1	Shodmon Ghissar
1995	Pamir Dushanbe	67	Istravshan	57	Sitora Dushanbe	52		Pakhtakor Dzh'lovsk	0-0 3-2p	Regar TadAZ
1996	Dinamo Dushanbe	73	Sitora Dushanbe	71	Khojent	64		Not played		
1997	Vakhsh Qurgonteppa	59	Ranjbar Vosse	55	Khujand	52		Vakhsh Qurgonteppa	4-0	Khujand
1998	Varzob Dushanbe	56	Khujand	44	Saddam Sarband	42		Khujand	2-1	Ranjbar Vose
1999	Varzob Dushanbe	57	Khuja Gazimalik	49	Ravshan Kulyab	46		Varzob Dushanbe	4-2p	Regar TadAZ
2000	Varzob Dushanbe	87	Regar TadAZ	77	Khujand	68		Not played		
2001	Regar TadAZ	50	Panjsher Kolk'bad	38	Pamir Dushanbe	32		Regar TadAZ	4-2	Varzob Dushanbe
2002	Regar TadAZ	58	Khujand	53	Farrukh Ghissar	44		Khujand	3-0	Vakhsh Qurgonteppa
2003	Regar TadAZ	81	Khujand	72	Aviator	71		Vakhsh Qurgonteppa		
2004	Regar TadAZ	86	Vakhsh Qurgonteppa	85	Aviator	71		Aviator B. Gafurov	5-0	Uroteppa
2005	Vakhsh Qurgonteppa	47	Regar Tursunzoda	42	Parvoz B. Gafurov	34		Regar TadAZ	1-1 4-2p	Vakhsh Qurgonteppa
2006	Regar TadAZ	55	Khima Dushanbe	54	Vakhsh Qurgonteppa	47		Regar TadAZ	2-1	Khima Dushanbe

Tajik clubs took part in the Soviet league until the end of the 1991 season

TKM – TURKMENISTAN

NATIONAL TEAM RECORD
JULY 10TH 2006 TO JULY 12TH 2010

PL	W	D	L	F	A	%
1	0	0	1	0	1	0

FIFA/COCA-COLA WORLD RANKING

1993	1994	1995	1996	1997	1998	1999	2000	2001	2002	2003	2004	2005	2006	High	Low
-	108	133	141	134	122	129	125	114	134	99	98	116	155	**86** 04/04	**169** 10/06

2006–2007											
08/06	09/06	10/06	11/06	12/06	01/07	02/07	03/07	04/07	05/07	06/07	07/07
158	162	169	151	155	155	155	158	163	163	163	164

With the national team pulling out of the regional Alma TV Cup due to the non-availability of players, Turkmenistan were restricted to just one match during the season, a 1-0 defeat at the hands of Qatar in Doha in a warm up match for the Qataris as they prepared for the AFC Asian Cup finals. With Turkmenistan's under–23 team also pulling out of the Asian Games in Doha, club football was the main focus of the season with defending champions MTTU Ashgabat once again the form team. In October 2006 they beat traditional giants Köpetdag Ashgabat in the Turkmenistan Cup Final in Turkmenbashi on penalties after the match had finished scoreless. Maksim Kazankov had squandered

INTERNATIONAL HONOURS
None

a golden chance for Köpetdag when he missed a penalty in the 57th minute as his team missed out on silverware for the fifth season running. MTTU then won the Championship ahead of Nebitchi Balkanabat, securing the double with two rounds to spare with a 5-1 victory over Merv Mary. Normally the Cup winners qualify for the AFC Cup but with MTTU winning the double, League runners-up Nebitchi qualified. Grouped with holders Al Faysali of Jordan, Nebitch finished bottom of the four-team group, six points behind third placed Al Ansar of Lebanon. MTTU managed to finish third in their group but were well off the pace set by group winners Al Wihdat of Jordan.

THE FIFA BIG COUNT OF 2006

	Male	Female		Total
Number of players	90 355	10 060	Referees and Assistant Referees	65
Professionals	280		Admin, Coaches, Technical, Medical	130
Amateurs 18+	615		Number of clubs	15
Youth under 18	310		Number of teams	98
Unregistered	23 000		Clubs with women's teams	0
Total players	100 415		Players as % of population	1.99%

Football Association of Turkmenistan (FFT)
15 A. Niyazova Street, Stadium Kopetdag, Ashgabat 744 001, Turkmenistan
Tel +993 12 477470   Fax +993 12 3632355
footballtkm@mail.ru   www.none
President: YUSUPOV Aman   General Secretary: SATYLOV Meret
Vice-President: SAPAEV Allabergen   Treasurer: LEONOVA Natalya   Media Officer: IVANNIKOV Evgeniy
Men's Coach: KURBANMAMEDOV Rakhim   Women's Coach: MAMEDOV Atamyrad
FFT formed: 1992   AFC: 1994   FIFA: 1994
Green shirts, White shorts, Green socks

RECENT INTERNATIONAL MATCHES PLAYED BY TURKMENISTAN

2002	Opponents	Score		Venue	Comp	Scorers	Att	Referee
	No international matches played in 2002							
2003								
19-10	United Arab Emirates	W	1-0	Ashgabat	ACq	Bayramov.V [43]		
30-10	United Arab Emirates	D	1-1	Sharjah	ACq	Bayramov.V [40]		
9-11	Sri Lanka	W	1-0	Balkanabat	ACq	Agabaev [9]		
12-11	Sri Lanka	W	3-0	Ashgabat	ACq	Agayev 2 [25 70], Bayramov.V [45]		
19-11	Afghanistan	W	11-0	Ashgabat	WCq	Ovekov 2 [6 35], Kuliev 3 [8 22 81], Bayramov.N [27] Berdyev [42], Agabaev 3 [49 65 67], Urazov [90]	12 000	Busurmankulov KGZ
23-11	Afghanistan	W	2-0	Kabul	WCq	Kuliev 2 [85 91+]	6 000	Khan PAK
28-11	Syria	D	1-1	Damascus	ACq	Urazov [16]		Sadeq KUW
3-12	Syria	W	3-0	Ashgabat	ACq	Not played. Turkmenistan awarded match 3-0		
2004								
18-02	Sri Lanka	W	2-0	Ashgabat	WCq	Ovekov [40], Bayramov.N [56]	11 000	Al Bannai UAE
17-03	Yemen	W	2-1	Sana'a	Fr			
31-03	Indonesia	W	3-1	Ashgabat	WCq	Bayramov.V 2 [10 74], Kuliev [35]	5 000	Sahib Shakir IRQ
28-04	Armenia	L	0-1	Yerevan	Fr		7 500	
31-05	Qatar	L	0-5	Doha	Fr			
9-06	Saudi Arabia	L	0-3	Riyadh	WCq		1 000	Khanthama THA
18-07	Saudi Arabia	D	2-2	Chengdu	ACrl	Bayramov.N [7], Kuliev [90]	12 400	Al Qahtani KSA
22-07	Iraq	L	2-3	Chengdu	ACrl	Bayramov.V [15], Kuliev [85]	22 000	Al Fadhli KUW
26-07	Uzbekistan	L	0-1	Chongqing	ACrl		34 000	Kousa SYR
8-09	Saudi Arabia	L	0-1	Ashgabat	WCq		5 000	Kwon Jong Chul KOR
9-10	Sri Lanka	D	2-2	Colombo	WCq	Bayramov.D [20], Nazarov [70]	4 000	Al Bannai UAE
17-11	Indonesia	L	1-3	Jakarta	WCq	Durdiyev [25]	15 000	Shaban KUW
2005								
29-01	Saudi Arabia	L	0-1	Riyadh	Fr			
3-08	Bahrain	L	0-5	Manama	Fr			
2006								
	No international matches played in 2006							
2007								
25-06	Qatar	L	0-1	Doha	Fr			

Fr = Friendly match • AC = AFC Asian Cup • WC = FIFA World Cup • q = qualifier • rl = first round group

TURKMENISTAN NATIONAL TEAM RECORDS AND RECORD SEQUENCES

Records			Sequence records					
Victory	11-0	AFG 2003	Wins	4	2003, 2003-2004	Clean sheets	4	2003
Defeat	1-6	KUW 2000	Defeats	4	2004-2007	Goals scored	14	2001-2004
Player Caps	n/a		Undefeated	13	2001-2004	Without goal	3	2004, 2005-2007
Player Goals	n/a		Without win	12	2004-2007	Goals against	14	2004-2007

TURKMENISTAN COUNTRY INFORMATION

Capital	Ashgabat	Independence	1991 from the USSR	GDP per Capita	$5 800
Population	4 863 169	Status	Republic	GNP Ranking	113
Area km²	488 100	Language	Turkmen, Russian, Uzbek	Dialling code	+993
Population density	10 per km²	Literacy rate	98%	Internet code	.tm
% in urban areas	45%	Main religion	Muslim	GMT +/–	+5
Cities/Towns ('000)	Ashgabat 979; Turkmenabat 234; Dasoguz 199; Mary 114; Balkanabat 87; Bayramali 75				
Neighbours (km)	Uzbekistan 1 621; Afghanistan 744; Iran 992; Kazakhstan 379; Caspian Sea 1 768				
Main stadia	Olympic Stadium – Ashgabat 30 000; Köpetdag – Ashgabat 26 000				

TURKMENISTAN 2006
FIRST DIVISION

	Pl	W	D	L	F	A	Pts
MTTU Ashgabat ‡	28	16	7	5			55
Nebitchi Balkanabat ‡	28	14	9	5			51
FK Ashgabat	28	14	6	8			48
Sagadam Turkmenbasy	28	12	5	11			41
Köpetdag Ashgabat	28	10	9	9			39
Turan Dasoguz	28	9	6	13			33
Merv Mary	28	7	4	17			25
Nisa Ashgabat	28	5	4	19			19

15/04/2006 - 3/12/2006 • ‡ Qualified for the 2006 AFC Cup

TURKMENISTAN CUP 2006

Preliminary Round	Quarter–finals	Semi–finals	Final
MTTU Ashgabat			
	MTTU Ashgabat 0 6		
	Shagadam Türk'bashy* 0 1		
Shagadam Türk'bashy		MTTU Ashgabat * 1 2	
FK Ashgabat		Nebitchi Balkanabat 1 0	
	FK Ashgabat		
	Nebitchi Balkanabat *		
Nebitchi Balkanabat			MTTU Ashgabat 0 7p
Nisa Ashgabat			Köpetdag Ashgabat 0 6p
	Nisa Ashgabat		
	Turan Dashoguz *		**CUP FINAL**
Turan Dashoguz		Nisa Ashgabat * 1 0 3p	
Merv Mary		Köpetdag Ashgabat 1 0 4p	Türkmenbashy
	Merv Mary 0 2		28-10-2006
	Köpetdag Ashgabat * 1 1		
Köpetdag Ashgabat			

* Home team in the first leg • ‡ Qualified for the 2006 AFC Cup

RECENT LEAGUE AND CUP RECORD

	Championship						Cup		
Year	Champions	Pts	Runners-up	Pts	Third	Pts	Winners	Score	Runners-up
1992	Köpetdag Ashgabat	54	Nebitchi Balkanabat	47	Akhal Akdashayak	46			
1993	Köpetdag Ashgabat	14	Byuzmeyin	11	Nebitchi Balkanabat	9	Köpetdag Ashgabat	4-0	Merv Mary
1994	Köpetdag Ashgabat	31	Nisa Ashgabat	24	Merv Mary	20	Köpetdag Ashgabat	2-0	Turan Dasoguz
1995	Köpetdag Ashgabat	84	Nisa Ashgabat	79	Nebitchi Balkanabat	61	Turan Dasoguz	4-3	Köpetdag Ashgabat
1996	Nisa Ashgabat	83	Köpetdag Ashgabat	74	Exkavatorshchik	60	No tournament due to season re-adjustment		
1997	No tournament due to season re-adjustment						Köpetdag Ashgabat	2-0	Nisa Ashgabat
1998	Köpetdag Ashgabat		Nisa Ashgabat				Nisa Ashgabat	3-0	Nebitchi Balkanabat
1999	Nisa Ashgabat	78	Köpetdag Ashgabat	67	Dagdan Ashgabat	60	Köpetdag Ashgabat	3-1	Nebitchi Balkanabat
2000	Köpetdag Ashgabat	56	Nebitchi Balkanabat	41	Nisa Ashgabat	37	Köpetdag Ashgabat	5-0	Nisa Ashgabat
2001	Nisa Ashgabat	77	Köpetdag Ashgabat	68	Nebitchi Balkanabat	60	Köpetdag Ashgabat	2-0	Nebitchi Balkanabat
2002	Sagadam Turk'basy	67	Nisa Ashgabat	63	Garagam Turk'abat	59	Garagam Turk'abat	0-0 4-2p	Sagadam Turk'basy
2003	Nisa Ashgabat	92	Nebitchi Balkanabat	79	Sagadam Turk'basy	76	Nebitchi Balkanabat	2-1	Nisa Ashgabat
2004	Nebitchi Balkanabat	84	Nisa Ashgabat	78	Merv Mary	67	Nebitchi Balkanabat	1-0	Asudalyk Ashgabat
2005	MTTU Ashgabat	72	Gazcy Gazojak	62	Nebitchi Balkanabat	58	Merv Mary	1-1 3-1p	Köpetdag Ashgabat
2006	MTTU Ashgabat	55	Nebitchi Balkanabat	51	FK Ashgabat	48	MTTU Ashgabat	0-0 7-6p	Köpetdag Ashgabat

Turkmen clubs took part in the Soviet league until the end of the 1991 season

TLS – TIMOR-LESTE

NATIONAL TEAM RECORD
JULY 10TH 2006 TO JULY 12TH 2010

PL	W	D	L	F	A	%
4	0	0	4	5	17	0

FIFA/COCA-COLA WORLD RANKING

1993	1994	1995	1996	1997	1998	1999	2000	2001	2002	2003	2004	2005	2006	High		Low	
-	-	-	-	-	-	-	-	-	-	-	-	-	198	198	12/06	199	07/07

2006–2007											
08/06	09/06	10/06	11/06	12/06	01/07	02/07	03/07	04/07	05/07	06/07	07/07
-	-	-	198	198	199	199	199	199	199	199	199

As one of FIFA's newest members, East Timor are finding the going tough as they seek to establish a foothold in world football. The four games played during the season in the ASEAN Football Federation Championship brought to a total of ten games that the national team has now played - all of which have been lost. Captain of the team is Portugal-born defender Alfredo Esteves who holds dual citizenship but chose to play for East Timor. His experience in the USL with Minnesota Thunder will be crucial as East Timor have entered the FIFA World Cup for the first time. Although they lost all four matches in the ASEAN qualifying group in Bacolod in the

INTERNATIONAL HONOURS
None

Philippines, East Timor did score five goals and they gave both Brunei and Laos a good run for their money before losing both matches 3-2. A critical stage in the development of football in the country will come with the establishment of regular club competition at home. That has been hampered by political instability in the country since it gained independence in May 2002 which spilled over into violence in the streets in 2006. Fima Sporting had beaten Esperança on penalties in early 2006 in the final of the Piala Kemederkaan, and the football federation will be hoping that the fragile peace that followed the violence will continue after the elections of July 2007.

THE FIFA BIG COUNT OF 2006

	Male	Female		Total
Number of players	15 500	0	Referees and Assistant Referees	0
Professionals	0		Admin, Coaches, Technical, Medical	100
Amateurs 18+	200		Number of clubs	10
Youth under 18	300		Number of teams	20
Unregistered	0		Clubs with women's teams	0
Total players	15 500		Players as % of population	1.46%

Federaçao Futebol Timor-Leste (FFTL)
Rua 12 de Novembro Sta. Cruz, PO Box 1031, Dili, Timor-Leste
Tel +670 3322231   Fax +670 3317430
federacao_futebol@yahoo.com   www.none
President: LAY Francisco Kalbuadi   General Secretary: SAMENTO Amandio
Vice-President: CABRAL FERNANDES Filomeno Pedro   Treasurer: FEREIRA Jesuina M.   Media Officer: TIMOTIO Antonio
Men's Coach: PAULO Joao   Women's Coach: DE ARAUJO Marcos
FFTL formed: 2002   AFC: 2002   FIFA: 2005
Red shirts, Black shorts, Red socks

RECENT INTERNATIONAL MATCHES PLAYED BY TIMOR–LESTE

2002 Opponents	Score	Venue	Comp	Scorers	Att	Referee
No international matches played before 2003						
2003						
21-03 Sri Lanka	L 2-3	Colombo	ACq			
23-03 Chinese Taipei	L 0-3	Colombo	ACq			
2004						
8-12 Malaysia	L 0-5	Kuala Lumpur	TCr1			
12-12 Thailand	L 0-8	Kuala Lumpur	TCr1			
14-12 Philippines	L 1-2	Kuala Lumpur	TCr1	Anai [14]		
16-12 Myanmar	L 1-3	Kuala Lumpur	TCr1	Simon Diamantino [15p]		
2005						
No international matches played in 2005						
2006						
12-11 Brunei	L 2-3	Bacolod	TCr1	Adelio Maria Costa [33], Anatacio Belo [77]		
14-11 Philippines	L 0-7	Bacolod	TCr1			
16-11 Laos	L 2-3	Bacolod	TCr1	Antonio Ximenes [82], Adelio Maria Costa [89]		
20-11 Cambodia	L 1-4	Bacolod	TCr1	Adelio Maria Costa [63]		
2007						
No international matches played in 2007 before August						

AC = AFC Asian Cup • TC = Tiger Cup/ASEAN Football Federation Championship
q = qualifier • r1 = first round group • Matches played before September 2005 are not full internationals

TIMOR–LESTE NATIONAL TEAM RECORDS AND RECORD SEQUENCES

Records			Sequence records				
Victory	-	Never won a match	Wins	0		Clean sheets	0
Defeat	0-8	THA 2004	Defeats	10	2003-	Goals scored	3	2004-2006
Player Caps	n/a		Undefeated	0		Without goal	3	2003-2004
Player Goals	n/a		Without win	10	2003-	Goals against	10	2003-

TIMOR–LESTE COUNTRY INFORMATION

Capital	Dili	Independence	2002 from Indonesia	GDP per Capita	$400
Population	1 040 880	Status	Republic	GNP Ranking	143
Area km²	15 077	Language	Tetum, Portuguese	Dialling code	+670
Population density	69 per km²	Literacy rate	58%	Internet code	.tp
% in urban areas	8%	Main religion	Christian 93%	GMT + / –	+8
Towns/Cities ('000)	Dili 159; Dare 18; Los Palos 17; Baucau 14; Ermera 12; Maliana 12				
Neighbours (km)	Indonesia 228; Timor Sea, Savu Sea and Banda Sea 706				
Main stadia	Estadio Nacional, Dili 5 000				

TOG – TOGO

NATIONAL TEAM RECORD
JULY 10TH 2006 TO JULY 12TH 2010

PL	W	D	L	F	A	%
9	3	3	3	10	12	50

FIFA/COCA-COLA WORLD RANKING

1993	1994	1995	1996	1997	1998	1999	2000	2001	2002	2003	2004	2005	2006	High		Low	
113	86	92	87	78	68	87	81	71	86	94	89	56	60	**46**	08/06	**123**	06/94

	2006–2007											
	08/06	09/06	10/06	11/06	12/06	01/07	02/07	03/07	04/07	05/07	06/07	07/07
	46	48	54	61	60	66	69	71	66	66	63	59

The fall-out from the controversy that surrounded Togo at the World Cup in Germany continued to overshadow football in the following 12 months, topped up by an embarrassing ban for the football federation president Tata Avlessi, who was handed an eight year ban by CAF after he had tried to fix a result in the African under–17 championship, which Togo hosted in March 2007. Togo finished as runners-up to Nigeria, thereby qualifying for the FIFA U-17 World Cup in South Korea but CAF found that Avlessi had passed on money to try and bribe referee Pa Abdou Sarr and slapped him with a harsh ban, which in turn saw him lose his job as the head of the TFF. The

INTERNATIONAL HONOURS
Qualified for the FIFA World Cup finals 2006

federation was also embroiled in a continuing dispute with Togo's only genuine world star, the Arsenal striker Emmanuel Adebayor. He and a handful of teammates boycotted several of the country's 2008 African Nations Cup qualifiers in a bid to force the federation to stump up promised World Cup bonuses. Former Nigeria captain Stephen Keshi, who engineered Togo's rise from obscurity, returned as coach as Togo battled with Mali for a place at the 2008 Nations Cup finals in neighbouring Ghana. Tragedy struck after the match against Sierra Leone in June 2007, when the Togolese Minister of Sport was among those killed in a helicopter crash in Freetown.

THE FIFA BIG COUNT OF 2006

	Male	Female		Total
Number of players	230 900	11 500	Referees and Assistant Referees	600
Professionals	100		Admin, Coaches, Technical, Medical	2 700
Amateurs 18+	5 200		Number of clubs	100
Youth under 18	4 500		Number of teams	620
Unregistered	15 600		Clubs with women's teams	0
Total players	242 400		Players as % of population	4.37%

Fédération Togolaise de Football (FTF)
Stade Municipal de Lomé, Case postale 5, Lome, Togo
Tel +228 2212698   Fax +228 2221413
eperviers@ftf.tg   www.ftf.tg
President: TBD   General Secretary: ASSOGBAVI Komlan
Vice-President: DOGBATSE Winny   Treasurer: ADJETE Tino   Media Officer: ATTOLOU Messan
Men's Coach: KESHI Stephen   Women's Coach: ZOUNGBEDE Paul
FTF formed: 1960   CAF: 1963   FIFA: 1962
Yellow shirts with green trimmings, Green shorts, White socks or Green shirts with white trimmings, Green shorts, White socks

RECENT INTERNATIONAL MATCHES PLAYED BY TOGO

2005	Opponents	Score		Venue	Comp	Scorers	Att	Referee
27-03	Mali	W	2-1	Bamako	WCq	Salifou [78], Mamam [91+]	45 000	Agbenyega GHA
29-05	Burkina Faso	W	1-0	Lomé	Fr			
5-06	Zambia	W	4-1	Lomé	WCq	Adebayor 2 [12 88], Toure.S [44], Kader Coubadja [65]	15 000	Guezzaz MAR
18-06	Senegal	D	2-2	Dakar	WCq	Olufade [11], Adebayor [71]	50 000	Guirat TUN
17-08	Morocco	W	1-0	Rouen	Fr	Dogbe [20]		
4-09	Liberia	W	3-0	Lomé	WCq	Adebayor 2 [52 93+], Mamam [69]	28 000	Abdel Rahman SUD
8-10	Congo	W	3-2	Brazzaville	WCq	Adebayor [40], Kader Coubadja 2 [60 70]	20 000	Shelmani LBY
11-11	Paraguay	L	2-4	Tehran	Fr	Mamam [33], Soulieman [34]		
13-11	Iran	L	0-2	Tehran	Fr			
2006								
7-01	Guinea	L	0-1	Viry-Chatillon	Fr			
11-01	Ghana	W	1-0	Monastir	Fr	Olufade [77]	2 500	Piccirillo FRA
21-01	Congo DR	L	0-2	Cairo	CNr1		6 000	Daami TUN
25-01	Cameroon	L	0-2	Cairo	CNr1		3 000	Sowe GAM
29-01	Angola	L	2-3	Cairo	CNr1	Kader Coubadja [24], Maman [67]	4 000	El Arjoun MAR
14-05	Saudi Arabia	L	0-1	Sittard	Fr		400	Braamhaar NED
2-06	Liechtenstein	W	1-0	Vaduz	Fr	Kader Coubadja [52]	2 700	Schorgenhofer AUT
13-06	Korea Republic	L	1-2	Frankfurt	WCr1	Kader Coubadja [31]	48 000	Poll ENG
19-06	Switzerland	L	0-2	Dortmund	WCr1		65 000	Amarilla PAR
23-06	France	L	0-2	Cologne	WCr1		45 000	Larrionda URU
15-08	Ghana	L	0-2	London	Fr			Dean ENG
29-08	Niger	D	1-1	Lomé	Fr	Amewou [55]		
3-09	Benin	W	2-1	Lomé	CNq	Dossevi [13], Amewou [78]		Louzaya CGO
8-10	Mali	L	0-1	Bamako	CNq			Benouza ALG
15-11	Luxembourg	D	0-0	Luxembourg	Fr		1 417	Richards WAL
2007								
7-02	Cameroon	D	2-2	Lomé	Fr	Olufade [25], Adebayor [40]		
25-03	Sierra Leone	W	3-1	Lomé	CNq	Adebayor 2 [38 85], Olufade [62]		
3-06	Sierra Leone	W	1-0	Freetown	CNq	Senaya Yao [78]		
17-06	Benin	L	1-4	Cotonou	CNq	Olufade [76]		

Fr = Friendly match • CN = CAF African Cup of Nations • WC = FIFA World Cup • q = qualifier • r1 = first round group

TOGO NATIONAL TEAM RECORDS AND RECORD SEQUENCES

Records			Sequence records					
Victory	4-0	Six times	Wins	5	2004-2005	Clean sheets	3	Six times
Defeat	0-7	MAR 1979, TUN 2000	Defeats	5	1977-79, 1999-00	Goals scored	12	1956-1957
Player Caps	n/a		Undefeated	12	2004-2005	Without goal	5	2002
Player Goals	n/a		Without win	14	1992-94, 1999-00	Goals against	9	1983-1984

RECENT LEAGUE AND CUP RECORD

	Championship						Cup		
Year	Champions	Pts	Runners-up	Pts	Third	Pts	Winners	Score	Runners-up
2001	Dynamic Togolais	17	Maranatha Fiokpo	16	ASKO Kara Lomé	14	Dynamic Togolais	3-0	Sara Sport Bafilo
2002	AS Douanes	63	Maranatha Fiokpo	63	Dynamic Togolais	51	Dynamic Togolais	2-0	Doumbé
2003	No tournament due to season readjustment						Maranatha Fiokpo		
2004	Dynamic Togolais	59	Maranatha Fiokpo	54	Kakadle Defale	51	AS Douanes	2-1	Foadam Dapaong
2005	AS Douanes	31	Dynamic Togolais	26	Togo Télécom	20	Dynamic Togolais	1-0	Agaza Lomé
2006	Maranatha Fiokpo	61	AS Douanes	50	Etoile Filante	47	AS Togo-Port	1-1 5-4p	ASKO Kara

TOGO COUNTRY INFORMATION

Capital	Lomé	Independence	1960 from France	GDP per Capita	$1 500
Population	5 556 812	Status	Republic	GNP Ranking	149
Area km²	56 785	Language	French	Dialling code	+228
Population density	97 per km²	Literacy rate	60%	Internet code	.tg
% in urban areas	31%	Main religion	Indigenous 51% Christian 29%	GMT +/−	0
Towns/Cities ('000)	Lomé 726; Kpalimé 110; Sokodé 108; Kara 94; Atakpamé 92; Bassar 55; Tsévié 55; Aného 47				
Neighbours (km)	Benin 644; Ghana 877; Burkina Faso 126; Atlantic Ocean/Bight of Benin 56				
Main stadia	Stade General Eyadema (Kegue) – Lomé 20 000				

TPE – CHINESE TAIPEI

NATIONAL TEAM RECORD
JULY 10TH 2006 TO JULY 12TH 2010

PL	W	D	L	F	A	%
10	3	1	6	19	30	35

FIFA/COCA-COLA WORLD RANKING

1993	1994	1995	1996	1997	1998	1999	2000	2001	2002	2003	2004	2005	2006	High	Low
161	170	178	174	154	169	174	162	170	166	150	155	156	166	144 08/06	180 07/96

2006–2007											
08/06	09/06	10/06	11/06	12/06	01/07	02/07	03/07	04/07	05/07	06/07	07/07
144	154	158	163	166	166	166	168	167	167	164	154

The record of the Chinese Taipei national team during the 2006-07 season perfectly illustrates the challenge that football faces in the country as it struggles for acceptance. On the one hand they are no match for the mainstream nations in Asia, with all six matches in the AFC Asian Cup qualifiers lost - and some heavily, notably the 8-0 thrashing at the hands of South Korea. Two months after that defeat, Chinese Taipei were on the end of a record 10-0 defeat by Kuwait, and yet in the same season they bizarrely managed their biggest ever win when they beat Guam 10-0 in the East Asian Championship qualifiers. With just 10 paying spectators, the match against Guam also set the

INTERNATIONAL HONOURS
Asian Games 1954 1958

world record for the lowest attendance at an international match. In the East Asian Championship qualifiers, the win over Guam proved to be in vain after Hong Kong secured a 15-1 win over the same opponents with goal difference proving to be the decisive factor after Chinese Taipei and Hong Kong drew their match 1-1. Tatung retained their title in the Football League but only on their head to head record with Taipower after the pair finished level on points. That meant Tatung qualified for the AFC President's Cup again but any hope of improving on their semi-final appearance in 2006 was put on hold after the 2007 tournament was postponed to September.

THE FIFA BIG COUNT OF 2006

	Male	Female		Total
Number of players	424 400	34 060	Referees and Assistant Referees	102
Professionals	0		Admin, Coaches, Technical, Medical	374
Amateurs 18+	5 960		Number of clubs	60
Youth under 18	6 600		Number of teams	600
Unregistered	75 900		Clubs with women's teams	0
Total players	458 460		Players as % of population	1.99%

Chinese Taipei Football Association (CTFA)
2F No. Yu Men St., 104 Taipei, Taiwan 104
Tel +886 2 25961184   Fax +886 2 25951594
ctfa7155@ms59.hinet.net   www.ctfa.com.tw
President: CHIOU I-Jen   General Secretary: LIN Der Chia
Vice-President: SHI Hwei-Yow   Treasurer: LIN Shiu Yi   Media Officer: BEARE Alexander James
Men's Coach: TOSHIAKI Imai   Women's Coach: CHOU Tai Ying
CTFA formed: 1924   AFC: 1954-75, 1990   FIFA: 1954
Blue shirts, Blue shorts, White socks

RECENT INTERNATIONAL MATCHES PLAYED BY CHINESE TAIPEI

2005	Opponents	Score		Venue	Comp	Scorers	Att	Referee
5-03	Guam	W	9-0	Taipei	EAq	Tu Ming Feng [8], Kuo Yin Hung 3 [10 20 69], Chiang Shih Lu 2 [56 70], He Ming Chan 3 [66 83 93+]		
9-03	Korea DPR	L	0-2	Taipei	EAq			
11-03	Hong Kong	L	0-5	Taipei	EAq			
13-03	Mongolia	D	0-0	Taipei	EAq			
2006								
22-02	Iran	L	0-4	Tehran	ACq		5 000	AK Nema IRQ
1-03	Syria	L	0-4	Taipei	ACq		700	O Il Son PRK
1-04	Philippines	W	1-0	Chittagong	CCr1	Chuang Wei Lun [20]	4 000	Lee Gi Young KOR
3-04	Afghanistan	D	2-2	Chittagong	CCr1	Chuang Wei Lun [48], Liang Chien Wei [73]	2 500	Lee Gi Young KOR
5-04	India	D	0-0	Chittagong	CCr1		2 000	Gosh BAN
8-04	Sri Lanka	L	0-3	Chittagong	CCqf		2 500	Al Ghatrifi OMA
9-08	Macau	W	1-0	Macau	Fr	Lee Yu Shan [64]		
16-08	Korea Republic	L	0-3	Taipei	ACq		1 300	Sarkar IND
6-09	Korea Republic	L	0-8	Suwon	ACq		21 053	Arambakade SRI
11-10	Iran	L	0-2	Taipei	ACq		2 000	Shamsuzzaman BAN
9-11	Kuwait	L	0-10	Al Ain	Fr			
15-11	Syria	L	0-3	Damascus	ACq		1 000	Al Hilali OMA
2007								
24-03	Uzbekistan	L	0-1	Taipei	Fr			
17-06	Guam	W	10-0	Macau	EAq	Lo Chih En 4 [7 28 72 88], Tsai Hui Kai [20], Feng Pao Hsing 2 [25 38], Chen Po Liang 2 [52 68], Huang Cheng Tsung [74]	10	Wan Daxue CHN
19-06	Hong Kong	D	1-1	Macau	EAq	Huang Wei Yi [51]	200	Kim Eui Soo KOR
24-06	Macau	W	7-2	Macau	EAq	Huang Wei Yi [3], Feng Pao Hsing [42], Kuo Chun Yi [52], Chen Po Liang [56], Lo Chih En 2 [57 90], Lo Chih An [71]	200	Kim Eui Soo KOR

Fr = Friendly match • EA = East Asian Championship • AC = AFC Asian Cup • CC = AFC Challenge Cup • WC = FIFA World Cup • q = qualifier

CHINESE TAIPEI NATIONAL TEAM RECORDS AND RECORD SEQUENCES

Records			Sequence records					
Victory	10-0	GUM 2007	Wins	8	1958-1960	Clean sheets	3	1981
Defeat	0-10	KUW 2006	Defeats	9	1988-92, 1992-96	Goals scored	15	1966-1967
Player Caps	n/a		Undefeated	11	1957-1960	Without goal	12	2000-2002
Player Goals	n/a		Without win	19	1988-1996	Goals against	15	1867-1968

CHINESE TAIPEI 2006
FUBON ENTERPRISE FOOTBALL LEAGUE

	Pl	W	D	L	F	A	Pts	Ta	TP	CS	FF
Tatung	9	5	3	1	16	9	18		2-1 0-1	3-3 1-1	1-0 1-0
Taipower	9	6	0	3	17	10	18	0-4		1-2 2-0	4-2 3-0
China Steel	9	2	2	5	12	15	8	1-2	0-2		4-1 1-2
Fubon Financial	9	2	1	6	8	19	7	2-2	0-3	1-0	

9/06/2006 - 21/07/2006 • † Qualified for the AFC President's Cup • Tatung champions due to head to head record • Matches played in Fongshan, Taipei and Tainan

RECENT LEAGUE RECORD

Year	Champions
1997	Taiwan Power Company Taipei
1998	Taiwan Power Company Taipei
1999	Taiwan Power Company Taipei
2000	Not played
2001	Taiwan Power Company Taipei
2002	Taiwan Power Company Taipei
2003	Taiwan Power Company Taipei
2004	Taiwan Power Company Taipei
2005	Tatung
2006	Tatung

CHINESE TAIPEI COUNTRY INFORMATION

Capital	Taipei	Independence	1949	GDP per Capita	$23 400
Population	22 749 838	Status	Republic	GNP Ranking	16
Area km²	35 980	Language	Mandarin, Min	Dialling code	+886
Population density	632 per km²	Literacy rate	96%	Internet code	.tw
% in urban areas	69%	Main religion	Buddhist, Confucian, Taoist	GMT +/–	+8
Towns/Cities ('000)	Taipei 2 514; Kaoshiung 1 512; Taichung 1 083; Tainan 734; Panchiao 491; Hsinchu 413				
Neighbours (km)	Taiwan Strait, East China Sea, Philippine Sea & South China Sea 1 566				
Main stadia	Chung Shan Soccer Stadium – Taipei 25 000				

TRI – TRINIDAD AND TOBAGO

NATIONAL TEAM RECORD
JULY 10TH 2006 TO JULY 12TH 2010

PL	W	D	L	F	A	%
16	6	2	8	26	27	43.7

FIFA/COCA-COLA WORLD RANKING

1993	1994	1995	1996	1997	1998	1999	2000	2001	2002	2003	2004	2005	2006	High		Low	
88	91	57	41	56	51	44	29	32	47	70	63	50	91	25	06/01	95	04/94

2006–2007											
08/06	09/06	10/06	11/06	12/06	01/07	02/07	03/07	04/07	05/07	06/07	07/07
61	56	80	90	91	87	68	68	66	67	73	65

The Soca Warriors used their new-found fame to good effect following their appearance at the 2006 FIFA World Cup finals as they proved to be a popular attraction with friendly matches in the Far-East and in Europe, but the team was back into serious competition very quickly with the Digicel Caribbean Cup finals being staged in Trinidad in January 2007. Aiming to win a record ninth title, Trinidad looked on course after easily winning their group and then beating Cuba in the semi-finals. In the final they met a strangely resilient Haiti team which had only just managed to qualify for the finals and early in the second half the Soca Warriors found themselves two goals

INTERNATIONAL HONOURS
Qualified for the FIFA World Cup finals 2006 **Caribbean Cup** 1981 1989 1992 1994 1995 1996 1997 1999 2001 **Champions Cup** Defence Force 1978 1985

down. Nigel Daniel did pull a goal back midway through the half but they couldn't break Haiti down. A week after that defeat, Trinidad's leading club Williams Connection restored some pride by winning the Caribbean club championship. In the final they beat compatriots San Juan Jabloteh 1-0 to win the title for the first time. In the Pro League Williams Connection had failed to defend their title after losing out to Joe Public on goal difference although they did win the FCB Cup. The season ended with the national team appearing in the Gold Cup in America, but they were knocked out in the first round.

THE FIFA BIG COUNT OF 2006

	Male	Female		Total
Number of players	71 150	13 450	Referees and Assistant Referees	250
Professionals	250		Admin, Coaches, Technical, Medical	650
Amateurs 18+	4 250		Number of clubs	95
Youth under 18	11 600		Number of teams	380
Unregistered	16 000		Clubs with women's teams	3
Total players	84 600		Players as % of population	7.94%

Trinidad and Tobago Football Federation (TTFF)
24-26 Dundonald Street, PO Box 400, Port of Spain, Trinidad and Tobago
Tel +1 868 6237312   Fax +1 868 6238109
admin@tttff.com   www.socawariorstt.com
President: CAMPS Oliver   General Secretary: GRODEN Richard
Vice-President: TIM KEE Raymond   Treasurer: TBD   Media Officer: FUENTES Shaun
Men's Coach: RIJSBERGEN Wim   Women's Coach: CHARLES Marlon
TTFF formed: 1908   CONCACAF: 1964   FIFA: 1963
Red shirts with white trimmings, Red shorts, Red socks or White shirts with red trimmings, White shorts, White socks

RECENT INTERNATIONAL MATCHES PLAYED BY TRINIDAD AND TOBAGO

2005	Opponents		Score	Venue	Comp	Scorers	Att	Referee
9-02	USA	L	1-2	Port of Spain	WCq	Eve [87]	11 000	Archundia MEX
20-02	Jamaica	L	1-2	Bridgetown	CC	Pierre.N [37]	5 000	Callender BRB
22-02	Cuba	L	1-2	Bridgetown	CC	Glen 13	2 100	Lancaster GUY
24-02	Barbados	W	3-2	Bridgetown	CC	Smith.C 11, Glenn 30, Eve 84	3 000	Prendergast JAM
26-03	Guatemala	L	1-5	Guatemala City	WCq	Edwards 32	22 506	Stott USA
30-03	Costa Rica	D	0-0	Port of Spain	WCq		8 000	Navarro CAN
25-05	Bermuda	W	4-0	Port of Spain	Fr	OG 34, Jones.K 46, Lawrence 51, John 65	400	
27-05	Bermuda	W	1-0	Marabella	Fr	John 17		
4-06	Panama	W	2-0	Port of Spain	WCq	John 34, Lawrence 71		Prendergast JAM
8-06	Mexico	L	0-2	Monterrey	WCq			
6-07	Honduras	D	1-1	Miami	GCr1	Birchall 28	10 311	Navarro CAN
10-07	Panama	D	2-2	Miami	GCr1	Andrews 17, Glen 91+	17 292	Wyngaarde SUR
12-07	Colombia	L	0-2	Miami	GCr1		11 000	Rodriguez MEX
17-08	USA	L	0-1	Hartford	WCq		25 500	Rodriguez MEX
3-09	Guatemala	W	3-2	Port of Spain	WCq	Latapy [48], John 2 [85 86]	15 000	Archundia MEX
7-09	Costa Rica	L	0-2	San Jose	WCq		17 000	Batres GUA
8-10	Panama	W	1-0	Panama City	WCq	John [61]	1 000	Navarro CAN
12-10	Mexico	W	2-1	Port of Spain	WCq	John 2 [43 69]	23 000	Pineda HON
12-11	Bahrain	D	1-1	Port of Spain	WCpo	Birchall [76]	24 991	Shield AUS
16-11	Bahrain	W	1-0	Manama	WCpo	Lawrence [49]	35 000	Ruiz COL
2006								
28-02	Iceland	W	2-0	London	Fr	Yorke 2 [9 52p]	7 890	
10-05	Peru	D	1-1	Port of Spain	Fr	Jones [74]	20 000	Prendergast JAM
27-05	Wales	L	1-2	Graz	Fr	John [32]	8 000	Messner AUT
31-05	Slovenia	L	1-3	Celje	Fr	Birchall [26]	2 500	Tanovic SCG
3-06	Czech Republic	L	0-3	Prague	Fr		15 910	Johannesson SWE
10-06	Sweden	D	0-0	Dortmund	WCr1		62 959	Maidin SIN
15-06	England	L	0-2	Nuremberg	WCr1		41 000	Kamikawa JPN
20-06	Paraguay	L	0-2	Kaiserslautern	WCr1		46 000	Rosetti ITA
9-08	Japan	L	0-2	Tokyo	Fr		47 482	Sun Baojie CHN
7-10	St Vincent/Grenadines	W	5-0	Port of Spain	Fr	Birchall [13], John 2 [24 46], Yorke [67], Baptiste [79]	4 116	
11-10	Panama	W	2-1	Port of Spain	Fr	Jones [33], Samuel [40]		
15-11	Austria	L	1-4	Vienna	Fr	Samuel [23]	13 100	Matejek CZE
2007								
12-01	Barbados	D	1-1	Port of Spain	CCr1	Glasgow [31]		
15-01	Martinique	W	5-1	Port of Spain	CCr1	Roberts [3], Baptiste 2 [36 75], Glasgow 2 [47 83]		Moreno PAN
17-01	Haiti	W	3-1	Port of Spain	CCr1	Jemmott [15], Glasgow 2 [67 85]		Campbell JAM
20-01	Cuba	W	3-1	Port of Spain	CCsf	OG [41], Glasgow [57], Theobald [73]		
23-01	Haiti	L	1-2	Port of Spain	CCf	Daniel [66]		Moreno PAN
31-01	Panama	L	1-2	Panama City	Fr	Jack [46]	5 000	Vidal PAN
4-02	Costa Rica	L	0-4	Alajuela	Fr			Porras CRC
28-05	Haiti	W	1-0	Port of Spain	Fr			
2-06	Honduras	L	1-3	San Pedro Sula	Fr	Thomas [17]	1 907	Soriano HON
7-06	El Salvador	L	1-2	Carson	GCr1	Spann [8]	21 334	Arredondo MEX
9-06	USA	L	0-2	Carson	GCr1		27 000	Moreno PAN
12-06	Guatemala	D	1-1	Foxboro	GCr1	McFarlane [87]	26 523	Pineda HON

Fr = Friendly match • GC = CONCACAF Gold Cup • WC = FIFA World Cup
q = qualifier • po = play-off • r1 = first round group • sf = semi-final • f = final

TRINIDAD AND TOBAGO NATIONAL TEAM RECORDS AND RECORD SEQUENCES

Records			Sequence records					
Victory	11-0	ARU 1989	Wins	8	1996, 1999	Clean sheets	5	2000, 2004
Defeat	0-7	MEX 2000	Defeats	6	1955-1957	Goals scored	19	1998-1999
Player Caps	118	EVE Angus	Undefeated	9	1996, 1999	Without goal	5	2006
Player Goals	64	JOHN Stern	Without win	13	1983-1985	Goals against	15	1976-1979

TRINIDAD AND TOBAGO COUNTRY INFORMATION

Capital	Port of Spain	Independence	1962 from the UK	GDP per Capita	$9 500
Population	1 096 585	Status	Republic	GNP Ranking	96
Area km²	5 128	Language	English, Hindi	Dialling code	+1 868
Population density	213 per km²	Literacy rate	98%	Internet code	.tt
% in urban areas	72%	Main religion	Christian 43%, Hindu 23%	GMT + / –	+4
Towns/Cities ('000)	Chaguanas 72; San Juan 56; San Fernando 56; Port of Spain 49; Arima 35; Marabella 26				
Neighbours (km)	Caribbean Sea & Atlantic Ocean 362				
Main stadia	Hasely Crawford Stadium – Port of Spain 27 000; Manny Ramjohn Stadium – Marabella 10 000; Marvin Lee Stadium – Tunapuna 8 000; Dr João Havelange Centre of Excellence – Macoya				

TRINIDAD AND TOBAGO 2006

PROFESSIONAL LEAGUE

	Pl	W	D	L	F	A	Pts	Joe Public	Vibe CT WC	Jabloteh	Caledonia	NE Stars	Rangers	Defence	Petrotin	Strikers	Tobago Utd
Joe Public	32	19	8	5	58	22	65		1-0 0-0	0-0 0-1	0-1 1-0	0-0 1-2	0-0 1-0	3-0 1-0	2-0 3-0	3-1 3-0	2-2
Williams Connection	32	19	8	5	59	24	65	2-3 3-1		0-1 1-0	3-0 2-1	3-0 2-2	5-0 1-0	2-1 1-1	3-0 7-0	0-0 4-2	3-1
San Juan Jabloteh	32	18	8	6	58	25	62	0-0 3-3	1-1 0-1		2-0 1-1	4-2 4-1	4-2 2-1	4-0 0-1	0-0 0-0	1-0	5-0 4-1
Caledonia AIA	32	16	5	11	50	43	53	1-0 2-4	2-2 1-1	2-1 0-2		2-3 1-0	2-1 1-0	1-0 1-2	2-2 3-2	0-1 4-1	1-0
North East Stars	32	16	2	14	53	45	50	1-2 0-1	2-1 1-1	0-1 0-0	1-2 1-2		0-1 1-3	3-1	1-0 2-1	1-0 5-0	5-0 5-1
Superstar Rangers	32	11	7	14	40	50	40	0-4 0-0	1-1 0-1	1-4 2-5	2-4 1-2	4-1 3-2		2-1	1-0	1-1	2-0 1-0
Defence Force	27	9	5	13	33	39	32	0-1	1-2	1-1	1-2	0-2 3-2	1-0 1-2		0-2 0-0	5-1	3-1 3-1
United Petrotin	27	8	8	11	22	34	32	0-1	0-1	2-1	0-3	2-1	0-0 1-1	1-1		2-0	1-1 2-0
San Fernando Strikers	27	5	4	18	27	55	19	1-5	0-1	0-1 1-2	3-1	0-1	3-3 1-2	1-1 1-3	0-1 0-1		4-1
Tobago United	27	0	3	24	21	84	3	1-7 1-5	0-3 1-2	0-3	2-2 1-5	2-4	0-3	1-2	0-2	1-2 2-3	

8/04/2006 - 2/12/2006 • Top scorers: Roan NELSON, Joe Public 16; Anthony WOLFE, San Juan 16

TRINIDAD AND TOBAGO 2006 SPORTWORLD NATIONAL SUPER LEAGUE (2)

	Pl	W	D	L	F	A	Pts
Police	18	13	1	4	36	26	40
Defence Force	18	11	2	5	33	17	35
Phoenix Tobago	18	9	3	5	31	21	30
WASA	18	8	5	5	38	29	29
The Harvard Club	18	8	3	6	31	23	27
Crab Connection	18	7	5	6	37	28	26
House of Dread	18	7	2	9	25	29	23
Caroni	18	6	3	9	31	26	21
Couva Players United	18	3	2	13	18	55	11
TSTT	18	2	4	12	18	44	10

20/07/2006 - 4/12/2006

FA TROPHY 2006

Quarter-finals		Semi-finals		Final	
WASA	4				
Phoenix	2	WASA	3		
W. Connection	0	Police	2		
Police	1			WASA	3 4p
Caledonia AIA	9			North East Stars 3 2p
St Clair	4	Caledonia AIA	1 2p		
SJ Jabloteh	0	North East Stars	1 3p	Ato Boldon, 13-12-2006
North East Stars	1				

FIRST CITIZENS BANK CUP 2006

Quarter-finals		Semi-finals		Final	
W. Connection	4				
S'star Rangers	0	W. Connection	2		
United Petrotin	1	SJ Jabloteh	0		
SJ Jabloteh	2			W. Connection	3
SF Strikers	4			North East Stars	1
Joe Public	3	SF Strikers	1 2p	29-09-2006
Caledonia AIA	1	North East Stars	1 3p	Scorers - Toussaint [57], Oliveira [57], Hector [89] for WC; Jeffrey [7] for NE Stars
North East Stars	3				

RECENT LEAGUE AND CUP RECORD

	Championship						Cup		
Year	Champions	Pts	Runners-up	Pts	Third	Pts	Winners	Score	Runners-up
1999	Defence Force	64	Joe Public	55	Williams Connection	55	Williams Connection		Joe Public
2000	Williams Connection	52	Defence Force	51	San Juan Jabloteh	47	Williams Connection	1-1 5-4p	Joe Public
2001	Williams Connection	37	Joe Public	35	Defence Force	24	Joe Public	1-0	Carib
2002	San Juan Jabloteh	65	Williams Connection	62	Joe Public	48	Williams Connection	5-1	Arima Fire
2003	San Juan Jabloteh	92	Williams Connection	80	North East Stars	64	North East Stars	2-2 4-1p	Williams Connection
2004	North East Strikers	57	Williams Connection	51	San Juan Jabloteh	51	Not played		
2005	Williams Connection	54	San Juan Jabloteh	39	Caledonia AIA/Fire	34	San Juan Jabloteh	2-1	Defence Force
2006	Joe Public	65	Williams Connection	65	San Juan Jabloteh	62	WASA	3-3 4-2p	North East Stars

TUN – TUNISIA

NATIONAL TEAM RECORD
JULY 10TH 2006 TO JULY 12TH 2010

PL	W	D	L	F	A	%
8	5	2	1	13	2	75

FIFA/COCA-COLA WORLD RANKING

1993	1994	1995	1996	1997	1998	1999	2000	2001	2002	2003	2004	2005	2006	High		Low	
32	30	22	23	23	21	31	26	28	41	45	35	28	32	19	02/98	46	05/07

2006–2007											
08/06	09/06	10/06	11/06	12/06	01/07	02/07	03/07	04/07	05/07	06/07	07/07
30	31	28	32	32	32	45	46	44	46	45	40

After seven successive seasons of finishing as runners-up, Etoile du Sahel finally got their hands on the Tunisian Championship after a grueling campaign which saw them slowly overtake Club Africain to eventually finish five points clear. But the success was tarnished by the immediate departure of Faouzi Benzarti, with the Etoile coach claiming he had never enjoyed positive support from officials and that he would have been fired anyway. It was Etoile's second success of the season after a controversy ridden win in the CAF Confederation Cup, where they beat FAR Rabat of Morocco on away goals in the final. The second leg in Sousse ended in a massive brawl as the

INTERNATIONAL HONOURS
Qualified for the FIFA World Cup finals 1978 1998 2002 2006 CAF African Cup of Nations 2004
CAF Champions League Club Africain 1991, Esperance 1994

Moroccan visitors protested the disallowing of a late effort that would have seen them win the trophy. CS Sfaxien reached the final of the African Champions League and had success snatched from them in a dramatic finish after Egypt's Al Ahly won the second leg of the final 1-0 with a injury time goal for a 2-1 aggregate triumph. Tunisia's national side had little trouble qualifying for the 2008 Nations Cup in Ghana, albeit from a relatively easy group. Roger Lemerre's side, with more of a local look about his team, did not concede a single goal in their first five qualifying matches.

THE FIFA BIG COUNT OF 2006

	Male	Female		Total
Number of players	500 636	24 628	Referees and Assistant Referees	998
Professionals	1 075		Admin, Coaches, Technical, Medical	6 626
Amateurs 18+	29 404		Number of clubs	250
Youth under 18	20 950		Number of teams	1 512
Unregistered	42 435		Clubs with women's teams	24
Total players	525 264		Players as % of population	5.16%

Fédération Tunisienne de Football (FTF)
Stade annexe d'El Menzah, Cité Olympique, Tunis 1003, Tunisia
Tel +216 71 793760   Fax +216 71 783843
directeur@ftf.org.tn   www.ftf.org.tn
President: SIOUD Tahar   General Secretary: KRAIEM Ridha
Vice-President: BEN AMOUR Kamel   Treasurer: HAMMAMI Mahmoud   Media Officer: CHAOUACHI Mindher
Men's Coach: LEMERRE Roger   Women's Coach: LANDOULSI Samir
FTF formed: 1956   CAF: 1960   FIFA: 1960
Red shirts with white trimmings, White shorts, Red socks or White shirts with red trimmings, White shorts, White socks

RECENT INTERNATIONAL MATCHES PLAYED BY TUNISIA

2004	Opponents	Score		Venue	Comp	Scorers	Att	Referee
24-01	Rwanda	W	2-1	Radès/Tunis	CNr1	Jaziri [26], Santos [56]	60 000	Evehe CMR
28-01	Congo DR	W	3-0	Radès/Tunis	CNr1	Santos 2 [55 87], Braham [65]	20 000	Damon RSA
1-02	Guinea	D	1-1	Radès/Tunis	CNr1	Ben Achour [58]	18 000	Tessema ETH
7-02	Senegal	W	1-0	Radès/Tunis	CNqf	Mnari [65]	57 000	Ali Bujsaim UAE
11-02	Nigeria	D	1-1	Radès/Tunis	CNsf	Badra [82p], W 5-3p	56 000	Codjia BEN
14-02	Morocco	W	2-1	Radès/Tunis	CNf	Santos [5], Jaziri [52]	60 000	Ndoye SEN
31-03	Côte d'Ivoire	L	0-2	Tunis	Fr		10 000	Haimoudi ALG
28-04	Mali	W	1-0	Sfax	Fr	Jedidi [56]	8 000	Shelmani LBY
30-05	Italy	L	0-4	Radès/Tunis	Fr		30 000	Duhamel FRA
5-06	Botswana	W	4-1	Radès/Tunis	WCq	Ribabro [9], Hagui 2 [35 79], Zitouni [74]	2 844	Abdel Rahman SUD
20-06	Guinea	L	1-2	Conakry	WCq	Braham [67]	15 300	Codjia BEN
18-08	South Africa	L	0-2	Tunis	Fr		4 000	Zekrini ALG
4-09	Morocco	D	1-1	Rabat	WCq	Santos [11]	45 000	Auda EGY
9-10	Malawi	D	2-2	Blantyre	WCq	Jaziri [82], Ghodhbane [89]	20 000	Awuye UGA
2005								
26-03	Malawi	W	7-0	Radès/Tunis	WCq	Guemamdia [3], Santos 4 [12 52 75 77], Clayton [60p], Ghodbane [80]	30 000	Abdel Rahman SUD
27-05	Angola	W	4-1	Tunis	Fr	Zitouni 2 [20 70], Mehedhebi 2 [51 89]	4 000	
4-06	Botswana	W	3-1	Gaborone	WCq	Nafti [20], Santos [44], Wissem [76]	20 000	Mana NGA
11-06	Guinea	W	2-0	Tunis	WCq	Clayton [36p], Chadli [78]	30 000	Lim Kee Chong MRI
15-06	Argentina	L	1-2	Cologne	CCr1	Guemamdia [72p]	28 033	Rosetti ITA
18-06	Germany	L	0-3	Cologne	CCr1		44 377	Prendergast JAM
21-06	Australia	W	2-0	Leipzig	CCr1	Santos 2 [26 70]	23 952	Chandia CHI
17-08	Kenya	W	1-0	Radès/Tunis	WCq	Guemamdia [2]	60 000	Evehe CMR
3-09	Kenya	W	2-0	Nairobi	WCq	Guemamdia [2], Jomaa [85]		Sowe GAM
8-10	Morocco	D	2-2	Radès/Tunis	WCq	Clayton [18], Chadli [69]	60 000	Abd El Fatah EGY
11-11	Congo DR	D	2-2	Paris	Fr	Ben Saada [19], Santos [65]		Garibian FRA
16-11	Egypt	W	2-1	Cairo	Fr	Guemamdia 2 [55 57]		
2006								
12-01	Libya	W	1-0	Radès/Tunis	Fr	Ltifi [73]		
15-01	Ghana	W	2-0	Radès/Tunis	Fr	Melliti [60], Ghodhbane [75p]	25 000	Wahid Salah
22-01	Zambia	W	4-1	Alexandria	CNr1	Santos 3 [35 82 90], Bouazizi [51]	16 000	Maillet SEY
26-01	South Africa	W	2-0	Alexandria	CNr1	Santos [32]	10 000	Evehe CMR
30-01	Guinea	L	0-3	Alexandria	CNr1		18 000	Maidin SIN
4-02	Nigeria	D	1-1	Port Said	CNqf	Hagui [49]	15 000	Maillet SEY
1-03	Serbia & Montenegro	L	0-1	Radès/Tunis	Fr		6 000	Haimoudi ALG
30-05	Belarus	W	3-0	Radès/Tunis	Fr	Namouchi [34p], Santos [46], Jomaa [90]	20 000	
2-06	Uruguay	D	0-0	Radès/Tunis	Fr	L 1-3p		
14-06	Saudi Arabia	D	2-2	Munich	WCr1	Jaziri [23], Jaidi [92+]	66 000	Shield AUS
19-06	Spain	L	1-3	Stuttgart	WCr1	Mnari [8]	52 000	Simon BRA
23-06	Ukraine	L	0-1	Berlin	WCr1		72 000	Amarilla PAR
16-08	Mali	L	0-1	Narbonne	Fr			
3-09	Mauritius	D	0-0	Curepipe	CNq			Ncobo RSA
7-10	Sudan	W	1-0	Radès/Tunis	CNq	Lado OG [79]		Coulibaly MLI
15-11	Libya	W	2-0	Radès/Tunis	Fr	Lachkhem [15], Zouaghi [55]		Zekrini ALG
2007								
7-02	Morocco	D	1-1	Casablanca	Fr	Jomaa [62]		
24-03	Seychelles	W	3-0	Victoria	CNq	Jomaa 3 [14 75 79]		Ssegonga UGA
2-06	Seychelles	W	4-0	Radès/Tunis	CNq	Jomaa [15], Zaïem 2 [41 56], Chermiti [84]		
16-06	Mauritius	W	2-0	Radès/Tunis	CNq	Jomaa [44], Nafti [50]		

Fr = Friendly match • CN = CAF African Cup of Nations • CC = FIFA Confederations Cup • WC = FIFA World Cup
q = qualifier • r1 = first round group • qf = quarter-final • sf = semi-final • f = final

TUNISIA NATIONAL TEAM RECORDS AND RECORD SEQUENCES

Records			Sequence records					
Victory	7-0	TOG 2000, MWI 2005	Wins	7	1963	Clean sheets	6	1965
Defeat	1-10	HUN 1960	Defeats	5	1988	Goals scored	14	1961-1963
Player Caps	n/a		Undefeated	11	1975-1977	Without goal	7	2002
Player Goals	n/a		Without win	14	2002	Goals against	13	1960-1962

TUNISIAN REPUBLIC; AL JUMHURIYAH AT TUNISIYAH

Capital	Tunis	Language	Arabic, French			Independence	1956
Population	10 276 158	Area	163 610 km²	Density	61 per km²	% in cities	57%
GDP per cap	$6 900	Dailling code	+216	Internet	.tn	GMT + / -	+1

MEDALS TABLE

			Overall			League			Cup			Europe			City	Stadium	Cap'ty	DoF
			G	S	B	G	S	B	G	S	B	G	S	B				
1	Espérance Sportive de Tunis	EST	35	19	11	20	10	8	12	6		3	3	3	Tunis	El Menzah	45 000	1919
2	Club Africain	CA	21	32	14	9	18	12	11	12		1	2	2	Tunis	El Menzah	45 000	1920
3	Etoile Sportive du Sahel	ESS	20	25	13	8	14	13	7	7		5	4		Sousse	Stade Olympique	28 000	1925
4	Stade Tunisien	ST	11	8	6	4	3	6	7	5					Tunis	Stade Zouiten	18 000	1948
5	Club Sportif Sfaxien	CSS	11	7	6	7	1	5	3	5		1	1	1	Sfax	Stade Taïeb-Mhiri	22 000	1928
6	Avenir Sportif de la Marsa	ASM	5	8	2		1	2	5	7					Marsa, Tunis	Stade Chtioui	6 000	1939
7	Club Athlétique Bizertin	CAB	4	3	2	1	2	1	2	1		1		1	Bizerte	Stade Municipal	20 000	1928
8	Club Sportif de Hammam Lif	CSHL	3	1	2	1		1	2	1				1	Hammam Lif	Stade Boui Kournine	8 000	1944
9	Jeunesse Sportive Kairouan	JSK	1	2		1	1		1						Kairouan	Stade Zouaoui	15 000	1942
	Olympique de Béjà	OB	1	2					1	2					Béjà	Stade Municipal	8 000	1929
	Sfax Railways Sport	SRS	1	2		1				2					Sfax	Stade Taïeb-Mhiri	22 000	
12	Club Olympique Transports	COT	1	1	2	1	2		1						Tunis	Stade Zouiten	18 000	
13	Espérance Sportive de Zarzis	ESZ	1						1						Zarzis	Stade Jlidi	7 000	1934
14	Stade Soussien	SS		2		1			1						Sousse	Stade Maarouf	5 000	
15	EM Mehdia	EMM	1						1						Mehdia			
	Etoile Sportive Beni Khalled	ESBK	1						1						Beni Khalled	Stade Habib Tajouri	5 000	
17	US Tunisien	UST		2		2									Tunis			

RECENT LEAGUE AND CUP RECORD

	Championship							Cup		
Year	Champions	Pts	Runners-up	Pts	Third	Pts		Winners	Score	Runners-up
1995	CS Sfaxien	38	Espérance Tunis	37	Etoile du Sahel	37		CS Sfaxien	2-1	Olympique Béja
1996	Club Africain	63	Etoile du Sahel	58	Espérance Tunis	52		Etoile du Sahel	2-1	JS Kairouan
1997	Etoile du Sahel	64	Espérance Tunis	61	CS Sfaxien	45		Espérance Tunis	1-0	CS Sfaxien
1998	Espérance Tunis	69	Cub Africain	59	Etoile du Sahel	48		Club Africain	1-1 4-2p	Olympique Béja
1999	Espérance Tunis	38	CA Bizertin	25	CS Sfaxien	24		Espérance Tunis	2-1	Club Africain
2000	Espérance Tunis	60	Etoile du Sahel	53	CS Sfaxien	35		Club Africain	0-0 4-2p	CS Sfaxien
2001	Espérance Tunis	57	Etoile du Sahel	38	Club Africain	36		CS Hammam-Lif	1-0	Etoile du Sahel
2002	Espérance Tunis	46	Etoile du Sahel	39	Club Africain	35		Tournament not finished		
2003	Espérance Tunis	57	Etoile du Sahel	38	Club Africain	35		Stade Tunisien	1-0	Club Africain
2004	Espérance Tunis	53	Etoile du Sahel	44	Club Africain	42		CS Sfaxien	2-0	Espérance Tunis
2005	CS Sfaxien	58	Etoile du Sahel	58	Club Africain	56		ES Zarzis	2-0	Espérance Tunis
2006	Espérance Tunis	56	Etoile du Sahel	55	Club Africain	47		Espérance Tunis	2-2 5-4p	Club Africain
2007	Etoile du Sahel	54	Club Africain	49	Espérance Tunis	49		Espérance Tunis	2-1	CA Bizertin

TUNISIA 2006–07

LIGUE NATIONALE A

	Pl	W	D	L	F	A	Pts	Etoile	Club Africain	Espérance T	Monastir	Sfaxien	Stade	Gafsa	Olymp. Béja	Hammam Lif	Marsa	ES Zarzis	Bizertin	Kram	Ha'm-Sousse
Etoile du Sahel †	26	15	8	3	43	18	54		1-0	3-1	1-1	5-0	2-1	2-1	3-2	2-0	1-1	4-2	1-2	3-0	1-1
Club Africain †	26	13	10	3	38	22	49	1-0		1-0	3-0	2-1	0-0	2-0	4-1	0-2	4-2	1-0	1-1	2-0	1-0
Espérance Tunis ‡	26	13	10	3	40	26	49	1-0	1-1		1-3	2-1	2-1	1-1	0-0	3-1	3-1	2-1	4-1	2-1	2-0
US Monastir ‡	26	13	8	5	34	24	47	0-0	4-4	1-1		2-1	1-2	1-1	3-0	1-0	3-0	1-0	2-2	1-0	1-0
CS Sfaxien	26	10	8	8	37	28	38	1-2	1-2	0-0	1-1		1-0	2-2	4-1	2-1	2-1	3-0	4-0	4-0	2-1
Stade Tunisien	26	8	8	10	25	26	32	0-0	0-1	2-3	2-1	0-0		4-0	3-0	0-3	2-1	0-0	2-1	1-3	1-1
EGS Gafsa	26	6	12	8	25	32	30	1-1	2-2	2-2	0-1	1-1	2-1		2-1	0-0	2-2	0-2	2-1	1-0	1-1
Olympique Béjà	26	7	9	10	23	35	30	1-1	1-1	1-2	2-1	1-1	0-0	0-0		2-1	1-2	1-0	1-0	2-1	1-0
CS Hammam Lif	26	6	11	9	22	26	29	1-1	0-0	1-1	2-0	1-2	0-0	1-2	0-0		0-0	1-1	2-2	2-2	1-0
AS Marsa	26	7	6	13	22	34	27	0-1	0-0	0-2	0-1	0-3	3-1	1-0	1-1	0-1		2-0	2-1	0-1	0-0
Espérance Zarzis	26	6	8	12	20	25	26	0-2	0-0	1-1	0-1	2-0	0-0	0-1	1-0	3-0	0-1		2-1	0-0	1-0
CA Bizertin	26	5	10	11	28	37	25	0-0	0-2	1-1	1-2	0-0	0-1	1-1	4-2	2-0	3-1	1-1		1-2	1-1
EOG Kram	26	5	9	12	15	27	24	0-1	1-1	0-1	0-1	1-1	0-0	1-0	0-0	0-0	0-0	0-1	2-1		0-0
ES Hammam-Sousse	26	4	11	11	14	26	23	0-4	4-2	1-1	0-0	0-0	0-1	1-0	0-1	0-1	1-0	0-3	0-0	2-1	

19/08/2006 - 27/05/2007 • † Qualified for the CAF Champions League • ‡ Qualified for the CAF Confederation Cup • Match in bold awarded

TUNISIA 2006–07 LIGUE NATIONAL B (2)

	Pl	W	D	L	F	A	Pts
Jendouba Sport	26	13	9	4	36	23	48
Stade Gabésien	26	13	9	4	38	21	48
Olympique Kef	26	11	7	8	30	24	40
AS Ariana	26	10	6	10	24	24	36
ES Jerba	26	9	8	9	28	27	35
El Makarem Mahdia	26	9	8	9	30	34	35
CS Korba	26	9	7	10	30	35	34
AS Kasserine	26	7	13	6	25	27	34
AS Djerba	26	9	6	11	25	29	33
ES Béni Khalled	26	9	5	12	25	36	32
JS Kairouan	26	8	7	11	33	30	31
Stir Zarzouna Bizerte	26	7	10	9	35	34	31
AS Gabés	26	7	10	9	27	27	31
CO Médenine	26	4	9	13	17	32	21

10/09/2006 - 13/05/2007

COUPE NATIONALE 2006–07

Fourth Round

Espérance Tunis	2
Olympique Béja *	1
CS Hazgui *	1
Jendouba Sports	3
Espérance Zarzis *	1
US Boussalem	0
ES Menzel Témime *	1
US Monastir	4
CS Hammam Lif	1 5p
SC Moknine *	1 3p
Stade Tunisien *	2
Etoile du Sahel	3
OC Kerkennah	0 5p
MS Manouba *	0 3p
Olympique Kef *	1
CA Bizertin	2

Quarter–finals

Espérance Tunis *	3
Jendouba Sports	0
Espérance Zarzis *	0
US Monastir	2
CS Hammam Lif *	0 4p
Etoile du Sahel	0 3p
OC Kerkennah *	2
CA Bizertin	3

Semi–finals

Espérance Tunis	2
US Monastir	0
CS Hammam Lif	0
CA Bizertin	1

Final

Espérance Tunis ‡	2
CA Bizertin	1

CUP FINAL

Stade 7 Novembre, Radès, 20-05-2007
Att: 51 000, Ref: Iturralde Gonzalez ESP

Scorers - Michael Enramo [36p],
Arbi Jabeur [49] for EST;
Jihed Zarrouk [61] for CAB

* Home team • ‡ Qualified for the CAF Confederation Cup

TUR – TURKEY

NATIONAL TEAM RECORD
JULY 10TH 2006 TO JULY 12TH 2010

PL	W	D	L	F	A	%
10	5	3	2	18	8	65

FIFA/COCA-COLA WORLD RANKING

1993	1994	1995	1996	1997	1998	1999	2000	2001	2002	2003	2004	2005	2006	High		Low	
52	48	30	31	43	57	29	30	23	9	8	14	11	26	5	06/04	67	10/93

2006–2007											
08/06	09/06	10/06	11/06	12/06	01/07	02/07	03/07	04/07	05/07	06/07	07/07
28	28	21	25	26	27	26	27	17	19	21	24

Turkey made a strong start to their UEFA Euro 2008 qualifying campaign with four straight wins, two of them in their 'home from home' in Frankfurt, Germany, as the national team served out their three-match ban from playing matches in Turkey. The 4-1 victory over eternal rivals Greece was particularly satisfying but a 3-2 defeat at the hands of Bosnia wasn't the ideal way for Fatih Terim's side to finish the season as they attempt to qualify for their first major finals since 2002. It wasn't a very successful year for Turkish clubs in European competition with Galatasaray finishing bottom of their UEFA Champions League group and Fenerbahçe not even making it to that stage. Under

INTERNATIONAL HONOURS
Qualified for the FIFA World Cup finals 2002   **UEFA European U-17 Championship** 1994 2005

new coach Zico, Fenerbahçe did have a good season at home, winning a record 17th title in their centenary season and also banishing memories of the capitulation on the final day of the previous year. Both Eric Gerets at Galatasaray and Jean Tigana at Besiktas parted company with their clubs at the end of a season, this despite Tigana leading Besiktas to victory in the Turkish Cup Final against Kayseri Erciyesspor. Kayseri were subsequently relegated but still qualified for the UEFA Cup whilst Bursapor became only the third club to beat all of the leading quartet of Galatasaray, Fenerbahçe, Besiktas and Trabzonspor in the same season since the League began in 1959.

THE FIFA BIG COUNT OF 2006

	Male	Female		Total
Number of players	2 402 838	345 819	Referees and Assistant Referees	802
Professionals	4 491		Admin, Coaches, Technical, Medical	20 725
Amateurs 18+	59 980		Number of clubs	4 298
Youth under 18	131 916		Number of teams	9 823
Unregistered	847 000		Clubs with women's teams	152
Total players	2 748 657		Players as % of population	3.90%

Türkiye Futbol Federasyonu (TFF)
Konaklar Mah. Ihlamurlu Sok. 9, 4. Levent, Istanbul, Turkey
Tel +90 212 2827020   Fax +90 212 2827016
tff@tff.org.tr   www.tff.org
President: ULUSOY Haluk   General Secretary: ARIBOGAN Lütfi
Vice-President: KAPULLUOGLU Kemal   Treasurer: BATMAZ Erdal   Media Officer: UGUR Ilker
Men's Coach: TERIM Fatih   Women's Coach: KIZILET Ali
TFF formed: 1923   UEFA: 1962   FIFA: 1923
White shirts with red trimmings, White shorts, White socks or Red shirts with white trimmings, Red shorts, Red socks

RECENT INTERNATIONAL MATCHES PLAYED BY TURKEY

2004	Opponents	Score	Venue	Comp	Scorers	Att	Referee
18-02	Denmark	L 0-1	Adana	Fr		15 000	Wack GER
31-03	Croatia	D 2-2	Zagreb	Fr	Zafer Biryol [73], Cagdas Atan [78]	12 000	Lopes Ferreira POR
28-04	Belgium	W 3-2	Brussels	Fr	Basturk [43], Tolga Seyhan [68], Karadeniz [89]	25 000	Van Egmond NED
21-05	Australia	W 3-1	Sydney	Fr	Umit Ozat [42], Hakan Sukur 2 [69 76]	28 326	Kamikawa JPN
24-05	Australia	W 1-0	Melbourne	Fr	Nihat Kahveci [45]	28 953	Rugg NZL
2-06	Korea Republic	W 1-0	Seoul	Fr	Hakan Sukur [22]	51 185	Maidin SIN
5-06	Korea Republic	L 1-2	Daegu	Fr	Hakan Sukur [44]	45 284	Yoshida JPN
18-08	Belarus	W 2-1	Denizli	Fr	Hakan Sukur [14]	18 000	Mrkovic BIH
4-09	Georgia	D 1-1	Trabzon	WCq	Fatih Tekke [49], Malkhaz Asatiani [85]	10 169	Medina Cantalejpo ESP
8-09	Greece	D 0-0	Piraeus	WCq		32 182	Frisk SWE
9-10	Kazakhstan	W 4-0	Istanbul	WCq	Karadeniz [17], Nihat Kahveci [50], Fatih Tekke 2 [90 93+]	39 900	Hrinak SVK
13-10	Denmark	D 1-1	Copenhagen	WCq	Nihat Kahveci [70]	41 331	De Santis ITA
17-11	Ukraine	L 0-3	Istanbul	WCq		40 468	Cardoso Batista POR
2005							
26-03	Albania	W 2-0	Istanbul	WCq	Necati Ates [3p], Basturk [5]	32 000	Plautz AUT
30-03	Georgia	W 5-2	Tbilisi	WCq	Tolga Seyhan [12], Fatih Tekke 2 [20 35], Koray Avci [72], Tuncay Sanli [89]	10 000	Hauge NOR
4-06	Greece	D 0-0	Istanbul	WCq		26 700	Merk GER
8-06	Kazakhstan	W 6-0	Almaty	WCq	Fatih Tekke 2 [13 85], Ibrahim Toraman [15], Tuncay Sanli 2 [41 90], Halil Altintop [88]	20 000	Kassai HUN
17-08	Bulgaria	L 1-3	Sofia	Fr	Fatih Tekke [21]	25 000	Zografos GRE
3-09	Denmark	D 2-2	Istanbul	WCq	Okan Buruk [47], Tumer Metin [81]	29 721	Mejuto Gonzalez ESP
7-09	Ukraine	W 1-0	Kyiv	WCq	Tumer Metin [55]	67 000	Sars FRA
8-10	Germany	W 2-1	Istanbul	Fr	Halil Altintop [25], Nuri [89]	25 000	Messina ITA
12-10	Albania	W 1-0	Tirana	WCq	Tumer Metin [58]	8 000	Dauden Ibanez ESP
12-11	Switzerland	L 0-2	Berne	WCpo		31 130	Michel SVK
16-11	Switzerland	W 4-2	Istanbul	WCpo	Tuncay Sanli 3 [22 36 89], Necati Ates [52p]	42 000	De Bleeckere BEL
2006							
1-03	Czech Republic	D 2-2	Izmir	Fr	Umit Karan 2 [89 90]	58 000	Meyer GER
12-04	Azerbaijan	D 1-1	Baku	Fr	Hasan Kabze [78]		Paniashvili GEO
24-05	Belgium	D 3-3	Genk	Fr	Necati Ates [2], Hasan Kabze [27], Tuncay Sanli [75]	15 000	Stuchlik AUT
26-05	Ghana	D 1-1	Bochum	Fr	Nihat Kahveci [17]	9 738	Meier GER
31-05	Saudi Arabia	W 1-0	Offenbach	Fr	Necati Ates [59]	9 000	Fleischer GER
2-06	Angola	W 3-2	Arnhem	Fr	Necati Ates [53], Nihat Kahveci [71], Halil Altintop [85]	1 200	Wegereef NED
4-06	FYR Macedonia	L 0-1	Krefeld	Fr		7 000	
16-08	Luxembourg	W 1-0	Luxembourg	Fr	Fatih Tekke [26]	3 353	Weiner GER
6-09	Malta	W 2-0	Frankfurt	ECq	Nihat Kahveci [56], Tümer Metin [77]	BCD	Vázquez ESP
7-10	Hungary	W 1-0	Budapest	ECq	Tuncay Sanli [41]	6 800	Hamer LUX
11-10	Moldova	W 5-0	Frankfurt	ECq	Hakan Sükür 4 [35 37p 43 73], Tuncay Sanli [68]	BCD	Vollquartz DEN
15-11	Italy	D 1-1	Bergamo	Fr	Materazzi OG [42]	24 386	Busacca SUI
2007							
7-02	Georgia	L 0-1	Tbilisi	Fr		50 000	Lajuks LVA
24-03	Greece	W 4-1	Piraeus	ECq	Tuncay Sanli [27], Gökhan Unal [55], Tümer Metin [70], Gökdeniz [81]	31 405	Stark GER
28-03	Norway	D 2-2	Frankfurt	ECq	Hamit Altintop 2 [72 90]	BCD	Farina ITA
2-06	Bosnia-Herzegovina	L 2-3	Sarajevo	ECq	Hakan Sükür [13], Sabri [39]	13 800	Fröjdfeldt SWE
5-06	Brazil	D 0-0	Dortmund	Fr		26 700	Meyer GER

Fr = Friendly match • EC = UEFA EURO 2004/2008 • CC = FIFA Confederation Cup • WC = FIFA World Cup • q = qualifier • po = play-off

TURKEY NATIONAL TEAM RECORDS AND RECORD SEQUENCES

Records			Sequence records		
Victory	7-0	SYR, KOR, SMR	Wins	5	1995, 2002
Defeat	0-8	POL, ENGx2	Defeats	8	1980-1982
Player Caps	114	RUSTU Reçber	Undefeated	15	1998-1999
Player Goals	51	HAKAN Sükür	Without win	17	1989-1992

Clean sheets	4	1958-1959
Goals scored	15	1925-1931
Without goal	8	1980-1982
Goals against	19	1923-1931

REPUBLIC OF TURKEY; TURKIYE CUMHURIYETI

Capital Ankara	Language Turkish		Formation 1923
Population 71 158 647	Area 780 580 km²	Density 88 per km²	% in cities 69%
GDP per cap $6700	Dailling code +90	Internet .tr	GMT + / - +2

MEDALS TABLE

		Overall			League			Cup			Europe			City	Stadium	Cap'ty	DoF
		G	S	B	G	S	B	G	S	B	G	S	B				
1	Galatasaray SK	31	14	16	16	9	15	14	5		1		1	Istanbul	Ali Sami Yen	23 785	1905
2	Fenerbahçe SK	21	22	6	17	15	6	4	7					Istanbul	Sükrü Saracoglu	50 509	1907
3	Besiktas JK	17	20	7	10	14	7	7	6					Istanbul	Inönü Stadi	32 750	1903
4	Trabzonspor	13	12	5	6	7	5	7	5					Trabzon	Hüseyin Avni Aker	21 700	1967
5	Altay SK	2	5	2		2		2	5					Izmir	Alsancak Stadi	17 500	1914
6	MKE Ankaragücü	2	3					2	3					Ankara	19 Mayis Stadi	21 250	1910
7	Gençlerbirligi SK	2	2	2		2		2	2					Ankara	19 Mayis Stadi	21 250	1923
8	Göztepe AS	2	1	2		1		2	1			1		Izmir	Alsancak Stadi	17 500	1925
9	Kocaelispor	2		1		1		1	2					Izmit	Ismet Pasa	15 000	1966
10	Eskisehirspor	1	5	2	3	2		1	2					Eskisehir	Atatürk Stadi	18 413	1965
11	Bursaspor	1	3					1	3					Bursa	Atatürk Stadi	19 700	1963
12	Sakaryaspor	1						1						Sakarya	Atatürk Stadi	14 500	1965
13	Samsunspor	1	2			2		1						Samsun	19 Mayis Stadi	13 500	1965
14	Boluspor	1	1			1		1						Boluspor	Atatürk Stadi	8 000	1965
15	Adana Demirspor	1						1						Adana	5 Ocak Stadi	19 000	1940
	Adanaspor	1			1									Adana	5 Ocak Stadi	19 000	1954
	Kayseri Erciyesspor	1						1						Kayseri	Atatürk Stadi	26 500	1966
	Mersin Idman Yurdu	1						1						Mersin	Tevfik Sirri Gür	17 500	1925
	Antalyaspor	1						1						Antalya	Atatürk Stadi	12 000	1966

RECENT LEAGUE AND CUP RECORD

	Championship						Cup		
Year	Champions	Pts	Runners-up	Pts	Third	Pts	Winners	Score	Runners-up
1995	Besiktas	79	Trabzonspor	76	Galatasaray	69	Trabzonspor	3-2 1-0	Galatasaray
1996	Fenerbahçe	84	Trabzonspor	82	Besiktas	69	Galatasaray	1-0 1-1	Fenerbahçe
1997	Galatasaray	82	Besiktas	74	Fenerbahçe	73	Kocaelispor	1-0 1-1	Trabzonspor
1998	Galatasaray	75	Fenerbahçe	71	Trabzonspor	66	Besiktas	1-1 1-1 4-2p	Galatasaray
1999	Galatasaray	78	Besiktas	77	Fenerbahçe	72	Galatasaray	0-0 2-0	Besiktas
2000	Galatasaray	79	Besiktas	75	Gaziantepspor	62	Galatasaray	5-3	Antalyaspor
2001	Fenerbahçe	76	Galatasaray	73	Gaziantepspor	68	Gençlerbirligi	2-2 4-1p	Fenerbahçe
2002	Galatasaray	78	Fenerbahçe	75	Besiktas	62	Kocaelispor	4-0	Besiktas
2003	Besiktas	85	Galatasaray	77	Gençlerbirligi	66	Trabzonspor	3-1	Gençlerbirligi
2004	Fenerbahçe	76	Trabzonspor	72	Besiktas	62	Trabzonspor	4-0	Gençlerbirligi
2005	Fenerbahçe	80	Trabzonspor	77	Galatasaray	76	Galatasaray	5-1	Fenerbahçe
2006	Galatasaray	83	Fenerbahçe	81	Besiktas	54	Besiktas	3-2	Fenerbahçe
2007	Fenerbahçe	70	Besiktas	61	Galatasaray	56	Besiktas	1-0	Kayseri Erciyesspor

TURKEY 2006-07

SUPER LIG

	Pl	W	D	L	F	A	Pts	Fenerbahçe	Besiktas	Galatasaray	Trabzonspor	Kayserispor	Gençlerbirligi	Sivasspor	Ankaraspor	Konyaspor	Bursaspor	Gaziantepspor	Manisaspor	Ankaragücü	Denizlispor	Caukur	Antalyaspor	K.Erciyesspor	Sakaryaspor
Fenerbahçe †	34	20	10	4	65	31	70		0-0	2-1	2-2	4-1	2-1	2-2	2-1	3-0	0-1	4-1	0-0	3-1	2-2	2-1	4-2	6-0	1-0
Besiktas †	34	18	7	9	43	32	61	0-1		2-1	2-3	2-1	1-0	0-1	2-1	3-1	3-1	2-1	3-1	2-1	2-0	1-0	1-0	1-0	0-0
Galatasaray ‡	34	15	11	8	58	37	56	1-2	1-0		2-1	4-0	1-0	3-1	2-0	3-3	3-1	2-2	4-0	1-1	1-1	3-1	1-1	0-1	4-0
Trabzonspor	34	15	7	12	54	44	52	1-2	3-2	3-1		0-0	4-3	2-0	3-0	1-1	3-1	2-0	1-1	0-1	1-0	0-1	0-0	3-1	5-2
Kayserispor	34	13	12	9	54	43	51	2-2	3-0	0-0	1-0		0-0	1-1	3-3	2-1	2-0	1-2	2-2	2-1	1-0	1-0	4-4	1-0	2-0
Gençlerbirligi	34	14	6	14	43	42	48	0-2	0-2	1-3	3-0	2-2		0-1	2-1	4-1	1-0	0-0	0-5	1-2	3-1	2-1	1-0	1-2	1-0
Sivasspor	34	14	6	14	41	44	48	1-1	0-1	1-1	3-2	1-2		0-2	1-3	3-1	3-1	3-2	2-1	0-2	1-0	0-1	2-1	0-2
Ankaraspor	34	10	17	7	43	38	47	2-2	0-0	1-1	2-1	1-1	1-2	2-1		4-2	0-0	2-0	1-1	1-0	1-1	2-1	1-1	2-2	1-0
Konyaspor	34	12	9	13	42	44	45	0-1	2-1	2-2	1-2	1-1	2-1	2-0	2-2		1-0	0-2	1-0	2-0	5-1	2-0	0-0	1-1	1-1
Bursaspor	34	12	9	13	36	42	45	0-4	3-0	2-0	2-1	0-3	0-0	1-3	0-0	1-0		1-1	4-0	0-0	1-0	1-0	0-0	0-0	3-1
Gaziantepspor	34	11	10	13	31	39	43	0-2	0-0	1-0	2-1	1-2	2-0	1-0	0-2	1-0	1-2		0-0	2-1	1-1	1-0	0-0	0-1	1-0
Vestel Manisaspor	34	11	9	14	41	45	42	2-3	1-0	2-2	0-0	1-0	0-3	1-0	1-3	0-1	4-1	4-1		0-1	0-0	2-0	3-2	5-1	0-3
MKE Ankaragücü	34	11	9	14	32	39	42	0-1	0-1	1-2	2-2	0-4	0-0	1-4	1-1	2-0	1-1	2-1	0-1		0-0	2-0	1-0	4-1	1-0
Denizlispor	34	9	14	11	33	40	41	0-0	0-2	1-1	3-4	2-1	3-2	2-0	1-1	0-1	0-0	0-2	0-0	1-0		2-0	1-1	2-1	1-0
Caykur Rizespor	34	11	7	16	34	40	40	0-1	0-1	2-1	3-2	2-1	0-1	1-1	1-1	1-0	1-2	2-0	3-1	3-1	2-2		1-0	0-0	3-1
Antalyaspor	34	8	15	11	32	36	39	1-0	4-4	0-1	1-2	1-0	1-3	1-2	1-1	1-0	3-2	0-0	0-0	1-1	0-0		3-1	1-0
Kayseri Erciyesspor ‡	34	9	10	15	29	49	37	1-1	1-1	1-2	0-1	0-4	0-2	0-0	1-0	1-2	2-1	1-1	1-0	0-1	2-0	1-1	0-0		2-0
Sakaryaspor Adapazari	34	4	10	20	25	51	22	2-1	1-1	0-3	1-0	3-3	1-1	1-3	0-0	1-1	1-3	1-2	0-1	0-0	1-2	1-1	0-0	1-2	

4/08/2006 - 26/05/2007 • † Qualified for the UEFA Champions League • ‡ Qualified for the UEFA Cup

TURKEY 2006-07 2. LIG A

	Pl	W	D	L	F	A	Pts
Gençlerbirligi Oftas	34	19	9	6	48	29	66
Istanbul BB	34	19	8	7	56	27	65
Malatyaspor †	34	18	7	9	66	41	61
Diyarbakirspor †	34	14	10	10	39	32	52
Kasimpasa †	34	14	10	10	53	41	52
Altay Izmir †	34	14	9	11	51	51	51
Elazigspor	34	14	8	12	52	49	50
Orduspor	34	14	7	13	50	43	49
Istanbulspor	34	10	13	11	39	46	43
Samsunspor	34	11	10	13	31	38	43
Kocaelispor	34	9	15	10	42	45	42
Gaziantep BB	34	10	12	12	47	48	42
Eskisehirspor	34	10	10	14	33	39	40
Karsiyaka Izmir	34	10	10	14	35	39	40
Mardinspor	34	9	11	14	27	44	38
Türk Telecom Ankara	34	8	11	15	43	54	35
Sebatspor Akçaabat	34	8	8	18	40	65	32
Usakspor	34	7	8	19	33	54	29

19/05/2007 - 14/05/2006 • † Qualified for the play-offs

Play-off semi-finals: Altay Izmir 1-0 Malatyaspor; Kasimpasa 2-1 Diyarbakirspor
Play-off final: Kasimpasa 3-3 4-3p Altay Izmir (All matches in Ankara)

TURKIYE KUPASI 2006-07

Third round groups (Five teams in each group)

Quarter–finals		

Group A — Pts
Galatasaray 9
Kayseri Erciyesspor 7

Besiktas * 4 0
VESTEL Manisa 0 2

Group B — Pts
VESTEL Manisa 7
Trabzonspor 6

Gençlerbirligi 1 0
Fenerbahçe * 2 1

Group C — Pts
Fenerbahçe 12
Gaziantepspor 9

Trabzonspor * 1 1
Gaziantepspor 0 1

Group D — Pts
Gençlerbirligi 9
Besiktas 9

Galatasaray 0 1
Kayseri Erciyesspor * 0 1

Semi–finals

Besiktas * 1 1
Fenerbahçe 0 1

Trabzonspor * 0 1 4p
Kayseri Erciyesspor 1 0 5p

Final

Besiktas 1
Kayseri Erciyesspor ‡ 0

CUP FINAL
Attaturk Stadium, Izmir
9-05-2007

Scorer - Bobo 102 for Besiktas

* Home team in the first leg • ‡ Qualified for the UEFA Cup

UAE – UNITED ARAB EMIRATES

NATIONAL TEAM RECORD
JULY 10TH 2006 TO JULY 12TH 2010

PL	W	D	L	F	A	%
21	9	2	10	26	32	47.6

FIFA/COCA-COLA WORLD RANKING

1993	1994	1995	1996	1997	1998	1999	2000	2001	2002	2003	2004	2005	2006	High		Low	
51	46	75	60	50	42	54	64	60	89	75	82	85	87	42	11/98	111	10/03

	2006–2007										
08/06	09/06	10/06	11/06	12/06	01/07	02/07	03/07	04/07	05/07	06/07	07/07
88	88	91	83	87	88	87	92	91	90	94	106

2007 proved to be a year of mixed fortunes for the UAE national team. It started off in dramatic fashion with Abu Dhabi hosting the Gulf Cup, a tournament the UAE had never won since first taking part in 1972. They started badly, losing to Oman, but then three straight wins saw them through to the final where they faced Oman again. It may have taken 35 years but the UAE finally got their hands on the trophy thanks to a goal from the player of the tournament, Ismael Matar, in a 1-0 victory. In contrast the AFC Asian Cup finals were a big disappointment. Qatar were beaten in the third match but by then the UAE were already out, having lost to Japan and hosts Vietnam.

INTERNATIONAL HONOURS
Qualified for the FIFA World Cup finals 1990   Gulf Cup 2007

After spending the best part of a decade in the doldrums, Al Wasl completed a domestic double on the last day of the season with a 6-2 win over relegated Dubai. The Brazilian Anderson was the hero with a hat-trick as the Dubai based club won their first title since 1997 after a close fought battle with Al Wahda and Al Jazeera. The previous month they had had an equally emphatic victory over Al Ain to win the President's Cup - the first time they had won the tournament since 1987. Once again the Brazilian influence was strong with Oliveira scoring twice to add to goals by Anderson and Tariq Hassan.

THE FIFA BIG COUNT OF 2006

	Male	Female		Total
Number of players	82 776	0	Referees and Assistant Referees	150
Professionals	67		Admin, Coaches, Technical, Medical	836
Amateurs 18+	1 020		Number of clubs	31
Youth under 18	6 689		Number of teams	156
Unregistered	11 000		Clubs with women's teams	0
Total players	82 776		Players as % of population	3.18%

United Arab Emirates Football Association (UAEFA)
PO Box 916, Abu Dhabi, United Arab Emirates
Tel +971 2 4445600   Fax +971 4 2944344
uaefa@uae-football.org.ae   www.uaefootball.org
President: AL SERKAL Yousuf   General Secretary: BIN DAKHAN Mohammed
Vice-President: AL ROAMITHI Mohamed   Treasurer: AL KHOURI Younes Haji   Media Officer: None
Men's Coach: MESTU Bruno   Women's Coach: None
UAEFA formed: 1971   AFC: 1974   FIFA: 1972
White shirts with red trimmings, White shorts, White socks

RECENT INTERNATIONAL MATCHES PLAYED BY THE UNITED ARAB EMIRATES

2004 Opponents	Score	Venue	Comp	Scorers	Att	Referee
11-11 Jordan	W 4-0	Abu Dhabi	Fr			
17-11 Korea DPR	W 1-0	Dubai	WCq	Saleh Obeid 58	2 000	Abdul Hamid MAS
22-11 Belarus	L 2-3	Dubai	Fr	Saleh Obeid 21, Fahed Masoud 75	600	Kaliq BHR
27-11 Kuwait	L 0-1	Abu Dhabi	Fr			
3-12 Kuwait	D 1-1	Dubai	Fr	Basheer Saeed 26		
10-12 Qatar	D 2-2	Doha	GCr1	Subait Khatir 41p, Ismail Matar 83		
13-12 Oman	L 1-2	Doha	GCr1	Fahed Masoud 46+		
16-12 Iraq	D 1-1	Doha	GCr1	Faisal Khalil 68		
2005						
9-02 Switzerland	L 1-2	Dubai	Fr	Ismail Matar 21	1 000	Al Hilali OMA
24-05 Peru	D 0-0	Tokyo	Fr		6 536	
27-05 Japan	W 1-0	Tokyo	Fr	Haidar Ali 68		Lubos SVK
29-07 Kuwait	D 1-1	Geneva	Fr	Salam Saad 10, W 7-6p		
31-07 Egypt	D 0-0	Geneva	Fr	L 4-5p		
23-09 Benin	D 0-0	Dubai	Fr			
11-10 Oman	D 2-2	Al Ain	Fr	Ismail Matar 2 19 85		
12-11 Brazil	L 0-8	Abu Dhabi	Fr		50 000	Abd El Fatah EGY
16-11 Syria	W 3-0	Damascus	Fr	Saeed Alkas 23, Ismail Matar 34, Faisal Khalil 88		
2-12 Libya	D 1-1	Sharjah	Fr	Abdul Rahman Juma 60		
2006						
18-01 Korea Republic	W 1-0	Dubai	Fr	Faisal Khalil 22		Al Hilali OMA
22-02 Oman	W 1-0	Dubai	ACq	Ismail Matar 15	15 000	Al Ghamdi KSA
1-03 Pakistan	W 4-1	Karachi	ACq	Subait Al Mekhaini 68, Ismail Matar 78, Salam Saad 81, Saeed Alkas 88	10 000	Tongkhan THA
2-05 Syria	W 2-1	Dubai	Fr	Nawaf Mubarak 40, Faisal Khalil 90		
8-08 Iran	L 0-1	Tehran	Fr		4 000	
16-08 Jordan	W 2-1	Amman	ACq	Mohammed Omar 52, Subait Khater 68	18 000	Al Hamdan KSA
27-08 Saudi Arabia	L 0-1	Jeddah	Fr			
6-09 Jordan	D 0-0	Dubai	ACq		9 000	Al Fadhli KUW
11-10 Oman	L 1-2	Muscat	ACq	Mohammed Omar 57	28 000	Huang Junjie CHN
15-11 Pakistan	W 3-2	Abu Dhabi	ACq	Ali Abbas 54, Mohammed Omar 2 58 72	6 000	Sarkar IND
6-12 Poland	L 2-5	Abu Dhabi	Fr	Subait Khater 26, Mohamed Srour 86	1 000	Al Hilali OMA
10-12 Slovakia	L 1-2	Abu Dhabi	Fr	Ismael Matar 90		Ibrahim QAT
2007						
12-01 Iran	L 0-2	Abu Dhabi	Fr		9 000	Omar UAE
17-01 Oman	L 1-2	Abu Dhabi	GCr1	Ismail Matar 63		
20-01 Yemen	W 2-1	Abu Dhabi	GCr1	Mohammed Omar 2p, Basher Saeed 65		
23-01 Kuwait	W 3-2	Abu Dhabi	GCr1	Ismail Matar 2 1 91+, Faisal Khalil 33		
27-01 Saudi Arabia	W 1-0	Abu Dhabi	GCsf	Ismail Matar 91+		
30-01 Oman	W 1-0	Abu Dhabi	GCf	Ismail Matar 73		
21-06 Malaysia	W 3-1	Kelana Jaya	Fr	Faisal Khalil 8, Ismael Matar 52, Al Shehi 67	2 000	Shaharul MAS
24-06 Saudi Arabia	L 0-2	Singapore	Fr			
27-06 Bahrain	D 2-2	Petaling Jaya	Fr	Al Shehi 35, Yousef Jaber 50		
1-07 Korea DPR	W 1-0	Singapore	Fr	Yousef Jaber 52		
8-07 Vietnam	L 0-2	Hanoi	ACr1		39 450	Najm LIB
13-07 Japan	L 1-3	Hanoi	ACr1	Saeed Alkas 66	5 000	Tongkhan THA
16-07 Qatar	W 2-1	Ho Chi Minh City	ACr1	Saeed Alkas 59, Faisal Khalil 90	3 000	Moradi IRN

Fr = Friendly match • AC = AFC Asian Cup • GC = Gulf Cup • WC = FIFA World Cup
q = qualifier • r1 = first round group • sf = semi-final • f = final

UNITED ARAB EMIRATES NATIONAL TEAM RECORDS AND RECORD SEQUENCES

Records			Sequence records				
Victory	12-0	BRU 2001	Wins	5	1993, 1998, 2007	Clean sheets	4	1985, 1993, 1996
Defeat	0-8	BRA 2005	Defeats	9	1990-1992	Goals scored	18	1999-2000
Player Caps	164	AL TALYANI Adnan	Undefeated	16	1996-1997	Without goal	4	1974-1976, 1980
Player Goals	53	AL TALYANI Adnan	Without win	14	1974-1979	Goals against	14	2002-2003

		Population '000
1	Dubai	1 422
2	Abu Dhabi	633
3	Sharjah	584
4	Al Ain	444
5	Ajman	250
6	Ras Al Khaima	121
7	Al Fujairah	69
8	Umm al Quwain	47
9	Khor Fakkan	35

UNITED ARAB EMIRATES; AL IMARAT AL ARABIYAH AL MUTTAHIDAH

Capital	Abu Dhabi	Language	Arabic			Independence	1971
Population	4 444 011	Area	82 880 km²	Density	30 per km²	% in cities	84%
GDP per cap	$23 200	Dailling code	+971	Internet	.ae	GMT + / -	+4

MEDALS TABLE

		Overall			Lge	Cup	Asia			City	Stadium	Cap'ty	DoF
		G	S	B	G	G	G	S	B				
1	Al Ain	14	1	1	9	4	1	1	1	Al Ain	Tahnoon Bin Mohammed	10 000	1968
2	Sharjah FC	13			5	8				Sharjah	Sharjah Stadium	12 000	1966
3	Al Ahli	10			4	6				Dubai	Rashed	18 000	1970
4	Al Wasl	9	1		7	2			1	Dubai	Zabeel	18 000	1960
5	Al Shabab	6	1		2	4			1	Dubai	Al Maktoum	12 000	1958
6	Al Nasr	6			3	3				Dubai	Al Maktoum	12 000	1945
7	Al Wahda	4			3	1				Abu Dhabi	Al Nahyan	12 000	1974
8	Al Sha'ab	1	1			1		1		Sharjah	Khalid Bin Mohammed	10 000	1974
9	Ajman	1								Ajman			
10	Bani Yas	1								Abu Dhabi			
11	Emirates Club									Ras Al Khaima	Al Emarat	3 000	1929
	Al Fujairah									Al Fujairah			1972
	Al Jazeera									Abu Dhabi	Mohammed Bin Zayed	40 000	1974

RECENT LEAGUE AND CUP RECORD

	Championship							Cup		
Year	Champions	Pts	Runners-up	Pts	Third	Pts		Winners	Score	Runners-up
1995	Al Shabab	29	Al Ain	23	Al Wasl	18		Sharjah	0-0 5-4p	Al Ain
1996	Sharjah	39	Al Wasl	35	Al Ain	25		Al Ahli	4-1	Al Wahda
1997	Al Wasl	19	Al Nasr	16	Al Wahda	16		Al Shabab	1-1 5-4p	Al Nasr
1998	Al Ain	32	Sharjah	30	Al Wasl	23		Sharjah	3-2	Al Wasl
1999	Al Wahda	65	Al Ain	57	Al Nasr	56		Al Ain	1-0	Al Shabab
2000	Al Ain	47	Al Nasr	46	Al Wahda	45		Al Wahda	1-1 8-7p	Al Wasl
2001	Al Wahda	50	Al Ahly	42	Al Jazeera	38		Al Ain	3-2	Al Sha'ab
2002	Al Ain	47	Al Jazeera	38	Al Sha'ab	37		Al Ahli	3-1	Al Jazeera
2003	Al Ain	48	Al Wahda	43	Al Ahli	34		Sharjah	1-1 6-5p	Al Wahda
2004	Al Ain	15	Al Ahli	13	Al Shabab	7		Al Ahli	2-1	Al Sha'ab
2005	Al Wahda	62	Al Ain	57	Al Jazeera	53		Al Ain	3-1	Al Wahda
2006	Al Ahli	47	Al Wahda	47	Al Jazeera	45		Al Ain	2-1	Sharjah
2007	Al Wasl	47	Al Wahda	43	Al Jazeera	41		Al Wasl	4-1	Al Ain

UNITED ARAB EMIRATES 2006–07

PREMIER LEAGUE

	Pl	W	D	L	F	A	Pts	Wasl	Wahda	Jazeera	Sharjah	Sha'ab	Shabab	Ahli Dubai	Nasr	Ain	Emirates	Ahli Fujeira	Dubai
Al Wasl †	22	13	8	1	45	24	47		1-1	2-1	1-0	1-1	2-2	3-1	1-0	4-2	3-1	4-2	1-1
Al Wahda	22	13	4	5	40	34	43	0-3		2-1	2-2	2-0	4-3	2-0	2-1	1-0	4-3	4-1	2-1
Al Jazeera	22	13	2	7	40	24	41	0-1	3-0		4-1	3-0	3-0	1-0	1-3	0-2	4-1	2-1	1-1
Sharjah	22	9	5	8	37	33	32	1-1	1-2	0-1		1-2	1-0	2-0	0-0	1-0	2-1	3-1	1-1
Al Sha'ab	22	9	4	9	40	37	31	5-2	1-0	1-3	2-1		0-2	4-1	3-1	3-3	0-2	0-2	4-1
Al Shabab	22	9	4	9	37	34	31	0-1	1-1	1-4	3-1	2-2		0-1	3-1	3-1	0-1	2-1	2-1
Al Ahli Dubai	22	10	0	12	33	34	30	1-3	4-1	3-1	3-5	2-1	1-2		2-0	0-1	2-0	1-3	1-2
Al Nasr	22	7	7	8	30	32	28	1-1	1-1	1-1	3-1	3-2	2-2	1-4		0-1	2-2	1-0	1-0
Al Ain	22	7	7	8	22	26	28	0-0	2-3	2-1	0-3	1-0	2-1	0-1	0-0		0-0	1-1	3-1
Emirates	22	6	5	11	29	40	23	2-2	2-0	2-3	1-1	0-3	1-3	0-2	1-2	2-0		0-0	3-1
Al Ahli Fujeira	22	5	4	13	27	41	19	0-2	2-3	0-1	2-3	2-2	3-1	0-2	3-2	0-0	1-3		0-3
Dubai	22	4	4	14	31	52	16	2-6	1-3	0-1	3-6	2-4	0-4	2-1	1-4	1-1	5-1	1-2	

21/09/2006 - 27/05/2007 • † Qualified for the AFC Champions League

UNITED ARAB EMIRATES 2006–07
SECOND DIVISION

	Pl	W	D	L	F	A	Pts
Dhafra	30	20	6	4	67	22	66
Hatta	30	20	5	5	77	36	65
Al Ittihad	30	19	7	4	72	30	64
Ajman	30	18	7	5	62	27	61
Ras Al Khaima	30	18	3	9	62	34	57
Bani-Yas	30	17	3	10	60	32	54
Al Khaleej	30	16	6	8	60	34	54
Dibba Al Hisn	30	13	6	11	56	49	45
Dibba	30	10	5	15	43	58	35
Al Arabi	30	9	7	14	54	65	34
Hamra Island	30	9	4	17	40	73	31
Thaid	30	7	7	16	42	72	28
Himriya	30	5	8	17	27	52	23
Al Urooba	30	7	2	21	32	72	23
Masafi	30	4	7	19	35	72	19
Ramms	30	5	3	22	37	98	18

21/09/2006 - 11/05/2007

PRESIDENT'S CUP 2006–07

Round of 16		Quarter-finals		Semi-finals		Final	
Al Wasl	2 4p						
Emirates	2 2p	Al Wasl *	1				
Hamra Island	1	Al Ittihad	0				
Al Ittihad	2			Al Wasl	2		
Al Jazeera	0 4p			Al Ahli Dubai *	1		
Dibba Al Hisn	0 2p	Al Jazeera	1				
Ajman	0	Al Ahli Dubai *	2				
Al Ahli Dubai	1					Al Wasl	4
Al Ahli Fujeira	2					Al Ain	1
Shabab	2	Al Ahli Fujeira	2 4p				
Bani Yas	1	Al Nasr *	2 2p				
Al Nasr	2			Al Ahli Fujeira	0		
Al Sha'ab	3			Al Ain *	1		
Al Wahda	2	Al Sha'ab	2				
Ras Al Khaimah	2	Al Ain *	3				
Al Ain	5					* Home team	

CUP FINAL

3-04-2007

Scorers - Oliveira 2 [12 60], Anderson [44], Tariq Hassan [51] for Al Wasl; Frank Ongfieng [26] for Al Ain

UGA – UGANDA

NATIONAL TEAM RECORD
JULY 10TH 2006 TO JULY 12TH 2010

PL	W	D	L	F	A	%
16	5	9	2	16	10	59.3

FIFA/COCA-COLA WORLD RANKING

1993	1994	1995	1996	1997	1998	1999	2000	2001	2002	2003	2004	2005	2006	High		Low	
94	93	74	81	109	105	108	103	119	102	103	109	101	103	66	04/95	121	07/02

2006–2007											
08/06	09/06	10/06	11/06	12/06	01/07	02/07	03/07	04/07	05/07	06/07	07/07
99	99	103	102	103	102	102	102	106	106	91	99

Uganda stand on the brink of possible qualification for the 2008 African Nations Cup final, potentially ending a lengthy absence from the continent's top tournament. A dramatic 2-1 home win over Nigeria in the middle of qualifying campaign allowed Uganda to chase one of the three qualifying berths reserved for the best runners-up in the 12 qualifying groups. They needed to win at home against Niger in their last Group Two qualifiers to stand any chance but a goalless draw at Lesotho in their penultimate match came as a blow to their hopes. The Cranes have shown much progress under the tutelage of Hungarian-born coach Laszlo Csaba and their improving success has

INTERNATIONAL HONOURS
CECAFA Cup 1973 1976 1977 1989 1990 1992 1996 2000 2003

seen a new-found commitment from occasionally errant players in the past, the likes of Ibrahim Ssekagya and Asani Bajope returning to add mettle to the team's spine. Uganda lost two successive penalty shootouts in the CECAFA Cup to finish fourth in December's tournament in Ethiopia. They were beaten in the semifinals by Sudan, who won 6-5 on kicks after a 2-2 draw, and then by Rwanda, who won 4-2 on penalties after a goalless draw in the third place play-off. The taxmen won the league again in July with Uganda Revenue Authority ending with a healthy eight point advantage over second placed SC Villa. Earlier in the season, Express had won the Cup

THE FIFA BIG COUNT OF 2006

	Male	Female		Total
Number of players	1 186 014	5 500	Referees and Assistant Referees	600
Professionals	14		Admin, Coaches, Technical, Medical	5 000
Amateurs 18+	28 000		Number of clubs	400
Youth under 18	18 500		Number of teams	2 000
Unregistered	60 000		Clubs with women's teams	2
Total players	1 191 514		Players as % of population	4.23%

Federation of Uganda Football Associations (FUFA)
FUFA House, Plot No. 879, Kyadondo Block 8, Mengo Wakaliga Road, PO Box 22518, Kampala, Uganda
Tel +256 41 272702   Fax +256 41 272702
fufaf@yahoo.com   www.fufa.co.ug
President: MULINDWA Lawrence   General Secretary: MASEMBE Charles
Vice-President: BARIGYE Richard   Treasurer: KYEYAGO Jowali   Media Officer: MULINDWA Rogers
Men's Coach: CSABA Laszlo   Women's Coach: None
FUFA formed: 1924   CAF: 1959   FIFA: 1959
Yellow shirts, Yellow shorts, Yellow socks

RECENT INTERNATIONAL MATCHES PLAYED BY UGANDA

2004	Opponents	Score		Venue	Comp	Scorers	Att	Referee
6-06	Congo DR	W	1-0	Kampala	WCq	Sekajja [75]	45 000	Maillet SEY
19-06	Cape Verde Islands	L	0-1	Praia	WCq		5 000	Coulibaly MLI
3-07	Ghana	D	1-1	Kampala	WCq	Obua [46+]	20 000	El Beltagy EGY
7-08	Kenya	D	1-1	Kampala	Fr	Obua [27p]	25 000	
14-08	Rwanda	L	1-2	Kampala	Fr	Sebalata		
18-08	Kenya	L	1-4	Nairobi	Fr	Tabula [55]	5 000	
22-08	Zimbabwe	L	0-2	Harare	Fr		3 000	
4-09	Burkina Faso	L	0-2	Ouagadougou	WCq		30 000	Ould Lemghambodj MTN
10-10	South Africa	L	0-1	Kampala	WCq		50 000	Gasingwa RWA
12-12	Somalia	W	2-0	Addis Abeba	CCr1	Kalungi 2 [30 42]		
14-12	Sudan	L	1-2	Addis Abeba	CCr1	Mwesigwa [83]		
18-12	Kenya	D	1-1	Addis Abeba	CCr1	Obua [77p]		
2005								
8-01	Egypt	L	0-3	Cairo	Fr			
26-03	South Africa	L	1-2	Johennesburg	WCq	Obua [63p]	20 000	Chukwujekwu NGA
5-06	Congo DR	L	0-4	Kinshasa	WCq		80 000	Daami TUN
18-06	Cape Verde Islands	W	1-0	Kampala	WCq	Serunkuma [36]	5 000	Kidane ERI
4-09	Ghana	L	0-2	Kumasi	WCq		45 000	Hicuburundi BDI
8-10	Burkina Faso	D	2-2	Kampala	WCq	Masaba [30], Serunkuma [71]	1 433	Benouza ALG
27-11	Ethiopia	D	0-0	Kigali	CCr1			
30-11	Djibouti	W	6-1	Kigali	CCr1	Masaba [12p], Nsereko 2 [27 29], Serunkuma [47], Mawejje [85], Muganga [89]		
1-12	Somalia	W	7-0	Kigali	CCr1	Massa 2 [15 24], Nsereko 18, Mubiru 2 [64 73], Vincent [78], Ryekwassa [88]		
3-12	Sudan	W	3-0	Kigali	CCr1	Massa [4], Serunkuma [35], Mubiru [92+]		
8-12	Rwanda	L	0-1	Kigali	CCsf			
10-12	Zanzibar †	D	0-0	Kigali	CC3p	L 4-5p		
27-12	Egypt	L	0-2	Cairo	Fr			
29-12	Ecuador	W	2-1	Cairo	Fr	Massa [47], Mwanga [54]		
2006								
26-07	Rwanda	D	1-1	Kigali	Fr	Serunkuma [88]		
5-08	Botswana	D	0-0	Kampala	Fr	W 3-1p		
16-08	Libya	L	2-3	Tripoli	Fr	Bongole [46], Serunkuma [69]		
29-08	Burkina Faso	D	0-0	Kampala	Fr			
2-09	Lesotho	W	3-0	Kampala	CNq	Massa 2 [29 42], Obua [57p]		Abdelrahman SUD
8-10	Niger	D	0-0	Niamey	CNq			Abdou Diouf SEN
27-11	Sudan	W	2-1	Addis Abeba	CCr1	Serunkuma [72], Masaba [87p]		
30-11	Rwanda	W	1-0	Addis Abeba	CCr1	Serunkuma [60]		
3-12	Somalia	W	2-0	Addis Abeba	CCr1	Wagaluka [11], Kadogo [17]		
6-12	Malawi	D	0-0	Addis Abeba	CCqf	W 4-2p		
8-12	Sudan	D	2-2	Addis Abeba	CCsf	Kayizi [15], Serunkuma [72]. L 5-6p		
10-12	Rwanda	D	0-0	Addis Abeba	CC3p	L 2-4p		
2007								
24-03	Nigeria	L	0-1	Abeokuta	CNq			Diatta SEN
26-05	Tanzania	D	1-1	Kampala	Fr	Kadogo [2]		
2-06	Nigeria	W	2-1	Kampala	CNq	Obua [52p], Sekajja [65p]		
19-06	Lesotho	D	0-0	Maseru	CNq			

Fr = Friendly match • CN = CAF African Cup of Nations • CC = CECAFA Cup • WC = FIFA World Cup
q = qualifier • r1 = first round group • qf = quarter-final • sf = semifinal • 3p = third place play-off • f = final • † Not a full international

UGANDA NATIONAL TEAM RECORDS AND RECORD SEQUENCES

Records			Sequence records					
Victory	13-1	KEN 1932	Wins	7	1932-1940	Clean sheets	5	1996-1998
Defeat	0-6	TUN 1999	Defeats	5	1978-1979, 2004	Goals scored	19	1931-1952
Player Caps	n/a		Undefeated	15	1996-1998	Without goal	4	1995, 1999
Player Goals	n/a		Without win	11	1995-1996	Goals against	15	1999-2000

UGANDA COUNTRY INFORMATION

Capital	Kampala	Independence	1962 from the UK	GDP per Capita	$1 400
Population	26 404 543	Status	Republic	GNP Ranking	106
Area km²	236 040	Language	English, Ganda	Dialling code	+3
Population density	111 per km²	Literacy rate	69%	Internet code	.ug
% in urban areas	13%	Main religion	Christian 66%, Muslim 16%	GMT + / −	+3
Towns/Cities ('000)	Kampala 1 353; Gulu 146; Lira 119; Jinja 93; Mbarara 79; Mbale 76; Mukono 67; Kasese 67				
Neighbours (km)	Kenya 933; Tanzania 396; Rwanda 169; Congo DR 765; Sudan 435;				
Main stadia	National Stadium – Kampala 40 000				

UGANDA 2006 SUPER LEAGUE

	Pl	W	D	L	F	A	Pts
URA Kampala †	28	19	8	1	47	13	65
Police Jinja	28	16	7	5	42	13	55
Express RE Kampala	28	15	9	4	32	16	54
Kampala City Council	28	15	8	5	34	17	53
SC Villa Kampala	28	13	10	5	39	19	49
Victor FC	28	14	7	7	28	20	49
SC Simba	28	12	11	5	36	21	47
Kinyara Sugar	28	7	13	8	26	26	34
Mbale Heroes	28	8	8	12	18	25	32
Maji FC Kampala	28	7	9	12	23	27	30
Bunamwaya Wakiso	28	7	8	13	26	35	29
Masaka Local Council	28	6	9	13	20	31	27
Kampala United	28	5	10	13	22	31	25
KB Lions	28	2	5	21	14	68	11
Super Cubs Kampala	28	0	6	22	10	55	6

28/01/2006 - 13/08/2006 • † Qualified for Champions League

KAKUNGULU CUP 2006

Quarter-finals		Semi-finals		Final	
Express RE *	0 1				
Kinyara Sugar	0 1	Express RE	1 2		
Kampala Utd *		Victor FC *	0 0		
Victor FC				Express RE	2
SC Simba *	2 0			Maji FC	0
URA Kampala	2 1	SC Simba	0 3	23-09-2006	
Entebbe Utoda *	2 0	Maji FC *	2 1	Scorers - David Zziwa, Tony Odur for Express	
Maji FC	1 2	‡ Qualified for the CAF Confederation Cup			

UGANDA 2006-07 SUPER LEAGUE

	Pl	W	D	L	F	A	Pts
URA Kampala †	32	22	7	3	54	18	73
SC Villa Kampala	32	19	8	5	49	20	65
Police Jinja	32	17	10	5	40	15	61
Kampala City Council	32	17	6	9	51	33	57
Bunamwaya Wakiso	32	15	8	9	38	29	53
Kinyara Sugar	32	12	13	7	37	29	49
Victor FC	32	12	11	9	34	33	47
SC Simba	32	13	6	13	34	25	45
Express RE Kampala	32	8	15	9	22	30	39
Masaka Local Council	32	8	13	11	22	30	36
Maji FC Kampala	32	8	12	12	36	45	36
Boroboro Holy Hill	32	9	9	14	26	37	36
Iganga Town Council	32	7	13	12	17	32	34
Mbale Heroes	31	8	7	16	30	38	31
Kanoni Mukono Utd	31	8	6	17	30	45	30
City Lads Kampala	32	5	8	19	28	49	23
Masindi Town Counvil	32	2	10	20	17	57	16

25/11/2006 - 18/07/2007 • † Qualified for Champions League

KAKUNGULU CUP 2007

Quarter-finals		Semi-finals		Final	
Express RE	1 1				
Kinyara	0 1	Express RE	1 0		
Ex-Villa	2 1	URA Kampala	1 0		
URA Kampala	5 2			Express RE	0 4p
Police	2 0			Kampala CC	0 2p
Villa	2 0	Police		10-08-2007	
Mutundwe Lions	0 0	Kampala CC			
Kampala CC	2 1	‡ Qualified for the CAF Confederation Cup			

RECENT LEAGUE AND CUP RECORD

	Championship						Cup		
Year	Champions	Pts	Runners-up	Pts	Third	Pts	Winners	Score	Runners-up
2000	SC Villa	75	Kampala CC	70	Express	65	SC Villa	1-0	Military Police
2001	SC Villa	70	Kampala CC	65	Mbale Heroes	48	Express	3-1	SC Villa
2002	SC Villa	79	Express	63	Kampala CC	61	SC Villa	2-1	Express
2003	SC Villa	72	Express	72	Kampala CC	53	Express	3-1	Police
2004	SC Villa	67	Express	57	URA Kampala	57	Kampala CC	1-1 3-2	Express
2005	Police Jinja	3-1	SC Villa				URA Kampala	2-1	Kampala CC
2006	URA Kampala	65	Police Jinja	55	Express	54	Express	2-0	Maji FC
2007	URA Kampala	73	SC Villa	65	Police Jinja	61			

UKR – UKRAINE

NATIONAL TEAM RECORD
JULY 10TH 2006 TO JULY 12TH 2010

PL	W	D	L	F	A	%
8	5	1	2	15	7	68.7

FIFA/COCA-COLA WORLD RANKING

1993	1994	1995	1996	1997	1998	1999	2000	2001	2002	2003	2004	2005	2006	High	Low
90	77	71	59	49	47	27	34	45	45	60	57	40	13	11 05/07	132 09/93

2006–2007											
08/06	09/06	10/06	11/06	12/06	01/07	02/07	03/07	04/07	05/07	06/07	07/07
15	13	13	13	13	13	11	11	11	11	13	17

Ukraine may have beaten Italy when it came to choosing the host country for Euro 2012, but the Italians look likely to have the last laugh when it comes to qualifying for Euro 2008. Even though Ukraine finished in the top eight of the last World Cup, they found themselves grouped with Italy and France - the two World Cup Finalists - as well as a resurgent Scotland, and going into the summer 2007 recess they found themselves trailing in fourth place behind their rivals. By winning the right to host Euro 2012, along with neighbours Poland, football in the country now has a focus around which to develop the undoubted potential that exists in Ukraine both on and off the field.

INTERNATIONAL HONOURS
Qualified for the FIFA World Cup finals 2006

Club football could benefit hugely with the League already boasting a number of top class international players from around the world and more could follow like Italy's Cristiano Lucarelli who joined Shakhtar Donetsk in July 2007. Signings like this may enable both Shakhtar and Dynamo Kyiv to challenge for honours on the European scene whereas at the moment they operate on a level just below the top clubs. Of the two it was Dynamo who took the honours at home during the season, going through both their League and Cup campaigns undefeated, finishing 11 points ahead of Shakhtar in the League and beating them 2-1 in the Cup Final.

THE FIFA BIG COUNT OF 2006

	Male	Female		Total
Number of players	2 040 756	232 261	Referees and Assistant Referees	7 530
Professionals	2 427		Admin, Coaches, Technical, Medical	8 050
Amateurs 18+	25 500		Number of clubs	68
Youth under 18	658 540		Number of teams	6 500
Unregistered	314 700		Clubs with women's teams	2
Total players	2 273 017		Players as % of population	4.87%

Football Federation of Ukraine (FFU)
Laboratorna Str. 1, PO Box 293, Kyiv 03150, Ukraine
Tel +380 44 5210521   Fax +380 44 5210550
ffu@ffu.org.ua   www.ffu.org.ua
President: SURKIS Grigoriy   General Secretary: BANDURKO Oleksandr
Vice-President: BANDURKO Oleksandr   Treasurer: MISCHENKO Lyudmyla   Media Officer: NYKONENKO Valeriy
Men's Coach: BLOKHIN Oleg   Women's Coach: KULAYER Volodymyr
FFU formed: 1991   UEFA: 1992   FIFA: 1992
Yellow shirts with blue trimmings, Yellow shorts, Yellow socks or Blue shirts with yellow trimming, Blue shorts, Blue socks

RECENT INTERNATIONAL MATCHES PLAYED BY UKRAINE

2003	Opponents	Score		Venue	Comp	Scorers	Att	Referee
20-08	Romania	L	0-2	Donetsk	Fr		28 000	Egorov RUS
6-09	Northern Ireland	D	0-0	Donetsk	ECq		24 000	Stark GER
19-09	Spain	L	1-2	Elche	ECq	Shevchenko [84]	38 000	Hauge NOR
11-10	FYR Macedonia	D	0-0	Kyiv	Fr		13 000	Orlic MDA
2004								
18-02	Libya	D	1-1	Tripoli	Fr	Pukanych [14]	40 000	El Arjoun MAR
31-03	FYR Macedonia	L	0-1	Skopje	Fr		16 000	Karagic SCG
28-04	Slovakia	D	1-1	Kyiv	Fr	Venhlynskyi [13]	18 000	Ryszka POL
6-06	France	L	0-1	Paris	Fr		66 646	Ceferin SVN
18-08	England	L	0-3	Newcastle	Fr		35 387	McCurry SCO
4-09	Denmark	D	1-1	Copenhagen	WCq	Husin [56]	36 335	Meier SUI
8-09	Kazakhstan	W	2-1	Almaty	WCq	Byelik [14], Rotan [90]	23 000	Oliveira POR
9-10	Greece	D	1-1	Kyiv	WCq	Shevchenko [48]	56 000	Mejuto Gonzalez ESP
13-10	Georgia	W	2-0	Lviv	WCq	Byelik [12], Shevchenko [79]	28 000	Stark GER
17-11	Turkey	W	3-0	Istanbul	WCq	Husyev [8], Shevchenko 2 [17 88]	40 468	Cardoso Batista POR
2005								
9-02	Albania	W	2-0	Tirana	WCq	Rusol [40], Gusin [59]	12 000	Bennett ENG
30-03	Denmark	W	1-0	Kyiv	WCq	Voronin [68]	60 000	Michel SVK
4-06	Kazakhstan	W	2-0	Kyiv	WCq	Shevchenko [18], Avdeyev OG [83]	45 000	Lehner AUT
8-06	Greece	W	1-0	Piraeus	WCq	Gusin [82]	33 500	Temmink NED
15-08	Israel	D	0-0	Kyiv	Fr	L 3-5p		Mikulski POL
17-08	Serbia & Montenegro	W	2-1	Kyiv	Fr	Rebrov [61], Nazarenko [72]		
3-09	Georgia	D	1-1	Tbilisi	WCq	Rotan [43]	BCD	Ovrebo NOR
7-09	Turkey	L	0-1	Kyiv	WCq		67 000	Sars FRA
8-10	Albania	D	2-2	Dnipropetrovsk	WCq	Shevchenko [45], Rotan [86]	24 000	Verbist BEL
12-10	Japan	W	1-0	Kyiv	Fr	Husin [89p]		Lajuks LVA
2006								
28-02	Azerbaijan	D	0-0	Baku	Fr			Sipailo LVA
28-05	Costa Rica	W	4-0	Kyiv	Fr	Nazarenko [27], Vorobei [33], Kalinichenko [38], Bielik [56]	25 000	Ivanov.N RUS
2-06	Italy	D	0-0	Lausanne	Fr		10 000	Nobs SUI
5-06	Libya	W	3-0	Gossau	Fr	Yezerskyi [49], Bielik [87], Vorobei [89]	2 500	Wilzhaber SUI
8-06	Luxembourg	W	3-0	Luxembourg	Fr	Voronin [55], Shevchenko [83], Kalinichenko [84]		Vervecken BEL
14-06	Spain	L	0-4	Leipzig	WCr1		43 000	Busacca SUI
19-06	Saudi Arabia	W	4-0	Hamburg	WCr1	Rusol [4], Rebrov [36], Shevchenko [46], Kalinichenko [84]	50 000	Poll ENG
23-06	Tunisia	W	1-0	Berlin	WCr1	Shevchenko [70p]	72 000	Amarilla PAR
26-06	Switzerland	D	0-0	Cologne	WCr2		45 000	Archundia MEX
30-06	Italy	L	0-3	Hamburg	WCqf		50 000	De Bleeckere BEL
15-08	Azerbaijan	W	6-0	Kyiv	Fr	Voronin [3], Nazarenko [12], Rotan [25], Husiyev [45], Vorobei [71], Bielik [91+]	6 000	Sukhina RUS
6-09	Georgia	W	3-2	Kyiv	ECq	Shevchenko [31], Rotan [62], Rusol [80]	35 000	Jara CZE
7-10	Italy	L	0-2	Rome	ECq		49 149	Vassaras GRE
11-10	Scotland	W	2-0	Kyiv	ECq	Kucher [60], Shevchenko [90p]	50 000	Hansson SWE
2007								
7-02	Israel	D	1-1	Tel Aviv	Fr	Kalinichenko [73]	12 000	Rodriguez ESP
24-03	Faroe Islands	W	2-0	Toftir	ECq	Yezerskiy [20], Gusev [57]	717	Skomina SVN
28-03	Lithuania	W	1-0	Odessa	ECq	Gusev [47]	33 600	Meyer GER
2-06	France	L	0-2	Paris	ECq		79 000	Medina Cantalejo ESP

Fr = Friendly match • EC = UEFA EURO 2004/2008 • WC = FIFA World Cup
q = qualifier • r1 = first round group • r2 = second round • qf = quarter-final • BCD = Behind closed doors

UKRAINE NATIONAL TEAM RECORDS AND RECORD SEQUENCES

Records			Sequence records				
Victory	6-0	AZE 2006	Wins	6	2004-2005	Clean sheets	7	2004-2005
Defeat	0-4	CRO 1995, ESP 2006	Defeats	2	Six times	Goals scored	10	1995-1996
Player Caps	79	SHOVKOVSKYI Oleksandr	Undefeated	13	1998-1999	Without goal	3	2003
Player Goals	33	SHEVCHENKO Andriy	Without win	11	2003-2004	Goals against	8	2004

MAJOR CITIES/TOWNS
Population '000

	City	Population
1	Kyiv	2 469
2	Kharkiv	1 412
3	Dnipropetrovsk	1 017
4	Odessa	988
5	Donetsk	973
6	Zaporizhzhya	787
7	Lviv	710
8	Kryvyi Rih	644
9	Mykolayiv	509
10	Mariupol	477
11	Luhansk	446
12	Makiyivka	370
13	Vinnytsia	350
14	Simferopol	342
15	Sevastopol	328
16	Kherson	318
17	Poltava	318
18	Chernihiv	309
19	Cherkasy	298
20	Sumy	295
21	Zhytomyr	281
22	Horlivka	272
23	Lutsk	216
24	Uzhgorod	118

UKRAINE; UKRAYINA

Capital Kyiv	Language Ukrainian, Russian	Independence 1991
Population 46 299 862	Area 603 700 km²	% in cities 70%
GDP per cap $5400	Dailling code +380	Internet .ua	GMT +/- +2	Density 79 per km²

MEDALS TABLE

		Overall			League			Cup		Europe			City	Stadium	Cap'ty	DoF
		G	S	B	G	S	B	G	S	G	S	B				
1	Dynamo Kyiv	21	5		12	4		9	1				Kyiv	Valeriy Lobanovskyi	16 888	1927
2	Shakhtar Donetsk	8	12		3	9		5	3				Donetsk	RSK Olimpiyskiy	31 547	1936
3	Chernomorets Odessa	2	2	3		2	3	2					Odesa	Tsentralnyi	30 767	1936
4	Tavriya Simferopol	1	1		1				1				Simferopol	Lokomotiv	20 013	1958
5	Dnipro Dnipropetrovsk		4	4		1	4		3				Dnipropetrovsk	Meteor	26 345	1925
6	Karpaty Lviv		2	1			1		2				Lviv	Ukrainia	29 004	1963
7	CSCA Kyiv		2						2				Kyiv			
8	Kryvbas Kryvyi Rih		1	2			2		1				Kryvyi Rih	Metalurh	29 782	1959
9	Metallist Kharkiv		1	1			1		1				Kharkiv	Metallist	28 000	1925
10	Metalurh Zaporizhya		1						1				Zaporizhya	Slavutych Arena	11 983	1935
11	Nyva Vinnytsia		1						1				Vinnytsia			

UKRAINIAN TEAMS IN SOVIET FOOTBALL

		Overall			League			Cup		Europe		
1	Dynamo Kyiv	24	13	5	13	11	3	9	2	2		2
7	Shakhtar Donetsk	4	6	2		2	2	4	4			
9	Dnipro Dnipropetrovsk	3	2	2	2	2	2	1				
13	Zorya Luhansk	1	2		1				2			
15	Metallist Kharkiv	1	1					1	1			
16	Karpaty Lviv	1						1				

RECENT LEAGUE AND CUP RECORD

	Championship						Cup		
Year	Champions	Pts	Runners-up	Pts	Third	Pts	Winners	Score	Runners-up
1995	Dynamo Kyiv	83	Ch'morets Odesa	73	Dn. Dnipropetrovsk	65	Shakhtar Donetsk	1-1 7-6p	Dn. Dnipropetrovsk
1996	Dynamo Kyiv	79	Ch'morets Odesa	73	Dn. Dnipropetrovsk	63	Dynamo Kyiv	2-0	Nyva Vinnitsa
1997	Dynamo Kyiv	73	Shakhtar Donetsk	62	Vorskla Poltava	58	Shakhtar Donetsk	1-0	Dn. Dnipropetrovsk
1998	Dynamo Kyiv	72	Shakhtar Donetsk	67	Karpaty L'viv	57	Dynamo Kyiv	2-1	CSCA Kyiv
1999	Dynamo Kyiv	74	Shakhtar Donetsk	65	Kryvbas Kryvyi Rih	59	Dynamo Kyiv	3-0	Karpaty L'viv
2000	Dynamo Kyiv	84	Shakhtar Donetsk	66	Kryvbas Kryvyi Rih	60	Dynamo Kyiv	1-0	Kryvbas Kryvyi Rih
2001	Dynamo Kyiv	64	Shakhtar Donetsk	63	Dn. Dnipropetrovsk	55	Shakhtar Donetsk	2-1	CSCA Kyiv
2002	Shakhtar Donetsk	66	Dynamo Kyiv	65	Metalurh Donetsk	42	Shakhtar Donetsk	3-2	Dynamo Kyiv
2003	Dynamo Kyiv	73	Shakhtar Donetsk	70	Metalurh Donetsk	60	Dynamo Kyiv	2-1	Shakhtar Donetsk
2004	Dynamo Kyiv	73	Shakhtar Donetsk	70	Dn. Dnipropetrovsk	57	Shakhtar Donetsk	2-0	Dn. Dnipropetrovsk
2005	Shakhtar Donetsk	80	Dynamo Kyiv	73	Metalurh Donetsk	49	Dynamo Kyiv	1-0	Shakhtar Donetsk
2006	Shakhtar Donetsk	75	Dynamo Kyiv	75	Ch'morets Odesa	45	Dynamo Kyiv	1-0	Metalurh Zapor'hja
2007	Dynamo Kyiv	74	Shakhtar Donetsk	63	Metallist Kharkiv		Dynamo Kyiv	2-1	Shakhtar Donetsk

UKRAINE 2006–07

VYSCHA LIHA

	Pl	W	D	L	F	A	Pts	Dynamo Kyiv	Shakhtar	Metalist	Dnipro	Tavriya	Chernomorets	Metalurh Z.	Karpaty	Metalurh D.	Kryvbas	Zorja	Kharkiv	Vorskla	Arsenal	Illychivets	Stal Alchevsk
Dynamo Kyiv †	30	22	8	0	67	23	74		1-0	2-0	2-0	2-1	4-1	3-1	3-1	0-0	3-1	4-0	2-0	1-1	5-2	1-0	3-1
Shakhtar Donetsk †	30	19	6	5	57	20	63	2-2		5-0	2-3	3-0	2-0	0-2	4-1	2-1	5-0	3-0	1-2	2-1	0-1	3-1	3-1
Metalist Kharkiv ‡	30	18	7	5	40	20	61	0-2	0-1		1-0	1-0	4-0	1-0	1-1	1-0	0-0	1-0	2-0	2-1	5-1	2-0	1-0
Dnipro Dnipropetrovsk ‡	30	11	14	5	32	24	47	0-2	1-1	0-2		2-0	1-0	1-1	2-2	2-0	1-1	3-0	1-0	1-0	1-1	1-1	0-0
Tavriya Simferopol	30	12	6	12	32	30	42	2-4	1-3	2-0	0-0		1-1	5-1	0-1	2-0	3-1	1-2	2-0	1-0	1-3	1-0	2-1
Chernomorets Odessa	30	11	8	11	36	33	41	2-3	0-0	1-3	0-1	0-0		1-1	1-0	2-0	2-3	2-0	4-2	2-0	2-0	2-1	3-0
Metalurh Zaporizhya	30	10	10	10	25	32	40	0-5	0-3	0-0	1-1	1-0	1-0		1-2	2-0	1-1	1-0	3-1	0-0	2-1	2-1	1-0
Karpaty Lviv	30	9	10	11	26	32	37	1-1	0-0	0-3	0-1	0-2	0-1	0-0		0-0	1-1	1-0	1-0	1-2	1-1	1-0	3-1
Metalurh Donetsk	30	9	9	12	26	35	36	1-1	0-0	0-2	1-1	1-2	1-0	1-0	3-3		2-1	3-2	1-2	0-0	2-1	2-1	2-1
Kryvbas Kryvyi Rih	30	7	14	9	29	36	35	1-1	0-1	0-3	1-1	0-0	2-2	1-1	3-0	1-1		2-0	3-1	0-0	1-0	0-0	1-0
Zorja Luhansk	30	9	7	14	23	43	34	1-2	0-2	2-2	0-3	1-0	0-4	0-0	1-0	1-0	2-1		0-1	0-0	2-1	1-1	1-0
FC Kharkiv	30	8	9	13	26	38	33	0-2	0-3	0-0	0-0	1-1	1-0	0-0	1-2	0-0	2-0	2-2		3-2	2-0	2-0	0-0
Vorskla Poltava	30	7	10	13	23	28	31	1-1	0-1	2-2	0-1	0-0	0-0	2-1	1-2	2-0	2-1	1-1	0-1		0-1	3-0	1-0
Arsenal Kyiv	30	7	9	14	28	44	30	0-1	1-2	0-0	1-1	0-1	1-1	1-0	1-0	0-2	1-1	2-2	1-1	1-0		2-0	1-3
Illychivets Mariupil	30	6	7	17	23	39	25	2-3	1-1	0-3	1-1	1-0	0-0	1-0	1-2	0-2	0-1	0-1	2-1	2-0	4-1		0-0
Stal Alchevsk	30	5	6	19	22	38	21	1-1	0-2	0-1	3-1	0-1	2-1	0-1	0-1	3-0	0-0	0-1	4-2	0-1	1-1	0-2	

21/07/2006 - 17/06/2007 • † Qualified for the UEFA Champions League • ‡ Qualified for the UEFA Cup
Top scorers: Oleksandr HLADKIY, FC Kharkiv 13; Vasil GIGIADZE, Kryvbas 11; BATISTA, Karpaty 10; Sergei KORNILENKO, Dnipro 10; Serhiy NAZARENKO, Dnipro 10; BRANDAO, Shakhtar 9; Maksim SHATSKIKH, Dynamo 9

UKRAINE 2006–07 PERSHA LIHA (2)

	Pl	W	D	L	F	A	Pts
Naftovyk-Ukrnafta	36	27	2	7	58	29	83
Zakarpattya Uzhgorod	36	25	5	6	50	22	80
Obolon Kyiv	36	23	4	9	47	27	73
Krymteplytsja	36	21	7	7	53	37	70
FK Oleksandrija	36	19	4	13	37	37	61
Dynamo Kyiv-2	36	17	8	11	53	37	59
Helios Kharkiv	36	17	7	12	45	36	58
Enerhetyk Burshtyn	36	15	11	10	44	33	56
Stal Dniprodzerzhinsk	36	15	8	13	42	37	53
Dynamo-IhroServis	36	14	9	13	46	44	51
FK Lviv	36	13	8	15	45	45	47
Volyn Lutsk	36	13	7	16	40	48	46
MFK Mykolajiv	36	12	10	14	33	40	46
Desna Chernihiv	36	11	8	17	51	58	41
Dnipro Cherkasy	36	10	9	17	31	46	39
CSCA Kyiv	36	10	8	18	24	44	38
Spartak Ivano-Franksk	36	10	3	23	24	50	33
Podillja Khmelnytskyj §3	36	5	6	25	20	62	18
Borysfen Boryspil §6	36	1	4	31	10	29	1

21/07/2006 - 21/06/2007 • § = points deducted
Spartak Sumy withdrew in November

FFU CUP 2006–07

Third Round		Quarter–finals		Semi–finals		Final	
Dynamo Kyiv	2						
FC Kharkiv *	0	Dynamo Kyiv *	1 2				
Tytan Armjansk *	0	Dnipro Dnipropetrovsk	1 1				
Dnipro Dnipropetrovsk	2			Dynamo Kyiv	1 4		
Illychivets Mariupil	2			Metalist Kharkiv *	0 2		
Kryvbas Kryvyi Rih *	0	Illychivets Mariupil *	0 0				
FK Lviv *	2 6p	Metalist Kharkiv	0 2				
Metalist Kharkiv	2 7p					Dynamo Kyiv	2
Tavriya Simferopol	2					Shakhtar Donetsk	1
Krymteplytsja *	1	Tavriya Simferopol	4 1				
Stal Alchevsk	1 4p	Stal Dniprodzerzhinsk *	1 0				
Stal Dniprodzerzhinsk *	1 5p			Tavriya Simferopol	0 2		
FK Sevastopol *	4			Shakhtar Donetsk *	0 2		
Metalurh Donetsk	1	FK Sevastopol *	0 1				
Borysfen Boryspil *	0	Shakhtar Donetsk	1 6				
Shakhtar Donetsk	2						

* Home team/home team in the 1st leg • ‡ Qualified for the UEFA Cup

CUP FINAL

NSK Olimpiyskiy, Kyiv
27-05-2007, Att: 64 500

Scorers - Kleber [58], Oleg Gusev [80] for Dynamo; Elano [89] for Shakhter

URU – URUGUAY

NATIONAL TEAM RECORD
JULY 10TH 2006 TO JULY 12TH 2010

PL	W	D	L	F	A	%
13	7	2	4	21	14	61.5

It has become fashionable to speculate about which nation in South America should be ranked third on the continent behind Argentina and Brazil. Paraguay are mentioned most often, along with Colombia and Chile, but very rarely nowadays does Uruguay get a mention. For many years there was no debate, Uruguay occupying a place in the top three by right and at the 2007 Copa América, the national team proved that there is still life in the old dog yet by reaching the semi-finals for the fourth tournament running. On their day La Celeste can be a match for any team in the world and they were only knocked out of the Copa América in Venezuela on penalties after their semi-final against Brazil had finished level at 2-2. Having also lost to Brazil on penalties in the semi-finals of the previous tournament in 2004, the disappointment was difficult to take for the Uruguayans, although by beating Argentina in the final, Brazil did preserve Uruguay's status as the leading nation in the tournament with 14 titles, along with the Argentines. It looked as if the Uruguayans would struggle in Venezuela after a disastrous opening 3-0 defeat at the hands of Peru, but a 1-0 victory over Bolivia and then a draw with the hosts saw them through to the quarter-finals as one

INTERNATIONAL HONOURS
FIFA World Cup 1930 1950   Olympic Gold 1924 1928
Qualified for the FIFA World Cup finals 1930 (hosts) 1950 1954 1962 1966 1970 1986 1990 2002
Copa América 1916 1917 1920 1923 1924 1926 1935 1942 1956 1959 1967 1983 1987 1995
Panamerican Games 1983 Juventud de América 1954 1958 1964 1975 1977 1979 1981
Copa Toyota Libertadores Peñarol 1960 1961 1966 1982 1987 Nacional 1971 1980 1988

of the best third place teams. Bizarrely Uruguay then faced Venezuela again and thanks to a commanding second-half performance in a 4-1 victory, they knocked the hosts out to set up the meeting with Brazil. Uruguayan clubs also restored some pride with better-than-usual performances in the in South American club competitions. In the second half of 2006, Nacional had reached the last eight of the Copa Sudamericana where they lost to Brazil's Atlético Paranaense, having knocked out Boca Juniors on the way. In the 2007 Copa Libertadores they also reached the quarter-finals, consigning holders Internacional to third place in the group before losing to Colombia's Cucuta. Defensor also qualified from their group and then beat Flamengo before losing to Grêmio on penalties in the quarter-finals. Surprisingly, however, the form team of the season, Danubio, didn't get past the qualifiers for the Copa Libertadores but they did have a very successful season in the Uruguayan Championship, winning both the Apertura and the Clausura. In both they were involved in a very tight race with Peñarol and they needed a play-off and a penalty shoot-out to win the latter. By winning both titles, Danubio were automatic champions for the season.

Asociación Uruguaya de Fútbol (AUF)
Guayabo 1531, Montevideo 11200, Uruguay
Tel +59 82 4004814   Fax +59 82 4090550
auf@auf.org.uy   www.auf.org.uy
President: CORBO Jose Luis   General Secretary: LEIZA Adrian
Vice-President: RAMOS Júan José   Treasurer: ACHE Eduardo   Media Officer: GONZALEZ Heber
Men's Coach: TABAREZ Oscar   Women's Coach: DUARTE Juan
AUF formed: 1900   CONMEBOL: 1916   FIFA: 1923
Sky blue with white trimmings, Black shorts, Black socks

RECENT INTERNATIONAL MATCHES PLAYED BY URUGUAY

2004	Opponents	Score		Venue	Comp	Scorers	Att	Referee
18-02	Jamaica	L	0-2	Kingston	Fr		27 000	Gordon TRI
31-03	Venezuela	L	0-3	Montevideo	WCq		40 094	Ortube BOL
1-06	Peru	L	1-3	Montevideo	WCq	Forlan [72]	30 000	Selman CHI
6-06	Colombia	L	0-5	Barranquilla	WCq		7 000	Amarilla PAR
7-07	Mexico	D	2-2	Chiclayo	CAr1	Bueno [42], Montero [87]	25 000	Hidalgo PER
10-07	Ecuador	W	2-1	Chiclayo	CAr1	Forlán [61], Bueno [79]	25 000	Brand VEN
13-07	Argentina	L	2-4	Piura	CAr1	Estoyanoff [7], Sanchez.V [39]	24 000	Selman CHI
18-07	Paraguay	W	3-1	Tacna	CAqf	Bueno [40p], Silva 2 [65 88]	20 000	Baldassi ARG
21-07	Brazil	D	1-1	Lima	CAsf	Sosa [22]. L 3-5p	10 000	Rodríguez Moreno MEX
24-07	Colombia	W	2-1	Cusco	CA3p	Estoyanoff [4], Sanchez.V [88]	35 000	Ortube BOL
5-09	Ecuador	W	1-0	Montevideo	WCq	Bueno [57]	28 000	Hidalgo PER
9-10	Argentina	L	2-4	Buenos Aires	WCq	Rodriguez.C [63], Chevanton [86]	50 000	Souza BRA
12-10	Bolivia	D	0-0	La Paz	WCq		24 349	Rezende BRA
17-11	Paraguay	W	1-0	Montevideo	WCq	Montero [78]	35 000	Simon BRA
2005								
26-03	Chile	D	1-1	Santiago	WCq	Regueiro [4]	55 000	Ruiz COL
30-03	Brazil	D	1-1	Montevideo	WCq	Forlán [48]	60 000	Baldassi ARG
4-06	Venezuela	D	1-1	Maracaibo	WCq	Forlán [2]	12 504	Brazenas ARG
7-06	Peru	D	0-0	Lima	WCq		31 515	Baldassi ARG
17-08	Spain	L	0-2	Gijon	Fr		25 885	Benquerenca POR
4-09	Colombia	W	3-2	Montevideo	WCq	Zalayeta 3 [42 51 86]	60 000	Elizondo ARG
8-10	Ecuador	D	0-0	Quito	WCq		37 270	Rezende BRA
12-10	Argentina	W	1-0	Montevideo	WCq	Recoba [46]	55 000	Souza BRA
26-10	Mexico	L	1-3	Guadalajara	Fr	Abreu [17]	45 000	Guajardo MEX
12-11	Australia	W	1-0	Montevideo	WCpo	Rodriguez.D [37]	55 000	Larsen DEN
16-11	Australia	L	0-1	Sydney	WCpo		82 698	Medina Cantalejo ESP
2006								
1-03	England	L	1-2	Liverpool	Fr	Pouso [26]	40 013	Farina ITA
21-05	Northern Ireland	W	1-0	New Jersey	Fr	Estoyanoff [33]	4 152	
23-05	Romania	W	2-0	Los Angeles	Fr	Vargas 2 [46 59]	10 000	Stott USA
27-05	Serbia & Montenegro	D	1-1	Belgrade	Fr	Godin [82]	30 000	Kos SVN
30-05	Libya	W	2-1	Radès/Tunis	Fr	Vigneri [15], Abreu [34]		
4-06	Tunisia	D	0-0	Radès/Tunis	Fr	W 3-1p		
16-08	Egypt	W	2-0	Alexandria	Fr	Godin [67], OG [83]	10 000	Benouza ALG
27-09	Venezuela	L	0-1	Maracaibo	Fr		28 000	Manzur VEN
18-10	Venezuela	W	4-0	Montevideo	Fr	Sánchez.V [12], Godin [14], Abreu [51], Blanco [88]	7 000	Silvera URU
15-11	Georgia	L	0-2	Tbilisi	Fr		12 000	Godulyan UKR
2007								
7-02	Colombia	W	3-1	Cucuta	Fr	Abreu 2 [16p 59p], Vargas [84]	26 000	Hoyos COL
24-03	Korea Republic	W	2-0	Seoul	Fr	Bueno 2 [19 37]	42 159	Ogiya JPN
2-06	Australia	W	2-1	Sydney	Fr	Forlán [40], Recoba [77]	61 795	Rosetti ITA
26-06	Peru	L	0-3	Merida	CAr1		23 000	Amarilla PAR
30-06	Bolivia	W	1-0	San Cristobal	CAr1	Sánchez.V [58]	18 000	Toledo USA
3-07	Venezuela	D	0-0	Merida	CAr1		42 000	Simon BRA
7-07	Venezuela	W	4-1	San Cristobal	CAqf	Forlán 2 [38 90], Garcia.P [65], Rodriguez.C [87]	42 000	Chandia CHI
10-07	Brazil	D	2-2	Maracaibo	CAsf	Forlán [36], Abreu [70]. L 4-5p	40 000	Ruiz COL
14-07	Mexico	L	1-3	Caracas	CA3p	Abreu [22]	30 000	Reinoso ECU

Fr = Friendly match • CA = Copa América • WC = FIFA World Cup
q = qualifier • po = play-off • r1 = first round group • qf = quarter-final • sf = semi-final • 3p = third place play-off

URUGUAY NATIONAL TEAM RECORDS AND RECORD SEQUENCES

Records			Sequence records					
Victory	9-0	BOL 1927	Wins	7	1941-42, 1980-81	Clean sheets	6	1969-1970
Defeat	0-6	ARG 1902	Defeats	5	1916	Goals scored	20	1953-1956
Player Caps	78	RODRIGUEZ Rodolfo	Undefeated	14	1967-1968	Without goal	4	1925, 1968. 1976
Player Goals	31	SCARONE Héctor	Without win	9	1986	Goals against	18	1961-1963

ARG

BRA

Salto

Paysandu

Las Piedras

Montevideo   Ciudad de la Costa

ATLANTIC OCEAN

ORIENTAL REPUBLIC OF URUGUAY; REPUBLICA ORIENTAL DEL URUGUAY

Capital	Montevideo	Language	Spanish			Independence	1828
Population	3 460 607	Area	176 220 km²	Density	19 per km²	% in cities	90%
GDP per cap	$12 800	Dailling code	+598	Internet	.uy	GMT +/ -	-3

MAJOR CITIES/TOWNS
Population '000

1	Montevideo	1 272
2	Salto	101
3	Ciudad de la Costa	91
4	Paysandu	73
5	Las Piedras	70
6	Rivera	65
7	Maldonado	57
8	Tacuarembó	53
9	Melo	51
10	Mercedes	43
11	Artigas	42
12	Minas	38
13	San José	36
14	Durazno	34
15	Florida	32
16	Treinta y Tres	25
17	Rocha	25
18	San Carlos	25
19	Pando	24
20	Fray Bentos	23
21	Colonia	21
22	Trinidad	21
23	El Pinar	20
24	La Paz	20

MEDALS TABLE

		Overall			League			Sth Am			City	Stadium	Cap'ty	DoF
		G	S	B	G	S	B	G	S	B				
1	CA Peñarol	52	44	18	47	38	5	5	6	13	Montevideo	Estadio Centenario	65 000	1891
2	Club Nacional de Football	44	44	21	41	40	12	3	4	9	Montevideo	Parque Central	20 000	1899
3	Montevideo Wanderers FC	4	4	14	4	6	14				Montevideo	Parque Alfredo Victor Viera	12 000	1902
4	River Plate FC	4	1	1	4	1	1				Montevideo			1902-20
5	Defensor SC	3	5	8	3	5	8				Montevideo	Luis Franzini	18 000	1913
6	Danubio FC	3	4	5	3	4	4			1	Montevideo	Jardines del Hipodromo	16 000	1932
7	Rampla Juniors FC	1	5	13	1	5	14				Montevideo	Estadio Olimpico	9 500	1914
8	CA Bella Vista	1	1	2	1	1	2				Montevideo	Jose Nasazzi	15 000	1920
9	Central Español FC	1		4	1		4				Montevideo	Parque Palermo	9 000	1905
10	CA Progreso	1			1						Montevideo	Parque Abraham Paladino	8 000	1917
11	CA Cerro		1	6		1	6				Montevideo	Luis Tróccoli	30 000	1922
12	Universal		1	4		1	4							
13	CA River Plate		1	2		1	2				Montevideo	Federico Saroldi	12 000	1932
14	Albion		1	1		1	1							
15	Rocha FC		1			1					Rocha	Mario Sobrero	8 000	1999
16	CA Fénix			3			3				Montevideo	Parque Capurro	10 000	1916
	Liverpool FC			3			3				Montevideo	Estadio Belvedere	9 500	1915

URUGUAY LEAGUE RECORD

Year	Winners	Score	Runners-up
1995	Peñarol	1-0 1-2 3-1	Nacional
1996	Peñarol	1-0 1-1	Nacional
1997	Peñarol	1-0 3-0	Defensor Sporting
1998	Nacional	†	
1999	Peñarol	1-1 1-1 2-1	Nacional
2000	Nacional	1-0 1-1	Peñarol
2001	Nacional	2-2 2-1	Danubio
2002	Nacional	2-1 2-1	Danubio
2003	Peñarol	1-0	Nacional
2004	Danubio	1-0	Nacional
2005	Nacional	w-o	Defensor Sporting
2006	Nacional	4-1 2-0	Rocha
2007	Danubio	†	Peñarol

† Automatic champions as winners of both the Apertura and Clausura

URUGUAY 2006–07

PRIMERA DIVISION PROFESSIONAL — TABLA ANUAL

	Pl	W	D	L	F	A	Pts	Danubio	Peñarol	Defensor	Wanderers	Bella Vista	Nacional	Liverpool	Tacuarémbo	River Plate	Miramar	C. Español	Rampla J.	Progreso	Rocha	Cerrito	Rentistas
Danubio †	30	21	3	6	62	27	66		0-1	0-2	3-0	2-1	3-0	2-0	1-1	3-1	5-2	6-0	2-1	0-0	3-0	0-2	5-1
Peñarol	30	19	7	4	64	38	64	1-4		0-1	0-2	2-1	4-1	1-1	3-3	3-1	1-1	1-2	2-2	4-0	4-2	4-2	4-2
Defensor	30	17	8	5	57	32	59	0-2	2-2		2-2	1-0	3-0	3-2	2-1	2-2	0-0	2-3	2-1	3-2	0-1	3-1	2-2
Wanderers †	30	16	5	9	53	39	53	2-0	1-2	3-4		3-1	2-1	0-0	0-2	0-1	5-2	2-1	4-1	3-2	1-1	2-0	2-0
Bella Vista	30	16	3	11	48	38	51	3-2	2-5	0-2	3-1		0-0	1-0	2-0	2-1	0-1	1-0	3-1	3-0	4-0	2-0	3-2
Nacional †	30	13	6	11	42	44	45	0-1	0-3	1-4	1-1	1-1		2-1	2-2	1-0	4-0	0-0	5-1	1-0	3-0	1-3	0-1
Liverpool	30	12	6	12	47	44	42	3-3	1-1	2-1	2-3	2-4	1-2		2-0	1-4	2-1	2-0	0-0	4-0	4-0	2-2	1-0
Tacuarembó	30	8	12	10	40	39	36	0-1	0-1	0-0	0-0	0-3	3-0	2-1		1-1	3-2	4-0	3-3	2-1	0-1	3-0	1-1
River Plate	30	9	9	12	41	47	36	1-2	3-3	2-3	0-1	3-1	1-1	3-2	1-1		2-1	0-1	2-2	2-4	3-0	0-3	1-0
Miramar Misiones	30	9	7	14	36	46	34	2-1	0-1	1-0	1-4	1-2	2-0	1-2	3-1	2-3		2-0	0-1	2-2	0-0	1-1	2-2
Central Español	30	10	4	16	31	48	34	0-1	1-2	0-3	2-1	1-0	1-3	3-0	1-0	1-1	0-2		0-1	1-1	2-3	1-1	2-1
Rampla Juniors	30	8	8	14	35	47	32	0-1	0-2	2-2	2-0	2-1	1-3	1-2	0-0	0-1	3-2	0-1		3-2	0-2	1-0	3-4
Progreso	30	7	10	13	38	52	31	1-2	0-1	0-4	2-3	2-2	1-2	2-1	2-2	3-1	1-1	3-2	1-1		0-1	1-1	0-0
Rocha	30	9	4	17	24	44	31	1-2	1-2	0-1	0-1	0-1	2-3	0-2	1-0	3-0	1-0	0-1	1-0	1-2		2-1	1-2
Cerrito	30	6	9	15	33	48	24	1-3	0-1	0-3	2-0	0-2	1-2	0-1	3-3	0-0	1-0	0-2	1-2	1-1	0-0		1-1
Rentistas	30	5	9	16	33	54	24	0-2	2-0	1-0	0-3	2-0	1-4	3-0	1-2	1-2	1-1	1-2	0-2	1-2	1-1	2-1	

19/08/2006 - 19/05/2007 • † Qualified for the Copa Libertadores • Danubio are champions having won both the Apertura and Clausura
Apertura matches are in the shaded boxes • Relegation play-off: Rocha 0-2 0-3 Progreso
Top scorers: Aldo DIAZ, Tacuarembó 15; Manuel ABREU, Liverpool 14; Ignacio GONZALEZ, Danubio 13; Nicolás VIGNERI, Peñarol 13

URUGUAY 2006–07 — TORNEO APERTURA

	Pl	W	D	L	F	A	Pts
Danubio	15	11	1	3	36	17	34
Peñarol	15	10	2	3	30	18	32
Defensor	15	9	4	2	28	13	31
Bella Vista	15	10	1	4	25	15	31
Nacional	15	8	3	4	28	22	27
Wanderers	15	8	3	4	22	18	27
Liverpool	15	6	4	5	24	20	22
Central Español	15	7	1	7	21	25	22
Tacuarembó	15	4	4	7	15	18	16
Rocha	15	4	3	8	15	21	15
River Plate	15	4	3	8	15	25	15
Miramar Misiones	15	3	5	7	17	26	14
Cerrito	15	4	4	7	16	21	13
Progreso	15	3	4	8	16	31	13
Rampla Juniors	15	3	3	9	15	23	12
Rentistas	15	1	5	9	13	23	8

19/08/2006 - 10/12/2006 • §3 = three points deducted

URUGUAY 2006–07 — TORNEO CLAUSURA

	Pl	W	D	L	F	A	Pts
Danubio	15	10	2	3	26	10	32
Peñarol	15	9	5	1	34	20	32
Defensor	15	8	4	3	29	19	28
Wanderers	15	8	2	5	31	21	26
River Plate	15	5	6	4	26	22	21
Tacuarembó	15	4	8	3	25	21	20
Bella Vista	15	6	2	7	23	23	20
Liverpool	15	6	2	7	23	24	20
Miramar Misiones	15	6	2	7	19	20	20
Rampla Juniors	15	5	5	5	20	24	20
Progreso	15	4	6	5	22	21	18
Nacional	15	5	3	7	14	22	18
Rentistas	15	4	4	7	20	28	16
Rocha	15	5	1	9	9	23	16
Central Español	15	3	3	9	10	23	12
Cerrito	15	2	5	8	17	27	11

17/02/2007 - 19/05/2007 • Play-off: Danubio 1-1 4-3p Peñarol

FIFA/COCA-COLA WORLD RANKING

1993	1994	1995	1996	1997	1998	1999	2000	2001	2002	2003	2004	2005	2006	High		Low	
17	37	32	43	40	76	46	32	22	28	21	16	18	29	**14**	08/06	**76**	12/98

2006–2007											
08/06	09/06	10/06	11/06	12/06	01/07	02/07	03/07	04/07	05/07	06/07	07/07
14	15	17	29	29	30	24	26	23	23	30	19

THE FIFA BIG COUNT OF 2006

	Male	Female		Total
Number of players	214 000	27 300	Referees and Assistant Referees	400
Professionals	1 100		Admin, Coaches, Technical, Medical	2 200
Amateurs 18+	30 000		Number of clubs	1 210
Youth under 18	8 000		Number of teams	2 200
Unregistered	94 500		Clubs with women's teams	10
Total players	241 300		Players as % of population	7.03%

USA – UNITED STATES OF AMERICA

NATIONAL TEAM RECORD
JULY 10TH 2006 TO JULY 12TH 2010

PL	W	D	L	F	A	%
13	9	1	3	24	13	73.1

With so much written and said about David Beckham's transfer to America, one could have been forgiven for thinking that football was an entirely new game to the country. His arrival was of course significant for the future of football in the USA, but it came just days after the national team had defeated Mexico in the final of the CONCACAF Gold Cup to win the title for a record-equalling fourth time. Beckham may be joining a League in its infancy but the average attendance in Major League Soccer is now almost on a par with Italy's Serie A - a sobering statistic for those who like to mock MLS from both within as well as outside of the USA. Having Tom Cruise as your friend and choosing Los Angeles instead of, say, Columbus, may have played straight into the hands of the cynics, but Beckham proved in his final season at Real Madrid that he is still a world class player and that he could be worth every cent of the $250m he stands to earn from the five-year deal he signed with LA Galaxy. Beckham in not in the USA to help establish football as many in the European press have claimed - Pele, Beckenbauer, Best and Cruijff did that in the 1970s. His job it to help take it to a level where it can start to compete with the top European nations on a

INTERNATIONAL HONOURS
FIFA Women's World Cup 1991 1999   Women's Olympic Gold 1996 2004   FIFA U-19 Women's World Championship 2002
Qualified for the FIFA World Cup 1930 1934 1950 1990 1994 1998 2002 2006
CONCACAF Gold Cup 1991 2002 2005   CONCACAF Women's Gold Cup 1991 1993 1994 2000 2002
Panamerican Games 1991   CONCACAF U-17 1983 1992
CONCACAF Champions Cup DC United 1998 Los Angeles Galaxy 2000

more or less equal footing. Many would argue that the national team is not far off that already as 2007 proved to be another successful year for the senior side. Not only did America win the Gold Cup but the win over Mexico in the final set a new record of seven consecutive victories and had it not been for a tame draw against Guatemala in a friendly played in March, that record would have extended to 10. Just four days after the Gold Cup Final, the Americans were facing Argentina in the Copa América in Venezuela with an experimental team, but the tournament wasn't a success; all three matches were lost, leaving the USA rooted to the bottom of their group. The 2006 season in MLS saw newly formed Houston Dynamo crowned as champions after beating New England Revolution on penalties in the final after a 1-1 draw. Taylor Twellman had given New England the lead deep into extra-time but Brian Ching levelled straight after. Jay Heaps missed the crucial penalty, consigning his team to the runners-up spot for the second year running. 2006 was also the year in which the game in America lost one of its great pioneers, Lamar Hunt. He died two and a half months after Chicago Fire won the Cup that bears his name.

US Soccer Federation (USSF)
US Soccer House, 1801 S. Prairie Avenue, Chicago IL 60616, USA
Tel +1 312 8081300   Fax +1 312 8081301
communications@ussoccer.org   www.ussoccer.com
President: GULATI Sunil   General Secretary: FLYNN Dan
Vice-President: EDWARDS Mike   Treasurer: GOAZIOU Bill   Media Officer: MOORHOUSE Jim
Men's Coach: BRADLEY Bob   Women's Coach: RYAN Greg
USSF formed: 1913   CONCACAF: 1961   FIFA: 1914
White shirts with a red and blue panel on the left, Blue shorts, White socks

RECENT INTERNATIONAL MATCHES PLAYED BY THE USA

2005 Opponents	Score	Venue	Comp	Scorers	Att	Referee
9-02 Trinidad and Tobago	W 2-1	Port of Spain	WCq	Johnson [23], Lewis [53]	11 000	Archundia MEX
9-03 Colombia	W 3-0	Fullerton	Fr	Noonan [25], Marshall [33], Mathis [66]	7 086	Rodriguez MEX
19-03 Honduras	W 1-0	Albuquerque	Fr	Johnson [45]	9 222	Navorro CAN
27-03 Mexico	L 1-2	Mexico City	WCq	Lewis [58]	84 000	Sibrian SLV
30-03 Guatemala	W 2-0	Birmingham	WCq	Johnson [11], Ralston [69]	31 624	Ramdhan TRI
28-05 England	L 1-2	Chicago	Fr	Dempsey [79]	47 637	Archundia MEX
4-06 Costa Rica	W 3-0	Salt Lake City	WCq	Donovan 2 [10 62], McBride [87]	40 576	Batres GUA
8-06 Panama	W 3-0	Panama City	WCq	Bocanegra [6], Donovan [19], McBride [39]	15 000	Navarro CAN
7-07 Cuba	W 4-1	Seattle	GCr1	Dempsey [44], Donovan 2 [87 92+], Beasley [89]	15 831	Pineda HON
9-07 Canada	W 2-0	Seattle	GCr1	Hutchinson OG [48], Donovan [90]	15 109	Brizan TRI
12-07 Costa Rica	D 0-0	Boston	GCr1		15 211	Archundia MEX
16-07 Jamaica	W 3-1	Boston	GCqf	Wolff [6], Beasley 2 [42 83]	22 108	Batres GUA
21-07 Honduras	W 2-1	New Jersey	GCsf	O'Brien [86], Onyewu [92+]	41 721	Prendergast JAM
24-07 Panama	D 0-0	New Jersey	GCf		31 018	Batres GUA
17-08 Trinidad & Tobago	W 1-0	Hartford	WCq	McBride [2]	25 500	Rodriguez MEX
3-09 Mexico	W 2-0	Columbus	WCq	Ralston [53], Beasley [57]	24 685	Batres GUA
7-09 Guatemala	D 0-0	Guatemala City	WCq		27 000	Rodriguez MEX
8-10 Costa Rica	L 0-3	San Jose	WCq		18 000	Archundia MEX
12-10 Panama	W 2-0	Boston	WCq	Martino [51], Twellman [57]	2 500	Alcala MEX
12-11 Scotland	D 1-1	Glasgow	Fr	Wolff [9p]	26 708	Undiano Mallenco ESP
2006						
22-01 Canada	D 0-0	San Diego	Fr		6 077	Archundia MEX
29-01 Norway	W 5-0	Carson	Fr	Twellman 3 [5 18 76], Pope [67], Klein [87]	16 366	Ruiz COL
10-02 Japan	W 3-2	San Francisco	Fr	Pope [24], Dempsey [39], Twellman [50]	37 365	Elizondo ARG
19-02 Guatemala	W 4-0	Frisco	Fr	Olsen [38], Ching [45], Johnsen [47], Klein [71]	14 453	Navarro CAN
1-03 Poland	W 1-0	Kaiserslautern	Fr	Dempsey [48]	13 395	Kinhofer GER
22-03 Germany	L 1-4	Dortmund	Fr	Cherundolo [85]	64 500	Frojdfeldt SWE
11-04 Jamaica	D 1-1	Cary	Fr	Olsen [25]	8 093	Gasso MEX
23-05 Morocco	L 0-1	Nashville	Fr		26 141	Navarro CAN
26-05 Venezuela	W 2-0	Cleveland	Fr	Ching [36], Dempsey [69]	29 745	Morales MEX
28-05 Latvia	W 1-0	Hartford	Fr	McBride [43]	24 636	Dipiero CAN
12-06 Czech Republic	L 0-3	Gelsenkirchen	WCr1		52 000	Amarilla PAR
17-06 Italy	D 1-1	Kaiserslautern	WCr1	OG [27]	46 000	Larrionda URU
22-06 Ghana	L 1-2	Nuremberg	WCr1	Dempsey [43]	41 000	Merk GER
2007						
7-02 Mexico	W 2-0	Glendale	Fr	Conrad [52], Donovan [91+]	62 462	Navarro CAN
25-03 Ecuador	W 3-1	Tampa	Fr	Donovan 3 [1 66 67]	31 547	Petrescu CAN
28-03 Guatemala	D 0-0	Frisco	Fr		10 932	Archundia MEX
2-06 China PR	W 4-1	San Jose	Fr	Beasley [10p], Feilhaber [28], Dempsey [75], Onyewu [79]	20 821	Guajardo MEX
7-06 Guatemala	W 1-0	Carson	GCr1	Dempsey [26]	21 334	Pineda HON
9-06 Trinidad and Tobago	W 2-0	Carson	GCr1	Ching [29], Johnson [54]	27 000	Moreno PAN
12-06 El Salvador	W 4-0	Foxboro	GCr1	Beasley 2 [34 89], Donovan [45p], Twellman [72]	26 523	Archundia MEX
16-06 Panama	W 2-1	Foxboro	GCqf	Donovan [60p], Bocanegra [62]	22 412	Brizan TRI
21-06 Canada	W 2-1	Chicago	GCsf	Hejduk [39], Donovan [45p]	50 760	Archundia MEX
24-06 Mexico	W 2-1	Chicago	GCf	Donovan [62p], Feilhaber [73]	60 000	Batres GUA
28-06 Argentina	L 1-4	Maracaibo	CAr1	Johnson [9p]	34 500	Chandia CHI
2-07 Paraguay	L 1-3	Barinas	CAr1	Clark [40]	23 000	Rivera PER
5-07 Colombia	L 0-1	Barquisimeto	CAr1		37 000	Andarcia VEN

Fr = Friendly match • GC = CONCACAF Gold Cup • CA = Copa América • WC = FIFA World Cup
q = qualifier • r1 = first round group • qf = quarter-final • sf = semi-final • 3p = third place play-off • f = final

USA NATIONAL TEAM RECORDS AND RECORD SEQUENCES

Records			Sequence records				
Victory	8-1	CAY 1993	Wins	7	2007	Clean sheets	5	2003
Defeat	0-11	NOR 1948	Defeats	13	1973-1975	Goals scored	23	2004-2005
Player Caps	164	JONES Cobi	Undefeated	16	2004-2005	Without goal	5	1990-1991
Player Goals	34	WYNALDA Eric	Without win	16	1973-1976	Goals against	14	1973-1976

MAJOR CITIES/TOWNS

Population '000

1	New York	22 747
2	Los Angeles	17 989
3	Chicago	9 510
4	Washington	8 197
5	San Francisco	7 719
6	Philadelphia	6 268
7	Dallas	6 175
8	Boston	6 167
9	Detroit	5 925
10	Houston	5 406
11	Atlanta	4 973
12	San Diego	4 922
13	Miami	4 825
14	Phoenix	4 026
15	Seattle	3 852
16	Minneapolis	3 237
17	Cleveland	2 954
18	Denver	2 722
19	Tampa	2 653
20	Saint Louis	2 632
21	Kansas City	1 885
22	Salt Lake City	1 793
23	Columbus	1 656
24	Rochester	1 107

UNITED STATES OF AMERICA

Capital	Washington DC	Language	English, Spanish	Independence	1776
Population	301 139 947	Area	9 631 418 km²	Density	30 per km²	% in cities	76%
GDP per cap	$37 800	Dailling code	+1	Internet	.us	GMT +/-	-6/11

MEDALS TABLE

		Overall			Lge		Cup		CON'CAF			City	Stadium	Cap'ty	DoF
		G	S	B	G	S	G	S	G	S	B				
1	DC United	6	2	4	4	1	1	1	1		4	Washington	RFK Memorial	56 454	1995
2	Los Angeles Galaxy	5	6		2	3	2	2	1	1		Carson/Los Angeles	Home Depot Centre	27 000	1995
3	Chicago Fire	5	3	2	1	2	4	1			2	Chicago	Soldier Field	20 000	1997
4	Kansas City Wizards	2	1	1	1	1	1				1	Kansas City	Arrowhead	79 451	1995
5	San Jose Earthquakes	2			2							San Jose	Spartan Stadium	26 000	1995-'05
6	Columbus Crew	1	1				1	1				Columbus	Crew Stadium	22 555	1994
7	FC Dallas	1	1				1	1				Dallas	Pizza Hut Park	21 193	1996
8	Rochester Raging Rhinos	1	1				1	1				Rochester	PAETEC Park	13 500	1996
9	Houston Dynamo	1			1							Houston	Robertson Stadium	33 000	2005
10	New England Revolution	4			3		1					Foxboro/Boston	Gillette Stadium	68 756	1995
11	Colorado Rapids	2			1		1					Denver	Dick's Sporting Goods Park	18 086	1995
12	Miami Fusion	1					1					Fort Lauderdale	Lockhart Stadium	20 450	1998-'01
13	Red Bull New York	1					1					New York	Giants Stadium	80 242	1995
14	Chivas USA											Carson/Los Angeles	Home Depot Centre	27 000	2004
	Real Salt Lake											Salt Lake	Rice-Eccles	46 500	2004
	Toronto FC											Toronto	BMO Field	20 148	2006
	Tampa Bay Mutiny											Tampa	Raymond James Stadium	66 321	1996-'01

RECENT LEAGUE AND CUP RECORD

	MLS				Cup		
Year	Champions	Score	Runners-up	Winners	Score	Runners-up
1996	DC United	3-2	Los Angeles Galaxy	DC United	3-0	Rochester Rhinos
1997	DC United	2-1	Colorado Rapids	Dallas Burn	0-0 5-3p	DC United
1998	Chicago Fire	2-0	DC United	Chicago Fire	2-1	Columbus Crew
1999	DC United	2-0	Los Angeles Galaxy	Rochester Rhinos	2-0	Colorado Rapids
2000	Kansas City Wizards	1-0	Chicago Fire	Chicago Fire	2-1	Miami Fusion
2001	San Jose Earthquakes	2-1	Los Angeles Galaxy	Los Angeles Galaxy	2-1	New England Revolution
2002	Los Angeles Galaxy	1-0	New England Revolution	Columbus Crew	1-0	Los Angeles Galaxy
2003	San Jose Earthquakes	4-2	Chicago Fire	Chicago Fire	1-0	MetroStars
2004	DC United	3-2	Kansas City Wizards	Kansas City Wizards	1-0	Chicago Fire
2005	Los Angeles Galaxy	1-0	New England Revolution	Los Angeles Galaxy	1-0	FC Dallas
2006	Houston Dynamo	0-0 4-3p	New England Revolution	Chicago Fire	3-1	Los Angeles Galaxy

USA 2006

MAJOR LEAGUE SOCCER REGULAR SEASON

Eastern Conference

	Pl	W	D	L	F	A	Pts	DC United	NE Revs	Chicago Fire	New York	Wizards	Crew	Dallas	Houston	Chivas	Rapids	LA Galaxy	Salt Lake
DC United †	32	15	10	7	52	38	55		1-0 1-2	0-2 3-2	2-4 3-2	4-3 2-1	1-0 5-1 3-2	1-1	2-0	2-0	1-1	2-5	1-1
New England Revs †	32	12	12	8	39	35	48	1-1 1-1		1-2 0-1	3-2 1-0	0-0 1-1	1-0 1-0	1-0	1-1	3-1	3-1	4-0	1-3
Chicago Fire †	32	13	8	11	43	41	47	1-1 0-3	3-1 2		2-0 2-1	1-0 3-0	0-0 1-4	2-3	2-2	1-2	1-0	2-1	2-1
New York Red Bulls †	32	9	12	11	41	41	39	1-4 0-0	0-0 2-1	1-1 1-0		1-0 3-2	0-0 1-0	1-2	1-1	5-4	1-0	2-1	6-0
Kansas City Wizards	32	10	8	14	43	45	38	1-3 2-3	1-0 1-1	1-1 3-2	1-1 2-2		3-1 4-0	1-0	2-3	2-1	4-1	0-2	3-3
Columbus Crew	32	8	9	15	30	42	33	1-1 0-1	1-1 3-0	1-1 1-2	0-2 1-0	0-1 0-1		3-1	1-1	1-1	1-0	1-1	1-2

Western Conference

	Pl	W	D	L	F	A	Pts	DC United	NE Revs	Chicago Fire	New York	Wizards	Crew	Dallas	Houston	Chivas	Rapids	LA Galaxy	Salt Lake
FC Dallas †	32	16	4	12	48	44	52	0-1	4-0	3-2	2-1	2-1	1-2		1-1 1-0	2-1 0-1	1-0 4-1	1-0 2-1	2-1
Houston Dynamo †	32	11	13	8	44	40	46	1-0	1-1	0-1	1-1	1-2	1-1	4-3 1-0		3-1 0-0	5-2 3-3	2-1 0-1	2-1 2-1
Chivas USA †	32	10	13	9	45	42	43	1-2	1-1	1-0	0-0	1-1	2-0	3-0 1-1	1-3 2		4-1 1-0	1-2 0-0	3-0 1-1
Los Angeles Galaxy	32	11	6	15	37	37	39	1-1	0-1	1-1	1-0	2-1	0-1	2-0 5-2	0-0 1-2	1-2 3-0	0-1 0-0		0-3 2-0
Colorado Rapids †	32	11	8	13	36	49	41	2-1	3-2	1-0	1-1	1-0	3-1	2-2 0-2	0-1 1-0	1-3 3-3		1-0 1-0	1-0 1-4
Real Salt Lake	32	10	9	13	45	49	39	2-1	0-0	3-1	1-1	2-1	0-1	0-1 3-2	3-1 1-1	0-0 3-2	2-0 1-2	3-1 0	

1/04/2006 - 14/10/2006 • † Qualified for the play-offs • Top scorers: Jeff CUNNINGHAM, RSL 16; Christian GOMEZ, DC 14; Ante RAZOV, Chivas 14

MLS PLAY-OFFS 2006

Conference semi-finals

Houston Dynamo	1	2
Chivas USA *	2	0
FC Dallas	2	2 4p
Colorado Rapids *	1	3 5p
DC United	1	1
New York Red Bulls *	0	1
Chicago Fire *	1	1 2p
New England Revolution	0	2 4p

Conference finals

Houston Dynamo *	3
Colorado Rapids	1
DC United *	0
New England Revolution	1

MLS Cup

Houston Dynamo	0 4p
New England Revolution	0 3p

* Home team/home team in the first leg

MLS CUP 2006

Pizza Hut Park, Dallas, 12-11-2006, Att: 22 427, Ref: Jair Marrufo

Houston Dynamo 1 4p Ching [114]
New England Revolution 1 3p Twellman [113]

Houston - Pat ONSTAD - Craig WAIBEL, Ryan COCHRANE (Kelly GRAY 11), Eddie ROBINSON, Wade BARRETT, Brian MULLEN, Dwayne DE ROSARIO, Adrian SERIOUX (Stuart HOLDEN 12), Brad DAVIS, Brian CHING, Paul DALGLISH (Alejandro MORENO 81). Tr: Dominic KINNEAR
Revs - Matt REIS - Jay HEAPS, Michael PARKHURST, Avery JOHN, Andy DORMAN (Clint DEMPSEY 62), Steve RALSTON, Daniel HERNANDEZ (Jeff LARENTOWICZ 12), Shalrie JOSEPH, Joe FRANCHINO (Khano SMITH 53), Pat NOONAN, Taylor TWELLMAN. Tr: Steve NICHOL
Penalties: Gray ✓, Joseph ✓, Holden ✓, Reis ✓, De Rosario ✓, Noonan ✖, Davis ✖, Twellman ✓, Ching ✓, Heaps ✖

USA 2006 USL FIRST DIVISION (2)

	Pl	W	D	L	F	A	Pts
Montreal Impact ‡	28	14	9	5	31	15	51
Rochester Rhinos ‡	28	13	11	4	34	21	50
Charleston Battery ‡	28	13	7	8	33	25	46
Vancouver Whitecaps ‡	28	12	10	6	40	28	46
Miami FC ‡	28	11	6	11	47	44	39
Puerto Rico Islanders ‡	28	10	8	10	38	36	38
Seattle Sounders	28	11	4	13	42	48	37
Atlanta Silverbacks	28	10	5	13	36	42	35
Virginia Beach M'ners	28	8	8	12	26	37	32
Toronto Lynx	28	8	8	12	30	36	32
Portland Timbers	28	7	6	15	25	39	27
Minnesota Thunder	28	7	6	15	34	45	27

‡ Qualified for the play-offs

USL FIRST DIVISION PLAY-OFFS

Quarter-finals: Puerto Rico 2-2 0-1 **Charleston**; Miami 1-4 0-2 **Vancouver**
Semi-finals: Montreal 0-0 0-2 **Vancouver**; Charleston 0-1 0-0 **Rochester**
Final: **Vancouver Whitecaps** 3-0 Rochester Taging Rhinos

FIFA/COCA-COLA WORLD RANKING

1993	1994	1995	1996	1997	1998	1999	2000	2001	2002	2003	2004	2005	2006	High	Low
22	23	19	18	26	23	22	16	24	10	11	11	8	31	4 04/06	35 10/97

2006–2007

08/06	09/06	10/06	11/06	12/06	01/07	02/07	03/07	04/07	05/07	06/07	07/07
23	29	29	31	31	31	28	30	29	29	16	14

LAMAR HUNT US OPEN CUP 2006

Third Round		Fourth Round	Quarter-finals	Semi-finals	Final

Third Round

Des Moines Menace	1	
Kansas City Wizards	2	
Rochester Rhinos	5	
New Hampshire Ph'toms	1	
Atlanta Silverbacks	1	
Willimington Ham'heads	2	
Columbus Crew	4	
Michigan Bucks	1	
Seattle Sounders	2	
Carolina Dynamo	3	
Charleston Battery	3	
Portland Timbers	1	
Virginia Beach Mariners	1	
Real Salt Lake	2	
Dallas Roma	0 4p	
Chivas USA	0 2p	

Fourth Round

Chicago Fire	2	
Kansas City Wizards	0	
Rochester Rhinos	0 4p	
New England Revolution	0 5p	
New York Red Bulls	2	
Wilmington Ham'heads	1	
Columbus Crew	1	
DC United	2	
Houston Dynamo	4	
Carolina Dynamo	2	
Charleston Battery	3 3p	
FC Dallas	3 5p	
Colorado Rapids	1	
Real Salt Lake	0	
Dallas Roma	0	
Los Angeles Galaxy	2	

Quarter-finals

Chicago Fire	2	
New England Revolution	1	
New York Red Bulls	1	
DC United	3	
Houston Dynamo	3	
FC Dallas	0	
Colorado Rapids	1	
Los Angeles Galaxy	3	

* Home team

Semi-finals

Chicago Fire	3	
DC United	0	
Houston Dynamo	1	
Los Angeles Galaxy	3	

Final

Chicago Fire	3	
Los Angeles Galaxy	1	

CUP FINAL

Toyota Park, Chicago
27-09-2006, Att: 8.185. Ref: Terry Vaughn
Scorers - Jaqua 10, Herron 1º, Thiago 88 for Fire;
Gordon 51 for Galaxy

Fire - Matt Pickers, C.J. Brown, Tony Sanneh, Gonzalo Segares, Nate Jaqua, Diego Gutierrez, Justin Mapp (Thiago 85), Logan Pause, Ivan Guerrero, Chris Rolfe (Jim Curtin 91+), Andy Herron (Dasan Robinson 82). Tr: Dave Sarachan

Galaxy - Kevin Hartman, Chris Albright, Ugo Ihemelu (Herculez Gomez 77), Tyrone Marshall, Ante Jazic, Cobi Jones (Quavas Kirk 72), Paulo Nagamura, Peter Vagenas, Santino Quaranta (Josh Gardner 88), Alan Gordon, Landon Donovan. Tr: Frank Yallop

UZB – UZBEKISTAN

NATIONAL TEAM RECORD
JULY 10TH 2006 TO JULY 12TH 2010

PL	W	D	L	F	A	%
16	7	4	5	30	13	56.2

FIFA/COCA-COLA WORLD RANKING

1993	1994	1995	1996	1997	1998	1999	2000	2001	2002	2003	2004	2005	2006	High	Low
-	78	97	109	79	66	55	71	62	98	81	47	59	45	**45** 12/06	**119** 11/96

2006–2007											
08/06	09/06	10/06	11/06	12/06	01/07	02/07	03/07	04/07	05/07	06/07	07/07
54	57	59	45	45	45	50	53	60	58	58	54

For the second Asian Cup running, Uzbekistan bowed out at the quarter-final stage and that about sums up their position in Asian football - better than most of the pack but falling just short of the likes of Japan, Saudi Arabia, Iran and South Korea at the top of the pile. Until they manage to raise their game to that level, they will find these major tournaments and World Cup qualifiers a frustrating experience. Having said that, the Uzbeks were desperately unlucky in their 2-1 quarter-final defeat at the hands of Saudi Arabia, after hitting the woodwork five times during the match. It was also a tale of missed opportunities in the 2007 AFC Champions League where for the

INTERNATIONAL HONOURS
Asian Games 1994

third year running Pakhtakor Tashkent finished as runners-up in their group, with Saudi's Al Hilal qualifying for the knock-out rounds instead, while a final-round defeat at the hands of Syria's Al Karama saw Neftchi Fergana overtaken by their opponents for the top spot in their group. Pakhtakor had qualified for the Champions League thanks to yet another very successful season at home in Uzbekistan. By winning both the League and the Cup, they secured a fifth consecutive double and are now just one short of the world record held by Georgia's Dinamo Tbilisi. Their 2-0 win over Mashal Muborak in the Cup Final was actually their sixth Cup triumph in a row.

THE FIFA BIG COUNT OF 2006

	Male	Female		Total
Number of players	692 500	37 700	Referees and Assistant Referees	350
Professionals	1 580		Admin, Coaches, Technical, Medical	975
Amateurs 18+	4 460		Number of clubs	216
Youth under 18	30 500		Number of teams	24 000
Unregistered	470 300		Clubs with women's teams	0
Total players	730 200		Players as % of population	2.67%

Uzbekistan Football Federation (UFF)

O'zbekiston Futbol Federatsiyasi, Massiv Almazar, Furkat Street 15/1, Tashkent 700 003, Uzbekistan

Tel +998 71 1441684   Fax +998 71 1441683

info@uzfootball.com   www.uzfootball.com

President: USMANOV Mirabror   General Secretary: RAKHMATULLAEV Sardor

Vice-President: RAKHIMOV Bakhtier   Treasurer: ISKHAKOVA Zemfira   Media Officer: RIZAEV Sanjar

Men's Coach: INILEYEV Rauf   Women's Coach: YUMANGULOV Abdurahman

UFF formed: 1946   AFC: 1994   FIFA: 1994

White shirts with blue trimmings, White shorts, White socks or Blue shirts with white trimmings, Blue shorts, Blue socks

RECENT INTERNATIONAL MATCHES PLAYED BY UZBEKISTAN

2003	Opponents	Score		Venue	Comp	Scorers	Att	Referee
17-11	Tajikistan	W	4-1	Bangkok	ACq	Shishelov 2 [8 36], Kapadze [50], Koshekev [61]		
19-11	Hong Kong	W	1-0	Bangkok	ACq	Shirshov [32]		
21-11	Thailand	L	1-4	Bangkok	ACq	Koshekev [88]		
2004								
18-02	Iraq	D	1-1	Tashkent	WCq	Soliev [78]	24 000	Srinivasan IND
31-03	Chinese Taipei	W	1-0	Taipei	WCq	Koshekev [59]	2 500	Midi Nitrorejo IDN
28-05	Azerbaijan	L	1-3	Baku	Fr	Tadjiyev [45]	12 000	
9-06	Palestine	W	3-0	Tashkent	WCq	Soliev [93+]	45 000	Kamikawa JPN
18-07	Iraq	W	1-0	Chengdu	ACr1	Kasimov [22]	12 400	Kwon Jong Chul KOR
22-07	Saudi Arabia	W	1-0	Chengdu	ACr1	Geynrikh [11]	22 000	Codjia BEN
26-07	Turkmenistan	W	1-0	Chongqing	ACr1	Koshekev [57]	34 000	Kousa SYR
30-07	Bahrain	D	2-2	Chengdu	ACqf	Geynrikh [60], Shishelov [86], L 3-4p	18 000	Salmeen BHR
8-09	Palestine	W	3-0	Rayyan	WCq	Kasimov [9], Djeparov [32], Bikmoev [78]	400	Maidin SIN
13-10	Iraq	W	2-1	Amman	WCq	Shatskikh [10], Geynrikh [22]	10 000	Maidin SIN
17-11	Chinese Taipei	W	6-1	Tashkent	WCq	Geynrikh [5], Kasimov 3 [12 45 85], Shatskikh [18], Koshekev [34]	20 000	Basma SYR
2005								
9-02	Saudi Arabia	D	1-1	Tashkent	WCq	Soliev [93+]	45 000	Kamikawa JPN
25-03	Kuwait	L	1-2	Kuwait City	WCq	Geynrikh [77]	12 000	Sun Baojie CHN
30-03	Korea Republic	L	1-2	Seoul	WCq	Geynrikh [78]	62 857	Najm LIB
3-06	Korea Republic	D	1-1	Tashkent	WCq	Shatskikh [63]	40 000	Moradi IRN
8-06	Saudi Arabia	L	0-3	Riyadh	WCq		72 000	Huang Junjie CHN
17-08	Kuwait	W	3-2	Tashkent	WCq	Djeparov [41p], Shatskikh [51], Soliev [76]	40 000	Mohd Saleh MAS
3-09	Bahrain †	W	1-0	Tashkent	WCpo	Kasimov [12]		
8-10	Bahrain	D	1-1	Tashkent	WCpo	Shatskikh [19]	55 000	Busacca SUI
12-10	Bahrain	D	0-0	Manama	WCpo		25 000	Poll ENG
2006								
22-02	Bangladesh	W	5-0	Tashkent	ACq	Geynrikh 2 [10 52], Djeparov [24], Shatskikh 2 [34 84]	12 000	Ebrahim BHR
1-03	Qatar	L	1-2	Doha	ACq	OG [20]	7 000	Sun Baoje CHN
16-08	Hong Kong	D	2-2	Tashkent	ACq	Soliev [18], Shatskikh [35]	15 000	Shaban KUW
6-09	Hong Kong	D	0-0	Hong Kong	ACq		7 608	Lee Gi Young KOR
11-10	Bangladesh	W	4-0	Dhaka	ACq	Zeytullaev [11], Bakaev [18], Djeparov [22], Shatskikh [39p]	120	Tan Hai CHN
15-11	Qatar	W	2-0	Tashkent	ACq	Koshelev [31], Zeytullaev [52]	14 000	Al Saeedi UAE
2007								
7-02	Uzbekistan	D	0-0	Karshi	Fr			
7-03	Azerbaijan	L	0-1	Shymkent	Fr			
9-03	Kyrgyzstan	W	6-0	Shymkent	Fr	Soliev [2], Bakaev 3 [7p 43 89], Mandzukas [63], Shishelov [80]		
11-03	Kazakhstan	D	1-1	Shymkent	Fr	Geynrikh [34]		
24-03	Chinese Taipei	W	1-0	Taipei	Fr	Khoshimov [53]		
27-03	China PR	L	1-3	Macau	Fr	Shishelov [76]		
2-07	Iraq	W	2-0	Paju	Fr	Ibragimov [3], Bakaev [30]		
5-07	Korea Republic	L	1-2	Seoul	Fr	Djeparov [59p]	21 019	Prayoon THA
11-07	Iran	L	1-2	Kuala Lumpur	ACr1	Rezaei OG [16]	1 863	Ghalehnoy IRN
14-07	Malaysia	W	5-0	Kuala Lumpur	ACr1	Shatskikh 2 [10 89], Kapadze [30], Bakaev [45p], Ibragimov [85]	7 137	Abdou QAT
18-07	China PR	W	3-0	Kuala Lumpur	ACr1	Shatskikh [72], Kapadze [86], Geynrikh [90]	2 200	Al Fadhli KUW
22-07	Saudi Arabia	L	1-2	Jakarta	ACqf	Solomin [82]	12 000	Kwon Jong Chul KOR

Fr = Friendly match • AC = AFC Asian Cup • WC = FIFA World Cup • † Matched annulled due to referee error
q = qualifier • po = play-off • r1 = first round group • qf = quarter-final • po = play-off

UZBEKISTAN NATIONAL TEAM RECORDS AND RECORD SEQUENCES

Records			Sequence records				
Victory	15-0	MGL 1998	Wins	8	1994	Clean sheets	4	2004, 2006-2007
Defeat	1-8	JPN 2000	Defeats	4	2000-2001	Goals scored	18	2003-2005
Player Caps	65	KASIMOV Mirdzhal	Undefeated	11	1994, 2001	Without goal	3	2000-2001
Player Goals	29	KASIMOV Mirdzhal	Without win	6	1997	Goals against	9	2004-2005

REPUBLIC OF UZBEKISTAN; OZBEKISTON RESPUBLIKASI

Capital	Tashkent	Language	Uzbek, Russian			Independence	1991
Population	27 780 059	Area	447 400 km²	Density	59 per km²	% in cities	41%
GDP per cap	$1 700	Dailling code	+7	Internet	.uz	GMT + / -	+5

MAJOR CITIES/TOWNS

Population '000

1	Tashkent	1 959
2	Namangan	446
3	Andijan	321
4	Samarkand	312
5	Bukhara	249
6	Nukus	240
7	Karshi	231
8	Kukon	187
9	Chirchik	168
10	Fergana	161
11	Jizak	159
12	Urganch	152
13	Termiz	147
14	Margilan	132
15	Navoiy	131
16	Angren	127
17	Olmalik	120
18	Bekobod	86
19	Khujayli	76
20	Denov	73
21	Shahrihan	67
22	Chust	66
23	Kagan	65
24	Zarafshon	65

MEDALS TABLE

		Overall			League			Cup		Europe			City	Stadium	Cap'ty	DoF
		G	S	B	G	S	B	G	S	G	S	B				
1	Pakhtakor Tashkent	15	3	2	7	2		8	1			2	Tashkent	Pakhtakor Markaziy	55 000	1956
2	Neftchi Fergana	7	14	1	5	9		2	5			1	Fergana	Fergana	20 000	1962
3	Navbahor Namangan	4	1	8	1		8	3	1				Namangan	Markaziy	35 000	1978
4	Dustlik Tashkent	3			2			1					Tashkent			
5	MHSK Tashkent	1	2	1	1	1	1		1				Tashkent			
6	Mashal Muborak	2					1		1				Muborak	Bahrom Vafoev	10 000	1991
7	Nasah Karshi	1	4			4		1					Karshi	Markaziy	20 000	1978
8	Nurafshon Bukhara	1			1								Bukhara	Markaziy	40 000	
	Samarkand Dinamo	1							1				Samarkand	Dinamo	12 500	1960
	Temirulchi Kukon	1							1				Kukon			
	Traktor Tashkent	1							1				Tashkent	Traktor	6 400	1968
	FK Yangier	1							1				Yangier			
13	Kizilgum Zarafshon		1			1							Zarafshon	Kizilgum		1994
	Sogdiana Jizak		1			1							Jizak	Markaziy	10 000	1970

RECENT LEAGUE AND CUP RECORD

	Championship						Cup		
Year	Champions	Pts	Runners-up	Pts	Third	Pts	Winners	Score	Runners-up
1995	Neftchi Fergana	76	MHSK Tashkent	74	Navbahor Nam'gan	72	Navbahor Nam'gan	1-0	MHSK Tashkent
1996	Navbahor Nam'gan	74	Neftchi Fergana	72	MHSK Tashkent	62	Neftchi Fergana	0-0 5-4p	Pkhtakor Tashkent
1997	MHSK Tashkent	90	Neftchi Fergana	81	Navbahor Nam'gan	68	Pakhtakor Tashkent	3-2	Neftchi Fergana
1998	Pakhtakor Tashkent	76	Neftchi Fergana	70	Navbahor Nam'gan	59	Navbahor Nam'gan	2-0	Neftchi Fergana
1999	Dustlik Tashkent	64	Neftchi Fergana	63	Navbahor Nam'gan	61	No tournament		
2000	Dustlik Tashkent	94	Neftchi Fergana	90	Nasaf Karshi	85	Dustlik Tashkent	4-1	Samarkand Dinamo
2001	Neftchi Fergana	84	Pakhtakor Tashkent	72	Nasaf Karshi	71	Pakhtakor Tashkent	2-1	Neftchi Fergana
2002	Pakhtakor Tashkent	74	Neftchi Fergana	69	Kizilgum Zarafshon	59	Pakhtakor Tashkent	6-3	Neftchi Fergana
2003	Pakhtakor Tashkent	77	Neftchi Fergana	71	Navbahor Nam'gan	63	Pakhtakor Tashkent	3-1	Nasaf Karshi
2004	Pakhtakor Tashkent	69	Neftchi Fergana	65	Navbahor Nam'gan	57	Pakhtakor Tashkent	3-2	Traktor Tashkent
2005	Pakhtakor Tashkent	65	Mashal Muborak	59	Nasaf Karshi	51	Pakhtakor Tashkent	1-0	Neftchi Fergana
2006	Pakhtakor Tashkent	77	Neftchi Fergana	71	Nasaf Karshi	70	Pakhtakor Tashkent	2-0	Mashal Muborak

UZBEKISTAN 2006

O'ZBEKISTON CHEMPIONATI OLIY LIGA

	Pl	W	D	L	F	A	Pts	Pak	Nef	Nas	Mas	Tra	Kiz	Nav	Sam	Lok	And	Buk	Shu	Top	Met	Sog	Hor
Pakhtakor Tashkent †	30	25	2	3	84	12	77		3-0	2-0	3-0	3-1	2-1	3-0	3-0	7-1	6-1	2-0	2-1	4-0	6-0	4-0	1-0
Neftchi Fergana †	30	23	2	5	60	23	71	1-1		1-1	1-1	0-0	4-0	2-0	1-0	4-1	2-0	2-1	2-1	2-1	1-0	2-0	6-0
Nasaf Karshi	30	22	4	4	63	33	70	1-0	1-2		3-1	2-0	1-0	1-0	1-0	5-1	3-2	1-0	3-2	3-2	3-2	4-2	9-3
Mashal Muborak	30	18	6	6	50	28	60	0-2	1-0	1-1		0-0	2-3	3-0	4-1	4-1	3-1	1-1	2-0	2-0	2-1	3-0	2-0
Traktor Tashkent	30	15	4	11	51	46	49	0-3	0-1	2-1	1-1		0-1	1-1	2-1	0-1	3-2	1-3	4-1	4-1	1-1	1-0	1-0
Kizilgum Zarafshon	30	14	6	10	51	37	48	0-1	2-3	0-0	1-1	2-3		3-0	2-0	1-0	5-1	1-0	3-0	0-1	5-0	2-1	5-3
Navbahor Namangan	30	13	5	12	46	35	44	1-0	0-2	2-3	0-1	4-1	1-1		0-0	3-0	2-1	1-0	3-2	1-0	2-1	1-0	10-0
Samarkand Dinamo	30	12	4	14	39	39	40	2-0	0-1	2-0	0-1	0-1	1-1	2-0		2-2	6-1	2-1	4-1	2-0	1-0	2-0	1-0
Lokomotiv Tashkent	30	10	8	12	39	55	38	0-1	1-0	0-2	2-3	1-2	1-1	2-1	4-3		2-0	1-0	1-0	2-2	1-0	1-0	5-1
FK Andijan	30	10	5	15	46	52	35	1-1	0-1	0-1	0-0	2-3	5-3	2-1	3-0	5-0		1-1	1-0	3-1	0-0	2-0	7-1
FK Bukhara	30	9	7	14	35	34	34	0-2	2-0	0-0	0-3	0-3	0-0	2-1	4-0	1-1	0-0		1-2	2-1	0-0	3-0	5-0
Shurton Guzor	30	10	2	18	43	55	32	0-6	1-2	2-3	1-2	3-2	3-1	1-2	1-0	2-1	3-1	1-0		6-1	1-0	0-1	5-0
Topolon Sariosia	30	9	4	17	40	58	31	0-3	2-3	1-2	2-0	1-6	1-3	1-1	1-0	2-2	1-0	2-4	3-0		2-1	3-1	4-0
Metallgum Bekobod	30	7	7	16	36	45	28	0-1	2-1	1-2	1-2	1-2	4-1	1-1	1-1	3-3	3-0	2-1	2-1	1-0		1-2	6-0
Sogdiana Jizak	30	7	3	20	23	48	24	0-3	0-3	0-2	0-1	4-3	0-2	0-2	0-1	1-1	0-1	2-0	0-0	0-0	1-0		4-0
Horezm Urganch	30	0	3	27	21	127	3	1-9	2-8	2-4	2-4	1-3	0-1	0-5	0-4	1-1	0-3	1-3	2-2	0-4	1-1	0-4	

11/03/2006 - 12/11/2006 • † Qualified for the AFC Champions League
Top scorers: Pavel SOLOMIN, Traktor 21; Nasir OTAQOZIYEV, Neftchi 19; Arif MIRZOYEV, Navbahor 18; Server DJEPAROV, Pakhtakor 18

UZBEKISTAN 2006 BIRINCHI LIGA (2)

	Pl	W	D	L	F	A	Pts
Khurovchi Tashkent	38	27	5	6	94	32	86
FK Vobkent	38	25	5	8	95	53	80
Mashal Muborak	38	23	9	6	63	30	78
Osiyo Tashkent	38	24	1	13	67	54	73
Sementchi Kuvasoy	38	21	8	9	65	35	71
OTMK Olmalik	38	20	9	9	58	35	69
Gallakor Gallaorol	38	17	10	11	63	45	61
UDJ Andijan	38	19	3	16	53	44	60
Kimyogar Chirchik	38	17	5	16	69	64	56
Lochin Shorchi	38	15	4	19	71	76	49
Oktepa Tashkent	38	14	6	18	57	63	48
Kosonsoy Zakovat §3	38	14	8	16	51	54	47
FK Hazorasp §6	38	16	4	18	54	55	46
FK Shahrixon §3	38	14	6	18	60	64	45
Miyonkol Kattagorgon	38	14	2	22	51	78	44
Zarafshon Navai	38	13	3	22	42	76	42
Shakhontohur Tashkent	38	10	9	19	49	65	39
FK Qo'qon 1912 §6	38	9	3	26	58	89	24
Surhom Termiz §6	38	8	5	25	34	79	23
Sidaryo Guliston §6	38	6	3	29	36	99	15

9/04/2006 - 1/11/2006 • § = points deducted

UZBEKISTAN CUP 2006

Second Round

Pakhtakor Tashkent	1	7
FK Vobkent *	0	0
Samarkand Dinamo *	3	0
Metallurg Bekobod	0	4
Aktobe Tashkent	1	1
FK Shorchi *	0	1
Nasaf Karshi *	1	0
Traktor Tashkent	0	4
Neftchi Fergana	3	5
FK Shahrihan *	1	0
Lokomotiv Tashkent *	2	1
Shurton Guzor	1	3
FK Bukhara *	2	1
Navabor Namangan	0	1
Kizilgum Zarafshon	0	2
Mashal Muborak *	1	1

Quarter-finals

Pakhtakor Tashkent	4	6
Metallurg Bekobod *	1	0
Aktobe Tashkent	0	1
Traktor Tashkent *	3	0
Neftchi Fergana	1	4
Shurton Guzor *	1	1
FK Bukhara	1	1
Mashal Muborak *	4	0

Semi-finals

Pakhtakor Tashkent	6	7
Traktor Tashkent *	2	1
Neftchi Fergana	0	2
Mashal Muborak *	2	2

Final

Pakhtakor Tashkent	2
Mashal Muborak	0

CUP FINAL

Pakhtakor, Tashkent
8-11-2006, Att: 17 000, Ref: Lutfullin

Scorers - Renat Bayramov 46+, Uche Iheruome 83

* Home team/home team in the first leg

VAN – VANUATU

NATIONAL TEAM RECORD
JULY 10TH 2006 TO JULY 12TH 2010

PL	W	D	L	F	A	%
2	1	0	1	5	5	50

FIFA/COCA-COLA WORLD RANKING

1993	1994	1995	1996	1997	1998	1999	2000	2001	2002	2003	2004	2005	2006	High	Low
164	172	179	180	186	177	184	167	168	156	160	143	146	167	**139** 08/04	**188** 04/00

2006–2007											
08/06	09/06	10/06	11/06	12/06	01/07	02/07	03/07	04/07	05/07	06/07	07/07
162	165	165	168	167	167	168	167	162	159	175	177

By the end of 2007, Tafea FC from the capital Port Vila could be celebrating a world record because by winning the Championship for the 13th season in a row in October 2006, they set themselves up for a tilt at the world record of 14 consecutive championships held by Latvia's Skonto Riga. The biggest threat to their ambitions could come from Tupuji Imere who gave them a good run for their money in 2006. There was general disappointment at Vanuatu's absence from the inaugural O–League in 2007, especially given their record in past OFC Champions Cup campaigns, notably in 2005 when Tafea were runners-up. Port Vila Sharks were due to enter but

INTERNATIONAL HONOURS
Melanesian Cup 1990

had to pull out after failing to secure an international standard venue to host matches. Tafea more than made up for that, however, by qualifying for the 2007-08 tournament. They easily beat University of Papua New Guinea 5-1 and then beat New Caledonia's JS Baco 5-0 to top a qualifying group played in June 2007. They then avoided both New Zealand teams when the draw for the group stage was made, and will be hoping to overcome the champions of both Fiji and the Solomon Islands to qualify for the final. What a story it would be if Tafea won a world record 14th consecutive title and then celebrated that by qualifying for the FIFA Club World Cup!

THE FIFA BIG COUNT OF 2006

	Male	Female		Total
Number of players	25 600	1 800	Referees and Assistant Referees	110
Professionals	0		Admin, Coaches, Technical, Medical	206
Amateurs 18+	4 050		Number of clubs	200
Youth under 18	1 250		Number of teams	400
Unregistered	21 000		Clubs with women's teams	30
Total players	27 400		Players as % of population	13.12%

Vanuatu Football Federation (VFF)
PO Box 266, Port Vila, Vanuatu
Tel +678 27239   Fax +678 25236
jimmy_nipo@yahoo.com   www.sportingpulse.com.au
President: TRONQUET Jacques   General Secretary: IAPSON George
Vice-President: MALTOCK Lambert   Treasurer: WARSAL Leon Katty   Media Officer: None
Men's Coach: ALWIN Job   Women's Coach: ALWIN Job
VFF formed: 1934   OFC: 1988   FIFA: 1988
Gold shirts, Black shorts, Gold socks

RECENT INTERNATIONAL MATCHES PLAYED BY VANUATU

2002	Opponents	Score	Venue	Comp	Scorers	Att	Referee
12-07	New Zealand	L 0-3	Auckland	OCsf		1 000	Breeze AUS
14-07	Tahiti	L 0-1	Auckland	OC3p		1 000	Rakaroi FIJ
2003							
30-06	Fiji	D 0-0	Suva	SPr1			Ariiotima TAH
1-07	Solomon Islands	D 2-2	Suva	SPr1	Mermer 22, Qorig 47		Shah FIJ
3-07	Tuvalu †	W 1-0	Suva	SPr1	Tabe 86	700	Bayung PNG
7-07	Kiribati †	W 18-0	Lautoka	SPr1	Mermer 4 4 15 51 53, Chillia 4 10 22 29 30, Iwai 5 27 40 41 63 64, Tabe 35, Vava 47, Thomsen 54, Demas 62, Pita 83	2 000	Bayung PNG
9-07	New Caledonia	D 1-1	Lautoka	SPsf	Laki 54, L 3-4p	7 000	Shah FIJ
11-07	Tahiti	W 1-0	Suva	SP3p	Mermer 57	6 000	Rakaroi FIJ
2004							
3-04	Solomon Islands	L 1-2	Port-Vila	Fr	Chillia 41	4 000	Fred VAN
6-04	Solomon Islands	L 1-2	Port-Vila	Fr			
10-05	Papua New Guinea	D 1-1	Apia	WCq	Lauru 92+	500	Breeze AUS
12-05	American Samoa	W 9-1	Apia	WCq	Qorig 2 30 47+, Mermer 3 37 56 91+, Poida 55, Chilea 65, Maleb 2 80 92+	400	Fox NZL
15-05	Samoa	W 3-0	Apia	WCq	Mermer 13, Chillia 55, Maleb 57	650	Breeze AUS
19-05	Fiji	W 3-0	Apia	WCq	Thomsen 46+, Lauru 2 63 65	200	Breeze AUS
29-05	Solomon Islands	L 0-1	Adelaide	WCq		200	Shield AUS
31-05	Fiji	L 0-1	Adelaide	WCq		500	Ariiotima TAH
2-06	New Zealand	W 4-2	Adelaide	WCq	Chillia 37, Bibi 64, Maleb 72, Qoriz 88	356	Farina ITA
4-06	Australia	L 0-3	Adelaide	WCq		4 000	Ariiotima TAH
6-06	Tahiti	L 1-2	Adelaide	WCq	Iwai 23	300	Rakaroi FIJ
2005							
No international matches played in 2005							
2006							
No international matches played in 2006							
2007							
17-07	New Caledonia	L 3-5	Noumea	Fr	Gete 34, Masauvakalo 83, Soromon 92+		
19-07	New Caledonia	W 2-0	Noumea	Fr			

Fr = Friendly match • OC = OFC Oceania Cup • SP = South Pacific Games • WC = FIFA World Cup
q = qualifier • r1 = first round group • sf = semi-final • 3p = third place play-off • † Not a full international

VANUATU NATIONAL TEAM RECORDS AND RECORD SEQUENCES

Records			Sequence records				
Victory	13-1	SAM 1981	Wins	3	2004	Clean sheets	2	Five times
Defeat	0-9	NZL 1951	Defeats	6	Three times	Goals scored	13	1996-2000
Player Caps	n/a		Undefeated	6	2003	Without goal	3	1992, 2003-2004
Player Goals	n/a		Without win	9	1979-1981	Goals against	23	1951-1979

RECENT LEAGUE RECORD

Year	Port Vila Football League
2003	Tafea FC
2004	Tafea FC
2005	Tafea FC
2006	Tafea FC

VANUATU COUNTRY INFORMATION

Capital	Port-Vila	Independence	1980 from UK and France	GDP per Capita	$2 900
Population	202 609	Status	Republic	GNP Ranking	183
Area km²	12 200	Language	English, French, Bislama	Dialling code	+678
Population density	16 per km²	Literacy rate	53%	Internet code	.vu
% in urban areas	19%	Main religion	Christian	GMT +/–	+11
Towns/Cities ('000)	Port-Vila 35; Luganville 13; Norsup 3; Port Olry 2; Isangel ; Sola 1				
Neighbours (km)	South Pacific Ocean 2 528				
Main stadia	Korman Stadium – Port-Vila				

VEN – VENEZUELA

NATIONAL TEAM RECORD
JULY 10TH 2006 TO JULY 12TH 2010

PL	W	D	L	F	A	%
17						

FIFA/COCA-COLA WORLD RANKING

1993	1994	1995	1996	1997	1998	1999	2000	2001	2002	2003	2004	2005	2006	High	Low
93	110	127	111	115	129	110	111	81	69	57	62	67	73	**48** 04/04	**129** 12/98

					2006–2007						
08/06	09/06	10/06	11/06	12/06	01/07	02/07	03/07	04/07	05/07	06/07	07/07
65	80	72	73	73	73	66	74	71	70	70	56

March 31, 2004 will be remembered as the day that football in Venezuela arrived on the scene. That was when the national team beat the four-times world champions Uruguay in a FIFA World Cup qualifier in Montevideo. In the future, however, historians may look back on Venezuela's hosting of the Copa América in 2007 as the time when football really caught the imagination of the Venezuelan people. It was an fantastic tournament, with big crowds watching some excellent football. Venezuela also won a Copa América match for only the second time, 40 years on from the first, when they beat Peru 2-0 in San Cristóbal, while the following game in Merida saw the Vinotinto

INTERNATIONAL HONOURS
None

not only qualify for the quarter-finals but also break their record for the longest undefeated run - a record that had stood since 1956. There was obvious disappointment with the defeat to Uruguay in the quarter-finals but the legacy of the tournament for football in the country could be far reaching. The domestic season was dominated by the duel between Caracas and Unión Maracaibo. Both the Apertura and Clausura were decided on the final day with matches between the two, with Caracas winning the former thanks to a 3-1 win whilst Unión won the latter by beating Caracas 3-1. That meant a play-off for the championship, which was won 1-0 on aggregate by Caracas.

THE FIFA BIG COUNT OF 2006

	Male	Female		Total
Number of players	1 270 894	219 679	Referees and Assistant Referees	832
Professionals	546		Admin, Coaches, Technical, Medical	8 300
Amateurs 18+	9 897		Number of clubs	717
Youth under 18	28 172		Number of teams	2 449
Unregistered	516 400		Clubs with women's teams	203
Total players	1 490 573		Players as % of population	5.79%

Federación Venezolana de Fútbol (FVF)
Avda. Santos Erminy Ira, Calle las Delicias Torre Mega II, P.H. Quitar P.H., Caracas 1050, Venezuela
Tel +58 212 7624472   Fax +58 212 7620596
sec_presidencia_fvf@cantv.net   www.federacionvenezolanadefutbol.org
President: ESQUIVEL Rafael   General Secretary: GARCIA-REGALADO Jesus
Vice-President: CABEZAS Temistocles   Treasurer: SANGLADE Luis Ignacio   Media Officer: GOUSSOT Zaiddy
Men's Coach: PAEZ Richard   Women's Coach: ALONSO Lino
FVF formed: 1926   CONMEBOL: 1965   FIFA: 1952
Burgundy shirts with white trimmings, White shorts, White socks

RECENT INTERNATIONAL MATCHES PLAYED BY VENEZUELA

2004	Opponents	Score		Venue	Comp	Scorers	Att	Referee
18-02	Australia	D	1-1	Caracas	Fr	Arango [91+]	16 000	Ruiz COL
10-03	Honduras	W	2-1	Maracaibo	Fr	Vera [35p], Noriega [53]	24 000	Manzur VEN
31-03	Uruguay	W	3-0	Montevideo	WCq	Urdaneta [19], González.H [67], Arango [77]	40 094	Ortube BOL
28-04	Jamaica	L	1-2	Kingston	Fr	Arango [27]	10 000	Ford BRB
1-06	Chile	L	0-1	San Cristobal	WCq		23 040	Torres PAR
6-06	Peru	D	0-0	Lima	WCq		40 000	Larrionda URU
6-07	Colombia	L	0-1	Lima	CArl		45 000	Rezende BRA
9-07	Peru	L	1-3	Lima	CArl	Margiotta [74]	43 000	Selman CHI
12-07	Bolivia	D	1-1	Trujillo	CArl	Moran [27]	25 000	Mattus CRC
18-08	Spain	L	2-3	Las Palmas	Fr	Rojas.J [46+], Castellín [92+]	32 000	Rodomonti ITA
5-09	Paraguay	L	0-1	Asuncion	WCq		30 000	Mendez URU
9-10	Brazil	L	2-5	Maracaibo	WCq	Moran 2 [79 90]	26 133	Chandia CHI
14-10	Ecuador	W	3-1	San Cristobal	WCq	Urdaneta [20p], Moran 2 [72 80]	13 800	Lecca PER
17-11	Argentina	L	2-3	Buenos Aires	WCq	Moran [31], Vielma [72]	30 000	Hidalgo PER
21-12	Guatemala	L	0-1	Caracas	Fr		6 000	Solorzano VEN
2005								
9-02	Estonia	W	3-0	Maracaibo	Fr	Paez [20], Margiotta [33], Maldonado [83]	12 000	Vazquez ECU
26-03	Colombia	D	0-0	Maracaibo	WCq		18 000	Simon BRA
29-03	Bolivia	L	1-3	La Paz	WCq	Maldonado [71]	7 908	Lecca PER
25-05	Panama	D	1-1	Caracas	Fr	Maldonado [4]	15 000	Brand VEN
4-06	Uruguay	D	1-1	Maracaibo	WCq	Maldonado [74]	12 504	Brazenas ARG
8-06	Chile	L	1-2	Santiago	WCq	Moran [82]	35 506	Torres PAR
17-08	Ecuador	L	1-3	Loja	Fr	Torrealba [70]	10 000	Vasco ECU
3-09	Peru	W	4-1	Maracaibo	WCq	Maldonado [17], Arango [68], Torrealba 2 [73 79]	6 000	Rezende BRA
8-10	Paraguay	L	0-1	Maracaibo	WCq		13 272	Elizondo ARG
12-10	Brazil	L	0-3	Belem	WCq		47 000	Baldassi ARG
2006								
1-03	Colombia	D	1-1	Maracaibo	Fr	Gomez [48]	15 000	Carpio ECU
5-05	Mexico	L	0-1	Pasadena	Fr		57 000	Vaughn USA
26-05	USA	L	0-2	Cleveland	Fr		29 745	Morales MEX
16-08	Honduras	D	0-0	Maracay	Fr		9 000	Brandt VEN
2-09	Switzerland	L	0-1	Basel	Fr		12 500	Hamer LUX
6-09	Austria	W	1-0	Basel	Fr	De Ornelas [8]	1 453	Bertolini SUI
27-09	Uruguay	W	1-0	Maracaibo	Fr	Arismendi [81]	28 000	Manzur VEN
18-10	Uruguay	L	0-4	Montevideo	Fr		7 000	Silvera URU
15-11	Guatemala	W	2-1	Caracas	Fr	Villafraz [4], Rey [52]	9 000	Andarcia VEN
2007								
14-01	Sweden	W	2-0	Maracaibo	Fr	Guerra [17], Arismendi [91+]	14 000	Buitrago COL
7-02	Chile	L	0-1	Maracaibo	Fr		9 000	Buitrago COL
28-02	Mexico	L	1-3	San Diego	Fr	Arismendi [83]	63 328	Stott USA
24-03	Cuba	W	3-1	Merida	Fr	Arango [11], Torrealba [33], González.C [64]	12 000	Andarcia VEN
28-03	New Zealand	W	5-0	Maracaibo	Fr	Páez [7], De Ornelas 2 [30 75], Fedor [84p], Moran [91+]	12 000	
25-05	Honduras	W	2-1	Merida	Fr	Vielma [18], Arismendi [38]	42 000	Gomez VEN
1-06	Canada	D	2-2	Maracaibo	Fr	Cichero [22], Maldonado [25]		Lopez COL
26-06	Bolivia	D	2-2	San Cristobal	CArl	Maldonado [21], Páez [56]	42 000	Reinoso ECU
30-06	Peru	W	2-0	San Cristobal	CArl	Cichero [49], Arismendi [79]	42 000	Archundia MEX
3-07	Uruguay	D	0-0	Merida	CArl		42 000	Simon BRA
7-07	Uruguay	L	1-4	San Cristobal	CAqf	Arango [41]	42 000	Chandia CHI

Fr = Friendly match • CA = Copa América • WC = FIFA World Cup • q = qualifier • r1 = first round group • qf = quarter-final

VENEZUELA NATIONAL TEAM RECORDS AND RECORD SEQUENCES

Records			Sequence records					
Victory	6-0	PUR 1946	Wins	4	2001	Clean sheets	4	2002
Defeat	0-11	ARG 1975	Defeats	9	1989-1991	Goals scored	8	1946-1956
Player Caps	79	REY José Manuel	Undefeated	7	2007	Without goal	5	1990-1991
Player Goals	16	MORAN Ruberth	Without win	26	1989-1993	Goals against	21	1993-96, 1999-01

CARIBBEAN SEA

BOLIVARIAN REPUBLIC OF VENEZUELA; REPUBLICA BOLIVARIANA DE VENEZUELA

Capital	Caracas	Language	Spanish	Independence	1821
Population	26 023 528	Area	912 050 km²	% in cities	93%
GDP per cap	$4 800	Dailling code	+58	Internet	.ve	GMT +/-	-4

MAJOR CITIES/TOWNS
Population '000

1	Maracaibo	2 054
2	Caracas	1 801
3	Valencia	1 457
4	Barquisimeto	833
5	Ciudad Guayana	792
6	Barcelona	459
7	Maturin	445
8	Maracay	399
9	Petare	386
10	Turmero	373
11	Barinas	306
12	Santa Teresa	305
13	Ciudad Bolivar	300
14	Cumaná	263
15	Baruta	252
16	San Cristóbal	249
17	Puerto la Cruz	227
18	Mérida	221
19	Guatire	208
20	Coro	205
21	Cabimas	205
22	Cúa	199
23	Acarigua	116
24	Valera	92

MEDALS TABLE

		Overall			Lge			Sth Am			City	Stadium	Cap'ty	DoF
		G	S	B	G	S	B	G	S	B				
1	Caracas FC	9	1	1	9	1				1	Caracas	Estadio Olimpico	25 000	1967
2	Unión SC	7	3		7	3								
3	Dos Caminos SC	6	7		6	7								
4	Deportivo Tachira	5	7		5	7					San Cristobal	Polideportivo de Pueblo Nuevo	30 000	1974
5	Deportivo Italia	5	6		5	6					Caracas	Brigido Iriarte	15 000	1948
6	Portuguesa FC	5	3	1	5	3				1	Acarígua	José Antonio Paez	20 000	1972
7	Centro Atlético	4	7		4	7								
8	Deportivo Galicia	4	5		4	5					Caracas	Brigido Iriarte	15 000	
	Loyola SC	4	5		4	5								
10	Deportivo Portugués	4	2		4	2								
11	CS Maritimo	4	1		4	1					Caracas			1959
12	Deportivo Venezuela	4			4									
13	Universidad Central	3	3		3	3								
14	Universidad de Los Andes	3	1	1	3	1				1	Merida	Guillermo Soto Rosas	15 000	1977
15	Estudiantes Merida	2	7		2	7					Merida	Guillermo Soto Rosas	15 000	1971

RECENT LEAGUE RECORD

	Championship							Championship Play-off		
Year	Champions	Pts	Runners-up	Pts	Third	Pts		Winners	Score	Runners-up
1995	Caracas FC	17	Minervén	16	Trullianos	14				
1996	Minervén	22	Mineros de Guayana	20	Caracas FC	19				
1997	Caracas FC							Caracas	3-1 5-0	Atlético Zulia
1998	Atlético Zulia							Atlético Zulia	1-0 4-0	Estudiantes
1999	ItalChalcao							ItalChalcao	5-1 2-1	Unión At. Táchira
2000	Deportivo Táchira	15	ItalChacao	7	Estudiantes	6				
2001	Caracas FC	35	Trujillanos	33	ItalChacao	32				
2002	Nacional Táchira							Nacional Táchira	3-3 0-0 5-3p	Estudiantes
2003	Caracas FC							Caracas FC	1-1 3-0	Unión At. Maracaibo
2004	Caracas FC	†								
2005	Unión At. Maracaibo	†								
2006	Caracas FC							Caracas FC	1-1 3-0	Unión At. Maracaibo
2007	Caracas FC							Caracas FC	1-0 0-0	Unión At. Maracaibo

† Automatic champions as winners of both the Apertura and Clausura

VENEZUELA 2006-07

PRIMERA DIVISION TORNEO APERTURA 2006

	Pl	W	D	L	F	A	Pts	Caracas	Unión	Mineros	Táchira	Zamora	Portuguesa	Carabobo	Aragua	Trujillanos	Monagas
Caracas FC	18	10	6	2	27	12	36		3-1	2-0	1-0	0-0	2-0	1-1	2-0	1-1	1-0
Unión At. Maracaibo	18	10	6	2	28	17	36	0-0		2-0	1-1	1-1	3-1	2-1	2-0	2-1	1-0
Mineros de Guyana	18	7	6	5	27	24	27	3-2	2-2		2-0	0-1	3-2	0-0	2-1	2-0	2-0
Deportivo Táchira	18	6	7	5	22	19	25	2-1	3-1	0-2		3-2	1-1	1-0	2-0	5-2	1-1
Zamora FC	18	5	8	5	24	22	23	1-1	1-2	3-3	1-0		2-2	4-0	2-2	2-1	2-1
Portuguesa FC	18	5	8	5	23	23	23	0-1	1-1	4-3	0-0	2-0		1-1	1-1	3-1	1-0
Carabobo FC	18	4	9	5	17	22	21	1-3	0-3	1-1	0-0	1-0	2-0		3-1	1-0	1-1
Aragua FC	18	4	7	7	21	24	19	2-2	0-1	0-0	2-2	1-0	1-1	0-0		4-2	4-0
Trujillanos FC	18	3	5	10	21	31	14	0-1	1-1	3-1	1-0	1-1	1-3	1-1	0-1		1-1
Monagas SC	18	1	8	9	14	30	11	0-3	1-2	1-1	1-1	1-1	0-0	3-3	2-1	1-4	

6/08/2006 - 17/12/2006 • ‡ Qualified for the overall championship final • Top scorer: Robinson RENTERIA, Trujillanos 11

VENEZUELA 2006-07

PRIMERA DIVISION TORNEO CLAUSURA 2007

	Pl	W	D	L	F	A	Pts	Unión	Caracas	Mineros	Zamora	Carabobo	Monagas	Aragua	Táchira	Portuguesa	Trujillanos
Unión At. Maracaibo	18	9	5	4	28	19	32		3-1	3-2	2-1	1-0	2-2	2-1	3-0	4-0	1-1
Caracas FC	18	8	8	2	25	16	32	1-1		3-1	1-1	1-1	1-0	3-0	0-0	1-0	2-0
Mineros de Guyana	18	7	6	5	26	24	27	2-1	1-3		1-0	2-1	1-2	3-3	1-1	2-0	2-0
Zamora FC	18	7	5	6	24	18	26	1-1	0-0	1-2		3-1	2-2	1-0	1-0	3-2	0-1
Carabobo FC	18	6	7	5	17	15	25	3-0	0-0	1-2	2-0		1-0	1-3	1-0	1-0	1-0
Monagas SC	18	5	6	7	13	21	21	1-0	0-1	1-1	0-2	1-1		0-0	1-3	0-1	1-0
Aragua FC	18	4	8	6	19	22	20	0-1	2-2	1-1	1-0	1-1	0-1		2-1	1-0	1-1
Deportivo Táchira	18	3	10	5	22	25	19	0-0	1-1	0-0	2-2	1-1	0-0	2-2		2-2	5-3
Portuguesa FC	18	5	4	9	19	26	19	2-0	1-3	1-0	0-4	0-0	5-0	0-0	2-3		2-1
Trujillanos FC	18	4	5	9	20	27	17	1-3	4-1	2-2	0-2	0-0	0-1	2-1	3-1	1-1	

7/01/2007 - 29/04/2007 • ‡ Qualified for the overall championship final • Top scorer: Alex SINISTERRA, Zamora 11
Championship Final: Unión At. Maracaibo 0-1 0-0 Caracas FC • Caracas FC are Venezuelan champions in 2006

PRIMERA DIVISION AGGREGATE

	Pl	W	D	L	F	A	Pts
Caracas FC †	36	18	14	4	52	28	68
Unión At. Maracaibo †	36	19	11	6	56	36	68
Mineros de Guyana †	36	14	12	10	53	48	54
Zamora ‡	36	12	13	11	48	40	49
Carabobo ‡	36	10	16	10	34	37	46
Deportivo Táchira	36	9	17	10	44	44	44
Portuguesa FC	36	10	12	14	42	49	42
Aragua FC	36	8	15	13	40	46	39
Monagas SC	36	6	14	16	27	51	32
Trujillanos FC	36	7	10	19	41	58	31

† Qualified for Copa Libertadores 2007 • ‡ Qualified for Copa Sudamericana • Top scorer: Robinson RENTERIA, Truj'nos 18

VENEZUELA 2006-07 ASCENSO APERTURA (2) GRUPO CENTRO-OCCIDENTE

	Pl	W	D	L	F	A	Pts
Llaneros de Guanare †	16	10	3	3	28	17	33
Unión At. Maracaibo B	16	8	3	5	27	15	27
Atlético El Vigía	16	6	5	5	22	16	23
Guaros de Lara	16	6	5	5	25	24	23
Estudiantes Mérida	16	5	5	6	27	35	20
Sport Zulia	16	4	6	6	21	23	18
Atlético Turén	16	4	6	6	19	24	18
UCLA Barquisimeto	16	3	3	10	20	27	12

12/08/2006 - 26/11/2006 • † Qualified for Apertura final

VENEZUELA 2006-07 ASCENSO APERTURA (2) GRUPO CENTRO-ORIENTE

	Pl	W	D	L	F	A	Pts
Deportivo Anzoátegui †	16	10	4	2	35	17	34
Unión Lara	16	10	3	3	27	13	33
Caracas FC B	16	8	3	5	28	20	27
Estrella Roja Caracas	16	7	3	6	20	21	24
Deportivo Italia	16	5	6	5	16	13	21
Iberoamericano	16	5	6	5	21	22	21
Deportivo Galicia	16	2	3	11	12	28	9
Escuela San Tomé	16	2	2	12	9	42	8

12/08/2006 - 26/11/2006 • † Qualified for Apertura final
Apertura final: Anzoátegui 2-1 Llaneros

VENEZUELA 2006-07 ASCENSO CLAUSURA (2)

	Pl	W	D	L	F	A	Pts
Atlético El Vigía	18	9	6	3	33	20	33
Guaros de Lara	18	9	6	3	29	18	33
Estudiantes Mérida	18	9	6	3	29	17	33
Unión Lara	18	9	5	4	30	20	32
Deportivo Anzoátegui	18	7	5	6	36	25	29
Llaneros de Guanare	18	6	6	6	24	25	25
Deportivo Italia	18	6	4	8	21	32	22
Caracas FC B	18	5	3	10	24	33	18
Estrella Roja Caracas	18	4	5	9	20	31	17
Unión At. Maracaibo B	18	3	0	15	14	39	9

6/01/2007 - 29/04/2007 • Clubs in bold promoted

VGB – BRITISH VIRGIN ISLANDS

NATIONAL TEAM RECORD
JULY 10TH 2006 TO JULY 12TH 2010

PL	W	D	L	F	A	%
0	0	0	0	0	0	0

FIFA/COCA-COLA WORLD RANKING

1993	1994	1995	1996	1997	1998	1999	2000	2001	2002	2003	2004	2005	2006	High	Low
-	-	-	-	180	187	161	172	163	161	175	165	171	190	**160** 03/00	**192** 01/07

2006–2007											
08/06	09/06	10/06	11/06	12/06	01/07	02/07	03/07	04/07	05/07	06/07	07/07
167	171	171	173	190	192	188	184	178	179	177	179

The British Virgin Islands was one of just four nations that didn't enter the 2006-07 Digicel Caribbean Cup, a decision which left the national team without any competitive football since the end of 2004. The only international action came in the CONCACAF Youth Tournament where the under–20 side lost all three matches in their qualifying group - two of them heavily. A 3-0 defeat against neighbours US Virgin Islands was followed by a 9-0 thrashing at the hands of Bermuda and culminated in an even worse mauling by the Bahamas, who scored 15 goals without reply. Only the previous season the BVI's women's under–20 side had lost by a staggering 25-0 against

INTERNATIONAL HONOURS
None

Dominica and it's an overall record which doesn't inspire much confidence for the future of the game on the islands. FIFA's Goal project is financing a new technical centre but a lack of suitable land held up the scheme until a plot was found on government-owned land. In preparation for their qualifying campaign, the men's under–21 team had taken part in the League on Virgin Gorda and had finished fourth out of the eight teams. Virgin Gorda was the only League played in 2006 after the League in Tortola was cancelled, and after losing their title in 2005, Rangers were back to their winning ways, beating Guy Boys 4-3 in the final of the play-offs.

THE FIFA BIG COUNT OF 2006

	Male	Female		Total
Number of players	1 240	315	Referees and Assistant Referees	5
Professionals	0		Admin, Coaches, Technical, Medical	16
Amateurs 18+	190		Number of clubs	0
Youth under 18	245		Number of teams	14
Unregistered	120		Clubs with women's teams	0
Total players	1 555		Players as % of population	6.73%

British Virgin Islands Football Association (BVIFA)
Botanic Station Road, Road Town, PO Box 4269, Tortola, British Virgin Islands
Tel +1 284 4945655   Fax +1 284 4948968
bvifa@surfbvi.com   www.bvifa.com
President: DASENT Llewellyn   General Secretary: GRANT Kenrick
Vice-President: LIBURD Aubrey   Treasurer: DASENT Llewellyn   Media Officer: GRANT Kenrick
Men's Coach: PATRICK Mitchell   Women's Coach: SAMUEL Vincent
BVIFA formed: 1974   CONCACAF: 1996   FIFA: 1996
Gold shirts, Green shorts, Green socks

RECENT INTERNATIONAL MATCHES PLAYED BY THE BRITISH VIRGIN ISLANDS

2002	Opponents	Score	Venue	Comp	Scorers	Att	Referee
6-07	Anguilla	W 2-1	Tortola	Fr	Baptiste [42], Huggins [44]		
14-07	St Lucia	L 1-3	Tortola	CCq	Huggins [53]		
28-07	St Lucia	L 1-8	Castries	CCq	Azile [36]		
2003							
No international matches played in 2003							
2004							
28-01	Dominica	L 0-1	Tortola	Fr			Matthew SKN
30-01	US Virgin Islands	W 5-0	Tortola	Fr	OG [18], Williams [24], Morris 2 [26 56], Ferron [88]		
1-02	Dominica	L 1-2	Tortola	Fr	Morris [28]		
22-02	St Lucia	L 0-1	Tortola	WCq		800	Charles DMA
20-03	St Kitts and Nevis	L 0-4	Basseterre	Fr			Stewart JAM
28-03	St Lucia	L 0-9	Vieux Fort	WCq		665	Corrivault CAN
25-09	US Urgin Islands	W 2-1	Tortola	Fr	Heileger [48], Ettienne [55]		
24-11	St Vincent/Grenadines	D 1-1	Kingstown	CCq	Haynes [53]	300	Prendergast JAM
26-11	Cayman Islands	L 0-1	Kingstown	CCq			
28-11	Bermuda	W 2-0	Kingstown	CCq	James 2 [12 24]	400	Matthews SKN
12-12	Trinidad and Tobago	L 0-4	Tortola	CCq		16 000	Arthur LCA
19-12	Tinidad and Tobago	L 0-2	Tunapuna	CCq			Lancaster GUY
2005							
No international matches played in 2005							
2006							
No international matches played in 2006							
2007							
No international matches played in 2007 before August							

Fr = Friendly match • CC = Digicel Caribbean Cup • WC = FIFA World Cup • q = qualifier

BRITISH VIRGIN ISLANDS NATIONAL TEAM RECORDS AND RECORD SEQUENCES

Records			Sequence records					
Victory	5-0	PUR, AIA, VIR	Wins	2	1999	Clean sheets	2	1999, 2001
Defeat	0-12	JAM 1994	Defeats	8	1997-1998	Goals scored	6	1999-2000
Player Caps	n/a		Undefeated	6	2000-2001	Without goal	3	Five times
Player Goals	n/a		Without win	10	1991-1997	Goals against	18	1992-1999

RECENT LEAGUE RECORD

	Tortola	Virgin Gorda
Year	Champions	Champions
1996	Black Lions	Spice United
1997	No tournament	Beverly Hills
1998	BDO Binder Stingers	United Kickers
1999	Veterans	
2000	HBA Panthers	Rangers
2001	HBA Panthers	Rangers
2001	Future Stars United	Rangers
2002	HBA Panthers	No tournament
2003	Old Madrid	Rangers
2004	Valencia	Rangers
2005	Not finished	Hairoun
2006	No tournament	Rangers

BRITISH VIRGIN ISLANDS 2006 VIRGIN GORDA PLAY-OFFS

Semi–finals

Rangers	7
Wolves	2

Under–21	1
Rangers	3

Final

Rangers	4
Guy Boys	3

5-11-2006
Scorers - Rohan Lennon 2 [6 25],
Avondale Williams 2 [40 43] for Rangers;
Dwayne Ross [30p], Eldon Williams [79],
Lionel Grimes [90] for Guy Boys

BRITISH VIRGIN ISLANDS COUNTRY INFORMATION

Capital	Road Town	Status	Overseas territory of the UK	GDP per Capita	$16 000
Population	22 187			GNP Ranking	n/a
Area km²	153	Language	English	Dialling code	+1284
Population density	145 per km²	Literacy rate	97%	Internet code	.vg
% in urban areas	NA	Main religion	Christian	GMT +/–	-4
Towns/Cities	Road Town 8 449; Spanish Town 355				
Neighbours (km)	Caribbean Sea & Atlantic Ocean 80				
Main stadia	Shirley Recreational Field – Road Town, Tortola 2 000				

VIE - VIETNAM

NATIONAL TEAM RECORD
JULY 10TH 2006 TO JULY 12TH 2010

PL	W	D	L	F	A	%
15	6	4	5	29	21	53.3

FIFA/COCA-COLA WORLD RANKING

1993	1994	1995	1996	1997	1998	1999	2000	2001	2002	2003	2004	2005	2006	High		Low	
135	151	122	99	104	98	102	99	105	108	98	103	120	172	84	09/98	172	12/06

2006-2007											
08/06	09/06	10/06	11/06	12/06	01/07	02/07	03/07	04/07	05/07	06/07	07/07
143	151	151	160	172	134	135	139	140	139	142	117

Of the quartet of host nations at the 2007 AFC Asian Cup, only the Vietnamese made it past the group stage, although they only just managed that thanks to the UAE coming from behind to beat Qatar in the final group game. In front of a passionate crowd in Hanoi, Vietnam had started well with a 2-0 victory over the UAE. They then drew against Qatar, and had Qatar beaten their Arab rivals, Vietnam's 4-1 defeat at the hands of Japan would have proved costly. Instead they qualified for the quarter-finals, although having finished behind Japan in the group there was the bizarre situation of the hosts playing their quarter-final against Iraq away from home in Bangkok. Had the

INTERNATIONAL HONOURS
South East Asian Games 1959

match been played in Hanoi there might have been a different outcome to the 2-0 defeat although coach Alfred Riedl believed the physical superiority of the Iraq team was the crucial difference. In domestic football in 2006, Gach Dong Tam Long An just missed out on securing what would have been an historic consecutive double. A fine run of form in the second half of the season, culminating in an away win over Binh Duong, had seen GDT finish a point ahead of their rivals to win the League, but at the end of the season they lost 2-1 to Hoa Phat in the Cup Final - the first team from Hanoi to win the Cup in the 15-year history of the competition.

THE FIFA BIG COUNT OF 2006

	Male	Female		Total
Number of players	1 755 000	119 350	Referees and Assistant Referees	152
Professionals	100		Admin, Coaches, Technical, Medical	10 500
Amateurs 18+	20 850		Number of clubs	27
Youth under 18	2 800		Number of teams	10 000
Unregistered	793 200		Clubs with women's teams	8
Total players	1 874 350		Players as % of population	2.22%

Vietnam Football Federation (VFF)
Liên Doàn Bong Dá Viêt Nam, 18 Ly van Phuc, Dong Da District, Hanoi 844, Vietnam
Tel +84 4 8452480   Fax +84 4 8233119
vff@hn.vnn.vn   www.vff.org.vn
President: NGUYEN Trong Hy   General Secretary: TRAN Quoc Tuan
Vice-President: LE The Tho   Treasurer: LE Hung Dung   Media Officer: NGUYEN Trung Lan
Men's Coach: RIEDL Alfred   Women's Coach: TRAN Ngoc
VFF formed: 1962   AFC: 1954   FIFA: 1964
Red shirts, Red shorts, Red socks

RECENT INTERNATIONAL MATCHES PLAYED BY VIETNAM

2003	Opponents	Score	Venue	Comp	Scorers	Att	Referee
12-02	Albania	L 0-5	Bastia Umbra	Fr			Nicoletti ITA
25-09	Korea Republic	L 0-5	Incheon	ACq			
27-09	Nepal	W 5-0	Incheon	ACq	Pham Van Quyen 3 14 22 36, Nguyen Huu Thang 23, Phan Thanh Binh 90		
29-09	Oman	L 0-6	Incheon	ACq			
19-10	Korea Republic	W 1-0	Muscat	ACq	Pham Van Quyen 73		
21-10	Nepal	W 2-0	Muscat	ACq	Nguyen Minh Phuong 49, Phan Thanh Binh 51		
24-10	Oman	L 0-2	Muscat	ACq			
2004							
18-02	Maldives	W 4-0	Hanoi	WCq	Phan Van Tai Em 2 9 60, Nguyen Minh Hai 13, Pham Van Quyen 80p	25 000	Fong HKG
31-03	Lebanon	L 0-2	Nam Dinh	WCq		25 000	Irmatov UZB
9-06	Korea Republic	L 0-2	Daejeon	WCq		40 019	Al Mehannah KSA
20-08	Myanmar	W 5-0	Ho Chi Minh City	Fr	Le Cong Vinh 2, Thach Boa Khanh, Nguyen Minh Phuong, Pham Van Quyen		
24-08	India	W 2-1	Ho Chi Minh City	Fr	Le Cong Vinh 21, Thach Boa Khanh 57		
8-09	Korea Republic	L 1-2	Ho Chi Minh City	WCq	Phan Van Tai Em 49	25 000	Yoshida JPN
13-10	Maldives	L 0-3	Male	WCq		10 000	Haq IND
17-11	Lebanon	D 0-0	Beirut	WCq		1 000	Ebrahim BHR
7-12	Singapore	D 1-1	Ho Chi Minh City	TCr1	Thach Boa Khanh 51	20 000	Sun Baojie CHN
9-12	Cambodia	W 9-1	Ho Chi Minh City	TCr1	Thach Boa Khanh 2 8 23, Le Cong Vinh 3 58 87 89, OG 63, Dang Van Thanh 2 71 83, Nguyen Huu Thang 83	8 000	Supian MAS
11-12	Indonesia	L 0-3	Hanoi	TCr1		40 000	Sun Baojie CHN
15-12	Laos	W 3-0	Hanoi	TCr1	Le Cong Vinh 9, Nguyen Minh Phuong 41 Thach Bao Khanh 74	20 000	Rungklay THA
2005							
No international matches played in 2005							
2006							
24-12	Thailand	L 1-2	Bangkok	Fr	Phan Thanh Binh 35		
26-12	Kazakhstan	W 2-1	Bangkok	Fr	Le Hong Minh 21, Le Cong Vinh 90		
28-12	Singapore	W 3-2	Bangkok	Fr	Phan Thanh Binh 7, Nguyen Vu Phong 53, Le Cong Vinh 90		
30-12	Thailand	L 1-3	Bangkok	Fr	Phan Tan Binh 68		
2007							
13-01	Singapore	D 0-0	Singapore	TCr1		20 000	Sananwai THA
15-01	Indonesia	D 1-1	Singapore	TCr1	Supardi OG 35	4 500	Shahbuddin
17-01	Laos	W 9-0	Singapore	TCr1	Le Cong Vinh 3 1 28 58, Phan Thanh Binh 4 29 73p 81 84, Nguyen Van Bien 2 45 90	1 005	
24-01	Thailand	L 0-2	Hanoi	TCsf		40 000	Napitupulu IDN
28-01	Thailand	D 0-0	Bangkok	TCsf		35 000	Srinivasan IND
24-06	Jamaica	W 3-0	Hanoi	Fr	Le Cong Vinh 8, Tran Duc Dong 66, Nguyen Anh Duc 90		
30-06	Bahrain	W 5-3	Hanoi	Fr	Le Cong Vinh 2 11 17, Mai Tien Thanh 53, Phan Thanh Binh 77, Nguyen Anh Duc 87		
8-07	UAE	W 2-0	Hanoi	ACr1	Hyung Quang Thanh 63, Le Cong Vinh 73	39 450	Najm LIB
12-07	Qatar	D 1-1	Hanoi	ACr1	Phan Thanh Binh 32	40 000	Moradi IRN
16-07	Japan	L 1-4	Hanoi	ACr1	Suzuki OG 8	40 000	Breeze AUS
21-07	Iraq	L 0-2	Bangkok	ACqf		9 720	Nishimura JPN

Fr = Friendly match • TC = Tiger Cup/ASEAN Football Federation Championship • AC = AFC Asian Cup • WC = FIFA World Cup
q = qualifier • r1 = first round game • sf = semi-final • 3p = third place play-off

VIETNAM NATIONAL TEAM RECORDS AND RECORD SEQUENCES

Records			Sequence records					
Victory	11-0	GUM 2000	Wins	6	1966	Clean sheets	6	1999
Defeat	1-9	IDN 1971	Defeats	10	1997	Goals scored	23	1949-1958
Player Caps	n/a		Undefeated	8	1954-1956	Without goal	4	1997
Player Goals	n/a		Without win	12	1974-1993	Goals against	22	1956-1959

VIETNAM COUNTRY INFORMATION

Capital	Hanoi	Independence	1954 from France	GDP per Capita	$2 500
Population	82 689 518	Status	Republic	GNP Ranking	58
Area km²	329 560	Language	Vietnamese	Dialling code	+84
Population density	251 per km²	Literacy rate	90%	Internet code	.vn
% in urban areas	21%	Main religion	Buddhist, Hoa Hao, Cao Dai	GMT + / −	+7
Towns/Cities ('000)	Ho Chi Minh City 3 467; Hanoi 1 431; Hai Phong 602; Da Nang 472; Bien Hoa 407; Hue 287				
Neighbours (km)	Cambodia 1 228; China 1 281; Laos 2 130; South China Sea & Gulf of Tonkin 3 444				
Main stadia	My Dinh – Hanoi 40 000; San Chi Lang – Da Nang 28 000; Thong Nhat – Ho Chi Minh City 25 000				

VIETNAM 2006

V-LEAGUE

	Pl	W	D	L	F	A	Pts	GDT	Binh Duong	Binh Dinh	HAGL	SLNA	Khanh Hoa	Da Nang	Hanoi ABC	Nam Dinh	TMNC	HPHN	Hai Phong	TPTG
Gach Dong Tam †	24	12	4	8	38	32	40		2-2	0-0	0-1	0-0	3-1	2-1	0-1	3-0	4-3	1-1	2-1	3-0
Binh Duong	24	11	6	7	33	25	39	1-2		0-3	0-0	0-0	1-0	2-0	3-1	2-0	0-0	3-0	2-3	2-0
Binh Dinh	24	9	9	6	32	22	36	0-1			1-0	3-0	1-0	0-0	4-1	1-1	1-3	1-0		1-0
Hoang Anh Gia Lai	24	10	6	8	24	21	36	3-0	1-2	1-1		3-0	1-1	3-2	3-2	1-0	1-0	1-0	2-0	0-0
Song Lam Nghe An	24	9	9	6	27	27	36	0-2	2-1	2-2	1-0		3-1	2-1	2-1	1-1	1-1	1-1	2-1	1-0
Khatoco Khanh Hoa	24	10	5	9	30	25	35	1-0	0-1	3-3	3-0	3-1		2-0	0-0	1-1	0-2	3-2	3-1	1-0
Da Nang	24	9	7	8	32	27	34	4-0	2-1	3-1	1-0	1-1	2-1		1-0	1-2	1-1	0-0	2-2	2-0
Hanoi ABC	24	9	6	9	28	31	33	1-3	2-0	0-0	1-1	0-3	1-0	1-0		1-2	4-2	2-1	1-1	2-1
Nam Dinh	24	9	5	10	22	28	32	1-2	0-1	1-0	2-0	2-0	1-0	0-0	0-1		3-2	0-1	1-1	0-0
TMN-Cang Saigon	24	7	8	9	35	38	29	2-1	2-4	1-1	0-0	2-1	0-0	1-4	0-2	4-1		2-0	1-3	1-0
Hoa Phat Hanoi	24	7	6	11	30	41	27	2-5	1-0	0-0	2-1	1-3	0-1	1-2	1-0	4-3	3-1		2-2	
Mitsu Haier Hai Phong	24	5	9	10	31	36	24	1-3	1-1	2-1	0-0	1-0	1-3	2-2	1-1	0-1	1-3	5-1		0-0
Thep Pomina Tien Giang	24	5	8	11	17	26	23	0-1	3-3	1-0	2-0	0-0	0-2	2-0	1-0	1-2	1-1	2-1	1-1	

15/01/2006 - 20/08/2006 • † Qualified for the AFC Champions League • Top scorer: ELENILDO, Thep Mien 18

VIETNAM CUP 2006

Round of 16	Quarter-finals	Semi-finals	Final
Hoa Phat Hanoi **1**			
Song Lam Nghe An 0	Hoa Phat Hanoi **1**		
Halida Thanh Hoa 0	MH Hai Phong 0		
MH Hai Phong **1**		Hoa Phat Hanoi **4**	
Nam Dinh **3**		Da Nang 3	
Hoang Anh Gia Lai 1	Nam Dinh **2**		
Hanoi ABC 1 5p	Da Nang **3**		
Da Nang **1 6p**			Hoa Phat Hanoi **2**
Binh Dinh bye			Gach Dong Tam 0
	Binh Dinh **2**		
Binh Duong 1	Khatoco Khanh Hoa 1	Binh Dinh 1 2p	
Khatoco Khanh Hoa **2**		Gach Dong Tam **1 4p**	
TMN-Cang Saigon **1 5p**			
An Giang 1 4p	TMN-Cang Saigon 0		
Dong Thap 0	Gach Dong Tam **2**		
Gach Dong Tam **1**			

CUP FINAL
3-09-2006
Scorers – Da Silva 25, Vo Duc Lam 75 for Hoa Phat; Antonio Carlos 21 for GDT

RECENT LEAGUE AND CUP RECORD

Championship

Year	Champions	Pts	Runners-up	Pts	Third	Pts
2000	Song Lam Nghe An	43	Cong An HCMC	42	Cong An Hanoi	37
2001	Song Lam Nghe An	36	Nam Dinh	34	The Cong	29
2002	Cang Saigon	32	Song Lam Nghe An	28	Ngan Hang Dong	26
2003	Hoang Anh Gia Lai	43	Gach Dong Tam	40	Nam Dinh	36
2004	Hoang Anh Gia Lai	46	Nam Dinh	44	Gach Dong Tam	38
2005	Gach Dong Tam	42	Da Nang	38	Binh Duong	38
2006	Gach Dong Tam	40	Bin Duong	39	Binh Dinh	36

Cup

Year	Winners	Score	Runners-up
2000	Cang Saigon	2-1	Cong An HCMC
2001	Cong An HCMC	2-1	Cong An Hanoi
2002	Song Lam Nghe An	1-0	Thua Thien
2003	Binh Dinh	2-1	Ngan Hang Dong
2004	Binh Dinh	2-0	The Cong
2005	Gach Dong Tam	5-0	Hai Phong
2006	Hoa Phat Hanoi	2-0	Gach Dong Tam

Cong An = Police • The Cong = Army • Cang Saigon = Saigon Port • HCMC = Ho Chi Minh City

VIN – ST VINCENT AND THE GRENADINES

NATIONAL TEAM RECORD
JULY 10TH 2006 TO JULY 12TH 2010

PL	W	D	L	F	A	%
15	6	2	7	25	27	46.6

FIFA/COCA-COLA WORLD RANKING

1993	1994	1995	1996	1997	1998	1999	2000	2001	2002	2003	2004	2005	2006	High		Low	
129	144	95	93	122	138	141	127	125	144	169	137	130	85	**80**	08/96	**170**	02/04

2006–2007												
08/06	09/06	10/06	11/06	12/06	01/07	02/07	03/07	04/07	05/07	06/07	07/07	
131	129	85	87	85	104	100	100	102	100	106	103	

The national team of St Vincent and the Grenadines is fast building a reputation as a team to treat with caution and that was proved in the Digicel Caribbean Cup as they pulled off a couple of shock results. In their first round qualifying group, most thought St Vincent and St Lucia would just be making up the numbers, with hosts Jamaica as well as Haiti expected to go through with ease. After the first round of matches that looked to be on the cards as St Vincent lost 3-0 to Haiti, but they then pulled off the shock of the entire tournament by beating Jamaica with Wesley John and Kendal Velox the goalscoring heroes in a 2-1 victory. Shandel Samuel then scored five in an 8-0 demolition

INTERNATIONAL HONOURS
None

of St Lucia, and Vincy Heat were through to the next round on goal difference ahead of the Jamaicans. That saw them travel to Barbados where they qualified for the finals for the first time since 1996 courtesy of victories over the Bahamas and Bermuda. In the finals in Trinidad, St Vincent got off to a sensational start when they ended Guyana's 14-match unbeaten run with a 2-0 victory, but after defeats against Cuba and then Guadeloupe, the adventure was over. With ten goals over the nine games played in the Digicel Caribbean Cup, Samuel finished as joint top scorer with Guyana's Nigel Codrington to crown an excellent season for SVG.

THE FIFA BIG COUNT OF 2006

	Male	Female		Total
Number of players	8 600	900	Referees and Assistant Referees	5
Professionals	0		Admin, Coaches, Technical, Medical	500
Amateurs 18+	1 100		Number of clubs	50
Youth under 18	3 300		Number of teams	300
Unregistered	1 300		Clubs with women's teams	2
Total players	9 500		Players as % of population	8.06%

Saint Vincent and the Grenadines Football Federation (SVGFF)
Murray's Road, PO Box 1278, Saint George, St Vincent and the Grenadines
Tel +1 784 4561092   Fax +1 784 4572193
svgfootball@vincysurf.com   www.svgvincyheat.com
President: LEACOCK St Clair   General Secretary: BENNETT Earl
Vice-President: DOPWELL Leopold   Treasurer: HUGGINS Trevor   Media Officer: WILLIAMS Asberth
Men's Coach: VRANES Zoran   Women's Coach: McCARTHY Seamus
SVGFF formed: 1979   CONCACAF: 1988   FIFA: 1988
Green shirts, Blue shorts, Green socks

RECENT INTERNATIONAL MATCHES PLAYED BY ST VINCENT AND THE GRENADINES

2004	Opponents	Score		Venue	Comp	Scorers	Att	Referee
13-06	Nicaragua	D	2-2	Diriamba	WCq	Haynes [9], Samuel [43]	7 500	Delgado CUB
20-06	Nicaragua	W	4-1	Kingstown	WCq	Samuel 2 [14 79], James [15], Alonso OG [86]	5 000	Brohim DMA
18-08	Trinidad and Tobago	L	0-2	Kingstown	WCq		5 000	Vaughn USA
10-09	St Kitts and Nevis	W	1-0	Kingstown	WCq	Jack [23]	4 000	Delgado CUB
6-10	Mexico	L	0-7	Pachuca	WCq		21 000	Liu CAN
10-10	Mexico	L	0-1	Kingstown	WCq		2 500	Alfaro SLV
13-10	St Kitts and Nevis	W	3-0	Basseterre	WCq	Velox 2 [19 85], Samuel [65]	500	Whittaker CAY
13-11	Grenada	W	6-2	Kingstown	Fr	James 2 [1227], John [19], Joseph [71], Gonsalves [74], Velox [88]		Moss VIN
17-11	Trinidad and Tobago	L	1-2	Port of Spain	WCq	Haynes [49]	10 000	Batres GUA
20-11	Grenada	L	2-3	Gouyave	Fr	Gonsalves [18], Haynes [58]	3 000	Bedeau CAN
24-11	British Virgin Islands	D	1-1	Kingstown	CCq	Forde [69]	300	Prendergast JAM
26-11	Bermuda	D	3-3	Kingstown	CCq	Pierre [7], Haynes [52], Samuel [54]		Prendergast JAM
28-11	Cayman Islands	W	4-0	Kingstown	CCq	Samuel [20], Forde [43p], Haynes [51], Gonsalves [80]	850	Prendergast JAM
12-12	Grenada	W	3-1	Kingstown	CCq	Samuel [10], Guy [23], Velox [64]		Fanus LCA
19-12	Grenada	W	1-0	St George's	CCq	Francis [6]	1 000	Small BRB
2005								
9-01	Trinidad and Tobago	L	1-3	Port of Spain	CCq	Haynes [25]	1 688	Chance ATG
16-01	Trinidad and Tobago	W	1-0	Kingstown	CCq	Forde [66p]	1 450	Pine JAM
30-01	Barbados	L	1-3	Bridgetown	Fr	Guy [14]		
2006								
27-08	Antigua and Barbuda	L	0-1	St John's	Fr			Willett ATG
10-09	Barbados	D	1-1	Bridgetown	Fr	Marshall [65]		Small BRB
27-09	Haiti	L	0-4	Kingston	CCq		3 000	Forde BRB
29-09	Jamaica	W	2-1	Kingston	CCq	John [48], Velox [70]	3 000	Brizan TRI
1-10	St Lucia	W	8-0	Kingston	CCq	Douglas [11], Samuel 5 [26 42 56 76 90], John [52], Haynes [84]	3 000	Tamayo CUB
7-10	Trinidad and Tobago	L	0-5	Port of Spain	Fr		4 116	
1-11	Grenada	W	4-1	Kingstown	Fr			
5-11	Antigua and Barbuda	D	2-2	Kingstown	Fr	Douglas [1], Francis [17]		
19-11	Bermuda	W	3-0	Bridgetown	CCq	James [58], Samuel 2 [66 77]		
21-11	Barbados	L	0-3	Bridgetown	CCq			
23-11	Bahamas	W	3-2	Bridgetown	CCq	Samuel 2 [57 61], Charles [80]		
2007								
14-01	Guyana	W	2-0	Marabella	CCr1	Samuel [4], Glynn [85]		Angela ARU
16-01	Cuba	L	0-3	Marabella	CCr1			
18-01	Guadeloupe	L	0-1	Marabella	CCr1			Brizan TRI
30-05	Haiti	L	0-3	Port of Spain	Fr			

Fr = Friendly match • CC = Digicel Caribbean Cup • WC = FIFA World Cup • q = qualifier • r1 = first round group

ST VINCENT AND THE GRENADINES NATIONAL TEAM RECORDS AND RECORD SEQUENCES

Records			Sequence records				
Victory	9-0	MSR 1995, VIR 2000	Wins	5	1999-2000	Clean sheets	4	1995
Defeat	0-11	MEX 1992	Defeats	7	1992-1993, 2000	Goals scored	21	1996-2000
Player Caps	n/a		Undefeated	8	1995	Without goal	7	1992-1993
Player Goals	n/a		Without win	10	1996	Goals against	12	1996-1998

ST VINCENT AND THE GRENADINES COUNTRY INFORMATION

Capital	Kingstown	Independence	1979 from the UK	GDP per Capita	$2 900
Population	117 193	Status	Parliamentary Democracy	GNP Ranking	176
Area km²	389	Language	English	Dialling code	+1809
Population density	301 per km²	Literacy rate	96%	Internet code	.vc
% in urban areas	46%	Main religion	Christian	GMT +/–	-4
Towns/Cities ('000)	Kingstown 17; Barroualie 2; Georgetown 2; Layou 2; Byera 1; Biabou 1				
Neighbours (km)	Caribbean Sea & Atlantic Ocean 84				
Main stadia	Arnos Vale Playing Ground – Kingstown 18 000				

VIR – US VIRGIN ISLANDS

NATIONAL TEAM RECORD
JULY 10TH 2006 TO JULY 12TH 2010

PL	W	D	L	F	A	%
2	0	0	2	1	12	0

FIFA/COCA-COLA WORLD RANKING

1993	1994	1995	1996	1997	1998	1999	2000	2001	2002	2003	2004	2005	2006	High		Low	
-	-	-	-	-	-	194	198	198	197	199	196	196	198	190	04/99	200	09/04

2006–2007											
08/06	09/06	10/06	11/06	12/06	01/07	02/07	03/07	04/07	05/07	06/07	07/07
197	198	198	198	198	199	199	199	199	199	199	199

Charlotte Amalie, on the island of St Thomas in the US Virgin Islands, hosted a Digicel Caribbean Cup qualifying group for the for the first time in 2006, although home advantage didn't bring about a change in fortunes for the national team, which slipped to an 18th straight defeat in full internationals. Not since their first match - a 1-0 victory over the British Virgin Islands in 1998, have the US Virgin Island savoured a win, and as that match was played before they joined FIFA later in the year, they have yet officially to win a match. Against Bermuda, a country with half the population of the US Virgin Islands, they were soundly beaten 6-0, while against the Dominican

INTERNATIONAL HONOURS
None

Republic, another country with a far greater interest in American sports, they did at least manage to get a goal in a 6-1 defeat. Club football has seen the most rapid progress with both Positive Vibes and New Vibes sufficiently confident to enter the CFU Caribbean Club Championship. Positive Vibes managed to beat Haiti's Aigle Noir 3-2 and finished third in their group as did New Vibes, who hosted a group won by Trinidad's San Juan Jabloteh. In domestic football, Helenites won the San Croix Championship and then beat New Vibes 4-3, and Positive Vibes 1-0, in the four-team play-off between the two islands, to win the USVI Championship for the first time.

THE FIFA BIG COUNT OF 2006

	Male	Female		Total
Number of players	5 800	900	Referees and Assistant Referees	1
Professionals	0		Admin, Coaches, Technical, Medical	100
Amateurs 18+	200		Number of clubs	10
Youth under 18	700		Number of teams	20
Unregistered	1 000		Clubs with women's teams	0
Total players	6 700		Players as % of population	6.17%

U.S.V.I. Soccer Federation Inc. (USVISA)
AQ Building Contant, Suite 205, PO Box 306627, St Thomas VI 0080-6627, US Virgin Islands
Tel +1 340 7142828   Fax +1 340 7142830
usvisoccer@vipowernet.net   www.none
President: MARTIN Derrick   General Secretary: MONTICEUX Glen
Vice-President: FAHIE Collister   Treasurer: TBD   Media Officer: none
Men's Coach: WILLIAMS Clifton   Women's Coach: WOREDE Yohannes
USVISA formed: 1992   CONCACAF: 1998   FIFA: 1998
Royal blue shirts, Royal blue shorts, Royal blue socks

RECENT INTERNATIONAL MATCHES PLAYED BY THE US VIRGIN ISLANDS

2002	Opponents	Score		Venue	Comp	Scorers	Att	Referee
16-08	Dominican Republic	L	1-6	Santo Domingo	CCq	Sheppard [44]		Forde BRB
18-08	Dominican Republic	L	1-5	Santo Domingo	CCq	Sheppard [69]		Jean Lesly HAI
2003								
No international matches played in 2003								
2004								
30-01	British Virgin Islands	L	0-5	Road Town	Fr			
31-01	Dominica	L	0-5	Road Town	Fr			Matthew SKN
18-02	St Kitts and Nevis	L	0-4	Charlotte Amalie	WCq		225	Brizan TRI
31-03	St Kitts and Nevis	L	0-7	Basseterre	WCq		800	Recinos SLV
25-09	British Virgin Islands	L	1-2	Road Town	Fr	Challenger [65]		
24-11	Haiti	L	0-11	Kingston	CCq		250	Piper TRI
26-11	Jamaica	L	1-11	Kingston	CCq	Lauro [72]	4 200	Piper TRI
28-11	St Martin †	D	0-0	Kingston	CCq		200	Brizan TRI
2005								
No international matches played in 2005								
2006								
27-09	Bermuda	L	0-6	Charlotte Amalie	CCq		150	Small BRB
1-10	Dominican Republic	L	1-6	Charlotte Amalie	CCq	Pierre [7]	250	Davis TRI
2007								
No international matches played in 2007 before August								

Fr = Friendly match • CC = Digicel Caribbean Cup • WC = FIFA World Cup • q = qualifier • † Not a full international

US VIRGIN ISLANDS NATIONAL TEAM RECORDS AND RECORD SEQUENCES

Records			Sequence records					
Victory	1-0	BVI 1998	Wins	1	1998	Clean sheets	1	1998, 1999
Defeat	1-14	LCA 2001	Defeats	19	2000-	Goals scored	3	2001-2002
Player Caps	n/a		Undefeated	3	1998-1999	Without goal	4	1999-2000, 2004
Player Goals	n/a		Without win	20	1999-	Goals against	18	2000-2006

RECENT LEAGUE RECORD

	Overall Championship			St Thomas/St John	St Croix
Year	Champions	Score	Runners-up	Champions	Champions
1998				MI Roc Masters	Helenites
1999				MI Roc Masters	Unique FC
2000	United We Stand Upsetters	5-1	Helenites	United We Stand Upsetters	Helenites
2001		Not played			Not played
2002	Hatian Stars	1-0	United We Stand Upsetters	Waitikubuli United	Helenites
2003		Not played		Waitikubuli United	Helenites
2004		Not played			Helenites
2005	Positive Vibes	2-0	Helenites	Positive Vibes	Helenites
2006	New Vibes	4-2	Positive Vibes	Positive Vibes	Helenites
2007	Helenites	1-0	Positive Vibes	Positive Vibes	Helenites

US VIRGIN ISLANDS COUNTRY INFORMATION

Capital	Charlottte Amalie	Status	US Unincorpoated Territory	GDP per Capita	$17 500
Population	108 775			GNP Ranking	n/a
Area km²	352	Language	English, Spanish, Creole	Dialling code	+1340
Population density	309 per km²	Literacy rate	n/a	Internet code	.vi
% in urban areas	n/a	Main religion	Christian	GMT + / –	-4
Towns/Cities ('000)	Charlotte Amalie 10; Anna's Retreat 8; Charlotte Amalie West 5; Frederiksted Southeast 3				
Neighbours (km)	Caribbean Sea & Atlantic Ocean 188				
Main stadia	Lionel Roberts – Charlotte Amalie, St Thomas 9 000				

WAL – WALES

NATIONAL TEAM RECORD
JULY 10TH 2006 TO JULY 12TH 2010

PL	W	D	L	F	A	%
11	3	4	4	14	13	45.4

FIFA/COCA-COLA WORLD RANKING

1993	1994	1995	1996	1997	1998	1999	2000	2001	2002	2003	2004	2005	2006	High		Low	
29	41	61	80	102	97	98	109	100	52	66	68	71	73	27	08/93	113	09/00

2006–2007											
08/06	09/06	10/06	11/06	12/06	01/07	02/07	03/07	04/07	05/07	06/07	07/07
56	62	77	73	73	74	75	77	74	75	75	74

Manager John Toshack endured another difficult season as the national team struggled to make an impact in their Euro 2008 qualifying group. The 5-1 defeat at home to Slovakia was a particularly embarrassing experience for everyone involved. A lack of first team football for some players has made the transition to international level difficult, while the retirement of Ryan Giggs after the home draw against the Czech Republic won't make matters any easier. Not one member of the squad plays in the Welsh League but that doesn't detract from the efforts of the Welsh FA to try and foster a competitive club scene away from the clubs playing in England. TNS Llansantffraid

INTERNATIONAL HONOURS
Qualified for the FIFA World Cup finals 1958

secured a hat-trick of League titles in 2007 and they will be looking to equal Barry Town's record of four straight titles set from 1996 to 1999. Having lost their sponsor Total Network Solutions, the club failed to secure another on E-bay and so decided to keep the designation TNS by adopting the name The New Saints. Having merged with Oswestry Town in 2003, there are plans to move to the English town eight miles away in order to develop a bigger ground and wider supporter base. TNS also won the FAW Premier Cup after beating Newport County 1-0 in the final while Carmarthen Town won the Welsh Cup and Caersws beat Rhyl on penalties in the League Cup Final.

THE FIFA BIG COUNT OF 2006

	Male	Female		Total
Number of players	157 550	16 000	Referees and Assistant Referees	1 120
Professionals	550		Admin, Coaches, Technical, Medical	10 200
Amateurs 18+	35 800		Number of clubs	1 900
Youth under 18	31 200		Number of teams	4 500
Unregistered	41 000		Clubs with women's teams	20
Total players	173 550		Players as % of population	5.91%

The Football Association of Wales, Ltd (FAW)

11/12 Neptune Court, Vanguard Way, Cardiff, CF24 5PJ, United Kingdom
Tel +44 29 20435830   Fax +44 29 20496953
info@faw.co.uk   www.faw.org.uk
President: REES Peter   General Secretary: COLLINS David
Vice-President: PRITCHARD Philip   Treasurer: HUGHES Trevor Lloyd   Media Officer: COLLINS David
Men's Coach: TOSHACK John MBE   Women's Coach: BEATTIE Andy
FAW formed: 1876   UEFA: 1954   FIFA: 1910-20, 1924-28, 1946
Red shirts, Red shorts, Red socks or White shirts, White shorts, White socks

RECENT INTERNATIONAL MATCHES PLAYED BY WALES

2002	Opponents	Score		Venue	Comp	Scorers	Att	Referee
21-08	Croatia	D	1-1	Varazdin	Fr	Davies.S [11]	6 000	Frohlich GER
7-09	Finland	W	2-0	Helsinki	ECq	Hartson [30], Davies.S [72]	35 833	Plautz AUT
6-10	Italy	W	2-1	Cardiff	ECq	Davies.S [11], Bellamy [70]	70 000	Vessiere FRA
20-11	Azerbaijan	W	2-0	Baku	ECq	Speed [10], Hartson [70]	8 000	Huyghe BEL
2003								
12-02	Bosnia-Herzegovina	D	2-2	Cardiff	Fr	Earnshaw [8], Hartson [74]	25 000	Malcolm NIR
29-03	Azerbaijan	W	4-0	Cardiff	ECq	Bellamy [1], Speed [40], Hartson [44], Giggs [52]	72 500	Leuba SUI
26-05	USA	L	0-2	San Jose	Fr		12 282	Archundia MEX
20-08	Serbia & Montenegro	L	0-1	Belgrade	ECq		25 000	Frisk SWE
6-09	Italy	L	0-4	Milan	ECq		68 000	Merk GER
10-09	Finland	D	1-1	Cardiff	ECq	Davies.S [3]	72 500	Dauden Ibanez ESP
11-10	Serbia & Montenegro	L	2-3	Cardiff	ECq	Hartson [24p], Earnshaw [90]	72 514	Stuchlik AUT
15-11	Russia	D	0-0	Moscow	ECpo		29 000	Cortez Batista POR
19-11	Russia	L	0-1	Cardiff	ECpo		73 062	Mejuto Gonzalez ESP
2004								
18-02	Scotland	W	4-0	Cardiff	Fr	Earnshaw 3 [1 35 58], Taylor [78]	47 124	Ross NIR
31-03	Hungary	W	2-1	Budapest	Fr	Koumas [20], Earnshaw [81]	10 000	Meyer GER
27-05	Norway	D	0-0	Oslo	Fr		14 137	Hansson SWE
30-05	Canada	W	1-0	Wrexham	Fr	Parry [21]	10 805	McKeon IRL
18-08	Latvia	W	2-0	Riga	Fr	Hartson [80], Bellamy [89]	10 000	Ivanov RUS
4-09	Azerbaijan	D	1-1	Baku	WCq	Speed [47]	8 000	Trivkovic CRO
8-09	Northern Ireland	D	2-2	Cardiff	WCq	Hartson [32], Earnshaw [74]	63 500	Messina ITA
9-10	England	L	0-2	Manchester	WCq		65 224	Hauge NOR
13-10	Poland	L	2-3	Cardiff	WCq	Earnshaw [56], Hartson [90]	56 685	Sars FRA
2005								
9-02	Hungary	W	2-0	Cardiff	Fr	Bellamy 2 [63 80]	16 672	Richmond SCO
26-03	Austria	L	0-2	Cardiff	WCq		47 760	Allaerts BEL
30-03	Austria	L	0-1	Vienna	WCq		29 500	Mejuto Gonzalez ESP
17-08	Slovenia	D	0-0	Swansea	Fr		10 016	Stokes IRL
3-09	England	L	0-1	Cardiff	WCq		70 715	Ivanov.V RUS
7-09	Poland	L	0-1	Warsaw	WCq		13 500	Larsen DEN
8-10	Northern Ireland	W	3-2	Belfast	WCq	Davies [27], Robinson [37], Giggs [81]	13 451	Bossen NED
12-10	Azerbaijan	W	2-0	Cardiff	WCq	Giggs 2 [3 51]	32 628	Hansson SWE
16-11	Cyprus	L	0-1	Limassol	Fr		1 000	Jakov ISR
2006								
1-03	Paraguay	D	0-0	Cardiff	Fr		12 324	McDonald SCO
27-05	Trinidad and Tobago	W	2-1	Graz	Fr	Earnshaw 2 [38 87]	8 000	Messner AUT
15-08	Bulgaria	D	0-0	Swansea	Fr		8 200	Attard MLT
2-09	Czech Republic	L	1-2	Teplice	ECq	Jiránek OG [85]	16 200	Eriksson SWE
5-09	Brazil	L	0-2	London	Fr		22 008	Riley ENG
7-10	Slovakia	L	1-5	Cardiff	ECq	Bale [37]	28 415	Van Egmond NED
11-10	Cyprus	W	3-1	Cardiff	ECq	Koumas [33], Earnshaw [39], Bellamy [72]	20 456	Granat POL
14-11	Liechtenstein	W	4-0	Wrexham	Fr	Koumas 2 [8 14], Bellamy [76], Llewellyn [89]	8 752	Wilmes LUX
2007								
6-02	Northern Ireland	D	0-0	Belfast	Fr		13 500	Richmond SCO
24-03	Republic of Ireland	L	0-1	Dublin	ECq		72 539	Hauge NOR
28-03	San Marino	W	3-0	Cardiff	ECq	Giggs [3], Bale [20], Koumas [63p]	18 752	Tchagharyan ARM
26-05	New Zealand	D	2-2	Wrexham	Fr	Bellamy 2 [18 38]	7 819	Skjerven NOR
2-06	Czech Republic	D	0-0	Cardiff	ECq		30 174	Allaerts BEL

Fr = Friendly match • EC = UEFA EURO 2004/2008 • WC = FIFA World Cup • q = qualifier

WALES NATIONAL TEAM RECORDS AND RECORD SEQUENCES

Records			Sequence records					
Victory	11-0	NIR 1888	Wins	6	1980-1981	Clean sheets	4	1981, 1991
Defeat	0-9	SCO 1878	Defeats	8	1897-1900	Goals scored	16	1950-1954
Player Caps	92	SOUTHALL Neville	Undefeated	8	1980-1981	Without goal	6	1971-72, 1973-74
Player Goals	28	RUSH Ian	Without win	12	1896-00, 1999-01	Goals against	28	1891-1900

WALES (PART OF THE UNITED KINGDOM)

Capital	Cardiff	Language	English, Welsh	Independence	n/a
Population	2 935 283	Area	20 798 km²	Density 141 per km²	% in cities 89%
GDP per cap	$22 160	Dialling code	+44	Internet .uk	GMT +/- 0

MAJOR CITIES/TOWNS
Population '000

1	Cardiff	307
2	Swansea	171
3	Newport	117
4	Rhondda	59
5	Barry	52
6	Cwmbran	48
7	Llanelli	47
8	Neath	46
9	Wrexham	44
10	Bridgend	42
11	Port Talbot	34
12	Aberdare	33
13	Merthyr Tydfil	30
14	Rhyl	26
15	Aberystwyth	19
16	Connah's Quay	16
17	Carmarthen	15
18	Bangor	15
19	Haverfordwest	13
20	Newtown	10
21	Caernarfon	9
22	Welshpool	5
23	Porthmadog	3
24	Llansantffraid	1

MEDALS TABLE

		Overall			League			Cup			LC		PC		Europe			City	Stadium	Cap'ty	DoF
		G	S	B	G	S	B	G	S	B	G	S	G	S	G	S	B				
1	Wrexham AFC	28	25					23	22				5	3				Wrexham	Racecourse Ground	15 500	1872
2	Cardiff City	23	12	1				22	10				1	2			1	Cardiff	Ninian Park	22 008	1899
3	Barry Town	18	3		7	1		6	1		4	1	1					Barry	Jenner Park	3 500	1912
4	Swansea City	12	10					10	8				2	2				Swansea	Liberty Stadium	20 532	1912
5	TNS Llantsantffraid	9	5		4	3		2	2		2		1					Llansantffraid	Recreation Ground	2 000	1959
6	NEWI Cefn Druids	8	5					8	5									Wrexham	Plaskynaston Lane	2 500	1992
7	Bangor City	7	13	3	2		3	5	8		5							Bangor	Farrar Road	2 200	1876
8	Rhyl	7	9	1	1	2	1	4	4		2	2	1					Rhyl	Belle Vue	4 000	1883
10	Chirk	5	1					5	1									Chirk			
12	Merthyr Tydfil	3	3					3	3									Merthyr Tydfil	Penydarren Park	10 000	1945
13	Oswestry Town	3	1					3	1									Oswestry	Park Hall		1860
	Caersws	3	1										3	1				Caersws	Recreation Ground	2 500	1887
16	Newtown	2	6		2			2	4									Newtown	Latham Park	5 000	1875
17	Carmarthen Town	2	3	1			1	1	2		1	1						Carmarthen	Richmond Park	2 300	1948
19	Afan Lido	2	2		1			1			2							Port Talbot	The Marston's	4 200	1967
20	Cwmbran Town	1	5	2	1	1	2	3			1							Cwmbran	Cwmbran Stadium	7 877	1951
21	Newport County	1	4					1	2						2			Newport	Newport Stadium	4 300	1912

RECENT LEAGUE AND CUP RECORD

	Championship						Cup		
Year	Champions	Pts	Runners-up	Pts	Third	Pts	Winners	Score	Runners-up
1996	Barry Town	97	Newtown	80	Conwy United	76	TNS Llansantffraid	3-3 3-2p	Barry Town
1997	Barry Town	105	Inter Cardiff	84	Ebbw Vale	78	Barry Town	2-1	Cwmbran Town
1998	Barry Town	104	Newtown	78	Ebbw Vale	77	Bangor City	1-1 4-2p	Nomads
1999	Barry Town	76	Inter Cardiff	63	Cwmbran Town	57	Inter Cardiff	1-1 4-2p	Carmarthen Town
2000	TNS Llansantffraid	76	Barry Town	74	Cwmbran Town	69	Bangor City	1-0	Cwmbran Town
2001	Barry Town	77	Cwmbran Town	74	Carmarthen Town	58	Barry Town	2-0	TNS Llansantffraid
2002	Barry Town	77	TNS Llansantffraid	70	Bangor City	69	Barry Town	4-1	Bangor City
2003	Barry Town	83	TNS Llansantffraid	80	Bangor City	71	Barry Town	2-2 4-3	Cwmbran Town
2004	Barry Town	77	TNS Llansantffraid	76	Haverfordwest Cty	62	Rhyl	1-0	TNS Llansantffraid
2005	TNS Llansantffraid	78	Rhyl	74	Bangor City	67	TNS Llansantffraid	1-0	Carmarthen Town
2006	TNS Llansantffraid	86	Llanelli	68	Rhyl	64	Rhyl	2-0	Bangor City
2007	TNS Llansantffraid	76	Rhyl	69	Llanelli	63	Carmarthen Town	3-2	Afan Lido

WALES 2006-07

	Pl	W	D	L	F	A	Pts	TNS	Rhyl	Llanelli	Welshpool	Nomads	Port Talbot	Carmarthen	Aberystwyth	Bangor	Haver west	Portmadog	Airbus	Druids	Caersws	Caernarfon	Newtown	Cwmbran
TNS Llansantffraid †	32	24	4	4	81	20	76		2-0	0-2	6-0	4-0	2-0	4-1	4-1	5-2	2-1	3-0	7-0	3-1	2-1	1-3	4-0	4-0
Rhyl ‡	32	20	9	3	67	35	69	0-0		2-2	0-0	2-1	2-0	1-0	3-0	3-1	3-2	2-1	4-0	2-2	4-0	0-0	2-2	1-0
Llanelli	32	18	9	5	72	33	63	1-2	6-0		2-3	1-1	0-0	1-1	1-3	3-0	3-2	3-0	4-0	3-1	0-0	4-2	3-2	5-1
Welshpool Town	32	17	9	6	54	33	60	1-0	1-1	0-2		0-0	0-1	1-1	1-0	1-1	0-0	3-1	6-3	4-2	1-0	3-0	1-0	1-1
Connah's Quay Nomads	32	16	8	8	49	40	56	0-0	0-2	0-1	1-3		2-1	4-1	1-0	3-0	5-3	1-0	1-2	1-0	4-3	2-2	2-1	2-2
Port Talbot Town	32	15	6	11	42	39	51	2-1	3-2	1-0	0-0	0-1		1-0	1-3	0-5	1-4	1-2	0-2	1-1	0-0	7-1	2-1	2-0
Carmarthen Town ‡	32	14	8	10	57	50	50	0-0	1-1	0-2	2-4	1-3	1-0		1-0	2-2	1-3	1-1	2-1	4-0	2-0	4-1	2-0	1-0
Aberystwyth Town	32	13	9	10	47	37	48	0-0	2-3	1-1	0-0	1-1	0-2	4-2		0-2	2-2	0-1	1-1	3-0	1-0	2-0	4-2	3-1
Bangor City	32	14	6	12	55	47	48	0-2	1-3	4-0	1-0	3-1	0-0	1-3	1-4		4-1	2-1	3-1	6-0	1-2	0-0	5-2	1-1
Haverfordwest County	32	10	9	13	49	46	39	0-3	0-1	1-1	0-1	0-0	1-2	0-1	1-1	2-0		1-1	5-1	0-1	1-0	2-1	3-2	2-0
Porthmadog	32	8	11	13	40	52	32	0-5	1-2	1-1	2-1	1-2	1-1	3-0	0-4	1-1	0-3		1-1	3-0	4-0	2-2	2-3	2-2
Airbus UK	32	7	8	17	40	67	29	0-1	0-2	1-4	1-4	2-3	3-0	2-2	0-0	4-1	2-0	1-1		0-1	0-3	2-3	1-2	3-1
NEWI Cefn Druids	32	7	7	18	41	66	28	2-3	2-3	0-1	1-3	2-2	0-3	1-2	1-2	0-3	2-2	3-0	3-1		2-2	3-2	1-3	1-0
Caersws	32	6	9	17	34	59	27	0-2	1-1	0-3	1-3	2-1	1-4	1-7	0-1	3-3	0-1	0-0	2-1			1-1	0-1	3-3
Caernarfon Town	32	6	8	18	41	73	26	1-3	2-6	2-6	2-0	0-2	1-2	3-5	1-3	0-1	1-4	2-2	0-2	1-1	2-2		1-0	0-1
Newtown	32	6	6	20	30	63	24	0-4	0-6	0-2	0-4	0-1	1-2	1-1	1-1	2-1	1-0	0-0	1-1	0-2	0-1	0-1		2-3
Cwmbran Town	32	4	8	20	36	75	20	0-5	2-3	2-2	1-4	0-1	1-2	4-5	2-0	0-1	0-0	2-3	2-2	3-2	2-5	0-3	0-2	

18/08/2006 - 21/04/2007 • † Qualified for the UEFA Champions League • ‡ Qualified for the UEFA Cup

FAW PREMIER CUP 2006-07

Quarter-finals

TNS Llansantffraid	3
Porthmadog *	1
Carmarthen Town *	2
Cardiff City	3
Port Talbot Town *	2
Swansea City	1
Wrexham	1
Newport County *	2

Semi-finals

TNS Llansantffraid	1
Cardiff City *	0
Port Talbot Town	1
Newport County *	2

Final

TNS Llansantffraid	1
Newport County *	0

Spytty Park, Newport, 21-03-2007
Scorer - Steve Beck for TNS

* Home team

WELSH CUP 2006-07

Eighth-finals

Carmarthen Town *	0 5p
Caersws	0 4p
TNS Llansantffraid	2 2p
Portmadog	2 3p
Connah's Q. Nomads *	3
Llandudno	1
Newtown	0
Llanelli *	7
Welshpool Town *	3
Neath Athletic	0
Bridgend Town	1
Holyhead Hotspur *	2
Port Talbot Town *	3
Ton Pentre	1
Ely Rangers *	1
Afan Lido	2

Quarter-finals

Carmarthen Town *	1 4p
Portmadog	1 3p
Connah's Q. Nomads	2
Llanelli *	6
Welshpool Town	5
Holyhead Hotspur *	1
Port Talbot Town *	0
Afan Lido	1

Semi-finals

Carmarthen Town †	1
Llanelli	0
Welshpool Town	1 6p
Afan Lido ††	1 7p

Final

Carmarthen Town ‡	3
Afan Lido	2

CUP FINAL

Stebonheath Park, Llanelli
5-05-2007

Scorers - Kaid Mohamed 2, Sacha Walters for Carmarthen Town; Ian Jones 2 for Afan Lido

‡ Qualified for the UEFA Cup

* Home team • † Played in Haverfordwest • †† Played in Aberystwyth

YEM – YEMEN

NATIONAL TEAM RECORD
JULY 10TH 2006 TO JULY 12TH 2010

PL	W	D	L	F	A	%
14	4	2	8	16	23	35.7

FIFA/COCA-COLA WORLD RANKING

1993	1994	1995	1996	1997	1998	1999	2000	2001	2002	2003	2004	2005	2006	High		Low	
91	103	123	139	128	146	158	160	135	145	132	124	139	141	**90**	08/93	**163**	07/00

2006–2007											
08/06	09/06	10/06	11/06	12/06	01/07	02/07	03/07	04/07	05/07	06/07	07/07
125	136	144	138	141	140	143	137	135	134	137	138

After playing only two matches in the previous 18 months, it was a busy season for the Yemen as the national team completed their AFC Asian Cup qualifiers under coach Ahmed Al Raei and then travelled to Abu Dhabi under new Egyptian coach Mohsen Saleh take part in the Gulf Cup. In the Asian Cup there were victories home and away against India, and although Yemen were only denied a draw against Japan in Sana'a by an injury-time goal, they were comprehensively beaten by neighbours Saudi Arabia. In the Gulf Cup a draw in the opening match with Kuwait held out the promise of better things, but those hopes were dashed with defeats at the hands of both the hosts

INTERNATIONAL HONOURS
None

UAE and Oman. With a number of friendlies played in between, Yemen did achieve something of note: winning four consecutive matches, having never won more than two in a row since playing their first international in 1965. Yemeni clubs returned for the 2007 edition of the AFC Cup having been absent from the 2005 and 2006 tournaments, with champions Al Saqer and Cup runners-up Al Hilal Hudayda representing the country, although both finished a long way off the pace at the bottom of their respective groups. The 2007 Championship, which finished at the beginning of August, was won by Al Ahly from the capital Sana'a.

THE FIFA BIG COUNT OF 2006

	Male	Female		Total
Number of players	355 200	28 100	Referees and Assistant Referees	252
Professionals	0		Admin, Coaches, Technical, Medical	250
Amateurs 18+	7 190		Number of clubs	110
Youth under 18	1 910		Number of teams	220
Unregistered	50 100		Clubs with women's teams	0
Total players	383 300		Players as % of population	1.79%

Yemen Football Association (YFF)
Quarter of Sport Al Jeraf, (Stadium Ali Mushen), PO Box 908, Sanaa-Yemen, Al Thawra City, Yemen
Tel +967 1 310923   Fax +967 1 310921
S.G@yemenfootball.org   www.yemenfootball.org
President: AL-EISSI Ahmed Saleh   General Secretary: SHAIBANI Hammed
Vice-President: AL AWAEJ Najeeb   Treasurer: AL NADRY Khaled   Media Officer: None
Men's Coach: SALEH Mohsen   Women's Coach: None
YFF formed: 1962   AFC: 1972   FIFA: 1980
Green shirts, Green shorts, Green socks

RECENT INTERNATIONAL MATCHES PLAYED BY YEMEN

2003	Opponents	Score		Venue	Comp	Scorers	Att	Referee
10-10	Bhutan	W	8-0	Jeddah	ACq	Al Qassayi 3 [20 25 82], Al Habishi [36], Al Shiri [60], Al Salmi 2 [67 88], Al Hijam [74]		
13-10	Saudi Arabia	L	1-3	Jeddah	ACq	Al Qassayi [12]		
15-10	Indonesia	D	2-2	Jeddah	ACq	Al Salmi [31p], Al Omqi [59]		
17-10	Bhutan	W	4-0	Jeddah	ACq	Al Hijam 2 [3 20], Al Omqi [33], Al Salmi [81]		
28-12	Oman	D	1-1	Kuwait City	GC	Fawzi Bashir [65]		Abdul Sadeq KUW
30-12	Bahrain	L	1-5	Kuwait City	GC	Al Salmi [14p]		Al Hamdan KSA
2004								
1-01	Kuwait	L	0-4	Kuwait City	GC			
5-01	Qatar	L	0-3	Kuwait City	GC			
8-01	Saudi Arabia	L	0-2	Kuwait City	GC			
11-01	United Arab Emirates	L	0-3	Kuwait City	GC			
18-02	Korea DPR	D	1-1	Sana'a	WCq	Al Selwi [73]	15 000	Husain BHR
17-03	Turkmenistan	L	1-2	Sana'a	Fr	Saleh Al Shekri [40p]		
31-03	Thailand	L	0-3	Sana'a	WCq		25 000	Mansour LIB
9-06	United Arab Emirates	L	0-3	Al Ain	WCq		5 000	Sapaev TKM
26-08	Syria	L	1-2	Sana'a	Fr			
28-08	Syria	W	2-1	Sana'a	Fr			
8-09	United Arab Emirates	W	3-1	Sana'a	WCq	Al Nono 2 [22 77], Abduljabar [49]	17 000	Al Ghamdi KSA
13-10	Korea DPR	L	1-2	Pyongyang	WCq	Jaber [76]	15 000	Vo Minh Tri VIE
1-11	Zambia	D	2-2	Dubai	Fr	Al Nono [83], Al Qaar [90]		
17-11	Thailand	D	1-1	Bangkok	WCq	Al Shehri [69]	15 000	Baskar IND
3-12	Iraq	L	1-3	Dubai	Fr	Nashwan Abdulaziz [28]		
5-12	Qatar	L	0-3	Doha	Fr			
11-12	Bahrain	D	1-1	Doha	GCr1	Nasser Ghazi [47]		
14-12	Saudi Arabia	L	0-2	Doha	GCr1			
17-12	Kuwait	L	0-3	Doha	GCr1			
2005								
No international matches played in 2005								
2006								
22-02	Saudi Arabia	L	0-4	Sana'a	ACq		55 000	Al Fadhli KUW
1-03	India	W	3-0	New Delhi	ACq	Salem Abdullah [6], Al Hubaishi [43], Al Nono [56p]	8 000	Torky IRN
17-07	Ethiopia	L	0-1	Addis Abeba	Fr			
16-08	Japan	L	0-2	Niigata	ACq		40 913	Lee Gi Young KOR
26-08	Libya	L	0-1	Sana'a	Fr			
29-08	Libya	D	1-1	Sana'a	Fr			
6-09	Japan	L	0-1	Sana'a	ACq		7 000	Al Ghatrifi OMA
11-10	Saudi Arabia	L	0-5	Jeddah	ACq		1 500	Nema IRQ
15-11	India	W	2-1	Sana'a	ACq	Al Haggam [60], Al Nono [82]	5 500	Marshoud JOR
14-12	Comoros	W	2-0	Sana'a	Fr	Al Haggam 2 [73 90]		
20-12	Djibouti	W	4-1	Sana'a	Fr	Al Sasi [9], Al Sahhed [50], Al Hubaishi [52], Al Tahoos [85]		
2007								
7-01	Eritrea	W	4-1	Sana'a	Fr	Al Worafi [54], Al Hubaishi [71], Basuki [73], Al Haggam [79]		
12-01	Bahrain	L	0-4	Dubai	Fr			
17-01	Kuwait	D	1-1	Abu Dhabi	GCr1	Al Omqy [16]		
20-01	UAE	L	1-2	Abu Dhabi	GCr1	Al Sasi [90]		
23-01	Oman	L	1-2	Abu Dhabi	GCr1	Mohammed Salem [9]		

Fr = Friendly match • GC = Gulf Cup • AC = AFC Asian Cup • WC = FIFA World Cup • q = qualifier • r1 = first round group

YEMEN NATIONAL TEAM RECORDS AND RECORD SEQUENCES

Records			Sequence records				
Victory	11-2	BHU 2000	Wins	4	2006-2007	Clean sheets	4	1989-1990
Defeat	1-15	ALG 1973	Defeats	10	1965-1975	Goals scored	7	2001
Player Caps	n/a		Undefeated	5	2001	Without goal	5	1994-1996
Player Goals	n/a		Without win	12	1981-1989	Goals against	17	1976-1990

YEMEN COUNTRY INFORMATION

Capital	Sana'a	Unification	1990	GDP per Capita	$800
Population	20 024 867	Status	Republic	GNP Ranking	93
Area km²	527 970	Language	Arabic	Dialling code	+967
Population density	38 per km²	Literacy rate	50%	Internet code	.ye
% in urban areas	34%	Main religion	Muslim	GMT + / −	+3
Towns/Cities ('000)	Sana'a 1 937; Hudayda 617; Taizz 615; Aden 550; Mukalla 258; Ibb 234; Damar 158;				
Neighbours (km)	Oman 288; Saudi Arabia 1 458; Red Sea & Arabian Sea 1 906				
Main stadia	Ali Moshen – Sana'a 25 000				

YEMEN 2007

PREMIER LEAGUE

	Pl	W	D	L	F	A	Pts	Ahly	Hassan	Saqr	Sha'ab Ibb	Sha'ab H	Yarmuk	Hilal	Rasheed	Shula	Tilal	Wahda	Ittihad	Shabab B	Nasir
Al Ahly Sana'a †	26	12	12	2	39	9	47		5-1	2-0	0-0	2-0	1-1	4-2	1-0	1-1	1-1	0-0	4-0	2-0	8-0
Hassan Abyan	26	14	3	9	31	36	45	1-0		1-1	0-3	2-1	1-0	3-0	1-0	2-0	1-0	1-0	3-1	1-0	1-0
Al Saqr Taizz	26	12	7	7	41	25	43	0-0	4-1		4-1	8-1	2-0	2-1	3-2	1-1	0-0	1-2	2-0	3-0	1-1
Al Sha'ab Ibb	26	11	6	9	32	27	39	1-1	1-1	0-3		3-1	1-2	1-2	0-1	1-0	4-0	2-0	2-0	2-0	2-0
Al Sha'ab Hadramaut	26	11	4	11	27	28	37	0-0	1-2	3-0	3-1		0-0	2-0	2-0	4-0	0-0	2-0	0-0	2-1	1-0
Al Yarmuk Sana'a	26	8	12	6	26	18	36	0-0	3-1	1-1	0-1	2-0		0-1	0-1	1-1	0-0	1-0	1-1	0-1	3-0
Al Hilal Hudayda	26	10	6	10	35	32	36	0-1	1-1	1-0	0-0	1-0	0-3		1-1	1-2	2-1	4-0	0-0	5-2	5-0
Al Rasheed Taizz	26	9	8	9	21	19	35	0-1	2-1	0-1	1-1	1-0	1-1	0-0		0-0	1-1	2-0	0-0	2-0	2-0
Shula Aden	26	8	11	7	27	30	35	1-0	3-1	2-1	0-1	2-0	0-0	3-2	2-1		0-0	0-0	1-1	1-1	1-1
Al Tilal Aden	26	8	10	8	29	23	34	0-2	3-0	1-2	1-0	0-1	1-2	2-2	0-2	1-1		2-1	2-0	2-0	3-1
Al Wahda Sana'a	26	10	4	12	31	34	34	0-0	3-1	0-1	3-0	2-1	0-2	0-1	2-0	3-2	0-3		2-1	5-2	4-1
Al Ittihad Ibb	26	8	9	9	27	27	33	0-0	0-1	2-0	2-1	0-1	1-1	0-1	1-0	3-0	1-1	2-1		6-0	2-1
Al Shabab Al Baydaa	26	5	7	14	28	45	22	0-3	0-0	4-0	0-0	0-1	1-0	2-2	3-2	0-0	1-2	0-0	1-3		6-1
Al Nasir Al Dalaa	26	4	5	17	16	57	17	0-3	0-2	2-0	2-2	0-1	0-0	1-0	0-1	2-1	0-5	1-1	0-1	2-1	

25/01/2007 - 3/08/2007 • † Qualified for the AFC Cup • See page 1047 for the table and results of the 2006 season

PRESIDENTS CUP 2006

First Round

Al Sha'ab Hadramaut	1 4p	
Shula Aden	1 1p	
Al Taawun Badan	Bye	
Yarmuk Al Rawda	1	
Al Rasheed Taizz	0	
Al Saqr Taizz	0	
Al Sha'ab Ibb	1	
Al Ahly Sana'a	1	
Al Tadamun Shabwa	0	
Hassan Abyan	0 4p	
Shabab Al Jeel	0 5p	
Al Tilal Aden	Bye	
May 22 Sana'a	0	
Al Hilal Hudayda	1	

Quarter–finals

Al Sha'ab Hadramaut	0 4p
Al Taawun Badan	0 3p
Yarmuk Al Rawda	1 p
Al Sha'ab Ibb	1 p
Al Ahly Sana'a	1 4p
Shabab Al Jeel	1 3p
Al Tilal Aden	1 7p
Al Hilal Hudayda	1 8p

Semi–finals

Al Sha'ab Hadramaut	1 4p
Al Sha'ab Ibb	1 3p
Al Ahly Sana'a	1
Al Hilal Hudayda	2

Final

Al Sha'ab Hadramaut	2
Al Hilal Hudayda †	1

CUP FINAL

Al Ahly Sana'a	1
Al Hilal Hudayda	2

12-12-2006

* Home team • † Qualified for the AFC Cup

RECENT LEAGUE AND CUP RECORD

	Championship							Cup		
Year	Champions	Pts	Runners-up	Pts	Third	Pts		Winners	Score	Runners-up
2001	Al Ahly Sana'a							Al Ahly Sana'a	2-1	Al Tilal Aden
2002	Al Wahda Sana'a	63	Al Ahly Sana'a	50	Al Hilal Hudayda	39		Al Sha'ab Ibb	4-0	Al Tadamun
2003	Al Sha'ab Ibb	46	Al Tilal Aden	43	Al Hilal Hudayda	36		Al Sha'ab Ibb	2-1	Al Sha'ab Mukalla
2004	Al Sha'ab Ibb	46	Al Ahly Sana'a	44	Al Tilal Aden	39		Al Ahly Sana'a	2-0	Al Sha'ab Ibb
2005	Al Tilal Aden	54	Al Saqr Taizz	47	Al Ahli Sana'a	45		Hilal Al Sahely	3-1	Al Rasheed Taizz
2006	Al Saqr Taizz	55	Al Sha'ab Ibb	48	Al Tilal Aden	43		Sha'ab Hadramaut	2-1	Al Hilal Hudayda
2007	Al Ahly Sana'a	47	Hassan Abyan	45	Al Saqr Taizz	43				

ZAM – ZAMBIA

NATIONAL TEAM RECORD
JULY 10TH 2006 TO JULY 12TH 2010

PL	W	D	L	F	A	%
16	9	5	2	21	8	71.8

FIFA/COCA-COLA WORLD RANKING

1993	1994	1995	1996	1997	1998	1999	2000	2001	2002	2003	2004	2005	2006	High	Low
27	21	25	20	21	29	36	49	64	67	68	70	58	62	15 02/96	80 05/04

2006–2007											
08/06	09/06	10/06	11/06	12/06	01/07	02/07	03/07	04/07	05/07	06/07	07/07
59	55	60	60	62	63	65	67	69	68	60	61

Zambia triumphed in two regional competitions in 2006 and lost only two of the 16 internationals they played, yet qualification for the 2008 Cup of Nations was far from assured. In October 2006, Zambia won a third COSAFA Cup when they ended Angola's reign with a 2-0 triumph in the final in Lusaka. It was achieved with a mainly home-based side, which then went on to win the East African CECAFA in Addis Ababa as invited guests, after eliminating hosts Ethiopia in the quarter-finals and then winning the final on post-match penalties after a 0-0 draw with Sudan. Bizarrely, however, the trophy was awarded to the losers as they were deemed to be the top regional team.

INTERNATIONAL HONOURS
CECAFA Cup 1984   COSAFA Castle Cup 1997 1998

A rare home defeat by rivals South Africa was the cause of the troubled Nations Cup qualifying campaign, and further ground was lost in June 2007 as bottom-placed Chad picked up their first points with a draw in Chililabombwe. Tragedy had struck just a fortnight earlier with 12 spectators crushed in a stampede after Zambia's 3-0 triumph over Congo at the same venue, in the far north of the country. In the league, Zanaco won the Premier League title again but in keeping with recent form did not progress far in the early stages of the 2007 African Champions League. Zanaco also won the Top–8 Cup whilst ZESCO United and Kabwe Warriors won the other Cups on offer in 2006.

THE FIFA BIG COUNT OF 2006

	Male	Female		Total
Number of players	992 786	32 031	Referees and Assistant Referees	524
Professionals	101		Admin, Coaches, Technical, Medical	11 035
Amateurs 18+	19 560		Number of clubs	470
Youth under 18	9 050		Number of teams	2 350
Unregistered	975 606		Clubs with women's teams	448
Total players	1 024 817		Players as % of population	8.91%

Football Association of Zambia (FAZ)
Football House, Alick Nkhata Road, Long Acres, PO Box 34751, 34751 Lusaka, Zambia
Tel +260 1 250940   Fax +260 1 250946
faz@zamnet.zm   www.faz.co.zm
President: MULONGA Teddy   General Secretary: MUSONDA John Brig Gen
Vice-President: BWALYA Kalusha   Treasurer: MWEEMBA Rix   Media Officer: MWANSA Mbulakulima
Men's Coach: PHIRI Patrick   Women's Coach: BANDA E.
FAZ formed: 1929   CAF: 1964   FIFA: 1964
Copper shirts, Black shorts, Copper socks

RECENT INTERNATIONAL MATCHES PLAYED BY ZAMBIA

2004	Opponents	Score		Venue	Comp	Scorers	Att	Referee
31-07	Mauritius	W	3-1	Lusaka	CCqf	Mulenga [11], Numba [55], Bwalya.K [68]		Manuel ZIM
28-08	Rwanda	W	2-1	Kitwe	Fr	Kaposa [8], Mwamdila [38]	15 000	Mwanza ZAM
4-09	Liberia	W	1-0	Lusaka	WCq	Bwalya.K [91+]	30 000	Nchengwa BOT
30-09	Botswana	L	0-1	Gaborone	Fr			Chidoda BOT
10-10	Congo	W	3-2	Brazzaville	WCq	Mbesuma 3 [2 37 65]	20 000	Yacoubi TUN
24-10	Zimbabwe	D	0-0	Harare	CCsf	W 5-4p	25 000	Simisse MRI
1-11	Yemen	D	2-2	Dubai	Fr	Mwale [32], Nsofwa [58]		
20-11	Angola	D	0-0	Lusaka	CCf	L 4-5p		Lwanja MWI
2005								
26-02	Botswana	D	0-0	Gaborone	Fr			
26-03	Congo	W	2-0	Chililabombwe	WCq	Tana [1], Mbesuma [44]	20 000	Maillet SEY
5-06	Togo	L	1-4	Lome	WCq	Kampamba [15]	15 000	Guezzaz MAR
11-06	Swaziland	W	3-0	Lusaka	CCrl	Mbesuma 2 [44 46], Kalaba [56]		Chidoda BOT
12-06	Malawi	W	2-1	Lusaka	CCrl	Mbesuma 2 [79 85]		Nhlapo RSA
18-06	Mali	W	2-1	Chililabombwe	WCq	Chalwe [26], Mbesuma [85]	29 000	Colembi ANG
13-08	South Africa	D	2-2	Mmabatho	CCsf	Chamanga [18], Chris Katongo [24]. W 9-8p		Raolimanana MAD
14-08	Zimbabwe	L	0-1	Mmabatho	CCf			Massango MOZ
3-09	Senegal	L	0-1	Chililabombwe	WCq		20 000	Abd El Fatah EGY
25-09	Congo DR	D	2-2	Chililabombwe	Fr	Mweetwa [41], Luipa [57]		
27-09	Congo DR	D	0-0	Lubumbashi	Fr			
1-10	Liberia	W	5-0	Monrovia	WCq	Lwipa 2 [50 82], Mweetwa 2 [51 63], Numba [61]	BCD	Evehe CMR
11-12	Congo DR	D	1-1	Lubumbashi	Fr	Numba [15]		
14-12	Congo DR	W	4-1	Chingola	Fr	Milanzi 2 [2 62], Dube Phiri [10], Kasonde [13]		
31-12	Zimbabwe	D	1-1	Harare	Fr	Dube Phiri [84]		
2006								
22-01	Tunisia	L	1-4	Alexandria	CNrl	Chamanga [9]	16 000	Maillet SEY
26-01	Guinea	L	1-2	Alexandria	CNrl	Tana [34]	24 000	Imeire NGA
30-01	South Africa	W	1-0	Alexandria	CNrl	Chris Katongo [75]	4 000	Abd El Fatah EGY
14-05	Botswana	D	0-0	Gaborone	Fr	L 4-5p		
15-07	Zimbabwe	D	0-0	Lusaka	Fr			
22-07	Malawi	W	3-1	Katutura	CCrl	Dube Phiri [84], Kalaba [85], Chris Katongo [88]		Katjimune NAM
23-07	Seychelles	W	2-0	Katutura	CCrl	Chamanga [33], Lwipa [44]		Ngobo RSA
19-08	Botswana	W	1-0	Lusaka	CCsf	Singuluma [53]		Mnkantjo ZIM
3-09	Chad	W	2-0	N'Djamena	CNq	Chamanga [46], Dube Phiri [59]		Shelmani LBY
8-10	South Africa	L	0-1	Lusaka	CNq			Maillet SEY
21-10	Angola	W	2-0	Lusaka	CCf	Dube Phiri [76], Nsofwa [89]		Raolimanana MAD
26-11	Burundi	L	2-3	Addis Abeba	CErl	Kalaba [61], Dube Phiri [87]		
2-12	Zanzibar †	W	4-0	Addis Abeba	CErl	Dube Phiri 2 [34 37], Felix Katongo [69], Kalaba [73]		
5-12	Ethiopia	W	1-0	Addis Abeba	CEqf	Sakuwaha [87]		
8-12	Rwanda	W	1-0	Addis Abeba	CEsf	Lwipa [24]		
10-12	Sudan	D	0-0	Addis Abeba	CEf	W 11-10p		
2007								
25-03	Congo	D	0-0	Brazzaville	CNq			Coulibaly MLI
26-05	Namibia	W	2-1	Windhoek	Fr	Sakala 2 [25 78]		
2-06	Congo	W	3-0	Chililabombwe	CNq	Mulenga [18], Nog OG [69], Chalwe [82]		
9-06	Tanzania	D	1-1	Morogoro	Fr	Kalaba [81]		
16-06	Chad	D	1-1	Chililabombwe	CNq	Mbesuma [56]		

Fr = Friendly match • CC = COSAFA Cup • CE = CECAFA Cup • CN = CAF African Cup of Nations • WC = FIFA World Cup • BCD = Behind closed doors
q = qualifier • rl = first round group • qf = quarter-final • sf = semi-final • f = final • † Not an official international

ZAMBIA NATIONAL TEAM RECORDS AND RECORD SEQUENCES

Records			Sequence records					
Victory	9-0	KEN 1978	Wins	8	1964-1966	Clean sheets	7	1997-1998, 2000
Defeat	1-10	COD 1969	Defeats	4	Four times	Goals scored	19	1966-1971
Player Caps	n/a		Undefeated	11	Three times	Without goal	4	2001
Player Goals	n/a		Without win	11	1999-2000	Goals against	10	1966-1968

REPUBLIC OF ZAMBIA

Capital	Lusaka	Language	English, Bemba, Kaonda	Independence	1964
Population	11 477 447	Area	752 614 km²	Density 14 per km²	% in cities 43%
GDP per cap	$800	Dailling code	+260	Internet .zm	GMT + / - +2

MEDALS TABLE

		Overall			Lg	C	T8	LC	Africa			City	Stadium	Cap'ty	DoF
		G	S	B	G	G	G	G	G	S	B				
1	Mufulira Wanderers	27		3	9	9	9				3	Mufulira	Shinde	12 000	
2	Nkana	24	1	5	11	6	7			1	5	Kitwe	Scriveners	12 000	
3	Kabwe Warriors	18			5	5	7	1				Kabwe	Railways Stadium	10 000	
4	Power Dynamos	16	1		5	7	2	1	1	1		Kitwe	Arthur Davies	10 000	1977
5	Green Buffaloes	12			6	1	5					Lusaka	Independence	50 000	
6	Zanaco	10			4	1	3	2				Lusaka	Sunset Stadium	20 000	
7	Roan United	8			1	4	3					Luanshya	Kafubu	10 000	
8	Nchanga Rangers	6	1		2	1	3				1	Chingola	Nchanga Stadium	15 000	
9	City of Lusaka	5			1	2	2					Lusaka	Woodlands	10 000	

RECENT LEAGUE AND CUP RECORD

	Championship						Cup		
Year	Champions	Pts	Runners-up	Pts	Third	Pts	Winners	Score	Runners-up
1997	Power Dynamos	66	Nkana	64	Nchanga Rangers	56	Power Dynamos	1-0	City of Lusaka
1998	Nchanga Rangers	56	Kabwe Warriors	49	Nkana	48	Konkola Blades	2-1	Zanaco
1999	Nkana	57	Zamsure	55	Nchanga Rangers	54	Zamsure		Power Dynamos
2000	Power Dynamos	56	Nkana	52	Zanaco	50	Nkana	0-0 7-6p	Green Buffaloes
2001	Nkana	60	Zanaco	57	Kabwe Warriors	55	Power Dynamos	1-0	Kabwe Warriors
2002	Zanaco	61	Power Dynamos	60	Green Buffaloes	60	Zanaco	2-2 3-2p	Power Dynamos
2003	Zanaco	69	Green Buffaloes	59	Kabwe Warriors	57	Power Dynamos	1-0	Kabwe Warriors
2004	Red Arrows	62	Green Buffaloes	55	Zanaco	53	Lusaka Celtic	2-1	Kabwe Warriors
2005	Zanaco	65	Zesco United	54	Power Dynamos	52	Green Buffaloes	2-1	Red Arrows
2006	Zanaco	71	Green Buffaloes	57	Power Dynamos	51	Zesco United	2-0	Red Arrows

BP TOP-8 CUP 2006

First Round		Semi-finals		Final	
Zanaco	2 3p				
Green Buffaloes	2 2p	**Zanaco**	4		
ZESCO United	0	Chambishi	1		
Chambishi	1			**Zanaco**	3
Kitwe United	1			Nchanga Rangers	1
Red Arrows	0	Kitwe United	1	Nkolama, Lusaka, 18-11-2006
Power Dynamos	0	**Nchanga Rangers**	2	Scorers - Kelvin Kaindu [2],
Nchanga Rangers	1			Winstone Kalengo 2 [40] [78] for Zanaco;
				Thomas Chisha [4] for Nchanga

ZAMBIA 2006

KONKOLA COPPER MINES PREMIER LEAGUE

	Pl	W	D	L	F	A	Pts	Zanaco	Buffaloes	Power Dy.	Kabwe	Forest Ran.	Konkola	Nakambala	ZESCO	Lusaka Dy.	Red Arrows	Nat. Ass'bly	Nchanga	Nkwazi	Celtic	Kitwe Utd	Chambishi
Zanaco †	30	21	8	1	57	18	71		1-1	3-1	2-0	1-2	1-0	3-1	2-1	7-1	2-1	2-1	2-0	1-1	1-0	4-0	1-0
Green Buffaloes ‡	30	17	6	7	44	24	57	0-1		2-1	1-2	0-0	3-0	1-1	2-1	2-1	2-0	2-0	4-3	3-1	3-1	3-0	1-0
Power Dynamos	30	14	9	7	40	30	51	0-2	0-1		0-2	0-0	1-0	3-1	1-2	4-1	2-1	2-1	1-0	4-2	0-1	0-0	1-1
Kabwe Warriors	30	11	12	7	33	23	45	1-2	0-0	1-1		1-1	1-1	1-1	0-0	1-2	1-1	1-1	2-0	1-0	2-1	2-0	2-1
Forest Rangers	30	10	15	5	24	20	45	0-0	1-0	0-0	1-0		1-1	1-0	0-1	1-1	1-1	0-0	1-1	2-1	0-0	2-0	2-0
Konkola Blades	30	11	11	8	28	21	44	0-0	0-2	1-2	0-0	0-1		0-1	1-1	3-0	2-1	3-0	3-0	2-1	1-0	1-0	2-0
Nakambala Leopards	30	11	7	12	30	37	40	2-2	1-0	1-1	0-3	1-0	0-1		1-0	4-2	3-1	2-1	0-2	1-0	2-0	1-0	2-3
ZESCO United	30	9	12	9	25	22	39	1-2	1-1	0-1	1-0	0-0	1-1	1-0		0-0	0-0	2-0	4-0	1-1	1-0	1-1	0-1
Lusaka Dynamos	30	10	8	12	35	39	38	0-1	0-0	2-3	2-1	1-1	1-1	1-0	0-1		3-2	0-1	0-0	0-1	4-0	2-0	1-1
Red Arrows	30	10	7	13	44	40	37	2-3	3-0	3-4	0-1	4-0	1-1	1-1	0-1	0-3		3-2	2-1	4-0	2-1	0-1	2-1
National Assembly	30	9	10	11	30	31	37	1-1	2-0	0-1	0-0	0-0	0-1	1-2	2-2	3-0	0-0		1-4	0-0	1-0	0-0	2-1
Nchanga Rangers	30	9	9	12	26	34	36	0-2	0-1	1-2	0-0	2-1	0-0	1-0	1-0	0-1	0-2	1-0		1-0	1-2	1-2	2-0
Nkwazi	30	9	9	12	27	36	36	0-0	2-1	1-1	2-1	3-1	1-0	3-2	2-0	0-2	0-2	1-3	2-2		0-0	0-0	1-0
Lusaka Celtic	30	6	8	16	20	38	26	1-4	0-3	1-1	0-3	0-1	0-1	4-0	1-0	1-0	1-2	1-1	1-2	1-0		1-1	1-1
Kitwe United	30	3	14	13	9	31	23	0-0	1-3	0-0	1-1	0-0	0-0	0-0	1-0	0-2	2-2	0-3	0-0	0-1	0-0		1-0
Chambishi	30	4	7	19	16	44	19	0-4	0-2	0-2	1-2	1-3	1-1	1-0	0-1	0-3	0-3	0-1	0-0	1-1	0-0	1-0	

18/03/2006 - 2/12/2006 • † Qualified for the CAF Champions League • ‡ Qualified for the CAF Confederation Cup • Top scorers: Winstone KALENGO, Zanaco 28; Mumamba NUMBA, Zanaco 19; Ignatius Lwipa, Zanaco 15; Sebastian MWANSA, Buffaloes 15; Dube PHIRI, Red Arrows 15

COCA-COLA LEAGUE CUP 2006

First Round

Kabwe Warriors	1	
Young Arrows *	0	
Green Buffaloes	0	
City of Lusaka *	1	
Roan United *	1	
Power Dynamos	0	
Irwin Rangers *	0	
Zanaco	4	
Lusaka Dynamos	0 3p	
Ndola United *	0 0p	
Lima Stars *	0	
Konkola Blades	1	
National Assembly	0 4p	
Mufulira Wanderers *	0 2p	
Muchindu Blue Eagles*	0	
Forest Rangers	2	

Quarter-finals

Kabwe Warriors	1
City of Lusaka *	0
Roan United *	1 8p
Zanaco	1 9p
Lusaka Dynamos	2
Konkola Blades *	0
National Assembly	0
Forest Rangers *	2

Semi-finals

Kabwe Warriors ‡	2
Zanaco	1
Lusaka Dynamos	0 2p
Forest Rangers †	0 3p

Final

Kabwe Warriors	2
Forest Rangers	0

CUP FINAL
23-09-2006
Scorers - Musonda Mweuke [30], Siloni Jere [70] for Kabwe

* Home team • ‡ Held in Lusaka • † Held in Kitwe

MOSI CUP 2006

Round of 16

ZESCO United	5
Kambuku Warriors *	0
Kabwe Warriors *	0 5p
Power Dynamos	0 6p
Forest Rangers *	0 4p
Nkana	0 3p
Zanaco	0
Lusaka Dynamos *	2
Nkwazi	1 5p
National Assembly *	1 4p
Zamtel *	2 6p
Young Arrows	2 7p
Lusaka City Council *	1 5p
Lusaka Celtic	1 4p
Nakambala Leopards	1
Red Arrows *	2

Quarter-finals

ZESCO United *	1
Power Dynamos	0
Forest Rangers *	0
Lusaka Dynamos	2
Nkwazi *	2
Young Arrows	0
Lusaka City Council	1
Red Arrows *	5

Semi-finals

ZESCO United ‡	1
Lusaka Dynamos	0
Nkwazi	0
Red Arrows ‡	3

Final

ZESCO United	2
Red Arrows	0

CUP FINAL
Woodlands, Lusaka
25-11-2006
Scorer - Clifford Chipala 2 [53][62] for ZESCO

* Home team • ‡ Both semis held at Woodlands • Nkwazi won third place match 1-0

ZIM – ZIMBABWE

NATIONAL TEAM RECORD
JULY 10TH 2006 TO JULY 12TH 2010

PL	W	D	L	F	A	%
10	2	5	3	8	10	45

FIFA/COCA-COLA WORLD RANKING

1993	1994	1995	1996	1997	1998	1999	2000	2001	2002	2003	2004	2005	2006	High		Low	
46	51	59	71	74	74	67	68	68	57	53	60	53	76	**40**	04/95	**96**	07/07

2006–2007											
08/06	09/06	10/06	11/06	12/06	01/07	02/07	03/07	04/07	05/07	06/07	07/07
70	73	82	76	76	72	94	91	82	84	90	96

The destiny of the 2006 League title in Zimbabwe was never in doubt after Highlanders started the campaign at a blistering pace, winning their first 10 matches. It was a first triumph since 2002 for the Bulawayo side and capped a miserable season for Harare, whose clubs ended the season without a trophy for only the second season since the start of the decade. The once-powerful Dynamos are symbolic of the capital's fall from grace. Dembare, as they are also known, last won the title in 1997, despite being able to attract the biggest support in the country. Football remains very popular despite the hyper-inflation that is bringing the country to its knees although a number of clubs have

INTERNATIONAL HONOURS
CECAFA Cup 1985 **COSAFA Castle Cup** 2000 2003

warned that they could soon go out of business. Just organising and paying for transport to away games is proving an ever more difficult task. The Football Association even suffered the embarrassment of not being able to get enough of the scare foreign currency to pay for travel to a friendly in Lesotho in early 2007 and had to cancel the trip. Little surprise then that the national team had a poor season, losing in the semi-final of the 2006 COSAFA Cup to Angola and then crashing out of the 2007 tournament on penalties to Mozambique in the first round. Zimbabwe will be absent from the 2008 Nations Cup finals after failing to overcome Morocco in their qualifying group.

THE FIFA BIG COUNT OF 2006

	Male	Female		Total
Number of players	622 300	29 100	Referees and Assistant Referees	800
Professionals	100		Admin, Coaches, Technical, Medical	2 300
Amateurs 18+	28 600		Number of clubs	350
Youth under 18	5 900		Number of teams	1 250
Unregistered	46 800		Clubs with women's teams	0
Total players	651 400		Players as % of population	5.32%

Zimbabwe Football Association (ZIFA)
53 Livingstone Avenue, Causeway, PO Box CY 114, Harare, Zimbabwe
Tel +263 4 798631   Fax +263 4 798626
zifa@africaonline.co.zw   www.zimbabwesoccer.com
President: NYATHANGA Wellington   General Secretary: RUSHWAYA Henrietta
Vice-President: MADZORERA Tendai   Treasurer: TBD   Media Officer: None
Men's Coach: MHLAURI Charles   Women's Coach: BOWERS Vernon
ZIFA formed: 1965   CAF: 1965   FIFA: 1965
Green shirts, Yellow shorts, Green socks

RECENT INTERNATIONAL MATCHES PLAYED BY ZIMBABWE

2004	Opponents	Score		Venue	Comp	Scorers	Att	Referee
25-01	Egypt	L	1-2	Sfax	CNr1	Ndlovu.P [46]	22 000	Pare BFA
29-01	Cameroon	L	3-5	Sfax	CNr1	Ndlovu.P 2 [8 47p], Nyandoro [89]	15 000	Aboubacar CIV
3-02	Algeria	W	2-1	Sousse	CNr1	Luphahala 2 [65 71]	10 000	Maillet SEY
1-05	Zambia	D	1-1	Lusaka	Fr	Ndlovu.B [89]		
16-05	Zambia	D	0-0	Harare	Fr			
24-05	Egypt	L	0-2	Cairo	Fr		10 000	
5-06	Gabon	D	1-1	Libreville	WCq	Kaondera [82]	25 000	Quartey GHA
20-06	Algeria	D	1-1	Harare	WCq	Raho OG [60]	65 000	Ntambidila COD
27-06	Swaziland	W	5-0	Mbabane	CCqf	Kasinuayo [7], Ndlovu.P 3 [41 58 81], OG [54]. Abandoned 83'		Infante MOZ
3-07	Rwanda	W	2-0	Kigali	WCq	Ndlovu.P [41], Nengomasha [79]		Chilinda MWI
18-08	Botswana	W	2-0	Bulawayo	Fr	Ncube [67], Sibanda [87]	5 000	
22-08	Uganda	W	2-0	Harare	Fr	Moyo [28], Ncube [81]	3 000	
5-09	Nigeria	L	0-3	Harare	WCq		60 000	Mandzioukouta COD
10-10	Angola	L	0-1	Luanda	WCq		17 000	Lwanja MWI
24-10	Zambia	D	0-0	Harare	CCsf	L 4-5p	25 000	Simisse MRI
2005								
27-02	Malawi	L	1-2	Blantyre	Fr	Tsipa [54]		
16-03	Botswana	D	1-1	Harare	Fr	Chimedza [53]	3 000	
27-03	Angola	W	2-0	Harare	WCq	Kawondera [60], Mwaruwari [69]		Codjia BEN
16-04	Mozambique	W	3-0	Windhoek	CCr1	Chimedza 2 [66p 78], Sandaka [82]		Mufeti NAM
17-04	Botswana	W	2-0	Windhoek	CCr1	Badza [21], Sandaka [58]		Braga Mavunza ANG
5-06	Gabon	W	1-0	Harare	WCq	Ndlovu.P [52]	55 000	Ssegonga UGA
19-06	Algeria	D	2-2	Oran	WCq	Kawondera [33], Ndlovu.P [87]	15 000	Pare BFA
13-08	Angola	W	2-1	Mmabatho	CCsf	Chandida [59], Sandaka [76]		Kapanga MWI
14-08	Zambia	W	1-0	Mmabatho	CCf	Chandida [84]		Massango MOZ
28-08	Mozambique	D	0-0	Mutare	Fr			
4-09	Rwanda	W	3-1	Harare	WCq	Kawondera [4], Mwaruwari [43], Rambanapasi [78]	55 000	Ssegona UGA
8-10	Nigeria	L	1-5	Abuja	WCq	Mwaruwari [70]	45 000	Pare BFA
31-12	Zambia	D	1-1	Harare	Fr	Mbwando [63]		
2006								
5-01	Egypt	L	0-2	Alexandria	Fr			
14-01	Morocco	L	0-1	Marrakech	Fr			
23-01	Senegal	L	0-2	Port Said	CNr1		15 000	Abdel Rahman SUD
27-01	Nigeria	L	0-2	Port Said	CNr1		10 000	Coulibaly MLI
31-01	Ghana	W	2-1	Ismailia	CNr1	Chimedza [60], Mwaruwari [68]	14 000	Louzaya CGO
24-06	Malawi	D	1-1	Maputo	Fr	Gwekwerere [28p], L 1-2p		
25-06	Swaziland	W	2-1	Maputo	Fr	Gwekwerere [14], Matema [73]		
15-07	Zambia	D	0-0	Lusaka	Fr			
17-09	Angola	L	1-2	Harare	CCsf	Chandida [64]		Kaoma ZAM
7-10	Malawi	L	0-1	Blantyre	CNq			Seechun MRI
15-11	Namibia	W	3-2	Harare	Fr	Gwekwerere [11], Mushangazhike [17], Matawu [50]		
2007								
25-03	Morocco	D	1-1	Harare	CNq	Nyandoro [81]		Damon RSA
28-04	Madagascar	W	1-0	Maputo	CCr1	Nkata [8]		Faduco MOZ
29-04	Mozambique	D	0-0	Maputo	CCr1	L 4-5p		Seechun MRI
25-05	Lesotho	D	1-1	Masvingo	Fr	Antipas [57]		
29-05	Burkina Faso	D	1-1	Masvingo	Fr	Kawondera [45]		
2-06	Morocco	L	0-2	Casablanca	CNq			

Fr = Friendly match • CN = CAF African Cup of Nations • CC = COSAFA Cup • WC = FIFA World Cup
q = qualifier • r1 = first round group • qf = quarter-final • sf = semi-final • f = final

ZIMBABWE NATIONAL TEAM RECORDS AND RECORD SEQUENCES

Records			Sequence records					
Victory	7-0	BOT 1990	Wins	6	2003	Clean sheets	5	2002-2003
Defeat	0-5	CIV 1989, COD 1995	Defeats	5	1997-1998	Goals scored	12	2003-2004
Player Caps	n/a		Undefeated	13	1981-1982	Without goal	4	1988, 2006
Player Goals	n/a		Without win	9	1995-96, 1997-98	Goals against	11	1995-1996

REPUBLIC OF ZIMBABWE

Capital	Harare	Language	English, Shona, Sindebele	Independence	1980
Population	12 311 143	Area	390 580 km²	Density	32 per km²	% in cities	32%
GDP per cap	$1 900	Dialling code	+263	Internet	.zw	GMT +/-	+2

MEDALS TABLE

		Overall			Lg	C	IT	LC	Africa			City	Stadium	Cap'ty	DoF
		G	S	B	G	G	G	G	G	S	B				
1	Dynamos	31	1		17	7	5	2	1			Harare	Rufaro	45 000	1963
2	CAPS United	21			4	8	4	5				Harare	National Stadium	60 000	1973
3	Highlanders	15			7	2	5	1				Bulawayo	Barbourfields	35 000	1926
4	Zimbabwe Saints	6			2	3	1					Bulawayo	Barbourfields	35 000	
5	Black Rhinos	5			2	1	2					Harare			1983
6	Masvingo United	4				2	2					Masvingo	Mucheke	5 000	
7	Amazulu	3			1	1	1					Bulawayo			
8	Arcadia United	3			1	2						Harare			
9	Bulawayo Rovers	3			2	1						Bulawayo			
10	Chibuku	3			1	2						Harare			
11	Sailisbury Callies	3				3						Harare			
12	Hwange (ex Wankie)	3				3						Hwange			
13	Black Aces	2			1			1				Harare			
14	Bulawayo Sables	2			2							Bulawayo			
15	Chapungu United	2				1	1					Gweru	Ascot	5 000	
16	Mangula	2				2						Mangula			
17	Salisbury Sables	2			2							Harare			

RECENT LEAGUE AND CUP RECORD

	Championship						Cup		
Year	Champions	Pts	Runners-up	Pts	Third	Pts	Winners	Score	Runners-up
1995	Dynamos	58	Blackpool	58	Black Aces	53	Chapungu United		
1996	CAPS United	71	Dynamos	68	Blackpool	54	Dynamos		
1997	Dynamos	68	CAPS United	57	Black Aces	50	CAPS United	3-2	Dynamos
1998	No championship due to calender reorganisation						CAPS United		
1999	Highlanders	72	Dynamos	71	Zimbabwe Saints	54	Amazulu		
2000	Highlanders	78	AmaZulu	76	Dynamos	66	No tournament		
2001	Highlanders	62	AmaZulu	59	Shabanie Mine	51	Highlanders	4-1	Shabanie Mine
2002	Highlanders	72	Black Rhinos	52	AmaZulu	50	Masvingo United	2-2 4-3p	Railstars
2003	AmaZulu	51	Highlanders	50	Dynamos	48	Dynamos	2-0	Highlanders
2004	CAPS United	79	Highlanders	64	Shabanie Mine	51	CAPS United	1-0	Wankie
2005	CAPS United	58	Masvingo United	56	Highlanders	51	Masvingo United	1-1 3-1p	Highlanders
2006	Highlanders	65	Motor Action	54	Masvingo United	49	Mwana Africa	1-0	Chapungu

ZIMBABWE 2006

NATIONAL PREMIER SOCCER LEAGUE

	Pl	W	D	L	F	A	Pts	Highlanders	Motor	Masvingo	CAPS Utd	Hwange	Dynamos	Chapungu	Mono'tapa	Rhinos	Mwana	Buymore	Lanc. Steel	Sh. Stars	Railstars	Shabanie	Saints
Highlanders †	30	20	5	5	56	26	65		0-0	2-0	1-0	4-1	2-0	5-1	4-2	0-0	3-1	0-1	3-0	3-2	2-2	3-0	1-0
Motor Action	30	15	9	6	41	29	54	1-0		2-0	2-2	0-1	1-1	3-2	0-3	1-1	0-2	2-0	0-0	1-0	3-2	1-0	4-1
Masvingo United	30	14	7	9	37	31	49	0-1	3-1		2-0	1-1	2-2	2-1	1-0	1-0	2-1	0-0	1-3	1-0	2-1	1-1	2-0
CAPS United	30	13	8	9	36	33	47	2-1	1-2	2-1		3-0	2-1	1-1	0-1	0-3	2-1	3-0	1-0	1-1	3-2	1-1	2-1
Hwange	30	14	5	11	40	43	47	2-4	2-2	2-1	0-0		3-2	2-1	1-0	0-2	0-1	2-1	1-2	4-2	3-0	3-3	2-1
Dynamos	30	12	10	8	41	30	46	0-1	1-0	0-0	1-1	2-0		1-0	1-1	3-1	3-1	0-0	3-1	1-0	1-1	3-0	4-1
Chapungu United	30	14	3	13	46	37	45	1-2	2-3	1-3	4-2	0-0	0-1		1-0	0-1	5-0	2-0	1-0	2-1	3-2	1-0	2-0
Monomatapa United	30	11	10	9	39	31	43	1-2	2-2	0-1	0-0	3-1	2-1	1-2		2-2	0-0	2-2	2-1	1-0	1-2	3-1	2-1
Black Rhinos	30	12	7	11	34	34	43	1-3	0-2	1-0	1-0	0-1	2-1	0-2	1-2		0-2	2-1	1-0	3-4	1-0	3-0	1-0
Mwana Africa	30	12	7	11	35	37	43	1-2	0-2	0-1	2-0	2-0	1-1	2-1	1-0	0-0		2-1	3-1	2-1	3-1	1-1	1-1
Buymore Chitungwiza	30	9	10	11	24	28	37	0-0	0-0	2-1	1-2	0-1	0-0	0-0	0-1	1-0			1-0	3-1	1-1	2-0	2-0
Lancashire Steel	29	8	9	12	27	34	33	1-0	0-0	1-1	0-2	2-1	2-1	1-2	1-1	2-2	3-0	0-0		1-1	1-0	0-0	n/p
Shooting Stars	30	8	8	14	39	47	32	0-0	3-2	3-1	0-1	1-3	3-0	1-0	2-2	0-0	1-1	2-3	0-4		3-1	1-0	0-0
Railstars Bulawayo	30	8	7	15	41	48	31	1-3	0-2	2-3	1-1	2-0	0-0	0-4	0-3	3-1	1-1	2-0	4-0	1-2		4-1	2-0
Shabanie Mine	30	6	9	15	28	44	27	4-1	0-1	1-1	2-0	1-2	1-2	2-1	0-1	2-2	2-1	1-0	0-0	2-2	2-0		0-1
Zimbabwe Saints	29	5	2	22	23	55	17	1-3	0-1	0-2	0-1	0-1	1-4	1-3	1-4	2-1	1-2	1-2	2-0	3-2	1-3	2-1	

25/03/2006 - 16/12/2006 • † Qualified for the CAF Champions League • Top scorers: Ralph MATEMA, Highlanders 11; Master MASITARA, Railstars 11

INDEPENDENCE CUP 2006

Semi-finals

Masvingo United	1
Highlanders	0

Dynamos	1 4p
CAPS United	1 5p

Final

Masvingo United	1 3p
CAPS United	1 0p

National Stadium, Harare, 18-04-2006
Scorers - Wonder Sithole [49] for Masvingo;
Malvern Nyakabangwe [59] for CAPS

CBZ CUP 2006

Second Round

Mwana Africa	0 5p
Dynamos *	0 4p
Black Rhinos *	0
Monomatapa United	1
Motor Action *	2
Shooting Stars	1
Lengthens *	2 2p
Buymore	2 3p
Hwange	1 3p
Railstars *	1 2p
Masvingo United	0
Shabanie Mine *	2
Lancashire Steel *	2
Zisco Steel	0
Border Strikers	0
Chapungu United *	2

Quarter-finals

Mwana Africa	1
Monomatapa United *	0
Motor Action	0
Buymore *	1
Hwange *	2
Shabanie Mine	1
Lancashire Steel *	0
Chapungu United	1

Semi-finals

Mwana Africa *	2
Buymore	1
Hwange	0
Chapungu United *	1

Final

Mwana Africa ‡	1
Chapungu United	0

CUP FINAL

Harare, 10-12-2006

Scorer - Benjamin Marere [81] for Mwana

* Home team • ‡ Qualified for the CAF Confederation Cup

PART THREE

THE
CONTINENTAL
CONFEDERATIONS

AFC

ASIAN FOOTBALL CONFEDERATION

The AFC Asian Cup provided the most compelling football story of the year, with Iraq's victory over Saudi Arabia in the final making headline news the world over. It really was a remarkable triumph. Not only did the Iraqis play all of their qualifying matches away from home, coach Jorvan Vieira then had to contend with frequent disruptions to his pre-finals training camp in Amman, Jordan, as his players made regular land trips back to Iraq to play for their club sides in a championship coming to its climax. Yet Iraq's triumph in Southeast Asia was no fluke, with impressive wins over Australia and Vietnam on the way to the final. Tragedy followed the semi-final victory over South Korea when celebrating crowds provided an easy target for a suicide bomber who left 50 people dead. But that didn't stop people pouring onto the streets again to celebrate the win in the final, when thankfully there were no casualties. In light of Iraq's triumph, the Asian Cup has to be considered a success despite disappointing crowds in Malaysia and in games not involving

THE FIFA BIG COUNT OF 2006 FOR ASIA

	Male	Female		Total
Number of players	80 075 000	5 102 000	Referees and Assistant Referees	263 000
Professionals	11 000		Admin, Coaches, Technical, Medical	410 000
Amateurs 18+	1 531 000		Number of clubs	20 000
Youth under 18	2 322		Number of teams	145 000
Unregistered	81 136 000		Clubs with women's teams	3 000
Total involved in football	85 849		Players as % of population	2.22%

Indonesia, Thailand and Vietnam, the other three co-hosts. These are still early days in the revolution that Mohamed Bin Hamman, President of the Asian Football Confederation (AFC), hopes will transform the game in Asia. The AFC has promised that stadiums will be full when Qatar hosts the tournament in 2011. Certainly the AFC Champions League is increasing its profile, with Japanese clubs starting to take the competition seriously and Australian clubs making their long awaited debut in the 2007 tournament. The 2006 Champions League was won by South Korea's Jeonbuk Motors who beat Syria's Al Karama in the final. With Jordan's Al Faysali retaining the AFC Cup by beating Al Muharraq from Bahrain in the final, and three Jordanian teams already qualified from the group stage of the 2007 tournament, it surely can't be long before Jordan is accepted into the Champions League circle. Finally, 2006 was also a good year for North Korea, winners of the Asian Youth Championship and the women's U-16 championship.

Asian Football Confederation (AFC)
AFC House, Jalan 1/155B, Bukit Jalil, 57000 Kuala Lumpur, Malaysia
Tel +60 3 89943388   Fax +60 3 89946168
media@the-afc.com   www.the-afc.com
President: BIN HAMMAM Mohamed QAT   General Secretary: SAMUEL Dato' Paul Mony MAS
AFC Formed: 1954

AFC EXECUTIVE COMMITTEE

President: BIN HAMMAM Mohamed QAT   Vice-President: ZHANG Jilong CHN   Vice-President: FERNANDO V. Manilal SRI
Vice-President: TENGKU Abdullah Ahmad Shah MAS   Vice-President: AL SERKAL Yousuf UAE   Hon Treasurer: BOUZO Farouk, Gen SYR
FIFA Vice-President: CHUNG Mong Joon, Dr KOR   FIFA Executive Member: MAKUDI Worawi   FIFA Executive Member: OGURA Junji

MEMBERS OF THE EXECUTIVE COMMITTEE

RAKHIMOV BaKhtier UZB   TAHIR Dali IDN   AL MEDLEJ Hafez, Dr KSA
THAPA Ganesh NEP   HUSSAIN Mohammed Saeed IRQ   NAM SANG John Koh SIN
FARAHANI Mohsen Safai IRN   DAS MUNSHI Priya Ranjan IND   LAI Richard GUM
AL MASKERY Saif Hasil Rashid OMA   ZAW Zaw MYA

MAP OF AFC MEMBER NATIONS

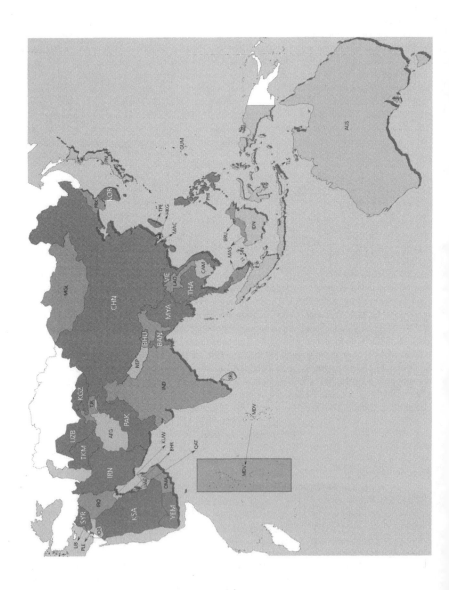

ASIAN TOURNAMENTS

AFC ASIAN CUP

Year	Host Country	Winners	Score	Runners-up	Venue
1956	Hong Kong	Korea Republic	2-1	Israel	Government Stadium, Hong Kong
1960	Korea Republic	Korea Republic	3-0	Israel	Hyochang Park, Seoul
1964	Israel	Israel	2-0	India	Bloomfield, Jaffa
1968	Iran	Iran	3-1	Burma	Amjadieh, Tehran
1972	Thailand	Iran	2-1	Korea Republic	Suphachalasai, Bangkok
1976	Iran	Iran	1-0	Kuwait	Azadi, Tehran
1980	Kuwait	Kuwait	3-0	Korea Republic	Kuwait City
1984	Singapore	Saudi Arabia	2-0	China PR	National Stadium, Singapore
1988	Qatar	Saudi Arabia	0-0 4-3p	Korea Republic	Khalifa, Doha
1992	Japan	Japan	1-0	Saudi Arabia	Main Stadium, Hiroshima
1996	UAE	Saudi Arabia	0-0 4-2p	United Arab Emirates	Zayed, Abu Dhabi
2000	Lebanon	Japan	1-0	Saudi Arabia	Camille Chamoun, Beirut
2004	China PR	Japan	3-1	China PR	Workers' Stadium, Beijing
2007	ASEAN co-hosts	Iraq	1-0	Saudi Arabia	Gelora Bung Karno, Jakarta

From 1956 to 1968 the tournament was played as a league. The result listed is that between the winners and runners-up.

AFC ASIAN CUP MEDALS TABLE

	Country	G	S	B	F	SF
1	Saudi Arabia	3	3		6	6
2	Iran	3		4	2	7
3	Japan	3			3	4
4	Korea Republic	2	3	3	3	5
5	Israel	1	2	1		
6	Kuwait	1	1	1	2	4
7	Iraq	1			1	2
8	China PR		2	2	2	6
9	Utd Arab Emirates		1		1	2
10	India			1		
	Myanmar			1		
12	Thailand			1		1
13	Chinese Taipei			1		
	Hong Kong			1		
15	Bahrain					1
	Cambodia					1
	Korea DPR					1
		14	14	14	20	40

This table represents the Gold (winners), Silver (runners-up) and
Bronze (semi-finalists) placings of countries in the AFC Asian Cup,
along with the number of appearances in the final and semi-finals

The AFC Asian Cup is the continent's premier competition for national teams. The first tournament was held in Hong Kong in 1956 and was won by South Korea who also triumphed four years later at home. Despite appearing in three more finals the Koreans have failed in their efforts to add a third title. Israel were the winners in 1964, again on home soil, but from the late 1960s to the late 1970s Iran were the undisputed kings of Asia, winning every game they played on the way to a hat-trick of titles. Kuwait were the first Arab nation to win the tournament, in 1980, and were followed by Saudi Arabia, who with three titles between 1984 and 1996, dominated for over a decade, and have appeared in six of the last seven finals. Just once since 1980 has the home nation won - in 1992 when Japan won for the first time. Coinciding with the explosion of interest in football there, the Japanese went on to win two more titles in the next four tournaments. Traditionally held every four years, the cycle was changed in 2007 to avoid clashing with other continental championships and there was another first when four nations - Indonesia, Malaysia, Thailand and Vietnam - hosted a tournament sensationally won by Iraq as civil war raged back home.

AFC WOMEN'S CHAMPIONSHIP

Year	Host Country	Winners	Score	Runners-up	Venue
1975	Hong Kong	New Zealand	3-1	Thailand	Hong Kong
1977	Chinese Tapei	Chinese Taipei	3-1	Thailand	Taipei
1979	India	Chinese Taipei	2-0	India	Calicut
1981	Hong Kong	Chinese Taipei	5-0	Thailand	Hong Kong
1983	Thailand	Thailand	3-0	India	Bangkok
1986	Hong Kong	China PR	2-0	Japan	Hong Kong
1989	Hong Kong	China PR	1-0	Chinese Taipei	Hong Kong
1991	Japan	China PR	5-0	Japan	Fukuoka
1993	Malaysia	China PR	3-0	Korea DPR	Sarawak
1995	Malaysia	China PR	2-0	Japan	Sabah
1997	China PR	China PR	2-0	Korea DPR	Guangdong
1999	Philippines	China PR	3-0	Chinese Taipei	Bacalod
2001	Chinese Taipei	Korea DPR	2-0	Japan	Taipei
2003	Thailand	Korea DPR	2-1	China PR	Bangkok
2006	Australia	China PR	2-2 4-2p	Australia	Adelaide

The AFC Women's Championship is the longest running of all the continental championships for women, though unsurprisingly it has remained the preserve of East Asia with the countries of the Middle East yet to enter a single tournament. China has emerged as the most successful nation with seven consecutive titles between 1986 and 1999. 2001 saw North Korea win the title for the first time to become the fifth different winners along with Thailand, Chinese Taipei and New Zealand. Australia look certain to present a strong challenge in the future and they reached the final in 2006 when they hosted their first AFC tournament since joining the confederation earlier in the year. Japan have made it to four finals but have yet to win.

FOOTBALL TOURNAMENT OF THE ASIAN GAMES

Year	Host Country	Winners	Score	Runners-up	Venue
1951	India	India	1-0	Iran	New Delhi
1954	Philippines	Chinese Taipei	5-2	Korea Republic	Manilla
1958	Japan	Chinese Taipei	3-2	Korea Republic	Tokyo
1962	Indonesia	India	2-1	Korea Republic	Djakarta
1966	Thailand	Burma	1-0	Iran	Bangkok
1970	Thailand	Burma	0-0 †	Korea Republic	Bangkok
1974	Iran	Iran	1-0	Israel	Tehran
1978	Thailand	Korea Republic	0-0 †	Korea DPR	Bangkok
1982	India	Iraq	1-0	Kuwait	New Dehli
1986	Korea Republic	Korea Republic	2-0	Saudi Arabia	Seoul
1990	China PR	Iran	0-0 4-1p	Korea DPR	Beijing
1994	Japan	Uzbekistan	4-2	China PR	Hiroshima
1998	Thailand	Iran	2-0	Kuwait	Bangkok
2002	Korea Republic	Iran	2-1	Japan	Busan
2006	Qatar	Qatar	1-0	Iraq	Doha

† Gold medal shared in 1970 and 1978

For many years the Football Tournament of the Asian Games rivalled the Asian Cup in importance, meaning the continent had a major championship every other year. Football was included at the very first Asiad, in New Delhi in 1951, where the matches were contested over two halves of 40 minutes. India were the first gold medalists and since then the range of winners has been more diverse than in the Asian Cup with Japan and Saudi Arabia yet to the title. Iran is the most successful nation in the tournament with four golds followed by South Korea with three. Qatar became the eighth different winners when they won the Doha games in 2006. The Asian Games operate as a regional version of the Olympics so in the amateur days this was not an issue given the lack of professional players on the continent. In 2002, as with the Olympics, the football tournament was turned into a U–23 tournament with three older players allowed.

WOMEN'S FOOTBALL TOURNAMENT OF THE ASIAN GAMES

Year	Host Country	Winners	Score	Runners-up	Venue
1990	China PR	China PR	5-0	Japan	Beijing
1994	Japan	China PR	2-0	Japan	Hiroshima
1998	Thailand	China PR	1-0	Korea DPR	Bangkok
2002	Korea Republic	Korea DPR	0-0	China PR	Busan
2006	Qatar	Korea DPR	0-0 4-2p	Japan	Doha

In 1990, 1994 and 2002 the tournament was played as a league. The result listed is that between the winners and runners-up

Given the strength of women's football in East Asia, it was a natural progression to introduce the sport to the Games when Beijing was host in 1990. The Chinese won that year and they, along with North Korea, are the only nations to have come away with gold medals.

AFC CHALLENGE CUP

Year	Host Country	Winners	Score	Runners-up	Venue
2006	Bangladesh	Tajikistan	4-0	Sri Lanka	Bangabandhu, Dhaka

The AFC Challenge Cup for national teams was launched in 2006 for the lower ranked nations on the continent in order to give these nations the realistic prospect of winning competitive honours in what is effectively the second division of Asian nations.

AFC YOUTH CHAMPIONSHIP WINNERS

Year	Host Country	Winners	Score	Runners-up	Venue
1959	Malaysia	Korea Republic	2-1	Malaysia	Kuala Lumpur
1960	Malaysia	Korea Republic	4-0	Malaysia	Kuala Lumpur
1961	Thailand	Burma	0-0†	Indonesia	Bangkok
1962	Thailand	Thailand	2-1	Korea Republic	Bangkok
1963	Malaysia	Burma	2-2†	Korea Republic	Penang
1964	Vietnam	Burma	0-0†	Israel	Saigon
1965	Japan	Israel	5-0	Burma	Tokyo
1966	Philippines	Burma	1-1	Israel	Manila
1967	Thailand	Israel	3-0	Indonesia	Bangkok
1968	Korea Republic	Burma	4-0	Malaysia	Seoul
1969	Thailand	Burma	2-2†	Thailand	Bangkok
1970	Philippines	Burma	3-0	India	Manila
1971	Japan	Israel	1-0	Korea Republic	Tokyo
1972	Thailand	Israel	1-0	Korea Republic	Bangkok
1973	Iran	Iran	2-0	Japan	Tehran
1974	Thailand	Iran	2-2†	India	Bangkok
1975	Kuwait	Iran	0-0†	Iraq	Kuwait City
1976	Thailand	Iran	0-0†	Korea DPR	Bangkok
1977	Iran	Iraq	4-3	Iran	Tehran
1978	Bangladesh	Iraq	1-1†	Korea Republic	Dhaka
1980	Thailand	Korea Republic	4-1‡	Qatar	Bangkok
1982	Thailand	Korea Republic	1-1‡	China PR	Bangkok
1984	UAE	China PR	2-2‡	Saudi Arabia	Abu Dhabi
1986	Saudi Arabia	Saudi Arabia	2-0	Bahrain	Riyadh
1988	Qatar	Iraq	1-1 5-4p	Syria	Doha
1990	Indonesia	Korea Republic	0-0 4-3p	Korea DPR	Jakarta
1992	UAE	Saudi Arabia	2-0	Korea Republic	Dubai
1994	Indonesia	Syria	2-1	Japan	Jakarta
1996	Korea Republic	Korea Republic	3-0	China PR	Suwon
1998	Thailand	Korea Republic	2-1	Japan	Chiang Mai
2000	Iran	Iraq	2-1	Japan	Tehran
2002	Qatar	Korea Republic	1-0	Japan	Doha
2004	Malaysia	Korea Republic	2-0	China PR	Kuala Lumpur
2006	India	Korea DPR	1-1 5-3p	Japan	

† Title shared between both finalists • ‡ Played on a league system so the match indicated was not a final

AFC UNDER 17 CHAMPIONSHIP WINNERS

Year	Host Country	Winners	Score	Runners-up	Venue
1984	Qatar	Saudi Arabia		Qatar	Doha
1986	Qatar	Korea Republic		Qatar	Doha
1988	Thailand	Saudi Arabia		Bahrain	Bangkok
1990	UAE	Qatar		UAE	Dubai
1992	Saudi Arabia	China PR		Qatar	Riyadh
1994	Qatar	Japan		Qatar	Doha
1996	Thailand	Oman		Thailand	Bangkok
1998	Qatar	Thailand		Qatar	Doha
2000	Vietnam SR	Oman		Iran	Danang
2002	UAE	Korea Republic		Yemen	Abu Dhabi
2004	Japan	China PR		Korea DPR	Shizuoka
2006	Singapore	Japan		Korea DPR	Singapore

AFC UNDER 19 WOMEN'S CHAMPIONSHIP WINNERS

Year	Host Country	Winners	Score	Runners-up	Venue
2002	India	Japan	2-1	Chinese Taipei	
2006	Malaysia	China PR	1-0	Korea DPR	
2007	China				

AFC UNDER 16 WOMEN'S CHAMPIONSHIP WINNERS

Year	Host Country	Winners	Score	Runners-up	Venue
2005	Korea Republic	Japan	1-1 3-1p	China PR	Namhae
2007	Malaysia	Korea DPR	3-0	Japan	MPPJ Stadium, Petaling Jaya

Asia has a long history of youth tournaments dating back to the 1950s and the AFC now runs tournaments at both under 17 and under 19 level for both men and women. These act as qualifiers for the FIFA tournaments held the year after for the under 17 and under 20 age groups.

ASEAN FOOTBALL FEDERATION CHAMPIONSHIP

Year	Host Country	Winners	Score	Runners-up	Venue
1996		Thailand	1-0	Malaysia	
1998	Vietnam	Singapore	1-0	Vietnam	Hanoi Stadium, Hanoi
2000	Thailand	Thailand	4-1	Indonesia	Bangkok
2002	Indonesia/Sin'pore	Thailand	2-2 4-2p	Indonesia	Gelora Senayan, Jakarta
2004	Malaysia/Vietnam	Singapore	3-1 2-1	Indonesia	Jakarta, Singapore
2007	Sin'pore/Thailand	Singapore	2-1 1-1	Thailand	Singapore, Bangkok

SOUTH ASIAN FOOTBALL FEDERATION CUP

Year	Host Country	Winners	Score	Runners-up	Venue
1993	Pakistan	India	2-0	Sri Lanka	Lahore
1995	Sri Lanka	Sri Lanka	1-0	India	Colombo
1997	Nepal	India	5-1	Maldives	Dasharath Rangashala, Kathmandu
1999	Goa	India	2-0	Bangladesh	Margao
2003	Bangladesh	Bangladesh	1-1 5-3p	Maldives	Bangabandu, Dhaka
2005	Pakistan	India	2-0	Bangladesh	Karachi

EAST ASIAN CHAMPIONSHIP

Year	Host Country	Winners	Score	Runners-up	Venue
2003	Japan	Korea Republic	0-0	Japan	International, Yokohama
2005	Korea Republic	China PR	2-2	Japan	World Cup Stadium, Daejeon

The 2003 tournament was played as a league. The result listed is that between the winners and runners-up

WEST ASIAN FOOTBALL FEDERATION CHAMPIONSHIP

Year	Host Country	Winners	Score	Runners-up	Venue
2000	Jordan	Iran	1-0	Syria	Malek Abdullah, Amman
2002	Syria	Iraq	3-2	Jordan	Al Abbassiyyine, Damascus
2004	Iran	Iran	4-1	Syria	Tehran
2007	Jordan	Iran	2-1	Iraq	International, Amman

GULF CUP

Year	Host Country	Winners	Runners-up
1970	Bahrain	Kuwait	Bahrain
1972	Saudi Arabia	Kuwait	Saudi Arabia
1974	Kuwait	Kuwait	Saudi Arabia
1976	Qatar	Kuwait	Iraq
1979	Iraq	Iraq	Kuwait
1982	UAE	Kuwait	Bahrain
1984	Oman	Iraq	Qatar
1986	Bahrain	Kuwait	UAE
1988	Saudi Arabia	Iraq	UAE

GULF CUP

Year	Host Country	Winners	Runners-up
1990	Kuwait	Kuwait	Qatar
1992	Qatar	Qatar	Bahrain
1994	UAE	Saudi Arabia	UAE
1996	Oman	Kuwait	Qatar
1998	Bahrain	Kuwait	Saudi Arabia
2002	Saudi Arabia	Saudi Arabia	Qatar
2004	Kuwait	Saudi Arabia	Bahrain
2005	Qatar	Qatar	Oman
2007	UAE	UAE	Oman

Regional tournaments in Asia are particularly strong and they play a hugely important role given the vast size of the continent. Each of the four regional federations - ASEAN for South-East Asia, EAF for East Asia, SAFF for Southern Asia and WAFF for West Asia - runs a tournament, whilst the Gulf Cup is held for the nations bordering the Arabian Gulf.

FOOTBALL TOURNAMENT OF THE SOUTH EAST ASIAN GAMES

Year	Host Country	Winners	Score	Runners-up	Venue
1959	Thailand	Vietnam	3-1	Thailand	Bangkok
1961	Burma	Malaysia	2-0	Burma	Rangoon
1965	Malaysia	Burma	2-2†	Thailand	Kuala Lumpur
1967	Thailand	Burma	2-1	South Vietnam	Bangkok
1969	Burma	Burma	3-0	Thailand	Rangoon
1971	Malaysia	Burma	2-1	Malaysia	Kuala Lumpur
1973	Singapore	Burma	2-1	South Vietnam	Singapore
1975	Thailand	Thailand	2-1	Malaysia	Bangkok
1977	Malaysia	Malaysia	2-0	Thailand	Kuala Lumpur
1979	Indonesia	Malaysia	1-0	Indonesia	Jakarta
1981	Philippines	Thailand	2-1	Malaysia	Manila
1983	Singapore	Thailand	2-1	Singapore	Singapore
1985	Thailand	Thailand	2-0	Singpaore	Bangkok
1987	Indonesia	Indonesia	1-0	Malaysia	Jakarta
1989	Malaysia	Malaysia	3-1	Singapore	Merdeka, Kuala Lumpur
1991	Philippines	Indonesia	0-0 4-3p	Thailand	Manila
1993	Singapore	Thailand	4-3	Myanmar	Singapore
1995	Thailand	Thailand	4-0	Vietnam	Chiang Mai
1997	Indonesia	Thailand	1-1 4-2p	Indonesia	Jakarta
1999	Brunei	Thailand	2-0	Vietnam	Bandar Seri Begawan
2001	Malaysia	Thailand	1-0	Malaysia	Kuala Lumpur
2003	Vietnam	Thailand	2-1	Vietnam	Hanoi
2005	Philippines	Thailand	3-0	Vietnam	Manila

† Gold medal shared • Until 2001 the SEA Games featured full national teams but is now a U-23 event

FOOTBALL TOURNAMENT OF THE EAST ASIAN GAMES

Year	Host Country	Winners	Score	Runners-up	Venue
1993	China PR	Korea Republic	1-1†	Korea DPR	Shanghai
1997	Korea Republic	Korea Republic	0-1†	Japan	Pusan
2001	Japan	Japan	2-1	Australia	Nagai, Osaka
2005	Macao	China PR	1-0	Korea DPR	Macau Stadium, Macau

† Played on a league basis. The result listed is between the top two teams, both of which occurred in the last round of games

FOOTBALL TOURNAMENT OF THE WEST ASIAN GAMES

Year	Host Country	Winners	Score	Runners-up	Venue
1997	Iran	Iran			Tehran
2002	Kuwait	Kuwait	0-0†	Iran	Al Qadisiya, Kuwait
2005	Qatar	Iraq	2-2 4-3p	Syria	Doha

† Played on a league basis. The result listed is between the top two teams which occurred in the last round of games. Syria shared second place

FOOTBALL TOURNAMENT OF THE SOUTH ASIAN GAMES

Year	Host Country	Winners	Score	Runners-up	Venue
1984	Nepal	Nepal	4-2	Bangladesh	Dasharath Rangashala, Kathmandu
1985	Bangladesh	India	1-1 4-1p	Bangladesh	Dhaka
1987	India	India	1-0	Nepal	Salt Lake, Calcutta
1989	Pakistan	Pakistan	1-0	Bangladesh	Islamabad
1991	Sri Lanka	Pakistan	2-0	Maldives	Colombo
1993	Bangladesh	Nepal	2-2 4-3p	India	Dhaka
1995	India	India	1-0	Bangladesh	Madras
1999	Nepal	Bangladesh	1-0	Nepal	Dasharath Rangashala, Kathmandu
2004	Pakistan	Pakistan	1-0	India	Jinnah Stadium, Islamabad
2006	Sri Lanka	Oakistan	1-0	Sri Lanka	Colombo

Football tournaments as part of regional games in Asia can trace their roots back to 1911 when the Far East Olympics were first held. That tournament saw the first international match ever played on Asian soil when the Philippines beat China 2-1 in Manila. The football tournament of the SEA Games is the longest established of the current tournaments, dating back to 1959, followed by the South Asian Games in 1984. The football tournaments of the East Asian Games and the West Asian Games are relative newcomers, having first been played in the 1990s.

ASIAN CHAMPIONS CUP AND AFC CHAMPIONS LEAGUE FINALS

Year	Winners	Country	Score	Country	Runners-up
1967	Hapoel Tel Aviv	ISR	2-1	MAS	Selangor
1968	Maccabi Tel Aviv	ISR	1-0	KOR	Yangzee
1970	Taj Club	IRN	2-1	ISR	Hapoel Tel Aviv
1971	Maccabi Tel Aviv	ISR	W-O	IRQ	Police Club
1986	Daewoo Royals	KOR	3-1	KSA	Al Ahly
1987	Furukawa	JPN	4-3	KSA	Al Hilal
1988	Yomiuri	JPN	W-O	KSA	Al Hilal
1989	Al Saad	QAT	2-3 1-0	IRQ	Al Rasheed
1990	Liaoning	CHN	2-1 1-1	JPN	Nissan
1991	Esteghlal SC	IRN	2-1	CHN	Liaoning
1992	Al Hilal	KSA	1-1 4-3p	IRN	Esteghlal SC
1993	Pas	IRN	1-0	KSA	Al Shabab
1994	Thai Farmers Bank	THA	2-1	OMA	Omani Club
1995	Thai Farmers Bank	THA	1-0	QAT	Al Arabi
1996	Ilhwa Chunma	KOR	1-0	KSA	Al Nasr
1997	Pohang Steelers	KOR	2-1	KOR	Ilhwa Chunma
1998	Pohang Steelers	KOR	0-0 6-5p	CHN	Dalian
1999	Jubilo Iwata	JPN	2-1	IRN	Esteghlal SC
2000	Al Hilal	KSA	3-2	JPN	Jubilo Iwata
2001	Suwon Samsung Bluewings	KOR	1-0	JPN	Jubilo Iwata
2002	Suwon Samsung Bluewings	KOR	0-0 4-2p	KOR	Anyang LG Cheetahs
2003	Al Ain	UAE	2-0 0-1	THA	BEC Tero Sasana
2004	Al Ittihad	KSA	1-3 5-0	KOR	Seongnam Ilhwa Chunma
2005	Al Ittihad	KSA	1-1 4-2	UAE	Al Ain
2006	Jeonbuk Hyundai Motors	KOR	2-0 1-2	SYR	Al Karama

AFC CUP

Year	Winners	Country	Score	Country	Runners-up
2004	Al Jaish	SYR	3-2 0-1	SYR	Al Wahda
2005	Al Faysali	JOR	1-0 3-2	LIB	Al Nejmeh
2006	Al Faysali	JOR	3-0 2-4	BHR	Muharraq

AFC PRESIDENT'S CUP

Year	Winners	Country	Score	Country	Runners-up
2005	Regar TadAZ	TJK	3-0	KGZ	Dordoy-Dinamo
2006	Dordoy-Dinamo	KGZ	2-1	TJK	Vakhsh

ASIAN CUP WINNERS' CUP FINALS

Year	Winners	Country	Score	Country	Runners-up
1991	Pirouzi	IRN	0-0 1-0	BHR	Al Muharraq
1992	Nissan	JPN	1-1 5-0	KSA	Al Nasr
1993	Nissan	JPN	1-1 1-0	IRN	Pirouzi
1994	Al-Qadisiyah	KSA	4-2 2-0	HKG	South China
1995	Yokohama Flugels	JPN	2-1	UAE	Al Shaab
1996	Bellmare Hiratsuka	JPN	2-1	IRQ	Al Talaba
1997	Al Hilal	KSA	3-1	JPN	Nagoya Grampus Eight
1998	Al Nasr	KSA	1-0	KOR	Suwon Samsung Bluewings
1999	Al Ittihad	KSA	3-2	KOR	Chunnam Dragons
2000	Shimizu S-Pulse	JPN	1-0	IRQ	Al Zawra
2001	Al Shabab	KSA	4-2	CHN	Dalian Shide
2002	Al Hilal	KSA	2-1	KOR	Chonbuk Hyundai Motors

Discontinued after 2002 following the creation of the AFC Champions League

As part of his bold Vision Asia development strategy, AFC President Mohamed bin Hammam has placed the growth of club football at the heart of his plan to raise standards in the game across the continent. The launch of the AFC Champions League in 2002 was a key element and it replaced both the old Asian Champion Team's Cup and Asian Cup Winners' Cup. Entry to the AFC Champions League is restricted to the top tier of nations where club football was seen as most developed. In order to foster development in the other nations, two new competitions were also introduced - the AFC Cup and the President's Cup, with the former open to middle ranking nations and the latter for countries where football is least developed. These two tournaments aimed at increasing the competitive nature of the club game by holding out the real prospect of honours for nations unlikely ever to win the Champions League. Historically Saudi Arabian and Korean clubs have been the most successful in the Champions Teams' Cup and the AFC Champions League with 11 titles between them, while Iran, Japan and China PR have underachieved given the strength of their domestic leagues. No team has ever won the title more than twice.

AFC CHAMPIONS LEAGUE MEDALS TABLE

	Country	G	S	B	F	SF
1	Korea Republic	7	4	4	11	18
2	Saudi Arabia	4	5	1	9	10
3	Japan	3	3	2	6	9
4	Iran	3	2	5	5	12
5	Israel	3	1		4	4
6	Thailand	2	1	1	3	4
7	China PR	1	2	3	3	8
8	UAE	1	1	2	2	5
9	Qatar	1	1	1	2	3
10	Iraq		2		2	4
	Syria		1	1	1	2
12	Malaysia		1		1	1
	Oman		1		1	1
14	Uzbekistan			3		4
15	Indonesia			1		3
16	Lebanon			1		1
	Korea DPR			1		1
	Kuwait			1		1
19	India					1
	Kazakstan					1
		25	25	27	50	93

This table represents the Gold (winners), Silver (runners-up) and Bronze (semi-finalists) placings of clubs representing the above countries in the AFC Champions League, along with the number of appearances in the final and semi-finals

ASIAN CHAMPIONS LEAGUE MEDALS TABLE

	Country		G	S	B
1	Esteghlal SC (Taj)	IRN	2	2	3
2	Al Hilal	KSA	2	2	1
3	Thai Farmers Bank	THA	2		1
4	Al Ittihad	KSA	2		
	Maccabi Tel Aviv	ISR	2		
	Pohang Steelers	KOR	2		
	Suwon Samsung Bluewings	KOR	2		
8	Jubilo Iwata	JPN	1	2	
	Seongnam Ilhwa Chunma	KOR	1	2	
10	Al Ain	UAE	1	1	1
	Liaoning	CHN	1	1	1
12	Hapoel Tel Aviv	ISR	1	1	
13	Busan I'Park	KOR	1		1
	Jeonbuk Hyundai Motors	KOR	1		1
	Verdy Kawasaki (Yomiuri)	JPN	1		1
16	Al Saad	QAT	1		
	JEF United (Furukawa)	JPN	1		
	Pass	IRN	1		
19	Dalian	CHN		1	1
20	Al Ahly	KSA		1	
	Al Arabi	QAT		1	
	Al Karama	SYR		1	
	Al Nasr	KSA		1	
	Al Rasheed	IRQ		1	
	Al Shabab	KSA		1	
	Anyang LG Cheetahs	KOR		1	
	BEC Tero Sasana	THA		1	
	Omani Club	OMA		1	
	Police	IRQ		1	
	Selangor	MAS		1	
	Yangzee	KOR		1	
	Yokohama Marinos (Nissan)	JPN		1	
33	Pirouzi	IRN			3
34	Pakhtakor Tashkent	UZB			2
35	Al Qadisiya	KUW			1
	Al Rayyan	QAT			1
	Al Wasl	UAE			1
	April 25th	PRK			1
	Homenetmen	LIB			1
	Neftchi Fergana	UZB			1
	Sanfrecce Hiroshima (Toyo)	JPN			1
	Shenzhen	CHN			1
	Tiga Berlian	IDN			1
	Tungsten Mining	KOR			1
	Ulsan Hyundai Horang-i	KOR			1
			25	25	27

AFC CUP MEDALS TABLE

	Country	G	S	B	F	SF
1	Jordan	2		1	2	3
2	Syria	1	1		2	2
3	Lebanon		1	1	1	2
4	Bahrain		1		1	1
5	Singapore			2		2
6	Hong Kong			1		1
7	Maldives			1		1
		3	3	6	6	12

This table represents the Gold (winners), Silver (runners-up) and Bronze (semi-finalists) placings of clubs representing the above countries in the AFC Cup, along with the number of appearances in the final and semi-finals

AFC CUP MEDALS TABLE

	Country		G	S	B
1	Al Faysali	JOR	2		
2	Al Jaish	SYR	1		
3	Al Nijmeh	LIB		1	1
4	Al Wahda	SYR		1	
	Muharraq	BHR		1	
6	Al Wahdat	JOR			1
	Geylang United	SIN			1
	Home United	SIN			1
	New Radiant	MDV			1
	Sun Hei	HKG			1
			3	3	6

AFC PRESIDENT'S CUP MEDALS TABLE

	Country	G	S	B	F	SF
1	Kyrgyzstan	1	1		2	2
	Tajikistan	1	1		2	2
3	Cambodia			1		1
	Chinese Taipei			1		1
	Nepal			1		1
	Sri Lanka			1		1
		2	2	2	4	8

This table represents the Gold (winners), Silver (runners-up) and Bronze (semi-finalists) placings of clubs representing the above countries in the AFC President's Cup, along with the number of appearances in the final and semi-finals

AFC PRESIDENT'S CUP MEDALS TABLE

	Country		G	S	B
1	Dordoy-Dinamo	KGZ	1	1	
2	Regar TadAZ	TJK	1		
3	Vakhsh Qurgonteppa	TJK		1	
4	Blue Star Club	SRI			1
	Khmera	CAM			1
	Tatung	TPE			1
	Three Star Club	NEP			1
			2	2	4

AFC ASIAN CUP 2007 QUALIFIERS

QUALIFYING GROUPS

Group A		Pts	Group B		Pts	Group C		Pts	Group D		Pts
Japan	JPN	15	Iran	IRN	14	UAE	UAE	13	Australia	AUS	9
Saudi Arabia	KSA	15	Korea Republic	KOR	11	Oman	OMA	12	Bahrain	BHR	4
Yemen	YEM	6	Syria	SYR	8	Jordan	JOR	10	Kuwait	KUW	4
India	IND	0	Chinese Taipei	TPE	0	Pakistan	PAK	0	Lebanon withdrew		

Group E		Pts	Group F		Pts
Iraq	IRQ	11	Qatar	QAT	15
China PR	CHN	11	Uzbekistan	UZB	11
Singapore	SIN	4	Hong Kong	HKG	8
Palestine	PLE	4	Bangladesh	BAN	0

Indonesia, Malaysia, Thailand and Vietnam qualified automatically as hosts • The top two in each qualifying group qualify for the finals • Bangladesh and Pakistan met in a preliminary round but both teams made it to the group stage after the withdrawl of Sri Lanka

GROUP A

	GROUP A	PL	W	D	L	F	A	GD	PTS	JPN	KSA	YEM	IND
1	Japan	6	5	0	1	15	2	+13	15		3-1	2-0	6-0
2	Saudi Arabia	6	5	0	1	21	4	+17	15	1-0		5-0	7-1
3	Yemen	6	2	0	4	5	13	-8	6	0-1	0-4		2-1
4	India	6	0	0	6	2	24	-22	0	0-3	0-3	0-3	

Salt Lake, Kolkata		
16-08-2006, 15:00, 10 000, Tongkhan THA		
IND	**0 3**	**KSA**
		Sulaimani 2,
		Yasser Al Kahtani 2 [18] [52]

INDIA		SAUDI ARABIA	
1 NANDY Sandip		KHOJAH Mohammad	42
3 NANJANGUD SHIVA. Manju		AL DOSARI Ahmed Dokhi	2
17 SINGH Irungbam Surkumar		FALLATAH Redha Tukar	3
41 PRADEEP Naduparampil	74	AL QADI Naif Ali	5
42 MANDAL Deepak Kumar		63 AL KATHRAN Abdulaziz	12
4 WADOO Mehrajuddin		SULAIMANI Hussein Abdul Gani	24
6 VENKATESH Shanmugam	86	60 AL DOSARI Saleh Bashar	43
9 SINGH Manjit		HAIDAR Mohammed	7
12 DIAS Steven		76 AL KHARIRI Saud	14
53 SINGH Renedy Potsangbam	68	AL GHAMDI Omar	37
15 BHUTIA Baichung		AL KAHTANI Yasser	20
Tr: HOUGHTON Bob		Tr: PAQUETA	
5 NAIK Samir Subash	68	63 AL GHANNAM Abdullatif	8
33 D'CUNHA CORREIA Alvito	74	76 AL MAHYANI Eysa	19
47 SARKAR Anupam	86	60 AL KWYKBI Alaa Ahmed	32

Nigata Stadium, Nigata		
16-08-2006, 19:20, 40 913, Lee Gi Young KOR		
JPN	**2 0**	**YEM**
Abe 70, Sato 91+		

JAPAN		YEMEN	
23 KAWAGUCHI Yoshikatsu		SAEED Salem	25
14 SANTOS Alessandro		SALEM Mohammed	2
20 TSUBOI Keisuke		SAEED ABDULLAH Salem	6
21 KAJI Akira		AL WADI Ahmed	13
31 KOMANO Yuichi	46	AL QOR Wasim	37
45 TANAKA Marcus Tulio		76 AL OMQY Ali	14
4 ENDO Yasuhito	71	81 AL WORAFI Akram	15
30 ABE Yuki		MUNASSAR Mohanad	16
55 SUZUKI Keita		AL WAH Mohammed	23
36 MAKI Seiichiro		AL NONO Ali	10
38 TANAKA Tatsuya	89	62 AL HUBAISHI Fekri	40
Tr: OSIM Ivica		Tr: AL RAEAI Ahmed	
37 SATO Hisato	89	76 YAHYA Radwan	9
51 HANYU Naotake	46	81 AL SHEHRI Saleh	41
57 SATO Yuto	71	62 AL MANG Mohammed	43

Prince Abdullah Al Faisal, Jeddah
3-09-2006, 20:30, 15 000, Maidin SIN

KSA **1 0** **JPN**

Saleh Al Dosari 73

SAUDI ARABIA			JAPAN		
42	KHOJAH Mohammad		KAWAGUCHI Yoshikatsu		23
2	AL DOSARI Ahmed Dokhi		SANTOS Alessandro		14
3	FALLATAH Redha Tukar		TSUBOI Keisuke		20
5	AL QADI Naif Ali		KAJI Akira		21
12	AL KATHRAN Abdulaziz	59	KOMANO Yuichi		31
24	SULAIMANI Hussein Abdul Gani		TANAKA Marcus Tulio		45
43	AL DOSARI Saleh Bashar		ENDO Yasuhito		4
7	HAIDAR Mohammed		ABE Yuki		30
14	AL KHARIRI Saud		81	SUZUKI Keita		55
19	AL MAHYANI Eysa	71	74	MAKI Seiichiro		36
37	AL GHAMDI Omar	46	66	TANAKA Tatsuya		38
	Tr: PAQUETA			Tr: OSIM Ivica		
27	AUTEF Abdoh	59	66	SATO Hisato		37
31	AL SUWAILH Ahmed	71	81	HANYU Naotake		51
46	AL HAGBANI Bader	46	74	GANAHA Kazuki		65

Ali Moshen, Sana'a
6-09-2006, 15:20, 7000, Al Ghatrifi OMA

YEM **0 1** **JPN**

Ganaha 91+

YEMEN			JAPAN		
25	SAEED Salem		KAWAGUCHI Yoshikatsu		23
2	SALEM Mohammed		SANTOS Alessandro		14
6	SAEED ABDULLAH Salem		TSUBOI Keisuke		20
13	AL WADI Ahmed		KAJI Akira		21
37	AL QOR Wasim		TANAKA Marcus Tulio		45
14	AL OMQY Ali	77	ENDO Yasuhito		4
15	AL WORAFI Akram		ABE Yuki		30
16	MUNASSAR Mohanad		73	HANYU Naotake		51
23	AL WAH Mohammed	84	SUZUKI Keita		55
41	AL SHEHRI Saleh	46	93	MAKI Seiichiro		36
10	AL NONO Ali		46	TANAKA Tatsuya		38
	Tr: AL RAEAI Ahmed			Tr: OSIM Ivica		
9	YAHYA Radwan	77	46	SATO Hisato		37
26	BASUHAI Yaser	46	73	GANAHA Kazuki		65
43	AL MANG Mohammed	84	93	UMESAKI Tsukasa		72

Prince Abdullah Al Faisal, Jeddah
6-09-2006, 20:30, 3000, Al Saeedi UAE

KSA **7 1** **IND**

Saleh Al Dosari 2 31 46, Al Mahyani 34, Haidar 57, Nanjangud 22
Al Hagbani 62, Al Suwailh 2 79 86

SAUDI ARABIA			INDIA		
42	KHOJAH Mohammad		NANDY Sandip		1
3	FALLATAH Redha Tukar		81	NANJANGUD SHIVA. Manju		3
5	AL QADI Naif Ali		SINGH Irungbam Surkumar		17
24	SULAIMANI Hussein Abdul Gani		PRADEEP Naduparampil		41
43	AL DOSARI Saleh Bashar	53	MANDAL Deepak Kumar		42
45	FALLATAH Hassan		SARKAR Anupam		47
7	HAIDAR Mohammed	65	WADOO Mehrajuddin		4
14	AL KHARIRI Saud		64	SINGH Manjit		9
19	AL MAHYANI Eysa	77	DIAS Steven		12
27	AUTEF Abdoh		SINGH Renedy Potsangbam		53
46	AL HAGBANI Bader		BHUTIA Baichung		15
	Tr: PAQUETA			Tr: HOUGHTON Bob		
31	AL SUWAILH Ahmed	77	64	NABI Syed Rahim		10
32	AL KWYKBI Alaa Ahmed	53	81	KUMAR MARIA Sanjeev		23
33	AL MOWALLAD Moh'd Massad	65			

Sree Kanterava, Bangalore
11-10-2006, 17:40, 5000, Chan Siu Kee HKG

IND **0 3** **JPN**

Bando 2 22 43, Nakamura 81

INDIA			JAPAN		
1	NANDY Sandip		KAWAGUCHI Yoshikatsu		23
3	NANJANGUD SHIVA. Manju		SANTOS Alessandro		14
17	SINGH Irungbam Surkumar		KOMANO Yuichi		31
23	KUMAR MARIA Sanjeev		46	MIZUMOTO Hiroki		69
41	PRADEEP Naduparampil		KONNO Yasuyuki		26
42	MANDAL Deepak Kumar	14	ABE Yuki		30
6	VENKATESH Shanmugam	84	NAKAMURA Kengo		53
9	SINGH Manjit	66	SUZUKI Keita		55
12	DIAS Steven		YAMAGISHI Satoshi		60
53	SINGH Renedy Potsangbam		65	MAKI Seiichiro		36
15	BHUTIA Baichung		68	BANDO Ryuji		74
	Tr: HOUGHTON Bob			Tr: OSIM Ivica		
33	D'CUNHA CORREIA Alvito	84	46	HASEBE Makoto		35
47	SARKAR Anupam	14	68	SATO Hisato		37
58	CHHETRI Sunil	66	65	GANAHA Kazuki		65

Prince Abdullah Al Faisal, Jeddah
11-10-2006, 22:15, 1500, Abdul Kadir Nema IRQ

KSA **5 0** **YEM**

Saleh Al Dosari 22, Haidar 27,
Fallatah 66, Al Mahyani 2 68 92+

SAUDI ARABIA			YEMEN		
21	ZAID Mabrouk		SAEED Salem		25
4	AL MONTASHARI Hamad		SALEM Mohammed		2
5	AL QADI Naif Ali	68	73	SAEED ABDULLAH Salem		6
24	SULAIMANI Hussein Abdul Gani		AL WADI Ahmed		13
43	AL DOSARI Saleh Bashar	65	AL QOR Wasim		37
45	FALLATAH Hassan		74	AL OMQY Ali		14
7	HAIDAR Mohammed		AL WORAFI Akram		15
19	AL MAHYANI Eysa		MUNASSAR Mohanad		16
46	AL HAGBANI Bader		AL WAH Mohammed		23
49	AL DOSSARI Abdullah	76	AL NONO Ali		10
10	AL SHALHOUB Mohammed		85	BASUHAI Yaser		26
	Tr: PAQUETA			Tr: AL RAEAI Ahmed		
15	AL BAHRI Ahmed	76	74	YAHYA Radwan		9
31	AL SUWAILH Ahmed	65	85	AL SHEHRI Saleh		41
47	HAWSAWI Osama	68	73	AL TAHESH Khaled		42

Ali Moshen, Sana'a
15-11-2006, 16:00, 5500, Marshoud JOR

YEM **2 1** **IND**

Al Haggam 60, Al Nono 82 — Pradeep 54

YEMEN			INDIA		
1	ABDULWALI Muaad		NANDY Sandip		1
5	AL BAADANI Yaser		NANJANGUD SHIVA. Manju		3
6	SAEED ABDULLAH Salem		RAHMAN Habibur Mondal		30
13	AL WADI Ahmed		PRADEEP Naduparampil		41
14	AL OMQY Ali		5	SINGH Narinder		48
16	MUNASSAR Mohanad		ROY Debabrata		51
41	AL SHEHRI Saleh	69	81	SINGH Manjit		9
43	AL MANG Mohammed	47	DIAS Steven		12
8	AL TAHOOS Mohammed	58	SINGH Goura. Moirangthem		61
10	AL NONO Ali	71	NABI Syed Rahim		10
29	AL HAGGAM Nashwan		BHUTIA Baichung		15
	Tr: AL RAEAI Ahmed			Tr: HOUGHTON Bob		
15	AL WORAFI Akram	47	5	SINGH Irungbam Surkumar		17
37	AL QOR Wasim	58	81	SAIKH Tarif Ahamed		59
38	OMAR Awsam	69	71	SINGH Bungo Thokchom		63

Sapporo Dome, Sapporo
15-11-2006, 19:00, 40 965, Shield AUS

JPN 3 1 KSA

Tanaka [20], Ganaha 2 [29 50]   Al Qahtani [33p]

JAPAN		SAUDI ARABIA	
23	KAWAGUCHI Yoshikatsu		AL MOSAILEM Yasser 41
14	SANTOS Alessandro 65	77	AL DOSARI Ahmed Dokhi 2
21	KAJI Akira		FALLATAH Redha Tukar 3
31	KOMANO Yuichi	92	AL MONTASHARI Hamad 4
45	TANAKA Marcus Tulio		SULAIMANI Hussein Abdul Gani 24
26	KONNO Yasuyuki	63	HAIDAR Mohammed 7
30	ABE Yuki		AL THAKER Khaled Aziz 16
53	NAKAMURA Kengo	56	AL MAHYANI Eysa 19
55	SUZUKI Keita		AL GHAMDI Omar 37
36	MAKI Seiichiro 87		AL SAQRI Saleh 51
65	GANAHA Kazuki 74		AL KAHTANI Yasser 20
	Tr: OSIM Ivica		Tr: PAQUETA
51	HANYU Naotake 87	63	AL SHALHOUB Mohammed 10
60	YAMAGISHI Satoshi 65	56	AL SUWAILH Ahmed 31
80	TAKAMATSU Daiki 74	77	FALLATAH Hassan 45

GROUP B

GROUP B		PL	W	D	L	F	A	GD	PTS	IRN	KOR	SYR	TPE
1	Iran	6	4	2	0	12	2	+10	14		2-0	1-1	4-0
2	Korea Republic	6	3	2	1	15	5	+10	11	1-1		1-1	8-0
3	Syria	6	2	2	2	10	6	+4	8	0-2	1-2		3-0
4	Chinese Taipei	6	0	0	6	0	24	-24	0	0-2	0-3	0-4	

Chungsan, Taipei
16-08-2006, 18:00, 1300, Sarkar IND

TPE 0 3 KOR

Ahn Jung Hwan [32], Jung Jo Gook [55],
Kim Do Heon [81]

CHINESE TAIPEI		KOREA REPUBLIC	
1	LU Kun Chi		KIM Young Kwang 31
2	KAO Hao Chieh		KIM Jin Kyu 6
4	KUO Chun Yi		JANG Hack Young 11
24	LIN Che Min 73		KIM Sang Sik 13
45	TU Chu Hsien		KIM Nam Il 7
6	FENG Pao Hsing		SONG Chong Gug 12
23	LIANG Chien Wei 87	92	KIM Jung Woo 15
43	LIN Tsung Jen		LEE Eul Yong 38
19	CHUANG Wei Lun	65	LEE Chun Soo 14
30	CHEN Po Liang		JUNG Jo Gook 19
42	HUANG Wei Yi 85	71	AHN Jung Hwan 37
	Tr: IMAI Toshiaki		Tr: VERBEEK Peter
28	LEE Yu Shan 85	71	KIM Do Heon 8
29	HSIEH Meng Hsuan 73	65	PARK Chu Young 10
41	CHIANG Shih Lu 87	92	OH Beom Seok 30

Azadi, Tehran
16-08-2006, 18:00, 40 000, Irmatov UZB

IRN 1 1 SYR

Nekounam [72]   Chaabo [88]

IRAN		SYRIA	
30	TALEBLOO Vahid		BALHOWSS Mowsaab 25
28	SADEGHI Amirhossein		MOHAMMAD Rafat 2
41	SHAKOURI Hadi		JENYAT Aatef 13
2	MAHDAVIKIA Mehdi 68		DYAB Ali 30
6	NEKOUNAM Javad		AL JABBAN Tarek 33
11	VAHEDI NIKBAKHT Alireza		MANSOR AL BABA Khaled 36
24	TIMOTIAN Andranik	66	AL ALMENA Mahmoud 8
36	MADANCHI Mehrzad 69	77	AL RACHED Moh'd Yhya 19
16	ENAYATI Gholamreza	84	ALAYA Mootassem 21
40	PAKIKHATIBI Rasoul 87		AL SAYAD Maher 9
45	FEKRI JOYBARI Mahmoud		CHAABO Zyad 20
	Tr: GHALEHNCY Ardeshir		Tr: IBRAHIM Fajr
17	MOBALI Iman 69	77	AL HAJ Majed 14
23	KAZEMIAN Javad 68	66	AYAN Wael 34
47	KAZEMI Hossein 87	84	TARAB Bakri 38

World Cup Stadium, Seoul
2-09-2006, 20:00, 63 113, Breeze AUS

KOR 1 1 IRN

Seol Ki Hyeon [46]
Hashemian [93+]

KOREA REPUBLIC				IRAN
31	KIM Young Kwang			MIRZAPOUR Ebrahim 1
3	KIM Dong Jin			REZAEI Rahman 5
13	KIM Sang Sik			NOSRATI Mohammad 20
17	LEE Ho			MAHDAVIKIA Mehdi 2
7	KIM Nam Il			NEKOUNAM Javad 6
8	KIM Do Heon	79		KARIMI Ali 8
12	SONG Chong Gug	81	68	VAHEDI NIKBAKHT Alireza 11
33	PARK Ji Sung		90	TIMOTIAN Andranik 24
34	LEE Young Pyo		55	MADANCHI Mehrzad 36
9	CHO Jae Jin			HASHEMIAN Vahid 9
35	SEOL Ki Hyeon			FEKRI JOYBARI Mahmoud 45
	Tr: VERBEEK Peter			Tr: GHALEHNCY Ardeshir
23	CHO Won Hee	81	68	KAEBI Hossein 13
38	LEE Eul Yong	79	90	AKBARPOUR Siyavash 29
			55	MAJIDI Farhad 50

Abbasiyyin, Damascus
6-09-2006, 19:00, 10 000, Matsumura JPN

SYR 0 2 IRN

Nosrati [27], Nekounam [55]

SYRIA				IRAN
25	BALHOWSS Mowsaab			MIRZAPOUR Ebrahim 1
2	MOHAMMAD Rafat			REZAEI Rahman 5
13	JENYAT Aatef	14		NOSRATI Mohammad 20
30	DYAB Ali	86		MAHDAVIKIA Mehdi 2
33	AL JABBAN Tarek			NEKOUNAM Javad 6
36	MANSOR AL BABA Khaled		90	KARIMI Ali 8
6	AL HOUSSAIN Jehad			VAHEDI NIKBAKHT 11
21	ALAYA Mootassem	69		TIMOTIAN Andranik 24
9	AL SAYAD Maher		76	HASHEMIAN Vahid 9
10	AL KHATIB Firas	59		ENAYATI Gholamreza 16
20	CHAABO Zyad		28	FEKRI JOYBARI Mahmoud 45
	Tr: IBRAHIM Fajr			Tr: GHALEHNCY Ardeshir
14	AL HAJ Majed	59	28 92	SADEGHI Amirhossein 28
19	AL RACHED Moh'd Yhya	69	90	MADANCHI Mehrzad 36
34	AYAN Wael	14	76	MAJIDI Farhad 50

World Cup Stadium, Seoul
6-09-2006, 20:00, 21 053, Arambakade Gedara SRI

KOR 8 0 TPE

Seol Ki Hyeon 2 [4 43], Jung Jo Gook 3 [5 46+ 88],
Cho Jae Jin 2 [64 83p], Kim Do Heon [78]

KOREA REPUBLIC				CHINESE TAIPEI
1	LEE Woon Jae			LU Kun Chi 1
3	KIM Dong Jin			KAO Hao Chieh 2
13	KIM Sang Sik			KUO Chun Yi 4
7	KIM Nam Il			CHENG Yung Jen 5
8	KIM Do Heon			LIN Che Min 24
12	SONG Chong Gug			TU Chu Hsien 45
33	PARK Ji Sung	56		FENG Pao Hsing 6
34	LEE Young Pyo	55	75	LIANG Chien Wei 23
9	CHO Jae Jin		46	HUNG Kai Chun 25
19	JUNG Jo Gook			CHIANG Shih Lu 41
35	SEOL Ki Hyeon	78		LIN Tsung Jen 43
	Tr: VERBEEK Peter			Tr: IMAI Toshiaki
11	JANG Hack Young	55	75	TAI Hung Hsu 8
21	BAEK Ji Hoon	78	46	CHUANG Wei Lun 19
40	CHOI Sung Kuk	56		

Municipal Stadium, Taipei
11-10-2006, 18:00, 2000, Shamsuzzaman BAN

TPE 0 2 IRN

Karimi 2 [11 58]

CHINESE TAIPEI				IRAN
1	LU Kun Chi			RODBARIAN Hassan 12
2	KAO Hao Chieh	75		REZAEI Rahman 5
4	KUO Chun Yi		60	KAEBI Hossein 13
5	CHENG Yung Jen			NOSRATI Mohammad 20
33	CHEN Yu Lin			MAHDAVIKIA Mehdi 2
45	TU Chu Hsien			NEKOUNAM Javad 6
6	FENG Pao Hsing			KARIMI Ali 8
7	HUANG Cheng Tsung	84		TIMOTIAN Andranik 24
23	LIANG Chien Wei			NOURI RODSARI Pejman 56
19	CHUANG Wei Lun	69	78	ENAYATI Gholamreza 16
42	HUANG Wei Yi	76		PAKIKHATIBI Rasoul 40
	Tr: IMAI Toshiaki			Tr: GHALEHNCY Ardeshir
29	HSIEH Meng Hsuan	84	60	KAZEMIAN Javad 23
30	CHEN Po Liang	76	78	MAJIDI Farhad 50
41	CHIANG Shih Lu	69		

World Cup Stadium, Seoul
11-10-2006, 20:00, 24 140, Kunsuta THA

KOR 1 1 SYR

Cho Jae Jin [9]
Al Sayed [18]

KOREA REPUBLIC				SYRIA
31	KIM Young Kwang			BALHOWSS Mowsaab 25
3	KIM Dong Jin			BARAKAT Adeb 5
13	KIM Sang Sik			JENYAT Aatef 13
7	KIM Nam Il			AL KOUJA Anas 15
8	KIM Do Heon			DAKKA Abdelkader 17
12	SONG Chong Gug			AL JABBAN Tarek 33
15	KIM Jung Woo			TARAB Bakri 38
34	LEE Young Pyo			AL ALMENA Mahmoud 8
9	CHO Jae Jin			AYAN Wael 34
35	SEOL Ki Hyeon			AL SAYAD Maher 9
40	CHOI Sung Kuk			CHAABO Zyad 20
	Tr: VERBEEK Peter			Tr: IBRAHIM Fajr
				HOMSI Majd 3
				AOUAD Samer 27
				AL AGA Abdel Fatah 37

Abbasiyyin, Damascus
15-11-2006, 14:00, 1000, Al Hilali OMA

SYR 3 0 TPE

Al Jaban [50], Al Khatib 2 [61 80]

SYRIA				CHINESE TAIPEI
25	BALHOWSS Mowsaab			LU Kun Chi 1
5	BARAKAT Adeb			KUO Chun Yi 4
13	JENYAT Aatef			CHENG Yung Jen 5
17	DAKKA Abdelkader			CHEN Yu Lin 33
33	AL JABBAN Tarek			TU Chu Hsien 45
38	TARAB Bakri			FENG Pao Hsing 6
8	AL ALMENA Mahmoud	46	65	HUANG Cheng Tsung 7
21	ALAYA Mootassem			LIANG Chien Wei 23
34	AYAN Wael	85		HSIEH Meng Hsuan 29
9	AL SAYAD Maher	57		CHUANG Wei Lun 19
20	CHAABO Zyad	46	85	HUANG Wei Yi 42
	Tr: IBRAHIM Fajr			Tr: IMAI Toshiaki
6	AL HOUSSAIN Jehad	46	65	LEE Meng Chian 18
10	AL KHATIB Firas	46	85	WU Pai Ho 34
11	AL HAMWI Mohammad	85	57	CHIANG Shih Lu 41

Azadi, Tehran		
15-11-2006, 15:30, 30 000, Ebrahim BHR		
IRN	**2 0**	**KOR**

Enayati [48], Badamaki [91+]

	IRAN			KOREA REPUBLIC	
12	RODBARIAN Hassan			KIM Young Kwang	31
20	NOSRATI Mohammad			KIM Dong Jin	3
28	SADEGHI Amirhossein			KIM Jin Kyu	6
6	NEKOUNAM Javad			LEE Ho	17
8	KARIMI Ali		87	CHO Won Hee	23
11	VAHEDI NIKBAKHT Alireza		41	KIM Chi Woo	56
23	KAZEMIAN Javad	77		KIM Jung Woo	15
24	TIMOTIAN Andranik			LEE Chun Soo	14
9	HASHEMIAN Vahid	88		JUNG Jo Gook	19
16	ENAYATI Gholamreza	69	77	CHOI Sung Kuk	40
45	FEKRI JOYBARI Mahmoud			KIM Dong Hun	59
	Tr: GHALEHNCY Ardeshir			Tr: VERBEEK Peter	
40	PAKIKHATIBI Rasoul	69	87	CHO Sung Hwan	42
41	SHAKOURI Hadi	88	41	YANG Sang Min	54
57	BADAMAKI Gholamhossein	77	77	YEOM Ki Hun	58

GROUP C

	GROUP C	PL	W	D	L	F	A	GD	PTS	UAE	OMA	JOR	PAK
1	United Arab Emirates	6	4	1	1	11	6	+5	13		1-0	0-0	3-2
2	Oman	6	4	0	2	14	6	+8	12	2-1		3-0	5-0
3	Jordan	6	3	1	2	10	5	+5	10	1-2	3-0		3-0
4	Pakistan	6	0	0	6	4	22	-18	0	1-4	1-4	0-3	

Jinnah Stadium, Islamabad		
16-08-2006, 19:00, 4000, Torky IRN		
PAK	**1 4**	**OMA**

Essa [79p]

Bader Mubarak 2 [15p 35],
Amad Ali [27], Al Ajmi [90]

	PAKISTAN			OMAN	
1	KHAN Jaffar			AL MAZROEI Suleiman	41
2	AKRAM Mohd Naveed		80	AL WAHAIBI Juma Abdullah	3
5	ISHAQ Samar			AL RAGADI Said Ashoon	4
14	IMRAN Mohammed			AL GHEILANI Hasan Yousuf	17
27	AHMED Tanveer			AL MUKHAINI Moh'd Hamed	6
8	SHAH Farooq	70		AL MUKHAINI Ahmed Hadid	21
11	AZIZ Abdul			AL NAUFALI Khalifa Ayil	25
29	AHMED Saeed	36	87	AL MAIMANI Badar Mubarak	8
32	AHMED Adeel			AL AJMI Ismail	15
35	MASIH Akram	47	73	AL HINAI Mohamed Mubarak	16
10	ESSA Muhammad			AL HOSNI Amad Ali	20
	Tr: SHAREEDA Salman			Tr: MACALA Milan	
7	HAMEED Zahid	36	73	AL BALUSHI Hashim	9
30	AHMED Shahid	47	87	AL BUSAIDY Yousuf Shaaban	11
33	RASOOL Muhammad	70	80	AL FARSI Ali	42

International Stadium, Amman		
16-08-2006, 18 000, Al Hamdan KSA		
JOR	**1 2**	**UAE**

Rafat Ali [88]

Omar [52], Subait Khater [68]

	JORDAN			UAE	
1	SABBAH Amer Shafi			AL BADRANI Waleed Salem	17
5	KHAMEES Mohammad			SALEH Mohammed Khamis	3
6	BANI YASEEN Bashar			MOHAMED Haidar Ali	8
16	SULEIMAN Faisal Ibrahim			AL BALOOSHI Mohamed Qassim	25
18	MAHMOUD Hasan Abdel	55		AL RADIMI Adil Abdelaziz	35
37	MATALKA Ala			AL JENAIBI Ab'raheem Jumaa	2
4	ABU ALIEH Qusai			AL JUNAIBI Ismaeil Matar	10
7	KHALIL Amer Deeb			AL SAEDI Helal Saeed	12
13	JABER Rafat Ali		66	AL DARMAKI Nawaf Mubarak	32
21	IBRAHIM Ahmad Hayel	70	75	AHMED Mohammed Omar	7
31	MANSOUR Mooyad Salim		85	AL JUNAIBI Faisal Khalil	11
	Tr: EL GOHARY Mahmoud			Tr: METSU Bruno	
10	ABU KESHEK Moayad	55	85	AL KAS Saeed Hassan	19
29	AL TALL Siraj	70	75	AL ABADLA Salem Saad	23
			66	AL MEKHAINI Subait Khater	24

Al Shabab, Dubai
6-09-2006, 19:15, 9000, Al Fadhli KUW

UAE 0 0 JOR

UAE			JORDAN		
17	AL BADRANI Waleed Salem		SABBAH Amer Shafi	1	
14	AL HAMMADI Basheer Saeed		AL MALTA'AH Khaled	3	
21	MAJEED Humaid Fakher		KHAMEES Mohammad	5	
25	AL BALOOSHI Mohamed Qassim		BANI YASEEN Bashar	6	
35	AL RADIMI Adil Abdelaziz		SULEIMAN Faisal Ibrahim	16	
2	AL JENAIBI Ab'raheem Jumaa		OTHMAN Basem Fathi	23	
10	AL JUNAIBI Ismaeil Matar		ABU ALIEH Qusai	4	
12	AL SAEDI Helal Saeed		KHALIL Amer Deeb	7	
24	AL MEKHAINI Subait Khater	57	SHEIKH QASEM Hassouneh	8	
7	AHMED Mohammed Omar	66	60	JABER Rafat Ali	13
23	AL ABADLA Salem Saad	71	73	MANSOUR Moayad Salim	31
	Tr: METSU Bruno		Tr: EL GOHARY Mahmoud		
11	AL JUNAIBI Faisal Khalil	66	73	AL TALL Siraj	29
18	AL WEHAIBI Ali	71	60	AL MAHARMEH Abdelhadi	50
32	AL DARMAKI Nawaf Mubarak	57			

Sultan Qaboos, Muscat
6-09-2006, 20:00, 10 000, Abdul Kadir Nema IRQ

OMA 5 0 PAK

Amad Ali [7], Fawzi Bashir 2 [36] [58],
Al Ajmi [47+], Al Touqi [88]

OMAN			PAKISTAN		
26	AL HABSI Ali Abdulla		KHAN Jaffar	1	
2	AL NOOBI Mohamed Rabia		ISHAQ Samar	5	
3	AL WAHAIBI Juma Abdullah		IMRAN Mohammed	14	
4	AL RAGADI Said Ashoon		AHMED Tanveer	27	
17	AL GHEILANI Hasan Yousuf	68	IRFAN Muhammad	47	
12	AL MAHAURI Ahmed Mubarak		65	HAMEED Zahid	7
21	AL MUKHAINI Ahmed Hadid		AZIZ Abdul	11	
8	AL MAIMANI Badar Mubarak		AHMED Saeed	29	
10	DOORBEEN Fawzi Bashir		AHMED Adeel	32	
15	AL AJMI Ismail	83	65	ALI Abbas	45
20	AL HOSNI Amad Ali	75	ESSA Muhammad	10	
	Tr: MACALA Milan		Tr: SHAREEDA Salman		
7	AL TOUQI Mohamed Sultan	83	65	AKRAM Mohd Naveed	2
14	AL MUSHAIFRI Younis Khalifa	75	65	NIAZI Imran	46
16	AL HINAI Mohamed Mubarak	68			

Punjab Stadium, Lahore
11-10-2006, 21:00, 4000, Orzuev TJK

PAK 0 3 JOR

Al Maharmeh [16], Rafat Ali [37],
Khaled Saed [85]

PAKISTAN			JORDAN		
48	SHAHZAD Muhammad		SABBAH Amer Shafi	1	
5	ISHAQ Samar		AL MALTA'AH Khaled	3	
14	IMRAN Mohammed		KHAMEES Mohammad	5	
27	AHMED Tanveer		SULEIMAN Faisal Ibrahim	16	
44	AHMED Ejaz		88	MAHMOUD Hasan Abdel	18
32	AHMED Adeel	71	OTHMAN Basem Fathi	23	
43	HUSSAIN Mubashar		ABU HASHHASH Shadi	45	
46	NIAZI Imran	75	KHALIL Amer Deeb	7	
10	ESSA Muhammad		SHEIKH QASEM Hassouneh	8	
30	AHMED Shahid	46	JABER Rafat Ali	13	
33	RASOOL Muhammad		72	AL MAHARMEH Abdelhadi	50
	Tr: SHAREEDA Salman		Tr: EL GOHARY Mahmoud		
9	HUSSAIN Imran	71	88	AL SHUAIBI Amjad	15
16	WASEEM Muhammad	46	72	MANSOUR Moayad Salim	31
45	ALI Abbas	75			

Sultan Qaboos, Muscat
11-10-2006, 22:00, 28 000, Huang Junjie CHN

OMA 2 1 UAE

Hassan Yousuf [24], Al Ajmi [28]   Omar [57]

OMAN			UAE		
26	AL HABSI Ali Abdulla		AL BADRANI Waleed Salem	17	
2	AL NOOBI Mohamed Rabia		SALEH Mohammed Khamis	3	
4	AL RAGADI Said Ashoon		84	MOHAMED Haidar Ali	8
17	AL GHEILANI Hasan Yousuf		AL BALOOSHI Mohamed Qassim	25	
12	AL MAHAURI Ahmed Mubarak		AL RADIMI Adil Abdelaziz	35	
21	AL MUKHAINI Ahmed Hadid	65	AL JENAIBI Ab'raheem Jumaa	2	
25	AL NAUFALI Khalifa Ayil		AL HAWASIN Ali Abbas	5	
8	AL MAIMANI Badar Mubarak	91	77	AL JUNAIBI Ismaeil Matar	10
10	DOORBEEN Fawzi Bashir	85	64	AL DARMAKI Nawaf Mubarak	32
15	AL AJMI Ismail		AHMED Mohammed Omar	7	
20	AL HOSNI Amad Ali		AL JUNAIBI Faisal Khalil	11	
	Tr: MACALA Milan		Tr: METSU Bruno		
5	MUSTAHIL RABIA Hussain	91	84	MAJEED Humaid Fakher	21
7	AL TOUQI Mohamed Sultan	65	77	AL ABADLA Salem Saad	23
16	AL HINAI Mohamed Mubarak	85	64	AL MEKHAINI Subait Khater	24

International Stadium, Amman
15-11-2006, 17:00, 3000, Najm LIB

JOR 3 0 OMA

Amer Deeb [80], Rafat Ali [83],
Al Shiekh [87]

JORDAN			OMAN		
1	SABBAH Amer Shafi		AL MAZROEI Suleiman	41	
3	AL MALTA'AH Khaled		AL NOOBI Mohamed Rabia	2	
5	KHAMEES Mohammad		AL RAGADI Said Ashoon	4	
6	BANI YASEEN Bashar		AL TOUQI Mohamed Sultan	7	
16	SULEIMAN Faisal Ibrahim	71	AL MAHAURI Ahmed Mubarak	12	
23	OTHMAN Basem Fathi		AL MUKHAINI Ahmed Hadid	21	
4	ABU ALIEH Qusai		AL NAUFALI Khalifa Ayil	25	
7	KHALIL Amer Deeb		64	AL MAIMANI Badar Mubarak	8
8	SHEIKH QASEM Hassouneh		DOORBEEN Fawzi Bashir	10	
13	JABER Rafat Ali		AL AJMI Ismail	15	
50	AL MAHARMEH Abdelhadi		75	AL GHAILANI Ibrahim	29
	Tr: EL GOHARY Mahmoud		Tr: MACALA Milan		
31	MANSOUR Moayad Salim	71	64	AL HINAI Mohamed Mubarak	16
			75	AL MAGHNI Hassan Zaher	27

Mohamed Bin Zayid, Abu Dhabi
15-11-2006, 18:15, 6000, Sarkar IND

UAE 3 2 PAK

Ali Abbas [54], Omar 2 [58] [72]   Naveed Akram [22],
Tanveer Ahmed [67]

UAE			PAKISTAN		
30	MAQDEMI Majed Naser		KHAN Jaffar	1	
3	AL AREEFI Saleh Obaid	62	AKRAM Mohd Naveed	2	
13	AL AREEFI Saleh Obaid		ISHAQ Samar	5	
21	MAJEED Humaid Fakher		IMRAN Mohammed	14	
25	AL BALOOSHI Mohamed Qassim		AHMED Tanveer	27	
5	AL HAWASIN Ali Abbas		AZIZ Abdul	11	
10	AL JUNAIBI Ismaeil Matar		52	AHMED Adeel	32
26	ALEM Salem Kahmis		75	HUSSAIN Mubashar	43
43	AL BALOOSHI Hasan Ali		ALI Abbas	45	
48	AL BALOOSHI Khaled Darwish	76	NIAZI Imran	46	
7	AHMED Mohammed Omar	80	ESSA Muhammad	10	
	Tr: METSU Bruno		Tr: SHAREEDA Salman		
23	AL ABADLA Salem Saad	80	75	WASEEM Muhammad	16
27	AL SAEEDI Yousef Abdulaziz	76	52	RASOOL Muhammad	33
33	BIN MADI Faisal Ali	62			

GROUP D

GROUP D	PL	W	D	L	F	A	GD	PTS	AUS	BHR	KUW	LIB
1 Australia	4	3	0	1	7	3	+4	9		2-0	2-0	
2 Bahrain	4	1	1	2	3	6	-3	4	1-3		2-1	
3 Kuwait	4	1	1	2	3	4	-1	4	2-0	0-0		
4 Lebanon					Withdrew						1-1	

Aussie Stadium, Sydney
16-08-2006, 19:30, 32 000, Huang Junjie CHN

AUS 2 0 KUW

Dodd [75], Petrovski [86]

AUSTRALIA				KUWAIT	
51	BOLTON Clint			AL KHALDI Nawaf	22
27	CECCOLI Alvin			ABDULLAH Yaqoub	2
33	MILLIGAN Mark			AL SHAMARI Nohayr	5
35	NORTH Jade			AL EIDAN Ahmad	12
38	VALKANIS Michael			SHAHEEN Fahad	30
46	MUSCAT Kevin			AL DAWOOD Abdul Rahman	8
44	CORICA Steve	90		AL ATAIQI Jarah	18
45	DODD Travis		88	AL MUTAIRI Nawaf	19
19	WILKSHIRE Luke	56	79	AL MUTAIRI Khalaf	10
22	THOMPSON Archie	69		AL MUTWA Bader	17
30	CARNEY Dave		84	AL HAMAD Fahad	20
	Tr: ARNOLD Graham			Tr: STOICHITA Mihai	
28	BROSQUE Alex	69	79	JUMAH Walied	15
29	PETROVSKI Saso	56	88	AL OTAIBI Nawaf	38
49	MCKAY Matt	90	84	AL RASHIDI Fahad Aidh	46

Kuwait SC, Kuwait City
6-09-2006, 20:30, 8000, Kamikawa JPN

KUW 2 0 AUS

Khalaf Al Mutairi [55], Al Mutwa [60]

KUWAIT				AUSTRALIA	
22	AL KHALDI Nawaf			SCHWARZER Mark	1
2	ABDULLAH Yaqoub			MILICEVIC Ljubo	24
5	AL SHAMARI Nohayr			BEAUCHAMP Michael	26
12	AL EIDAN Ahmad			MCKAIN Jonathan	36
30	SHAHEEN Fahad	38		SKOKO Josip	8
8	AL DAWOOD Abdul Rahman			CHIPPERFIELD Scott	14
18	AL ATAIQI Jarah		62	WILKSHIRE Luke	20
19	AL MUTAIRI Nawaf		30	ELRICH Ahmad	21
10	AL MUTAIRI Khalaf	82		STERJOVSKI Mile	39
17	AL MUTWA Bader			ALOISI John	15
20	AL HAMAD Fahad	40		HOLMAN Brett	25
	Tr: STOICHITA Mihai			Tr: ARNOLD Graham	
4	AL HAJERI Naser	82	62	MCDONALD Scott	31
15	JUMAH Walied	38	30	GRIFFITHS Ryan	60
49	SAEED Farag	49			

Aussie Stadium, Sydney
11-10-2006, 19:30, 37 000, Al Marzouqi UAE

AUS 2 0 BHR

Aloisi [17], Bresciano [23]

AUSTRALIA			BAHRAIN	
1	SCHWARZER Mark		SABT ABBAS Sayed Mohd	21
2	NEILL Lucas		AL CHUBAN Jasim	32
26	BEAUCHAMP Michael		MESHKHAS Ebrahim	40
4	CAHILL Tim	81	AYYAD Abbas	53
7	EMERTON Brett		AAISH Faouzi Mubraken	25
13	GRELLA Vince		MUSAIFER Ali Aamer	27
14	CHIPPERFIELD Scott		ABDUL RAHMAN Mahmood	43
17	CULINA Jason	61	MOHAMED Mahmood	49
23	BRESCIANO Marco	67 68	AL SHEKAR Husain	51
39	STERJOVSKI Mile	75	AYYAD Mahmood Abbas	52
15	ALOISI John	88	HASAN Ismaeel	28
	Tr: ARNOLD Graham		Tr: KRESO Senad	
8	SKOKO Josip	81 68	MAHMOOD Mohamed Noordin	38
22	THOMPSON Archie	75 88	AL MUQLA Ebrahim	44
45	DODD Travis	67 61	HASAN Fahad Al Hardan	46

National Stadium, Manama
15-11-2006, 18:00, 20 000, Kwon Jong Chul KOR

BHR 2 1 KUW

Talal Yusuf [34], Salman Issa [43]   Faraj Laheeb [70]

BAHRAIN				KUWAIT	
22	AHMED Abdul Rahman			AL KHALDI Nawaf	22
2	HASAN Mohamed			ABDULLAH Yaqoub	2
14	ALI Salman Isa Ghuloom			AL SHAMARI Nohayr	5
16	MOHAMED HUSAIN Sayed Adnan			AL EIDAN Ahmad	12
40	MESHKHAS Ebrahim		54	SHAHEEN Fahad	30
8	AL DOSARI Rashed			JARRAGH Mohammad	3
10	SALMEEN Mohamed Ahmed	86		AL ATAIQI Jarah	18
13	MAHMOOD Talal Yusuf			AL MUTAIRI Nawaf	19
25	AAISH Faouzi Mubraken	60	80	AL MUTAIRI Khalaf	10
9	ABDULLA Husain Ali			AL MUTWA Bader	17
30	HUBAIL A'ala	72	58	AL HAMAD Fahad	20
	Tr: BRIEGEL Hans-Peter			Tr: STOICHITA Mihai	
18	HABIB Husain Maki	86	54	JUMAH Walied	15
28	HASAN Ismaeel	72	80	AL OTAIBI Nawaf	38
43	ABDUL RAHMAN Mahmood	60	58	SAEED Farag	49

GROUP E

GROUP E	PL	W	D	L	F	A	GD	PTS	IRQ	CHN	SIN	PLE
1 Iraq	6	3	2	1	12	8	+4	11		2-1	4-2	2-2
2 China PR	6	3	2	1	7	3	+4	11	1-1		1-0	2-0
3 Singapore	5	1	1	3	4	6	-2	4	2-0	0-0		n/p
4 Palestine	5	1	1	3	3	9	-6	4	0-3	0-2	1-0	

Tianjin Teda, Tianjin
16:08-2006, 20:00, 27 000, Ebrahim BHR

CHN   **1   0**   **SIN**

Shao Jiayi [93+p]

CHINA PR			SINGAPORE	
1	LI Lei Lei		LIONEL Lewis	18
3	SUN Xiang		SAHAK Aide Iskandar	5
5	LI Weifeng		SHUNMUGHAM Subramani	14
13	CAO Yang	76	MUSTAFIC Fahrudin	15
40	XU Yunlong		BENNETT Daniel	16
44	XU Liang	66	EMUEJERAYE Precious	21
6	SHAO Jiayi	82	ABDUL HALIM Mohd Isa	23
11	TAO Wei	52	KHAMARUDIN Ahmad Latiff	41
15	ZHAO Junzhe		90 KAMAREZAMAN Noh Alam Shah	8
32	HAO Junmin		EDHEREFE Itimi Dickson	25
29	LI Jinyu	87	GONCALVES Egmar	44
	Tr: ZHU Guanghu		Tr: AVRAMOVIC Radojko	
24	ZHAO Xuri	64 52	87 SHI Jiayi	2
28	DONG Fangzhuo	76	90 SHARIFF Ashrin	9
41	DU Zhenyu	66	82 ISHAK Mohammad Shahril	17

King Abdullah International, Amman
17-08-2006, 20:00, 5000, Basma SYR

PLE   **0   3**   **IRQ**

Younis Mahmoud 2 [59 61],
Mohammad Nasser [90]

PALESTINE			IRAQ	
21	SALEH Ramzi		NADIR Sarhang Muhsen	37
3	ESHBAIR Hamada		MOHAMMED Yasser Raad	4
5	JENDEYA Saeb		HASSAN Haidar Abdul-Amir	14
11	ABULATIFA Fady		REHEMA Ali Hussein	15
15	ABUSIDU Majed	46	MEJIBEL Samal Saeed	16
18	AL AMOUR Ismail	87	HAJI Jasim Mohammed	27
8	AL SWEIRKI Ibrahim	46	ISMAIL Khalid Mushir	32
12	SALEM Fady	92	AL SADWIN Salih Sadir	6
34	KHALIL Omar	70	TAHER Hawar Mulla Md	11
35	AL HOLI Jamal		62 RIDHA Emad Mohammed	7
17	AMER Taysir		KHALEF Younes Mahmoud	10
	Tr: NASSAR Azmi		Tr: SALMAN Akram	
10	AL WAARA Khaldun	87	46 AJEEL Mahdi Kareem	18
14	OMAR Mohanad	46	92 TAHIR Haitham Khadim	19
47	BADRASAWI Bahaa	70	62 SHAKROUN Mohammad Nasser	25

National Stadium, Singapore
6-09-2006, 19:30, 38 824, Shamsuzzaman BAN

SIN   **0   0**   **CHN**

SINGAPORE			CHINA PR	
18	LIONEL Lewis		LI Lei Lei	1
5	SAHAK Aide Iskandar		ZHANG Yaokun	4
14	SHUNMUGHAM Subramani		LI Weifeng	5
15	MUSTAFIC Fahrudin	46	ZHENG Zhi	9
16	BENNETT Daniel		CAO Yang	13
21	EMUEJERAYE Precious		SHAO Jiayi	6
41	KHAMARUDIN Ahmad Latiff	57	LI Tie	8
17	ISHAK Mohammad Shahril		TAO Wei	11
8	KAMAREZAMAN Noh Alam Shah	69	ZHENG Bin	12
19	MOHAMMAD Khairul Amri	80	WANG Dong	31
25	EDHEREFE Itimi Dickson	86	HAN Peng	27
	Tr: AVRAMOVIC Radojko		Tr: ZHU Guanghu	
9	SHARIFF Ashrin	71	86 DONG Fangzhuo	28
11	SHAHUL HAMEED Fazrul	57	80 HAO Junmin	32
23	ABDUL HALIM Mohd Isa	46	69 DU Zhenyu	41

Khalifa Bin Zayed, Al Ain
6-09-2006, 20:30, 1000, Mujghef JOR

IRQ   **2   2**   **PLE**

Saleh Sadir [70], Hawar Taher [75]   Taysir Amer [13],
Ismail Al Amour [78]

IRAQ			PALESTINE	
37	NADIR Sarhang Muhsen		SALEH Ramzi	21
4	MOHAMMED Yasser Raad		ESHBAIR Hamada	3
14	HASSAN Haidar Abdul-Amir		JENDEYA Saeb	5
15	REHEMA Ali Hussein		ABULATIFA Fady	11
32	ISMAIL Khalid Mushir		ABUSIDU Majed	15
36	ABD ALRADA Alaa	46	75 BARBAKH Ihmeidan	40
6	AL SADWIN Salih Sadir		AL SWEIRKI Ibrahim	8
11	TAHER Hawar Mulla Md		SALEM Fady	12
19	TAHIR Haitham Khadim	61	KHALIL Omar	34
7	RIDHA Emad Mohammed		ATTAL Fahad	16
10	KHALEF Younes Mahmoud		AMER Taysir	17
	Tr: SALMAN Akram		Tr: SABAH Mohammed	
17	ALWAN Ahmad Salah	61	66 AL AMOUR Ismail	18
25	SHAKROUN Mohammad Nasser	46	75 ABUSELEISEL Ammar	19
			43 NASSAR Ali	32

Khalifa Bin Zayed, Al Ain
11-10-2006, 21:30, 3000, Mamedov TKM

IRQ 4 2 SIN

Younis Mahmoud 2 [35] [68],
Mahdi Kareem [60], Hawar Taher [93+]

Egmar Goncalves [9],
Khairul Amri [62]

IRAQ			SINGAPORE	
22	ABBAS Noor Sabri		LIONEL Lewis	18
2	ESAD Ahmed Kadhim		SAHAK Aide Iskandar	5
14	HASSAN Haidar Abdul-Amir		SHUNMUGHAM Subramani	14
27	HAJI Jasim Mohammed		MUSTAFIC Fahrudin	15
32	ISMAIL Khalid Mushir		BENNETT Daniel	16
5	ALI Nashat Akram	93	EMUEJERAYE Precious	21
6	AL SADWIN Salih Sadir	73	25 KHAMARUDIN Ahmad Latiff	41
11	TAHER Hawar Mulla Md	57	SHI Jiayi	2
18	AJEEL Mahdi Kareem		ISHAK Mohammad Shahril	17
7	RIDHA Emad Mohammed	71	MOHAMMAD Khairul Amri	19
10	KHALEF Younes Mahmoud		74 GONCALVES Egmar	44
	Tr: SALMAN Akram		Tr: AVRAMOVIC Radojko	
4	MOHAMMED Yasser Raad	73	74 SHARIFF Ashrin	9
19	TAHIR Haitham Khadim	71	57 ABDUL HALIM Mohd Isa	23
25	SHAKROUN Mohammad Nasser	93	25 EDHEREFE Itimi Dickson	25

King Abdullah International, Amman
11-10-2006, 22:00, 3000, Al Fadhli KUW

PLE 0 2 CHN

Mao Jianqing [27], Sun Xiang [64]

PALESTINE			CHINA PR	
21	SALEH Ramzi		LI Lei Lei	1
2	ATURA ALAM Francisco		SUN Xiang	3
3	ESHBAIR Hamada		ZHANG Yaokun	4
4	ROJAS PESCE Bruno		ZHENG Zhi	9
5	JENDEYA Saeb		CAO Yang	13
11	ABULATIFA Fady		XU Yunlong	40
15	ABUSIDU Majed		ZHAO Junzhe	15
25	ADAUY BISHARA Roberto	57	79 WANG Dong	31
9	ZAATARA Imad	57	HAN Peng	27
16	ATTAL Fahad	61	82 LI Jinyu	29
33	BESHE Roberto Kettlun		65 MAO Jianqing	50
	Tr: SABAH Mohammed		Tr: ZHU Guanghu	
8	AL SWEIRKI Ibrahim	57	79 LI Tie	8
18	AL AMOUR Ismail	57	82 DONG Fangzhuo	28
49	KESHKESH Ahmed	61	65 ZHU Ting	52

Changsha Helong Sports Centre, Changsha
15-11-2006, 19:30, Mohd Salleh MAS

CHN 1 1 IRQ

Han Peng [40]

Alwan Ahmad [65]

CHINA PR			IRAQ	
1	LI Lei Lei		ABBAS Noor Sabri	22
3	SUN Xiang		ESAD Ahmed Kadhim	2
4	ZHANG Yaokun		HASSAN Haidar Abdul-Amir	14
9	ZHENG Zhi		REHEMA Ali Hussein	15
13	CAO Yang		MEJIBEL Samal Saeed	16
40	XU Yunlong		HAJI Jasim Mohammed	27
15	ZHAO Junzhe		ISMAIL Khalid Mushir	32
31	WANG Dong	65	ALI Nashat Akram	5
41	DU Zhenyu	75	61 TAHIR Haitham Khadim	19
27	HAN Peng	82	74 ABDULLAH Wisam Zaki	28
29	LI Jinyu		87 RIDHA Emad Mohammed	7
	Tr: ZHU Guanghu		Tr: SALMAN Akram	
10	CHEN Tao	65	74 MOHAMMED Yasser Raad	4
44	XU Liang	75	61 ALWAN Ahmad Salah	17
52	ZHU Ting	82	87 HAFIDH Wisam	26

National Stadium, Singapore
15-11-2006

SIN   PLE

Match not played

SINGAPORE	PALESTINE

GROUP F

GROUP F		PL	W	D	L	F	A	GD	PTS	QAT	UZB	HKG	BAN
1	Qatar	6	5	0	1	14	4	+10	15		2-1	2-0	3-0
2	Uzbekistan	6	3	2	1	14	4	+10	11	2-0		2-2	5-0
3	Hong Kong	6	2	2	2	5	7	-2	8	0-3	0-0		2-0
4	Bangladesh	6	0	0	6	1	19	-18	0	1-4	0-4	0-1	

Ma Aziz Stadium, Chittagong
16-08-2006, 16:00, 7000, Al Yarimi YEM

BAN 1   4 QAT

Mohamad Arman 23

Wesam Rizik 7p, Adel Lamy 36, Khalfan Ibrahim 2 38 74

BANGLADESH			QATAR	
1	HOQUE Md Aminul	18	ABDULLA Abdulaziz Ali	22
3	AHMED Abu Faysal		ADAM Maaz	2
4	BARMAN Rajani		AL GHANIM Ibrahim	14
5	ISLAM Kazi Nazrul		RAJAB Bilal Mohammed	30
14	PARVEZ Mostofa Anwar		AL SHAMMRI Saad	8
38	HASAN Mahmudul	42	ABDULMAJID Wesam Rizki	17
7	MUNNA Motiur		AL KHALFAN Ibrahim	26
8	MIA ARMAN Mohammed	59	RAHMATI Younes Ali	27
13	KHAN JOY Arif		SIDDIQ Majadi Abdullah	5
10	AHMAD Md Alfaz		23 ABDULLA Meshaal	11
36	MONI Mohammed		MOHD Adel Lamy	16
	Tr: KHAN Hassan Jamal		Tr: MUSOVIC Dzemaludin	
9	FARHAD Ariful Kabir	59	23 AL DOSARI Amer	24
16	HOSSAIN Md Abul	42		

Pakhtakor, Tashkent
16-08-2006, 19:00, 15 000, Shaban KUW

UZB 2   2 HKG

Soliev 18, Shatskikh 35

Sham Kwok Keung 2 66 87

UZBEKISTAN			HONG KONG	
1	SAFONOV Evgene		FAN Chun Yip	19
5	ALIQULOV Asror		LEE Wai Lun	5
17	NIKOLAEV Alexey		CHAN Wai Ho	15
33	RADKEVICH Vladimir		LEE Wai Man	18
6	KOSHELEV Leonid	84	POON Yiu Cheuk	20
7	BAYRAMOV Renat	46	CHU Siu Kei	7
8	DJEPAROV Server	41	CHEUNG Sai Ho	8
9	SOLIEV Anvarjon	69	55 LAW Chun Bong	11
10	KARPENKO Victor		88 LO Chi Kwan	14
18	KAPADZE Timur		LEUNG Chun Pong	39
16	SHATSKIKH Maksim		AMBASSA GUY Gerard	23
	Tr: NEPOMNIASTCHI Valeri		Tr: LAI SUN CHEUNG Kenny	
15	GEYNRIKH Alexander	46	55 SHAM Kwok Keung	12
20	BAKAEV Ulugbek	69	88 POON Man Tik	24
25	DENISOV Vitaliy	84	41 LEE Sze Ming	41

Al Gharafa, Doha
6-09-2006, 20:00, 500, Najm LIB

QAT 3   0 BAN

Hussain Yasser 25, Adel Lamy 30, Saad Al Shammari 52

QATAR			BANGLADESH	
33	BURHAN Qasem		HOQUE Md Aminul	1
2	ADAM Maaz	78	BARMAN Rajani	4
10	ABDULRAHMAN Hussain Yaser		ISLAM Kazi Nazrul	5
30	RAJAB Bilal Mohammed		PARVEZ Mostofa Anwar	14
40	AL MEAMARI Abdulrahman		ISLAM Md Ariful	29
4	AL BERIK Abdulla	68	HASAN Mahmudul	38
8	AL SHAMMRI Saad		MUNNA Motiur	7
17	ABDULMAJID Wesam Rizki	60	KHAN JOY Arif	13
5	SIDDIQ Majadi Abdullah	81	HOSSAIN Md Abul	16
9	BECHIR Sayd Ali Baba	70	AHMAD Md Alfaz	10
16	MOHD Adel Lamy	57	MONI Mohammed	36
	Tr: MUSOVIC Dzemaludin		Tr: KHAN Hassan Jamal	
14	AL GHANIM Ibrahim	78	60 AZIZ Arman	15
35	ALI Yusef Ahmed	68	57 AMELI Mohammed	21
46	AL HAMAD Mohd Salem	70	81 HOSSAIN Md Zahid	30

Hong Kong Stadium, Hong Kong
6-09-2006, 20:00, 7608, Lee Gi Young KOR

HKG 0   0 UZB

HONG KONG			UZBEKISTAN	
19	FAN Chun Yip		SAFONOV Evgene	1
5	LEE Wai Lun		FEDOROV Andrey	3
15	CHAN Wai Ho		KLETSOV Aleksandr	4
18	LEE Wai Man		ALIQULOV Asror	5
8	CHEUNG Sai Ho	58	84 NIKOLAEV Alexey	17
20	POON Yiu Cheuk		KOSHELEV Leonid	6
39	LEUNG Chun Pong	64	DJEPAROV Server	8
7	CHU Siu Kei		70 KIRYAN Vladislav	14
9	CHAN Siu Ki		KAPADZE Timur	18
14	LO Chi Kwan	46	69 TADJIYEV Zaynitdin	31
23	AMBASSA GUY Gerard		81 SOLOMIN Pavel	42
	Tr: LAI SUN CHEUNG Kenny		Tr: NEPOMNIASTCHI Valeri	
12	SHAM Kwok Keung	46	70 KARPENKO Victor	10
24	POON Man Tik	64	81 BIKMOEV Marat	13
41	LEE Sze Ming	58	69 GEYNRIKH Alexander	15

Army Stadium, Dhaka
11-10-2006, 15:00, 120, Tan Hai CHN

BAN 0   4 UZB

Zeytullaev 11, Bakaev 18, Djeparov 22, Shatskikh 39p

BANGLADESH			UZBEKISTAN	
1	HOQUE Md Aminul		JURAEV Temur	21
4	BARMAN Rajani		FEDOROV Andrey	3
5	ISLAM Kazi Nazrul		ALIQULOV Asror	5
14	PARVEZ Mostofa Anwar		SUYUNOV Ilhomjon	19
23	FAISAL Md Waly	62	ZEYTULLAEV Ilyas	46
29	ISLAM Md Ariful	46	KOSHELEV Leonid	6
7	MUNNA Motiur	69	DJEPAROV Server	8
15	AZIZ Arman		KAPADZE Timur	18
16	HOSSAIN Md Abul		INNOMOV Islom	24
10	AHMAD Md Alfaz	55	SHATSKIKH Maksim	16
36	MONI Mohammed	55	76 BAKAEV Ulugbek	20
	Tr: KHAN Hassan Jamal		Tr: NEPOMNIASTCHI Valeri	
17	UZZAL Mehedi	69	76 GEYNRIKH Alexander	15
21	AMELI Mohammed	55	46 DENISOV Vitaliy	25
30	HOSSAIN Md Zahid	55	62 MAGDEEV Ildar	43

Al Gharafa, Doha
11-10-2006, 21:00, 1000, Kousa SYR

QAT 2   0 HKG

Bilal Rajab 43, Hussain Yasser 53

QATAR			HONG KONG	
1	AHMED Mohamed Saqr		FAN Chun Yip	19
7	NASSER Ali Saleh	79	LEE Wai Lun	5
10	ABDULRAHMAN Hussain Yaser		CHAN Wai Ho	15
21	KONI Abdulla Obaid		CORDEIRO Cristiano	30
30	RAJAB Bilal Mohammed		36 LAU Chi Keung Sanvel	6
40	AL MEAMARI Abdulrahman		CHU Siu Kei	7
17	ABDULMAJID Wesam Rizki		LAW Chun Bong	11
26	AL KHALFAN Ibrahim		70 CHEUNG Kin Fung	13
27	RAHMATI Younes Ali	70	52 LO Chi Kwan	14
11	ABDULLA Meshaal	65	LEUNG Chun Pong	39
16	MOHD Adel Lamy		AMBASSA GUY Gerard	23
	Tr: MUSOVIC Dzemaludin		Tr: LAI SUN CHEUNG Kenny	
12	HASSAN Magid Mohd	65	52 SHAM Kwok Keung	12
13	AL SULAITY Mohammed	79	70 TSE Man Wing	36
15	AL BLOUSHI Talal	70	36 LEE Sze Ming	41

Pakhtakor, Tashkent
15-11-2006, 16:00, 14 000, Al Saeedi UAE

UZB 2 0 **QAT**

Koshelev [31], Zeytullaev [52]

UZBEKISTAN				QATAR	
12	NESTEROV Ignatiy			AHMED Mohamed Saqr	1
3	FEDOROV Andrey		80	NASSER Ali Saleh	7
5	ALIQULOV Asror			ABDULRAHMAN Hussain Yaser	10
17	NIKOLAEV Alexey			AL GHANIM Ibrahim	14
25	DENISOV Vitaliy			RAJAB Bilal Mohammed	30
46	ZEYTULLAEV Ilyas	71	58	AL BERIK Abdulla	4
6	KOSHELEV Leonid	82	67	AL BLOUSHI Talal	15
8	DJEPAROV Server			ABDULMAJID Wesam Rizki	17
14	KIRYAN Vladislav			AL KHALFAN Ibrahim	26
18	KAPADZE Timur	88	46	ALHAMAD Mesaad	48
16	SHATSKIKH Maksim		58	QUINTANA Andres	49
	Tr: NEPOMNIASTCHI Valeri			Tr: MUSOVIC Dzemaludin	
10	KARPENKO Victor	71	67	HASSAN Magid Mohd	12
15	GEYNRIKH Alexander	82	80	RAHMATI Younes Ali	27
20	BAKAEV Ulugbek	88	46	AL MEAMARI Abdulrahman	40

Mongkok, Hong Kong
15-11-2006, 20:00, 1273, Kim Dong Jin KOR

HKG 2 0 **BAN**

Guy Ambassa 2 [43] [74p]

HONG KONG				BANGLADESH	
19	FAN Chun Yip		77	HOQUE Md Aminul	1
5	LEE Wai Lun			BARMAN Rajani	4
18	LEE Wai Man			ISLAM Kazi Nazrul	5
30	CORDEIRO Cristiano			PARVEZ Mostofa Anwar	14
7	CHU Siu Kei	39		FAISAL Md Waly	23
13	CHEUNG Kin Fung			ISLAM Md Ariful	29
14	LO Chi Kwan	88	71	MUNNA Motiur	7
27	WONG Chun Yue	69		AZIZ Arman	15
39	LEUNG Chun Pong		64	HOSSAIN Md Abul	16
9	CHAN Siu Ki		78	AHMAD Md Alfaz	10
23	AMBASSA GUY Gerard			AMELI Mohammed	21
	Tr: LAI SUN CHEUNG Kenny			Tr: KHAN Hassan Jamal	
12	SHAM Kwok Keung	69	64	MAHMOOD Md Faisal	24
41	LEE Sze Ming	39	71	HOSSAIN Md Zahid	30
43	ZECH Colly Barnes	88	78	ISLAM Md Mazharul	33

AFC ASIAN CUP 2007 FINALS

FINAL TOURNAMENT

AFC ASIAN CUP INDONESIA, MALAYSIA, THAILAND, VIETNAM 2007

First round groups	Pts	Quarter-finals		Semi-finals		Final	
Iraq	5						
Australia	4	Iraq	2				
Thailand	4	Vietnam	0				
Oman	2						
				Iraq	0 4p		
	Pts			Korea Republic	0 3p		
Japan	7						
Vietnam	4	Iran	0 2p				
UAE	3	Korea Republic	0 4p				
Qatar	2						
						Iraq	1
	Pts					Saudi Arabia	0
Iran	7						
Uzbekistan	6	Japan	1 4p				
China PR	4	Australia	1 3p				
Malaysia	0						
				Japan	2		
	Pts			Saudi Arabia	3		
Saudi Arabia	7						
Korea Republic	4	Uzbekistan	1			3rd Place Play-off	
Indonesia	3	Saudi Arabia	2			Korea Republic	0 6p
Bahrain	3					Japan	0 5p

GROUP A	PL	W	D	L	F	A	PTS		AUS	THA	OMA
1 Iraq	3	1	2	0	4	2	5		3-1	1-1	0-0
2 Australia	3	1	1	1	6	4	4			4-0	1-1
3 Thailand	3	1	1	1	3	5	4				2-0
4 Oman	3	0	2	1	1	3	2				

Rajamangala, Bangkok, Thailand
7-07-2007, 19:35, 30 000, Kwon Jong Chul KOR

THA 1 1 IRQ

Sutee Suksomkit [6p]　　　　　　　　　Younis Mahmoud [32]

THAILAND			IRAQ	
18 Kosin HATHAIRATANAKUL			HASSAN Noor Sabri Abbas	22
2 Suree SUKHA			AL HAMD Jassim Gholam	2
4 Jetsada JITSAWAD			GATEA Bassim Abbas	3
5 Niweat SIRIWONG		91	ALI Nashat Akram	5
6 Nataporn PHANRIT		66	AL SADWN Salih Sadir	6
7 Datsakorn THONGLAO			KHALEF Younis Mahmoud	10
9 Therdsak CHAIMAN	72		TAHER Hawar Mohammed	11
10 Tawan SRIPAN			HUSSAIN Haidar Abdul	14
12 Nirut SURASIANG			REHEMA Ali Hussein	15
13 Kiatisuk SENAMUANG	72		AJEEL Mahdi Karim	18
17 Sutee SUKSOMKIT	86		TAHIR Haitham Khadir	19
Tr: PHALAJIVIN Chanvit			Tr: VIEIRA Jorvan	
8 Suchao NUTNUM	72	91	MUHAMED Karrar Jassim	13
14 Teerathep WINOTHAI	72	66	ABOUDY Qusay Munir	24
21 Teerasil DANGDA	86			

Rajamangala, Bangkok, Thailand
12-07-2007, 17:20, 19 000, Lee Gi Young KOR

OMA 0 2 THA

Pipat Thonkanya 2 [70 78]

OMAN			THAILAND	
26 AL HABSI Ali			Kosin HATHAIRATANAKUL	18
2 AL NOOBI Mohamed Rabia			Suree SUKHA	2
3 AL WAHAIBI Juma			Niweat SIRIWONG	5
4 SUWAILIM Said Shoon			Nataporn PHANRIT	6
8 AL-MAIMANI Badar Mubarak	78		Datsakorn THONGLAO	7
10 DOORBEEN Fawzi Basheer		58	Therdsak CHAIMAN	9
12 AL MAHAURI Ahmed Mubarak			Tawan SRIPAN	10
15 AL AJMI Ismail			Nirut SURASIANG	12
17 AL GHEILANI Hassan Yousuf		67	Kiatisuk SENAMUANG	13
20 AL HOSNI Imad Ali			Kiatprawut SAIWAEO	16
21 AL MUKHANI Ahmed Hadid		73	Sutee SUKSOMKIT	17
Tr: CALDERON Gabriel			Tr: PHALAJIVIN Chanvit	
14 AL MUSHAIFRI Younis	78	73	Suchao NUTNUM	8
		67	Teerathep WINOTHAI	14
		58	Pipat THONKANYA	23

Supachalasai, Bangkok, Thailand
16-07-2007, 19:35, 500, Maillet SEY

OMA 0 0 IRQ

OMAN			IRAQ	
26 AL HABSI Ali			HASSAN Noor Sabri Abbas	22
2 AL NOOBI Mohamed Rabia			AL HAMD Jassim Gholam	2
6 AL SINANI Issam Fayel			GATEA Bassim Abbas	3
8 AL-MAIMANI Badar Mubarak			M. KHALDOUN Ibrahim	4
10 DOORBEEN Fawzi Basheer	69		ALI Nashat Akram	5
11 AL-BUSAIDI Yousuf Sha'ban		71	M. AHMED Abid Ali	8
12 AL MAHAURI Ahmed Mubarak			KHALEF Younis Mahmoud	10
15 AL AJMI Ismail	67	45	TAHER Hawar Mohammed	11
17 AL GHEILANI Hassan Yousuf			REHEMA Ali Hussein	15
20 AL HOSNI Imad Ali			AJEEL Mahdi Karim	18
21 AL MUKHANI Ahmed Hadid	81		ABOUDY Qusay Munir	24
Tr: CALDERON Gabriel			Tr: VIEIRA Jorvan	
14 AL MUSHAIFRI Younis	67	71	MSHEHID Ali Abbas	7
24 AL MAHYUARI Younis Mubarak	81	45	MUHAMED Karrar Jassim	13
28 AL HADRI Hussain Ali	69			

Rajamangala, Bangkok, Thailand
8-07-2007, 17:20, 5000, Maillet SEY

AUS 1 1 OMA

Cahill [91+]　　　　　　　　　　　Badar Mubarak [32]

AUSTRALIA			OMAN	
1 SCHWARZER Mark			AL HABSI Ali	26
2 NEILL Lucas			AL NOOBI Mohamed Rabia	2
3 KISNORBO Patrick	78		AL WAHAIBI Juma	3
5 CULINA Jason			SUWAILIM Said Shoon	4
7 EMERTON Brett		60	AL MAIMANI Badar Mubarak	8
8 WILKSHIRE Luke		65	AL BUSAIDI Yousuf Sha'ban	11
9 VIDUKA Mark			AL MAHAURI Ahmed Mubarak	12
10 KEWELI Harry			AL AJMI Ismail	15
13 GRELLA Vince	62		AL GHEILANI Hassan Yousuf	17
21 STERJOVSKI Mile	46	80	AL HOSNI Imad Ali	20
23 BRESCIANO Mark			AL MUKHANI Ahmed Hadid	21
Tr: ARNOLD Graham			Tr: CALDERON Gabriel	
4 CAHILL Tim	62	60	DOORBEEN Fawzi Basheer	10
14 HOLMAN Brett	78	65	AL GHASSANI Mohamed Saleh	13
15 ALOISI John	46	80	AL MAHYUARI Younis Mubarak	24

Rajamangala, Bangkok, Thailand
13-07-2007, 17:20, 7884, Karim BHR

IRQ 3 1 AUS

Nashat Akram [22], Hawar
Mohammed [60], Karrar Jassim [86]　　　Viduka [47]

IRAQ			AUSTRALIA	
22 HASSAN Noor Sabri Abbas			SCHWARZER Mark	1
2 AL HAMD Jassim Gholam		93+	NEILL Lucas	2
3 GATEA Bassim Abbas		71	KISNORBO Patrick	3
5 ALI Nashat Akram		64	CULINA Jason	5
6 AL SADWN Salih Sadir	49		EMERTON Brett	7
10 KHALEF Younis Mahmoud	91+		WILKSHIRE Luke	8
11 TAHER Hawar Mohammed			VIDUKA Mark	9
14 HUSSAIN Haidar Abdul			KEWELI Harry	10
15 REHEMA Ali Hussein			GRELLA Vince	13
18 AJEEL Mahdi Karim		46	HOLMAN Brett	14
19 TAHIR Haitham Khadir	74		BRESCIANO Mark	23
Tr: VIEIRA Jorvan			Tr: ARNOLD Graham	
9 SHAKROWN Moh'd Naser	91+	46	CAHILL Tim	4
13 MUHAMED Karrar Jassim	74	64	THOMPSON Archie	11
24 ABOUDY Qusay Munir	49	71	ALOISI John	15

Rajamangala, Bangkok, Thailand
16-07-2007, 19:35, 46 000, Kwon Jong Chul KOR

THA 0 4 AUS

Beauchamp [20], Viduka 2 [80 83],
Kewell [90]

THAILAND			AUSTRALIA	
18 Kosin HATHAIRATANAKUL			SCHWARZER Mark	1
2 Suree SUKHA			CULINA Jason	5
5 Niweat SIRIWONG			BEAUCHAMP Michael	6
6 Nataporn PHANRIT			EMERTON Brett	7
8 Suchao NUTNUM			WILKSHIRE Luke	8
10 Tawan SRIPAN		84	VIDUKA Mark	9
12 Nirut SURASIANG			GRELLA Vince	13
13 Kiatisuk SENAMUANG		61	ALOISI John	15
14 Teerathep WINOTHAI	60		CARNEY David	20
16 Kiatprawut SAIWAEO	56		MILLIGAN Mark	22
17 Sutee SUKSOMKIT	54	74	BRESCIANO Mark	23
Tr: PHALAJIVIN Chanvit			Tr: ARNOLD Graham	
4 Jetsada JITSAWAD	56	74	CAHILL Tim	4
7 Datsakorn THONGLAO	54	61	KEWELI Harry	10
23 Pipat THONKANYA	60	84	HOLMAN Brett	14

	GROUP B	PL	W	D	L	F	A	PTS
1	Japan	3	2	1	0	8	3	7
2	Vietnam	3	1	1	1	4	5	4
3	UAE	3	1	0	2	3	6	3
4	Qatar	3	0	2	1	3	4	2

	VIE	UAE	QAT
	4-1	3-1	1-1
		2-0	1-1
			2-1

MY Dinh Stadium, Hanoi, Vietnam
8-07-2007, 19:35, 39 450, Najm LIB

VIE 2 0 UAE

Huynh Quang Thanh 63,
Le Cong Vinh 73

VIETNAM			UAE	
22 DUONG Hong Son			MAQDEMI Majed Nasser	1
2 PHUNG Van Nhien			AL JENAIBI Jumaa	2
3 NGUYEN Huy Hoang			AL HOSANI Abdul Rahman	6
7 VU Nhu Thanh			MOHAMED Haidar Alo Ali	8
9 LE Cong Vinh	95+		AL JUNAIBI Ismail Matar	10
12 NGUYEN Minh Phuong	77		AL JUNAIBI Faisal Khalil	11
14 LE Tan Tai		70	AL MAHRI Ahmed Mubarak	13
16 HUYNH Quang Thanh			AL HAMMADI Basheer Saeed	14
17 NGUYEN Vu Phong			AL SHEHHI Mohamed Saeed	15
18 PHAN Thanh Binh	84		AL HAMMADI Yousef Jaber	17
19 PHAN Van Tai Em		80	AL SAEDI Helal Saeed	20
Tr: RIEDL Alfred			Tr: METSU Bruno	
10 HUYNH Phuc Hiep	95+	70	ALBALOOSHI Darwish	7
15 NGUYEN Minh Chuyen	77	80	AL HAMMADI Amir Mubarak	18
21 NGUYEN Anh Duc	84			

MY Dinh Stadium, Hanoi, Vietnam
9-07-2007, 17:20, 5000, Breeze AUS

JPN 1 1 QAT

Takahara 60
Sebastian Quintana 88

JAPAN			QATAR	
1 KAWAGUCHI Yoshikatsu			AHMED Mohamed Saqr	1
21 KAJI Akira		46	AL HAMAD Mesaad Hamad	2
22 NAKAZAWA Yuji			BUDAWOOD Meshal Mubarak	6
2 KONNO Yasuyuki			AL SHAMMARI Saad	8
6 ABE Yuki			ABDULLA Mostafa Abdulla	13
7 ENDO Yashuhito			KONI Abdullah Koni	21
9 YAMAGISHI Satoru	74		AL BLOUSHI Talal	15
10 NAKAMURA Shunsuke		75	ABDULMAJID Wesam Rizik	17
13 SUZUKI Keita		92+	AB'RAHMAN Hussain Yasser	10
14 NAKAMURA Kengo	81	66	ABDULLA Waleed Jassim	18
19 TAKAHARA Naohiro			QUINTANA Sebastian	23
Tr: OSIM Ivica			Tr: MUSOVIC Dzemaludin	
8 HANYU Naotake	74	46	SIDDIQ Majadi Siddiq	5
24 HASHIMOTO Hideo	81	75	HASSAN Magid Mohamed	12
		66	MOHD Adel Lamy	20

MY Dinh Stadium, Hanoi, Vietnam
12-07-2007, 19:35, 40 000, Moradi IRN

QAT 1 1 VIE

Sebastian Quintana 79
Phan Thanh Binh 32

QATAR			VIETNAM	
1 AHMED Mohamed Saqr			DUONG Hong Son	22
6 BUDAWOOD Meshal Mubarak			PHUNG Van Nhien	2
8 AL SHAMMARI Saad			NGUYEN Huy Hoang	3
13 ABDULLA Mostafa Abdulla	55		VU Nhu Thanh	7
21 KONI Abdullah Koni			HUYNH Quang Thanh	16
15 AL BLOUSHI Talal			NGUYEN Minh Phuong	12
17 ABDULMAJID Wesam Rizik			LE Tan Tai	14
12 HASSAN Magid Mohamed	78		NGUYEN Vu Phong	17
18 ABDULLA Waleed Jassim	58	82	PHAN Van Tai Em	19
20 MOHD Adel Lamy	73		LE Cong Vinh	9
23 QUINTANA Sebastian	94+		PHAN Thanh Binh	18
Tr: MUSOVIC Dzemaludin			Tr: RIEDL Alfred	
5 SIDDIQ Majadi Siddiq	78	55	PHAM Hung Dung	6
9 BECHIR Seyd	58	82	NGUYEN Minh Chuyen	15
11 YAHYA Ali Afef	73	94+	NGUYEN Anh Duc	21

MY Dinh Stadium, Hanoi, Vietnam
13-07-2007, 20:35, 5000, Tongkhan THA

UAE 1 3 JPN

Saeed Alkas 66
Takahara 2 22 27, Nakamura.S 42p

UAE			JAPAN	
1 MAQDEMI Majed Nasser			KAWAGUCHI Yoshikatsu	1
6 AL HOSANI Abdul Rahman			KOMANO Yuichi	3
8 MOHAMED Haidar Alo Ali			KAJI Akira	21
14 AL HAMMADI Basheer Saeed	53		NAKAZAWA Yuji	22
21 MAJEED Humaid Fakher			ABE Yuki	6
2 AL JENAIBI Jumaa			ENDO Yashuhito	7
5 HUSSAIN Essa Ali	46	71	NAKAMURA Shunsuke	10
20 AL SAEDI Helal Saeed		77	SUZUKI Keita	13
7 AL BALOOSHI Darwish	46		NAKAMURA Kengo	14
10 AL JUNAIBI Ismail Matar		66	TAKAHARA Naohiro	19
15 AL SHEHHI Mohamed Saeed	56		MAKI Seiichiro	12
Tr: METSU Bruno			Tr: OSIM Ivica	
13 AL MAHRI Ahmed Mubarak	46	77	KONNO Yasuyuki	2
19 ALKAS Saeed	46	66	HANYU Naotake	8
22 AL BALOOSHI Qassim	56	71	MIZUNO Koki	15

MY Dinh Stadium, Hanoi, Vietnam
16-07-2007, 17:20, 40 000, Breeze AUS

VIE 1 4 JPN

Suzuki OG 7
Maki 2 12 59, Endo 31,
Nakamura.S 52

VIETNAM			JAPAN	
22 DUONG Hong Son			KAWAGUCHI Yoshikatsu	1
2 PHUNG Van Nhien			KOMANO Yuichi	3
3 NGUYEN Huy Hoang			KAJI Akira	21
7 VU Nhu Thanh			NAKAZAWA Yuji	22
16 HUYNH Quang Thanh			ABE Yuki	6
12 NGUYEN Minh Phuong	80	68	ENDO Yashuhito	7
14 LE Tan Tai	74	61	NAKAMURA Shunsuke	10
15 NGUYEN Minh Chuyen			SUZUKI Keita	13
17 NGUYEN Vu Phong			NAKAMURA Kengo	14
19 PHAN Van Tai Em	65		TAKAHARA Naohiro	19
9 LE Cong Vinh		68	MAKI Seiichiro	12
Tr: RIEDL Alfred			Tr: OSIM Ivica	
4 DOAN Viet Cuong	74	61	HANYU Naotake	8
11 PHUNG Cong Minh	65	68	SATO Hisato	11
18 PHAN Thanh Binh	80	68	MIZUNO Koki	15

Army Stadium, Ho Chi Minh City, Vietnam
16-07-2007, 17:20, 3000, Moradi IRN

QAT 1 2 UAE

Sebastian Quintana 42
Saeed Alkas 59, Faisal Khalil 94+

QATAR			UAE	
1 AHMED Mohamed Saqr			AL BADRANI Waleed Salem	12
3 RAJAB Bilal			AL HOSANI Abdul Rahman	6
13 ABDULLA Mostafa Abdulla	72		AL HAMMADI Yousef Jaber	17
21 KONI Abdullah Koni			AL BALOOSHI Qassim	22
6 BUDAWOOD Meshal Mubarak			AL JENAIBI Jumaa	2
5 SIDDIQ Majadi Siddiq			AL DHAHERI Ali Msarri	4
15 AL BLOUSHI Talal			AL MAHRI Ahmed Mubarak	13
17 ABDULMAJID Wesam Rizik	79	91	AL HAMMADI Amir Mubarak	18
10 AB'RAHMAN Hussain Yasser		81	AL DARMAKI Nawaf Mubarak	9
11 YAHYA Ali Afef	69		AL JUNAIBI Ismail Matar	10
23 QUINTANA Sebastian	78		ALKAS Saeed	19
Tr: MUSOVIC Dzemaludin			Tr: METSU Bruno	
2 AL HAMAD Mesaad	72	78	AL JUNAIBI Faisal Khalil	11
12 HASSAN Magid Mohamed	69	81	AL SHEHHI Mohamed Saeed	15
20 MOHD Adel Lamy	79	91	AL SAEDI Helal Saeed	20

GROUP C	PL	W	D	L	F	A	PTS
1 Iran	3	2	1	0	6	3	7
2 Uzbekistan	3	2	0	1	9	2	6
3 China PR	3	1	1	1	7	6	4
4 Malaysia	3	0	0	3	1	12	0

	UZB	CHN	MAS
	2-1	2-2	2-0
		3-0	5-0
			5-1

National Stadium, Bukit Jalil, Kuala Lumpur, Malaysia
10-07-2007, 20:35, 20 000, Basma SYR

MAS   1   5   CHN

Indra Putra [72]

Han Peng 2 [15 55], Shao Jiayi [36],
Wang Dong 2 [51 93+]

MALAYSIA		CHINA PR	
1 Azizon ABDUL KADIR		LI Lei Lei	1
3 Fauzi NAN		SUN Xiang	3
7 Khaironnisam HUSSAIN		ZHANG Yaokun	4
19 Rosdi TALIB		LI Weifeng	5
5 Norhafiz Zamani MISBAH		ZHENG Zhi	10
10 Mohd Hardi JAAFAR	67	SHAO Jiayi	6
12 Shukor ADAN		SUN Jihai	7
15 Sharulnizam MUSTAPHA	46	WANG Dong	15
18 Mohd Fadzli SAARI	58	ZHOU Haibin	18
14 Akmal Rizal RAKHIL	62	72	HAN Peng	9
20 Hairuddin OMAR		88	MAO Jianqing	20
Tr: BAKAR Norizan		Tr: ZHU Guanghu	
9 Eddy Helmi ABD MANAN	46	67	LI Tie	8
13 Indra Putra MAHAYUDDIN	62	72	DONG Fangzhuo	11
17 Nantha K. KALLIAPPAN	58	88	ZHENG Bin	19

National Stadium, Bukit Jalil, Kuala Lumpur, Malaysia
14-07-2007, 18:20, 7137, Abdou QAT

UZB   5   0   MAS

Shatskikh 2 [10 89], Kapadze [30],
Bakaev [47+], Ibragimov [85]

UZBEKISTAN		MALAYSIA	
12 NESTEROV Ignatiy		Azizon ABDUL KADIR	1
2 KARIMOV Hayrulla		Thirumurugan VEERAN	6
6 ISMAILOV Anzur	50	Khaironnisam HUSSAIN	7
17 NIKOLAEV Aleksey		Nantha K. KALLIAPPAN	17
23 DENISOV Vitaliy	68	Rosdi TALIB	19
8 DJEPAROV Server	83	Mohd Hardi JAAFAR	10
18 KAPADZE Timur		Shukor ADAN	12
19 INOMOV Islom		Sharulnizam MUSTAPHA	15
26 KARPENKO Victor	55	Ivan MOHD YUSOFF	22
10 BAKAEV Ulugbek	63	Indra Putra MAHAYUDDIN	13
16 SHATSKIKH Maksim	71	Hairuddin OMAR	20
Tr: INILEEV Rauf		Tr: BAKAR Norizan	
4 IBRAGIMOV Aziz	50	55	Nor Farhan MUHAMMAD	11
9 SOLOMIN Pavel	68	71	Akmal Rizal RAKHIL	14
15 GEYNRIKH Alexander	63	83	Mohd Fadzli SAARI	18

National Stadium, Bukit Jalil, Kuala Lumpur, Malaysia
18-07-2007, 20:35, 4520, Basma SYR

MAS   0   2   IRN

Nekonam [29p], Teymourian [77]

MALAYSIA		IRAN	
1 Azizon ABDUL KADIR		RODBARIAN Hassan	1
2 Hamzani OMAR	73	REZAEI Rahman	5
6 Thirumurugan VEERAN		HOSSEINI Seyed Jalal	12
7 Khaironnisam HUSSAIN		MAHDAVIKIA Mehdi	2
17 Nantha K. KALLIAPPAN		TIMOTIAN Andranik	4
19 Rosdi TALIB		NEKOUNAM Javad	6
23 Mohamad AIDIL ZAFUAN		ZANDI Fereydoon	7
12 Shukor ADAN		KARIMI Ali	8
15 Sharulnizam MUSTAPHA	68	52	MOBALI Eman	14
8 Safee SALI	53	79	HASHEMIAN Vahid	9
13 Indra Putra MAHAYUDDIN	46	ENAYATI Gholam Reza	16
Tr: BAKAR Norizan		Tr: GHALEHNOY Ardeshir	
3 Fauzi NAN	73	46	PAKI KHATIBI Rasoul	10
10 Mohd Hardi JAAFAR	53	52	KAZEMIAN Javad	17
11 Nor Farhan MUHAMMAD	68	79	RAJABZADEH Mehdi	18

National Stadium, Bukit Jalil, Kuala Lumpur, Malaysia
11-07-2007, 18:20, 1863, Al Fadhli KUW

IRN   2   1   UZB

Hosseini [55], Kazemeyan [78]

Rezaei OG [16]

IRAN		UZBEKISTAN	
1 RODBARIAN Hassan		BUGALO Pavel	1
5 REZAEI Rahman		KARIMOV Hayrulla	2
12 HOSSEINI Seyed Jalal		IBRAGIMOV Aziz	4
2 MAHDAVIKIA Mehdi		NIKOLAEV Aleksey	17
4 TIMOTIAN Andranik		DENISOV Vitaliy	23
6 NEKOUNAM Javad	61	HAYDAROV Azizbek	7
7 ZANDI Fereydoon		DJEPAROV Server	8
8 KARIMI Ali	90	KAPADZE Timur	18
9 HASHEMIAN Vahid	73	INOMOV Islom	19
10 PAKI KHATIBI Rasoul	46	64	SOLOMIN Pavel	9
16 ENAYATI Gholam Reza	81	BAKAEV Ulugbek	10
Tr: GHALEHNOY Ardeshir		Tr: INILEEV Rauf	
11 MADANCHI Mehrzad	72	64	BIKMAEV Marat	11
15 AGHILY ANVAR Seyed	90	61	KHOSHIMOV Khikmatdjon	13
17 KAZEMIAN Javad	46	81	GEYNRIKH Alexander	15

National Stadium, Bukit Jalil, Kuala Lumpur, Malaysia
15-07-2007, 18:20, 5938, Al Ghamdi KSA

CHN   2   2   IRN

Shao Jiayi [6], Mao Jianqing [33]

Zandi [45], Nekoam [73]

CHINA PR		IRAN	
1 LI Lei Lei		RODBARIAN Hassan	1
3 SUN Xiang		REZAEI Rahman	5
4 ZHANG Yaokun		HOSSEINI Seyed Jalal	12
5 LI Weifeng	46	KAEBI Hossein	13
10 ZHENG Zhi		MAHDAVIKIA Mehdi	2
6 SHAO Jiayi		TIMOTIAN Andranik	4
7 SUN Jihai		NEKOUNAM Javad	6
15 WANG Dong	61	89	ZANDI Fereydoon	7
18 ZHOU Haibin	46	KARIMI Ali	8
20 MAO Jianqing	68	HASHEMIAN Vahid	9
9 HAN Peng	79	ENAYATI Gholam Reza	16
Tr: ZHU Guanghu		Tr: GHALEHNOY Ardeshir	
2 DU Wei	79	89	MADANCHI Mehrzad	11
12 ZHAO Xuri	61	46	MOBALI Eman	14
14 ZHU Ting	68	46	KAZEMIAN Javad	17

Shah Alam, Kuala Lumpur, Malaysia
18-07-2007, 20:35, 2200, Al Fadhli KUW

UZB   3   0   CHN

Shatskikh [72], Kapadze [86],
Geynrikh [94+]

UZBEKISTAN		CHINA PR	
12 NESTEROV Ignatiy		YANG Jun	22
2 KARIMOV Hayrulla		DU Wei	2
4 IBRAGIMOV Aziz	93+	SUN Xiang	3
17 NIKOLAEV Aleksey		ZHANG Yaokun	4
23 DENISOV Vitaliy	63	78	ZHANG Shuai	13
28 GAFUROV Anvar		SHAO Jiayi	6
7 HAYDAROV Azizbek		SUN Jihai	7
8 DJEPAROV Server		ZHOU Haibin	18
18 KAPADZE Timur		HAN Peng	9
10 BAKAEV Ulugbek	46	70	DONG Fangzhuo	11
16 SHATSKIKH Maksim	41	MAO Jianqing	20
Tr: INILEEV Rauf		Tr: ZHU Guanghu	
9 SOLOMIN Pavel	93+	70	ZHAO Xuri	12
15 GEYNRIKH Alexander	46	78	ZHU Ting	14
26 KARPENKO Victor	63	41	WANG Dong	15

	GROUP D	PL	W	D	L	F	A	PTS
1	Saudi Arabia	3	2	1	0	7	2	7
2	Korea Republic	3	1	1	1	3	3	4
3	Indonesia	3	1	0	2	3	4	3
4	Bahrain	3	1	0	2	3	7	3

	KOR	IDN	BHR
KOR		1-1	2-1	4-0
IDN	1-0		1-2
BHR	2-1		

Gelora Bung Karna Main Stadium, Jakarta, Indonesia
10-07-2007, 17:20, 60 000, Nishimura JPN

IDN 2 1 BHR

Budi Sudarsono [14]
Bambang Pamungkas [64]
Sayed Mahmood Jalal [27]

INDONESIA			BAHRAIN	
1 Yandri Christian PITOY			AHMED Abdulrahman 21	
2 Muhammaed RIDWAN		3	MARZOOQ Abdulla 3	
4 Ricardo SALAMPESSY			MOHAMED Husain Baba 17	
5 Maman ABDURACHMAN			AL WADAEI Sayed Jalal 7	
6 Charis YULIANTO		83	AL DOSARI Rashed 8	
9 Mahyadi PANGGABEAN	31	66	OMAR Abdullah 15	
8 Elie AIBOY	85		AAISH Faouzi 25	
11 Ponaryo ASTAMAN	34		ABDUL RAHMAN Mahmoud 27	
15 Firman UTINA		80	HUBAIL Mohamed 29	
13 Budi SUDARSONO			OKWUNWANNE Jaycee John 26	
20 Bambang PAMUNGKAS			HUBAIL A'ala 30	
Tr: KOLEV Ivan			Tr: MACALA Milan	
7 Eka RAMDANI	31	80	ABDULLA Husain Ali 9	
16 Syamsul BACHRI	34	83	FATADI Abdulla Baba 12	
22 SUPARDI	85	66	MAHMOOD Talal Yusuf 13	

Gelora Bung Karna Main Stadium, Jakarta, Indonesia
11-07-2007, 19:35, 15 000, Shield AUS

KOR 1 1 KSA

Choi Sung Kuk [65]
Yasser Al Kahtani [77p]

KOREA REPUBLIC			SAUDI ARABIA	
1 LEE Woon Jae			AL MOSAILEM Yasser 1	
3 KIM Jin Kyu			HAWSAWI Osama 3	
14 KIM Sang Sik			AL MOUSA Kamil 7	
15 KIM Chi Woo			AL BAHRI Ahmed 15	
16 OH Beom Seok			JAHDALI Walid 19	
22 KANG Min Soo			KHARIRI Saud 14	
17 KIM Jung Woo			KHALED Aziz 16	
20 SON Dae Ho		56	AL KAHTANI Abdulrahman 18	
7 CHOI Sung Kuk	66	80	AL KAHTANI Yasser 20	
9 CHO Jae Jin	81		AL MOUSA Ahmed 30	
19 YEOM Ki Hun			ALHAWSAWI Malek Maaz 9	
Tr: VERBEEK Peter			Tr: HELIO DOS ANJOS	
10 LEE Chun Soo	66	80	AL HARTHI Saad 11	
12 LEE Dong Gook	81	56	AUTEF Abdoh 28	

Gelora Bung Karna Main Stadium, Jakarta, Indonesia
14-07-2007, 19:35, 87 000, Al Badwawi UAE

KSA 2 1 IDN

Yasser Al Kahtani [12],
Saad Al Harthi [89]
Elie Aiboy [17]

SAUDI ARABIA			INDONESIA	
1 AL MOSAILEM Yasser			Yandri Christian PITOY 1	
3 HAWSAWI Osama			Muhammaed RIDWAN 2	
7 AL MOUSA Kamil			Ricardo SALAMPESSY 4	
15 AL BAHRI Ahmed			Maman ABDURACHMAN 5	
19 JAHDALI Walid			Charis YULIANTO 6	
14 KHARIRI Saud	66		Eka RAMDANI 7	
16 KHALED Aziz		80	Elie AIBOY 8	
18 AL KAHTANI Abdulrahman		84	Firman UTINA 15	
20 AL KAHTANI Yasser	89		Syamsul BACHRI 16	
30 AL MOUSA Ahmed	56	89	Budi SUDARSONO 13	
9 ALHAWSAWI Malek Maaz			Bambang PAMUNGKAS 20	
Tr: HELIO DOS ANJOS			Tr: KOLEV Ivan	
11 AL HARTHI Saad	89	89	Ismet SOFYAND 14	
17 AL JASSAM Taiseer	66	84	ATEP 17	
28 AUTEF Abdoh	56	80	SUPARDI 22	

Gelora Bung Karna Main Stadium, Jakarta, Indonesia
15-07-2007, 19:35, 9000, Sun Baojie CHN

BHR 2 1 KOR

Salman Isa [43]
Ismaeel Abdullatif [85]
Kim Do Heon [4]

BAHRAIN			KOREA REPUBLIC	
21 AHMED Abdulrahman			LEE Woon Jae 1	
2 HASAN Mohamed			SONG Chong Gug 2	
3 MARZOOQ Abdulla			KIM Jin Kyu 3	
14 ALI Salman Isa	78		KIM Dong Jin 4	
16 HUSSAIN Sayed Adnan			KIM Sang Sik 14	
7 AL WADAEI Sayed Jalal			KANG Min Soo 22	
8 AL DOSARI Rashed			LEE Ho 6	
25 AAISH Faouzi			KIM Do Heon 8	
29 HUBAIL Mohamed		68	LEE Chun Soo 10	
11 HASAN Ismaeel Abdullatif	87	66	LEE Dong Gook 12	
30 HUBAIL A'ala			YEOM Ki Hun 19	
Tr: MACALA Milan			Tr: VERBEEK Peter	
10 SALMEEN Mohamed	87	66	CHO Jae Jin 9	
27 ABDUL RAHMAN Mahmoud	78	68	KIM Jung Woo 17	

Gelora Bung Karna Main Stadium, Jakarta, Indonesia
18-07-2007, 17:20, 87 000, Shield AUS

IDN 0 1 KOR

Kim Jung Woo [34]

INDONESIA			KOREA REPUBLIC	
23 Markus RIRIHINA			LEE Woon Jae 1	
2 Muhammaed RIDWAN		88	KIM Jin Kyu 3	
4 Ricardo SALAMPESSY			KIM Sang Sik 14	
5 Maman ABDURACHMAN			KIM Chi Woo 15	
6 Charis YULIANTO			OH Beom Seok 16	
8 Elie AIBOY			KANG Min Soo 22	
11 Ponaryo ASTAMAN	76		KIM Jung Woo 17	
7 Firman UTINA		89	SON Dae Ho 20	
16 Syamsul BACHRI			CHOI Sung Kuk 7	
13 Budi SUDARSONO			CHO Jae Jin 9	
20 Bambang PAMUNGKAS			LEE Chun Soo 10	
Tr: KOLEV Ivan			Tr: VERBEEK Peter	
3 Erol IBA	76	88	LEE Dong Gook 12	
		89	OH Jang Eun 27	

Jaka Baring Stadium, Jakarta, Indonesia
18-07-2007, 17:20, 500, Nishimura JPN

KSA 4 0 BHR

Ahmed Al Mousa [18], Abdulrahman
Al Kahtani [45], Taisser Al Jassam 2 [68 79]

SAUDI ARABIA			BAHRAIN	
1 AL MOSAILEM Yasser			AHMED Abdulrahman 21	
3 HAWSAWI Osama			HASAN Mohamed 2	
7 AL MOUSA Kamil			MARZOOQ Abdulla 3	
15 AL BAHRI Ahmed			ALI Salman Isa 14	
19 JAHDALI Walid			HUSSAIN Sayed Adnan 16	
14 KHARIRI Saud		81	AL WADAEI Sayed Jalal 7	
18 AL KAHTANI Abdulrahman	56		AL DOSARI Rashed 8	
20 AL KAHTANI Yasser	77	73	MAHMOOD Talal Yusuf 13	
30 AL MOUSA Ahmed	71		AAISH Faouzi 25	
9 ALHAWSAWI Malek Maaz			HASAN Ismaeel Abdullatif 11	
17 AL JASSAM Taiseer		67	HUBAIL A'ala 30	
Tr: HELIO DOS ANJOS			Tr: MACALA Milan	
6 AL GHAMDI Omar	71	73	FATADI Abdulla Baba 12	
11 AL HARTHI Saad	77	81	HABIB Husain 18	
28 AUTEF Abdoh	56	67	OKWUNWANNE Jaycee John 26	

QUARTER-FINALS

Rajamangala, Bangkok, Thailand
21-07-2007, 9720, Nishimura JPN

IRQ 2 0 VIE

Younis Mahmoud 2 [2] [65]

	IRAQ			VIETNAM	
22	HASSAN Noor Sabri Abbas			DUONG Hong Son	22
2	AL HAMD Jassim Gholam		83	NGUYEN Huy Hoang	3
3	GATEA Bassim Abbas			VU Nhu Thanh	7
14	HUSSAIN Haidar Abdul	84		HUYNH Quang Thanh	16
15	REHEMA Ali Hussein			CHAU Phong Hoa	29
5	ALI Nashat Akram		46	PHUNG Cong Minh	11
11	TAHER Hawar Mohammed			NGUYEN Minh Phuong	12
13	MUHAMED Karrar Jassim	66		LE Tan Tai	14
18	AJEEL Mahdi Karim			NGUYEN Vu Phong	17
19	TAHIR Haitham Khadir	32		LE Cong Vinh	9
10	KHALEF Younis Mahmoud		70	NGUYEN Anh Duc	21
	Tr: VIEIRA Jorvan			Tr: RIEDL Alfred	
4	M. KHALDOUN Ibrahim	84	83	PHAM Hung Dung	6
8	M. AHMED Abid Ali	32	46	NGUYEN Minh Chuyen	15
9	SHAKROWN Moh'd Naser	66	70	PHAN Thanh Binh	18

National Stadium, Bukit Jalil, Kuala Lumpur, Malaysia
22-07-2007, 18:20, 8629, Al Badwawi UAE

IRN 0 0 KOR

2 [p] 4

	IRAN			KOREA REPUBLIC	
1	RODBARIAN Hassan	120		LEE Woon Jae	1
5	REZAEI Rahman			KIM Jin Kyu	3
12	HOSSEINI Seyed Jalal			KIM Sang Sik	14
20	NOSRATI Mohammad			KIM Chi Woo	15
2	MAHDAVIKIA Mehdi			OH Beom Seok	16
4	TIMOTIAN Andranik			KANG Min Soo	22
6	NEKOUNAM Javad			KIM Jung Woo	17
8	KARIMI Mohammad		106	SON Dae Ho	20
11	MADANCHI Mehrzad	62		LEE Chun Soo	10
9	HASHEMIAN Vahid	87	46	LEE Dong Gook	12
10	PAKI KHATIBI Rasoul		78	YEOM Ki Hun	19
	Tr: GHALEHNOY Ardeshir			Tr: VERBEEK Peter	
7	ZANDI Fereydoon	62	78	CHOI Sung Kuk	7
16	ENAYATI Gholam Reza	87	106	KIM Do Heon	8
22	TALEBLOO Vahid	120	46	CHO Jae Jin	9

MY Dinh Stadium, Hanoi, Vietnam
21-07-2007, 17:20, 25 000, Al Fadhli KUW

JPN 1 1 AUS

Takahara [72]   4 [p] 3   Aloisi [69]

	JAPAN			AUSTRALIA	
1	KAWAGUCHI Yoshikatsu			SCHWARZER Mark	1
3	KOMANO Yuichi			NEILL Lucas	2
21	KAJI Akira	88		CULINA Jason	5
22	NAKAZAWA Yuji			BEAUCHAMP Michael	6
6	ABE Yuki			EMERTON Brett	7
7	ENDO Yashuhito			MILLIGAN Mark	22
10	NAKAMURA Shunsuke		75	GRELLA Vince	13
13	SUZUKI Keita		82	ALOISI John	15
14	NAKAMURA Kengo	115		CARNEY David	20
12	MAKI Seiichiro	102	71	BRESCIANO Mark	23
19	TAKAHARA Naohiro		61	VIDUKA Mark	9
	Tr: OSIM Ivica			Tr: ARNOLD Graham	
2	KONNO Yasuyuki	88	71	CAHILL Tim	4
11	SATO Hisato	102	61	KEWELI Harry	10
20	YANO Kisho	115	82	CARLE Nicky	19

Gelora Bung Karna Main Stadium, Jakarta, Indonesia
22-07-2007, 20:20, 12 000, Kwon Jong Chul KOR

KSA 2 1 UZB

Yasser Al Kahtani [2],
Ahmad Al Mousa [75]   Solomin [80]

	SAUDI ARABIA			UZBEKISTAN	
1	AL MOSAILEM Yasser			NESTEROV Ignatiy	12
3	HAWSAWI Osama			KARIMOV Hayrulla	2
7	AL MOUSA Kamil			IBRAGIMOV Aziz	4
15	AL BAHRI Ahmed			NIKOLAEV Aleksey	17
19	JAHDALI Walid			DENISOV Vitaliy	23
14	KHARIRI Saud	89	46	GAFUROV Anvar	28
16	AL THAKER Khaled Aziz		78	HAYDAROV Azizbek	7
18	AL KAHTANI Abdulrahman	63		DJEPAROV Server	8
20	AL KAHTANI Yasser	90	57	KAPADZE Timur	18
9	ALHAWSAWI Malek Maaz			INOMOV Islom	19
17	AL JASSAM Taiseer			SHATSKIKH Maksim	16
	Tr: HELIO DOS ANJOS			Tr: INILEEV Rauf	
6	AL GHAMDI Omar	89	78	SOLOMIN Pavel	9
11	AL HARTHI Saad	90	46	GEYNRIKH Alexander	15
30	AL MOUSA Ahmed	63	57	KARPENKO Victor	26

SEMI-FINALS

National Stadium, Bukit Jalil, Kuala Lumpur, Malaysia
25-07-2007, 18:20, 12 500, Al Fadhli KUW

IRQ 0 0 KOR

4 [p] 3

	IRAQ			KOREA REPUBLIC	
22	HASSAN Noor Sabri Abbas			(c) LEE Woon Jae	1
2	AL HAMD Jassim Gholam			KIM Jin Kyu	3
3	GATEA Bassim Abbas		58	KIM Sang Sik	14
14	HUSSAIN Haidar Abdul			KIM Chi Woo	15
15	REHEMA Ali Hussein			OH Beom Seok	16
5	ALI Nashat Akram			KANG Min Soo	22
11	TAHER Hawar Mohammed		106	SON Dae Ho	20
13	MUHAMED Karrar Jassim	108	87	CHOI Sung Kuk	7
18	AJEEL Mahdi Karim			CHO Jae Jin	9
24	ABOUDY Qusay Munir			LEE Chun Soo	10
10	KHALEF Younis Mahmoud			YEOM Ki Hun	19
	Tr: VIEIRA Jorvan			Tr: VERBEEK Peter	
16	ABBAS Ahmed Menajed	108	87	LEE Dong Gook	12
			58	KIM Jung Woo	17
			106	OH Jang Eun	27

MY Dinh Stadium, Hanoi, Vietnam
25-07-2007, 20:20, 10 000, Breeze AUS

JPN 2 3 KSA

Nakazawa [37], Abe [53]   Yasser Al Kahtani 35,
Malek Maaz 2 47 57

	JAPAN			SAUDI ARABIA	
1	KAWAGUCHI Yoshikatsu (c)			AL MOSAILEM Yasser	1
3	KOMANO Yuichi			HAWSAWI Osama	3
21	KAJI Akira			AL MOUSA Kamil	7
22	NAKAZAWA Yuji			AL BAHRI Ahmed	15
6	ABE Yuki		77	JAHDALI Walid	19
7	ENDO Yashuhito	75	86	KHARIRI Saud	14
10	NAKAMURA Shunsuke			AL THAKER Khaled Aziz	16
13	SUZUKI Keita		60	AL KAHTANI Abdulrahman	18
14	NAKAMURA Kengo	87		AL KAHTANI Yasser	20
12	MAKI Seiichiro	68		ALHAWSAWI Malek Maaz	9
19	TAKAHARA Naohiro			AL JASSAM Taiseer	17
	Tr: OSIM Ivica			Tr: HELIO DOS ANJOS	
8	HANYU Naotake	75	86	AL GHAMDI Omar	6
11	SATO Hisato	68	77	FALLATAH Redha Tukar	25
20	YANO Kisho	87	60	AL MOUSA Ahmed	30

THIRD PLACE PLAY-OFF

Jaka Baring Stadium, Palembang, Indonesia
28-07-2007, 19:35, 10 000, Al Badwawi UAE

KOR   0   0   JPN

6 ^P_S 5

KOREA REPUBLIC				JAPAN	
1	LEE Woon Jae (c)			(c) KAWAGUCHI Yoshikatsu	1
3	KIM Jin Kyu			KOMANO Yuichi	3
15	KIM Chi Woo			KAJI Akira	21
16	OH Beom Seok			NAKAZAWA Yuji	22
22	KANG Min Soo	56		ABE Yuki	6
8	KIM Do Heon	65		ENDO Yashuhito	7
17	KIM Jung Woo		78	YAMAGISHI Satoru	9
27	OH Jang Eun	86		NAKAMURA Shunsuke	10
9	CHO Jae Jin			SUZUKI Keita	13
10	LEE Chun Soo		72	NAKAMURA Kengo	14
19	YEOM Ki Hun	39		TAKAHARA Naohiro	19
	Tr: VERBEEK Peter			Tr: OSIM Ivica	
6	LEE Ho	86	72	HANYU Naotake	8
11	LEE Keun Ho	39	78	SATO Hisato	11
13	KIM Chi Gon	65			

AFC ASIAN CUP 2007 FINAL

Gelora Bung Karno Main Stadium, Jakarta, Indonesia

29-07-2007, 19:35, 60 000

IRAQ   1   0   SAUDI ARABIA

Younis Mahmoud [73]

		IRAQ			MATCH OFFICIALS		SAUDI ARABIA		
22	GK	HASSAN Noor Sabri Abbas					AL MOSAILEM Yasser	GK	1
2	DF	AL HAMD Jassim Gholan			REFEREE		HAWSAWI Osama	DF	3
3	DF	GATEA Bassim Abbas	89		SHIELD Mark AUS		AL MOUSA Kamil	DF	7
14	DF	HUSSAIN Haidar Abdul Amer			ASSISTANTS	84	AL BAHRI Ahmed	DF	15
15	DF	REHEMA Ali Hussein			SAEED Mohamed MDV		JAHDALI Walid Abdrabh	DF	19
5	MF	ALI Nashat Akram			ALLABERDIYEV Begench TKM		KHARIRI Saud	MF	14
11	MF	TAHER Hawar Mohammed			4TH OFFICIAL		AL THAKER Khaled Aziz	MF	16
13	MF	MUHAMED Karrar Jassim	83		AL FADHLI Saad KUW	46	AL KAHTANI Abdulrahman	MF	18
18	MF	AJEEL Mahdi Karim	90				(c) AL KAHTANI Yasser	MF	20
24	MF	ABOUDY Qusay Munir					ALHAWSAWI Malek Maaz	FW	9
10	FW	KHALEF Younis Mahmoud (c)				76	AL JASSAM Taiseer	FW	17
		Tr: VIEIRA Jorvan					Tr: HELIO DOS ANJOS		
		Substitutes					Substitutes		
7	MF	MSHEHID Ali Abbas	89			84	AL HARTHI Saad	FW	11
8	MF	MOHAMED Ahmed Abid Ali	90			76	AUTEF Abdoh	MF	28
16	FW	ABBAS Ahmed Menajed	83			46	AL MOUSA Ahmed	MF	30

The Iraqi players are fantastic people but you have to understand their difficulties. I can feel when I'm going to lose a match but today I felt well and was sure that we could do something because of my relationship with the players. They have so much confidence, they were so sure and they wanted to win because it was very important for their country.

Jorvan Vieira

We knew that Iraq would be a very difficult team to play in the final. Because of the political situation in Iraq, they were very motivated to do well and they also had the support of the crowd here and all around the world. I am very happy for the Iraqi team, for all of their staff and especially for all of the people in Iraq because they deserve to be happy.

Helio dos Anjos

AFC U-17 CHAMPIONSHIP SINGAPORE 2006

Qualifying Group A

(In Jordan)	Pl	W	D	L	F	A	Pts	JOR	PLE
Iraq	2	2	0	0	4	0	**6**	1-0	3-0
Jordan	2	1	0	1	2	1	**3**		2-0
Palestine	2	0	0	2	0	5	**0**		

Qualifying Group B

(In Qatar)	Pl	W	D	L	F	A	Pts	QAT	BHR
Yemen	2	2	0	0	6	3	**6**	2-0	4-3
Qatar	2	1	0	1	2	3	**3**		2-1
Bahrain	2	0	0	2	4	6	**0**		

Qualifying Group C

(In Oman)	Pl	W	D	L	F	A	Pts	OMA	LIB
Saudi Arabia	2	2	0	0	8	1	**6**	4-0	4-1
Oman	2	1	0	1	5	5	**3**		5-1
Lebanon	2	0	0	2	2	9	**0**		

Qualifying Group D

(In Syria)	Pl	W	D	L	F	A	Pts	UAE	KUW
Syria	2	1	1	0	2	0	**4**	2-0	0-0
UAE	2	1	0	1	2	2	**3**		2-0
Kuwait	2	0	1	1	0	2	**1**		

Qualifying Group E

(Home/Away)	Pl	W	D	L	F	A	Pts	BAN	SRI
Bangladesh	2	1	0	1	3	1	**3**		3-0
Sri Lanka	2	1	0	1	1	3	**3**	1-0	

Qualifying Group F

(In Nepal)	Pl	W	D	L	F	A	Pts	UZB	KGZ
Nepal	2	2	0	0	4	1	**6**	2-0	2-1
Uzbekistan	2	1	0	1	2	2	**3**		2-0
Kyrgyzstan	2	0	0	2	1	4	**0**		

Qualifying Group G

(In India)	Pl	W	D	L	F	A	Pts	IND	PAK
Tajikistan	2	2	0	0	4	2	**6**	3-2	1-0
India	2	1	0	1	11	3	**3**		9-0
Pakistan	2	0	0	2	0	10	**0**		

Qualifying Group H

(Home/Away)	Pl	W	D	L	F	A	Pts	IRN	TKM
Iran	2	2	0	0	10	2	**6**		5-0
Turkmenistan	2	0	0	2	2	10	**0**	2-5	

Qualifying Group I

(In Laos)	Pl	W	D	L	F	A	Pts	AUS	IDN
Laos	2	1	1	0	5	0	**4**	0-0	5-0
Australia	2	1	1	0	3	1	**4**		3-1
Indonesia	2	0	0	2	1	8	**0**		

Qualifying Group J

(In Thailand)	Pl	W	D	L	F	A	Pts	THA	MDV
Myanmar	2	1	1	0	13	1	**4**	1-1	10-0
Thailand	2	1	1	0	11	1	**4**		12-0
Maldives	2	0	0	2	0	22	**0**		

Qualifying Group K

(Home/Away)	Pl	W	D	L	F	A	Pts	VIE	MAS
Vietnam	2	2	0	0	2	0	**6**		1-0
Malaysia	2	0	0	2	0	2	**0**	0-1	

Qualifying Group L

(In Korea Rep)	Pl	W	D	L	F	A	Pts	KOR	MAC
Japan	2	1	1	0	27	1	**4**	1-1	26-0
Korea Republic	2	1	1	0	15	1	**4**		14-0
Macau	2	0	0	2	0	40	**0**		

Qualifying Group M

(In China PR)	Pl	W	D	L	F	A	Pts	TPE	MGL
China PR	2	2	0	0	20	0	**6**	9-0	11-0
Chinese Taipei	2	1	0	1	2	10	**3**		2-1
Mongolia	2	0	0	2	1	13	**0**		

Play-off in Kuala Lumpur

Korea Republic	1
Thailand	0

Qualifying Group N

(In Korea DPR)	Pl	W	D	L	F	A	Pts	HKG	GUM
Korea DPR	2	2	0	0	21	2	**6**	4-0	17-2
Hong Kong	2	0	1	1	2	6	**1**		2-2
Guam	2	0	1	1	4	19	**1**		

AFC U-17 CHAMPIONSHIP SINGAPORE 2006

First round groups

Group A	Pl	W	D	L	F	A	Pts	KOR	SIN	NEP
Japan	3	2	1	0	10	3	**7**	3-2	1-1	6-0
Korea Republic	3	2	0	1	7	4	**6**		3-1	2-0
Singapore	3	0	2	1	2	4	**2**			0-0
Nepal	3	0	1	2	0	8	**1**			

Group B	Pl	W	D	L	F	A	Pts	IRN	IRQ	YEM
Tajikistan	3	3	0	0	7	4	**9**	2-1	1-0	4-3
Iran	3	1	1	1	2	2	**4**		0-0	1-0
Iraq	3	0	2	1	1	2	**2**			1-1
Yemen	3	0	1	2	4	6	**1**			

Group C	Pl	W	D	L	F	A	Pts	PRK	MYA	LAO
Saudi Arabia	2	2	0	0	7	1	**6**	2-1	5-0	
Korea DPR	2	1	0	1	7	4	**3**		6-2	
Myanmar	2	0	0	2	2	11	**0**			
Laos				Disqualified						

Group D	Pl	W	D	L	F	A	Pts	SYR	VIE	BAN
China PR	3	2	1	0	9	3	**7**	1-0	3-3	5-0
Syria	3	2	0	1	9	1	**6**		2-0	7-0
Vietnam	3	1	1	1	5	5	**4**			2-0
Bangladesh	3	0	0	3	0	14	**0**			

Quarter-finals

Japan		1 8p
Iran		1 7p
Saudi Arabia		1
Syria		2
Tajikistan		1
Korea Republic		0
China PR		1
Korea DPR		2

Semi-finals

Japan	2
Syria	0
Tajikistan	0
Korea DPR	3

Final

Japan	4
Korea DPR	2

Third Place Play-off

Tajikistan	3 5p
Syria	3 4p

Held in Singapore from 3-09-2006 to 17-09-2006 • Japan, Korea DPR, Tajikistan and Syria qualified for the FIFA U-17 World Cup Korea 2007

AFC YOUTH CHAMPIONSHIP INDIA 2006

Qualifying Group A

(In Kuwait)	Pl	W	D	L	F	A	Pts	KUW	LIB
Iraq	2	2	0	0	3	0	6	1-0	2-0
Kuwait	2	1	0	1	4	2	3		4-1
Lebanon	2	0	0	2	1	6	0		

Qualifying Group B

(In Saudi)	Pl	W	D	L	F	A	Pts	SYR	OMA
Saudi Arabia	2	2	0	0	7	3	6	3-1	4-2
Syria	2	1	0	1	3	3	3		2-0
Oman	2	0	0	2	2	6	0		

Qualifying Group C

(In UAE)	Pl	W	D	L	F	A	Pts	YEM	PLE
UAE	2	2	0	0	8	0	6	2-0	6-0
Yemen	2	1	0	1	3	2	3		3-0
Palestine	2	0	0	2	0	9	0		

Qualifying Group D

(In Jordan)	Pl	W	D	L	F	A	Pts	BHR	QAT
Jordan	2	1	0	1	4	3	3	0-2	4-1
Bahrain	2	1	0	1	2	2	3		0-2
Qatar	2	1	0	1	3	4	3		

Qualifying Group E

(In Tajikistan)	Pl	W	D	L	F	A	Pts	UZB	PAK
Tajikistan	2	1	1	0	8	0	4	0-0	8-0
Uzbekistan	2	1	1	0	3	0	4		3-0
Pakistan	2	0	0	2	0	11	0		

Qualifying Group F

(Home/Away)	Pl	W	D	L	F	A	Pts	KGZ	NEP
Kyrgyzstan	2	2	0	0	3	0	6		2-0
Nepal	2	0	0	2	0	3	0	0-1	

Qualifying Group G

(In Sri Lanka)	Pl	W	D	L	F	A	Pts	SRI	TKM
Australia	2	2	0	0	7	0	6	4-0	3-0
Sri Lanka	2	1	0	1	2	5	3		2-1
Turkmenistan	2	0	0	2	1	5	0		

Qualifying Group H

(Home/Away)	Pl	W	D	L	F	A	Pts	IRN	BAN
Iran	2	2	0	0	7	0	6		5-0
Bangladesh	2	0	0	2	0	7	0	0-2	

Qualifying Group I

(Home/Away)	Pl	W	D	L	F	A	Pts	MAS	MYA
Malaysia	2	1	0	1	4	3	3		4-2
Myanmar	2	1	0	1	3	4	3	1-0	

Qualifying Group J

(In Singapore)	Pl	W	D	L	F	A	Pts	IDN	SIN
Thailand	2	2	0	0	5	1	6	3-1	2-0
Indonesia	2	0	1	1	2	4	1		1-1
Singapore	2	0	1	1	3	1	1		

Qualifying Group K

(In Vietnam)	Pl	W	D	L	F	A	Pts	LAO	MDV
Vietnam	2	1	1	0	5	2	4	1-1	4-1
Laos	2	1	1	0	2	1	4		1-0
Maldives	2	0	0	2	1	5	0		

Qualifying Group L

(In Macau)	Pl	W	D	L	F	A	Pts	GUM	MAC
China PR	2	2	0	0	26	1	6	17-0	9-1
Guam	2	1	0	1	2	17	3		2-0
Macau	2	0	0	2	1	11	0		

Qualifying Group M

(In Korea Rep)	Pl	W	D	L	F	A	Pts	HKG	MGL
Korea Republic	2	2	0	0	15	0	6	2-0	13-0
Hong Kong	2	1	0	1	4	5	3		4-3
Mongolia	2	0	0	2	3	17	0		

Play-off

Korea DPR	W-0
Myanmar	

Qualifying Group N

(In Japan)	Pl	W	D	L	F	A	Pts	PRK	TPE
Japan	2	2	0	0	6	0	6	1-0	5-0
Korea DPR	2	1	0	1	5	1	3		5-0
Chinese Taipei	2	0	0	2	0	10	0		

AFC YOUTH CHAMPIONSHIP INDIA 2006

First round groups

Group A	Pl	W	D	L	F	A	Pts	JOR	KGZ	IND
Korea Republic	3	3	0	0	13	0	9	3-0	7-0	3-0
Jordan	3	1	1	1	3	5	4		0-0	3-2
Kyrgyzstan	3	0	2	1	1	8	2			1-1
India	3	0	1	2	3	7	1			

Group B	Pl	W	D	L	F	A	Pts	AUS	THA	UAE
China PR	3	3	0	0	4	1	9	1-0	1-0	2-1
Australia	3	2	0	1	5	2	6		3-1	2-0
Thailand	3	1	0	2	3	5	3			2-1
UAE	3	0	0	3	2	6	0			

Group C	Pl	W	D	L	F	A	Pts	PRK	IRN	TJK
Japan	3	2	0	1	7	2	6	2-0	1-2	4-0
Korea DPR	3	2	0	1	6	2	6		5-0	1-0
Iran	3	2	0	1	5	7	6			3-1
Tajikistan	3	0	0	3	1	8	0			

Group D	Pl	W	D	L	F	A	Pts	KSA	VIE	MAS
Iraq	3	2	1	0	8	3	7	2-2	3-1	3-0
Saudi Arabia	3	2	1	0	6	2	7		2-0	2-0
Vietnam	3	1	0	2	3	6	3			2-1
Malaysia	3	0	0	3	1	7	0			

Quarter-finals

Korea DPR	2
Iraq	0
China PR	1
Jordan	2
Korea Republic	2
Australia	1
Saudi Arabia	1
Japan	2

Semi-finals

Korea DPR	1	
Jordan	0	
Korea Republic	1	2p
Japan	1	3p

Final

Korea DPR	1	5p
Japan	1	3p

Third Place Play-off

Korea Republic	2
Jordan	0

Played in India from 29-10-2006 to 12-11-2006 • Korea DPR, Japan, Korea Republic and Jordan qualified for the FIFA U-20 World Cup Canada 2007

AFC WOMEN'S U–16 CHAMPIONSHIP 2007

AFC WOMEN'S U-16 CHAMPIONSHIP MALAYSIA 2007

Preliminary groups

	IND	JOR	Pts
Korea DPR	3-0	6-0	6
India		3-1	3
Jordan			0

	MYA	HKG	Pts
Korea Republic	4-2	12-0	6
Myanmar		7-0	3
Hong Kong			0

	VIE	SIN	Pts
Australia	4-0	9-0	6
Vietnam		6-0	3
Singapore			0

	TPE	MDV	Pts
Thailand	2-2	7-0	4
Taiwan		6-0	4
Maldives			0

First round groups

	KOR	AUS	Pts
China PR	3-1	0-0	4
Korea Republic		3-1	3
Australia			1

	JPN	THA	Pts
Korea DPR	1-0	7-1	6
Japan		2-1	3
Thailand			0

Semi-finals

Korea DPR	4
Korea Republic	1

China PR	1
Japan	3

Final

Korea DPR †	3
Japan †	0

3rd Place Play-off

Korea Republic †	1	4p
China PR	1	2p

Final tournament held in Malaysia from 8-03-2007 to 17-03-2007 • † Qualified for the FIFA U-17 Women's World Cup New Zealand 2008

AFC WOMEN'S U–19 CHAMPIONSHIP 2007

AFC WOMEN'S U-19 CHAMPIONSHIP 2007

Preliminary 1

A - in KGZ	IRN	KGZ	Pts
Jordan	1-0	6-0	6
Iran		2-0	3
Kyrgyzstan			0

B - in SIN	BAN	BHR	Pts
Singapore	0-0	2-1	4
Bangladesh		1-0	4
Bahrain			0

C - in TPE	UZB	TJK	Pts
Hong Kong	1-2	3-1	3
Uzbekistan		2-3	3
Tajikistan			3

D - MAS	MDV	IDN	Pts
Guam	1-1	2-0	4
Maldives		1-0	4
Indonesia			0

Preliminary 2

A - in MAS	MYA	IND	JOR	SIN	Pts
Thailand	3-3	5-1	5-0	17-0	10
Myanmar		2-1	2-0	11-1	10
India			4-0	7-0	6
Jordan				7-0	3
Singapore					0

B - in TPE	VIE	GUM	HKG	Pts
Taiwan	1-0	5-0	8-0	9
Vietnam		3-0	3-0	6
Guam			3-0	3
Hong Kong				0

First Round Groups — Pts

Semi-finals — Pts

Final

Preliminary 1 held 17-10-2006 to 21-10-2006 • Preliminary 2 held 7-11-2006 to 15-11-2006 • Final tournament moved from Malaysia to China PR and delayed until October 2007 • Acts as U-20 Women's World Cup qualifiers

ASIAN GAMES DOHA 2006

ASIAN GAMES DOHA 2006 MEN'S FOOTBALL TOURNAMENT

Preliminary groups

	KGZ	TJK	MAC	Pts
Jordan	0-0	0-0	13-0	5
Kyrgyzstan		2-2	7-0	5
Tajikistan			5-1	5
Macao				0

	SYR	SIN	IDN	Pts
Iraq	0-0	2-0	6-0	7
Syria		0-0	4-1	5
Singapore			1-1	2
Indonesia				1

First round groups

	QAT	UAE	JOR	Pts
Uzbekistan	1-0	2-1	3-1	9
Qatar		4-1	3-0	6
UAE			1-1	1
Jordan				1

	BHR	VIET	BAN	Pts
Korea Rep	1-0	2-0	3-0	9
Bahrain		2-1	5-1	6
Vietnam			5-1	3
Bangladesh				0

	KUW	KGZ	PLE	Pts
Thailand	1-0	2-0	1-0	9
Kuwait		3-0	2-0	6
Kyrgyzstan			3-0	3
Palestine				0

	HKG	IND	MDV	Pts
Iran	2-1	2-0	3-1	9
Hong Kong		1-1	1-0	4
India			2-1	4
Maldives				0

	IRQ	OMA	MAS	Pts
China PR	1-0	2-1	3-1	9
Iraq		2-0	4-0	6
Oman			3-1	3
Malaysia				0

	JPN	SYR	PAK	Pts
Korea DPR	2-1	0-0	1-0	7
Japan		1-0	3-2	6
Syria			2-0	4
Pakistan				0

Quarter-finals

Qatar	3
Thailand	0

China PR	2 7p
Iran	2 8p

Korea Rep	3
Korea DPR	0

Uzbekistan	1
Iraq	2

Semi-finals

Qatar	2
Iran	0

Korea Rep	0
Iraq	1

Final

Qatar	1
Iraq	0

3rd Place Play-off

Iran	1
Korea Rep	0

Played in Doha, Al Wakra and Al Rayyan in Qatar from 18-11-2006 to 15-12-2006 • Played as a U-23 tournament

ASIAN GAMES DOHA 2006 WOMEN'S FOOTBALL TOURNAMENT

First Round Group Stage

	Pl	W	D	L	F	A	Pts	CHN	THA	JOR
Japan	3	3	0	0	18	0	9	1-0	4-0	13-0
China PR	3	2	0	1	19	1	6		7-0	12-0
Thailand	3	1	0	2	5	11	3			5-0
Jordan	3	0	0	3	0	30	0			

	Pl	W	D	L	F	A	Pts	KOR	TAI	VIE
Korea DPR	3	3	0	0	13	1	9	4-1	4-0	5-0
Korea Republic	3	2	0	1	6	5	6		2-0	3-1
Taiwan	3	1	0	2	3	7	3			3-1
Vietnam	3	0	0	3	2	11	0			

Semi-finals

Korea DPR	3
China PR	1

Korea Republic	1
Japan	3

Final

Korea DPR	0 4p
Japan	0 2p

3rd Place Play-off

China PR	2
Korea Republic	0

Held in Doha and Al Rayyan in Qatar from 30-11-2006 to 13-12-2006 • Full national team tournament

REGIONAL TOURNAMENTS IN ASIA 2006–07

ASEAN FOOTBALL FEDERATION CHAMPIONSHIP 2006-07

Preliminary group

First round groups

Group A	MAS	MYA	PHI	Pts
Thailand	1-0	1-1	4-0	**7**
Malaysia		0-0	4-0	**4**
Myanmar			0-0	**3**
Philippines				**1**

	PHI	CAM	BRU	TLS	Pts
Laos	2-1	2-2	4-1	3-2	**10**
Philippines		1-0	4-1	7-0	**9**
Cambodia			1-1	4-1	**5**
Brunei				3-2	**4**
Timor-Leste					**0**

Group B	VIE	IDN	LAO	Pts
Singapore	0-0	2-2	11-0	**5**
Vietnam		1-1	9-0	**5**
Indonesia			3-1	**5**
Laos				**0**

Semi-finals

Singapore	1	1	5p
Malaysia	1	1	4p

Vietnam	0	0
Thailand	2	0

Final

Singapore	2	1
Thailand	1	1

Preliminary round held in Bacolod, Philippines from 12-11-2006 to 20-11-2006 • Group A of the final tournament held in Bangkok, Thailand from 13-01-2007 to 16-01-2007 • Group B of the final tournament held in Singapore from 13-01-2007 to 17-01-2007 • Semi-finals and final held home and away from 23-01-2007 to 4-02-2007

ASEAN Cup Final, National Stadium, Singapore
1st leg. 31-01-2007, 20:00, 55 000, Ravichandran MAS

SIN	2 1	THA

Noh Alam Shah [17], Fahrudin [90p] | Pipat Thonkanya [50]

SINGAPORE			THAILAND	
18	Lionel LEWIS		Kittisak RAWANGPA	22
16	Daniel BENNETT		Jetsada JITSAWAD	4
21	Precious EMUEJERAYE		Nataporn PHANRIT	6
5	Aide ISKANDAR		Niweat SIRIWONG	5
20	Mohamed Noh RAHMAN		Suree SUKKA	2
15	Mustafic FAHRUDIN		Nirut SURASIANG	21
7	SI Jia Yi		Datsakorn THONGLAO	7
2	Muhammad RIDHUAN	79	Sarayoot CHAIKAMDEE	9
8	Noh Alam SHAH		Suchao NUTNUM	14
11	Fazrul NAWAZ	66	Sutee SUKSOMKIT	17
10	Indra SAHDAN	45	Pipat THONKANYA	23
	Tr: Radojko AVRAMOVIC		Tr: Chanvit PHALAJIVIN	
17	Shahril ISHAK	79	35 Natthaphomg SAMANA	19
19	Khairul AMRI	45	90 Khwanchai PHUANGPRAKOB	25
22	Itimi DICKSON	66		

ASEAN Cup Final, Suphachalasai, Bangkok
2nd leg. 4-02-2007, 20:00, 30 000, Napitupulu IDN

THA	1 1	SIN

Pipat Thonkanya [37] | Khairul Amri [81]

THAILAND			SINGAPORE	
22	Kittisak RAWANGPA		Lionel LEWIS	18
4	Jetsada JITSAWAD		Daniel BENNETT	16
19	Natthaphomg SAMANA		Precious EMUEJERAYE	21
5	Niweat SIRIWONG		Aide ISKANDAR	5
2	Suree SUKKA		Mohamed Noh RAHMAN	20
8	Hadthporn SUWAN	79	56 Itimi DICKSON	22
12	Pichitpong CHOELCHEW	90	Mustafic FAHRUDIN	15
7	Datsakorn THONGLAO		Shahril ISHAK	17
14	Suchao NUTNUM		SI Jia Yi	7
17	Sutee SUKSOMKIT		88 Muhammad RIDHUAN	2
23	Pipat THONKANYA		Noh Alam SHAH	8
	Tr: Chanvit PHALAJIVIN		Tr: Radojko AVRAMOVIC	
15	BUNKHAM	79	88 Shunmughan SUBRAMANI	14
25	Khwanchai PHUANGPRAKOB	90	56 Khairul AMRI	19

SOUTH ASIAN FEDERATION GAMES COLOMBO 2006

First Round Group Stage

	Pl	W	D	L	F	A	Pts	PAK	MDV	BHU
Sri Lanka	3	2	0	1	5	1	6	0-1	1-0	4-0
Pakistan	3	2	0	1	6	3	6		1-3	4-0
Maldives	3	2	0	1	4	2	6			1-0
Bhutan	3	0	0	3	0	9	0			

	Pl	W	D	L	F	A	Pts	IND	BAN	AFG
Nepal	3	1	2	0	7	3	5	1-1	1-1	5-1
India	3	1	2	0	3	2	5		2-1	0-0
Bangladesh	3	0	2	1	2	3	2			0-0
Afghanistan	3	0	2	1	1	5	2			

Held in Colombo, Sri Lanka from 14-08-2006 to 26-08-2006 • U-23 event

Semi-finals

Pakistan	2
Nepal	1

India	1 5p
Sri Lanka	1 6p

Final

Pakistan	1
Sri Lanka	0

3rd Place Play-off

Nepal	2
India	0

GULF CUP ABU DHABI 2007

First Round Group Stage

	Pl	W	D	L	F	A	Pts	UAE	KUW	YEM
Oman	3	3	0	0	6	3	9	2-1	2-1	2-1
UAE	3	2	0	1	6	5	6		3-2	2-1
Kuwait	3	0	1	2	4	6	1			1-1
Yemen	3	0	1	2	3	5	1			

	Pl	W	D	L	F	A	Pts	BHR	IRQ	QAT
Saudi Arabia	3	2	1	0	4	2	7	2-1	1-0	1-1
Bahrain	3	1	1	1	4	4	4		1-1	2-1
Iraq	3	1	1	1	2	2	4			1-0
Qatar	3	0	1	2	2	4	1			

Held in Abu Dhabi, UAE, from 17-01-2007 to 30-01-2007

Semi-finals

UAE	1
Saudi Arabia	0

Bahrain	0
Oman	1

Final

UAE	1
Oman	0

WEST ASIAN FEDERATION CHAMPIONSHIP JORDAN 2007

First Round Group Stage

	Pl	W	D	L	F	A	Pts	JOR	LIB
Syria	2	2	0	0	2	0	6	1-0	1-0
Jordan	2	1	0	1	3	1	3		3-0
Lebanon	2	0	0	2	0	4	0		

	Pl	W	D	L	F	A	Pts	IRQ	PLE
Iran	2	1	1	0	2	0	4	0-0	2-0
Iraq	2	1	1	0	1	0	4		1-0
Palestine	2	0	0	2	0	3	0		

Held in Amman, Jordan, from 16-06-2007 to 24-06-2007

Semi-finals

Iran	1
Jordan	0

Syria	0
Iraq	3

Final

Iran	2
Iraq	1

AFC CHAMPIONS LEAGUE 2006

AFC CHAMPIONS LEAGUE 2006

Group Stage			Quarter-finals		Semi-finals		Final	

Group A — Pts

		Pts
Al Qadisiya	KUW	11
Pakhtakor Tashkent	UZB	10
Al Ittihad	SYR	8
Foolad	IRN	4

Group B — Pts

		Pts
Al Ain	UAE	13
Al Hilal	KSA	10
Mash'al	UZB	8
Al Mina'a	IRQ	2

Quarter-final:
Jeonbuk Motors   0 4
Shanghai Shenhua *   1 2

Group C — Pts

		Pts
Al Karama	SYR	12
Saba Battery	IRN	10
Al Wahda	UAE	7
Al Gharafa	QAT	6

Quarter-final:
Al Shabab   0 0
Ulsan Horang-i *   6 1

Semi-final:
Jeonbuk Motors *   2 4
Ulsan Horang-i   3 1

Group D — Pts

		Pts
Al Shabab	KSA	13
Al Sadd	QAT	13
Al Quwa Al Jawiya	IRQ	6
Al Arabi	KUW	3

Final:
Jeonbuk Motors *   2 1
Al Karama   0 2

Group E — Pts

		Pts
Jeonbuk Motors	KOR	13
Dalian	CHN	12
Gamba Osaka	JPN	10
Da Nang	VIE	0

Quarter-final:
Al Qadisiya *   2 3
Al Ain   2 0

Semi-final:
Al Qadisiya *   0 0
Al Karama   0 1

Group F — Pts

		Pts
Ulsan Hyundai	KOR	6
Tokyo Verdy	JPN	0

Quarter-final:
Al Ittihad *   2 0
Al Karama   0 4

Group G — Pts

		Pts
Shanghai Shenhua	CHN	6
Dong Tam	VIE	0

† Al Ittihad (KSA) given a bye to the quarter-finals as holders • * Home team in the first leg • For results and match details from the group stage see **Almanack of World Football 2007** pages 901–906

QUARTER-FINALS

Yuan Shen, Shanghai
13-09-2006, 20:00, 5000, Kamikawa JPN

Shanghai Shenhua 1

Gao Lin [32]

Zhou Yajun - Ng Wai Chiu● (Li Chengming 74),
Cheng Liang●, Sun Xiang, Li Weifeng, Sun Ji●, Zheng
Kewei, Shen Longyuan●, Luis Ramirez (Jancker 70),
Mao Jianqing (Wang Ke 81), Gao Lin

Jeonbuk Motors 0

Kwoun Sun Tae - Choi Chul Soon, Choi Jin Cheul, Kim
Young Sun●, Wang Jun Hyun●, Kim Jae Young, Jeon
Kwang Hwan, Kwon Jip, Kim Hyeung Bum●36, Cho Jin
Soo (Botti 66●76), Ze Carlo

Jeonju World Cup Stadium, Jeonju
20-09-2006, 19:00, 9000, Kunsuta THA

Jeonbuk Motors 4

Ze Carlo 2 [44 62], Yeom KH [69], Chung JK [78]

Kwoun Sun Tae - Choi Chul Soon, Choi Jin Cheul (Kim In
Ho 60), Kim Young Sun, Wang Jun Hyun (Cho Jin Soo 86),
Kim Jae Young, Chung Jung Kwan, Yeom Ki Hun, Kwon
Jip (Lee Hyun Seung 51), Jang Ji Hyun, Ze Carlo●

Shanghai Shenhua 2

Gao Lin [35], Jancker [90]

Zhou Yajun - Ng Wai Chiu, Cheng Liang, Sun Xiang,
Li Weifeng●37, Sun Ji●, Zheng Kewei, Shen Longyuan
(Jancker 78), Luis Ramirez (Yu Tao 65), Mao
Jianqing● (Li Chengming 41), Gao Lin

Ulsan Munsu, Ulsan
13-09-2006, 19:00, 3873, Irmatov UZB

Ulsan Horang-i 6

Lee Chun Soo [22], Lee Sang Ho [28], Leandro [69],
Choi Sung Kuk 2 [35 78], Machado [87]

Kim Jee Hyuk - Park Byung Gyu, Cho Se Kwon (Byun Sung
Hwan 66), Park Dong Hyuk, Park Kyu Seon, Lee Sang Ho,
Lee Jong Min, Kim Young Sam, Lee Chun Soo (Jang Sang
Won 79), Choi Sung Kuk, Leandro● (Machado 77)

Al Shabab 0

M.Khojah - A.Al Dosari, S.Sadeeq, H.Maaz
(A.Al Astaa 46), A.Shuhail, A.Autef, S.Shrahilee
(H.Fllath 66), A.Ateef, Y.Al Muwaine, H.Antchouet
(A.bin Saran 46), F.Fallata

King Fahad International, Riyadh
20-09-2006, 20:15, 2000, Mohd Salleh MAS

Al Shabab 0

S.Al Harbi - A.Al Dosari, S.Sadeeq, H.Maaz,
S.Shrahilee, N.Ousmane, A.Ateef● (M.Al Dosari 67),
Y.Al Muwaine, N.Akram (A.Autef 62), H.Antchouet●
(F.bin Sultan 63), N.Majrashi

Ulsan Horang-i 1

Park Dong Hyuk [50]

Kim Jee Hyuk - Park Byung Gyu, You Kyoung Youl, Park
Dong Hyuk●, Jang Sang Won (Lee Hyun Min 87), Byun
Sung Hwan, Lee Sang Ho, Lee Jong Min, Kim Young Sam,
Machado (Yang Dong Hyen 61), Leandro (Cho Se Kwon 88)

Friendship & Peace, Kuwait City
13-09-2006, 19:45, 9000, Maidin SIN

Al Qadisiya 2

Khalaf Salama 2 [45 48]

N.Al Khaldi - A.Al Shamali, M.Neda● (S.Al Shammari
81), N.Al Shammari, J.Mubarak, B.Keita, A.Mussa
(S.Al Hendi 72), F.Basheer, K.Salama, M.Mubarak
(N.Al Mutairi 81), B.Al Mutwa

Al Ain 2

Jestrovic [23], Dodo [66]

Waleed Salem● - Ali Msarri (Gharib Harib 43),
Abdulla Ali●, Fahad Ali (Juma Khater 71), Humaid
Fakher, Juma Abdulla, Rami Yaslam, Helal Saeed,
Subait Khater (Shehab Ahmed 90), Jestrovic, Dodo

Khalifa Bin Zayed, Al Ain
20-09-2006, 19:25, 10 000, Shield AUS

Al Ain 0

Waleed Salem - Ali Ahmed (Faisal Ali 75), Abdulla Ali,
Fahad Ali, Humaid Fakher, Juma Abdulla●95+, Rami
Yaslam (Shehab Ahmed 46), Helal Saeed● (Gharib
Harib 68), Subait Khater●, Jestrovic, Dodo

Al Qadisiya 3

Basheer 2 [26 91+], M.Mubarak [94+]

N.Al Khaldi - A.Al Shamali●, M.Neda, N.Al Shammari,
J.Mubarak, S.Al Hendi, B.Keita●, N.Al Mutairi●,
F.Basheer●, K.Salama● (M.Mubarak● 68), B.Al Mutwa
(M.Al Otaibi 92+)

Prince Abdullah Al Faisal, Jeddah
13-09-2006, 20:20, 20 000, Ebrahim BHR

Al Ittihad 2

Alhassane Keita [43], Borgetti [46]

Mabrouk Zaid - Ahmed Dokhi, Redha Tukar●, O.Al Harbi,
M.Al Saeed, Mohammed Noor (Mohammed Haidar 84),
Acimovic (Ibrahim Sowed 71), S.Al Khariri, Alhassane
Keita, Manaf Abushgeer, Borgetti (Hamzah Idris● 53)

Al Karama 0

M.Balhous (A.Al Hafez 30) - N.Al Sebai, Fabio Santos●,
H.Abbas●, J.Kassab, A.Al Khouja (A.Akkari 76), J.Al
Hussein, AK.Refai, M.Al Hamwi (M.Ibrahim 82),
I.Mando, A.Al Omeir

KB Al Waleed Stadium, Homs
20-09-2006, 21:30, 25 000, Torky IRN

Al Karama 4

Mando [41], Al Omeir [49], Ibrahim 2 [105 108]

M.Balhous● - Fabio Santos, H.Abbas, J.Kassab,
B.Abduldaim● (T.Taearah 90) (N.Al Sebai 115),
A.Al Khouja, J.Al Hussein, AK.Refai, M.Al Hamwi●,
I.Mando, A.Al Omeir● (M.Ibrahim● 97)

Al Ittihad 0

Mabrouk Zaid - Ahmed Dokhi●, Redha Tukar (A.Al
Shahrani● 11) (S.Al Aboud 78), O.Al Harbi●, M.Al Saeed,
Mohammed Noor, S.Al Saqri, Acimovic (M.Al Otaibi 53),
S.Al Khariri●●113, Alhassane Keita, Manaf Abushgeer

SEMI-FINALS

Jeonju World Cup Stadium, Jeonju
27-09-2006, 19:00, 12 473, Breeze AUS

Jeonbuk Motors 2

Ze Carlo [26p], Yeom Ki Hun [46]

Kwoun Sun Tae - Choi Chul Soon, Choi Jin Cheul, Kim
Young Sun, Kim Jae Young (Wang Jung Hyun 42),
Chung Jung Kwan (Cho Jin Soo 83), Botti, Yeom Ki Hun,
Jeon Kwang Hwan (Kim In Ho 46), Kwon Jip●, Ze Carlo●

Ulsan Horang-i 3

You Kyoung Youl [6], Vinicius [37], Choi Sung Kuk [82]

Kim Jee Hyuk - Vinicius, Park Byung Gyu, You Kyoung
Youl●, Park Dong Hyuk●, Park Kyu Seon●, Lee Sang Ho
(Machado 66), Lee Jong Min, Kim Young Sam, Choi Sung
Kuk (Jang Sang Won 92+), Leandro (Cho Se Kwon 91+)

Ulsan Munsu, Ulsan
18-10-2006, 19:30, Maidin SIN

Ulsan Horang-i 1

Lee Chun Soo [70]

Kim Jee Hyuk - Vinicius (Jang Sang Won 59), Park Byung
Gyu, You Kyoung Youl●, Park Dong Hyuk●●90, Park Kyu
Seon (Machado 67), Lee Jong Min●, Kim Young Sam (Lee
Sang Ho 43), Lee Chun Soo, Choi Sung Kuk●, Leandro

Jeonbuk Motors 4

Choi JC [10], Chung JK [20], Lim YH [68], Lee KH [81]

Kwoun Sun Tae● - Choi Chul Soon, Choi Jin Cheul, Kim
Young Sun, Kim In Ho (Lim You Hwan 52), Chung Jung
Kwan, Botti (Lee Kwang Hyeon 53), Yeom Ki Hun, Kwon
Jip● (Kim Hyun Su 89), Kim Hyeung Bum, Ze Carlo

KB Al Waleed Stadium, Homs
27-09-2006, 21:30, 35 000, S Keun Soo KOR

Al Karama 0

M.Balhous - Fabio Santos, H.Abbas, J.Kassab●,
A.Al Khouja, J.Al Hussein, AK.Refai, M.Al Hamwi,
I.Mando, A.Jenyat (M.Ibrahim 61), A.Al Omeir
(A.Akkari 81)

Al Qadisiya 0

N.Al Khaldi● - A.Al Shamali, M.Neda,
N.Al Shammari●, J.Mubarak●, S.Al Hendi, B.Keita,
N.Al Mutairi, F.Basheer (M.Al Otaibi 84), K.Salama
(B.Al Mutwa 62), M.Mubarak● (A.Mussa 76)

Friendship & Peace, Kuwait City
18-10-2006, 21:30, 20 000, Nishimura JPN

Al Qadisiya 0

N.Al Khaldi - M.Neda, N.Al Shammari, A.Al Zahamil
(M.Mubarak 56), J.Mubarak, B.Keita, N.Al Mutairi,
A.Mussa (M.Al Otaibi 74), F.Basheer, K.Salama
(S.Al Hendi 61), B.Al Mutwa

Al Karama 1

Aatef Jenyat [15]

M.Balhous - Fabio Santos, J.Kassab, A.Al Khouja,
J.Al Hussein (M.Eid 73), AK.Refai●, M.Al Hamwi,
I.Mando●, A.Jenyat, A.Akkari● (M.Ibrahim 58),
A.Al Omeir (N.Al Sebai 73)

AFC CHAMPIONS LEAGUE FINAL FIRST LEG
Jeonju World Cup Stadium, Jeonju
1-11-2006, 19:00, 25 830, Mohd Salleh MAS

JEONBUK   2   0   AL KARAMA

Yeom Ki Hun [59], Botti [90]

Jeonbuk Motors			Al Karama	
21	KWOUN Sun Tae		BALHOUS Mosab	1
4	CHOI Jin Cheul		FABIO SANTOS	3
5	KIM Young Sun		KASSAB Jehad	5
6	KIM Hyun Su	51	AL KHOUJA Anas	14
16	LIM You Hwan		AL HUSSEIN Jehad	6
28	WANG Jung Hyun	57 86	REFAI Abdul Kader	7
8	CHUNG Jung Kwan		AL HAMWI Mohamad	9
11	YEOM Ki Hun	87	MANDO Iyad	10
22	KIM Hyeung Bum		JENYAT Aatef	21
26	JANG Ji Hyun	66	IBRAHIM Mohanad	8
15	ZE CARLO	80	AL OMEIR Ahmed	20
	Tr: CHOI Kang Hee		Tr: KWID Mohammed	
	Substitutes		Substitutes	
10	BOTTI	51	AL SEBAI Naser	2 66
12	JEON Kwang Hwan	57	EID Mohamad	15 86
20	KIM In Ho	87	SLEMAN Youssef	17 80

AFC CHAMPIONS LEAGUE FINAL SECOND LEG
Khaled Bin Al Waleed Stadium, Homs
8-11-2006, 19:00, 40 000, Shield AUS

AL KARAMA   2   1   JEONBUK

Iyad Mando [54],
Mohanad Ibrahim [61]   Ze Carlo [86]

Al Karama			Jeonbuk Motors	
1	BALHOUS Mosab		KWOUN Sun Tae	21
3	FABIO SANTOS		CHOI Jin Cheul	4
5	KASSAB Jehad		KIM Young Sun	5
13	ABDULDAIM Belal	86	KIM Hyun Su	6
14	AL KHOUJA Anas		LIM You Hwan	16
6	AL HUSSEIN Jehad		HAN Je Kwang	9
7	REFAI Abdul Kader		YEOM Ki Hun	11
9	AL HAMWI Mohamad	64 66	JEON Kwang Hwan	12
10	MANDO Iyad	56	KWON Jip	19
21	JENYAT Aatef		JANG Ji Hyun	26
8	IBRAHIM Mohanad	88	ZE CARLO	15
	Tr: KWID Mohammed		Tr: CHOI Kang Hee	
	Substitutes		Substitutes	
19	AKKARI Abdalrahman	86 66	KIM In Ho	20
20	AL OMEIR Ahmed	64 56	KIM Hyeung Bum	22
		88	WANG Jung Hyun	28

AFC CHAMPIONS LEAGUE 2007

ADELAIDE UTD		
	Goalkeepers	
1	Daniel Beltrame	AUS
20	Robert Bajic	AUS
	Defenders	
2	Richie Alagich	AUS
3	Kristian Rees	AUS
4	Angelo Costanzo	AUS
5	Michael Valkanis	AUS
14	Aaron Goulding	AUS
17	Adam Van Dommele	AUS
18	Robert Cornthwaite	AUS
	Midfielders	
6	Ross Aloisi	AUS
7	Lucas Pantelis	AUS
9	Matthew Kemp	AUS
12	Greg Owens	AUS
13	Travis Dodd	AUS
16	Bobby Petta	NED
21	Jason Spagnuolo	AUS
22	Diego Walsh	BRA
	Forwards	
8	Carl Veart	AUS
10	Fernando Rech	BRA
11	Dez Giraldi	AUS
15	Nathan Burns	AUS
19	Bruce Djite	AUS

AL AIN		
	Goalkeepers	
1	Mutaz Abdulla	UAE
12	Waleed Salem	UAE
30	Abdulla Sultan	UAE
	Defenders	
2	Fabricio Al Cantara	BRA
3	Juma Khater	UAE
4	Musallem Fayez	UAE
6	Ali Msarri	UAE
7	Ali Ahmed	UAE
16	Abdulla Ali	UAE
18	Fawzi Fayez	UAE
19	Fahad Ali	UAE
25	Humaid Fakher	UAE
26	Abdulla Mousa	UAE
28	Mahboub Juma	UAE
29	Juma Abdulla	UAE
	Midfielders	
5	Sultan Rashed	UAE
8	Ahmed Khalfan	UAE
13	Rami Yaslam	UAE
20	Helal Saeed	UAE
21	Gharib Harib	UAE
23	Shehab Ahmed	UAE
24	Ahmed Abdulla	UAE
	Forwards	
9	Faisal Ali	UAE
10	Frank Ongfiang	
11	Hawar Mohammed	IRQ
14	Nassib Ishaq	UAE
15	Nasser Khamis	
17	Abdulla Al Jaberi	
22	Adnan Mohammed	
27	Salem Abdulla	UAE

AL ARABI		
	Goalkeepers	
1	Yousef Al Thuwaini	KUW
22	Mahmod Husain	KUW
26	Muhamaad Ghanem	KUW
	Defenders	
2	Ali Al Maqseed	KUW
3	Abdulaziz Fadhel	KUW
5	Musaed Abdullah	KUW
6	Fahad Dabes	KUW
16	Ahmad Al Najjar	KUW
23	Ebrahim Meshkhas	BHR
27	Naser Al Shatti	KUW
28	Hussain Al Qhareeb	KUW
29	Hamdi Marzouki	TUN
	Midfielders	
4	Mohammad Jarragh	KUW
11	Muhammad Ashkanani	KUW
12	Abdullah Al Shamali	KUW
14	Mubarak Kamshad	KUW
15	Nawaf Al Shuwaye	KUW
18	Jasem Al Owisi	KUW
19	Malek Al Qallaf	KUW
20	Fahad Al Farhan	KUW
21	Ahmad Mousa	KUW
30	Homoud Majed	KUW
	Forwards	
7	Khaled Abdulkuddous	KUW
8	Ahmad Al Dhuwaihi	KUW
9	Jarrah Al Zuhair	KUW
10	Firas Al Khatib	SYR
13	Abdullah Al Mutawa	KUW
17	Khaled Khalaf	KUW
24	Yousef Al Khelifi	KUW
25	Husain Al Mosawi	KUW

AREMA MALANG		
	Goalkeepers	
1	Hendro Kartiko	IDN
3	Achmad Kurniawan	IDN
20	Hengky Oba	IDN
	Defenders	
2	Alexander Pulalo	IDN
4	Bruno Casimir	CMR
6	Suroso	IDN
8	Elie Aiboy	IDN
16	Rasmoyo	IDN
24	Richie Hari Pravita	IDN
26	Ortisan Salossa	IDN
28	Agung Yudha Kurniawan	IDN
29	Sunar Sulaiman	IDN
	Midfielders	
11	Ponaryo Astaman	IDN
14	Arif Suyono	IDN
17	Akbar Rasyid	IDN
27	Sutaji	IDN
	Forwards	
7	Setyo Prastowo	IDN
13	Jaenal Ichwan	IDN
19	Basile Essa Mvondo	IDN
21	Patricio Morales	CHI

BANGKOK UNIV.

Goalkeepers

1	Weera Koedpudsa	THA
18	Manteeva Lamsombat	THA
22	Phansa Meesattham	THA

Defenders

2	Sanit Soonki	THA
3	Apiwat Sriburin	THA
4	Kriangkrai Chasang	THA
5	Punnarat Klinsukon	THA
6	Thanayut Kaewjoho	THA
7	Polkrit Boonyasejtha	THA
19	Jeera Jarernsuk	THA
23	Narong Pram-On	THA
24	Rawin Nontagate	THA
28	Patiparn Phetphun	THA

Midfielders

8	Tanapat Na Tarue	THA
10	Ramthep Chaipan	THA
11	Kittisak Siriwaen	THA
12	Atthaphol Phunarae	THA
14	Teerayoot Seubsin	THA
15	Masahiro Fukasawa	JPN
20	Chatchai	THA
25	Pornpong Pornjamsai	THA
26	Benjapol Kloy-Eiam	THA
27	Thada Thongthuam	THA
29	Suppasek Kaikaew	THA

Forwards

9	Ekkaphan Petvises	THA
13	Kraisorn Pancharoen	THA
16	Suriya Domtaisong	THA
17	Nopphon Phon-Udom	THA
21	Ponlawat Pinkong	THA
30	Nattawut Kingpila	THA

CHUNNAM DRAG.

Goalkeepers

1	Cho Min Hyuck	KOR
21	Yeom Dong Gyun	KOR
29	Song You Gual	KOR

Defenders

2	Lee Wan	KOR
3	Hong Sung Yo	KOR
4	Kang Min Soo	KOR
5	Park Ji Yong	KOR
6	Kim Jin Kyu	KOR
17	Lee Jun Ki	KOR
23	Kim Jin Hyun	KOR
26	Song Tae Lim	KOR

Midfielders

8	Kim Tae Su	KOR
9	Song Jung Hyun	KOR
10	Park Chun Sin	KOR
12	Lee Sang Il	KOR
13	Yoo Hong Youl	KOR
14	Kim Chi Woo	KOR
15	Baek Seung Min	KOR
16	Lim Kwan Sik	KOR
18	Cho Se Kwon	KOR
19	Kim Seung Hyun	KOR
22	Kim Seong Jae	KOR
24	Chang Dong Hyok	KOR
25	Lee Kyu Ro	KOR
28	Yang Sang Min	KOR
30	Song Han Bok	KOR

Forwards

7	Ju Kwang Youn	KOR
11	Sandro	BRA
20	Leandro	BRA
27	Sandro Cardoso	BRA

DONG TAM LA

Goalkeepers

1	Santos	BRA
25	Nguyen Tien Phong	VIE
26	Nguyen Huu Quang	VIE

Defenders

2	Thai Duong	VIE
3	Phan Van Giau	VIE
4	Nguyen Van Hung	VIE
5	Le Quang Trai	VIE
12	Luu Minh Tri	VIE
18	Doan Nhat Tien	VIE
23	Vo Phi Thuong	VIE

Midfielders

7	Nguyen Minh Phuong	VIE
10	Phan Van Tai Em	VIE
15	Nguyen Tuan Phong	VIE
16	Phan Thanh Giang	VIE
19	Nguyen Thanh Truc	VIE
20	Nguyen Hoang Thuong	VIE
22	Nguyen Xuan Hoang	VIE
24	Ly Lam Huy	VIE

Forwards

6	Nguyen Van Khai	VIE
8	Nguyen Viet Thang	VIE
9	Antonio	BRA
11	Kabanga Tshamala	CGO

ESTEGHLAL

Esteghlal were expelled from the tournament after failing to register their players on time

AL HILAL

Goalkeepers

1	Mohammed Al Daeyea	KSA
22	Fahad Al Shammari	KSA
30	Hasan Al Otaibi	KSA

Defenders

2	Abdulaziz Abdulsalam	KSA
3	Marcelo Tavares	BRA
4	Ahmad Al Dossary	KSA
7	Yasser Al Yas	KSA
12	Saad Al Theyab	KSA
15	Khalid Al Angrie	KSA
16	Abdulaziz Hulayyil	KSA
17	Fahad Al Mefareg	KSA
19	Abdulaziz Kahthran	KSA
25	Majed Al Marshadi	KSA
28	Badr Al Dosari	KSA
29	Ahmed Al Jari	KSA

Midfielders

5	Abdullatif Al Ghannam	KSA
6	Khaled Al Thaker	KSA
10	Mohammad Al Shlhoub	KSA
11	Nawaf Al Temyat	KSA
13	Omar Al-Ghamdi	KSA
14	Tareq El Taib	LBY
20	Yasser Al Qahtani	KSA
21	Sultan Al Bargan	KSA
24	Ahmed Al Harbi	KSA

Forwards

8	Rodrigo	BRA
9	Sami Al Jaber	KSA
18	Ahmed Al Suwaileh	KSA
23	Bader Al Kharashi	KSA
26	Mohammed Al Anbar	KSA
27	Sultan Al Saud	KSA

AL ITTIHAD

Goalkeepers

1	Mahmoud Karkar	SYR
24	Yasser Jarkas	SYR
30	Khaled Othman	SYR

Defenders

2	Maan Al Rashad	SYR
3	Majd Homsi	SYR
4	Hossen Kelawi	SYR
5	Omar Hemidi	SYR
6	Ibrahim Aziza	SYR
12	Zakaria Al Kaddour	SYR
13	Zakaria Bek	SYR
14	Wael Aian	SYR
20	Salah Shahrour	SYR
21	Hayder Kadham	IRQ
22	Bakri Tarrab	SYR
27	Rami Hameda	SYR
28	Ahmed Kilasi	SYR

Midfielders

7	Ammar Rihawi	SYR
8	Anatolii Matkevych	UKR
10	Osama Haddad	SYR
17	Mahmoud Al Amena	SYR
19	Yahia Al Rached	SYR
23	Ayman Habal	SYR

Forwards

9	Mohamed Al Damen	SYR
10	Abdul Aga	SYR
11	Dumitru Popovich	MDA
15	Ahmed Al Hussein	SYR
18	Anas Sari	SYR
25	Mohd Tamer Rashed	SYR
29	Mahmoud Al Beef	SYR

KAWASAKI FRON.

Goalkeepers

1	Eiji Kawashima	JPN
21	Takashi Aizawa	JPN
22	Yuki Uekusa	JPN
28	Rikihiro Sugiyama	JPN

Defenders

2	Hiroki Ito	JPN
3	Hideki Shinoda	JPN
4	Yusuke Igawa	JPN
5	Yoshinobu Minowa	JPN
8	Jun Sonoda	JPN
13	Shuhei Terada	JPN

Midfielders

6	Takahiro Kawamura	JPN
11	Magnum Tavares	BRA
14	Kengo Nakamura	JPN
15	Taku Harada	JPN
17	Masayuki Ochiai	JPN
18	Satoshi Hida	JPN
19	Yusuke Mori	JPN
20	Yuji Yabu	JPN
24	Masahiro Ohashi	JPN
25	Tatsuya Suzuki	JPN
26	Kazuhiro Marakami	JPN
29	Hiroyuki Taniguchi	JPN

Forwards

7	Marsaru Kurotsu	JPN
9	Kazuki Ganaha	JPN
10	Carlos Juninho	BRA
12	Takahisa Nishiyama	JPN
16	Jong Tae-se	PRK
23	Satoshi Kukino	JPN
27	Ken Tokura	JPN
30	Yuji Kimura	JPN

AL KARAMA

Goalkeepers

1	Mosab Balhous	SYR
22	Adnan Al Hafez	SYR
30	Fahd Saleh	SYR

Defenders

2	Naser Al Sebai	SYR
3	Fabio Santos	BRA
4	Hassan Abbas	SYR
13	Jehad Kassab	SYR
14	Belal Abduldaim	SYR
16	Anas Al Khouja	SYR
23	Tarek Al Hourani	SYR
28	Tawfek Taearah	SYR
	Mohamad Hamwia	SYR

Midfielders

6	Jehad Al Hussien	SYR
7	Abdul Kader Refai	SYR
9	Mohamad Al Hamwi	SYR
10	Iyad Mando	SYR
11	Fahd Aodi	SYR
12	Mohamad Hayan	SYR
15	Mohamad Eid	SYR
18	Mahmoud Al Mallul	SYR
21	Aatef Jenyat	SYR
24	Mohamad Abdulkader	SYR
25	Firas Issmael	SYR
26	Ahmad Swidan	SYR
27	Tammam Zarour	SYR

Forwards

8	Mohanad Ibrahim	SYR
17	Youssef Sleman	SYR
19	Abdalrahman Akkari	SYR
20	Senghor Koupouleni	SEN

AL KUWAIT

Goalkeepers
1	Musab Al Kandari
22	Bader Al Azami
23	Khaled Fadhli

Defenders
2	Yaqoub Al Taher
3	Fahad Shaheen
4	Yousef Zayed
5	Mubarak Al Enezi
14	Khaled Saleh
20	Husain Al Shammari
24	Mohammad Al Rashidi
25	Ahmad Al Shammari
29	Samer Al Martah

Midfielders
6	Ebrahim Shehab	
7	Abdulrahman Al Awadhi	
8	Andre Valentim	POR
10	Adel Al Anezi	
11	Khaled Al Azemi	
12	Obaid Al Otaibi	
13	Talal Yusuf	BHR
15	Waleed Ali	
16	Nawaf Al Owisi	
18	Jarah Al Ataiqi	
21	Abdul Aziz Al Ahmad	
26	Hassan Al Khaldi	
27	Saud Al Otaibi	
28	Abdul Razaq Al Buti	
30	Husain Baba	BHR

Forwards
9	Abdullah Nahar
17	Ahmad Mubarak
19	Faraj Laheeb

AL NAJAF

Goalkeepers
1	Hadi Jaber	IRQ
19	Jassim Mohammed	IRQ
20	Mohammed Abdulzahra	IRQ

Defenders
2	Qassim Faraj	IRQ
3	Ali Al Fatla	IRQ
4	Haeder Aboudi	IRQ
7	Nabeel Abbas	IRQ
7	Jassib Sultan	IRQ
8	Falah Hassan	IRQ
13	Ali Abduljabbar	IRQ
14	Ayad Sadir	IRQ
26	Hamed Al Bohid	IRQ
28	Hassanain Khodair	IRQ

Midfielders
6	Karrar Jassim	IRQ
9	Suhail Naim	IRQ
11	Mohammed Hadi	IRQ
12	Qais Issa	IRQ
15	Dhayaa Abbas	IRQ
18	Dheiaa Faleh	IRQ
22	Said Mohsen Ali	IRQ
26	Hattam Saheb	IRQ
27	Maytham Anad	IRQ

Forwards
10	Foad Jawad	IRQ
16	Abbas Rashed	IRQ
17	Yasir Abdulrazaaq	IRQ
23	Ali Mohammed	IRQ
24	Aqeel Mohammed	IRQ

NEFTCHI

Goalkeepers
1	Hislatjon Chilmatov	UZB
16	Kazbek Artikbayev	UZB
21	Gayratjon Hasanov	UZB

Defenders
2	Aleksandr Tokov	UZB
3	Masod Toirov	UZB
4	Maksim Usmanov	UZB
5	Nasim Shoimov	UZB
12	Gayrat Amanmuradov	UZB
13	Ruslan Melziddinov	UZB
14	Azamat Juramuradov	UZB
15	Muhsin Nizametdinov	UZB
27	Farruh Zakirov	UZB
28	Ulugbek Hoshimov	UZB
29	Ikboljon Bobohonov	UZB

Midfielders
6	Bahtiyorjon Yakubov	UZB
7	Mansurjon Saidov	UZB
8	Akmal Holmatov	UZB
11	Aziz Alijonov	UZB
17	Akbarjon Abdulrahmonov	UZB
19	Sherzod Hakimov	UZB
20	Nodirbek Kuziboyev	UZB
22	Iqboljon Akramov	UZB
23	Sandjar Askaraliev	UZB
24	Umidjon Booiev	UZB

Forwards
9	Nosirbek Otakuziev	UZB
10	Anvar Berdiev	UZB
18	Ilya Kovalenko	UZB
25	Azizjon Ibragimov	UZB
26	Mukh'damin Vakhidov	UZB
30	Islom Choriev	UZB

PAKHTAKOR

Goalkeepers
1	Eldor Tadjibaev	UZB
12	Ignatiy Nesterov	UZB
30	Temur Juraev	UZB

Defenders
2	Bakhtiyor Ashurmatov	UZB
3	Rahm'llo Berdimurodov	UZB
5	Asror Aliqulov	UZB
13	Aleksander Kletskov	UZB
21	Komoloddin Tadjiev	UZB
26	Maxim Belykh	RUS
27	Ilhomjon Suyunov	UZB

Midfielders
4	Anvar Berdiev	UZB
6	Leonid Koshelev	UZB
14	Vladislav Kiryan	UZB
15	Islom Inomov	UZB
17	Vyacheslav Ponomarev	UZB
18	Timur Kapadze	UZB
20	Ildar Magdeev	UZB
22	Renat Bayramov	UZB
24	Anzur Ismailov	UZB
25	Odil Ahmedov	UZB

Forwards
7	Uche Iheruome	NGA
8	Server Djeperov	UZB
9	Anvarjon Soliev	UZB
10	Zaynitdin Tadjiev	UZB
11	Shakhboz Erkinov	UZB
16	Pavel Purishkin	UZB
23	Alisher Azizov	UZB
28	Pavel Solomin	UZB
29	Farhodjon Usmanov	UZB

PERSIK KEDIRI

Goalkeepers
1	Kurnia Sandy	IDN
20	Adi Gesang Saputra	IDN
27	Wahyudi	IDN

Defenders
4	Aris Indarto	IDN
6	Zainuri	IDN
15	Sulis Budi Prasetyo	IDN
18	Aris Budi Prasetiya	IDN
23	Restu Setyo Kartiko	IDN

Midfielders
2	Yohanes Yantara	IDN
3	Erol Iba	IDN
7	Bertha Yuana Putra	IDN
8	Jefri Dwi Hadi	IDN
11	Deca	BRA
12	Harianto	IDN
17	Dwi Prio Utomo	IDN
19	Suswanto	IDN
25	Khusnul Yuli Kurniawan	IDN
28	Ronald Fagundez	URU
30	Danillo Fernando	BRA

Forwards
9	Johan Prasetyo Wibowo	IDN
10	Christian Gonzalez	URU
13	Budi Sudarsono	IDN
22	Musikan	IDN

AL RAYYAN

Goalkeepers
1	Qasem Burhan	QAT
18	Aman Salam	QAT
26	Soud Al Hajri	QAT

Defenders
2	Selman Mesbeh	QAT
3	Abdulrahman Mesbeh	QAT
4	Abdulrahman Al Kuwari	QAT
5	Abdulaziz Eisa	QAT
6	Jacek Bak	POL
8	Dahi Al Naami	QAT
12	Shami Suwaid	QAT
16	Nayef Al Khater	QAT
17	Mohammed Al Hajj	QAT
19	Khalid Mohammed	QAT
20	Ismaiel Muhammed	QAT
23	Khaled Jaberti	QAT
24	Mehsin Al Marri	QAT
29	Sadiq Taj	QAT

Midfielders
7	Adel Lamy	QAT
10	Waleed Jassim	QAT
11	Ali Al Marri	QAT
13	Talal Al Qahtani	QAT
14	Sabri Lamouchi	FRA
21	Fahad Al Ajmi	QAT
28	Mubarak Al Baloushi	QAT

Forwards
9	Thiago Cardoso	BRA
15	Mohammed Majed	QAT
22	Hussain Yasser	QAT
25	Abdulrahman Tariq	QAT
27	Jaralla Al Marri	QAT
30	Saoud Khames	QAT

AL SADD

Goalkeepers
1	Saad Al Sheeb	QAT
22	Basel Samih	QAT
25	Khalifa Al Dosari	QAT
30	Mohamed Saqr	QAT

Defenders
2	Jafal Al Kuwari	QAT
3	Essa Al Kuwari	QAT
4	Abdullah Al Bareek	QAT
5	Tahir Zakariya	QAT
13	Hamad Al Shamari	QAT
21	Abdullah Koni	QAT
27	Hasan Al Haydos	QAT
28	Ali Al Nuaimi	QAT
29	Mohammed Al Yazidi	QAT

Midfielders
6	Ali Nasser Saleh	QAT
7	Wesam Rizik	QAT
8	Mased Al Hamad	QAT
9	Ibrahim Abdulmaged	QAT
12	Magid Mohammed	QAT
14	Khalfan Ibrahim	QAT
15	Talal Al Bloushi	QAT
17	Hamood Abdulla	QAT
18	Bakhit Al Marri	QAT
19	Nasser Saad	QAT
20	Meqbel Meshaal	QAT

Forwards
10	Emerson	BRA
11	Carlos Tenorio	ECU
16	Mohamed Gholam	QAT
23	Felipe	BRA
24	Ali Afef	QAT
26	Yusuf Ahmed	QAT

SEONGNAM IC

Goalkeepers
1	Kim Hae-woon	KOR
21	Park Sang-chul	KOR
30	Kim Yong-dae	KOR

Defenders
2	Park Jin-sub	KOR
3	Cho Yong-hyung	KOR
4	Kim Tae-youn	KOR
5	Cho Byung-kuk	KOR
18	Park Jae-yong	KOR
20	Kim Young Chul	KOR
22	Jang Hack-yong	KOR
29	Koh Bum-soo	KOR

Midfielders
6	Son Dae-ho	KOR
8	Kim Do-heon	KOR
13	Seo Dong-won	KOR
14	Kim Sang Sik	KOR
16	Lee Jeong-yong	KOR
17	Kim Cheol-ho	KOR
19	Shin Young-chol	KOR
23	Park Woo-hyon	KOR
26	Choi Sang-hun	KOR
27	Park Kwang-min	KOR
28	Do Jae-joon	KOR

Forwards
7	Choi Sung-kuk	KOR
9	Kim Dong-hun	KOR
10	Itamar	BRA
11	Mota	BRA
12	Nam Ki-il	KOR
15	Han Dong-won	KOR
24	Kim Min-ho	KOR
25	Adrian Neaga	ROU

SEPAHAN

Goalkeepers
1	Armenak Petrosyan	ARM
22	Mohammad Savari	IRN
24	Masoud Homami	IRN

Defenders
2	Hamid Azizadeh	IRN
5	Hadi Aghily	IRN
8	Mohsen Bengar	IRN
15	Mojtaba Saedi	IRN
19	Mahmoud Mansouri	IRN

Midfielders
3	Seyed Mohammadpour	IRN
4	Moharram Navidkia	IRN
6	Jalal Akbari	IRN
7	Farshad Bahadorani	IRN
9	Hadi Jafari	IRN
12	Abdul Wahab Al Hail	IRQ
14	Mohammad Nori	IRN
16	Javad Maheri	IRN
17	Meysam Soleimani	IRN
21	Saeid Bayat	IRN
25	Ebrahim Lovinian	IRN
27	Ghader Afkari	IRN
28	Ehsan Hajysafi	IRN
29	Mohammadreza Zare	IRN
30	Hossein Papi	IRN

Forwards
10	Hamid Shafiei	IRN
11	Rasoul Khatibi	IRN
13	Mahmoud Karimi	IRN
18	Hamed Rasouli	IRN
20	Emad Mohammed	IRQ
23	Seyed Mohamad Salehi	IRN
26	Jalalaldin Ali Mohamadi	IRN

AL SHABAB

Goalkeepers
1	Hussain Shaian	KSA
22	Saeid Al Harbi	KSA
23	Waleed Ali	KSA
30	Mohammad Khojah	KSA

Defenders
2	Abdullah Al Astaa	KSA
3	Abdulmohsen Al Dosari	KSA
4	Saleh Sadeeq	KSA
5	Mohammed bin Hamdan	KSA
6	Safwan Al Mowalad	KSA
13	Hassan Maaz	KSA
14	Abdullah Shuhail	KSA
15	Abdoh Autef	KSA
16	Amir Megahed	EGY
17	Zaid Al Mowalad	KSA
20	Faisal Al Obili	KSA
24	Sanad Shrahilee	KSA
26	Saeed Ismail	KSA
29	Hosein Fllath	KSA

Midfielders
7	Mansour Al Dossari	KSA
8	Abdullah Al Dosari	KSA
11	Ahmed Ateef	KSA
19	Yousef Al Muwaine	KSA
25	Nashat Akram	IRQ
28	Bader Al Hagbani	KSA

Forwards
9	Waleed Al Gizani	KSA
10	Naji Majrashi	KSA
12	Fahad Fallata	KSA
18	Godwin Attram	GHA
21	Abdulaziz bin Saran	KSA
27	Fisal bin Sultan	KSA

SHANDONG L.

Goalkeepers
1	Li Leilei	CHN
22	Yang Cheng	CHN
23	Guan Zhen	CHN

Defenders
3	Wang Chao	CHN
5	Shu Chang	CHN
14	Yuan Weiwei	CHN
15	Nikola Malbasa	SRB
25	Jiao Zhe	CHN
27	Wang Liang	CHN

Midfielders
2	Liu Jindong	CHN
4	Branko Bakovic	SRB
8	Aleksandar Zivkovic	SRB
11	Wang Xiaolong	CHN
12	Li Wei	CHN
16	Gao Yao	CHN
17	Wan Cheng	CHN
18	Zhou Haibin	CHN
20	Cui Peng	CHN
24	Lu Zheng	CHN

Forwards
6	Han Peng	CHN
13	Wang Yongpo	CHN
21	Liu Zhao	CHN
29	Li Jinyu	CHN

SHANGHAI SHEN.

Goalkeepers
1	Wang Dalei	CHN
12	Zhang Chen	CHN
22	Dong Lei	CHN

Defenders
2	Yao Lijun	CHN
3	Dong Yang	CHN
5	Du Wei	CHN
11	Zhang Xiaorui	CHN
13	Cheng Liang	CHN
19	Li Chengming	CHN
21	Jiang Kun	CHN
23	Li Weifeng	CHN
24	Li Gang	CHN
30	Lu Xin	CHN

Midfielders
4	Chang Lin	CHN
6	Liu Zhiqing	CHN
7	Xiao Zhanbo	CHN
10	Fernando Correa	URU
14	Shen Longyuan	CHN
15	Wang Ke	CHN
16	Yu Tao	CHN
17	Sun Ji	CHN
18	Zheng Kewei	CHN
25	Yin Xifu	CHN
26	Wang Hongliang	CHN
28	Qu Shaoyan	CHN

Forwards
8	Sergio Blanco	URU
9	Diego Alonso	URU
20	Xie Hui	CHN
27	Mao Jianqing	CHN
29	Gao Lin	CHN

SYDNEY FC

Goalkeepers
1	Clint Bolton	AUS
20	Dean Bouzanis	AUS
23	Justin Pasfield	AUS

Defenders
2	Iain Fyfe	AUS
3	Nikolas Tsattalios	AUS
4	Mark Rudan	AUS
11	Nikolai Topor-Stanley	AUS
16	Mark Milligan	AUS
17	Jacob Timpano	AUS

Midfielders
5	Noel Spencer	AUS
6	Ufuk Talay	AUS
7	Robbie Middleby	AUS
8	Ruben Zadkovich	AUS
10	Steve Corica	AUS
12	David Carney	AUS
13	Jeremy Brockie	NZL
15	Terry McFlynn	NIR

Forwards
9	David Zdrilic	AUS
14	Alex Brosque	AUS
18	Adam Casey	AUS
19	Luka Glavas	AUS

URAWA REDS

Goalkeepers
1	Norihiro Yamagishi	JPN
23	Ryota Tsuzuki	JPN
28	Nabuhiro Kato	JPN
29	Koko Otani	JPN

Defenders
2	Keisuke Tsuboi	JPN
4	Marcus Tulio Tanaka	JPN
5	Fabio Nene	BRA
12	Shunsuke Tsutsumi	JPN
19	Hideki Uchidate	JPN
20	Satoshi Horinouchi	JPN
24	Kazuya Sakamoto	JPN

Midfielders
3	Hajime Hosogai	JPN
6	Nobuhisa Yamada	JPN
7	Tomoyuki Sakai	JPN
8	Shinji Ono	JPN
10	Robson Ponte	BRA
13	Keita Suzuki	JPN
14	Tadaaki Hirakawa	JPN
16	Takahito Soma	JPN
17	Makoto Hasebe	JPN
22	Yuki Abe	JPN
25	Takafumi Akahoshi	JPN
26	Yuya Nakamura	JPN
27	Yoshiya Nishizawa	JPN
30	Masayuki Okano	JPN

Forwards
9	Yuchiro Nagai	JPN
11	Tatsuya Tanaka	JPN
18	Junki Koike	JPN
21	Washington	BRA

AL WAHDA

Goalkeepers
1	Shaiban Saleh	UAE
17	Nadir Lamyaghri	MAR
22	Abdulbaset Al Hammadi	UAE

Defenders
3	Abdulla Salem	UAE
4	Ali Jumaa	UAE
8	Omar Ali	UAE
12	Marwan Mohamed	UAE
13	Talal Abdulla	UAE
21	Basheer Saeed	UAE
25	Yaser Abdulla	UAE
30	Hamdan Ismaeel	UAE

Midfielders
2	Tawfeeq Abdul Razzaq	UAE
5	Abdul Salam Jumaa	UAE
6	Yaser Matar	UAE
9	Abdulla Belal	UAE
15	Fahed Masoud	UAE
16	Mohamed Othman	UAE
18	Abdulla Al Ameri	UAE
23	Haidar Alo Ali	UAE
24	Abdulraheem Jumaa	UAE
26	Mahmoud Khamis	UAE
28	Eisa Ahmed	UAE

Forwards
7	Maurito	ANG
10	Ismail Matar	UAE
11	Saleh Al Menhali	UAE
14	Mamadou Bagayoko	FRA
19	Saeed Salem	UAE
20	Mohamed Saeed	UAE
27	Abdulla Ali	UAE
29	Abdulrahim Al Hosani	UAE

AL ZAWRA'A

Goalkeepers
1	Ahmed Ali Jaber	IRQ
21	Osama Hussein	IRQ
30	Sarmad Rasheed	IRQ

Defenders
2	Mohammed Ali	IRQ
3	Dergham Jaseem	IRQ
4	Ahmed Muhsin	IRQ
6	Wisam Kadhim	IRQ
15	Ghaith Abdulghani	IRQ
17	Mousa Hashem	IRQ
18	Amar Abd Al Zahra	IRQ
22	Amar Ali	IRQ
23	Haidar Imad	IRQ

Midfielders
5	Ahmed Abid Ali	IRQ
7	Ali Yousif	IRQ
11	Aus Ibrahim	IRQ
12	Hassan Zabon	IRQ
13	Nawaf Lafy	IRQ
16	Mohanad Nassir	IRQ
19	Akram Jabbar	IRQ
20	Senann Fawzi	IRQ
25	Ahmad Abrahim	IRQ

Forwards
8	Hayder Sabbah	IRQ
9	Abdulsalam Abboud	IRQ
10	Muslim Mubarak	IRQ

AFC CHAMPIONS LEAGUE 2007

Group Stage			Quarter-finals	Semi-finals	Final

Group A		Pts
Al Wahda	UAE	13
Al Zawra'a	IRQ	11
Al Arabi	KUW	7
Al Rayyan	QAT	2

Group B		Pts
Al Hilal	KSA	8
Pakhtakor Tashkent	UZB	6
Al Kuwait	KUW	2
Esteghlal	IRN	0

Quarter-finals:
Sepahan *
Kawasaki Frontale

Group C		Pts
Al Karama	SYR	11
Neftchi Fergana	UZB	10
Al Najaf	IRQ	8
Al Sadd	QAT	4

Quarter-finals:
Al Wahda *
Al Hilal

Group D		Pts
Sepahan	IRN	13
Al Shabab	KSA	10
Al Ain	UAE	6
Al Ittihad	SYR	3

Group E		Pts
Urawa Reds	JPN	10
Sydney FC	AUS	9
Persik Kediri	IDN	7
Shanghai Shenhua	CHN	5

Quarter-finals:
Seongnam Chunma*
Al Karama

Group F		Pts
Kawasaki Frontale	JPN	16
Chunnam Dragons	KOR	10
Arema Malang	IDN	4
Bangkok University	THA	3

Quarter-finals:
Urawa Reds *
Jeonbuk Motors

Group G		Pts
Seongnam Chunma	KOR	13
Shandong Luneng	CHN	13
Adelaide United	AUS	8
Dong Tam Long An	VIE	0

† Jeonbuk Hyundai Motors (KOR) given a bye to the quarter-finals as holders • * Home team in the first leg • On February 17, 2007, Esteghlal were thrown out of the tournament after failing to register their players on time

Remaining ties: Quarter-finals 19/09/2007 & 26/09/2007; Semi-finals 3/10/2007 & 24/10/2007; Final 7/11/2007 & 14/11/2007

GROUP A

		Pl	W	D	L	F	A	Pts	UAE	IRQ	KUW	QAT
Al Wahda	UAE	6	4	1	1	13	6	13		1-1	4-1	3-0
Al Zawra'a	IRQ	6	3	2	1	9	6	11	1-2		3-2	0-0
Al Arabi	KUW	6	2	1	3	10	12	7	3-2	0-1		1-1
Al Rayyan	QAT	6	0	2	4	3	11	2	0-1	1-3	1-3	

GROUP A MATCHDAY 1
Al Rayyan Sports Club, Doha
7-03-2007, 18:00, 3000, Yang Zhiqiang CHN

Al Rayyan 0

Qasem Burhan – Selman Mesbeh, Abdulrahman Mesbeh, Jacek Bak, Nayef Al Khater, Mohammed Al Hajj, Waleed Jassim, Ali Al Marri, Sabri Lamouchi, Hussain Yasser (Adel Lamy 70), Thiago Cardoso.

Al Wahda 1
Mohamed Saeed [81]

Nadir Lamyaghri – Omar Ali, Basheer Saeed, Yaser Abdulla, Abdul Salam Jumaa (Tawfeeq Abdul Razzaq 53), Fahed Masoud, Haidar Alo Ali, Abdulraheem Jumaa, Maurito (Mohamed Saeed 75), Ismail Matar●87, Mamadou Bagayoko.

GROUP A MATCHDAY 2
Al Rayyan Sports Club, Doha
21-03-2007, 20:30, 1500, Lee Gi Young KOR

Al Zawra'a 0

Ahmed Ali Jaber – Mohammed Ali, Wisam Kadhim, Ahmed Abid Ali, Ali Yousif, Aus Ibrahim, Nawaf Lafy (Abdulsalam Abboud 84), Mohanad Nassir (Akram Jabbar 90), Ahmad Abrahim, Hayder Sabbah, Muslim Mubarak.

Al Rayyan 0

Qasem Burhan – Selman Mesbeh (Abdulrahman Mesbeh 69), Dahi Al Naami, Nayef Al Khater, Mohammed Al Hajj, Adel Lamy, Ali Al Marri, Sabri Lamouchi, Mubarak Al Baloushi, Thiago Cardoso (Saoud Khames 78), Hussain Yasser.

GROUP A MATCHDAY 4
Al Rayyan Sports Club, Doha
25-04-2007, 18:25, 1000, Al Mutlaq KSA

Al Rayyan 1
Thiago Cardoso [44p]

Soud Al Hajri – Selman Mesbeh, Abdulrahman Al Kuwari (Walled Jassim 57) Abdulaziz Eisa (Mohammed Al Hajj 46), Shami Suwaid, Khalid Mohammed, Ismaiel Muhammed, Thiago Cardoso, Jaralla Al Marri, Saoud Khames.

Al Arabi 3
Khaled Khalaf [25], Firas Al Khatib 2 [63 69]

Yousef Al Thuwaini – Ali Al Maqseed (Malek Al Qallaf 57), Musaed Abdullah (Ahmad Mousa 57), Fahad Dabes, Ebrahim Meshkhas, Hussain Al Qhareeb, Hamdi Marzouki (Muhammad Ashkanani 65), Fahad Al Farhan, Khaled Abdulkuddous, Firas Al Khatib, Khaled Khalaf.

GROUP A MATCHDAY 5
Al Rayyan Sports Club, Doha
9-05-2007, 20:50, 500, Torky IRN

Al Zawra'a 3
Wisam Kadhim [21], Abrahim [70], Nawaf Lafy [78]

Ahmed Ali Jaber – Ahmed Muhsin (Ali Yousef 80), Wisam Kadhim, Ghaith Abdulghani, Ahmed Abid Ali, Aus Ibrahim (Mohammed Ali 88), Nawaf Lafy, Mohanad Nassir, Ahmad Abrahim (Akram Jabbar 79), Hayder Sabbah, Muslim Mubarak.

Al Arabi 2
Firas Al Khatib 2 [50 84]

Yousef Al Thuwaini – Ali Al Maqseed, Abdulaziz Fadhel, Fahad Dabes (Jarrah Al Zuhair 72), Ebrahim Meshkhas, Hamdi Marzouki, Abdullah Al Shamali (Khaled Khalaf 81), Fahad Al Farhan (Mubarak Kamshad 86), Khaled Abdulkuddous, Firas Al Khatib.

GROUP A MATCHDAY 1
Sabah Al Salem, Kuwait City
7-03-2007, 18:30, 3000, Basma SYR

Al Arabi 0

Yousef Al Thuwaini – Ali Al Maqseed, Musaed Abdullah, Ebrahim Meshkhas, Hamdi Marzouki, Mohammad Jarragh, Malek Al Qallaf, Ahmad Al Dhuwaihi (Jarrah Al Zuhair 72), Firas Al Khatib, Abdullah Al Mutawa (Khaled Khalaf 78), Husain Al Mosawi (Khaled Abdulkuddous 63).

Al Zawra'a 1
Mouslim Mubarak [66]

Ahmed Ali Jaber – Mohammed Ali, Wisam Kadhim, Ahmed Abid Ali, Ali Yousif (Ahmed Muhsin 34), Aus Ibrahim, Mohanad Nassir, Ahmad Abrahim (Akram Jabbar 90+1), Hayder Sabbah, Abdulsalam Abboud (Nawaf Lafy 53), Muslim Mubarak.

GROUP A MATCHDAY 3
Sabah Al Salem, Kuwait City
11-04-2007, 20:00, 2000, Al Ghafary JOR

Al Arabi 1
Jarrah Al Zuhair [60]

Yousef Al Thuwaini – Ali Al Maqseed, Abdulaziz Fadhel, Musaed Abdullah (Jarrah Al Zuhair 58), Ebrahim Meshkhas, Mohammad Jarragh, Malek Al Qallaf, Ahmad Mousa (Jasem Al Owisi 90), Khaled Abdulkuddous, Ahmad Al Dhuwaihi (Muhammad Ashkanani 84), Firas Al Khatib.

Al Rayyan 1
Adel Lamy [52]

Qasem Burhan – Selman Mesbeh, Abdulrahman Mesbeh (Nayef Al Khater 91+), Nayef Al Khater, Mohammed Al Hajj, Ismaiel Muhammed, Adel Lamy, Waleed Jassim, Ali Al Marri (Saoud Lhames 32), Mubarak Al Baloushi, Thiago Cardoso (Abdulrahman Tariq 85).

GROUP A MATCHDAY 4
Al Nahyan, Abu Dhabi
25-04-2007, 19:40, 3000, Karim BHR

Al Wahda 1
Abdulraheem Jumaa [57]

Nadir Lamyaghri – Basheer Saeed, Yaser Abdulla (Talal Abdulla 77), Hamdan Ismaeel, Fahed Masoud, Mohamed Othman, Haidar Alo Ali, Abdulraheem Jumaa, Maurito, Ismail Matar (Abdulla Belal 55), Mohamed Saeed.

Al Zawra'a 1
Haidar Sabah [75]

Ahmed Ali Jaber – Mohammed Ali (Aus Ibrahim 66), Ahmed Muhsin (Ali Yousif 74; Akram Jabbar 86), Wisam Kadhim, Ghaith Abdulghani, Ahmed Abid Ali, Nawaf Lafy (Abdulsalam Abboud 81), Mohanad Nassir, Ahmad Abrahim, Hayder Sabbah, , Muslim Mubarak

GROUP A MATCHDAY 6
Al Gharafa, Doha
23-05-2007, 18:35,

Al Rayyan 1
Saoud Khames [75]

Soud Al Hajri (Qasem Burhan 46) – Selman Mesbeh, Abdulrahman Mesbeh, Jacek Bak (Ismaiel Muhhamed 57), Shami Suwaid (Ali Al Marri 86), Nayef Al Khater, Mohammed Al Hajj, Khalid Mohammed, Thiago Cardoso, Mohammed Majed, Abdulrahman Tariq (Saoud Khames 75).

Al Zawra'a 3
Mesbeh [13], Abboud [26], Haidar Sabah [34]

Ahmed Ali Jaber – Ahmed Muhsin, Wisam Kadhim, Ghaith Abdulghani, Ahmed Abid Ali, Ali Yousif, Mohanad Nassir, Ahmad Abrahim (Senann Fawzi 90), Hayder Sabbah, Abdulsalam Abboud (Mousa Hashem 76), Muslim Mubarak

GROUP A MATCHDAY 2
Al Nahyan, Abu Dhabi
21-03-2007, 19:20, 3500, Nishimura JPN

Al Wahda 4
Bagayoko 2 [40 56], Al Menhali [63], Basheer [68]

Nadir Lamyaghri – Omar Ali, Basheer Saeed (Mohamed Othman 88), Yaser Abdulla, Tawfeeq Abdul Razzaq, Fahed Masoud, Haidar Alo Ali, Abdulraheem Jumaa, Mahmoud Khamis (Saleh Al Menhali 52), Mamadou Bagayoko (Yaser Matar 73), Mohamed Saeed.

Al Arabi 1
Mohammad Jarragh [35]

Muhamaad Ghanem – Ali Al Maqseed, Abdulaziz Fadhel (Nawaf Al Shuwaye 73), Musaed Abdullah, Ebrahim Meshkhas, Hamdi Marzouki, Mohammad Jarragh, Khaled Abdulkuddous (Khaled Khalaf 61), Ahmad Al Dhuwaihi, Firas Al Khatib, Abdullah Al Mutawa (Jarrah Al Zuhair 60).

GROUP A MATCHDAY 3
Al Rayyan Sports Club, Doha
11-04-2007, 20:30, 500, Najm LIB

Al Zawra'a 1
Ahmed Abid Ali [47]

Ahmed Ali Jaber – Mohammed Ali, Wisam Kadhim, Ghaith Abdulghani, Ahmed Abid Ali, Ali Yousif (Ahmed Muhsin 55), Mohanad Nassir, Ahmad Abrahim, Hayder Sabbah, Abdulsalam Abboud, Muslim Mubarak (Nawaf Lafy 77).

Al Wahda 2
Abulraheem Jumaa [13], Basheer Saeed [74]

Nadir Lamyaghri – Omar Ali, Talal Abdulla (Yaser Abdulla 46), Basheer Saeed, Fahed Masoud, Tawfeeq Abdul Razzaq (Yaser Matar 60), Haidar Alo Ali, Abdulraheem Jumaa, Maurito (Abdulla Al Ameri 69), Mamadou Bagayoko, Mohamed Saeed.

GROUP A MATCHDAY 5
Al Nahyan, Abu Dhabi
9-05-2007, 19:45, Shield AUS

Al Wahda 3
Maurito [8], Haidar Alo Ali [30p], Bagayoko [76p]

Nadir Lamyaghri – Omar Ali, Basheer Saeed, Hamdan Ismaeel, Tawfeeq Abdul Razzaq, Abdulla Belal (Eisa Ahmed 46), Mohamed Othman, Haidar Alo Ali (Mahmoud Khamis 64), Abdulraheem Jumaa (Mohamed Saeed 68), Maurito, Mamadou Bagayoko.

Al Rayyan 0

Qasem Burhan – Selman Mesbeh, Abdulrahman Mesbeh, Jacek Bak (Ismaiel Muhhamed 57), Shami Suwaid (Ali Al Marri 86), Nayef Al Khater, Khalid Mohammed, Mubarak Al Baloushi, Thiago Cardoso, Mohammed Majed, Abdulrahman Tariq.

GROUP A MATCHDAY 6
Sabah Al Salem, Kuwait City
23-05-2007, 20:30,

Al Arabi 3
K.Abdulkuddous [6], K.Khalaf [55], J.Al Zahair [87]

No details available

Al Wahda 2
Saeed Salem [23], Yaser Matar [90]

No details available

GROUP B

		Pl	W	D	L	F	A	Pts	KSA	UZB	KUW	IRN
Al Hilal	KSA	4	2	2	0	5	1	8		2-0	1-1	-
Pakhtakor Tashkent	UZB	4	2	0	2	3	5	6	0-2		2-1	-
Al Kuwait	KUW	4	0	2	2	2	4	2	0-0	0-1		-
Esteghlal	IRN	0	0	0	0	0	0	0	-	-	-	

GROUP B MATCHDAY 1
King Fahad International, Riyadh
7-03-2007, 20:30, 50 000, Mohd Salleh MAS

Al Hilal   **1**
Rodrigo [16]

Mohammed Al Daeyea – Tavares, Khalid Al Angrie, Fahad Al Mefareg, Abdulaziz Kahthran, Khaled Al Thakar (Badr Al Dosari 46), Mohammad Al Shlhoub, Omar Al-Ghamdi, Tareq El Taib, Yasser Al Qahtani (Nawaf Al Temyat 81), Rodrigo (Ahmed Al Suwaileh 81).

Al Kuwait   **1**
Fahad Shaheen [90]

Khaled Fadhil – Yaqoub Al Taher, Fahad Shaheen, Samer Al Martah, Ebrahim Shehab (Tala Yusuf 56), Andre Valentim, Waleed Ali, Jarah Al Ataiqi, Husain Baba, Abdullah Nahar (Abdulrahman Al Awadhi 76), Faraj Laheeb.

GROUP B MATCHDAY 2
Kuwait Stadium, Kuwait City
21-03-2007. 18:30, 2000, Tongkhan THA

Al Kuwait   **0**

Khaled Fadhil – Yaqoub Al Taher, Fahad Shaheen (Abdulrahman Al Awadhi 74), Samer Al Martah (Yousef Zayed 69), Andre Valentim, Tala Yusuf, Waleed Ali, Jarah Al Ataiqi, Husain Baba (Ebrahim Shehab 83), Abdullah Nahar, Faraj Laheeb.

Pakhtakor Tashkent   **1**
Magdeev 68

Nesterov – Aliqulov, Kletskov, Suyunov, Koshelev, Kiryan (Magdeev 46), Inomov, Kapadze, Ahmedov (Bayramov 78), Iheruome (Soliev 87), Djeperov.

GROUP B MATCHDAY 3
Army Stadium, Tashkent
11-04-2007, 17:00, 10 000, Huang Junjie CHN

Pakhtakor Tashkent   **0**

Nesterov – Aliqulov, Kletskov, Djeperov, Kiryan (Erkinov 77), Inomov, Kapadze (Koshelev 67), Magdeev, Bayramov (Soliev 60), Ahmedov, Iheruome.

Al Hilal   **2**
Omar Al Ghamdi [53], Rodrigo [59]

Mohammed Al Daeyea – Tavares, Khalid Al Angrie, Fahad Al Mefareg, Abdulaziz Kahthran (Abdulaziz Hulayyil 83) , Khaled Al Thakar, Rodrigo, Mohammad Al Shlhoub, Omar Al-Ghamdi, Yasser Al Qahtani, Ahmed Al Harbi (Yasser Al Yas 46).

GROUP B MATCHDAY 4
King Fahad International, Riyadh
25-04-2007, 20:45, 40 000, Lee Gi Young KOR

Al Hilal   **2**
Rodrigo 2 [30] [90p]

Mohammed Al Daeyea – Tavares, Khalid Al Angrie, Fahad Al Mefareg, Abdulaziz Kahthran, Khaled Al Thakar, Rodrigo, Mohammad Al Shlhoub, Omar Al-Ghamdi (Abdulaziz Hulayyil 80), Tareq El Taib (Abdullatif Al Ghannam 60), Yasser Al Qahtani (Yasser Al Yas 68).

Pakhtakor Tashkent   **0**

Nesterov – Aliqulov, Ismailov, Koshelev, Djeperov, Inomov, Kapadze, Magdeev (Kiryan 83), Bayramov (Ahmedov 73), Iheruome, Soliev (Erkinov 67).

GROUP B MATCHDAY 5
Kuwait Stadium, Kuwait City
9-05-2007, 18:45, 7000, Karim BHR

Al Kuwait   **0**

Khaled Fadhil – Yaqoub Al Taher, Fahad Shaheen (Abdullah Nahar 67), Hussain Al Shammari, Samer Al Martah, Andre Valentim, Tala Yusuf (Abdulrahman Al Awadhi 70), Waleed Ali, Jarah Al Ataiqi, Husain Baba (Yousef Zayed 73), Faraj Laheeb.

A Hilal   **1**
Magdeev 68

Mohammed Al Daeyea – Tavares, Khalid Al Angrie (Yasser Al Yas 74), Fahad Al Mefareg, Abdulaziz Kahthran, Abdullatif Al Ghannam, Khaled Al Thakar, Nawaf Al Temyat, Omar Al-Ghamdi, Tareq El Taib, Yasser Al Qahtani.

GROUP B MATCHDAY 6
Army Stadium, Tashkent
23-05-2007, 18:00, 3000, Maidin SIN

Pakhtakor Tashkent   **2**
Iheruome [45], Erkinov [59]

Nesterov – Aliqulov, Kletskov, Tadjiev, Ismailov, Koshelev, Djeperov (Kapadze 57), Magdeev (Kiryan 75), Ahmedov, Iheruome (Soliev 66), Erkinov.

Al Kuwait   **1**
Faraj Laheeb [71]

Khaled Fadhil – Fahad Shaheen, Yousef Zayed (Husain 46), Khaled Saleh, Hussain Al Shammari, Samer Al Martah, Abdulrahman Al Awadhi, Valentim (Jarah Al Ataiqi 52), Talal Yusuf (Ahmad Mubarak 64), Abdul Razaq Al Buti, Faraj Laheeb.

GROUP C

		Pl	W	D	L	F	A	Pts	SYR	UZB	IRQ	QAT
Al Karama	SYR	6	3	2	1	11	7	11		2-0	1-1	2-1
Neftchi Fergana	UZB	6	3	1	2	6	7	10	2-1		1-1	2-1
Al Najaf	IRQ	6	2	2	2	9	8	8	2-4	0-1		1-0
Al Sadd	QAT	6	1	1	4	6	10	4	1-1	2-0	1-4	

GROUP C MATCHDAY 1
Khaled Ibn Al Waleed, Homs
7-03-2007, 19:00, 30 000, Al Badwawi UAE

Al Karama 2
Koupouleni [70], Abdalrahman Akkari [85]

Mosab Balhous – Fabio Santos, Hassan Abbas, Belal Abdulaim, Anas Al Khouja, Jehad Al Hussien, Fahd Aodi (Koupouleni 69), Aatef Jenyat (Mohamad Al Hamwi 79), Firas Issmael, Mohanad Ibrahim (Iyad Mando 60), Abdalrahman Akkari.

Al Sadd 1
Magid Mohammed [22]

Basel Samih – Jafal Al Kuwari, Abdullah Al Bareek, Ali Nasser Saleh (Yusuf Ahmed 81), Mased Al Hamad (Hamood Abdulla 89), Ibrahim Abdulmaged, Magid Mohammed (Khalfan Ibrahim 73), Bakhit Al Marri, Tenorio, Mohamed Gholam, Felipe.

GROUP C MATCHDAY 2
Al Sadd, Doha
21-03-2007, 18:30, 5000, Williams AUS

Al Sadd 1
Talal Al Bloushi [45]

Basel Samih – Jafal Al Kuwari, Abdullah Al Bareek, Ali Nasser Saleh, Mased Al Hamad, Ibrahim Abdulmaged•26, Magid Mohammed (Yusuf Ahmed 79), Khalfan Ibrahim (Hamood Abdulla 53), Talal Al Bloushi, Tenorio, Felipe•45.

Al Najaf 4
Aqeel [47], Karrar Jassim [70p], Mohsen Ali 2 [55] [84p]

Hadi Jaber – Haeder Aboudi, Nabeel Abbas, Jassib Sultan, Falah Hassan, Ayad Sadir (Hattam Saheb 46), Karrar Jassim, Dheiaa Faleh, Said Mohsen Ali (Ali Abduljabbar 88), Ali Mohammed, Aqeel Mohammed (Suhail Naim 64).

GROUP C MATCHDAY 4
Fergana Stadium, Fergana
25-04-2007, 16:00, 14 600, Matsumura JPN

Neftchi Fergana 2
Akramov [1], Shoimov [41]

Hasanov – Toirov, Usmanov, Kuziboyev, Akramov (Nizametdinov 90), Holmatov, Kuziboyev, Akramov (Alijonov 72), Askaraliev, Otakuziev, Ibragimov (Melzidinov 69).

Al Sadd 1
Emerson [17]

Mohamed Saqr – Jafal Al Kuwari, Abdullah Al Bareek, Ali Al Nuaimi, Ali Nasser Saleh, Ibrahim Abdulmaged (Mohammed Al Yazidi 83), Magid Mohammed, Meqbel Meshaal (Ali Afef 58), Emerson, Tenorio, Mohamed Gholam.

GROUP C MATCHDAY 5
Al Sadd, Doha
9-05-2007, 18:50, 2000, Kunsuta THA

Al Sadd 1
Ali Nasser Saleh [16]

Basel Samih (Saad Al Sheeb 69) – Essa Al Kuwari, Abdullah Koni (Hamad Al Shamari 69), Mohammed Al Yazidi, Ali Nasser Saleh, Ibrahim Abdulmaged, Magid Mohammed, Talal Al Bloushi, Meqbel Meshaal, Mohamed Gholam (Abdullah Al Bareek 54), Yusuf Ahmed.

Al Karama 1
Iyad Mando [44]

Mosab Balhous – Fabio Santos, Hassan Abbas, Belal Abdulaim, Anas Al Khouja, Jehad Al Hussien (Mohanad Ibrahim 90), Iyad Mando, Fahd Aodi (Abdalrahman Akkari 59), Aatef Jenyat (Naser Al Sebai 82), Firas Issmael, Senghor Koupouleni.

GROUP C MATCHDAY 1
Sabah Al Salem, Kuwait City
7-03-2007, 21:30, 500, Mombini IRN

Al Najaf 0

Hadi Jaber – Haeder Aboudi, Nabeel Abbas, Jassib Sultan, Falah Hassan, Ayad Sadir (Hattam Saheb 79), Karrar Jassim, Dheiaa Faleh, Said Mohsen Ali, Yasir Abdulrazaaq (Ali Mohammed 73), Aqeel Mohammed (Suhail Naim 83).

Neftchi Fergana 1
Holmatov [71]

Hasanov – Toirov, Usmanov, Shoimov, Saidov, Holmatov, Kuziboyev, Akramov (Nizametdinov 85), Askaraliev, Berdiev, Kovalenko.

GROUP C MATCHDAY 3
Al Sadd, Doha
11-04-2007, 18:30, 2000, Tan Hai CHN

Al Sadd 2
Khalfan Ibrahim [65], Emerson [72]

Mohamed Saqr – Jafal Al Kuwari, Abdullah Al Bareek, Ali Nasser Saleh, Mased Al Hamad, Khalfan Ibrahim (Meqbel Meshaal 75), Talal Al Bloushi (Magid Mohammed 42), Hamood Abdulla, Emerson (Bakhit Al Marri 89), Tenorio, Mohamed Gholam.

Neftchi Fergana 0

Hasanov – Toirov, Usmanov, Melziddinov, Juramuradov, Saidov (Otakuziev 81), Holmatov, Akramov (Alijonov 71), Askaraliev, Berdiev, Kovalenko.

GROUP C MATCHDAY 4
Sabah Al Salem, Kuwait City
25-04-2007, 19:00, 400, Al Fadhli KUW

Al Najaf 2
Mohsen Ali [7p], Qassim Faraj [86p]

Hadi Jaber – Nabeel Abbas, Jassib Sultan, Falah Hassan, Ali Abduljabbar, Ayad Sadir, Karrar Jassim, Dheiaa Faleh, Said Mohsen Ali, Ali Mohammed, Aqeel Mohammed.

Al Karama 4
Fahd Aodi [50], J.Al Hussien 2 [46] [52], Koupouleni [65]

Adnan Al Hafez•85 – Fabio Santos, Hassan Abbas, Belal Abdulaim, Anas Al Khouja, Jehad Al Hussien (Mohanad Ibrahim 82), Iyad Mando, Aatef Jenyat (Mohamad Al Hamwi 90), Firas Issmael, Mohanad Ibrahim, Senghor Koupouleni (Mosab Balhous 85).

GROUP C MATCHDAY 6
Sabah Al Salem, Kuwait City
23-05-2007, 17:30,

Al Najaf 1
Mohsen Ali [78]

Mohammed Abdulzahra – Haeder Aboudi, Nabeel Abbas, Jassib Sultan, Falah Hassan, Ayad Sadir, Karrar Jassim, Said Mohsen Ali, Hattam Saheb, Ali Mohammed, Aqeel Mohammed.

Al Sadd 0

Saad Al Sheeb – Abdullah Al Bareek, Hamad Al Shamari, Ali Al Nuaimi, Mohammed Al Yazidi, Mased Al Hamad, Ibrahim Abdulmaged, Hamood Abdulla, Bakhit Al Marri, Meqbel Meshaal, Yusuf Ahmed.

GROUP C MATCHDAY 2
Fergana Stadium, Fergana
21-03-2007, 15:00, 16 500, Shamsuzzaman BAN

Neftchi Fergana 2
Berdiev [26], Otakuziev [77]

Hasanov – Toirov, Usmanov, Shoimov, Saidov (Nizametdinov 90), Holmatov, Kuziboyev, Akramov, Askaraliev, Berdiev, Kovalenko (Otakuziev 54).

Al Karama 1
Firas Issmael [33]

Mosab Balhous – Fabio Santos, Hassan Abbas, Belal Abdulaim, Anas Al Khouja, Jehad Al Hussien, Fahd Aodi (Abdul Kader Refai 78), Aatef Jenyat (Iyad Mando 73), Firas Issmael, Abdalrahman Akkari, Senghor Koupouleni (Mohanad Ibrahim 78).

GROUP C MATCHDAY 3
Khaled Ibn Al Waleed, Homs
11-04-2007, 20:00, 30 000, Karim BHR

Al Karama 1
Fahd Aodi [90p]

Mosab Balhous – Naser Al Sebai, Fabio Santos, Belal Abdulaim, Abdul Kader Refai (Hassan Abbas 68), Mohamad Al Hamwi (Fahd Aodi 73), Iyad Mando, Aatef Jenyat, Firas Issmael, Mohanad Ibrahim (Senghor Koupouleni 58), Abdalrahman Akkari.

Al Najaf 1
Falah Hassan [71]

Hadi Jaber – Nabeel Abbas, Jassib Sultan, Falah Hassan, Ali Abduljabbar, Ayad Sadir, Karrar Jassim (Ali Al Fatla 96+), Dheiaa Faleh, Said Mohsen Ali (Qais Issa 92+), Ali Mohammed, Aqeel Mohammed (Hattam Saheb 65).

GROUP C MATCHDAY 5
Fergana Stadium, Fergana
9-05-2007, 16:30,

Neftchi Fergana 1
Holmatov [43]

Hasanov – Toirov, Usmanov, Shoimov, Saidov (Nizametdinov 90), Holmatov, Kuziboyev (Otakuziev 66), Akramov, Askaraliev, Berdiev, Kovalenko (Ibragimov 76)

Al Najaf 1
Ali Mohammed [60]

Hadi Jaber – Nabeel Abbas, Jassib Sultan, Falah Hassan, Ali Abduljabbar, Ayad Sadir, Karrar Jassim (Ali Al Fatla 86), Qais Issa (Hattam Saheb 56), Dheiaa Faleh (Ali Abduljabbar 65), Said Mohsen Ali, Ali Mohammed, Aqeel Mohammed.

GROUP C MATCHDAY 6
Khaled Ibn Al Waleed, Homs
23-05-2007, 20:00, 35 000, Al Mutlaq KSA

Al Karama 2
Iyad Mando 2 [12] [50]

Mosab Balhous – Fabio Santos, Hassan Abbas, Belal Abdulaim, Anas Al Khouja, Jehad Al Hussien, Iyad Mando, Fahd Aodi (Abdalrahman Akkari 75), Aatef Jenyat, Firas Issmael, Senghor Koupouleni.

Neftchi Fergana 0

Hasanov – Shoimov, Melziddinov, Juramuraov, Nizametdinov, Yakubov (Akramov 78), Saidov, Holmatov, Alijonov, Askaraliev (Ibragimov 57) (Hakimov 69), Berdiev.

GROUP D

		Pl	W	D	L	F	A	Pts	IRN	KSA	UAE	SYR
Sepahan	IRN	6	4	1	1	12	5	13			1-1	2-1
Al Shabab	KSA	6	3	1	2	9	3	10	0-1			4-0
Al Ain	UAE	6	1	3	2	5	8	6	3-2	0-2		
Al Ittihad	SYR	6	0	3	3	3	13	3	0-5	1-1	0-0	

GROUP D MATCHDAY 1
Foolad Shahr, Esfahan
7-03-2007, 15:00, 15 000, Al Fadhli KUW

Sepahan 2
Seyed M. Salehi 2 [20] [30]

Petrosyan – Azizadeh, Aghily, Bengar, Bahadorani, Abu Al Hail, Nori, Soleimani (Bayat 66), Lovinian, Emad Mohammed (Shafiei 85), Salehi.

Al Ittihad 1
Anas Sari [13]

Mahmoud Karkar – Majd Homsi, Omar Hemidi, Wael Aian, Hayder Kadham, Bakri Tarrab, Mahmoud Al Amena (Abdul Aga 60), Yahia Al Rached, Anatolii Matkvych (Ammar Rihawi 76), Dumitru Popovich (Osama Haddad 82), Anas Sari.

GROUP D MATCHDAY 1
Khalifa Bin Zayed Al Nahyan, Al Ain
7-03-2007, 19:30, 5000, Al Hilali OMA

Al Ain 0

Walled Salem – Fabricio Al Cantara, Ali Ahmed (Nassib Ishaq 60)m Abdulla Ali, Humaid Fakher, Helal Saeed (Rami Yaslam 74), Gharib Harib, Faisal Ali (Shehab Ahmed 46), Frank Ongfiang, Hawar Mohammed.

Al Shabab 2
Godwin Attram [45], Waleed Al Gizani [73]

Saeid Al Harbi – Abdulmohsen Al Dosari, Saleh Sadeeq, Hassan Maaz, Abdoh Autef, Zaid Al Mowalad (Abdullah Shuhail 62), Ahmed Ateef, Yousef Al Muwaine, Bader Al Hagbani (Amir Megahed 80), Waleed Al Gizani, Godwin Attram (Nashat Akram 61).

GROUP D MATCHDAY 2
Al Hamadania, Aleppo SYR
21-03-2007, 19:20, 15 000, Kadir Nema IRQ

Al Ittihad 0

Mahmoud Karkar – Majd Homsi, Omar Hemidi, Wael Aian, Hayder Kadham, Bakri Tarrab, Ammar Rihawi (Ayman Habal 90), Anatolii Matkvych, Mahmoud Al Amena (Dumitru Popovich 82), Yahia Al Rached (Abdul Aga 58), Anas Sari.

Al Ain 0

Mutaz Abdulla – Musallem Fayez, Abdulla Ali, Fahad Ali, Humaid Fakher, Ahmed Khalfan (Sultan Rashed 73), Rami Yaslam (Hawar Mohammed 65), Helal Saeed, Gharib Harib, Nassib Ishaq (Ali Msarri 80), Nasser Khamis.

GROUP D MATCHDAY 2
King Fahad International, Riyadh
21-03-2007, 16:30, 12 000, Irmatov UZB

Al Shabab 1

Mohammad Khojah – Abdulmohnsen Al Dosari, Saleh Sadeeq, Hassan Maaz, Abdullah Shuhail, Abdoh Autef (Fisal bin Sultan 81), Ahmed Ateef, Yousef Al Muwaine, Nashat Akram (Naji Majrashi 60), Bader Al Hagbani (Abdulaziz bin Saran 88), Godwin Attram.

Sepahan 1
Seyed M. Salehi [83]

Petrosyan – Azizadeh, Aghily, Akbari, Bahadorani, Abu Al Hail, Nori (Soleimani 46), Bayat (Hamid Shafiei 69), Lovinian, Emad Mohammed, Salehi (Hadi Jafari 87).

GROUP D MATCHDAY 3
Khalifa Bin Zayed Al Nahyan, Al Ain
11-04-2007, 19:45, 7 000, Kunsuta THA

Al Ain 3

Mutaz Abdulla – Fabricio Al Cantara (Faisal Ali 70), Musallem Fayez, Ali Msarri, Ali Ahmed, Abdulla Ali, Fahad Ali, Rami Yaslam, Frank Ondfiang, Hawar Mohammed, Nasser Khamis (Gharib Harib 46).

Sepahan 2
Seyed M. Salehi [8], Emad Mohammed [65]

Petrosyan – Azizadeh, Aghily, Akbari, Abu Al Hail, Nori, Bayat (Navidikia 60), Lovinian, Hamid Shafiei, Emad Mohammed, Salehi.

GROUP D MATCHDAY 3
King Fahad International, Riyadh
11-04-2007, 20:35, 4000, Maidin SIN

Al Shabab 4
Abdulmohsen Al Dosari 2 [33] [48],
Naji Majrashi [60p], Waleed Al Gizani [79]

Mohammad Khojah – Abdullah Al Astaa, Abdulmohnsen Al Dosari, Saleh Sadeeq, Hassan Maaz, Abdoh Autef (Waleed Al Gizani 79), Ahmed Ateef, Yousef Al Muwaine, Nashat Akram, Naji Majrashi (Fisal bin Sultan 78), Godwin Attram (Bader Al Hagbani 74).

Al Ittihad 0

Mahmoud Karkar – Maan Al Rashad, Majd Homsi, Omar Hemidi•33, Wael Aian, Bakri Tarrab, Obada Al Said (Hayder Kadham 40), Mahmoud Al Amena (Ammar Rihawi 64), Anatolii Matkvych•57, Abdul Aga (Dumitru Popovich 74), Anas Sari.

GROUP D MATCHDAY 4
Foolad Shahr, Esfahan
25-04-2007, 16:00, 25 000, Shield AUS

Sepahan 1
Hossein Papi [49]

Petrosyan – Aghily, Bengar, Akbari, Bahadorani (Mahmoud Karimi 89), Abu Al Hail, Nori, Bayat, Hamid Shafiei (Papi 46), Emad Mohammed (Hadi Jafari 83), Salehi.

Al Ain 1
Hawar Mohammed [86]

Waleed Salem – Musallem Fayez, Ali Msarri, Ali Ahmed (Ahmed Khalfan 55), Abdulla Ali (Nassib Ishaq 55), Fahad Ali, Humaid Fakher, Helal Saeed (Juma Khater 90), Gharib Harib, Hawar Mohammed, Frank Ongfiang.

GROUP D MATCHDAY 4
Al Hamadania, Aleppo SYR
25-04-2007, 18:45, 8000, Najm LIB

Al Ittihad 1
Ammar Rihawi [36]

Mahmoud Karkar – Maan Al Rashad, Majd Homsi, Mohammed Ibrahim, Hayder Kadham, Bakri Tarrab, Ammar Rihawi, Mahmoud Al Amena (Moahamed Al Damen 66; Obada Al Said 73), Yahia Al Rached, Abdul Aga, Anas Sari (Dumitru Popovich 46).

Al Shabab 1
Ahmed Ateef [65]

Mohammad Khojah – Abdullah Al Astaa, Saleh Sadeeq, Hassan Maaz, Faisal Al Obili, Abdoh Autef, Ahmed Ateef, Yousef Al Muwaine, Nashat Akram, Naji Majrashi, Waleed Al Gizani (Fisal bin Sultan 66).

GROUP D MATCHDAY 5
Al Hamadania, Aleppo SYR
9-05-2007, 19:00, 2000, Lee Gi Young KOR

Al Ittihad 0

Mahmoud Karkar – Maan Al Rashad, Majd Homsi, Omar Hemidi, Wael Aian, Bakri Tarrab, Osama Haddad, Mahmoud Al Amena, Yahia Al Rached (Ammar Rihawi 46), Abdul Aga, Anas Sari (Dumitru Popovich 32).

Sepahan 5
Abdulwahab Al Hail [10], Mohammad Nori 2 [40] [55]
Emad Mohammed 2 [70] [90]

Petrosyan – Aghily (Azizadeh 74), Bengar, Akbari (Mohammadpour 84), Hadi Jafari, Abu Al Hail, Nori, Bayat•81, Hajysafi (Papi 74), Emad Mohammed, Salehi.

GROUP D MATCHDAY 5
King Fahad International, Riyadh
9-05-2007, 18:45, 6000, Kwon KOR

Al Shabab 2
Abdullah Al Astaa [59], Waleed Al Gizani [88]

Mohammad Khojah – Abdullah Al Astaa (Abdullah Shuhail 79), Abdulmohsen Al Dosari, Saleh Sadeeq, Hassan Maaz, Abdoh Autef (Waleed Al Gizani 65), Ahmed Ateef, Yousef Al Muwaine, Nashat Akram, Naji Majrashi, Godwin Attram (Bader Al Hagbani 83).

Al Ain 0

Waleed Salem – Musallem Fayez, Ali Ahmed (Salem Abdulla 85), Abdulla Ali, Fahad Ali, Humaid Fakher, Sultan Rashed (Faisal Ali 74), Ahmed Khalfan (Rami Yaslam 64), Gharib Harib, Hawar Mohammed, Frank Ongfiang.

GROUP D MATCHDAY 6
Foolad Shahr, Esfahan
23-05-2007, 16:30, 30 000, Nishimura JPN

Sepahan 1
Seyed M. Salehi [33]

Savari – Aghily, Bengar, Akbari, Bahadorani, Hadi Jafari, Abu Al Hail, Nori (Maheri 83), Hajysafi (Lovinian 66), Emad Mohammed (Papi 90), Salehi.

Al Shabab 0

Mohammad Khojah – Abdulmohsen Al Dosari, Saleh Sadeeq, Hassan Maaz•81, Shuhail (Fisal bin Sultan 65), Abdoh Autef (Waleed Al Gizani 46), Ahmed Ateef, Yousef Al Muwaine, Nashat Akram, Naji Majrashi (Faisal Al Obili 68), Godwin Attram.

GROUP D MATCHDAY 6
Khalifa Bin Zayed Al Nahyan, Al Ain
23-05-2007, 19:30,

Al Ain 1
Gharib Harib [53]

Waleed Salem – Musallem Fayez, Ali Msarri, Ali Ahmed, Abdulla Mousa (Juma Khater 79), Sultan Rashed, Ahmed Khalfan, Fawzi Fayez (Humaid Fakher 70), Shehab Ahmed (Gharib Harib 52), Frank Ongfiang, Nasser Khamis.

Al Ittihad 1
Anas Sari [90]

Mahmoud Karkar – Maan Al Rashad, Majd Homsi, Omar Hemidi (Mahmoud Al Beef 69), Hayder Kadham, Bakri Tarrab, Osama Haddad, Mahmoud Al Amena, Yahia Al Rached (Obada Al Said 83), Abdul Aga, Anas Sari.

GROUP E

		Pl	W	D	L	F	A	Pts	JPN	AUS	IDN	CHN
Urawa Reds	JPN	6	2	4	0	9	5	10		0-0	3-0	1-0
Sydney FC	AUS	6	2	3	1	8	5	9	2-2		3-0	0-0
Persik Kediri	IDN	6	2	1	3	6	16	7	3-3	2-1		1-0
Shanghai Shenhua	CHN	6	1	2	3	7	4	5	0-0	1-2	6-0	

GROUP E MATCHDAY 1
Yuanshen Stadium, Shanghai
7-03-2007, 19:00, 8000, Lee Gi Young KOR

Shanghai Shenhua 1
Xie Hui [78]

Wang Dalei – Du Wei, Chang Lin, Sun Ji, Zheng Kewei (Li Gang 39), Jiang Kun (Xie Hui 71), Qu Shaoyan, Blanco, Alonso, Correa (Yu Tao 46), Mao Jianqing.

Sydney FC 2
Corica [8], Ufuk Talay [23]

Bolton – Fyfe, Rudan, Topor-Stanley, Milligan, Talay, Middleby (Spencer 69), Corica, Carney, Zdrilic, Brosque.

GROUP E MATCHDAY 1
Saitama 2002, Saitama
7-03-2007, 19:30, 31 303, Kim Dong Jin KOR

Urawa Reds 3
Yamada [12], Nagai [45], Ono [76]

Tsuzuki – Tsuboi, Nene, Yamada, Ono, Ponte, Suzuki.K, Soma (Hirakawa 81), Abe, Nagai, Washington (Okano 69)

Persik Kediri 0

Wahyudi – Indarto, Zainuri, Prasetiya, Iba, Harianto, Kurniawan, Fagundez, Fernando (Suswanto 75), Gonzalez, Sudarsono.

GROUP E MATCHDAY 2
Manahan Stadium, Solo City
21-03-2007, 15:30, 5000, Ebrahim BHR

Persik Kediri 1
Bertha Yuana Putra [71]

Sandy – Indarto, Zainuri, Prasetiya, Yantara, Utomo, Kurniawan, Fagundez, Fernando, Gonzalez, Sudarsono (Putra 58).

Shanghai Shenhua 0

Zhang Chen – Du Wei, Chang Lin, Yu Tao (Wang Ke 77), Sun Ji, Li Gang, Qu Shaoyan, Correa (Jiang Kun 46), Xie Hui, Mao Jianqing, Gao Lin (Blanco 46).

GROUP E MATCHDAY 2
Aussie Stadium, Sydney
21-03-2007, 20:00, 21 010, Mohd Salleh MAS

Sydney FC 2
Carney [1], Ufuk Talay [22]

Bolton – Fyfe, Rudan, Topor-Stanley, Milligan, Talay, Middleby (Zadkovich 43), Corica, Carney, Zdrilic (McFlynn 46), Brosque.

Urawa Reds 2
Robson Ponte [30], Nagai [54]

Tsuzuki – Tsuboi, Tanaka, Nene (Hasebe 38), Yamada (Hirakawa 61; Hosogai 85), Ono, Ponte, Suzuki.K, Abe, Nagai, Washington.

GROUP E MATCHDAY 3
Saitama 2002, Saitama
11-04-2007, 19:30, 28 828, Moradi IRN

Urawa Reds 1
Abe [42]

Tsuzuki – Tsuboi, Tanaka, Abe, Yamada, Ono, Ponte (Hosogai 84), Suzuki.K, Hasebe, Nagai (Okano 69), Washington.

Shanghai Shenhua 0

Zhang Chen – Chang Lin, Liu Zhiqing, Li Weifeng, Yu Tao (Blanco 74), Zheng Kewei, Qu Shaoyan (Dong Yang 13), Lu Xin, Correa, Xie Hui, Mao Jianqing (Jiang Kun 60)

GROUP E MATCHDAY 3
Manahan Stadium, Solo City
12-04-2007, 10:30, 15 000, Balideh QAT

Persik Kediri 2
Aris Budi Prasetiya [25], Budi Sudarsono [70]

Sandy – Indarto (Kartiko 64), Zainuri, Prasetiya, Iba (Yantara 86), Putra (Sudarsono 68), Harianto, Kurniawan, Fagundez, Fernando, Gonzalez.

Sydney FC 1
Corica [8]

Bolton – Fyfe, Rudan, Topor-Stanley, Talay, Zadkovich•61, Corica, Carney (Tsattalios 84), McFlynn (Casey 65), Zdrilic (Glavas 74), Brosque.

GROUP E MATCHDAY 4
Yuanshen Stadium, Shanghai
25-04-2007, 16:00, 10 000, Ghatrifi OMA

Shanghai Shenhua 0

Wang Dalei – Dong Yang, Du Wei, Chang Lin, Liu Zhiqing (Li Weifeng 73), Xiao Zhanbo, Shen Longyuan, Zheng Kewei (Lu Xin 46), Jiang Kun, Correa (Blanco 46), Xie Hui.

Urawa Reds 0

Tsuzuki – Tsuboi, Tanaka, Yamada•75, Ono (Hirakawa 60), Ponte, Suzuki.K, Hasebe, Abe, Washington (Okano 80).

GROUP E MATCHDAY 4
Parramatta Stadium, Sydney
25-04-2007, 20:00, 10 075, Vo VIE

Sydney FC 3
Brosque [73], Corica 2 [54] [90]

Bolton – Fyfe, Rudan, Topor-Stanley, Milligan, Talay, Middleby, Corica, McFlynn, Zdrilic (Casey 76), Brosque.

Persik Kediri 0

Sandy (Wahyudi 64) – Indarto, Zainuri, Prasetiya, Iba, Hadi (Putra 79), Harianto, Kurniawan, Fagundez, Gonzalez, Sudarsono.

GROUP E MATCHDAY 5
Manahan Stadium, Solo City
9-05-2007, 15:30,

Persik Kediri 3
Christian Gonzalez 2 [23p] [31], Budi Sudarsono [83]

Sandy – Indarto, Prasetyo, Kartiko, Iba, Putra (Sudarsono 61), Harianto, Kurniawan, Fagundez, Fernando, Gonzalez.

Urawa Reds 3
Ono [9p], Robson Ponte [50], Abe [62]

Tsuzuki – Tsuboi, Nene, Ono, Ponte, Suzuki.K, Hirakawa (Hosogai 22), Soma (Okano 46), Horinouchi, Abe (Hasebe 85), Nagai.

GROUP E MATCHDAY 5
Aussie Stadium, Sydney
9-05-2007, 19:30, 14 786, Bashir SIN

Sydney FC 0

Bolton – Fyfe, Rudan, Topor-Stanley, Milligan, Talay (Casey 73), Middleby, Corica, Carney, Zdrilic (Glavas 81), Brosque.

Shanghai Shenhua 0

Zhang Chen – Yao Lijun (Yin Xifu 83), Dong Yang, Du Wei, Liu Zhiqing, Xiao Zhanbo, Wang Ke (Kewei 65), Li Gang, Blanco, Alonso, Correa (Hongliang 58).

GROUP E MATCHDAY 6
Yuanshen Stadium, Shanghai
23-05-2007, 19:00,

Shanghai Shenhua 6
Xie Hui [8], Gao Lin [25], Blanco [86], Alonso 3 [79] [87] [90]

Wang Dalei – Yao Lijun, Xiao Zhanbo, Cheng Liang, Wang Ke, Yin Xifu, Wang Hongliang, Lu Xin, Xie Hui (Blanco 55), Mao Jianqing (Alonso 55), Gao Lin (Jiang Kun 55).

Persik Kediri 0

Sandy – Indarto, Zainuri, Prasetiya, Kurniawan, Iba, Putra, Hadi, Fernando, Harianto, Musikan (Suswanto 53•62).

GROUP E MATCHDAY 6
Saitama 2002, Saitama
23-05-2007, 19:30, 44 793, Al Marzouqi UAE

Urawa Reds 0

Tsuzuki – Tsuboi, Nene, Yamada, Ono (Nagai 85), Ponte (Okano 90), Suzuki.K, Soma (Hasebe 62), Horinouchi, Abe, Washington.

Sydney 0

Bolton – Fyfe, Rudan, Topor-Stanley, Milligan, Talay (Casey 70), Zadkovich, Corica, Carney, Zdrilic, Brosque.

GROUP F

		Pl	W	D	L	F	A	Pts	JPN	KOR	IDN	THA
Kawasaki Frontale	JPN	6	5	1	0	15	4	16		3-0	3-0	1-1
Chunnam Dragons	KOR	6	3	1	2	7	8	10	1-3		2-0	3-2
Arema Malang	IDN	6	1	1	4	2	9	4	1-3	0-1		1-0
Bangkok University	THA	6	0	3	3	4	7	3	1-2	0-0	0-0	

GROUP F MATCHDAY 1
Gajayana Stadium, Malang
7-03-2007, 15:30, 26 000, Al Ghafary JOR
Arema Malang   1
Elie Aiboy [12]

Kartiko – Pulalo, Casimir, Aiboy (Ichwan 75), Sulaiman (Kurniawan 76), Astaman, Suyono (Rasmoyo 84), Rasyid, Sutaji, Mvondo, Morales.

Kawasaki Frontale   3
Tavares 2 [1] [73], Kengo Nakamura [82]

Kawashima – Ito, Minowa, Terada, Taniguchi (Ochiai 90), Juninho, Tavares (Ohashi 85), Nakamura, Mori, Marakami, Ganaha (Kurotsu 66).

GROUP F MATCHDAY 1
Thai-Japanese Stadium, Bangkok
7-03-2007, 18:00, 4000, Breeze AUS
Bangkok University   0

Koedpudsa – Klinsukon, Boonyasejtha, Jarernsuk, Phetphun, Tarue, Chaipan (Pcichtchaiphotchanat 86), Siriwaen (Seubsin 66), Fukasawa, Pancharoen, Domtaisong (Phon–Udom 83).

Chunnam Dragons   0

Yeom Dong Gyun – Kang Min Soo, Kim Jin Kyu, Lee Jun Ki, Kim Tae Su, Song Sung Hyun (Ju Kwang Youn 81), Kim Chi Woo, Chang Dong Hyok, Yang Sang Min, Sandro (Song Tae Lim 65), Sandro Cardoso (Baek Seung Min 46).

GROUP F MATCHDAY 2
Kawasaki Todoroki, Kawasaki
21-03-2007, 14:00, 10 816, Maidin SIN
Kawasaki Frontale   1
Patiparn Phetphun OG [77]

Kawashima – Ito, Igawa (Taniguchi 73), Minowa, Terada, Kawamura (Ganaha 64), Juninho, Tavares (Tae-Se 85), Nakamura, Marakami, Kurotsu.

Bangkok University   1
Suriya Domaisong [7]

Koedpudsa – Kaewjoho, Boonyasejtha, Jarernsuk, Phetphun, Tarue (Pornjamsai 87), Chaipan•57, Siriwaen (Phon–Udom 46), Pancharoen (Pcichtchaiphotchanat 63), Fukasawa, Domtaisong.

GROUP F MATCHDAY 2
Gwangyang Football Stadium
21-03-2007, 19:00, 1500, Huang Junjie CHN
Chunam Dragons   2
Kim Tae Su [48], Cardoso [82]

Yeom Dong Gyun – Lee Wan (Baek Seung Min 46), Kang Min Soo, Kim Jin Kyu, Kim Tae Su, Kim Chi Woo, Lim Kwan Sik (Leandro 46), Kim Seong Jae, Ju Kwang Youn (Song Dong Hyun 46), Sandro, Sandro Cardoso.

Arema Malang   0

Kurniawan – Pulalo, Casimir, Aiboy (Ichwan 89), Kurniawan, Astaman, Suyono, Rasyid, Sutaji (Rasmoyo 87), Mvondo, Morales.

GROUP F MATCHDAY 3
Royal Thai Army Stadium, Bangkok
11-04-2007, 18:00, 1500, Chynybekov KGZ
Bangkok University   0

Koedpudsa – Klinsukon, Boonyasejtha, Jarernsuk, Phetphun, Tarue, Siriwaen (Petvises 82)), Kloy-Eiam, Pancharoen (Seubsin 81), Fukasawa (Thongthuam 84), Domtaisong.

Arema Malang   0

Oba – Pulalu, Casimir, Aiboy, Provita, Kurniawan, Astaman, Suyono, Sutaji, Prastowo (Salossa 86), Morales.

GROUP F MATCHDAY 3
Gwangyang Football Stadium
11-04-2007, 19:00, 5703, Al Ghamdi KSA
Chunnam Dragons   1
Kang Min Soo [90]

Yeom Dong Gyun – Kang Min Soo, Park Ji Yong, Kim Jin Kyu, Lee Jun Ki (Ju Kwang Youn 34), Kim Tae Su, Song Jung Hyun, Baek Seung Min, Chang Dong Hyok (Kim Seong Jae 72), Sandro, Leandro (Sandro Cardoso 46).

Kawasaki Frontale   3
Tavares [57], Carlos Juninho 2 [29] [70]

Kawashima – Ito, Minowa, Terada, Taniguchi, Juninho (Ochiai 75), Tavares (Tae-Se 87), Nakamura, Mori, Marakami (Igawa 68), Ganaha.

GROUP F MATCHDAY 4
Gajayana Stadium, Malang
25-04-2007, 15:30, 10 000, Sun Baojie CHN
Arema Malang   1
Bruno Casimir [56]

Kartiko – Casimir, Suroso•61, Aiboy, Rasmoyo (Pulalo 46), Salossa, Astaman, Suyono, Rasyid (Sulaiman 63), Sutaji, Mvondo•90.

Bangkok University   0

Lamsombat – Klinsukon, Boonyasejtha, Jarernsuk (Soonki 65), Phetphun, Chaipan, Pcichtchaiphotchanat (Seubsin 65), Pancharoen, Fukasawa, Domtaisong, Phon-Udom (Siriwaen 48).

GROUP F MATCHDAY 4
Kawasaki Todoroki, Kawasaki
25-04-2007, 19:00, 10 070, Williams AUS
Kawasaki Frontale   3
Carlos Juninho [25], Jong Tae Se 2 [81] [87]

Kawashima – Ito, Minowa, Terada, Taniguchi (Ochiai 88), Juninho, Tavares (Ohashi 90), Nakamura, Mori, Marakami (Igawa 84), Tae-Se.

Chunnam Dragons   0

Yeom Dong Gyun – Kang Min Soo, Kim Jin Kyu, Lee Jun Ki (Lee Kyu Ro 65), Song Jung Hyun, Park Chun Sin (Kim Jin Hyun 56), Kim Chi Woo, Baek Seung Min, Kim Seong Jae, Chang Dong Hyok (Sandro 31), Leandro.

GROUP F MATCHDAY 5
Kawasaki Todoroki, Kawasaki
9-05-2007, 19:00, 9453, Vo VIE
Kawasaki Frontale   3
Kengo Nakamura 2 [4] [70], Harada [80]

Kawashima – Ito, Minowa, Terada (Sahara 74), Taniguchi, Kawamura (Harada 59), Juninho, Tavares (Ohashi 90), Nakamura, Mori, Tae-Se (Kurotsu 71).

Arema Malang   0

Kartiko – Rasmoyo, Pravita, Sulaiman, Astaman, Suyono, Rasyid, Sutaji, Prastowo, Ichwan, Morales.

GROUP F MATCHDAY 5
Gwangyang Football Stadium
9-05-2007, 19:00, 1000, Neman
Chunnam Dragons   3
Kim Seung Hyun [28], Song Tae Lim 2 [79] [90]

Song You Gual – Hong Sung Yo, Park Ji Yong, Kim Jin Hyun, Park Chun Sin, Baek Seung Min, Lim Kwan Sik (Lee Wan 46), Kim Seung Hyun (Song Tae Lim 60), Chang Dong Hyok, Lee Kyu Ro, Leandro (Ju Kwang Youn 46).

Bangkok University   2
Kittisak Siriwaen [11], Kraisorn Pancharoen [39]

Koedpudsa – Klinsukon, Kaewjoho, Boonyasejtha, Jarernsuk (Thongthuam 84), Tarue (Phunarae 88), Chaipan (Pornjamsi 46), Siriwaen, Pancharoen, Fukasawa, Domtaisong.

GROUP F MATCHDAY 6
Gajayana Stadium, Malang
23-05-2007, 15:30, 5000, Al Ghatrifi OMA
Arema Malang   0

Kurniawan – Pulalo, Casimir, Suroso, Aiboy (Prastowo 76), Rasmoyo, Astaman, Suyono (Ichwan 27), Sutaji, Mvondo, Morales.

Chunnam Dragons   1
Ju Kwang Youn [47]

Cho Min Hyuck – Lee Wan, Park Ji Yong, Lee Jun Ki, Kim Jin Hyun, Park Chun Sin (Lee Kyu Ro 80), Baek Seung Min, Lim Kwan Sik (Cho Se Kwon 86), Chang Dong Hyok, Song Han Bok, Ju Kwang Youn.

GROUP F MATCHDAY 6
Royal Thai Army Stadium, Bangkok
23-05-2007, 18:00,
Bangkok University   1
Ekkaphan Petvises [40]

Koedpudsa – Klinsukon (Chasang 67), Kaewjoho, Boonyasejtha (Nontagate 66), Phetphun, Tarue, Phunarae (Phon-Udom 64), Seubsin, Kloy-Eiam, Thongthuam, Petvises.

Kawasaki Frontale   2
Harada [14], Nishiyama [63]

Aizawa – Sahara (Sonoda 38), Igawa, Kawamura, Harada, Hida, Ohashi (Yabu 65), Suzuki, Nishiyama (Yuji Kimura 90), Tae-Se, Kukino.

GROUP G

		Pl	W	D	L	F	A	Pts	KOR	CHN	AUS	VIE
Seongnam Ilhwa Chunma	KOR	6	4	1	1	13	6	13		3-0	1-0	4-1
Shandong Luneng	CHN	6	4	1	1	12	8	13	2-1		2-2	4-0
Adelaide United	AUS	6	2	2	2	9	6	8	2-2	0-1		3-0
Dong Tam Long An	VIE	6	0	0	6	4	18	0	1-2	2-3	0-2	

GROUP G MATCHDAY 1
Seongnam Tancheon Sports Complex
7-03-2007, 19:00, 877, Orzuev TJK

Seongnam Ilhwa Chunma   **4**
Mota 2 9 69p, Kim Dong Hun 70, Neaga 81

Kim Yong Dae – Park Jin Sub (Cho Yong Hyung 60), Cho Byung Kuk, Kim Young Chul, Jang Hack Yong, Kim Do Heon, Kim Sang Sik, Choi Sung Kuk (Kim Dong Hun 46), Itamar, Mota (Nam Ki Il 72), Adrian Neaga.

Dong Tam Long An   **1**
Tshamala 89

Santos – Phan Van Giau, Le Quang Trai, Luu Minh Tri, Nguyen Minh Phuong, Phan Van Tai Em, Nguyen Thanh Truc, Ly Lam Huy, Nguyen Viet Thang, Antonio (Vo Phi Thuong 46), Kabanga Tshamala.

GROUP G MATCHDAY 2
Shandong Sports Center, Jinan
21-03-2007, 19:00, 25 000, Najm LIB

Shandong Luneng   **2**
Zivkovic 62p, Wang Yongpo 79

Li Leilei – Wang Chao (Yuan Weiwei 59), Shu Chang, Malbasa, Jiao Zhe, Zivkovic, Wang Yongpo (Bakovic 90), Zho Haibin, Cui Peng, Han Peng, Li Jinyu (Liu Jindong 84)

Seongnam Ilhwa Chunma   **1**
Cho Byung Kuk 78

Kim Yong Dae – Park Jin Sub, Cho Byung Kuk, Kim Young Chul, Jang Hack Yong, Kim Do Heon, Kim Sang Sik, Kim Dong Won (Choi Sung Kuk 46), Itamar (Nam Ki Il 85), Mota, Adrian Neaga (Nam Ki Il 72).

GROUP G MATCHDAY 4
Long An Stadium, Long An
25-04-2007, 18:00, 10 000, Al Saeedi UAE

Dong Tam Long An   **2**
Tshamala 14, Nguyen Hoang Thuong 36

Santos – Luu Minh Tri, Doan Nhat Tien, Vo Phi Thuong, Phan Van Tai Em, Nguyen Tuan Phong, Phan Thanh Giang, Nguyen Thanh Truc (Nguyen Van Hung 63), Nguyen Hoang Thuong●41, Nguyen Viet Thang (Nguyen Van Khai 74), Kabanga Tshamala.

Shandong Luneng   **3**
Wang Yongpo 29, Li Jinyu 2 49 90

Li Leilei – Shu Chang, Yuan Weiwei, Malbasa, Jiao Zhe, Liu Jindong (Li Wei 74) Zivkovic, Wang Yongpo, Cui Peng, Han Peng, Li Jinyu.

GROUP G MATCHDAY 5
Shandong Sports Center, Jinan
9-05-2007, 19:30, 30 000, Al Ghamdi KSA

Shandong Luneng   **2**
Li Wei 35, Shu Chang 56

Li Leilei – Wang Chao (Yuan Weiwei 86), Shu Chang, Malbasa, Jiao Zhe, Zivkovic, Li Wei (Lu Zheng 54), Zho Haibin (Wang Xiaolong 74), Cui Peng, Han Peng, Li Jinyu.

Adelaide United   **2**
Fernando 36p, Burns 48

Beltrame – Alagich, Rees, Costanzo, Valkanis, Van Dommele, Kemp (Petta 84), Rech (Pantelis 60), Dodd, Burns, Djite.

GROUP G MATCHDAY 1
Hindmarsh, Adelaide
7-03-2007, 19:30, 7645, Tongkhan THA

Adelaide United   **0**

Beltrame – Alagich, Rees (Giraldi 82), Costanzo, Valkanis, Goulding, Kemp, Rech (Veart 65), Dodd, Burns, Djite.

Shandong Luneng   **1**
Valkanis OG 47

Li Leilei – Wang Chao (Yuan Weiwei 78), Shu Chang, Malbasa, Jiao Zhe, Zivkovic, Wang Yongpo, Zho Haibin, Cui Peng (Bakovic 80), Han Peng (Lu Zheng 76), Li Jinyu.

GROUP G MATCHDAY 3
Shandong Sports Center, Jinan
11-04-2007, 19:00, 15 000, Win Cho MAS

Shandong Luneng   **4**
Han Peng 2 42 53, Wang Yongpo 56, Li Jinyu 75

Li Leilei – Shu Chang, Yuan Weiwei, Malbasa, Jiao Zhe, Zivkovic (Wang Xiaolong 77), Wang Yongpo (Li Wei 64), Zho Haibin, Cui Peng, Han Peng (Lu Zheng 67), Li Jinyu.

Dong Tam Long An   **0**

Santos – Phan Van Giau●86, Le Quang Trai, Luu Minh Tri, Nguyen Minh Phuong, Phan Van Tai Em, Nguyen Tuan Phong, Phan Thanh Giang, Nguyen Hoang Thuong, Nguyen Viet Thang (Nguyen Van Khai 70), Kabanga Tshamala.

GROUP G MATCHDAY 4
Seongnam Tancheon Sports Complex
25-04-2007, 19:00, 30 000, Basma SYR

Seongnam Ilhwa Chunma   **1**
Choi Sung Kuk 29

Kim Yong Dae – Park Jin Sub (Park Jae Yong 46), Cho Byung Kuk, Kim Young Chul, Jang Hack Yong, Son Dae Ho, Kim Do Heon, Kim Sang Sik, Choi Sung Kuk, Kim Dong Hun, Mota.

Adelaide United   **0**

Bajic – Alagich, Rees, Costanzo, Valkanis, Van Dommele, Rech, Dodd, Walsh (Kemp 71), Burns (Pantelis 66), Djite.

GROUP G MATCHDAY 6
Seongnam Tancheon Sports Complex
23-05-2007, 19:00, 13 243, Moradi IRN

Seongnam Ilhwa Chunma   **3**
Kim Dong Hun 37, Son Dae Ho 42, Mota 71

Kim Yong Dae – Park Jin Sub, Cho Byung Kuk, Kim Young Chul, Jang Hack Yong, Son Dae Ho, Kim Do Heon (Cho Yong Hyung 80), Kim Sang Sik, Choi Sung Kuk (Nam Ki Il 80), Kim Dong Hun (Kim Tae Youn 90), Mota.

Shandong Luneng   **0**

Yang Cheng – Shu Chang, Yuan Weiwei, Malbasa, Jiao Zhe, Zivkovic, Gao Yao, Zho Haibin, Cui Peng, Han Peng, Lu Zheng.

GROUP G MATCHDAY 2
Long An Stadium, Long An
21-03-2007, 18:00, 10 460, Saleem MDV

Dong Tam Long An   **0**

Santos – Phan Van Giau, Le Quang Trai, Luu Minh Tri (Nguyen Van Khai 67), Nguyen Minh Phuong, Phan Van Tai Em, Nguyen Tuan Phong, Nguyen Hoang Thuong (Thai Duong 35), Ly Lam Huy, Nguyen Viet Thang, Kabanga Tshamala.

Adelaide United   **2**
Fernando 18, Dodd 31

Beltrame – Alagich, Rees, Costanzo, Valkanis, Goulding, Kemp (Veart 68), Rech, Dodd, Burns (Pantelis 89), Djite (Giraldi 70).

GROUP G MATCHDAY 3
Hindmarsh, Adelaide
11-04-2007, 19:30, 9093, Subkhiddin MAS

Adelaide United   **2**
Fernando 48, Djite 55

Beltrame – Alagich (Cornthwaite 71), Rees, Costanzo, Valkanis, Goulding, Rech (Spagnuolo 74), Dodd, Walsh (Giraldi 84), Burns, Djite.

Seongnam Ilhwa Chunma   **2**
Kim Dong Hun 56, Mota 75

Kim Yong Dae – Park Jin Sub, Cho Byung Kuk, Kim Young Chul, Jang Hack Yong, Son Dae Ho (Han Dong Won 64), Kim Sang Sik, Choi Sung Kuk (Adrian Neaga 76), Itamar (Kim Dong Hun 46), Mota.

GROUP G MATCHDAY 5
Long An Stadium, Long An
9-05-2007, 18:00,

Dong Tam Long An   **1**
Phan Van Tai Em 45

Santos – Phan Van Giau, Luu Minh Tri, Doan Nhat Tien, Nguyen Minh Phuong, Phan Van Tai Em, Nguyen Tuan Phong, Phan Thanh Giang (Antonio 27), Nguyen Thanh Truc, Nguyen Viet Thang (Nguyen Van Khai 86), Kabanga Tshamala.

Seongnam Ilhwa Chunma   **2**
Mota 17, Choi Sung Kuk 83

Kim Yong Dae – Park Jin Sub, Kim Young Chul, Jang Hack Yong, Son Dae Ho, Kim Do Heon, Kim Sang Sik, Shin Young Chol (Choi Sung Kuk 46), Itamar (Han Dong Won 69), Mota, Adrian Neaga (Kim Dong Hun 46).

GROUP G MATCHDAY 6
Hindmarsh, Adelaide
23-05-2007, 19:30, 6 917, Bashir SIN

Adelaide United   **3**
Dodd 3 7 22 49

Bajic – Alagich, Rees, Costanzo, Valkanis, Van Dommele, Pantelis, Kemp (Cornthwaite 81), Dodd, Veart (Goulding 60). Giraldi (Petta 65).

Dong Tam Long An   **0**

Santos – Thai Duong (Luu Minh Tri 58), Phan Van Giau, Nguyen Van Hung (Nguyen Viet Thang 25), Nguyen Minh Phuong, Nguyen Tuan Phong, Phan Thanh Giang, Nguyen Thanh Truc (Phan Van Tai Em 63), Nguyen Hoang Thuong, Antonio, Kabanga Tshamala.

AFC CUP 2006

AFC CUP 2006

Group Stage			Quarter-finals			Semi-finals			Final		
Group A		Pts	Al Faysali *	1 1 5p							
Al Muharraq	BHR	11	Sun Hei	1 1 4p							
Al Ahed	LIB	10									
Mahindra United	IND	9									
Brothers Union	BAN	2									
						Al Faysali *	1 1				
Group B		Pts				Al Wihdat	0 1				
Al Nasr	OMA	12									
Dempo SC	IND	4									
Merv Mary	TKM	1									
			Tampines Rovers	0 0							
Group C		Pts	Al Wihdat	1 4							
Al Wihdat	JOR	6									
Mohemmedan SC	BAN	0						Al Faysali *	3 2		
								Al Muharraq	0 4		
Group D		Pts									
Al Faysali	JOR	7									
Al Nijmeh	LIB	7									
MTTU	TKM	2	Selangor *	0 0							
			Al Nijmeh	1 0							
Group E		Pts									
Sun Hei	HKG	13									
Perlis	MAS	11				Al Nijmeh *	1 2				
Home United	SIN	6				**Al Muharraq**	2 4				
New Radiant	MDV	4									
Group F		Pts	Al Nasr *	2 1							
Tampines Rovers	SIN	15	**Al Muharraq**	3 0							
Selangor	MAS	15									
Happy Valley	HKG	4									
Hurriyya	MDV	1									

* Home team in the first leg • For results and match details from the group stage see **Almanack of World Football 2007** pages 911–912

QUARTER-FINALS

Amman International, Amman
12-09-2006, 19:00, 3000, Shamsuzzaman BAN

Al Faysali	1

Hatem Aqel [54]

Loai - Khamees●, Khaled Sa'ed, Hatem Aqel● - Isam (Moayad Abukeshek 46), Qusai Abu Alieh, Qais Al Otabe (Haitham Alshboul 46), Haider Abdulamir - Almaharmeh (Abdulelah 73), Moayad Mansour●, Siraj Al Tall

Sun Hei	1

Lee Kin Wo [44]

Chan Ka Ki - Tseng Siu Wing●, Chung Kin Hei, Lee Wai Lun●, Cordeiro - Chan Yiu Lun (Lau Chi Keung 61), Lo Chi Kwan, Lai Kai Cheuk, Freitas - Marcio●, Chan Ho Man (Lee Kin Wo● 43) (Tse Man Wing 90)

Hong Kong Stadium, Hong Kong
19-09-2006, 20:00, 2722, O Il Son PRK

Sun Hei	1 5p

Lo Chi Kwan [21p]

Chan Ka Ki - Tseng Siu Wing, Chung Kin Hei, Lee Wai Lun, Cordeiro - Lau Chi Keung, Chu Siu Kei (Chan Ho Man 86), Chan Yiu Lun● (Lee Kin Wo 67), Lo Chi Kwan, Freitas - Marcio

Al Faysali	1 4p

Abukeshek [60]

Loai - Khamees, Khaled Sa'ed●, Hatem Aqel - Qusai Abu Alieh●, Sharif Nassar, Abdulelah (Haitham Alshboul 46), Haider Abdulamir, Moayad Abukeshek (Qais Al Otabe 109) - Almaharmeh (Siraj Al Tall 97●120), Moayad Mansour

---

Tampines Stadium, Singapore
12-09-2006, 19:30, 3000, Tan Hai CHN

Tampines Rovers	0

Rezal● - Aide Iskandar●, Satria (Mirko Grabovac 56), Sead Muratovic● (Noraidit Mahat 83), Nazri●, Zul - Santi, Rafi● - Noh Alam Shah, Peres, Ahmad Latiff (Shahdan 74)

Al Wihdat	1

Alzugheir [49]

Qandil - Basem Fathi, Faisal Ibrahim, Haitham Semrin, Alzugheir - Hasan Abdel-Fattah, Amer Deeb● - Mahmoud Deeb (Mosa Hammad 89), Musab Al Rifae● - Mahmoud Shelbaieh, Abdallah Ata (Issa Alsapah 64)

Amman International, Amman
19-09-2006, 20:00, 5000, Kwon Jong Chul KOR

Al Wihdat	4

Alzugheir [14], Shelbaieh 2 [46+] [47], Mosa [69]

Qandil - Basem Fathi, Faisal Ibrahim (Fadi Shahin 80), Haitham Semrin, Alzugheir - Hasan Abdel-Fattah, Amer Deeb (Khalil Fetian 72), Abdallah Deeb, Musab Al Rifae - Mahmoud Shelbaieh●, Abdallah Ata (Hammad Mosa 46)

Tampines Rovers	0

Rezal (Hafez Mawasi 52) - Aide Iskandar●, Sead Muratovic, Nazri, Zul - Santi, Rafi (Naufal Ashiblie 74) - Noh Alam Shah●, Mirko Grabovac, Peres, Ahmad Latiff (Shahdan 46)

Shah Alam Stadium, Shah Alam
12-09-2006, 20:45, 4500, Sarkar IND

Selangor	0

Shahrizan - Tharmini Saiban (Razman Roslan 79), Wan Rohaimi● (Rajan Koran 58●78), Sanba●, Ba Cheikh● - Elie Aiboy (Sritharan Raju 67), Gunalan Padathan, Amri Yahyah, Surendran, Shukor Adan - Bambang Pamungkas

Al Nijmeh	1

Ali Mohamad [24]

Sakr - Zaher, Ali Mohamad●, Hamieh, El Najjarine - Hachem, Abbas Atwi (Charara 86), El Naamani●, Ahmad Moghrabi - Ghaddar (Nassereddine 55), Akram Moghrabi (Hayssam Atwi 81)

Sports City, Beirut
19-09-2006, 20:00, 3500, Al Saeedi UAE

Al Nijmeh	0

Sakr - Zaher, Ali Mohamad (Fattal 89), Hamieh, El Najjarine - Hachem, Abbas Atwi (Charara 93+), El Naamani, Ahmad Moghrabi - Akram Moghrabi●, Nassereddine (Ghaddar 85)

Selangor	0

Shahrizan - Tharmini Saiban●, Mohd Fadil●, Sanba●, Ba Cheikh - Elie Aiboy (Sritharan Raju● 80), Gunalan Padathan●, Amri Yahyah, Surendran●, Shukor Adan● - Bambang Pamungkas

---

Salalah Sports Complex, Salalah
12-09-2006, 19:30, 1000, Shaban KUW

Al Nasr	2

Adil Matar [22], Nabil Ashoor [55]

Abdul Fael - Hussain Rabia, Adil Matar, Hani Said (Haitham Tabook 62) - Hamdi Hoobees, Bilal Zayid, Nabil Ashoor, Mohammed Salim (Imad Jamil 46), Ben Teekloh (Radhawan Nairooz 71) - Ghazi Ahmed, Montyre Donald●

Al Muharraq	3

Leandson 2 [13] [64], Massolin [58]

Ali Hasan - Sadeq Jaafar, Massolin, Yusuf Salmeen (Meshkhas 64), Mohamed Abdulla - Anwar Yusuf, Mahmood Abdulrahman, Ali Aamer, Fatai Baba (Almuqla 94+) - Leandson (Fahad 84), Okwunwanne

---

National Stadium, Manama
19-09-2006, 18:40, 2000, Al Ghamdi KSA

Al Muharraq	0

Ali Hasan● - Sadeq Jaafar●, Massolin, Meshkhas, Mohamed Abdulla (Reyadh Bader 89) - Anwar Yusuf, Mahmood Abdulrahman, Ali Aamer, Fatai Baba● (Fahad 75) - Leandson, Okwunwanne (Jaafar 61)

Al Nasr	1

Adil Matar [56p]

Al Alawi - Imad Jamil● (Hani Said 69), Ashraf Taysir, Hussain Rabia, Adil Matar - Hamdi Hoobees, Nabil Ashoor, Ben Teekloh (Radhawan Nairooz 81) - Haitham Tabook (Razaqallah 46), Ghazi Ahmed●, Montyre Donald

SEMI-FINALS

Amman International, Amman
26-09-2006, 21:30, 17 000, Mansour LIB

Al Faysali	1

Almaharmeh [9]

Loai● - Khamees, Khaled Sa'ed, Hatem Aqel● - Qusai Abu Alieh, Haitham Alshboul (Qais Al Otabe 81), Nassar, Haider Abdulamir, Moayad Abukeshek (Halasa 67) - Almaharmeh (Khaled Nemer 74), Moayad Mansour●

Al Wihdat	0

Qandil - Basem Fathi, Faisal Ibrahim●, Haitham Semrin●, Alzugheir (Alsapah 72) - Hasan Abdel-Fattah, Amer Deeb●, Abdallah Deeb (Rafat Ali 51), Musab Al Rifae - Mahmoud Shelbaieh, Abdallah Ata (Shatat 51)

King Abdullah, Amman
17-10-2006, 21:00, 10 000, Moradi IRN

Al Wihdat	1

Shelbaieh [53]

Qandil● - Basem Fathi, Faisal Ibrahim● (Ragheb 81), Haitham Semrin●●●90, Alzugheir - Hasan Abdel-Fattah, Shatat●, Amer Deeb, Rafat Ali●, Musab Al Rifae (Abdallah Deeb 71) - Mahmoud Shelbaieh

Al Faysali	1

Abukeshek [66]

Loai - Khamees, Khaled Sa'ed●●●90, Hatem Aqel, Baha (Zuhair 77) - Qusai Abu Alieh, Haitham Alshboul (Moayad Mansour● 77), Sharif●, Haider Abdulamir, Moayad Abukeshek - Almaharmeh (Odtalah 91+)

Sports City, Beirut
26-09-2006, 21:00, 2000, Shaban KUW

Al Nijmeh	1

Nassereddine [21]

Sakr - Zaher●, Ali Mohamad, Hamieh, El Najjarine - Hachem●95+, Abbas Atwi (Ghaddar 72), El Naamani●, Ahmad Moghrabi - Akram Moghrabi (Charara 80), Nassereddine (Haitham Fattal 72)

Al Muharraq	2

Fatai Baba [54], Okwunwanne [75]

Ali Hasan - Sadeq Jaafar, Massolin, Meshkhas●, Mohamed Abdulla (Alchuban 83) - Anwar Yusuf (Abdulla Omar 46), Mahmood Abdulrahman●, Ali Aamer, Fatai Baba (Hadi 72) - Leandson, Okwunwanne

---

National Stadium, Manama
17-10-2006, 21:00, 1500, Al Ghamdi KSA

Al Muharraq	4

Leandson 2 [21p] [76p], Omar [29], Massolin [92+p]

Ali Hasan - Sadeq Jaafar, Massolin, Meshkhas●, Mohamed Abdulla - Mahmood Abdulrahman● (Faouzi Aaish 86), Ali Aamer, Fatai Baba - Abdulla Omar, Leandson (Aldakeel 80), Okwunwanne (Hadi 70)

Al Nijmeh	2

Ghaddar 2 [41] [46+]

Sakr●90 - Dokmak, Ali Mohamad●●82, Hamieh, El Najjarine● - Abbas Atwi, El Naamani●90, Fadlallah●, Ahmad Moghrabi - Ghaddar (Nassereddine 55), Akram Moghrabi● (Charara 72●84)

AFC CUP FINAL First LEG

Amman International, Amman
27-10-2006, 18:00, 7000, Kousa SYR

AL FAYSALI 3 0 MUHARRAQ

Almaharmeh 2 [54] [83], Odtallah [60]

Al Faysali			Al Muharraq	
1	ELAMAIREH Lo'ai		AL THANI Ali Hasan	1
7	KHAMEES Mohammad	54	ALI Sadeq Jaafar	2
17	AQEL Hatem		RASHAD Richard Massolin	3
13	ABU ALIEH Qusai		AL CHUBAN Jasim	5
14	ALSHBOUL Haitham	85	ABDULRAHMAN Mohamed	26
15	NASSAR Sharif Adnan		53 AL DOSERI Rashed	8
28	HUSSAIN Haider Abdulamir		MUSAIFER Ali Amer	16
29	ABUKESHEK Moayad	87	ABIODUN Fatai Baba	29
30	ODTALLAH Hussein Zaid		OMAR Abdulla	17
11	ALMAHARMEH Abdelhadi	67	DA SILVA Leandson	19
27	AL TALL Siraj	59	OKWUNWANNE Jaycee	22
	Tr: HAMD Adnan		Tr: CARLOS ELINHO	
	Substitutes		Substitutes	
5	NEMER Khaled	59	54 ALBASRI Reyadh Bader	6
9	HALASA Saman	87	67 AL DAKEEL Abdulla	10
24	AL OTABE Qais	85	53 AAISH Faouzi	28

AFC CUP FINAL SECOND LEG

National Stadium, Manama
3-11-2006, 18:00, 3000, Al Saeedi UAE

MUHARRAQ 4 2 AL FAYSALI

Omar [18], Da Silva [52],
Meshkhas [60], Abdulrahman [62]

Haider [35], Al Tall [91+]

Al Muharraq				Al Faysali	
1	AL THANI Ali Hasan			ELAMAIREH Lo'ai	1
3	RASHAD Richard Massolin	81		KHAMEES Mohammad	7
4	MESHKHAS Ebrahim			ALMALTA'AH Khaled Sa'ed	12
5	AL CHUBAN Jasim			AQEL Hatem	17
8	AL DOSERI Rashed	75		ABU ALIEH Qusai	13
13	ABDULRAHMAN Mahmood	87	63	ALSHBOUL Haitham	14
16	MUSAIFER Ali Amer			NASSAR Sharif Adnan	15
28	AAISH Faouzi			HUSSAIN Haider Abdulamir	28
17	OMAR Abdulla		87	ABUKESHEK Moayad	29
19	DA SILVA Leandson			ALMAHARMEH Abdelhadi	11
22	OKWUNWANNE Jaycee		57	MANSOUR Moayad Salim	19
	Tr: AL ZAYANI Khalifa			Tr: HAMD Adnan	
	Substitutes			Substitutes	
9	AL ZAIN Mohamed Jaafar	87	63	NEMER Khaled	5
10	AL DAKEEL Abdulla	81	57	SHAWISH Mohammad	20
29	ABIODUN Fatai Baba	75	87	AL TALL Siraj	27

AFC CUP 2007

AFC CUP 2007

Group Stage			Quarter-finals	Semi-finals	Final
Group A		Pts			
Al Nijmeh	LIB	15	Mahindra United *		
Shabab Al Ordun	JOR	13	Al Nijmeh		
Muscat Club	OMA	4			
Al Saqr	YEM	2			
Group B		Pts			
Al Wihdat	JOR	14			
Al Muharraq	BHR	11			
MTTU Ashgabat	TKM	6			
Al Hilal Hudayda	YEM	2			
			Shabab Al Ordun *		
Group C		Pts	Sing. Armed Forces		
Al Faysali	JOR	11			
Dhofar Club	OMA	10			
Al Ansar	LIB	9			
Nebitchi Balkanabat	TKM	2			
Group D		Pts			
Sun Hei	HKG	15			
Negeri Sembilan	MAS	7			
Victory SC	MDV	6	Tampines Rovers *		
Hoa Phat Hanoi	VIE	3	Al Faysali		
Group E		Pts			
Sing. Armed Forces	SIN	15			
Mahindra United	IND	12			
Happy Valley	HKG	9			
New Radiant	MDV	0			
Group F		Pts			
Tampines Rovers	SIN	13	Sun Hei *		
Mohun Bagan	IND	11	Al Wihdat		
Osotpa M-150	THA	10			
Pahang	MAS	0			

* Home team in the first leg
Remaining ties: Quarter-finals 18-09-2007 & 25-09-2007; Semi-finals 2-10-2007 & 23-10-2007; Final 2-11-2007 & 9-11-2007

GROUP A

King Abdullah, Amman, 6-03-2007, 17:00, 300, Abdou QAT

Shabab Al Ordun	2	Rafat Mohammad [39], Ahmad Alomier [92+]
Al Saqr	0	

Sports City, Beirut, 6-03-2007, 19:30, 500, Al Mutlaq KSA

Al Nijmeh	1	Abbas Atwi [18]
Muscat Club	0	

Al Thawra Sports City, Sana'a, 20-03-2007, 15:45, 5000, Recho SYR

Al Saqr	1	Ali Al Omqi [61]
Al Nijmeh	2	Khaled Hamieh [46+], Ali Nassereddine [89]

Sultan Qaboos, Muscat, 20-03-2007, 19:00, 109, Al Saeedi UAE

Muscat Club	0	
Shabab Al Ordun	1	Saher Adi [50]

Al Thawra Sports City, Sana'a, 10-04-2007, 16:00, 6000, Lazim IRQ

Al Saqr	2	Fahd Rashed [6], Fahman Mousa [54]
Muscat Club	2	Azzan Surror [4], Ibrahim Al Fazari [69]

King Abdullah, Amman, 10-04-2007, 19:00, 1000, Mombini IRN

Shabab Al Ordun	2	Esam Abo Touk [18], Odai Alsaify [19]
Al Nijmeh	0	

Sports City, Beirut, 24-04-2007, 17:00, 3000, Orzuev TJK

Al Nijmeh	2	Ali Wassef [51], Ramos [86]
Shabab Al Ordun	1	Saher Adi [77]

Sultan Qaboos, Muscat, 24-04-2007, 19:00, 200, Saidov UZB

Muscat Club	2	Mohammed Taqi [18], Azzan Suroor [89]
Al Saqr	0	

Al Thawra Sports City, Sana'a, 8-05-2007, 15:45, 2500, H. Junjie CHN

Al Saqr	1	Mohammed Al Mang [38]
Shabab Al Ordun	1	Waseem Albzoor [10]

Sultan Qaboos, Muscat, 8-05-2007, 19:15, 150, Al Fadhli KUW

Muscat Club	0	
Al Nijmeh	1	Mohamad Ghaddar [74]

King Abdullah, Amman, 22-05-2007, 19:00, 100, Kunsuta THA

Shabab Al Ordun	1	Odai Alsaify [73]
Muscat Club	0	

Sports City, Beirut, 22-05-2007, 17:00, 800, Chynybekov KGZ

Al Nijmeh	2	Abbas Atwi [15], Mohamad Ghaddar [77]
Al Saqr	1	

GROUP B

Al Thawra Sports City, Sana'a, 6-03-2007, 16:00, 4500, Shaharul MAS

Al Hilal Hudayda	3	Al Dhaheri 2 [55 69], Al Shehri [91+]
Al Wihdat	3	Alsapah [39], Alzugheir [49], Shelbaieh [78]

National Stadium, Manama, 6-03-2007, 18:30, 1000, Recho SYR

Al Muharraq	3	Leandson [20], Omar [46+], Jaafar Alzain [57]
MTTU Ashgabat	1	Arazov [13]

Olympic Stadium, Ashgabat, 20-03-2007, 19:00, 300, Saidov UZB

MTTU Ashgabat	3	Shamuradov [44], Karadanov 2 [63 82]
Al Hilal Hudayda	1	Al Shehri [11]

King Abdullah, Amman, 20-03-2007, 20:00, 6000, Mansour LIB

Al Wihdat	1	Awad Ragheb [66]
Al Muharraq	1	Abdulla Al Dakeel [45]

Olympic Stadium, Ashgabat, 10-04-2007, 19:00, 1000, Sarkar IND

MTTU Ashgabat	1	Karadanov [76]
Al Wihdat	2	Hasan Abdel-Fattah [30], Al Zugheir [66p]

National Stadium, Manama, 10-04-2007, 18:45, 2000, Bashir SIN

Al Muharraq	2	Mahmood Abdulrahman 2 [5 66]
Al Hilal Hudayda	1	Anas Salem [31]

Al Thawra Sports City, Sana'a, 24-04-2007, 16:00, 3000, Torky IRN

Al Hilal Hudayda	1	Nasser Ghazi [52]
Al Muharraq	1	Leandson [23]

King Abdullah, Amman, 24-04-2007, 20:00, 7000, Abdou QAT

Al Wihdat	4	Awad Ragheb [29], Hasan Abdel-Fattah 2 [54 68], Shelbaieh [71]
MTTU Ashgabat	2	Shamuradov 2 [23 40]

King Abdullah, Amman, 8-05-2007, 20:00, 5000, Al Saeedi UAE

Al Wihdat	4	Basem Fathi [17], Abdallah Salim Deeb [67], Awad Ragheb [73], Rafat Ali [85]
Al Hilal Hudayda	0	

Olympic Stadium, Ashgabat, 8-05-2007, 19:00, 200, Yang CHN

MTTU Ashgabat	1	Arazov [9]
Al Muharraq	2	Abdulla Al Dakeel [36], Jaafar Alzin [GG]

Al Thawra Sports City, Sana'a, 21-05-2007, 16:00, 3000, Saleem MDV

Al Hilal Hudayda	0	
MTTU Ashgabat	2	Karadanov [3], Bayramov [58]

National Stadium, Manama, 22-05-2007, 19:00, 2000, Al Enezi KUW

Al Muharraq	1	Abdulla Al Dakeel [79]
Al Wihdat	2	Shelbaieh [51], Awad Ragheb [72]

Group A	Pl	W	D	L	F	A	Pts
Al Nijmeh	6	5	0	1	8	5	15
Shabab Al Ordun	6	4	1	1	8	3	13
Muscat Club	6	1	1	4	4	6	4
Al Saqr	6	0	2	4	5	11	2

Group B	Pl	W	D	L	F	A	Pts
Al Wihdat	6	4	2	0	16	8	14
Al Muharraq	6	3	2	1	10	7	11
MTTU Ashgabat	6	2	0	4	10	12	6
Al Hilal Hudayda	6	0	2	4	6	15	2

GROUP C

Sultan Qaboos, Muscat, 6-03-2007, 19:00, 400, Karim BHR

Dhofar Club	0
Al Ansar	0

Nisa Stadium, Ashgabat, 6-03-2007, 15:30, 100, Al Enezi KUW

Nebitchi B'abat	0
Al Faysali	0

Sports City, Beirut, 20-03-2007, 18:00, 2500, Moradi IRN

Al Ansar	3	Ghosson [3], Saleh Al Sadwn [45], Basma [71]
Nebitchi B'abat	1	Guljagazov [80]

International, Amman, 20-03-2007, 17:00, 2000, Al Baloshi QAT

Al Faysali	2	Abdelhadi Almaharmeh [28], Zuhair [58]
Dhofar Club	1	Salah Abdul Latif [53]

Sports City, Beirut, 10-04-2007, 18:00, 3500, Al Marqouqi UAE

Al Ansar	0	
Al Faysali	2	Moayad Mansour [14], Anas Hijah [66]

Sultan Qaboos, Muscat, 10-04-2007, 19:00, 200, Tongkhan THA

Dhofar Club	1	Abdelmajid Dine [39]
Nebitchi B'abat	0	

Olympic Stadium, Ashgabat, 24-07-2007, 15:30, 200, Sarkar IND

Nebitchi B'abat	0	
Dhofar Club	1	Hani Al Dhabit [81]

International, Zeqra, 24-07-2007, 18:00, 2000, Gosh BAN

Al Faysali	1	Abdelhadi Almaharmeh [90]
Al Ansar	1	Fadi Ghosson [36]

Sports City, Beirut, 8-05-2007, 18:00, 2100, Auda Lazim IRQ

Al Ansar	3	Malek Hassoun [10], Fadi Ghosson [44], Nasrat Al Jamal [79]
Dhofar Club	0	

International, Zeqra, 8-05-2007, 19:00, 300, Al Badawi UAE

Al Faysali	2	Haitham Shboul [48], Anas Hijah [88]
Nebitchi B'abat	0	

Olympic Stadium, Ashgabat, 22-05-2007, 17:30, 150, Saidov UZB

Nebitchi B'abat	1	Begjanov [82]
Al Ansar	1	Ahmed Abbas [50]

Sultan Qaboos, Muscat, 22-05-2007, 19:15, 400, Basma SYR

Dhofar Club	1	Fahad Ba-Masilah [11]
Al Faysali	0	

GROUP D

Mongkok, Hong Kong, 6-03-2007, 19:30, 369, Matsumura JPN

Sun Hei	2	Inegbenoise [17], Colly Ezeh [49]
Victory SC	0	

Abdul Rahman, Paroi, 6-03-2007, 20:45, 1500, Al Yarimi YEM

Negeri Sembilan	0
Hoa Phat Hanoi	0

National Stadium, Male, 20-03-2007, 16:00, 8000, Sarkar IND

Victory SC	2	Ashad Ali [7], Izzath Abdul Baree [22]
Negeri Sembilan	2	Freddy Santos 2 [17 94+]

Hang Day, Hanoi, 20-03-2007, 16:00, 1500, Win MYA

Hoa Phat Hanoi	1	Xuan Thanh Trinh [58]
Sun Hei	2	Miguel Da Silva [24], Lo Chi Kwan [60]

National Stadium, Male, 10-04-2007, 16:00, 6000, Mujghef JOR

Victory SC	2	Shiyam [73], Pham Hai Nam OG [90]
Hoa Phat Hanoi	2	Juselio Da Silva [14], Willians Santos [77]

Mongkok, Hong Kong, 10-04-2007, 19:30, 200, Al Enezi KUW

Sun Hei	2	Inegbenoise 2 [6 69]
Negeri Sembilan	0	

Abdul Rahman, Paroi, 24-04-2007, 20:45, 1100, Al Badwawi UAE

Negeri Sembilan	1	Freddy Santos [88]
Sun Hei	0	

Hang Day, Hanoi, 24-04-2007, 16:00, 500, Tan Hai CHN

Hoa Phat Hanoi	0	
Victory SC	2	Ashad Ali 2 [37 81]

Hang Day, Hanoi, 8-05-2007, 16:00, 3000, Gosh BAN

Hoa Phat Hanoi	0
Negeri Sembilan	0

National Stadium, Male, 9-05-2007, 16:00, 4000, Williams AUS

Victory SC	0	
Sun Hei	2	Colly Ezeh [14], Freiras [33]

Abdul Rahman, Paroi, 22-05-2007, 20:45, 600, Mansour LIB

Negeri Sembilan	1	Shahrizam [45]
Victory SC	1	Shaffaz [22]

Mongkok, Hong Kong, 22-05-2007, 19:30, 208, Tongkhan THA

Sun Hei	7	Freitas 3 [5 61 73], Colly Ezeh 2 [15 65], Chu Siu Kei 2 [25 41]
Hoa Phat Hanoi	4	Cao Sy Cuong [10p], Nguyen Ngoc Tu [33], Vu Hong Viet [54p], Nguyen Anh Cuong [75]

Group C	Pl	W	D	L	F	A	Pts
Al Faysali	6	3	2	1	7	3	11
Dhofar Club	6	3	1	2	4	5	10
Al Ansar	6	2	3	1	8	5	9
Nebitchi Balkanabat	6	0	2	4	2	8	2

Group D	Pl	W	D	L	F	A	Pts
Sun Hei	6	5	0	1	15	6	15
Negeri Sembilan	6	1	4	1	4	5	7
Victory SC	6	1	3	2	7	9	6
Hoa Phat Hanoi	6	0	3	3	7	13	3

GROUP E

Choa Chu Kang, Singapore, 6-03-2007, 19:30, 2288, Al Baloshi QAT
S. Armed Forces   0
Mahindra United   2   Yakubu [36p], Pomeyie [83]

National Stadium, Male, 6-03-2007, 16:00, 7000, Chynybekov UZB
New Radiant   0
Happy Valley   2   Gerard Ambassa [12], Poon Yiu Cheuk [81]

Nehru Stadium, Goa, 20-03-2007, 16:00, 3000, Al Ghatrifi OMA
Mahindra United   1   Yakubu [94+]
New Radiant   0

Mongkok, Hong Kong, 20-03-2007, 19:30, 391, Gosh BAN
Happy Valley   1   Lee Sze Ming [22]
S. Armed Forces   4   Chaiman [7], Noor Ali [61], Duric 2 [79 89]

Nehru Stadium, Goa, 10-04-2007, 16:00, 2000, Recho SYR
Mahindra United   3   Venkatesh [40], Pomeyie 2 [73 77]
Happy Valley   1   Gerard Ambassa [54]

Choa Chu Kang, Singapore, 10-04-2007, 19:30, 2309, Kim Dong Jin KOR
S. Armed Forces   3   Duric [10], Ashrin Shariff 2 [68 84]
New Radiant   1   Idris Kasirye [72]

National Stadium, Male, 24-04-2007, 16:00, 3000, Win MYA
New Radiant   2   Ilyas Ibrahim [9], Ali Ashfaq [71]
S. Armed Forces   3   Mustaqim [33], Kenji Arai [38], Duric [65]

Mongkok, Hong Kong, 24-04-2007, 19:30, 100, Shaharul MAS
Happy Valley   2   Law Chun Bong 2 [21 23]
Mahindra United   1   Yakubu [68]

Nehru Stadium, Goa, 8-05-2007, 16:00, 500, Mujghef JOR
Mahindra United   0
S. Armed Forces   1   Chaiman [7]

Mongkok, Hong Kong, 8-05-2007, 19:30, 400, Al Ghatrifi OMA
Happy Valley   2   Monteiro [19], Gerard Ambassa [63]
New Radiant   1   Assad Abdul Gani [86p]

Choa Chu Kang, Singapore, 22-05-2007, 19:15, 2326, Shield AUS
S. Armed Forces   2   Ashrin Shariff 2 [62 81]
Happy Valley   1   Monteiro [2]

National Stadium, Male, 22-05-2007, 16:15, 2500, Nema IRQ
New Radiant   0
Mahindra United   2   Rafi Madambillath [16], Steven Dias [63]

GROUP F

RT Army Stadium, Bangkok, 6-03-2007, 16:00, 150, Torky IRN
Osotpa M-150   4   Kittisak Jaihan [15], Wuttichai Khookaew [54], Kritsada Kemden [70], Jessada Puanakunmee [78]
Pahang   0

Salt Lake, Kolkata, 6-03-2007, 17:00, 20 000, Vo VIE
Mohun Bagan   0
Tampines Rovers   0

Darul Makmur, Pahang, 20-03-2007, 20:30, 1000, Lazim IRQ
Pahang   1   Tarik El Janaby [61]
Mohun Bagan   2   Puia Pachuau [30], Baichung Bhutia [74]

Tampines Stadium, Singapore, 20-03-2007, 19:30, 2668, Al Marzouqi
Tampines Rovers   2   Peres [25], Noh Alam Shah [79]
Osotpa M-150   1   Worawut Wangsawat [76]

MPPJ Stadium, Selangor, 10-04-2007, 20:30, 100, Williams AUS
Pahang   1   Kamal Rodiarjat [80]
Tampines Rovers   4   Mohamed Rafi [2], Muhammad Ridhuan [45+], Aliff Safie'e [65], Sutee Suksomkit [78]

RT Army Stadium, Bangkok, 10-04-2007, 16:00, 2000, Yang CHN
Osotpa M-150   0
Mohun Bagan   0

Salt Lake, Kolkata, 24-04-2007, 17:00, 18 000, Kwon Jong Chul KOR
Mohun Bagan   1   Barreto [43]
Osotpa M-150   0

Tampines Stadium, Singapore, 24-04-2007, 19:30, 2942, Al Yarimi YEM
Tampines Rovers   2   Muhammad Ridhuan [32], Grabovic [70]
Pahang   0

Shah Alam, Selangor, 8-05-2007, 20:30, 100, Abdou QAT
Pahang   0
Osotpa M-150   4   Sumanya Purisay [29], Kittisak Jaihan 2 [38p 51], Apipoo Suntornpanavej [77]

Tampines Stadium, Singapore, 8-05-2007, 19:30, 2500, Ebrahim BHR
Tampines Rovers   2   Noh Alam Shah 2 [34 66]
Mohun Bagan   0

RT Army Stadium, Bangkok, 22-05-2007, 16:00, 200, Takayama JPN
Osotpa M-150   3   Apipoo Suntornpanavej 3 [64 82 92+]
Tampines Rovers   0

Salt Lake, Kolkata, 22-05-2007, 17:00, 15 000, Orzuev TJK
Mohun Bagan   2   Lal Kamal Bhowmick [12], Puia Pachuau [69]
Pahang   0

Group E	Pl	W	D	L	F	A	Pts
Singapore Armed Forces	6	5	0	1	13	7	**15**
Mahindra United	6	4	0	2	9	4	**12**
Happy Valley	6	3	0	3	9	11	**9**
New Radiant	6	0	0	6	4	13	**0**

Group F	Pl	W	D	L	F	A	Pts
Tampines Rovers	6	4	1	1	10	5	**13**
Mohun Bagan	6	3	2	1	5	3	**11**
Osotpa M-150	6	3	1	2	12	3	**10**
Pahang	6	0	0	6	2	18	**0**

CAF

CONFEDERATION AFRICAINE DE FOOTBALL

With both Asia and South America bringing forward their continental championships by a year to avoid clashing with the European Championship, the African Football Confederation courted controversy by refusing to change the dates of the 2008 Africa Cup of Nations in order to avoid clashing with the European club season. While their stance may be understandable, the implications could be far-reaching if African players find it harder to sign for European clubs or elect in even greater numbers to qualify for the national team of the country in which they play their club football. That cannot be in the best interests of African football. Most of the major nations had relatively easy passages to the finals of the 2008 Africa Cup of Nations, with Nigeria, Tunisia, Cameroon, Angola and Morocco all making sure of their places by mid 2007. But there were also a number of outstanding achievements, not least the success of Sudan, a former winner, making it to the finals for the first time since 1976. Club football was once again dominated by Egypt's Al Ahly

THE FIFA BIG COUNT OF 2006 FOR AFRICA

	Male	Female		Total
Number of players	44 940 000	1 361 000	Referees and Assistant Referees	50 000
Professionals	7 000		Admin, Coaches, Technical, Medical	580 000
Amateurs 18+	926 000		Number of clubs	12 000
Youth under 18	2 156 000		Number of teams	71 000
Unregistered	43 199 000		Clubs with women's teams	1 000
Total involved in football	46 930 000		Players as % of population	5.16%

who won their fifth continental title, the African Champions League, in 2006, equalling the record held by their fierce rivals Zamalek. In a very close final they beat Tunisia's CS Sfaxien, who, deep into injury-time in the second leg, were winning on away goals until Mohamed Aboutrika scored for Ahly. That goal meant that Ahly became only the third club to retain the title and they will be out to win an unprecedented hat-trick in 2007. The 2006 Confederation Cup final was also an all north African affair with Tunisia's Etoile du Sahel beating Morocco's FAR Rabat in controversial circumstances. Etoile won on away goals but FAR had a stoppage time 'winner' disallowed for offside, a decision which provoked an attack by some of the players on South African referee David Bennett. Other winners during the season included Congo, who won the African Youth Championship and the regional CEMAC Cup; Nigeria, winners of the African U–17 Championship; and Zambia, who won both the COSAFA and CECAFA Cups.

Confédération Africaine de Football (CAF)

PO Box 23, 3 Abdel Khalek Sarwat Street, El Hay El Motamayez, 6th October City, Egypt

Tel +20 2 8371000   Fax +20 2 8370006

info@cafonline.com   www.cafonline.com

President: HAYATOU Issa CMR   General Secretary: FAHMY Mustapha EGY

CAF Formed: 1957

CAF EXECUTIVE COMMITTEE

President: HAYATOU Issa CMR	1st Vice-President: MEMENE Seyi TOG	2nd Vice-President: OLIPHANT Molefi RSA

ORDINARY MEMBERS OF THE EXECUTIVE COMMITTEE

DIAKITE Amadou MLI	DJIBRINE Adoum CHA	ADAMU Amos Dr. NGA
RAOURAOUA Mohamed ALG	BARANSANANIYE Moses BDI	PATEL Suketu SEY
REDA Hani Abu EGY	KAMACH Thierry CTA	CAMARA Almamy Kabele GUI
	MUSABYIMANA Celestin RWA	
Co-opted: ALOULOU Slim	FIFA Exco: CHIBOUB Slim TUN	General Secretary: FAHMY Mustapha EGY

MAP OF CAF MEMBER NATIONS

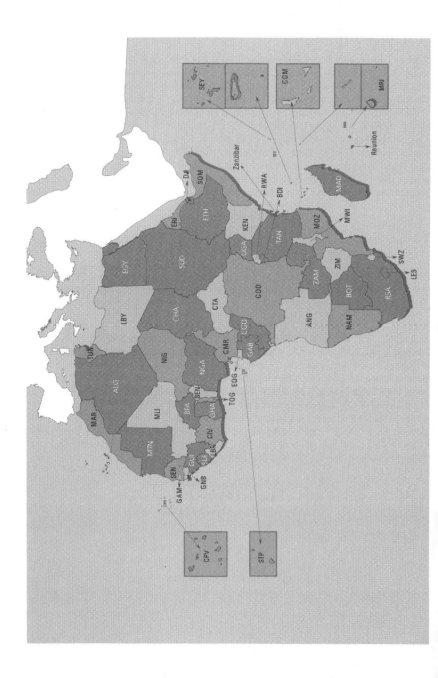

AFRICAN TOURNAMENTS

CAF AFRICA CUP OF NATIONS

Year	Host Country	Winners	Score	Runners-up	Venue
1957	Sudan	Egypt	4-0	Ethiopia	Municipal, Khartoum
1959	Egypt	Egypt	2-1	Sudan	Al Ahly Stadium, Cairo
1962	Ethiopia	Ethiopia	2-0	Egypt	Haile Selassie, Addis Abeba
1963	Ghana	Ghana	3-0	Sudan	Accra Stadium, Accra
1965	Tunisia	Ghana	3-2	Tunisia	Zouiten, Tunis
1968	Ethiopia	Congo Kinshasa	1-0	Ghana	Haile Selassie, Addis Abeba
1970	Sudan	Sudan	1-0	Ghana	Municipal, Khartoum
1972	Cameroon	Congo	3-2	Mali	Omnisports, Yaoundé
1974	Egypt	Zaire	2-2 2-0	Zambia	International, Cairo
1976	Ethiopia	Morocco	1-1	Guinea	Addis Abeba Stadium
1978	Ghana	Ghana	2-0	Uganda	Accra Stadium, Accra
1980	Nigeria	Nigeria	3-0	Algeria	Surulere, Lagos
1982	Libya	Ghana	1-1 7-6p	Libya	11th June Stadium, Tripoli
1984	Côte d'Ivoire	Cameroon	3-1	Nigeria	Houphouët Boigny, Abidjan
1986	Egypt	Egypt	0-0 5-4p	Cameroon	International, Cairo
1988	Morocco	Cameroon	1-0	Nigeria	Mohamed V, Casablanca
1990	Algeria	Algeria	1-0	Nigeria	Stade Olympique, Algiers
1992	Senegal	Côte d'Ivoire	0-0 11-10p	Ghana	Stade de l'Amite, Dakar
1994	Tunisia	Nigeria	2-1	Zambia	El Menzah, Tunis
1996	South Africa	South Africa	2-0	Tunisia	Soccer City, Johannesburg
1998	Burkina Faso	Egypt	2-0	South Africa	Stade du 4 Août, Ouagadougou
2000	Ghana/Nigeria	Cameroon	2-2 4-3p	Nigeria	Surulere, Lagos
2002	Mali	Cameroon	0-0 3-2p	Senegal	Stade du 26 Mars, Bamako
2004	Tunisia	Tunisia	2-1	Morocco	Rades, Tunis
2006	Egypt	Egypt	0-0 4-2p	Côte d'Ivoire	International, Cairo

Thirteen different countries have triumphed at the 25 CAF Africa Cup of Nations tournaments and this lack of domination by one country and the fact that it is played every two years means the competition gives a very good indication of the footballing prowess on the continent. The great teams from the past have all managed to inscribe their name on the trophy - Egypt team of the late 1950s; Ghana at the time of independence in the 1960s; Zaire in the early 1970s; Cameroon in the 1980s; and the Nigerians of the mid-1990s. Fifteen nations have hosted the tournament, which has grown from a three team round robin in the early years into a 16 team spectacular. For the 2006 edition the FIFA World Cup qualifiers doubled up as Nations Cup qualifiers to ease the fixture load and this remains the plan for those editions played in future FIFA World Cup years. In 2006 Egypt hosted the tournament for the fourth time and won a record fifth title, moving one ahead of Ghana who will hope to draw level again when they host the tournament in 2008. Remarkably the other previous joint record holders, Cameroon, have won all their four titles away from home.

CAF AFRICAN WOMEN'S CHAMPIONSHIP

Year	Host Country	Winners	Score	Runners-up	Venue
1991		Nigeria	2-0 4-0	Cameroon	
1995		Nigeria	4-1 7-1	South Africa	
1998	Nigeria	Nigeria	2-0	Ghana	Abeokuta
2000	South Africa	Nigeria	2-0	South Africa	Johannesburg
2002	Nigeria	Nigeria	2-0	Ghana	Lagos
2004	South Africa	Nigeria	5-0	Cameroon	Johannesburg
2006	Nigeria	Nigeria	1-0	Ghana	Warri

With women's football not particulary widespread in Africa, the chance of a place in the FIFA Women's World Cup provided the spur for CAF to introduce a women's Championship. To date Nigeria has won all seven tournaments played with Ghana losing in the final three times.

AFRICAN YOUTH CHAMPIONSHIP

Year	Host Country	Winners	Score	Runners-up	Venue
1979		Algeria	2-1 2-3	Guinea	Algiers, Conakry
1981		Egypt	1-1 2-0	Cameroon	Douala, Cairo
1983		Nigeria	2-2 2-1	Côte d'Ivoire	Abidjan, Lagos
1985		Nigeria	1-1 2-1	Tunisia	Tunis, Lagos
1987		Nigeria	2-1 3-0	Togo	Lomé, Lagos
1989		Nigeria	2-1 2-0	Mali	Bamako, Lagos
1991	Egypt	Egypt	2-1	Côte d'Ivoire	Cairo
1993	Mauritius	Ghana	2-0	Cameroon	Bellevue
1995	Nigeria	Cameroon	4-0	Burundi	Lagos
1997	Morocco	Morocco	1-0	South Africa	Meknès
1999	Ghana	Ghana	1-0	Nigeria	Accra
2001	Ethiopia	Angola	2-0	Ghana	Addis Abeba
2003	Burkina Faso	Egypt	4-3	Côte d'Ivoire	Ouagadougou
2005	Benin	Nigeria	2-0	Egypt	Cotonou
2007	Congo	Congo	1-0	Nigeria	Brazzaville

AFRICAN U–17 CHAMPIONSHIP

Year	Host Country	Winners	Score	Runners-up	Venue
1995	Mali	Ghana	3-1	Nigeria	Bamako
1997	Botswana	Egypt	1-0	Mali	Gaborone
1999	Guinea	Ghana	3-1	Burkina Faso	Conakry
2001	Seychelles	Nigeria	3-0	Burkina Faso	Victoria
2003	Swaziland	Cameroon	1-0	Sierra Leone	Mbabane
2005	Gambia	Gambia	1-0	Ghana	Bakau
2007	Togo	Nigeria	1-0	Togo	Lome

AFRICAN WOMEN'S U–19 CHAMPIONSHIP

Year	Host Country	Winners	Score	Runners-up	Venue
2002		Nigeria	6-0 3-2	South Africa	
2004		Nigeria	1-0 0-0	South Africa	

Africa's youth tournaments came from the need to play qualifiers for the FIFA age-restricted competitions. Until the 1990s they were played on a home and away basis but since 1991 in the Youth Championship and 1995 in the U-17s, there has been a final tournament in a designated country. This has given those countries unlikely to host the CAF Africa Cup of Nations a chance to organise a major football tournament.

FOOTBALL TOURNAMENT OF THE AFRICAN GAMES

Year	Host Country	Winners	Score	Runners-up	Venue
1965	Congo	Congo	0-0 †	Mali	Brazzaville
1973	Nigeria	Nigeria	2-0	Guinea	Lagos
1978	Algeria	Algeria	1-0	Nigeria	Algiers
1987	Kenya	Egypt	1-0	Kenya	Nairobi
1991	Egypt	Cameroon	1-0	Tunisia	Cairo
1995	Zimbabwe	Egypt	3-1	Zimbabwe	Harare
1999	South Africa	Cameroon	0-0 4-3p	Zambia	Johannesburg
2003	Nigeria	Cameroon	2-0	Nigeria	Abuja

† Decided on number of corner-kicks awarded. Congo won 7-2

WOMEN'S FOOTBALL TOURNAMENT OF THE AFRICAN GAMES

Year	Host Country	Winners	Score	Runners-up	Venue
2003	Nigeria	Nigeria	1-0	South Africa	Abuja

At one time the football tournament of the African Games carried enormous prestige but it is only since 1987 that it has been played on a regular basis and it is now an age restricted tournament.

GOSSAGE CUP

Year	Host Country	Winners
1926	Kenya	Kenya
1928	Uganda	Uganda
1929	Kenya	Uganda
1930	Uganda	Uganda
1931	Kenya	Kenya
1932	Uganda	Uganda
1935	Uganda	Uganda
1936	Kenya	Uganda
1937	Uganda	Uganda
1938	Kenya	Uganda
1939	Uganda	Uganda
1940	Kenya	Uganda
1941	Uganda	Kenya
1942	Kenya	Kenya
1943	Uganda	Uganda
1944	Kenya	Kenya
1945	Uganda	Uganda
1946	Kenya	Kenya
1947	Tanzania	Uganda
1948	Uganda	Uganda
1949	Zanzibar	Tanzania
1951	Kenya	Tanzania

GOSSAGE CUP (CONT'D)

Year	Host Country	Winners
1952	Uganda	Uganda
1953	Zanzibar	Kenya
1954	Kenya	Uganda
1955	Uganda	Uganda
1956	Tanzania	Uganda
1957	Zanzibar	Uganda
1958	Kenya	Kenya
1959	Tanzania	Kenya
1960	Uganda	Kenya
1961	Kenya	Kenya
1962	Home and away	Uganda
1963	Kenya	Uganda
1964	Tanzania	Tanzania
1965	Uganda	Tanzania
1966	Zanzibar	Kenya

CHALLENGE CUP

Year	Host Country	Winners
1967	Kenya	Kenya
1968	Tanzania	Uganda
1969	Uganda	Uganda
1970	Zanzibar	Uganda
1971	Kenya	Kenya

CECAFA CUP

Year	Host Country	Winners	Score	Runners-up	Venue
1973	Uganda	Uganda	2-1	Tanzania	
1974	Tanzania	Tanzania	1-1 5-3p	Uganda	
1975	Zambia	Kenya	0-0 5-4p	Malawi	
1976	Zanzibar	Uganda	2-0	Zambia	
1977	Somalia	Uganda	0-0 5-3p	Zambia	
1978	Malawi	Malawi	3-2	Zambia	
1979	Kenya	Malawi	3-2	Kenya	
1980	Sudan	Sudan	1-0	Tanzania	
1981	Tanzania	Kenya	1-0	Tanzania	
1982	Uganda	Kenya	1-1 5-3p	Uganda	
1983	Kenya	Kenya	1-0	Zimbabwe	
1984	Uganda	Zambia	0-0 3-0p	Malawi	Kampala
1985	Zimbabwe	Zimbabwe	2-0	Kenya	Rufaro, Harare
1986	Sudan	Not held			
1987	Ethiopia	Ethiopia	1-1 5-4p	Zimbabwe	
1988	Malawi	Malawi	3-1	Zambia	
1989	Kenya	Uganda	3-3 2-1	Malawi	Nyayo, Nairobi
1990	Zanzibar	Uganda	2-0	Sudan	
1991	Uganda	Zambia	2-0	Kenya	Kampala
1992	Tanzania	Uganda	1-0	Tanzania	Mwanza
1993	Uganda	Not held			
1994	Kenya	Tanzania	2-2 4-3p	Uganda	Nairobi
1995	Uganda	Zanzibar	1-0	Uganda	
1996	Sudan	Uganda	1-0	Sudan	
1997		Not held			
1998		Not held			
1999	Rwanda	Rwanda B	3-1	Kenya	Amahoro, Kigali
2000	Uganda	Uganda	2-0	Uganda B	Nakivubo, Kampala
2001	Rwanda	Ethiopia	2-1	Kenya	Amahoro, Kigali
2002	Tanzania	Kenya	3-2	Tanzania	Memorial, Arusha
2003	Sudan	Uganda	2-0	Rwanda	Khartoum
2004	Ethiopia	Ethiopia	3-0	Burundi	Addis Abeba
2005	Rwanda	Ethiopia	1-0	Rwanda	Amahoro, Kigali
2006	Ethiopia	Zambia	0-0 11-10p	Sudan	Addis Abeba

COSAFA CUP

Year	Host Country	Winners	Score	Runners-up	Venue
1997	Home and away	Zambia	1-1	Namibia	Windhoek
1998	Home and away	Zambia	1-0	Zimbabwe	Harare
1999	Home and away	Angola	1-0 1-1	Namibia	Luanda & Windhoek
2000	Home and away	Zimbabwe	3-0 3-0	Lesotho	Maseru & Bulawayo
2001	Home and away	Angola	0-0 1-0	Zimbabwe	Luanda & Harare
2002	Home and away	South Africa	3-1 1-0	Malawi	Blantyre & Durban
2003	Home and away	Zimbabwe	2-1 2-0	Malawi	Blantyre & Harare
2004	Home and away	Angola	0-0 5-4p	Zambia	Lusaka
2005	Home and away	Zimbabwe	1-0	Zambia	Mafikeng
2006	Home and away	Zambia	2-0	Angola	Lusaka

COUPE CEMAC

Year	Host Country	Winners	Score	Runners-up	Venue
2003	Congo	Cameroon	3-2	Central African Rep.	Brazzaville
2005	Gabon	Cameroon	1-0	Chad	Libreville
2006	Equat. Guinea	Equatorial Guinea	1-1 4-2p	Cameroon	Bata
2007	Chad	Congo	1-0	Gabon	N'Djamena

COPA AMILCAR CABRAL

Year	Host Country	Winners	Score	Runners-up	Venue
1979	Guinea-Bissau	Senegal	1-0	Mali	Bissau
1980	Gambia	Senegal	1-0	Gambia	Banjul
1981	Mali	Guinea	0-0 6-5p	Mali	Bamako
1982	Cape Verde	Guinea	3-0	Senegal	Praia
1983	Mauritania	Senegal	3-0	Guinea-Bissau	Nouakchott
1984	Sierra Leone	Senegal	0-0 5-3p	Sierra Leone	Freetown
1985	Gambia	Senegal	1-0	Gambia	Banjul
1986	Senegal	Senegal	3-1	Sierra Leone	Dakar
1987	Guinea	Guinea	1-0	Mali	Conakry
1988	Guinea-Bissau	Guinea	3-2	Mali	Bissau
1989	Mali	Mali	3-0	Guinea	Bamako
1991	Senegal	Senegal	1-0	Cape Verde Islands	Dakar
1993	Sierra Leone	Sierra Leone	2-0	Senegal	Freetown
1995	Mauritania	Sierra Leone	0-0 4-2p	Mauritania	Nouakchott
1997	Gambia	Mali	1-0	Senegal	Banjul
2000	Cape Verde	Cape Verde Islands	1-0	Senegal	Praia
2001	Mali	Senegal	3-1	Gambia	Bamako
2005	Guinea	Guinea	1-0	Senegal	Conakry

There is a long and rich history of regional tournaments in Africa dating back to 1926 when William Gossage sponsored an annual competition between Kenya and Uganda. From 1945 it was extended to include Tanganyika and then Zanzibar from 1949 and was a popular feature of the football calendar. With independence the name of the competition was changed to the Challenge Cup in 1967. With the creation in 1973 of CECAFA – the Confederation of East and Central African Football Associations – the tournament was renamed as the CECAFA Cup and expanded to include Zambia and Somalia; Malawi joined in 1975, Sudan in 1980, Zimbabwe in 1982, Ethiopia in 1983, Seychelles in 1992, Eritrea and Djibouti in 1994, Rwanda in 1995 and finally Burundi in 1998. The Southern African contingent left to join COSAFA in the aftermath of South Africa's return to international football with the first COSAFA Castle Cup held in 1997 and contested since by Angola, Botswana, Lesotho, Madagascar, Malawi, Mauritius, Mozambique, Namibia, Seychelles, South Africa, Swaziland, Zambia and Zimbabwe. The situation in West Africa has been much more fragmented, although the Copa Amilcar Cabral has stood the test of time unlike many other tournaments in the region. The Coupe CEMAC is the latest addition to the list of tournaments. Introduced in 2003 entries come from the member states of the Communauté Economique et Monétaire de l'Afrique Central.

CAF CHAMPIONS LEAGUE

Year	Winners	Country	Score	Country	Runners-up
1965	Oryx Douala	CMR	2-1	MLI	Stade Malien
1966	Stade Abidjan	CIV	1-3 4-1	MLI	AS Real Bamako
1967	Tout Puissant Englebert	COD	1-1 2-2	GHA	Asante Kotoko
1968	Tout Puissant Englebert	COD	5-0 1-4	TOG	Etoile Filante
1969	Al Ismaili	EGY	2-2 3-1	COD	Tout Puissant Englebert
1970	Asante Kotoko	GHA	1-1 2-1	COD	Tout Puissant Englebert
1971	Canon Yaoundé	CMR	0-3 2-0 1-0	GHA	Asante Kotoko
1972	Hafia FC Conakry	GUI	4-2 3-2	UGA	Simba FC
1973	AS Vita Kinshasa	COD	2-4 3-0	GHA	Asante Kotoko
1974	CARA Brazzaville	CGO	4-2 2-1	EGY	Mehalla Al Kubra
1975	Hafia FC Conakry	GUI	1-0 2-1	NGA	Enugu Rangers
1976	Mouloudia d'Algiers	ALG	3-0 0-3 4-1p	GUI	Hafia FC Conakry
1977	Hafia FC Conakry	GUI	1-0 3-2	GHA	Hearts of Oak
1978	Canon Yaoundé	CMR	0-0 2-0	GUI	Hafia FC Conakry
1979	Union Douala	CMR	0-1 1-0 5-3p	GHA	Hearts of Oak
1980	Canon Yaoundé	CMR	2-2 3-0	COD	AS Bilima
1981	JE Tizi-Ouzou	ALG	4-0 1-0	COD	AS Vita Kinshasa
1982	Al Ahly Cairo	EGY	3-0 1-1	GHA	Asante Kotoko
1983	Asante Kotoko	GHA	0-0 1-0	EGY	Al Ahly Cairo
1984	Zamalek	EGY	2-0 1-0	NGA	Shooting Stars
1985	FAR Rabat	MAR	5-2 1-1	COD	AS Bilima
1986	Zamalek	EGY	2-0 0-2 4-2p	CIV	Africa Sports
1987	Al Ahly Cairo	EGY	0-0 2-0	SUD	Al Hilal
1988	Entente Setif	ALG	0-1 4-0	NGA	Iwuanyanwu Owerri
1989	Raja Casablanca	MAR	1-0 0-1 4-2p	ALG	Mouloudia d'Oran
1990	JS Kabylie	ALG	1-0 0-1 5-3p	ZAM	Nkana Red Devils
1991	Club Africain	TUN	5-1 1-1	UGA	Nakivubo Villa
1992	Wydad Casablanca	MAR	2-0 0-0	SUD	Al Hilal
1993	Zamalek	EGY	0-0 0-0 7-6p	GHA	Asante Kotoko
1994	Espérance Tunis	TUN	0-0 3-1	EGY	Zamalek
1995	Orlando Pirates	RSA	2-2 1-0	CIV	ASEC Mimosas
1996	Zamalek	EGY	1-2 2-1 4-2p	NGA	Shooting Stars
1997	Raja Casablanca	MAR	0-1 1-0 5-4p	GHA	Obuasi Goldfields
1998	ASEC Mimosas	CIV	0-0 4-1	ZIM	Dynamos
1999	Raja Casablanca	MAR	0-0 0-0 4-3p	TUN	Espérance Tunis
2000	Hearts of Oak	GHA	2-1 3-1	TUN	Espérance Tunis
2001	Al Ahly Cairo	EGY	1-1 3-0	RSA	Pretoria Sundowns
2002	Zamalek	EGY	0-0 1-0	MAR	Raja Casablanca
2003	Enyimba	NGA	2-0 0-1	EGY	Al Ismaili
2004	Enyimba	NGA	1-2 2-1 5-3p	TUN	Etoile du Sahel
2005	Al Ahly Cairo	EGY	0-0 3-0	TUN	Etoile du Sahel
2006	Al Ahly Cairo	EGY	1-1 1-0	TUN	CS Sfaxien

Previously known the African Cup of Champion Clubs, the CAF Champions League is unpredictable and never short of controversy, but it remains hugely entertaining despite the growing number of African players who will never compete in it thanks to moves to Europe at increasingly young ages. The heart of the rivalry in the tournament lies between the Arab North African countries and the sub-Saharan countries. Until the 1980s the latter held the upper hand but for 17 years between 1981 and 1997 only Ghana's Asante Kotoko and Orlando Pirates from South Africa managed to prise the Cup from the north. Since 1995 the honours have been more evenly spread. It has proved difficult for any club, however, to maintain a consistant presence in the tournament with the possible exception of the two Egyptian giants and record title holders Al Ahly and Zamalek. In 2004 Enyimba became only the second club to retain the title and the first since 1968. They were also the 19th different club from 13 different countries to have won the title. No other continent has such a range of winners. Amongst the early powers were clubs from Cameroon and Guinea, notably three times winners Canon Yaoundé and Hafia Conakry. Before the 1980s, North African clubs won the tournament just twice. Since the triumph of JS Kabylie (then called Tizi-Ouzou) it has been a very different story. Al Ahly won the cup for the first time in 1982 and had they not decided to defend their Cup Winners Cup title twice in the mid 1980s, they may well have won more than their current haul of five titles. They were clearly the best team on the continent and having suceeded in their aim of a hat trick of titles in the Cup Winners Cup, they then won the Champions Cup to make it four titles in a row and five in six seasons. Their next triumph was not until 2001, leaving the field open for rivals Zamalek. They won a record fourth title in 1996 with Ismail Youssef part of the squad in all four campaigns and then added a fifth in 2002. Raja Casablanca also made their mark, winning three titles in eleven years thanks largely to their excellent youth set up, helping to establish Morocco as the second most successful nation in the tournament after Egypt. In 1997 the tournament was rebranded as the CAF Champions League although the group stage has always been held in the closing stages of the competition rather than early on. In 2004, again following the European example, a second club from the top nations was allowed entry. The turn of the century saw Al Ahly emerge once again as the most powerful club on the continent and in 2006 they matched Zamalek's five titles.

CAF CONFEDERATION CUP

Year	Winners	Country	Score	Country	Runners-up
2004	Hearts of Oak	GHA	1-1 1-1 8-7p	GHA	Asante Kotoko
2005	FAR Rabat	MAR	0-1 3-0	NGA	Dolphin Port Harcourt
2006	Etoile du Sahel	TUN	1-1 0-0	MAR	FAR Rabat

CAF CUP WINNERS' CUP

Year	Winners	Country	Score	Country	Runners-up
1975	Tonnerre Yaoundé	CMR	1-0 4-1	CIV	Stella Abidjan
1976	Shooting Stars	NGA	4-1 0-1	CMR	Tonnerre Yaoundé
1977	Enugu Rangers	NGA	4-1 1-1	CMR	Canon Yaoundé
1978	Horoya AC Conakry	GUI	3-1 2-1	ALG	MA Hussein-Dey
1979	Canon Yaoundé	CMR	2-0 6-0	KEN	Gor Mahia
1980	TP Mazembe	COD	3-1 1-0	CIV	Africa Sports
1981	Union Douala	CMR	2-1 0-0	NGA	Stationery Stores
1982	Al Mokaoulum	EGY	2-0 2-0	ZAM	Power Dynamos
1983	Al Mokaoulum	EGY	1-0 0-0	TOG	Agaza Lomé
1984	Al Ahly Cairo	EGY	1-0 0-1 4-2p	CMR	Canon Yaoundé
1985	Al Ahly Cairo	EGY	2-0 0-1	NGA	Leventis United
1986	Al Ahly Cairo	EGY	3-0 0-2	GAB	AS Sogara
1987	Gor Mahia	KEN	2-2 1-1	TUN	Espérance Tunis
1988	CA Bizerte	TUN	0-0 1-0	NGA	Ranchers Bees
1989	Al Merreikh	SUD	1-0 0-0	NGA	Bendel United
1990	BCC Lions	NGA	3-0 1-1	TUN	Club Africain
1991	Power Dynamos	ZAM	2-3 3-1	NGA	BCC Lions
1992	Africa Sports	CIV	1-1 4-0	BDI	Vital'O
1993	Al Ahly Cairo	EGY	1-1 1-0	CIV	Africa Sports
1994	DC Motema Pembe	COD	2-2 3-0	KEN	Kenya Breweries
1995	JS Kabylie	ALG	1-1 2-1	NGA	Julius Berger
1996	Al Mokaoulum	EGY	0-0 4-0	COD	Sodigraf
1997	Etoile du Sahel	TUN	2-0 0-1	MAR	FAR Rabat
1998	Espérance Tunis	TUN	3-1 1-1	ANG	Primeiro Agosto
1999	Africa Sports	CIV	1-0 1-1	TUN	Club Africain
2000	Zamalek	EGY	4-1 0-2	CMR	Canon Yaoundé
2001	Kaiser Chiefs	RSA	1-1 1-0	ANG	Inter Luanda
2002	Wydad Casablanca	MAR	1-0 1-2	GHA	Asante Kotoko
2003	Etoile du Sahel	TUN	0-2 3-0	NGA	Julius Berger

Discontinued after the 2003 tournament and replaced by the CAF Confederation Cup

CAF CUP

Year	Winners	Country	Score	Country	Runners-up
1992	Shooting Stars	NGA	0-0 3-0	UGA	Nakivubo Villa
1993	Stella Abidjan	CIV	0-0 2-0	TAN	SC Simba
1994	Bendel Insurance	NGA	0-1 3-0	ANG	Primeiro de Maio
1995	Etoile du Sahel	TUN	0-0 2-0	GUI	Kaloum Star
1996	Kawkab Marrakech	MAR	1-3 2-0	TUN	Etoile du Sahel
1997	Esperance Tunis	TUN	0-1 2-0	ANG	Petro Atlético
1998	CS Sfaxien	TUN	1-0 3-0	SEN	ASC Jeanne d'Arc
1999	Etoile du Sahel	TUN	1-0 1-2	MAR	Wydad Casablanca
2000	JS Kabylie	ALG	1-1 0-0	EGY	Al Ismaili
2001	JS Kabylie	ALG	1-2 1-0	TUN	Etoile du Sahel
2002	JS Kabylie	ALG	4-0 0-1	CMR	Tonnerre Youndé
2003	Raja Casablanca	MAR	2-0 0-0	CMR	Cotonsport Garoua

Discontinued after the 2003 tournament and replaced by the CAF Confederation Cup

With the decision to allow more than one team from each country into the CAF Champions League, CAF decided in 2003 to discarded the Cup Winners' Cup and the CAF Cup in favour of a 'best of the rest' tournament - the CAF Confederation Cup. Teams knocked out in early rounds of the Champions League enter the Confederation Cup at the intermediate stage after which there is a group stage with the winners of each group contesting the final.

CECAFA CLUB CHAMPIONSHIP

Year	Winners	Country	Score	Country	Runners-up
1974	Simba SC	TAN	1-0 †	KEN	Abaluhya FC
1975	Young Africans	TAN	2-0	TAN	Simba SC
1976	Luo Union	KEN	2-1	TAN	Young Africans
1977	Luo Union	KEN	2-1	SOM	Horsed
1978	Kamapala City Council	UGA	0-0 3-2p	TAN	Simba SC
1979	Abaluhya FC	KEN	1-0	UGA	Kampala City Council
1980	Gor Mahia	KEN	3-2	KEN	Abaluhya FC
1981	Gor Mahia	KEN	1-0	TAN	Simba SC
1982	AFC Leopards	KEN	1-0	ZIM	Rio Tinto
1983	AFC Leopards	KEN	2-1	MWI	Admarc Tigers
1984	AFC Leopards	KEN	2-1	KEN	Gor Mahia
1985	Gor Mahia	KEN	2-0	KEN	AFC Leopards
1986	El Merreikh	SUD	2-2 4-2p	TAN	Young Africans
1987	Nakivubo Villa	UGA	1-0	SUD	El Merreikh
1988	Kenya Breweries	KEN	2-0	SUD	El Merreikh
1989	Kenya Breweries	KEN	3-0	TAN	Coastal Union
1990	Not held				
1991	Simba SC	TAN	3-0	UGA	Nikivubo Villa
1992	Simba SC	TAN	1-1 5-4p	TAN	Young Africans
1993	Young Africans	TAN	2-1	UGA	Nakivubo Villa
1994	El Merreikh	SUD	2-1	UGA	Express FC
1995	Simba SC	TAN	1-1 5-3p	UGA	Express FC
1996	Simba SC	TAN	1-0	RWA	APR FC
1997	AFC Leopards	KEN	1-0	KEN	Kenya Breweries
1998	Rayyon Sport	RWA	2-1	ZAN	Mlandege
1999	Young Africans	TAN	1-1 4-1p	UGA	SC Villa
2000	Tusker FC	KEN	3-1	RWA	APR FC
2001	Tusker FC	KEN	0-0 3-0p	KEN	Oserian
2002	Simba SC	TAN	1-0	BDI	Prince Louis
2003	SC Villa	UGA	1-0	TAN	Simba SC
2004	APR FC	RWA	3-1	KEN	Ulinzi Stars
2005	SC Villa	UGA	3-0	RWA	APR FC
2006	Police FC	UGA	2-1	TAN	Moro United

CAF AFRICA CUP OF NATIONS MEDALS TABLE

	Country	G	S	B	F	SF
1	Egypt	5	1	3	5	9
2	Ghana	4	3		7	6
3	Cameroon	4	1	1	5	7
4	Nigeria	2	4	6	6	11
5	Zaire	2		1	2	4
6	Tunisia	1	2	1	3	5
7	Sudan	1	2	1	3	2
8	Côte d'Ivoire	1	1	4	2	6
9	Algeria	1	1	2	2	5
10	South Africa	1	1	1	2	3
11	Morocco	1	1	1	1	4
12	Ethiopia	1	1	1	1	3
13	Congo	1			1	2
14	Zambia		2	3	2	5
15	Mali		1		1	4
16	Senegal		1		1	3
17	Uganda		1		1	2
18	Libya		1		1	1
19	Guinea		1			
20	Burkina Faso					1
		25	25	25	46	83

This table represents the Gold (winners), Silver (runners-up) and Bronze (semi-finalists) placings of nations in the CAF Africa Cup of Nations, along with the number of appearances in the final and semi-finals inclusive of 2006

CAF CHAMPIONS LEAGUE MEDALS TABLE

	Country	G	S	B	F	SF
1	Egypt	11	4	8	15	23
2	Morocco	5	1	3	6	7
3	Cameroon	5		6	5	11
4	Algeria	4	1	4	5	9
5	Ghana	3	8	6	11	15
6	Congo DR	3	5	5	8	13
7	Guinea	3	2	3	5	8
8	Tunisia	2	5	4	7	9
9	Nigeria	2	4	7	6	13
10	Côte d'Ivoire	2	2	6	4	9
11	South Africa	1	1	1	2	3
12	Congo	1			1	1
13	Mali		2	1	2	3
	Sudan		2	1	2	3
	Uganda		2	1	2	3
16	Zambia		1	6	1	7
17	Togo		1	3	1	4
18	Zimbabwe		1		1	
19	Senegal			5		5
20	Ethiopia			2		2
	Kenya			2		2
22	Angola			1		1
23	Tanzania			1		1
		42	42	76	84	152

This table represents the Gold (winners), Silver (runners-up) and Bronze (semi-finalists) placings of clubs representing the above countries in the CAF Champions League, along with the number of appearances in the final and semi-finals inclusive of 2006

CAF CHAMPIONS LEAGUE MEDALS TABLE

	Country		G	S	B
1	Al Ahly Cairo	EGY	5	1	2
	Zamalek	EGY	5	1	2
3	Hafia FC Conakry	GUI	3	2	
4	Raja Casablanca	MAR	3	1	1
5	Canon Yaoundé	CMR	3		2
6	Asante Kotoko	GHA	2	5	3
7	TP Mazembe	ZAI	2	2	2
8	Jeunesse Sportive Kabylie	ALG	2		2
9	Enyimba	NGA	2		
10	Esperance Tunis	TUN	1	2	3
11	Hearts of Oak	GHA	1	2	1
12	ASEC Mimosas	CIV	1	1	5
13	Ismaily	EGY	1	1	3
14	AS Vita Club Kinshasa	ZAI	1	1	1
15	FAR Rabat	MAR	1		2
16	Oryx Douala	CMR	1		1
	Union Douala	CMR	1		1
18	CARA Brazzaville	CGO	1		
	Mouloudia Alger	ALG	1		
	Club Africain	TUN	1		
	Entente Setif	ALG	1		
	Orlando Pirates	RSA	1		
	Stade Abidjan	CIV	1		
	Wydad Casablanca	MAR	1		
25	Al Hilal	SUD		2	1
26	AS Bilima	ZAI		2	
	Etoile du Sahel	TUN		2	
	Shooting Stars	NGR		2	
29	Nkana Red Devils	ZAM		1	5
30	Enugu Rangers	NGR		1	3
31	Iwuanyanwu Owerri	NGR		1	2
32	Ghazl Al Mehalla	EGY		1	1
	Mouloudia Oran	ALG		1	1
	CS Sfaxien	TUN		1	1
35	Africa Sports	CIV		1	
	Dynamos	ZIM		1	
	Etoile Filante	TOG		1	
	Nakivubo Villa	UGA		1	
	AS Real Bamako	MLI		1	
	Obuasi Goldfields	GHA		1	
	Mamelodi Sundowns	RSA		1	
	Simba FC	UGA		1	
	Stade Malien	MLI		1	
44	US Goree	SEN			2
	AS Kaloum Star	GUI			2
	Lomé I	TOG			2
	Jeanne d'Arc	SEN			2
48	Bendel Insurance	NGR			1
	Kenya Breweries	KEN			1
	Cotton Club	ETH			1
	ASC Diaraf	SEN			1
	Djoliba AC	MLI			1
	Express FC	UGA			1
	Great Olympics	GHA			1
	CS Imana	ZAI			1
	Kakimbo FC	GUI			1

CAF CHAMPIONS LEAGUE MEDALS TABLE (CONT'D)

Country		G	S	B
AFC Leopards	KEN			1
Leopard Douala	CMR			1
FC Lupopo	ZAI			1
Mufulira Wanderers	ZAM			1
Petro Atlético	ANG			1
Real Republicans	GHA			1
St. Georges	ETH			1
Semassi Sokode	TOG			1
SC Simba	TAN			1
Stationery Stores	NGR			1
Tonnerre Yaoundé	CMR			1
USM Alger	ALG			1
		42	42	76

PAST AFRICAN PLAYER OF THE YEAR AWARDS

There have been four seperate awards for African football, the first of which was awarded by *France Football* magazine from 1970 until 1994. In 1992, CAF introduced an annual award and this is now the major award available to African players. From 1991 until 2003 *Afrique Football* magazine also made an annual award but their winners replicated those of CAF, with the addition of Abedi Pele in 1991. Since 1992 the BBC has also made an annual award, voted for by listeners to the BBC World Service's *Fast Track* programme.

FF PLAYER OF THE YEAR 1970

KEITA Salif	Saint-Étienne	MLI	54
POKOU Laurent	ASEC Abidjan	CIV	28
ABOUGREISHA Ali	Ismaili	EGY	28
KALALA Pierre	TP Englebert	ZAI	19
LALMAS Hacène	CR Belcourt	ALG	15
SORY Petit	Hafia	GUI	9
ALLAL Ben Kassou	FAR Rabat	MAR	5
MENSAH Robert	Asante Kotoko	GHA	5
KOFI Osei	Asante Kotoko	GHA	5
Four players with four votes			

FF PLAYER OF THE YEAR 1971

SUNDAY Ibrahim	Asante Kotoko	GHA	29
MENSAH Robert	Asante Kotoko	GHA	15
OBENGUE Lea	Canon	CMR	13
POKOU Laurent	ASEC Abidjan	CIV	8
ATTOUGA Sadok	Club Africain	TUN	8
KIBONGE Mafu	Victoria Club	ZAI	6
M'PELE Francois	Ajaccio	CGO	6
KOUM Emmanuel	Monaco	CMR	6
LALMAS Hacène	CR Belcourt	ALG	6
KALLET BIALY Ernest	Africa Sports	CIV	6

FF PLAYER OF THE YEAR 1972

SOULEYMANE Cherif	Hafia	GUI	21
BWANGA Tshimen	TP Mazembe	ZAI	16
SORY Petit	Hafia	GUI	14
HANY Moustafa	Al Ahly	EGY	12
FARRAS Ahmed	Mohammedia	MAR	11
HADEFI Miloud	MO Oran	ALG	11
MALIK Jabir	Asante Kotoko	GHA	10
ABOUGREISHA Ali	Ismaili	EGY	8
MINGA Jean-Noel	CARA	CGO	8
N'TUMBA Kalala	Vita	ZAI	8

FF PLAYER OF THE YEAR 1973

BWANGA Tshimen	TP Mazembe	ZAI	49
KAZADI Mwamba	TP Mazembe	ZAI	44
POKOU Laurent	ASEC Abidjan	CIV	41
KAKOKO Etepe	Imana	ZAI	29
FARRAS Ahmed	Mohammedia	MAR	18
SAM Yaw	Asante Kotoko	GHA	16
KEMBO Kembo Uba	Vita	ZAI	15
SOULEYMANE Cherif	Hafia	GUI	9
Three players with eight votes			

FF PLAYER OF THE YEAR 1974

MOUKILA Paul	CARA	CGO	57
LOBILO Boba	Vita	ZAI	32
SHEHATA Hassan	Zamalek	EGY	28
CHAMA Dickson	Gr'n Buffaloes	ZAM	16
FARRAS Ahmed	Mohammedia	MAR	14
N'DAYE Mulamba	Vita	ZAI	10
KAKOKO Etepe	Imana	ZAI	8
Five players with six votes			

FF PLAYER OF THE YEAR 1975

FARRAS Ahmed	Mohammedia	MAR	28
N'JO LEA Mamadou	Hafia	GUI	24
MILLA Roger	Canon	CMR	24
DHIAB Tarak	Esperance	TUN	16
SAGNA Christophe	Jeanne d'Arc	SEN	15
SORY Petit	Hafia	GUI	10
LARBI Ahardane	Wydad	MAR	9
GAAFAR Farouk	Zamalek	EGY	7
ATTOUGA Sadok	Club Africain	TUN	7
Three players with five votes			

FF PLAYER OF THE YEAR 1976

MILLA Roger	Tonnerre	CMR	33
CAMARA Papa	Hafia	GUI	32
BENCHEIKH Ali	MC Alger	ALG	27
SYLLA Bengally	Hafia	GUI	26
FARRAS Ahmed	Mohammedia	MAR	12
BETROUNI Rachid	MC Alger	ALG	12
LARBI Ahardane	Wydad	MAR	11
ATTOUGA Sadok	Club Africain	TUN	11
DHIAB Tarak	Espérance	TUN	10
SORY Petit	Hafia	GUI	10

FF PLAYER OF THE YEAR 1977

DHIAB Tarak	Espérance	TUN	45
CAMARA Papa	Hafia	GUI	33
ODEGBAMI Segun	Shooting Stars	NGA	29
POLO Mohamed	Olympics	GHA	15
BWALYA Thomas	Mufulira	ZAM	6
BENCHEIKH Ali	MC Alger	ALG	5
ATTOUGA Sadok	Club Africain	TUN	4
GAAFAR Farouk	Zamalek	EGY	3
BAHAMBOULA Jonas	Diable Noir	CGO	3
SOULEYMANE Cherif	Hafia	GUI	3

FF PLAYER OF THE YEAR 1978

ABDUL RAZAK Karim	Asante Kotoko	GHA	58
BENCHEIKH Ali	MP Algiers	ALG	33
N'KONO Thomas	Canon	CMR	29
CHUKWU Christian	Enugu Rangers	NGA	25
SYLLA Bengally	Hafia	GUI	20
DHIAB Tarak	Al Ahly Jeddah	TUN	18
LAHZANI Temime	Espérance	TUN	12
MANGA-ONGUENE J	Canon	CMR	10
OMONDI Philip	Kampala CC	UGA	9
Four players with four votes			

FF PLAYER OF THE YEAR 1979

N'KONO Thomas	Canon	CMR	55
ARMAH Adolf	Hearts of Oak	GHA	23
BANGOURA Kerfalla	Horoya	GUI	15
CAMPAORE Abdoulaye	Bobo Dioulasso	BFA	13
OLUOCH Nahashion	Gor Mahia	KEN	9
KIYIKA Tokodia	Imana	ZAI	8
AGBONIFO Felix	Shooting Stars	NGA	7
MIEZAN Pascal	ASEC Abidjan	CIV	6
LAWAL Muda	Shooting Stars	NGA	5
Four players with four votes			

FF PLAYER OF THE YEAR 1980

MANGA-ONGUENE J	Canon	CMR	64
ODEGBAMI Segun	Shooting Stars	NGA	41
ABEGA Théophile	Canon	CMR	18
BELLOUMI Lakhdar	GCR Mascara	ALG	13
MAYELE Ayel	AS Bilima	ZAI	12
N'KONO Thomas	Canon	CMR	12
KOUICI Mustapha	CR Belcourt	MAR	11
MASSENGO Elunga	TP Mazembe	ZAI	7
BENSAOULA Tadj	MC Oran	ALG	6
KAZADI Mwamba	TP Mazembe	ZAI	6

FF PLAYER OF THE YEAR 1981

BELLOUMI Lakhdar	GCR Mascara	ALG	78
N'KONO Thomas	Canon	CMR	54
FERGANI Ali	JE Tizi-Ouzou	ALG	26
EKOULE Eugène	Union Douala	CMR	18
ABEGA Théophile	Canon	CMR	16
BOUDERBALA Aziz	Wydad	MAR	16
ODEGBAMI Segun	Shooting Stars	NGA	8
KEITA Cheik	Kaloum Stars	GUI	6
KOUADIO Koffi	ASEC Abidjan	CIV	4
ZAKI Badou	Wydad	MAR	4

FF PLAYER OF THE YEAR 1982

N'KONO Thomas	Español	CMR	83
ASSAD Salah	Mulhouse	ALG	54
BELLOUMI Lakhdar	GCR Mascara	ALG	36
EL KHATIB Mahmoud	Al Ahly Cairo	EGY	28
ABEGA Théophile	Canon	CMR	23
KAUMBA Peter	Power Dynamos	ZAM	23
ASASE Albert	Asante Kotoko	GHA	22
AFRIYIE Opoku	Asante Kotoko	GHA	13
MADJER Rabah	Hussein Dey	ALG	9
MERZEKANE Chaabane	Hussein Dey	ALG	8

FF PLAYER OF THE YEAR 1983

EL KHATIB Mahmoud	Al Ahly Cairo	EGY	98
N'TI Opoku	Asante Kotoko	GHA	89
MOUTAIROU Rafiou	Agaza Lomé	TOG	19
ABEGA Théophile	Canon	CMR	18
BELL Joseph Antoine	Al Mokaouloum	CMR	18
ABDUL RAZAK Karim	Al Mokaouloum	GHA	18
SECK Cheikh	Diaraf Dakar	SEN	11
NASSER Mohamed Ali	Al Ahly Cairo	EGY	7
HADDAOUI Mustapha	Rajan	MAR	7
MADJER Rabah	Racing Paris	ALG	7

FF PLAYER OF THE YEAR 1984

ABEGA Théophile	Toulouse	CMR	124
YOUSSEF Ibrahim	Zamalek	EGY	65
BELL Joseph Antoine	Al Mokaouloum	CMR	65
NWOSU Henry	Nigerian Bank	NGA	47
ABOU ZEID Taher	Al Ahly Cairo	EGY	28
FOFANA Youssouf	Cannes	CIV	28
EL KHATIB Mahmoud	Al Ahly Cairo	EGY	28
KESHI Stephen	Nigerian Bank	NGA	16
BELLOUMI Lakhdar	GCR Mascara	ALG	12
MSIYA Clifton	Berrick Power	MWI	12

FF PLAYER OF THE YEAR 1985

TIMOUMI Mohamed	FAR Rabat	MAR	113
MADJER Rabah	Porto	ALG	45
MENAD Djamel	JE Tizi-Ouzou	ALG	39
YOUSSEF Ibrahim	Zamalek	EGY	39
ZAKI Badou	Wydad	MAR	33
FOFANA Youssouf	Monaco	CIV	31
BELLOUMI Lakhdar	GCR Mascara	ALG	20
PELE Abedi	Dragons	GHA	19
BOCANDE Jules	Metz	SEN	17
Two players with 16 votes			

FF PLAYER OF THE YEAR 1986

ZAKI Badou	Real Mallorca	MAR	125
BOUDERBALA Aziz	Sion	MAR	88
MILLA Roger	Montpellier	CMR	80
ABOU ZEID Taher	Al Ahly	EGY	47
TIMOUMI Mohamed	Real Murcia	MAR	35
BOCANDE Jules	PSG	SEN	13
DOLMY Abdelmajid	Raja	MAR	13
PELE Abedi	Niort	GHA	13
CHABALA Efford	Nkana	ZAM	11
DRID Nacer	MP Oran	ALG	11

FF PLAYER OF THE YEAR 1987

MADJER Rabah	Porto	ALG	130
FOFANA Youssouf	Monaco	CIV	63
OMAM BIYIK François	Laval	CMR	52
ABDELGHANI Magdi	Al Ahly Cairo	EGY	37
ABOU ZEID Taher	Al Ahly Cairo	EGY	25
MALUNGA Kennedy	Club Brugge	MWI	24
DAWO Peter	Gor Mahia	KEN	21
PELE Abedi	Marseille	GHA	17
AYOYI Ambrose	AFC Leopards	KEN	15
MILLA Roger	Montpellier	CMR	14

FF PLAYER OF THE YEAR 1988

BWALYA Kalusha	Cercle Brugge	ZAM	111
MILLA Roger	Montpellier	CMR	68
FOFANA Youssouf	Monaco	CIV	40
WEAH George	Monaco	LBR	32
BOUDERBALA Aziz	Racing Paris	MAR	27
RUFAI Peter	Lokeren	NGA	27
KESHI Stephen	Anderlecht	NGA	14
KUNDE Emmanuel	Reims	CMR	14
KINGAMBO Jacques	St Truidense	ZAI	13
BELL Joseph Antoine	Toulon	CMR	12

FF PLAYER OF THE YEAR 1989

WEAH George	Monaco	LBR	133
BELL Joseph Antoine	Bordeaux	CMR	105
BWALYA Kalusha	PSV	ZAM	49
PELE Abedi	Lille OSC	GHA	40
OMAM BIYIK François	Laval	CMR	31
ABDELGHANI Magdi	Beira Mar	EGY	30
SHOUBEIR Ahmed	Al Ahly Cairo	EGY	28
TATAW Stephen	Tonnerre	CMR	19
KESHI Stephen	Anderlecht	NGA	18
HASSAN Hossam	Al Ahly Cairo	EGY	17

FF PLAYER OF THE YEAR 1990

MILLA Roger	No Club	CMR	209
EL OUAZANI Cherif	Aydinspor	ALG	64
MADJER Rabah	Porto	ALG	60
OMAM BIYIK François	Stade Rennais	CMR	60
SHOUBEIR Ahmed	Al Ahly Cairo	EGY	49
RAMZY Hany	Neuchâtel	EGY	41
MAKANAKY Cyrille	Málaga	CMR	34
WEAH George	Monaco	LBR	26
PELE Abedi	Marseille	GHA	23
HASSAN Hossam	PAOK	EGY	22

FF PLAYER OF THE YEAR 1991

PELE Abedi	Marseile	GHA	159
WEAH George	Monaco	LBR	106
OMAM BIYIK François	Cannes	CMR	52
BWALYA Kalusha	PSV	ZAM	30
LAMPETY Nii	Anderlecht	GHA	29
YEBOAH Anthony	Ein. Frankfurt	GHA	20
MENDY Roger	Monaco	SEN	18
TRAORE Abdoulaye	ASEC Abidjan	CIV	16
FOFANA Youssouf	Monaco	CIV	14
BOUDERBALA Aziz	Lyon	EGY	13

FF PLAYER OF THE YEAR 1992

PELE Abedi	Marseille	GHA	198
WEAH George	PSG	LBR	161
YEBOAH Anthony	Ein. Frankfurt	GHA	64
TRAORE Abdoulaye	ASEC Abidjan	CIV	36
GOUAMENE Alain	Raja	CIV	33
N'DORAM Japhet	Nantes	CHA	30
NDLOVU Peter	Coventry City	ZIM	24
YEKINI Rashidi	Vitoria Setubal	NGA	20
BWALYA Kalusha	PSV	ZAM	15
DAOUDI Rachid	Wydad	MAR	14

FF PLAYER OF THE YEAR 1993

PELE Abedi	Lyonnais	GHA	119
YEBOAH Anthony	Ein. Frankfurt	GHA	117
YEKINI Rashidi	Vitoria Setubal	NGA	104
IKPEBA Victor	Monaco	NGA	57
WEAH George	PSG	LBR	56
BWALYA Kalusha	PSV	ZAM	48
OMAM BIYIK François	RC Lens	CMR	28
DAOUDI Rachid	Wydad	MAR	20
NDLOVU Peter	Coventry City	ZAM	19
TRAORE Abdoulaye	ASEC Abidjan	CIV	16

FF PLAYER OF THE YEAR 1994

WEAH George	PSG	LBR	148
AMUNIKE Emmanuel	Sporting CP	NGA	133
AMOKACHI Daniel	Everton	NGA	99
YEKINI Rashidi	Olympiakos	NGA	87
BWALYA Kalusha	América	ZAM	37
YEBOAH Anthony	Ein. Frankfurt	GHA	32
GEORGE Finidi	Ajax	NGA	31
TIEHI Joël	Le Havre	CIV	22
N'DORAM Japhet	Nantes	CHA	18
OKOCHA Jay-Jay	Ein. Frankfurt	NGA	18

CAF PLAYER OF THE YEAR 1992

PELE Abedi	Marseille	GHA
GOUAMENE Alain	Raja	CIV
YEKINI Rashidi	Vitoria Setubal	NGA
WEAH George	PSG	LBR
DAOUDI Rachid	Wydad	MAR
MAGUY Serge Alain	Africa Sports	CIV
YEBOAH Anthony	Ein. Frankfurt	GHA
RAMZY Hany	Neuchatel	EGY
NDAW Moussa	Wydad	SEN
AMOKACHI Daniel	Club Brugge	NGA

CAF PLAYER OF THE YEAR 1993

YEKINI Rashidi	Vitoria Setubal	NGA
PELE Abedi	Marseille	GHA
WEAH George	PSG	LBR
YEBOAH Anthony	Ein. Frankfurt	GHA
OMAM BIYIK François	RC Lens	CMR
NAYBET Nouredine	Nantes	MAR
IKPEBA Victor	Monaco	NGA
BELL Joseph Antoine	Saint-Etienne	CMR
Three players in 9th place		

CAF PLAYER OF THE YEAR 1994

AMUNIKE Emmanuel	Sporting CP	NGA
WEAH George	PSG	LBR
YEKINI Rashidi	Olympiakos	NGA
GEORGE Finidi	Ajax	NGA
AMOKACHI Daniel	Everton	NGA
N'DORAM Japhet	Nantes	CHA
TIEHI Joel	Le Havre	CIV
OKOCHA Jay-Jay	Ein. Frankfurt	NGA
MAGUY Serge Alain	Africa Sports	CIV
OLISEH Sunday	FC Liège	NGA

CAF PLAYER OF THE YEAR 1995

WEAH George	Milan	LBR
N'DORAM Japhet	Nantes	CHA
GEORGE Finidi	Ajax	NGA
YEBOAH Anthony	Leeds	GHA
KANU Nwankwo	Ajax	NGA
AMUNIKE Emmanuel	Sporting CP	NGA
AMOKACHI Daniel	Everton	NGA
TIEHI Joel	Martigues	CIV
ONDO Valery	Mbilinga	GAB
Two players in 10th place		

CAF PLAYER OF THE YEAR 1996

KANU Nwankwo	Internazionale	NGA
WEAH George	Milan	LBR
AMOKACHI Daniel	Besiktas	NGA
FISH Mark	Lazio	RSA
GEORGE Finidi	Betis	NGA
N'DORAM Japhet	Nantes	CHA
BWALYA Kalusha	América	ZAM
AMUNIKE Emmanuel	Sporting CP	NGA
OLISEH Sunday	1.FC Köln	NGA
YEBOAH Anthony	Leeds United	GHA

CAF PLAYER OF THE YEAR 1997

IKPEBA Victor	Monaco	NGA	56
N'DORAM Japhet	Monaco	CHA	40
WEST Taribo	Internazionale	NGA	35
OLISEH Sunday	Ajax	NGA	24
SONGO'O Jacques	Deportivo LC	CMR	17
WEAH George	Milan	LBR	15
SELLIMI Adel	Nantes	TUN	12
GEORGE Finidi	Betis	NGA	9
PAULAO	Coimbra	ANG	7
M'BOMA Patrick	Gamba Osaka	CMR	6

CAF PLAYER OF THE YEAR 1998

HADJI Mustapha	Deportivo LC	MAR	76
OKOCHA Jay-Jay	PSG	NGA	74
OLISEH Sunday	Ajax	NGA	58
HASSAN Hossam	Al Ahly Cairo	EGY	34
MCCARTHY Benni	Ajax	RSA	24
GUEL Tchiressoua	ASEC Abidjan	CIV	16
AKONNOR Charles	Fortuna Köln	GHA	12
FOE Marc-Vivien	RC Lens	CMR	10
GEORGE Finidi	Betis	NGA	8
SONG Rigobert	Salernitana	CMR	6

CAF PLAYER OF THE YEAR 1999

KANU Nwankwo	Arsenal	NGA	46
KUFFOUR Samuel	Bayern	GHA	44
BAKAYOKO Ibrahima	Marseille	CIV	42
WEAH George	Milan	LBR	40
OKOCHA Jay-Jay	PSG	NGA	30
DINDANE Aruna	ASEC Abidjan	CIV	28
IKPEBA Victor	Dortmund	NGA	26
BENARBIA Ali	PSG	ALG	24
HADJI Mustapha	Coventry City	MAR	24
BADRA Khaled	Espérance	TUN	22

CAF PLAYER OF THE YEAR 2000

M'BOMA Patrick	Parma	CMR	123
LAUREN Etame-Mayer	Arsenal	CMR	36
ETO'O Samuel	Real Mallorca	CMR	29
GEREMI Njitap	Real Madrid	CMR	27
KANU Nwankwo	Arsenal	NGA	21
NAYBET Nouredine	Deportivo LC	MAR	20
HASSAN Hossam	Zamalek	EGY	17
NONDA Shabani	Monaco	COD	11
BARTLETT Shaun	Charlton	RSA	10
RAMY Hani	Werder	EGY	10

CAF PLAYER OF THE YEAR 2001

DIOUF El-Hadji	RC Lens	SEN	93
KUFFOUR Samuel	Bayern	GHA	66
ETO'O Samuel	Real Mallorca	CMR	34
KALLON Mohamed	Internazionale	SLE	28
NAYBET Nouredine	Deportivo LC	MAR	26
FADIGA Khalilou	Auxerre	SEN	22
BAGAYOKO Mamadou	Strasbourg	MLI	16
M'BOMA Patrick	Sunderland	CMR	15
RAMY Hani	Werder	EGY	12
Two players with 10 votes			

CAF PLAYER OF THE YEAR 2002

DIOUF El-Hadji	Liverpool	SEN	93
DIOP Papa Bouba	RC Lens	SEN	46
HOSSAM Ahmed	Celta Vigo	EGY	42
FADIGA Khalilou	Auxerre	SEN	41
LAUREN Etame-Mayer	Arsenal	CMR	35
CAMARA Henri	Sedan	SEN	20
AGHAHOWA Julius	Shakhtar	NGA	19
TRABELSI Hatem	Ajax	TUN	19
DIAO Salif	Liverpool	SEN	17
KEITA Seydou	RC Lens	MLI	16

CAF PLAYER OF THE YEAR 2003

ETO'O Samuel	Mallorca	CMR

CAF PLAYER OF THE YEAR 2004			
ETO'O Samuel	Barcelona	CMR	116
DROGBA Didier	Chelsea	CIV	90
OKOCHA Jay-Jay	Bolton	NGA	68
MCCARTHY Benni	Porto	RSA	31
ADEBAYOR Emmanuel	Monaco	TOG	21

CAF PLAYER OF THE YEAR 2005			
ETO'O Samuel	Barcelona	CMR	108
DROGBA Didier	Chelsea	CIV	106
ESSIEN Michael	Chelsea	GHA	50

CAF PLAYER OF THE YEAR 2006			
DROGBA Didier	Chelsea	CIV	79
ETO'O Samuel	Barcelona	CMR	74
ESSIEN Michael	Chelsea	GHA	36

CAF AFRICA CUP OF NATIONS GHANA 2008

QUALIFYING GROUPS

Group 1		Pts		Group 2		Pts		Group 3		Pts		Group 4		Pts
Côte d'Ivoire	CIV	9		Egypt	EGY	8		**Nigeria**	NGA	12		**Tunisia**	TUN	13
Gabon	GAB	6		Botswana	BOT	7		Uganda	UGA	8		**Sudan**	SUD	12
Madagascar	MAD	0		Burundi	BDI	6		Niger	NIG	4		Seychelles	SEY	3
Djibouti withdrew				Mauritania	MTN	4		Lesotho	LES	4		Mauritius	MRI	1

Group 5		Pts		Group 6		Pts		Group 7		Pts		Group 8		Pts
Cameroon	CMR	15		**Angola**	ANG	13		Senegal	SEN	8		Guinea	GUI	8
Equat'rial Guinea	EQG	7		Eritrea	ERI	8		Tanzania	TAN	8		Algeria	ALG	8
Liberia	LBR	4		Kenya	KEN	4		Mozambique	MOZ	6		Gambia	GAM	5
Rwanda	RWA	3		Swaziland	SWZ	2		Burkina Faso	BFA	4		Cape Verde Isl	CPV	5

Group 9		Pts		Group 10		Pts		Group 11		Pts		Group 12		Pts
Mali	MLI	9		Congo DR	COD	8		South Africa	RSA	11		**Morocco**	MAR	10
Togo	TOG	9		Namibia	NAM	7		Zambia	ZAM	8		Malawi	MWI	3
Benin	BEN	8		Libya	LBY	7		Congo	CGO	6		Zimbabwe	ZIM	1
Sierra Leone	SLE	1		Ethiopia	ETH	6		Chad	CHA	1				

Tables as of August 15, 2007 • Teams in bold have qualified • Ghana qualified automatically as hosts • The final tournament will be held in Accra, Kumasi, Tamale and Sekondi-Takoradi, Ghana from 20-01-2008 to 10-02-2008 • The group winners and best three runners-up from the groups of four qualify for the finals.
Match details for both the qualifying matches and final tournament will be included in next year's Almanack of World Football

REGIONAL TOURNAMENTS IN AFRICA 2006–07

COSAFA CASTLE CUP 2006							
First Round		**First Round finals**		**Semi-finals**		**Final**	
Zambia	3						
Malawi	1	**Zambia**	2				
Namibia	1 2p	Seychelles	0				
Seychelles	1 4p			**Zambia** *	1		
South Africa	1			Botswana	0		
Swaziland	0	South Africa	0 5p			**Zambia** *	2
Madagascar	0	**Botswana**	0 6p			Angola	0
Botswana	2			Zimbabwe *	1		
Lesotho	0 5p			**Angola**	2		
Mozamqique	0 4p	Lesotho	1				
Mauritius	1	**Angola**	3				
Angola	5						

Group A between Angola, Mauritius, Mozambique and Lesotho was played in Maseru, Lesotho from 29-04-2006 to 30-04-2006. Mozambique beat Mauritius 5-4 on penalties, after a 0-0 draw, in a third place play-off • Group B between Botswana, Madafascar, Swaziland and South Africa was played in Gaborone, Botswana from 20-05-2006 to 21-05-2006. Swaziland beat Madagascar 2-0 in a third place play-off • Group C between Zambia, Malawi, Namibia and the Seychelles was played in Windhoek, Namibia from 22-07-2006 to 23-07-2006. Namibia beat Malawi 3-2 in a third place play-off • * Home team • The holders Zimbabwe received a bye to the semi-finals

CECAFA CUP ETHIOPIA 2006

First round groups | **Quarter-finals** | **Semi-finals** | **Final**

Group A	Pl	W	D	L	F	A	Pts	ETH	MWI	DJI
Tanzania	3	3	0	0	7	2	9	2-1	2-1	3-0
Ethiopia	3	2	0	1	6	2	6		1-0	4-0
Malawi	3	1	0	2	4	3	3			3-0
Djibouti	3	0	0	3	0	10	0			

Quarter-finals:
Zambia 1
Ethiopia 0

Semi-finals:
Zambia 1
Rwanda 0

Group B	Pl	W	D	L	F	A	Pts	ZAM	ZAN
Burundi	2	1	1	0	3	2	4	3-2	0-0
Zambia	2	1	0	1	6	3	3		4-0
Zanzibar	2	0	1	1	0	4	1		

Quarter-finals:
Tanzania 1
Rwanda 2

Final:
Zambia 0 11p
Sudan 0 10p

Quarter-finals:
Uganda 0 4p
Malawi 0 2p

Semi-finals:
Uganda 2 5p
Sudan 2 6p

Group C	Pl	W	D	L	F	A	Pts	SUD	RWA	SOM
Uganda	3	3	0	0	5	1	9	2-1	1-0	2-0
Sudan	3	1	1	1	4	2	4		0-0	3-0
Rwanda	3	1	1	1	3	1	4			3-0
Somali	3	0	0	3	0	8	0			

Quarter-finals:
Burundi 0
Sudan 1

Third place play-off:
Rwanda 0 4p
Uganda 0 2p

Played in Addis Abeba, Ethiopia from 25-11-2006 to 10-12-2006 • As Zambia were invited guests, Sudan were awarded the trophy

COUPE DE LA CEMAC EQUATORIAL GUINEA 2007

First Round Group Stage | **Semi-finals** | **Final**

Group A	Pl	W	D	L	F	A	Pts	CTA	CMR
Chad	2	2	0	0	5	3	6	3-2	2-1
Central African Rep	2	0	1	1	2	3	1		0-0
Cameroon	2	0	1	1	1	2	1		

Semi-finals:
Congo 4
Central African Rep 1

Final:
Congo 1
Gabon 0

Group B	Pl	W	D	L	F	A	Pts	GAB	EQG
Congo	2	1	1	0	4	3	4	2-2	2-1
Gabon	2	0	2	0	3	3	2		1-1
Equatorial Guinea	2	0	1	1	2	3	1		

Semi-finals:
Chad 0
Gabon 2

Third place play-off:
Chad 1
Central African Rep 0

Played in N'Djamena, Chad from 4-03-2007 to 16-03-2007 • Cameroon did not send their full senior team

COSAFA CASTLE CUP 2007

First Round | **First Round finals** | **Semi-finals** | **Final**

First Round		First Round finals	
Mozambique	2		
Seychelles	0	Mozambique	0 5p
Madagascar	0	Zimbabwe	0 4p
Zimbabwe	1		
Mauritius	0 6p		
Swaziland	0 5p	Mauritius	0
Malawi	0 5p	South Africa	2
South Africa	0 6p		
Angola	2		
Lesotho	0	Namibia	0 1p
Namibia	0	Botswana	0 3p
Botswana	1		

Group A between Mozambique, the Seychelles, Madagascar and Zimbabwe was played in Maputo, Mozambique from 28-04-2007 to 29-04-2007.
Madagascar beat Seychelles 5-0 in a third place play-off • Group B between South Africa, Malawi, Swaziland and Mauritius was played in Somhlolo, Swaziland from 26-05-2007 to 27-05-2007. Swaziland beat Malawi 1-0 in a third place play-off • Group C between Angola, Lesotho, Namibia and Botswana was played in Gaborone, Botswana from 28-07-2007 to 29-07-2007. Namibia beat Lesotho 3-2 in a third place play-off
The holders Zambia received a bye to the semi-finals • The semi-finals and final to be held in the latter part of 2007

CAF AFRICAN YOUTH CHAMPIONSHIP 2007

AFRICAN YOUTH CHAMPIONSHIP 2007 QUALIFIERS

Preliminary Round			First Round			Second Round		
Equatorial Guinea	0	2	**Nigeria**	3	0			
Gabon	0	1	Equatorial Guinea	0	2	**Nigeria** †	5	1
Rwanda	2	0	**Rwanda**	1	1	Rwanda	0	0
Ethiopia	1	0	Kenya	0	0			
Kenya		1	**Mali**	1	1			
Djibouti		0	Guinea	0	0	Mali	1	1
Mauritania	0	1	Morocco	2	0	**Gambia** †	1	2
Guinea	0	4	**Gambia**	2	2			
Sierra Leone	1	0	**South Africa**	1	3			
Gambia	1	4	Zimbabwe	0	3	South Africa	2	0
Madagascar	1	2	**Zambia**	4	1	**Zambia** †	1	2
Mauritius	1	2	Madagascar	1	1			
Congo DR	3	1	**Burkina Faso**	w-o				
Namibia	0	1	Congo DR			**Burkina Faso** †	1 0	4p
			Ghana	2	2	Ghana	0 1	3p
			Senegal	0	1			
			Burundi	1	1			
			Mozambique	0	1	Burundi	0	0
Libya	0	1	**Egypt**	4	0	**Egypt** †	1	2
Algeria	2	1	Algeria	0	2			
Sudan	1	0	Benin					
Tunisia	3	3	**Tunisia**	w-o		Tunisia	1	0
			Angola	0	2	**Côte d'Ivoire** †	1	2
			Côte d'Ivoire	0	3			
Niger	2	1	**Cameroon**	1	1			
Togo	0	3	Niger	0	2	**Cameroon** †	2	2
Malawi	2	1	Lesotho	2	0	Malawi	0	0
Botswana	0	0	**Malawi**	1	2			

† Qualified for the finals in Congo • Congo qualified as hosts • Home teams in the first legs are listed above their opponents • w-o = walk over after opponents withdrew • Matches played between 15-04-2006 and 22-10-2006

CAF AFRICAN YOUTH CHAMPIONSHIP CONGO 2007

First Round Group Stage

Group A	Pl	W	D	L	F	A	Pts	CGO	BFA	CIV
Gambia	3	3	0	0	4	0	**9**	1-0	2-0	1-0
Congo	3	2	0	1	3	1	**6**		1-0	2-0
Burkina Faso	3	1	0	2	2	3	**3**			2-0
Côte d'Ivoire	3	0	0	3	0	5	**0**			

Group B	Pl	W	D	L	F	A	Pts	NGA	EGY	CMR
Zambia	3	2	0	1	8	6	**6**	2-4	3-0	3-2
Nigeria	3	1	1	1	5	5	**4**		1-1	0-2
Egypt	3	1	1	1	2	4	**4**			1-0
Cameroon	3	1	0	2	4	4	**3**			

Semi-finals

Congo	1
Zambia	0

Gambia	0
Nigeria	1

Final

Congo	1
Nigeria	0

Third place play-off

Gambia	3
Zambia	1

Tournament played in Brazzaville, Congo from 20-01-2007 to 3-02-2007
Congo, Nigeria, Gambia and Zambia qualified for the FIFA U–20 World Cup in Canada

CAF AFRICAN U-17 CHAMPIONSHIP 2007

AFRICAN U-17 CHAMPIONSHIP 2007 QUALIFIERS

Preliminary Round			First Round			Second Round		
Rwanda	2		Nigeria	3	3			
Somalia	0		Rwanda	0	2	Nigeria †	5	0
			Sierra Leone			Morocco	0	1
			Morocco	w-o				
			Côte d'Ivoire	w-o				
			Benin			Côte d'Ivoire	3	0
			Ghana	3	1	Ghana †	1	2
			Guinea	1	1			
Algeria	0	0	Tunisia	1	1			
Mauritania	0	4	Mauritania	1	0	Tunisia †	1 0	4p
			Gambia	0	0	Senegal	0 1	2p
			Senegal	2	2			
			South Africa	6	3			
			Botswana	0	1	South Africa †	5	2
Reunion	4	0	Zimbabwe	1 1	4p	Zimbabwe	1	2
Mauritius	1	0	Reunion	1 1	2p			
Lesotho	0	2	Mali	3	2			
Malawi	3	1	Malawi	0	0	Mali	1	0
			Burkina Faso	1	2	Burkina Faso †	6	0
			Ethiopia	0	2			
Chad	1	1	Angola	1	0			
Gabon	0	3	Gabon	1	4	Gabon †	1	2
Congo DR ‡	1		Cameroon	0	1	Central African Rep.	2	0
Central African Rep.	1		Central African Rep.	1	1			
Libya	2	0	Egypt	1	0			
Eritrea	1	2	Eritrea	1	1	Eritrea †	1	2
Sudan	4		Sudan	0	1	Zambia	0	0
Djibouti	2		Zambia	3	3			
Mozambique	1	0						
Zambia	2	2						

† Qualified for the finals in Togo • Togo qualified as hosts • Home teams in the first legs are listed above their opponents • w-o = walk over after opponents withdrew • ‡ Congo DR withdrew after the first leg • Matches played between 14-07-2006 and 10-12-2006

CAF AFRICAN U-17 CHAMPIONSHIP TOGO 2007

First Round Group Stage

Group A	Pl	W	D	L	F	A	Pts	TUN	RSA	GAB
Togo	3	2	0	1	4	4	6	0-3	2-0	2-1
Tunisia	3	1	2	0	5	2	5		2-1	0-0
South Africa	3	1	1	1	5	5	4			3-1
Gabon	3	0	1	2	2	5	1			

Group B	Pl	W	D	L	F	A	Pts	GHA	BFA	ERI
Nigeria	3	3	0	0	12	1	9	2-0	2-1	8-0
Ghana	3	2	0	1	9	3	6		3-1	6-0
Burkina Faso	3	1	0	2	5	5	3			3-0
Eritrea	3	0	0	3	0	17	0			

Semi-finals

Nigeria	2
Tunisia	0

Ghana	1
Togo	2

Final

Nigeria	1
Togo	0

Third place play-off

Ghana	1
Tunisia	0

Tournament played in Kegue and Lome, Togo, from 10-03-2007 to 25-03-2007
Nigeria, Togo, Ghana and Tunisia qualified for the FIFA U-17 World Cup in Korea Republic

MTN CAF CHAMPIONS LEAGUE 2006

First Round

Al Ahly	EGY	Bye	
Red Sea FC Asmara	ERI	1	0
Tusker *	KEN	3	1
Stade Malien *	MLI	3	2
Satellite FC	GUI	0	2
Africa Sports	CIV	0	2
Renacimiento *	EQG	0	2
USCAFOOT	MAD	1	2
Excelsior *	REU	3	0
Likhopo *	LES	0	0
Mamelodi Sundowns	RSA	1	3
Ferroviário Maputo	MOZ	0	2
La Passe *	SEY	0	0
Aigle Royal Menoua *	CMR	1	0
Asante Kotoko	GHA	1	3
JS Kabylie	ALG	1	4
Al Ittihad Tripoli *	LBY	1	0
Young Africans *	TAN	2	0
Zanaco	ZAM	1	2
Inter Star *	BDI	3	0
CAPS United ‡	ZIM	3	0
NASR Sebkha	MTN		
Raja Casablanca	MAR	w-o	
Port Autonome Dakar	SEN	0	3
AS Douanes Lomé *	TOG	0	2
Rail Club Kadiogo *	BFA	1	0
USM Alger	ALG	1	1
Civics *	NAM	4	1
Sagrada Esperança	ANG	0	2
East End Lions *	SLE	0	0
ASEC Mimosas	CIV	4	3
Orlando Pirates	RSA	5	2
Mbabane Swallows *	SWZ	0	2
Coin Nord	COM	0	
AS Port Louis 2000 *	MRI	1	
Enugu Rangers	NGA	2	1
Police XI *	BOT	2	0
Police *	UGA	0	0
Al Hilal Omdurman	SUD	0	3
FC St Eloi Lupopo *	COD	2	2
AS Police Pointe-Noire	CGO	0	1
Renaissance *	CHA	1	0
Cotonsport	CMR	1	1
ASC Diaraf Dakar	SEN	0	3
LPRC Oilers *	LBR	0	2
Mangasport	GAB	1	0
Enyimba	NGA	0	2
Hearts of Oak	GHA	w-o	
Wallidan	GAM		
ENPPI *	EGY	0	0
St George	ETH	0	1
AS Polisi	ZAN	w-o	
Civo United	MWI		
Etoile du Sahel	TUN	Bye	
FAR Rabat	MAR	Bye	
Atlético Aviação	ANG	2	0
APR FC *	RWA	3	1
DC Motema Pembe	COD	0	2
Anges de Fatima *	CTA	0	0
AS-FNIS Niamey *	NIG	1	0
CS Sfaxien	TUN	3	4

Second Round

Al Ahly	2	3
Tusker *	0	0
Stade Malien *	2	0
Renacimiento	1	1
USCAFOOT *	1	2
Mamelodi Sundowns	1	2
Ferroviário Maputo *	0	1
Asante Kotoko	0	2
JS Kabylie	0	3
Zanaco *	1	0
Inter Star	0	2
Raja Casablanca *	7	1
Port Autonome Dakar *	2	2
USM Alger	1	3
Civics	0	0
ASEC Mimosas *	3	1
Orlando Pirates	5	4
AS Port Louis 2000 *	0	0
Enugu Rangers *	1	0
Al Hilal Omdurman	0	4
FC St Eloi Lupopo *	1	0
Cotonsport	0	0
ASC Diaraf Dakar *	0	0
Enyimba	0	2
Hearts of Oak	0	†
St George *	4	†
AS Polisi *	0	0
Etoile du Sahel	2	3
FAR Rabat	1	1
APR FC *	2	0
DC Motema Pembe	1	0
CS Sfaxien *	1	1

Third Round

Al Ahly	0	4
Renacimiento *	0	0
USCAFOOT	0	1
Asante Kotoko *	6	0
JS Kabylie *	3	0
Raja Casablanca	1	1
Port Autonome Dakar *	1	0
ASEC Mimosas	0	6
Orlando Pirates *	2	1
Al Hilal Omdurman	0	3
FC St Eloi Lupopo	0	0
Enyimba *	2	1
Hearts of Oak *	1	0 6p
Etoile du Sahel	0	1 5p
FAR Rabat	1	0
CS Sfaxien *	1	1

CAF CHAMPIONS LEAGUE 2006

MTN CAF CHAMPIONS LEAGUE 2006

Champions League Stage   **Semi-finals**   **Final**

Group A		Pts	TUN	EGY	GHA	ALG
CS Sfaxien	TUN	12		1-0	2-1	2-0
Al Ahly	EGY	11	2-1		4-0	2-0
Asante Kotoko	GHA	7	4-2	0-0		2-1
JS Kabylie	ALG	4	0-1	2-2	1-0	

Al Ahly *	2	1
ASEC Mimosas	0	2

Al Ahly *	1	1
CS Sfaxien	1	0

Orlando Pirates *	0	0
CS Sfaxien	0	1

Group B		Pts	CIV	RSA	NGA	GHA
ASEC Mimosas	CIV	12		4-0	3-0	3-0
Orlando Pirates	RSA	9	1-1		1-0	0-0
Enyimba	NGA	8	0-0	1-1		1-0
Hearts of Oak	GHA	2	0-0	0-1	0-2	

* Home team in the first leg • Losing teams in the second round enter the CAF Confederation Cup
† St George walked off at the end of the first leg and were disqualified • ‡ CAPS Utd disqualified were disqualified after using an ineligible player, despite having played, and lost 0-1, their second round first leg match against Raja

GROUP A

		Pl	W	D	L	F	A	Pts	TUN	EGY	GHA	ALG
CS Sfaxien	TUN	6	4	0	2	9	7	12		1-0	2-1	2-0
Al Ahly	EGY	6	3	2	1	10	4	11	2-1		4-0	2-0
Asante Kotoko	GHA	6	2	1	3	7	10	7	4-2	0-0		2-1
Jeunesse Kabylie	ALG	6	1	1	4	4	9	3	0-1	2-2	1-0	

GROUP A MATCHDAY 1
Sfax
15-07-2006, 20:30, Coulibaly MLI

CS Sfaxien — **1**
Issam Merdassi [44]

Jaouachi - Garbi, Aimen Ben Amor, El Abdi, Merdassi, Boujelbene, Bergaoui, Nafti (Essafi 89), Kadri•, Shaibu (Ziadi• 63) (Younes 81), Kouassi.
Tr: Mrad Mahjoub

Al Ahly — **0**

Al Hadari - El Shater (Riad 78), Al Nahhas, El Sayed, Wael Gomaa, Tarek Said, Shawky•, Hassan Mostafa (Ahmed Sedik 68), Aboutrika, Moteab, Flavio (Ashour 43). Tr: Manuel Jose

---

GROUP A MATCHDAY 1
Algiers
16-06-2006, 21:00, Damon RSA

Jeunesse Kabylie — **1**
Cheikh Oumar Dabo [12p]

Chaouch - Mohamed Meftah, Djouder, Herkat, Zafour•, Rahim Meftah, Daoud•, Hamlaoui, Oladipikpo (Marek 84), Dabo (Saibi 71), Hemani (Oussalah 76). Tr: Jean-Yves Chay

Asante Kotoko — **0**

Nii Baah - Ofosu-Appiah, Yeboah, Acquah, Addo, Asante (Kwame 69), Yamoah, Owusu-Ansah, Adu Amofa, Arhin-Duah, Sandje Betah•.
Tr: Emmanuel Afranie

GROUP A MATCHDAY 2
Obuasi
29-07-2006, 14:00, Mbera GAB

Asante Kotoko — **4**
Ahmed Toure [8], Edmund Owusu-Ansah [36], Osei Kwame [76], Nana Arhin-Duah [79]

Nii Baah - Ansah, Yeboah (Kwame 44), Shilla, Acquah, Asante (Adu Amofa 46'), Owusu-Ansah, Chibsah, Yamoah (Ofosu-Appiah 67'), Arhin-Duah, Toure. Tr: Emmanuel Afranie

CS Sfaxien — **2**
Blaise Kouassi [5], Mohamed Kadri [24]

Jaouachi - Garbi, Massaoud, Merdassi, El Abdi•, Mrabet•, Boujelbene, Berguagi (Shaibu 44), Kadri (Younes 84), Kouassi•, Nafti• (Essafi 68).
Tr: Mrad Mahjoub

GROUP A MATCHDAY 2
Cairo
29-07-2006, 19:30, Codjia BEN

Al Ahly — **2**
Ahmed Sedik [35], Osama Hosni [44]

Al Hadari - El Shater, Qanawi, Wael Gomaa, Mohamed Sedik, Ashour, Shawky, Hassan Mostafa, Ahmed Sedik (Mensah 84), Hosni (Riad 89), Samaka (Ahmed Hassan 72). Tr: Manuel Jose

Jeunesse Kabylie — **0**

Gaouaoui - Zafour•, Herkat, Mohamed Meftah• (Oussalah 81), Rahim Meftah, Djouder, Marek• (Saibi 70), Hamlaoui, Oladikpikpo (Hemani• 46), Yacef, Dabo. Tr: Jean-Yves Chay

---

GROUP A MATCHDAY 3
Obuasi
13-08-2006, 13:45, Maillet SEY

Asante Kotoko — **0**

Alhassan - Ofosu Appiah, Yeboah, Acquah, Addo, Chibsah, Ansah (Yamoah 62) (Owusu Ansah, Toure (Amofa 68), Arhin Duah (Darko 55), Kwame.
Tr: Emmanuel Afranie

Al Ahly — **0**

Al Hadari - Wael Gomaa, Tarek Said, El Shater (Ahmed Sedik 46), Shady Mohamed, Shawky (Mensah 85), Hassan Mostafa, Mohamed Sedik, Ashour, Osama Hosni, Flavio. Tr:: Manuel Jose

---

GROUP A MATCHDAY 3
Algiers
13-08-2006, 21:00, Imiere NGA

Jeunesse Kabylie — **0**

Gaouaoui - Herkat, Rahim Meftah, Hemani•, Djouder, Hamlaoui, Daoud, Douicher (Anwar Boudjakdji 74), Oladikpikpo (Marek 85), Yacef, Dabo (Saibi 79).
Tr: Jean-Yves Chay

CS Sfaxien — **1**
Hamza Younes [76]

Bejaoui - Berguagi, Massaoud, Merdassi, Hammami, Aimen Ben Amor•, Mrabet•, Boujelbene, Shaibu (Younes 64), Frimpong, Nafti (Karim Ben Amor 89).
Tr: Mrad Mahjoub

GROUP A MATCHDAY 4
Cairo
26-08-2006, Kidane ERI

Al Ahly — **4**
Mohamed Aboutrika [8p], Osama Hosni [11], Mohamed Shawky [17], Flavio [20]

Al Hadari - El Shater, Said, Wael Gomaa, Mohamed Sedik, Shady Mohamed, Shawki (Ahmed Sedik 76), Ashour, Aboutrika, Osama Hosni (Moteab 46), Flavio (Hassan Mostafa 61). Tr: Manuel Jose

Asante Kotoko — **0**

Alhassan - Ansah, Yeboah, Murtala Mohamed, Addo, Owusu-Ansah, Chibsah (Ofosu-Appiah 81), Kwame, Arhin-Duah• (Toure 60'), Darko, Adu Amofa.
Tr: Emmanuel Afranie

GROUP A MATCHDAY 4
Sfax
16-08-2006, 18:30, Abdelrahmane SUD

CS Sfaxien — **2**
Abdelkrim Nafti [8], Joetex Frimpong [31]

Jaouachi - Berguagi•, Haj Massaoud, El Abdi, Merdassi, Hammami, Boujelbene, Shaibu (Ziadi 7), Frimpong, Kouassi• (Aimen Ben Amor 82), Nafti. Coach: Tr: Mrad Mahjoub

Jeunesse Kabylie — **0**

Gaouaoui - Zafou, Mohamed Meftah•, Djouder, Daoud (Douicher 46), Rahim Meftah (Saibi 82), Boudjakdji•, Yacef•, Hamlaoui, Oladikpikpo• (Marek 76'), Dabo. Tr: Lyes Izri

---

GROUP A MATCHDAY 5
Obuasi
9-09-2006, 14:00, Shelmani LBY

Asante Kotoko — **2**
Nana Arhin Duah 2 [39] [74]

Nii Bah - Mohamed, Addo, Kwame (Ansah 70), Ofosu-Appiah, Owusu-Ansah, Asante, Yamoah, Arhin-Duah, Adu Amofa• (Darko• 62), Nkrumah (Akoto 77). Tr: Emmanuel Afranie

Jeunesse Kabylie — **1**
Hamza Yacef [3]

Gaouaoui - Zafour•, Daoud, Mohamed Meftah•, Djouder, Rahim Meftah, Boudjakdji (Douicher 66), Hamlaoui, Oladikpikpo (Marek 82), Yacef (Saibi 82), Dabo. Tr: Lyes Izri

---

GROUP A MATCHDAY 5
Cairo
9-09-2006, 19:30, Samba Diouf SEN

Al Ahly — **2**
Mohamed Aboutrika [29], Flavio [39]

Al Hadari - El Shater (Ahmed Sedik 78), Tarek Said, Wael Gomaa, Mohamed Sedik• (Mohamed Abdellah 68), Hassan Mostafa (Ahmed Hassan 76), Shady Mohamed, Shawki, Aboutrika, Osama Hosni, Flavio. Tr: Manuel Jose

CS Sfaxien — **1**
Tarak Ziadi [85]

Jaouachi - Gharbi, Massaoud, El Abdi•, Merdassi•, Berguagi• (Karim Ben Amor), Boujelbene, Shaibu• (Hammami 43), Frimpong, Kouassi (Ziadi 62), Nafti.
Tr: Mrad Mahjoub

GROUP A MATCHDAY 6
Algiers
17-09-2006, Guezzaz MAR

Jeunesse Kabylie — **2**
Cheikh Oumar Dabo 2 [64p] [81]

Gaouaoui - Douicher•, Djouder (Marek 69), Rahim Meftah, Zafour, Hamlaoui, Boudjakdji (Sofiane Herkat 89), Oladikpikpo•, Yacef•, Hemani, Dabo. Tr: Carlos Roberto da Cunha

Al Ahly — **2**
Mohamed Aboutrika 2 [14] [89p]

Al Hadari - El Shater (Mohamed Abdellah 76), Tarek Said (Samaka 83), Shady Mohamed•, Wael Gomaa, Mohamed Sedik•, Hassan Mostafa, Ashour (Wael Riad 76), Aboutrika•, Flavio•. Tr: Manuel Jose

---

GROUP A MATCHDAY 6
Sfax
17-09-2006, 21:00, Sowe GAM

CS Sfaxien — **2**
Joetex Frimpong [7], Chadi Hammami [84]

Bejaoui - Garbi (Aimen Ben Amor 64), Mrabet•, El Abdi, Massaoud, Karim Ben Amor, Hammami, Boujelbene, Nafti (Kadri 73), Ziadi•, Frimpong (Kouassi 74). Tr: Mrad Mahjoub

Asante Kotoko — **1**
Murtala Mohamed [44]

Nii Bah - Yeboah, Murtala Mohamed, Thompson, Ofosu-Appiah, Addo•, Owusu-Ansah•, Yamoah (Adu Amofa 88), Arhin-Duah, Nkrumah (Akoto 77), Toure (Ansah 83). Tr: Emmanuel Afranie

GROUP B

		Pl	W	D	L	F	A	Pts	CIV	RSA	NGA	GHA
ASEC Abidjan	CIV	6	3	3	0	1	1	12		4-0	3-3	3-0
Orlando Pirates	RSA	6	2	3	1	6	6	9	1-1		1-0	0-0
Enyimba	NGA	6	2	2	2	5	5	8	0-0	1-1		1-0
Hearts of Oak	GHA	6	0	2	4	0	7	2	0-0	0-1	0-2	

GROUP B MATCHDAY 1
Obuasi
16-07-2006, 15:00, Evehe CMR
Hearts of Oak 0

Quartey - Amankwah Mireku, Coleman, Boafo, Quaye, Gawu, Senyo, Ato Afedzie (Andoh 80), Annan, Louis, Dong Bortey (Bossman 42). Tr: Francis Oti-Akenten

Enyimba 2
Ekene Emigo [14], Boafo OG [82]
Aiyenugba - Okpara, Odita, Omolade, Baleria●, Mangut (Ledor 61), Adegoke, Johnson, Emigo, Amadi (Sakibu, 46), Tyavkase (Ezenwa● 79). Tr: Alphonsus Dike

---

GROUP B MATCHDAY 1
Johannesburg
18-07-2006, 18:00, Hicuburundi BDI
Orlando Pirates 1
Blaise Mbele [44]
Francis Chansa - Thwala, Malinga, Lekgwathi, Mabe, Twala, Mathe, Isaac Chansa, Okonkwo, Arendse, Leremi (Makhanya 63), Mbele (Manenzhe 79). Tr: Tebeho Moloi

ASEC Mimosas 1
Emmanuel Umoh [89]
Kante - Adenon, Akes Goore●, Doumbia, Soro, Kocou, Kone (Diomande 82), Maglorie Kouame, Ya Konan, Modibo Diarra (Konan 62), Yao Kouassi (Umoh 79). Tr: Patrick Liewig

---

GROUP B MATCHDAY 2
Aba
30-07-2006, 14:00, Louzaya CGO
Enyimba 1
Chidozie Johnson [66]
Aiyenugba - Okpara, Odita, Baleria, Omolade (76), Adegoke, Mbwas Mangut (Ledor 55), Johnson, Emigo, Amadi (Sakibu 42), Akueme. Tr: Alphonsus Dike

Orlando Pirates 1
Lucky Lekgwathi [33]
Francis Chansa● - Mabe, Lekgwathi, Chabalala, Malinga, Sibeko● (Leremi 64), Mathe (Mokoena 83), Okonkwo, Isaac Chansa, Makhanya●, Arendse (Mbele 55). Tr: Milutin Sredojevic

---

GROUP B MATCHDAY 2
Abidjan
30-07-2006, 16:00, El Arjoun MAR
ASEC Mimosas 3
Didier Ya Konan 2 [42] [64p], Emmanuel Kone [70]
Kabore● - Ndri Alli, Akes Goore, Doumbia, Kocou (Ali Diarra 65'), Ya Konan (Umoh 86), Kouame, Kone, Konan (Die 76'), Yao Kouassi. Tr: Patrick Liewig

Hearts of Oak 0

Quartey - Vardis, Boafo, Ofei●, Annan, Donkor, Bossman (Tekyi Mensah 41), Louis (Andoh 74), Nyarko, Gawu, Gansah (Senyo, 59). Tr: Francis Oti-Akenten

---

GROUP B MATCHDAY 3
Johannesburg
12-08-2006, 18:00, Ssegonga UGA
Orlando Pirates 0

Francis Chansa - Mabe (Vilakazi 62), Chabalala, Malinga, Seema (Sibeko 72), Lekgwathi, Okonkwo, Isaac Chansa, Leremi (Pule 77), Mbele, Arendse. Tr: Milutin Sredojevic

Hearts of Oak 0

Sanni - Boafo (Coleman● 46), Amankwah Mireku, Vardis, Tekyi Mensah (Afedzi 46): Nyarko●, Annan, Donkor●, Senyo, Gawu, Louis (Bossman 78). Tr: Atto Hammond

---

GROUP B MATCHDAY 3
Abidjan
13-08-2006, 16:00, Lwanja MWI
ASEC Mimosas 3
Didier Ya Konan [66], Bakary Soro [68], Emmanuel Umoh [87]
Kabore - Ndri Alli, Adenon, Akes Goore, Soro, Ali Diarra, Ya Konan (Kocou 85), Maglorie Kouame, Kone●, Ouedraogo (Yao 46), Konan (Umoh● 65). Tr: Patrick Liewig

Enyimba 0

Aiyenugba - Okpara, Odita●, Ogar, Adegoke, Mangut (Agbo 73), Johnson, Olomu, Emigo (Elvis 57), Akueme (Sakibu 41), Ezenwa. Tr: Alphonsus Dike

---

GROUP B MATCHDAY 4
Aba
27-08-2007, 15:00, Abd El Fatah EGY
Enyimba 0

Aiyenugba - Odita, Elvis, Omolade●, Ogar, Adegoke (Gwar 77), Johnson (Ledor 48), Olomu, Emigo, Sakibu, Anjembe (Agbo 53). Tr: Alphonsus Dike

ASEC Mimosas 0

Kabore - Ndri Alli, Adenon, Akes Goore, Soro●, Kocou (Ali Diarra 61), Ya Konan, Maglorie Kouame●, Yao Kouassi●, Kone●, Umoh (Konan 61). Tr: Patrick Liewig

---

GROUP B MATCHDAY 4
Obuasi
27-08-2006, 16:30, Daami TUN
Hearts of Oak 0

Saani - Vardis, Quaye, Mireku Amankwah, Coleman, Ato Afedzie (Tagoe 46), Annan, Donkor, Louis (Bawa 81), Andoh (Nii Larbi 61), Gawu. Tr: Atto Hammond

Orlando Pirates 1
Blaise Mbele [57]
Francis Chansa - Mabe, Seema●, Malinga (Arendse 25), Chabalala, Lekgwathi, Vilakazi, Leremi (Mokoena● 63), Makhanya (Pule 58), Okonkwo●, Mbele. Tr: Milutin Sredojevic

---

GROUP B MATCHDAY 5
Abidjan
10-09-2006, 13:30, Benouza ALG
ASEC Mimosas 4
Fone Die 2 [43] [53], Dacosta Akes Goore [58], Koffi Konan [89]
Mohamed Kabore - Ndri Alli, Adenon, Akes Goore, Soro, Kocou, Maglorie Kouame, Diomande, Yao (Modibo Diarra 19), Umoh (Fofana 39), Die (Konan 76). Coach: Patrick Liewig

Orlando Pirates 0

Francis Chansa - Thwala, Seema, Malinga, Chabalala●, Lekgwathi, Vilakazi, Leremi (Mokoena 55), Isaac Chansa●, Makhanya● (Pule 55●61), Mbele (Sibeko 73). Tr: Milutin Sredojevic

---

GROUP B MATCHDAY 5
Aba
10-09-2006, 14:00, Pare BFA
Enyimba 1
Louis Otawa [89]
Aiyenugba - Odita●, Elvis, Ogar, Adegoke, Ledor (Olumu 58), Emigo, Otanwa, Mba, Akueme (Gwar 62), Agbo (Amadi 75). Tr: Alphonsus Dike

Hearts of Oak 0

Abubakari● - Vardis, Muntari, Kofi Egyiri, Coleman, Mireku Amankwah●, Ato Afedzie● (Nyarko 65), Tekyi ensah (Bossman 22), Ofei (Nii Larbi (Bawu 80'), Gawu. Tr: Mitko Kostadinov Dobrev

---

GROUP B MATCHDAY 6
Obuasi
16-09-2006
Hearts of Oak 0

Sulemana Abubakari - Coleman, Egyiri, Muntari (Louis 35), Quaye, Efei, Annan, Bossman, Afedzi● (Nyarko 78), Gawu, Nii Larbi (Bawa 57). Tr: Mitko Kostadinov Dobrev

ASEC Abidjan 0

Kabore - Youan Bi, Ndri Alli, Adenon●, Ali Diarra, Ya Konan, Kone, Kocou, Die (Donan 59'), Diomande (Fofana 74'), Coulibaly. Tr: Patrick Liewig

---

GROUP B MATCHDAY 6
Johannesburg
16-09-2006, 18:00, Bisingu COD
Orlando Pirates 1
Onyekachi Okonkwo [30]
Phadi - Thwala, Malinga, Chabalala, Lekgwathi, Seema, Vilakazi (Manenzhe 89), Okonkwo, Makhanya (Leremi 78), Mokoena, Mbele● (Sibeko 89). Tr: Milutin Sredojevic

Enyimba 0

Aiyenugba - Adegoke, Okammor●, Elvis, Ogar, Omolade (Akueme 49), Otanwa● (Gwar 71), Mba, Emigo, Olomu, Agbo (Ledor 81). Tr: Alphonsus Dike

SEMI-FINALS

Cairo
1-10-2006, 21:30, Pare BFA
Al Ahly   **2**
Mohamed Aboutrika [25], Emad Moteab [38]
Al Hadari - El Shater (Ahmed Sedik 76), Galal, Shady Mohamed, Wael Gomaa•, Shawky•, Hossam Ashour, Tarek Said, Aboutrika, Moteab, Osama Hosni (Samaka 17) (Ahmed Hassan 81). Tr: Manuel Jose
ASEC Mimosas   **0**

Kabore - Ndri Alli, Adenon, Akes Goore, Soro, Kocou•, Maglorie Kouame• (Ali Diarra 50), Yao, Ya Konan, Die (Diomande 59), Kone (Fofana 82). Tr: Patrick Liewig

Houphouet-Boigny, Abidjan
15-10-2006, 17:30, Haimoudi ALG
ASEC Mimosas   **2**
Didier Ya Konan 2 [58] [72]
Kabore - Ndri Alli, Adenon, Akes Goore, Soro, Kocou (Umoh 83), Maglorie Kouame, Yao Kouassi (Fofana 60), Ya Konan, Die, Kone (Kouadio 79). Tr: Patrick Liewig
Al Ahly   **1**
Flavio [38]
Al Hadari - El Shater (Mensah 75), Mohamed Sedik, Shady Mohamed, Wael Gomaa, Shawky, Ashour, Tarek Said, Aboutrika (Wael Riad 87), Moteab, Flavio (Barakat 63). Tr: Manuel Jose

Johannesburg
30-09-2006, 18:00, Lwanja MWI
Orlando Pirates   **0**

Phadi - Thwala, Malinga, Chabalala, Lekgwathi•, Sibeko, Vilakazi (Manenzhe 75), Okonkwo, Leremi, Mokoena (Pule 56), Mbele. Tr: Milutin Sredojevic

CS Sfaxien   **0**

Jaouachi - Garbi, Mrabet•, El Abdi•, Massaoud, Karim Ben Amor, Hammami, Boujelbene, Nafti (Kadri 77), Kouassi•, Frimpong• (Younes 80). Tr: Mrad Mahjoub

Stade Taïeb-Mhiri, Sfax
14-10-2006, 20:30, Diatta SEN
CS Sfaxien   **1**
Tarak Ziadi [40]
Jaouachi - Garbi, Mrabet, El Abdi, Massaoud, Merdassi (Mechergui 82), Boujelbene, Nafti, Ziadi (Kadri 80), Kouassi (Hammami 40), Frimpong. Tr: Mrad Mahjoub
Orlando Pirates   **0**

Phad - Thwala, Malinga, Chabalala, Lekgwathi, Seema, Sibeko•, Vilakazi (Mbele 61), Okonkwo• (Pule 51), Leremi• (Mokoena• 77), Manenzhe. Tr: Milutin Sredojevic

---

CAF CHAMPIONS LEAGUE FINAL 1ST LEG
International Stadium, Cairo
19-10-2006, 19:30, Sowe GAM

| AL AHLY | 1 | 1 | CS SFAXIEN |

Mohamed Aboutrika [27]   Joetex Frimpong [53]

	Al Ahly				CS Sfaxien	
1	Essam AL HADARI				Ahmed JAOUACHI	1
20	Mohamed SEDIK				Fateh GARBI	2
26	Wael GOMAA				Amir Haj MASSAOUD	23
7	Shady MOHAMED				Wissem EL ABDI	15
25	Hossam ASHOUR				Issam MERDASSI	24
17	Mohamed SHAWKY		89		Anis BOUJELBENE	17
29	Ahmed QANAWI	70			Haitham MRABET	3
22	Mohamed ABOUTRIKA				Chadi HAMMAMI	13
8	Mohamed BARAKAT	81			Abdelkrim NAFTI	10
23	FLAVIO		75		Tarak ZIADI	25
9	Emad MOTEAB	80	90		Joetex FRIMPONG	7
	Tr: MANUEL Jose				Tr: MAJHOUBI Mrab	
	Substitutes				Substitutes	
2	Islam EL SHATER	70	90		Chaker BERGUAGI	4
10	Wael RIAD	80	75		Blaise KOUASSI	9
24	Ahmed HASSAN	81	89		Bechir MECHREGUI	16

CAF CHAMPIONS LEAGUE FINAL 2ND LEG
Stade 7 Novembre, Rades, Tunis
11-11-2006, 17:00,

| CS SFAXIEN | 0 | 1 | AL AHLY |

                          Mohamed Aboutrika [92+]

	CS Sfaxien				Al Ahly	
1	Ahmed JAOUACHI				Essam AL HADARI	1
2	Fateh GARBI		70		Mohamed SEDIK	20
23	Amir Haj MASSAOUD		65		Mohamed ABDELLAH	21
16	Bechir MECHREGUI				Wael GOMAA	26
24	Issam MERDASSI				Shady MOHAMED	7
17	Anis BOUJELBENE				Hossam ASHOUR	25
3	Haitham MRABET				Ahmed QANAWI	29
13	Chadi HAMMAMI	89			Hassan MOSTAFA	14
10	Abdelkrim NAFTI		43		Akwetey MENSAH	19
25	Tarak ZIADI	80			Mohamed ABOUTRIKA	22
7	Joetex FRIMPONG				FLAVIO	23
	Tr: MAJHOUBI Mrab				Tr: MANUEL Jose	
	Substitutes				Substitutes	
9	Blaise KOUASSI	89	65		Islam EL SHATER	2
21	Hamza Younes	80	43		Emad MOTEAB	9
			70		Wael RIAD	10

AL AHLY

Goalkeepers
1	Essam AL HADARI	EGY
27	Amir ABDELHAMID	EGY
28	Nader EL SAYED	EGY

Defenders
2	Islam EL SHATER	EGY
3	Mohamed ADELWAHAB	EGY
4	Emad AL NAHHAS	EGY
5	Ahmed EL SAYED	EGY
6	Ahmed SEDIK	EGY
13	Amr EL HALAWANI	EGY
16	Amro SAMAKA	EGY
19	Akwety MENSAH	GHA
20	Mohamed SEDIK	EGY
26	Wael GOMAA	EGY
29	Ahmed SHADID	EGY
30	Rami ADEL	EGY

Midfielders
7	Shady MOHAMED	EGY
8	Mohamed BARAKAT	EGY
10	Wael RIAD	EGY
11	Haitham EL FAZANI	EGY
12	Tarek SAID	EGY
14	Hassan MOSTAFA	EGY
15	Abdellah ABDELHAMID	EGY
17	Mohamed SHAWKY	EGY
18	Osama HOSNI	EGY
21	Mohamed ABDELLAH	EGY
22	Mohamed ABOUTRIKA	EGY
24	Ahmed HASSAN	EGY
25	Hossam ASHOUR	EGY

Forwards
9	Emad MOTEAB	EGY
23	FLAVIO	ANG

ASANTE KOTOKO

Goalkeepers
1	Habib MOHAMMED	GHA
16	Mohamed ALHASSAN	GHA
23	Eric Nii BAAH	GHA

Defenders
2	Aziz ANSAH	GHA
3	Godfred YEBOAH	GHA
4	Kenneth ABABIO	GHA
5	Shilla ILLIASU	GHA
8	Edmund OWUSU-ANSAH	GHA
14	Osei Kwame JUNIOR	GHA
19	Frank OSEI	GHA
26	Murtala MOHAMED	GHA

Midfielders
6	Kobina DODZIE	GHA
7	Nana ARHIN-DUAH	GHA
10	Osei AKOTO	GHA
12	Douglas NKRUMAH	GHA
13	Imbola Sandje BETAH	GHA
17	Yusif CHIBSAH	GHA
18	John KUDJOE	GHA
20	Samuel Adjei ADDO	GHA
21	Gabriel Issah AHMED	GHA
22	Daniel ACQUAH	GHA
24	Kwame Obeng DARKO	GHA
27	Mark Adu AMOFA	GHA
28	Michael ASANTE	GHA
30	Michael OFOSU-APPIAH	GHA

Forwards
9	Oga Willie THOMPSON	GHA
15	Ahmed TOURE	GHA
25	Tawfik Alolo ALHASSAN	GHA
29	Charles TAYLOR	GHA

ASEC MIMOSAS

Goalkeepers
1	Guyan Joe KANTE	CIV
16	Mohamed KABORE	BFA
21	Sylvain KOMENAN	CIV

Defenders
2	Ndri ALLI	CIV
3	Abdou ADENON	CIV
4	Adou Peter TAYORO	CIV
5	Bakary SORO	CIV
6	Bi Gaman YOUAN	CIV
12	Dacosta Akes GOORE	CIV
13	Arthur KOCOU	CIV
15	Mamadou DOUMBIA	CIV
27	Tiecoura COULIBALY	CIV

Midfielders
7	Ali DIARRA	CIV
8	Didier YA KONAN	CIV
10	Emmanuel KONE	CIV
11	LEANDRO	CIV
14	Désiré KOUAME	CIV
18	Modibo DIARRA	CIV
20	Aboubacar DIOMANDE	CIV
22	Abdramane DIABY	CIV
24	Anlioun TOURE	CIV
25	Abdul OUEDRAOGO	CIV
29	Patrick NDOUA	CIV
30	Pacome KOUADIO	CIV

Forwards
9	Emmanuel UMOH	NGA
17	Foneye DIE	CIV
19	Beko FOFANA	CIV
23	Serge KOUADIO	CIV
26	Koffi KONAN	CIV
28	Martial Yao KOUASSI	CIV

ENYIMBA

Goalkeepers
1	Ambrose VANZEKIN	NGA
17	Dele AIYENUGBA	NGA
18	John GAADI	NGA

Defenders
2	Mutiu ADEGOKE	NGA
3	Ilga OKPARA	NGA
4	Okey ODITA	NGA
5	Francis OKAMMOR	NGA
20	Ekene EMIGO	NGA
23	Benedict ATULE	NGA
24	Odey OGAR	NGA
25	Baleria ABUBAKAR	NGA
29	Oliver AGBO	NGA

Midfielders
6	Charles OMOKARO	NGA
7	Louis OTAWA	NGA
8	Sam LEDOR	NGA
10	Sunday MBA	NGA
11	Atanda SAKIBU	NGA
12	Ajibade OMOLADE	NGA
14	Chukwuma EZIAGWU	NGA
15	Foster AMADI	NGA
19	Emeka AKUEME	NGA
21	Kingsley ELVIS	NGA
22	Chidozie JOHNSON	NGA
26	Prince Wilson OLOMU	NGA
28	Mbwas MANGUT	NGA
30	Simi GWAR	NGA

Forwards
9	Timothy ANJEMBE	NGA
13	Nnaemeka ONOVO	NGA
16	David TYAVKASE	NGA
27	Ekene EZENWA	NGA

HEARTS OF OAK

Goalkeepers
1	Collins ADDO	GHA
22	Suleiman ABUBAKARI	GHA
30	Laud QUARTEY	GHA

Defenders
2	Charles VARDIS	GHA
4	Daniel QUAYE	GHA
5	Saliu MUNTARI	GHA
6	Yaw Mireku AMANKWA	GHA
13	Kwabena BOAFO	GHA
17	Michael DONKOR	GHA
24	Stephen OFEI	GHA
24	Nana Kofi EGYIRI	GHA
28	Mohamed Saani	GHA

Midfielders
3	Francis BOSSMAN	GHA
7	Mohamed BAWU	GHA
8	Anthony ANNAN	GHA
10	Eric GAWU	GHA
12	Eric NYARKO	GHA
14	Joe LOUIS	GHA
15	Abraham ANNAN	GHA
16	Alfred Nii LARBI	GHA
19	Joseph TAGOE	GHA
20	Joseph Tekyi MENSAH	GHA
21	Robert ARYEE	GHA
23	Stanley Ato AFEDZIE	GHA
25	Daniel COLEMAN	GHA
29	Obed ANSAH	GHA

Forwards
9	Moses ANDOH	GHA
11	Bernard Dong BORTEY	GHA
26	Ekow GANSAH	GHA
27	Ruben SENYO	GHA

JS KABYLIE

Goalkeepers
1	Lounes GAOUAOUI	ALG
12	Nabil MAZARI	ALG
13	Mourad BERREFANE	ALG

Defenders
2	Slimane RAHO	ALG
3	Brahim ZAFOUR	ALG
4	Kamel HABRI	ALG
5	Sofiane HERKAT	ALG
6	Nassim HAMLAOUI	ALG
15	Samir ZAZOU	ALG
17	Omar DAOUD	ALG
19	Samir DJOUDER	ALG
20	Rahim MEFTAH	ALG
21	Kamel MAREK	ALG
22	Nourdine DRIOUECHE	ALG
23	Mohamed BOUDJAKDJI	ALG
30	Mohamed MEFTAH	ALG

Midfielders
8	Lounes BENDAHMANE	ALG
10	Moh. BENHADJ-DJILLALI	ALG
14	Boubakeur ATHMANI	ALG
18	Lamara DOUICHER	ALG
24	Fahem OUSLATI	ALG
25	Ouslati FAHEM	ALG
26	Faouzi CHAOUCH	ALG
27	Wassiou OLADIKPIKPO	ALG
29	Cheikh Oumar DABO	ALG

Forwards
7	Hamza YACEF	ALG
9	Khaled SAIBI	ALG
11	Nabil HEMANI	ALG
16	Abdelhamid BERGUIGA	ALG
24	Nassim OUSSALAH	ALG

ORLANDO PIRATES

Goalkeepers
1	Thabang STEMMER	RSA
11	Robert Senzo MEYIWA	RSA
21	Francis CHANSA	COD
29	Avril PHADI	RSA

Defenders
2	Kelebogile MABE	RSA
3	Themba MNGUNI	RSA
4	Thabang MOLEFE	RSA
8	Edward MALINGA	RSA
14	Lucky LEKGWATHI	RSA
16	Lucas THWALA	RSA
19	Innocent MDLEDLE	RSA
25	Tonic CHABALALA	RSA
28	Lehlohonolo SEEMA	LES

Midfielders
7	Gift LEREMI	RSA
8	Isaac CHANSA	ZAM
10	Benedict VILAKAZI	RSA
12	Solomon MATHE	RSA
13	Onyekachi OKONKWO	NGA
15	Perry MUTAPA	RSA
17	Daniel TSHABALALA	RSA
20	Edelbert DINHA	ZIM
24	Joseph MAKHANYA	RSA
26	Cavaan SIBEKO	RSA
27	Jabu MAHLANGU	RSA

Forwards
6	Blaise Lelo MBELE	COD
9	Davies Mwape	ZAM
18	Tyren ARENDSE	RSA
22	Phumudzo MANENZHE	RSA
23	Lebohang MOKOENA	RSA

CS SFAXIEN

Goalkeepers
1	Ahmed JAOUACHI	TUN
16	Hassen BEJAOUI	TUN
27	Ali EL KALAI	TUN
30	Walid BEN HASSAN	TUN

Defenders
2	Fateh GARBI	TUN
5	Aimen BEN AMOR	TUN
6	Bechir MECHREGUI	TUN
15	Wissem EL ABDI	TUN
18	Karim BEN AMAR	TUN
23	Amir Haj MASSAOUD	TUN
24	Issam MERDASSI	TUN
29	Wajih SGHAIER	TUN

Midfielders
3	Haitham MRABET	TUN
4	Chaker BERGUAGI	TUN
8	Mohamed ABIDI	TUN
10	Abdelkrim NAFTI	TUN
11	GIVALDO	TUN
12	Ikpotor KINGS	NGA
13	Chadi HAMMAMI	TUN
17	Anis BOUJELBENE	TUN
22	ARMANDO	TUN
26	Jamel KCHAREM	TUN
28	Ishola SHAIBU	NGA

Forwards
7	Joetex FRIMPONG	GHA
9	Blaise KOUASSI	CIV
14	Hamza SALLEMI	TUN
19	Mohamed KADRI	TUN
20	Zoubeir ESSAFI	TUN
21	Hamza YOUNES	TUN
25	Tarek ZIADI	TUN

MTN CAF CHAMPIONS LEAGUE 2007

First Round

Etoile du Sahel	TUN	Bye
Sporting da Praia	CPV	0 ‡
Fello Star Labé *	GUI	0 ‡
APR FC	RWA	2 2
St Eloi Lupopo *	COD	1 0
ASC Diaraf Dakar *	SEN	1 0
Marantha Fiokpo	TOG	0 3
TP Mazembe *	COD	3 4
Police XI	BOT	0 2
ANSE Réunion	SEY	0 0
Adema Antananarivo *	MAD	0 3
AshantiGold	GHA	1 1
Renacimiento *	EQG	0 0
FAR Rabat	MAR	Bye
Al Ittihad Tripoli *	LBY	3 1
Mogas 90	BEN	0 0
USM Alger *	ALG	3 0
AS FNIS Niamey	NIG	1 2
St George	ETH	w-o
Escom United	MWI	
Canon Yaoundé *	CMR	1 0
Etoile du Congo	CGO	0 2
Cotonsport Garoua *	CMR	3 0
URA Kampala	UGA	0 0
Mighty Barolle	LBR	1 1
Séwé Sport *	CIV	3 0
Mangasport	GAB	1 1
Primeiro de Agosto *	ANG	0 1
Os Balantas	GNB	1 1
Jeunesse Kabylie *	ALG	3 2
Al Ahly	EGY	Bye
Pamplemousse SC	MRI	0 1 8p
Highlanders *	ZIM	1 0 9p
Desportivo Maputo	MOZ	w-o
St Pierroise	REU	
Royal Leopards	SWZ	2 0
Mamelodi Sundowns *	RSA	4 2
Wydad Casablanca *	MAR	4 1
ASC Mauritel	MTN	0 2
AS Douanes Dakar ‡	SEN	2 2
Stade Malien *	MLI	1 0
FC Kallon	SLE	0 1
Ocean Boys *	NGA	0 0
ASEC Mimosas	CIV	Bye
Espérance Tunis *	TUN	4 2
Rennaisance	CHA	0 1
Likhopo Maseru *	LES	0 0
Zanaco	ZAM	0 1
Petro Atlético *	ANG	1 1
Civics	NAM	0 1
AJSM Mutsamudu	COM	1
Young Africans *	TAN	5
Nasarawa United	NGA	1 2
ASFA/Yennenga *	BFA	1 0
Asante Kotoko *	GHA	1 0 2p
Gambia Ports Authority	GAM	0 1 4p
Zamalek *	EGY	4 1
Vital'O	BDI	1 0
Polisi SC	ZAN	0 0
Al Hilal Omdurman *	SUD	4 2

Second Round

Etoile du Sahel	1	4
Fello Star Labé *	0	1
APR FC * ‡	2	0
Marantha Fiokpo	0	2
TP Mazembe	2	4
Adema Antananarivo *	2	1
AshantiGold *	2 0	6p
FAR RAbat	0 2	7p
Al Ittihad Tripoli *	4	1
AS FNIS Niamey	1	0
St George *	1	0
Etoile du Congo	0	2
Cotonsport Garoua	0	4
Séwé Sport *	1	0
Mangasport *	3	0
Jeunese Kabylie	1	3
Al Ahly	0	2
Highlanders *	0	0
Desportivo Maputo *	1	0
Mamelodi Sundowns	1	2
Wydad Casablanca	0	3
Stade Malien *	0	1
FC Kallon *	0	1
ASEC Mimosas	1	2
Espérance Tunis *	2	4
Zanaco	0	1
Petro Atlético	0	2
Young Africans *	3	0
Nasarawa United *	3	1
Gambia Ports Authority	0	2
Zamalek	0	2
Al Hilal Omdurman *	2	2

Third Round

Etoile du Sahel	0	3
Marantha Fiokpo *	0	0
TP Mazembe *	1	0
FAR Rabat	0	2
Al Ittihad Tripoli	1	2
Etoile du Congo *	3	0
Cotonsport Garoua *	1	0
Jeunesse Kabylie	0	2
Al Ahly	2	2
Mamelodi Sundowns *	2	0
Wydad Casablanca	0	0
ASEC Mimosas *	2	0
Espérance Tunis *	3	0
Young Africans	0	0
Nasarawa United *	3 0	2p
Al Hilal Omdurman	0 3	3p

‡ Sporting, Douanes & APR disqualified

* Home team in the first leg • Losing teams in the second round enter the Confederation Cup

CAF CHAMPIONS LEAGUE 2007

MTN CAF CHAMPIONS LEAGUE 2007

Champions League Stage   Semi-finals   Final

Group A		Pts	TUN	LBY	ALG	MAR
Etoile du Sahel	TUN	10		0-0	3-0	
Al Ittihad Tripoli	LBY	7			1-0	2-0
Jeunesse Kabylie	ALG	3	0-2			2-0
FAR Rabat	MAR	3	0-1	1-0		

Group B		Pts	EGY	SUD	CIV	TUN
Al Ahly	EGY	9		2-0		3-0
Al Hilal Omdurman	SUD	6			2-1	2-0
ASEC Mimosas	CIV	4	0-1	1-0		
Espérance Tunis	TUN	4	1-0		0-0	

Remaining two rounds in the groups to be played 17-19/08/2007 and 31/08-2/09/2007 • Semi-finals to be played on 21-23/09/2007 and 5-7/10/2007 • Final to be played on 26-28/10/2007 and 9-11/11/2007

FIRST ROUND

Conakry, 28-01-2007, Yarsiah LBR
Fello Stars Labe **0**
Sporting da Praia **0**

Kinshasa, 27-01-2007, Abimni CMR
St Eloi Lupopo **1** Bayiya [62]
APR FC **2** Twite [41], Bwalya [76]

Kigali, 10-02-2007, Niyongabo BDI
APR FC **2** Kizito [10], Kayiizi [60]
St Eloi Lupopo **0**

Dakar, 27-01-2007, Bourge MTN
ASC Diaraf Dakar **1** Thioune [44]
Marantha Fiokpo **0**

Lomé, 11-02-2007, Odeniran NGA
Marantha Fiokpo **3** Assiongbon [11p], Sapoul [58], Adzima [71]
ASC Diaraf Dakar **0**

Kinshasa, 28-01-2007, Roopnah MRI
TP Mazembe **3** Mputu 3 [17 68 71]
Police XI **0**

Gaborone, 10-02-2007
Police XI **2** Letsholathebe, Kaelo
TP Mazembe **4** Ngandu, Mputu 2, Nkulukuta

Antananarivo, 28-01-2007, Roopnah MRI
AS Adema **0**
ANSE Réunion **0**

Victoria, 10-02-2007, Mhlapo RSA
ANSE Réunion **0**
AS Adema **3** Randriamalala [25], Kennedy [46], Niasexe [74]

Malabo, 28-01-2007, Wam CMR
Renacimiento **0**
AshantiGold **1** Quartey [53]

Obuasi, 11-02-2007, Sanusie SLE
AshantiGold **1** Arthur [29]
Renacimiento **0**

Tripoli, 27-01-2007, Rouaissi MAR
Al Ittihad Tripoli **3** Koulibaly [44], Shibani 2 [52 75]
Mogas 90 **0**

Cotonou, 11-02-2007, Djaoupe TOG
Mogas 90 **0**
Al Ittihad Tripoli **1** Reweni [89]

Algiers, 27-01-2007, Saadallah TUN
USM Alger   3 Mintou Doucoure 3 [6 57], Dziri [83]
AS FNIS Niamey 1 Hamidou Djibu [89]

Niamey, 11-02-2007, Dipama BFA
AS FNIS Niamey 2 Hamidou Djibo 2 [60p 79]
USM Alger   0

Yaoundé, 28-01-2007
Canon Yaoundé   1 Ngambe [32]
Etoile du Congo 0

Brazzaville, 11-02-2007, Ndume GAB
Etoile du Congo 2 Lebally 2 [27 31]
Canon Yaoundé   0

Garoua, 28-01-2007
Cotonsport   3 Hamadama [14], Litsingui [55p], Nimely [70]
URA Kampala 0

Kampala, 11-02-2007
URA Kampala 0
Cotonsport   0

Abidjan, 28-01-2007, Jallow GAM
Séwé Sport   3 Siaka [17], Jimmy Jerry [75], Dioumacy [78]
Mighty Barolle 1 Ben Martin [2]

Monrovia, 11-02-2007, Fall SEN
Mighty Barolle 1 Amagashi [7]
Séwé Sport   0

Luanda, 28-01-2007, Buenkadila COD
Primeiro Agosto 0
Mangasport   1 Lolo [18]

Moanda, 11-02-2007, Ojo-Oba NGA
Mangasport   1
Primeiro Agosto 1 Milanzi [7]

Algiers, 27-01-2007, Younes EGY
Jeunesse Kabylie 3 Oussalah [10], Saibi 2 [41 51]
Os Balantas   1 Emerson [71]

Bissau, 11-02-2007, Kaba GUI
Os Balantas   1 Pinto [50]
Jeunesse Kabylie 2 Dabo 2 [4 81]

Bulawayo, 28-01-2007, Massango MOZ
Highlanders   1 Tarumbwa [40]
Pamplemousse   0

Curepipe, 11-02-2007
Pamplemousse   1 Sophie [57]
Highlanders   0 Highlanders W 9-8p

Pretoria, 27-01-2007, Mufeti NAM
M'lodi Sundowns 4 Jose Torrealba 3 [38 53 79], Moriri [75]
Royal Leopards   2 Mmaba [44], Dlamini [89]

Somholo, 11-02-2007
Royal Leopards   0
M'lodi Sundowns 2 Chabangu [63], Peter Ndlovu [84]

Casablanca, 28-01-2007
WAC Casablanca 4 Menkari [47], Ajraoui [67], Rafik 2 [75 80]
ASC Mauritel   0

Nouakchott, 10-02-2007, Traore MLI
ASC Mauritel   2 Cheikh Sao [41], Babakar Sy [88]
WAC Casablanca 1 Rafik [72]

Bamako, 28-01-2007
Stade Malien   1 Sogoba [20]
Douanes Dakar   2 Diene 2 [42 44]

Dakar, 10-02-2007, Hama NIG
Douanes Dakar   2 Diene 2 [16 39]
Stade Malien   0

Yenagoa, 28-01-2007, Cabi GNB
Ocean Boys   0
FC Kallon   0

Freetown, 10-02-2007, Agbovi GHA
FC Kallon   1 Foday [49]
Ocean Boys   0

Tunis, 27-01-2007, El Achiri MAR
Espérance Tunis 4 Moyin Chaabani [7], Ltifi 3 [16 22 47]
Rennaisance   0

N'Djamena, 10-02-2007
Rennaisance   1 Ahmed Brahim [82]
Espérance Tunis 2 Aboucherouane 2 [23 75]

Maseru, 28-01-2007, Dlamini SWZ
Likhopo Maseru 0
Zanaco   0

Lusaka, 11-02-2007
Zanaco   1 Kalengo [48]
Likhopo Maseru 0

Luanda, 27-01-2007, Poungui CGO
Petro Atlético 1 Manucho [23]
Civics   0

Windhoek, 10-02-2007, Sikazwe ZAM
Civics   1 Brendell [89]
Petro Atlético 1 Manucho [12]

Dar es Salaam, 27-01-2007, Kapanga MWI
Young Africans 5 Kassim [30], Mwaikimba [37], Malulid [43],
AJSM Mutsamudu 1 Houmad [47]   Mwalala 2 [54 62]

Ouagadougou, 27-01-2007, Tokpeme BEN
ASFA/Yennenga   1 Ismael Alhassane [80p]
Nasarawa United 1 Nasiru Salisu [41]

Lafia, 11-02-2007, Seck SEN
Nasarawa United 2 Femi Thomas [44p], Shehu Dauda [70]
ASFA/Yennenga   0

Obuasi, 3-02-2007
Asante Kotoko   1 Acquah p
Ports Authority 0

Banjul, 11-02-2007
Ports Authority 1 Camara [75]
Asante Kotoko   0 Ports W 4-2p

Cairo, 28-01-2007, Abdalla LBY
Zamalek   4 Amr Zaki [4], Hazem Imam [42], Tarek El Sayed [63],
Vital'O   1 Ndizeye [80]   Mostafa Gafar [73]

Bujumbura, 10-02-2007, Mwandike TAN
Vital'O   0
Zamalek   1 Hazem Imam [19]

Khartoum, 28-01-2007, Girma ETH
Al Hilal 4
Polisi   0

Zanzibar, 10-02-2007, Batte UGA
Polisi   0
Al Hilal 2 Yousef Allaedin [36], Mohamed Tahir [72]

SECOND ROUND

Conakry, 11-03-2007, Mendy GAM
Fello Star Labé 0
Etoile du Sahel 1 Ja [44]

Sousse, 17-03-2007, Bichari ALG
Etoile du Sahel 4 Amine Chermiti 2 [4 84], OG [60], Soltani [89]
Fello Star Labé 1 Lamine Camara [77]

Kigali, 3-03-2007, Ould Lemghambodj MTN
APR FC   2 Abbas Rassou [55], Joseph Bwalya [60]
Marantha Fiokpo 0

Lomé, 18-03-2007
Marantha Fiokpo 2 Daouda [44], Assiongbon [85p]
APR FC   0 Abandoned 87' after APR walked-off

Antananarivo, 4-03-2007, Mpopo LES
AS Adema   2 Mbomboko OG [29], Randriamihaja [66]
TP Mazembe   2 Mputu [17], Basisila [58]

Kinshasa, 18-03-2007, Antonio de Sousa ANG
TP Mazembe   4 Bedi Mbenza [4], Mputu 3 [52 73 81]
AS Adema   1 Tsaralaza [62]

Obuasi, 4-03-2007, Chaibou NIG

AshantiGold	2	Shaibu Yakubu [51p], Asamoah [89]
FAR Rabat	0	

Rabat, 17-03-2007, Khelifi ALG

FAR Rabat	2	Ouaddouch [15], Naoum [42]
AshantiGold	0	FAR Rabat W 7-6p

Tripoli, 5-03-2007, Boukar CHA

Al Ittihad Tripoli	4	Rewani [25], Shibani [41p], Camara [43],
AS FNIS Niamey	1	Awalu [8] Feranandes [89]

Niamey, 18-03-2007, Younes EGY

AS FNIS Niamey	0	
Al Ittihad Tripoli	1	Alexis Enam [16]

Addis Abeba, 4-03-2007, Mwandike TAN

St George	1	Chinyere [58]
Etoile du Congo	0	

Brazzaville, 18-03-2007, Kotey GHA

Etoile du Congo	2	Ockakas [55], Ibara [60]
St George	0	

Abidjan, 3-03-2007, Faial CPV

Séwé Sport	1	Miezan Aka [55]
Cotonsport	0	

Garoua, 18-03-2007, Ndoubangar CHA

Cotonsport	4	Hamadama [19], Litsingi [53], Nassourou [83],
Séwé Sport	0	Nimely [85]

Moanda, 4-03-2007, Kazubu Kakonde COD

Mangasport	3	Paupol 2 [10 39], Lolo [62]
Jeunesse Kabylie	1	Dabo [57]

Algiers, 16-03-2007, El Achiri MAR

Jeunesse Kabylie	3	Hamza Yacef [1], Dabo [65], Hemani [86]
Mangasport	0	

Bulawayo, 4-03-2007, Mlangeni SWZ

Highlanders	0	
Al Ahly	0	

Cairo, 18-03-2007, Jedidi TUN

Al Ahly	2	Shady Mohamed [13], Flavio [57]
Highlanders	0	

Maputo, 4-03-2007, Ram MRI

GD Maputo	1	Maurito [69]
M'lodi Sundowns	1	Moriri [14]

Johannesburg, 17-03-2007, Lwanja MWI

M'lodi Sundowns	2	Dladla [10], Moriri [87]
GD Maputo	0	

Bamako, 4-03-2007, Keita GUI

Stade Malien	0	
WAC Casablanca	0	

Casablanca, 18-03-2007, Tamuni LBY

WAC Casablanca	3	Rafik [72p], Ajraoui [84], Mansour [87]
Stade Malien	1	Leigh Saja [89p]

Freetown, 4-03-2007, Wam CMR

FC Kallon	0	
ASEC Mimosas	1	Kassiati Gildas [32]

Abidjan, 18-03-2007, Barhmi MAR

ASEC Mimosas	2	Wawa [8], Umoh [55]
FC Kallon	1	Foday [46]

Tunis, 2-03-2007, Ould Lemghambodj MTN

Espérance Tunis	2	Chakib Lachkham [26], Kamel Zaiem [60p]
Zanaco	0	

Lusaka, 17-03-2007, Katjimune NAM

Zanaco	1	Kaindu [55p]
Espérance Tunis	4	Ltifi [35], Lachkham [39], Kasdaoui 2 [62 73]

Dar es Salaam, 4-03-2007, Faduco MOZ

Young Africans	3	Renato OG [77], Kassim [83], Ngasa [88]
Petro Atlético	0	

Luanda, 18-03-2007

Petro Atlético	2	Manucho [83], Kembua [89]
Young Africans	0	

Lafia, 4-03-2007

Nasarawa United	3	Falogun [19], Saviour [70], Salisu [89]
Ports Authority	0	

Banjul, 16-03-2007, Sedjro TOG

Ports Authority	2	Mandou Bojang [60], Modou Sarr [79p]
Nasarawa United	1	Onuh [44]

Omdurman, 4-03-2007, Kayindi-Ngobi UGA

Al Hilal	2	Abdelwaheb OG [59], Mohamed Tahir [84]
Zamalek	0	

Cairo, 17-03-2007, Bekele ETH

Zamalek	2	Amr Zaki [39], Gamal Hamza [87]
Al Hilal	2	Ndubuisi Eze [78], Kelechi Osunwa [89]

THIRD ROUND

Lomé, 8-04-2007, Pare BFA

Marantha Fiokpo	0	
Etoile du Sahel	0	

Sousse, 21-04-2007, Ousmane Diouf SEN

Etoile du Sahel	3	Amine Chermite [15], Soltani [34], Afaoune [90]
Marantha Fiokpo	0	

Kinshasa, 8-04-2007, Ncobo RSA

TP Mazembe	1	Kaluyituka Diogo [66]
FAR Rabat	0	

Rabat, 21-04-2007

FAR Rabat	2	Bourji [62], Al Marooroufi [83]
TP Mazembe	0	

Brazzaville, 8-04-2007, Imiere NGA

Etoile du Congo	3	Ibara [30], Bayema 2 [58 69]
Al Ittihad Tripoli	1	Naje Shushan [60]

Tripoli, 22-04-2007, Daami TUN

Al Ittihad Tripoli	2	Salem Rewani 2 [45 74]
Etoile du Congo	0	

Garoua, 8-04-2007, Kotey GHA

Cotonsport	1	Litsingi [36]
Jeunesse Kabylie	0	

Algiers, 20-04-2007, Guezzaz MAR

Jeunesse Kabylie	2	Dabo [65], Hamlaoui [92]
Cotonsport	0	

Pretoria, 7-04-2007, Maillet SEY

M'lodi Sundowns	2	Ntwagae [78], Torrealba [88]
Al Ahly	2	Barakat [27], Flavio [54]

Cairo, 20-04-2007, Ssegonga UGA

Al Ahly	2	Shady Mohamed [69], Aboutrika [81]
M'lodi Sundowns	0	

Abidjan, 8-04-2007, Louzaya CGO

ASEC Mimosas	2	Abdul Nafiu 2 [26 93+]
WAC Casablanca	0	

Casablanca, 22-04-2007, Djaoupe TOG

WAC Casablanca	0	
ASEC Mimosas	0	

Tunis, 6-04-2007, Pare

Espérance Tunis	3	Zaiem [28], Ltaief [66], Tayeb [77]
Young Africans	0	

Mwanza, 21-04-2007, Marange ZIM

Young Africans	0	
Espérance Tunis	0	

Lafia, 8-04-2007, Coulibaly MLI

Nasarawa United	3	Dawda [44], Onuh [71], Stephen [83]
Al Hilal	0	

Khartoum, 20-04-2007, Guezzaz MAR

Al Hilal	3	Khan [39], Kelechi [56], Bashir Osman [85]
Nasarawa United	0	Al Hilal W 3-2p

CAF CONFEDERATION CUP 2006

First Round

Moro United	TAN	Bye
TP Mazembe	COD	Bye
Ferroviária Beira *	MOZ	2
Elan Club	COM	1
JKU *	ZAN	0 1
USJF Ravinala	MAD	0 2
Berekum Arsenal	GHA	Bye
Tourbillon *	CHA	2 1
Diables Noirs	CGO	2 3
Les Astres Douala	CMR	3 2
TP USCA Bangui *	CTA	1 0
Petro Atlético	ANG	Bye
Inter Clube	ANG	Bye
AS Kabasha Goma *	COD	0 0
Sogéa	GAB	0 2
Zesco United *	ZAM	3 1
Pointe-aux-Sables	MRI	0 0
Sechelles MB *	SEY	0 0
Township Rollers	BOT	2 1
Lobi Stars	NGA	Bye
Impôts FC Yaoundé	CMR	0 0 4p
FC Akonangui *	EQG	0 0 5p
Espérance Zarzis *	TUN	2 0
USO Ouagadougou	BFA	0 0
Olympique Khouribga	MAR	Bye
Espérance Tunis	TUN	Bye
Mighty Blackpool *	SLE	2 0
CSS Richard-Toll	SEN	1 2
Rayon Sports *	RWA	1 1
Awassa City	ETH	0 0
Al Ittihad Alexandria	EGY	Bye
Sawahel	EGY	0 4
Al Akhdar Darnah *	LBY	1 0
AS Kaloum Star	GUI	Bye
Jeunesse Abidjan	CIV	w-o
Bakau United *	GAM	
Heartland Owerri	NGA	Bye
Al Merreikh	SUD	Bye
World Hope *	KEN	1 0
URA Kampala	UGA	1 1
King Faisal Babies	GHA	Bye
Dynamic Togolais *	TOG	0 0
AS Bamako	MLI	0 5
AS Douanes Dakar	SEN	Bye
ASC Entente Sebkha	MTN	
ASO Chlef	ALG	w-o
Séwé Sport San Pedro	CIV	0 3
Sahel SC *	NIG	0 1
NA Hussein-Dey	ALG	Bye

Second Round

Moro United	w-o	
TP Mazembe		
Ferroviário Beira	0 0 5p	
USJF Ravinala	0 0 6p	
Berekum Arsenal	1 1	
Diables Noirs *	2 0	
Les Astres Douala	1 2	
Petro Atético	2 2	
Inter Clube	0 2	
Sogéa *	1 0	
Zesco United *	2 0	
Township Rollers	1 2	
Lobi Stars	0 1 6p	
FC Akonangui *	1 0 5p	
Espérance Zarzis *	1 0	
Olympique Khouribga	0 6	
Espérance Tunis	1 3	
CSS Richard-Toll *	0 0	
Rayon Sports *	1 0	
Al Ittihad Alexandria	0 3	
Sawahel *	6 1	
AS Kaloum Star	0 0	
Jeunesse Abidjan *	0 0	
Heartland Owerri	0 2	
Al Merreikh	1 2	
URA Kampala *	2 0	
King Faisal Babies	0 0	
AS Bamako *	1 0	
AS Douanes Dakar	0 1	
ASO Chlef *	0 0	
Séwé Sport San Pedro *	0 1	
NA Hussein-Dey	0 3	

Third Round

Moro United	2 3	
USJF Ravinala *	1 1	
Berekum Arsenal *	0 0	
Petro Atlético	0 2	
Inter Clube	1 1	
Township Rollers *	1 0	
Lobi Stars *	1 1	
Olympique Khouribga	1 2	
Espérance Tunis *	1 0 4p	
Al Ittihad Alexandria	0 1 3p	
Sawahel *	0 2	
Heartland Owerri	0 3	
Al Merreikh	0 3 4p	
AS Bamako *	3 0 3p	
AS Douanes Dakar	0 1	
NA Hussein-Dey	2 1	

CAF CONFEDERATION CUP 2006

CAF CONFEDERATION CUP 2006

Intermediate Round

Etoile du Sahel †*	TUN	4	3
Moro United	TAN	1	0

Port Autonome †*	SEN	0	0
Petro Atlético	ANG	1	1

Inter Clube	ANG	0	1
USCAFOOT †*	MAD	0	0

Al Hilal Omdurman†*	SUD	0	1
Olympique Khouribga	MAR	0	2

Espérance Tunis	TUN	0	2
Raja Casablanca †*	MAR	0	0

Heartland Owerri	NGA	0	4
Renacimiento †*	EQG	5	0

St Eloi Lupopo †*	COD	2	1
Al Merreikh	SUD	0	2

NA Hussein-Dey	ALG	0	1
FAR Rabat †*	MAR	2	0

Group Stage

Group A	Pts	MAR	MAR	ANG	ANG
FAR Rabat	13		2-1	2-1	2-0
Olympique Khouribga	10	2-0		1-0	1-0
Petro Atlético	8	1-1	1-1		4-1
Inter Clube	3	0-2	1-0	1-3	

Group B	Pts	TUN	TUN	COD	EQG
Etoile du Sahel	18		1-0	4-1	4-1
Espérance Tunis	8	1-3		1-0	5-0
St Eloi Lupopo	4	0-1	2-2		5-1
Renacimiento	4	0-2	1-1	3-0	

Final

Etoile du Sahel	1	0
FAR RAbat *	1	0

† Champions League second round losers that entered at the Intermediate round
* Home team in the first leg • ‡ Team withdrew • w–o = walk over

GROUP A

Rabat, 12-08-2006		
FAR Rabat	2	Allaoui [31], Benkassou [76]
OC Khouribga	1	Falah [36]

Luanda, 12-08-2006		
Inter Clube	1	Zinga [73]
Petro Atlético	3	Mbiyananga [31], Mateus Alberto [54], Da Costa [59]

Khouribga, 26-08-2006		
OC Khouribga	1	Fellah [89]
Inter Clube	0	

Luanda, 26-08-2006		
Petro Atlético	1	
FAR Rabat	1	

Rabat, 9-09-2006		
FAR Rabat	2	
Inter Clube	0	

Khouribga, 10-09-2006		
OC Khouribga	1	Fellah [20]
Petro Atlético	0	

Luanda, 24-09-2006		
Inter Clube	0	
FAR Rabat	2	Ahmed [21], Ouaddouch [38]

Luanda, 24-09-2006		
Petro Atlético	1	David [64]
OC Khouribga	1	Amzil [70]

Khouribga, 14-10-2006,		
OC Khouribga	2	Fellah [79], Ouganna [92+]
FAR Rabat	0	

Luanda, 15-10-2006		
Petro Atlético	4	Mateus Alberto 3 [5 36 76], Jose Alberto [39]
Inter Clube	1	Hendriques [75]

Luanda, 28-10-2006		
Inter Clube	1	Hendriques [81]
OC Khouribga	0	

Rabat, 28-10-2006		
FAR Rabat	2	Ouaddouch [29], Benkassou [66]
Petro Atlético	1	Joaodo [79]

Group A	Pl	W	D	L	F	A	Pts
FAR Rabat	6	4	1	1	9	5	13
Olympique Khouribga	6	3	1	2	6	4	10
Petro Atlético Luanda	6	2	2	2	10	7	8
Inter Club Luanda	6	1	0	5	3	12	3

GROUP B

Lubumbashi, 13-08-2006		
St Eloi Lupopo	5	Lukoji [20], Bayiya 2 [66 83], Pambani [80], Sunda [89]
Renacimiento	1	Ondobo [64]

Souse, 12-08-2006		
Etoile du Sahel	1	Ben Frej [75]
Espérance Tunis	0	

Tunis, 26-08-2006		
Espérance Tunis	1	Chaabani [30]
St Eloi Lupopo	0	

Malabo, 27-08-2006		
Renacimiento	0	
Etoile du Sahel	2	

Tunis, 10-09-2006		
Espérance Tunis	5	
Renacimiento	0	

Souse, 9-09-2006		
Etoile du Sahel	4	
St Eloi Lupopo	1	

Malabo, 24-09-2006		
Renacimiento	1	Ndong [19]
Espérance Tunis	1	Zitouni [28]

Lubumbashi, 24-09-2006		
St Eloi Lupopo	0	
Etoile du Sahel	1	Fredj [64]

Tunis, 13-10-2006		
Espérance Tunis	1	Mahjoubi [18]
Etoile du Sahel	3	Nafkha 2 [16 61], Chikhaoui [81]

Malabo, 15-10-2006		
Renacimiento	3	
St Eloi Lupopo	0	

Lubumbashi, 27-10-2006		
St Eloi Lupopo	2	Ndume, Twite
Espérance Tunis	2	Hamdi, Zitouni

Souse, 28-10-2006		
Etoile du Sahel	4	Moussa [44], Ogunbiyi [47], Gilson [68], Micon [89]
Renacimiento	1	El Hadj [27]

Group B	Pl	W	D	L	F	A	Pts
Etoile du Sahel	6	6	0	0	15	3	18
Espérance Tunis	6	2	2	2	10	7	8
St Eloi Lupopo	6	1	1	4	8	12	4
Renacimiento	6	1	1	4	6	17	4

Stade Moulay Abdellah, Rabat
18-11-2007, 30 000, Auda EGY

FAR RABAT 1 1 ETOILE SAHEL

Ben Frej OG [72]   Gilson [33]

FAR Rabat			Etoile du Sahel	
12 Tarek EL JARMOUNI			Aymen MATHLOUTHI	1
10 Ahmed AJEDDOU			Saber BEN FREJ	13
3 Chihab ATIK	†		Mehdi MERIAH	11
27 Youssef RABEH			Saif GHEZAL	2
8 Mounir BENKASSOU		69	Mejdi BEN MOHAMED	21
15 Adil SERRAJ		1	Mohamed NAFKHA	19
Zouheir HAFID			Moussa NARRY	24
25 Yassine NAOUM	‡		Muri OGUNBIYI	25
28 Adil LOUTFI			Yassine CHIKHAOUI	17
23 Ali JAAFARI			GILSON	7
24 Jawad OUADOUCH			Emeka OPARA	
Tr: STAMBOULI Henri			Tr: BENZARTI Faouzi	
Substitutes			Substitutes	
6 Brahim EL BAHRI	†	1	Khaled MELLITI	20
Hakim AJRAOUI	‡			

Stade Olympique, Sousse
2-12-2007, 20 000, Bennett RSA

ETOILE SAHEL 0 0 FAR RABAT

Etoile du Sahel			FAR Rabat	
1 Aymen MATHLOUTHI			Tarek JARMOUNI	12
13 Saber BEN FREJ			Mounir BENKASSOU	8
11 Mehdi MERIAH			Ahmed AJEDDOU	10
2 Saif GHEZAL			Khaled MAAROUFI	13
15 Lotfi SELLAMI			Youssef EL BASRI	14
19 Mohamed NAFKHA		55	Khalid EL HIRECH	17
24 Moussa NARRY			Abdesadek HAFID	21
25 Muri OGUNBIYI	85		Ali JAAFARI	23
17 Yassine CHIKHAOUI			Jawad OUADOUCH	24
7 GILSON			Youssef RABEH	27
Emeka OPARA		77	Adil LOUTFI	28
Tr: BENZARTI Faouzi			Tr: STAMBOULI Henri	
Substitutes			Substitutes	
20 Khaled MELLITI	85	55	Khaled EL BAHRI	
		77	Hakim AJRAOUI	

CAF CONFEDERATION CUP 2007

First Round				Second Round			Third Round		
Les Astres Douala	CMR	2	1						
JS Talangai *	CGO	0	0	Les Astres Douala	w-o				
				Tema Youth ‡			Les Astres Douala	0	1
Tema Youth	GHA	Bye					Benfica Luanda * ‡	3	1
DC Motema Pembe	COD	Bye							
				DC Motema Pembe	1	0			
San Pedro Claver *	EQG	1	0	Benfica Luanda *	4	0			
Benfica Luanda	ANG	5	2						
Atraco	RWA	0	3						
Prince Louis FC *	BDI	0	0	Atraco	0	2			
Notwane FC *	BOT	1	0	Mekelakeya *	1	0			
Mekelakeya	ETH	1	1				Atraco *	2	1
Ports Authority *	SLE	2	1				EGS Gafsa	2	1
AS Bamako	MLI	0	0	Ports Authority *	3	1			
AS Togo-Port Lomé *	TOG	1	0	EGS Gafsa	2	4			
EGS Gafsa	TUN	1	2						
Mwana Africa	ZIM	3	3						
Mundu FC *	ZAN	0	1	Mwana Africa *	2	0			
				Inter Clube	0	0			
Inter Clube	ANG	Bye					Mwana Africa	0	3
US Ouakam	SEN	Bye					Etoile Filante *	2	0
				US Ouakam	0	1 3p			
Sahel SC Niamey *	NIG	2	1	Etoile Filante *	1	0 4p			
Etoile Filante	BFA	2	1						
Issia Wazzi	CIV	Bye							
				Issia Wazzi	2	5			
Delta Téléstar *	GAB	1	0	OC Bukavu Dawa *	0	0			
OC Bukavu Dawa	COD	0	2				Issia Wazzi *	1	0
Satelitte Conakry	GUI	3					CS Sfaxien	0	2
Benfica *	GNB	1		Satelitte Conakry *	1	0			
				CS Sfaxien	3	4			
CS Sfaxien	TUN	Bye							
Dolphin	NGA	Bye							
				Dolphin	0	1			
AS Denguélé	CIV	0	1	Hawks *	0	0			
Hawks *	GAM	0	1				Dolphin *	1	0 5p
US Gorée	SEN	3	1				HUS Agadir	0	1 3p
NPA Anchors *	LBR	2	0	US Gorée *	0	2			
				HUS Agadir	0	3			
HUS Agadir	MAR	Bye							
Green Buffaloes	ZAM	Bye							
				Green Buffaloes	0	2			
St Michael United *	SEY	2	0	St Pauloise *	0	0			
St Pauloise	REU	1	1				Green Buffaloes	1	1
Ajesaia	MAD	0	4				Ismaily *	2	1
Curepipe Starlight SC *	MRI	1	0	Ajesaia *	2	1			
				Ismaily	2	6			
Ismaily	EGY	Bye							
Kwara United	NGA	1	2						
AS Dragons *	BEN	0	0	Kwara United *	3	0 7p			
				MC Alger	0	3 6p			
MC Alger	ALG	Bye					Kwara United	1	3
Têxtile Pungué *	MOZ	1	1 3p				Union Douala *	1	2
Simba SC	TAN	1	1 1p	Têxtile Pugué *	0	0			
				Union Douala	3	3			
Union Douala	CMR	Bye							
ASO Chlef	ALG	1	2						
ASAC Concorde *	MTN	0	1	ASO Chlef *	0	1			
				ENPPI	0	0			
ENPPI	EGY	Bye					ASO Chlef *	1	0
AS Coton Tchad	CHA	1	1				Al Merreikh	0	3
Al Ahly Tripoli *	LBY	2	0	AS Coton Tchad *	2	0			
				Al Merreikh	0	5			
Al Merreikh	SUD	Bye							

CAF CONFEDERATION CUP 2007

CAF CONFEDERATION CUP 2007

Intermediate Round				Group Stage	Final

Les Astres Douala CMR 1 2
Etoile du Congo † * CGO 2 0

EGS Gafsa TUN 1 1
Mam'di Sundowns † * RSA 2 1

Group A — Pts

Les Astres Douala — 1-1
Mamelodi Sundowns — 3-2
TP Mazembe
CS Sfaxien

TP Mazembe † * COD 1 3
Mwana Africa ZIM 0 1

Cotonsport Garoua † * CMR 2 0
CS Sfaxien TUN 1 4

Dolphin NGA 2 2
Marantha Fiokpo † * TOG 1 0

Wydad Casablanca † * MAR 0 0
Ismaily EGY 1 2

Group B — Pts

Dolphin — 2-0
Ismaily — 1-1
Kwara United
Al Merreikh

Kwara United NGA 1 1
Nasarawa United † * NGA 1 0

Young Africans † * TAN 0 0
Al Merreikh SUD 0 2

† Champions League second round losers that entered at the Intermediate round
* Home team in the first leg • ‡ Tema failed to show for their match against Astres. Benfica fielded an ineligible player in their second leg match against Astres. Both Tema and Benfica were disqualified
Remaining four rounds in the groups to be played 17-19/08/2007, 31/08-2/09/2007, 21-23/09/2007 and 5-7/10/2007
Final to be played on 2-4/11/2007 and 23-25/11/2007

FIRST ROUND

Brazzaville, 28-01-2007

| JS Talangai | 0 | |
| Les Astres Douala | 2 | Enama Okouda 2 [37 68] |

Stade de la Reunification, Douala, 10-02-2007, Djaoupe TOG

| Les Astres Douala | 1 | Enama Okouda [89] |
| JS Talangai | 0 | |

Malabo, 28-01-2007

| San Pedro Claver | 1 | |
| Benfica Luanda | 5 | Mputu 2 [23 70], Toto [37], Avex [89], Erick [90] |

Estádio dos Coqueiros, Luanda, 11-02-2007

| Benfica Luanda | 2 | Avex [18], Vado [56] |
| San Pedro Claver | 0 | |

Bujumbura, 28-01-2007, Kalyango UGA

| Prince Louis FC | 0 | |
| Atraco | 0 | |

Kigali, 11-02-2007, Chiganga SUD

| Atraco | 3 | Kabagande [44], Kudra [68], Nuhanimana [83] |
| Prince Louis FC | 0 | |

Gaborone, 28-01-2006, Mnkantso ZIM

| Notwane FC | 1 | Molwantna [47] |
| Mekelakeya | 1 | Gebreegziabher [68] |

Addis Abeba, 11-02-2007

| Mekelakeya | 1 | Nasser [72] |
| Notwane FC | 0 | |

Freetown, 27-01-2007

| Ports Authority | 2 | Muwahid Sesay [1], Daniel Foday [56] |
| AS Bamako | 0 | |

Modibo Keita, Bamako, 11-02-2007

| AS Bamako | 0 | |
| Ports Authority | 1 | Abdul Din Sesay [83] |

Lomé, 28-01-2007

| Togo-Port Lomé | 1 | Cherif [49p] |
| EGS Gafsa | 1 | Ben Ouanes [75] |

Gafsa, 10-02-2007

| EGS Gafsa | 2 | Khanchil [48], Baghouli [74p] |
| Togo-Port Lomé | 0 | |

Zanzibar, 27-01-2007

| Mundu FC | 0 | |
| Mwana Africa | 3 | Tawanda Mareya [27], OG [70], Kamunenga [81] |

Harare, 11-02-2007, Ramocha BOT

| Mwana Africa | 3 | Tawanda Mareya 3 [19 41 70] |
| Mundu FC | 1 | Victor Mwamba [47p] |

Niamey, 28-01-2007, Moeketsi LES

| Sahel SC Niamey | 2 | Moussa Hamani [4], Issoufou Kamilou [82] |
| Etoile Filante | 2 | Fousseni Traore [6], Dela Sakou [34] |

Stade 4 Aout, Ouagadougou, 10-02-2007, Jo GNB

| Etoile Filante | 1 | Sandaogo [12] |
| Sahel SC Niamey | 1 | Youssoufou Ibrahim [87] |

Libreville, 27-01-2007, Ebatta CGO

| Delta Téléstar | 1 | Nzue Nguema [31] |
| OC Bukavu Dawa | 0 | |

Stade des Martyrs, Kinshasa, 11-02-2007

| OC Bukavu Dawa | 2 | Godefroid Osama [7], Albert Omba [66] |
| Delta Téléstar | 0 | |

Bissau, 27-01-2007, Sidibe MLI

| Benfica Bissau | 1 | Da Silva Santos [85] |
| Satelitte Conakry | 3 | Ela Camara 2 [35 50], Barry [61] |

Banjul, 28-01-2007, Soussou TOG

| Hawks | 0 | |
| AS Denguélé | 0 | |

Abidjan, 11-02-2007, Konah LBR

| AS Denguélé | 1 | Koffi Kouassi [38] |
| Hawks | 1 | Ousman Jatta [89] |

Monrovia, 28-01-2007, Wokoma NGA

| NPA Anchors | 2 | Melvin George [43], Jesper Kun [83] |
| US Gorée | 3 | Ndione [1], Gassama [11], Blamo [76] |

Demba Diop, Dakar, 10-02-2007

| US Gorée | 1 | Ndione [60] |
| NPA Anchors | 0 | |

Victoria, 27-01-2007, Moeketsi LES

| St Michael Utd | 2 | Leonnie Nastinan [24], Alex Nibourette [57] |
| St Pauloise | 1 | Paulin Voavy [20] |

St Paul, 11-02-2007

| St Pauloise | 1 | Romain Tossem [75] |
| St Michael Utd | 0 | |

Curepipe, 28-01-2007, Andre SEY

| Curepipe Starlight | 1 | Samuel Rebet [28] |
| Ajesaia | 0 | |

Antananarivo, 11-02-2007, Bibi SEY

| Ajesaia | 4 | Nomenjanahary [7], Rakotondramanana 2 [44 64], Rabeariniala [46] |
| Curepipe Starlight | 0 | |

Cotonou, 28-01-2007

| AS Dragons | 0 | |
| Kwara United | 1 | Akombo Ukeyima [15] |

Kwara Stadium, Ilorin, 11-02-2007

| Kwara United | 2 | Shedrach Francis [35], Nkoro Ndubuisi [44] |
| AS Dragons | 0 | |

Maputo, 28-01-2007, Manuel ZIM

| Têxtile Pungué | 1 | Jossias [70p] |
| Simba SC | 1 | Kaniki [89] |

Dar-es-Salaam, 11-02-2007

| Simba SC | 1 | Akilimali [88] |
| Têxtile Pungué | 1 | Castigo [65]. Têxtile won 3-1p |

Nouakchott, 27-01-2007, Lopes CPV

| ASAC Concorde | 0 | |
| ASO Chlef | 1 | Zaoueche [50] |

Chlef, 11-02-2007

| ASO Chlef | 2 | Aissaoui [1], Kechamli [35] |
| ASAC Concorde | 1 | Bahid [80] |

Tripoli, 28-01-2007, Faruk EGY

| Al Ahly Tripoli | 2 | Ahmed Osman [33], Muybel [63] |
| AS Coton Tchad | 1 | David Mbajhouloum [28] |

Idriss Mhtouk, N'Djamena, 11-02-2007, Lagandzi RSA

| AS Coton Tchad | 1 | Lucien Tekor [89] |
| Al Ahly Tripoli | 0 | |

SECOND ROUND

Luanda, 3-03-2007, Rembangouet GAB

| Benfica Luanda | 4 | Erick 2 [5 18], Toto 2 [67 71] |
| Motema Pembe | 1 | Salambo [44] |

Kinshasa, 16-03-2007

| Motema Pembe | 0 | |
| Benfica Luanda | 0 | |

Addis Abeba, 3-03-2007, Nhlapo RSA

| Mekelakeya | 1 | Merkeb Gebregziabher [40] |
| Atraco | 0 | |

Kigali, 17-03-2007, El Nigomi SUD

| Atraco | 2 | Muhayimana [22], Hitimana [26] |
| Mekelakeya | 0 | |

Freetown, 4-03-2007, Igue BEN

| Ports Authority | 3 | Abdul Din Sesay 3 [34 38 79] |
| EGS Gafsa | 2 | Bakari Dao [67], Hamdi Jabnoun [72] |

Gafsa, 17-03-2007, Tahri MAR

| EGS Gafsa | 4 | Ben Ouanes [21], Khammar [53], Bakari Dao [62], Alusine [30] |
| Ports Authority | 1 | Khanchil [68] |

Harare, 3-03-2007, Jovinala MWI

| Mwana Africa | 2 | Svesve [19], Marere [77] |
| Inter Clube | 0 | |

Luanda, 18-03-2007, Mwanza ZAM

| Inter Clube | 0 |
| Mwana Africa | 0 |

Ouagadougou, 5-03-2007, Mahamat CHA

| Etoile Filante | 1 | Dela Sakou [50] |
| US Ouakam | 0 | |

Dakar, 17-03-2007, Karembe MLI

| US Ouakam | 1 | Moussa Dione [67p] |
| Etoile Filante | 0 | Etoile won 4-3p |

Kinshasa, 4-03-2007, Bodo Ndzomo CMR

| OC Bukavu Dawa | 0 | |
| Issia Wazzi | 2 | Wilfried Boli 2 [36 73] |

Abidjan, 17-03-2007, Nelson CPV

| Issia Wazzi | 5 | Lacina Serifou 3 [14 83 88], Wilfried Boli 3 [59 89] |
| OC Bukavu Dawa | 0 | |

Conakry, 10-03-2007, Jallow GAM

| Satelitte Conakry | 1 | Sekou Camara [4] |
| CS Sfaxien | 3 | Kouassi [12], Merdassi [26], Ziadi [39] |

Taïeb-Mhiri, Sfax, 17-03-2007, Djaballah ALG

| CS Sfaxien | 4 | Kouassi 2 [9 25], Merdassi 2 [15 89p] |
| Satelitte Conakry | 0 | |

Banjul, 3-03-2007, Fagla TOG

| Hawks | 0 |
| Dolphin | 0 |

Port Harcourt, 18-03-2007, Tokpeme BEN

| Dolphin | 1 | Gbenga Ajala [6] |
| Hawks | 0 | |

Dakar, 3-03-2007, Ilboudo BFA

| US Gorée | 0 |
| HUS Agadir | 0 |

Agadir, 17-03-2007, Shaaban EGY

| HUS Agadir | 3 | Alouli [33], El Fathi [42], Najdi [78] |
| US Gorée | 2 | Thiaw [19], Diop [86] |

St Pierre, 3-03-2007, Randriatsarafihavy MAD

| St Pauloise | 0 |
| Green Buffaloes | 0 |

Lusaka, 18-03-2007, Lebaka LES

| Green Buffaloes | 2 | Ngosa [31], Mwansa [85] |
| St Pauloise | 0 | |

Antananarivo, 3-03-2007, Benstrong SEY

| Ajesaia | 2 | Tsiry Rakotondramanana [13], Njaka [85] |
| Ismaily | 2 | Soliman [41], Mohsen Abugreisha [43] |

Ismailiya, 18-03-2007, Lebaka LES

| Ismaily | 6 | Gamal 2 [13 83], Mohsen Abugreisha 2 [29 41], |
| Ajesaia | 1 | Nomenjanahary [9]   Sayed Moawad 2 [42 85] |

Kwara Stadium, Ilorin, 4-03-2007, Doue CIV

| Kwara United | 3 | Ukeyima 2 [15 39], Akabueze [64] |
| MC Alger | 0 | |

Algiers, 18-03-2007, Saadallah TUN

| MC Alger | 3 | Zemit [15], Badache [19], Sidibie [77] |
| Kwara United | 0 | Kwara won 7-6p |

Beira, 4-03-2007,

| Têxtile Pungué | 0 | |
| Union Douala | 3 | Mbila [23], Belle [64], Djidda [89] |

Douala, 18-03-2007

| Union Douala | 3 | Same [44], Djidda [78], Eyoum [88] |
| Têxtile Pungué | 0 | |

Chlef, 2-03-2007, Fall SEN

| ASO Chlef | 0 |
| ENPPI | 0 |

Cairo, 18-03-2007, Abdel Gadir SUD

| ENPPI | 0 | |
| ASO Chlef | 1 | Boukhari [22] |

Idriss Mhtouk, N'Djamena, 2-03-2007, Mamane NIG

| AS Coton Tchad | 2 | Esai Djikeloum 2 [6 43p] |
| Al Merreikh | 0 | |

Khartoum, 17-03-2007, Nduwarugira BDI

| Al Merreikh | 5 | Tambal 2, Idahor 2, Soudey |
| AS Coton Tchad | 0 | |

THIRD ROUND

Luanda, 7-04-2007

| Benfica Luanda | 3 | Serge Mputu 3 [31p 51 70] |
| Les Astres Douala | 0 | |

Douala, 21-04-2007

| Les Astres Douala | 1 | Ojobong [46] |
| Benfica Luanda | 1 | Paito [16] |

Kigali, 6-04-2007, Ngosi MWI

| Atraco | 2 | Magumba [18], Mulenda [60] |
| EGS Gafsa | 2 | Bakari Dao [32], Ben Ouanes [84] |

Gafsa, 21-04-2007, Haimoudi ALG

| EGS Gafsa | 1 | Bakari Dao [5] |
| Atraco | 1 | Muhayimana [81] |

Ouagadougou, 7-04-2007, Keita GUI

| Etoile Filante | 2 | Ouattara [44], Sanou.V [66] |
| Mwana Africa | 0 | |

Harare, 21-04-2007, Seechurn MRI

| Mwana Africa | 3 | Tsodzo [7], Kondowe [43], Huronda [72] |
| Etoile Filante | 0 | |

Abidjan 7-04-2007, Aguidissou BEN

| Issia Wazzi | 1 | Wilfried Boli [43p] |
| CS Sfaxien | 0 | |

Taïeb-Mhiri, Sfax, 21-04-2007, Auda EGY

| CS Sfaxien | 2 | Sellami [9], Kouassi [89] |
| Issia Wazzi | 0 | |

Port Harcourt, 8-04-2007, Evehe CMR

| Dolphin | 1 | Kula Anubi [20] |
| HUS Agadir | 0 | |

Agadir, 22-04-2007, Ould Lemghaifry MTN

| HUS Agadir | 1 | Issiaka Zale [58] |
| Dolphin | 0 | Dolphin won 5-3p |

Ismailiya, 6-04-2007, Abdel Rahman SUD

| Ismaily | 2 | Abdullah Said [77], Omar Gamal [89] |
| Green Buffaloes | 1 | Morgan Hanjeeme [36] |

Lusaka, 21-04-2007, Katjimune MAN

| Green Buffaloes | 1 | Mwanza [43] |
| Ismaily | 1 | Mohsen Abugreisha [56] |

Douala, 6-04-2007, Abdou Diouf SEN

| Union Douala | 1 | Same [17] |
| Kwara United | 1 | Chukwuma Akabueze [13] |

Kwara Stadium, Ilorin, 18-04-2007, Mendy GAM

| Kwara United | 3 | Ukeyima [6], Okwu 2 [63 89p] |
| Union Douala | 2 | Woukone [1], Djidda [72] |

Chlef, 8-04-2007, Doue CIV

| ASO Chlef | 1 | Al Hassane Issoufou [23] |
| Al Merreikh | 0 | |

Khartoum, 21-04-2007, Gasingwa RWA

| Al Merreikh | 3 | Idahor [32], Tambal [39], Faisal Agab [81] |
| ASO Chlef | 0 | |

INTERMEDIATE ROUND

Brazzaville, 13-05-2007, Gasingwa RWA

| Etoile du Congo | 2 | Ngono Ambono [8], Ngassilat Lebally [16] |
| Les Astres Douala | 1 | Riwou Bessong [56] |

Douala, 19-05-2007, Ncobo RSA

| Les Astres Douala | 2 | Narcisse Ekanga [31], Paul Ncha [41] |
| Etoile du Congo | 0 | |

Polokwane, 5-05-2007, Matela RSA

| M'lodi Sundowns | 2 | Chabangu [40], Sapula [57] |
| EGS Gafsa | 1 | Khanchil [2] |

INTERMEDIATE ROUND (CONT'D)

Gafsa, 19-05-2007, El Arjoune MAR

EGS Gafsa	1	Ben Ouanes [4]
M'lodi Sundowns	1	Peter Ndlovu [14]

Kinshasa, 6-05-2007, Louzaya CGO

TP Mazembe	1	Mputu [16]
Mwana Africa	0	

Harare, 19-05-2007, Chiganga TAN

Mwana Africa	1	Muronda [32]
TP Mazembe	3	Kaluytukadioko [38], Mputu 2 [53p 89]

Garoua, 6-05-2007, Mana NGA

Cotonsport	2	Kanilou Daouda [76], Gaha [89]
CS Sfaxien	1	Ben Amar [75]

Stade Taïeb-Mhiri, Sfax, 19-05-2007, Benouza ALG

CS Sfaxien	4	Nafti [5], Hamza Younes 2 [11 57], Sellami [84]
Cotonsport	0	

Womé, 6-05-2007, Aguidissou BEN

Marantha Fiokpo	1	Allassani Daouda [27]
Dolphin	2	Bola Bello 2 [15 31]

Port Harcourt, 20-05-2007, Banao BFA

Dolphin	2	Bola Bello [7], Eze Nwabika [70]
Marantha Fiokpo	0	

Casablanca, 6-05-2007, Bennaceur TUN

WAC Casablanca	0	
Ismaily	1	Omar Gamal [13]

Ismailiya, 18-05-2007, Bennaceur TUN

Ismaily	2	Samir Farag [75], Abdelwahed [89]
WAC Casablanca	0	

Lafia, 6-05-2007, Aboubacar CIV

Nasarawa United	1	Onuh [47]
Kwara United	1	Obada [3]

Kwara Stadium, Ilorin, 20-05-2007, Agbovi GHA

Kwara United	1	Ahmed Mohamed [68]
Nasarawa United	0	

Mwanza, 6-05-2007, Kapanga MWI

Young Africans	0	
Al Merreikh	0	

Khartoum, 19-05-2007, Niyongabo BDI

Al Merreikh	2	Faisal Agab [27], Abdelhamid Soudey [36]
Young Africans	0	

REGIONAL CLUB TOURNAMENTS IN AFRICA 2006–07

CECAFA KAGAME INTER-CLUB CUP RWANDA 2007

First round groups

Group A		Pl	W	D	L	F	A	Pts	UGA	TAN	BDI	DJI
APR FC	RWA	4	3	0	1	7	4	9	0-3	1-0	3-0	3-1
URA Kampala	UGA	4	2	1	1	8	3	7		2-2	3-0	0-1
Young Africans	TAN	4	1	2	1	7	4	5			1-1	4-0
Vital'O	BDI	4	1	1	2	5	7	4				4-0
CDE	DJI	4	1	0	3	2	11	3				

Group B		Pl	W	D	L	F	A	Pts	RWA	UGA	ZAN
St George	ETH	3	3	0	0	11	3	9	4-2	4-0	3-1
Atraco	RWA	3	2	0	1	4	4	6		1-0	1-0
Police FC	UGA	3	1	0	2	2	5	3			2-0
Polisi	ZAN	3	0	0	3	1	6	0			

Semi–finals

APR FC	2
Atraco	0

St George	1
URA Kampala	2

Final

APR FC	2
URA Kampala	1

Third place play-off

St George	2
Atraco	0

The tournament took place in Rwanda from 6-01-2007 to 20-01-2007 and was played in Kigali
Final: Stade Amahoro, Kigali, 20-01-2007, Ref: Niyongabo BDI. Scorers: Abbas Rasou [5], Twite Mbuyu [11] for APR; David Kiwanuka [95+] for Revenue

CONCACAF

CONFEDERATION OF NORTH, CENTRAL AMERICAN AND

CARIBBEAN ASSOCIATION FOOTBALL

It was a busy year of international football with regional championships in Central America as well as the Caribbean, both of which served as qualifiers for the CONCACAF Gold Cup at the end of the season. There were a huge number of entrants for the Caribbean Cup as the competition continued its revival under the sponsorship of regional communications giant Digicel. There were also plenty of surprises, especially with Jamaica falling in the first qualifying round after finishing third in their group behind Haiti and St Vincent. Trinidad hosted the tournament finals at the beginning of 2007, but for the first time they failed to win on home soil. They did reach the final but lost 2-1 to a Haiti team that returned home to an ecstatic reception. It was the first time Haiti had won the tournament, and the first time since 1993 that a country other than Trinidad or Jamaica had been crowned as Caribbean champions. February 2007 saw the Central American nations travel to El Salvador for the UNCAF Cup where, despite winning their first round group, the hosts failed in

THE FIFA BIG COUNT OF 2006 FOR NORTH AND CENTRAL AMERICA AND THE CARIBBEAN

	Male	Female		Total
Number of players	33 071 000	10 038 000	Referees and Assistant Referees	172 000
Professionals	9 000		Admin, Coaches, Technical, Medical	961 000
Amateurs 18+	884 000		Number of clubs	17 000
Youth under 18	5 163 000		Number of teams	490 000
Unregistered	36 988 000		Clubs with women's teams	7 000
Total involved in football	44 242 000		Players as % of population	8.53%

their bid to win the title for the first time. In reaching the final Panama continued the impressive gains they have made in recent years, but it was old hands Costa Rica who won a sixth title as Panama's bad run of luck in penalty shoot-outs continued. Big crowds were attracted to many of the games in the Gold Cup in the USA in June, where USA and Mexico met in the final for the first time since 1998. A 2-1 victory meant USA equalled Mexico's haul of four titles, but many of the headlines during the tournament involved tiny Guadeloupe who, inspired by former French international Jocelyn Angloma, progressed as far as the semi-finals. In club football it was a great year for Mexican teams generally, and for Pachuca in particular. In December 2006 they won South America's Copa Sudamerica and then beat compatriots Guadalajara on penalties in the final to win the CONCACAF Champions' Cup. Costa Rica's Municipal Puntarenas had earlier won the UNCAF club championship while Trinidad's Williams Connection won the Caribbean championship.

Confederation of North, Central American and Caribbean Association Football (CONCACAF)
725, Fifth Avenue, Trump Tower, 17th Floor, New York, NY 1022, USA
Tel +1 212 3080 044   Fax +1 212 3081 851
mail@concacaf.net   www.concacaf.com
President: WARNER Jack A. TRI   General Secretary: BLAZER Chuck USA
CONCACAF Formed: 1961

CONCACAF EXECUTIVE COMMITTEE
President: WARNER Jack A. TRI
Vice-President: AUSTIN Lisle BRB   Vice-President: BANEGAS Alfredo Hawit HON   Vice-President: CANEDO WHITE Guillermo MEX
ORDINARY MEMBERS OF THE EXECUTIVE COMMITTEE
BURRELL Horace Capt. JAM   ALVARADO Ariel PAN   GULATI Sunil USA
FIFA Exco: SALGUERO Rafael GUA   FIFA Exco: BLAZER Chuck USA

MAP OF CONCACAF MEMBER NATIONS

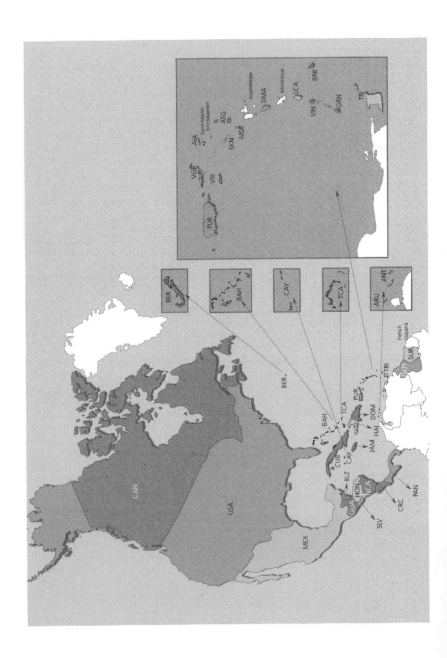

CENTRAL AMERICAN, NORTH AMERICAN AND CARIBBEAN TOURNAMENTS

CCCF CHAMPIONSHIP

Year	Host Country	Winners	Score	Runners-up	Venue
1941	Costa Rica	Costa Rica	3-1	El Salvador	San José
1943	El Salvador	El Salvador	2-1	Guatemala	San Salvador
1946	Costa Rica	Costa Rica	1-4	Guatemala	San José
1948	Guatemala	Costa Rica	2-3	Guatemala	Guatemala City
1951	Panama	Panama	2-0	Costa Rica	Panama City
1953	Costa Rica	Costa Rica	4-1	Honduras	San José
1955	Honduras	Costa Rica	2-1	Netherlands Antilles	Tegucigalpa
1957	Curaçao	Haiti	3-1	Curaçao	Willemstad
1960	Cuba	Costa Rica	4-1†	Netherlands Antilles	Havana
1961	Costa Rica	Costa Rica	4-0	El Salvador	San José

All tournaments played on a league basis. The result listed is the match played between the top two • † Play-off after both teams finished level

CONCACAF NATIONS CUP

Year	Host Country	Winners	Score	Runners-up	Venue
1963	El Salvador	Costa Rica	4-1	El Salvador	San Salvador
1965	Guatemala	Mexico	2-1	Guatemala	Guatemala City
1967	Honduras	Guatemala	1-0	Mexico	Tegucigalpa
1969	Costa Rica	Costa Rica	1-1	Guatemala	San José
1971	Trinidad & T	Mexico	0-0	Haiti	Port of Spain

All tournaments played on a league basis. The result listed is the match played between the top two

CONCACAF NATIONS CUP/FIFA WORLD CUP QUALIFIERS

Year	Host Country	Winners	Score	Runners-up	Venue
1973	Haiti	Haiti	2-1	Trinidad	Port-au-Prince
1977	Mexico	Mexico	4-1	Haiti	Mexico City
1981	Honduras	Honduras	0-0	El Salvador	Tegucigalpa
1985	Home & Away	Canada	2-1	Honduras	Saint John's
1989	Home & Away	Costa Rica	1-0	USA	San José

All tournaments played on a league basis. The result listed is the match played between the top two

CONCACAF GOLD CUP

Year	Host Country	Winners	Score	Runners-up	Venue
1991	USA	USA	0-0 4-3p	Honduras	Coliseum, Los Angeles
1993	Mexico/USA	Mexico	4-0	USA	Azteca, Mexico City
1995	USA	Mexico	2-0	Brazil	Coliseum, Los Angeles
1998	USA	Mexico	1-0	USA	Coliseum, Los Angeles
2000	USA	Canada	2-0	Colombia	Coliseum, Los Angeles
2002	USA	USA	2-0	Costa Rica	Rose Bowl, Pasadena
2003	Mexico/USA	Mexico	1-0	Brazil	Azteca, Mexico City
2005	USA	USA	0-0 3-1p	Panama	Giants Stadium, New Jersey
2007	USA	USA	2-1	Mexico	Soldier Field, Chicago

Not until the introduction of the CONCACAF Gold Cup in 1991 did Central America, North America and the Caribbean have a proper continental championship. Prior to 1963 there had been a Central American tournament with the occasional Caribbean entrant, a competition dominated by Costa Rica. 1963 saw the introduction of the CONCACAF Nations Cup, staged every other year until 1971, but the Americans and Mexicans failed to take it seriously and from 1973 until 1981 the Nations Cup was incorporated into the FIFA World Cup qualifiers. Since the creation of the CONCACAF Gold Cup in 1991, the USA has hosted every tournament (twice in conjunction with Mexico) and the two have provided the winners, with the exception of Canada in 2000.

CONCACAF WOMEN'S GOLD CUP

Year	Host Country	Winners	Score	Runners-up	Venue
1991	Haiti	USA	5-0	Canada	Port au Prince
1993	USA	USA	1-0	Canada	Long Island
1994	Canada	USA	6-0	Canada	Montreal
1998	Canada	Canada	1-0	Mexico	Toronto
2000	USA	USA	1-0	Brazil	Foxboro, Boston
2002	USA/Canada	USA	2-1	Canada	Rose Bowl, Pasadena
2006	USA	USA	2-1	Canada	Home Depot Center, Los Angeles

CONCACAF UNDER 20 WOMEN'S TOURNAMENT

Year	Host Country	Winners	Score	Runners-up	Venue
2004	Canada	Canada	2-1	USA	Frank Clair, Ottawa
2006	Mexico	USA	3-2	Canada	Veracruz

If there is one area in which CONCACAF can claim to be world beaters it is in women's football, with both the USA and Canada ranked at the highest level of the game. The Women's Gold Cup coincided with the launch of the men's competition and since then the USA have won six of the seven tournaments played, beating Canada in the final of five of them. Canada won on home soil in 1998, beating the USA in an historic semi-final before defeating Mexico in the final, the only other team from the CONCACAF area to reach the final. It is hard to imagine any nation seriously threatening the North American dominance at this or U-19 level.

CONCACAF UNDER 20 TOURNAMENT

Year	Host Country	Winners	Score	Runners-up	Venue
1954	Costa Rica	Costa Rica	3-1†	Panama	San José
1956	El Salvador	El Salvador	1-1†	Netherlands Antilles	San Salvador
1958	Guatemala	Guatemala	1-0†	Honduras	Guatemala City
1960	Honduras	Costa Rica	0-4†	Honduras	Tegucigalpa
1962	Panama	Mexico	1-1†	Guatemala	Panama City
1964	Guatemala	El Salvador			Guatemala City
1970	Cuba	Mexico	0-0†	Cuba	Havana
1973	Mexico	Mexico	2-0	Guatemala	Puebla
1974	Canada	Mexico	1-0	Cuba	
1976	Puerto Rico	Mexico	4-3	Honduras	
1978	Honduras	Mexico	1-0	Canada	
1980	USA	Mexico	2-0	USA	Giants Stadium, New Jersey
1982	Guatemala	Honduras	1-0	USA	Guatemala City
1984	Trinidad	Mexico	2-1	Canada	
1986	Trinidad	Canada	1-1†	USA	
1988	Guatemala	Costa Rica	3-0†	Mexico	
1990	Guatemala	Mexico	2-1†	Trinidad	Guatemala City
1992	Canada	Mexico	3-0†	USA	Victoria
1994	Honduras	Honduras	1-0†	Costa Rica	
1996	Mexico	Canada	2-2†	Mexico	Saltillo

† Final tournament played as a league. The match listed is between the top two • Played as the CCCF youth championship from 1954 to 1960

CONCACAF UNDER 17 TOURNAMENT

Year	Host Country	Winners	Score	Runners-up	Venue
1983	Trinidad	USA		Trinidad	
1985	Mexico	Mexico	1-1†	Costa Rica	
1987	Honduras	Mexico	3-1†	USA	
1988	Trinidad	Cuba	0-1†	USA	Port of Spain
1991	Trinidad	Mexico	1-1†	USA	Port of Spain
1992	Cuba	USA	3-4†	Mexico	
1994	El Salvador	Costa Rica	1-2†	USA	Flor Blanca, San Salvador
1996	Trinidad	Mexico	3-1†	USA	Port of Spain

† All final tournaments played as a league. The match listed is between the top two.

At both U-19 and U-17 levels CONCACAF tournaments have served as qualifiers for the FIFA events but since 1996, once the qualifying nations have been identified, the principle of determining the champions at each level has been abandoned.

CARIBBEAN CUP

Year	Host Country	Winners	Score	Runners-up	Venue
1989	Barbados	Trinidad & Tobago	2-1	Grenada	Bridgetown
1990	Trinidad	Not completed			
1991	Jamaica	Jamaica	2-0	Trinidad & Tobago	Kingston
1992	Trinidad	Trinidad & Tobago	3-1	Jamaica	Port of Spain
1993	Jamaica	Martinique	0-0 6-5p	Jamaica	Kingston
1994	Trinidad	Trinidad & Tobago	7-2	Martinique	Port of Spain
1995	Cayman/Jamaica	Trinidad & Tobago	5-0	St Vincent/Grenadines	George Town
1996	Trinidad	Trinidad & Tobago	2-0	Cuba	Port of Spain
1997	Antigua/St Kitts	Trinidad & Tobago	4-0	St Kitts and Nevis	St John's
1998	Jamaica/Trinidad	Jamaica	2-1	Trinidad & Tobago	Port of Spain
1999	Trinidad	Trinidad & Tobago	2-1	Cuba	Port of Spain
2001	Trinidad	Trinidad & Tobago	3-0	Haiti	Port of Spain
2005	Barbados	Jamaica	1-0†	Cuba	Waterford
2007	Trinidad	Haiti	2-1	Trinidad & Tobago	Port of Spain

† Final tournament played as a league. The match listed is between the top two.

UNCAF CUP

Year	Host Country	Winners	Score	Runners-up	Venue
1991	Costa Rica	Costa Rica	2-0†	Honduras	San José
1993	Honduras	Honduras	2-0†	Costa Rica	Tegucigalpa
1995	El Salvador	Honduras	3-0	Guatemala	San Salvador
1997	Guatemala	Costa Rica	1-1†	Guatemala	Mateo Flores, Guatemala City
1999	Costa Rica	Costa Rica	1-0†	Guatemala	San José
2001	Honduras	Guatemala	2-0†	Costa Rica	Tegucigalpa
2003	Panama	Costa Rica	1-1†	Guatemala	Rommel Fernández, Panama City
2005	Guatemala	Costa Rica	1-1 7-6p	Honduras	Mateo Flores, Guatemala City
2007	El Salvador	Costa Rica	1-1 4-1p	Panama	Cuscatlán, San Salvador

† Final tournament played as a league. The match listed is between the top two.

The UNCAF Cup, played between the nations of Central America, is a prestigious event that doubles as a qualifying competition for the Gold Cup, as does the Caribbean Cup. Trinidad and Tobago along with Jamaica have dominated the latter competition with Martinique in 1993 and Haiti in 2007 the only countries to break the duopoly while Costa Rica have won six UNCAF championships.

UNCAF CLUB CHAMPIONSHIP

Year	Winners	Country	Score	Country	Runners-up
1999	Olimpia	HON	2-0 †	CRC	LD Alajuelense
2000	Olimpia	HON	0-0 †	CRC	LD Alajuelense
2001	Municipal	GUA	1-1 †	CRC	Deportivo Saprissa
2002	LD Alajuelense	CRC	4-0 †	PAN	Arabe Unido
2003	Deportivo Saprissa	CRC	3-2	GUA	Comunicaciones
2004	Municipal	GUA	1-0 †	CRC	Deportivo Saprissa
2005	LD Alajuelense	CRC	1-0 0-1 4-2p	HON	Olimpia
2006	Municipal Puntarenas	CRC	3-2 0-1 3-1p	HON	Olimpia

† Played on a league system. The match listed was between the top two

CARIBBEAN CLUB TOURNAMENT

Year	Winners	Country	Score	Country	Runners-up
2003	San Juan Jabloteh	TRI	2-1 1-2 4-2p	TRI	Vibe CT Williams Connection
2004	Harbour View	JAM	1-1 2-1	JAM	Tivoli Gardens
2005	Portmore United	JAM	1-2 4-0	SUR	Robinhood
2006	Vibe CT Williams Connection	TRI	1-0	TRI	San Juan Jabloteh

Not an official tournament

CONCACAF CHAMPIONS' CUP

Year	Winners	Country	Score	Country	Runners-up
1962	Guadalajara	MEX	1-0 5-0	GUA	Comunicaciones
1963	Racing Club Haïtienne	HAI	W-0	MEX	Guadalajara
1964	Not completed				
1965	Not completed				
1966	Not held				
1967	Alianza	SLV	1-2 3-0 5-3	ANT	Jong Colombia
1968	Toluca	MEX	W-0 †		
1969	Cruz Azul	MEX	0-0 1-0	GUA	Comunicaciones
1970	Cruz Azul	MEX	W-0 †		
1971	Cruz Azul	MEX	5-1	CRC	LD Alajuelense
1972	Olimpia	HON	0-0 2-0	SUR	Robinhood
1973	Transvaal	SUR	W-0 †		
1974	Municipal	GUA	2-1 2-1	SUR	Transvaal
1975	Atletico Español	MEX	3-0 2-1	SUR	Transvaal
1976	Aguila	SLV	6-1 2-1	SUR	Robinhood
1977	América	MEX	1-0 0-0	SUR	Robinhood
1978	UAG Tecos	MEX	W-0 †		
1979	Deportivo FAS	SLV	1-0 8-0	ANT	Jong Colombia
1980	UNAM Pumas	MEX	2-0 ‡	HON	Universidad de Honduras
1981	Transvaal	SUR	1-0 1-1	SLV	Atlético Marte
1982	UNAM Pumas	MEX	2-2 3-0	SUR	Robinhood
1983	Atlante	MEX	1-1 5-0	SUR	Robinhood
1984	Violette	HAI	W-0 †		
1985	Defence Force	TRI	2-0 0-1	HON	Olimpia
1986	LD Alajuelense	CRC	4-1 1-1	SUR	Transvaal
1987	América	MEX	2-0 1-1	TRI	Defence Force
1988	Olimpia	HON	2-0 2-0	TRI	Defence Force
1989	UNAM Pumas	MEX	1-1 3-1	CUB	Piñar del Rio
1990	América	MEX	2-2 6-0	CUB	Piñar del Rio
1991	Puebla	MEX	3-1 1-1	TRI	Police FC
1992	América	MEX	1-0	CRC	LD Alajuelense
1993	Deportivo Saprissa	CRC	2-2 ‡	MEX	Leon
1994	Cartagines	CRC	3-2	MEX	Atlante
1995	Deportivo Saprissa	CRC	1-0 ‡	GUA	Municipal
1996	Cruz Azul	MEX	1-1 ‡	MEX	Necaxa
1997	Cruz Azul	MEX	5-3	USA	Los Angeles Galaxy
1998	DC United	USA	1-0	MEX	Toluca
1999	Necaxa	MEX	2-1	CRC	LD Alajuelense
2000	LA Galaxy	USA	3-2	HON	Olimpia
2001	Not completed				
2002	Pachuca	MEX	1-0	MEX	Monarcas Morelia
2003	Toluca	MEX	3-3 2-1	MEX	Monarcas Morelia
2004	LD Alajuelense	CRC	1-1 4-0	CRC	Deportivo Saprissa
2005	Deportivo Saprissa	CRC	2-0 1-2	MEX	UNAM Pumas
2006	América	MEX	0-0 2-1	MEX	Toluca
2007	Pachuca	MEX	2-2 0-0 7-6p	MEX	Guadalajara

† 1968 Toluca were declared champions after Aurora GUA and Transvaal SUR were disqualified • 1970 Cruz Azul were declared champions after Deportivo Saprissa CRC and Transvaal SUR withdrew • 1973 Transvaal were declared champions after LD Alajuelense CRC and Deoprtivo Saprissa CRC withdrew • 1978 UAG Tecos were joint winners with Comunicaciones GUA and Defence Force TRI • 1984 Violette were declared champions after Guadalajara and New York Freedoms were disqualified • ‡ 1980 1993 1995 & 1996 finals played as a league with the match listed between the top two

The entry of MLS clubs in the late 1990's and, more significantly, the prospect of a place at the FIFA Club World Cup has given the CONCACAF Champions' Cup a significant boost in recent years. Without these two events, the competition was in danger of dying a death, especially given the fact that since 1998 Mexican clubs have entered South America's Copa Libertadores. First played in 1962, the CONCACAF Champions' Cup has always been dominated by Mexico. Their

CONCACAF CHAMPIONS' CUP MEDALS TABLE

	Country	G	S	B	F	SF
1	Mexico	23	10	11	33	44
2	Costa Rica	6	4	11	10	21
3	El Salvador	3	1	2	4	6
4	Surinam	2	8	3	10	13
5	Guatemala	2	3	7	5	12
6	Honduras	2	3	3	5	8
7	Trinidad and Tobago	2	3	2	5	7
8	USA	2	1	10	3	13
9	Haiti	2			2	2
10	Netherlands Antilles		2	4	2	6
11	Cuba		2		2	2
12	Martinique			3		3
13	Bermuda			1		1
		44	37	57	81	138

This table represents the Gold (winners), Silver (runners-up) and Bronze (semi-finalists) placings of clubs representing the above countries in the CONCACAF Champions' Cup, along with the number of appearances in the final and semi-finals.

22 titles is more than the number won by clubs from the rest of the clubs in the confederation combined. Had they taken the competition more seriously over the years, the number of titles won by Mexican clubs would surely have been even greater. Organising the tournament has never been easy for CONCACAF given the diverse nature of the confederation members - tiny Montserrat has a population of just 5000 whilst the USA has almost 300 million. Geographically the region has also traditionally been divided into three seperate groupings of the Caribbean, Central America and North America, the latter comprising Mexico, Canada and the USA. In the early years of the tournament all three regions held qualifying tournaments, which left an awkward numbers of teams for a final tournament and on nine ocassions over the years the competition has remained unfinished. Since the turn of the century, however, a regular format has been kept, with the winner of a Caribbean tournament and the top three from a Central American tournament joining two American and two Mexican clubs in the quarter-finals. Costa Rican clubs have provided an unexpected challenge in recent years and both Deportivo Saprissa and LD Alajuelense are in the all-time top five most successful clubs. Cruz Azul and América remain the most successful teams with five titles, but spare a thought for Suriname's Robinhood who have lost all five finals they have played in.

CONCACAF CHAMPIONS' CUP MEDALS TABLE

	Country		G	S	B
1	América	MEX	5		1
2	Cruz Azul	MEX	5		
3	Deportivo Saprissa	CRC	3	1	6
4	UNAM Pumas	MEX	3	1	
5	LD Alajuelense	CRC	2	3	4
6	Transvaal	SUR	2	3	
7	Toluca	MEX	2	2	1
8	Olimpia	HON	2	2	1
9	Defence Force	TRI	2	2	
10	Pachuca	MEX	2	1	1
11	Comunicaciones	GUA	1	2	3
	Guadalajara	MEX	1	2	1
	Municipal	GUA	1	1	1
14	Necaxa	MEX	1	1	1
	Atlante	MEX	1	1	
16	Los Angeles Galaxy	USA	1	1	
17	DC United	USA	1		5
18	Alianza	SLV	1		2
19	Aguila	SLV	1		
	Atlético Español	MEX	1		
	CS Cartagines	CRC	1		
	Deportivo FAS	SLV	1		
	Puebla	MEX	1		
	Racing Club Haïtienne	HAI	1		
	UAG Tecos	MEX	1		
	Violette	HAI	1		
27	Robinhood	SUR		5	3
28	Jong Colombia	ANT		2	1
29	Piñar del Rio	CUB		2	
	Monarcas Morelia	MEX		2	
31	Leon	MEX		1	2
32	Atlético Marte	SLV		1	
	Police FC	TRI		1	
	Universidad de Honduras	HON		1	
35	Monterrey	MEX			3
36	Chicago Fire	USA			2
	SUBT	ANT			2
	Trintoc	TRI			2
39	Aurora	GUA			1
	Herediano	CRC			1
	Houston Dynamo	USA			1
	Kansas City Wizards	USA			1
	L'Aiglon	MTQ			1
	Marathon	HON			1
	Pembrooke	BER			1
	Philidelphia Ukrainians	USA			1
	Real España	HON			1
	Riviere-Pilote	MTQ			1
	US Robert	MTQ			1
	Sithoc	ANT			1
	Suchitepequez	GUA			1
	Tigres UANL	MEX			1
	Xelaju	GUA			1
			44	37	57

CONCACAF GOLD CUP 2007 QUALIFIERS

UNCAF CUP EL SALVADOR 2007

First Round Group Stage

Group A	Pl	W	D	L	F	A	Pts	GUA	NCA	BLZ
El Salvador	3	2	1	0	4	2	7	0-0	2-1	2-1
Guatemala	3	2	1	0	2	0	7		1-0	1-0
Nicaragua	3	1	0	2	5	5	3			4-2
Belize	3	0	0	3	3	7	0			

Group B	Pl	W	D	L	F	A	Pts	CRC	HON
Panama	2	1	1	0	2	1	4	1-0	1-1
Costa Rica	2	1	0	1	3	2	3		3-1
Honduras	2	0	1	1	2	4	1		

Held in San Salvador from 8-02-2007 to 18-02-2007
The top five qualified for the CONCACAF Gold Cup 2007

Semi-finals

Costa Rica	2
El Salvador	0

Guatemala	0
Panama	2

Final

Costa Rica	1	4p
Panama	1	1p

Fifth place play-off

Honduras	9
Nicaragua	1

Third place play-off

Guatemala	1
El Salvador	0

DIGICEL CARIBBEAN CUP QUALIFYING ROUNDS 2006–07

First Round Groups

Group A	Pl	W	D	L	F	A	Pts	SUR	GRN	ANT
Guyana	3	3	0	0	11	0	9	5-0	1-0	5-0
Surinam	3	2	0	1	2	5	6		1-0	1-0
Grenada	3	0	1	2	1	3	1			1-1
Netherlands Antilles	3	0	1	2	1	7	1			

Group B	Pl	W	D	L	F	A	Pts	ATG	SKN	AIA
Barbados	3	2	1	0	11	3	7	3-1	1-1	7-1
Antigua & Barbuda	3	2	0	1	7	6	6		1-0	5-3
St Kitts & Nevis	3	1	1	1	7	3	4			6-1
Anguilla	3	0	0	3	5	18	0			

Group C	Pl	W	D	L	F	A	Pts	DOM	VIR
Bermuda	2	2	0	0	9	1	6	3-1	6-0
Dominican Republic	2	1	0	1	7	4	3		6-1
US Virgin Islands	2	0	0	2	1	12	0		

Group D	Pl	W	D	L	F	A	Pts	VIN	JAM	LCA
Haiti	3	2	0	1	11	3	6	4-0	0-2	7-1
St Vincent/Grenadines	3	2	0	1	10	5	6		2-1	8-0
Jamaica	3	2	0	1	7	2	6			4-0
St Lucia	3	0	0	3	1	19	0			

Group E	Pl	W	D	L	F	A	Pts	BAH	TCA	CAY
Cuba	3	3	0	0	19	0	9	6-0	6-0	7-0
Bahamas	3	2	0	1	6	9	6		3-2	3-1
Turks & Caicos Islands	3	1	0	2	4	9	3			2-0
Cayman Islands	3	0	0	3	1	12	0			

Group F	Pl	W	D	L	F	A	Pts	MTQ	SMA	DMA
Guadeloupe	3	3	0	0	6	0	9	4-0	1-0	1-0
Martinique	3	2	0	1	5	4	6		1-0	4-0
Saint Martin	3	0	1	2	0	2	1			0-0
Dominica	3	0	1	2	0	5	1			

Second Round Groups

Group G	Pl	W	D	L	F	A	Pts	VIN	BER	BAH
Barbados	3	2	1	0	6	2	7	3-0	1-1	2-1
St Vincent/Grenadines	3	2	0	1	6	5	6		3-0	3-2
Bermuda	3	1	1	1	5	4	4			4-0
Bahamas	3	0	0	3	3	9	0			

Group H	Pl	W	D	L	F	A	Pts	GLP	DOM	ATG
Guyana	3	3	0	0	13	2	9	3-2	4-0	6-0
Guadeloupe	3	2	0	1	8	4	6		3-0	3-1
Dominican Republic	3	1	0	2	2	7	3			2-0
Antigua & Barbuda	3	0	0	3	1	11	0			

Group I	Pl	W	D	L	F	A	Pts	MTQ	HAI	SUR
Cuba	3	2	1	0	5	2	7	0-0	2-1	3-1
Martinique	3	2	1	0	2	0	7		1-0	1-0
Haiti	3	0	1	2	2	4	1			1-1
Surinam	3	0	1	2	2	5	1			

The top two from the second round groups qualified for the finals whilst Bermuda, Dominican Republic and Haiti qualified for a play-off to decide the final place. The Dominican Republic then withdrew

Play-off: Haiti 2-0 3-0 Bermuda. Haiti qualified, along with hosts Trinidad and Tobago

DIGICEL CARIBBEAN CUP FINALS TRINIDAD AND TOBAGO 2007

First Round Group Stage

Group A	Pl	W	D	L	F	A	Pts	HAI	MTQ	BRB
Trinidad & Tobago	3	2	1	0	9	3	**7**	3-1	5-1	1-1
Haiti	3	2	0	1	4	3	**6**		1-0	2-0
Martinique	3	1	0	2	4	8	**3**			3-2
Barbados	3	0	1	2	3	6	**1**			

Group B	Pl	W	D	L	F	A	Pts	CUB	GUY	VIN
Guadeloupe	3	2	0	1	6	4	**6**	2-1	3-4	1-0
Cuba	3	1	1	1	4	2	**4**		0-0	3-0
Guyana	3	1	1	1	4	5	**4**			0-2
St Vincent/Grenadines	3	1	0	2	2	4	**3**			

Held in Trinidad & Tobago from 12-01-2007 to 23-01-2007

Haiti, Trinidad & Tobago, Cuba and Guadeloupe qualified for the CONCACAF Gold Cup 2007

Semi-finals

Haiti	3
Guadeloupe	1

Cuba	1
Trinidad & Tobago	3

Final

Haiti	2
Trinidad & Tobago	1

Third place play-off

Cuba	2
Guadeloupe	1

CONCACAF GOLD CUP USA 2007

CONCACAF GOLD CUP USA 2007

First round groups

Group A	Pts
Canada	6
Costa Rica	4
Guadeloupe	4
Haiti	2

Group B	Pts
USA	9
Guatemala	4
El Salvador	3
Trinidad and Tobago	1

Group C	Pts
Honduras	6
Mexico	6
Panama	4
Cuba	1

Quarter-finals

USA	2
Panama	1

Guatemala	0
Canada	3

Guadeloupe	2
Honduras	1

Costa Rica	0
Mexico	1

Semi-finals

USA	2
Canada	1

Guadeloupe	0
Mexico	1

Final

USA	2
Mexico	1

GROUP A	PL	W	D	L	F	A	PTS		CRC	GLP	HAI
1 Canada	3	2	0	1	5	3	6		2-1	1-2	2-0
2 Costa Rica	3	1	1	1	3	3	4			1-0	1-1
3 Guadeloupe	3	1	1	1	3	3	4				1-1
4 Haiti	3	0	2	1	2	4	2				

Orange Bowl, Miami
6-06-2007, 17 420, Wijngaarde SUR

CRC 1 2 CAN

Centeno 56
DeGuzman 2 57 73

COSTA RICA			CANADA		
18 PORRAS Jose (c)			ONSTAD Patrick 22		
2 DRUMMOND Jervis			HAINAULT Andrew 5		
3 CORDERO Victor			† DEGUZMAN Julian 6		
7 FONSECA Rolando			JAZIC Ante 3		
8 RODRIGUEZ Rodolfo			(c) STALTERI Paul 7		
10 CENTENO Walter	54	72	NASH Martin 16		
11 BARRANTES Michael			BERNIER Patrice 15		
12 GONZALEZ Leonardo	67		HASTINGS Richard 11		
15 WALLACE Harold			HUTCHINSON Atiba 12		
17 BADILLA Gabriel	75		DEROSARIO Dwayne 14		
19 SABORIO Alvaro		90	FRIEND Robert 9		
Tr: MEDFORD Hernan			Tr: HART Stephen		
14 AZOFEIFA Randall	54	90	GERBA Ali 10		
16 BOLANOS Christian	67	72	HARMSE Kevin 8		
21 GABRIEL Windell	75				

Orange Bowl, Miami
6-07-2007, 17 420, Vaughn USA

GLP 1 1 HAI

Fiston 53
Chery 35p

GUADELOUPE			HAITI		
1 GRANDEL Franck			FENELON Gabart 1		
2 COMMINGES Miguel			GILLES Frantz 3		
6 VERTOT Alain (c)			PIERRE Jean Jaques 5		
14 SOMMEIL David			GUILLAUME Stephane 6		
20 TACALFRED Michael			BRUNY Pierre-Richard 13		
21 FLEURIVAL David		59	GERMAIN Peter 4		
22 LOVAL Loic	83		FUCIEN Brunel 7		
8 AUVRAY Stephane			CHERY Mones 14		
19 SOCRIER Richard		66	MARCELIN James 12		
10 CAPOUE Aurelien	78	77	ELIPHENE Cadet 9		
12 FISTON Cedrick	66		† BOUCICAUT Alexandre 10		
Tr: SALNOT Roger			Tr: GARCIA Luis Armelio		
11 RADDAS Fabien	78	59	ALCENAT Jean Sony 2		
7 MOCKA Dominique	66	66	FABRICE Noel 11		
18 QUISTIN Ludovic	83	66	ROMULUS Turlien 8		

Orange Bowl, Miami
9-06-2007, 22 529, Brizan TRI

CAN 1 2 GLP

Ali Gerba 35
Angloma 10, Fleurival 38

CANADA			GUADELOUPE		
1 SUTTON Greg			GRANDEL Franck 1		
5 HAINAULT Andrew			COMMINGES Miguel 2		
6 DEGUZMAN Julian			(c) VERTOT Alain 6		
3 JAZIC Ante			SOMMEIL David 14		
7 STALTERI Paul (c)			TACALFRED Michael 20		
16 NASH Martin	72		FLEURIVAL David 21		
15 BERNIER Patrice	83		LOVAL Loic 22		
11 HASTINGS Richard			AUVRAY Stephane 8		
12 HUTCHINSON Atiba			SOCRIER Richard 19		
14 DEROSARIO Dwayne		93+	CAPOUE Aurelien 10		
10 GERBA Ali	68	88	† ANGLOMA Jocelyn 15		
Tr: HART Stephen			Tr: SALNOT Roger		
20 POZNIAK Chris	72	93+	FISTON Cedrick 12		
8 HARMSE Kevin	83	88	LAMBOURDE Jean Luc 13		
17 HUME Iain	68				

Orange Bowl, Miami
9-06-2007, 22 529, Campbell JAM

HAI 1 1 CRC

Centeno 14

HAITI			COSTA RICA		
1 FENELON Gabart †			(c) PORRAS Jose 18		
3 GILLES Frantz			DRUMMOND Jervis 2		
5 PIERRE Jean Jaques			CORDERO Victor 3		
6 GUILLAUME Stephane		78	FONSECA Rolando 7		
13 BRUNY Pierre-Richard(c)			NUNEZ Andres 6		
2 ALCENAT Jean Sony	53		CENTENO Walter 10		
7 FUCIEN Brunel	73		BARRANTES Michael 11		
14 CHERY Mones			GONZALEZ Leonardo 12		
17 VUBERT Alain	67		AZOFEIFA Randall 14		
9 ELIPHENE Cadet		62	BADILLA Gabriel 17		
10 BOUICAUT Alexandre			SABORIO Alvaro 19		
Tr: SALNOT Roger			Tr: MEDFORD Hernan		
15 ROMULUS Turlien	53	78	CUBERO Johnny 9		
15 RAYMOND Ednerson	73	62	CAMACHO Mario 22		
19 PIERRE-LOUIS Ricardo	67				

Orange Bowl, Miami
11-06-2007, 15 892, Wijngaarde SUR

CRC 1 0 GLP

Centeno 14

COSTA RICA			GUADELOUPE		
18 PORRAS Jose (c)			GRANDEL Franck 1		
2 DRUMMOND Jervis			DURPES Philippe 4		
3 CORDERO Victor			(c) VERTOT Alain 6		
13 ALEMAN Allan	81		SOMMEIL David 14		
6 NUNEZ Andres			TACALFRED Michael 20		
10 CENTENO Walter †			FLEURIVAL David 21		
11 BARRANTES Michael	74	86	LOVAL Loic 22		
15 WALLACE Harold			AUVRAY Stephane 8		
14 AZOFEIFA Randall			SOCRIER Richard 19		
17 BADILLA Gabriel			CAPOUE Aurelien 10		
19 SABORIO Alvaro	62	65	FISTON Cedrick 12		
Tr: MEDFORD Hernan			Tr: SALNOT Roger		
7 FONSECA Rolando	74	65	ANGLOMA Jocelyn 15		
21 GABRIEL Windell	81	86	RADDAS Fabien 11		
9 CUBERO Johnny	62				

Orange Bowl, Miami
11-06-2007, 15 892,

HAI 0 2 CAN

DeRosario 2 32 35p

HAITI			CANADA		
1 FENELON Gabart			ONSTAD Patrick 22		
3 GILLES Frantz			HAINAULT Andrew 5		
5 ROMULUS Turlien		78	DEGUZMAN Julian 6		
6 GUILLAUME Stephane			JAZIC Ante 3		
13 BRUNY Pierre-Richard(c)	81		POZNIAK Chris 20		
4 GERMAIN Peter			(c) STALTERI Paul 7		
7 FUCIEN Brunel	67	83	NAKAJIMA-Farran Issey 18		
20 CHERY Mones			HASTINGS Richard 11		
19 PIERRE-LOUIS Ricardo			HUTCHINSON Atiba 12		
9 ELIPHENE Cadet			† DEROSARIO Dwayne 14		
10 BOUICAUT Alexandre			FRIEND Robert 9		
Tr: SALNOT Roger			Tr: HART Stephen		
21 JEAN-JAQUES Jamil	67	83	BERNIER Patrice 15		
		78	HARMSE Kevin 8		

GROUP B		PL	W	D	L	F	A	PTS		GUA	SLV	TRI
1	USA	3	3	0	0	7	0	9		1-0	4-0	2-0
2	Guatemala	3	1	1	1	2	2	4			1-1	1-1
3	El Salvador	3	1	0	2	2	6	3				2-1
4	Trinidad and Tobago	3	0	1	2	2	5	1				

Home Depot Center, Carson, Los Angeles
7-06-2007, 21 334, Pineda HON

USA 1 0 GUA

Dempsey [26]

USA			GUATEMALA	
1	HOWARD Tim		TRIGUENO Ricardo	1
2	HEJDUK Frankie	89	NORIEGA Leonel	2
3	BOCANEGRA Carlos (c)		MELGAR Pablo	3
13	BORNSTEIN Jonathan		MEDINA Henry Alexander	5
22	ONYEWU Oguchi	73	(c) CABRERA Gustavo	6
6	BRADLEY Michael		ALBIZURIS Claudio	7
5	FEILHABER Benny	81	CONTRERAS Jose	8
7	BEASLEY DaMarcus	81	AVILA Marvin Tomas	11
8	DEMPSEY Clint †	61 71	GOMEZ Rigoberto	14
20	TWELLMAN Taylor	71	QUINONES Carlos	18
10	DONOVAN Landon		RUIZ Carlos	20
	Tr: BRADLEY Bob		Tr: GOMEZ Hernan Dario	
12	DEMERIT Jay	81 89	SWISHER Luis	15
14	RALSTON Steve	71 81	FIGUEROA Carlos	12
9	JOHNSON Eddie	61 71	RODRIGUEZ Mario	19

Home Depot Center, Carson, Los Angeles
7-06-2007, 21 334, Arredondo MEX

SLV 2 1 TRI

Sanchez [38], Alas [81]   Spann [8]

EL SALVADOR			TRINIDAD & TOBAGO	
1	GOMEZ Juan Jose		WILLIAMS Jan Michael	21
2	GUEVARA Leonel		NICKOLSON Thomas	6
5	HENRIQUEZ Jose		NOREIGA Anthony	20
7	MERINO Victor Hugo		THOMAS Keyeno	5
8	MENJIVAR Carlos Alberto	8	POWER Seon	17
17	ALAS Dennis †		AGUILLERA Romauld	2
19	PACHECO Alfredo (c)		PACHECO Andrei	15
18	ESCOBAR Alexander	73	SPANN Silvio	16
21	QUINTANILLA Eliseo		THEOBALD Densill	18
11	CERRITOS Ronald	67	GLASGOW Gary	12
16	LARIOS Cesar Alexander	63	ROBERTS Darryl	14
	Tr: DE LOS COBOS Carlos		Tr: RIJSBERGEN Wim	
14	SANCHEZ Ramon Alfredo	8 84	MCFARLANE Errol	9
23	MARTINEZ Jose Orlando	63 73	BAPTISTE Kerry	8
		67	TOUSSAINT Andre	11

Home Depot Center, Carson, Los Angeles
9-06-2007, 27 000, Jauregui ATG

GUA 1 0 SLV

Contreras [69]

GUATEMALA			EL SALVADOR	
1	TRIGUENO Ricardo	44	(c) GOMEZ Juan Jose	1
2	NORIEGA Leonel		GUEVARA Leonel	2
3	MELGAR Pablo		HENRIQUEZ Jose	5
5	MEDINA Henry Alexander	14	MERINO Victor Hugo	7
6	CABRERA Gustavo (c)		ESCOBAR Alexander	18
7	ALBIZURIS Claudio		ALAS Dennis	17
8	CONTRERAS Jose †		PACHECO Alfredo	19
12	FIGUEROA Carlos	58	CAMPOS Juan Alexander	9
19	RODRIGUEZ Mario	46	QUINTANILLA Eliseo	21
18	QUINONES Carlos		CERRITOS Ronald	11
20	RUIZ Carlos	80	SANCHEZ Ramon Alfredo	14
	Tr: GOMEZ Hernan Dario		Tr: DE LOS COBOS Carlos	
11	AVILA Marvin Tomas	46 44	GAMERO Dagoberto	22
17	PEZZAROSSI Dwight	58 14	MARTINEZ Jose Orlando	23
27	ARREOLA Jairo	80 78	ALVAREZ Francisco Jovel	20

Home Depot Center, Carson, Los Angeles
9-06-2007, 27 000, Moreno PAN

TRI 0 2 USA

Ching [29], Johnson [54]

TRINIDAD & TOBAGO			USA	
21	WILLIAMS Jan Michael		(c) KELLER Kasey	18
6	NICKOLSON Thomas	24	DEMERIT Jay	12
20	NOREIGA Anthony	20	PARKHURST Michael	16
5	THOMAS Keyeno		SPECTOR Jonathan	17
17	POWER Seon		SIMEK Frank	15
2	AGUILLERA Romauld		RALSTON Steve	14
15	PACHECO Andrei	81	FEILHABER Benny	5
16	SPANN Silvio		CLARK Ricardo	19
18	THEOBALD Densill (c)		MAPP Justin	21
11	TOUSSAINT Andre		JOHNSON Eddie	9
14	ROBERTS Darryl		† CHING Brian	11
	Tr: RIJSBERGEN Wim		Tr: BRADLEY Bob	
8	BAPTISTE Kerry	24	DONOVAN Landon	10
7	NOEL Trent	81	TWELLMAN Taylor	20
13	BAPTISTE Christon	20	BRADLEY Michael	6

Gillette Stadium, Foxboro, Boston
12-06-2007, 26 523, Archundia MEX

USA 4 0 SLV

Beasley 2 [34 89], Donovan [45p],
Twellman [72]

USA			EL SALVADOR	
1	HOWARD Tim		MONTES Miguel Angel	25
17	SPECTOR Jonathan	81 46	GUEVARA Leonel	2
22	ONYEWU Oguchi		HENRIQUEZ Jose	5
16	PARKHURST Michael	46	CARBALLO Ramiro	12
13	BORNSTEIN Jonathan		ESCOBAR Alexander	18
6	BRADLEY Michael	64	SANCHEZ Ramon Alfredo	14
4	MASTROENI Pablo		(c) PACHECO Alfredo	19
5	FEILHABER Benny		ALAS Dennis	17
7	BEASLEY DaMarcus †	77	MARTINEZ Jose Orlando	23
8	DEMPSEY Clint		CERRITOS Ronald	11
10	DONOVAN Landon (c)	46	CAMPOS Juan Alexander	9
	Tr: BRADLEY Bob		Tr: DE LOS COBOS Carlos	
15	SIMEK Frank	81 46	SALAZAR Manuel	15
11	CHING Brian	64 46	MARTINEZ Julio Enrique	13
20	TWELLMAN Taylor	46 77	LARIOS Cesar Alexander	16

Gillette Stadium, Foxboro, Boston
12-06-2007, 26 523, Pineda HON

TRI 1 1 GUA

McFarlane [87]   Ruiz [84]

TRINIDAD & TOBAGO			GUATEMALA	
21	WILLIAMS Jan Michael		† TRIGUENO Ricardo	1
3	WOLFFE Glenton		MELGAR Pablo	3
4	JACK Dwayne		MEDINA Henry Alexander	5
5	THOMAS Keyeno	77	(c) CABRERA Gustavo	6
7	NOEL Trent		MARTINEZ Nestor	13
17	POWER Seon		NORIEGA Leonel	2
18	THEOBALD Densill (c)	53	FIGUEROA Carlos	12
16	SPANN Silvio	59	CONTRERAS Jose	8
2	ROBERTS Darryl		QUINONES Carlos	18
12	GLASGOW Gary	69 90	RUIZ Carlos	20
11	TOUSSAINT Andre		AVILA Marvin Tomas	11
	Tr: RIJSBERGEN Wim		Tr: GOMEZ Hernan Dario	
13	BAPTISTE Christon	77 53	RODRIGUEZ Mario	19
9	MCFARLANE Errol	69 90	SANDOVAL Hernan	23
8	BAPTISTE Kerry	59		

GROUP C	PL	W	D	L	F	A	PTS		MEX	PAN	CUB
1 Honduras	3	2	0	1	9	4	6		2-1	2-3	5-0
2 Mexico	3	2	0	1	4	3	6			1-0	2-1
3 Panama	3	2	1	1	5	5	4				2-2
4 Cuba	3	0	1	2	3	9	1				

Giants Stadium, East Rutherford, New York
8-06-2007, 20 230, Navarro CAN

PAN 3 2 HON

Rivera 33, Blas Perez 42, Garces 82 | Guevara 40, Costly 92+

PANAMA			HONDURAS		
1 PENEDO Jaime			VALLECILLO Orlin Jared 12		
23 BALOY Felipe (c)			GARCIA Oscar Bonieck 14		
3 MORENO Luis			CABALLEROS Jorge 4		
2 RIVERA Carlos			FIGUEROA Maynor 3		
21 HENRIQUEZ Amilcar	28	76	ALVAREZ Edgar 17	76	
6 GOMEZ Gabriel			MENDOZA Sergio 6		
4 PEREZ Juan	85		CLAROS Jorge Aron 18		
8 BLANCO Alberto	63		GUEVARA Amado 20		
7 PEREZ Blas †		29	PALACIOS Wilson 8		
5 TORRES Roman			MARTINEZ Emil 7		
19 MUNOZ Nicolas	60	66	(c) PAVON Carlos 9		
Tr: GUIMARAES Alexandre			Tr: RUEDA Reinaldo		
9 GARCES Jose Luis	63	76	VALLECILO Erick 5	76	
22 HERRERA Victor	60	85	RODRIGUEZ Mario 19	85	
15 PHILLIPS Ricardo	28	66	COSTLY Carlos 13	66	

Giants Stadium, East Rutherford, New York
8-06-2007, 20 230, Aguilar SLV

MEX 2 1 CUB

Borgetti 37, Castillo 55 | Alcantara 22

MEXICO			CUBA		
13 OCHOA Guillermo			MOLINA Odelin 1		
15 CASTRO Jose Antonio			FERNANDEZ Reysander 16		
2 MAGALLON Jonny			MINOSO Silvio Pedro 2		
22 RODRIGUEZ Francisco			COLOME Jaime 14		
16 LOZANO Jaime	61		DUARTE Leonel 19	61	
8 PARDO Pavel (c)			(c) MARQUEZ Yenier 3		
20 ARCE Fernando			MORALES Gisbel 15		
18 GUARDADO Andres	86	78	ALONSO Osvaldo 6	78	
21 CASTILLO Nery †			ALCANTARA Reynier 18	88	
23 BAUTISTA Adolfo	46		CERVANTES Alain 9		
9 BORGETTI Jared	78		FAIFE Pedro Adriani 17		
Tr: SANCHEZ Hugo			Tr: GONZALEZ Raul		
3 SALCIDO Carlos	86	78	VILLAURRUTIA Enrique 11		
17 FONSECA Jose Francisco	46	88	MORE Lester 10		
6 TORRADO Gerrardo	78	61	RAMOS Adonis 13		

Giants Stadium, East Rutherford, New York
10-06-2007, 68 123, Quesada CRC

HON 2 1 MEX

Costly 2 60 91+ | Blanco 29p

HONDURAS			MEXICO		
12 VALLECILLO Orlin Jared			SANCHEZ Oswaldo 1		
21 IZAGUIRRE Emilio			OSORIO Ricardo 5		
3 FIGUEROA Maynor			MAGALLON Jonny 2		
4 CABALLEROS Jorge			SALCIDO Carlos 3		
14 GARCIA Oscar Bonieck			TORRADO Gerrardo 6		
17 ALVAREZ Edgar	63		MORALES Ramon 11	63	
7 MARTINEZ Emil	75		(c) PARDO Pavel 8		
20 GUEVARA Amado	84		MEDINA Alberto 7		
18 CLAROS Jorge Aron	46	72	GUARDADO Andres 18	72	
9 PAVON Carlos (c)	84		BRAVO Omar 19	84	
13 COSTLY Carlos		49	BLANCO Cuauhtemoc 10		
Tr: RUEDA Reinaldo			Tr: SANCHEZ Hugo		
11 MARTINEZ Jairo	75	63	RODRIGUEZ Francisco 22	63	
16 OLIVA Carlos	84	72	ARCE Fernando 20	72	
19 RODRIGUEZ Mario	46	84	FONSECA Jose Francisco 17	84	

Giants Stadium, East Rutherford, New York
10-06-2007, 68 123

PAN 2 2 CUB

Garces 16, Blas Perez 47 | Colome 29, Alcantara 78

PANAMA			CUBA		
1 PENEDO Jaime			MOLINA Odelin 1		
21 HENRIQUEZ Amilcar	64		MINOSO Silvio Pedro 2		
23 BALOY Felipe (c)			MARQUEZ Yenier 3		
2 RIVERA Carlos			FERNANDEZ Reysander 16		
8 BLANCO Alberto	46		COLOME Jaime 14		
6 GOMEZ Gabriel	65		DUARTE Leonel 19	65	
4 PEREZ Juan			ALONSO Osvaldo 6		
22 HERRERA Victor			MORALES Gisbel 15		
7 PEREZ Blas †			ALCANTARA Reynier 18		
5 TORRES Roman			FAIFE Pedro Adriani 17		
9 GARCES Jose Luis	78	85	CERVANTES Alain 9		
Tr: GUIMARAES Alexandre			Tr: GONZALEZ Raul		
3 MORENO Luis	64	85	MARTINEZ Ariel 7	85	
15 PHILLIPS Ricardo	46	65	RAMOS Adonis 13	65	
20 MITRE Engin	78				

Reliant Stadium, Houston
13-06-2007, 68 417

CUB 0 5 HON

| | Pavon 4 3 12 43 53, Guevara 89

CUBA			HONDURAS		
1 MOLINA Odelin			VALLECILLO Orlin Jared 12		
3 MARQUEZ Yenier			FIGUEROA Maynor 3		
5 CLAVELO Jorge Luis			CABALLEROS Jorge 4		
14 COLOME Jaime			GARCIA Oscar Bonieck 14		
16 FERNANDEZ Reysander		71	ALVAREZ Edgar 17	71	
15 MORALES Gisbel			IZAGUIRRE Emilio 21		
11 VILLAURRUTIA Enrique	57	66	LEON Julio Cesar 10	66	
17 FAIFE Pedro Adriani			RODRIGUEZ Mario 19		
13 RAMOS Adonis	57		GUEVARA Amado 20		
18 ALCANTARA Reynier			COSTLY Carlos 13		
9 CERVANTES Alain	87	62	(c) PAVON Carlos 9	62	
Tr: GONZALEZ Raul			Tr: RUEDA Reinaldo		
7 MARTINEZ Ariel	57	62	PALACIOS Wilson 8	62	
19 DUARTE Leonel	57	66	MARTINEZ Emil 7	66	
			OLIVA Carlos 16	71	

Reliant Stadium, Houston
13-06-2007, 68 417

MEX 1 0 PAN

Salcido 60

MEXICO			PANAMA		
1 SANCHEZ Oswaldo			PENEDO Jaime 1		
5 OSORIO Ricardo		80	MORENO Luis 3	80	
2 MAGALLON Jonny			(c) BALOY Felipe 23		
22 RODRIGUEZ Francisco			RIVERA Carlos 2		
3 SALCIDO Carlos			PEREZ Juan 4		
8 PARDO Pavel (c)			GOMEZ Gabriel 6		
7 MEDINA Alberto	76	66	HERRERA Victor 22		
6 TORRADO Gerrardo	89	80	ESCOBAR Rolando 10	80	
18 GUARDADO Andres	90		GARCES Jose Luis 9		
21 CASTILLO Nery	81		PEREZ Blas 7		
9 BORGETTI Jared		83	TORRES Roman 5		
Tr: SANCHEZ Hugo			Tr: GUIMARAES Alexandre		
20 ARCE Fernando	76	80	TEJADA Luis ?	80	
16 LOZANO Jaime	89	66	PHILLIPS Ricardo 15	66	
17 FONSECA Jose Francisco	81	90	HENRIQUEZ Luis 17	90	

QUARTER-FINALS

Gillette Stadium, Foxboro, Boston
16-06-2007, 22 412, Campbell JAM

CAN	3	0	GUA

DeRosario [17], Ali Gerba 2 [33] [44]

CANADA		GUATEMALA	
22 ONSTAD Patrick		TRIGUENO Ricardo 1	
5 HAINAULT Andrew		MELGAR Pablo 3	
10 GERBA Ali †	67	MEDINA Henry Alexander 5	
6 DEGUZMAN Julian		(c) CABRERA Gustavo 6	
7 STALTERI Paul (c)	54	ALBIZURIS Claudio 7	
3 JAZIC Ante		CONTRERAS Jose 8	
11 HASTINGS Richard	27	SWISHER Luis 15	
16 NASH Martin		GOMEZ Rigoberto 14	
13 HUTCHINSON Atiba	92+	QUINONES Carlos 18	
15 BERNIER Patrice	75	AVILA Marvin Tomas 11	
14 DEROSARIO Dwayne	89	RUIZ Carlos 20	
Tr: HART Stephen		Tr: GOMEZ Hernan Dario	
18 NAKAJIMA-FARRAN Issey	89 54	MARTINEZ Nestor 13	
20 POZNIAK Chris	92+ 75	FIGUEROA Carlos 12	
17 HUME Iain	67 27	RODRIGUEZ Mario 19	

Gillette Stadium, Foxboro, Boston
16-06-2007, 22 412, Brizan TRI

USA	2	1	PAN

Donovan [60p], Bocanegra [62]   Blas Perez [84]

USA		PANAMA	
1 HOWARD Tim		PENEDO Jaime 1	
2 HEJDUK Frankie		RIVERA Carlos 2	
22 ONYEWU Oguchi		MORENO Luis 3	
3 BOCANEGRA Carlos (c)		HENRIQUEZ Amilcar 21	78
13 BORNSTEIN Jonathan		(c) BALOY Felipe 23	
6 BRADLEY Michael		HERRERA Victor 22	78
4 MASTROENI Pablo		PEREZ Juan 4	
7 BEASLEY DaMarcus		TORRES Manuel 14	76
8 DEMPSEY Clint	84	PHILLIPS Ricardo 15	
20 TWELLMAN Taylor	71	MITRE Engin 20	63
10 DONOVAN Landon †	89	PEREZ Blas 7	
Tr: BRADLEY Bob		Tr: GUIMARAES Alexandre	
19 CLARK Ricardo	89 63	MUNOZ Nicolas 19	
14 RALSTON Steve	71 78	HENRIQUEZ Luis 17	
11 CHING Brian	84 78	BLANCO Alberto 8	

Reliant Stadium, Houston
17-06-2007, 70 092, Vaughn USA

MEX	1	0	CRC

Borgetti [97]

MEXICO		COSTA RICA	
1 SANCHEZ Oswaldo		(c) PORRAS Jose 18	
2 MAGALLON Jonny		DRUMMOND Jervis 2	
22 RODRIGUEZ Francisco		CORDERO Victor 3	
5 OSORIO Ricardo	89	WALLACE Harold 15	
4 SALCIDO Carlos	43	ALEMAN Allan 13	
6 TORRADO Gerrardo	76	BADILLA Gabriel 17	
7 MEDINA Alberto		NUNEZ Andres 6	
16 LOZANO Jaime	115	AZOFEIFA Randall 14	
18 GUARDADO Andres	102	BARRANTES Michael 11	
19 BRAVO Omar	91+ 46	GABRIEL Windell 21	
9 BORGETTI Jared †	103	SABORIO Alvaro 19	
Tr: SANCHEZ Hugo		Tr: MEDFORD Hernan	
10 BLANCO Cuauhtemoc	76 89	FONSECA Rolando 7	
20 ARCE Fernando	115 46	GONZALEZ Leonardo 12	
23 BAUTISTA Adolfo	91+ 120 102	CAMACHO Mario 22	

Reliant Stadium, Houston
17-06-2007, 70 092, Navarro CAN

HON	1	2	GLP

Pavon [71]   Angloma [17], Socrier [21]

HONDURAS		GUADELOUPE	
12 VALLECILLO Orlin Jared		GRANDEL Franck 1	
17 ALVAREZ Edgar		COMMINGES Miguel 2	
3 FIGUEROA Maynor		(c) VERTOT Alain 6	
4 CABALLEROS Jorge		TACALFRED Michael 20	
14 GARCIA Oscar Bobieck		SOMMEIL David 14	
21 IZAGUIRRE Emilio		FLEURIVAL David 21	
20 GUEVARA Amado		AUVRAY Stephane 8	
10 LEON Julio Cesar	60	ANGLOMA Jocelyn 15	
19 RODRIGUEZ Mario	59	HANNANY Lery 17	
13 COSTLY Carlos	67 71	SOCRIER Richard 19	
9 PAVON Carlos (c)	89	LOVAL Loic 22	
Tr: RUEDA Reinaldo		Tr: SALNOT Roger	
23 GUERRO Ivan	60 59	RADDAS Fabien 11	
8 PALACIOS Wilson	67 71	LAMBOURDE Jean Luc 13	
	89	FISTON Cedrick 12	

SEMI-FINALS

Soldier Field, Chicago
21-06-2007, 50 760, Archundia MEX

CAN	1	2	USA

Hume [76]   Hejduk [39], Donovan [45p]

CANADA		USA	
22 ONSTAD Patrick		(c) KELLER Kasey 18	
5 HAINAULT Andrew		HEJDUK Frankie 2	
10 GERBA Ali	81	BOCANEGRA Carlos 3	
3 JAZIC Ante		ONYEWU Oguchi 22	
6 DEGUZMAN Julian		BORNSTEIN Jonathan 13	
7 STALTERI Paul (c)	89	MASTROENI Pablo 4	
11 HASTINGS Richard	89	BRADLEY Michael 6	
13 HUTCHINSON Atiba	88	DEMPSEY Clint 8	
15 BERNIER Patrice		BEASLEY DaMarcus 7	
16 NASH Martin	64 80	JOHNSON Eddie 9	
14 DEROSARIO Dwayne		† DONOVAN Landon 10	
Tr: HART Stephen		Tr: BRADLEY Bob	
18 NAKAJIMA-FARRAN Issey	81 89	CLARK Ricardo 19	
17 HUME Iain	64 80	FEILHABER Benny 5	
	88	TWELLMAN Taylor 20	

Soldier Field, Chicago
21-06-2007, 50 760, Moreno PAN

GLP	0	1	MEX

Pardo [70]

GUADELOUPE		MEXICO	
1 GRANDEL Franck		SANCHEZ Oswaldo 1	
2 COMMINGES Miguel		MAGALLON Jonny 2	
6 VERTOT Alain (c)		OSORIO Ricardo 5	
14 SOMMEIL David		SALCIDO Carlos 3	
20 TACALFRED Michael		RODRIGUEZ Francisco 22	
21 FLEURIVAL David	89 70	TORRADO Gerrardo 6	
8 AUVRAY Stephane		MEDINA Alberto 7	
15 ANGLOMA Jocelyn		† (c) PARDO Pavel 8	
10 CAPOUE Aurelien		GUARDADO Andres 18	46
19 SOCRIER Richard	78	BLANCO Cuauhtemoc 10	85
22 LOVAL Loic	82	BORGETTI Jared 9	
Tr: SALNOT Roger		Tr: SANCHEZ Hugo	
12 FISTON Cedrick	78 70	ARCE Fernando 20	
13 LAMBOURDE Jean Luc	89 85	BRAVO Omar 19	
11 RADDAS Fabien	82 46	BAUTISTA Adolfo 23	

CONCACAF GOLD CUP FINAL 2007

Soldier Field, Chicago
24-06-2007, 60 000, Batres GUA

USA   2   1   MEX

Donovan 62p, Feilhaber 73   Guardado 44

		USA			MATCH STATS				MEXICO	
1	GK	HOWARD Tim						SANCHEZ Oswaldo	GK	1
17	DF	SPECTOR Jonathan	72	13	Shots	16		MAGALLON Jonny	DF	2
22	DF	ONYEWU Oguchi			Shots on Goal			SALCIDO Carlos	DF	3
3	DF	BOCANEGRA Carlos (c)		21	Fouls Committed	9		MARQUEZ Rafael	DF	4
13	DF	BORNSTEIN Jonathan		2	Corner Kicks	10		OSORIO Ricardo	DF	5
8	MF	DEMPSEY Clint	69	0	Caught offside	6	78	MEDINA Alberto	MF	7
5	MF	FEILHABER Benny †			Possession %			(c) PARDO Pavel	MF	8
4	MF	MASTROENI Pablo	46		(C)Captain † Man of the Match		81	LOZANO Jaime	MF	16
7	MF	BEASLEY DaMarcus			MATCH OFFICIALS			GUARDADO Andres	MF	18
11	FW	CHING Brian			REFEREE	40		BORGETTI Jared	FW	9
10	FW	DONOVAN Landon			BATRES Carlos GUA			CASTILLO Nery	FW	21
		Tr: BRADLEY Bob			ASSISTANTS			Tr: SANCHEZ Hugo		
		Substitutes			LEAL Leonel CRC			Substitutes		
15	DF	SIMEK Frank	72		TORRES William CRC		78	BLANCO Cuauhtemoc	FW	10
19	MF	CLARK Ricardo	46		4TH OFFICIAL	40		BRAVO Omar	FW	19
20	FW	TWELLMAN Taylor	69		QUESADA Walter CRC		81	BAUTISTA Adolfo	FW	23

*This is the kind of effort on the inside of our team
that we keep talking about. A result that didn't come
easy, a result where we had to come from behind, a
result that comes from the effort of our entire group.
We are proud to have defended the Gold Cup and to
keep the trophy in the United States*

Bob Bradley

*It's not a painful loss when you leave a good image. I
think that the game, the image, our attack and every-
thing we showed on the field was magnificent. When
your rival takes advantage of their opportunities, you
must congratulate your rival. The US were more prac-
tical but we deserved a better result.*

Hugo Sanchez

CONCACAF WOMEN'S GOLD CUP 2006

CONCACAF WOMEN'S GOLD CUP 2006 QUALIFYING

Caribbean Preliminary Qualifying Rounds

		Group A	Pl	W	D	L	F	A	Pts	BER	VIR	TCA
British Virgin Isl.	1 0	**Dominican Republic**	3	3	0	0	11	2	**9**	3-1	3-1	5-0
US Virgin Islands	3 5	Bermuda	3	2	0	1	9	4	**6**		4-1	4-0
		US Virgin Islands	3	1	0	2	4	7	**3**			2-0
Turks & Caicos Isl.	w-o	Turks & Caicos Isl.	3	0	0	3	0	11	**0**			
Bahamas												

		Group B	Pl	W	D	L	F	A	Pts	ANT	ARU	HAI
Cayman Islands	1 0	**Surinam**	2	2	0	0	10	1	**6**	7-1	3-0	0-3
Neth. Antilles	2 1	Netherlands Antilles	2	1	0	1	3	8	**3**	2-1		
		Aruba	2	0	0	2	1	5	**0**			
		Haiti qualified after beating Surinam in a play-off										

		Group C	Pl	W	D	L	F	A	Pts	LCA	SKN	ATG
St Kitts & Nevis	w-o	**Jamaica**	3	3	0	0	26	0	**9**	5-0	11-0	10-0
Montserrat		St Lucia	3	2	0	1	5	8	**6**		3-2	2-1
		St Kitts & Nevis	3	1	0	2	5	16	**3**			3-2
Barbados	0 0	Antigua & Barbuda	3	0	0	3	3	15	**0**			
Antigua & Barbuda	1 0											

		Group D	Pl	W	D	L	F	A	Pts	VIN	DMA	GRN
		Trinidad & Tobago	3	3	0	0	20	1	**9**	4-1	6-0	10-0
		St Vincent & Gren.	3	2	0	1	8	4	**6**		2-0	5-0
Grenada	w-o	Dominica	3	0	1	2	2	10	**1**			2-2
Guyana		Grenada	3	0	1	2	2	17	**1**			

Caribbean Qualifying Finals

Group A	Pl	W	D	L	F	A	Pts	DOM	SUR
Trinidad & Tobago	2	2	0	0	12	1	**6**	7-0	5-1
Dominican Republic	2	1	0	1	2	7	**3**		2-0
Surinam	2	0	0	2	1	7	**0**		

Group B	Pl	W	D	L	F	A	Pts	HAI	BER
Jamaica	2	2	0	0	10	0	**6**	3-0	7-0
Haiti	2	1	0	1	5	3	**3**		5-0
Bermuda	2	0	0	2	0	12	**0**		

Central America Qualifying Finals

Group A	Pl	W	D	L	F	A	Pts	NCA	SLV
Mexico	2	2	0	0	17	0	**6**	9-0	8-0
Nicaragua	2	1	0	1	2	10	**3**		2-1
El Salvador	2	0	0	2	1	10	**0**		

Group B	Pl	W	D	L	F	A	Pts	GUA	CRC
Panama	2	2	0	0	5	0	**6**	3-0	2-0
Guatemala	2	1	0	1	2	4	**3**		2-1
Costa Rica	2	0	0	2	1	4	**0**		

CONCACAF WOMEN'S GOLD CUP 2006

First round	Semi-finals	Final

USA	2
Mexico	0

Trinidad & Tobago	0
Mexico	3

USA	2
Canada	1

Jamaica	2
Panama	0

Jamaica	0
Canada	4

1ST ROUND. Tropical Park Stadium, Miami
19-11-2006, 17:00, 800; Seitz USA

PAN   0   2   JAM

Sullivan 4, Reid 59

PANAMA			JAMAICA		
12	BENIS Lineth			JACKSON Paula	13
2	DE LA ROSA Mayra			WILSON Alicia	4
3	AGUILAR Steffany	57	72	SULLIVAN Audia	6
4	CHAVARRIA Kendra		88	REID Venicia	7
5	EVANS Phanilka	87		MANYAN Natalya	9
6	GUTIERREZ Raiza (c)			PARKER Kimmia	11
7	SAMUELS Sumara			SOMAN Peta-Gaye	12
8	PEREZ Yoraidil			(c) BELL Nicola	15
11	VALDERRAMA Diana			HUE Diane	17
13	GUANTE Ymara	28		JOHNSON Stacy-Ann	18
17	BEDOYA Maritzenia		55	BRYAN Rochelle	19
	Tr: BARBARAN Lizandro			Tr: BLAINE Vin	
15	ROMERO Ruth	57	72	MURRAY Christina	3
18	DEMERA Amarelis	28	55	McHARDY Lianne	8

1ST ROUND. Tropical Park Stadium, Miami
19-11-2006, 19:30, 3 135, Ortega SLV

MEX   3   0   TRI

Perez.P 20, Gonzalez 45
Dominguez 67

MEXICO			TRINIDAD & TOBAGO		
20	PEREZ Sophia		75	RAMKISSOON Lisa-Jo	1
2	GOMEZ Elizabeth			RUSSELL Ayana	2
3	SANDOVAL Rubi Marlene		63	MEYER Katrina	4
4	GONZALEZ Monica		58	(c) JAMES Nadia	5
5	CASTILLO Maria de Jesus			JAMES Leslie Ann	6
7	LOPEZ Juana Evelyn	73		REYES Niasha	7
8	LEYVA Fatima			MASCALL Dernelle	9
9	DOMINGUEZ Maribel (c)			ST LOUIS Tasha	10
10	MORA Iris Adriana	61		MOLLON Ahkeela Darcel	12
11	PEREZ Patricia	65		MAHABIRSINGH Micah	15
15	SAUCEDO Luz del Rosario			NICHOLSON Mauricia	20
	Tr: CUELLAR Leonardo			Tr: CHARLES Marlon	
16	PADILLA Carmen	73	63	DOUGLAS Aveann	11
17	OCAMPO Monica	61	58	CORDNER Kennya	19
18	WORBIS Teresa	65	75	FORBES Kimika	21

SEMI-FINAL. Home Depot Center, Carson, Los Angeles
22-11-2006, 19:00, 6 128, Ferreira-James GUY

USA   2   0   MEX

Wambach 2 10 64

USA			MEXICO		
18	SOLO Hope			PEREZ Sophia	20
2	MITTS Heather			GOMEZ Elizabeth	2
3	RAMPONE Christine			SANDOVAL Rubi Marlene	3
4	WHITEHILL Cat		77	GONZALEZ Monica	4
5	TARPLEY Lindsay	64	54	CASTILLO Maria de Jesus	5
10	WAGNER Aly		82	LOPEZ Juana Evelyn	7
11	LLOYD Carli			LEYVA Fatima	8
12	OSBOURNE Leslie			(c) DOMINGUEZ Maribel	9
13	LILLY Kristine (c)			SAUCEDO Luz del Rosario	15
17	CHALUPNY Lori			OCAMPO Monica	17
20	WAMBACH Abby	88		WORBIS Teresa	18
	Tr: RYAN Greg			Tr: CUELLAR Leonardo	
6	KAI Natasha	88	77	VERGARA Monica	6
9	O'REILLY Heather	64	54	MORA Iris Adriana	10
			82	GORDILLO Maria	13

SEMI-FINAL. Home Depot Center, Carson, Los Angeles
22-11-2006, 16:30, 6 128, Desilva TRI

CAN   4   0   JAM

Sinclair 2 40 71, Wilkinson 51,
Booth 88

CANADA			JAMAICA		
22	McLEOD Erin			JACKSON Paula	13
2	KISS Kristina	77		WILSON Alicia	4
3	BOOTH Melanie			SULLIVAN Audia	6
8	MATHESON Diana			MANYAN Natalya	9
9	CHAPMAN Candace			PARKER Kimmia	11
10	FRANKO Martina			SOMAN Peta-Gaye	12
11	HERMUS Randee			(c) BELL Nicola	15
12	SINCLAIR Christine (c)	75		HAMILTON Yolanda	16
13	WALSH Amy			HUE Diane	17
16	WILKINSON Rhian		72	JOHNSON Stacy-Ann	18
17	TIMKO Brittany	83	57	BRYAN Rochelle	19
	Tr: PELLERUD Evan			Tr: BLAINE Vin	
5	NEIL Andrea	83	57	DAVIS Omolyn	10
7	MORNEAU Isabelle	75	72	FALCONER Hishamar	14
18	GAYLE Robyn	77			

3RD PLACE. Home Depot Center, Carson, Los Angeles
26-11-2006, 15:00, Seitz USA

MEX	3	0	JAM

Ocampo 2 [19p 37], Dominguez [22]

MEXICO			JAMAICA	
20 PEREZ Sophia			JACKSON Paula	13
2 GOMEZ Elizabeth			WILSON Alicia	4
3 SANDOVAL Rubi Marlene			SULLIVAN Audia	6
4 GONZALEZ Monica			REID Venicia	7
5 CASTILLO Maria de Jesus			MANYAN Natalya	9
8 LEYVA Fatima	63		DAVIS Omolyn	10
9 DOMINGUEZ Maribel (c)			SOMAN Peta-Gaye	12
10 MORA Iris Adriana	70		FALCONER Hishamar	14
15 SAUCEDO Luz del Rosario	57		(c) BELL Nicola	15
17 OCAMPO Monica			HAMILTON Yolanda	16
18 WORBIS Teresa			HUE Diane	17
Tr: CUELLAR Leonardo			Tr: BLAINE Vin	
7 LOPEZ Juana Evelyn	63	31	MURRAY Christina	3
11 PEREZ Patricia	57	51	McHARDY Lianne	8
19 CORRAL Verónica	70	46	PARKER Kimmia	11

FINAL. Home Depot Center, Carson, Los Angeles
26-11-2006, 17:30, Tovar MEX

USA	2	1	CAN

Osborne [6], Lilly [120p]   Hermus [44]

USA			CANADA	
18 SOLO Hope			McLEOD Erin	22
2 MITTS Heather			BOOTH Melanie	3
3 RAMPONE Christine		55	MORNEAU Isabelle	7
4 WHITEHILL Cat		78	MATHESON Diana	8
6 KAI Natasha			CHAPMAN Candace	9
7 MILLER Marci			FRANKO Martina	10
12 OSBOURNE Leslie	91		HERMUS Randee	11
13 LILLY Kristine (c)			(c) SINCLAIR Christine	12
15 MARKGRAF Kate	91	118	WALSH Amy	13
16 HUCLES Angela	57		WILKINSON Rhian	16
20 WAMBACH Abby			GAYLE Robyn	18
Tr: RYAN Greg			Tr: PELLERUD Evan (86)	
10 WAGNER Aly	57	118	KISS Kristina	2
11 LLOYD Carli	91	78	NEIL Andrea	5
14 LOPEZ Stephanie	91	55	TIMKO Brittany	17

CONCACAF U–20 TOURNAMENT 2007

CONCACAF U–20 TOURNAMENT 2007

First Round	Second Round	Final Round

CFU Group A

	BAH	VIR	VGB	Pts
Bermuda	2-0	7-0	9-0	9
Bahamas	3-3		15-0	4
US Virgin Islands		3-0		4
British Virgin Islands				0

CFU Group B

	CUB	CAY	AIA	Pts
Dominican Republic	1-0	2-0	12-0	9
Cuba	2-0		11-0	6
Cayman Islands		2-0		3
Anguilla				0

CFU Group F - in TRI

	TRI	DOM	VIN	Pts
St Kitts & Nevis	1-0	2-1	0-1	6
Trinidad & Tobago		1-1	3-0	4
Dominican Republic			3-1	4
St Vincent				3

CFU Group C

	ATG	SMA	DMA	Pts
St Kitts & Nevis	2-0	9-1	2-0	9
Antigua & Barbuda	1-1		4-3	4
Saint–Martin		1-1		2
Dominica				1

CONCACAF Group A	Pl	W	D	L	F	A	Pts	PAN	HAI	GUA
USA	3	2	1	0	9	1	7	5-0	4-1	0-0
Panama	3	1	1	1	4	8	4		3-2	1-1
Haiti	3	1	0	2	5	7	3			2-0
Guatemala	3	0	2	1	1	3	2			

Played in Panama City from 17-01-2007 to 21-01-2007

CFU Group D

	GRN	LCA	BRB	Pts
St Vincent	3-1	2-1	2-0	9
Grenada	2-0		1-0	6
St Lucia		1-1		1
Barbados				1

CFU Group G - in HAI

	JAM	ANT	BER	Pts
Haiti	0-0	5-0	11-0	7
Jamaica		2-0	3-1	7
Neth. Antilles			5-1	3
Bermuda				0

CONCACAF Group B	Pl	W	D	L	F	A	Pts	CRC	SKN	JAM
Mexico	3	2	1	0	5	1	7	1-1	2-0	2-0
Costa Rica	3	2	1	0	6	3	7		3-2	2-0
St Kitts & Nevis	3	0	1	2	3	6	1			1-1
Jamaica	3	0	1	2	1	5	1			

Played in Culiacán, Mexico from 21-02-2007 to 25-02-2007

CFU Group E

	SUR	GUY	ARU	Pts
Neth. Antilles	2-1	1-2	2-0	6
Surinam	4-2		2-0	6
Guyana		1-1		4
Aruba				1

Play-off: **Jamaica** 2-0 0-1 Trinidad

UNCAF Group 1

	SLV	BLZ	Pts
Guatemala	6-1	5-0	6
El Salvador		5-1	3
Belize			0

UNCAF Group 2

	HON	NCA	Pts
Costa Rica	2-2	7-1	4
Honduras		4-3	4
Nicaragua			0

USA, Panama and Mexico qualified automatically for the final round, the latter two as final round group hosts

USA, Mexico, Panama and Costa Rica qualified for the FIFA U–20 World Cup Canada 2007

CONCACAF U-17 TOURNAMENT 2007

CONCACAF U-17 TOURNAMENT 2007

First Round	Second Round	Final Round

First Round

Group A	SLV BER PXI	Pts
Canada	2-1 10-0 7-0	9
El Salvador	1-1 17-0	6
Bermuda	1-0	3
President's XI		0

Group B	PUR LCA AIA	Pts
Panama	8-0 6-0 12-0	9
Puerto Rico	2-0 5-0	6
St Lucia	3-1	3
Anguilla		0

Group C	SUR ANT VIN	Pts
Barbados	1-1 4-1 3-1	7
Surinam	3-2 4-2	7
Neth. Antilles	3-1	3
St Vincent		0

Group D	CAY SMA	Pts
Haiti	5-0 10-0	6
Cayman Islands	5-2	3
Saint-Martin		0

Group E	GUY GRN ARU	Pts
Trinidad & Tobago	3-0 5-0 8-1	9
Guyana	2-0 3-0	6
Grenada	1-1	1
Aruba		1

Group F	CUB BAH DMA	Pts
Jamaica	2-1 6-2 8-0	9
Cuba	10-0 10-0	6
Bahamas	4-3	3
Dominica		0

Group G	SKN VIR ATG	Pts
Mexico	5-0 13-0 4-0	9
St Kitts & Nevis	2-0 3-0	6
US Virgin Islands	2-1	3
Antigua/Barbuda		0

UNCAF Group	SLV PAN NCA GUA	Pts
Costa Rica	2-0 0-1 5-1 5-0	9
El Salvador	1-0 3-0 2-1	9
Panama	1-1 3-2	7
Nicaragua	1-1	2
Guatemala		1

Second Round

Group A	TRI SUR BRB	Pts
Haiti	1-0 7-1 5-0	9
Trinidad & Tobago	4-0 1-1	4
Surinam	3-0	3
Barbados		1

Group B	JAM PAN CAN	Pts
Mexico	2-1 2-1 2-1	9
Jamaica	1-1 3-0	4
Panama	2-2	2
Canada		1

Final Round

Group A	Pl	W	D	L	F	A	Pts	HON	MEX	SLV
Haiti	3	1	2	0	4	1	5	1-1	0-0	3-0
Honduras	3	1	2	0	2	1	5		0-0	1-0
Mexico	3	0	3	0	2	2	3			2-2
El Salvador	3	0	1	2	1	5	1			

Played in Tegucigalpa, HON from 17-01-2007 to 21-01-2007

Group B	Pl	W	D	L	F	A	Pts	CRC	TRI	CAN	JAM
USA	4	3	0	1	9	5	9	2-1	3-0	2-1	2-3
Costa Rica	4	2	1	1	4	2	7		2-0	0-0	1-0
Trinidad & Tobago	4	2	0	2	3	6	6			2-1	1-0
Canada	4	1	1	2	5	4	4				3-0
Jamaica	4	1	0	3	3	7	3				

Played in Kingston, JAM from 21-02-2007 to 25-02-2007

Haiti, USA, Honduras, Costa Rica and Trinidad & Tobago qualified for the FIFA U-17 World Cup Korea 2007

USA and Honduras qualified directly for the final round, Honduras as group hosts. Trinidad played host to the first and second rounds apart from the UNCAF group which was played in El Salvador • Mexico beat Haiti 3-0 in a play-off between the winners of groups A & B in the second round whilst Trinidad beat Jamaica 2-0 in a 3rd place play-off

CONCACAF CHAMPIONS' CUP 2006-07 REGIONAL ROUNDS

TORNEO INTERCLUBES DE UNCAF

First Round			
Mun. Puntarenas *	CRC	5	1
Hankook Verdes	BLZ	0	1
Vista Hermosa	SLV	0	1
LD Alajuelense *	CRC	1	2
Marathón *	HON	2	1
Aguila	SLV	0	1
Plaza Amador	PAN	0	0
Dep. Marquense *	GUA	3	0
Victoria Ceiba	HON	1	3
San Francisco *	PAN	0	1
Real Estelí *	NCA	1	0
Deportivo Saprissa	CRC	1	1
Municipal	GUA	2	8
Wagiya *	BLZ	0	0
Diriangén *	NCA	0	1
Olimpia ††	HON	3	2

Quarter-Finals

Mun. Puntarenas	3	2
LD Alajuelense *	0	0

Marathón *	1	0
Dep. Marquense	1	1

Victoria Ceiba	0	2
Deportivo Saprissa *	1	0

Municipal *	1	0
Olimpia	1	3

Semi-finals

Mun. Puntarenas *	2	0
Dep. Marquense	0	0

Victoria Ceiba *	0	1
Olimpia	3	1

Final

Mun. Puntarenas *	3 0 3p
Olimpia	2 1 1p

Third place play-off

Dep. Marquense *	3	1
Victoria Ceiba	0	1

†† Olimpia awarded first match 3-0 • * Home team in the first leg

CFU CARIBBEAN CHAMPIONSHIP

First Round Groups

Group A (in Kingston, JAM)	Pl	W	D	L	F	A	Pts	ANT	VIR	HAI
Harbour View	JAM	3	3	0	0	8	0	9	2-0	5-0	1-0
Centro Barber	ANT	3	2	0	1	4	2	6		2-0	2-0
Positive Vibes	VIR	3	1	0	2	3	9	3			3-2
Aigle Noir	HAI	3	0	0	3	2	6	0			

Group B (in Kingston, JAM)	Pl	W	D	L	F	A	Pts	JAM	ANT
Baltimore St Marc	HAI	2	2	0	0	6	0	6	2-0	4-0
Waterhouse	JAM	2	0	1	1	1	3	1		1-1
Undeba	ANT	2	0	1	1	1	5	1		

Group C (in Bayamon, PUR)	Pl	W	D	L	F	A	Pts	PUR	ATG
W Connection	TRI	2	2	0	0	6	0	6	1-0	5-0
PR Islanders	PUR	2	1	0	1	3	2	3		3-1
Hoppers	ATG	2	0	0	2	1	8	0		
Fruta Conquerors	GUY		Withdrew							

Group D (in St Thomas, VIR)	Pl	W	D	L	F	A	Pts	ATG	VIR	ARU
San Juan Jabloteh	TRI	3	3	0	0	17	0	9	4-0	5-0	8-0
SAP	ATG	3	2	0	1	10	6	6		3-1	7-1
New Vibes	VIR	3	0	1	2	2	9	1			1-1
SV Britannia	ARU	3	0	1	2	2	16	1			

Semi-finals and final played in Trinidad

Semi-finals

W. Connection	3
Harbour View	2

Baltimore St Marc	0
San Juan Jabloteh	2

Final

W. Connection	1
San Juan Jabloteh	0

CONCACAF CHAMPIONS' CUP 2006–07

CONCACAF CHAMPIONS' CUP 2006–07

Quarter-Finals

Pachuca *	MEX	2	1
Deportivo Marquense	GUA	0	0

Municipal Puntarenas *	CRC	1	0
Houston Dynamo	USA	0	2

DC United	USA	4	3
Olimpia *	HON	1	2

Williams Connection *	TRI	2	0
Guadalajara	MEX	1	3

Semi-finals

Pachuca	0	5
Houston Dynamo *	2	2

DC United *	1	1
Guadalajara	1	2

Final

Pachuca	2 0 7p
Guadalajara *	2 0 6p

* Home team in the first leg
American and Mexican teams qualified directly for the quarter-finals

FIRST ROUND
UNCAF

Miguel Lito Pérez, Puntarenas, 24-08-2006, 15:00, Guerrero NCA
Mun. Puntarenas 5 Camacho [34], Macotelo [59], Bernard [64p],
Hankook Verdes 0 Sancho [65], Barbosa [85]

Norman Broaster, San Ignacio, 31-08-2006, 19:30, 1100, Lopez GUA
Hankook Verdes 1 Benavides [13]
Mun. Puntarenas 1 Villegas [15]

Alejandro Morera Soto, Alajuela, 24-08-2006, 20:00, Vidal PAN
LD Alajuelense 1 Salazar [70]
Vista Hermosa 0

Estadio Barraza, San Miguel, 30-08-2006, 15:00, Pineda HON
Vista Hermosa 1 Alvarez [78]
LD Alajuelense 2 Jiménez [26], Fonseca [76]

Francisco Morazán, San Pedro Sula, 24-08-2006, 19:00, 2863, Rodas GUA
Marathón 2 Martínez.W [9], Martínez.E [30]
Aguila 0

Estadio Barraza, San Miguel, 31-08-2006, 19:00, Batres GUA
Aguila 1 Amaya [83]
Marathón 1 Martínez.E [9]

Estadio Marquesa, San Marcos, 23-08-2006, 12:00, Zelaya HON
Dep. Marquense 3 Alegría 2 [31 50], Gutiérrez [48]
Plaza Amador 0

Rommel Férnandez, Panama City, 29-08-2006, 20:00, 200, Aguilar SLV
Plaza Amador 0
Dep. Marquense 0

Agustín Muquita, La Chorrera, 23-08-2006, 20:30, Rodriguez CRC
San Francisco 0
Victoria Ceiba 1 De Souza [4]

Ceibeños, La Ceiba, 30-08-2006, 19:30, 2407, Mena CRC
Victoria Ceiba 3 Brooks [19], Grant [53], Morán [68]
San Francisco 1 Gamboa [61]

Independencia, Esteli, 23-08-2006, 16:30, Moreno PAN
Real Esteli 1 Sanchez.V [22]
Dep. Saprissa 1 Solís [76]

Ricardo Saprissa, San Jose, 29-08-2006, 20:00, BCD, Rodriguez HON
Dep. Saprissa 1 Centeno [53]
Real Esteli 0

Carl Ramos, Dangriga, 22-08-2006, 19:30, Mendoza CRC
Wagiya 0
Municipal 2 Villatoro 2 [12 72]

El Trébol, Guatemala City, 31-08-2006, 12:30, Campos NCA
Municipal 8 Villatoro 4 [16 60 79 81], Albizurzis [46],
Wagiya 0 Motta 2 [55 74], OG [90]

Caciques Diriangen, Diriamba, 24-08-2006, 16:30, 2500, Cerdas CRC
Diriangen 1 Valenzuela [4]. Olimpia awarded match 3-0
Olimpia 2 Emilio 2 [39 87]

Tiburcio Andino, Tegucigalpa, 30-08-2006, 19:00, 1128, Rodriguez PAN
Olimpia 2 Palacios [8], Emilio [72]
Diriangen 1 Valenzuela [4]

QUARTER-FINALS
UNCAF

Alejandro Morera Soto, Alajuela, 20-09-2006, 20:00, Bardalez HON
LD Alajuelense 0
Mun. Puntarenas 3 Camacho [15], Macotelo [78], Guerrero [89]

Miguel Lito Pérez, Puntarenas, 27-09-2006, 2000, Batres GUA
Mun. Puntarenas 2 Bernard [26p], Macotelo [77]
LD Alajuelense 0

Francisco Morazán, San Pedro Sula, 28-09-2006, 5057, Quesada CRC
Marathón 1 Segales [38]
Dep. Marquense 1 Alegría [37]

Estadio Marquesa, San Marcos, 3-10-2006, 12:00, 7000, Vidal PAN
Dep. Marquense 1 Cayeta [86p]
Marathón 0

Ricardo Saprissa, San Jose, 26-09-2006, 20:00, Rodas GUA
Dep. Saprissa 1 Badilla [27]
Victoria Ceiba 0

Ceibeños, La Ceiba, 5-10-2006, 19:30, 5384, Moreno PAN
Victoria Ceiba 2 Flores [3], De Souza [74]
Dep. Saprissa 0

Mateo Flores, Guatemala City, 27-09-2006, 20:00, 5000, Jimenez CRC
Municipal 1 Figueroa [59]
Olimpia 1 Emilio [78]

Tiburcio Andino, Tegucigalpa, 4-10-2006, 19:00, 5370, Aguilar SLV
Olimpia 3 Velásquez [15], Palacios [79], Morales [90]
Municipal 0

SEMI-FINALS
UNCAF

Miguel Lito Pérez, Puntarenas, 25-10-2006, 12:00, Aguilar SLV
Mun. Puntarenas 2
Dep. Marquense 0

Estadio Marquesa, San Marcos, 31-10-2006, 12:00, 6500, Pineda HON
Dep. Marquense 0
Mun. Puntarenas 0

Ceibeños, La Ceiba, 24-10-2006, 19:00, 7915, Quesada CRC
Victoria Ceiba 2 Anthony [10], Flores [70]
Olimpia 2 Emilio 2 [5 66]

Tiburcio Andino, Tegucigalpa, 31-10-2006, 20:00, 4766, Batres GUA
Olimpia 2 Palacios [32], Emilio [73]
Victoria Ceiba 0

THIRD PLACE
UNCAF

Estadio Marquesa, San Marcos, 21-11-2006, 12:00, Quesada CRC
Dep. Marquense 3 Priego 2 [8 38], Gutiérrez [88]
Victoria Ceiba 0

Ceibeños, La Ceiba, 28-11-2006, 19:30, 1245, Aguilar SLV
Victoria Ceiba 1 Morán [2]
Dep. Marquense 1 Alegría [61]

Deportivo Marquense qualified for the CONCACAF Champion's Cup
quarter-finals

FINAL
UNCAF

Miguel Lito Pérez, Puntarenas, 22-11-2006, 15:00, Vidal PAN
Mun. Puntarenas 3 Bernard [43], Guerrero 2 [77 89]
Olimpia 2 Avila [27], Palacios [76]

Tiburcio Carias Andino, Tegucigalpa, 29-11-2006, 20:00, Batres GUA
Olimpia 1 Emilio [13]
Mun. Puntarenas 0

Puntarenas won 3-1 on penalties to win UNCAF Championship. Both
qualified for the CONCACAF Champion's Cup quarter-finals

FIRST ROUND GROUPS
CFU

Group A

Harbour View Stadium, Kingston, 1-12-2006, 18:00, Davis TRI

Centro Barber   2   Molina [11], Perez.E [38]
Positive Vibes   0

Harbour View Stadium, Kingston, 1-12-2006, 20:00, Brizan TRI

Harbour View   1   Taylor [13]
Aigle Noir   0

Harbour View Stadium, Kingston, 3-12-2006, 18:00, Stennet JAM

Aigle Noir   0
Centro Barber   2   Perez.E [6], Bermandus [75]

Harbour View Stadium, Kingston, 3-12-2006, 20:00, Piper TRI

Harbour View   5   Bryan 2 [5 56], Taylor [22], Thomas 2 [67 80]
Positive Vibes   0

Harbour View Stadium, Kingston, 5-12-2006, 18:00, Davis TRI

Positive Vibes   3   Baron [20], Fahie [31], Francis [64]
Aigle Noir   2   Bernard [85], Anselme [89]

Harbour View Stadium, Kingston, 5-12-2006, 20:00, Brizan TRI

Harbour View   2   Bryan [11], Smith.O [57]
Centro Barber   0

Group B

Waterhouse Stadium, Kingston, 8-12-2006, Piper TRI

Waterhouse   0
Baltimore   2   Saint-Pierre [18], Dumel [49]

Waterhouse Stadium, Kingston, 10-12-2006, 15:30

Baltimore   4   Dumel 3 [6 26 45], Lesca [61]
UNDEBA   0

Waterhouse Stadium, Kingston, 12-12-2006, 18:00

Waterhouse   1   Williams [64]
UNDEBA   1   Stone OG [6]

Group C

Juan Ramon Loubriel, Bayamon, 9-12-2006, 3800, Morales MEX

PR Islanders   3   Morales 2 [7 23], González.A [44]
Hoppers   1   Hernández.A [5]

Juan Ramon Loubriel, Bayamon, 11-12-2006, 20:00

W. Connection   5
Hoppers   0

Juan Ramon Loubriel, Bayamon, 13-12-2006, 20:00

PR Islanders   0
W. Connection   1   Toussaint [5]

Group D

Lionel Roberts Stadium, St Thomas, 10-12-2006

San Juan Jab'teh   4
Sap   0

Lionel Roberts Stadium, St Thomas, 10-12-2006

SV Britannia   1
New Vibes   1

Lionel Roberts Stadium, St Thomas, 12-12-2006

SV Britannia   0   Noel [16], Baptiste [18], Marcano 2 [21 51],
San Juan Jab'teh   8   Joseph [35], Peltier [45], Michael [74], Guevara [79]

Lionel Roberts Stadium, St Thomas, 12-12-2006

New Vibes   1   Wilton [35]
Sap   3   Williams [20], Simon [54], Challenger [74]

Lionel Roberts Stadium, St Thomas, 14-12-2006

SV Britannia   1
Sap   7

Lionel Roberts Stadium, St Thomas, 14-12-2006

New Vibes   0
San Juan Jab'teh   5   Peltier 2 [2 26], Noel 2 [14 23], Alexis [90]

SEMI-FINALS CFU

Manny Ramjohn, Marabella, 26-01-2007, 20:30, Moreno PAN

W. Connection   3   Toussaint [43], Jean 2 [45 70]
Harbour View   2   Stewart [83], Taylor [89]

Manny Ramjohn, Marabella, 26-01-2007, 18:30, Jauregui ANT

San Juan Jab'teh   2   Prosper [27], Joseph [59]
Baltimore   0

FINAL CFU

Manny Ramjohn, Marabella, 28-01-2007, Jauregui ANT

W. Connection   1   Pacheco [11]
San Juan Jab'teh   0

QUARTER-FINALS

Estadio Hidalgo, Pachuca
22-02-2007, 20:05, Rodriguez CRC

Pachuca   2
Alvarez [12], Caballero [57]

Calero - Cabrera, López.L, Mosquera, Pinto, Salazar (Rodriguez.G● 56), Correa, Caballero● (Arrelano 79), Cacho (Landín 56), Chitiua, Alvarez. Tr: Meza

Deportivo Marquense   0

Trigueño● - Donis, Flores, Martínez.N, Hernández.R, Quiñónez (Soria 68), Gutiérrez.R, Hurtarte (Alegría 61), Aguilar, Hulse, Cacho (Pezzarossi 73). Tr: Melgar

---

Estadio Marquesa, San Marcos
28-02-2007, 18:15, 7000, Zelaya HON

Deportivo Marquense   0

Trigueño - Martínez.N●, Donis, Flores (Jiménez● 32), Aceituno, Quiñónez, Noriega (Gutiérrez.R 45), Aguilar, Hulse, Cacho (Pezzarossi 57), Alegría. Tr: Melgar

Pachuca   1
Landín [16]

Calero - López.L, Mosquera, Pérez.M, Caballero (Martínez.R 76), Landín, Correa, Chitiva (Álvarez 58), Salazar, Cabrera, Jiménez (Fernández.H 76). Tr: Meza

---

Miguel Lito Perez, Puntarenas
21-02-2007, 13:35, Arredondo MEX

Municipal Puntarenas   1
Bernard [90]

Orio – Gomez.E, Nuñez, Wong, Viquez, Arnaez.R (Ocamica 59), Sanchez.M, Sancho (DaCosta 75), Bernard, Barboza, Camacho (Rocella 68). Tr: Arnaez.L

Houston Dynamo   0

Onstad (Wells 23) – Robinson●●71, Cochrane, Dalglish (Gray 68), Mullan, Davis (Wondolowski 51), Clark, DeRosario, Moreno, Waibel●, Barrett●. Tr: Kinnear

---

Aggie SC, College Station
1-03-2007, 20:05, 4200, Archundia MEX

Houston Dynamo   2
Dalglish [27], Gray [74]

Wells – Moreno (Ching 71), Waibel, Barrett, Cochrane, Gray, Dalglish● (Wondolowski● 85), Mullan●, Davis, Clark, DeRosario● (Goldthwaite 73). Tr: Kinnear

Municipal Puntarenas   0

Orio – Gómez.E, Nuñez (Portuguez 89), Wong, Viquez, Sánchez.M, Macotelo (Guerrero 79), Garro, Bernard●, Camacho● (Rocella 83), Barboza. Tr: Espinoza

---

Tiburcio Carias Andino, Tegucigalpa
21-02-2007, 20:00, Gasso MEX

Olimpia   1
Carcamo [33]

James – Avila, Palacios, Morales, Figueroa (Avila●), Barahona, Garcia●, Mendoza (Tilguath), Palacios●, Velasquez, Carcamo. Tr: Espinoza

DC United   4
Gomez.C 2 [29 59], Emilio [44], Erpen [74]

Perkins – Erpen, Gomez.C (Moose), Emilio, Olsen● (McTavish), Carroll●, Cros, Simms, Namoff, Boswell, Moreno● (Walker). Tr: Soehn

---

RFK Stadium, Washington
1-03-2007, 19:05, 8181, Navarro CAN

DC United   3
Emilio 2 [37 83], Gomez [48p]

Perkins (Nolly 67) – Erpen, Gomez.C, Emilio, Carroll (Olsen 46), Gros, McTavish, Simms, Namoff●, Boswell, Moreno (Walker 46). Tr: Soehn

Olimpia   2
Thomas [39p], Pacini [76]

Valladares – Avila●, Figueroa, Barahona●, Cruz, Palacios● (Navas 76), Cárcamo (Pacini 67), Tilguath (Lopez.W 46), Avila, Mendoza●, Thomas. Tr: Espinoza

Manny Ramjohn, Marabella
13-02-2007, 4000, Campbell JAM
Williams Connection   **2**
Jean [80], Seabra [87]
Williams•20 - Jean, Oliveira, Joseph, Goulart, Thomas, Hector (Toussaint 65), Pacheco (Seabra 59), Scott (Beckles 21), Drayton, Viveros. Tr: Charles-Fevrier
Guadalajara   **1**
Bravo [61]
Michel - Morales, Rivera (Pineda• 70), Patlan (Medina• 42), Martinez.D, Sol, Reynoso, Ledezma, Bravo•, Santana, Magallón. Tr: De La Torre

Jalisco Stadium, Guadalajara
28-02-2007, 20:45, 5765, Pineda HON
Guadalajara   **3**
Santana 2 [21 47], Bautista [74]
Michel - Mejia, Reynoso•, Rodriguez.F, Martinez.D, Araujo (Hernandez.J 45) (Ledesma 68), Pineda, Bautista, Bravo, Santana (Sol 76), Medina. Tr: De La Torre
Williams Connection   **0**
Beckles• - Oliveira•, Cupid• (Ocoro 45), Joseph, Seabra (Pacheco 67), Jean, Goulart, Thomas, DeLeon, Hector (Toussaint 45), Drayton. Tr: Charles-Fevrier

SEMI-FINALS

Robertson Stadium, Houston
15-03-2007, 19:35, Brizan TRI
Houston Dynamo   **2**
Ching [57], Wondolowski [84]
Wells - Robinson, Gray, Dalglish (DeRosario 77), Mullan, Davis•, Clark, Moreno, Waibel, Barrett, Ching (Wondolowski 82). Tr: Kinnear
Pachuca   **0**
Calero - López.L, Mosquera•, Correa, Landín (Cacho 46), Chitiva, Salazar• (Alvarez 62), Rodriguez.C, Giménez.C•, Pinto, Aguilar (Caballero 75). Tr: Meza

Estadio Hidalgo, Pachuca
5-04-2007, 20:35, 32 000, Navarro CAN
Pachuca   **5**
Caballero 2 [3 85], Giménez.C 3 [15 58 104]
Calero - López.L, Mosquera, Correa, Alvarez, Caballero•, Chitiva (Pérez.M 114), Cacho• (Landín 74), Cabrera (Aguilar 77), Giménez.C, Pinto. Tr: Meza
Houston Dynamo   **2**
Mullan [53], Ching [78]
Wells• - Robinson•, Cochrane, Gray•, Mullan, Davis (Goldthwaite• 76), DeRosario (Dalglish• 107), Moreno, Waibel (Holden 56), Barrett, Ching. Tr: Kinnear

RFK Stadium, Washington
15-03-2007, 20:15, 26 528, Petrescu CAN
DC United   **1**
Emilio [90]
Perkins - Erpen, Gomez.C•, Emilio, Olsen, Carroll (DeRoux 60), Gros, Simms, Namoff, Boswell•, Moreno (Walker 70). Tr: Soehn
Guadalajara   **1**
Bravo [63]
Michel - Magallón, Reynoso, Rodriguez.F, Martinez.D•, Mejia, Pineda, Morales, Santana• (Medina 71), Bravo• (Araujo 88), Bautista. Tr: De La Torre

Estadio Jalisco, Guadalajara
3-04-2007, 20:35, 21 000, Morneo PAN
Guadalajara   **2**
Bautista [42], Pineda [51]
Michel - Magallón, Reynoso, Rodriguez.F, Martinez.D• (Patlán 84), Mejia, Pineda, Morales, Santana, Medina, Bautista. Tr: De La Torre
DC United   **1**
Moreno [35]
Perkins - Erpen, Gomez.C, Emilio, Olsen•, Gros (DeRoux 31) (Carreiro 66), Simms, Namoff, Boswell, Moreno (Walker 76). Tr: Soehn

CONCACAF CHAMPIONS CUP FINAL 1ST LEG

Estadio Jalisco, Guadalajara
18-04-2007, 20:35, 30 000, Arredondo MEX

GUADALAJARA   2   2   PACHUCA

Bravo 2 [44 67]   Cacho [21], Cabrera [82]

Guadalajara			Pachuca
MICHEL Luis Ernesto			CALERO Miguel
RODRIGUEZ Francisco			LOPEZ Leobardo
REYNOSO Héctor			MOSQUERA Aquivaldo
ESPARZA Omar			CORREA Jaime
PINEDA Gonzalo		74	CHITIVA Andrés
BRAVO Omar	80	67	CACHO Juan Carlos
MEDINA Alberto		64	SALAZAR Fernando
MORALES Ramón	87		CABRERA Marvin
MAGALLON Jonny			RODRIGUEZ Gerardo
MEJIA Edgar			GIMENEZ Christian
BAUTISTA Adolfo			PINTO Fausto
Tr: DE LA TORRE José Manuel			Tr: MEZA Enrique
Substitutes			Substitutes
SANTANA Sergio	80	64	ALVAREZ Damián
PATLAN Antonio	87	67	LANDIN Luis Angel
		74	ARELLANO Omar

CONCACAF CHAMPIONS CUP FINAL 2ND LEG

Estadio Hidalgo, Pachuca
25-04-2007, 20:35, 30 000, Archundia MEX

PACHUCA   0   0   GUADALAJARA

7 P S O 6

Pachuca			Guadalajara
CALERO Miguel			MICHEL Luis Ernesto
LOPEZ Leobardo			RODRIGUEZ Francisco
CORREA Jaime			REYNOSO Héctor
CABALLERO Gabriel			ESPARZA Omar
CHITIVA Andrés			PINEDA Gonzalo
CACHO Juan Carlos	62		BRAVO Omar
SALAZAR Fernando			MEDINA Alberto
CABRERA Marvin	87	65	MORALES Ramón
RODRIGUEZ Gerardo			MAGALLON Jonny
GIMENEZ Christian			MEJIA Edgar
PINTO Fausto		104	BAUTISTA Adolfo
Tr: MEZA Enrique			Tr: DE LA TORRE José Manuel
Substitutes			Substitutes
ALVAREZ Damián	62	65	MARTINEZ Diego
LANDIN Luis Angel	87	104	BAEZ Xavier Ivan

CONMEBOL

CONFEDERACION SUDAMERICANA DE FUTBOL

In the 1980s the Copa América was in very real danger of disappearing from the calendar. In an effort to revive its fortunes, the South American football confederation decided that, from 1987, the tournament would do a tour of the continent with all ten members of the South American confederation taking a turn to host the competition. It was a decision that saved the Copa América, and in 2007 Venezuela brought that cycle to an end as hosts for the first time in their history. The tournament was a resounding success with capacity crowds enjoying some of the most entertaining football in the history of the Copa América. Argentina, in particular, were a joy to watch, scoring 16 goals in their first five games as they set out to win the title for the first time since 1993. In the final they faced a Brazil team under new coach Carlos Dunga, and without Kaká and Ronaldinho, but that made little difference as the Brazilians ran out comfortable 3-0 winners, countering Argentina's flair with the kind of pragmatic football that won Brazil the World Cup in 1994 when

THE FIFA BIG COUNT OF 2006 FOR SOUTH AMERICA

	Male	Female		Total
Number of players	24 703	3 074	Referees and Assistant Referees	32 000
Professionals	25 000		Admin, Coaches, Technical, Medical	136 000
Amateurs 18+	980 000		Number of clubs	47 000
Youth under 18	2 346 000		Number of teams	162 000
Unregistered	24 018 000		Clubs with women's teams	1 000
Total involved in football	27 946 000		Players as % of population	7.47%

Dunga was captain. For Argentina, defeat left a famous generation of players, including Veron, Crespo, Ayala and Zanetti, without a single international trophy to show for their efforts. There was better news for Argentina in the Copa Libertadores when Boca Juniors beat Grêmio in the final to move to within one win of Independiente's record haul of seven titles. Boca have now established themselves as the top club on the continent with four victories in eight editions of the Copa Libertadores since the start of the decade, the most sustained period of success that any club has managed to achieve since the early 1970s. South America's other major club tournament was won by Pachuca who beat Chile's Colo Colo in the final of the Copa Sudamericana - the first time a Mexican club has won a South American club title since they were first invited to compete in 1998. On the world stage there was success for Argentina in the FIFA U–20 World Cup and for Internacional in the FIFA Club World Cup, where they beat European champions Barcelona 1-0 in the final.

Confederación Sudamericana de Fútbol (CONMEBOL)

Autopista Aeropuerto Internacional y Leonismo Luqueño, Luque, Gran Asuncion, Paraguay

Tel +595 21 645781   Fax +595 21 645791

conmebol@conmebol.com.py   www.conmebol.com

President: LEOZ Nicolás, Dr PAR   General Secretary: DELUCA Eduardo ARG

CONMEBOL Formed: 1916

MAP OF CONMEBOL MEMBER NATIONS

SOUTH AMERICAN TOURNAMENTS

COPA AMERICA

Year	Host Country	Winners	Score	Runners-up	Venue
1910	Argentina ††	Argentina	4-1	Uruguay	‡ Racing Club, Buenos Aires
1916	Argentina †	Uruguay	0-0	Argentina	‡ Racing Club, Buenos Aires
1917	Uruguay	Uruguay	1-0	Argentina	‡ Parque Pereira, Montevideo
1919	Brazil	Brazil	1-0	Uruguay	§ Laranjeiras, Rio de Janeiro
1920	Chile	Uruguay	1-1	Argentina	* Sporting Club, Vina del Mar
1921	Argentina	Argentina	1-0	Brazil	* Sportivo Barracas, Buenos Aires
1922	Brazil	Brazil	3-0	Paraguay	§ Laranjeiras, Rio de Janeiro
1923	Uruguay	Uruguay	2-0	Argentina	‡ Parque Central, Montevideo
1924	Uruguay	Uruguay	0-0	Argentina	‡ Parque Central, Montevideo
1925	Argentina	Argentina	2-2	Brazil	‡ Bombonera, Buenos Aires
1926	Chile	Uruguay	2-0	Argentina	* Sport de Nunoa, Santiago
1927	Peru	Argentina	3-2	Uruguay	* Estadio Nacional, Lima
1929	Argentina	Argentina	4-1	Paraguay	* San Lorenzo, Buenos Aires
1935	Peru †	Uruguay	3-0	Argentina	‡ Estadio Nacional, Lima
1937	Argentina	Argentina	2-0	Brazil	‡ San Lorenzo, Buenos Aires
1939	Peru	Peru	2-1	Uruguay	‡ Estadio Nacional, Lima
1941	Chile †	Argentina	1-0	Uruguay	* Estadio Nacional, Santiago
1942	Uruguay	Uruguay	1-0	Argentina	‡ Centenario, Montevideo
1945	Chile †	Argentina	3-1	Brazil	* Estadio Nacional, Santiago
1946	Argentina †	Argentina	2-0	Brazil	‡ Monumental, Buenos Aires
1947	Ecuador	Argentina	6-0	Paraguay	* Estadio Capwell, Guayaquil
1949	Brazil	Brazil	7-0	Paraguay	§ Sao Januario, Rio de Janeiro
1953	Lima	Paraguay	3-2	Brazil	§ Estadio Nacional, Lima
1955	Chile	Argentina	1-0	Chile	‡ Estadio Nacional, Santiago
1956	Uruguay †	Uruguay	1-0	Argentina	‡ Centenario, Montevideo
1957	Peru	Argentina	3-0	Brazil	‡ Estadio Nacional, Lima
1959	Argentina	Argentina	1-1	Brazil	‡ Monumental, Buenos Aires
1959	Ecuador †	Uruguay	5-0	Argentina	* Modelo, Guayaquil
1963	Bolivia	Bolivia	5-4	Brazil	‡ Felix Capriles, Cochabamba
1967	Uruguay	Uruguay	1-0	Argentina	‡ Centenario, Montevideo
1975		Peru	0-1 2-0 1-0	Colombia	Bogota, Lima, Caracas
1979		Paraguay	3-0 0-1 0-0	Chile	Asuncion, Santiago, Buenos Aires
1983		Uruguay	2-0 1-1	Brazil	Montevideo & Salvador
1987	Argentina	Uruguay	1-0	Chile	Monumental, Buenos Aires
1989	Brazil	Brazil	1-0	Uruguay	‡ Maracana, Rio de Janeiro
1991	Chile	Argentina	3-2	Brazil	* Estadio Nacional, Santiago
1993	Ecuador	Argentina	2-1	Mexico	Monumental, Guayaquil
1995	Uruguay	Uruguay	1-1 5-3p	Brazil	Centenario, Montevideo
1997	Bolivia	Brazil	3-1	Bolivia	Hernando Siles, La Paz
1999	Paraguay	Brazil	3-0	Uruguay	Defensores del Chaco, Asuncion
2001	Colombia	Colombia	1-0	Mexico	El Campin, Bogota
2004	Peru	Brazil	2-2 4-2p	Argentina	Estadio Nacional, Lima
2007	Venezuela	Brazil	3-0	Argentina	Pachencho Romero, Maracaibo

† Extraordinario tournaments are recognised as official tournaments though the teams did not compete for the Copa America • †† Unofficial tournament that is not part of the official records • ‡ Tournament played on a league system. The final game was between the top two teams
** Tournament played on a league system. The game listed between the top two teams was not the final match in the tournament • § Tournament played on a league system. The game listed was a play-off after the top two teams finished level on points.

Following the demise of the British International Championship, the Copa América is now the longest-running international competition in the world, dating back to 1916 though some historians like to point to a tournament played in 1910 that was referred to at the time as the "South American Championship". Argentina and Uruguay have always been the most enthusiastic proponents of the Copa América and each has been champions 14 times lending credence to the belief among many

South Americans that the real home of football on the continent lies around the River Plate estuary and the cities of Montevideo and Buenos Aires and not further north in Brazil. In the first 33 editions spanning 73 years the Brazilians won the title just three times and never outside of Rio de Janeiro. Aside from these three, Peru in 1939 and 1975, and Paraguay in 1953 and 1979, have been champions twice while Bolivia in 1963 and Colombia in 2001 have both won the title once. Only Venezuela, Ecuador and Chile have failed to win it. Historically the tournament has usually been played on a league system although since the 1970s a group stage followed by knock-out rounds has been the preferred format. Another innovation has been the invitation extended to Mexico to take part since 1993, along with another guest, most commonly Costa Rica or the USA. Now held every two years the Copa América has finally caught the imagination of the Brazilians and in recent years they have been the most successful nation winning three of the past four editions and their 1997 triumph in Bolivia was their first away from home. The past three FIFA World Cup qualifying campaigns in South America, in which each of the ten nations plays each other home and away, has to a certain extent cast a shadow over the Copa América. It is difficult to argue against the fact that the top team, at the end of what amounts to a three-year campaign, should be regarded as the best team on the continent rather than the Copa America champions. However, the Copa América remains an important landmark in the fixture list and it rarely fails to entertain.

SOUTH AMERICAN WOMEN'S CHAMPIONSHIP

Year	Host Country	Winners	Score	Runners-up	Venue
1991	Brazil	Brazil	6-1	Chile	‡ Maringá
1995	Brazil	Brazil	2-0	Argentina	Uberlândia
1998	Argentina	Brazil	7-1	Argentina	Mar del Plata
2003	Peru	Brazil	3-2	Argentina	** Lima
2006	Argentina	Argentina	2-0	Brazil	‡ Mar de Plata

‡ Tournament played on a league system. The final game was between the top two teams • ** Tournament played on a league system. The game listed between the top two teams was not the final match in the tournament.

SOUTH AMERICAN WOMEN'S U-20 CHAMPIONSHIP

Year	Host Country	Winners	Score	Runners-up	Venue
2004		Brazil	5-2	Paraguay	
2006	Chile	Brazil	1-0	Argentina	Sausalito, Viña del Mar

‡ Tournament played on a league system. The final game was between the top two teams

The South American Women's Championship was introduced in 1991 as a qualifying tournament for the FIFA Women's World Cup and has been played as such ever since. Brazil have dominated since the start, a pattern that has continued in the under 20 competition which was introduced in 2004 to tie in with the FIFA U-20 Women's World Cup.

SOUTH AMERICA PRE-OLIMPICO

Year	Host Country	Winners	Runners-up
1960	Peru	Argentina	Peru
1964	Peru	Argentina	Brazil
1968	Colombia	Brazil	Colombia
1971	Colombia	Brazil	Colombia
1976	Brazil	Brazil	Uruguay
1980	Colombia	Argentina	Colombia
1984	Ecuador	Brazil	Chile
1987	Bolivia	Brazil	Argentina
1992	Paraguay	Paraguay	Colombia
1996	Argentina	Brazil	Argentina
2000	Brazil	Brazil	Chile
2004	Chile	Argentina	Paraguay

Open to non-professionals only prior to 1984 • The 1987 tournament was open to any player who had not played in a FIFA World Cup™ match • Since 1992 it has been an U-23 tournament

SUDAMERICANA SUB-17

Year	Host Country	Winners	Runners-up
1985	Argentina	Argentina	Brazil
1986	Peru	Bolivia	Brazil
1988	Ecuador	Brazil	Argentina
1991	Paraguay	Brazil	Uruguay
1993	Colombia	Colombia	Chile
1995	Peru	Brazil	Argentina
1997	Paraguay	Brazil	Argentina
1999	Uruguay	Brazil	Paraguay
2002	Peru	Brazil	Argentina
2003	Bolivia	Argentina	Brazil
2005	Venezuela	Brazil	Uruguay
2007	Ecuador	Brazil	Colombia

From 1985-1988 the championship was a U-16 tournament but since 1991 it has operated as an U-17 championship

SUDAMERICANA SUB-20

Year	Host Country	Winners	Runners-up
1954	Venezuela	Uruguay	Brazil
1958	Chile	Uruguay	Argentina
1964	Colombia	Uruguay	Paraguay
1967	Paraguay	Argentina	Paraguay
1971	Paraguay	Paraguay	Uruguay
1974	Chile	Brazil	Uruguay
1975	Peru	Uruguay	Chile
1977	Venezuela	Uruguay	Brazil
1979	Uruguay	Uruguay	Argentina
1981	Ecuador	Uruguay	Brazil
1983	Bolivia	Brazil	Uruguay
1985	Paraguay	Brazil	Paraguay

SUDAMERICANA SUB-20

Year	Host Country	Winners	Runners-up
1987	Colombia	Colombia	Brazil
1988	Argentina	Brazil	Colombia
1991	Venezuela	Brazil	Argentina
1992	Colombia	Brazil	Uruguay
1995	Bolivia	Brazil	Argentina
1997	Chile	Argentina	Brazil
1999	Argentina	Argentina	Uruguay
2001	Ecuador	Brazil	Argentina
2003	Uruguay	Argentina	Brazil
2005	Colombia	Colombia	Brazil
2007	Paraguay	Brazil	Argentina

SUPERCOPA JOAO HAVELANGE

Year	Winners	Country	Score	Country	Runners-up
1988	Racing Club	ARG	2-1 1-1	BRA	Cruzeiro
1989	Boca Juniors	ARG	0-0 0-0 5-3p	ARG	Independiente
1990	Olimpia	PAR	3-0 3-3	URU	Nacional Montevideo
1991	Cruzeiro	BRA	0-2 3-0	ARG	River Plate
1992	Cruzeiro	BRA	4-0 0-1	ARG	Racing Club
1993	São Paulo FC	BRA	2-2 2-2 5-3p	BRA	Flamengo
1994	Independiente	ARG	1-1 1-0	ARG	Boca Juniors
1995	Independiente	ARG	2-0 0-1	BRA	Flamengo
1996	Velez Sarsfield	ARG	1-0 2-0	BRA	Cruzeiro
1997	River Plate	ARG	0-0 2-1	BRA	São Paulo FC

COPA MERCOSUR

Year	Winners	Country	Score	Country	Runners-up
1998	Palmeiras	BRA	1-2 3-1 1-0	BRA	Cruzeiro
1999	Flamengo	BRA	4-3	BRA	Palmeiras
2000	Vasco da Gama	BRA	2-0 0-1 4-3	BRA	Palmeiras
2001	San Lorenzo	ARG	0-0 1-1 4-3p	BRA	Flamengo

COPA MERCONORTE

Year	Winners	Country	Score	Country	Runners-up
1998	Atlético Nacional Medellin	COL	3-1 1-0	COL	Deportivo Cali
1999	América Cali	COL	1-2 1-0	COL	Independiente Santa Fé
2000	Atlético Nacional Medellin	COL	0-0 2-1	COL	Millonarios
2001	Millonários	COL	1-1 1-1 3-1p	ECU	Emelec

COPA CONMEBOL

Year	Winners	Country	Score	Country	Runners-up
1992	Atlético Mineiro	BRA	2-0 0-1	PAR	Olimpia
1993	Botafogo	BRA	1-1 2-2 3-1p	URU	Peñarol
1994	São Paulo FC	BRA	6-1 0-3	URU	Peñarol
1995	Rosario Central	ARG	0-4 4-0 4-3p	BRA	Atlético Mineiro
1996	Lanús	ARG	2-0 0-1	COL	Independiente Santa Fé
1997	Atlético Mineiro	BRA	4-1 1-1	ARG	Lanús
1998	Santos	BRA	1-0 0-0	ARG	Rosario Central
1999	Talleres Córdoba	ARG	2-4 3-0	BRA	CSA

COPA SUDAMERICANA

Year	Winners	Country	Score	Country	Runners-up
2002	San Lorenzo	ARG	4-0 0-0	COL	Atlético Nacional Medellin
2003	Cienciano	PER	3-3 1-0	ARG	River Plate
2004	Boca Juniors	ARG	0-1 2-0	BOL	Bolivar
2005	Boca Juniors	ARG	1-1 1-1 4-3p	MEX	Pumas UNAM
2006	Pachuca	MEX	1-1 2-1	CHI	Colo Colo

COPA LIBERTADORES DE AMERICA

Year	Winners	Country	Score	Country	Runners-up
1960	Peñarol	URU	1-0 1-1	PAR	Olimpia
1961	Peñarol	URU	1-0 1-1	BRA	Palmeiras
1962	Santos	BRA	2-1 2-3 3-0	URU	Peñarol
1963	Santos	BRA	3-2 2-1	ARG	Boca Juniors
1964	Independiente	ARG	0-0 1-0	URU	Nacional Montevideo
1965	Independiente	ARG	1-0 1-3 4-1	URU	Peñarol
1966	Peñarol	URU	2-0 2-3 4-2	ARG	River Plate
1967	Racing Club	ARG	0-0 0-0 2-1	URU	Nacional Montevideo
1968	Estudiantes LP	ARG	2-1 1-3 2-0	BRA	Palmeiras
1969	Estudiantes LP	ARG	1-0 2-0	URU	Nacional Montevideo
1970	Estudiantes LP	ARG	1-0 0-0	URU	Peñarol
1971	Nacional Montevideo	URU	0-1 1-0 2-0	ARG	Estudiantes LP
1972	Independiente	ARG	0-0 2-1	PER	Universitario
1973	Independiente	ARG	1-1 0-0 2-1	CHI	Colo Colo
1974	Independiente	ARG	1-2 2-0 1-0	BRA	São Paulo FC
1975	Independiente	ARG	0-1 3-1 2-0	CHI	Union Española
1976	Cruzeiro	BRA	4-1 1-2 3-2	ARG	River Plate
1977	Boca Juniors	ARG	1-0 0-1 0-0 5-4p	BRA	Cruzeiro
1978	Boca Juniors	ARG	0-0 4-0	COL	Deportivo Cali
1979	Olimpia	PAR	2-0 0-0	ARG	Boca Juniors
1980	Nacional Montevideo	URU	0-0 1-0	BRA	Internacional PA
1981	Flamengo	BRA	2-1 0-1 2-0	CHI	Cobreloa
1982	Peñarol	URU	0-0 1-0	CHI	Cobreloa
1983	Grêmio	BRA	1-1 2-1	URU	Peñarol
1984	Independiente	ARG	1-0 0-0	BRA	Grêmio
1985	Argentinos Juniors	ARG	1-0 0-1 1-1 5-4p	COL	América Cali
1986	River Plate	ARG	2-1 1-0	COL	América Cali
1987	Peñarol	URU	0-2 2-1 1-0	COL	América Cali
1988	Nacional Montevideo	URU	0-1 3-0	ARG	Newell's Old Boys
1989	Atlético Nacional Medellín	COL	0-2 2-0 5-4p	PAR	Olimpia
1990	Olimpia	PAR	2-0 1-1	ECU	Barcelona
1991	Colo Colo	CHI	0-0 3-0	PAR	Olimpia
1992	São Paulo FC	BRA	1-0 0-1 3-2p	ARG	Newell's Old Boys
1993	São Paulo FC	BRA	5-1 0-2	CHI	Universidad Catolica
1994	Velez Sarsfield	ARG	1-0 0-1 5-3p	BRA	São Paulo FC
1995	Grêmio	BRA	3-1 1-1	COL	Atlético Nacional Medellin
1996	River Plate	ARG	0-1 2-0	COL	América Cali
1997	Cruzeiro	BRA	0-0 1-0	PER	Sporting Cristal
1998	Vasco da Gama	BRA	2-0 2-1	ECU	Barcelona
1999	Palmeiras	BRA	0-1 2-1 4-3p	COL	Deportivo Cali
2000	Boca Juniors	ARG	2-2 0-0 4-2p	BRA	Palmeiras
2001	Boca Juniors	ARG	1-0 0-1 3-1p	MEX	Cruz Azul
2002	Olimpia	PAR	0-1 2-1 4-2p	BRA	São Caetano
2003	Boca Juniors	ARG	2-0 3-1	BRA	Santos
2004	Once Caldas	COL	0-0 1-1 2-0p	ARG	Boca Juniors
2005	São Paulo FC	BRA	1-1 4-0	BRA	Atlético Paranaense
2006	Internacional	BRA	2-1 2-2	BRA	São Paulo FC
2007	Boca Juniors	ARG	3-0 2-0	BRA	Grêmio

There are currently two club tournaments held in South America with the Copa Libertadores held in the first half of the year and the Copa Sudamericana towards the end. The Copa Libertadores is the senior of the two and has been held annually since 1960. The Copa Sudamericana is the latest in a long line of secondary tournaments following on from the Supercopa João Havelange, the Copa Mercosur and the Copa Merconorte. In the 1990s there was even a third tournament, the Copa CONMEBOL, but that lasted just eight years.

COPA AMERICA MEDALS TABLE

	Country	G	S	B	F	SF
1	Argentina	14	12	4	3	4
2	Uruguay	14	6	7	4	8
3	Brazil	8	11	7	6	8
4	Paraguay	2	5	8	1	2
5	Peru	2		4	1	4
6	Colombia	1	1	3	2	6
7	Bolivia	1	1		1	1
8	Chile			4	5	2	3
9	Mexico		2	3	2	5
10	Honduras				1		1
11	Ecuador					1
	United States					1
		42	42	42	22	42

This table represents the Gold (winners), Silver (runners-up) and Bronze (semi-finalists) placings of nation in the Copa América, along with the number of appearances in the final and semi-finals. It does not include the 1910 tournament and does not distinguish between official and extraordinario tournaments

COPA LIBERTADORES MEDALS TABLE

	Country	G	S	B	F	SF
1	Argentina	21	8	30	29	59
2	Brazil	13	13	20	26	46
3	Uruguay	8	7	17	15	32
4	Paraguay	3	3	13	6	19
5	Colombia	2	7	18	9	27
6	Chile	1	5	13	6	19
7	Peru		2	6	2	8
8	Ecuador		2	9	2	11
9	Mexico		1	4	1	5
9	Bolivia			3		3
	Venezuela			3		3
		48	48	136	96	232

This table represents the Gold (winners), Silver (runners-up) and Bronze (semi-finalists) placings of clubs representing the above countries in the Copa Libertadores, along with the number of appearances in the final and semi-finals

COPA LIBERTADORES MEDALS TABLE

	Country		G	S	B
1	Independiente	ARG	7		5
2	Boca Juniors	ARG	6	3	3
3	Peñarol	URU	5	4	10
4	Nacional Montevideo	URU	3	3	6
5	Olimpia	PAR	3	3	5
6	São Paulo FC	BRA	3	3	2
7	Estudiantes La Plata	ARG	3	1	1
8	River Plate	ARG	2	1	11
9	Grêmio	BRA	2	2	2
10	Santos FC	BRA	2	1	3
11	Cruzeiro	BRA	2	1	2

COPA LIBERTADORES MEDALS TABLE (CONT'D)

	Country		G	S	B
12	SE Palmeiras	BRA	1	3	2
13	Colo Colo	CHI	1	1	3
14	At. Nacional Medellín	COL	1	1	2
15	Internacional PA	BRA	1	1	2
16	Flamengo	BRA	1		2
	Racing Club Avellaneda	ARG	1		2
18	Argentinos Juniors	ARG	1		1
	Vélez Sarsfield	ARG	1		1
20	Once Caldas	COL	1		
	Vasco da Gama	BRA	1		
22	América Cali	COL		4	6
23	Barcelona	ECU		2	5
24	Deportivo Cali	COL		2	2
25	Cobreloa	CHI		2	1
26	Newell's Old Boys	ARG		2	
27	Universidad Catolica	CHI		1	4
28	Universitario	PER		1	3
29	Union Española	CHI		1	1
30	Atlético Paranaense	BRA		1	
	Cruz Azul	MEX		1	
	São Caetano	BRA		1	
	Sporting Cristal	PER		1	
34	Cerro Porteño	PAR			5
35	Millonarios	COL			3
	San Lorenzo de Almagro	ARG			3
37	Alianza	PER			2
	America CF	MEX			2
	Botafogo	BRA			2
	Chivas Guadalajara	MEX			2
	LDU Quito	ECU			2
	Rosario Central	ARG			2
	Universidad de Chile	CHI			2
	Libertad	PAR			2
45	Atlético Junior	COL			1
	Atlético Mineiro	BRA			1
	Atlético San Cristobal	VEN			1
	Blooming	BOL			1
	Bolivar	BOL			1
	Corinthians	BRA			1
	Cúcuta Deportiva	COL			1
	Danubio	URU			1
	Defensor Lima	PER			1
	Deportes Tolima	COL			1
	Emelec	ECU			1
	Guarani Asuncion	PAR			1
	Guarani Campinas	BRA			1
	Huracán	ARG			1
	Independiente Medellin	COL			1
	Independiente Santa Fé	COL			1
	Jorge Wilsterman	BOL			1
	Nacional Quito	ECU			1
	O'Higgins	CHI			1
	Palestino	CHI			1
	Portuguesa	VEN			1
	ULA Merida	VEN			1
			48	48	136

COPA SUDAMERICANA MEDALS TABLE

	Country	G	S	B	F	SF
1	Argentina	3	1	1	4	5
2	Mexico	1	1	1	2	3
3	Peru	1			1	1
4	Bolivia		1	1	1	2
	Colombia		1	1	1	2
	Chile		1	1	1	2
7	Brazil			3		3
8	Ecuador			1		1
	Uruguay			1	1	1
		5	5	10	10	20

This table represents the Gold (winners), Silver (runners-up) and Bronze (semi-finalists) placings of clubs representing the above countries in the Copa Merconorte, along with the number of appearances in the final and semi-finals

COPA SUDAMERICANA MEDALS TABLE

	Country		G	S	B
1	Boca Juniors	ARG	2		
2	Cienciano	PER	1		
	Pachuca	MEX	1		
4	San Lorenzo	ARG	1		
5	Atlético Nacional Medellin	COL		1	1
	Bolivar	BOL		1	1
7	Colo Colo	CHI		1	
	Pumas UNAM	MEX		1	
	River Plate	ARG		1	
10	Atlético Paranaense	BRA			1
	Internacional	BRA			1
	LDU Quito	ECU			1
	Nacional Montevideo	URU			1
	São Paulo FC	BRA			1
	Universidad Catolica	CHI			1
	Toluca	MEX			1
	Velez Sarsfield	ARG			1
			5	5	10

PAST SOUTH AMERICAN
PLAYER OF THE YEAR AWARDS

Historically there have been two different awards for South American Footballer of the Year. From 1971 until 1992 *El Mundo* newspaper in Caracas awarded the accolade which was open to South Americans playing anywhere in the world. Since 1986 *El Pais* of Montevideo has given the award to the best South American playing within the Americas.

PLAYER OF THE YEAR 1971

TOSTAO	Cruzeiro	BRA	24
PASTORIZA Omar	Independiente	ARG	21
ARTIME Luis	Nacional	ARG	19
CUBILLAS Teófilo	Alianza	PER	17
GERSON	São Paulo FC	BRA	16
PELE	Santos	BRA	15
MAZURKIEWICZ Lad.	Atlético MG	URU	13
JAIRZINHO	Botafogo	BRA	11
RIVELINO Roberto	Corinthians	BRA	10
CHUMPITAZ Hector	Universitario	PAR	9

PLAYER OF THE YEAR 1972

CUBILLAS Teófilo	Alianza	PER	41
PELE	Santos	BRA	32
JAIRZINHO	Botafogo	BRA	28
TOSTAO	Vasco	BRA	16
ADEMIR da Guia	Palmeiras	BRA	15
M. CASTILLO Julio	Peñarol	URU	15
ALONSO Norberto	River Plate	ARG	11
FIGUEROA Elias	Internacional	CHI	11
FISCHER Rodolfo	Botafogo	ARG	9
REINOSO Carlos	América, Mex	CHI	6

PLAYER OF THE YEAR 1973

PELE	Santos	BRA	54
BRINDISI Miguel	Huracán	ARG	43
RIVELINO Roberto	Corinthians	BRA	33
MORENA Fernando	Peñarol	URU	19
CASZELY Carlos	Colo Colo	CHI	17
FIGUEROA Elias	Internacional	CHI	10
JAIRZINHO	Botafogo	BRA	6
SOTIL Hugo	CF Barcelona	PER	6
AYALA Ruben	Atlético Madrid	ARG	6
Two players with five votes			

PLAYER OF THE YEAR 1974

FIGUEROA Elias	Internacional	CHI	39
MARINHO Francisco	Botafogo	BRA	24
BABINGTON Carlos	Wattenschied	ARG	22
PEREIRA Luis	Palmeiras	BRA	20
PELE	Santos	BRA	15
MORENA Fernando	Peñarol	URU	14
BOCHINI Ricardo	Independiente	ARG	14
HOUSEMAN Rene	Huracán	ARG	11
CASZELY Carlos	Levante	CHI	8
RIVELINO	Fluminense	BRA	7

PLAYER OF THE YEAR 1975

FIGUEROA Elias	Internacional	CHI	50
ALONSO Norberto	River Plate	ARG	24
MORENA Fernando	Peñarol	URU	23
NELINHO	Cruzeiro	BRA	20
PEREIRA Luis	Atlético Madrid	BRA	16
SOTIL Hugo	CF Barcelona	ARG	12
SCOTTA Horacio	San Lorenzo	ARG	11
CUBILLAS Teófilo	FC Porto	PER	10
BOCHINI Ricardo	Independiente	ARG	10
LEIVINHA	Atlético Madrid	BRA	7

PLAYER OF THE YEAR 1976

FIGUEROA Elias	Palestino	CHI	51
ZICO	Flamengo	BRA	34
RIVELINO Roberto	Fluminense	BRA	31
GATTI Hugo	Boca Juniors	ARG	29
PEREIRA Luis	Atlético Madrid	BRA	19
MORENA Fernando	Peñarol	URU	12
PASSARELLA Daniel	River Plate	ARG	10
PAULO CESAR	Fluminense	BRA	10
ALONSO Norberto	River Plate	ARG	10
LEIVINHA	Atlético Madrid	BRA	9

PLAYER OF THE YEAR 1977

ZICO	Flamengo	BRA
RIVELINO Roberto	Fluminense	BRA
FIGUEROA Elias	Palestino	CHI
PELE	NY Cosmos	BRA
FILLOL Ubaldo	River Plate	ARG
BOCHINI Ricardo	Independiente	ARG
CUBILLAS Teófilo	Alianza	PER
GATTI Hugo	Boca Juniors	ARG
BERTONI Daniel	Independiente	ARG
HOUSEMAN Rene	Huracán	ARG

PLAYER OF THE YEAR 1978

KEMPES Mario	Valencia	ARG	78
FILLOL Ubaldo	River Plate	ARG	59
DIRCEU Guimaraes	América, Mex	BRA	48
PASSARELLA Daniel	River Plate	ARG	29
CUBILLAS Teófilo	Alianza	PER	19
FIGUEROA Elias	Palestino	CHI	7
BOCHINI Ricardo	Independiente	ARG	6
CUETO César	Alianza	PER	5
RIVELINO Roberto	Fluminense	BRA	4
ARDILES Osvaldo	Tottenham	ARG	3

PLAYER OF THE YEAR 1979

MARADONA Diego	Argentinos J	ARG	80
ROMERO Julio Cesar	Sp. Luqueño	PAR	40
FALCAO Roberto	Internacional	BRA	29
FILLOL Ubaldo	River Plate	ARG	26
ZICO	Flamengo	BRA	15
MORENA Fernando	Rayo Vallecano	URU	13
CASZELY Carlos	Colo Colo	CHI	11
PASSARELLA Daniel	River Plate	ARG	9
KEMPES Mario	Valencia	ARG	9
DIAZ Ramón	River Plate	ARG	7

PLAYER OF THE YEAR 1980

MARADONA Diego	Argentinos J	ARG
ZICO	Flamengo	BRA
VICTORINO Waldemar	Nacional	URU
FILLOL Ubaldo	River Plate	ARG
PAZ Ruben	Peñarol	URU
PASSARELLA Daniel	River Plate	ARG
TONINHO CEREZO	Atlético MG	BRA
SOCRATES	Corinthians	BRA
RODRIGUES Rodolfo	Nacional	URU
ROMERO Julio Cesar	NY Cosmos	PAR

PLAYER OF THE YEAR 1981

ZICO	Flamengo	BRA
MARADONA Diego	Boca Juniors	ARG
JUNIOR	Flamengo	BRA
URIBE Julio	Sporting Cristal	PER
YANEZ Patricio	San Luis	CHI
PASSARELLA Daniel	River Plate	ARG
FALCAO Roberto	Roma	BRA
SOCRATES	Corinthians	BRA
FIGUEROA Elias	Ft Lauderdale	CHI
PAZ Ruben	Peñarol	URU

PLAYER OF THE YEAR 1982

ZICO	Flamengo	BRA
FALCAO Roberto	Roma	BRA
MARADONA Diego	Barcelona	ARG
MORENA Fernando	Peñarol	URU
JUNIOR	Flamengo	BRA
SOCRATES	Corinthians	BRA
PASSARELLA Daniel	Fiorentina	ARG
SANCHEZ Hugo	Atlético Madrid	MEX

PLAYER OF THE YEAR 1983

SOCRATES	Corinthians	BRA	59
FILLOL Ubaldo	Argentinos J	ARG	30
EDER	Atlético MG	BRA	29
MORENA Fernando	Peñarol	URU	25
DIOGO Victor	Peñarol	URU	17
GARECA Ricardo	Boca Juniors	ARG	15
RODRIGUEZ Rodolfo	Santos	URU	13
AGUILERA Ramon	Nacional	URU	10
JUNIOR	Flamengo	BRA	9
PAZ Ruben	Peñarol	URU	8

PLAYER OF THE YEAR 1984

FRANCESCOLI Enzo	River Plate	URU	43
FILLOL Ubaldo	Flamengo	ARG	36
BOCHINI Ricardo	Independiente	ARG	25
RODRIGUEZ Rodolfo	Santos	URU	20
GARECA Ricardo	Boca Juniors	ARG	17
DE LEON Hugo	Grêmio	URU	17
BURRUCHAGA Jorge	Independiente	ARG	13
MARCICO Alberto	FC Oeste	ARG	11
DIOGO Victor	Palmeiras	URU	8
MORENA Fernando	Peñarol	URU	7

PLAYER OF THE YEAR 1985

ROMERO Julio Cesar	Fluminense	PAR
FRANCESCOLI Enzo	River Plate	URU
BORGHI Claudio	Argentinos J	ARG
CABANAS Roberto	América Cali	PAR
CASAGRANDE Walter	Corinthians	BRA
FERNANDEZ Roberto	América Cali	PAR
ZICO	Flamengo	BRA
BATISTA Daniel	Argentinos J	ARG
RENATO GAUCHO	Grêmio	BRA
RODRIGUEZ Rodolfo	Santos	URU

PLAYER OF THE YEAR 1986

MARADONA Diego	Napoli	ARG
CARECA	São Paulo FC	BRA
SANCHEZ Hugo	Real Madrid	MEX
BURRUCHAGA Jorge	FC Nantes	ARG
ROMERO Julio Cesar	Fluminense	PAR
VALDANO Jorge	Real Madrid	ARG
FRANCESCOLI Enzo	Racing Paris	URU
JOSIMAR	Botafogo	BRA
RUGGERI Oscar	River Plate	ARG
NEGRETE Manuel	Sporting CL	MEX

PLAYER OF THE YEAR 1987

VALDERRAMA Carlos	Deportivo Cali	COL
CABANAS Roberto	América Cali	PAR
ALZAMENDI Antonio	River Plate	URU
AGUIRRE Diego	Peñarol	URU
ROJAS Roberto	Colo Colo	CHI
MARANGONI Claudio	Independiente	ARG
PERDOMO Jose	Peñarol	URU
LETELIER Juan Carlos	Cobreloa	CHI
REDIN Bernardo	Deportivo Cali	COL
RODRIGUEZ Rodolfo	Santos	URU

PLAYER OF THE YEAR 1988

PAZ Ruben	Racing Club	URU
DE LEON Hugo	Nacional	URU
GEOVANI SILVA	Vasco	BRA
TAFFAREL Claudio	Internacional	BRA
FABBRI Nestor	Racing Club	ARG
REDIN Bernardo	Deportivo Cali	COL
BATISTA Daniel	River Plate	ARG
URIBE Julio	Sporting Cristal	PER
POLILLA	River Plate	BRA

PLAYER OF THE YEAR 1989

MARADONA Diego	Napoli	ARG
SOSA Ruben	Lazio	URU
BEBETO	Vasco	BRA
ROMARIO	PSV	BRA
CARECA	Napoli	BRA
HIGUITA Rene	At. Nacional	COL
BATISTA Daniel	River Plate	ARG
ALEMAO	Napoli	BRA
DUNGA Carlos	Fiorentina	BRA
REDIN Bernardo	Deportivo Cali	COL

PLAYER OF THE YEAR 1990

MARADONA Diego	Napoli	ARG
CANIGGIA Claudio	Atalanta	ARG
HIGUITA Rene	At. Nacional	COL
CARECA	Napoli	BRA
ALEMAO	Napoli	BRA
GOYCOECHEA Sergio	Racing Club	ARG
SANCHEZ Hugo	Real Madrid	MEX
CONEJO Luis	Albacete	CRC
VALDERRAMA Carlos	Montpellier	COL

PLAYER OF THE YEAR 1991

BATISTUTA Gabriel	Fiorentina	ARG
CANIGGIA Claudio	Atalanta	ARG
ZAMORANO Ivan	Sevilla	CHI
ROCHA Ricardo	Real Madrid	BRA
RUGGERI Oscar	Vélez	ARG
RODRIGUEZ Leonardo	Toulon	ARG
LATORRE Diego	Boca Juniors	ARG
VALDERRAMA Carlos	Real Valladolid	COL

PLAYER OF THE YEAR 1992

MARADONA Diego	Sevilla	ARG	32
BEBETO	Deportivo LC	BRA	31
RAI	São Paulo FC	BRA	25
BATISTUTA Gabriel	Fiorentina	ARG	24
CANIGGIA Claudio	Roma	ARG	21
FONSECA Daniel	Napoli	URU	18
ROMARIO	PSV	BRA	17
CABANAS Roberto	Boca Juniors	PAR	14
ZAMORANO Ivan	Real Madrid	CHI	13
MULLER	São Paolo FC	BRA	10

PLAYER OF THE YEAR 1986

ALZAMENDI Antonio	River Plate	URU
CARECA	São Paulo FC	BRA
ROMERO Julio Cesar	Fluminense	PAR

PLAYER OF THE YEAR 1987

VALDERRAMA Carlos	Deportivo Cali	COL	56
TRASANTE Obdulio	Peñarol	URU	27
PERDOMO José	Peñarol	URU	25
DOMINGUEZ Alfonso	Peñarol	URU	23
ALZAMENDI Antonio	River Plate	URU	23
JOSIMAR	Flamengo	BRA	18
GUTIERREZ Nelson	River Plate	URU	17
AGUIRRE Diego	Peñarol	URU	15
PAZ Ruben	Racing Club	URU	10
2 players with 9 votes			

PLAYER OF THE YEAR 1988

PAZ Ruben	Racing Club	URU
DE LEON Hugo	Nacional	URU
SALDANHA José	Nacional	URU

PLAYER OF THE YEAR 1989

BEBETO	Vasco	BRA	74
MAZINHO	Vasco	BRA	42
HIGUITA Rene	At. Nacional	COL	34
OSTOLAZA Santiago	Nacional	URU	32
BATISTA Sergio	River Plate	ARG	30
DE LEON Hugo	Nacional	URU	29
AGUINAGA Alex	Necaxa	ECU	28
SIMON Juan	Boca Juniors	ARG	23
DOMINGUEZ Alfonso	Peñarol	URU	22
MORENO Carlos	Independiente	ARG	21

PLAYER OF THE YEAR 1990

AMARILLA Raúl	Olimpia	PAR	57
DA SILVA Ruben	River Plate	URU	32
ALVAREZ Leonel	At. Nacional	COL	25
HIGUITA René	At. Nacional	COL	25
BASUALDO Fabian	River Plate	ARG	23

PLAYER OF THE YEAR 1991

RUGGERI Oscar	ARG	44
DIAZ Ramón	ARG	28
TOLEDO Patricio	CHI	23
ASTRADA Leonardo	ARG	21
BORRELLI Juan José	ARG	18
TILICO Mario	BRA	18
MENDOZA Gabriel	CHI	15
BASUALDO Fabian	ARG	13
DEL SOLAR José	PER	13
Three players with 12 votes		

PLAYER OF THE YEAR 1992

RAI	São Paulo FC	BRA	55
GOYCOECHEA Sergio	Olimpia	ARG	24
ACOSTA Alberto	Newell's OB	ARG	20
GAMBOA Fernando	San Lorenzo	ARG	20
CAFU	São Paulo FC	BRA	18
RENATO Gaúcho	Cruzeiro	BRA	17
JUNIOR	Flamengo	BRA	14
BOIADEIRO	Boca Juniors	BRA	13
MARCICO Alberto	Cruzeiro	ARG	13
ISLAS Luis	Independiente	ARG	10

PLAYER OF THE YEAR 1993

VALDERRAMA Carlos	Atlético Junior	COL	46
ETCHEVERRY Marco	Colo Colo	BOL	30
CAFU	São Paulo FC	BRA	28
RINCON Freddy	Palmeiras	COL	28
ALVAREZ Leonel	América Cali	COL	18
MULLER	São Paulo FC	BRA	18
GOYCOECHEA Sergio	Olimpia	ARG	12
PEREA Luis Carlos	Ind. Medellin	COL	11
KANAPKIS Fernando	Mandiyu	URU	11
MARADONA Diego	Newell's OB	ARG	11

PLAYER OF THE YEAR 1994

CAFU	São Paulo FC	BRA	36
CHILAVERT Jose Luis	Vélez	PAR	35
LOPEZ Gustavo	Independiente	ARG	22
RAMBERT Sebastian	Independiente	ARG	21

PLAYER OF THE YEAR 1995

FRANCESCOLI Enzo	River Plate	URU	34
MARADONA Diego	Boca Juniors	ARG	28
EDMUNDO	Flamengo	BRA	24
ROMARIO	Flamengo	BRA	23
CHILAVERT Jose Luis	Vélez	PARA	21

PLAYER OF THE YEAR 1996

CHILAVERT Jose Luis	Vélez	PAR	80
FRANCESCOLI Enzo	River Plate	URU	69
ORTEGA Ariel	River Plate	ARG	41
VALDERRAMA Carlos	Tampa Bay	COL	41
ARCE Francisco	Grêmio	PAR	27
GAMARRA Carlos	Cerro Porteño	PAR	26
SALAS Marcelo	River Plate	CHI	23
ACUNA Roberto	Independiente	PAR	18
SORIN Juan Pablo	River Plate	ARG	18
AYALA Celso	River Plate	PAR	17

PLAYER OF THE YEAR 1997

SALAS Marcelo	River Plate	CHI	87
SOLANO Nolberto	Boca Juniors	PER	39
CHILAVERT Jose Luis	Vélez	PAR	37
AYALA Celso	River Plate	PAR	35
GALLARDO Marcelo	River Plate	ARG	35
FRANCESCOLI Enzo	River Plate	URU	28
DENILSON	São Paulo FC	BRA	27
BERMUDEZ Jorge	Boca Juniors	COL	26
ASTRADA Leonardo	River Plate	ARG	23
EDMUNDO	Vasco	BRA	23

PLAYER OF THE YEAR 1998

PALERMO Martin	Boca Juniors	ARG	73
GAMARRA Carlos	Corinthians	PAR	70
CHILAVERT Jose Luis	Vélez	PAR	63
ARCE Francisco	Palmeiras	PAR	44
SERNA Mauricio	Boca Juniors	COL	41
FELIPE	Vasco	BRA	27
GALLARDO Marcelo	River Plate	ARG	27
MARCELINO	Corinthians	BRA	24
BERMUDEZ Jorge	Boca Juniors	COL	22
CAGNA Diego	Boca Juniors	ARG	21

PLAYER OF THE YEAR 1999

SAVIOLA Javier	River Plate	ARG	55
ARCE Francisco	Palmeiras	PAR	45
RIQUELME Juan	Boca Juniors	ARG	42
CHILAVERT Jose Luis	Vélez	PAR	36
Cordoba Ivan	San Lorenzo	COL	33
ALEX	Palmeiras	BRA	28
AIMAR Pablo	River Plate	ARG	27
VAMPETA	Corinthians	BRA	23
Three players with 22 votes			

PLAYER OF THE YEAR 2000

ROMARIO	Vasco	BRA	67
RIQUELME Juan	Boca Juniors	ARG	64
CORDOBA Oscar	Boca Juniors	COL	53
PALERMO Martin	Boca Juniors	ARG	53
AIMAR Pablo	River Plate	ARG	38
SERNA Mauricio	Boca Juniors	COL	38
SORIN Juan Pablo	Cruzeiro	ARG	37
ARCE Francisco	Palmeiras	PAR	36
BERMUDEZ Jorge	Boca Juniors	COL	36
GAMARRA Carlos	Flamengo	PAR	32

PLAYER OF THE YEAR 2001

RIQUELME Juan	Boca Juniors	ARG	88
CORDOBA Oscar	Boca Juniors	COL	59
ROMARIO	Vasco	BRA	41
ARCE Francisco	Palmeiras	PAR	39
SORIN Juan Pablo	Cruzeiro	ARG	37
YEPES Mario	River Plate	COL	36
ORTEGA Ariel	River Plate	ARG	31
LEMBO Alejandro	Nacional	URU	29
SERNA Mauricio	Boca Juniors	COL	27
Two players with 20 votes			

PLAYER OF THE YEAR 2002

CARDOZO José	Toluca	PAR	39
ORTEMAN Sergio	Olimpia	URU	32
LEMBO Alejandro	Nacional	URU	30
D'ALESSANDRO Andrés	River Plate	ARG	29
KAKA	São Paulo FC	BRA	27
MILITO Gabriel	Independiente	ARG	25
ARCE Francisco	Palmeiras	PAR	24
SAJA Sebastian	San Lorenzo	ARG	23
DELGADO Marcelo	Boca Juniors	ARG	18
ROBINHO	Santos	BRA	16

PLAYER OF THE YEAR 2003

TEVEZ Carlos	Boca Juniors	ARG	73
CARDOZO José	Toluca	PAR	39
DIEGO	Santos	BRA	33
BATTAGLIA Sebastián	Boca Juniors	ARG	26
RODRIGUEZ Clemente	Boca Juniors	ARG	18
SCHIAVI Rolando	Boca Juniors	ARG	17
ALEX	Cruzeiro	BRA	16
ROBINHO	Santos	BRA	14
ABBONDANZIERI Rob.	Boca Juniors	ARG	14
SOSA Marcelo	Danubio	URU	13

PLAYER OF THE YEAR 2004

TEVEZ Carlos	Boca Juniors	ARG	76
MASCHERANO Javier	River Plate	ARG	56
GONZALEZ Luis	River Plate	ARG	37
ROBINHO	Santos	BRA	37
HENAO Juan Carlos	Once Caldas	COL	32
CARDOZO José	Toluca	PAR	26
LEO	Santos	BRA	24
ELANO	Santos	BRA	23
LUGANO Diego	São Paulo FC	URU	22
SCHIAVI Rolando	Boca Juniors	ARG	22

PLAYER OF THE YEAR 2005

TEVEZ Carlos	Corinthians	ARG	77
LUGANO Diego	São Paulo FC	URU	54
CICINHO	São Paulo FC	BRA	37
ROGERIO Ceni	São Paulo FC	BRA	31
PALACIO Rodrigo	Boca Juniors	ARG	36
GAGO Fernando	Boca Juniors	ARG	25
GUSTAVO NERY	Corinthians	BRA	25
GAMARRA Carlos	Palmeiras	PAR	22
BILOS Daniel	Boca Juniors	ARG	21
MASCHERANO Javier	Corinthians	ARG	21

PLAYER OF THE YEAR 2006

FERNANDEZ Matías	Colo Colo	CHI	62
PALACIO Rodrigo	Boca Juniors	ARG	53
GAGO Fernando	Boca Juniors	ARG	50
ROGERIO CENI	São Paulo FC	BRA	45
FERNANDAO	Internacional	BRA	36
SUAZO Humberto	Colo Colo	CHI	36
VERON Juan Seb.	Estudiantes	ARG	29
IBARRA Hugo	Boca Juniors	ARG	24
DIAZ Daniel	Boca Juniors	ARG	23
HIGUAIN Gonzalo	River Plate	ARG	23

COPA AMERICA VENEZUELA 2007

COPA AMERICA VENEZUELA 2007

First round groups		Quarter-finals		Semi-finals			Final	
Group A	Pts							
Venezuela	5							
Peru	4	Brazil	6					
Uruguay	4	Chile	1					
Bolivia	2							
				Brazil	2	5p		
				Uruguay	2	4p		
		Venezuela	1					
Group B	Pts	Uruguay	4					
Mexico	7						Brazil	3
Brazil	6						Argentina	0
Chile	4							
Ecuador	0							
		Mexico	6					
		Paraguay	0					
				Mexico	0			
Group C	Pts			Argentina	3			
Argentina	9							
Paraguay	6	Peru	0					
Colombia	3	Argentina	4					
USA	0							

GROUP A	PL	W	D	L	F	A	PTS
1 Venezuela	3	1	2	0	4	2	5
2 Peru	3	1	1	1	5	4	4
3 Uruguay	3	1	1	1	1	3	4
4 Bolivia	3	0	2	1	4	5	2

	PER	URU	BOL
	2-0	0-0	2-2
		3-0	2-2
			1-0

Metropolitano, Mérida
26-06-2007, 18:05, 23 000, Amarilla PAR

URU 0 3 PER

Villalta [27], Mariño [70], Guerrero [89]

URUGUAY			PERU	
1 CARINI Fabián			BUTRON Leao	1
14 DIOGO Carlos			VILLALTA Miguel	2
2 LUGANO Diego (c)			RODRIGUEZ Alberto	5
8 GODIN Diego			ACASIETE Santiago	3
6 RODRIGUEZ Darío			GALLIQUIO John	22
15 PEREZ Diego			BAZALAR Juan Carlos	8
5 GARCIA Pablo			VILCHEZ Walter	4
18 CANOBBIO Fabián	46	55	GARCIA Pedro	18
11 ESTOYANOFF Fabián	80	80	FARFAN Jefferson	17
21 FORLAN Diego			GUERRERO Paolo	9
22 SANCHEZ Vicente	66	77	(c) PIZARRO Claudio	14
Tr: TABAREZ Oscar			Tr: URIBE Julio Cesar	
9 VARGAS Gonzalo	80	55	MARINO Juan Carlos	10
13 ABREU Sebastián	66	80	DE LA HAZA Paolo	13
7 RODRIGUEZ Christian	46	77	MENDOZA Andrés	16

Pueblo Nuevo, San Cristóbal
30-06-2007, 16:05, 18 000, Toledo USA

BOL 0 1 URU

Sánchez [58]

BOLIVIA			URUGUAY	
12 GALARZA Sergio			CARINI Fabián	1
14 HOYOS Miguel Angel		56	DIOGO Carlos	14
16 RALDES Ronald			(c) LUGANO Diego	2
2 PENA Juan Manuel (c)			SCOTTI Andrés	19
4 ALVAREZ Lorgio			RODRIGUEZ Darío	6
5 REYES Leonel	71		PEREIRA Maximiliano	16
6 GARCIA Ronald	29		PEREZ Diego	15
8 MOJICA Gualberto			GARCIA Pablo	5
10 VACA Joselito	62	89	RODRIGUEZ Christian	7
17 ARCE Juan Carlos		82	FORLAN Diego	21
9 MORENO Jaime	71	56	SANCHEZ Vicente	21
Tr: SANCHEZ Erwin			Tr: TABAREZ Oscar	
11 CABRERA Diego	62	89	GODIN Diego	8
20 LIMA Sacha	29	82	ESTOYANOFF Fabián	11
22 PENA Darwin	71	56	GONZALEZ Ignacio	20

Metropolitano, Mérida
3-07-2007, 18:35, 35 000, Chandia CHI

PER 2 2 BOL

Pizarro 2 [34 85]

Moreno [24], Campos [45]

PERU			BOLIVIA	
1 BUTRON Leao			SUAREZ Hugo	1
22 GALLIQUIO John	55		HOYOS Miguel Angel	14
5 RODRIGUEZ Alberto			(c) PENA Juan Manuel	2
15 VILLAMARIN Edgar			RALDES Ronald	16
4 VILCHEZ Wálter			ALVAREZ Lorgio	4
13 DE LA HAZA Paolo			REYES Leonel	5
10 MARINO Juan Carlos		80	MOJICA Gualberto	8
19 ISMODES Damián	70	67	CAMPOS Jhasmany	21
17 FARFAN Jefferson	44		VACA Joselito	10
14 PIZARRO Claudio (c)		58	ANDAVERIS Augusto	19
9 GUERRERO Paolo			MORENO Jaime	9
Tr: URIBE Julio Cesar			Tr: SANCHEZ Erwin	
6 HERRERA Jhoel	55	78 80	ORTIZ Jorge Antonio	15
11 ZUNIGA Ysrael	44	58	ARCE Juan Carlos	17
20 JIMENEZ Roberto	70	67	GALINDO Gonzalo	18

Pueblo Nuevo, San Cristóbal
26-06-2007, 20:50, 42 000, Reinoso ECU

VEN 2 2 BOL

Maldonado [20], Páez [55]

Moreno [38], Arce [84]

VENEZUELA			BOLIVIA	
1 VEGA Renny			GALARZA Sergio	12
3 REY José Manuel			HOYOS Miguel Angel	14
5 MEA VITALI Miguel			RALDES Ronald	16
6 CICHERO Alejandro			(c) PENA Juan Manuel	2
8 VERA Luis (c)			ALVAREZ Lorgio	4
9 MALDONADO Giancarlo	77	59	REYES Leonel	5
11 PAEZ Ricardo	72		GARCIA Ronald	6
15 DE ORNELAS Fernando	59		MOJICA Gualberto	8
17 ROJAS Jorge		70	VACA Joselito	10
18 ARANGO Juan			ARCE Juan Carlos	17
20 GONZALEZ Héctor		74	MORENO Jaime	9
Tr: PAEZ Richard			Tr: SANCHEZ Erwin	
13 VIELMA Leonel	72	74	CABRERA Diego	11
14 GUERRA Alejandro	59	70	GALINDO Gonzalo	18
7 TORREALBA José	77	59	PENA Darwin	22

Pueblo Nuevo, San Cristóbal
30-06-2007, 18:20, 42 000, Archundia MEX

VEN 2 0 PER

Cichero [48], Arismendi [79]

VENEZUELA			PERU	
1 VEGA Renny			BUTRON Leao	1
20 GONZALEZ Héctor			ACASIETE Santiago	3
3 REY José Manuel		51	VILLALTA Miguel	2
6 CICHERO Alejandro			RODRIGUEZ Alberto	5
21 ROUGA Andrés	37	75	GALLIQUIO John	22
5 MEA VITALI Miguel		14	GARCIA Pedro	18
8 VERA Luis (c)			BAZALAR Juan Carlos	8
18 ARANGO Juan	74		FARFAN Jefferson	17
11 PAEZ Ricardo	78		VILCHEZ Walter	4
9 MALDONADO Giancarlo			GUERRERO Paolo	9
15 DE ORNELAS Fernando	63	67	(c) PIZARRO Claudio	14
Tr: PAEZ Richard			Tr: URIBE Julio Cesar	
10 GONZALEZ César	74	51	MARINO Juan Carlos	10
16 PEREZ Edder	37	67	ISMODES Damián	19
19 ARISMENDI Daniel	63	75	MENDOZA Andrés	16

Metropolitano, Mérida
3-07-2007, 20:50, 42 000, Simon BRA

VEN 0 0 URU

VENEZUELA			URUGUAY	
1 VEGA Renny			CARINI Fabián	1
20 GONZALEZ Héctor			FUCILE Jorge	4
6 CICHERO Alejandro			(c) LUGANO Diego	2
3 REY José Manuel			SCOTTI Andrés	19
16 PEREZ Edder			RODRIGUEZ Darío	6
8 VERA Luis (c)			PEREIRA Maximiliano	16
5 MEA VITALI Miguel	75		PEREZ Diego	15
10 GONZALEZ César			GARCIA Pablo	5
18 ARANGO Juan			RODRIGUEZ Christian	7
15 DE ORNELAS Fernando	65	67	SANCHEZ Vicente	22
9 MALDONADO Giancarlo	57	79	FORLAN Diego	21
Tr: PAEZ Richard			Tr: TABAREZ Oscar	
14 GUERRA Alejandro	65	79	ABREU Sebastián	13
7 TORREALBA José	57	67	RECOBA Alvaro	10
22 FERNANDEZ Pedro	75			

	GROUP B	PL	W	D	L	F	A	PTS
1	Mexico	3	2	1	0	4	1	7
2	Brazil	3	2	0	1	4	2	6
3	Chile	3	1	1	1	3	5	4
4	Ecuador	3	0	0	3	3	6	0

	BRA	CHI	ECU
	2-0	0-0	2-1
		3-0	1-0
			3-2

Polideportivo Cachamay, Puerto Ordaz
27-06-2007, 18:35, 35 000, Ruiz COL

ECU 2 3 CHI

Valencia [16], Benítez [23]   Suazo 2 [20 80], Villanueva [86]

	ECUADOR			CHILE	
12	MORA Cristhian			BRAVO Claudio	1
4	DE LA CRUZ Ulises			PETRIC Nicolás	2
3	HURTADO Iván (c)			ITURRA Manuel	13
15	BAGUI Oscar			(c) VALDIVIA Jorge	15
17	ESPINOZA Giovanny			GONZALEZ Mark	11
14	CASTILLO Segundo			CABION José	17
20	TENORO Edwin	72		VILLANUEVA Carlos	18
8	MENDEZ Edison			RIFFO Miguel	10
16	VALENCIA Luis Antonio	46		SANUEZA Arturo	14
11	BENITEZ Christian			FUENTES Ismael	8
21	TENORIO Carlos	75	46	ROCO Sebastian	9
	Tr: SUAREZ Luis Fernando			Tr: ACOSTA Nelson	
10	CAICEDO Felipe	75	46	ORMENO Alvaro	5
			72	FIERRO Gonzalo	21
			46	LORCA Juan	22

Polideportivo Cachamay, Puerto Ordaz
27-06-2007, 20:50, 40 000, Pezzotta ARG

BRA 0 2 MEX

Castilo [23], Morales [28]

	BRAZIL			MEXICO	
12	DONI			OCHOA Guillermo	13
2	MAICON	78	74	CASTRO Israel	5
3	ALEX COSTA			MAGALLON Jonny	2
4	JUAN			(c) MARQUEZ Rafael	4
5	MINERO			PINTO Fausto	3
6	GILBERTO			ARCE Fernando	20
7	ELANO	45		CORREA Jaime	8
8	GILBERTO SILVA (c)			TORRADO Gerardo	6
9	VAGNER LOVE		78	MORALES Ramón	11
10	DIEGO	45	69	CACHO Juan Carlos	12
11	ROBINHO			CASTILLO Nery	21
	Tr: DUNGA Carlos			Tr: SANCHEZ Hugo	
13	DANIEL ALVES	78	74	CASTRO José Antonio	15
20	ANDERSON	45	69	BRAVO Omar	19
21	AFONSO	45	78	LOZANO Jaime	16

Monumental, Maturín
1-07-2007, 16:05, 42 000, Torres PAR

BRA 3 0 CHI

Robinho 3 [36p 84 87]

	BRAZIL			CHILE	
12	DONI			BRAVO Claudio	1
2	MAICON	19		ORMENO Alvaro	2
4	JUAN		54	RIFFO Miguel	5
3	ALEX COSTA			FUENTES Ismael	8
6	GILBERTO			CONTREREAS Pablo	15
8	GILBERTO SILVA (c)		46	JARA Gonzalo	19
5	MINERO			SANUEZA Arturo	14
7	ELANO	77	26	MELENDEZ Rodrigo	18
20	ANDERSON	46		GONZALEZ Mark	11
11	ROBINHO			(c) VALDIVIA Jorge	10
9	VAGNER LOVE			SUAZO Humberto	8
	Tr: DUNGA Carlos			Tr: ACOSTA Nelson	
13	DANIEL ALVES	19	54	VARGAS Jorge	13
17	JOSUE	77	26	ITURRA Manuel	16
19	JULIO BAPTISTA	46	46	LORCA Juan	22

José Antonio Anzoátegui, Puerto La Cruz
4-07-2007, 18:35, 30 000, Amarilla PAR

MEX 0 0 CHI

	MEXICO			CHILE	
13	OCHOA Guillermo			BRAVO Claudio	1
15	CASTRO José Antonio			CONTERAS Pablo	15
2	MAGALLON Jonny			FUENTES Ismael	4
14	PINEDA Gonzalo	81		ROCO Sebastián	3
22	RODRIGUEZ Francisco			TELLO Rodrigo	7
8	CORREA Jaime			FIERRO Gonzalo	20
18	GUARDADO Andres	46		ITURRA Manuel	16
16	LOZANO Jaime			(c) SANUEZA Arturo	14
7	MEDINA Alberto		70	VILLANUEVA Carlos	21
10	BLANCO Cuauhtémoc (c)		77	LORCA Juan	22
19	BRAVO Omar	75		SUAZO Humberto	8
	Tr: SANCHEZ Hugo			Tr: ACOSTA Nelson	
17	BAUTISTA Adolfo	46	70	Fernandez Matias	14
9	LANDIN Luis Angel	75	77	GONZALEZ Mark	11
20	ARCE Fernando	81			

Monumental, Maturín
1-07-2007, 18:20, 42 000, Ortube BOL

MEX 2 1 ECU

Castillo [21], Bravo [79]   Méndez [84]

	MEXICO			ECUADOR	
1	SANCHEZ Oswaldo			MORA Cristhian	12
5	CASTRO Israel			DE LA CRUZ Ulises	4
2	MAGALLON Jonny			(c) HURTADO Iván	3
4	MARQUEZ Rafael (c)			ESPINOZA Giovanny	17
3	PINTO Fausto		71	BAGUI Oscar	15
20	ARCE Fernando			CASTILLO Segundo	14
8	CORREA Jaime		46	TENORIO Edwin	20
6	TORRADO Gerardo			MENDEZ Edison	8
11	MORALES Ramón	83		VALENCIA Luis Antonio	16
12	CACHO Juan Carlos	64		BENITEZ Christian	11
21	CASTILLO Nery	78	78	TENORIO Carlos	21
	Tr: SANCHEZ Hugo			Tr: SUAREZ Luis Fernando	
14	PINEDA Gonzalo	83	78	BORJA Felix	9
10	BLANCO Cuauhtémoc	78	46	REASCO Neicer	18
19	BRAVO Omar	64	71	AYOVI Walter	19

José Antonio Anzoátegui, Puerto La Cruz
4-07-2007, 20:50, 34 000, Pezzotta ARG

BRA 1 0 ECU

Robinho [56p]

	BRAZIL			ECUADOR	
12	DONI			ELIZAGA Marcelo	1
13	DANIEL ALVES	80		BAGUI Oscar	15
3	ALEX COSTA			GUAGUA Jorge Daniel	2
4	JUAN			ESPINOZA Giovanny	17
6	GILBERTO	58		REASCO Neicer	18
8	GILBERTO SILVA (c)			(c) MENDEZ Edison	8
5	MINERO			CASTILLO Segundo	14
17	JOSUE		76	AYOVI Walter	19
19	JULIO BAPTISTA	73		VALENCIA Luis Antonio	16
11	ROBINHO		60	BORJA Felix	9
9	VAGNER LOVE			BENITEZ Christian	11
	Tr: DUNGA Carlos			Tr: SUAREZ Luis Fernando	
14	ALEX SILVA	80	76	CAICEDO Feipe	10
10	DIEGO	73	60	TENORIO Carlos	21
16	KLEBER	58			

GROUP C	PL	W	D	L	F	A	PTS
1 Argentina	3	3	0	0	9	3	9
2 Paraguay	3	2	0	1	8	2	6
3 Colombia	3	1	0	2	3	9	3
4 USA	3	0	0	3	2	8	0

	PAR	COL	USA
PAR		1-0	4-2	4-1
COL			5-0	3-1
USA				1-0

José Encarnación 'Pachencho' Romero, Maracaibo
28-06-2007, 18:35, 30 000, Larrionda URU

PAR 5 0 COL

Santa Cruz 3 $^{30\ 46\ 80}$,
Cabañas 2 $^{84\ 88}$

PARAGUAY			COLOMBIA	
1 VILLAR Justo (c)			(c) CALERO Miguel	1
2 VERON Darío			VALLEJO Gerardo	4
5 CACERES Julio César			CORDOBA Iván	2
14 DA SILVA Paulo			YEPES Mario	3
6 BONET Carlos			ARIZALA Javier	5
3 MOREL Claudio			VARGAS Fabián	6
8 BARRTEO Edgar			VIAFARA Jhon	15
16 RIVEROS Cristian		63	DOMINGUEZ Alvaro	9
19 SANTANA Jonathan	78	56	FERREIRA David	8
18 CARDOZO Oscar	70	76	RODALLEGA Hugo	11
9 SANTA CRUZ Roque	83		PEREA Edixon	7
Tr: MARTINO Gerardo			Tr: PINTO Jorge Luis	
7 CABANAS Salvador	70	63	MARIN Vladimir	13
17 LOPEZ Dante	83	76	REY Luis Gabriel	18
20 VERA Enrique	78	56	TORRES Macnelly	20

José Encarnación 'Pachencho' Romero, Maracaibo
28-06-2007, 20:50, 34 500, Chandia CHI

ARG 4 1 USA

Crespo 2 $^{11\ 60}$, Aimar ^{76}, Tevez ^{84}
Johnson ^{9p}

ARGENTINA			USA	
1 ABBONDANZIERI Roberto			(c) KELLER Kasey	18
8 ZANETTI Javier			WYNNE Marvell	2
2 AYALA Roberto (c)			DEMERIT Jay	3
15 MILITO Gabriel			FEILHABER Benny	5
6 HEINZE Gabriel			CONRAD Jimmy	12
14 MASCHERANO Javier			BORNSTEIN Jonathan	13
19 CAMBIASSO Esteban	58	62	OLSEN Ben	14
20 VERON Juan Sebastián	87	80	CLARK Ricardo	19
10 RIQUELME Juan Román			MAPP Justin	21
18 MESSI Lionel		79	JOHNSON Eddie	9
9 CRESPO Hernán		69	TWELLMAN Taylor	20
Tr: BASILE Alfio			Tr: BRADLEY Bob	
5 GAGO Fernando	87	69	GOMEZ Herculez	8
11 TEVEZ Carlos	79	62	GAVEN Eddie	11
16 AIMAR Pablo	58	80	BECKERMAN Kyle	17

La Carolina, Barinas
2-07-2007, 18:35, 23 000, Rivera PER

USA 1 3 PAR

Clark ^{35}
Barreto ^{29}, Cardozo ^{56},
Cabañas $^{92+}$

USA			PARAGUAY	
18 KELLER Kasey (c)		54	(c) VILLAR Justo	1
15 MOOR Drew			VERON Darío	2
3 DEMERIT Jay	64		CACERES Julio César	5
5 FEILHABER Benny			DA SILVA Paulo	14
12 CONRAD Jimmy			BONET Carlos	6
13 BORNSTEIN Jonathan			MOREL Claudio	3
14 OLSEN Ben	71		BARRTEO Edgar	8
19 CLARK Ricardo			RIVEROS Cristian	16
6 KLJESTAN Sacha	80	77	SANTANA Jonathan	19
9 JOHNSON Eddie		73	CARDOZO Oscar	18
20 TWELLMAN Taylor			SANTA CRUZ Roque	9
Tr: BRADLEY Bob			Tr: MARTINO Gerardo	
7 CALIFF Danny	64	73	CABANAS Salvador	7
21 MAPP Justin	71	77	VERA Enrique	20
25 NGUYEN Lee	80	54	BOBADILLA Aldo	22

Pachencho Romero, Maracaibo
2-07-2007, 20:50, 35 000, Simon BRA

ARG 4 2 COL

Crespo ^{20p}, Riquelme 2 $^{34\ 45}$,
Milito.D $^{91+}$
Perea ^{10}, Castrillón ^{76}

ARGENTINA			COLOMBIA	
1 ABBONDANZIERI Roberto			(c) CALERO Miguel	1
8 ZANETTI Javier			VALLEJO Gerardo	4
2 AYALA Roberto (c)			CORDOBA Iván	2
15 MILITO Gabriel			PEREA Luis	14
6 HEINZE Gabriel			ARIZALA Javier	5
14 MASCHERANO Javier		90	VARGAS Fabián	6
19 CAMBIASSO Esteban		61	VIAFARA Jhon	15
20 VERON Juan Sebastián	80		BANGUERO Jorge	21
10 RIQUELME Juan Román		76	FERREIRA David	8
18 MESSI Lionel	84		RODALLEGA Hugo	11
9 CRESPO Hernán	21	67	PEREA Edixon	7
Tr: BASILE Alfio			Tr: PINTO Jorge Luis	
21 MILITO Diego	21	67	CHITIVA Andrés	10
13 GONZALEZ Luis	80	61	CASTRILLON Jaime	17
11 TEVEZ Carlos	84	76	TORRES Macnelly	20

Metropolitano, Barquisimeto
5-07-2007, 18:35, 37 000, Andarcia VEN

COL 1 0 USA

Castrillón ^{15}

COLOMBIA			USA	
12 ZAPATA Robinson	87		GUZAN Brad	23
22 ZUNIGA Juan Camilo			BOSWELL Bobby	4
14 PEREA Luis (c)			PEARCE Heath	6
3 YEPES Mario			MOOR Drew	15
5 ARIZALA Javier			(c) CALIFF Danny	7
21 BANGUERO Jorge		65	MAPP Justin	21
15 VIAFARA Jhon	55		BECKERMAN Kyle	17
17 CASTRILLON Jaime			CLARK Ricardo	19
20 TORRES Macnelly	85		KLJESTAN Sacha	6
19 VALOYES César	78	46	GOMEZ Herculez	8
11 RODALLEGA Hugo		72	JOHNSON Eddie	9
Tr: PINTO Jorge Luis			Tr: BRADLEY Bob	
13 MARIN Vladimir	55	65	DAVIES Charlie	10
8 FERREIRA David	85	46	GAVEN Eddie	11
10 CHITIVA Andres	78	72	NGUYEN Lee	25

Metropolitano, Barquisimeto
5-07-2007, 20:50, 37 000, Larrionda URU

ARG 1 0 PAR

Mascherano ^{79}

ARGENTINA			PARAGUAY	
1 ABBONDANZIERI Roberto			BOBADILLA Aldo	22
4 IBARRA Hugo			VERON Darío	2
17 BURDISSO Nicolás			(c) CACERES Julio César	5
3 DIAZ Daniel			MANZUR Julio	4
8 ZANETTI Javier (c)			GONZALEZ Edgar	15
13 GONZALEZ Luis	66		VERA Enrique	20
5 GAGO Fernando		81	SANTANA Jonathan	19
19 CAMBIASSO Esteban	67		TORRES Aureliano	11
16 AIMAR Pablo	85	69	DOS SANTOS Julio	10
7 PALACIO Rodrigo			CABANAS Salvador	7
11 TEVEZ Carlos		58	CUEVAS Nelson	21
Tr: BASILE Alfio			Tr: MARTINO Gerardo	
2 AYALA Roberto	85	69	BARRTEO Edgar	8
14 MASCHERANO Javier	66	58	LOPEZ Dante	17
18 MESSI Lionel	67	81	SANTA CRUZ Roque	9

QUARTER-FINALS

José Antonio Anzoátegui, Puerto La Cruz
7-07-2007, 20:50, 25 000, Larrionda URU

CHI 1 6 BRA

Suazo 76

Juan 16, Baptista 23, Robinho 2 27 50, Josué 68, Vágner Love 85

CHILE			BRAZIL
1 BRAVO Claudio			DONI 12
2 ORMEÑO Alvaro	71		MAICON 2
15 CONTREREAS Pablo			ALEX COSTA 3
4 FUENTES Ismael	73		JUAN 4
19 JARA Gonzalo			GILBERTO 6
20 FIERRO Gonzalo	46		MINERO 5
16 ITURRA Manuel			(c) GILBERTO SILVA 8
11 GONZALEZ Mark	66		JOSUE 17
17 SANUEZA Arturo (c)			JULIO BAPTISTA 19
8 SUAZO Humberto	65		ROBINHO 11
22 LORCA Juan	56		VAGNER LOVE 9
Tr: ACOSTA Nelson			Tr: DUNGA Carlos
6 CABION José	56	71	ELANO 7
10 VALDIVIA Jorge	46	73	NALDO 15
14 FERNANDEZ Matías	66	65	AFONSO 21

Pueblo Nuevo, San Cristóbal
7-07-2007, 18:05, 42 000, Chandia CHI

VEN 1 4 URU

Arango 41

Forlán 2 38 91+, García 64, Rodriguez 86

VENEZUELA			URUGUAY
1 VEGA Renny			CARINI Fabián 1
20 GONZALEZ Héctor			(c) LUGANO Diego 2
3 REY José Manuel			SCOTTI Andrés 19
6 CICHERO Alejandro	89		RODRIGUEZ Darío 6
17 ROJAS Jorge			PEREIRA Maximiliano 16
5 MEA VITALI Miguel	76		GARCIA Pablo 5
8 VERA Luis (c)			PEREZ Diego 15
18 ARANGO Juan			RODRIGUEZ Christian 7
11 PAEZ Ricardo David			FUCILE Jorge 4
9 MALDONADO Giancarlo	71		FORLAN Diego 21
15 DE ORNELAS Fernando	46	79	RECOBA Alvaro 10
Tr: PAEZ Richard			Tr: TABAREZ Oscar
14 GUERRA Alejandro	76	89	GODIN Diego 8
10 GONZALEZ Cesar	71	79	GONZALEZ Ignacio 20
19 ARISMENDI Daniel	46		

Monumental, Maturín
8-07-2007, 16:05, 50 000, Pezzotta ARG

MEX 6 0 PAR

Castillo 2 5p 38, Torrado 27, Arce 79, Blanco 87p, Bravo 91+

MEXICO			PARAGUAY
1 SANCHEZ Oswaldo		3	BOBADILLA Aldo 22
5 CASTRO Israel		46	VERON Darío 2
4 MARQUEZ Rafael (c)			(c) CACERES Julio Cesar 5
2 MAGALLON Jonny			DA SILVA Paulo 14
3 PINTO Fausto			BONET Carlos 6
20 ARCE Fernando	80		RIVEROS Cristian 16
8 CORREA Jaime			MOREL Claudio 3
6 TORRADO Gerardo			BARRTEO Edgar 8
18 GUARDADO Andrés		4	SANTANA Jonathan 19
21 CASTILLO Nery	54	67	CARDOZO Oscar 18
12 CACHO Juan Carlos	65		SANTA CRUZ Roque 9
Tr: SANCHEZ Hugo			Tr: MARTINO Gerardo
10 BLANCO Cuauhtémoc	80	4	ZAYAS Joel 12
17 BAUTISTA Adolfo	54	67	CABANAS Salvador 7
19 BRAVO Omar	65	46	VERA Enrique 20

Metropolitano, Barquisimeto
8-07-2007, 18:50, 37 000, Simon BRA

ARG 4 0 PER

Riquelme 2 47 85, Messi 61, Mascherano 75

ARGENTINA			PERU
1 ABBONDANZIERI Roberto			BUTRON Leao 1
8 ZANETTI Javier			VILLALTA Miguel Angel 2
2 AYALA Roberto (c)			ACASIETE Santiago 3
15 MILITO Gabriel		64	VILLAMARIN Edgar 15
6 HEINZE Gabriel			GALLIQUIO John 22
14 MASCHERANO Javier			DE LA HAZA Paolo 13
13 CAMBIASSO Esteban	83		BAZALAR Juan Carlos 8
20 VERON Juan Sebastián	71		VILCHEZ Wálter 4
10 RIQUELME Juan Román		74	MARINO Juan Carlos 10
18 MESSI Lionel			(c) PIZARRO Claudio 14
21 MILITO Diego	46	55	GUERRERO Paolo 9
Tr: BASILE Alfio			Tr: URIBE Julio Cesar
5 GAGO Fernando	71	64	ZUNIGA Ysrael 11
11 TEVEZ Carlos	46	74	MENDOZA Andrés 16
16 AIMAR Pablo	83	55	GARCIA Pedro 18

SEMI-FINALS

José Encarnación 'Pachencho' Romero, Maracaibo
10-07-2007, 20:50, 40 000, Ruiz COL

URU 2 2 BRA

Forlán 45, Abreu 70   4 p 8 5   Maicon 13, Baptista 45

URUGUAY			BRAZIL
1 CARINI Fabián			DONI 12
2 LUGANO Diego (c)			MAICON 2
19 SCOTTI Andrés			JUAN 4
6 RODRIGUEZ Darío	46		ALEX COSTA 3
16 PEREIRA Maximiliano			GILBERTO 6
5 GARCIA Pablo			(c) GILBERTO SILVA 8
15 PEREZ Diego	75		MINERO 5
7 RODRIGUEZ Christian		73	JOSUE 17
4 FUCILE Jorge		73	JULIO BAPTISTA 19
21 FORLAN Diego			ROBINHO 11
10 RECOBA Alvaro	46	79	VAGNER LOVE 9
Tr: TABAREZ Oscar			Tr: DUNGA Carlos
3 GARGANO Walter	75	73	DIEGO 10
13 ABREU Sebastián	46	73	FERNANDO 18
20 GONZALEZ Ignacio	46	79	AFONSO 21

Polideportivo Cachamay, Puerto Ordaz
11-07-2007, 20:50, 40 000, Chandia CHI

MEX 0 3 ARG

Heinze 44, Messi 61, Riquelme 66p

MEXICO			ARGENTINA
1 SANCHEZ Oswaldo			ABBONDANZIERI Roberto 1
5 CASTRO Israel			ZANETTI Javier 8
4 MARQUEZ Rafael (c)			(c) AYALA Roberto 2
2 MAGALLON Jonny			MILITO Gabriel 15
3 PINTO Fausto			HEINZE Gabriel 6
20 ARCE Fernando			MASCHERANO Javier 14
6 TORRADO Gerardo	46		CAMBIASSO Esteban 19
8 CORREA Jaime	83	78	VERON Juan Sebastián 20
18 GUARDADO Andrés		86	RIQUELME Juan Román 10
21 CASTILLO Nery			MESSI Lionel 18
12 CACHO Juan Carlos	46	78	TEVEZ Carlos 11
Tr: SANCHEZ Hugo			Tr: BASILE Alfio
7 MEDINA Alberto	46	78	GAGO Fernando 5
14 PINEDA Gonzalo	83	78	PALACIO Rodrigo 7
19 BRAVO Omar	46	86	AIMAR Pablo 16

SEMI-FINAL PENALTY SHOOT-OUT URUGUAY V BRAZIL
BRAZIL WON 5-4

Robinho ✓; Forlán ✖; Juan ✓; Scotti ✓; Gilberto Silva ✓; González ✓; Afonso ✖;
Rodríguez ✓; Diego ✓; Abreu ✓; Fernando ✖; García ✖; Gilberto ✓; Lugano ✖

THIRD PLACE PLAY-OFF

Olímpico, Caracas
14-07-2007, 17:05, 30 000, Reinoso ECU

URU 1 3 MEX

Abreu 22   Blanco 38p, Bravo 68, Guardado 76

URUGUAY				MEXICO
1	CARINI Fabián			OCHOA Guillermo 13
17	VALDEZ Carlos			CASTRO José Antonio 15
2	LUGANO Diego (c)	36		MAGALLON Jonny 2
19	SCOTTI Andrés			RODRIGUEZ Francisco 22
5	GARCIA Pablo	79	64	PINTO Fausto 3
16	PEREIRA Maximiliano			(c) BLANCO Cuauhtémoc 10
20	GONZALEZ Ignacio	74		TORRADO Gerardo 6
7	RODRIGUEZ Cristian		78	LOZANO Jaime 16
4	FUCILE Jorge			MORALES Ramón 11
21	FORLAN Diego	74		CASTILLO Nery 21
13	ABREU Sebastián		88	BRAVO Omar 19
	Tr: TABAREZ Oscar			Tr: SANCHEZ Hugo
8	GARGANO Walter	79	78	CORREA Jaime 8
18	CANOBBIO Fabián	74	88	LANDIN Luis Angel 9
22	SANCHEZ Vicente	74	64	GUARDADO Andrés 18

COPA AMERICA 2007 FINAL

José Encarnación 'Pachencho' Romero, Maracaibo
15-07-2007, 17:05, 42 000

BRAZIL   3 0   ARGENTINA

Julio Baptista 4, Ayala OG 40, Daniel Alves 69

BRAZIL				MATCH STATS			ARGENTINA		
12	GK	DONI					ABBONDANZIERI Roberto	GK	1
2	DF	MAICON		3	Shots	5	ZANETTI Javier	DF	8
3	DF	ALEX COSTA		2	Shots on Goal	1	(c) AYALA Roberto	DF	2
4	DF	JUAN (c)		37	Fouls Committed	21	MILITO Gabriel	DF	15
6	DF	GILBERTO		4	Corner Kicks	9	HEINZE Gabriel	DF	6
7	MF	ELANO	34	1	Caught offside	3	MASCHERANO Javier	MF	14
5	MF	MINEIRO			Possession %		67	VERON Juan Sebastián	MF	20
17	MF	JOSUE			(C)Captain		RIQUELME Juan Román	MF	10
19	FW	JULIO BAPTISTA			MATCH OFFICIALS		59	CAMBIASSO Esteban	MF	19
11	FW	ROBINHO	91+		REFEREE		MESSI Lionel	FW	18
9	FW	VAGNER LOVE	90		AMARILLA Carlos PAR		TEVEZ Carlos	FW	11
		Tr: DUNGA Carlos			ASSISTANTS		Tr: BASILE Alfio		
		Substitutes			RIAL Walter URU		Substitutes		
10	MF	DIEGO	91+		SANCHEZ Luis VEN		67	GONZALEZ Luis	MF	13
13	MF	DANIEL ALVES	34		4TH OFFICIAL		59	AIMAR Pablo	MF	16
18	MF	FERNANDO	90						

My players demonstrated that they're capable of great things. Argentina were the favourites of the press and everyone but the game is decided over 90 minutes. We came to the rescue of the Brazilian worker, who wakes up in the morning and returns home late at night, whose only satisfaction is seeing Brazil win a football match.

Carlos Dunga

We knew we had to be awake today, but instead we were caught falling asleep. It makes you angry being unable to win and close out an exceptional tournament.

Carlos Tevez

We are totally ruined. A loss like this you feel deep in your soul.

Esteban Cambiasso

COPA TOYOTA LIBERTADORES 2007

COPA TOYOTA LIBERTADORES 2007

Preliminary Round

CF América *	MEX	5	1
Sporting Cristal	PER	0	2
Deportes Tolima	COL	2	2
Deportivo Táchira *	VEN	1	0
Vélez Sarsfield *	ARG	3	2
Danubio	URU	0	1
Paraná	BRA	2	1
Cobreloa *	CHI	0	1
LDU Quito	ECU	1	3
Tacuary *	PAR	1	0
Santos	BRA	1	5
Blooming *	BOL	0	0

* Home team in the first leg

Group Stage

Grupo 1

		Pts	PAR	MEX	ARG	ECU
Libertad	PAR	13		1-2	1-0	1-0
CF América	MEX	12	1-4		4-0	2-1
Banfield	ARG	9	0-1	3-1		4-1
El Nacional Quito	ECU	1	1-1	1-2	0-1	

Grupo 2

		Pts	MEX	BRA	CHI	PER
Necaxa	MEX	12		2-1	2-0	2-0
São Paulo FC	BRA	11	3-0		2-2	4-0
Audax Italiano	CHI	11	2-1	0-0		1-0
Alianza Lima	PER	0	1-2	0-1	1-3	

Grupo 3

		Pts	BRA	COL	COL	PAR
Grêmio	BRA	10		0-0	1-0	1-0
Cúcuta Deportiva	COL	9	3-1		0-0	1-1
Deportes Tolima	COL	7	1-0	3-4		1-0
Cerro Porteño	PAR	7	0-1	2-1	1-0	

Grupo 4

		Pts	ARG	URU	BRA	ECU
Vélez Sarsfield	ARG	11		1-1	3-0	1-0
Nacional	URU	10	2-0		3-1	3-1
Internacional	BRA	10	0-0	1-0		3-0
Emelec	ECU	3	0-1	1-0	1-2	

Grupo 5

		Pts	BRA	BRA	BOL	VEN
Flamengo	BRA	16		1-0	1-0	3-1
Paraná	BRA	9	0-1		2-0	2-1
Real Potosí	BOL	6	2-2	3-1		2-2
Unión At. Maracaibo	VEN	2	1-2	2-4	1-1	

Grupo 6

		Pts	CHI	VEN	ECU	ARG
Colo Colo	CHI	9		2-1	4-0	1-2
Caracas FC	VEN	9	0-4		1-0	3-1
LDU Quito	ECU	8	3-1	3-1		1-1
River Plate	ARG	8	1-0	0-1	0-0	

Grupo 7

		Pts	MEX	ARG	PER	BOL
Toluca	MEX	12		2-0	3-0	1-2
Boca Juniors	ARG	10	3-0		1-0	7-0
Cienciano	PER	9	1-2	3-0		5-1
Bolívar	BOL	4	0-2	0-0	2-3	

Grupo 8

		Pts	BRA	URU	ARG	COL
Santos	BRA	18		1-0	3-0	3-0
Defensor Sporting	URU	9	0-2		3-0	3-0
Gimnasia Y Esgrima LP	ARG	9	1-2	3-0		3-2
Deportivo Pasto	COL	0	0-1	1-2	0-2	

COPA TOYOTA LIBERTADORES 2007

Round of 16			Quarter–finals			Semi–finals			Final		
Boca Juniors *	3	1									
Vélez Sarsfield	0	3									
			Boca Juniors *	1	2						
			Libertad	1	0						
Paraná *	1	1									
Libertad	2	1									
						Boca Juniors	1	3			
						Cúcuta Deportivo *	3	0			
Nacional Mont'deo *	3	1									
Necaxa	2	0									
			Nacional Mont'deo	0	2						
			Cúcuta Deportivo *	2	2						
Toluca	1	2									
Cúcuta Deportivo *	5	0									
									Boca Juniors *	3	2
									Grêmio	0	0
Santos	2	3									
Caracas FC *	2	2									
			Santos	0	2						
			CF América *	0	1						
Colo Colo	0	2									
CF América *	3	1									
						Santos	0	3			
						Grêmio *	2	1			
Defensor Sporting *	3	0									
Flamengo	0	2									
			Defensor Sporting *	2 0	2p						
			Grêmio	0 2	4p						
São Paulo FC *	1	0									
Grêmio	0	2	* Home team in the first leg								

PRELIMINARY ROUND

Nemesio Diez, Toluca
24-01-2007, 21:15, 13 138, Selman CHI

CF América	5
Rojas [20], Cabañas 3 [42 66 81], Blanco [48]	

Ochoa – Rodriguez, Castro, Rojas.O, Davino, Cervantes, Cabanas, Blanco, Villa, Arguello (Mosqueda 64), Cuevas (Torres 87). Tr: Luis Fernando Tena

Sporting Cristal	0

Delgado – Fassi•, Rebosio, Villalta, Mendoza, Prado•, Alvarez•, Chara (Lobaton 57), Cominges, Hernandez (Ismodes 72), Orejuela (Bonnet 81).
Tr: Jorge Sampaoli

Estadio Nacional, Lima
31-01-2007, 21:15, Hoyos COL

Sporting Cristal	2
Villalta [77], Rebosio [79]	

Delgado – Prado•59, Villalta•, Rebosio•, Fassi, Alvarez (Torres 46), Mendoza, Lobaton (Soto 73), Ismodes•, Orejuela, Bonnet (Garcia 73). Tr: Jorge Sampaoli

CF América	1
Saritama [84]	

Ochoa – Rodriguez•, Rojas.O, Cervantes•, Cabanas, Blanco (Mosqueda 64), Salinas (Infante• 55), Rojas.R, Villa•, Arguello, Cuevas (Saritama 30).
Tr: Luis Fernando Tena

José Pachencho Romero, Maracaibo
30-01-2007, 20:30, 250, Garay PER

Deportivo Táchira	1
Morán [37]	

Martinez• – Boada, Lancken (Perez 86), Perozo, Chacon, Villafraz (Fernandez 80), Cuevas (Guerrero 46), Campos, Moran, Rondon, Gonzalez•. Tr: Manuel Plasencia

Deportes Tolima	2
Perlaza [44], Charría [75p]	

Julio – Vallejo•, Cuenu, Martinez, Alvarez, Patino•, Gonzalez•, Escobar (Ramirez 74), Anchico, Charria (Bustos 87), Perlaza (Rivas 59). Tr: Jaime De La Pava

Manuel Murillo Toro, Ibagué
8-02-2007, 19:00, Carpio ECU

Deportes Tolima	2
Savoia [19], Perlaza [67]	

Julio – Cuenu, Martinez (Ayr 64), Vallejo (Gonzalez 35), Escobar, Savoia• (Cochas 69), Charria, Perlaza, Sinisterra, Anchico, Patino•. Tr: Jaime De La Pava

Deportivo Táchira	0

Martinez – Chacon, Boada, Perozo, Lancken, Villafraz, Guerrero•, Fernandez (Campos 82), Perez (Gonzalez 80), Velazco (Arias 56), Moran.
Tr: Manuel Plasencia

José Amalfitani, Buenos Aires
30-01-2007, 19:15, Lopes BRA

Vélez Sarsfield	3
Zárate.M [13], Balvorín [48], Pellegrino [75]	

Sessa• – Pellerano, Pellegrino, Mendez, Bustamante• (Broggi• 46), Papa, Castroman (Robles• 36), Bustos, Moreno Y Fabianesi (Escudero 73), Balvorin•, Zarate.M. Tr: Ricardo La Volpe

Danubio	0

Conde – Ferro, Lima, Vidal Da Silva (Mena 50), Gonzalez, Garcia (Noble 81), Rodriguez, Viera Castro, Ricard•••39, Grossmuller, Malrrechauffe.
Tr: Gustavo Matosas

Parque Central, Montevideo
6-02-2007, 21:15, Chandia CHI

Danubio	1
Stuani [45]	

Conde – Lima, Abelenda (Mena 60), Stuani• (Peralta 69), Gonzalez•••57, Garcia, Rodriguez•, Viera Castro, Grossmuller (Ferro 86), Malrrechauffe, Gargano. Tr: Gustavo Matosas

Vélez Sarsfield	2
Castromán [38], Moreno y Fabianesi [75]	

Sessa – Pellerano, Pellegrino, Bustamante, Mendez, Bustos, Papa (Uglessich 75), Robles (Broggi 46), Moreno Y Fabianesi, Castroman•, Zarate.M (Ocampo 78). Tr: Ricardo La Volpe

Estadio Municipal, Calama
1-02-2007, 18:15, 9765, Ortubé BOL

Cobreloa	0

Hurtado – Gonzalez, Fuentes, Perez• (Arias 68), Osorio (Delgado 68), Diaz, Mannara, Rios (Aranguiz 68), Paredes, Barrios•, Olguin. Tr: Gustavo Huerta

Paraná	2
Henrique [15], Josiel [88]	

Flavio – Daniel Marques, Aderaldo•, Goiano, Egidio (Joao Vitor• 70), Beto•, Gerson•, Henrique (Xaves 70), Dinelson (Josiel 70), Neguete•, Andre Luiz. Tr: Zetti

Durival de Britto e Silva, Curitiba
7-02-2007, 21:45, 14 953, Arias PAR

Paraná	1
Lima [75]	

Flavio – Daniel Marques•, Goiano•28, Egidio, Beto•, Gerson (Joelson 74), Henrique, Dinelson (Xaves 65), Neguete, Josiel (Lima 71), Andre Luiz. Tr: Zetti

Cobreloa	1
Mannara [89]	

Hurtado – Osorio•••61, Fuentes, Olguin, Perez, Gonzalez, Rios (Beausejour• 59), Diaz, Paredes (Aranguiz 63), Mannara•, Barrios. Tr: Gustavo Huerta

Defensores del Chaco, Asunción
1-02-2007, 20:30, 1316, Fagundes BRA

Tacuary	1
Villalba [38]	

Silva – Gonzalez (Silva• 64), Aguayo, Martinez (Paez 75), Villalba, Ortiz (Ibarra 70), Paniagua, Samusio, Palacios, Luzardi•, Oviedo. Tr: Oscar Paulin

LDU Quito	1
Urrutia [64]	

Mora – Araujo, Ambrossi, Ayovi.A•, Urrutia, Escalada, Lara• (Bolanos 83), Larrea (Obregon 76), Guerron (Salas 90), Vera, Campos. Tr: Edgardo Bauza

La Casa Blanca, Quito
6-02-2007, 20:45, 11 686, Vázquez URU

LDU Quito	3
Guerrón [24], Samudio OG [54], Ambrossi [70]	

Mora – Ayovi.A, Campos, Araujo, Ambrossi•, Vera, Obregon• (Larrea 67), Urrutia, Lara•, Guerron (Salas 72), Escalada (Vizcarra 77). Tr: Edgardo Bauza

Tacuary	0

Silva – Paniagua, Vera, Aguayo•, Samudio (Paez 56), Oviedo, Villalba (Ortiz 66), Silva, Luzardi (Sanabria• 77), Ibarra, Palacios. Tr: Oscar Paulin

Estadio Ramón, Santa Cruz
31-01-2007, 19:45, 11 901, Prudente URU

Blooming	0

Salazar – Jauregui, Dos Santos• (Wernly• 60), Gomez•, Alexandre, Fierro (Mendez 46), Vaca, Dimas•, Ortiz, Suarez.D (Alex Da Rosa 53), Mendez•.
Tr: Alvaro Pena

Santos	1
Pedro [48]	

Fabio Costa – Adailton•, Kleber, Pedro•, Rodrigo Souto, Antonio Carlos•, Maldonado (Avalos 82), Fabiano (Marcos Aurelio 62), Ze Roberto, Cleber Santa•75, Rodrigo Tiui (Rodrigo Tabata 71). Tr: Luxembourgo

Vila Belmiro, Santos
7-02-2007, 21:45, 11 005, Pezzotta ARG

Santos	5
Cléber 2 [2 28], Rodrigo T. 2 [36 83], Marcos A. [76]	

Fabio Costa – Adailton, Kleber (Carlinhos 79), Pedro•, Rodrigo Souto• (Pedrinho 45), Antonio Carlos, Marcos Aurelio, Maldonado, Rodrigo Tuli, Ze Roberto, Cleber Santana (Rodrigo Tabata 64). Tr: Luxembourgo

Blooming	0

Salazar – Ortiz•, Jauregui•, Dos Santos, Mendez.G, Mendez.L (Suarez.C 41), Alexandre, Angulo, Vaca Diez• (Da Rosa 41), Dimas (Gomez 65), Suarez.D•.
Tr: Alvaro Pena

GRUPO 1

		Pl	W	D	L	F	A	Pts	PAR	MEX	ARG	ECU
Libertad	PAR	6	4	1	1	9	4	13		1-2	1-0	1-0
CF América	MEX	6	4	0	2	12	10	12	1-4		4-0	2-1
Banfield	ARG	6	3	0	3	8	8	9	0-1	3-1		4-1
El Nacional Quito	ECU	6	0	1	5	4	11	1	1-1	1-2	0-1	

GROUP 1 MATCHDAY 1
Olímpico Atahualpa, Quito
20-02-2007, 17:15, 6246, Duarte COL

El Nacional   **1**

Benítez [27]

Ibarra – De Jesus.E, De Jesus.O, Castro•, Caicedo, Cagua (Quiroz• 46), Sanchez.W (Ordonez 53), Hidalgo•••76, Benitez•, Kaviedes• (Ayovi 83), Calderon. Tr: Ever Almeida

CF América   **2**

Fernández [41], Villa [46]

Ochoa• – Rodriguez, Castro, Cervantes, Saritama• (Salinas 46), Fernandez, Mosqueda (Torres 59), Villa•, Arguello•, Mendoza, Inigo (Cuevas• 46). Tr: Luis Fernando Tena

GROUP 1 MATCHDAY 1
Defensores del Chaco, Asunción
20-02-2007, 21:30, 1457, Lopes BRA

Libertad   **1**

Riveros [85]

Bava – Benitez.P, Balbuena (Benitez.E 66), Guinazu•, Riveros, Marin, Lopez, Bonet, Sarabia, Aquino (Martinez.O 72), Bareiro (Romero 71). Tr: Sergio Markarian

Banfield   **0**

Lucchetti – Maidana•, Pages (Schmidt 68), Barraza, Villarreal, Sanguinetti, Quinteros, Chatruc (Galarza 68), Cvitanich, Andrizzi, Vitti (Lujambio 58). Tr: Patricio Hernandez

GROUP 1 MATCHDAY 2
Florencia Sola, Buenos Aires
27-02-2007, 19:00, 5773, Gaciba BRA

Banfield   **4**

Cvitanich [8], Andrizzi 2 [24 29], Lucchetti [65p]

Lucchetti – Maidana, Pages• (Galvan 73), Barraza, Villarreal, Sanguinetti•, Chatruc (Salvatierra 69), Quinteros, Cvitanich, Andrizzi, Lujambio (Vitti 44). Tr: Patricio Hernandez

El Nacional   **1**

Calderon [22]

Ibarra – De Jesus.O, Castro, Caicedo•, De Jesus.E•, Sanchez.W, Morales (Quiroz 46), Quinonez•••85, Ayovi (Figueroa 46), Kaviedes, Calderon. Tr: Ever Almeida

GROUP 1 MATCHDAY 2
Azteca, Mexico City
1-03-2007, 20:30, Silvera URU

CF América   **1**

Cuevas [41]

Navarrete – Davino, Cervantes (Cuevas 29) (Torres 54), Cabanas, Fernandez, Mosqueda, Infante•, Rojas.R, Pena (Saritama 46), Arguello•, Mendoza•. Tr: Luis Fernando Tena

Libertad   **4**

Aquino [3], Benítez 2 [20 79], López [45+]

Bava – Benitez.P, Balbuena, Guinazu, Riveros•, Marin (Benitez.E 89), Lopez, Martinez.O (Pittoni 74), Bonet, Sarabia, Aquino• (Romero 78). Tr: Sergio Markarian

GROUP 1 MATCHDAY 3
Olímpico Atahualpa, Quito
6-03-2007, 17:00, Ruiz COL

El Nacional   **1**

Calderón [68]

Ibarra – De Jesus.O, Castro•, Caicedo•••80, De Jesus.O, Hidalgo, Quiroz, Sanchez.W (Ayovi• 42), Kaviedes (Figueroa 64), Benitez, Calderon. Tr: Ever Almeida

Libertad   **1**

López [78]

Bava – Benitez.P, Balbuena• (Benitez.E 66), Guinazu, Riveros•, Marin, Lopez, Martinez.O•, Bonet, Sarabia, Aquino. Tr: Sergio Markarian

GROUP 1 MATCHDAY 3
Azteca, Mexico City
7-03-2007, 20:30, Chandia CHI

CF América   **4**

Rojas [20], Cabañas 2 [23 48], Mosqueda [52]

Ochoa – Rodriguez, Castro, Rojas.O, Davino, Cabanas, Blanco, Mosqueda (Fernandez 70), Rojas.R (Mendoza 56),Villa, Arguello (Torres• 75). Tr: Luis Fernando Tena

Banfield   **0**

Lucchetti – Maidana, Barraza•, Pages•, Villarreal, Sanguinetti, Quinteros•, Chatruc (Vitti 63), Cvitanich, Morales (Schmidt 53), Andrizzi (Esteban 46). Tr: Patricio Hernandez

GROUP 1 MATCHDAY 4
Florencia Sola, Buenos Aires
21-03-2007, 19:30, 4903, Grance PAR

Banfield   **3**

Lujambio 2 [24 39], Cvitanich [70]

Lucchetti• – Barraza, Galvan, Sanguinetti, Schmidt•, Chatruc (Morales• 63), Villarreal, Quinteros, Andrizzi (Salvatierra 84), Cvitanich, Lujambio (Bardaro 46). Tr: Pablo Sanchez & Hernan Lisi

CF América   **1**

Cabañas [89]

Ochoa – Rojas.R, Cervantes, Rodriguez (Salinas 26), Castro, Arguello (Bilos 46), Mosqueda (Fernandez• 73), Rojas.O•, Villa•, Saritama, Cabanas. Tr: Luis Fernando Tena

GROUP 1 MATCHDAY 4
Defensores del Chaco, Asunción
22-03-2007, 18:00, Baldassi ARG

Libertad   **1**

Bonet [10]

Bava – Benitez.P, Balbuena (Benitez.E 66), Guinazu, Riveros, Lopez, Martinez.O (Marin 82), Bonet, Sarabia, Aquino (Pittoni 87), Bareiro (Romero 68). Tr: Sergio Markarian

El Nacional   **0**

Corozo – Cuerro (Checa 79), De Jesus.O, Castro, Cagua, De Jesus.E•, Quiroz (Calderon 46), Hidalgo, Quinonez, Ayovi (Kaviedes 77), Benitez. Tr: Ever Almeida

GROUP 1 MATCHDAY 5
Olímpico Atahualpa, Quito
3-04-2007, 21:30, Buitrago COL

El Nacional   **0**

Corozo – De Jesus.O (Minda 80), Castro, Caicedo•, Cagua•, Ayovi, Quiroz (Ordonez 46), Quinonez, Sanchez, Calderon, Kaviedes. Tr: Ever Almeida

Banfield   **1**

Quinteros [79]

Lucchetti• – Barraza, Galvan, Sanguinetti, Civelli, Chatruc (Vitti 60), Quinteros, Villarreal, Andrizzi, Lujambio• (Santana 83), Cvitanich• (Morales 88). Tr: Pablo Sanchez & Hernan Lisi

GROUP 1 MATCHDAY 5
Defensores del Chaco, Asunción
11-04-2007, 18:30, Larrionda URU

Libertad   **1**

López [7p]

Bava – Balbuena, Guinazu•••44, Lopez, Martinez.O, Bonet, Sarabia (Barone• 17), Martinez.R•, Aquino• (Marin 82), Caceres, Benitez.E (Pittoni 58). Tr: Sergio Markarian

CF América   **2**

Cabañas 2 [63 75]

Navarrete – Rodriguez, Bilos•84, Saritama (Cabanas 46), Fernandez (Rojas.R 80), Infante (Cuevas 46), Salinas, Torres, Pena, Mendoza, Inigo. Tr: Luis Fernando Tena

GROUP 1 MATCHDAY 6
Azteca, Mexico City
18-04-2007, 17:30, Andarcia VEN

CF América   **2**

Cabañas [30], Fernández [67]

Ochoa – Rodriguez, Castro, Davino, Cabanas, Blanco, Fernandez (Torres 87), Rojas.R, Villa, Arguello, Mendoza. Tr: Luis Fernando Tena

El Nacional   **1**

Ayovi [17]

Ibarra – De Jesus.O (Minda 80), Castro, Gomez•, Caicedo•, Cagua, Minda (Ordonez 71), Quinonez, Ayovi, Kaviedes (Morales 71), Benitez. Tr: Ever Almeida

GROUP 1 MATCHDAY 6
Florencia Sola, Buenos Aires
18-04-2007, 19:30, 6570, Simon BRA

Banfield   **0**

Lucchetti – Galvan•, Civelli (Morales 85), Salvatierra (Bardaro 61), Villarreal•, Sanguinetti, Quinteros, Chatruc, Cvitanich, Andrizzi (Vitti 76), Lujambio•••35. Tr: Pablo Sanchez & Hernan Lisi

Libertad   **1**

Marín [55]

Gonzalez – Balbuena, Lopez, Martinez.O (Damiani 85), Bonet, Sarabia, Martinez.R, Aquino, Caceres, Barone• (Marin 46), Gamarra (Robles 46). Tr: Sergio Markarian

GRUPO 2

		Pl	W	D	L	F	A	Pts	MEX	BRA	CHI	PER
Necaxa	MEX	6	4	0	2	9	7	12		2-1	2-0	2-0
São Paulo FC	BRA	6	3	2	1	11	4	11	3-0		2-2	4-0
Audax Italiano	CHI	6	3	2	1	8	6	11	2-1	0-0		1-0
Alianza Lima	PER	6	0	0	6	2	13	0	1-2	0-1	1-3	

GROUP 2 MATCHDAY 1
San Carlos de Apoquindo, Santiago
14-02-2007, 20:45, 3413, Silvera URU

Audax Italiano 0

Peric – Rieloff, Carrasco, Gonzalez, Cereceda, Garrido, Scotti•, Romero•, Villanueva, Moya (Medina• 75), Di Santo (Orellana 75). Tr: Raul Toro

São Paulo FC 0

Rogerio Ceni – Andre Dias, Miranda•, Josue, Leandro, Reasco, Aloisio, Alex Silva•, Jadilson, Fredson•, Lenilson (Hugo 58). Tr: Muricy Ramalho

GROUP 2 MATCHDAY 1
Alejandro Villavueva, Lima
20-02-2007, 21:45, Gamboa BOL

Alianza 1
Ligüera [57]

Forsyth (Pizarro 43) – Salas, Salazar•, Poroso, Yglesias, Jayo, Ciurlizza, Zegarra (Sanchez 75), Liguera, Benavides• (Sotil 66), Maestri. Tr: Gerardo Pelusso

Necaxa 2
Moreno [17], Salgueiro [32]

Alvarez – Quattrocchi, Beltran, Cervantes•, Salgueiro (Gimenez 84), Moreno• (Marchant 73), Everaldo Barbosa•, Hernandez•, Galindo, Lucas, Kleber Boas (Padilla.A 85). Tr: Jose Luis Trejo

GROUP 2 MATCHDAY 2
Estadio Victoria, Aguascalientes
28-02-2007, 21:00, Vázquez URU

Necaxa 2
Kléber Boas [8], Padilla [69]

Alvarez – Quattrocchi, Cervantes, Cabrera• (Padilla.A 46), Moreno, Everaldo Barbosa, Hernandez, Perez•, Ruiz (Morales• 82), Lucas (Oviedo 56), Kleber Boas. Tr: Jose Luis Trejo

Audax Italiano 0

Peric• – Rieloff•, Carrasco•, Gonzalez, Cereceda•, Garrido, Scotti, Romero, Villanueva (Medina 77), Moya (Di Santo 80), Santis (Orellana 67). Tr: Raul Toro

GROUP 2 MATCHDAY 2
Morumbi, São Paulo
28-02-2007, 21:45, Pezzotta ARG

São Paulo FC 4
Alex Silva 2 [14 70], Leandro [57], Júnior [87]

Rogerio Ceni – Ilsinho, Andre Dias•, Miranda, Josue, Leandro, Souza• (Fredson 90), Hugo, Aloisio, Alex Silva (Edcarlos 84), Jadilson (Junior 82). Tr: Muricy Ramalho

Alianza 0

Forsyth – Salas•, Poroso, Alvarado, Yglesias•, Herrera, Ciurlizza, Zegarra (Maestri 62), Viza•, Liguera (Sotil 82), Silva (Hernandez 62). Tr: Gerardo Pelusso

GROUP 2 MATCHDAY 3
Alejandro Villavueva, Lima
13-03-2007, 21:30, Reinoso ECU

Alianza 1
Silva [67]

Pinto – Salas, Arakaki, Heerrera, Jayo (Torres 19), Ciurlizza, Olcese (Viza 59), Liguera•, Poroso, Sanchez, Maestri• (Silva 66). Tr: Gerardo Pelusso

Audax Italiano 3
Villanueva [44], Cereceda [81], Moya [88]

Peric – Rieloff, Carrasco, Gonzalez, Cereceda•, Garrido, Leal•, Romero, Villanueva (Santis 77), Moya (Cabrera 92), Medina (Di Santo 61). Tr: Raul Toro

GROUP 2 MATCHDAY 3
Estadio Victoria, Aguascalientes
21-03-2007, 19:00, Pezzotta ARG

Necaxa 2
Kléber Boas [61], Salgueiro [68]

Alvarez – Cervantes•, Lucas, Moreno (Gimenez 87), Quattrocchi, Kleber Boas, Galindo•, Beltran, Salgueiro (Ruiz 79), Everaldo Barbosa•, Hernandez (Perez 37). Tr: Jose Luis Trejo

São Paulo FC 1
Jadilson [40]

Rogerio Ceni•41 – Ilsinho, Andre Dias (Edcarlos 84) (Marcel 75), Miranda, Josue•, Leandro•, Souza•, Aloisio, Alex Silva, Jadilson, Lenilson. Tr: Muricy Ramalho

GROUP 2 MATCHDAY 4
Estadio Nacional, Santiago
27-03-2007, 18:30, 1606

Audax Italiano 1
Moya [26]

Peric – Cabrera •, Carrasco, Gonzalez, Cereceda, Garrido•, Leal•, Romero, Villanueva (Santis 63), Moya, Di Santo. Tr: Raul Toro

Alianza 0

Pinto – Salas, Arakaki, Salazar•, Yglesias, Ciurlizza, Hernandez• (Zegarra 79), Liguera, Ross, Silva (Benavides 46), Viza (Sotil 73). Tr: Gerardo Pelusso

GROUP 2 MATCHDAY 4
Morumbi, São Paulo
4-04-2007, 21:45, 30 992, Baldassi ARG

São Paulo FC 3
Souza [11], Miranda [57], Hugo [73]

Rogerio Ceni – Ilsinho• (Reasco• 70), Alex Silva, Miranda, Jadilson• (Junior 77), Josue, Richarylson, Souza, Hugo, Leandro, Aloisio (Borges 84). Tr: Muricy Ramalho

Necaxa 0

Alvarez – Quattrocchi, Beltran•, Hernandez (Salgueiro 54), Lucas, Cervantes•••61, Everaldo Barbosa, Ruiz (Perez 74), Galindo, Kleber Boa, Giminez (Marchant 77). Tr: Jose Luis Trejo

GROUP 2 MATCHDAY 5
Monumental, Santiago
11-04-2007, 20:45, Favale ARG

Audax Italiano 2
Moya [23], Romero [62]

Peric – Rieloff, Rivera, Gonzalez, Cereceda, Garrido, Leal, Romero•, Villanueva (Medina 86), Moya, Di Santo (Orellana 86). Tr: Raul Toro

Necaxa 1
Salgueiro [53]

Alvarez – Quattrocchi, Beltran, Gutierrez• (Lucas 80), Salgueiro, Everaldo Barbosa, Galindo•, Hernandez•, Perez (Ruiz 46), Giminez (Marchant 75), Kleber Boas. Tr: Jose Luis Trejo

GROUP 2 MATCHDAY 5
Alejandro Villavueva, Lima
18-04-2007, 20:30, 288, Intriago ECU

Alianza 0

Forsyth – Salazar, Arakaki•, Alvarado, Herrera, Yglesias, Jayo (Viza 83), Ciurlizza, Liguera (Olcese 73), Ross, Silva (Benavides 65). Tr: Gerardo Pelusso

São Paulo FC 1
Borges [46+]

Rogerio Ceni – Andre Dias, Miranda•, Junior, Jorge Wagner, Josue, Souza, Reasco, Aloisio (Lenitso 77), Alex Silva, Borges. Tr: Muricy Ramalho

GROUP 2 MATCHDAY 6
Estadio Victoria, Aguascalientes
25-04-2007, 19:45, Osses CHI

Necaxa 2
Kléber Boas [7], Salgueiro [48]

Alvarez – Quattrocchi, Beltran•, Cervantes•, Salgueiro (Morales 72), Everaldo Barbosa, Galindo•, Kleber Boas, Giminez (Moreno 63), Ruiz, Marchant (Hernandez 85). Tr: Jose Luis Trejo

Alianza 0

Pinto – Herrera, Salazar, Arakaki, Yglesias, Jayo, Zegarra, Hernandez• (Olcese 61), Viza, Ross (Sotil 76), Benavides (Silva 65). Tr: Gerardo Pelusso

GROUP 2 MATCHDAY 6
Morumbi, São Paulo
25-04-2007, 21:45, 20 795, Amarilla PAR

São Paulo FC 2
Richarylson [6], Aloisio [67]

Rogerio Ceni – Ilsinho•, Miranda, Junior, Josue, Leandro•, Souza, Hugo (Jorge Wagner 83), Aloisio• (Marcel 85), Alex Silva, Richarylson•. Tr: Muricy Ramalho

Audax Italiano 2
Di Santo [59], Moya [71]

Peric – Rieloff (Leal 46), Rivera• (Cabrera• 46), Gonzalez•, Santis (Di Santo 46), Garrido, Scotti•, Romero, Villanueva, Moya•, Cereceda•. Tr: Raul Toro

GRUPO 3

		Pl	W	D	L	F	A	Pts	BRA	COL	COL	PAR
Grêmio	BRA	6	3	1	2	4	4	10		0-0	1-0	1-0
Cúcuta Deportiva	COL	6	2	3	1	9	7	9	3-1		0-0	1-1
Deportes Tolima	COL	6	2	1	3	5	6	7	1-0	3-4		1-0
Cerro Porteño	PAR	6	2	1	3	4	5	7	0-1	2-1	1-0	

GROUP 3 MATCHDAY 1
General Santander, Cúcuta
13-02-2007, 19:15, 15 412, Hoyos COL

Cúcuta Deportivo 0

Zapata – Bustos, Moreno, Hurtado•, Ragua, Flores (Del Castillo 73), Castro (Henry 83), Torres, Cordoba (Bobadilla 73), Perez•, Cortes•. Tr: Jorge Luis Bernal

Deportes Tolima 0

Julio• – Cuenu•, Martinez•••58, Sinisterra•, Patino, Gonzalez, Anchico, Escobar, Charria, Perlaza (Ayr 61) (Bustos 77), Savoia• (Rivas 73). Tr: Jaime de la Pava

GROUP 3 MATCHDAY 1
La Olla, Asunción
15-02-2007, 21:45, Baldassi ARG

Cerro Porteño 0

Navarro – Perez, Rodrigo Costa, Britez (Giminez 73), Ramirez•89, Gonzalez, Alvarez•, Nunez (Cristaldo• 82), Moringo• (Godoy 58), Da Silva, Salcedo. Tr: Gustavo Costas

Grêmio 1

Lucas 52

Saja – Patricio, Schiavi, William, Edmilson, Diego Souza•, Lucas (Sandro Goiano 93+), Tuta (Douglas 21), Tcheco, Carlos Eduardo (Ramon 69), Teco. Tr: Mano Menezes

GROUP 3 MATCHDAY 2
Olímpico, Porto Alegre
27-02-2007, 22:15, 36 373, Pozo CHI

Grêmio 0

Saja – Patricio, Schiavi•, William•, Diego Souza (Aloisio 85), Lucas, Tcheco, Carlos Eduardo, Lucio, Ramon (Sandro Goiano 66), Douglas (Everton 64). Tr: Mano Menezes

Cúcuta Deportivo 0

Zapata• – Hurtado, Moreno, Flores, Castro, Cortes (Martinez 73), Perez, Torres•, Bustos (Garcia 78), Ragua•, Rueda• (Del Castillo 46). Tr: Jorge Luis Bernal

GROUP 3 MATCHDAY 2
Manuel Murillo Toro, Ibagué
7-03-2007, 19:15, 6110, Rivera PER

Deportes Tolima 1

Quintero 63

Julio – Vallejo, Cuenu, Cambindo, Sinisterra, Patino, Escobar, Charria• (Gonzalez 83), Anchico, Perlaza (Rivas 76), Savoia (Quintero 61). Tr: Jaime de la Pava

Cerro Porteño 0

Navarro – Alvarez•, Perez, Cabrera, Nunez, Britez (Hobecker 58), Gonzalez•, Salcedo, Cristaldo (Giminez 74), Ramirez• (Godoy 79), Da Silva. Tr: Gustavo Costas

GROUP 3 MATCHDAY 3
General Santander, Cúcuta
13-03-2007, 19:15, 16 789, Lunati ARG

Cúcuta Deportivo 1

Pérez 81

Zapata – Ragua (Gaonzalez 78), Moreno, Hurtado, Bustos•, Rueda•, Flores (Cordoba 60), Bobadilla (Cortes 56), Torres, Martinez, Perez. Tr: Jorge Luis Bernal

Cerro Porteño 1

Ramírez 46

Navarro• – Alvarez, Perez, Cabrera, Nunez••• 65, Gamarra•, Gonzalez, Giminez (Godoy 24), Salcedo•, Ramirez (Cristaldo• 68), Da Silva (Achucarro 87). Tr: Gustavo Costas

GROUP 3 MATCHDAY 3
Manuel Murillo Toro, Ibagué
15-03-2007, 19:30, Furchi ARG

Deportes Tolima 1

Perlaza 33

Julio• – Vallejo, Cambindo, Cuenu, Sinisterra, Patino•, Anchico, Escobar, Charria (Gonzalez• 87), Perlaza (Savoia 86), Quintero (Roong 76). Tr: Jaime de la Pava

Grêmio 0

Saja – Patricio, Schiavi, William•, Diego Souza (Carlos Eduardo 46), Lucas, Tcheco, Lucio, Ramon (Aloisio 83), Everton, Nunes. Tr: Mano Menezes

GROUP 3 MATCHDAY 4
Estadio Sarubbi, Ciudad del Este
20-03-2007, 20:45, Pompei ARG

Cerro Porteño 2

Ramírez 52, Da Silva 65

Navarro – Alvarez, Perez, Cabrera, Ramirez, Gonzalez•, Cristaldo•, Gamarra (Achucarro 46), Godoy (Moringo 62), Da Silva (Britez 75), Salcedo. Tr: Gustavo Costas

Cúcuta Deportivo 1

Pérez 35p

Zapata – Bustos, Moreno, Hurtado, Ragua, Castro• (Cordoba 68), Flores, Rueda• (Del Castillo 72), Torres, Martinez• (Cortes 74), Perez•. Tr: Jorge Luis Bernal

GROUP 3 MATCHDAY 4
Olímpico, Porto Alegre
27-03-2007, 21:45, Vázquez URU

Grêmio 1

Tuta 21

Saja – Patricio, Schiavi•, William•, Edmilson•, Lucas•, Tuta (Douglas 69), Tcheco•, Carlos Eduardo (Teco 85), Lucio•, Ramon (Diego Souza 77). Tr: Mano Menezes

Deportes Tolima 0

Julio – Cuenu•, Cambindo, Vallejo, Escobar, Charria, Perlaza, Patino•, Sinisterra, Gonzalez• (Rolong 64), Anchico (Quintero 82). Tr: Jaime de la Pava

GROUP 3 MATCHDAY 5
Defensores del Chaco, Asunción
10-04-2007, 20:15, Silvera URU

Cerro Porteño 1

Moríngo 81

Navarro – Perez, Cabrera•, Britez (Achucarro• 53), Ramirez (Nunez 88), Gonzalez, Alvarez (Godoy 69), Moringo, Da Silva•, Rojas, Salcedo. Tr: Gustavo Costas

Deportes Tolima 0

Julio• – Vallejo•, Cuenu, Cambindo, Sinisterra, Patino•, Anchico•••58, Escobar, Charria, Savoia (Quintero 46), Perlaza (Rolong 76). Tr: Jaime de la Pava

GROUP 3 MATCHDAY 5
General Santander, Cúcuta
11-04-2007, 19:45, Ortubé BOL

Cúcuta Deportivo 3

Bustos 43, Pérez 73, Del Castillo 87

Zapata – Bustos•, Portocarrero, Moreno•, Ragua•, Rueda•, Castro (Cortes 59), Flores (Del Castillo 59), Torres•, Martinez• (Garcia 78), Perez. Tr: Jorge Luis Bernal

Grêmio 1

Moreno OG 51

Saja – Patricio, Schiavi, William•, Diego Souza (Carlos Eduardo 76), Lucas, Tuta•, Tcheco• (Everton 83), Lucio, Ramon, William Antunes. Tr: Mano Menezes

GROUP 3 MATCHDAY 6
Manuel Murillo Toro, Ibagué
24-04-2007, 19:15, Ruiz COL

Deportes Tolima 3

Charría 2 38 63, Quintero 49

Julio – Cambindo, Cuenu, Sinisterra, Gonzalez (Rivas 46), Patino, Escobar•, Charria•, Perlaza (Bolivar 74), Quintero (Rolong 83), Vallejo. Tr: Hernan Torres

Cúcuta Deportivo 4

Del Castillo 19, Martínez 41, Pérez 2 70 86

Zapata – Bustos•, Hurtado• (Portocarrero 46), Moreno, Rueda, Castro• (Cortes• 55), Ragua, Del Castillo (Cordoba 69), Torres, Martinez, Perez. Tr: Jorge Luis Bernal

GROUP 3 MATCHDAY 6
Olímpico, Porto Alegre
24-04-2007, 21:15, 40 620, Pezzotta ARG

Grêmio 1

Everton 69

Saja – Patricio•, William•, Diego Souza•, Tuta•, Tcheco (William Antunes 84), Carlos Eduardo (Edmilson 74), Teco, Sandro Goiano, Lucio, Nunes (Everton 64). Tr: Mano Menezes

Cerro Porteño 0

Navarro• – Perez•, Cabrera•, Britez (Cristaldo 81), Ramirez, Gonzalez, Alvarez, Moringo (Da Silva 72), Achucarro• (Godoy 75), Rojas, Salcedo•. Tr: Gustavo Costas

GRUPO 4

		Pl	W	D	L	F	A	Pts	ARG	URU	BRA	ECU
Vélez Sarsfield	ARG	6	3	2	1	6	3	11		1-1	3-0	1-0
Nacional	URU	6	3	1	2	9	5	10	2-0		3-1	3-1
Internacional	BRA	6	3	1	2	7	7	10	0-0	1-0		3-0
Emelec	ECU	6	1	0	5	3	10	3	0-1	1-0	1-2	

GROUP 4 MATCHDAY 1
George Capwell, Guayaquil
13-02-2007, 21:30, Arias PAR

Emelec 0

Elizaga – Quinonez.C, Corozo●, Quinonez.M, Estacio●, Quinonez.J, Arroyo●, Rivera (Caicedo.J● 78), Rodriguez, Hernandez (Ladines 61), Morales Neumann (Asis 61). Tr: Carlos Torres Garces

Vélez Sarsfield 1
Bustamante [13]

Sessa● – Mendez, Castroman (Ocampo 81), Zarate.M (Balvorin 71), Papa, Moreno Y Fabianesi, Pellegrino, Pellerano, Bustamante, Bustos●, Escudero (Broggi 66). Tr: Ricardo La Volpe

GROUP 4 MATCHDAY 1
Parque Central, Montevideo
21-02-2007, 21:45, 9582, Pezzotta ARG

Nacional 3
Vera [72], Delgado [75], Martínez [92+]

Viera – Godin●, Rodriguez●●●61, Alvarez.P, Viana, Vanzini (Sosa 65), Broli (Martinez● 41), Delgado, Tejera (Castro 65), Marquez, Vera. Tr: Daniel Carreno

Internacional 1
Hidalgo [37]

Clemer – Rafael Santos, Wellington Monteiro●●●74, Hidalgo, Alex (Perdigao 74), Edinho, Iarley, Elder Granja, Edigle●, Adriano (Michel 82), Luiz Adriano (Fernandao 64). Tr: Abel Braga

GROUP 4 MATCHDAY 2
José Amalfitani, Buenos Aires
28-02-2007, 19:15, 8661, Fagundes BRA

Vélez Sarsfield 1
Escudero [45]

Sessa – Pellerano, Pellegrino, Mendez●, Papa (Bustamante 78), Escudero, Moreno Y Fabianesi● (Robles 60), Bustos●, Sena (Broggi 60), Zarate.M, Balvorin. Tr: Ricardo La Volpe

Nacional 1
Vera [46]

Viera – Jaume●, Godin, Broli● (Vanzini 84), Alvarez.P, Cardaccio (Arismendi● 62), Sosa●, Vera, La Luz● (Castro 46), Martinez, Viana●. Tr: Daniel Carreno

GROUP 4 MATCHDAY 2
Beira-Rio, Porto Alegre
28-02-2007, 21:45, 34 327, Selman CHI

Internacional 3
Perdigão [26], Indio [55], Alexandre Pato [66]

Clemer – Ceara, Indio (Wilson 76), Rafael Santos, Hidalgo, Alex (Maycon 68), Edinho, Fernandao, Iarley, Alexandre Pato (Adriano 80), Perdigao. Tr: Abel Braga

Emelec 0

Elizaga – Quinonez.C, Caicedo.R (Rodriguez 56), Quinonez.M, Estacio, Corozo●, Quinonez.J●, Caicedo.J●, Rivera, Hernandez (Arroyo 70), Morales Neumann● (Ladines 77). Tr: Carlos Torres Garces

GROUP 4 MATCHDAY 3
José Amalfitani, Buenos Aires
14-03-2007, 19:30, Amarilla PAR

Vélez Sarsfield 3
Castromaán [16], Escudero 2 [21 81]

Sessa – Uglessich, Pellerano, Pellegrino, Bustamante, Papa (Montero 75), Moreno Y Fabianesi, Mendez●, Castroman (Ocampo 66), Zarate.M (Balvorin 85), Escudero. Tr: Ricardo La Volpe

Internacional 0

Clemer – Ceara●, Indio, Hidalgo, Edinho●, Fernadao, Iarley (Alexandre Pato 46), Adriano (Christian 46), Wilson●, Michel (Vargas 75), Maycon●. Tr: Abel Braga

GROUP 4 MATCHDAY 3
George Capwell, Guayaquil
22-03-2007, 21:30, Selman CHI

Emelec 1
Quiñónez [89]

Elizaga – Quinonez.C, Zambrano, Caicedo.R●90, Quinonez.M●67, Hernandez (Estacio 73), Rivera, Quinonez.J, Minda (Arroyo 63), Morales Neumann (Ladines 66), Viatri. Tr: Carlos Torres Garces

Nacional 0

Viera – Jaume●67, Godin, Broli, Alvarez.P, Cardaccio (Delgado 77), Sosa, Vera (Castro 79), La Luz (Rodriguez 71), Martinez, Viana. Tr: Daniel Carreno

GROUP 4 MATCHDAY 4
Beira-Rio, Porto Alegre
28-03-2007, 21:45, 35 258, Larrionda URU

Internacional 0

Clemer – Ceara, Indio, Rubens Cardoso, Hidalgo, Edinho, Maycon, Alex (Perdigao 74), Iarley● (Alexandre Pato 46), Fernadao (Adriano 77), Christian●●●27. Tr: Abel Braga

Vélez Sarsfield 0

Sessa – Uglessich●, Pellegrino●, Pellerano, Bustamante (Broggi 27), Mendez, Moreno Y Fabianesi (Sena 81), Bustos, Papa, Escudero●, Zarate.M (Balvorin 71). Tr: Ricardo La Volpe

GROUP 4 MATCHDAY 4
Parque Central, Montevideo
3-04-2007, 19:00, 10 246, Amarilla PAR

Nacional 3
Viana [19], Delgado [30], Juárez [46+]

Muslera – Godin●, Da Rosa, Alvarez.P, Viana, Vanzini● (Cardaccio 72), Sosa, Delgado, Martinez, Castro (Tejera 82), Juarez● (Marquez 72). Tr: Daniel Carreno

Emelec 1
Morales Neumann [92+]

Elizaga – Quinonez.C, Corozo●, Quinonez.J, Estacio, Minda, Caicedo.J, Rivera (Ayovi 59), Arroyo●, Hernandez (Mercado 46), Viatri (Morales Neumann 74). Tr: Carlos Torres Garces

GROUP 4 MATCHDAY 5
George Capwell, Guayaquil
10-04-2007, 21:30, Rivera PER

Emelec 1
Arroyo [45]

Angulo – Mercado, Caicedo.R (Corozo 76), Quinonez.J, Estacio, Caicedo.J, Rivera, Hernandez, Arroyo●●●87, Morales Neumann (Ladines 70), Viatri (Ayovi 61). Tr: Carlos Torres Garces

Internacional 2
Iarley [36], Alexandre Pato [52]

Clemer – Indio (Edigle 70), Edinho, Hidalgo●, Ceara, Wellington Monteiro, Vargas, Fernadao, Rubens Cardoso, Iarley (Michel 83), Alexandre Pato (Maycon 90). Tr: Abel Braga

GROUP 4 MATCHDAY 5
Parque Central, Montevideo
12-04-2007, 20:15, Chandia CHI

Nacional 2
Godín [33], Castro [75]

Muslera – Alvarez.P, Godin, Jaume, Viana, Vanzini (Cardaccio● 50), Sosa, Delgado, Martinez, Vera, Castro (Broli 78). Tr: Daniel Carreno

Vélez Sarsfield 0

Sessa● – Uglessich, Pellegrino, Pellerano (Papa 46), Torsiglieri, Mendez (Ereros 78), Moreno Y Fabianesi●, Bustos, Escudero●, Ocampo, Balvorin (Sena● 46). Tr: Ricardo La Volpe

GROUP 4 MATCHDAY 6
Beira-Rio, Porto Alegre
19-04-2007, 19:15, 38 853, Selman CHI

Internacional 1
Fernandão [80]

Clemer – Ceara, Indio●65, Wellington Monteiro, Hidalgo, Edinho, Fernandao, Iarley●, Alexandre Pato, Rubens Cardoso (Perdigao 63), Vargas (Michel 70). Tr: Abel Braga

Nacional 0

Muslera – Jaume, Godin, Alvarez.P, Vanzini● (Arismendi 81), Romero●, Sosa, Castro (Vera 56), Delgado● (Cardaccio● 46), Martinez, Viana. Tr: Daniel Carreno

GROUP 4 MATCHDAY 6
José Amalfitani, Buenos Aires
19-04-2007, 19:15, Grance PAR

Vélez Sarsfield 1
Escudero [64]

Sessa – Uglessich (Ocampo 46), Pellegrino, Pellerano, Bustamante, Mendez, Bustos, Moreno Y Fabianesi● (Sena 80), Zarate.M. Tr: Ricardo La Volpe

Emelec 0

Angulo● – Mercado, Corozo, Caicedo.R●, Estacio, Quinonez.M●, Caicedo.J, Rivera (Ayovi 80), Quinonez.J●, Hernandez● (Morales Neumann● 69), Viatri. Tr: Carlos Torres Garces

GRUPO 5

		Pl	W	D	L	F	A	Pts	BRA	BRA	BOL	VEN
Flamengo	BRA	6	5	1	0	10	4	16		1-0	1-0	3-1
Paraná	BRA	6	3	0	3	8	8	9	0-1		2-0	2-1
Real Potosí	BOL	6	1	3	2	8	9	6	2-2	3-1		2-2
Unión At. Maracaibo	VEN	6	0	2	4	8	14	2	1-2	2-4	1-1	

GROUP 5 MATCHDAY 1
Estadio Guzmán, Potosí
14-02-2007, 19:45, Rivera PER

Real Potosí 2
Monteiro [13], Aguilera [43]

Burtovoy – Ribiero, Rodriguez, Amador•, Garcia
(Colque 86), Calustro• (Brandan 75), Suarez, Paz.M,
Pena, Monteiro, Aguilera (Paz.L 61). Tr: Felix Berdeja

Flamengo 2
Roni [48], Obina [66]

Bruno – Leo Moura, Moises•, Paulinho, Juan (Roni 46),
Obina (Souza• 72), Claiton, Renato Augusto, Renato,
Thiago (Juninho 61), Ronaldo Angelim. Tr: Ney Franco

GROUP 5 MATCHDAY 1
Estadio Pachencho, Maracaibo
15-02-2007, 18:30, Haro ECU

Unión At. Maracaibo 2
Arismendi [44], Cásseres [66]

Angelucci – Martinez, Fuenmayor, Bovaglio•,
Valenilla, Fernandez, Mea Vitali.M, Urdaneta
(Almeida 75), Figueroa (Renteria 58), Arismendi•
(Ballesteros 69), Casseres. Tr: Jorge Pellicer

Paraná 4
Josiel [38], Dinelson [55], Henrique [56], Gerson [68]

Flavio – Daniel Marques•, Egidio, Beto, Gerson•,
Henrique (Joelson 72), Dinelson (Alex 85), Neguete•,
Xaves, Josiel (Lima 79), Andre Luiz. Tr: Zetti

GROUP 5 MATCHDAY 2
Durival Britto e Silva, Curitiba
21-02-2007, 19:30, Laverni ARG

Paraná 2
Dinelson [62], Daniel Marques [73]

Flavio – Daniel Marques•, Goiano (Vinicius 67),
Egidio•, Beto•, Gerson•, Henrique (Xaves 80),
Dinelson (Joelson 85), Joao Paulo, Josiel, Andre Luiz.
Tr: Zetti

Real Potosí 0

Burtovoy – Ribiero•, Rodriguez, Amador•, Colque,
Calustro, Suarez, Paz.M•••60, Pena, Monteiro, Paz.M
(Brandan 67). Tr: Felix Berdeja

GROUP 5 MATCHDAY 2
Maracanã, Rio de Janeiro
21-02-2007, 21:45, 31 240, Osses CHI

Flamengo 3
Renato [16], Souza [36], Obina [45]

Bruno – Leo Moura, Moises, Irineu, Paulinho (Juninho
77), Juan, Obina (Roni 46), Claiton, Souza, Renato
Augusto (Salino 76), Renato•. Tr: Ney Franco

Unión At. Maracaibo 1
Arismendi [89]

Angelucci – Fernandez, Fuenmayor, Mea Vitali.R,
Martinez, Mea Vitali.M•, Gonzalez•, Suanno
(Figueroa 45), Urdaneta•, Renteria (Arismendi 67),
Casseres (Laffatigue 58). Tr: Jorge Pellicer

GROUP 5 MATCHDAY 3
Estadio Pachencho, Maracaibo
13-03-2007, 18:00, Hoyos COL

Unión At. Maracaibo 1
Fernández [72]

Angelucci – Fernandez•, Fuenmayor, Mea Vitali.R,
Martinez, Gonzalez (Vallenilla• 46), Mea Vitali.M,
Figueroa, Galvan (Laffatigue• 70), Casseres,
Arismendi (Ballesteros 32). Tr: Jorge Pellicer

Real Potosí 1
Peña [64]

Burtovoy• – Ribiero•, Rodriguez, Garcia, Pena, Ortiz
(Yecerotte 80), Calustro, Suarez, Brandan•
(Cuellar 75), Paz.L, Aguilera• (Monteiro 73).
Tr: Felix Berdeja

GROUP 5 MATCHDAY 3
Durival Britto e Silva, Curitiba
14-03-2007, 21:45, 15 614, Gaciba BRA

Paraná 0

Flavio – Daniel Marques, Egidio, Beto•, Gerson,
Henrique (Lima 60), Neguete•88, Joao Vitor
(Joelson 22), Xaves (Vinicius 60), Josiel, Andre Luiz.
Tr: Zetti

Flamengo 1
Renato [24]

Bruno – Leo Moura, Ronaldo Angelim, Irineu,
Paulinho, Juan, Roni (Leo Medeiros 87), Juninho•
(Salino 58), Souza• (Leonardo 77), Renato Augusto,
Renato. Tr: Ney Franco

GROUP 5 MATCHDAY 4
Estadio Guzmán, Potosí
20-03-2007, 20:45, Carpio ECU

Real Potosí 2
Monteiro 2 [12p 40]

Burtovoy – Ribiero, Rodriguez, Amador•, Garcia,
Calustro (Paz.L 58), Suarez, Paz.M, Pena, Monteiro,
Aguilera (Brandan 67). Tr: Felix Berdeja

Unión At. Maracaibo 2
Cásseres [36], Ballesteros [55]

Sanhouse – Martinez•, Fuenmayor•, Mea Vitali.R•,
Machado, Fernandez, Mea Vitali.M, Galvan•
(Figueroa 55), Vallenilla, Casseres (Laffatigue 91+),
Ballesteros (Renteria 75). Tr: Jorge Pellicer

GROUP 5 MATCHDAY 4
Maracanã, Rio de Janeiro
21-03-2007, 21:50, Simon BRA

Flamengo 1
Souza [87]

Bruno – Leo Moura, Ronaldo Angelim, Irineu,
Paulinho•, Juan•, Roni (Leonardo 70), Renato
Augusto, Souza• (Leo Medeiros 90), Juninho
(Jailton 89), Renato. Tr: Ney Franco

Paraná 0

Flavio – Daniel Marques, Egidio, Beto•, Gerson
(Vinicus 69), Henrique (Alex 74), Dinelson (Lima 79),
Joao Paulo, Xaves•, Josiel, Andre Luiz•. Tr: Zetti

GROUP 5 MATCHDAY 5
Estadio Pachencho, Maracaibo
4-04-2007, 20:45, Carrillo PER

Unión At. Maracaibo 1
Paulinho OG [77]

Sanhouse – Martinez (Rodriguez 62), Fuenmayor, Mea
Vitali.R, Machado, Vallenilla (Diaz 62), Mea Vitali.M,
Fernandez, Figueroa (Beraza 69), Casseres,
Ballesteros. Tr: Jorge Pellicer

Flamengo 2
Renato [12], Renato Augusto [81]

Bruno – Leo Moura, Irineu, Ronaldo Angelim,
Paulinho, Juan, Claiton (Moises 85), Juninho
(Gerson 92), Souza, Renato Augusto (Jailton 90),
Renato. Tr: Ney Franco

GROUP 5 MATCHDAY 5
Estadio Guzmán, Potosí
10-04-2007, 18:00, Grance PAR

Real Potosí 3
Rodríguez [23], Brandán [70], Monteiro [75]

Burtovoy – Eguino, Paz.M•, Rodriguez (Paz.L• 68),
Colque, Ribeiro (Aguilera 89), Suarez, Calustro,
Brandan, Pena (Yecerotte• 79), Monteiro.
Tr: Mauricio Soria

Paraná 1
Gerson [29]

Flavio – Daniel Marques, Aderaldo, Goiano
(Vinicius 75), Egidio, Beto•, Gerson• (Alex 66),
Henrique, Dinelson (Joelson• 85), Joao Paulo, Xaves.
Tr: Zetti

GROUP 5 MATCHDAY 6
Maracanã, Rio de Janeiro
18-04-2007, 21:45, 14 964, Prudente URU

Flamengo 1
Souza [12]

Bruno – Leo Moura, Irineu, Ronaldo Angelim,
Paulinho, Juan, Roni, Claiton (Salino 77), Souza
(Leo Medeiros 46), Renato Augusto, Renato.
Tr: Ney Franco

Real Potosí 0

Burtovoy – Eguino, Paz.M• (Amador 70), Rodriguez,
Colque (Paz.L 86), Ribeiro, Suarez•, Calustro,
Brandan (Aguilera 76), Pena, Monteiro.
Tr: Mauricio Soria

GROUP 5 MATCHDAY 6
Durival Britto e Silva, Curitiba
18-04-2007, 21:45, 6551, Pompei ARG

Paraná 2
Egidio [7], Beto [14]

Flavio – Alex, Daniel Marques, Egidio, Beto, Gerson,
Dinelson (Goiano 63), Vinicius (Joelson 87), Joao Vitor,
Xaves, Josiel (Lima 69). Tr: Zetti

Unión At. Maracaibo 1
Machado [70]

Sanhouse – Rodriguez, Mea Vitali.R•, Bovaglio
(Vallenilla 46), Machado, Diaz, Fernandez, Urdaneta,
Beraza, Renteria (Ballesteros 66), Arismendi
(Casseres• 66). Tr: Jorge Pellicer

GRUPO 6		PI	W	D	L	F	A	Pts	CHI	VEN	ECU	ARG
Colo Colo	CHI	6	3	0	3	12	7	9		2-1	4-0	1-2
Caracas FC	VEN	6	3	0	3	7	10	9	0-4		1-0	3-1
LDU Quito	ECU	6	2	2	2	7	8	8	3-1	3-1		1-1
River Plate	ARG	6	2	2	2	5	6	8	1-0	0-1	0-0	

GROUP 6 MATCHDAY 1
Brígido Iriarte, Caracas
22-02-2007, 17:45, Carrillo PER

Caracas FC 1
Guerra [75]

Toyo – Vielma, Rey, Vizcarrondo, Perez, Vera•, Rojas, Guerra (Rouga 88), Gonzalez (Olivares• 63), Carpintero, Velasquez (Castellin 61).
Tr: Noel Sanvicente

LDU Quito 0

Mora – Ayovi.A•, Araujo, Campos, Vera, Obregon (Bolanos 81), urrutia, Ambrossi, Lara, Guerron (Salas 70), Escalada. Tr: Edgardo Bauza

GROUP 6 MATCHDAY 1
Monumental, Santiago
22-02-2007, 21:00, Torres PAR

Colo Colo 1
Suazo [60]

Cejas – Riffo•, Vidal, Henriquez, Gonzalez (Mena 57•••89), Melendez•, Sanhueza•, Jerez (Gimenez 57), Hernandez•, Suazo•, Sanchez (Lorca• 78). Tr: Claudio Borghi

River Plate 2
Ponzio [45], Farías [54]

Carrizo – Ferrari•, Gerlo, Rivas•, Tuzzio, Galvan (Ahumada 75), Ponzio, Belluschi, Sambueza (Zapata• 66), Farias•, Garcia•65.
Tr: Daniel Passarella

GROUP 6 MATCHDAY 2
La Casa Blanca, Quito
7-03-2007, 17:00, Duarte COL

LDU Quito 3
Obregón [46], Salas [74p], Guerrón [85]

Mora – Ayovi.A, Araujo, Calderon, Larrea• (Guerron 75), Ambrossi, Obregon (Bolanos 63), Vera•, Lara•80, Salas (Ortiz 84), Escalada. Tr: Edgardo Bauza

Colo Colo 1
Suazo [32]

Cejas – Riffo, Vidal•, Henriquez•••74, Fierro•, Melendez•, Sanhueza•, Jerez (Gonzalez 58), Hernandez (Lorca 81), Suazo, Sanchez (Gimenez 72). Tr: Claudio Borghi

GROUP 6 MATCHDAY 2
Monumental, Buenos Aires
8-03-2007, 21:30, Pozo CHI

River Plate 0

Carrizo – Ferrari (Rios 84), Gerlo, Rivas, Tuzzio, Galvan• (Fernandez 46), Ahumada•, Belluschi•, Zapata (Sambueza 75), Farias, Ruben•.
Tr: Daniel Passarella

Caracas FC 1
Velásquez [9]

Toyo – Vielma, Rey, Vizcarrondo•, Perez• (Rouga 66), Vera•, Rojas, Guerra•, Gonzalez (Bustamante 86), Velasquez (Lucena 71), Carpintero. Tr: Noel Sanvicente

GROUP 6 MATCHDAY 3
La Casa Blanca, Quito
15-03-2007, 17:15, Chandia CHI

LDU Quito 1
Vera [15]

Mora – Ayovi.A, Araujo•, Calderon, Obregon (Guerron 56), Larrea• (Putan 81), Vera•, Ambrossi, Bolanos (Escalada•••50, Salas.
Tr: Edgardo Bauza

River Plate 2
Farías [54]

Carrizo – Ferrari•, Gerlo, Lussenhoff, Villagra, Ponzio• (Zapata 89), Ahumada•, Belluschi•, Sambueza•40, Farias, Ruben (Lima• 73).
Tr: Daniel Passarella

GROUP 6 MATCHDAY 3
General Santander, Cúcuta
20-03-2007, 18:30, Buitrago COL

Caracas FC 0

Toyo – Vielma, Rey, Vizcarrondo (Lucena 46), Perez•, Vera, Rojas, Guerra, Gonzalez (Castellin• 67), Velasquez (Escobar 63), Carpintero.
Tr: Noel Sanvicente

Colo Colo 1
Sánchez 3 [21 60 88], Giménez [27]

Cejas – Riffo, Mena, Vidal, Fierro, Melendez, Villarroel•, Jerez (Acevedo 87), Hernandez (Millar 82), Sanchez, Gimenez (Jara 53). Tr: Claudio Borghi

GROUP 6 MATCHDAY 4
Monumental, Buenos Aires
29-03-2007, 21:00, 15 707, Simon BRA

River Plate 0

Carrizo – Ferrari•, Gerlo, Rivas, Villagra, Fernandez, Ponzio•, Belluschi, Zapata, Rosales (Ortega 82), Farias (Ruben 71). Tr: Daniel Passarella

LDU Quito 0

Mora• – Araujo, Ayovi.A, Campos•, Calderon, Bolanos (Guerron 62), Larrea (Obregon 79), Vera•, Ambrossi, Lara, Salas (Vizcarra 86). Tr: Edgardo Bauza

GROUP 6 MATCHDAY 4
Monumental, Santiago
30-03-2007, 18:15, 11 310, Garay PER

Colo Colo 2
Fierro [43], Suazo [92+p]

Cejas – Riffo, Mena, Vidal, Fierro, Melendez•, Villarroel• (Millar 75), Jerez (Suazo 55), Hernandez, Sanchez, Gimenez (Sanhueza 55). Tr: Claudio Borghi

Caracas FC 1
González [67]

Toyo – Vielma, Rey, Rouga, Perez•, Vera•, Rojas, Guerra (Lucena• 84), Gonzalez (Olivares• 68), Velasquez• (Escobar 46), Carpintero.
Tr: Noel Sanvicente

GROUP 6 MATCHDAY 5
Monumental, Santiago
3-04-2007, 20:15, Silvera URU

Colo Colo 4
Fierro 2 [50p 72], Suazo [65], Millar [78]

Cejas – Riffo, Mena, Vidal• (Jara 80), Fierro, Melendez•, Sanhueza, Jerez, Hernandez (Villarroel 87), Sanchez (Millar 77), Suazo. Tr: Claudio Borghi

LDU Quito 0

Mora – Araujo, Ayovi.A, Campos•, Calderon• (Guerron 57), Larrea•, Vera (Bolanos 34), Ambrossi, Lara (Ortiz 77), Escalada, Salas•. Tr: Edgardo Bauza

GROUP 6 MATCHDAY 5
General Santander, Cúcuta
5-04-2007, 20:15, Larrionda URU

Caracas FC 3
Rey [15], Escobar 2 [32 36]

Toyo – Rey, Vizcarrondo, Vielma, Rouga, Olivares, Lucena•42, Gonzalez (Pinango 46), Guerra (Bustamante 87), Carpintero, Escobar (Caraballo 67).
Tr: Noel Sanvicente

River Plate 1
Farías [28]

Carrizo – Ferrari, Gerlo, Rivas, Villagra, Fernandez, Ponzio (Lima 82), Belluschi, Zapata•42, Rosales (Ruben 46), Farias (Galvas 73). Tr: Daniel Passarella

GROUP 6 MATCHDAY 6
La Casa Blanca, Quito
25-04-2007, 17:30, Buckley PER

LDU Quito 3
Ayovi [23], Campos [40], Guerrón [55]

Mora – Calle• (Araujo 69), Campos, Calderon, Vera, Larrea, Urrutia•, Ambrossi, Bolanos• (Obregon 77), Guerron (Putan 73), Ayovi.O•. Tr: Edgardo Bauza

Caracas FC 1
González [63]

Toyo – Bustamante, Rouga, Rivero (Vizcarrondo 46), Vielma, Pinango (Gonzalez 46), Olivares•, Rojas, Caraballo• (Vera 69), Escobar, Carpintero.
Tr: Noel Sanvicente

GROUP 6 MATCHDAY 6
Monumental, Buenos Aires
25-04-2007, 19:30, Oliveira BRA

River Plate 1
Galván [62]

Ojeda – Villagra (Ferrari 68), Gerlo, Lussenhoff•, Rivas, Galvan•, Ahumada (Belluschi 46), Sambueza, Ortega•, Rios, Ruben (Lima 46). Tr: Daniel Passarella

Colo Colo 0

Cejas – Jara (Arenas 70), Melendez, Vidal•, Fierro•, Villarroel, Sanhueza•, Jerez (Acevedo 64), Millar, Suazo, Gimenez (Lorca 64). Tr: Claudio Borghi

GRUPO 7											
		Pl	W	D	L	F	A	Pts	MEX	ARG	PER	BOL
Toluca	MEX	6	4	0	2	10	6	12		2-0	3-0	1-2
Boca Juniors	ARG	6	3	1	2	11	5	10	3-0		1-0	7-0
Cienciano	PER	6	3	0	3	12	9	9	1-2	3-0		5-1
Bolívar	BOL	6	1	1	4	5	18	4	0-2	0-0	2-3	

GROUP 7 MATCHDAY 1
Hernando Siles, La Paz
14-02-2007, 17:30, 3413, Grance PAR

Bolívar 0

Zayas – Flores, Vaca•, Tordoya•, Garcia.I, Reyes, Viglianti•, Sillero, Baldivieso, Leitao Polieri, Saucedo (Meza 70). Tr: Victor Antelo

Boca Juniors 0

Caranta – Maidana•, Morel•, Ibarra•, Battaglia, Diaz, Palacio (Marioni 62), Orteman, Palermo, Cardozo (Barros Schelotto 84), Banega (Ledesma 69). Tr: Miguel Angel Russo

GROUP 7 MATCHDAY 1
Estadio Inca, Cusco
21-02-2007, 21:00, Reinoso ECU

Cienciano 1
Hernández.J [37]

Flores – De La Haza, Pisano, Hernandez•, Fernandez.C, Bazalar, Torres, Garcia• (Mostto 46), Marino, Uribe (Guizasola• 62), Saraz (Ruiz 46). Tr: Julio Cesar Uribe

Toluca 2
De La Torre [71], Velasco [87]

Lozano – Arias, De La Torre.M, Esquivel, Espinosa•, Almazan, Castillejos.J (Velasco• 62), Garcia, De La Torre.D, Valadez (Viades 82), Cruzalta• (Nunez 46). Tr: Pablo Marino

GROUP 7 MATCHDAY 2
Nemesio Diez, Toluca
27-02-2007, 20:30, Andarcia VEN

Toluca 1
Da Silva [2]

Cristante – Da Silva, Rosada, De La Torre.M, Esquivel, Avalos (Velasco 45), Zinha•, Sanchez, Almazan, Ponce (Valadez 61), De La Torre.D. Tr: Americo Gallego

Bolívar 2
Viglianti [55], Sillero [58]

Zayas• – Juarez•, Salvatierra, Tordoya, Garcia.I, Reyes, Viglianti, Melgar (Camacho 88), Sillero (Guatia 91+), Leitao Polieri•, Cuellar (Meza 67). Tr: Victor Antelo

GROUP 7 MATCHDAY 2
La Bombonera, Buenos Aires
1-03-2007, 21:15, 11 800, Lopes BRA

Boca Juniors 1
Ibarra [81]

Caranta – Ibarra, Maidana, Diaz, Morel (Rodriguez 85), Banega, Orteman (Marino 68•••81), Cardozo (Ledesma 90), Riquelme, Palermo, Marioni. Tr: Miguel Angel Russo

Cienciano 0

Flores• – De La Haza, Pisano, Hernandez, Fernandez.C (Villamarin 46), Bazalar, Torres (Mostto 46), Garcia, Marino, Uribe (Huertas 67), Saraz. Tr: Julio Cesar Uribe

GROUP 7 MATCHDAY 3
Estadio Inca, Cusco
8-03-2007, 17:15, Haro ECU

Cienciano 5
Mostto 2 [63] [79], Mariño 2 [69p] [82], Ruiz [88]

Flores – De La Haza, Pisano, Hernandez, Villamarin•, Bazalar, Torres• (Mostto• 36), Garcia (Chiroque 64), Marino, Uribe, Saraz (Ruiz• 46). Tr: Julio Cesar Uribe

Bolívar 1
Cuellar [16]

Zayas – Juarez (Saucedo 80), Salvatierra (Garcia.F 75), Tordoya, Garcia.I•, Reyes, Viglianti•, Melgar•••68, Sillero, Leitao Polieri•, Cuellar (Baldivieso 66). Tr: Victor Antelo

GROUP 7 MATCHDAY 3
Nemesio Diez, Toluca
14-03-2007, 21:00, Larrionda URU

Toluca 2
Ponce [7], Sánchez [57]

Cristante – Da Silva, Viades (Zinha 46), Rosada, Espinosa, Sanchez, Ponce (Esquivel 64), Morales, De La Torre.D•, Cruzalta, Zinha (Avalos 76). Tr: Americo Gallego

Boca Juniors 0

Caranta – Ibarra, Maidana•, Diaz•22, Morel• (Rodriguez 72), Banega, Ledesma, Battaglia• (Orteman 84), Cardozo, Boselli (Silvestre 24), Marioni. Tr: Miguel Angel Russo

GROUP 7 MATCHDAY 4
José Amalfitani, Buenos Aires
22-03-2007, 21:15, Amarilla PAR

Boca Juniors 3
Maidana [15], Riquelme [23], Boselli [82]

Caranta – Ibarra, Maidana, Morel•, Rodriguez, Ledesma•, Banega, Cardozo (Datolo 84), Riquelme, Mondaini (Marioni 75), Palermo (Boselli 82). Tr: Miguel Angel Russo

Toluca 0

Cristante• – Cruzalta•••40, Da Silva, Arias• (Almazan 46), Ponce, Rosada, Espinosa, Morales (Esquivel 59), De La Torre.D (Avalos 66), Zinha, Sanchez. Tr: Americo Gallego

GROUP 7 MATCHDAY 4
Hernando Siles, La Paz
28-03-2007, 18:30, Laverni ARG

Bolívar 2
Leitão Polieri 2 [12] [66]

Zayas – Juarez (Montano 88), Vaca, Tordoya, Camacho, Reyes•, Salvatierra• (Flores 46), Viglianti, Leitao Polieri•, Garcia.F (Cuellar 53), Saucedo. Tr: Victor Antelo

Cienciano 3
Mariño [33], González Vigil [63], Uribe [81p]

Flores• – Pisano•, Salazar.J•, Guizaola, Bazalar, Chiroque (Uribe 67), De La Haza•, Marino, Guevara• (Fernandez.C 56), Mostto (Ruiz 75), Gonzalez. Tr: Jose Basualdo

GROUP 7 MATCHDAY 5
Estadio Inca, Cusco
4-04-2007, 17:30, Ruiz COL

Cienciano 3
González Vigil [48], Mostto [79], Torres [91+]

Flores – Guevara (Torres• 59), Pisano•, Salazar.J, Villamarin•, De La Haza, Bazalar, Chiroque (Huertas 68), Marino, Fernandez.C 23), Gonzalez Vigil, Mostto•••83. Tr: Jose Basualdo

Boca Juniors 0

Caranta – Rodriguez, Maidana (Silvestre 81), Diaz, Morel•, Orteman (Banega 64), Battaglia• (Datolo 72), Ledesma, Cardozo•••38, Marioni, Boselli. Tr: Miguel Angel Russo

GROUP 7 MATCHDAY 5
Hernando Siles, La Paz
12-04-2007, 21:30, Arias PAR

Bolívar 0

Zayas – Juarez•, Salvatierra (Meza 65), Vaca, Tordoya, Camacho, Reyes•, Melgar (Cuellar 83), Viglianti, Leitao Polieri•, Saucedo. Tr: Marco Antonio Sandy

Toluca 2
Ponce [14], Sánchez [88]

Cristante – Arias, Da Silva, Viades, Rosada•, Esquivel (Avalos 82), Espinosa, Zinha (Castillejos.J 63), Sanchez•, Ponce•, De La Torre.D (De La Torre.M 68). Tr: Americo Gallego

GROUP 7 MATCHDAY 6
Nemesio Diez, Toluca
26-04-2007, 19:15, Chandia CHI

Toluca 3
Morales 2 [32] [48], Sánchez [70]

Cristante – Da Silva, Viades•, Rosada, Esquivel (De La Torre.M 82), Zinha•, Sanchez, Ponce, Morales (Espinosa 80), De La Torre.D (Avalos 75), Cruzalta. Tr: Americo Gallego

Cienciano 0

Flores• – Pisano, Salazar.J•, Villamarin, De La Haza•, Torres, Bazalar, Chiroque, Gonzalez Vigil, Saraz (Ruiz 52), Guevara• (Guizasola 62). Tr: Jose Basualdo

GROUP 7 MATCHDAY 6
La Bombonera, Buenos Aires
26-04-2007, 21:15, Grance PAR

Boca Juniors 7
Palacio 2 [32] [45], Palermo [37p], Tordoya OG [51], Datolo [57], Marioni 2 [64] [85]

Caranta – Ibarra, Diaz, Morel, Rodriguez•, Ledesma, Banega•, Datolo•, Riquelme (Marino 75), Palacio (Boselli 63), Palermo (Marioni 63). Tr: Miguel Angel Russo

Bolívar 0

Zayas – Vaca•, Tordoya, Salvatierra, Juarez, Melgar•, Bustillos•, Camacho•, Reyes, Leitao Polieri (Viglianti• 46), Saucedo (Sillero 70). Tr: Marco Antonio Sandy

GRUPO 8

		Pl	W	D	L	F	A	Pts	BRA	URU	ARG	COL
Santos	BRA	6	6	0	0	12	1	18		1-0	3-0	3-0
Defensor Sporting	URU	6	3	0	3	8	7	9	0-2		3-0	3-0
Gimnasia Y Esgrima LP	ARG	6	3	0	3	9	10	9	1-2	3-0		3-2
Deportivo Pasto	COL	6	0	0	6	3	14	0	0-1	1-2	0-2	

GROUP 8 MATCHDAY 1
Centenario, Montevideo
13-02-2007, 20:00, 7385, Pozo CHI

Defensor Sporting 3
Ariosa [36], Morales [63], Pereira [72]

Silva – Martinez, Fadeuille• (Amado 68), De Souza, Morales (Fernandez.S 76), Villa•, Gonzalez, Ariosa, Caceres, Pereira (Diaz 74), Maulella.
Tr: Jorge da Silva

Gimnasia y Esgrima LP 0

Kletnicki – Basualdo, Herner, San Esteban, Landa, Ormeno (Pierguidi 46), Piatti, Escobar•, Romero (Chaves 46), Pacheco (Leguizamon 51), Silva.
Tr: Pedro Troglio

GROUP 8 MATCHDAY 2
Ciudad de La Plata, La Plata
6-03-2007, 21:15, Selman CHI

Gimnasia y Esgrima LP 3
Leal [28], Pacheco [49], Piergüidi [86]

Kletnicki – Basualdo•, Semino, Landa, Romero (Silva 73), Piatti, Alderete•, Cornejo, Pacheco (San Esteban 88), Pierguidi, Leal (Ormeno 73).
Tr: Pedro Troglio

Deportivo Pasto 0
Rodas [19], Valencia [70]

Barahona – Ramos.J, Mera•, Diaz, Monroy, Vidal•, Rodriguez•, Jaramillo•, Villamil• (Valencia 64), Garcia (Martinez 69), Rodas. Tr: Alvaro Gomez

GROUP 8 MATCHDAY 4
Ciudad de La Plata, La Plata
22-03-2007, 19:00, 11 799, Silvera URU

Gimnasia y Esgrima LP 1
Leal [88]

Kletnicki – Basualdo, Semino, Landa, Alderete•, Romero• (Leal 77), Piatti, Dubarbier, Pierguidi, Pacheco (Leguizamon• 67), Silva. Tr: Pedro Troglio

Santos 2
Marcos Aurélio [3], Zé Roberto [90]

Fabio Costa• – Adailton, Kleber, Denis (Pedro• 74), Rodrigo Souto•, Antonio Carlos, Marcus Aurelio (Pedrinho 63), Leonardo (Marcelo 63), Rodrigo Tiui•, Ze Roberto, Cleber Santana. Tr: Luxemburgo

GROUP 8 MATCHDAY 5
Estadio Libertad, Pasto
5-04-2007, 21:30, Intriago ECU

Deportivo Pasto 0

Ramos.N – Viveros (Villamil 56), Saa•, Vargas, Lora•, Martinez, Rodriguez (Ramos.J 56•58), Rosero, Valencia, Salazar• (Buelvas 75), Hidalgo.
Tr: Alvaro Gomez

Gimnasia y Esgrima LP 2
Pacheco [15], Leal [75]

Bangardino• – Semino, Crosa, San Esteban, Basualdo, Franco, Alderete•, Romero, Pacheco (Cornejo 85), Pierguidi (Chaves 65), Leguizamon (Leal• 52). Tr: Victor Bernay

GROUP 8 MATCHDAY 1
Estadio Libertad, Pasto
21-02-2007, 21:15, Andarcia VEN

Deportivo Pasto 0

Barahona – Ramos.J•, Mera, Diaz•, Monroy, Jaramillo, Rodriguez• (De La Cruz• 66), Vidal, Villamil (Valencia 70), Rodas, Garcia (Martinez 65).
Tr: Alvaro Gomez

Santos 1
Maldonado [61]

Fabio Costa – Adailton, Kleber, Pedro•, Avalos•, Antonio Carlos, Marcos Aurelio (Rodrigo Tabata 85), Maldonado, Rodrigo Tiui (Jonas 65), Ze Roberto (Pedrinho 78), Rodrigo Tabata 85), Cleber Santana. Tr: Luxemburgo

GROUP 8 MATCHDAY 3
Vila Belmiro, Santos
14-03-2007, 21:45, 6855, Grance PAR

Santos 3
Basualdo OG [6], Cléber Santana [52], Zé Roberto [69]

Fabio Costa• – Denis, Adailton•, Antonio Carlos•, Kleber, Cleber Santana (Pedrinho 77), Maldonado, Rodrigo Souto, Ze Roberto, Marcus Aurelio (Rodrigo Tabata 70•92), Rodrigo Tiui• (Avalos 59). Tr: Luxemburgo

Gimnasia y Esgrima LP 0

Kletnicki – Semino•, San Esteban•, Genriletti, Basualdo, Ormeno, Escobar (Romero 72), Cornejo (Silva 57), Pacheco, Pierguidi, Leal (Dubarbier 57).
Tr: Pedro Troglio

GROUP 8 MATCHDAY 4
Centenario, Montevideo
28-03-2007, 21:45, Gaciba BRA

Defensor Sporting 3
Ithurralde [16], Morales [26p], Peinado [93+]

Silva – Martinez•, Fadeuille, De Souza (Pezzolano 74), Morales (Diaz 62), Gonzalez (Viudez 62), Ariosa, Ithurralde, Peinado, Caceres, Pereira.
Tr: Jorge da Silva

Deportivo Pasto 0

Barahona – Viveros (Rosero 85), Mera, Vargas•, Monroy•, Vidal, Villamil, De La Cruz•, Salazar (Hidalgo 88), Rodas, Garcia (Martinez 54).
Tr: Alvaro Gomez

GROUP 8 MATCHDAY 6
Ciudad de La Plata, La Plata
19-04-2007, 21:30, Fagundes BRA

Gimnasia y Esgrima LP 3
Leguizamón 2 [24,72], Ithurralde OG [44]

Olave – Franco, Crosa, Semino•, Romero•, Cornejo (Silva• 58), Alderete, Chaves (Dubarbier 66), Pacheco, Leguizamon, Leal (Basualdo 58).
Tr: Ricardo Kuzemka

Defensor Sporting 0

Silva• – Gonzalez, Ithurralde, Martinez, Caceres•, Diaz (Pereira 74), Fadeuille, Ariosa, De Souza (Pezzolano• 79), Morales (Villa 59), Peinado.
Tr: Jorge da Silva

GROUP 8 MATCHDAY 2
Vila Belmiro, Santos
1-03-2007, 19:00, 9409, Baldassi ARG

Santos 1
Zé Roberto [48]

Fabio Costa – Adailton, Kleber, Denis•, Rodrigo Souto, Antonio Carlos•, Marcus Aurelio (Jonas 87), Maldonado, Rodrigo Tiui (Pedrinho 72), Ze Roberto, Cleber Santana (Avalos 71). Tr: Luxemburgo

Defensor Sporting 0

Silva – Ithurralde, Martinez•, Caceres•, Pereira• (Ariosa 65), Diaz (Morales 77), Fadeuille, Gonzalez, Pezzolano (Ariosa 65), Fernandez.S, Peinado.
Tr: Jorge da Silva

GROUP 8 MATCHDAY 3
Estadio Libertad, Pasto
15-03-2007, 21:45, Rivera PER

Deportivo Pasto 1
Rodas [26]

Barahona – Ramos.J•65, Mera, Vargas•, Monroy (Martinez 84), Vidal, Villamil, Jaramillo•••46, Valencia (Rosero 51), Rodas (Viveros 79), Hidalgo.
Tr: Alvaro Gomez

Defensor Sporting 2
Martinez [80], De Souza [91+]

Silva – Caceres, Ithurralde (Villa 70•71), Martinez, Pereira, Gonzalez, Fadeuille, Diaz• (Peinado 59), Ariosa (De Souza 64), Fernandez.S•56, Morales.
Tr: Jorge da Silva

GROUP 8 MATCHDAY 5
Centenario, Montevideo
5-04-2007, 19:00, 33 848, Arias PAR

Defensor Sporting 0

Silva – Ithurralde, Martinez (Viudez 73), Caceres, Gonzalez, Fadeuille (Peinado 73), Diaz, Ariosa (Pereira 64), De Souza, Morales, Villa. Tr: Jorge da Silva

Santos 2
Marcos Aurélio [68], Rodrigo Tabata [84]

Fabio Costa – Denis (Pedro• 46), Marcelo, Adailton, Kleber, Rodrigo Souto•, Cleber Santana (Pedrinho 67), Ze Roberto, Maldonado, Marcus Aurelio, Jonas (Rodrigo Tabata 67). Tr: Luxemburgo

GROUP 8 MATCHDAY 6
Vila Belmiro, Santos
19-04-2007, 21:30, 3253, Maldonado BOL

Santos 3
Carlinhos [7], Pedrinho [45], Rodrigo Tiuí [84]

Fabio Costa – Adailton, Carlinhos, Denis, Rodrigo Tabata, Marcelo, Jonas•, Maldonado (Rodrigo Souto 46), Marcos Aurelio (Rodrigo Tiui 61), Pedrinho, Cleber Santana (Ze Roberto 46). Tr: Luxemburgo

Deportivo Pasto 0

Barahona (Ramos.N 82) – Viveros, Saa, Vargas, Lora, Rosero (Martinez 56), De La Cruz, Rebolledo•, Valencia, Rodas (Villamil 56), Garcia.
Tr: Alvaro Gomez

ROUND OF SIXTEEN

La Bombonera, Buenos Aires
2-05-2007, 21:45, 28 657, Baldassi ARG

Boca Juniors   **3**

Riquelme [9], Palermo [60], Rodriguez [89]

Caranta – Ibarra, Silvestre, Morel•, Rodriguez, Ledesma•, Banega• (Bertolo 87), Cardozo, Riquelme, Palacio•, Palermo (Boselli 86). Tr: Miguel Angel Russo

Vélez Sarsfield   **0**

Sessa•25 – Uglessich, Pellegrino•, Pellerano, Bustamante, Mendez•, Bustos•, Moreno Y Fabianesi (Papa 72), Escudero (Cabral 72), Castroman•, Zarate.M• (Peratta• 28). Tr: Ricardo La Volpe

José Amalfitani, Buenos Aires
9-05-2007, 19:15, 10 232, Laverni ARG

Vélez Sarsfield   **3**

Zárate.M 2 [14 36], Ocampo [79]

Peratta – Pellerano, Pellegrino, Bustamante (Balvorin• 60), Mendez••92+, Bustos, Cabral (Broggi• 60), Escudero, Ocampo, Zarate, Castroman•82 (Moreno Y Fabianesi 63). Tr: Ricardo La Volpe

Boca Juniors   **1**

Riquelme [32]

Caranta• – Ibarra, Silvestre, Morel, Rodriguez•, Ledesma•34, Banega•, Cardozo (Bertolo 46), Riquelme, Palacio (Boselli 82), Palermo (Orteman 86). Tr: Miguel Angel Russo

Durival Britto e Silva, Curitiba
3-05-2007, 19:00, 8393, Silvera URU

Paraná   **1**

Josiel [51]

Flavio – Daniel Marques, Egidio, Beto•, Gerson• (Adriano 71), Dinelson, Neguete•77, Leo Matos, Xaves, Josiel, Lima (Joao Paulo 79). Tr: Zetti

Libertad   **2**

Marín [71], Barone [89]

Gonzalez – Balbuena• (Damiani 24), Guinazu•, Lopez•, Martinez.O (Bareiro 68), Bonet, Martinez.R•, Aquino, Caceres, Barone, Gamarra (Marin 46). Tr: Sergio Markarian

Defensores del Chaco, Asunción
10-05-2007, 20:00, 1554, Selman CHI

Libertad   **1**

Gamarra.R [12]

Bava – Balbuena•, Guinazu (Bareiro 89), Riveros, Lopez, Bonet, Sarabia, Martinez.R, Aquino (Marin 79), Caceres, Gamarra (Martinez.O 56). Tr: Sergio Markarian

Paraná   **1**

Joelson [84]

Flavio – Daniel Marques•, Toninho, Egidio (Joao Paulo 33), Beto•, Dinelson (Lima 46), Vinicius•86, Leo Matos•, Xaves, Joelson•, Josiel. Tr: Zetti

Parque Central, Montevideo
3-05-2007, 21:15, 13 204, Fagundes BRA

Nacional   **3**

Vera [7], Godín [23], Martínez.J [55]

Muslera – Jaume, Godin, Alvarez.P, Vanzini (Caballero 79), Cardaccio (Romero 89), Sosa, Vera•82, Delgado• (Castro 73), Martinez•, Viana. Tr: Daniel Carreno

Necaxa   **2**

Kléber Boas [10], Godín OG [53]

Alvarez – Quattrocchi, Beltran, Cervantes, Rojas, Moreno (Salgueiro 64), Everaldo Barbosa•82, Galindo• (Hernandez 60), Ruiz, Giminez (Gracian 46), Kleber Boas. Tr: Jose Luis Trejo

Azteca, Mexico City
10-05-2007, 21:30, 21 314, Pezzotta ARG

Necaxa   **0**

Vilar– Quattrocchi, Beltran, Cervantes•, Rojas (Moreno• 53), Salgueiro (Gracian 55), Hernandez (Sanchez 46), Galindo, Ruiz, Giminez, Kleber Boas. Tr: Jose Luis Trejo

Nacional   **1**

Martínez.J [88]

Muslera• – Jaume, Godin•, Alvarez.P, Cardaccio, Romero, Sosa•, Castro (Marquez 59), Delgado• (Caballero 66), Martinez, Viana. Tr: Daniel Carreno

General Santander, Cúcuta
3-05-2007, 21:30, 26 304, Laverni ARG

Cúcuta Deportivo   **5**

Martinez.J 3 [33 42 45], Castro [34], Del Castillo [89]

Zapata – Gonzalez•, Moreno, Hurtado, Bustos, Castro, Rueda• (Flores 75), Torres, Del Castillo, Perez, Martinez (Pajoy 80). Tr: Jorge Luis Bernal

Toluca   **1**

Sánchez [1]

Cristante – Da Silva, Rosada, Zinha, Sanchez, Duenas (Scocco 68), Ponce, Morales•26, Viades•, Palencia• (Esquivel 46), Cruzalta (De La Torre.D 46). Tr: Americo Gallego

Nemesio Diez, Toluca
8-05-2007, 21:45, 6557, Andarcia VEN

Toluca   **2**

Zinha [21], Scocco [90]

Cristante – Arias, Da Silva, Rosada•, Esquivel (Castillejos.I 74), Zinha•, Sanchez, Ponce•, Scocco•, De La Torre.D (De La Torre.M 64), Palencia (Avalos 56). Tr: Americo Gallego

Cúcuta Deportivo   **0**

Zapata• – Gonzalez, Moreno•, Hurtado, Bustos, Rueda•, Castro, Torres (Pajoy 87), Del Castillo, Martinez (Flores 67), Perez• (Cortes 80). Tr: Jorge Luis Bernal

Olímpico Universitario, Caracas
2-05-2007, 16:15, 16 087, Reinoso ECU

Caracas FC   **2**

Velásquez [55], Vielma [87]

Toyo – Rey, Rouga, Vielma•, Perez•, Vera, Olivares, Rojas• (Caraballo 71), Gonzalez, Velasquez, Escobar (Carpintero 68). Tr: Noel Sanvicente

Santos   **2**

Zé Roberto [16], Kléber [64]

Fabio Costa• – Adailton, Kleber, Denis (Dionisio 5•••53), Rodrigo Souto, Antonio Carlos (Avalos 42), Marcus Aurelio (Rodrigo Tabata 75), Maldonado, Marcelo•, Ze Roberto•, Cleber Santana. Tr: Luxemburgo

Vila Belmiro, Santos
10-05-2007, 18:30, 10 826, Amarilla PAR

Santos   **3**

Adailton [34], Zé Roberto 2 [40 66]

Fabio Costa – Adailton•92+, Kleber, Pedrinho (Rodrigo Tabata 63), Rodrigo Souto, Avalos, Jonas (Renatinho 63), Maldonado, Marcus Aurelio (Marcelo 71), Ze Roberto, Cleber Santana. Tr: Luxemburgo

Caracas FC   **2**

Rey [23], Carpintero [30]

Toyo – Vizcarrondo•, Rey, Olivares (Jiminez 83), Carpintero, Vera• (Guerra 71), Rojas•, Gonzalez•, Perez, Velasquez (Castellin 78), Rouga. Tr: Noel Sanvicente

Azteca, Mexico City
2-05-2007, 17:30, 47 307, Arias PAR

CF América   **3**

Cabañas [26], Fernández.S [29], Rojas.R [53]

Ochoa – Rodgriguez, Castro, Davino•80, Cabanas (Bilos 87), Blanco•, Fernandez (Baloy 81), Rojas.R, Villa•, Arguello•, Mendoza•. Tr: Luis Fernando Tena

Colo Colo   **0**

Cejas – Riffo, Mena, Jara (Jerez 46), Fierro, Melendez•, Sanhueza, Vidal, Hernandez (Gonzalez 63), Suazo, Sanchez (Gimenez 56). Tr: Claudio Borghi

Monumental, Santiago
8-05-2007, 19:45, 12 569, Larrionda URU

Colo Colo   **2**

Castro.J OG [70], Suazo [88]

Cejas – Riffo, Mena• (Gimenez 75), Vidal•, Fierro•, Melendez•92+, Sanhueza, Villarroel (Lorca 57), Hernandez, Sanchez (Arenas 84), Suazo. Tr: Claudio Borghi

CF América   **1**

Infante [86]

Ochoa – Castro•, Perez• (Billos 72), Cabanas, Fernandez (Cuevas 74), Baloy•, Rojas.R, Torres, Arguello, Mendoza (Infante 78), Inigo. Tr: Luis Fernando Tena

Centenario, Montevideo
2-05-2007, 21:45, 26 921, Chandia CHI

Defensor Sporting   **3**

Navarro 2 [5p 75], González.A [49]

Silva – Sorondo•, Martinez, Fadeuille, De Souza (Amado 87), Pezzolano (Fernandez.S 74), Gonzalez, Navarro, Peinado (Morales• 82), Caceres, Pereira. Tr: Jorge da Silva

Flamengo   **0**

Bruno – Leo Moura, Moises, Irineu•, Paulinho• (Jailton 84), Juan, Salino• (Leo Lima 56), Juninho (Roni 46), Souza, Renato Augusto•, Renato. Tr: Ney Franco

Maracanã, Rio de Janeiro
9-05-2007, 21:45, 57 767, Baldassi ARG

Flamengo   **2**

Renato 2 [35 47]

Bruno – Leo Moura•, Ronaldo Angelim, Irineu, Paulinho (Leo Lima 77), Juan, Roni•, Claiton (Paulo Sergio 69), Souza•, Renato Augusto, Renato. Tr: Ney Franco

Defensor Sporting   **0**

Silva – Caceres, Sorondo•, Martinez•, Arioso, Amado•, Gonzalez, Fadeuille•, De Souza, Peinado (Morales 65), Pezzolano (Fernandez.S 46). Tr: Jorge da Silva

Morumbí, São Paulo
2-05-2007, 21:45, 33 387, Tardelli BRA

São Paulo FC 1
Miranda [56]
Rogerio Ceni – Ilsinho (Marcel 86), Miranda, Josue•, Leandro• (Dagoberto 46), Souza, Hugo•, Aloisio• (Andre Dias 86), Alex Silva, Jadilson•, Richarylson. Tr: Muricy Ramalho

Grêmio 0

Saja – Patricio•, William•, Edmilson, Diego Souza, Tuta• (Everton 85), Tcheco•, Carlos Eduardo (Amoroso 66), Teco, Sandro Goiano (Gavilan• 57), Lucio. Tr: Mano Menezes

Olímpico, Porto Alegre
9-05-2007, 21:45, 42 669, Chandia CHI

Grêmio 2
Tcheco [17], Diego Souza [75]
Saja – Patricio, William•, Edmilson, Diego Souza•, Tuta•, Tcheco (Gavilan 42), Carlos Eduardo (Sciavi 87), Teco, Sandro Goiano• (Amoroso 66), Lucio. Tr: Mano Menezes

São Paulo FC 0

Rogerio Ceni – Ilsinho (Marcel 86), Miranda•, Josue, Leandro (Marcel 87), Souza•, Hugo (Dagoberto 46), Aloisio•, Alex Silva, Jadilson (Jorge Wagner 46), Richarylson. Tr: Muricy Ramalho

QUARTER-FINALS

La Bombonera, Buenos Aires
17-05-2007, 21:15, 31 397, Ruiz COL

Boca Juniors 1
Palermo [90]
Caranta – Ibarra, Silvestre, Morel, Rodriguez, Bertolo (Datolo 58), Banega•, Cardozo, Riquelme, Palacio, Palermo. Tr: Miguel Angel Russo

Libertad 1
Martínez.O [82]
Bava – Bonet, Sarabia, Martinez.R•, Balbuena•, Aquino (Robles 73), Riveros, Caceres, Guinazu•, Marin• (Martinez.O 64), Lopez (Bareiro 91). Tr: Sergio Markarian

Defensores del Chaco, Asunción
24-05-2007, 20:15, 27 137, Chandia CHI

Libertad 0
Bava – Balbuena, Guinazu, Riveros (Martinez.O 74), Lopez, Bonet, Sarabia•, Aquino (Marin 65), Martinez.R, Caceres, Gamarra (Bareiro 74). Tr: Sergio Markarian

Boca Juniors 2
Riquelme [61], Palacio [71]
Caranta – Ibarra, Diaz, Morel (Silvestre 84), Rodriguez, Ledesma•, Banega• (Datolo 56), Cardozo (Orteman 75), Riquelme, Palacio, Palermo•. Tr: Miguel Angel Russo

General Santander, Cúcuta
15-05-2007, 21:00, 32 400, Simon BRA

Cúcuta Deportivo 2
Torres [65], Pérez.B [89]
Zapata – Bustos, Moreno, Hurtado, Gonzalez, Castro (Cordoba 46), Rueda• (Flores 75), Del Castillo, Torres•, Perez•, Martinez (Cortes 78). Tr: Jorge Luis Bernal

Nacional 1
Muslera – Godin, Alvarez.P, Cardaccio (Caballero 56), Romero, Sosa, Vera (Marquez 81), Delgado• (Broli 75), Pallas•••30, Martinez, Viana. Tr: Daniel Carreno

Parque Central, Montevideo
22-05-2007, 20:15, 13 842, Pezzota ARG

Nacional 2
Castro.G [11], Vera [84]
Muslera – Jaume, Godin, Alvarez.P, Viana, Sosa•, Cardaccio (Martinez 46), Delgado•, Marquez (Caballero 51), Vera, Castro (Juarez 63). Tr: Daniel Carreno

Cúcuta Deportivo 2
Bustos [21], Pajoy [90]
Zapata – Bustos, Moreno•, Hurtado, Gonzalez, Castro (Garcia• 87), Rueda, Del Castillo•, Torres (Cordoba• 73), Perez, Martinez (Pajoy 69). Tr: Jorge Luis Bernal

Azteca, Mexico City
16-05-2007, 19:45, 69 157, Silvera URU

CF América 0
Ochoa – Infante, Baloy, Cervantes, Rojas.O, Pena, Inigo (Cabanas 58) Torres•, Mosqueda (Blanco 58), Perez (Fernandez 67), Cuevas•. Tr: Luis Fernando Tena

Santos 0
Fabio Costa – Alessandro, Kleber, Avalos, Domingos•, Marcelo•, Rodrigo Souto (Pedrinho• 75), Cleber Santana, Maldonado, Ze Roberto•, Marcus Aurelio (Rodrigo Tabata 75). Tr: Luxemburgo

Vila Belmiro, Santos
23-05-2007, 21:45, 11 925, Ruiz COL

Santos 2
Jonas [65], Rodrigo Souto [71]
Fabio Costa – Adailton, Kleber, Alessandro (Pedrinho 46), Rodrigo Souto, Avalos, Jonas (Dionisio 79), Maldonado, Marcos Aurelio, Ze Roberto•, Cleber Santana (Marcelo 75). Tr: Luxemburgo

CF América 1
Bilos [32]
Navarrete – Rojas.O, Cervantes, Bilos, Mosqueda (Perez 70), Infante•, Baloy, Torres, Pena, Mendoza, Inigo (Marquez 74). Tr: Luis Fernando Tena

Centenario, Montevideo
16-05-2007, 19:30, 28 468, Selman CHI

Defensor Sporting 2
Sorondo [1], Martinez.W [34]
Silva• – Gonzalez••37, Sorondo, Martinez, Caceres, Pereira, Fadeuille, De Souza• (Diaz 77), Vila (Fernandez.S• 66), Morales (Amado 43), Peinado. Tr: Jorge da Silva

Grêmio 0
Saja – Patricio, William, Teco•, Lucio, Nunes (Amoroso 46), Gavilan, Diego Souza, Tcheco•, Carlos Eduardo (Everton• 76), Tuta (Ramon 83). Tr: Mano Menezes

Olímpico, Porto Alegre
23-05-2007, 19:15, 42 387, Amarilla PAR

Grêmio 2 4p
Tcheco [23], Teco [45]
Saja – Patricio•, William, Teco, Lucio, Gavilan (Douglas 62), Sandro Goiano•, Tcheco• (Ramon 60), Carlos Eduardo, Amoroso•90, Tuta (Everton 84). Tr: Mano Menezes

Defensor Sporting 0 2p
Silva – Sorondo (Lamas 15), Caceres (Vila 61), Martinez•, Ariosa, Pereira•, Fadeuille, Amado (Diaz 46••90), De Souza, Peinado, Fernandez•. Tr: Jorge da Silva

PENALTIES (GREMIO WON 4-2)

Fadeuille ✗; Patricio ✓; Peinado ✗;
Lucio ✓; De Souza ✓; Douglas ✓;
Pereira ✓; Ramon ✓

SEMI-FINALS

General Santander, Cúcuta
31-05-2007, 19:00, 42 000, Amarilla PAR

Cúcuta Deportivo	3

Pérez.B 2 [39] [65], Bustos [83]

Zapata – Bustos, Hurtado, Moreno, Gonzalez, Rueda•
(Pajoy 77), Castro (Cordoba 32; Flores 72),
Del Castillo, Torres, Perez, Martinez.
Tr: Jorge Luis Bernal

Boca Juniors	1

Ledesma [27]

Caranta (Bobadilla 46) – Ibarra, Diaz, Morel,
Rodriguez (Silvestre 77), Ledesma•, Banega, Cardozo
(Datolo 66), Riquelme, Palacio, Palermo.
Tr: Miguel Angel Russo

La Bombonera, Buenos Aires
7-06-2007, 19:15, 37 488, Silvera URU

Boca Juniors	3

Riquelme [44], Palermo [61], Battaglia [90]

Bobadilla – Ibarra•, Diaz, Morel (Silvestre 84),
Rodriguez•, Ledesma•, Banega, Cardozo
(Battaglia 85), Riquelme, Palacio, Palermo•.
Tr: Miguel Angel Russo

Cúcuta Deportivo	0

Zapata – Bustos•, Hurtado, Moreno, Gonzalez, Torres,
Flores (Cordoba• 67), Rueda• (Garcia 91),
Del Castillo• (Cortes 79), Pajoy•, Martinez.
Tr: Jorge Luis Bernal

Olímpico, Porto Alegre
30-05-2007, 21:45, 44 646, Pezzotta ARG

Grêmio	2

Tcheco [35]p, Carlos Eduardo [37]

Saja – Patricio•, William, Diego Souza (Edmilson 80),
Tuta•, Tcheco (Ramon 46), Carlos Eduardo, Teco,
Sandro Goiano•, Lucio•, Gavilan. Tr: Mano Menezes

Santos	0

Fabio Costa – Adailton, Kleber, Alessandro (Pedrinho 46),
Rodrigo Souto, Avalos•, Jonas (Rodrigo Tabata• 46),
Maldonado, Marcos Aurelio, Ze Roberto, Cleber
Santana (Moraes 66). Tr: Luxemburgo

Vila Belmiro, Santos
6-06-2007, 21:45, 19 788, Torres PAR

Santos	3

Renatinho 2 [45] [61], Zé Roberto [77]

Fabio Costa – Adailton, Kleber, Alessandro (Rodrigo
Tabata 58), Rodrigo Souto, Dominos, Marcos Aurelio•,
Pedrinho (Moraes 50), Renatinho (Jonas 72), Ze
Roberto, Cleber Santana• (Moraes 66). Tr: Luxemburgo

Grêmio	1

Diego Souza [24]

Saja• – Patricio, William, Diego Souza, Tcheco
(Edmilson 81), Carlos Eduardo (Ramon 28), Teco,
Sandro Goiano•, Lucio, Douglas (Lucas 62) Gavilan.
Tr: Mano Menezes

COPA LIBERTADORES FINAL 1ST LEG
La Bombonera, Buenos Aires
13-06-2007, 21:45, 39 993, Larrionda URU

BOCA JUNIORS	3	0		GREMIO

Palacio [18], Riquelme [73],
Patricio OG [89]

	BOCA JUNIORS			GREMIO	
12	CARANTA Mauricio			SAJA Diego	1
4	IBARRA Hugo			PATRICIO	2
6	DIAZ Daniel			WILLIAM	4
3	MOREL Claudio			TECO	14
21	RODRIGUEZ Clemente			LUCIO	16
8	LEDESMA Pablo		58	SANDRO GOIANO	15
24	BANEGA Ever	81		GAVILAN Diego	22
19	CARDOZO Neri	67	80	TCHECO	10
11	RIQUELME Juan			DIEGO SOUZO	7
14	PALACIO Rodrigo			CARLOS EDUARDO	11
9	PALERMO Martín	72		TUTA	9
	Tr: RUSSO Miguel Angel			Tr: MANO MENEZES	
	Substitutes			Substitutes	
5	BATTAGLIA Sebastián	81	72	LUCAS	8
23	DATOLO Jesús Alberto	67	80	DOUGLAS	20

COPA LIBERTADORES FINAL 2ND LEG
Olímpico, Porto Alegre
20-06-2007, 21:45, 43 952, Ruiz COL

GREMIO		0	2	BOCA JUNIORS

Riquelme 2 [68] [80]

	GREMIO			BOCA JUNIORS	
1	SAJA Diego			CARANTA Mauricio	12
2	PATRICIO			IBARRA Hugo	4
4	WILLIAM			DIAZ Daniel	6
14	TECO	35		MOREL Claudio	3
16	LUCIO			RODRIGUEZ Clemente	21
7	DIEGO SOUZO			LEDESMA Pablo	8
8	LUCAS		82	BANEGA Ever	24
22	GAVILAN Diego		59	CARDOZO Neri	19
10	TCHECO			RIQUELME Juan	10
11	CARLOS EDUARDO		87	PALACIO Rodrigo	14
9	TUTA	70		PALERMO Martín	9
	Tr: MANO MENEZES			Tr: RUSSO Miguel Angel	
	Substitutes			Substitutes	
3	SCHIAVI Rolando	35	59	BATTAGLIA Sebastián	5
19	EVERTON	70	82	ORTEMAN Sergio	16
21	AMOROSO	46	87	BOSELLI Mauro	17

ALIANZA

Goalkeepers
1 FORSYTH George Patrick
12 PIZARRO Francisco
21 PINTO Joel Ademir

Defenders
3 SALAZAR Santiago Roberto
4 ARAKAKI Ernesto Seiko
18 ALVARADO Ismael Enrique
24 POROSO Augusto Jesús

Midfielders
2 HERRERA Jhoel Alexander
5 SALAS Guillermo Sandro
6 VIZA César Junior
7 CIURLIZZA Marko Gustavo
8 JAYO Juan José
10 LIGÜERA Martín Ricardo
13 SÁNCHEZ Alexander Gustavo
14 TORRES Erick Omar
15 HERNÁNDEZ Luis Alberto
17 ZEGARRA Carlos Alberto
19 VIRVIESCAS Kilian Edwin
20 OLCESE Aldo Italo
23 YGLESIAS Jorge Jair

Forwards
9 MAESTRI Flavio Francisco
11 BENAVIDES Renzo Émerson
16 SOTIL Johan Joussep
22 ROSS Douglas Junior
25 SILVA Roberto Enrique

CF AMERICA

Goalkeepers
1 OCHOA Francisco Guillermo
12 BECERRA Alberto
21 NAVARRETE Armando

Defenders
2 RODRÍGUEZ Ismael de Jesús
3 CASTRO José Antonio
4 ROJAS Óscar Adrián
5 DAVINO Duilio César
6 CERVANTES Diego Alberto
14 INFANTE Carlos Jesús
15 BALOY Felipe Abdiel
16 ROJAS Ricardo Francisco
24 IÑIGO Rodrigo

Midfielders
7 BILOS Daniel Rubén
8 PÉREZ Luis Ernesto
8 SARITAMA Luis Fernando
13 MOSQUEDA Juan Carlos
17 TORRES Ignacio
18 VILLA Germán
19 PEÑA Fabián
20 ARGÜELLO Alejandro
22 MENDOZA Raúl Alvin

Forwards
9 CABAÑAS Salvador
10 BLANCO Cuauhtémoc
11 FERNÁNDEZ Santiago
23 CUEVAS Nelson Rafael
25 CARIGNANO César Andrés
25 GÓMEZ Marco Antonio

AUDAX ITALIANO

Goalkeepers
1 LOYOLA Víctor Jesús
12 LEMA Jorge Antonio
22 PERIC Nicolás Miroslav

Defenders
3 CARRASCO Jorge Antonio
4 CERECEDA Roberto Andres
5 GONZÁLEZ Juan Claudio
15 RIELOFF Boris Alexis
18 RIVERA Eladio Felipe
19 SANTIS César Elias
21 GUTIÉRREZ Fernando Antonio

Midfielders
2 LEAL Braulio Antonio
6 GARRIDO Carlos Alberto
7 ROMERO Miguel Ángel
8 SCOTTI Diego
10 VILLANUEVA Carlos Andrés
13 CABRERA Enzo Carlo
14 ORELLANA Fabián Ariel
17 VALDIVIA Claudio Andrés
24 DOMÍNGUEZ Sebastián Isaías
25 MEDEL Marco Antonio

Forwards
9 MOYA Rodolfo Antonio
11 MEDINA Leonardo Andrés
16 CAMPOS Matías Daniel
20 DI SANTO Franco Matías
23 TOLEDO Oliver Adrián

BANFIELD

Goalkeepers
1 LUCCHETTI Cristian David

Defenders
2 MAIDANA Julián Edgardo
3 GALVÁN Carlos Alberto
4 PAGÉS Ricardo Hernán
6 SANGUINETTI Javier Esteban
13 BARRAZA Julio Eduardo
22 ESTEBAN Guillermo Adolfo
24 GALARZA Marcos Adrián

Midfielders
5 QUINTEROS Daniel Eduardo
7 SANTANA Fabián Ernesto
8 VILLARREAL Javier Alejandro
10 ANDRIZZI Martín Ezequiel
11 SALVATIERRA Roberto Hernán
14 SCHMIDT Gastón Ezequiel
15 CIVELLI Luciano
19 CHATRUC José Manuel
20 MORALES Ángel Alejandro

Forwards
9 CVITANICH Darío
12 SANTILLO Pablo Ariel
16 VITTI Pablo Ernesto
17 LUJAMBIO Josemir
18 BARRALES Jerónimo
21 BOLOGNA Enrique Alberto
23 GONZÁLEZ Silvio Augusto
25 BARDARO Cristian Pedro

BOCA JUNIORS

Goalkeepers
1 BOBADILLA Aldo Antonio
12 CARANTA Mauricio Ariel
25 MIGLIORE Pablo Alejandro

Defenders
2 SILVESTRE Matías Agustín
3 MOREL Claudio Marcelo
4 IBARRA Hugo Benjamín
6 DÍAZ Daniel Alberto
13 VILLAFAÑE Santiago
20 MAIDANA Jonatan Ramón
21 RODRÍGUEZ Clemente Juan
22 CAHAIS Matías

Midfielders
5 BATTAGLIA Sebastián Alejandro
7 CHÁVEZ Cristián Manuel
8 LEDESMA Pablo Martín
10 RIQUELME Juan Román
13 BERTOLO Nicolás Santiago
15 MARINO Guillermo Andrés
16 ORTEMAN Sergio Daniel
19 CARDOZO Neri Raúl
23 DATOLO Jesús Alberto
24 BANEGA Ever Maximiliano

Forwards
7 BARROS SCHELOTTO Guillermo
9 PALERMO Martín
11 MARIONI Bruno
14 PALACIO Rodrigo Sebastián
17 BOSELLI Mauro
18 MONDAINI Marcos Gustavo

BOLIVAR

Goalkeepers
1 ZAYAS Joel Fernando
12 TORO Elliotth Alejandro
25 ISSA Diego Gabriel

Defenders
2 SALVATIERRA Diego Esteban
3 VACA Juan Doile
4 CAMACHO Carlos Oswaldo
5 TORDOYA Carlos Hugo
14 GUATÍA Ovidio
15 JUÁREZ Ariel
16 GARCÍA Ignacio Awad
17 GARCÍA Faustino Abraham

Midfielders
6 REYES Leonel Alfredo
8 VIGLIANTI Gabriel Alejandro
9 LEITÃO POLIERI Thiago
10 BALDIVIESO Julio César
13 BUSTILLOS Juan Enrique
20 PACHI Daner Jesús
22 ALPIRE Dany Daniel
24 MELGAR Rubén

Forwards
7 CUELLAR Adalberto
11 SILLERO Luis Hernán
18 SAUCEDO Carlos
19 MONTAÑO Rudy David
21 MEZA Justo Rolando
23 FLORES Zackary

CARACAS FC

Goalkeepers
1 TOYO Javier Eduardo
12 ROSALES Vicente
22 LIEBESKIND Alan

Defenders
2 VIZCARRONDO Oswaldo
3 REY José Manuel
4 GODOY Daniel José
5 VIELMA Leonel
13 RIVERO Jobanny
15 PÉREZ Edder Alfonso
17 BUSTAMANTE Jaime Andrés
21 ROUGA Enrique Andrés
25 LUCENA Franklin

Midfielders
6 OLIVARES Weymar Franck
8 VERA Luis Enrique
10 ROJAS Jorge Alberto
11 GONZÁLEZ César Eduardo
16 PIÑANGO Bremer
18 GUERRA Alejandro Abraham
23 JIMÉNEZ Édgar
23 DEPABLOS Pedro Javier
24 CARABALLO José

Forwards
7 CARPINTERO Wilson Alberto
9 CASTELLÍN Rafael
14 CASANOVA Jorge Francisco
19 VELÁSQUEZ Iván
20 ESCOBAR Habinson

CERRO PORTENO

Goalkeepers
1 AURRECOCHEA Pablo
12 NAVARRO Hilario Bernardo
25 FERNÁNDEZ Roberto Junior

Defenders
2 CÁCERES Marcos Antonio
3 PÉREZ Fidel Amado
4 CABRERA Nelson David
5 BARBOSA Rodrigo
11 CRISTALDO Ernesto Rubén
22 MENDOZA David Bernardo
23 ROJAS Alfredo David

Midfielders
6 BRÍTEZ Jorge Orlando
8 GONZÁLEZ Édgar Daniel
13 ÁLVAREZ Lorgio
14 NÚÑEZ Jorge Martín
15 MORÍNIGO Gustavo Eliseo
16 HOBECKER Osvaldo
18 GAMARRA Oscar Moisés
19 GODOY Eder Ricardo
21 ESTIGARRIBIA Marcelo
24 SALCEDO José Domingo

Forwards
7 RAMÍREZ César
9 ALDAVE Mauro Esteban
10 GIMÉNEZ Pablo Junior
17 ACHUCARRO Jorge Daniel
20 DA SILVA Alejandro Damián

CIENCIANO

Goalkeepers
1 CISNEROS Jesús
12 DRAGO Ignacio
21 FLORES Juan Ángel
Defenders
4 HERNÁNDEZ Juan Francisco
5 GAMARRA Sandro
6 PISANO Nicolás Osvaldo
17 SALAZAR Javier
19 GUIZASOLA Guillermo
25 DE LA HAZA Paolo
Midfielders
2 HUERTAS Miguel Ángel
3 VILLAMARÍN Edgar Harry
8 BAZALAR Juan Carlos
10 GARCÍA Julio César
14 FERNÁNDEZ Carlos Oswaldo
16 SALAZAR Yosiro Abelardo
20 GUEVARA Cristian
23 MARIÑO Juan Carlos
24 URIBE Julio Edson
Forwards
7 MOSTTO Miguel Ángel
9 SARAZ Rodrigo
11 FERNÁNDEZ José Carlos
13 RUIZ Jaime Alfonso
15 GONZÁLEZ VIGIL Juan Diego
18 TORRES Miguel Ángel
22 CHIROQUE Willian

COLO COLO

Goalkeepers
1 CEJAS Christian Sebastian
12 WIRTH Rainer Klaus
25 LEYTON Richard
Defenders
2 JARA Gonzalo
3 MENA Luis arturo
4 HENRÍQUEZ David Andrés
5 RIFFO Miguel Augusto
6 VELÁSQUEZ Gilberto Ariel
15 VILLARROEL Moisés Fermín
17 SANHUEZA Arturo
18 MELÉNDEZ Rodrigo
21 ACEVEDO Gerson Elías
23 VIDAL Arturo Erasmo
24 GONZALEZ Boris Igor
Midfielders
8 JEREZ José Luis
9 MILLAR Rodrigo Javier
11 FIERRO Gonzalo Antonio
14 ABARCA Cristian Felipe
19 ARENAS Juan Pablo
Forwards
7 SÁNCHEZ Alexis Alejandro
13 REYES César Alejandro
16 SUAZO Humberto Andrés
20 GIMÉNEZ Édison
22 LORCA Juan Gonzalo

CUCUTA

Goalkeepers
1 ZAPATA Robinson
12 CASTELLANOS Andrés Leandro
22 VALENCIA Williers
Defenders
2 HURTADO Julián
3 MORENO Wálter José
5 PORTOCARRERO Pedro Paulo
13 BUSTOS Rubén Darío
14 VÁSQUEZ César Alberto
15 RAGUA Joe Louis
17 GARCIA Braynner Yesid
21 GONZÁLEZ Elvis Javier
Midfielders
4 FLORES Nelson Alfonso
6 CASTRO Charles
8 HENRY Lin Carlos
10 TORRES Macnelly
16 CASTILLO José Rodrigo
19 DEL CASTILLO Alexander
20 BOBADILLA Roberto Carlos
24 RUEDA Dúmar Ricardo
25 CÓRDOBA David Camilo
Forwards
7 CORTÉS Víctor Javier
9 PÉREZ Blas Antonio
11 PAJOY Lionard Fernando
18 RIVAS Elvis Antonio
23 MARTÍNEZ Juan Manuel

DEFENSOR

Goalkeepers
1 SILVA Martín
12 NANNI Mauricio
17 RODRÍGUEZ Fernando
Defenders
2 SORONDO Gonzalo
3 SEMPERENA Nelson
3 MARTÍNEZ Williams
6 LAMAS Andrés
13 SUÁREZ Damián
19 ITHURRALDE Ignacio
22 CÁCERES José Martín
24 MAULELLA Gonzalo
Midfielders
4 FADEUILLE Fernando
5 DÍAZ Carlos
7 DE SOUZA Diego
8 AMADO Miguel
10 VIUDEZ Tabaré
13 FERREIRA Diego
15 GONZÁLEZ Álvaro
16 FERNÁNDEZ Ruben
18 ARIOSA Sebastián
23 PEREIRA Maximiliano
Forwards
9 MORALES Carlos María
11 PEZZOLANO Paulo César
14 VILLA Mauro
20 NAVARRO Álvaro
21 PEINADO Danilo
25 FERNÁNDEZ Sebastián

EMELEC

Goalkeepers
1 ELIZAGA Marcelo Ramón
12 ANGULO Robert Andrés
22 GUAMÁN Xavier Humberto
Defenders
2 MORANTE Eduardo Xavier
3 QUIÑÓNEZ Marco Antonio
4 COROZO Facundo Jesús
6 QUIÑÓNEZ Carlos Andrés
9 ESTACIO Silvano
13 MERCADO Lorenzo Javier
23 CAICEDO Ranner Geovanny
24 MINDA Tilson Oswaldo
25 ZAMBRANO Luis Alberto
Midfielders
5 QUIÑÓNEZ José Luis
14 HERNÁNDEZ Sebastián
15 RIVERA Luis Guillermo
16 ARROYO Michael Antonio
17 CAICEDO Jaime Ramiro
18 GUERRERO Wimper Orlando
19 AYOVÍ Jaime Javier
Forwards
7 LADINES Jorge Washington
11 RODRÍGUEZ Israel Rodrigo
14 ASÍS Óscar Maximiliano
20 VIATRI Lucas Ezequiel
21 MORALES NEUMANN Jerónimo

FLAMENGO

Goalkeepers
1 BRUNO
12 DIEGO
24 MARCELO LOMBA
Defenders
3 MOISES
4 IRINEU
15 RODRIGO ARROZ
16 THIAGO
21 RONALDO ANGELIM
25 MARLON
Midfielders
2 LEO MOURA
5 PAULINHO
6 JUAN
7 LÉO LIMA
8 CLAITON
10 RENATO AUGUSTO
11 RENATO
13 LUIZINHO
14 GERSON
19 LEO MEDEIROS
20 JAILTON
22 SALINO
23 JUNINHO
Forwards
7 OBINA
9 SOUZA
14 PAULO SERGIO
17 RONI
18 LEONARDO

GIMNASIA Y E LP

Goalkeepers
1 OLAVE Juan Carlos
12 KLETNICKI Carlos José
13 BANGARDINO Pablo Martín
Defenders
2 SAN ESTEBAN Jorge Hector
3 HERNER Diego Armando
4 SEMINO Gustavo Adrián
6 LANDA Lucas León
14 FRANCO Horacio Ariel
15 CROSA Fernando Javier
17 ROMERO Héctor Daniel
19 GENTILETTI Santiago Juan
Midfielders
5 ESCOBAR Matías Leonardo
10 CORNEJO Oscar Roberto
11 PACHECO Antonio
18 ALDERETE Reinaldo Andrés
20 BASUALDO Germán Rodrigo
22 PIATTI Ignacio
23 CUEVAS Juan Ezequiel
24 CHAVES Jonatan Daniel
25 ORMEÑO Álvaro Andrés
Forwards
7 LEAL Sergio Willian
8 LEGUIZAMÓN Félix Luciano
9 SILVA Santiago Martin
16 DUBARBIER Sebastián
21 PIERGÜIDI Antonio

GREMIO

Goalkeepers
1 SAJA Diego Sebastián
12 GALATTO
24 MARCELO GROHE
Defenders
2 PATRICIO
3 SCHIAVI Rolando Carlos
4 WILLIAM
6 BRUNO TELES
13 PEREIRA
14 TECO
16 LUCIO
22 JUCEMAR
Midfielders
5 EDMÍLSON
7 DIEGO SOUZA
8 LUCAS
10 TCHECO
11 CARLOS EDUARDO
13 SANDRO GOIANO
18 RAMÓN
21 ADILSON
22 GAVILÁN Diego Antonio
23 WILLIAM ANTUNES
25 NUNES
Forwards
9 TUTA
17 KELLY
17 ALOÍSIO
19 EVERTON
20 DOUGLAS
21 AMOROSO

INTERNACIONAL	LDU QUITO	LIBERTAD	NACIONAL
Goalkeepers	**Goalkeepers**	**Goalkeepers**	**Goalkeepers**
1 CLEMER	1 PRETTI Luis Humberto	1 BAVA Jorge Rodrigo	1 MUSLERA Fernando
12 RENÁN	12 MORA Cristian Rafael	12 GONZÁLEZ Horacio Javier	12 ÁLVAREZ Lucero
22 MARCELO BOECK	22 DOMÍNGUEZ Alexander	25 ACOSTA Roberto Carlos	25 VIERA Alexis
Defenders	**Defenders**	**Defenders**	**Defenders**
3 ÍNDIO	2 ARAUJO Norberto Carlos	2 BENÍTEZ Pedro Juan	2 JAUME Diego
4 RAFAEL SANTOS	3 CALLE Renán	3 BALBUENA Édgar Gabriel	3 GODÍN Diego
14 EDIGLÉ	3 JÁCOME Rolando Santiago	4 VERA Arnaldo Andres	4 RODRÍGUEZ Alejandro
17 WILSON	6 AYOVÍ Arlin Segundo	11 BONET Carlos	5 DA ROSA Jorge
Midfielders	23 CAMPOS Jairo Rolando	14 SARABIA Pedro Alcides	21 PALLAS José
2 CEARÁ	**Midfielders**	15 MARTÍNEZ Ricardo Julián	**Midfielders**
5 WELLINGTON MONTEIRO	4 AMBROSSI Paul Vicente	20 DAMIANI Raúl Hernán	6 BROLI Marcelo
6 HIDALGO Emilio Martín	5 OBREGÓN Alfonso Andrés	21 ROMÁN Adalberto	7 ÁLVAREZ Pablo
7 ALEX	8 URRUTIA Patricio Javier	22 BARONE Deivis	8 VANZINI Marco
8 EDINHO	10 LARA Christian Rolando	**Midfielders**	10 CABALLERO Pablo
13 ELDER GRANJA	13 LARREA Pedro Sebastián	5 GUIÑAZÚ Pablo Horacio	10 TEJERA Marcelo
15 RUBENS CARDOSO	14 CHALÁ Victor Manuel	6 RIVEROS Cristian Miguel	13 CARDACCIO Mathias
16 ADRIANO	15 ORTIZ Luis Alberto	7 ROBLES Édgar Arnulfo	15 ROMERO Adrián
20 VARGAS Fabián Andrés	16 CALDERÓN Diego Armando	8 MARÍN Vladimir	16 SOSA Marcelo
21 MICHEL	17 MONAR Jhonatan Stalin	10 MARTÍNEZ Osvaldo David	17 ARISMENDI Diego
24 PERDIGÃO	18 AYOVI Orlando	13 PITTONI Wilson Osmar	20 DELGADO Javier
25 MAYCON	20 VERA Enrique Daniel	16 AQUINO Sergio Daniel	21 LA LUZ Ignacio
Forwards	25 VILLALVA Jonathan Mauricio	18 CÁCERES Víctor Javier	23 MARTÍNEZ Jorge
9 FERNANDÃO	**Forwards**	21 BENÍTEZ Milton Rodrigo	24 VIANA Agustín
10 IARLEY	7 VIZCARRA José Nicolás	**Forwards**	**Forwards**
11 ALEXANDRE PATO	9 ESCALADA Luis Miguel	9 LÓPEZ Hernán Rodrigo	9 DA SILVA Giancarlo
18 LUIZ ADRIANO	11 SALAS Franklin Agustín	17 BAREIRO Fredy José	11 MÁRQUEZ Andrés
19 CHRISTIAN	19 GUERRÓN Joffre David	19 ROMERO Nelson David	14 CAUTERUCCIO Martín
23 JEAN	21 BOLAÑOS Luis Alberto	23 BENÍTEZ Édgar	18 VERA Diego
	24 PUTÁN Ángel Enrique	24 GAMARRA Roberto	19 CASTRO Gonzalo
			22 JUÁREZ Carlos

EL NACIONAL	NECAXA	PARANA	PASTO
Goalkeepers	**Goalkeepers**	**Goalkeepers**	**Goalkeepers**
1 COROZO Rixon Javier	1 VÁZQUEZ Edmundo Iván	1 FLÁVIO	1 GÓMEZ Diego Fernando
12 IBARRA Oswaldo Johvani	14 VILAR Federico	12 MARCOS LEANDRO	12 BARAHONA Carlos Alberto
22 SÁNCHEZ Robinson Geovanny	25 ÁLVAREZ Alexandro	22 GABRIEL	22 RAMOS Nelson Fernando
Defenders	**Defenders**	**Defenders**	**Defenders**
2 CASTRO Carlos Ernesto	2 QUATTROCCHI Pablo Javier	3 DANIEL MARQUES	2 MONROY Fernando
3 GÓMEZ Bolívar Efren	3 BELTRÁN Joaquín	4 ADERALDO	3 VIVEROS Einer
4 DE JESÚS Omar Andrés	12 PADILLA Luis Alberto	9 NEGUETE	4 VARGAS Walden Alexis
6 CAICEDO Pavel Cipriano	13 HERNÁNDEZ Luis Omar	14 JOÃO PAULO	5 MERA José Hermes
16 CAGUA Jhon Patricio	14 PÉREZ Mario	15 JOÃO VITOR	13 LORA Luis Eduardo
19 DE JESÚS Érik Rolando	18 NAVARRO Ricardo	**Midfielders**	15 DÍAZ Wilmer
20 CHECA Luis Armando	20 LUCAS Osvaldo	2 ALEX	19 RAMOS Jamell Orlando
24 CUERO Willian Ángelis	**Midfielders**	5 GOIANO	24 SAA Carlos Alfredo
Midfielders	4 CERVANTES Horacio Javier	6 EGIDIO	**Midfielders**
5 HIDALGO Carlos Ramón	5 GUTIÉRREZ Víctor Manuel	7 BETO	8 REBOLLEDO Juan Fernando
7 QUIROZ Mario David	6 CABRERA Salvador	8 GERSON	10 VILLAMIL Ferley Raúl
15 SÁNCHEZ Wellington Eduardo	7 MARCHANT Julio Javier	9 ADRIANO	11 VALENCIA Luis Omar
17 AYOVÍ Wálter Orlando	11 DE ASSIS BARBOSA Everaldo	10 DINELSON	16 RODRÍGUEZ Harold Antonio
18 QUIÑÓNEZ Pedro Ángel	15 ZEA Óscar Uriel	15 LÉO MATOS	17 SALAZAR Carlos Eduardo
23 MORALES Santiago Damián	16 GALINDO Gerardo Gabriel	16 SERGINHO	18 DE LA CRUZ Rolan
25 MINDA Jhon Stalin	17 RUIZ Jaime	17 XAVES	20 VIDAL Jorge Hernando
Forwards	19 SÁNCHEZ Emmanuel	18 JOÉLSON	23 ROSERO Jhonatan René
8 ORDÓÑEZ Ebelio Agustín	21 GRACIÁN Leandro	24 DIGÃO	25 JARAMILLO Jhon Alexander
9 CALDERÓN Wálter Richard	21 OVIEDO Franky	25 ANDRÉ LUIZ	**Forwards**
10 CHALÁ Cléver Manuel	24 MORALES Fernando	**Forwards**	6 GARCÍA Juan Enrique
11 BENÍTEZ Christian Rogelio	**Forwards**	9 HENRIQUE	7 BUELVAS Amir
13 MERCADO Ríchar Luis	5 ROJAS Óscar	11 VINICIUS	9 MARTÍNEZ Oscar Darío
14 KAVIEDES Iván	8 SALGUEIRO Juan Manuel	19 JOSIEL	14 RODAS Carlos Andrés
21 FIGUEROA Gustavo Omar	9 PADILLA Aarón	20 LIMA	21 HIDALGO Carlos Daniel
	10 MORENO Alfredo David	21 ZUMBI	
	22 GIMÉNEZ Héctor Horacio	23 JEFFERSON	
	23 BOAS PEREIRA Kléber João		

REAL POTOSI

Goalkeepers
1 GOIS DE LIRA Gustavo
12 BURTOVOY José Pablo
22 BARRIENTOS Hamlet Israel

Defenders
3 RODRÍGUEZ Edemir
4 VERA Oscar Luis
5 AMADOR Santos
8 YECEROTTE Gerardo César
16 EGUINO Ronald
25 BARRIENTOS Ever

Midfielders
6 SUÁREZ Nicolás
7 PAZ Marco David
10 PEÑA Darwin
11 COLQUE Percy
13 MUÑOZ Edgar Gerardo
14 GARCÍA Gerson Luis
15 HUALLPA Dino
19 BRANDÁN Fernando Ariel
20 ORTIZ Eduardo
21 RIBEIRO Luis Gatty
24 CALUSTRO Franz Álvaro

Forwards
9 AGUILERA Rubén Darío
17 CUÉLLAR Adrián
18 MONTEIRO Carlos Eduardo
23 PAZ Lider

RIVER PLATE

Goalkeepers
1 CARRIZO Juan Pablo
12 LEYENDA Bernardo Alejandro
17 OJEDA Juan Marcelo

Defenders
2 TUZZIO Eduardo Nicolás
4 LUSSENHOFF Federico
14 GERLO Danilo Telmo
20 NASUTTI Cristian Javier
23 RIVAS Nelson Enrique

Midfielders
3 DOMÍNGUEZ Federico Hernán
4 FERRARI Paulo
5 AHUMADA Oscar Adrián
8 BELLUSCHI Fernando Daniel
10 ORTEGA Ariel Arnaldo
15 LIMA René Martín
16 ZAPATA Víctor Eduardo
19 GALVÁN Diego Alberto
22 VILLAGRA Cristian Carlos
24 FERNÁNDEZ Augusto Matías
25 PONZIO Leonardo Daniel

Forwards
7 ROSALES Mauro Damián
9 FARÍAS Ernesto Antonio
11 GARCÍA Radamel Falcao
13 RÍOS Andrés Lorenzo
21 RUBÉN Marco Antonio

SANTOS

Goalkeepers
1 FÁBIO COSTA
12 ROGER
24 FELIPE

Defenders
2 ADAÍLTON
4 ANTÔNIO CARLOS
13 AVALOS
14 DOMINGOS
19 MARCELO
23 LEONARDO

Midfielders
3 KLÉBER
4 PEDRO
5 RODRIGO SOUTO
8 MALDONADO Claudio Andrés
10 ZÉ ROBERTO
11 CLÉBER SANTANA
15 DÊNIS
16 CARLINHOS
18 PEDRINHO
20 RODRIGO TABATA
23 ADRIANO
25 DIONISIO

Forwards
7 JONAS
9 FABIANO
17 MARCOS AURÉLIO
21 JÚNIOR
22 RENATINHO
25 RODRIGO TIUÍ

SAO PAULO

Goalkeepers
1 ROGÉRIO CENI
22 BOSCO
24 MATEUS

Defenders
3 ANDRÉ DIAS
4 EDCARLOS
5 MIRANDA
15 ALEX SILVA
25 ALEX

Midfielders
2 ILSINHO
6 JÚNIOR
7 JORGE WAGNER
8 JOSUÉ
11 HUGO
12 HERNANES
12 MAURINHO
13 REASCO Néicer
16 JADÍLSON
18 FREDSON
20 RICHARYLSON
21 RAFINHA
23 LENILSON

Forwards
9 LEANDRO
14 ALOÍSIO
17 BORGES
19 MARCEL
25 DAGOBERTO

TOLIMA

Goalkeepers
1 JULIO Agustín
12 SERPA Janner Alberto
22 QUIÑÓNEZ Enrique Arístides

Defenders
2 ÁLVAREZ Ricardo Adolfo
3 MARTÍNEZ Yesid
4 CUENU Hilario
5 CAMBINDO Roller
14 SINISTERRA Jesús Brahman
21 BUSTOS Darío Alberto
24 AYR Nicolás Nahuel

Midfielders
6 VALLEJO Gerardo Enrique
7 COCHAS Diego Emilio
8 ESCOBAR Juan Carlos
10 CHARRÍA John Jairo
13 PATIÑO Hernando
15 GONZÁLEZ Franklin Emir
16 ANCHICO Yulian José
18 RAMÍREZ Andrés Camilo
20 BOLÍVAR Gustavo Adolfo
23 ROLONG Leiner Concepción

Forwards
9 SAVOIA Gustavo Humberto
11 PERLAZA Jorge Isaacs
17 RIVAS César Augusto
19 CASTILLO John Jairo
25 QUINTERO Carlos Darwin

TOLUCA

Goalkeepers
1 CRISTANTE Rolando Hernán
12 LOZANO César Amado
25 GALLEGO Jeremías

Defenders
2 ARIAS Jonathan
3 DA SILVA Paulo César
4 VIADES Emilio Hassam
6 DE LA TORRE Manuel
13 ALMAZÁN Miguel Ángel
14 DUEÑAS Édgar Esteban
17 GARCÍA José
24 CRUZALTA José Manuel

Midfielders
5 ROSADA Ariel Javier
8 ESPINOSA Erik Osvaldo
10 MATIAS Antonio Naelson
15 CASTILLEJOS Josué
16 PONCE Sergio Amaury
18 MORALES Carlos Adrián
19 CASTILLEJOS Iván
20 VELASCO Moisés Adrián
21 DE LA TORRE Diego Javier
22 NÚÑEZ Juan Carlos

Forwards
7 ESQUIVEL Carlos
9 ÁVALOS Érwin Lorenzo
11 SÁNCHEZ Vicente Martín
17 SCOCCO Ignacio
23 PALENCIA Juan Francisco
23 VALADEZ Ismael

UA MARACAIBO

Goalkeepers
1 ANGELUCCI Gilberto
12 SANHOUSE Manuel
22 ANGULO Alexis

Defenders
2 RODRÍGUEZ Renier
3 MEA VITALI Rafael
13 FUENMAYOR Juan
24 BOVAGLIO Lucas Alfredo
25 MARTÍNEZ Juan

Midfielders
4 GALVÁN Rubén Gastón
5 MACHADO Julio César
6 FERNÁNDEZ Pedro
7 BERAZA Guillermo
8 MEA VITALI Miguel
10 URDANETA Gabriel
14 DÍAZ Dickson
16 SUANNO Vicente
17 ALMEIDA Wilton
18 FIGUEROA Dario Damián
20 GONZÁLEZ Andrée
21 VALLENILLA Luis

Forwards
9 LAFFATIGUE Julio
11 BALLESTEROS Orlando
15 ARISMENDI Daniel
19 RENTERÍA Emilio
23 CÁSSERES Cristian

VELEZ

Goalkeepers
2 SESSA Gastón Alejandro
14 CACACE Ezequiel Damián
21 PERATTA Sebastián Darío

Defenders
3 UGLESSICH Mariano Esteban
5 TORSIGLIERI Marco Natanel
7 BUSTAMANTE Marcelo Hernán
13 MONTERO Gastón Eduardo
16 CORONEL Leandro Gastón
16 PELLERANO Hernán Darío
17 PELLEGRINO Maximiliano

Midfielders
4 BROGGI Ariel Esteban
6 BUSTOS Andrés Maximiliano
6 MORENO Y FABIANESI Iván
11 ESCUDERO Damián Ariel
19 RAZZOTTI Franco
20 PAPA Emiliano Ramiro
22 ROBLES Javier Sebastián
23 SENA Sergio Román
24 MÉNDEZ Mario
25 CORIA Facundo Gabriel
25 OCAMPO Ramón Dario

Forwards
9 CASTROMÁN Lucas Martín
10 ZÁRATE Mauro Matías
12 BALVORÍN Gustavo Alberto
18 EREROS Sebastián Adolfo
25 CABRAL Alejandro Ariel

COPA NISSAN SUDAMERICANA 2006

Preliminary Round				First Round				Round of 16		
				Pachuca	MEX	Bye				
								Pachuca		1 5
Mineros de Guyana *	VEN	3	3					Deportes Tolima *		2 1
Carabobo	VEN	0	1	Mineros de Guyana	VEN	0	2			
				Deportes Tolima *	COL	0	2			
Deportes Tolima *	COL	3	1							
Independiente Medellín	COL	1	1							
				Corinthians	BRA	1	3			
				Vasco da Gama *	BRA	0	1			
								Corinthians *		0 2
								Lanús		0 4
				Vélez Sarsfield	ARG	0	0			
				Lanús *	ARG	2	1			
Nacional Montevideo	URU	1	0							
Central Español *	URU	0	0	Nacional Montevideo	URU	2	2			
				Libertad *	PAR	1	1			
Libertad *	PAR	3	1					Nacional Montevideo *		2 1 3p
Cerro Porteño	PAR	1	0					Boca Juniors		1 2 1p
				Boca Juniors	ARG	Bye				
				River Plate	ARG	Bye				
								River Plate *		0 2
								Atlético Paranaense		1 2
				Paraná *	BRA	1	0			
				Atlético Paranaense	BRA	3	1			
				Toluca	MEX	Bye				
Universitario Sucre *	BOL	2	3					Toluca *		1 2
Bolívar	BOL	2	2					El Nacional Quito		0 0
				Universitario Sucre *	BOL	1	1			
LDU Quito *	ECU	2	1	El Nacional Quito	ECU	3	2			
El Nacional Quito	ECU	3	1							
				Santos *	BRA	1 0 4p				
				Cruzeiro	BRA	0 1 3p				
								Santos		0 1
								San Lorenzo *		3 0
				Banfield	ARG	1	0			
				San Lorenzo *	ARG	2	0			
				Gimnasia y Esgrima LP	ARG	Bye				
								Gimnasia y Esgrima LP		1 2
								Fluminense *		1 0
				Botafogo *	BRA	1 1 2p				
				Fluminense	BRA	1 1 4p				
				LD Alajuelense	CRC	Bye				
Coronel Bolognesi *	PER	1	2					LD Alajuelense *		0 2
Univ. San Martín	PER	0	3					Colo Colo		4 7
				Coronel Bolognesi *	PER	2	0			
Huachipato *	CHI	1 2 3p		Colo Colo	CHI	1	1			
Colo Colo	CHI	2 1 4p						* Home team in the first leg		

COPA NISSAN SUDAMERICANA 2006

COPA NISSAN SUDAMERICANA 2006

Quarter–finals			Semi–finals			Final		
Pachuca	3	2						
Lanús *	0	2						
			Pachuca	1	4			
			Atlético Paranaense *	0	1			
Nacional Montevideo *	1	1						
Atlético Paranaense	2	4						
						Pachuca *	1	2
						Colo Colo	1	1
Toluca	1	2						
San Lorenzo *	3	0						
			Toluca	1	0			
			Colo Colo *	2	2			
Gimnasia y Esgrima LP	1	0						
Colo Colo *	4	2						

PRELIMINARY ROUND

Brígido Iriarte, Caracas, 22-08-2006, 18:00, Soto VEN

Mineros Guyana	3	Santo [7], García.J [36], Chad [38]
Carabobo	0	

Misael Delgado, Valencia, 30-08-2006, 17:30, Brand VEN

Carabobo	1	Arismendi [87]
Mineros Guyana	3	García.J 2 [13 51], Santo [44]

Manuel Murillo Toro, Ibagué, 23-08-2006, 21:30, Buitrago COL

Deportes Tolima	3	Escobar.JC [19], Charría [66], Quintero [67]
Indep. Medellín	1	Molina [40]

Atanasio Girardot, Medellín, 29-08-2006, 21:30, Hoyos COL

Indep. Medellín	1	Domínguez.E [83]
Deportes Tolima	1	Mera OG [11]

Centenario, Montevideo, 23-08-2006, 19:00, 2371, Viera URU

Central Español	0	
Nacional	1	Vázquez [60]

Parque Central, Montevideo, 29-08-2006, 18:30, 3269, Prudente URU

Nacional	0	
Central Español	0	

Defensores de Chaco, Asunción, 23-08-2006, 20:15, Arias PAR

Libertad	3	Guiñazú [45], Cabrera OG [50], López.H [88]
Cerro Porteño	1	Da Silva [63]

La Olla, Asunción, 29-08-2006, 20:00, Torres PAR

Cerro Porteño	0	
Libertad	1	López.H [79]

Patria, Sucre, 24-08-2006, 18:00, Gamboa BOL

Universit. Sucre	2	Gomes.J 2 [31 45]
Bolívar	2	Gutiérrez.L 2 [29 56]

Hernando Siles, La Paz, 31-08-2006, 19:00, 15 785, Paniagua BOL

Bolívar	2	Reyes [2], Gutiérrez.L [90p]
Universit. Sucre	3	Salaberry 2 [23 45], Gomes.J [78]

La Casa Blanca, Quito, 22-08-2006, 14:45, Haro ECU

LDU Quito	2	Delgado.A [53], Candelario [76]
El Nacional	3	Calle [45], Ordóñez [45], Caicedo [81]

Olímpico Atahualpa, Quito, 30-08-2006, 14:00, Carpio ECU

El Nacional	1	Ordóñez [50]
LDU Quito	1	Candelario [22]

Modelo, Tacna, 24-08-2006, 21:30, Carrillo PER

Coron. Bolognesi	1	Fano [70]
Univ. San Martín	0	

Monumental, Lima, 31-08-2006, 15:30, Buckley PER

Univ. San Martín	3	Del Solar 2 [13 40], Villarreal [69]
Coron. Bolognesi	2	Vásquez [32], Fano [58]

Municipal, Concepción, 24-08-2006, 20:15, 16 696, Osorio CHI

Huachipato	1	Ruiz.D [22]
Colo Colo	2	Fernández.M [32], Fierro [75p]

Monumental, Santiago, 31-08-2006, 21:30, Osses CHI

Colo Colo	1	Fernández.M [9]	Colo Colo W 5-3p
Huachipato	2	Peralta [46], Ruiz.D [49]	

FIRST ROUND

Manuel Murillo Toro, Ibagué, 5-09-2006, 20:30, Rivera PER

Deportes Tolima	0	
Mineros Guyana	0	

Brígido Iriarte, Caracas, 21-09-2006, 19:00, Reinoso ECU

Mineros Guyana	2	Chad [9], Cuenú OG [23]
Deportes Tolima	2	Charría [12], Quintero [36]

São Januario, Rio de Janeiro, 6-09-2006, 1221, Pena BRA

Vasco da Gama	0	
Corinthians	1	Gustavo Nery [49]

Canindé, São Paulo, 13-09-2006, 22:00, Gaciba BRA

Corinthians	3	Amoroso [5], Rafael Moura [27], Magrão [42]
Vasco da Gama	1	Diego [32]

La Fortaleza, Buenos Aires, 30-08-2006, 21:00, 5841, Lunati ARG

Lanús	2	Archubi 2 [47 82]
Vélez Sarsfield	0	

José Amalfitani, Buenos Aires, 20-09-2006, 21:15, 8089, Furchi ARG

Vélez Sarsfield	0	
Lanús	1	Archubi [63]

Defensores del Chaco, Asunción, 5-09-2006, 19:15, Baldassi ARG

Libertad	1	Samudio [14]
Nacional	2	Tejera [46], Martínez.J [80]

Parque Central, Montevideo, 19-09-2006, 12 376, Chandía CHI

Nacional	2	Garcés [35], Castro [85]
Libertad	1	Bonet [65]

Pinheirão, Curitiba, 6-09-2006, 19:30, 3322, Fagundes BRA

Paraná	1	Cristiano [3]
At. Paranaense	3	Cristian [7], Marcos Aurélio [25], Ferreira [67]

Kyocera Arena, Curitiba, 13-09-2006, 19:15, 8295, Lopes BRA

At. Paranaense	1	Denis Marques [77]
Paraná	0	

Patria, Sucre, 12-09-2006, 18:00, Arias PAR

Universit. Sucre	1	Palacios [79]
El Nacional	3	Caicedo 2 [9 18], Quiroz [72]

Olímpico Atahualpa, Quito, 21-09-2006, 20:30, 5892, Andarcia VEN

El Nacional	2	Ordóñez [8], Vera [80]
Universit. Sucre	1	Salaberry [35]

Vila Belmiro, Santos, 6-09-2006, 22:00, 7819, Gaciba BRA

Santos	1	André [81]
Cruzeiro	0	

Mineirão, Belo Horizonte, 13-09-2006, 22:00, 4278, Souza BRA

Cruzeiro	1	Wagner [51]
Santos	0	Santos W 4-3p

Nuevo Gasómetro, Buenos Aires, 22-08-2006, 21:15, 6878, Pezzotta ARG

San Lorenzo	2	Jiménez.R [24], González.H [33p]
Banfield	1	Morales.A [78]

Florencio Sola, Buenos Aires, 12-09-2006, 21:15, 7316, Favale ARG

Banfield	0	
San Lorenzo	0	

Maracanã, Rio de Janeiro, 7-09-2006, 19:00, 14 418, Tardelli BRA

Botafogo	1	Reinaldo [52]
Fluminense	1	Arouca [29]

Maracanã, Rio de Janeiro, 14-09-2006, 19:00, 6921, Beltrame BRA

Fluminense	1	Marcão [93+]
Botafogo	1	Júnior César [81]

Modelo, Tacna, 12-09-2006, 21:30, Brand VEN

Coron. Bolognesi	2	Fano [62], Mazakatsu [80]
Colo Colo	1	Jerez [50]

Monumental, Santiago, 19-09-2006, 21:30, Pezzotta ARG

Colo Colo	1	Vidal [45]
Coron. Bolognesi	0	

Pachuca, Boca Juniors, River Plate, Toluca, Gimnasia y Esgrima and LD Alajuelense all received byes to the round of 16

ROUND OF 16

Manuel Murillo Toro, Ibagué, 26-09-2006, 18:00, Andarcia VEN

Deportes Tolima	2	Charría [2], Rueda [61]
Pachuca	1	Caballero [34]

Hidalgo, Pachuca, 10-10-2006, 21:00, 20 000, Reinoso ECU

Pachuca	5	Aguilar [10], Cacho [46], Mosquera [62], Chitiva [78], Cabrera [83]
Deportes Tolima	1	Rivas [61]

Morumbí, São Paulo, 27-09-2006, 22:00, 7125, Torres PAR

Corinthians 0

Lanús 0

La Fortaleza, Buenos Aires, 11-10-2006, 22:00, 22 000, Chandía CHI

Lanús 4 Romero [16], Velásquez [17], Aguirre [36], Archubi [74]

Corinthians 2 Nadson [1], Renato [55]

Centenario, Montevideo, 28-09-2006, 21:45, Selman CHI

Nacional 2 Tejera [19], Alonso [21]

Boca Juniors 1 Palacio [45]

Ernesto Martearena, Salta, 12-10-2006, 21:45, 22 000, Simon BRA

Boca Juniors 2 Palacio [55], Bertolo [83]

Nacional 1 Perrone [15] Nacional W 3-1p

Monumental, Buenos Aires, 27-09-2006, 19:15, Vázquez URU

River Plate 0

At. Paranaense 1 Marcos Aurélio [25]

Kyocera Arena, Curitiba, 12-10-2006, 19:15, Torres PAR

At. Paranaense 2 Jancarlos [7]

River Plate 2 Gallardo [50p], Gerlo [79]

La Bombonera, Toluca, 26-09-2006, 20:15, Silvera URU

Toluca 1 Esquivel [71]

El Nacional 0

Olímpico Atahualpa, Quito, 10-10-2006, 16:00, Rivera PER

El Nacional 0

Toluca 2 Zinha [21], Sánchez [34]

Nuevo Gasómetro, Buenos Aires, 27-09-2006, 22:00, Chandía CHI

San Lorenzo 3 González.A [7], Jiménez.R [52], Lavezzi [66]

Santos 0

Vila Belmiro, Santos, 11-10-2006, 19:30, 6824, Larrionda URU

Santos 1 Wellington Paulista [37]

San Lorenzo 0

Maracanã, Rio de Janeiro, 28-09-2006, 19:15, 4191, Ruiz COL

Fluminense 1 Pitbull [89]

Gimnasia y E. LP 1 Herner [83]

Ciudad de La Plata, La Plata, 11-10-2006, 22:00, 38 000, Selman CHI

Gimnasia y E. LP 2 Tuta OG [45], Silva [66]

Fluminense 0

Alejandro Sota, Alajuela, 4-10-2006, 19:15, Baldassi ARG

LD Alajuelense 0

Colo Colo 4 Fernández.M 2 [36 80p], Jerez [65], Suazo [67]

Monumental, Santiago, 10-10-2006, 19:30, Gamboa BOL

Colo Colo 7 Suazo 2 [3 12], Vidal 2 [16 47], Sánchez.A [63], Fernández.M [79], Aceval [86]

LD Alajuelense 2 Fonseca.R 2 [10 34]

QUARTER-FINALS

18-10-2006, 21:45, 21 000, Simon BRA

Lanús 0

Bossio - Graieb, Hoyos, Ribonetto, Velásquez, Aguirre, Fritzler•, Pelletieri•, Archubi, Biglieri (Manicero 46), Lagos (Acosta 81). Tr: Cabrero

Pachuca 3 Cacho 2 [16 89], Giménez.C [79]

Calero - López.L (Salazar 62), Mosquera, Pinto•, Caballero, Correa, Salazar (Rodríguez.C 75), Chitiva (Alvarez 62), Giménez.C• (Alfaro 81), Cacho. Tr: Meza

---

31-10-2006, 19:15, 8906, Silvera URU

Pachuca 2 Giménez.C [58], Alvarez [93+]

Calero - López.L (Salazar 62), Mosquera, Pinto•, Cabrera, Rodríguez.C•, Caballero, Correa, Chitiva (Alvarez 64), Giménez.C, Landin (Cacho 67). Tr: Meza

Lanús 2 Valeri [55], Graf [62]

Bossio - Hoyos•, Ribonetto, Almirón (Lagos 90), Benítez (Archubi 77), Valeri•, Fritzler (Martínez.R 46), Pelletieri•, Acosta, Biglieri•, Graf. Tr: Cabrero

---

19-10-2006, 17:00, Baldassi ARG

Nacional Montevideo 1 Alonso [55]

Viera - Caballero•, Jaume•, Romero, Viana (Martínez.J 79), Vázquez• (Juárez 84), Brítez•, Delgado, Tejera, Perrone•, Alonso (Castro.G 69). Tr: Lasarte

Atlético Paranaense 2 Pedro Oldoni [74], Marcos Aurélio [89p]

Navarro Montoya - César, Danilo, João Leonardo, William, Alan Bahia, Cristian, Ferreira (Marcos Aurélio 70), Michel•, Denis Marques• (Pedro Oldoni 70), Paulo Rink• (Válber 70•77). Tr: Alvarez

---

25-10-2006, 22:00, 20 017, Chandía CHI

Atlético Paranaense 2 João Leonardo [29], Denis Marques [36], Marcos Aurélio [56], Danilo [68]

Cleber - Jancarlos, Danilo, João Leonardo•, Michel, Alan Bahia, Cristian, Denis Marques• (Pedro Oldoni 80), Ferreira (William 74), Marcos Aurélio (Paulo Rink 78). Tr: Alvarez

Nacional Montevideo 1 Brítez [50]

Viera - Jaume•, Godín•, Romero•72, Brítez, Viana, Vázquez•, Delgado, Tejera (Leites 74), Perrone (Juárez 65), Castro.G. Tr: Lasarte

---

25-10-2006, 19:30, 12 000, Amarilla PAR

San Lorenzo 3 Quatrocchi [17], Silvera 2 [51 56]

Orión - González.A•, Quatrocchi, Méndez.S•, Hirsig, Bottinelli.J, Silvera, Rivero (Acevedo 29), Bottinelli.D (Ferreyra• 77), Lavezzi (Jiménez.R 89), Tula•. Tr: Ruggeri

Toluca 1 Marioni [74]

Cristante - Da Silva•, Viades, Rosada•, Esquivel, Espinosa (De la Torre 46), Marioni, Zinha•, Sánchez.V•, Dueñas•, Ponce. Tr: Gallego

---

1-11-2006, 19:15, Larrionda URU

Toluca 2 Morales [5], Da Silva [69]

Cristante - Da Silva, Viades• (Almazán 33), Rosada•, Esquivel, Marioni, Zinha•68, Sánchez.V, Dueñas, Morales (Castillejos 66), Cruzalta (De la Torre 57). Tr: Gallego

San Lorenzo 0

Orión - González.A (Botero 72), Quatrocchi, Méndez.S, Tula• (Bottinelli.D 83), Bottinelli.J•, Silvera, Rivero•72, Hirsig, Ferreyra, Lavezzi. Tr: Ruggeri

---

19-10-2006, 21:15, Torres PAR

Colo Colo 4 Fernández.M [23p], Suazo 3 [46 66 75]

Cejas - González.A, Riffo, Henríquez•, Ormeño, Meléndez•, Sanhueza, Vidal•, Fernández.M, Sánchez.A (Cáceres 86), Suazo. Tr: Borghi

Gimnasia y Esgrima La Plata 1 Escobar [38]

Olave• - Herner, San Esteban, Goux•, Cabrera, Escobar, González.E, Basualdo•, Cuevas (Guglielminpietro 46), Leguizamón•, Cardetti (Cornejo 61) (Semino 80). Tr: Troglio

---

26-10-2006, 21:15, 38 438, Ruiz COL

Gimnasia y Esgrima La Plata 0

Olave - San Esteban, Goux, Landa, Cabrera, Escobar (Semino 73), González.E• (Cuevas 54•90), Basualdo, Leguizamón• (Guglielminpietro 54), Silva•, Dubarbier•70. Tr: Troglio

Colo Colo 2 Suazo [47p], Fierro [78]

Cejas• - González.A, Riffo, Henríquez, Ormeño•, Meléndez (Mena 81), Sanhueza, Vidal•, Fernández.M, Sánchez.A (Fierro 59), Suazo• (Cáceres 84). Tr: Borghi

SEMI-FINALS

1st leg. Kyocera Arena, Curitiba
15-11-2006, 15:30, 19 872, Martín ARG

Atlético Paranaense   **0**

Cleber - Jancarlos, Danilo, Michel• (Grando 83), Alan Bahia, Cristian (William 70), Denis Marques, Ferreira, Marcos Aurélio (Dagoberto• 62), Erandir, César•. Tr: Alvarez

Pachuca   **1**

Alvarez [86]

Calero - Cabrera (Rodríguez.C 65), López.L, Mosquera•, Pinto•, Salazar•, Correa, Cabballero, Chitiva• (Alfaro 75), Cacho (Alvarez 68), Giménez. Tr: Meza

2nd leg. Hidalgo, Pachuca
22-11-2006, 20:00, Reinoso ECU

Pachuca   **4**

Giménez.C 2 [57] [63], Alvarez [75], Cacho [80]

Calero - Cabrera, López.L, Mosquera, Pinto, Salazar, Correa, Cabballero, Landin (Cacho• 52), Chitiva (Alvarez 68), Giménez.C (Arellano 78). Tr: Meza

Atlético Paranaense   **1**

Ferreira [41]

Cleber - Jancarlos•64, Danilo, João Leonardo, Michel, Alan Bahia, Cristian (Válber 62), Denis Marques, Ferreira, Marcos Aurélio (William 67), Erandir• (Marcelo Silva 69). Tr: Alvarez

1st leg. Monumental, Santiago
16-11-2006, 21:15, Rivera PER

Colo Colo   **2**

Suazo [13p], Fernández [31p]

Cejas - Riffo, González.A (Sánchez.A 55), Henriquez•, Ormeño, Meléndez•, Sanhueza, Vidal, Fernández.M, Fierro (Cáceres 85), Suazo. Tr: Borghi

Toluca   **1**

Marioni [24]

Cristante• - Da Silva, Viades (Mira 46), Morales•, Marioni (De la Torre 85), Rosada, Espinosa•, Ponce• (Esquivel• 67), Dueñas, Almazán, Sánchez.V. Tr: Gallego

2nd leg. La Bombonera, Toluca
21-11-2006, 19:15, Brand VEN

Toluca   **0**

Cristante - Da Silva, Viades (Castillejos 69), Marioni, Rosada, Esquivel, Zinha•, Dueñas (Morales 35), González.E (De la Torre 46), Cruzalta, Sánchez.V. Tr: Gallego

Colo Colo   **2**

Fernández 2 [14] [58]

Cejas - Riffo, Henriquez•, Vidal, Ormeño, Meléndez•, Sanhueza, Fierro, Fernández.M (Mena 91), Sánchez.A (Villarroel 58), Suazo• (Cáceres 82). Tr: Borghi

FINAL

COPA SUDAMERICANA FINAL 1ST LEG
Estadio Hidalgo, Pachuca
30-11-2006, 19:15, 35 000, Silvera URU

PACHUCA   **1   1**   **COLO COLO**

Chitiva [27]   Suazo [50]

PACHUCA			COLO COLO	
1	CALERO Miguel		CEJAS Christian	1
13	SALAZAR Fernando		RIFFO Miguel Augusto	5
2	LOPEZ Leobardo	71	HENRIQUEZ David	4
3	MOSQUERA Aquivaldo		VIDAL Arturo Erasmo	23
21	PINTO Fausto	78	ORMENO Alvaro	2
22	AGUILAR Paul	46	MELENDEZ Andrés	19
6	CORREA Jaime		SANHUEZA Arturo	17
8	CABALLERO Gabriel	58	88	FIERRO Gonzalo	11
10	CHITIVA Andrés		FERNANDEZ Matías	14
19	GIMENEZ Christian	60	SANCHEZ Alexis	7
11	CACHO Juan Carlos		SUAZO Humberto Andrés	16
	Tr: MEZA Enrique		Tr: BORGHI Claudio	
	Substitutes		Substitutes	
7	ALVAREZ Damián	58	88	MENA Luis	3
16	RODRIGUEZ Carlos	46	78	VILLARROEL Moisés	6
20	SAUCEDO Roberto	71	60	GONZALEZ Andrés	18

COPA SUDAMERICANA FINAL 2ND LEG
Estadio Nacional, Santiago
13-12-2006, 21:30, 70 000, Baldassi ARG

COLO COLO   **1   2**   **PACHUCA**

Suazo [35]   Caballero [53], Giménez.C [72]

COLO COLO			PACHUCA	
1	CEJAS Christian		CALERO Miguel	1
5	RIFFO Miguel Augusto		LOPEZ Leobardo	2
23	VIDAL Arturo Erasmo		MOSQUERA Aquivaldo	3
4	HENRIQUEZ David		PINTO Fausto	21
2	ORMENO Alvaro	79	CABRERA Marvin	14
19	MELENDEZ Andrés	86	46	SALAZAR Fernando	13
17	SANHUEZA Arturo		CORREA Jaime	6
11	FIERRO Gonzalo	76	CABALLERO Gabriel	8
14	FERNANDEZ Matías		76	CHITIVA Andrés	10
16	SUAZO Humberto Andrés	83	GIMENEZ Christian	19
7	SANCHEZ Alexis	83	46	CACHO Juan Carlos	11
	Tr: BORGHI Claudio		Tr: MEZA Enrique	
	Substitutes		Substitutes	
9	CACERES Mario	79	46	ALVAREZ Damián	7
10	CANEO Miguel	83	46	RODRIGUEZ Carlos	16
18	GONZALEZ Andrés	86	83	ALFARO Juan	23

CONMEBOL WOMEN'S TOURNAMENTS 2006

SUDAMERICANO FEMININO ARGENTINA 2006

First Round Group Stage

Group A	Pl	W	D	L	F	A	Pts	URU	ECU	COL	CHI
Argentina	4	4	0	0	17	1	12	2-1	1-0	6-0	8-0
Uruguay	4	2	0	2	4	4	6		1-0	0-1	2-1
Ecuador	4	1	1	2	4	5	4			2-2	2-1
Colombia	4	1	1	2	4	11	4				1-3
Chile	4	1	0	3	5	13	3				

Group B	Pl	W	D	L	F	A	Pts	PAR	VEN	PER	BOL
Brazil	4	4	0	0	18	2	12	4-1	6-0	2-0	6-1
Paraguay	4	3	0	1	11	7	9		3-1	2-1	5-1
Venezuela	4	1	1	2	4	10	4			2-0	1-1
Peru	4	1	0	3	3	7	3				2-1
Bolivia	4	0	1	3	4	14	1				

Final Round Group

	Pl	W	D	L	F	A	Pts	BRA	URU	PAR
Argentina	3	2	1	0	4	0	7	2-0	2-0	0-0
Brazil	3	2	0	1	12	2	6		6-0	6-0
Uruguay	3	1	0	2	3	10	3			3-2
Paraguay	3	0	1	2	2	9	1			

Argentina and Brazil qualified for the FIFA Women's World Cup China PR 2007
Tournament played in Mar del Plata, Argentina from 10-11-2006 to 26-11-2006

SUDAMERICANO FEMININO SUB-20 CHILE 2006

First Round Group Stage

Group A	Pl	W	D	L	F	A	Pts	PER	CHI	VEN	URU
Brazil	4	4	0	0	28	1	12	5-0	8-1	7-0	8-0
Peru	4	2	1	1	6	9	7		4-3	1-1	1-0
Chile	4	1	1	2	9	15	4			2-2	3-1
Venezuela	4	0	3	1	5	12	3				2-2
Uruguay	4	0	1	3	3	14	1				

Group B	Pl	W	D	L	F	A	Pts	PAR	COL	BOL	ECU
Argentina	4	3	1	0	11	3	10	3-2	3-1	0-0	5-0
Paraguay	4	3	0	1	10	6	9		3-1	3-1	2-1
Colombia	4	2	0	2	10	8	6			7-2	1-0
Bolivia	4	1	1	2	5	11	4				2-1
Ecuador	4	0	0	4	2	10	0				

Final Round Group

	Pl	W	D	L	F	A	Pts	ARG	PAR	PER
Brazil	3	2	1	0	9	1	7	1-0	1-1	7-0
Argentina	3	1	1	1	4	1	4		4-0	0-0
Paraguay	3	1	1	1	3	5	4			2-0
Peru	3	0	1	2	0	9	1			

Brazil and Argentina qualified for the FIFA U-20 Women's World Championship Russia 2006
Tournament played in Viña del Mar and Valparaíso, Chile from 4-01-2006 to 20-01-2006

CONMEBOL YOUTH TOURNAMENTS 2007

SUDAMERICANO SUB-20 PARAGUAY 2007

First Round Group Stage

Group A	Pl	W	D	L	F	A	Pts	PAR	CHI	BOL	PER
Brazil	4	3	1	0	10	4	10	1-1	4-2	3-0	2-1
Paraguay	4	2	2	0	3	1	8		1-0	0-0	1-0
Chile	4	2	0	2	10	7	6			4-0	4-2
Bolivia	4	1	1	2	4	8	4				4-1
Peru	4	0	0	4	4	11	0				

Group B	Pl	W	D	L	F	A	Pts	URU	ARG	ECU	VEN
Colombia	4	3	0	1	5	3	9	0-1	2-1	1-0	2-1
Uruguay	4	2	1	1	6	5	7		3-3	2-1	0-1
Argentina	4	1	2	1	11	6	5			1-1	6-0
Ecuador	4	1	1	2	5	5	4				3-1
Venezuela	4	1	0	3	3	11	3				

Final Round Group

	Pl	W	D	L	F	A	Pts	ARG	URU	CHI	PAR	COL
Brazil	5	3	2	0	10	5	11	2-2	3-1	2-2	1-0	2-0
Argentina	5	2	3	0	4	2	9		1-0	0-0	1-0	2-0
Uruguay	5	2	1	2	7	6	7			1-1	3-1	2-0
Chile	5	1	3	1	10	6	6				2-3	5-0
Paraguay	5	2	0	3	7	9	6					3-2
Colombia	5	0	1	4	2	12	1					

Brazil, Argentina, Uruguay and Chile qualified for the FIFA U-20 World Cup Canada 2007
Brazil and Argentina qualified for the 2008 Beijing Olympic Football Tournament
Tournament played in Pedro Juan Caballero, Ciudad del Este, Asunción and Luque, Paraguay from 7-01-2001 to 28-01-2007

SUDAMERICANO SUB-17 ECUADOR 2007

First Round Group Stage

Group A	Pl	W	D	L	F	A	Pts	ECU	BRA	BOL	CHI
Peru	4	2	1	1	7	5	7	0-0	2-1	4-1	1-3
Ecuador	4	2	1	1	6	5	7		5-4	0-1	1-0
Brazil	4	2	0	2	14	9	6			7-2	2-0
Bolivia	4	2	0	2	5	11	6				1-0
Chile	4	1	0	3	3	5	3				

Group B	Pl	W	D	L	F	A	Pts	COL	VEN	URU	PAR
Argentina	4	2	2	0	7	2	8	0-0	1-1	2-1	4-0
Colombia	4	2	2	0	5	2	8		2-2	1-0	2-0
Venezuela	4	1	2	1	6	8	5			1-4	2-1
Uruguay	4	1	1	2	7	6	4				2-2
Paraguay	4	0	1	3	3	10	1				

Final Round Group

	Pl	W	D	L	F	A	Pts	COL	ARG	PER	VEN	ECU
Brazil	5	4	1	0	15	2	13	0-0	2-0	4-0	5-2	
Colombia	5	3	1	1	11	3	10		1-2	3-0	5-0	2-1
Argentina	5	2	2	1	6	5	8			1-1	1-1	2-0
Peru	5	1	2	2	5	11	5				2-1	2-2
Venezuela	5	1	1	3	3	12	4					1-0
Ecuador	5	0	1	4	5	12	1					

Brazil, Colombia, Argentina and Peru qualified for the FIFA U-17 World Cup Korea Republic 2007
All six final round teams qualified for the Panamerican Games Rio de Janeiro 2007
Tournament played in Riobamba, Ambato, Latacunga, Azogues, Cuenca, Ibarra and Quito, Ecuador from 4-03-2007 to 25-03-2007

OFC

OCEANIA FOOTBALL CONFEDERATION

Oceania may not have seen much international action during the 2006-07 season, but the 13th South Pacific Games, played in Samoa over the course of two weeks from 25 August 2007, saw not only the OFC Nations Cup kick-off but also the qualifiers for the 2010 FIFA World Cup in South Africa. With all of the OFC members except New Zealand and Papua New Guinea taking part, the Games have become a major feature in the Oceania calendar with the additional reward for the three medallists of joining New Zealand in a group challenging for both the OFC Nations Cup and a possible place in the World Cup Finals. In an effort to bring international football to the different countries in Oceania, that group contest is taking place on a home and away basis with the winners not only crowned Oceania Champions but also earning the right to play off against an Asian nation for a place in the World Cup finals. The promise of a more level playing field after Australia's departure to the Asian Football Confederation seems to have given the members of the Oceania confederation a new lease of life, and although New Zealand is emerging as the dominant

THE FIFA BIG COUNT OF 2006 FOR OCEANIA

	Male	Female		Total
Number of players	486 000	56 000	Referees and Assistant Referees	3 000
Professionals	n/a		Admin, Coaches, Technical, Medical	29 000
Amateurs 18+	59 000		Number of clubs	2 000
Youth under 18	175 000		Number of teams	13 000
Unregistered	301 000		Clubs with women's teams	n/a
Total involved in football	573 000		Players as % of population	4.68%

power, countries like Fiji and the Solomon Islands are now playing with a real prospect of honours. Nowhere was that more evident than in the inaugural O–League, Oceania's version of the various Champions Leagues around the world. The first tournament was fairly limited in its scope, with clubs from just five of the OFC members taking part and New Zealand entering two teams. Matches in the two groups of three teams were, however, played on a home and away basis meaning that supporters in all five nations were able to experience the tournament first hand, something that did not happen often in the past due to the practice of choosing one venue to host the entire competition. Fijian club Ba won a group containing Tahiti's Temanava and Marist from the Solomon Islands and they almost beat the winners of the other group, Waitakere United from New Zealand, in the final, losing only on away goals over the two legs. The 2007–08 O–League kicked off in June 2007 with a three-team preliminary group, bringing the number of competing countries up to seven out of the 11 OFC members.

Oceania Football Confederation (OFC)

Ericsson Stadium, 12 Maurice Road, Penrose, PO Box 62 586, Auckland 6, New Zealand

Tel +64 9 5258161   Fax +64 9 5258164

info@ofcfoot.org.nz   www.oceaniafootball.com

President: TEMARII Reynald TAH

General Secretary: NICHOLAS Tai COK

Vice-President: LULU Johnny VAN   Treasurer: HARMON Lee COK

OFC Formed: 1966

OFC EXECUTIVE COMMITTEE

President: TEMARII Reynald TAH

Senior Vice-President: LULU Johnny VAN   1st Vice-President: BURGESS Mark NZL   2nd Vice-President: WICKHAM Adrian SOL

3rd Vice-President: OTT Richard ASA   Treasurer: HARMON Lee COK   CHUNG David PNG

FOURNIER Claude NCL   HARERAAROA Eugene TAH   General Secretary NICHOLAS Tai COK

MAP OF OFC MEMBER NATIONS

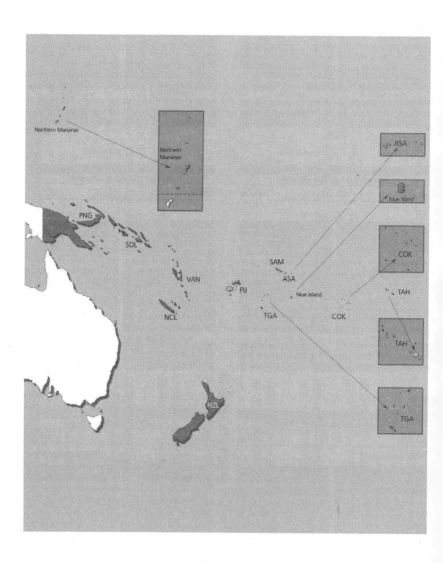

OCEANIA TOURNAMENTS

OCEANIA NATIONS CUP

Year	Host Country	Winners	Score	Runners-up	Venue
1973	New Zealand	New Zealand	2-0	Tahiti	Auckland
1980	New Caledonia	Australia	4-2	Tahiti	Nouméa
1996	Home & away	Australia	6-0 5-0	Tahiti	Papeete & Canberra
1998	Australia	New Zealand	1-0	Australia	Brisbane
2000	Tahiti	Australia	2-0	New Zealand	Stade de Pater, Papeete
2002	New Zealand	New Zealand	1-0	Australia	Ericsson Stadium, Auckland
2004	Home & away	Australia	5-1 6-0	Solomon Islands	Honaria & Sydney

OCEANIA WOMEN'S CHAMPIONSHIP

Year	Host Country	Winners	Score	Runners-up	Venue
1983	New Caledonia	New Zealand	3-2	Australia	Nouméa
1986	New Zealand	Chinese Taipei	4-1	Australia	Christchurch
1989	Australia	Chinese Taipei	1-0	New Zealand	Brisbane
1991	Australia	New Zealand	1-0 0-1 †	Australia	Sydney
1995	Papua N. Guinea	Australia	1-2 1-0 †	New Zealand	Port Moresby
1998	New Zealand	Australia	3-1	New Zealand	Mount Smart, Auckland
2003	Australia	Australia	2-0 †	New Zealand	Belconnen, Canberra
2007	Papua N. Guinea	New Zealand	7-0	Papua New Guinea	Lae

† The 1991, 1995, 2003 and 2007 tournaments were played as leagues • The results shown are those between the top two teams

OCEANIA YOUTH CHAMPIONSHIP

Year	Host Country	Winners	Score	Runners-up	Venue
1974	Tahiti	Tahiti	2-0	New Zealand	Papeete
1978	New Zealand	Australia	5-1 †	Fiji	Auckland
1980	Fiji	New Zealand	2-0	Australia	Suva
1982	Papua New Guinea	Australia	4-3	New Zealand	Port Moresby
1985	Australia	Australia	3-2 †	Israel	Sydney
1987	New Zealand	Australia	1-1 †	Israel	Auckland
1988	Fiji	Australia	1-0	New Zealand	Suva
1990	Fiji	Australia	6-0 †	New Zealand	Suva
1992	Tahiti	New Zealand	1-0 †	Tahiti	Papeete
1994	Fiji	Australia	1-0	New Zealand	Suva
1996	Tahiti	Australia	2-1	New Zealand	Papeete
1998	Samoa	Australia	2-0	Fiji	Apia
2001	New Cal/Cook Is	Australia	1-2 3-1	New Zealand	Auckland & Coffs Harbour
2003	Vanuatu/Fiji	Australia	11-0 4-0	Fiji	Melbourne & Ba
2005	Solomon Islands	Australia	3-0	Solomon Islands	Honiara
2007	New Zealand	New Zealand	3-2	Fiji	Waitakere

† The 1978, 1985, 1987, 1990, 1992 and 2007 tournaments were played as leagues • The results shown are those between the top two teams

OCEANIA U–17 CHAMPIONSHIP

Year	Host Country	Winners	Score	Runners-up	Venue
1983	New Zealand	Australia	2-1	New Zealand	Mount Smart, Auckland
1986	Chinese Taipei	Australia	0-1	New Zealand	CKF Stadium, Kaohsiung
1989	Australia	Australia	5-1	New Zealand	
1991	New Zealand	Australia	1-1 1-0	New Zealand	Napier
1993	New Zealand	Australia	3-0	Soloman Islands	
1995	Vanuatu	Australia	1-0	New Zealand	
1997	New Zealand	New Zealand	1-0	Australia	
1999	Fiji	Australia	5-0	Fiji	Churchill Park, Lautoka
2001	Samoa/Cook Isl	Australia	3-0 6-0	New Zealand	Canberra & Auckland
2003	Home & away	Australia	3-1 4-0	New Caledonia	Nouméa
2005	New Caledonia	Australia	1-0	Vanuatu	Nouméa
2007	Tahiti	New Zealand	2-1	Tahiti	Papeete

From 1983 to 1991 and in 2007 the tournaments were played as leagues • The results shown are those between the top two teams

OCEANIA WOMEN'S U-19 CHAMPIONSHIP

Year	Host Country	Winners	Score	Runners-up	Venue
2002	Tonga	Australia	6-0	New Zealand	Nuku'alofa
2004	Papua New Guinea	Australia	14-1	Papua New Guinea	Lloyd Robson Oval, Port Moresby

SOUTH PACIFIC GAMES WINNERS

Year	Host Country	Winners	Runners-up
1963	Fiji	New Caledonia	Fiji
1966	New Caledonia	Tahiti	New Caledonia
1969	Papua New Guinea	New Caledonia	Tahiti
1971	Tahiti	New Caledonia	Tahiti
1975	Guam	Tahiti	New Caledonia
1979	Fiji	Tahiti	Fiji
1983	Western Samoa	Tahiti	Fiji
1987	New Caledonia	New Caledonia	Tahiti
1991	Papua New Guinea	Fiji	Solomon Isl
1995	Tahiti	Tahiti	Solomon Isl
1999	Guam	Not played	
2003	Fiji	Fiji	New Caledonia

MELANESIAN CUP WINNERS

Year	Host Country	Winners	Runners-up
1988	Solomon Islands	Fiji	Solomon Isl
1989	Fiji	Fiji	New Caledonia
1990	Vanuatu	Vanuatu	New Caledonia
1992	Vanuatu	Fiji	New Caledonia
1994	Solomon Islands	Solomon Isl	Fiji
1996	Papua New Guinea	Papua NG	Solomon Isl
1998	Vanuatu	Fiji	Vanuatu
2000	Fiji	Fiji	Solomon Isl

SOUTH PACIFIC MINI GAMES WINNERS

Year	Host Country	Winners	Runners-up
1981	Solomon Islands	Tahiti	New Caledonia
1985	Cook Islands	Tahiti	
1989	Tonga	Papua NG	
1993	Vanuatu	Tahiti	Fiji

POLYNESIAN CUP WINNERS

Year	Host Country	Winners	Runners-up
1994	Samoa	Tahiti	Tonga
1996	Tonga	Tonga	Samoa
1998	Cook Islands	Tahiti	Cook Islands
2000	Tahiti	Tahiti	Cook Islands

O–LEAGUE

Year	Winners	Country	Score	Country	Runners-up
1987	Adelaide City	AUS	1-1 4-1p	NZL	Mount Wellington
1999	South Melbourne	AUS	5-1	FIJ	Nadi
2001	Wollongong City Wolves	AUS	1-0	VAN	Tafea FC
2005	Sydney FC	AUS	2-0	NCL	AS Magenta
2006	Auckland City	NZL	3-1	TAH	AS Piraé
2007	Waitakere United	NZL	1-2 1-0	FIJ	Ba

OFC YOUTH TOURNAMENTS 2007

OFC U-17 CHAMPIONSHIP, TAHITI 2007

	Pl	W	D	L	F	A	Pts	TAH	FIJ	NCL
New Zealand	3	3	0	0	9	2	9	2-1	3-1	4-0
Tahiti	3	0	2	1	1	2	2		0-0	0-0
Fiji	3	0	2	1	2	4	2			1-1
New Caledonia	3	0	2	1	1	5	2			

New Zealand qualified for the FIFA U–17 World Cup 2007 in Korea Republic

OFC U-20 CHAMPIONSHIP, NEW ZEALAND 2007

	Pl	W	D	L	F	A	Pts	FIJ	SOL	NCL	TAH	VAN	SAM
New Zealand	6	5	1	0	21	4	16	3-2	1-1	1-0	2-0	7-0	7-1
Fiji	6	4	0	2	16	6	12		3-0	2-1	0-2	2-0	7-0
Solomon Islands	6	3	2	1	14	8	11			1-0	2-1	2-2	8-1
New Caledonia	6	3	0	3	11	6	9				2-1	3-1	5-0
Tahiti	6	2	1	3	9	9	7					2-2	3-1
Vanuatu	6	1	2	3	8	17	5						3-1
Samoa	6	0	0	6	4	33	0						

New Zealand qualified for the FIFA U–20 World Cup 2007 in Canada

O-LEAGUE 2007

GROUP A		Pl	W	D	L	F	A	Pts	NZL	NZL	NCL
Waitakere United	NZL	4	2	2	0	13	5	8		2-2	6-1
Auckland City	NZL	4	2	2	0	10	4	8	2-2		4-0
AS Mont Dore	NCL	4	0	0	4	1	15	0	0-3	0-2	

GROUP B		Pl	W	D	L	F	A	Pts	FIJ	TAH	SOL
Ba	FIJ	4	3	1	0	7	3	10		1-0	3-2
AS Temanava	TAH	4	1	1	2	3	5	4	1-1		2-1
Marist	SOL	4	1	0	3	5	7	3	0-2	2-0	

GROUP A

Stade Noumea Daly, Noumea, 21-01-2007
AS Mont Dore   0
Auckland City   2   Urlovic 2 [19 31p]

Trusts Stadium, Waitakere, 24-01-2007
Waitakere United   2   Hay [25], Menapi [48]
Auckland City   2   Urlovic [73], Young [89]

Fred Taylor Park, Waitakere, 20-02-2007
Waitakere United   6   Menapi 2 [5 87], Edwards [8], Koprivcic 2 [57 64]
AS Mont Dore   1   Diaike [57]   Pearce [55]

Sandringham, 22-02-2007
Auckland City   4   Young 2 [12 26], Bryan Little 2 [41 65]
AS Mont Dore   0

Stade Noumea Daly, Noumea, 31-03-2007
AS Monte Dore   0
Waitakere United   3   Menapi [11], Gwyther [39], Wylie [50]

Kiwitea Street, Auckland, 4-04-2006
Auckland City   2   Jordan 2 [20 94+]
Waitakere United   2   Koprivcic 2 [32 35]

GROUP B

Lawson Tama, Honiara, 19-02-2007
Marist   0
Ba   2   Vakatalesau [36], Tuba [57p]

Stade Pater, Papeete, 23-02-2007
AS Temanava   1   Kabeu [78p]
Ba   1   Kumar [28]

Govind Park, Ba, 12-03-2007
Ba   3   Tuba [15p], Doi Doi 2 [32 48]
Marist   2   Luwi [85], OG [87]

Stade Pater, Papeete, 16-03-2007
AS Temanava   2   Poiroi [12], Araparii [58p]
Marist   1   Luwi [28p]

Churchill Park, Lautoka, 20-03-2007
Ba   1   Manuca [72]
AS Temanava   0

Lawson Tama, Honiara, 22-03-2007
Marist   2   Luwi [48], Naka [51]
AS Temanava   0

FINAL

Govind Park, Ba
21-04-2007, 15:00, 10 000, Minan PNG
Ba   **2**
                    Chandra [8], Bukalidi [74]
Laisenia Tuba - Shalen Lal, Roneel Kumar• (c), Jone
Vesikula, Keni Doidoi (Kiniviliame Kainehewe 63),
Josaia Bukalidi, Ronald Chandra (Osea Vakatalesau 55)
(Leone Vurukania 92+), Robert Wise, Luke Vidovi,
Malakai Tiwa, Malakai Kainihewe. Tr: Yogendra Dutt
Waitakere United   **1**
                    Menapi [54]
Michael Utting - George Suri, Danny Hay (c),
Commins Menapi, Allan Pearce, Craig Wylie (Hone
Fowler 72), Jakub Sinkora, Daniel Koprivcic (Michael
Gwyther 81), Hoani Edwards (Pedro Santos 73),
Rupesh Puna, Jeff Campbell. Tr: Steve Cain

Mount Smart, Auckland
29-04-2007, 14:00, 9000, Averii TAH
Waitakere United   **1**
                    Allan Pearce [55]
Michael Utting - Craig Wylie•••94+, George
Suri•••51, Graham Pearce (Rupesh Puna 85), Sam
Jasper, Hoani Edwards, Pedro Santos (Hone Fowler 59),
Jeff Campbell, Allan Pearce, Commins Menapi, Daniel
Koprivcic (Jakub Sinkora 73). Tr: Steve Cain
Ba   **0**
Laisenia Tuba - Shalen Lal (Avinesh Swamy 68),
Roneel Kumar, Jone Vesikula, Josaia Bukalidi, Robert
Wise•, Peni Finau, Kiniviliame Turagalailai•, Osea
Vakatalesau• (Ronald Chandra 82), Malakai Tiwa,
Malakai Kainihewe. Tr: Yogendra Dutt

UEFA

UNION DES ASSOCIATIONS EUROPEENNES DE FOOTBALL

Aime Jacquet, the French World Cup-winning coach in 1998, once warned that "the day the business side of football overtakes the sporting side, football will no longer exist. It will be like boxing. It will be finished." Football may not have reached that point yet, but some would argue that the danger signs are not being heeded. Prompted by his desire to protect the sporting principles of the game, Michel Platini chose to stand in the UEFA presidential election in January 2007, an election in which he beat the incumbent, Lennart Johansson, by 27 votes to 23. UEFA has made great strides in helping to maintain fair competition amongst national teams, but at club level the task is far more daunting. As a select handful of clubs become ever richer, critics point to the decreasing competitiveness of the various national leagues in which they play and it can be no-coincidence that American sports entrepreneurs, sensing rich pickings, are circling like sharks to follow in the footsteps of Tom Hicks and George Gillett who bought Liverpool in February 2007. While America

THE FIFA BIG COUNT OF 2006 FOR EUROPE

	Male	Female		Total
Number of players	55 283 000	6 364 000	Referees and Assistant Referees	322 000
Professionals	60 000		Admin, Coaches, Technical, Medical	2 100 000
Amateurs 18+	11 101 000		Number of clubs	202 000
Youth under 18	9 386 000		Number of teams	872 000
Unregistered	40 622 000		Clubs with women's teams	13 000
Total involved in football	64 069 000		Players as % of population	7.59%

may be the centre of unbridled capitalism, sport there is run on almost communist lines in order to protect competition. By contrast, European football, and football in England in particular, offers no such constraints. Those riches seem to be helping English clubs in Europe with Manchester United, Chelsea and Liverpool all reaching the semi-finals of the UEFA Champions League. But it was Milan, however, who emerged triumphant with their 2-1 victory over Liverpool in the final in Athens, laying to rest some of the ghosts of their dramatic defeat at the hands of the same opponents two years earlier. Spanish football showed its strength in depth when both Sevilla and Espanyol made it through to the final of the UEFA Cup, with Sevilla retaining their title on penalties after an excellent game in Glasgow. The other winners during the European season included the German U–19 women's team, the Spanish U–17 and U–19 teams, and the Dutch U–21 team, all of whom won their respective European championships, as well as Arsenal Ladies who won the UEFA Women's Cup.

Union des associations européennes de football (UEFA)

Route de Genève 46, 1260 Nyon, Switzerland

Tel +41 22 9944444   Fax +41 22 9944488

info@uefa.com   www.uefa.com

President: PLATINI Michel FRA   Chief Executive: INFANTINO Gianni ITA (Interim)

UEFA Formed: 1954

UEFA EXECUTIVE COMMITTEE

President: PLATINI Michel FRA   Vice-President: ERZIK Senes TUR   Vice-President: THOMPSON Geoffrey ENG
Vice-President: VILLAR LLONA Angel Maria ESP   Vice-President: MAYER-VORFELDER Gerhard GER   Treasurer: LEFKARITIS Marios CYP

ORDINARY MEMBERS OF THE EXECUTIVE COMMITTEE

CARRARO Franco ITA	KOLOSKOV Viacheslav, Dr RUS	MADAIL Gilberto, Dr POR
MIFSUD Joseph, Dr MLT	OMDAL Per Ravn NOR	SANDU Mircea ROU
SPRENGERS Mathieu, Drs NED	SURKIS Grigory UKR	Chief Executive: INFANTINO Gianni ITA (Interim)
Co-opted: STICKLER Friedrich AUT	Co-opted: SPIESS Giangiorgio SUI	Hon President: JOHANSSON Lennart SWE
FIFA Exco member: D'HOOGHE Michel, Dr BEL		FIFA Exco member: BECKENBAUER Franz GER

MAP OF UEFA MEMBER NATIONS

EUROPEAN TOURNAMENTS

UEFA EUROPEAN CHAMPIONSHIP

Year	Host Country	Winners	Score	Runners-up	Venue
1960	France	Soviet Union	2-1	Yugoslavia	Parc des Princes, Paris
1964	Spain	Spain	2-1	Soviet Union	Bernabeu, Madrid
1968	Italy	Italy	1-1 2-0	Yugoslavia	Stadio Olimpico, Roma
1972	Belgium	Germany FR	3-0	Soviet Union	Heysel, Brussels
1976	Yugoslavia	Czechoslovakia	2-2 5-4p	Germany FR	Crvena Zvezda, Belgrade
1980	Italy	Germany FR	2-1	Belgium	Stadio Olimpico, Rome
1984	France	France	2-0	Spain	Parc des Princes, Paris
1988	Germany FR	Netherlands	2-0	Soviet Union	Olympiastadion, Munich
1992	Sweden	Denmark	2-0	Germany	Nya Ullevi, Gothenburg
1996	England	Germany	2-1	Czech Republic	Wembley, London
2000	Belgium/Netherlands	France	2-1	Italy	Feijenoord Stadion, Rotterdam
2004	Portugal	Greece	1-0	Portugal	Stadio da Luz, Lisbon

The UEFA European Championship is the second youngest of the Confederation championships after the Oceania Nations Cup. At first there was a patchy response to the tournament and it was not until the third edition that the Germans, the most succesful nation to date with three titles, bothered to enter. The French are the only other team to have been European Champions more than once, and the wide range of winners has been a prominent feature and one of the major reasons for the continued success of the tournament. Only England of the traditional powers have failed to win the title but it has been the triumphs of the smaller nations such as Czechoslovakia, the Netherlands, Denmark and most recently Greece that have caught the imagination. Only since 1980 has the European Championship had a finals tournament along the lines of the current system. From 1980 to 1992 the finals had eight teams which grew to 16 in 1996 in no small part because UEFA's membership had grown from 32, which it had been for much of the post-war period, to beyond 50 as the political boundaries of Europe were redrawn. Eleven nations have hosted the finals but home advantage has never been a serious factor. On seven occasions the hosts have been beaten in the semi-finals, and in only three of the 12 tournaments have they actually won the title – and not since 1984 – while in 2004 Portugal became the first host nation to lose the final itself. The most recent fashion has been co-hosting - Belgium and the Netherlands in 2000, with Austria and Switzerland scheduled for 2008 and Poland and the Ukraine for 2012.

UEFA EUROPEAN WOMEN'S CHAMPIONSHIP

Year	Host Country	Winners	Score	Runners-up	Venue
1984		Sweden	1-0 0-1 4-3p	England	Gothenburg & Luton
1987	Norway	Norway	2-1	Sweden	Ullevål, Oslo
1989	Germany FR	Germany FR	4-1	Norway	Osnabrück
1991	Denmark	Germany	3-1	Norway	Aalborg Stadion
1993	Italy	Norway	1-0	Italy	Dino Manuzzi, Cesena
1995	Germany	Germany	3-2	Sweden	Fritz Walter Stadion, Kaiserslautern
1997	Norway/Sweden	Germany	2-0	Italy	Ullevål, Oslo
2001	Germany	Germany	1-0	Sweden	Donaustadion, Ulm
2005	England	Germany	3-1	Norway	Ewood Park, Blackburn

The UEFA Women's Championship is now a flourishing event in its own right, drawing good crowds into the stadiums and earning widespread coverage in the media. An unofficial European Championship was played in Italy in 1979 but since then there have been nine official tournaments, six of which have been won by Germany. The Scandinavian countries remain strong and provided the two other winners in Norway and Sweden. The eight-team final tournament was introduced for 1997 in Norway and Sweden. Although early editions often doubled up as FIFA Women's World Cup qualifiers, these are now held separately.

UEFA EUROPEAN UNDER–21 CHAMPIONSHIP

Year	Host Country	Winners	Score	Runners-up	Venue
1978		Yugoslavia	1-0 4-1	German DR	Halle & Mostar
1980		Soviet Union	0-0 1-0	German DR	Rostock & Moscow
1982		England	3-1 2-3	Germany FR	Sheffield & Bremen
1984		England	1-0 2-0	Spain	Seville & Sheffield
1986		Spain	1-2 2-1 3-0p	Italy	Rome & Valladolid
1988		France	0-0 3-0	Greece	Athens & Besançon
1990		Soviet Union	4-2 3-1	Yugoslavia	Sarajevo & Simferopol
1992		Italy	2-0 0-1	Sweden	Ferrara & Växjö
1994	France	Italy	1-0	Portugal	Montpellier
1996	Spain	Italy	1-1 4-2p	Spain	Barcelona
1998	Romania	Spain	1-0	Greece	Bucharest
2000	Slovakia	Italy	2-1	Czech Republic	Bratislava
2002	Switzerland	Czech Republic	0-0 3-1p	France	St Jakob Park, Basel
2004	Germany	Italy	3-0	Serbia & Montenegro	Ruhrstadion, Bochum
2006	Portugal	Netherlands	3-0	Ukraine	Bessa, Oporto
2007	Netherlands	Netherlands	4-1	Serbia	Euroborg, Groningen

UEFA EUROPEAN UNDER–19 CHAMPIONSHIP

Year	Host Country	Winners	Score	Runners-up	Venue
1981	West Germany	Germany FR	1-0	Poland	Düsseldorf
1982	Finland	Scotland	3-1	Czechoslovakia	Helsinki
1983	England	France	1-0	Czechoslovakia	White Hart Lane, London
1984	Soviet Union	Hungary	0-0 3-2p	Soviet Union	Zentralny, Moscow
1986	Yugoslavia	German DR	3-1	Italy	Subotica
1988	Czechoslovakia	Soviet Union	3-1	Portugal	Frydek-Mistek
1990	Hungary	Soviet Union	0-0 4-2p	Portugal	Bekescsaba
1992	Germany	Turkey	2-1	Portugal	Bayreuth
1993	England	England	1-0	Turkey	City Ground, Nottingham
1994	Spain	Portugal	1-1 4-1p	Germany	Merida
1995	Greece	Spain	4-1	Italy	Katerini
1996	France/Luxemb	France	1-0	Spain	Besançon
1997	Iceland	France	1-0	Portugal	Reykjavík
1998	Cyprus	Republic of Ireland	1-1 4-3p	Germany	Larnaca
1999	Sweden	Portugal	1-0	Italy	Norrköping
2000	Germany	France	1-0	Ukraine	Nürnberg
2001	Finland	Poland	3-1	Czech Republic	Helsinki
2002	Norway	Spain	1-0	Germany	Ullevaal, Oslo
2003	Liechtenstein	Italy	2-0	Portugal	Rheinpark Stadion, Vaduz
2004	Switzerland	Spain	1-0	Turkey	Colovray, Nyon
2005	Nth. Ireland	France	3-1	England	Windsor Park, Belfast
2006	Poland	Spain	2-1	Scotland	Miejski, Poznan
2007	Austria	Spain	1-0	Greece	Linzer, Linz

Played as an U-18 tournament from 1981 to 2001

UEFA EUROPEAN WOMEN'S UNDER–19 CHAMPIONSHIP

Year	Host Country	Winners	Score	Runners-up	Venue
1998		Denmark	2-0 2-3	France	Aabenraa & Niederbronn-les-Bains
1999	Sweden	Sweden	1-0	Germany	Bromölla
2000	France	Germany	4-2	Spain	La Libération, Boulogne
2001	Norway	Germany	3-2	Norway	Aråsen, Lillestrom
2002	Sweden	Germany	3-1	France	Olympia, Helsingborg
2003	Germany	France	2-0	Norway	Alfred Kunze Sportpark, Leipzig
2004	Finland	Spain	2-1	Germany	Pohjola Stadion, Vantaa
2005	Hungary	Russia	2-2 6-5p	France	ZTE, Zalaegerszeg
2006	Switzerland	Germany	3-0	France	Neufeld, Berne
2007	Iceland	Germany	2-0	England	Laugardalsvöllur, Reykjavík

The first three tournaments were played as U-18 championships

UEFA EUROPEAN UNDER-17 CHAMPIONSHIP

Year	Host Country	Winners	Score	Runners-up	Venue
1982	Italy	Italy	1-0	Germany FR	Falconara
1984	Germany FR	Germany FR	2-0	Soviet Union	Ulm
1985	Hungary	Soviet Union	4-0	Greece	Budapest
1986	Greece	Spain	2-1	Italy	Athens
1987	France	Italy	1-0	Soviet Union	Paris
1988	Spain	Spain	0-0 4-2p	Portugal	Teresa Rivero, Madrid
1989	Denmark	Portugal	4-1	German DR	Vejle
1990	East Germany	Czechoslovakia	3-2	Yugoslavia	Erfurt
1991	Switzerland	Spain	2-0	Germany	Wankdorf, Berne
1992	Cyprus	Germany	2-1	Spain	Ammokostos, Larnaca
1993	Turkey	Poland	1-0	Italy	Inönü, Istanbul
1994	Rep. Ireland	Turkey	1-0	Denmark	Tolka Park, Dublin
1995	Belgium	Portugal	2-0	Spain	Brussels
1996	Austria	Portugal	1-0	France	Wien
1997	Germany	Spain	0-0 5-4p	Austria	Celle
1998	Scotland	Republic of Ireland	2-1	Italy	McDiarmid Park, Perth
1999	Czech Republic	Spain	4-1	Poland	Olomouc
2000	Israel	Portugal	2-1	Czech Republic	Ramat Gan
2001	England	Spain	1-0	France	Stadium of Light, Sunderland
2002	Denmark	Switzerland	0-0 4-2p	France	Farum Park, Farum
2003	Portugal	Portugal	2-1	Spain	Fontelo Municipal, Viseu
2004	France	France	2-1	Spain	Gaston Petit, Chateauroux
2005	Italy	Turkey	2-0	Netherlands	E. Mannucci, Pontedera
2006	Luxembourg	Russia	2-2 5-3p	Czech Republic	Josy Barthel, Luxembourg
2007	Belgium	Spain	1-0	England	RFC Tournai, Tournai

Played as an U-16 tournament prior to 2002

Europe has a long history of youth football dating back to the launch of the International Youth Tournament by the English FA in 1948. UEFA took over the running of that event in 1956 and it remained largely unaltered until 1980 when it was replaced by two new tournaments, for players under 16 and players under 18. These have since changed to Under-17 and Under-19 Championships to tie in with the systems used by FIFA for their World Championships at these levels. In 1998 UEFA launched their Under-19 Championship for women which, like the men's events, doubles up when required as a qualifying tournament for the FIFA World Championships. UEFA has one other age-restricted event, the UEFA European Under-21 Championship which mirrors the qualifying groups of the senior men's team, with games often played the previous day. Tournaments are played over two years and since 1992 every second edition has doubled up as a qualifing tournament for the Olympic Games.

UEFA WOMEN'S CUP

Year	Winners	Country	Score	Country	Runners-up
2002	1.FFC Frankfurt	GER	2-0	SWE	Umeå IK
2003	Umeå IK	SWE	4-1 3-0	DEN	Fortuna Hjørring
2004	Umeå IK	SWE	3-0 5-0	GER	1.FFC Frankfurt
2005	1.FFC Turbine Potsdam	GER	2-0 3-1	SWE	Djurgården/Alvsjö
2006	1.FFC Frankfurt	GER	4-0 3-2	GER	1.FFC Turbine Potsdam
2007	Arsenal	ENG	1-0 0-0	SWE	Umeå IK

Of all of the recent additions to the UEFA calendar the UEFA Women's Cup is potentially the most interesting. Whereas women's football in the USA has had its foundations in the college system, in Europe the link with men's clubs has been stronger and could develop further if the UEFA Women's Cup fulfils its potential and prompts clubs to become more serious about funding their female sections. For the 2005 tournament 42 of UEFA's 52 members entered teams, up from 22 in the first tournament in 2001, although it is the German and Scandinavian teams that have so far been the most successful.

UEFA CHAMPIONS LEAGUE

Year	Winners	Country	Score	Country	Runners-up
1956	Real Madrid	ESP	4-3	FRA	Stade de Reims
1957	Real Madrid	ESP	2-0	ITA	Fiorentina
1958	Real Madrid	ESP	3-2	ITA	Milan
1959	Real Madrid	ESP	2-0	FRA	Stade de Reims
1960	Real Madrid	ESP	7-3	FRG	Eintracht Frankfurt
1961	Benfica	POR	3-2	ESP	Barcelona
1962	Benfica	POR	5-3	ESP	Real Madrid
1963	Milan	ITA	2-1	POR	Benfica
1964	Internazionale	ITA	3-1	ESP	Real Madrid
1965	Internazionale	ITA	1-0	POR	Benfica
1966	Real Madrid	ESP	2-1	YUG	Partizan Beograd
1967	Celtic	SCO	2-1	ITA	Internazionale
1968	Manchester United	ENG	4-1	POR	Benfica
1969	Milan	ITA	4-1	NED	Ajax
1970	Feyenoord	NED	2-1	SCO	Celtic
1971	Ajax	NED	2-0	GRE	Panathinaikos
1972	Ajax	NED	2-0	ITA	Internazionale
1973	Ajax	NED	1-0	ITA	Juventus
1974	Bayern München	FRG	1-1 4-0	ESP	Atlético Madrid
1975	Bayern München	FRG	2-0	ENG	Leeds United
1976	Bayern München	FRG	1-0	FRA	AS Saint-Étienne
1977	Liverpool	ENG	3-1	FRG	Borussia Mönchengladbach
1978	Liverpool	ENG	1-0	BEL	Club Brugge
1979	Nottingham Forest	ENG	1-0	SWE	Malmö FF
1980	Nottingham Forest	ENG	1-0	FRG	Hamburger SV
1981	Liverpool	ENG	1-0	ESP	Real Madrid
1982	Aston Villa	ENG	1-0	FRG	Bayern München
1983	Hamburger SV	FRG	1-0	ITA	Juventus
1984	Liverpool	ENG	1-1 4-2p	ITA	Roma
1985	Juventus	ITA	1-0	ENG	Liverpool
1986	Steaua Bucuresti	ROU	0-0 2-0p	ESP	Barcelona
1987	FC Porto	POR	2-1	FRG	Bayern München
1988	PSV Eindhoven	NED	0-0 6-5p	POR	Benfica
1989	Milan	ITA	4-0	ROU	Steaua Bucuresti
1990	Milan	ITA	1-0	POR	Benfica
1991	Crvena Zvezda Beograd	YUG	0-0 5-3p	FRA	Olympique Marseille
1992	Barcelona	ESP	1-0	ITA	Sampdoria
1993	Olympique Marseille	FRA	1-0	ITA	Milan
1994	Milan	ITA	4-0	ESP	Barcelona
1995	Ajax	NED	1-0	ITA	Milan
1996	Juventus	ITA	1-1 4-2p	NED	Ajax
1997	Borussia Dortmund	GER	3-1	ITA	Juventus
1998	Real Madrid	ESP	1-0	ITA	Juventus
1999	Manchester United	ENG	2-1	GER	Bayern München
2000	Real Madrid	ESP	3-0	ESP	Valencia
2001	Bayern München	GER	1-1 5-4p	ESP	Valencia
2002	Real Madrid	ESP	2-1	GER	Bayer Leverkusen
2003	Milan	ITA	0-0 3-2p	ITA	Juventus
2004	FC Porto	POR	3-0	FRA	Monaco
2005	Liverpool	ENG	3-3 3-2p	ITA	Milan
2006	Barcelona	ESP	2-1	ENG	Arsenal
2007	Milan	ITA	2-1	ENG	Liverpool

FAIRS CUP

Year	Winners	Country	Score	Country	Runners-up
1958	Barcelona	ESP	2-2 6-0	ENG	London Select XI
1960	Barcelona	ESP	0-0 4-1	ENG	Birmingham City
1961	Roma	ITA	2-2 2-0	ENG	Birmingham City
1962	Valencia	ESP	6-2 1-1	ESP	Barcelona
1963	Valencia	ESP	2-1 2-0	YUG	Dinamo Zagreb
1964	Real Zaragoza	ESP	2-1	ESP	Valencia
1965	Ferencváros	HUN	1-0	ITA	Juventus
1966	Barcelona	ESP	0-1 4-2	ESP	Real Zaragoza
1967	Dinamo Zagreb	YUG	2-0 0-0	ENG	Leeds United
1968	Leeds United	ENG	1-0 0-0	HUN	Ferencváros
1969	Newcastle United	ENG	3-0 3-2	HUN	Ujpesti Dózsa
1970	Arsenal	ENG	1-3 3-0	BEL	RSC Anderlecht
1971	Leeds United	ENG	2-2 1-1	ITA	Juventus

UEFA CUP

Year	Winners	Country	Score	Country	Runners-up
1972	Tottenham Hotspur	ENG	2-1 1-1	ENG	Wolverhampton Wanderers
1973	Liverpool	ENG	3-0 0-2	FRG	Borussia Mönchengladbach
1974	Feyenoord	NED	2-2 2-0	ENG	Tottenham Hotspur
1975	Borussia Mönchengladbach	FRG	0-0 5-1	NED	FC Twente Enschede
1976	Liverpool	ENG	3-2 1-1	BEL	Club Brugge
1977	Juventus	ITA	1-0 1-2	ESP	Athletic Bilbao
1978	PSV Eindhoven	NED	0-0 3-0	FRA	SEC Bastia
1979	Borussia Mönchengladbach	FRG	1-1 1-0	YUG	Crvena Zvezda Beograd
1980	Eintracht Frankfurt	FRG	2-3 1-0	FRG	Borussia Mönchengladbach
1981	Ipswich Town	ENG	3-0 2-4	NED	AZ 67 Alkmaar
1982	IFK Göteborg	SWE	1-0 3-0	FRG	Hamburger SV
1983	RSC Anderlecht	BEL	1-0 1-1	POR	Benfica
1984	Tottenham Hotspur	ENG	1-1 1-1 4-3p	BEL	RSC Anderlecht
1985	Real Madrid	ESP	3-0 0-1	HUN	Videoton SC
1986	Real Madrid	ESP	5-1 0-2	FRG	1.FC Köln
1987	IFK Göteborg	SWE	1-0 1-1	SCO	Dundee United
1988	Bayer Leverkusen	FRG	0-3 3-0 3-2p	ESP	Español
1989	Napoli	ITA	2-1 3-3	FRG	VfB Stuttgart
1990	Juventus	ITA	3-1 0-0	ITA	Fiorentina
1991	Internazionale	ITA	2-0 0-1	ITA	Roma
1992	Ajax	NED	2-2 0-0	ITA	Torino
1993	Juventus	ITA	3-1 3-0	GER	Borussia Dortmund
1994	Internazionale	ITA	1-0 1-0	AUT	Austria Salzburg
1995	Parma	ITA	1-0 1-1	ITA	Juventus
1996	Bayern München	GER	2-0 3-1	FRA	Bordeaux
1997	Schalke 04	GER	1-0 0-1 4-1p	ITA	Internazionale
1998	Internazionale	ITA	3-0	ITA	Lazio
1999	Parma	ITA	3-0	FRA	Olympique Marseille
2000	Galatasaray	TUR	0-0 4-1p	ENG	Arsenal
2001	Liverpool	ENG	5-4	ESP	CD Alavés
2002	Feyenoord	NED	3-2	GER	Borussia Dortmund
2003	FC Porto	POR	3-2	SCO	Glasgow Celtic
2004	Valencia	ESP	2-0	FRA	Olympique Marseille
2005	CSKA Moskva	RUS	3-1	POR	Sporting CP
2006	Sevilla	ESP	4-0	ENG	Middlesbrough
2007	Sevilla	ESP	2-2 3-1p	ESP	Espanyol

Europe's top club competition needs little introduction, although how it is referred to may need a little explanation. Launched in 1955 as the European Champion Clubs' Cup, it was often known simply as the European Cup. In 1992 it was rebranded as the UEFA Champions League, although technically speaking many of the teams taking part are not the champions of their respective leagues and half of the competition is actually run on a knock-out basis and not a league system. There are few higher honours for a footballer than lifting the European Champions Clubs' Cup, as the trophy itself is still known, and the Final in May remains one of the major highlights of the year. Before 1955 clubs from different countries only met in friendly matches with two major exceptions. The annual Mitropa Cup, which started in 1927, brought together the top teams from Italy, Czechoslovakia, Hungary, Austria, Switzerland and Yugoslavia and was at its most powerful before the Second World War; and the Latin Cup, played in the post-war period between the champions of Spain, Portugal, France and Italy. Ironically the 1955 Latin Cup final was contested by Real Madrid and Stade de Reims, the two teams which a year later made it to the final of the first European Cup. The southern European nations benefited from the competitive edge that the Latin Cup had given them and it wasn't until Celtic's victory in 1967 that a club from outside of Spain, Italy or Portugal won the Cup. Most notable was Real Madrid's achievement in winning the first five tournaments and with nine triumphs they remain the most successful team. Milan are second with six although their titles have been more widespread over time than Real's, showing slightly more consistency than their rivals. 1967 marked a complete shift in the balance of power with clubs from northern Europe completely dominating the competition for most of the next two decades. English clubs won six titles in a row from 1977 to 1982 while Bayern München and Ajax each won a hat-trick of titles. Heysel in 1985 marked the next watershed. That one of the worst disasters in European football should come in the European Cup Final was difficult to take but it meant that UEFA could ban English clubs and the fans that had followed them abroad. It also meant the balance of power shifted south once again, coinciding with the rise of the great Milan team of the late 1980s and early 1990s, a team that, in the eyes of many, rivals the Real Madrid of the 1950s as the greatest in the history of the competition. The 1991-92 season saw the first shake-up in the European Cup with two groups of four replacing the quarter-finals, the winners of which qualified for the final, while the following year it was rebranded the UEFA Champions League. Since then the format has been tinkered with on a number of occasions, with four first round groups introduced for the 1994-95 season, six first round groups for the 1997-98 season and finally eight first round groups and four second round groups for the 1999-2000 season. Most dramatically of all perhaps was the decision taken for the 1997-98 season which allowed more than the champions from each country to take part. For the top countries that now means entry for the top four teams, a situation which has led to some criticism, but it does satisfy the needs of the clubs whilst balancing the integrity of the national leagues. It has often been said that a European League is inevitable one day, but in many respects it is already with us in the form of the UEFA Champions League and much to UEFA's credit it has come without the clubs breaking away to form an independent body. Since the formation of the UEFA Champions League there has been a remarakble leveling of standards with no one team able to dominate the competition. Only a revived Real Madrid have come close but the past 17 tournaments have been won by 12 different clubs from eight countries. There was a time when winning the UEFA Cup was seen as a more challenging task than winning the European Champions Clubs' Cup. With up to three or four clubs from the top nations taking part, compared to just one in the European Cup, the depth and quality of opposition was often stronger. Rather whimsically the tournament was at first restricted to teams from cities that had staged a major international trade fair. Renamed in 1971 the UEFA Cup now finds itself in a crisis. Qualifying for the UEFA Cup and not the UEFA Champions League is now seen by the top clubs as a major disaster, hardly good for the credibility of the tournament. Furthermore, the problem is exacerbated by the clubs finishing third in the Champions League groups then playing in the UEFA Cup and more often than not going on to win it. This decline in prestige has had one good side effect; perhaps because the pressure is not so intense or the fear of failure so great, every final in recent years has been an entertaining extravaganza.

UEFA EUROPEAN CHAMPIONSHIP MEDALS TABLE

	Country	G	S	B	F	SF
1	Germany	3	2	1	5	6
2	France	2		1	2	4
3	Soviet Union	1	3		4	5
4	Czechoslovakia	1	1	2	2	3
5	Italy	1	1	1	2	3
6	Spain	1	1		2	2
7	Netherlands	1		4	1	5
8	Denmark	1		1	1	3
9	Greece	1			1	1
10	Yugoslavia		2		2	3
11	Portugal		1	2	1	3
12	Belgium		1	1	1	2
13	England			2		2
14	Hungary			1		2
15	Czech Republic			1		1
	Sweden			1		1
		12	12	18	24	46

This table represents the Gold (winners), Silver (runners-up) and Bronze (semi-finalists) placings in the UEFA European Championship, along with the number of appearances in the final and semi-finals

UEFA CHAMPIONS LEAGUE MEDALS TABLE

	Country	G	S	B	F	SF
1	Italy	11	14	8	25	33
2	Spain	11	9	18	20	38
3	England	10	4	15	14	29
4	Germany	6	7	10	13	23
5	Netherlands	6	2	5	8	13
6	Portugal	4	5	2	9	11
7	France	1	5	7	6	13
8	Scotland	1	1	6	2	8
9	Romania	1	1	2	2	4
	Serbia	1	1	2	2	4
11	Belgium		1	3	1	4
12	Greece		1	2	1	3
13	Sweden		1	1	1	2
14	Hungary			3		3
	Switzerland			3		3
	Ukraine			3		3
17	Austria			2		2
	Bulgaria			2		2
	Poland			2		2
20	Czech Republic			1		1
	Russia			1		1
	Slovakia			1		1
	Turkey			1		1
		52	52	100	104	204

This table represents the Gold (winners), Silver (runners-up) and Bronze (semi-finalists) placings of clubs representing the above countries in the UEFA Champions League, along with the number of appearances in the final and semi-finals

FAIRS/UEFA CUP MEDALS TABLE

	Country	G	S	B	F	SF
1	Spain	11	7	11	18	29
2	Italy	10	8	15	18	33
3	England	10	8	9	18	27
4	Germany	6	7	23	13	36
5	Netherlands	4	2	3	6	9
6	Sweden	2			2	2
7	Belgium	1	3	5	4	9
8	Hungary	1	3	3	4	7
9	Portugal	1	2	2	3	5
10	Croatia	1	1	1	2	3
11	Turkey	1		1	1	2
11	Russia	1		1	1	2
13	France		4	5	4	9
14	Scotland		2	4	2	6
15	Serbia		1	3	1	4
16	Austria		1	1	1	2
17	Czech Republic			2		2
17	German DR			2		2
17	Switzerland			2		2
17	Romania			2		2
21	Bosnia-Herzegovina			1		1
21	Denmark			1		1
21	Greece			1		1
		49	49	98	98	196

This table represents the Gold (winners), Silver (runners-up) and Bronze (semi-finalists) placings of clubs representing the above countries in the UEFA Cup, along with the number of appearances in the final and semi-finals

CUP WINNERS CUP MEDALS TABLE

	Country	G	S	B	F	SF
1	England	8	5	8	13	21
2	Spain	7	7	5	14	19
3	Italy	7	4	9	11	20
4	Germany	4	4	9	8	17
5	Belgium	3	4	5	7	12
6	Scotland	2	2	4	4	8
7	Ukraine	2	-	-	2	2
8	France	1	2	6	3	9
9	German DR	1	2	3	3	6
10	Netherlands	1	1	6	2	8
11	Portugal	1	1	3	2	5
12	Georgia	1		1	1	2
13	Czechoslovakia	1			1	1
14	Austria		3	1	3	4
15	Hungary		2	1	2	3
16	Russia		1	5	1	6
17	Poland		1	1	1	2
18	Czech Republic			3		3
19	Croatia			2		2
19	Serbia			2		2
19	Bulgaria			2		2
22	Romania			1		1
22	Wales			1		1
		39	39	78	78	156

This table represents the Gold (winners), Silver (runners-up) and Bronze (semi-finalists) placings of clubs representing the above countries in the Cup Winners Cup, along with the number of appearances in the final and semi-finals

UEFA CHAMPIONS LEAGUE MEDALS TABLE

	Country		G	S	B
1	Real Madrid	ESP	9	3	9
2	Milan	ITA	7	4	2
3	Liverpool	ENG	5	2	1
4	Bayern München	GER	4	3	5
5	Ajax	NED	4	2	2
6	Juventus	ITA	2	5	3
7	Benfica	POR	2	5	1
8	Barcelona	ESP	2	3	4
9	Internazionale	ITA	2	2	3
10	Manchester United	ENG	2		7
11	FC Porto	POR	2		1
12	Nottingham Forest	ENG	2		
13	Glasgow Celtic	SCO	1	1	2
14	Hamburger SV	GER	1	1	1
	Olympique Marseille	FRA	1	1	1
	Steaua Bucuresti	ROU	1	1	1
17	Borussia Dortmund	GER	1		2
	Crvena Zvezda Beograd	SER	1		2
	PSV Eindhoven	NED	1		2
20	Feyenoord	NED	1		1
21	Aston Villa	ENG	1		
22	Stade de Reims	FRA		2	
	Valencia	ESP		2	
24	Atlético Madrid	ESP		1	2
	Leeds United	ENG		1	2
	AS Monaco	FRA		1	2
	Panathinaikos	GRE		1	2
28	Borussia Mönchengladbach	GER		1	1
	AS Saint-Étienne	FRA		1	1
30	Arsenal	ENG		1	
	Bayer Leverkusen	GER		1	
	Club Brugge	BEL		1	
	Eintracht Frankfurt	GER		1	
	Fiorentina	ITA		1	
	Malmö FF	SWE		1	
	Partizan Beograd	SRB		1	
	Roma	ITA		1	
	Sampdoria	ITA		1	
39	Chelsea	ENG			3
	Dynamo Kyiv	UKR			3
41	RSC Anderlecht	BEL			2
	CSKA Sofia	BUL			2
	FC Zürich	SUI			2
44	FK Austria	AUT			1
	Girondins Bordeaux	FRA			1
	Deportivo La Coruna	ESP			1
	Derby County	ENG			1
	Dinamo Bucuresti	ROU			1
	Dukla Praha	CZE			1
	Dundee	SCO			1
	Dundee United	SCO			1
	Galatasaray	TUR			1
	IFK Göteborg	SWE			1
	Hibernian Edinburgh	SCO			1
	1.FC Köln	GER			1
	Legia Warszawa	POL			1

UEFA CHAMPIONS LEAGUE MEDALS TABLE (CONTD)

Country		G	S	B
FC Nantes	FRA			1
Paris Saint-Germain	FRA			1
Rába ETO Györ	HUN			1
Glasgow Rangers	SCO			1
SK Rapid Wien	AUT			1
Real Sociedad	ESP			1
Spartak Moskva	RUS			1
Spartak Trnava	SVK			1
Standard CL	BEL			1
Tottenham Hotspur	ENG			1
Ujpesti TE	HUN			1
Vasas Budapest	HUN			1
Villarreal	ESP			1
Widzew Lódz	POL			1
Young Boys Berne	SUI			1
		52	52	100

FAIRS/UEFA CUP MEDALS TABLE

	Country		G	S	B
1	Juventus	ITA	3	3	1
2	Internazionale	ITA	3	1	5
3	Barcelona	ESP	3	1	4
4	Valencia	ESP	3	1	
5	Liverpool	ENG	3		1
6	Borussia Mönchengladbach	GER	2	2	1
7	Leeds United	ENG	2	1	2
8	Tottenham Hotspur	ENG	2	1	1
9	Parma	ITA	2		1
	Real Madrid	ESP	2		1
11	Feyenoord	NED	2		
	IFK Göteborg	SWE	2		
	Sevilla	ESP	2		
14	RSC Anderlecht	BEL	1	2	
15	Ferencváros	HUN	1	1	2
16	Roma	ITA	1	1	1
17	Arsenal	ENG	1	1	
	Dinamo Zagreb	CRO	1	1	
	Real Zaragoza	ESP	1	1	
20	Bayern München	GER	1		2
21	Ajax	NED	1		1
	Bayer Leverkusen	GER	1		1
	Eintracht Frankfurt	GER	1		1
	Newcastle United	ENG	1		1
	FC Schalke 04	GER	1		1
26	CSKA Moskva	RUS	1		
	Galatasaray	TUR	1		
	Ipswich Town	ENG	1		
	Napoli	ITA	1		
	FC Porto	POR	1		
	PSV Eindhoven	NED	1		
32	Birmingham City	ENG		2	1
	Borussia Dortmund	GER		2	1
34	RCD Español	ESP		2	
	Olympique Marseille	FRA		2	
36	1.FC Köln	GER		1	5
37	VfB Stuttgart	GER		1	2
38	AZ Alkmaar	NED		1	1
	Club Brugge	BEL		1	1
	Crvena Zvezda Beograd	SRB		1	1
	Hamburger SV	GER		1	1
	Lazio	ITA		1	1
	Sporting CP	POR		1	1
	Twente Enschede	NED		1	1
45	Austria Salzburg	AUT		1	
	CD Alavés	ESP		1	
	Athletic Bilbao	ESP		1	
	SEC Bastia	FRA		1	
	Benfica	POR		1	
	Girondins Bordeaux	FRA		1	
	Glasgow Celtic	SCO		1	
	Dundee United	SCO		1	
	Fiorentina	ITA		1	
	London Select XI	ENG		1	
	Middlesbrough	ENG		1	
	Torino	ITA		1	

FAIRS/UEFA CUP MEDALS TABLE

	Country		G	S	B
	Ujpesti TE	HUN		1	
	Videoton SC	HUN		1	
	Wolverhampton Wanderers	ENG		1	
60	Atlético Madrid	ESP			3
	Werder Bremen	GER			3
62	Bologna	ITA			2
	1.FC Kaiserslautern	GER			2
	Milan	ITA			2
65	AEK Athens	GRE			1
	AJ Auxerre	FRA			1
	Belgrade Select XI	SRB			1
	Boavista	POR			1
	Brondbyernes IF	DEN			1
	Cagliari	ITA			1
	Chelsea	ENG			1
	MSV Duisburg	GER			1
	Bohemians Praha	CZE			1
	Dundee	SCO			1
	1.FC Dynamo Dresden	GDR			1
	Genoa 1893	ITA			1
	Grasshopper-Club	SUI			1
	Göztepe Izmir	TUR			1
	Hibernian Edinburgh	SCO			1
	Hajduk Split	CRO			1
	Hertha BSC Berlin	GER			1
	Karlsruher SC	GER			1
	Kilmarnock	SCO			1
	RFC Liège	BEL			1
	Lausanne-Sports	SUI			1
	VfB Leipzig	GDR			1
	Racing Club Lens	FRA			1
	Manchester United	ENG			1
	AS Monaco	FRA			1
	MTK-VM Budapest	HUN			1
	RWD Molenbeek	BEL			1
	Nottingham Forest	ENG			1
	Osasuna	ESP			1
	Paris Saint-Germain	FRA			1
	Radnicki Nis	SRB			1
	Glasgow Rangers	SCO			1
	Slavia Praha	CZE			1
	FC Sochaux	FRA			1
	Spartak Moskva	RUS			1
	Steaua Bucureşti	ROU			1
	Tenerife	ESP			1
	FC Tirol	AUT			1
	Universitatea Craiova	ROU			1
	Union St. Gilloise	BEL			1
	Villarreal	ESP			1
	KSV Waregem	BEL			1
	Zeljeznicar Sarajevo	BIH			1
			48	48	96

CUP WINNERS CUP MEDALS TABLE

	Country		G	S	B
1	Barcelona	ESP	4	2	
2	RSC Anderlecht	BEL	2	2	
3	Milan	ITA	2	1	
4	Chelsea	ENG	2		2
5	Dynamo Kyiv	UKR	2		
6	Atlético Madrid	ESP	1	2	2
7	Arsenal	ENG	1	2	
	Glasgow Rangers	SCO	1	2	
9	Sampdoria	ITA	1	1	1
	West Ham United	ENG	1	1	1
	Fiorentina	ITA	1	1	1
	Paris Saint-Germain	FRA	1	1	1
13	Ajax	NED	1	1	
	Hamburger SV	GER	1	1	
	Parma	ITA	1	1	
16	Bayern München	GER	1		3
17	Juventus	ITA	1		2
	Real Zaragoza	ESP	1		2
19	Aberdeen	SCO	1		1
	Dinamo Tbilisi	GEO	1		1
	Manchester City	ENG	1		1
	Manchester United	ENG	1		1
	KV Mechelen	BEL	1		1
	Sporting CP	POR	1		1
	Tottenham Hotspur	ENG	1		1
26	Borussia Dortmund	GER	1		
	Everton	ENG	1		
	Lazio	ITA	1		
	1.FC Magdeburg	GDR	1		
	Slovan Bratislava	SVK	1		
	Valencia	ESP	1		
	Werder Bremen	GER	1		
33	Real Madrid	ESP		2	
	SK Rapid Wien	AUT		2	
35	Dinamo Moskva	RUS		1	2
36	FK Austria	AUT		1	1
	Carl Ziess Jena	GDR		1	1
	AS Monaco	FRA		1	1
	Standard CL	BEL		1	1
	Liverpool	ENG		1	1
41	Ferencváros	HUN		1	
	Fortuna Düsseldorf	GER		1	
	Górnik Zabrze	POL		1	
	Leeds United	ENG		1	
	VfB Leipzig	GDR		1	
	Real Mallorca	ESP		1	
	MTK-VM Budapest	HUN		1	
	TSV München 1860	GER		1	
	FC Porto	POR		1	
	Royal Antwerp FC	BEL		1	
	VfB Stuttgart	GER		1	
52	Feyenoord	NED			3
53	Benfica	POR			2
	Glasgow Celtic	SCO			2
	Lokomotiv Moskva	RUS			2
	PSV Eindhoven	NED			2

CUP WINNERS CUP MEDALS TABLE

	Country		G	S	B
57	Atalanta	ITA			1
	Baník Ostrava	CZE			1
	Bayer Uerdingen	GER			1
	SK Beveren	BEL			1
	Girondins Bordeaux	FRA			1
	Borussia Mönchengladbach	GER			1
	Cardiff City	WAL			1
	Club Brugge	BEL			1
	CSKA Sofia	BUL			1
	Deportivo La Coruña	ESP			1
	1.FC Köln	GER			1
	Dukla Praha	CZE			1
	Dunfermline Athletic	SCO			1
	Berliner FC	GDR			1
	Dinamo Bucuresti	ROU			1
	Dinamo Zagreb	CRO			1
	Eintracht Frankfurt	GER			1
	Hajduk Split	CRO			1
	Legia Warszawa	POL			1
	Olympique Lyonnais	FRA			1
	Olympique Marseille	FRA			1
	FC Nantes	FRA			1
	Napoli	ITA			1
	1.FC Nürnberg	GER			1
	OFK Beograd	SRB			1
	Crvena Zvezda Beograd	SRB			1
	Roma	ITA			1
	FSV Zwickau	GDR			1
	FC Schalke 04	GER			1
	Slavia Sofia	BUL			1
	Sparta Praha	CZE			1
	Spartak Moskva	RUS			1
	Torino	ITA			1
	FC Twente Enschede	NED			1
	Ujpesti TE	HUN			1
	Racing Club Genk	BEL			1
	Vicenza	ITA			1
	Wolverhampton Wanderers	ENG			1
			39	39	78

PAST UEFA AWARDS

MOST VALUABLE PLAYER

1998	RONALDO	BRA	Internazionale
1999	BECKHAM David	ENG	Manchester United
2000	REDONDO Fernando	ARG	Real Madrid
2001	EFFENBERG Stefan	GER	Bayern München
2002	ZIDANE Zinedine	FRA	Real Madrid
2003	BUFFON Gianluigi	ITA	Juventus
2004	DECO	POR	FC Porto
2005	GERRARD Steven	ENG	Liverpool
2006	RONALDINHO	BRA	Barcelona

BEST GOALKEEPER

1998	SCHMEICHEL Peter	DEN	Manchester United
1999	KAHN Oliver	GER	Bayern München
2000	KAHN Oliver	GER	Bayern München
2001	KAHN Oliver	GER	Bayern München
2002	KAHN Oliver	GER	Bayern München
2003	BUFFON Gianluigi	ITA	Juventus
2004	BAIA Vitor	POR	FC Porto
2005	CECH Petr	CZE	Chelsea
2006	LEHMANN Jens	GER	Arsenal

BEST DEFENDER

1998	HIERRO Fernando	ESP	Real Madrid
1999	STAM Jaap	NED	Manchester United
2000	STAM Jaap	NED	Manchester United
2001	AYALA Fabian	ARG	Valencia
2002	ROBERTO CARLOS	BRA	Real Madrid
2003	ROBERTO CARLOS	BRA	Real Madrid
2004	CARVALHO Ricardo	POR	FC Porto
2005	TERRY John	ENG	Chelsea
2006	PUYOL Carles	ESP	Barcelona

BEST MIDFIELDER

1998	ZIDANE Zinedine	FRA	Juventus
1999	BECKHAM David	ENG	Manchester United
2000	MENDIETA Gaizka	ESP	Valencia
2001	MENDIETA Gaizka	ESP	Lazio
2002	BALLACK Michael	GER	Bayern München
2003	NEDVED Pavel	CZE	Juventus
2004	DECO	POR	FC Porto
2005	KAKA	BRA	Milan
2006	DECO	POR	Barcelona

BEST FORWARD

1998	RONALDO	BRA	Internazionale
1999	SHEVCHENKO Andriy	UKR	Milan
2000	RAUL	ESP	Real Madrid
2001	RAUL	ESP	Real Madrid
2002	VAN NISTELROOIJ Ruud	NED	Manchester United
2003	RAUL	ESP	Real Madrid
2004	MORIENTES Fernando	ESP	Monaco
2005	RONALDINHO	BRA	Barcelona
2006	ETO'O Samuel	CMR	Barcelona

COACH OF THE YEAR

1998	LIPPI Marcelo	ITA	Juventus
1999	FERGUSON Alex	SCO	Manchester United
2000	CUPER Hector	ARG	Valencia
2001	HITZFELD Ottmar	GER	Bayern München
2002	DEL BOSQUE Vicente	ESP	Real Madrid
2003	ANCELOTTI Carlo, ITA, Milan & MOURINHO Jose, POR, FC Porto
2004	MOURINHO Jose, POR, FC Porto & BENITEZ Raffa, ESP, Valencia
2005	BENITEZ Raffa, ESP, Valencia & GAZZAEV Valeri, RUS, CSKA
2006	RIJKAARD Frank, NED, Barcelona & RAMOS Juande, ESP, Sevilla

PAST EUROPEAN PLAYER OF THE YEAR AWARDS

The Ballon d'Or is awarded by *France Football* magazine and since 1995 has been also open to non Europeans playing with European clubs

BALLON D'OR 1956

MATTHEWS Stanley	Blackpool	ENG	47
DI STEFANO Alfredo	Real Madrid	ESP	44
KOPA Raymond	Reims	FRA	33
PUSKAS Ferenc	Honved	HUN	32
YACHIN Lev	Dyn. Moskva	URS	19
BOZSIK Jozsef	Honved	HUN	15
OCWIRK Ernst	Sampdoria	AUT	9
KOCSIS Sandor	Honved	HUN	6
Three players with four votes			

BALLON D'OR 1957

DI STEFANO Alfredo	Real Madrid	ESP	72
WRIGHT Billy	Wolves	ENG	19
KOPA Raymond	Real Madrid	FRA	16
EDWARDS Duncan	Man United	ENG	16
KUBALA Laszlo	Barcelona	ESP	15
CHARLES John	Juventus	WAL	14
STRELTSOV Eduard	Torp. Moskva	URS	12
TAYLOR Tommy	Man Utd	ENG	10
BOZSIK Jozsef	Honved	HUN	9
NETTO Igor	Dyn. Moskva	URS	9

BALLON D'OR 1958

KOPA Raymond	Real Madrid	FRA	71
RAHN Helmut	RW Essen	FRG	40
FONTAINE Just	Reims	FRA	23
HAMRIN Kurt	Fiorentina	SWE	15
CHARLES John	Juventus	WAL	15
WRIGHT Billy	Wolves	ENG	9
HAYNES Johnny	Fulham	ENG	7
GREGG Harry	Man United	NIR	6
SZYMANIAK Horst	Wuppertaler SV	FRG	6
LIEDHOLM Nils	Milan	SWE	6

BALLON D'OR 1959

DI STEFANO Alfredo	Real Madrid	ESP	80
KOPA Raymond	Reims	FRA	42
CHARLES John	Juventus	WAL	24
SUAREZ Luis	Barcelona	ESP	22
SIMONSSON Agne	Örgryte IS	SWE	20
TICHY Lajos	Honved	HUN	18
PUSKAS Ferenc	Real Madrid	HUN	16
GENTO Francisco	Real Madrid	ESP	12
RAHN Helmut	1.FC Köln	FRG	11
SZYMANIAK Horst	Karlsruher SC	FRG	8

BALLON D'OR 1960

SUAREZ Luis	Barcelona	ESP	54
PUSKAS Ferenc	Real Madrid	HUN	37
SEELER Uwe	Hamburger SV	FRG	33
DI STEFANO Alfredo	Real Madrid	ESP	32
YASHIN Lev	Dyn. Moskva	URS	28
KOPA Raymond	Reims	FRA	14
CHARLES John	Juventus	WAL	11
CHARLTON Bobby	Man United	ENG	11
SIVORI Omar	Juventus	ITA	9
SZYMANIAK Horst	Karlsruher SC	FRG	9

BALLON D'OR 1961

SIVORI Omar	Juventus	ITA	46
SUAREZ Luis	Internazionale	ESP	40
HAYNES Johnny	Fulham	ENG	22
YASHIN Lev	Dyn. Moskva	URS	21
PUSKAS Ferenc	Real Madrid	ESP	16
DI STEFANO Alfredo	Real Madrid	ESP	13
SEELER Uwe	Hamburger SV	FRG	13
CHARLES John	Juventus	WAL	10
GENTO Francisco	Real Madrid	ESP	8
Seven players with five votes			

BALLON D'OR 1962

MASOPUST Josef	Dukla Praha	CZE	65
EUSEBIO	Benfica	POR	53
SCHNELLINGER K-H	1.FC Köln	FRG	33
SEKULARAC Dragoslav	Crvena Zvezda	YUG	26
JURION Jef	Anderlecht	BEL	15
RIVERA Gianni	Milan	ITA	14
GREAVES Jimmy	Tottenham	ENG	11
GALIC Milan	Partizan	YUG	10
CHARLES John	Roma	WAL	9
GOROCS Janos	Ujpesti Dózsa	HUN	6

BALLON D'OR 1963

YACHIN Lev	Dyn. Moskva	URS	73
RIVERA Gianni	Milan	ITA	56
GREAVES Jimmy	Tottenham	ENG	51
LAW Denis	Man United	SCO	45
EUSEBIO	Benfica	POR	19
SCHNELLINGER K-H	Mantova	FRG	16
SEELER Uwe	Hamburger SV	FRG	9
SUAREZ Luis	Internazionale	ESP	5
TRAPATTONI Giovanni	Milan	ITA	5
CHARLTON Bobby	Man United	ENG	5

BALLON D'OR 1964

LAW Denis	Man United	SCO	61
SUAREZ Luis	Internazionale	ESP	43
AMANCIO	Real Madrid	ESP	38
EUSEBIO	Benfica	POR	31
VAN HIMST Paul	Anderlecht	BEL	28
GREAVES Jimmy	Tottenham	ENG	19
CORSO Mario	Internazionale	ITA	17
YACHIN Lev	Dyn. Moskva	URS	15
RIVERA Gianni	Milan	ITA	14
VORONIN Valery	Torp. Moskva	URS	13

BALLON D'OR 1965

EUSEBIO	Benfica	POR	67
FACCHETTI Giacinto	Internazionale	ITA	59
SUAREZ Luis	Internazionale	ITA	45
VAN HIMST Paul	Anderlecht	BEL	25
CHARLTON Bobby	Man United	ENG	19
ALBERT Florian	Ferencváros	HUN	14
RIVERA Gianni	Milan	ITA	10
ASPARUCHOV Georgi	Levski Sofia	BUL	9
MAZZOLA Sandro	Internazionale	ITA	9
VORONIN Valerie	Torp. Moskva	URS	9

BALLON D'OR 1966

CHARLTON Bobby	Man United	ENG	81
EUSEBIO	Benfica	POR	80
BECKENBAUER Franz	Bayern	FRG	59
MOORE Bobby	West Ham Utd	ENG	31
ALBERT Florian	Ferencváros	HUN	23
BENE Ferenc	Ujpesti Dózsa	HUN	8
YACHIN Lev	Dyn. Moskva	URS	6
BALL Alan	Everton	ENG	6
FARKAS János	Vasas	HUN	6
TORRES José	Benfica	POR	5

BALLON D'OR 1967

ALBERT Florian	Ferencváros	HUN	68
CHARLTON Bobby	Man United	ENG	40
JOHNSTONE Jimmy	Celtic	SCO	39
BECKENBAUER Franz	Bayern	FRG	37
EUSEBIO	Benfica	POR	26
GEMMELL Tommy	Celtic	SCO	21
MULLER Gerd	Bayern	FRG	19
BEST George	Man United	NIR	18
CHISLENKO Igor	Torp. Moskva	URS	9
Three players with eight votes			

BALLON D'OR 1968

BEST George	Man United	NIR	61
CHARLTON Bobby	Man United	ENG	53
DZAJIC Dragan	Crvena Zvezda	YUG	46
BECKENBAUER Franz	Bayern	FRG	36
FACCHETTI Giacinto	Internazionale	ITA	30
RIVA Gigi	Cagliari	ITA	22
AMANCIO	Real Madrid	ESP	18
EUSEBIO	Benfica	POR	15
RIVERA Gianni	Milan	ITA	13
Two players with eight votes			

BALLON D'OR 1969

RIVERA Gianni	Milan	ITA	83
RIVA Gigi	Cagliari	ITA	79
MULLER Gerd	Bayern	FRG	38
CRUIJFF Johan	Ajax	NED	30
KINDVALL Ove	Feyenoord	SWE	30
BEST George	Man United	ENG	21
BECKENBAUER Franz	Bayern	FRG	18
PRATI Pierino	Milan	ITA	17
JEKOV Peter	CSKA Sofia	BUL	14
CHARLTON Jack	Leeds United	ENG	10

BALLON D'OR 1970

MULLER Gerd	Bayern	FRG	77
MOORE Bobby	West Ham Utd	ENG	69
RIVA Gigi	Cagliari	ITA	65
BECKENBAUER Franz	Bayern	FRG	32
Wolfgang Overath	1.FC Köln	FRG	29
DZAJIC Dragan	Crvena Zvezda	YUG	24
CRUIJFF Johan	Ajax	NED	13
BANKS Gordon	Stoke City	ENG	8
MAZZOLA Sandro	Internazionale	ITA	8
Four players with seven votes			

BALLON D'OR 1971

CRUIJFF Johan	Ajax	NED	116
MAZZOLA Sandro	Internazionale	ITA	57
BEST George	Man United	NIR	56
NETZER Gunter	Gladbach	FRG	30
BECKENBAUER Franz	Bayern	FRG	27
MULLER Gerd	Bayern	FRG	18
SKOBLAR Josip	Marseille	YUG	18
CHIVERS Martin	Tottenham	ENG	13
KEIZER Piet	Ajax	NED	9
Two players with seven votes			

BALLON D'OR 1972

BECKENBAUER Franz	Bayern	FRG	81
MULLER Gerd	Bayern	FRG	79
NETZER Gunter	Gladbach	FRG	79
CRUIJFF Johan	Ajax	NED	73
KEIZER Piet	Ajax	NED	13
DEYNA Kazimierz	Legia	POL	6
BANKS Gordon	Stoke City	ENG	4
HULSHOFF Barry	Ajax	NED	4
LUBANSKI Wlodzmierz	Gornik Zabrze	POL	4
MOORE Bobby	West Ham Utd	ENG	4

BALLON D'OR 1973

CRUIJFF Johan	Barcelona	NED	96
ZOFF Dino	Juventus	ITA	47
MULLER Gerd	Bayern	FRG	44
BECKENBAUER Franz	Bayern	FRG	30
BREMNER Billy	Leeds United	SCO	22
DEYNA Kazimierz	Legia	POL	16
EUSEBIO	Benfica	POR	14
RIVERA Gianni	Milan	ITA	12
EDSTROM Ralf	Eindhoven	SWE	11
HOENESS Uli	Bayern	FRG	11

BALLON D'OR 1974

CRUIJFF Johan	Barcelona	NED	116
BECKENBAUER Franz	Bayern	FRG	105
DEYNA Kazimierz	Legia	POL	35
BREITNER Paul	Real Madrid	FRG	32
NEESKENS Johan	Barcelona	NED	21
LATO Grzegorz	Stal Mielec	POL	16
MULLER Gerd	Bayern	FRG	14
GADOCHA Robert	Legia	POL	11
BREMNER Billy	Leeds United	SCO	9
Three players with four votes			

BALLON D'OR 1975

BLOKHIN Oleg	Dynamo Kiev	URS	122
BECKENBAUER Franz	Bayern	FRG	42
CRUIJFF Johan	Barcelona	NED	27
VOGTS Berti	Gladbach	FRG	25
MAIER Sepp	Bayern	FRG	20
GEELS Ruud	Ajax	NED	18
HEYNCKES Jupp	Gladbach	FRG	14
BREITNER Paul	Real Madrid	FRG	14
TODD Colin	Derby County	ENG	12
GEORGESCU Dudu	Din. Bucuresti	ROM	11

BALLON D'OR 1976

BECKENBAUER Franz	Bayern	FRG	91
RENSENBRINK Rob	Anderlecht	NED	75
VIKTOR Ivo	Dukla Praha	CZE	52
KEEGAN Kevin	Liverpool	ENG	32
PLATINI Michel	AS Nancy	FRA	19
ONDRUS Anton	Slovan	CZE	16
CRUIJFF Johan	Barcelona	NED	12
CURKOVIC Ivan	Saint-Etienne	YUG	12
Three players with nine votes			

BALLON D'OR 1977

SIMONSEN Allan	Gladbach	DEN	74
KEEGAN Kevin	Liverpool	ENG	71
PLATINI Michel	AS Nancy	FRA	70
BETTEGA Roberto	Juventus	ITA	39
CRUYFF Johan	Barcelona	NED	23
FISCHER Klaus	Schalke 04	FRG	21
NYILASI Tibor	Ferencváros	HUN	13
RENSENBRINK Rob	Anderlecht	NED	13
GEORGESCU Dudu	Din. Bucuresti	ROU	6
3 players with 5 votes			

BALLON D'OR 1978

KEEGAN Kevin	Hamburger SV	ENG	87
KRANKL Hans	Rapid Wien	AUT	81
RENSENBRINK Rob	Anderlecht	NED	50
BETTEGA Roberto	Juventus	ITA	28
ROSSI Paolo	Vicenza	ITA	23
HELLSTROM Ronnie	Kaiserslautern	SWE	20
KROL Ruud	Ajax	NED	20
DALGLISH Kenny	Liverpool	SCO	10
SIMONSEN Allan	Gladbach	DEN	10
SHILTON Peter	Nottm Forest	ENG	9

BALLON D'OR 1979

KEEGAN Kevin	Hamburger SV	ENG	118
RUMMENIGGE K-H	Bayern	FRG	52
KROL Ruud	Ajax	NED	41
KALTZ Manni	Hamburger SV	FRG	27
PLATINI Michel	Saint-Etienne	FRA	23
ROSSI Paolo	Perugia	ITA	16
BRADY Liam	Arsenal	IRL	13
FRANCIS Trevor	Nottm Forest	ENG	13
BONIEK Zbigniew	Wisla Krakow	POL	9
NEHODA Zdenek	Dukla Praha	CZE	9

BALLON D'OR 1980

RUMMENIGGE K-H	Bayern	FRG	122
SCHUSTER Bernd	Barcelona	FRG	34
PLATINI Michel	Saint-Etienne	FRA	33
VAN MOER Wilfried	SK Beveren	BEL	27
CEULEMANS Jan	Club Brugge	BEL	20
HRUBESCH Horst	Hamburger SV	FRG	18
PROHASKA Herbert	Internazionale	AUT	16
MULLER Hansi	VfB Stuttgart	FRG	11
BRADY Liam	Juventus	IRL	11
KALTZ Manni	Hamburger SV	FRG	10

BALLON D'OR 1981

RUMMENIGGE K-H	Bayern	FRG	106
BREITNER Paul	Bayern	FRG	64
SCHUSTER Bernd	Barcelona	FRG	39
PLATINI Michel	Saint-Etienne	FRA	36
BLOKHIN Oleg	Dynamo Kyiv	URS	14
ZOFF Dino	Juventus	ITA	13
SHENGELIA Ramas	Dynamo Tbilisi	URS	10
CHIVADZE Alexander	Dynamo Tbilisi	URS	9
BRADY Liam	Juventus	IRL	7
WARK John	Ipswich Town	SCO	7

BALLON D'OR 1982

ROSSI Paolo	Juventus	ITA	115
GIRESSE Alain	Bordeaux	FRA	64
BONIEK Zbigniew	Juventus	POL	53
RUMMENIGGE K-H	Bayern	FRG	51
CONTI Bruno	Roma	ITA	48
DASAYEV Rinat	Spartak Moskva	URS	17
LITTBARSKI Pierre	1.FC Köln	FRG	10
ZOFF Dino	Juventus	ITA	9
PLATINI Michel	Juventus	FRA	5
SCHUSTER Bernd	Barcelona	FRG	4

BALLON D'OR 1983

PLATINI Michel	Juventus	FRA	110
DALGLISH Kenny	Liverpool	SCO	26
SIMONSEN Allan	Vejle BK	DEN	25
STRACHAN Gordon	Aberdeen	SCO	24
MAGATH Felix	Hamburger SV	FRG	20
DASAYEV Rinat	Spartak Moskva	URS	15
PFAFF Jean-Marie	Bayern	BEL	15
OLSEN Jesper	Ajax	DEN	14
RUMMENIGGE K-H	Bayern	FRG	14
ROBSON Bryan	Man United	ENG	13

BALLON D'OR 1984

PLATINI Michel	Juventus	FRA	128
TIGANA Jean	Bordeaux	FRA	57
ELKJAER Preben	Hellas Verona	DEN	48
RUSH Ian	Liverpool	WAL	44
FERNANDO	Bordeaux	POR	18
SOUNESS Graeme	Sampdoria	SCO	16
SCHUMACHER Harald	1.FC Köln	FRG	12
RUMMENIGGE K-H	Internazionale	FRG	10
GIRESSE Alain	Bordeaux	FRA	9
ROBSON Bryan	Man United	ENG	7

BALLON D'OR 1985

PLATINI Michel	Juventus	FRA	127
ELKJAER Preben	Hellas Verona	DEN	71
SCHUSTER Bernd	Barcelona	FRG	46
LAUDRUP Michael	Juventus	DEN	14
RUMMENIGGE K-H	Internazionale	FRG	13
BONIEK Zbigniew	Roma	POL	12
PROTASOV Oleg	Dnepr	URS	10
BRIEGEL Hans-Peter	Hellas Verona	FRG	9
DASAYEV Rinat	Spartak Moskva	URS	8
ROBSON Bryan	Man United	ENG	8

BALLON D'OR 1986

BELANOV Igor	Dynamo Kyiv	URS	84
LINEKER Gary	Barcelona	ENG	62
BUTRAGUENO Emilio	Real Madrid	ESP	59
AMOROS Manuel	Monaco	FRA	22
ELKJAER Preben	Hellas Verona	DEN	22
RUSH Ian	Liverpool	WAL	20
ZAVAROV Alexander	Dynamo Kyiv	URS	20
VAN BASTEN Marco	Ajax	NED	10
DUCKADAM Helmuth	Steaua	ROU	10
ALTOBELLI Alessandro	Internazionale	ITA	9

BALLON D'OR 1987

GULLIT Ruud	Milan	NED	106
FUTRE Paolo	Atlético Madrid	POR	91
BUTRAGUENO Emilio	Real Madrid	ESP	61
MICHEL Gonzales	Real Madrid	ESP	29
LINEKER Gary	Barcelona	ENG	13
BARNES John	Liverpool	ENG	10
VAN BASTEN Marco	Milan	NED	10
VIALLI Gianluca	Sampdoria	ITA	9
ROBSON Bryan	Man United	ENG	7
ALLOFS Klaus	Marseille	FRG	6

BALLON D'OR 1988

VAN BASTEN Marco	Milan	NED	129
GULLIT Ruud	Milan	NED	88
RIJKAARD Frank	Milan	NED	45
MIKHAILICHENKO Alex	Dynamo Kyiv	URS	41
KOEMAN Ronald	PSV	NED	39
MATTHAUS Lothar	Bayern	FRG	10
VIALLI Gianluca	Sampdoria	ITA	7
BARESI Franco	Milan	ITA	5
KLINSMANN Jürgen	VfB Stuttgart	FRG	5
ZAVAROV Aleksandr	Juventus	URS	5

BALLON D'OR 1989

VAN BASTEN Marco	Milan	NED	119
BARESI Franco	Milan	ITA	80
RIJKAARD Frank	Milan	NED	43
MATTHAUS Lothar	Internazionale	FRG	24
SHILTON Peter	Derby County	ENG	22
STOJKOVIC Dragan	Crvena Zvezda	YUG	19
GULLIT Ruud	Milan	NED	16
HAGI Gheorghe	Steaua	ROU	11
KLINSMANN Jürgen	Internazionale	FRG	11
Two players with 10 votes			

BALLON D'OR 1990

MATTHAUS Lothar	Internazionale	FRG	137
SCHILLACI Salvadore	Juventus	ITA	84
BREHME Andreas	Internazionale	FRG	68
GASCOIGNE Paul	Tottenham	ENG	43
BARESI Franco	Milan	ITA	37
KLINSMANN Jürgen	Internazionale	FRG	12
SCIFO Enzo	AJ Auxerre	BEL	12
BAGGIO Roberto	Juventus	ITA	8
RIJKAARD Frank	Milan	NED	7
BUCHWALD Guido	VfB Stuttgart	FRG	6

BALLON D'OR 1991

PAPIN Jean-Pierre	Marseille	FRA	141
PANCEV Darko	Crvena Zvezda	YUG	42
SAVICEVIC Dejan	Crvena Zvezda	YUG	42
MATTHAUS Lothar	Internazionale	FRG	42
PROSINECKI Robert	Real Madrid	YUG	34
LINEKER Gary	Tottenham	ENG	33
VIALLI Gianluca	Sampdoria	ITA	18
BELODEDICI Miodrag	Crvena Zvezda	YUG	15
HUGHES Mark	Man United	WAL	12
WADDLE Chris	Marseille	ENG	11

BALLON D'OR 1992

Player	Club	Nat	Pts
VAN BASTEN Marco	Milan	NED	98
STOICHKOV Hristo	Barcelona	BUL	80
BERGKAMP Dennis	Ajax	NED	53
HASSLER Thomas	Roma	GER	42
SCHMEICHEL Peter	Man United	DEN	41
LAUDRUP Brian	Fiorentina	DEN	32
LAUDRUP Michael	Barcelona	DEN	22
KOEMAN Ronald	Barcelona	NED	14
CHAPUISAT Stéphane	Dortmund	SUI	10
Two players with eight votes			

BALLON D'OR 1993

Player	Club	Nat	Pts
BAGGIO Roberto	Juventus	ITA	142
BERGKAMP Dennis	Internazionale	NED	83
CANTONA Eric	Man United	FRA	34
BOKSIC Alen	Lazio	CRO	29
LAUDRUP Michael	Barcelona	DEN	27
BARESI Franco	Milan	ITA	24
MALDINI Paolo	Milan	ITA	19
KOSTADINOV Emil	FC Porto	BUL	11
CHAPUISAT Stéphane	Dortmund	SUI	9
GIGGS Ryan	Man United	WAL	9

BALLON D'OR 1994

Player	Club	Nat	Pts
STOICHKOV Hristo	Barcelona	BUL	210
BAGGIO Roberto	Juventus	ITA	136
MALDINI Paolo	Milan	ITA	109
BROLIN Tomas	Parma	SWE	68
HAGI Gheorghe	Barcelona	ROU	68
KLINSMANN Jürgen	Tottenham	GER	43
RAVELLI Thomas	IFK Göteborg	SWE	21
LITMANEN Jari	Ajax	FIN	12
DESAILLY Marcel	Milan	FRA	8
SAVICEVIC Dejan	Milan	YUG	8

BALLON D'OR 1995

Player	Club	Nat	Pts
WEAH George	Milan	LBR	144
KLINSMANN Jürgen	Bayern	GER	108
LITMANEN Jari	Ajax	FIN	67
DEL PIERO Alex	Juventus	ITA	57
KLUIVERT Patrick	Ajax	NED	47
ZOLA Gianfranco	Parma	ITA	41
MALDINI Paolo	Milan	ITA	36
OVERMARS Marc	Ajax	NED	33
SAMMER Matthias	Dortmund	GER	18
LAUDRUP Michael	Real Madrid	DEN	17

BALLON D'OR 1996

Player	Club	Nat	Pts
SAMMER Matthias	Dortmund	GER	144
RONALDO	Barcelona	BRA	141
SHEARER Alan	Newcastle Utd	ENG	109
DEL PIERO Alex	Juventus	ITA	65
KLINSMANN Jürgen	Bayern	GER	60
SUKER Davor	Real Madrid	CRO	38
CANTONA Eric	Man United	FRA	24
DESAILLY Marcel	Milan	FRA	22
DJORKAEFF Youri	Internazionale	FRA	20
WEAH George	Milan	LBR	17

BALLON D'OR 1997

Player	Club	Nat	Pts
RONALDO	Internazionale	BRA	222
MIJATOVIC Predrag	Real Madrid	YUG	72
ZIDANE Zinedine	Juventus	FRA	63
BERGKAMP Dennis	Arsenal	NED	53
ROBERTO CARLOS	Real Madrid	BRA	47
MOLLER Andreas	Dortmund	GER	40
RAUL	Real Madrid	ESP	35
SCHMEICHEL Peter	Man United	DEN	19
KOHLER Jürgen	Dortmund	GER	17
Two players with 16 votes			

BALLON D'OR 1998

Player	Club	Nat	Pts
ZIDANE Zinedine	Juventus	FRA	244
SUKER Davor	Real Madrid	CRO	68
RONALDO	Internazionale	BRA	66
OWEN Michael	Liverpool	ENG	51
RIVALDO	Barcelona	BRA	45
BATISTUTA Gabriel	Fiorentina	ARG	43
THURAM Lilian	Parma	FRA	36
BERGKAMP Dennis	Arsenal	NED	28
DAVIDS Edgar	Juventus	NED	28
DESAILLY Marcel	Chelsea	FRA	19

BALLON D'OR 1999

Player	Club	Nat	Pts
RIVALDO	Barcelona	BRA	219
BECKHAM David	Man United	ENG	154
SHEVCHENKO Andriy	Milan	UKR	64
BATISTUTA Gabriel	Fiorentina	ARG	48
FIGO	Barcelona	POR	38
KEANE Roy	Man United	IRL	38
VIERI Christian	Internazionale	ITA	33
VERON Juan Seb.	Lazio	ARG	30
RAUL	Real Madrid	ESP	27
MATTHAUS Lothar	Bayern	GER	16

BALLON D'OR 2000

Player	Club	Nat	Pts
FIGO	Real Madrid	POR	197
ZIDANE Zinedine	Juventus	FRA	181
SHEVCHENKO Andriy	Milan	UKR	85
HENRY Thierry	Arsenal	FRA	57
NESTA Alessandro	Lazio	ITA	39
RIVALDO	Barcelona	BRA	39
BATISTUTA Gabriel	Roma	ARG	26
MENDIETA Gaizka	Valencia	ESP	22
RAUL	Real Madrid	ESP	18
Two players with 10 votes			

BALLON D'OR 2001

Player	Club	Nat	Pts
OWEN Michael	Liverpool	ENG	176
RAUL	Real Madrid	ESP	140
KAHN Oliver	Bayern	GER	114
BECKHAM David	Man United	ENG	102
TOTTI Francesco	Roma	ITA	57
FIGO	Real Madrid	POR	56
RIVALDO	Barcelona	BRA	20
SHEVCHENKO Andriy	Milan	UKR	18
HENRY Thierry	Arsenal	FRA	14
ZIDANE Zinedine	Real Madrid	FRA	14

BALLON D'OR 2002

Player	Club	Nat	Pts
RONALDO	Real Madrid	BRA	171
ROBERTO CARLOS	Real Madrid	BRA	145
KAHN Oliver	Bayern	GER	114
ZIDANE Zinedine	Real Madrid	FRA	78
BALLACK Michael	Bayern	GER	67
HENRY Thierry	Arsenal	FRA	54
RAUL	Real Madrid	ESP	38
RIVALDO	Milan	BRA	29
BASTURK Yildiray	Leverkusen	TUR	13
DEL PIERO Alex	Juventus	ITA	12

BALLON D'OR 2003

Player	Club	Nat	Pts
NEDVED Pavel	Juventus	CZE	190
HENRY Thierry	Arsenal	FRA	128
MALDINI Paolo	Milan	ITA	123
SHEVCHENKO Andriy	Milan	UKR	67
ZIDANE Zinedine	Real Madrid	FRA	64
VAN NISTELROOU Ruud	Man United	NED	61
RAUL	Real Madrid	ESP	32
ROBERTO CARLOS	Real Madrid	BRA	27
BUFFON Gianluigi	Juventus	ITA	19
BECKHAM David	Real Madrid	ENG	17

BALLON D'OR 2004

Player	Club	Nat	Pts
SHEVCHENKO Andriy	Milan	UKR	175
DECO	Barcelona	POR	139
RONALDINHO	Barcelona	BRA	133
HENRY Thierry	Arsenal	FRA	80
ZAGORAKIS Theodoros	Bologna	GRE	44
ADRIANO	Internazionale	BRA	23
NEDVED Pavel	Juventus	CZE	23
ROONEY Wayne	Man United	ENG	22
RICARDO CARVALHO	Chelsea	POR	18
VAN NISTELROOU Ruud	Man United	NED	18

BALLON D'OR 2005

Player	Club	Nat	Pts
RONALDINHO	Barcelona	BRA	225
LAMPARD Frank	Chelsea	ENG	148
GERRARD Steven	Liverpool	ENG	142
HENRY Thierry	Arsenal	FRA	41
SHEVCHENKO Andriy	Milan	UKR	33
MALDINI Paolo	Milan	ITA	23
ADRIANO	Internazionale	BRA	22
IBRAHIMOVIC Zlatan	Juventus	SWE	21
KAKA	Milan	BRA	19
Two players with 18 votes			

BALLON D'OR 2006

Player	Club	Nat	Pts
CANNAVARO Fabio	Real Madrid	ITA	173
BUFFON Gianluigi	Juventus	ITA	124
HENRY Thierry	Arsenal	FRA	121
RONALDINHO	Barcelona	BRA	73
ZIDANE Zinedine	Real Madrid	FRA	71
ETO'O Samuel	Barcelona	CMR	67
KLOSE Miroslav	Werder Bremen	GER	29
DROGBA Didier	Chelsea	CIV	25
PIRLO Andrea	Milan	ITA	17
LEHMAN Jens	Arsenal	GER	13

UEFA EURO 2008 QUALIFIERS

QUALIFYING GROUPS

Group A		Pts	Group B		Pts	Group C		Pts	Group D		Pts
Poland	POL	19	France	FRA	18	Greece	GRE	18	Germany	GER	19
Serbia	SRB	14	Italy	ITA	16	Bosnia-H'cegovina	BIH	13	Czech Republic	CZE	14
Portugal	POR	14	Scotland	SCO	15	Turkey	TUR	13	Rep. of Ireland	IRL	13
Finland	FIN	14	Ukraine	UKR	12	Norway	NOR	13	Slovakia	SVK	9
Belgium	BEL	7	Lithuania	LTU	7	Hungary	HUN	6	Wales	WAL	7
Armenia	ARM	7	Georgia	GEO	6	Malta	MLT	4	Cyprus	CYP	4
Kazakhstan	KAZ	6	Faroe Islands	FRO	0	Moldova	MDA	2	San Marino	SMR	0
Azerbaijan	AZE	5									

Group E		Pts	Group F		Pts	Group G		Pts
Croatia	CRO	17	Sweden	SWE	16	Romania	ROU	17
Israel	ISR	17	Spain	ESP	15	Bulgaria	BUL	15
Russia	RUS	15	Northern Ireland	NIR	13	Netherlands	NED	14
England	ENG	14	Denmark	DEN	11	Albania	ALB	9
FYR Macedonia	MKD	7	Iceland	ISL	4	Belarus	BLR	7
Estonia	EST	0	Liechtenstein	LIE	4	Slovenia	SVN	4
Andorra	AND	0	Latvia	LVA	3	Luxembourg	LUX	0

Tables as of August 15, 2006 • Austria and Switzerland qualified automatically as hosts • The final tournament will be held in both countries from June 7 to June 29, 2008, with the final in Vienna • The top two in each qualifying group qualify for the finals

GROUP A

Constant Vanden Stock, Brussels				Crvena Zvezda, Belgrade			
16-08-2006, 20:45, 15 495, Courtney NIR				2-09-2006, 20:15, BCD, Kircher GER			
BEL	**0**	**0**	**KAZ**	**SRB**	**1**	**0**	**AZE**

Zigic [72]

BELGIUM				KAZAKHSTAN			SERBIA				AZERBAIJAN		
1	STIJNEN Stijn			LORIA David	1		1	STOJKOVIC Vladimir			VELIYEV Farkhad	1	
15	VERMAELEN Thomas			KUCHMA Aleksandr	3		21	MARKOVIC Marjan			GASHIMOV Zaur	2	
3	SIMONS Timmy			SMAKOV Samat	5		5	STEPANOV Milan			ABBASOV Ruslan	15	
4	VAN BUYTEN Daniel			AZOVSKIY Yegor	2		20	KRSTAJIC Mladen			KERIMOV Aslan	8	
27	KOMPANY Vincent	38	54	KARPOVITCH Andrei	6		3	LUKOVIC Aleksandar			SOKOLOV Sergei	5	
5	VAN DAMME Jelle	60		SERGIENKO Eduard	7		4	DULJAJ Igor			BAKHSHIEV Elmar	6	
13	HOEFKENS Carl	74		KHOKHLOV Nikita	8		7	KOROMAN Ognjen	64	77	LADAGA Andre	4	
8	GOOR Bart			BYAKOV Dmitriy	9		10	STANKOVIC Dejan		62	MUZIKA Yuri	17	
10	BUFFEL Thomas			BALTIEV Ruslan	10		8	LAZOVIC Danko	74		IMAMALIEV Emin	19	
22	GERAERTS Karel			ZHALMAGAMBETOV Maksim	4		9	PANTELIC Marko	81		CHERTOGANOV Aleksandr	22	
18	DEMBELE Moussa			ZHUMASKALIYEV Nurbol	11		19	ZIGIC Nikola		72	ISMAYLOV Farrukh	16	
	Tr: VANDEREYCKEN René			Tr: PIJPERS Arno				Tr: CLEMENTE Javier			Tr: DINIYEV Shakhin		
16	PIERONI Luigi	60	54	TRAVIN Andrei	16		2	ERGIC Ivan	74	72	MUSAEV Samir	9	
17	HUYSEGEMS Stein	38					22	ILIC Sasa	64	62	GURBANOV Ilgar	18	
20	VANDEN BORRE Anthony	74					11	LJUBOJA Danijel	81	77	DZAVADOV Vagif	20	

The Krzyszkowiak, Bydgoszcz
2-09-2006, 20:30, 13 000, Duhamel FRA

POL	1	3	FIN

Gargula [89]
Litmanen 2 [54 76p], Väyrynen [84]

#	POLAND		
1	DUDEK Jerzy		
3	WASILEWSKI Marcin		
5	GLOWACKI Arkadiusz		
6	BAK Jacek		
2	ZEWLAKOW Michal		
15	BLASZCZYKOWSKI Jakub	46	
10	SZYMKOWIAK Miroslaw	46	
16	RADOMSKI Arkadiusz	75	78
8	KRZYNOWEK Jacek		86
9	ZURAWSKI Maciej		66
11	FRANKOWSKI Tomasz	73	
	Tr: JANAS Pawel		
7	SMOLAREK Euzebiusz	46	78
13	GARGULA Lukasz	73	86
20	JELEN Ireneusz	46	66

#	FINLAND		
22	JAASKELAINEN Jussi		
5	TIHINEN Hannu		
4	HYYPIA Sami		
19	KALLIO Toni		
6	TAINIO Teemu		
2	PASANEN Petri		
23	HEIKKINEN Markus		
11	KOLKKA Joonas		
10	LITMANEN Jari		
21	JOHANSSON Jonatan		
8	VAYRYNEN Mika		
	Tr: HODGSON Roy		
7	NURMELA Mika		78
9	FORSSELL Mikael		86
20	EREMENKO Jr Alexei		66

Tofikh Bakhramov, Baku
6-09-2006, 19:00, 8500, Szabó HUN

AZE	1	1	KAZ

Ladaga [16]
Byakov [36]

#	AZERBAIJAN		
1	VELIYEV Farkhad		
8	KERIMOV Aslan		
5	SOKOLOV Sergei	58	
15	ABBASOV Ruslan	46	
4	LADAGA Andre		
10	SULTANOV Dzeykhun	65	
16	CHERTOGANOV Aleksandr		
19	IMAMALIEV Emin		
20	DZAVADOV Vagif		
18	GURBANOV Ilgar		
7	GOMES Leandro		
	Tr: DINIYEV Shakhin		
9	MUSAEV Samir	65	
17	MUZIKA Yuri	58	
20	MELIKOV Rail	46	

	KAZAKHSTAN		#
	LORIA David		1
	AZOVSKIY Yegor		2
	KUCHMA Aleksandr		3
	ZHALMAGAMBETOV Maksim		4
	SMAKOV Samat		5
66	KARPOVITCH Andrei		6
	SERGIENKO Eduard		7
	KHOKHLOV Nikita		8
	BYAKOV Dmitriy		9
	BALTIEV Ruslan		10
74	ZHUMASKALIYEV Nurbol		11
	Tr: PUPERS Arno		
74	UTABAYEV Kairat		15
66	TRAVIN Andrei		16

Olympiastadion, Helsinki
6-09-2006, 20:00, 38 010, Plautz AUT

FIN	1	1	POR

Johansson [22]
Nuno Gomes [42]

#	FINLAND		
22	JAASKELAINEN Jussi		
19	KALLIO Toni		
4	HYYPIA Sami		
5	TIHINEN Hannu		
2	PASANEN Petri		
11	KOLKKA Joonas	81	
6	TAINIO Teemu		
8	VAYRYNEN Mika		85
10	LITMANEN Jari		56
23	HEIKKINEN Markus		
21	JOHANSSON Jonatan	63	75
	Tr: HODGSON Roy		
18	KUQI Shefki	63	
20	EREMENKO Jr Alexei	81	

	PORTUGAL		#
	RICARDO		1
	MARCO CANEIRA		3
53	RICARDO COSTA		4
	RICARDO CARVALHO		16
	NUNO VALENTE		14
	COSTINHA		6
	PETIT		8
85	DECO		20
56	NANI		32
	CRISTIANO RONALDO		17
75	NUNO GOMES		21
	Tr: SCOLARI Luiz Felipe		
85	TIAGO		19
75	JOAO MOUTINHO		28
56	RICARDO ROCHA		29

Wojska Polskiego, Warsaw
6-09-2006, 20:30, 4918, Poll ENG

POL	1	1	SRB

Matusiak [30]
Lazovic [71]

#	POLAND		
1	KOWALEWSKI Wojciech		
4	GOLANSKI Pawel	72	
2	JOP Mariusz		
6	BAK Jacek		
14	ZEWLAKOW Michal		
11	JELEN Ireneusz	73	67
18	LEWANDOWSKI Mariusz		
16	RADOMSKI Arkadiusz		
8	KRZYNOWEK Jacek		60
9	ZURAWSKI Maciej		82
19	MATUSIAK Radoslaw		
	Tr: BEENHAKKER Leo		
3	WASILEWSKI Marcin	72	67
15	BLASZCZYKOWSKI Jakub	73	

	SERBIA		#
	STOJKOVIC Vladimir		1
	MARKOVIC Marjan		21
	STEPANOV Milan		5
	BISEVAC Milan		6
	KRSTAJIC Mladen		20
67	DULJAJ Igor		4
	KOVACEVIC Nenad		16
	STANKOVIC Dejan		10
	TRISOVIC Aleksandar		14
	PANTELIC Marko		9
	ZIGIC Nikola		19
	Tr: CLEMENTE Javier		
67	ERGIC Ivan		2
82	KOROMAN Ognjen		7
60	LAZOVIV Danko		8

Republican, Yerevan
6-09-2006, 21:00, 4122, Lehner AUT

ARM	0	1	BEL

Van Buyten [41]

#	ARMENIA		
1	KASPAROV Gevorg		
4	HOVSEPYAN Sargis		
5	ARZUMANYAN Robert		
3	DOKHOYAN Karen		
2	MELIKYAN Egishe		
6	KHACHATRYAN Romik		66
15	ALEKSANYAN Karen		
7	MKRTCHYAN Agvan	76	57
9	MIKHITARYAN Hamlet	81	
14	MELKONYAN Samvel		77
10	SHAHGELDYAN Armen	72	
	Tr:		
8	HAKOBYAN Feliks	72	66
11	KARAMYAN Arman	76	77
17	PETROSYAN Galust	81	59

	BELGIUM		#
	STIJNEN Stijn		1
	HOEFKENS Carl		13
	SIMONS Timmy		3
	VAN DAMME Jelle		4
	VAN BUYTEN Daniel		5
66	DAERDEN Koen		7
	ENGLEBERT Gaetan		11
57	COLLEN Pieter		2
	GERAERTS Karel		22
77	DEMBELE Moussa		18
	PIERONI Luigi		16
	Tr: VANDEREYCKEN René		
66	GOOR Bart		8
77	DEFOUR Steven		14
59	VANDEN BORRE Anthony		20

Crvena Zvezda, Belgrade
7-10-2006, 20:15, 16 901, Messina ITA

SRB	1	0	BEL

Zigic [54]

#	SERBIA		
1	STOJKOVIC Vladimir		
21	MARKOVIC Marjan		
5	VIDIC Nemanja		
20	KRSTAJIC Mladen		
3	DRAGUTINOVIC Ivica		
16	KOVACEVIC Nenad		
10	STANKOVIC Dejan		
7	KOROMAN Ognjen	71	75
14	TRISOVIC Aleksandar	58	84
9	PANTELIC Marko	91+	
19	ZIGIC Nikola		
	Tr: CLEMENTE Javier		
4	DULJAJ Igor	91+	62
2	ERGIC Ivan	71	75
8	LAZOVIC Danko	58	84

	BELGIUM		#
	STIJNEN Stijn		1
	KOMPANY Vincent		27
	HOEFKENS Carl		13
	SIMONS Timmy		3
	VERMAELEN Thomas		4
	VAN BUYTEN Daniel		5
	GERAERTS Karel		22
75	MUDINGAYI Gaby		6
84	GOOR Bart		8
62	DEMBELE Moussa		18
	Tr: VANDEREYCKEN René		
75	MPENZA Mbo		11
84	PIERONI Luigi		16
62	VANDENBERGH Kevin		19

Estádio do Bessa, Porto
7-10-2006, 21:00, 14 000, Halsey ENG

POR	3	0	AZE

Ronaldo 2 [25][63], Carvalho [31]

PORTUGAL			AZERBAIJAN	
1 RICARDO			VELIYEV Farkhad	1
13 LUIS MIGUEL			GASHIMOV Zaur	2
16 RICARDO CARVALHO			PEREIRA Ernani	3
33 RICARDO ROCHA			SOKOLOV Sergei	5
14 NUNO VALENTE	45		KERIMOV Aslan	8
6 COSTINHA			LADAGA Andre	4
18 MANICHE	64		CHERTOGANOV Aleksandr	22
20 DECO			IMAMALIEV Emin	19
17 CRISTIANO RONALDO	73	66	MUZIKA Yuri	17
21 NUNO GOMES		64	SULTANOV Dzeykhun	10
11 SIMAO		76	GOMES Leandro	7
Tr: SCOLARI Luiz Felipe			Tr: DINIYEV Shakhin	
3 MARCO CANEIRA	45	64	ISMAYLOV Farrukh	16
19 TIAGO	64	66	GURBANOV Ilgar	18
32 NANI	73	76	DZAVADOV Vagif	20

Republican, Yerevan
7-10-2006, 12:00, 2800, Skomina SVN

ARM	0	0	FIN

ARMENIA			FINLAND	
1 KASPAROV Gevorg			JAASKELAINEN Jussi	22
4 HOVSEPYAN Sargis			PASANEN Petri	2
5 ARZUMANYAN Robert			HYYPIA Sami	4
3 DOKHOYAN Karen			TIHINEN Hannu	5
2 MELIKYAN Egishe		73	VAYRYNEN Mika	6
14 MELKONYAN Samvel			LITMANEN Jari	10
6 TIGRANYAN Armen			KOLKKA Joonas	11
15 ALEKSANYAN Karen	54	66	KUQI Shefki	18
11 KARAMYAN Arman	45		KALLIO Toni	19
10 SHAHGELDYAN Armen		83	JOHANSSON Jonatan	21
9 MANUCHARYAN Edgar	78		HEIKKINEN Markus	23
Tr: PORTERFIELD Ian			Tr: HODGSON Roy	
7 HAKOBYAN Ara	78	73	NURMELA Mika	7
13 HAKOBYAN Aram	54	66	FORSSELL Mikael	9
17 MKRTCHYAN Agvan	45	83	RIIHILATI Aki	16

Centralny, Almaty
7-10-2006, 21:00, 22 000, Trivkovic CRO

KAZ	0	1	POL

Smolarek [52]

KAZAKHSTAN			POLAND	
1 LORIA David			KOWALEWKI Wojciech	1
2 AZOVSKIY Yegor			BRONOWICKI Grzegorz	3
3 Kuchma Aleksandr			GOLANSKI Pawel	4
4 ZHALMAGAMBETOV Maksim		87	BLASZCZYKOWSKI Jakub	5
5 SMAKOV Samat			BAK Jacek	6
6 KARPOVITCH Andrei	59		SMOLAREK Euzebiusz	7
7 SERGIENKO Eduard	81		SOBOLEWSKI Radoslaw	8
8 KHOKHLOV Nikita		71	ZURAWSKI Maciej	9
9 BYAKOV Dmitriy			RASIAK Grzegorz	11
10 ZHUMASKALIYEV Nurbol			RADOMSKI Arkadiusz	16
11 UTABAYEV Kairat	68	30	LEWANDOWSKI Mariusz	18
Tr: PIJPERS Arno			Tr: BEENHAKKER Leo	
15 ASHIRBEKOV Kairat	68	87	GRZELAK Rafal	13
17 LARIN Sergey	81	30	KAZMIERCZAK Przemyslaw	17
16 TRAVIN Andrei	59	71	MATUSIAK Radoslaw	19

Crvena Zvezda, Beograd
11-10-2006, 20:15, 10 987, Kasnaferis GRE

SRB	3	0	ARM

Stankovic [54p], Lazovic [62], Zigic [92+]

SERBIA			ARMENIA	
1 STOJKOVIC Vladimir			KASPAROV Gevorg	1
3 DRAGUTINOVIC Ivica			HOVSEPYAN Sargis	4
15 STEPANOV Milan			ARZUMANYAN Robert	5
20 KRSTAJIC Mladen			DOKHOYAN Karen	3
4 DULIAJ Igor		76	NAZARYAN Rafael	8
16 KOVACEVIC Nenad			MELIKYAN Egishe	2
10 STANKOVIC Dejan			MELKONYAN Samvel	14
7 KOROMAN Ognjen	72		MKRTCHYAN Agvan	17
14 TRISOVIC Aleksandar	45	69	HAKOBYAN Aram	13
9 PANTELIC Marko	45	79	MANUCHARYAN Edgar	9
19 ZIGIC Nikola		65	SHAHGELDYAN Armen	10
Tr: CLEMENTE Javier			Tr: PORTERFIELD Ian	
2 ERGIC Ivan	72	79	TIGRANYAN Armen	6
22 ILIC Sasa	45	69	MINASYAN Arthur	15
8 LAZOVIC Danko	45	65	ERZRUMYAN Nshan	16

Slaski, Chorzow
11-10-2006, 20:30, 38 199, Stark GER

POL	2	1	POR

Smolarek 2 [9][18]   Nuno Gomes [92+]

POLAND			PORTUGAL	
1 KOWALEWKI Wojciech			RICARDO	1
3 BRONOWICKI Grzegorz			LUIS MIGUEL	13
4 GOLANSKI Pawel			NUNO VALENTE	14
6 BAK Jacek			RICARDO CARVALHO	16
18 LEWANDOWSKI Mariusz			RICARDO ROCHA	33
5 BLASZCZYKOWSKI Jakub	65	83	DECO	20
7 SMOLAREK Euzebiusz		68	PETIT	8
14 SOBOLEWSKI Radoslaw		45	COSTINHA	6
16 RADOMSKI Arkadiusz			SIMAO	11
9 ZURAWSKI Maciej			NUNO GOMES	21
11 RASIAK Grzegorz	73		CRISTIANO RONALDO	17
Tr: BEENHAKKER Leo			Tr: SCOLARI Luiz Felipe	
8 KRZYNOWEK Jacek	65	45	TIAGO	19
19 MATUSIAK Radoslaw	73	83	MANICHE	18
		68	NANI	32

Constant Vanden Stock, Brussels
11-10-2006, 20:45, 11 917, Lajuks LVA

BEL	3	0	AZE

Simons [24p], Vandenbergh [47],
Dembélé [82]

BELGIUM			AZERBAIJAN	
1 STIJNEN Stijn			VELIYEV Farkhad	1
3 SIMONS Timmy		77	GASHIMOV Zaur	2
4 VERMAELEN Thomas			SOKOLOV Sergei	5
20 VANDEN BORRE Anthony	77		KERIMOV Aslan	8
14 LEONARD Philippe			PEREIRA Ernani	3
5 VAN BUYTEN Daniel			LADAGA Andre	4
13 HOEFKENS Carl		33	MUZIKA Yuri	17
22 GERAERTS Karel		55	SULTANOV Dzeykhun	10
8 GOOR Bart			IMAMALIEV Emin	19
9 MPENZA Emile	70		CHERTOGANOV Aleksandr	22
19 VANDENBERGH Kevin	86		GOMES Leandro	7
Tr: VANDEREYCKEN René			Tr: DINIYEV Shakhin	
11 MPENZA Mbo	77	33	GURBANOV Ilgar	18
16 PIERONI Luigi	86	77	NADYROV Vugar	15
18 DEMBELE Moussa	70 [87]	55	DZAVADOV Vagif	20

Centralny, Almaty
11-10-2006, 22:00, 17 863, Briakos GRE

KAZ 0 2 FIN

Litmanen [27], Hyypia [62]

KAZAKHSTAN			FINLAND		
1 LORIA David			JAASKELAINEN Jussi	22	
5 SMAKOV Samat			PASANEN Petri	2	
3 KUCHMA Aleksandr			HYYPIA Sami	4	
4 ZHALMAGAMBETOV Maksim			TIHINEN Hannu	5	
2 AZOVSKIY Yegor			LITMANEN Jari	10	
10 BALTIEV Ruslan			KOLKKA Joonas	11	
8 KHOKHLOV Nikita			ILOLA Jari	15	
6 TRAVIN Andrei	82	92+	VAYRYNEN Mika	6	
7 SERGIENKO Eduard	76		NURMELA Mika	7	
11 ZHUMASKALIYEV Nurbol	63	72	FORSSELL Mikael	9	
9 BYAKOV Dmitriy			KALLIO Toni	19	
Tr: PIJPERS Arno			Tr: HODGSON Roy		
14 ASHIRBEKOV Kairat	63	92+	RIIHILATI Aki	16	
16 AZOVSKIY Maksim	82	72	KUQI Shefki	18	
17 LARIN Sergey	76				

Finnair, Helsinki
15-11-2006, 19:00, 9445, Thomson SCO

FIN 1 0 ARM

Nurmela [10]

FINLAND			ARMENIA		
22 JAASKELAINEN Jussi			KASPAROV Gevorg	1	
4 HYYPIA Sami		46	DOKHOYAN Karen	3	
28 NYMAN Ari			HOVSEPYAN Sargis	4	
5 TIHINEN Hannu			TADEVOSYAN Aleksandr	18	
23 HEIKKINEN Markus			PACHAJYAN Levon	15	
19 KALLIO Toni		75	MKHITARYAN Hamlet	9	
11 KOLKKA Joonas			KHACHATRYAN Romik	6	
20 EREMENKO Jr Alexei	88		MKRTCHYAN Agvan	17	
6 VAYRYNEN Mika	47		KARAMYAN Artavazd	13	
21 JOHANSSON Jonatan		78	ZEBELYAN Robert	14	
7 NURMELA Mika			SHAHGELDYAN Armen	10	
Tr: HODGSON Roy			Tr: PORTERFIELD Ian		
15 ILOLA Jari	47	75	HAKOBYAN Ara	7	
18 KUQI Shefki	88	46	ALEKSANYAN Valeri	5	
		78	KARAMYAN Arman	11	

Roi Baudouin, Brussels
15-11-2006, 20:30, 37 928, Dougal SCO

BEL 0 1 POL

Matusiak [19]

BELGIUM			POLAND		
1 STIJNEN Stijn			BORUC Artur	1	
2 VERMAELEN Thomas		79	DUDKA Dariusz	2	
3 SIMONS Timmy			BRONOWICKI Grzegorz	3	
5 VAN BUYTEN Daniel			WASILEWSKI Marcin	13	
13 HOEFKENS Carl			BAK Jacek	6	
14 LEONARD Philippe	80		ZEWLAKOW Michal	14	
20 VANDEN BORRE Anthony	45		SOBOLEWSKI Radoslaw	8	
8 GOOR Bart			BLASZCZYKOWSKI Jakub	5	
22 GERAERTS Karel			SMOLAREK Euzebiusz	7	
9 MPENZA Emile		62	ZURAWSKI Maciej	9	
19 VANDENBERGH Kevin	62	89	MATUSIAK Radoslaw	11	
Tr: VANDEREYCKEN René			Tr: BEENHAKKER Leo		
6 MUDINGAYI Gaby	80	89	KAZMIERCZAK Przemyslaw	17	
10 PIERONI Luigi	62	62	GARGULA Lukasz	18	
17 HUYSEGEMS Stein	45	79	MURAWSKI Rafal	15	

Cidade de Coimbra, Coimbra
15-11-2006, 21:00, 29 500, Rogalla SUI

POR 3 0 KAZ

Simão 2 [8 86], Ronaldo [30]

PORTUGAL			KAZAKHSTAN		
1 RICARDO			LORIA David	1	
13 LUIS MIGUEL			KUCHMA Aleksandr	3	
2 PAULO FERREIRA			ZHALMAGAMBETOV Maksim	4	
16 RICARDO CARVALHO			SMAKOV Samat	5	
36 TONEL	77		AZOVSKIY Yegor	2	
19 TIAGO			TRAVIN Andrei	6	
20 DECO	63	74	SERGIENKO Eduard	7	
25 RAUL MEIRELES			KHOKHLOV Nikita	8	
17 CRISTIANO RONALDO	58		BYAKOV Dmitriy	9	
11 SIMAO			BALTIEV Ruslan	10	
21 NUNO GOMES			ZHUMASKALIYEV Nurbol	11	
Tr: SCOLARI Luiz Felipe			Tr: PIJPERS Arno		
30 CARLOS MARTINS	63	74	LARIN Sergey	15	
27 RICARDO QUARESMA	58				
4 JORGE ANDRADE	77				

Wojska Polskiego, Warsaw
24-03-2007, 18:00, 13 000, Jakobsson ISL

POL 5 0 AZE

Bak [3], Dudka [6], Lobodzinski [34], Krzynówek [58], Kázmierczak [84]

POLAND			AZERBAIJAN		
1 BORUC Artur			HASANZADE Jahangir	12	
13 WASILEWSKI Marcin			KERIMOV Aslan	8	
2 DUDKA Dariusz			ABBASOV Samir	9	
6 BAK Jacek			PEREIRA Ernani	3	
14 ZEWLAKOW Michal			BAKHSHIEV Elmar	6	
15 LOBODZINSKI Wojciech			GURBANOV Ilgar	18	
9 GARGULA Lukasz	65		IMAMALIEV Emin	19	
18 LEWANDOWSKI Mariusz	67		KERIMOV Kanan	21	
8 KRZYNOWEK Jacek	79		CHERTOGANOV Aleksandr	22	
7 ZURAWSKI Maciej		62	GOMES Leandro	11	
11 MATUSIAK Radoslaw	69		SUBASIC Branimir	15	
Tr: BEENHAKKER Leo			Tr: DINIYEV Shakhin		
7 JELEN Ireneusz	79	62	LADAGA Andre	4	
16 KAZMIERCZAK Przemyslaw	69	65	AGHAKISHIYEV Murad	14	
		67	DZAVADOV Vagif	20	

Centralny, Almaty
24-03-2007, 19:00, 19 600, Hrinák SVK

KAZ 2 1 SRB

Ashirbekov [47], Zhumaskaliyev [61] Zigic [68]

KAZAKHSTAN			SERBIA		
1 LORIA David			STOJKOVIC Vladimir	1	
5 SMAKOV Samat			MARKOVIC Marjan	21	
3 KUCHMA Aleksandr			STEPANOV Milan	15	
4 ZHALMAGAMBETOV Maksim			VIDIC Nemanja	5	
5 IRISMETOV Farkhadbek			TOSIC Dusko	11	
6 SKORYKH Sergey			KOVACEVIC Nenad	16	
7 SERGIENKO Eduard	58	70	ERGIC Ivan	2	
8 BALTIEV Ruslan			JANKOVIC Bosko	18	
9 SUYUMAGAMBETOV Murat	80		KRASIC Milos	17	
10 ZHUMASKALIYEV Nurbol		69	PANTELIC Marko	9	
11 ASHIRBEKOV Kairat	71	94+	ZIGIC Nikola	19	
Tr: PIJPERS Arno			Tr: CLEMENTE Javier		
15 CHICHULIN Anton	58	70	KOROMAN Ognjen	7	
14 BYAKOV Dmitriy	71	69	LAZOVIC Danko	8	
17 FINONCHENKO Andrey	80				

José Alvalade, Lisbon
24-03-2007, 21:00, 47 009, Vassaras GRE

POR 4   0 BEL

Nuno Gomes 53, Ronaldo 2 55 75, Quaresma 69

PORTUGAL				BELGIUM
1	RICARDO			STUNEN Stijn 1
13	LUIS MIGUEL	64		HOEFKENS Carl 13
16	RICARDO CARVALHO			CLEMENT Philippe 3
4	JORGE ANDRADE			VAN BUYTEN Daniel 5
2	PAULO FERREIRA			VAN DER HEYDEN Peter 16
19	TIAGO			FELLAINI Marouane 17
8	PETIT	76		MUDINGAYI Gaby 6
28	JOAO MOUTINHO			DE MAN Mark 15
17	CRISTIANO RONALDO	78		DEFOUR Steven 25
21	NUNO GOMES		56	MARTENS Maarten 10
27	RICARDO QUARESMA	70	81	MPENZA Mbo 11
	Tr: SCOLARI Luiz Felipe			Tr: VANDEREYCKEN René
5	FERNANDO MEIRA	76	81	VAN DAMME Jelle 4
10	VIANA Hugo	78	64	STERCHELE Francois 14
32	NANI	70	56	CHATELLE Thomas 18

Tofik Bakhramov, Baku
28-03-2007, 20:00, 14 500, Messina ITA

AZE 1   0 FIN

Imamaliev 83

AZERBAIJAN				FINLAND
1	VELIYEV Farkhad			JAASKELAINEN Jussi 22
3	PEREIRA Ernani			PASANEN Petri 2
4	LADAGA Andre	66		HYYPIA Sami 4
7	GULIYEV Ramin			TIHINEN Hannu 5
8	KERIMOV Aslan			VAYRYNEN Mika 6
9	ABBASOV Samir			LITMANEN Jari 10
10	SULTANOV Dzeykhun	76	85	KOLKKA Joonas 11
11	GOMES Leandro	10		KALLIO Toni 19
14	AGHAKISHIYEV Murad			EREMENKO Jr Alexei 20
15	SUBASIC Branimir		86	JOHANSSON Jonatan 21
22	CHERTOGANOV Aleksandr			HEIKKINEN Markus 23
	Tr: DINIYEV Shahin			Tr: HODGSON Roy
17	NADYROV Vugar	10	86	FORSSELL Mikael 9
18	GURBANOV Ilgar	76	85	KUQI Shefki 18
19	IMAMALIEV Emin	66		

Korona Kielce, Kielce
28-03-2007, 20:30, 13 450, Undiano Mallenco ESP

POL 1   0 ARM

Zurawski 26

POLAND				ARMENIA
1	BORUC Artur			BEREZOVSKY Roman 1
2	DUDKA Dariusz			MELIKYAN Egishe 2
6	BAK Jacek			DOKHOYAN Karen 3
13	WASILEWSKI Marcin			HOVSEPYAN Sargis 4
14	ZEWLAKOW Michal			ARZUMANYAN Robert 5
8	KRZYNOWEK Jacek	83		KHACHATRYAN Romik 6
17	BLASZCZYKOWSKI Jakub	45		NAZARYAN Rafael 8
18	LEWANDOWSKI Mariusz	68		KARAMYAN Artavazd 13
19	GARGULA Lukasz			PACHAJYAN Levon 16
9	ZURAWSKI Maciej	75		SHAHGELDYAN Armen 10
16	KAZMIERCZAK Przemyslaw	61		ZEBELYAN Robert 18
	Tr: BEENHAAKER Leo			Tr: PORTERFIELD Ian
7	JELEN Ireneusz	83	75	MKHITARYAN Hamlet 9
20	SOBOLEWSKI Radoslaw	61	68	MELKONYAN Samvel 14
			45	MANUCHARYAN Edgar 15

Crvena Zvezda, Belgrade
28-03-2007, 20:30, 46 810, Layec FRA

SRB 1   1 POR

Jankovic 37 | Tiago 5

SERBIA				PORTUGAL
1	STOJKOVIC Vladimir			RICARDO 1
11	TOSIC Dusko	84		PAULO FERREIRA 2
5	VIDIC Nemanja			JORGE ANDRADE 4
3	DRAGUTONVIC Ivica		72	LUIS MIGUEL 13
20	KRSTAJIC Mladen			RICARDO CARVALHO 16
4	DULJAJ Igor			PETIT 8
18	JANKOVIC Bosko	68	77	JOAO MOUTINHO 28
16	KOVACEVIC Nenad			TIAGO 19
17	KRASIC Milos			CRISTIANO RONALDO 17
10	STANKOVIC Dejan	78	82	NUNO GOMES 21
9	PANTELIC Marko			SIMAO 11
	Tr: CLEMENTE Javier			Tr: SCOLARI Luiz Felipe
21	MARKOVIC Marjan	78	72	MARCO CANEIRA 3
7	KOROMAN Ognjen	68	77	RAUL MEIRELES 25
8	LAZOVIC Danko	84	82	RICARDO QUARESMA 27

Olympiastadion, Helsinki
2-06-2007, 19:15, 33 615, Mejuto Gonzalez ESP

FIN 0   2 SRB

Jankovic 3, Jovanovic 86

FINLAND				SERBIA
22	JAASKELAINEN Jussi			STOJKOVIC Vladimir 1
19	KALLIO Toni			DRAGUTONVIC Ivica 3
4	HYYPIA Sami			KRSTAJIC Mladen 20
5	TIHINEN Hannu			VIDIC Nemanja 5
2	PASANEN Petri			RUKAVINA Antonio 6
23	HEIKKINEN Markus			STANKOVIC Dejan 10
15	ILOLA Jari			KOVACEVIC Nenad 16
6	VAYRYNEN Mika			KUZMANOVIC Zdravko 22
8	TAINIO Teemu	28	67	JANKOVIC Bosko 18
18	KUQI Shefki	70	60	PANTELIC Marko 9
9	FORSSELL Mikael	62	85	KRASIC Milos 17
	Tr: HODGSON Roy			Tr: CLEMENTE Javier
10	LITMANEN Jari	70	85	DULJAJ Igor 4
11	KOLKKA Joonas	28	60	JOVANOVIC Milan 14
21	JOHANSSON Jonatan	62	67	LAZOVIC Danko 8

Centralny, Almaty
2-06-2007, 18:00, 17 100, Kralovec CZE

KAZ 1   2 ARM

Baltiev 88p | Arzumanyan 31, Hovsepyan 39p

KAZAKHSTAN				ARMENIA
1	LORIA David			KASPAROV Gevorg 12
2	SMAKOV Samat			HOVSEPYAN Sargis 4
3	KUCHMA Aleksandr			ARZUMANYAN Robert 5
4	ZHALMAGAMBETOV Maksim			TADEVOSYAN Aleksandr 18
5	IRISMETOV Farkhadbek			MKRTCHYAN Agvan 17
6	CHICHULIN Anton			MINASYAN Vahagn 16
7	SERGIENKO Eduard	36	80	ARAKELYAN Ararat 6
8	BALTIEV Ruslan			VOSKANYAN Artur 7
11	KUKEYEV Zhambyl	57		MELIKYAN Egishe 2
9	SUYUMAGAMBETOV Murat		75	MKHITARYAN Hamlet 9
10	ZHUMASKALIYEV Nurbol	78	90	MELKONYAN Samvel 14
	Tr: PIJPERS Arno			Tr: PORTERFIELD Ian
14	BYAKOV Dmitriy	36	80	HAKOBYAN Aram 13
17	TIESHEV Murat	57	75	SHAHGELDYAN Armen 10
19	KORNIENKO Oleg	78	90	KARAMYAN Arman 11

Tofik Bakhramov, Baku
2-06-2007, 21:00, 25 800, Kapitanis CYP

AZE 1 3 **POL**

Subasic [6]   Smolarek [63], Krzynówek 2 [66 90]

AZERBAIJAN			POLAND	
1 VELIYEV Farkhad			BORUC Artur	1
7 GULIYEV Ramin			WASILEWSKI Marcin	13
9 ABBASOV Samir			DUDKA Dariusz	2
5 GULIYEV Emin			BAK Jacek	6
16 GURBANOV Alim	65		ZEWLAKOW Michal	14
19 IMAMALIEV Emin	70	57	BLASZCZYKOWSKI Jakub	5
22 CHERTOGANOV Aleksandr			LEWANDOWSKI Mariusz	18
8 KERIMOV Aslan			KRZYNOWEK Jacek	8
21 MAMEDOV Khagani	53		SMOLAREK Euzebiusz	7
11 ABBASOV Ramazan		81	RASIAK Grzegorz	11
15 SUBASIC Branimir		57	ZURAWSKI Maciej	9
Tr: DINIYEV Shahin			Tr: BEENHAAKER Leo	
2 GASHIMOV Zaur	70	57	LOBODZINSKI Wojciech	15
20 DZAVADOV Vagif	53	57	SAGANOWSKI Marek	10
18 GURBANOV Ilgar	65	81	SOBOLEWSKI Radoslaw	16

Roi Baudouin, Brussels
2-06-2007, 20:45, 45 383, Hansson SWE

BEL 1 2 **POR**

Fellaini [55]   Nani [43], Hélder Postiga [64]

BELGIUM			PORTUGAL	
1 STIJNEN Stijn			RICARDO	1
17 FELLAINI Marouane			JORGE ANDRADE	4
3 SIMONS Timmy			PAULO FERREIRA	2
13 HOEFKENS Carl	47+		FERNANDO MEIRA	5
24 VERMAELEN Thomas		53	LUIS MIGUEL	13
7 CLEMENT Philippe			DECO	20
16 VERTONGHEN Jan			PETIT	8
6 MUDINGAYI Gaby	76		TIAGO	19
9 MPENZA Emile		79	HELDER POSTIGA	23
14 STERCHELE Francois	61	86	NANI	32
25 DEFOUR Steven			RICARDO QUARESMA	27
Tr: VANDEREYCKEN René			Tr: SCOLARI Luiz Felipe	
15 DE MAN Mark	47+	53	BOSINGWA	31
22 GERAERTS Karel	76	94+ 79	HUGO ALMEIDA	26
23 DE MUL Tom	61	86	DUDA	33

Olympiastadion, Helsinki
6-06-2007, 20:15, 34 818, Riley ENG

FIN 2 0 **BEL**

Johansson [27], Eremenko Jr [71]

FINLAND			BELGIUM	
22 JAASKELAINEN Jussi			STIJNEN Stijn	1
19 KALLIO Toni		47+	VERMAELEN Thomas	24
2 PASANEN Petri			SIMONS Timmy	3
28 NYMAN Ari			CLEMENT Philippe	7
5 TIHINEN Hannu			DE MAN Mark	15
11 KOLKKA Joonas			VAN DAMME Jelle	4
23 HEIKKINEN Markus			VAN DER HEYDEN Peter	16
32 EREMENKO Roma		52	FELLAINI Marouane	17
6 VAYRYNEN Mika			DEFOUR Steven	25
20 EREMENKO Jr Alexei	89	55	DE MUL Tom	23
21 JOHANSSON Jonatan		86	MPENZA Emile	9
Tr: HODGSON Roy			Tr: VANDEREYCKEN René	
9 FORSSELL Mikael	89	55	HAROUN Faris	8
		47+	MAERTENS Birger	10
		86	STERCHELE Francois	14

Centralny, Almaty
6-06-2007, 19:00, 11 800, Toussaint LUX

KAZ 1 1 **AZE**

Baltiev [53]   Nadyrov [30]

KAZAKHSTAN			AZERBAIJAN	
1 LORIA David			HASANZADE Jahangir	12
2 SMAKOV Samat			GASHIMOV Zaur	2
3 KUCHMA Aleksandr			GULIYEV Emin	5
4 ZHALMAGAMBETOV Maksim	45		GULIYEV Ramin	7
5 IRISMETOV Farkhadbek			ABBASOV Samir	9
6 CHICHULIN Anton		74	SULTANOV Dzeykhun	10
10 BALTIEV Ruslan			CHERTOGANOV Aleksandr	22
8 KARPOVITCH Andrei			ABBASOV Ramazan	11
9 OSTAPENKO Sergey	79		SUBASIC Branimir	15
7 BYAKOV Dmitriy		84	NADYROV Vugar	17
11 ZHUMASKALIYEV Nurbol	93+	58	KERIMOV Kanan	8
Tr: PUPERS Arno			Tr: DINIYEV Shahin	
15 UTABAYEV Kairat	93+	74	GURBANOV Alim	16
16 TIESHEV Murat	79	58	IMAMALIEV Emin	19
		84	MAMEDOV Khagani	21

Republican, Yerevan
6-06-2007, 20:30, 9800, Balaj ROU

ARM 1 0 **POL**

Mkhitaryan [66]

ARMENIA			POLAND	
1 KASPAROV Gevorg			BORUC Artur	1
4 HOVSEPYAN Sargis			DUDKA Dariusz	2
5 ARZUMANYAN Robert			BRONOWICKI Grzegorz	3
2 MELIKYAN Egishe			WASILEWSKI Marcin	13
14 MINASYAN Vahagn	78		ZEWLAKOW Michal	14
18 TADEVOSYAN Aleksandr			LEWANDOWSKI Mariusz	18
17 MKRTCHYAN Agvan		65	BAK Jacek	6
7 VOSKANYAN Artur		60	SMOLAREK Euzebiusz	7
6 ARAKELYAN Ararat			KRZYNOWEK Jacek	8
9 MKHITARYAN Hamlet	70	60	LOBODZINSKI Wojciech	15
10 SHAHGELDYAN Armen	46		SAGANOWSKI Marek	10
Tr: PORTERFIELD Ian			Tr: BEENHAAKER Leo	
11 KARAMYAN Arman	70	60	BLASZCZYKOWSKI Jakub	5
13 HAKOBYAN Aram	46	60	ZURAWSKI Maciej	9
16 PACHAJYAN Levon	78	65	SOBOLEWSKI Radoslaw	16

GROUP B

Svangaskard, Toftir
16-08-2006, 19:00, 2114, Ross NIR

FRO 0 6 GEO

Mujiri 16, Iashvili 18, Arveladze 3 37 62 82, Kobiashvili 51p

FAROE ISLANDS				GEORGIA		
1	MIKKELSEN Jakup			CHANTURIA Grigol		34
3	JOENSEN Janus			SHASHIASHVILI Georgi		37
4	DANIELSEN Atil			ASATIANI Malkhaz		16
13	JOHANNESEN Oli		66	KANDELAKI Ilia		35
5	JORGENSEN Claus	45		KOBIASHVILI Levan		10
7	BENJAMINSEN Frodi		71	ALADASHVILI Kakhaber		6
8	BORG Jakup		57	GOGIA Gogita		14
12	NIELSEN Kari			KANKAVA Jaba		22
8	SAMUELSEN Simun	60		MUJIRI David		20
10	JACOBSEN Christian			IASHVILI Aleksandr		9
6	JACOBSEN Rogvi	71		ARVELADZE Shota		11
	Tr: OLSEN Jøgvan Martin			Tr: TOPPMOLLER Klaus		
2	HANSEN Pauli	45	66	KVIRKVELIA David		5
11	FREDRIKSBERG Jonhard	71	71	GAKHOKIDZE Georgi		8
14	SAMUELSEN Hans	60	57	DEMETRADZE Georgi		24

Celtic Park, Glasgow
2-09-2006, 15:00, 50 059, Egorov RUS

SCO 6 0 FRO

Fletcher 7, McFadden 10, Boyd 2 24p 38, Miller.K 30p, O'Connor 85

SCOTLAND				FAROE ISLANDS		
1	GORDON Craig			MIKKELSEN Jakup		1
2	DAILLY Christian			HANSEN Pauli		2
5	WEIR David			JOHANNESEN Oli		13
4	PRESSLEY Steven			DANIELSEN Atil		4
3	NAYSMITH Gary			JOENSEN Janus		3
7	FLETCHER Darren	45		BENJAMINSEN Frodi		7
8	HARTLEY Paul		76	JOHNSSON Julian		8
6	QUASHIE Nigel	84		BORG Jakup		9
9	MILLER Kenny	61	60	FREDRIKSBERG Jonhard		15
10	BOYD Kris			JACOBSEN Christian		10
11	MCFADDEN James		84	JACOBSEN Rogvi		6
	Tr: SMITH Walter			Tr: OLSEN Jøgvan Martin		
16	SEVERIN Scott	84	76	SAMUELSEN Simun		5
17	O'CONNOR Garry	61	84	NIELSEN Kari		12
18	TEALE Gary Stewart	45	60	THORLIEFSON Hanus		18

Bori Paichadze, Tbilisi
2-09-2006, 20:00, 54 000, Wegereef NED

GEO 0 3 FRA

Malouda 7, Saha 16, Asatiani OG 47

GEORGIA				FRANCE		
34	CHANTURIA Grigol			COUPET Gregory		23
13	KHIZANISHVILI Zurab			SAGNOL Willy		19
10	KOBIASHVILI Levan			THURAM Lilian		15
16	ASATIANI Malkhaz			GALLAS William		5
22	KANKAVA Jaba			ABIDAL Eric		3
6	ALADASHVILI Kakhaber	39		VIEIRA Patrick		4
14	GOGIA Gogita		58	MAKELELE Claude		6
9	IASHVILI Aleksandr	45	69	RIBERY Frank		22
30	DEMETRADZE Georgi			MALOUDA Florent		7
20	MUJIRI David	82	86	SAHA Louis		14
11	ARVELADZE Shota			HENRY Thierry		12
	Tr: TOPPMOLLER Klaus			Tr: DOMENECH Raymond		
5	KVIRKVELIA David	45	58	MAVUBA Rio Antonio		8
18	MENTESHASHVILI Zurab	82	86	WILTORD Sylvain		11
35	KANDELAKI Ilia	39	69	GOVOU Sidney		9

San Paolo, Naples
2-09-2006, 20:50, 43 440, Hansson SWE

ITA 1 1 LTU

Inzaghi 30   Danilevicius 21

ITALY				LITHUANIA		
1	BUFFON Gianluigi			KARCEMARSKAS Zydrunas		1
22	ODDO Massimo			STANKEVICIUS Marius		2
5	CANNAVARO Fabio			DZIAUKSTAS Rolandas		3
6	BARZAGLI Andrea			SKERLA Andrius		5
3	GROSSO Fabio			PREIKSAITIS Aidas		14
21	PIRLO Andrea			ZVIRGZDAUSKAS Tomas		6
4	DE ROSSI Daniele	61	65	SAVENAS Mantas		7
8	GATTUSO Genaro		82	MIKOLIUNAS Saulius		13
20	PERROTTA Simone	72		CESNAUSKIS Deividas		18
10	CASSANO Antonio		79	POSKUS Robertas		11
9	INZAGHI Filippo		86	DANILEVICIUS Tomas		9
	Tr: DONADONI Roberto			Tr: LIUBINSKAS Algimantas		
23	MARCHIONNI Marco	61	79	LABUKAS Tadas		8
11	GILARDINO Alberto	72	65	KALONAS Mindaugas		10
17	DI MICHELE David	86	82	TAMOSAUSKAS Tomas		17

NSC Olympiyskiy, Kyiv
6-09-2006, 19:00, 35 000, Jara CZE

UKR 3 2 GEO

Shevchenko 31, Rotan 62, Rusol 80   Arveladze 38, Demetradze 61

UKRAINE				GEORGIA		
1	SHOVKOVSKIY Olexandr			CHANTURIA Grigol		34
2	NESMACHNIY Andriy			KOBIASHVILI Levan		10
6	RUSOL Andriy			ASATIANI Malkhaz		16
4	TYMOSCHUK Anatoliy			KHIZANISHVILI Zurab		13
21	ROTAN Ruslan		35	IMEDASHVILI David		36
8	SHELAYEV Oleh			KANKAVA Jaba		22
9	GUSEV Oleh			GOGIA Gogita		14
11	REBROV Serghiy	57	85	KVIRKVELIA David		5
14	HUSIN Andriy	45	81	MENTESHASHVILI Zurab		18
17	TKACHENKO Serhiy	63		DEMETRADZE Georgi		30
7	SHEVCHENKO Andriy			ARVELADZE Shota		11
	Tr: BLOKHIN Oleg			Tr: TOPPMOLLER Klaus		
5	YEZERSKIY Volodymyr	45	85	MUJIRI David		20
10	VORONIN Andriy	57	81	ASHVETIA Mikheil		32
16	VOROBEY Andriy	63	35	KANDELAKI Ilia		35

S. Darius & S. Girenas, Kaunas
6-09-2006, 19:30, 8000, Hrinák SVK

LTU 1 2 SCO

Miceika 85   Dailly 46, Miller.K 62

LITHUANIA				SCOTLAND		
1	KARCEMARSKAS Zydrunas			GORDON Craig		1
2	STANKEVICIUS Marius			DAILLY Christian		2
3	DZIAUKSTAS Rolandas			WEIR David		5
5	SKERLA Andrius			CALDWELL Gary		6
6	ZVIRGZDAUSKAS Tomas			NAYSMITH Gary		3
7	SAVENAS Mantas	50		PRESSLEY Steven		4
10	KALONAS Mindaugas			FLETCHER Darren		7
13	MIKOLIUNAS Saulius	66	43	QUASHIE Nigel		10
14	PREIKSAITIS Aidas	81	21	MCFADDEN James		11
11	POSKUS Robertas		88	HARTLEY Paul		8
9	DANILEVICIUS Tomas			MILLER Kenny		9
	Tr: LIUBINSKAS Algimantas			Tr: SMITH Walter		
8	LABUKAS Tadas	66	21	ALEXANDER Graham		13
16	MICEIKA Darius	81	43	BOYD Kris		16
17	TAMOSAUSKAS Tomas	50	88	SEVERIN Scott		17

Stade de France, Paris
6-09-2006, 21:00, 78 831, Fandel GER

FRA	3	1		ITA

Govou 2 [2 55], Henry [18]   Gilardino [20]

FRANCE			ITALY	
23 COUPET Gregory			BUFFON Gianluigi	1
19 SAGNOL Willy			ZAMBROTTA Gianluca	19
5 GALLAS William			CANNAVARO Fabio	5
15 THURAM Lilian			BARZAGLI Andrea	6
3 ABIDAL Eric			GROSSO Fabio	3
22 RIBERY Frank	88	54	SEMIOLI Franco	7
4 VIEIRA Patrick			PIRLO Andrea	21
6 MAKELELE Claude			GATTUSO Genaro	8
7 MALOUDA Florent			PERROTTA Simone	20
9 GOVOU Sidney	75	73	CASSANO Antonio	10
12 HENRY Thierry		87	GILARDINO Alberto	11
Tr: DOMENECH Raymond			Tr: DONADONI Roberto	
11 WILTORD Sylvain	75	87	DE ROSSI Daniele	4
14 SAHA Louis	88	73	INZAGHI Filippo	9
		54	DI MICHELE David	17

Tórsvøllur, Tórshavn
7-10-2006, 15:00, 1982, Buttimer IRL

FRO	0	1		LTU

                           Skerla [89]

FAROE ISLANDS			LITHUANIA	
1 MIKKELSEN Jakup			KARCEMARSKAS Zydrunas	1
3 MORTENSEN Vagnur			STANKEVICIUS Marius	2
4 DANIELSEN Atil			PAULAUSKAS Gediminas	4
17 THOMASSEN Mikkjal			SKERLA Andrius	5
7 BENJAMINSEN Frodi			ZVIRGZDAUSKAS Tomas	6
2 HANSEN Pauli	90	45	SAVENAS Mantas	7
9 BORG Jakup			MICEIKA Darius	16
14 DJURHUUS Marni			CESNAUSKIS Deividas	18
5 SAMUELSEN Simun	73	62	MIKOLIUNAS Saulius	13
6 JACOBSEN Rogvi	81		DANILEVICIUS Tomas	9
10 JACOBSEN Christian		70	POSKUS Robertas	11
Tr: OLSEN Jøgvan Martin			Tr: LIUBINSKAS Algimantas	
11 FREDRIKSBERG Jonhard	73	45	KALONAS Mindaugas	10
12 NIELSEN Kari	81	70	BENIUSIS Ricardas	15
18 HANSEN Arnbjorn	90	62	KAVALIAUSKAS Vitalijus	17

Hampden Park, Glasgow
7-10-2006, 17:00, 50 456, Busacca SUI

SCO	1	0		FRA

Caldwell.G [67]

SCOTLAND			FRANCE	
1 GORDON Craig			COUPET Gregory	23
2 DAILLY Christian			ABIDAL Eric	3
4 PRESSLEY Steven			THURAM Lilian	15
5 WEIR David			BOUMSONG Jean-Alain	2
3 ALEXANDER Graham			SAGNOL Willy	19
7 FLETCHER Darren		74	RIBERY Frank	22
6 FERGUSON Barry			VIEIRA Patrick	4
8 CALDWELL Gary			MAKELELE Claude	6
10 HARTLEY Paul			MALOUDA Florent	7
11 MCCULLOCH Lee	58	62	TREZEGUET David	20
9 MCFADDEN James	72		HENRY Thierry	12
Tr: SMITH Walter			Tr: DOMENECH Raymond	
16 O'CONNOR Garry	72	74	WILTORD Sylvain	11
17 TEALE Gary Stewart	58	62	SAHA Louis	14

Stadio Olimpico, Rome
7-10-2006, 20:50, 49 149, Vassaras GRE

ITA	2	0		UKR

Oddo [71p], Toni [79]

ITALY			UKRAINE	
1 BUFFON Gianluigi			SHOVKOVSKIY Olexandr	1
22 ODDO Massimo			RUSOL Andriy	6
5 CANNAVARO Fabio			SHERSHUN Bohdan	3
23 MATERAZZI Marco			YEZERSKIY Volodymyr	5
19 ZAMBROTTA Gianluca			NESMACHNIY Andriy	2
8 GATTUSO Genaro		59	NAZARENKO Serhiy	18
21 PIRLO Andrea			GUSEV Oleh	9
10 DE ROSSI Daniele			SHELAYEV Oleh	8
15 IAQUINTA Vicenzo	76		TYMOSCHUK Anatoliy	4
9 TONI Luca	85	73	VOROBEY Andriy	16
7 DEL PIERO Alessandro	62		VORONIN Andriy	10
Tr: DONADONI Roberto			Tr: BLOKHIN Oleg	
16 CAMORANESI Mauro	76	59	KALYNYCHENKO Maxym	19
18 INZAGHI Filippo	85	73	MILEVSKIY Artem	15
11 DI NATALE Antonio	62			

NSC Olympiyskiy, Kyïv
11-10-2006, 20:00, 50 000, Hansson SWE

UKR	2	0		SCO

Kucher [60], Shevchenko [90p]

UKRAINE			SCOTLAND	
1 SHOVKOVSKIY Olexandr			GORDON Craig	1
2 NESMACHNIY Andriy		89	NEILSON Robbie	2
22 SVIDERSKIY Vyacheslav			WEIR David	5
17 KUCHER Olexandr		86	PRESSLEY Steven	4
6 RUSOL Andriy			ALEXANDER Graham	3
4 TYMOSCHUK Anatoliy			CALDWELL Gary	8
8 SHELAYEV Oleh			FERGUSON Barry	6
9 GUSEV Oleh	62		FLETCHER Darren	7
19 KALYNYCHENKO Maxym	76		HARTLEY Paul	10
7 SHEVCHENKO Andriy			MILLER Kenny	9
10 VORONIN Andriy	93+	73	MCFADDEN James	11
Tr: BLOKHIN Oleg			Tr: SMITH Walter	
3 SHERSHUN Bohdan	93+	89	MCMANUS Stephen	13
15 MILEVSKIY Artem	62	73	BOYD Kris	14
16 VOROBEY Andriy	76			

Stade Bonal, Sochaux-Montbéliard
11-10-2006, 21:00, 19 314, Corpodean ROU

FRA	5	0		FRO

Saha [1], Henry [22], Anelka [77],
Trezeguet 2 [78 84]

FRANCE			FAROE ISLANDS	
1 LANDREAU Mickael			MIKKELSEN Jakup	1
19 SAGNOL Willy	79		DJURHUUS Marni	2
5 GALLAS William			MORTENSEN Vagnur	3
15 THURAM Lilian			DANIELSEN Atil	4
17 ESCUDE Julien			SAMUELSEN Simun	5
22 RIBERY Frank			JACOBSEN Rogvi	6
4 VIEIRA Patrick			BENJAMINSEN Frodi	7
8 TOULALAN Jeremy			THOMASSEN Mikkjal	8
7 MALOUDA Florent		87	BORG Jakup	9
14 SAHA Louis	61		JACOBSEN Christian	10
12 HENRY Thierry	61	47	HANSEN Pauli	11
Tr: DOMENECH Raymond			Tr: OLSEN Jøgvan Martin	
13 CLERC Francois	79	47	NIELSEN Kari	12
20 TREZEGUET David	61	87	FREDRIKSBERG Jonhard	14
39 ANELKA Nicolas	61			

Boris Paichadze, Tbilisi
11-10-2006, 22:00, 48 000, Riley ENG

GEO	1	3	ITA

Shashiashvili [26]

De Rossi [18], Camoranesi [63], Perrotta [71]

GEORGIA			ITA
1 LOMAIA GEORGI			BUFFON Gianluigi 1
13 KHIZANISHVILI Zurab			ODDO Massimo 22
3 KHIZANEISHVILI Otar		74	CANNAVARO Fabio 5
4 KALADZE Kakha			NESTA Alessandro 13
37 SHASHIASHVILI Georgi		64	PIRLO Andrea 21
22 KANKAVA Jaba	70		DE ROSSI Daniele 10
7 TSKITISHVILI Levan	74		PERROTTA Simone 20
18 MENTESHASHVILI Zurab			ZAMBROTTA Gianluca 19
21 MARTSVALADZE Otar	85	87	CAMORANESI Mauro 16
5 KVIRKVELIA David			TONI Luca 9
32 ASHVETIA Mikheil			DI NATALE Antonio 11
Tr: TOPPMÖLLER Klaus			Tr: DONADONI Roberto
9 IASHVILI Aleksandr	70	74	MATERAZZI Marco 23
18 GIGADZE Vasil	85	64	MAURI Stefan 24
35 KANDELAKI Ilia	74	87	IAQUINTA Vicenzo 15

Hampden Park, Glasgow
24-03-2007, 15:00, 52 063, Vollquartz DEN

SCO	2	1	GEO

Boyd [11], Beattie [89]

Arveladze [41]

SCOTLAND			GEORGIA
1 GORDON Craig			LOMAIA Georgi 1
2 ALEXANDER Graham			SHASHIASHVILI Georgi 37
4 WEIR David			KHIZANISHVILI Zurab 13
5 MCMANUS Stephen			SALUKVADZE Lasha 23
3 NAYSMITH Gary			ELIAVA Zaali 25
7 TEALE Gary Stewart	60	57	BURDULI Vladimer 41
6 FERGUSON Barry		92+	TSKITISHVILI Levan 7
8 HARTLEY Paul		45	MENTESHASHVILI Zurab 18
11 MCCULLOCH Lee			KOBIASHVILI Levan 10
9 MILLER Kenny	92+		DEMETRADZE Georgi 30
10 BOYD Kris	76		AVERLADZE Shota 11
Tr: MCLEISH Alex			Tr: TOPPMÖLLER Klaus
16 BEATTIE Craig	76	45	GOGUA Gogita 14
17 MALONEY Shaun	92+	92+	MUJIRI David 20
18 BROWN Scott	60	57	SIRADZE David 43

Svangaskard, Toftir
24-03-2007, 15:00, 717, Skomina SVN

FRO	0	2	UKR

Yezerskiy [20], Gusev [57]

FAROE ISLANDS			UKRAINE
1 MIKKELSEN Jakup			SHOVKOVSKIY Olexandr 1
2 OLSEN Suni	74		YEZERSKIY Volodymyr 5
3 DJURHUUS Marni			CHYGRYNSKIY Dmytro 13
4 DANIELSEN Atli			RUSOL Andriy 6
5 SAMUELSEN Simun	66		NESMACHNIY Andriy 2
6 JACOBSEN Rogvi		65	GUSEV Oleh 9
7 BENJAMINSEN Frodi		82	TYMOSCHUK Anatoliy 4
8 THOMASSEN Mikkjal	78		MIKHALIK Taras 17
9 BORG Jakup			KALYNYCHENKO Maxym 19
10 JACOBSEN Christian			BIELIK Olexiy 20
13 JOHANNESEN Oli		75	VORONIN Andriy 10
Tr: OLSEN Jøgvan Martin			Tr: BLOKHIN Oleg
12 JOENSEN Samal	78	82	SHELAYEV Oleh 8
14 HOLST Christian	66	65	VOROBEY Andriy 16
15 HANSEN Tem	74	75	NAZARENKO Serhiy 18

S. Darius & S. Girenas, Kaunas
24-03-2007, 19:00, 8 740, Webb ENG

LTU	0	1	FRA

Anelka [73]

LITHUANIA			FRANCE
1 KARCEMARSKAS Zydrunas			COUPET Gregory 23
15 KLIMAVICIUS Arunas			SAGNOL Willy 19
5 SKERLA Andrius			THURAM Lilian 15
6 ZVIRGZDAUSKAS Tomas			GALLAS William 5
13 PAULAUSKAS Gediminas			ABIDAL Eric 3
2 SEMBERAS Deividas		89	MALOUDA Florent 7
14 MORINAS Igoris	82		MAKELELE Claude 6
7 SAVENAS Mantas	77		TOULALAN Jeremy 8
4 STANKEVICIUS Marius			DIARRA Lassana 4
11 POSKUS Robertas	86	62	GOVOU Sidney 9
9 DANILEVICIUS Tomas			ANELKA Nicolas 39
Tr: LIUBINSKAS Algimantas			Tr: DOMENECH Raymond
8 BENIUSIS Ricardas	82	62	CISSE Djibril 10
10 KALONAS Mindaugas	77	89	DIABY Abou 12
18 RADZINEVICIUS Tomas	86		

Centralny, Odessa
28-03-2007, 18:00, 33 600, Meyer GER

UKR	1	0	LTU

Gusev [47]

UKRAINE			LITHUANIA
1 SHOVKOVSKIY Olexandr			GRYBAUSKAS Paulius 12
2 NESMACHNIY Andriy			SEMBERAS Deividas 2
3 KUCHER Olexandr			KLIMAVICIUS Arunas 15
5 YEZERSKIY Volodymyr			PAULAUSKAS Gediminas 13
6 RUSOL Andriy			STANKEVICIUS Marius 4
9 GUSEV Oleh	79		SKERLA Andrius 5
4 TYMOSCHUK Anatoliy			ZVIRGZDAUSKAS Tomas 6
19 KALYNYCHENKO Maxym	82	51	SAVENAS Mantas 7
17 MIKHALIK Taras	70	56	MORINAS Igoris 14
7 SHEVCHENKO Andriy		64	POSKUS Robertas 11
10 VORONIN Andriy			DANILEVICIUS Tomas 9
Tr: BLOKHIN Oleg			Tr: LIUBINSKAS Algimantas
13 CHYGRYNSKIY Dmytro	82	51	KALONAS Mindaugas 10
16 VOROBEY Andriy	79	56	GEDGAUDAS Andrius 16
8 SHELAYEV Oleh	70	64	RADZINEVICIUS Tomas 18

Boris Paichadze, Tbilisi
28-03-2007, 20:00, 12 000, Saliy KAZ

GEO	3	1	FRO

Siradze [25], Iashvili 2 [46 95+p]

Rógvi Jacobsen [57]

GEORGIA			FAROE ISLANDS
1 LOMAIA Georgi			MIKKELSEN Jakup 1
5 KVIRKVELIA David			OLSEN Suni 2
7 TSKITISHVILI Levan			DJURHUUS Marni 3
9 IASHVILI Aleksandr			DANIELSEN Atli 4
10 KOBIASHVILI Levan	61		JACOBSEN Rogvi 6
20 MUJIRI David		65	BENJAMINSEN Frodi 7
22 KANKAVA Jaba			THOMASSEN Mikkjal 8
23 SALUKVADZE Lasha		91+	BORG Jakup 9
30 DEMETRADZE Georgi			JACOBSEN Christian 10
37 SHASHIASHVILI Georgi		43	FLOTUM Andrew 11
43 SIRADZE David			JOHANNESEN Oli 13
Tr: TOPPMÖLLER Klaus			Tr: OLSEN Jøgvan Martin
18 MENTESHASHVILI Zurab	61	91+	SAMUELSEN Simun 5
		43	HOLST Christian 14

San Nicola, Bari
28-03-2007, 20:50, 37 600, De Bleeckere BEL

ITA	2	0		SCO

Toni 2 [12] [70]

	ITALY			SCOTLAND	
1	BUFFON Gianluigi			GORDON Craig	1
22	ODDO Massimo			ALEXANDER Graham	2
5	CANNAVARO Fabio			NAYSMITH Gary	3
23	MATERAZZI Marco			WEIR David	4
19	ZAMBROTTA Gianluca			MCMANUS Stephen	5
8	GATTUSO Genaro			FERGUSON Barry	6
10	DE ROSSI Daniele		66	TEALE Gary Stewart	7
16	CAMORANESI Mauro			HARTLEY Paul	8
20	PERROTTA Simone	77	86	BROWN Scott	10
17	DI NATALE Antonio	66	81	MCCULLOCH Lee	11
9	TONI Luca	87		MILLER Kenny	9
	Tr: DONADONI Roberto			Tr: MCLEISH Alex	
21	PIRLO Andrea	77	81	BOYD Kris	15
7	DEL PIERO Alessandro	66	86	BEATTIE Craig	16
15	QUAGLIARELLA Fabio	87	66	MALONEY Shaun	17

Tórsvøllur, Torshavn
2-06-2007, 19:45, 5800, Malek POL

FRO	1	2		ITA

Rógvi Jacobsen [77]   Inzaghi 2 [12] [48]

	FAROE ISLANDS			ITALY	
1	MIKKELSEN Jakup			BUFFON Gianluigi	1
4	DANIELSEN Atil			ODDO Massimo	22
3	DJURHUUS Marni			TONETTO Max	3
5	JACOBSEN Jon			CANNAVARO Fabio	5
13	JOHANNESEN Oli		66	MATERAZZI Marco	23
9	BORG Jakup	73		DIANA Aimo	16
8	THOMASSEN Mikkjal			GATTUSO Genaro	8
19	OLSEN Suni			PIRLO Andrea	21
10	JACOBSEN Christian			DEL PIERO Alessandro	7
6	JACOBSEN Rogvi		86	ROCCHI Tommaso	11
11	FLOTUM Andrew	56	58	INZAGHI Filippo	9
	Tr: OLSEN Jøgvan Martin			Tr: DONADONI Roberto	
7	SAMUELSEN Simun	73	66	BARZAGLI Andrea	6
14	HOLST Christian	56	58	LUCARELLI Cristiano	18
			86	QUAGLIARELLA Fabio	27

Darius & Girenas, Kaunas
2-06-2007, 21:00, 6400, Circhetta SUI

LTU	1	0		GEO

Mikoliunas [78]

	LITHUANIA			GEORGIA	
1	KARCEMARSKAS Zydrunas			LOMAIA Georgi	1
2	SEMBERAS Deividas			KHIZANEISHVILI Otar	3
4	STANKEVICIUS Marius			KALADZE Kakha	4
5	SKERLA Andrius			ELIAVA Zaali	25
6	ZVIRGZDAUSKAS Tomas			KOBIASHVILI Levan	10
15	KLIMAVICIUS Arunas			KHIZANISHVILI Zurab	13
13	PAULAUSKAS Gediminas		80	TSKITISHVILI Levan	7
7	SAVENAS Mantas	55	64	MENTESHASHVILI Zurab	18
14	MORINAS Igoris	62		KVIRKVELIA David	5
8	BENIUSIS Ricardas	75		IASHVILI Aleksandr	9
9	DANILEVICIUS Tomas			DEMETRADZE Georgi	30
	Tr: LIUBINSKAS Algimantas			Tr: TOPPMOLLER Klaus	
18	LABUKAS Tadas	75	80	MUJIRI David	20
23	MIKOLIUNAS Saulius	62	64	MARTSVALADZE Otar	21
10	KALONAS Mindaugas	55			

Stade de France, Paris
2-06-2007, 21:00, 79 000, Medina Cantalejo ESP

FRA	2	0		UKR

Ribéry [57], Anelka [71]

	FRANCE			UKRAINE	
23	COUPET Gregory			SHOVKOVSKIY Olexandr	1
3	ABIDAL Eric			NESMACHNIY Andriy	2
5	GALLAS William		78	YEZERSKIY Volodymyr	5
13	CLERC Francois			RUSOL Andriy	6
15	THURAM Lilian			CHYGRYNSKIY Dmytro	13
6	MAKELELE Claude			GAY Olexiy	3
7	MALOUDA Florent			TYMOSCHUK Anatoliy	4
8	TOULALAN Jeremy			GUSEV Oleh	9
11	NASRI Samir	81		MIKHALIK Taras	15
22	RIBERY Franck		64	KALYNYCHENKO Maxym	19
39	ANELKA Nicolas	77	72	VORONIN Andriy	10
	Tr: DOMENECH Raymond			Tr: BLOKHIN Oleg	
4	DIARRA Lassana	81	78	LEVCHENKO Evgen	14
9	CISSE Djibril	77	64	ROTAN Ruslan	21
			72	VOROBEY Andriy	16

Abbé-Deschamps, Auxerre
6-06-2007, 21:00, 19 345, Batista POR

FRA	1	0		GEO

Nasri [33]

	FRANCE			GEORGIA	
1	LANDREAU Mickael			LOMAIA Georgi	1
3	ABIDAL Eric			KHIZANEISHVILI Otar	3
13	CLERC Francois			KALADZE Kakha	4
5	GALLAS William			KHIZANISHVILI Zurab	13
6	MAKELELE Claude			GHVINIANDZE Mate	17
7	MALOUDA Florent	65	12	SALUKVADZE Lasha	23
11	NASRI Samir		62	ELIAVA Zaali	25
22	RIBERY Franck	94+		KVIRKVELIA David	5
15	THURAM Lilian		89	KANKAVA Jaba	22
8	TOULALAN Jeremy			BURDULI Vladimer	41
39	ANELKA Nicolas	93+		IASHVILI Aleksandr	9
	Tr: DOMENECH Raymond			Tr: TOPPMOLLER Klaus	
20	BENZEMA Karim	93+	12	MUJIRI David	20
9	CISSE Djibril	65	62	MARTSVALADZE Otar	21
10	GOVOU Sidney	94+	89	SHASHIASHVILI Georgi	37

S. Darius & S. Girenas, Kaunas
6-06-2007, 21:45, 7800, Vink NED

LTU	0	2		ITA

Quagliarella 2 [31] [45]

	LITHUANIA			ITALY	
1	KARCEMARSKAS Zydrunas			BUFFON Gianluigi	1
2	SEMBERAS Deividas			ODDO Massimo	22
4	STANKEVICIUS Marius			CANNAVARO Fabio	5
5	SKERLA Andrius			MATERAZZI Marco	23
6	ZVIRGZDAUSKAS Tomas			ZAMBROTTA Gianluca	19
15	KLIMAVICIUS Arunas			PIRLO Andrea	21
13	PAULAUSKAS Gediminas	46	65	DE ROSSI Daniele	10
7	SAVENAS Mantas	61	71	PERROTTA Simone	20
10	KALONAS Mindaugas			QUAGLIARELLA Fabio	27
14	MORINAS Igoris	39		INZAGHI Filippo	9
9	DANILEVICIUS Tomas		74	DI NATALE Antonio	15
	Tr: LIUBINSKAS Algimantas			Tr: DONADONI Roberto	
18	LABUKAS Tadas	61	65	GATTUSO Genaro	8
23	MIKOLIUNAS Saulius	39	71	AMBROSINI Massimo	4
16	GEDGAUDAS Andrius	46	74	DEL PIERO Alessandro	7

GROUP C

Ta'Qali, Ta'Qali
2-09-2006, 19:15, 2000, Vejlgaard DEN

MLT 2 5 BIH

Pace 6, Mifsud 85 — Barbarez 4, Hrgovic 10, Bartolovic 46+, Muslimovic 48, Misimovic 51

No	MALTA					BOSNIA-HER'GOVINA	No
1	HABER Justin					HASAGIC Kenan	1
2	CIANTAR Ian	45				BERBEROVIC Dzemal	2
3	AZZOPARDI Ian					MUSIC Vednin	3
4	SAID Brian					SPAHIC Emir	4
6	DIMECH Luke					BAJRAMOVIC Zlatan	5
7	AGIUS Gilbert	82	61			PAPAC Sasa	6
8	MATTOCKS Claude	65	66			BARBAREZ Sergej	9
9	MIFSUD Michael					MISIMOVIC Zvjezdan	10
13	SCHEMBRI Andre					MUSLIMOVIC Zlatan	13
18	PACE Jamie					HRGOVIC Mirko	18
20	SAMMUT Kevin	53			53	BARTOLOVIC Mladen	19
	Tr: FITZEL Dusan					Tr: SLISKOVIC Blaz	
14	SCIBERRAS Gareth	82	66			GRUJIC Vladan	11
15	PULLICINO Peter	65	53			BESLIJA Mirsad	14
10	WOODS Ivan	45	61			MILENKOVIC Ninoslav	17

Megyeri úti, Budapest
2-09-2006, 20:00, 12 283, Braamhaar NED

HUN 1 4 NOR

Gera 90p — Solskjær 2 15 54, Strømstad 32, Pedersen 41

No	HUNGARY					NORWAY	No
1	KIRALY Gabor					MYHRE Thomas	1
2	FEHER Csaba					RAMBEKK Anders	17
3	LOW Zsolt					HAGEN Eric	3
4	JUHASZ Roland	66				HANGELAND Brede	5
5	EGER Laszlo					JOHNSON Marius	15
6	SOWUNMI Thomas	80			62	STROMSTAD Fredrik	7
7	MOLNAR Balazs					ANDRESEN Martin	8
8	DARDAI Pal				85	HAESTAD Kristofer	22
9	HORVATH Andras	61				PEDERSEN Morten Gamst	11
10	GERA Zoltan					SOLSKIAER Ole Gunnar	20
11	HUSZTI Szabolcs				76	CAREW John	10
	Tr: BOZSIK Peter					Tr: HAREIDE Age	
14	TORGHELLE Sandor	80			85	LARSEN Tommy Svindal	2
15	VANCZAK Vilmos	66			76	IVERSEN Steffen	14
18	KISS Zoltan	61			62	BRAATEN Daniel	26

Zimbru, Chisinau
2-09-2006, 21:15, 10 500, Trefoloni ITA

MDA 0 1 GRE

Liberopoulos 77

No	MOLDOVA					GREECE	No
1	PASCENCO Serghei					NIKOPOLIDIS Antonios	1
2	LASCENCOV Serghei					SEITARIDIS Giourkas	2
3	CORNEENCOV Andrei					FYSSAS Panagiotis	14
4	TESTIMITANU Ion	89			89	DELLAS Traianos	5
5	IEPUREANU Serghei	65				KYRGIAKOS Sotirios	25
6	REBEJA Radu					KATSOURANIS Konstantinos	21
7	COVALCIUC Serghei				45	BASINAS Angelos	6
8	OLEXIC Ghenadie				45	ZAGORAKIS Theodoros	7
9	BERCO Victor					KARAGOUNIS Georgios	10
10	ROGACIOV Serghei	78	45		45	CHARISTEAS Angelos	9
11	IVANOV Stanislav					AMANATIDIS Ioannis	20
	Tr: TESLEV Anatol					Tr: REHHAGEL Otto	
15	CLESCENCO Serghei	65	89		89	ANATOLAKIS Georgios	32
17	DADU Serghei	78	45		45	LIBEROPOULOS Nikolaos	33
					45	SALPINGIDIS Dimitrios	22

Ullevål, Oslo
6-09-2006, 19:00, 23 848, Ristoskov BUL

NOR 2 0 MDA

Strømstad 73, Iversen 79

No	NORWAY					MOLDOVA	No
1	MYHRE Thomas					PASCENCO Serghei	1
3	HAGEN Eric				77	LASCENCOV Serghei	2
5	HANGELAND Brede					CORNEENCOV Andrei	3
15	JOHNSON Marius	65				TESTIMITANU Ion	4
7	STROMSTAD Fredrik	90				REBEJA Radu	5
8	ANDRESEN Martin					EPUREANU Alexandru	6
11	PEDERSEN Morten Gamst					COVALCIUC Serghei	7
17	RAMBEKK Anders					IVANOV Stanislav	8
22	HAESTAD Kristofer	46			46	BERCO Victor	9
10	CAREW John	72			72	ROGACIOV Serghei	10
24	JOHNSEN Frode	45				OLEXIC Ghenadie	11
	Tr: HAREIDE Age					Tr: TESLEV Anatol	
2	LARSEN Tommy Svindal	90	77		77	CLESCENCO Serghei	15
14	IVERSEN Steffen	65	72		72	DADU Serghei	17
20	SOLSKIAER Ole Gunnar	45					

Commerzbank Arena, Frankfurt am Main
6-09-2006, 20:00, BCD, Vázquez ESP

TUR 2 0 MLT

Nihat 56, Tümer Metin 77

No	TURKEY					MALTA	No
1	RUSTU Recber					HABER Justin	1
3	MEHMET Topuz					CIANTAR Ian	2
4	CAN Arat					WELLMAN Stephen	5
5	GOKHAN Zan					SAID Brian	4
7	MARCO Aurelio					DIMECH Luke	6
9	FATIH Tekke	45	87			AGIUS Gilbert	7
10	YILDIRAY Basturk	45	81			SAMMUT Kevin	11
11	TUMER Metin					MIFSUD Michael	9
13	ERGUN Penbe					WOODS Ivan	10
20	HAKAN Sukur	85	89			SCHEMBRI Andre	13
22	HAMIT Altintop					PACE Jamie	18
	Tr: Fatih TERIM					Tr: FITZEL Dusan	
8	NIHAT Kahveci	45	87		87	SCIBERRAS Gareth	14
14	ARDA Turan	45	89		89	SCERRI Terence	15
16	NURI Sahin	85	81		81	PULLICINO Peter	16

Bilino Polje, Zenica
6-09-2006, 20:15, 11 800, Kapitanis CYP

BIH 1 3 HUN

Misimovic 64 — Huszti 36p, Gera 46, Dárdai 49

No	BOSNIA-HER'GOVINA					HUNGARY	No
1	HASAGIC Kenan					KIRALY Gabor	1
4	SPAHIC Emir	39	82		82	FEHER Csaba	2
3	MUSIC Vednin	46	65		65	LOW Zsolt	3
6	PAPAC Sasa	90			90	TORGHELLE Sandor	9
9	BARBAREZ Sergej					EGER Laszlo	5
15	KERKEZ Dusan					TOTH Balazs	6
5	BAJRAMOVIC Zlatan					MOLNAR Balazs	7
18	HRGOVIC Mirko	73				DARDAI Pal	8
19	BARTOLOVIC Mladen	63				HUSZTI Szabolcs	11
10	MISIMOVIC Zvjezdan					GERA Zoltan	10
7	BOLIC Elvir					VANCZAK Vilmos	4
	Tr: SLISKOVIC Blaz					Tr: BOZSIK Peter	
13	MUSLIMOVIC Zlatan	46	90		90	KABAT Péter	14
14	BESLIJA Mirsad	73	65		65	JUHASZ Roland	13
20	TRIVUNOVIC Vule	63	82		82	KISS Zoltan	18

Zimbru, Chisinau
7-10-2006, 19:00, 7114, Piccirillo FRA

MDA 2 2 BIH

Rogaciov 2 [13 32p] Misimovic [62], Grlic [68]

MOLDOVA			BOSNIA-HER'GOVINA	
1	PASCENCO Serghei		HASAGIC Kenan	1
2	LASCENCOV Serghei		TRIVUNOVIC Vule	20
3	CATINSUS Valeriu		PAPAC Sasa	6
11	GATCAN Alexandru	93+	VIDIC Velimir	16
6	EPUREANU Alexandru		SILIC Dalibor	3
8	OLEXIC Ghenadie	77	BAJRAMOVIC Zlatan	5
4	TESTIMITANU Ion	86	HRGOVIC Mirko	18
5	REBEJA Radu		BARBAREZ Sergej	9
7	IVANOV Stanislav		MISIMOVIC Zvjezdan	10
9	IEPUREANU Serghei	72	45	DAMJANOVIC Dario	13
10	ROGACIOV Serghei	71	BARTOLOVIC Mladen	19
	Tr: TESLEV Anatol		Tr: SLISKOVIC Blaz	
14	CORNEENCOV Andrei	72	86	SMAJIC Sulejman	2
15	CLESCENCO Serghei	93+	45	GRLIC Ivicia	8
16	DADU Serghei	71	77	GRUJIC Vladan	11

Ferenc Puskás, Budapest
7-10-2006, 19:45, 6800, Hamer LUX

HUN 0 1 TUR

Tuncay Sanli [41]

HUNGARY			TURKEY	
1	KIRALY Gabor		RUSTU Recber	1
2	FEHER Csaba		HAMIT Altintop	22
3	VANCZAK Vilmos		SERVET Cetin	2
4	JUHASZ Roland		GOKHAN Zan	5
5	EGER Laszlo		MARCO Aurelio	7
6	TOTH Balazs	63	GOKDENIZ Karadeniz	10
7	HALMOSI Peter	45	91+	ARDA Turan	14
8	DARDAI Pal		IBRAHIM Uzülmez	24
9	TORGHELLE Sandor	83	SABRI Sarioglu	25
10	GERA Zoltan		93+	TUNCAY Sanli	17
11	HUSZTI Szabolcs		HAKAN Sukur	20
	Tr: BOZSIK Peter		Tr: Fatih TERIM	
13	KABAT Péter	76 45	91+	MEHMET Topuz	3
14	SZABICS Imre	83	93+	CAN Arat	4
15	KOMLOSI Adam	76	63	HUSEYIN Cimsir	15

Karaiskaki, Piraeus
7-10-2006, 22:20, 21 189, Michel SVK

GRE 1 0 NOR

Katsouranis [33]

GREECE			NORWAY	
1	NIKOPOLIDIS Antonios		MYHRE Thomas	1
2	SEITARIDIS Giourkas	85	RAMBEKK Anders	17
14	FYSSAS Panagiotis		HAGEN Eric	3
32	ANATOLAKIS Georgios		HANGELAND Brede	5
25	KYRGIAKOS Sotirios		RIISE John Arne	6
6	BASINAS Angelos	61	STROMSTAD Fredrik	7
21	KATSOURANIS Konstantinos		ANDRESEN Martin	8
10	KARAGOUNIS Georgios	90	HAESTAD Kristofer	22
8	GIANNAKOPOLOUS Stelios	45	PEDERSEN Morten Gamst	11
27	SAMARAS Georgios		IVERSEN Steffen	14
33	LIBEROPOULOS Nikolaos	71	SOLSKJAER Ole Gunnar	20
	Tr: REHHAGEL Otto		Tr: HAREIDE Age	
20	AMANATIDIS Ioannis	71	61	BRAATEN Daniel	26
9	CHARISTEAS Angelos	45	85	ARST Ole Martin	9
3	PATSATZOGLOU Christos	90			

Ta'Qali, Ta'Qali
11-10-2006, 19:15, 3600, Ver Eecke BEL

MLT 2 1 HUN

Schembri 2 [14 53] Torghelle [19]

MALTA			HUNGARY	
1	HABER Justin		KIRALY Gabor	1
8	SCICULUNA Kenneth	76	FEHER Csaba	2
5	WELLMAN Stephen		TOTH Balazs	6
4	SAID Brian		JUHASZ Roland	4
6	DIMECH Luke	38	VANCZAK Vilmos	3
11	MALLIA George	64	46	LEANDRO	5
10	SAMMUT Kevin		HUSZTI Szabolcs	11
18	PACE Jamie		DARDAI Pal	8
13	SCHEMBRI Andre	72	TORGHELLE Sandor	9
9	MIFSUD Michael	60	SZABICS Imre	7
7	AGIUS Gilbert	82	GERA Zoltan	10
	Tr: FITZEL Dusan		Tr: BOZSIK Peter	
14	SCERRI Terence	72	76	HALMOSI Peter	14
15	PULLICINO Peter	82	60	CZVITKOVICS Peter	17
17	COHEN Andrew	64	46	KISS Zoltan	18

Commerzbank Arena, Frankfurt am Main
11-10-2006, 20:00, BCD, Vollquartz DEN

TUR 5 0 MDA

Hakan Sükür 4 [35 37p 43 73],
Tuncay Sanli [68]

TURKEY			MOLDOVA	
1	RUSTU Recber		PASCENCO Serghei	1
2	SERVET Cetin	45	EPUREANU Alexandru	2
22	HAMIT Altintop		CATINSUS Valeriu	3
5	GOKHAN Zan		OLEXIC Ghenadie	9
7	MARCO Aurelio		GATCAN Alexandru	11
10	GOKDENIZ Karadeniz	60	63	IEPUREANU Serghei	6
14	ARDA Turan	72	COVALCIUC Serghei	7
24	IBRAHIM Uzülmez		IVANOV Stanislav	8
25	SABRI Sarioglu		REBEJA Radu	5
17	TUNCAY Sanli		ROGACIOV Serghei	10
20	HAKAN Sukur	81	TESTIMITANU Ion	4
	Tr: Fatih TERIM		Tr: TESLEV Anatol	
11	TUMER Metin	60	45	CORNEENCOV Andrei	15
8	NIHAT Kahveci	72	63	DADU Serghei	16
21	HALIL Altintop	81			

Bilino Polje, Zenica
11-10-2006, 20:15, 8000, Baskakov RUS

BIH 0 4 GRE

Charisteas [8p], Patsatzoglou [82],
Samaras [85], Katsouranis [94+]

BOSNIA-HER'GOVINA			GREECE	
1	HASAGIC Kenan	45	NIKOPOLIDIS Antonios	1
3	SILIC Dalibor	79	ANATOLAKIS Georgios	32
4	SPAHIC Emir		KYRGIAKOS Sotirios	25
5	BAJRAMOVIC Zlatan		FYSSAS Panagiotis	14
6	PAPAC Sasa	50	57	SEITARIDIS Giourkas	2
8	GRLIC Ivicia	61	KATSOURANIS Konstantinos	21
10	MISIMOVIC Zvjezdan	36	KARAGOUNIS Georgios	10
18	HRGOVIC Mirko	89	GIANNAKOPOLOUS Stelios	8
19	BARTOLOVIC Mladen		BASINAS Angelos	6
21	SKORO Alen		SAMARAS Georgios	27
22	BAJIC Branimir		CHARISTEAS Angelos	9
	Tr: SLISKOVIC Blaz		Tr: REHHAGEL Otto	
12	TOLJA Almir	45	57	PATSATZOGLOU Christos	3
11	IBRICIC Senidad	79	36	ZAGORAKIS Theodoras	7
11	GRUJIC Vladan	61	89	AMANATIDIS Ioannis	20

Zimbru, Chisinau
24-03-2007, 19:00, 8033, Aliyev AZE

MDA 1 1 MLT

Epureanu 85 | Mallia 73

#	MOLDOVA	h	a	MALTA	#
1	PASCENCO Serghei			HABER Justin	1
2	GOLOVATENCO Victor			SAID Brian	4
3	EPUREANU Alexandru			BRIFFA Roderick	5
4	OLEXIC Ghenadie		87	DIMECH Luke	6
9	BORDIAN Vitalie			AGIUS Gilbert	7
5	REBEJA Radu		92+	MIFSUD Michael	9
6	COMLEONOC Victor	84	77	WOODS Ivan	10
8	NAMASCO Serghei			MALLIA George	11
10	FRUNZA Viorel	70	70	SCHEMBRI Andre	13
11	BUGALOV Igor			SCICULUNA Kenneth	17
7	ZMEU Denis	63		PACE Jamie	18
	Tr: DOBROVOLSKIY Igor			Tr: FITZEL Dusan	
17	IVANOV Stanislav	63	70	BOGDANOVIC Daniel	8
18	DADU Serghei	84 87	77	SAMMUT Kevin	14
			92+	SCIBERRAS Gareth	15

Ullevål, Oslo
24-03-2007, 20:05, 16 987, Riley ENG

NOR 1 2 BIH

Carew 50p | Misimovic 18, Muslimovic 33

#	NORWAY	h	a	BOSNIA-HER'GOVINA	#
1	MYHRE Thomas			GUSO Adnan	1
3	HAGEN Eric		58	BERBEROVIC Dzemal	2
5	HANGELAND Brede		47	NADAREVIC Safet	4
6	RIISE John Arne			BAJIC Branimir	5
7	STROMSTAD Fredrik	62		KRUNIC Branislav	6
8	ANDRESEN Martin			DAMJANOVIC Dario	8
10	CAREW John			MUSLIMOVIC Zvjezdan	9
11	PEDERSEN Morten Gamst			MISIMOVIC Zvjezdan	10
22	HAESTAD Kristofer			IBISEVIC Vedad	11
24	JOHNSEN Frode	46	82	CUSTOVIC Asim	15
34	STORBAEK Jarl Andre	79		HRGOVIC Mirko	18
	Tr: HAREIDE Age			Tr: MUZUROVIC Fuad	
14	IVERSEN Steffen	46	58	MUSIC Vednin	7
19	GRINDHEIM Christian	62	82	MALETIC Darko	14
30	BRENNE Simon	79	47	RADELJIC Ivan	16

Karaiskaki, Piraeus
24-03-2007, 21:30, 31 405, Stark GER

GRE 1 4 TUR

Kyrgiakos 5 | Tuncay Sanli 27, Gökhan Unal 55, Tümer Metin 70, Gökdeniz 81

#	GREECE	h	a	TURKEY	#
1	NIKOPOLIDIS Antonios			VOLKAN Demirel	23
5	DELLAS Traianos			SERVET Cetin	2
25	KYRGIAKOS Sotirios			HAMIT Altintop	22
2	SEITARIDIS Giourkas			GOKHAN Zan	4
14	FYSSAS Panagiotis	56	19	IBRAHIM Uzülmez	3
21	KATSOURANIS Konstantinos			MEHMET Aurelio	7
6	BASINAS Angelos		80	TUMER Metin	11
10	KARAGOUNIS Georgios			SABRI Sarioglu	25
8	GIANNAKOPOLOUS Stellios	72	57	GOKHAN Unal	18
9	CHARISTEAS Angelos	63		HAKAN Sukur	20
4	SAMARAS Georgios			TUNCAY Sanli	17
	Tr: REHHAGEL Otto			Tr: Fatih TERIM	
20	AMANATIDIS Ioannis	72	80	GOKDENIZ Karadeniz	10
15	VASSILIOS Torosidis	56	57	HUSEYIN Cimsir	15
17	GEKAS Theofanis	63	19	VOLKAN Yaman	16

Megyeri úti, Budapest
28-03-2007, 18:00, 6150, Ingvarsson SWE

HUN 2 0 MDA

Priskin 9, Gera 63

#	HUNGARY	h	a	MOLDOVA	#
1	VEGH Zoltan			PASCENCO Serghei	1
2	CSIZMADIA Csaba			GOLOVATENCO Victor	2
3	BODOR Boldizsar			COJOCARI Andrei	3
4	JUHASZ Roland			OLEXIC Ghenadie	4
5	BALOGH Bela	36		EPUREANU Alexandru	5
6	TOTH Balazs		45	IVANOV Stanislav	7
7	VADOCZ Krisztian			CORNEENCOV Andrei	8
8	TOZSER Daniel			BORDIAN Vitalie	9
9	PRISKIN Tamas	88	66	COMLEONOC Victor	6
10	HAJNAL Tamas	64	45	FRUNZA Viorel	10
11	GERA Zoltan			BUGAIOV Igor	11
	Tr: VARHIDI Peter			Tr: DOBROVOLSKIY Igor	
13	HUSZTI Szabolcs	64	45	ALEXEEV Serghei	14
15	VASKO Tamas	36	45	NAMASCO Serghei	17
16	TISZA Tibor	88	66	ZMEU Denis	18

Ta'Qali, Ta'Qali
28-03-2007, 19:30, 8700, Garcia POR

MLT 0 1 GRE

Basinas 66p

#	MALTA	h	a	GREECE	#
1	HABER Justin			CHALKAS Konstantinos	12
2	AZZOPARDI Ian		83	DELLAS Traianos	5
4	SAID Brian			VINTRA Loukas	14
5	BRIFFA Roderick	66		KYRGIAKOS Sotirios	25
6	SCICULUNA Kenneth			KAPSIS Michalis	19
7	AGIUS Gilbert			TOROSIDIS Vassilios	15
11	MALLIA George	91+		BASINAS Angelos	6
14	SAMMUT Kevin			KARAGOUNIS Georgios	10
18	PACE Jamie			KATSOURANIS Konstantinos	21
9	MIFSUD Michael	92+	92+	GEKAS Theofanis	
13	SCHEMBRI Andre	71	64	SALPINGIDIS Dimitrios	22
	Tr: FITZEL Dusan			Tr: REHHAGEL Otto	
17	BARBARA Etienne	91+	83	ANATOLKIS Georgios	32
20	BOGDANOVIC Daniel	71	64	LIBEROPOLOUS Nikolaos	33
			92+	SAMARAS Georgios	4

Commerzbank Arena, Frankfurt am Main
28-03-2007, 20:00, BCD, Farina ITA

TUR 2 2 NOR

Hamit Altintop 2 72 90 | Brenne 31, Andresen 40

#	TURKEY	h	a	NORWAY	#
23	VOLKAN Demirel			MYHRE Thomas	1
25	SABRI Sarioglu			RIISE John Arne	6
2	SERVET Cetin			HAGEN Eric	3
21	EMRE Asik			HANGELAND Brede	5
22	HAMIT Altintop			STORBAEK Jarl Andre	34
11	TUMER Metin	45		STROMSTAD Fredrik	7
6	EMRE Belozoglu			ANDRESEN Martin	8
10	GOKDENIZ Karadeniz	79	57	HAESTAD Kristofer	22
7	MEHMET Aurelio		85	BRENNE Simon	30
20	HAKAN Sukur	93+	63	HELSTAD Thorstein	32
17	TUNCAY Sanli			CAREW John	10
	Tr: Fatih TERIM			Tr: HAREIDE Age	
15	HUSEYIN Cimsir	93+	57	SKJELBRED Per Ciljan	39
16	VOLKAN Yaman	45	63	HOLM Daniel	31
26	MEHMET Yidiz	79	85	NEVLAND Erik	36

Ulleväl, Oslo
2-06-2007, 20:05, 16 364, Granat POL

NOR 4 0 MLT

Hæstad 31, Helstad 73, Iversen 79, Riise 91+

No	NORWAY				MALTA	No
23	OPDAL Hakon				MUSCAT Mario	1
3	HAGEN Eric				AZZOPARDI Ian	3
6	RIISE John Arne				SAID Brian	4
21	RIISE Bjorn				WELLMAN Stephen	6
8	ANDRESEN Martin				SCICULUNA Kenneth	17
22	HAESTAD Kristofer	82			AGIUS Gilbert	7
14	IVERSEN Steffen		46		SAMMUT Kevin	10
10	CAREW John	72			MALLIA George	11
11	PEDERSEN Morten Gamst	62			PACE Jamie	18
34	STORBAEK Jarl Andre		83		MIFSUD Michael	9
5	HANGELAND Brede		69		SCHEMBRI Andre	13
	Tr: HAREIDE Age				Tr: FITZEL Dusan	
26	BRAATEN Daniel	82	69		BOGDANOVIC Daniel	5
30	BRENNE Simon	62	46		WOODS Ivan	14
32	HELSTAD Thorstein	72	83		BARBARA Etienne	16

Olimpijski, Sarajevo
2-06-2007, 20:00, 13 800, Fröjdfeldt SWE

BIH 3 2 TUR

Muslimovic 27, Dzeko 47, Custovic 90 — Hakan Sükür 13, Sabri 39

No	BOSNIA-HER'GOVINA				TURKEY	No
1	GUSO Adnan				RUSTU Recber	1
5	BAJIC Branimir				HAMIT Altintop	22
7	MUSIC Vednin				SERVET Cetin	2
8	DAMJANOVIC Dario				GOKHAN Zan	4
4	RAHIMIC Elvir				IBRAHIM Uzulmez	3
18	HRGOVIC Mirko				MARCO Aurelio	7
10	MISIMOVIC Zvjezdan		77		SABRI Sarioglu	25
20	MALETIC Darko	84	46		GOKDENIZ Karadeniz	10
9	MUSLIMOVIC Zvjezdan	93+	64		ARDA Turan	14
11	DZEKO Edin	62			TUNCAY Sanli	17
12	ALAIM Muhamed				HAKAN Sukur	9
	Tr: MUZUROVIC Fuad				Tr: Fatih TERIM	
6	PANDZA Boris	93+	64		YILDIRAY Basturk	8
14	ZEBA Zajko	62	46		HUSEYIN Cimsir	15
15	CUSTOVIC Adnan	84	77		UMIT Karan	20

Pankritio, Irákleio
2-06-2007, 21:30, 17 244, Larsen DEN

GRE 2 0 HUN

Gekas 16, Seitaridis 29

No	GREECE				HUNGARY	No
12	CHALKAS Konstantinos				VEGH Zoltan	1
2	SEITARIDIS Giourkas				CSIZMADIA Csaba	2
15	TOROSIDIS Vassilios		40		BODOR Boldizsar	3
32	ANATOLKIS Georgios	53			JUHASZ Roland	4
25	KYRGIAKOS Sotirios				BALOGH Bela	5
21	KATSOURANIS Konstantinos				TOTH Balazs	6
10	KARAGOUNIS Georgios		73		VADOCZ Krisztian	7
6	BASINAS Angelos				TOZSER Daniel	8
17	GEKAS Theofanis	79			PRISKIN Tamas	9
20	AMANATIDIS Ioannis	87			HAJNAL Tamas	10
9	CHARISEAS Angelos		79		GERA Zoltan	11
	Tr: REHHAGEL Otto				Tr: VARHIDI Peter	
8	GIANNAKOPOLOUS Stelios	79	79		DZSUDZSAK Balazs	14
3	PATSATZOGLOU Christos	53	40		VANCZAK Vilmos	15
33	LIBEROPOLOUS Nikolaos	87	73		SZELESI Zoltan	18

Ulleväl, Oslo
6-06-2007, 19:00, 19 198, Iturralde Gonzalez ESP

NOR 4 0 HUN

Iversen 22, Braaten 57, Carew 2 60 78

No	NORWAY				HUNGARY	No
23	OPDAL Hakon				VEGH Zoltan	1
34	STORBAEK Jarl Andre				SZELESI Zoltan	2
3	HAGEN Eric				JUHASZ Roland	4
5	HANGELAND Brede				BALOGH Bela	5
6	RIISE John Arne				VANCZAK Vilmos	3
21	RIISE Bjorn		83		BUZSAKY Akos	7
8	ANDRESEN Martin				TOTH Balazs	6
19	GRINDHEIM Christian	46			TOZSER Daniel	8
14	IVERSEN Steffen	46			GERA Zoltan	11
10	CAREW John		71		PRISKIN Tamas	9
11	PEDERSEN Morten Gamst	82			HAJNAL Tamas	10
	Tr: HAREIDE Age				Tr: VARHIDI Peter	
22	HAESTAD Kristofer	46	71		TISZA Tibor	13
26	BRAATEN Daniel	46	83		VADOCZ Krisztian	17
32	HELSTAD Thorstein	82				

Pankritio, Irákleio
6-06-2007, 21:30, 22 000, Wegereef NED

GRE 2 1 MDA

Charisteas 30, Liberopoulos 95+ — Frunza 80

No	GREECE				MOLDOVA	No
1	NIKOPOLIDS Antonios				CALANCEA Nicolai	1
2	SEITARIDIS Giourkas				EPUREANU Alexandru	5
18	GOUMAS Ioannis				GOLOVATENCO Victor	2
25	KYRGIAKOS Sotirios				CATINSUS Valeriu	3
3	PATSATZOGLOU Christos	83			NAMASCO Serghei	6
15	TOROSIDIS Vassilios				BORDIAN Vitalie	11
10	KARAGOUNIS Georgios		82		COMLEONOC Victor	17
21	KATSOURANIS Konstantinos				JOSAN Nicolae	4
20	AMANATIDIS Ioannis	71			GATCAN Alexandru	8
9	CHARISEAS Angelos		64		ALEXEEV Serghei	7
17	GEKAS Theofanis	63	57		BUGAIOV Igor	9
	Tr: REHHAGEL Otto				Tr: DOBROVOLSKIY Igor	
4	SAMARAS Georgios	71	64		FRUNZA Viorel	18
8	GIANNAKOPOLOUS Stelios	83	82		TIGIRLAS Igor	15
33	LIBEROPOLOUS Nikolaos	63	57		ZMEU Denis	14

Olimpijski, Sarajevo
6-06-2007, 20:15, 10 500, Richards WAL

BIH 1 0 MLT

Muslimovic 6

No	BOSNIA-HER'GOVINA				MALTA	No
1	GUSO Adnan				MUSCAT Mario	1
7	MUSIC Vednin	91+			AZZOPARDI Ian	3
16	HRGOVIC Mirko				SAID Brian	4
28	PANDZA Boris		65		BOGDANOVIC Daniel	5
16	RADELJIC Ivan				DIMECH Luke	6
11	MALETIC Darko	80			AGIUS Gilbert	7
4	DAMJANOVIC Dario				BRIFFA Roderick	8
10	MISIMOVIC Zvjezdan				MIFSUD Michael	9
25	RAHIMIC Elvir		70		WOODS Ivan	10
9	MUSLIMOVIC Zvjezdan				SAMMUT Kevin	17
23	DZEKO Edin	56	82		PACE Jamie	18
	Tr: MUZUROVIC Fuad				Tr: SLISKOVIC Blaz	
8	MUHAREMOVIC Veldin	91+	65		SCHEMBRI Andre	13
19	BARTOLOVIC Mladen	80	82		BARBARA Etienne	14
20	ZEBA Zajko	56	70		MALLIA George	11

GROUP D

Na Stínadlech, Teplice
2-09-2006, 20:15, 16 200, Eriksson SWE

CZE	2	1		WAL
Lafata 2 76 89			Jiránek OG 85	

CZECH REPUBLIC			WALES	
1 CECH Petr			JONES Paul	1
21 UJFALUSI Tomas		78	DELANEY Mark	2
13 JIRANEK Martin			GABBIDON Daniel	4
22 ROZEHNAL David			COLLINS James	5
6 JANKULOVSKI Marek		79	RICKETTS Sam	3
8 STAJNER Jiri	47+		ROBINSON Carl	6
4 GALASEK Tomas	87	47	FLETCHER Carl	8
10 ROSICKY Tomas			DAVIES Simon	10
20 PLASIL Jaroslav			GIGGS Ryan	11
18 KULIC Marek	75		BELLAMY Craig	7
9 KOLLER Jan			NYATANGA Lewin	9
Tr: BRUCKNER Karel			Tr: TOSHACK John	
5 KOVAC Radoslav	87	78	COTTERRILL David	12
7 SIONKO Libor	47+	47	LEDLEY Jospeph	15
11 LAFATA David	75	79	EARNSHAW Robert	18

Tehelné Pole, Bratislava
2-09-2006, 20:15, 4723, Orekhov UKR

SVK	6	1		CYP
Skrtel 9, Mintál 2 33 56,				
Sebo 2 43 49, Karhan 52			Yiasoumis 90	

SLOVAKIA			CYPRUS	
1 CONTOFALSKY Kamil			MORPHIS Michael	12
2 ZABAVNIK Radoslav	45		THEODOTOU Georgos	2
3 SKRTEL Martin			LAMBROU Lambros	4
5 DURICA Jan		67	LOUKA Loukas	5
15 CECH Marek			MICHAIL Chrysostomous	13
4 HLINKA Peter			CHARALAMBIDES C'tinos	10
6 KARHAN Miroslav			MAKRIDIS Konstantinos	20
18 SVENTO Dusan		45	GARPOZIS Alexandros	19
11 MINTAL Marek			OKKAS Yiannis	9
8 NEMETH Szilard	45		YIASOUMIS Yiasoumi	18
9 SEBO Filip	56		ALEXANDROU Nektarios	16
Tr: GALIS Dusan			Tr: ANASTASIADIS Angelos	
16 KRAJCIK Matej	45	67	THEOFILOU Christos	21
14 HOLOSKO Filip	45	45	KRASSAS Asimakis	23
10 HODUR Ivan	56			

Gottlieb-Daimler, Stuttgart
2-09-2006, 20:45, 53 198, Medina Cantalejo ESP

GER	1	0		IRL
Podolski 57				

GERMANY			REP. OF IRELAND	
1 LEHMANN Jens			GIVEN Shay	1
16 LAHM Philipp			CARR Stephen	2
3 FRIEDRICH Arne			O'BRIEN Andy	4
24 FRIEDRICH Manuel			DUNNE Richard	5
2 JANSEN Marcel		83	KILBANE Kevin	7
19 SCHNEIDER Bernd	83		FINNAN Steve	3
8 FRINGS Torsten			REID Steven	8
13 BALLACK Michael			O'SHEA John	6
7 SCHWEINSTEIGER Bastian		77	DUFF Damien	11
20 PODOLSKI Lukas	76	79	DOYLE Kevin	9
11 KLOSE Miroslav			KEANE Robbie	10
Tr: LOW Joachim			Tr: STAUNTON Steve	
10 NEUVILLE Oliver	76	79	ELLIOTT Stephen	12
18 BOROWSKI Tim	83	83	O'BRIEN Alan	13
		77	McGEADY Aiden	18

Tehelné Pole, Bratislava
6-09-2006, 20:15, 27 684, Bennett ENG

SVK	0	3		CZE
			Sionko 2 10 21, Koller 57	

SLOVAKIA			CZECHOSLOVAKIA	
1 CONTOFALSKY Kamil			CECH Petr	1
4 HLINKA Peter			JANKULOVSKI Marek	6
3 SKRTEL Martin			JIRANEK Martin	13
5 DURICA Jan			UJFALUSI Tomas	21
7 VALACHOVIC Jozef	45		ROZEHNAL David	22
18 SVENTO Dusan		72	POLAK Jan	3
15 CECH Marek	24		GALASEK Tomas	4
16 KRAJCIK Matej		77	SIONKO Libor	7
6 KARHAN Miroslav			ROSICKY Tomas	10
11 MINTAL Marek			PLASIL Jaroslav	20
9 SEBO Filip	45		KOLLER Jan	9
Tr: GALIS Dusan			Tr: BRUCKNER Karel	
10 HODUR Ivan	45	72	KOVAC Radoslav	5
14 HOLOSKO Filip	45	77	STAJNER Jiri	8
8 NEMETH Szilard	24			

Olimpico, Serravalle
6-09-2006, 20:45, 5090, Dereli TUR

SMR	0	13		GER
			Podolski 4 11 43 64 72, Schweinsteiger 2 28 47, Klose 2 30 46+,	
			Ballack 35, Hitzlsperger 2 66 73, Friedrich.M 87, Schneider 90p	

SAN MARINO			GERMANY	
1 SIMONCINI Aldo			LEHMANN Jens	1
4 ALBANI Nicola			JANSEN Marcel	2
5 DELLA VALLE Alessandro			FRIEDRICH Arne	3
6 BACCIOCCHI Simone			LAHM Philipp	16
8 PALAZZI Mirko			SCHWEINSTEIGER Bastian	7
2 VALENTINI Carlo		62	FRINGS Torsten	8
3 VANNUCCI Damiano	68	46	BALLACK Michael	13
7 MARANI Michele	78		SCHNEIDER Bernd	19
11 DOMENICONI Marco	45		FRIEDRICH Manuel	24
9 MARANI Manuel		46	KLOSE Miroslav	11
10 SELVA Andy			PODOLSKI Lukas	20
Tr: MAZZA Giampaolo			Tr: LOW Joachim	
13 BONINI Giovanni	45	46	ASAMOAH Gerald	14
17 MASI Mattia	78	62	HITZLSPERGER Thomas	15
18 SIMONCINI Davide	68	46	ODONKOR David	22

Millennium Stadium, Cardiff
7-10-2006, 15:00, 28 415, Van Egmond NED

WAL	1	5		SVK
Bale 37			Svento 14, Mintál 2 32 38,	
			Karhan 51, Vittek 59	

WALES			SLOVAKIA	
1 JONES Paul			CONTOFALSKY Kamil	1
2 DUFFY Richard			KOZAK Jan	2
3 BALE Gareth			KRATOCHVIL Roman	3
4 GABBIDON Daniel			PETRAS Martin	4
5 NYATANGA Lewin			VARGA Stanislav	5
6 ROBINSON Carl		67	KARHAN Miroslav	6
8 EDWARDS Robert	58	71	MINTAL Marek	9
9 KOUMAS Jason		77	VITTEK Robert	11
10 DAVIES Simon	88		PETRAS Peter	15
7 BELLAMY Craig			SVENTO Dusan	18
11 EARNSHAW Robert	45		DURICA Jan	20
Tr: TOSHACK John			Tr: GALIS Dusan	
14 LEDLEY Jospeph	58	77	HOLOSKO Filip	8
15 PARRY Paul	45	71	HODUR Ivan	10
16 COTTERRILL David	88	67	KRAJCIK Matej	16

U Nisy, Liberec
7-10-2006, 17:15, 9514, Aliyev AZE

CZE 7 0 SMR

Kulic [15], Polák [22], Baros 2 [28 68],
Koller 2 [43 52], Jarolím [49]

CZECH REPUBLIC				SAN MARINO	
1	CECH Petr			VALENTINI Federico	1
21	UJFALUSI Tomas			ALBANI Nicola	4
2	GRYGERA Zdenek			DELLA VALLE Alessandro	5
22	ROZEHNAL David	45		BACCIOCCHI Simone	6
6	JANKULOVSKI Marek		82	ANDREINI Matteo	11
14	JAROLIM David			VALENTINI Carlo	2
3	POLAK Jan			VANNUCCI Damiano	3
10	ROSICKY Tomas	63	69	MASI Mattia	7
15	BAROS Milan			DOMENICONI Marco	8
18	KULIC Marek	45	54	MORETTI Michele	9
9	KOLLER Jan			SELVA Andy	10
	Tr: BRUCKNER Karel			Tr: MAZZA Giampaolo	
11	LAFATA David	45	69	CRESCENTINI Federico	15
19	ZAPOTOCNY Tomas	45	54	MARANI Michele	17
20	PLASIL Jaroslav	63	82	MARIOTTI Paolo	18

GSP, Nicosia
7-10-2006, 19:30, 5000, Batista POR

CYP 5 2 IRL

Konstantinou.M 2 [10 50p],
Garpozis [16], Charalambides 2 [60 75]

Ireland [8], Dunne [44]

CYPRUS				REP. OF IRELAND	
12	MORPHIS Michael			KENNY Paddy	1
17	STASIAS Marinos			FINNAN Steve	2
4	LAMBROU Lambros			O'SHEA John	3
5	LOUKA Loukas		71	O'BRIEN Andy	4
2	THEODOTOU Georgos		78	DUNNE Richard	5
13	MICHAIL Chrysostomous	46		KILBANE Kevin	6
19	GARPOZIS Alexandros	77	80	McGEADY Aiden	7
20	MAKRIDIS Konstantinos		83	IRELAND Stephen	8
9	OKKAS Yiannis	86		MORRISON Clinton	9
11	KONSTANTINOU Michalis			KEANE Robbie	10
7	ALONEFTIS Efstathios			DUFF Damien	11
	Tr: ANASTASIADIS Angelos			Tr: STAUNTON Steve	
3	CHARALAMBOUS Elias	77	83	DOUGLAS Jonathan	12
10	CHARALAMBIDES C'tinos	46	71	LEE Alan	15
18	YIASOUMIS Yiasoumi	86	80	O'BRIEN Alan	18

Lansdowne Road, Dublin
11-10-2006, 19:30, 35 500, Layec FRA

IRL 1 1 CZE

Kilbane [62]

Koller [64]

REP. OF IRELAND				CZECH REPUBLIC	
1	HENDERSON Wayne			CECH Petr	1
2	KELLY Stephen			POLAK Jan	3
4	McSHANE Paul			UJFALUSI Tomas	21
5	O'SHEA John			KOVAC Radoslav	5
3	FINNAN Steve			JANKULOVSKI Marek	6
6	CARSLEY Lee			JIRANEK Martin	13
7	REID Andy	72		ROSICKY Tomas	10
8	DOUGLAS Jonathan		85	PLASIL Jaroslav	20
9	KILBANE Kevin	79		ROZEHNAL David	22
11	DUFF Damien			KOLLER Jan	9
10	KEANE Robbie		82	BAROS Milan	15
	Tr: STAUNTON Steve			Tr: BRUCKNER Karel	
13	O'BRIEN Alan	79	85	GRYGERA Zdenek	2
14	QUINN Alan	72	82	JAROLIM David	14

Millennium Stadium, Cardiff
11-10-2006, 20:00, 20 456, Granat POL

WAL 3 1 CYP

Koumas [33], Earnshaw [39],
Bellamy [72]

Okkas [83]

WALES				CYPRUS	
1	PRICE Lewis			MORPHIS Michael	12
2	DUFFY Richard	78		THEODOTOU Georgos	2
4	GABBIDON Daniel			LAMBROU Lambros	4
5	NYATANGA Lewin			LOUKA Loukas	5
3	BALE Gareth		84	MICHAIL Chrysostomous	13
8	MORGAN Craig		45	GARPOZIS Alexandros	19
6	ROBINSON Carl		45	MAKRIDIS Konstantinos	20
10	KOUMAS Jason	76		ALONEFTIS Efstathios	7
7	BELLAMY Craig	91+		KONSTANTINOU Michalis	11
11	EARNSHAW Robert			OKKAS Yiannis	9
	Tr: TOSHACK John			Tr: ANASTASIADIS Angelos	
16	PARRY Paul	91+	45	CHARALAMBIDES C'tinos	10
17	LEDLEY Jospeph	76	84	YIASOUMIS Yiasoumi	18
12	EDWARDS Robert	78	45	CHARALAMBOUS Elias	3

Tehelné Pole, Bratislava
11-10-2006, 20:45, 27 580, Hauge NOR

SVK 1 4 GER

Varga [58]

Podolski 2 [13 72], Ballack [25],
Schweinsteiger [36]

SLOVAKIA				GERMANY	
1	CONTOFALSKY Kamil			LEHMANN Jens	1
15	PETRAS Peter	73		FRIEDRICH Arne	3
5	VARGA Stanislav			FRIEDRICH Manuel	24
3	SKRTEL Martin			FRITZ Clemens	27
20	DURICA Jan			LAHM Philipp	16
6	KARHAN Miroslav			BALLACK Michael	13
4	PETRAS Martin			FRINGS Torsten	8
18	SVENTO Dusan		75	SCHNEIDER Bernd	19
2	KOZAK Jan	65	77	SCHWEINSTEIGER Bastian	7
9	MINTAL Marek			KLOSE Miroslav	11
11	VITTEK Robert		85	PODOLSKI Lukas	20
	Tr: GALIS Dusan			Tr: LOW Joachim	
8	HOLOSKO Filip	73	75	ODONKOR David	22
10	HODUR Ivan	65	77	TROCHOWSKI Piotr	28
			85	HANKE Mike	9

Lansdowne Road, Dublin
15-11-2006, 19:30, 34 018, Isaksen FRO

IRL 5 0 SMR

Reid [7], Doyle [24], Keane 3 [31 58p 85]

REP. OF IRELAND				SAN MARINO	
1	GIVEN Shay			VALENTINI Federico	1
3	FINNAN Steve			BUGLI Matteo	8
4	McSHANE Paul			ALBANI Nicola	4
5	DUNNE Richard			BACCIOCCHI Simone	6
2	O'SHEA John		81	SIMONCINI Davide	5
6	CARSLEY Lee	50	72	VANNUCCI Damiano	3
9	KILBANE Kevin	79		VALENTINI Carlo	2
7	REID Andy			ANDREINI Matteo	7
11	DUFF Damien		59	MARIOTTI Paolo	11
8	DOYLE Kevin	63		MARANI Manuel	9
10	KEANE Robbie			SELVA Andy	10
	Tr: STAUNTON Steve			Tr: MAZZA Giampaolo	
14	DOUGLAS Jonathan	50	72	CRESCENTINI Federico	13
17	LEE Alan	79	59	MARANI Michele	16
18	McGEADY Aiden	63	81	BONINI Giovanni	18

GSP, Nicosia
15-11-2006, 21:00, 12 300, Fröjdfeldt SWE

CYP 1 1 GER

Okkas [43]   Ballack [16]

CYPRUS			GERMANY		
22	GEORGALLIDES Antonis		HILDEBRAND Timo	12	
8	ELIA Marios		FRIEDRICH Arne	3	
4	LAMBROU Lambros		LAHM Philipp	16	
5	LOUKA Loukas		SCHWEINSTEIGER Bastian	7	
2	THEODOTOU Georgos	79	FRINGS Torsten	8	
20	MAKRIDIS Konstantinos		BALLACK Michael	13	
10	CHARALAMBIDES C'tinos		FRITZ Clemens	27	
13	MICHAIL Chrysostomous	68	FRIEDRICH Manuel	24	
9	OKKAS Yiannis	72	79	ODONKOR David	22
7	ALONEFTIS Efstathios		KLOSE Miroslav	11	
11	KONSTANTINOU Michalis	62	NEUVILLE Oliver	10	
	Tr: ANASTASIADIS Angelos		Tr: LOW Joachim		
29	NICOLAOU Charis	72	79	HITZLSPERGER Thomas	15
3	CHARALAMBOUS Elias	79	62	HANKE Mike	9
23	KRASSAS Asimakis	68			

Olimpico, Serravalle
7-02-2006, 20:45, 3294, Rasmussen DEN

SMR 1 2 IRL

Marani [86]   Kilbane [49], Ireland [94+]

SAN MARINO			REP. OF IRELAND		
1	SIMONCINI Aldo		HENDERSON Wayne	1	
2	VALENTINI Carlo		FINNAN Steve	2	
9	MARANI Manuel		DUNNE Richard	5	
4	ALBANI Nicola	45	O'SHEA John	4	
5	SIMONCINI Davide	74	HARTE Ian	3	
6	MUCCIOLI Riccardo		DUFF Damien	7	
7	BONINI Giovanni	76	CARSLEY Lee	6	
8	DOMENICONI Marco	88	IRELAND Stephen	8	
3	MARANI Michele		KILBANE Kevin	11	
10	SELVA Andy	80	LONG Shane	9	
11	GASPERONI Alex	66	KEANE Robbie	10	
	Tr: MAZZA Giampaolo		Tr: STAUNTON Steve		
13	ANDREINI Matteo	66	74	HUNT Stephen	14
14	BUGLI Matteo	88	45	McSHANE Paul	17
17	VANNUCCI Damiano	76	80	STOKES Anthony	18

Croke Park, Dublin
24-03-2007, 15:00, 72 539, Hauge NOR

IRL 1 0 WAL

Ireland [39]

REP. OF IRELAND			WALES		
1	GIVEN Shay		COYNE Danny	1	
2	FINNAN Steve		RICKETTS Sam	2	
4	McSHANE Paul	74	BALE Gareth	3	
5	DUNNE Richard		COLLINS James	4	
2	O'SHEA John		EVANS Steve	5	
8	DOUGLAS Jonathan	80	NYATANGA Lewin	6	
6	CARSLEY Lee	45	LEDLEY Jospeph	8	
7	IRELAND Stephen	59	91+	ROBINSON Carl	9
9	KILBANE Kevin		DAVIES Simon	10	
10	KEANE Robbie	89	GIGGS Ryan	11	
11	DUFF Damien		BELLAMY Craig	7	
	Tr: STAUNTON Steve		Tr: TOSHACK John		
12	HUNT Stephen	80	74	COLLINS Danny	12
14	McGEADY Aiden	89	45	FLETCHER Carl	14
17	DOYLE Kevin	59	91+	EASTER Jermaine Mauric	18

GSP, Nicosia
24-03-2007, 20:00, 2696, Lehner AUT

CYP 1 3 SVK

Aloneftis [43]   Vittek [54], Skrtel [67], Jakubko [77]

CYPRUS			SLOVAKIA		
12	MORPHIS Michael	42	CONTOFALSKY Kamil	1	
17	STASIAS Marinos		46	SINGLAR Peter	9
4	LAMBROU Lambros		SKRTEL Martin	3	
5	LOUKA Loukas		DURICA Jan	5	
2	THEODOTOU Georgos	42	GRESKO Vratislav	2	
13	MICHAIL Chrysostomous		BORBELY Balazs	17	
10	CHARALAMBIDES C'tinos		KRAJCIK Matej	14	
19	GARPOZIS Alexandros	66	SVENTO Dusan	18	
20	MAKRIDIS Konstantinos	58	68	SAPARA Marek	7
18	YIASOUMIS Yiasoumi		VITTEK Robert	11	
7	ALONEFTIS Efstathios	79	JAKUBKO Martin	16	
	Tr: ANASTASIADIS Angelos		Tr: KOCIAN Jan		
22	GEORGALLIDES Antonis	42	68	KOZAK Jan	4
3	CHARALAMBOUS Elias	66	79	SESTAK Stanislav	19
8	ELIA Marios	58	46	ZOFCAK Igor	20

Strahov, Prague
24-03-2007, 20:45, 17 821, Rosetti ITA

CZE 1 2 GER

Baros [77]   Schweinsteiger [42], Kuranyi [62]

CZECH REPUBLIC			GERMANY		
1	CECH Petr		LEHMANN Jens	1	
21	UJFALUSI Tomas	84	LAHM Philipp	16	
13	JIRANEK Martin		MERTESACKE Per	17	
22	ROZEHNAL David		METZELDER Christoph	21	
6	JANKULOVSKI Marek		JANSEN Marcel	2	
7	SIONKO Libor	46	SCHNEIDER Bernd	19	
10	ROSICKY Tomas		FRINGS Torsten	8	
4	GALASEK Tomas	67	BALLACK Michael	13	
3	POLAK Jan		SCHWEINSTEIGER Bastian	7	
9	KOLLER Jan	89	PODOLSKI Lukas	20	
15	BAROS Milan		KURANYI Kevin	31	
	Tr: BRUCKNER Karel		Tr: LOW Joachim		
18	KULIC Marek	67	89	HITZLSPERGER Thomas	15
19	VICEK Stanislav	84			
20	PLASIL Jaroslav	46			

U Nisy, Liberec
28-03-2007, 17:25, 9310, Bebek CRO

CZE 1 0 CYP

Kovác [22]

CZECH REPUBLIC			CYPRUS		
1	CECH Petr		GEORGALLIDES Antonis	22	
21	UJFALUSI Tomas		STASIAS Marinos	17	
2	GRYGERA Zdenek	12	LAMBROU Lambros	4	
22	ROZEHNAL David		THEODOTOU Georgos	2	
6	JANKULOVSKI Marek		PASARESKEVAS Chrisou	31	
4	GALASEK Tomas	76	ELIA Marios	8	
10	ROSICKY Tomas	75	CHARALAMBIDES C'tinos	10	
3	POLAK Jan		MAKRIDIS Konstantinos	20	
14	JAROLIM David	72	YIASOUMIS Yiasoumi	18	
9	KOLLER Jan		OKKAS Yiannis	9	
15	BAROS Milan	77	ALONEFTIS Efstathios	7	
	Tr: BRUCKNER Karel		Tr: ANASTASIADIS Angelos		
5	KOVAC Radoslav	27	12	76	CHARALAMBOUS Elias	3
13	JIRANEK Martin	27	75	KRASSAS Asimakis	23
20	PLASIL Jaroslav	77	72	CHILI Kyriakos	32

Croke Park, Dublin
28-03-2007, 19:30, 71 257, Baskakov RUS

IRL	1 0	SVK

Doyle [13]

	REP. OF IRELAND			SLOVAKIA	
1	GIVEN Shay			CONTOFALSKY Kamil	1
2	O'SHEA John		79	SINGLAR Peter	9
3	FINNAN Steve			SKRTEL Martin	3
4	McSHANE Paul			KLIMPL Maros	10
5	DUNNE Richard			GRESKO Vratislav	2
6	CARSLEY Lee		87	SVENTO Dusan	18
7	IRELAND Stephen	70		ZOFCAK Igor	20
8	McGEADY Aiden	87		BORBELY Balazs	17
9	KILBANE Kevin	72		SAPARA Marek	7
11	DUFF Damien			VITTEK Robert	11
10	DOYLE Kevin	74		JAKUBKO Martin	16
	Tr: STAUNTON Steve			Tr: KOCIAN Jan	
12	HUNT Stephen	70	72	HOLOSKO Filip	13
15	QUINN Alan	84	79	SESTAK Stanislav	19
17	LONG Shane	74	87	MICHALIK Lubomir	5

Millennium Stadium, Cardiff
28-03-2007, 20:00, 18 752, Tchagharyan ARM

WAL	3 0	SMR

Giggs [3], Bale [20], Koumas [63p]

	WALES			SAN MARINO	
1	COYNE Danny			SIMONCINI Aldo	1
2	RICKETTS Sam		85	VALENTINI Carlo	2
5	EVANS Steve	63		ANDREINI Matteo	3
4	COLLINS James			ALBANI Nicola	4
3	BALE Gareth			MUCCIOLI Riccardo	5
6	FLETCHER Carl			BACCIOCCHI Simone	6
8	KOUMAS Jason		79	NEGRI Cristian	7
10	DAVIES Simon		67	DOMENICONI Marco	8
11	GIGGS Ryan	73		MARANI Manuel	9
7	BELLAMY Craig			SELVA Andy	10
9	EASTER Jermaine Mauric	49		GASPERONI Alex	11
	Tr: TOSHACK John			Tr: MAZZA Giampaolo	
14	NYATANGA Lewin	63	67	BUGLI Matteo	14
16	PARRY Paul	73	79	NANNI Federico	15
17	COTTERRILL David	49	85	TOCCACELI Alan	16

Frankenstadion, Nuremberg
2-06-2007, 19:00, 43 967, Asumaa FIN

GER	6 0	SMR

Kuranyi [45], Jansen [52], Frings [56p],
Gómez 2 [63] [65], Fritz [67]

	GERMANY			SAN MARINO	
1	LEHMANN Jens			SIMONCINI Aldo	1
16	LAHM Philipp	70		VALENTINI Carlo	2
17	MERTESACKE Per			VANNUCCI Damiano	3
21	METZELDER Christoph			ALBANI Nicola	4
2	JANSEN Marcel			DELLA VALLE Alessandro	5
8	FRINGS Torsten		54	SIMONCINI Davide	6
15	HITZLSPERGER Thomas			BACCIOCCHI Simone	7
19	SCHNEIDER Bernd		69	NEGRI Cristian	8
34	HILBERT Roberto	59	85	BUGLI Matteo	9
11	KLOSE Miroslav			GASPERONI Alex	11
31	KURANYI Kevin	59	76	MARANI Manuel	10
	Tr: LOW Joachim			Tr: MAZZA Giampaolo	
27	FRITZ Clemens	59	85	VITAIOLI Fabio	18
32	GOMEZ Mario	59	69	BONINI Giovanni	14
37	HELMES Patrick	70	76	DOMENICONI Marco	15

Millennium Stadium, Cardiff
2-06-2007, 15:00, 30 174, Allaerts BEL

WAL	0 0	CZE

	WALES			CZECH REPUBLIC	
1	HENNESSEY Wayne			CECH Petr	1
2	RICKETTS Sam			UJFALUSI Tomas	21
3	NYATANGA Lewin			KOVAC Radoslav	5
4	GABBIDON Daniel			JANKULOVSKI Marek	6
5	COLLINS James			ROZEHNAL David	2
6	ROBINSON Carl		65	POLAK Jan	3
8	LEDLEY Joseph		83	SLVOK Tomas	7
9	KOUMAS Jason			ROSICKY Tomas	10
10	DAVIES Simon			PLASIL Jaroslav	20
11	GIGGS Ryan	89		KOLLER Jan	9
7	BELLAMY Craig		46	BAROS Milan	15
	Tr: TOSHACK John			Tr: BRUCKNER Karel	
14	EARNSHAW Robert	89	83	MATEJOVSKY Marek	8
			65	JAROLIM David	14
			46	KULIC Marek	18

AOL Arena, Hamburg
6-06-2007, 20:30, 51 600, Benquerença POR

GER	2 1	SVK

Durica OG [10], Hitzlsperger [43]   Metzelder OG [20]

	GERMANY				SLOVAKIA	
1	LEHMANN Jens				CONTOFALSKY Kamil	1
2	JANSEN Marcel				SKRTEL Martin	3
16	LAHM Philipp				MANSYK Marek	8
17	MERTESACKE Per				DURICA Jan	5
21	METZELDER Christoph				KLIMPL Maros	10
27	FRITZ Clemens				SVENTO Dusan	18
8	FRINGS Torsten		83		STRBA Zdeno	6
15	HITZLSPERGER Thomas				KRAJCIK Matej	7
19	SCHNEIDER Bernd	92+	65		SAPARA Marek	9
11	KLOSE Miroslav	74	65		SESTAK Stanislav	16
31	KURANYI Kevin	65			VITTEK Robert	11
	Tr: LOW Joachim				Tr: KOCIAN Jan	
38	ROLFES Simon	92+	83		ORAVEC Tomas	14
32	GOMEZ Mario	65	65		ZOFCAK Igor	15
28	TROCHOWSKI Piotr	74	65		HOLOSKO Filip	13

GROUP E

A Le Coq Arena, Tallinn
16-08-2006, 19:00, 7500, Jakobsson ISL

EST 0 1 MKD

Sedloski [73]

ESTONIA			FYR MACEDONIA	
1 POOM Mart			NIKOLOVSKI Jane	1
2 JAAGER Enar			LAZAREVSKI Vlade	14
3 STEPANOV Andrei		87	PETROV Robert	3
4 PIIROJA Raio			SEDLOSKI Goce	4
5 KRUGLOV Dmitri			MITRESKI Igor	5
6 DMITRIJEV Aleksandr			NOVESKI Nikolce	2
7 TEREHHOV Sergei			SUMULIKOSKI Velice	8
8 KLAVAN Ragnar			JANCEVSKI Igor	17
10 LINDPERE Joel	74	82	PANDEV Goran	19
11 SIDORENKOV Andrei	67	71	NAUMOSKI Ilco	11
9 VIIKMAE Kristen	92+		MAZNOV Goran	9
Tr: GOES Jelle			Tr: KATANEC Srecko	
14 BARENGRUB Alo	92+	87	VASOSKI Aleksandar	15
17 TEEVER Ingemar	67	82	TASEVSKI Darko	16
18 NEEMELO Tarmo	74	71	STOJKOV Aco	18

Old Trafford, Manchester
2-09-2006, 17:00, 56 290, Brugger AUT

ENG 5 0 AND

Crouch 2 [5 66], Gerrard [13],
Defoe 2 [38 47]

ENGLAND			ANDORRA	
1 ROBINSON Paul			ALVAREZ Jesús 'Koldo'	1
2 NEVILLE Phil	65		LIMA Antoni	5
5 BROWN Wes			GARCIA José 'Txema'	7
6 TERRY John			AYALA Jose Manuel	2
3 COLE Ashley			SONEJEE Oscar	4
4 GERRARD Steven		45	SANCHEZ Javier	3
7 HARGEAVES Owen		77	SIVERA Toni	6
8 LAMPARD Frank			VIEIRA Marcio	8
11 DOWNING Stewart	64		SILVA Fernando	9
9 CROUCH Peter		49	PUJOL Marc	10
10 DEFOE Jermain	71		RUIZ Justo	11
Tr: McCLAREN Steve			Tr: RODRIGO David	
15 RICHARDSON Kieran	64	45	SANCHEZ Juli	12
16 LENNON Aaron	65	49	JIMENEZ Manolo	15
18 JOHNSON Andrew	71	77	GARCIA Genis	16

A Le Coq Arena, Tallinn
2-09-2006, 21:30, 7800, Verbist BEL

EST 0 1 ISR

Colautti [8]

ESTONIA			ISRAEL	
1 POOM Mart			AWAT Dudu	1
2 JAAGER Enar			GERSHON Shimon	5
3 STEPANOV Andrei			BEN HAIM Tal	3
4 PIIROJA Raio			BENAYOUN Yossi	15
5 KRUGLOV Dmitri		59	ZANDBERG Michael	17
11 TEREHHOV Sergei			AFEK Omri	18
8 KLAVAN Ragnar			BADIR Walid	10
6 DMITRIJEV Aleksandr	85		TAL Idan	11
7 VIIKMAE Kristen	69	72	KATAN Yaniv	20
5 SAHAROV Aleksandr	86		ZIV Yoav	2
10 OPER Andres			COLAUTTI Roberto	9
Tr: GOES Jelle			Tr: KASHTAN Dror	
14 BARENGRUB Alo	86	72	ALBERMAN Gal	19
17 VASSILJEV Konstantin	69	59	BEN SHUSHAN Amit	8
18 TEEVER Ingemar	85			

Lokomotiv, Moscow
6-09-2006, 19:00, 27 500, Mejuto Gonzalez ESP

RUS 0 0 CRO

RUSSIA			CROATIA	
1 AKINFEEV Igor			PLETIKOSA Stipe	1
6 IGNASHEVIC Sergei			KOVAC Robert	4
22 ANYUKOV Aleksandr			CORLUKA Vedran	5
25 KOLODIN Denis			SABLJIC Goran	13
27 BEREZUTSKIY Aleksei			SERIC Anthony	20
17 IZMAILOV Marat			KOVAC Niko	10
8 ALDONIN Evgeni			MODRIC Luka	14
20 SEMSHOV Igor			KRANJCAR Niko	19
15 BILYALETDINOV Diniyar		58	RAPAIC Milan	7
19 PAVLYUCHENKO Roman	53	88	KLASNIC Ivan	17
10 ARSHAVIN Andrei		71	DA SILVA Eduardo	22
Tr: HIDDINK Guus			Tr: BILIC Slaven	
13 POGREBNYAK Pavel	53	88	BABIC Marco	8
		71	LEKO Jerko	16
		58	PETRIC Mladen	21

De Goffert, Nijmegen
6-09-2006, 19:00, 400, Zrnic BIH

ISR 4 1 AND

Benayoun [9], Ben Shushan [11],
Gershon [43p], Tamuz [69]

Fernández [84]

ISRAEL			ANDORRA	
1 AWAT Dudu			ALVAREZ Jesús 'Koldo'	1
18 AFEK Omri			BERNAUS Marc	9
3 BEN HAIM Tal			GARCIA José 'Txema'	3
5 GERSHON Shimon			LIMA Antoni	5
14 ZIV Yoav			AYALA Jose Manuel	2
11 TAL Idan		77	SILVA Fernando	4
10 BADIR Walid	76		SONEJEE Oscar	6
15 BENAYOUN Yossi	69	67	VIEIRA Marcio	8
7 BEN SHUSHAN Amit			JIMENEZ Manolo	10
20 KATAN Yaniv	62	45	PUJOL Marc	9
9 COLAUTTI Roberto		54	RUIZ Justo	11
Tr: KASHTAN Dror			Tr: RODRIGO David	
16 GOLAN Omer	69	54	FERNANDEZ Juli	12
16 TAMUZ Toto	62	67	MORENO Sergio	16
19 ALBERMAN Gal	76	45	GARCIA Genis	18

Gradski, Skopje
6-09-2006, 21:00, 15 000, Layec FRA

MKD 0 1 ENG

Crouch [46]

FYR MACEDONIA			ENGLAND	
1 NIKOLOVSKI Jane			ROBINSON Paul	1
2 NOVESKI Nikolce			NEVILLE Phil	2
3 PETROV Robert			TERRY John	6
4 SEDLOSKI Goce			FERDINAND Rio	5
5 MITRESKI Igor			COLE Ashley	3
14 LAZAREVSKI Vlade			GERRARD Steven	4
17 JANCEVSKI Igor	52		HARGEAVES Owen	7
8 SUMULIKOSKI Velice		84	LAMPARD Frank	8
11 NAUMOSKI Ilco	74		DOWNING Stewart	11
9 MAZNOV Goran	56	87	DEFOE Jermain	9
19 PANDEV Goran		76	CROUCH Peter	10
Tr: KATANEC Srecko			Tr: McCLAREN Steve	
10 SAKIRI Artim	74	84	CARRICK Michael	15
18 TASEVSKI Darko	52	76	LENNON Aaron	16
20 STOJKOV Aco	56	87	JOHNSON Andrew	18

Old Trafford, Manchester
7-10-2006, 17:00, 72 060, Merk GER

ENG 0 0 MKD

	ENGLAND			FYR MACEDONIA	
1	ROBINSON Paul			NIKOLOVSKI Jane	1
2	NEVILLE Gary			NOVESKI Nikolce	2
6	TERRY John			PETROV Robert	3
5	KING Ledley			SEDLOSKI Goce	4
3	COLE Ashley			LAZAREVSKI Vlade	14
4	GERRARD Steven			MITRESKI Igor	5
8	LAMPARD Frank			MITRESKI Aleksandar	6
7	CARRICK Michael			SUMULIKOSKI Velice	8
11	DOWNING Stewart			MAZNOV Goran	9
9	ROONEY Wayne	45		NAUMOSKI Ilco	11
10	CROUCH Peter	83		PANDEV Goran	19
	Tr: McCLAREN Steve			Tr: KATANEC Srecko	
16	WRIGHT-PHILLIPS Shaun	70	83	TASEVSKI Darko	18
17	DEFOE Jermaine	74	45	STOJKOV Aco	20

Dinamo, Moscow
7-10-2006, 19:00, 22 000, Meyer GER

RUS 1 1 ISR

Arshavin [5]   Ben Shushan [84]

	RUSSIA				ISRAEL	
1	AKINFEEV Igor				AWAT Dudu	1
2	BEREZUTSKIY Vasili				BEN HAIM Tal	3
6	IGNASHEVIC Sergei		45		GERSHON Shimon	5
22	ANYUKOV Aleksandr				KEISE Adoram	6
27	BEREZUTSKIY Aleksei		45		SABAN Rahamin Klemi	21
4	SMERTIN Aleksei				AFEK Omri	18
8	ALDONIN Evgeni				BADIR Walid	10
10	ARSHAVIN Andrei				TAL Idan	11
15	BILYALETDINOV Diniyar	30	75		BENAYOUN Yossi	15
21	ZHIRKOV Yuri	77			ALBERMAN Gal	19
13	POGREBNYAK Pavel	57			COLAUTTI Roberto	9
	Tr: HIDDINK Guus				Tr: KASHTAN Dror	
7	IZMAILOV Marat	57	75		TAMUZ Toto	8
11	KERZHAKOV Aleksandr	30	45		BEN SHUSHAN Amit	7
20	SEMSHOV Igor	77	45		BEN-YOSEF Tomer	4

Maksimir, Zagreb
7-10-2006, 20:15, 17 618, Zammit MLT

CRO 7 0 AND

Petric 4 [12 37 48 50], Klasnic [58],
Balaban [62], Modric [83]

	CROATIA			ANDORRA	
1	PLETIKOSA Stipe			ALVAREZ Jesús 'Koldo'	1
2	SIMIC Dario			AYALA Jose Manuel	2
3	SIMUNIC Josip			RUBIO Jordi	3
4	KOVAC Robert			SONEJEE Oscar	4
5	CORLUKA Vedran			FERNANDEZ Juli	5
10	KOVAC Niko	69		ESCURA Jordi	6
14	MODRIC Luka	68		GARCIA Genis	7
17	KLASNIC Ivan			VIEIRA Marcio	8
19	KRANJCAR Niko	53		SANCHEZ Juli	9
21	PETRIC Mladen	60		PUJOL Marc	10
22	DA SILVA Eduardo	64	60	SILVERA Toni	11
	Tr: BILIC Slaven			Tr: RODRIGO David	
8	BABIC Marco	64	53	BELTRAN Juan Carlos	13
9	BALABAN Bosko	60	68	JIMENEZ Manolo	17
16	LEKO Jerko	69	60	RUIZ Justo	18

Estadi Comunal, Andorra La Vella
11-10-2006, 15:00, 300, Silagava GEO

AND 0 3 MKD

Pandev [13], Noveski [16],
Naumoski [31]

	ANDORRA			FYR MACEDONIA	
1	ALVAREZ Jesús 'Koldo'			NIKOLOVSKI Jane	1
5	GARCIA José 'Txema'			NOVESKI Nikolce	2
2	AYALA Jose Manuel			MITRESKI Igor	5
4	SONEJEE Oscar		70	SEDLOSKI Goce	4
3	RUBIO Jordi			PETROV Robert	3
7	GARCIA Genis			MITRESKI Aleksandar	6
6	VIEIRA Marcio			SUMULIKOSKI Velice	8
10	PUJOL Marc	87		LAZAREVSKI Vlade	14
11	BERNAUS Marc		32	NAUMOSKI Ilco	11
8	SILVERA Toni	26	55	PANDEV Goran	19
9	BELTRAN Juan Carlos	34		MAZNOV Goran	9
	Tr: RODRIGO David			Tr: KATANEC Srecko	
17	JIMENEZ Manolo	87	55	TASEVSKI Darko	18
18	RUIZ Justo	34	32	STOJKOV Aco	20
			70	SAKIRI Artim	10

Maksimir, Zagreb
11-10-2006, 19:00, 31 991, Rosetti ITA

CRO 2 0 ENG

Eduardo [61], Neville.G OG [69]

	CROATIA			ENGLAND	
1	PLETIKOSA Stipe			ROBINSON Paul	1
2	SIMIC Dario	73		CARRAGHER Jamie	4
3	SIMUNIC Josip			FERDINAND Rio	5
4	KOVAC Robert			TERRY John	6
5	CORLUKA Vedran			NEVILLE Gary	2
7	RAPAIC Milan	76		CARRICK Michael	7
10	KOVAC Niko		72	PARKER Scott	11
14	MODRIC Luka			LAMPARD Frank	8
19	KRANJCAR Niko	89		COLE Ashley	3
22	DA SILVA Eduardo	81		ROONEY Wayne	9
21	PETRIC Mladen	72		CROUCH Peter	10
	Tr: BILIC Slaven			Tr: McCLAREN Steve	
8	BABIC Marco	89	72	RICHARDSON Kieran	14
16	LEKO Jerko	81	73	WRIGHT-PHILLIPS Shaun	16
18	OLIC Ivica	76	72	DEFOE Jermaine	17

Petrovsky, St Petersburg
11-10-2006, 19:00, 21 517, Braamhaar NED

RUS 2 0 EST

Pogrebnyak [78], Sychev [91+]

	RUSSIA			ESTONIA	
1	AKINFEEV Igor			POOM Mart	1
27	BEREZUTSKIY Aleksei		81	ALLAS Teet	7
2	BEREZUTSKIY Vasili			JAAGER Enar	2
6	IGNASHEVIC Sergei			STEPANOV Andrei	3
22	ANYUKOV Aleksandr		90	PIIROJA Raio	4
14	BYSTROV Vladimir			KRUGLOV Dmitri	5
29	TITOV Yegor		81	TEREHHOV Sergei	11
15	BILYALETDINOV Diniyar	92+		DMITRIJEV Aleksandr	6
8	ALDONIN Evgeni	74		KLAVAN Ragnar	8
10	ARSHAVIN Andrei		81	TEEVER Ingemar	9
11	KERZHAKOV Aleksandr	45		OPER Andres	10
	Tr: HIDDINK Guus			Tr: GOES Jelle	
13	POGREBNYAK Pavel	45	81	SIDORENKOV Andrei	15
26	SYCHEV Dmitri	74	81	PURJE Ats	17
34	SAENKO Ivan	92+	81	GUSSEV Vladislav	18

Gradski, Skopje
15-11-2006, 17:00, 13 000, Allaerts BEL

MKD 0 2 RUS

Bystrov [18], Arshavin [32]

FYR MACEDONIA				RUSSIA	
1	NIKOLOVSKI Jane			AKINFEEV Igor	1
2	NOVESKI Nikolce			BEREZUTSKIY Vasili	2
3	PETROV Robert			BEREZUTSKIY Aleksei	27
4	SEDLOSKI Goce			KOLODIN Denis	25
5	MITRESKI Igor			BYSTROV Vladimir	14
14	LAZAREVSKI Vlade			BILYALETDINOV Diniyar	15
8	SUMULIKOSKI Velice			SEMSHOV Igor	20
10	SAKIRI Artim	35		ZHIRKOV Yuri	21
6	MITRESKI Aleksandar	45		TITOV Yegor	29
9	MAZNOV Goran		90	ARSHAVIN Andrei	10
20	STOJKOV Aco		57	POGREBNYAK Pavel	13
	Tr: KATANEC Srecko			Tr: HIDDINK Guus	
9	GROZDANOVSKI Vlatko	71	90	PAVLYUCHENKO Roman	19
17	JANCEVSKI Igor	71 45	57	SYCHEV Dmitri	26
18	TASEVSKI Darko	35			

Ramat Gan, Tel Aviv
15-11-2006, 19:00, 35 000, Iturralde González ESP

ISR 3 4 CRO

Colautti 2 [8 89], Benayoun [68]   Srna [35p], Eduardo 3 [39 54 72]

ISRAEL				CROATIA	
1	AWAT Dudu			RUNJE Vedran	23
18	AFEK Omri			CORLUKA Vedran	5
3	BEN HAIM Tal			SIMIC Dario	2
4	BEN-YOSEF Tomer			KOVAC Robert	4
6	KEISE Adoram			SIMUNIC Josip	3
19	ALBERMAN Gal		88	SRNA Darijo	11
10	BADIR Walid	45		KOVAC Niko	10
11	TAL Idan			MODRIC Luka	14
17	KATAN Yaniv	59	70	KRANJCAR Niko	19
15	BENAYOUN Yossi		81	DA SILVA Eduardo	22
9	COLAUTTI Roberto			PETRIC Mladen	21
	Tr: KASHTAN Dror			Tr: BILIC Slaven	
7	BEN SHUSHAN Amit	59	70	BABIC Marco	8
8	TAMUZ Toto	45	81	LEKO Jerko	16
			88	OLIC Ivica	18

Maksimir, Zagreb
24-03-2007, 20:15, 29 969, Plautz AUT

CRO 2 1 MKD

Srna [58], Eduardo [88]   Sedloski [38]

CROATIA				FYR MACEDONIA	
1	PLETIKOSA Stipe			NIKOLOVSKI Jane	1
2	SIMIC Dario			NOVESKI Nikolce	2
3	SIMUNIC Josip			POPOV Nikolce	3
5	CORLUKA Vedran		68	SEDLOSKI Goce	4
7	RAPAIC Milan	45		LAZAREVSKI Vlade	14
8	BABIC Marco		77	MITRESKI Aleksandar	6
9	BALABAN Bokso	79		SUMULIKOSKI Velice	8
10	KOVAC Niko		71	MAZNOV Goran	9
14	MODRIC Luka		60	NAUMOSKI Ilco	11
19	KRANJCAR Niko			PANDEV Goran	19
22	DA SILVA Eduardo			VASOSKI Aleksandar	5
	Tr: BILIC Slaven			Tr: KATANEC Srecko	
11	SRNA Darijo	45	71	VAJS Miroslav	16
20	BUDAN Igor	79	77	JANCEVSKI Igor	17
			60	TASEVSKI Darko	10

Ramat Gan, Tel Aviv
24-03-2007, 20:30, 38 000, Ovrebø NOR

ISR 0 0 ENG

ISRAEL				ENGLAND	
1	AWAT Dudu			ROBINSON Paul	1
3	BEN HAIM Tal		72	NEVILLE Phil	2
5	GERSHON Shimon			FERDINAND Rio	5
14	ZIV Yoav			TERRY John	6
4	BENADO Arik			CARRAGHER Jamie	3
2	SHPUNGIN Yuval			GERRARD Steven	4
10	BADIR Walid			LAMPARD Frank	8
15	BENAYOUN Yossi			HARGREAVES Owen	7
7	BEN SHUSHAN Amit	87	83	LENNON Aaron	11
8	TAMUZ Toto	75		ROONEY Wayne	9
17	BALALI Pini	69	80	JOHNSON Andrew	10
	Tr: KASHTAN Dror			Tr: McCLAREN Steve	
19	ALBERMAN Gal	87	72	RICHARDS Michah	12
9	SAHAR Ben	69	83	DOWNING Stewart	16
11	BARDA Elyaniv	75	80	DEFOE Jermaine	18

A Le Coq Arena, Tallinn
24-03-2007, 20:30, 8212, Ceferin SVN

EST 0 2 RUS

Kerzhakov.A 2 [66 78]

ESTONIA				RUSSIA	
1	POOM Mart			AKINFEEV Igor	1
2	SISOV Tinhon	80		SHISHKIN Roman	4
3	LEMSALU Marek			IGNASHEVICH Sergei	5
5	KRUGLOV Dmitri			ANYUKOV Aleksandr	22
4	SIDORENKO Andrei			TORBINSKIY Dmitri	7
6	DMITRIJEV Aleksandr			BILYALETDINOV Diniyar	15
8	LEETMA Liivo	69		ZYRYANOV Konstantin	17
10	LINDPERE Joel			ZHIRKOV Yuri	18
11	KLAVAN Ragnar		90	BYSTROV Vladimir	23
9	OPER Andres		83	KERZHAKOV Aleksandr	11
7	TEREHHOV Sergei	52		ARSHAVIN Andrei	10
	Tr: GOES Jelle			Tr: HIDDINK Guus	
15	KAMS Gert	52	83	SYCHEV Dmitri	26
16	KINK Tarmo	69	90	SAENKO Ivan	34
18	NEEMELO Tarmo	80			

Ramat Gan, Tel Aviv
28-03-2007, 19:00, 21 000, Cüneyt Cakir TUR

ISR 4 0 EST

Idan Tal [19], Colautti [29],
Sahar 2 [77 80]

ISRAEL				ESTONIA	
1	AWAT Dudu			POOM Mart	1
2	SHPUNGIN Yuval			SISOV Tinhon	2
3	BEN HAIM Tal			LEMSALU Marek	3
5	GERSHON Shimon			BARENGRUB Alo	4
14	ZIV Yoav			OPER Andres	7
11	TAL Idan	87		KRUGLOV Dmitri	5
10	BADIR Walid			DMITRIJEV Aleksandr	6
15	BENAYOUN Yossi		39	RAHN Taavi	8
7	BEN SHUSHAN Amit	70	80	LINDPERE Joel	10
8	TAMUZ Toto	64		KLAVAN Ragnar	11
9	COLAUTTI Roberto		61	NEEMELO Tarmo	9
	Tr: KASHTAN Dror			Tr: GOES Jelle	
16	SAHAR Ben	64	80	KAMS Gert	16
18	TOEMA Salim	87	61	KONSA Oliver	17
19	ALBERMAN Gal	70	39	KINK Tarmo	18

Olímpico de Montjuic, Barcelona
28-03-2007, 21:00, 12 800, Paixão POR

AND 0 3 ENG

Gerrard 2 [54 76], Nugent [92+]

#	ANDORRA			#	ENGLAND	
1	ALVAREZ Jesús 'Koldo'			1	ROBINSON Paul	
4	SONEJEE Oscar		61	2	RICHARDS Micah	
5	LIMA Antoni			6	TERRY John	
2	AYALA Jose Manuel			5	FERDINAND Rio	
3	BERNAUS Marc			3	COLE Ashley	
6	ESCURA Jordi			11	LENNON Aaron	
7	VIEIRA Marcio			7	HARGREAVES Owen	
8	GARCIA Genis			4	GERRARD Steven	
11	RUIZ Justo	88		8	DOWNING Stewart	
10	PUJOL Marc	69	79	10	JOHNSON Andrew	
9	BELTRAN Juan Carlos	93+	61	9	ROONEY Wayne	
	Tr: RODRIGO David				Tr: McCLAREN Steve	
15	MORENO Sergio	93+	61	15	DYER Kieron	
16	MARTINEZ Francisco	69	79	19	NUGENT David	
18	FERNANDEZ Juli	88	61		DEFOE Jermaine	61

A Le Coq Arena, Tallinn
2-06-2007, 21:30, 8651, Kassai HUN

EST 0 1 CRO

Eduardo [32]

#	ESTONIA			#	CROATIA	
1	POOM Mart			1	PLETIKOSA Stipe	
2	JAAGER Enar			3	SIMUNIC Josip	
3	STEPANOV Andrei			4	KOVAC Robert	
4	PIIROJA Raio			5	CORLUKA Vedran	
5	KRUGLOV Dmitri			8	BABIC Marco	
6	DMITRIJEV Aleksandr			10	KOVAC Niko	
11	LINDPERE Joel	78		11	SRNA Darijo	
8	KLAVAN Ragnar			14	MODRIC Luka	
10	VASSILJEV Konstantin		74	19	KRANJCAR Niko	
7	KONSA Oliver	71	54	21	PETRIC Mladen	
9	VOSKOBOINIKOV Vladimir		84	22	DA SILVA Eduardo	
	Tr: GOES Jelle				Tr: BILIC Slaven	
17	KINK Tarmo	78	84	9	BALABAN Bokso	
18	NEEMELO Tarmo	71	74	16	LEKO Jerko	
			54	18	OLIC Ivica	

Petrovsky, St Petersburg
2-06-2007, 19:00, 21 520, Skjerven NOR

RUS 4 0 AND

Kerzhakov.A 3 [8 16 49], Sychev [71]

#	RUSSIA				ANDORRA	#
16	MALAFEEV Vyacheslav			ALVAREZ Jesús 'Koldo'	1
2	BEREZUTSKI Vasili			GARCIA José 'Txema'	5
5	IGNASHEVICH Sergei		57	DA CUNHA Oscar Alfonso	7
27	BEREZUTSKI Aleksei	46		BERNAUS Marc	3
23	BYSTROV Vladimir			AYALA Jose Manuel	2
2	ZYRYANOV Konstantin			ESCURA Jordi	6
7	TORBINSKIY Dmitri			VIEIRA Marcio	6
20	SEMSHOV Igor			PUJOL Marc	8
3	ZHIRKOV Yuri	57	73	JIMINEZ Manolo	10
10	ARSHAVIN Andrei			RUIZ Justo	11
11	KERZHAKOV Aleksandr	54	88	MORENO Sergio	9
	Tr: HIDDINK Guus			Tr: RODRIGO David	
22	ANYUKOV Aleksandr	46	57	SANCHEZ Juli	14
28	BUDYANSKI Viktor	57	88	SOMOZA Alex	16
26	SYCHEV Dmitri	54	73	ANDORRA Xavi	17

Gradski, Skopje
2-06-2007, 19:30, 12 000, Kircher GER

MKD 1 2 ISR

Stojkov [13]   Itzhaki [11], Colautti [44]

#	FYR MACEDONIA				ISRAEL	#
1	NIKOLOVSKI Jane			AWAT Dudu	1
2	NOVESKI Nikolce			SHPUNGIN Yuval	2
3	PETROV Robert			ZIV Yoav	14
14	LAZAREVSKI Vlade	46		BENADO Arik	4
5	MITRESKI Igor			BADIR Walid	10
6	VASOSKI Aleksandar			TAL Idan	11
8	SUMULIKOSKI Velice		61	BALALI Pini	17
11	TASEVSKI Darko			ALBERMAN Gal	19
11	NAUMOSKI Ilco	46	81	COLAUTTI Roberto	9
19	PANDEV Goran	55	76	ITZHAKI Barak	7
20	STOJKOV Aco			KEINAN Dekel	5
	Tr: KATANEC Srecko			Tr: KASHTAN Dror	
13	POLOZANI Artim	55	81	GOLAN Omer	12
21	RISTIC Stevica	46	61	SAHAR Ben	18
7	GROZDANOVSKI Vlatko	46	76	ZANDBERG Michael	15

Maksimir, Zagreb
6-06-2007, 20:30, 36 194, Michel SVK

CRO 0 0 RUS

#	CROATIA				RUSSIA	#
1	PLETIKOSA Stipe			MALAFEEV Vyacheslav	16
5	CORLUKA Vedran			BEREZUTSKI Vasili	2
2	SIMIC Dario			IGNASHEVICH Sergei	5
4	KOVAC Robert			BEREZUTSKI Aleksei	27
3	SIMUNIC Josip		61	BYSTROV Vladimir	23
11	SRNA Darijo	8		ANYUKOV Aleksandr	22
10	KOVAC Niko			ZHIRKOV Yuri	18
14	MODRIC Luka			SEMSHOV Igor	20
19	KRANJCAR Niko	66	46	BUDYANSKI Viktor	28
22	DA SILVA Eduardo			ARSHAVIN Andrei	10
18	OLIC Ivica	83	73	KERZHAKOV Aleksandr	11
	Tr: BILIC Slaven			Tr: HIDDINK Guus	
16	LEKO Jerko	8	46	TORBINSKIY Dmitri	7
8	BABIC Marco	83	73	SYCHEV Dmitri	26
21	PETRIC Mladen	66	61	SAENKO Ivan	9

A Le Coq Arena, Tallinn
6-06-2007, 21:30, 9635, Gilewski POL

EST 0 3 ENG

Cole.J [37], Crouch [54], Owen [62]

#	ESTONIA				ENGLAND	#
1	POOM Mart			ROBINSON Paul	1
2	JAAGER Enar			BROWN Wes	2
3	STEPANOV Andrei			TERRY John	6
5	KRUGLOV Dmitri			KING Ledley	5
4	KLAVAN Ragnar			BRIDGE Wayne	3
6	DMITRIJEV Aleksandr		68	BECKHAM David	7
11	LINDPERE Joel			GERRARD Steven	4
10	VASSILJEV Konstantin			LAMPARD Frank	8
7	KONSA Oliver	46	75	COLE Joe	11
9	VOSKOBOINIKOV Vladimir			CROUCH Peter	9
11	TEREHHOV Sergei	64	88	OWEN Michael	10
	Tr: GOES Jelle			Tr: McCLAREN Steve	
17	KINK Tarmo	64	88	JENAS Jermaine	14
18	NEEMELO Tarmo	46	68	DYER Kieron	15
			75	DOWNING Stewart	16

GROUP F

Windsor Park, Belfast
2-09-2006, 15:00, 13 522, Skjerven NOR

NIR	0	3	ISL

Thorvaldsson [13], Hreidarsson [20], Gudjohnsen [37]

NORTHERN IRELAND			ICELAND	
1	TAYLOR Maik		ARASON Arni	1
2	BAIRD Chris		STEINSSON Gretar	2
3	CAPALDI Tony	76	SIGURDSSON Ingridi	3
18	HUGHES Aaron		INGIMARSSON Ivar	5
5	CRAIGAN Stephen		HREIDASSON Hermann	7
6	CLINGHAN Gary	75	GUNNARSSON Brynjar	4
7	GILLESPIE Keith	55	ARNASON Kari	8
11	ELLIOT Stuart	63	GUDJONSSON Johannes	10
8	DAVIS Steven		GUDJOHNSEN Eidur	9
9	HEALY David	64	SIGURDSSON Hannes	6
10	QUINN James	83	THORVALDSSON Gunnar	11
	Tr: SANCHEZ Lawrie		Tr: SVERRISSON Eyjólfur	
16	FEENEY Warren	83 55	DANIELSSON Helgi Valur	13
17	LAFFERTY Kyle	63 64	JONSSON Hjalmar	14
4	DUFF Michael	76 75	GISLASON Stefan	15

Skonto, Riga
2-09-2006, 21:00, 7500, Ceferin SVN

LVA	0	1	SWE

Källström [38]

LATVIA			SWEDEN	
1	KOLINKO Aleksandrs		SHAABAN Rami	1
2	STEPANOVS Igors		NILSSON Mikael	2
3	ASTAFJEVS Vitalis		MELLBERG Olof	3
4	ZIRNIS Dzintars	83	HANSSON Petter	4
5	LAIZANS Jurijs	84	EDMAN Erik	5
7	SMIRNOVS Maris		LINDEROTH Tobias	6
8	BLEIDELIS Imants		ALEXANDERSSON Niclas	7
9	VERPAKOVSKIS Maris	71	KALLSTROM Kim	8
10	RUBINS Andrejs		LJUNGBERG Fredrik	9
11	PROHORENKOVS Andrejs	57	IBRAHIMOVIC Zlatan	10
17	KLAVA Oskars	81	ELMANDER Johan	11
	Tr: ANDREJEVS Jurijs		Tr: LAGERBACK Lars	
16	VISNAKOVS Aleksejs	84 71	SVENSSON Anders	17
20	KARLSONS Girts	83 81	WILHELMSSON Christian	20
29	PAHARS Marians	57		

El Vivero, Badajoz
2-09-2006, 22:00, 13 876, Bozinovski MKD

ESP	4	0	LIE

Torres [20], Villa 2 [45 62], Luis García [66]

SPAIN			LIECHTENSTEIN	
1	CASILLAS Iker		JEHLE Peter	1
15	RAMOS Sergio	56	TELSER Martin	2
5	PUYOL Carles		MAIERHOFER Sandro	15
22	IBANEZ Pablo		HASLER Daniel	3
19	PERNIA Mariano		STOCKLASA Martin	6
6	ALBELDA David	69	BURGMEIR Franz	11
14	ALONSO Xabi		BUCHEL Martin	13
18	FABREGAS Cesc	63	RITZBERGER Marco	21
7	RAUL		D'ELIA Fabio	19
9	TORRES Fernando	69	BECK Thomas	9
21	VILLA David	63 86	FRICK Mario	10
	Tr: ARAGONES Luis		Tr: ANDERMATT Martin	
11	GARCIA Luis	63 69	BECK Roger	16
12	OUBINA Borja	69 86	ROHRER Raphael	20
16	INIESTA Andres	63 56	FISCHER Benjamin	7

Laugardalsvöllur, Reykjavík
6-09-2006, 18:05, 10 007, Ivanov.N RUS

ISL	0	2	DEN

Rommedahl [5], Tomasson [33]

ICELAND			DENMARK	
1	ARASON Arni		SORENSEN Thomas	1
2	STEINSSON Gretar		JACOBSEN Lars	8
3	SIGURDSSON Ingridi		GRAVGAARD Michael	3
7	HREIDASSON Hermann		AGGER Daniel	4
5	INGIMARSSON Ivar		POULSEN Christian	2
6	JONSSON Hjalmar	66 82	KAHLENBERG Thomas	6
4	GUNNARSSON Brynjar	76 70	GRAVESEN Thomas	7
8	ARNASON Kari	82	KRISTIANSEN Jan	5
10	GUDJONSSON Johannes		TOMASSON Jon Dahl	9
9	GUDJOHNSEN Eidur	91+	JORGENSEN Martin	10
11	THORVALDSSON Gunnar		ROMMEDAHL Dennis	11
	Tr: SVERRISSON Eyjólfur		Tr: OLSEN Morten	
15	GISLASON Stefan	76 91+	HELVEG Thomas	12
17	VIDARSSON Arnar	82 82	JENSEN Claus	14
18	GUNNARSSON Veigar	66 70	JENSEN Daniel	15

Ullevi, Gothenburg
6-09-2006, 19:30, 17 735, Banari MDA

SWE	3	1	LIE

Allbäck 2 [2 69], Rosenberg [89]   Frick.M [27]

SWEDEN			LIECHTENSTEIN	
1	SHAABAN Rami		JEHLE Peter	1
2	NILSSON Mikael		HASLER Daniel	4
3	HANSSON Petter		RITTER Christof	5
4	LUCIC Teddy	89	MAIERHOFER Sandro	15
5	EDMAN Erik		BUCHEL Martin	13
6	LINDEROTH Tobias		STOCKLASA Martin	6
7	ALEXANDERSSON Niclas	55	FISCHER Benjamin	7
8	KALLSTROM Kim	57	FRICK Daniel	17
9	LJUNGBERG Fredrik		RITZBERGER Marco	21
10	ALLBACK Marcus	42	BECK Thomas	9
11	ELMANDER Johan	82	FRICK Mario	10
	Tr: LAGERBACK Lars		Tr: ANDERMATT Martin	
15	SVENSSON Anders	57 55	BUCHEL Ronny	8
16	ROSENBERG Markus	82 42	BURGMEIR Franz	11
		89	D'ELIA Fabio	19

Windsor Park, Belfast
6-09-2006, 20:15, 13 885, De Bleeckere BEL

NIR	3	2	ESP

Healy 3 [20 64 80]   Xavi [14], Villa [52]

NORTHERN IRELAND			SPAIN	
1	CARROLL Roy	12	CASILLAS Iker	1
2	DUFF Michael	45	RAMOS Sergio	15
18	HUGHES Aaron		PUYOL Carles	5
5	CRAIGAN Stephen		IBANEZ Pablo	22
3	EVANS Jonny		LOPEZ Antonio	3
7	GILLESPIE Keith	29	ALBELDA David	6
6	CLINGHAN Gary		HERNANDEZ Xavi	8
8	DAVIS Steven		ALONSO Xabi	14
11	BAIRD Chris	63	TORRES Fernando	9
9	HEALY David	85	VILLA David	21
10	LAFFERTY Kyle	54	RAUL	7
	Tr: SANCHEZ Lawrie		Tr: ARAGONES Luis	
12	TAYLOR Maik	12 45	SALGADO Michel	2
13	FEENEY Warren	85 63	GARCIA Luis	11
16	QUINN James	54 29	FABREGAS Cesc	18

Råsunda, Stockholm
7-10-2006, 20:00, 41 482, Bennett ENG

SWE 2 0 ESP

Elmander 10, Allbäck 82

SWEDEN	No	Sub
SHAABAN Rami	1	
NILSSON Mikael	2	
MELLBERG Olof	3	
HANSSON Petter	4	
EDMAN Erik	5	
LINDEROTH Tobias	6	
ALEXANDERSSON Niclas	7	
LJUNBERG Fredrik	9	56
SVENSSON Anders	8	75
ELMANDER Johan	11	77
ALLBACK Marcus	10	
Tr: LAGERBACK Lars		
ANDERSSON Daniel	15	77
KALLSTROM Kim	16	75
WILHELMSSON Christian	18	56

SPAIN	Sub	No
CASILLAS Iker		1
RAMOS Sergio		4
PUYOL Carles		5
GUTIERREZ Juanito		20
CAPDEVILA Joan	52	10
ALBELDA David		6
ANGULO Miguel Angel	59	17
FABREGAS Cesc	45	18
HERNANDEZ Xavi		8
VILLA David		7
TORRES Fernando		9
Tr: ARAGONES Luis		
GARCIA Luis	59	11
INIESTA Andres	45	16
PUERTA Antonio	52	15

Parken Stadion, Copenhagen
7-10-2006, 20:00, 41 482, Plautz AUT

DEN 0 0 NIR

DENMARK	No	Sub
SORENSEN Thomas	1	68
JACOBSEN Lars	6	
GRAVGAARD Michael	3	
AGGER Daniel	4	
JENSEN Niclas	5	73
JENSEN Daniel	7	
POULSEN Christian	2	
KAHLENBERG Thomas	8	
TOMASSON Jon Dahl	9	
JORGENSEN Martin	10	
LOVENKRANDS Peter	11	55
Tr: OLSEN Morten		
JENSEN Claus	14	55
CHRISTIANSEN Jesper	16	68
BENDTNER Nicklas	18	73

NORTHERN IRELAND	Sub	No
TAYLOR Maik		1
DUFF Michael		2
HUGHES Aaron		18
CRAIGAN Stephen		5
BAIRD Chris		11
CLINGHAN Gary	56	6
DAVIS Steven		8
EVANS Jonny		3
GILLESPIE Keith		7
LAFFERTY Kyle	63	10
HEALY David	84	9
Tr: SANCHEZ Lawrie		
JONES Stephen	63	14
JOHNSON Damien	56	15
FEENEY Warren	84	17

Skonto, Riga
7-10-2006, 21:00, 6800, Kelly IRL

LVA 4 0 ISL

Karlsons.G 14, Verpakovskis 2 15 25, Visnakovs 52

LATVIA	No	Sub
KOLINKO Aleksandrs	1	
STEPANOVS Igors	2	
ASTAFJEVS Vitalis	3	
ZIRNIS Dzintars	4	
LAIZANS Jurijs	5	
KLAVA Oskars	17	82
SMIRNOVS Maris	7	
BLEIDELIS Imants	8	46
VERPAKOVSKIS Maris	9	57
SOLONICINS Genadijs	15	
KARLSONS Girts	20	
Tr: ANDREJEVS Jurijs		
VISNAKOVS Aleksejs	16	46
KACANOVS Deniss	25	82
PAHARS Marians	29	57

ICELAND	Sub	No
ARASON Arni		1
STEINSSON Gretar		2
SIGURDSSON Ingridi		3
GISLASON Stefan		4
INGIMARSSON Ivar		5
SIGURDSSON Hannes	71	6
HREIDASSON Hermann		7
GUNNARSSON Brynjar		8
GUDJOHNSEN Eidur		9
GUDJONSSON Johannes	46	10
ARNASON Kari	42	11
Tr: SVERRISSON Eyjolfur		
DANIELSSON Helgi Valur	42	13
HALLFREDSSON Emil	71	16
GUNNARSSON Veigar	46	18

Laugardalsvöllur, Reykjavík
11-10-2006, 18:05, 8725, Gilewski POL

ISL 1 2 SWE

Vidarsson 6 | Källström 8, Wilhelmsson 59

ICELAND	No	Sub
ARASON Arni	1	
INGIMARSSON Ivar	5	
STEINSSON Gretar	11	
HREIDASSON Hermann	7	
SIGURDSSON Kristjan	2	
SIGURDSSON Ingridi	3	51
GUDJONSSON Johannes	10	81
VIDARSSON Arnar	4	
HALLFREDSSON Emil	6	
SIGURDSSON Hannes	8	
GUDJOHNSEN Eidur	9	
Tr: SVERRISSON Eyjolfur		
JONSSON Hjalmar	14	51
BALDVINSSON Marel	18	81

SWEDEN	Sub	No
SHAABAN Rami		1
NILSSON Mikael		2
ANTONSSON Mikael		3
HANSSON Petter		4
EDMAN Erik		5
ALEXANDERSSON Niclas		7
ANDERSSON Daniel		6
KALLSTROM Kim		8
WILHELMSSON Christian		9
ALLBACK Marcus	79	10
ELMANDER Johan	90	11
Tr: LAGERBACK Lars		
MAJSTOROVIC Daniel	90	14
ROSENBERG Markus	79	18

Windsor Park, Belfast
11-10-2006, 20:00, 13 500, Fleischer GER

NIR 1 0 LVA

Healy 35

NORTHERN IRELAND	No	Sub
TAYLOR Maik	1	
BAIRD Chris	2	
CRAIGAN Stephen	5	
HUGHES Aaron	18	
EVANS Jonny	3	
GILLESPIE Keith	7	
DAVIS Steven	8	
JOHNSON Damien	11	
CLINGHAN Gary	6	
HEALY David	9	91+
LAFFERTY Kyle	10	88
Tr: SANCHEZ Lawrie		
QUINN James	16	88
FEENEY Warren	17	91+

LATVIA	Sub	No
KOLINKO Aleksandrs		1
STEPANOVS Igors		2
ASTAFJEVS Vitalis		3
ZIRNIS Dzintars		4
LAIZANS Jurijs		5
KACANOVS Deniss		25
SOLONICINS Genadijs	85	15
SMIRNOVS Maris	45	7
VERPAKOVSKIS Maris	78	9
KARLSONS Girts		20
PAHARS Marians		29
Tr: ANDREJEVS Jurijs		
GORKSS Kaspars	45	14
VISNAKOVS Aleksejs	85	16
KALNINS Gatis	78	19

Rheinpark, Vaduz
11-10-2006, 20:15, 2665, Richards WAL

LIE 0 4 DEN

Jensen.D 29, Gravgaard 32, Tomasson 2 51 64

LIECHTENSTEIN	No	Sub
JEHLE Peter	1	
TELSER Martin	2	
HASLER Daniel	4	
RITTER Christof	5	
STOCKLASA Martin	6	
FISCHER Benjamin	7	80
BECK Thomas	8	63
FRICK Mario	10	
BURGMEIER Franz	11	62
BUCHEL Martin	13	
OEHRI Yves	29	
Tr: ANDERMATT Martin		
FRICK Daniel	17	62
D'ELIA Fabio	19	80
RITZBERGER Marco	21	63

DENMARK	Sub	No
CHRISTIANSEN Jesper		1
POULSEN Christian		2
GRAVGAARD Michael		3
AGGER Daniel		4
JENSEN Niclas		5
JACOBSEN Lars		6
JENSEN Daniel	45	7
KAHLENBERG Thomas	65	8
TOMASSON Jon Dahl		9
JORGENSEN Martin		10
ROMMEDAHL Dennis	78	11
Tr: OLSEN Morten		
JENSEN Claus	45	14
SORENSEN Dennis	65	18
KROHN-DEHLI Michael	78	15

Rheinpark, Vaduz
24-03-2007, 20:15, 4340, Oriekhov UKR

LIE   1   4   NIR

Burgmeier 91+

Healy 3 52 75 83, McCann 92+

LIECHTENSTEIN				NORTHERN IRELAND
1	JEHLE Peter			TAYLOR Maik 1
29	OEHRI Yves	68		DUFF Michael 2
6	STOCKLASA Martin			CRAIGAN Stephen 5
5	RITTER Christof			HUGHES Aaron 18
3	STOCKLASA Michael			JOHNSON Damien 8
13	BUCHEL Martin	68	68	BRUNT Chris 11
8	BUCHEL Ronny	88		GILLESPIE Keith 7
11	BURGMEIR Franz			EVANS Jonny 3
9	BECK Thomas			DAVIS Steven 6
10	FRICK Mario		56	LAFFERTY Kyle 10
20	ROHRER Raphael	84	84	HEALY David 9
	Tr: ANDERMATT Martin			Tr: SANCHEZ Lawrie
2	TELSER Martin	68	68	McCANN Grant 4
17	FRICK Daniel	88	56	FEENEY Warren 14
28	BUCHEL Stefan	84	84	JONES Stephen 17

Bernabéu, Madrid
24-03-2007, 22:00, 73 575, Busacca SUI

ESP   2   1   DEN

Morientes 34, Villa 46+

Gravgaard 49

SPAIN				DENMARK
1	CASILLAS Iker			SORENSEN Thomas 1
2	NAVARRO Javi			AGGER Daniel 4
4	MARCHENA Carlos			GRAVGAARD Michael 3
17	CAPDEVILLA Joan			JACOBSEN Lars 7
19	LOPEZ Angel		20	JENSEN Niclas 5
8	HERNANDEZ Xavi	60		POULSEN Christian 2
16	INIESTA Andres			JENSEN Daniel 6
21	SILVA David		60	KAHLENBERG Thomas 8
6	ALBELDA David	60		ROMMEDAHL Dennis 11
10	MORIENTES Fernando	64	38	JORGENSEN Martin 10
7	VILLA David	76		TOMASSON Jon Dahl 9
	Tr: ARAGONES Luis			Tr: OLSEN Morten
9	TORRES Fernando	64	38 73	ANDREASEN Leon 13
11	ANGULO Miguel Angel	76	60	GRONKJAER Jesper 15
14	ALONSO Xabi	60	73	BENDTNER Nicklas 17

Rheinpark, Vaduz
28-03-2007, 19:30, 1680, Gumienny BEL

LIE   1   0   LVA

Frick.M 17

LIECHTENSTEIN				LATVIA
1	JEHLE Peter			KOLINKO Aleksandrs 1
2	TELSER Martin			KACANOVS Deniss 25
6	STOCKLASA Martin		79	GORKSS Kaspars 13
4	HASLER Daniel			STEPANOVS Igors 2
3	STOCKLASA Michael			KLAVA Oskars 17
13	BUCHEL Martin			BLEIDELIS Imants 8
8	BUCHEL Ronny		61	MOROZS Viktors 22
11	BURGMEIR Franz			LAIZANS Jurijs 5
10	FRICK Mario			VISNAKOVS Aleksejs 16
9	BECK Thomas	76	45	VERPAKOVSKIS Maris 9
20	ROHRER Raphael	91+		PAHARS Marians 29
	Tr: ANDERMATT Martin			Tr: ANDREJEVS Jurijs
7	FISCHER Benjamin	76	61	PEREPLYOTKIN Andrei 10
28	BUCHEL Stefan	91+	79	PROHORENKOVS Andrejs 11
			45	KARLSONS Girts 20

Windsor Park, Belfast
28-03-2007, 19:45, 13 500, Braamhaar NED

NIR   2   1   SWE

Healy 2 31 58

Elmander 26

NORTHERN IRELAND				SWEDEN
1	TAYLOR Maik			ISAKSSON Andreas 1
2	DUFF Michael			NILSSON Mikael 2
18	HUGHES Aaron		69	MELLBERG Olof 3
5	CRAIGAN Stephen			HANSSON Petter 4
3	EVANS Jonny			EDMAN Erik 5
8	JOHNSON Damien	92+	61	ALEXANDERSSON Niclas 7
4	McCANN Grant			ANDERSSON Daniel 6
6	DAVIS Steven		45	SVENSSON Anders 8
11	BRUNT Chris			LJUNBERG Fredrik 9
9	HEALY David	89		IBRAHIMOVIC Zlatan 10
10	FEENEY Warren	79		ELMANDER Johan 11
	Tr: SANCHEZ Lawrie			Tr: LAGERBACK Lars
7	WEBB Sean	89	69	MAJSTOROVIC Daniel 14
13	SPROULE Ivan	92+	45	KALLSTROM Kim 16
14	LAFFERTY Kyle	79	61	WILHELMSSON Christian 21

Son Moix, Palma de Mallorca
28-03-2007, 22:00, 18 326, Duhamel FRA

ESP   1   0   ISL

Iniesta 81

SPAIN				ICELAND
1	CASILLAS Iker			ARASON Arni 1
15	RAMOS Sergio			SIGURDSSON Kristjan 2
4	MARCHENA Carlos			BJARNASON Olafur Orn 4
5	PUYOL Carles			INGIMARSSON Ivar 5
17	CAPDEVILLA Joan	46		GUNNARSSON Gunnar 3
16	INIESTA Andres			STEINSSON Gretar 11
6	ALBELDA David	78	83	VIDARSSON Arnar 6
8	HERNANDEZ Xavi			GUNNARSSON Brynjar 8
21	SILVA David			HALLFREDSSON Emil 7
7	VILLA David		56	GUNNARSSON Veigar 10
10	MORIENTES Fernando	43		GUDJOHNSEN Eidur 9
	Tr: ARAGONES Luis			Tr: SVERRISSON Eyjólfur
9	TORRES Fernando	43	56	GISLASON Stefan 14
11	ANGULO Miguel Angel	46	83	SIGURDSSON Hannes 16
14	ALONSO Xabi	78		

Skonto Riga
2-06-2007, 21:30, 10 000, Thomson SCO

LVA   0   2   ESP

Villa 45, Xavi 60

LATVIA				SPAIN
1	KOLINKO Aleksandrs			CASILLAS Iker 1
4	ZIRNIS Dzintars			PUYOL Carles 5
17	KLAVA Oskars			RAMOS Sergio 15
6	IVANOVS Deniss			MARCHENA Carlos 4
19	ZAKRESEVSKIS Arturs	66		ALBELDA David 6
10	RUBINS Andrejs	65		INIESTA Andres 16
3	ASTAFJEVS Vitalis			HERNANDEZ Xavi 8
5	LAIZANS Jurijs		45	ANGULO Miguel Angel 11
8	BLEIDELIS Imants	85		CAPDEVILLA Joan 20
9	VERPAKOVSKIS Maris			VILLA David 7
20	KARLSONS Girts	89	56	GARCIA Luis 3
	Tr: STARKOVS Aleksandrs			Tr: ARAGONES Luis
15	SOLONICINS Genadijs	65	66 45	ALONSO Xabi 14
18	CAUNA Aleksandrs	89	45	SANCHEZ Joaquin 17
14	PEREPLYOTKIN Andrei	85	56	SOLDADO Roberto 10

Laugardalsvöllur, Reykjavík
2-06-2007, 16:00, 5139, Kaldma EST

ISL	1	1		LIE

Gunnarsson.B [27]   Rohrer [69]

ICELAND			LIECHTENSTEIN	
1 ARASON Arni			JEHLE Peter 1	
2 STEINSSON Gretar			STOCKLASA Michele 3	
3 GUNNARSSON Gunnar			HASLER Daniel 4	
4 SIGURDSSON Kristjan			STOCKLASA Martin 6	
5 INGIMARSSON Ivar			RITZBERGER Franz [21]	
6 GISLASON Stefan			BUCHEL Ronny 8	
7 HALLFREDSSON Emil	78		BURGMEIR Franz 11	
8 GUNNARSSON Brynjar	85		POLVERINO Michele 18	
11 GUDMUNDSSON Matthias	82	87	BECK Thomas 9	
10 GUNNARSSON Veigar	70		FRICK Mario 10	
9 GUDJOHNSEN Eidur	72		ROHRER Raphael 20	
Tr: SVERRISSON Eyjólfur			ZAUGG Hans-Peter	
13 SAEVARSSON Birkir	70	85	KIEBER Wolfgang 14	
17 BJARNASON Theodor	82	78	FRICK Daniel 17	
18 SIGURDSSON Hannes	72	87	BECK Roger 16	

Parken Stadion, Copenhagen
2-06-2007, 20:00, 42 083, Fandel GER

DEN	3	3		SWE

Agger [34], Tomasson [62],   Elmander 2 [7 26], Hansson [23]
Andreason [75]

DENMARK			SWEDEN	
1 SORENSEN Thomas			ISAKSSON Andreas 1	
3 GRAVGAARD Michael			NILSSON Mikael 2	
4 AGGER Daniel			MELLBERG Olof 3	
7 JACOBSEN Lars			HANSSON Petter 4	
2 POULSEN Christian	[89]		ALEXANDERSSON Niclas [5]	
5 KRISTIANSEN Jan	35		WILHELMSSON Christian 7	
6 JENSEN Daniel	63		LINDEROTH Tobias [6]	
8 KAHLENBERG Thomas	47		SVENSSON Anders 8	
11 ROMMEDAHL Dennis			LJUNGBERG Fredrik 9	
9 TOMASSON Jon Dahl		80	ALLBACK Marcus 10	
10 JORGENSEN Martin		74	ELMANDER Johan [11]	
Tr: OLSEN Morten			Tr: LAGERBACK Lars	
12 ANDREASEN Leon	35	80	BAKORCIOGLU Kennedy 16	
15 GRONKJAER Jesper	63	74	ROSENBERG Markus 18	
18 BENDTNER Nicklas	47			

Match abandoned after 89 minutes. Awarded 3-0 to Sweden

Rheinpark, Vaduz
6-06-2007, 20:30, 5739, Ivanov.N RUS

LIE	0	2		ESP

Villa 2 [8 14]

LIECHTENSTEIN			SPAIN	
1 JEHLE Peter			REINA Pepe 23	
3 STOCKLASA Michael	29		NAVARRO Javi 2	
4 HASLER Daniel			MARCHENA Carlos 4	
6 STOCKLASA Martin			RAMOS Sergio 15	
21 RITZBERGER Franz		52	CAPDEVILLA Joan 20	
8 BUCHEL Ronny			ALONSO Xabi 14	
11 BURGMEIR Franz			INIESTA Andres 16	
27 POLVERINO Michele			SANCHEZ Joaquin 17	
20 ROHRER Raphael	59	67	FABREGAS Cesc [18]	
10 FRICK Mario		77	SILVA David 21	
9 BECK Thomas	82		VILLA David 7	
ZAUGG Hans-Peter			Tr: ARAGONES Luis	
2 TELSER Martin	29	67	GARCIA Luis 9	
16 BECK Roger	82	77	SOLDADO Roberto 10	
17 FRICK Daniel	59	52	LOPEZ Angel 19	

Råsunda, Stockholm
6-06-2007, 20:15, 33 358, Hamer LUX

SWE	5	0		ISL

Allbäck 2 [11 51], Svensson.A [42],
Mellberg [45], Rosenberg [50]

SWEDEN			ICELAND	
1 ISAKSSON Andreas			ARASON Arni 1	
5 ALEXANDERSSON Niclas		92+	STEINSSON Gretar 2	
3 MELLBERG Olof			GUNNARSSON Gunnar [3]	
4 HANSSON Petter			BJARNASON Olafur Orn 4	
2 NILSSON Mikael	57		INGIMARSSON Ivar 5	
7 WILHELMSSON Christian			BJARNASON Theodor 10	
6 LINDEROTH Tobias	62		VIDARSSON Arnar [6]	
8 SVENSSON Anders		53	HALLFREDSSON Emil 7	
9 LJUNGBERG Fredrik			GUNNARSSON Brynjar 8	
11 ROSENBERG Markus			SIGURDSSON Hannes 9	
10 ALLBACK Marcus	73	65	SAEVARSSON Birkir 11	
Tr: LAGERBACK Lars			Tr: SVERRISSON Eyjólfur	
13 VON SCHLEBRUGGE Max	57	92+	SIGURDSSON Kristjan 13	
15 ANDERSSON Daniel	62	53	JONSSON Hjalmar 15	
17 IBRAHIMOVIC Zlatan	73	65	GUDMUNDSSON Matthias 17	

Skonto Riga
6-06-2007, 21:30, 7500, Trefoloni ITA

LVA	0	2		DEN

Rommedahl 2 [15 17]

LATVIA			DENMARK	
1 KOLINKO Aleksandrs			SORENSEN Thomas 1	
4 ZIRNIS Dzintars			JACOBSEN Lars 2	
17 KLAVA Oskars			LAURSEN Martin 3	
6 IVANOVS Deniss			AGGER Daniel 4	
2 STEPANOVS Igors			JENSEN Niclas 5	
10 RUBINS Andrejs	75		JENSEN Daniel [6]	
3 ASTAFJEVS Vitalis			JORGENSEN Martin 10	
5 LAIZANS Jurijs			TOMASSON Jon Dahl 9	
8 BLEIDELIS Imants	66	46	ROMMEDAHL Dennis [7]	
9 VERPAKOVSKIS Maris	60		BENDTNER Nicklas 11	
20 KARLSONS Girts	61		GRONKJAER Jesper 8	
Tr: STARKOVS Aleksandrs			Tr: OLSEN Morten	
29 PAHARS Marians	61	46	KAHLENBERG Thomas 14	
15 SOLONICINS Genadijs	66	60	WURTZ Rasmus 15	
18 CAUNA Aleksandrs	75			

GROUP G

Dinamo, Minsk
2-09-2006, 20:00, 23 000, Asumaa FIN

BLR 2 2 ALB

Kalachev 2, Romashchenko 24 | Skela 7p, Hasi 86

#	BELARUS			ALBANIA	#
1	KHOMUTOVSKI Vasili			LIKA Ilion	1
2	KULCHY Aleksandr			DALLKU Armend	4
3	KORYTHKO Vladimir			HASI Besnik	6
4	OMELYANCHUK Sergei		45	ALIAJ Adrian	11
5	SHTANIUK Sergei			BEQIRI Elvin	2
6	HLEB Vyacheslav	64		HAXHI Altin	23
6	KALACHEV Timofei	84	84	LALA Altin	14
7	KOVBA Denis			CANA Lorik	5
9	ROMASCHENKO Maksim		73	SKELA Ervin	13
10	HLEB Aleksandr			TARE Igil	17
11	KUTUZOV Vitali			BOGDANI Erion	22
	Tr: PUNTUS Yuri			Tr: BARIC Otto	
15	BULYGA Vitali	64	45	CURRI Debatik	24
18	LANKO Vitali	84	84	MUKAJ Devis	15
			73	KAPLLANI Edmond	9

Stade Josy Barthel, Luxembourg City
2-09-2006, 20:30, 8055, Lopes Ferreira POR

LUX 0 1 NED

| Mathijsen 18

#	LUXEMBOURG			NETHERLANDS	#
1	JOUBERT Jonathan			VAN DER SAR Edwin	1
7	STRASSER Jeff			HEITINGA Johnny	2
4	HOFFMANN Eric		46	OOIJER Andre	3
5	REITER Claude			MATHIJSEN Joris	4
2	KINTZIGER Kim			DE CLER Tim	5
8	BETTMER Gilles		46	SCHAARS Stijn	6
9	JOACHIM Aurelien			JANSSEN Theo	10
10	LOMBARDELLI Claudio	83		LANDZAAT Denny	8
17	MUTSCH Mario			HUNTELAAR Klaas Jan	9
16	REMY Sebastian		77	VAN PERSIE Robin	7
14	FERREIRA Carlos	88		KUYT Dirk	11
	Tr: HELLERS Guy			Tr: VAN BASTEN Marco	
17	FEDERSPIEL Ben	83	46	EMANUELSON Urby	13
18	HUSS Daniel	88	46	V. OF HESSELINK Jan	17
			77	BABEL Ryan	18

Stadionul Farul, Constanta
2-09-2006, 21:00, 12 620, Farina ITA

ROU 2 2 BUL

Rosu 40, Marica 44 | Petrov.M 2 82 84

#	ROMANIA			BULGARIA	#
1	LOBONT Bogdan			PETKOV Georgi	1
2	CONTRA Cosmin			TUNCHEV Aleksandar	15
3	RAT Razvan			ANGELOV Stanislav	6
4	TAMAS Gabriel	94+		TOPUZAKOV Elin	21
5	CHIVU Cristian			WAGNER Lucio	25
6	CODREA Paul			PETROV Stilian	19
7	PETRE Florentin	71	47	KISHISHEV Radostin	2
8	DICA Nicolae	59		PETROV Martin	17
9	MARICA Ciprian			JANKOVIC Zoran	14
10	MUTU Adrian		62	BERBATOV Dimitar	9
11	ROSU Laurentiu	79	47	PEEV Georgi	11
	Tr: PITURCA Victor			Tr: STOICHKOV Hristo	
14	NICOLITA Banel	71	47	GEORGIEV Blagoy	7
16	MAFTEI Vasile	79	47	YANKOV Chavdar	8
17	COCIS Razvan	59	62	BZHINOV Valeri	10

Qemal Stafa, Tirana
6-09-2006, 20:00, 12 000, Benquerença POR

ALB 0 2 ROU

| Dica 65, Mutu 75p

#	ALBANIA			ROMANIA	#
25	BEQAJ Arian			LOBONT Bogdan	1
2	BEQIRI Elvin			CONTRA Cosmin	2
4	DALLKU Armend			RAT Razvan	3
5	CANA Lorik			GHIONEA Sorin	4
6	HASI Besnik			CHIVU Cristian	5
13	SKELA Ervin	64		CODREA Paul	6
14	LALA Altin	78		PETRE Florentin	7
17	TARE Igil			DICA Nicolae	8
22	BOGDANI Erion	62	78	MARICA Ciprian	9
23	HAXHI Altin		85	MUTU Adrian	10
24	CURRI Debatik		89	ROSU Laurentiu	11
	Tr: BARIC Otto			Tr: PITURCA Victor	
8	KASTRATI Bekim	62	85	NICOLITA Banel	14
11	ALIAJ Adrian	64	78	GANEA Ioan	18
15	MUKAJ Devis	78	89	MARGARITESCU Andrei	17

Vasil Levski, Sofia
6-09-2006, 20:00, 14 491, Bo Larsen DEN

BUL 3 0 SVN

Bozhinov 58, Petrov.M 72, Telkiyski 81 |

#	BULGARIA			SLOVENIA	#
27	IVANKOV Dimitar			MAVRIC Borut	1
6	ANGELOV Stanislav			ILIC Branko	20
25	WAGNER Lucio			KNAVS Aleksander	6
15	TUNCHEV Aleksandar			JOKIC Bojan	15
21	TOPUZAKOV Elin			CESAR Bostjan	5
19	PETROV Stilian			ZLOGAR Anton	16
9	YANKOV Chavdar	69	76	KOREN Robert	8
7	GEORGIEV Blagoy	53		KOMAC Andrej	11
17	PETROV Martin			ACIMOVIC Milenko	18
10	BZHINOV Valeri	60	80	BIRSA Valter	14
14	JANKOVIC Zoran			NOVAKOVIC Milivoje	9
	Tr: STOICHKOV Hristo			Tr: OBLAK Branko	
2	KISHISHEV Radostin	69	76	LAVRIC Klemen	17
22	TELKIYSKI Dimitar	53	80	SEMLER Borut	13
11	YOVOV Hristo	60			

Philips Stadion, Eindhoven
6-09-2006, 20:30, 30 089, Webb ENG

NED 3 0 BLR

Van Persie 2 33 78, Kuyt 92+ |

#	NETHERLANDS			BELARUS	#
1	VAN DER SAR Edwin			KHOMUTOVSKI Vasili	1
2	HEITINGA Johnny	67		YUREVIC Aleksandr	2
3	OOIJER Andre			SHTANIUK Sergei	5
4	MATHIJSEN Joris			OMELYANCHUK Sergei	4
5	VAN BRONCKHORST Gio			LENTSEVICH Dmitri	8
6	DE JONG Nigel		73	KALACHEV Timofei	6
10	SNEIJDER Wesley			KOVBA Denis	7
8	LANDZAAT Denny	68	45	KORYTHKO Vladimir	3
9	HUNTELAAR Klaas Jan	76	69	ROMASCHENKO Maksim	9
7	VAN PERSIE Robin			HLEB Aleksandr	10
11	KUYT Dirk			KORNILENKO Sergei	11
	Tr: VAN BASTEN Marco			Tr: PUNTUS Yuri	
12	BOULAHROUZ Khalid	67	45	STRAKHANOVICH Oleg	13
14	SCHAARS Stijn	68	69	KONTSEVOY Artem	16
18	BABEL Ryan	76	73	LANKO Vitali	18

Stadionul Steaua, Bucharest
7-10-2006, 20:15, 12 000, Undiano Mallenco ESP

ROU 3 1 BLR

Mutu 7, Marica 10, Goian 76 | Kornilenko 20

	ROMANIA					BELARUS	
1	COMAN Danut					GAYEV Vladimir	1
3	RAT Razvan	65				KULCHY Aleksandr	2
4	TAMAS Gabriel				65	LENTSEVICH Dmitri	3
5	CHIVU Cristian					OMELYANCHUK Sergei	4
7	PETRE Florentin					SHTANIUK Sergei	5
9	MARICA Ciprian	92+	50			KALACHEV Timofei	8
10	MUTU Adrian	72				HLEB Aleksandr	13
11	ROSU Laurentiu					GURENKO Sergei	6
17	GOIAN Dorin					ROMASCHENKO Maksim	9
18	MARIN Petre	66				KORNILENKO Sergei	21
20	DICA Nicolae	88			66	YUREVIC Aleksandr	23
	Tr: PITURCA Victor					Tr: PUNTUS Yuri	
13	COCIS Razvan	88	66			KORYTHKO Vladimir	17
19	NICULESCU Claudiu	92+	65		66	STRAKHANOVICH Oleg	18
21	BUGA Mugurel	72	50		65	HLEB Vyacheslav	15
					50		

Arena Petrol, Celje
7-10-2006, 20:45, 3800, Kailis CYP

SVN 2 0 LUX

Novakovic 30, Koren 44

	SLOVENIA					LUXEMBOURG	
1	MAVRIC Borut				72	JOUBERT Jonathan	1
20	ILIC Branko					KINTZIGER Kim	2
4	MAVRIC Matej					HOFFMANN Eric	4
5	CESAR Bostjan					REITER Claude	5
15	JOKIC Bojan					PETERS Rene	6
10	CEH Nastja					STRASSER Jeff	7
18	ACIMOVIC Milenko	75				BETTMER Gilles	8
14	BIRSA Valter				66	JOACHIM Aurelien	9
8	KOREN Robert				42	LOMBARDELLI Claudio	10
9	NOVAKOVIC Milivoje					REMY Sebastian	16
17	LAVRIC Klemen	85				MUTSCH Mario	17
	Tr: OBLAK Branko					Tr: HELLERS Guy	
11	KOMAC Andrej	75			72	GILLET Stephane	12
19	BURGIC Miran	85			42	LEWECK Charles	3
					66	HUSS Daniel	18

Vasil Levski, Sofia
7-10-2006, 21:00, 30 547, Ovrebø NOR

BUL 1 1 NED

Petrov.M 12 | Van Persie 62

	BULGARIA					NETHERLANDS	
27	IVANKOV Dimitar					VAN DER SAR Edwin	1
6	ANGELOV Stanislav					BOULAHROUZ Khalid	2
21	TOPUZAKOV Elin					OOIJER Andre	3
5	ILIEV Valentin					MATHIJSEN Joris	4
25	WAGNER Lucio					VAN BRONCKHORST Gio	5
2	KISHISHEV Radostin					DE JONG Nigel	6
8	YANKOV Chavdar	82				LANDZAAT Denny	8
7	YOVOV Hristo	54			91+	SNEIJDER Wesley	10
19	PETROV Stilian					VAN PERSIE Robin	7
17	PETROV Martin	64			16	KUYT Dirk	9
9	BERBATOV Dimitar					ROBBEN Arjen	11
	Tr: STOICHKOV Hristo					Tr: VAN BASTEN Marco	
22	TELKIYSKI Dimitar	54			91+	SCHAARS Stijn	15
20	JANKOVIC Zoran	82			16	BABEL Ryan	18
10	BZHINOV Valeri	64					

Dinamo, Minsk
11-10-2006, 19:00, 21 150, Kassai HUN

BLR 4 2 SVN

Kovba 18, Kornilenko 2 52 60, Korythko 85 | Cesar 19, Lavric 43

	BELARUS					SLOVENIA	
1	GAYEV Vladimir					MAVRIC Borut	1
4	OMELYANCHUK Sergei					ILIC Branko	20
5	SHTANIUK Sergei					JOKIC Bojan	15
6	GURENKO Sergei					CESAR Bostjan	5
2	KULCHY Aleksandr					MAVRIC Matej	4
3	KOVBA Denis					KOREN Robert	8
8	KALACHEV Timofei				70	ACIMOVIC Milenko	18
9	ROMASCHENKO Maksim	50				ZLOGAR Anton	16
13	HLEB Aleksandr					BIRSA Valter	14
15	HLEB Vyacheslav	69			82	NOVAKOVIC Milivoje	9
21	KORNILENKO Sergei	90				LAVRIC Klemen	17
	Tr: PUNTUS Yuri					Tr: OBLAK Branko	
14	KONTSEVOY Artem	90			70	KOMAC Andrej	11
17	KORYTHKO Vladimir	50			82	BURGIC Miran	19
18	STRAKHANOVICH Oleg	69					

Stade Josy Barthel, Luxembourg City
11-10-2006, 20:15, 3156, Panic BIH

LUX 0 1 BUL

| Tunchev 26

	LUXEMBOURG					BULGARIA	
1	GILLET Stephane					IVANKOV Dimitar	27
5	REITER Claude					ANGELOV Stanislav	6
7	STRASSER Jeff					TUNCHEV Aleksandar	15
2	KINTZIGER Kim					TOPUZAKOV Elin	21
6	PETERS Rene	61				WAGNER Lucio	25
8	BETTMER Gilles				77	YANKOV Chavdar	8
17	MUTSCH Mario				45	LAZAROV Zdravko	11
16	REMY Sebastian					PETROV Stilian	19
9	JOACHIM Aurelien	52				TELKIYSKI Dimitar	22
10	LOMBARDELLI Claudio	69			68	BZHINOV Valeri	10
4	FERREIRA Carlos					BERBATOV Dimitar	9
	Tr: HELLERS Guy					Tr: STOICHKOV Hristo	
3	LEWECK Charles	69			77	KISHISHEV Radostin	2
11	PAYAL Ben	61			45	YOVOV Hristo	7
18	HUSS Daniel	52			68	JANKOVIC Zoran	20

Amsterdam ArenA, Amsterdam
11-10-2006, 20:30, 40 085, Yefet ISR

NED 2 1 ALB

Van Persie 15, Beqaj OG 42 | Curri 67

	NETHERLANDS					ALBANIA	
1	VAN DER SAR Edwin					BEQAJ Arian	25
2	BOULAHROUZ Khalid					DEDE Nevil	3
3	OOIJER Andre					DALLKU Armend	4
4	MATHIJSEN Joris				65	ALIAJ Adrian	5
5	VAN BRONCKHORST Gio	68				HASI Besnik	6
6	DE JONG Nigel	50				HAXHI Altin	23
10	SNEIJDER Wesley	80				CURRI Debatik	24
8	LANDZAAT Denny					SKELA Ervin	13
7	BABEL Ryan	47+				LALA Altin	14
9	VAN PERSIE Robin					TARE Igil	17
11	ROBBEN Arjen	79				BOGDANI Erion	22
	Tr: VAN BASTEN Marco					Tr: BARIC Otto	
14	DE CLER Tim	80			65	MURATI Edvin	7
15	SCHAARS Stijn	50			47+	MUKAJ Devis	15
17	EMANUELSON Urby	68			79	BERISHA Besart	8

Stade Josy Barthel, Luxembourg City
24-03-2007, 17:00, 2021, Whitby WAL

LUX 1 – 2 BLR

Sagramola 68 | Kalachev 25, Kutuzov 54

#	LUXEMBOURG			BELARUS	#
1	JOUBERT Jonathan			ZHENOV Yuri	12
7	STRASSER Jeff			YUREVIC Aleksandr	3
4	HOFFMANN Eric			SHTANIUK Sergei	5
5	REITER Claude			KULCHY Aleksandr	2
2	KINTZIGER Kim			KORYTHKO Vladimir	6
6	PETERS Rene		58	STRAKHANOVICH Oleg	18
8	BETTMER Gilles			HLEB Aleksandr	13
9	PAYAL Ben	67		KALACHEV Timofei	9
10	LOMBARDELLI Claudio	58		HLEB Vyacheslav	10
16	REMY Sebastian		74	KORNILENKO Sergei	8
11	COLLETTE Dan	64	80	KUTUZOV Vitali	11
	Tr: HELLERS Guy			Tr: PUNTUS Yuri	
3	BIGARD Jerome	58	58	CHELYADINSKI Artyom	14
13	FERREIRA Carlos	67	74	BLIZNYUK Gennadi	17
14	SAGRAMOLA Chris	64	80	RADKOV Artyom	15

Loro Boriçi, Shkoder
24-03-2007, 17:00, 7000, Attard MLT

ALB 0 – 0 SVN

#	ALBANIA			SLOVENIA	#
1	BEQAJ Arian			HANDANOVIC Samir	1
4	DALLKU Armend			MAVRIC Matej	4
2	BEQIRI Elvin			JOKIC Bojan	15
28	DEDE Nevil			CESAR Bostjan	5
5	CANA Lorik			ILIC Branko	20
23	HAXHI Altin			KOREN Robert	8
14	LALA Altin			ZLOGAR Anton	16
10	DURO Klodian		90	KOMAC Andrej	11
20	MUKAJ Devis	86	80	CEH Nastja	10
9	KAPLLANI Edmond	58		LAVRIC Klemen	17
22	BOGDANI Erion	89	63	RAKOVIC Ermin	14
	Tr: BARIC Otto			Tr: OBLAK Branko	
8	BUSHAJ Alban	58	90	CIPOT Fabijan	2
18	SALIHI Hamdi	89	63	BIRSA Valter	19
11	BERISHA Besart	86	80	ACIMOVIC Milenko	18

De Kuip, Rotterdam
24-03-2007, 20:30, 48 000, Merk GER

NED 0 – 0 ROU

#	NETHERLANDS			ROMANIA	#
1	STEKELENBURG Maarten			LOBONT Bogdan	1
2	JALIENS Kew			CONTRA Cosmin	2
4	BOUMA Wilfred			GOIAN Dorin	15
3	MATHIJSEN Joris			TAMAS Gabriel	4
5	VAN BRONCKHORST Gio	78		RAT Razvan	3
6	LANDZAAT Denny	79		COCIS Razvan	19
8	SNEIJDER Wesley			NICOLITA Banel	8
7	BABEL Ryan			RADOI Mirel	6
10	VAN DER VAART Rafael	86	87	CODREA Paul	5
9	HUNTELAAR Klaas Jan	64	64	MARICA Ciprian	9
11	ROBBEN Arjen			MUTU Adrian	10
	Tr: VAN BASTEN Marco			Tr: PITURCA Victor	
14	EMANUELSON Urby	79	87	ROSU Laurentiu	11
16	SEEDORF Clarence	86	64	NICULAE Daniel	21
			78	RADU Stefan	22

Vasil Levski, Sofia
28-03-2007, 18:00, 19 800, Eriksson SWE

BUL 0 – 0 ALB

#	BULGARIA			ALBANIA	#
27	IVANKOV Dimitar			BEQAJ Arian	1
2	KISHISHEV Radostin			DALLKU Armend	4
3	TUNCHEV Aleksandar			DEDE Nevil	28
4	TOMASIC Igor			BEQIRI Elvin	2
25	WAGNER Lucio			CURRI Debatik	24
14	YANKOV Chavdar			LALA Altin	14
19	PETROV Stilian		68	DURO Klodian	10
13	PEEV Georgi	65	54	HAXHI Altin	23
18	YOVOV Hristo	45		CANA Lorik	5
20	JANKOVIC Zoran	45	79	BERISHA Besart	11
9	BERBATOV Dimitar			BOGDANI Erion	22
	Tr: STOICHKOV Hristo			Tr: BARIC Otto	
22	TELKIYSKI Dimitar	45	68	BULKU Ervin	29
14	TODOROV Svetoslav	45	54	KAPLLANI Edmond	9
10	BZHINOV Valeri	65	79	BUSHAJ Alban	8

Stadionul Ceahlaul, Piatra Neamt
28-03-2007, 18:30, 9120, Lajuks LVA

ROU 3 – 0 LUX

Mutu 26, Contra 56, Marica 90

#	ROMANIA			LUXEMBOURG	#
1	LOBONT Bogdan			JOUBERT Jonathan	1
2	CONTRA Cosmin			STRASSER Jeff	7
4	TAMAS Gabriel	87		BIGARD Jerome	3
15	GOIAN Dorin			HOFFMANN Eric	4
22	RADU Stefan			REITER Claude	5
6	RADOI Mirel			PETERS Rene	6
7	ZICU Ianis	50	50	BETTMER Gilles	8
11	ROSU Laurentiu	53	81	LOMBARDELLI Claudio	10
19	COCIS Razvan			REMY Sebastian	16
21	NICULAE Daniel	65		MUTSCH Mario	17
10	MUTU Adrian		49	COLLETTE Dan	11
	Tr: PITURCA Victor			Tr: HELLERS Guy	
9	MARICA Ciprian	65	50	PAYAL Ben	2
13	STOICA Dorel	87	49	SAGRAMOLA Chris	9
20	CRISTEA Adrian	53	81	FERREIRA Carlos	14

Arena Petrol, Celje
28-03-2007, 20:45, 10 000, Mejuto González ESP

SVN 0 – 1 NED

Van Bronckhorst 86

#	SLOVENIA			NETHERLANDS	#
1	HANDANOVIC Samir			VAN DER SAR Edwin	1
20	ILIC Branko		74	HEITINGA Johnny	2
15	JOKIC Bojan			MATHIJSEN Joris	3
4	MAVRIC Matej			BOUMA Wilfred	4
5	CESAR Bostjan			EMANUELSON Urby	5
10	CEH Nastja		85	AFELLAY Ibrahim	6
11	KOMAC Andrej		73	BABEL Ryan	7
8	KOREN Robert			VAN BRONCKHORST Gio	8
18	ACIMOVIC Milenko	61		KUYT Dirk	9
17	LAVRIC Klemen	83		SNEIJDER Wesley	10
14	RAKOVIC Ermin	65		ROBBEN Arjen	11
				Tr: VAN BASTEN Marco	
7	SUKALO Goran	61	74	De ZEEUW Denny	13
9	NOVAKOVIC Milivoje	65	85	SEEDORF Clarence	15
19	BIRSA Valter	83	73	KOEVERMANS Danny	18

Qemal Stafa, Tirana
2-06-2007, 20:30, 3000, Silgava GEO

ALB 2 0 LUX

Kapllani [38], Haxhi [57]

	ALBANIA			LUXEMBOURG	
1	BEQAJ Arian			JOUBERT Jonathan	1
4	DALLKU Armend			KINZIGER Kim	2
5	CANA Lorik		60	BIGARD Jerome	3
8	BUSHAJ Alban	76		HOFFMANN Eric	4
9	KAPLLANI Edmond			STRASSER Jeff	7
10	DURO Klodian			PETERS Rene	6
11	BERISHA Besart	45		BETTMER Gilles	8
13	SKELA Ervin		82	PAYAL Ben	10
23	HAXHI Altin	74	70	COLLETTE Dan	11
24	CURRI Debatik			REMY Sebastian	16
29	DEDE Nevil			MUTSCH Mario	17
	Tr: BARIC Otto			Tr: HELLERS Guy	
21	VANGJELI Kristi	74	82	FERREIRA Carlos	14
20	MUKAJ Devis	45	60	DA MOTA Daniel	9
18	SALIHI Hamdi	76	70	SAGRAMOLA Chris	15

Dinamo, Minsk
2-06-2007, 21:00, 29 000, Jara CZE

BLR 0 2 BUL

Berbatov 2 [28 46]

	BELARUS			BULGARIA	
12	ZHENOV Yuri			IVANKOV Dimitar	27
4	OMELYANCHUK Sergei	71		TUNCHEV Aleksandar	3
5	SHTANIUK Sergei			TOMASIC Igor	4
21	TIGOREV Yan		93+	ANGELOV Stanislav	6
2	KULCHY Aleksandr			WAGNER Lucio	25
3	KALACHEV Timofei			TELKIYSKI Dimitar	22
6	KORYTHKO Vladimir			KISHISHEV Radostin	2
7	KOVBA Denis			PETROV Stilian	19
10	HLEB Aleksandr		79	YOVOV Hristo	18
8	KORNILENKO Sergei	59	91+	PETROV Martin	17
11	KUTUZOV Vitali	46		BERBATOV Dimitar	9
	Tr: PUNTUS Yuri			Tr: STOILOV Stanimir	
13	STRAKHANOVICH Oleg	71	79	MANCHEV Vladimir	11
14	VASILYUK Roman	59	93+	DOMOVCHIYSKI Valeri	14
20	HLEB Vyacheslav	46	91+	GENKOV Tsvetan	15

Arena Petrol, Celje
2-06-2007, 20:45, 6500, Dougal SCO

SVN 1 2 ROU

Vrsic [94+]

Tamas [52], Nicolita [69]

	SLOVENIA			ROMANIA	
1	HANDANOVIC Samir			LOBONT Bogdan	1
5	CESAR Bostjan	80		CHIVU Cristian	5
20	ILIC Branko			CONTRA Cosmin	2
15	JOKIC Bojan			RAT Razvan	3
4	MAVRIC Matej			TAMAS Gabriel	4
7	SUKALO Goran	83		CODREA Paul	6
10	CEH Nastja			NICOLITA Banel	16
11	KOMAC Andrej	63		ROSU Laurentiu	11
8	KOREN Robert	53	74	MARICA Ciprian	9
17	LAVRIC Klemen			MUTU Adrian	10
14	RAKOVIC Ermin	61	77	STOICA Dorei	13
	Tr: KEK Matjaz			Tr: PITURCA Victor	
13	VRSIC Dare	83	77	MURESAN Mireca	18
19	BIRSA Valter	53	80 74	NICULAE Daniel	21
9	NOVAKOVIC Milivoje	61	63	ZICU Ianis	8

Stade Josy Barthel, Luxembourg City
6-06-2007, 20:15, 4325, Malzinskas, LTU

LUX 0 3 ALB

Skela [25], Kapllani 2 [36 72]

	LUXEMBOURG			ALBANIA	
1	JOUBERT Jonathan			BEQAJ Arian	1
7	STRASSER Jeff			DEDE Nevil	28
3	BIGARD Jerome	46		HAXHI Altin	23
4	HOFFMANN Eric			DALLKU Armend	4
2	KINZIGER Kim			CURRI Debatik	24
10	PAYAL Ben	64	60	SKELA Ervin	13
6	PETERS Rene			CANA Lorik	5
8	BETTMER Gilles		77	MUKAJ Devis	20
16	REMY Sebastian			KAPLLANI Edmond	9
17	MUTSCH Mario		67	BUSHAJ Alban	8
11	COLLETTE Dan	79		BOGDANI Erion	22
	Tr: HELLERS Guy			Tr: BARIC Otto	
13	SAGRAMOLA Chris	79	60	DURO Klodian	10
9	DA MOTA Daniel	64	77	XHAFAJ Daniel	19
10	LOMBARDELLI Claudio	46	67	BERISHA Besart	11

Vasil Levski, Sofia
6-06-2007, 20:00, 10 501, Jakobsson ISL

BUL 2 1 BLR

Petrov.M [10], Yankov [40]

Vasilyuk [5p]

	BULGARIA			BELARUS	
27	IVANKOV Dimitar			ZHENOV Yuri	12
2	KISHISHEV Radostin			SHTANIUK Sergei	5
3	TUNCHEV Aleksandar			RADKOV Artyom	15
4	TOMASIC Igor			TIGOREV Yan	22
25	WAGNER Lucio			YUREVIC Aleksandr	18
8	YANKOV Chavdar	93+	44	KALACHEV Timofei	3
19	PETROV Stilian			KORYTHKO Vladimir	6
22	TELKIYSKI Dimitar			KOVBA Denis	7
18	YOVOV Hristo	68		HLEB Aleksandr	10
9	BERBATOV Dimitar		64	STRAKHANOVICH Oleg	13
17	PETROV Martin	84	55	VASILYUK Roman	14
	Tr: STOILOV Stanimir			Tr: PUNTUS Yuri	
16	SIRAKOV Zaharin	93+	55	KORNILENKO Sergei	8
6	ANGELOV Stanislav	68	64	HLEB Vyacheslav	20
11	MANCHEV Vladimir	84	44	KUTUZOV Vitali	11

Dan Paltinisanu, Timisoara
6-06-2007, 21:00, 17 850, Yefet ISR

ROU 2 0 SVN

Mutu [40], Contra [70]

	ROMANIA			SLOVENIA	
1	LOBONT Bogdan			HANDANOVIC Samir	1
3	RAT Razvan			MAVRIC Matej	4
4	TAMAS Gabriel			MOREC Mitja	6
19	GOLAN Dorin		84	JOKIC Bojan	15
2	CONTRA Cosmin			ILIC Branko	20
8	ZICU Ianis	60		CEH Nastja	10
5	CHIVU Cristian			KOMAC Andrej	11
6	CODREA Paul	78		VRSIC Dare	13
7	PETRE Florentin	75	77	ZLOGAR Anton	16
9	MARICA Ciprian			LAVRIC Klemen	17
10	MUTU Adrian		54	BIRSA Valter	19
	Tr: PITURCA Victor			Tr: KEK Matjaz	
11	ROSU Laurentiu	60	84	FILEKOVIC Suad	3
16	NICOLITA Banel	75	77	SUKALO Goran	7
17	PLESAN Mihaita	78	54	NOVAKOVIC Milivoje	9

UEFA CHAMPIONS LEAGUE 2006–07

First Qualifying Round

Sioni Bolnisi *	GEO	2	0
FK Baku	AZE	0	1
Pyunik Yerevan *	ARM	0	0
Sheriff Tiraspol	MDA	0	2
TVMK Tallinn *	EST	2	1
FH Hafnarfjördur	ISL	3	1
Linfield *	NIR	1	2
ND Gorica	SVN	3	2
Liepajas Metalurgs*	LVA	1	1
Aktobe Lento	KAZ	0	1
Birkirkara *	MLT	0	2
B'36 Tórshavn	FRO	3	2
MyPa-47 *	FIN	1	1
TNS Llansantffraid	WAL	0	0
Elbasani *	ALB	1	0
Ekranas Panevezys	LTU	0	3
Cork City *	IRL	1	1
Apollon Limassol	CYP	0	1
F'91 Dudelange *	LUX	0	0
Rabotnicki Skopje	MKD	1	0
Shakhtyor Soligorsk*	BLR	0	0
Siroki Brijeg	BIH	1	1

Second Qualifying Round

Levski Sofia *	BUL	2	2
Sioni Bolnisi	GEO	0	0
Spartak Moskva *	RUS	1	0
Sheriff Tiraspol	MDA	1	0
Mladá Boleslav *	CZE	3	2
Vålerenga IF	NOR	1	2
FC Zürich *	SUI	2	0
Salzburg	AUT	1	2
FH Hafnarfjördur *	ISL	0	0
Legia Warszawa	POL	1	2
ND Gorica *	SVN	0	0
Steaua Bucuresti	ROU	2	3
Liepajas Metalurgs*	LVA	1	0
Dynamo Kyiv	UKR	4	4
Fenerbahçe *	TUR	4	5
B'36 Tórshavn	FRO	0	0
FC København *	DEN	2	2
MyPa-47	FIN	0	2
Ekranas Panevezys*	LTU	1	2
Dinamo Zagreb	CRO	4	5
Djurgårdens IF *	SWE	1	1
MFK Ruzomberok	SVK	0	3
Cork City *	IRL	0	0
Crvena Zvezda	SRB	1	3
Debreceni VSC *	HUN	1	1
Rabotnicki Skopje	MKD	1	4
Heart of Midlothian*	SCO	3	0
Siroki Brijeg	BIH	0	0

Third Qualifying Round

Levski Sofia *	BUL	2	2
Chievo Verona	ITA	0	2
Slovan Liberec *	CZE	0	1
Spartak Moskva	RUS	0	2
Liverpool *	ENG	2	1
Maccabi Haifa	ISR	1	1
Galatasaray *	TUR	5	1
Mladá Boleslav	CZE	2	1
Salzburg *	AUT	1	0
Valencia	ESP	0	3
Shakhtar Donetsk *	UKR	1	3
Legia Warszawa	POL	0	2
Standard CL *	BEL	2	1
Steaua Bucuresti	ROU	2	2
Dynamo Kyiv *	UKR	3	2
Fenerbahce	TUR	1	2
FK Austria *	AUT	1	0
Benfica	POR	1	3
FC København *	DEN	1	2
Ajax	NED	2	0
Dinamo Zagreb *	CRO	0	1
Arsenal	ENG	3	2
CSKA Moskva *	RUS	3	2
MFK Ruzomberok	SVK	0	0
Hamburger SV *	GER	0	1
Osasuna	ESP	0	1
Milan *	ITA	1	2
Crvena Zvezda	SRB	0	1
Lille OSC *	FRA	3	1
Rabotnicki Skopje	MKD	0	0
Heart of Midlothian*	SCO	1	0
AEK Athens	GRE	2	3

Group Stage

Group A		Pts
Chelsea	ENG	13
Barcelona	ESP	11
Werder Bremen	GER	10
Levski Sofia	BUL	0

Group B		Pts
Bayern München	GER	12
Internazionale	ITA	10
Spartak Moskva	RUS	5
Sporting CP	POR	5

Group C		Pts
Liverpool	ENG	13
PSV Eindhoven	NED	10
Girondins Bordeaux	FRA	7
Galatasaray	TUR	4

Group D		Pts
Valencia	ESP	13
Roma	ITA	10
Shakhtar Donetsk	UKR	6
Olympiacos	GRE	3

Group E		Pts
Olymp. Lyonnais	FRA	14
Real Madrid	ESP	11
Steaua Bucuresti	ROU	5
Dynamo Kyiv	UKR	2

Group F		Pts
Manchester United	ENG	12
Celtic	SCO	9
Benfica	POR	7
FC København	DEN	7

Group G		Pts
Arsenal	ENG	11
FC Porto	POR	11
CSKA Moskva	RUS	8
Hamburger SV	GER	3

Group H		Pts
Milan	ITA	10
Lille OSC	FRA	9
AEK Athens	GRE	8
RSC Anderlecht	BEL	4

* Home team in the first leg • Teams placed third in the group stage
qualify for the UEFA Cup as do the third qualifying round losers

UEFA CHAMPIONS LEAGUE 2006–07

UEFA CHAMPIONS LEAGUE 2006–07

Round of Sixteen			Quarter-finals			Semi-finals			Final		
Milan	0	1									
Celtic *	0	0									
			Milan *	2	2						
			Bayern München	2	0						
Real Madrid *	3	1									
Bayern München	2	2									
						Milan	2	3			
						Manchester United *	3	0			
Roma *	0	2									
Olympique Lyonnais	0	0									
			Roma *	2	1						
			Manchester United	1	7						
Lille OSC *	0	0									
Manchester United	1	1									
									Milan		2
									Liverpool		1
Chelsea	1	2									
FC Porto *	1	1									
			Chelsea *	1	2						
			Valencia	1	1						
Internazionale *	2	0									
Valencia	2	0									
						Chelsea *	1 0 1p				
						Liverpool	0 1 4p				
PSV Eindhoven *	1	1									
Arsenal	0	1									
			PSV Eindhoven *	0	0						
			Liverpool	3	1						
Barcelona *	1	1									
Liverpool	2	0									

* Home team in first leg

FIRST QUALIFYING ROUND

1st leg. Mikheil Meshki, Tbilisi
11-07-2006, 19:00, 4000, Kinhöfer GER
Sioni Bolnisi 2
Boyomo 69, Ugrekhelidze 88
Batiashvili – Kobauri, Tchelidze, Chichveishvili, Rakviashvili (Chelidze 46), Bajelidze•, Shavgulidze, Alavidze, Kutsurua (Ugrekhelidze 76), Mikuchadze, Memedji (Boyomo• 46). Tr: Tskhadadze
FK Baku 0

Diallo – Ladaga• (Amirbekov 93), Guliyev.R, Guliyev.V•33, Megrealadze (Ionescu• 55), Sultanov, Abbasov.R•36, Abbasov.A, Jovandic•, Melikov, Bangoura. Tr: Hajiyev

---

2nd leg. Tofikh Bakhramov, Baku
18-07-2006, 19:00, 5500, Berezka UKR
FK Baku 1
Guliyev.F 63
Diallo – Ladaga, Abdullayev, Guliyev.R, Megrealadze (Guliyev.F 46), Sultanov, Abbasov.A, Jovandic, Ionescu, Melikov (Amirbekov 46), Bangoura•. Tr: Hajiyev
Sioni Bolnisi 0

Batiashvili – Kobauri• (Alavidze• 30), Tchelidze, Chichveishvili, Boyomo, Rakviashvili, Ugrekhelidze, Shavgulidze, Bajelidze (Chelidze 46), Kutsurua (Memedji 79), Chassem. Tr: Tskhadadze

---

1st leg. Republican, Yerevan
11-07-2006, 19:00, 5000, Rogalla SUI
Pyunik Yerevan 0
Kasparov – Hovsepyan (Melkonyan 46), Tadevosyan, Aleksanyan, Voskanyan (Tigranyan• 33), Khachatryan, Mkrtchyan•, Pachajyan (Sahakyan 73), Nazaryan•, Petrosyan, Avetisyan•. Tr: Petrosyan
Sheriff Tiraspol 0

Hutan – Mamah, Tarkhinshvilli, Corneencov, Kuchuk (Omotoyossi 63), Florescu, Arbanas, Epureanu, Cocis (Suvorov 73), Pirsa (Gumenuk 36), Gnanou. Tr: Koutchouck

---

2nd leg. Sheriff, Tiraspol
18-07-2006, 20:00, 6500, Halsey ENG
Sheriff Tiraspol 2
Cocis 30, Gumenuk 90
Hutan – Mamah, Tarkhinshvilli, Corneencov• (Suvorov 87), Kuchuk (Omotoyossi 70), Florescu, Arbanas, Epureanu, Cocis, Pirsa (Gumenuk• 61), Gnanou. Tr: Koutchouck.
Pyunik Yerevan 0

Kasparov – Hovsepyan, Tadevosyan, Khachatryan, Arzumanyan, Tigranyan, Safaryan• (Avetisyan 38), Mkrtchyan•, Pachajyan, Melkonyan (Nazaryan 68), Petrosyan (Sahakyan 57). Tr: Petrosyan

---

1st leg. Kadriorg, Tallinn
11-07-2006, 18:00, 400, Staberg NOR
TVMK Tallinn 2
Haavistu.K 70, Dobrecovs 76p
Teles – Gabovs (Sarajev• 8), Rimas, Kacanovs•, Haavistu (Masitsev 80), Borisov, Sirmelis, Dobrecovos, Seero, Kostin (Zenjov 55), Gussev. Tr: Bulavin
FH Hafnarfjördur 3
Gudmundsson.T 33, Olafsson 69, Gudnason.At 92+
Lárusson – Nielsen•, Ásgeirsson, Vidarsson, Gudmundsson, Olafsson•, Sævarsson, Björnsonn, Albertsson, Snorrason (Gudnadson 83), Vilhjalmsson (Dyring 83). Tr: Johannesson

---

2nd leg. Kaplakrikavöllur, Hafnarfjördur
19-07-2006, 19:15, 1004, Vuorela FIN
FH Hafnarfjördur 1
Gudnason.At 91+
Lárusson – Bett, Ásgeirsson, Vidarsson•, Gudmundsson.T Olafsson (Gudnason.Ar 93+), Sævarsson, Björnsonn, Albertsson, Snorrason (Gudnadson.At 84), Vilhjalmsson (Dyring 68). Tr: Johannesson
TVMK Tallinn 1
Dobrecovs 60p
Teles – Zenjov (Gussev 57), Rimas, Kacanovs (Kostin 82), Haavistu, Borisov, Sirmelis•, Dobrecovos Sarajev, Seero, Kuvsinovs (Masitsev 74). Tr: Bulavin

---

1st leg. Windsor Park, Belfast
11-07-2006, 18:00, 1906, Coue FRA
Linfield 1
Dickson 58p
Mannus – Ervin (Douglas 46), McShane (McCann 25), Mulgrew, Murphy•, O'Kane, Thompson•, Magennis (Mouncey 32), Dickson, McAreavey, Bailie. Tr: Jeffrey
ND Gorica 3
Demirovic 2 14 27, Sturm 66
Pirih• – Srebrnic (Jogan 84), Jokic, Zivec•, Kovacevic, Dedic, Demirovic, Burgic, Sturm• (Rexhay 75), Pitamic• (Nikolic 63), Suler•. Tr: Nielsen

---

2nd leg. Sportni Park, Nova Gorica
19-07-2006, 20:05, 1391, Papila TUR
ND Gorica 2
Burgic 2 31 83
Pirih – Srebrnic•, Jokic, Zivec (Jogan 75), Kovacevic, Dedic, Demirovic, Burgic (Matavz 85), Sturm (Rezhay 55), Nikolic, Suler. Tr: Nielsen
Linfield 2
Thompson 28, McAreavey 90
Mannus – Douglas (Ervin 65), McCann, Mulgrew (McAreavey• 51), Murphy, O'Kane, Thompson, Kingsberry, Dickson (Garrett 82), Mouncey•, Bailie. Tr: Jeffrey

---

1st leg. Daugava, Liepaja
12-07-2006, 20:00, 3500, Supraha CRO
Liepajas Metalurgs 1
Tamosauskas 14
Krucs – Klava•, Zirnis•, Ivanovs, Surnins, Petrenko, Miceika• (Katasonov 46), Kalonas, Tamosauskas•, Solonicins, Karlsons (Astrauskas 67). Tr: Zelkevicius
Aktobe Lento 0

Nesterenko – Samchenko, Nizovtsev, Malkov, Yaskovich, Aksenov, Nikolaev, Shkurin, Rogaciov, Golovskoy, Kitsak. Tr: Mukhanov

---

2nd leg. Centralny, Aktobe
19-07-2006, 20:00, 13 000, Bossen NED
Aktobe Lento 1
Nikolaev 17
Nesterenko – Samchenko•, Aksenov (Ashirbekov 60), Nizovtsev, Yaskovich, Kitsak, Nikolaev, Shkurin, Rogaciov•83, Golovskoy•, Malkov (Logvinenko 75). Tr: Mukhanov
Liepajas Metalurgs 1
Ivanovs 59p
Krucs – Klava, Zirnis•, Ivanovs, Surnins, Petrenko, Karlsons, Kalonas, Tamosauskas, Solonicins, Astrauskas (Grebis 59) (Kets 90). Tr: Zelkevicius

---

1st leg. Ta'Qali, Ta'Qali
11-07-2006, 18:30, 805, Shmolik BLR
Birkirkara 0
Bledzewski – Sammut• (Sadowski 65), Gallovich, Scicluna, Galea, Camenzulli•, Mallia, Calascione (Tabone 71), Paradiso, Sbai (Paris.T 52), Triganza•. Tr: Azzopardi
B'36 Tórshavn 3
Davy 2 15 32, Thorleifson 92+
Mikkelsen – Alex, Thorleifson, Thomassen•, Benjaminsen, Ellingsgaard• (Gunnarsson 63), Jacobsen.K•, Midjord (Hansen.S 88), Matras, Davy (Ekeke• 75), Jacobsen.H. Tr: Clementsen

---

2nd leg. Tórsvøllur, Tórshavn
19-07-2006, 19:00, 1810, Matejek CZE
B'36 Tórshavn 2
Matras 44, Ekeke 80
Mikkelsen – Alex, Thorleifson (Joensen.N 62), Thomassen•72, Benjaminsen, Ellingsgaard (Ekeke 67), Jacobsen.K (Joensen.B 81), Midjord, Matras, Davy, Jacobsen.H. Tr: Clementsen
Birkirkara 2
Mallia 59, Scicluna 83
Bledzewski – Bonnici, Sammut, Camenzulli•83, Briffa (Calascione 19), Sbai• (Tabone 81), Scicluna, Paradiso (Paris.T 73), Triganza•, Mallia, Gallovich•. Tr: Azzopardi

---

1st leg. Jalkapallokenttä, Anjalankosken
12-07-2006, 19:00, 1850, Stanisic SRB
MyPa-47 Anjalankoski 1
Adriano 58
Korhonen – Timoska, Taipale, Lindstöm, Kuparinen (Puhakainen 62), Manso, Karhu, Kangaskolkka (Pellonen 70), Miranda, Kansikas, Adriano (Leguizamon 75). Tr: Mäkelä
TNS Llansanttfraid 0

Doherty• – Baker, King, Jackson, Holmes, Ruscoe (Leah 76), Hogan, Wilde (Carter 65), Beck, Ward (Toner 87), Stones. Tr: McKenna

---

1st leg. Latham Park, Newtown
19-07-2006, 19:30, 864, Vervecken BEL
TNS Llansanttfraid 0
Doherty – Baker, King (Carter 61), Jackson, Holmes, Ruscoe (Toner 46), Hogan (Leah 80), Wilde, Beck, Ward, Stones. Tr: McKenna
MyPa-47 Anjalankoski 1
Puhakainen 5
Korhonen – Timoska, Taipale, Lindstöm, Kuparinen, Puhakainen (Kangaskolkka 57), Manso (Huttunen 69), Leguizamon (Hernesniemi 78), Miranda, Kansikas, Adriano. Tr: Mäkelä

1st leg. Ruzhdi Bizhuta, Elbasan
11-07-2006, 17:30, 7000, Gonzalez V ESP
Elbasani 1
Stojku 79
Kotorri – Brahja, Dede, Vrapi, Alenchenu, Kaçi (Xhafaj 59), Çapja• (Stojku 69), Osja, Qorri, Bylykbashi, Dalipi (Norra 74). Tr: Daja
Ekranas Panevezys 0

Skrupskis – Klimavicius, Banevicius, Skrobias, Paulauskas, Kucys (Gardzijauskas 82), Savenas, Tomkevicius, Mikhalchuk• (Saulenas 89), Kavaliauskas• (Slekys 60), Luksys. Tr: Liubsys

2nd leg. Aukstaitija, Panevezys
18-07-2006, 18:00, 2570, Malcolm NIR

Ekranas Panevezys	3
	Luksys 2 [13 70], Tomkevicius [48]

Skrupskis – Klimavicius, Banevicius, Gardzijauskas●,
Paulauskas, Kucys (Petrauskas 78), Slekys
(Kavaliauskas 46), Savenas, Tomkevicius
(Saulenas 68), Mikhalchuk, Luksys. Tr: Liubsys

Elbasani	0

Kotorri – Brahja (Tetova● 46), Dede●, Alenchenu,
Vrapi, Norra, Osja, Çapja (Stijku 63), Qorri
(Dalipi 46), Bylykbashi, Xhafaj. Tr: Daja

1st leg. Turner's Cross, Cork
12-07-2006, 19:30, 3882, Einwaller AUT

Cork City	1
	Woods [62]

Devine – Murphy, Bennett, Murray, O'Brien, Fenn,
Woods●, O'Donovan, Gamble, Behan (Lordan 93+),
Horgan. Tr: Richardson

Apollon Limassol	0

Chvalovsky – Barun, Alvarez, Merkis, Michalski,
Andone (Machado● 80), Ajeel, Solomou (Taher 65),
Arig, Sosin●, Hamadi● (Paiva 58). Tr: Stange

2nd leg. GSP, Nicosia
19-07-2006, 21:00, 5563, Johannésson SWE

Apollon Limassol	1
	Sosin [51]

Chvalovsky – Barun (Hamadi 78●90), Alvarez●,
Merkis●90, Michalski●, Andone, Ajeel, Machado
(Solomou 78), Arig, Sosin, Paiva (Taher 59).
Tr: Stange

Cork City	1
	Murray.D [75]

Devine – Murphy●●90, Bennett, Murray●, O'Brien●,
Fenn, Woods (Softic 90), O'Donovan (Lordan 92+),
Gamble●90, Behan (Sullivan 87), Horgan.
Tr: Richardson

1st leg. Jos Nosbaum, Dudelange
11-07-2006, 19:00, 1100, Levi ISR

F'91 Dudelange	0

Joubert – Borbiconi, Mouny●, Crapa (Gruszczynski 82),
Di Gregorio (Lecomte 69), Martine, Bellini (Joly● 72),
Kabongo, Remy, Hug, Zeghdane. Tr: Leflochmoan

Rabotnicki Skopje	1
	Velkoski [77]

Pacovski – Jovanoski●, Ilievski, Vajs, Stepanovski,
Lazarevski (Karcev 80), Stojanov, Ignatov, Trajcev
(Jankep 72), Pejcic, Velkoski (Aleksovski 83). Tr:
Jovanovski

2nd leg. Gradski, Skopje
18-07-2006, 20:00, 2000, Sukhina RUS

Rabotnicki Skopje	0

Pacovski – Jovanoski, Ilievski, Vajs●, Stepanovski●,
Lazarevski, Stojanov (Abrilio 86), Mihajlovic
(Jankep 68) Trajcev, Pejcic, Velkoski (Aleksovski 90).
Tr: Jovanovski

F'91 Dudelange	0

Joubert – Borbiconi, Mouny●, Crapa●, Bellini
(Di Gregorio 75), Kabongo, Remy (Lecomte 80), Hug,
Helder (Joly 54), Gruszczynski, Zeghdane.
Tr: Leflochmoan

1st leg. Centralny, Gomel
12-07-2006, 20:00, 6000, Stokes IRL

Shakhtyor Soligorsk	1

Makauchyk – Budaev (Goncharik 63), Yurevich,
Leonchik, Klimenko● (Barel● 81), Nikiforenko,
Martsinovich, Sobal●, Plaskonny, Kavalchuk,
Beganski (Bychanok 37). Tr: Verheichyk

Siroki Brijeg	1
	Bubalo [29]

Basic● – Anic, Silic●, Pandza, Landeka, Lago,
Carvalho●, Gomes, Celson, Karoglan (Kovacic 84),
Bubalo (Lukacevic 56) (Galic 89)

2nd leg. Pecara, Siroki Brijeg
19-07-2006, 20:30, 4500, Pieri ITA

Siroki Brijeg	1
	Ronelle [29p]

Basic – Anic (Doci 77), Silic, Pandza, Landeka,
Carvalho (Papic 87), Lago, Bubalo (Lukacevic● 61),
Gomes, Karoglan, Celson

Shakhtyor Soligorsk	0

Makauchyk – Budaev●27, Yurevich, Leonchik,
Klimenko (Novik 75), Nikiforenko●, Martsinovich,
Sobal (Barel 82), Plaskonny●, Kavalchuk, Bychanok
(Goncharik 64). Tr: Verheichyk

SECOND QUALIFYING ROUND

1st leg. Georgi Asparuhov, Sofia
26-07-2006, 20:30, 11 075, Stuchlik AUT

Levski Sofia	2
	Angelov.E [20], Borimirov [82p]

Petkov – Tomasic, Eromoigbe●, Borimirov, Yovov
(Koprivarov 67), Angelov.S, Telkiyski (Domovchiyski 67),
Wagner, Bardon (Ivanov 84), Angelov.E, Topuzakov.
Tr: Stoilov

Sioni Bolnisi	0

Batiashvili● – Boyomo, Tchelidze, Chichveishvili
(Ocropiridze 87), Alavidze, Rakviashvili, Bajelidze,
Shavgulidze (Chelidze 65), Katsurua● (Kobauri● 65),
Ugrekhelidze 65), Chassem. Tr: Tskhadadze

2nd leg. Mikheil Meskhi, Tbilisi
2-08-2006, 19:00, 6900, Dereli TUR

Sioni Bolnisi	0

Batiashvili – Rakviashvili, Boyomo, Chichveishvili,
Shavgulidze●, Chelidze●, Bajelidze (Katsurua 46),
Ugrekhelidze, Alavidze●●●65, Memdeji (Kardava 58),
Chassem (Ocropiridze 75). Tr: Tskhadadze

Levski Sofia	2
	Domovchiyski [18], Angelov.E [91+]

Petkov – Milanov, Eromoigbe (Bornosuzov 77),
Borimirov, Domovchiyski●, Ivanov, Angelov.S, Telkiyski
(Angelov.E 71), Wagner, Bardon● (Koprivarov 68),
Topuzakov. Tr: Stoilov

1st leg. Sheriff, Tiraspol
26-07-2006, 20:00, 12 000, Malek POL

Sheriff Tiraspol	1
	Omotoyossi [92+]

Hutan – Mamah, Tarkhinshvilli, Corneencov, Kuchuk
(Omotoyossi 63), Florescu, Arbanas●, Epureanu●,
Cocis (Suvorov 83), Pirsa (Gumenuk 66), Gnanou●.
Tr: Koutchouck

Spartak Moskva	1
	Kovác [77]

Kowalewski – Jiránek, Kovác, Stranzl, Rodríguez,
Bystrov, Mozart, Covalciuc (Torbinskiy 60), Titov,
Pavlyuchenko (Owusu-Abeyie 52), Pjanovic
(Bazhenov 75). Tr: Fedotov

2nd leg. Luzhniki, Moscow
2-08-2006, 19:00, 22 000, Gumienny BEL

Spartak Moskva	0

Kowalewski – Jiránek, Kovác, Stranzl, Rodríguez,
Mozart, Bystrov (Torbinskiy 58), Kalynychenko, Titov
(Owusu-Abeyie 51) (Covalciuc 67), Pavlyuchenko●,
Cavenaghi●. Tr: Fedotov

Sheriff Tiraspol	0

Hutan – Mamah, Gumenuk● (Suvorov 81)
Tarkhinshvilli, Corneencov, Florescu, Arbanas,
Epureanu, Pirsa● (Balima 61), Omotoyossi (Kuchuk 62)
Gnanou. Tr: Koutchouck

1st leg. Mestsky, Mladá Boleslav
26-07-2006, 20:45, 5000, Oliveira POR

Mladá Boleslav	3
	Pecka [7], Palát [10], Matejovsky [18]

Kucera – Sevinsky, Vaculik, Palát●, Matejovsky,
Brezinsky, Kulic● (Ordos 85), Polácek (Riegel 72)
(Kysela 87), Pecka, Vit, Abrahám. Tr: Uhrin

Válerenga IF	1
	Gashi [67]

Arason – Jepsen, Holm.T, Dos Santos, Holm.D, Berre
(Sørensen 59), Storbæk, Grindheim, Hovi, Johnsen●,
Muri (Gashi 24). Tr: Rekdal

2nd leg. Ullevål, Oslo
2-08-2006, 20:45, 9639, Thomson SCO

Válerenga IF	2
	Vit OG [73], Holm.D [86]

Arason – Jepsen, Holm.T●, Dos Santos (Sørensen 64),
Holm.D, Gashi, Storbæk, Grindheim● (Berre 64),
Johnsen (Lange 68), Flo●, Wæhler. Tr: Rekdal

Mladá Boleslav	2
	Brezinsky [41], Kulic [83]

Kucera – Sevinsky●, Vaculik (Holub 92+), Palát●,
Matejovsky, Brezinsky, Kulic (Sedlácek 84), Polácek
(Riegel 74), Pecka, Vit, Abrahám●66. Tr: Uhrin

1st leg. Hardturm, Zürich
26-07-2006, 20:15, 11 200, Kelly IRL

FC Zürich 2

Keita [2], Clederson [20]

Leoni – Von Bergen, Margairaz (Alphonse 75), Dzemaili, Inler, Keita• (Stanic 83), Stahel, Araujo, Cesar (Abdi 86), Scheider, Tihinen. Tr: Favre

Austria Salzburg 1

Vonlanthen [32]

Ochs – Bodnár, Dudic•, Linke, Kovac, Jezek (Piták 84), Tiffert•, Vonlanthen• (Carboni 40), Janko (Zickler• 46), Aufhauser••36, Vargas. Tr: Trapattoni

2nd leg. Wals-Siezenheim, Salzburg
2-08-2006, 20:15, 16 168, Vink NED

Austria Salzburg 2

Tiffert [39], Zickler [56p]

Ochs – Bodnár, Dudic, Linke, Carboni•, Kovac•, Zickler, Jezek (Piták 72), Tiffert•, Janocko• (Meyer 86), Vargas. Tr: Trapattoni

FC Zürich 0

Leoni – Von Bergen, Margairaz (Stanic 76), Dzemaili• (Alphonse• 72), Inler, Keita (Pouga 83), Stahel, Araujo•, Cesar, Scheider, Tihinen. Tr: Favre

1st leg. Kaplakrikavöllur, Hafnarfjördur
26-07-2006, 18:30, 1910, Ingvarsson SWE

FH Hafnarfjördur 0

Lárusson – Asgeirsson, Vidarsson (Vilhjalmsson 54), Gudmundsson.T•, Sævarsson, Björnsonn, Bett, Olafsson (Gudnadson.A 87), Albertsson, Snorrason, Lindbæk (Dyring 77). Tr: Johannesson

Legia Warszawa 1

Elton [83]

Fabiański – Szala, Choto, Alcantara, Guerreiro, Kielbowicz, Vukovic, Janczyk (Korzym 67), Szalachowski• (Radovic 70), Gottwald (Elton 46). Tr: Wdowczyk

2nd leg. Wojska Polskiego, Warsaw
2-08-2006, 20:30, 6400, Briakos GRE

Legia Warszawa 2

Vukovic [38], Edson [78]

Fabiański – Szala, Choto, Alcantara•, Guerreiro, Wlodarczyk (Janczyk 53), Kielbowicz (Burkhardt 46), Vukovic•, Janczyk (Korzym 67), Szalachowski (Radovic 53), Edson, Elton. Tr: Wdowczyk

FH Hafnarfjördur 0

Lárusson – Asgeirsson (Gudnadsson.Ar 82), Gudmundsson.T, Sævarsson, Björnsonn•, Olafsson, Albertsson•, Lindbæk•, Nielsen, Snorrason (Gudnason.At 84), Bett (Vilhjalmsson 65). Tr: Johannesson

1st leg. Sportni Park, Nova Gorica
26-07-2006, 21:00, 1548, Messner AUT

ND Gorica 0

Simcic – Srebrnic, Jokic, Zivec (Jogan 75), Kovacevic, Dedic, Demirovic, Sturm (Velikonja 89), Pitamic, Ranic (Rexhay 74), Suler•. Tr: Nielsen

Steaua Bucureşti 2

Dica [54], Iacob [65]

Fernandes – Marin•, Ghionea, Goian, Nesu, Nicolita, Paraschiv• (Cristocea 70), Lovin, Bostina (Oprita 70), Dica, Iacob (Badea 85). Tr: Olarolu

2nd leg. Lia Manoliu, Bucharest
2-08-2006, 21:00, 16 763, Kralovec CZE

Steaua Bucureşti 3

Bostina [43], Iacob [70], Ochirosli [87p]

Cerna – Dica (Oprita 59), Bostina, Cristocea, Nesu, Nicolita (Badea 59), Baciu, Iacob (Ochirosil 76), Lovin, Saban, Ghionea•. Tr: Olarolu

ND Gorica 0

Simcic – Srebrnic, Jokic, Zivec (Jogan 60), Nikolic•, Kovacevic, Dedic, Demirovic (Rexhay 77), Sturm (Velikonja 82), Pitamic, Ranic. Tr: Nielsen

1st leg. Daugava, Liepaja
26-07-2006, 20:00, 4573, Courtney NIR

Liepajas Metalurgs 1

Kalonas [87]

Krucs – Zuravlovs, Klava, Jemelins, Surnins, Tamosauskas•, Miceika•, Rimkevicius, Solonicins, Kalonas, Karlsons (Astrauskas 54). Tr: Zelkevicius

Dynamo Kyiv 4

Diogo Rincon [20], Shatskikh [29], Verpakovskis [32], Gavrancic [82]

Shovkovskiy – Rebrov (Rotan• 66), Corrêa (Belkevich 59), Rincón (Cernat 76), Shatskikh, Mikhalik•, Gusev, Verpakovskis, El Kaddouri, Gavrancic, Yussuf. Tr: Demyaneko

2nd leg. Valery Lobanovskiy, Kyiv
2-08-2006, 19:00, 9470, Weiner GER

Dynamo Kyiv 4

Rotan 2 [37] [90], Corrêa [66], Rebrov [85]

Rybka – Belkevich, Cernat, Rotan•, Shatskikh (Rebrov 45), Mikhalik, Gusev (Corrêa 58), Verpakovskis•, El Kaddouri, Gavrancic, Rodrigo (Mandzyuk 73). Tr: Demyaneko

Liepajas Metalurgs 0

Krucs – Zuravlovs, Klava, Jemelins, Surnins, Rimkevicius•, Solonicins (Grebis 79), Kalonas (Kets 85), Karlsons, Zirnis, Katasonov. Tr: Zelkevicius

1st leg. Sükrü Saraçoglu, Istanbul
26-07-2006, 21:00, 34 500, Trivkovic CRO

Fenerbahçe 4

Appiah 26, Tümer Metin [39], Tuncay Sanli [54], Onder Turaci [93]

Rüstü Recber – Appiah, Umit Ozat, Tuncay Sanli•, Tümer Metin (Ugur Boral 69), Aurélio, Can Arat, Onder Turaci, Alex, Serkan Balci• (Kerim Zengin 78), Anelka•. Tr: Zico

B'36 Tórshavn 0

Mikkelsen – Alex, Joensen.N• (Hansen.J 72), Thorleifson, Ekeke (Gunnarson.J 62), Benjaminsen, Jacobsen.K•, Midjord, Matras, Davy (Hansen.S• 76), Jacobsen.H. Tr: Clementsen

2nd leg. Jalkapallokenttä, Anjalankosken
2-08-2006, 20:00, 2443, Egorov RUS

MyPa-47 2

Pellonen [41], Puhakainen [79]

Korhonen – Timoska•, Taipale•, Lindstöm, Kuparinen, Huttunen, Kangaskolkka (Oksanen 90), Miranda, Kansikas, Pellonen (Muinonen 73), Adriano (Manso 78). Tr: Mäkelä

FC København 2

Berglund [12], Linderoth [73]

Christiansen – Jacobsen, Hangeland, Linderoth, Silberbauer (Bernburg 80), Berglund (Bergvold 64), Grønkjær, Allbäck, Hutchinson, Gravgaard (Thomassen 76), Bergdølmo. Tr: Solbakken

2nd leg. Tórsvøllur, Tórshavn
1-08-2006, 18:30, 1548, Richards WAL

B'36 Tórshavn 0

Mikkelsen – Alex, Joensen.N (Jacobsen.R 87), Thorleifson (Ellingsgaard 62), Thomassen•, Benjaminsen, Gunnarsson.J, Midjord, Matras, Davy (Joensen.B 75), Jacobsen.H. Tr: Clementsen

Fenerbahçe 5

Tuncay Sanli [44], Mehmet Yozgatli [49], Can Arat [79], Semih Sentürk [83], Murat [90]

Rüstü Recber – Umit Ozat, Mehmet Yozgatli, Tuncay Sanli (Murat Hacioglu 65), Aurélio, Can Arat, Onder Turaci, Alex (Olcan Adin 82), Semih Sentürk, Ugur Boral, Serkan Balci (KerimZengin 70). Tr: Zico

1st leg. Parken, Copenhagen
26-07-2006, 20:45, 17 523, Megia Davila ESP

FC København 2

Bergdølmo [64p], Gravgaard [93]

Christiansen – Jacobsen, Hangeland, Santos (Berglund 71), Endiroth, Grønkjær, Allbäck, Hutchinson, Gravgaard•, Bergdølmo, Pimpong (Bergvold 73). Tr: Solbakken

MyPa-47 0

Korhonen – Timoska•, Taipale, Lindstöm, Kuparinen•, Manso (Pellonen 58), Huttunen, Kangaskolkka (Puhakainen 71), Miranda•, Kansikas, Adriano• (Hernesniemi 82). Tr: Mäkelä

1st leg. Aukstaitija, Panevezys
25-07-2006, 18:00, 2700, Asumaa FIN

Ekranas Panevezys 1

Luksys [14]

Skrupskis – Klimavicius, Banevicius, Paulauskas, Gardzijauskas, Tomkevicius, Savenas, Slekys (Kucys• 61), Mikhalchuk (Kavaliauskas• 68), Varnas (Petrauskas 86), Luksys. Tr: Liubsys

Dinamo Zagreb 4

Eduardo 2 [51], Buljat [32], Vugrinec [69]

Turina – Buljat, Cale, Corluka, Cvitanovic, Etto, Modric, Agic (Drpic 74), Da Silva (Carlos• 87), Mamic (Vukojevic 80), Vugrinec. Tr: Kuze

2nd leg. Maksimir, Zagreb
2-08-2006, 20:30, 6270, Styles ENG

Dinamo Zagreb 5

Ljubojevic 3 [2] [62] [91+], Vukojevic [48], Vugrinec [90]

Turina – Buljat, Corluka, Tomic (Vugrinec 79), Costa (Da Silva 79), Modric (Grgurovic 65), Agic, Carlos, Vukojevic, Drpic, Ljubojevic. Tr: Kuze

Ekranas Panevezys 2

Savenas [65], Luksys [69]

Skrupskis – Klimavicius, Banevicius, Paulauskas, Gardzijauskas, Tomkevicius, Savenas, Petrauskas (Galkevicius 83), Kucys (Slekys 46), Varnas (Pogreban 58), Luksys. Tr: Liubsys

1st leg. Råsunda, Stockholm
26-07-2006, 20:00, 8161, Tudor ROU

Djurgårdens IF 1

Enrico [70]

Tourray – Storm, Kuivsto, Arneng, Hysén (Enrico 67), Kusi-Asare (Thiago 80), Sjölund, Jonson, Johannesson, Komac, Barsom. Tr: Jonevret

MFK Ruzomberok 0

Hajdúch – Sedlak, Nezmar, Zofcák, Tomcák (Dovicovic 89), Pospisil, Laurinc, Bozok• (Rychilk 76), Dvornik, Siva, Sapara (Zosák 88). Tr: Komnacky

2nd leg. MFK, Ruzomberok
2-08-2006, 20:00, 4800, Piccirillo FRA

MFK Ruzomberok	3
	Zofcák [14], Tomcák [18], Nezmar [88]

Hajdúch – Sedlak•, Nezmar, Zofcák, Tomcák (Dovicovic 89), Pospisil (Jendrisek 77), Laurinc, Bozok (Zosák 86), Dvornik, Siva, Sapara. Tr: Komnacky

Djurgårdens IF	1
	Kusi-Asare [75]

Tourray – Concha (Thiago 86), Storm•, Kuivsto, Arneng, Hysén (Enrico 60), Kusi-Asare (Árnason 78), Sjölund, Jonson•, Johannesson•66, Komac.
Tr: Jonevret

1st leg. Oláh Gábor, Debrecen
26-07-2006, 20:45, 6124, Oriekhov UKR

Debreceni VSC	1
	Zsolnai [47]

Csernyánszki – Máté•, Szatmári (Dzsudzsák 46), Vukmir, Dombi (Sidibe 78), Sándor, Bogdanovic, Brnovic (Zsolnai• 20), Bernáth, Halmosi, Éger.
Tr: Supka

Rabotnicki Skopje	1
	Stankovski [45]

Pacovski – Stojanov, Jeremic•, Stepanovski•, Jovanoski (Karcev 46), Vajs, Trajcev, Nedzipi (Jankep 78), Stankovski•, Pejcic, Velkoski (Abrilio 70).
Tr: Jovanovski

1st leg. Turner's Cross, Cork
26-07-2006, 19:45, 5442, Mikulski POL

Cork City	0

Devine – Bennett, Murray•, O'Brien, Fenn, Woods, O'Donovan, Lordan (Callaghan 86), Softic, Behan (McCarthy 84), Horgan. Tr: Richardson

Crvena Zvezda Beograd	1
	Behan OG [37]

Randjelovic – Pantic (Djokic 68), Bisevac, Jankovic (Milijas 60), Perovic, Joksimovic, Kovacevic, Georgiev•, Zigic• (Purovic 93+), Basta, Milovanovic.
Tr: Bajevic

2nd leg. Gradski, Skopje
2-08-2006, 20:00, 5500, Skomina SVN

Rabotnicki Skopje	4
	Nedzipi [21], Pejcic [35], Trajcev [42], Abrilio [56]

Pacovski – Jovanovski, Vajs, Abrilio, Jeremic• (Lazarevski 68), Karcev, Ignatov (Stojanov 69), Trajcev, Nedzipi, Stankovski (Velkoski 60), Pejcic.
Tr: Jovanovski

Debreceni VSC	1
	Sidibe [20]

Csernyánszki – Vukmir (Virág 77), Dombi, Sándor (Kiss 46), Bogdanovic (Szatmári 46), Komlósi, Dzsudzsák•, Bernáth•, Sidibe•50, Halmosi•••43, Éger•. Tr: Supka

2nd leg. Pecara, Siroki Brijeg
2-08-2006, 20:30, 5000, Kassai HUN

Siroki Brijeg	0

Vasilj – Anic•, Silic•, Lago, Papic (Studenovic 88), Pandza•, Landeka, Gomes, Kovacic (Erceg 70), Karoglan, Celson (Carvalho 75).

Heart of Midlothian	0

Gordon – Neilson (Tall 61), Fyssas, Pressley, McCann (Mikoliunas• 61), Aguiar, Pospisil, Bednár•, Cesnauskis (Beslija 84), Berra, Brellier.
Tr: Ivanauskas

2nd leg. Maracana, Belgrade
2-08-2006, 20:15, 25 858, Kircher GER

Crvena Zvezda Beograd	3
	Milovanovic [3], Zigic 2 [34 59]

Randjelovic – Pantic, Bisevac, Djokic (Jankovic 70), Perovic (Milijas 60), Joksimovic, Kovacevic, Georgiev, Zigic (Purovic 64), Basta, Milovanovic. Tr: Bajevic

Cork City	0

Devine – Bennett•, Callaghan, O'Brien, Fenn•, Woods, O'Donovan•, Lordan, Softic, Behan (Sullivan 80), Horgan. Tr: Richardson

1st leg. Murrayfield, Edinburgh
26-07-2006, 19:45, 28 486, Berntsen NOR

Heart of Midlothian	3
	Carvalho OG [53], Tall [79], Bednár [85]

Gordon – Neilson, Fyssas, Pressley, Tall, McCann (Pospisil 56), Aguiar (Brellier 89), Jankauskas (Mikoliunas 56), Bednár, Cesnauskis, Berra.
Tr: Ivanauskas

Siroki Brijeg	0

Basic – Anic, Silic, Pandza, Landeka, Lago•, Carvalho (Papic 90), Bubalo (Doci 59), Gomes•, Karoglan (Kovacic 84), Celson•

THIRD QUALIFYING ROUND

1st leg. Vasil Levski, Sofia
9-08-2006, 20:30, 18 949, Jara CZE

Levski Sofia	2
	Domovchiyski [8], Bardon [86p]

Petkov – Tomasic, Eromoigbe, Borimirov, Yovov (Milanov 90), Domovchiyski (Angelov.E 75), Angelov.S, Telkiyski (Ivanov 83), Wagner, Bardon, Topuzakov•.
Tr: Stoilov

Chievo Verona	0

Sicignand – Mantovani, Semioli, Giunti, Zanchetta (Marcolini 62), Amauri, Lanna, Scurto•, Moro, Brighi•, Tribocchi (Pellissier 68). Tr: Pillon

2nd leg. Luzhniki, Moscow
23-08-2006, 19:00, 24 000, Medina C. ESP

Spartak Moskva	2
	Mozart [23], Pavlyuchenko [79]

Kowalewski – Stranzl, Jiránek•, Kovác, Rodríguez, Shishkin, Covalciuc, Bystrov (Kalynychenko• 75), Mozart•, Pavlyuchenko, Cavenaghi (Bazhenov 87).
Tr: Fedotov

Slovan Liberec	1
	Hodúr [73p]

Cech – Zápotocny•••56, Kostál•, Janu (Matula 76), Singlár, Bílek, Hodúr, Pospěch, Frejlach (Ancic 62), Holenda (Blazek 54), Pudil•.

2nd leg. Bentegodi, Verona
23-08-2006, 21:00, 23 517, Cardoso POR

Chievo Verona	2
	Amauri 2 [48 81]

Sicignand – Mantovani, Malago, Lanna•83, Mandelli, Semioli (Luciano 72), Giunti (Marcolini• 65), Zanchetta, Sammarco•, Amauri, Pellissier (Tribocchi 59). Tr: Pillon

Levski Sofia	2
	Telkiyski [34], Bardon [46]

Petkov• – Tomasic•, Borimirov, Telkiyski (Angelov.S 76), Bardon, Milanov, Eromoigbe, Domovchiyski (Angelov.E 72), Wagner•••92+, Topuzakov, Yovov (Koprivarov 92+). Tr: Stoilov

1st leg. Anfield, Liverpool
9-08-2006, 20:05, 40 058, Stark GER

Liverpool	2
	Bellamy [32], González [87]

Reina – Finnan, Hyypiä, Riise, Gerrard (González 86), Alonso, Pennant, Bellemay (Crouch 65), Sissoko•, Carragher, Zenden (Garcia 55). Tr: Benitez

Maccabi Haifa	1
	Boccoli [29]

Davidovich – Harazi, Anderson, Boccoli, Colautti•, Masudi (Meshumar 89), Xavir, Magrashvilli•, Olarra, Katan (Melikson 86), Keinan. Tr: Levy

1st leg. U Nisy, Liberec
9-08-2006, 20:15, 8130, Hamer LUX

Slovan Liberec	0

Cech – Zápotocny, Bílek•, Hodúr, Pospěch (Parks 81), Kostál•, Janu, Singlár, Frejlach (Papousek 46), Pudil, Blazek (Holenda 52).

Spartak Moskva	0

Kowalewski – Shishkin, Jiránek, Stranzl, Rodríguez, Mozart, Kovác•, Kalynychenko•, Covalciuc, Pavlyuchenko (Boyarinstev 72), Cavenaghi (Bazhenov 87). Tr: Fedotov

2nd leg. Valery Lobanovskiy, Kyiv
22-08-2006, 21:35, 15 000, Rosetti ITA

Maccabi Haifa	1
	Colautti [63]

Davidovich – Harazi, Magrashvilli, Olarra, Keinan (Meshumar• 65), Anderson• (Melikson 71), Xavir, Boccoli, Masudi (Arbaitman 80), Colautti, Katan.
Tr: Levy

Liverpool	1
	Crouch [54]

Reina – Finnan, Hyypiä•, Agger, Warnock (Aurélio 28), González, Alonso•, Sissoko (Gerrard 67), Pennant (Bellamy 86), Garcia, Crouch. Tr: Benitez

1st leg. Ali Sami Yen, Istanbul
9-08-2006, 20:30, 17 715, Plautz AUT

Galatasaray 5
Ilic [7p], Arda 2 [43 60], Hakan Sükür [49], Sabri [90]
Mondragón – Cihan Haspolatli, Tomas, Song, Orhan Ak (Ergün Penbe 70), Sabri Sarioglu, Okan Buruk (Mehmet Güven 75), Ayhan Akman•, Arda Turan, Ilic (Hasan Sas 85), Hakan Sükür. Tr: Gerets

Mladá Boleslav 2
Brezinsky [82], Kulic [83]
Kucera• – Sevinsky, Vit, Brezinsky, Smerda•, Vaculik (Sedlácek 59), Matejovsky•, Riegel, Polácek (Mikolanda 69), Kulic•, Pecka. Tr: Uhrin

2nd leg. Mestsky, Mladá Boleslav
23-08-2006, 19:30, 4680, Hansson SWE

Mladá Boleslav 1
Palát [88]
Miller – Sevinsky, Rolko, Vaculik, Pelát, Holub (Riegel 74), Matejovsky, Brezinsky, Polácek (Sedlácek 46), Pecka, Smerda (Mikolanda 68). Tr: Uhrin

Galatasaray 1
Hasan Sas [73]
Mondragón – Cihan Haspolatli, Song, Tomas, Orhan Ak (Ugur Uçar 76), Sabri Sarioglu•, Ayhan Akman, Okan Buruk•, Hasan Sas•, Ilic (Arda Turan 71), Hakan Sükür (Ozcan 84). Tr: Gerets

1st leg. Wals-Siezenheim, Salzburg
9-08-2006, 20:45, 15 000, Fröjdfeldt SWE

Austria Salzburg 1
Piták [73]
Ochs – Bodnár, Dudic, Linke, Carboni, Kovac, Zickler, Jezek (Winklhofer 78), Piták, Janocko (Aufhauser 51), Vargas•. Tr: Trapattoni

Valencia 0
Cañizares – Albelda, Baraja, Morientes, Angulo, Regueiro (Villa 62), Rodríguez (Silva 73), Navarro, Albiol, Torres, Moretti. Tr: Flores

2nd leg. Mestalla, Valencia
22-08-2006, 22:00, 50 283, Michel SVK

Valencia 3
Morientes [13], Villa [33], Silva [94+]
Cañizares• – Moretti, Navarro, Albiol, Albelda, Edu (Marchena 88), Silva, Rodríguez (Gavilán 72), Angulo•, Morientes (Regueiro 72), Villa. Tr: Flores

Austria Salzburg 0
Ochs – Linke, Bodnár•, Dudic, Vargas•, Aufhauser, Kovac (Jezek 65), Piták, Tiffert• (Vonlanthen 57), Carboni, Orosz (Lokvenc 46). Tr: Trapattoni

1st leg. RSC Olympiyskiy, Donetsk
9-08-2006, 19:30, 24 000, De Bleeckere BEL

Shakhtar Donetsk 1
Elano [39p]
Shutkov – Rat, Lewandowski, Hübschman, Srna, Matuzalem, Fernandinho•, Agahowa (Marica 63), Tymoschuk, Elano• (Jadson 57), Brandão (Bielik 80). Tr: Lucescu

Legia Warszawa 1
Jadson [2]
Fabiański – Szala•, Choto, Alcantara, Guerreiro, Surma, Wlodarczyk, (Radovic 74), Vukovic (Balde• 83), Szalachowski, Edson, Elton (Gottwald 64). Tr: Wdowczyk

2nd leg. Wojska Polskiego, Warsaw
23-08-2006, 20:30, 8700, Riley ENG

Legia Warszawa 2
Wlodarczyk 2 [19 88]
Fabiański – Radovic, Choto, Balde, Edson, Szalachowski, Guerreiro•, Surma (Burkhardt 74), Gottwald (Korzym 46), Elton (Janczyk 65), Wlodarczyk. Tr: Wdowczyk

Shakhtar Donetsk 3
Marica 2 [25 50+], Fernandinho [29]
Shutkov – Hübschman, Tymoschuk, Fernandinho•, Matuzalem• (Jadson 75), Lewandowski, Brandão (Okoduwa 71), Rat, Marcia (Vorobey 71), Sviderskiy, Elano. Tr: Lucescu

1st leg. Sclessin, Liège
9-08-2006, 20:30, 15 613, Ivanov.V RUS

Standard CL 2
Rapaic 2 [17 51]
Renard – Deflandre, Andre, Defour (Pelaic 79), Rapaic, Sarr, Rogério, Geraerts•, Jovanovic, Fellaini•, Sá Pinto. Tr: Boskamp

Steaua Bucuresti 2
Paraschiv [8], Marin [79]
Fernandes – Goian, Oprita (Baciu 91+), Badea (Cristocea 62), Dica, Nesu•, Nicolita (Bostina 79), Marin, Lovin, Paraschiv, Ghionea•. Tr: Olarolu

2nd leg. Lia Manoliu, Bucharest
23-08-2006, 20:30, 44 234, Poll ENG

Steaua Bucuresti 2
Badea 2 [35 51]
Fernandes• – Goian•, Badea (Oprita 83), Dica, Cristocea, Nesu (Bostina 88), Nicolita, Baciu, Marin•, Lovin, Paraschiv (Coman 70). Tr: Olarolu

Standard CL 1
Jovanovic [2]
Renard – Deflandre (Bouchouari 7), Onyewu (Andre 64), Defour, Rapaic•, Sarr, Rogério, Geraerts, Jovanovic•, Fellaini•, Sá Pinto•••82. Tr: Boskamp

1st leg. Valery Lobanovskiy, Kyiv
9-08-2006, 19:00, 16 873, Ceferin SVN

Dynamo Kyiv 3
Diogo Rincón 2 [1 67], Yussuf [83]
Shovkovskiy – Rebrov (Milevskiy 62), Sabljic•, Corrêa, Rincón, Shatskikh, Gusev (Belkevich 78), El Kaddouri, Yussuf•, Rodrigo, Markovic. Tr: Demyaneko

Fenerbahçe 1
Marco Aurélio [48]
Rüstü Reçber – Appiah•, Umit Ozat•, Tuncay Sanli, Tümer Metin (Ugur Boral 72), Aurélio, Can Arat (Servet Çetin 80), Onder Turaci, Alex, Serkan Balci•••75, Anelka (Semih Sentürk 72). Tr: Zico

2nd leg. Sükrü Saraçoglu, Istanbul
23-08-2006, 21:00, 42 836, Bennett ENG

Fenerbahçe 2
Appiah [36], Kerim Zengin [57]
Rüstü Reçber – Umit Ozat•, Can Arat, Onder Turaci (Mehmet Yozgatli 84), Appiah•, Aurélio, Alex, Tuncay Sanli, Kerim Zengin, Semih Sentürk (Murat Hacioglu 64), Tümer Metin (Ugur Boral 76). Tr: Zico

Dynamo Kyiv 2
Shatskikh 2 [5 42]
Shovkovskiy – Sabljic•, Corrêa, Rodrigo, Rotan (Verpakovskis 86), Gusev (Gavrancic 66), El Kaddouri, Yussuf, Rebrov, Shatskikh•, Markovic. Tr: Demyaneko

1st leg. Ernst Happel, Vienna
8-08-2006, 20:45, 19 600, Farina ITA

FK Austria 1
Blanchard [36]
Safar – Troyansky, Tokic, Wallner, Radomski, Vachousek, Aigner (Ceh 46), Lasnik (Pichlmann 82), Blanchard, Wimmer (Mila 46), Papac. Tr: Schinkels

Benfica 1
Nuno Gomes [16]
Quim – Anderson, Luisão, Petit, Katsouranis, Rui Costa, Paulo Jorge (Nuno Assis 89), Manú (Ferreira 70), Nuno Gomes (Kikin 80), Nélson, Ricardo Rocha. Tr: Fernando Santos

2nd leg. Estadio da Luz, Lisbon
22-08-2006, 20:15, 58 110, Hauge NOR

Benfica 3
Rui Costa [21], Nuno Gomes [48•], Petit [57]
Quim – Anderson, Luisão, Petit (Beto 74), Katsouranis, Rui Costa (Kikin 66), Paulo Jorge (Mantorras 85), Manú, Nuno Gomes, Nélson, Ricardo Rocha. Tr: Fernando Santos

FK Austria 1
Safar – Troyansky, Hill, Tokic•, Wallner, Radomski•, Blanchard, Ceh (Pichlmann 54), Wimmer•, Papac (Schicker• 29), Mila• (Lasnik 46). Tr: Schinkels

1st leg. Parken, Copenhagen
9-08-2006, 20:30, 40 000, Mejuto G. ESP

FC København 1
Hangeland [47]
Christiansen – Jacobsen•, Hangeland, Linderoth, Silberbauer (Kvist 79), Berglund (Pimpong 69), Grønkjær, Allbäck•, Hutchinson•, Gravgaard, Bergdølmo. Tr: Solbakken

Ajax 2
Huntelaar 2 [37 84]
Stekelenburg – Heitinga•, Stam, Vermaelen, Emanuelson•, Maduro, Rosales (Rosenberg 77), Huntelaar•, Sneijder, Perez• (Babel 68), Gabri. Tr: Ten Cate

2nd leg. Amsterdam ArenA, Amsterdam
23-08-2006, 20:30, 35 617, Fandel GER

Ajax 0
Stekelenburg – Heitinga, Stam•, Vermaelen, Emanuelson, Maduro (Vertonghen 61), Rosales (Rosenberg 85), Babel, Huntelaar, Sneijder•, Gabri. Tr: Ten Cate

FC København 2
Silberbauer [59], Vermaelen OG [77]
Christiansen – Jacobsen, Hangeland, Linderoth, Silberbauer• (Thomassen 89), Allbäck•, Hutchinson, Gravgaard, Bergdølmo, Kvist, Pimpong (Berglund 58). Tr: Solbakken

1st leg. Maksimir, Zagreb
8-08-2006, 21:05, 31 120, Vassaras GRE

Dinamo Zagreb 0
Turina – Buljat (Vukojevic 91+), Cale (Carlos 91+), Nowotny, Corluka•, Cvitanovic, Etto, Modric, Da Silva, Mamic, Vugrinec (Agic 27). Tr: Kuze

Arsenal 3
Fabregas 2 [63 78], Van Persie [64]
Almunia – Fabregas, Touré, Rosicky (Flamini 82), Van Persie, Hleb•, Gilberto, Djourou, Adebayor (Aliadière 82), Eboué, Hoyte•. Tr: Wenger

2nd leg, Emirates Stadium, London
23-08-2006, 20:05, 52 498, Layec FRA

Arsenal   **2**
Ljungberg [77], Flamini [91+]

Almunia – Eboué, Touré, Djourou•, Hoyte, Hleb (Gilberto 70), Fabregas, Flamini•, Ljungberg, van Persie (Walcott• 81), Adebayor (Henry 65). Tr: Wenger

Dinamo Zagreb   **1**
Eduardo [12]

Turina – Corluka, Cvitanovic, Mamic, Drpic•, Etto (Tomic 92+), Vukojevic (Ljubojevic 89), Agic• (Buljat• 69), Carlos, Modric, Da Silva. Tr: Kuze

1st leg, Lokomotiv, Moscow
9-08-2006, 20:00, 9947, Meyer GER

CSKA Moskva   **3**
Olic 2 [58 65], Vágner Love [83]

Akinfeev – Semberas•, Ignashevich, Berezutskiy.A•, Daniel Carvalho (Gusev 86), Olic (Dudu 73), Jô (Vágner Love 60), Krasic, Zhirkov, Aldonin•, Rahimic. Tr: Gazzaev

MFK Ruzomberok   **0**

Hajdúch – Sedlak, Nezmar, Zofcák•, Pospisil, Laurinc•, Bozok (Tomcák 63), Dvornik, Siva, Rák (Rychlik 84), Sapara. Tr: Komnacky

2nd leg, MFK, Ruzomberok
23-08-2006, 20:15, 4715, Benquerença POR

MFK Ruzomberok   **0**

Hajdúch – Sedlak (Dovicovic 70), Nezmar (Babnic 78), Zofcák, Pospisil, Laurinc, Bozok (Tomcák 70), Dvornik, Siva, Rák, Sapara. Tr: Komnacky

CSKA Moskva   **2**
Daniel Carvalho [8], Vágner Love [32]

Akinfeev – Semberas, Ignashevich, Berezutskiy, Daniel Carvalho (Olic 70), Jô, Vágner Love (Zhirkov 46), Krasic (Gusev 86), Dudu, Aldonin, Rahimic. Tr: Gazzaev

1st leg, AOL Arena, Hamburg
9-08-2006, 20:30, 47 458, Ovrebo NOR

Hamburger SV   **0**

Kirschstein – Mahdavikia, Guerrero, Kompany, Jarolím, Trochowski• (Lauth 73), Sanogo, Demel, Reinhardt, van der Vaart, de Jong. Tr: Doll

Osasuna   **0**

Ricardo López – Cuéllar, Garcia•, Milosevic (Nekunam 89), Puñal, Romero•, David López•, Flaño, Soldado (Romeo 79), Delporte• (Valdo 70), Monreal. Tr: Ziganda

2nd leg, Reyno de Navarra, Pamplona
22-08-2006, 20:45, 18 768, Busacca SUI

Osasuna   **1**
Cuéllar [6]

Ricardo López – Cuéllar, Romero, Flaño (Valdo 80), Monreal, Garcia, Puñal•, David López, Delporte, Milosevic, Soldado (Webó 68). Tr: Ziganda

Hamburger SV   **1**
De Jong [74]

Kirschstein – Reinhardt, Kompany (Benjamin 11), Demel•, Wicky (Guerrero• 66), Mahdavikia, Jarolím, van der Vaart, de Jong, Lauth (Trochowski 79), Sanogo. Tr: Doll

1st leg, San Siro, Milan
9-08-2006, 20:45, 70 510, Wegereef NED

Milan   **1**
Inzaghi [22]

Dida – Cafu (Brocchi 78), Costacurta, Gattuso, Inzaghi, Seedorf, Gilardino (Ambrosini 72), Simic, Pirlo (Gourcuff 81), Kaká, Sginho. Tr: Ancelotti

Crvena Zvezda Beograd   **0**

Randjelovic – Pantic, Bisevac, Jankovic (Krivokapic 90), Perovic• (Tutoric 66), Kovacevic, Georgiev, Gueye•, Zigic, Basta, Milovanovic (Djokic 81). Tr: Bajevic

2nd leg, Maracana, Belgrade
22-08-2006, 21:00, 49 604, Larsen DEN

Crvena Zvezda Beograd   **1**
Djokic [80]

Randjelovic – Pantic (Purovic 61), Basta, Gueye•, Bisevac, Kovacevic, Milovanovic (Andjelkovic 71), Georgiev, Jankovic (Perovic 53), Djokic, Zigic. Tr: Bajevic

Milan   **2**
Inzaghi [29], Seedorf [79]

Dida – Cafu (Favalli 82), Costacurta, Simic, Serginho, Gattuso, Kaká•, Pirlo, Seedorf, Inzaghi (Ambrosini 68), Gilardino (Borriello 88). Tr: Ancelotti

1st leg, Métropole, Villeneuve d'Ascq
9-08-2006, 18:00, 9560, Hrinak SVK

Lille OSC   **3**
Jovanoski OG [60], Bastos [70p], Fauvergue [72]

Sylva – Schmitz, Cabaye, Bastos, Youla (Odemwingie 52), Fauvergue, Makoun, Tafforeau, Keita (Mirallas 76), Plestan, Lichtsteiner (Chalmé• 45). Tr: Puel

Rabotnicki Skopje   **0**

Pacovski – Vajs, Jovanoski, Ilievski, Lazarevski• (Stepanovski• 60), Trajcev•, Ignatov• (Stojanov 86), Nedzipi (Jankep 66), Abrilio, Stankovski, Pejcic. Tr: Jovanovski

2nd leg, Gradski, Skopje
23-08-2006, 20:00, 6 500, Kapitanis CYP

Rabotnicki Skopje   **0**

Pacovski – Abrilio, Jeremic, Jovanoski•••83, Vajs• (Karcev 60), Trajcev, Nedzipi, Jankep, Velkoski (Aleksovski 76), Stankovski, Pejcic. Tr: Jovanovski

Lille OSC   **1**
Audel [18]

Malicki – Lichtsteiner•, Tavlaridis•, Schmitz, Tafforeau, Makoun• (Chalmé 62), Dumont, Cabaye (Robail 76), Mirallas, Youla, Audel. Tr: Puel

1st leg, Murrayfield, Edinburgh
9-08-2006, 20:45, 32 450, Vollquartz DEN

Heart of Midlothian   **1**
Mikoliunas [62]

Gordon – Neilson, Fyssas, Pressley, McCann•, Aguiar•••66, Pospisil (Elliot 83), Bednár (Wallace 69), Mikoliunas, Berra, Karipidis (Jankauskas 55). Tr: Ivanauskas

AEK Athens   **2**
Kapetanos [89], Fyssas OG [92+]

Sorrentino – Pautasso (Tziortziopoulos 81), Dellas, Cirillo, Georgeas•, Emerson, Ivic, Lagos (Lakis 65), Liberopoulos, Kapetanos•, César (Tozsér 94+). Tr: Serrer Férrer

2nd leg, Olympic, Athens
23-08-2006, 21:45, 42 925, Baskakov RUS

AEK Athens   **3**
Júlio César 2 [79p 86], Liberopoulos [82]

Chiotis – Pautasso (Tozsér 72), Cirillo, Dellas, Georgeas•, Emerson, Ivic, Lagos (Lakis 54), César•, Liberopoulos• (Kampantias 84), Kapetanos. Tr: Serrer Ferrer

Heart of Midlothian   **0**

Gordon – Neilson•, Pressley, Berra, Fyssas•, Brellier•••30, Mikoliunas•, McCann•63, Cenauskis (Wallace 81), Hartley (Jankauskas 61), Mole (Pinilla 89). Tr: Ivanauskas

GROUP A

		Pl	W	D	L	F	A	Pts	ENG	ESP	GER	BUL
Chelsea	ENG	6	4	1	1	10	4	13		1-0	2-0	2-0
Barcelona	ESP	6	3	2	1	12	4	11	2-2		2-0	5-0
Werder Bremen	GER	6	3	1	2	7	5	10	1-0	1-1		2-0
Levski Sofia	BUL	6	0	0	6	1	17	0	1-3	0-2	0-3	

GROUP A MATCHDAY 1
Stamford Bridge, London
12-09-2006, 19:45, 32 135, Vassaras GRE

Chelsea 2
Essien [24], Ballack [68p]
Cech – Boulahrouz, Terry•, Ricardo Carvalho, Cole.A, Essien, Makalele, Ballack (Mikel 90), Lampard•, Shevchenko (Cole.J• 81), Drogba (Kalou 86). Tr: Mourinho

Werder Bremen 0

Reinke – Fritz, Pasanen, Naldo, Wome, Frings, Baumann• (Zidan 86), Diego, Borowski, Klose, Klasnic (Hugo Almeida 66). Tr: Schaaf

---

GROUP A MATCHDAY 1
Camp Nou, Barcelona
12-09-2006, 20:45, 62 839, Plautz AUT

Barcelona 5
Iniesta [7], Giuly [39], Puyol [49], Eto'o [58], Ronaldinho [93+]
Valdes – Belletti, Puyol, Thuram (Oleguer 80), Van Bronkhorst, Guily (Gudjohnsen 63), Iniesta (Xavi 72), Motta, Ronaldinho, Deco, Eto'o. Tr: Rijkaard

Levski Sofia 0

Petkov – Milanov•, Topuzakov, Tomasic, Angelov.S, Borimirov (Minev 63), Bardon, Eromoigbe, Telkiyski, Angelov.A (Ivanov.G• 46), Yovov (Ivanov.M 70). Tr: Stoilov

---

GROUP A MATCHDAY 2
Weserstadion, Bremen
27-09-2006, 20:45, 37 000, Rosetti ITA

Werder Bremen 1
Puyol OG [56]
Wiese – Fritz, Mertesacke, Naldo•, Schulz, Borowski, Baumann•, Diego, Frings•, Klose (Klasnic 90), Hunt (Owomoyela 90). Tr: Schaaf

Barcelona 1
Messi [89]
Valdes – Oleguer, Thuram, Puyol, Silvinho (Zambrotta 83), Iniesta, Motta, Deco, Guily (Messi 65), Eto'o (Gudjohnsen 65), Ronaldinho. Tr: Rijkaard

---

GROUP A MATCHDAY 2
Vasil Levski, Sofia
27-09-2006, 21:45, 42 226, Duhamel FRA

Levski Sofia 1
Ognyanov [89]
Petkov – Milanov, Topuzakov, Tomasic, Lucio Wagner, Telkiyski (Ivanov.G 67), Borimirov (Koprivarov 79), Bardon (Ognyanov 71, Eromoigbe, Angelov.S•), Yovov. Tr: Stoilov

Chelsea 3
Drogba 3 [39] [52] [68]
Cech – Paulo Ferreira, Terry, Ricardo Carvalho, Bridge, Mikel• (Kalou 63) Essien, Ballack, Lampard, Shevchenko (Wright-Phillips 83), Drogba (Robben 70). Tr: Mourinho

---

GROUP A MATCHDAY 3
Stamford Bridge, London
18-10-2006, 19:45, 40 599, De Bleeckere BEL

Chelsea 1
Drogba [47]
Hilario – Boulahtouz, Ricardo Carvalho, Terry, Cole.A, Essien, Makalele, Ballack, Lampard•, Shevchenko (Robben 77), Drogba (Kalou 90). Tr: Mourinho

Barcelona 0

Valdes – Zambrotta, Puyol (Oleguer 74), Marquez, Van Bronkhorst• (Iniesta 57), Xavi•, Edmilson, Deco•, Messi, Gudjohnsen (Guily 60), Ronaldinho. Tr: Rijkaard

---

GROUP A MATCHDAY 3
Weserstadion, Bremen
18-10-2006, 20:45, 36 246, Allaerts BEL

Werder Bremen 2
Naldo [46+], Diego [73]
Wiese – Fritz•, Mertesacke, Naldo, Wome (Klasnic 46), Vranjes (Andreasen 73), Frings, Schulz, Diego, Klose (Hugo Almeida 82), Hunt. Tr: Schaaf

Levski Sofia 0

Petkov – Angelov.S, Topuzakov, Tomasic•, Lucio Wagner, Telkiyski (Koprivarov 79), Borimirov•, Bardon, Eromoigbe, Yovov (N Dimitrov 79), Domovchiyski (Ivanov.M 64). Tr: Stoilov

---

GROUP A MATCHDAY 4
Camp Nou, Barcelona
31-10-2006, 20:45, 90 166, Farina ITA

Barcelona 2
Deco [3], Gudjohnsen [58]
Valdes – Zambrotta, Marquez, Puyol, Van Bronkhorst, Xavi (Iniesta 83), Motta• (Edmilson• 57), Deco, Messi•, Gudjohnsen• (Guily 77), Ronaldinho. Tr: Rijkaard

Chelsea 2
Lampard [52], Drogba [93+]
Hilario – Boulahtouz (Cole.J• 75), Ricardo Carvalho, Terry•, Cole.A•, Essien•, Makalele, Ballack (Paulo Ferreira 90), Lampard•, Drogba, Robben• (Kalou 72). Tr: Mourinho

---

GROUP A MATCHDAY 4
Vasil Levski, Sofia
31-10-2006, 21:45, 25 862, Trefoloni ITA

Levski Sofia 0

Mihaylov (Mitrev 46) – Milanov, Topuzakov, Tomasic (Angelov.E 57), Lucio Wagner•, Borimirov, Angelov.S, Eromoigbe, Telkiyski (Dimitrov.N 69), Yovov, Bardon. Tr: Stoilov

Werder Bremen 3
Mihaylov OG [33], Baumann [35], Frings [37]
Wiese – Fritz, Mertesacke, Naldo, Wome• (Pasanen 85), Frings, Baumann• (Andreasen 78), Vranjes•, Diego, Klose, Hunt (Klasnic 74). Tr: Schaaf

---

GROUP A MATCHDAY 5
Weserstadion, Bremen
22-11-2006, 20:45, 36 908, Michel SVK

Werder Bremen 1
Mertesacker [27]
Wiese – Fritz, Mertesacke, Naldo, Wome, Borowski•, Frings, Jensen.D (Hunt 78), Diego, Klose (Klasnic 90), Hugo Almeida (Schulz 87). Tr: Schaaf

Chelsea 0

Cudicini – Geremi, Terry•, Boulahrouz, Cole.A, Essien, Makalele, Ballack (Wright-Phillips 77), Cole.J, Drogba (Shevchenko 59), Mikel (Robben 59). Tr: Mourinho

---

GROUP A MATCHDAY 5
Vasil Levski, Sofia
22-11-2006, 21:45, 41 423, Baskakov RUS

Levski Sofia 0

Petkov – Milanov•, Topuzakov, Tomasic, Lucio Wagner, Borimirov, Angelov.S (Telkiyski 58), Bardon, Yovov (Ognyanov 73), Domovchiyski (Ivanov.G 57). Tr: Stoilov

Barcelona 2
Giuly [5], Iniesta [65]
Valdes – Zambrotta, Puyol, Marquez (Oleguer 63), Silvinho, Borimirov•, Eromoigbe, Angelov.S (Telkiyski 58), Guily (Xavi 58), Motta, Deco, Iniesta (Ezqueiro 81), Gudjohnsen, Ronaldinho. Tr: Rijkaard

---

GROUP A MATCHDAY 6
Stamford Bridge, London
5-12-2006, 19:45, 33 358, Hamer LUX

Chelsea 2
Shevchenko [27], Wright-Phillips [83]
Hilario – Paulo Ferreira (Diarra 58), Boulahrouz, Ricardo Carvalho, Bridge, Lampard, Essien, Ballack, Shevchenko (Kalou 69), Drogba, Robben (Wright-Phillips 69). Tr: Mourinho

Levski Sofia 0

Mitrev – Milanov, Topuzakov, Tomasic, Angelov.S, Borimirov, Eromoigbe, Dimitrov.N (Baltanov 59), Bardon, Yovov (Koprivarov 70), Domovchiyski (Ivanov.G 75). Tr: Stoilov

---

GROUP A MATCHDAY 6
Camp Nou, Barcelona
5-12-2006, 20:45, 95 824, Busacca SUI

Barcelona 2
Ronaldinho [13], Gudjohnsen [18]
Valdes – Zambrotta, Puyol•, Marquez, Van Bronkhorst, Iniesta (Xavi 73), Motta• (Thuram 62), Deco, Guily (Ezqueiro 85), Gudjohnsen, Ronaldinho. Tr: Rijkaard

Werder Bremen 0

Wiese – Fritz, Mertesacke, Naldo, Wome• (Hunt 80), Jensen.D, Frings•, Borowski, Diego•, Klose, Hugo Almeida (Klasnic 71). Tr: Schaaf

GROUP B

		Pl	W	D	L	F	A	Pts	GER	ITA	RUS	POR
Bayern München	GER	6	3	3	0	10	3	12		1-1	4-0	0-0
Internazionale	ITA	6	3	1	2	5	5	10	0-2		2-1	1-0
Spartak Moskva	RUS	6	1	2	3	7	11	5	2-2	0-1		1-1
Sporting CP	POR	6	1	2	3	3	6	5	0-1	1-0	1-3	

GROUP B MATCHDAY 1
José Alvalade, Lisbon
12-09-2006, 19:45, 30 222, Hamer LUX

Sporting CP 1
Caneira [64]

Ricardo – Abel, Tonel, Anderson, Polga, Naneira, Nani (Tello 83), Miguel Veloso, Romagnoli (Alecsandro 66), Joao Moutinho•, Yannick, Liedson•. Tr: Paulo Bento

Internazionale 0

Toldo• – Macion, Cordoba•, Samuel, Grosso (Zanetti 80), Figo (Gonzalez 66), Vieira••68, Dacourt, Stankovic, Adriano (Crespo 71), Ibrahimovic. Tr: Mancini

---

GROUP B MATCHDAY 1
Allianz Arena, Munich
12-09-2006, 20:45, 63 000, Undiano ESP

Bayern München 4
Pizarro [48], Santa Cruz [52], Schweinsteiger [71], Salihamidzic [84]

Kahn – Sagnol, Lucio•, Van Buyten, Lahm, Hargreaves, Santa Cruz (Karimi 81), Van Bommel (Scholl 74), Schweinsteiger, Pizarro (Salihamidzic 70), Podolski. Tr: Magath

Spartak Moskva 0

Kowalewski – Jiránek (Shishkin 31), Geder, Stranzl, Rodríguez, Bystrov•, Kováč (Bazhenov 62), Mozart, Covalciuc (Torbinsky 77), Titov, Pavlyuchenko. Tr: Fedotov

---

GROUP B MATCHDAY 2
Luzhniki, Moscow
27-09-2006, 20:30, 36 000, Hansson SWE

Spartak Moskva 1
Boyarintsev [5]

Kowalewski – Jiránek, Geder, Stranzl•, Shishkin, Kovac, Mozart (Rebko 80), Bystov, Titov, Boyarinstev, Pavlyuchenko (Owusu-Abeyie 80). Tr: Fedotov

Sporting CP 1
Nani [59]

Ricardo – Miguel Garcia (Alecsandro 46), Tonel• (Parades 58), Anderson Polga, Caneira, Joao Moutinho, Miguel Veloso•, Nani, Tello, Yannick (Joao Alves 82), Liedson. Tr: Paulo Bento

---

GROUP B MATCHDAY 2
San Siro, Milan
27-09-2006, 20:45, 36 460, Bennett ENG

Internazionale 0

Julio Cesar – Macion, Cordoba, Materazzi•, Grosso•85, Zanetti, Dacourt, Stankovic (Solari 77), Figo (Gonzalez 67), Ibrahimovic••58, Crespo (Adriano 77). Tr: Mancini

Bayern München 2
Pizarro [81], Podolski [91+]

Kahn – Sagnol•, Lucio, Van Buyten, Lahm, Salihamidzic (Scholl• 70), Ottl•, Van Bommel, Schweinsteiger, Makaay (Santa Cruz 82), Pizarro (Podolski 89). Tr: Magath

---

GROUP B MATCHDAY 3
José Alvalade, Lisbon
18-10-2006, 19:45, 36 500, Hauge NOR

Sporting CP 0

Ricardo – Caneira, Tonel, Anderson Polga, Tello•, Joao Moutinho, Miguel Veloso• (Parades 70), Nani, Carlos Martins (Yannick 46), Alecsandro (Bueno 57), Liedson•. Tr: Paulo Bento

Bayern München 1
Schweinsteiger [19]

Kahn – Sagnol, Lucio, Van Buyten, Lahm, Van Bommel•, Ottl• (Demichelis 46), Santa Cruz (Salihamidzic 59), Schweinsteiger•••47, Pizarro, Podolski (Dos Santos• 65). Tr: Magath

---

GROUP B MATCHDAY 3
San Siro, Milan
18-10-2006, 20:45, 21 945, Layec FRA

Internazionale 2
Cruz 2 [1] [9]

Julio Cesar – Macion, Cordoba, Materazzi, Zanetti, Figo• (Adriano 69), Vieira, Dacourt, Stankovic, Recoba (Burdisso 58), Cruz (Samuel 90). Tr: Mancini

Spartak Moskva 1
Pavlyuchenko [54]

Kowalewski – Shishkin, Jiránek, Geder, Rodriguez•, Mozart (Owusu-Abeyie 80), Kovac, Bystrov (Kalinichenko• 75), Titov, Boyarinstev, Pavlyuchenko•. Tr: Fedotov

---

GROUP B MATCHDAY 4
Luzhniki, Moscow
31-10-2006, 20:30, 45 000, Larsen DEN

Spartak Moskva 0

Kowalewski – Shishkin, Jiránek, Stranzl, Rodriguez (Cavenaghi 46), Bystrov (Covalciuc 54), Kovac, Titov, Mozart, Boyarinstev, Pavlyuchenko. Tr: Fedotov

Internazionale 1
Cruz [I]

Julio Cesar – Macion, Cordoba, Materazzi, Burdisso, Figo (Grosso 72), Zanetti, Dacourt, Stankovic, Ibrahimovic, Cruz (Solari 84). Tr: Mancini

---

GROUP B MATCHDAY 4
Allianz Arena, Munich
31-10-2006, 20:45, 66 000, Busacca SUI

Bayern München 0

Kahn – Sagnol, Demichelis•, Van Buyten•, Lahm, Lell (Dos Santos 46), Ottl, Salihamidzic, Santa Cruz (Karimi 80), Pizarro, Makaay. Tr: Magath

Sporting CP 0

Ricardo – Caneira, Tonel, Anderson Polga, Tello, Parades (Farnerud 52), Custodio•, Joao Moutinho, Carlos Martins (Nani 46), Yannick (Alecsandro 78), Liedson•. Tr: Paulo Bento

---

GROUP B MATCHDAY 5
Luzhniki, Moscow
22-11-2006, 20:30, 25 000, Gilewski POL

Spartak Moskva 2
Kalynychenko [16], Kováč [72]

Zuev – Jiránek, Geder (Rebko 87), Stranzl, Shishkin, Bystrov•, Kovac, Titov, Mozart•, Kalinichenko, Pavlyuchenko. Tr: Fedotov

Bayern München 2
Pizarro 2 [22] [39]

Kahn – Sagnol, Demichelis, Van Buyten, Lell, Van Bommel, Ottl, Salihamidzic (Scholl 84), Schweinsteiger, Pizarro, Makaay. Tr: Magath

---

GROUP B MATCHDAY 5
San Siro, Milan
22-11-2006, 20:45, 36 935, De Bleeckere BEL

Internazionale 1
Crespo [36]

Julio Cesar – Macion•, Cordoba, Materazzi, Grosso (Cambiasso 82), Zanetti, Dacourt (Burdisso 90), Vieira, Stankovic•, Ibrahimovic, Crespo. Tr: Mancini

Sporting CP 0

Ricardo – Caneira (Abel 15; Miguel Veloso), Tonel, Anderson Polga, Tello, Parades•, Joao Moutinho, Custodio•, Nani•, Farnerud (Carlos Martins 57), Alecsandro. Tr: Paulo Bento

---

GROUP B MATCHDAY 6
José Alvalade, Lisbon
5-12-2006, 19:45, 17 000, Vollquartz DEN

Sporting CP 1
Carlos Bueno [31]

Ricardo – Miguel Garcia (Miguel Veloso 28), Tonel, Anderson Polga•, Ronny, Joao Moutinho, Parades (Nani 60), Yannick, Tello, Bueno (Alecsandro 68), Liedson. Tr: Paulo Bento

Spartak Moskva 3
Pavlyuchenko [7], Kalynychenko [16], Boyarintsev [89]

Zuev• – Jiránek, Geder•, Stranzl, Shishkin, Bystrov (Dzyuba 90), Kovac, Titov, Mozart, Kalynychenko (Boyarintsev 64), Pavlyuchenko (Owusu-Abeyie 74). Tr: Fedotov

---

GROUP B MATCHDAY 6
Allianz Arena, Munich
5-12-2006, 20:45, 66 000, M. Cantalejo ESP

Bayern München 1
Makaay [62]

Kahn – Sagnol, Lucio, Van Buyten, Lahm, Van Bommel• (Demichelis 72), Ottl, Schweinsteiger, Salihamidzic (Deisler 79), Pizarro, Makaay (Santa Cruz 83). Tr: Magath

Internazionale 1
Vieira [91+]

Toldo – Macion, Andreolli, Samuel•, Maxwell, Solari (Grosso 83), Vieira, Figo (Recoba 70), Zanetti, Gonzalez, Ibrahimovic (Crespo 46). Tr: Mancini

GROUP C

		Pl	W	D	L	F	A	Pts	ENG	NED	FRA	TUR
Liverpool	ENG	6	4	1	1	11	5	13		2-0	3-0	3-2
PSV Eindhoven	NED	6	3	1	2	6	6	10	0-0		1-3	2-0
Girondins Bordeaux	FRA	6	2	1	3	6	7	7	0-1	0-1		3-1
Galatasaray	TUR	6	1	1	4	7	12	4	3-2	1-2	0-0	

GROUP C MATCHDAY 1
Philips Stadion, Eindhoven
12-09-2006, 20:45, 32 000, Busacca SUI
PSV Eindhoven 0

Gomes – Kromkamp, Alex, Reiziger, Salcido, Simons, Mendez, Afellay (Varyrynen 74), Culina (Aissati 63), Farfan, Kone. Tr: Koeman

Liverpool 0

Reina – Finnan, Carragher, Agger, Fabio Aurellio (González 82), Warnock, Sissoko (Xabi Alonso 62), Pennant, Bellemay (Gerrard 72), Kuyt, Zenden. Tr: Benítez

---

GROUP C MATCHDAY 1
Olympiyat, Istanbul
12-09-2006, 21:45, 71 230, Rosetti ITA
Galatasaray 0

Mondragon – Sabri Sarioglu, Song, Tomas, Ferhat Oztorun, Hasan Sas (Cihan Haspolatli 76), Inamoto, Ilic (Mehmet Topal 76), Arda Turan, Umit Karan (Hasan Kabze 61), Necati Ates. Tr: Gerets

Girondins Bordeaux 0

Rame – Jurietti, Jemmali, Planus, Marange, Faubert, Ducasse•, Micoud, Wendel, Darcheville (Laslandes 85), Chamakh (Perea 85). Tr: Ricardo Gomes

---

GROUP C MATCHDAY 2
Anfield, Liverpool
27-09-2006, 19:45, 41 976, M.Cantalejo ESP
Liverpool 3
Crouch 2 9 52, Luis García 14

Reina – Finnan•, Carragher, Agger, Fabio Aurellio, Pennant (Sissoko 78), Gerrard, Xabi Alonso•, Luis Garcia, Kuyt (Gonzalez 66), Crouch (Bellamy 90). Tr: Benítez

Galatasaray 2
Umit Karan 2 59 65

Mondragon – Cihan Haspolatli (Umit Karan 46), Song, Tomas, Orhan Ak, Ayhan Akman•, Mehmet Topal (Hasan Sas• 46), Sabri Sarioglu, Ilic, Arda Turan (Carrusco 86), Hakan Sükür. Tr: Gerets

---

GROUP C MATCHDAY 2
Chaban-Delmas, Bordeaux
27-09-2006, 20:45, 23 587, Benquerença POR
Girondins Bordeaux 0

Rame – Jemmali (Laslandes 89), Henrique, Enakarhire, Jurietti (Dalmat 74), Fernando, Mavuba, Faubert, Micoud (Chamakh 46), Wendel, Darcheville. Tr: Ricardo Gomes

PSV Eindhoven 1
Väyrynen 65

Gomes – Kromkamp•, Alex, Salcido•, Lamey•85, Mendez, Simons, Varyrynen• (Addo 79), Afellay (Aissati 72), Kone, Diego Tardelli (Beerens 85). Tr: Koeman

---

GROUP C MATCHDAY 3
Chaban-Delmas, Bordeaux
18-10-2006, 20:45, 31 471, Ovrebo NOR
Girondins Bordeaux 0

Rame• – Jurietti•, Henrique, Jemmali, Wendel, Alonso (Faubert 63), Mavuba, Fernando, Micoud, Laslandes (Chamakh 63), Darcheville (Perea 71). Tr: Ricardo Gomes

Liverpool 1
Crouch 58

Reina – Finnan, Hyypia, Carragher, Riise, Luis Garcia, Xabi Alonso, Zenden•, Gonzalez (Sissoko 68), Crouch (Kuyt• 65), Bellamy (Warnock 87). Tr: Benítez

---

GROUP C MATCHDAY 3
Olympiyat, Istanbul
18-10-2006, 21:45, 50 389, Baskakov RUS
Galatasaray 1
Ilic 19

Mondragon – Sabri Sarioglu, Song, Tomas•, Orhan Ak•, Aydin Yilmaz (Cihan Haspolatli 67), Ayhan Akman•, Inamoto, Arda Turan, Umit Karan (Hakan Sükür 70), Ilic (Necati Ates 70). Tr: Gerets

PSV Eindhoven 2
Kromkamp 59, Arouna Koné 72

Gomes – Kromkamp, Alex, Salcido•, Reiziger, Culina (Aissati 90), Mendez (Varyrynen 62), Simons, Cocu, Kone, Farfan. Tr: Koeman

---

GROUP C MATCHDAY 4
Anfield, Liverpool
31-10-2006, 19:45, 41 978, Merk GER
Liverpool 3
Luis García 2 23 76, Gerrard 72

Reina – Finnan, Hyypia, Carragher, Riise, Gerrard, Xabi Alonso (Zenden 58), Sissoko•, Luis Garcia (Fowler 78), Crouch (Pennant 73), Kuyt. Tr: Benítez

Girondins Bordeaux 0

Rame – Faubert, Jemmali, Cid, Marange, Fernando•67, Ducasse, Micoud (Mavuba 75), Wendel, Darcheville (Obertan 60), Chamakh (Perea 12). Tr: Ricardo Gomes

---

GROUP C MATCHDAY 4
Philips Stadion, Eindhoven
31-10-2006, 20:45, 34 500, Hansson SWE
PSV Eindhoven 2
Simons 59, Arouna Koné 84

Gomes – Kromkamp (Culina 46), Alex, Da Costa, Salcido, Mendez, Simons, Afellay (Varyrynen 76), Cocu, Farfan, Kone (Aissati 86). Tr: Koeman

Galatasaray 0

Mondragon – Sabri Sarioglu, Song, Tomas•38, Orhan Ak, Hasan Sas, Inamoto•, Ayhan Akman, Arda Turan• (Cihan Haspolatli• 66), Umit Karan (Hakan Sükür 79), Ilic (Necati Ates 70). Tr: Gerets

---

GROUP C MATCHDAY 5
Anfield, Liverpool
22-11-2006, 19:45, 41 948, Messina ITA
Liverpool 2
Gerrard 65, Crouch 89

Reina – Finnan, Carragher, Agger, Riise, Pennant (Bellamy 79), Xabi Alonso (Zenden 21), Gerrard, Gonzalez (Luis Garcia 36), Crouch, Kuyt. Tr: Benítez

PSV Eindhoven 0

Gomes – Kromkamp, Da Costa, Alex, Salcido, Mendez (Beerens 81), Simons, Feher (Tardelli 68), Afellay, Kone, Farfan. Tr: Koeman

---

GROUP C MATCHDAY 5
Chaban-Delmas, Bordeaux
22-11-2006, 20:45, 22 834, Hrinak SVK
Girondins Bordeaux 3
Alonso 22, Laslandes 47, Faubert 50

Rame – Faubert, Enakarhire•, Planus, Jurietti, Alonso, Mavuba, Micoud (Dalmat 79), Wendel• (Ducasse 68), Laslandes, Darcheville (Obertan 46). Tr: Ricardo Gomes

Galatasaray 1
Inamoto 73

Mondragon – Sabri Sarioglu•, Song, Tolga Seyhan, Cihan Haspolatli, Hasan Sas• (Ergun Penbe 69), Inamoto•, Ayhan Akman, Arda Turan•59, Hakan Sükür (Mehmet Topal 63), Ilic (Umit Karan 46). Tr: Gerets

---

GROUP C MATCHDAY 6
Philips Stadion, Eindhoven
5-12-2006, 20:45, 30 000, I.Gonzalez ESP
PSV Eindhoven 1
Alex 87

Gomes – Kromkamp, Alex, Addo (Kluivert 46), Reiziger, Mendez•, Simons, Cocu, Aissati (Culina 62), Farfan, Tardelli (Kone 46). Tr: Koeman

Girondins Bordeaux 3
Faubert 7, Dalmat 25, Darcheville 37

Rame – Jemmali, Enakarhire, Cid, Marange, Faubert•, Mavuba, Ducasse, Dalmat (Obertan 80), Darcheville• (Perea 70), Laslandes. Tr: Ricardo Gomes

---

GROUP C MATCHDAY 6
Olympiyat, Istanbul
5-12-2006, 21:45, 22 434, Benquerença POR
Galatasaray 3
Necati 24, Okan 28, Ilic 39

Mondragon – Sabri Sarioglu, Cihan Haspolatli, Tomas, Emre Asik (Tolga Seyhan 80), Ergun Penbe, Inamoto•, Okan Buruk, Carrusca (Mehmet Güven 75), Umit Karan, Necati Ates (Ilic 46+). Tr: Gerets

Liverpool 2
Fowler 2 22 90

Dudek – Peltier, Carragher, Agger, Riise, Pennant•, Xabi Alonso (Miki 84), Paletta, Guthrie (Luis Garcia 66), Bellamy (Crouch 74), Fowler. Tr: Benítez

GROUP D

		Pl	W	D	L	F	A	Pts	ESP	ITA	UKR	GRE
Valencia	ESP	6	4	1	1	12	6	13		2-1	2-0	2-0
Roma	ITA	6	3	1	2	8	4	10	1-0		4-0	1-1
Shakhtar Donetsk	UKR	6	1	3	2	6	11	6	2-2	1-0		2-2
Olympiacos	GRE	6	0	3	3	6	11	3	2-4	0-1	1-1	

GROUP D MATCHDAY 1
Olimpico, Rome
12-09-2006, 20:45, 34 035, Layec FRA

Roma   4
Taddei [67], Totti [76], De Rossi [79], Pizarro [89]

Doni – Panucci, Ferrari, Chivu, Tonetto, De Rossi, Aquilani• (Pizarro 62), Taddei, Perrotta, Mancini (Cassetti 87), Totti (Montella 80). Tr: Spalletti

Shakhtar Donetsk   0

Shutkov – Srna, Hubschman•, Lewandowski, Rat, Matuzalem (Gay 72; Jadson 81), Tymoschuk•, Duljaj, Marica•, Brandao (Agahowa 63), Elano. Tr: Lucescu

GROUP D MATCHDAY 1
Karaiskaki, Piraeus
12-09-2006, 21:45, 31 490, Hauge NOR

Olympiacos   2
Konstantinou.M [28], Castillo [66]

Nikopolidis – Zewlakow (Pantos 46), Anatolakis (Julio Cesar 69), Ouddou•, Domi, Kafes, Stoltidis, Rivaldo, Castillo, Constantinou, Djordjevic. Tr: Sollied

Valencia   4
Morientes 3 [34] [39] [90], Albiol [85]

Canizares – Miguel, Ayala•, Albiol, Moretti, Angulo, Edu•, Marchena, Gavilan (Silva 72), Morientes (Jorge Lopez 90), Villa (Reguerio 81). Tr: Flores

GROUP D MATCHDAY 2
Mestalla, Valencia
27-09-2006, 20:45, 40 593, Fandel GER

Valencia   2
Angulo [13], Villa [29]

Canizares – Miguel, Ayala•, Albiol, Moretti, Angulo, Albelda•, Edu, Vicente (Gavilan 90), Villa (Silva 72), Morientes (Reguerio 87). Tr: Flores

Roma   1
Totti [18p]

Doni – Panucci, Ferrari•, Chivu, Tonetto, Cassetti (Okaka Chuka 64), Pizarro•, De Rossi•, Aquilani (Montella 46), Perrotta, Totti. Tr: Spalletti

GROUP D MATCHDAY 2
RSC Olympiyskiy, Donetsk
27-09-2006, 21:45, 26 500, Braamhaar NED

Shakhtar Donetsk   2
Matuzalem [34], Marica [70]

Shust – Srna, Hubschman•, Lewandowski•, Rat, Fernandinho, Tymoschuk•, Matuzalem, Elano (Jadson 76), Marica (Agahowa 89), Brandao (Vorobei 76). Tr: Lucescu

Olympiacos   2
Konstantinou.M [24], Castillo [68]

Nikopolidis – Pantos• (Rivaldo 85), Kostoulas, Julio Cesar, Anatolakis (Patsatzoglou 46), Georgatos•, Castillo, Maric•, Stoltidis, Djordjevic, Constantinou (Okkas 90). Tr: Sollied

GROUP D MATCHDAY 3
Mestalla, Valencia
18-10-2006, 20:45, 33 540, Riley ENG

Valencia   2
Villa 2 [31] [45]

Canizares – Miguel, Albiol, David Navarro, Moretti, Joaquin, Albelda•, Edu (Jorge Lopez 53), Reguerio (Gavilan 64), Morientes, Villa (Silva 77). Tr: Flores

Shakhtar Donetsk   0

Pletikosa – Sviderskyi•••[76], Chygrynskyi, Leonardo, Rat, Fernandinho (Vorobei 46), Tymoschuk•, Jadson (Hubschman 46), Matuzalem, Marica•, Agahowa (Brandao• 46). Tr: Lucescu

GROUP D MATCHDAY 3
Karaiskaki, Piraeus
18-10-2006, 21:45, 31 009, Poll ENG

Olympiacos   0

Nikopolidis – Zewlakow, Anatolakis, Julio Cesar, Georgatos, Castillo, Kafes (Maric 59), Stoltidis, Djordjevic (Okkas 70), Rivaldo (Borja 83), Constantinou. Tr: Sollied

Roma   1
Perrotta [76]

Doni – Panucci, Ferrari, Chivu, Tonetto•, De Rossi, Cassetti (Rosi 66), Faty (Aquilani 77), Perrotta, Taddei (Defendi 90), Totti. Tr: Spalletti

GROUP D MATCHDAY 4
Olimpico, Rome
31-10-2006, 20:45, 28 828, Benquerença POR

Roma   1
Totti [66]

Doni – Panucci, Ferrari (Perotta 46), Mexes, Chivu, De Rossi, Taddei, Pizarro•, Aquilani (Vucinic 63), Tonetto, Totti•=[32]. Tr: Spalletti

Olympiacos   1
Júlio César [19]

Nikopolidis• – Zewlakow, Kostoulas•, Julio Cesar•, Domi, Stoltidis, Patsatzoglou (Anatolakis 65), Maric (Kafes 90), Rivaldo, Djordjevic• (Borja 86), Constantinou•. Tr: Sollied

GROUP D MATCHDAY 4
RSC Olympiyskiy, Donetsk
31-10-2006, 21:45, 25 800, Fröjdfeldt SWE

Shakhtar Donetsk   2
Jadson [2], Fernandinho [28]

Shust – Srna•, Chygrynskyi, Hubschmann•, Rat, Fernandinho (Duljaj 89), Lewandowski•, Matuzalem•, Jadson, Agahowa, Brandao• (Marica 75). Tr: Lucescu

Valencia   2
Morientes [18], Ayala [68]

Canizares – Miguel, Ayala, David Navarro (Hugo Viana 87), Moretti, Angulo•, Albiol•, Edu, Silva, Morientes (Joaquin 77), Villa• (Reguerio 90). Tr: Flores

GROUP D MATCHDAY 5
Mestalla, Valencia
22-11-2006, 20:45, 33 407, Duhamel FRA

Valencia   2
Angulo [45], Morientes [46]

Canizares – Miguel, Albiol•, Ayala•, Curro Torres, Joaquin, Baraja (Hugo Viana 86), Pallardo•, Silva, Villa (Morientes 22), Angulo (Tavano 75). Tr: Flores

Olympiacos   0

Nikopolidis – Pantos•, Julio Cesar, Kostoulas, Zewlakow•, Okkas, Stoltidis (Babangida 62), Rivaldo, Djordjevic, Castillo• (Borja 70), Constantinou (Maric• 17). Tr: Sollied

GROUP D MATCHDAY 5
RSC Olympiyskiy, Donetsk
22-11-2006, 21:45, 23 900, Stark GER

Shakhtar Donetsk   1
Marica [61]

Shust – Srna, Kucher, Chygrynskyi, Rat, Fernandinho (Gay 76), Duljaj, Matuzalem, Jadson (Elano 81), Marica (Agahowa 75), Brandao.
Tr: Lucescu

Roma   0

Doni – Cassetti•, Mexes•, Ferrari (Pizarro• 69), Panucci, Perotta•, De Rossi, Aquilani (Montella 78), Taddei, Totti, Mancini (Vucinic 78). Tr: Spalletti

GROUP D MATCHDAY 6
Olimpico, Rome
5-12-2006, 20:45, 38 898, Plautz AUT

Roma   1
Panucci [13]

Doni – Panucci, Mexes, Chivu, Tonetto, De Rossi (Perotta 75), Virga (Rosi 83), Cassetti, Taddei, Mancini, Vucinic (Okaka Chuka 90). Tr: Spalletti

Valencia   0

Butelle– Curro Torres, David Navarro, Albiol, Cerrajeria•, Joaquin, Hugo Viana, Pallardo (Corcoles 90), Jorge Lopez (Romero 74), Aaron (Nacho Insa 27), Tavano. Tr: Flores

GROUP D MATCHDAY 6
Karaiskaki, Piraeus
5-12-2006, 21:45, 30 805, Bennett ENG

Olympiacos   1
Castillo [54]

Nikopolidis – Pantos (Constantinou• 75), Zewlakow, Julio Cesar, Domi (Georgatos 83), Maric•, Stoltidis, Rivaldo, Djordjevic, Babangida (Borja 83), Castillo. Tr: Sollied

Shakhtar Donetsk   1
Matuzalem [27]

Shust – Srna, Chygrynskyi, Kucher•, Rat•••[90], Jadson, Matuzalem (Duljaj 77), Tymoschuk, Fernandinho (Elano 81), Brandao•, Marica (Agahowa 66). Tr: Lucescu

GROUP E

		Pl	W	D	L	F	A	Pts	FRA	ESP	ROU	UKR
Olympique Lyonnais	FRA	6	4	2	0	12	3	14		2-0	1-1	1-0
Real Madrid	ESP	6	3	2	1	14	8	11	2-2		1-0	5-1
Steaua Bucureşti	ROU	6	1	2	3	7	11	5	0-3	1-4		1-1
Dynamo Kyiv	UKR	6	0	2	4	5	16	2	0-3	2-2	1-4	

GROUP E MATCHDAY 1
Stade de Gerland, Lyon
13-09-2006, 20:45, 40 013, Stark GER

Olympique Lyonnais 2
Fred [11], Tiago [31]

Coupet – Reveillere●, Cris, Muller, Abidal, Tiago, Toulalan, Juninho (Kallstrom 73), Govou (Clerc 82), Fred (Wiltord 78), Malouda. Tr: Houllier

Real Madrid 0

Casillas – Cicinho, Cannavaro●, Sergio Ramos●, Roberto Carlos●, Diarra●, Emerson, Beckham (Guti 55), Raul (Robinho 69), Cassano (Reyes 46), Van Nistelrooy. Tr: Capello

---

GROUP E MATCHDAY 2
Stadionul Steaua, Bucharest
26-09-2006, 21:45, 25 169, Webb ENG

Steaua Bucureşti 0

Carlos – Marin, Goian, Ghionea, Nesu, Nicolita●, Lovin (Thereau 76), Paraschiv (Petre● 57), Bostina (Oprita● 55), Dica, Badea. Tr: Olaroiu

Olympique Lyonnais 3
Fred [43], Tiago [55], Benzema [89]

Coupet – Clerc, Cris, Muller, Abidal (Reveillere 76), Tiago (Kallstrom 82), Toulalan●, Juninho, Wiltord, Fred (Benzema 85), Malouda. Tr: Houllier

---

GROUP E MATCHDAY 4
Bernabéu, Madrid
1-11-2006, 20:45, 69 105, Plautz AUT

Real Madrid 1
Nicolita OG [70]

Casillas – Sergio Ramos, Ivan Helguera, Cannavaro, Roberto Carlos, Emerson, Diarra (Beckham 59), Raul, Guti, Robinho (Reyes 87), Van Nistelrooy●73 (Ronaldo 74). Tr: Capello

Steaua Bucureşti 0

Cernea● – Stancu, Goian●, Ghionea, Marin, Nicolita●, Paraschiv (Thereau 79), Petre●, Oprita (Coman 84), Dica, Badea (Lovin 79). Tr: Olaroiu

---

GROUP E MATCHDAY 5
Stadionul Steaua, Bucharest
21-11-2005, 21;45, 23 172, Jara CZE

Steaua Bucureşti 1
Dica [69]

Cernea● – Stancu, Ghionea●, Goian, Marin, Nicolita, Petre, Paraschiv (Radoi 66), Oprita● (Cristocea 55), Dica (Lovin 90), Thereau. Tr: Olaroiu

Dynamo Kyiv 1
Cernat [29]

Shovkovskyi – Markovic, Rodrigo●, Rodolfo (Gavrancic● 46), El Kaddouri, Gusev●, Yussuf●, Bialkevich, Cernat (Diogo Rincon● 78), Shatskikh, Kleber● (Milevskyi 67). Tr: Demyanenko

---

GROUP E MATCHDAY 1
NSC Olympiyskiy, Kyiv
13-09-2006, 21;45, 49 500, Allaerts BEL

Dynamo Kyiv 1
Rebrov [16]

Shovkovskiy – Markovic (Moreno 61), Rodolfo, Rodrigo, Nesmachnyi, Gusev, Yussuf, Rebrov (Otalvaro 73), Corrêa (Bialkevich 59), Diogo Rincón, Shatskikh. Tr: Demyanenko

Steaua Bucureşti 4
Ghionea [3], Badea [24], Dica 2 [43 79]

Carlos● – Saban, Goian, Ghionea●, Nesu●, Nicolita, Paraschiv, Lovin, Cristocea (Oprita 74), Dica (Petre 82), Badea (Thereau 70). Tr: Olaroiu

---

GROUP E MATCHDAY 3
Stadionul Steaua, Bucharest
17-10-2006, 21;45, 24 123, Rosetti ITA

Steaua Bucureşti 1
Badea [64]

Carlos – Saban (Thereau 59), Goian●, Ghionea, Marin, Nicolita, Paraschiv (Oprita 78), Lovin (Petre 62), Bostina, Dica●, Badea. Tr: Olaroiu

Real Madrid 4
Sergio Ramos [9], Raúl [34], Robinho [56], Van Nistelrooij [76]

Casillas – Sergio Ramos, Ivan Helguera, Cannavaro, Roberto Carlos, Robinho, Emerson, Diarra, Guti (Beckham 71), Van Nistelrooy (Ronaldo 78), Raul. Tr: Capello

---

GROUP E MATCHDAY 4
Stade de Gerland, Lyon
1-11-2006, 20:45, 40 520, Vink NED

Olympique Lyonnais 1
Benzema [14]

Coupet – Clerc, Squillaci, Cris, Abidal, Tiago, Toulalan, Juninho (Kallstrom79), Govou (Diarra 88), Benzema (Wiltord 75), Malouda●. Tr: Houllier

Dynamo Kyiv 0

Shovkovskyi – Gusev●, Rodolfo, Gavrancic (Rodrigo 46), El Kaddouri●, Yussuf, Cernat (Bialkevich 77), Mikhalik, Rebrov (Shatskikh 66), Milevskyi, Kleber. Tr: Demyanenko

---

GROUP E MATCHDAY 6
Stade de Gerland, Lyon
6-12-2006, 20:45, 39 351, Ceferin SVN

Olympique Lyonnais 1
Diarra [12]

Coupet – Reveillere, Cacapa●, Muller, Berthod, Tiago (Toulalan 65), Diarra, Kallstrom, Govou (Remy 80), Carew (Wiltord 65), Ben Arfa. Tr: Houllier

Steaua Bucureşti 1
Dica [2]

Cernea – Stancu, Ghionea, Goian, Marin, Nicolita, Radoi● (Petre 78), Paraschiv●, Cristocea (Oprita 82), Dica●, Thereau (Badea 73). Tr: Olaroiu

---

GROUP E MATCHDAY 2
Bernabéu, Madrid
26-09-2006, 20:45, 68 105, Poll ENG

Real Madrid 5
Van Nistelrooij 2 [20 70p], Raul 2 [27 61], Reyes [46+]

Casillas – Mejia, Cannavaro, Sergio Ramos●, Roberto Carlos, Emerson, Diarra, Reyes (Beckham 46), Guti, Raul (Robinho 84), Van Nistelrooy (Ronaldo 72). Tr: Capello

Dynamo Kyiv 1
Milevskiy [47]

Shovkovskyi●68 – Gusev, Sablic, Gavrancic, Nesmachnyi, Diogo Rincon (Aliyev 81), Correa (Mikhalik 74), Yussuf, Bialkevich (Rybka 70), Milevskyi, Shatskikh●. Tr: Demyanenko

---

GROUP E MATCHDAY 3
NSC Olympiyskiy, Kyiv
17-10-2006, 21;45, 35 500, Messina ITA

Dynamo Kyiv 0

Lutsenko – Markovic, Rodolfo, Gavrancic, El Kaddouri, Mikhalik, Correa (Gusev 46), Yussuf●, Diogo Rincon, Rebrov (Shatskikh 46), Milevskyi● (Kleber 85). Tr: Demyanenko

Olympique Lyonnais 3
Juninho [31], Källström [38], Malouda [50]

Vercoutre – Clerc, Squillaci, Cris, Abidal (Reveillere 69), Kallstrom●, Diarra (Tiago 80), Juninho (Toulalan 58), Wiltord, Fred, Malouda●. Tr: Houllier

---

GROUP E MATCHDAY 5
Bernabéu, Madrid
21-11-2006, 20:45, 69 906, Hauge NOR

Real Madrid 2
Diarra [39], Van Nistelrooij [83]

Casillas – Sergio Ramos●, Ivan Helguera, Cannavaro●, Roberto Carlos●, Diarra, Emerson (Cassano 76), Raul●, Guti (Reyes 21), Robihno, Van Nistelrooy●89. Tr: Capello

Olympique Lyonnais 2
Carew [11], Malouda [31]

Coupet – Reveillere●, Cris, Squillaci, Abidal, Tiago, Toulalan● (Diarra 90), Juninho●, Clerc, Carew, Malouda●. Tr: Houllier

---

GROUP E MATCHDAY 6
NSC Olympiyskiy, Kyiv
6-12-2006, 21;45, 32 000, Riley ENG

Dynamo Kyiv 2
Shatskikh 2 [13 27]

Shovkovski – Markovic, Rodrigo●, Rodolfo (Mandzyuk 34), Nesmachnyi, Gusev, Yussuf, Mikhalik, Bialkevich, Milevskiy (Rotan 85), Shatskikh. Tr: Demyanenko

Real Madrid 2
Ronaldo 2 [86 88p]

Diego Lopez – Michel Salgado, Torres, Meija, Roberto Carlos, Nieto (Valero 74), Beckham, De la Red (Javi Garcia 70), Diarra, Ronaldo●, Cassano. Tr: Capello

GROUP F

		Pl	W	D	L	F	A	Pts	ENG	SCO	POR	DEN
Manchester United	ENG	6	4	0	2	10	5	12		3-2	3-1	3-0
Celtic	SCO	6	3	0	3	8	9	9	1-0		3-0	1-0
Benfica	POR	6	2	1	3	7	8	7	0-1	3-0		3-1
FC København	DEN	6	2	1	3	5	8	7	1-0	3-1	0-0	

GROUP F MATCHDAY 1
Old Trafford, Manchester
13-09-2006, 19:45, 74 031, Michel SVK

Manchester United 3

Saha 2 $^{30p\ 40}$, Solskjær ^{47}

Van der Sar – Neville, Ferdinand, Brown, Silvestre•, Fletcher, Scholes (O'Shea 80), Carrick, Giggs (Solskjær 33), Rooney (Richardson 86), Saha. Tr: Ferguson

Celtic 2

Vennegoor ^{21}, Nakamura ^{43}

Boruc• – Wilson (Telfer 52), Caldwell, McManus, Naylor, Lennon, Nakamura, Gravesen, Jarosik (Miller• 56), McGeady (Maloney 70), Vennegoor of Hesselink. Tr: Strachan

GROUP F MATCHDAY 1
Parken, Copenhagen
13-09-2006, 20:45, 40 085, Baskakov RUS

FC København 0

Christiansen – Jacobsen, Hangeland, Gravgaard, Bergdolmo, Silberbauer, Norregaard•, Linderoth, Hutchinson, Gronkjær (Kvist 44), Berglund (Pimpong 74). Tr: Solbakken

Benfica 0

Quim – Alcides•, Ricardo Rocha, Luisao, Leo, Paulo Jorge, Katsouranis, Petit, Simao (Manu 81), Nuno Gomes (Fonseca 90), Nuno Assis. Tr: Fernando Santos

GROUP F MATCHDAY 2
Estadio da Luz, Lisbon
26-09-2006, 19:45, 53 000, De Bleeckere BEL

Benfica 0

Quim – Alcides, Luisao, Anderson (Mantorras 82), Leo, Katsouranis•, Karagounis (Nuno Assis 62), Petit•, Paulo Jorge (Miccoli 65), Nuno Gomes, Simao. Tr: Fernando Santos

Manchester United 1

Saha ^{60}

Van der Sar – Neville, Vidic, Ferdinand, Heinze•, O'Shea, Carrick•, Scholes•, Rooney (Fletcher 85), Cristiano Ronaldo, Saha (Smith 85). Tr: Ferguson

GROUP F MATCHDAY 2
Celtic Park, Glasgow
26-09-2006, 19:45, 58 000, Meyer GER

Celtic 1

Miller.K ^{36p}

Boruc – Telfer, Caldwell, McManus, Naylor, Nakamura, Lennon, Gravesen, McGeady (Pearson 88), Zurawski (Beattie 73), Miller.K (Maloney 82). Tr: Strachan

FC København 0

Christiansen – Jacobsen, Hangeland, Gravgaard, Bergdolmo (Thomassen 75), Silberbauer, Linderoth, Norregaard, Hutchinson, Berglund (Kvist 55), Allback. Tr: Solbakken

GROUP F MATCHDAY 3
Celtic Park, Glasgow
17-10-2006, 19:45, 58 313, Braamhaar NED

Celtic 3

Miller.K 2 $^{56\ 66}$, Pearson ^{90}

Boruc – Telfer, Caldwell, McManus, Naylor, Maloney, Lennon, Sno• (Pearson 88) Nakamura, Zurawski (Jarosik 84), Miller. Tr: Strachan

Benfica 0

Quim – Alcides, Luisao, Ricardo Rocha, Leo, Katsouranis• (Nelson 72), Petit, Miccoli, Nuno Assis, Simao, Nuno Gomes (Fonseca 78) Tr: Fernando Santos

GROUP F MATCHDAY 3
Old Trafford, Manchester
17-10-2006, 19:45, 72 020, Wegereef NED

Manchester United 3

Scholes ^{39}, O'Shea ^{46}, Richardson ^{83}

Van der Sar – O'Shea, Brown, Vidic, Evra•, Cristiano Ronaldo, Carrick (Solskjær 60), Scholes (Richardson 76), Fletcher, Saha (Smith 60), Rooney. Tr: Ferguson

FC København 0

Christiansen – Jacobsen, Hangeland, Gravgaard, Wendt, Silberbauer (Berglund 57), Linderoth, Norregaard (Kvist 57), Hutchinson, Berglund (Pimpong 57), Allback. Tr: Solbakken

GROUP F MATCHDAY 4
Estadio da Luz, Lisbon
1-11-2006, 19:45, 47 574, Vassaras GRE

Benfica 3

Caldwell.G OG ^{10}, Nuno Gomes ^{22}, Karyaka ^{76}

Quim – Nelson, Luisao, Ricardo Rocha•, Leo•, Katsouranis, Petit (Beto 84), Nuno Assis, Simao, Nuno Gomes (Mantorras 89), Miccoli (Karyaka 67). Tr: Fernando Santos

Celtic 0

Boruc – Telfer, Caldwell, McManus, Naylor, Nakamura, Sno• (Zurawski 72), Lennon, Pearson•, Maloney• (McGeady 65), Miller. Tr: Strachan

GROUP F MATCHDAY 4
Parken, Copenhagen
1-11-2006, 20:45, 40 308, Stark GER

FC København 1

Allbäck ^{73}

Christiansen – Jacobsen, Hangeland•, Gravgaard, Wendt, Silberbauer (Kvist 71), Linderoth, Norregaard, Bergvold (Berglund 68), Allback (Thomassen 89), Hutchinson. Tr: Solbakken

Manchester United 0

Van der Sar – Brown, Vidic (Ferdinand 46), Silvestre, Heinze (Evra 80), Fletcher (Scholes 71), Carrick, O'Shea, Cristiano Ronaldo•, Rooney, Solskjær. Tr: Ferguson

GROUP F MATCHDAY 5
Celtic Park, Glasgow
21-11-2006, 19:45, 59 179, M.Gonzalez ESP

Celtic 1

Nakamura ^{81}

Boruc – Telfer, Balde, McManus•, Naylor, Nakamura (Miller 85), Gravesen, Lennon•, Sno, (Jarosik 46), Venegoor of Hesselink, Zurawski (Maloney• 46). Tr: Strachan

Manchester United 0

Van der Sar – Neville, Ferdinand, Vidic, Heinze (Evra 87), Cristiano Ronaldo, Carrick (O'Shea 87), Scholes•, Giggs, Saha•90, Rooney. Tr: Ferguson

GROUP F MATCHDAY 5
Estadio da Luz, Lisbon
21-11-2006, 19:45, 37 199, Rosetti ITA

Benfica 3

Léo ^{14}, Miccoli 2 $^{16\ 37}$

Quim – Nelson•, Anderson, Ricardo Rocha, Leo, Katsouranis (Mantorras 86), Petit, Nuno Assis (Karagounis 80), Simao, Nuno Gomes, Micoli• (Karyaka 70). Tr: Fernando Santos

FC København 1

Allbäck ^{89}

Christiansen – Jacobsen, Hangeland, Gravgaard, Wendt• (Bergvold 80), Silberbauer• (Kvist 59), Linderoth•, Norregaard (Berglund 59) Hutchinson, Gronkjær, Allback. Tr: Solbakken

GROUP F MATCHDAY 6
Old Trafford, Manchester
6-12-2006, 19:45, 74 955, Fandel GER

Manchester United 3

Vidic $^{46•}$, Giggs ^{61}, Saha ^{75}

Van der Sar – Neville, Ferdinand, Vidic, Evra (Heinze 67), Cristiano Ronaldo, Carrick, Scholes (Solskjær 79), Giggs (Fletcher• 74), Saha, Rooney•. Tr: Ferguson

Benfica 1

Nélson ^{27}

Quim – Nelson, Luisao, Ricardo Rocha•, Leo, Katsouranis, Petit, Simao, Nuno Assis (Karagounis 73), Nuno Gomes, Micoli (Paulo Jorge 64). Tr: Fernando Santos

GROUP F MATCHDAY 6
Parken, Copenhagen
6-12-2006, 20:45, 38 647, Layec FRA

FC København 3

Hutchinson ^{2}, Grønkjær ^{27}, Allbäck ^{57}

Christiansen – Jacobsen (Norregaard 56), Hangeland, Gravgaard, Wendt, Silberbauer, Linderoth, Kvist, Gronkjær• (Berglund 90), Allback (Bergvold 81), Hutchinson. Tr: Solbakken

Celtic 1

Jarosik ^{75}

Boruc – Wilson, Balde, McManus• (O'Dea 73), Naylor, Gravesen (Nakamura 69), Lennon, Jarosik•, McGeady (Pearson 69), Zurawski, Miller•. Tr: Strachan

GROUP G

		Pl	W	D	L	F	A	Pts	ENG	POR	RUS	GER
Arsenal	ENG	6	3	2	1	7	3	11		2-0	0-0	3-1
FC Porto	POR	6	3	2	1	9	4	11	0-0		0-0	4-1
CSKA Moskva	RUS	6	2	2	2	4	5	8	1-0	0-2		1-0
Hamburger SV	GER	6	1	0	5	7	15	3	1-2	1-3	3-2	

GROUP G MATCHDAY 1
Estadio do Dragão, Porto
13-09-2006, 19:45, 37 123, Ovrebo NOR

FC Porto 0

Helton – Besingwa, Pepe, Bruno Alves, Ezequias, Gonzalez, Paulo Assuncao, Anderson, Sektioui (Helder Posiga 46), Adriano (Lopez 71), Quaresma (Alan 61). Tr: Ferreira

CSKA Moskva 0

Akinfeev – Ignashevich, Semberas, Berezutsky.A, Krasic, Rahimic•, Aldonin, Zhirkov•, Daniel Carvalho (Gusev 90), Vágner Love (Olic 76), Dudu Cearense• (Berezutskiy.V 87). Tr: Gazzaev

---

GROUP G MATCHDAY 1
AOL Arena, Hamburg
13-09-2006, 20:45, 50 389, Fröjdfeldt SWE

Hamburger SV 1
Sanogo [91+]

Kirschstein•10 – Demel (Mahdavikia 54), Reinhardt, Kompany, Mathijesen, Jarolim, De Jong, Trochowski, Wicky (Wachte 12), Sanogo, Ljuboja (Guerrero 82). Tr: Doll

Arsenal 2
Gilberto [12p], Rosicky [53]

Lehmann – Eboue, Toure (Hoyte 29), Djourou, Gallas, Hleb (Flamini 70), Fabregas, Gilberto Silva, Rosicky, Adebayor, Van Persie (Julio Baptista 70). Tr: Wenger

---

GROUP G MATCHDAY 2
Emirates Stadium, London
26-09-2006, 19:45, 59 861, Farina ITA

Arsenal 2
Henry [38], Hleb [48]

Lehmann – Eboue, Toure, Gallas (Song 90), Hoyte, Hleb (Walcott 86), Fabregas, Gilberto Silva•, Rosicky•, Henry, Van Persie (Ljunberg 74). Tr: Wenger

FC Porto 0

Helton – Besingwa, Pepe, Bruno Alves, Cech, Gonzalez, Paulo Assuncao, Ricardo Costa• (Raul Meireles 46), Anderson (Adriano 66), Helder Posiga (Lopez 46), Quaresma. Tr: Ferreira

---

GROUP G MATCHDAY 2
Lokomotiv, Moscow
26-09-2006, 20:30, 23 000, Wegereef NED

CSKA Moskva 1
Dudu [59]

Akinfeev – Berezutsky.V, Ignashevich, Berezutsky.A, Dudu Cearense, Semberas (Krasic 46), Daniel Carvalho (Jô 85), Rahimic, Zhirkov, Vágner Love•, Olic (Aldonin 76). Tr: Gazzaev

Hamburger SV 0

Kirschstein – Mahdavikia, Reinhardt, Kompany, Mathijesen•, Jarolim•, Wicky, De Jong (Trochowski 70), Sorin• (Guerrero 69), Ljuboja (Lauth 80•85), Sanogo. Tr: Doll

---

GROUP G MATCHDAY 3
Estadio do Dragão, Porto
17-10-2006, 19:45, 31 109, Hamer LUX

FC Porto 4
López 2 [14 81], González [48+p], Postiga [69]

Helton – Fucile•, Pepe, Bruno Alves, Cech, Gonzalez, Raul Meireles, Anderson (Jorginho 43), Quaresma• (Vierinha 80), Helder Posiga (Bruno Moraes 75), Lopez. Tr: Ferreira

Hamburger SV 1
Trochowski [89]

Kirschstein – Benjamin (Fillinger 86), Wicky (Klingbell 54), Mathijesen, Atouba (Guerrero 68), Mahdavikia•, De Jong•, Trochowski, Sorin, Ljuboja•, Sanogo. Tr: Doll

---

GROUP G MATCHDAY 3
Lokomotiv, Moscow
17-10-2006, 20:30, 28 800, M.Gonzalez ESP

CSKA Moskva 1
Carvalho [24]

Akinfeev – Berezutsky.V, Semberas, Berezutsky.A, Ignashevich•, Rahimic•, Aldonin (Krasic 90), Dudu Cearense, Zhirkov, Vágner Love• (Olic 86) Daniel Carvalho (Taranov 89). Tr: Gazzaev

Arsenal 0

Lehmann – Hoyte, Toure, Djourou (Clichy 75), Gallas, Hleb, Fabregas, Gilberto Silva, Rosicky (Walcott 80), Henry•, Van Persie (Adebayor 68). Tr: Wenger

---

GROUP G MATCHDAY 4
Emirates Stadium, London
1-11-2006, 19:45, 60 003, Michel SVK

Arsenal 0

Lehmann – Hoyte, Toure, Gallas, Clichy, Van Persie (Aliadiere 82), Fabregas (Flamini 89), Gilberto Silva, Hleb• (Walcott 71), Rosicky, Henry•. Tr: Wenger

CSKA Moskva 0

Akinfeev – Ignashevich, Semberas•, Berezutsky.A, Berezutsky.V•, Rahimic, Krasic (Aldonin 40), Zhirkov, Daniel Carvalho (Taranov 90), Dudu Cearense, Vágner Love (Olic 85). Tr: Gazzaev

---

GROUP G MATCHDAY 4
AOL Arena, Hamburg
1-11-2006, 20:45, 51 000, Duhamel FRA

Hamburger SV 1
Van der Vaart [62]

Kirschstein – Mahdavikia, Kompany (Klingbell 71), Mathijesen, Atouba (Berisha 65), Trochowski, Feilhaber, Sorin, Van der Vaart•, Ljuboja (Guerrero 58), Sanogo. Tr: Doll

FC Porto 3
González [44], López [61], Moraes [87]

Helton – Bosingwa, Pepe, Bruno Alves, Fucile, Gonzalez, Paulo Assuncao, Raul Meireles• (Cech 90), Quaresma, Helder Posiga (Bruno Moraes• 70), Lopez (Jorginho 82). Tr: Ferreira

---

GROUP G MATCHDAY 5
Emirates Stadium, London
21-11-2006, 19:45, 59 962, Larsen DEN

Arsenal 3
Van Persie [52], Eboué [83], Baptista [88]

Lehmann – Eboue, Toure, Senderos•, Clichy•, Hleb• (Julio Baptista 81), Fabregas, Flamini, Van Persie (Adebayor 70), Ljunberg (Walcott 75), Henry•. Tr: Wenger

Hamburger SV 1
Van der Vaart [4]

Wachter – Benjamin•, Reinhardt, Mathijesen, Atouba (Ljuboja 67), Mahdavikia (Feilhaber 45), Wicky (Lauth 87), Trochowski, Van der Vaart•, Fillinger•, Sanogo•. Tr: Doll

---

GROUP G MATCHDAY 5
Lokomotiv, Moscow
21-11-2006, 20:30, 21 853, Vassaras GRE

CSKA Moskva 0

Akinfeev – Berezutsky.V, Semberas, Berezutsky.A, Krasic (Olic 66), Rahimic•, Dudu Cearense (Kochubey• 27), Aldonin, Zhirkov•, Vágner Love•, Daniel Carvalho. Tr: Gazzaev

FC Porto 2
Quaresma [2], González [61]

Helton – Bosingwa, Pepe•, Bruno Alves•, Fucile, Gonzalez, Paulo Assuncao•, Raul Meireles (Jorginho 70), Quaresma (Alan 88), Helder Posiga (Bruno Moraes 77), Lopez. Tr: Ferreira

---

GROUP G MATCHDAY 6
Estadio do Dragão, Porto
6-12-2006, 19:45, 45 609, Merk GER

FC Porto 0

Helton – Bosingwa, Pepe, Bruno Alves, Fucile, Gonzalez, Pablo Assuncao, Raul Meireles (Ibson 86), Lopez, Helder Posiga (Bruno Moraes 81), Quaresma. Tr: Ferreira

Arsenal 0

Lehmann – Eboue, Toure, Djourou, Clichy, Hleb, Ljunberg, Gilberto Silva, Fabregas, Flamini, Adebayor (Van Persie 79). Tr: Wenger

---

GROUP G MATCHDAY 6
AOL Arena, Hamburg
6-12-2006, 20:45, 49 649, Farina ITA

Hamburger SV 3
Berisha [28], Van der Vaart [84], Sanogo [90]

Wachter – Mahdavikia, Reinhardt, Mathijesen, Atouba•-•69 (Feilhaber 69), Jarolim (Sanogo 83), Laas, Trochowski, Van der Vaart, Ljuboja (Guerrero 75), Berisha. Tr: Doll

CSKA Moskva 2
Olic [23p], Zhirkov [65]

Akinfeev – Berezutsky.V•, Semberas, Berezutsky.A, Krasic, Taranov (Odiah 77, Kochubey 86), Aldonin, Zhirkov, Dudu Cearense• (Grigoryev 9), Olic, Daniel Carvalho. Tr: Gazzaev

GROUP H

		Pl	W	D	L	F	A	Pts	ITA	FRA	GRE	BEL
Milan	ITA	6	3	1	2	8	4	10		0-2	3-0	4-1
Lille OSC	FRA	6	2	3	1	8	5	9	0-0		3-1	2-2
AEK Athens	GRE	6	2	2	2	6	9	8	1-0	1-0		1-1
RSC Anderlecht	BEL	6	0	4	2	7	11	4	0-1	1-1	2-2	

GROUP H MATCHDAY 1
Constant Vanden Stock, Brussels
13-09-2006, 20:45, 21 071, Dougal SCO
RSC Anderlecht 1
Pareja [41]

Zitka – Vanden Borre, Pereja, Deschacht, Van Damme, Vanderhaeghe, Biglia (Juhasz 68), Goor●, Boussoufa●, Hassan, Tchite. Tr: Vercauteren

Lille OSC 1
Fauvergue [80]

Sylva – Chalme, Plestan, Schmitz, Tafforeau, Cabaye● (Fauvergue 60), Makoun, Keita, Bodmer, Bastos (Youla● 60), Odemwingie (Lichsteiner 88). Tr: Puel

---

GROUP H MATCHDAY 1
San Siro, Milan
13-09-2006, 20:45, 31 836, Riley ENG
Milan 3
Inzaghi [17], Gourcuff [41], Kaká [76p]

Dida – Cafu, Simic, Maldini●, Favalli (Jankulovski 79), Gattuso, Brocchi (Ambrosini 75), Gourcuff, Kaká, Inzaghi, Ricardo Oliveira (Seedorf 71). Tr: Ancelotti

AEK Athens 0

Sorrentino – Pautasso, Dellas (Ivic 55), Cirillo●, Tziortziopoulos, Kapetanos (Lagos 46), Emerson (Tozser 70), Moras●, Julio Cesar, Delibasic, Limberopolous. Tr: Serra Ferrer

---

GROUP H MATCHDAY 2
Félix-Bollaert, Lens
26-09-2006, 20:45, 33 302, M.Gonzalez ESP
Lille OSC 0

Sylva – Chalme, Plestan, Tavlaridis (Schmitz 85), Vitakic, Keita, Bodmer, Makoun, Tafforeau, Fauvergue (Cabaye● 62), Odemwingie. Tr: Puel

Milan 0

Dida – Cafu, Nesta, Kaladze, Jankulovski●, Gattuso, Pirlo, Ambrosini, Kaká, Seedorf, Gilardino (Inzaghi 76). Tr: Ancelotti

---

GROUP H MATCHDAY 2
Olympic, Athens
26-09-2006, 21:45, 35 618, Larsen DEN
AEK Athens 1
Júlio César [28]

Sorrentino – Georgeas, Moras, Cirillo●, Udeze, Lagos, Kiriakidis, Tozser (Lakis 55), Julio Cesar● (Lakis 55), Hetemaj (Delibasic 70), Kapetanos (Limberopolous 46). Tr: Serra Ferrer

RSC Anderlecht 1
Frutos [25]

Zitka – Vanden Borre●, Pereja, Deschacht, Van Damme, Biglia, Levia, Goor●, Boussoufa (Legear 81), Frutos, Tchite●. Tr: Vercauteren

---

GROUP H MATCHDAY 3
Félix-Bollaert, Lens
17-10-2006, 20:45, 32 145, Meyer GER
Lille OSC 3
Robail.M [64], Gygax [82], Makoun [91+]

Sylva – Chalme, Tavlaridis●, Plestan●, Tafforeau, Keita●, Cabaye (Mirallas 64), Bodmer, Makoun, Robail.M● (Gygax 78), Odemwingie (Youla 78). Tr: Puel

AEK Athens 1
Ivic [68]

Sorrentino – Udeze●, Papastathopolous●, Cirillo, Georgeas, Emerson, Tozser (Ivic 56) (Kiriakidis 77), Lakis (Delibasic 71), Julio Cesar●, Limberopolous●. Tr: Serra Ferrer

---

GROUP H MATCHDAY 3
Constant Vanden Stock, Brussels
17-10-2006, 20:45, 21 845, M.Cantalejo ESP
RSC Anderlecht 0

Zitka – Juhasz, De Man, Deschacht, Vanden Borre● (Legear 84), Vanderhaege (Hassan 70), Biglia, Goor, Tchite, Frutos, Boussoufa (Serhat 84). Tr: Vercauteren

Milan 1
Kaká [58]

Dida – Bonera●●●47, Nesta, Kaladze●, Jankulovski, Gattuso, Pirlo, Seedorf (Brocchi 81), Kaká, Inzaghi (Gilardino 72), Ricardo Oliveira (Cafu 50). Tr: Ancelotti

---

GROUP H MATCHDAY 4
San Siro, Milan
1-11-2006, 20:45, 37 768, Fandel GER
Milan 4
Kaká [3 6p 22 56], Gilardino [88]

Dida – Simic, Nesta (Cafu 19), Maldini, Jankulovski, Gourcuff (Gattuso● 66), Brocchi, Seedorf, Kaká, Ricardo Oliveira (Pirlo 73), Gilardino●. Tr: Ancelotti

RSC Anderlecht 1
Juhász [61]

Zitka – Vanden Borre (Legear 85), De Man, Juhasz, Deschacht, Hassan Ahmed●, Vanderhaege (Serhat Akin 39), Biglia●, Boussoufa (Mpenza 80), Tchite, Goor. Tr: Vercauteren

---

GROUP H MATCHDAY 4
Olympic, Athens
1-11-2006, 21:45, 31 148, Bennett ENG
AEK Athens 1
Liberopoulos [74]

Sorrentino – Moras, Dellas●, Crillo, Georgeas, Emerson (Kapetanos● 47), Tozser, Zikos, Julio Cesar (Manduca 58), Limberopolous, Hetemaj (Kiriakidis 88). Tr: Serra Ferrer

Lille OSC 0

Sylva – Chalme, Tavlaridis●●●22, Plestan, Tafforeau, Keita●, Cabaye●, Bodmer, Makoun● (Fauvergue 77), Robail.M (Debuchy 57), Odemwingie (Youla 57). Tr: Puel

---

GROUP H MATCHDAY 5
Félix-Bollaert, Lens
21-11-2006, 20:45, 40 001, Ovrebo NOR
Lille OSC 2
Odemwingie [28], Fauvergue [47]

Sylva – Chalme, Plestan, Schmitz, Tafforeau●, Keita, Makoun, Bodmer, Robail.M (Debuchy 55), Fauvergue (Bastos 71), Odemwingie (Mirallas 75). Tr: Puel

RSC Anderlecht 2
Mbo Mpenza [2 38 48]

Schollen – Vanden Borre, De Man, Van Damme●●●88, Deschacht, Pareja●, Biglia (Juhasz 90), Hassan Ahmed● (Vanderhaege 83), Goor, Tchite, Mpenza (Boussoufa 66). Tr: Vercauteren

---

GROUP H MATCHDAY 5
Olympic, Athens
21-11-2006, 21:45, 56 203, Braamhaar NED
AEK Athens 1
Júlio César [32]

Sorrentino – Cirillo, Dellas, Papastathopolous, Tziortziopolous●, Emerson, Zikos, Manduca, Tozser● (Kiriakidis 66), Limberopolous, Julio Cesar (Hetemaj 86). Tr: Serra Ferrer

Milan 0

Dida (Kalac 78) – Brocchi, Costacurta (Jankulovski 46), Maldini, Bonera, Gourcuff, Pirlo, Seedorf●, Kaká, Ricardo Oliveira● (Borriello 70), Inzaghi. Tr: Ancelotti

---

GROUP H MATCHDAY 6
Constant Vanden Stock, Brussels
6-12-2006, 20:45, 21 845, Fröjdfeldt SWE
RSC Anderlecht 2
Vanden Borre [38], Frutos [63]

Zitka – Pereja, De Man, Juhasz, Deschacht, Vanden Borre, Biglia, Hassan (Boussoufa 65), Goor, Frutos (Legear 79), Tchite. Tr: Vercauteren

AEK Athens 2
Lakis [75], Cirillo [81]

Sorrentino – Pautasso, Cirillo, Papastathopolous, Georgeas, Kiriakidis (Lakis 50), Zikos, Manduca (Delibasic 58), Tozser, Limberopolous, Julio Cesar (Hetemaj 58). Tr: Serra Ferrer

---

GROUP H MATCHDAY 6
San Siro, Milan
6-12-2006, 20:45, 27 067, Poll ENG
Milan 0

Kalac – Bonera, Simic, Kaladze, Jankulovski, Brocchi (Seedorf 46), Pirlo, Ambrosini (Kaká 54), Gourcuff, Inzaghi, Borriello (Ricardo Oliveira 72). Tr: Ancelotti

Lille OSC 2
Odemwingie [7], Keita [67]

Malicki – Chalme, Plestan, Tavlaridis, Tafforeau, Keita● (Youla 83), Cabaye, Makoun, Debuchy, Bodmer (Fauvergue 89), Odemwingie (M Robail 73). Tr: Puel

ROUND OF SIXTEEN

Celtic Park, Glasgow
20-02-2007, 19:45, 58 785, Hauge NOR
Celtic   **0**

Boruc – Wilson, McManus, O'Dea, Naylor, Nakamura•, Sno, Lennon (Gravesen 81), McGeady, Vennegoor of Hesselink, Miller (Jarosik 63). Tr: Strachan

Milan   **0**

Kalac – Oddo, Kaladze (Bonera 63), Maldini•, Jankulovski, Gourcuff, Gattuso, Pirlo, Ambrosini, Kaká, Gilardino• (Ricardo Oliveira 77). Tr: Ancelotti

---

San Siro, Milan
7-03-2007, 20:45, 52 914, Plautz AUT
Milan   **1**
                                          Kaka [93]

Dida – Oddo (Simic 116), Bonera, Maldini, Jankulovski, Gattuso, (Brocchi 79), Pirlo, Ambrosini•, Seedorf, Kaká, Inzaghi (Gilardino 73). Tr: Ancelotti

Celtic   **0**

Boruc – Telfer, McManus•, O'Dea, Naylor•, Nakamura (Miller 106), Lennon•, Sno (Beattie 97), McGeady•, Jarosik (Gravesen 62), Vennegoor of Hesselink.
Tr: Strachan

Bernabéu, Madrid
20-02-2007, 20:45, 70 928, De Bleeckere BEL
Real Madrid   **3**
                           Raúl 2 [10] [28], Van Nistelrooy [34]

Casillas – Torres, Cannavaro, Ivan Helguera, Roberto Carlos (Raul Bravo 59), Beckham, Gago, Guti, Raul, Higuain (Robinho 53), Van Nistelrooy. Tr: Capello

Bayern München   **2**
                                  Lucio [23], Van Bommel [88]

Kahn – Sagnol, Lucio, Van Buyten, Lahm, Van Bommel, Hargreaves, Demichelis (Salihamidzic 46), Schweinsteiger (Scholl 79), Makaay, Podolski (Pizarro 61). Tr: Hitzfeld

---

Allianz-Arena, Munich
7-03-2007, 20:45, 66 000, Michel SVK
Bayern München   **2**
                                  Makaay [1], Lucio [66]

Kahn – Sagnol (Gorlitz 85), Lucio, Van Buyten, Lahm, Salihamidzic, Van Bommel••[82], Hargreaves, Schweinsteiger, Makaay (Pizarro 69), Podolski• (Demichelis 88). Tr: Hitzfeld

Real Madrid   **1**
                                     Van Nistelrooy [83p]

Casillas – Torres, Sergio Ramos•, Ivan Helguera, Roberto Carlos, Emerson (Guti• 32), Gago (Robinho 75), Diarra••[82], Raul, Higuain (Cassano 46), Van Nistelrooy. Tr: Capello

---

Stadio Olimpico, Rome
21-02-2007, 20:45, 60 053, Riley ENG
Roma   **0**

Doni – Panucci•, Mexes•, Ferrari, Tonetto•, Taddei• (Vucinic 86), De Rossi•, Perrotta, Pizarro•, Mancini• (Wilhelmsson 76), Totti•. Tr: Spalletti

Olympique Lyonnais   **0**

Coupet – Clerc, Cris, Squillaci, Abidal, Tiago, Toulalan•, Juninho•, Govou•, Fred (Baros 74), Malouda. Tr: Houllier

---

Stade Gerland, Lyon
6-03-2007, 20:45, 39 260, Mejuto G. ESP
Olympique Lyonnais   **0**

Coupet – Reveillere (Benzema 69), Squillaci, Cris•, Abidal, Tiago•, Diarra (Kallstrom• 46), Juninho, Govou (Wiltord 46), Fred•, Malouda. Tr: Houllier

Roma   **2**

Doni – Cassetti, Mexes, Chivu, Tonetto, De Rossi, Pizarro•, Taddei, Perrotta•, Mancini (Faty 90), Totti.
Tr: Spalletti

Stade Félix-Bollaert, Lens
20-02-2007, 20:45, 40 725, Braamhaar NED
Lille OSC   **0**

Sylva• – Chalme, Plestan, Tavlaridis, Tafforeau, Bodmer, Makoun, Debuchy•, Fauvergue• (Cabaye 57), Obraniak (Bastos 90), Odemwingie (Audel 75).
Tr: Puel

Manchester United   **1**
                                        Giggs [83]

Van der Sar – Neville, Ferdinand, Vidic•, Evra•, Cristiano Ronaldo (Saha 67), Carrick, Scholes (O'Shea 90), Giggs, Rooney, Larsson. Tr: Ferguson

---

Old Trafford, Manchester
7-03-2007, 19:45, 75 182, Medina C. ESP
Manchester United   **1**
                                      Larsson [72]

Van der Sar – Neville, Ferdinand, Vidic, Silvestre, Carrick, Scholes, O'Shea, Cristiano Ronaldo• (Richardson• 74), Larsson (Smith 81), Rooney (Park 81). Tr: Ferguson

Lille OSC   **0**

Sylva – Chalmé•, Tavlaridis, Plestan•, Tafforeau•, Makoun•, Dumont (Fauvergue 74), Keita, Obraniak, Bastos (Debuchy 46), Odemwingie (Mirallas 74).
Tr: Puel

Estádio do Dragão, Porto
21-02-2007, 19:45, 50 216, Busacca SUI
FC Porto   **1**
                                    Raul Meireles [12]

Helton – Bosingwa, Pepe•, Bruno Alves, Fucile (Bruno Moaes 65), Gonzalez, Paulo Assuncao, Raul Meireles (Cech 56), Lopez, Helder Postiga (Adriano 77), Quaresma. Tr: Ferreira

Chelsea   **1**
                                     Shevchenko [16]

Cech• – Diarra, Terry (Robben 13; Mikel 46), Ricardo Carvalho, Bridge, Essien•, Makelele•, Ballack•, Lampard, Shevchenko (Kalou 88), Drogba.
Tr: Mourinho

Stamford Bridge, London
6-03-2007, 19:45, 39 113, Rosetti ITA
Chelsea   **2**
                                 Robben [48], Ballack [79]

Cech – Diarra• (Paulo Ferreira 66), Ricardo Carvalho, Essien, Cole.A, Robben•, Makelele (Mikel 46), Ballack, Lampard, Shevchenko (Kalou 84), Drogba. Tr: Mourinho

FC Porto   **1**
                                      Quaresma [15]

Helton – Fucile•, Pepe, Bruno Alves, Cech (Adriano• 56), Gonzalez, Ricardo Costa, Paulo Assuncao, Raul Meireles (Ibson 56), Lopez (Bruno Moraes 82), Quaresma•. Tr: Ferreira

---

San Siro, Milan
21-02-2007, 20:45, 25 269, Hansson SWE
Internazionale   **2**
                                 Cambiasso [29], Maicon [76]

Julio Cesar – Maicon, Cordoba, Materazzi, Burdisso•, Stankovic, Cambiasso (Dacourt 31), Figo (Solari 89), Zanetti•, Crespo (Cruz 68), Ibrahimovic. Tr: Mancini

Valencia   **2**
                                   Villa [64], Silva [86]

Canizares – Miguel, Ayala, Albiol, Moretti, Angulo (Joaquin 83), Marchena• Albelda•, Silva (Jorge Lopez 990), Morientes (Hugo Viana 76), Villa.
Tr: Flores

Mestalla, Valencia
6-03-2007, 20:45, 48 109, Stark GER
Valencia   **0**

Canizares• – Miguel, Ayala, Albiol, Moretti, Angulo• (Joaquin 77), Baraja (Hugo Viana 38), Marchena, Silva, Morientes (Vicente 67), Villa. Tr: Flores

Internazionale   **0**

Julio Cesar – Maicon•, Cordoba, Materazzi•, Maxwell (Grosso 75), Zanetti, Burdisso, Stankovic, Dacourt (Figo 64), Crespo (Cruz 58), Ibrahimovic•.
Tr: Mancini

Philips Stadion, Eindhoven
20-02-2007, 20:45, 35 100, Ovrebo NOR
PSV Eindhoven   **1**
                                        Méndez [61]

Gomes – Kromkamp, Alex, Da Costa (Sun 66), Salcido, Culina, Simons, Cocu, Méndez, Kone, Diego Tardelli (Vayrynen 75). Tr: Koeman

Arsenal   **0**

Lehmann – Gallas, Toure, Senderos•, Clichy, Hleb (Julio Baptista 76), Gilberto Silva, Fabregas, Rosicky, Henry, Adebayor. Tr: Wenger

---

Emirates Stadium, London
7-03-2007, 19:45, 50 073, Hamer LUX
Arsenal   **1**
                                       Alex OG [58]

Lehmann – Toure, Gilberto Silva, Gallas, Clichy (Walcott 85), Hleb, Fabregas•, Denilson, Ljunberg (Diaby 76), Adebayor, Julio Baptista (Henry 66).
Tr: Wenger

PSV Eindhoven   **1**
                                         Alex [83]

Gomes – Feher•, Alex, Salcido, Sun, Mendez (Vayrynen 90), Simons, Cocu, Culina, Kone (Afellay 41), Farfan (Addo 89). Tr: Koeman

---

Camp Nou, Barcelona
21-02-2007, 20:45, 93 641
Barcelona   **1**
                                         Deco [14]

Valdes – Belletti•, Marquez, Puyol, Zambrotta•, Xavi (Giuly 65), Motta (Iniesta 54), Deco, Messi, Saviola (Gudjohnsen 82), Ronaldinho. Tr: Rijkaard

Liverpool   **2**
                                   Bellamy [43], Riise [74]

Reina – Arbeloa, Carragher, Agger•, Riise, Finnan, Sissoko• (Zenden 84), Gerrard, Xabi Alonso, Bellamy• (Pennant 80), Kuyt• (Crouch 90). Tr: Benitez

Anfield, Liverpool
6-03-2007, 19:45, 42 579, Fandel GER

Liverpool	0

Reina• – Finnan, Carragher, Agger, Arbeloa•, Gerrard, Sissoko•, Xabi Alonso, Riise (Fabio Aurelio 77), Bellamy (Pennant• 68), Kuyt (Crouch 89). Tr: Benitez

Barcelona	1
	Gudjohsen 75

Valdes – Thuram• (Gudjohnsen 71), Marquez, Puyol, Oleguer, Xavi, Iniesta, Deco, Messi, Eto'o (Giuly 61), Ronaldinho. Tr: Rijkaard

QUARTER-FINALS

San Siro, Milan
3-04-2007, 20:45, 67 500, Baskakov RUS

Milan	2
	Pirlo 40, Kaká 84p

Dida – Oddo, Nesta, Maldini, Jankulovski (Kaladze 87), Gattuso, Pirlo, Ambrosini, Seedorf (Gourcuff 85), Kaka, Gilardino• (Inzaghi 71). Tr: Ancelotti

Bayern München	2
	Van Buyten 2 78 93+

Rensing – Sagnol (Lell 68), Lucio•, Van Buyten, Lahm, Salihamidzic•, Hargreaves, Ottl, Schweinsteiger, Makaay (Santa Cruz 86), Podolski (Pizarro 68). Tr: Hitzfeld

Allianz-Arena, Munich
11-04-2007, 20:45, 66 000, Mejuto G. ESP

Bayern München	0

Kahn – Salihamidzic•, Lucio, Van Buyten, Lahm, Ottl (Santa Cruz 46), Hargreaves, Van Bommel•, Lell (Gorlitz 77), Makaay (Pizarro 69), Podolski. Tr: Hitzfeld

Milan	2
	Seedorf 27, Inzaghi 31

Dida – Oddo, Nesta, Maldini, Jankulovski, Gattuso (Cafu 87), Pirlo, Ambrosini, Seedorf (Gourcuff 80), Kaka, Inzaghi (Serginho 70). Tr: Ancelotti

Stadio Olimpico, Rome
4-04-2007, 20:45, 68 389, Fandel GER

Roma	2
	Taddei 44, Vucinic 66

Doni – Cassetti, Mexes, Chivu, Panucci, De Rossi, Wilhelmsson (Vucinic 62), Taddei (Rosi 82), Perrotta•, Mancini, Totti. Tr: Spalletti

Manchester United	1
	Rooney 60

Van der Sar – Brown, O'Shea, Ferdinand, Heinze•, Cristiano Ronaldo, Carrick, Scholes••34, Giggs (Saha 77), Rooney, Solskjaer• (Fletcher 72). Tr: Ferguson

Old Trafford, Manchester
10-04-2007, 19:45, 74 476, Michel SVK

Manchester United	7
	Carrick 2 11 60, Smith 17, Rooney 19,
	Cristiano Ronaldo 2 44 49, Evra 81

Van der Sar – O'Shea (Evra 52), Ferdinand•, Brown, Heinze, Cristiano Ronaldo, Carrick (Richardson 73), Fletcher, Giggs (Solskjaer 61), Smith•, Rooney. Tr: Ferguson

Roma	1
	De Rossi 69

Doni – Cassetti, Mexes•, Chivu, Panucci, Pizarro, De Rossi (Faty 86), Wilhelmsson (Rosi 88), Vucinic, Mancini, Okaka (Chuka 90), Totti. Tr: Spalletti

Stamford Bridge, London
4-04-2007, 19:45, 38 065, De Bleeckere BEL

Chelsea	1
	Drogba 53

Cech – Diarra•, Ricardo Carvalho, Terry, Cole.A, Ballack, Mikel (Cole.J 75), Lampard, Kalou (Wright-Phillips 75), Shevchenko, Drogba•. Tr: Mourinho

Valencia	1
	Silva 30

Canizares – Miguel, Ayala•, Moretti, Del Horno, Joaquin (Hugo Viana 87), Albiol, Albelda•, Vicente (Angulo 58), Silva•, Villa (Jorge Lopez 90). Tr: Flores

Mestalla, Valencia
10-04-2007, 20:45, 47 280, Vassaras GRE

Valencia	1
	Morientes 32

Canizares – Miguel, Ayala•, Moretti, Del Horno•, Joaquin, Albelda•, Albiol, (Hugo Viana 72), Silva, Villa, Morientes (Angulo 65). Tr: Flores

Chelsea	2
	Shevchenko 52, Essien 90

Cech – Diarra (Cole.J 75), Ricardo Carvalho, Terry, Cole.A, Essien•, Mikel, Ballack•, Lampard (Makelele 90), Drogba, Shevchenko (Kalou 90). Tr: Mourinho

Philips Stadion, Eindhoven
3-04-2007, 20:45, 35 100, Layec FRA

PSV Eindhoven	0

Gomes – Kromkamp (Feher• 68), Da Costa, Simons, Salcido, Mendez (Kluivert• 51), Vayrynen, Cocu, Culina, Farfan (Sun Xiang 46), Diego Tardelli. Tr: Koeman

Liverpool	3
	Gerrard 27, Riise 49, Crouch 63

Reina – Finnan, Carragher, Agger, Riise (Zenden 66), Gerrard, Mascherano•, Xabi Alonso, Fabio Aurelio (Gonzalez 75), Crouch (Pennant 85), Kuyt•. Tr: Benitez

Anfield, Liverpool
11-04-2007, 19:45, 41 447, Rosetti ITA

Liverpool	1
	Crouch 67

Reina – Arbeloa, Hyypia, Agger (Paletta 79), Riise, Pennant, Sissoko, Xabi Alonso (Gonzalez 75), Zenden, Crouch, Bellamy (Fowler 17). Tr: Benitez

PSV Eindhoven	0

Gomes – Marcellis•64, Simons, Addo, Salcido•, Feher (Sun Xiang 63), Cocu, Vayrynen, Culina, Farfan (Kluivert 63), Kone (Van Eljden 72). Tr: Koeman

SEMI-FINALS

Old Trafford, Manchester
24-04-2007, 19:45, 73 820, Vassaras GRE

Manchester United	3
	Cristiano Ronaldo 5, Rooney 2 59 91+

Van der Sar – O'Shea, Brown, Heinze, Evra•, Fletcher, Carrick, Scholes, Cristiano Ronaldo, Rooney, Giggs•. Tr: Ferguson

Milan	2
	Kaká 2 22 37

Dida – Oddo, Nesta, Maldini (Bonera• 46), Jankulovski, Gattuso (Cafu 53), Pirlo, Ambrosini, Seedorf, Kaká•, Gilardino (Gourcuff 84). Tr: Ancelotti

San Siro, Milan
2-05-2007, 20:45, 67 500, De Bleeckere BEL

Milan	3
	Kaká 11, Seedorf 30, Gilardino 78

Dida – Oddo, Nesta, Kaladze, Jankulovski, Gattuso• (Cafu 84), Pirlo, Seedorf, Ambrosini•, Kaká (Favalli 86), Inzaghi (Gilardino 67). Tr: Ancelotti

Manchester United	0

Van der Sar – O'Shea (Saha 77), Brown, Vidic, Heinze, Fletcher, Scholes, Carrick, Cristiano Ronaldo•, Rooney, Giggs. Tr: Ferguson

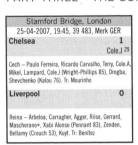

Stamford Bridge, London
25-04-2007, 19:45, 39 483, Merk GER

Chelsea 1

Cole.J [29]

Cech – Paulo Ferreira, Ricardo Carvalho, Terry, Cole.A,
Mikel, Lampard, Cole.J (Wright-Phillips 85), Drogba,
Shevchenko (Kalou 76). Tr: Mourinho

Liverpool 0

Reina – Arbeloa, Carragher, Agger, Riise, Gerrard,
Mascherano●, Xabi Alonso (Pennant 83), Zenden,
Bellamy (Crouch 53), Kuyt. Tr: Benitez

Anfield, Liverpool
1-05-2007, 19:45, 42 554, Mejuto G. ESP

Liverpool 1

Agger [22]

Reina – Finnan, Carragher, Agger●, Riise, Pennant
(Xabi Alonso 78), Gerrard, Mascherano (Fowler 118),
Zenden●, Kuyt, Crouch (Bellamy 106). Tr: Benitez

Chelsea 0

Cech – Paulo Ferreira, Essien, Terry, Cole.A●, Mikel,
Makelele (Geremi 118), Lampard, Cole.J (Robben 98),
Drogba, Kalou (Wright-Phillips 107). Tr: Mourinho

PENALTIES (LIVERPOOL WON 4-1)

Kuyt ✓; Geremi ✘; Gerrard ✓; Lampard ✓;
Xabi Alonso ✓; Robben ✘; Zenden ✓

UEFA CHAMPIONS LEAGUE FINAL 2007

OACA Spyro Louis, Athens
23–05–2007, 21:45, 63 800

MILAN   2 1   LIVERPOOL

Inzaghi 2 [45] [82]   Kuyt [89]

MILAN				MATCH STATS			LIVERPOOL			
1	GK	DIDA		4	Shots	10	88	REINA Pepe	GK	25
44	DF	ODDO Massimo		3	Shots on Goal	4		FINNAN Steve	DF	3
13	DF	NESTA Alessandro		15	Fouls Committed	27		CARRAGHER Jamie	DF	23
3	DF	MALDINI Paolo		4	Corner Kicks	6		AGGER Daniel	DF	5
18	DF	JANKULOVSKI Marek	80	3	Offside	3		RIISE John Arne	DF	6
8	MF	GATTUSO Gennaro		53	Possession %	47		PENNANT Jermaine	MF	16
21	MF	PIRLO Andrea						XABI ALONSO	MF	14
23	MF	AMBROSINI Massimo					78	MASCHERANO Javier	MF	20
10	MF	SEEDORF Clarence	92+		MATCH OFFICIALS		59	ZENDEN Boudewijn	MF	32
22	FW	KAKA			REFEREE			GERRARD Steven	MF	8
9	FW	INZAGHI Filippo	88		Herbert FANDEL GER			KUYT Dirk	FW	18
		Tr: ANCELOTTI Carlo			ASSISTANTS			Tr: BENITEZ Rafael		
		Substitutes			Carsten KADACH GER			Substitutes		
4	DF	KALADZE Kakha	80		Volker WEZEL GER		88	ARBELOA Alvaro	DF	2
11	FW	GILARDINO Alberto	88		4TH OFFICIAL		59	KEWELL Harry	MF	7
19	DF	FAVALLI Giuseppe	92+		Florian MEYER Ger		78	CROUCH Peter	FW	15

*It is the greatest victory we've had. Few people
believed we could do it, but we've done something extraordinary. Nobody expected it. When
I think back to December, we had to overcome
so many hurdles so that makes it a very special
victory. We maintained great harmony despite
the troubles. What I've achieved is due to the
fact that I feel I belong to Milan.*

Carlo Ancelotti

*In the first half we controlled the game, pushing
forward, creating chances, but we conceded a
bad goal, a deflection, at the end. In football
you need to take your chances. The problem
when you play Milan is that they are very well
organised and good on the counter. You need to
attack with balance and when you lose that
balance, one opportunity can kill you.*

Rafael Benitez

AEK ATHENS

Goalkeepers

22	Dionisis Chiotis	GRE
28	Stefano Sorrentino	ITA
84	Ioannis Arabatzis	GRE

Defenders

4	Evangelos Moras	GRE
5	Bruno Cirillo	ITA
13	Martin Pautasso	ARG
14	Stavros Tziortziopoulos	GRE
15	Socratis Papastathopoulos	GRE
24	Ifeanyi Udeze	NGA
31	Nikolaos Georgeas	GRE
55	Traianos Dellas	GRE

Midfielders

7	Ilias Kiriakidis	GRE
10	Panagiotis Kone	GRE
16	Akis Zikos	GRE
17	Vladimir Iviç	SRB
19	Panagiotis Lagos	GRE
23	Vassilios Lakis	GRE
25	Emerson	BRA
56	Perparim Hetemaj	FIN
88	Dániel Tõzsér	HUN

Forwards

9	Andrija Delibasiç	SRB
11	Gustavo Manduca	BRA
33	Nikolaos Liberopoulos	GRE
35	Pantelis Kapetanos	GRE
99	Júlio César	BRA

ANDERLECHT

Goalkeepers

1	Daniel Zítka	CZE
13	Silvio Proto	BEL
22	Davy Schollen	BEL
25	Jan Van Steenberghe	BEL

Defenders

3	Olivier Deschacht	BEL
6	Jelle Van Damme	BEL
23	Roland Juhász	HUN
26	Nicolas Pareja	ARG
31	Mark De Man	BEL
32	Cor Gillis	BEL
33	Hervé Kage	BEL
34	Sven Kums	BEL
37	Anthony Vanden Borre	BEL

Midfielders

4	Yves Vanderhaeghe	BEL
5	Lucas Biglia	ARG
8	Cristian Leiva	ARG
10	Hassan Ahmed	EGY
14	Bart Goor	BEL
30	Gérard Lifondja	BEL
42	Sébastien Siani	CMR
43	Cédric Ciza	BEL

Forwards

7	Mohamed Tchite	CGO
9	Mbo Mpenza	BEL
11	Mbark Boussoufa	MOR
17	Dieudonné Mbokani Bezua	CGO
18	Sami Allagui	GER
24	Serhat Akin	TUR
29	Nicolas Frutos	ARG
38	Roland Lamah	BEL

ARSENAL

Goalkeepers

1	Jens Lehmann	GER
21	Mart Poom	EST
24	Manuel Almunia	ESP
36	Vito Mannone	ITA

Defenders

5	Kolo Touré	CIV
6	Philippe Senderos	SUI
10	William Gallas	FRA
20	Johan Djourou	SUI
22	Gaël Clichy	FRA
27	Emmanuel Eboué	CIV
31	Justin Hoyte	ENG
33	Matthew Connolly	ENG
34	Ryan Garry	ENG
45	Armand Traoré	FRA

Midfielders

2	Abou Diaby	FRA
4	Cesc Fàbregas	ESP
7	Tomáš Rosický	CZE
8	Fredrik Ljungberg	SWE
9	Julio Baptista	BRA
13	Aleksandr Hleb	BLR
15	Denilson	BRA
16	Mathieu Flamini	FRA
19	Gilberto	BRA
42	Francisco Perez	ESP
43	Mark Randall	ENG

Forwards

11	Robin van Persie	NED
14	Thierry Henry	FRA
25	Emmanuel Adebayor	TOG
30	Jérémie Aliadière	FRA
32	Theo Walcott	ENG

BARCELONA

Goalkeepers

1	Víctor Valdés	ESP
25	Albert Jorquera	ESP
28	Ruben Martínez	ESP

Defenders

2	Juliano Belletti	BRA
4	Rafael Márquez	MEX
5	Carles Puyol	ESP
11	Gianluca Zambrotta	ITA
12	Giovanni van Bronckhorst	NED
15	Edmílson	BRA
16	Sylvinho	BRA
21	Lilian Thuram	FRA
23	Oleguer Presas	ESP
26	Jesus Olmo Lozano	ESP
29	Marc Valiente	ESP

Midfielders

3	Thiago Motta	BRA
6	Xavi Hernández	ESP
20	Deco	POR
24	Andrés Iniesta	ESP
27	Jordi Gómez	ESP
30	Lluis Sastre	ESP
32	Marc Crosas	ESP

Forwards

7	Eidur Gudjohnsen	ISL
9	Ludovic Giuly	FRA
9	Samuel Eto'o	CMR
10	Ronaldinho	BRA
18	Santiago Ezquerro	ESP
19	Lionel Messi	ARG
22	Javier Saviola	ARG
31	Giovani Dos Santos	MEX

BAYERN MUNCHEN

Goalkeepers

1	Oliver Kahn	GER
22	Michael Rensing	GER
29	Bernd Dreher	GER

Defenders

2	Willy Sagnol	FRA
3	Lucio	BRA
6	Daniel Van Buyten	BEL
6	Martín Demichelis	ARG
18	Andreas Görlitz	GER
21	Philipp Lahm	GER
25	Valérien Ismaël	FRA
30	Christian Lell	GER
37	Christian Saba	GHA

Midfielders

7	Mehmet Scholl	GER
8	Ali Karimi	IRN
17	Mark van Bommel	NED
19	Julio dos Santos	PAR
20	Hasan Salihamidžiç	BIH
23	Owen Hargreaves	ENG
26	Sebastian Deisler	GER
31	Bastian Schweinsteiger	GER

Forwards

10	Roy Makaay	NED
11	Lukas Podolski	GER
11	Claudio Pizarro	PER
24	Roque Santa Cruz	PAR
34	Stefan Maierhofer	AUT

BENFICA

Goalkeepers

1	José Moreira	POR
12	Quim	POR
31	Moretto	BRA

Defenders

2	Pedro Correia	POR
3	Anderson	BRA
4	Luisão	BRA
6	Léo	BRA
11	Miguelito	POR
13	Alcides	BRA
16	Nélson	POR
33	Ricardo Rocha	POR

Midfielders

6	Petit	POR
7	Marco Ferreira	POR
8	Konstantinos Katsouranis	GRE
10	Rui Costa	POR
14	Diego Souza	BRA
15	Paulo Jorge	POR
16	Beto	BRA
18	Manú	POR
19	Andrei Karyaka	RUS
20	Nuno Assis	POR
26	Georgios Karagounis	GRE
28	João Coimbra	POR

Forwards

9	Mantorras	ANG
17	Kikin	MEX
20	Simão	POR
21	Nuno Gomes	POR
30	Fabrizio Miccoli	ITA

BORDEAUX

Goalkeepers

1	Kévin Olimpa	FRA
16	Ulrich Ramé	FRA
30	Mathieu Valverde	FRA

Defenders

2	Paul Baysse	FRA
3	Henrique	BRA
5	Fernando Menegazzo	BRA
6	Franck Jurietti	FRA
13	David Jemmali	TUN
21	Joseph Enakarhire	NGA
23	Florian Marange	FRA
25	Gérald Cid	FRA
27	Marc Planus	FRA
28	Benoît Tremoulinas	FRA
31	Bruno Ecuele Manga	GAB

Midfielders

8	Alejandro César Alonso	ARG
11	Vladimír Šmicer	CZE
14	Johan Micoud	FRA
17	Geraldo Mauricio Wendel	BRA
18	Julien Faubert	FRA
19	Pierre Ducasse	FRA
20	Stéphane Dalmat	FRA
24	Rio Antonio Mavuba	FRA
32	Abdou Traore	MLI

Forwards

7	Lilian Laslandes	FRA
9	Jean-Claude Darcheville	FRA
10	Juan Pablo Francia	ARG
12	Edixon Perea	COL
26	Gabriel Obertan	FRA
29	Marouane Chamakh	MAR
34	Cheick Tidiane Diabate	MLI

CELTIC

Goalkeepers

1	Artur Boruc	POL
21	Mark Brown	SCO
47	Michael McGovern	NIR

Defenders

3	Lee Naylor	ENG
5	Gary Caldwell	SCO
6	Dianbobo Balde	FRA
12	Mark Wilson	SCO
24	Jean-Joël Perrier Doumbé	FRA
41	John Kennedy	SCO
44	Stephen McManus	SCO
48	Darren O'Dea	IRL
49	Scott Cuthbert	SCO

Midfielders

2	Paul Telfer	SCO
15	Evander Sno	NED
16	Thomas Gravesen	DEN
18	Neil Lennon	NIR
20	Jiří Jarošík	CZE
25	Shunsuke Nakamura	JPN
42	Michael McGlinchey	SCO
46	Aiden McGeady	IRL
52	Simon Ferry	SCO
54	Ryan Conroy	SCO

Forwards

7	Maciej Żurawski	POL
9	Kenny Miller	SCO
10	Jan Vennegoor of Hesselink	NED
14	Derek Riordan	SCO
37	Craig Beattie	SCO
51	Nicholas Riley	SCO

CHELSEA

Goalkeepers

1	Petr Cech	CZE
22	Magnus Hedman	SWE
23	Carlo Cudicini	ITA
40	Hilário	POR

Defenders

3	Ashley Cole	ENG
6	Ricardo Carvalho	POR
9	Khalid Boulahrouz	NED
18	Wayne Bridge	ENG
20	Paulo Ferreira	POR
26	John Terry	ENG
33	Nuno Morais	POR

Midfielders

4	Claude Makelele	FRA
5	Michael Essien	GHA
8	Frank Lampard	ENG
10	Joe Cole	ENG
12	John Obi Mikel	NGA
13	Michael Ballack	GER
14	Geremi	CMR
16	Arjen Robben	NED
19	Lassana Diarra	FRA
24	Shaun Wright-Phillips	ENG
44	Michael Mancienne	ENG
46	James Smith	ENG

Forwards

7	Andriy Shevchenko	UKR
11	Didier Drogba	CIV
21	Salomon Kalou	CIV

CSKA MOSKVA

Goalkeepers

1	Veniamin Mandrykin	RUS
35	Igor Akinfeev	RUS
77	Vladimir Gabulov	RUS

Defenders

2	Deividas Semberas	LTU
4	Sergei Ignashevich	RUS
6	Aleksei Berezutskiy	RUS
15	Chidi Odiah	NGA
24	Vasili Berezutskiy	RUS
39	Ivan Taranov	RUS
50	Anton Grigoryev	RUS
57	Sergei Gorelov	RUS

Midfielders

7	Daniel Carvalho	BRA
8	Rolan Gusev	RUS
17	Milos Krasic	SRB
18	Yuri Zhirkov	RUS
20	Dudu	BRA
22	Evgeni Aldonin	RUS
25	Elvir Rahimic	BIH
37	Kirill Kochubei	RUS

Forwards

9	Ivica Olic	CRO
10	Jô	BRA
11	Vágner Love	BRA
40	Aleksandr Salugin	RUS

DYNAMO KYIV

Goalkeepers

1	Olexandr Shovkovskiy	UKR
21	Taras Lutsenko	UKR
55	Olexandr Rybka	UKR

Defenders

4	Rodolfo	BRA
6	Goran Sabljic	CRO
26	Andriy Nesmachniy	UKR
27	Vladyslav Vaschuk	UKR
32	Goran Gavrancic	SRB
39	Denys Dedechko	UKR
44	Rodrigo	BRA
81	Marjan Markovic	SRB

Midfielders

7	Carlos Corrêa	BRA
8	Valentin Belkevich	BLR
10	Florin Cernat	ROU
14	Ruslan Rotan	UKR
15	Diogo Rincón	BRA
17	Taras Mikhalik	UKR
20	Oleh Gusev	UKR
29	Vitaliy Mandzyuk	UKR
30	Badr El Kaddouri	MAR
37	Ayila Yussuf	NGA
40	Harrison Otalvaro	COL

Forwards

5	Serhiy Rebrov	UKR
9	Kleber	BRA
11	José Moreno	COL
16	Maksim Shatskikh	UZB
23	Maris Verpakovskis	LVA
25	Artem Milevskiy	UKR
78	Volodymyr Lysenko	UKR
88	Olexandr Aliyev	UKR

GALATASARAY

Goalkeepers

1	Faryd Mondragón	COL
12	Aykut Erçetin	TUR
17	Fevzi Elmas	TUR

Defenders

2	Stjepan Tomas	CRO
4	Rigobert Song	CMR
5	Orhan Ak	TUR
19	Cihan Haspolatlı	TUR
21	Emre Asık	TUR
28	Tolga Seyhan	TUR
67	Ergün Penbe	TUR

Midfielders

7	Okan Buruk	TUR
11	Hasan Sas	TUR
14	Mehmet Topal	TUR
16	Marcelo Adrian Carrusca	ARG
18	Ayhan Akman	TUR
22	Sasa Ilic	SRB
23	Junichi Inamoto	JPN
24	Mehmet Güven	TUR
25	Ferhat Öztorun	TUR
26	Aydın Yılmaz	TUR
35	Oguz Sabankay	TUR
55	Sabri Sarıoglu	TUR
66	Arda Turan	TUR

Forwards

9	Hakan Sükür	TUR
10	Necati Ates	TUR
27	Ozgürcan Ozcan	TUR
58	Hasan Kabze	TUR
99	Umit Karan	TUR

HAMBURGER SV

Goalkeepers

1	Stefan Wachter	GER
12	Sascha Kirschstein	GER
29	Wolfgang Hesl	GER

Defenders

2	Juan Pablo Sorin	ARG
3	Thimothée Atouba	CMR
4	Bastian Reinhardt	GER
8	Joris Mathijsen	NED
10	Vincent Kompany	BEL
16	René Klingbeil	GER
20	Guy Demel	FRA

Midfielders

6	Raphael Wicky	SUI
7	Mehdi Mahdavikia	IRN
13	Mario Fillinger	GER
14	David Jarolim	CZE
15	Piotr Trochowski	GER
18	Oliver Hampel	GER
23	Rafael van der Vaart	NED
27	Alexander Laas	GER
28	Nigel de Jong	NED
30	Collin Benjamin	NAM
33	Benny Feilhaber	USA

Forwards

9	José Paolo Guerrero	PER
11	Benjamin Lauth	GER
17	Boubacar Sanogo	CIV
22	Besart Berisha	ALB
34	Sidney Sam	GER
37	Rouwen Hennings	GER
38	Danijel Ljuboja	SRB

INTERNAZIONALE

Goalkeepers

1	Francesco Toldo	ITA
12	Júlio César	BRA
22	Paolo Orlandoni	ITA
35	Paolo Tornaghi	ITA

Defenders

2	Iván Córdoba	COL
4	Javier Zanetti	ARG
6	Maxwell	BRA
11	Fabio Grosso	ITA
13	Maicon	BRA
16	Nicolás Burdisso	ARG
23	Marco Materazzi	ITA
25	Walter Samuel	ARG
36	Simone Fautario	ITA
46	Dennis Esposito	ITA
77	Marco Andreolli	ITA

Midfielders

5	Dejan Stankovic	SRB
7	Luís Figo	POR
14	Patrick Vieira	FRA
15	Olivier Dacourt	FRA
19	Esteban Cambiasso	ARG
21	Santiago Solari	ARG
47	Francesco Bolzoni	ITA
54	Gabriele Puccio	ITA
91	Mariano González	ARG

Forwards

8	Zlatan Ibrahimovic	SWE
9	Julio Cruz	ARG
10	Adriano	BRA
18	Hernán Crespo	ARG
20	Alvaro Recoba	URU
58	Jonathan Biabiany	FRA

KØBENHAVN

Goalkeepers

1	Jesper Christiansen	DEN
21	Thomas Villadsen	DEN
31	Benny Gall	DEN

Defenders

2	Lars Jacobsen	DEN
5	Brede Hangeland	NOR
14	Michael Gravgaard	DEN
15	André Bergdølmo	NOR
16	Dan Thomassen	DEN
17	Oscar Wendt	SWE
25	Jamil Fearrington	DEN
26	Nikolaj Hansen	DEN

Midfielders

4	Hjalte Nørregaard	DEN
6	Tobias Linderoth	SWE
8	Michael Silberbauer	DEN
10	Jesper Grønkjær	DEN
13	Atiba Hutchinson	CAN
23	William Kvist	DEN
24	Jeppe Brandrup	DEN
28	Martin Bergvold	DEN

Forwards

9	Fredrik Berglund	SWE
11	Marcus Allbäck	SWE
20	Razak Pimpong	GHA
27	Martin Bernburg	DEN

LEVSKI SOFIA

Goalkeepers

1	Georgi Petkov	BUL
12	Bozhidar Mitrev	BUL
47	Lazar Ivanov	BUL
88	Nikolay Mihaylov	BUL

Defenders

3	Zhivko Milanov	BUL
4	Igor Tomasic	BUL
5	Borislav Hristov	BUL
11	Elin Topuzakov	BUL
14	Veselin Minev	BUL
20	Stanislav Angelov	BUL
25	Lucio Wagner	BUL
36	Borislav Iliev	BUL
44	Todor Stoev	BUL

Midfielders

6	Richard Eromoigbe	NGA
7	Daniel Borimirov	BUL
15	Georgi Sarmov	BUL
18	Miroslav Ivanov	BUL
19	Atanas Bornosuzov	BUL
21	Dimitar Telkiyski	BUL
27	Cédric Bardon	FRA
39	Dimitar Dimitrov	BUL
43	Spas Bayraktarov	BUL
45	Hristo Lemperov	BUL
46	Shenol Galip	BUL

Forwards

9	Georgi Ivanov	BUL
10	Hristo Yovov	BUL
16	Maryan Ognyanov	BUL
17	Valeri Domovchiyski	BUL
24	Nikolay Dimitrov	BUL
28	Emil Angelov	BUL
30	Lachezar Baltanov	BUL

LILLE OSC

Goalkeepers
1	Tony Sylva	SEN
16	Grégory Malicki	FRA
30	Laurent Pichon	FRA
40	Alexandre Oukidja	FRA

Defenders
4	Efstathios Tavlaridis	GRE
5	Rafael Schmitz	BRA
19	Peter Franquart	FRA
20	Grégory Tafforeau	FRA
22	Milivoje Vitakic	SRB
25	Nicolas Plestan	FRA
26	Stephan Lichtsteiner	SUI
36	Emerson	BRA

Midfielders
2	Mathieu Debuchy	FRA
7	Yohan Cabaye	FRA
8	Michel Bastos	BRA
9	Johan Audel	FRA
12	Mathieu Bodmer	FRA
17	Jean II Makoun	CMR
18	Mathieu Robail	FRA
21	Matthieu Chalmé	FRA
29	Stéphane Dumont	FRA
31	Jerry Van Dam	FRA
34	Henry Ewane Elong	CMR
35	Ludovic Obraniak	FRA
37	Aurélien Chedjou	CMR

Forwards
11	Souleymane Youla	GUI
13	Nicolas Fauvergue	FRA
14	Peter Odemwingie	NGA
23	Kader Keita	CIV
27	Kevin Mirallas	BEL
32	Chris Makiese	FRA

LIVERPOOL

Goalkeepers
1	Jerzy Dudek	POL
25	Pepe Reina	ESP
30	Daniele Padelli	ITA
40	David Martin	ENG

Defenders
2	Álvaro Arbeloa	ESP
3	Steve Finnan	IRL
4	Sami Hyypiä	FIN
5	Daniel Agger	DEN
6	John Arne Riise	NOR
12	Fabio Aurelio	BRA
23	Jamie Carragher	ENG
29	Gabriel Paletta	ARG

Midfielders
7	Harry Kewell	AUS
8	Steven Gerrard	ENG
11	Mark González	CHI
14	Xabi Alonso	ESP
16	Jermaine Pennant	ENG
20	Javier Mascherano	ARG
22	Mohamed Sissoko	FRA
24	Paul Anderson	ENG
32	Boudewijn Zenden	NED

Forwards
9	Robbie Fowler	ENG
15	Peter Crouch	ENG
17	Craig Bellamy	WAL
18	Dirk Kuyt	NED

MAN UNITED

Goalkeepers
1	Edwin van der Sar	NED
29	Tomasz Kuszczak	POL
38	Thomas Heaton	ENG
39	Ron Robert Zieler	GER

Defenders
2	Gary Neville	ENG
3	Patrice Evra	FRA
4	Gabriel Heinze	ARG
5	Rio Ferdinand	ENG
6	Wes Brown	ENG
15	Nemanja Vidic	SRB
22	John O'Shea	IRL
27	Mikaël Silvestre	FRA
32	Craig Cathcart	NIR
34	Ryan Shawcross	ENG
35	Kieran Lee	ENG

Midfielders
11	Ryan Giggs	WAL
13	Park Ji Sung	KOR
16	Michael Carrick	ENG
18	Paul Scholes	ENG
23	Kieran Richardson	ENG
24	Darren Fletcher	SCO
33	Chris Eagles	ENG
49	Richard Jones	ENG

Forwards
7	Cristiano Ronaldo	POR
8	Wayne Rooney	ENG
9	Louis Saha	FRA
14	Alan Smith	ENG
17	Henrik Larsson	SWE
20	Ole Gunnar Solskjær	NOR
21	Dong Fangzhuo	CHN

MILAN

Goalkeepers
1	Dida	BRA
16	Zeljko Kalac	AUS
26	Marco Storari	ITA
29	Valerio Fiori	ITA

Defenders
2	Cafu	BRA
3	Paolo Maldini	ITA
4	Kakha Kaladze	GEO
5	Alessandro Costacurta	ITA
13	Alessandro Nesta	ITA
17	Dario Simic	CRO
18	Marek Jankulovski	CZE
19	Giuseppe Favalli	ITA
25	Daniele Bonera	ITA
27	Serginho	BRA
31	Luca Antonelli	ITA
32	Cristian Brocchi	ITA
36	Matteo Darmiani	ITA
44	Massimo Oddo	ITA

Midfielders
8	Gennaro Gattuso	ITA
10	Clarence Seedorf	NED
20	Yoann Gourcuff	FRA
21	Andrea Pirlo	ITA
22	Kaká	BRA
23	Massimo Ambrosini	ITA
28	Alex Guerci	ITA
33	Davide Di Gennaro	ITA

Forwards
7	Ricardo Oliveira	BRA
9	Filippo Inzaghi	ITA
11	Alberto Gilardino	ITA
15	Marco Borriello	ITA

OL. LYONNAIS

Goalkeepers
1	Grégory Coupet	FRA
25	Joan Hartock	FRA
30	Rémy Vercoutre	FRA
35	Jérémy Aymes	FRA

Defenders
2	François Clerc	FRA
3	Cris	BRA
4	Patrick Müller	SUI
5	Claudio Caçapa	BRA
12	Anthony Réveillère	FRA
20	Eric Abidal	FRA
23	Jérémy Berthod	FRA
29	Sébastien Squillaci	FRA
32	Sandy Paillot	FRA

Midfielders
6	Kim Källström	SWE
8	Juninho Pernambucano	BRA
10	Florent Malouda	FRA
15	Alou Diarra	FRA
21	Tiago	POR
24	Romain Beynie	FRA
26	Fábio Santos	BRA
28	Jérémy Toulalan	FRA
40	Loosemy Karaboue	FRA
41	Damien Plessis	FRA

Forwards
7	Milan Baros	CZE
11	Fred	BRA
14	Sidney Govou	FRA
18	Hatem Ben Arfa	FRA
19	Karim Benzema	FRA
22	Sylvain Wiltord	FRA
27	Anthony Mounier	FRA
34	Loïc Remy	FRA

OLYMPIACOS

Goalkeepers
34	Kleopas Giannou	GRE
71	Antonios Nikopolidis	GRE
74	Tomislav Butina	CRO
87	Leonidas Panagopoulos	GRE

Defenders
2	Christos Patsatzoglou	GRE
3	Didier Domi	FRA
14	Michal Zewlakow	POL
19	Athanasios Kostoulas	GRE
27	Abdeslam Ouaddou	MOR
30	Anastasios Pantos	GRE
32	Georgios Anatolakis	GRE
55	Júlio César	BRA

Midfielders
1	Pantelis Kafes	GRE
6	Ieroklis Stoltidis	GRE
7	Nery Alberto Castillo	URU
8	Milos Maric	YUG
10	Rivaldo	BRA
11	Predrag Djordjevic	YUG
16	Marco Né	CIV
17	Yiannis Taralidis	GRE
21	Grigoris Georgatos	GRE
28	Konstantinos Mendrinos	GRE

Forwards
9	Yiannis Okkas	CYP
18	Félix Borja	ECU
23	Michalis Konstantinou	CYP
40	Haruna Babangida	NGA
77	Charilaos Pappas	GRE

PORTO

Goalkeepers
1	Helton	BRA
24	Paulo Ribeiro	POR
32	Hugo Ventura	POR
99	Vítor Baía	POR

Defenders
2	Ricardo Costa	POR
3	Pepe	BRA
5	Marek Cech	SVK
12	Bosingwa	POR
13	Fucile	URU
14	Bruno Alves	POR
25	Lucas Buccolini	ITA
26	João Paulo	POR

Midfielders
6	Ibson	BRA
7	Ricardo Quaresma	POR
8	Lucho González	ARG
10	Anderson	BRA
14	Raul Meireles	POR
18	Paulo Assunção	BRA
21	Alan	BRA
30	Fabinho	POR
35	André Castro	POR
36	Rui Pedro	POR

Forwards
9	Lisandro López	ITA
17	Vieirinha	POR
19	Tomislav Šokota	CRO
20	Jorginho	BRA
22	Renteria Cuesta	COL
23	Hélder Postiga	POR
28	Adriano	BRA
29	Bruno Moraes	BRA
33	Daniel Candeias	POR

PSV

Goalkeepers
1	Heurelho Gomes	BRA
21	Oscar Moens	NED
31	Ruud Boffin	BEL
46	Gino Mommers	NED

Defenders
2	Jan Kromkamp	NED
3	Michael Reiziger	NED
4	Alex	BRA
5	Michael Ball	ENG
14	Manuel Da Costa	POR
18	Eric Addo	GHA
19	Michael Lamey	NED
22	Csaba Fehér	HUN
23	Carlos Salcido	MEX
28	Sun Xiang	CHN
32	Jelle De Bock	BEL

Midfielders
6	Timmy Simons	BEL
7	Mika Väyrynen	FIN
8	Phillip Cocu	NED
11	Edison Méndez	ECU
20	Ibrahim Afellay	NED
29	Arvid Smit	NED
36	Marten Boverhof	NED
50	Jasper Waalkens	NED

Forwards
9	Patrick Kluivert	NED
10	Arouna Koné	CIV
15	Jason Culina	AUS
16	Ismaïl Aissati	NED
17	Jefferson Farfán	PER
26	Tardelli Diego	BRA
33	Roy Beerens	NED

REAL MADRID

Goalkeepers
1	Iker Casillas	ESP
13	Diego López	ESP
28	Antonio Adán	ESP
29	Francisco Casilla	ESP

Defenders
2	Michel Salgado	ESP
3	Roberto Carlos	BRA
4	Sergio Ramos	ESP
5	Fabio Cannavaro	ITA
11	Cicinho	BRA
12	Marcelo	BRA
15	Raúl Bravo	ESP
21	Iván Helguera	ESP
22	Paco Pavón	ESP
24	Álvaro Mejía	ESP
38	Miguel Torres	FSP

Midfielders
6	Mahamadou Diarra	MLI
8	Emerson	BRA
14	Guti	ESP
16	Fernando Gago	ARG
23	David Beckham	ENG
27	Rubén de la Red	ESP
36	Miguel Nieto	ESP
39	Borja Valero	ESP

Forwards
7	Raúl González	ESP
10	Robinho	BRA
17	Ruud Van Nistelrooij	NED
18	Antonio Cassano	ITA
19	José Antonio Reyes	ESP
20	Gonzalo Higuaín	ARG
26	Javi García	ESP

ROMA

Goalkeepers
1	Gianluca Curci	ITA
24	Carlo Zotti	ITA
27	Julio Sergio Bertagnoli	BRA
32	Doni	BRA

Defenders
2	Christian Panucci	ITA
3	Gilberto Martínez	CRC
5	Philippe Mexes	FRA
13	Cristian Chivu	ROU
19	Rodrigo Defendi	BRA
21	Matteo Ferrari	ITA
22	Max Tonetto	ITA
77	Marco Cassetti	ITA

Midfielders
4	Christian Wilhelmsson	SWE
7	David Pizarro	CHI
8	Alberto Aquilani	ITA
11	Taddei	BRA
14	Ricardo Faty	FRA
16	Daniele De Rossi	ITA
18	Valerio Virga	ITA
19	Simone Perrotta	ITA
28	Aleandro Rosi	ITA

Forwards
9	Vincenzo Montella	ITA
10	Francesco Totti	ITA
23	Mirko Vucinic	SRB
30	Mancini	BRA
35	Stefano Okaka Chuka	NGA
39	Claudio Della Penna	ITA

SHAKHTAR

Goalkeepers
1	Stipe Pletikosa	CRO
12	Dmytro Shutkov	UKR
35	Bohdan Shust	UKR

Defenders
3	Tomás Hübschman	CZE
5	Olexandr Kucher	UKR
8	Leonardo	BRA
13	Vyacheslav Shevchuk	UKR
26	Razvan Rat	ROU
27	Dmytro Chygrynskiy	UKR
32	Vyacheslav Sviderskiy	UKR

Midfielders
4	Anatoliy Tymoschuk	UKR
6	Igor Duljaj	SRB
7	Fernandinho	BRA
9	Matuzalem	BRA
10	Zvonimir Vukic	SRB
18	Mariusz Lewandowski	POL
19	Olexiy Gay	UKR
33	Darijo Srna	CRO
36	Elano Blumer	BRA
37	Serhiy Tkachenko	UKR
38	Jadson Rodriguez	BRA
40	Olexandr Miroshnychenko	UKR
41	Serhiy Shevchuk	UKR
42	Andriy Shybko	UKR

Forwards
11	Andriy Vorobey	UKR
15	Emmanuel Okoduwa	NGA
17	Julius Aghahowa	NGA
20	Olexiy Bielik	UKR
25	Brandão	BRA
29	Ciprian Marica	ROU

SPARTAK

Goalkeepers
1	Dmitri Khomich	RUS
12	Ivan Komissarov	RUS
30	Wojciech Kowalewski	POL
46	Aleksei Zuev	RUS

Defenders
2	Geder	BRA
3	Martin Stranzl	AUT
5	Adrian Iencsi	ROU
13	Martin Jiránek	CZE
15	Radoslav Kovác	CZE
17	Clemente Rodríguez	ARG
35	Sergei Kabanov	RUS
49	Roman Shishkin	RUS
59	Andrei Ivanov	RUS
77	Eugeni Shpedt	RUS

Midfielders
7	Denis Boyarintsev	RUS
9	Yegor Titov	RUS
11	Aleksandr Pavlenko	RUS
14	Dmitri Torbinskiy	RUS
21	Quincy Owusu-Abeyie	NED
23	Vladimir Bystrov	RUS
24	Mozart	BRA
25	Maxym Kalynychenko	UKR
27	Serghei Covalciuc	MDA
39	Aleksei Rebko	RUS

Forwards
10	Roman Pavlyuchenko	RUS
18	Mihailo Pjanovic	SRB
19	Fernando Cavenaghi	ARG
32	Nikita Bazhenov	RUS
40	Artem Dzyuba	RUS
58	Artem Fomin	RUS

SPORTING CP

Goalkeepers
1	Ricardo	POR
16	Tiago	POR
22	Rui Patrício	POR

Defenders
4	Anderson Polga	BRA
8	Ronny	BRA
12	Marco Caneira	POR
15	Tonel	POR
24	Miguel Garcia	POR
24	Miguel Veloso	POR
78	Abel	POR

Midfielders
10	Carlos Martins	POR
11	Rodrigo Tello	CHI
18	Nani	POR
21	Pontus Farnerud	SWE
27	Custódio	POR
28	João Moutinho	POR
30	Leandro Romagnoli	ITA
34	João Alves	BRA
76	Carlos Paredes	PAR

Forwards
19	Alecsandro	BRA
20	Yannick Djaló	POR
31	Liedson	BRA
80	Carlos Bueno	URU

STEAUA

Goalkeepers
12	Cornel Cernea	ROU
13	Carlos Fernandes	POR
31	Marius Toma	ROU

Defenders
3	Dorin Goian	ROU
4	Daniel Panait	ROU
6	Mirel Radoi	ROU
15	Mihai Nesu	ROU
17	Eugen Baciu	ROU
18	Petre Marin	ROU
23	Rahamin Klemi Saban	ISR
24	Sorin Ghionea	ROU
27	Stelian Stancu	ROU

Midfielders
8	Ovidiu Petre	ROU
10	Nicolae Dica	ROU
11	Gabriel Bostina	ROU
14	Vasilica Cristocea	ROU
16	Banel Nicolita	ROU
22	Sorin Paraschiv	ROU
28	Gigel Coman	ROU
30	Iulian Ochirosii	ROU

Forwards
7	Daniel Oprita	ROU
9	Valentin Badea	ROU
19	Victoras Iacob	ROU
21	Cyril Thereau	FRA

VALENCIA

Goalkeepers
1	Santiago Cañizares	ESP
13	Juan Luis Mora	ESP
25	Ludovic Butelle	FRA

Defenders
2	Luis Miguel	POR
3	Asier del Horno	ESP
4	Roberto Ayala	ARG
5	Carlos Marchena	ESP
17	David Navarro	ESP
20	Raúl Albiol	ESP
23	Cristobal Curro Torres	ESP
24	Emiliano Moretti	ITA
26	David Cerrajería	ESP

Midfielders
6	David Albelda	ESP
8	Rubén Baraja	ESP
14	Vicente Rodríguez	ESP
15	Joaquín Sánchez	ESP
16	Hugo Viana	POR
18	Jorge López	ESP
22	Edu	BRA

Forwards
7	David Villa	ESP
9	Fernando Morientes	ESP
10	Miguel Ángel Angulo	ESP
11	Mario Regueiro	URU
12	Francesco Tavano	ITA
21	David Silva	ESP

WERDER BREMEN

Goalkeepers
1	Andreas Reinke	GER
18	Tim Wiese	GER
30	Kasper Jensen	DEN
33	Christian Vander	GER

Defenders
3	Petri Pasanen	FIN
4	Naldo	BRA
5	Pierre Wome	CMR
8	Clemens Fritz	GER
15	Patrick Owomoyela	GER
16	Leon Andreasen	DEN
26	Florian Mohr	GER
27	Christian Schulz	GER
29	Per Mertesacker	GER

Midfielders
6	Frank Baumann	GER
7	Jurica Vranjes	CRO
10	Diego	BRA
19	Jérôme Polenz	GER
20	Daniel Jensen	DEN
22	Torsten Frings	GER
24	Tim Borowski	GER

Forwards
9	Mohamed Zidan	EGY
11	Miroslav Klose	GER
14	Aaron Hunt	GER
17	Ivan Klasnic	CRO
23	Hugo Almeida	POR

UEFA CUP 2006–07

UEFA CUP 2006-07 EARLY ROUNDS FOR TEAMS IN GROUPS A TO D

First Qualifying Round

Jeunesse d'Esch	LUX	0	0
Skonto Riga	LVA	2	3
NK Rijeka	CRO	2	1
Omonia Nicosia	CYP	2	2
NK Koper	SVN	0	0
Litex Lovech	BUL	1	5
Karvan Yevlakh	AZE	1	1
Spartak Trnava	SVK	0	0
Hibernians	MLT	0	1
Dinamo Bucuresti	ROU	4	5
Dinamo Tiranë	ALB	0	1
CSKA Sofia	BUL	1	4
Rhyl	WAL	0	1
Suduva Marij'pole	LTU	0	2
Varteks Varazdin	CRO	1	0
SK Tirana	ALB	1	2
Glentoran	NIR	0	0
SK Brann Bergen	NOR	1	1
Atvidabergs FF	SWE	4	3
Etzella Ettelbruck	LUX	0	0
FC Fehérvár	HUN	1	1
Kairat Almaty	KAZ	0	2
BATE Borisov	BLR	2	1
Nistru Otaci	MDA	0	0
APOEL Nicosia	CYP	3	4
Murata	SMR	1	0
Vardar Skopje	MKD	1	1
KSV Roeselare	BEL	2	5
Ameri Tbilisi	GEO	0	2
Banants Yerevan	ARM	1	1
Gefle IF	SWE	1	0
Llanelli	WAL	2	0

Second Qualifying Round

Molde FK	NOR	0	2
Skonto Riga	LVA	0	1
Omonia Nicosia	CYP	0	1
Litex Lovech	BUL	0	2
OFK Belgrade	SRB	1	1
AJ Auxerre	FRA	0	5
Partizan Beograd	SRB	2	1
NK Maribor	SVN	1	1
Karvan Yevlakh	AZE	0	0
Slavia Praha	CZE	2	0
Dinamo Bucuresti	ROU	1	1
Beitar Jerusalem	ISR	0	1
SV Ried	AUT	0	0
FC Sion	SUI	0	1
CSKA Sofia	BUL	0	1
Hajduk Kula	SRB	0	1
Suduva Marij'pole	LTU	0	2
Club Brugge	BEL	2	5
SK Tirana	ALB	0	1
Kayserispor	TUR	2	3
SK Brann Bergen	NOR	3	1
Atvidabergs FF	SWE	3	1
FC Fehérvár	HUN	1	2
Grasshopper-Club	SUI	1	2
Rubin Kazan	RUS	3	2
BATE Borisov	BLR	0	0
APOEL Nicosia	CYP	1	0
Trabzonspor	TUR	1	1
KSV Roeselare	BEL	2	0
Ethnikos Achnas	CYP	1	5
Hertha Berlin	GER	1	2
Ameri Tbilisi	GEO	0	2
OB Odense	DEN	1	5
Llanelli	WAL	0	1

First Round

Molde FK	NOR	0	0
Rangers	SCO	0	2
Maccabi Haifa	ISR	1	3
Litex Lovech	BUL	1	1
Livorno	ITA	2	1
SV Pasching	AUT	0	0
Dinamo Zagreb	CRO	1	1
AJ Auxerre	FRA	2	3
Partizan Beograd	SRB	4	0
FC Groningen	NED	2	1
Slavia Praha	CZE	0	0
Tottenham H'spur	ENG	1	1
Xánthi	GRE	3	1
Dinamo Bucuresti	ROU	4	4
FC Sion	SUI	0	1
Bayer Leverkusen	GER	0	3
Besiktas	TUR	2	2
CSKA Sofia	BUL	0	2
MFK Ruzemerok	SVK	0	1
Club Brugge	BEL	1	1
AZ Alkmaar	NED	3	1
Kayserispor	TUR	2	1
Atromitos	GRE	1	0
Sevilla	ESP	2	4
Sporting Braga	POR	2	1
Chievo Verona	ITA	0	2
Slovan Liberec	CZE	2	2
Crvena Zvezda	SRB	0	1
Atvidabergs FF	SWE	0	0
Grasshopper-Club	SUI	3	5
Rubin Kazan	RUS	0	0
Parma	ITA	1	1
Trabzonspor	TUR	2	0
Osasuna	ESP	2	0
Ethnikos Achnas	CYP	0	1
RC Lens	FRA	0	3
Hertha Berlin	GER	2	0
OB Odense	DEN	2	1
Vitória Setúbal	POR	0	3
SC Heerenveen	NED	3	0

Group Stage

Group A		Pts
Rangers	SCO	10
Maccabi Haifa	ISR	7
Livorno	ITA	5
AJ Auxerre	FRA	4
Partizan Beograd	SRB	1

Group B		Pts
Tottenham Hotspur	ENG	12
Dinamo Bucuresti	ROU	7
Bayer Leverkusen	GER	4
Besiktas	TUR	3
Club Brugge	BEL	2

Group C		Pts
AZ Alkmaar	NED	10
Sevilla	ESP	7
Sporting Braga	POR	6
Slovan Liberec	CZE	5
Grasshopper-Club	SUI	0

Group D		Pts
Parma	ITA	9
Osasuna	ESP	7
RC Lens	FRA	4
OB Odense	DEN	4
SC Heerenveen	NED	4

In each preliminary and first round tie the home team in the first leg is listed above their opponent

UEFA CUP 2006-07 EARLY ROUNDS FOR TEAMS IN GROUPS E TO H

First Qualifying Round

Lokomotiv Sofia	BUL	2	1
Makedonija Skopje	MKD	0	1
FC Basel	SUI	3	0
Tobol Kostanai	KAZ	1	0
Ujpesti TE	HUN	0	1
FC Vaduz	LIE	4	0
Artmedia Bra'lava	SVK	2	1
WIT Georgia	GEO	0	2
Zaglebie Lubin	POL	1	0
Dinamo Minsk	BLR	1	0
Skála	FRO	0	0
IK Start Kris'sand	NOR	1	3
HJK Helsinki	FIN	1	1
Drogheda United	IRL	1	3

Zimbru Chisinau	MDA	1	2
Karabakh Agdam	AZE	1	1

IFK Göteborg	SWE	0	0
Derry City	IRL	1	1
Orasje	BIH	0	0
Domzale	SVN	2	5
FK Sarajevo	BIH	3	2
Ranger's FC	AND	0	0
Rapid Bucuresti	ROU	5	1
Sliema Wanderers	MLT	0	0
Mika Ashtarak	ARM	1	0
Young Boys Berne	SUI	3	1
Levadia Tallinn	EST	2	0
Haka Valkeakoski	FIN	0	1
FK Ventspils	LVA	2	2
Gl Gøtu	FRO	1	0
Randers FC	DEN	1	1
IA Akranes	ISL	0	2
Portadown	NIR	1	0
FBK Kaunas	LTU	3	1
Lyn Oslo	NOR	1	0
Flora Tallinn	EST	1	0
Brøndby IF	DEN	3	0
Valur Reykjavik	ISL	1	0

Second Qualifying Round

Bnei Yehuda	ISR	0	0
Lokomotiv Sofia	BUL	2	4
SV Mattersburg	AUT	1	0
Wisla Krakow	POL	1	1
FC Basel	SUI	1	1
FC Vaduz	LIE	0	2

Artmedia Bra'lava	SVK	2	3
Dinamo Minsk	BLR	1	2
IK Start Kris'sand	NOR	1 0 11p
Drogheda United	IRL	0 1 10p

Zimbru Chisinau	MDA	0	0
Metalurh Zap'hya	UKR	0	3
Gretna	SCO	1	2
Derry City	IRL	5	2
Chernomorets O.	UKR	0	1
Wisla Plock	POL	0	1
Hapoel Tel Aviv	ISR	1	3
Domzale	SVN	2	0
FK Sarajevo	BIH	1	0
Rapid Bucuresti	ROU	0	2
Young Boys Berne	SUI	3	0
Olymp. Marseille	FRA	3	0
Twente Enschede	NED	1	0
Levadia Tallinn	EST	1	1
FK Ventspils	LVA	0	0
Newcastle United	ENG	1	0

Randers FC	DEN	3	0
FBK Kaunas	LTU	1	1
Flora Tallinn	EST	0	0
Brøndby IF	DEN	0	4

First Round

SV Salzburg	AUT	2	0
Blackburn Rovers	ENG	2	2
Schalke 04	GER	1	1
AS Nancy-L'raine	FRA	0	3
Lokomotiv Sofia	BUL	2	0
Feyenoord	NED	2	0
Wisla Krakow	POL	0	2
Iraklis Thess'niki	GRE	1	0
FC Basel	SUI	6	1
Rabotniki Skopje	MKD	2	0

Artmedia Bra'lava	SVK	2	1
Espanyol	ESP	2	3
IK Start Krist'sand	NOR	2	0
Ajax	NED	5	4
Lokomotiv Moskva	RUS	2	0
Zulte Waregem	BEL	1	2
Heart of Mid'thian	SCO	0	0
Sparta Praha	CZE	0	2
Legia Warzsawa	POL	1	0
FK Austria Wien	AUT	1	1

Panathinaikos	GRE	1	1
Metalurh Zap'zhya	UKR	1	0
Derry City	IRL	0	0
Paris St-Germain	FRA	0	2
Chernomorets O.	UKR	0	1
Hapoel Tel Aviv	ISR	1	3
Rapid Bucuresti	ROU	1	2
Nacional Funchal	POR	0	1
Olymp. Marseille	FRA	1	2
Mladá Boleslav	CZE	0	4

Levadia Tallinn	EST	0	1
Newcastle United	ENG	1	2
Standard CL	BEL	0	0
Celta Vigo	ESP	1	3
Fenerbahçe	TUR	2	3
Randers FC	DEN	1	0
West Ham United	ENG	0	0
Palermo	ITA	1	3
Eint'cht Frankfurt	GER	4	2
Brøndby IF	DEN	0	2

Group Stage

Group E		Pts
Blackburn Rovers	ENG	10
AS Nancy-Lorraine	FRA	7
Feyenoord	NED	5
Wisla Krakow	POL	3
FC Basel	SUI	2

Group F		Pts
Espanyol	ESP	12
Ajax	NED	7
Zulte Waregem	BEL	6
Sparta Praha	CZE	4
FK Austria Wien	AUT	0

Group G		Pts
Panathinaikos	GRE	7
Paris Saint-Germain	FRA	5
Hapoel Tel Aviv	ISR	5
Rapid Bucuresti	ROU	4
Mladá Boleslav	CZE	3

Group H		Pts
Newcastle United	ENG	10
Celta Vigo	ESP	5
Fenerbahçe	TUR	4
Palermo	ITA	4
Eintracht Frankfurt	GER	3

In each preliminary and first round tie the home team in the first leg is listed above their opponents

UEFA CUP 2006-07 FINAL ROUNDS

Round of Thirty-two	Round of Sixteen	Quarter-Final	Semi-Final	Final
Sevilla 2 1				
Steaua Buc'sti * 0 0				
	Sevilla * 2 3			
	Shak. Donetsk 2 2			
Nancy-Lorraine 1 0				
Shak. Donetsk * 1 1				
		Sevilla * 2 2		
		Tottenham H. 1 2		
Sporting Braga * 1 1				
Parma 0 0				
	Sporting Braga * 2 2			
	Tottenham H. 3 3			
Feyenoord *				
Tottenham H. ‡ w-o				
			Sevilla 0 2	
			Osasuna * 1 0	
B. Leverkusen * 3 0				
Blackburn Rov. 2 0				
	B. Leverkusen 1 3			
	RC Lens * 2 0			
Panathinaikos 1 0				
RC Lens * 3 0				
		B. Leverkusen * 0 0		
		Osasuna 3 1		
Rangers 1 4				
Hapoel Tel Aviv* 2 0				
	Rangers * 1 0			
	Osasuna 1 1			
Gir. Bordeaux * 0 0				
Osasuna 0 1				
				Sevilla 2 3p
				Espanyol 2 1p
Werder Bremen* 3 1				
Ajax 0 3				
	Werder Bremen 1 2			
	Celta Vigo * 0 0			
Spartak Moskva* 1 1				
Celta Vigo 1 2				
		Werder Bremen 0 4		
		AZ Alkmaar * 0 1		
Newcastle Utd 3 1				
Zulte Waregem * 1 0				
	Newcastle Utd * 4 0			
	AZ Alkmaar 2 2			
Fenerbahçe * 3 2				
AZ Alkmaar 3 2				
			Werder Bremen 0 1	
			Espanyol * 3 2	
Benfica * 1 2				
Dinamo Buc'sti 0 1				
	Benfica 1 3			
	Paris S-G * 2 1			
AEK Athens * 0 0				
Paris S-G 2 2				
		Benfica 2 0		
		Espanyol * 3 0		
Maccabi Haifa 0 1				
CSKA Moskva 0 0				
	Maccabi Haifa * 0 0			
	Espanyol 0 4			
Livorno * 1 0				
Espanyol 2 2				

* Home team in the first leg • ‡ Feyenoord expelled due to crowd problems during their group match with Nancy

FIRST QUALIFYING ROUND

La Frontière, Esch-sur-Alzette, 13-07-2006, 18:00, 850, Kailis CYP
Jeunesse d'Esch   0
Skonto Riga   2 Piacek [48], Stolcers [79]
  Skonto, Riga, 27-07-2006, 18:00, 2193, Stavrev MKD
Skonto Riga   3
Jeunesse d'Esch   0
  Kantrida, Rijeka, 13-07-2006, 20:45, 4622, Borski POL
NK Rijeka   2 Bule [9], Kerkez [50p]
Omonia Nicosia   2 Vakouftsis [31p], Grozdanovski [54]
  GSP, Nicosia, 27-07-2006, 14 000, Clattenburg ENG
Omonia Nicosia   2 Mguni 2 [61 88]
NK Rijeka   1 Lukunic [78]
  Sportni Park, Domzale, 13-07-2006, 20:00, 610, Casha MLT
FC Koper   0
Litex Lovech   1 Kirilov [17]
  Gradski, Lovech, 27-07-2006, 20:45, 2719, Trattou CYP
Litex Lovech   5 Sandrinho [20p], Novakovic [62], Jelenkovic [85],
FC Koper   0   Lyubenov [91+], Genchev [93+]
  Shafa, Baku, 13-07-2006, 20:00, 2000, Spirkoski MKD
Karvan Yevlakh   1 Muradov [82]
Spartak Trnava   0
  National, Senec, 27-07-2006, 19:00, 1842, McCourt NIR
Spartak Trnava   0
Karvan Yevlakh   1 Camara [12]
  National Stadium, Ta'Qali, 13-07-2006, 21:00, 252, Zakharov RUS
Hibernians   0
Dinamo Bucuresti   4 Danciulescu [4], Niculescu 2 [57 58], Radu [83]
  Dinamo, Bucharest, 27-07-2006, 21:00, 4500, Svilokos CRO
Dinamo Bucuresti   5 Cristea [54], Danciulescu 2 [61 84], Munteanu [91+],
Hibernians   1 Buzurovic [86]   Buzurovic OG [93+]
  Selman Stermazi, Tirana, 13-07-2006, 17:30, 1000, Jakov ISR
Dinamo Tiranë   0
CSKA Sofia   1 Trica [86]
  Balgarska Armia, Sofia, 27-07-2006, 20:00, 4321, Megyebiro HUN
CSKA Sofia   4 Trica 2 [36 53], Furtado [49], Petre.F [75]
Dinamo Tiranë   1 Kastel [12]
  Belle Vue, Rhyl, 13-07-2006, 19:30, 1475, Isaksen FRO
Rhyl   0
Suduva Marij'pole   0
  Suduva, Marijampole, 27-07-2006, 18:00, 2000, Mihaljevic SRB
Suduva Marij'pole   2 Maciulevicius [18p], Mikuckis [25]
Rhyl   1 Grigas OG [80]
  Varteks, Varazdin, 13-07-2006, 18:00, 1500, Kuipers NED
Varteks Varazdin   1 Novinic [47]
SK Tirana   1 Mukaj [21]
  Selman Stermazi, Tirana, 27-07-2006, 17:00, 3500, Tsikinis GRE
SK Tirana   2 Salihi [16], Merkoci [90]
Varteks Varazdin   0
  The Oval, Belfast, 13-07-2006, 19:30, 1743, Hermansen DEN
Glentoran   0
SK Brann Bergen   1 Memelli [69]
  Brann, Bergen, 27-07-2006, 19:30, 3584, Laperriere SUI
SK Brann Bergen   1 Bjarnason [85p]
Glentoran   0
  Idrottspark, Norrköping, 13-07-2006, 20:00, 1020, Zhukov UKR
Atvidabergs FF   4 Johansson [12], Karlsson.P 3 [41 47 55]
Etzella Ettelbrück   0
  Deich, Ettelbrück, 27-07-2007, 18:00, 354, Rossi SMR
Etzella Ettelbrück   0
Atvidabergs FF   3 Jönsson [61], Johansson [70p], Karlsson.Ch [80p]
  Sóstói, Székesfehérvár, 13-07-2006, 20:00, 2721, Laursen DEN
FC Fehérvár   1 Dvéri [8]
Kairat Almaty   0

  Tsentralny, Almaty, 27-07-2006, 19:30, 7500, Constantin ROU
Kairat Almaty   2 Bulashev [75], Smakov [86p]
FC Fehérvár   1 Sitku [34]
  Gradski, Borisov, 13-07-2006, 19:00, 4000, Kaldma EST
BATE Borisov   2 Stasevich [55], Molosh [76p]
Nistru Otaci   0
  Republika, Chisinau, 27-07-2006, 19:00, 1000, Kovarik CZE
Nistru Otaci   0
BATE Borisov   1 Bliznyuk [30]
  GSP, Nicosia, 13-07-2006, 20:00, 6489, Coltescu ROU
APOEL Nicosia   3 Neophytou [34p], Georgiou [58], Eleftheriou [82]
SS Murata   1 Protti [51]
  Olimpico, Serravalle, 27-07-2006, 21:00, 667, Amirkhanyan ARM
SS Murata   0   Michail [91p]
APOEL Nicosia   4 Georgiou [15], Fernandes [22], Neophytou [25],
  Gradski, Skopje, 13-07-2006, 18:00, 2000, Bede HUN
Vardar Skopje   1 Ristovski [1]
KSV Roeselare   2 Sabah [32], Oyen [39]
  Schiervelde, Roeselare, 27-07-2006, 20:00, 3731, Guliyev AZE
KSV Roeselare   5 Sabah [13], Dufoor 3 [20 30 76], Vanderbiest [64p]
Vardar Skopje   1 Wandeir [52]
  Mikheil Meshki, Tbilisi, 13-07-2006, 20:000, 2000, Toussaint LUX
Ameri Tbilisi   0
Banants Yerevan   1 Vahe Tadevosyan [10]
  Republican, Yerevan, 27-07-2006, 19:00, 4000, Ristoskov BUL
Banants Yerevan   1 Vahe Tadevosyan [38]
Ameri Tbilisi   2 Tsinamdzgvrishvili [60], Dobrovolski [62]
  Råsunda, Stockholm, 13-07-2006, 19:00, 839, Tsaregradskiyi KAZ
Gefle IF   1 Viikmäe [24]
Llanelli   2 Griffiths [82], Mingorance [87]
  Stradey Park, Llanelli, 27-07-2006, 19:30, 3250, Kulbakov BLR
Llanelli   0
Gefle IF   0
  Balgarska Armia, Sofia, 13-07-2006, 20:30, 1800, Vejlgaard DEN
Lokomotiv Sofia   2 Paskov [60p], Karadzinov [86]
Makedonija Skopje   0
  Gradski, Skopje, 27-07-2006, 19:30, 5000, Da Silva POR
Makedonija Skopje   1 Ismaili [25]
Lokomotiv Sofia   1 Genkov [69]
  St Jakob-Park, Basel, 27-07-2006, 20:00, 11 643, De Sousa POR
FC Basel   3
Tobol Kostanay   1
  Tsentralny, Kostanai, 27-07-2006, 19:00, 8000, Wilmes LUX
Tobol Kostanai   0
FC Basel   0
  Ferenc Puskás, Budapest, 13-07-2006, 19:00, 3763, Moen NOR
Ujpesti TE   0
FC Vaduz   4 Omar 2 [14 63], Akdemir [31], Sara [90]
  Rheinpark, Vaduz, 27-07-2006, 19:30, 1150, Cakir TUR
FC Vaduz   0
Ujpesti TE   1 Norbert Tóth [55]
  Tehelné Pole, Bratislava, 13-07-2006, 18:00, 861, Krajnc SVN
Artmedia Bra'lava   2 Hartig [10], Reiter [51]
WIT Georgia   0
  Mikheil Meshkhi, Tbilisi, 27-07-2006, 18:00, Tsachilidis GRE
WIT Georgia   2 Lomaia [44], Razmadze [88p]
Artmedia Bra'lava   1 Halenár [48]
  Zaglebia, Lubin, 13-07-2006, 17:30, 3526, Arzumen TUR
Zaglebie Lubin   1 Lobodzinski [67]
Dinamo Minsk   1 Kovel [73]
  Dinamo, Minsk, 27-07-2006, 18:30, 3586, Aliyev AZE
Dinamo Minsk   0
Zaglebie Lubin   0
  Toftir, Toftir, 13-07-2006, 19:00, 720, Lawlor WAL
Skála   0
IK Start   1 Johnson.M [3]

Kristiansand, Kristiansand, 27-07-2006, 19:00, 1470, Dimitrov BUL

IK Start	3	Bärlin [42], Pedersen.S [51], Wright [78]
Skála	0	

Finnair, Helsinki, 13-07-2006, 19:00, 2467, Zuta LTU

HJK Helsinki	1	Halsti [83]
Drogheda United	1	Robinson [41]

Dalymount Park, Dublin, 13-07-2006, 19:45, 3750, Prades AND

Drogheda United	3	Gartland [57], Lynch 2 [96 114]
HJK Helsinki	1	Ghazi [36]

Zimbru, Chisinau, 13-07-2006, 20:00, 2000, Delevic SRB

Zimbru Chisinau	1	Petrosyan [75]
Karabakh Agdam	1	Samir Musaev [68]

Shafa, Baku, 27-07-2006, 20:00, 8000, Mrkovic BIH

Karabakh Agdam	1	Samir Musaev [23]
Zimbru Chisinau	2	Chirilov [52], Balasa [100]

Ullevi, Gothenburg, 13-07-2006, 19:00, 3350, Sidenco MDA

IFK Göteborg	0	
Derry City	1	Hargan [80]

Brandywell, Londonderry, 27-07-2006, 19:30, 2650, Hinriksson ISL

Derry City	1	O'Flynn [32p]
IFK Göteborg	0	

GOAL, Orasje, 13-07-2006, 17:00, 2200, Deaconu ROU

NK Orasje	0	
NK Domzale	2	Juninho [30], Aljancic [39]

Sportni Park, Domzale, 27-07-2006, 20:15, 1100, Yildirim TUR

NK Domzale	5	Ljubijankic 2 [13 75], Djukic 2 [21 41], Rakovic [61]
NK Orasje	0	

Kosevo, Sarajevo, 13-07-2006, 18:00, 2023, Havrilla SVK

FK Sarajevo	3	Obuca 2 [20 30], Duro.S [45]
Ranger's FC	0	

Comunal, Andorra La Vella, 27-07-2006, 18:00, 200, Podeschi SMR

Rangers FC	0	
FK Sarajevo	2	Hadzic [10], Obuca [45]

Giulesti, Bucharest, 13-07-2006, 20:30, 6000, Kenan ISR

Rapid Bucuresti	5	Grigore [5], Carabott OG [15], Constantin.N 2 [22 42]
Sliema Wanderers	0	Said OG [44]

National Stadium , Ta'Qali, 27-07-2006, 18:00, 200, Karadzic SRB

Sliema Wanderers	0	
Rapid Bucuresti	1	Buga [11]

Republican, Yerevan, 13-07-2006, 20:00, 7500, Saliy KAZ

MIKA Ashtarak	1	Grigoryan.D [90]
BSC Young Boys	3	Dos Santos [22], Raimondi [50], Sermeter [86]

Stade de Suisse, Berne, 27-07-2006, 19:30, 6432, Jareci ALB

BSC Young Boys	1	Häberli [85]
MIKA Ashtarak	0	

Kadriorg, Tallinn, 13-07-2006, 18:30, 2150, Todorov BUL

Levadia Tallinn	2	Purje 2 [32 36]
Haka Valkeakoski	0	

Tehtaan Kenttä, Valkeakoski, 27-07-2006, 19:00, 1234, Shandor UKR

Haka Valkeakoski	1	Innanen [4]
Levadia Tallinn	0	

Ventspils Pilsetas, Ventspils, 13-07-2006, 18:30, 550, Silagava GEO

FK Ventspils	2	Ndeki 2 [23 65]
Gl Gøtu	1	Simun Jacobsen [29]

Toftir, Toftir, 27-07-2006, 18:00, 386, Kaasik EST

Gl Gøtu	0	
FK Ventspils	2	Rimkus 2 [75 77]

Randers, Randers, 13-07-2006, 19:00, 4680, Vialichka BLR

Randers FC	1	Da Silva [64]
IA Akranes	0	

Akranesvöllur, Akranes, 27-07-2006, 18:00, 650, Drabek AUT

IA Akranes	2	Hjartarson [27], Gudjónsson.B [92+p]
Randers FC	1	Johansen [29]

Shamrock Park, Portadown, 13-07-2006, 19:30, 548, Stalhammar SWE

Portadown	1	McCutcheon [65]
FBK Kaunas	3	Manchkhava [2], Pehlic [9], Velicka [46]

S.Darius & S.Girena, Kaunas, 27-07-2006, 20:00, 3060, Valgeirsson ISL

FBK Kaunas	1	Ivaskevicius [43]
Portadown	0	

Ullevål, Oslo, 13-07-2006, 19:00, 510, Murray SCO

FC Lyn Oslo	1	Tessem [42p]
Flora Tallinn	1	Lindpere [81]

A Le Coq Arena, Tallinn, 27-07-2006, 18:45, 1500, Sapi HUN

Flora Tallinn	0	
FC Lyn Oslo	0	

Brøndby, Copenhagen, 13-07-2006, 20:45, 6338, Kovacic CRO

Brøndby IF	3	Rasmussen.T [8], Rasmussen.M [32], Ericsson [34]
Valur Retkjavík	1	Gunnlaugsson [83]

Laugardalsvöllur, Reykjavík, 27-07-2006, 18:45, 1627, Buttimer IRL

Valur Retkjavík	0	
Brøndby IF	0	

SECOND QUALIFYING ROUND

Molde, Molde, 10-08-2006, 19:00, 1495, Ross NIR

Molde FK	0	
Skonto Riga	0	

Skonto, Riga, 24-08-2006, 19:00, 3500, Banari MDA

Skonto Riga	1	Astafjevs [68]
Molde FK	2	Mavric.M [42], Ohr [61]

GSP, Nicosia, 8-08-2006, 19:00, 13 447, Lopes Ferreira POR

Omonia Nicosia	0	
Litex Lovech	0	

Gradski, Lovech, 24-08-2006, 20:45, 3600, Lajuks LVA

Litex Lovech	2	Zlatinov [42], Manolev [45]
Omonia Nicosia	1	Berberovic OG [32]

Omladinski, Belgrade, 8-08-2006, 17:00, 2000, Georgiev BUL

OFK Beograd	1	Bajalica [31]
AJ Auxerre	0	

Abbé-Deschamps, Auxerre, 24-08-2006, 20:00, 3951, Perez Burrull ESP

AJ Auxerre	5	Mignot [23], Jelen [44], Pieroni 3 [82 86 89]
OFK Beograd	1	Pilipovic [31]

Partizan, Belgrade, 10-08-2006, 20:00, 8000, Slupik POL

Partizan Beograd	2	Odita 2 [28 30]
NK Maribor	1	Mihelic [64]

Ljudski vrt, Maribor, 24-08-2006, 21:00, 8600, Kalt FRA

NK Maribor	1	Zajc [63]
Partizan Beograd	1	Zajic [30]

Shafa, Baku, 10-08-2006, 20:00, 6700, Stanisic SRB

Karvan Yevlakh	0	
Slavia Praha	2	Hrdlicka [15], Fort [93+]

Evzena Rosického, Prague, 24-08-2006, 20:45, 2512, Hermansen DEN

Slavia Praha	0	
Karvan Yevlakh	0	

Dinamo, Bucharest, 10-08-2006, 21:00, 5300, Godulyan UKR

Dinamo Bucuresti	1	Munteanu [77]
Beitar Jerusalem	0	

Georgi Asparuhov, Sofia, 24-08-2006, 21:00, 500, Ver Eecke BEL

Beitar Jerusalem	1	Itzhaki [5]
Dinamo Bucuresti	1	Gershon OG [23]

Fill Metallbau, Ried/Innkreis, 10-08-2006, 18:30, 3033, Zammit MLT

SV Ried	0	
FC Sion	0	

Stade de Genève, Geneva, 24-08-2006, 20:00, 7500, Svendson DEN

FC Sion	1	Kuljic [34p]
SV Ried	0	

Balgarska Armia, Sofia, 10-08-2006, 19:30, 3128, Stokes IRL

CSKA Sofia	0	
Hajduk Kula	0	

Crvena Zvezda, Belgrade, 24-08-2006, 20:30, 584, Ishchenko UKR
Hajduk Kula 1 Stancic [100]
CSKA Sofia 1 Tunchev [119]
S.Darius & S.Girena, Kaunas, 10-08-2006, 21:00, 2100, Kos SVN
Suduva Marij'pole 0
Club Brugge 2 Daerden [19], Roelandts [70]
Jan Breydel, Bruges, 24-08-2006, 20:30, 6800, Bertolini SUI
Club Brugge 5 Roelandts [9], Balaban 2 [39 69], Gvozdenovic [58],
Suduva Marij'pole 2 Otavio [51], Chigladze.D [57p]   Dufer [67]
Selman Stermasi, Tirana, 10-08-2006, 17:30, 3500, Bede HUN
SK Tirana 0
Kayserispor 2 Akagündüz 2 [26 45]
Kayseri Atatürk, Kayseri, 24-08-2006, 19:00, 11 887, Kaldma EST
Kayserispor 3 Mehmet Topuz [5], Akagündüz [46], Gökhan [48]
SK Tirana 1 Salihi [52]
Brann, Bergen, 10-08-2006, 19:00, 2684, Havrilla SVK
SK Brann Bergen 3 Memelli 3 [4 26 59]
Atvidabergs FF 3 Haglund [27], Bergström [48], Karlsson.P [83]
Vårendsvallen, Växjö, 24-08-2006, 19:30, 786, Mikolajewski POL
Atvidabergs FF 1 Haglund [35]
SK Brann Bergen 1 Dahl [85]
Sóstói, Szekesfehérvár, 10-08-2006, 20:00, 3970, Dean ENG
FC Fehérvár 1 Horváth [93+]
Grasshopper-Club 1 Roberto Pinto [70]
Hardturm, Zürich, 24-08-2006, 19:30, 2600, Kuipers NED
Grasshopper-Club 2 Sutter [5], Antonio [24]
FC Fehérvár 0
Tsentralnyi, Kazan, 10-08-2006, 19:00, 10 000, Sipailo LVA
Rubin Kazan 3 Bazaev [37], Ashvetia 2 [57 68]
BATE Borisov 0
Gradski, Borisov, 24-08-2006, 19:30, 2700, Zrnic BIH
BATE Borisov 0
Rubin Kazan 2 Dominguez 2 [37 44]
GSP, Nicosia, 10-08-2006, 21:00, 17 048, Rodriguez Santiago ESP
APOEL Nicosia 1 Fernandes [2]
Trabzonspor 1 Yattara [90]
Hüseyin Avni Aker, Trabzon, 24-08-2006, 20:45, 13 993, Weiner GER
Trabzonspor 1 Omer Riza [87]
APOEL Nicosia 0
Schiervelde, Roeselare, 10-08-2006, 18:00, 2986, Nalbandyan ARM
KSV Roeselare 2 Dufoor [40], Oris [82]
Ethnikos Achnas 1 Stjepanovic [79p]
GSP, Nicosia, 24-08-2006, 18:00, 1300, Tanovic SRB
Ethnikos Achnas 5 Poyiatzis 2 [3 17], Stjepanovic 2 [47p 65], Belic [88]
KSV Roeselare 0
FL Jahn Sportpark, Berlin, 10-08-2006, 19:00, 7377, Zografos GRE
Hertha Berlin 1 Okoronkwo [92+]
Ameri Tbilisi 0
Mikheil Meskhi, Tbilisi, 24-08-2006, 21:00, 5800, Olsiak SVK
Ameri Tbilisi 2 Davitindze [17], Davitashvili [47]
Hertha Berlin 1 Lakic [35], Pantelic [83]
Fionia Park, Odense, 10-08-2006, 19:00, 2744, Markusson ISL
OB Odense 1 Bechara [29]
Llanelli 0
Liberty Stadium, Swansea, 24-08-2006, 19:45, 2759, Delevic SRB
Llanelli 1 Corbisiero [10]   Bechara [91+]
OB Odense 5 Timm [17], Hansen [33], Sørensen [58], Ophaug [65],
National, Senec, 10-08-2006, 18:00, 500, Attard MLT
Bnei Yehuda TA 0
Lokomotiv Sofia 2 Davtchev [30], Genkov [57p]
Balgarska Armia, Sofia, 24-08-2006, 20:30, 881, Stalhammar SWE
Lokomotiv Sofia 4 Dobrev [21], Genkov [43], Karadzinov 2 [61 81]
Bnei Yehuda TA 0
Ernst Happel, Vienna, 10-08-2006, 20:45, 7200, Staberg NOR
SV Mattersburg 1 Naumoski [20]
Wisla Kraków 1 Zienczuk [14]

Wisly, Kraków, 24-08-2006, 20:30, 12 817, Malzinskas LTU
Wisla Kraków 1 Brozek.P [23]
SV Mattersburg 0
St Jakob-Park, Basel, 10-08-2006, 20:00, 14 296, Matejek CZE
FC Basel 1 Majstorovic [58]
FC Vaduz 0
Rheinpark, Vaduz, 24-08-2006, 19:30, 3660, Clattenburg ENG
FC Vaduz 2 Sara [49], Ritzberger [63]
FC Basel 1 Kuzmanovic [56]
Petrzalka, Bratislava, 10-08-2006, 17:30, 4500, McDonald SCO
Artmedia Bra'lava 2 Reiter [73], Cisovsky [76]
Dinamo Minsk 1 Edu [22]
Dinamo, Minsk, 24-08-2006, 19:00, 1850, Paniashvili GEO
Dinamo Minsk 2 Kovel [76], Marcio [92+]
Artmedia Bra'lava 3 Halenár [31], Gajdos [38], Burák [61]
Kristiansand, Kristiansand, 10-08-2006, 19:00, 1433, Jareci ALB
Start Kristiansand 1 Strømstad [66]
Drogheda United 0
Dalymount Park, Dublin, 24-08-2006, 19:45, 4142, Germanakos GRE
Drogheda United 1 Zayed [84]
Start Kristiansand 0   Start won 11-10 on pens
Zimbru, Chisinau, 24-08-2006, 20:00, 8000, Levi ISR
Zimbru Chisinau 0
Metalurh Zap'hya 0
Metalurh, Zaporizhya, 24-08-2006, 20:00, 5500, Kari FIN
Metalurh Zap'hya 3 Tasevski 2 [16 54], Kvirkvelia [70]
Zimbru Chisinau 0
Fir Park, Motherwell, 10-08-2006, 19:45, 6040, Strahonja CRO
Gretna 1 McGuffie [12]
Derry City 5 Kelly [23], Deery 2 [54 56], Martyn 2 [63 75]
Brandywell, Londonderry, 24-08-2006, 19:30, 2850, Rasmussen DEN
Derry City 2 Farren [37], Oman [69]
Gretna 2 Graham [17], Baldacchino [77]
Chernomorets, Odessa, 24-08-2006, 18:00, 14 500, Sapi HUN
Chern'ets. Odessa 0
Wisla Plock 0
Wisly, Plock, 24-08-2006, 17:30, 4400, Aydinus TUR
Wisla Plock 1 Geworgyan [63]
Chern'ets. Odessa 1 Shyshchenko [30]
Willem II, Tilburg, 24-08-2006, 19:00, 180, Gonchar RUS
Hapoel Tel Aviv 1 De Bruno [42]
NK Domzale 2 Ljubijankic 2 [65p 91+]
Sportni Park, Domzale, 24-08-2006, 18:30, 2300, Collum SCO
NK Domzale 0
Hapoel Tel Aviv 3 Jolic [70], Vermouth [91+], Ogbona [93+]
Kosevo, Sarajevo, 24-08-2006, 20:00, 8000, Pereira Gomes POR
FK Sarajevo 2 Obuca [92]
Rapid Bucuresti 0
Giulesti, Bucharest, 24-08-2006, 19:30, 6700, Van de Velde BEL
Rapid Bucuresti 2 Buga [39], Moldovan.V [91+]
FK Sarajevo 0
Stade de Suisse, Bern, 10-08-2006, 19:30, 18 274, Brugger AUT
BSC Young Boys 3 Hakan Yakin [20], Daniel [49], Dos Santos [73]
Olymp. Marseille 3 Zubar [18], Niang 2 [44 57]
Vélodrome, Marseille, 24-08-2006, 20:45, 35 764, Bozinovski MKD
Olymp. Marseille 0
BSC Young Boys 0
Arke, Enschede, 10-08-2006, 19:30, 8421, Kinhöfer GER
Twente Enschede 1 Heubach [53]
Levadia Tallinn 1 Andreev [24]
A Le Coq Arena, Tallinn, 24-08-2006, 21:00, 3000, Salomir ROU
Levadia Tallinn 1 Nahk [36]
Twente Enschede 0
Skonto, Riga, 24-08-2006, 20:50, 6000, Lannoy FRA
FK Ventspils 0
Newcastle United 1 Bramble [67]

St James' Park, Newcastle, 24-08-2006, 19:45, 30 498, Einwaller AUT
Newcastle United 0
FK Ventspils 0

Randers, Randers, 10-08-2006, 19:00, 4200, Whitby WAL
Randers FC 3 Fall [59], Ahmed [82], Pedersen.K [92+p]
FBK Kaunas 1 Juska [80]

S.Darius & S.Girenas, Kaunas, 24-08-2006, 19:00, 3000, Gvardis RUS
FBK Kaunas 1 Velicka [72p]
Randers FC 0

A Le Coq Arena, Tallinn, 10-08-2006, 21:00, 2500, Hietala FIN
Flora Tallinn 0
Brøndby IF 0

Brøndby, Copenhagen, 24-08-2006, 20:45, 8899, Circhetta SUI
Brøndby IF 4 Jensen [49], Agger 2 [64 87], Lorentzen [78]
Flora Tallinn 0

FIRST ROUND

Molde, Molde, 14-09-2006, 20:05, 6452, Granat POL
Molde FK 0
Rangers 0

Ibrox, Glasgow, 28-09-2006, 19:45, 44 624, Kircher GER
Rangers 2 Buffel [12], Ferguson [45]
Molde FK 0

De Goffert, Nijmegan, 14-09-2006, 20:30, 390, Halsey ENG
Maccabi Haifa 1 Katan [7]
Litex Lovech 1 Zanev [51]

Gradski, Lovech, 28-09-2006, 21:00, 3000, Kelly IRL
Litex Lovech 1 Sandrinho [37]
Maccabi Haifa 3 Xavir [19], Masudi [33], Colautti [67]

Armando Picchi, Livorno, 14-09-2006, 20:45, 7671, Kalt FRA
Livorno 2 Danilevicius [43], Lucarelli [49]
SV Pasching 0

Waldstadion, Pasching, 28-09-2006, 18:30, 4100, Kassai HUN
SV Pasching 0
Livorno 1 Bakayoko [56]

Maksimir, Zagreb, 14-09-2006, 20:15, 24 200, Dondarini ITA
Dinamo Zagreb 1 Eduardo [69]
AJ Auxerre 2 Jelen [43], Niculae [72]

Abbé-Deschamps, Auxerre, 28-09-2006, 19:30, 4591, Yefet ISR
AJ Auxerre 3 Jelen 2 [35 41], Mathis [70]
Dinamo Zagreb 1 Eduardo [61p]

Partizan, Belgrade, 14-09-2006, 19:00, 10 000, Lajuks LVA
Partizan Beograd 4 Marinkovic.Neb 2 [49 43], Zajic 2 [16 90]
FC Groningen 2 Fledderus [58], Luis Suárez [92+]

Euroborg, Groningen, 28-09-2006, 20:00, 19 230, Balaj ROU
FC Groningen 1 Van De Laak [59p]
Partizan Beograd 0

Evzena Rosického, Prague, 14-09-2006, 20:00, 14 869, Piccirillo FRA
Slavia Praha 0
Tottenham H'spur 1 Jenas [37]

White Hart Lane, London, 28-09-2006, 20:00, 35 191, Skjerven NOR
Tottenham H'spur 1 Keane [79]
Slavia Praha 0

Xanthis, Xanthi, 14-09-2006, 19:00, 3380, Panic BIH
Xanthi 3 Quintana 2 [8 45], Kazakis [66]
Dinamo Bucuresti 4 Niculescu 2 [18 35], Danciulescu [25], Pulhac [85]

Dinamo, Bucharest, 28-09-2006, 20:00, 5442, Egorov RUS
Dinamo Bucuresti 4 Niculescu 2 [12 82], Cristea [47], Danciulescu [79]
Xanthi 1 Paviot [51]

Stade de Genève, Geneva, 14-09-2006, 20:30, 11 000, Malek POL
FC Sion 0
Bayer Leverkusen 0

BayArena, Leverkusen, 28-09-2006, 20:30, 16 986, Eriksson SWE
Bayer Leverkusen 3 Voronin [26], Ramelow [76], Schneider [86p]
FC Sion 1 Fernandes [75]

Inönü, Istanbul, 14-09-2006, 19:45, 22 602, Duarte Paixao POR
Besiktas 2 Kleberson [81], Gökhan Güleç [91+]
CSKA Sofia 0

Balgarska Armia, Sofia, 28-09-2006, 19:30, 14 000, Van Egmond
CSKA Sofia 2 Iliev.V [60], Tunchev [69]
Besiktas 2 Márcio [95], Deivson [103]

MFK Ruzomberok, Ruzomberok, 14-09-2006, 20:45, 4200, Trivkovic CRO
MFK Ruzomberok 0
Club Brugge 1 Balaban [38]

Jan Breydel, Bruges, 28-09-2006, 20:30, 8425, Dereli TUR
Club Brugge 1 Balaban [89]
MFK Ruzomberok 1 Rák [29]

DSB, Alkmaar, 14-09-2006, 20:00, 12 200, Rodriguez Santiago ESP
AZ Alkmaar 3 Koevermans [6p], Molhoek [32], Arveladze.S [64]
Kayserispor 2 Bülent [25], Ragip [67]

Kayseri Atatürk, Kayseri, 28-09-2006, 20:00, 16 332, Kralovec CZE
Kayserispor 1 Gökhan [11]
AZ Alkmaar 1 Dembélé [54]

Georgios Kamaras, Athens, 28-09-2006, 22:00, 3500, Messner AUT
Atromitos 1 Korakis [64]
Sevilla 2 Kepa [16], Valente [43]

Sánchez-Pizjuan, Seville, 28-09-2006, 21:30, 30 644, Hrinak SVK
Sevilla 4 Luis Fabiano 2 [2 29], Ioannou OG [10], Kepa [86]
Atromitos 0

Municipal, Braga, 14-09-2006, 19:00, 9753, Verbist BEL
Sporting Braga 2 Paulo Jorge [5], Wender [91p]
Chievo Verona 0

Bentegodi, Verona, 28-09-2006, 20:45, 4722, Megía Davila ESP
Chievo Verona 2 Tiribocchi [38], Godeas [67]
Sporting Braga 1 Wender [104]

U Nisy, Liberec, 14-09-2006, 17:30, 7215, Thomson SCO
Slovan Liberec 2 Frejlach [43], Blazek [90]
Crvena Zvezda 0

Crvena Zvezda, Belgrade, 28-09-2006, 20:00, 14 000, Circhetta SUI
Crvena Zvezda 1 Ailton [43]
Slovan Liberec 2 Bílek [2], Holenda [67]

Idrottspark, Norrköping, 14-09-2006, 19:30, 5130, Courtney NIR
Atvidabergs FF 0
Grasshopper-Club 3 León [12], Eduardo [28], Sutter [57]

Hardturm, Zürich, 28-09-2006, 19:30, 4800, Paniashvili GEO
Grasshopper-Club 5 Blumer [29], Sutter [31], Schweiger [57],
Atvidabergs FF 0 Eduardo [60], Renggli [67]

Tsentralnyi, Kazan, 14-09-2006, 17:30, 23 000, Briakos GRE
Rubin Kazan 0
Parma 1 Dessena [79]

Ennio Tardini, Parma, 28-09-2006, 18:30, 2070, Weiner GER
Parma 1 Paponi [49]
Rubin Kazan 0

Hüseyin Avni Aker, Trabzon, 14-09-2006, 20:00, 100, Jara CZE
Trabzonspor 2 Gökdeniz [55], Umut [89]
Osasuna 2 Valdo [21], Juanlu [53]

Reyno de Navarra, Pamplona, 28-09-2006, 20:45, 14 918, Gumienny BEL
Osasuna 0
Trabzonspor 0

GSP, Nicosia, 14-09-2006, 19:00, 1169, Messina ITA
Ethnikos Achnas 0
Racing Club Lens 0

Félix-Bollaert, Lens, 28-09-2006, 18:00, 27 870, Batista POR
Racing Club Lens 3 Dindane [10], Jemaa [63], Cousin [64]
Ethnikos Achnas 1 Belic [69]

Olympiastadion, Berlin, 28-09-2006, 17:00, 12 814, Kassai HUN
Hertha Berlin 2 Giménez [38], Boateng [51]
OB Odense 2 Simunic OG [6], Bechara [53]

Fionia Park, Odense, 28-09-2006, 15:30, 11 466, Brines SCO
OB Odense   1   Timm [62]
Hertha Berlin   0

José Alvalade, Lisbon, 14-09-2006, 21:00, 3027, Fleischer GER
Vitória Setúbal   0
SC Heerenveen   3   Alves 2 [59 66], Nilsson [92+]

Abe Lenstra, Heerenveen, 28-09-2006, 18:45, 16 800, Bozinovski MKD
SC Heerenveen   0
Vitória Setúbal   0

Wals-Siezenheim, Salzburg, 14-09-2006, 20:45, 16 140, Mikulski POL
SV Salzburg   2   Zickler [30], Janko [92+]
Blackburn Rovers   2   Savage [32], McCarthy [39]

Ewood Park, Blackburn, 28-09-2006, 19:45, 18 888, Lopes POR
Blackburn Rovers   2   McCarthy [32], Bentley [56]
SV Salzburg   0

Veltins Arena, Gelsenkirchen, 14-09-2006, 19:00, 45 878, Vollquartz DEN
Schalke 04   1   Larsen [86]
AS Nancy   0

Marcel Picot, Nancy, 28-09-2006, 18:00, 18 029, Iturralde ESP
AS Nancy   3   Andre Luiz [18], Curbelo [25], Dia [70]
Schalke 04   1   Kuranyi [78]

Balgarska Armia, Sofia, 14-09-2006, 21:20, 3000, Sandmoen NOR
Lokomotiv Sofia   2   Geknov [5], Davtchev [29]
Feyenoord   2   Lucius [49p], Greene [60]

De Kuip, Rotterdam, 28-09-2006, 19:45, 20 000, Bebek CRO
Feyenoord   0
Lokomotiv Sofia   0

Wisly, Krakow, 14-09-2006, 20:30, 13 377, Asumaa FIN
Wisla Krakow   0
Iraklis Th'saloniki   1   Prittas [8]

Kaftanzoglio, Thessalonica, 28-09-2006, 21:30, 6331, Brugger AUT
Iraklis Th'saloniki   0
Wisla Krakow   2   Mijailovic [94+], Cantoro [100]

St Jakob-Park, Basel, 14-09-2006, 20:00, 11 945, Tudor ROU
FC Basel   6   Kuzmanovic [2], Petric 2 [6 40], Majstorovic [34p],
Rabotnicki Skopje   2   Pejcic [89], Buckley OG [94+]   Cristiano 2 [71 73]

Gradski, Skopje, 28-09-2006, 19:30, 1500, Richards WAL
Rabotnicki Skopje   0
FC Basel   1   Sterjovski [74]

Tehelné Pole, Bratislava, 28-09-2006, 18:45, 3480, Ivanov.N RUS
Artmedia Bra'lava   2   Halenár [36], Tchur [41]
Espanyol   2   Riera [31], Pandiani [53]

Olimpico, Barcelona, 28-09-2006, 21:30, 8100, Kapitanis CYP
Espanyol   3   Pandiani 2 [19 79], Luis García [67]
Artmedia Bra'lava   1   Burýan [13]

Aråsen, Lillestrom, 14-09-2006, 18:15, 1840, Gilewski POL
Start Kristiansand   1   Johnson.M [27], Fevang [55]   García [67]
Ajax   5   Huntelaar 2 [17 87], Rosenberg [42], Sneijder [63],

Amsterdam ArenA, Amsterdam, 28-09-2006, 20:45, 24 000, Ceferin SVN
Ajax   4   Rosenberg 2 [6 26], Grygera [43], Babel [68]
Start Kristiansand   0

Lokomotiv, Moscow, 14-09-2006, 20:15, 11 023, McDonald SCO
Lokomotiv Moskva   2   Loskov [35], Ivanovic [73]
Zulte Waregem   1   Vandemarliere [93]

Jules Otten, Gent, 28-09-2006, 19:00, 4800, Hyytiä FIN
Zulte Waregem   2   Matthys [57], Sergeant [82]
Lokomotiv Moskva   0

Murrayfield, Edinburgh, 14-09-2006, 19:45, 25 000, Bertini ITA
Heart of Midl'thian   0
Sparta Praha   2   Kolár [34], Matusovic [71]

Sparta, Prague, 28-09-2006, 21:00, 16 505, Sippel GER
Sparta Praha   0
Heart of Midl'thian   0

Legia, Warsaw, 14-09-2006, 17:30, 8000, Skomina SVN
Legia Warszawa   1   Junior [45]
FK Austria Wien   1   Mair [26]

Ernst Happel, Vienna, 28-09-2006, 20:45, 12 100, Sukhina RUS
FK Austria Wien   1   Wallner [65]
Legia Warszawa   0

Pampeloponnisiako, Patras, 14-09-2006, 21:45, 15 649, Gomes POR
Panathinaikos   1   Salpingidis [10]
Metalurh Zap'hya   1   Godin [47]

Metalurh, Zaporizhya, 28-08-2006, 21:45, 11 000, Slupik POL
Metalurh Zap'hya   0
Panathinaikos   1   Papadopoulos [14]

Brandywell, Londonderry, 14-09-2006, 19:00, 3000, Havrilla SVK
Derry City   0
Paris St-Germain   0

Parc des Princes, Paris, 21:00, 22 213, Oriekhov UKR
Paris St-Germain   2   Cissé [7], Pauleta [42]
Derry City   0

Chernomorets, Odessa, 14-09-2006, 19:00, 18 500, Corpodean ROU
Chernomorets O.   0
Hapoel Tel Aviv   1   De Bruno [74]

Bloomfield, Tel Aviv, 28-09-2006, 19:30, 12 000, Stuchlik AUT
Hapoel Tel Aviv   3   Toema [24], Barda [74], De Bruno [88]
Chernomorets O.   1   Nizhegorodov [82]

Giulesti, Bucharest, 14-09-2006, 20:00, 7050, Matejek CZE
Rapid Bucuresti   1   Moldovan.V [43]
Nacional Funchal   0

Dos Barreiros, Funchal, 28-09-2006, 20:00, 6833, Szabo HUN
Nacional Funchal   1   Juliano Spadacio [29]
Rapid Bucuresti   2   Rada [91], Burdujan [101]

Vélodrome, Marseille, 14-09-2006, 20:45, 15 077, Berntsen NOR
Olymp. Marseille   1   Bamogo [31]
Mladá Boleslav   0

Mestsky, Mladá Boleslav, 28-09-2006, 17:30, 5000, Bossen NED
Mladá Boleslav   4   Pecka [34], Holub 2 [62p 82], Sedlácek [92+]
Olymp. Marseille   2   Maoulida [14], Taiwo [56]

A Le Coq Arena, Tallinn, 14-09-2006, 17:55, Ingvarsson SWE
Levadia Tallinn   0
Newcastle United   1   Sibierski [10]

St James' Park, Newcastle, 28-09-2006, 19:30, 27 012, Jakobsson ISL
Newcastle United   2   Martins 2 [47 50]
Levadia Tallinn   1   Zelinski [65]

Sclessin, Liège, 14-09-2006, 20:30, 10 646, Lehner AUT
Standard Liège   0
Celta Vigo   1   Gustavo López [38]

Balaídos, Vigo, 28-09-2006, 21:00, 7751, Trefoloni ITA
Celta Vigo   3   Baiano 2 [22 83], Canobbio [70]
Standard Liège   0

Sükrü Saraçoglu, Istanbul, 14-09-2006, 21:45, 32 893, Wack GER
Fenerbahçe   2   Pedersen.R OG [24], Kezman [54]
Randers FC   1   Fall [13]

Atletion, Aarhus, 28-09-2006, 20:30, 14 282, Oliveira POR
Randers FC   0
Fenerbahçe   3   Deivid [61], Tuncay Sanli [64], Kezman [70]

Upton Park, London, 14-09-2006, 20:00, 33 322, Johannesson SWE
West Ham United   0
Palermo   1   Caracciolo [45]

Renzo Barbera, Palermo, 28-09-2006, 20:45, 20 000, Kasnaferis GRE
Palermo   3   Simplicio 2 [35 62], Di Michele [67]
West Ham United   0

Commerzbank Arena, Frankfurt, 14-09-2006, 20:45, 40 000, Styles ENG
Eintracht Frankfurt   4   Thurk 3 [51p 71p 78], Köhler [90]
Brøndby IF   0

Brøndby, Copenhagen, 28-09-2006, 18:05, 14 067, Vink NED
Brøndby IF   2   Ericsson [20], Rasmussen.T [65]
Eintracht Frankfurt   2   Vasoski 2 [6 52]

GROUP A

Armando Picchi, Livorno, 19-10-2006, 20:45, 13 199, Santiago ESP

Livorno 2 Lucarelli 2 [34p 90]
Rangers 3 Adam [27], Boyd [30p], Novo [35]

Bloomfield, Tel Aviv, 19-10-2006, 20:45, 14 300, Batista POR

Maccabi Haifa 3 Masudi [13], Boccoli [56], Colautti [58]
AJ Auxerre 1 Niculae [29]

Partizan, Belgrade, 2-11-2006, 19:00, 12 746, Sippel GER

Partizan Beograd 1 Mirosavljevic [70]
Livorno 1 Amelia [88]

Ibrox, Glasgow, 2-11-2006, 19:45, 43 062, Kapitanis CYP

Rangers 2 Novo [5], Adam [89p]
Maccabi Haifa 0

Abbé-Deschamps, Auxerre, 23-11-2006, 19:30, 8305, Eriksson SWE

AJ Auxerre 2 Jelen [31], Niculae.D [75]
Rangers 2 Novo [62], Boyd [84]

Bloomfield, Tel Aviv, 23-11-2006, 20:45, 13 500, Granat POL

Maccabi Haifa 1 Anderson [21]
Partizan Beograd 0

Partizan, Belgrade, 29-11-2006, 20:45, 4121, Sandmoen NOR

Partizan Beograd 1 Marinkovic.Neb [5]
AJ Auxerre 4 Cheyrou [18], Niculae.N [24], Akalé [36], Pieroni [82]

Armando Picchi, Livorno, 29-11-2006, 20:45, 7780, Vink NED

Livorno 1 Lucarelli [20]
Maccabi Haifa 1 Colautti [93+]

Ibrox, Glasgow, 14-12-2006, 19:45, 43 129, Bossen NED

Rangers 1 Hutton [55]
Partizan Beograd 0

Abbé-Deschamps, Auxerre, 14-12-2006, 20:45, 4330, Bebek CRO

AJ Auxerre 0
Livorno 1 Lucarelli [59]

Group A	Pl	W	D	L	F	A	Pts
Rangers	4	3	1	0	8	4	10
Maccabi Haifa	4	2	1	1	5	4	7
Livorno	4	1	2	1	5	5	5
AJ Auxerre	4	1	1	2	7	7	4
Partizan Beograd	4	0	1	3	2	7	1

GROUP B

Inönü, Istanbul, 19-10-2006, 20:00, 23 100, Vollquartz DEN

Besiktas 0
Tottenham H'spur 2 Ghaly [31], Berbatov [63]

Jan Breydel, Bruges, 19-10-2006, 20:45, 17 769, Kasnaferis GRE

Club Brugge 1 Clement [47]
Bayer Leverkusen 1 Schneider [35]

White Hart Lane, London, 2-11-2006, 20:00, 35 716, Undiano ESP

Tottenham H'spur 3 Berbatov 2 [17 73], Keane [63]
Club Brugge 1 Ibrahim [14]

Dinamo, Bucharest, 2-11-2006, 20:30, 7419, Ceferin SVN

Dinamo Bucuresti 2 Cristea [21], Niculescu [87p]
Besiktas 1 Deivson [58]

BayArena, Leverkusen, 23-11-2006, 20:30, 22 500, Hansson SWE

Bayer Leverkusen 0
Tottenham H'spur 1 Berbatov [36]

Jan Breydel, Bruges, 23-11-2006, 20:30, 18 713, Ingvarsson SWE

Club Brugge 1 Vermant [62p]
Dinamo Bucuresti 1 Niculescu [33]

Dinamo, Bucharest, 29-11-2006, 21:45, 8223, Lopes Ferreira POR

Dinamo Bucuresti 2 Niculescu 2 [37 74]
Bayer Leverkusen 1 Barbarez [22]

Inönü, Istanbul, 29-11-2006, 21:45, 19 668, Szabo HUN

Besiktas 2 Ibrahim Akin [32], Ricardinho [70p]
Club Brugge 1 Balaban [14p]

White Hart Lane, London, 14-12-2006, 19:45, 34 004, Brugger AUT

Tottenham H'spur 3 Berbatov [16], Defoe 2 [39 50]
Dinamo Bucuresti 1 Mendy [91+]

BayArena, Leverkusen, 14-12-2006, 20:30, 19 500, Paparesta ITA

Bayer Leverkusen 2 Schneider [78], Barbarez [87]
Besiktas 1 Ricardinho [91+p]

Group B	Pl	W	D	L	F	A	Pts
Tottenham Hotspur	4	4	0	0	9	2	12
Dinamo Bucuresti	4	2	1	1	6	6	7
Bayer Leverkusen	4	1	1	2	4	5	4
Besiktas	4	1	0	3	4	7	3
Club Brugge	4	0	2	2	4	7	2

GROUP C

DSB, Alkmaar, 19-10-2006, 20:15, 13 534, Stuchlik AUT

AZ Alkmaar 3 Arveladze.S [37], Koevermans [75], Schaars [82]
Sporting Liberec 0

U Nisy, Liberec, 19-10-2006, 21:00, 7023, Tudor ROU

Slovan Liberec 0
Sevilla 0

Hardturm, Zürich, 2-11-2006, 19:00, 5500, Briakos GRE

Grasshopper-Club 2 Mbala Mbuta [29], Eduardo [62] Marten [93+]
AZ Alkmaar 5 Arveladze [48], De Zeeuw [56], Dembélé 2 [78 95+],

Municipal, Braga, 2-11-2006, 20:30, 8859, Styles ENG

Sporting Braga 4 Chaves [30], Marcel [33], Césinha [54p], Gama [91+]
Slovan Liberec 0

U Nisy, Liberec, 23-11-2006, 18:15, 7662, Verbist BEL

Slovan Liberec 4 Blazek [7], Zápotocny [21], Papousek [68],
Grasshopper-Club 1 Schwegler [9] Frejlach [91+]

Sánchez-Pizjuan, Sevilla, 23-11-2006, 20:45, 28 225, Fleischer GER

Sevilla 2 Luis Fabiano [40], Chevantón [76]
Sporting Braga 0

Hardturm, Zürich, 29-11-2006, 20:45, 7300, Genov BUL

Grasshopper-Club 0
Sevilla 4 Daniel 2 [12 53], Chevantón [62], Kepa [84]

DSB, Alkmaar, 29-11-2006, 20:45, 16 000, Brines SCO

AZ Alkmaar 2 Steinsson [70], Jenner [89]
Slovan Liberec 2 Zápotocny [26], Papousek [85]

Municipal, Braga, 14-12-2006, 19:45, 11 048, Ivanov.N RUS

Sporting Braga 2 João Pinto [61], Castanheira [91+]
Grasshopper-Club 0

Sánchez-Pizjuan, Sevilla, 14-12-2006, 20:45, 29 373, Skjerven NOR

Sevilla 1 Chevantón [52p]
AZ Alkmaar 2 Arveladze.S 2 [62 93+]

Group C	Pl	W	D	L	F	A	Pts
AZ Alkmaar	4	3	1	0	12	5	10
Sevilla	4	2	1	1	7	2	7
Sporting Braga	4	2	0	2	6	5	6
Slovan Liberec	4	1	2	1	6	7	5
Grasshopper-Club	4	0	0	4	3	15	0

GROUP D

Reyno de Navarra, Pamplona, 19-10-2006, 20:45, 13 500, Skomina SVN

Osasuna 0
SC Heerenveen 0

Fionia Park, Odense, 19-10-2006, 20:45, 12 559, Gumienny BEL

OB Odense 1 Hansen [7]
Parma 2 Dessena [41], Budan [51]

Abe Lenstra, Heerenveen, 2-11-2006, 18:45, 18 000, Asumaa FIN
SC Heerenveen 0
OB Odense 2 Lekic 2 [45] [60]

Félix-Bollaert, Lens, 2-11-2006, 20:00, 33 954, Lehner AUT
Racing Club Lens 3 Dindane [15], Cousin [74p], Boukari [88]
Osasuna 1 Valdo [46]

Ennio Tardini, Parma, 23-11-2006, 20:45, 2461, Halsey ENG
Parma 2 Budan 2 [24] [73]
Heerenveen 1 Pranjic [21]

Fionia Park, Odense, 23-11-2006, 20:45, 7701, Yefet ISR
OB Odense 1 Grahn [58]
Racing Club Lens 1 Jemaa [87]

Félix-Bollaert, Lens, 29-11-2006, 20:45, 32 341, Dougal SCO
Racing Club Lens 1 Cousin [19]
Parma 2 Dedic [77], Paponi [92+]

Reyno de Navarra, Pamplona, 29-11-2006, 20:45, 13 115, Sippel GER
Osasuna 3 Puñal 2 [29] [67], Romeo [87]
OB Odense 1 Puñal OG [75]

Ennio Tardini, Parma, 14-12-2006, 20:45, 1972, Dereli TUR
Parma 0
Osasuna 3 David López 2 [33] [44], Juanfran [82]

Abe Lenstra, Heerenveen, 14-12-2006, 20:45, 22 000, Kapitanis CYP
SC Heerenveen 1 Alves [93+]
Racing Club Lens 0

Group D	Pl	W	D	L	F	A	Pts
Parma	4	3	0	1	6	6	9
Osasuna	4	2	1	1	7	4	7
Racing Club Lens	4	1	1	2	5	5	4
OB Odense	4	1	1	2	5	6	4
SC Heerenveen	4	1	1	2	2	4	4

GROUP E

Wisly, Kraków, 19-10-2006, 16:45, 10 500, Johannesson SWE
Wisla Kraków 1 Cantoro [28]
Blackburn Rovers 2 Savage [56], Bentley [90]

St Jakob Park, Basel, 20:15, 15 480, McDonald SCO
FC Basel 1 Eduardo [60]
Feyenoord 1 Huysegems [76]

Ewood Park, Blackburn, 2-11-2006, 20:00, 13 789, Oriekhov UKR
Blackburn Rovers 3 Tugay [75], Jeffers [89p], McCarthy [92+]
FC Basel 0

Marcel Picot, Nancy, 2-11-2006, 20:00, 17 509, Kralovec CZE
AS Nancy-Lorraine 2 Kim [10], Berenguer [58]
Wisla Kraków 1 Brozek [32]

St Jakob Park, Basel, 23-11-2006, 20:15, 14 497, Duarte Paixao POR
FC Basel 2 Chipperfield [32], Sterjovski [56]
AS Nancy-Lorraine 2 Kim [31], Berenguer [34]

De Kuip, Rotterdam, 23-11-2006, 20:45, 28 000, Kircher GER
Feyenoord 0
Blackburn Rovers 0

Marcel Picot, Nancy, 30-11-2006, 20:45, 19 048, Berntsen NOR
AS Nancy-Lorraine 3 Puygrenier [22], Kim [42], Zerka [66p]
Feyenoord 0

Wisly, Kraków, 3-11-2006, 20:45, 5580, Kassai HUN
Wisla Kraków 3 Brozek 2 [11] [83], Paulista [71]
FC Basel 1 Petric [8]

Ewood Park, Blackburn, 13-12-2006, 19:45, 12 568, Lehner AUT
Blackburn Rovers 1 Neill [93+]
AS Nancy-Lorraine 0

De Kuip, Rotterdam, 13-12-2006, 20:45, 20 459, Dondarini ITA
Feyenoord 3 Hofs [16], De Guzman [41], Charisteas [67]
Wisla Kraków 1 Brozek [23]

Group E	Pl	W	D	L	F	A	Pts
Blackburn Rovers	4	3	0	1	6	1	10
AS Nancy-Lorraine	4	2	1	1	7	4	7
Feyenoord	4	1	2	1	4	5	5
Wisla Kraków	4	1	0	3	6	8	3
FC Basel	4	0	2	2	4	9	2

GROUP F

Ernst Happel, Vienna, 19-10-2006, 19:30, 11 100, Jakobsson ISL
FK Austria Wien 1 Lasnik [22]
Zulte Waregem 4 Matthys 3 [33] [56] [69], Vandendriessche [90]

Sparta, Prague, 19-10-2006, 20:15, 11 020, Webb ENG
Sparta Praha 0
Espanyol 2 Luis Garcia [17p], Riera [85]

Jules Otten, Gent, 2-11-2006, 20:30, 7542, Szabo HUN
Zulte Waregem 3 Roussel [4], Meert [17], Repka OG [72]
Sparta Praha 1

Amsterdam ArenA, 2-11-2006, 20:45, 32 285, Corpodean ROU
Ajax 3 Huntelaar 2 [35] [68], Manucharyan [65]
FK Austria Wien 0

Sparta, Prague, 23-11-2006, 18:30, 12 230, Piccirillo FRA
Sparta Praha 0
Ajax 0

Olímpico, Barcelona, 23-11-2006, 21:30, 9250, Balaj ROU
Espanyol 6 Coro [9], Pandiani 2 [14] [83], Luis Garcia 3 [19] [27p] [73]
Zulte Waregem 2 Matthys [17], D'Haene [62]

Amsterdam ArenA, 30-11-2006, 20:45, 42 000, Bertini ITA
Ajax 0
Espanyol 2 Pandiani [36], Coro [78]

Ernst Happel, Vienna, 30-11-2006, 20:45, 8600, Lajuks LVA
FK Austria Wien 0
Sparta Praha 1 Repka [11]

Olímpico, Barcelona, 13-12-2006, 20:45, 6000, Slupik POL
Espanyol 1 Pandiani [57]
FK Austria Wien 0

Jules Otten, Gent, 13-12-2006, 20:45, 11 603, Trivkovic CRO
Zulte Waregem 0
Ajax 3 Huntelaar 2 [4] [57], Heitinga [83]

Group F	Pl	W	D	L	F	A	Pts
Espanyol	4	4	0	0	11	2	12
Ajax	4	2	1	1	6	2	7
Zulte Waregem	4	2	0	2	9	11	6
Sparta Praha	4	1	1	2	2	5	4
FK Austria Wien	4	0	0	4	1	9	0

GROUP G

OACA Spyro Louis, Athens, 19-10-2006, 19:00, Itturalde ESP
Panathinaikos 2 Chen OG [47], Romero [64]
Hapoel Tel Aviv 0

Giulesti, Bucharest, 19-10-2006, 21:00, 8500, Ivanov.N RUS
Rapid Bucuresti 0
Paris St-Germain 0

Bloomfield, Tel Aviv, 2-11-2006, 18:30, 6106, Hrinak SVK
Hapoel Tel Aviv 2 Ogbona [10], Badir [33]
Rapid Bucuresti 2 Moldovan.V [14], Buga [53]

Mestsky, Mladá Boleslav, 2-11-2006, 20:15, 4280, Kelly IRL
Mladá Boleslav 0
Panathinaikos 1 Salpingidis [64]

Giulesti, Bucharest, 23-11-2006, 20:15, 6600, Messner AUT
Rapid Bucuresti　1　Constantin.M [52]
Mladá Boleslav　1　Rajnoch [42]

Parc des Princes, Paris, 23-11-2006, 20:45, 22 836, Weiner GER
Paris St-Germain　2　Frau [14], Pauleta [25]
Hapoel Tel Aviv　4　Toema 2 [2 6], Badir [44], Barda [57]

Mestsky, Mladá Boleslav, 30-11-2006, 20:45, 4840, Panic BIH
Mladá Boleslav　0
Paris St-Germain　0

OACA Spyro Louis, Athens, 30-11-2006, 21:45, 18 033, Trefoloni ITA
Panathinaikos　0
Rapid Bucuresti　0

Parc des Princes, Paris, 13-12-2006, 20:45, 17 371, Megia Davila ESP
Paris St-Germain　4　Pauleta 2 [29 47], Kalou.B 2 [52 54]
Panathinaikos　0

Bloomfield, Tel Aviv, 13-12-2006, 21:45, 7889, Meyer GER
Hapoel Tel Aviv　1　Barda [27]
Mladá Boleslav　1　Kysela [39]

Group G	Pl	W	D	L	F	A	Pts
Panathinaikos	4	2	1	1	3	4	7
Paris Saint-Germain	4	1	2	1	6	4	5
Hapoel Tel Aviv	4	1	2	1	7	7	5
Rapid Bucuresti	4	0	4	0	3	3	4
Mladá Boleslav	4	0	3	1	2	3	3

GROUP H

Commerzbank Arena, Frankfurt, 19-10-2006, 18:15, 45 000, Yefet ISR
Eintracht Frankfurt　1　Streit [46+]
Palermo　2　Brienza [50], Zaccardo [88]

St James' Park, Newcastle, 19-10-2006, 20:00, 30 035, Gilewski POL
Newcastle United　1　Sibierski [79]
Fenerbahçe　0

Renzo Barbera, Palermo, 2-11-2006, 20:45, 17 000, Jara CZE
Palermo　0
Newcastle United　1　Luque [37]

Balaídos, Vigo, 2-11-2006, 21:00, 9372, Dougal SCO
Celta Vigo　1　Perera [11]
Eintracht Frankfurt　1　Huber [17]

St James' Park, Newcastle, 23-11-2006, 19:45, 25 079, Van Egmond NED
Newcastle United　2　Sibierski [37], Taylor [86]
Celta Vigo　1　Cannobbio [9]

Sükrü Saraçoglu, Istanbul, 23-11-2006, 20:00, 39 071, Batista POR
Fenerbahçe　3　Appiah [20], Lugano [62], Tuncay Sanli [83]
Palermo　0

Balaídos, Vigo, 30-11-2006, 20:45, 7666, Allaerts BEL
Celta Vigo　1　Cannobbio [77]
Fenerbahçe　0

Commerzbank Arena, Frankfurt, 30-11-2006, 20:45, 47 000, Oliveira POR
Eintracht Frankfurt　0
Newcastle United　0

Renzo Barbera, Palermo, 13-12-2006, 20:45, 10 222, Thomson SCO
Palermo　1　Tedesco [70]
Celta Vigo　1　Baiano [59]

Sükrü Saraçoglu, Istanbul, 13-12-2006, 21:45, 44 123, Wegereef NED
Fenerbahçe　2　Tuncay Sanli [64], Semih Sentürk [83]
Eintracht Frankfurt　2　Takahara 2 [7 52]

Group H	Pl	W	D	L	F	A	Pts
Newcastle United	4	3	1	0	4	1	10
Celta Vigo	4	1	2	1	4	4	5
Fenerbahçe	4	1	1	2	5	4	4
Palermo	4	1	1	2	3	6	4
Eintracht Frankfurt	4	0	3	1	4	5	3

ROUND OF THIRTY-TWO

Steaua, Bucharest, 15-02-2007, 20:30, 23 927, Meyer GER
Steaua Bucuresti　0
Sevilla　2　Poulsen [41], Kanouté [77p]

Sánchez-Pizjuan, Seville, 22-02-2007, 20:45, 19 336, Dougal SCO
Sevilla　1　Kerzhakov [48+]
Steaua Bucuresti　0

RSC Olympiyskiy, Donetsk, 14-02-2007, 19:00, 24 800, Briakos GRE
Shakhtar Donetsk　1　Srna [84]
Nancy-Lorraine　1　Fortune [81]

Marcel Picot, Nancy, 22-02-2007, 19:00, 16 564, Gilewski POL
Nancy-Lorraine　0
Shakhtar Donetsk　1　Fernandinho [71]

Municipal, Braga, 15-02-2007, 19:00, 6046, Skomina SVN
Sporting Braga　1　Zé Carlos [81]
Parma　0

Ennio Tardini, Parma, 22-02-2007, 20:45, 2773, Hrinak SVK
Parma　0
Sporting Braga　1　Diego [90]

BayArena, Leverkusen, 14-02-2007, 18:15, 17 906, Vink NED
Bayer Leverkusen　3　Callsen-Bracker [18], Ramelow [43], Schneider [56]
Blackburn Rovers　2　Bentley [38], Nonda [87]

Ewood Park, Blackburn, 22-02-2007, 18:05, 25 124, Undiano ESP
Blackburn Rovers　0
Bayer Leverkusen　0

Félix-Bollaert, Lens, 15-02-2007, 20:45, 29 532, Eriksson SWE
Racing Club Lens　3　Jemaa 2 [50 70], Dindane [90p]
Panathinaikos　1　Salpingidis [65]

OACA Spyro Louis, Athens, 22-02-2007, 21:45, 40 914, Jara CZE
Panathinaikos　0
Racing Club Lens　0

Bloomfield, Tel Aviv, 14-02-2007, 21:05, 11 175, Oliveira POR
Hapoel Tel Aviv　2　Toema [43], Dego [76]
Rangers　1　Novo [53]

Ibrox, Glasgow, 22-02-2007, 20:05, 46 213, Trefoloni ITA
Rangers　4　Ferguson 2 [24 73], Boyd [35], Adam [95+]
Hapoel Tel Aviv　0

Chaban-Delmas, Bordeaux, 14-02-2007, 18:00, 17 676, Yefet ISR
Girond. Bordeaux　0
Osasuna　0

Reyno de Navarra, Pamplona, 22-02-2007, 20:45, 17 475, Messina ITA
Osasuna　1　Nekunam [120]
Girond. Bordeaux　0

Weserstadion, Bremen, 14-02-2007, 20:30, 37 500, Batista POR
Werder Bremen　3　Mertesacker [48], Naldo [54], Frings [71]
Ajax　0

Amsterdam ArenA, 22-02-2007, 21:00, 35 227, Webb ENG
Ajax　3　Leonardo [4], Huntelaar [60], Babel [74]
Werder Bremen　1　Almeida [14]

Luzhniki, Moscow, 15-02-2007, 19:00, 19 500, Kapitanis CYP
Spartak Moskva　1　Kalynychenko [65]
Celta Vigo　1　Núñez [41]

Balaídos, Vigo, 22-02-2007, 20:45, 6189, Duhamel FRA
Celta Vigo　2　Nené [19], Jonathan [78]
Spartak Moskva　1　Titov [88]

Jules Otten, Gent, 15-02-2007, 20:45, 8015, Genov BUL
Zulte Waregem　1　D'Haene [69]
Newcastle United　3　Dindeleux OG [47], Martins [59p], Sibierski [76]

St James' Park, Newcastle, 22-02-2007, 19:45, 30 083, Ivanov.N RUS
Newcastle United　1　Martins [68]
Zulte Waregem　0

Sükrü Saraçoglu, Istanbul, 14-02-2007, 20:00, 38 711, Iturralde ESP
Fenerbahçe　3　Tümer Metin 2 [27 73], Tuncay Sanli [65]
AZ Alkmaar　3　De Zeeuw [15], Boukhari [62], Jenner [63]

DSB, Alkmaar, 22-02-2007, 18:45, 16 118, Kircher AUT

AZ Alkmaar   2   Martens [63], Opdam [86]
Fenerbahçe   2   Tümer Metin [21], Alex [34]

Estádio da Luz, Lisbon, 14-02-2007, 20:00, 35 197, Bebek CRO

Benfica   1   Miccoli [90]
Dinamo Bucuresti   0

Dinamo, Bucharest, 22-02-2007, 20:45, 12 480, Vollquartz DEN

Dinamo Bucuresti   1   Munteanu [24]
Benfica   2   Anderson [50], Katsouranis [64]

OACA Spyro Louis, Athens, 14-02-2007, 21:45, 26 120, Thomson SCO

AEK Athens   0
Paris St-Germain   2   Traoré [46+], Mendy [88]

Parc des Princes, Paris, 22-02-2007, 20:45, 22 670, Paparesta ITA

Paris St-Germain   2   Frau [42], Mendy [91+]
AEK Athens   0

Republican, Vladikavkaz, 14-02-2007, 20:00, 25 000, Ceferin SVN

CSKA Moskva   0
Maccabi Haifa   0

Bloomfield, Tel Aviv, 22-02-2007, 20:45, 13 500, Lehner AUT

Maccabi Haifa   1   Colautti [13]
CSKA Moskva   0

Armando Picchi, Livorno, 14-02-2007, 20:45, 400, Lannoy FRA

Livorno   1   Galante [82]
Espanyol   2   Pandiani [28p], Moha [59]

Olímpico, Barcelona, 22-02-2007, 21:30, 12 134, Allaerts BEL

Espanyol   2   Lacruz [15], Coro [49]
Livorno   0

ROUND OF SIXTEEN

Sánchez-Pizjuan, Seville, 8-03-2007, 20:45, 25 599, Kassai HUN

Sevilla   2   Marti [8p], Maresca [88p]
Shakhtar Donetsk   2   Hübschman [19], Matuzalem [60p]

RSC Olymiyskiy, Donetsk, 25-03-2007, 20:30, 25 500, Paparesta ITA

Shakhtar Donetsk   2   Matuzalem [49], Elano [83]
Sevilla   3   Maresca [53], Palop [94+], Chevanton [105]

Municipal, Braga, 8-03-2007, 21:35, 12 904, Baskakov RUS

Sporting Braga   2   Paulo Jorge [76], Zé Carlos [81]
Tottenham H'spur   3   Keane 2 [57 92+], Malbranque [72]

White Hart Lane, London, 14-03-2007, 20:15, 33 761, Duhamel FRA

Tottenham H'spur   3   Berbatov 2 [28 42], Malbranque [76]
Sporting Braga   2   Huddlestone OG [24], Andrade [61]

Félix-Bollaert, Lens, 8-03-2007, 19:00, 29 200, Webb ENG

Racing Club Lens   2   Monterrubio [16], Cousin [69p]
Bayer Leverkusen   1   Haggui [51]

BayArena, Leverkusen, 14-03-2007, 18:15, 17 944, Benquerença POR

Bayer Leverkusen   3   Voronin [36], Barbarez [56], Juan [70]
Racing Club Lens   0

Ibrox, Glasgow, 8-03-2007, 20:05, 50 290, Wegereef NED

Rangers   1   Hemdani [92+]
Osasuna   1   Raúl Garcia [17]

Reyno de Navarra, Pamplona, 14-03-2007, 20:45, 19 126, Larsen

Osasuna   1   Webó [71]
Rangers   0

Balaídos, Vigo, 8-03-2006, 20:45, 9236, Malek POL

Celta Vigo   0
Werder Bremen   1   Almeida [84]

Weserstadion, Bremen, 14-03-2007, 20:45, 35 278, Farina ITA

Werder Bremen   2   Almeida [49], Fritz [61]
Celta Vigo   0

St James' Park, Newcastle, 8-03-2007, 19:30, 28 452, Busacca SUI

Newcastle United   4   Steinsson OG [7], Dyer [22], Martins 2 [23 37]
AZ Alkmaar   2   Arveladze.S [31], Koevermans [73]

DSB, Alkmaar, 15-03-2007, 20:35, 16 100, Layec FRA

AZ Alkmaar   2   Arveladze.S [14], Koevermans [56]
Newcastle United   0

Parc des Princes, Paris, 8-03-2007, 20:45, 33 962, Poll ENG

Paris St-Germain   2   Pauleta [35], Frau [39]
Benfica   1   Simão [10]

Estádio da Luz, Lisbon, 15-03-2007, 21:00, 58 800, Meyer GER

Benfica   3   Simão 2 [12 89p], Petit [27]
Paris St-Germain   1   Pauleta [32]

Bloomfield, Tel Aviv, 8-03-2007, 20:45, 14 700, Bebek CRO

Maccabi Haifa   0
Espanyol   0

Olímpico, Barcelona, 15-03-2007, 21:30, 16 150, Fröjdfeldt SWE

Espanyol   4   De la Peña [53], Tamudo [59], Luis García [61],
Maccabi Haifa   0   Pandiani [93+]

QUARTER-FINALS

Sánchez-Pizjuan, Seville, 5-04-2007, 20:45, 32 738, Hamer LUX

Sevilla   2   Kanouté [19p], Kerzhakov [36]
Tottenham H'spur   1   Keane [2]

White Hart Lane, London, 12-04-2007, 19:45, 35 234, Plautz AUT

Tottenham H'spur   2   Defoe [65], Lennon [66]
Sevilla   2   Malbranque OG [3], Kanouté [8]

BayArena, Leverkusen, 5-04-2007, 19:00, 22 500, Hauge NOR

Bayer Leverkusen   0
Osasuna   3   Cuéllar [1], David López [71], Webó [73]

Reyno de Navarra, Pamplona, 12-04-2007, 20:45, 17 450, Fröjdfeldt SWE

Osasuna   1   Juanlu Gómez [62]
Bayer Leverkusen   0

DSB, Alkmaar, 5-04-2007, 20:45, 16 800, Benquerença POR

AZ Alkmaar   0
Werder Bremen   0

Weserstadion, Bremen, 12-04-2007, 20:45, 35 000, Riley ENG

Werder Bremen   4   Borowski [16], Klose 2 [36 62], Diego [82]
AZ Alkmaar   1   Dembélé [32]

Olímpico, Barcelona, 5-04-2007, 20:45, 25 100, Braamhaar NED

Espanyol   3   Tamudo [15], Riera [33], Pandiani [58]
Benfica   2   Nuno Gomes [63], Simão [65]

Estádio da Luz, Lisbon, 12-04-2007, 19:45, 51 102, Larsen DEN

Benfica   0
Espanyol   0

SEMI-FINALS

Reyno de Navarra, Pamplona
26-04-2007, 20:45, 18 134, Braamhaar NED

Osasuna	**1**
	Soldado 55

Ricardo López - Izquierdo, Cuéllar●, Cruchaga, Corrales - Raúl García, Patxi Puñal, David López - Milosevic (Valdo López 81), Juanfran, Soldado● (Webó 74). Tr: Ziganda

Sevilla	**0**

Cobeño - Javi Navarro, Escude, Dragutinovic - Alves, Adriano (Puerta 83), Poulsen●, Martí (Hinkel 72) - Luis Fabiano● (Kerzhakov 61), Kanouté●, Navas●. Tr: Ramos

Sánchez-Pizjuan, Seville
3-05-2007, 20:45, 38 497, Poll ENG

Sevilla	**2**
	Luis Fabiano 37, Renato 53

Palop - Javi Navarro, Escude●, Puerta - Alves, Adriano (Duda● 27), Poulsen, Renato (Aitor Ocio 88), Martí - Luis Fabiano (Kerzhakov 73), Kanouté. Tr: Ramos

Osasuna	**0**

Ricardo López - Izquierdo (Muñoz● 83), Cuéllar●, Cruchaga, Corrales - Raúl García, Patxi Puñal (Valdo López 61), David López, Nekunam● - Juanfran (Delporte 71), Webó. Tr: Ziganda

Olímpico, Barcelona
26-04-2007, 20:45, 40 250, Ovrebø NOR

Espanyol	**3**
	Moisés 20, Pandiani 50, Coro 88

Iraizoz - David García, Lacruz, Torrejón, Jarque, Moisés● - De La Peña (Jônatas 79) - Pandiano● (Ito 73), Riera, Rufete (Corominas 83), Tamudo. Tr: Valverde

Werder Bremen	**0**

Wiese●58 - Pasanen, Naldo, Fritz●, Owomoyela - Baumann● (Vranjes 79), Diego, Jensen (Reinke 60), Frings - Klose (Almeida 74), Hunt. Tr: Schaaf

Weserstadion, Bremen
3-05-2007, 20:45, 37 000, Layec FRA

Werder Bremen	**1**
	Almeida 4

Reinke - Pasanen, Naldo, Owomoyela (Schindler 46), Schulz - Diego, Jensen (Wome 70), Frings (Baumann 75) - Klose●●●19, Hunt, Almeida●. Tr: Schaaf

Espanyol	**2**
	Coro 50, Lacruz 60

Iraizoz - David García, Lacruz, Torrejón, Jarque - Zabaleta● (Martínez 65), Ito - Luis García●, Riera (Rufete 71), Corominas●, Tamudo (Julián 79). Tr: Valverde

FINAL

Hampden Park, Glasgow
16-05-2007, 19:45, 47 602, Busacca SUI, Arnet SUI, Cuhat SUI

ESPANYOL	**2**	**2**	**SEVILLA**
Riera 28, Jônatas 115	**1**	P S O **3**	Adriano 18, Kanoute 105

		ESPANYOL			SEVILLA		
1	GK	IRAIZOZ Gorka			PALOP Andrés	GK	1
3	DF	DAVID GARCIA			(c) JAVI NAVARRO	DF	2
19	DF	TORREJON Marc			PUERTA Antonio	DF	16
21	DF	JARQUE Daniel			DRAGUTINOVIC Ivica	DF	19
22	DF	MOISES Hurtado	68		DANIEL ALVES	MF	4
8	MF	ZABALETA Pablo Javier		76	ADRIANO Correia	MF	6
9	MF	DE LA PEÑA Iván	87		POULSEN Christian	MF	8
10	FW	LUIS GARCIA			MARTI José Luis	MF	18
11	FW	RIERA Albert		46	MARESCA Enzo	MF	25
18	FW	RUFETE Francisco	56	64	LUIS FABIANO	FW	10
23	FW	TAMUDO Raúl (c)	73		KANOUTE Frédéric	FW	12
		Tr: VALVERDE Ernesto			Tr: RAMOS Juande		
4	DF	LACRUZ Jesús María	73		DAVID Castedo	DF	3
6	MF	EDUARDO COSTA			CHEVANTON Ernesto	FW	7
7	FW	PANDIANI Walter	56	64	KERZHAKOV Aleksandr	FW	9
16	MF	JONATAS	87	76	RENATO	MF	11
20	FW	COROMINAS Ferrán			COBENO David	GK	13
25	GK	KAMENI Idriss		46	Jesús NAVAS	FW	15
30	DF	CHICA Francisco			AITOR OCIO	DF	20

PENALTIES (SEVILLA WON 3-1)

Sevilla first: Kanoute ✓; Luis Garcia ✗; Dragutinovic ✓; Pandiani ✓; Daniel Alves ✗; Jônatas ✗; Puerta ✓; Torrejón ✗

UEFA WOMEN'S CUP 2006–07

SEMI-FINALS

Brøndby, Copenhagen
4-11-2006, 13:00, 682, Brohet BEL

Brøndby	2
	Pape [16], Jensen.L [59]

Cederkvist - Andersen, Nielsen.A, Sørensen, Jensen.S,
Bukh, Olsen, Jensen.L (Konge 85), Falk, Pedersen.S*
(Nielsen.K 70), Pape. Tr: Henrik Jensen

Arsenal	2
	Smith 2 [9 51]

Byrne - Scott, Ludlow, Asante, Phillip - Grant,
Chapman, Yankey (Carney 72) - Smith**79,
Sanderson, Fleeting (Davison 88). Tr: Akers

Borehamwood FC, Borehamwood
11-11-2006, 14:00, 1293, Avdonchenko RUS

Arsenal	3
	Yankey [33], Carney [53], Fleeting [90]

Byrne - Scott, Ludlow, Asante, Phillip - Grant,
Chapman, Carney (Davison 80), Yankey* -
Sanderson, Fleeting*. Tr: Akers

Brøndby	0

Cederkvist - Andersen, Nielsen.A, Sørensen*,
Jensen.S, Bukh, Olsen, Jensen.L (Konge 66), Falk*,
Nielsen.K (Løvendorf 66), Pape. Tr: Henrik Jensen

Sofiemyr, Oslo
4-11-2006, 14:00, 792, Toms ENG

Kolbotn	1
	Rønning [35]

Bye - Stangeland, Stensland, Lindblom, Rønning,
Gulbrandsen (Schjelderup 81), Huse, Andersen,
Hansen (Isaksen 72), Blystad-Bjerke (Herlovsen 62),
Berg-hansen. Tr: Bergo

Umeå IK	5

Ljungberg 2 [2 77], Klaveness [54], Marta 2 [68 89]

Lundgren - Paulsson, Westberg, Bergqvist, Moström,
Mäkinen, Sjöström (Dahlkvist 77), Klaveness,
Valkonen, Marta, Ljungberg. Tr: Jeglertz

Gammliavallen, Umeå
12-11-2006, 14:00, 762, Petignat SUI

Umeå IK	6

Marta 2 [12 77], Ljungberg 2 [24 92+],
Mäkinen [48], Moström [55]

Lundgren - Paulsson, Frisk, Westberg (Dahlkvist 62),
Bergqvist, Moström, Mäkinen, Sjöström (Pedersen 72),
Klaveness (Karlsson 83), Marta, Ljungberg.
Tr: Jeglertz

Kolbotn	0

Bye - Stangeland, Stensland, Lindblom (Berge 46),
Rønning, Gulbrandsen, Huse, Andersen, Hansen
(Isaksen 72), Blystad-Bjerke (Herlovsen 46),
Berg-hansen. Tr: Bergo

Gammliavallen, Umeå
21-04-2007, 14:00, 6265, Beck GER

UMEA IK	0	1	ARSENAL
			Scott [91+]

UMEA IK			ARSENAL	
53 SOBERG Carola			BYRNE Emma	1
2 PAULSSON Anna			PHILLIP Mary	23
3 FRISK Johanna			SCOTT Alex	12
89 BERGQVIST Maria			GRANT Clara	7
4 WESTBERG Karolina			LUDLOW Jayne	4
7 DAHLKVIST Lisa	76		ASANTE Anita	18
20 MOURA Elaine			CHAPMAN Katie	17
10 LJUNGBERG Hanna	63	89	CARNEY Karen	14
13 EDLUND Madelaine			YANKEY Rachel	11
60 MARTA			SANDERSON Lianne	9
14 KLAVENESS Lise			FLEETING Julie	10
Tr: JEGLERTZ Andrée			Tr: AKERS Victor	
30 RONNLUND Ulla-Karin			SPENCER Rebecca	24
6 BERGLUND Emma			TRACY Yvonne	3
12 PEDERSEN June			CHAMP Leanne	5
18 MA Xiaoxu	63		WHITE Faye	6
19 BACHMANN Ramona	76	89	LARKIN Sian	16
77 KONRADSSON Emmelie			DAVISON Gemma	20
11 KARLSSON Erika			FLAHERTY Gilly	26

Borehamwood FC, Borehamwood
29-04-2007, 12:00, 3467, Petignat SUI

ARSENAL	0	0	UMEA IK

ARSENAL			UMEA IK	
1 BYRNE Emma			SOBERG Carola	53
12 SCOTT Alex			PAULSSON Anna	2
4 LUDLOW Jayne	90		WESTBERG Karolina	4
18 ASANTE Anita			FRISK Johanna	3
23 PHILLIP Mary			BERGQVIST Maria	89
14 CARNEY Karen		55	DAHLKVIST Lisa	7
17 CHAPMAN Katie			MOURA Elaine	20
7 GRANT Clara		72	MA Xiaoxu	18
11 YANKEY Rachel			KLAVENESS Lise	14
10 FLEETING Julie			MARTA	60
9 SANDERSON Lianne			LJUNGBERG Hanna	10
Tr: AKERS Victor			Tr: JEGLERTZ Andrée	
24 SPENCER Rebecca			RONNLUND Ulla-Karin	30
3 TRACY Yvonne			BERGLUND Emma	6
5 CHAMP Leanne			KARLSSON Erika	11
6 WHITE Faye	90		PEDERSEN June	12
16 LARKIN Sian		55	EDLUND Madelaine	13
20 DAVISON Gemma		72	BACHMANN Ramona	19
26 FLAHERTY Gilly			KONRADSSON Emmelie	77

UEFA WOMEN'S CUP 2006-07

First round Groups

Group 1 - Zagreb — Saestum (NED), Cardiff City (WAL), Maksimir (CRO), Dundalk (IRL)

	Pl	W	D	L	F	A	Pts	WAL	CRO	IRL
NED	3	3	0	0	15	1	9	2-0	7-0	6-1
WAL	3	2	0	1	5	4	6		3-2	2-0
CRO	3	1	0	2	10	10	3			8-0
IRL	3	0	0	3	1	16	0			

Group 2 - Livingston — Espanyol (ESP), Juvisy (FRA), Hibernian (SCO), KÍ Klaksvík (FRO)

	Pl	W	D	L	F	A	Pts	FRA	SCO	FRO
ESP	3	3	0	0	12	1	9	1-0	4-1	7-0
FRA	3	2	0	1	12	1	6		6-0	6-0
SCO	3	1	0	2	3	11	3			2-1
FRO	3	0	0	3	1	15	0			

Group 3 - Neulengbach — Breidablik (ISL), Neulengbach (AUT), 1.Dezembro (POR), Newtownabbey (NIR)

	Pl	W	D	L	F	A	Pts	AUT	POR	NIR
ISL	3	3	0	0	14	0	9	3-0	4-0	7-0
AUT	3	2	0	1	8	4	6		3-0	5-1
POR	3	1	0	2	7	8	3			7-1
NIR	3	0	0	3	2	19	0			

Group 4 - Strumica — HJK Helsinki (FIN), AZS Wroclaw (POL), Zuchwil (SUI), Shkiponjat (MKD)

	Pl	W	D	L	F	A	Pts	POL	SUI	MKD
FIN	3	3	0	0	10	0	9	1-0	2-0	7-0
POL	3	1	1	1	6	4	4		2-2	4-1
SUI	3	1	1	1	5	5	4			3-1
MKD	3	0	0	3	2	14	0			

Group 5 - Siauliai — Universitet Vitebsk (BLR), Flammamonza (ITA), SFK 2000 Sarajevo (BIH), Gintra Universitetas (LTU)

	Pl	W	D	L	F	A	Pts	ITA	BIH	LTU
BLR	3	2	0	1	4	1	6	0-1	1-0	3-0
ITA	3	2	0	1	3	1	6		0-1	2-0
BIH	3	1	1	1	2	2	4			1-1
LTU	3	0	1	2	1	6	1			

Group 6 - Murska Sub. — Wezemaal (BEL), Masinac Nis (SRB), Pomurje (SVN), Pärnu (EST)

	Pl	W	D	L	F	A	Pts	SRB	SVN	EST
BEL	3	3	0	0	18	1	9	6-1	5-0	7-0
SRB	3	2	0	1	10	9	6		3-2	6-1
SVN	3	1	0	2	9	9	3			7-1
EST	3	0	0	3	2	20	0			

Group 7 - Mocenok — Rossiyanka (RUS), Alma (KAZ), Slovan Duslo Sal'a (SVK), Clujana (ROU)

	Pl	W	D	L	F	A	Pts	KAZ	SVK	ROU
RUS	3	3	0	0	18	0	9	7-0	6-1	5-2
KAZ	3	2	0	1	11	4	6		4-2	5-2
SVK	3	1	0	2	4	11	3			4-0
ROU	3	0	0	3	2	12	0			

Group 8 - Chernigov — Legend Chernigov (UKR), Maccabi Holon (ISR), PAOK Tessaloniki (GRE), AEK Kokkinochorion (CYP)

	Pl	W	D	L	F	A	Pts	ISR	GRE	CYP
UKR	3	3	0	0	12	0	9	2-0	4-0	6-0
ISR	3	1	1	1	6	4	4		2-2	4-0
GRE	3	1	1	1	6	8	4			4-2
CYP	3	0	0	3	2	14	0			

Group 9 - Pravetz — 1.FC Femina Budapest (HUN), NSA Sofia (BUL), Narta Chisinau (MDA), Gömrükçü Baku (AZE)

	Pl	W	D	L	F	A	Pts	BUL	MDA	AZE
HUN	3	3	0	0	15	1	9	4-1	4-0	7-0
BUL	3	2	0	1	10	6	6		3-1	5-2
MDA	3	1	0	2	3	11	3			3-1
AZE	3	0	0	3	2	16	0			

Second Round Groups

Group 1 - Helsinki

	Pl	W	D	L	F	A	Pts	ISL	FIN	BLR
1.FFC Frankfurt (GER)	3	3	0	0	12	0	9	5-0	2-0	5-0
Breidablik (ISL)	3	2	0	1	3	6	6		2-1	1-0
HJK Helsinki (FIN)	3	0	1	2	1	4	1			0-0
Universitet Vitebsk (BLR)	3	0	1	2	0	6	1			

Group 2 - Askim

	Pl	W	D	L	F	A	Pts	NOR	ESP	UKR
Umeå (SWE)	3	3	0	0	7	1	9	2-1	3-0	2-0
Kolbotn (NOR)	3	2	0	1	7	5	6		4-2	2-1
Espanyol (ESP)	3	1	0	2	7	7	3			5-0
Legend Chernigov (UKR)	3	0	0	3	1	9	0			

Group 3 - Zeist

	Pl	W	D	L	F	A	Pts	NED	BEL	CZE
1.FFC Turb. Potsdam (GER)	3	2	1	0	7	2	7	2-2	1-0	4-0
Saestum (NED)	3	2	1	0	7	3	7		2-0	3-1
Wezemaal (BEL)	3	1	0	2	4	5	3			4-2
Sparta Praha (CZE)	3	0	0	3	3	11	0			

Group 4 - Krasnoarmeysk

	Pl	W	D	L	F	A	Pts	DEN	RUS	HUN
Arsenal (ENG)	3	3	0	0	12	4	9	1-0	5-4	6-0
Brøndby (DEN)	3	2	0	1	7	3	6		2-1	5-1
Rossiyanka (RUS)	3	1	0	2	9	9	3			4-2
1.FC Femina Budapest (HUN)	3	0	0	3	3	15	0			

Knockout phase

Quarter-finals		Semi-finals		Final	
Arsenal	5 · 4				
Breidablik *	0 · 1	Arsenal	2 · 3		
1.FFC Turbine Potsdam	0 · 2	Brøndby *	2 · 0		
Brøndby *	3 · 1			Arsenal	1 · 0
Kolbotn *	2 · 2			Umeå *	0 · 0
1.FFC Frankfurt	1 · 3	Kolbotn *	1 · 0		
Saestum *	1 · 2	Umeå	5 · 6		
Umeå	6 · 5				

Seven clubs - Arsenal, Brøndby, 1.FC Frankfurt, Kolbotn, Potsdam, Sparta Praha, Umeå - received byes to the second round • * Home team in the first leg

UEFA EUROPEAN WOMEN'S U–19 CHAMPIONSHIP 2007

First Qualifying Round Group 1

	Pl	W	D	L	F	A	Pts	SWE	FRO	KAZ
France	3	3	0	0	20	1	9	2-1	7-0	11-0
Sweden	3	2	0	1	15	2	6		7-0	7-0
Faroe Islands	3	1	0	2	6	14	3			6-0
Kazakhstan	3	0	0	3	0	24	0	Played in SWE		

First Qualifying Round Group 2

	Pl	W	D	L	F	A	Pts	POL	LVA	ARM
Spain	3	3	0	0	21	0	9	4-0	14-0	3-0
Poland	3	2	0	1	9	4	6		7-0	2-0
Latvia	3	1	0	2	1	21	3			1-0
Armenia	3	0	0	3	0	6	0	Played in POL		

First Qualifying Round Group 3

	Pl	W	D	L	F	A	Pts	BEL	GRE	EST
England	3	3	0	0	15	2	9	5-2	2-0	8-0
Belgium	3	2	0	1	12	5	6		1-0	9-0
Greece	3	0	1	2	1	4	1			1-1
Estonia	3	0	1	2	1	18	1	Played in EST		

First Qualifying Round Group 4

	Pl	W	D	L	F	A	Pts	AUT	MKD	GEO
Germany	3	3	0	0	30	1	9	5-1	7-0	18-0
Austria	3	2	0	1	18	6	6		7-1	10-0
FYR Macedonia	3	0	1	2	3	16	1			2-2
Georgia	3	0	1	2	2	30	1	Played in MKD		

First Qualifying Round Group 5

	Pl	W	D	L	F	A	Pts	NED	CRO	LTU
Norway	3	3	0	0	19	3	9	4-2	6-0	9-1
Netherlands	3	2	0	1	17	5	6		8-1	7-0
Croatia	3	1	0	2	4	14	3			3-0
Lithuania	3	0	0	3	1	19	0	Played in LTU		

First Qualifying Round Group 6

	Pl	W	D	L	F	A	Pts	HUN	POR	TUR
Switzerland	3	2	1	0	10	2	7	3-0	2-2	5-0
Hungary	3	2	0	1	6	6	6		3-1	3-2
Portugal	3	0	2	1	3	5	2			0-0
Turkey	3	0	1	2	2	8	1	Played in TUR		

First Qualifying Round Group 7

	Pl	W	D	L	F	A	Pts	UKR	ROU	MDA
Wales	3	3	0	0	16	0	9	1-0	5-0	10-0
Ukraine	3	1	1	1	6	3	4		1-1	5-1
Romania	3	1	1	1	5	6	4			4-0
Moldova	3	0	0	3	1	19	0	Played in MDA		

First Qualifying Round Group 8

	Pl	W	D	L	F	A	Pts	SRB	AZE	NIR
Denmark	3	3	0	0	12	1	9	5-0	3-1	4-0
Serbia	3	2	0	1	5	5	6		2-0	3-0
Azerbaijan	3	1	0	2	4	6	3			3-1
Northern Ireland	3	0	0	3	1	10	0	Played in AZE		

First Qualifying Round Group 9

	Pl	W	D	L	F	A	Pts	RUS	SVN	ISR
Scotland	3	3	0	0	14	5	9	2-1	6-1	6-3
Russia	3	2	0	1	6	4	6		1-0	2-0
Slovenia	3	1	0	2	2	7	3			1-0
Israel	3	0	0	3	3	9	0	Played in SVN		

First Qualifying Round Group 10

	Pl	W	D	L	F	A	Pts	ITA	SVK	BUL
Republic of Ireland	3	3	0	0	10	1	9	1-0	4-0	5-1
Italy	3	2	0	1	11	1	6		5-0	6-0
Slovakia	3	1	0	2	2	9	3			2-0
Bulgaria	3	0	0	3	1	13	0	Played in SVK		

First Qualifying Round Group 11

	Pl	W	D	L	F	A	Pts	CZE	BLR	BIH
Finland	3	2	1	0	13	2	7	1-1	4-1	8-0
Czech Republic	3	2	1	0	10	3	7		3-1	6-1
Belarus	3	1	0	2	5	7	3			3-0
Bosnia-Herzegovina	3	0	0	3	1	17	0	Played in BIH		

Second Qualifying Round Group 1

	Pl	W	D	L	F	A	Pts	UKR	CZE	AUT
England	3	2	1	0	6	1	7	1-1	2-0	3-0
Ukraine	3	1	2	0	3	2	5		1-1	1-0
Czech Republic	3	0	2	1	2	4	2			1-1
Austria	3	0	1	2	1	5	1	Played in AUT		

Second Qualifying Round Group 2

	Pl	W	D	L	F	A	Pts	IRL	NED	POR
France	3	3	0	0	11	0	9	2-0	4-0	5-0
Republic of Ireland	3	2	0	1	2	2	6		1-0	1-0
Netherlands	3	0	1	2	3	8	1			3-3
Portugal	3	0	1	2	3	9	1	Played in FRA		

Second Qualifying Round Group 3

	Pl	W	D	L	F	A	Pts	HUN	SCO	SWE
Germany	3	3	0	0	13	1	9	6-0	3-0	4-1
Hungary	3	1	1	1	6	10	4		3-3	3-1
Scotland	3	0	2	1	3	6	2			0-0
Sweden	3	0	1	2	2	7	1	Played in GER		

Second Qualifying Round Group 4

	Pl	W	D	L	F	A	Pts	NOR	ROU	BEL
Denmark	3	1	2	0	9	2	5	1-1	7-0	1-1
Norway	3	1	2	0	11	1	6		2-0	0-0
Romania	3	1	0	2	1	9	3			1-0
Belgium	3	0	2	1	1	2	2	Played in ROU		

Second Qualifying Round Group 5

	Pl	W	D	L	F	A	Pts	RUS	WAL	FIN
Poland	3	2	1	0	5	0	7	1-0	4-0	0-0
Russia	3	1	1	1	1	1	4		1-0	0-0
Wales	3	1	0	2	2	6	3			2-1
Finland	3	0	2	1	1	2	2	Played in WAL		

Second Qualifying Round Group 6

	Pl	W	D	L	F	A	Pts	ITA	SUI	SRB
Spain	3	2	1	0	15	2	7	1-1	3-1	11-0
Italy	3	2	1	0	10	3	7		3-2	6-0
Switzerland	3	1	0	2	8	6	3			5-0
Serbia	3	0	0	3	0	22	0	Played in ITA		

UEFA EUROPEAN WOMEN'S U-19 CHAMPIONSHIP 2007

First Round Group Stage

Group A	Pl	W	D	L	F	A	Pts	NOR	DEN	ISL
Germany	3	3	0	0	7	2	9	2-0	1-0	4-2
Norway	3	2	0	1	7	3	6		2-1	5-0
Denmark	3	1	0	2	3	4	3			2-1
Iceland	3	0	0	3	3	11	0			

Semi-finals

Germany	4
France	2

Final

Germany	2
England	0

Group B	Pl	W	D	L	F	A	Pts	FRA	ESP	POL
England	3	2	1	0	5	2	7	3-1	1-0	1-1
France	3	2	0	1	6	3	6		1-0	4-0
Spain	3	1	0	2	2	2	3			2-0
Poland	3	0	1	2	1	7	1			

Norway	0
England	3

Finals held in Iceland from 18-07-2007 to 29-07-2007

UEFA EUROPEAN U-17 CHAMPIONSHIP 2007

Qualifying Round Group 1

	Pl	W	D	L	F	A	Pts	BLR	KAZ	SMR
Ukraine	3	3	0	0	12	1	9	4-1	2-0	6-0
Belarus	3	1	1	1	8	5	4		1-1	6-0
Kazakhstan	3	1	1	1	5	3	4			4-0
San Marino	3	0	0	3	0	16	0	Played in BLR		

Qualifying Round Group 2

	Pl	W	D	L	F	A	Pts	CZE	LUX	SVN
Turkey	3	2	1	0	8	3	7	3-1	1-1	4-1
Czech Republic	3	1	1	1	3	3	4		2-0	0-0
Luxembourg	3	0	2	1	1	3	2			0-0
Slovenia	3	0	2	1	1	4	2	Played in CZE		

Qualifying Round Group 3

	Pl	W	D	L	F	A	Pts	ISL	ROU	LTU
France	3	3	0	0	10	3	9	3-1	3-0	4-2
Iceland	3	1	1	1	6	5	4		1-1	4-1
Romania	3	1	1	1	4	4	4			3-0
Lithuania	3	0	0	3	3	11	0	Played in ROU		

Qualifying Round Group 4

	Pl	W	D	L	F	A	Pts	SRB	MLT	AND
Italy	3	2	1	0	8	0	7	0-0	4-0	4-0
Serbia	3	2	1	0	6	0	7		2-0	4-0
Malta	3	1	0	2	1	6	3			1-0
Andorra	3	0	0	3	0	9	0	Played in MLT		

Qualifying Round Group 5

	Pl	W	D	L	F	A	Pts	RUS	GEO	MKD
Germany	3	3	0	0	11	2	9	3-1	1-0	7-1
Russia	3	2	0	1	9	6	6		2-1	6-2
Georgia	3	1	0	2	6	3	3			5-0
FYR Macedonia	3	0	0	3	3	18	0	Played in GEO		

Qualifying Round Group 6

	Pl	W	D	L	F	A	Pts	AZE	DEN	LVA
Republic of Ireland	3	2	1	0	4	0	7	2-0	0-0	2-0
Azerbaijan	3	1	1	1	2	3	4		0-0	2-1
Denmark	3	0	3	0	2	2	3			2-2
Latvia	3	0	1	2	3	6	1	Played in AZE		

Qualifying Round Group 7

	Pl	W	D	L	F	A	Pts	SWE	AUT	LIE
Greece	3	2	0	1	6	4	6	0-2	2-1	4-1
Sweden	3	1	2	0	5	3	5		2-2	1-1
Austria	3	1	1	1	13	4	4			10-0
Liechtenstein	3	0	1	2	2	15	1	Played in GRE		

Qualifying Round Group 8

	Pl	W	D	L	F	A	Pts	NOR	CRO	EST
Netherlands	3	3	0	0	11	2	9	1-0	5-1	5-1
Norway	3	2	0	1	10	2	6		5-0	5-1
Croatia	3	1	0	2	8	11	3			7-1
Estonia	3	0	0	3	3	17	0	Played in EST		

Qualifying Round Group 9

	Pl	W	D	L	F	A	Pts	FIN	ISR	ALB
Poland	3	3	0	0	7	0	9	2-0	3-0	2-0
Finland	3	1	1	1	5	4	4		1-1	4-1
Israel	3	0	2	1	2	5	2			1-1
Albania	3	0	1	2	2	7	1	Played in FIN		

Qualifying Round Group 10

	Pl	W	D	L	F	A	Pts	SCO	ARM	BUL
Hungary	3	2	1	0	5	2	7	1-1	1-0	3-1
Scotland	3	1	2	0	2	1	5		0-0	1-0
Armenia	3	1	1	1	4	3	4			4-2
Bulgaria	3	0	0	3	3	8	0	Played in ARM		

Qualifying Round Group 11

	Pl	W	D	L	F	A	Pts	BIH	WAL	MDA
Slovakia	3	2	1	0	5	3	6	2-1	1-2	2-0
Bosnia-Herzegovina	3	2	0	1	5	3	6		2-0	2-1
Wales	3	2	0	1	4	3	6			2-0
Moldova	3	0	0	3	1	6	0	Played in SVK		

Qualifying Round Group 12

	Pl	W	D	L	F	A	Pts	SUI	FRO	CYP
Northern Ireland	3	3	0	0	5	0	9	1-0	1-0	3-0
Switzerland	3	2	0	1	3	1	6		1-0	2-0
Faroe Islands	3	0	1	2	1	3	1			1-1
Cyprus	3	0	1	2	1	6	1	Played in NIR		

Elite Round Group 1

	Pl	W	D	L	F	A	Pts	IRL	SCO	GRE
Germany	3	3	0	0	11	2	9	3-0	4-1	4-1
Republic of Ireland	3	2	0	1	3	4	6		2-1	1-0
Scotland	3	0	1	2	2	6	1			0-0
Greece	3	0	1	2	1	5	1	Played in GER		

Elite Round Group 2

	Pl	W	D	L	F	A	Pts	ITA	CZE	SVK
Ukraine	3	3	0	0	8	2	9	1-0	5-2	2-0
Italy	3	2	0	1	4	2	6		2-1	2-0
Czech Republic	3	1	0	2	6	7	3			3-0
Slovakia	3	0	0	3	0	7	0	Played in ITA		

Elite Round Group 3

	Pl	W	D	L	F	A	Pts	SRB	AZE	BIH
England	3	3	0	0	8	1	9	2-1	1-0	5-0
Serbia	3	2	0	1	8	3	6		5-1	2-0
Azerbaijan	3	1	0	2	2	6	3			1-0
Bosnia-Herzegovina	3	0	0	3	0	8	0	Played in BIH		

Elite Round Group 4

	Pl	W	D	L	F	A	Pts	BLR	TUR	WAL
Netherlands	3	3	0	0	7	0	9	5-0	1-0	1-0
Belarus	3	2	0	1	4	5	6		1-0	3-0
Turkey	3	1	0	2	3	2	3			3-0
Wales	3	0	0	3	0	7	0	Played in TUR		

Elite Round Group 5

	Pl	W	D	L	F	A	Pts	NOR	HUN	FIN
France	3	2	1	0	5	1	7	2-0	0-0	3-1
Norway	3	1	1	1	3	4	4		1-0	2-2
Hungary	3	1	1	1	3	3	4			3-2
Finland	3	0	1	2	5	8	1	Played in FRA		

Elite Round Group 6

	Pl	W	D	L	F	A	Pts	POR	RUS	NIR
Iceland	3	1	2	0	8	7	5	0-0	6-5	2-2
Portugal	3	1	2	0	2	1	5		0-0	2-1
Russia	3	1	1	1	8	7	4			3-1
Northern Ireland	3	0	1	2	4	7	1	Played in POR		

Elite Round Group 7

	Pl	W	D	L	F	A	Pts	SUI	POL	SWE
Spain	3	3	0	0	5	1	9	1-0	1-0	3-1
Switzerland	3	2	0	1	5	2	6		2-0	3-1
Poland	3	1	0	2	3	4	3			3-1
Sweden	3	0	0	3	3	9	0	Played in ESP		

UEFA EUROPEAN U-17 CHAMPIONSHIP 2007

First Round Group Stage

Group A	Pl	W	D	L	F	A	Pts	FRA	GER	UKR
Spain	3	2	1	0	5	1	7	2-0	0-0	3-1
France	3	1	1	1	4	5	4		2-1	2-2
Germany	3	1	1	1	3	2	4			2-0
Ukraine	3	0	1	2	3	7	1			

Semi-finals

Spain	1 7p
Belgium	1 6p

Final

Spain	1
England	0

Group B	Pl	W	D	L	F	A	Pts	BEL	NED	ISL
England	3	2	1	0	7	3	7	1-1	4-2	2-0
Belgium	3	1	2	0	8	4	5		2-2	5-1
Netherlands	3	1	1	1	7	6	4			3-0
Iceland	3	0	0	3	1	10	0	Finals held in Belgium from 2-05-2007 to 13-05-2007		

Semi-finals

France	0
England	1

5th place play-off

Germany	3
Netherlands	2

UEFA EUROPEAN U–19 CHAMPIONSHIP 2007

Qualifying Round Group 1

	Pl	W	D	L	F	A	Pts	BUL	UKR	KAZ
Greece	3	2	0	1	6	5	6	2-0	2-1	2-4
Bulgaria	3	1	1	1	4	2	4		0-0	4-0
Ukraine	3	1	1	1	3	2	4			2-0
Kazakhstan	3	1	0	2	4	8	3	Played in BUL		

Qualifying Round Group 2

	Pl	W	D	L	F	A	Pts	SUI	SVN	LIE
Israel	3	3	0	0	11	1	9	2-1	3-0	6-0
Switzerland	3	2	0	1	6	3	6		2-1	3-0
Slovenia	3	1	0	2	6	5	3			5-0
Liechtenstein	3	0	0	3	0	14	0	Played in SVN		

Qualifying Round Group 3

	Pl	W	D	L	F	A	Pts	NED	BLR	MKD
Republic of Ireland	3	3	0	0	8	1	9	2-0	4-1	2-0
Netherlands	3	2	0	1	4	3	6		3-1	1-0
Belarus	3	1	0	2	3	7	3			1-0
FYR Macedonia	3	0	0	3	0	4	0	Played in MKD		

Qualifying Round Group 4

	Pl	W	D	L	F	A	Pts	GEO	BEL	NIR
Romania	3	3	0	0	10	2	9	3-0	4-2	3-0
Georgia	3	2	0	1	5	4	6		3-2	1-0
Belgium	3	1	0	2	8	9	3			4-2
Northern Ireland	3	0	0	3	2	8	0	Played in ROU		

Qualifying Round Group 5

	Pl	W	D	L	F	A	Pts	SVK	ALB	AND
Russia	3	2	0	1	4	1	6	0-1	2-0	2-0
Slovakia	3	2	0	1	6	3	6		2-3	3-0
Albania	3	2	0	1	5	4	6			2-0
Andorra	3	0	0	3	0	7	0	Played in AND		

Qualifying Round Group 6

	Pl	W	D	L	F	A	Pts	SWE	ISL	FRO
Poland	3	2	0	1	5	4	6	3-1	0-2	2-1
Sweden	3	2	0	1	7	4	6		2-0	4-1
Iceland	3	2	0	1	5	3	6			3-1
Faroe Islands	3	0	0	3	3	9	0	Played in SWE		

Qualifying Round Group 7

	Pl	W	D	L	F	A	Pts	AZE	ARM	CYP
Hungary	3	3	0	0	12	2	9	5-0	4-1	3-1
Azerbaijan	3	1	1	1	3	7	4		2-1	1-1
Armenia	3	1	0	2	3	6	3			1-0
Cyprus	3	0	1	2	2	5	1	Played in CYP		

Qualifying Round Group 8

	Pl	W	D	L	F	A	Pts	DEN	MLT	FIN
France	3	3	0	0	8	2	9	1-0	4-2	3-0
Denmark	3	1	1	1	5	4	4		1-1	4-2
Malta	3	0	2	1	4	6	2			1-1
Finland	3	0	1	2	3	8	1	Played in DEN		

Qualifying Round Group 9

	Pl	W	D	L	F	A	Pts	GER	EST	BIH
Scotland	3	3	0	0	11	0	9	1-0	4-0	6-0
Germany	3	2	0	1	12	3	6		7-2	5-0
Estonia	3	1	0	2	5	12	3			3-1
Bosnia-Herzegovina	3	0	0	3	1	14	0	Played in SCO		

Qualifying Round Group 10

	Pl	W	D	L	F	A	Pts	TUR	LUX	WAL
Czech Republic	3	2	1	0	8	1	7	2-0	1-1	5-0
Turkey	3	2	0	1	8	4	6		4-1	4-1
Luxembourg	3	1	1	1	3	5	4			1-0
Wales	3	0	0	3	1	10	0	Played in LUX		

Qualifying Round Group 11

	Pl	W	D	L	F	A	Pts	POR	LVA	SMR
Norway	3	2	1	0	9	3	7	2-2	2-1	5-0
Portugal	3	2	1	0	8	2	7		1-0	5-0
Latvia	3	1	0	2	6	3	3			5-0
San Marino	3	0	0	3	0	15	0	Played in NOR		

Qualifying Round Group 12

	Pl	W	D	L	F	A	Pts	CRO	MDA	LTU
Serbia	3	2	1	0	7	2	7	2-2	4-1	4-0
Croatia	3	2	1	0	7	2	7		3-0	2-0
Moldova	3	1	0	2	3	7	3			2-0
Lithuania	3	0	0	3	0	8	0	Played in LTU		

Elite Round Group 1

	Pl	W	D	L	F	A	Pts	IRL	HUN	BUL
Germany	3	2	1	0	3	0	7	1-0	0-0	2-0
Republic of Ireland	3	2	0	1	5	1	6		2-0	3-0
Hungary	3	0	2	1	1	3	2			1-1
Bulgaria	3	0	1	2	1	6	1	Played in IRL		

Elite Round Group 2

	Pl	W	D	L	F	A	Pts	CRO	ITA	SWE
Greece	3	2	1	0	8	2	7	2-2	2-0	4-0
Croatia	3	1	2	0	6	4	5		3-1	1-1
Italy	3	1	0	2	6	7	3			5-2
Sweden	3	0	1	2	3	10	1	Played in GRE		

Elite Round Group 3

	Pl	W	D	L	F	A	Pts	NED	ENG	CZE
Russia	3	2	1	0	5	1	7	0-0	2-0	3-1
Netherlands	3	2	1	0	4	1	7		2-1	2-0
England	3	1	0	2	3	4	3			2-0
Czech Republic	3	0	0	3	1	7	0	Played in ENG		

Elite Round Group 4

	Pl	W	D	L	F	A	Pts	TUR	SCO	GEO
Portugal	3	2	1	0	5	2	7	1-0	4-2	0-0
Turkey	3	1	1	1	3	3	4		2-1	1-1
Scotland	3	1	0	2	5	7	3			2-1
Georgia	3	0	2	1	2	3	2	Played in SCO		

Elite Round Group 5

	Pl	W	D	L	F	A	Pts	ISL	NOR	AZE
Spain	3	3	0	0	12	4	9	3-2	5-2	4-0
Iceland	3	1	0	2	10	9	3		3-4	5-2
Norway	3	1	0	2	7	10	3			1-2
Azerbaijan	3	1	0	2	4	10	3	Played in NOR		

Elite Round Group 6

	Pl	W	D	L	F	A	Pts	ISR	POL	SVK
France	3	2	0	1	6	3	6	3-1	3-1	0-1
Israel	3	2	0	1	11	4	6		4-1	6-0
Poland	3	1	0	2	4	8	3			2-1
Slovakia	3	1	0	2	2	8	3	Played in ISR		

Elite Round Group 7

	Pl	W	D	L	F	A	Pts	ROU	SUI	DEN
Serbia	3	3	0	0	5	1	9	2-0	1-0	2-1
Romania	3	2	0	1	7	5	6		4-2	3-1
Switzerland	3	1	0	2	4	5	3			2-0
Denmark	3	0	0	3	2	7	0	Played in SUI		

UEFA EUROPEAN U-19 CHAMPIONSHIP 2007

First Round Group Stage

Group A

	Pl	W	D	L	F	A	Pts	GRE	POR	AUT
Spain	3	1	2	0	3	1	5	0-0	1-1	2-0
Greece	3	1	2	0	2	1	5		1-0	1-1
Portugal	3	1	1	1	3	2	4			2-0
Austria	3	0	1	2	1	5	1			

Group B

	Pl	W	D	L	F	A	Pts	FRA	SRB	RUS
Germany	3	2	1	0	7	5	7	1-1	3-2	3-2
France	3	1	2	0	6	3	5		5-2	0-0
Serbia	3	1	0	2	10	10	3			6-2
Russia	3	0	1	2	4	9	1			

Semi-finals

Spain	0 4p
France	0 2p

Germany	2
Greece	3

Final

Spain	1
Greece	0

Finals held in Austria from 16-07-2007 to 27-07-2007

UEFA EUROPEAN U–21 CHAMPIONSHIP 2007

Preliminary Round		
Home team first leg	Score	Home team second leg
Malta	1-2 1-2	Georgia
Liechtenstein	1-4 0-4	Northern Ireland
Luxembourg	0-3 0-2	FYR Macedonia
Andorra	0-0 0-2	Iceland
Estonia	0-2 1-5	Wales
Azerbaijan	0-3 0-3	Republic of Ireland
San Marino	3-0 0-4	Armenia
Kazakhstan	0-0 0-1	Moldova

Qualifying Round Group 1

	Pl	W	D	L	F	A	Pts	ARM	NOR
Bosnia-Herzegovina	2	1	1	0	4	3	4	3-2	1-1
Armenia	2	1	0	1	3	3	3		1-0
Norway	2	0	1	1	1	2	1		

Qualifying Round Group 2

	Pl	W	D	L	F	A	Pts	SVK	ALB
Spain	2	2	0	0	7	2	6	4-2	3-0
Slovakia	2	0	1	1	2	4	1		0-0
Albania	2	0	1	1	0	3	1		

Qualifying Round Group 3

	Pl	W	D	L	F	A	Pts	LTU	GEO
Serbia	2	2	0	0	5	1	6	2-0	3-1
Lithuania	2	1	0	1	1	2	3		1-0
Georgia	2	0	0	2	1	4	0		

Qualifying Round Group 4

	Pl	W	D	L	F	A	Pts	IRL	GRE
Belgium	2	2	0	0	3	1	6	1-0	2-1
Republic of Ireland	2	1	0	1	2	1	3		2-0
Greece	2	0	0	2	1	4	0		

Qualifying Round Group 5

	Pl	W	D	L	F	A	Pts	AUT	ISL
Italy	2	2	0	0	2	0	6	1-0	1-0
Austria	2	0	1	1	0	1	1		0-0
Iceland	2	0	1	1	0	1	1		

Qualifying Round Group 6

	Pl	W	D	L	F	A	Pts	HUN	FIN
Russia	2	2	0	0	8	2	6	3-1	5-1
Hungary	2	1	0	1	6	3	3		5-0
Finland	2	0	0	2	1	10	0		

Qualifying Round Group 7

	Pl	W	D	L	F	A	Pts	POL	LVA
Portugal	2	2	0	0	4	0	6	2-0	2-0
Poland	2	1	0	1	3	3	3		3-1
Latvia	2	0	0	2	1	5	0		

Qualifying Round Group 8

	Pl	W	D	L	F	A	Pts	SUI	MDA
England	2	1	1	0	5	4	4	3-2	2-2
Switzerland	2	1	0	1	5	4	3		3-1
Moldova	2	0	1	1	3	5	1		

Qualifying Round Group 9

	Pl	W	D	L	F	A	Pts	BLR	CYP
Czech Republic	2	2	0	0	4	1	6	2-1	2-0
Belarus	2	1	0	1	2	2	3		1-0
Cyprus	2	0	0	2	0	3	0		

Qualifying Round Group 10

	Pl	W	D	L	F	A	Pts	ROU	NIR
Germany	2	2	0	0	8	3	6	5-1	3-2
Romania	2	1	0	1	4	5	3		3-0
Northern Ireland	2	0	0	2	2	6	0		

Qualifying Round Group 11

	Pl	W	D	L	F	A	Pts	DEN	MKD
Sweden	2	2	0	0	5	1	6	2-0	3-1
Denmark	2	1	0	1	3	2	3		3-0
FYR Macedonia	2	0	0	2	1	6	0		

Qualifying Round Group 12

	Pl	W	D	L	F	A	Pts	UKR	CRO
Bulgaria	2	2	0	0	5	1	6	3-0	2-1
Ukraine	2	1	0	1	2	4	3		2-1
Croatia	2	0	0	2	2	4	0		

Qualifying Round Group 13

	Pl	W	D	L	F	A	Pts	TUR	WAL
Israel	2	1	1	0	3	2	4	0-0	3-2
Turkey	2	0	2	0	0	0	2		0-0
Wales	2	0	1	1	2	3	1		

Qualifying Round Group 14

	Pl	W	D	L	F	A	Pts	SVN	SCO
France	2	2	0	0	5	1	6	2-0	3-1
Slovenia	2	1	0	1	1	2	3		1-0
Scotland	2	0	0	2	1	4	0		

Play-offs		
Home team first leg	Score	Home team second leg
Serbia	0-3 5-0	Sweden
Czech Republic	2-1 1-1	Bosnia-Herzegovina
Russia	4-1 0-3	Portugal
England	1-0 2-0	Germany
Italy	0-0 2-1	Spain
Belgium	1-1 4-1	Bulgaria
France	1-1 0-1	Israel

Netherlands qualify automatically as hosts

UEFA EUROPEAN UNDER 21 CHAMPIONSHIP 2006-07

First Round Group Stage

Group A	Pl	W	D	L	F	A	Pts	BEL	POR	ISR
Netherlands	3	2	1	0	5	3	7	2-2	2-1	1-0
Belgium	3	1	2	0	3	2	5		0-0	1-0
Portugal	3	1	1	1	5	2	4			4-0
Israel	3	0	0	3	0	6	0			

Group B	Pl	W	D	L	F	A	Pts	ENG	ITA	CZE
Serbia	3	2	0	1	2	2	6	0-2	1-0	1-0
England	3	1	2	0	4	2	5		2-2	0-0
Italy	3	1	1	1	5	4	4			3-1
Czech Republic	3	0	1	2	1	4	1			

Semi-finals

Netherlands	1 13p
England	1 12p

Belgium	0
Serbia	2

Final

Netherlands	4
Serbia	1

Play-off for the Beijing Olympics: **Italy** 0-0 4-3p Portugal
Tournament held in The Netherlands from 10-06-2007 to 23-06-2007

REGIONAL CLUB TOURNAMENTS IN EUROPE

ROYAL LEAGUE 2006-07

First round groups

Group A		Pl	W	D	L	F	A	Pts	DEN	NOR	SWE	NOR
OB Odense	DEN	6	4	1	1	13	7	13		3-2	3-0	5-3
Brann Bergen	NOR	6	2	3	1	13	11	9	1-1		2-2	3-2
Helsingborgs IF	SWE	6	2	3	1	7	8	9	1-0	2-2		3-1
Rosenborg BK	NOR	6	0	1	5	8	15	1	0-1	1-3	0-0	

Group B		Pl	W	D	L	F	A	Pts	NOR	DEN	DEN	SWE
Lillestrøm SK	NOR	6	3	3	0	7	3	12		1-1	1-0	2-0
Brøndby IF	DEN	6	3	2	1	10	8	11	1-1		1-3	3-1
FC Kobenhavn	DEN	6	3	0	3	9	5	9	0-1	0-1		4-0
Hammarby IF	SWE	6	0	1	5	5	15	1	1-1	2-3	1-2	

Group C		Pl	W	D	L	F	A	Pts	NOR	SWE	SWE	DEN
Vålerenga IF	NOR	6	4	2	0	13	8	14		2-1	4-2	1-0
Elfsborg IF	SWE	6	2	2	2	11	8	8	2-3		4-0	1-0
AIK Stockholm	SWE	6	1	3	2	7	12	6	1-1	1-1		1-1
Viborg FF	DEN	6	0	3	3	6	9	3	2-2	2-2	1-2	

The tournament took place from 10-11-2005 to 6-04-2006 • * Home team in the first leg

Quarter-finals

Brøndby IF	3
Brann Bergen	0

Lillestrøm SK	2 1p
OB Odense	2 3p

Helsingborgs IF	2
Vålerenga IF	1

Elfsborg IF	1
FC København	2

Semi-finals

Brøndby IF	2
OB Odense	1

Helsingborgs IF	1
FC København	3

Final

Brøndby IF	1
FC København	0

FINAL

Brøndby, Copenhagen
15-03-2007, Att: 17 914
Ref: Ovrebø NOR

Scorer - Ericsson 38p

BALTIC CHAMPIONS CUP 2006

		Pl	W	D	L	F	A	Pts	LVA	EST
Ekranas Panevezys	LTU	2	1	1	0	7	5	4	1-1	6-4
Metalurgs Liepaja	LVA	2	1	1	0	3	1	4		2-0
TVMK Tallinn	EST	2	0	0	2	4	8	0		

Held in Liepaja from 10-08-2006 to 12-08-2006

APPENDIX 1 – MISCELLANEOUS

MALAYSIA FA CUP 2006

Second Round		Quarter-finals		Semi-finals		Final	
Pahang *	1 2						
Selangor	0 2	Pahang *	6 2				
PDRM	1 0	Pulau Pinang	0 2				
Pulau Pinang *	1 1			Pahang	0 3		
Terengganu	3 2			Negri Sembilan *	0 2		
Selangor MPPJ *	0 1	Terengganu *	0 1				
Melaka Telekom *	0 1	Negri Sembilan	0 2				
Negri Sembilan	3 1					Pahang †	0 4p
Singapore U-23 *	2 3					Perlis	0 2p
Johor	2 1	Singapore U-23 *	7 1				
Selangor PKNS *	1 0	Sarawak	2 4				
Sarawak	3 1			Singapore U-23 *	3 0		
Perak	0 3			Perlis	2 2		
Kelantan *	1 1	Perak	0 1				
ATM	0 2	Perlis *	2 0				
Perlis *	0 5						

CUP FINAL
20-05-2006

* Home team in the first leg • † Qualified for the AFC Cup

YEMEN 2006

PREMIER LEAGUE

	Pl	W	D	L	F	A	Pts	Saqr	Sha'ab Ibb	Tilal	Ahly	Hilal	Hassan	Rasheed	Sha'ab H	Shula	Yarmuk	Tadamun	Shabab	May 22	Taawun
Al Saqr Taizz †	26	16	7	3	49	20	55		1-1	3-0	2-0	1-1	2-0	1-2	5-1	5-1	0-0	7-3	2-1	2-1	2-0
Al Sha'ab Ibb	26	14	6	6	51	32	48	3-0		2-1	1-0	2-2	2-2	1-0	5-0	2-1	1-0	2-1	4-2	5-4	6-1
Al Tilal Aden	26	13	4	9	42	35	43	0-1	2-0		3-3	1-3	0-1	0-3	3-0	1-0	2-0	2-1	4-2	5-1	3-2
Al Ahly Sana'a	26	12	6	8	44	35	42	1-2	1-0	1-0		2-3	2-0	0-1	4-0	2-2	2-2	4-3	3-1	3-1	3-1
Al Hilal Hudayda †	26	11	7	8	45	37	40	0-1	1-1	2-4	0-0		0-2	3-0	4-5	1-0	1-0	1-0	2-3	5-1	2-2
Hassan Abyan	26	11	7	8	29	25	40	2-2	2-0	1-2	3-0	1-1		0-0	2-1	1-0	1-2	1-0	1-2	3-2	2-0
Al Rasheed Taizz	26	11	4	11	27	30	37	0-1	2-0	1-3	1-1	1-2	1-0		2-2	1-1	1-0	2-0	1-3	2-0	3-1
Al Sha'ab Hadramaut	26	10	5	11	31	45	35	0-0	1-0	1-2	0-1	1-0	1-2	3-0		1-1	3-1	2-1	0-3	2-1	2-1
Shula Aden	26	8	10	8	31	29	34	1-0	1-1	0-1	1-1	2-1	1-1	4-0	0-0		2-2	4-1	1-0	1-0	3-2
Al Yarmuk Sana'a	26	9	7	10	28	37	34	0-0	0-4	0-1	0-2	0-1	3-0	2-1	3-1	1-0		2-1	2-1	0-0	2-2
Al Tadamun Shabwa	26	10	2	14	35	45	32	0-5	2-3	1-1	3-1	2-1	0-1	1-0	2-0	1-2	3-0		1-0	1-0	4-3
Shabab Al Jeel	26	7	6	13	29	37	27	0-1	2-2	1-1	2-1	1-2	0-0	1-0	0-1	1-1	0-0	0-1		0-0	2-0
May 22 Sana'a	26	5	5	16	29	49	20	2-2	2-0	3-0	1-3	1-3	1-0	0-1	2-2	0-0	0-3	0-1	3-1		3-1
Al Taawun Badan	26	4	6	16	33	52	18	0-1	1-3	0-0	2-3	3-3	0-0	0-1	0-1	2-1	2-1	1-1	3-0	3-0	

21/04/2006 - 4/08/2006 • † Qualified for the AFC Cup • Matches in bold were awarded

FIFA/COCA-COLA WORLD RANKING FOR MEXICO

1993	1994	1995	1996	1997	1998	1999	2000	2001	2002	2003	2004	2005	2006	High		Low	
16	15	12	11	5	10	10	12	9	8	7	7	5	20	**4**	02/98	**26**	06/07

						2006–2007						
08/06	09/06	10/06	11/06	12/06	01/07	02/07	03/07	04/07	05/07	06/07	07/07
16	17	19	20	20	21	19	21	18	20	26	10

THE FIFA BIG COUNT OF 2006 FOR MEXICO

	Male	Female		Total
Number of players	7 151 688	1 327 907	Referees and Assistant Referees	4 885
Professionals	4 593		Admin, Coaches, Technical, Medical	80 904
Amateurs 18+	186 954		Number of clubs	302
Youth under 18	129 006		Number of teams	19 957
Unregistered	7 000 000		Clubs with women's teams	9
Total players	8 479 595		Players as % of population	7.89%

FIFA/COCA-COLA WORLD RANKING FOR SOUTH AFRICA

1993	1994	1995	1996	1997	1998	1999	2000	2001	2002	2003	2004	2005	2006	High		Low	
95	56	40	19	31	26	30	20	35	30	36	38	49	67	**16**	08/96	**109**	08/93

						2006–2007						
08/06	09/06	10/06	11/06	12/06	01/07	02/07	03/07	04/07	05/07	06/07	07/07
76	76	65	66	67	69	59	60	61	59	57	64

THE FIFA BIG COUNT OF 2006 FOR SOUTH AFRICA

	Male	Female		Total
Number of players	4 423 300	117 110	Referees and Assistant Referees	4 020
Professionals	1 000		Admin, Coaches, Technical, Medical	16 537
Amateurs 18+	165 560		Number of clubs	450
Youth under 18	1 300 400		Number of teams	3 200
Unregistered	2 025 000		Clubs with women's teams	450
Total players	4 540 410		Players as % of population	10.28%

THE FIFA BIG COUNT OF 2006 FOR THE USA

	Male	Female		Total
Number of players	17 416 859	7 055 919	Referees and Assistant Referees	140 000
Professionals	1 513		Admin, Coaches, Technical, Medical	656 300
Amateurs 18+	260 928		Number of clubs	5 000
Youth under 18	3 907 065		Number of teams	400 000
Unregistered	13 466 000		Clubs with women's teams	4 000
Total players	24 472 778		Players as % of population	8.20%

ARAB CHAMPIONS LEAGUE 2006-07

First Round

Entente Sétif	ALG	0	3
Al Merreikh *	SUD	2	0
OC Khouribga	MAR	1 3	0p
Al Ittihad Jeddah *	KSA	3 1	3p
Ismaily *	EGY	2	4
Arbil	IRQ	0	2
Al Ahly Manama	BHR	1	0
Bordj Bou Arreridj	ALG	0	2
Al Qadisiya *	KUW	2	3
Al Ansar Beirut	LIB	1	1
Al Wahda Damascus	SYR	0	1
Club Africain *	TUN		
Raja Casablanca *	MAR	8	6
Al Markaz Tulkarem	PLE	0	0
US Monastir	TUN	0 0	8p
Al Ahly Jeddah *	KSA	0 0	9p
Zamalek *	EGY	1	2
COD Meknès	MAR	0	2
Al Nahda	OMA	0	2
Al Ittihad Tripoli *	LBY	4	4
Mouloudia Alger	ALG	0	2
Al Tilal Aden *	YEM	0	1
SID Kartljen	DJI	1	0
Al Nasr Riyadh *	KSA	12	9
Al Kuwait SC	KUW	2 1	4p
Al Ahli Dubai *	UAE	1 2	3p
Al Ahly Doha *	QAT	0	2
Al Shabab Ordon	JOR	2	1
ENPPI *	EGY	3	1
Al Jaish Damascus	SYR	1	0
ASC Nasr Sebkha *	MTN	0	1
Al Faysali	JOR	0	2

Second Round

Entente Sétif *	4	1
Al Ittihad Jeddah	1	3
Ismaily	0 0	3p
Bordj Bou Arreridj *	0 0	5p
Al Qadisiya *	1	1
Club Africain	0	1
Raja Casablanca	1	3
Al Ahly Jeddah *	1	3
Zamalek *	1 0	4p
Al Ittihad Tripoli	0 1	1p
Mouloudia Alger	1	2
Al Nasr Riyadh *	2	2
Al Kuwait SC	2	2
Al Shabab Ordon *	2	1
ENPPI *	2	1
Al Faysali	1	1

Group Stage

Group A

	Pl	W	D	L	F	A	Pts	Zamalek	Al Ahly	CABBA	Al Qadisya
Zamalek	6	3	2	1	10	7	11		1-0	2-2	4-2
Al Ahly Jeddah	6	3	1	2	12	5	10	1-1		6-0	2-1
Bordj Bou Arreridj	6	2	2	2	7	7	8	0-1	1-0		2-1
Al Qadisya	6	1	1	4	7	17	4	2-1	1-3	1-1	

Group B

	Pl	W	D	L	F	A	Pts	ES Sétif	Al Faysali	Al Nasr	Al Kuwait
Entente Sétif	6	3	2	1	4	2	11		0-0	1-0	0-0
Al Faysali	6	3	1	2	4	4	10	1-0		1-0	0-1
Al Nasr Riyadh	6	3	0	3	9	5	9	1-2	3-1		3-0
Al Kuwait SC	6	1	1	4	1	7	4	0-1	0-1	0-2	

Semi-finals

Entente Sétif	0	2
Al Ahly Jeddah *	1	0
Zamalek	0	1
Al Faysali *	0	2

Final

Entente Sétif *	1	1
Al Faysali	1	0

* Home team in the first leg • Tournament held from 9/09/2006 - 17/05/2007

REVIEW OF WOMEN'S LEAGUE FOOTBALL

CHINA PR 2006 SUPER LEAGUE

	Pl	W	D	L	F	A	Pts
Shanghai SVA	14	10	0/2	2	24	10	32
Tianjin Huisen	14	7	3/3	1	24	9	30
Dalian Shide	13	8	1/2	2	21	6	28
Jiangsu Huatai	12	6	1/0	5	14	14	20
Beijing Tiaotai	14	4	2/2	6	11	13	18
Hebei Huayao	13	2	3/1	7	10	17	13
Guangdong Haiyin	13	2	2/3	6	7	23	13
Sichuan Jiannanchun	11	0	1/0	10	4	23	2

CZECH REPUBLIC 2006–07 FIRST DIVISION

	Pl	W	D	L	F	A	Pts
Sparta Praha	22	20	2	0	143	7	62
Slavia Praha	22	16	2	4	85	15	50
Slovácko	22	15	4	3	83	16	49
Plzen	22	12	6	4	41	21	42
Brno	21	12	3	6	67	31	39
Hradec Králóve	21	12	2	7	42	24	38
Teplice	22	8	2	12	28	53	26
Krásná Studánka	22	6	2	14	18	58	20
Hlucín	22	6	1	15	17	75	19
Redice	22	4	1	17	16	97	13
Holecov	22	3	3	16	16	87	12
Karlatejn	22	2	2	18	21	93	8

DENMARK 2006–07 FIRST DIVISION

	Pl	W	D	L	F	A	Pts
Brøndby	21	19	0	2	97	9	57
Fortuna Hjørring	21	16	3	2	77	9	51
Skovlunde	21	14	2	5	46	23	44
Vejle	21	11	2	8	54	44	35
Skovbakken	21	5	3	13	34	52	18
BK Skjold	21	4	4	13	20	64	16
Varde	21	3	3	15	20	77	12
Team Viborg	21	3	1	17	11	81	10

ENGLAND 2006–07 PREMIER LEAGUE

	Pl	W	D	L	F	A	Pts
Arsenal LFC	22	22	0	0	119	10	66
Everton LFC	22	17	1	4	56	15	52
Charlton Athletic LFC	22	16	2	4	63	32	50
Bristol Academy WFC	22	13	1	8	53	41	40
Leeds United LFC	22	12	1	9	50	44	37
Blackburn Rovers LFC	22	10	2	10	37	36	32
Birmingham City LFC	22	8	4	10	34	29	28
Chelsea LFC	22	8	4	10	33	34	28
Doncaster Rov. Belles	22	7	2	13	29	54	23
Cardiff City LFC	22	3	3	16	26	64	12
Sunderland WFC	22	3	2	17	15	72	11
Fulham Women FC	22	1	2	19	12	96	5

Cup Final: Arsenal LFC 4-1 Charlton Athletic LFC
League Cup: Arsenal LFC 1-0 Leeds United LFC

FINLAND 2006 FIRST DIVISION

	Pl	W	D	L	F	A	Pts
Honka	18	15	2	1	65	9	47
FC United Pietarsaari	18	13	3	2	62	8	42
HJK Helsinki	18	12	5	1	50	9	41
Aland United	18	8	3	7	40	35	27
Ilves Tampere	18	8	2	8	34	36	26
TiPS Vantaa	18	6	4	8	31	32	22
Sport	18	5	2	11	23	40	17
SCR Raisio	18	5	2	11	24	45	17
KMF	18	5	2	11	22	52	17
FC Espoo	18	0	1	17	10	95	1

Cup Final: HJK Helsinki 3-0 United Pietarsaari

FRANCE 2006–07 DIVISION 1

	Pl	W	D	L	F	A	Pts
Olympique Lyonnais	22	20	1	1	116	9	83
Montpellier HSC	22	17	3	2	64	12	76
FCF Juvisy	22	17	2	3	54	18	75
ASJ Soyaux	22	11	5	6	30	28	60
CNFE FF	22	9	3	10	43	43	52
Saint-Brieuc	22	8	3	11	27	47	49
Paris St-Germain	22	6	8	8	37	33	48
Toulouse FC	22	7	3	12	30	41	46
ESOF La Roche	22	6	1	15	15	51	41
FCF Hénin-Beaumont	22	5	3	14	31	81	40
USCCO Compiègne	22	5	1	16	31	71	38
FC Condé	22	4	1	17	32	76	35

Cup Final: Montpellier HSC 0-0 3-0p Olympique Lyonnais

GERMANY 2006–07 FIRST DIVISION

	Pl	W	D	L	F	A	Pts
1. FFC Frankfurt	22	19	3	0	91	17	60
FCR 2001 Duisburg	22	16	3	3	76	25	51
FFC Turbine Potsdam	22	13	5	4	51	23	44
FC Bayern München	22	12	2	8	35	29	38
SC 07 Bad Neuenahr	22	10	3	9	45	45	33
SG Essen-Schönebeck	22	10	2	10	45	42	32
TSV Crailsheim	22	9	3	10	33	37	30
VfL Wolfsburg	22	8	3	11	20	49	27
Hamburger SV	22	7	5	10	34	34	26
SC Freiburg	22	8	1	13	36	57	25
FFC Heike Rheine	22	4	2	16	24	57	14
FFC Brauweiler Pulheim	22	0	0	22	15	100	0

Cup Final: 1.FFC Frankfurt 5-2 FCR 2001 Duisburg

ICELAND 2005 FIRST DIVISION

	Pl	W	D	L	F	A	Pts
Valur Reykjavík	14	13	0	1	90	8	39
Breidablik	14	12	0	2	64	14	36
KR Reykjavík	14	10	0	4	81	23	30
Stjarnan	14	8	0	6	36	25	24
Keflavík	14	7	0	7	43	34	21
Fylkir	14	4	0	10	15	82	12
Thor/KA	14	1	0	13	15	68	3
FH Hafnarfjördur	14	1	0	13	6	96	3

Cup Final: Valur 3-3 4-2p Breidablik

ITALY 2006–07
FIRST DIVISION

	Pl	W	D	L	F	A	Pts
Bardolino	22	18	3	1	71	19	57
Torino	22	13	5	4	57	28	44
Fiammamonza	22	8	11	3	33	16	35
Torres Terra Sarda	22	9	7	6	49	39	34
Reggiana	22	9	6	7	42	24	33
Milan	22	7	7	8	20	29	28
Tavagnacco	22	8	4	10	35	54	28
Atalanta	22	7	5	10	27	33	26
Aircargo Agliana	22	5	9	8	25	31	25
Firenze	22	6	6	10	28	35	24
Vigor Senigallia	22	5	5	12	37	58	20
Porto Mantovano	22	2	2	18	19	77	8

Cup Final: Bardolino 3-1 1-3 3-2p Torino

JAPAN 2006
NADESHIKO LEAGUE

	Pl	W	D	L	F	A	Pts
NTV Beleza	17	14	2	1	57	11	44
Urawa Reds Ladies	17	12	2	3	28	16	38
TASAKI Perule FC	17	10	3	4	31	19	33
Okayama Yunogo	17	7	2	8	18	23	23
INAC Leonessa	17	4	4	9	25	37	16
Iga FC Kunoichi	17	5	1	11	12	31	16
Speranza Takatsuki	17	3	4	10	19	33	13
TEPCO Mareeze	17	1	6	10	13	33	9

28th All Japan Women's Football Championship Final 2006
TASAKI Perule 2-0 Okayama Yunogo Belle

NORWAY 2006
FIRST DIVISION

	Pl	W	D	L	F	A	Pts
Kolbotn	18	13	3	2	76	17	42
Trondheim/Orn	18	13	3	2	47	10	42
Røa	18	12	3	3	69	24	39
Team Strømmen	18	11	3	4	46	25	36
Arna-Bjørnar	18	11	2	5	60	26	35
Amazon Grimstad	18	7	2	9	42	32	23
Fløya	18	4	2	12	24	57	14
Sandviken	18	4	2	12	25	62	14
Klepp	18	3	2	13	17	61	11
Liungen	18	1	0	17	10	102	3

RUSSIA 2006
FIRST DIVISION

	Pl	W	D	L	F	A	Pts
Rossiyanka MO	16	14	2	0	99	14	44
Spartak Moskva	16	11	4	1	54	10	37
Nadezhda Noginsk	16	10	4	2	56	12	34
FK Ryazan VDV	16	10	2	4	41	33	32
Prialit Reutov	16	5	4	7	18	32	19
Lada Togliatti	16	5	2	9	25	38	17
Chertanovo Moskva	16	5	1	10	27	42	16
Aurora St Petersburg	16	2	1	13	14	61	7
Victoria Belgorod	16	0	0	16	2	94	0

Cup Final: Rossiyanka 3-0 1-1 Spartak Moskva

SCOTLAND 2006–07
FIRST DIVISION

	Pl	W	D	L	F	A	Pts
Hibernian LFC	22	22	0	0	115	17	66
Glasgow City LFC	22	19	1	2	92	19	58
Edinburgh City	22	16	0	6	73	31	48
Newburgh JFCL	22	13	5	4	67	41	44
Kilmarnock Ladies	22	10	4	8	51	38	34
Aberdeen FCL	22	8	4	10	55	55	28
Hamilton Academical	22	8	4	10	42	55	28
Raith Rovers LFC	22	9	1	12	33	54	28
Forfar Farmington LFC	22	7	2	13	37	62	23
Arsenal North LFC	22	3	3	16	45	79	12
Lochee United	22	4	0	18	22	79	12
Hutchison Vale	22	1	0	21	10	112	3

Cup Final: Hibernian LFC 5-1 Glasgow City

SPAIN 2006–07
FIRST DIVISION

	Pl	W	D	L	F	A	Pts
Espanyol	26	20	3	3	87	29	63
Athletic Bilboko	26	19	5	2	77	25	62
Levante	26	16	7	3	76	25	55
Rayo Vallecano	26	16	5	5	61	40	53
Sevilla	26	13	6	7	58	35	45
Torrejón	26	11	4	11	42	39	37
Puebla	26	10	6	10	32	40	36
Atlético Madrid	26	8	7	11	31	46	31
Real Sociedad	26	7	6	13	30	51	27
Sporting de Huelva	26	5	9	12	28	58	24
Oviedo Moderno	26	5	7	14	29	58	22
T. Alcaine	26	5	5	16	20	50	20
Barcelona	26	4	4	18	26	58	16
SD Lagunak	26	4	4	18	28	72	16

SWITZERLAND 2006–07
LIGUE NATIONALE A

	Pl	W	D	L	F	A	Pts
FFC Zuchwil 05	14	13	0	1	41	17	39
FFC Zürich Seebach	14	7	3	4	27	19	24
SC LUwin.ch	14	7	2	5	35	27	23
FFC Bern	14	5	5	4	27	26	20
Yverdon-Sport	14	4	4	6	33	32	17
FC Schwerzenbach	14	3	5	6	25	28	14
FC Rot-Schwarz Thun	14	3	3	8	26	42	12
FC Rapid Lugano	14	1	4	9	20	43	7

Cup Final: FFC Zürich-Seebach 2-1 FFC Zuchwil 05

SWEDEN 2006
DAMALLSVENSKAN

	Pl	W	D	L	F	A	Pts
Umeå IK	22	21	1	0	74	11	64
Djurgården/Alvsjö	22	13	4	5	61	23	43
Linköpings FC	22	12	5	5	43	25	41
Malmö FF DFF	22	11	7	4	41	23	40
Kopparbergs/Göteborg	22	10	5	7	44	36	35
KIF Orebro DFF	22	8	5	9	33	33	29
Hammarby IF DFF	22	8	5	9	34	43	29
Sunnanå SK	22	8	3	11	26	33	27
Bälinge IF	22	4	7	11	16	41	19
QBIK	22	2	9	11	18	51	15
Jitex BK Mölndal	22	2	7	13	17	59	13
Mallbackens IF Lysvik	22	3	2	17	15	44	11

Cup Final: Linköpings 3-2 Umeå IK

USA 2006
W-LEAGUE

Central Conference Atlantic Division

	Pl	W	D	L	F	A	Pts
Atlanta Silverbacks †	12	9	1	2	25	10	28
Richmond Kickers †	12	9	1	2	25	10	28
Charlotte Lady Eagles	12	8	2	2	31	10	26
Cocoa Expos	11	5	3	3	20	8	18
Hampton Roads	11	2	1	8	9	22	7
Bradenton Athletics	11	1	1	9	9	32	4
Fredricksburg Gunners	11	1	1	9	6	33	4

Central Conference Midwest Division

	Pl	W	D	L	F	A	Pts
Minnesota Lightening †	12	10	1	1	27	8	31
Michigan Hawks †	12	8	1	3	27	13	25
Cleveland Internationals	12	8	0	4	30	16	24
Chicago Gaels	12	7	1	4	39	17	22
London Gryphons	12	4	0	8	19	41	12
Fort Wayne Fever	12	1	2	9	8	27	5
West Michigan Firewomen	12	1	1	10	7	35	4

Conference play-off semi-finals: **Atlanta** 4-0 Michigan;
Minnesota 4-2 Richmond
Final: **Atlanta** 5-2 Minnesota

Eastern Conference Northeast Division

	Pl	W	D	L	F	A	Pts
Washington Freedom †	14	12	1	1	48	10	37
Jersey Sky Blue †	14	12	0	2	48	6	36
Nth Virginia Majestics	14	7	1	6	28	26	22
Boston Renegades	14	7	0	7	19	31	21
New Jersey Wildcats	14	5	4	5	16	13	19
Long Island Riders	14	5	2	7	20	24	17
New York Magic	14	1	3	10	8	32	6
Western Mass Pioneers	14	1	1	12	9	54	4

Eastern Conference Northern Division

	Pl	W	D	L	F	A	Pts
Ottawa Fury †	12	11	1	0	47	9	34
Toronto Lynx †	12	7	2	3	29	16	23
Laval Comets	12	7	1	4	35	10	22
Rochester Rhinos	12	5	0	7	21	28	15
Hamilton Avalanche	12	2	0	10	11	42	6
Vermont Voltage	12	2	0	10	9	47	6

Conference semi-finals: **Ottawa** 4-0 Jersey;
Washington 6-1 Toronto
Final: **Washington** 1-0 Ottawa

Western Conference

	Pl	W	D	L	F	A	Pts
San Diego Sunwaves †	12	8	1	3	28	12	25
Seattle Sounders †	12	7	1	4	21	14	22
Vancouver Whitecaps †	12	6	3	3	24	17	21
Fort Collins Force	12	4	1	7	18	31	13
Mile High Edge	12	3	2	7	16	26	11
Real Colorado Cougars	12	3	2	7	11	18	11

Conference final: Seattle 2-1 San Diego;

Championship Finals

Semi-finals: **Washington** 3-0 Rochester; **Atlanta** 4-1 Seattle
Third place: Seattle 2-1 Rochester
Final: **Washington** 3-1 Atlanta
Washington Freedom are the 2007 W-League champions

† Qualified for the play-offs

USA 2006
WPSL

West Conference

	Pl	W	D	L	F	A	Pts
Ajax America ‡	14	14	0	0	63	6	42
San Diego Sea Lions	14	9	1	4	43	14	28
California Storm	14	9	1	4	46	14	28
Sonoma County Sol	14	6	3	5	29	18	21
Claremont Stars	14	5	4	5	35	19	20
San Fran. Nighthawks	14	2	5	7	22	36	11
Lamorinda East Bay	13	1	1	11	14	67	4
Sacramento Pride	13	1	0	12	5	80	3

Southwest Conference

	Pl	W	D	L	F	A	Pts
Denver Diamonds †	8	5	1	2	14	16	16
Rush Salt Lake City	8	5	0	3	13	8	15
Utah Spiders	8	4	2	2	23	11	14
Alburquerque Asylum	8	4	0	4	20	12	12
Colorado Springs Utd	8	0	1	6	7	30	1

Midwest Conference

	Pl	W	D	L	F	A	Pts
FC Indiana ‡	8	7	0	1	33	3	21
River Cities	8	7	0	1	37	2	21
FC Twente	8	2	0	6	11	23	6
FC St Louis	8	2	0	6	12	37	6
Chicago Utd Breeze	8	2	0	6	10	36	6

South Conference

	Pl	W	D	L	F	A	Pts
Tampa Bay Elite †	8	6	2	0	29	5	20
Central Florida Strikers	8	4	3	1	19	9	15
Palm Beach United	8	4	1	3	19	10	13
Orlando Falcons	8	1	2	5	9	27	5
Miami Kickers	8	0	2	6	5	30	2

Southwest/South play-off: **Tampa** 2-1 Denver

Eastern Conference North Division

	Pl	W	D	L	F	A	Pts
New England Mutiny †	10	7	3	0	34	3	24
Long Island Fury †	10	7	2	1	34	6	23
SP Connecticut †	10	6	3	1	27	12	21
Adirondack Lynx	10	6	0	4	26	15	18
Massachusetts Stingers	10	6	0	4	17	14	18
Boston Aztecs	10	5	1	4	20	12	16
New York AC	10	4	0	6	11	22	12
Bay State Select	10	2	1	7	13	26	7

East play-off: **Long Island** 3-2 Connecticut

Eastern Conference South Division

	Pl	W	D	L	F	A	Pts
Atlantic City Diablos †	10	8	0	2	35	9	24
Northampton Laurels †	10	5	0	5	12	23	15
Philadelphia Liberty	10	3	1	6	11	19	10
Real Shore	10	2	0	8	5	26	6
Central Delaware SA	10	1	1	8	13	31	4
Maryland Pride	10	1	0	9	6	39	3

Eastern semi-finals: **New England** 6-1 Northampton;
Atlantic City 33-1 Long Island
Final: **New England** 2-1 Atlantic City

Championship Finals

Semi-finals: **FC Indiana** 1-1 4-3p Ajax;
New England 1-1 5-4p Tampa Bay
Final: **FC Indiana** 3-0 New England
FC Indiana are the 2007 WPSL champions

† Qualified for the play-offs • ‡ Qualified for the finals

THE (VERY) UNOFFICIAL WORLD CHAMPIONSHIP

Many Scots would tell you that the proudest moment for their national team was on April 15, 1967, the day they beat world champions England at Wembley. Working on the basis that if you beat the world champions then you must be the best in the world, this unofficial world championship builds on that theory, adopting the system boxing uses to decide its world champions. Therefore when the Scots lost to the Soviet Union in May 1967, the Soviets then became unofficial world champions and so on. The series starts in 1908 when the England amateur team, playing as Great Britain, won the first official Olympic title, at that time the world championship of football. In many cases the sequence leads naturally to the FIFA World Cup final, but where it doesn't - in 1938, 1950, 1954, 1962, 1970, 1994, 2002 and 2006 - the title is vacated and the final is used to restart the sequence.

THE (VERY) UNOFFICIAL WORLD CHAMPIONSHIP

Champions	Opponents	Score	Venue	Date
England	Denmark	2-0	London	24-10-1908
Denmark	England	2-1	Copenhagen	5-05-1910
England	Denmark	3-0	London	21-10-1911
Netherlands	England	2-1	The Hague	24-03-1913
England	Netherlands	2-1	Hull	15-11-1913
Denmark	England	3-0	Copenhagen	5-06-1914
Sweden	Denmark	4-0	Stockholm	8-10-1916
Denmark	Sweden	2-1	Stockholm	14-10-1917
Norway	Denmark	3-1	Oslo	16-06-1918
Denmark	Norway	4-0	Copenhagen	6-10-1918
Norway	Denmark	3-2	Oslo	21-09-1919
Sweden	Norway	3-0	Oslo	27-06-1920
Netherlands	Sweden	5-4	Antwerp	29-08-1920
Belgium	Netherlands	3-0	Antwerp	31-08-1920
Italy	Belgium	3-2	Antwerp	5-05-1921
Czechoslovakia	Italy	5-1	Prague	27-05-1923
Switzerland	Czechoslovakia	1-0	Paris	30-05-1924
Uruguay	Switzerland	3-0	Paris	9-06-1924
Argentina	Uruguay	3-2	Montevideo	31-08-1924
Uruguay	Argentina	1-0	Montevideo	16-11-1924
Argentina	Uruguay	1-0	Buenos Aires	5-01-1925
Uruguay	Argentina	2-0	Santiago	24-10-1926
Argentina	Uruguay	1-0	Montevideo	14-07-1927
Uruguay	Argentina	1-0	Buenos Aires	30-08-1927
Argentina	Uruguay	3-2	Lima	20-11-1927
Uruguay	Argentina	2-1	Amsterdam	13-06-1928
Paraguay	Uruguay	3-1	Asuncion	15-08-1928
Argentina	Paraguay	4-1	Buenos Aires	10-11-1929
Uruguay	Argentina	4-2	Montevideo	30-07-1930
Brazil	Uruguay	2-0	Rio de Janeiro	6-09-1931
Spain	Brazil	3-1	Genoa	27-05-1934
Italy	Spain	1-0	Florence	1-06-1934
England	Italy	3-2	London	14-11-1934
Scotland	England	2-0	Glasgow	6-04-1935
Wales	Scotland	2-1	Dundee	2-12-1936
England	Wales	2-1	Middlesbrough	17-11-1937
Scotland	England	1-0	London	9-04-1938
Vacated				
Italy	Hungary	4-2	Paris	19-06-1938
Switzerland	Italy	3-1	Zurich	12-11-1939
Hungary	Switzerland	3-0	Budapest	31-03-1940
Germany	Hungary	7-0	Cologne	6-04-1941
Switzerland	Germany	2-1	Berne	20-04-1941
Hungary	Switzerland	2-1	Zurich	16-11-1941
Germany	Hungary	5-3	Budapest	3-05-1942

THE (VERY) UNOFFICIAL WORLD CHAMPIONSHIP

Champions	Opponents	Score	Venue	Date
Sweden	Germany	3-2	Berlin	20-09-1942
Switzerland	Sweden	3-1	Zurich	15-11-1942
Hungary	Switzerland	3-1	Geneva	16-05-1943
Sweden	Hungary	7-2	Budapest	7-11-1943
Switzerland	Sweden	3-0	Geneva	25-11-1945
England	Switzerland	4-1	London	11-05-1946
France	England	2-1	Paris	19-05-1946
England	France	3-0	London	3-05-1947
Switzerland	England	1-0	Zurich	18-05-1947
France	Switzerland	2-1	Lausanne	8-06-1947
Italy	France	3-1	Paris	4-04-1948
England	Italy	4-0	Turin	16-05-1948
Scotland	England	3-1	London	9-04-1949
England	Scotland	1-0	Glasgow	15-04-1950
USA	England	1-0	Belo Horizonte	29-06-1950
Chile	USA	5-2	Recife	2-07-1950
Vacated				
Uruguay	Brazil	2-1	Rio de Janeiro	16-07-1950
Chile	Uruguay	2-0	Santiago	13-04-1952
Brazil	Chile	3-0	Santiago	20-04-1952
Peru	Brazil	1-0	Lima	19-03-1953
Uruguay	Peru	3-0	Lima	28-03-1953
Paraguay	Uruguay	4-1	Montevideo	10-04-1954
Vacated				
West Germany	Hungary	3-2	Berne	4-07-1954
Belgium	West Germany	2-0	Brussels	26-09-1954
Italy	Belgium	1-0	Bari	16-01-1955
Yugoslavia	Italy	4-0	Turin	29-05-1955
Austria	Yugoslavia	2-1	Vienna	30-10-1955
France	Austria	3-1	Paris	25-03-1956
Hungary	France	2-1	Paris	7-10-1956
Norway	Hungary	2-1	Oslo	12-06-1957
Denmark	Norway	2-0	Tammerfors	19-06-1957
Sweden	Denmark	2-1	Copenhagen	30-06-1957
West Germany	Sweden	1-0	Hamburg	20-11-1957
Czechoslovakia	West Germany	3-2	Prague	2-04-1958
Nth. Ireland	Czechoslovakia	1-0	Halmstad	8-06-1958
Argentina	Nth. Ireland	3-1	Halmstad	11-06-1958
Czechoslovakia	Argentina	6-1	Helsingborg	15-06-1958
Nth. Ireland	Czechoslovakia	2-1	Malmö	17-06-1958
France	Nth. Ireland	4-0	Norrkoping	19-06-1958
Brazil	France	5-2	Stockholm	24-06-1958
Uruguay	Brazil	3-0	Guayaquil	12-12-1959
Argentina	Uruguay	4-0	Buenos Aires	17-08-1960
Spain	Argentina	2-0	Seville	11-06-1961

THE (VERY) UNOFFICIAL WORLD CHAMPIONSHIP

Champions	Opponents	Score	Venue	Date
Czechoslovakia	Spain	1-0	Viña del Mar	31-05-1962
Mexico	Czechoslovakia	3-1	Viña del Mar	7-06-1962
Vacated				
Brazil	Czechoslovakia	3-1	Santiago	17-06-1962
Paraguay	Brazil	2-0	La Paz	17-03-1963
Bolivia	Paraguay	2-0	Cochabamba	24-03-1963
Paraguay	Bolivia	2-0	Asuncion	25-07-1965
Argentina	Paraguay	3-0	Buenos Aires	1-08-1965
Italy	Argentina	3-0	Turin	22-06-1966
Soviet Union	Italy	1-0	Sunderland	16-07-1966
West Germany	Soviet Union	2-1	Liverpool	25-07-1966
England	West Germany	4-2	London	30-07-1966
Scotland	England	3-2	London	15-04-1967
Soviet Union	Scotland	2-0	Glasgow	10-05-1967
Austria	Soviet Union	1-0	Vienna	15-10-1967
Soviet Union	Austria	3-1	Leningrad	16-06-1968
Sweden	Soviet Union	1-0	Moscow	6-08-1969
France	Sweden	3-0	Paris	1-11-1969
Switzerland	France	2-1	Basle	3-05-1970
Vacated				
Brazil	Italy	4-1	Mexico City	21-06-1970
Italy	Brazil	2-0	Rome	9-06-1973
Poland	Italy	2-1	Stuttgart	23-06-1974
West Germany	Poland	1-0	Frankfurt	3-07-1974
England	West Germany	2-0	London	12-03-1975
Czechoslovakia	England	2-1	Bratislava	30-10-1975
West Germany	Czechoslovakia	2-0	Hanover	17-11-1976
France	West Germany	1-0	Paris	23-02-1977
Rep. Ireland	France	1-0	Dublin	30-03-1977
Bulgaria	Rep. Ireland	2-0	Sofia	1-06-1977
France	Bulgaria	3-1	Paris	16-11-1977
Italy	France	2-1	Mar del Plata	2-06-1978
Netherlands	Italy	2-1	Buenos Aires	21-06-1978
Argentina	Netherlands	3-1	Buenos Aires	25-06-1978
Bolivia	Argentina	2-1	La Paz	18-07-1979
Paraguay	Bolivia	2-0	Asuncion	1-08-1979
Chile	Paraguay	1-0	Santiago	5-12-1979
Brazil	Chile	2-1	Belo Horizonte	24-06-1980
Uruguay	Brazil	2-1	Montevideo	10-01-1981
Peru	Uruguay	2-1	Montevideo	23-08-1981
Chile	Peru	2-1	Santiago	23-03-1982
Peru	Chile	1-0	Lima	30-03-1982
Poland	Peru	5-1	La Coruna	22-06-1982
Italy	Poland	2-0	Barcelona	8-07-1982
Switzerland	Italy	1-0	Rome	27-10-1982
Soviet Union	Switzerland	1-0	Lausanne	13-04-1983
Portugal	Soviet Union	1-0	Lisbon	13-11-1983
Yugoslavia	Portugal	3-2	Lisbon	2-06-1984
Belgium	Yugoslavia	2-0	Lens	13-06-1984
France	Belgium	5-0	Nantes	16-06-1984
Bulgaria	France	2-0	Sofia	2-05-1985
Netherlands	Bulgaria	1-0	Heerenveen	4-09-1985
Belgium	Netherlands	1-0	Brussels	16-10-1985
Netherlands	Belgium	2-1	Rotterdam	20-11-1985
West Germany	Netherlands	3-1	Dortmund	14-05-1986
Denmark	West Germany	2-0	Queretaro	13-06-1986
Spain	Denmark	5-1	Queretaro	18-06-1986
Belgium	Spain	1-1 5-4p	Puebla	22-06-1986
Argentina	Belgium	2-0	Mexico City	25-06-1986
Italy	Argentina	3-1	Zurich	10-06-1987

THE (VERY) UNOFFICIAL WORLD CHAMPIONSHIP

Champions	Opponents	Score	Venue	Date
Wales	Italy	1-0	Brescia	4-06-1988
Netherlands	Wales	1-0	Amsterdam	14-09-1988
Italy	Netherlands	1-0	Rome	16-11-1988
Romania	Italy	1-0	Sibiu	29-03-1989
Poland	Romania	2-1	Warsaw	12-04-1989
England	Poland	3-0	London	3-06-1989
Uruguay	England	2-1	London	22-05-1990
Belgium	Uruguay	3-1	Verona	17-06-1990
Spain	Belgium	2-1	Verona	21-06-1990
Yugoslavia	Spain	2-1	Verona	26-06-1990
Argentina	Yugoslavia	0-0 3-2p	Florence	30-06-1990
West Germany	Argentina	1-0	Rome	8-07-1990
Wales	Germany	1-0	Cardiff	5-06-1991
Germany	Wales	4-1	Nuremberg	16-10-1991
Italy	Germany	1-0	Turin	25-03-1992
Switzerland	Italy	1-0	Berne	1-05-1993
Portugal	Switzerland	1-0	Oporto	13-10-1993
Italy	Portugal	1-0	Milan	17-11-1993
France	Italy	1-0	Naples	6-02-1994
Vacated				
Brazil	Italy	0-0 3-2p	Los Angeles	17-07-1994
Norway	Brazil	4-2	Oslo	30-05-1997
Italy	Norway	1-0	Marseille	27-06-1998
France	Italy	0-0 4-3p	Paris	3-07-1998
Russia	France	3-2	Paris	5-06-1999
Israel	Russia	4-1	Haifa	23-02-2000
Czech Republic	Israel	4-1	Prague	26-04-2000
Germany	Czech Republic	3-2	Nuremberg	3-06-2000
England	Germany	1-0	Charleroi	17-06-2000
Romania	England	3-2	Charleroi	20-06-2000
Italy	Romania	2-0	Brussels	24-06-2000
France	Italy	2-1	Rotterdam	2-07-2000
Spain	France	2-1	Valencia	28-03-2001
Netherlands	Spain	1-0	Rotterdam	27-03-2002
Vacated				
Brazil	Germany	2-0	Yokohama	30-06-2002
Paraguay	Brazil	1-0	Fortaleza	21-08-2002
Costa Rica	Paraguay	2-1	Alajuela	29-03-2003
Chile	Costa Rica	1-0	Santiago	30-04-2003
Costa Rica	Chile	1-0	San José	8-06-2003
Canada	Costa Rica	1-0	Foxboro	12-07-2003
Cuba	Canada	2-0	Foxboro	14-07-2003
Costa Rica	Cuba	3-0	Foxboro	16-07-2003
Mexico	Costa Rica	2-0	Mexico City	24-07-2003
Peru	Mexico	3-1	New Jersey	20-08-2003
Chile	Peru	2-1	Santiago	9-09-2003
Uruguay	Chile	2-1	Montevideo	15-11-2003
Jamaica	Uruguay	2-0	Kingston	18-02-2004
Nigeria	Jamaica	2-0	London	31-05-2004
Angola	Nigeria	1-0	Luanda	20-06-2004
Zimbabwe	Angola	2-0	Harare	27-03-2005
Nigeria	Zimbabwe	5-1	Abuja	8-10-2005
Romania	Nigeria	3-0	Bucharest	16-11-2005
Uruguay	Romania	2-0	Los Angeles	23-05-2006
Vacated				
Italy	France	1-1 5-3p	Berlin	9-07-2006
Croatia	Italy	2-0	Livorno	16-08-2006

APPENDIX 5 – HOW TO USE THE ALMANACK

① ⇨ | **Estadio Centenario, Montevideo** |
7-09-2003, 16:00, 39 253, Zamora PER ⇦②

URU   **5   0**   **BOL** ⇦③

④ ⇨ Forlan [17], Chevanton 2 [40 61] ⇦⑤
Abeijon [83], Bueno [88]

① Stadium and city/town where the match was played.

② *From left to right:* Date, kick-off time, attendance, name and nationality of referee. Assistant referees are included for FIFA tournaments.

③ Teams (using FIFA abbreviations) and scores.

④ Name of goal scorer and the time that the goal was scored.

⑤ Indicates that 2 goals were scored by Chevanton followed by the times of the goals.

BOLIVIA

① ⇨	FERNANDEZ Leonardo	21	⇦②
	PENA Juan Manuel	2	⇦③
	HOYOS Miguel	4	
	SANCHEZ Oscar	5	
	ROJAS Richard	6	
	CRISTALDO Luis	7	
	MENDEZ Limberg	9	
	CASTILLO Jose	11	
④ ⇨ 67	RICALDI Alvaro	15	⇦⑤
46	RIBEIRO Luis	17	
⑥ ⇨ 46	MOREJON Limber	19	
	Tr: ACOSTA Nelson		⇦⑦
46	BALDIVIESO Julio	10	
46	JUSTINIANO Raul	16	⇦⑧

⇔

Estadio Centenario, Montevideo		
7-09-2003, 16:00, 39 253, Zamora PER		

URU   **5   0**   **BOL**

Forlan [17], Chevanton 2 [40 61]
Abeijon [83], Bueno [88]

	URUGUAY				BOLIVIA	
1	MUNUA Gustavo				FERNANDEZ Leonardo	21
5	SOSA Marcelo	69			PENA Juan Manuel	2
6	LOPEZ Diego				HOYOS Miguel	4
9	BUENO Carlos				SANCHEZ Oscar	5
10	LIGUERA Martin	77			ROJAS Richard	6
11	NUNEZ Richard				CRISTALDO Luis	7
14	GONZALEZ Cristian				MENDEZ Limberg	9
17	LAGO Eduardo				CASTILLO Jose	11
19	CHEVANTON Ernesto		67		RICALDI Alvaro	15
20	RECOBA Alvaro		46		RIBEIRO Luis	17
21	FORLAN Diego	76	46		MOREJON Limber	19
	Tr: CARRASCO Juan Ramon				Tr: ACOSTA Nelson	
8	ABEIJON Nelson	69	46		BALDIVIESO Julio	10
15	SANCHEZ Vicente	76	46		JUSTINIANO Raul	16
16	OLIVERA Ruben	77				

① Family name in capitals, followed by the player's given name.

② Shirt number.

③ A shaded box indicates that the player was cautioned.

④ A shaded box next to a player who has been sent off (see below), indicates a dismissal for two yellow cards.
A blacked-out box indicates a straight red card.

⑤ A blacked-out box indicates the player was dismissed at the time shown in the centre column.

⑥ Substitution time.

⑦ Team coach/trainer.

⑧ Substitute. The time of the substitution corresponds with the player listed in the starting line-up.

EXPLANATION OF OTHER TERMS USED IN THE ALMANACK

In the Champions League match reports:
* • indicates a booking.
* •85 indicates a player was sent off (with minute).

≠90 indicates a player missed a penalty.
2✘ indicates the second penalty in a penalty shoot-out was missed (or scored 2✓)

MEDALS TABLE

		Overall			League			Cup			Europe			City		Stadium	Cap'ty		DoF	
		G	S	B	G	S	B	G	S	G	S	B								
1	Bayern München	39	12	14	20	7	4	13	2	6	3	10	Munich		Allianz-Arena	69 901		1900	
2	1.FC Nürnberg	14	5	1	9	3		5	2			1	Nuremburg		Frankenstadion	46 780		1900	
3	Schalke 04	12	16	3	7	9	1	4	7	1		2	Gelsenkirchen		Veltins Arena	61 524		1904	

③ ④ ⑤ ← above Overall, League, Cup columns
② ← above City
⑦ ← pointing to 1900 (Bayern)
⑥ ← below Europe column

① Indicates that Bayern are the most successful team in the history of German football, above
   1.FC Nürnberg in second place and Schalke in third place.
② Indicates that Bayern play in the city of Munich and use the 69,901 capacity Allianz-Arena.
③ Column G (gold) lists the total number of trophies Bayern have won – 39; Column S (silver)
   lists the number of times Bayern have been runners-up in the League or losing Cup Finalists -
   12; Column B (bronze) lists the number of times Bayern have been finished third in the
   League or have been losing Cup semi-finalists.
④ This column follows the same principle as column ③ but refers only to the League.
⑤ This column follows the same principle as column ③ but refers only to the Cup.
⑥ This column follows the same principle as column ③ but refers to all three European
   competitions (the UEFA Champions League, the UEFA Cup and the Cup Winners Cup).
⑦ Indicates that Bayern were formed in 1900.

CHINA PR 2004

① SUPER LEAGUE	② Pl	③ W	④ D	⑤ L	⑥ F	⑦ A	⑧ Pts	Shenzhen	Shandong	Shanghai I	Liaoning	Dalian	Tianjin	Beijing	Shenyang	Sichuan	Shanghai S	Qingdao	Chongqing
Shenzhen Jianlibao †	22	11	9	2	30	13	42		2-1	1-0	3-0	2-2	0-1	2-0	0-0	1-1	3-1	1-0	0-0
Shandong Luneng Tai.	22	10	6	6	44	29	36	1-1		4-2	3-1	2-3	3-1	5-2	4-1	1-2	2-1	1-1	4-1
Shanghai International	22	8	8	6	39	31	32	2-2	2-1		2-1	4-0	3-0	1-1	3-1	3-2	1-1	1-0	1-2
Liaoning Zhongyu	22	10	2	10	39	40	32	1-2	2-3	2-1		1-5	1-5	1-1	1-0	0-0	5-2	3-1	3-0

⇐ ⑨ (pointing to Liaoning Zhongyu 3-0 Chongqing)

15/05/2004 - 5/12/2004 • † Teams qualifying for the AFC Champions League

① Chinese champions of 2004.
   All champions are listed in bold. If the
   club at the top of the table is not listed in
   bold it means that the table shown represents only part of a season. Relegated
   clubs are also shown in bold.
② Number of games played.
③ Number of wins.
④ Number of draws.
⑤ Number of losses.

⑥ Number of goals scored.
⑦ Number of goals conceded.
⑧ Number of points gained in the season.
⑨ This result represents the match between
   Liaoning Zhongyu at home and
   Chongqing, the away club. The home
   team score is listed first so Liaoning
   Zhongyu won 3-0 at home to Chongqing.
⑩ Dates for the season.

BRAZIL NATIONAL TEAM RECORDS AND RECORD SEQUENCES

Records			Sequence records						
Victory	10-1	BOL 1949	①	Wins	14	1997	⑤ Clean sheets	8	1989
Defeat	0-6	URU 1920	②	Defeats	4	2001	⑥ Goals scored	47	1994-1997
Player Caps	126	CAFU	③	Undefeated	43	1993-1997	⑦ Without goal	5	1990
Player Goals	77	PELE	④	Without win	7	1983-84, 1990-91	⑧ Goals against	24	1937-1944

① Number of consecutive wins.
② Number of consecutive defeats.
③ Number of consecutive games played
   without defeat.
④ Number of consecutive games played
   without a win.
⑤ Number of consecutive games played

without conceding a goal.
⑥ Number of consecutive games played in
   which Brazil scored.
⑦ Number of consecutive games played
   without scoring.
⑧ Number of consecutive games played
   with opponent scoring.

CALENDAR FOR THE 2007–08 SEASON

Week starting

Month	Week	Events
September 2007	Sat 1	
	Sat 8	8-09 & 12-09 International match days; 8-09 South Pacific Games Final in Samoa; 9-09 FIFA U-17 World Cup Final in Seoul; 10-09 to 30-09 FIFA Women's World Cup in China; 11-09 SA R2
	Sat 15	18-09 UEFA CL matchday 1; 18-09 AFC Cup QF1; 19-09 AFC CL QF1; 20-09 to 30-09 AFC President's Cup in Lahore; 20-09 UEFA Cup R1
	Sat 22	22-09 CAF CC SF1; 22-09 CAF CC group matchday 5; 25-09 AFC Cup QF2; 26-09 AFC CL QF2
	Sat 29	2-10 UEFA CL matchday 2; 2-10 AFC Cup SF1; 3-10 AFC CL SF1; 4-10 SA R2; 4-10 UEFA Cup R1
October 2007	Sat 6	6-10 to 16-10 AFC U-19 Women's Championship in China; 6-10 CAF CL SF2; 6-10 CAF CC group matchday 6; 9-10 SA QF1
	Sat 13	13-10 & 17-10 International match days
	Sat 20	23-10 UEFA CL matchday 3; 23-10 AFC Cup SF2; 24-10 AFC CL SF2; 25-10 UEFA Cup matchday 1
	Sat 27	27-10 CAF CL F1; 1-11 SA QF2; 2-11 AFC Cup F1; 27-10 O-League matchday 1; 31-10 O-League matchday 2; 1-11 to 11-11 FIFA Beach Soccer World Cup in Rio
November 2007	Sat 3	3-11 CAF CC F1; 6-11 UEFA CL matchday 4; 7-11 AFC CL F1; 8-11 SA SF1; 9-11 AFC Cup F2; 8-11 UEFA Cup matchday 2
	Sat 10	10-11 CAF CL F2; 14-11 AFC CL F2; 15-11 SA SF2
	Sat 17	17-11 & 21-11 International match days;
	Sat 24	24-11 CAF CC F2; 25-11 Preliminary draw for the 2010 FIFA World Cup in Durban; 27-11 UEFA CL matchday 5; 28-11 SA F1; 29-11 UEFA Cup matchday 3; 25-11 to 11-12 CECAFA Cup in Dar es Salaam
December 2007	Sat 1	2-12 draw for UEFA Euro 2008 finals in Lucerne; 5-12 UEFA Cup matchday 4; TBC FIFA Club World Cup in Japan
	Sat 8	11-12 UEFA CL matchday 6
	Sat 15	15-12 SA F2; 17-12 FIFA World Player Gala; 19-12 UEFA Cup matchday 5
	Sat 22	
	Sat 29	
January 2008	Sat 5	
	Sat 12	
	Sat 19	20-01 to 10-02 CAF Africa Cup of Nations in Ghana
	Sat 26	
February 2008	Sat 2	6-02 International match day
	Sat 9	13-02 UEFA Cup R2; TBC Start of the Copa Libertadores; TBC Start of the CAF Champions League and Confederation Cup
	Sat 16	17-02 O-League matchday 3; 19-02 UEFA CL R2; 20-02 O-League matchday 4; 21-02 UEFA Cup R2
	Sat 23	
March 2008	Sat 1	5-03 UEFA CL R2; 6-03 UEFA Cup R3
	Sat 8	13-03 UEFA Cup R3
	Sat 15	
	Sat 22	26-03 O-League matchday 5
	Sat 29	29-03 O-League matchday 6; 1-04 UEFA CL QF1; 3-04 UEFA Cup QF1
April 2008	Sat 5	9-04 UEFA CL QF2; 10-04 UEFA Cup QF2
	Sat 12	
	Sat 19	22-04 UEFA CL SF1; 24-04 UEFA Cup SF1
	Sat 26	26-04 O-League F1; 30-04 UEFA CL SF2; 1-05 UEFA Cup SF2
May 2008	Sat 3	4-05 O-League F2
	Sat 10	14-05 UEFA Cup F
	Sat 17	21-05 UEFA CL F
	Sat 24	
	Sat 31	
June 2008	Sat 7	7-06 to 29-06 UEFA Euro 2008 in Austria/Switzerland; 7-06 to 10-06 Euro 2008 first matchdays; 11-06 to 14-06 Euro 2008 second matchdays
	Sat 14	15-06 to 18-06 Euro 2008 third matchdays; 19-06 to 22-06 Euro 2008 quarter-finals
	Sat 21	25-06 to 26-06 Euro 2008 semi-finals
	Sat 28	29-06 Euro 2008 final in Vienna

CL = Champions League (according to the confederation indicated) • SA = Copa Sudamericana • CC = Confederation Cup
r1 = first round • r2 = second round • r3 = third round • qf = quarter-final • sf = semi-final • f = final
1 = first leg • 2 = second leg • TBC = dates to be confirmed